The World Book Atlas

The World Book

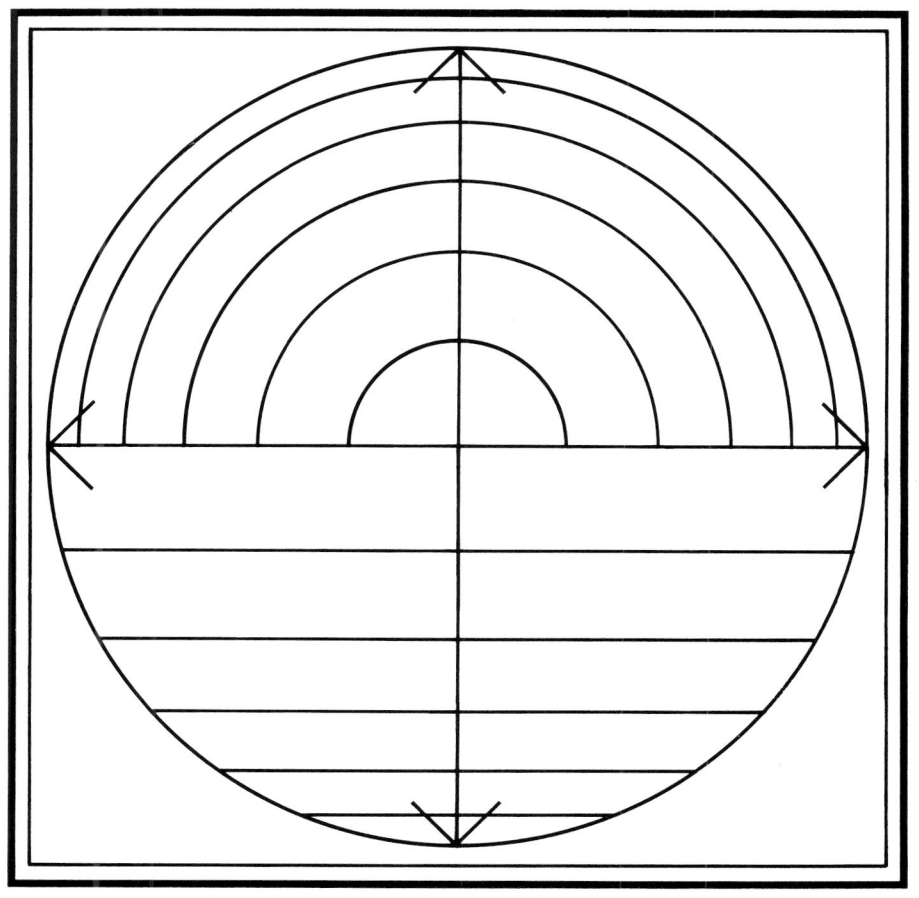

Atlas

World Book, Inc.
a Scott Fetzer company
Chicago

Staff

World Book Staff

President *Peter Mollman*

Publisher *William H. Nault*

Editorial

Editor in chief
Robert O. Zeleny

Executive editor
Dominic J. Miccolis

Associate editor
Maureen Mostyn Liebenson

Senior editor
Lisa Klobuchar

Rights and permissions
Janet T. Peterson

Art

Art director
Roberta Dimmer

Assistant art director
Joe Gound

Photography director
John S. Marshall

Designer
Chestnut House

Product production

Manufacturing
Henry Koval, director
Sandra Van den Broucke, manager

Pre-press services
Jerry Stack, director
Randi Park
Barbara Podczerwinski

The World Book Atlas
Revised 1990 edition
Copyright © 1986 World Book, Inc.
United States and Canada Map Section from
Atlas of the United States
Copyright © 1983, Rand McNally & Company
and
Cosmopolitan World Atlas
Copyright © 1981, Rand McNally & Company
Thematic Maps on pages 68-91 and some
illustrative material on pages 8-96 from
Goode's World Atlas
Copyright © 1986, Rand McNally & Company
Maps of the World and Index, and some
illustrative material on pages 8-96 from
The Great Geographical Atlas
Copyright © 1982 Istituto Geografico
De Agostini, S.p.A., Novara, Italy

Printed in the United States of America
ISBN 0-7166-3228-4
Library of Congress Catalog Card Number 90-70620
e/ij

Maps of the World credits

Cartographic and geographic director
Giuseppe Motta

Geographic research
G. Baselli
M. Colombo

Terrain illustration
S. Andenna
E. Ferrari

Cartographic production
F. Tosi
G. Capitini
A. Carnero

Coordination
S. Binda
L. Pasquali
G. Zanetta

Consultants

Lawrence C. Bliss, B.S., M.S., Ph.D.
  Professor and Chairman
  Department of Botany
  University of Washington

Kempton E. Webb, A.B., M.A., Ph.D.
  Professor
  Department of Geography
  Columbia University

James S. Sweitzer, B.S., M.S., Ph.D.
  Astronomer
  Chicago, Illinois

Mark Elison, M.S.
  Department of Geological Sciences
  Northwestern University

Rand McNally & Company Staff

Product director
Russell L. Voisin

Managing editor
Jon M. Leverenz

Geographic research
V. Patrick Healy

Research coordinator
Susan K. Hudson

Cartographic production
Ronald F. Peters

Acknowledgments

Illustration credits read from top to bottom and from left to right on each page. Illustrations that extend over two pages are credited to the left-hand page.

8, NASA. 9, John Shaw, Bruce Coleman Ltd.; © Marty Snyderman; Phil Degginger from E. R. Degginger. 10, Artwork © Mitchell Beazley Pub. Ltd. 1973 as The Good Earth. 11, © John Eastcott/ Yva Momatiuk, Woodfin Camp, Inc.; © Marty Snyderman; © Jeff Foott, Bruce Coleman Ltd. 12, © Leo Touchet, Woodfin Camp, Inc.; Henry Ausloss, World Wildlife Fund from Bruce Coleman Ltd. 13, WORLD BOOK diagrams; Terraphotographics/BPS; Carlos Elmer, Shostal; Robert Glaze; © Loren McIntyre. 14, Artwork Brian Delf. 15, Ronald Thompson/Frank W. Lane, Bruce Coleman Ltd.; © Jim Brandenburg, Woodfin Camp, Inc.; Charlie Ott, Bruce Coleman Ltd. 16, © David Muench; WORLD BOOK artwork. 17, © Dwight Kuhn; Artwork © Mitchell Beazley Pub. Ltd. 1973 as The Good Earth. 18, Norman Tomalin, Bruce Coleman Ltd. 19, © David Muench; © Jeff Foott. 20, Animals Coral Mula; trees Donald Myall. 21, E. R. Degginger; Mike Price, Bruce Coleman Ltd. 22, Hutchison Library; Artwork Bob Bampton/ The Garden Studio. 23, G. R. Plage, Bruce Coleman Ltd. 24, © Jodi Cobb, Woodfin Camp, Inc.; Artwork, Jim Robins. 26, © Dwight R. Kuhn; © J. Alsop, Bruce Coleman Inc.; © Dwight R. Kuhn. 27, E. R. Degginger; Artwork, Donald Myall. 28, W. E. Ruth, Bruce Coleman Inc. 29, Phil Degginger from E. R. Degginger; © Jim Brandenburg, Woodfin Camp, Inc.; Wolf Jean Hellmer for WORLD BOOK, other animals Coral Mula. 30, WORLD BOOK artwork; © B. and C. Alexander. 31, © Paul Drummond from B. and C. Alexander; U.S. Naval Photographic Center; Artwork Jim Robins. 32,

© Loren McIntyre, Woodfin Camp, Inc. 33, Hutchison Library; Photri; Shostal. 34, © Odyssey Productions. 35, Robert Glaze; © Odyssey Productions. 36, Cameramann International Ltd. 37, © Enrique Shore, Woodfin Camp, Inc.; © Steve Vidler, The Stock House Ltd.; Pedro Luis Roata, Shostal. 38, © DPA from Photoreporters. 39, Eric Carle, Shostal; © Alon Reininger, Woodfin Camp, Inc. 40, © Marc F. Bernheim, Woodfin Camp, Inc. 41, © Robert Azzi, Woodfin Camp, Inc.; © D. and J. Heaton, The Stock House Ltd.; © Malcolm Holmes, The Stock House Ltd. 42, © Robert Azzi, Woodfin Camp, Inc. 43, Masood Qureshi, Bruce Coleman Ltd.; S. Trevor/D. B., Bruce Coleman Inc.; © Carl Frank, Photo Researchers. 44, Fritz Prenzel, Bruce Coleman Ltd. 45, © Odyssey Productions; Shostal; © Robin Smith, The Stock House Ltd. 46, Cameramann International, Ltd. 47, Cameramann International, Ltd.; © N. Devore III, Bruce Coleman Inc. 48, TASS from Sovfoto. 49, Chris Bonington, Bruce Coleman Ltd.; Shostal. 50, NASA; 51, © Harold Sund; E. R. Degginger. 52, WORLD BOOK diagram. 53, WORLD BOOK diagrams; © David F. Malin, Anglo-Australian Telescope Board. 54, NASA. 55, WORLD BOOK diagrams; Illustrations from Album of Astronomy © 1981 by Rand McNally & Company. 56, WORLD BOOK diagram. 57, WORLD BOOK diagram; John S. Shelton. 58-59, Artwork © Mitchell Beazley Pub. Ltd. 1973 as The Good Earth. 59, © George Hall, Woodfin Camp, Inc. 60, Gene Ahrens; Artwork © Mitchell Beazley Pub. Ltd. 1973 as The Good Earth. 61, © Odyssey Productions; John S. Shelton. 62-63, Map Librairie Hachette; Artwork © Mitchell Beazley Pub. Ltd. 1973 as The Good Earth. 64, John S. Shelton; E. R. Degginger. 65, Smithsonian Collection from E. R. Degginger; WORLD BOOK photo; Smithsonian Collection from E. R. Degginger; Smithsonian Collection from E. R. Degginger;

© Lee Boltin. 66, © Craig Aurness, West Light. 67, Map from Goode's World Atlas; G. R. Roberts. 68, © Jim Brandenburg. 69, Grant Heilman; © Craig Aurness, Woodfin Camp, Inc. 70, John Shaw, Bruce Coleman Ltd. 75, Jeff Foott; © Thomas Nebbia, Woodfin Camp, Inc. 77, E. R. Degginger; N. G. Blake, Bruce Coleman Ltd. 79, © Mike Yamashita, Woodfin Camp, Inc.; © Craig Aurness, Woodfin Camp, Inc.; © Tsang Yan-sau, The Stock House Ltd. 81, © Mike Yamashita, Woodfin Camp, Inc.; © William Strode, Woodfin Camp, Inc.; © Lincoln Potter, The Stock House Ltd. 83, © Odyssey Productions; WORLD BOOK photo. 84, E. R. Degginger. 85, E. R. Degginger. 86, E. R. Degginger. 87, Standard Oil Company of California; The Gas Council. 91, © Loren McIntyre, Woodfin Camp, Inc.; © Thomas Hopker, Woodfin Camp, Inc. 92, NASA. 93, © Scala, Art Resource; Hunting Surveys Ltd. 94, British Museum; Harvard Semitic Museum, Cambridge, Mass.; British Library. 95, Michael Holford, Science Museum, London; Diagrams Creative Cartography Ltd.; NASA. 96, Map Istituto Geografico De Agostini; WORLD BOOK diagram.

Locator maps on pages 20, 22, 25, 27, 28, 31, 34, 36, 38, 40, 42, 44, 46, 48 were created exclusively for The World Book Atlas.

Structure and Contents

Structure of The World Book Atlas

The World Book Atlas is arranged according to the structure that follows.

Looking at Earth's Features   8-31

Looking at Earth's People and Their Lands   32-49

Looking at Earth as a Planet   50-65

Thematic Maps   66-91

Understanding Maps   92-96

Maps of the World   97-224

Maps of the United States and Canada   225-288

Geographical Information and Maps of the World Index   289-432

Contents of The World Book Atlas

Looking at Earth's Features   8
The Ocean   10
Mountains   12
Rivers and Streams   14
Lakes and Ponds   16
Swamps, Marshes, and Bogs   18
Tropical Forests   20
Deserts   22
Grasslands   24
Midlatitude Forests   26
Subarctic Cold Lands   28
Polar Caps   30

Looking at Earth's People and Their Lands   32
North America   34
South America   36
Europe   38
Asia   40
Africa   42
Australia and New Zealand   44
Pacific Islands   46
Polar Regions   48

Looking at Earth as a Planet   50
Earth in the Solar System   52
Earth's Atmosphere and Motion   54
Earth's Structure   56
Earthquakes and Volcanoes   58
Earth's Changing Surface   60
Beneath the Ocean   62
Earth's Minerals   64

Thematic Maps   66
Land and Water   68
Temperature   70
Precipitation, Winds, and Ocean Currents   72
Climatic Regions   74
Natural Vegetation   76
Agricultural Regions   78
Land Use   80
Distribution of Important Minerals   82
Distribution of Important Fuels   86
Energy   88
Languages and Religions   89
Population   90

Understanding Maps   92
The History of Maps   94
How to Read Maps   96

Maps of the World   97
Legend   98
Index Maps   100
World, Physical   102
World, Political   104
The Oceans   106
World Transportation and Time Zones   108
Europe, Physical   110
Europe, Political   112
Northern Europe   114
Baltic Region   116
British Isles   118
Central Europe   120
France and Benelux   122
Belgium, Netherlands and Luxembourg   124
Spain and Portugal   126
Italy, Austria and Switzerland   128
Southeastern Europe   130
Southwestern U.S.S.R.   132
The Urals   134
South-Central U.S.S.R.   135
Western U.S.S.R.   136
Eastern U.S.S.R.   138
Asia, Physical   140
Asia, Political   142
Southwestern Asia   144
Middle East   146
South-Central Asia   148
Southeast Asia   150
China and Mongolia   152
Northeastern China, Korea and Japan   154
Japan   156
Africa, Physical   158
Africa, Political   160
Northwestern Africa   162
Northeastern Africa   164
West-Central Africa   166
East-Central Africa   168
Equatorial Africa   170
Southern Africa   172
North America, Physical   174
North America, Political   176
Alaska   178
Greenland   179
Canada   180
United States   182
Eastern United States   184
Central United States   186
Western United States   188
Middle America   190
Mexico   192
Central America and Western Caribbean   194
Eastern Caribbean   196
Caribbean Islands   197

South America, Physical   198
South America, Political   200
Northern South America   202
East-Central South America   204
Southern South America   206
Australia and Oceania, Physical   208
Australia and Oceania, Political   210
Australia   212
The North Pacific   214
The South Pacific   216
New Zealand   218
Islands of Melanesia   219
Islands of Micronesia-Polynesia   220
Islands of Polynesia   221
Antarctic Region, Physical   222
Arctic Region, Physical   224

**Maps of the United States
and Canada**   225
Legend   225
United States   226
Alabama   228
Alaska   229
Arizona   230
Arkansas   231
California   232
Colorado   233
Connecticut   234
Delaware   235
Florida   236
Georgia   237
Hawaii   238
Idaho   239
Illinois   240
Indiana   241
Iowa   242
Kansas   243
Kentucky   244
Louisiana   245
Maine   246
Maryland   247
Massachusetts   248
Michigan   249
Minnesota   250
Mississippi   251
Missouri   252
Montana   253
Nebraska   254
Nevada   255
New Hampshire   256
New Jersey   257
New Mexico   258
New York   259
North Carolina   260
North Dakota   261
Ohio   262
Oklahoma   263

Oregon   264
Pennsylvania   265
Rhode Island   266
South Carolina   267
South Dakota   268
Tennessee   269
Texas   270
Utah   271
Vermont   272
Virginia   273
Washington   274
West Virginia   275
Wisconsin   276
Wyoming   277
Canada   278
Alberta   280
British Columbia   281
Manitoba   282
Maritime Provinces   283
Newfoundland   284
Ontario   285
Quebec   286
Saskatchewan   287
The United States and
Canada/Facts in Brief   288

**Geographical Information and Maps
of the World Index**   289
World Nations and Other
Political Units   290
World Geographical Tables   297
Populations of Major Cities   300
Sources   302
Transliteration Systems   304
Geographical Glossary   305
Maps of the World Index   313

Looking at Earth's

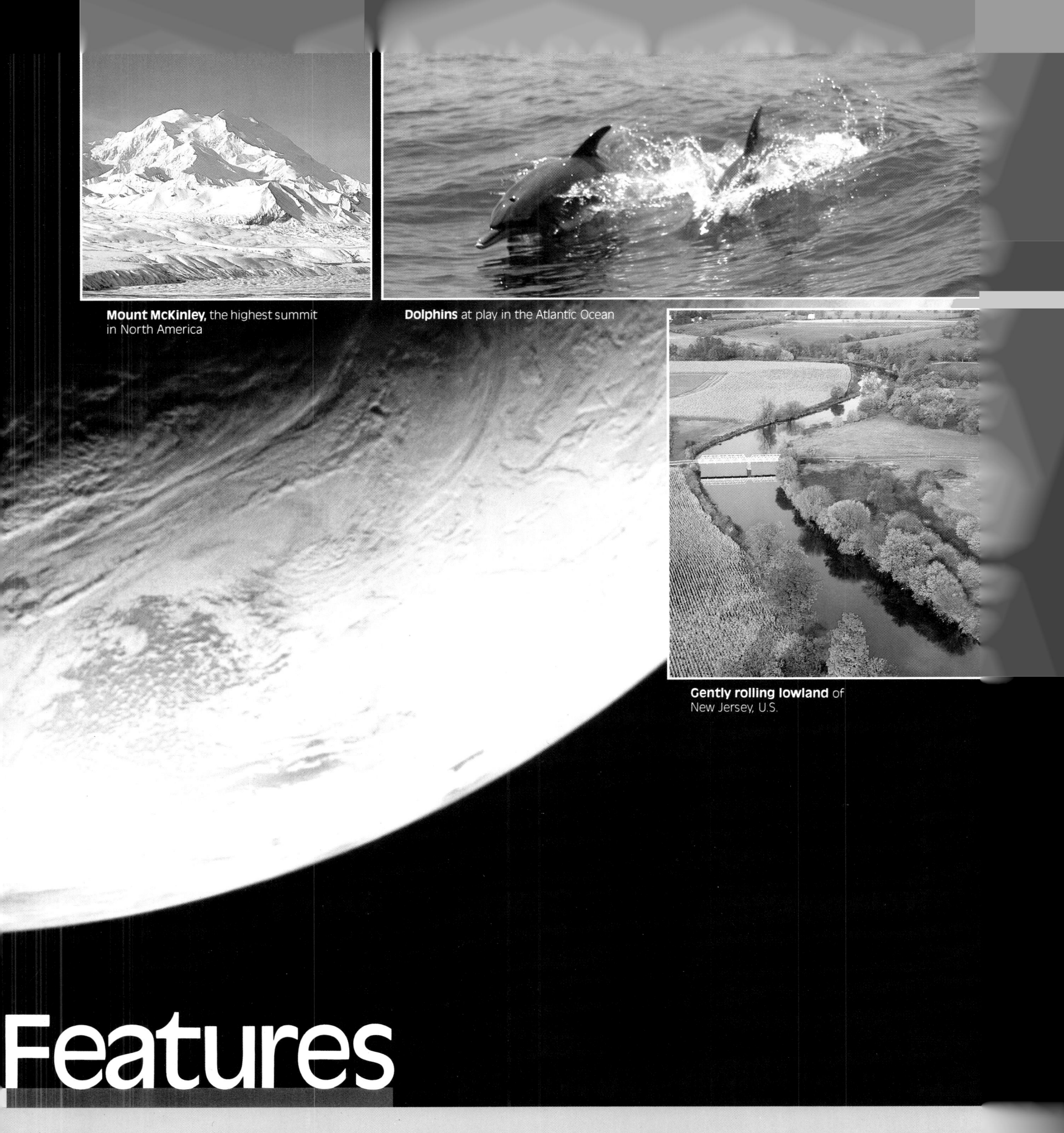

Mount McKinley, the highest summit in North America

Dolphins at play in the Atlantic Ocean

Gently rolling lowland of New Jersey, U.S.

Features

EARTH POSSESSES a vast ocean of water, flowing rivers, bright lakes, great forests, green plains, towering mountains, windswept deserts, and snowy polar caps. This combination of features makes earth unique among all the planets and moons in the solar system.

The Ocean

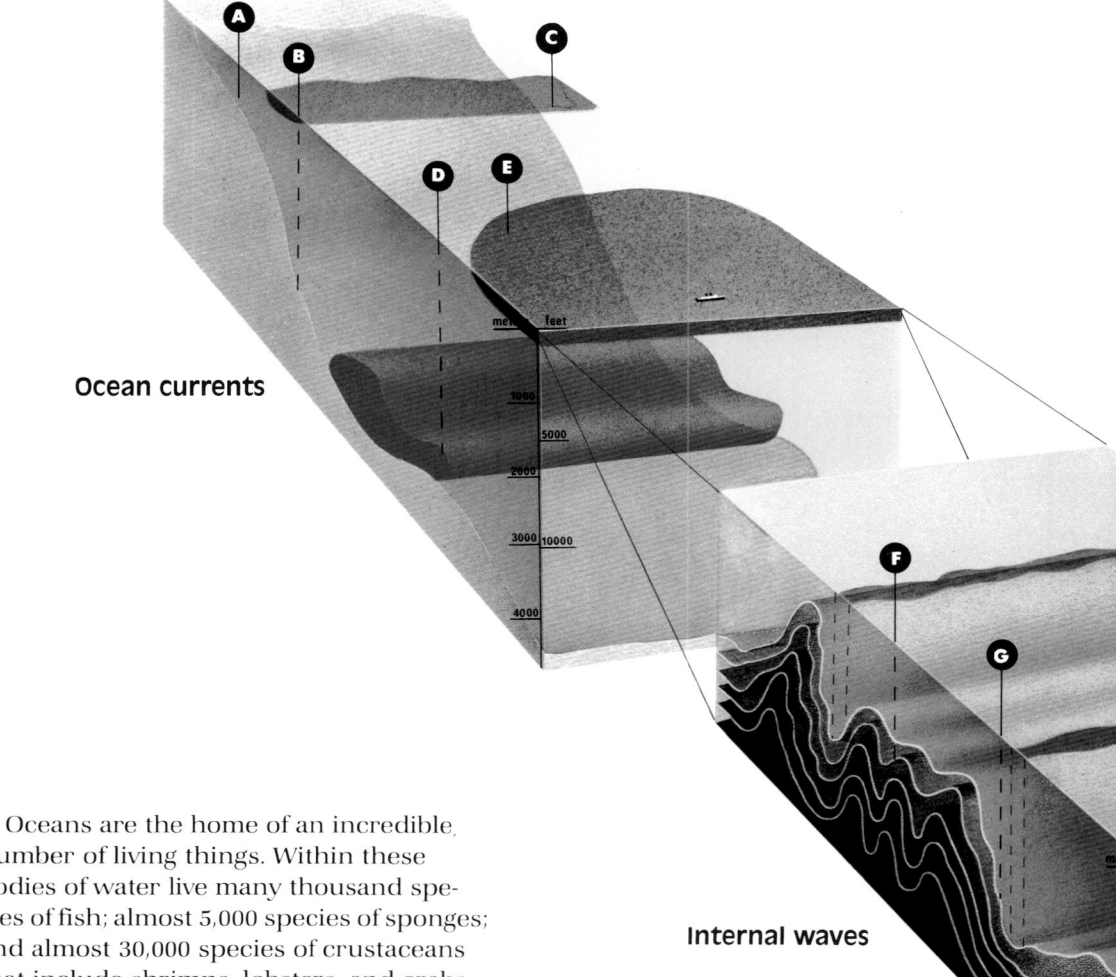

Ocean currents

Internal waves

More than 70 per cent of the world's surface is covered by oceans. Oceans have been given different names, such as Atlantic and Pacific, but they are actually all one large interconnected body of water, swept by winds that create waves, and moved by tides caused by the tug of the moon.

Oceans, often known as seas, are deep as well as vast. The bottoms of some seas lie more than 6 miles (10 kilometers) below their surfaces. Great mountains can rise from their floors and stick out above the water as islands.

Oceans are very important parts of the earth. The action of the sun's heat pouring down on an ocean turns enormous amounts of its surface into water vapor. This vapor rises into the air, cools, and forms clouds, which are carried by wind. When clouds are cooled even more, much of the water vapor forming them turns back into water and falls as rain or snow. This moisture creates the fresh water of rivers and lakes. It also provides the ground water that helps plants to grow, and thus animal life to exist.

Ocean water moves constantly in streams called currents. Currents are caused by a combination of the wind, the sun's heat, the salinity of the water, and the earth's rotation. The temperature of a current affects the temperature of the air above it. Therefore, warm currents bring warm air and water to some places, and cool currents bring cool air and water to other places. Without the help of the Equatorial Current, the Gulf Stream, and other currents, the air around the planet would be hotter both day and night near the equator and cooler both day and night at high latitudes.

Ocean water is salty. There is enough salt in the sea to cover every bit of dry land with a layer of salt 150 feet (45 meters) high. Actually, much of this salt originally came from the land. For countless millions of years, rivers that were supplied by rainfall runoff moved down mountainsides and across rolling lands. These rivers washed millions of tons of minerals out of the channels through which they flowed. The minerals, mainly various kinds of salts, were carried along by the rivers. Eventually, the rivers flowed into the ocean and released their cargoes of mud and salt. This accumulation of salt in its water keeps the ocean salty. Only pure water evaporates from its surface when water vapor forms.

Oceans are the home of an incredible number of living things. Within these bodies of water live many thousand species of fish; almost 5,000 species of sponges; and almost 30,000 species of crustaceans that include shrimps, lobsters, and crabs. Among the ocean mammals are whales, dolphins, seals, walruses, manatees, and otters. Reptiles, including turtles and snakes, and thousands of species of worms also live in the sea. Oceans do differ from one another in their species of plants and animals. That is because the seas vary in terms of climate.

All these animals, together with ocean plants, are members of complex ecological systems. The ocean food chain begins with microscopic green plants. These plants, called phytoplankton, drift in masses near the sunlit surfaces and give the water a greenish tint. Like all green plants, they use sunlight to manufacture food for themselves. As a by-product of this process, the plants produce tiny amounts of oxygen. This oxygen is used by sea animals and plants. It also helps replenish the oxygen in the earth's air.

Floating among the phytoplankton are trillions of microscopic animals called zooplankton. These creatures cannot make their own food. Instead they feed on phytoplankton. Zooplankton themselves are eaten by small fish and crustaceans, which are eaten by bigger fish and other creatures. They, in turn, are food for still larger animals, such as 60-foot-long sperm whales. But without the tiny phytoplankton, the earth's oceans could not support this complex food chain.

A continental shelf is the land around a continent that slopes deeply underwater (**A**). Farther offshore, the continental slope (**B**) plunges to the ocean bottom. Ocean characteristics vary greatly. Below the warm Gulf Stream (**C**) off the United States east coast moves a cold current (**D**). Near its source, the Gulf Stream borders the Sargasso Sea (**E**), a region of slow ocean currents surrounded by a boundary of fast-moving currents. Waves beneath the ocean surface (**F**) are caused by differences in salt content, density, and temperature. These internal waves move up and down like surface waves (**G**). Sometimes a dark band (**H**) on the surface marks an internal wave. The internal wave motion (**I**) shows how deep water is held back while surface waves lunge forward. A beach's breakpoint and foreshore determine where waves break. For example, a breakpoint at position (**J**) and foreshore at position (**K**) would cause waves to break at position (**L**). When the moon is full or new, incoming tides are at their highest and outgoing tides at their lowest. These tides are called spring tides. In the diagram, (**M-M**) shows the spring tidal range. At the quarters of the moon, tides are neither high nor low. Such tides are called neap tides. The neap tidal range is shown at (**N-N**). Location (**O**) shows the average tide level. Strong ocean waves wear away shoreline rocks, producing sand. Sand can be dry (**P**) or permanently wet (**Q**). Surface sand often has ripple marks (**R**) created when water recedes after each wave.

Wind action on the water produces surface waves. Waves travel forward in the direction of the wind.

In the ocean, fish often travel in schools—large groups of the same species. Here a school of grunts passes by coral formations. Grunts are known for making grunting sounds when taken from the water.

Waves on a beach

The sea otter swims, often on its back, in the North Pacific Ocean and near the shores of western North America and Siberia. This brown, furry animal floats in masses of seaweed called kelp.

Mountains

Mount Saint Elias, Alaska, is one of the highest peaks in North America. It stands in the Saint Elias Mountains, a rugged series of the highest coastal mountains in the world.

An ibex climbs a rocky slope in the Italian Alps. The thinness of the forest shows that the animal is nearing the timber line.

About one-fifth of the earth's land surface is made up of mountains. Mountains are composed of rock formations that rise 2,000 feet (610 meters) or more above the surrounding land. There are also mountains underwater. Those rock formations, called submarine mountains, form islands or are part of the ocean floor.

On land, mountains may be rocky and barren, or they may be green with vegetation. They may have high pointed peaks and narrow ridges. Their sides, or slopes, are long, broad, or slanting. Often mountains are cut by deep, wide indentations called canyons or valleys. Due to the decrease in temperature as elevation increases, mountainsides are made up of several different environments.

Mountains are formed over enormous amounts of time by movements of the earth's rocky crust. In some places, sideways shifts of the crust make huge wavelike wrinkles or folds. These movements result in folded mountains such as the Jura Mountains of Europe and the Appalachian Mountains of eastern North America. In other places, the crust is broken into gigantic blocks that are pushed upward to form block mountains. The Sierra Nevada of California is an example of block mountains. Dome mountains such as the Harlech Dome in Wales are created when molten rock called magma is forced upward under the surface rock to form a blisterlike swelling. The volcanic mountains of Washington and Oregon were created by volcanic activity.

The top of a very high mountain is generally covered with ice and snow. But a little farther down the slope, melted snow can provide moisture for lichens, mosses, and

low-growing flowering plants that flourish where soil develops. This region is called the alpine zone. A number of species of insects, particularly springtails and bristle-tails, thrive in this region. Brightly colored butterflies flit among the flowers. The American Rocky Mountain goat and the European ibex live here too. Small animals such as conies, chipmunks, and mountain ground hogs also make their homes near a mountain's top.

The animals of the high mountain regions are especially fitted for their environment. Many have enlarged hearts and lungs, and their blood contains extra oxygen-bearing red corpuscles. These features help the animals survive in a mountaintop's thin air. When winter comes, most of the smaller creatures take shelter in burrows and live on seeds and hay stored during summer. Larger animals and even some birds simply move a short way down the mountain-side. There the temperature is not as cold and food is still available.

A little below the alpine region is the timber line. This is the highest point at which a tree can survive without freezing. The tallest trees in this region are often bush-size dwarf willows, birches, aspens, spruces, firs, and pines. Each winter they are mostly covered by snow, which actually protects them from the terrible freezing wind of the mountaintop. These trees may, however, have some shoots that reach above the snow. At lower levels of mountains, the same kinds of trees can reach full size and form forests. Birds, squirrels, deer, and bears are at home in openings in these wooded areas.

The lower the elevation, the higher the temperature. If a mountain is in a place that gets plenty of rainfall, there will generally be a forest growing on its lower slopes. But if the mountain is in a dry region, its lower slopes will be covered with grassy meadow or maybe even desert. The animals that live here are not true "mountain animals." The same kinds of creatures may be found in other environments that feature similar conditions.

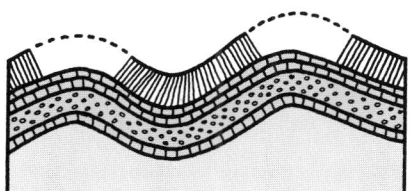

Folded mountains include the European Alps, *right*. The valleys and ridges that are characteristic of folded mountains are shown in the diagram, *above*.

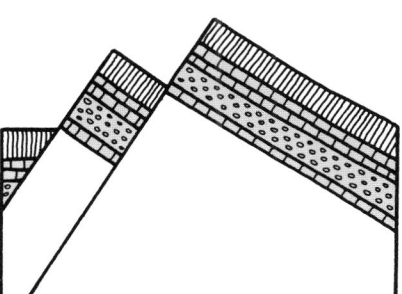

Block mountains are found in the desert land, *right*, near Las Vegas, Nevada. The diagram, *above*, shows the layers of cleanly broken sedimentary rock that are characteristic of block mountains.

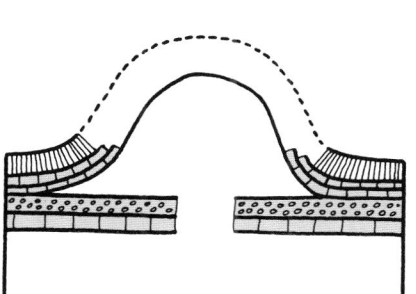

Dome mountains, such as Harlech Dome in Wales, *right*, are formed when the earth's crust rises into domes. The diagram, *above*, indicates that a dome's softer rock is eventually eroded.

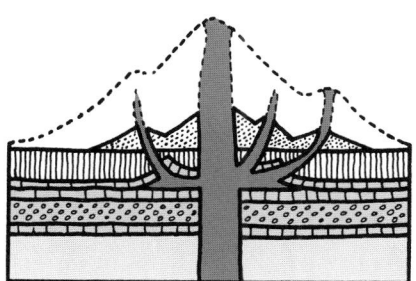

Volcanic mountains are the remains of volcanoes. The diagram, *above*, shows the pipeline vents through which lava moves inside a volcano. The material piles up and results in volcanic mountains such as the Cascade Mountains of Washington and Oregon, *right*.

Rivers and Streams

Rivers and streams are bodies of water that flow through land in long passages called channels. As they flow, always downhill, they are fed by other waters that enrich them and increase their size. Eventually they flow into another body of water, such as a larger river, a lake, or the ocean.

A river or stream channel is formed by the wearing away, or friction, of flowing water. The bottom of a channel is called the bed, and the sides are known as the banks. The channel of a small stream can be a few feet wide and less than a mile long. The channel of a large river, however, can be miles wide and extend for thousands of miles.

A river often begins high on a mountain. It can start as trickles of water from melting snow, as a spring bubbling out of rocks, or as a stream flowing from a mountain lake. As the water flows along, it is fed by streams and smaller rivers. It becomes deeper and wider, and its size is increased further by rainfall.

A river or stream is a habitat for plant and animal life. The character of that life depends upon the temperature, depth, and speed of the water. A swift-moving, shallow mountain stream is bare of most plant life. The exception is the jellylike algae that coat the rocky bottom. Black fly larvae use their tiny hooks to anchor themselves to the stream's rocks. These creatures have their food — microscopic plants and animals — delivered to them by the swift-flowing water. The larvae, in turn, are a source of nourishment for different species of birds such as dippers, or water ouzels, of western North America. These birds spend much of their time wading in swift streams and feeding on the insect life present.

A larger, slow-moving river that is far from its mountain beginnings is a very different environment. Unlike a swift-flowing stream that sweeps its floor clean, the bed of a slow-moving river is filled with mud and silt. These materials form soil for plant life. "Forests" of algae or eelgrass often cover a sluggish river's bottom. Cattails and bulrushes grow thickly along the banks. Water lilies and similar plants float on the surface. Fish such as pike and bass lurk among the bottom greenery and dart out to snap up frogs and smaller fishes. Muskrats use cattails and other plants both as food and to line the insides of riverbank burrows. Frogs attach their eggs to plants and rocks. Insects rely on the river plants as resting places.

Many kinds of insects lurk and burrow in the mud below the water. They are food for fish such as carp. Many kinds of predatory swimming insects, including dragonfly nymphs and diving beetles, often thrive in surface waters where light is more plentiful. Small fish, frogs, otters, and birds such as kingfishers are also among the creatures that make these waters their regular hunting place. And in parts of Africa, warm, slow rivers are the natural habitat of hippopotamuses.

The place where a river empties into the sea is called the mouth. A low plain made up of clay, gravel, sand, and other sediments at a river's mouth is known as a delta, and a deep, broad mouth is called an estuary. In an estuary there is a mingling of fresh water and salt water. This mixing creates a new and different kind of environment for life. The most common kind of estuary animal is the oyster. Hundreds of thousands of oysters may cover an estuary's bottom. Shrimps, crabs, and fish such as flounder are typical dwellers of this environment. Sea plants such as turtle grass and sea lettuce can also thrive in the quiet, shallow, salty environment where a river and the ocean meet.

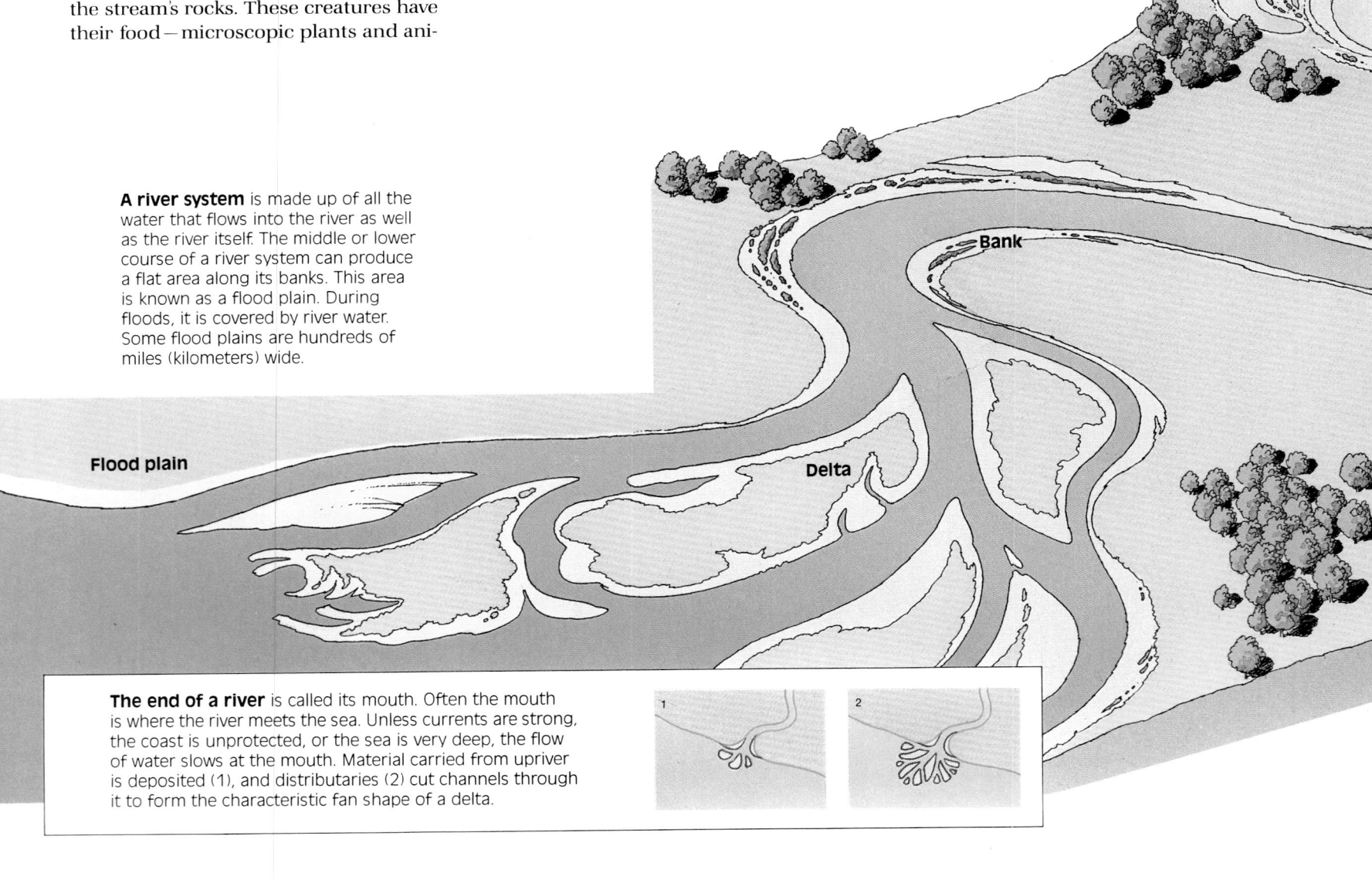

A river system is made up of all the water that flows into the river as well as the river itself. The middle or lower course of a river system can produce a flat area along its banks. This area is known as a flood plain. During floods, it is covered by river water. Some flood plains are hundreds of miles (kilometers) wide.

Flood plain

Bank

Delta

The end of a river is called its mouth. Often the mouth is where the river meets the sea. Unless currents are strong, the coast is unprotected, or the sea is very deep, the flow of water slows at the mouth. Material carried from upriver is deposited (1), and distributaries (2) cut channels through it to form the characteristic fan shape of a delta.

The flow of water in most rivers is fastest in the upper courses. Salmon have to fight to reach their upstream spawning grounds.

A river's slope tends to flatten near the mouth, and the water slows down. Painted turtles are at home in this environment.

Oxbow lake

The muddy Klamath River enters the clean, blue water of the Pacific Ocean north of Redwood National Park in northern California.

Lakes and Ponds

Lakes and ponds are bodies of standing water that are surrounded by land.

Lakes, which are larger than ponds, may be formed in many ways. Some lakes are made by stranded blocks of ice and blocked rivers that result when glaciers melt. Others are formed by the slow accumulation of rain water in volcanic craters. Still others are caused by the gradual filling in of sinkholes with ground water. Sinkholes are depressions in the earth caused by the collapse of underground rock.

Lakes can be fed in many ways. Some lakes are fed by rivers and mountain streams. Others are supplied by underground springs or streams, as well as ground water replenishment. Some lakes have inlets but no outlets. The excess waters of these kinds of lakes do not drain away. Instead, they slowly evaporate.

The presence of a large lake can affect weather conditions for the land around it. In summer, a lake will not get as warm as the surrounding land. Cool winds blowing off the water will help hold down the temperature. In winter, a lake will not cool off as fast as the land does. This will help keep the nearby land warmer, at least until the lake freezes. Then the lake acts the same way as a cold land surface.

Crater Lake is located in an inactive volcano in the Cascade Mountains of Oregon. It is the deepest lake in the United States, measuring 1,932 feet (589 meters).

Lake waters are divided into distinct layers, which are determined by the amount of penetrating sunlight. Each descending layer receives less sunlight than the one above it, unless the water is very clear. Therefore, the deeper a layer is, the colder and darker its waters.

The different layers of a lake are inhabited by distinct communities of animal and plant life. These communities depend on one another for food. For example, microscopic plants that drift in a lake's upper waters are eaten by microscopic animals. Both the tiny plants and the tiny animals are called plankton. Plankton is eaten by fish that live near a lake's surface.

Many kinds of insects live in the upper water of a lake. Whirligig beetles swim in this region. Their divided eyes look both above and below the water. Backswimmers, another type of insect, reside just at the surface, and they swim faceup. Water striders actually walk *upon* the water, which for them is like solid ground. All these insects feed on other insects that fall or alight upon the quiet surface water.

Many of a lake's plants and animals live near the shore, in what is called the littoral zone. Here snails and worms creep on plant stems, and predatory fish lurk among bulrushes and other water plants. In the shallows near the shore, water birds often hunt and use bits of plants as nesting material.

Few of the littoral zone animals or water animals are found on the lake bottom.

There is also little if any plant life there. The main inhabitants include snails and shrimplike crustaceans. These creatures eat the remains of dead plants and animals that drift down from the upper regions of the lake.

A pond is basically a miniature lake that is shallow enough for sunlight to reach the bottom and enable plants to grow there. Many ponds are formed naturally, but a great many are made by people. Most of the same creatures that are found in lakes are also found in ponds. Such creatures include fish, frogs, and water insects. In many cases, eggs and larvae of these animals are brought from one lake or pond to another by water birds. The birds carry the transported material on their feet or in their feathers. The wind is another transporter. It carries plant seeds from one water home to another. The seeds of water plants can also float to new locations.

Many ponds and small, shallow lakes are temporary features. Over time, the build-up of material on the water's floor and the spread of vegetation will fill in a small pond. Eventually it will become a marsh or swamp. Over many hundreds or many thousands of years, climate change, sediment accumulation, and vegetation growth will turn even a large, shallow lake into a wetland.

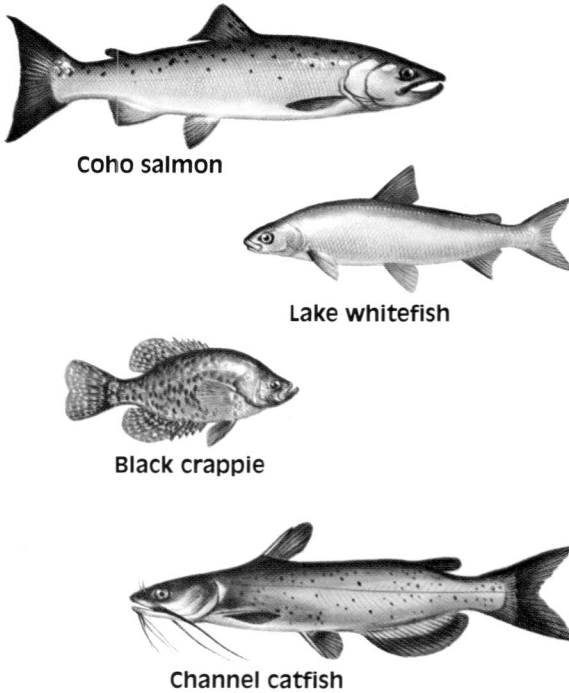

Many species of fish are found in lakes. If a lake freezes over in winter, the fish that live there can swim down to warmer water near the bottom until spring.

Coho salmon

Lake whitefish

Black crappie

Channel catfish

Pond animal and plant life

In a pond, the primary food producers are microscopic plants that use sunlight to make food for primary consumers, such as tadpoles. A fish (secondary consumer) may eat the tadpole. Decomposers complete the food chain by cleaning up the waste and producing chemicals that primary producers use to make food.

The pond environment

The pond environment
1   Common frog (male, x0.5)
2   Starwort (x0.5)
3   Water crowfoot (x0.25)
4   Aplecta hypnorum (x2)
5   Wandering snail (x0.75)
6   Keeled ramshorn snail (x0.5)
7   Curled pondweed (x0.25)
8   Bithynia (x1)
9   Ramshorn snail (x0.3)
10   Water lily root (x0.25)
11   Great pond snail (x0.8)

Near the surface
12   Pond skater (x0.5)
13   Whirligig beetle (x0.25)
14   Water boatman (x1)
15   Nonbiting midge (x5)
16   Mosquito pupa (x5)
17   Dragonfly (male, x0.65)
18   China-marks moth (x0.75)
19   Mayfly (female, x0.2)

Middle depths
20   Water flea (Daphnia, x2.5)
21   Smooth newt (male, x0.5)
22   Cyclops (typical of species, x8)
23   Flagellate (x650)
24   Great diving beetle (male, x1)
25   Hydra (x4)
26   Stickleback (male, x0.5)
27   Common frog tadpole (x1.5)
28   Flagellate (Euglena, x180)
29   Water mite (x5)

The bottom
30   Caddis-fly larva in case
31   Chaetonotus (x150)
32   Horny-orb shell (x1)
33   Tubifex worms (x0.2)
34   Midge larva (x3.5)
35   Pond sponge (x0.2)
36   Leech (Helobdella sp., x4)
37   Water hog-louse (x2.5)
38   Flatworm (x2)

Near the surface

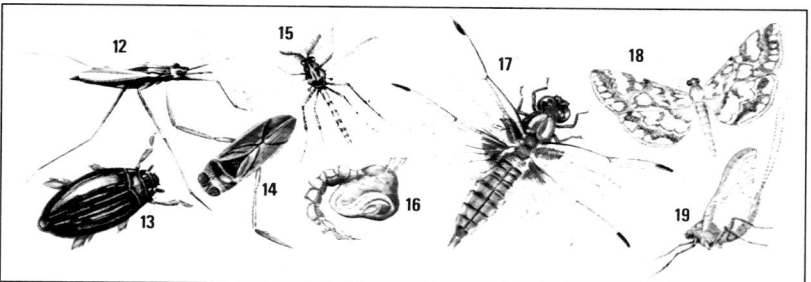

Middle depths

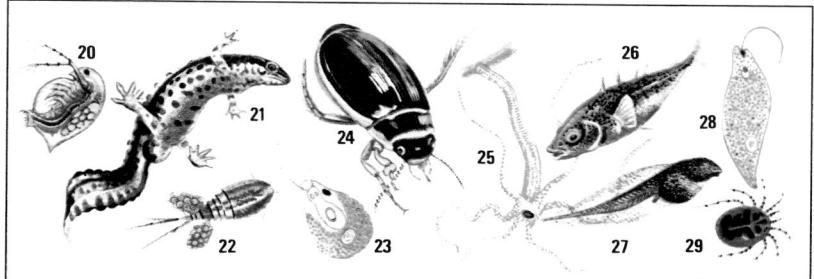

The bottom

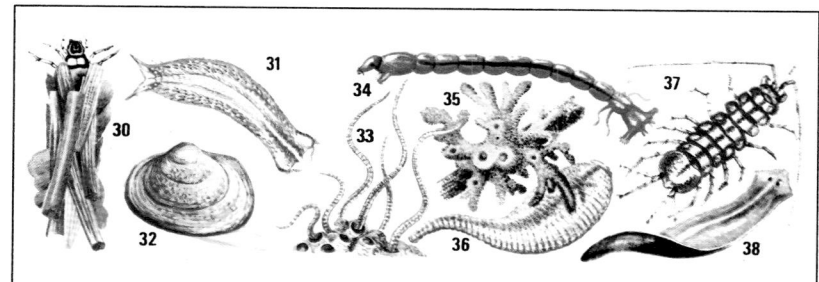

Swamps, Marshes, and Bogs

Okefenokee Swamp, in southeastern Georgia and northeastern Florida, is the home of many animals, including deer, bears, wildcats, otters, raccoons, opossums, and alligators. About two-thirds of the swamp is a government wildlife preserve.

Swamps, marshes, and bogs are known as the earth's wetlands. A wetland is a land area where the water level remains near or above the surface of the ground for most of the year.

Swamps, the first type of wetland, are areas of muddy, watery land covered by trees and bushes. The major kinds of swamps are deepwater, shallow-water, and mangrove.

Deepwater swamps are near large, slow-flowing rivers that flood regularly. These floods spread water over adjoining land. Bald cypress and black gum trees, which thrive in muddy soil, grow easily in such areas. The thick foliage of these trees blocks out much of the sunlight. Thus, only certain kinds of plants can grow on the muddy ground.

Shallow-water swamps are usually found in areas where soil stays moist or water-covered for only part of the year. Bushes and trees such as willows, oaks, and maples, flourish there. Water lilies and similar plants cover the surface of the standing water in springtime.

Unlike the other deepwater and shallow-water swamps that have fresh water, mangrove swamps have salt water. These swamps lie along tropical seacoasts and are named for the mangrove shrubs that grow there.

Swamp water swarms with insects, frogs, and fish. These creatures are food for long-legged birds such as herons and egrets. The birds wade in the water and use their beaks to spear prey. In the tropics and subtropics, swamps are home to alligators, crocodiles, turtles, and snakes. Such animals prefer the combination of hot weather and watery conditions.

Many animals are equally at home in swamps and in inland marshes. Marshes, the second kind of wetland, are flat, treeless areas covered with water. There are, however, animals such as American red-winged blackbirds and muskrats that prefer marshes. Blackbirds nest among the cattails, bulrushes, and other water plants that grow thickly in this environment. Those same plants are food for muskrats and also nesting places for many kinds of waterfowl. Like muskrats, these birds are prey for mink, which live on marshland edges.

An inland marsh is also a major source of food for animals that do not actually inhabit it. Raccoons visit marshes to hunt fish and crayfish in the shallow water. Raccoons also dig up nests of turtle eggs and search for the egg-filled nests of ducks and

other waterfowl. Deer also visit marshes. There, they browse on water lilies, marsh marigolds, grasses, and grasslike plants called sedges.

In addition to inland marshes, there are also saltwater marshes. These form where river deltas empty into the sea. Fish, crabs, oysters, and mussels flourish in salt marshes where salt grasses are abundant. Diving birds such as ospreys are salt marsh dwellers, and gulls are frequent visitors.

Bogs, the third type of wetland, are wet, spongy areas. They are filled with mosses and large amounts of partly decayed plant matter called peat. These environments are usually found in the colder, northern parts of the world. Bogs generally evolve from deep lakes that have become filled with dead, compacted plant material. Sphagnum moss and sedges form a thick mat on the surface of the water. There, wild cranberries, other berry bushes, and a few dwarf trees may grow. Other species of plants that thrive in and around bogs are carnivorous plants such as the sundew, pitcher plant, and Venus's-flytrap. Aside from insects and frogs, few animals live permanently in this type of wetland. But many animals, among them moose and bear, visit bogs in search of food.

In addition to supporting plant and animal communities, wetlands are ecologically valuable in other ways. They can store large amounts of water for long periods of time. And because they hold back water, they help prevent floods.

Bogs, with their acidic soil and water, favor the growth of mosses— especially sphagnum moss, which absorbs water like a sponge.

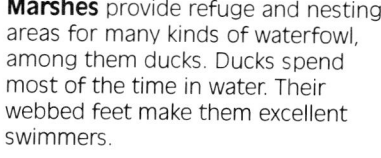

Marshes provide refuge and nesting areas for many kinds of waterfowl, among them ducks. Ducks spend most of the time in water. Their webbed feet make them excellent swimmers.

Tropical Forests

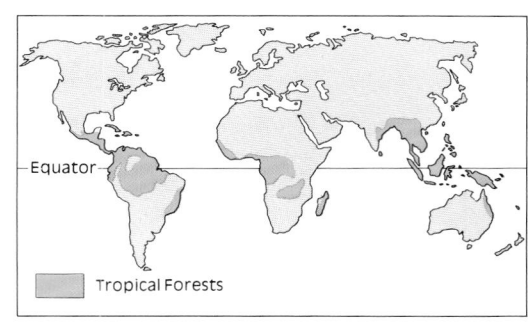

Equator

Tropical Forests

A broad band around the middle of the earth receives the planet's greatest amount of sunlight. This zone, known as the tropics, generally features year-round summer conditions. Humidity and temperatures are constantly high. Days are long and sunny, and many tropical regions are frequently rainy. In this climate, huge forests flourish. They are called tropical rain forests, and they almost always lie near the equator. These forests cover the tropical portions of Africa, Asia, Australia, Central and South America, and the Pacific islands.

Unlike a midlatitude forest, a tropical rain forest has few seasonal temperature changes. Because of the unending summer conditions, most trees in a tropical forest stay green all year. Such trees gradually lose old leaves as they grow new ones. However, there are some deciduous trees in tropical forests that shed all their leaves briefly during the dry season.

Generally all the trees in a tropical rain forest have tall, straight trunks with branches only at the very top. The tops of the trees are called the crowns, and they merge to form a covering of leaves high in the air. This covering is known as the upper canopy. Its thickness blocks most of the sunlight from reaching the forest floor. Because the floor is so dim, few plants can grow there. Mushrooms and other fungi that need little light flourish in this environment.

Orchids, wild pineapples, other flowering plants, and ferns grow high up on the trunks of tropical trees. These plants begin as seeds that are carried by the wind. The seeds lodge within crevices in the tree bark, and are warmed by sunlight. For water, the seeds soak up moisture from the air and rain that runs down the tree trunks.

Forest vines are rooted in the ground. Often they wind up tree trunks and other vines until they reach the treetops. There they can spread out among the leafy branches of the upper canopy. Extremely tall trees called emergents thrust through the upper canopy's vines and branches. Many kinds of insects and insect-eating birds live in the emergents. Large, predatory birds live there too. Such birds include harpy eagles, which prey on the monkeys that live below in the upper canopy.

Monkeys and many other creatures are attracted by the upper canopy's abundance of fruit and nuts. Fruit-eating birds, such as toucans, and leaf-eating mammals, such as sloths, also thrive in the crowns of tall trees. Hummingbirds and brilliantly colored butterflies flutter between the canopy's leaves and flowers. Tree frogs and lizards creep through the upper canopy branches, hunting insects. Snakes lurk among the leaves to capture these creatures. Other residents of the upper canopy include gliding animals such as large bats called flying foxes and flying dragons, a type of lizard.

Not all trees are tall enough to reach the upper canopy. Some full-grown trees can thrive at lower levels in the forest because they do not require an abundance of light. The crowns of these trees form one or two lower canopies that are generally quite sturdy. The lower canopies are inhabited by larger forest animals such as apes and leopards. These animals live both in trees and on the forest floor.

In many parts of a tropical rain forest, tree trunks are spread far apart and few plants grow on the ground. But in places where abundant sunlight is able to reach the ground, there is a thick, tangled growth of bushes and low plants. Such areas are called jungles, and they grow frequently in former clearings and along the banks of wide rivers in the tropical regions of the world.

Upper canopy

Abundant fruits and nuts at this level, from 100 to 150 feet (30 to 45 meters) high, provide food for monkeys, birds, leaf-eating mammals, snakes, tree frogs, and lizards. Well adapted to treetop life, they seldom touch the ground.

Royal python

Tree shrew

Sacred langur

Lower canopy

The crowns of shorter trees support larger creatures that also spend time on the ground. Plants such as orchids and mosses are abundant in the lower canopy, or understory, which rises from 16 to 100 feet (5 to 30 meters) from the forest floor.

Leopard

Orangutan

Pouched tree frog

Shrub layer

Woody shrubs at this layer rarely reach higher than 16 feet (5 meters). The plants spring up to fill the space available between larger, taller trees.

Four-striped squirrel

Oriental civet

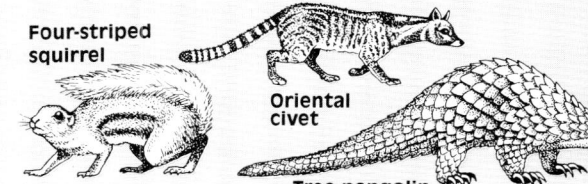

Tree pangolin

Forest floor

The ground layer of the forest is dark. It receives less than 1 per cent of sunlight. Only ferns and other shade-loving plants can survive here. Animals that live here must be able to tolerate high humidity, so insects abound. Many ground-layer mammals have compact bodies that help them move through dense undergrowth.

Okapi

Forest buffalo

Indian tiger

Malayan tapir

Congo forest mouse

Short-eared elephant shrew

Orange-rumped agouti

Mandrill

Emergent layer

The tallest trees in a tropical forest form the emergent layer at around 130 feet (40 meters) or higher. Animal life at this level is mostly birds and insects.

Demidoff's bushbaby

Flying fox

Gray parrot

Flying squirrel

Gold Coast turaco

Chameleon

Chimpanzee

Orchids, which thrive in humid conditions, abound in tropical forests. They range in size from small flowers to huge vines as long as 100 feet (30 meters).

In the dim light near the edge of a Sumatra rain forest, the forest floor is relatively free of plant life.

Layers of the forest

Living conditions at different heights determine what creatures inhabit different layers of the forest. The topmost layers are so high up that only birds and insects are found there. To survive in the dense canopy and middle layer, animals must be streamlined and adapted for climbing. In the high humidity and gloom of the ground layer, insects and fungi break down rotting fruit and leaves from above. These decomposers enrich the soil that feeds the forest.

Deserts

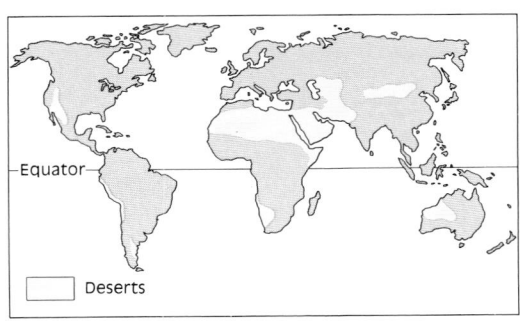

About one-seventh of the earth's land is covered by deserts. In general, deserts are any areas that have little rainfall, dry soil, and a limited amount of very special kinds of plants. But there is no "typical" desert. Some, such as parts of the Sahara, consist mainly of lifeless, rocky surfaces and smaller areas of shifting piles of sand called dunes. Others are limited to rocky, dry areas full of plant and animal life. Those deserts, located in the subtropics, remain searingly hot throughout the year. But others such as the Great Basin and the Gobi Desert are bitterly cold in winter and very hot in summer.

Often a desert will gradually merge with a fertile grassland. But unlike the neighboring grasses, desert plants must cope with a minimal supply of water. Some of these plants have long roots that probe far underground to find water. Others have shallow, widespread roots that absorb the tiniest amounts of dew and rain that soak down from the surface. The leaves of these plants are small, and they often fall off during the dry season.

Many types of desert vegetation flourish only when there is a little rain. After a rainfall, previously inactive seeds quickly germinate and grow into plants. These plants—known as annuals—flower, form more seeds, then die. The new seeds lie dormant until it rains again. The next rainfall, however, may be years away.

Desert plants vary in form from the prickly pear cactus to giant cacti. Many shrub and low tree species also grow in deserts. Such desert plants enable wildlife to live among them. They do this by providing animals with food and moisture. Some desert plants also provide animals with shelter. For example, North American Gila woodpeckers drill holes in giant cacti. In these hollows, the birds raise their families. When they leave, the holes are taken over by other kinds of birds or by lizards, rats, or mice.

Extreme heat can kill an animal. That is why desert creatures must be able to keep their bodies from becoming too hot. There are various ways animals can control their body temperatures. Small creatures, among them insects, snakes, and tiny mammals, hide from the heat. They dig down into the sand and stay there. Or they keep cool in underground burrows or dark crevices in the rocks. Some creatures pant to cool themselves. Others escape the heat by going into a kind of hibernation for days or weeks. During this time, their bodies stay cool. Some desert animals have special body features that help them lose heat. The big ears of a desert fox or jack rabbit are examples of these features. Blood carries body heat up into the thin skin of these animals' ears. From the ears, heat radiates into the dry, hot air of the desert. Thus the body temperature of the animals is lowered.

In addition to surviving the heat, desert animals must be adapted for an environment that has very little water. Desert larks of the Sahara, for example, can thrive for weeks without a drink. Camels and little furry dassies of South Africa can often live without drinking for months. These birds and mammals get moisture from the food they eat. They are also able to store this moisture in their bodies for a long time. There are also desert creatures, among them the kangaroo rat, that never need to drink. Their food gives them all the moisture they require.

Some desert dwellers, however, must find water each day. One such animal is the red kangaroo of the Australian Desert. This large mammal is known for grazing in the dry grasslands that border the desert. Each day, in search of water, the kangaroo must travel from the grasslands to one of the few watering holes in the almost waterless environment of the desert.

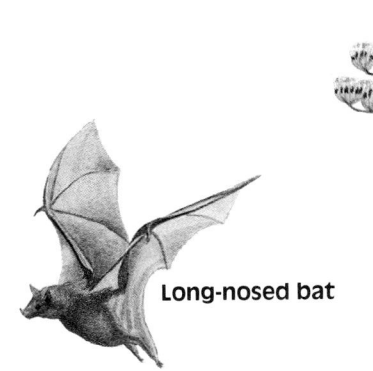

Long-nosed bat

Different deserts are home to different species of plants and animals. All desert creatures and vegetation, however, share the need to obtain and conserve water.

Scattered throughout the world's largest desert, the Sahara, are fertile areas known as oases. The water for Saharan oases comes mainly from springs or underground streams.

Agave

Esparto grass

Monument Valley, Utah, gets bitter-ly cold in winter. Red sandstone formations rise 1,000 feet (300 meters) from the desert floor.

Gila monster

Elf owl

Great horned owl

Fennec fox

Roadrunner

Desert hedgehog

Saguaro cactus

Kangaroo rat

Desert tortoise

Fat sand rat

Dorcas gazelle

Welwitschia

Addax antelope

Grasslands

Between humid forests and arid deserts lie the earth's sun-filled grasslands. These areas, which may be flat or hilly, are literally seas of grasses.

The three types of grasslands are steppes, prairies, and savannas. A grassland is classified into one of these three types according to the average height of the grass that grows there. Plant height depends upon the amount of rainfall received.

Steppes, which are the driest grassland, are covered mainly by short grasses. Most plants in a steppe do not grow over 1 foot (30 centimeters) high. In North America, steppes cover most of the Great Plains. In the Soviet Union, they reach from the southern Ukraine to central Asia.

Prairies, which receive moderate rainfall, are blanketed chiefly by tall grasses. In moist prairies, grass may grow 6 feet (1.8 meters) high or even taller. The North American prairie reaches from central Texas to southern Saskatchewan. Saskatchewan, Alberta, and Manitoba are called Canada's "Prairie Provinces." Other prairies include the Pampa of Argentina.

Savannas are grasslands with widely scattered trees and shrubs. Most savannas are in the tropics, but some are in temperate regions. This type of grassland covers more than two-fifths of Africa and large parts of Australia, South America, and India.

One of the main types of grassland animals is the grazer, or grass-eater. The larger grazers are generally animals that live in herds, such as the American bison and antelope and the African gnu and zebra. In many places, however, wild grazers have been replaced by domesticated grazers such as sheep and cattle. The herds of grass-eaters roam across a grassland, eating as they go. The area they move across looks like a mowed lawn for a time, but the grass quickly grows again unless it is the dry season.

Actually, there are many more small grazers than big ones. Small grazers include many kinds of grasshoppers, ants, aphids, leaf hoppers, and other insects. Just as large predators prey on large grazers, small predators such as birds and mice prey on small grazers.

Many kinds of flowering plants such as sunflowers, prairie clover, and cornflowers grow in grasslands. They produce seeds and leaves that are eaten by the region's wildlife, which includes jack rabbits and colonies of prairie dogs. There are many predators of these seed- and leaf-eaters. All grasslands contain snakes, which hunt for prey among the grass stems. But in addition to being the hunter, snakes are also the hunted. The sky over a grassland is the natural range for hawks and other birds of prey that will swoop down to seize snakes, as well as rabbits.

In tropical savannas, the temperature stays hot all year, so life goes on unchanged, except for alternating rainy and dry seasons. But the steppes and prairies have warm summers and cool to cold winters. In most of these regions the grassland life is curtailed by cold weather. The ground freezes and the grass stops growing. Much of the insect life dies or burrows underground. The insect-eating birds migrate to other regions. Most of the smaller animals hibernate or remain in burrows through the cold season, living on stored food. But with the coming of spring and the thawing of the ground, the grasslands quickly return to life.

Much of the world's grasslands have been turned into farmland where wheat and corn, which are actually grasses, are grown. Even in man-made grasslands, however, much of the same life which may be found in a natural grassland exists. Insects, birds, small mammals, and other creatures thrive among the cultivated grasses.

American buffalo, or bison, live in herds and graze on the grasses and small plants found on American prairies.

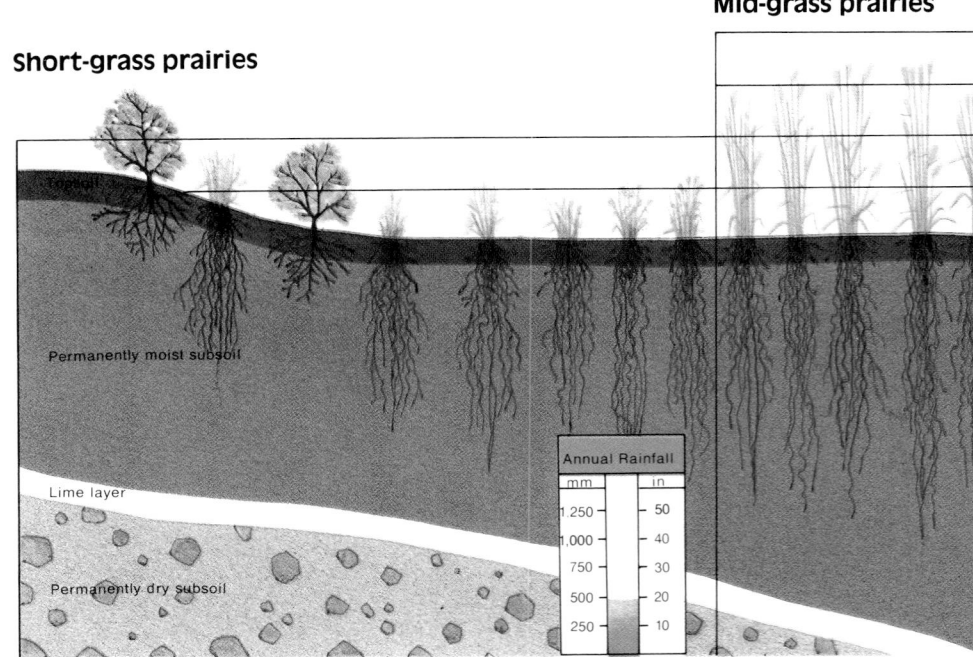

Short-grass prairies

Mid-grass prairies

Topsoil

Permanently moist subsoil

Lime layer

Permanently dry subsoil

Annual Rainfall

mm	in
1,250	50
1,000	40
750	30
500	20
250	10

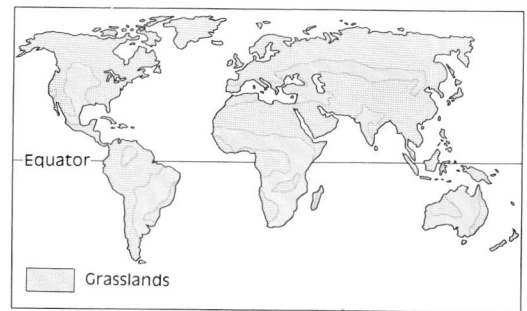

Equator

Grasslands

Red-tailed hawk

Western meadowlark

Burrowing owl

Grassland creatures solve the problem of survival by adapting to the environment in various ways. Many, such as small burrowing animals and certain invertebrates, seek protection underground. The marsupial mole lives almost entirely underground, while the prairie dog surfaces to eat. Snakes, of course, are well adapted for the pursuit of burrowing creatures. Small carnivores like the pampas cat often surprise their victims. Certain grassland predators rely on speed for catching prey—as do some of the creatures they hunt in the race for survival. The sharp-eyed hawk rides thermal winds in search of food, while the meadowlark adapts to a mostly treeless environment by singing to declare its territory. Camouflage protects many insects.

Rainfall determines what grasses grow where on the North American prairies. In general, the drier the climate, the shorter the grasses. In regions where annual rainfall is no more than 20 inches (500 millimeters), only short grass—with short root systems—can survive in the relatively narrow layer of permanently moist subsoil. As the depth of the subsoil increases, it can support the longer root systems of mid-grass and tall-grass prairies. Tall bluestem and Indian grass predominate in the regions where annual rainfall measures 40 inches (1,000 millimeters). The North American prairie includes most of Oklahoma, Kansas, Nebraska, Iowa, Illinois, South Dakota, and North Dakota, and parts of neighboring states and provinces. Alberta, Saskatchewan, and Manitoba are the "Prairie Provinces" of Canada.

Saiga

American bison

European hare

Guanaco

Springhaas

Marbled polecat

Pampas cat

Gopher snake

Marsupial mole

Prairie dog

European souslik

Viscacha

Lubber grasshopper

Praying mantis

Tumble bug

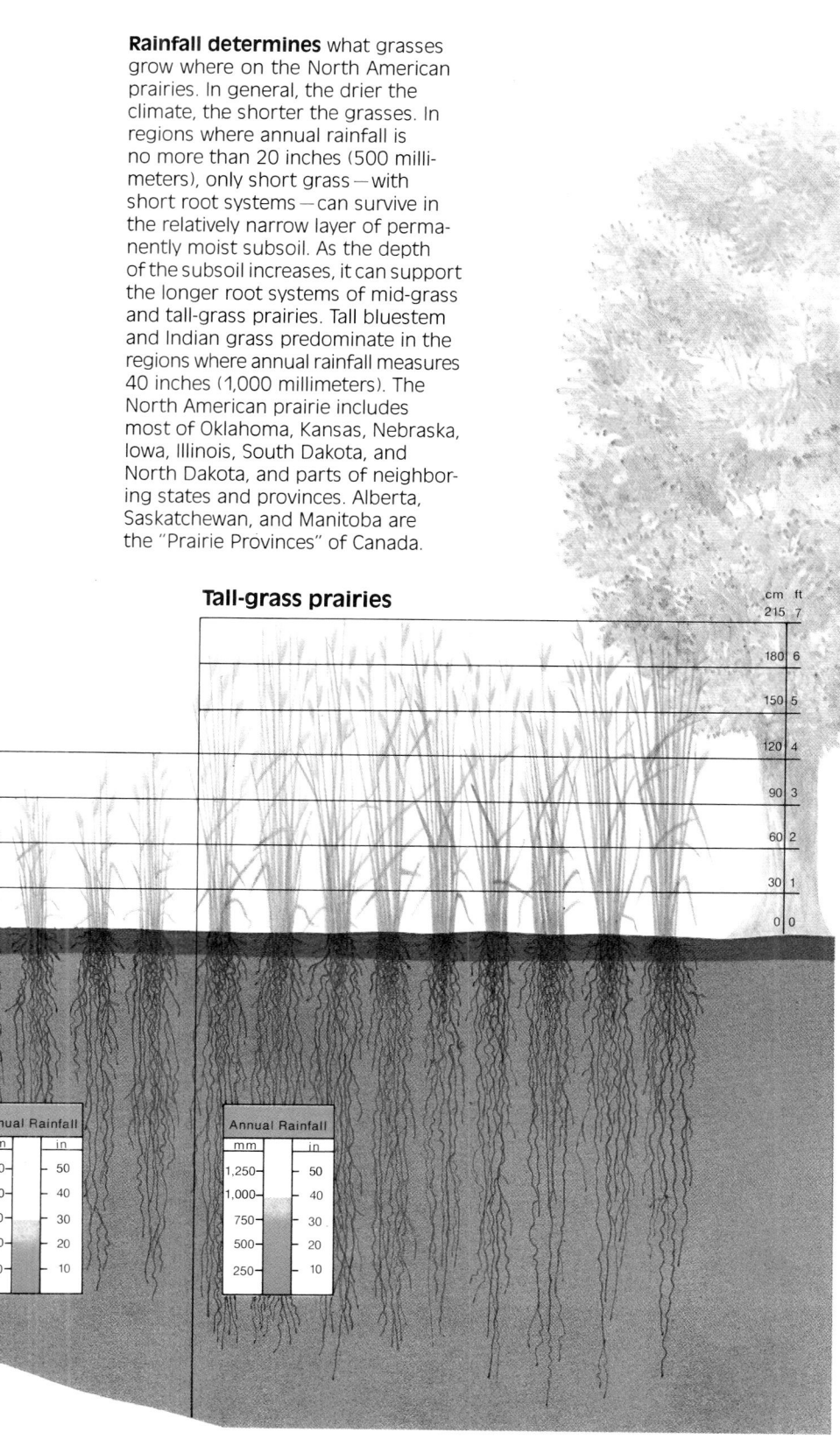

Tall-grass prairies

cm	ft
215	7
180	6
150	5
120	4
90	3
60	2
30	1
0	0

Annual Rainfall	
mm	in
1,250	50
1,000	40
750	30
500	20
250	10

Annual Rainfall	
mm	in
1,250	50
1,000	40
750	30
500	20
250	10

Midlatitude Forests

The earth's midlatitude regions lie between the polar circles and the tropics. Here, the seasonal climate ranges from warm summers to cold winters and, in some places, offers distinct dry and rainy seasons.

Deciduous trees, those with broad leaves shed annually, grow best in midlatitude regions where it is warm and moist at least four to five months a year. They are the main trees of most midlatitude forests, but many kinds of needle-leaved or broad-leaved evergreens also thrive in such a climate.

Midlatitude forests once covered eastern North America, western Europe, and eastern Asia. Changes in climate, together with activities such as forestry and farming, have reduced these forests to small areas.

Ground water generally freezes in midlatitude regions during winter. Thus, deciduous trees cannot draw up water into their leaves, and the leaves cannot tolerate freezing. This is why trees shed their leaves in autumn and stand bare during winter. However, evergreens can hold water in their needles throughout wintertime. This is how they can remain green all year.

In spring, when the ground begins to thaw, small flowers of the forest floor are first to bloom. Buds soon appear on trees and bushes, and burst into pastel-colored flowers and tiny, pale-green leaves. Hibernating creatures stir. Birds return from the warm lands where they spent winter. Insect and spider eggs, produced in autumn, now hatch by the millions.

Summer days are long and filled with sunshine and frequent rain. During this season, the tree leaves grow and become dark green with the substance called chlorophyll. Leaves are a tree's foodmakers. Using sunlight for power, their chlorophyll turns water absorbed by the roots and carbon dioxide from the air into sugars.

To get at this food in the leaves, leaf-eating insects, such as aphids, grasshoppers, and caterpillars, swarm among the upper branches of the trees. Many predatory insects and spiders live there too, preying on the leaf-eaters. And such a plentiful supply of insects and spiders attracts a variety of insect-eating birds.

The tops of the taller deciduous trees form the roof, or canopy, of the forest. The canopy is the home of insects, spiders, songbirds, squirrels, and nocturnal flying squirrels. Beneath the canopy is a second "layer" of trees called the understory. Some young trees in this layer must grow into the sunlight or they will die. Others are low-growing trees that do not need as much sunlight.

Beneath the understory is a layer of shrubs. These shrubs produce berries and seeds that are a source of food for mice and chipmunks. Under the bushes, upon the forest floor, are low-growing flowering plants, ferns, and mosses, which do not need much sunlight to make their food. Mushrooms also grow there. They need little sunlight, for they take their food from the rotting, decaying things on which they grow. Grouse, woodcocks, and pheasants feed on this vegetation. Deer also browse on the forest floor, and insects swarm there and are hunted by mice, frogs, and toads. They in turn are preyed upon by snakes, foxes, and raccoons.

In late summer, deciduous trees begin to prepare for winter. A layer of corklike substance grows where each leaf stem is attached to the branch. No more water can reach the leaves. Their green color fades, and their true color, generally yellow or orange, is seen. After chlorophyll breaks down, red or purple pigments form in a dying leaf.

With no water, the leaves die, turn brown, and wither. Autumn wind and rains tear them loose to swirl to the ground. There, they become food for mushrooms, other fungi, and tiny animals. These will help turn the leaves into the soil of the forest floor. The seasonal cycle is now complete, and winter is approaching.

Seasonal climate is an important feature of midlatitude forests. Deciduous trees, which lose their leaves each autumn, flourish in such an environment.

Mushrooms get their nourishment from dead matter, such as fallen leaves.

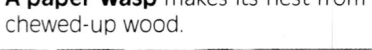
A paper wasp makes its nest from chewed-up wood.

A flying squirrel can spread its legs and glide through the air from tree to tree.

Midlatitude forests provide food and shelter for many animals and for a variety of plants.

Hazel Mouse

Acorn Woodpecker

American Black Bear

European Woodcock

Stag Beetle

Bluebell

Hepatica

Equator

Midlatitude Forests

Subarctic Cold Lands

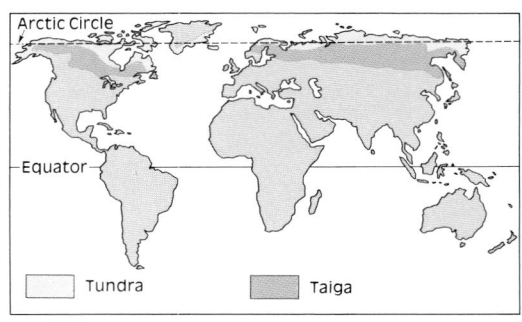

The transitional area between tundra and taiga is marked by shrubs, grasses, and the shoots of deciduous trees.

The dry, treeless, subarctic cold lands that lie near the Arctic Ocean are called arctic tundras. They include the northern parts of North America, Europe, and Asia. For three to four months a year, the sky over arctic tundras is dark both day and night. Beneath the darkened sky, snow blankets the frozen ground.

Change occurs on the tundra in spring, when the northern part of the earth is tilted toward the sun. This causes the tundra sky to lighten. Sunlight melts the snow and thaws the land's upper layer of soil, which is about one-foot (30 centimeters) deep. Below this layer is the perpetually frozen ground known as permafrost.

Plants that have been dormant through the months of darkness abruptly burst into bloom in springtime. These plants are tough, low-growing, and ground-hugging. They include mosses, lichens, grasses, and small flowering plants such as bilberries and bearberries. The very cold winters with strong winds prevent plants from growing higher than the depth of the protective snow. Therefore, no full-size trees can survive on the tundra. Some willow shrubs, however, grow 3 to 10 feet (91 to 305 centimeters) high on slopes and valleys where winter snows are deep.

In spring and summer, the many flowering plants of the tundra turn the region into a sea of color. Arctic foxes, ermines, and snowy owls prey on the little mouselike lemming and arctic hare that search the tundra for tender leaves. Birds such as the willow ptarmigan nest and raise their young among the flowers. Mosquitoes, midges, and black flies are everywhere. Polar bears may leave the icepack and come on land to find food. Caribou, reindeer, and musk oxen browse on plants and are hunted by packs of wolves.

When earth tilts away from the sun, winter returns suddenly. In late August or early September, the ground freezes and snow begins to fall. Most birds and animals migrate southward during winter, but some live year-round on the tundra. Lemmings spend the winter in nests of leaves and feed on the green shoots of flowering plants and mosses. In winter, herds of shaggy musk oxen use their broad hoofs to search for grasses buried beneath the snow in patches.

The tundra regions spread southward for hundreds of miles until they reach regions that are slightly warmer. There, where the ground thaws more in summer, short trees grow far apart from one anoth-

er. A little farther south, taller trees grow closer and closer together until they form vast, thick stretches of forest. This is the northern, boreal forest, or taiga. It covers much of Canada and the northern parts of the Scandinavian countries and the Soviet Union.

The trees of the taiga are mainly needle-leaf evergreens, such as the white spruce. A few species of hardy deciduous trees, among them birches, are also present. Mosses, lichens, and very few flowering plants cover the forest floor.

Throughout winter, trees in the taiga stand heaped with snow. Elk, caribou, reindeer, and moose graze through the forests. As they go, they eat shrubs, grasses, and shoots of deciduous trees. Snowshoe hare, squirrels, and ptarmigan are abundant and preyed on by lynxes, martins, and wolves. Bears spend their winters in the taiga in long periods of sleep or in complete hibernation.

In spring, the snow melts, soaking into the ground. This provides the taiga with a new supply of water for all the trees. Mosquitoes and horseflies swarm. Birds arrive. Hibernating animals become active. Like the tundra, the taiga teems with life through the short, warm summer.

Flowers, mosses, and lichens carpet the tundra when springtime relieves the long months of darkness. To survive, they must reproduce before the first snows come in September.

With the spring thaws, bears emerge from their winter hibernation to forage along the banks of the McNeil River in Alaska.

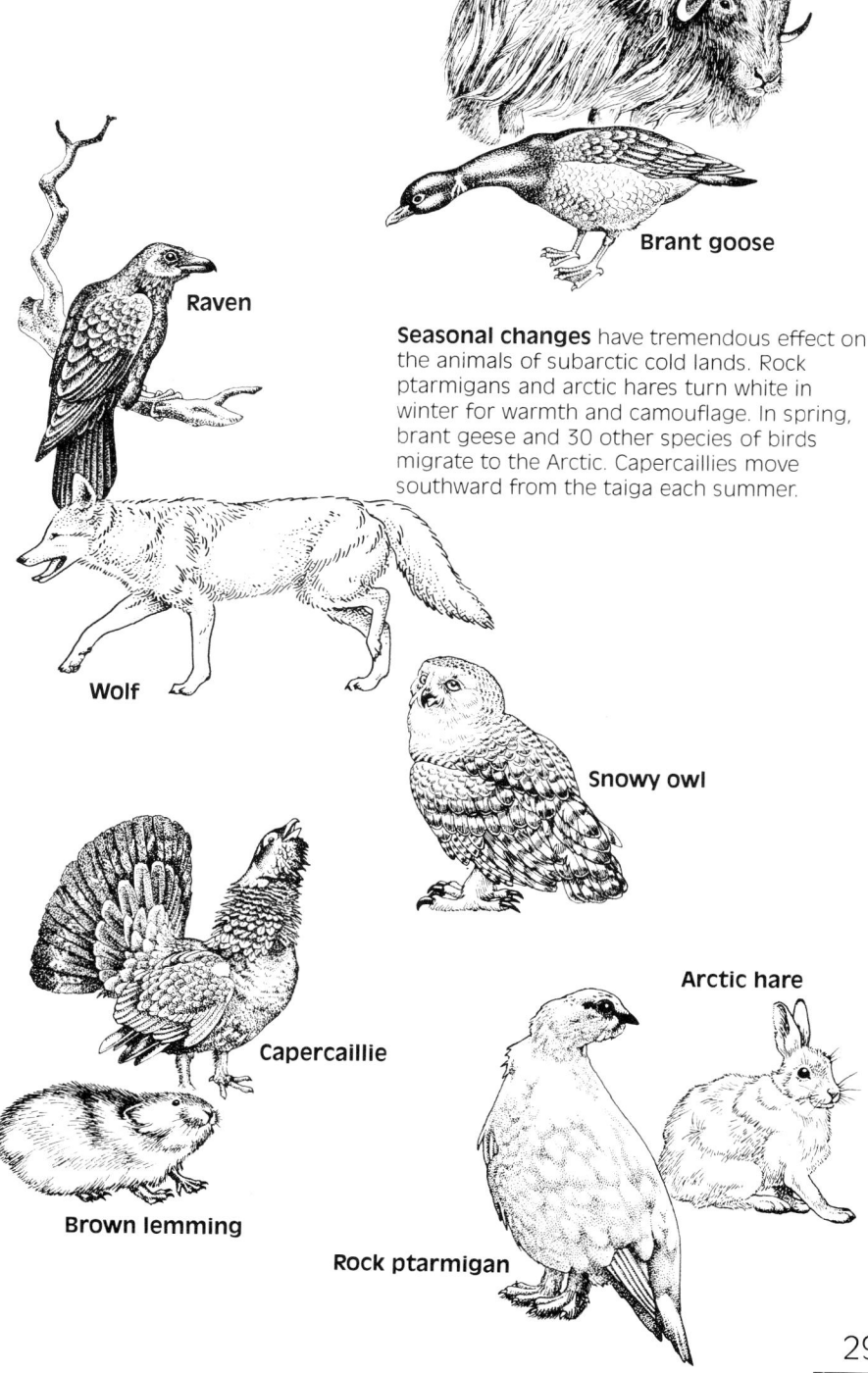

Musk ox

Brant goose

Raven

Seasonal changes have tremendous effect on the animals of subarctic cold lands. Rock ptarmigans and arctic hares turn white in winter for warmth and camouflage. In spring, brant geese and 30 other species of birds migrate to the Arctic. Capercaillies move southward from the taiga each summer.

Wolf

Snowy owl

Capercaillie

Arctic hare

Brown lemming

Rock ptarmigan

Polar Caps

The polar caps are regions of permanent ice and snow located at earth's North and South Poles. These regions are the parts of the planet that receive the least sunlight. During four months of winter, no sunlight touches either pole. In summer, much of the continuous light that does reach the poles is reflected into space by the glare of snow.

The two polar caps are very different from one another. The North Pole lies on a frozen sea, the Arctic Ocean. The South Pole sits upon the continent of Antarctica, which is covered by a layer of ice and snow at least a mile (1.6 kilometers) deep. The ice at the North Pole is frozen salty seawater, but the ice covering Antarctica is frozen fresh water — the largest concentration of fresh water in the world.

These frozen regions are deserts for plants. Animal life, however, does exist in the seas at both polar caps. Many kinds of fish, including the 8- to 14-foot (2.4- to 4.2-meter) long polar shark, live beneath the ice in the Arctic Ocean waters. Seals and walruses are also at home in the sea, and it is there that they find their food. Seals eat mainly fish, while walruses dive to the ocean floor to scoop up clams and other shellfish. Even in the coldest waters, these large mammals are kept warm by their extremely thick skin and layer of blubber. Of course, seals and walruses are air breathers. Thus, they must find or make openings in the ice so they can put their noses above water and breathe.

At the north polar cap, polar bears roam over the ice hunting for seals and other animals. These bears are excellent swimmers, and their thick, dense fur keeps them warm in freezing water. The fur's white color helps the animals blend in against their environment. Thus camouflaged, a bear can wait on ice near a seal's breathing hole and seize an unsuspecting victim when it comes up for air.

Several kinds of whales also make the Arctic Ocean their home. Such whales include the beluga, or white whale, and the narwhal. The narwhal is a small whale that has a maximum length of 18 feet (5.4 meters). Male narwhals have long, spiral tusks that jut from the mammals' upper jaw. The much larger bowhead whale is also an inhabitant of the Arctic Ocean.

The sea around Antarctica is the summer home of several species of whales that feed on small, shrimplike creatures called krill. These include blue, fin, humpback, and right whales. Southern bottlenose and southern fourtooth whales, which feed on squid and fish, are also Antarctic residents. Killer whales swim year-round in the cold Antarctic waters, preying on penguins, seals, and smaller whales in addition to fish and squid. A number of seal species, including krill-eating Antarctic fur seals and crabeater seals, aggressive leopard seals, and massive southern elephant seals, nest on the Antarctic coastline or on nearby islands.

The main creature found on land at the southern pole cap is the penguin, a flightless bird that walks with a clumsy waddle. One species of penguin, the emperor penguin, lays eggs and rears its young on the snow-covered slopes of Antarctica during winter. The birds' feathers and layers of fat keep them warm. To keep their eggs warm, the male birds hold them on their feet and cover them with their bellies.

Although they are at home on land for several months of the year, penguins are primarily sea creatures. Emperor penguins are superb swimmers that live on fish, and the birds spend months at a time in cold, polar waters.

A mother polar bear usually has twin cubs. Most cubs stay with their mother for about two years.

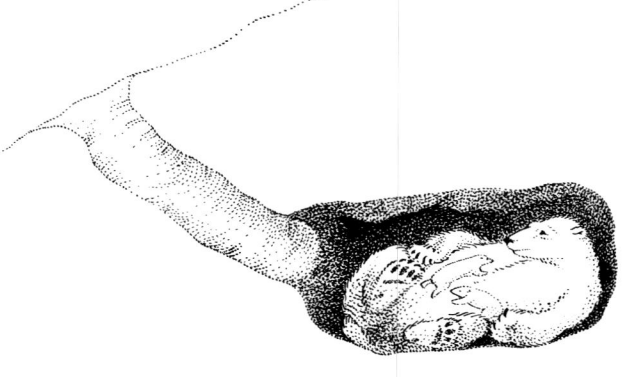

Polar bears live in underground shelters called dens during the colder months. Bears usually dig their dens in deep snowbanks.

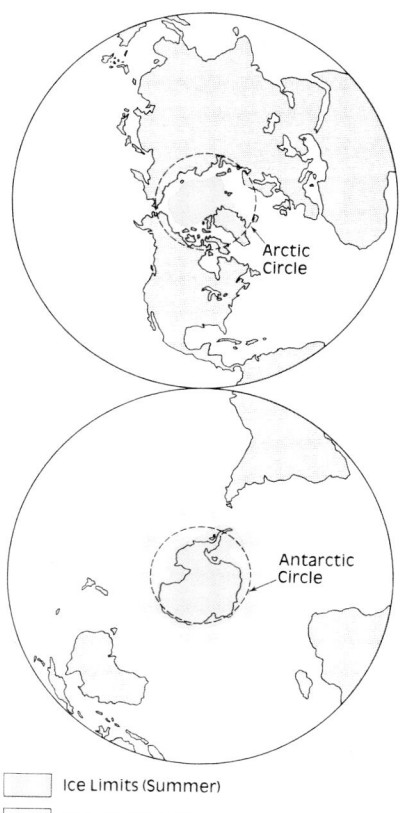

Arctic
Circle

Antarctic
Circle

Ice Limits (Summer)
Ice Limits (Winter)

Penguins have adapted to Antarctic
conditions with short, dense feathers,
thick layers of fat, webbed feet, and
wings that serve as flippers.

The Antarctic landscape is made up
of mountains, glaciers, and dry valleys,
like those shown at the left. A dry
valley is an ice-free rocky area carved
out by a glacier that has retreated.
Wind sweeps away most of the snow
that falls in dry valleys.

Blue whales and crabeater seals eat
millions of tons of krill, the Antarctic's
chief food source. Leopard seals
and killer whales prey on penguins.

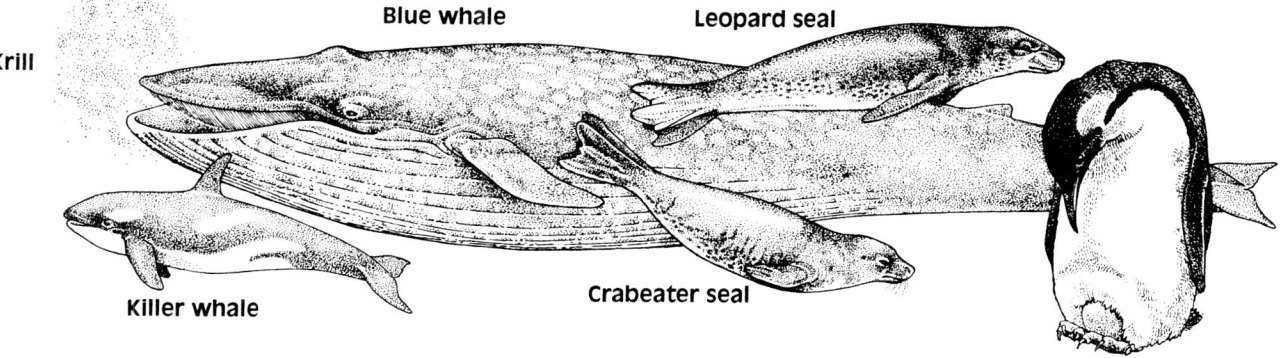

Krill

Blue whale

Leopard seal

Killer whale

Crabeater seal

Emperor penguin

Looking at Earth's

Rockefeller Center Plaza in New York City, New York, U.S.

Rice fields in the Yangtze Valley, China

Supermarket in Luanda, Angola

People and Their Land

BILLIONS OF PEOPLE live on earth. They live on all the planet's land, from frozen polar caps to tropical regions. Their ways of life range from simple cultures to complex societies. People are the most adaptable of earth's creatures.

North America

The continent of North America extends from islands in the frozen Arctic Ocean southward to the tropical country of Panama, the connecting link to South America. North America includes Greenland, Canada, the United States, Mexico, Guatemala, Honduras, Nicaragua, Costa Rica, Panama, El Salvador, Belize, and the islands of the West Indies. These places are home to people who speak many different languages and have vastly different ways of life.

Greenland, the world's largest island, has been the home of Inuit people, or Eskimos, for about 5,000 years. Eric the Red, a Norse chieftain, discovered Greenland about A.D. 982. In 1721, Norwegians established a mission and trading center on the island. Today, Greenland is a province of Denmark, and Greenlanders are mostly a mixture of Danish and Inuit. They speak an Inuit language called Greenlandic, but many also speak Danish.

American Indians and Inuit were living in what is now Canada when the first European settlers arrived from France in the 1600's. For a time, Canada was a colony of France, but Great Britain gained control of most of it in 1763. Thousands of English, Scottish, and Irish colonists then began to arrive. In the late 1800's and in the 1900's, especially after World War II, people from other parts of Europe came to Canada.

Those people were chiefly from Germany, Italy, and Hungary. Today, about forty per cent of all Canadians are of British or Irish descent. About a fourth have French ancestry, and another fourth are from other parts of Europe. There are also still about 350,000 American Indians and 25,000 Inuit in Canada. The language most widely spoken in the world's second-largest country is English. French, however, is spoken by most people in the province of Quebec.

The United States has been called a "melting pot" because its people are a mixture from all over the world. The first permanent European settlement in what is now the United States was founded by Spaniards in 1565. In the 1600's and 1700's, many people from England, as well as some from the Netherlands, Sweden, and France, founded colonies on the east coast. Some of these people brought with them black slaves from Africa. During the 1600's, 1700's, and 1800's, many people from all parts of Europe migrated to the new land, but since most of the first colonists had been British, English became the main language. In the 1800's, many Chinese men were brought to help work on the railroads, and eventually they sent for their families. During the 1900's, immigrants from Japan, India, Pakistan, and other parts of Asia came to the United States. Also in the 1900's, people from Mexico and Latin America immigrated to the United States. And the country is

still the home of about 1,400,000 American Indians.

Mexico, Guatemala, Honduras, Nicaragua, Costa Rica, Panama, and El Salvador were all colonized in the 1500's and 1600's by people from Spain. The colonists intermarried with the American Indians who were already living there. Thus, the people of these countries are nearly all a mixture of Spanish and American Indian. There are also, however, some black people whose ancestors were from Africa.

The languages of all these countries settled by Spain is Spanish, but many people, especially in the small towns, still speak American Indian languages. English is the official language of Belize, another country that has a racially mixed population. About half the people have full or partial black African ancestry, about two-fifths have American Indian ancestry, and most of the rest of the people are of European, East Indian, Chinese, or Lebanese descent.

In the 1500's and 1600's, most of the West Indies islands were colonized by people from Spain, England, France, and the Netherlands. Most of the people now on many other islands are descendants of black Africans originally brought there as slaves. Others are descendants of European colonists. Depending on who were the original colonists of an island, the main spoken language is Spanish, English, or French.

A jungle village in Mexico's Chiapas Highlands climbs steeply up the mountainside. The area has great blocklike mountains cut by broad, deep valleys.

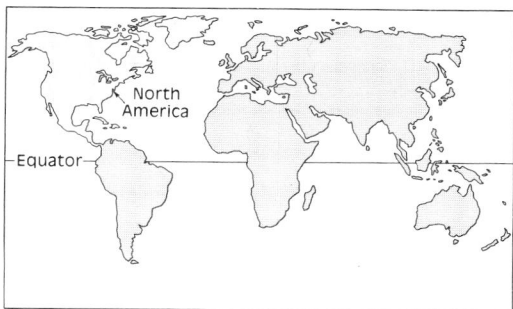

Schoolchildren in Chicago, Illinois, reflect the city's rich ethnic variety.

The city of Quebec is the capital of the province of Quebec, Canada. Street signs on Rue Champlain in the old section of the city are in French, the language of most of Quebec's residents.

South America

The continent of South America extends from a northernmost corner of land in the warm Caribbean Sea southward to a cold, tiny island only some 600 miles from the tip of snow-covered Antarctica. Between those points lie the continent's 12 independent countries. In order of size, those countries are: Brazil, Argentina, Peru, Colombia, Bolivia, Venezuela, Chile, Paraguay, Ecuador, Guyana, Uruguay, and Suriname. South America also includes French Guiana, an overseas department (administrative district) of France, and the Falkland Islands, a British dependency.

The equator runs through the northern part of South America, and more than three-fourths of the continent is in the tropics. A huge tropical rain forest covers more than one-third of the land mass, and the world's longest mountain range above sea level, the Andes, spans the entire west coast.

South America was inhabited by millions of American Indians for about 15,000 years before the first European explorers arrived. Some of the ancient peoples were quite primitive, but others achieved a fairly high degree of civilization. For example, the Inca established a great empire.

In the 1500's and 1600's, South America was explored and colonized by Europeans, chiefly from Spain and Portugal. For 300 years, the parts of South America that are now the nations of Argentina, Bolivia, Chile, Colombia, Ecuador, Paraguay, Peru, Uruguay, and Venezuela, were Spanish colonies. Many people in these countries today are descendants of Spanish colonists, and a great many are descended from Spaniards and American Indians who intermarried. The main language in these countries is Spanish. But there are still many American Indians, especially in Bolivia, Ecuador, and Peru, who speak their ancient languages. Peru, in fact, has two official languages. One is Spanish, and the other is Quechua, the country's chief Indian tongue.

Brazil covers almost half the continent. The country was settled by colonists from Portugal, and the main language of Brazil today is Portuguese. About half of South America's people live in Brazil. It is the world's sixth largest nation in population. Many Brazilians are descended from Portuguese colonists and other Europeans. Many others are descendants of Europeans and American Indians, or of Europeans and black African slaves. Still others are Asians, chiefly Japanese.

The small country of Suriname was ruled by the Netherlands during most of the period from 1667 until 1975, when it gained independence. Today Suriname is officially a Dutch-speaking country. Its population is made up of people of a great many backgrounds. Many of these people are Hindustanis, descendants of people from India. Others are of mixed European and black African ancestry. The population also includes blacks, Chinese, and Indonesians. A few American Indian tribes still live in the rain forests that cover much of the nation.

The country of Guyana was a British colony from 1831 to 1966, and its official language is English. But more than half of Guyana's population is made up of East Indians whose ancestors were brought from India to work on plantations. The rest of the country's people are blacks, American Indians, Europeans, and Chinese. Many of these people speak their own language, as well as English.

French Guiana became an overseas department of France in 1946. French is the district's official language. Most of the people's ancestors were black African, European, or both.

The Falkland Islands are a dependency of Great Britain, but the islands are also claimed by Argentina. Most of the islanders, however, are British people, and the main language is English.

A farmer inspects his sugar cane field in Brazil, one of the fastest-growing nations in the world.

Buenos Aires, Argentina, is the nation's capital and largest city, as well as its chief port and leading industrial center.

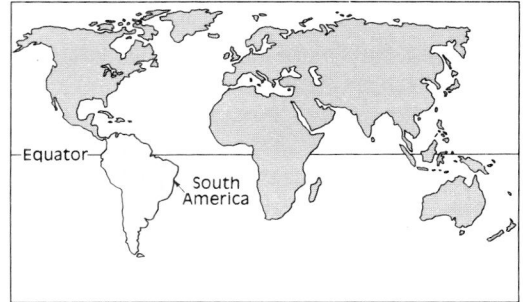

Markets like this one in the Peruvian highlands are a main source of both income and recreation for farmers. Conversation is exchanged along with goods and money.

Argentina's gauchos are typically people of mixed Amerindian and European ancestry. Gauchos chiefly work as ranch hands on estates or large ranches known as estancias.

Europe

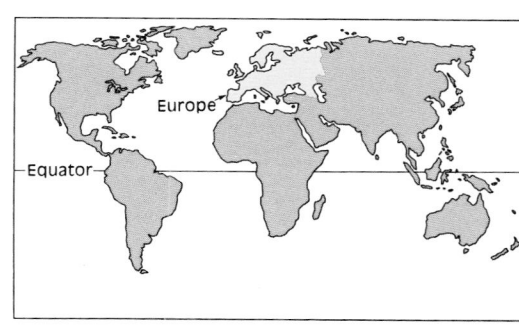

The land mass known as the continent of Europe is actually a huge peninsula — a piece of land nearly surrounded by water — that extends westward from the continent of Asia. Geographers say that Europe begins at the Ural Mountains in the Soviet Union and reaches into the Atlantic Ocean. There it includes the British Isles, Iceland, and a large number of small islands. From north to south, Europe extends from the Arctic Ocean to the Mediterranean Sea. In terms of area, Europe is smaller than any other continent, except Australia. In terms of population, it is packed with more people than any other continent, except Asia.

Europe currently includes 34 countries. These range in size from the world's biggest country, the Soviet Union, to its smallest one, Vatican City. Vatican City, which is the administrative center of the Roman Catholic Church, consists of only 0.17 of a square mile (0.44 square kilometer).

Europe is often called the birthplace of Western civilization. Most of the major scientific, philosophical, and political ideas affecting the Western world were developed by Europeans.

The majority of the people living in Europe today are descended from primitive tribes that lived there thousands of years ago. The members of these tribes and their descendants did not always remain in the same areas. Throughout the centuries of European history, various groups of people have moved around and settled in different countries. As a result, many European countries are inhabited by several ethnic groups — people who share a common ancestry, language, religion, and way of life. For example, there are the Flemings and the Walloons in Belgium and the Czechs and the Slovaks in Czechoslovakia. The members of the various ethnic groups within a country may all think of themselves as citizens of the same country. Still, they are likely to associate mainly with the people of their own ethnic group and to marry members of that same group.

About 50 different languages are spoken in Europe. Often, people in various parts of a country speak a dialect of that country's language. Every dialect has its own pronunciation and sentence structure and may even have its own vocabulary. The same language, then, may be spoken differently in different parts of a country. There are more than 100 different dialects among the languages of Europe.

In many European countries, more than one language is spoken. Ireland, for example, has two official languages — English and Gaelic. Everyone in Ireland speaks English, and about 30 per cent of the Irish people can speak Gaelic too. Gaelic is a form of the language spoken by the ancient Celts, from whom many of the Irish are descended. Switzerland has three official languages and four national languages. The official languages are German, French, and Italian. The national languages are the three official languages plus Romansh. Romansh, which is similar to Latin, is spoken by only about 1 per cent of the Swiss population.

Throughout Europe, many people can speak a second language, usually the language of the foreign country nearest to them. In the western part of Europe, a great number of people also speak English.

Europeans are generally light-skinned, and many are light-haired. However, in recent years, people of other racial groups from other continents have moved to Europe, chiefly to find jobs. Those people are now Europeans. Just as the Americas may be viewed as "melting pots," so has Europe become a place where people of various national and cultural backgrounds live together.

The Berlin Wall, built in 1961 to separate Communist East Berlin from West Berlin, was opened in November 1989 by the East German government. Thousands of Berliners gathered at the wall to celebrate East Germany's new freedom. Several other Eastern European countries began the process of democratic reform in 1989.

Crowds gather for the pope's weekly audience in the Square of Saint Peter in Vatican City. Vatican City is the world's smallest independent state. It lies entirely within the city of Rome, Italy.

Agriculture employs more Romanians than any other activity. Families work together on the nation's collective farms. To a large extent, the farmers rely on old-fashioned farm equipment.

Asia

The largest continent, Asia, includes almost one-third of all the earth's land. The northernmost part of the continent, which is the tip of Siberia in the Soviet Union, lies in the bitter cold of the Arctic Circle. The southernmost part, the islands of Indonesia, lies in the simmering tropics near the equator. From west to east, Asia stretches across the earth from Africa and Europe to the Pacific Ocean. Examples of every known kind of plant-and-animal habitat, from tundra to tropical rain forest, can be found in Asia.

This vast area houses about 60 per cent of all the world's people. A variety of races and many different ethnic groups inhabit Asia. The population of the continent is divided among 41 independent nations and three other political units—the British dependency, Hong Kong; the Portuguese territory, Macao; and the Egyptian military administration, the Gaza Strip. The smallest unit is the Maldives, a group of islands in the Indian Ocean, with a population of about 215,000. The largest is gigantic China, with a population of more than one billion.

Few people live in large areas of Asia because those areas are either too cold, too hot, too mountainous, or too dry. The result is that Asians are jammed tightly into the places where the climate and the physical features of the land are more agreeable. Most of these people live in valleys, near rivers, or on the seacoast.

Different groups of Asians often differ greatly from each other in appearance. Most of the people in Southwest Asian countries such as Saudi Arabia and Turkey resemble Europeans. Some Asians, however, have darker skin and hair. People of southern India have dark skins and straight hair. Inhabitants of the Indonesian part of New Guinea and other islands of Southeast Asia have brown or yellow skins and curly hair. The people of most of East Asia, those who live in countries such as China and Japan, have yellowish to brownish skin and dark straight hair.

Numerous languages and dialects are spoken throughout Asia. Often, many different languages are spoken within the same country. In India alone, there are 16 major languages and more than 1,000 minor languages and dialects. Thus, the people of one village may not speak the same language as the people of the neighboring village. These language differences often cause serious problems in matters of education and commerce.

Ways of life, too, are often very different in various parts of Asia. In Southwest Asia, about half of the people are farmers. Most of them live, dress, and work in much the same way as their ancestors have always done. On the other hand, about 77 per cent of the people of Japan live and work in or near cities that resemble those of Western countries. Many of these urban dwellers work in tall office buildings and ride modern elevated and subway trains. But in Central Asian Mongolia, Sinkiang, and Tibet, life is simpler. Most people live by herding sheep, goats, cattle, horses, camels, or yaks on the vast dry plains. The few inhabitants of New Guinea also live uncomplicated lives in tiny primitive villages that lie within tropical rain forests. Most New Guineans supply all their own needs. Some live in isolated mountain valleys and never have contact with the outside world.

Asia has played an important part in human history. It was the ancient people of Southeast Asia who developed the world's first civilization some 5,500 years ago. Asia was also the site of a number of significant inventions, such as movable type and gunpowder. And it was in Asia that all the major religions of the world began— Christianity, Judaism, Islam, Buddhism, Hinduism, Shinto, and Taoism.

Raising livestock has long been the chief economic activity in Mongolia, though few Mongolians still follow the traditional nomadic way of life.

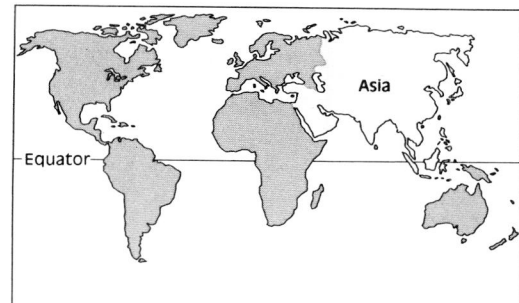

At floating markets in Bangkok, baskets of produce and other goods are exchanged from boat to boat..

At a used-car market in Saudi Arabia, a hawker sporting both Arab and Western dress uses a modern bullhorn to attract customers.

The Ganges River in India is sacred to Hindus. Each year, thousands of pilgrims climb down stairways called ghats to bathe in the river's waters.

Africa

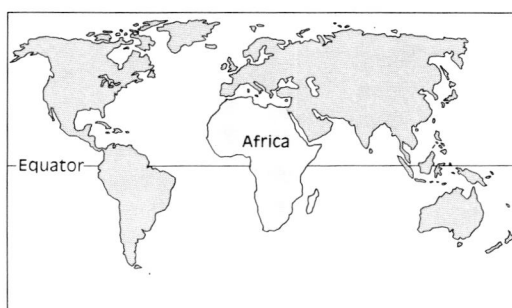

The Nile River is the world's longest river. It flows northward from Burundi, through Sudan, Ethiopia, and Egypt to the Mediterranean Sea.

Africa, the second largest continent, occupies about one-fifth of the earth's land. The continent is an immense plateau, a region of striking contrasts. Less than one-fifth of the land is covered by great forests, most of them tropical rain forests. Although much of the continent is grassland, the world's largest desert, the Sahara, lies across 3½ million square miles (9 million square kilometers) of the northern region. The world's longest river, the Nile, flows through Africa's northeastern section.

The equator passes through almost the exact middle of the continent. Thus, about 90 per cent of Africa is in the tropic zones. The parts of the continent that lie at low elevations are hot all year long. Rain falls year-round in the Congo Basin and in some of the coastal areas, where the rain forests are located. But most of Africa has long, dry seasons with only one or two spells of heavy rainfall.

Many different kinds of people inhabit Africa. In northern Africa, mainly in Algeria and Morocco, live a group of people called Berbers. Most Berbers are light-skinned, dark-haired people. Their ancestors can be traced back thousands of years in Africa. Also living in this region are Arabs whose ancestors came from the Arabian Peninsula more than 1,300 years ago. Another group, people of European descent whose ancestors settled in Africa in the 1600's, live along the Mediterranean coast.

Black Africans make up almost 75 per cent of all the African people. They are dark-skinned and have black, curly hair. Most of the people of the Sahara are black Africans.

Black African people also inhabit much of the land south of the Sahara. Their ancestors lived in the north many thousands of years ago, when the Sahara was a fertile grassland. Many began moving southward when the Sahara started to become a desert.

A group of small people called Pygmies dwell in the rain forests of central Africa. Pygmies have reddish-brown skin and tightly curled brown hair. They live primarily in small bands of fewer than 50 members. Each Pygmy band has its own territory in the forest. These people look on the forest as the giver of life, because it provides them with food, clothing, protection, and shelter.

In southwest Africa live two groups of people who have yellowish-brown skins and black, tightly coiled hair. These people, known as Bushmen and Khoikhoi, are mem-

Nairobi, the capital of Kenya, is the most important commercial center in eastern Africa. The central area of the city has many modern buildings and tree-lined streets.

bers of the African Khoisan culture. Some of these Africans gather wild plant food and hunt animals. Others work on rural reserves, cattle ranches, or farms.

The major groups living in the far south are descendants of Europeans who came to Africa during the last four hundred years and of East Indians who came during the last century. The African island of Madagascar is home to many people whose ancestors came there from Indonesia about 2,000 years ago.

All these people make up hundreds of different ethnic groups, each with its own language or dialect. There are more than 800 different languages and many dialects in Africa. The fact that European nations had at one time established colonies throughout Africa is reflected in the official languages of Africa's 51 nations. French is an official language of 20 nations; English of 17; and Portuguese of 3. Arabic is the official language of seven African nations. While many citizens can speak their country's official language, most people speak mainly the language or dialect of their own ethnic group.

In Africa, as in Asia, a great many people still live in rural areas in exactly the same way that their ancestors lived for hundreds of years. However, some Africans live very modernized lives in large cities that in many ways are similar to ones found in North America and Europe. Most urban dwellers have a higher standard of living than rural people. Better schools and medical facilities, as well as other attractions, lead more and more rural people to move into the cities.

A Bushman in the Kalahari Desert of Botswana, Africa, drinks water that has been stored in an ostrich egg container.

Berber women perform a ceremonial dance in Morocco. There are about 20 million Berbers living in northwest Africa and the Sahara.

Australia and New Zealand

Australia, the smallest continent, lies entirely in the Southern Hemisphere between the Indian and the South Pacific oceans. The northern third of Australia is in the tropics and stays hot all year long. The other two-thirds have warm summers and mild winters. About one-third of the total land area of the continent is covered by desert.

All of Australia is a single nation, the Commonwealth of Australia, which is composed of six states. It is an independent nation with its own government, but it is a member of the Commonwealth of Nations. Australia regards the British monarch as its head of state.

Two groups of people make up most of Australia's population of about 16,000,000. Nearly all are European immigrants or descendants of European immigrants—mainly British—who came to Australia during the last 200 years. Some are more recent arrivals, having immigrated during the last 40 years. These people are all white-skinned, and many are fair-haired and have light-colored eyes. All speak English.

About 1 per cent of the Australian population is made up of a group of people known as Aborigines. Aborigines are descendants of a people who came to Australia at least 40,000 years ago, probably from somewhere in Southeast Asia. While all Aborigines are dark-skinned, some have dark brown hair and others have light brown or blond hair.

At one time, there were 300,000 Aborigines, separated into hundreds of tribes. Each of those tribes had its own language. Today, there are some 206,000 Australians who are classed as Aborigines. Most of them, however, are actually a mixture of Aborigine and European as a result of intermarriage among their ancestors. Aborigines now generally speak English, although many can also speak their ancient language.

Although these two groups make up most of Australia's population, several other groups are represented. Since the 1970's, an increasing number of immigrants from New Zealand and Southeast Asia have settled in Australia. There are also a small number of persons from both Canada and the United States.

Most Australians of European descent live in the southeastern quarter of the continent. They have settled largely in cities along the coast, where it is cooler and there is more rainfall. Some live along the extreme southwest coast. The way of life of these people is much like that of people in the United States and Canada. Although some Aborigines have moved into the cit-

ies, most live in the forested lands of central and northern Australia.

About 1,000 miles (1,600 kilometers) southeast of Australia in the Southwest Pacific Ocean lie two large islands and several dozen small ones. This cluster of islands forms the nation of New Zealand. Located far south of the equator, New Zealand has a mild climate with a good deal of rainfall. Much of the land is green and fertile, with numerous lakes, rivers, and snow-capped mountains.

Like Australia, New Zealand is a member of the Commonwealth of Nations and regards the British monarch as its head of state. Also like Australia, New Zealand's population, which is over 3 million, is made up primarily of two groups of people. Most of them are descendants of the British who settled in New Zealand during the 1800's. The other group, the Maoris, are descendants of a people who came to New Zealand about 1,000 years ago from some other South Pacific islands. Maoris, who belong to the Polynesian race, have light brown skin, dark hair, and dark eyes.

New Zealanders live much as people do in Great Britain. Their language is, of course, English. Many Maoris, however, can also speak the language of their ancestors.

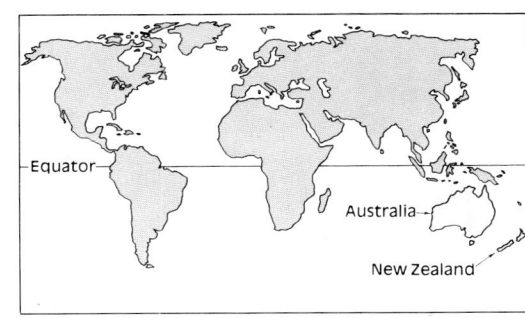

The Opera House in Sydney, Australia, has facilities for opera, concerts, and theater. The building, which is internationally known, was completed in 1973.

A sheep farmer in New Zealand uses a minibike to round up his herd. Lamb and wool are among the nation's chief exports.

The ancestors of these Aboriginal stockmen were the first people to live in Australia. Most Aborigines today live in the rural areas of the continent.

New Zealanders love outdoor sports and activities in all kinds of weather. Skiing is becoming increasingly popular.

Pacific Islands

A vast portion of the Pacific Ocean is dotted with many thousands of big and little islands. This region of ocean and islands is known as the Pacific Islands, or Oceania. Not all islands in the Pacific Ocean, however, are a part of Oceania. For example, islands near the mainland of Asia are considered part of Asia, and islands near North and South America are grouped with those continents.

Geographers divide the Pacific Islands into three parts. Scattered across the central Pacific are thousands of islands that make up the portion called Polynesia, meaning "many islands." Polynesia includes Hawaii, New Zealand, and Midway Island. North and east of Australia lie groups of islands that form what is called Melanesia, meaning "black islands." Fiji, the Solomon Islands, and New Caledonia are Melanesian islands. Between Melanesia and Japan lie islands that form Micronesia, meaning "small islands." Some of the Micronesian islands are Guam, Wake Island, and the Caroline Islands.

All these islands fall into one of two types. High Islands, such as the main islands of Hawaii, are hilly and mountainous and often have volcanoes. Low Islands such as the Marshall Islands are formed of coral reefs that are generally just above sea level. Most of Oceania lies in the tropics. There-fore, the weather on the islands is quite warm year-round. Although the area, in general, gets plenty of rainfall, some islands may receive little rain.

Generally, a different kind of people lives in each part of the Pacific Islands. In Melanesia, the people are rather short, with dark skins and coarse, curly black hair. They resemble the black people of Africa. Scientists believe that the ancestors of the Melanesians came from somewhere in Asia many thousands of years ago.

The people of Micronesia are a little tall-er than the Melanesians and have lighter skins. Most also have coarse, curly, or wavy black hair. Their ancestors, too, prob-ably came from Asia, but at a later time than the ancestors of the Melanesians.

Polynesians are taller than both other groups. All have light brown skins, but some have wavy hair and others have straight hair. Their ancestors probably came from Melanesia or Micronesia.

There have been other influences on the people of the Pacific Islands. For example, many people from other lands have settled on the Polynesian islands in the past. Thus, many Polynesians have Asian and Euro-pean ancestors. A large number of people living on Fiji are descended from East Indians who came there to work about 100 years ago. And people of European and Asian descent live on many of the other Pacific Islands.

The Melanesians, Micronesians, and Polynesians all have similar ways of life. There are, however, some differences in language, law, dress, and religion. Many hundreds of languages are spoken through-out Oceania. The people of Melanesia, particularly, speak a number of different languages. English is spoken on a great many of the islands that were once colonies of Great Britain or that are now governed by Great Britain or the United States. French is spoken on a number of islands that are governed by France.

Many of the islands of Oceania are inde-pendent and have their own governments. Hawaii, American Samoa, Guam, Midway Island, and Wake Island, however, belong to the United States. Pitcairn Island comes under the authority of Great Britain. France, Chile, and New Zealand all govern islands. And a part of New Guinea is governed by Indonesia.

Of all the Pacific Islands, only Hawaii and New Zealand have large, modern cities and towns. Most Pacific Islanders live in small villages and make their livings by farming or fishing, much as their ancestors have done for hundreds of years.

For a village feast in Leone, American Samoa, a woman prepares food. Kinship groups play a major role in Polynesian village life.

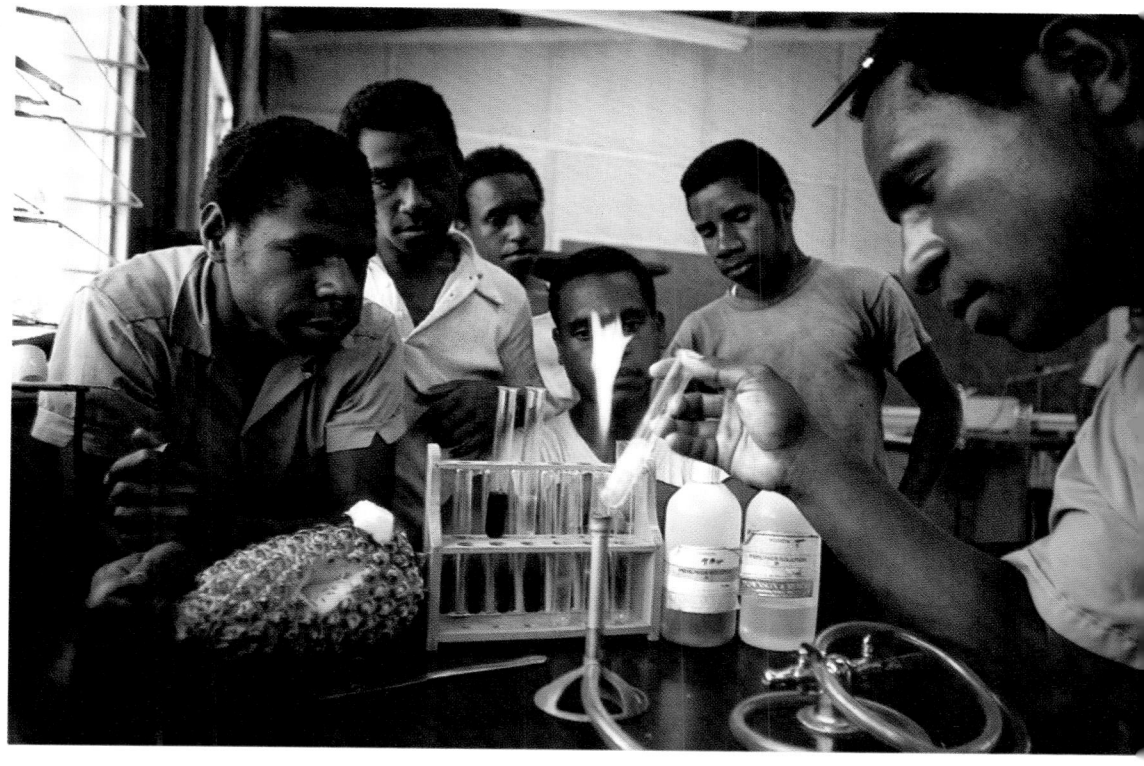

Off the Caroline Islands in Micronesia, some fishermen still travel in hand-hewn sailing canoes.

Melanesian students study pineapple extract in their school laboratory.

Polar Regions

The earth's north polar region, the Arctic, does not seem a likely place for people to live. Nevertheless, large numbers of people do live in the parts of North America, Europe, and Asia that lie within the Arctic Circle.

Large supplies of oil, uranium, titanium, and other valuable minerals have been found in the Arctic. This has caused the settlement of some areas by communities of scientists, technicians, miners, and oil field workers. Modern technology enables these settlements to survive in the Arctic's hostile environment.

Most Arctic residents, however, live simpler lives. Many follow the traditions of their ancestors.

In North America, about 117,000 of the people known as Inuit, or Eskimos, live in the northern parts of Greenland, Canada, and Alaska. Inuit are stocky people with short arms and legs. They resemble the Mongoloid people of Asia, and scientists believe they came to North America about 10,000 years ago via a land connection that once existed between Alaska and northeastern Asia. Inuit throughout the Arctic speak essentially the same language.

For thousands of years, Inuit followed a traditional way of life that had been developed to meet the needs of living in the Arctic. They lived mainly on the meat of seals and caribou, which they hunted with harpoons. During the short Arctic summer, they stayed in tents of sealskin or caribou skin, and they fished for arctic trout called char. In winter, the Inuit made temporary dome-shaped houses of snow. They traveled by means of dog sleds and boats made of wood, bone, and skins. Today, that way of life is largely gone. Most Inuit now hunt with rifles, travel by snowmobile and motorboat, and live in heated houses in settlements.

About 1,500 Inuit also live in Siberia, the Asian part of the Soviet Union. Several tribes of people who greatly resemble Amerindians of the Pacific Northwest live in northeastern Siberia. These tribes— the Kamchadals, the Koryaks, and the Chukchi—live by hunting and fishing. They number about 20,000 people. Tribes of Mongoloid people—the Yakuts, Tungus, and Samoyeds—reside in north-central Siberia and live mainly by raising reindeer. There are nearly 420,000 of these people.

The European part of the Arctic lies across the northern parts of the Soviet Union, Finland, Norway, and Sweden. In the Arctic part of the European Soviet Union, live some 250,000 people called Zyrians. These people, who are related to modern Finlanders, are hunters, fishermen, and reindeer herders.

The Arctic part of Norway, Sweden, and Finland, together with a bit of the Soviet Union, has long been known as Lapland, the home of people called Lapps. Lapps are short and muscular, with slightly yellowish skin and straight black hair. Scientists think the Lapps may have come to Lapland from central Asia many thousands of years ago.

There are nearly 45,000 Lapps. Some are nomadic. They raise herds of reindeer that they follow from place to place as the animals search for edible vegetation. Other Lapps live near the sea and make their living mainly by fishing. Still others hunt, fish, and raise reindeer. All Lapps speak a language that is much like Finnish, but it is spoken with different dialects in different parts of Lapland.

People have never settled in the earth's south polar region, the Antarctic, as they have in the Arctic. People *do* live in Antarctica today, but they are mainly scientists studying the continent for various reasons. These people are really only visitors, however. They live in temporary housing, and their supplies are delivered by ship or by airplane.

Murmansk is the Soviet Union's chief port on the Arctic Ocean and the world's largest city north of the Arctic Circle.

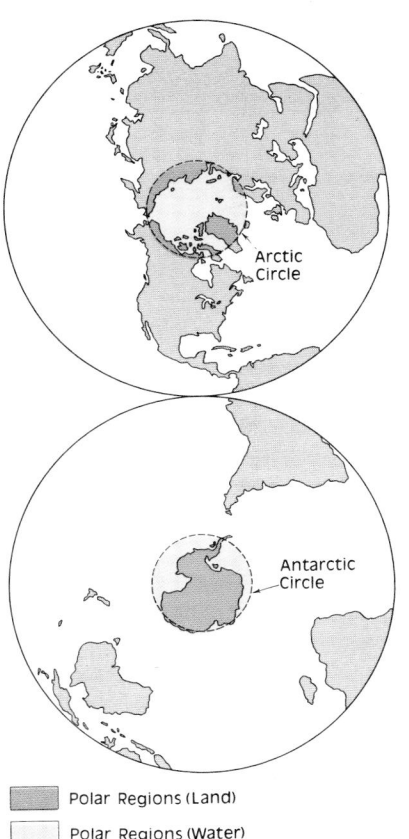

Polar Regions (Land)
Polar Regions (Water)

Most Inuit today live in wooden or prefabricated housing, instead of in tents or houses made of snow or sod.

Lapps wear brightly trimmed traditional wool and reindeer fur costumes on special occasions. Most of the time, however, they wear Western-style clothing.

Looking at Earth

Earthrise over the moon

Glaciers in southeastern Alaska, U.S.

Kilauea in southeastern Hawaii, U.S.

As a Planet

EARTH IS ONE of the four rocky inner planets of the solar system. It is a ball of molten stone and metal enclosed by a shell of rock. The features of this active planet are in constant change from the action of volcanoes, earthquakes, water, and wind.

Earth in the Solar System

The planet Earth is a huge ball covered with water, rock, and soil. It travels in an orbit—an oval-shaped path—around a star, the sun. The sun, in turn, moves in an orbit around the center of a vast system of stars called a galaxy.

There are at least 100 billion galaxies scattered throughout the observable universe. Each consists of from less than a billion to a trillion or more stars. The galaxy in which Earth and the sun are located is known as the Milky Way.

The Milky Way is a spiral-shaped galaxy of hundreds of billions of stars. All these stars are at incredible distances from one another. The nearest star to the sun and to Earth is approximately 25 million million miles (40 million million kilometers) away.

All stars within a galaxy revolve around the center of the galaxy. The stars that are farthest from the center naturally take longer to make the journey. Both the sun and Earth are located far from the center of the Milky Way. It would take the sun and Earth about 250 million years to make one complete revolution around the center.

Earth is only one of a number of objects that orbit the sun. There are eight other major planets and their moons. There are also some very small minor planets, called asteroids. In addition, various-sized chunks of rock called meteoroids orbit the sun. And there are comets and clouds of dust and gas. All these things, together with the sun, make up what is known as the solar system.

The nine known planets of the solar system orbit the sun at various distances. In order of distance from the sun, these planets are Mercury, Venus, Earth, Mars, Jupiter, Saturn, Uranus, Neptune, and Pluto. Although Pluto is normally the outermost planet, it crossed inside Neptune's orbit in 1979 and will remain there until 1999.

Mercury, Venus, Earth, and Mars are essentially balls of rock and metal. Jupiter, Saturn, Uranus, and Neptune, called the giant planets, are made up chiefly of gases that are compressed into fluids and contain little iron and rock. Pluto's composition is still unknown. Scientists, however, believe Pluto is like a ball of ice, similar to the satellites of the giant planets.

Earth, the third planet from the sun, circles it at an average distance of 93 million miles (150 million kilometers). The closest planet to Earth is Venus, the second planet from the sun. Venus approaches to within 25 million miles (approximately 40 million kilometers) of Earth during its orbit.

But the closest to Earth of all solar-system bodies is its own moon. The moon's mean distance from Earth is only about 238,857 miles (384,403 kilometers). The moon is held in orbit around Earth by the pull of the planet's gravity. Earth's moon is a barren, airless ball of rock. It is about one-fourth the size of Earth. The moon's surface has mountains, valleys, and plains. It is pitted with billions of craters, caused by

The solar system, *below,* contains nine planets and their satellites, plus numerous comets, meteorites, and interplanetary dust. The planets orbit the sun, a rather ordinary star lying about 30,000 light years from the center of the Milky Way.

Distances from the sun (Figures in millions)

Sun	Mercury	Venus	Earth	Mars
	36 miles	67.3 miles	93 miles	141.7 miles
	57.9 kilometers	109 kilometers	150 kilometers	228 kilometers

Mercury is the planet closest to the sun. It also moves around the sun faster than any other planet—once every 88 Earth days. Like Venus, Mercury does not have a moon.

Venus is almost the same size and mass as Earth. But its atmosphere is mostly carbon dioxide, and its temperature is too high to allow life to exist.

Earth, like Pluto, has only one moon. The gravitational pull of Earth keeps the moon in its orbit. Without this pull from Earth, the moon would fly off into space.

Mars has surface conditions that are closer to Earth's than any other planet's. In spite of experiments conducted by space probes, scientists have not been able to determine whether life exists on Mars.

the impact of pieces of rock that have smashed into its surface.

Earth's moon shines because sunlight reflects off its surface. The amount of light-reflecting surface visible from Earth varies when the moon is in different positions as it moves around the planet. These differences account for the phases of the moon, such as first quarter and full moon.

An eclipse of the moon occurs when Earth is directly between the sun and the full moon, casting its shadow on the moon's surface. An eclipse of the sun occurs when the moon passes directly between the sun and Earth, blocking off the sun's light and casting a shadow on Earth.

The spiral galaxy, *above,* like the Milky Way, resembles an enormous pinwheel. However, because of Earth's position in the Milky Way, its pinwheel shape cannot be seen from Earth. Instead, the galaxy appears as a broad, hazy band of starlight stretching across the sky.

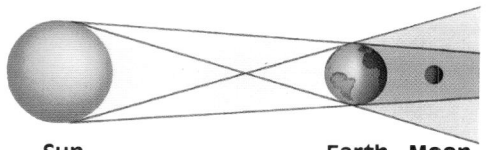

Sun	**Earth Moon**

A lunar eclipse takes place when Earth passes between the sun and moon.

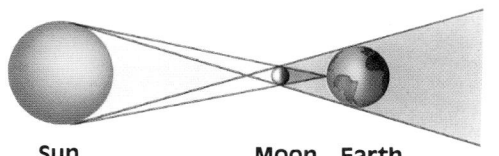

Sun	**Moon Earth**

A solar eclipse occurs when the moon passes between the sun and Earth.

Jupiter	Saturn	Uranus	Neptune	Pluto
483.7 miles	885.2 miles	1,781 miles	2,793 miles	3,660 miles
777 kilometers	1,424 kilometers	2,869 kilometers	4,495 kilometers	5,890 kilometers

Pluto, which has a moon more than one-third its size, is the most distant planet from the sun. At some point in its oval-shaped orbit, Pluto enters Neptune's orbit and stays there for about 20 years. This event occurs every 248 years.

Jupiter, the largest planet, has the fastest spin in the solar system. It rotates once every 9 hours 55 minutes. The rapid spin flattens the planet at the poles. Jupiter has 16 known satellites.

Saturn, the second largest planet, is circled by seven major rings. Jupiter, Neptune, and Uranus are the only other planets known to have rings, but theirs are much fainter than Saturn's.

Uranus is believed to be basically featureless and surrounded by clouds. Little is known about the planet's surface.

Neptune, like Pluto, cannot be seen without a telescope. Neptune has eight moons. One of them, Triton, is the only large satellite in the solar system that travels from east to west.

Earth's Atmosphere and Motion

Like the moon, Earth also glows with reflected sunlight. Seen from space, the planet appears to be a large, dark blue and brown ball covered with wispy white patches. The brown areas are Earth's continents, and the vast blue expanses are its oceans. Of all the planets in the solar system, only Earth has water in liquid form. Oceans, which contain most of Earth's water, cover about 70 per cent of the planet's surface. The white patches are the clouds that drift in Earth's atmosphere.

Earth's atmosphere is the layer of gases that surrounds the planet. The atmosphere of Earth is a mixture of 78 per cent nitrogen, 21 per cent oxygen, and small amounts of several other gases. The atmosphere extends 1,000 miles (1,600 kilometers) from the planet's surface. Earth's atmosphere is thickest within the first 50 miles (80 kilometers) of the planet, and it becomes progressively thinner thereafter.

Venus and Mars also have an atmosphere. The atmosphere of Venus is a thick mixture of mainly carbon dioxide and other gases. It is filled with clouds formed largely of droplets of sulfuric acid and sulfur. The atmosphere of Mars is a thin mixture of carbon dioxide and other gases.

Earth is fifth in size among all the planets and the largest of the rocky inner planets. The Earth's diameter, or distance from one side to the other through its center, is about 7,900 miles (12,713 kilometers) measured from North Pole to South Pole. Earth's circumference, or distance around the planet, is about 24,901.5 miles (40,075.16 kilometers) measured at the equator.

Venus is only slightly smaller than Earth. Mars is about half the size of Earth, and Mercury is about two-fifths as big. However, the diameter of Jupiter—the solar system's largest planet—is more than 11 times the length of Earth's.

Earth rotates on its axis, an imaginary line through the center of the planet from the North Pole to the South Pole. This

Earth is the only planet in the solar system that has enough oxygen surrounding it and enough water on its surface to support life as it is known today. About 70 per cent of Earth's surface is water; the rest is land. All Earth's animals and plants live on or close to the planet's surface.

rotation causes day and night on Earth. As the planet rotates, half of it faces the sun. There it is daytime. The other half faces away from the sun into the blackness of space, and on that half it is nighttime. The planet makes one complete rotation every 23 hours 56 minutes 4.09 seconds. This is the length of Earth's day.

As Earth rotates, it also moves in an orbit around the sun. Earth moves through space at an average speed of 66,600 miles (107,200 kilometers) an hour. One orbit, or revolution around the sun, takes 365 days 6 hours 9 minutes 9.54 seconds. This is the length of Earth's year.

Earth's axis is tilted, rather than straight up and down. This tilt and Earth's orbit around the sun cause the seasons. During part of the orbit, the northern half of the planet is tilted toward the sun. In this position, the northern half receives more light and heat than the southern half. This is summer for the northern portion of the planet and winter for the southern portion, which is tilted away from the sun. During another part of the orbit, the southern half of the planet is tilted toward the sun, and seasons are reversed.

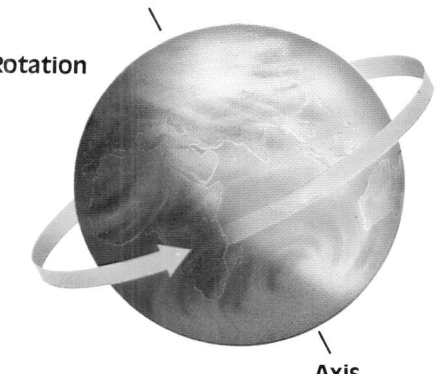

Rotation

Axis

Earth spins eastward around its axis once every 23 hours 56 minutes and 4.09 seconds. Earth circles the sun once every 365 days 6 hours 9 minutes and 9.54 seconds.

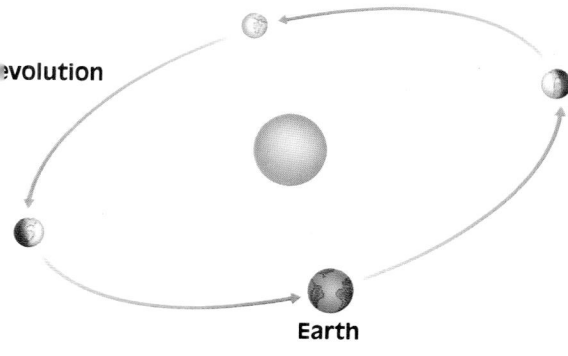

Revolution

Earth

Altitude

Divisions of the Atmosphere

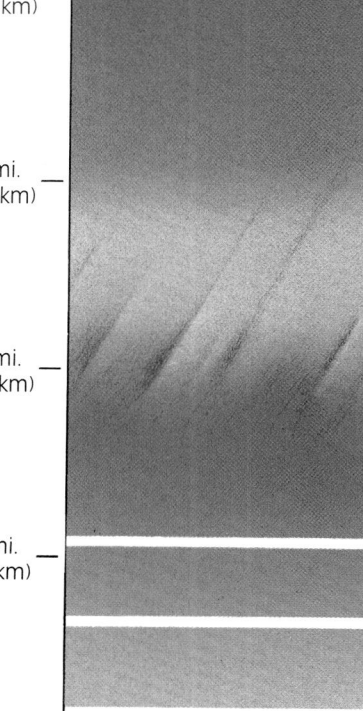

600 mi. (960 km)

550 mi. (890 km)

500 mi. (800 km)

450 mi. (720 km)

400 mi. (640 km)

350 mi. (560 km)

300 mi. (480 km)

250 mi. (400 km)

200 mi. (320 km)

150 mi. (240 km)

100 mi. (160 km)

50 mi. (80 km)

0 mi./km

Earth's atmosphere consists of four layers, the troposphere, the stratosphere, the mesosphere, and the thermosphere. The diagram on the right shows a detailed enlargement of the first three layers and the lower 70 miles (112 kilometers) of the thermosphere. More than 75 per cent of Earth's air and almost all its weather occurs in the troposphere. The stratosphere contains the ozone layer, which absorbs harmful rays from the sun. Meteor trails can be seen in the mesosphere. Auroral displays, or northern and southern lights, occur in the lower thermosphere.

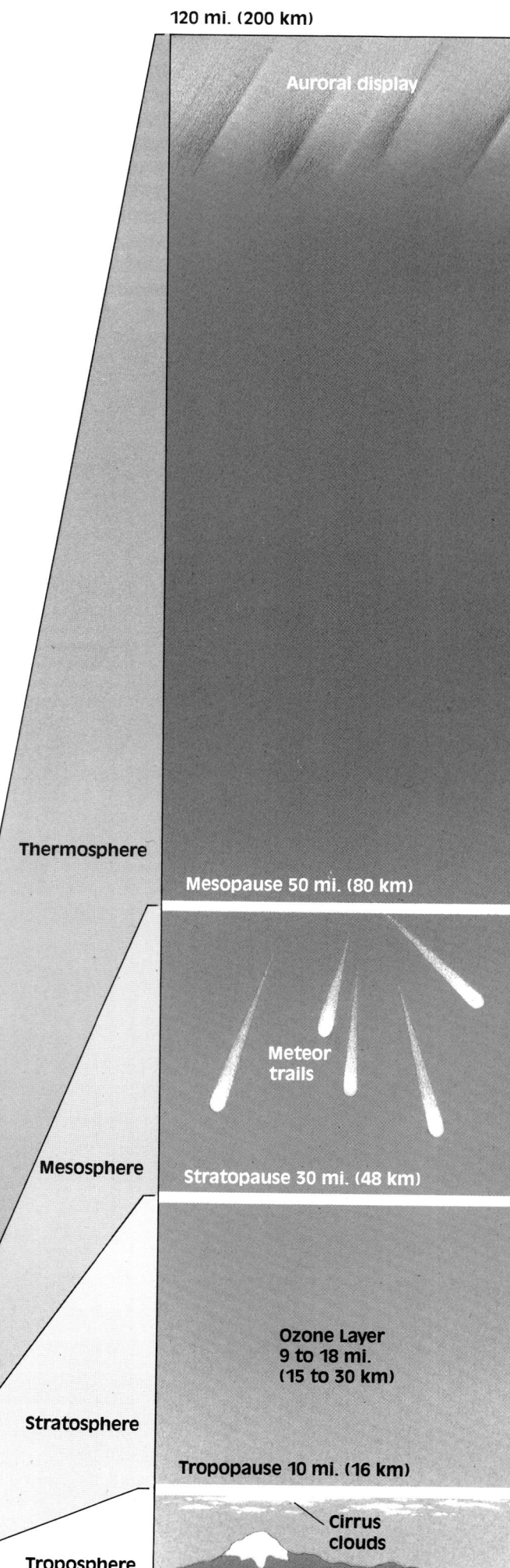

120 mi. (200 km)

Auroral display

Thermosphere

Mesopause 50 mi. (80 km)

Meteor trails

Stratopause 30 mi. (48 km)

Mesosphere

Ozone Layer 9 to 18 mi. (15 to 30 km)

Stratosphere

Tropopause 10 mi. (16 km)

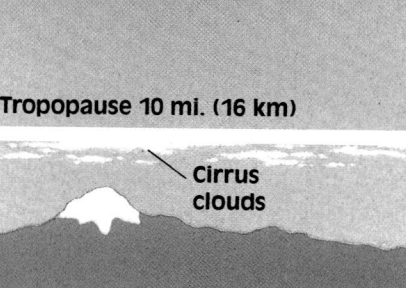

Cirrus clouds

Troposphere

Earth's Structure

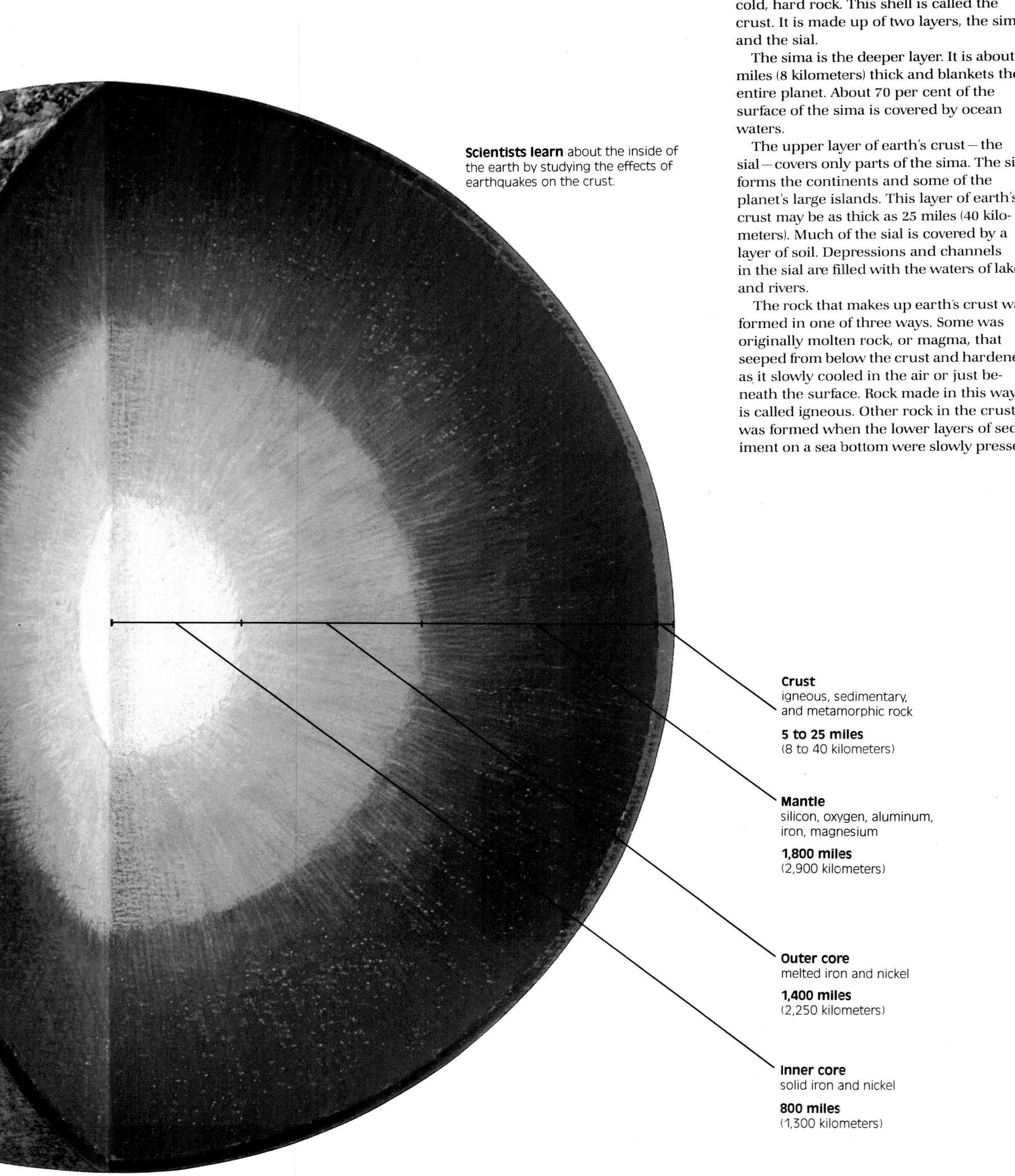

Scientists learn about the inside of the earth by studying the effects of earthquakes on the crust.

The earth is covered by a thin shell of cold, hard rock. This shell is called the crust. It is made up of two layers, the sima and the sial.

The sima is the deeper layer. It is about 5 miles (8 kilometers) thick and blankets the entire planet. About 70 per cent of the surface of the sima is covered by ocean waters.

The upper layer of earth's crust — the sial — covers only parts of the sima. The sial forms the continents and some of the planet's large islands. This layer of earth's crust may be as thick as 25 miles (40 kilometers). Much of the sial is covered by a layer of soil. Depressions and channels in the sial are filled with the waters of lakes and rivers.

The rock that makes up earth's crust was formed in one of three ways. Some was originally molten rock, or magma, that seeped from below the crust and hardened as it slowly cooled in the air or just beneath the surface. Rock made in this way is called igneous. Other rock in the crust was formed when the lower layers of sediment on a sea bottom were slowly pressed

Crust
igneous, sedimentary, and metamorphic rock

5 to 25 miles
(8 to 40 kilometers)

Mantle
silicon, oxygen, aluminum, iron, magnesium

1,800 miles
(2,900 kilometers)

Outer core
melted iron and nickel

1,400 miles
(2,250 kilometers)

Inner core
solid iron and nickel

800 miles
(1,300 kilometers)

together by the tremendous weight of sediment and water from above. This pressure formed the sediment into the kind of rock called sedimentary. Still other rock was formed when igneous and sedimentary rocks were changed by tremendous heat and pressure deep within earth's crust. Later, this rock was pushed to the surface. Such rock is called metamorphic.

Although much of the rock in earth's crust was formed long ago, the process of rock formation continues. Igneous rock is still formed by the cooling of magma. Sedimentary rock is still formed in shallow seas. Metamorphic rock is still pushed up from the lower layer of earth's crust.

Beneath the crust lies a layer of rock called the mantle. This layer extends to a depth of 1,800 miles (2,900 kilometers) thick. The temperatures of rock within the earth get progressively higher toward the center of the planet. The deepest part of the mantle reaches a temperature of 4000° F. (2200° C).

Beneath the mantle is the earth's outer core, which scientists believe is made of melted iron and nickel 1,400 miles (2,250 kilometers) thick. In the outer core, temperatures range from about 4000° F. (2200° C) at the upper level to about 9000° F. (5000° C) at the deepest level. Earth's magnetic field is generated by electricity in the outer core. It is the magnetic field that allows compasses to function.

At the very center of earth lies the inner core. Some scientists believe that this layer is a solid ball of iron and nickel about 800 miles (1,300 kilometers) thick. The temperature of the inner core is about 9000° F. (5000° C). Although the metal of the inner core is hot enough to be melted, the atoms of the metal are pressed together so tightly by gravity that melting is impossible.

Igneous rocks are formed when melted rock deep inside the crust cools and hardens.

Metamorphic rocks are formed when igneous and sedimentary rocks are chemically and physically changed by heat and pressure.

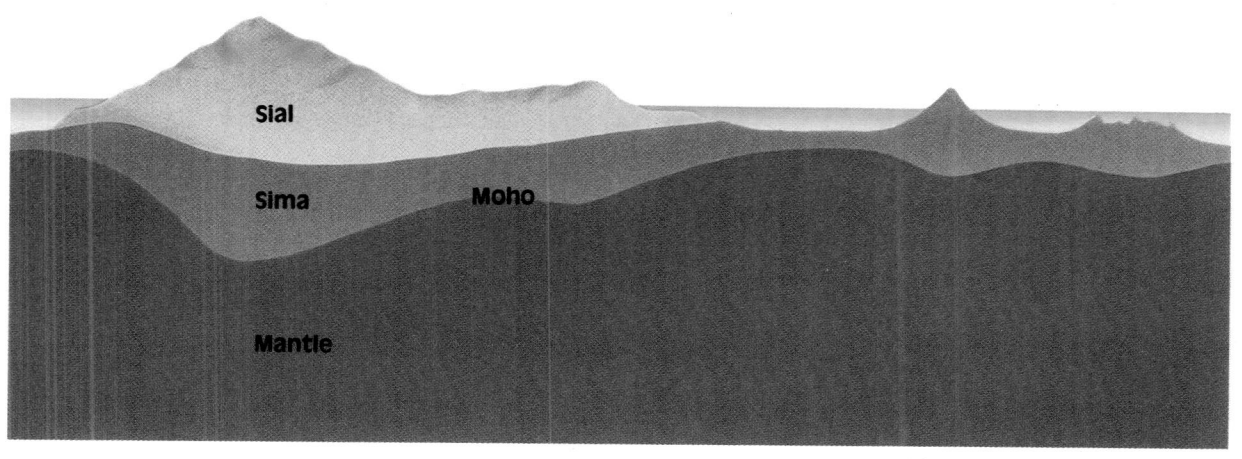

Sedimentary rocks are developed from material worn away from the land. These rocks may contain fossils—shells, bones, and other remains of living things.

Sial

Sima   Moho

Mantle

The earth's crust has two layers — the sial, made up of granitelike rocks, and the sima, similar to hardened lava. The moho is the boundary between the crust and the mantle.

Earthquakes and Volcanoes

The earth's crust is continually changing. Most of the time, this change is so gradual that only the most sophisticated scientific equipment can detect it. But sometimes tremendous forces inside the earth unleash their power in sudden events that cause dramatic changes in the earth's surface. These events include volcanic eruptions and earthquakes.

An earthquake is the sometimes violent shaking of the earth's surface that happens as a result of the movement of the materials in the crust and mantle beneath it. The strongest earthquakes can tumble buildings, change the course of rivers, or shift parts of the ocean floor and send giant tidal waves charging across the sea. A volcano is an opening in the earth's surface where red-hot molten rock, called magma, escapes from deep inside the earth. Volcanic eruptions can create mountains and islands and cover hundreds of square miles (kilometers) with flowing lava or ash.

Most earthquakes and volcanoes occur at the boundaries between giant sections of the earth's outermost layer, called plates. These plates are in constant motion in relation to one another. They slowly glide over a zone of partially melted rock in the earth's mantle at a rate of ½ to 4 inches (1.3 to 10 centimeters) a year. Most earthquakes and volcanoes occur as a result of this movement.

Earthquakes occur along faults, which are breaks in the earth's crust. The rock that makes up the earth's crust is cold and rigid. As a result, it does not glide along smoothly as does the hot rock at deeper levels. The movement of the plates past each other combined with the resistance of the rock on each side of the fault create a build-up of stress at the fault. Eventually, the stress exceeds the rock's strength. Each side of the fault snaps to a new position to "catch up" with the plate it is attached to, and an earthquake occurs.

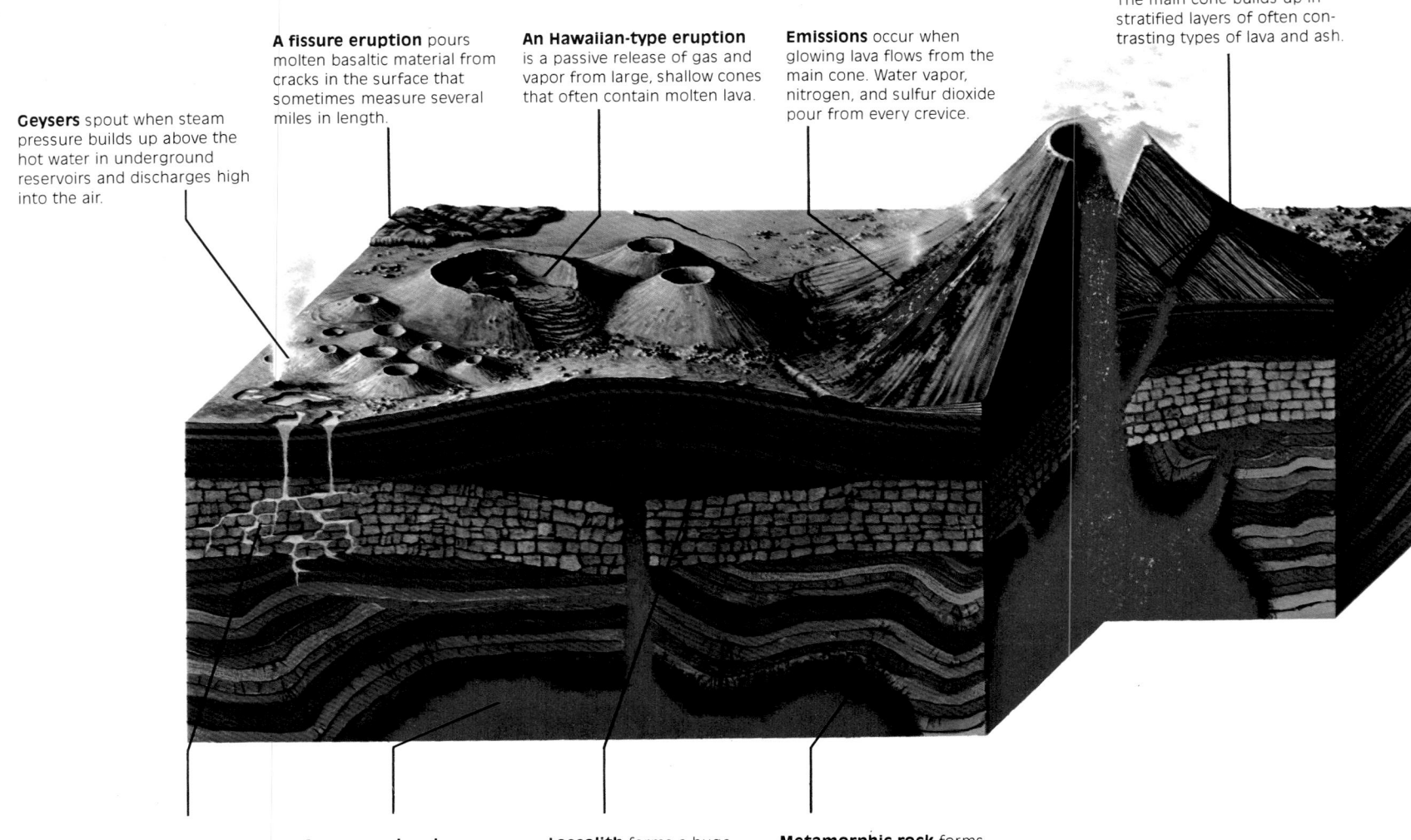

Layering is the product of millions of years of eruptions. The main cone builds up in stratified layers of often contrasting types of lava and ash.

A fissure eruption pours molten basaltic material from cracks in the surface that sometimes measure several miles in length.

An Hawaiian-type eruption is a passive release of gas and vapor from large, shallow cones that often contain molten lava.

Emissions occur when glowing lava flows from the main cone. Water vapor, nitrogen, and sulfur dioxide pour from every crevice.

Geysers spout when steam pressure builds up above the hot water in underground reservoirs and discharges high into the air.

Underground water, heated under pressure to beyond the normal boiling point, rushes out whenever pressure is relieved.

A magma chamber contains intensely hot magma under high pressure. Every volcano has one.

Laccolith forms a huge lens of cooled rock above the hot magma chamber.

Metamorphic rock forms near the magma chamber when heat and intense pressure create chemical and physical changes in sedimentary and igneous strata.

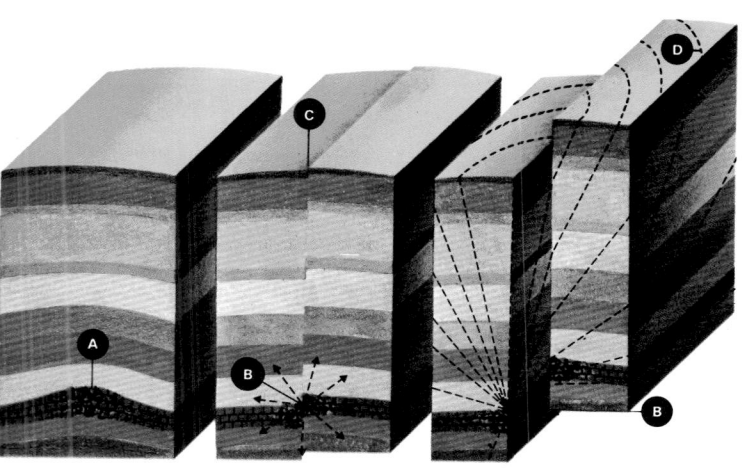

How earthquakes happen.
Stresses build over many years until the breaking strength of some part of the rock along a fault line or other line of potential movement is exceeded (**A**). Shock waves move out in all directions (**B**). The epicenter (**C**) is on the surface directly above the break. The most damage is done by the earthquake when the shock waves reach the surface (**D**).

The San Andreas Fault, a major break in the earth's crust, extends more than 750 miles (1,210 kilometers) through California and produces a major quake every few hundred years.

The snapping of the rock causes vibrations called seismic waves to move out in all directions. The waves move like ripples in a pond after a stone is dropped into it. It is these waves that cause the damage to the earth's surface and to objects on it.

Earthquakes may occur at the surface of the earth or at depths of up to 400 miles (640 kilometers) below the surface. The point of an earthquake's origin is called its focus. The quake's epicenter is the place on the surface of the earth directly above the focus.

Many volcanoes form where the edge of one plate overlaps another and pushes it down into the mantle. There, portions of the plate melt to form magma and large amounts of gas. The mixture rises toward the surface and eventually collects in a magma chamber just beneath the earth's surface. The pressure of the surrounding rock forces the mixture in the magma chamber up through the surface of the earth, creating an opening called a central vent. Magma that has penetrated the earth's surface is called lava.

Lava builds up around the central vent. As the lava cools, it forms a cone-shaped volcanic mountain. Volcanic mountains can be either low and broad or tall and pointed.

Some volcanoes also form when the edges of two plates move apart from each other, allowing magma from the mantle to seep up between them. Most of this type of volcanic activity occurs on the ocean floor. The tops of some of these volcanoes become islands, such as Iceland.

A few volcanoes have developed near the center of plates far from the edges. Scientists think this happens when huge magma columns, called plumes, push up into the crust. The Hawaiian Islands were formed by this type of volcanic action, which continues today at Kilauea, a famous volcano on the island of Hawaii.

Seismographic stations throughout the Pacific watch for earthquake shocks and oceanic tidal waves that sometimes follow. Here concentric rings show the time necessary for a tidal wave to travel from the point above the earthquake's center in Hawaii.

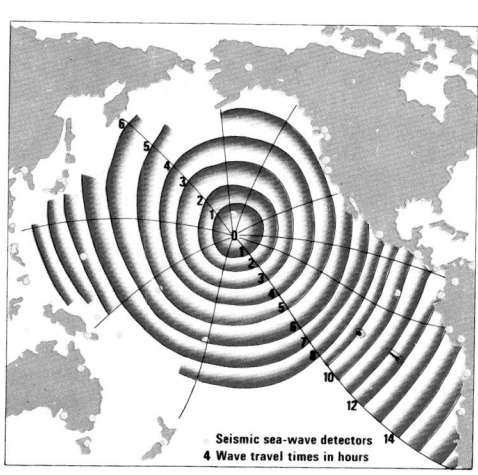

Earth's Changing Surface

The earth's surface is constantly undergoing changes. Some changes are rapid, such as those caused by landslides, earthquakes, and volcanic eruptions. But other changes are slow and steady. Mountains are worn flat. Deep canyons are carved. Fertile lands lose their rich soil. Coastlines change shape.

One of the chief causes of the slow and steady changes in earth's surface is erosion, or the breaking down and movement of the planet's rock and soil by natural forces. A major factor in erosion is water, both in its liquid and in its solid form — ice.

Erosion begins with weathering, a process in which various environmental factors break down soil and rock and release them from earth's surface. Ice is a primary factor in weathering. Ice forms when water trapped inside the cracks of rocks freezes. As water becomes ice, it expands and can break the rock into fragments. Melting snow and rain that beats down on weathered rocks washes away billions of dust-sized particles. These bits of rock are carried into streams and rivers. As rivers move along, they tear more tiny bits of rock out of the channels through which they flow. After many thousands or millions of years, the action of flowing water can form a deep canyon or flatten a mountain.

Coastlines and lake shores are also altered by the force of water. Waves crashing against cliffs break away loose pieces of rock. The constant beating of the waves causes a crushing and grinding that breaks boulders into pebbles and pebbles into sand. In some places, the shoreline is slowly pushed back, and the sea takes its place. In other places, waves combine with wind, another major factor in erosion, to increase the land by moving sand from one location to another. This process helps build up beaches.

Wind can carry particles of earth great distances. If there are no trees or grasses to protect the land, wind may pick up tons of dry, dusty soil. This can rob farmland of rich soil. In time, the area may become almost a desert.

Wind that carries sand or sandy soil can also cause erosion in rocky places. A steady stream of wind-blown sand striking against stone can rub off or sandblast tiny particles and carry them away. Rocks that have been eroded in this way are common in many deserts.

The effects of water erosion can be as spectacular as the gooseneck canyons cut by the San Juan River in Utah.

Wind erosion: (1) parabolic blowout, (2) parabolic hairpin, (3) longitudinal ridge.

Sea erosion: (1) dunes, (2) deposition, (3) spit, (4) arch, (5) stack, (6) raised beach, (7) caves.

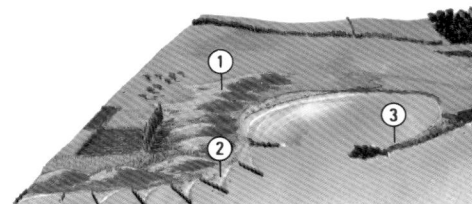

River erosion: (A) youthful stage, (B) mature stage, (C) old age stage, (1) pothole, (2) oxbow, (3) meander.

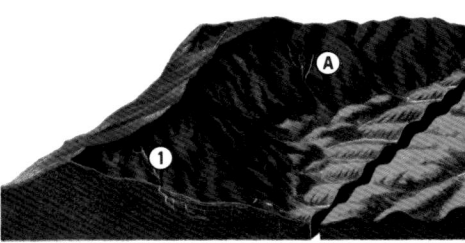

Glacial erosion: (1) preglacial rock, (2) valley, (3) bergschrund, (4) crevasses, (5) longitudinal moraine, (6) valley-floor moraines, (7) peaks and (8) valley carved by tributary, (9) terminal moraine.

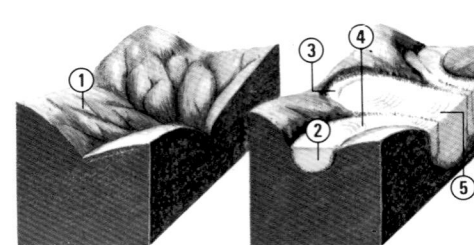

Ice, in the form of glaciers, has been responsible for enormous changes on earth's surface in the past. Glaciers are huge rivers of ice that move at very slow rates and flow over anything in their paths. Some glaciers are still at work. They form when deep snow turns to ice on mountaintops. The ice, which can move slowly downward, may widen an old valley or gouge out a new one. It can also pick up and carry tons of soil or rock and deposit them hundreds of miles (kilometers) away. When a glacier melts, it can fill a depression with fresh water, thus creating a new lake. If the Antarctic icecap, which is a glacier, would melt, it could drastically raise the level of ocean waters. This would cause floods that could change the coastlines of continents.

The Australian rock formation, *above,* shows the sculptural effects of wind carrying sand and other debris.

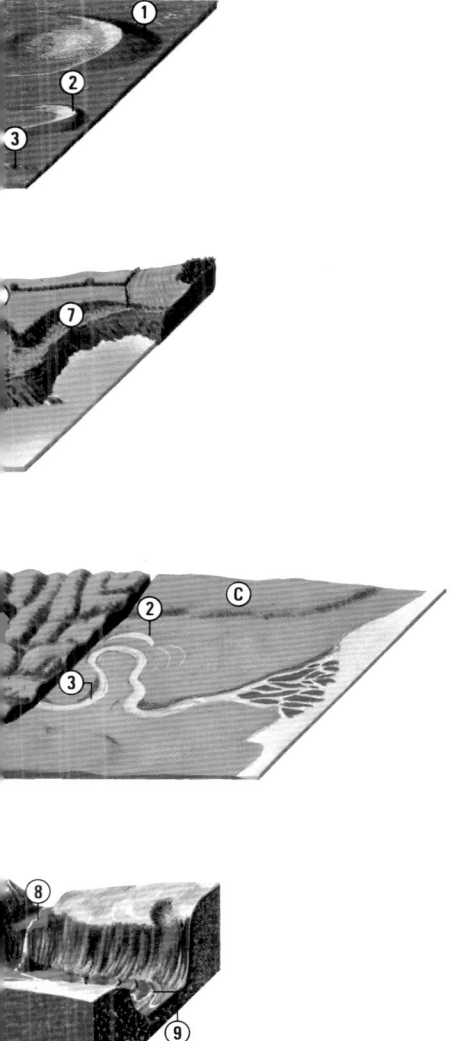

Glaciated valleys and terraces such as those in Ortnevik, Norway, are typically formed over thousands of years.

Beneath the Ocean

If all earth's ocean water would suddenly vanish, the planet would present a new landscape. There would be vast plains, slopes, deep valleys, and ranges of towering mountains never seen before. These features now lie beneath the water, forming the sea bottom.

Along the coasts of the continents, from the edges of the shores, the muddy or rocky ocean bottom slopes gently out beneath the water. This submerged land is known as the continental shelves. They are coated by thick layers of sediment that were carried to the coasts by rivers.

From the edges of the continental shelves, the ocean bottom slants downward more sharply, forming what are called the continental slopes. Deep canyons cut through the slopes in some places. Far below the surface of the water, the continental slopes merge with the abyss, or deep ocean bottom. The depth of the abyss ranges from 10,000 feet (3,040 meters) to 18,000 feet (5,472 meters). The abyssal plains are broad, almost completely flat areas that make up 30 per cent of earth's total surface. Most of the plains are covered with thick sediment.

A range of towering submarine mountains, known as the Mid-Atlantic Ridge, stretches north to south along the middle of the Atlantic Ocean bottom for 10,000 miles (16,000 kilometers). The peaks of a number of mountains in this range stick up above the water. They create islands in the Atlantic Ocean, such as the Azores

All submarine landscapes follow the same general pattern, although details vary from ocean to ocean. The layout includes a volcanic ridge, which may break the surface in places, broad abyssal plains with occasional deep trenches, and continents bordered by shallow slopes and shelves.

A — Volcano in midocean ridge
B — Deep oceanic trench
C — Continental shelf
D — Abyssal plain
E — Midocean ridge
F — Guyots
G — Oceanic islands
X1 — Upper granitic crust and sediments
X2 — Lower granitic crust
Y — Basaltic crust
S — Sediment
Z — Mantle

Features of the ocean floor

Feature	Col	No	Feature	Col	No	Feature	Col	No
Aleutian Basin	B	8	Canada Plain	A	8	East Pacific Rise	E	9
Aleutian Trench	B	8	Canary Basin	C	2	Eltanin		
Angola Basin	D	3	Challenger			Fracture Zone	E	9
Arabian Basin	D	5	Fracture Zone	E	9	Emperor Seamounts	C	8
Argentine Basin	E	2	Clarion			Falkland Trough	E	2
Atlantic-Indian			Fracture Zone	C	9	Grand Banks	B	2
Basin	F	4	Clipperton			Hawaiian Ridge	C	8
Atlantic-Indian			Fracture Zone	D	9	Japan Trench	C	7
Ridge	F	4	Diamantina			Kerguelen		
Baffin Basin	A	1	Fracture Zone	E	6	Plateau	F	5
Bermuda Rise	C	1	Dogger Bank	B	3	Kermadec Trench	E	8

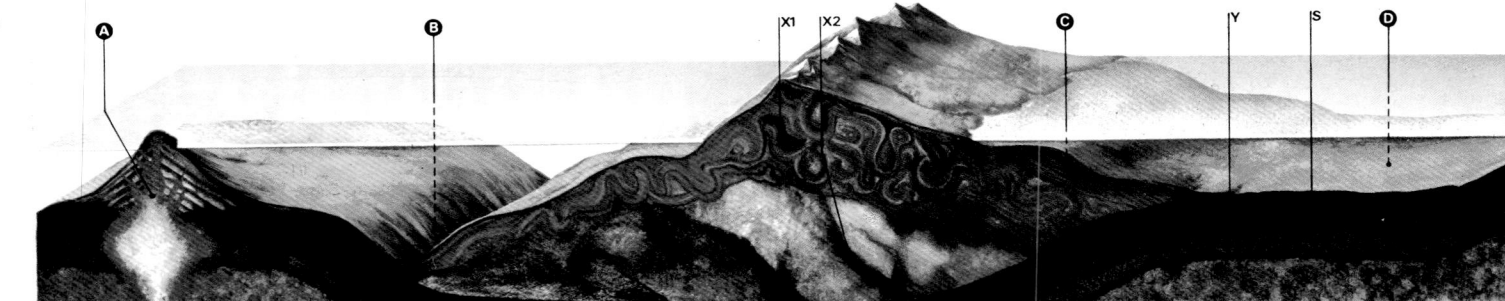

The ocean floor consists of narrow valleys, broad plains, and huge mountain ranges. Major undersea landforms are shown on the map, *below.* The map index indicates their locations.

and Ascension. A continuation of the Mid-Atlantic Ridge circles the southern tip of Africa and extends beneath the Indian Ocean. Underwater mountains also extend between Australia and Antarctica, as well as beneath the Pacific Ocean to Mexico.

The deepest parts of the ocean bottom are long, narrow trenches, or valleys. These trenches are filled with sediment that is often hundreds of feet (meters) thick. The earth's deepest trench is the Mariana Trench. It is 43 miles (68.8 kilometers) wide and 1,580 miles (2,550 kilometers) long. Its bottom is 36,198 feet (11,033 meters) below the surface of the Pacific Ocean.

Many of earth's resources, such as minerals, oil, and gas, are found beneath the ocean waters. The continental shelves are particularly rich in oil. In fact, about 20 per cent of the world's oil supply comes from offshore drilling in modern or ancient river deltas. Rocks containing manganese, a mineral that is important in the production of steel, are scattered all over the ocean floor. There are large deposits of metals, among them nickel and cobalt, on some parts of the sea floor. It seems likely that additional deposits of minerals and other useful substances will be discovered beneath the sea. Exploration of the riches beneath earth's ocean water has really just begun.

Kuril Trench	C	7
Labrador Basin	B	2
Lord Howe Rise	E	7
Mariana Trench	C	7
Mendocino Fracture Zone	C	8
Mid-Atlantic Ridge	D 2, E	3
Mid-Indian Ridge	E	5
Middle America Trench	D	10
Molokai Fracture Zone	C	9
Murray Fracture Zone	C	9
Nazca Ridge	D	10
Ninetyeast Ridge	D	5
Pacific-Antarctic Ridge	F	8
Peru-Chile Trench	E	10
Puerto Rico Trench	C	1
Reykjanes Ridge	B	2
Rockall Rise	B	3
South Indian Basin	F	6
Southeast Indian Rise	E	6
Southeast Pacific Basin	F	9
Southwest Indian Ridge	E	5
Tasman Basin	E	7
Tonga Trench	D	8
Walvis Ridge	E	3

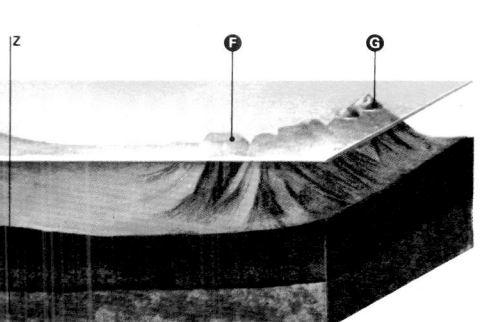

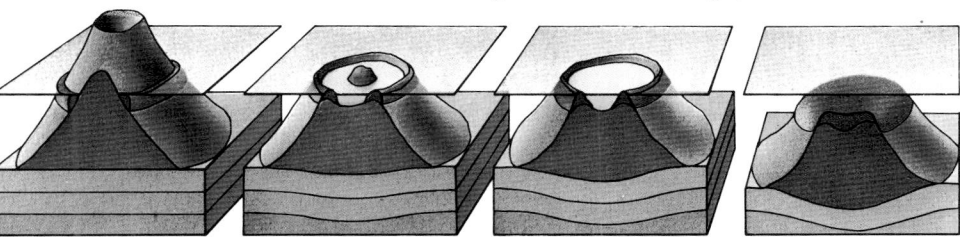

Stages of a coral island are shown here from left to right. First, a volcanic peak on a submarine ridge starts to sink beneath the sea. Next, coral grows, forming a shallow saltwater lagoon. When the original island disappears, the coral continues its upward growth and fills in the lagoon. Eventually the coral atoll sinks beneath the surface. The submerged island is called a guyot.

Earth's Minerals

All the rock on earth is formed of materials known as minerals. These substances are inorganic, which means they are made of matter that was never living. Some minerals such as gold are one single chemical element. Others are mixtures of elements. For example, hematite, also known as iron ore, consists of iron and oxygen.

The word "mineral" means something that is mined, or dug out of the earth. Nearly all minerals are formed inside the earth and can be removed only by mining. However, not all substances that are mined are minerals. Coal and oil are mined from the earth, but these substances are not minerals because they were formed from the remains of living things.

Atoms are incredibly tiny basic units of matter. In minerals, atoms are always arranged in repeated, three-dimensional patterns of flat surfaces and angles. These patterns of square or triangular shapes are called crystals. Its crystalline pattern deter-

mines one of the chief characteristics of a mineral—hardness. For example, a crystalline pattern formed of loosely packed atoms is softer than one formed of tightly packed atoms. Thus, some minerals, among them talc, are soft enough to be scratched by a fingernail. Other minerals, however, such as diamonds are extremely hard.

In addition to hardness, three other main characteristics of a mineral are its luster, cleavage, and color. The luster of a mineral may be shiny like metal, or it may be nonmetallic. A mineral's cleavage is the way it splits into pieces that have flat surfaces. The color of a mineral can result from its chemical composition or from chemical impurities in its crystals.

Minerals form in different ways. Many are brought into earth's crust in the hot, molten rock that seeps up from the mantle. The atoms of the various elements and compounds that make up the hot liquid are far apart and moving rapidly. As the liquid cools, the atoms slow down and come together, settling into crystalline patterns and forming minerals.

Some minerals form when hot gases erupt from volcanoes and vents in the earth's crust. The hot gases carry steam and particles of dust into the air. The gases cool suddenly when they reach the surface, and the atoms of certain elements join to form crystals that fall to the ground.

Still other minerals form by the slow evaporation of water in which the minerals are dissolved. As some of the water evaporates, the atoms of mineral elements move together in the remaining waters. Finally the atoms form into their crystalline shape.

There are about 3,000 different minerals. Many are highly useful to people, and some are essential. Minerals are used in food preparation, art, manufacturing, building, agriculture, and medicine. Many countries make their coins out of the metal minerals silver and nickel. Gold is a highly valued mineral used as international currency. Other minerals form valuable gemstones such as emeralds, rubies, and sapphires.

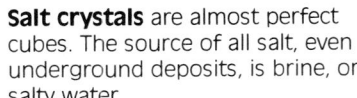

Most salt deposits of the United States Gulf Coast occur in formations called salt domes. The interior of a mine in a salt dome is actually a series of rooms made of salt.

Salt crystals are almost perfect cubes. The source of all salt, even underground deposits, is brine, or salty water.

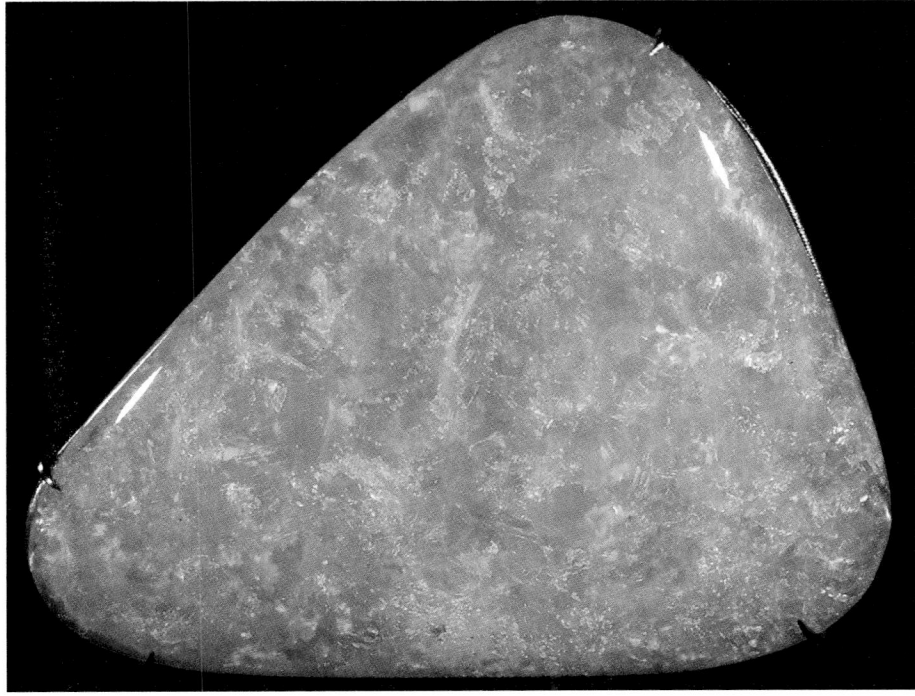

Opal is a gem made of silica that contains water. The water in an opal breaks the light that strikes it into brilliant internal colors.

An azure-blue color is characteristic of azurite, a copper mineral chiefly used as jewelry.

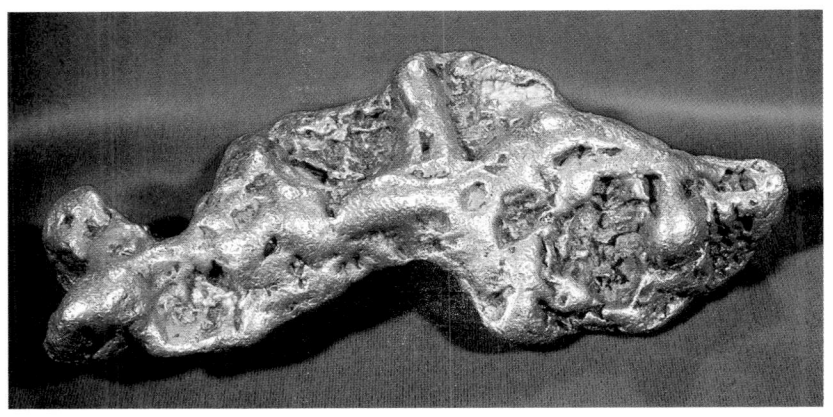

The metallic luster of gold does not tarnish. Gold, one of the first known metals, is prized for its beauty and scarcity.

Mica cleaves along specific planes — that is, it splits in one direction and forms thin sheets.

The hardest mineral is the diamond. It has a hardness of 10 on a hardness scale developed by Friedrich Mohs in 1822. A fingernail has a hardness of about 2 on the scale.

Natural vegetation in
New Mexico, U.S.

A map of the earth's pattern of natural vegetation

Natural vegetation in central Australia

Thematic Maps

THEMATIC MAPS graphically present and document information about aspects of the earth's land and its uses, and the earth's people and their cultures.

Land and Water

This map of the world provides an overview of the earth's basic geographic features. The map's primary purpose is to convey general information about the relative size and location of various land forms and bodies of water. Color is used to depict height above and depth below sea level of the earth's various features. More precise information is provided in the bar graphs below.

The Namib Desert meets the Atlantic at the Namibian coast. Wind creates surface "waves" on both land and sea.

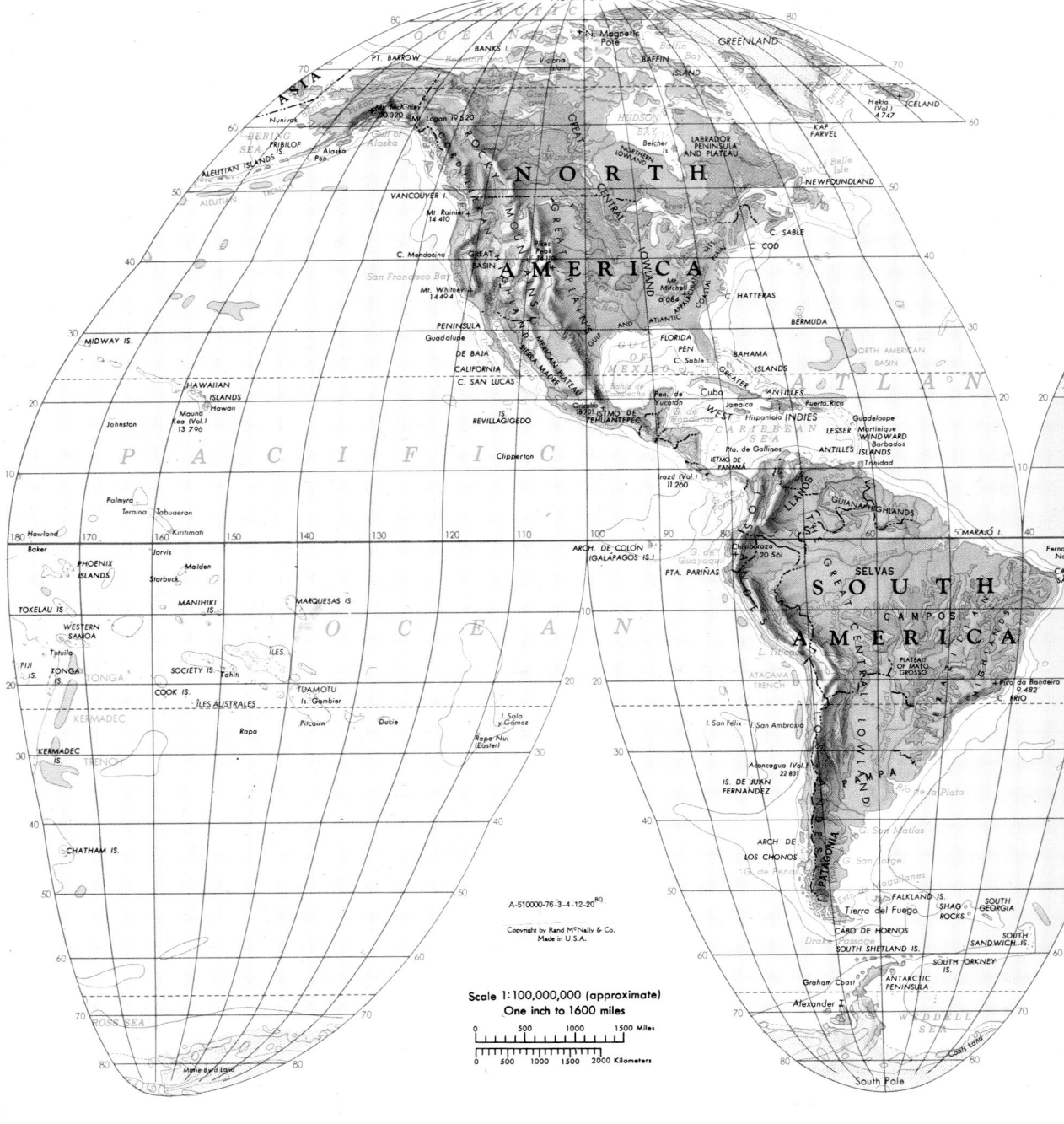

Scale 1:100,000,000 (approximate)
One inch to 1600 miles

Copyright by Rand McNally & Co.
Made in U.S.A.

Land Elevations in Profile

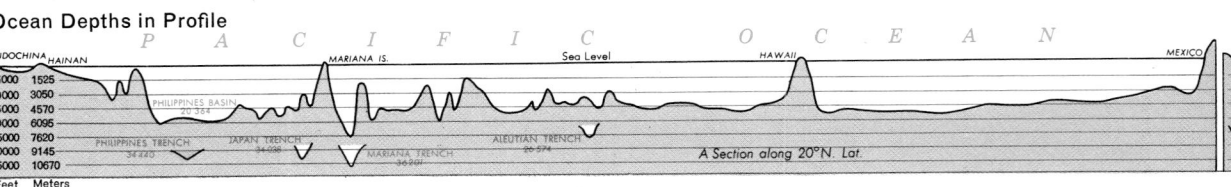

Ocean Depths in Profile

Vast farmlands occupy much of the interior plains of the United States.

The Sierra Nevada is a huge granite mountain range that extends from north to south for 400 miles (640 kilometers) in eastern California. The range's highest point is Mount Whitney.

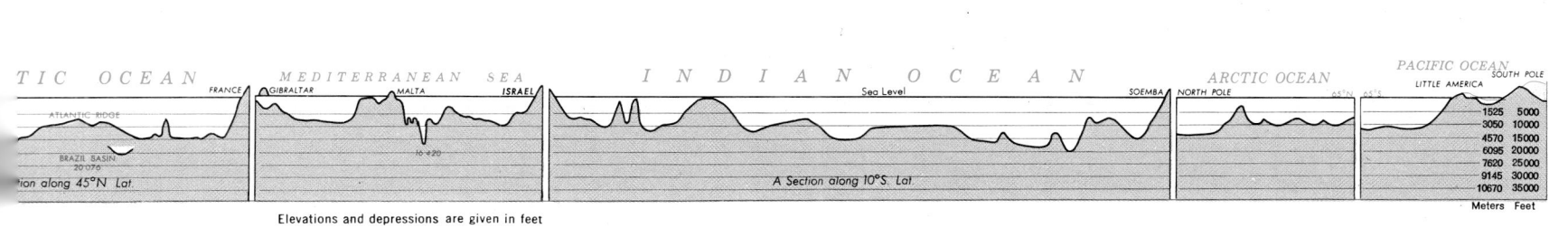

Goode's Homolosine Equal Area Projection

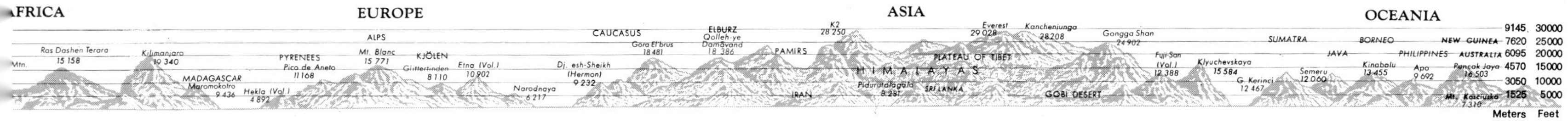

Elevations and depressions are given in feet

A Section along 45°N. Lat.

A Section along 10°S. Lat.

Temperature

In these maps, color is used to present general information about the temperatures in different parts of the world at different times of the year. As you can see from the map below, there are few parts of the earth where the temperature is always mild. The greatest swings in temperature are found in northeastern Siberia, where highs and lows may vary by more than 190° F. (106° C).

Surface temperature regions

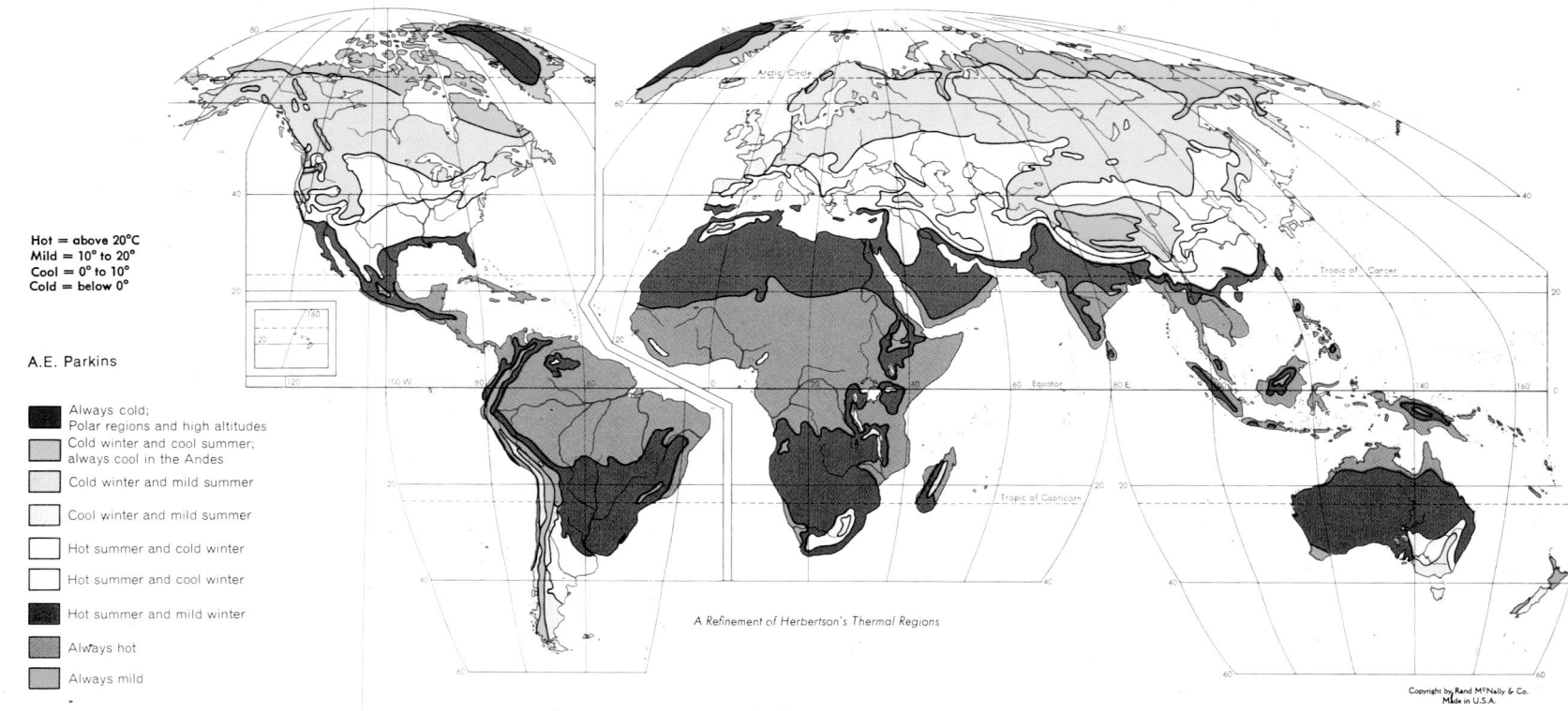

Hot = above 20°C
Mild = 10° to 20°
Cool = 0° to 10°
Cold = below 0°

A.E. Parkins

- Always cold; Polar regions and high altitudes
- Cold winter and cool summer; always cool in the Andes
- Cold winter and mild summer
- Cool winter and mild summer
- Hot summer and cold winter
- Hot summer and cool winter
- Hot summer and mild winter
- Always hot
- Always mild

A Refinement of Herbertson's Thermal Regions

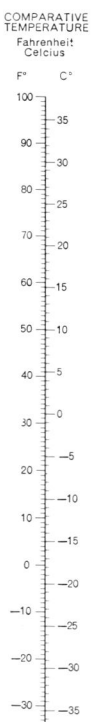

COMPARATIVE TEMPERATURE
Fahrenheit
Celsius

The temperature of a region is determined by the total amount of sunlight that it receives. Temperature greatly affects a region's weather.

January normal temperature

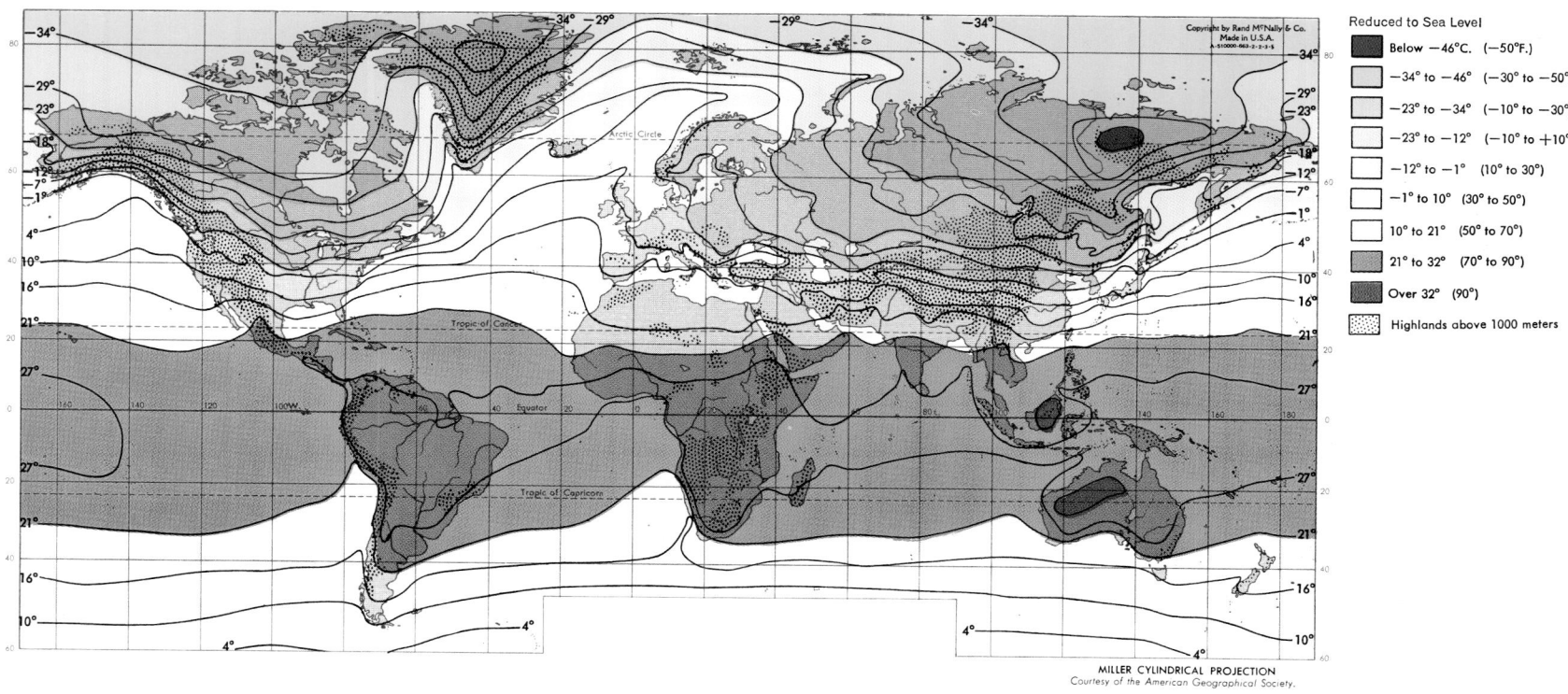

Reduced to Sea Level

- Below −46°C. (−50°F.)
- −34° to −46° (−30° to −50°)
- −23° to −34° (−10° to −30°)
- −23° to −12° (−10° to +10°)
- −12° to −1° (10° to 30°)
- −1° to 10° (30° to 50°)
- 10° to 21° (50° to 70°)
- 21° to 32° (70° to 90°)
- Over 32° (90°)
- Highlands above 1000 meters

MILLER CYLINDRICAL PROJECTION
Courtesy of the American Geographical Society.

July normal temperature

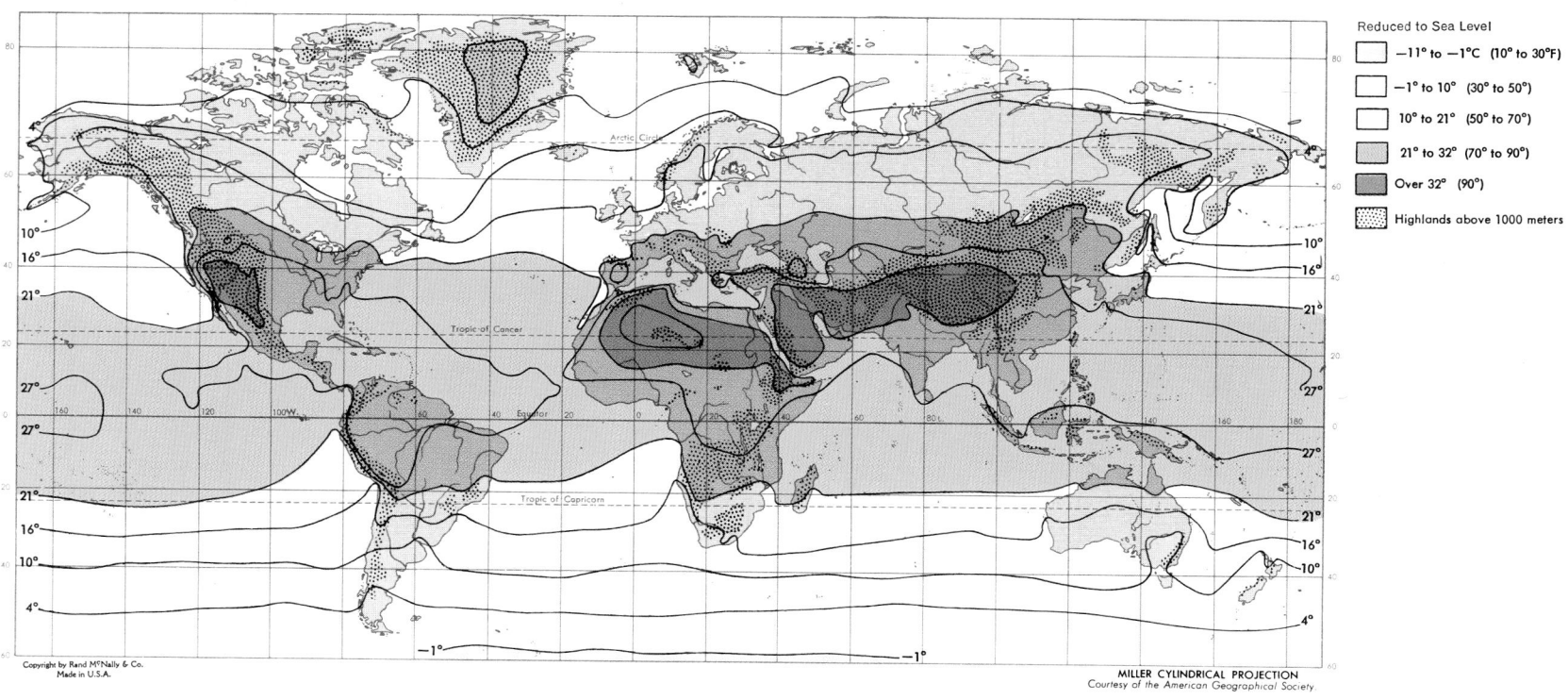

Reduced to Sea Level

- −11° to −1°C. (10° to 30°F.)
- −1° to 10° (30° to 50°)
- 10° to 21° (50° to 70°)
- 21° to 32° (70° to 90°)
- Over 32° (90°)
- Highlands above 1000 meters

MILLER CYLINDRICAL PROJECTION
Courtesy of the American Geographical Society.

Normal annual range of temperature

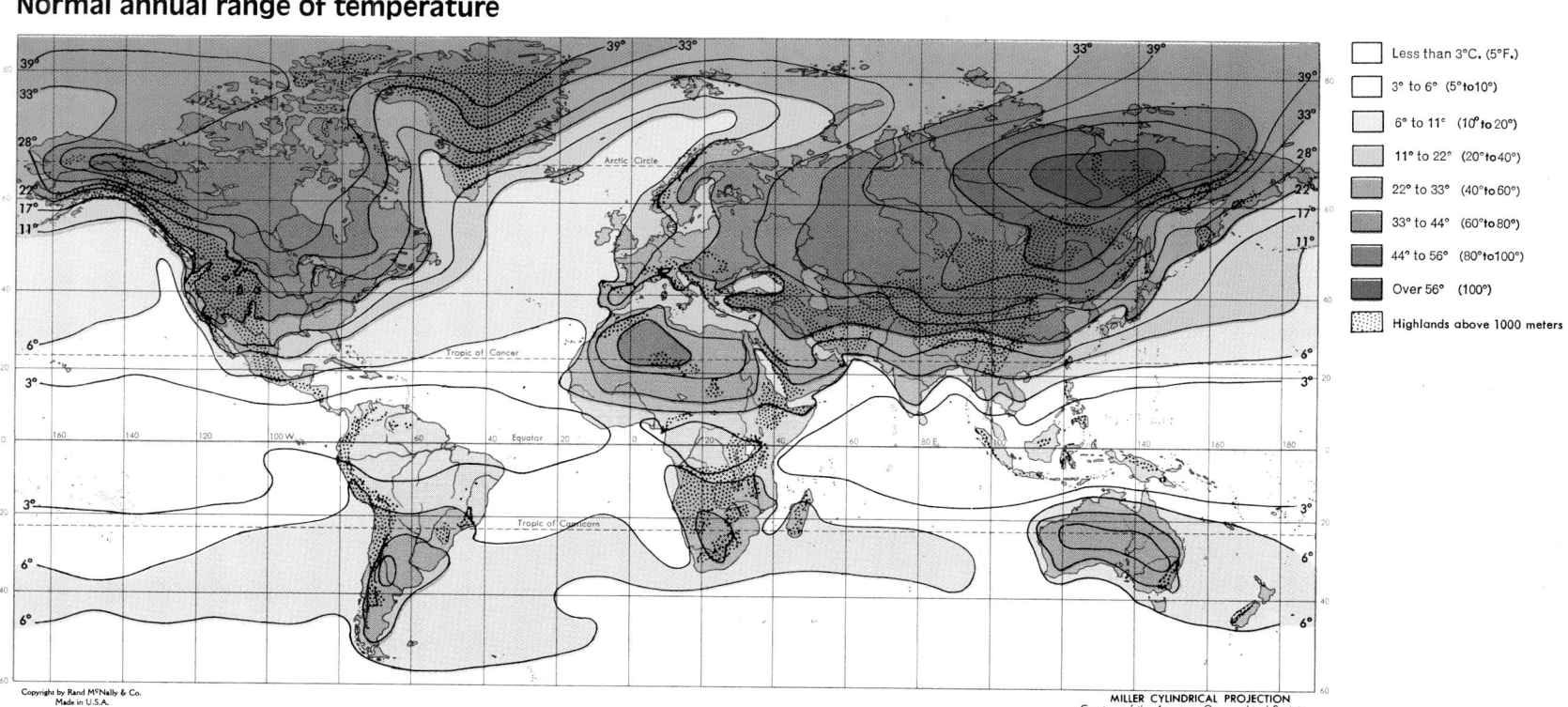

- Less than 3°C. (5°F.)
- 3° to 6° (5° to 10°)
- 6° to 11° (10° to 20°)
- 11° to 22° (20° to 40°)
- 22° to 33° (40° to 60°)
- 33° to 44° (60° to 80°)
- 44° to 56° (80° to 100°)
- Over 56° (100°)
- Highlands above 1000 meters

MILLER CYLINDRICAL PROJECTION
Courtesy of the American Geographical Society.

Precipitation, Winds, and Ocean Currents

Seasonal precipitation and air pressure are indicated by color in these thematic maps. Arrows on the two smaller maps show the direction and force of predominant winds. Longer arrows indicate steadier winds, while the thickness of the arrow is proportional to wind speed. The swirls of ocean currents are also shown by arrows on the large map.

Annual precipitation and ocean currents

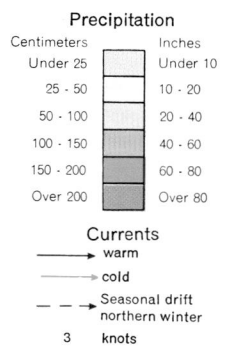

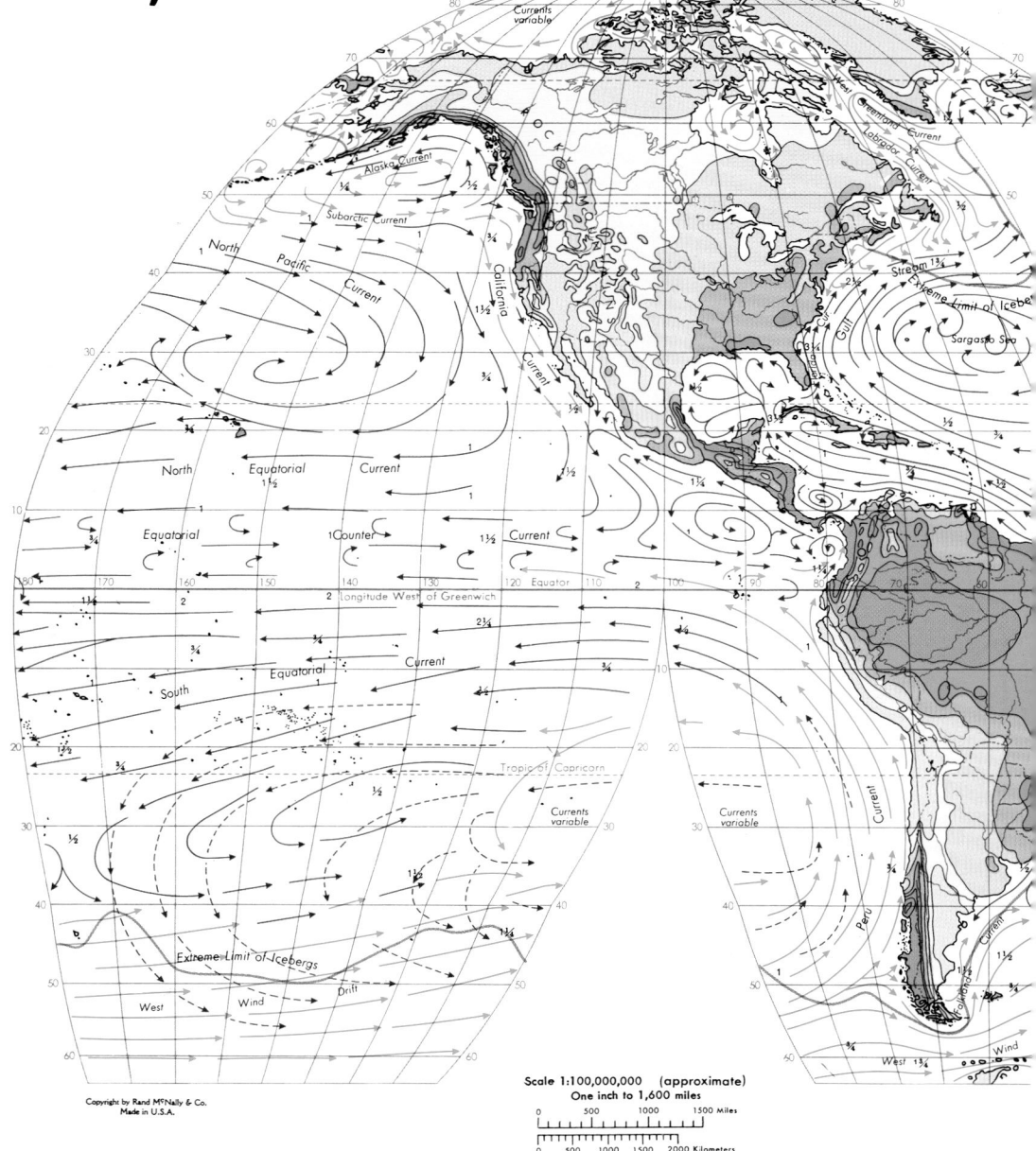

Scale 1:100,000,000 (approximate)
One inch to 1,600 miles

Copyright by Rand M\cNally & Co.
Made in U.S.A.

January pressure and predominant winds

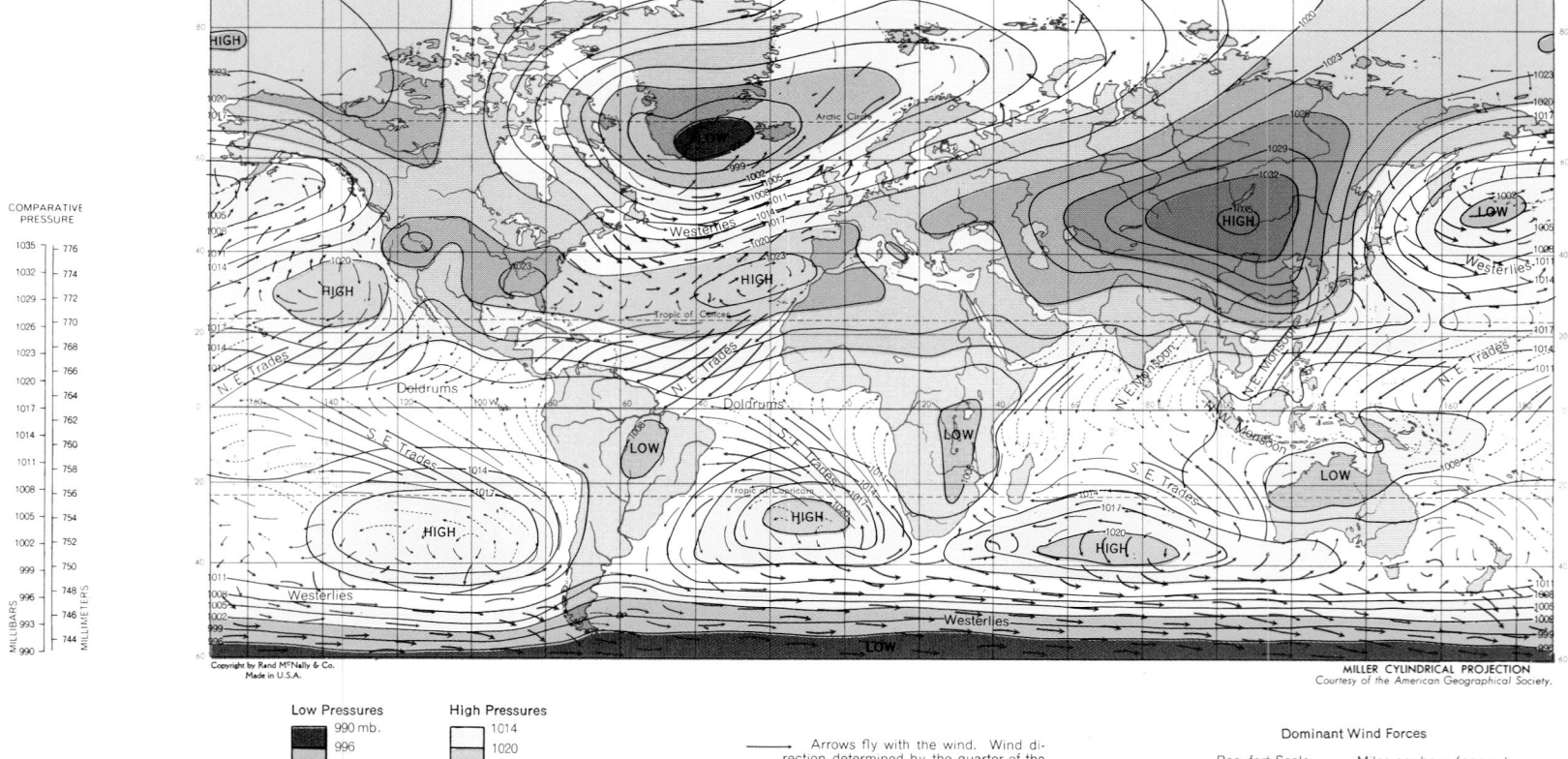

MILLER CYLINDRICAL PROJECTION
Courtesy of the American Geographical Society.

Copyright by Rand M\cNally & Co.
Made in U.S.A.

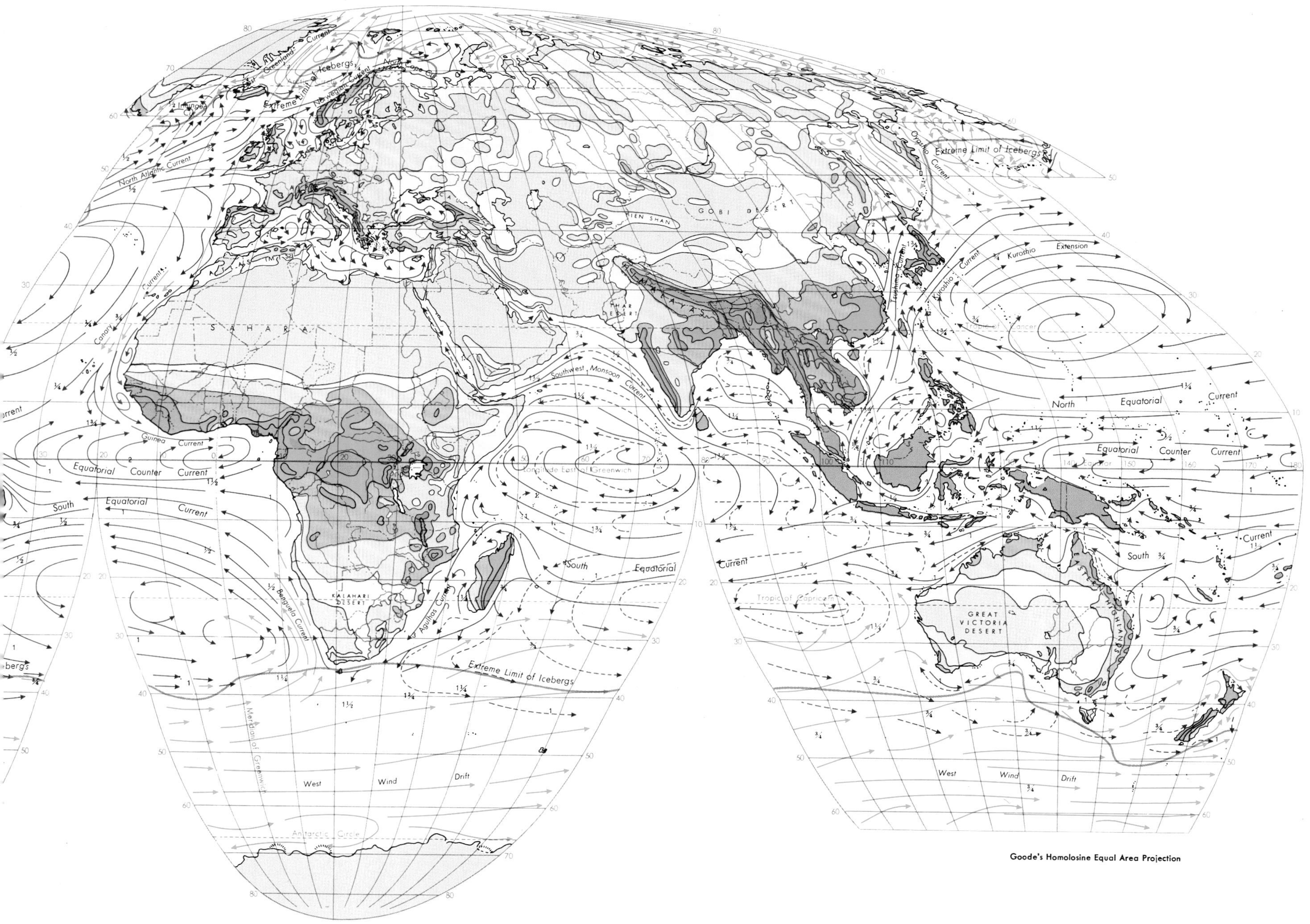

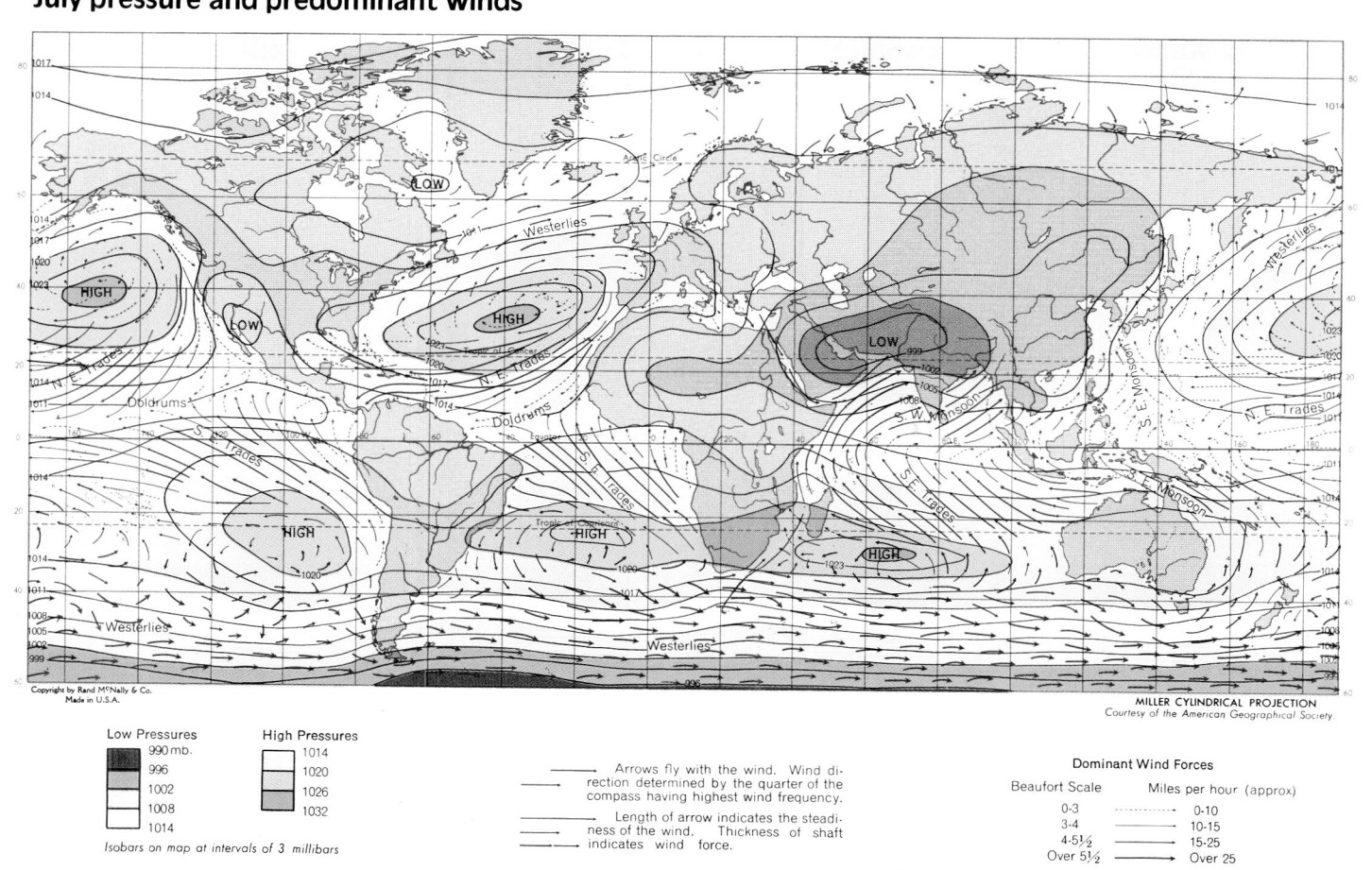

Goode's Homolosine Equal Area Projection

July pressure and predominant winds

MILLER CYLINDRICAL PROJECTION
Courtesy of the American Geographical Society.

Copyright by Rand McNally & Co.
Made in U.S.A.

Low Pressures		High Pressures	
	990 mb.		1014
	996		1020
	1002		1026
	1008		1032
	1014		

Isobars on map at intervals of 3 millibars

Arrows fly with the wind. Wind direction determined by the quarter of the
compass having highest wind frequency.

Length of arrow indicates the steadi-
ness of the wind.   Thickness of shaft
indicates wind force.

Dominant Wind Forces

Beaufort Scale	Miles per hour (approx)
0-3	0-10
3-4	10-15
4-5½	15-25
Over 5½	Over 25

Climatic Regions

Temperature, winds, precipitation—the interaction of these and other forces with the surface of the earth creates distinctive climates in different regions. The hottest, wettest countries of the world are found along the equator. Areas along the equator feature tropical rain forests and savannas. The Tropic of Capricorn passes mostly through dry climates, except for very small parts of Australia and Africa and the stretch between Brazil and Paraguay. There is more climatic variety along the Tropic of Cancer. While the map provides qualitative information, the graphs below supply quantitative information on rainfall and temperature.

Glenn T. Trewartha
The scheme of classification is modified and simplified from Köppen.

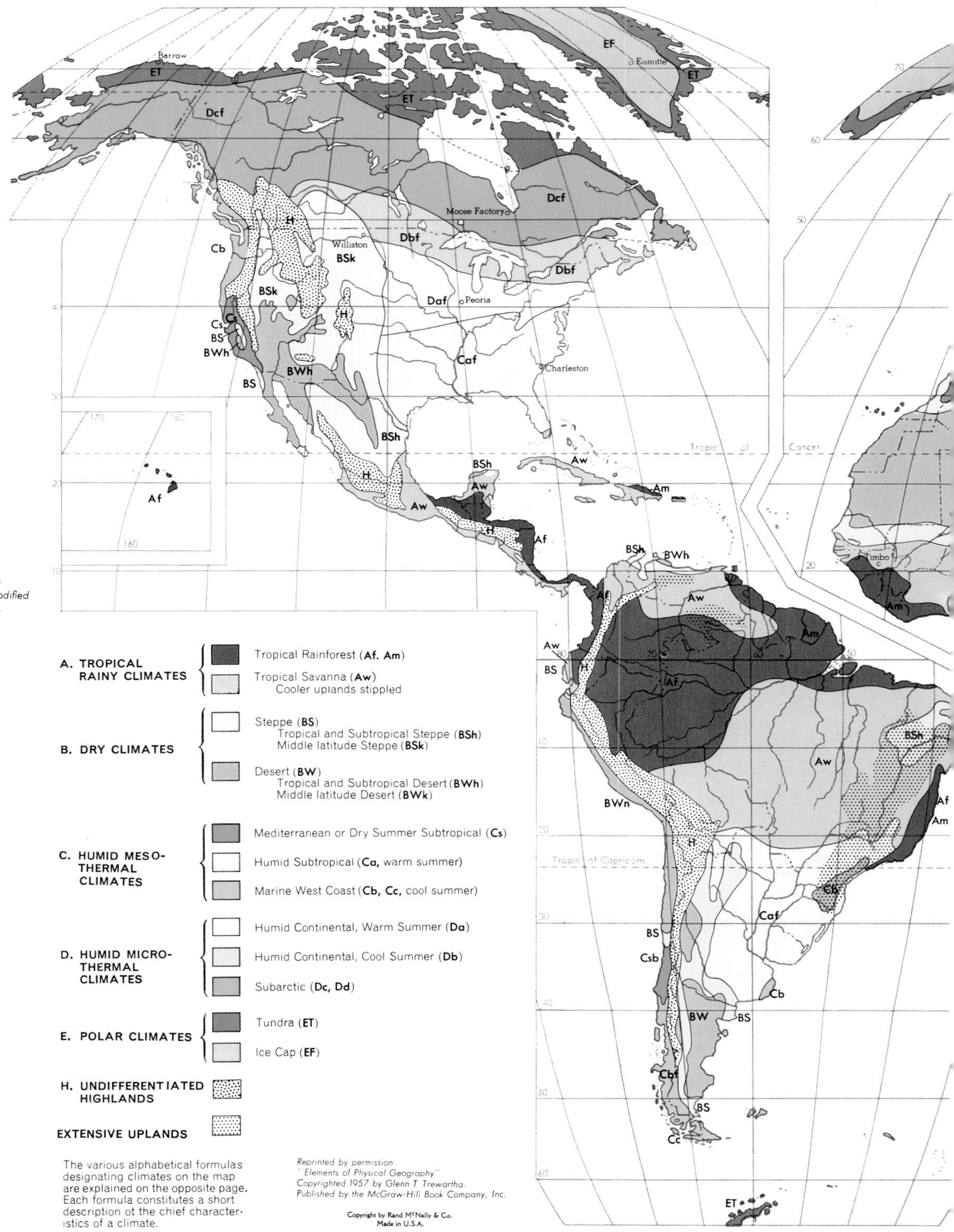

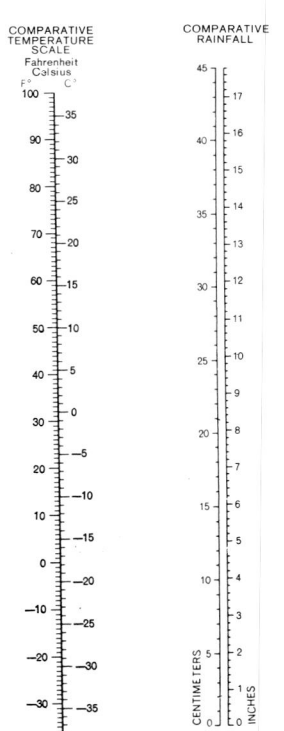

A. TROPICAL RAINY CLIMATES
- Tropical Rainforest (**Af, Am**)
- Tropical Savanna (**Aw**) Cooler uplands stippled

B. DRY CLIMATES
- Steppe (**BS**) Tropical and Subtropical Steppe (**BSh**) Middle latitude Steppe (**BSk**)
- Desert (**BW**) Tropical and Subtropical Desert (**BWh**) Middle latitude Desert (**BWk**)

C. HUMID MESO-THERMAL CLIMATES
- Mediterranean or Dry Summer Subtropical (**Cs**)
- Humid Subtropical (**Ca**, warm summer)
- Marine West Coast (**Cb, Cc**, cool summer)

D. HUMID MICRO-THERMAL CLIMATES
- Humid Continental, Warm Summer (**Da**)
- Humid Continental, Cool Summer (**Db**)
- Subarctic (**Dc, Dd**)

E. POLAR CLIMATES
- Tundra (**ET**)
- Ice Cap (**EF**)

H. UNDIFFERENTIATED HIGHLANDS

EXTENSIVE UPLANDS

The various alphabetical formulas designating climates on the map are explained on the opposite page. Each formula constitutes a short description of the chief character-istics of a climate.

Reprinted by permission.
"Elements of Physical Geography".
Copyrighted 1957 by Glenn T. Trewartha.
Published by the McGraw-Hill Book Company, Inc.

Copyright by Rand McNally & Co.
Made in U.S.A.

COMPARATIVE TEMPERATURE SCALE
Fahrenheit Celsius

COMPARATIVE RAINFALL

CENTIMETERS
INCHES

CURVES SHOW FAHRENHEIT TEMPERATURE
VERTICAL BARS SHOW RAINFALL IN INCHES

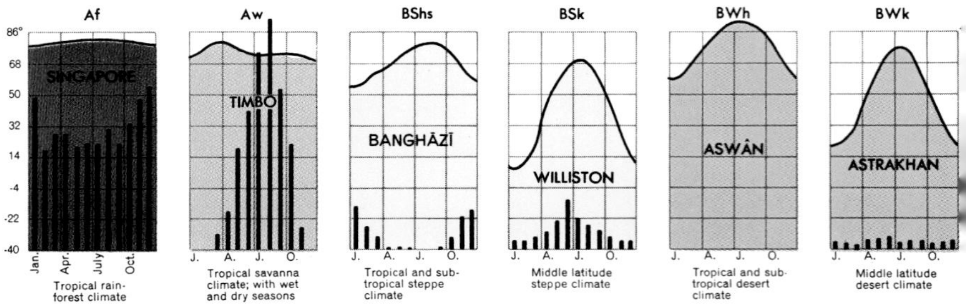

Af — SINGAPORE — Tropical rain-forest climate

Aw — TIMBO — Tropical savanna climate; with wet and dry seasons

BShs — BANGHÃZĨ — Tropical and sub-tropical steppe climate

BSk — WILLISTON — Middle latitude steppe climate

BWh — ASWÃN — Tropical and sub-tropical desert climate

BWk — ASTRAKHAN — Middle latitude desert climate

The climate of a given region has a great effect on people's life style. Climate helps determine the kinds of crops that grow, the kinds of housing in which people live, and the kinds of clothes that are worn.

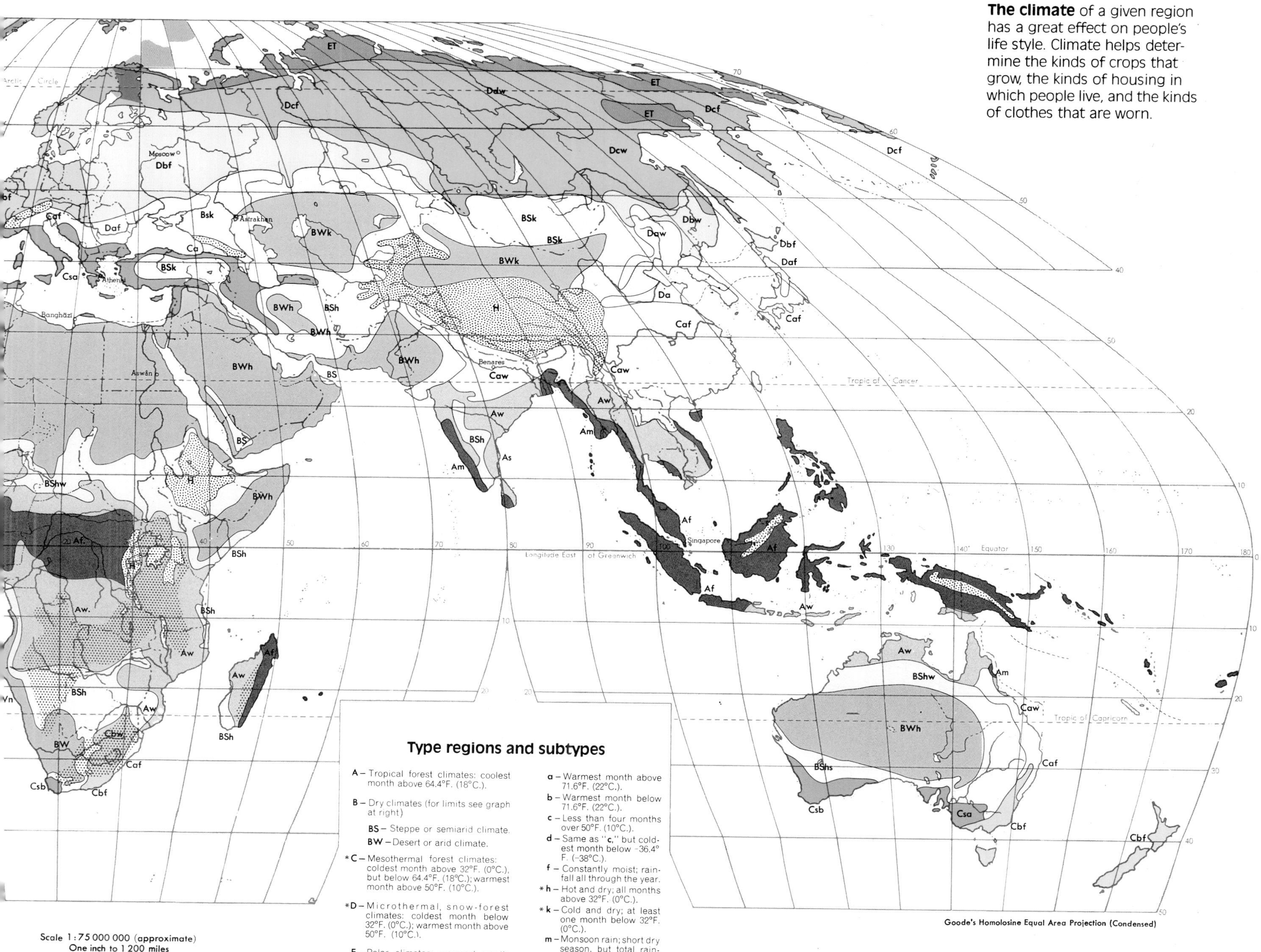

<!-- Climate map with labels -->
ET · Ddw · ET · Dcf · Dcw · Dcf · Dbf · Dbw · Daw · Daf · Da · Dbf · Caf · Caf · Caw · Aw · Am · As · Af · Singapore · Af · Aw · Aw · Am · BShw · Caw · BShw · BWh · BSh · Csb · Cbf · Caf · Cbf · Csa

Moscow · Dbf · Caf · BSk · Astrakhan · BWk · BSk · BSk · Ca · BWk · Csa · Athenai · H · BSh · Banghāzi · BWh · BSh · BWh · Aswān · BWh · BS · BSh · H · BWh · BSh · Benares · Caw · BSh · BShw · Af · Aw · BSh · Af · Aw · BW · Cbw · Caf · Csb · Cbf · Vn

Type regions and subtypes

A – Tropical forest climates: coolest month above 64.4°F. (18°C.).

B – Dry climates (for limits see graph at right)

   BS – Steppe or semiarid climate.

   BW – Desert or arid climate.

*****C** – Mesothermal forest climates: coldest month above 32°F. (0°C.), but below 64.4°F. (18°C.); warmest month above 50°F. (10°C.).

*****D** – Microthermal, snow-forest climates: coldest month below 32°F. (0°C.); warmest month above 50°F. (10°C.).

E – Polar climates: warmest month below 50°F. (10°C.).

   ET – Tundra climate: warmest month below 50°F. (10°C.) but above 32°F. (0°C.).

   EF – Perpetual frost: all months below 32°F. (0°C.).

a – Warmest month above 71.6°F. (22°C.).

b – Warmest month below 71.6°F. (22°C.).

c – Less than four months over 50°F. (10°C.).

d – Same as "c," but coldest month below -36.4°F. (-38°C.).

f – Constantly moist; rainfall all through the year.

*****h** – Hot and dry; all months above 32°F. (0°C.).

*****k** – Cold and dry; at least one month below 32°F. (0°C.).

m – Monsoon rain; short dry season, but total rainfall sufficient to support rainforest.

n – Frequent fog.

n′ – Infrequent fog, but high humidity and low rainfall.

s – Dry season in summer.

w – Dry season in winter.

* Modification of Köppen definition

Scale 1:75 000 000 (approximate)
One inch to 1 200 miles
0 500 1000 1500 Miles
0 500 1000 1500 2000 Kilometers

Goode's Homolosine Equal Area Projection (Condensed)

Limits of the regions of dry climate

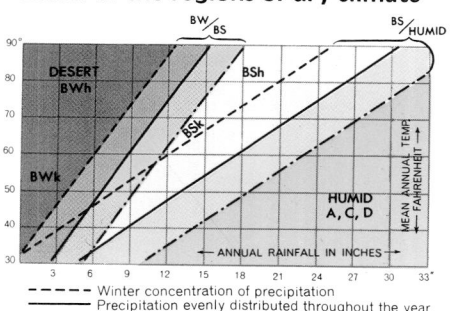

DESERT BWh · BSh · BWk · HUMID A, C, D · BW/BS · BS/HUMID · BSk

MEAN ANNUAL TEMP. FAHRENHEIT
ANNUAL RAINFALL IN INCHES

--- Winter concentration of precipitation
— Precipitation evenly distributed throughout the year
-·- Summer concentration of precipitation

Csa

ATHENAI

Mild climate; summer drouth and winter rain

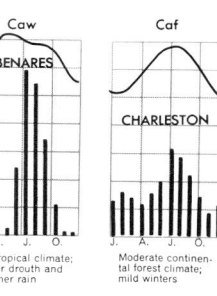

Caw

BENARES

Subtropical climate; winter drouth and summer rain

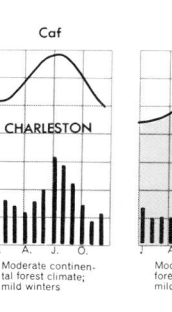

Caf

CHARLESTON

Moderate continental forest climate; mild winters

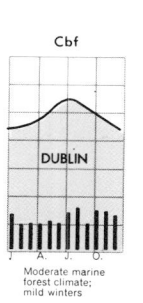

Cbf

DUBLIN

Moderate marine forest climate; mild winters

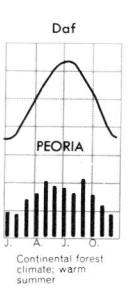

Daf

PEORIA

Continental forest climate; warm summer

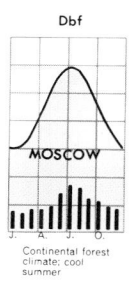

Dbf

MOSCOW

Continental forest climate; cool summer

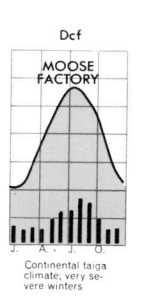

Dcf

MOOSE FACTORY

Continental taiga climate; very severe winters

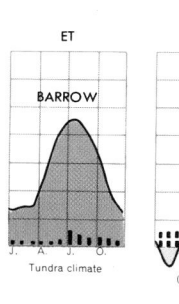

ET

BARROW

Tundra climate

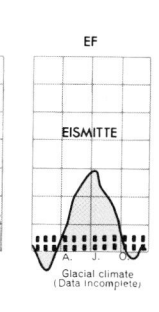

EF

EISMITTE

Glacial climate (Data incomplete)

Natural Vegetation

This map focuses on natural, not man-made, vegetation. Explanations of the formulas used to designate types of vegetation are provided. The key to the map's use of color and pattern is on the lower right.

As one would expect, vegetation is largely or entirely absent from the coldest extremes of our planet—the Arctic and Antarctic circles. As one moves toward the equator from either of the polar caps, vegetation becomes increasingly profuse.

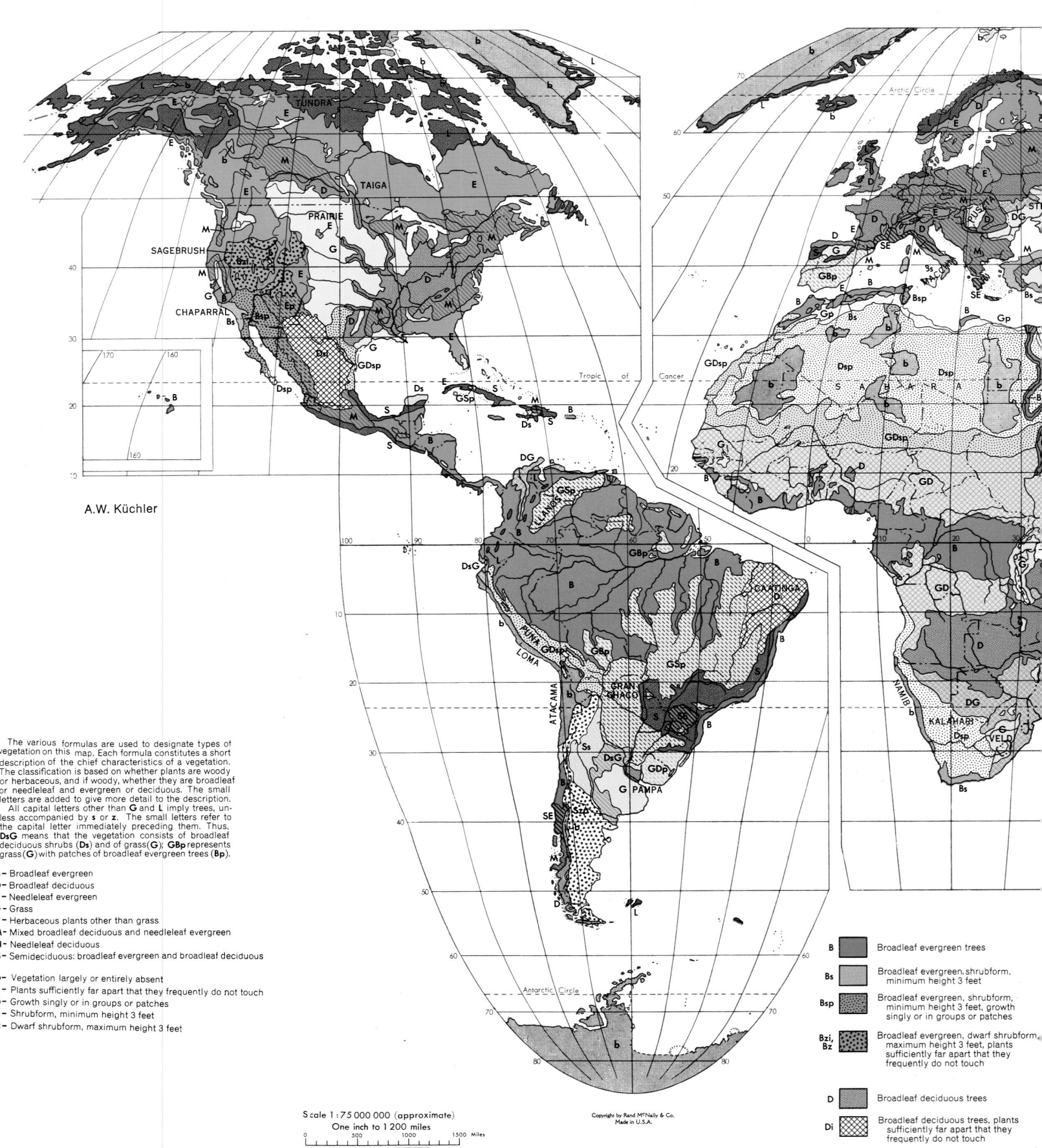

A.W. Küchler

The various formulas are used to designate types of vegetation on this map. Each formula constitutes a short description of the chief characteristics of a vegetation. The classification is based on whether plants are woody or herbaceous, and if woody, whether they are broadleaf or needleleaf and evergreen or deciduous. The small letters are added to give more detail to the description. All capital letters other than **G** and **L** imply trees, unless accompanied by **s** or **z**. The small letters refer to the capital letter immediately preceding them. Thus, **DsG** means that the vegetation consists of broadleaf deciduous shrubs (**Ds**) and of grass (**G**); **GBp** represents grass (**G**) with patches of broadleaf evergreen trees (**Bp**).

B – Broadleaf evergreen
D – Broadleaf deciduous
E – Needleleaf evergreen
G – Grass
L – Herbaceous plants other than grass
M – Mixed broadleaf deciduous and needleleaf evergreen
N – Needleleaf deciduous
S – Semideciduous: broadleaf evergreen and broadleaf deciduous

b – Vegetation largely or entirely absent
i – Plants sufficiently far apart that they frequently do not touch
p – Growth singly or in groups or patches
s – Shrubform, minimum height 3 feet
z – Dwarf shrubform, maximum height 3 feet

B	Broadleaf evergreen trees
Bs	Broadleaf evergreen, shrubform, minimum height 3 feet
Bsp	Broadleaf evergreen, shrubform, minimum height 3 feet, growth singly or in groups or patches
Bzi, Bz	Broadleaf evergreen, dwarf shrubform, maximum height 3 feet, plants sufficiently far apart that they frequently do not touch
D	Broadleaf deciduous trees
Di	Broadleaf deciduous trees, plants sufficiently far apart that they frequently do not touch

Scale 1:75 000 000 (approximate)
One inch to 1 200 miles
0   500   1000   1500 Miles
0 500 1000 1500 2000 Kilometers

The Australian outback is dry most of the year and comes to life only after a heavy rain.

Broadleaf deciduous trees are the prevailing natural vegetation in much of Great Britain. Here, sunlight filters through the trees in Simonshyde Wood, Saint Albans.

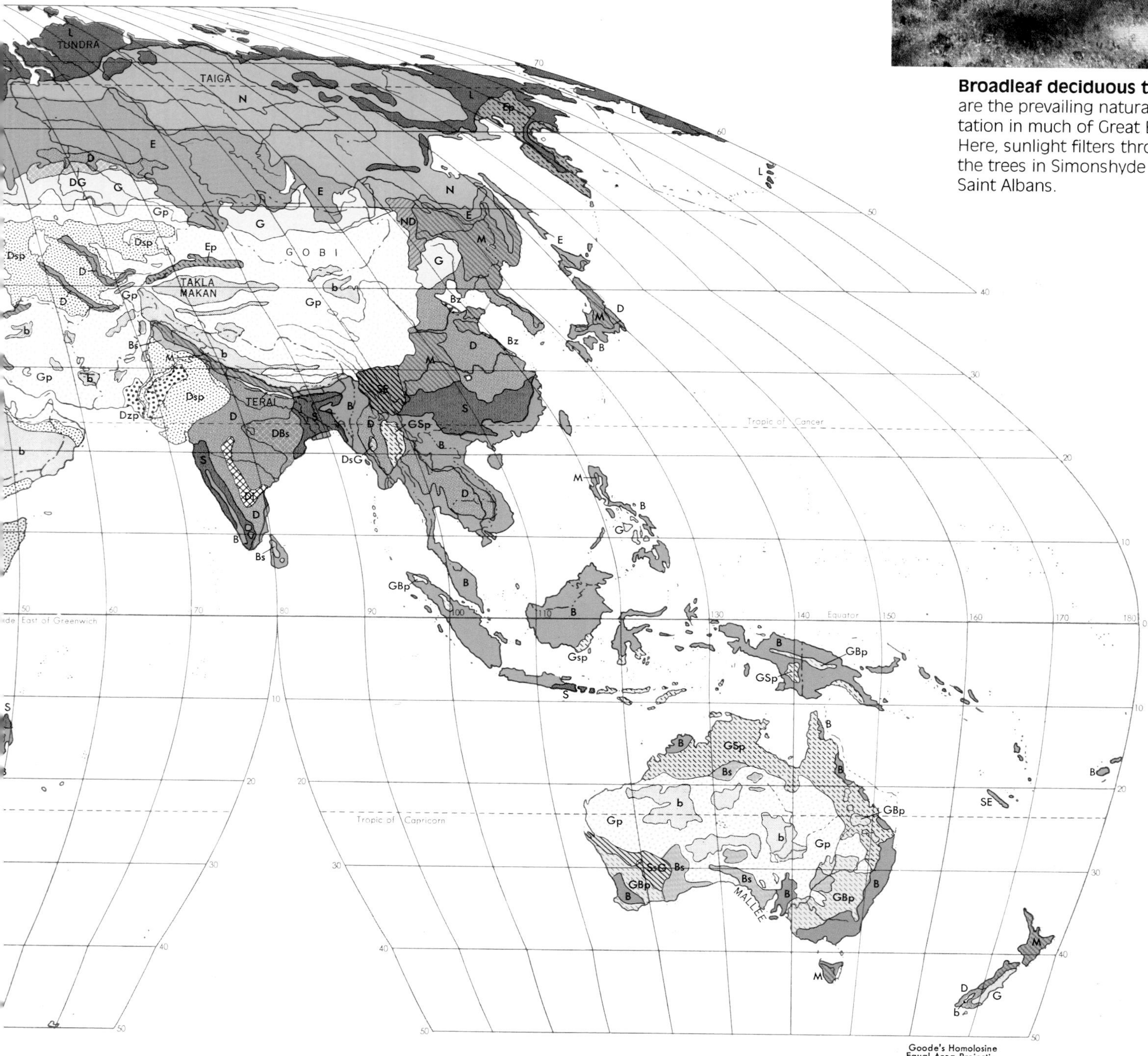

Goode's Homolosine
Equal Area Projection
(Condensed)

Ds		Broadleaf deciduous, shrubform, minimum height 3 feet
Dsi		Broadleaf deciduous, shrubform, minimum height 3 feet, plants sufficiently far apart that they frequently do not touch
Dsp		Broadleaf deciduous, shrubform, minimum height 3 feet, growth singly or in groups or patches
Dzp		Broadleaf deciduous, dwarf shrubform, maximum height 3 feet, growth singly or in groups or patches
DsG		Broadleaf deciduous, shrubform, minimum height 3 feet Grass and other herbaceous plants
DG		Broadleaf deciduous trees Grass and other herbaceous plants
DBs		Broadleaf deciduous trees Broadleaf evergreen, shrubform, minimum height 3 feet

E		Needleleaf evergreen trees
Ep		Needleleaf evergreen trees, growth singly or in groups or patches
G		Grass and other herbaceous plants
Gp		Grass and other herbaceous plants, growth singly or in groups or patches
GBp		Grass and other herbaceous plants Broadleaf evergreen trees, growth singly or in groups or patches
GD		Grass and other herbaceous plants Broadleaf deciduous trees
GDp		Grass and other herbaceous plants Broadleaf deciduous trees, growth singly or in groups or patches

GDsp		Grass and other herbaceous plants Broadleaf deciduous, shrubform, minimum height 3 feet, growth singly or in groups or patches
GSp		Grass and other herbaceous plants Semideciduous: broadleaf evergreen and broadleaf deciduous trees, growth singly or in groups or patches
L		Herbaceous plants other than grass
M		Mixed: broadleaf deciduous and needleleaf evergreen trees
N		Needleleaf deciduous trees
ND		Needleleaf deciduous trees Broadleaf deciduous trees

S		Semideciduous: broadleaf evergreen and broadleaf deciduous trees
Ss		Semideciduous: broadleaf evergreen and broadleaf deciduous, shrubform, minimum height 3 feet
SsG		Semideciduous: broadleaf evergreen and broadleaf deciduous, shrubform, minimum height 3 feet Grass and other herbaceous plants
Szp		Semideciduous: broadleaf evergreen and broadleaf deciduous, dwarf shrubform, maximum height 3 feet, growth singly or in groups or patches
SE		Semideciduous: broadleaf evergreen and broadleaf deciduous trees Needleleaf evergreen trees
b		Vegetation largely or entirely absent

Agricultural Regions

This thematic map shows qualitative, not quantitative, information. One can use the map to discover the types of agriculture that are practiced in various parts of the world, rather than to learn about agricultural output.

A look at North America reveals that much of the northern part of the continent is nonagricultural. The predominant types of agriculture in the United States are commercial livestock ranching and crop farming. Plantation agriculture and rudimental sedentary cultivation are common in Central America.

Shifting cultivation occurs in much of northern South America and central Africa. In large areas in northern Africa and central and northern Asia, nomadic herding is the norm. Intensive subsistence farming is practiced in Japan, Korea, much of China, most of Indochina, and India.

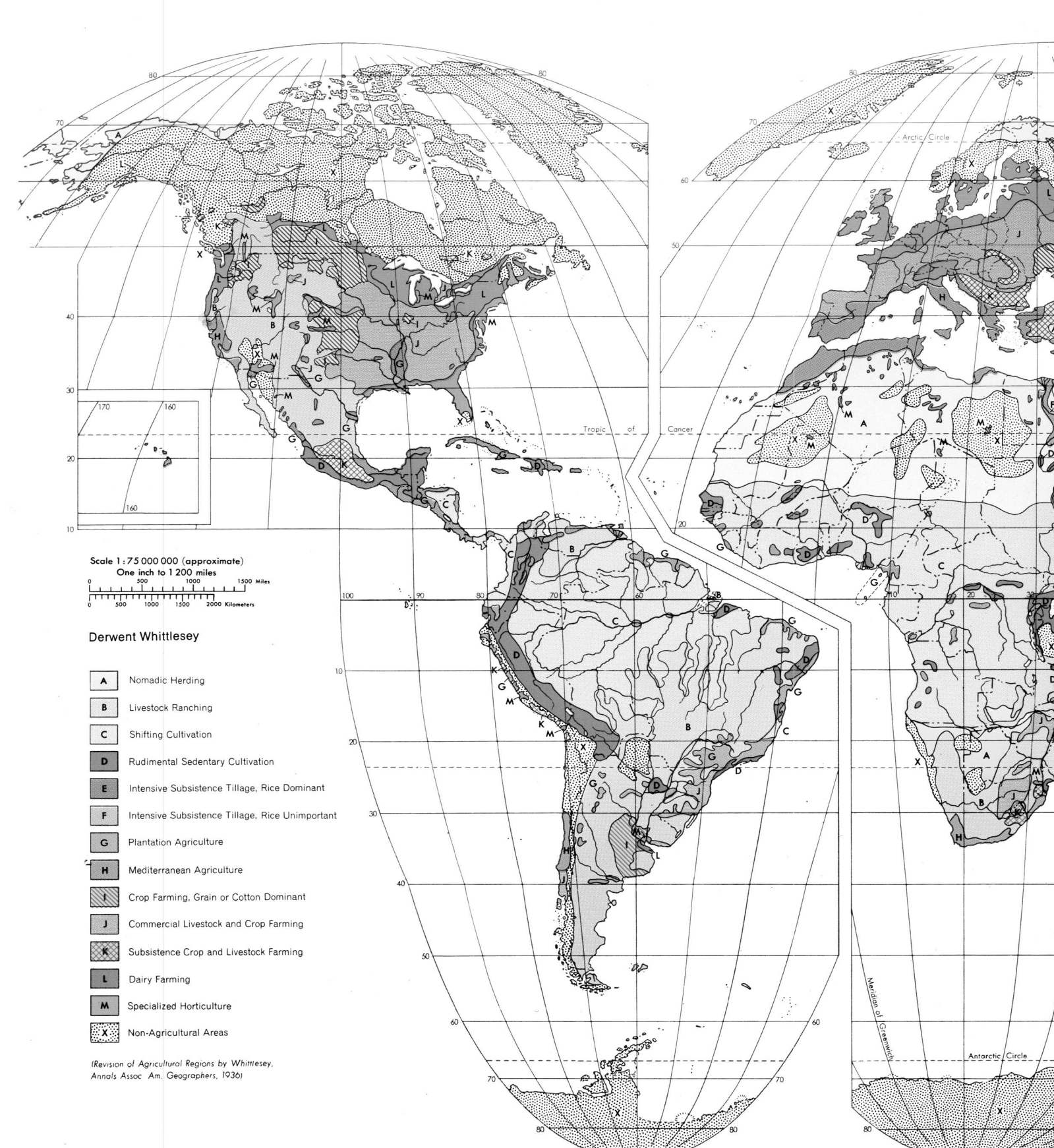

Scale 1 : 75 000 000 (approximate)
One inch to 1 200 miles

Derwent Whittlesey

A	Nomadic Herding
B	Livestock Ranching
C	Shifting Cultivation
D	Rudimental Sedentary Cultivation
E	Intensive Subsistence Tillage, Rice Dominant
F	Intensive Subsistence Tillage, Rice Unimportant
G	Plantation Agriculture
H	Mediterranean Agriculture
	Crop Farming, Grain or Cotton Dominant
J	Commercial Livestock and Crop Farming
	Subsistence Crop and Livestock Farming
L	Dairy Farming
M	Specialized Horticulture
X	Non-Agricultural Areas

(Revision of Agricultural Regions by Whittlesey,
Annals Assoc. Am. Geographers, 1936)

The type of agriculture in different parts of the world depends on conditions such as soil and climate. Terraced rice farming, *far left*, is seen in Bali; wheat farming in Saskatchewan, Canada; and nomadic herding in India.

Copyright by Rand McNally & Co.
Made in U.S.A.

Goode's Homolosine Equal Area Projection (Condensed)

Land Use

The main economies of various regions are shown here through the use of color and symbols. This map makes it easy to draw comparisons between regions and to study the distribution of certain economic activities. For example, while mining sites are scattered over many parts of the United States, most mining in South America is found in the continent's western and northern regions. The pie charts below complement the map by offering occupational information.

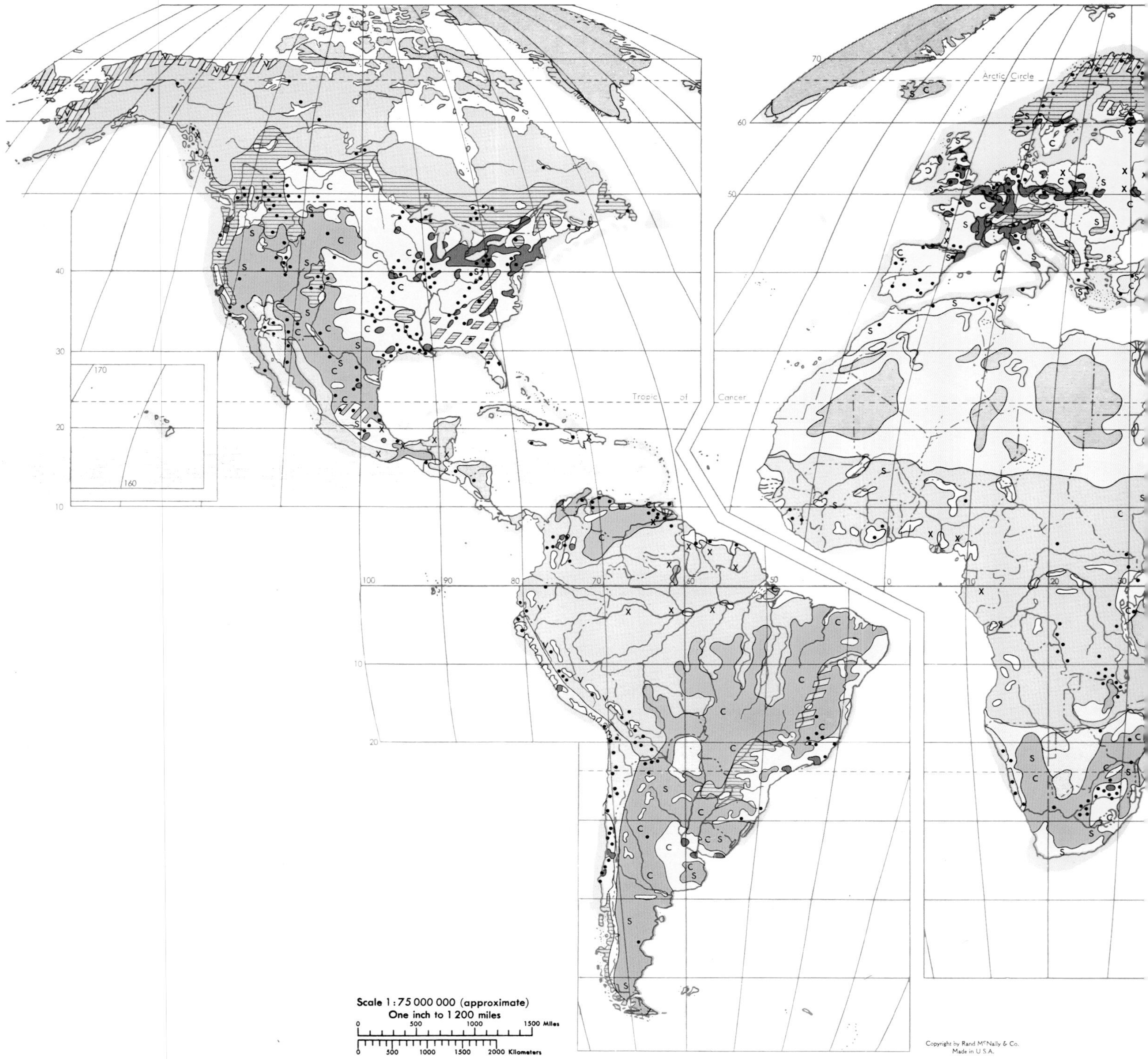

Arctic Circle
Tropic of Cancer
Scale 1 : 75 000 000 (approximate)
One inch to 1 200 miles
Copyright by Rand McNally & Co.
Made in U.S.A.

Occupational structure of selected areas

A—Agriculture
B—Manufacturing
C—Handicrafts
D—Mining
E—Construction
F—Trade and Commerce
G—Transportation and Communication
H—Service and Others

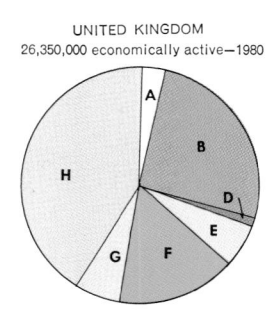

UNITED KINGDOM
26,350,000 economically active—1980

A
B
D
E
F
G
H

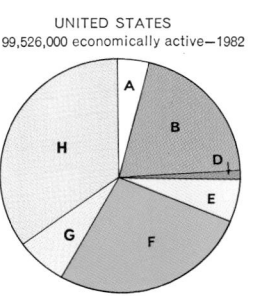

UNITED STATES
99,526,000 economically active—1982

A
B
D
E
F
G
H

CANADA
11,897,000 economically active—1983

A
B
D
E
F
G
H

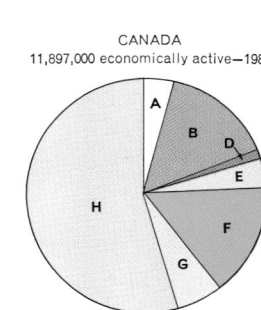

Most of the world's cultivated land is used to produce food, livestock, or forest products. Only in the last few centuries have mass-production methods become common.

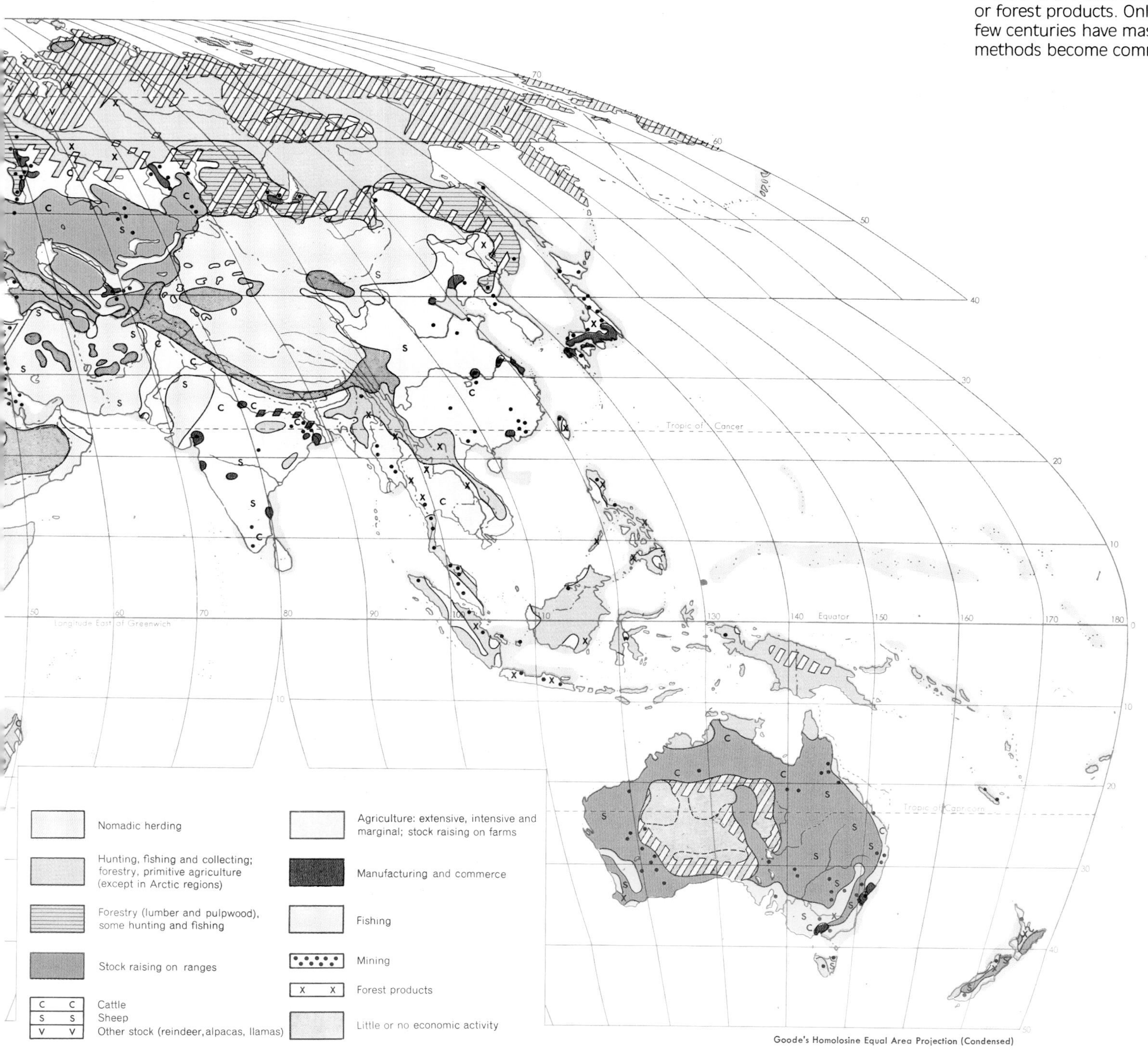

Nomadic herding	Agriculture: extensive, intensive and marginal; stock raising on farms
Hunting, fishing and collecting; forestry, primitive agriculture (except in Arctic regions)	Manufacturing and commerce
Forestry (lumber and pulpwood), some hunting and fishing	Fishing
Stock raising on ranges	Mining
C C Cattle	X X Forest products
S S Sheep	
V V Other stock (reindeer, alpacas, llamas)	Little or no economic activity

Goode's Homolosine Equal Area Projection (Condensed)

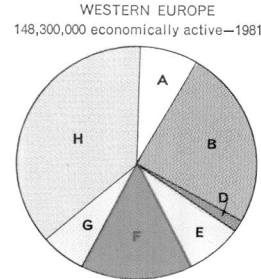

WESTERN EUROPE
148,300,000 economically active—1981

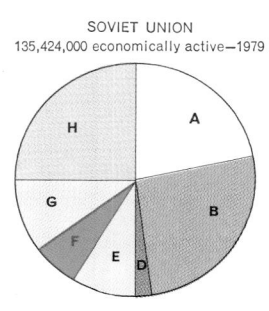

SOVIET UNION
135,424,000 economically active—1979

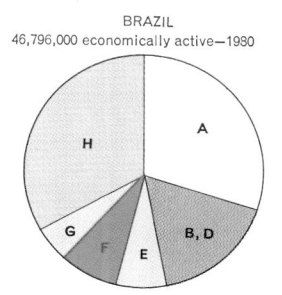

BRAZIL
46,796,000 economically active—1980

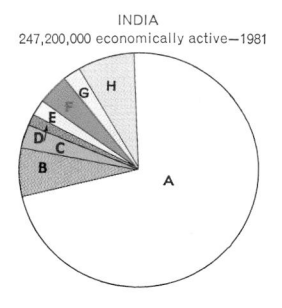

INDIA
247,200,000 economically active—1981

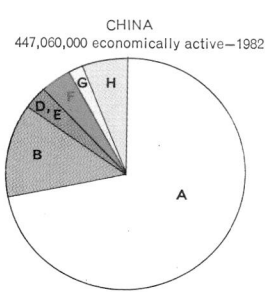

CHINA
447,060,000 economically active—1982

Distribution of Important Minerals

Ferrous Minerals

Ferrous minerals are minerals that contain iron. This thematic map shows the centers of production (mining) of ferrous minerals. The map also shows the commercial flow of iron ore. The wider the flow lines on the map, the greater the tonnage of ore. As the flow lines to Japan suggest, that country is the world's premier iron ore importer. A look at the pie chart reveals that Japan imports more than 37 per cent of the world's production of iron ore, while the nations of Europe account for more than 50 per cent.

The bar graphs below show the major producers of various ferrous minerals and their percentage of world production. Not surprisingly, the Soviet Union, which produces more than a quarter of the world's iron ore, is also the leader in iron ore reserves.

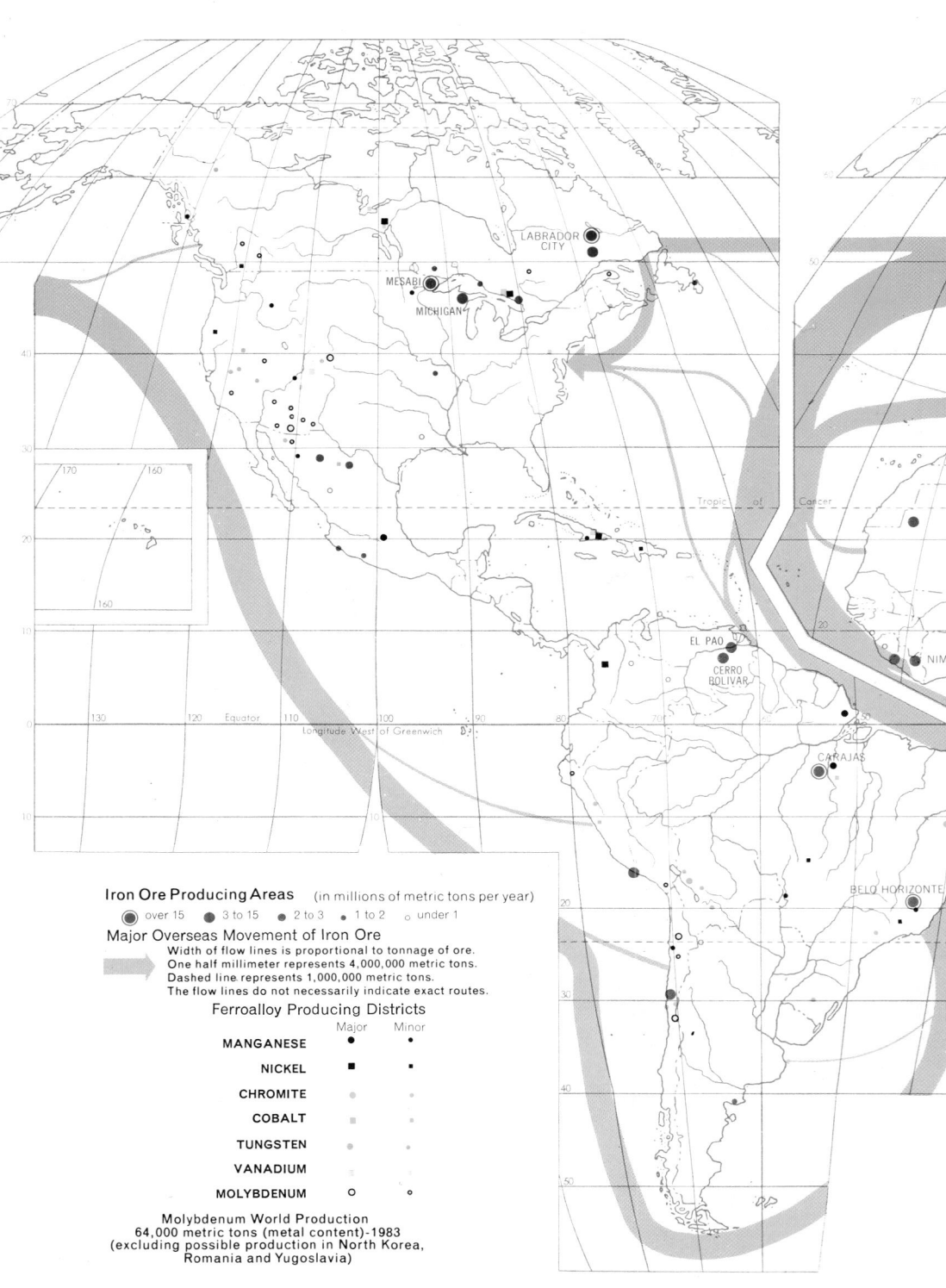

Iron Ore Producing Areas (in millions of metric tons per year)
⦿ over 15   ● 3 to 15   ● 2 to 3   • 1 to 2   ∘ under 1

Major Overseas Movement of Iron Ore
Width of flow lines is proportional to tonnage of ore.
One half millimeter represents 4,000,000 metric tons.
Dashed line represents 1,000,000 metric tons.
The flow lines do not necessarily indicate exact routes.

Ferroalloy Producing Districts

	Major	Minor
MANGANESE	●	•
NICKEL	■	▪
CHROMITE	○	∘
COBALT	○	∘
TUNGSTEN	○	∘
VANADIUM		
MOLYBDENUM	○	∘

Molybdenum World Production
64,000 metric tons (metal content)-1983
(excluding possible production in North Korea,
Romania and Yugoslavia)

Manganese World Production-7,961,000* metric tons (metal content)-1983

SOVIET UNION 40.6%	SOUTH AFRICA 14.1	GABON 11.9	BRAZIL 11.5	AUSTL. 7.6	INDIA 5.3	CHINA 4.0	ALL OTH. 2.9

←————AFRICA————→ ←S. AMER.→ ←ASIA→

*Excluding possible production in Cuba and Namibia

Nickel World Production-689,000 metric tons (metal content)-1983

SOVIET UNION 24.6%	CANADA 17.7	CUBA 5.4	DOM. REP. 2.9	AUSTRALIA 13.1	NEW CALEDONIA 9.1	INDON. 6.8	PHIL. 2.8	S. AFR. 3.0	BOTS. 2.5	GREECE 2.2	OTHER 4.1	COL. 2.0

←——NORTH AMERICA——→ ←——OCEANIA——→ ←—ASIA—→ AFR. EUR. S.A

Tungsten World Production-39,000 metric tons (metal content)-1982

CHINA 32.1%	SOUTH KOREA 5.9	BURMA 2.4	OTHER 4.6	SOVIET UNION 23.4	BOLIVIA 6.2	BRAZIL 3.1	AUSTL. 5.3	PORT. 2.9	AUS. 4.1	OTHER 2.5	U.S.A. 2.5

←———ASIA———→ ←S. AMER.→ ←OC.→ ←EUR.→ N.A.

Vanadium World Mine Production-29,000 metric tons (metal content)-1983

SOVIET UNION 33.1%	SOUTH AFRICA 28.0	CHINA 15.8	JAPAN 2.4	FINLAND 11.1	UNITED STATES 9.7

←———AFRICA———→ ←—ASIA—→ ←EUROPE→ N. AMER.

Open-pit iron mining in Australia is concentrated in the west and south of the continent.

Steel tubing

Pig iron

Pellets of iron ore

Iron ore

Steelmakers convert pellets of concentrated ore into pig iron, which is refined into steel.

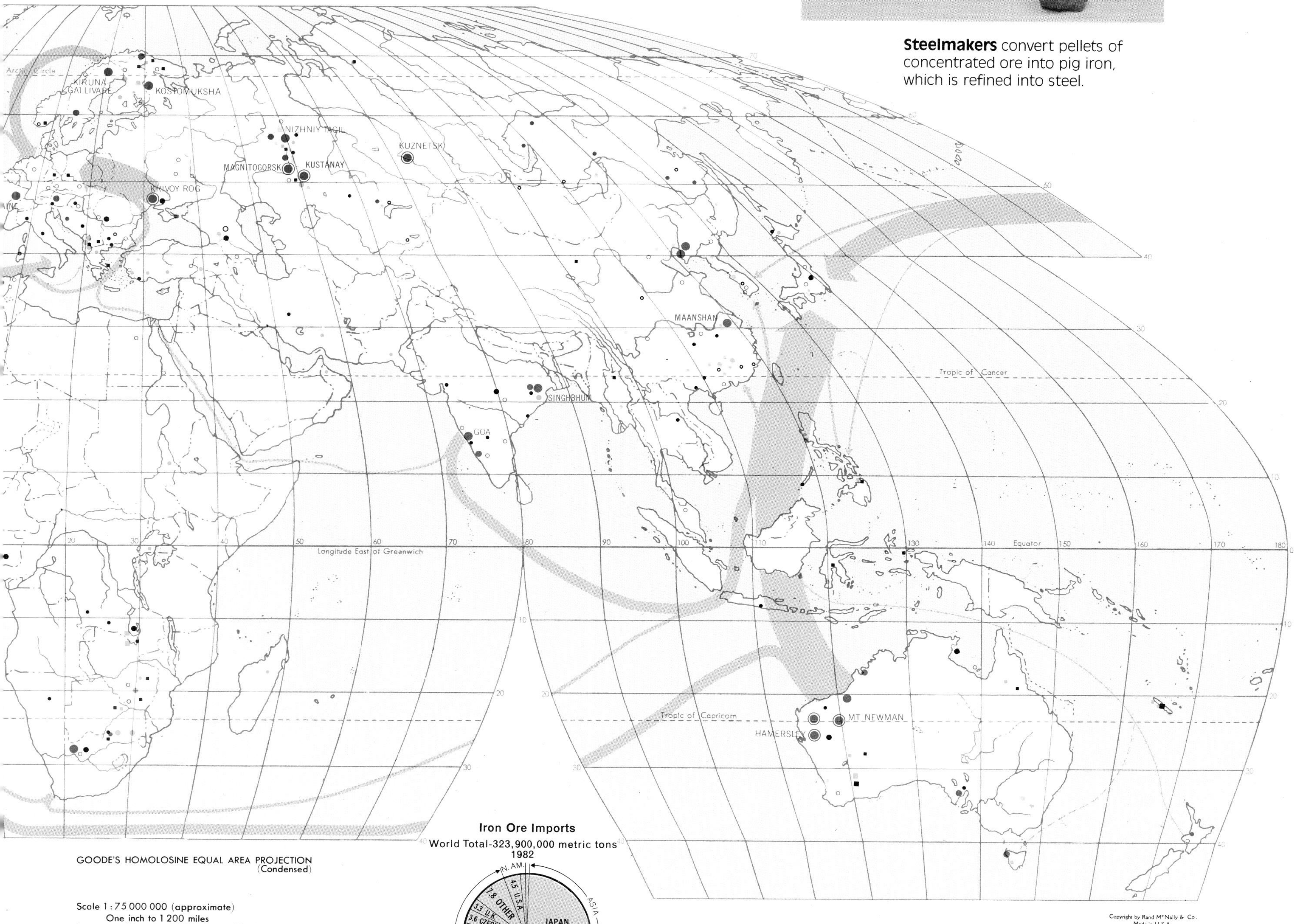

GOODE'S HOMOLOSINE EQUAL AREA PROJECTION
(Condensed)

Scale 1 : 75 000 000 (approximate)
One inch to 1 200 miles

Iron Ore Imports
World Total–323,900,000 metric tons
1982

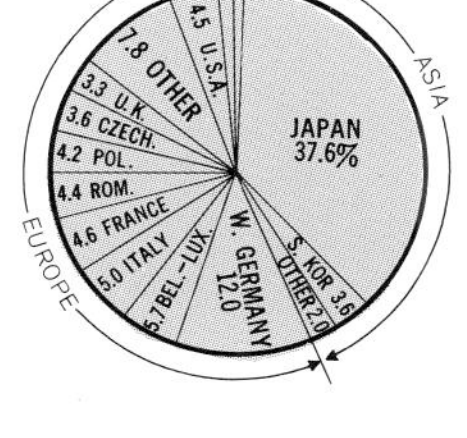

- N. AM.
- 4.5 U.S.A.
- 3.3 U.K.
- 3.6 OTHER
- 3.6 CZECH.
- 4.2 POL.
- 4.4 ROM.
- 4.6 FRANCE
- 5.0 ITALY
- 7 BEL.-LUX.
- W. GERMANY 12.0
- JAPAN 37.6%
- ASIA

Chromite   World Production–8,093,000** metric tons–1983

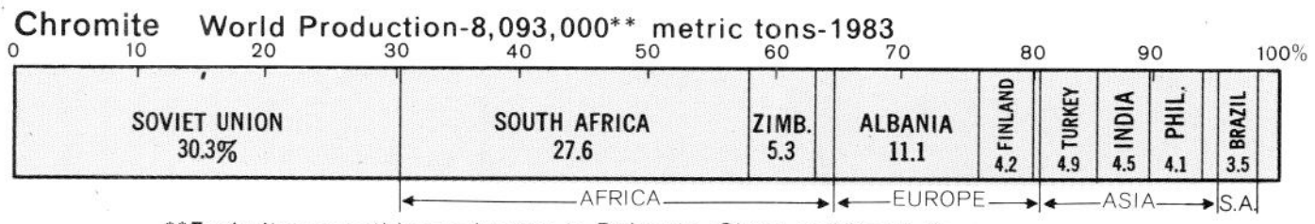

0	10	20	30	40	50	60	70	80	90	100%

SOVIET UNION 30.3%	SOUTH AFRICA 27.6	ZIMB. 5.3	ALBANIA 11.1	FINLAND 4.2	TURKEY 4.9	INDIA 4.5	PHIL. 4.1	BRAZIL 3.5

AFRICA — EUROPE — ASIA — S.A.

**Excluding possible production in Bulgaria, China and North Korea

Iron Ore   World Production–422,954,000†† metric tons (metal content)–1983

0	10	20	30	40	50	60	70	80	90	100%

SOVIET UNION 31.3%	AUSTRALIA 11.1	CHINA 8.4	INDIA 5.7	BRAZIL 6.5	OTHER 10.3	UNITED STATES 5.8	CANADA 5.0	S. AFR. 2.5	LIBERIA 2.1	OTHER 2.0	SWEDEN	OTHER 4.1

OCEANIA — ASIA — S. AMERICA — N. AMER. — AFR. — EUR.

††Excluding possible production in Cuba and Vietnam

Cobalt   World Mine Production–24,000† metric tons (metal content)–1983

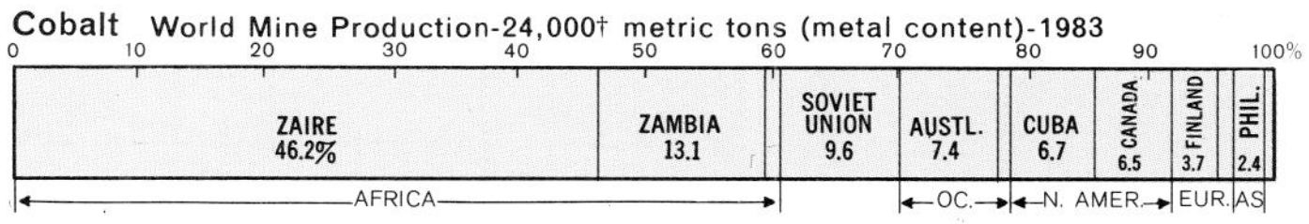

0	10	20	30	40	50	60	70	80	90	100%

ZAIRE 46.2%	ZAMBIA 13.1	SOVIET UNION 9.6	AUSTL. 7.4	CUBA 6.7	CANADA 6.5	FINLAND 3.7	PHIL. 2.4

AFRICA — OC. — N. AMER. — EUR. AS

†Excluding possible production in Bulgaria, Cyprus, East Germany, Greece, Indonesia, Poland, South Africa, Spain and Uganda

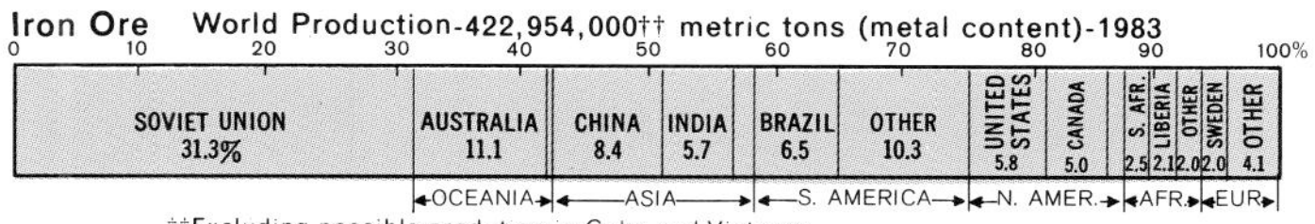

Iron Ore Reserves   World Total–65,500,000,000 metric tons (metal content)–1984

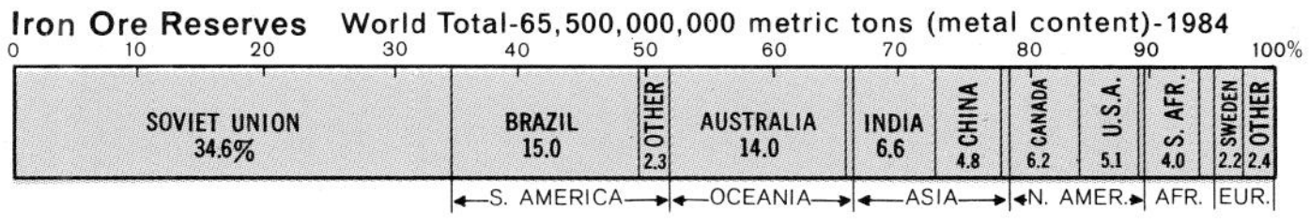

0	10	20	30	40	50	60	70	80	90	100%

SOVIET UNION 34.6%	BRAZIL 15.0	OTHER 2.3	AUSTRALIA 14.0	INDIA 6.6	CHINA 4.8	CANADA 6.2	U.S.A. 5.1	S. AFR. 4.0	OTHER 2.2	OTHER 2.4

S. AMERICA — OCEANIA — ASIA — N. AMER. — AFR. — EUR.

Distribution of Important Minerals

Nonferrous minerals

Copper

Copper is easy to shape, resistant to corrosion, and able to conduct electricity. Most copper comes from about seven kinds of ores that also may contain other metals.

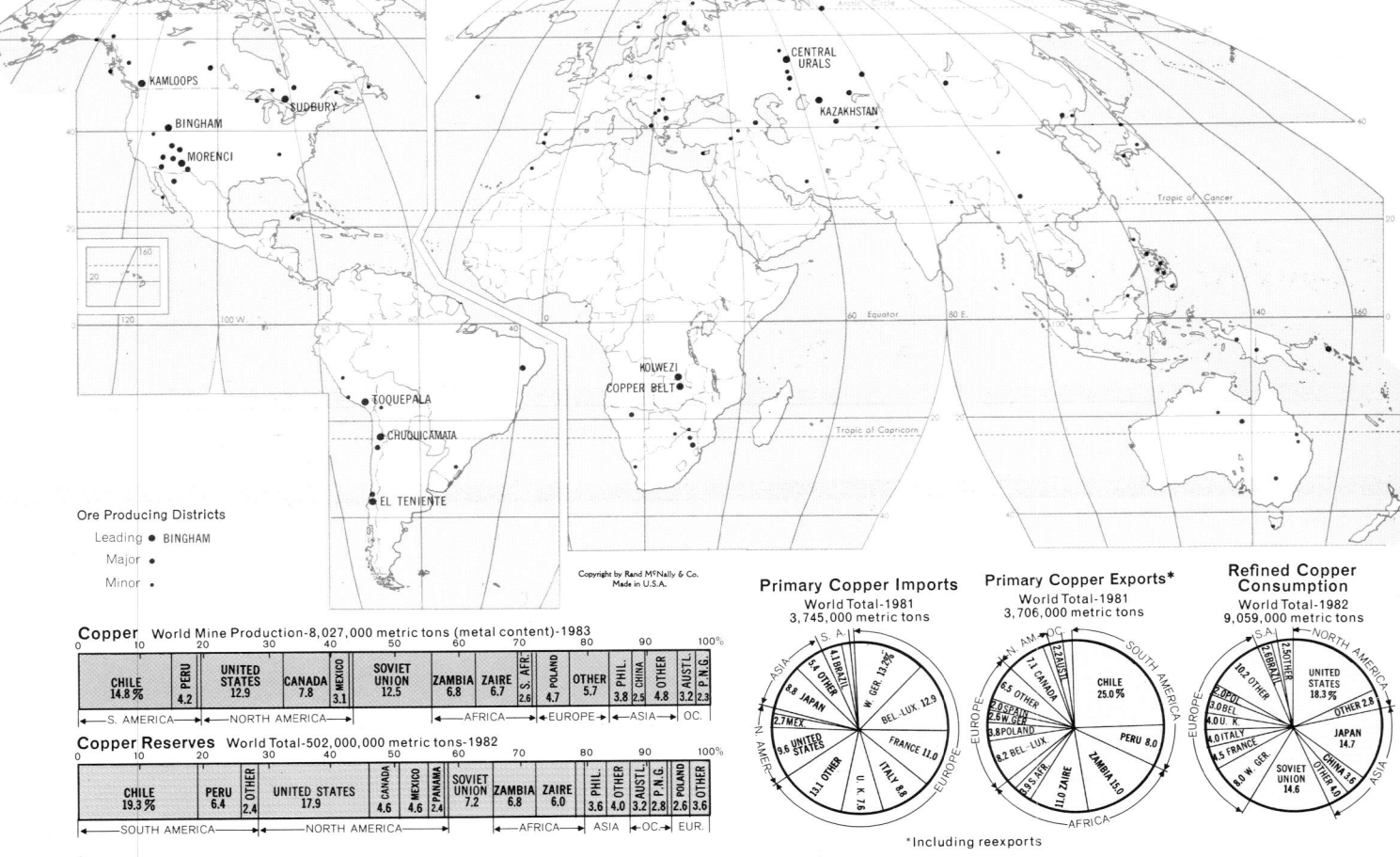

Ore Producing Districts
Leading ● BINGHAM
Major ●
Minor ·

Copyright by Rand McNally & Co.
Made in U.S.A.

Copper World Mine Production-8,027,000 metric tons (metal content)-1983

CHILE 14.8%	PERU 4.2	UNITED STATES 12.9	CANADA 7.8	MEXICO 3.1	SOVIET UNION 12.5	ZAMBIA 6.8	ZAIRE 6.7	S. AFR. 2.6	POLAND 4.7	OTHER 5.7	PHIL. 3.8	CHINA 2.5	OTHER 4.8	AUSTL. 3.2	P.N.G. 2.3
← S. AMERICA →	← NORTH AMERICA →					← AFRICA →			← EUROPE →		← ASIA →		OC.

Copper Reserves World Total-502,000,000 metric tons-1982

CHILE 19.3%	PERU 6.4	OTHER 2.4	UNITED STATES 17.9	CANADA 4.6	MEXICO 4.6	PANAMA 2.4	SOVIET UNION 7.2	ZAMBIA 6.8	ZAIRE 6.0	PHIL. 3.6	OTHER 4.0	AUSTL. 3.2	P.N.G. 2.8	POLAND 2.6	OTHER 3.6
← SOUTH AMERICA →			← NORTH AMERICA →				← AFRICA →			ASIA		OC.		EUR.

Primary Copper Imports
World Total-1981
3,745,000 metric tons

Primary Copper Exports*
World Total-1981
3,706,000 metric tons

Refined Copper Consumption
World Total-1982
9,059,000 metric tons

*Including reexports

Tin/Bauxite

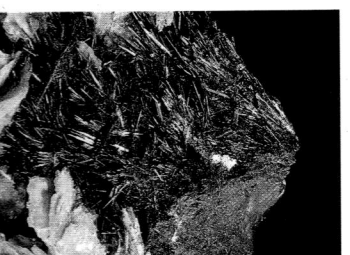

Stibnite, *above*, is the ore from which tin, a white metallic element, is made. Bauxite, *below*, is the ore from which most aluminum is made.

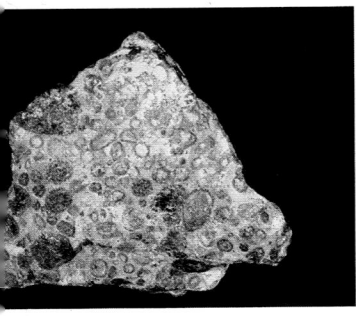
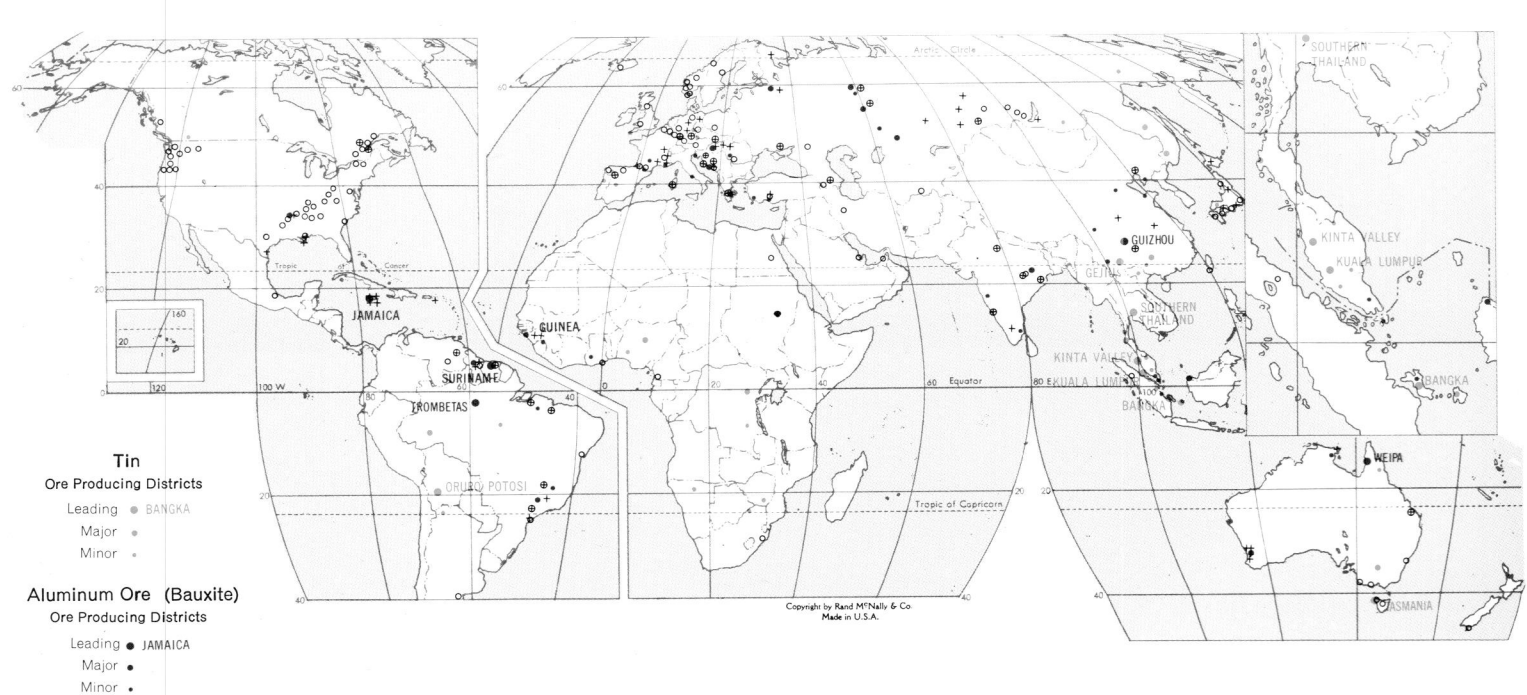

Tin
Ore Producing Districts
Leading ● BANGKA
Major ●
Minor ·

Aluminum Ore (Bauxite)
Ore Producing Districts
Leading ● JAMAICA
Major ●
Minor ·
Alumina refineries +
*Aluminum smelters o
*with capacities over 50,000 tons/year

Copyright by Rand McNally & Co.
Made in U.S.A.

Bauxite World Production-76,016,000 metric tons-1983

AUSTRALIA 32.2%	GUINEA 14.6	JAMAICA 9.6	BRAZIL 9.2	GUYANA 2.5	SURINAM	SOV. UN. 6.1	YUGO. 4.6	HUNG. 3.8	GREECE 2.5	FRANCE 2.6	INDIA 2.5	CHINA 2.0	OTHER
← OCEANIA →	← AFRICA →	← N. AM. →	← S. AMER. →			← EUROPE →						ASIA

Tin World Production-212,000 metric tons (metal content)-1983

MALAYSIA 19.8%	INDONESIA 12.8	THAILAND 9.4	CHINA 7.1	SOVIET UNION 17.5	BOLIVIA 11.5	BRAZIL 5.7	AUSTL. 4.6	AFRICA 5.5	EUROPE 3.4
← ASIA →					← S. AMER. →		OC.		

Aluminum World Production-13,870,000 metric tons-1983

UNITED STATES 24.2%	CANADA 7.9	SOVIET UNION 14.4	W. GER. 5.3	NORWAY 5.2	FRANCE 2.6	SPAIN 2.6	YUGO. 2.6	OTHER 11.3	AUSTL. 3.4	BRAZIL 2.9	VENZ. 2.5	CHINA 2.7	OTHER 6.9	AFRICA 2.8
← NORTH AMERICA →		← EUROPE →							OC.	S. A.		← ASIA →

The maps on these pages show the distribution of the world's copper, tin, bauxite, lead, and zinc centers of production (mining). More precise information on producers and consumers of these nonferrous minerals (containing no iron) is contained in the bar graphs and pie charts. For example, by viewing the pie charts that feature copper statistics, one can learn that the United States consumes more copper than any other nation on earth. West Germany, however, is the leading importer of copper, and Chile is the leading exporter of the mineral.

By looking at the bar graph of bauxite statistics, one can learn that Australia produces more bauxite than any other country. The second-largest producer of this nonferrous mineral is Guinea, and the third-largest is Jamaica.

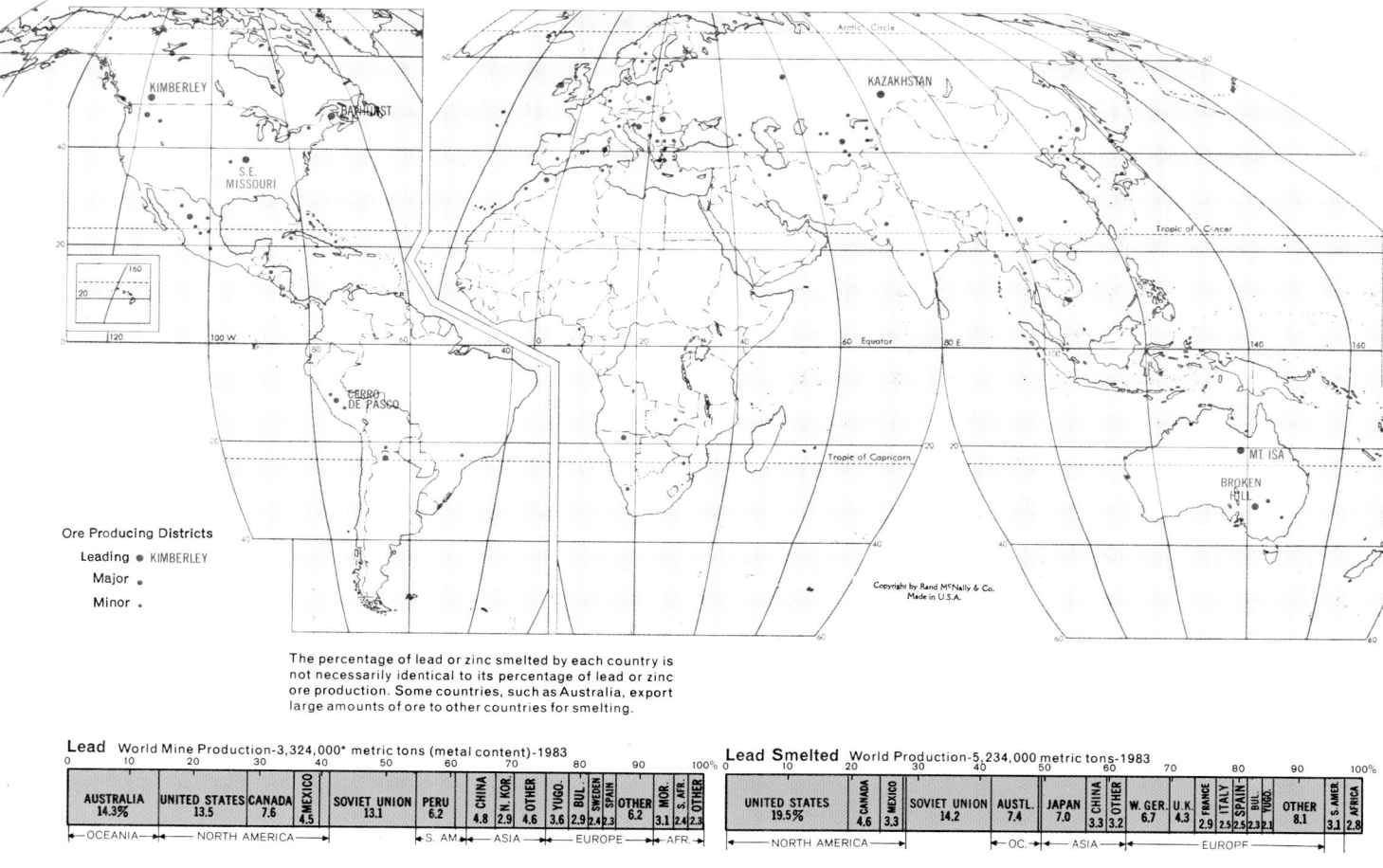

Ore Producing Districts
Leading ● KIMBERLEY
Major ₊
Minor ·

The percentage of lead or zinc smelted by each country is not necessarily identical to its percentage of lead or zinc ore production. Some countries, such as Australia, export large amounts of ore to other countries for smelting.

Lead

Galena is another name for lead ore. The Soviet Union is a leading producer of galena, a heavy, brittle mineral with a metallic luster.

Lead World Mine Production-3,324,000* metric tons (metal content)-1983

AUSTRALIA 14.3%	UNITED STATES 13.5	CANADA 7.6	MEXICO 4.5	SOVIET UNION 13.1	PERU 6.2	CHINA 4.8	N. KOR. 2.9	OTHER 4.6	YUGO. 3.6	BUL. 2.9	SWEDEN SPAIN 2.4 2.3	OTHER 6.2	MOR. 3.1	S. AFR. 2.4	OTHER 2.3
OCEANIA	NORTH AMERICA			S. AM.		ASIA			EUROPE				AFR.		

Lead Smelted World Production-5,234,000 metric tons-1983

UNITED STATES 19.5%	CANADA 4.6	MEXICO 3.3	SOVIET UNION 14.2	AUSTL. 7.4	JAPAN 7.0	CHINA 3.3	OTHER 3.2	W. GER. 6.7	U.K. 4.3	FRANCE 2.9	ITALY 2.5	SPAIN 2.5	BUL. 2.3	YUGO. 2.1	OTHER 8.1	S. AMER. 3.1	AFRICA 2.8
NORTH AMERICA			OC.	ASIA				EUROPE									

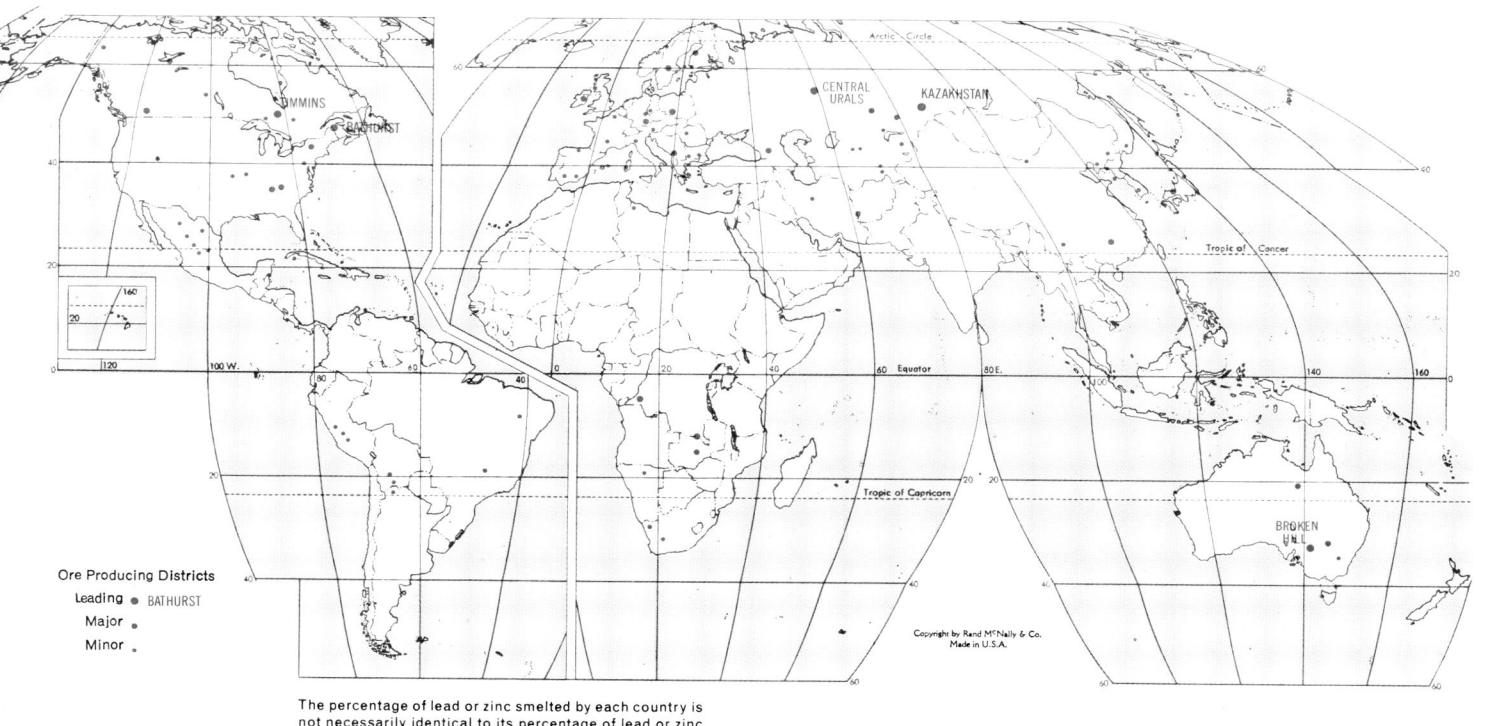

Ore Producing Districts
Leading ● BATHURST
Major ₊
Minor ·

The percentage of lead or zinc smelted by each country is not necessarily identical to its percentage of lead or zinc ore production. Some countries, such as Australia, export large amounts of ore to other countries for smelting.

Zinc

Zinc is a shiny metal that has many uses in industry. A coating of zinc applied to iron or steel prevents rust.

Zinc World Mine Production-6,246,000 metric tons (metal content)-1983

CANADA 17.1%	U.S.A. 4.4	MEXICO 4.1	SOVIET UNION 12.9	AUSTRALIA 11.1	PERU 8.9	OTHER 3.2	JAPAN 4.1	CHINA 2.2	N. KOR. 2.6	OTHER 2.6	SWEDEN 3.3	SPAIN POLAND 2.8 2.8	OTHER 8.5	AFRICA 5.0
NORTH AMERICA			OCEANIA	S. AMER.		ASIA					EUROPE			

Zinc Smelted World Production-6,176,000 metric tons-1983

SOVIET UNION 15.1%	JAPAN 11.4	CHINA 2.6	OTHER 4.9	CANADA 10.0	U.S.A. 4.9	MEXICO 2.9	W.GER. 5.8	BEL. 4.2	FRANCE 4.0	SPAIN 3.1	NETH. 3.0	POLAND 2.8	FINLAND 2.5	ITALY 2.4	OTHER 7.2	AUSTL. 4.9	PERU 2.5	OTHER 2.5	AFRICA 3.5
ASIA				N. AMERICA			EUROPE									OC.	S. A.		

Distribution of Important Fuels

This thematic map uses color and symbols to show the distribution of the world's important mineral and fossil fuels: coal and lignite, petroleum, natural gas, and uranium. Arrows indicate the movement of petroleum from exporting to importing countries. The thicker the line, the heavier the flow of petroleum. It is easy to see that Japan, Europe, and the United States are the world's major importers of petroleum. The Middle East exports the most petroleum.

Anthracite, *above,* is the hardest form of coal, a rock that can be ignited and burned.

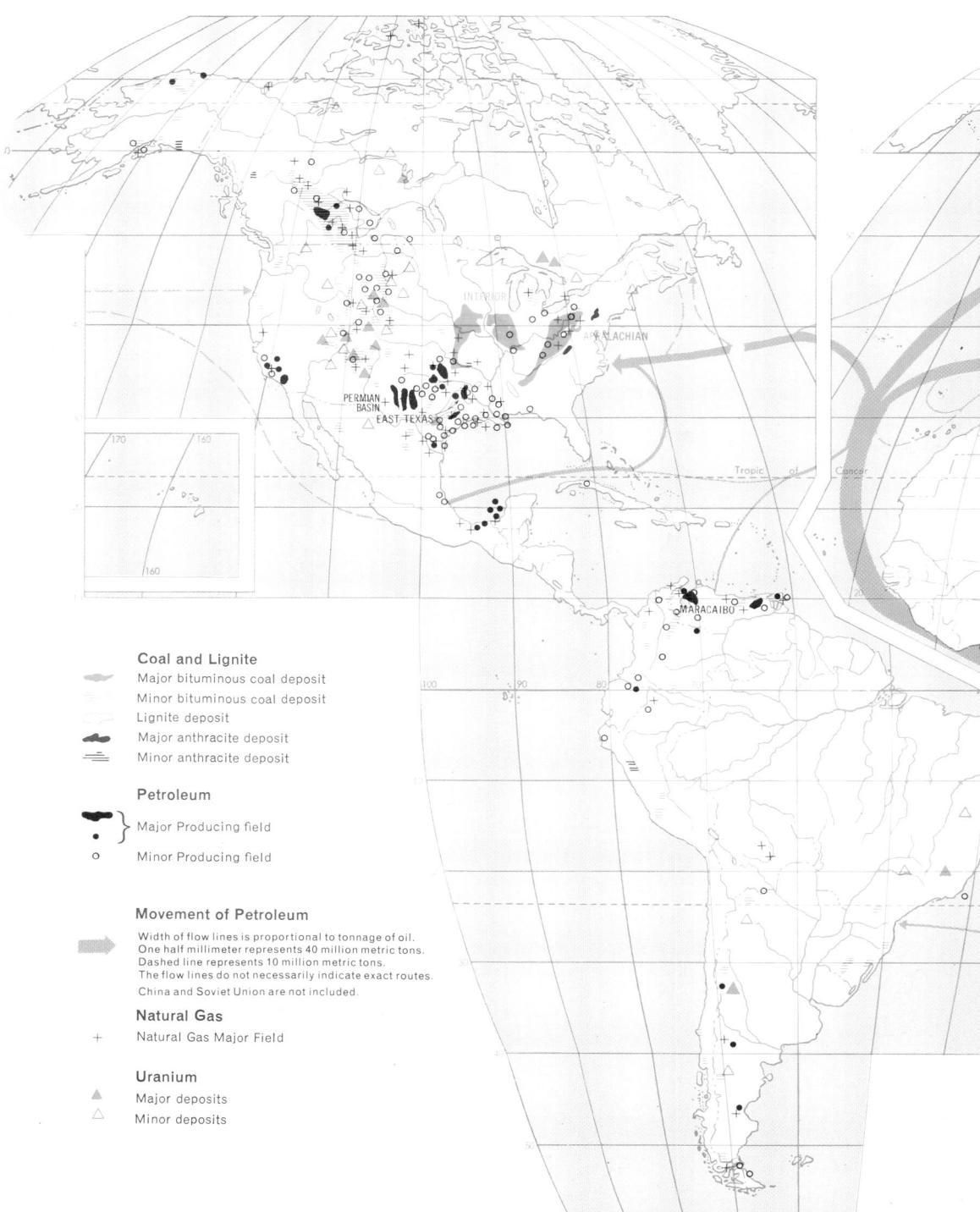

Coal and Lignite
- Major bituminous coal deposit
- Minor bituminous coal deposit
- Lignite deposit
- Major anthracite deposit
- Minor anthracite deposit

Petroleum
- Major Producing field
- Minor Producing field

Movement of Petroleum
Width of flow lines is proportional to tonnage of oil. One half millimeter represents 40 million metric tons. Dashed line represents 10 million metric tons. The flow lines do not necessarily indicate exact routes. China and Soviet Union are not included.

Natural Gas
+ Natural Gas Major Field

Uranium
▲ Major deposits
△ Minor deposits

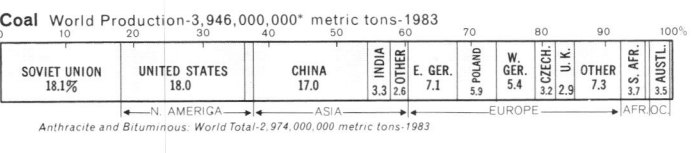

Coal World Production–3,946,000,000* metric tons–1983

SOVIET UNION 18.1%	UNITED STATES 18.0	CHINA 17.0	INDIA 3.3	OTHER 2.6	E. GER. 7.1	POLAND 5.9	W. GER. 5.4	CZECH. 3.2	U.K. 2.9	OTHER 7.3	S. AFR. 3.7	AUSTL. 3.5

←N. AMERICA→ ←ASIA→ ←EUROPE→ AFR OC
Anthracite and Bituminous: World Total–2,974,000,000 metric tons–1983

Coal Reserves World Total–894,974,000,000* metric tons–1981

UNITED STATES 28.7%	SOVIET UNION 26.8	CHINA 11.0	AUSTL. 7.3	W. GER. 7.3	POLAND 4.4	OTHER 4.6	SOUTH AFRICA 5.8

←NORTH AMERICA→ ←ASIA→ ←OC→ ←EUROPE→ AFR.
Anthracite and Bituminous: World Total–657,180,000,000 metric tons–1981
*Includes anthracite, subanthracite, bituminous, subbituminous, lignite and brown coal

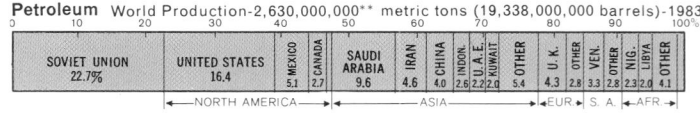

Petroleum World Production–2,630,000,000** metric tons (19,338,000,000 barrels)–1983

SOVIET UNION 22.7%	UNITED STATES 16.4	MEXICO 5.1	CANADA 2.7	SAUDI ARABIA 9.6	IRAN 4.6	CHINA	INDON. 2.6	U.A.E. 2.4	KUWAIT	OTHER	U.K. 4.3	OTHER 3.3	VEN. 3.5	NIG. 2.8	LIBYA 2.3	OTHER

←NORTH AMERICA→ ←ASIA→ EUR. S. A. AFR.

Petroleum Reserves (669,900,000,000 barrels)–1984
World Total–91,100,000,000** metric tons

SAUDI ARABIA 25.2%	KUWAIT 10.0	IRAN 7.6	IRAQ 6.4	U.A.E. 4.8	CHINA 2.9	OTHER 3.8	SOVIET UNION 9.4	MEXICO 7.2	U.S.A. 4.1	VEN. 3.7	LIBYA 3.2	NIG. 2.5	OTHER 2.8	U.K. 2.0

←ASIA→ ←N. AMER.→ S. A. AFR. EU.
**Crude Petroleum

Crude oil from Saudi Arabia

Crude oil from Australia

Crude oil from Venezuela

Tar sands from Canada

Oil shale from the United States

Petroleum has liquid and solid forms. Liquid crude oil occurs naturally in reservoirs. Tar sands and shale can be processed into oil.

Offshore wells for natural gas are drilled in water as much as 8,000 feet (2,400 meters) deep. The yields of natural gas fields off North Sea shores and in Yorkshire supply all Great Britain's gas needs.

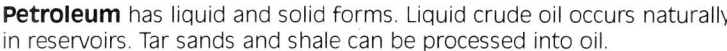

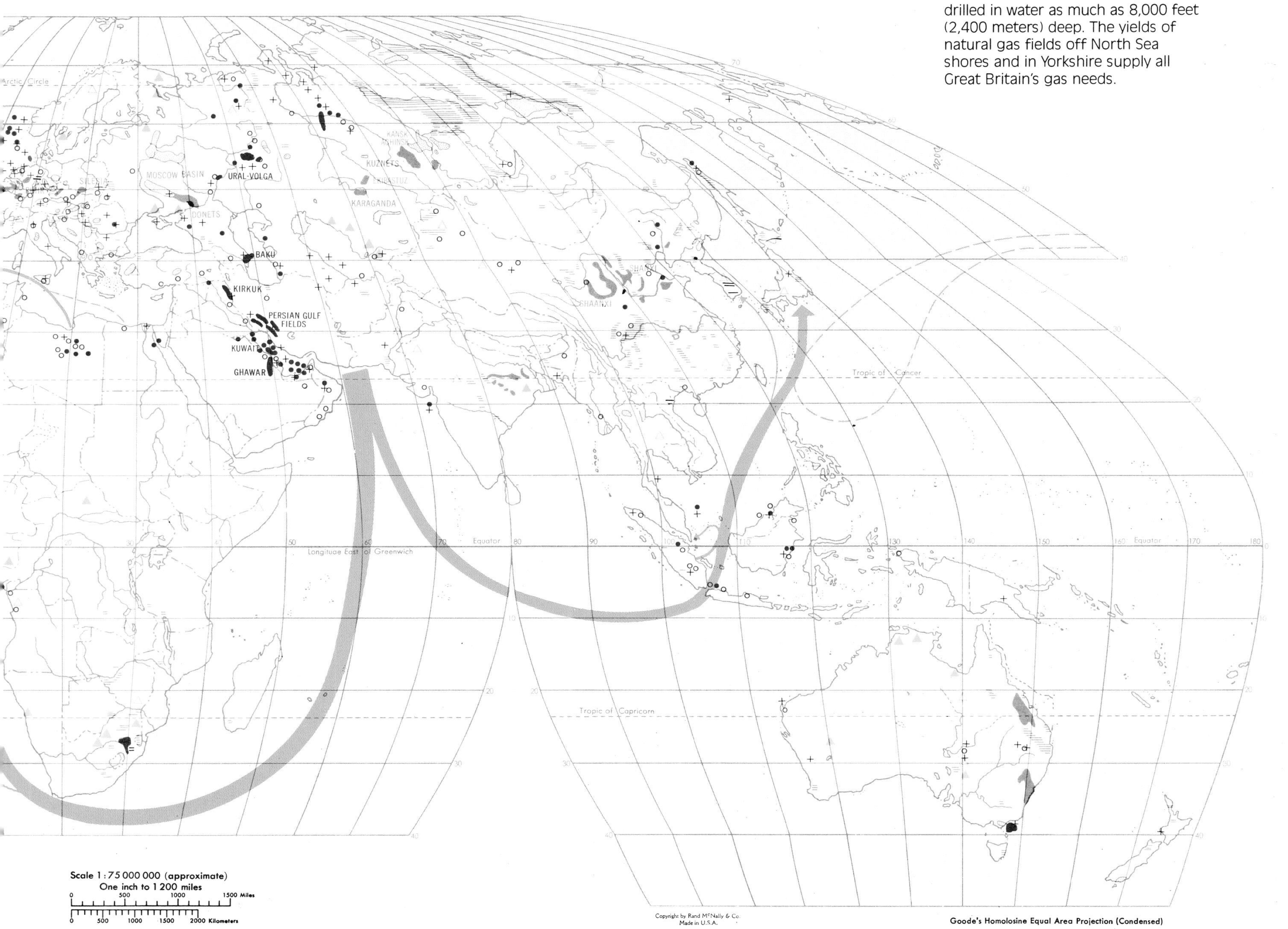

ARCTIC CIRCLE

MOSCOW BASIN

URAL-VOLGA

KUZNETS

KARAGANDA

DONETS

BAKU

KIRKUK

PERSIAN GULF FIELDS

KUWAIT

GHAWAR

KANSK-ACHINSK

KARAGANDUZ

SHAANXI

Tropic of Cancer

Longitude East of Greenwich

Equator

Equator

Tropic of Capricorn

Scale 1:75 000 000 (approximate)
One inch to 1 200 miles

1500 Miles
500   1000   1500

0   500   1000   1500   2000 Kilometers

Copyright by Rand McNally & Co.
Made in U.S.A.

Goode's Homolosine Equal Area Projection (Condensed)

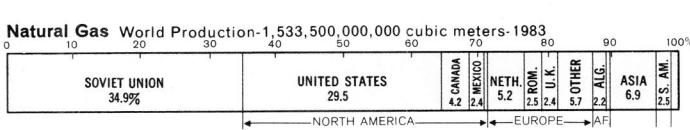

Natural Gas World Production-1,533,500,000,000 cubic meters-1983

SOVIET UNION 34.9%	UNITED STATES 29.5	CANADA 4.2	MEXICO 2.4	NETH. 5.2	ROM. 2.5	U.K. 2.4	OTHER 5.7	ASIA 6.9	S. AM. 2.5
		NORTH AMERICA		EUROPE				AF	

Natural Gas Reserves World Total-90,692,000,000,000 cubic meters-1983

SOVIET UNION 43.7%	IRAN 15.0	SAUDI ARABIA 3.9	OTHER 10.4	UNITED STATES 6.3	CANADA 2.4	MEXICO 2.4	ALG. 3.4	OTHER 2.5	EUROPE 5.5	S. AM. 3.1
	ASIA			N. AMER.			AFR.		

Uranium World Production-44,500† metric tons-1983

UNITED STATES 27.5%	CANADA 19.1	SOUTH AFRICA 16.0	NAMIBIA 10.0	NIGER 9.1	GABON 2.6	AUSTL. 7.5	FRANCE 6.7
NORTH AMERICA		AFRICA				OC.	EUR.

†Excluding possible production in China, India, Israel, Mexico, Soviet Union and Eastern Europe

Uranium Reserves World Total-2,000,000†† metric tons-1983

UNITED STATES 21.7%	CANADA 9.7	AUSRALIA 15.7	SOUTH AFRICA 15.6	NIGER 8.0	NAM. 6.7	OTHER 3.5	BRAZIL 8.2	INDIA 2.1	EUROPE 4.9
NORTH AMERICA		OCEANIA	AFRICA				S. AM.	AS.	

††Excluding possible reserves in China, Egypt, Israel, Libya, Soviet Union and Eastern Europe

Energy

The size of each circle on these thematic maps is proportional to the volume of energy produced or consumed by the nation in which the circle is located. Color is used to indicate the type of energy produced or consumed; for example, solid fuels, liquid fuels, and so on. The United States is one of the world's leading producers and consumers of energy.

Energy production

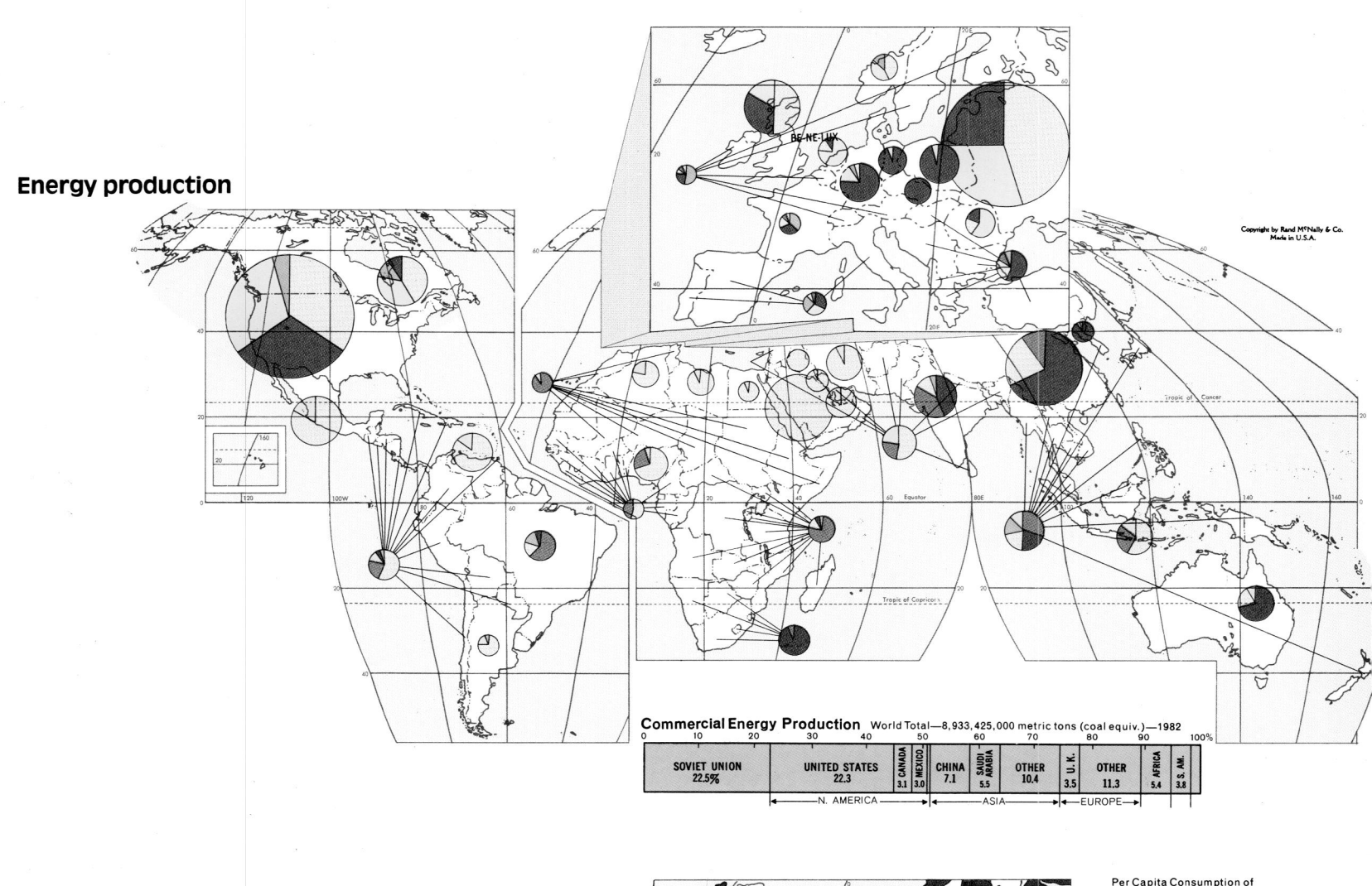

BE-NE-LUX
Copyright by Rand McNally & Co.
Made in U.S.A.
Tropic of Cancer
Equator
Tropic of Capricorn

Commercial Energy Production World Total—8,933,425,000 metric tons (coal equiv.)—1982
0 10 20 30 40 50 60 70 80 90 100%
SOVIET UNION 22.5%
UNITED STATES 22.3
CANADA 3.1
MEXICO 3.0
CHINA 7.1
SAUDI ARABIA 5.5
OTHER 10.4
U. K. 3.5
OTHER 11.3
AFRICA 5.4
S. AM. 3.8
N. AMERICA
ASIA
EUROPE

Energy consumption

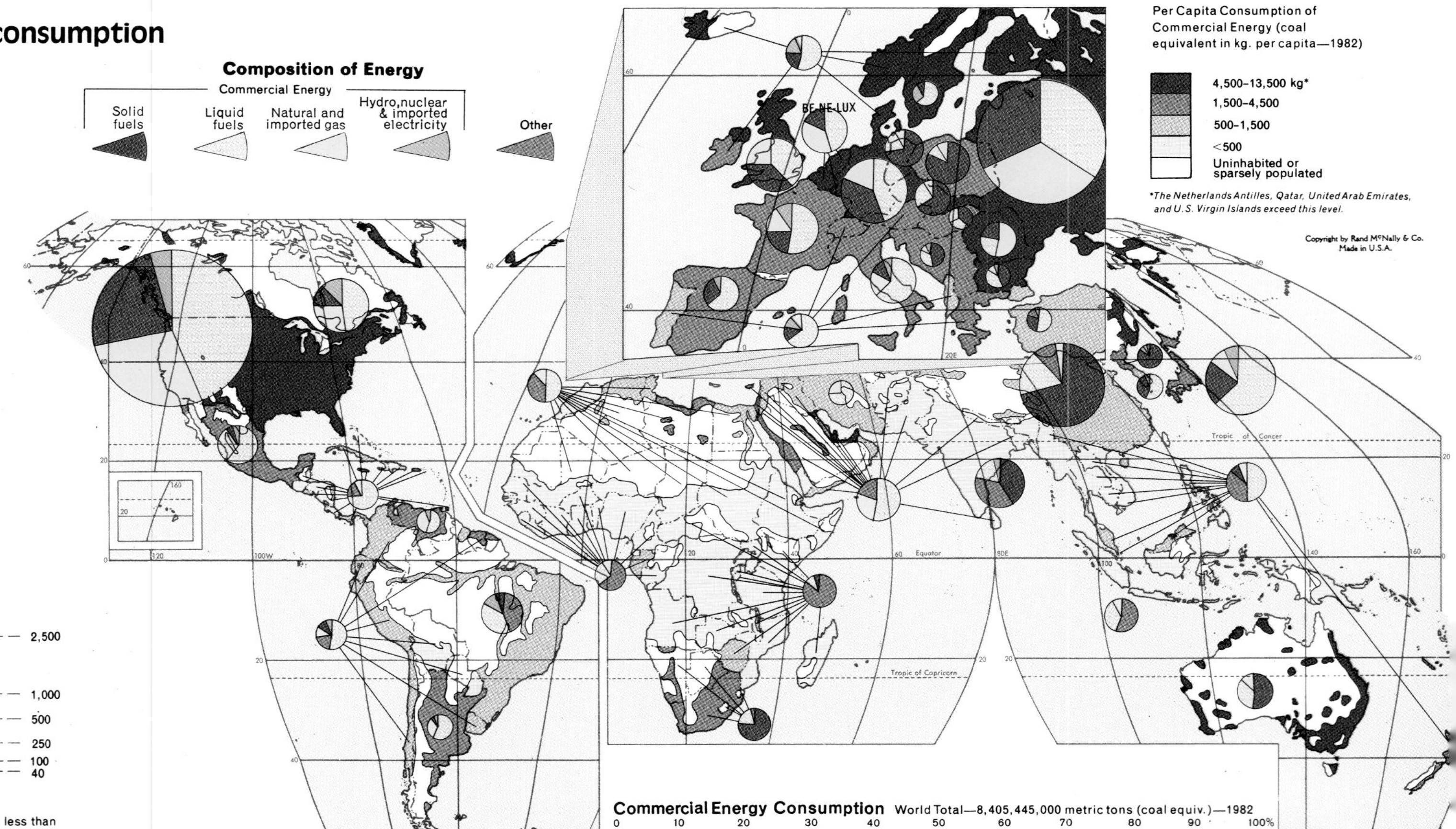

Composition of Energy
Commercial Energy
Solid fuels
Liquid fuels
Natural and imported gas
Hydro,nuclear & imported electricity
Other
Per Capita Consumption of Commercial Energy (coal equivalent in kg. per capita—1982)
4,500–13,500 kg*
1,500–4,500
500–1,500
<500
Uninhabited or sparsely populated
*The Netherlands Antilles, Qatar, United Arab Emirates, and U.S. Virgin Islands exceed this level.
BE-NE-LUX
Copyright by Rand McNally & Co.
Made in U.S.A.
Tropic of Cancer
Equator
Tropic of Capricorn

Volume of Energy
in millions of metric tons
(Coal equivalent)—1982
2,500
1,000
500
250
100
40

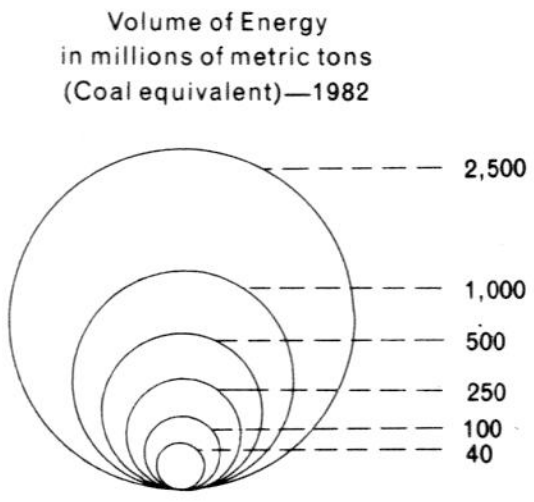

Volume data is not shown for countries with less than 1 million metric tons (coal equivalent)

Commercial Energy Consumption World Total—8,405,445,000 metric tons (coal equiv.)—1982
0 10 20 30 40 50 60 70 80 90 100%
UNITED STATES 26.0%
CANADA 2.8
OTHER 2.2
SOVIET UNION 18.6
CHINA 7.0
JAPAN 4.9
OTHER 7.3
W. GER. 4.0
U. K. 3.0
FRANCE 2.6
OTHER 14.7
S. AM. 3.0
AFRICA 2.4
NORTH AMERICA
ASIA
EUROPE

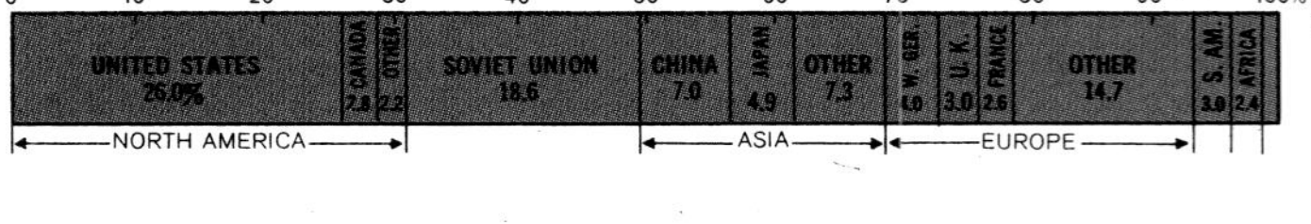

Languages
and Religions

These two thematic maps use color and pattern to show the differences between cultures that coexist in our world. Keys to the world's major religions and 50 major languages are found directly beneath the maps.

Languages

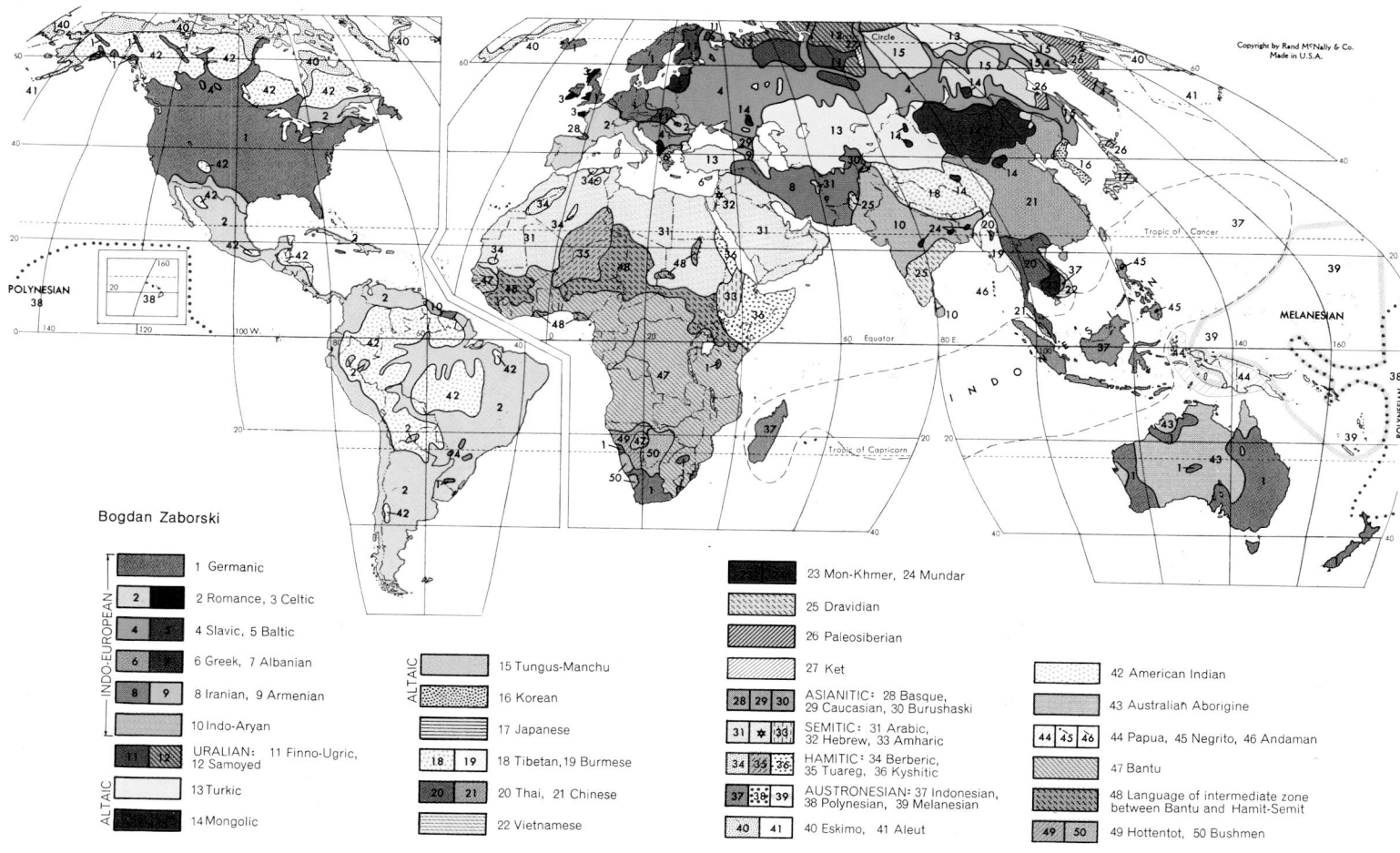

Bogdan Zaborski

INDO-EUROPEAN	1 Germanic
	2 Romance, 3 Celtic
	4 Slavic, 5 Baltic
	6 Greek, 7 Albanian
	8 Iranian, 9 Armenian
	10 Indo-Aryan
	URALIAN: 11 Finno-Ugric, 12 Samoyed
ALTAIC	13 Turkic
	14 Mongolic

ALTAIC	15 Tungus-Manchu
	16 Korean
	17 Japanese
	18 Tibetan, 19 Burmese
	20 Thai, 21 Chinese
	22 Vietnamese

	23 Mon-Khmer, 24 Mundar
	25 Dravidian
	26 Paleosiberian
	27 Ket
	ASIANITIC: 28 Basque, 29 Caucasian, 30 Burushaski
	SEMITIC: 31 Arabic, 32 Hebrew, 33 Amharic
	HAMITIC: 34 Berberic, 35 Tuareg, 36 Kyshitic
	AUSTRONESIAN: 37 Indonesian, 38 Polynesian, 39 Melanesian
	40 Eskimo, 41 Aleut

	42 American Indian
	43 Australian Aborigine
	44 Papua, 45 Negrito, 46 Andaman
	47 Bantu
	48 Language of intermediate zone between Bantu and Hamit-Semit
	49 Hottentot, 50 Bushmen

Religions

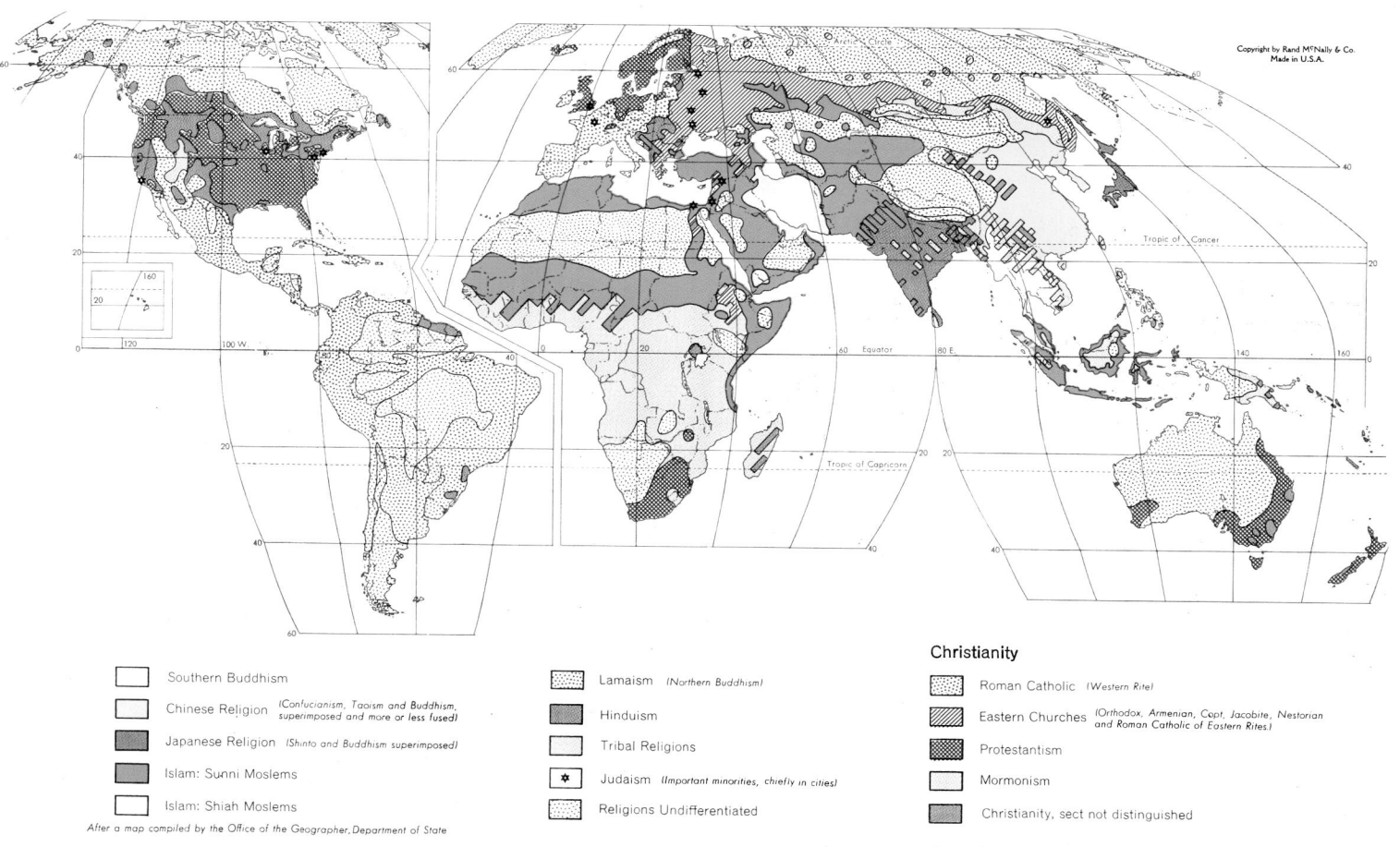

	Southern Buddhism
	Chinese Religion (Confucianism, Taoism and Buddhism, superimposed and more or less fused)
	Japanese Religion (Shinto and Buddhism superimposed)
	Islam: Sunni Moslems
	Islam: Shiah Moslems

	Lamaism (Northern Buddhism)
	Hinduism
	Tribal Religions
	Judaism (Important minorities, chiefly in cities)
	Religions Undifferentiated

Christianity

	Roman Catholic (Western Rite)
	Eastern Churches (Orthodox, Armenian, Copt, Jacobite, Nestorian and Roman Catholic of Eastern Rites)
	Protestantism
	Mormonism
	Christianity, sect not distinguished

After a map compiled by the Office of the Geographer, Department of State

Population

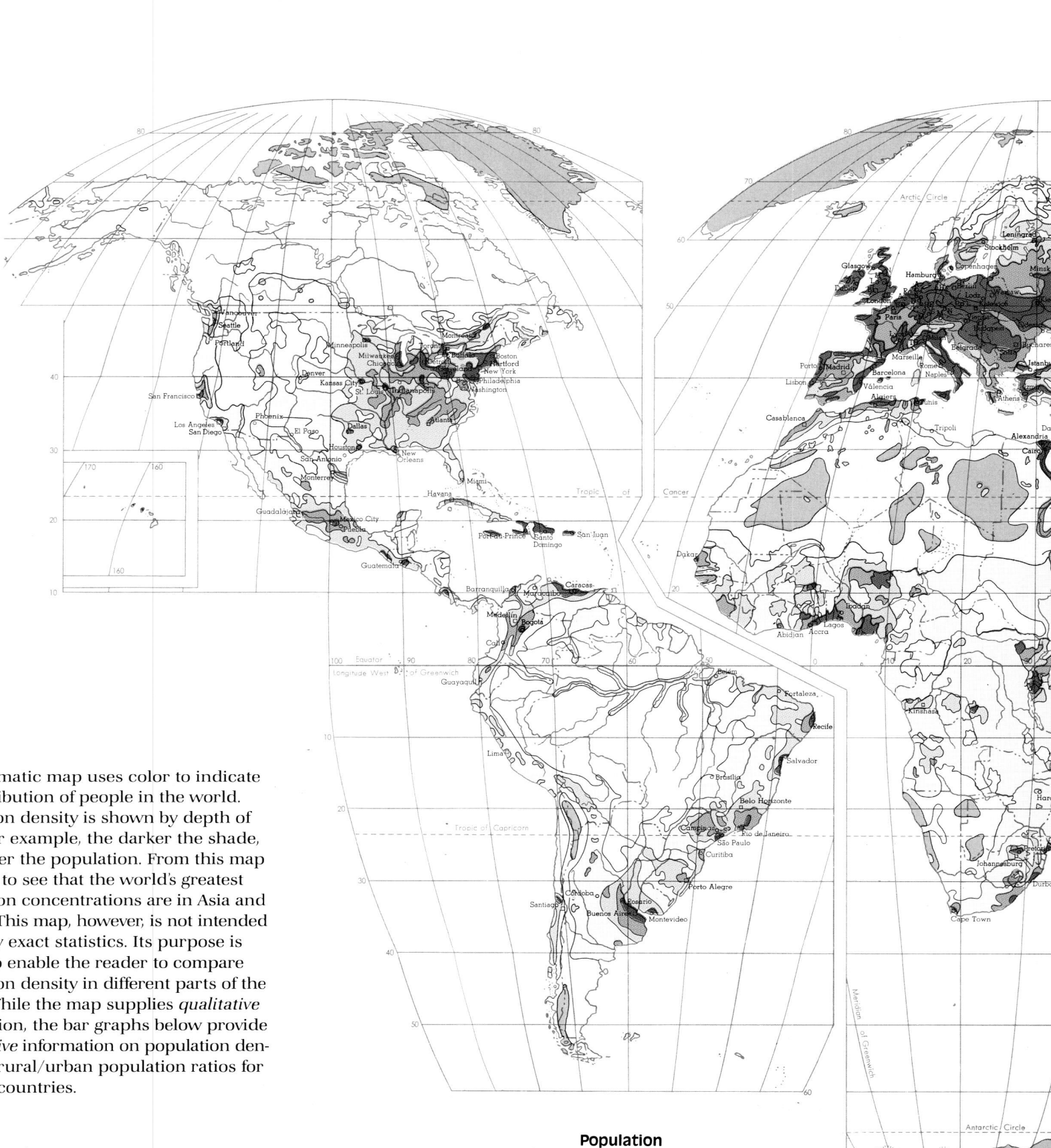

This thematic map uses color to indicate the distribution of people in the world. Population density is shown by depth of color. For example, the darker the shade, the denser the population. From this map it is easy to see that the world's greatest population concentrations are in Asia and Europe. This map, however, is not intended to supply exact statistics. Its purpose is simply to enable the reader to compare population density in different parts of the world. While the map supplies *qualitative* information, the bar graphs below provide *quantitative* information on population density and rural/urban population ratios for a dozen countries.

Population

Per Sq. Km.		Per Sq. Mile
Uninhabited		Uninhabited
Under 1		Under 2
1-10		2-25
10-25		25-60
25-50		60-125
50-100		125-250
Over 100		Over 250

□ Metropolitan areas over 2,000,000 population
○ Metropolitan areas 1,000,000 to 2,000,000 population

Some cities are identified by initial letter only.

Population density is not an issue among Amerindians of the Andes Mountains, *left*. But in Beijing (Peking), China, one of the world's largest cities, overcrowding is a problem. China has more people than any other country.

Sverdlovsk
Chelyabinsk
Omsk Novosibirsk

Qiqihar Harbin
Changchun
Shenyang
Pyongyang
Seoul Sapporo
Taegu Sendai
Pusan
Tōkyō-Yokohama
Qingdao
Ōsaka-Kyōto-Kōbe
Shanghai Kitakyūshū
Hangzhou

Tashkent
Alma-Ata

Mashhad
Kabul
Faisalabad
Ispahan
Delhi

Karachi
Ahmadabad Surat
Nagpur
Calcutta

Bombay
Pune
Hyderabad

T'aipei
Kaohsiung
Hong Kong

Madras
Bangalore
Coimbatore
Madurai
Colombo

Manila

Bangkok

Ho Chi Minh City

Kuala Lumpur
Singapore

Jakarta Surabaya
Bandung

Brisbane

Sydney

Melbourne

Copyright by Rand McNally & Co.
Made in U.S.A.

Scale 1 : 75 000 000 (approximate)
One inch to 1 200 miles

0   500   1000   1500 Miles

0   500   1000   1500   2000 Kilometers

Goode's Homolosine Equal Area Projection (Condensed)

Rural/urban population ratios

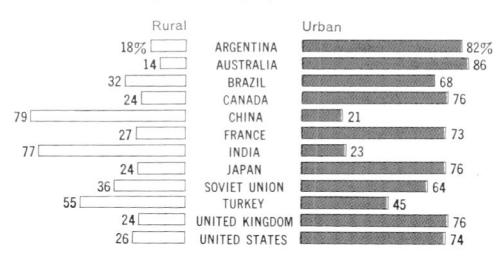

	Rural		Urban	
ARGENTINA	18%			82%
AUSTRALIA	14			86
BRAZIL	32			68
CANADA	24			76
CHINA	79			21
FRANCE	27			73
INDIA	77			23
JAPAN	24			76
SOVIET UNION	36			64
TURKEY	55			45
UNITED KINGDOM	24			76
UNITED STATES	26			74

Population density

per square kilometer (per square mile)

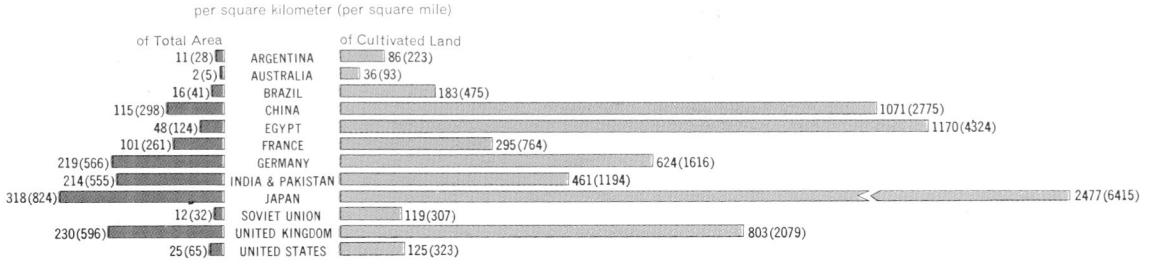

	of Total Area	of Cultivated Land
ARGENTINA	11 (28)	86 (223)
AUSTRALIA	2 (5)	36 (93)
BRAZIL	16 (41)	183 (475)
CHINA	115 (298)	1071 (2775)
EGYPT	48 (124)	1170 (4324)
FRANCE	101 (261)	295 (764)
GERMANY	219 (566)	624 (1616)
INDIA & PAKISTAN	214 (555)	461 (1194)
JAPAN	318 (824)	2477 (6415)
SOVIET UNION	12 (32)	119 (307)
UNITED KINGDOM	230 (596)	803 (2079)
UNITED STATES	25 (65)	125 (323)

Satellite imagery of the
Washington, D.C., area, U.S.

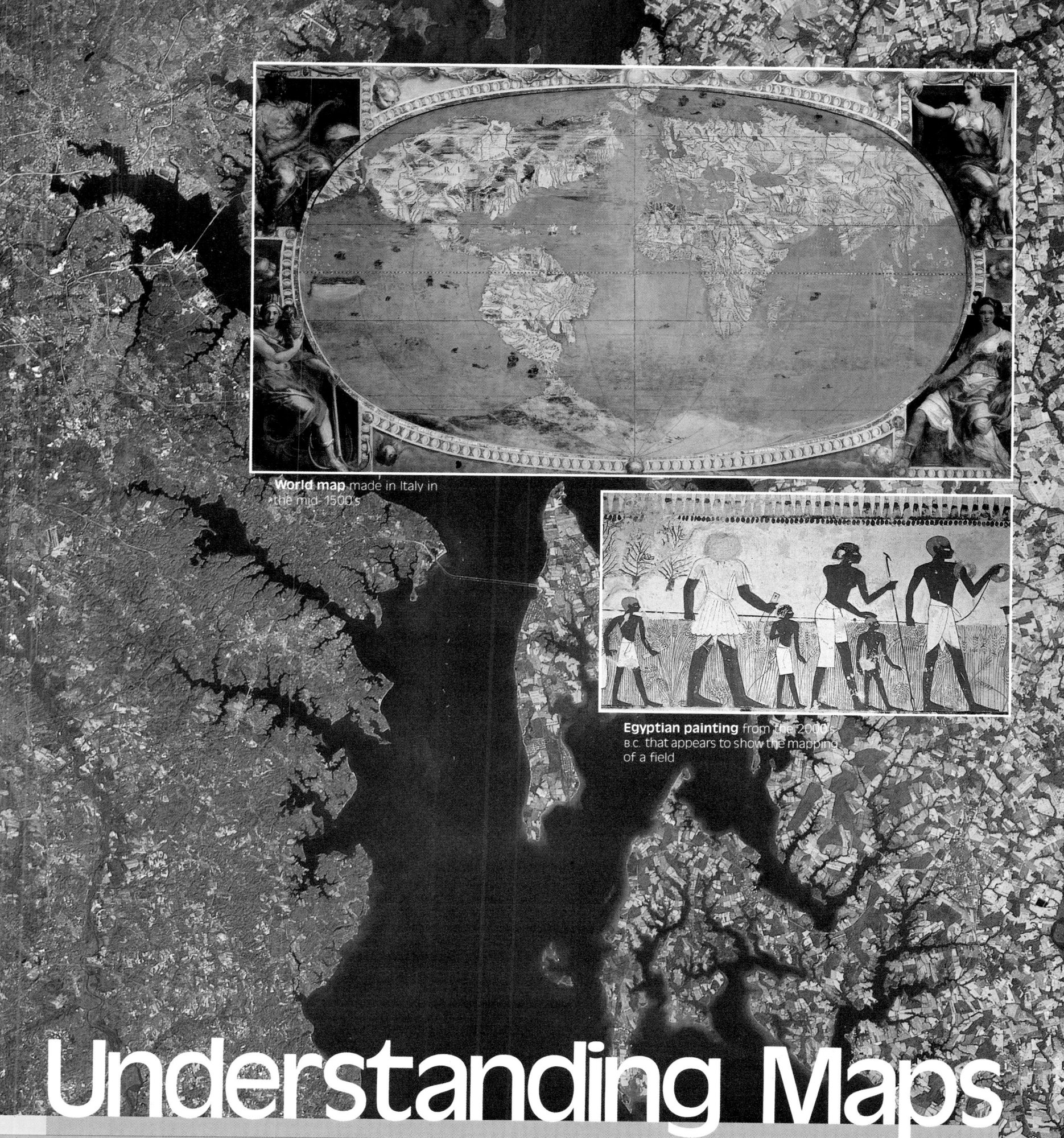

World map made in Italy in the mid-1500's

Egyptian painting from the 2000's B.C. that appears to show the mapping of a field

Understanding Maps

To UNDERSTAND the meanings of the lines, words, symbols, and colors on a map is to understand the distribution and arrangement of part or all of the earth's features.

The History of Maps

It is likely that some forms of maps were made as long ago as prehistoric times. There are archaeologists who believe that certain markings in cave paintings and other marks scratched onto bone tablets could have shown game routes and hunting trails.

The earliest map in existence that clearly shows features of land is a Babylonian clay tablet. It dates back to about 2500 B.C. In 1300 B.C., the Egyptians were also making maps of their surrounding area. It was not until the time of the Greek philosophers and geographers that people began to think about the nature of the earth as a whole. It was the Greeks who first projected the idea that the earth was round. It was they who developed a system of parallels and meridians and a method of projecting them.

The greatest geographer and mapmaker of the ancient world was Claudius Ptolemy, who lived in Alexandria, Egypt, about A.D. 150. Ptolemy wrote the eight-volume *Geographia*. This work includes Ptolemy's map of the world, as well as instructions for making maps.

The earliest surviving globe was made in 1623 by Jesuit missionaries. The long legend on the globe contains one of the earliest known references to the force of gravity.

The oldest known map, made about 2500 B.C., is on a clay tablet found in Iraq that seems to show a valley estate.

A map carved in rock, showing the Val Camonica, Italy, dates from the second and first millennia B.C.

Ptolemy made one error that had far-reaching effects. He showed Europe and Asia as taking up half the globe and being much closer to each other than they actually are. Ptolemy's influence was so strong that about 1,700 years later, Columbus thought he had to sail only about 2,400 nautical miles (4,400 kilometers) to reach Asia from Spain. The actual distance is about 11,000 nautical miles (20,400 kilometers). Instead of reaching Cathay and India as he planned to do, Columbus discovered America.

The Middle Ages saw little progress in mapmaking. However, toward the end of that period, about the year 1300, the portolan chart came into being. Drawn on sheepskin, portolan charts were much in demand by people involved in trade and shipping. Ships' pilots and captains from cities such as Genoa, Pisa, Venice, and Barcelona contributed information about sailing routes, ports, and anchorages.

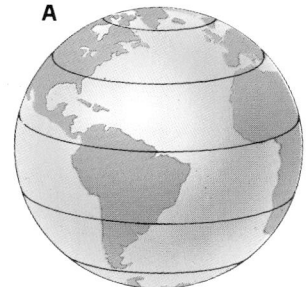
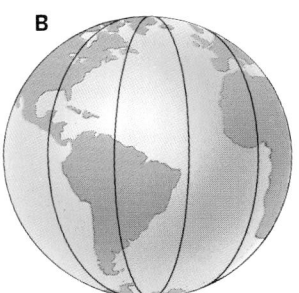
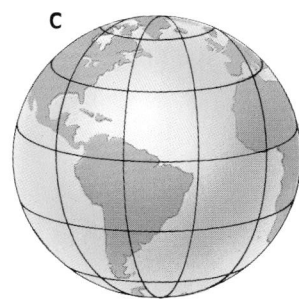

Lines of latitude (A) and longitude (B) are measured in degrees and enable every place on earth to be located by coordinates (C). The astrolabe, *left,* helped navigators in the Middle Ages establish latitude, or distance north and south from the equator, which has a latitude of 0 degrees. Longitude measures east-west distance from the prime meridian that passes through Greenwich, a borough of London, England. The longitude of the prime meridian is 0 degrees.

LandSat 1, a satellite, took the 46 infrared pictures that form this photomosaic of Italy.

Another thing that occurred in the Middle Ages also interested people in world maps and increased the sales of such maps. Marco Polo's travels to China gave people a desire to know the world. This desire probably helped lead to the great age of discovery and exploration.

The discoveries of explorers such as Columbus, da Gama, Vespucci, and Magellan changed the world maps during the 1400's and 1500's. The most important mapmaker of the period was Mercator of Flanders. He produced both globes and maps. Mercator also developed a map projection that was of great aid to sailors.

Mapmaking became more accurate and more scientific beginning in the 1700's. The use of new instruments such as the telescope and the chronometer—an instrument used in determining longitude at sea—made much more information available to mapmakers.

Great progress in mapping took place in the 1900's. Road maps for car travel first became widely used about 1910. Air travel, another form of transportation that developed in the early 1900's, required entirely different kinds of maps. Ever since World War I, aerial photography has played the major role in mapping. In 1940, after the U.S. Air Force reported that less than 10 per cent of the world was mapped sufficiently for the use of pilots, a major program was developed to map great areas of the world.

Much of the equipment still in use today had been developed by World War II. Since then, computers, satellites, and automation have made mapping even easier and more accurate.

How to Read Maps

Map language is a kind of code made up of elements such as scale, symbols, color, and grids. Understanding those elements allows the reader to break the map code.

Scale refers to the measurement on a map that represents a certain portion of the earth. A map scale may be shown as a representative fraction, in written form, or graphically.

As a representative fraction, a map scale might be written *1:3,300,000.* This means that one unit on the map represents 3,300,000 of the same units on the earth's surface (1 inch = 3,300,000 inches; 1 centimeter = 3,300,000 centimeters). In written form, the same proportion would be *1 inch = about 52 miles* or *1 centimeter = 33 kilometers.*

A graphic scale, also called a bar scale, is represented by a straight line on which distances have been marked off. Each mark represents a certain number of miles or kilometers.

Symbols allow mapmakers, or cartographers, to include a great deal of information clearly and concisely. Some symbols represent natural features of the land, such as mountains and lakes. Others represent cultural features such as cities and roads. Usually, a map contains a legend, which is a key that lists and explains the symbols used.

Color helps the map reader interpret what is shown. Mapmakers generally use blue for water, green for vegetation, and black or red for roads and place names.

Grid lines called meridians and parallels are used to mark longitude and latitude. Meridians are north-south lines drawn from pole to pole. Parallels are east-west lines drawn around a globe.

Learning to read maps is a skill. Like all skills, it requires practice. The ability to interpret a map will help the reader understand the earth, its features, and its people.

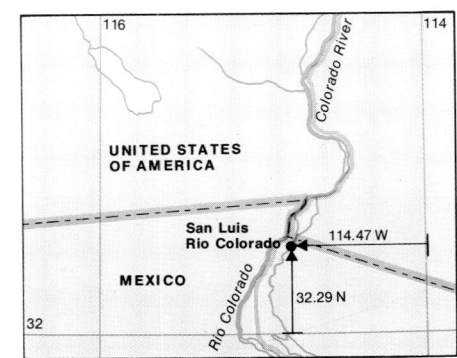

Any location can be expressed in terms of its latitude and longitude, the straight blue lines on the diagram above. San Luis on the Rio Colorado in Mexico is 32 degrees, 29 minutes (sixtieths of a degree) north of the equator and 114 degrees, 47 minutes west of Greenwich.

Maps often attempt to show what the surface of the earth looks like. For example, shading suggests that mountains rise above the land's surface. Detailed information about cities, boundaries, and roads can also appear on a map. The locations of various points of interest can be indicated as well.

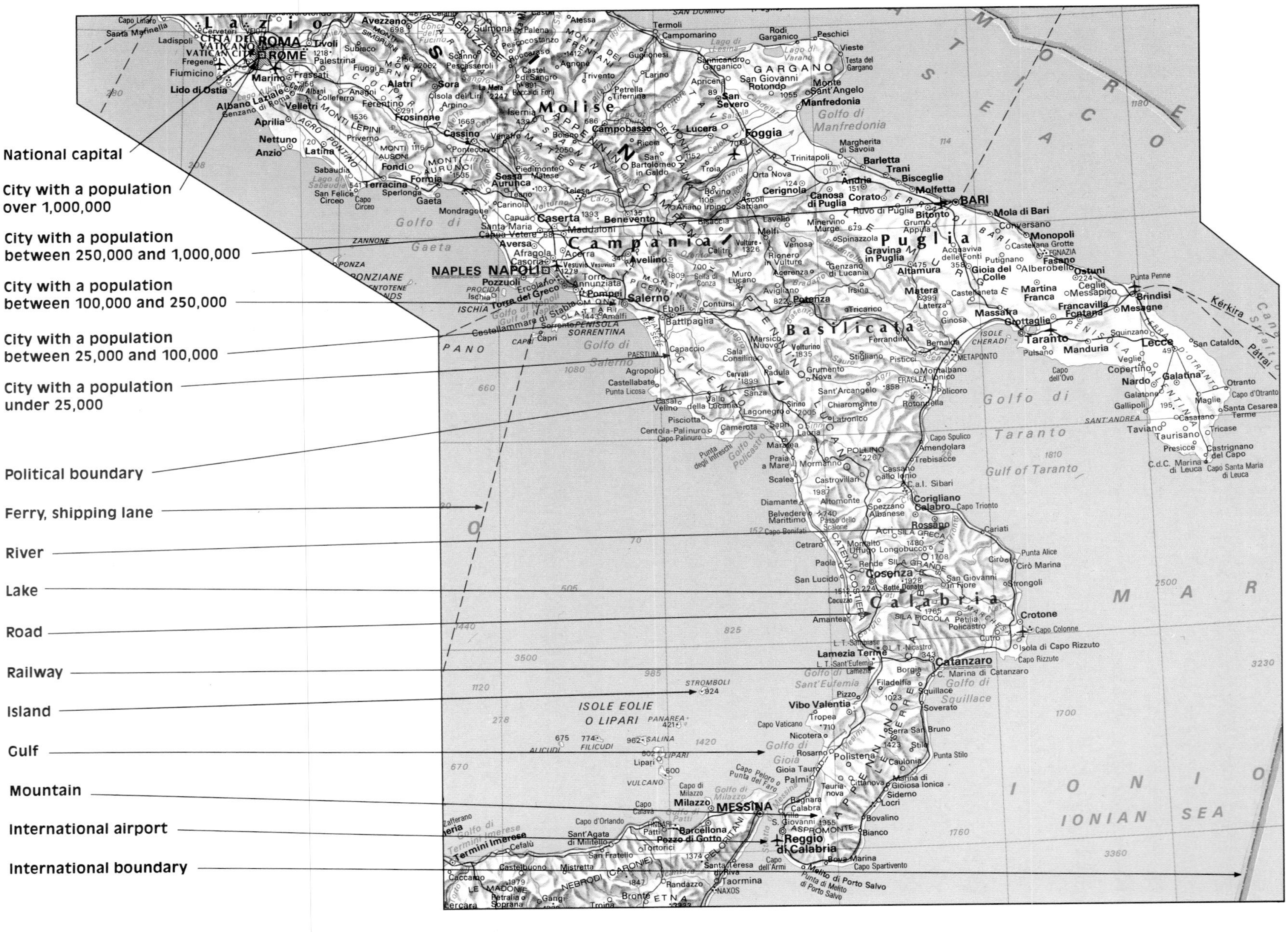

National capital
City with a population over 1,000,000
City with a population between 250,000 and 1,000,000
City with a population between 100,000 and 250,000
City with a population between 25,000 and 100,000
City with a population under 25,000
Political boundary
Ferry, shipping lane
River
Lake
Road
Railway
Island
Gulf
Mountain
International airport
International boundary

Maps of the World

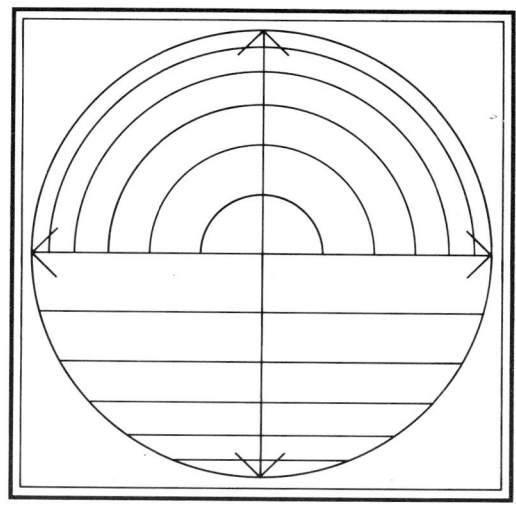

LEGEND

Hydrographic and Topographic Features
Symboles hydrographiques et morphologiques
Gewässer- und Geländeformen
Idrografia, Morfologia
Hidrografía y morfología

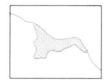
River, Stream
Cours d'eau permanent
Ständig wasserführender Fluß
Corso d'acqua perenne
Corriente de agua de régimen permanente

Lake
Lac d'eau douce
Süßwassersee
Lago d'acqua dolce
Lago de agua dulce

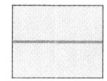
Rocks
Ecueils, Roches
Klippen, Felsriffe
Scogli, Rocce
Escollos, Rocas

Summer Limit of Pack-Ice
Limite du pack en été
Packeisgrenze im Sommer
Limite estivo del pack ghiacciato
Limite estival de banco de hielo

Intermittent Stream
Cours d'eau intermittent
Zeitweilig wasserführender Fluß
Corso d'acqua periodico
Corriente de agua intermitente

Intermittent Lake
Lac d'eau douce temporaire
Zeitweiliger Süßwassersee
Lago d'acqua dolce periodico
Lago de agua dulce intermitente

Reef, Atoll
Barrière, Atoll
Riff, Atoll
Barriera, Atollo
Barrera de arrecifes

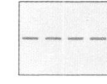
Winter Limit of Pack-Ice
Limite du pack en hiver
Packeisgrenze im Winter
Limite invernale del pack ghiacciato
Límite invernal de banco de hielo

Disappearing Stream
Perte de cours d'eau
Versickernder Fluß
Corso d'acqua che si inabissa
Corriente de agua que desaparece

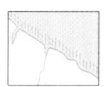
Salt Lake
Lac d'eau salée
Salzsee
Lago d'acqua salata
Lago de agua salada

Mangrove
Mangrove
Mangrove
Mangrovie
Manglar

Limit of Icebergs
Limite des glaces flottantes
Treibeisgrenze
Limite dei ghiacci alla deriva
Limite de hielo a la deriva

Undefined or Fluctuating River Course
Cours d'eau incertain
Fluß mit veränderlichem Lauf
Fiume dal corso incerto
Corriente de agua incerta

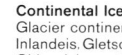
Intermittent Salt Lake
Lac d'eau salée temporaire
Zeitweiliger Salzsee
Lago d'acqua salata periodico
Lago de agua salada intermitente

Continental Ice-cap
Glacier continental
Inlandeis. Gletscher
Ghiacciaio continentale
Glaciar continental

Ice Shelf
Banquise
Schelfeis oder Eisschelf
Banchisa polare (Ice-shelf)
Banquisa

Waterfall, Rapids, Cataract
Chute, Rapide, Cataracte
Wasserfall, Stromschnelle, Katarakt
Cascata, Rapida, Cateratta
Cascada, Rapido, Catarata

Dry Lake Bed
Lac asséché
Trockener Seeboden
Alveo di lago asciutto
Lecho de lago seco

Glacial Tongue
Langue glaciaire
Gletscherzunge
Lingua di ghiaccio
Lengua de glaciar

Limit of Ice Shelf
Limite de la banquise
Schelfeisgrenze
Limite della banchisa
Límite de la banquisa

Canal
Canal
Kanal
Canale
Canal

Lake Surface Elevation
Cote du lac au-dessus du niveau de la mer
Höhe des Seespiegels
Altitudine del lago
Elevación de lago sobre el nivel del mar
315

Rocky Areas (Antarctica)
Région de roches (Antarctique)
Eisfreie Gebiete, Gebirge (Antarktika)
Aree rocciose (Antartide)
Area rocosa (Antártida)

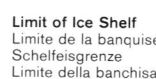
Contour Lines in Continental Ice
Courbes de niveau dans les régions glaciaires
Höhenlinien auf vergletschertem Gebiet
Curve altimetriche nelle aree ghiacciate
Curvas de nivel en aréas heladas

Navigable Canal
Canal navigable
Schiffbarer Kanal
Canale navigabile
Canal navegable

Lake Depth
Profondeur du lac
Seetiefe
Profondità del lago
Profundidad del lago

Defined Shoreline
Trait de côte définie
Küsten- oder Uferlinie
Linea di costa definita
Línea de costa definida

Bathymetric Contour
Courbe bathymétrique
Tiefenlinie
Curva batimetrica
Curva batimétrica

Swamp
Marais
Sumpf
Palude d'acqua dolce
Pantano

Sand Area
Région de sable, Désert
Sandgebiet, Sandwüste
Area sabbiosa, Deserto
Zona arenosa, desierto

Undefined or Fluctuating Shoreline
Trait de côte indéfinie
Unbestimmte oder veränderliche Uferlinie
Linea di costa indefinita
Línea de costa indefinida

Depth of Water
Valeur de sonde
Tiefenzahl
Quota batimetrica
Cota batimétrica

Salt Marsh
Marais d'eau salée
Salzsumpf
Palude d'acqua salata
Pantano de agua salada

Sandbank, Sandbar
Banc de sable
Sandbank
Bassofondo sabbioso
Banco submarino de arena

Mountain Range
Chaîne de montagnes
Bergkette
Catena di monti
Cadena montañosa

Mountain
Mont
Berg, Bergmassiv
Monte
Monte

Salt Pan
Marais salant
Salzpfanne
Salina
Salina

Port Facilities
Installations portuaires
Hafenanlagen
Impianti portuali
Instalaciones portuarias

Elevation
Cote, Altitude
Höhenzahl
Quota altimetrica
Cota altimétrica

Mountain Pass, Gap
Passage, Col, Port
Paß, Joch, Sattel
Passo, Colle, Valico
Paso, Collado, Puerto de montaña

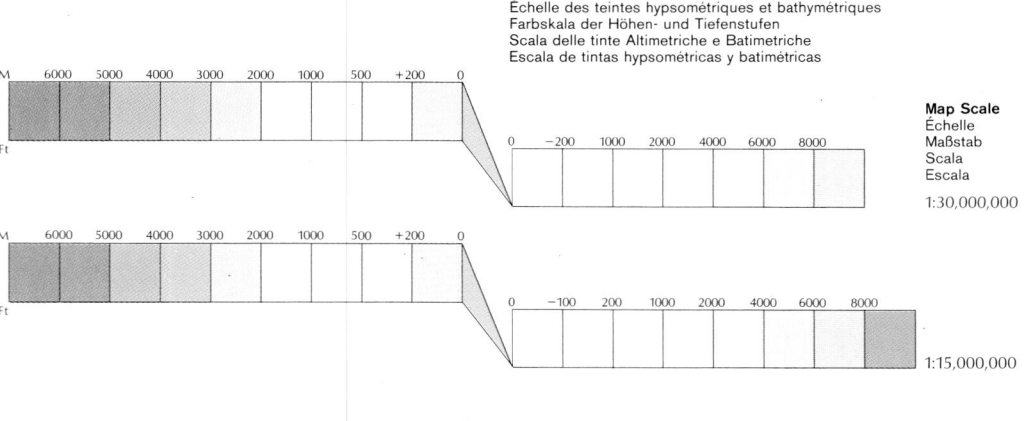

Scales in Metric and English Measures
Échelle des teintes hypsométriques et bathymétriques
Farbskala der Höhen- und Tiefenstufen
Scala delle tinte Altimetriche e Batimetriche
Escala de tintas hypsométricas y batimétricas

Map Scale
Échelle
Maßstab
Scala
Escala

1:30,000,000

1:15,000,000

Land Elevation Below Sea Level
Dépression et cote au-dessous du niveau de la mer
Senke mit Tiefenzahl unter dem Meeresspiegel
Depressione e quota sotto il livello del mare
Depresión y elevación bajo el nivel del mar
−155

Map Projections
Projections cartographiques
Kartennetzentwürfe
Proiezioni cartografiche
Proyecciones cartográficas

The projections appearing in this atlas have been plotted by computer

Les réseaux des projections ont été obtenus par élaboration automatique à partir de formules mathématiques

Die Kartennetze aller im Atlas vorkommenden Abbildungen wurden mit Hilfe der Datenverarbeitung (EDV) völlig neu errechnet

I disegni delle proiezioni presenti in quest'opera sono stati realizzati interamente ex-novo con l'uso del computer e del plotter a partire dalle formule matematiche

El reticulado de las proyecciones (redes geográficas) incluidas en esta obra han sido obtenidas por proceso automático a partir de las formulas matemáticas

The meanings of the symbols on the Legend pages are in English, French, German, Italian, and Spanish languages to permit the interpretation of the maps by a broad readership.

Boundaries, Capitals
Frontières, Soulignements
Grenzen, Unterstreichungen
Confini, Sottolineature
Límites, Subrayados

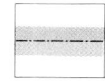
International Boundary
Frontière internationale
Staatsgrenze
Confine di Stato
Límite de Nación

Second-order Political Boundary
Frontière d'État fédéré, Région
Bundesstaats-, Regionsgrenze
Confine di Stato federato, Regione
Límite de Estado federado, Región

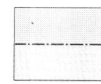
International Boundary (Continent Maps)
Frontière internationale (Continents)
Staatsgrenze (Erdteilkarten)
Confine di Stato (Carte dei Continenti)
Límite de Nación (Continentes)

Third-order Political Boundary
Frontière de Province, Comté, Bezirk
Provinz-, Grafschafts-, Bezirksgrenze
Confine di Provincia, Contea, Bezirk
Límite de Provincia, Condado, Bezirk

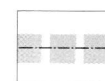
Undefined International Boundary
Frontière d'état internationale indéfinie
Nicht genau festgelegte Staatsgrenze
Confine di Stato indefinito
Límite de Nación indefinido

Administrative District Boundary (U.S.S.R.)
Frontière de Circonscription
Kreisgrenze
Confine di Circondario
Límite de Circunscripción administrativa

**International Ocean Floor Boundary
Defined by Treaty or Bilateral Agreement**
Frontière d'état eines définie par traités
et conventions bilatéraux
Durch Verträge festgelegte Staatsgrenze
im Meeresgebiet
Confine di Stato nel mare definito da
trattati e convenzioni bilaterali
Límite de Nación en el Mar definido por
los tratados bilaterales

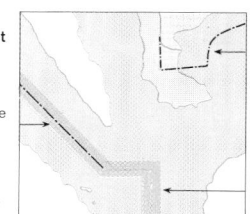

International Ocean Floor Boundary
Frontière d'état en mer
Staatsgrenze im Meeresgebiet
Confine di Stato nel mare
Límite de Nación en el mar

Undefined Ocean Floor Boundary
Frontière indéfinie d'état tracée en meer
Unbstimmte Staatsgrenze im Meeresgebiet
Confine di Stato indefinito nel mare
Límite indefinido de Nación en el mar

ROMA National Capital
Capitale d'État
Hauptstadt eines unabhängigen Staates
Capitale di Stato
Capital de Nación

Kristiansand Third - order Capital
Capitale de Province, Comté, Bezirk
Provinz-, Grafschafts-, Bezirkshauptstadt
Capoluogo di Provincia, Contea, Bezirk
Capital de Provincia, Condado, Bezirk

RIGA Dependency or Second-order Capital
Capitale d'État fédéré, Région
Bundesstaats-, Regionshauptstadt
Capitale di Stato federato, Regione
Capital de Estado federado, Región

Anadyr Administrative District Capital (U.S.S.R.)
Capitale de Circonscription
Kreishauptstadt
Capoluogo di Circondario
Capital de Circunscripción administrativa

Other Symbols
Symboles divers
Sonstige Zeichen
Simboli vari
Signos varios

LUTON AIRPORT International Airport
Aéroport international
Internationaler Flughafen
Aeroporto internazionale
Aeropuerto internacional

SANTAS CREUS Church, Monastery, Abbey
Monastère, Église, Abbaye
Kloster, Kirche, Abtei
Monastero, Chiesa, Abbazia
Monasterio, Iglesia, Abadía

Lighthouse
Phare
Leuchtturm
Faro
Faro

DAMPIERRE Castle
Château
Burg, Schloß
Castello
Castillo

BUI DAM Dam
Barrage
Staudamm, Staumauer
Diga artificiale, Sbarramento
Presa

PAESTUM Ruin, Archeological Site
Ruine, Centre archéologique
Ruine, Archäologisches Zentrum
Rovina, Zona archeologica
Ruina, Zona arqueológica

L.-GREENWICH
V.-IJmuiden Section of a City
Faubourg
Stadt- oder Ortsteil
Sobborgo urbano
Suburbio

MOLENS VAN KINDERDIJK Monument, Historic Site, etc.
Monument
Denkmal
Monumento
Monumento

Bidon V Uninhabited Locality, Hamlet
Ville inhabitée, Ferme, Hameau
Unbewohnte Stadt, Gehöft, Weiler
Città disabitata, Fattoria, Nucleo di case
Ciudad despoblada, Granja, Casar

HADRIAN'S WALL Wall
Muraille
Wall, Mauer
Vallo, Muraglia
Muralla

Bi'r Nāhid Periodically Inhabited Oasis
Oasis habitées périodiquement
Zeitweilig bewohnte Oase
Oasi periodicamente abitate
Oasis periodicamente habitados

GIANT'S CAUSEWAY Point of Interest
Curiosité
Sehenswürdigkeit
Curiosità
Curiosidad

Casey (Australia) Scientific Station
Base géophysique
Geophysikalische Beobachtungsstation
Base geofisica
Base geofísica

CUEVAS DE ARTÁ Cave
Grotte, Caverne
Höhle
Grotta, Caverna
Cueva, Gruta

Populated Places
Population
Bevölkerung
Popolazione
Población

Continent Maps
Cartes des Continents
Erdteilkarten
Carte dei Continenti
Mapas de Continentes

o < 25 000
⊙ 25 000-100 000
◎ 100 000-250 000
⊛ 250 000-1 000 000
⊡ > 1 000 000

Regional Maps
Cartes à plus grande échelle
Karten größeren Maßstabs
Carte di sviluppo
Mapas a gran escala

o < 10 000
o 10 000-25 000
⊙ 25 000-100 000
◎ 100 000-250 000
⊛ 250 000-1 000 000
⊡ > 1 000 000

Symbols represent population of inhabited localities
Les symboles représentent le nombre
d'habitants des localités
Die Signaturen entsprechen der
Einwohnerzahl des Ortes
I simboli sono relativi al valore
demografico dei centri abitati
Los símbolos son proporcionales
a la población del lugar

Town area symbol represents the shape of the urban area
Le petit plan de la ville reproduit la
configuration de l'aire urbaine
Die Plansignatur stellt die Gestalt
des Stadtgebietes dar
La piantina della città rappresenta la
configurazione dell'area urbana
El pequeño plano de la ciudad representa
la forma del área urbana

Transportation
Communications
Verkehrsnetz
Comunicazioni
Comunicaciones

Primary Railway
Chemin de fer principal
Hauptbahn
Ferrovia principale
Ferrocarril principal

Secondary Railway
Chemin de fer secondaire
Sonstige Bahn
Ferrovia secondaria
Ferrocarril secundario

Motorway, Expressway
Autoroute
Autobahn
Autostrada
Autopista

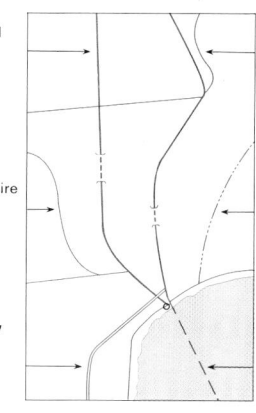

Road
Route de grande communication, Autres Routes
Fernverkehrsstraße, andere Straßen
Strada principale, Altre Strade
Carretera principal, Otras Carreteras

Trail, Caravan Route
Piste, Voie caravanière
Wüstenpiste, Karawanenweg
Pista nel deserto, Carovaniera
Pista en el desierto, Vía de Carabanas

Ferry, Shipping Lane
Bac, Ligne maritime
Fähre, Schiffahrtslinie
Traghetto, Linea di navigazione
Transbordador (Ferry), Línea de navegación

Type Styles
Caractères utilisés pour la toponymie
Zur Namenschreibung verwendete Schriftarten
Caratteri usati per la toponomastica
Caracteres utilizados para la toponimia

ITALY
Hessen RIBE

Political Units
Etat, Dépendance, Division administrative
Staat, abhängiges Gebiet, Verwaltungsgliederung
Stato, Dipendenza, Divisione amministrativa
Nación, Dependencia, División administrativa

Ankaratra	Monte Bianco
Tsiafajavona	Ngorongoro Crater
Nevado del Tolima	Kings Peak

Small Mountain Range, Mountain, Peak
Petit massif, Mont, Cime
Bergmassiv, Berg, Gipfel
Piccolo gruppo montuoso, Monte, Vetta
Macizo pequeño, Monte, Cima

LABRADOR SEA
Golfo Aragón

Sea, Gulf, Bay, Strait
Mer, Golfe, Baie, Détroit
Meer, Golf, Bucht, Meeresstraße
Mare, Golfo, Baia, Stretto
Mar, Golfo, Bahía, Estrecho

SAXONY
THRACE SUSSEX

Historical or Cultural Region
Région historique ou culturelle
Historische oder Kulturlandschaft
Regione storico - culturale
Región histórica y cultural

Cabo de São Vicente	Land's End
Mizen Head	Point Conception
Col de la Perche	Passo della Cisa

Cape, Point, Pass
Cap, Pointe, Passe
Kap, Landspitze, Paß
Capo, Punta, Passo
Cabo, Punta, Paso

West Mariana Basin
Galapagos Fracture Zone
Mid-Atlantic Ridge

Undersea Features
Formes du relief sous-marin
Formen des Meeresbodens
Forme del rilievo sottomarino
Formas del relieve submarino

PATAGONIA
BASSIN DE RENNES
PENÍNSULA DE YUCATAN

Physical Region (plain, peninsula)
Région physique (plaine, péninsule)
Landschaft (Ebene, Halbinsel)
Regione fisica (pianura, penisola)
Región natural (llanura, península)

MAHÉ	*ALDABRA ISLANDS*
CORSE	*CHANNEL ISLANDS*
SULU ARCHIPELAGO	

Island, Archipelago
Ile, Archipel
Insel, Archipel
Isola, Arcipelago
Isla, Archipiélago

Tarfaya
Tombouctou
Agadir
Nouakchott
BRAZZAVILLE
CASABLANCA

Size of type indicates relative importance of inhabited localities
La dimension des caractères indique
l'importance d'une localité
Die Schriftgröße entspricht der
Gesamtbedeutung des Ortes
La grandezza del carattere è proporzionale
all'importanza della località
La dimensión de los caracteres de imprenta
indica la importancia de la localidad

PYRENEES
CUMBRIAN MOUNTAINS
SIERRA DE GÁDOR   LA SILA

Mountain Range
Chaîne de montagnes
Bergkette, Gebirge
Catena di monti
Cadena montañosa

River, Waterfall, Cataract, Canal, Lake
Fleuve, Chute d'eau, Cataracte, Canal, Lac
Fluß, Wasserfall, Katarakt, Kanal, See
Fiume, Cascata, Cateratta, Canale, Lago
Río, Cascada, Catarata, Canal, Lago

INDEX MAPS

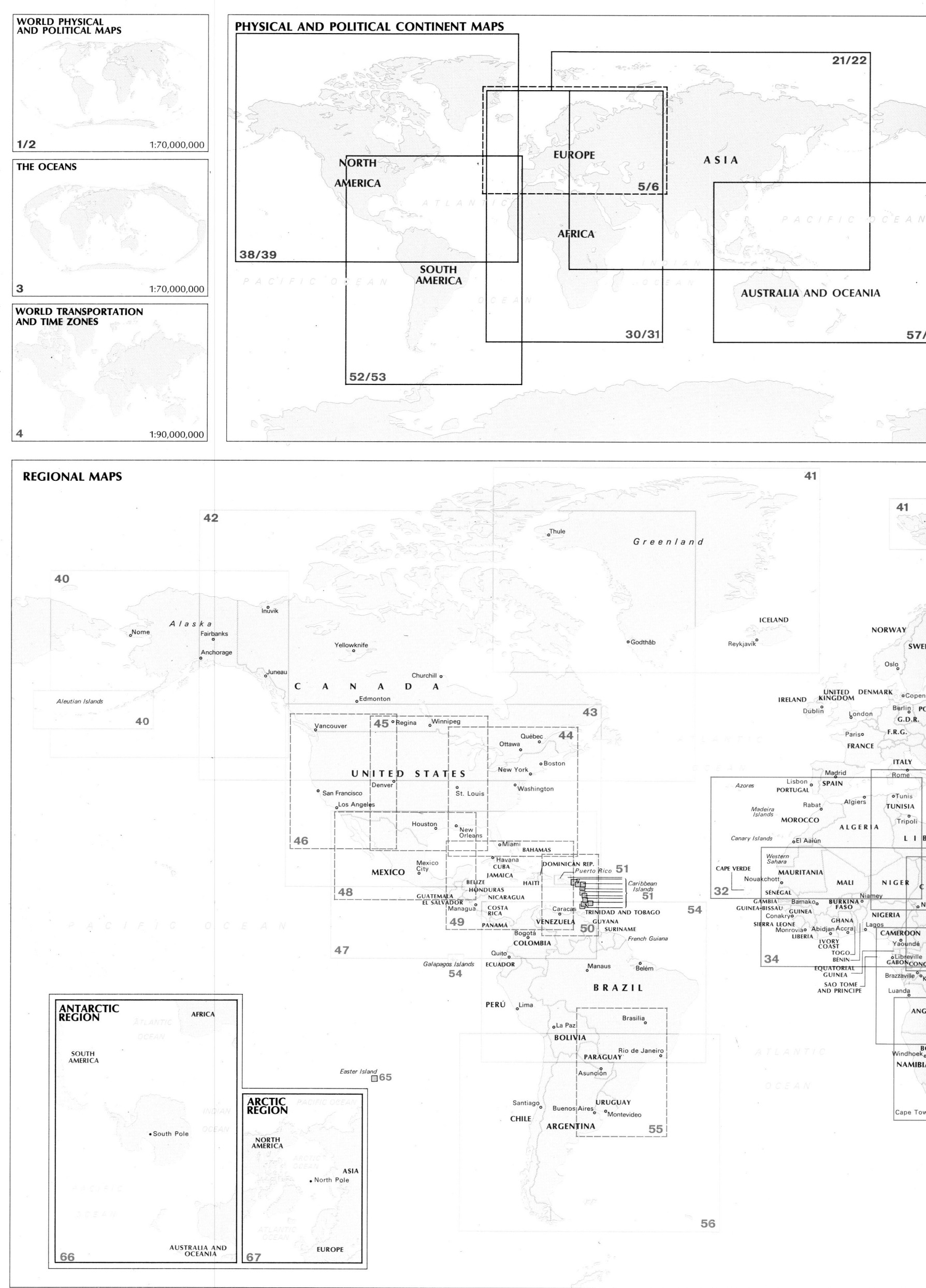

WORLD PHYSICAL AND POLITICAL MAPS

1/2   1:70,000,000

THE OCEANS

3   1:70,000,000

WORLD TRANSPORTATION AND TIME ZONES

4   1:90,000,000

PHYSICAL AND POLITICAL CONTINENT MAPS

21/22

NORTH AMERICA

EUROPE

5/6

ASIA

38/39

AFRICA

SOUTH AMERICA

AUSTRALIA AND OCEANIA

30/31

52/53

57/

REGIONAL MAPS

41

42

41

40

Alaska

Nome
Inuvik
Fairbanks
Anchorage
Juneau

Aleutian Islands

40

Yellowknife

C A N A D A

Churchill
Edmonton

43

Thule

Greenland

Godthåb

ICELAND

Reykjavík

NORWAY

SWE

Oslo

IRELAND   UNITED   DENMARK
           KINGDOM   Copenh
Dublin   Berlin   PO
           London   G.D.R.
                     F.R.G.
           Paris
FRANCE

45   Regina   Winnipeg
Vancouver

U N I T E D   S T A T E S

Québec
Ottawa   44
New York   Boston
Washington

San Francisco   Denver
Los Angeles

St. Louis

46

Houston
New Orleans

48

Mexico
City

MEXICO

Miami

BAHAMAS

Havana   CUBA
          JAMAICA
BELIZE   DOMINICAN REP.
HONDURAS HAITI   *Puerto Rico*   51
Managua   NICARAGUA
GUATEMALA
EL SALVADOR
          COSTA
          RICA
49   PANAMÁ

Caracas

VENEZUELA

50

Caribbean Islands   51

TRINIDAD AND TOBAGO
GUYANA
SURINAME
French Guiana

54

47

Bogotá
COLOMBIA

Quito

Galapagos Islands   ECUADOR
54

Manaus   Belém

B R A Z I L

ITALY
Rome

Madrid
Azores   Lisbon   SPAIN
            PORTUGAL
*Madeira   Algiers   Tunis
Islands*   Rabat   TUNISIA
            MOROCCO   Tripoli
Canary Islands   El Aaiún   A L G E R I A   L I B

            *Western
            Sahara*
CAPE VERDE   MAURITANIA
Nouakchott
32   SÉNÉGAL   MALI   NIGER
GAMBIA   Bamako   Niamey
GUINEA-BISSAU   BURKINA
Conakry   GUINEA   FASO
SIERRA LEONE   Abidjan Accra   NIGERIA
Monrovia   GHANA   Lagos
LIBERIA   IVORY   CAMEROON
            COAST   Yaoundé
            TOGO
34   BENIN
       EQUATORIAL   GABON CONG
       GUINEA   Libreville
       SAO TOME   Brazzaville   Ki
       AND PRINCIPE
                   Luanda

PERÚ   Lima

La Paz   Brasília

BOLIVIA

PARAGUAY   Rio de Janeiro

Asunción

Santiago   Buenos Aires   URUGUAY
            Montevideo
CHILE   ARGENTINA   55

56

ANG

Windhoek   BO

NAMIBIA

Cape Tow

ANTARCTIC REGION

AFRICA

SOUTH
AMERICA

South Pole

66   AUSTRALIA AND
      OCEANIA

Easter Island   65

ARCTIC REGION

NORTH
AMERICA

ASIA

North Pole

67   EUROPE

IONAL MAPS OF EUROPE

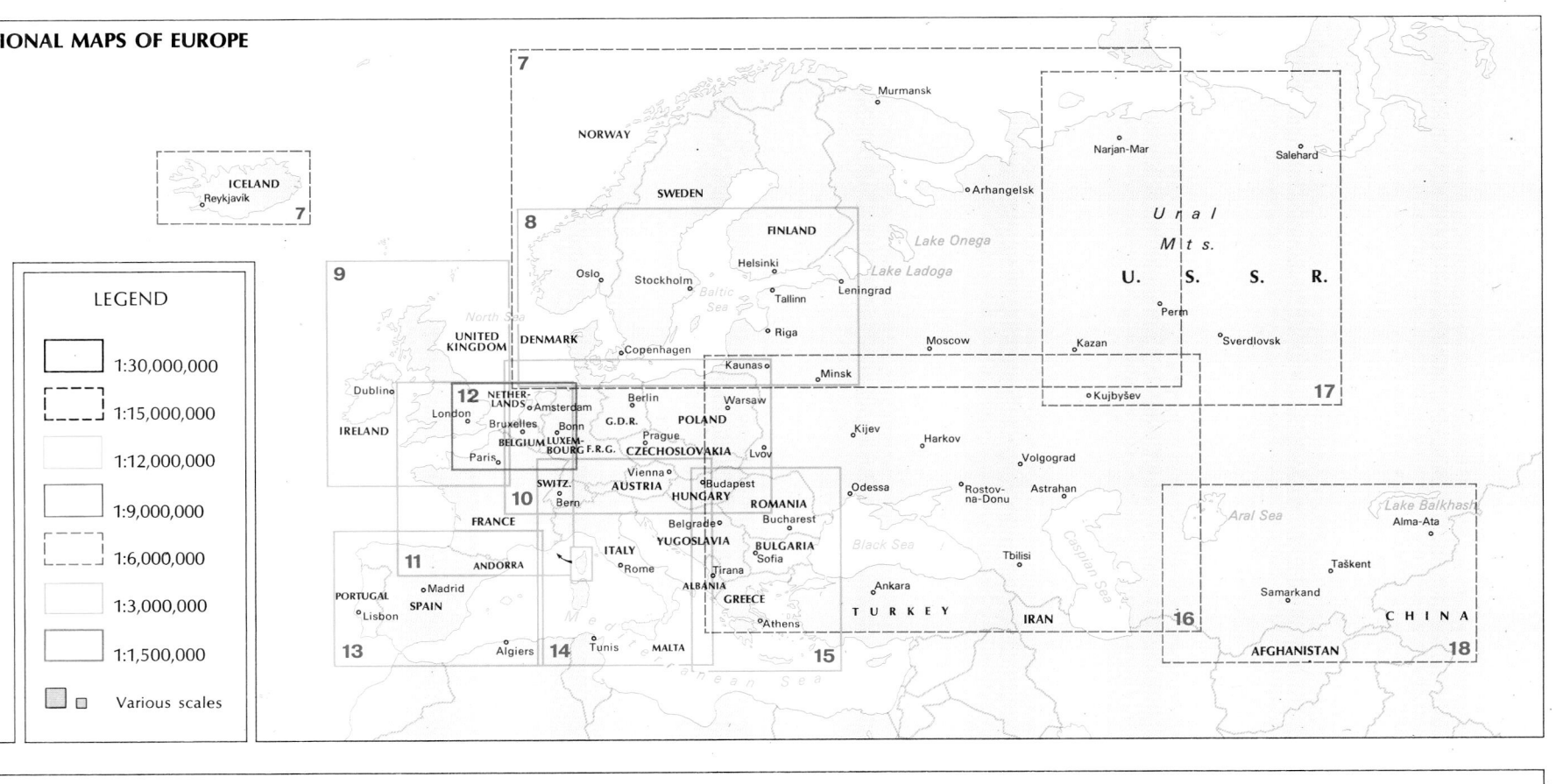

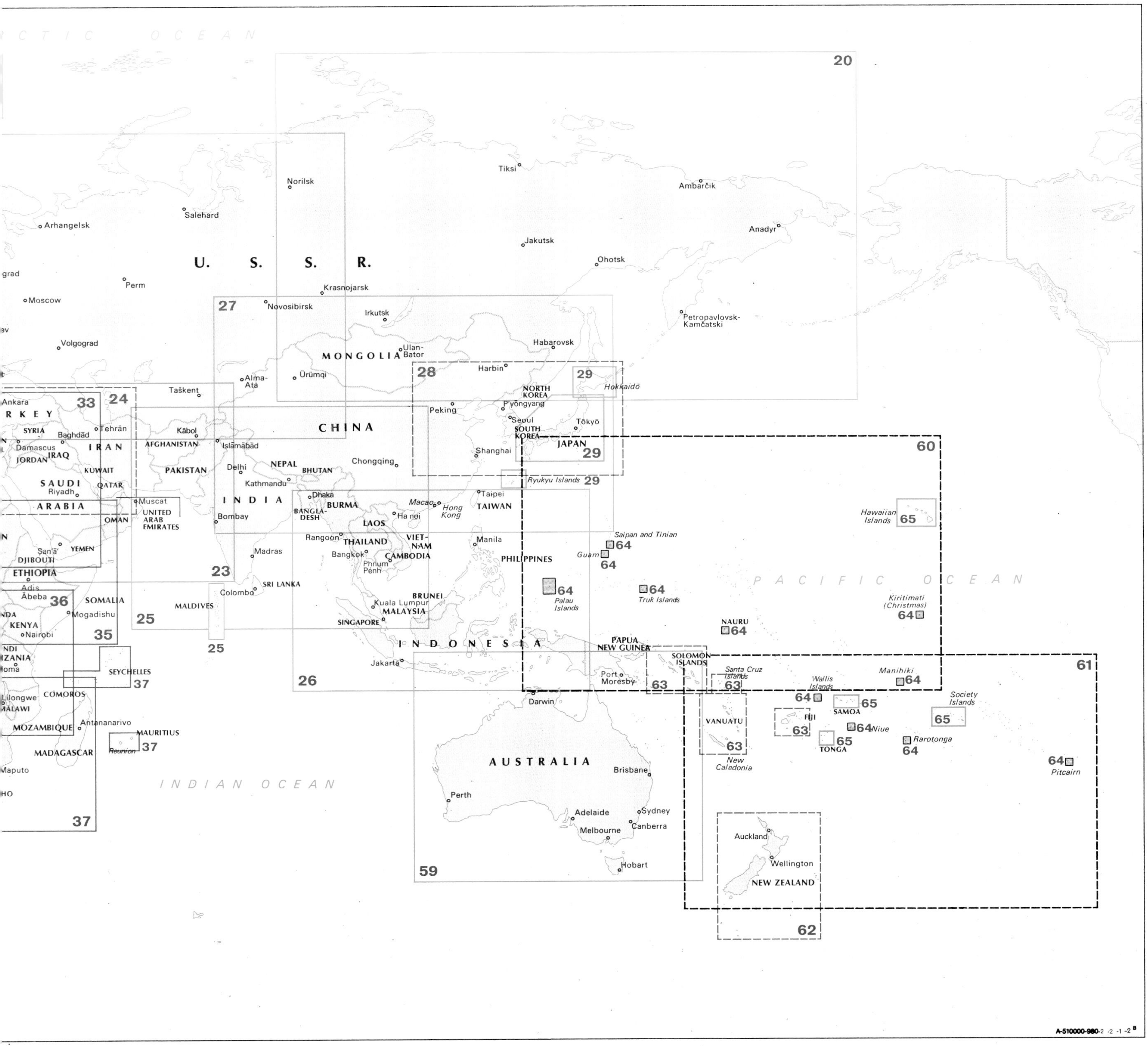

LEGEND

	1:30,000,000
	1:15,000,000
	1:12,000,000
	1:9,000,000
	1:6,000,000
	1:3,000,000
	1:1,500,000
	Various scales

Map 1 **WORLD, PHYSICAL**

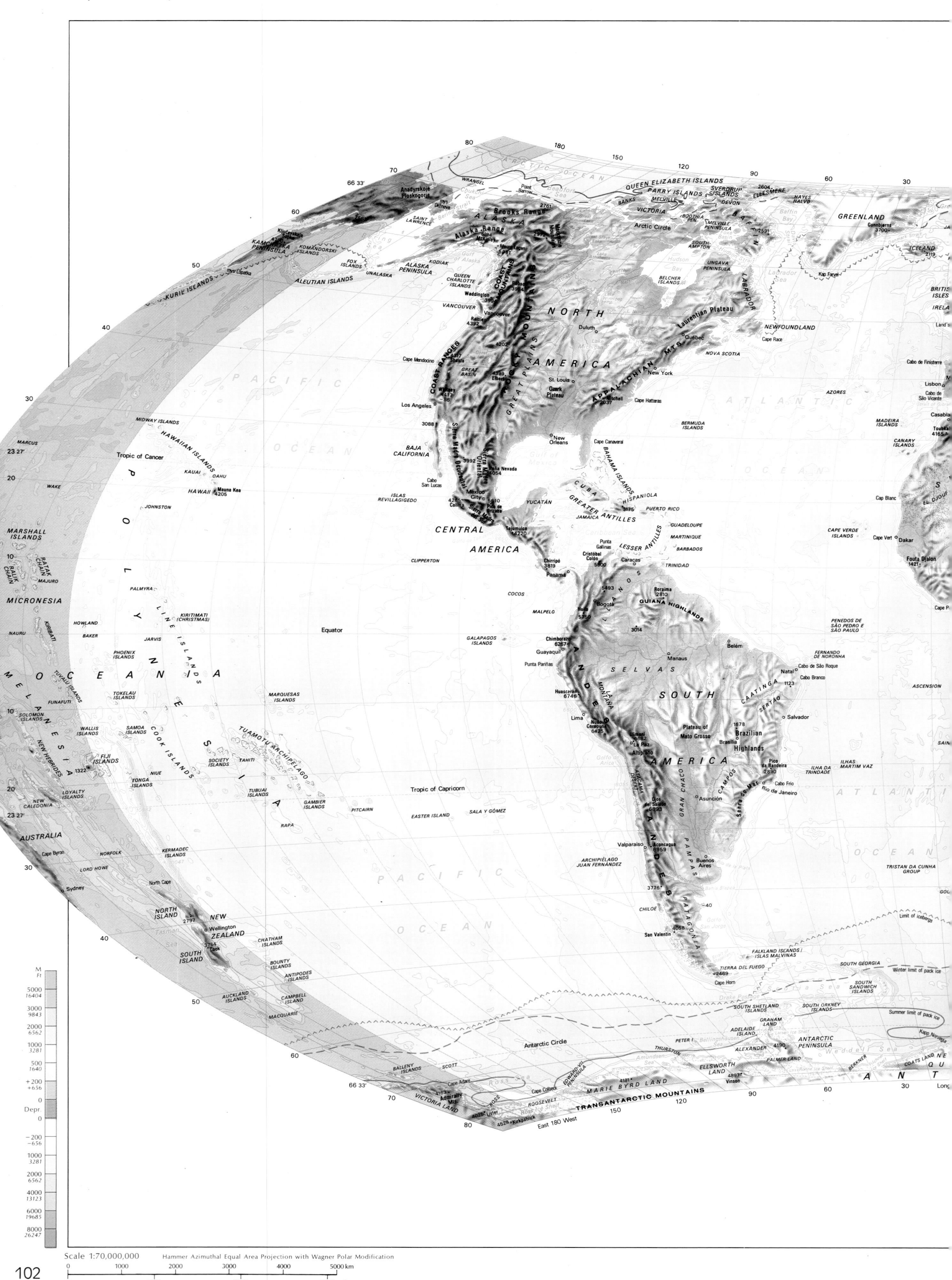

M
Ft

5000
16404

3000
9843

2000
6562

1000
3281

500
1640

+ 200
+656

Depr.
0

0

− 200
−656

1000
3281

2000
6562

4000
13123

6000
19685

8000
26247

Scale 1:70,000,000   Hammer Azimuthal Equal Area Projection with Wagner Polar Modification

0   1000   2000   3000   4000   5000 km

0   1000   2000   3000 miles

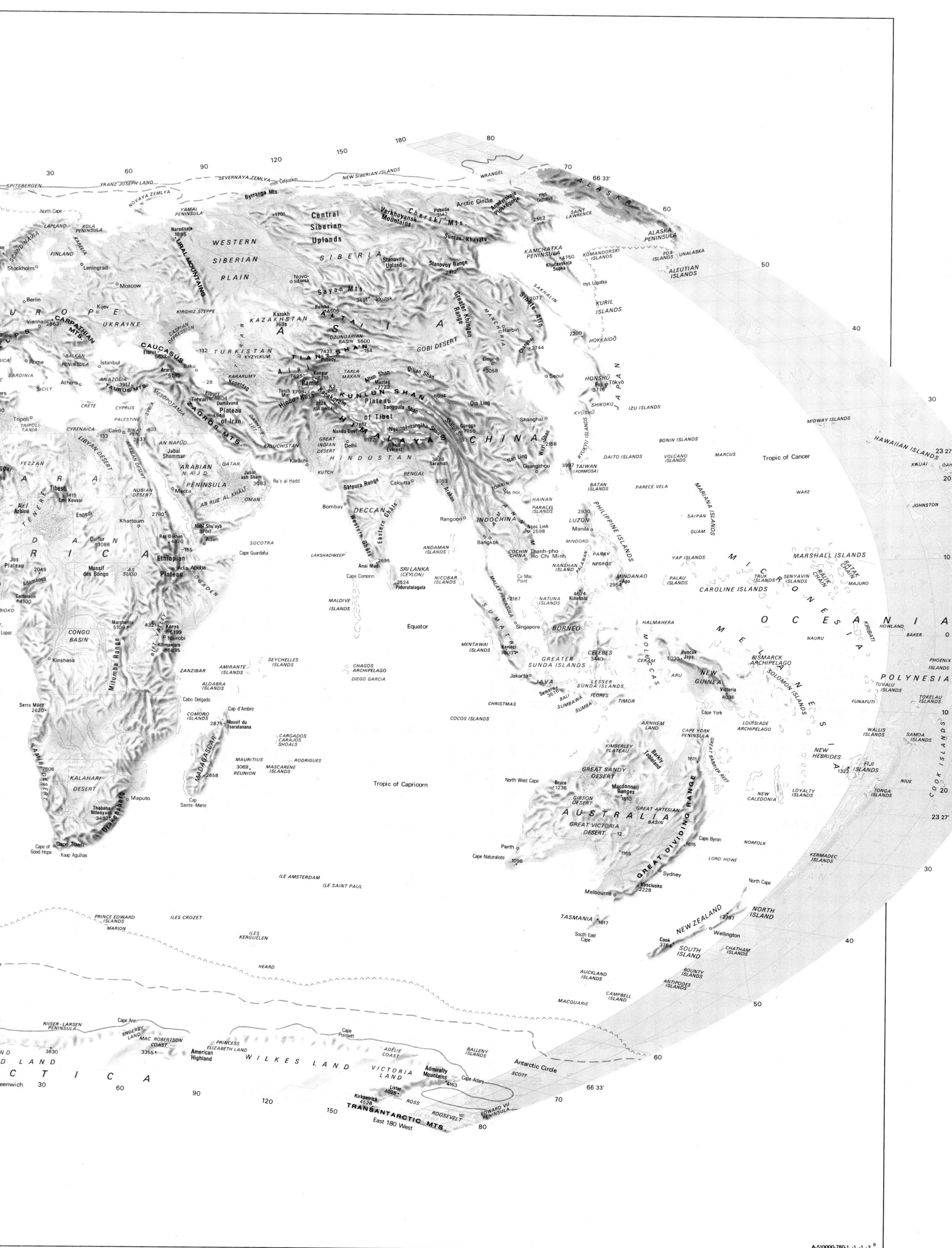

Map 2 **WORLD, POLITICAL**

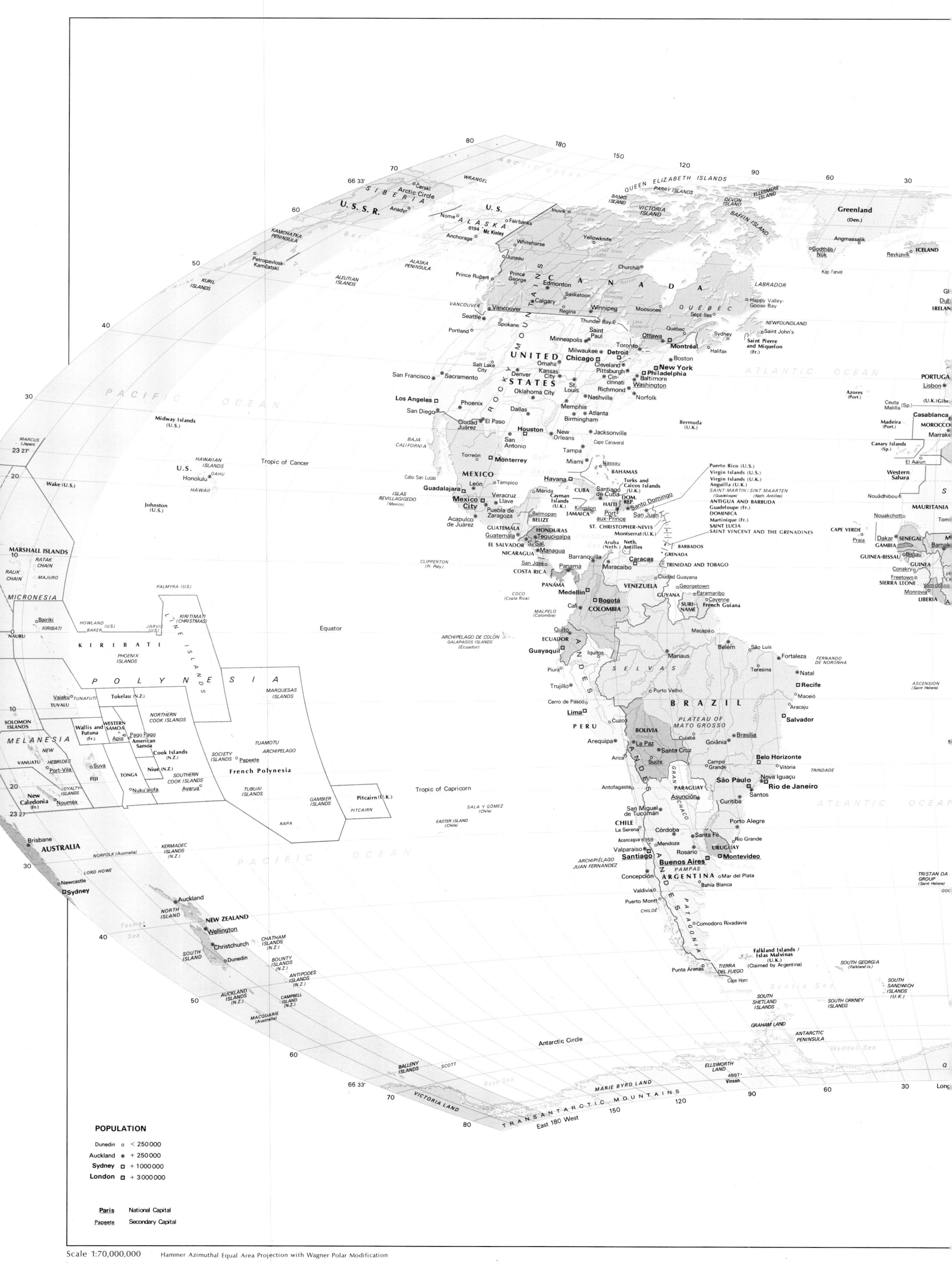

ARCTIC OCEAN

WRANGEL

U.S.S.R.

SIBERIA

KAMCHATKA
PENINSULA

Čerski
Arctic Circle
66 33'
Anadyr

Petropavlovsk-
Kamčatski

KURIL
ISLANDS

ALEUTIAN
ISLANDS

Nome
U.S.
ALASKA
6194
McKinley
Fairbanks
Inuvik

Anchorage
Whitehorse

QUEEN ELIZABETH ISLANDS

BANKS
ISLAND
PARRY ISLANDS
DEVON
ISLAND
ELLESMERE
ISLAND

VICTORIA
ISLAND
Greenland
(Den.)

BAFFIN ISLAND

Angmassalik

Godthåb /
Nûk
ICELAND
Reykjavik
Kap Farvel

Juneau
Yellowknife
Churchill

ALASKA
PENINSULA

Prince Rupert
Prince
George

VANCOUVER
Vancouver
Seattle
Calgary
Edmonton
Saskatoon
Regina
Winnipeg
Moosonee

C A N A D A
QUÉBEC
LABRADOR

Happy Valley-
Goose Bay
Sept-Îles

NEWFOUNDLAND

IRELAN

Spokane
Thunder Bay
Quebec
Saint John's
Saint Pierre
and Miquelon
(Fr.)

Portland
Minneapolis
Saint
Paul
Milwaukee
Toronto
Ottawa
Montréal
Sydney
Halifax

San Francisco
Sacramento
Salt Lake
City
Omaha
Kansas
City
Chicago
Detroit
Cleveland
Pittsburgh
Boston
New York
Philadelphia

Denver
UNITED
STATES
St.
Louis
Cincinnati
Baltimore
Washington
PORTUGA
Lisbon

Los Angeles
Phoenix
Oklahoma City
Nashville
Richmond
Norfolk
Azores
(Port.)

San Diego
Dallas
Memphis
Atlanta
Bermuda
(U.K.)
Ceuta
Melilla (Sp.)
(U.K.)Gibr

Ciudad
Juárez
El Paso
Birmingham
Casablanca
Madeira
(Port.)
MOROCCO
Marrake

Torreón
San
Antonio
New
Orleans
Jacksonville
Cape Canaveral
Canary Islands
(Sp.)
El Aaiun
Western
Sahara

BAJA
CALIFORNIA
Houston
Tampa
Miami
Nouâdhibou
MAURITANIA

MARCUS
(Japan)
23 27'
Midway Islands
(U.S.)
Cabo San Lucas
Monterrey
Nassau
BAHAMAS

HAWAIIAN
ISLANDS
OAHU
Tropic of Cancer
León
Tampico
Havana
Turks and
Caicos Islands
(U.K.)
Puerto Rico (U.S.)
Virgin Islands (U.S.)
Virgin Islands (U.K.)
Anguilla (U.K.)

Wake (U.S.)
U.S.
Honolulu
HAWAII
MEXICO
Veracruz
Llave
Mérida
CUBA
Cayman
Islands
(U.K.)
Santiago
de Cuba
HAITI
DOM.
REP.
Santo Domingo
SAINT-MARTIN / SINT MAARTEN
(Neth. Antilles)
ANTIGUA AND BARBUDA
(Guadeloupe)

Johnston
(U.S.)
ISLAS
REVILLAGIGEDO
(Mexico)
Guadalajara
Mexico
City
Puebla de
Zaragoza
Kingston
Port-
au-Prince
San Juan
Guadeloupe (Fr.)
DOMINICA
Martinique (Fr.)
SAINT LUCIA
SAINT VINCENT AND THE GRENADINES
CAPE VERDE

MARSHALL ISLANDS
10
RATAK
CHAIN
Acapulco
de Juárez
GUATEMALA
Guatemala
BELIZE
ST. CHRISTOPHER-NEVIS
Montserrat (U.K.)
Praia
Dakar
SENEGAL

RALIK
CHAIN
MAJURO
HONDURAS
Tegucigalpa
San
Sal.
BARBADOS
GUINEA-BISSAU
Bissau
GAMBIA

MICRONESIA
EL SALVADOR
NICARAGUA
Managua
Barranquilla
Aruba
(Neth.)
Neth.
Antilles
GRENADA
Conakry
SIERRA LEONE
Freetown
GUINEA

Bairiki
KIRIBATI
San José
COSTA RICA
PANAMA
Panamá
Maracaibo
Caracas
TRINIDAD AND TOBAGO
Monrovia
LIBERIA

NAURU
CLIPPERTON
(Fr. Poly.)
Medellín
VENEZUELA
Ciudad Guayana

HOWLAND
(U.S.)
BAKER
(U.S.)
JARVIS
(U.S.)
PALMYRA (U.S.)
KIRITIMATI
(CHRISTMAS)
Bogotá
COLOMBIA
Cali
GUYANA
Georgetown
Paramaribo
SURI-
NAME
Cayenne
French Guiana

K I R I B A T I
Quito
ECUADOR
Macapá
ASCENSION
(Saint Helena)

PHOENIX
ISLANDS
Equator
ARCHIPELAGO DE COLÓN
GALAPAGOS ISLANDS
(Ecuador)
Guayaquil
Iquitos
Manaus
Belém
São Luís
Fortaleza
FERNANDO
DE NORONHA

P O L Y N E S I A
Piura
SELVAS
Teresina
Natal

MARQUESAS
ISLANDS
Trujillo
Porto Velho
Aracaju
Recife

SOLOMON
ISLANDS
10
TUVALU
Vaiaku
FUNAFUTI
Tokelau (N.Z.)
NORTHERN
COOK ISLANDS
(N.Z.)
Cerro de Pasco
Lima
B R A Z I L
PLATEAU OF
MATO GROSSO
Maceió
Salvador

MELANESIA
WESTERN
SAMOA
Apia
Pago Pago
American
Samoa
PERU
Cuzco
BOLIVIA
La Paz
Cuiabá
Goiânia
Brasília
Belo Horizonte

VANUATU
NEW
HEBRIDES
Port-Vila
Wallis and
Futuna
(Fr.)
Suva
Cook Islands
(N.Z.)
Niue (N.Z.)
SOCIETY
ISLANDS
Papeete
SOUTHERN
COOK ISLANDS
Avarua
French Polynesia
Sucre
Santa Cruz
Campo
Grande
Vitória
TRINDADE

New
Caledonia
(Fr.)
Nouméa
LOYALTY
ISLANDS
FIJI
TONGA
Nuku'alofa
TUAMOTU
ARCHIPELAGO
Antofagasta
PARAGUAY
Asunción
CHACO
Curitiba
Nova Iguaçu
São Paulo
Rio de Janeiro
Santos

23 27'
GAMBIER
ISLANDS
Pitcairn (U.K.)
PITCAIRN
Tropic of Capricorn
SALA Y GÓMEZ
(Chile)
Arica
San Miguel
de Tucumán
Córdoba
Porto Alegre
ATLANTIC OCEAN

Brisbane
NORFOLK (Australia)
TUBUAI
ISLANDS
RAPA
EASTER ISLAND
(Chile)
CHILE
La Serena
PARAGUAY
Santa Fé
Rosario
URUGUAY
Montevideo
TRISTAN DA
GROUP
(Saint Helena)

AUSTRALIA
LORD HOWE
KERMADEC
ISLANDS
(N.Z.)
ARCHIPIÉLAGO
JUAN FERNANDEZ
Valparaíso
Santiago
Mendoza
Concepción
Buenos Aires
PAMPAS
ARGENTINA
Mar del Plata
Bahía Blanca

Newcastle
Sydney
Aconcagua 6959
Valdivia
Puerto Montt
CHILOÉ

Auckland
NORTH
ISLAND
Tasman
Sea
NEW ZEALAND
Wellington
Christchurch
CHATHAM
ISLANDS
(N.Z.)
Comodoro Rivadavia
PATAGONIA

SOUTH
ISLAND
Dunedin
BOUNTY
ISLANDS
(N.Z.)
Punta Arenas
TIERRA
DEL FUEGO
Cape Horn
Falkland Islands /
Islas Malvinas
(U.K.)
(Claimed by Argentina)
SOUTH GEORGIA
(Falkland Is.)

ANTIPODES
ISLANDS
(N.Z.)
Scotia Sea
SOUTH
SANDWICH
ISLANDS
(U.K.)

AUCKLAND
ISLANDS
(N.Z.)
CAMPBELL
ISLAND
(N.Z.)
SOUTH
SHETLAND
ISLANDS
SOUTH ORKNEY
ISLANDS

MACQUARIE
(Australia)
GRAHAM LAND
Weddell Sea

Antarctic Circle
ANTARCTIC
PENINSULA

BALLENY
ISLANDS
SCOTT
ELLSWORTH
LAND
4897
Vinsen
66 33'
70
VICTORIA LAND
MARIE BYRD LAND
120
60
30
Long

80
East 180 West
Ross Sea
T R A N S A N T A R C T I C   M O U N T A I N S
150
90

POPULATION

Dunedin	○ < 250 000
Auckland	◉ + 250 000
Sydney	□ + 1 000 000
London	▣ + 3 000 000

Paris	National Capital
Papeete	Secondary Capital

Scale 1:70,000,000 Hammer Azimuthal Equal Area Projection with Wagner Polar Modification

0 1000 2000 3000 4000 5000 km

0 1000 2000 3000 miles

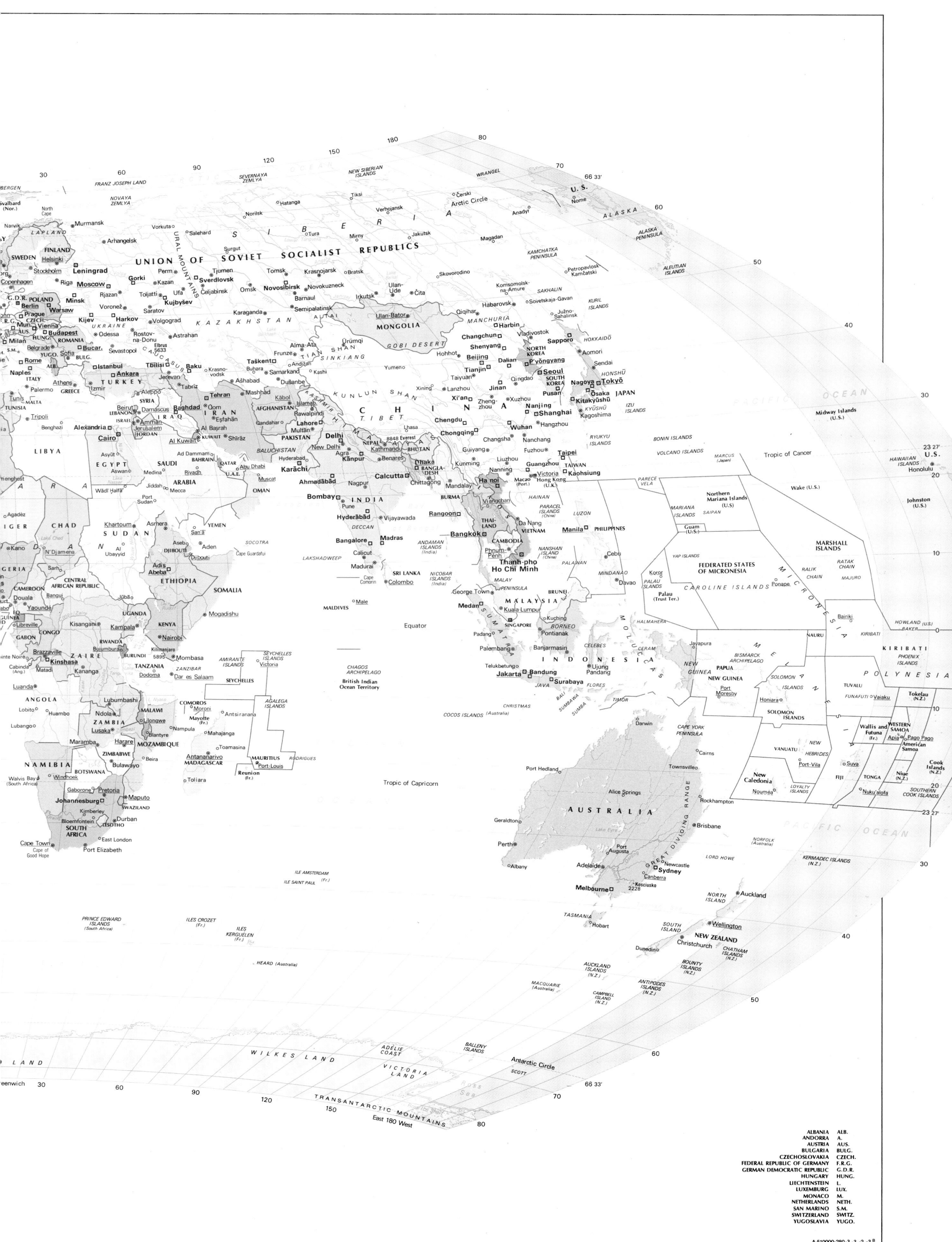

SVALBARD (Nor.)
FRANZ JOSEPH LAND
NOVAYA ZEMLYA
SEVERNAYA ZEMLYA
NEW SIBERIAN ISLANDS
WRANGEL
U.S.
Nome
Arctic Circle
66 33'
60
ALASKA
ALASKA PENINSULA
50
ALEUTIAN ISLANDS

North Cape
Narvik
Murmansk
Arhangelsk
Hatanga
Tiksi
Verhojansk
Čerski
Anadyr
LAPLAND
Vorkuta
Norilsk
Tura
Magadan
KAMCHATKA PENINSULA
Petropavlosk-Kamčatski
Komsomolsk-na-Amure

SWEDEN FINLAND
Helsinki
Leningrad
Salehard
S I B E R I A
Mirny
Jakutsk
Skovorodino
SAKHALIN
Sovetskaja-Gavan
KURIL ISLANDS

Stockholm
Gorki
U N I O N O F S O V I E T S O C I A L I S T R E P U B L I C S
Surgut
Tjumen
Tomsk
Krasnojarsk
Bratsk
Ulan-Ude
Čita
Habarovsk
Vladivostok
Južno-Sahalinsk
HOKKAIDŌ
Sapporo
50

Copenhagen
Riga
Moscow
Perm
Sverdlovsk
URAL MOUNTAINS
Omsk
Novosibirsk
Novokuzneck
Irkutsk
MANCHURIA
Harbin
Aomori
G.D.R. POLAND
Berlin
Minsk
Rjazan
Kazan
Ufa
Čeljabinsk
Barnaul
Semipalatinsk
ALTAI
Ulan-Bator
MONGOLIA
Changchun
NORTH KOREA
P'yŏngyang
Sendai
HONSHŪ
40

F.R.G.
Prague
Warsaw
Kijev
Harkov
Volgograd
K A Z A K H S T A N
Karaganda
Qiqihar
Hohhot
Shenyang
Beijing
Dalian
Seoul
Pusan
SOUTH KOREA
Nagoya
Tōkyō
KYŪSHŪ
CZECH.
Mün.
Vienna
Budapest
ROMANIA
Odessa
UKRAINE
Rostov-na-Donu
Astrahan
Frunze
Alma-Ata
TIAN SHAN
Ürümqi
SINKIANG
GOBI DESERT
Ulan-Bator
Changchun
Tianjin
Qingdao
Osaka
Kitakyūshū
Kagoshima
JAPAN
AUS. HUNG.
Milan
Belgrade
YUGO. Sofia
Bucar.
BULG.
Sevastopol
Elbrus 5633
Tbilisi
Baku
Bухara
Samarkand
Andižan
Kashi
KUNLUN SHAN
Xining
Lanzhou
Taiyuan
Jinan
Zheng-zhou
Xuzhou
Nanjing
Shanghai
Hangzhou
IZU ISLANDS
30

Rome
ITALY
Naples
ALB.
S.M.
Athens
GREECE
Istanbul
Ankara
TURKEY
Jerevan
Krasno-vodsk
Dušanbe
TIBET
Lhasa
8848 Everest
Chengdu
Chongqing
Changsha
Nanchang
Wuhan
Fuzhou
RYUKYU ISLANDS
BONIN ISLANDS
Midway Islands (U.S.)

Tunis
MALTA
Tripoli
TUNISIA
Izmir
Aleppo
SYRIA
Beirut
LEBANON
Damascus
Baghdad
Qom
Tehran
Tabriz
Mashhad
AFGHANISTAN
Kabol
Islamabad
Rawalpindi
Lahore
Multan
Kathmandu
NEPAL
BHUTAN
Benares
Guiyang
Kunming
Liuzhou
Nanning
Guangzhou
Victoria
TAIWAN
Taipei
Kaohsiung
Hong Kong (U.K.)
Macao (Port.)
VOLCANO ISLANDS
MARCUS (Japan)
Tropic of Cancer
23 27'
HAWAIIAN ISLANDS
U.S.
Honolulu
20

ISRAEL
Amman
JORDAN
Cairo
Alexandria
Benghazi
LIBYA
Tripoli
IRAQ
IRAN
Eşfahān
Shīrāz
Al Başrah
KUWAIT
Al Kuwait
BAHRAIN
QATAR
Abu Dhabi
U.A.E.
Qandahar
PAKISTAN
Delhi
Agra
KASHMIR
Kānpur
Dhākā
BANGLA-DESH
Chittagong
Mandalay
Ha noi
HAINAN
PARACEL ISLANDS (China)
NANSHAN ISLAND (China)
Wake (U.S.)
PARECE VELA
Johnston (U.S.)

Asyūţ
Aswān
EGYPT
Wādī Halfā
SAUDI
Medina
Riyadh
Ad Dammam
Muscat
OMAN
BALUCHISTAN
Hyderabad
Karāchi
Ahmadābād
Nagpur
Calcutta
Viahcham
BURMA
Da Nang
Manila
PHILIPPINES
Guam (U.S.)
SAIPAN
MARIANA ISLANDS
Northern Mariana Islands (U.S.)
MARSHALL ISLANDS
10

Port Sudan
Jiddah
Mecca
ARABIA
Bombay
Pune
INDIA
Hyderabad
DECCAN
Vijayawada
Rangoon
THAI-LAND
Bangkok
VIETNAM
Phnum Penh
CAMBODIA
Cebu
Davao
MINDANAO
KOROR
YAP ISLANDS
PALAU ISLANDS
FEDERATED STATES OF MICRONESIA
CAROLINE ISLANDS
RATAK CHAIN
MAJURO

Khartoum
Asmera
SUDAN
YEMEN
San'ā'
Aden
Cape Guardafui
SOCOTRA
Bangalore
Madras
ANDAMAN ISLANDS (India)
Thanh-pho Ho Chi Minh
NANSHAN ISLAND (China)
PALAWAN
RALIK CHAIN
M I C R O N E S I A

Agadez
CHAD
N'Djamena
Lake Chad
Aseb
Ubayyid
DJIBOUTI
Djibouti
Calicut
Madurai
SRI LANKA
NICOBAR ISLANDS (India)
MALAY PENINSULA
BRUNEI
Ponape
Bairiki
HOWLAND (U.S.)
BAKER (U.S.)

NIGER
Kano
Sarh
CENTRAL AFRICAN REPUBLIC
Bangui
Addis Ababa
ETHIOPIA
SOMALIA
Cape Comorin
Colombo
MALDIVES
Male
George Town
Medan
MALAYSIA
Kuala Lumpur
Kuching
BORNEO
CELEBES
HALMAHERA
CERAM
Jayapura
NAURU
KIRIBATI
PHOENIX ISLANDS
P O L Y N E S I A

CAMEROON
Douala
Yaounde
GUINEA
Libreville
GABON
CONGO
Kisangani
UGANDA
Kampala
KENYA
Nairobi
Equator
SINGAPORE
Padang
Pontianak
Banjarmasin
Ujung Pandang
Telukbetung
INDONESIA
MOLUCCAS
NEW GUINEA
PAPUA NEW GUINEA
BISMARCK ARCHIPELAGO
SOLOMON ISLANDS
TUVALU
FUNAFUTI
Vaiaku
Tokelau (N.Z.)

Pointe-Noire
Cabinda (Ang.)
Matadi
Brazzaville
Kinshasa
Kananga
ZAIRE
RWANDA
Bujumbura
BURUNDI
TANZANIA
Kilimanjaro 5895
Dodoma
Mombasa
ZANZIBAR
Dar es Salaam
SEYCHELLES
AMIRANTE ISLANDS
Victoria
Jakarta
Bandung
Surabaya
JAVA
BALI
SUMBAWA
FLORES
TIMOR
CHRISTMAS
Port Moresby
Honiara
SOLOMON ISLANDS
NEW HEBRIDES
Port-Vila
Suva
FIJI
WALLIS and FUTUNA (Fr.)
Apia
WESTERN SAMOA
Pago Pago
American Samoa
10

Luanda
ANGOLA
Lobito
Huambo
Lubumbashi
ZAMBIA
MALAWI
Moroni
COMOROS
Mayotte (Fr.)
Antsirañana
AGALEGA ISLANDS
CHAGOS ARCHIPELAGO
British Indian Ocean Territory
CHRISTMAS ISLANDS (Australia)
COCOS ISLANDS (Australia)
Darwin
CAPE YORK PENINSULA
VANUATU
NEW CALEDONIA
Nouméa
LOYALTY ISLANDS
TONGA
Nuku'alofa
Niue (N.Z.)
Cook Islands (N.Z.)
SOUTHERN COOK ISLANDS
20
23 27'

Lubango
Ndola
Lilongwe
ZIMBABWE
Harare
MOZAMBIQUE
Lusaka
Maramba
Blantyre
Nampula
Mahajanga
Toamasina
MADAGASCAR
Antananarivo
MAURITIUS
RODRIGUES
Port Hedland
Alice Springs
Lake Eyre
Cairns
Townsville
Rockhampton
NORFOLK (Australia)
KERMADEC ISLANDS (N.Z.)

NAMIBIA
Windhoek (South Africa)
Walvis Bay (South Africa)
BOTSWANA
Gaborone
Bulawayo
Beira
Reunion (Fr.)
Port-Louis
Toliara
Tropic of Capricorn
A U S T R A L I A
Geraldton
GREAT DIVIDING RANGE
Brisbane
30

Johannesburg
Kimberley
Pretoria
Maputo
SWAZILAND
LESOTHO
Durban
SOUTH AFRICA
Bloemfontein
ÎLE AMSTERDAM (Fr.)
ÎLE SAINT PAUL (Fr.)
Perth
Port Augusta
Newcastle
Sydney
Canberra
LORD HOWE

Cape Town
Cape of Good Hope
Port Elizabeth
East London
PRINCE EDWARD ISLANDS (South Africa)
ÎLES CROZET (Fr.)
ÎLES KERGUELEN (Fr.)
Albany
Adelaide
Kosciusko 2228
Melbourne
TASMANIA
Hobart
NORTH ISLAND
Auckland
40

HEARD (Australia)
WILKES LAND
MACQUARIE (Australia)
AUCKLAND ISLANDS (N.Z.)
CAMPBELL ISLAND (N.Z.)
ANTIPODES ISLANDS (N.Z.)
BOUNTY ISLANDS (N.Z.)
SOUTH ISLAND
Dunedin
Christchurch
Wellington
NEW ZEALAND
CHATHAM ISLANDS (N.Z.)
50

Greenwich
30
60
90
120
150
East 180 West
80
70
66 33'
ADÉLIE COAST
VICTORIA LAND
SCOTT
Antarctic Circle
BALLENY ISLANDS
60
T R A N S A N T A R C T I C M O U N T A I N S

ALBANIA	ALB.
ANDORRA	A.
AUSTRIA	AUS.
BULGARIA	BULG.
CZECHOSLOVAKIA	CZECH.
FEDERAL REPUBLIC OF GERMANY	F.R.G.
GERMAN DEMOCRATIC REPUBLIC	G.D.R.
HUNGARY	HUNG.
LIECHTENSTEIN	L.
LUXEMBURG	LUX.
MONACO	M.
NETHERLANDS	NETH.
SAN MARINO	S.M.
SWITZERLAND	SWITZ.
YUGOSLAVIA	YUGO.

A-510000-280-3 -3 -2 -3 B

Map 3 **THE OCEANS**

Continental Shelf

	0-200		200-1000		1000-2000
	0-656		*656-3281*		*3281-6562*

Scale 1:70,000,000   Hammer Azimuthal Equal Area Projection with Wagner Polar Modification

0   1000   2000   3000   4000   5000 km

0   1000   2000   3000 miles

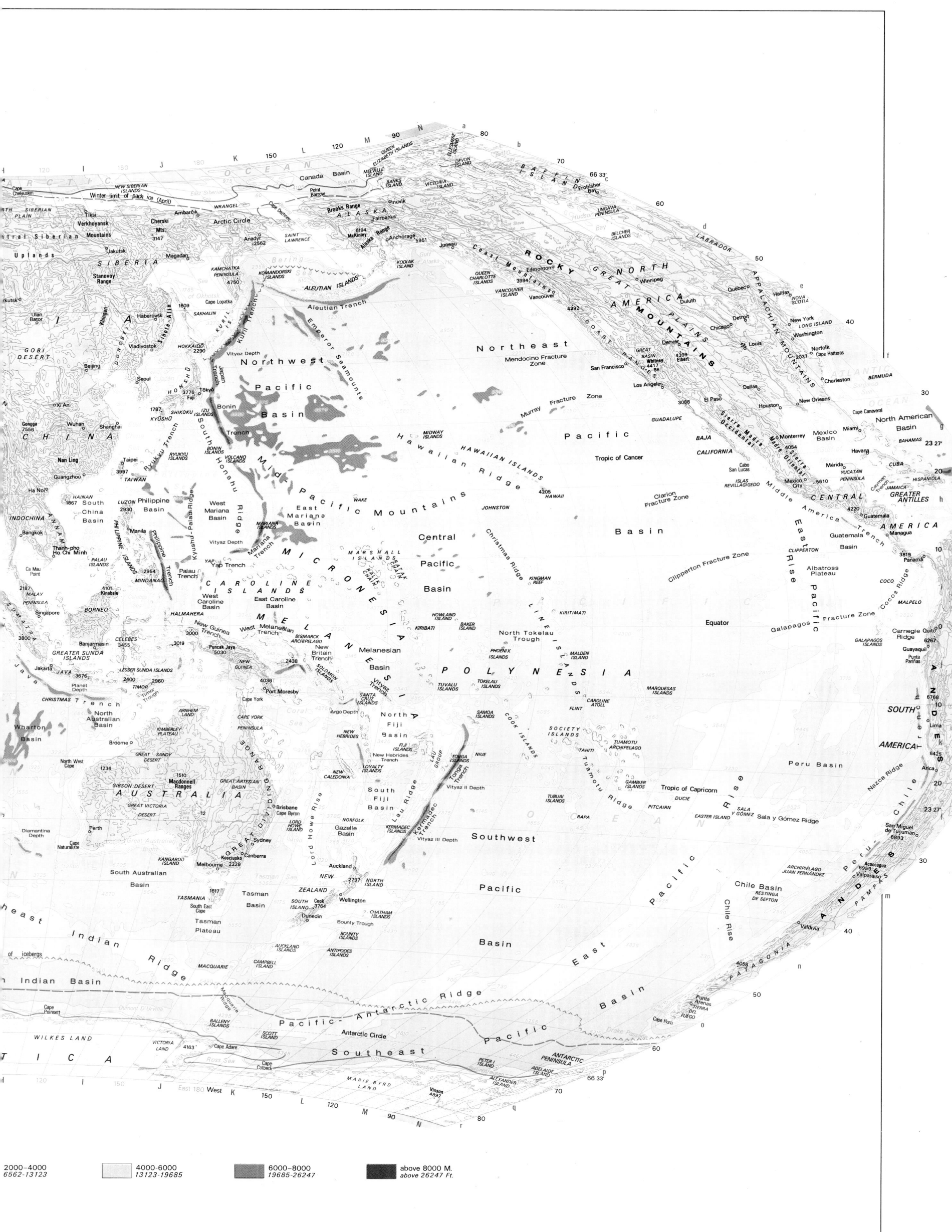

2000–4000
6562–13123

4000–6000
13123–19685

6000–8000
19685–26247

above 8000 M.
above 26247 Ft.

Map 4 **WORLD TRANSPORTATION AND TIME ZONES**

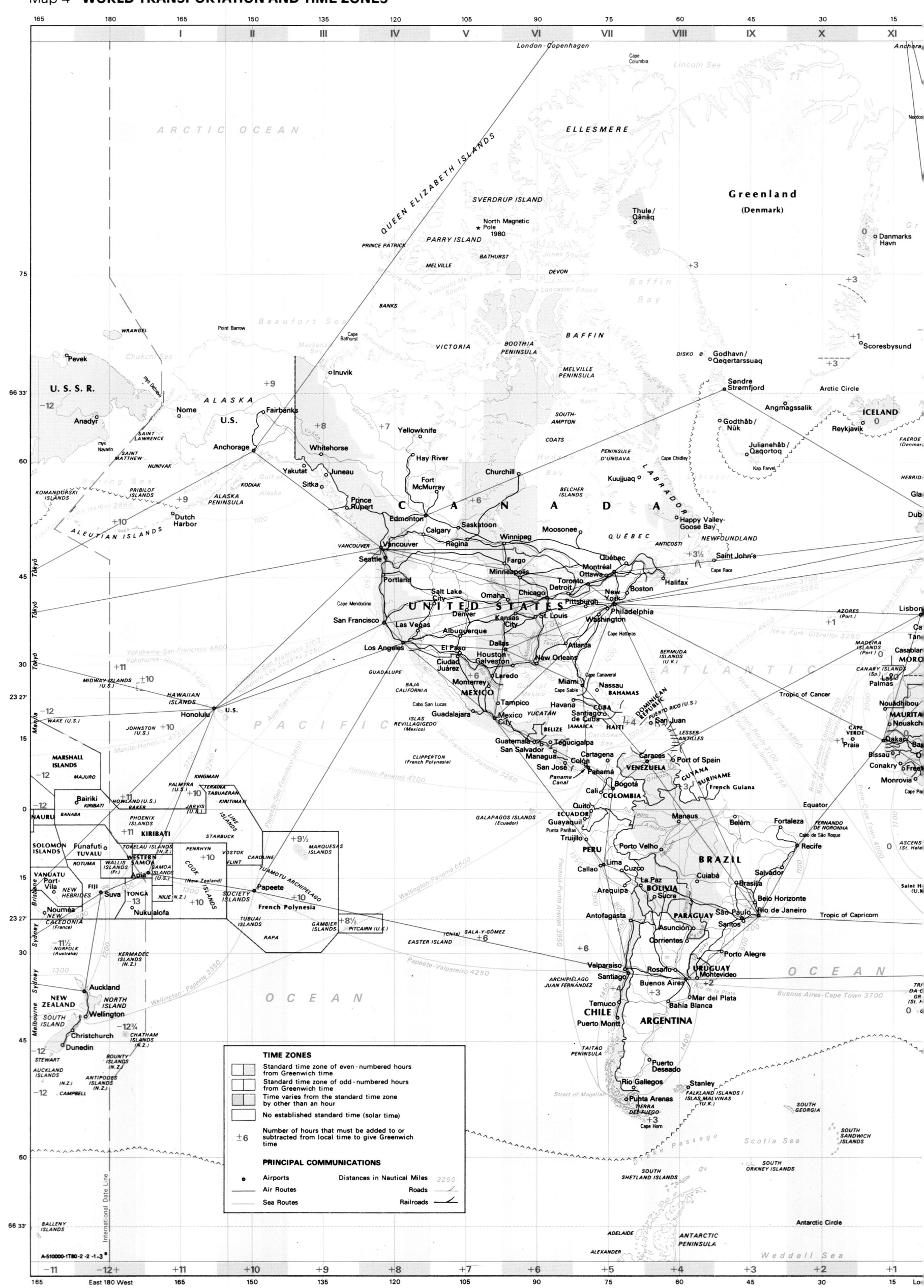

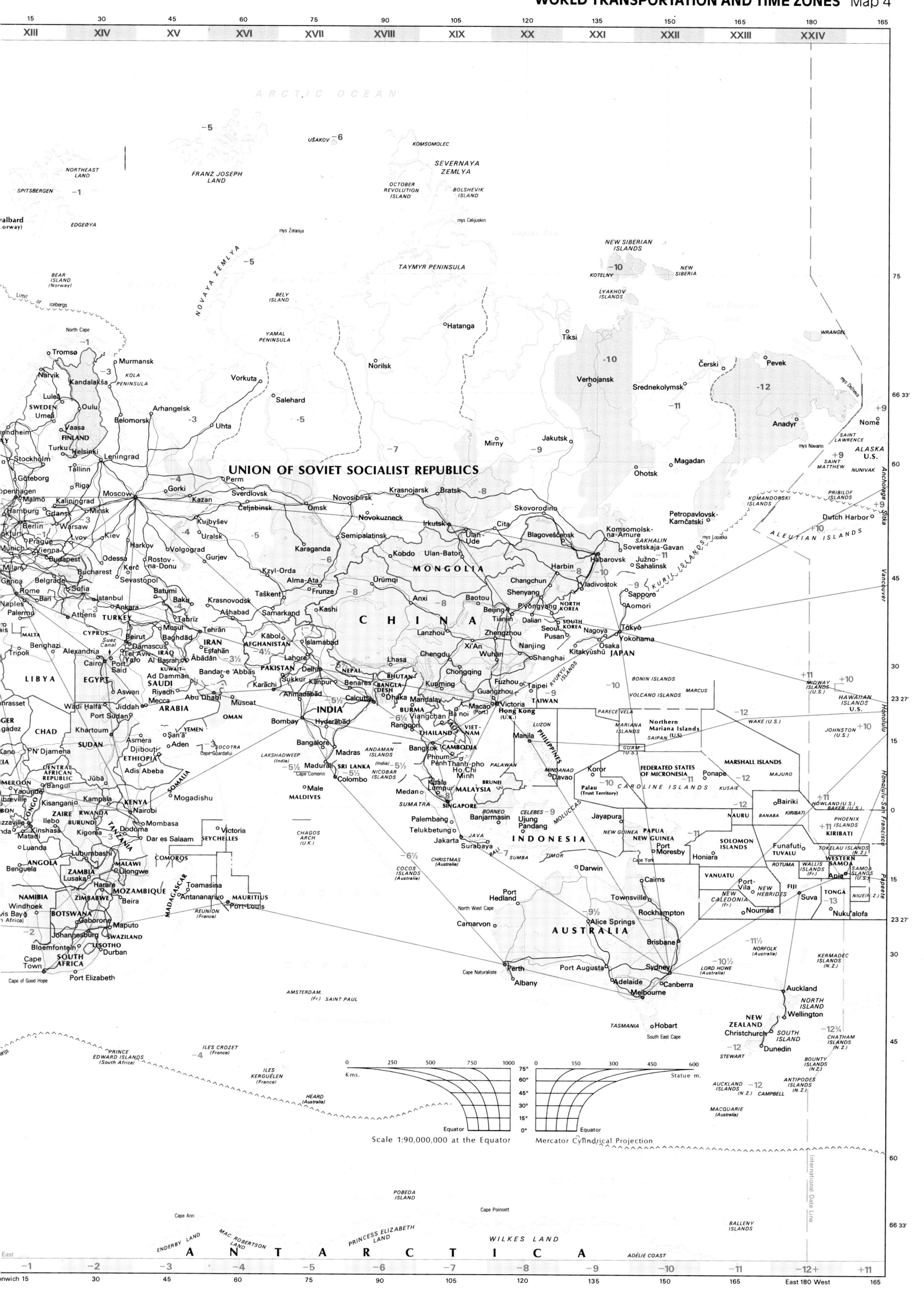

Scale 1:90,000,000 at the Equator

Mercator Cylindrical Projection

Map 5 **EUROPE, PHYSICAL**

GREENLAND

KING FREDERIK VI COAST

KING CHRISTIAN IX LAND

Denmark Strait

Limit of icebergs

Reykjanes Ridge

Iceland Basin

ICELAND

Reykjavik

VATNAJÖKULL

Arctic Circle

Faeroe-Iceland Ridge

FAEROE ISLANDS

JAN MAYEN

Mohns Ridge

Lofoten

GREENLAND SEA

NORWEGIAN SEA

Norwegian Basin

VESTERÅLEN

LOFOTEN

MID-ATLANTIC RIDGE

ATLANTIC OCEAN

West European Basin

Iberian Basin

Rockall Rise

Porcupine Bank

Faraday Seamounts

ROCKALL

HEBRIDES

SHETLAND ISLANDS

ORKNEY ISLANDS

Cape Wrath

Duncansby Head

LEWIS

SKYE

MULL

ISLAY

North-West Highlands

GRAMPIAN MTS

Aberdeen

Glasgow

Edinburgh

Southern Uplands

GREAT BRITAIN

NORTH SEA

Norwegian Trench

Trondheim

Ålesund

Dovrefjell

Jotunheimen

Bergen

Kristiansand

SVEALAND

GÖTALAND

Göteborg

SKAGERRAK

Ålborg

JYLLAND

København Copenhagen

Malmö

SKÅNE

BORNHOLM

FYN LAND

SJÆLLAND

LOLLAND

RÜGEN

POMERANIA

IRELAND

Belfast

Dublin

Cork

ANGLESEY

Liverpool

Kingston-upon-Hull

PENNINES

ENGLAND

MAN

CAMBRIAN

WALES

Birmingham

Bristol

London

Dover

CELTIC SEA

ST. GEORGE'S CHANNEL

Land's End

ISLES OF SCILLY

CORNWALL

Lizard Point

WIGHT

ENGLISH CHANNEL

CHANNEL ISLANDS

NORMANDY

Le Havre

Brest

Pointe de Saint-Mathieu

BRITTANY

Normandy Hills

Nantes

BELLE ILE

ÎLE DE RÉ

ÎLE D'OLÉRON

Bay of Biscay

Bordeaux

AQUITAINE BASIN

Toulouse

PARIS BASIN

Paris

Orléans

CHAMPAGNE

ARDENNES

Brussel Bruxelles

Amsterdam

Rotterdam

HOLLAND

FRIESLAND

FRISIAN ISLANDS

Hamburg

Kiel

NORTH GERMAN PLAIN

Berlin

Poznań

Leipzig

HARZ

Frankfurt

Bonn

Düsseldorf

Luxembourg

FRENCH SLATE MOUNTAINS

VOSGES

JURA

BLACK FOREST

SWABIAN JURA

BAVARIAN PLATEAU

BAVARIA

München Munich

SILESIA

Wrocław Breslau

BOHEMIA

Praha Prague

MORAVIA

Wien Vienna

Graz

ALPS

MASSIF CENTRAL

Monts Dore

Lyon

CÉVENNES

LANGUEDOC

PROVENCE

Marseille

RHÔNE VALLEY

Mont Blanc

Torino Turin

Milano Milan

PO VALLEY

Genova Genoa

Venezia Venice

LIGURIAN SEA

SLOVENIA

Zagreb

ISTRIA

DALMATIA

CORSICA

Ajaccio

CAP CORSE

ELBA

TUSCAN ARCHIPELAGO

Firenze Florence

Ancona

Bologna

APENNINES

GRAN SASSO D'ITALIA

ADRIATIC SEA

Cabo de Creus

Barcelona

CATALONIA

Valencia

Murcia

BALEARIC ISLANDS

IBIZA

MAJORCA

MINORCA

FORMENTERA

Cabo de la Nao

Cabo de Palos

GALICIA

La Coruña

Punta de la Estaca de Bares

Cabo de Peñas

Cabo de Finisterre

Picos de Europa

Bilbao

CANTABRIAN MTS

SUBMESETA NORTE

IBERIAN MOUNTAINS

ARAGON

PYRENEES

ANDORRA

SISTEMA CENTRAL

Madrid

SUBMESETA SUR

Serranía de Cuenca

SIERRA MORENA

LA MANCHA

BÉTICOS

SISTEMAS

SIERRA NEVADA

Mulhacén

ANDALUSIA

Sevilla Seville

ALGARVE

Cabo de São Vicente

Cádiz

Málaga

Cabo de Gata

Gibraltar

IBERIAN PENINSULA

Lisboa Lisbon

Cabo da Roca

Serra da Estrela

Portão

AZORES

GRACIOSA

SÃO JORGE

PICO

TERCEIRA

SÃO MIGUEL

Ponta Delgada

SANTA MARIA

Azores-Gibraltar Ridge

Josephine Seamount

Ampère Seamount

Seine Seamount

MADEIRA ISLANDS

PORTO SANTO

Funchal

ILHAS DESERTAS

ILHAS SELVAGENS

CANARY ISLANDS

LA PALMA

HIERRO

GOMERA

TENERIFE

Santa Cruz

GRAN CANARIA

Las Palmas

FUERTEVENTURA

LANZAROTE

Dacia Seamount

Casablanca

Rabat

Ras Beddouza

Safi

Meknès

Fès

Tangier

ISLA DE ALBORÁN

Oran

Cap des Trois Fourches

Cap Spartel

Oujda

RIF

MIDDLE ATLAS

HIGH ATLAS

Jbel Toubkal

Marrakech

Agadir

Cap Rhir

ANTI ATLAS

ATLAS MOUNTAINS

JBEL BANI

JBEL OUARKZIZ

HAMADA DU DRAA

Tindouf

El Aaiún

SAHARAN ATLAS

TELL ATLAS

Algiers

Al Jazā'ir

Constantine

MONTS DE LA MEDJERDA

Tunis

HAUTS PLATEAUX

MASSIF DE L'AURÈS

Cap Bon

HAMADA DU GUIR

ERG GRAND OCCIDENTAL

El Goléa

ERG GRAND ORIENTAL

Touggourt

SOUF

PELAGIE ISLANDS

SICILY

Etna

Palermo

Messina

Cape Spartivento

LIPARI ISLANDS

USTICA

EGADI ISLANDS

PANTELLERIA

MALTA

GOZO

Cape Corrente

KERKENNAH ISLANDS

DJERBA

GEFARA

Tarābulus Tripoli

JABAL NAFUSAH

TRIPOLITANIA

AL HAMĀDAH AL HAMRĀ

MEDITERRANEAN SEA

TYRRHENIAN SEA

Tyrrhenian Basin

SARDINIA

Cagliari

Gennargentu

ARCIPELAGO CAMPANO

Napoli Naples

Vesuvio

Roma Rome

Bari

Taranto

Napoli

SANT'ANTIOCO

ASINARA

ALGERIAN BASIN

Gulf of Lions

Golfe du Lion

Scale 1:15,000,000   Lambert Azimuthal Equal Area Projection

0   200   400   600   800   1000 km

0   250   500 miles

Longitude East 10 of Greenwich

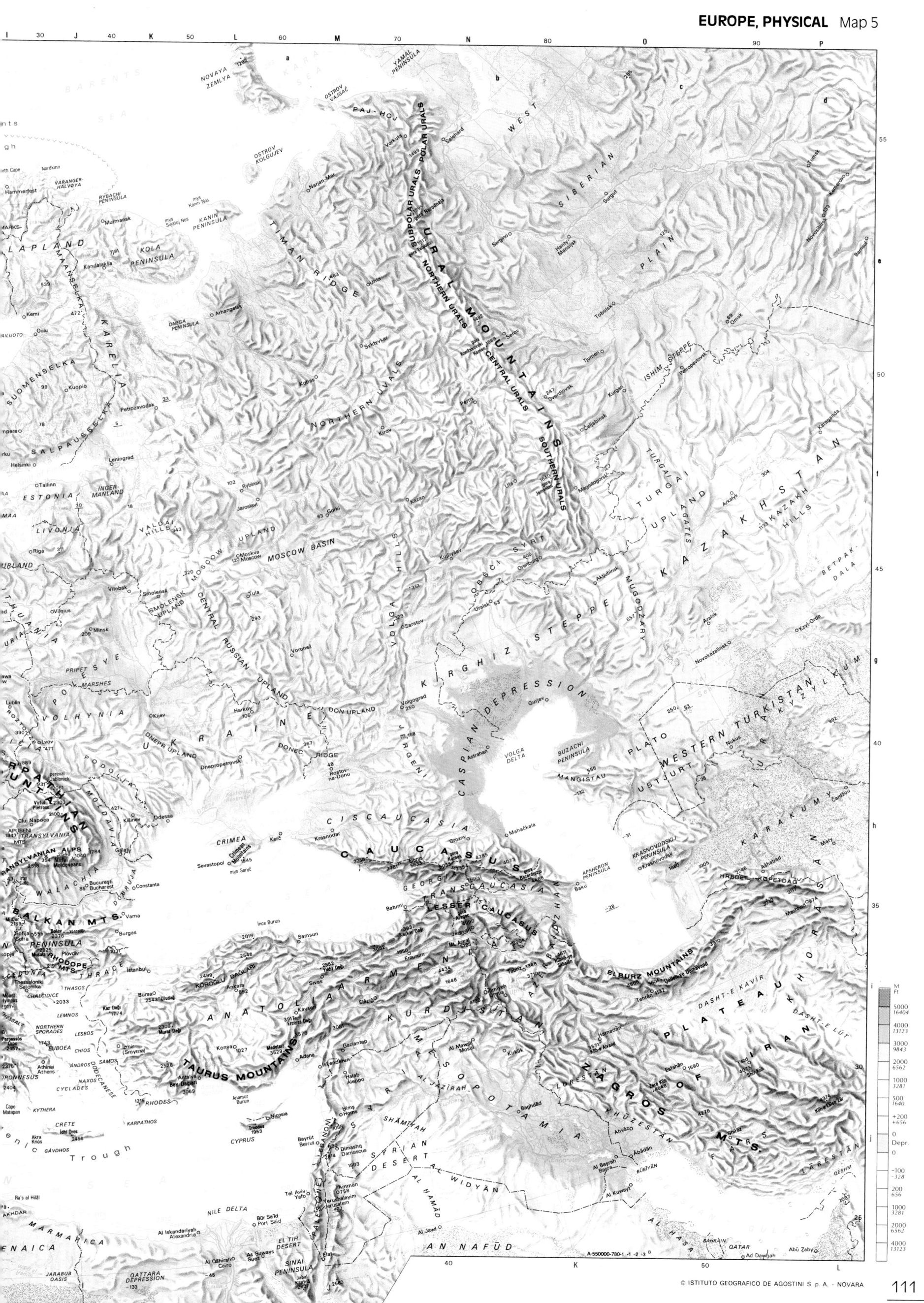

Map 6 **EUROPE, POLITICAL**

A 50 B 40 C 30 D 20 E 10 F 0 G 10

KING FREDERIK VI COAST
Angmagssalik
KING CHRISTIAN IX LAND
a
Nanortalik
Julianehåb
Narssaq
Frederiksdal
Skjoldungen
3700
Scoresbysund
Greenland Sea
Qaqortoq
Kap Farvel
Ivigtut
d
G r e e n l a n d
(Den.)

Denmark Strait

55

JAN MAYEN
(Norway)

VESTERÅLEN
LOFOTEN

Ísafjördur
Horn
Akureyri
Reykjavík
ICELAND
VATNAJÖKULL
2119
Hvannadalshnúkur
Seydisfjördur

Arctic Circle

e

Bodø
Mo i Rana

N o r w e g i a n   S e a

Thorshavn
Faeroe Islands
(Den.)
FØROYAR
FÆRØERNE

NORWAY
Kristiansund
Namsos
Molde
Trondheim
Ålesund
Dombås
Glittertinden 2472
Bergen
Gjøvik
Hamar
Haugesund
Stavanger
Skien
Drammen
Oslo
Moss
Kristiansand
Lindesnes

SWEDEN
Falun
Västerås
Karlstad
Örebro

50

SHETLAND ISLANDS

ROCKALL

Thurso
ORKNEY ISLANDS
Inverness
Aberdeen
HEBRIDES

N o r t h   S e a

Skagerrak
Göteborg
Jönköping

f

Londonderry
Glasgow
Dundee
Edinburgh
Newcastle upon Tyne
Carlisle
Sligo
Belfast
IRELAND
Galway
Middlesbrough
Manchester
Leeds
Kingston-upon-Hull
Liverpool
Sheffield
UNITED KINGDOM
Limerick
Dublin
Leicester
Nottingham
Waterford
Birmingham
Norwich
Cork
Wexford
Fishguard
Swansea
Oxford
Ipswich
Cardiff
Bristol
London
Southampton
Exeter
Brighton
Dover
Plymouth
Penzance
Land's End
ISLES OF SCILLY
English Channel
Calais

45

DENMARK
Herning
Ålborg
Frederikshavn
Växjö
Kalmar
Esbjerg
Århus
København
Copenhagen
Malmö
Helsingborg
Karlskrona
Kolding
Odense
BORNHOLM
(Den.)
Flensburg
Trelleborg
Kiel
Lübeck
Rostock
Stralsund
RÜGEN
Bremerhaven
Groningen
Hamburg
Szczecin
Stettin
Gdynia
Amsterdam
Bremen
GERMAN
Hannover
Berlin
Magdeburg
Poznań
s-Gravenhage
Den Haag
NETHERLANDS
Osnabrück
FED. REP.
Essen
Dortmund
Leipzig
DEM. REP.
Rotterdam
Antwerpen
Brussel
BELGIUM
Düsseldorf
Köln Cologne
OF
Dresden
Wrocław
Breslau
Bruxelles
Liège
Bonn
Erfurt
Cherbourg
Le Havre
Amiens
Lille
Luxembourg
Frankfurt
Karl-Marx-Stadt
Praha
Prague
Ostrava
Pointe de Saint-Mathieu
Brest
Caen
Rouen
Reims
LUXEMBOURG
Wiesbaden
Mainz
Würzburg
Nürnberg
Plzeň
Brno
CZECHOSLO
40
CHANNEL ISLANDS (U.K.)
Saint-Malo
Metz
Mannheim
GERMANY
Regensburg
Paris
Nancy
Saarbrücken
Rennes
Le Mans
Troyes
Strasbourg
Stuttgart
München
Munich
Wien
Vienna
Angers
Orléans
Augsburg
Linz
Nantes
Tours
Dijon
Mulhouse
Freiburg
Basel
Salzburg
Poitiers
Bourges
Besançon
Bern
Zürich
LIECHTENSTEIN
Innsbruck
Graz
La Rochelle
Limoges
Clermont-Ferrand
Lyon
Lausanne
Genève Geneva
SWITZERLAND
Mont Blanc 4807
AUSTRIA
Klagenfurt
Székesfehérv
Győr
Bordeaux
Saint-Étienne
Grenoble
Bolzano
Ljubljana
Zagreb
Bayonne
Toulouse
Nîmes
Milano
Milan
Brescia
Trieste
Rijeka
Gijón
Oviedo
Santander
San Sebastián
PYRENEES
Montpellier
Avignon
Nice
Verona
Venezia
Venice
La Coruña
Cabo de Finisterre
León
Pamplona
Pic d'Aneto 3404
ANDORRA
Andorra la Vella
Marseille
MONACO
Torino
Turin
Genova
Genoa
Parma
Bologna
Zadar
YUG
Vigo
Braga
Valladolid
Burgos
Zaragoza
Saragossa
Perpignan
Toulon
La Spezia
Livorno
Leghorn
SAN MARINO
Ancona
Split
Porto
Coimbra
Salamanca
Cabo de Creus
CORSICA (Fr.)
Bastia
Firenze
Florence
Perugia
PORTUGAL
Lisboa
Lisbon
SPAIN
Madrid
Barcelona
Ajaccio
VATICAN CITY
Roma
Rome
L'Aquila
Pescara
Dubrovnik
Setúbal
Toledo
Castellón de la Plana
Tarragona
Évora
Badajoz
ITALY
Foggia
Cabo de São Vicente
Albacete
Júcar
Valencia
Sassari
Olbia
Napoli
Naples
Bari
Brindisi
Faro
Huelva
Córdoba
BALEARIC ISLANDS
MINORCA
SARDINIA
Nuoro
Salerno
Taranto
Murcia
Palma
Tyrrhenian
Sevilla
Granada
Alicante
IBIZA
MAJORCA
Cosenza
Catanzaro
Cádiz
Almería
Cartagena
Cagliari
Algeciras
Málaga
ISLA DE ALBORAN (Sp.)
Sea
Palermo
Messina
Tanger
Gibraltar (U.K.)
Ceuta (Spain)
Mostaganem
Al Jazā'ir
Algiers
Oran
Reggio di Calabria
Larache
Tétouan
Melilla (Spain)
SICILY
Trapani
Mt. Etna 3323
Kenitra
Rabat
Ksar el Kebir
Sidi Bel Abbès
Saïda
Sétif
Blida
Tizi Ouzou
Bejaïa
Jijel
Skikda
Annaba
Túnis
Catania
Siracusa
Syracuse
Casablanca
Taza
Oujda
Bizerte
Cap Bon
Agrigento
El Jadida
Meknès
Fès
Cheliff
Relizane
Tiaret
Guelma
Constantine
Súsah
Sousse
PANTELLERIA (Italy)
Safi
Oued Zem
Beni Mellal
Batna
MOROCCO
ATLAS MOUNTAINS
Biskra
Tébessa
Al Qayrawān
Valletta
MALTA
Essaouira
Laghouat
Safāqis
Sfax
KERKENNAH ISLANDS
Agadir
Marrakech
4165
Jebel Toubkal
Ar Rachidiya
Figuig
Aïn Sefra
Al Aghwāt
Qafsah
Gábis
DJERBA
Sidi Ifni
Tiznit
ALGERIA
Madaniyīn
Goulimine
Zagora
Béchar
Ghardaïa
Touggourt
TUNISIA
Tarābulus
Tripoli
Cap Juby
Tarfaya
El Goléa
Ouargla
Al Khums
Abadla
Hassi Messaoud
Adh Dhahībāt
Az Zāwiyah
Nālūt
Gharyān
Ra's Misrātah
Misrātah
Western Sahara
GRAND ERG OCCIDENTAL
Beni Abbès
Timimoun
Mizdah
Banī Walīd
Qaryat al Qaddāhīyah
El Aaiún
GRAND ERG ORIENTAL
Ghadāmis
Surt
TRIPOLITANIA
LIB
Tindouf
Tabelbala
Gulf of Gabes
Gulf of

25

Semara
Dakhla

AZORES
GRACIOSA
SÃO JORGE
TERCEIRA
Angra do Heroísmo
PICO
FAIAL
Azores
(Portugal)
SÃO MIGUEL
Ponta Delgada
SANTA MARIA
h

MADEIRA ISLANDS
Funchal
PORTO SANTO
ILHAS DESERTAS
Madeira
(Portugal)

ILHAS SELVAGENS

LA PALMA
Canary Islands
(Spain)
GOMERA
TENERIFE
Santa Cruz de Tenerife
HIERRO
GRAN CANARIA
Las Palmas de Gran Canaria
LANZAROTE
FUERTEVENTURA

ATLANTIC OCEAN

Celtic Sea

Bay of Biscay

MEDITERRANEAN

Scale 1:15,000,000   Lambert Azimuthal Equal Area Projection
0   200   400   600   800   1000 km
0   250   500 miles

Longitude East 10 of Greenwich

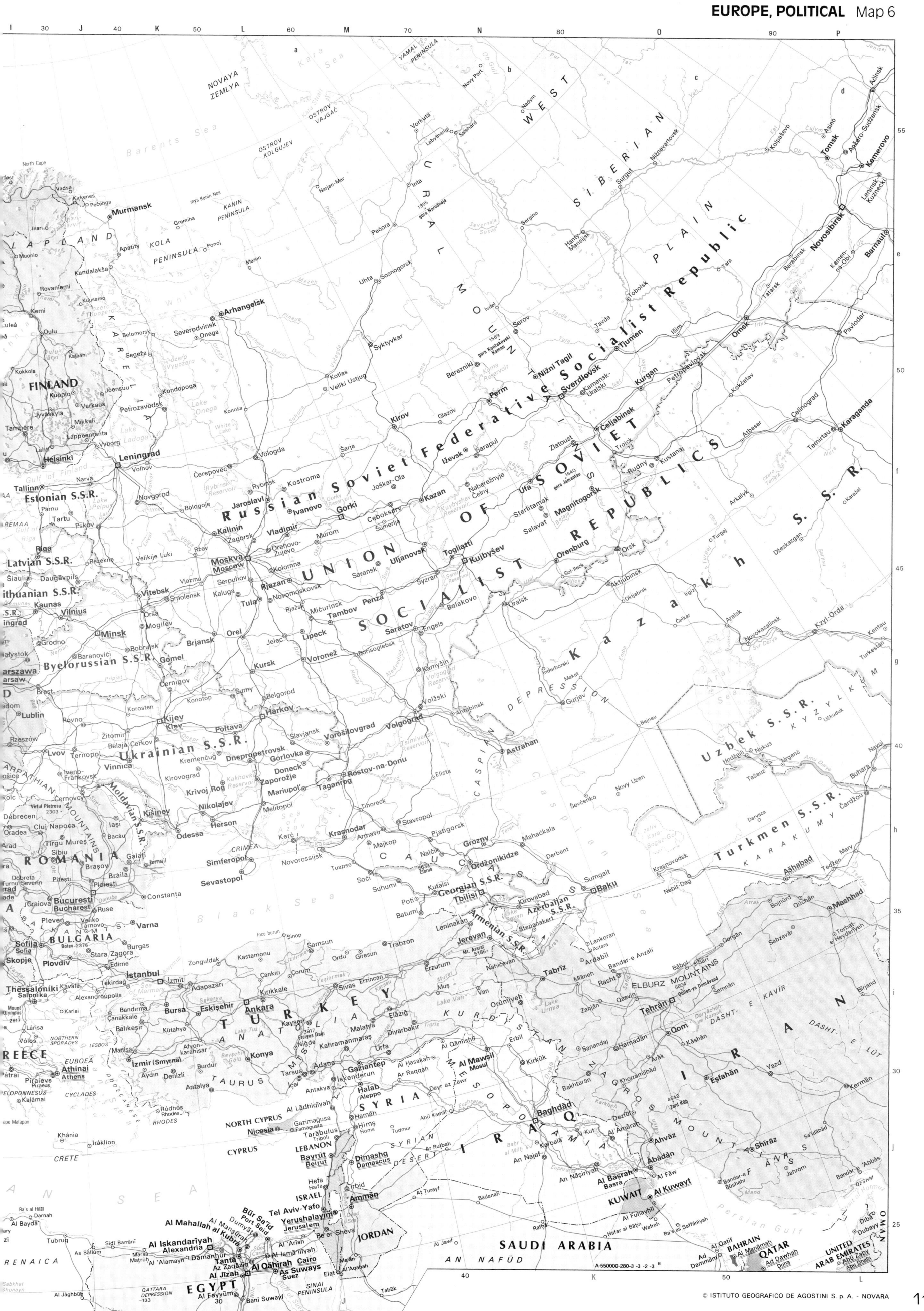

Map 7 **NORTHERN EUROPE**

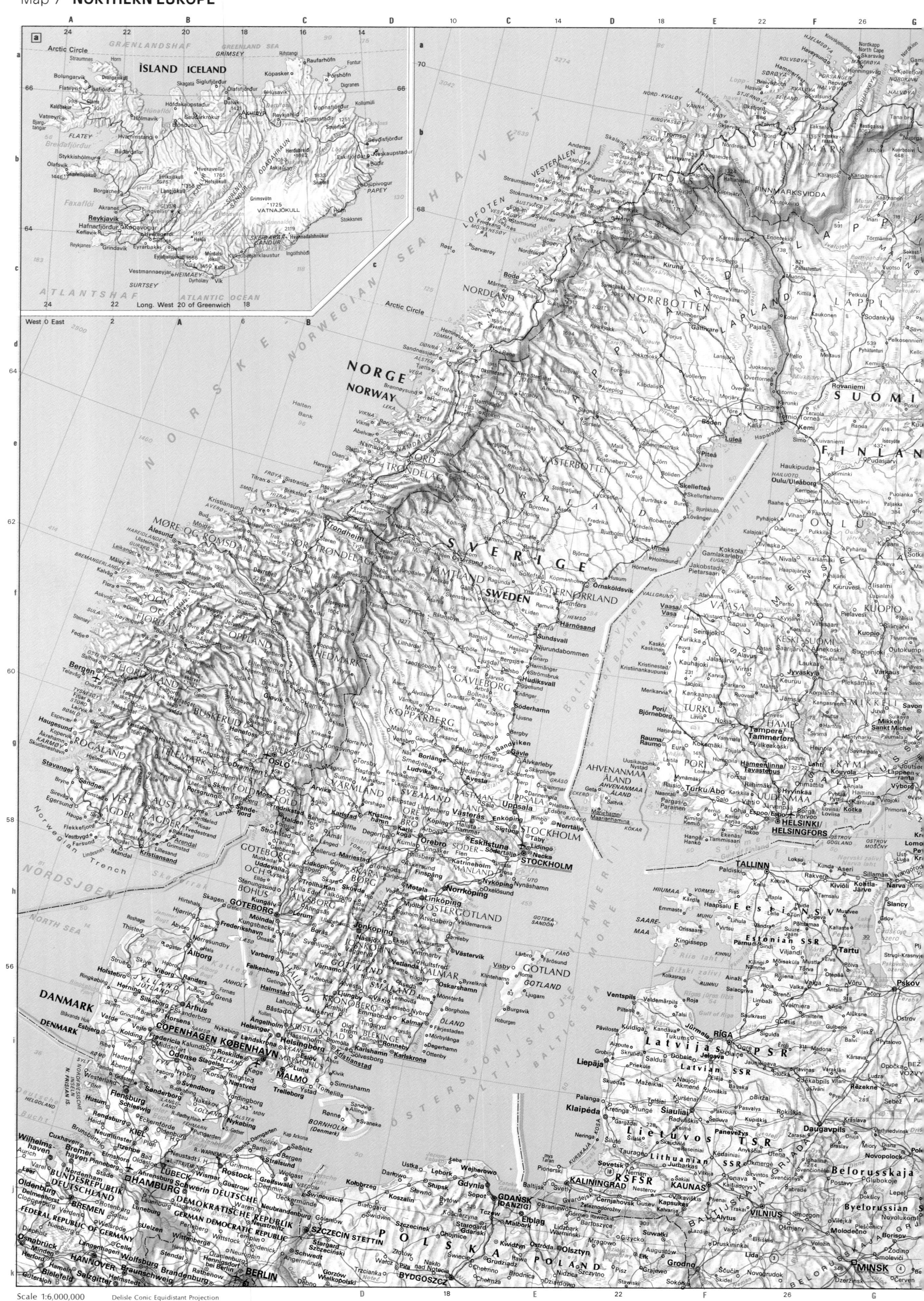

Scale 1:6,000,000   Delisle Conic Equidistant Projection

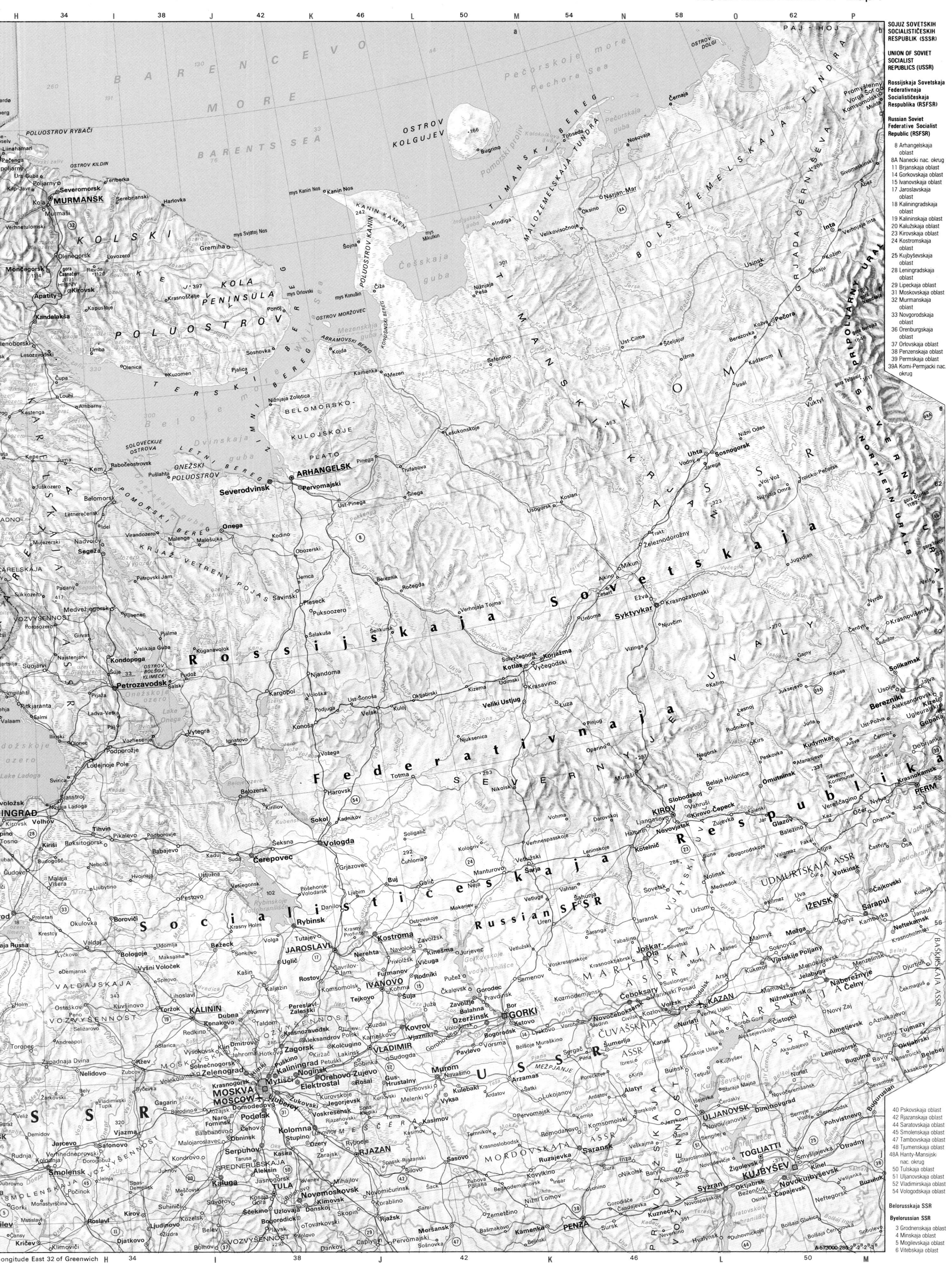

SOJUZ SOVETSKIH
SOCIALISTIČESKIH
RESPUBLIK (SSSR)

**UNION OF SOVIET
SOCIALIST
REPUBLICS (USSR)**

Rossijskaja Sovetskaja
Federativnaja
Socialističeskaja
Respublika (RSFSR)

**Russian Soviet
Federative Socialist
Republic (RSFSR)**

8 Arhangelskaja
   oblast
8A Nanecki nac. okrug
11 Brjanskaja oblast
14 Gorkovskaja oblast
15 Ivanovskaja oblast
17 Jaroslavskaja
   oblast
18 Kaliningradskaja
   oblast
19 Kalininskaja oblast
20 Kalužskaja oblast
23 Kirovskaja oblast
24 Kostromskaja
   oblast
25 Kujbyševskaja
   oblast
28 Leningradskaja
   oblast
29 Lipeckaja oblast
31 Moskovskaja oblast
32 Murmanskaja
   oblast
33 Novgorodskaja
   oblast
36 Orenburgskaja
   oblast
37 Orlovskaja oblast
38 Penzenskaja oblast
39 Permskaja oblast
39A Komi-Permjacki nac.
   okrug

40 Pskovskaja oblast
42 Rjazanskaja oblast
44 Saratovskaja oblast
45 Smolenskaja oblast
47 Tambovskaja oblast
48 Tjumenskaja oblast
48A Hanty-Mansijskij
   nac. okrug
50 Tulskaja oblast
51 Uljanovskaja oblast
52 Vladimirskaja oblast
54 Vologodskaja oblast

Belorusskaja SSR

Byelorussian SSR

3 Grodnenskaja oblast
4 Minskaja oblast
5 Mogilevskaja oblast
6 Vitebskaja oblast

Map 8 **BALTIC REGION**

Scale 1:3,000,000   Delisle Conic Equidistant Projection

0   50   100   150   200 km

0   50   100 miles

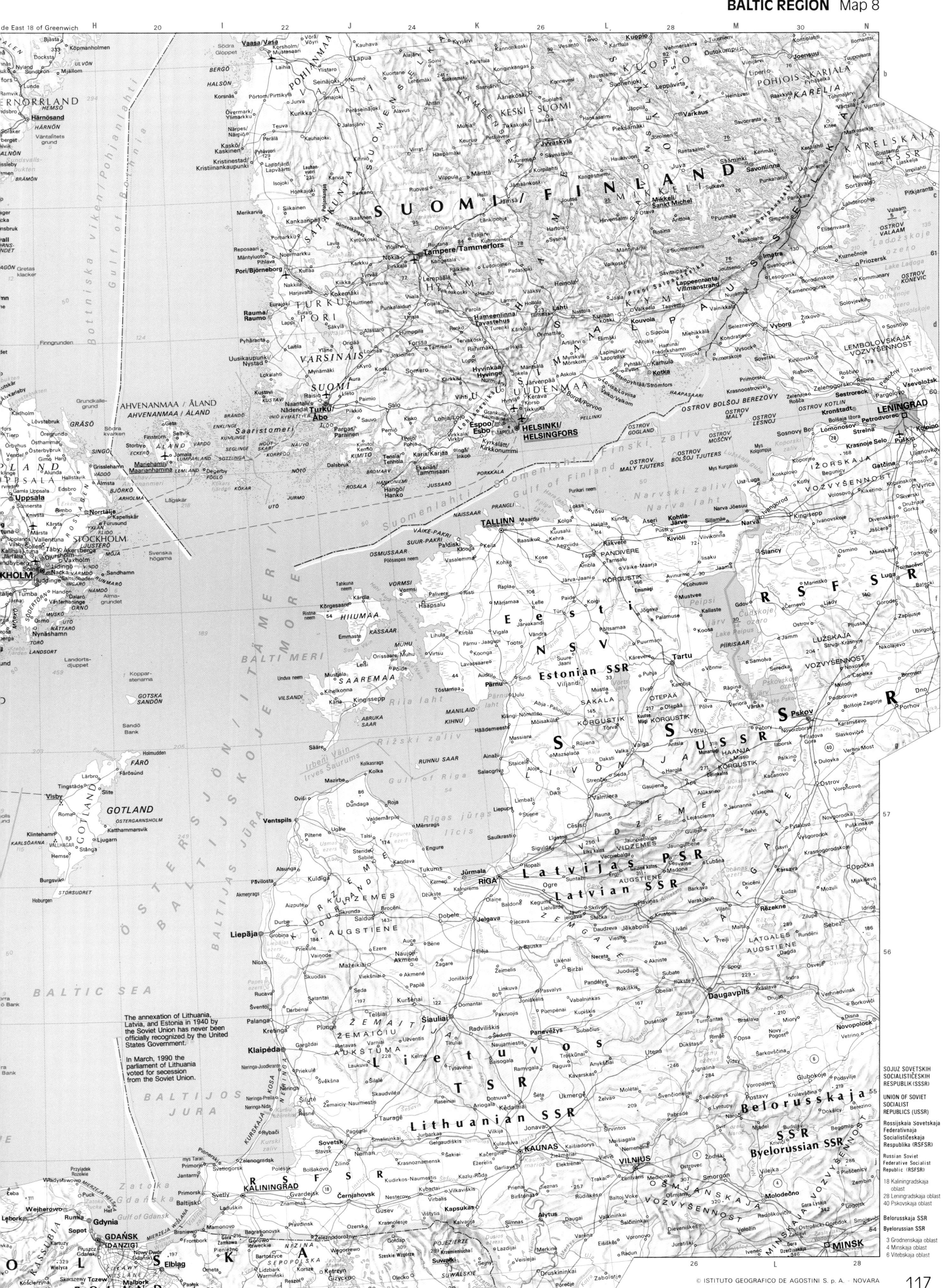

The annexation of Lithuania, Latvia, and Estonia in 1940 by the Soviet Union has never been officially recognized by the United States Government.

In March, 1990 the parliament of Lithuania voted for secession from the Soviet Union.

SOJUZ SOVETSKISH
SOCIALISTIČESKIH
RESPUBLIK (SSSR)

UNION OF SOVIET
SOCIALIST
REPUBLICS (USSR)

Rossijskaja Sovetskaja
Federativnaja
Socialističeskaja
Respublika (RSFSR)

Russian Soviet
Federative Socialist
Republic (RSFSR)

18 Kaliningradskaja
oblast

28 Leningradskaja oblast

40 Pskovskaja oblast

Belorusskaja SSR

Byelorussian SSR

3 Grodnenskaja oblast
4 Minskaja oblast
6 Vitebskaja oblast

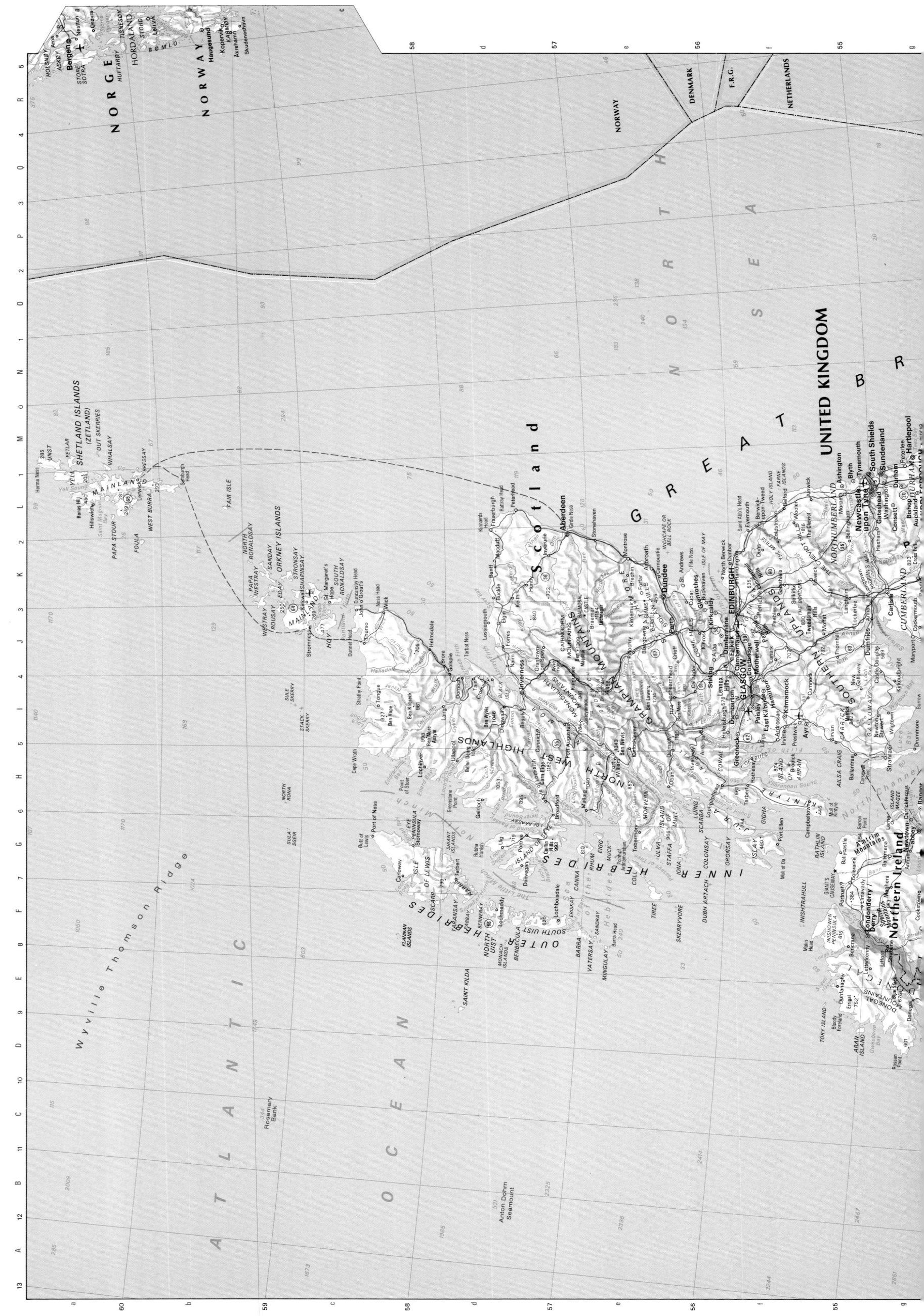

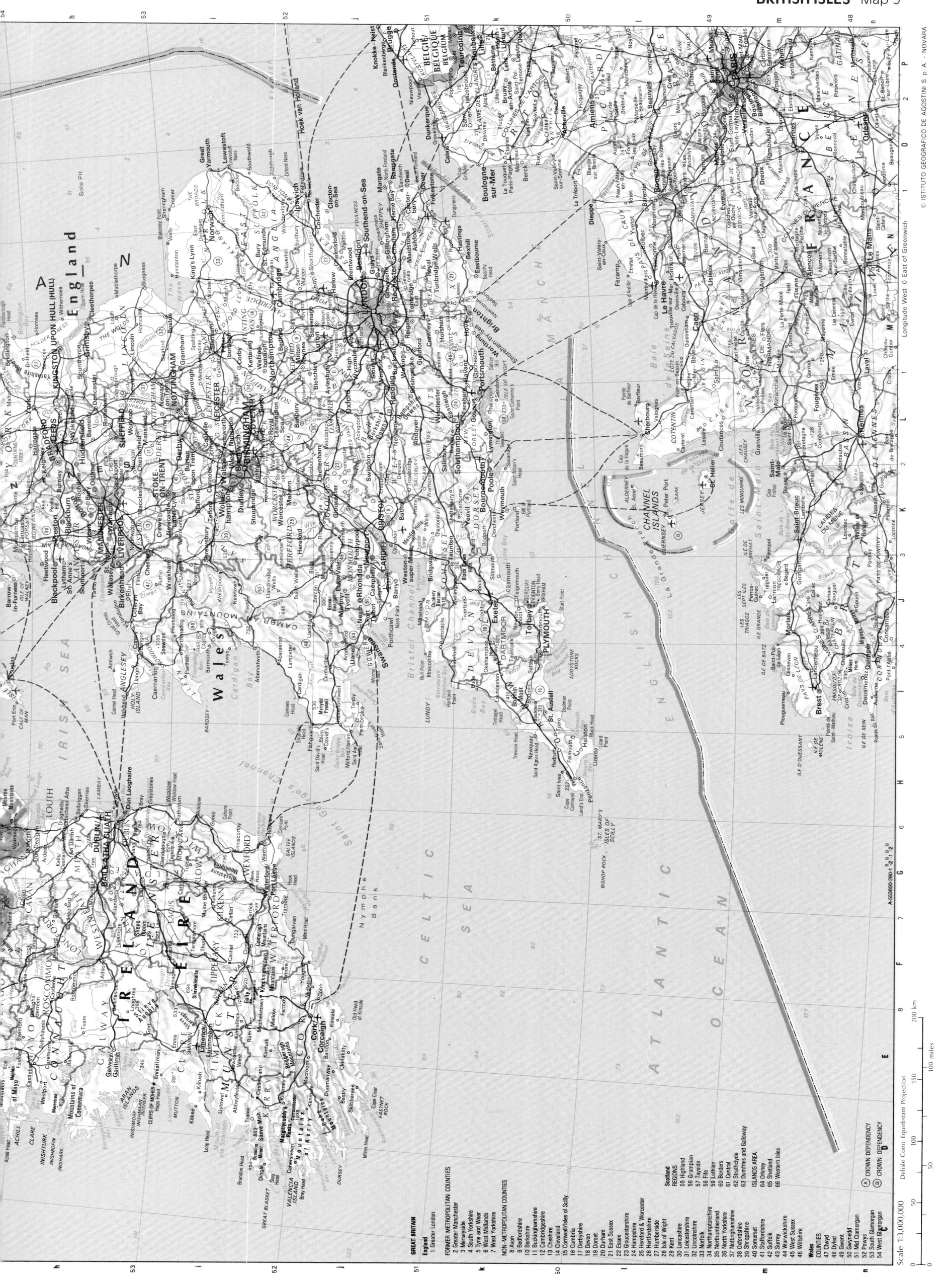

GREAT BRITAIN

England

FORMER METROPOLITAN COUNTIES
1 Greater London
2 Greater Manchester
3 Merseyside
4 South Yorkshire
5 Tyne and Wear
6 West Midlands
7 West Yorkshire

NON-METROPOLITAN COUNTIES
8 Avon
9 Bedfordshire
10 Berkshire
11 Buckinghamshire
12 Cambridgeshire
13 Cheshire
14 Cleveland
15 Cornwall
16 Cumbria
17 Derbyshire
18 Devon
19 Dorset
20 Durham
21 East Sussex
22 Essex
23 Gloucestershire
24 Hampshire
25 Hereford & Worcester
26 Hertfordshire
27 Humberside
28 Isle of Wight
29 Kent
30 Lancashire
31 Leicestershire
32 Lincolnshire
33 Norfolk
34 Northamptonshire
35 Northumberland
36 North Yorkshire
37 Nottinghamshire
38 Oxfordshire
39 Shropshire
40 Somerset
41 Staffordshire
42 Suffolk
43 Surrey
44 Warwickshire
45 West Sussex
46 Wiltshire

Wales

COUNTIES
47 Clwyd
48 Dyfed
49 Gwent
50 Gwynedd
51 Mid Glamorgan
52 Powys
53 South Glamorgan
54 West Glamorgan

Scotland

REGIONS
55 Highland
56 Grampian
57 Tayside
58 Fife
59 Lothian
60 Borders
61 Central
62 Strathclyde
63 Dumfries and Galloway

ISLANDS AREA
64 Orkney
65 Shetland
66 Western Isles

Ⓐ CROWN DEPENDENCY
Ⓑ CROWN DEPENDENCY

Scale 1:3,000,000

Delisle Conic Equidistant Projection

Longitude West 0 East of Greenwich

119

Map 10 **CENTRAL EUROPE**

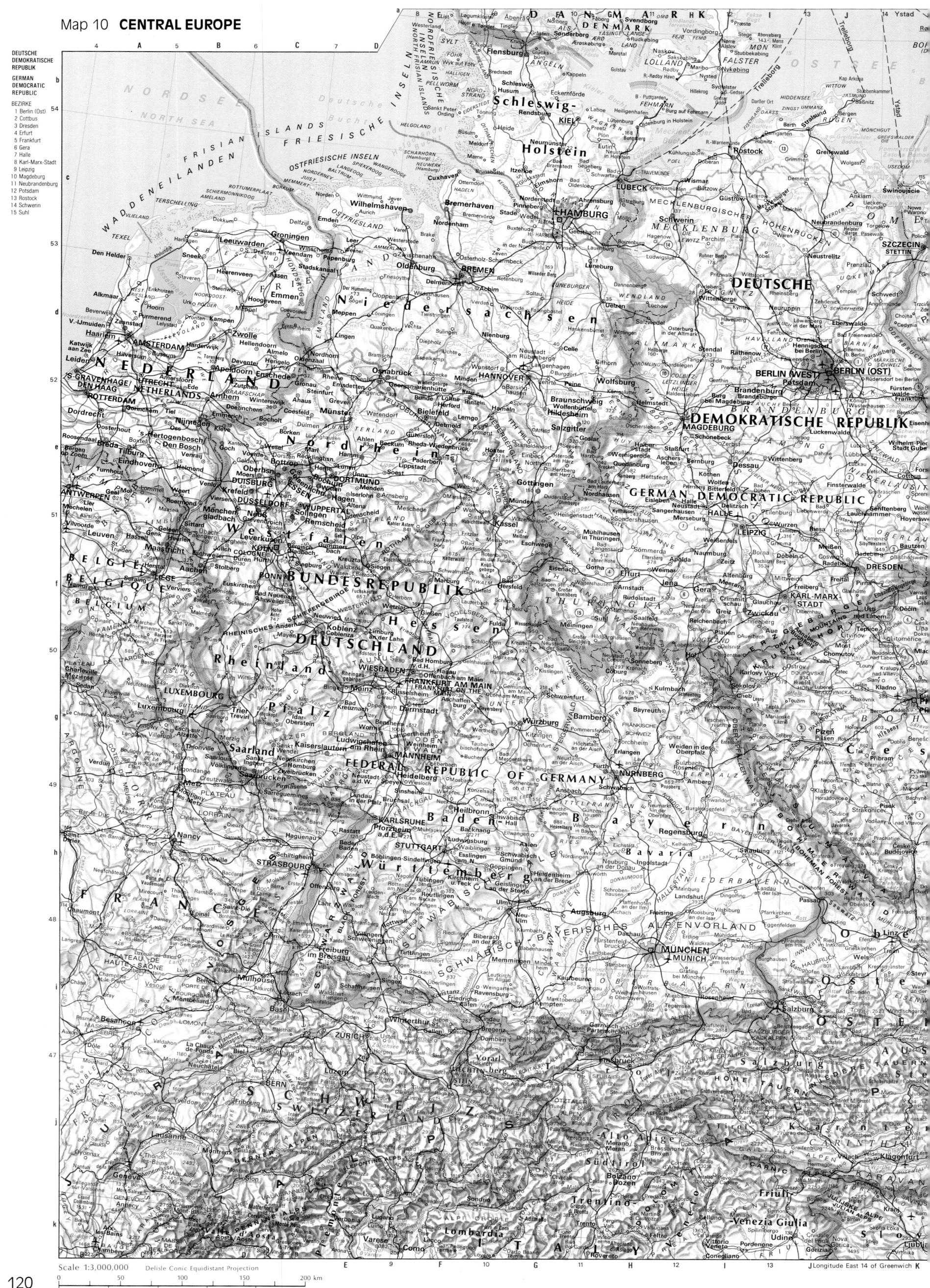

Scale 1:3,000,000   Delisle Conic Equidistant Projection

DEUTSCHE
DEMOKRATISCHE
REPUBLIK

GERMAN
DEMOCRATIC
REPUBLIK

BEZIRKE

1 Berlin (Ost)
2 Cottbus
3 Dresden
4 Erfurt
5 Frankfurt
6 Gera
7 Halle
8 Karl-Marx-Stadt
9 Leipzig
10 Magdeburg
11 Neubrandenburg
12 Potsdam
13 Rostock
14 Schwerin
15 Suhl

Map 11 FRANCE AND BENELUX

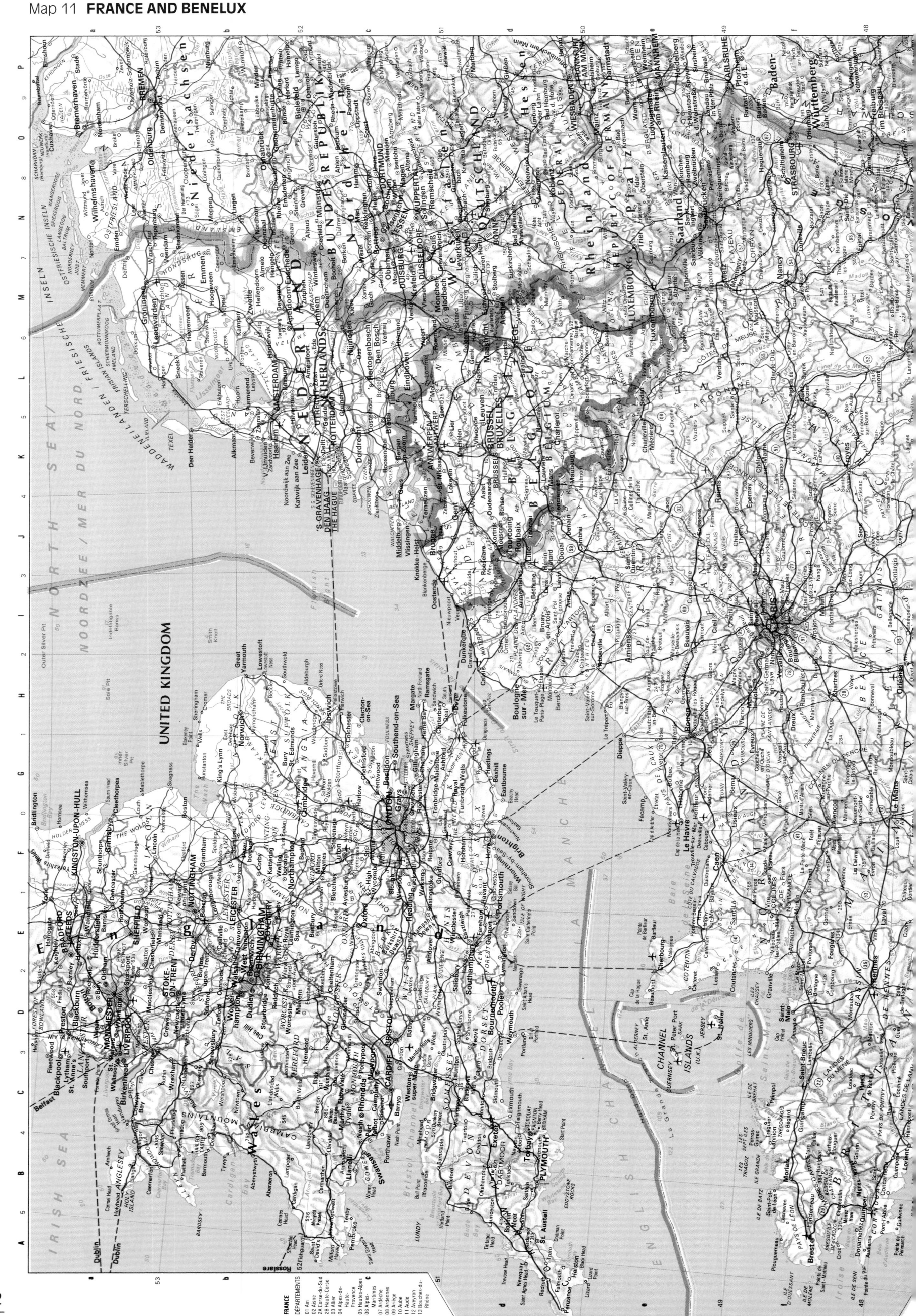

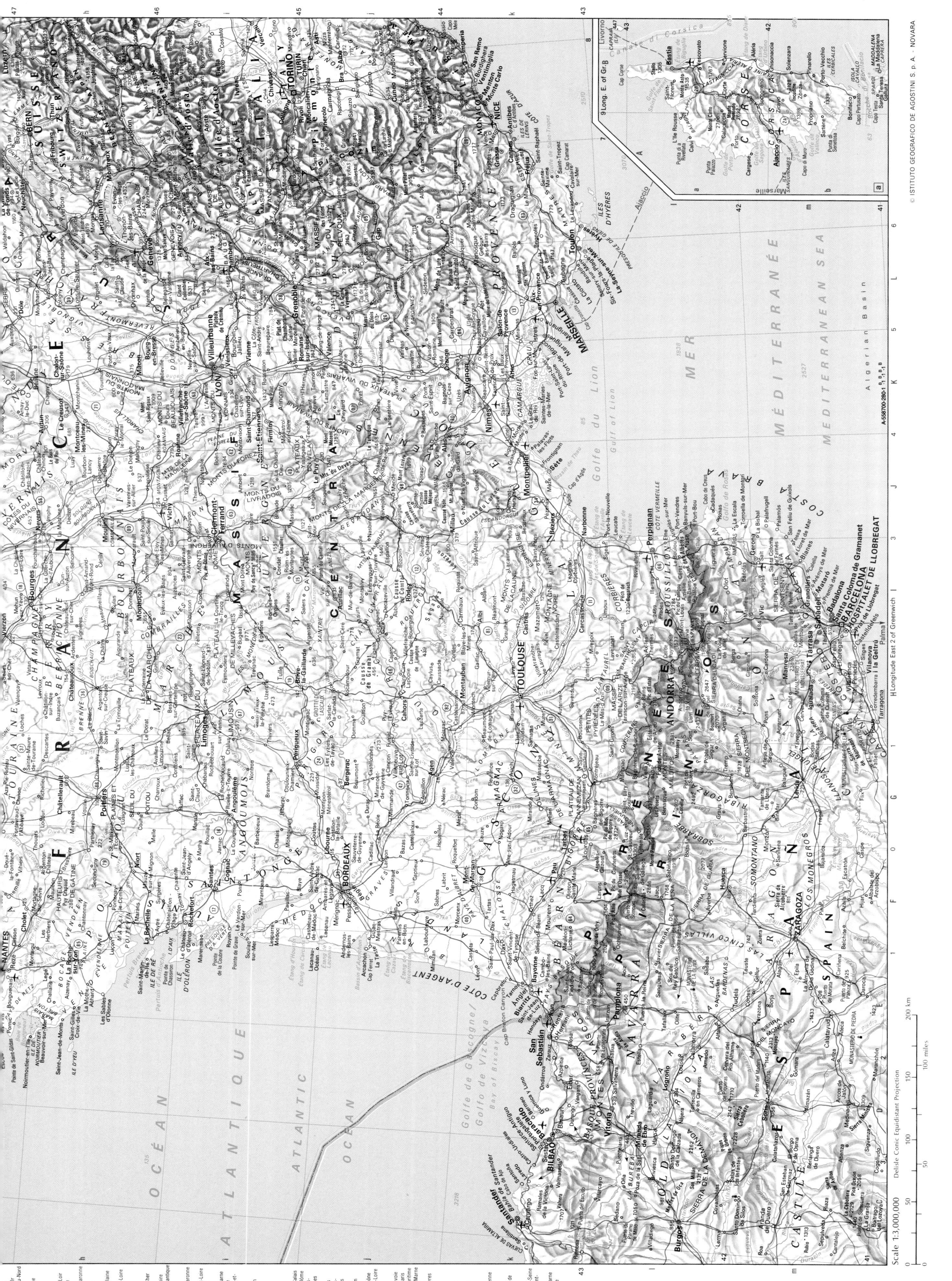

Scale 1:3,000,000

Delisle Conic Equidistant Projection

Map 12 **BELGIUM, NETHERLANDS AND LUXEMBOURG**

FRANCE

DÉPARTEMENTOS
75 Ville de Paris
92 Hauts-de-Seine
93 Seine-Saint-Denis
94 Val-de-Marne

Scale 1:1,500,000   Delisle Conic Equidistant Projection

Map 12

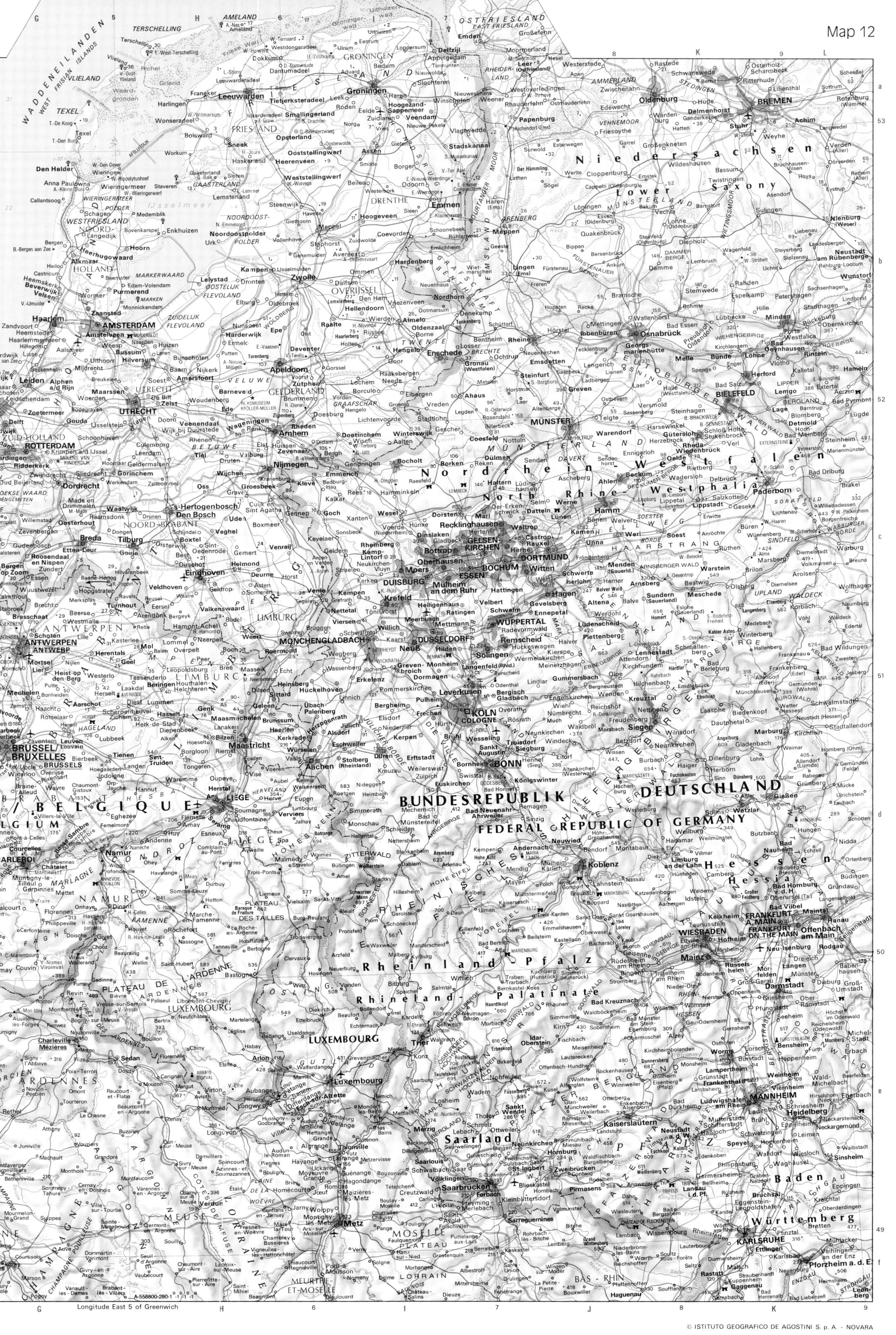

Map 13 **SPAIN AND PORTUGAL**

Longitude West 5 of Greenwich

Scale 1:3,000,000   Delisle Conic Equidistant Projection

0   50   100   150   200 km

0   50   100 miles

FRANCE

OCÉAN

CÔTE D'ARGENT

TOULOUSE

PYRÉNÉES

ANDORRA

PAMPLONA

NAVARRA

ARAGÓN

ZARAGOZA SARAGOSSA

HUESCA

LÉRIDA

BARCELONA
HOSPITALET DE LLOBREGAT
Badalona

TARRAGONA

COSTA BRAVA

GERONA

Perpignan

ROUSSILLON

Narbonne

MARSEILLE

Toulon

ÎLES D'HYÈRES

Golfe du Lion
Gulf of Lion

PROVENCE

Avignon

Nîmes

Montpellier

CAMARGUE

TERUEL

CASTELLÓN
Castellón de la Plana

ISLAS COLUMBRETES

VALENCIA

COSTA DEL AZAHAR

Sagunto

Gandia

ALICANTE
Elche

COSTA BLANCA

MURCIA
Cartagena
Cabo de Palos

COSTA BLANCA

ISLAS BALEARES
BALEARIC ISLANDS

MENORCA
MINORCA
Mahón
Ciudadela

MALLORCA
MAJORCA
PALMA
Manacor

IBIZA

FORMENTERA

ISLA CABRERA

BALEARES

Algerian Basin

MEDITERRANEAN SEA
MAR MEDITERRÁNEO

BAHR EL ABIAD EL MUTAWASSIT

ALGIERS
AL JAZÂ'IR

TIZI OUZOU

GRANDE KABYLIE
PETITE KABYLIE

Béjaia

Sétif

MOSTAGANEM

ORAN

AL JAZÂ'IR

ATLAS TELLIEN

ALGERIA

Blida

TLEMCEN

SIDI BEL ABBES

MASCARA

Tiaret

Map 14 **ITALY, AUSTRIA AND SWITZERLAND**

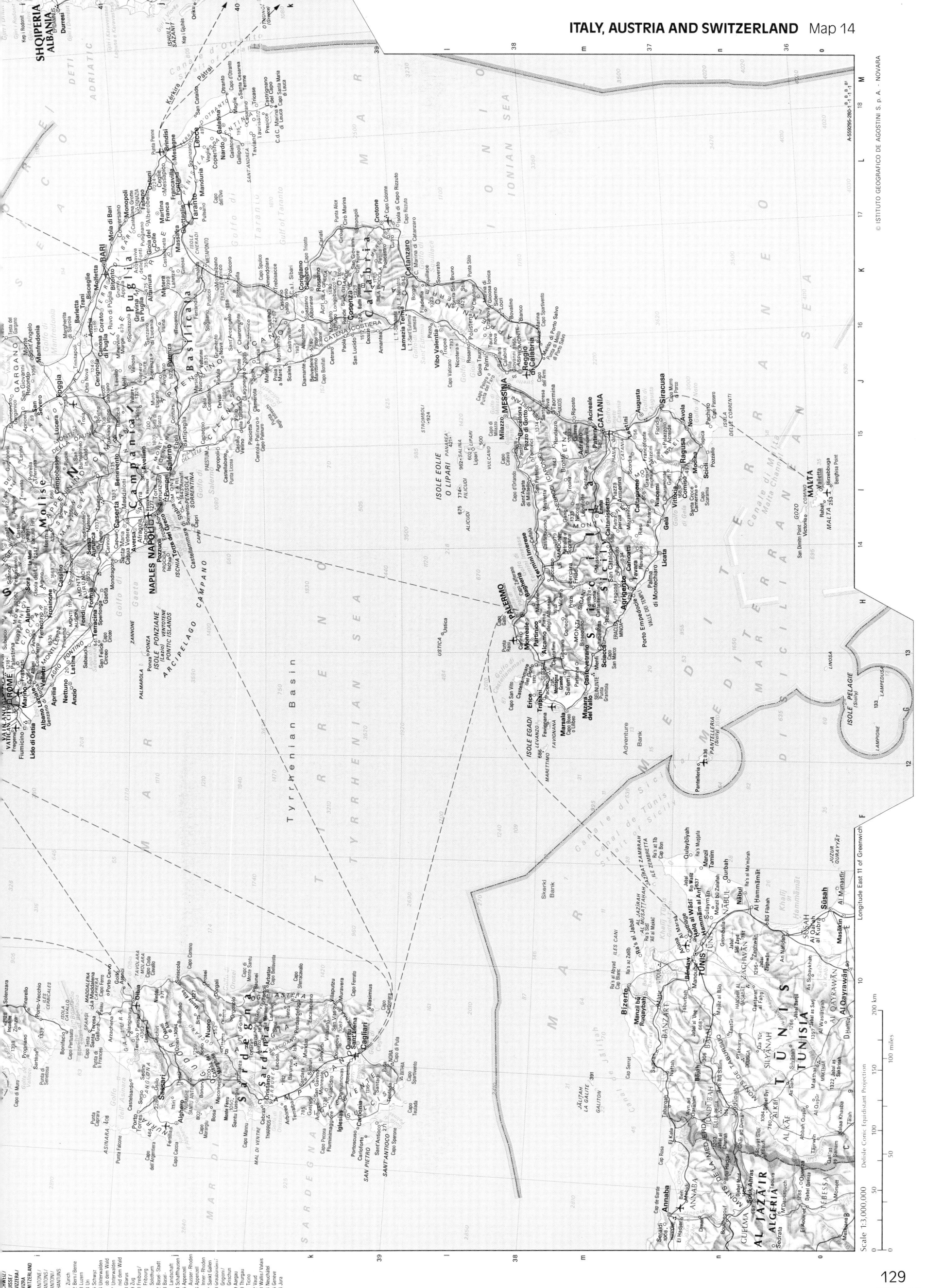

© ISTITUTO GEOGRAFICO DE AGOSTINI S. p. A. - NOVARA

A-550295-280/1-1¹-1²-1³-1⁴

SHQIPERIA
ALBANIA

Scale 1:3,000,000

Delisle Conic Equidistant Projection

Longitude East 11 of Greenwich

200 km

100 miles

Map 15 SOUTHEASTERN EUROPE

Map 15

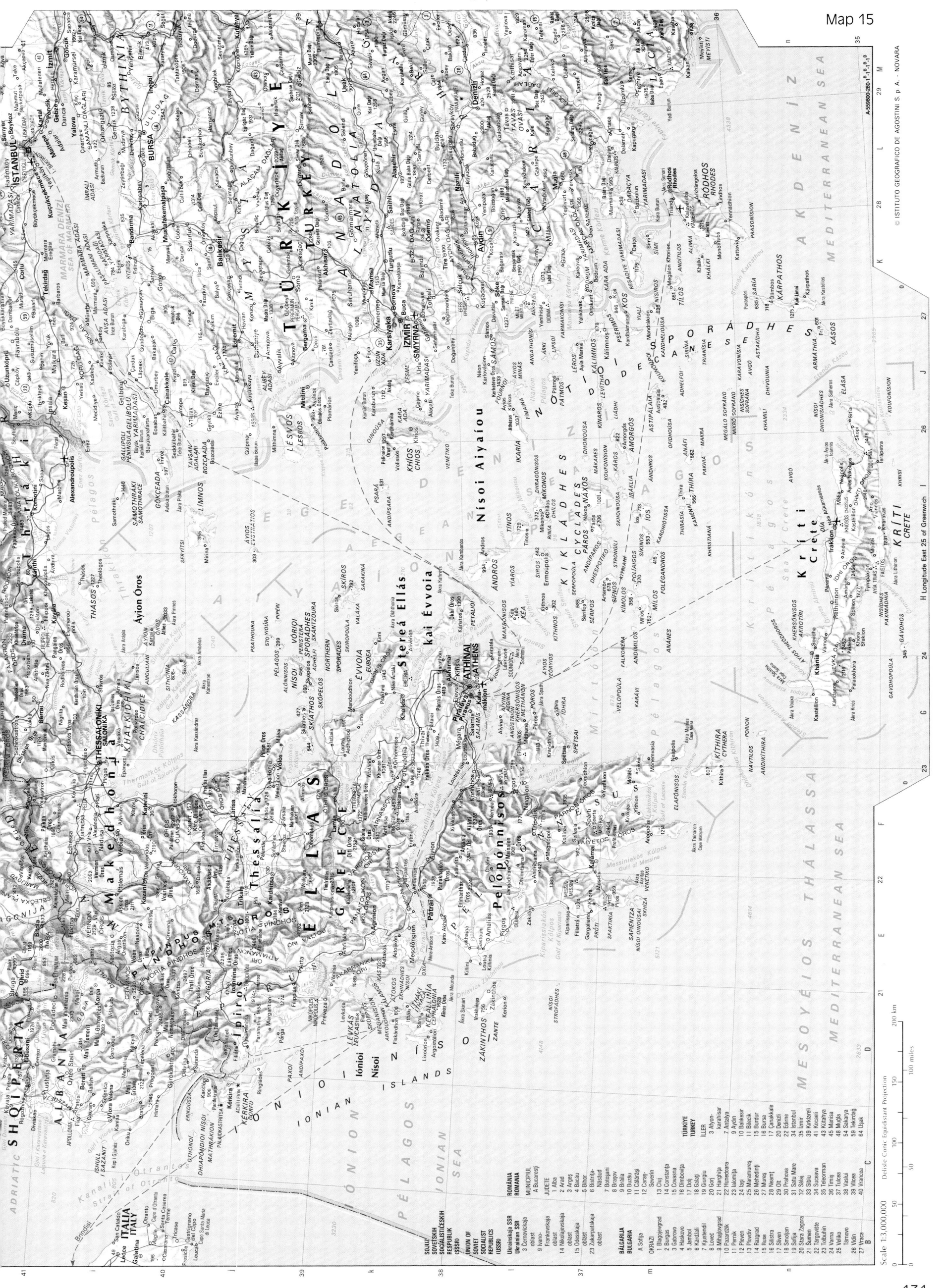

Scale 1:3,000,000

Delisle Conic Equidistant Projection

Map 16 **SOUTHWESTERN SOVIET UNION**

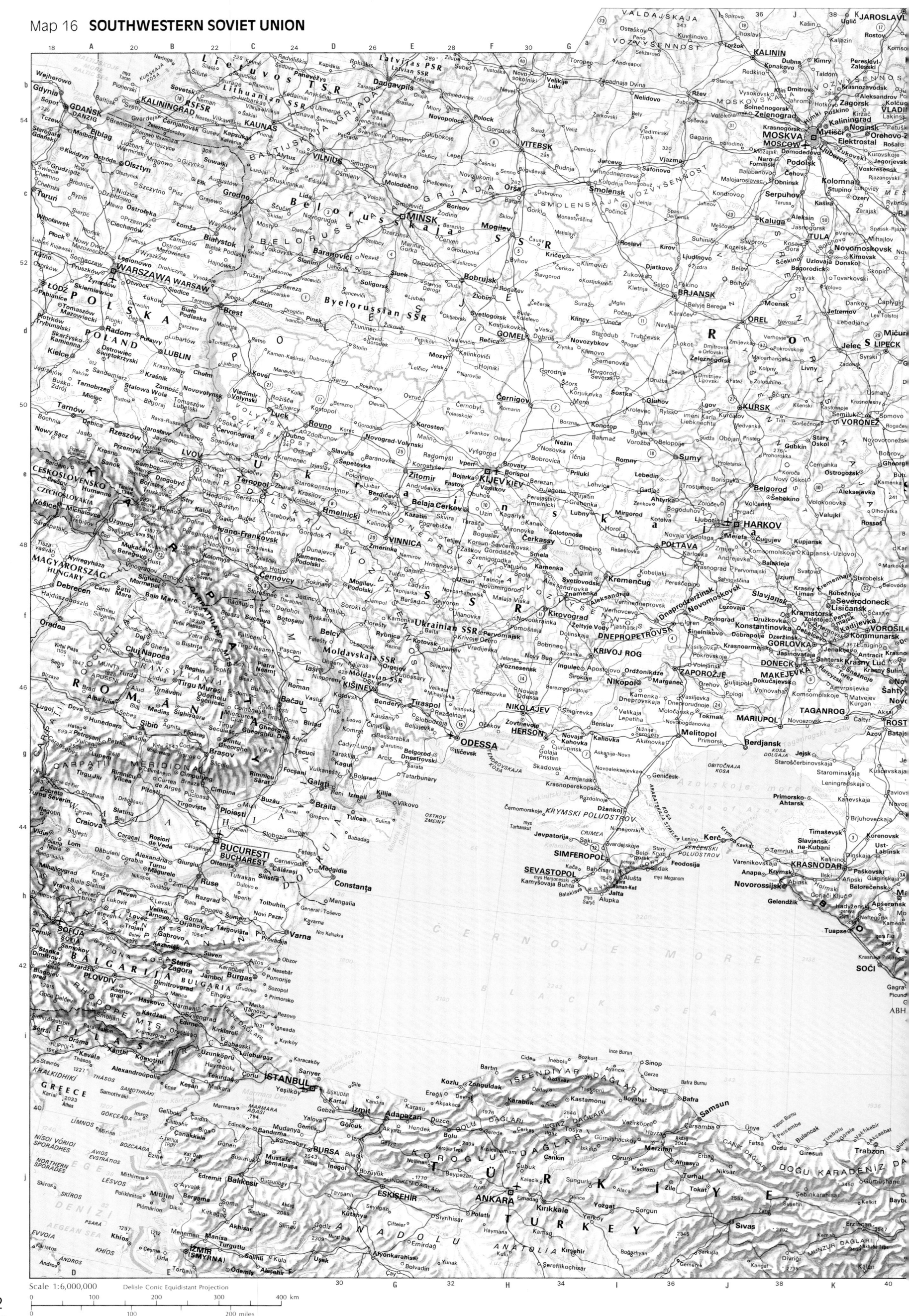

Scale 1:6,000,000   Delisle Conic Equidistant Projection

0   100   200   300   400 km

0   100   200 miles

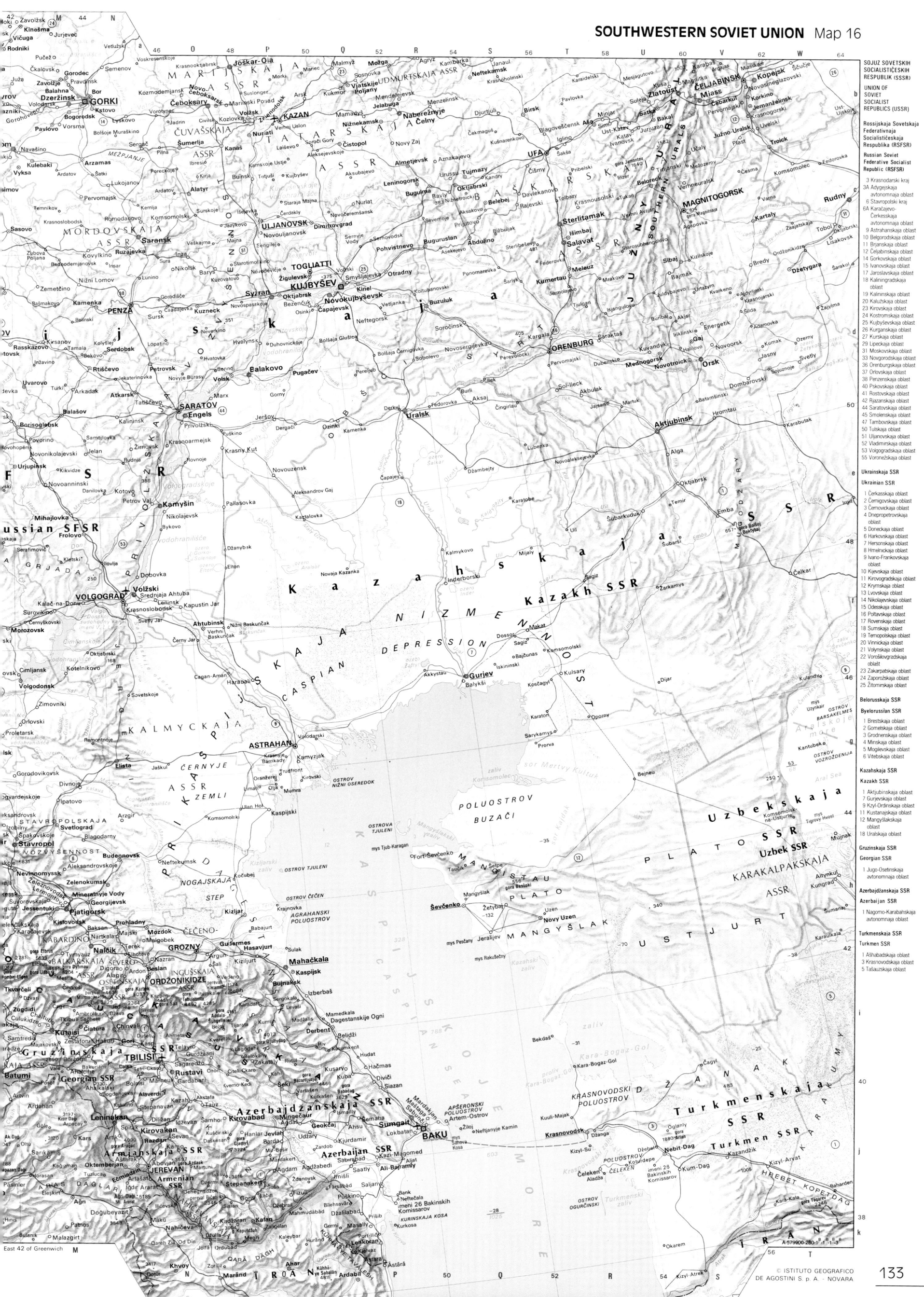

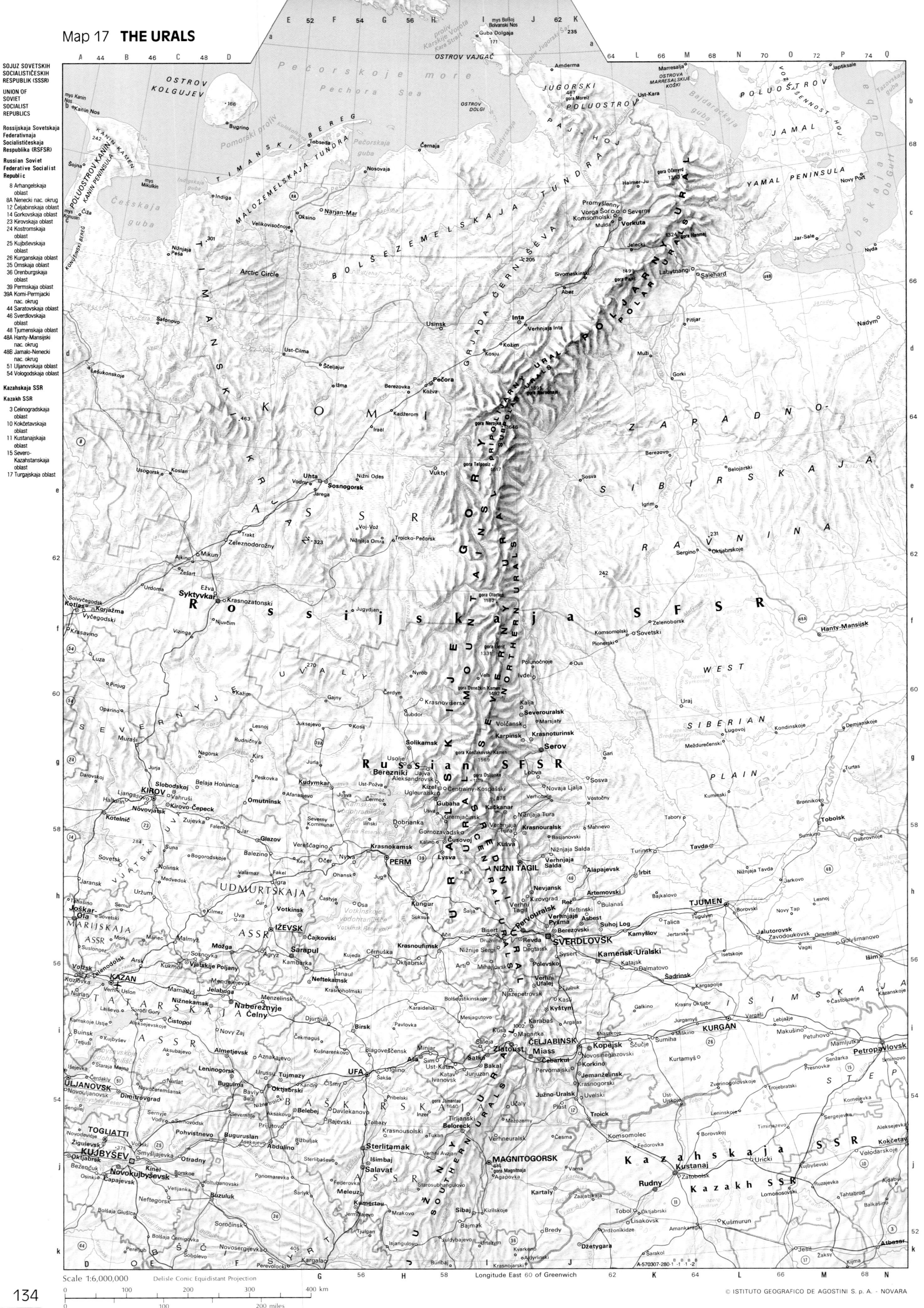

Map 17 THE URALS

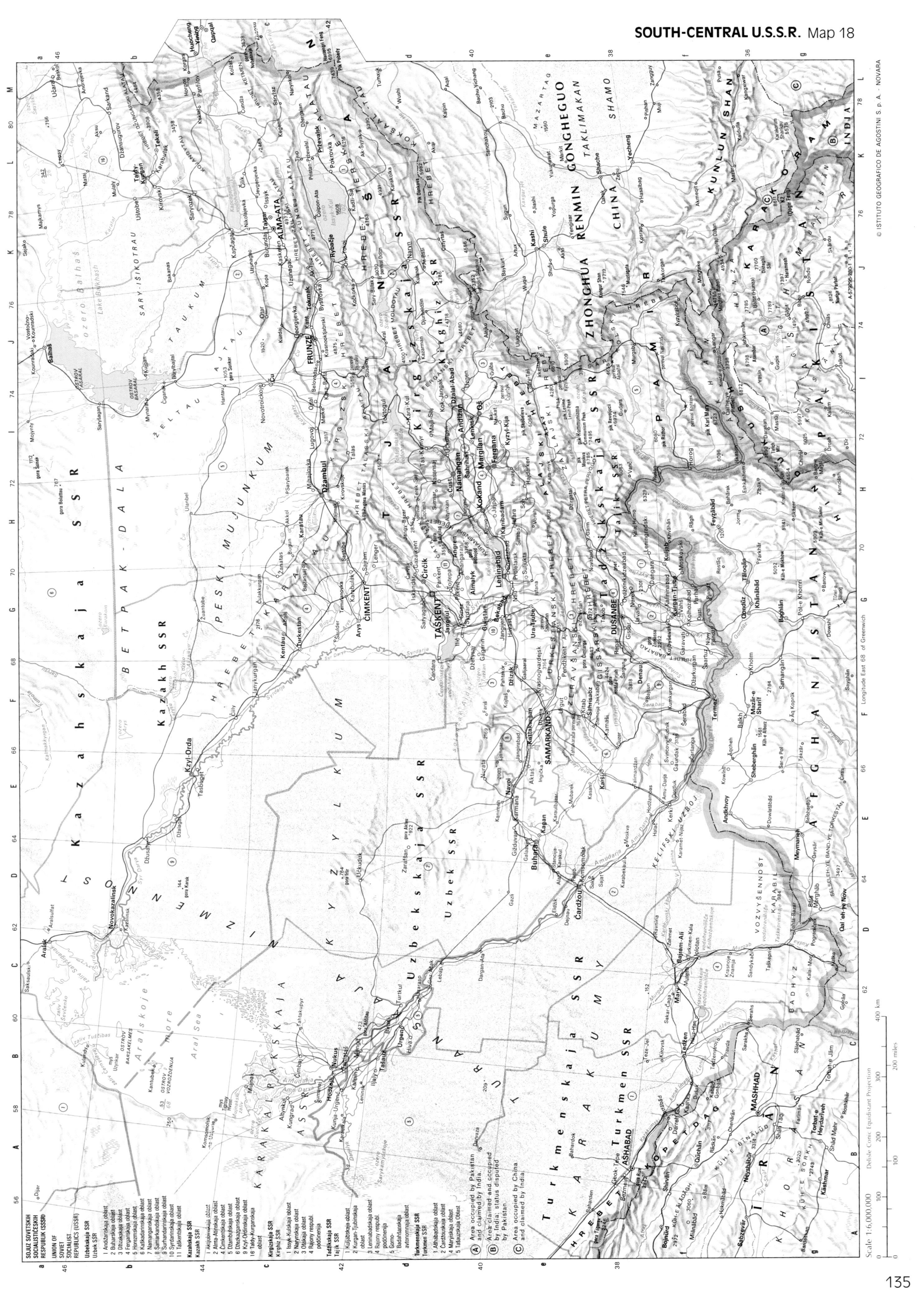

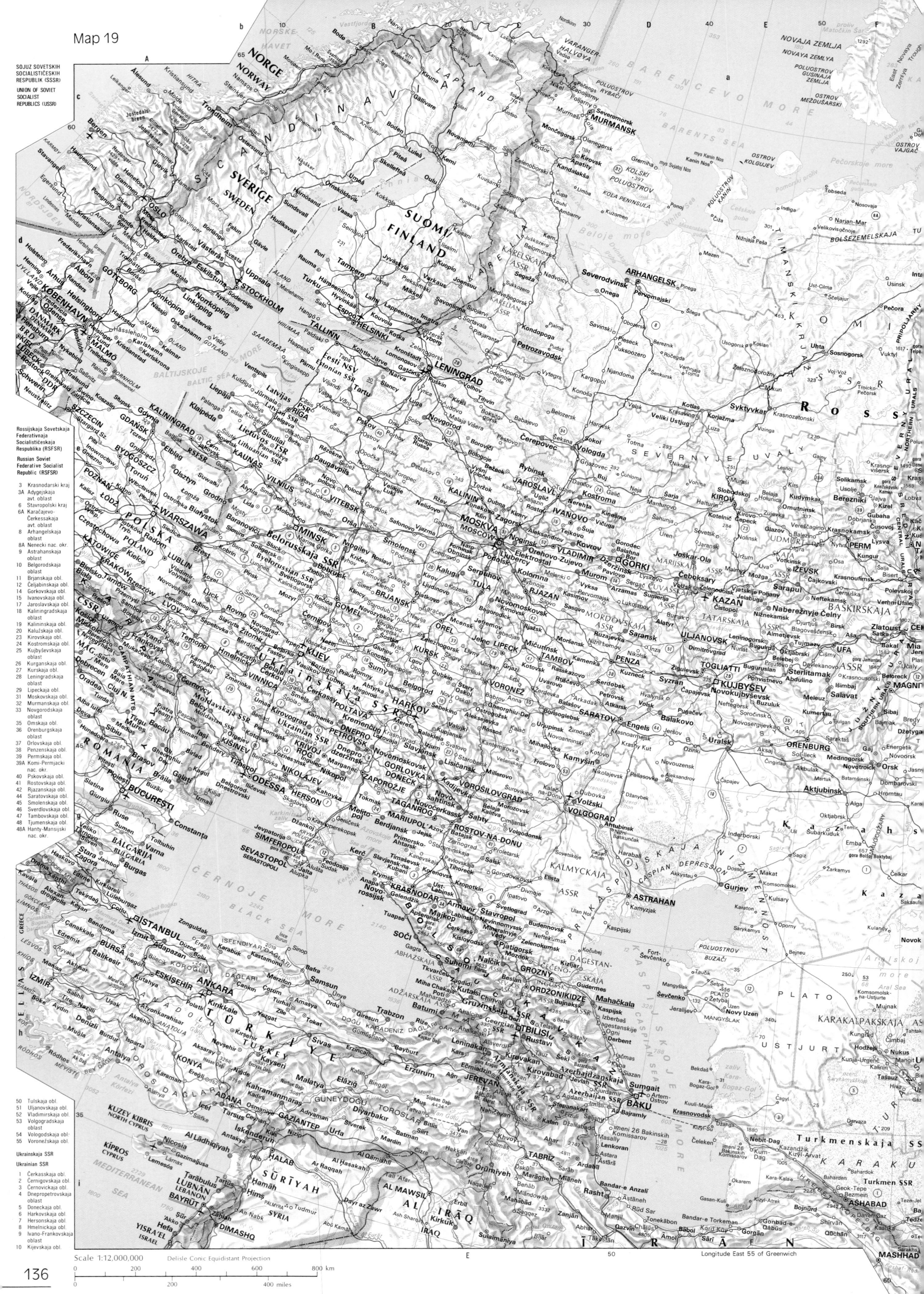

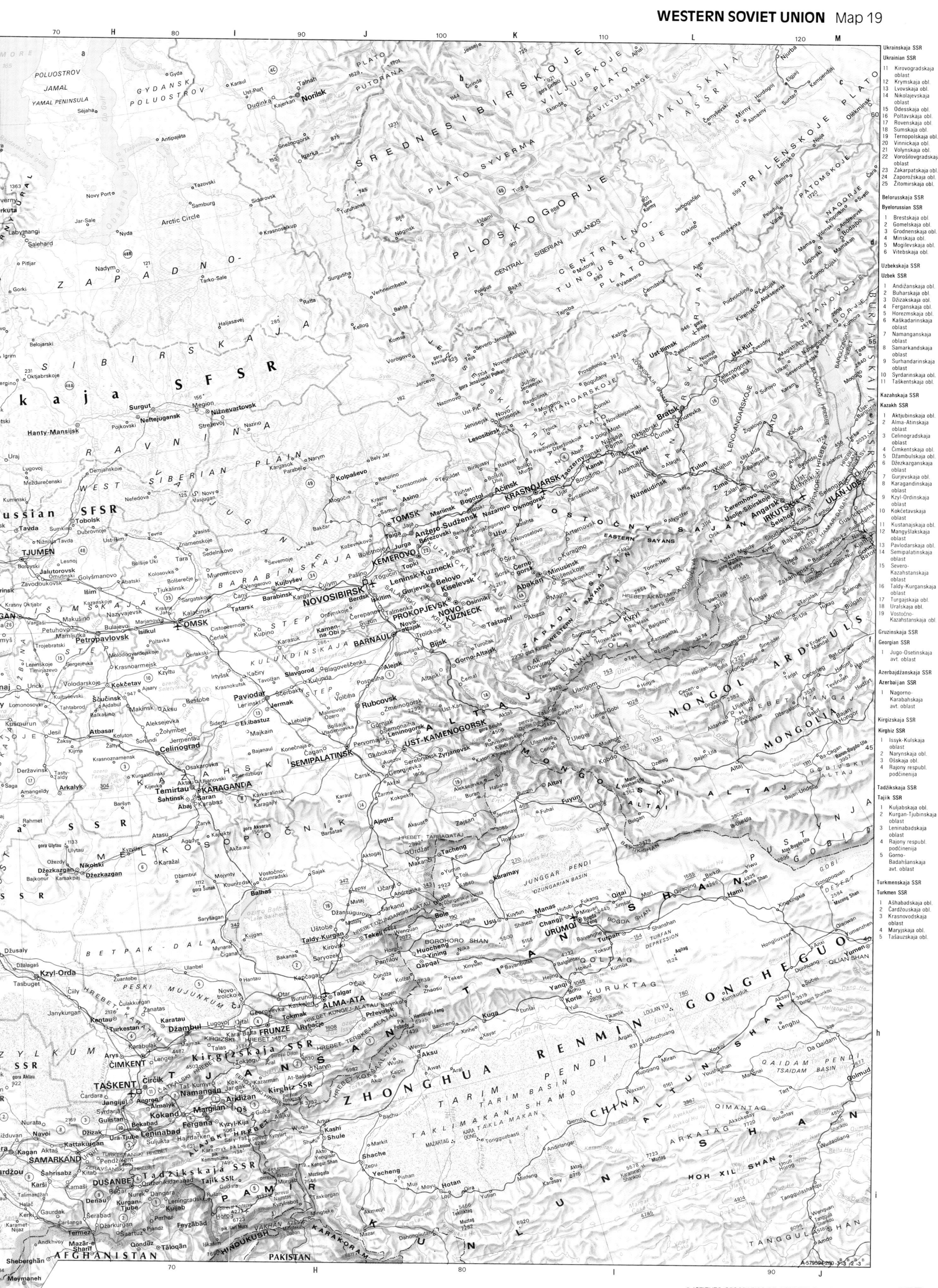

Ukrainskaja SSR
Ukrainian SSR
11 Kirovogradskaja oblast
12 Krymskaja obl.
13 Lvovskaja obl.
14 Nikolajevskaja oblast
15 Odesskaja obl.
16 Poltavskaja obl.
17 Rovenskaja obl.
18 Sumskaja obl.
19 Ternopolskaja obl.
20 Vinnickaja obl.
21 Volynskaja obl.
22 Vorošilovgradskaja oblast
23 Zakarpatskaja obl.
24 Zaporožskaja obl.
25 Žitomirskaja obl.

Belorusskaja SSR
Byelorussian SSR
1 Brestskaja obl.
2 Gomelskaja obl.
3 Grodnenskaja obl.
4 Minskaja obl.
5 Mogilevskaja obl.
6 Vitebskaja obl.

Uzbekskaja SSR
Uzbek SSR
1 Andižanskaja obl.
2 Buharskaja obl.
3 Džizakskaja obl.
4 Ferganskaja obl.
5 Horezmskaja obl.
6 Kaškadarinskaja oblast
7 Namanganskaja obl.
8 Samarkandskaja obl.
9 Surhandarinskaja oblast
10 Syrdarinskaja obl.
11 Taškentskaja obl.

Kazahskaja SSR
Kazakh SSR
1 Aktjubinskaja obl.
2 Alma-Atinskaja oblast
3 Celinogradskaja oblast
4 Čimkentskaja obl.
5 Džambulskaja obl.
6 Džezkazganskaja obl.
7 Gurjevskaja obl.
8 Karagandinskaja obl.
9 Kzyl-Ordinskaja obl.
10 Kokčetavskaja oblast
11 Kustanajskaja obl.
12 Mangyšlakskaja oblast
13 Pavlodarskaja obl.
14 Semipalatinskaja oblast
15 Severo-Kazahstanskaja oblast
16 Taldy-Kurganskaja oblast
17 Turgajskaja obl.
18 Uralskaja obl.
19 Vostočno-Kazahstanskaja obl.

Gruzinskaja SSR
Georgian SSR
1 Jugo-Osetinskaja avt. oblast

Azerbajdžanskaja SSR
Azerbaijan SSR
1 Nagorno-Karabahskaja avt. oblast

Kirgizskaja SSR
Kirghiz SSR
1 Issyk-Kulskaja oblast
2 Narynskaja obl.
3 Ošskaja obl.
4 Rajony respubl. podčinenija

Tadžikskaja SSR
Tajik SSR
1 Kuljabskaja obl.
2 Kurgan-Tjubinskaja oblast
3 Leninabadskaja obl.
4 Rajony respubl. podčinenija
5 Gorno-Badahšanskaja avt. oblast

Turkmenskaja SSR
Turkmen SSR
1 Ašhabadskaja obl.
2 Čardžouskaja obl.
3 Krasnovodskaja oblast
4 Maryjskaja obl.
5 Tašauzskaja obl.

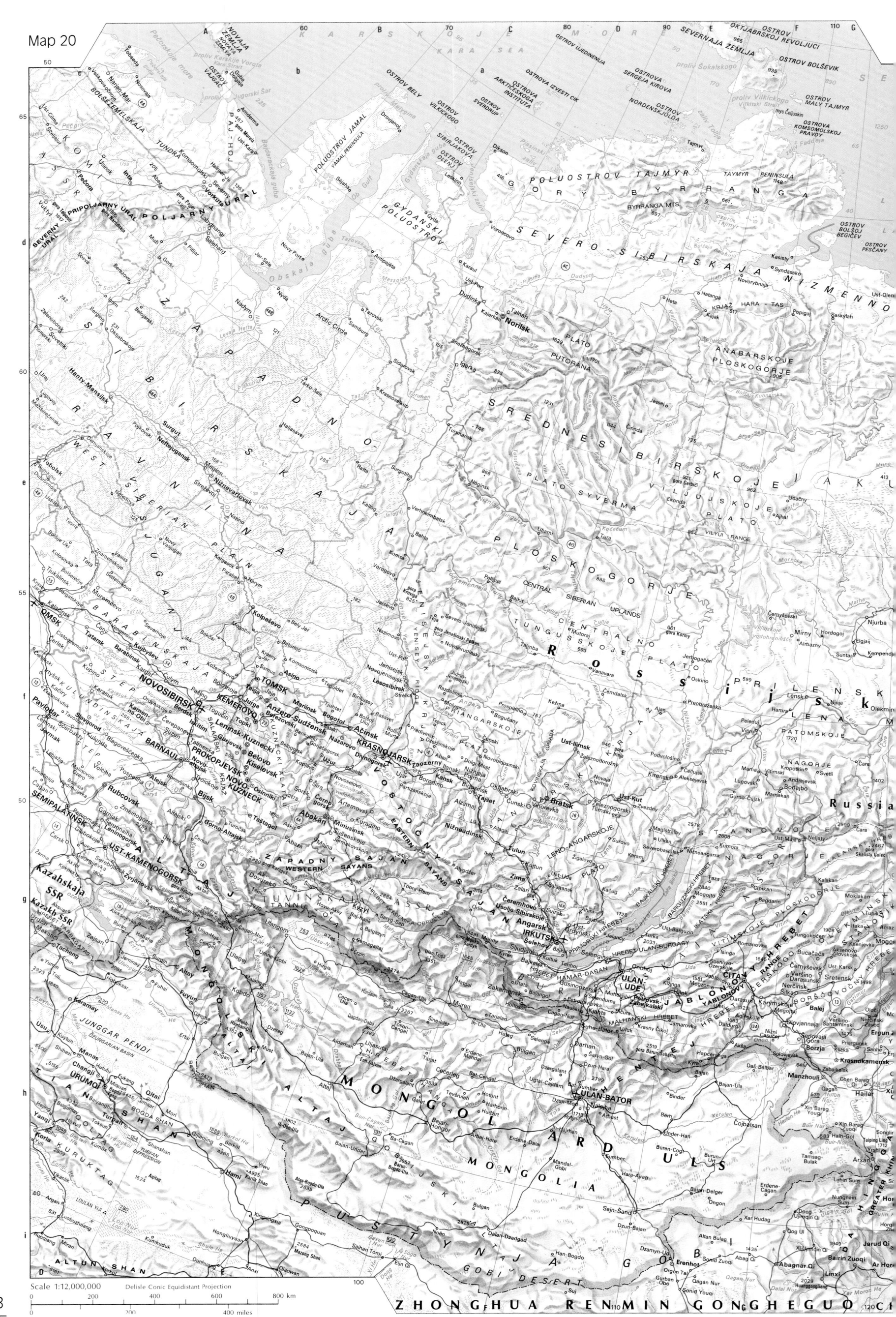

Map 20

Scale 1:12,000,000

Delisle Conic Equidistant Projection

0   200   400   600   800 km

0   200   400 miles

ZHONGHUA RENMIN GONGHEGUO

SOJUZ SOVETSKIH
SOCIALISTIĆESKIH
RESPUBLIK (SSSR)

UNION OF
SOVIET SOCIALIST
REPUBLICS (USSR)

Rossijskaja Sovetskaja
Federativnaja
Socialistićeskaja
Respublika (RSFSR)

Russian Soviet
Federative Socialist
Republic (RSFSR)

1 Altajski kraj
1A Gorno-Altajskaja
   avtonomnaja oblast
2 Habarovski kraj
2A Jevrejskaja
   avtonomnaja oblast
4 Krasnojarski kraj
4A Hakasskaja
   avtonomnaja oblast
4B Evenkijski nac.
   okrug
4C Tajmyrski (Dolgano-
   Nenecki) nac. okrug
5 Primorski kraj
7 Amurskaja oblast
8A Nenecki nac. okrug
13 Ćitinskaja oblast
13A Aginski Burjatski
   nac. okrug
16 Irkutskaja oblast
16A Ust-Ordynski
   Burjatski nac. okrug
21 Kamčatskaja oblast
21A Korjakski nac.
   okrug
22 Kemerovskaja
   oblast
30 Magadanskaja
   oblast
30A Ćukotski nac. okrug
34 Novosibirskaja
   oblast
35 Ōmskaja oblast
43 Sahalinskaja oblast
48 Tjumenskaja oblast
48A Hanty-Mansijski
   nac. okrug
48B Jamalo-Nenecki
   nac. okrug
49 Tomskaja oblast

Kazahskaja SSR

Kazakh SSR

13 Pavlodarskaja
   oblast
14 Semipalatinskaja
   oblast
19 Vostočno-
   Kazahstanskaja
   oblast

Ostrov Kunašir, ostrov Šikotan, ostrov
Iturup and Malaja Kurilskaja Grjada,
occupied by the U.S.S.R. since 1945,
are claimed by Japan pending a final
peace treaty.

A-579395-280-1

Map 21 **ASIA, PHYSICAL**

ALEUTIAN TRENCH
ALEUTIAN ISLANDS
FOX ISLANDS
ANDREANOF ISLANDS
RAT ISLANDS
NEAR ISLANDS
Kuril Trench
KURIL ISLANDS
HOKKAIDO
SAKHALIN
HONSHU
SHIKOKU
IZU ISLANDS
Bonin Trench

ALASKA PENINSULA
KENAI PENINSULA
ALASKA RANGE
ALASKA
SEWARD PENINSULA
BROOKS RANGE
YUKON PLATEAU

CHUKCHI PENINSULA
KAMCHATKA PENINSULA
SREDINNY
KORJAKSKOJE NAGORJE
KOLYMA RANGE
EASTERN SIBERIA
CHERSKI MOUNTAINS
VERKHOYANSK MOUNTAINS
SUNTAR-KHAYATA
STANOVOY RANGE
SIHOTE-ALIN
DZHUGDZHUR RANGE
LESSER KHINGAN RANGE
GREATER KHINGAN RANGE
MANCHURIA

ALASKA
ALEUTIAN RANGE

WRANGEL

BAFFIN
VICTORIA
BANKS
PARRY ISLANDS
QUEEN ELIZABETH ISLANDS
ELLESMERE
DEVON
Alpha Cordillera
Makarov Basin
Lomonosov Ridge
ARCTIC
Eurasia Basin
Nansen Basin
Fram Basin
North Pole
SEVERNAYA ZEMLYA
KOMSOMOLEC
BOLSHEVIK
OCTOBER REVOLUTION ISLAND
TAYMYR PENINSULA
BYRRANGA MOUNTAINS
NORTH SIBERIAN PLAIN
CENTRAL SIBERIAN UPLAND
PUTORANA PLATEAU
STANOVOY UPLAND
LENA MOUNTAINS
ALDAN PLATEAU
YABLONOVY RANGE
ORDOS
GOBI DESERT
ALTAI
KHANGAI
MONGOLIAN ALTAI
BEI SHAN
DZUNGARIAN BASIN
TARBAGATAY
KAZAKHSTAN
KAZAKH HILLS
TIAN SHAN

GREENLAND
KING FREDERIK VIII LAND
KING CHRISTIAN IX
KING CHRISTIAN X
KNUD RASMUSSEN LAND
PEARY LAND
FRANZ JOSEPH LAND
NOVAYA ZEMLYA
YAMAL PENINSULA
GYDA PENINSULA
WEST SIBERIAN
PLAIN
VASJUGANJE
ISHIM STEPPE
KAZAKH HILLS
KIRGHIZ STEPPE
WESTERN TURKISTAN

NORDAUSTLANDET
EDGEOYA
SPITSBERGEN
BEAR ISLAND
Barents Sea
KOLGUYEV
KANIN PENINSULA
TIMAN RIDGE
NORTHERN UVALS
URAL MOUNTAINS

ICELAND
Reykjavik
JAN MAYEN
Greenland Basin
Mohns Ridge
Norwegian Basin
FAEROE ISLANDS
SHETLAND ISLANDS
ORKNEY ISLANDS
HEBRIDES
GREAT BRITAIN
IRELAND
Dublin
London
BRITISH ISLES
Reykjanes Ridge
Iceland Basin
Rockall Rise

SCANDINAVIA
LAPLAND
KARELIA
KOLA PENINSULA
Murmansk
Archangel
North Cape

Stockholm
Helsinki
Oslo
Trondheim
Bergen
GOTLAND
SVEALAND
GOTALAND
Riga
Leningrad
Moscow
VALDAI HILLS
MOSCOW BASIN
CENTRAL RUSSIAN UPLAND
UKRAINE
VOLGA HILLS
CASPIAN DEPRESSION
Caspian Sea
CAUCASUS
CISCAUCASIA
TRANSCAUCASIA
LESSER CAUCASUS
KURA

POLAND
POMERANIA
Berlin
Hamburg
Amsterdam
FRIESLAND
FLANDERS
SILESIA
SUDETEN
BOHEMIA
BOHEMIAN FOREST
CARPATHIAN MTS.
BESKID
SLOVAKIA
Budapest
Vienna
Paris
MASSIF CENTRAL
VOSGES
JURA
ALPS
APENNINES
CORSICA
SARDINIA
BALKAN PENINSULA
BALKAN MTS.
MACEDONIA
THRACE
PINDUS MTS.
PELOPONNESUS
CRETE
Ionian Sea
Mediterranean Sea

ANATOLIA
TAURUS MTS.
CYPRUS
MESOPOTAMIA
SYRIAN DESERT
ZAGROS
KURDISTAN
ARMENIA
NILE DELTA

© ISTITUTO GEOGRAFICO DE AGOSTINI S. p. A. - NOVARA

AUSTRALIA

GREAT SANDY DESERT

GIBSON DESERT

GREAT VICTORIA DESERT

NULLARBOR PLAIN

ARCHIPELAGO OF THE RECHERCHE

KIMBERLEY PLATEAU

MOLUCCAS

NEW GUINEA

CERAM

PALAU ISLANDS

MINDANAO

PHILIPPINE ISLANDS

LUZON

SAMAR

LEYTE

CEBU

NEGROS

PANAY

MINDORO

PALAWAN

Philippine Trench

Philippine Basin

Ryukyu Trench

RYUKYU ISLANDS

TAIWAN (FORMOSA)

HAINAN

South China Basin

PARACEL ISLANDS

C H I N A

Daba Shan

Sichuan Pendi

Plateau of Yunnan

INDOCHINA

TONKIN

MEKONG DELTA

COCHIN CHINA

ANNAM

Annamite Range

KAMPUCHEA

Phnom Penh

MALAY PENINSULA

TENASSERIM

MERGUI ARCHIPELAGO

PHUKET

ISTHMUS OF KRA

Bilauktaung Range

Pegu Yoma

Arakan Yoma

NATUNA ISLANDS

RIAU ARCHIPELAGO

LINGGA ARCHIPELAGO

BANGKA

BELITUNG

SUMATRA

BARISAN MTS.

Palembang

Krakatau

GREATER SUNDA ISLANDS

K A L I M A N T A N

Banjarmasin

Pontianak

CELEBES

SULA ISLANDS

BUTUNG

FLORES

SUMBAWA

LOMBOK

BALI

MADURA

JAVA

LESSER SUNDA ISLANDS

SUMBA

SAWU

TIMOR

ALOR

SANGIHE ISLANDS

TALAUD ISLANDS

HALMAHERA

BURU

Java Trench

North Australian Basin

Wharton Basin

CHRISTMAS

COCOS ISLANDS

Broken Ridge

Ninetyeast Ridge

I N D I A N   O C E A N

Mid- Indian Basin

Mid- Indian Ridge

Nikitin Seamount

Bay of Bengal

ANDAMAN ISLANDS

Andaman Basin

NICOBAR ISLANDS

GREAT NICOBAR

LITTLE ANDAMAN

ENGGANO

MENTAWAI ISLANDS

PAGI ISLANDS

SIBERUT

NIAS

BATU ISLANDS

SIMEULUE

Medan

SRI LANKA (CEYLON)

Pidurutalagala

Colombo

Dondra Head

Cape Comorin

COROMANDEL COAST

EASTERN GHATS

DECCAN

India
n

Platea
u

MALDIVE ISLANDS

MALE ATOLL

SUVADIVA ATOLL

ADDU ATOLL

MINICOY

LAKSHADWEEP

Mid- Indian Ridge

CHAGOS ARCHIPELAGO

DIEGO GARCIA

Tropic of Capricorn

Mid- Indian Ridge

Arabian Basin

WESTERN GHATS

MALABAR COAST

Mangalore

Bombay

VINDHYA RANGE

SATPURA RANGE

GONDWANA

Chotanagpur Plateau

Calcutta

Kathmandu

PLATEAU OF TIBET

HIMALAYA

RANGE

HINDUSTAN

Delhi

PUNJAB

GUJARAT

KATHIAWAR

Ahmadabad

KIRTHAR RANGE

Karachi

BALUCHISTAN

CENTRAL MAKRAN RANGE

MAKRAN

DASHT-E LUT

IRAN

FARS

Murray Ridge

MASIRAH

KURIA MURIA ISLANDS

TRUCIAL COAST

JABAL AKHDAR

OMAN

Ras al Hadd

Masqat

ZUFAR

HADRAMAWT

AL HASA

Al Madinah

Makkah

HIJAZ

ARABIAN PENINSULA

AR-RUB' AL KHALI

NAFUD

ASIR

NAJD

SOCOTRA

ABD AL KURI

Aden

Mogadishu

OGADEN

ETHIOPIAN PLATEAU

Somali Basin

SEYCHELLES ISLANDS

MAHE

AMIRANTE ISLANDS

Amirante Basin

ALDABRA ISLANDS

COSMOLEDO GROUP

FARQUHAR GROUP

PROVIDENCE

ILES GLORIEUSES

NZWANI

NGAZIDJA

MAYOTTE

COMORO ISLANDS

Cap d'Ambre

MADAGASCAR

Antananarivo

Mascarene Plateau

Saya de Malha Bank

Mascarene Basin

CARGADOS CARAJOS ISLANDS

AGALEGA ISLANDS

TROMELIN

MASCARENE ISLANDS

MAURITIUS

REUNION

RODRIGUES

Madagascar Basin

Madagascar Plateau

Cap Sainte-Marie

Southwest Indian Ridge

Equator

Longitude East 80 of Greenwich

Lambert Azimuthal Equal Area Projection

Scale 1:30 000 000

Scale 1:30.000.000

500   1000   1500   2000 km

500   1000 miles

A-515200-780-1 -1 -2 -3 B

m	ft
6000	19685
5000	16404
4000	13123
3000	9843
2000	6562
500	1640
+200	+656
Depr.	0
-200	-656
1000	3281
2000	6562
4000	13123
6000	19685
8000	26247

Map 22 **ASIA, POLITICAL**

Map 23 **SOUTHWESTERN ASIA**

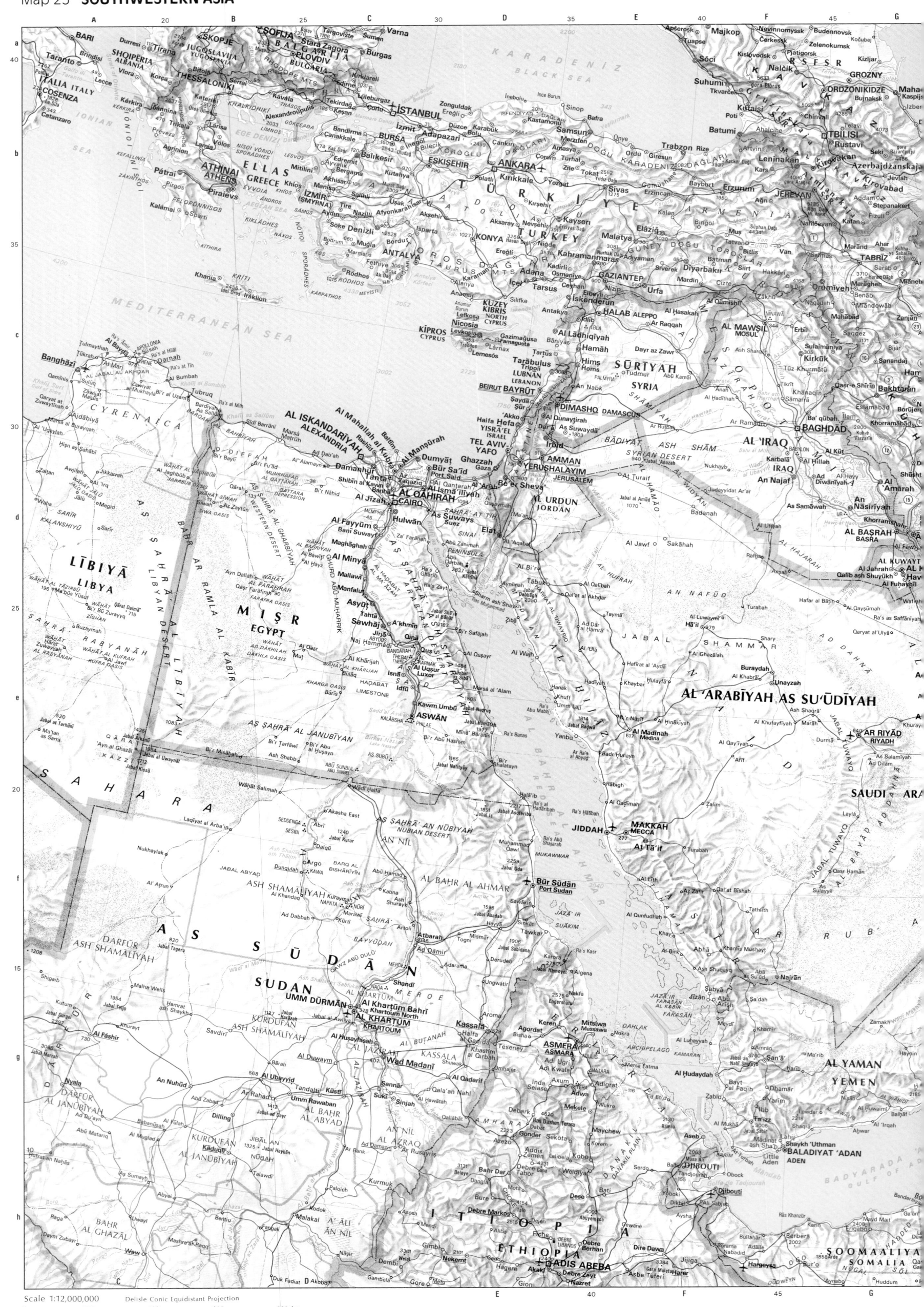

Scale 1:12,000,000   Delisle Conic Equidistant Projection

0   200   400   600   800 km

0   200   400 miles

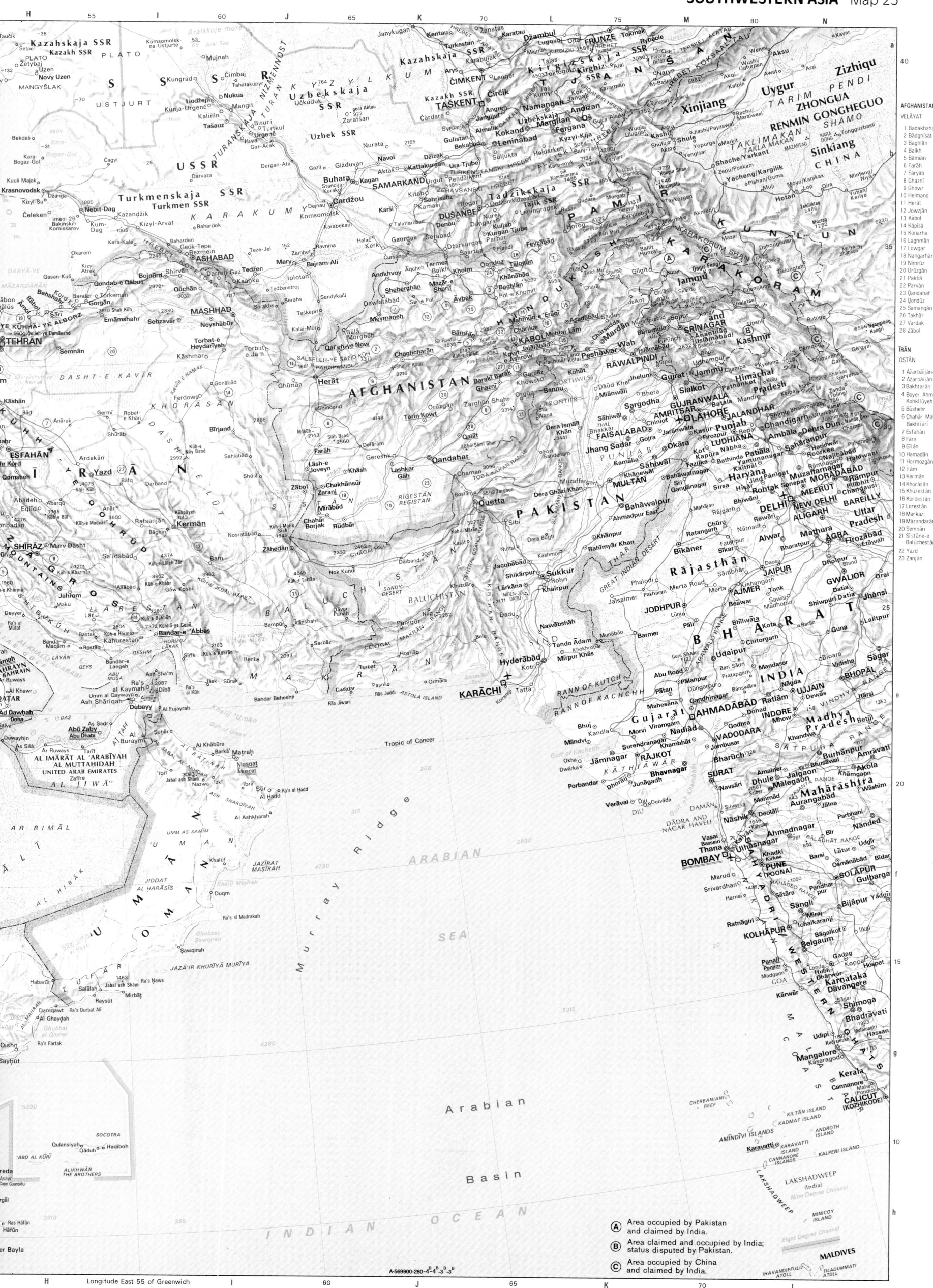

AFGHANISTAN
VELĀYAT

1 Badakhshan
2 Bādghīsāt
3 Baghlān
4 Balkh
5 Bāmiān
6 Farāh
7 Fāryāb
8 Ghazni
9 Ghowr
10 Helmand
11 Herāt
12 Jowzjān
13 Kābol
14 Kāpīsa
15 Konarha
16 Laghmān
17 Lowgar
18 Nangarhār
19 Nīmrūz
20 Orūzgān
21 Paktiā
22 Parvān
23 Qandahār
24 Qondūz
25 Samangān
26 Takhār
27 Vardak
28 Zābol

ĪRĀN
OSTĀN

1 Āzarbāijān-e Gharbi
2 Āzarbāijān-e Sharqi
3 Bakhtarān
4 Boyer Ahmadi-e
   Kohkīlūyeh
5 Būshehr
6 Chahār Mahāl-e
   Bakhtiāri
7 Esfahān
8 Fārs
9 Gīlān
10 Hamadān
11 Hormozgān
12 Īlām
13 Kermān
14 Kermānshāh
15 Khūzestān
16 Kordestān
17 Lorestān
18 Markazi
19 Māzandarān
20 Semnān
21 Sīstān-e
   Balūchestān
22 Yazd
23 Zanjān

Area occupied by Pakistan and claimed by India.

Area claimed and occupied by India; status disputed by Pakistan.

Area occupied by China and claimed by India.

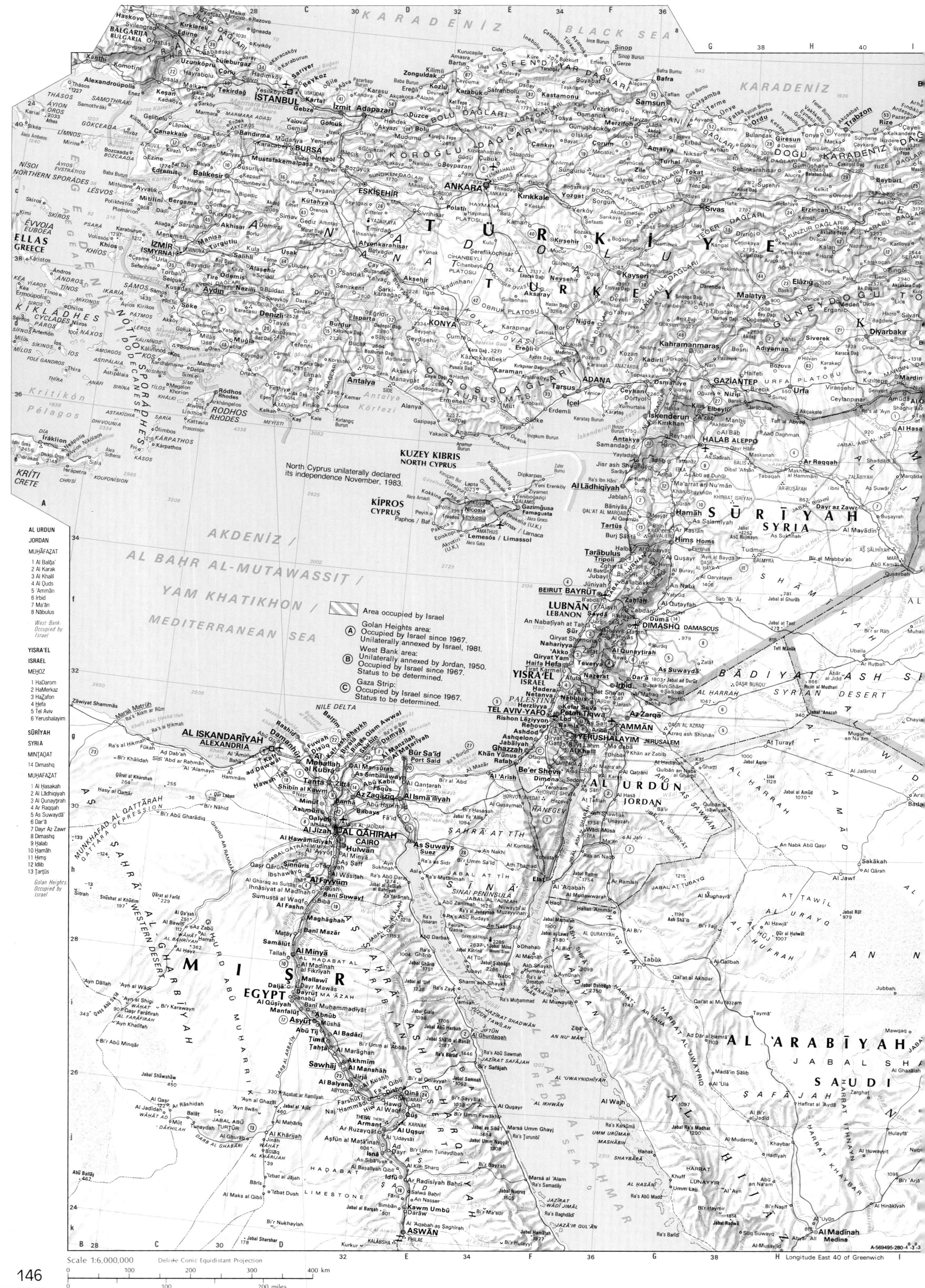

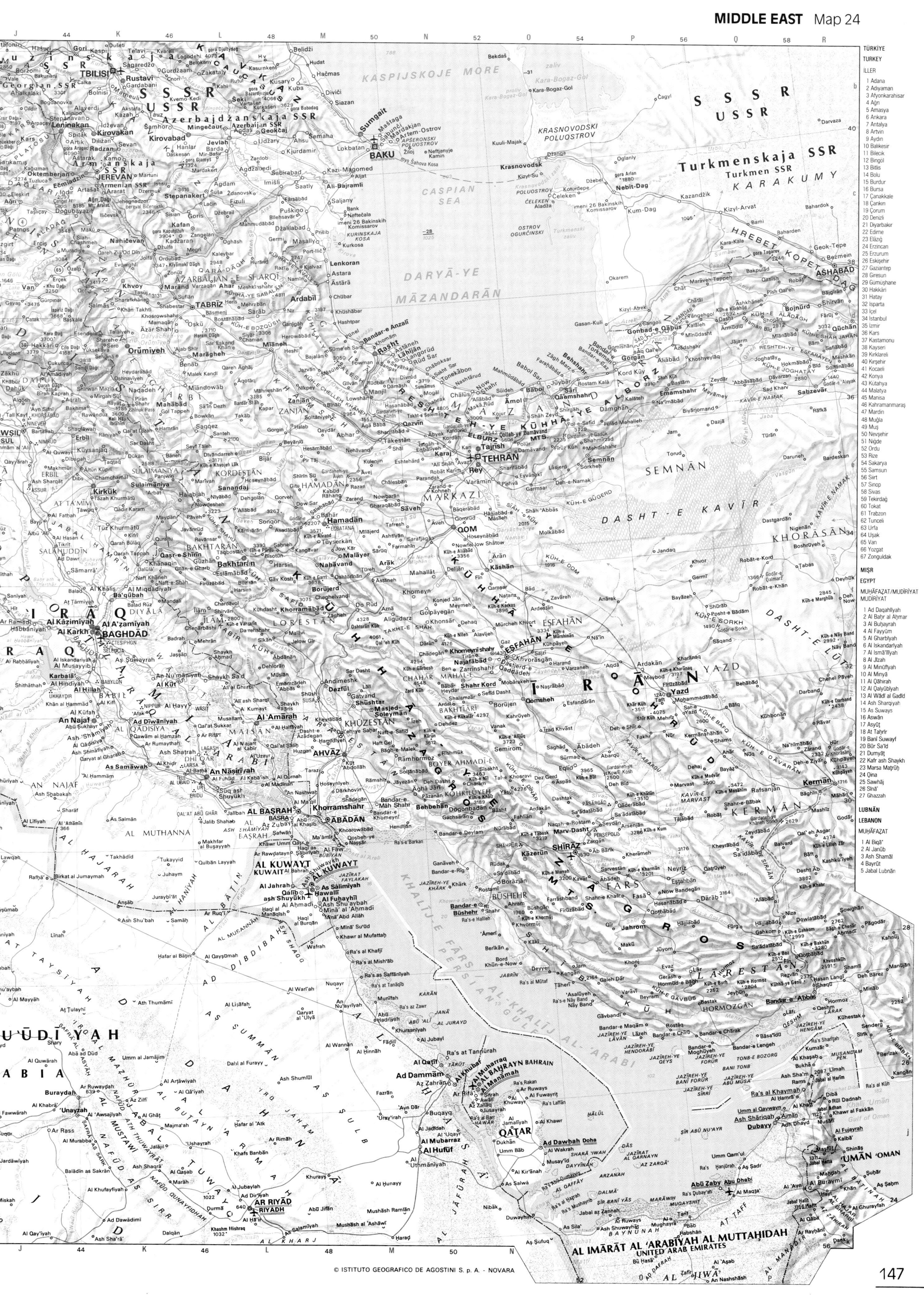

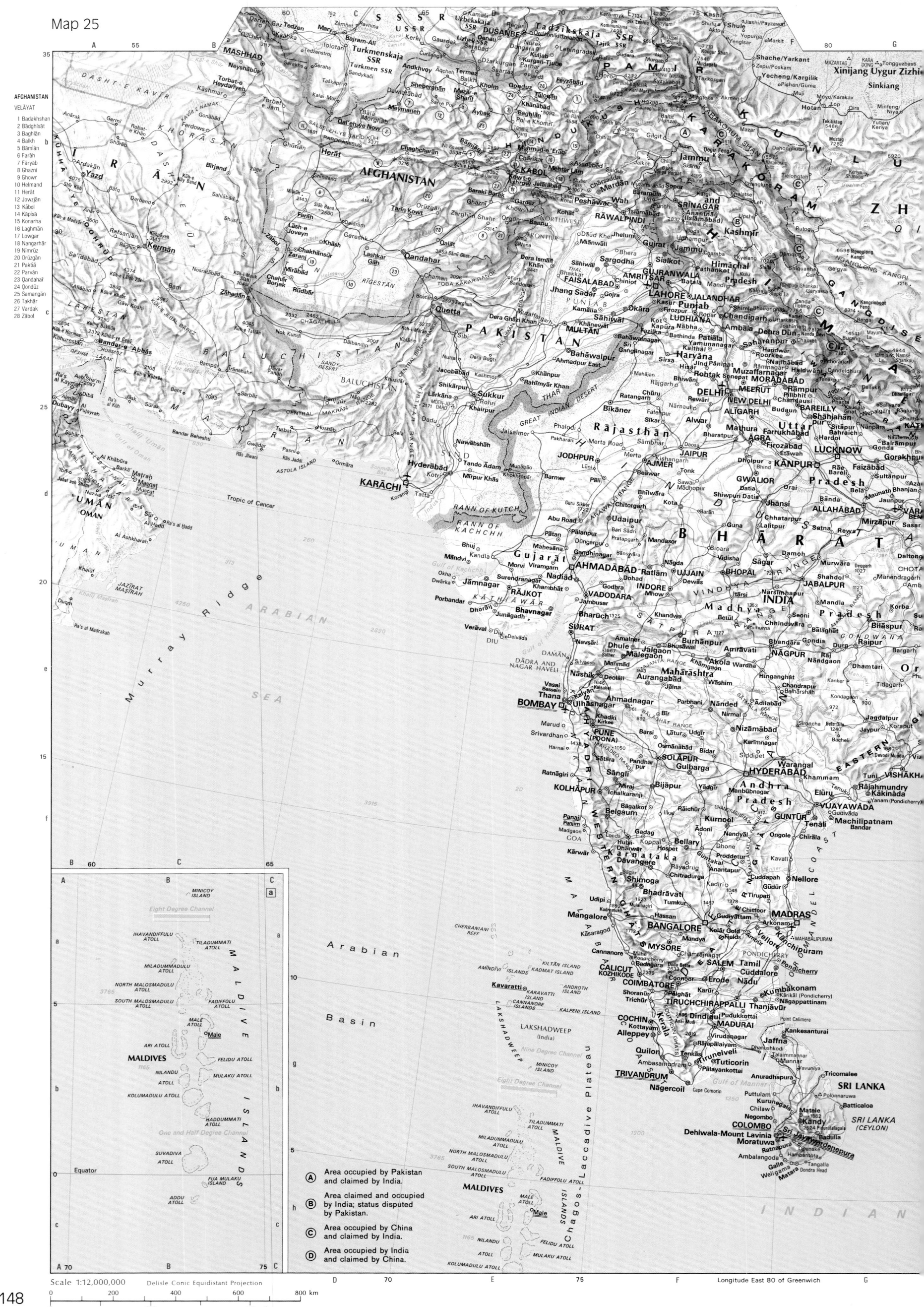

Map 25

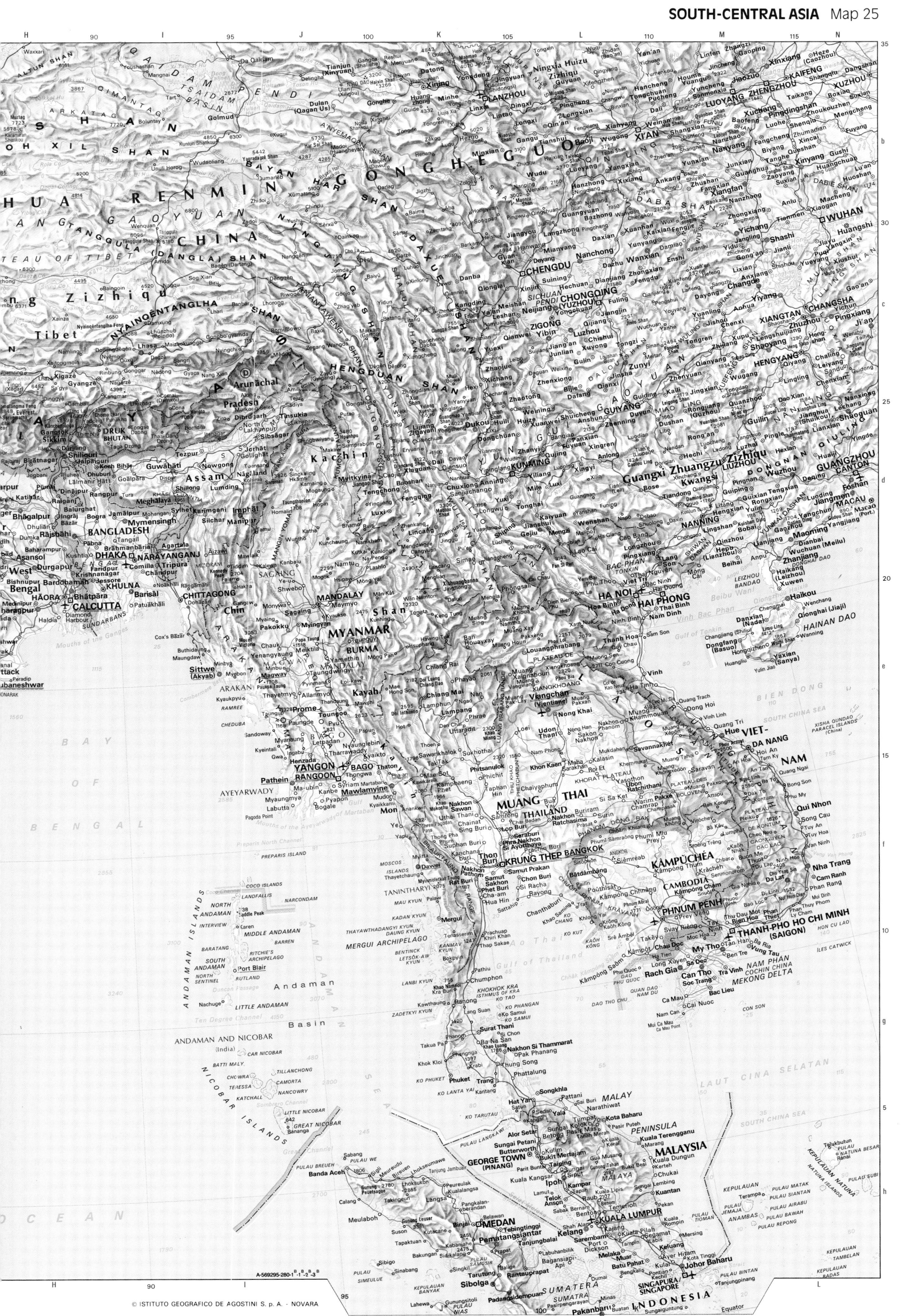

Map 26 **SOUTHEAST ASIA**

Scale 1:12,000,000 at the Equator   Mercator Cylindrical Projection   Longitude East 110 of Greenwich

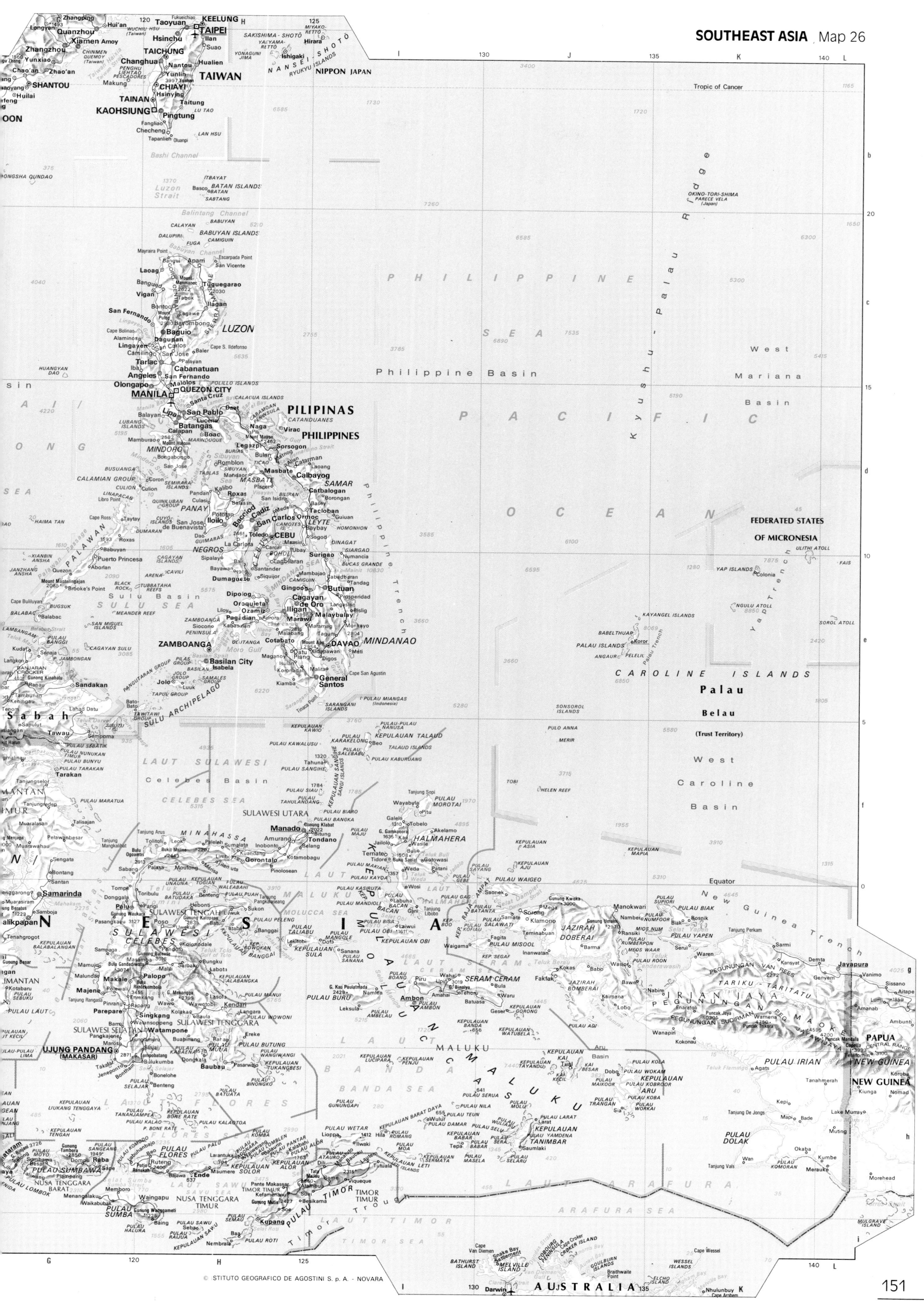

© ISTITUTO GEOGRAFICO DE AGOSTINI S. p. A - NOVARA

Map 27 **CHINA AND MONGOLIA**

Scale 1:12,000,000   Delisle Conic Equidistant Projection

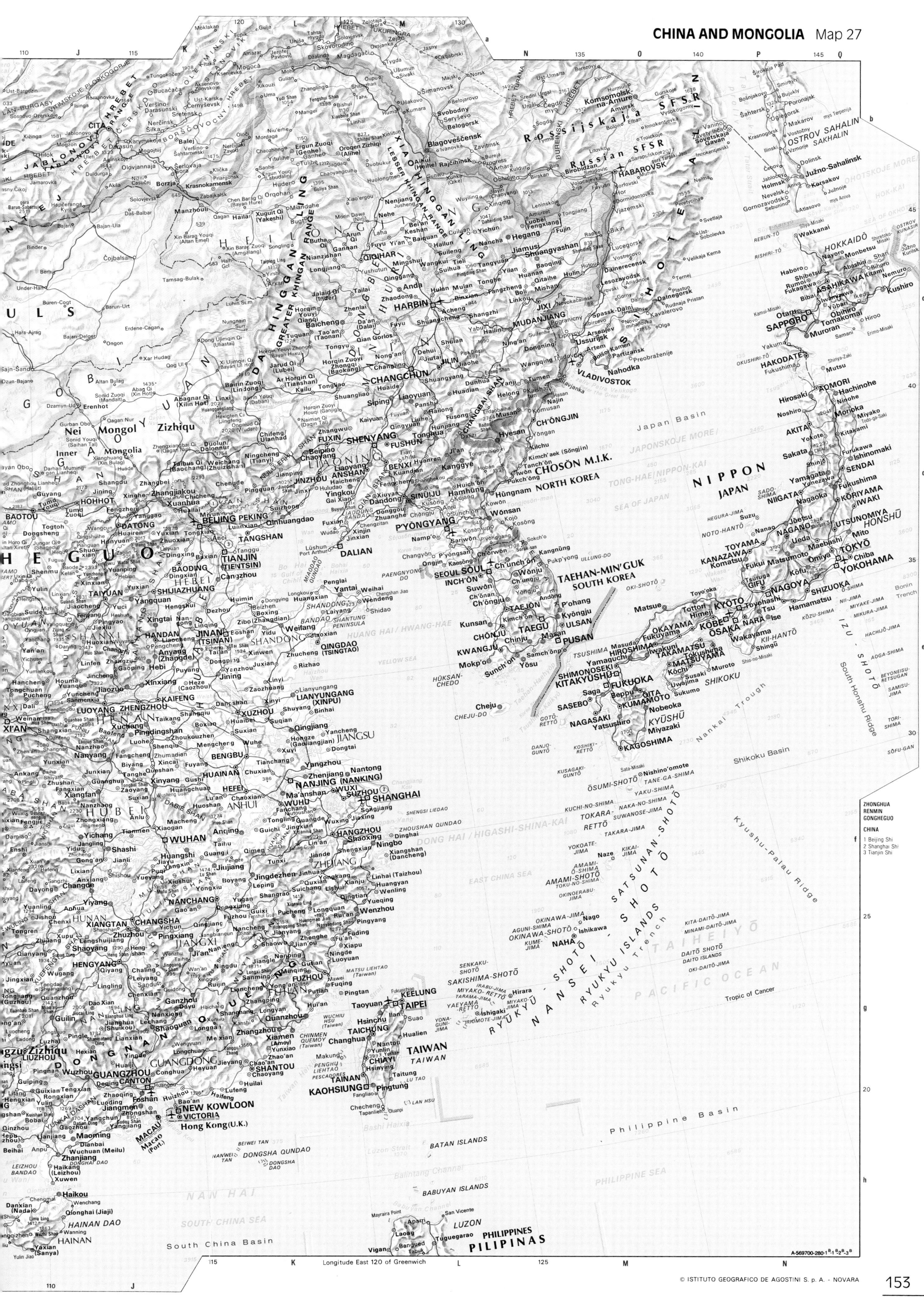

ROSSIJSKAJA SFSR
Russian SFSR

HEGUO

Nei Mongol Zizhiqu
Inner Mongolia

HEILONGJIANG

DA HINGGAN LING
GREATER KHINGAN RANGE

HARBIN

QIQIHAR

CHANGCHUN

JILIN

VLADIVOSTOK

SHENYANG
FUSHUN

ANSHAN

LIAONING

NORTH KOREA
CHOSÓN M.I.K.

PYONGYANG

HOHHOT

BAOTOU

DATONG

BEIJING PEKING

TANGSHAN

TIANJIN
(TIENTSIN)

HEBEI

BAODING

SHIJIAZHUANG

TAIYUAN

SHANXI

HANDAN

JINAN
(TSINAN)

SHANDONG

QINGDAO
(TSINGTAO)

SEOUL SOUL
INCH'ON

TAEHAN-MIN'GUK
SOUTH KOREA

TAEJON

TAEGU
PUSAN

NIPPON
JAPAN

HONSHŪ

SAPPORO

HOKKAIDŌ

XI'AN

LUOYANG ZHENGZHOU

HENAN

KAIFENG

XUZHOU

JIANGSU

HUBEI

WUHAN

ANHUI

HEFEI

NANJING (NANKING)

SUZHOU
SHANGHAI

HANGZHOU

ZHEJIANG

NANCHANG

HUNAN

JIANGXI

CHANGSHA

FUJIAN

FUZHOU

GUIZHOU

GUANGXI
ZHUANG

GUANGDONG

GUANGZHOU
CANTON

TAIPEI

TAICHUNG

TAIWAN
TAIWAN

KAOHSIUNG

NEW KOWLOON
VICTORIA
Hong Kong (U.K.)

MACAU
(Port.)

HAINAN

HAIKOU

HAINAN DAO

PACIFIC OCEAN

TAIHEIYŌ

RYUKYU ISLANDS
NANSEI-SHOTŌ

EAST CHINA SEA
DONG HAI / HIGASHI-SHINA-KAI

YELLOW SEA
HUANG HAI / HWANG-HAE

SEA OF JAPAN
JAPONSKOJE MORE

Japan Basin

SOUTH CHINA SEA
NAN HAI

PHILIPPINES
PILIPINAS

LUZON

Tropic of Cancer

ZHONGHUA
RENMIN
GONGHEGUO
CHINA

1 Beijing Shi
2 Shanghai Shi
3 Tianjin Shi

Map 28 **NORTHEASTERN CHINA, KOREA AND JAPAN**

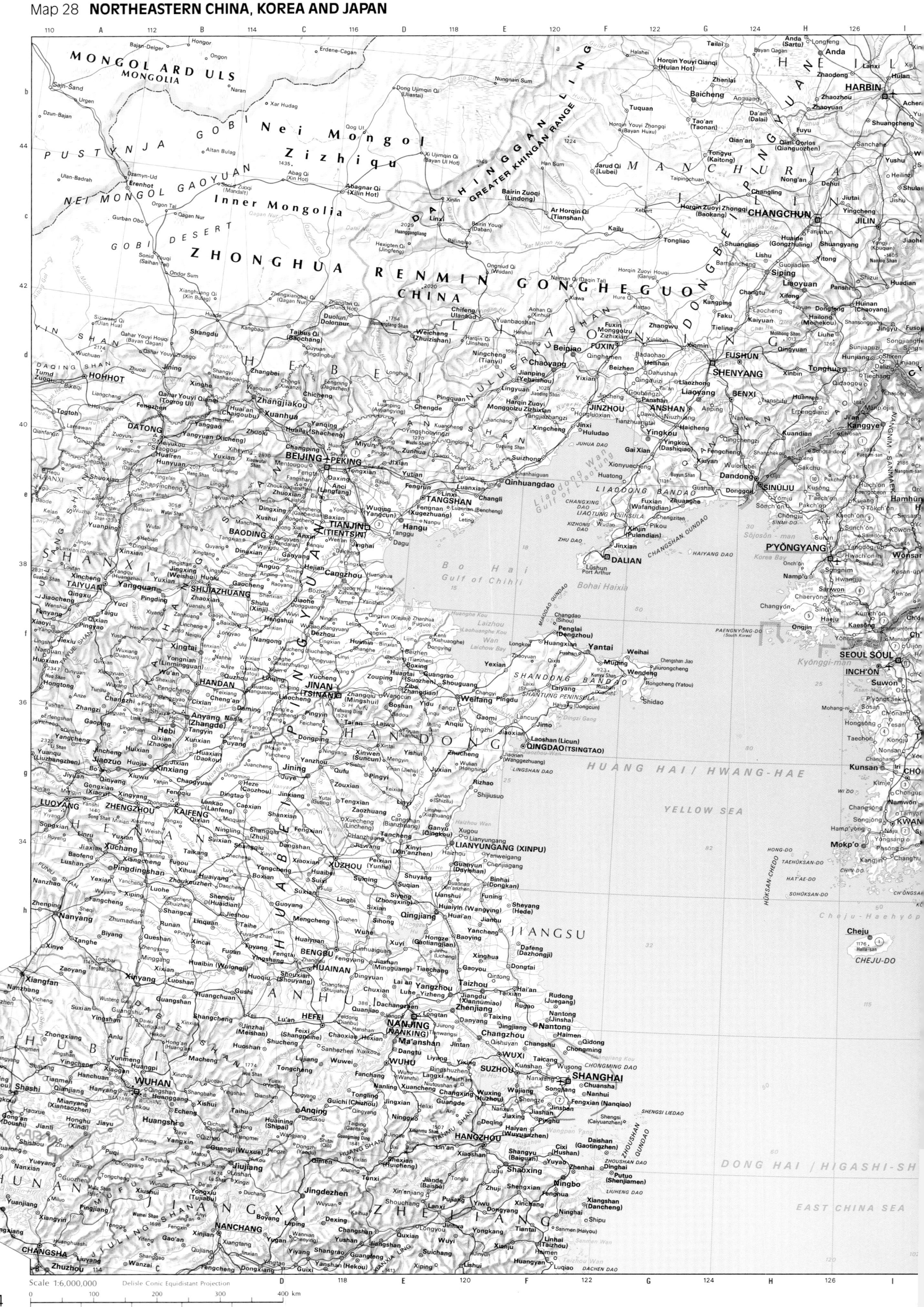

Scale 1:6,000,000   Delisle Conic Equidistant Projection

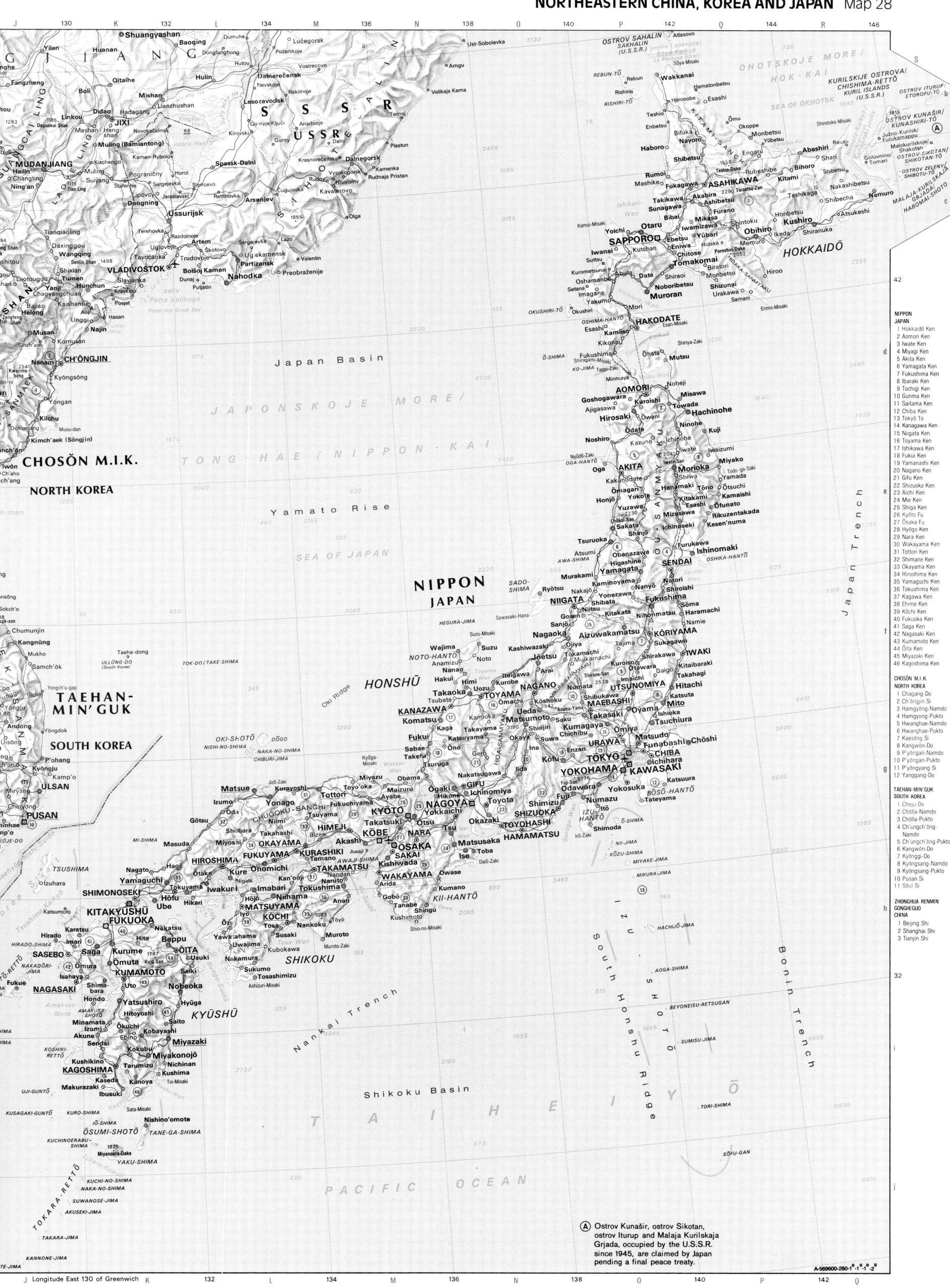

Map 29 **JAPAN**

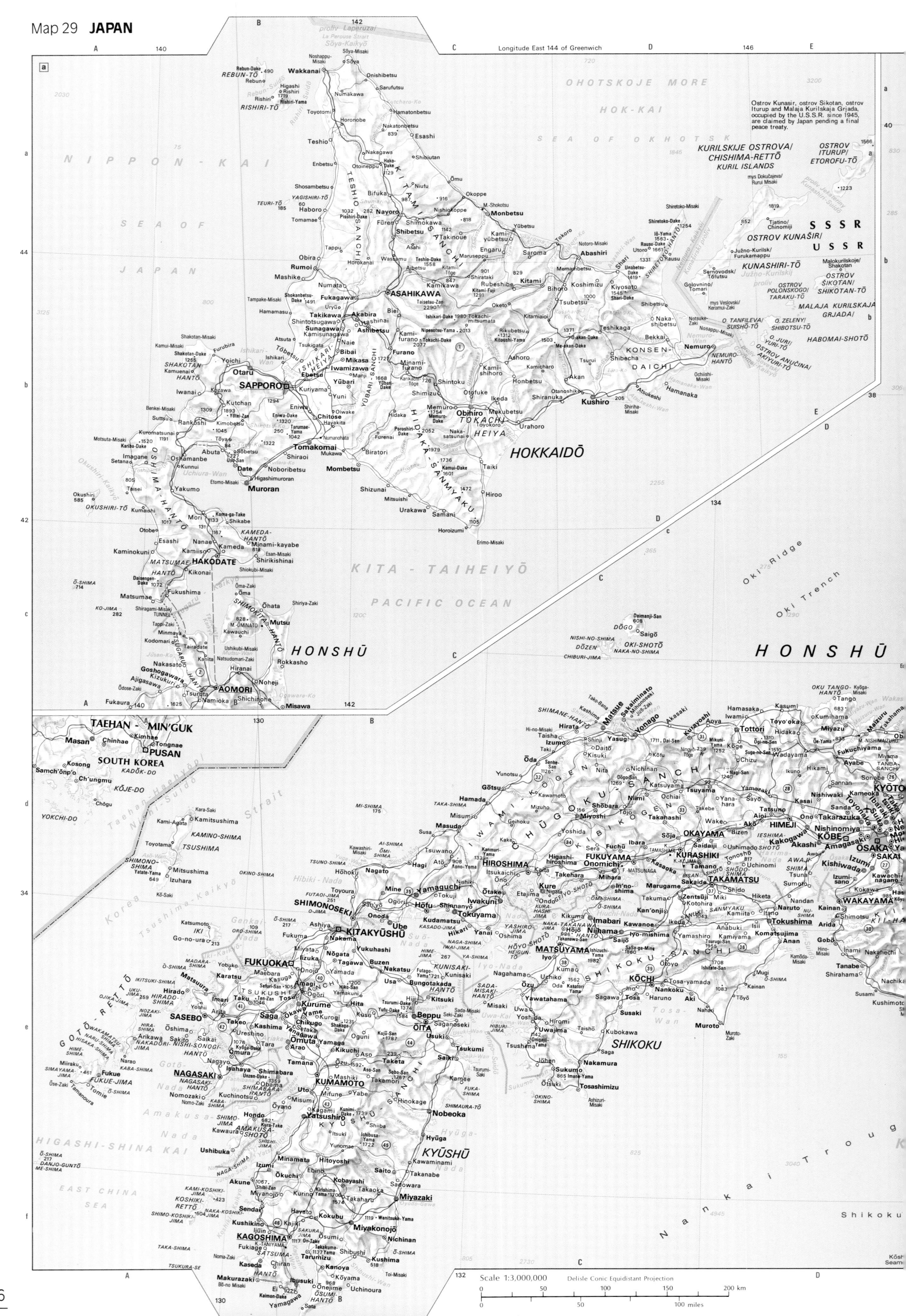

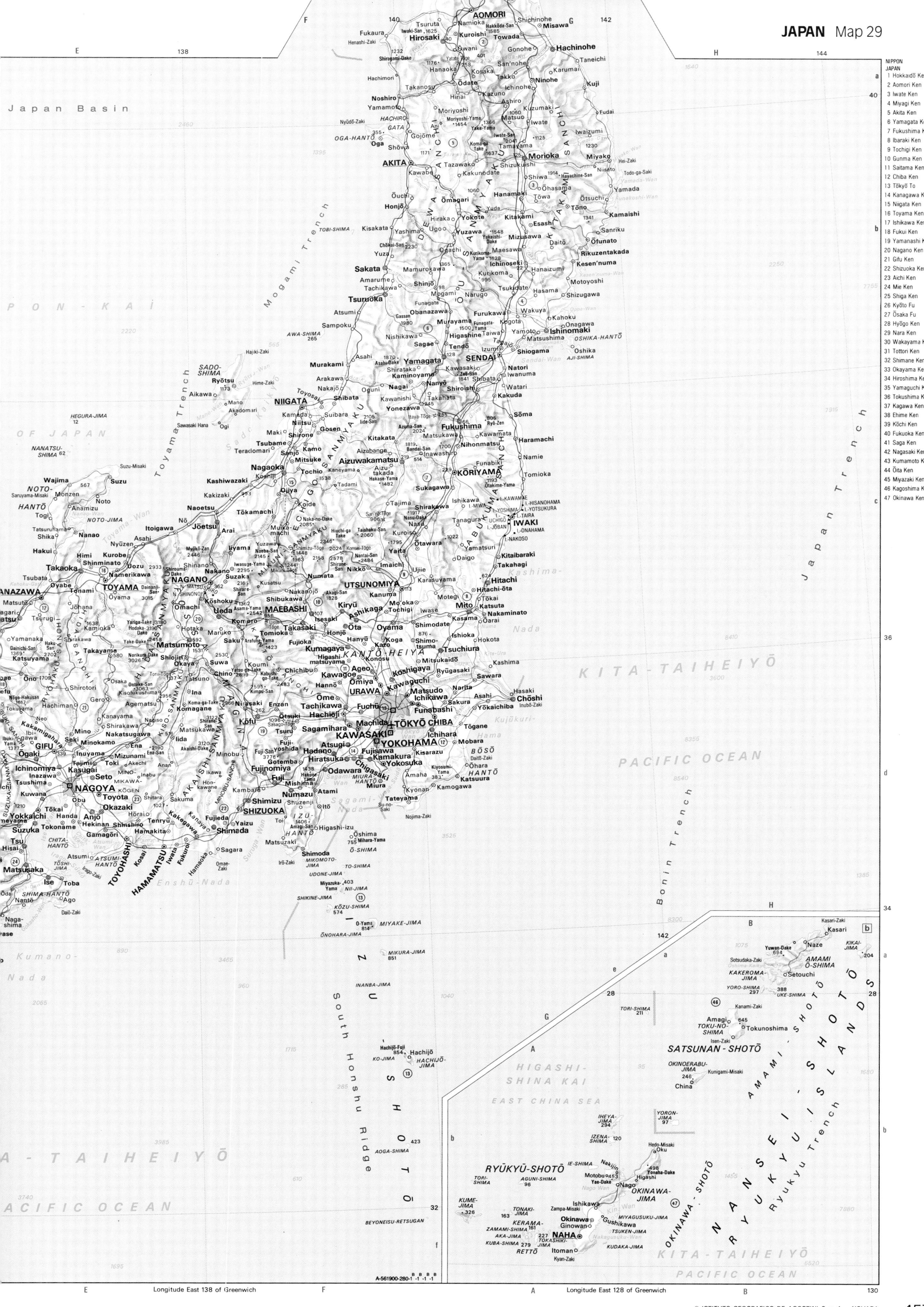

NIPPON
JAPAN
1 Hokkaidō Ken
2 Aomori Ken
3 Iwate Ken
4 Miyagi Ken
5 Akita Ken
6 Yamagata Ken
7 Fukushima Ken
8 Ibaraki Ken
9 Tochigi Ken
10 Gunma Ken
11 Saitama Ken
12 Chiba Ken
13 Tōkyō To
14 Kanagawa Ken
15 Niigata Ken
16 Toyama Ken
17 Ishikawa Ken
18 Fukui Ken
19 Yamanashi Ken
20 Nagano Ken
21 Gifu Ken
22 Shizuoka Ken
23 Aichi Ken
24 Mie Ken
25 Shiga Ken
26 Kyōto Fu
27 Ōsaka Fu
28 Hyōgo Ken
29 Nara Ken
30 Wakayama Ken
31 Tottori Ken
32 Shimane Ken
33 Okayama Ken
34 Hiroshima Ken
35 Yamaguchi Ken
36 Tokushima Ken
37 Kagawa Ken
38 Ehime Ken
39 Kōchi Ken
40 Fukuoka Ken
41 Saga Ken
42 Nagasaki Ken
43 Kumamoto Ken
44 Ōita Ken
45 Miyazaki Ken
46 Kagoshima Ken
47 Okinawa Ken

A-561900-280 -1 -1 -1

Map 30 **AFRICA, PHYSICAL**

Map 30

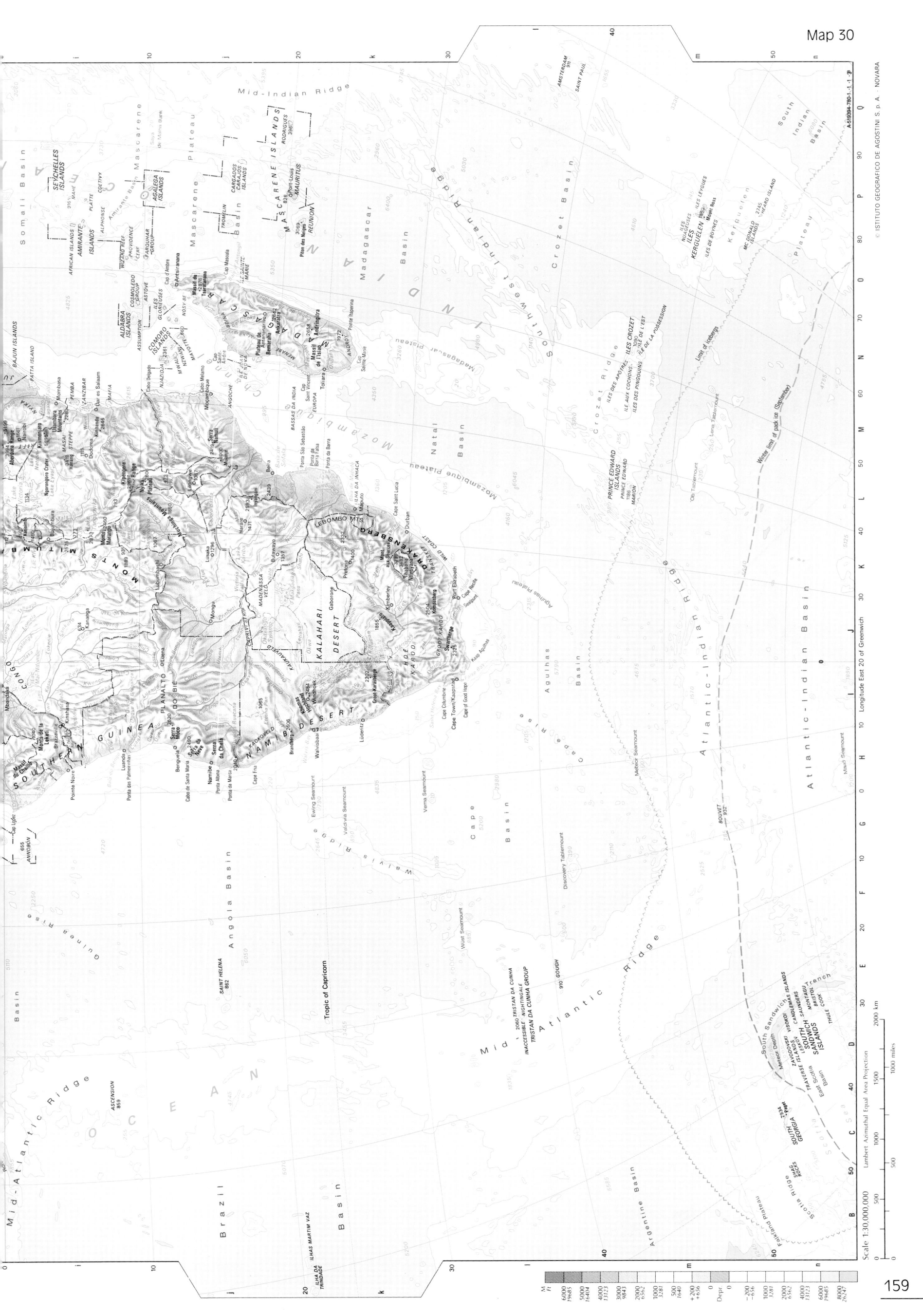

Map 31 **AFRICA, POLITICAL**

Map 31

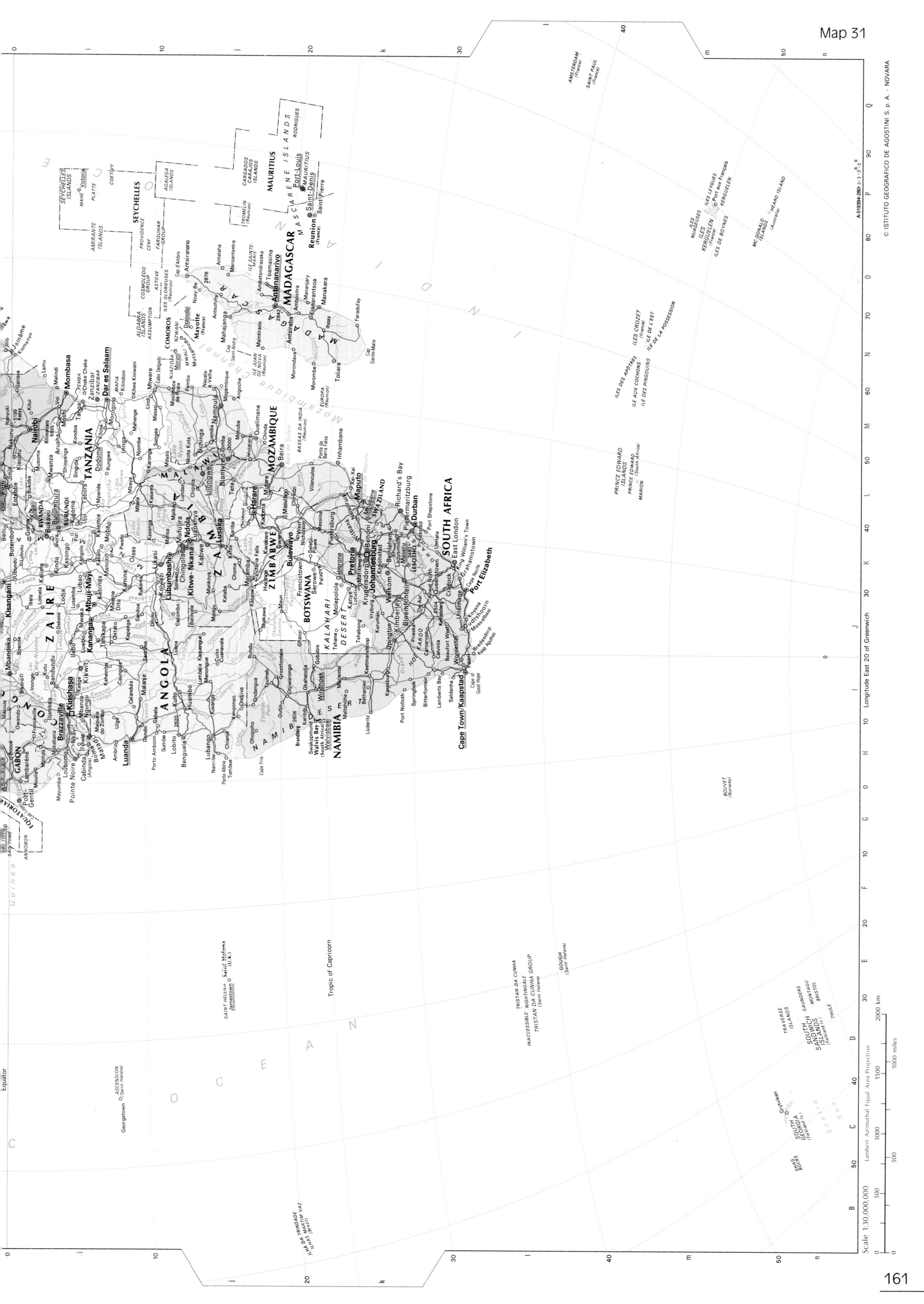

Map 32

AL JAZĀ'IR
ALGERIA

WILĀYATE
1 Adrar
2 Al Jazā'ir
3 Annaba
4 Batna
5 Béchar
6 Bejaia
7 Biskra
8 Blida
9 Bouira
10 Cheliff
11 Constantine
12 Djelfa
13 Guelma
14 Jijel
15 Laghouat
16 Mascara
17 Médéa
18 Mostaganem
19 M'Sila
20 Oran
21 Ouargla
22 Oum el Bouaghi
23 Saida
24 Setif
25 Sidi Bel Abbes
26 Skikda
27 Tamanrasset
28 Tebessa
29 Tiaret
30 Tizi Ouzou
31 Tlemcen

AL MAGHRIB
MOROCCO

PRÉFECTURES
A Casablanca
B Rabat-Salé

PROVINCES
1 Agadir
2 Al Hoceima
3 Ar Rachidiya
4 Azilal
5 Beni Mellal
6 Boulemane
7 Chechaouene
8 El Jadida
9 El Kelaa des Srarhna
10 Essaouira
11 Fes
12 Figuig
13 Kenitra
14 Khemisset
15 Khenifra
16 Khouribga
17 Marrakech
18 Meknes
19 Nador
20 Ouarzazate
21 Oujda
22 Safi
23 Settat
24 Tanger
25 Tan Tan
26 Taounate
27 Tata
28 Taza
29 Tetouan
30 Tiznit

TŪNIS
TUNISIA

WILĀYATE
1 Al Kāf
2 Al Mahdīyah
3 Al Munastīr
4 Al Qaşrayn
5 Al Qayrawān
6 Bājah
7 Bizerte
8 Jundūbah
9 Madanīyin
10 Nābul
11 Qābis
12 Qafşah
13 Qamūdah
14 Şafāqis
15 Silyānah
16 Sūsah
17 Tūnis
18 Zaghwān

CORVO
941 Santa Cruz
FLORES
ANGRA DO HEROÍSMO
HORTA
Santa Cruz
411 GRACIOSA
FAIAL Velas SÃO TERCEIRA
1021 2320 JORGE 1066
Horta PICO Lajes do Pico
Açores Angra do Heroísmo
(Portugal) Azores
SÃO MIGUEL
1105
Ponta Delgada
Vila Franca do Campo
PONTA DELGADA
FORMIGAS
590 SANTA MARIA
Vila do Porto

ARQUIPÉLAGO DOS AÇORES

Iberian Basin

OCEANO ATLÂNTICO/

Azores-Gibraltar Ridge

Josephine Seamount

Gettysburg Seamount

Ampère Seamount

Seewarte Seamounts

Seine Seamount

Great Meteor Tablemount

Porto Moniz
MADEIRA 1861 PORTO SANTO
Funchal ILHAS DESERTAS
ARQUIPÉLAGO DA MADEIRA
MADEIRA ISLANDS
Madeira
(Portugal)

Dacia Seamount

AL BAHR AL MUHĪT/

ILHAS SELVAGENS

Islas Canarias
Canary Islands
(Spain)

ALEGRANZA
GRACIOSA
676 LANZAROTE
Arrecife
LOBOS
Puerto del Rosario
FUERTEVENTURA
Gran Tarajal
Cap Juby

Los Llanos de Aridane
LA PALMA
Santa Cruz de la Palma
Santa Cruz de Tenerife
2423 TENERIFE 3715
SANTA CRUZ DE TENERIFE
GOMERA 1481 Puerto de la Cruz
Valverde San Sebastián de la Gomera
HIERRO
ISLAS CANARIAS
CANARY ISLANDS
Gáldar
LAS PALMAS
807
1949 Las Palmas de Gran Canaria
GRAN CANARIA

AL MAGHRIB
MOROCCO

Safi
Essaouira
Cap Sim
Agadir
Tiznit
Sidi Ifni
Goulimine
Cap Drâa
Tan Tan Plage
Tan Tan
Tarfaya

CA
Az
El Ja

Canary Basin

OCÉAN ATLANTIQUE

Echo Seamount

Tropic of Cancer

ATLANTIC OCEAN

El Aaiún
Hagunia
Edchera
SAGUIA EL-HAMRA
Hausa Echdeiria
Metmahag Semara
Bu Craa Bir Lehlú

Lemsid
Cabo Bojador
Cabo Bojador

Western
Sahara

ZEMMOUR
TIRIS ZEMMOUR

Taguersimet
Bir Enzarán
Dakhla RÍO DE ORO
Punta Durnford El Aargub
Imilili Bahía del Rio de Oro
Golfo de Cintra
Hási Ausert
Cabo Barbas Agüenit
Ederick Zoulrât
AGUERGUER Kedia d'Idjil
Bir Gandús Tourine
Tichla Touâjil
Zug Char
Boû Lahober
Nouâdhibou DAKHLET
Gǔera
Râs Nouâdhibou NOUÂDHIBOU
Cap Blanc
ÎLE TIDRA
Cap Timiris INCHIRI
Nouamrhar Akjoujt
Tiouilit Bennichab
Boû Rjeimat

Nouakchott
DISTRICT DE NOUAKCHOTT
Idini
Bella

MŪRĪTĀNIYĀ
MAURITANIA

TAGANT
Tamassoumit
Moudjéria
Nimjad Boutilimit
Nbâk Magta Lahjar
TRARZA Aleg
Tiguent
Mederdra BRAKNA
Keur Massène Boghé
Rosso Podor
Richard Toll Dagana
Saint-Louis Kaédi
GORGOL
Ngoui
Louga FOUTA Matam
Darou Khoudos Maghama
Kébémer Linguère Ranérou
Tivaouane Dahra
Thiès Mékhé
Bambey FERLO
Diourbel
DAKAR Mbacké
Rufisque Mbour
Fatick SÉNÉGAL
Joal-Fadiout
Kaolack Kaffrine
Guinguinéo
Koumpentoum

HODH
DAHR TICHIT
Ouadane
Chinguetti
Atar ADRAR
Oujeft
Chinguetti
620
Choūm
MAKTEÎR
Oualâta
HODH ECH CHARGUI
Néma
KOUMBI-SALEH
Mbout
Kankossa
Kiffa
ASSABA
Kobenni
Timbédra
Aïoun el 'Atroûs
Guerou
GUIDIMAKA
Sélibaby
Yélimané
Kayes
Nioro du Sahel
Nara

SANTO ANTÃO
1979 Ribeira Grande
Porto Novo BARLAVENTO
Mindelo SÃO VICENTE
SANTA LUZIA Ribeira Brava
BRANCO 1304 SÃO NICOLAU 406
RAZO Sal-Rei Pedra Lume
BOA VISTA SAL
387 Curral-Velho
Cape Verde Terrace
ILHAS DO CABO VERDE
CAPE VERDE ISLANDS
CAPE VERDE
ILHÉUS SECOS Tarrafal MAIO
Nova Sintra FOGO 436 Maio
2829 1423
BRAVA Praia
São Filipe SÃO TIAGO
SOTAVENTO
Cap Vert
Cape Verde

A Western Sahara is occupied by Morocco.

A-589791-280-1

Scale 1:9,000,000   Lambert Azimuthal Equal Area Projection
0   200   400   600 km
0   200 miles

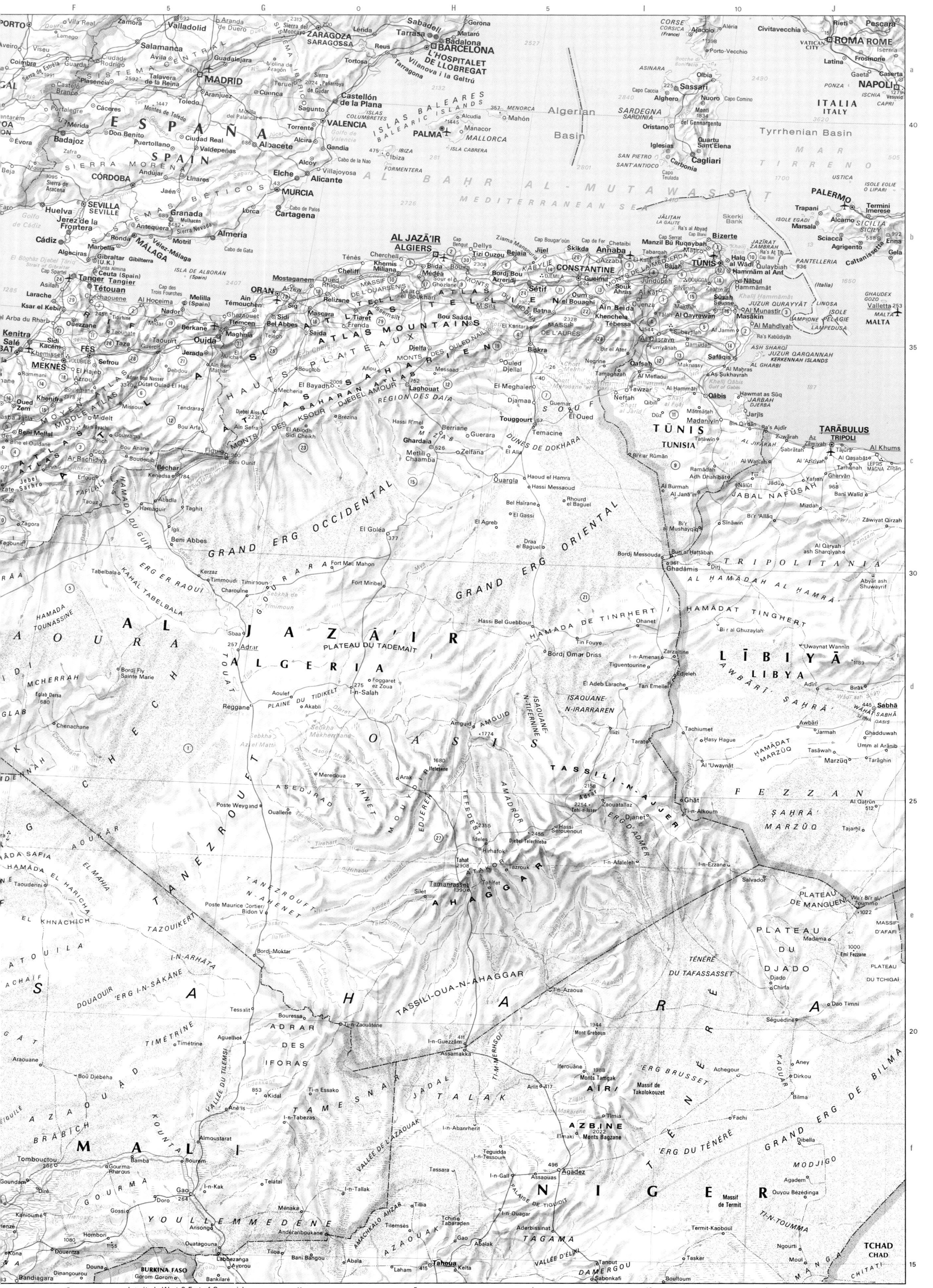

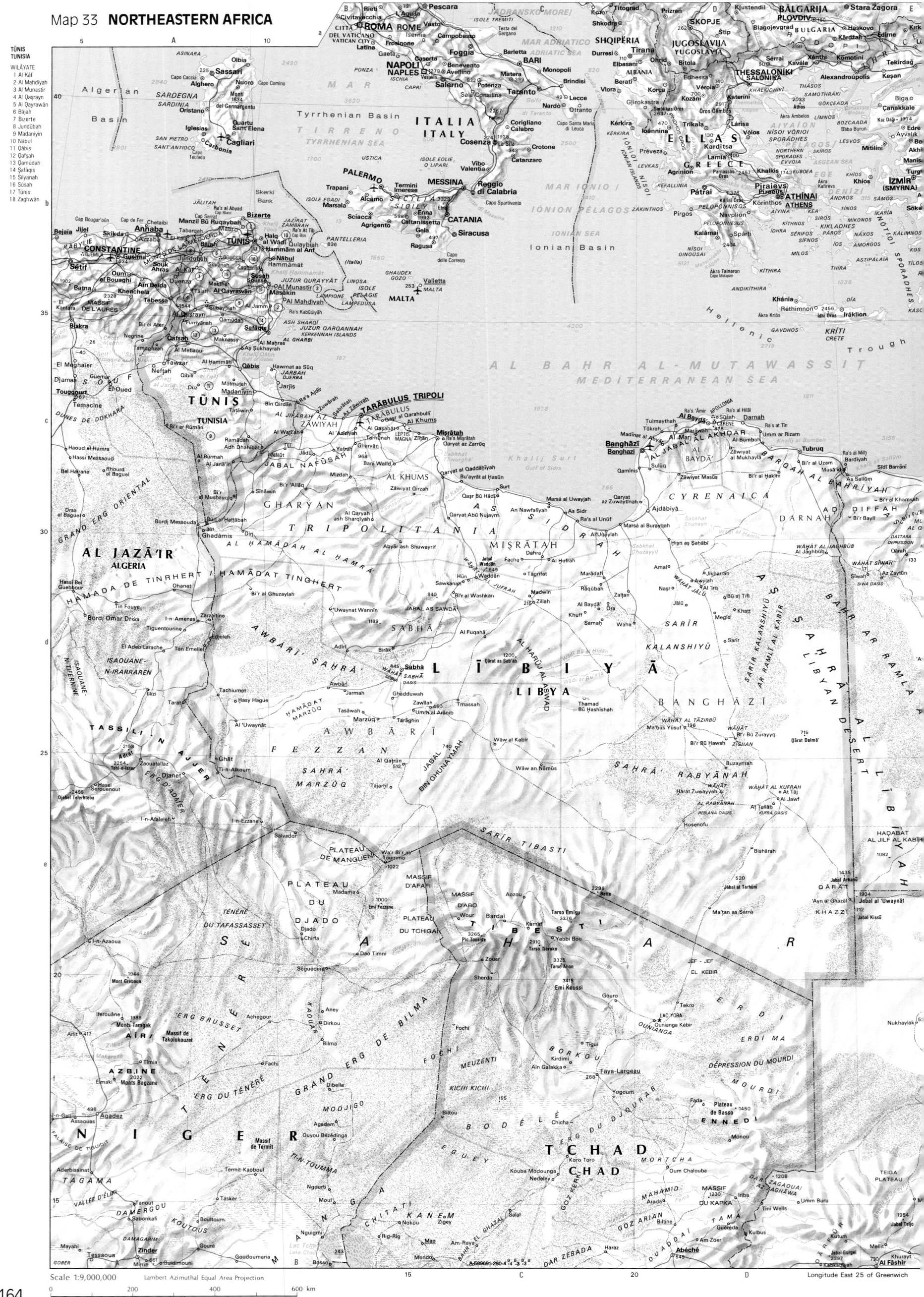

Map 33 **NORTHEASTERN AFRICA**

Scale 1:9,000,000 Lambert Azimuthal Equal Area Projection

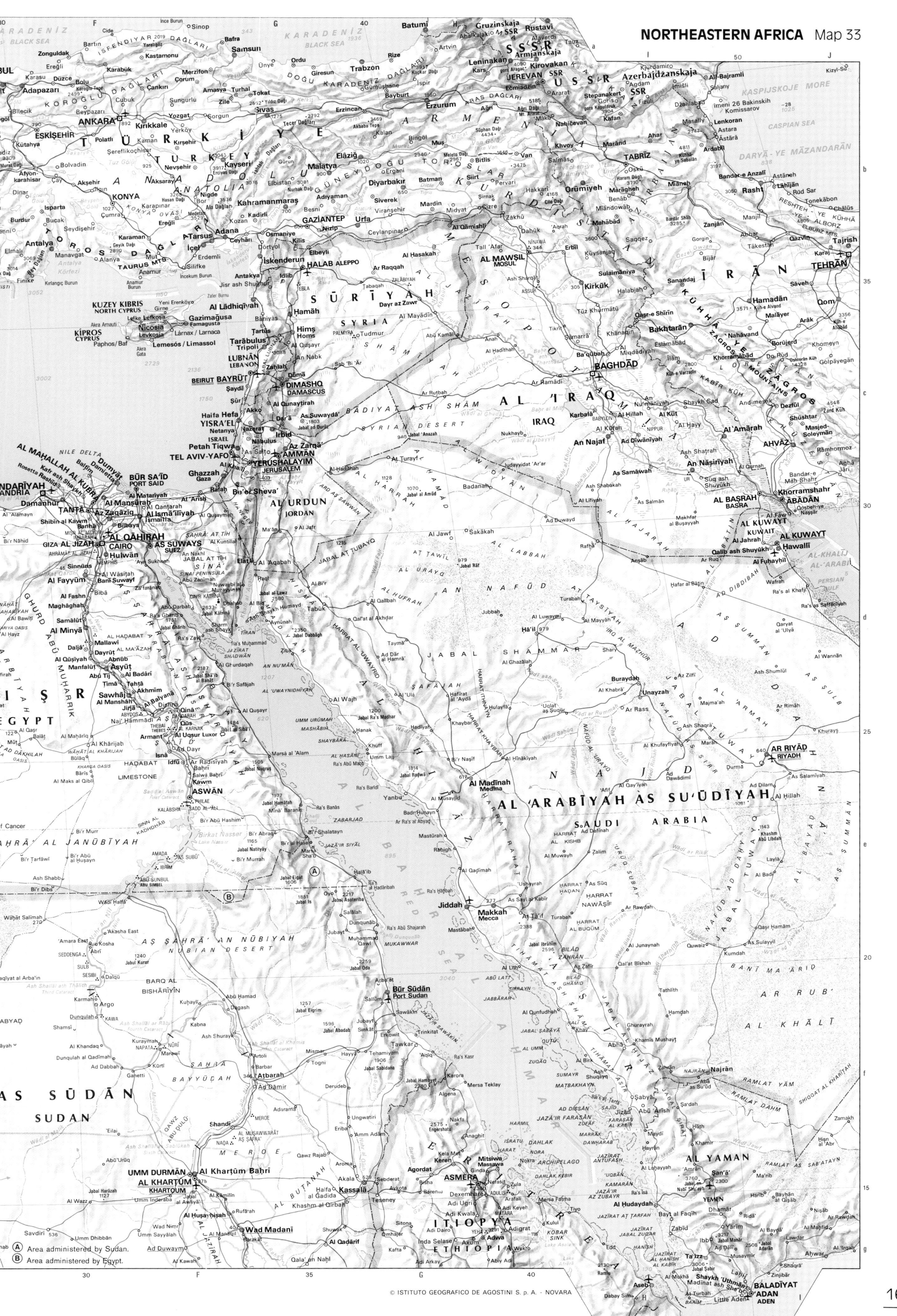

Ⓐ Area administered by Sudan.
Ⓑ Area administered by Egypt.

© ISTITUTO GEOGRAFICO DE AGOSTINI S.p.A. - NOVARA

Map 34 **WEST-CENTRAL AFRICA**

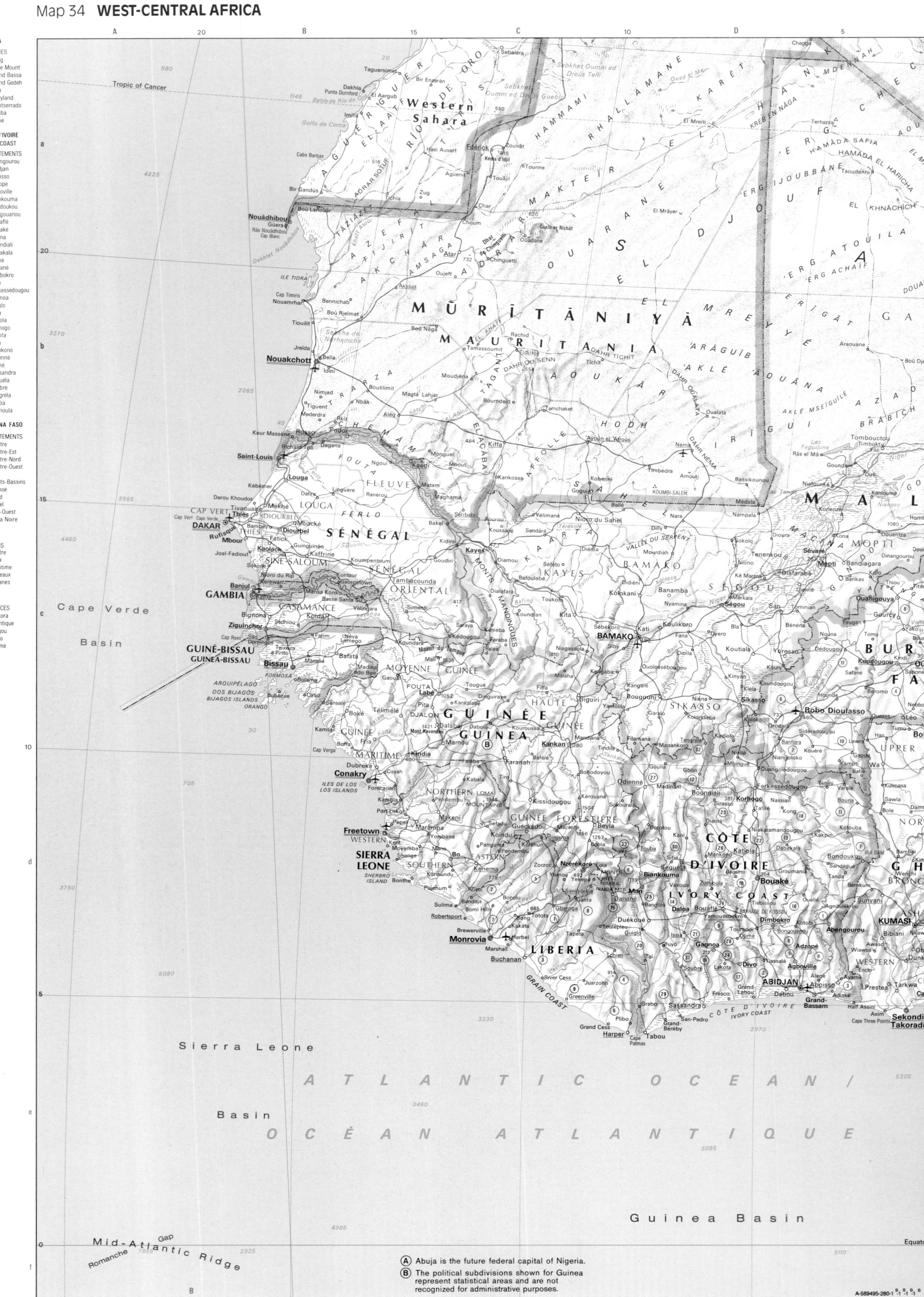

LIBERIA
COUNTIES
1 Bong
2 Cape Mount
3 Grand Bassa
4 Grand Gedeh
5 Lofa
6 Maryland
7 Montserrado
8 Nimba
9 Sinoe

CÔTE D'IVOIRE
IVORY COAST
DÉPARTEMENTS
1 Abengourou
2 Abidjan
3 Aboisso
4 Adzopé
5 Agboville
6 Biankouma
7 Bondoukou
8 Bongouanou
9 Bouaflé
10 Bouake
11 Bouna
12 Boundiali
13 Dabakala
14 Daloa
15 Danané
16 Dimbokro
17 Divo
18 Ferkessédougou
19 Gagnoa
20 Guiglo
21 Issia
22 Katiola
23 Korhogo
24 Lakota
25 Man
26 Mankono
27 Odienné
28 Oumé
29 Sassandra
30 Séguéla
31 Soubré
32 Tengréla
33 Touba
34 Zuenoula

BURKINA FASO
DÉPARTEMENTS
1 Centre
2 Centre-Est
3 Centre-Nord
4 Centre-Ouest
5 Est
6 Hauts-Bassins
7 Komoé
8 Nord
9 Sahel
10 Sud-Ouest
11 Volta Noire

TOGO
RÉGIONS
1 Centre
2 Kara
3 Maritime
4 Plateaux
5 Savanes

BÉNIN
PROVINCES
1 Atakora
2 Atlantique
3 Borgou
4 Mono
5 Ouémé
6 Zou

Ⓐ Abuja is the future federal capital of Nigeria.

Ⓑ The political subdivisions shown for Guinea represent statistical areas and are not recognized for administrative purposes.

Scale 1:9,000,000   Lambert Azimuthal Equal Area Projection

Longitude West 5 of Greenwich

A-589495-280-1

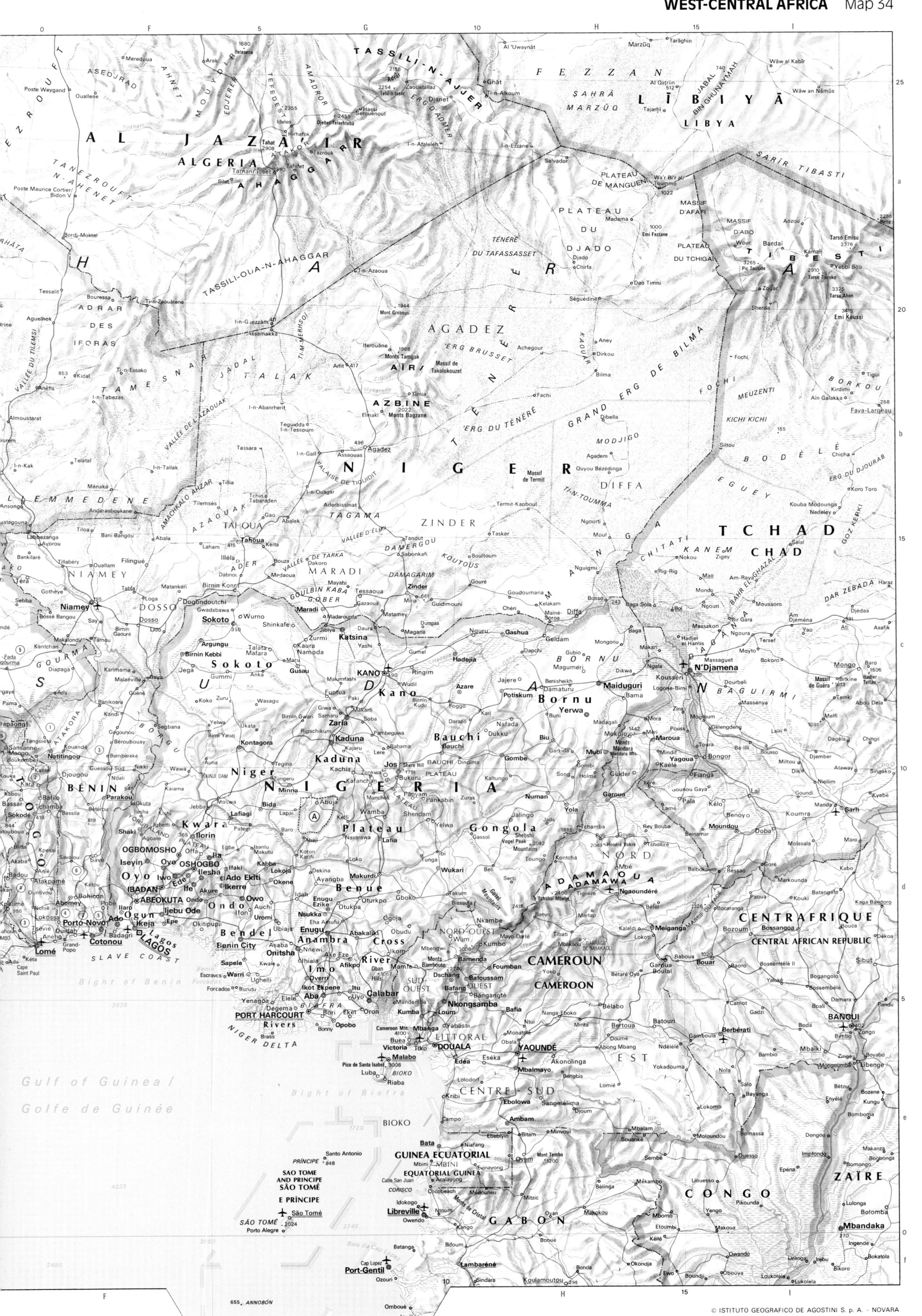

Map 35 **EAST-CENTRAL AFRICA**

Map 36 **EQUATORIAL AFRICA**

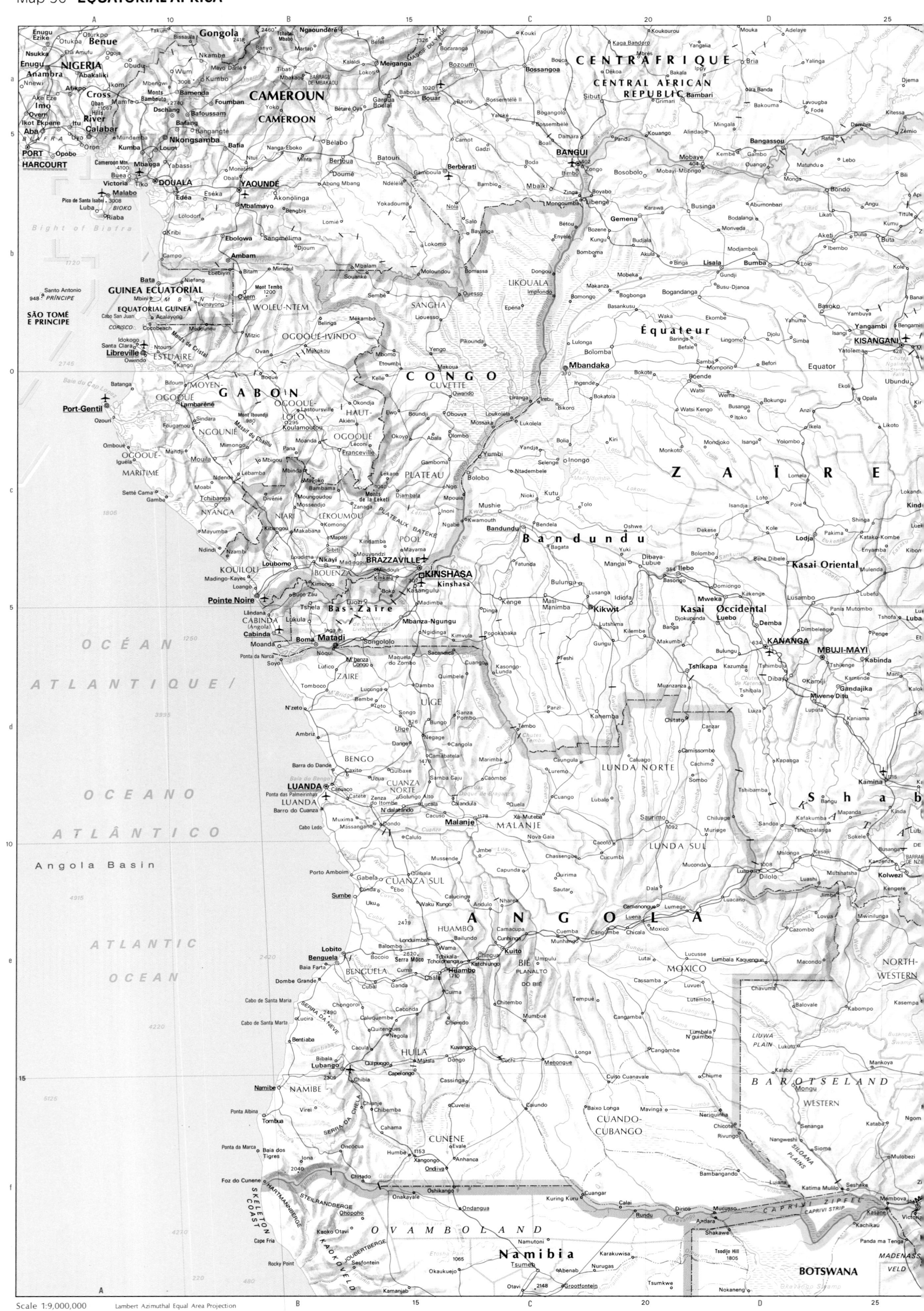

Scale 1:9,000,000   Lambert Azimuthal Equal Area Projection

0   200   400   600 km

0   200 miles

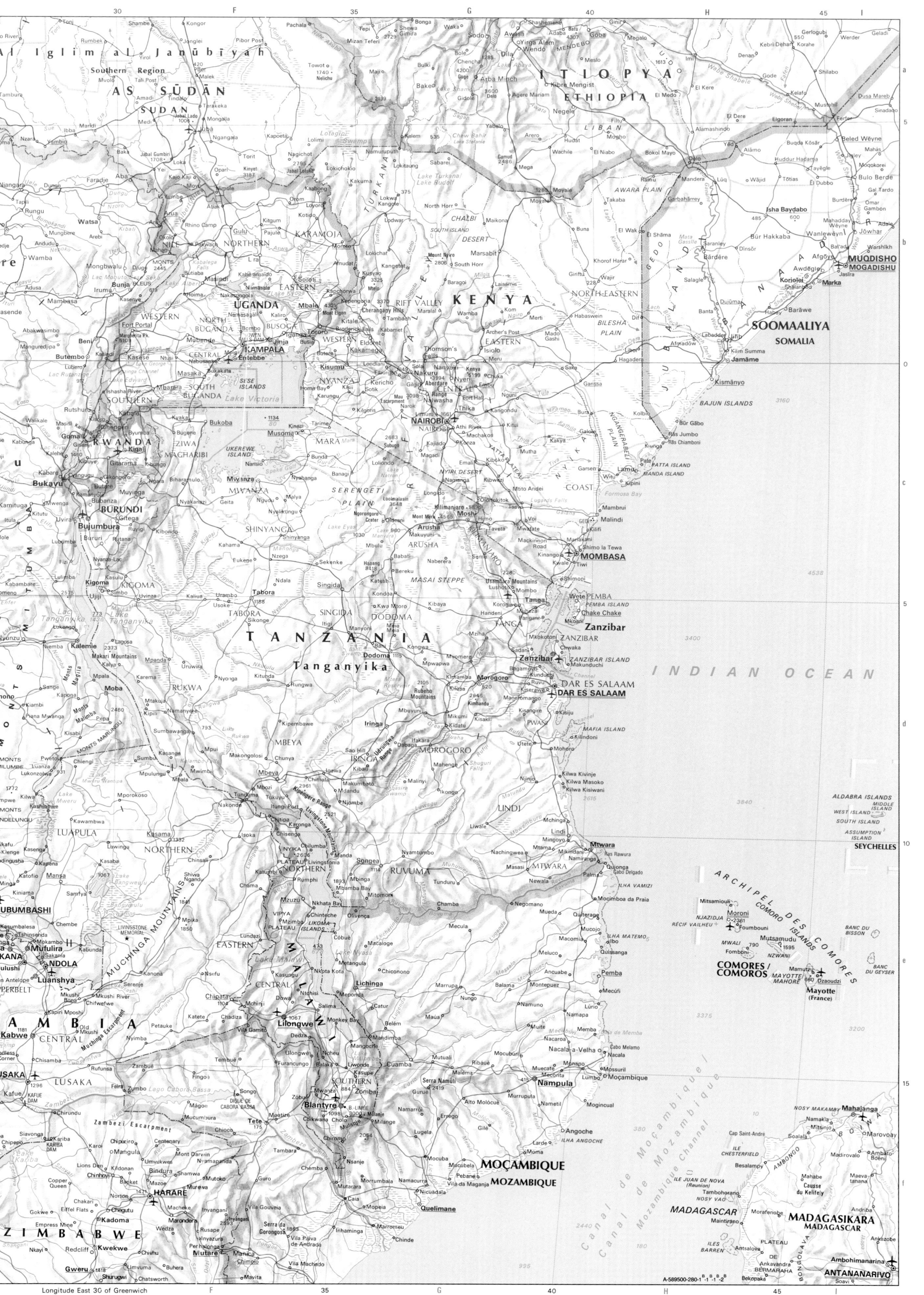

Map 37 **SOUTHERN AFRICA**

Scale 1:9,000,000   Lambert Azimuthal Equal Area Projection

Longitude East 25 of Greenwich

0   200   400   600 km

0   200 miles

OCEANO INDICO / OCÉAN INDIEN

INDIAN OCEAN / INDIESE OSEAAN

Natal Basin

Mozambique Plateau

Madagascar Plateau

MOÇAMBIQUE
MOZAMBIQUE

MADAGASCAR

MADAGASIKARA
MADAGASCAR

COMORES /
COMOROS

SEYCHELLES

Amirante Basin

INDIAN OCEAN

SEYCHELLES ISLANDS

SEYCHELLES

AMIRANTE ISLANDS

MAURITIUS

ILES MASCAREIGNES/
MASCARENE ISLANDS

Réunion
(France)

Longitude East 50 of Greenwich

Map 38 **NORTH AMERICA, PHYSICAL**

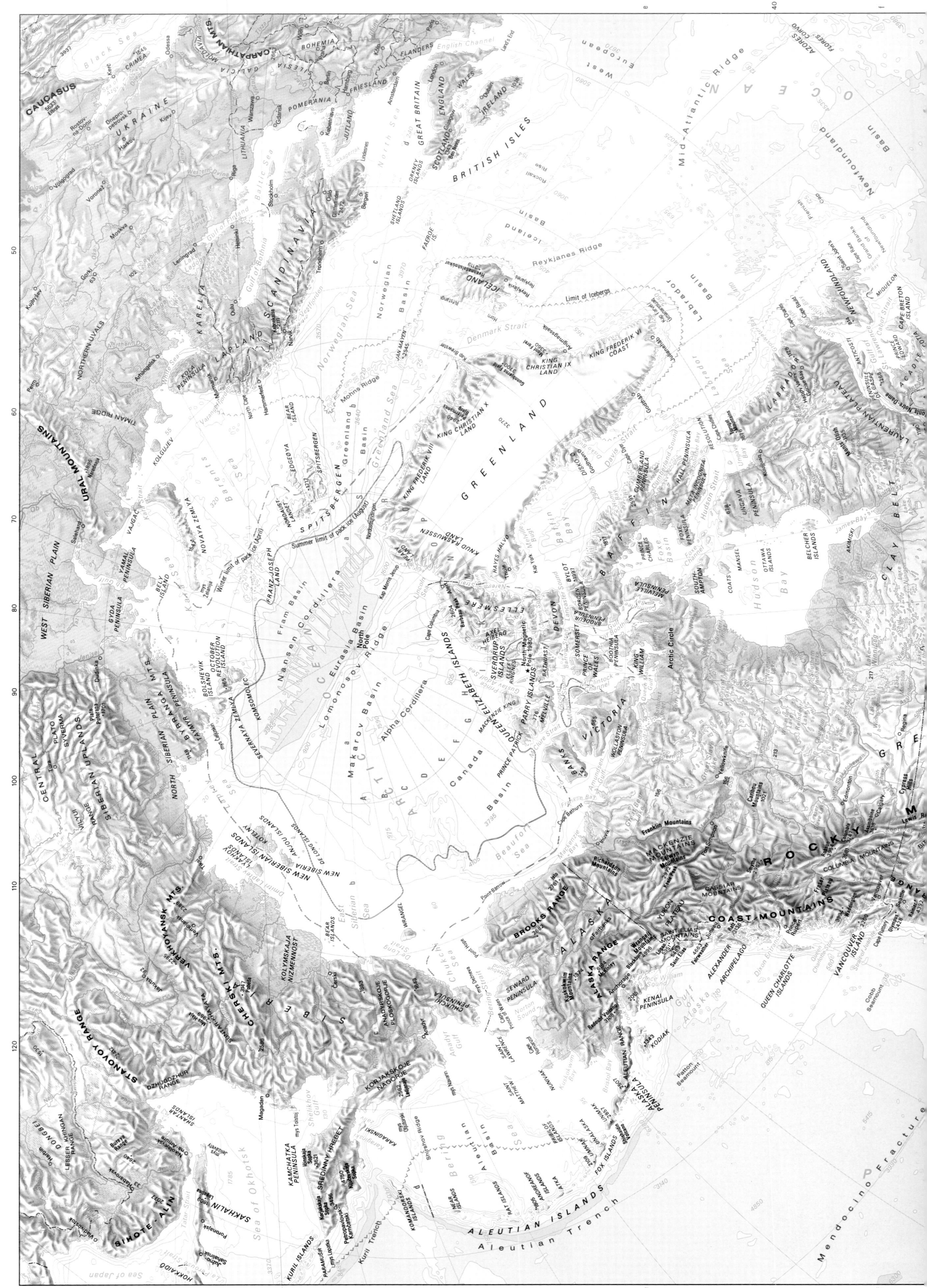

Map 39 **NORTH AMERICA, POLITICAL**

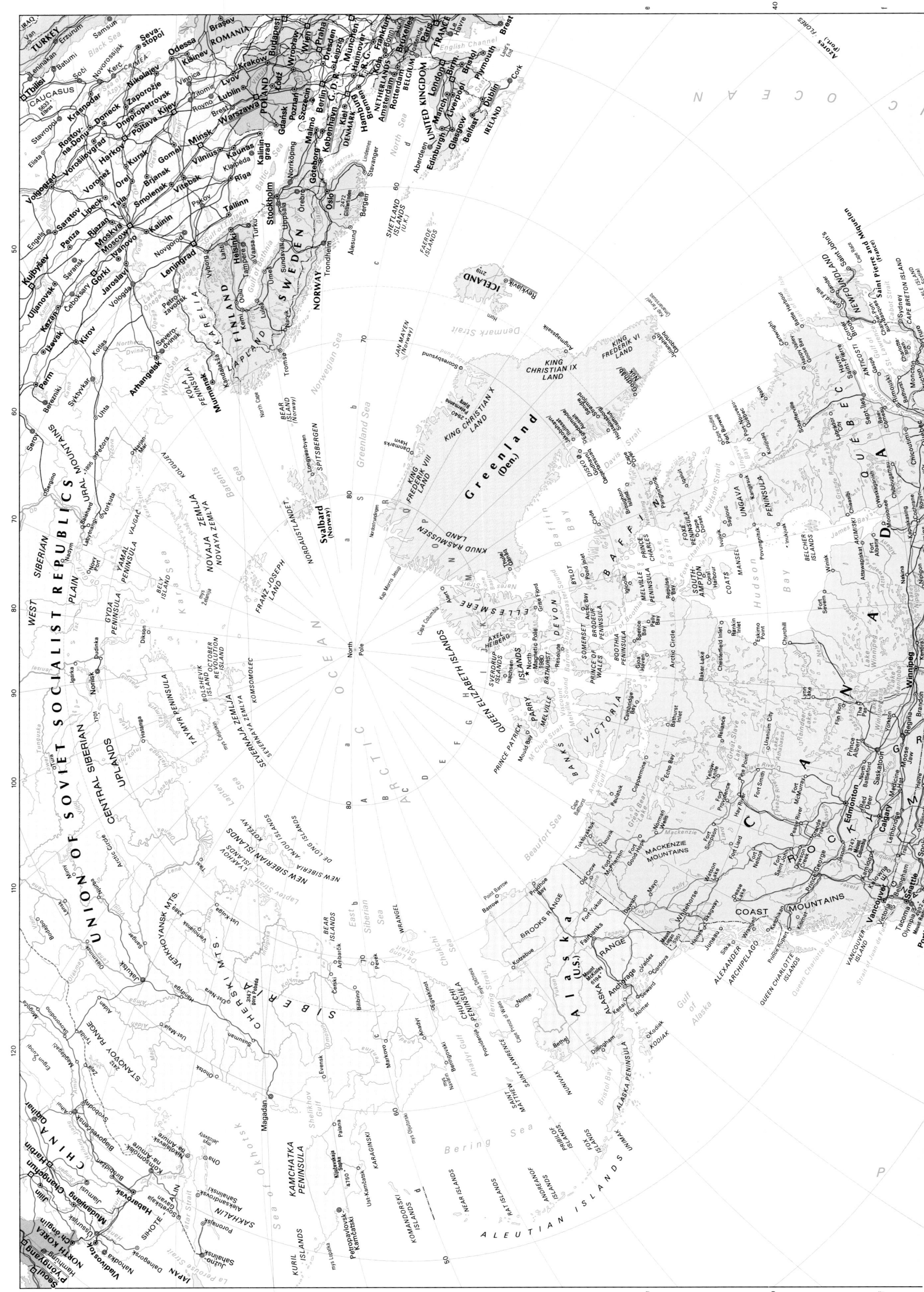

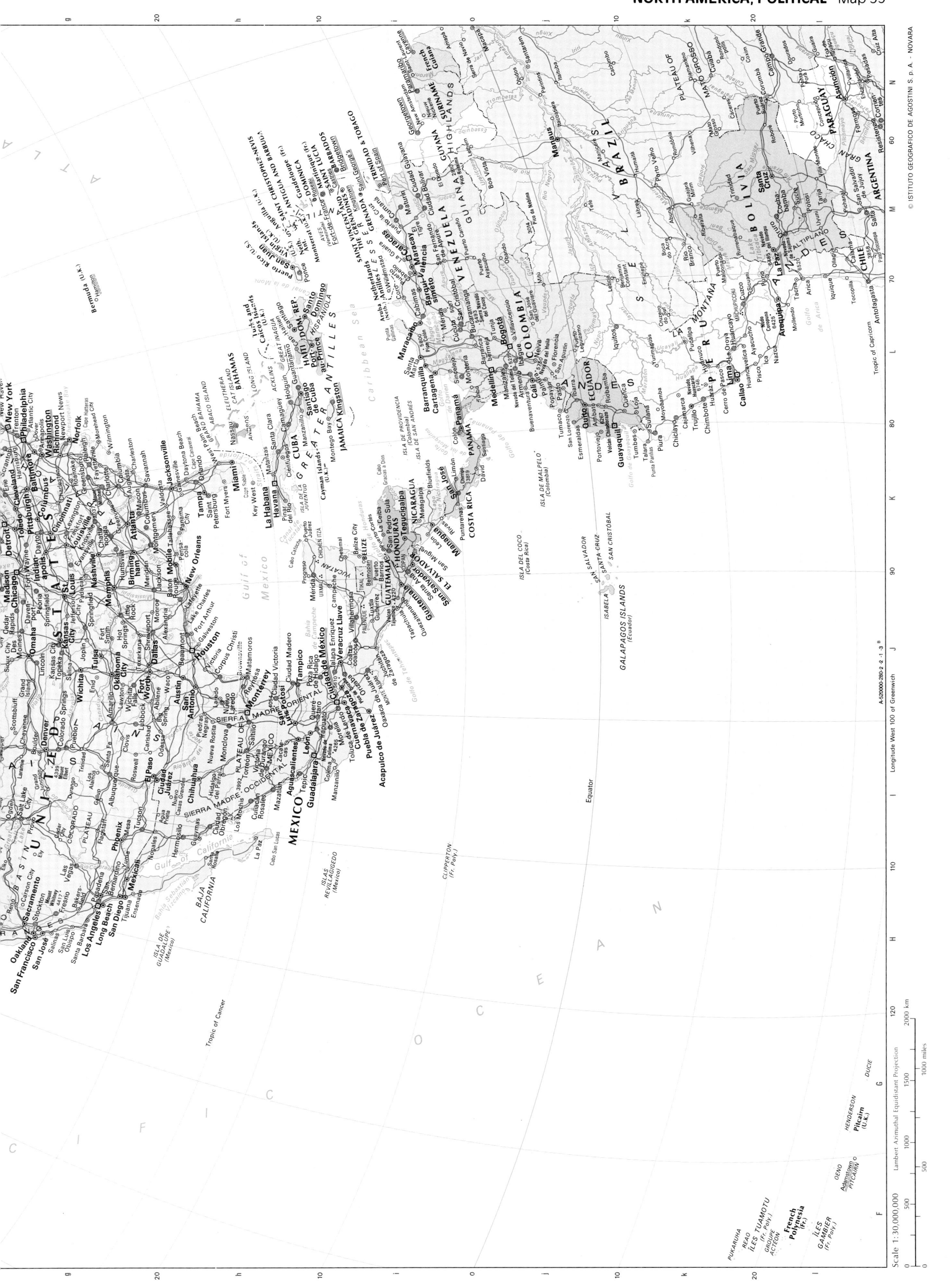

Scale 1:30,000,000

Lambert Azimuthal Equidistant Projection

Longitude West 100 of Greenwich

A-500000-280/2 -2 -1 -3 B

Map 40 **ALASKA**

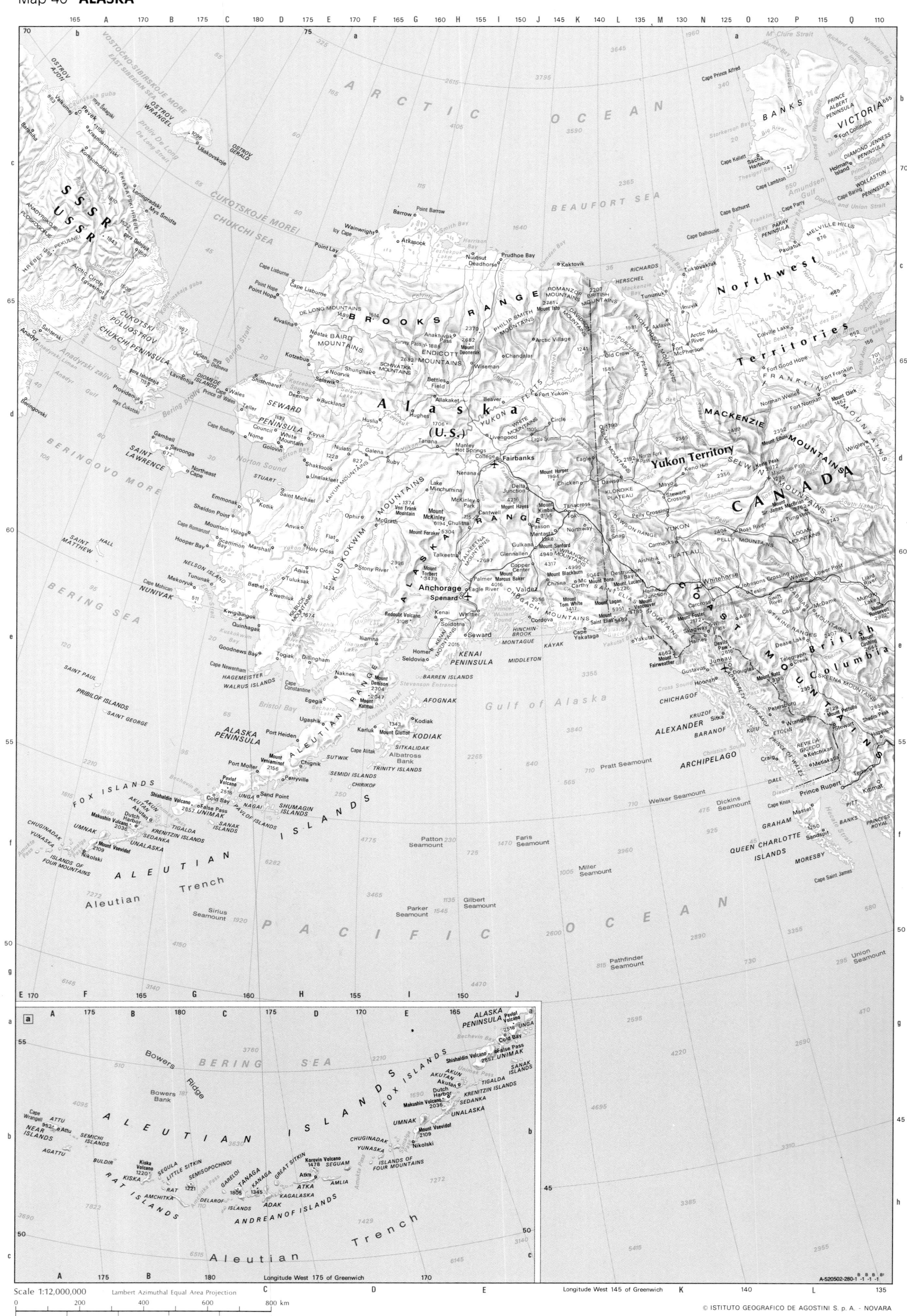

Scale 1:12,000,000   Lambert Azimuthal Equal Area Projection

0   200   400   600   800 km

0   200   400 miles

© ISTITUTO GEOGRAFICO DE AGOSTINI S. p. A. - NOVARA

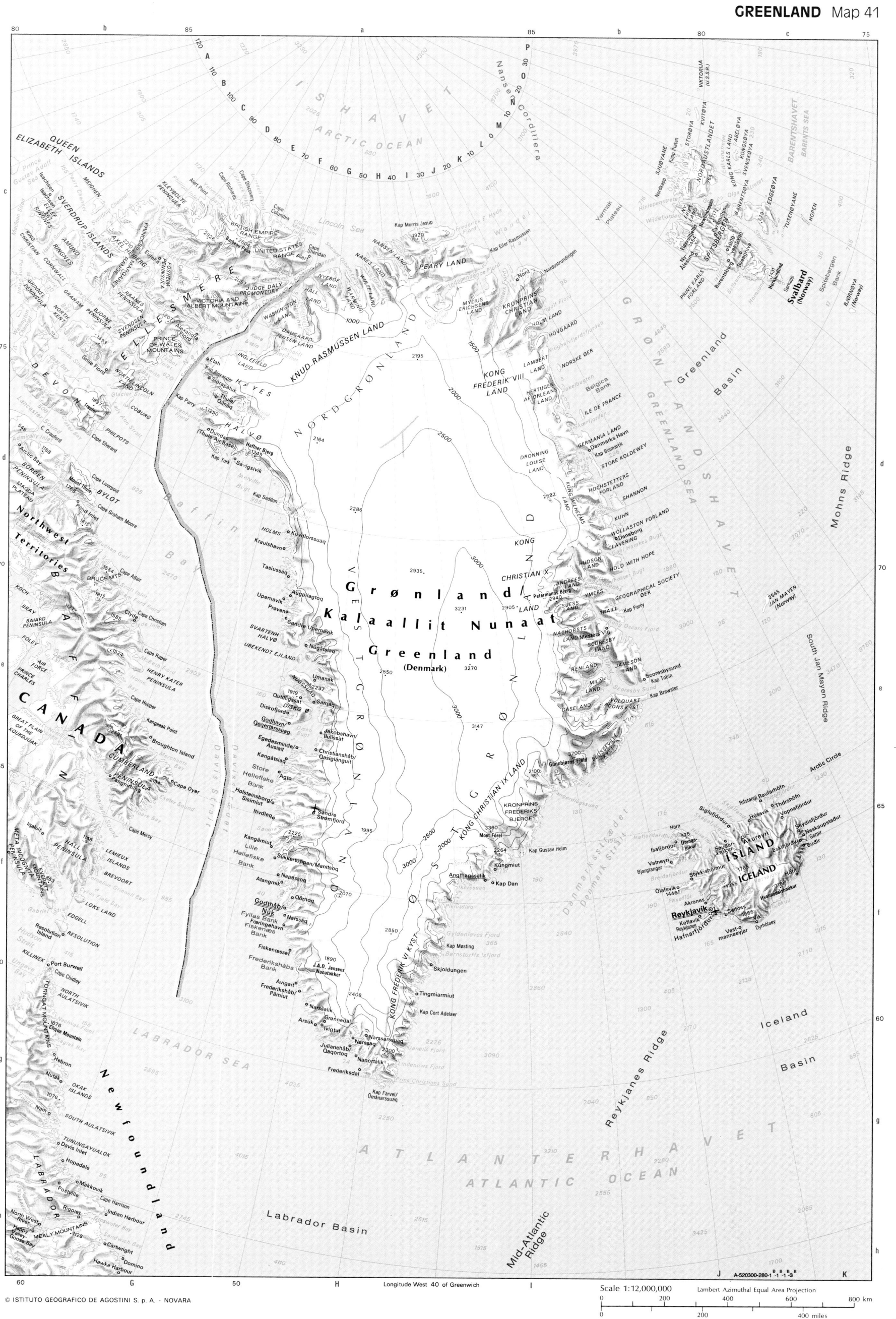

Scale 1:12,000,000   Lambert Azimuthal Equal Area Projection

Map 42 **CANADA**

Scale 1:12,000,000   Lambert Azimuthal Equal Area Projection

Longitude West 100 of Greenwich

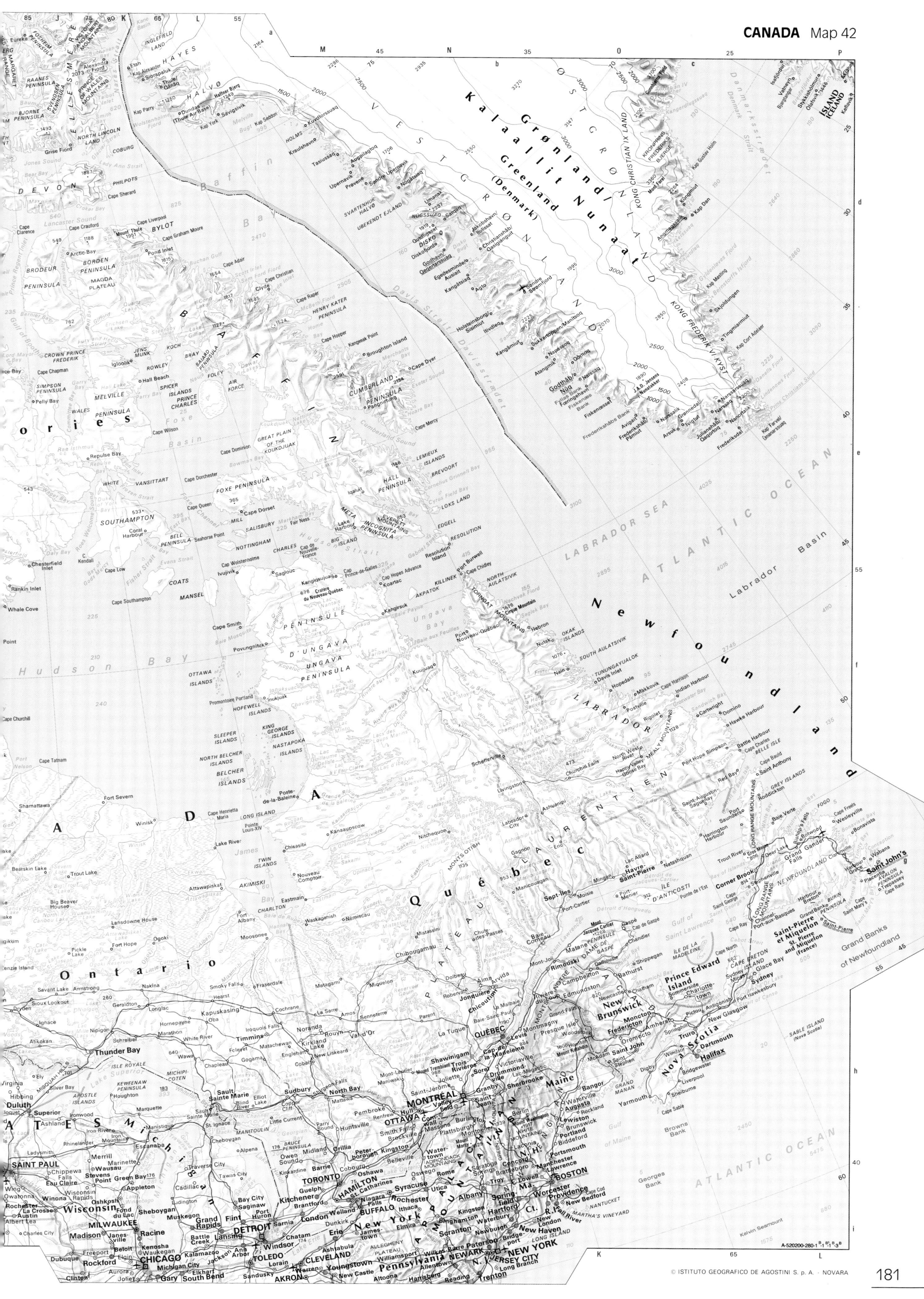

© ISTITUTO GEOGRAFICO DE AGOSTINI S. p. A · NOVARA

Map 43   **UNITED STATES**

Scale 1:12,000,000   Lambert Azimuthal Equidistant Projection

Longitude West 100 of Greenwich

0   200   400   600   800 km

0   200   400 miles

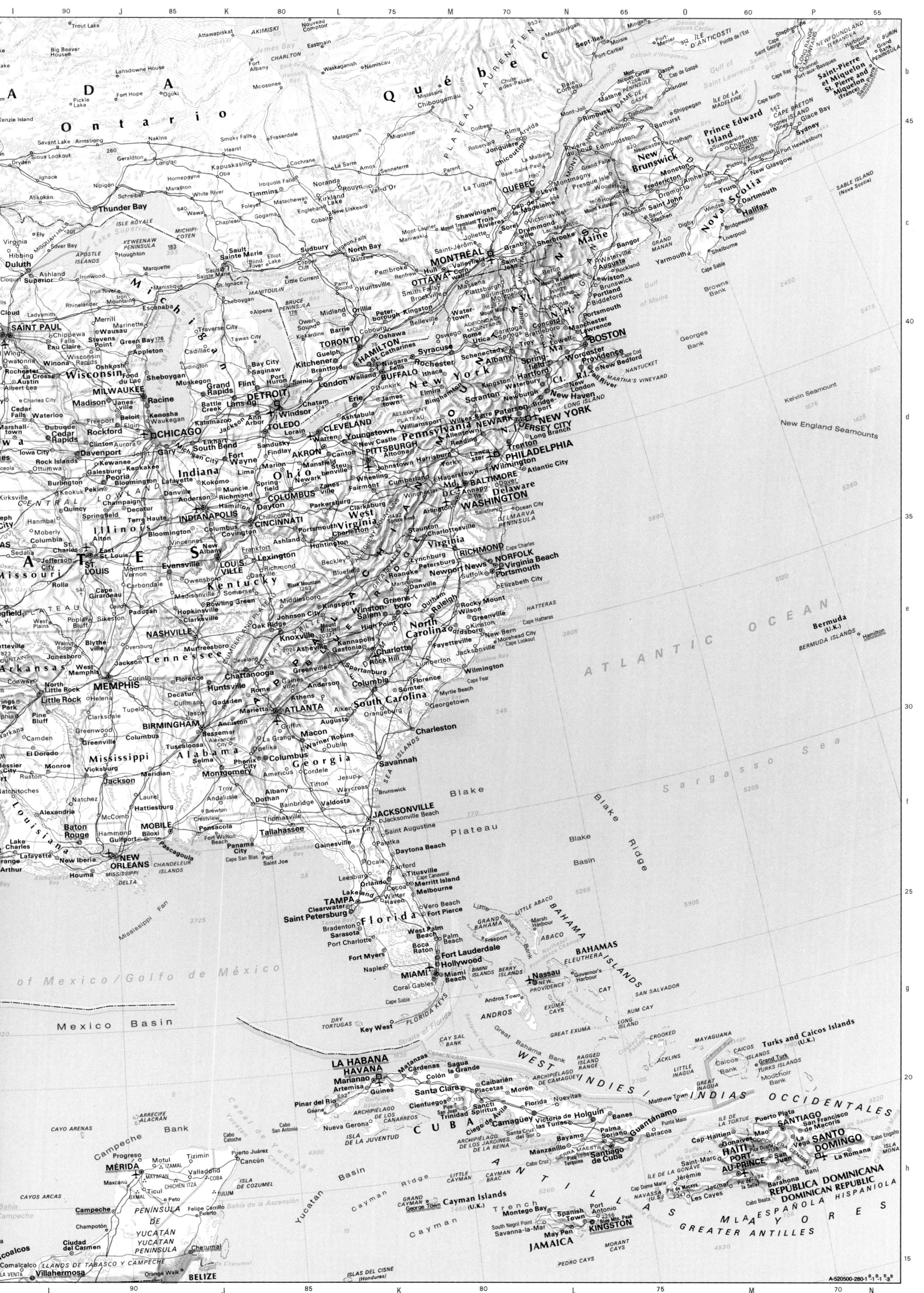

Map 44

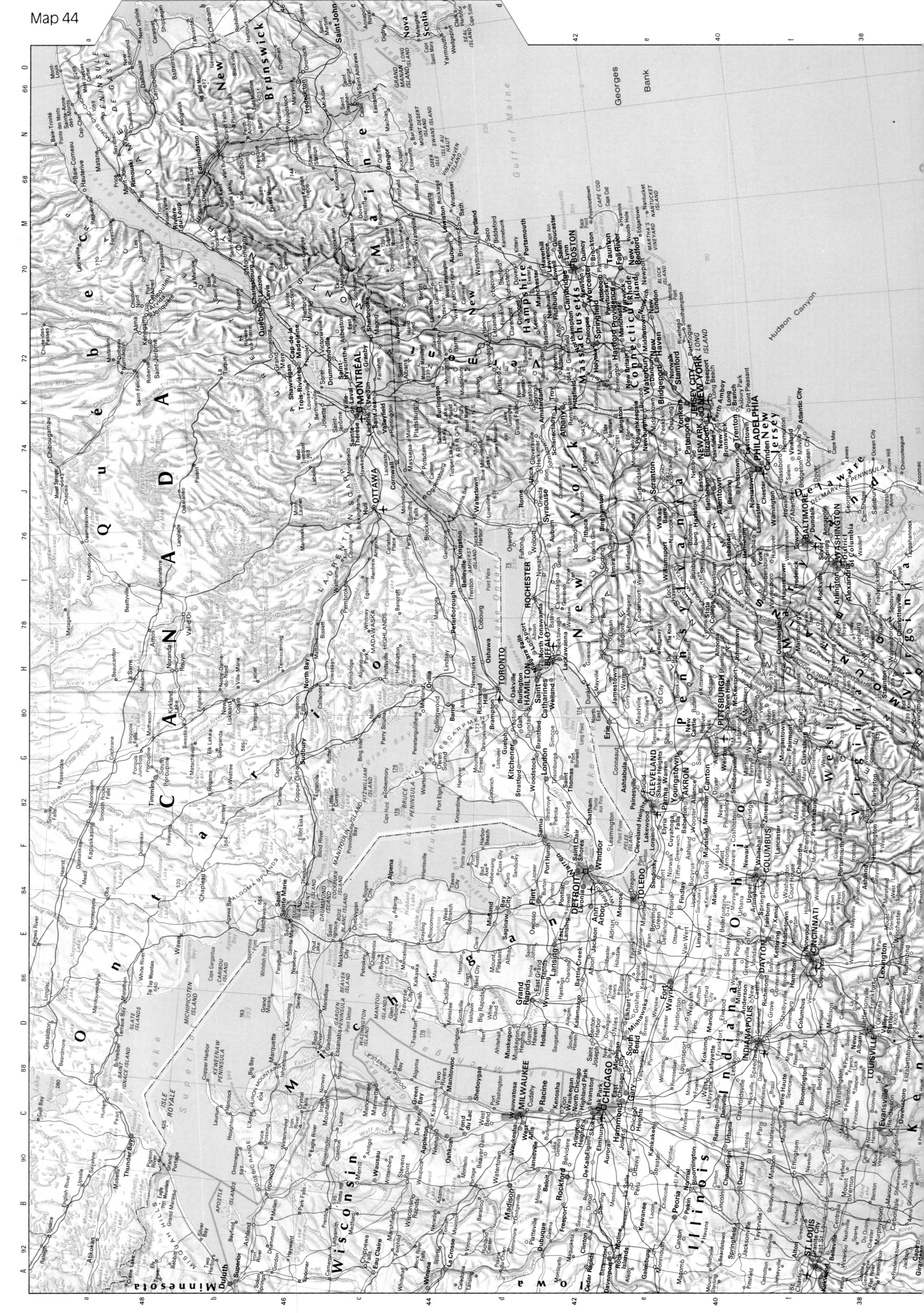

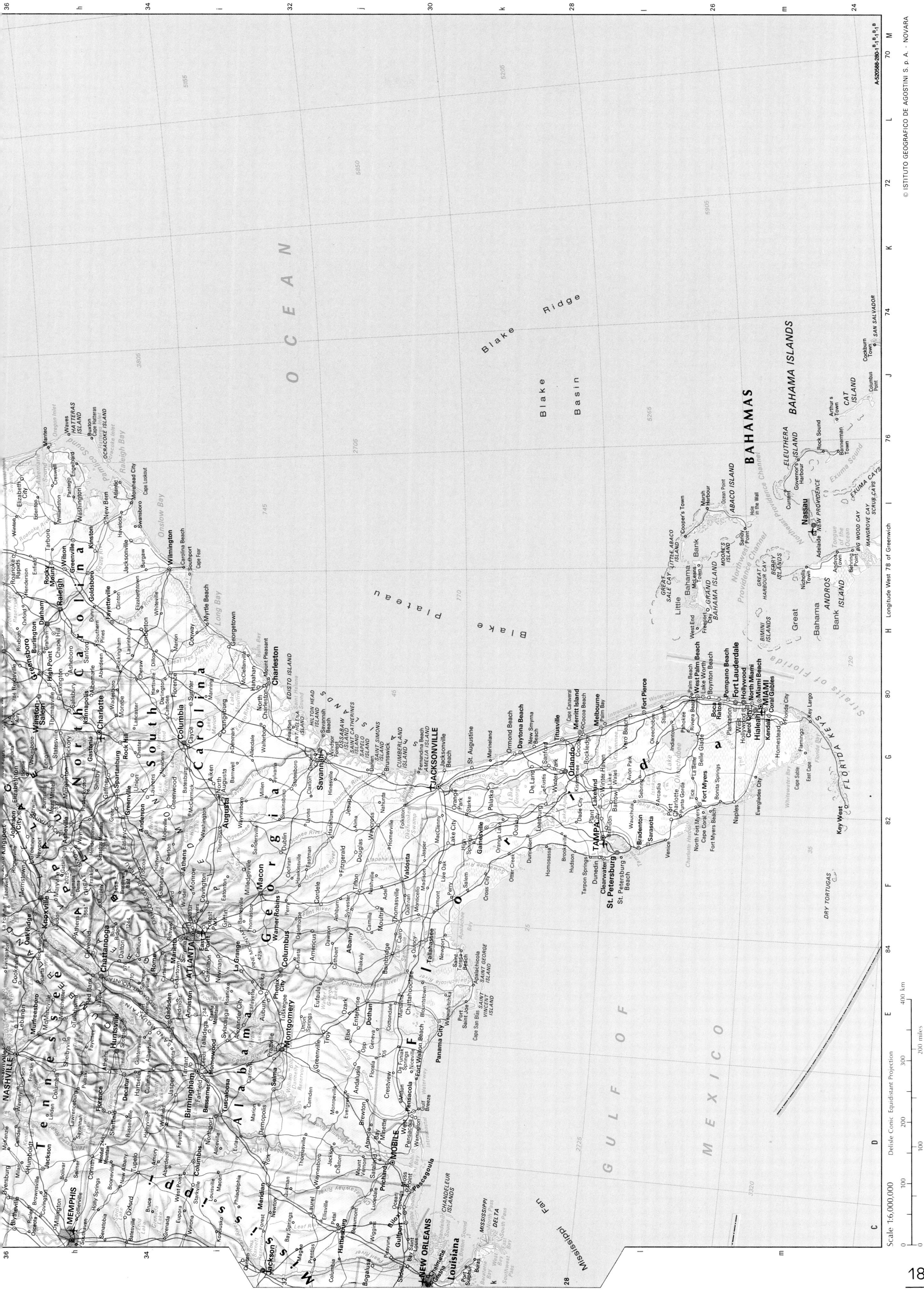

OCEAN

Blake Ridge

Blake Basin

Blake Plateau

GULF OF MEXICO

BAHAMAS

BAHAMA ISLANDS

GREAT ABACO ISLAND

LITTLE ABACO ISLAND

GRAND BAHAMA ISLAND

ANDROS ISLAND

ELEUTHERA

CAT ISLAND

SAN SALVADOR

NEW PROVIDENCE

BERRY ISLANDS

BIMINI ISLANDS

EXUMA CAYS

Northwest Providence Channel

Northeast Providence Channel

Straits of Florida

Tennessee

North Carolina

South Carolina

Georgia

Alabama

Mississippi

Florida

Louisiana

APPALACHIAN

MEMPHIS

NASHVILLE

Knoxville

Chattanooga

ATLANTA

Birmingham

Montgomery

Mobile

NEW ORLEANS

Jackson

Columbus

Macon

Columbia

Charlotte

Greensboro

Winston Salem

Raleigh

Wilmington

Charleston

Savannah

Augusta

JACKSONVILLE

Orlando

TAMPA

St. Petersburg

MIAMI

Fort Lauderdale

West Palm Beach

Key West

Nassau

HATTERAS ISLAND

OCRACOKE ISLAND

Cape Hatteras

Cape Lookout

Cape Fear

Myrtle Beach

Long Bay

Raleigh Bay

Onslow Bay

Albemarle Sound

Pamlico Sound

DRY TORTUGAS

FLORIDA KEYS

CHANDELEUR ISLANDS

MISSISSIPPI DELTA

Scale 1:6,000,000

Delisle Conic Equidistant Projection

0 100 200 300 400 km

0 100 200 miles

© ISTITUTO GEOGRAFICO DE AGOSTINI S. p. A. - NOVARA

185

Map 45

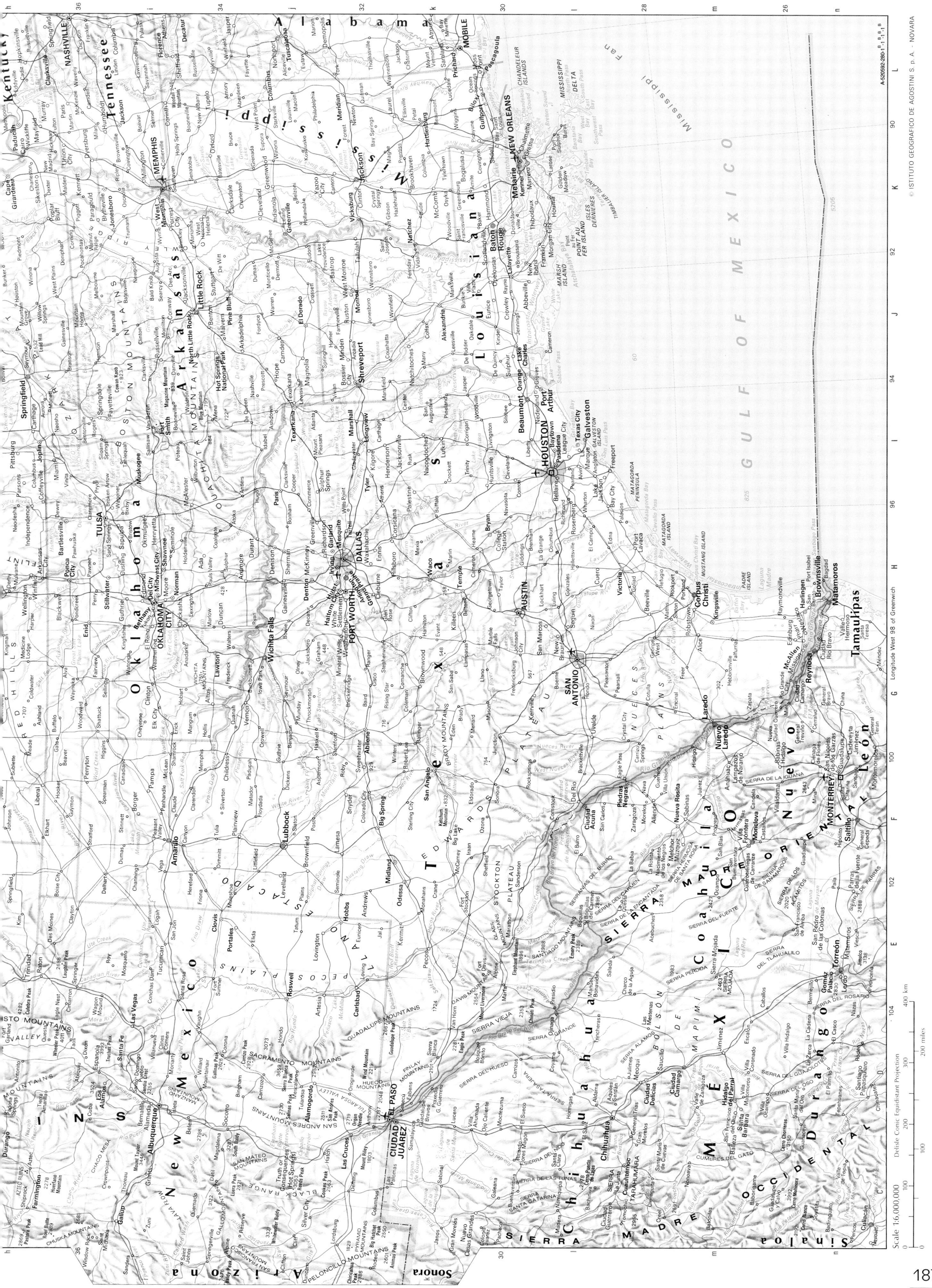

Kentucky
Tennessee
Alabama
Mississippi
Arkansas
Louisiana
Oklahoma
Texas
New Mexico
Arizona
Sonora
Chihuahua
Coahuila
Nuevo León
Tamaulipas
Durango
Sinaloa

SIERRA MADRE OCCIDENTAL
SIERRA MADRE ORIENTAL
MEXICO
GULF OF MEXICO

NASHVILLE
MEMPHIS
Little Rock
North Little Rock
NEW ORLEANS
Baton Rouge
MOBILE
Jackson
Shreveport
Vicksburg
Natchez
Alexandria
Lafayette
Lake Charles

TULSA
OKLAHOMA CITY
Norman
Lawton
Wichita Falls
FORT WORTH
DALLAS
Denton
Waco
Temple
AUSTIN
SAN ANTONIO
HOUSTON
Pasadena
Galveston
Beaumont
Port Arthur
Corpus Christi
Laredo
Nuevo Laredo
Brownsville
Matamoros
Reynosa
Ciudad Camargo

Amarillo
Lubbock
Midland
Odessa
Big Spring
San Angelo
Abilene
Roswell
Carlsbad
Hobbs
Clovis
Portales
EL PASO
CIUDAD JUAREZ
Las Cruces
Alamogordo
ALBUQUERQUE
Santa Fe
Las Vegas
Gallup
Farmington

MONTERREY
Saltillo
Torreón
Gómez Palacio
Chihuahua
Ciudad Delicias
Piedras Negras
Ciudad Acuña
Nueva Rosita
Del Rio

Springfield
Tulsa
Joplin
Fort Smith
Texarkana
Marshall
Longview
Tyler

BOSTON MOUNTAINS
OUACHITA MOUNTAINS
OZARK PLATEAU
SACRAMENTO MOUNTAINS
GUADALUPE MOUNTAINS
DAVIS MOUNTAINS
STOCKTON PLATEAU
EDWARDS PLATEAU
LLANO ESTACADO
STAKED PLAINS
BOLSÓN DE MAPIMÍ

MISSISSIPPI RIVER DELTA
CHANDELEUR ISLANDS
MATAGORDA ISLAND
PADRE ISLAND
MUSTANG ISLAND

Scale 16,000,000
Delisle Conic Equidistant Projection
Longitude West 98 of Greenwich

400 km
200 miles

© ISTITUTO GEOGRAFICO DE AGOSTINI S.p.A. - NOVARA

A-520592-280-1-1-1-1-B

187

Map 46 WESTERN UNITED STATES

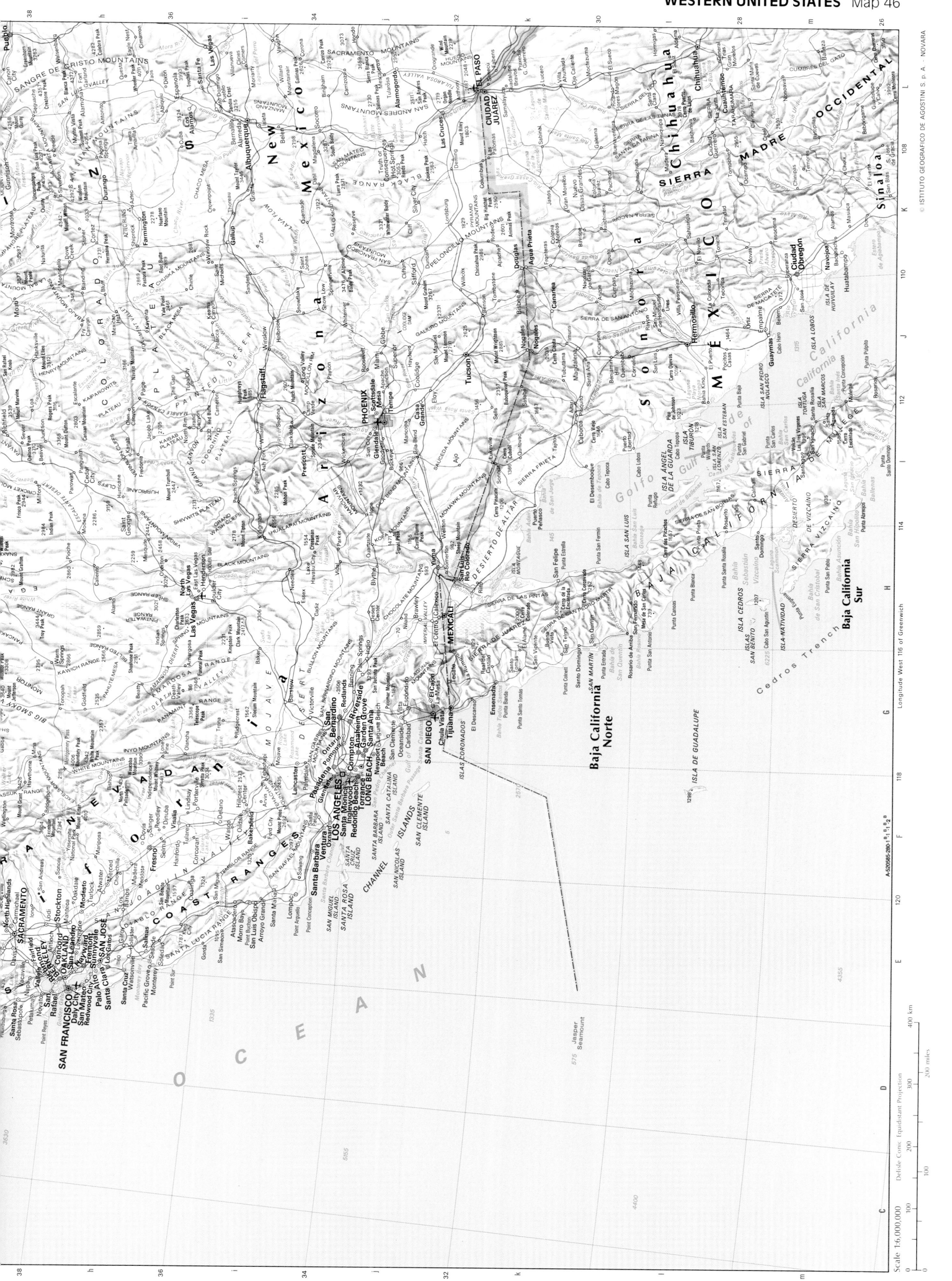

Scale 1:6,000,000

Delisle Conic Equidistant Projection

Longitude West 116 of Greenwich

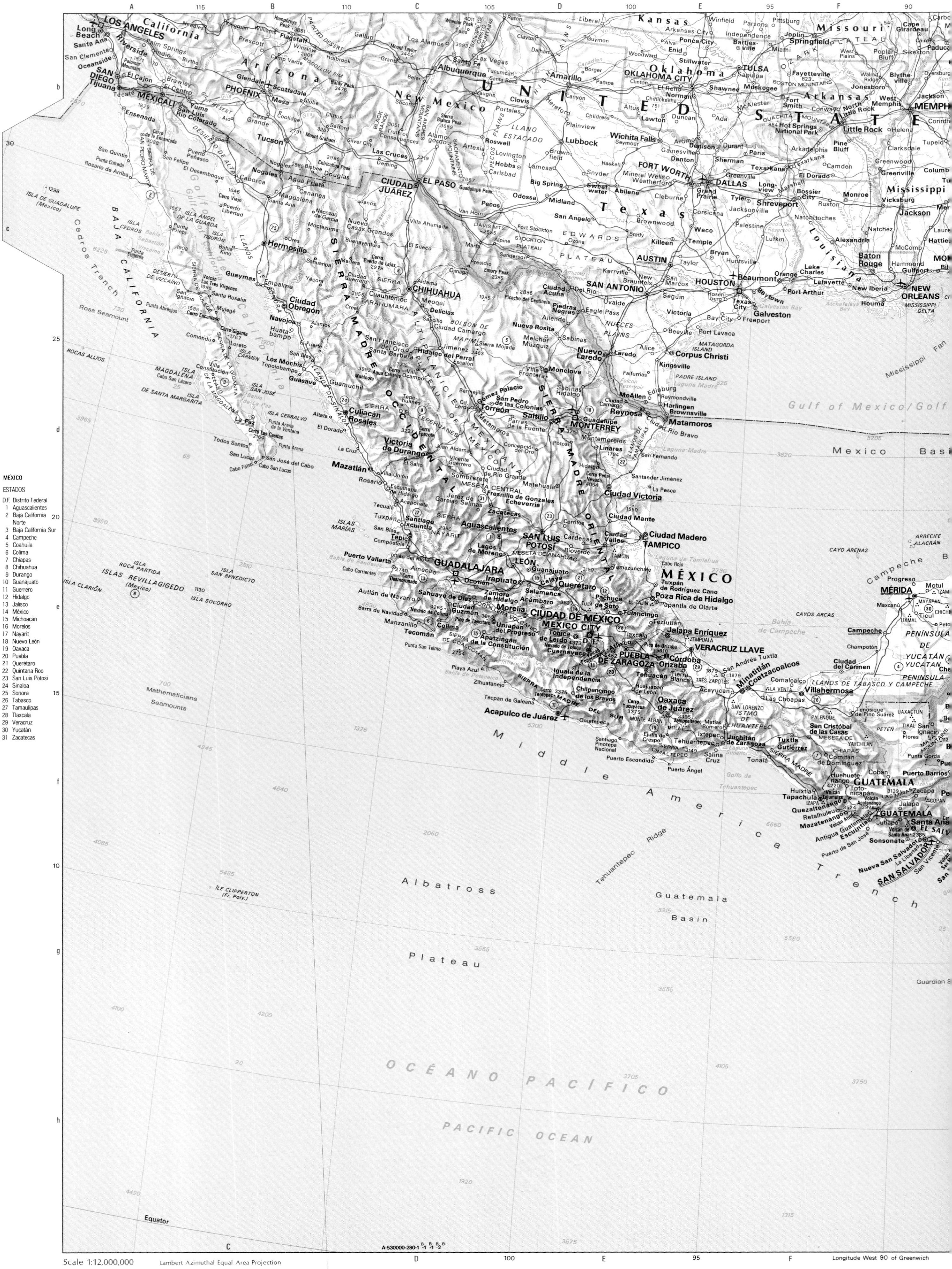

Map 47 **MIDDLE AMERICA**

MÉXICO

ESTADOS

D.F. Distrito Federal
1 Aguascalientes
2 Baja California
   Norte
3 Baja California Sur
4 Campeche
5 Coahuila
6 Colima
7 Chiapas
8 Chihuahua
9 Durango
10 Guanajuato
11 Guerrero
12 Hidalgo
13 Jalisco
14 México
15 Michoacán
16 Morelos
17 Nayarit
18 Nuevo León
19 Oaxaca
20 Puebla
21 Querétaro
22 Quintana Roo
23 San Luis Potosí
24 Sinaloa
25 Sonora
26 Tabasco
27 Tamaulipas
28 Tlaxcala
29 Veracruz
30 Yucatán
31 Zacatecas

Scale 1:12,000,000   Lambert Azimuthal Equal Area Projection

0   200   400   600   800 km

0   200   400 miles

A-530000-280-1-1-1-2

Longitude West 90 of Greenwich

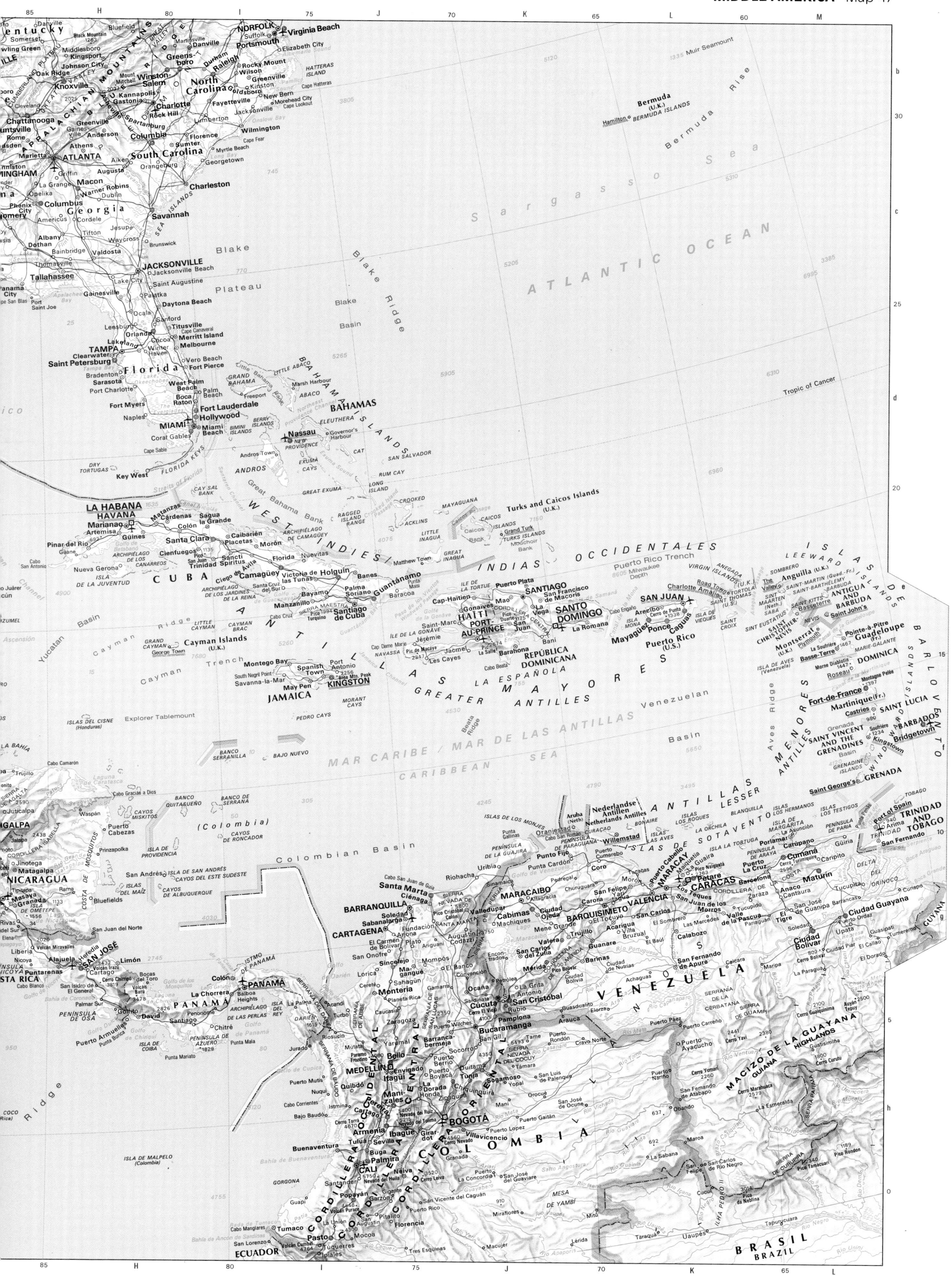

MÉXICO

GOLFO DE MÉXICO

GULF OF MEXICO

Mexico Basin

Texas

Louisiana

Mississippi

Alabama

Florida

Nuevo León

Tamaulipas

Luis Potosí

Hidalgo

Guerrero

Oaxaca

Morelos

Puebla

Tlaxcala

CIUDAD DE MEXICO / MEXICO CITY

Veracruz

Tabasco

Chiapas

Campeche

Yucatán

Quintana Roo

PENINSULA DE YUCATÁN

GUATEMALA

HONDURAS

BELIZE

ISTMO DE TEHUANTEPEC

Bahía de Campeche

Campeche Bank

© ISTITUTO GEOGRAFICO DE AGOSTINI S.p.A. - NOVARA

Map 49 **CENTRAL AMERICA AND WESTERN CARIBBEAN**

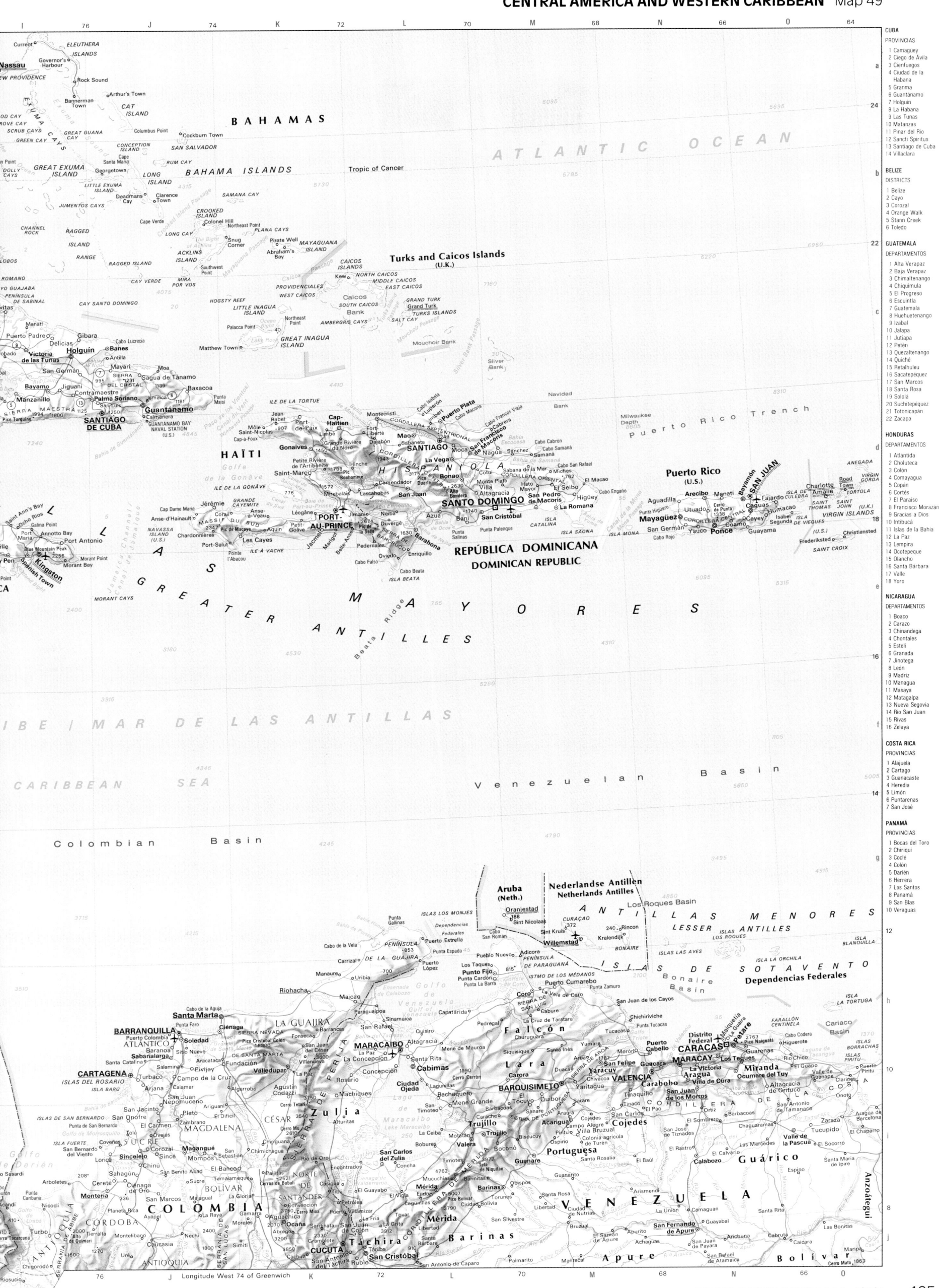

CUBA
PROVINCIAS
1 Camagüey
2 Ciego de Avila
3 Cienfuegos
4 Ciudad de la Habana
5 Granma
6 Guantánamo
7 Holguin
8 La Habana
9 Las Tunas
10 Matanzas
11 Pinar del Rio
12 Sancti Spiritus
13 Santiago de Cuba
14 Villaclara

BELIZE
DISTRICTS
1 Belize
2 Cayo
3 Corozal
4 Orange Walk
5 Stann Creek
6 Toledo

GUATEMALA
DEPARTAMENTOS
1 Alta Verapaz
2 Baja Verapaz
3 Chimaltenango
4 Chiquimula
5 El Progreso
6 Escuintla
7 Guatemala
8 Huehuetenango
9 Izabal
10 Jalapa
11 Jutiapa
12 Peten
13 Quezaltenango
14 Quiché
15 Retalhuleu
16 Sacatepéquez
17 San Marcos
18 Santa Rosa
19 Solalá
20 Suchitepéquez
21 Totonicapán
22 Zacapa

HONDURAS
DEPARTAMENTOS
1 Atlántida
2 Choluteca
3 Colon
4 Comayagua
5 Copán
6 Cortés
7 El Paraíso
8 Francisco Morazán
9 Gracias a Dios
10 Intibuca
11 Islas de la Bahia
12 La Paz
13 Lempira
14 Ocotepeque
15 Olancho
16 Santa Bárbara
17 Valle
18 Yoro

NICARAGUA
DEPARTAMENTOS
1 Boaco
2 Carazo
3 Chinandega
4 Chontales
5 Estelí
6 Granada
7 Jinotega
8 León
9 Madriz
10 Managua
11 Masaya
12 Matagalpa
13 Nueva Segovia
14 Rio San Juan
15 Rivas
16 Zelaya

COSTA RICA
PROVINCIAS
1 Alajuela
2 Cartago
3 Guanacaste
4 Heredia
5 Limón
6 Puntarenas
7 San José

PANAMÁ
PROVINCIAS
1 Bocas del Toro
2 Chiriqui
3 Coclé
4 Colón
5 Darien
6 Herrera
7 Los Santos
8 Panama
9 San Blas
10 Veraguas

Map 50 **EASTERN CARIBBEAN**

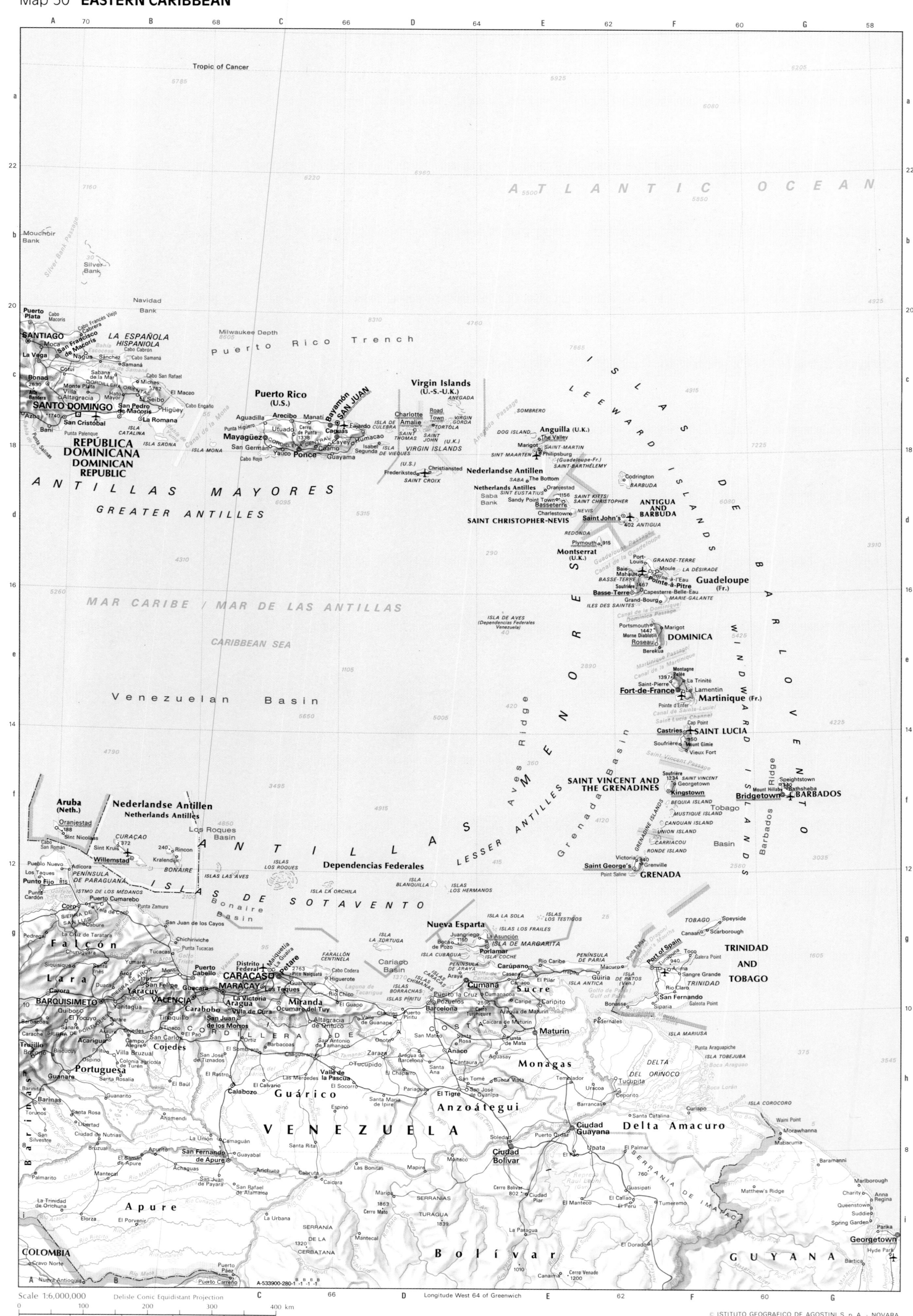

A 70   B   68   C   66   D   64   E   62   F   60   G   58

Tropic of Cancer

6285

5785   5925   6080

a

22   6220   6960   4760   4925   22

A T L A N T I C   O C E A N

5500   5850

7160   8310

b   Mouchoir
Bank   Silver Bank Passage   30   6095
Silver
Bank

*Navidad
Bank*   7665   4915   6080

20   Puerto
Plata   Cabo Francés Viejo
Cabo Cabrera   20
SANTIAGO   La Española
Moca   HISPANIOLA
La Vega   Nagua
Sánchez   Samaná   Milwaukee Depth
8605   *Puerto Rico Trench*   *I S*
L A
S
Cotuí   Cabo San Rafael
Miches   Cabo Samaná   Virgin Islands   *L*
E
E
W
c   Bonao   2630   CORDILLERA ORIENTAL   765   El Macao   (U.S.-U.K.)   ANEGADA   *A*
R   6295
Villa   Monte Plata   Cabo Engaño   Puerto Rico   SOMBRERO   *D*
Altagracia   San Pedro   (U.S.)   Charlotte   Road   VIRGIN   Anguilla (U.K.)   *I*
S
SANTO DOMINGO   Higüey   Bayamón   SAN JUAN   Amalie   Town   GORDA   The Valley   *L*
A
San Cristóbal   1740   La Romana   Aguadilla   Arecibo   Manatí   SAINT   TORTOLA   Marigot   SAINT-MARTIN   *N*
D
Azua   REPÚBLICA   Utuado   Caguas   THOMAS   SAINT   (U.K.)   (Guadeloupe-Fr.)   *S*
18   Baní   DOMINICANA   Mayagüez   Cayey   JOHN   Philipsburg   SAINT-BARTHÉLEMY   18
Punta Palenque   DOMINICAN   San Germán   Tauco   Humacao   SINT MAARTEN   Codrington
REPUBLIC   Ponce   Guayama   VIRGIN ISLANDS   (U.S.)   SABA   The Bottom   BARBUDA
Punta Salinas   Cabo Rojo   ISLA   SAINT CROIX   Nederlandse Antilles   Oranjestad   ANTIGUA
A N T I L L A S   M A Y O R E S   DE VIEQUES   Frederiksted   Christiansted   Netherlands Antilles   1156   SAINT KITTS/   AND   402 ANTIGUA
G R E A T E R   A N T I L L E S   SAINT CROIX   Saba   Basseterre   SAINT CHRISTOPHER   BARBUDA
Bank   Sandy Point Town   NEVIS   Saint John's
d   SAINT CHRISTOPHER-NEVIS   Charlestown   REDONDA   402 ANTIGUA   d
5315   290   Plymouth   915   GRANDE-TERRE   LA DÉSIRADE
4310   Montserrat   Port-   Moule
(U.K.)   Louis   Grande-Terre   Guadeloupe
5260   Baie-   Pointe-à-Pitre   (Fr.)
16   BASSE-TERRE   Mahault   1467   16
M A R   C A R I B E / M A R   D E   L A S   A N T I L L A S   Basse-Terre   Capesterre-Belle-Eau   MARIE-GALANTE
Soufrière   Grand-Bourg
CARIBBEAN SEA   ISLA DE AVES   ÎLES DES SAINTES
(Dependencias Federales   Portsmouth   Marigot
Venezuela)   1447   DOMINICA
40   Morse Diablotin   *W*
1105   Roseau   *I*
e   *V e n e z u e l a n   B a s i n*   Berekua   2890   *N*   e
5650   5005   Montagne   *D*
420   Pelée   *W*
Saint-Pierre   1397   *A*
4790   La Trinité   *R*
360   Fort-de-France   Le Lamentin   *D*
14   Martinique (Fr.)   4225   14
3495   Pointe d'Enfer   *I*
Cap Point   *S*
Castries   SAINT LUCIA   *L*
Soufrière   950   *A*
415   Mount Gimie   *N*
Vieux Fort   *D*
Aruba   Nederlandse Antillen   Soufrière   1234   SAINT VINCENT   Speightstown   *S*
f   (Neth.)   Netherlands Antilles   Georgetown   Bridgetown   BARBADOS   f
Oranjestad   Kingstown   Mount Hillaby   Bathsheba
188   CURAÇAO   372   Los Roques   BEQUIA ISLAND   Tobago
Sint Nicolaas   240   Basin   MUSTIQUE ISLAND
Willemstad   Kralendijk   4850   CANOUAN ISLAND   3910
12   BONAIRE   UNION ISLAND   12
Pueblo Nuevo   *A*   Victoria   CARRIACOU
Los Taques   Adícora   *N*   RONDE ISLAND   Basin   3035
Punto Fijo   *T*   Point Saline   GRENADA
Coro   Puerto Cumarebo   *I*   Saint George's   Grenville   2580
SIERRA   *L*   415   GRENADA
SAN LUIS   San Juan de los Cayos   *L*
g   Chichiriviche   *A*   Scarborough   g
ISLA LA SOLA   ISLAS   Speyside   TRINIDAD
Tucacas   LOS TESTIGOS   Canaan   AND
ISLA   Port of Spain   TOBAGO
Puerto   Maiquetía   LA TORTUGA   ISLA DE MARGARITA   Galera Point
Cabello   Distrito   Petare   Nueva Esparta   Asunción   Arima
CARACAS   Federal   Juangriego   1160   PENÍNSULA   Sangre Grande
MARACAY   Pico Naiguatá   Higuerote   DE PARIA   San Fernando
La Victoria   2763   Río   Carúpano   TRINIDAD
10   VALENCIA   Los Teques   Chico   Cariaco   Cumaná   Guíria   Galeota Point   10
BARQUISIMETO   Villa de Cura   El Guapo   Basin   Araya   El Pilar
Quíbor   Maracay   Barcelona   Guanta   Caripe   Sipario
San Juan   1370   Puerto la Cruz   Cariaco   Maturín
Acarigua   de los Morros   Clarines   Aragua de Maturín
Trujillo   Villa Bruzual   Ortiz   Píritu   Pedernales   ISLA MARIUSA
Guanare   Barbacoas   Onoto   375
Portuguesa   San José   Chaguaramas   Anaco   *M o n a g a s*   3545
de Tiznados   Valle de   Zaraza   DELTA
Barinas   la Pascua   El Socorro   San Tomé   DEL ORINOCO   ISLA TOBEJUBA
G u á r i c o   Santa María   El Tigre   San José   Tucupita
de Ipire   de Guanipa
San Fernando   Calabozo   Espino   Barrancas   *Delta Amacuro*
de Apure   *A n z o á t e g u i*   Ciudad   Wani Point
Guayaba   Las Bonitas   Ciudad   Guayana   ISLA COROCORO
Arichuna   San Juan   Maipoto   Guayana
de Payara   Cabruta   *V E N E Z U E L A*   Puerto Ordaz
i   Palmarito   San Rafael   Ciudad   i
de Atamaica   Bolívar   El Palmar
La Trinidad   San José   El Dorado   Marlborough
de Orichuna   Cerro Bolívar   El Callao   *G U Y A N A*   Anna Regina
Elorza   La Urbana   802   Ciudad   El Peru   Tumeremo   Matthew's Ridge   Queenstown
El Porvenir   Piar   Suddie
A p u r e   *B o l í v a r*   Georgetown
COLOMBIA   Nueva   Puerto   Cerro Venado   Canaimá   Parika
Antioquía   Páez   1200   Hyde Park
A   B   Puerto Carreño   C   66   D   *Longitude West 64 of Greenwich*   E   62   F   60   G   Bartica

Scale 1:6,000,000   Delisle Conic Equidistant Projection
0   100   200   300   400 km
0   100   200 miles

A-533900-280-1-1-1-1

© ISTITUTO GEOGRAFICO DE AGOSTINI S.p.A. - NOVARA

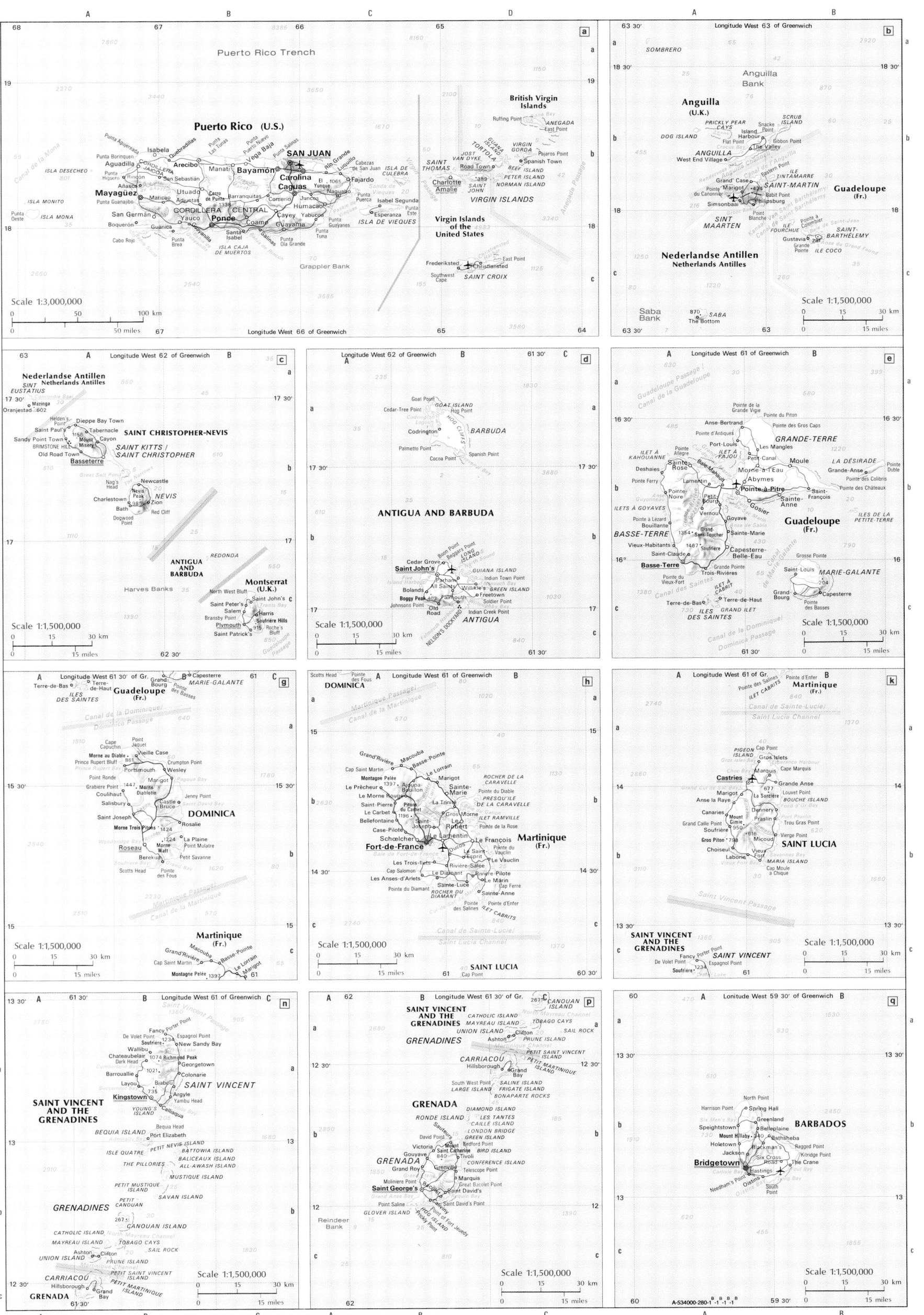

Mercator Cylindrical Projection

© ISTITUTO GEOGRAFICO DE AGOSTINI S.p.A. - NOVARA

Map 52

SOUTH AMERICA, PHYSICAL

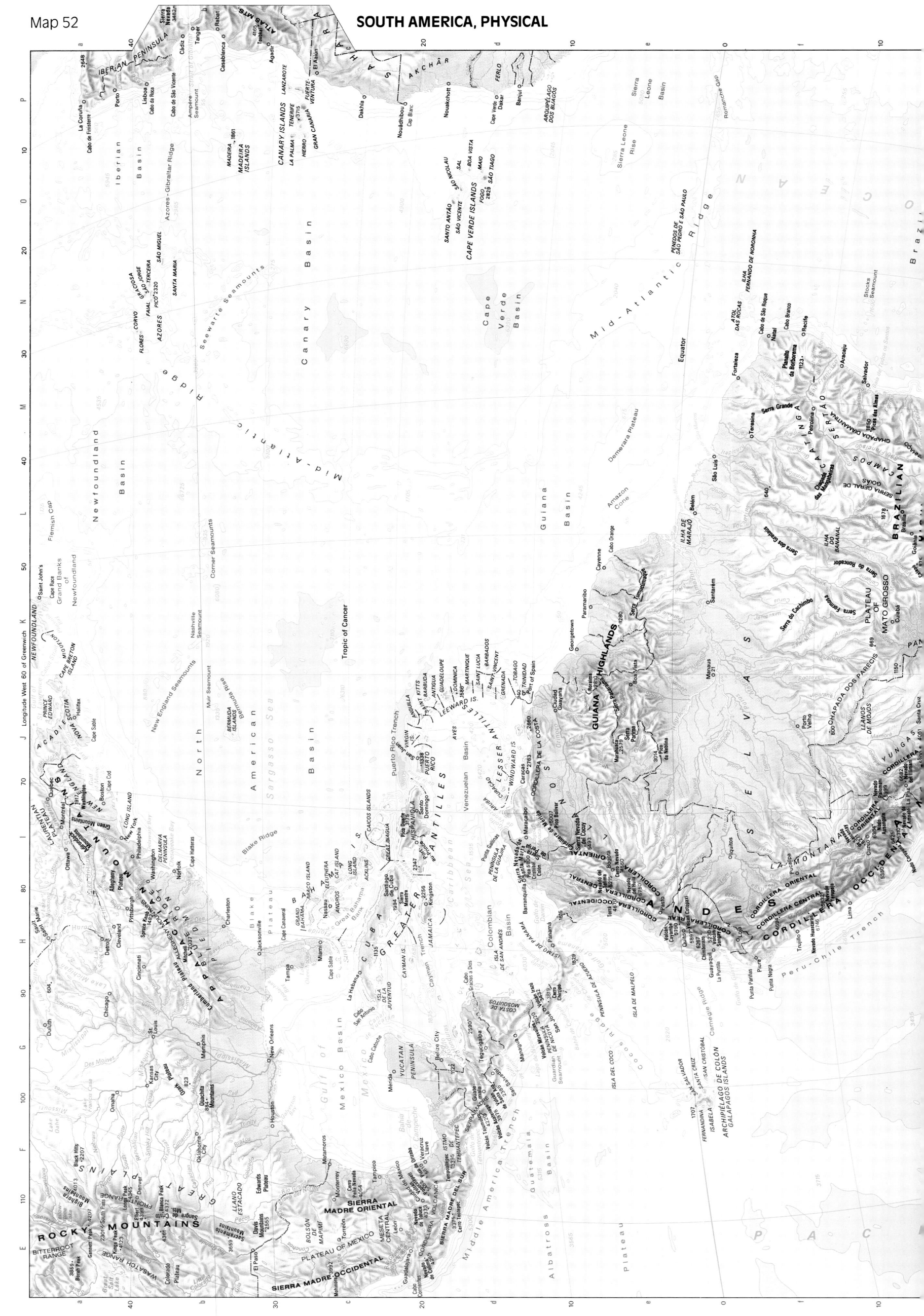

© ISTITUTO GEOGRAFICO DE AGOSTINI S. p. A. - NOVARA

Scale 1:30,000,000

Lambert Azimuthal Equal Area Projection

A-540000-780-1 -1 -1 -2 B

Map 53

SOUTH AMERICA, POLITICAL

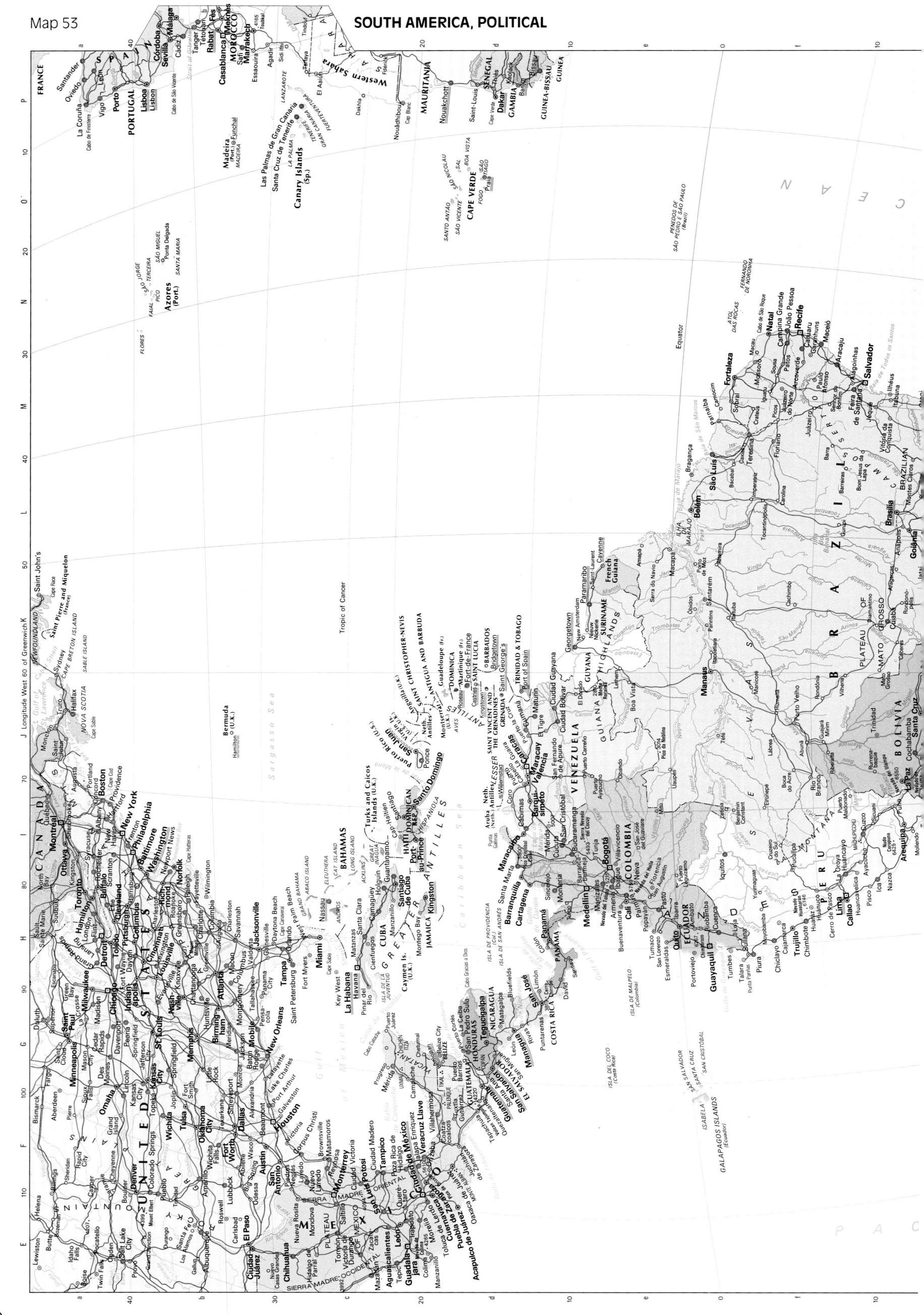

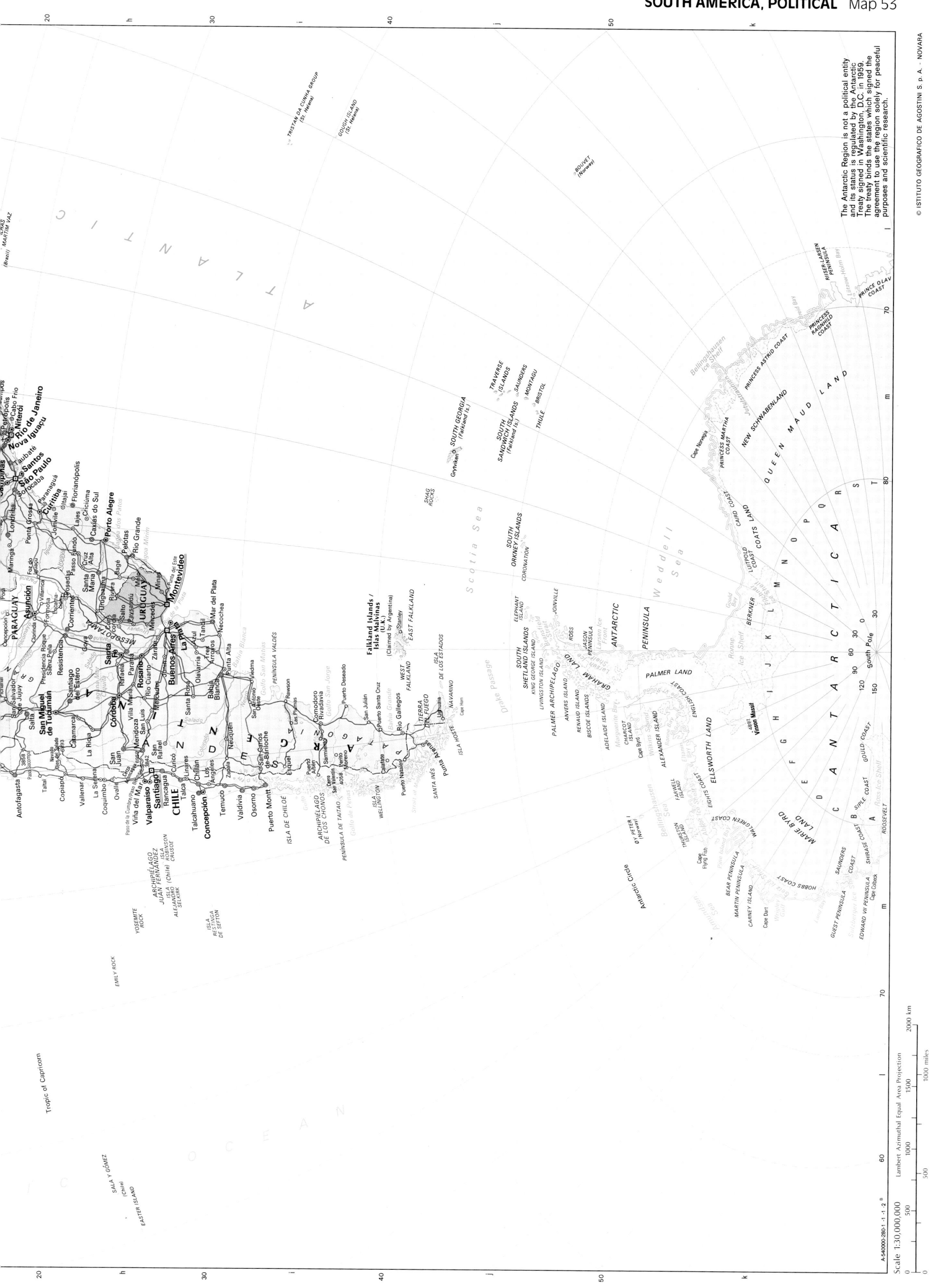

The Antarctic Region is not a political entity and its status is regulated by the Antarctic Treaty signed in Washington, D.C. in 1959. The treaty binds the states which signed the agreement to use the region solely for peaceful purposes and scientific research.

© ISTITUTO GEOGRAFICO DE AGOSTINI S. p. A. - NOVARA

A-540000-280-1-1-1-2 ®

Scale 1:30,000,000

Lambert Azimuthal Equal Area Projection

Map 54 **NORTHERN SOUTH AMERICA**

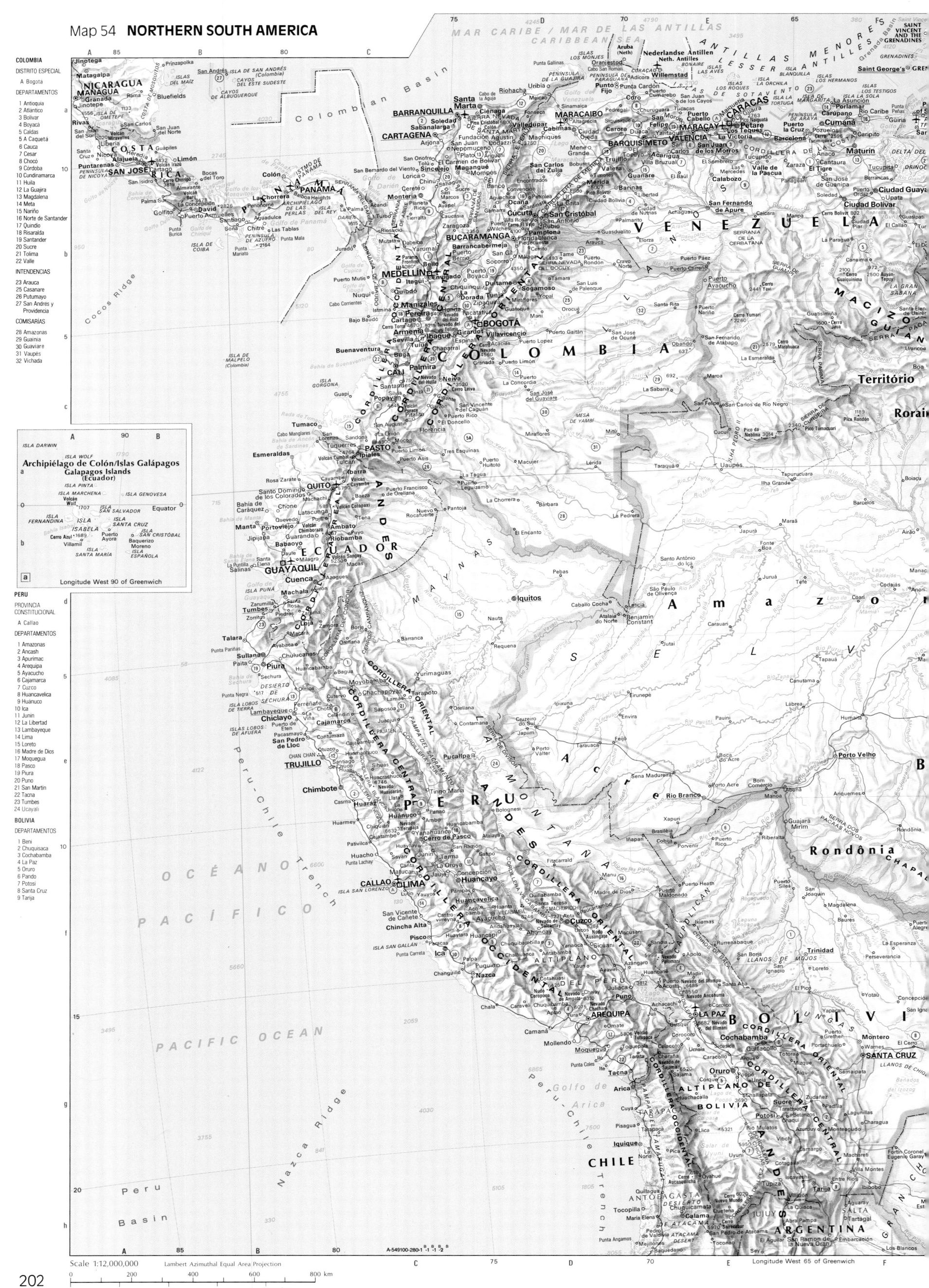

Map 55 **EAST-CENTRAL SOUTH AMERICA**

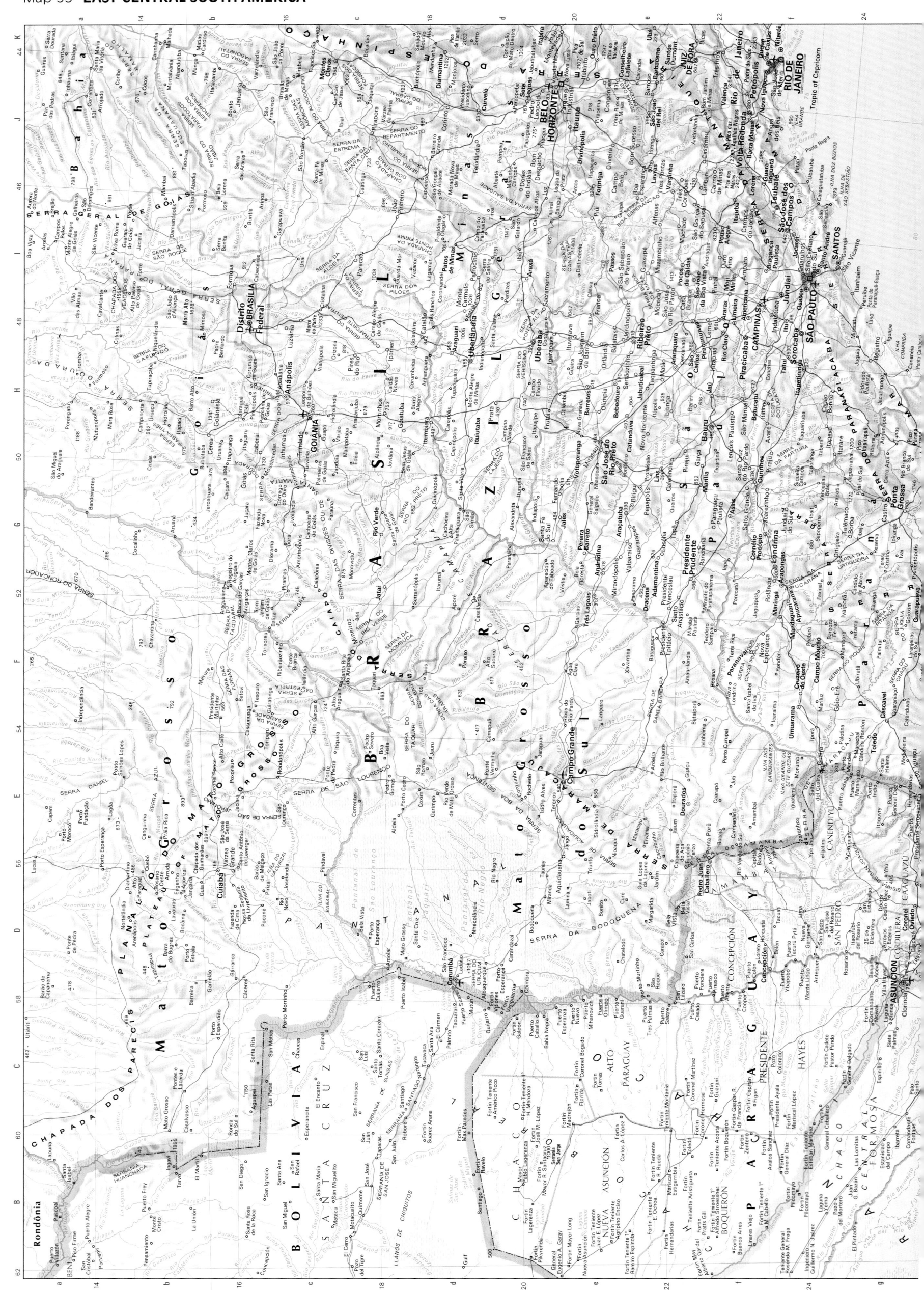

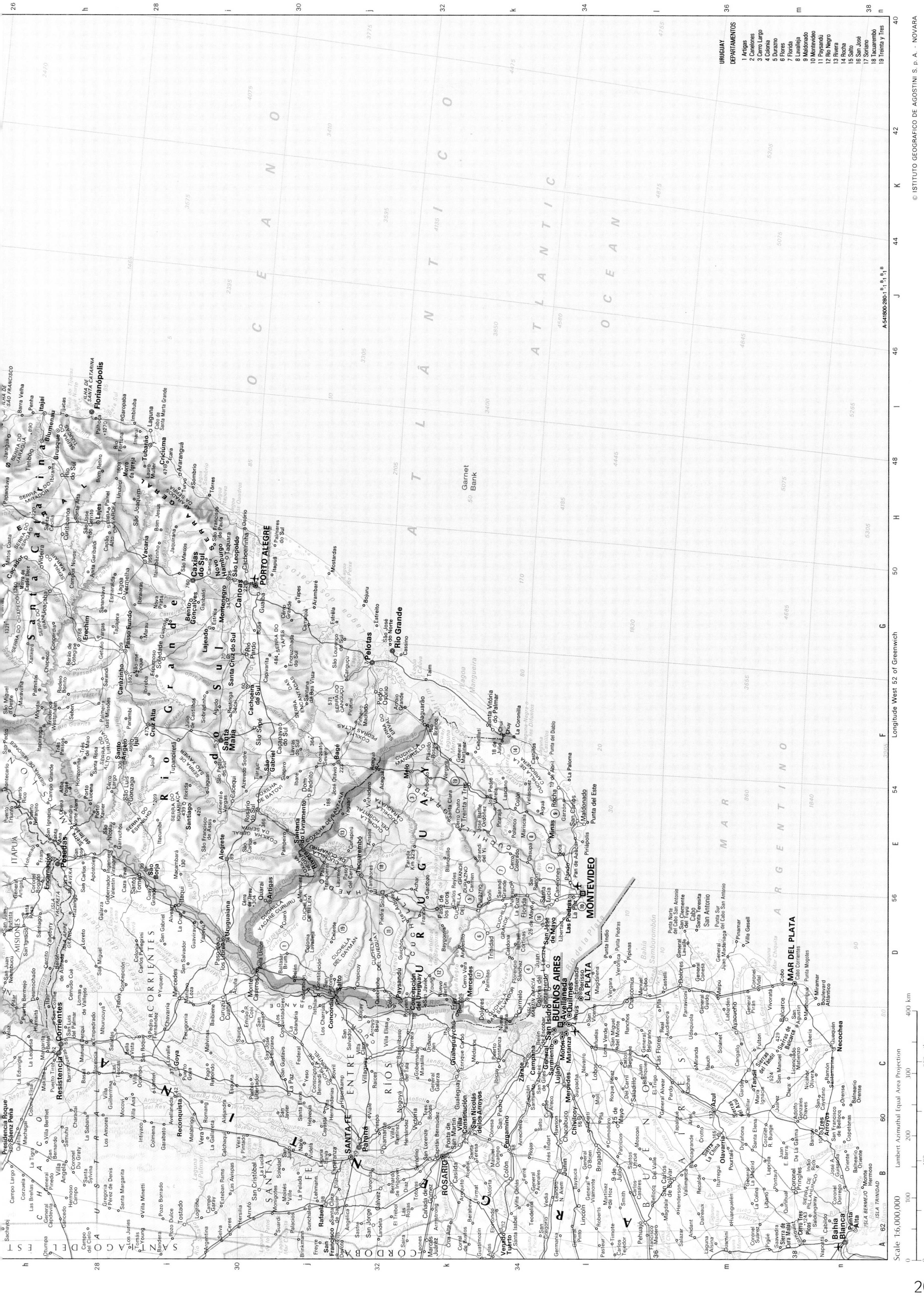

URUGUAY
DEPARTAMENTOS

1 Artigas
2 Canelones
3 Cerro Largo
4 Colonia
5 Durazno
6 Flores
7 Florida
8 Lavalleja
9 Maldonado
10 Montevideo
11 Paysandú
12 Río Negro
13 Rivera
14 Rocha
15 Salto
16 San José
17 Soriano
18 Tacuarembó
19 Treinta y Tres

A T L Â N T I C O

O C E A N O

A T L A N T I C   O C E A N

M A R   A R G E N T I N O

Garnet Bank

Florianópolis
Blumenau
PORTO ALEGRE
Caxias do Sul
São Leopoldo
Canoas
Montenegro
Pelotas
Rio Grande
Passo Fundo
Santa Maria
Cruz Alta
Santa Cruz do Sul
Cachoeira
Bagé
Melo
Santana do Livramento
Rivera
Tacuarembó
Artigas
Salto
Paysandú
Concepción del Uruguay
Concordia
Mercedes
Durazno
Florida
San José
Minas
Punta del Este
Maldonado
MONTEVIDEO
Las Piedras
Canelones
LA PLATA
BUENOS AIRES
Avellaneda
Quilmes
Lanús
San Isidro
Morón
La Matanza
Luján
Zárate
Campana
San Nicolás de los Arroyos
ROSARIO
SANTA FE
Paraná
Reconquista
Resistencia
Corrientes
Presidencia Roque Sáenz Peña
Goya
Encarnación
Posadas
MAR DEL PLATA
Tandil
Azul
Olavarría
Bahía Blanca
Punta Alta
Necochea

C H A C O
S A N T I A G O   D E L   E S T E R O
S A N T A   F E
C O R D O B A
C O R R I E N T E S
E N T R E   R I O S
B U E N O S   A I R E S
MISIONES
ITAPÚA
R I O   G R A N D E   D O   S U L
Santa Catarina
U R U G U A Y

Longitude West 52 of Greenwich

Lambert Azimuthal Equal Area Projection

Scale 1:6,000,000

0   100   200   300   400 km
0   100   200 miles

© ISTITUTO GEOGRAFICO DE AGOSTINI S. p. A. - NOVARA

205

Map 56 **SOUTHERN SOUTH AMERICA**

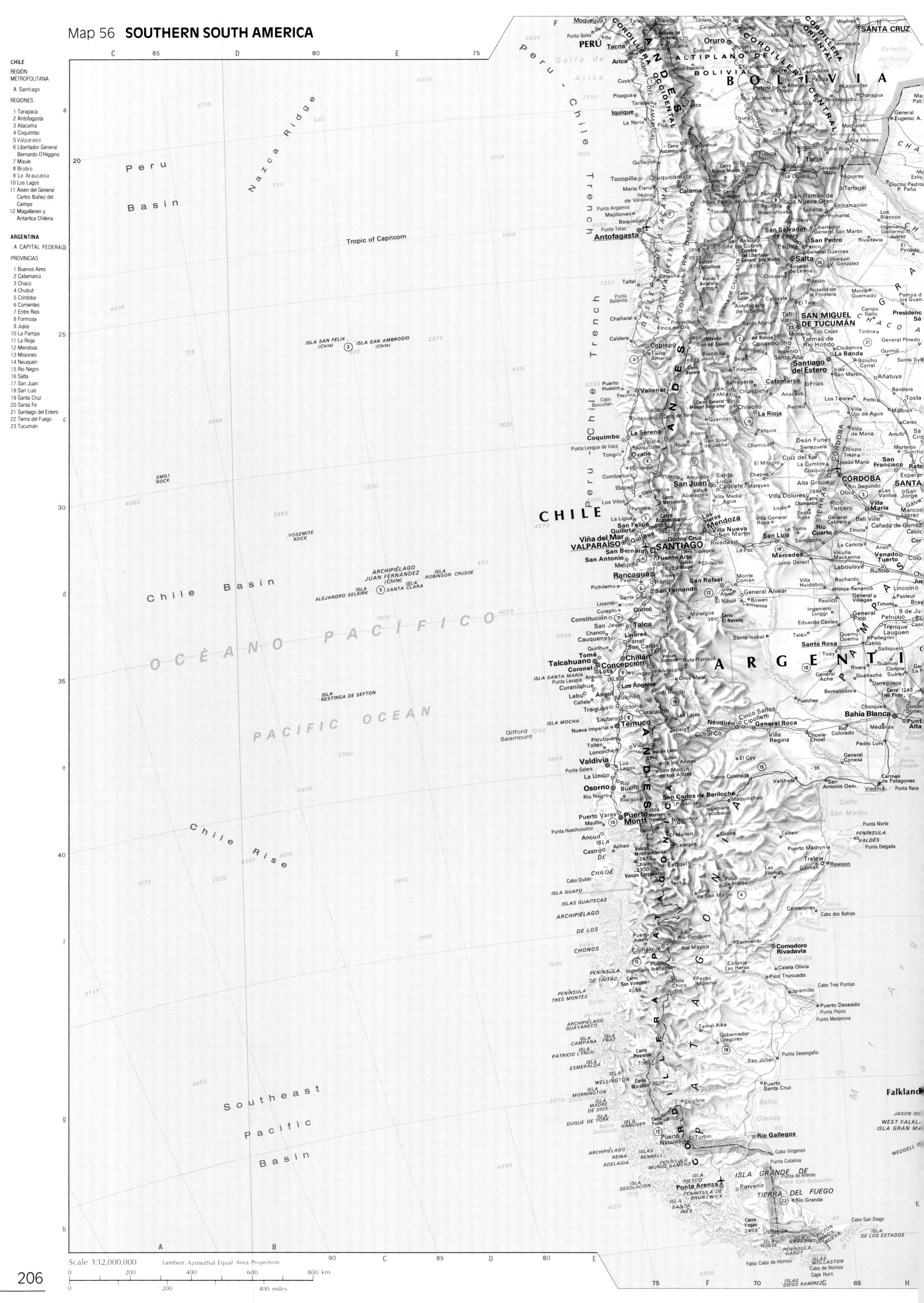

Map 57 **AUSTRALIA AND OCEANIA, PHYSICAL**

AUSTRALIA

CHINA

QIN LING
NAN LING
WUYI SHAN
DABA SHAN
SICHUAN PENDI
DALOU SHAN
WULING SHAN
TONKIN
HAINAN
LEIZHOU BANDAO
DONGSHA QUNDAO
PARACEL ISLANDS
KHORAT PLATEAU
INDOCHINA
ANNAM
COCHIN CHINA
MEKONG DELTA
Ca Mau Point

South China Sea
South China Basin
Yellow Sea
East China Sea
Sea of Japan

HONSHŪ
KYŪSHŪ
SHIKOKU
Tōkyō
Ōsaka
Nagasaki
RYUKYU ISLANDS
OKINAWA ISLANDS
AMAMI ISLANDS
TOKARA ISLANDS
SAKISHIMA
DAITO ISLANDS
TAIWAN (FORMOSA)
BATAN ISLANDS
BABUYAN ISLANDS

PHILIPPINE ISLANDS
LUZON
MINDORO
PANAY
SAMAR
LEYTE
CEBU
NEGROS
PALAWAN
MINDANAO
Davao
Manila
SULU ARCHIPELAGO
BASILAN
JOLO

BORNEO
KALIMANTAN
NATUNA ISLANDS
ANAMBAS ISLANDS
BANGKA
BELITUNG
GREATER SUNDA ISLANDS
SUMATRA
JAVA
Jakarta
Surabaya
MADURA
BALI
LOMBOK
SUMBAWA
FLORES
SUMBA
TIMOR
LESSER SUNDA ISLANDS

CELEBES
MINAHASSA PENINSULA
SANGIHE ISLANDS
TALAUD ISLANDS
HALMAHERA
MOLUCCAS
CERAM
BURU
Celebes Sea
Molucca Sea
Banda Sea
Flores Sea
Java Sea

Philippine Sea
Philippine Basin
Philippine Trench
West Mariana Basin
East Mariana Basin
Mariana Trench
Mariana Islands
GUAM
SAIPAN
TINIAN
ROTA
BONIN ISLANDS
VOLCANO ISLANDS
MARCUS ISLAND
WAKE

Northwest Pacific Basin
Mid-Pacific Mountains

MICRONESIA
CAROLINE ISLANDS
West Caroline Basin
East Caroline Basin
YAP ISLANDS
PALAU ISLANDS
TRUK ISLANDS
PONAPE
KUSAIE

MARSHALL ISLANDS
RALIK CHAIN
RATAK CHAIN
BIKINI
ENEWETAK
KWAJALEIN
MAJURO
JALUIT
MILI
NAURU
KIRIBATI (GILBERT ISLANDS)
TARAWA
BANABA
OCEAN

NEW GUINEA
Jayapura
Port Moresby
CENTRAL RANGE
OWEN STANLEY RANGE
New Guinea Trench
ARU ISLANDS
DOLAK

MELANESIA
BISMARCK ARCHIPELAGO
ADMIRALTY ISLANDS
NEW IRELAND
NEW BRITAIN
NEW HANOVER
BOUGAINVILLE
SOLOMON ISLANDS
CHOISEUL
SANTA ISABEL
NEW GEORGIA
MALAITA
GUADALCANAL
SAN CRISTOBAL
Solomon Sea
Coral Sea
Coral Sea Basin

SANTA CRUZ ISLANDS
NEW HEBRIDES
FIJI ISLANDS
VITI LEVU
NEW CALEDONIA
LOYALTY IS.
Melanesian Basin
New Caledonia Basin
Norfolk Ridge
LORD HOWE
NORFOLK
THREE KINGS ISLANDS

Arafura Sea
Timor Sea
Gulf of Carpentaria
ARNHEM LAND
CAPE YORK PENINSULA
GREAT BARRIER REEF
MELVILLE
BATHURST
Darwin
GROOTE EYLANDT
WESSEL ISLANDS
KIMBERLEY PLATEAU
ASHMORE
CARTIER
Broome
ROWLEY SHOALS
BARKLY TABLELAND
TANAMI DESERT
GREAT SANDY DESERT
GIBSON DESERT
GREAT VICTORIA DESERT
GREAT ARTESIAN BASIN
MACDONNELL RANGES
Alice Springs
SIMPSON DESERT
MUSGRAVE RANGES
GREAT DIVIDING RANGE
SELWYN RANGE
GREY RANGE
Lake Eyre
Lake Torrens
Lake Gairdner
Lake Frome
Lake Disappointment
Lake Mackay
Lake Amadeus
NULLARBOR PLAIN
Great Australian Bight
EYRE PENINSULA
FLINDERS RANGES
GAWLER RANGES
ARCHIPELAGO OF THE RECHERCHE
Perth
Albany
Cape Naturaliste
Cape Leeuwin
Cape Inscription
North West Cape
Brisbane
Cape Byron
Sydney
Canberra
Melbourne
Mount Kosciusko 2228
KANGAROO
Cape Howe
FLINDERS GROUP
KING
BASS STRAIT
TASMANIA
Mount Ossa 1617
Hobart
South East Cape

INDIAN OCEAN
Java Trench
North Australian Basin
South Australian Basin
Indian Ocean
Diamantina Depth
Planet Depth

Tasman Sea
Tasman Basin
NEW ZEALAND
NORTH ISLAND
SOUTH ISLAND
Mount Cook 3764
Christchurch
Dunedin
Cape Farewell
West Cape
STEWART
Southwest Cape
BANKS PENINSULA
AUCKLAND ISLANDS
Campbell Plateau

South Fiji Basin

Scale 1:30,000,000   Lambert Azimuthal Equal Area Projection
0 500 1000 1500 2000 km
0 500 1000 miles

Longitude East 170 of Greenwich

M
Ft
6000 / 19685
5000 / 16404
4000 / 13123
3000 / 9843
2000 / 6562
1000 / 3281
500 / 1640
+200 / +656
0
Depr.
0
−200 / −656
1000 / 3281
2000 / 6562
4000 / 13123
6000 / 19685
8000 / 26247

Point Conception
Mount Pines •2692
San Gorgonio •3506
•3267
El Paso
Edwards Plateau
CHANNEL ISLANDS
Los Angeles

Cerro de la Encantada 3088

Jasper Seamount

Isla de Guadalupe

Isla Cedros
Punta Eugenia 1996

Mohínora •3992
•2555
Torreón •3340

BAJA CALIFORNIA

DESIERTO DE VIZCAÍNO
SIERRA MADRE OCCIDENTAL
PLATEAU OF MEXICO
BOLSÓN DE MAPIMÍ

La Paz

Cabo San Lucas

ISLAS MARÍAS

Cabo Corrientes

ISLAS REVILLAGIGEDO

Murray Fracture Zone

Musicians Seamounts

MIDWAY ISLANDS
PEARL AND HERMES

Northeast

Pacific Basin

LISIANSKI   LAYSAN
Northampton Seamounts
MARO
GARDNER PINNACLES
HAWAIIAN ISLANDS

Wailian Ridge

FRENCH FRIGATE SHOALS
NECKER
NIHOA
KAUAI
Tropic of Cancer

NIIHAU
KAULA
OAHU
Honolulu
MOLOKAI
LANAI   MAUI
KAHOOLAWE
4205, Mauna Kea
HAWAII

Horizon Tablemount

Hess Tablemount

Pensacola Seamount

Cape Johnson Tablemount
JOHNSTON

Clarion Fracture Zone

PACIFIC   OCEAN

Christmas Ridge

Vityaz Seamount

Clipperton Fracture Zone

CLIPPERTON

KINGMAN
PALMYRA

TERAINA (WASHINGTON)
TABUAERAN (FANNING)

KIRITIMATI (CHRISTMAS)

BAKER
Equator

JARVIS

LINE ISLANDS

WINSLOW

PHOENIX ISLANDS
KANTON   ENDERBURY
North Tokelau Trough

MCKEAN   BIRNIE
ORONA (HULL)   RAWAKI (PHOENIX)
NIKUMARORO (GARDNER)   MANRA (SYDNEY)
CARONDELET

MALDEN

STARBUCK

P O L Y N E S I A

ATAFU   TOKELAU ISLANDS
NUKUNONU
FAKAOFO

Robbie Bank
SWAINS

PUKAPUKA

NASSAU

RAKAHANGA
MANIHIKI

PENRHYN

VOSTOK

CAROLINE

FLINT

EIAO   HATUTAA
NUKU HIVA
UA HUKA
UA POU   FATU HUTU
MARQUESAS   HIVA OA
ISLANDS   TAHUATA   ROCHER THOMASSET
FATU HIVA

NORTHERN COOK ISLANDS

SAMOA ISLANDS
SAVAI'I
UPOLU
MANUA ISLANDS
TUTUILA

SUWARROW

UVEA

NIUAFO'OU
TAFAHI
NIUATOPUTAPU

FONUALEI

TONGA ISLANDS
VAVA'U GROUP
HA'APAI GROUP
NOMUKA GROUP
KOTU GROUP

ANTIOPE

NIUE

BEVERIDGE

ATA
TONGATAPU GROUP

Vityaz II Depth

COOK ISLANDS

PALMERSTON

AITUTAKI
MANUAE
TAKUTEA
MITIARO
SOUTHERN COOK ISLANDS
ATIU   MAUKE
RAROTONGA

MANGAIA

MARIA

RIMATARA

TUBUAI ISLANDS

Tropic of Capricorn

RURUTU

TUBUAI

RAEVAVAE

President Thiers Seamount

RAPA
ILOTS DE BASS

MANUAE
MOTU ONE
MAUPITI
LEEWARD ISLANDS
ILES PALLISER

MAUPIHAA
TETIAROA
HUAHINE
BORA BORA
RAIATEA   MAKATEA
MAIAO
MOOREA   TAHITI
WINDWARD ISLANDS
SOCIETY ISLANDS

HEREHERETUE

RANGIROA   MANIHI
MATAIVA   AHE
APATAKI   TIKEHAU
ANAA   ARUTUA
KAUKURA   KAUEHI
NIAU   TAHANEA
FAKARAVA
MOTUTUNGA
REITORU
RAVAHERE
HARAIKI
NEGONEGO
MANUHANGI
PARAOA
AHUNUI
ILES DU DUC DE GLOUCESTER
TEMATANGI   MURUROA
FAGATAUFA
MORANE

ILES DU ROI GEORGES
RAPA
ILES DU DÉSAPPOINTEMENT
PUKAPUKA
TAKUME   TANGATAU
TAKAPOTO   FAKAHINA
NIHIRU
RAROIA
TENUATA
MARUTEA   TATAKOTO
NAO
AMANU
VAHITAHI   PUKARUHA
VAIRAATEA   REAO
PINAKI
TUREIA
VANAVANA
MARIA
MANGAREVA
GAMBIER ISLANDS   TEMOE

TUAMOTU ARCHIPELAGO

Tuamotu Ridge

GROUPE ACTÉON
MARUTEA

OENO
HENDERSON   DUCIE
PITCAIRN

East Pacific Rise

Wachusett Seamount

SALA Y GÓMEZ
EASTER ISLAND

ERNEST LEGOUVE

MARIA THERESA

Southwest

Pacific

Basin

CHATHAM ISLANDS

PACIFIC   OCEAN

A-590000-780-1 -1 -1 -2 ®

Map 58 **AUSTRALIA AND OCEANIA, POLITICAL**

CHINA
Chengdu
Chongqing
Kunming
Guiyang
Changsha
Wuhan
Nanjing
Shanghai
Hangzhou
Guangzhou
Canton
Hong Kong (U.K.)
Macao (Port.)
Hainan
Taipei
TAIWAN
Kaohsiung

SOUTH KOREA
Pusan
JAPAN
Tōkyō
Yokohama
Ōsaka
Kyōto
Nagoya
Hiroshima
Fukuoka
Nagasaki
Kagoshima
KYŪSHŪ
Sendai
Niigata

Ha noi
Hai phong
VIET-NAM
THAILAND
CAMBODIA
Phnum Penh
Ho Chi Minh (Saigon)

PHILIPPINES
LUZON
Manila
Quezon City
MINDORO
PANAY
Cebu
NEGROS
MINDANAO
Davao
Zamboanga

BRUNEI
MALAYSIA
KALIMANTAN
BORNEO
INDONESIA
SUMATRA
Jakarta
Bandung
Surabaya
CELEBES
HALMAHERA

Northern Mariana Islands (U.S.)
MARIANA ISLANDS
Guam (U.S.)
MARSHALL ISLANDS

FEDERATED STATES OF MICRONESIA
YAP ISLANDS
TRUK ISLANDS
Palau
Belau
(Trust Territory)
CAROLINE ISLANDS
MICRONESIA

NAURU / NAOERO
Bairiki
KIRIBATI

MELANESIA
NEW GUINEA
PAPUA NEW GUINEA
Port Moresby
BISMARCK ARCHIPELAGO
NEW BRITAIN
SOLOMON ISLANDS
Honiara
GUADALCANAL

VANUATU
NEW HEBRIDES
Port-Vila
NEW CALEDONIA (France)
Nouméa

TUVALU
FIJI ISLANDS

AUSTRALIA
GREAT SANDY DESERT
GIBSON DESERT
GREAT VICTORIA DESERT
SIMPSON DESERT
TANAMI DESERT
NULLARBOR PLAIN
Great Australian Bight
KIMBERLEY
ARNHEM LAND
Gulf of Carpentaria
CAPE YORK PENINSULA
Coral Sea

Darwin
Wyndham
Broome
Port Hedland
Karratha
Geraldton
Perth
Kalgoorlie
Esperance
Albany
Alice Springs
Coober Pedy
Port Augusta
Adelaide
Broken Hill
Melbourne
Geelong
Ballarat
Bendigo
Canberra
Wagga Wagga
Wollongong
Sydney
Newcastle
Brisbane
Gold Coast
Rockhampton
Mackay
Townsville
Cairns
Normanton
Mount Isa
Cloncurry
Longreach
Charleville
Bourke
Tamworth
Armidale

TASMANIA
Hobart
Launceston
Tasman Sea

NEW ZEALAND
NORTH ISLAND
SOUTH ISLAND
Auckland
Hamilton
Wellington
Nelson
Christchurch
Dunedin
Invercargill
Mount Cook

Norfolk
Kingston
(Australia)

INDIAN OCEAN

Scale 1:30,000,000
Lambert Azimuthal Equal Area Projection
500 1000 1500 2000 km
500 1000 miles
Longitude East 170 of Greenwich

San Luis
Obispo
Santa Barbara Bakersfield Pasadena Phoenix Mesa **UNITED STATES**
Los Angeles Barstow San Bernardino San Diego Yuma Tucson El Paso Odessa Big
Long Beach Mexicali Nogales Agua Casas Grandes Spring
San Bernardino Tijuana Ensenada Prieta Nueva Piedras
Nogales Casas Grandes Negras

ISLA DE
GUADALUPE
(Mexico)
BAJA
CALIFORNIA
Santa
Rosalía

MEXICO

La Paz
Cabo San Lucas

Ciudad
Juárez
Nuevo
Chihuahua
Hidalgo Monclova
del Parral
Nueva
Rosita
Hermosillo
Guaymas
Ciudad
Obregón
Los Mochis
Culiacán
Rosales
Durango
Victoria
de
Mazatlán

Tropic of Cancer

20

ISLAS
REVILLAGIGEDO
(Mexico)

Midway Islands
(U.S.)
PEARL AND HERMES

LISIANSKI

LAYSAN
MARO
GARDNER
PINNACLES

H A W A I I A N   I S L A N D S
FRENCH FRIGATE
SHOALS
NECKER
NIHOA
KAUAI

Hawaii
(U.S.)
KAULA *NIIHAU* *OAHU*
LANAI *MOLOKAI*
MAUI
KAHOOLAWE
Honolulu
Hawi
Hilo
HAWAII

c

Johnston
(U.S.)

P A C I F I C   *O C E A N*

CLIPPERTON
(French Polynesia)

10

KINGMAN
(U.S.)
PALMYRA
(U.S.)

d

TERAINA
(WASHINGTON)
TABUAERAN
(FANNING)

KIRITIMATI
(CHRISTMAS)

L I N E

JARVIS
(U.S.)

Equator

0

ND
BAKER
(U.S.)

WINSLOW

PHOENIX ISLANDS
KANTON
MCKEAN *BIRNIE* *ENDERBURY*
RAWAKI
(PHOENIX)
NIKUMARORO *ORONA* *MANRA*
(GARDNER) *(HULL)* *(SYDNEY)*
CARONDELET

K I R I B A T I

I S L A N D S

MALDEN

STARBUCK

e

C Y N E S I A

10

Tokelau *(New Zealand)*
ATAFU *TOKELAU*
NUKUNONU *ISLANDS*
FAKAOFO

WESTERN
SAMOA
SWAINS
SAMOA ISLANDS
SAVAI'I **Apia**
UPOLU
a
Mata-Utu
LLIS *UVEA*
UNA
PI

PUKAPUKA
NASSAU

RAKAHANGA
MANIHIKI
PENRHYN

NORTHERN
COOK ISLANDS

SUWARROW

VOSTOK

CAROLINE

FLINT

EIAO
NUKU HIVA *UA HUKA*
MARQUESAS
UA POU *HIVA OA*
TAHUATA
ISLANDS *FATU HIVA*

RANGIROA *ILES DU*
MATAIVA *MANIHI* *ROI GEORGES*
MOTU *APATAKI* *TAKUME* *FANGATAU*
ONE *LEEWARD* *ILES PALLISER* *ARATIKA*
MANUAE *ISLANDS* *KAUKURA* *TAKUME*
MAUPITI *HUAHINE* *KARAVA* *FAKAHINA*
MAUPIHAA *BORA-BORA* *TETIAROA* *TAHANEA* *MARUTEA*
RAIATEA *MOOREA* *MOTUTUNGA*
Papeete *HAO* *PUKARUHA*
TAHITI *RAVAHERE* *READ*
WINDWARD ISLANDS *VAHITAHI*
MANUANGI *AHUNUI*

TUAMOTU
ILES DU
DÉSAPPOINTEMENT
PUKAPUKA
A R C H I P E L A G O
AMANU
TATAKOTO

TAFAHI
NIUAFO'OU *NIUATO PUTAPU*

TONGA
FONUALEI

Cook Islands
(New Zealand)
PALMERSTON
AITUTAKI
MANUAE
TAKUTEA *MITIARO*
S O C I E T Y   I S L A N D S
MAUKE

American
Samoa
(U.S.)
ANTIOPE
Niue
(New Zealand)

VAVA'U
GROUP
HA'APAI GROUP
OTU GROUP **TONGA**
ISLANDS
NOMUKA GROUP
Nuku'alofa
TONGATAPU
GROUP
ATA
N REEFS

BEVERIDGE

SOUTHERN
COOK
ISLANDS
ATIU
Avarua *RAROTONGA*

MANGAIA

MARIA

RIMATARA

French
Polynesia

RURUTU

HEREHERETUE
ILES DU DUC
DE GLOUCESTER
MANUANGI
TUREIA
GROUPE
ACTEON
MARUTEA
MARIA
MANGAREVA
TEMOE
GAMBIER
ISLANDS

TEMATANGI
MURUROA
FAGATAUFA
MORANE

f

TUBUAI
ISLANDS *TUBUAI*
RAEVAVAE

20

OENO
PITCAIRN
HENDERSON
DUCIE
Adamstown
RAPA *ILOTS*
DE BASS
Pitcairn
(U.K.)

Tropic of Capricorn

UL
RMADEC
LANDS
w Zealand)
NCE ROCK

g

SALA Y GÓMEZ
(Chile)
EASTER ISLAND
(Chile)

ERNEST
LEGOUVÉ

MARIA THERESA

30

CHATHAM ISLANDS
(New Zealand)

h

i

A-590000-280-2 -2 -2 -3 B

Map 59 **AUSTRALIA**

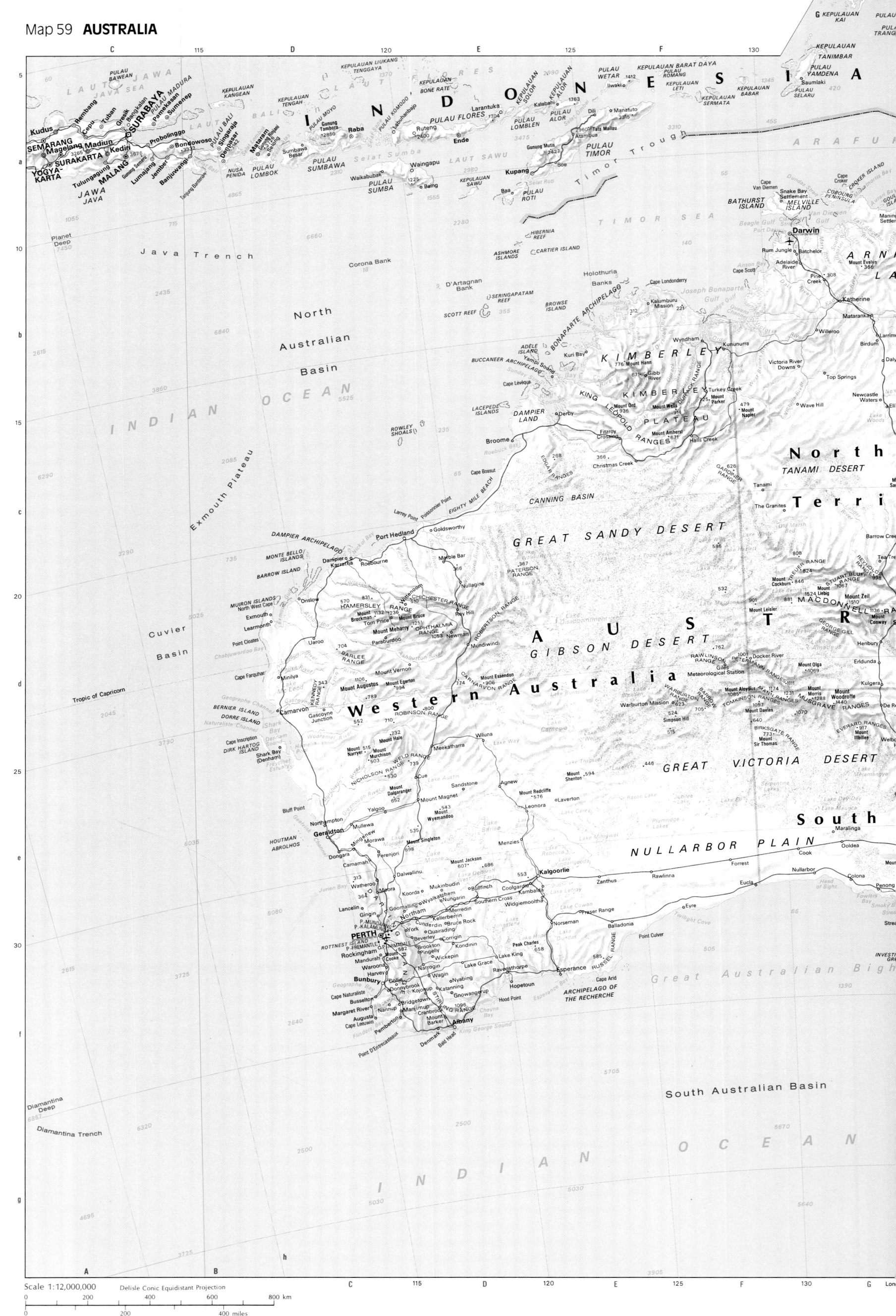

Scale 1:12,000,000   Delisle Conic Equidistant Projection

0   200   400   600   800 km

0   200   400 miles

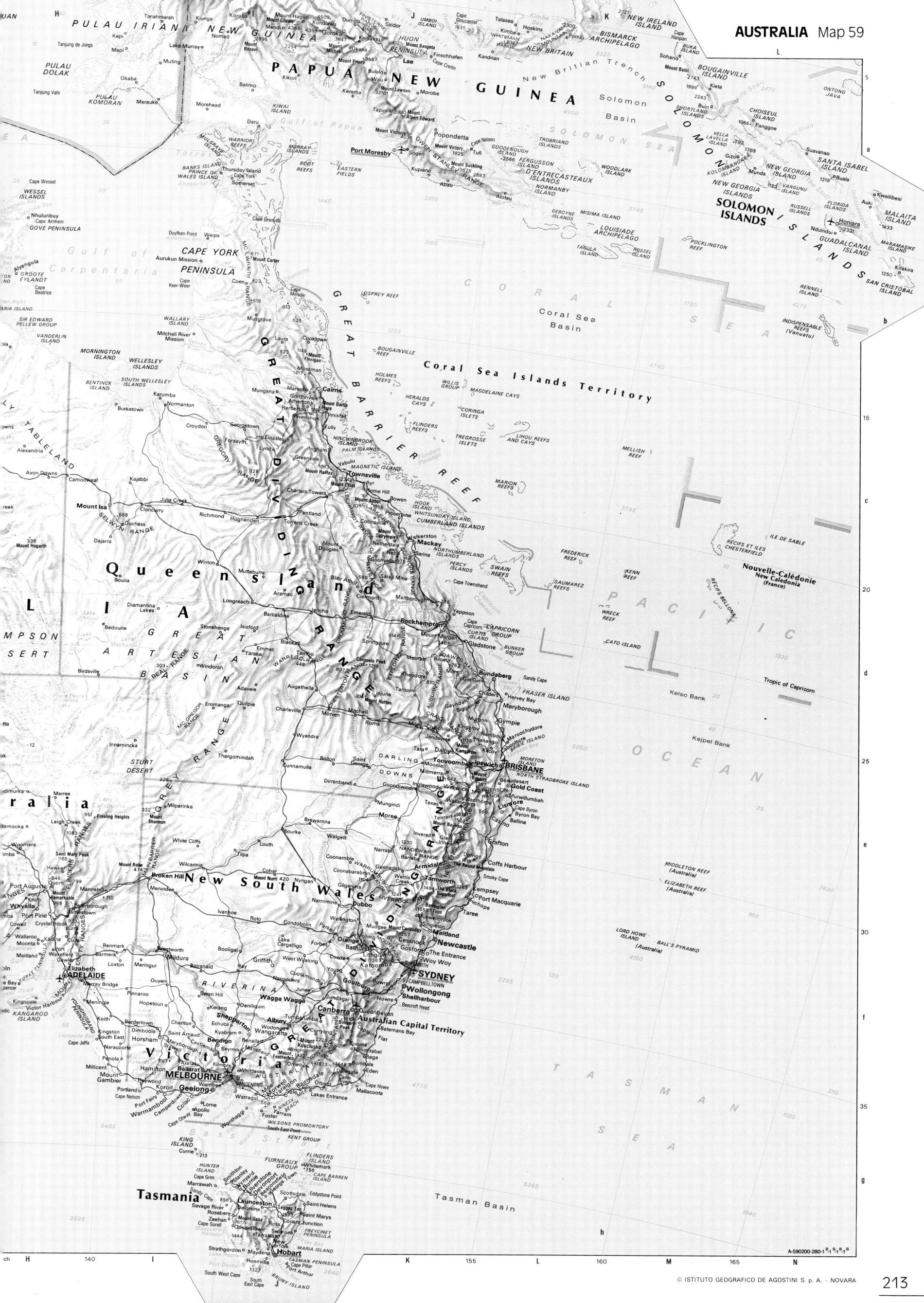

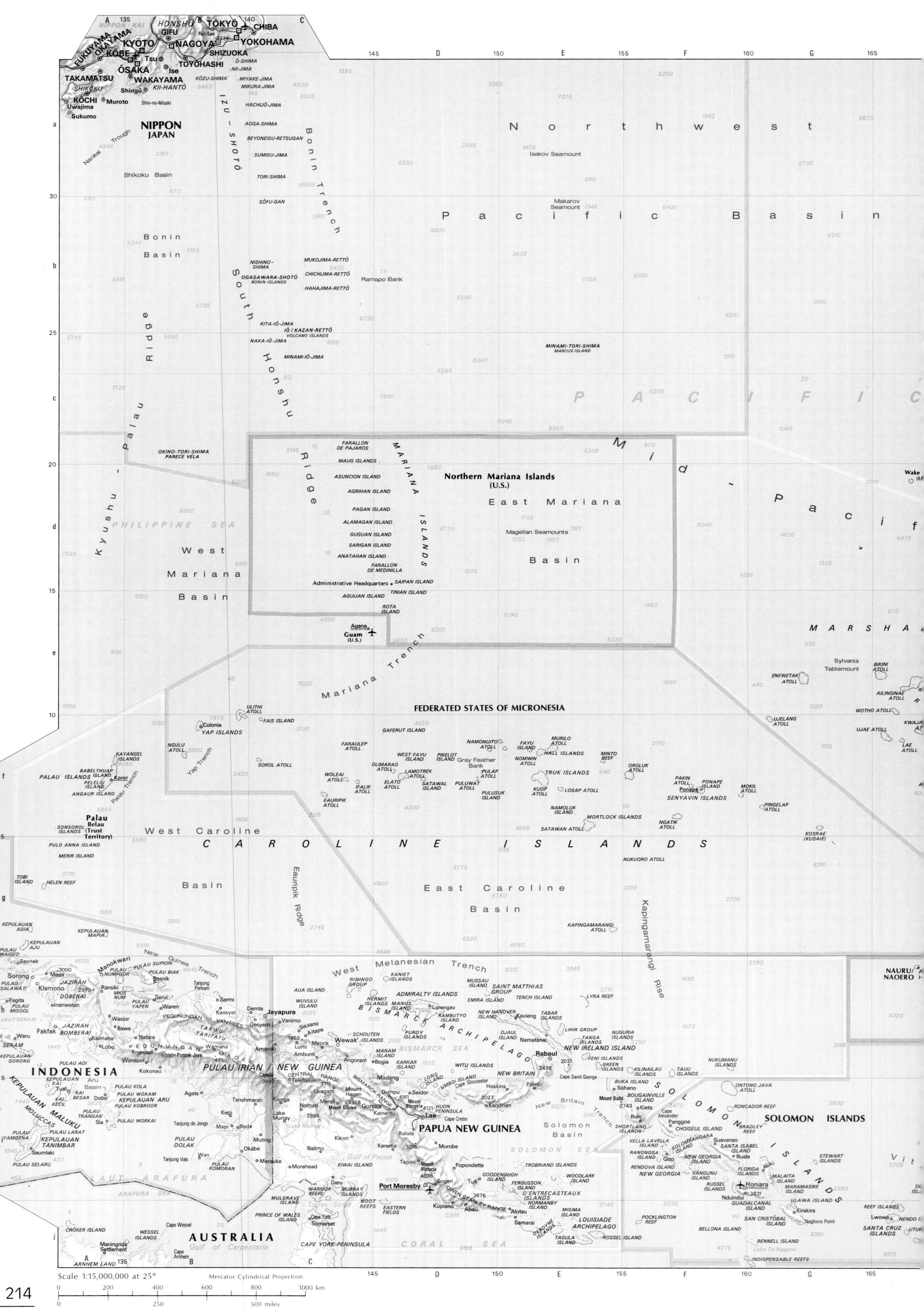

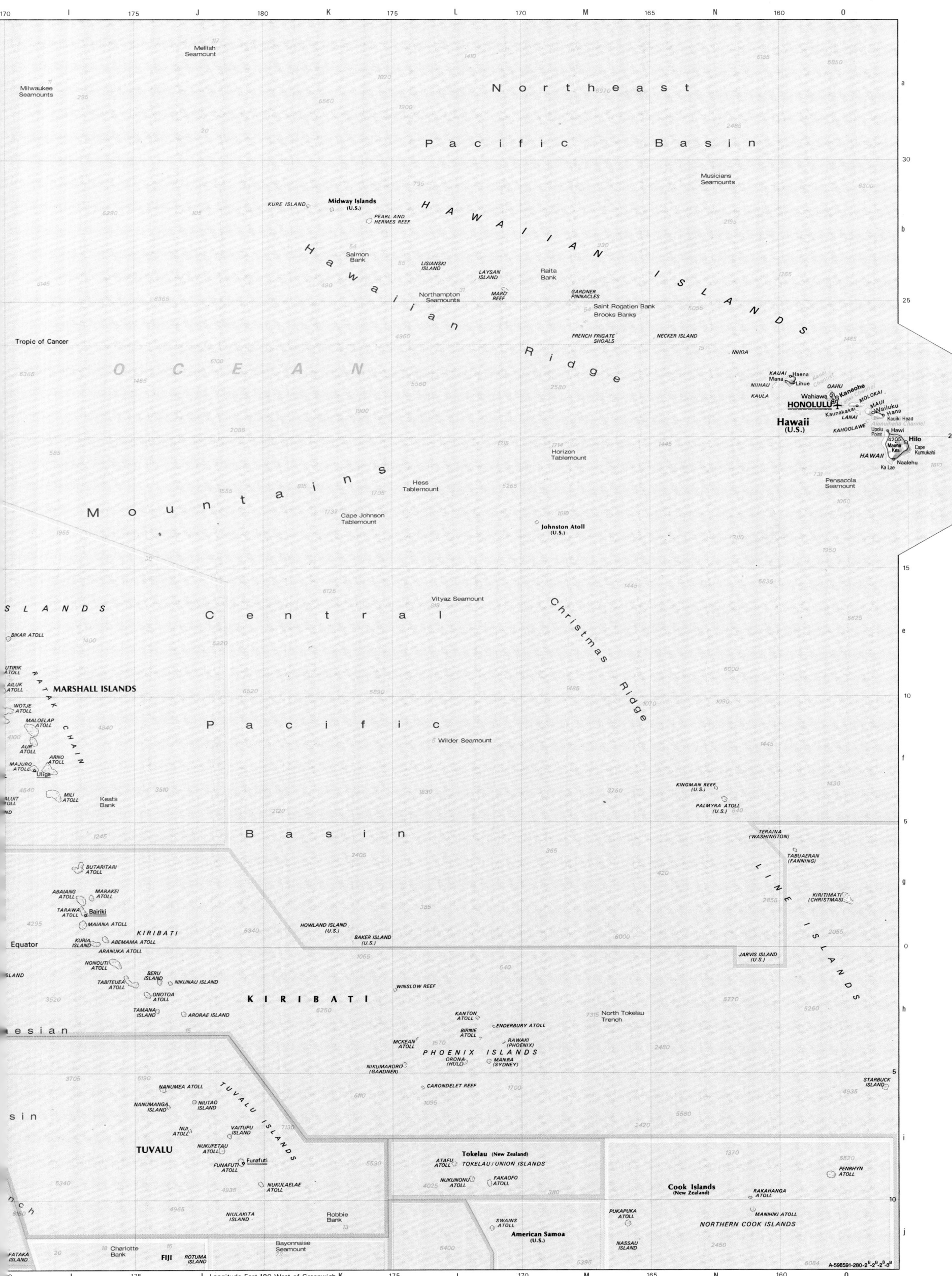

170 I 175 J 180 K 175 L 170 M 165 N 160 O

Mellish
Seamount

1410   6185   6850

Milwaukee
Seamounts   a
           295   2485

N o r t h e a s t
1020

6560   30
1900   *P a c i f i c   B a s i n*

Musicians
Seamounts

735   6300

KURE ISLAND   **Midway Islands**   b
           105   (U.S.)
6290   PEARL AND
                           HERMES REEF
                                                                        2195

Salmon
Bank   LISIANSKI   Raita
6245   ISLAND   LAYSAN   Bank   1755
           490   ISLAND

6365   Northampton   MARO   GARDNER
                       Seamounts   REEF   PINNACLES
                                                    Saint Rogatien Bank
                                                    Brooks Banks   5055

Tropic of Cancer   FRENCH FRIGATE   NECKER ISLAND
                                    4950   SHOALS   1465

6365   NIHOA

O C E A N   KAUAI   Haena   c
           1465   NIIHAU   Mana Lihue   OAHU
6365   Wahiawa Kaneohe
                       5560   KAULA   HONOLULU   MOLOKAI
                                                                                          LANAI MAUI Wailuku
1900   KAHOOLAWE   Hana
                                                                                          Kauiki Head
2095   **Hawaii**   Hawi
                                                                                  (U.S.)   Upolu 4205
1315   1714   Point Mauna Hilo
585   Horizon   1445   Kea
           Tablemount   *HAWAII* Cape
                                                                                                Kumukahi
                                                                        Pensacola   Naalehu
M o u n t a i n s   731   Seamount   Ka Lae   1810
815   1050
1555   Hess
           Tablemount   5265
M   1705   1950

1737   Cape Johnson   1510
        Tablemount
1955   d
                                            Johnston Atoll   3110
           30   (U.S.)
                                                                                    1950

15

8125   1445   5835
C e n t r a l
6220   Vityaz Seamount
                       813
BIKAR ATOLL   5625   e
1400
UTIRIK   8220
ATOLL
AILUK   5000
ATOLL   *R A T A K*   6820   5890
MARSHALL ISLANDS   1485
WOTJE   *P a c i f i c*   1070   1090
ATOLL   10
MALOELAP
ATOLL   4840
4100
AUR   5 Wilder Seamount   1445
ATOLL   *C H A I N*
ARNO   f
ATOLL
MAJURO   Uliga   KINGMAN REEF
ATOLL   (U.S.)   1430
MILI   3750
4640   ATOLL   3510
        Keats   PALMYRA ATOLL
        Bank   2120   (U.S.) 840

1245   5
                                            TERAINA
B a s i n   2406   (WASHINGTON)
                                                                        TABUAERAN   g
385   420   (FANNING)
                                                      2855   KIRITIMATI
BUTARITARI   (CHRISTMAS)
ATOLL   385   2055
ABAIANG   MARAKEI
ATOLL   ATOLL   *L I N E*
TARAWA   5340   HOWLAND ISLAND   6000
ATOLL   Bairiki   (U.S.)   *I S L A N D S*
4295   MAIANA ATOLL   BAKER ISLAND
        K I R I B A T I   (U.S.)   0
Equator   KURIA   JARVIS ISLAND
        ISLAND   ABEMAMA ATOLL   1055   (U.S.)
        ARANUKA ATOLL
NONOUTI   840
ATOLL   BERU
        ISLAND   WINSLOW REEF
TABITEUEA   NIKUNAU ISLAND
3520   ATOLL   8770   5260
        ONOTOA
        ATOLL   6250
TAMANA   **K I R I B A T I**   KANTON   7315   North Tokelau   h
ISLAND   ARORAE ISLAND   ATOLL   Trench
nesian   BIRNIE   ENDERBURY ATOLL   2480
                                ATOLL
        15   MCKEAN   1570   RAWAKI
                 ATOLL   (PHOENIX)
                 P H O E N I X   I S L A N D S   5
                 NIKUMARORO   ORONA   MANRA
                 (GARDNER)   (HULL)   (SYDNEY)
3705   6190   STARBUCK
        NANUMEA ATOLL   CARONDELET REEF   1700   ISLAND
NANUMANGA   NIUTAO   6110   4935
ISLAND   ISLAND   1095
                 T U V A L U   I S L A N D S   5580   i
        NUI   7130   2420
        ATOLL   VAITUPU
        NUKUFETAU   ISLAND
TUVALU   ATOLL   1370   5520
        FUNAFUTI   Funafuti   ATAFU   Tokelau (New Zealand)   PENRHYN
        ATOLL   5590   ATOLL   TOKELAU / UNION ISLANDS   ATOLL
sin   5340   NUKULAELAE   NUKUNONU   FAKAOFO   **Cook Islands**
        ATOLL   4935   ATOLL   ATOLL   3710   (New Zealand)
                                            RAKAHANGA
                 NIULAKITA   Robbie   4025   PUKAPUKA   ATOLL   ATOLL
nch   6160   4965   ISLAND   Bank   SWAINS   ATOLL   MANIHIKI ATOLL   10
                 13   American Samoa   *NORTHERN COOK ISLANDS*
                 Bayonnaise   (U.S.)   NASSAU   2450
FATAKA   Charlotte   Seamount   5400   ISLAND
ISLAND   Bank   29   5395   j
        20   16   85   ROTUMA
                 FIJI   ISLAND   A-59B591-280-2⁸-2⁸-2⁸-2⁸

170 I 175 J Longitude East 180 West of Greenwich K 175 L 170 M 165 N 160 O

Map 61　THE SOUTH PACIFIC

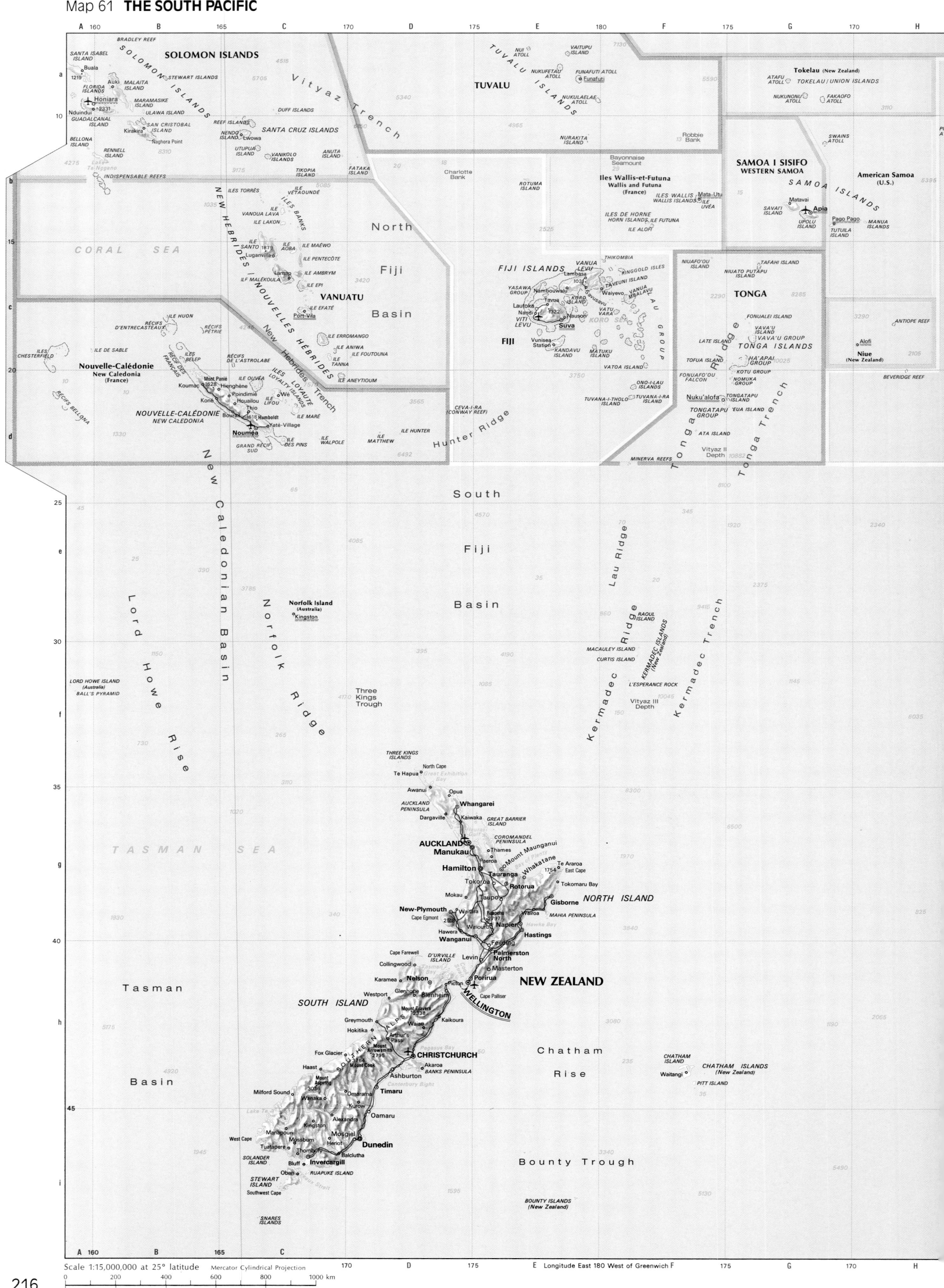

Scale 1:15,000,000 at 25° latitude　　Mercator Cylindrical Projection

Longitude East 180 West of Greenwich

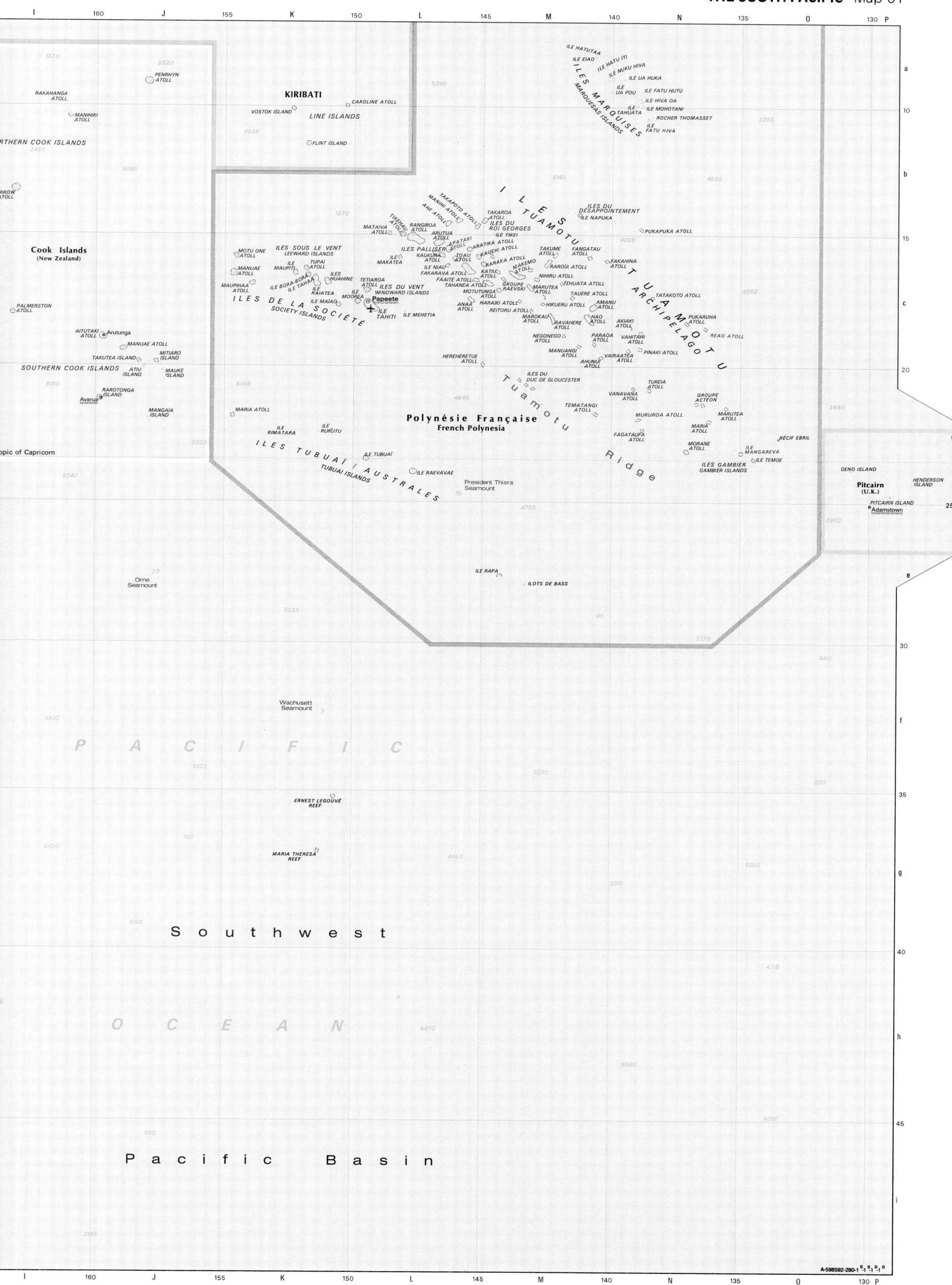

a

KIRIBATI

ILE HATUTAA
ILE EIAO
ILE HATU ITI
ILE NUKU HIVA
ILE UA HUKA
ILE UA POU   ILE FATU HUTU
ILE HIVA OA
ILE MOHOTANI
ROCHER THOMASSET
ILE FATU HIVA
ILES MARQUISES
MARQUESAS ISLANDS

RAKAHANGA ATOLL

PENRHYN ATOLL

VOSTOK ISLAND   CAROLINE ATOLL
LINE ISLANDS

MANIHIKI ATOLL

10

NORTHERN COOK ISLANDS

FLINT ISLAND

b

Cook Islands
(New Zealand)

TAKAPOTO ATOLL
MANIHI ATOLL
AHE ATOLL
TIKEHAU ATOLL   RANGIROA ATOLL
MATAIVA ATOLL
ARUTUA ATOLL
TAKAROA ATOLL
ILES DU ROI GEORGES
ILE TIKEI
ILES DU DESAPPOINTEMENT
ILE NAPUKA
PUKAPUKA ATOLL

I L E S   D U
T U A M O T U

MOTU ONE ATOLL
ILES SOUS LE VENT
LEEWARD ISLANDS
ILES PALLISER ATOLL
APATAKI
ARATIKA ATOLL
KAUEHI ATOLL
TAKUME ATOLL
FANGATAU ATOLL
FAKAHINA ATOLL

MANUAE ATOLL
ILE MAUPITI
TUPAI ATOLL
KAUKURA ATOLL
TOAU ATOLL
ARAKA ATOLL
MAKEMO ATOLL
RAROIA ATOLL

MAUPIHAA ATOLL
ILE BORA-BORA
ILE TAHAA
ILES HUAHINE
ILE NIAU
MAKATEA
FAKARAVA ATOLL
KATIU ATOLL
NIHIRU ATOLL
TEHUATA ATOLL

ILE RAIATEA
ILE MAIAO
TETIAROA ATOLL
ILES DU VENT
FAAITE ATOLL
TAHANEA ATOLL
MOTUTUNGA ATOLL
GROUPE RAEVRE
MARUTEA ATOLL

ILES DE LA SOCIÉTÉ
SOCIETY ISLANDS
ILE MOOREA
Papeete
WINDWARD ISLANDS
ANAA ATOLL
HARAIKI ATOLL
HIKUERU ATOLL
AMANU ATOLL

ILE TAHITI
ILE MEHETIA
REITORU ATOLL
MAROKAU ATOLL
HAO ATOLL
AKIAKI ATOLL
PUKARUHA ATOLL

PALMERSTON ATOLL
NEGONEGO ATOLL
RAVAHERE ATOLL
PARAOA ATOLL
VAHITAHI ATOLL
REAO ATOLL

AITUTAKI ATOLL   Arutunga
MANUAE ATOLL
HEREHERETUE ATOLL
MANUANGI ATOLL
PINAKI ATOLL

TAKUTEA ISLAND
MITIARO ISLAND
AHUNUI ATOLL
VAIRAATEA ATOLL

SOUTHERN COOK ISLANDS
ATIU ISLAND
MAUKE ISLAND
ILES DU DUC DE GLOUCESTER
TUREIA ATOLL

RAROTONGA ISLAND
Avarua
VANAVANA ATOLL
GROUPE ACTÉON

MANGAIA ISLAND
MARIA ATOLL
TEMATANGI ATOLL
MURUROA ATOLL
MARUTEA ATOLL

TATAKOTO ATOLL

Polynésie Française
French Polynesia
FAGATAUFA ATOLL
MARIA ATOLL

ILE RIMATARA
ILE RURUTU
MORANE ATOLL
RÉCIF EBRIL

Tropic of Capricorn
ILE TUBUAI
ILES TUBUAI / AUSTRALES
TUBUAI ISLANDS
ILES GAMBIER
GAMBIER ISLANDS
ILE MANGAREVA
ILE TEMOE

ILE RAEVAVAE
President Thiers Seamount
OENO ISLAND

Pitcairn
(U.K.)
HENDERSON ISLAND

25
PITCAIRN ISLAND
Adamstown

ILE RAPA
ILOTS DE BASS

e

Orne Seamount

30

Wachusett Seamount

P A C I F I C

f

ERNEST LEGOUVÉ REEF

35

MARIA THERESA REEF

g

S o u t h w e s t

40

O C E A N

h

45

P a c i f i c   B a s i n

i

A-598592-280-1

Map 62 **NEW ZEALAND**

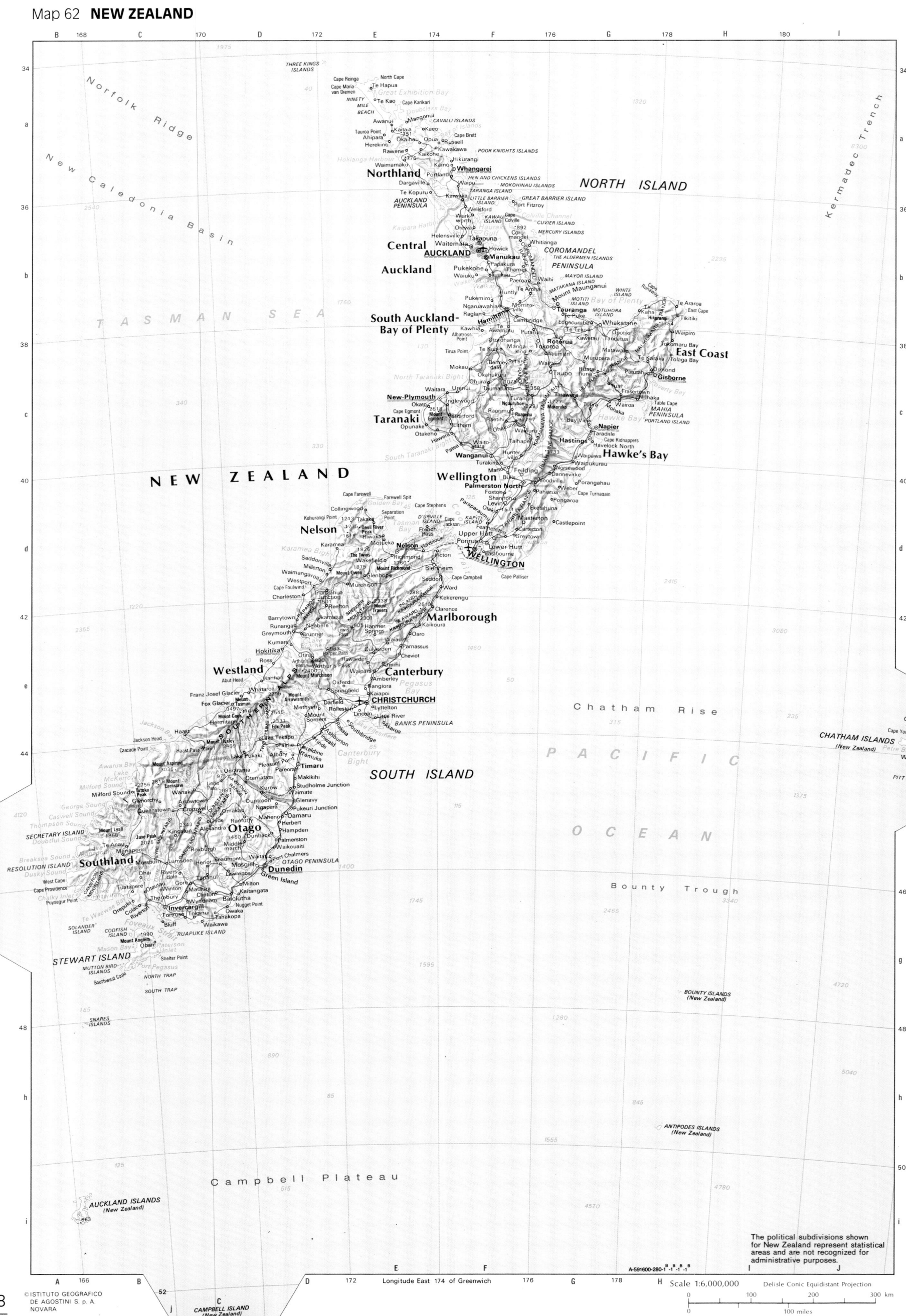

The political subdivisions shown
for New Zealand represent statistical
areas and are not recognized for
administrative purposes.

A-591600-280-1°-1°-1°-1°

Scale 1:6,000,000   Delisle Conic Equidistant Projection

Longitude East 174 of Greenwich

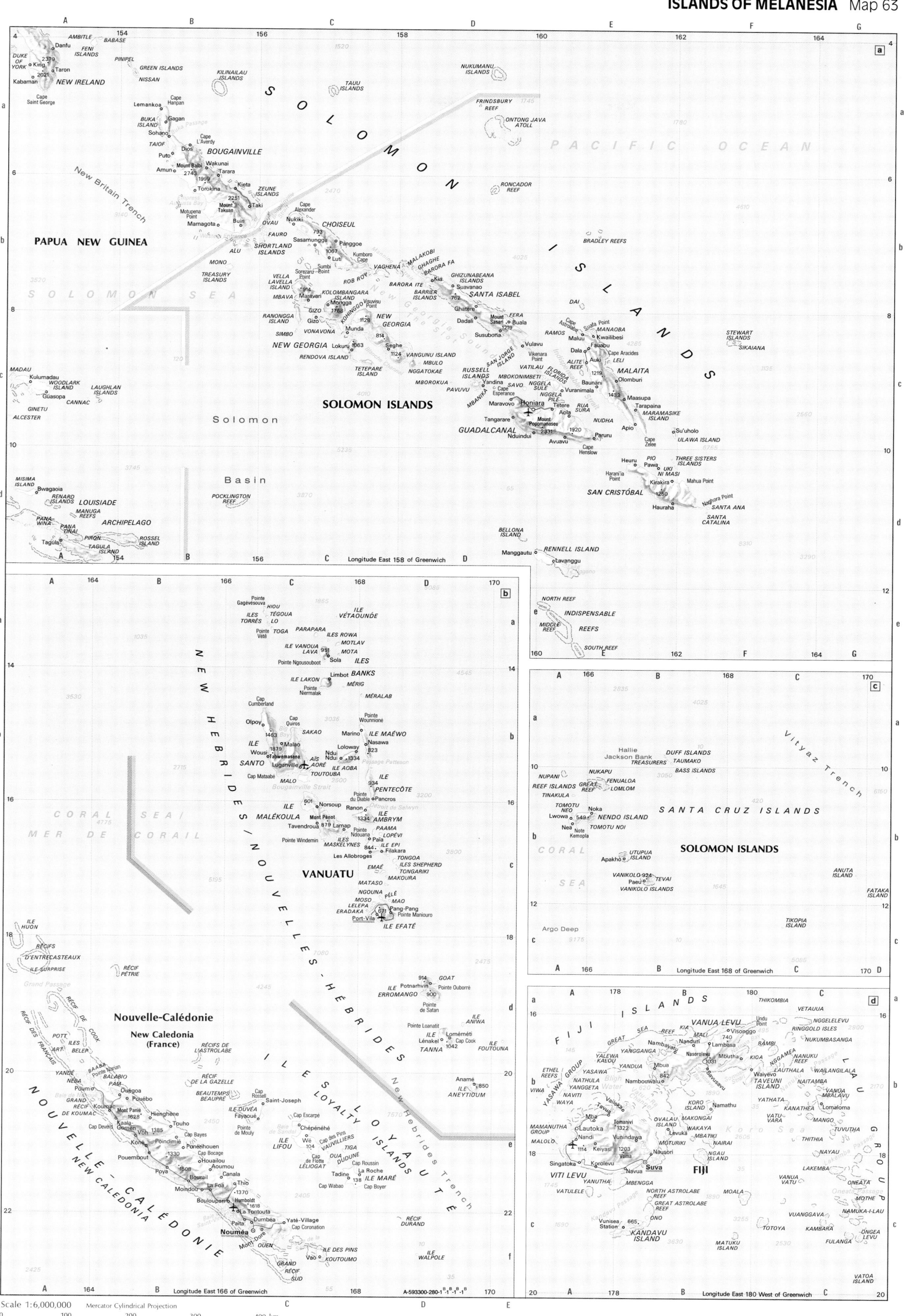

Map 64 **ISLANDS OF MICRONESIA-POLYNESIA**

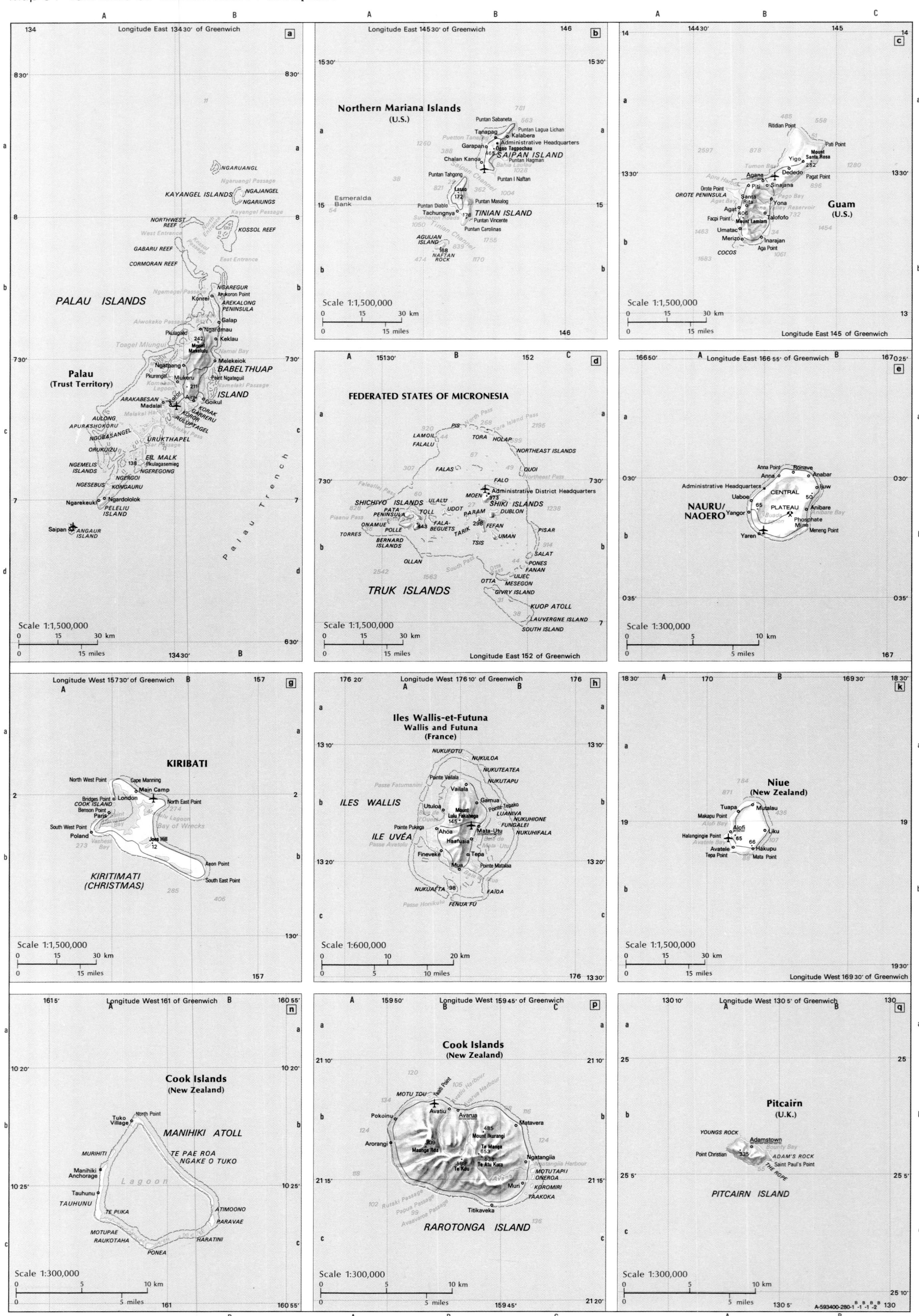

Northern Mariana Islands
(U.S.)

Guam
(U.S.)

PALAU ISLANDS

Palau
(Trust Territory)

**BABELTHUAP
ISLAND**

FEDERATED STATES OF MICRONESIA

TRUK ISLANDS

**NAURU/
NAOERO**

KIRIBATI

*KIRITIMATI
(CHRISTMAS)*

Iles Wallis-et-Futuna
Wallis and Futuna
(France)

ILES WALLIS

ILE UVÉA

Niue
(New Zealand)

Cook Islands
(New Zealand)

MANIHIKI ATOLL

Cook Islands
(New Zealand)

RAROTONGA ISLAND

Pitcairn
(U.K.)

PITCAIRN ISLAND

Scale 1:1,500,000
Scale 1:1,500,000
Scale 1:1,500,000
Scale 1:1,500,000
Scale 1:300,000
Scale 1:600,000
Scale 1:1,500,000
Scale 1:300,000
Scale 1:300,000
Scale 1:300,000

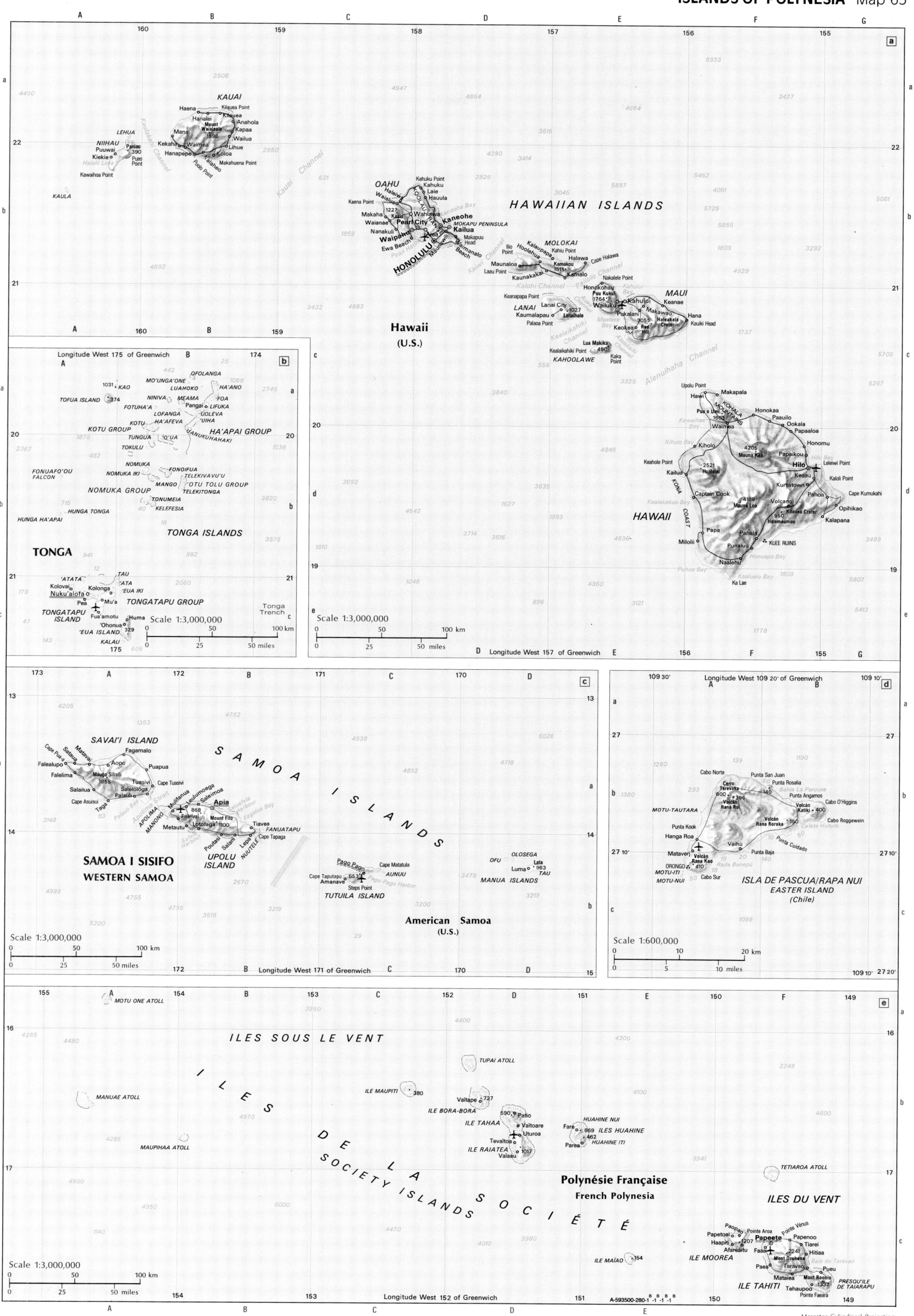

Mercator Cylindrical Projection

Map 66 **ANTARCTIC REGION, PHYSICAL**

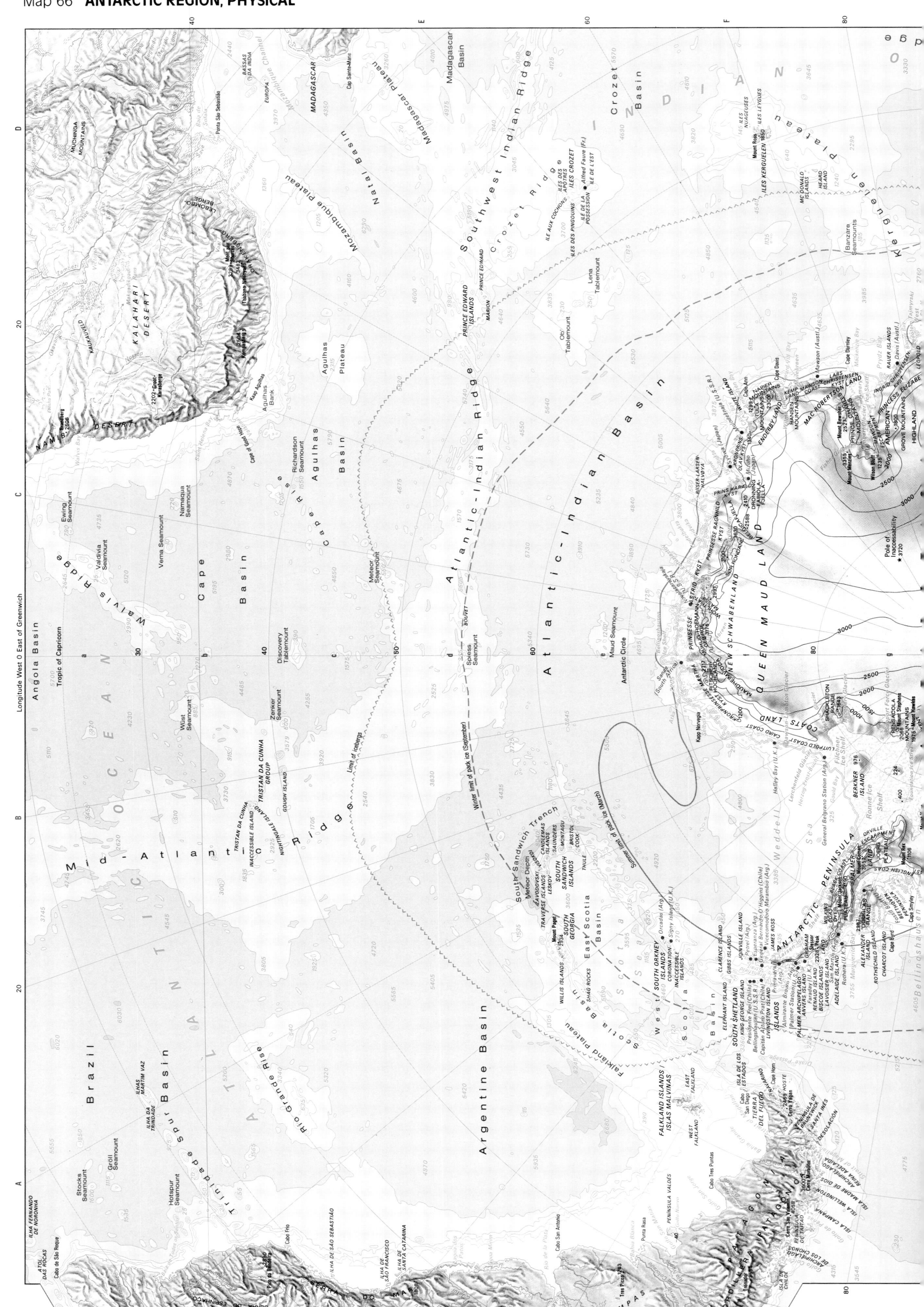

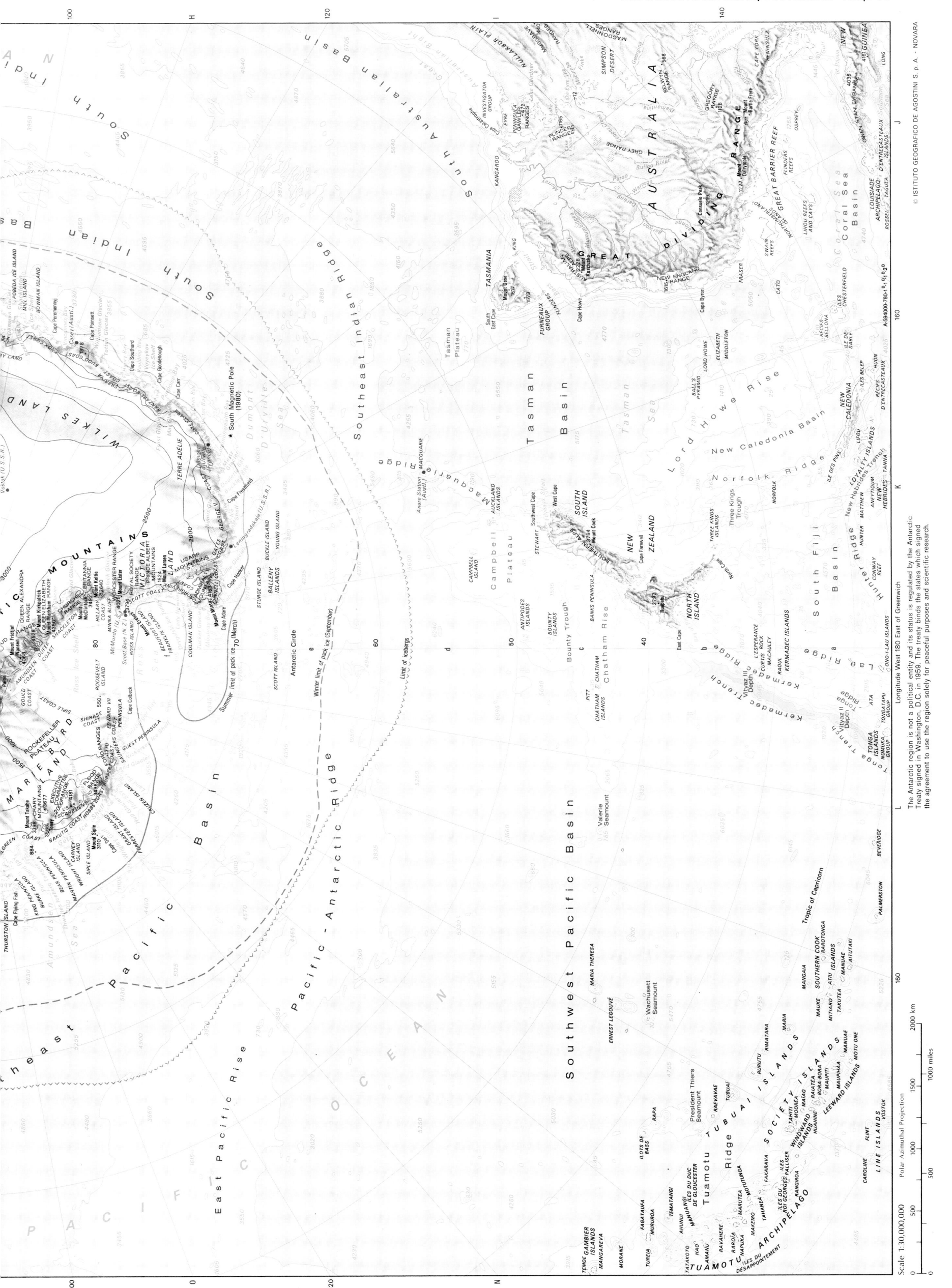

AUSTRALIA

TASMANIA

NEW ZEALAND

NORTH ISLAND

SOUTH ISLAND

WILKES LAND

VICTORIA LAND

BYRD LAND

MARIE

GREAT DIVIDING RANGE

NEW GUINEA

NEW CALEDONIA

Tasman Sea

Tasman Basin

Lord Howe Rise

New Caledonia Basin

Norfolk Ridge

South Fiji Basin

Kermadec Ridge

Tonga Trench

Kermadec Trench

South Australian Basin

Southeast Indian Ridge

South Indian Basin

Macquarie Ridge

Campbell Plateau

Chatham Rise

Bounty Trough

Pacific – Antarctic Ridge

Southwest Pacific Basin

Southeast Pacific Basin

East Pacific Rise

PACIFIC OCEAN

Tuamotu Ridge

Tubuai Islands

Society Islands

★ South Magnetic Pole (1980)

Antarctic Circle

Summer limit of pack ice (March)

Winter limit of pack ice (September)

Limit of icebergs

Tropic of Capricorn

D'Urville Sea

Ross Ice Shelf

SOUTHERN COOK ISLANDS

TUAMOTU ARCHIPELAGO

GAMBIER ISLANDS

Longitude West 180 East of Greenwich

The Antarctic region is not a political entity and its status is regulated by the Antarctic Treaty signed in Washington, D.C. in 1959. The treaty binds the states which signed the agreement to use the region solely for peaceful purposes and scientific research.

Scale 1:30,000,000   Polar Azimuthal Projection

500   1000   1500   2000 km

500   1000 miles

© ISTITUTO GEOGRAFICO DE AGOSTINI S.p.A. - NOVARA

Map 67 **ARCTIC REGION, PHYSICAL**

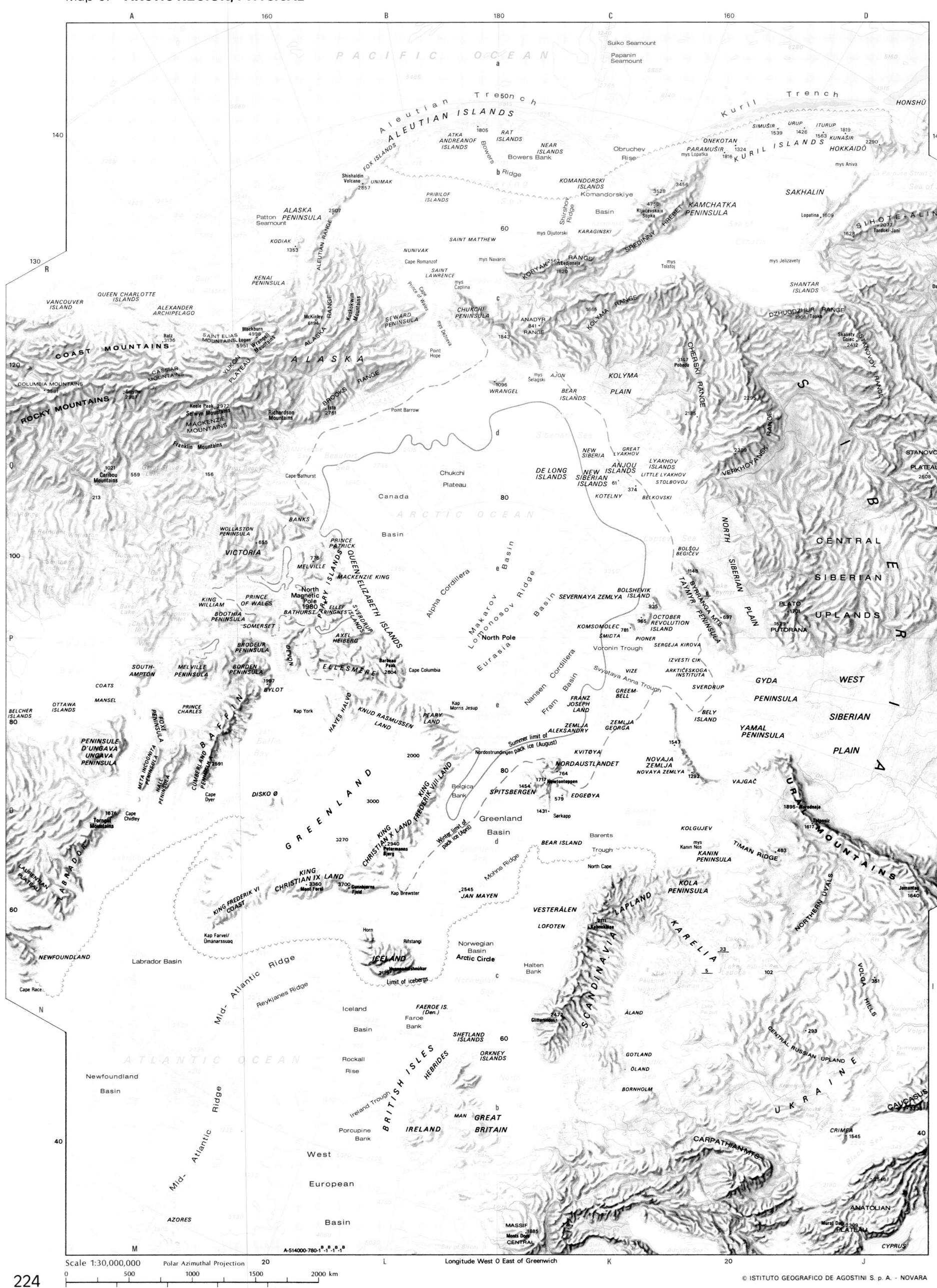

PACIFIC OCEAN

Suiko Seamount
Papanin Seamount

a

Aleutian Trench
ALEUTIAN ISLANDS
Bowers

Kuril Trench

1805
RAT
ISLANDS

ANDREANOF
ISLANDS

ATKA

NEAR
ISLANDS

Obruchev
Rise

ONEKOTAN
PARAMUŠIR

SIMUŠIR URUP ITURUP
1539 1426

1819
1563 KUNAŠIR 2290

HONSHŪ

FOX ISLANDS

Bowers Bank

b Ridge

KOMANDORSKI
ISLANDS

1324
mys Lopatka
1816

KURIL ISLANDS

HOKKAIDŌ

Shishaldin
Volcano
UNIMAK 2857

PRIBILOF
ISLANDS

Komandorskiye

Shirshov
Ridge

Basin

3528

475φ
Ključevskaja
Sopka

3456

KAMCHATKA
PENINSULA

mys Aniva

SAKHALIN

ALASKA
PENINSULA 2507
Patton
Seamount

SAINT MATTHEW

60

mys Oljutorski

KARAGINSKI

Lopatina 1609

SIHOTE-ALIN

2077
Tordoki-Jani

KODIAK 1353

NUNIVAK

Cape Romanzof

mys Navarin

mys
Tolstoj

1628

KENAI
PENINSULA

SAINT
LAWRENCE

mys Caplina

2562
KORYAK Ledjanaja
1826 RANGE

mys Jelizavety

SHANTAR
ISLANDS

McKinley
6194

ALEUTIAN RANGE

Kuskokwim
Mountains

SEWARD
PENINSULA

CHUKCHI
PENINSULA

ANADYR
841
RANGE

1665

KOLYMA RANGE

DZHUGDZHUR RANGE

1906 Topko

130
R

VANCOUVER
ISLAND

QUEEN CHARLOTTE
ISLANDS

ALEXANDER
ARCHIPELAGO

Ratz
3136

Blackburn
4998
Logan
5951 Mt.
Wrangell

SAINT ELIAS
MOUNTAINS

ALASKA
RANGE

Point Dension

1843

CHERSKI
RANGE

3147
Pobeda

2195

Skalisty
Golec 2412

STANOVOY RANGE

S
I
B
E
R

120

COAST MOUNTAINS

CASSIAR
MOUNTAINS

Sovphy
2987

YUKON
PLATEAU

ALASKA

Point
Hope

BROOKS RANGE

mys
Selagski

1096
WRANGEL

BEAR
ISLANDS

2185

VERKHOYANSK RANGE

STANOVOY
PLATEAU
2608

COLUMBIA MOUNTAINS 3581

Keele Peak 2972
Selwyn Mountains

Richardson
Mountains

Isto
2761

KOLYMA
PLAIN

2399

ROCKY MOUNTAINS

MACKENZIE
MOUNTAINS

Point Barrow

Franklin Mountains

Siberian Sea

CENTRAL

Q

1021
559
Caribou
Mountains

156

Beaufort

Chukchi
Plateau

DE LONG
ISLANDS

GREAT
LYAKHOV

NEW
SIBERIA

LYAKHOV
ISLANDS

SIBERIAN

213

Cape Bathurst

Canada
Basin

ARCTIC OCEAN

80

NEW
SIBERIAN
ISLANDS

ANJOU
ISLANDS

LITTLE LYAKHOV
STOLBOVOJ

374

UPLANDS

100

WOLLASTON
PENINSULA

655

BANKS

PRINCE
PATRICK

Canada
Basin

61

KOTELNY
BELKOVSKI

VICTORIA

MELVILLE 776

QUEEN ELIZABETH ISLANDS

MACKENZIE KING

Alpha Cordillera

Makarov
Basin

Lomonosov Ridge

BOLŠOJ
BEGIČEV

NORTH

1148

PLATO
1701
PUTORANA

STANOVOY
PLATEAU

KING
WILLIAM

PRINCE
OF WALES

North
Magnetic
Pole
1980 BATHURST

ELLEF
RINGNES
ISLAND

SVERDRUP

BOLSHEVIK
ISLAND

SEVERNAYA ZEMLYA

935

TAYMYR PENINSULA

BYRRANGA MTS.

SIBERIAN

697

P

BOOTHIA
PENINSULA

SOMERSET

AXEL
HEIBERG

ELLESMERE

Barbeau
Peak
2604

Cape Columbia

OCTOBER
REVOLUTION
ISLAND

KOMSOMOLEC
ŠMIDTA

965

781

PIONER

Voronin Trough

SERGEJA KIROVA

1629
PLAIN

SOUTH-
AMPTON

MELVILLE
PENINSULA

BORDEN
PENINSULA

1997
BYLOT

BRODEUR
PENINSULA

Kap Morris Jesup

PEARY
LAND

e

Nansen Cordillera

IZVESTI CIK

VIZE
ARKTIČESKOGA
INSTITUTA

SVERDRUP

GYDA
PENINSULA

WEST

COATS

MANSEL

PRINCE
CHARLES

Kap York

HAYES HALVØ

KNUD RASMUSSEN
LAND

Svyataya Anna Trough

Fram
Basin

FRANZ
JOSEPH
LAND

GREEM-
BELL

PIONER

BELY
ISLAND

SIBERIAN

BELCHER
ISLANDS

OTTAWA
ISLANDS

FOXE
PENINSULA

BAFFIN

Baffin
Bay

2000

Summer limit of
pack ice (August)

ZEMLJA
ALEKSANDRY

ZEMLJA
GEORGA

1541

YAMAL
PENINSULA

PLAIN

80

PENINSULE
D'UNGAVA
UNGAVA
PENINSULA

META INCOGNITA
PENINSULA

HALL
PENINSULA
2591

Nordostrundingen pack ice

Belgica
Bank

80

NORDAUSTLANDET
1712 Newtontoppen

764

ZEMLJA
GEORGA

NOVAJA
ZEMLJA
NOVAYA ZEMLYA

1292

VAJGAČ

O

TORNGAT
Mountains 1676
Cape
Chidley

PRINCE
CHARLES

DISKO Ø

3000

KING
FREDERIK VIII LAND

SPITSBERGEN

1454
579

EDGEØYA

BEAR ISLAND

1895 Narodnaja

U
R
A
L

MOUNTAINS

1617

GREENLAND

KING
CHRISTIAN X LAND FREDERIK

2940
Petermanns
Bjerg

3270

1431
Sørkapp

Greenland
Basin

d

Mohns Ridge

Barents
Trough

North Cape

KOLGUJEV

mys
Kanin Nos

TIMAN RIDGE

463

KANIN
PENINSULA

LAURENTIAN
PLATEAU

60

LABRADOR

KING FREDERIK VI
COAST

KING
CHRISTIAN IX LAND 3380
3700
Mont Forel

Gunnbjørns
Fjeld

2545
JAN MAYEN

VESTERÅLEN

KOLA
PENINSULA

LAPLAND

SCANDINAVIA

Jamantau
1640

NEWFOUNDLAND

Kap Farvel/
Ûmanarssuaq

Kap Brewster

LOFOTEN

2111
KJølen

KARELIA

NORTHERN URALS

N

Cape Race

Labrador Basin

Mid-Atlantic Ridge

Reykjanes Ridge

Horn
Rifstangi

ICELAND
2119
Hvannadalshnúkur

Limit of icebergs

Norwegian
Basin
Arctic Circle

Halten
Bank

c

2472
Glittertinden

ÅLAND

33
5

102

351

VOLGA
HILLS

Newfoundland
Basin

Mid-Atlantic Ridge

Iceland
Basin

FAEROE IS.
(Den.)
Faroe
Bank

SHETLAND
ISLANDS

60

293

CENTRAL RUSSIAN UPLAND

ATLANTIC OCEAN

Rockall
Rise

ORKNEY
ISLANDS

GOTLAND

ÖLAND

BRITISH ISLES

HEBRIDES

BORNHOLM

UKRAINE

Ireland Trough

MAN

b

CAUCASUS

Porcupine
Bank

IRELAND

GREAT
BRITAIN

CRIMEA
1545

40

West

CARPATHIAN MTS.

40

European

AZORES

Basin

MASSIF
1885
Monts Dore
CENTRAL

ANATOLIAN

Murat Dağı PLATEAU

CYPRUS

Scale 1:30,000,000   Polar Azimuthal Projection

20

Longitude West 0 East of Greenwich

20

© ISTITUTO GEOGRAFICO DE AGOSTINI S. p. A. - NOVARA

0   500   1000   1500   2000 km

0   500   1000 miles

A-514000-780-1

Maps of the United States and Canada

MAP LEGEND

CULTURAL FEATURES

Political Boundaries

International

Secondary (State)

County

Populated Places

Cities, towns, and villages

 Symbol size represents population of the place

Chicago
Gary
Racine
Glenview
Edgewood

Type size represents relative importance of the place

Major Urban Areas
Area of continuous commercial, industrial, and residential development in and around a major city

○ Community within a city

⊛ Capital of major political unit

✪ Capital of U.S. state

○ County Seat

▲ Military Installation

Transportation

Major Highway

Railroad

Tunnel

Miscellaneous

National Park

National Monument

Indian Reservation

△ Point of Interest

Dam

Bridge

Pier

LAND FEATURES

Mountain Ranges

Mountain Peak

Point of Elevation in Feet above Sea Level   + 11,278

Pass

Escarpment, Bluffs, Cliffs

Lava Flows

Plains, Flatlands

WATER FEATURES

Coastlines and Shorelines

Indefinite or Unsurveyed Coastlines and Shorelines

Lakes and Reservoirs

Canals

Rivers and Streams

Falls and Rapids

Intermittent or Unsurveyed Rivers and Streams

Swamps and Marshes

Directional Flow Arrow

Rocks, Shoals and Reefs

TYPE STYLES USED TO NAME FEATURES

Note: Size of type varies according to importance and available space. Letters for names of major features are spread across the extent of the feature.

CANADA	Country, State, or Province	U I N T A DESERT	Major Terrain Features
			NUNIVAK Island or Coastal Feature
Naval Air Station	Military Installation	MT. MORIAH	Individual Mountain
			Ocean Lake River Canal Hydrographic Features
CROCKETT	County	MESA VERDE SAN XAVIER	National Park or Monument, Indian Res.

Lambert Conformal Conic Projection
CALE 1:12,000,000   1 Inch = 189 Statute Miles

Cities and Towns

Albertville 12,039 A3
Alexander City 13,807 C4
Andalusia 10,415 D3
Anniston 29,523 B4
Arab 5,967 A3
Athens 14,558 A3
Atmore 8,789 D2
Auburn 28,471 C4
Bay Minette 7,455 E2
Bessemer 31,729 B3
Birmingham 286,799 B3
Bluff Park 12,000 g7
Boaz 7,151 A3
Brewton 6,680 D2
Center Point 23,317 f7
Childersburg 5,084 B3
Clanton 5,832 C3
Cullman 13,084 A3
Decatur 42,002 A3
Demopolis 7,678 C2
Dothan 48,750 D4
Enterprise 18,033 D4
Eufaula 12,097 D4
Fairfield 13,242 B3
Fayette 5,287 B2
Florence 37,029 A2
Fort Payne 11,485 A4
Gadsden 47,565 A3
Geneva 4,866 D4
Greenville 7,807 D3
Guntersville 7,041 A3
Haleyville 5,306 A2
Hamilton 5,093 A2
Hartselle 8,858 A3
Homewood 21,412 g7
Hueytown 13,478 g6
Huntsville 142,513 A3
Jackson 6,073 D2
Jacksonville 9,735 B4
Jasper 11,894 B2
Lanett 6,897 C4
Leeds 8,638 B3
Mobile 200,452 E1
Monroeville 5,674 D2
Montgomery 177,857 C3
Moundville 1,310 C2
Mountain Brook 19,718 g7
Muscle Shoals 8,911 A2
Northport 14,291 B2
Opelika 21,896 C4
Opp 7,204 D3
Ozark 13,188 D4
Pell City 6,616 B3
Phenix City 26,928 C4
Piedmont 5,544 B4
Prattville 18,647 C3
Prichard 39,541 E1
Roanoke 5,896 B4
Russellville 8,195 A2
Saraland 9,833 E1
Scottsboro 14,758 A3
Selma 26,684 C2
Sheffield 11,903 A2
Spanish Fort 3,415 E2
Sylacauga 12,708 B3
Talladega 19,128 B3
Tallassee 4,763 C4
Troy 12,945 D4
Tuscaloosa 75,211 B2
Tuscumbia 9,137 A2
Tuskegee 13,327 C4
Vestavia Hills 15,722 g7
Warrior 3,260 B3
Wetumpka 4,341 C3

228

Cities and Towns

Akiachak 438 **C7**
Alakanuk 522 **C7**
Anchorage 174,431 **C10**
Anderson 517 **C10**
Angoon 465 **D13**
Aniak 341 **C8**
Barrow 2,207 **A8**
Bethel 3,576 **C7**
Chevak 466 **C6**
Circle 81 **B11**
College 800 **B10**
Cordova 1,879 **C10**
Craig 527 **D13**
Delta Junction 945 **C10**
Dillingham 1,563 **D8**
Emmonak 567 **C7**
Fairbanks 22,645 **C10**
Fort Yukon 619 **B10**
Galena 765 **C8**
Gambell 445 **C5**
Glennallen 511 **119**
Haines 993 **D12**
Homer 2,209 **D9**
Hoonah 680 **D12**
Hooper Bay 627 **C6**
Juneau 19,528 **D13**
Kake 555 **D13**
Kenai 4,324 **C9**
Ketchikan 7,198 **D13**
King Cove 460 **E7**
King Salmon 545 **D8**
Kipnuk 371 **C7**
Kodiak 4,756 **D9**
Kotzebue 2,054 **B7**
Kwethluk 454 **C7**
McGrath 355 **C8**
Metlakatla 1,056 **D13**
Mountain Point 396 **n24**
Mountain Village 583 **C7**
Naknek 600 **D8**
Nenana 470 **C10**
Nikishka 1,109 **g16**
Nome 2,301 **C6**
Noorvik 492 **B7**
Nulato 350 **C8**
Old Harbor 340 **D9**
Palmer 2,141 **C10**
Petersburg 2,821 **D13**
Pilot Station 325 **C7**
Point Hope 464 **B6**
Prudhoe Bay 50 **A10**
Quinhagak 412 **C7**
St. Marys 382 **C7**
St. Paul 551 **D5**
Sand Point 625 **D7**
Savoonga 491 **C5**
Selawik 361 **B7**
Seldovia 479 **D9**
Seward 1,843 **C10**
Shishmaref 394 **B6**
Sitka 7,803 **D12**
Skagway 768 **D12**
Soldotna 2,320 **g16**
Sterling 919 **g16**
Tanana 388 **B9**
Togiak 470 **D7**
Tok 589 **C11**
Unalakleet 623 **C7**
Unalaska 1,322 **E6**
Valdez 3,079 **C10**
Wainwright 405 **A8**
Wasilla 1,559 **C10**
Wrangell 2,184 **D13**
Yakutat 3,478 **D12**

Polyconic Projection
SCALE 1:12,000,000 1 Inch = 189 Statute Miles

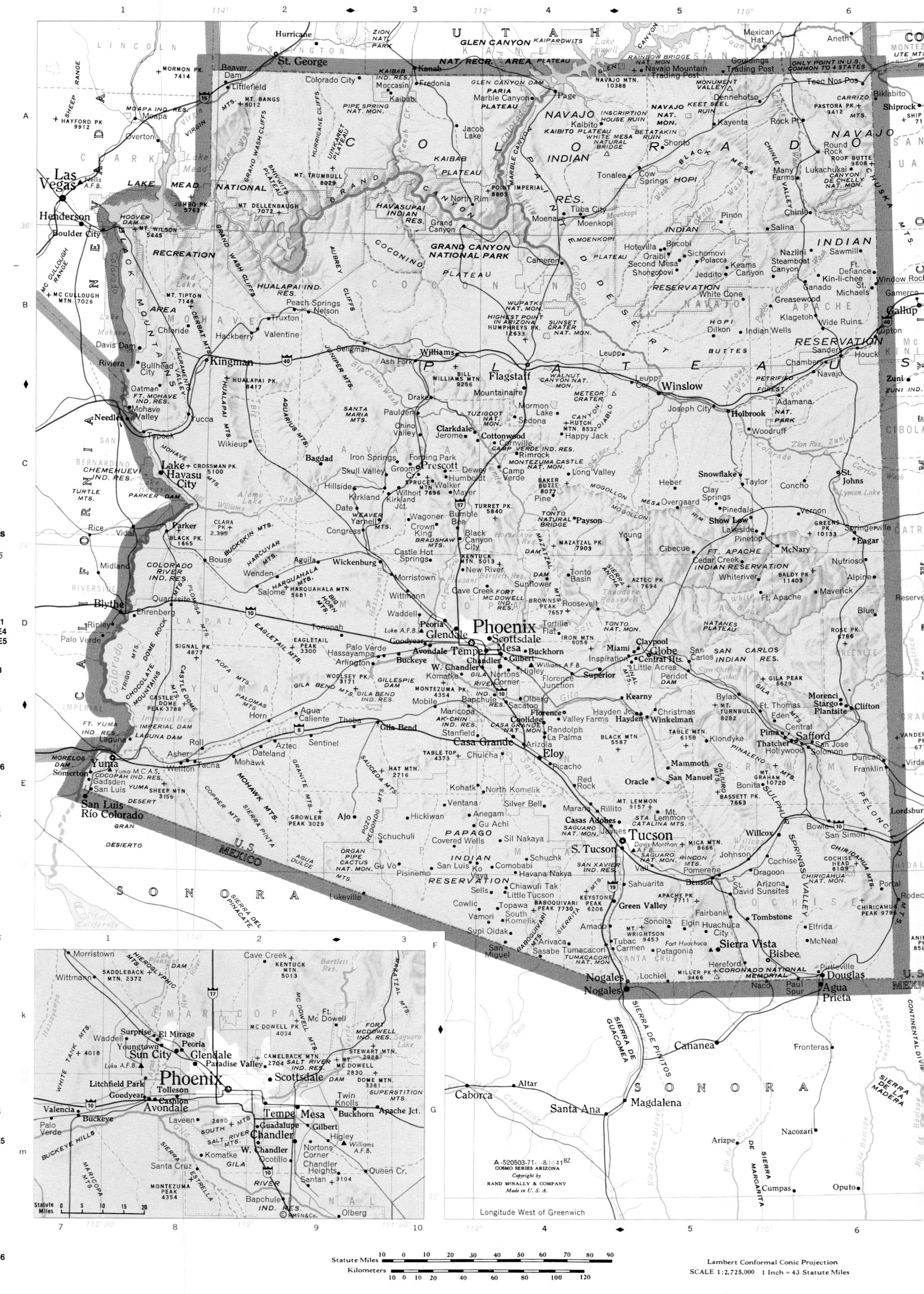

Cities and Towns

Ajo 5,189 **E3**
Apache Junction 9,935 **m9**
Avondale 8,168 **D3**
Bagdad 2,331 **C2**
Benson 4,190 **F5**
Bisbee 7,154 **F6**
Buckeye 3,434 **D3**
Bullhead City 5,000 **B1**
Casa Grande 14,971 **E4**
Casas Adobes 5,300 **E5**
Chandler 29,673 **D4**
Chinle 2,815 **A6**
Chino Valley 2,858 **C3**
Claypool 2,362 **D5**
Clifton 4,245 **D6**
Coolidge 6,851 **E4**
Cottonwood 4,550 **C3**
Douglas 13,058 **F6**
Eagar 2,791 **C6**
Eloy 6,240 **E4**
Flagstaff 34,743 **B4**
Florence 3,391 **D4**
Fort Defiance 3,431 **B6**
Gila Bend 1,585 **E3**
Gilbert 5,717 **D4**
Glendale 97,172 **D3**
Globe 6,886 **D5**
Green Valley 7,999 **F5**
Holbrook 5,785 **C5**
Kayenta 3,343 **A5**
Kearny 2,646 **D5**
Kingman 9,257 **B1**
Lake Havasu City 15,909 **C1**
Mammoth 1,906 **E5**
Mesa 152,453 **D4**
Miami 2,716 **D5**
Nogales 15,683 **F5**
Oracle 2,484 **E5**
Page 4,907 **A4**
Paradise Valley 11,085 **k9**
Parker 2,542 **C1**
Payson 5,068 **C4**
Peoria 12,307 **D3**
Phoenix 789,704 **D3**
Prescott 20,055 **C3**
Riviera 4,500 **B1**
Sacaton 1,951 **D4**
Safford 7,010 **E6**
St. Johns 3,368 **C6**
San Carlos 2,668 **D5**
San Luis 1,946 **E1**
San Manuel 5,443 **E5**
Scottsdale 88,622 **D4**
Sedona 5,368 **C4**
Sells 1,864 **F4**
Show Low 4,298 **C5**
Sierra Vista 24,937 **F5**
Snowflake 3,510 **C5**
Somerton 5,761 **E1**
South Tucson 6,554 **E5**
Sun City 40,505 **k8**
Superior 4,600 **D4**
Taylor 1,915 **C5**
Tempe 106,743 **D4**
Thatcher 3,374 **E6**
Tombstone 1,632 **F5**
Tuba City 5,041 **A4**
Tucson 330,537 **E5**
Wickenburg 3,535 **D3**
Willcox 3,243 **E6**
Williams 2,266 **B3**
Window Rock 2,230 **B6**
Winslow 7,921 **C5**
Yuma 42,481 **E1**

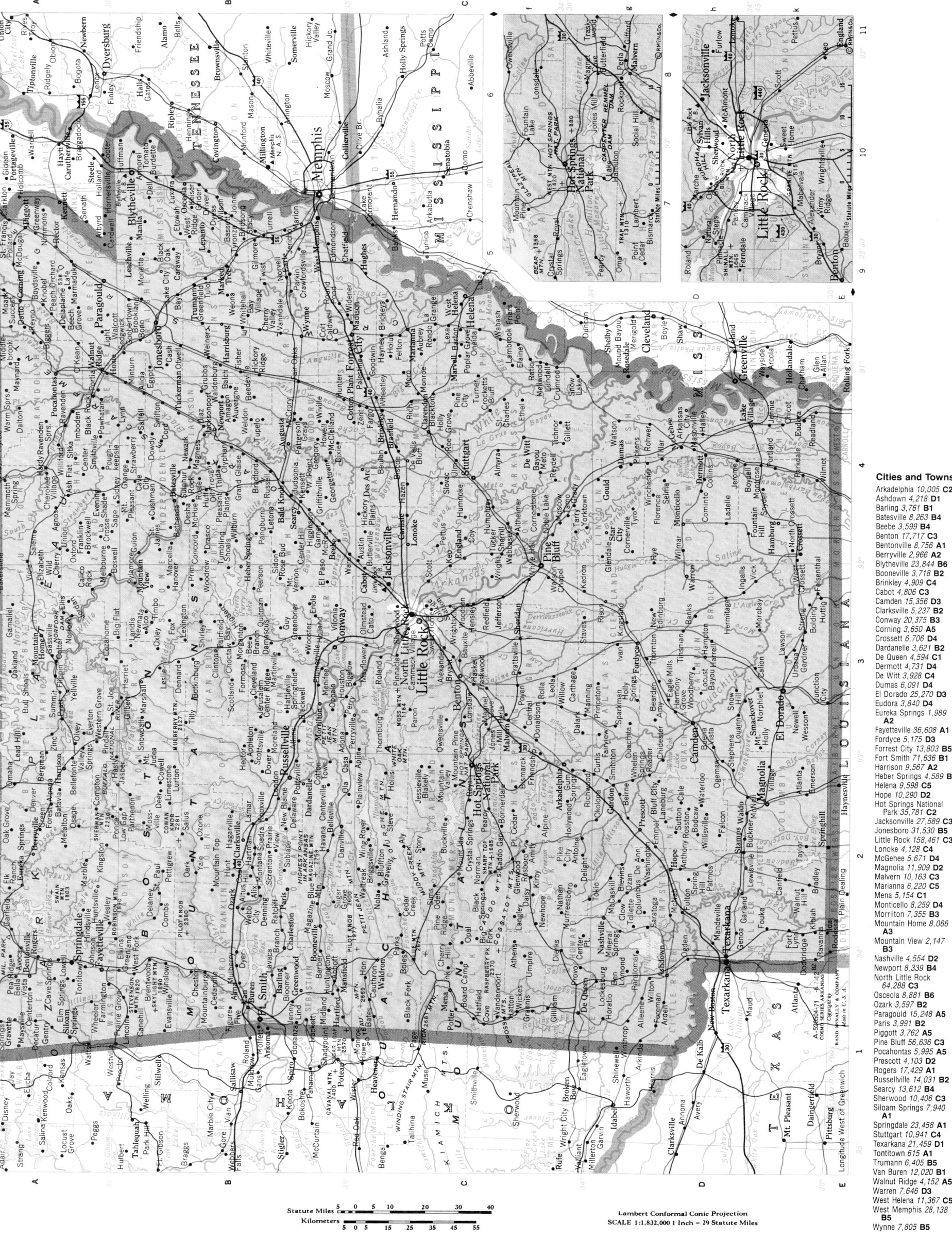

Statute Miles 5 0 5 10 20 30 40

Kilometers 5 0 15 25 35 45 55

Lambert Conformal Conic Projection
SCALE 1:1,832,000 1 Inch = 29 Statute Miles

Cities and Towns

Arkadelphia 10,005 **C2**
Ashdown 4,218 **D1**
Barling 3,761 **B1**
Batesville 8,263 **B4**
Beebe 3,599 **B4**
Benton 17,717 **C3**
Bentonville 8,756 **A1**
Berryville 2,966 **A2**
Blytheville 23,844 **B6**
Booneville 3,718 **B2**
Brinkley 4,909 **C4**
Cabot 4,806 **C3**
Camden 15,356 **D3**
Clarksville 5,237 **B2**
Conway 20,375 **B3**
Corning 3,650 **A5**
Crossett 6,706 **D4**
Dardanelle 3,621 **B2**
De Queen 4,594 **C1**
Dermott 4,731 **D4**
De Witt 3,928 **C4**
Dumas 6,091 **D4**
El Dorado 25,270 **D3**
Eudora 3,840 **D4**
Eureka Springs 1,989 **A2**
Fayetteville 36,608 **A1**
Fordyce 5,175 **D3**
Forrest City 13,803 **B5**
Fort Smith 71,636 **B1**
Harrison 9,567 **A2**
Heber Springs 4,589 **B3**
Helena 9,598 **C5**
Hope 10,290 **D2**
Hot Springs National
Park 35,781 **C2**
Jacksonville 27,589 **C3**
Jonesboro 31,530 **B5**
Little Rock 158,461 **C3**
Lonoke 4,128 **C4**
McGehee 5,671 **D4**
Magnolia 11,909 **D2**
Malvern 10,163 **C3**
Marianna 6,220 **C5**
Mena 5,154 **C1**
Monticello 8,259 **D4**
Morrilton 7,355 **B3**
Mountain Home 8,066
A3
Mountain View 2,147
B3
Nashville 4,554 **D2**
Newport 8,339 **B4**
North Little Rock
64,288 **C3**
Osceola 8,881 **B6**
Ozark 3,597 **B2**
Paragould 15,248 **A5**
Paris 3,991 **B2**
Piggott 3,762 **A5**
Pine Bluff 56,636 **C3**
Pocahontas 5,995 **A5**
Prescott 4,103 **D2**
Rogers 17,429 **A1**
Russellville 14,031 **B2**
Searcy 13,612 **B4**
Sherwood 10,406 **C3**
Siloam Springs 7,940
A1
Springdale 23,458 **A1**
Stuttgart 10,941 **C4**
Texarkana 21,459 **D1**
Tontitown 615 **A1**
Trumann 6,405 **B5**
Van Buren 12,020 **B1**
Walnut Ridge 4,152 **A5**
Warren 7,646 **D3**
West Helena 11,367 **C5**
West Memphis 28,138
B5
Wynne 7,805 **B5**

Cities and Towns

Anaheim 219,494 F5
Antioch 42,683 h9
Bakersfield 105,735 E4
Berkeley 103,328 D2
Beverly Hills 32,367 m12
Burbank 84,625 E4
Calexico 14,412 F6
Chico 26,603 C3
Chula Vista 83,927 F5
Concord 103,255 h8
Costa Mesa 82,562 n13
Davis 36,640 C3
East Los Angeles 110,017 m12
El Cajon 73,892 F5
El Centro 23,996 F6
Escondido 64,355 F5
Eureka 24,153 B1
Fairfield 58,099 C2
Fremont 131,945 D2
Fresno 217,289 D4
Fullerton 102,034 n13
Garden Grove 123,307 n13
Glendale 139,060 m12
Hayward 94,342 h8
Huntington Beach 170,505 F4
Indio 21,611 F5
Lancaster 48,027 E4
Lompoc 26,267 E3
Long Beach 361,334 F4
Los Angeles 2,966,850 E4
Marysville 9,898 C3
Menlo Park 26,369 k8
Merced 36,499 D3
Modesto 106,602 D3
Monterey 27,558 D3
Napa 50,879 C2
Newport Beach 62,556 n13
Oakland 339,337 D2
Oceanside 76,698 F5
Ontario 88,820 E5
Oxnard 108,195 E4
Palm Springs 32,366 F5
Palo Alto 55,225 D2
Pasadena 118,072 E4
Pomona 92,742 E5
Redding 41,995 B2
Redwood City 54,951 D2
Richmond 74,676 D2
Riverside 170,591 F5
Sacramento 275,741 C3
Salinas 80,479 D3
San Bernardino 118,794 E5
San Clemente 27,325 F5
San Diego 875,538 F5
San Francisco 678,974 D2
San Jose 629,546 D3
San Juan Capistrano 18,959 F5
San Luis Obispo 34,252 E3
Santa Ana 204,023 F5
Santa Barbara 74,414 E4
Santa Cruz 41,483 D2
Santa Maria 39,685 E3
Santa Monica 88,314 m12
Santa Rosa 83,320 C2
South Lake Tahoe 20,681 C4
Stockton 149,779 D3
Sunnyvale 106,618 k8
Torrance 129,881 n12
Tulare 22,526 D4
Turlock 26,287 D3
Vallejo 80,303 C2
Ventura 74,393 E4
Visalia 49,729 D4
Yuba City 18,736 C3

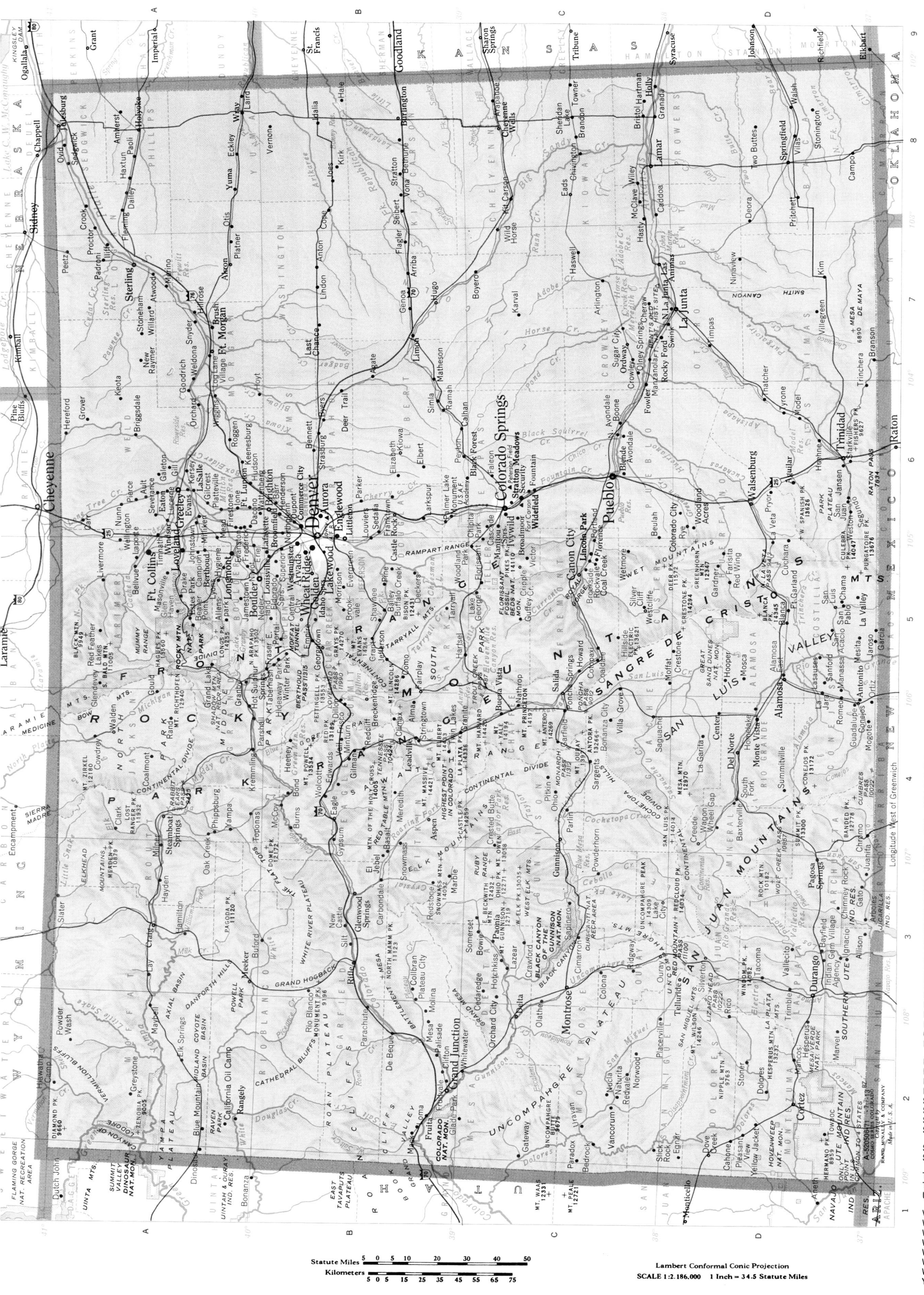

Statute Miles 5 0 5 10 20 30 40 50
Kilometers 5 0 5 15 25 35 45 55 65 75

Lambert Conformal Conic Projection
SCALE 1:2,186,000   1 Inch = 34.5 Statute Miles

Cities and Towns

Alamosa 6,830 **D5**
Arvada 84,576 **B5**
Aspen 3,678 **B4**
Aurora 158,588 **B6**
Black Forest 3,372 **C6**
Boulder 76,685 **A5**
Breckenridge 818 **B4**
Brighton 12,773 **B6**
Broomfield 20,730 **B5**
Burlington 3,107 **B8**
Canon City 13,037 **C5**
Castle Rock 3,921 **B6**
Central City 329 **B5**
Clifton 5,223 **B2**
Colorado Springs
    214,821 **C6**
Commerce City 16,234
    B6
Cortez 7,095 **D2**
Craig 8,133 **A3**
Delta 3,931 **C2**
Denver 492,365 **B6**
Durango 11,649 **D3**
Englewood 30,021 **B6**
Estes Park 2,703 **A5**
Evans 5,063 **A6**
Evergreen 6,376 **B5**
Fort Collins 65,092 **A5**
Fort Lupton 4,251 **A6**
Fort Morgan 8,768 **A7**
Fountain 8,324 **C6**
Glenwood Springs 4,637
    B3
Golden 12,237 **B5**
Grand Junction 27,956
    B2
Greeley 53,006 **A6**
Gunnison 5,785 **C4**
Holyoke 2,092 **A8**
Julesburg 1,528 **A8**
Lafayette 8,985 **B5**
La Junta 8,338 **D7**
Lakewood 113,808 **B5**
Lamar 7,713 **C8**
Las Animas 2,818 **C7**
Leadville 3,879 **B4**
Limon 1,805 **B7**
Littleton 28,631 **B6**
Longmont 42,942 **A5**
Louisville 5,593 **B5**
Loveland 30,244 **A5**
Meeker 2,356 **A3**
Monte Vista 3,902 **D4**
Montrose 8,722 **C3**
Northglenn 29,847 **B6**
Ouray 684 **C3**
Pagosa Springs 1,331
    D3
Pueblo 101,686 **C6**
Rangely 2,113 **A2**
Rifle 3,215 **B3**
Rocky Ford 4,804 **C7**
Salida 4,870 **C5**
Security 11,000 **C6**
Springfield 1,657 **D8**
Steamboat Springs
    5,098 **A4**
Sterling 11,385 **A7**
Stratton Meadows 6,223
    C6
Telluride 1,047 **D3**
Trinidad 9,663 **D6**
USAF Academy 8,000
    C6
Vail 2,261 **B4**
Walsenburg 3,945 **D6**
Westminster 50,211 **B5**
Wheat Ridge 30,293 **B5**
Widefield 7,500 **C6**
Windsor 4,277 **A6**
Wray 2,131 **A8**
Yuma 2,824 **A8**

CONNECTICUT

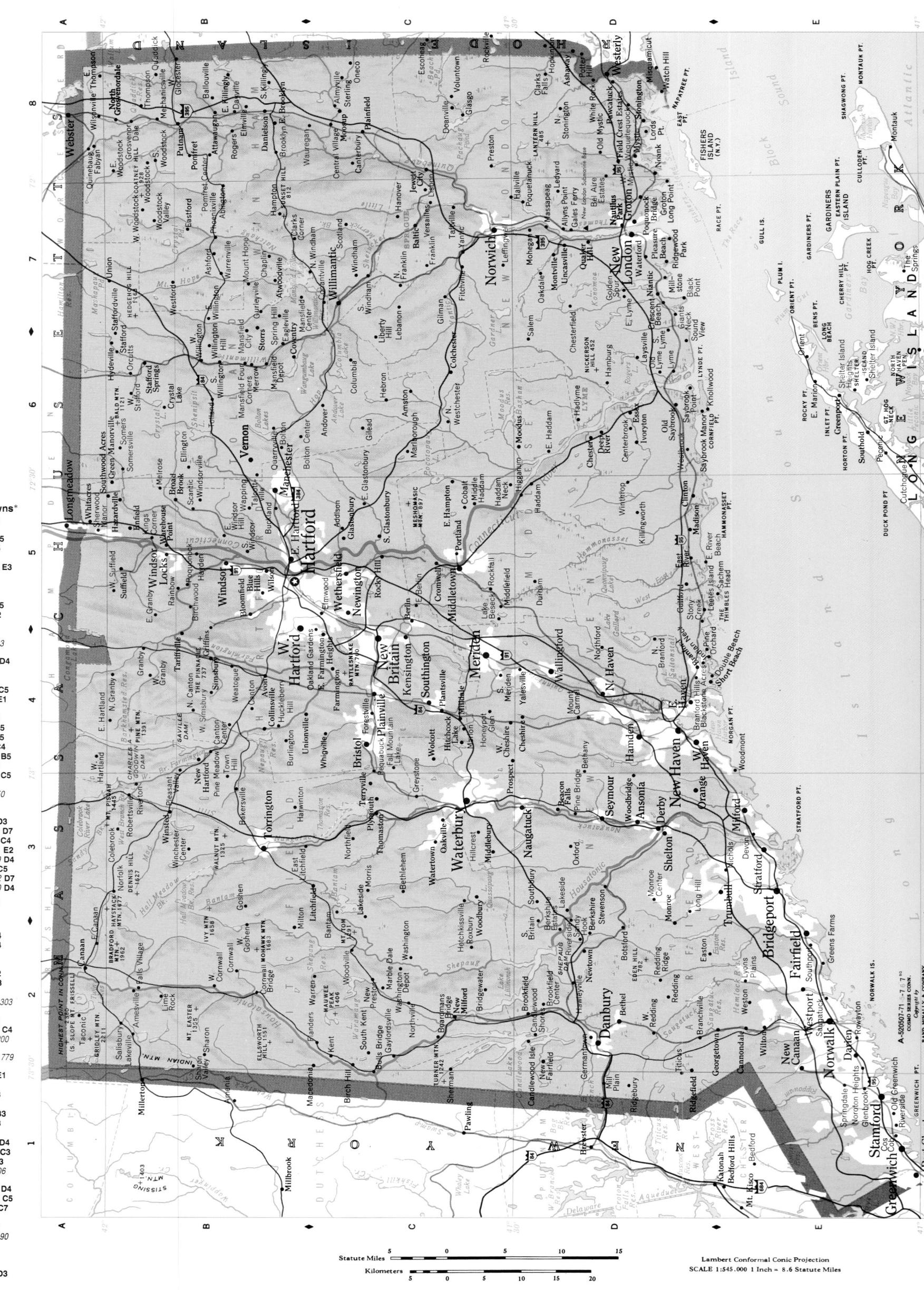

Cities and Towns*

Ansonia 19,039 **D3**
Bethel 8,755 **D2**
Bloomfield 7,400 **B5**
Blue Hills 6,600 **B5**
Branford 5,438 **D4**
Bridgeport 142,546 **E3**
Bristol 57,370 **C4**
Cheshire 5,722 **D4**
Clinton 11,195 **D5**
Cromwell 10,100 **C5**
Danbury 60,470 **D2**
Darien 18,892 **E2**
Derby 12,346 **D3**
East Hartford 52,563 **B5**
East Haven 25,028 **D4**
Enfield 8,151 **B5**
Fairfield 54,849 **E2**
Glastonbury 7,049 **C5**
Greenwich 59,578 **E1**
Groton 10,086 **D7**
Hamden 51,071 **D4**
Hartford 136,392 **B5**
Hazardville 5,436 **B5**
Kensington 7,502 **C4**
Manchester 49,761 **B5**
Meriden 57,118 **C4**
Middletown 39,040 **C5**
Milford 49,101 **E3**
Monroe Center 6,950 **D3**
Mystic 2,333 **D8**
Naugatuck 26,456 **D3**
Nautilus Park 6,500 **D7**
New Britain 73,840 **C4**
New Canaan 17,931 **E2**
New Haven 126,109 **D4**
Newington 28,841 **C5**
New London 28,842 **D7**
North Haven 22,080 **D4**
Norwalk 77,767 **E2**
Norwich 38,074 **C7**
Oakville 8,737 **C3**
Orange 13,237 **D3**
Plainville 16,401 **C4**
Plantsville 5,700 **C4**
Portland 8,383 **C5**
Putnam 6,855 **B8**
Ridgefield 6,066 **D2**
Seymour 13,434 **D3**
Shelton 31,314 **D3**
Sherwood Manor 6,303 **A5**
Simsbury 5,488 **B4**
Southington 17,400 **C4**
South Windsor 10,200 **B5**
Southwood Acres 9,779 **B5**
Stamford 102,453 **E1**
Storrs 11,394 **B7**
Stratford 50,541 **E3**
Terryville 5,234 **C3**
Torrington 30,987 **B3**
Trumbull 32,989 **E3**
Vernon 27,974 **B6**
Wallingford 37,274 **D4**
Waterbury 103,266 **C3**
Watertown 6,000 **C3**
West Hartford 61,306 **B4**
West Haven 53,184 **D4**
Wethersfield 26,013 **C5**
Willimantic 14,652 **C7**
Wilton 6,500 **E2**
Windsor 17,517 **B5**
Windsor Locks 12,190 **B5**
Winsted 8,092 **B3**
Wolcott 5,500 **C4**
Woodbridge 7,600 **D3**

*Populations are for localities, not incorporated towns.

Statute Miles

Kilometers

Lambert Conformal Conic Projection
SCALE 1:545,000 1 Inch = 8.6 Statute Miles

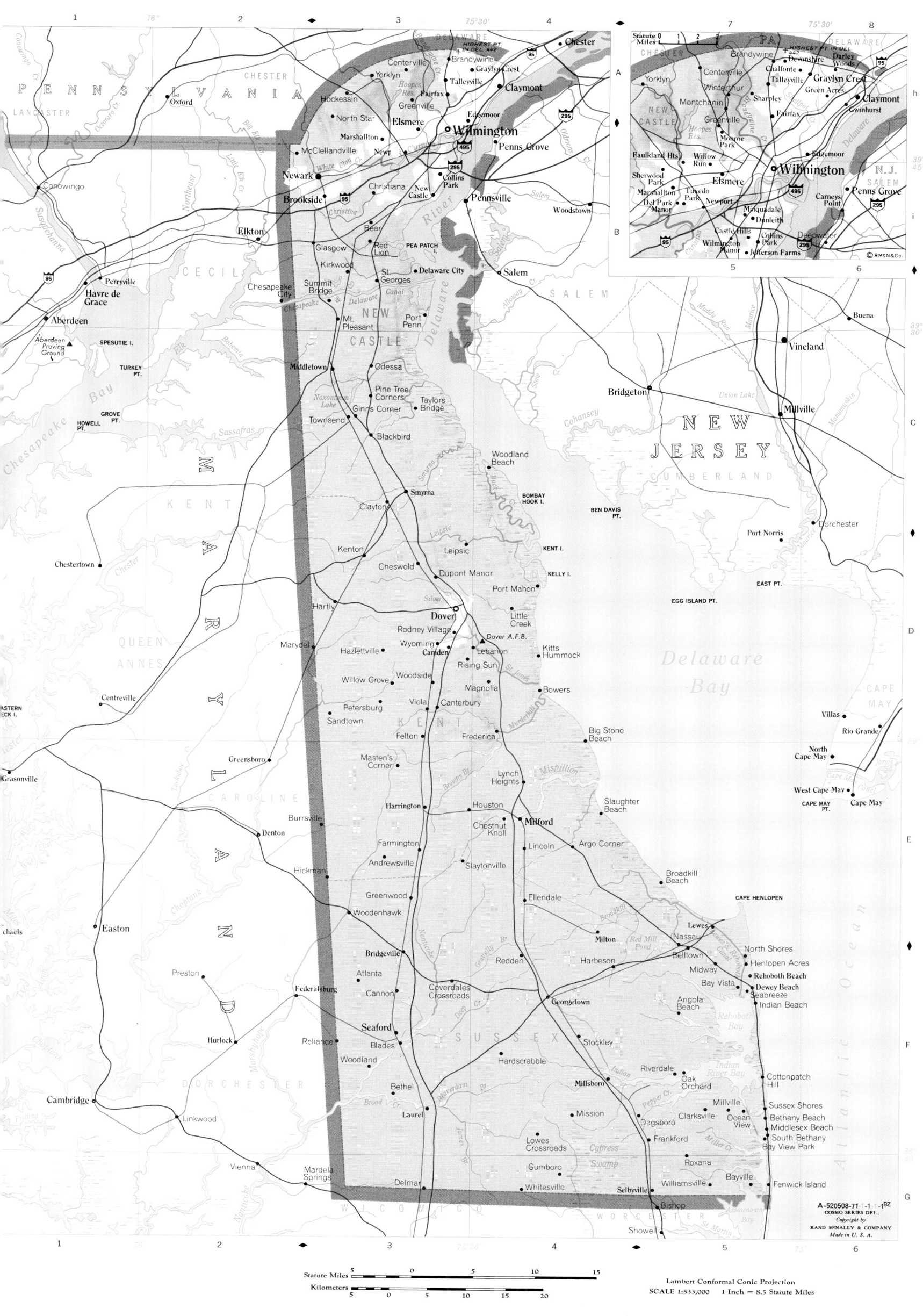

Cities and Towns

Bear 950 **B3**
Bethany Beach 330 **F5**
Blades 664 **F3**
Bridgeville 1,238 **F3**
Broadkill Beach 200 **E5**
Brookside 15,255 **B3**
Camden 1,757 **D3**
Canterbury 500 **D3**
Castle Hills 1,950 **I7**
Chalfonte 2,200 **h7**
Cheswold 269 **D3**
Christiana 500 **B3**
Clarksville 450 **F5**
Claymont 10,022 **A4**
Clayton 1,216 **C3**
Collins Park 2,850 **B3**
Dagsboro 344 **F5**
Delaware City 1,858 **B3**
Delmar 948 **G3**
Dewey Beach 1,500 **F5**
Dover 23,507 **D3**
Dunleith 2,700 **I7**
Dupont Manor 1,059 **D3**
Edgemoor 7,397 **A3**
Ellendale 361 **E4**
Elsmere 6,493 **B3**
Fairfax 2,850 **A3**
Felton 547 **D3**
Frankford 828 **F5**
Frederica 864 **D4**
Georgetown 1,710 **F4**
Graylyn Crest 5,000 **A3**
Greenwood 578 **E3**
Gumboro 200 **G4**
Gwinhurst 1,400 **h8**
Harbeson 250 **F4**
Harrington 2,405 **E3**
Hockessin 950 **A3**
Houston 357 **E3**
Jefferson Farms 2,400 **I7**
Kenton 243 **D3**
Kirkwood 400 **B3**
Laurel 3,052 **F3**
Leipsic 228 **D3**
Lewes 2,197 **E5**
Lincoln 500 **E4**
Little Creek 230 **D4**
Marshallton 3,950 **B3**
Middletown 2,946 **C3**
Midway 500 **F5**
Milford 5,366 **E4**
Millsboro 1,233 **F4**
Milton 1,359 **E4**
Minquadale 1,700 **I7**
Newark 25,247 **B3**
New Castle 4,907 **B3**
Newport 1,167 **B3**
Oak Orchard 250 **F5**
Ocean View 495 **F5**
Odessa 384 **C3**
Port Penn 300 **B3**
Rehoboth Beach 1,730 **F5**
Rodney Village 1,100 **D3**
St. Georges 500 **B3**
Seaford 5,256 **F3**
Selbyville 1,251 **G5**
Smyrna 4,750 **C3**
Talleyville 6,880 **A3**
Townsend 386 **C3**
Willow Run 1,950 **I7**
Wilmington 70,195 **B3**
Wilmington Manor 2,000 **I7**
Wyoming 960 **D3**
Yorklyn 600 **A3**

Cities and Towns

Bartow 14,780 **E5**
Belle Glade 16,535 **F6**
Boca Raton 49,505 **F6**
Boynton Beach 35,624 **F6**
Bradenton 30,170 **E4**
Brandon 29,100 **E4**
Cape Canaveral 5,733 **D6**
Cape Coral 32,103 **F5**
Carol City 47,349 **s13**
Clearwater 85,528 **E4**
Cocoa 16,096 **D6**
Coral Gables 43,241 **G6**
Daytona Beach 54,176 **C5**
Deerfield Beach 39,193 **F6**
De Land 15,354 **C5**
Delray Beach 34,325 **F6**
Dunedin 30,203 **D4**
Fort Lauderdale 153,279 **F6**
Fort Myers 36,638 **F5**
Fort Pierce 33,802 **E6**
Fort Walton Beach 20,829 **u15**
Gainesville 81,371 **C4**
Hallandale 36,517 **G6**
Hialeah 145,254 **G6**
Hollywood 121,323 **F6**
Homestead 20,668 **G6**
Immokalee 11,038 **F5**
Jacksonville 540,920 **B5**
Kendall 51,000 **s13**
Key Largo 7,447 **G6**
Key West 24,382 **H5**
Kissimmee 15,487 **D5**
Lake City 9,257 **B4**
Lakeland 47,406 **D5**
Lake Worth 27,048 **F6**
Largo 58,977 **E4**
Leesburg 13,191 **D5**
Marathon 7,508 **H5**
Margate 35,900 **F6**
Melbourne 46,536 **D6**
Merritt Island 30,708 **D6**
Miami 346,865 **G6**
Miami Beach 96,298 **G6**
Miramar 32,813 **s13**
Naples 17,581 **F5**
New Smyrna Beach 13,557 **C6**
North Miami 36,553 **G6**
North Miami Beach 36,481 **s13**
Ocala 37,170 **C4**
Orlando 128,291 **D5**
Panama City 33,346 **u16**
Pembroke Pines 35,776 **r13**
Pensacola 57,619 **u14**
Pinellas Park 32,811 **E4**
Plantation 48,653 **r13**
Plant City 17,064 **D4**
Pompano Beach 52,618 **F6**
Port Charlotte 25,770 **F4**
Riviera Beach 26,489 **F6**
St. Augustine 11,985 **C5**
St. Petersburg 238,647 **E4**
Sanford 23,176 **D5**
Sarasota 48,868 **E4**
Sebring 8,736 **E5**
Tallahassee 81,548 **B2**
Tampa 271,523 **E4**
Tarpon Springs 13,251 **D4**
Titusville 31,910 **D6**
Venice 12,153 **E4**
Vero Beach 16,176 **E6**
West Palm Beach 63,305 **F6**
West Pensacola 24,571 **u14**
Winter Haven 21,119 **D5**

Cities and Towns

Adel 5,592 **E3**
Albany 74,550 **E2**
Americus 16,120 **D2**
Athens 42,549 **C3**
Atlanta 425,022 **C2**
Augusta 47,532 **C5**
Bainbridge 10,553 **F2**
Blakely 5,880 **E2**
Brunswick 17,605 **E5**
Buford 6,578 **B2**
Cairo 8,777 **F2**
Calhoun 5,563 **B2**
Camilla 5,414 **E2**
Carrollton 14,078 **C1**
Cartersville 9,247 **B2**
Cedartown 8,619 **B1**
Cochran 5,121 **D3**
College Park 24,632 **C2**
Columbus 169,441 **D2**
Cordele 11,184 **E2**
Covington 10,586 **C2**
Dalton 20,939 **B2**
Dawson 5,699 **E2**
Decatur 18,404 **C2**
Douglas 10,980 **E4**
Douglasville 7,641 **C2**
Dublin 16,083 **D4**
Eastman 5,330 **D3**
East Point 37,486 **C2**
Elberton 5,686 **B4**
Fitzgerald 10,187 **E3**
Forest Park 18,782 **h8**
Fort Oglethorpe 5,443
   B1
Fort Valley 9,000 **D3**
Gainesville 15,280 **B3**
Griffin 20,728 **C2**
Hinesville 11,309 **E5**
Kennesaw 5,095 **B2**
La Fayette 6,517 **B1**
La Grange 24,204 **C1**
Lawrenceville 8,928 **C3**
Mableton 20,200 **h7**
Macon 116,896 **D3**
Marietta 30,829 **C2**
Martinez 16,472 **C4**
Milledgeville 12,176 **C3**
Monroe 8,854 **C3**
Moultrie 15,708 **E3**
Newnan 11,449 **C2**
North Atlanta 22,800 **h8**
Perry 9,453 **D3**
Quitman 5,188 **F3**
Rome 29,654 **B1**
Roswell 23,337 **B2**
St. Simons Island 6,566
   E5
Sandersville 6,137 **D4**
Sandy Springs 20,300
   h8
Savannah 141,390 **D5**
Smyrna 20,312 **C2**
Statesboro 14,866 **D5**
Stone Mountain 4,867
   C2
Swainsboro 7,602 **D4**
Sylvester 5,860 **E3**
Thomaston 9,682 **D2**
Thomasville 18,463 **F3**
Thomson 7,001 **C4**
Tifton 13,749 **E3**
Toccoa 9,104 **B3**
Tucker 18,200 **h8**
Valdosta 37,596 **F3**
Vidalia 10,393 **D4**
Warner Robins 39,893
   D3
Waycross 19,371 **E4**
Waynesboro 5,760 **C4**

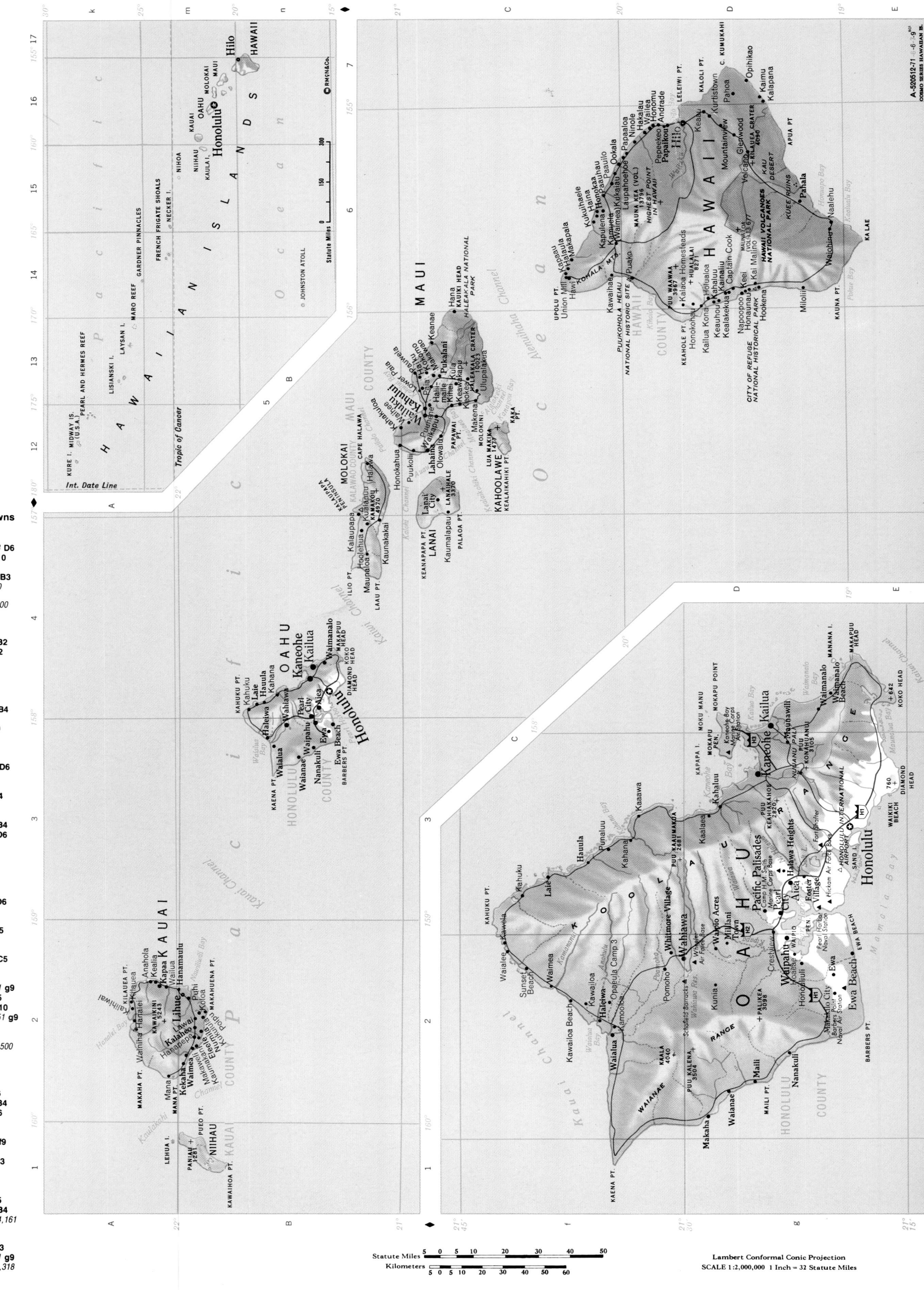

Cities and Towns

Aiea 15,200 **B4**
Anahola 915 **A2**
Captain Cook 2,008 **D6**
Crestview 1,000 **g10**
Ewa 2,637 **B3**
Ewa Beach 14,369 **B3**
Foster Village 3,700 **g10**
Halawa Heights 7,000 **g10**
Haleiwa 2,412 **B3**
Haliimaile 741 **C5**
Hanamaulu 3,227 **B2**
Hanapepe 1,417 **B2**
Hauula 2,997 **B4**
Hawi 795 **C6**
Hilo 35,269 **D6**
Holualoa 1,243 **D6**
Honokaa 1,936 **C6**
Honolulu 365,048 **B4**
Kaaawa 959 **f10**
Kahaluu 2,925 **g10**
Kahuku 935 **B4**
Kahului 12,978 **C5**
Kailua 35,812 **B4**
Kailua Kona 4,751 **D6**
Kalaheo 2,500 **B2**
Kamuela 1,179 **C6**
Kaneohe 29,919 **B4**
Kapaa 4,467 **A2**
Kaumakani 888 **B2**
Kaunakakai 2,231 **B4**
Kealakekua 1,033 **D6**
Kekaha 3,260 **B2**
Keokea 900 **C5**
Kihei 5,644 **C5**
Kilauea 895 **A2**
Koloa 1,457 **B2**
Kula 1,300 **C5**
Kurtistown 1,200 **D6**
Lahaina 6,095 **C5**
Laie 4,643 **B4**
Lanai City 2,092 **C5**
Lawai 950 **B2**
Lihue 4,000 **B2**
Lower Paia 1,500 **C5**
Maili 5,026 **g9**
Makaha 7,905 **g9**
Makakilo City 7,691 **g9**
Makawao 1,066 **C5**
Maunawili 2,200 **g10**
Mililani Town 20,351 **g9**
Naalehu 1,168 **D6**
Nanakuli 8,185 **B3**
Pacific Palisades 9,500 **g10**
Pahala 1,619 **D6**
Pahoa 923 **D7**
Paia 1,000 **C5**
Papaikou 1,567 **D6**
Pearl City 33,000 **B4**
Pepeekeo 1,800 **D6**
Puhi 991 **B2**
Pukalani 3,950 **C5**
Sunset Beach 800 **f9**
Volcano 900 **D6**
Wahiawa 16,911 **B3**
Waialua 4,051 **B3**
Waianae 5,000 **B3**
Wailua 1,587 **A2**
Wailuku 10,260 **C5**
Waimanalo 3,562 **B4**
Waimanalo Beach 4,161 **g11**
Waimea 1,569 **B2**
Waipahu 29,139 **B3**
Waipio Acres 4,091 **g9**
Whitmore Village 2,318 **f9**

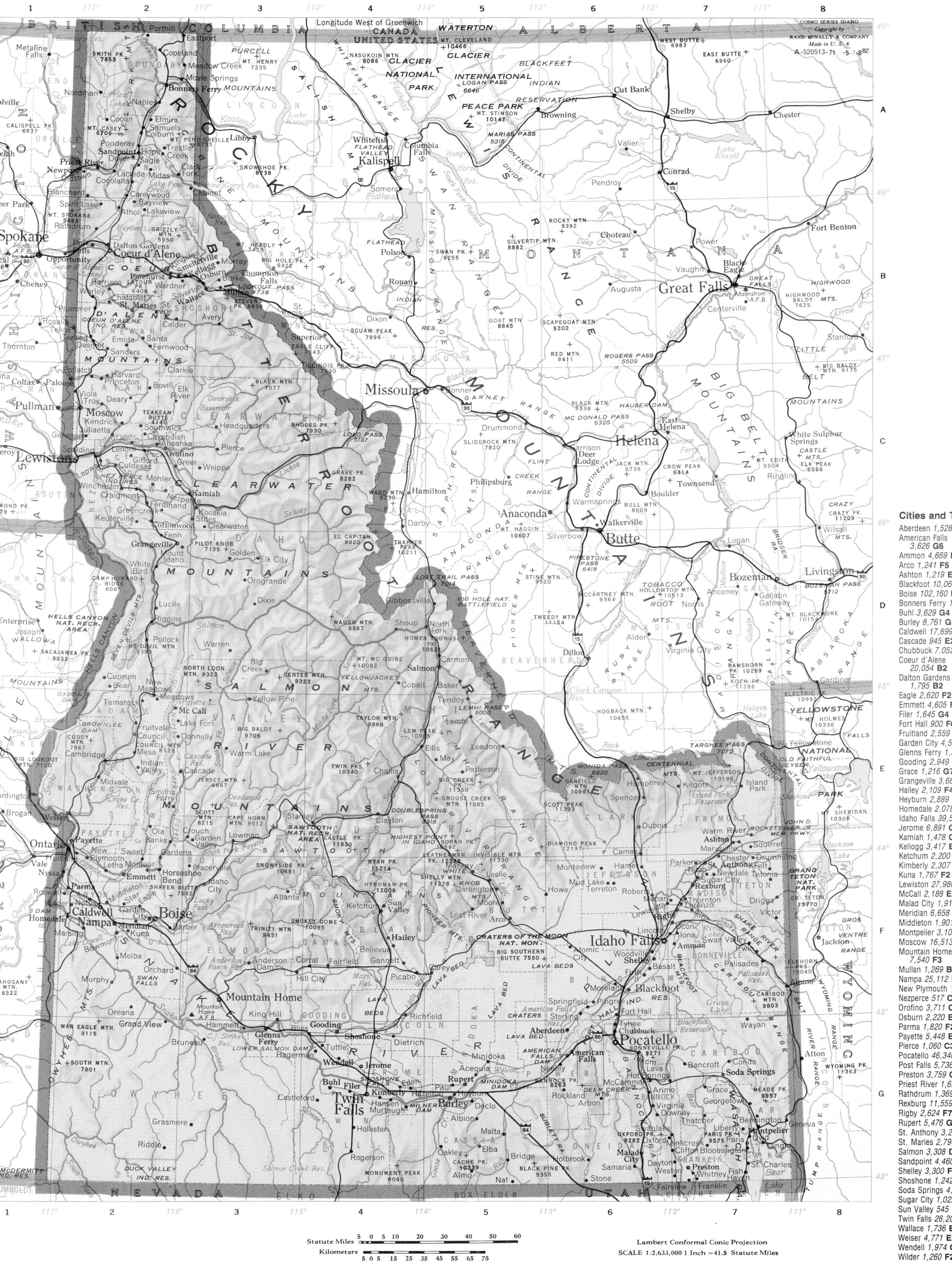

COSMO SERIES IDAHO
Copyright by
RAND McNALLY & COMPANY
Made in U.S.A.
A-520513-71 -5-7-8BZ

Statute Miles
5 0 5 10   20   30   40   50   60
Kilometers
5 0 5 15 25 35 45 55 65 75

Lambert Conformal Conic Projection
SCALE 1:2,633,000 1 Inch = 41.5 Statute Miles

Cities and Towns

Aberdeen 1,528 **G6**
American Falls
 3,626 **G6**
Ammon 4,669 **F7**
Arco 1,241 **F5**
Ashton 1,219 **E7**
Blackfoot 10,065 **F6**
Boise 102,160 **F2**
Bonners Ferry 1,906 **A2**
Buhl 3,629 **G4**
Burley 8,761 **G5**
Caldwell 17,699 **F2**
Cascade 945 **E2**
Chubbuck 7,052 **G6**
Coeur d'Alene
 20,054 **B2**
Dalton Gardens
 1,795 **B2**
Eagle 2,620 **F2**
Emmett 4,605 **F2**
Filer 1,645 **G4**
Fort Hall 900 **F6**
Fruitland 2,559 **F2**
Garden City 4,571 **F2**
Glenns Ferry 1,374 **G3**
Gooding 2,949 **G4**
Grace 1,216 **G7**
Grangeville 3,666 **D2**
Hailey 2,109 **F4**
Heyburn 2,889 **G5**
Homedale 2,078 **F2**
Idaho Falls 39,590 **F6**
Jerome 6,891 **G4**
Kamiah 1,478 **C2**
Kellogg 3,417 **B2**
Ketchum 2,200 **F4**
Kimberly 2,307 **G4**
Kuna 1,767 **F2**
Lewiston 27,986 **C1**
McCall 2,188 **E2**
Malad City 1,915 **G6**
Meridian 6,658 **F2**
Middleton 1,901 **F2**
Montpelier 3,107 **G7**
Moscow 16,513 **C2**
Mountain Home
 7,540 **F3**
Mullan 1,269 **B3**
Nampa 25,112 **F2**
New Plymouth 1,186 **F2**
Nezperce 517 **C2**
Orofino 3,711 **C2**
Osburn 2,220 **B3**
Parma 1,820 **F2**
Payette 5,448 **E2**
Pierce 1,060 **C3**
Pocatello 46,340 **G6**
Post Falls 5,736 **B2**
Preston 3,759 **G7**
Priest River 1,639 **A2**
Rathdrum 1,369 **B2**
Rexburg 11,559 **F7**
Rigby 2,624 **F7**
Rupert 5,476 **G5**
St. Anthony 3,212 **F7**
St. Maries 2,794 **B2**
Salmon 3,308 **D5**
Sandpoint 4,460 **A2**
Shelley 3,300 **F6**
Shoshone 1,242 **G4**
Soda Springs 4,051 **G7**
Sugar City 1,022 **F7**
Sun Valley 545 **F4**
Twin Falls 26,209 **G4**
Wallace 1,736 **B3**
Weiser 4,771 **E2**
Wendell 1,974 **G4**
Wilder 1,260 **F2**

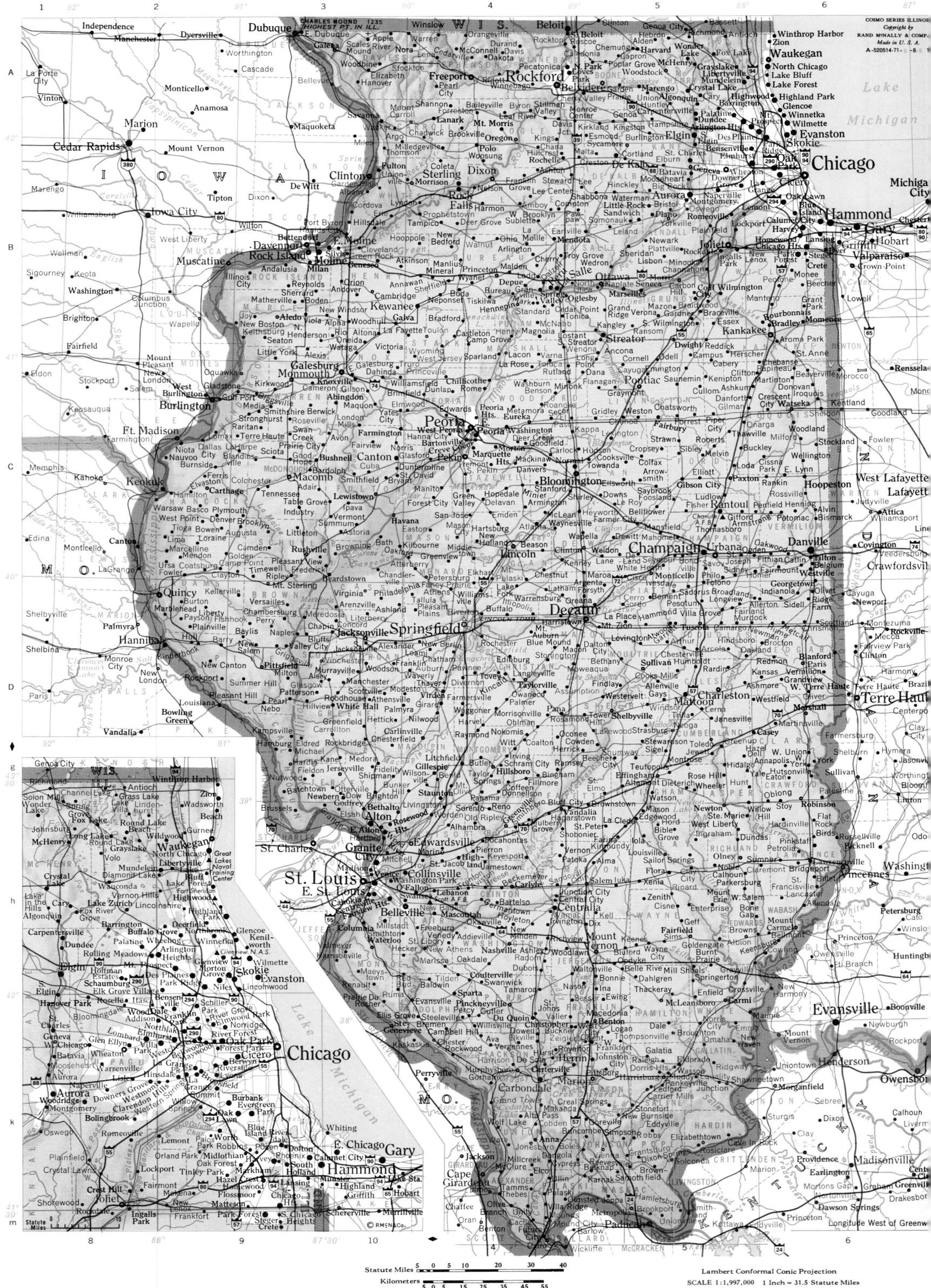

Cities and Towns

Alton 34,171 **E3**
Arlington Heights
  66,116 **A5**
Aurora 81,293 **B5**
Belleville 41,580 **E4**
Berwyn 46,849 **k9**
Bloomington 44,189 **C4**
Bourbonnais 13,280 **B6**
Brookfield 19,395 **k9**
Cahokia 18,904 **E3**
Cairo 5,931 **F4**
Calumet City 39,697 **B6**
Canton 14,626 **C3**
Carbondale 26,414 **F4**
Centralia 15,126 **E4**
Champaign 58,133 **C5**
Charleston 19,355 **D5**
Chicago 3,005,072 **B6**
Cicero 61,232 **B6**
Danville 38,985 **C6**
Decatur 94,081 **D5**
De Kalb 33,099 **B5**
Des Plaines 53,568 **A6**
Dixon 15,701 **B4**
Downers Grove
  42,572 **B5**
East St. Louis
  55,200 **E3**
Elgin 63,981 **A5**
Elmhurst 44,276 **B6**
Evanston 73,706 **A6**
Freeport 26,266 **A4**
Galena 3,876 **A3**
Galesburg 35,305 **C3**
Granite City 36,815 **E3**
Gurnee 7,179 **h9**
Highland Park
  30,611 **A6**
Jacksonville 20,284 **D3**
Joliet 77,956 **B5**
Kankakee 30,141 **B6**
Kewanee 14,508 **B4**
Lake Forest 15,245 **A6**
La Salle 10,347 **B4**
Lincoln 16,327 **C4**
Lombard 36,897 **k8**
Macomb 19,863 **C3**
Marion 14,031 **F5**
Mattoon 19,055 **D5**
Moline 46,278 **B3**
Monmouth 10,706 **C3**
Mount Prospect
  52,634 **A6**
Mount Vernon
  17,193 **E5**
Nauvoo 1,133 **C2**
Normal 35,672 **C5**
North Chicago
  38,774 **A6**
Oak Lawn 60,590 **B6**
Oak Park 54,887 **B6**
Ottawa 18,166 **B5**
Pekin 33,967 **C4**
Peoria 124,160 **C4**
Peru 10,886 **B4**
Pontiac 11,227 **C5**
Quincy 42,554 **D2**
Rockford 139,712 **A4**
Rock Island 46,928 **B3**
Salem 7,813 **E5**
Schaumburg 53,305 **h8**
Skokie 60,278 **A6**
Springfield 100,054 **D4**
Sterling 16,281 **B4**
Streator 14,795 **B5**
Taylorville 11,386 **D4**
Urbana 35,978 **C5**
Vandalia 5,338 **E4**
Waukegan 67,653 **A6**
Wheaton 43,043 **B5**
Zion 17,861 **A6**

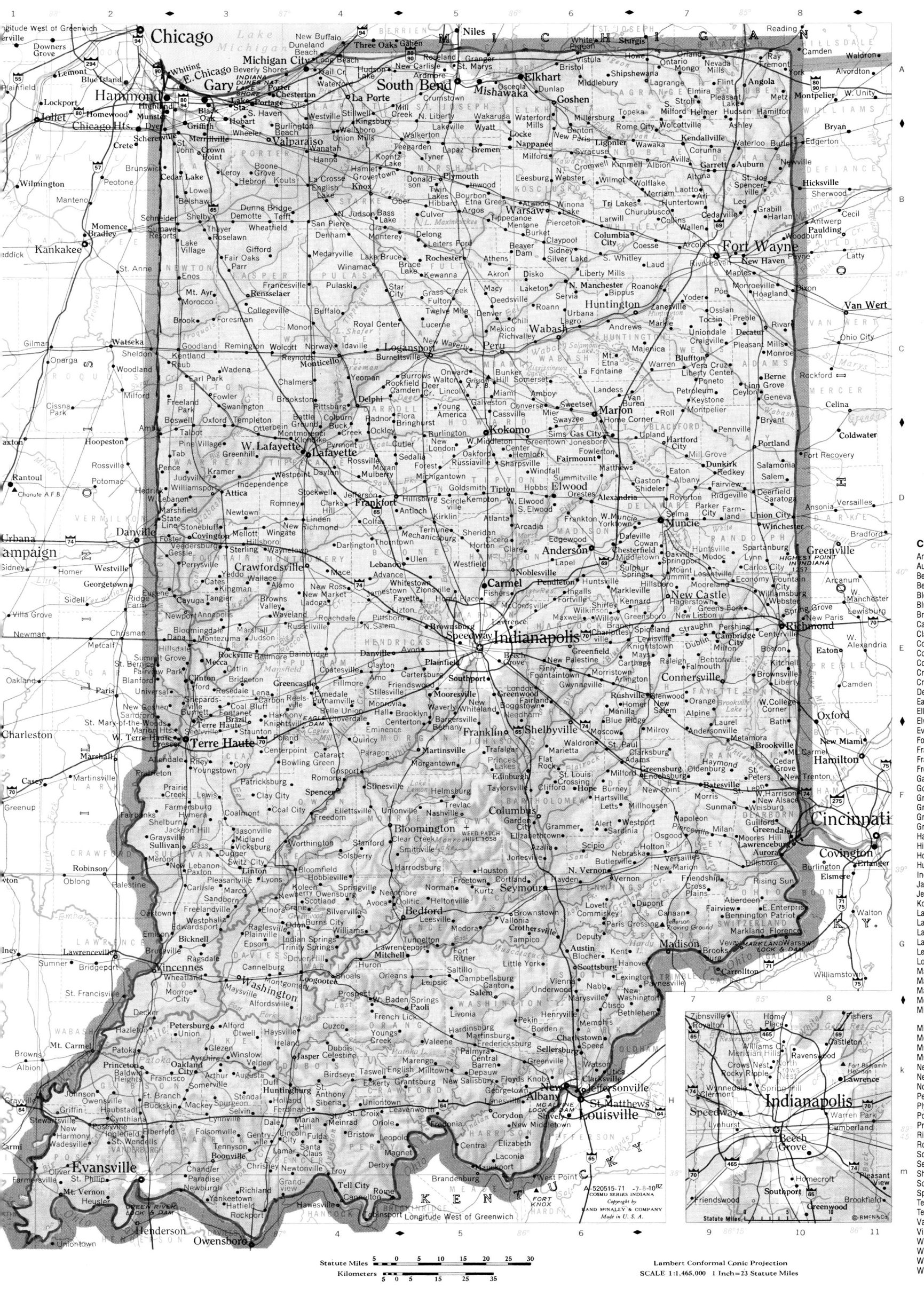

Cities and Towns
Anderson 64,695 **D6**
Auburn 8,122 **B7**
Bedford 14,410 **G5**
Beech Grove 13,196 **E5**
Bloomington 52,044 **F4**
Bluffton 8,705 **C7**
Brazil 7,852 **E3**
Carmel 18,272 **E5**
Clarksville 15,164 **H6**
Columbus 30,614 **F6**
Connersville 17,023 **E7**
Corydon 2,724 **H5**
Crawfordsville 13,325 **D4**
Crown Point 16,455 **B3**
Decatur 8,649 **C8**
East Chicago 39,786 **A3**
Elkhart 41,305 **A6**
Elwood 10,867 **D6**
Evansville 130,496 **I2**
Fort Wayne 172,028 **B7**
Frankfort 15,168 **D4**
Franklin 11,563 **F5**
French Lick 2,265 **G4**
Gary 151,953 **A3**
Goshen 19,665 **A6**
Greencastle 8,403 **E4**
Greensburg 9,254 **F7**
Greenwood 19,327 **E5**
Griffith 17,026 **A3**
Hammond 93,714 **A3**
Highland 25,935 **A3**
Hobart 22,987 **A3**
Huntington 16,202 **C7**
Indianapolis 700,807 **E5**
Jasper 9,097 **H4**
Jeffersonville 21,220 **H6**
Kokomo 47,808 **D5**
Lafayette 43,011 **D4**
Lake Station 14,294 **A3**
La Porte 21,796 **A4**
Lawrence 25,591 **E5**
Lebanon 11,456 **D5**
Logansport 17,731 **C5**
Madison 12,472 **G7**
Marion 35,874 **C6**
Martinsville 11,311 **F5**
Merrillville 27,677 **B3**
Michigan City
  36,850 **A4**
Mishawaka 40,201 **A5**
Mount Vernon 7,656 **I2**
Muncie 77,216 **D7**
Munster 20,671 **A2**
New Albany 37,103 **H6**
New Castle 20,056 **E7**
Noblesville 13,209 **B3**
Peru 13,764 **C5**
Plymouth 7,693 **B5**
Portage 27,409 **A3**
Princeton 8,976 **H2**
Richmond 41,349 **E8**
Rockville 2,785 **E3**
Schererville 13,209 **B3**
Seymour 15,050 **G6**
Shelbyville 14,989 **F6**
South Bend 109,727 **A5**
Speedway 12,641 **E5**
Tell City 8,704 **I4**
Terre Haute 61,125 **F3**
Valparaiso 22,247 **B3**
Vincennes 20,857 **G2**
Wabash 12,985 **C6**
Warsaw 10,647 **B6**
Washington 11,325 **G3**
West Lafayette
  21,247 **D4**

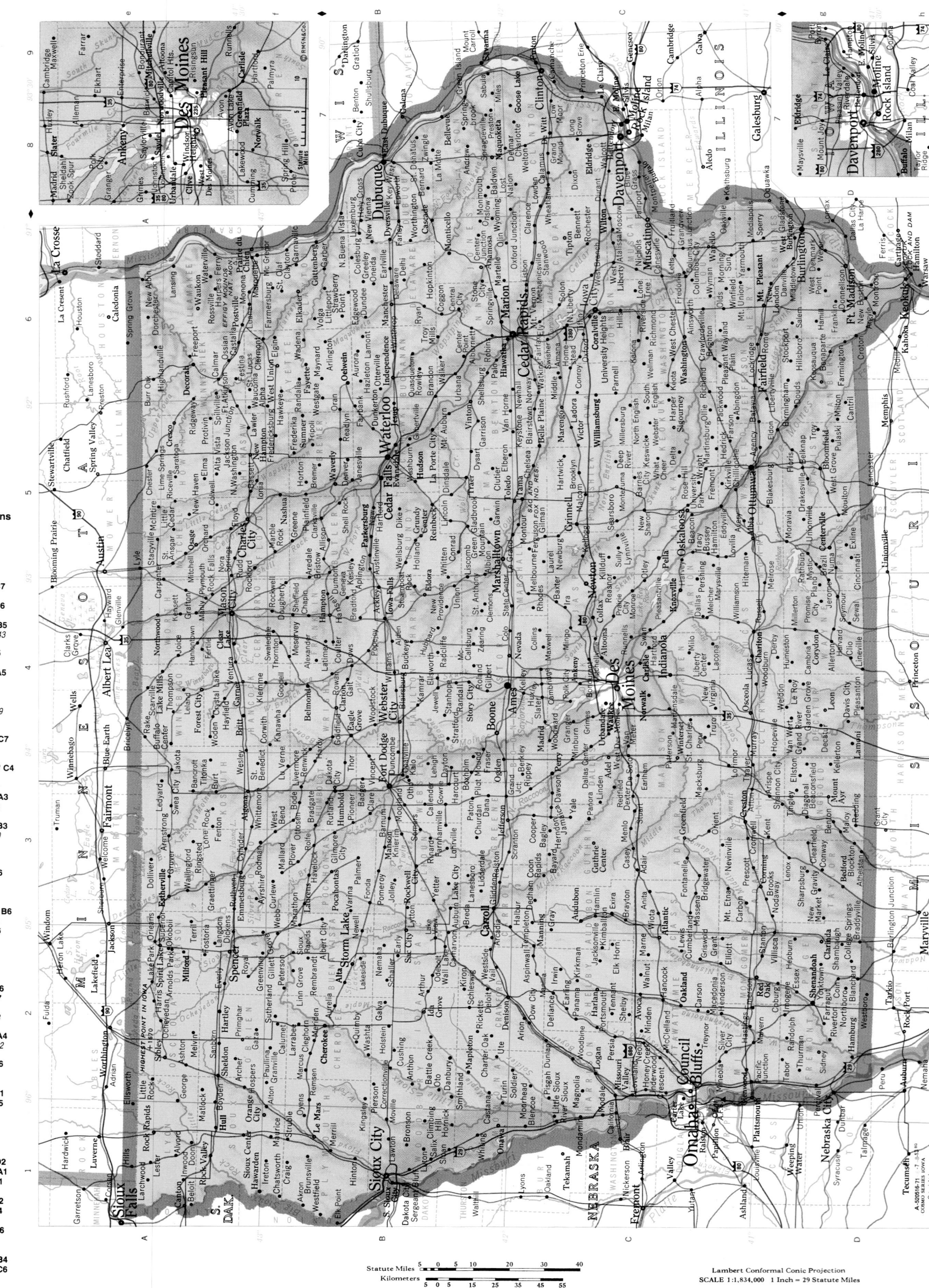

Cities and Towns

Algona 6,289 **A3**
Amana 600 **C6**
Ames 45,775 **B4**
Anamosa 4,958 **B6**
Ankeny 15,429 **C4**
Atlantic 7,789 **C2**
Bettendorf 27,381 **C7**
Boone 12,602 **B4**
Burlington 29,529 **D6**
Carroll 9,705 **B3**
Cedar Falls 36,322 **B5**
Cedar Rapids 110,243 **C6**
Centerville 6,558 **D5**
Chariton 4,987 **C4**
Charles City 8,778 **A5**
Cherokee 7,004 **B2**
Clarinda 5,458 **D2**
Clinton 32,828 **C7**
Council Bluffs 56,449 **C2**
Creston 8,429 **C3**
Davenport 103,264 **C7**
Decorah 7,991 **A6**
Denison 6,675 **B2**
Des Moines 191,003 **C4**
De Witt 4,512 **C7**
Dubuque 62,321 **B7**
Emmetsburg 4,621 **A3**
Estherville 7,518 **A3**
Fairfield 9,428 **C6**
Fort Dodge 29,423 **B3**
Fort Madison 13,520 **D6**
Glenwood 5,280 **C2**
Grinnell 8,868 **C5**
Guttenberg 2,428 **B6**
Hampton 4,630 **B4**
Harlan 5,357 **C2**
Humboldt 4,794 **B3**
Independence 6,392 **B6**
Indianola 10,843 **C4**
Iowa City 50,508 **C6**
Iowa Falls 6,174 **B4**
Jefferson 4,854 **B3**
Keokuk 13,536 **D6**
Knoxville 8,143 **C4**
Le Mars 8,276 **B1**
Manchester 4,942 **B6**
Maquoketa 6,313 **B7**
Marion 19,474 **B6**
Marshalltown 26,938 **B5**
Mason City 30,144 **A4**
Mount Pleasant 7,322 **D6**
Muscatine 23,467 **C6**
Newton 15,292 **C4**
Oelwein 7,564 **B6**
Orange City 4,588 **B1**
Oskaloosa 10,989 **C5**
Ottumwa 27,381 **C5**
Pella 8,349 **C5**
Perry 7,053 **C3**
Red Oak 6,810 **D2**
Sheldon 5,003 **A2**
Shenandoah 6,274 **D2**
Sioux Center 4,588 **A1**
Sioux City 82,003 **B1**
Spencer 11,726 **A2**
Storm Lake 8,814 **B2**
Urbandale 17,869 **C4**
Vinton 5,040 **B5**
Washington 6,584 **C6**
Waterloo 75,985 **B5**
Waverly 8,444 **B5**
Webster City 8,572 **B4**
West Branch 1,867 **C6**
West Des Moines 21,894 **C4**

See main index for complete listing.

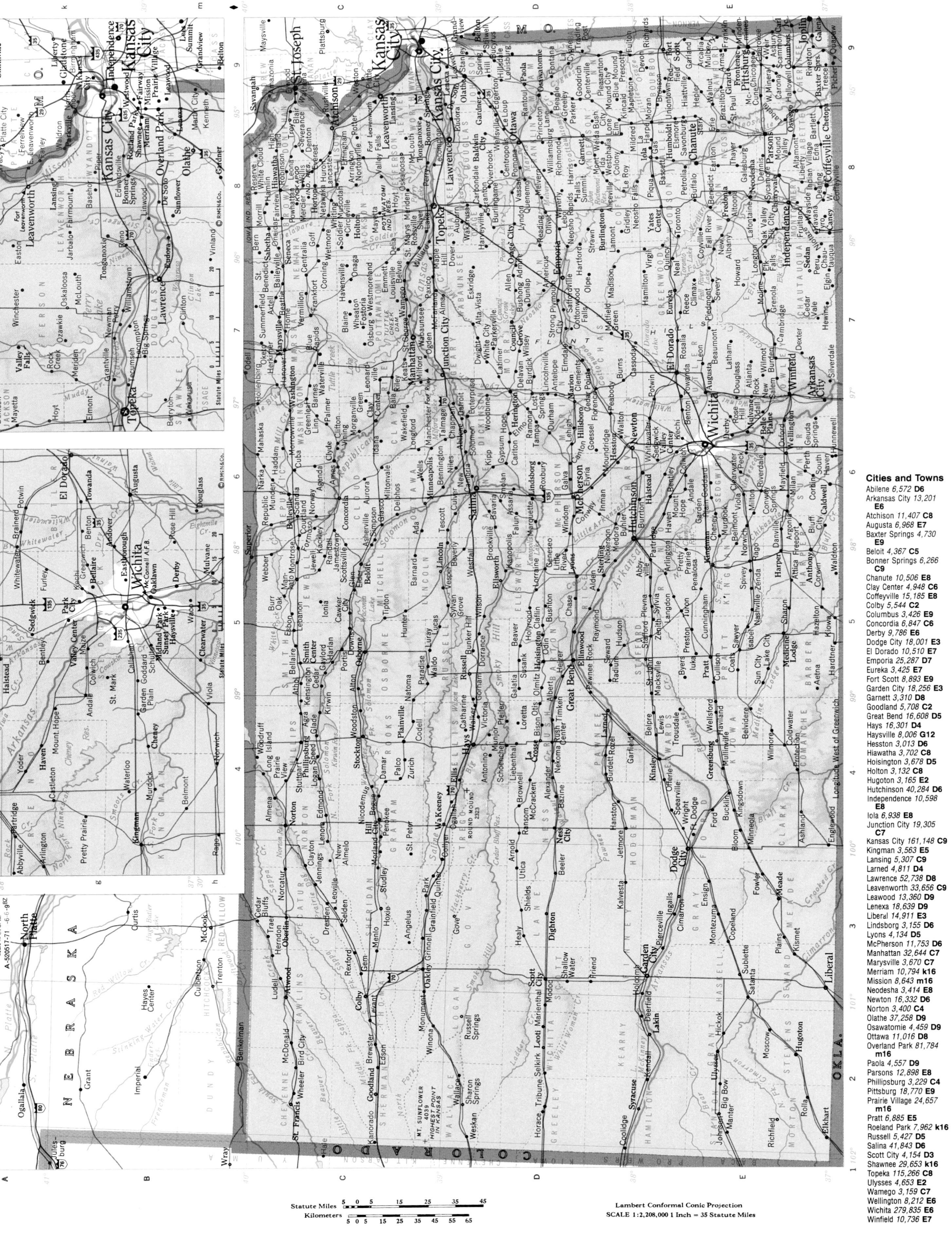

KENTUCKY

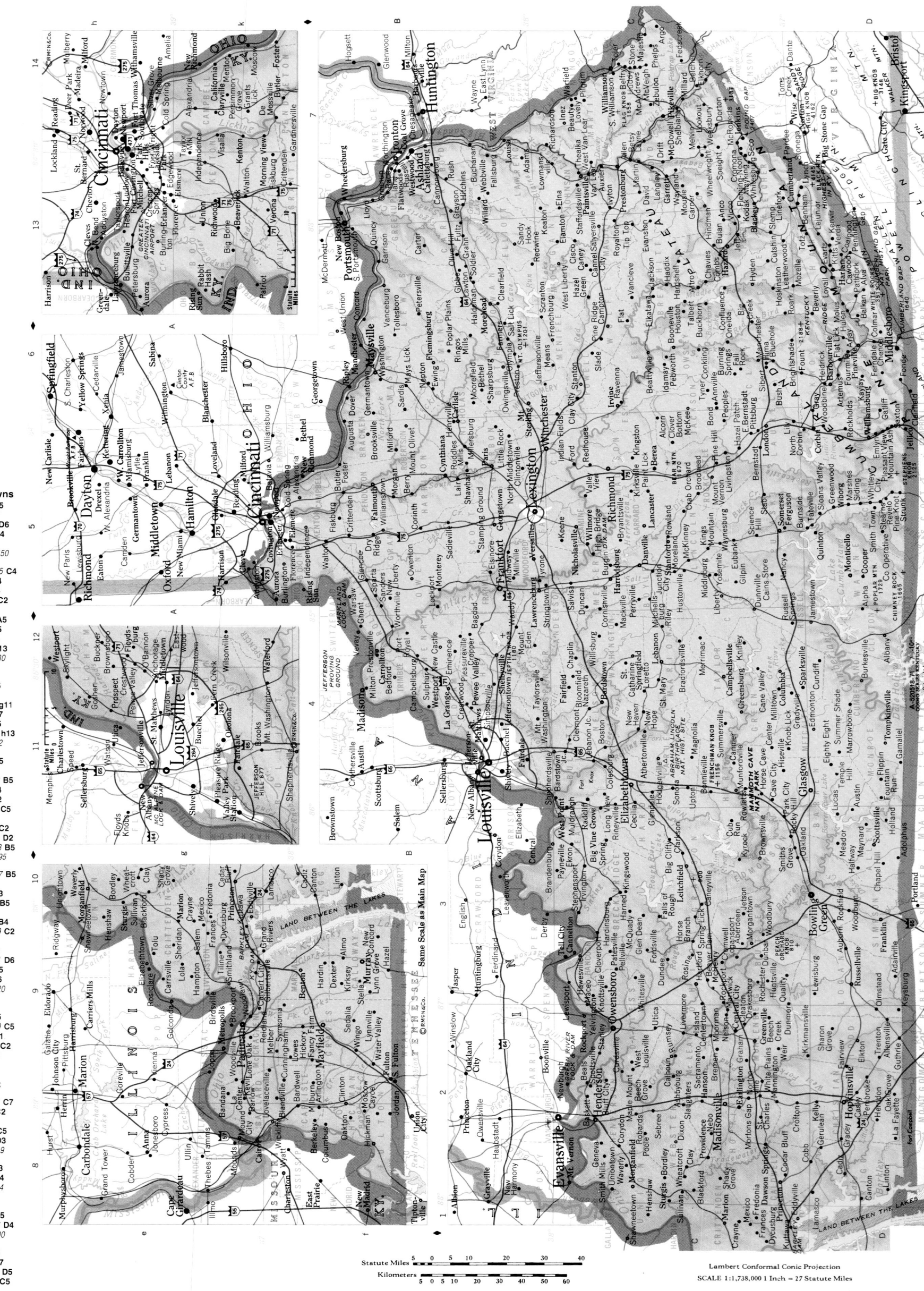

Cities and Towns

Alexandria *4,735* **B5**
Ashland *27,064* **B7**
Barbourville *3,333* **D6**
Bardstown *6,155* **C4**
Berea *8,226* **C5**
Bowling Green *40,450* **D3**
Campbellsville *8,715* **C4**
Carrollton *3,967* **B4**
Cave City *2,098* **C4**
Central City *5,214* **C2**
Corbin *8,075* **D5**
Covington *49,563* **A5**
Cynthiana *5,881* **B5**
Danville *12,942* **C5**
Edgewood *7,230* **h13**
Elizabethtown *15,380* **C4**
Elsmere *7,203* **B5**
Erlanger *14,433* **A5**
Fairdale *7,315* **B4**
Fern Creek *16,866* **g11**
Flatwoods *8,354* **B7**
Florence *15,586* **A5**
Fort Mitchell *7,297* **h13**
Fort Thomas *16,012* **h14**
Frankfort *25,973* **B5**
Franklin *7,738* **D3**
Georgetown *10,972* **B5**
Glasgow *12,958* **C4**
Greenville *4,631* **C2**
Harrodsburg *7,265* **C5**
Hazard *5,371* **C6**
Henderson *24,834* **C2**
Hopkinsville *27,318* **D2**
Independence *7,998* **B5**
Jeffersontown *15,795* **B4**
Lawrenceburg *5,167* **B5**
Lebanon *6,590* **C4**
Leitchfield *4,533* **C3**
Lexington *204,165* **B5**
London *4,002* **C5**
Louisville *298,840* **B4**
Madisonville *16,979* **C2**
Mayfield *10,705* **f9**
Maysville *7,983* **B6**
Middlesboro *12,251* **D6**
Monticello *5,677* **D5**
Morehead *7,789* **B6**
Mount Sterling *5,820* **B6**
Murray *14,248* **f9**
Newport *21,587* **A5**
Nicholasville *10,319* **C5**
Okolona *20,039* **g11**
Owensboro *54,450* **C2**
Paducah *29,315* **e9**
Paris *7,935* **B5**
Pikeville *4,756* **C7**
Pleasure Ridge Park *27,332* **g11**
Prestonsburg *4,011* **C7**
Providence *4,434* **C2**
Radcliff *14,519* **C4**
Richmond *21,705* **C5**
Russellville *7,520* **D3**
St. Matthews *13,519* **B4**
Scottsville *4,278* **D3**
Shelbyville *5,329* **B4**
Shepherdsville *4,454* **C4**
Shively *16,819* **B4**
Somerset *10,649* **C5**
Tompkinsville *4,366* **D4**
Valley Station *20,000* **g11**
Versailles *6,427* **B5**
Westwood *5,973* **B7**
Williamsburg *5,560* **D5**
Winchester *15,216* **C5**

See main index for complete listing.

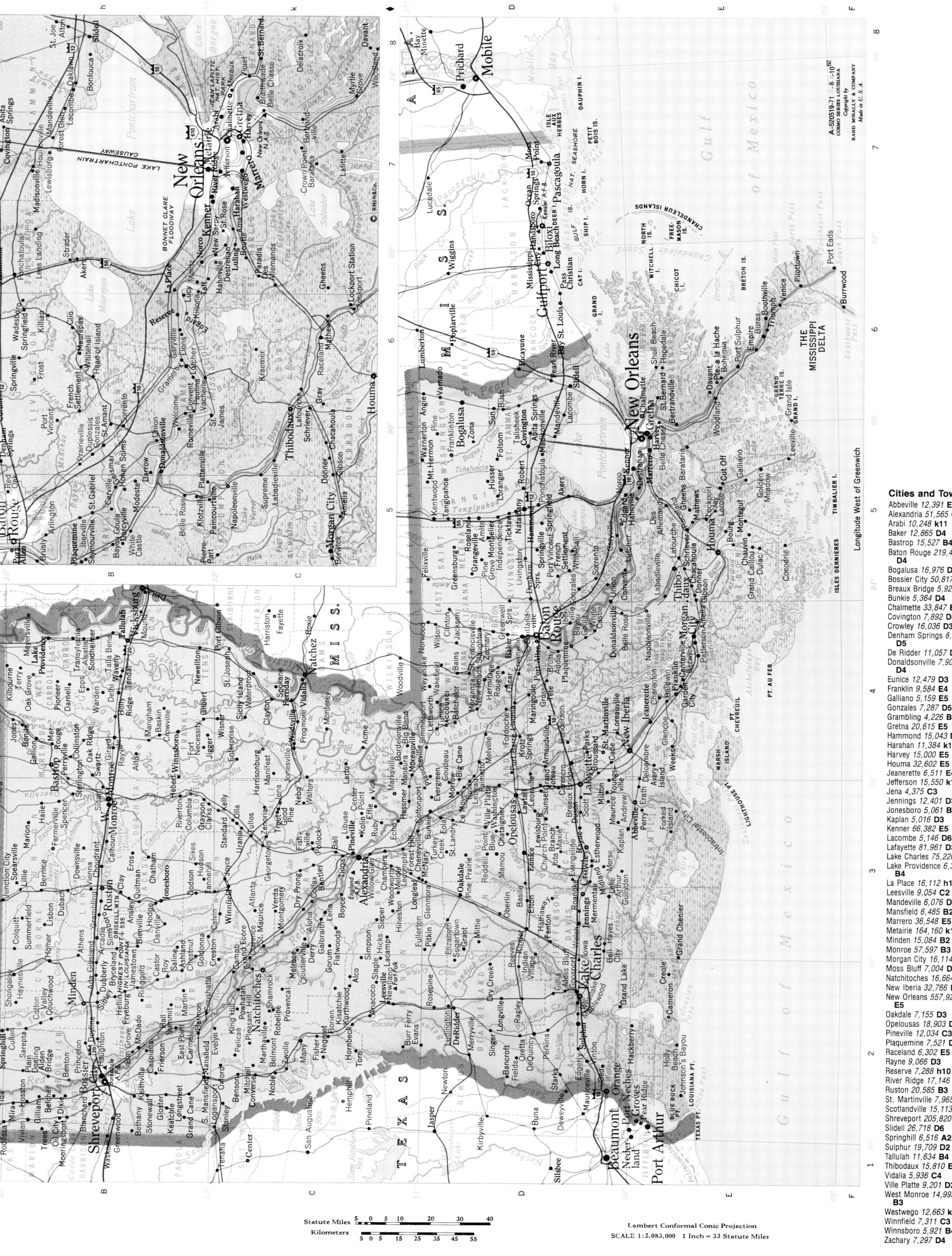

Lambert Conformal Conic Projection
SCALE 1:2,083,000   1 Inch = 33 Statute Miles

Statute Miles 5 0 5   20   30   40
Kilometers 5 0 5   15 25 35 45 55

Cities and Towns
Abbeville 12,391 **E3**
Alexandria 51,565 **C3**
Arabi 10,248 **k11**
Baker 12,865 **D4**
Bastrop 15,527 **B4**
Baton Rouge 219,419 **D4**
Bogalusa 16,976 **D6**
Bossier City 50,817 **B2**
Breaux Bridge 5,922 **D4**
Bunkie 5,364 **D4**
Chalmette 33,847 **E6**
Covington 7,892 **D5**
Crowley 16,036 **D3**
Denham Springs 8,563 **D5**
De Ridder 11,057 **D2**
Donaldsonville 7,901 **D4**
Eunice 12,479 **D3**
Franklin 9,584 **E4**
Galliano 5,159 **E5**
Gonzales 7,287 **D5**
Grambling 4,226 **B3**
Gretna 20,615 **E5**
Hammond 15,043 **D5**
Harahan 11,384 **k11**
Harvey 15,000 **E5**
Houma 32,602 **E5**
Jeanerette 6,511 **E4**
Jefferson 15,550 **k11**
Jena 4,375 **C3**
Jennings 12,401 **D3**
Jonesboro 5,061 **B3**
Kaplan 5,016 **D3**
Kenner 66,382 **E5**
Lacombe 5,146 **D6**
Lafayette 81,961 **D3**
Lake Charles 75,226 **D2**
Lake Providence 6,361 **B4**
La Place 16,112 **h11**
Leesville 9,054 **C2**
Mandeville 6,076 **D5**
Mansfield 6,485 **B2**
Marrero 36,548 **E5**
Metairie 164,160 **k11**
Minden 15,084 **B2**
Monroe 57,597 **B4**
Morgan City 16,114 **E4**
Moss Bluff 7,004 **D2**
Natchitoches 16,664 **C2**
New Iberia 32,766 **D4**
New Orleans 557,927 **E5**
Oakdale 7,155 **D3**
Opelousas 18,903 **D4**
Pineville 12,034 **C3**
Plaquemine 7,521 **D4**
Raceland 6,302 **E5**
Rayne 9,066 **D3**
Reserve 7,288 **h10**
River Ridge 17,146 **k11**
Ruston 20,585 **B3**
St. Martinville 7,965 **D4**
Scotlandville 15,113 **D4**
Shreveport 205,820 **B2**
Slidell 26,718 **D6**
Springhill 6,516 **A2**
Sulphur 19,709 **D2**
Tallulah 11,634 **B4**
Thibodaux 15,810 **E5**
Vidalia 5,936 **C4**
Ville Platte 9,201 **D3**
West Monroe 14,993 **B3**
Westwego 12,663 **k11**
Winnfield 7,311 **C3**
Winnsboro 5,921 **B4**
Zachary 7,297 **D4**

Longitude West of Greenwich

A-520519-71 · 8 -10
COSMO SERIES LOUISIANA
Copyright by
RAND M℡NALLY & COMPANY
Made in U.S.A.

MAINE

Cities and Towns*

Auburn 23,128 **D2**
Augusta 21,819 **D3**
Bangor 31,643 **D4**
Bar Harbor 2,685 **D4**
Bath 10,246 **E3**
Belfast 6,243 **D3**
Berwick 2,378 **E2**
Biddeford 19,638 **E2**
Boothbay Harbor 2,207 **E3**
Brewer 9,017 **D4**
Brunswick 10,990 **E3**
Bucksport 2,853 **D4**
Calais 4,262 **C5**
Camden 3,743 **D3**
Cape Elizabeth 7,838 **E2**
Caribou 9,916 **B5**
Cumberland Center 2,015 **g7**
Dexter 3,118 **C3**
Dover-Foxcroft 2,974 **C3**
East Millinocket 2,361 **C4**
Eastport 1,982 **D6**
Eliot 2,450 **E2**
Ellsworth 5,179 **D4**
Fairfield 3,169 **D3**
Falmouth 6,853 **E2**
Farmingdale 2,014 **D3**
Farmington 3,583 **D2**
Fort Fairfield 2,282 **B5**
Fort Kent 2,375 **A4**
Freeport 1,906 **E2**
Gardiner 6,485 **D3**
Gorham 4,052 **E2**
Hallowell 2,502 **D3**
Hampden 2,300 **D4**
Houlton 5,730 **B5**
Kennebunk 3,294 **E2**
Kittery 5,465 **E2**
Lewiston 40,481 **D2**
Lincoln 3,524 **C4**
Lisbon Falls 4,370 **E2**
Livermore Falls 2,441 **D2**
Madawaska 4,165 **A4**
Madison 2,788 **D3**
Mechanic Falls 2,616 **D2**
Mexico 3,207 **D2**
Millinocket 7,567 **C4**
Milo 2,255 **C4**
North Windham 5,492 **E2**
Norway 2,653 **D2**
Oakland 3,387 **D3**
Old Orchard Beach 6,291 **E2**
Orono 10,578 **D4**
Pittsfield 3,117 **D3**
Portland 61,572 **E2**
Presque Isle 11,172 **B5**
Rockland 10,268 **E2**
Rumford 6,256 **D2**
Saco 12,921 **E2**
Sanford 10,268 **E2**
Scarborough 2,280 **E2**
Skowhegan 6,517 **D3**
South Berwick 2,120 **E2**
South Paris 2,128 **D2**
South Portland 22,712 **E2**
Thomaston 2,348 **D3**
Topsham 4,657 **E3**
Van Buren 3,282 **A5**
Waterville 17,779 **D3**
Westbrook 14,976 **E2**
Wilton 2,262 **D2**
Winslow 5,903 **D3**
Winthrop 3,264 **D3**
Yarmouth 2,421 **E2**
York 3,130 **E2**

*Populations are for localities, not incorporated towns.

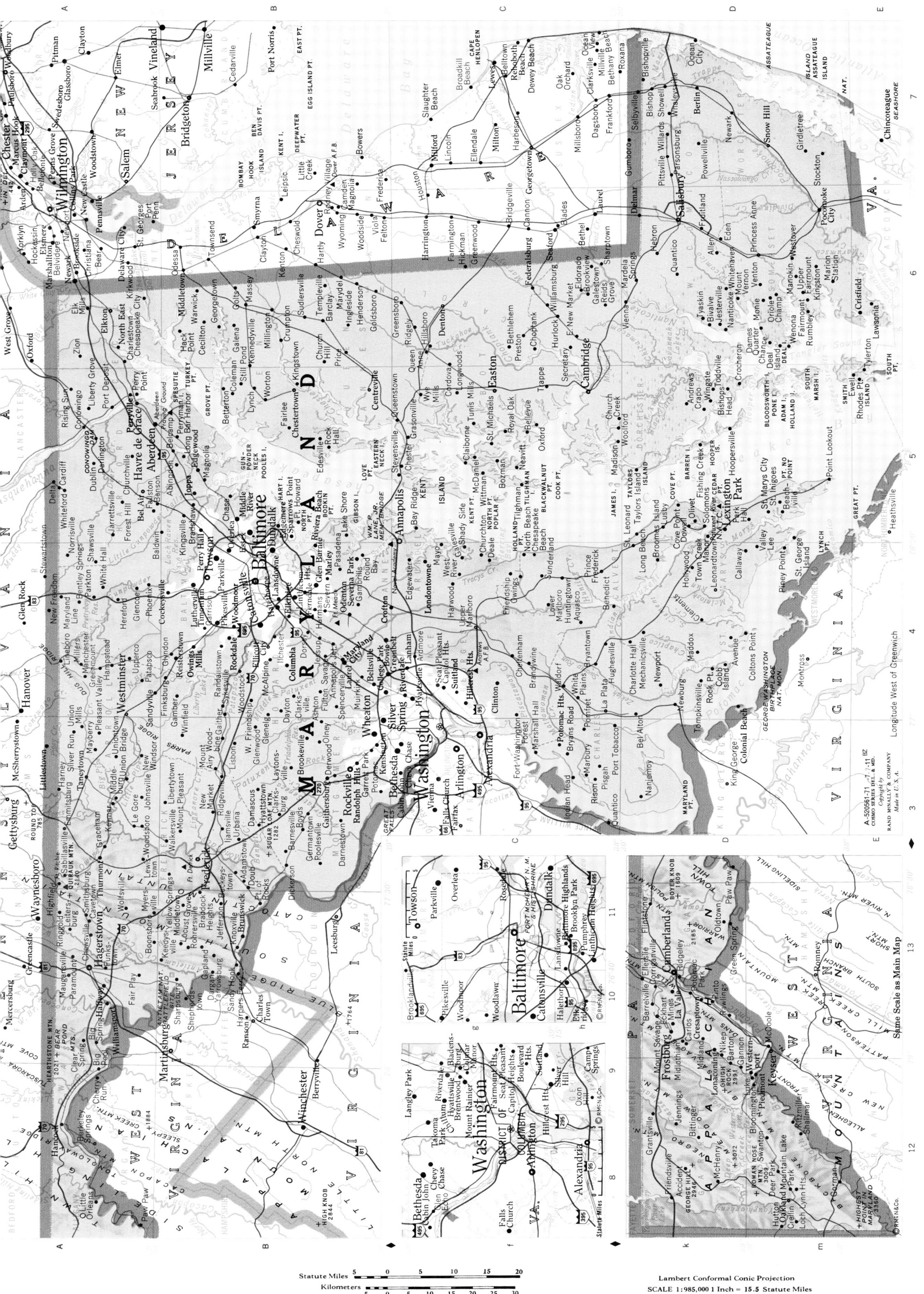

Cities and Towns

Aberdeen 11,533 **A5**
Annapolis 31,740 **C5**
Baltimore 786,775 **B4**
Bel Air 7,814 **A5**
Beltsville 12,760 **B4**
Bethesda 63,022 **C3**
Bladensburg 7,691 **f9**
Bowie 33,695 **B4**
Brunswick 4,572 **B2**
Cambridge 11,703 **C5**
Catonsville 33,208 **B4**
Chevy Chase 12,232 **C3**
Clinton 16,438 **C4**
Cockeysville 17,013 **B4**
College Park 23,614 **C4**
Columbia 52,518 **B4**
Crofton 12,009 **B4**
Cumberland 25,933 **k13**
Dundalk 71,293 **B4**
Easton 7,536 **C5**
Edgewood 19,455 **B5**
Elkton 6,468 **A6**
Essex 39,614 **B5**
Frederick 28,086 **B3**
Frostburg 7,715 **k13**
Gaithersburg 26,424 **B3**
Germantown 9,721 **B3**
Glen Burnie 30,000 **B4**
Greenbelt 17,332 **C4**
Hagerstown 34,132 **A2**
Halethorpe 20,163 **B4**
Halfway 8,659 **A2**
Havre de Grace 8,763
A5
Hillcrest Heights 17,021
C4
Hyattsville 12,709 **C4**
Joppa 11,348 **B5**
Langley Park 11,100 **f9**
Lansdowne 10,000 **B4**
Laurel 12,103 **B4**
Lexington Park 10,361
D5
Lutherville-Timonium
17,854 **B4**
Middle River 26,756 **B5**
Oakland 1,994 **m12**
Ocean City 4,946 **D7**
Olney 10,000 **B3**
Overlea 12,965 **B4**
Owings Mills 9,526 **B4**
Oxon Hill 8,100 **f9**
Parkville 35,159 **B4**
Perry Hall 13,455 **B5**
Pikesville 20,000 **B4**
Pocomoke City 3,558
D6
Potomac 22,800 **B3**
Randallstown 20,500
B4
Reisterstown 19,385 **B4**
Rockville 43,811 **B3**
Rosedale 19,956 **g11**
Salisbury 16,429 **D6**
Severn 20,147 **B4**
Severna Park 21,253
B4
Sharpsburg 721 **B2**
Silver Spring 64,100 **C3**
Snow Hill 2,192 **D7**
Suitland 24,800 **C4**
Takoma Park 16,231 **f8**
Towson 51,083 **B4**
Waldorf 9,782 **C4**
Westminster 8,808 **A4**
Wheaton 48,600 **B3**
White Plains 5,167 **C4**
Woodlawn 8,000 **g10**
Washington D.C.
638,432 **C3**

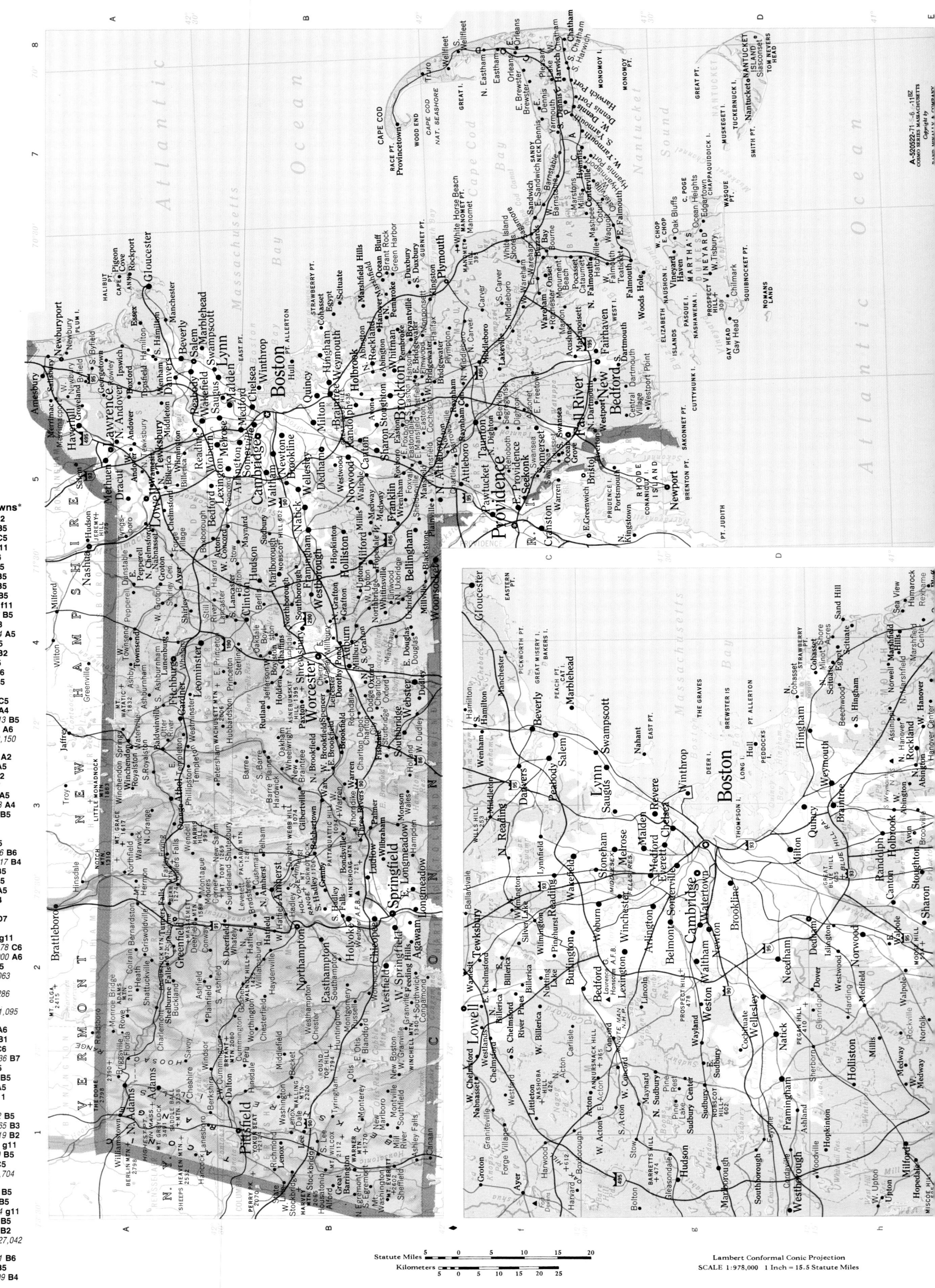

Cities and Towns*

Amherst 26,300 **B2**
Arlington 48,219 **B5**
Attleboro 34,196 **C5**
Belmont 26,100 **g11**
Beverly 37,655 **A6**
Boston 562,994 **B5**
Braintree 36,337 **B5**
Brockton 95,172 **B5**
Brookline 55,062 **B5**
Burlington 23,486 **f11**
Cambridge 95,322 **B5**
Chatham 1,922 **C8**
Chelmsford 31,174 **A5**
Chelsea 25,431 **B5**
Chicopee 55,112 **B2**
Concord 6,400 **B5**
Danvers 24,100 **A6**
Dedham 25,298 **B5**
Dracut 21,249 **A5**
Fall River 92,574 **C5**
Fitchburg 39,580 **A4**
Framingham 65,113 **B5**
Gloucester 27,768 **A6**
Great Barrington 3,150 **B1**
Greenfield 14,198 **A2**
Haverhill 46,865 **A5**
Holyoke 44,678 **B2**
Hyannis 8,000 **C7**
Lawrence 63,175 **A5**
Leominster 34,508 **A4**
Lexington 29,479 **B5**
Lowell 92,418 **A5**
Lynn 78,471 **B6**
Malden 53,386 **B5**
Marblehead 20,126 **B6**
Marlborough 30,617 **B4**
Medford 58,076 **B5**
Melrose 30,055 **B5**
Methuen 36,701 **A5**
Milford 23,390 **B4**
Milton 25,860 **B5**
Nantucket 3,229 **D7**
Natick 29,461 **B5**
Needham 27,901 **g11**
New Bedford 98,478 **C6**
Newburyport 15,900 **A6**
Newton 83,622 **B5**
North Adams 18,063 **A1**
Northampton 29,286 **B2**
North Attleboro 21,095 **C5**
Peabody 45,976 **A6**
Pittsfield 51,974 **B1**
Plymouth 7,232 **C6**
Provincetown 3,536 **B7**
Quincy 84,743 **B5**
Randolph 22,218 **B5**
Reading 22,678 **A5**
Revere 42,423 **g11**
Salem 38,220 **A6**
Somerville 77,372 **B5**
Southbridge 16,665 **B3**
Springfield 152,319 **B2**
Stoneham 21,424 **g11**
Stoughton 26,710 **B5**
Taunton 45,001 **C5**
Vineyard Haven 1,704 **D6**
Wakefield 24,895 **B5**
Waltham 58,200 **B5**
Watertown 34,384 **g11**
Wellesley 27,209 **B5**
Westfield 36,465 **B2**
West Springfield 27,042 **B2**
Weymouth 55,601 **B6**
Woburn 36,626 **B5**
Worcester 161,799 **B4**

*Populations are for localities, not incorporated towns.

Statute Miles

Kilometers

Lambert Conformal Conic Projection
SCALE 1:978,000   1 Inch = 15.5 Statute Miles

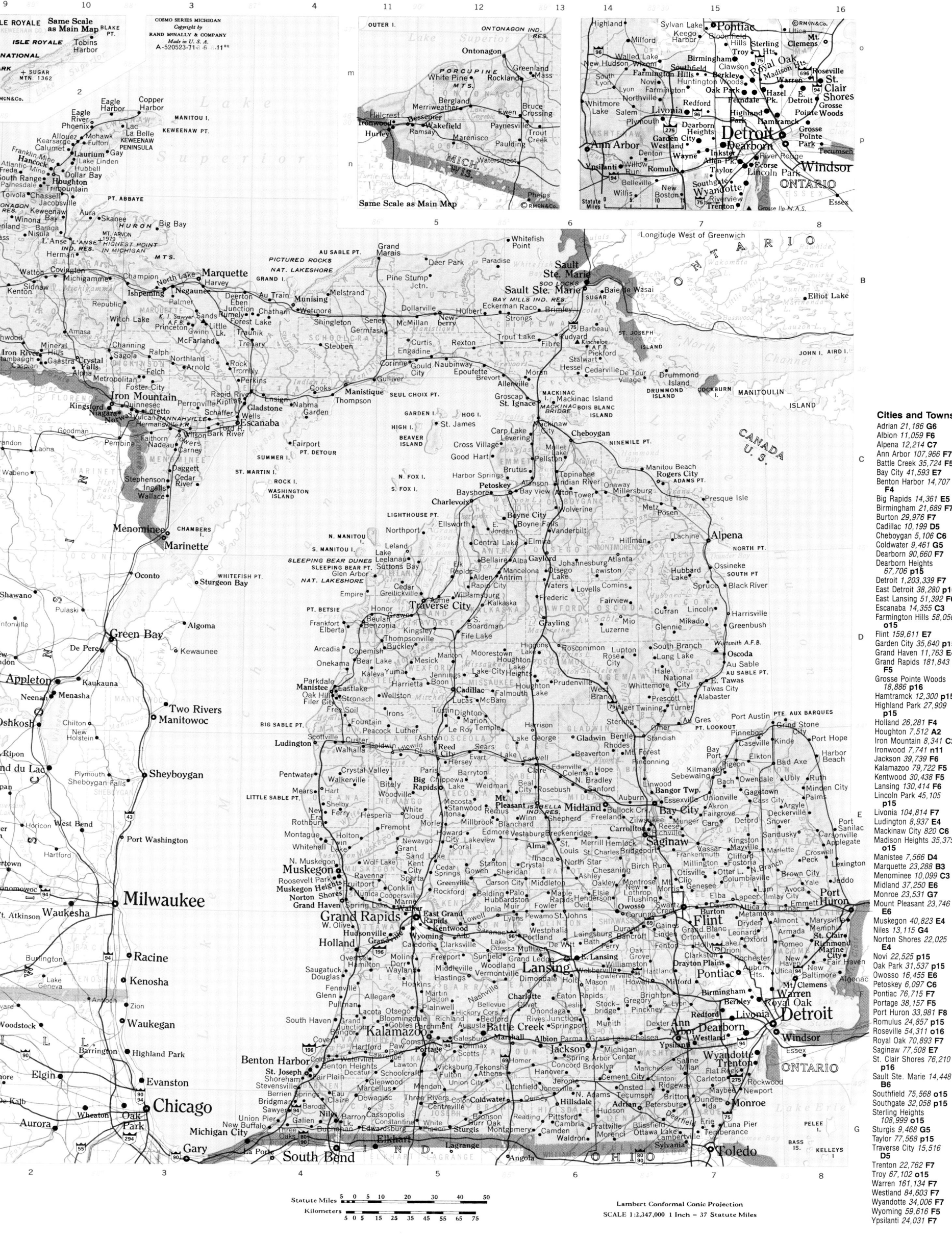

MINNESOTA

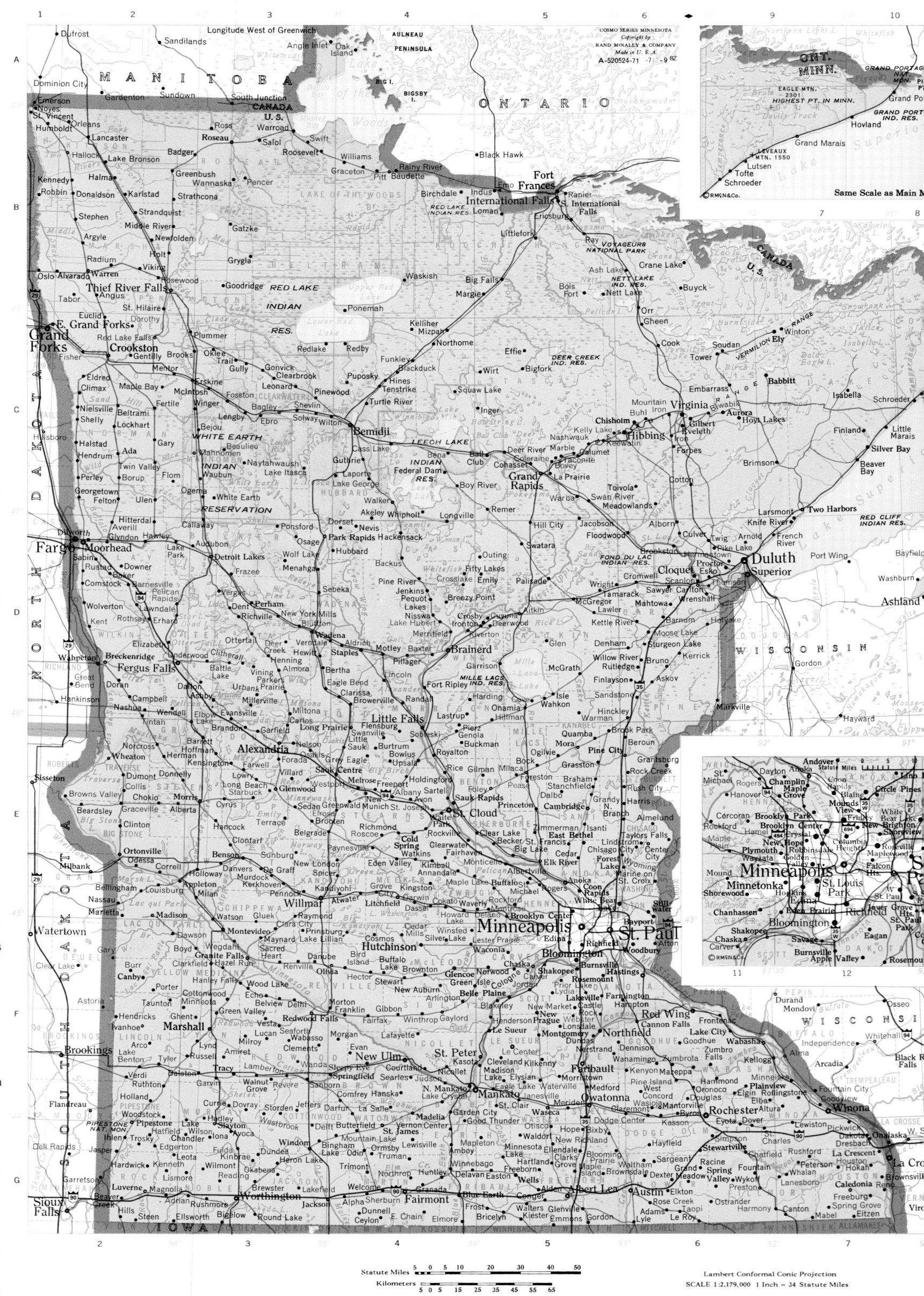

Cities and Towns
Albert Lea 19,200 **G5**
Alexandria 7,608 **E3**
Anoka 15,634 **E5**
Apple Valley 21,818 **n12**
Austin 23,020 **G6**
Bemidji 10,949 **C4**
Blaine 28,558 **m12**
Bloomington 81,831 **F5**
Brainerd 11,489 **D4**
Brooklyn Center 31,230 **E5**
Brooklyn Park 43,332 **m12**
Burnsville 35,674 **F5**
Chisholm 5,930 **C6**
Cloquet 11,142 **D6**
Columbia Heights 20,029 **m12**
Coon Rapids 35,826 **E5**
Cottage Grove 18,994 **n13**
Crookston 8,628 **C2**
Crystal 25,543 **m12**
Detroit Lakes 7,106 **D3**
Duluth 92,811 **D6**
Eagan 20,700 **n12**
East Bethel 6,626 **E5**
East Grand Forks 8,537 **C2**
Eden Prairie 16,263 **n12**
Edina 46,073 **F5**
Ely 4,820 **C7**
Fairmont 11,506 **G4**
Faribault 16,241 **F5**
Fergus Falls 12,519 **D2**
Fridley 30,228 **m12**
Golden Valley 22,775 **m12**
Grand Marais 1,289 **k9**
Grand Rapids 7,934 **C5**
Hibbing 21,193 **C6**
Hutchinson 9,244 **F4**
International Falls 5,611 **B5**
Inver Grove Heights 17,171 **n12**
Lakeville 14,790 **F5**
Litchfield 5,904 **E4**
Little Falls 7,250 **E4**
Mankato 28,651 **F5**
Maple Grove 20,525 **m12**
Maplewood 26,990 **n12**
Marshall 11,161 **F3**
Minneapolis 370,951 **F5**
Minnetonka 38,683 **n12**
Montevideo 5,845 **F3**
Moorhead 29,998 **D2**
Morris 5,367 **E3**
New Brighton 23,269 **m12**
New Hope 23,087 **m12**
New Ulm 13,755 **F4**
Northfield 12,562 **F5**
Owatonna 18,632 **F5**
Pipestone 4,887 **G2**
Plymouth 31,615 **m12**
Red Wing 13,736 **F6**
Redwood Falls 5,210 **F3**
Richfield 37,851 **F5**
Rochester 57,890 **F6**
Roseville 35,820 **m12**
St. Cloud 42,566 **E4**
St. Louis Park 42,931 **n12**
St. Paul 270,230 **F5**
St. Peter 9,056 **F5**
Shoreview 17,300 **m12**
South St. Paul 21,235 **n12**
Thief River Falls 9,105 **B2**
Virginia 11,056 **C6**
Waseca 8,219 **F5**
West St. Paul 18,527 **n12**
White Bear Lake 22,538 **E5**
Willmar 15,895 **E3**
Winona 25,075 **F7**
Worthington 10,243 **G3**

Statute Miles
Kilometers

Lambert Conformal Conic Projection
SCALE 1:2,179,000 1 Inch = 34 Statute Miles

Cities and Towns

Aberdeen 7,184 **B5**
Amory 7,307 **B5**
Baldwyn 3,427 **A5**
Batesville 4,692 **A4**
Bay Saint Louis 7,891 **E4**
Belzoni 2,982 **B3**
Biloxi 49,311 **E5**
Booneville 6,199 **A5**
Brandon 9,626 **C4**
Brookhaven 10,800 **D3**
Canton 11,116 **C3**
Carthage 3,453 **C4**
Clarksdale 21,137 **A3**
Cleveland 14,524 **B3**
Clinton 14,660 **C3**
Columbia 7,733 **D4**
Columbus 27,383 **B5**
Corinth 13,839 **A5**
Crystal Springs 4,902 **D3**
D'Iberville 9,000 **E5**
Ellisville 4,652 **D4**
Forest 5,229 **C4**
Fulton 3,238 **A5**
Gautier 8,917 **f8**
Greenville 40,613 **B2**
Greenwood 20,115 **B3**
Grenada 12,641 **B4**
Gulfport 39,676 **E4**
Hattiesburg 40,829 **D4**
Hazlehurst 4,437 **D3**
Hollandale 4,336 **B3**
Holly Springs 7,285 **A4**
Horn Lake 4,326 **A3**
Houston 3,747 **B4**
Indianola 8,221 **B3**
Jackson 202,895 **C4**
Kosciusko 7,415 **B4**
Laurel 21,897 **D4**
Leland 6,667 **B3**
Long Beach 7,967 **g7**
Louisville 7,323 **B4**
McComb 12,331 **D3**
Magee 3,497 **D4**
Meridian 46,577 **C5**
Morgantown 3,445 **D2**
Morton 3,303 **C4**
Moss Point 18,998 **E5**
Natchez 22,015 **D2**
New Albany 7,072 **A4**
Newton 3,708 **C4**
Ocean Springs 14,504 **E5**
Okolona 3,409 **B5**
Oxford 9,882 **A4**
Pascagoula 29,318 **E5**
Pass Christian 5,014 **E4**
Pearl 18,580 **C3**
Petal 8,476 **D4**
Philadelphia 6,434 **C4**
Picayune 10,361 **E4**
Pontotoc 4,723 **A4**
Ripley 4,271 **A5**
Ruleville 3,332 **B3**
Senatobia 5,013 **A4**
Southaven 16,071 **A3**
Starkville 15,169 **B5**
Tupelo 23,905 **A5**
Vicksburg 25,434 **C3**
Water Valley 4,147 **A4**
Waveland 4,186 **E4**
Waynesboro 5,349 **D5**
West Point 8,811 **B5**
Wiggins 3,205 **E4**
Winona 6,177 **B4**
Yazoo City 12,092 **C3**

Lambert Conformal Conic Projection
SCALE 1:1,837,000 1 Inch = 29 Statute Miles

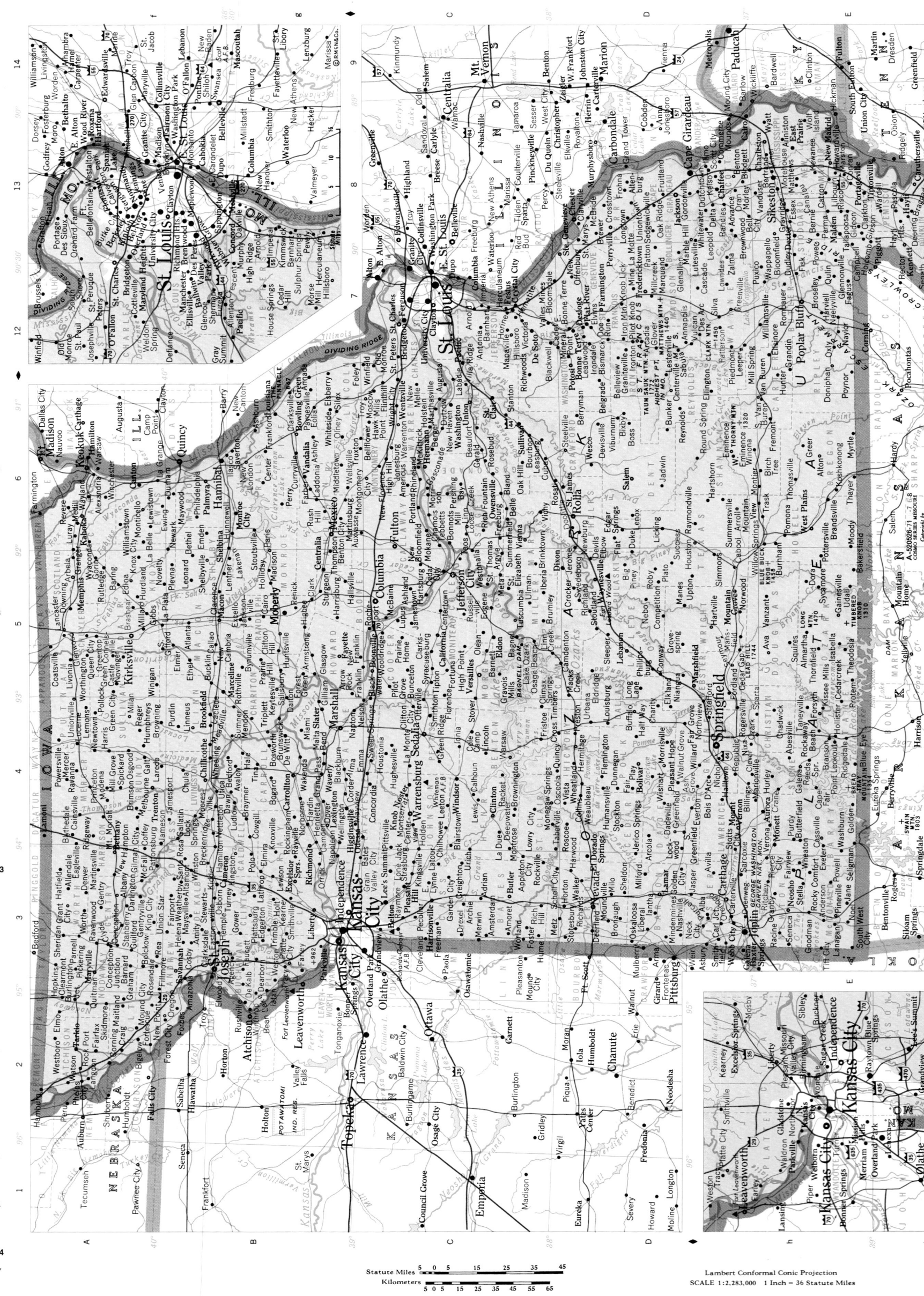

Cities and Towns

Arnold 19,141 C7
Aurora 6,437 E4
Ballwin 12,656 f12
Belton 12,708 C3
Berkeley 15,922 f13
Blue Springs 25,927 h11
Bolivar 5,919 D4
Boonville 6,959 C5
Branson 2,550 E4
Bridgeton 18,445 C7
Cape Girardeau 34,361 D8
Carthage 11,104 D3
Caruthersville 7,958 E8
Charleston 5,230 E8
Chillicothe 9,089 B4
Clayton 14,273 f13
Clinton 8,366 C7
Columbia 62,061 C5
Concord 20,896 f13
De Soto 5,993 C7
Dexter 7,043 E8
Eureka 3,862 f12
Excelsior Springs 10,424 B3
Farmington 8,270 D7
Ferguson 24,740 C7
Festus 7,574 C7
Florissant 55,372 f13
Fulton 11,046 C6
Gladstone 24,990 h10
Grandview 24,502 C3
Hannibal 18,811 B6
Independence 111,806 B3
Jackson 7,827 D8
Jefferson City 33,619 C5
Jennings 17,026 f13
Joplin 39,023 D3
Kansas City 448,159 B3
Kennett 10,145 E7
Kirksville 17,167 A5
Kirkwood 27,987 f13
Lebanon 9,507 D5
Lees Summit 28,741 C3
Liberty 16,251 B3
Malden 6,096 E8
Marshall 12,781 B4
Maryville 9,558 A3
Mehlville 22,900 f13
Mexico 12,276 B6
Moberly 13,418 B5
Monett 6,148 E4
Neosho 9,493 E3
Nevada 9,044 D3
Overland 19,620 f13
Perryville 7,343 D8
Poplar Bluff 17,139 E7
Raytown 31,759 h11
Richmond Heights 11,516 f13
Rolla 13,303 D6
St. Charles 37,379 C7
Ste. Genevieve 4,481 D7
St. Joseph 76,691 B3
St. Louis 453,085 C7
St. Peters 14,700 C7
Sappington 11,388 f13
Sedalia 20,927 C4
Sikeston 17,431 E8
Spanish Lake 20,632 f13
Springfield 133,116 D4
Sullivan 5,461 C6
Trenton 6,811 A4
University City 42,738 C7
Warrensburg 13,807 C4
Washington 9,251 C6
Webster Groves 23,097 f13
West Plains 7.741 E6

Statute Miles 5 0 5   15   25   35   45
Kilometers 5 0 5   15   25   35   45 55 65

Lambert Conformal Conic Projection
SCALE 1:2,283,000   1 Inch = 36 Statute Miles

252

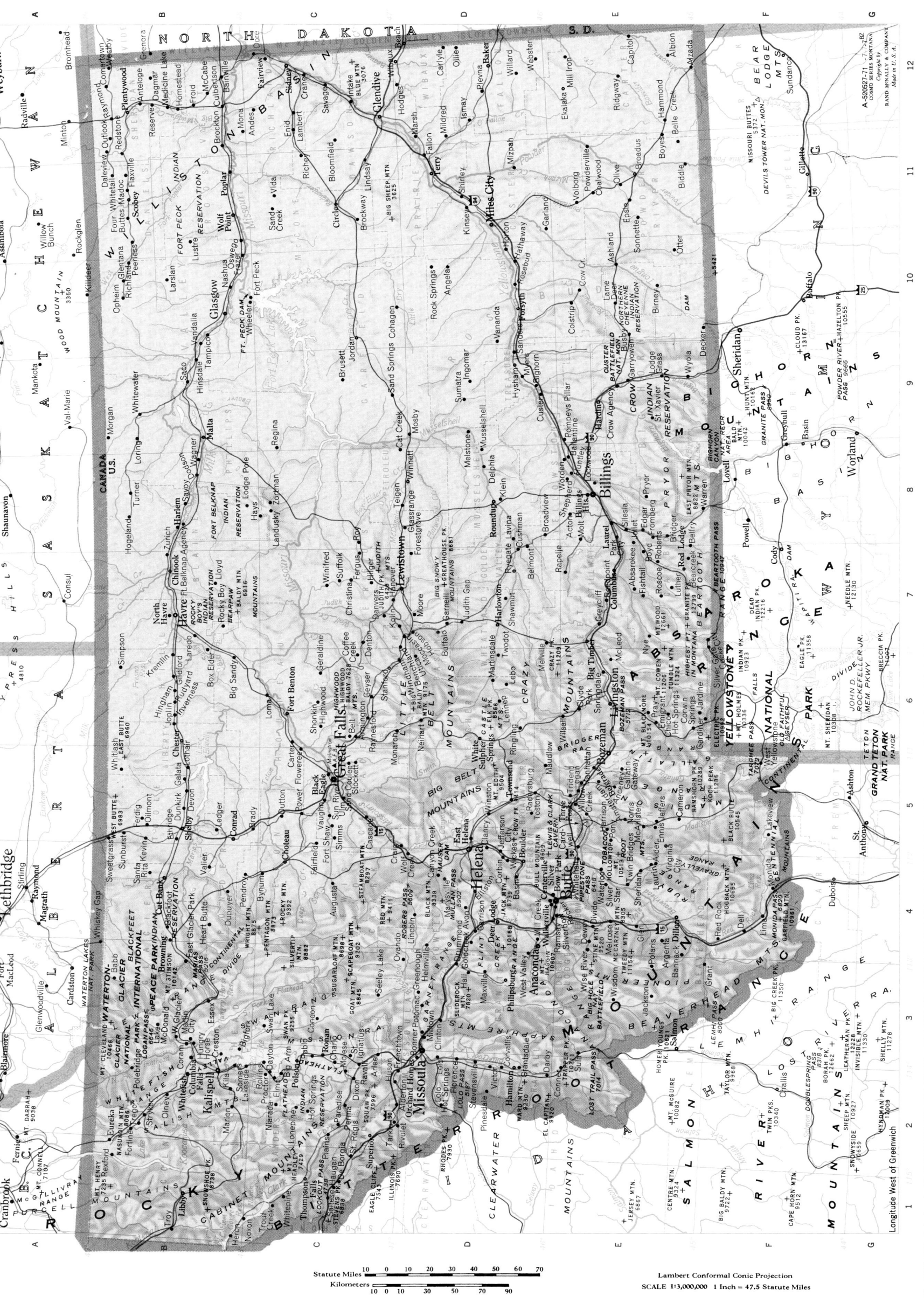

A-500597-71 7-7-BZ
Copyright by
RAND M*NALLY & COMPANY
Made in U.S.A.
COSMO SERIES MONTANA

Cities and Towns

Anaconda 12,518 **D4**
Baker 2,354 **D12**
Belgrade 2,336 **E5**
Bigfork 1,080 **B2**
Big Timber 1,690 **E7**
Billings 66,842 **E8**
Billings Heights 8,480 **E8**
Black Eagle 1,100 **C5**
Boulder 1,441 **D4**
Bozeman 21,645 **E5**
Browning 1,226 **B3**
Butte 37,205 **E4**
Chester 963 **B6**
Chinook 1,660 **B7**
Choteau 1,798 **C4**
Circle 931 **C11**
Colstrip 1,476 **E10**
Columbia Falls 3,112 **B2**
Columbus 1,439 **E7**
Conrad 3,074 **B5**
Crow Agency 750 **E9**
Cut Bank 3,688 **B4**
Deer Lodge 4,023 **D4**
Dillon 3,976 **E4**
East Glacier Park 500 **B3**
East Helena 1,647 **D5**
Eureka 1,119 **B1**
Fairview 1,366 **C12**
Forsyth 2,553 **D10**
Fort Benton 1,693 **C6**
Glasgow 4,455 **B10**
Glendive 5,978 **C12**
Great Falls 56,725 **C5**
Hamilton 2,661 **D2**
Hardin 3,300 **E9**
Harlem 1,023 **B8**
Harlowton 1,181 **D7**
Havre 10,891 **B7**
Helena 23,938 **D4**
Hungry Horse 900 **B2**
Kalispell 10,648 **B2**
Laurel 5,481 **E8**
Lewistown 7,104 **C7**
Libby 2,748 **B1**
Livingston 6,994 **E6**
Lockwood 1,600 **E8**
Lolo 2,418 **D2**
Malta 2,367 **B9**
Manhattan 988 **E5**
Miles City 9,602 **D11**
Missoula 33,388 **D2**
Orchard Homes 4,000 **D2**
Philipsburg 1,138 **D3**
Plains 1,116 **C2**
Plentywood 2,476 **B11**
Polson 2,798 **C2**
Poplar 995 **B11**
Red Lodge 1,896 **E7**
Ronan 1,382 **C2**
Roundup 2,119 **D8**
St. Ignatius 877 **C2**
Scobey 1,382 **B11**
Shelby 3,142 **B5**
Sidney 5,726 **C12**
Superior 1,054 **C2**
Terry 929 **D11**
Thompson Falls 1,478 **C1**
Three Forks 1,247 **E5**
Townsend 1,587 **D5**
Troy 1,088 **B1**
Vaughn 2,270 **C5**
Whitefish 3,703 **B2**
Whitehall 1,030 **E4**
White Sulphur Springs 1,302 **D6**
Wolf Point 3,074 **B11**

Statute Miles 10 0 10 20 30 40 50 60 70
Kilometers 10 0 10 30 50 70 90

Lambert Conformal Conic Projection
SCALE 1:3,000,000 1 Inch = 47.5 Statute Miles

NEBRASKA

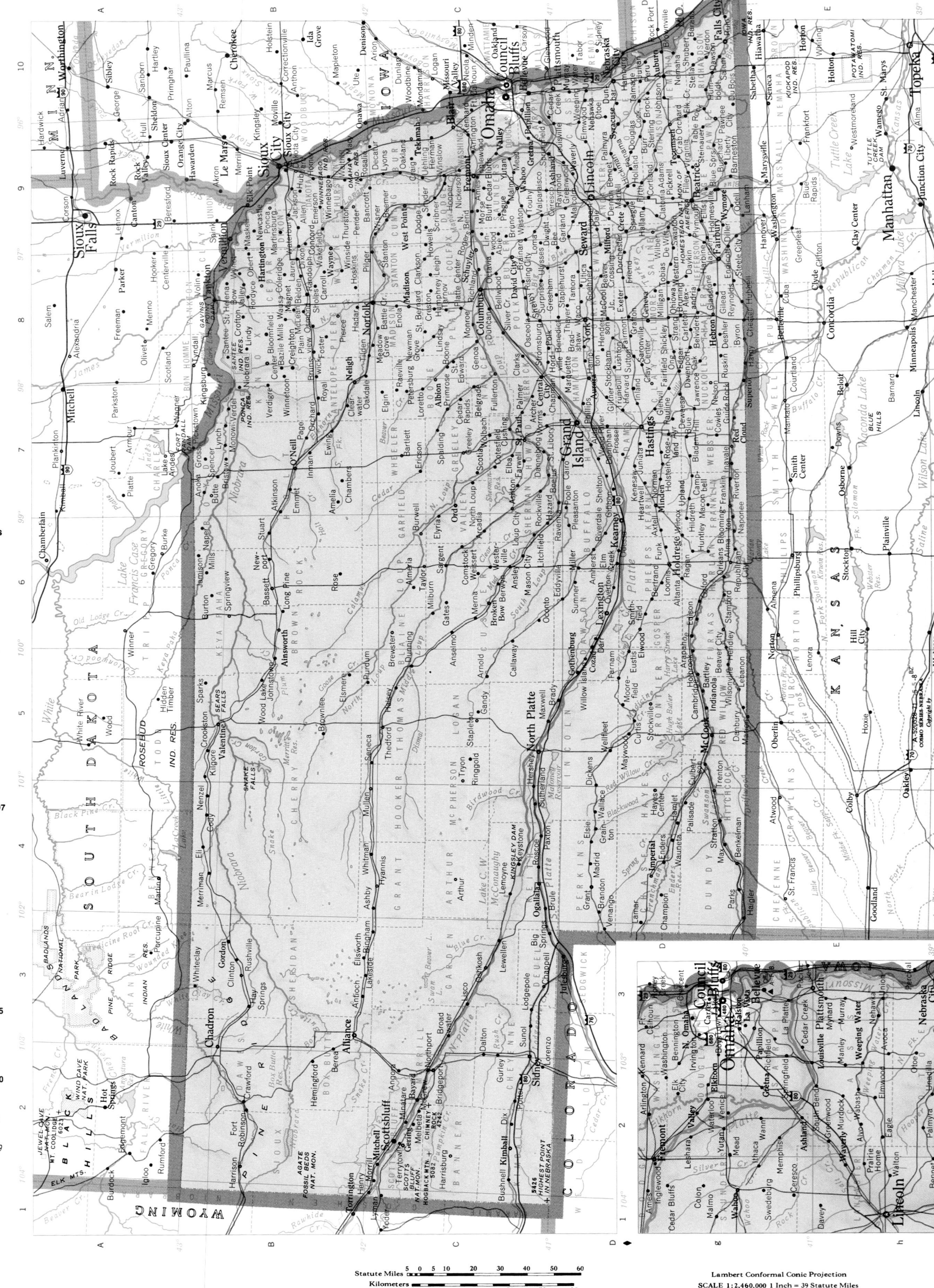

Cities and Towns

Ainsworth 2,256 **B6**
Albion 1,997 **C7**
Alliance 9,920 **B3**
Ashland 2,274 **C9**
Atkinson 1,521 **B7**
Auburn 3,482 **D10**
Aurora 3,717 **D7**
Beatrice 12,891 **D9**
Bellevue 21,813 **C10**
Blair 6,418 **C9**
Bridgeport 1,668 **C2**
Broken Bow 3,979 **C6**
Central City 3,083 **C7**
Chadron 5,933 **B3**
Columbus 17,328 **C8**
Cozad 4,453 **D6**
Crete 4,872 **D9**
David City 2,514 **C8**
Fairbury 4,885 **D8**
Falls City 5,374 **D10**
Fremont 23,979 **C9**
Fullerton 1,506 **C8**
Geneva 2,400 **D8**
Gering 7,760 **C2**
Gibbon 1,531 **D7**
Gordon 2,167 **B3**
Gothenburg 3,479 **D5**
Grand Island 33,180 **D7**
Gretna 1,609 **C9**
Hartington 1,730 **B8**
Hastings 23,045 **D7**
Hebron 1,906 **D8**
Holdrege 5,624 **D6**
Imperial 1,941 **D4**
Kearney 21,158 **D6**
Kimball 3,120 **C2**
La Vista 9,588 **g12**
Lexington 7,040 **D6**
Lincoln 171,932 **D9**
McCook 8,404 **D5**
Madison 1,950 **C8**
Milford 2,108 **D8**
Minden 2,939 **D7**
Mitchell 1,956 **C2**
Nebraska City 7,127 **D10**
Neligh 1,893 **B7**
Norfolk 19,449 **B8**
North Platte 24,509 **C5**
Ogallala 5,638 **C4**
Omaha 313,911 **C10**
O'Neill 4,049 **B7**
Ord 2,658 **C7**
Papillion 6,399 **C9**
Pierce 1,535 **B8**
Plattsmouth 6,295 **D10**
Ralston 5,143 **g12**
St. Paul 2,094 **C7**
Schuyler 4,151 **C8**
Scottsbluff 14,156 **C2**
Seward 5,713 **D8**
Sidney 6,010 **C3**
South Sioux City 9,339 **B9**
Stanton 1,603 **C8**
Superior 2,502 **D7**
Syracuse 1,638 **D9**
Tecumseh 1,926 **D9**
Tekamah 1,886 **C9**
Valentine 2,829 **B5**
Valley 1,716 **C9**
Wahoo 3,555 **C9**
Waverly 1,726 **D9**
Wayne 5,240 **B8**
West Point 3,609 **C9**
Wilber 1,624 **D9**
Wymore 1,841 **D9**
York 7,723 **D8**

Statute Miles

Kilometers

Lambert Conformal Conic Projection
SCALE 1:2,460,000 1 Inch = 39 Statute Miles

254

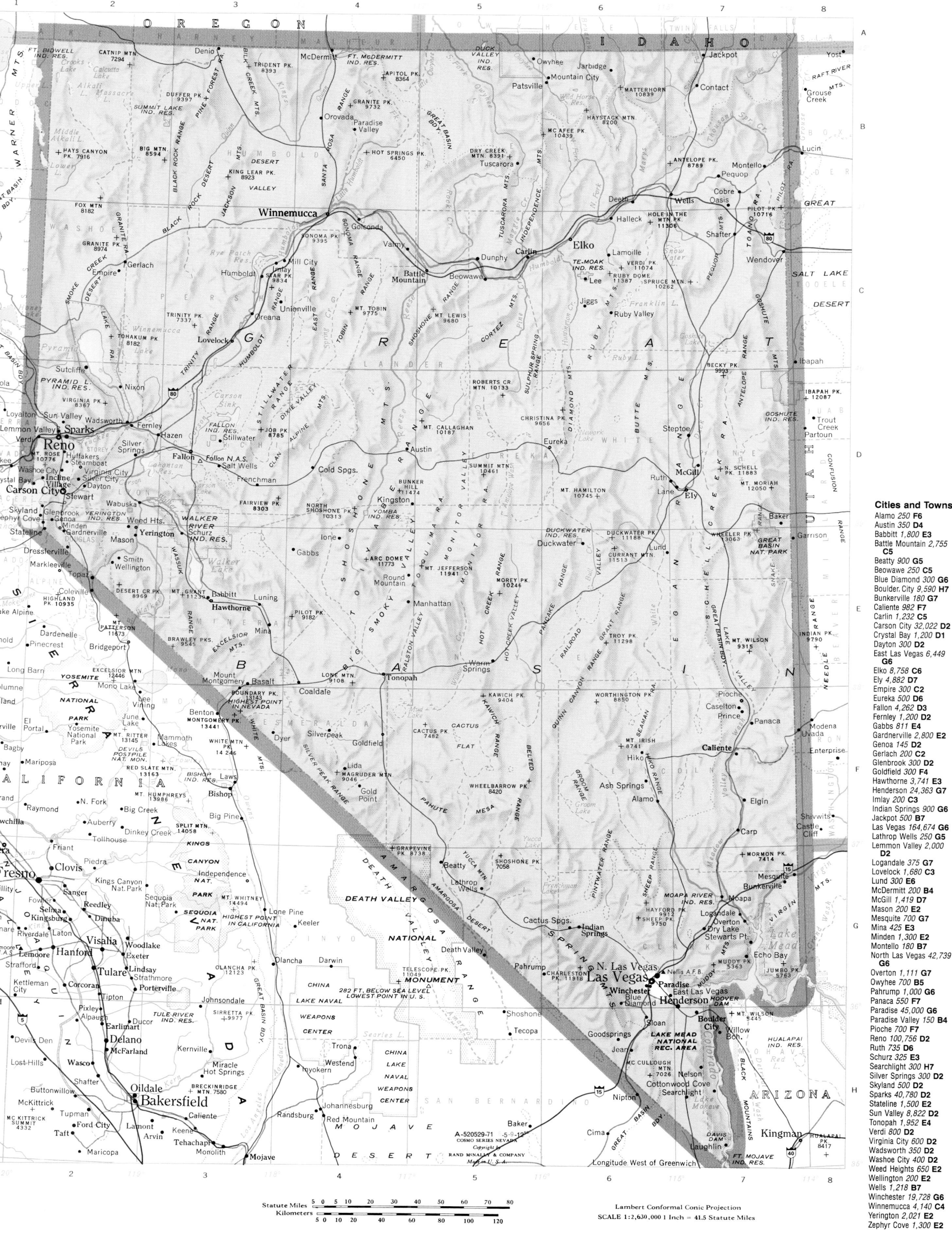

Cities and Towns

Alamo 250 **F6**
Austin 350 **D4**
Babbitt 1,800 **E3**
Battle Mountain 2,755 **C5**
Beatty 900 **G5**
Beowawe 250 **C5**
Blue Diamond 300 **G6**
Boulder City 9,590 **H7**
Bunkerville 180 **G7**
Caliente 982 **F7**
Carlin 1,232 **C6**
Carson City 32,022 **D2**
Crystal Bay 1,200 **D1**
Dayton 300 **D2**
East Las Vegas 6,449 **G6**
Elko 8,758 **C6**
Ely 4,882 **D7**
Empire 300 **C2**
Eureka 500 **D6**
Fallon 4,262 **D3**
Fernley 1,200 **D2**
Gabbs 811 **E4**
Gardnerville 2,800 **E2**
Genoa 145 **D2**
Gerlach 200 **C2**
Glenbrook 300 **D2**
Goldfield 300 **F4**
Hawthorne 3,741 **E3**
Henderson 24,363 **G7**
Imlay 200 **C3**
Indian Springs 900 **G6**
Jackpot 500 **B7**
Las Vegas 164,674 **G6**
Lathrop Wells 250 **G5**
Lemmon Valley 2,000 **D2**
Logandale 375 **G7**
Lovelock 1,680 **C3**
Lund 300 **E6**
McDermitt 200 **B4**
McGill 1,419 **D7**
Mason 200 **E2**
Mesquite 700 **G7**
Mina 425 **E3**
Minden 1,300 **E2**
Montello 180 **B7**
North Las Vegas 42,739 **G6**
Overton 1,111 **G7**
Owyhee 700 **B5**
Pahrump 1,000 **G6**
Panaca 550 **F7**
Paradise 45,000 **G6**
Paradise Valley 150 **B4**
Pioche 700 **F7**
Reno 100,756 **D2**
Ruth 735 **D6**
Schurz 325 **E3**
Searchlight 300 **H7**
Silver Springs 300 **D2**
Skyland 500 **D2**
Sparks 40,780 **D2**
Stateline 1,500 **E2**
Sun Valley 8,822 **D2**
Tonopah 1,952 **E4**
Verdi 800 **D2**
Virginia City 600 **D2**
Wadsworth 350 **D2**
Washoe City 400 **D2**
Weed Heights 650 **E2**
Wellington 200 **E2**
Wells 1,218 **B7**
Winchester 19,728 **G6**
Winnemucca 4,140 **C4**
Yerington 2,021 **E2**
Zephyr Cove 1,300 **E2**

Statute Miles 5 0 5 10 20 30 40 50 60 70 80
Kilometers 5 0 10 20 40 60 80 100 120

Lambert Conformal Conic Projection
SCALE 1:2,630,000 1 Inch = 41.5 Statute Miles

A-520529-71   5-9-12
COSMO SERIES NEVADA
Copyright by
RAND McNALLY & COMPANY
Made in U.S.A.

NEW HAMPSHIRE

Cities and Towns*
Antrim 1,142 **D3**
Ashland 1,479 **C3**
Bedford 1,300 **E3**
Berlin 13,084 **B4**
Bristol 1,258 **C3**
Charlestown 1,294 **D2**
Claremont 14,557 **D2**
Colebrook 1,131 **g7**
Concord 30,400 **D3**
Contoocook 1,499 **D3**
Conway 1,781 **C4**
Derry 12,248 **E4**
Dover 22,377 **D5**
Durham 8,448 **D5**
Enfield 1,581 **C2**
Epping 1,384 **D4**
Exeter 8,947 **E5**
Farmington 3,284 **D4**
Franconia 600 **B3**
Franklin 7,901 **D3**
Goffstown 2,500 **D3**
Gorham 2,180 **B4**
Greenville 1,447 **E3**
Groveton 1,389 **A3**
Hampton 6,779 **E5**
Hanover 6,861 **C2**
Henniker 1,538 **D3**
Hillsboro 1,797 **D3**
Hinsdale 1,546 **E2**
Hooksett 1,868 **D4**
Hudson 6,248 **E4**
Jaffrey 2,684 **E2**
Keene 21,449 **E2**
Laconia 15,575 **C4**
Lancaster 2,134 **B3**
Lebanon 11,134 **C2**
Lincoln 950 **B3**
Lisbon 1,151 **B3**
Littleton 4,480 **B3**
Manchester 90,936 **E4**
Marlborough 1,231 **E2**
Meredith 1,202 **C3**
Merrimack 1,200 **E4**
Milford 6,289 **E3**
Milton 1,000 **D5**
Nashua 67,865 **E4**
New Castle 975 **D5**
New London 1,335 **D3**
Newmarket 3,749 **D5**
Newport 4,388 **D2**
North Conway 2,184 **B4**
Northfield 1,340 **D3**
North Hampton 1,000 **E5**
North Walpole 950 **D2**
Peterborough 2,100 **E3**
Pinardville 4,500 **E3**
Pittsfield 1,584 **D4**
Plaistow 1,800 **E4**
Plymouth 3,628 **C3**
Portsmouth 26,254 **D5**
Raymond 1,192 **D4**
Rochester 21,560 **D5**
Salem 11,500 **E4**
Somersworth 10,350 **D5**
South Hooksett 1,200 **D4**
Suncook 4,698 **D4**
Tilton 1,230 **D3**
Troy 1,318 **E2**
West Swanzey 1,022 **E2**
Whitefield 1,005 **B3**
Wilton 1,310 **E3**
Winchester 1,732 **E2**
Wolfeboro 2,000 **C4**
Woodsville 1,195 **B2**

*Populations are for localities, not incorporated towns.

Statute Miles
Kilometers

Lambert Conformal Conic Projection
SCALE 1:792,000 1 Inch = 12.75 Statute Miles

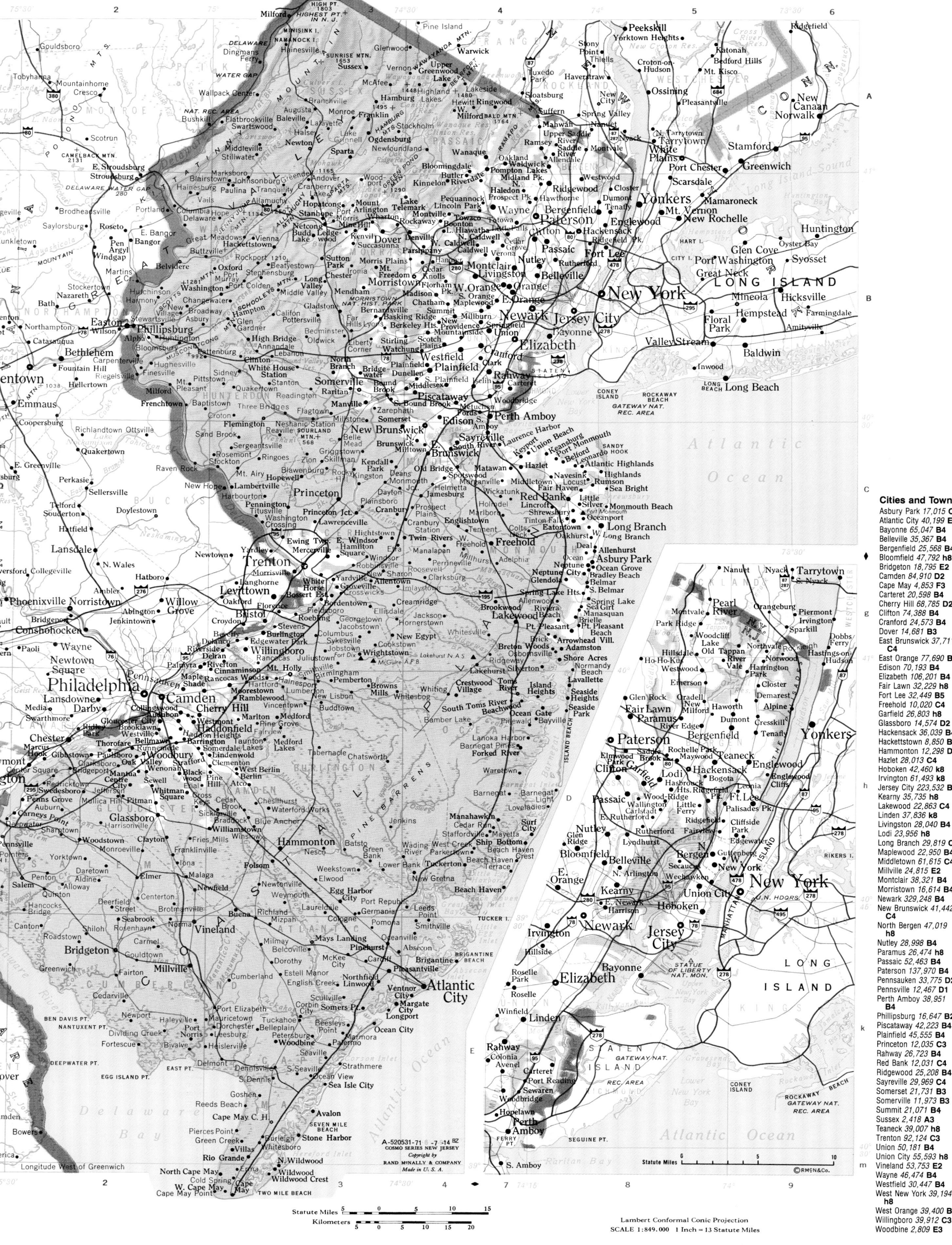

Cities and Towns

Asbury Park 17,015 **C4**
Atlantic City 40,199 **E4**
Bayonne 65,047 **B4**
Belleville 35,367 **B4**
Bergenfield 25,568 **B4**
◆ Bloomfield 47,792 **h8**
Bridgeton 18,795 **E2**
Camden 84,910 **D2**
Cape May 4,853 **F3**
Carteret 20,598 **B4**
Cherry Hill 68,785 **D2**
Clifton 74,388 **B4**
Cranford 24,573 **B4**
Dover 14,681 **B3**
East Brunswick 37,711 **C4**
East Orange 77,690 **B4**
Edison 70,193 **B4**
Elizabeth 106,201 **B4**
Fair Lawn 32,229 **h8**
Fort Lee 32,449 **B5**
Freehold 10,020 **C4**
Garfield 26,803 **h8**
Glassboro 14,574 **D2**
Hackensack 36,039 **B4**
Hackettstown 8,850 **B3**
Hammonton 12,298 **D3**
Hazlet 28,013 **C4**
Hoboken 42,460 **k8**
Irvington 61,493 **B4**
Jersey City 223,532 **B4**
Kearny 35,735 **h8**
Lakewood 22,863 **C4**
Linden 37,836 **k8**
Livingston 28,040 **B4**
Lodi 23,956 **h8**
Long Branch 29,819 **C5**
Maplewood 22,950 **B4**
Middletown 61,615 **C4**
Millville 24,815 **E2**
Montclair 38,321 **B4**
Morristown 16,614 **B4**
Newark 329,248 **B4**
New Brunswick 41,442 **C4**
North Bergen 47,019 **h8**
Nutley 28,998 **B4**
Paramus 26,474 **h8**
Passaic 52,463 **B4**
Paterson 137,970 **B4**
Pennsauken 33,775 **D2**
Pennsville 12,467 **D1**
Perth Amboy 38,951 **B4**
Phillipsburg 16,647 **B3**
Piscataway 42,223 **B4**
Plainfield 45,555 **B4**
Princeton 12,035 **C3**
Rahway 26,723 **B4**
Red Bank 12,031 **C4**
Ridgewood 25,208 **B4**
Sayreville 29,969 **C4**
Somerset 21,731 **B3**
Somerville 11,973 **B3**
Summit 21,071 **B4**
Sussex 2,418 **A3**
Teaneck 39,007 **h8**
Trenton 92,124 **C3**
Union 50,181 **B4**
Union City 55,593 **h8**
Vineland 53,753 **E2**
Wayne 46,474 **B4**
Westfield 30,447 **B4**
West New York 39,194 **h8**
West Orange 39,400 **B4**
Willingboro 39,912 **C3**
Woodbine 2,809 **E3**

A-520531-71 -7 -14 BZ
COSMO SERIES NEW JERSEY
Copyright by
RAND McNALLY & COMPANY
Made in U.S.A.

Lambert Conformal Conic Projection
SCALE 1:849,000   1 Inch = 13 Statute Miles

Cities and Towns

Alameda 7,800 **B3**
Alamogordo 24,024 **E4**
Albuquerque 331,767 **B3**
Anthony 3,285 **F3**
Armijo 18,900 **k7**
Artesia 10,385 **E5**
Aztec 5,512 **A2**
Bayard 3,036 **E1**
Belen 5,617 **C3**
Bernalillo 3,012 **B3**
Bloomfield 4,881 **A2**
Carlsbad 25,496 **E5**
Carizozo 1,222 **D4**
Central 1,968 **E1**
Chama 1,090 **A3**
Chimayo 1,993 **A4**
Clayton 2,968 **A6**
Clovis 31,194 **C6**
Crownpoint 1,134 **B1**
Deming 9,964 **E2**
Dulce 1,648 **A2**
Espanola 6,803 **B3**
Eunice 2,970 **E6**
Farmington 31,222 **A1**
Five Points 5,500 **B3**
Fort Sumner 1,421 **C5**
Gallup 18,167 **B1**
Grants 11,439 **B2**
Hatch 1,028 **E2**
Hobbs 29,153 **E6**
Hurley 1,616 **E1**
Isleta 1,246 **C3**
Jal 2,675 **E6**
Jemez Pueblo 1,503 **B3**
Kirtland 2,358 **A1**
La Luz 1,194 **D4**
Las Cruces 45,086 **E3**
Las Vegas 14,322 **B4**
Lordsburg 3,195 **E1**
Los Alamos 11,039 **B3**
Los Lunas 3,525 **C3**
Los Ranchos de
 Albuquerque 2,702
 B3
Loving 1,355 **E5**
Lovington 9,727 **E6**
Magdalena 1,022 **C2**
Mescalero 1,259 **D4**
Mesilla 2,029 **E3**
Milan 3,747 **B2**
Moriarty 1,276 **C3**
Mountain View 1,900
 C3
Paradise Hills 5,096 **B3**
Portales 9,940 **C6**
Questa 1,202 **A4**
Ranches of Taos 1,411
 A4
Raton 8,225 **A5**
Roswell 39,676 **D5**
Ruidoso 4,260 **D4**
Ruidoso Downs 949 **D4**
Santa Fe 48,953 **B4**
Santa Rosa 2,469 **C5**
Santo Domingo Pueblo
 2,082 **B3**
Shiprock 7,237 **A1**
Silver City 9,887 **E1**
Socorro 7,173 **C3**
Springer 1,657 **A5**
Sunland Park 3,377 **F3**
Taos 3,369 **A4**
Tesuque 1,014 **B4**
Thoreau 1,099 **B1**
Truth or Consequences
 5,219 **D2**
Tucumcari 6,765 **B6**
Tularosa 2,536 **D3**
University Park 4,383
 E3
Zuni 5,551 **B1**

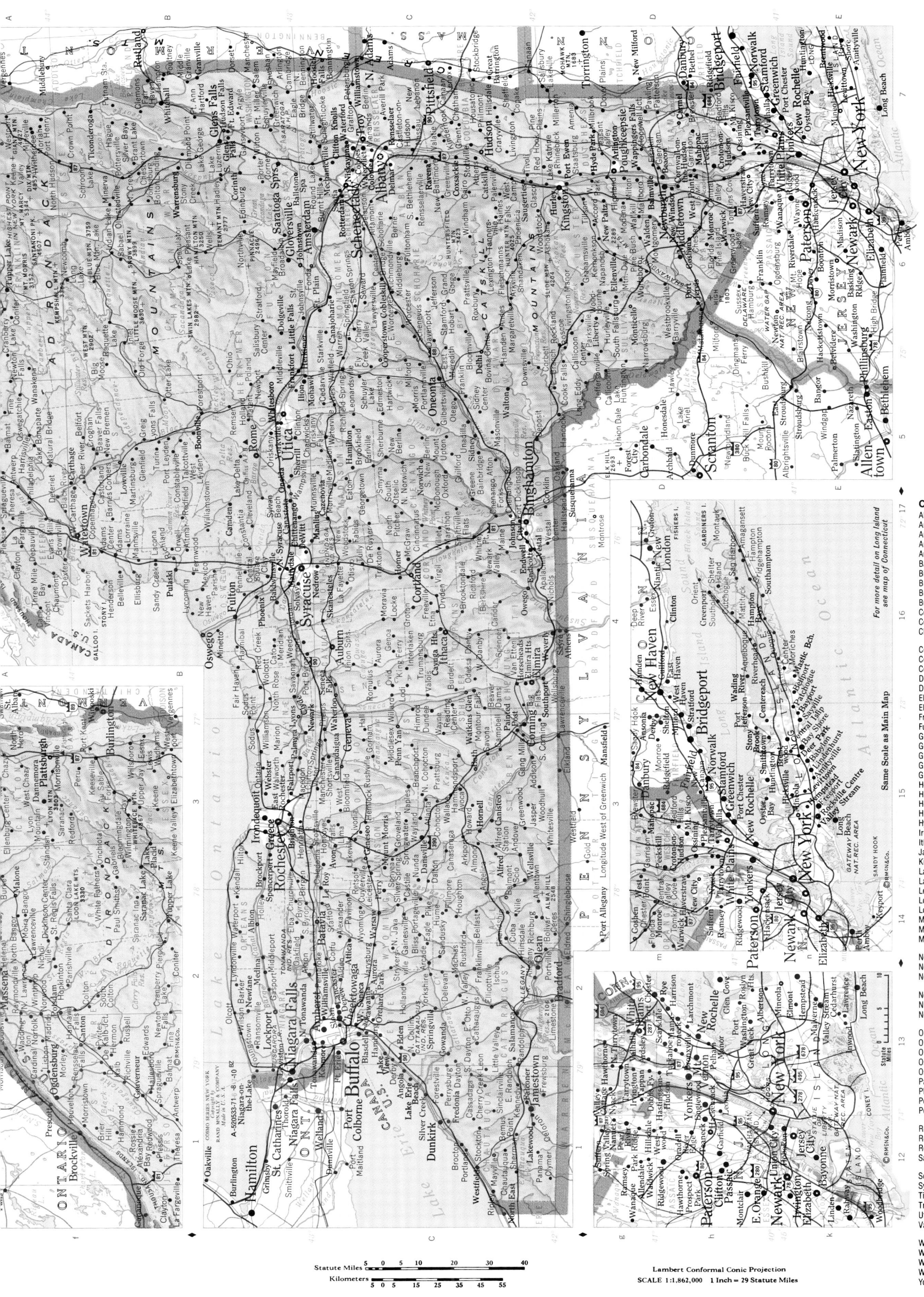

Cities and Towns

Albany 101,727 **C7**
Amherst 66,100 **C2**
Amityville 9,076 **E7**
Amsterdam 21,872 **C6**
Auburn 32,548 **C4**
Batavia 16,703 **C2**
Binghamton 55,860 **C5**
Brentwood 48,800 **E7**
Brighton 35,776 **B3**
Buffalo 357,870 **C2**
Centereach 34,600 **n15**
Central Islip 26,000 **n15**
Cheektowaga 100,400
   C2
Cooperstown 2,342 **C6**
Corning 12,953 **C3**
Cortland 20,138 **C4**
Deer Park 33,400 **n15**
Dunkirk 15,310 **C1**
Elmira 35,327 **C4**
Elmont 30,000 **k13**
Freeport 38,272 **n15**
Fulton 13,312 **B4**
Geneseo 6,746 **C3**
Geneva 15,133 **C4**
Glens Falls 15,897 **B7**
Gloversville 17,836 **B6**
Greece 63,700 **B3**
Hempstead 40,404 **n15**
Hicksville 50,000 **E7**
Hornell 10,234 **C3**
Hudson 7,986 **C7**
Hyde Park 2,805 **D7**
Irondequoit 57,648 **B3**
Ithaca 28,732 **C4**
Jamestown 35,775 **C1**
Kingston 24,481 **D6**
Lackawanna 22,701 **C2**
Lake Placid 2,490 **A7**
Levittown 65,400 **E7**
Lockport 24,844 **B2**
Long Beach 34,073 **E7**
Massena 12,851 **f10**
Middletown 21,454 **D6**
Mount Vernon 66,713
   h13
Newburgh 23,438 **D6**
New City 30,800 **D6**
New Rochelle 70,794
   E7
New York 7,071,639 **E7**
Niagara Falls 71,384 **B1**
North Tonawanda
   35,760 **B2**
Ogdensburg 12,375 **f9**
Olean 18,207 **C2**
Oneonta 14,933 **C5**
Ossining 20,196 **D7**
Oswego 19,793 **B4**
Palmyra 3,729 **B3**
Plattsburgh 21,057 **f11**
Port Chester 23,565 **E7**
Poughkeepsie 29,757
   D7
Rochester 241,741 **B3**
Rome 43,826 **B5**
Rotterdam 24,800 **C6**
Saratoga Springs
   23,906 **B7**
Schenectady 67,972 **C7**
Syracuse 170,105 **B4**
Ticonderoga 2,938 **B7**
Troy 56,638 **C7**
Utica 75,632 **B5**
Valley Stream 35,769
   n15
Watertown 27,861 **B5**
West Point 8,000 **D7**
West Seneca 51,210 **C2**
White Plains 46,999 **D7**
Yonkers 195,351 **E7**

Statute Miles 5 0 5 10 20 30 40
Kilometers 5 0 5 15 25 35 45 55

Lambert Conformal Conic Projection
SCALE 1:1,862,000   1 Inch = 29 Statute Miles

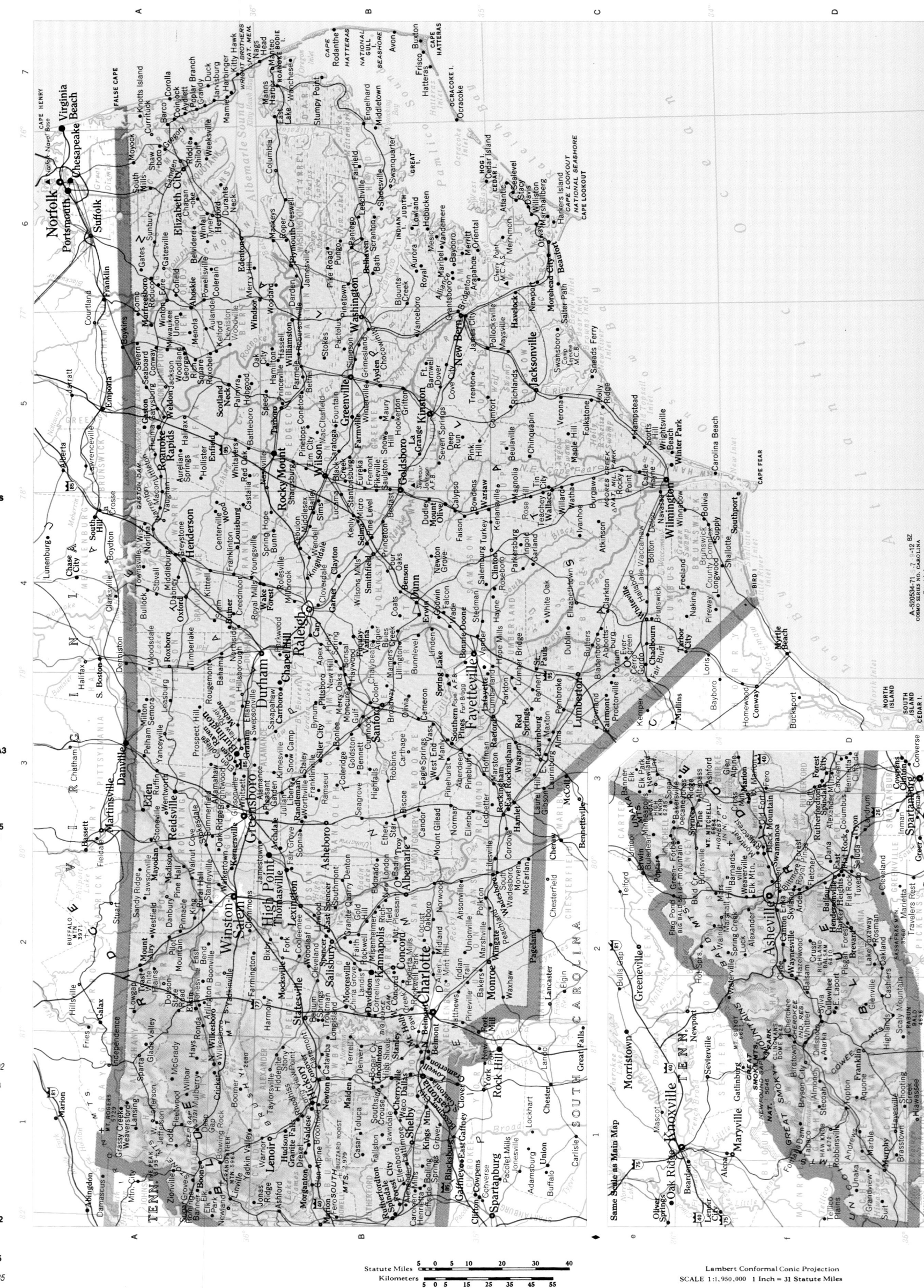

Cities and Towns
Albemarle 15,110 **B2**
Archdale 5,326 **B3**
Asheboro 15,252 **B3**
Asheville 53,583 **f10**
Boone 10,191 **A1**
Brevard 5,323 **f10**
Burlington 37,266 **A3**
Carrboro 7,336 **B3**
Chapel Hill 32,421 **B3**
Charlotte 314,447 **B2**
Clemmons 7,401 **A2**
Clinton 7,552 **C4**
Concord 16,942 **B2**
Dunn 8,962 **B4**
Durham 100,538 **B4**
Eden 15,672 **A3**
Edenton 5,357 **A6**
Elizabeth City 13,784
  A6
Fayetteville 59,507 **B4**
Forest City 7,688 **B1**
Garner 10,073 **B4**
Gastonia 47,333 **B1**
Goldsboro 31,871 **B5**
Graham 8,674 **A3**
Greensboro 155,642 **A3**
Greenville 35,740 **B5**
Havelock 17,718 **C6**
Henderson 13,522 **A4**
Hendersonville 6,862
  f10
Hickory 20,757 **B1**
High Point 63,808 **B2**
Jacksonville 18,237 **C5**
Kannapolis 34,564 **B2**
Kernersville 6,802 **A2**
Kings Mountain 9,080
  B1
Kinston 25,234 **B5**
Laurinburg 11,480 **C3**
Lenoir 13,748 **B1**
Lexington 15,711 **B2**
Lincolnton 4,879 **B1**
Lumberton 18,241 **C3**
Monroe 12,639 **C2**
Mooresville 8,575 **B2**
Morehead City 4,359
  C6
Morganton 13,763 **B1**
Mount Airy 6,862 **A2**
Mount Olive 4,876 **B4**
Nags Head 1,020 **B7**
New Bern 14,557 **B5**
Newton 7,624 **B1**
Oxford 7,603 **A4**
Plymouth 4,571 **B6**
Raleigh 150,255 **B4**
Reidsville 12,492 **A3**
Roanoke Rapids 14,702
  A5
Rockingham 8,300 **C3**
Rocky Mount 41,283
  B5
Roxboro 7,532 **A4**
Salisbury 22,677 **B2**
Sanford 14,773 **B3**
Selma 4,762 **B4**
Shelby 15,310 **B1**
Smithfield 7,288 **B4**
Southern Pines 8,620
  B3
Statesville 18,622 **B2**
Swannanoa 5,586 **f10**
Tarboro 8,634 **B5**
Thomasville 14,144 **B2**
Washington 8,418 **B5**
Whiteville 5,565 **C4**
Williamston 6,159 **B5**
Wilmington 44,000 **C5**
Wilson 34,424 **B5**
Winston-Salem 131,885
  A2

Statute Miles 5 0 5 10   20   30   40
Kilometers 5 0 5   15   25   35   45 55

Lambert Conformal Conic Projection
SCALE 1:1,950,000 1 Inch = 31 Statute Miles

Same Scale as Main Map

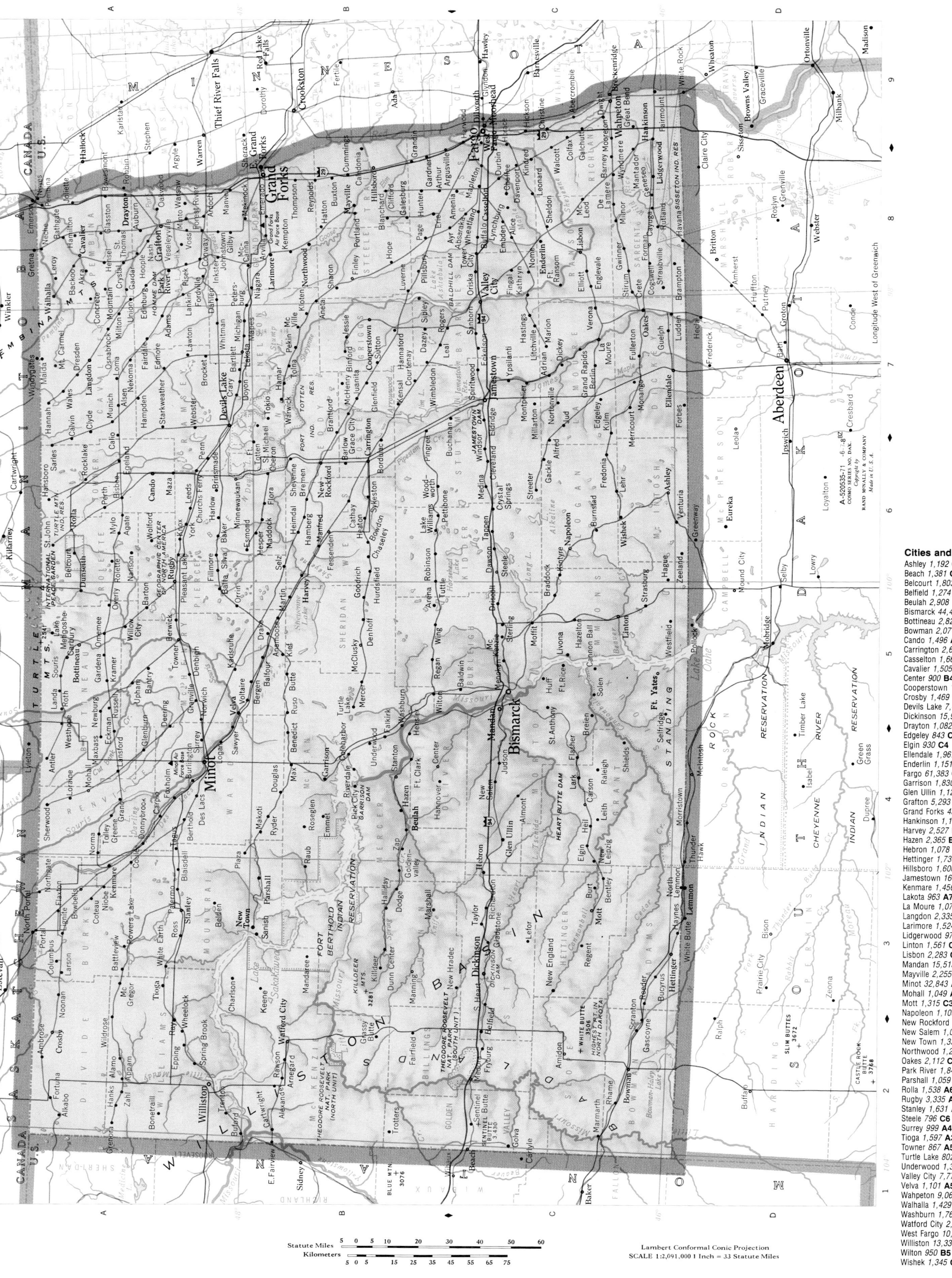

Cities and Towns

Ashley 1,192 **C6**
Beach 1,381 **C1**
Belcourt 1,803 **A6**
Belfield 1,274 **C2**
Beulah 2,908 **B4**
Bismarck 44,485 **C5**
Bottineau 2,829 **A5**
Bowman 2,071 **C2**
Cando 1,496 **A6**
Carrington 2,641 **B6**
Casselton 1,661 **C8**
Cavalier 1,505 **A8**
Center 900 **B4**
Cooperstown 1,308 **B7**
Crosby 1,469 **A2**
Devils Lake 7,442 **A7**
Dickinson 15,924 **C3**
Drayton 1,082 **A8**
Edgeley 843 **C7**
Elgin 930 **C4**
Ellendale 1,967 **C7**
Enderlin 1,151 **C8**
Fargo 61,383 **C9**
Garrison 1,830 **B4**
Glen Ullin 1,125 **C4**
Grafton 5,293 **A8**
Grand Forks 43,765 **B8**
Hankinson 1,158 **C9**
Harvey 2,527 **B6**
Hazen 2,365 **B4**
Hebron 1,078 **C3**
Hettinger 1,739 **D3**
Hillsboro 1,600 **B8**
Jamestown 16,280 **C7**
Kenmare 1,456 **A3**
Lakota 963 **A7**
La Moure 1,077 **C7**
Langdon 2,335 **A7**
Larimore 1,524 **B8**
Lidgerwood 971 **C8**
Linton 1,561 **C5**
Lisbon 2,283 **C8**
Mandan 15,513 **C5**
Mayville 2,255 **B8**
Minot 32,843 **A4**
Mohall 1,049 **A4**
Mott 1,315 **C3**
Napoleon 1,103 **C6**
New Rockford 1,791 **B6**
New Salem 1,081 **C4**
New Town 1,335 **B3**
Northwood 1,240 **B8**
Oakes 2,112 **C7**
Park River 1,844 **A8**
Parshall 1,059 **B3**
Rolla 1,538 **A6**
Rugby 3,335 **A6**
Stanley 1,631 **A3**
Steele 796 **C6**
Surrey 999 **A4**
Tioga 1,597 **A3**
Towner 867 **A5**
Turtle Lake 802 **B5**
Underwood 1,329 **B4**
Valley City 7,774 **C8**
Velva 1,101 **A5**
Wahpeton 9,064 **C9**
Walhalla 1,429 **A8**
Washburn 1,767 **B5**
Watford City 2,119 **B2**
West Fargo 10,099 **C9**
Williston 13,336 **A2**
Wilton 950 **B5**
Wishek 1,345 **C6**

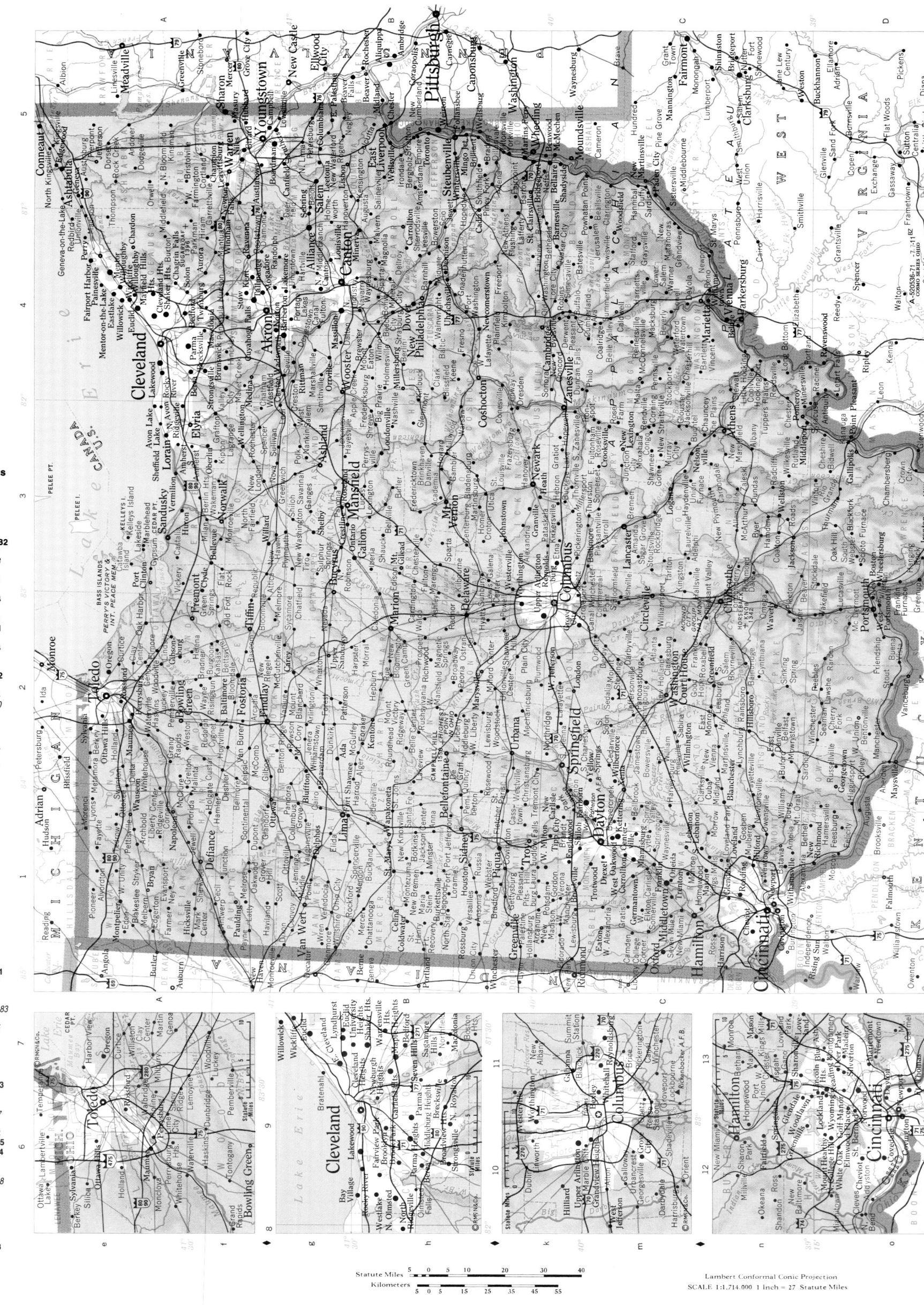

Cities and Towns

Akron 237,177 **A4**
Alliance 24,315 **B4**
Ashland 20,326 **B3**
Ashtabula 23,449 **A5**
Athens 19,743 **C3**
Barberton 29,751 **A4**
Bellefontaine 11,888 **B2**
Boardman 39,161 **A5**
Bowling Green 25,728
　A2
Brunswick 28,104 **A4**
Bucyrus 13,433 **B3**
Cambridge 13,573 **B4**
Canton 93,077 **B4**
Chillicothe 23,420 **C3**
Cincinnati 385,457 **C1**
Circleville 11,700 **C3**
Cleveland 573,822 **A4**
Cleveland Heights
　56,438 **A4**
Columbus 565,032 **C2**
Conneaut 13,835 **A5**
Coshocton 13,405 **B4**
Cuyahoga Falls 43,890
　A4
Dayton 193,444 **C1**
Defiance 16,810 **A1**
Delaware 18,780 **B2**
East Cleveland 36,957
　g9
East Liverpool 16,687
　B5
Elyria 57,538 **A3**
Euclid 59,999 **A4**
Findlay 35,594 **A2**
Fostoria 15,743 **A2**
Fremont 17,834 **A2**
Greenville 12,999 **B1**
Hamilton 63,189 **C1**
Ironton 14,290 **D3**
Kettering 61,186 **C1**
Lakewood 61,963 **A4**
Lancaster 34,953 **C3**
Lima 47,381 **B1**
Lorain 75,416 **A3**
Mansfield 53,927 **B3**
Marietta 16,467 **C4**
Marion 37,040 **B2**
Massillon 30,557 **B4**
Medina 15,268 **A4**
Mentor 42,065 **A4**
Middletown 43,719 **C1**
Mount Vernon 14,323
　B3
Newark 41,200 **B3**
New Philadelphia 16,883
　B4
North Olmsted 36,486
　h9
Norwalk 14,358 **A3**
Oxford 17,655 **C1**
Parma 92,548 **A4**
Piqua 20,480 **B1**
Portsmouth 25,943 **D3**
Salem 12,869 **B5**
Sandusky 31,360 **A3**
Shaker Heights 32,487
　A4
Springfield 72,563 **C2**
Steubenville 26,400 **B5**
Strongsville 28,577 **A4**
Tiffin 19,549 **A2**
Toledo 354,635 **A2**
Upper Arlington 35,648
　B2
Urbana 10,762 **B2**
Van Wert 11,035 **B1**
Warren 56,629 **A5**
Washington Court
　House 12,682 **C2**
Westerville 23,414 **B3**
Wooster 29,289 **B4**
Xenia 24,653 **C2**
Youngstown 115,436
　A5
Zanesville 28,655 **C4**

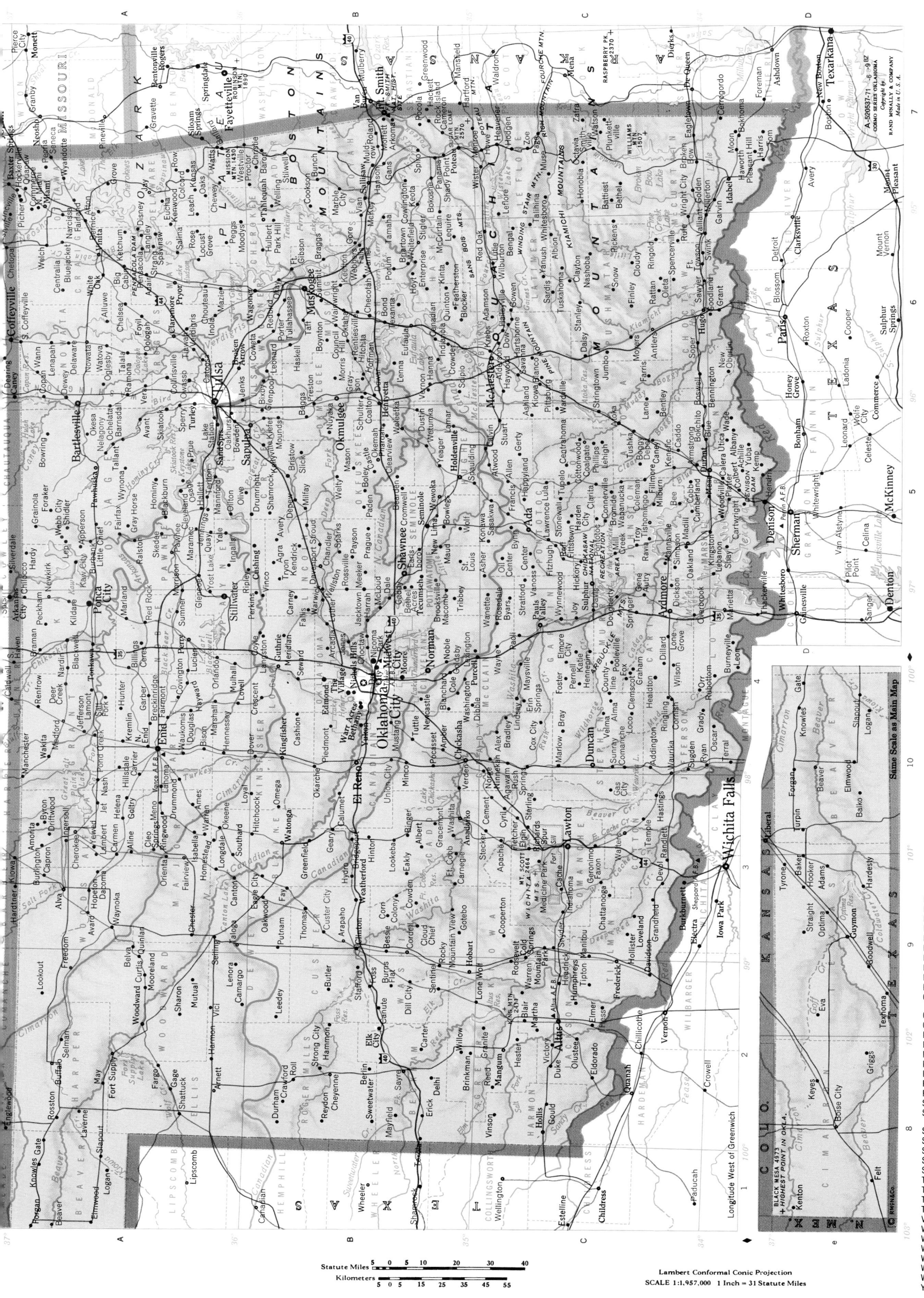

OKLAHOMA

Cities and Towns

Ada 15,902 **C5**
Altus 23,101 **C2**
Alva 6,416 **A3**
Anadarko 6,378 **B3**
Ardmore 23,689 **C4**
Bartlesville 34,568 **A6**
Bethany 22,130 **B4**
Bixby 6,969 **B6**
Blackwell 8,400 **A4**
Bristow 4,702 **B5**
Broken Arrow 35,761 **A6**
Broken Bow 3,965 **C7**
Chickasha 15,828 **B4**
Choctaw 7,520 **B4**
Claremore 12,085 **A6**
Clinton 8,796 **B3**
Coweta 4,554 **B6**
Cushing 7,720 **B5**
Del City 28,523 **B4**
Duncan 22,517 **C4**
Durant 11,972 **D5**
Edmond 34,637 **B4**
Elk City 9,579 **B2**
El Reno 15,486 **B4**
Enid 50,363 **A4**
Frederick 6,153 **C2**
Guthrie 10,312 **B4**
Guymon 8,492 **e9**
Henryetta 6,432 **B6**
Hobart 4,735 **B2**
Holdenville 5,469 **B5**
Hugo 7,172 **C6**
Idabel 7,622 **D7**
Kingfisher 4,245 **B4**
Lawton 80,054 **C3**
McAlester 17,255 **C6**
Madill 3,173 **C5**
Marlow 5,017 **C4**
Miami 14,237 **A7**
Midwest City 49,559 **B4**
Moore 35,063 **B4**
Muskogee 40,011 **B6**
Mustang 7,496 **B4**
Norman 68,020 **B4**
Nowata 4,270 **A6**
Oklahoma City 403,136 **B4**
Okmulgee 16,263 **B6**
Owasso 6,149 **A6**
Pauls Valley 5,664 **C4**
Pawhuska 4,771 **A5**
Perry 5,796 **A4**
Ponca City 26,238 **A4**
Poteau 7,089 **B7**
Pryor 8,483 **A6**
Purcell 4,638 **B4**
Sallisaw 6,403 **B7**
Sand Springs 13,121 **A5**
Sapulpa 15,853 **B5**
Seminole 8,590 **B5**
Shawnee 26,506 **B5**
Stillwater 38,268 **A4**
Sulphur 5,516 **C5**
Tahlequah 9,708 **B7**
Tecumseh 5,123 **B5**
The Village 11,049 **B4**
Tulsa 360,919 **A6**
Vinita 6,740 **A6**
Wagoner 6,191 **B6**
Warr Acres 9,940 **B4**
Watonga 4,139 **B3**
Weatherford 9,640 **B3**
Wewoka 5,480 **B5**
Woodward 13,610 **A2**
Yukon 17,112 **B4**

Statute Miles

Kilometers

Lambert Conformal Conic Projection
SCALE 1:1,957,000   1 Inch = 31 Statute Miles

263

OREGON

Cities and Towns

Albany 26,678 C3
Aloha 10,000 h12
Altamont 19,805 E5
Ashland 14,943 E4
Astoria 9,998 A3
Baker 9,471 C9
Beaverton 30,582 B4
Bend 17,263 C5
Burns 3,579 D7
Canby 7,659 B4
Central Point 6,357 E4
Coos Bay 14,424 D2
Coquille 4,481 D2
Corvallis 40,960 C3
Cottage Grove 7,148 D3
Crater Lake 25 E4
Dallas 8,530 C3
Eugene 105,624 C3
Florence 4,411 D2
Forest Grove 11,499 B3
Gladstone 9,500 B4
Grants Pass 15,032 E3
Gresham 33,005 B4
Hermiston 9,408 B7
Hillsboro 27,664 B4
Hood River 4,329 B5
Independence 4,024 C3
John Day 2,012 C8
Keizer 18,592 C3
Klamath Falls 16,661
 E5
La Grande 11,354 B8
Lake Oswego 22,527
 B4
Lakeview 2,770 E6
Lebanon 10,413 C4
Lincoln City 5,469 C3
McMinnville 14,080 B3
Medford 39,603 E4
Metzger 5,544 h12
Milton-Freewater 5,086
 B8
Milwaukie 17,931 B4
Monmouth 5,594 C3
Myrtle Creek 3,365 D2
Newberg 10,394 B4
Newport 7,519 C2
North Bend 9,779 D2
Oak Grove 11,640 B4
Ontario 8,814 C10
Oregon City 14,673 B4
Parkrose 21,103 B4
Pendleton 14,521 B8
Portland 366,383 B4
Prineville 5,276 C6
Redmond 6,452 C5
Reedsport 4,984 D2
River Road 10,370 C3
Roseburg 16,644 D3
St. Helens 7,064 B4
Salem 89,233 C4
Scappoose 3,213 B4
Seaside 5,193 B3
Silverton 5,168 C4
Springfield 41,621 C4
Stayton 4,396 C4
Sutherlin 4,560 D3
Sweet Home 6,921 C4
The Dalles 10,820 B5
Tigard 14,286 h12
Tillamook 3,981 B3
Tri City 3,439 E3
Umatilla 3,199 B7
West Linn 12,956 B4
West Slope 5,364 g12
White City 5,445 E4
Woodburn 11,196 B4

Statute Miles
Kilometers

Lambert Conformal Conic Projection
SCALE 1:2,329,000   1 Inch = 37 Statute Miles

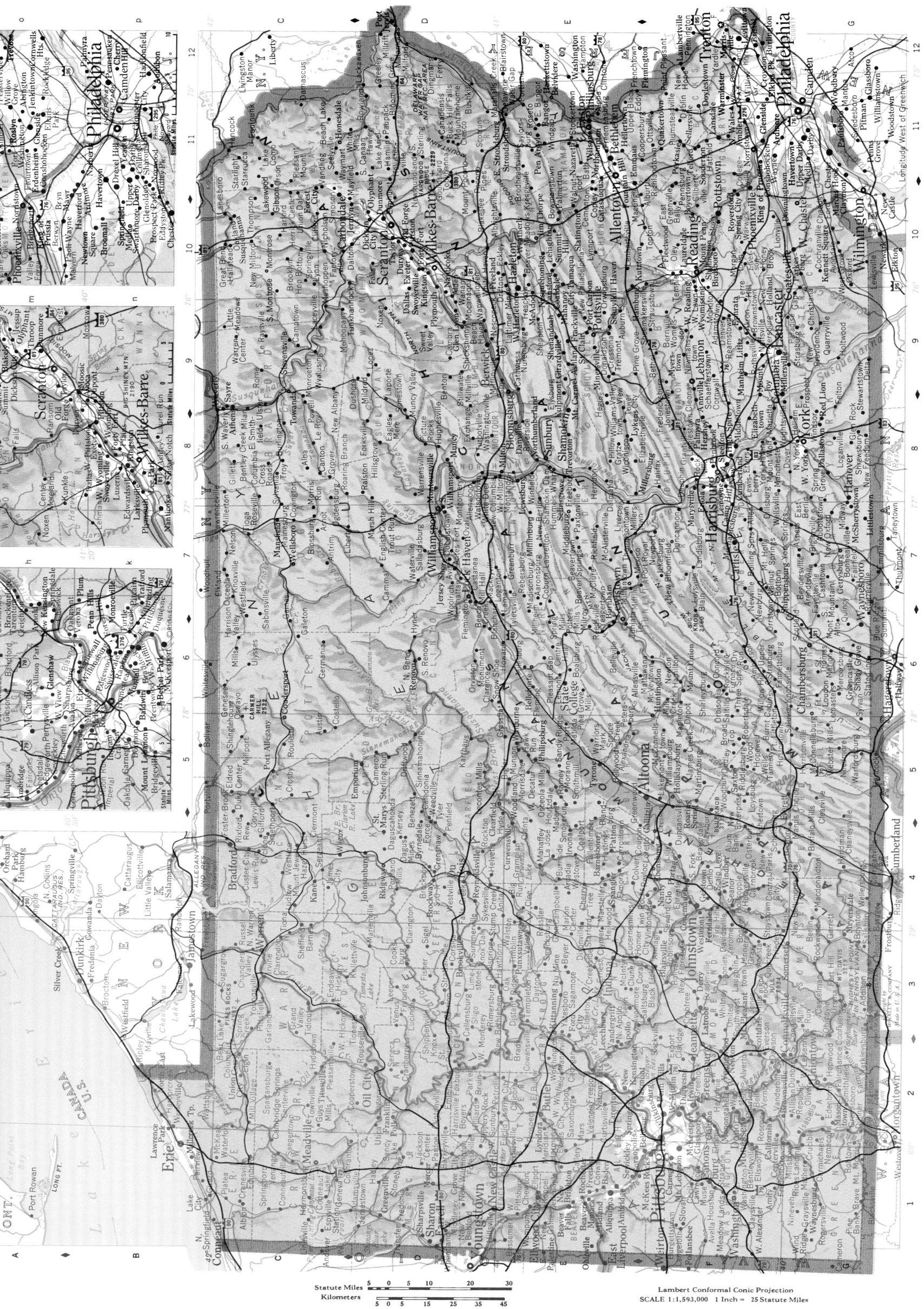

Cities and Towns

Aliquippa 17,094 **E1**
Allentown 103,758 **E11**
Altoona 57,078 **E5**
Beaver Falls 12,525 **E1**
Berwick 11,850 **D9**
Bethel Park 34,755 **k14**
Bethlehem 70,419 **E11**
Bloomsburg 11,717 **E9**
Bradford 11,211 **C4**
Broomall 23,642 **p20**
Butler 17,026 **E2**
Carbondale 11,255 **C10**
Carlisle 18,314 **F7**
Chambersburg 16,174 **G6**
Chester 45,794 **G11**
Coatesville 10,698 **G10**
Connellsville 10,319 **F2**
Du Bois 9,290 **D4**
Easton 26,027 **E11**
Ephrata 11,095 **F9**
Erie 119,123 **B1**
Gettysburg 7,194 **G7**
Greensburg 17,558 **F2**
Hanover 14,890 **G8**
Harrisburg 53,264 **F8**
Havertown 36,000 **G11**
Hazleton 27,318 **E10**
Hershey 9,000 **F8**
Indiana 16,051 **E3**
Jeannette 13,106 **F2**
Johnstown 35,496 **F4**
King of Prussia 18,200 **F11**
Lancaster 54,725 **F9**
Lansdale 16,526 **F11**
Latrobe 10,799 **F3**
Lebanon 25,711 **F9**
Levittown 78,600 **F12**
Lewistown 9,830 **E6**
Lock Haven 9,617 **D7**
McKeesport 31,012 **F2**
Meadville 15,544 **C1**
Middletown 10,122 **F8**
Millcreek Township 44,303 **B1**
Monroeville 30,977 **k14**
Mount Lebanon 34,414 **F1**
New Castle 33,621 **D1**
Norristown 34,684 **F11**
Oil City 13,881 **D2**
Penn Hills 57,632 **F2**
Philadelphia 1,688,210 **G11**
Pittsburgh 423,959 **F1**
Plum 25,390 **k14**
Pottstown 22,729 **F10**
Pottsville 18,195 **E9**
Punxsutawney 7,479 **E4**
Reading 78,686 **F10**
Scranton 88,117 **D10**
Shamokin 10,357 **D1**
Sharon 19,057 **D1**
Springfield 25,326 **p20**
State College 36,130 **E6**
Sunbury 12,292 **E8**
Uniontown 14,510 **G2**
Upper Darby 50,200 **G11**
Warminster 35,543 **F11**
Warren 12,146 **C3**
Washington 18,363 **F1**
Waynesboro 9,726 **G6**
West Chester 17,435 **G10**
West Mifflin 26,552 **F2**
Wilkes-Barre 51,551 **D10**
Wilkinsburg 23,669 **F2**
Williamsport 33,401 **D7**
Willow Grove 21,300 **F11**
York 44,619 **G8**

Statute Miles
Kilometers

Lambert Conformal Conic Projection
SCALE 1:1,593,000 1 Inch = 25 Statute Miles

RHODE ISLAND

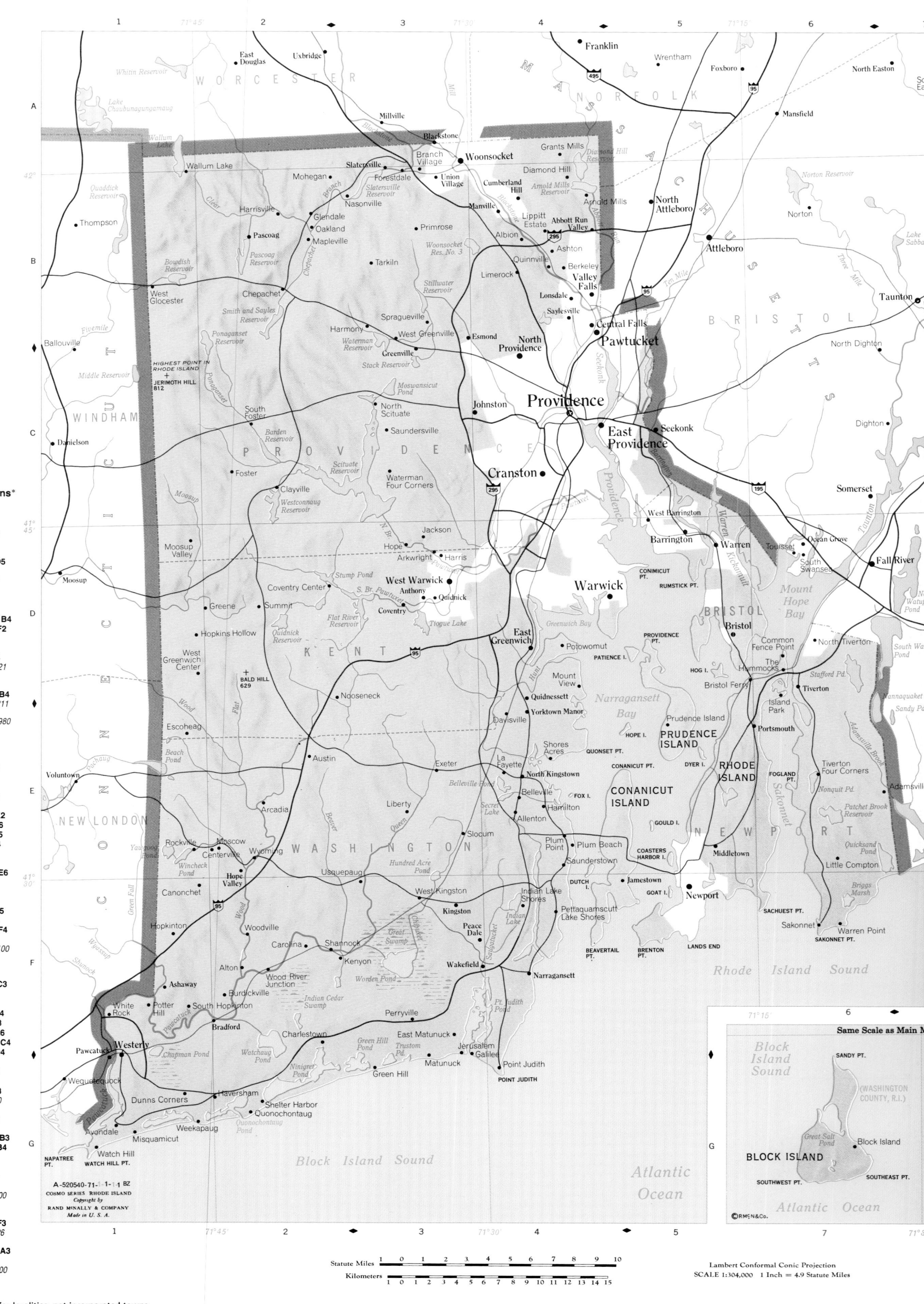

Cities and Towns*

Albion 1,200 **B4**
Allenton 600 **E4**
Anthony 4,500 **D3**
Arnold Mills 600 **B4**
Ashaway 1,747 **F1**
Ashton 875 **B4**
Barrington 16,174 **D5**
Berkeley 930 **B4**
Block Island 620 **h7**
Bradford 1,354 **F1**
Bristol 20,128 **D5**
Carolina 500 **F2**
Central Falls 16,995 **B4**
Charlestown 1,200 **F2**
Chepachet 900 **B2**
Coventry 8,000 **D3**
Cranston 71,992 **C4**
Cumberland Hill 5,421
   B4
Davisville 550 **E4**
Diamond Hill 1,150 **B4**
East Greenwich 10,211
   D4
East Providence 50,980
   C4
Esmond 3,500 **B4**
Forestdale 450 **B3**
Glendale 600 **B2**
Greenville 7,576 **C3**
Harmony 800 **B3**
Harris 1,000 **D3**
Harrisville 1,224 **B2**
Hope 490 **D3**
Hope Valley 1,414 **E2**
Island Park 1,000 **E6**
Jamestown 4,040 **F5**
Johnston 24,907 **C4**
Kingston 5,419 **F3**
La Fayette 680 **E4**
Little Compton 300 **E6**
Lonsdale 4,100 **B4**
Manville 3,100 **B4**
Mapleville 900 **B2**
Middletown 3,350 **E5**
Mount View 560 **D4**
Narragansett 3,342 **F4**
Newport 29,259 **F5**
North Kingstown 3,100
   E4
North Providence
   29,188 **C4**
North Scituate 325 **C3**
Oakland 500 **B2**
Pascoag 3,807 **B2**
Pawtucket 71,204 **C4**
Peace Dale 3,100 **F3**
Portsmouth 4,300 **E6**
Providence 156,804 **C4**
Quidnessett 3,300 **D4**
Quidnick 2,300 **D3**
Saylesville 3,200 **B4**
Shannock 600 **D2**
Slatersville 2,000 **A3**
South Hopkinton 500
   F1
Spragueville 430 **B3**
Tiverton 7,653 **D6**
Union Village 2,400 **B3**
Valley Falls 10,892 **B4**
Wakefield 3,400 **F3**
Warren 10,640 **D5**
Warwick 87,123 **D4**
Watch Hill 500 **G1**
West Barrington 3,700
   C5
Westerly 14,093 **F1**
West Kingston 700 **F3**
West Warwick 27,026
   D3
Woonsocket 45,914 **A3**
Wyoming 600 **E2**
Yorktown Manor 2,500
   E4

*Populations are for localities, not incorporated towns.

Statute Miles

Kilometers

Lambert Conformal Conic Projection
SCALE 1:304,000   1 Inch = 4.9 Statute Miles

A-520540-71-1-1-1 BZ
COSMO SERIES RHODE ISLAND
Copyright by
RAND McNALLY & COMPANY
Made in U.S.A.

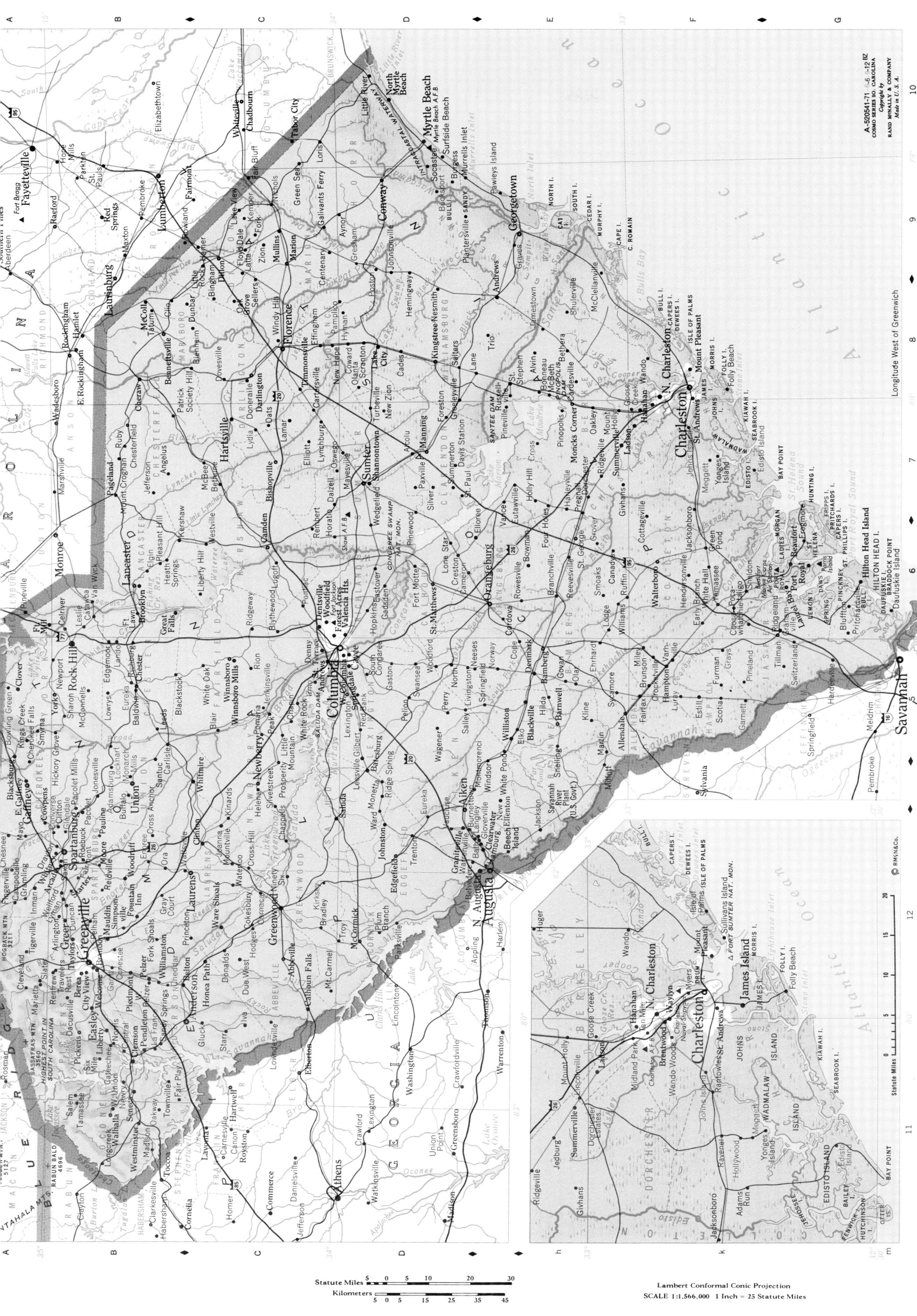

A-500541-71 -5,-6,-12 BZ
COSMO SERIES SO. CAROLINA
Copyright by
RAND McNALLY & COMPANY
Made in U.S.A.

Longitude West of Greenwich

Lambert Conformal Conic Projection
SCALE 1:1,566,000   1 Inch = 25 Statute Miles

Statute Miles 5 0 5 10   20   30
Kilometers 5 0 5 15 25 35 45

© RM&Co.

Cities and Towns

Abbeville 5,833 **C3**
Aiken 14,978 **D4**
Allendale 4,400 **E5**
Anderson 27,965 **B2**
Barnwell 5,572 **E5**
Batesburg 4,023 **D4**
Beaufort 8,634 **G6**
Belton 5,312 **B3**
Belvedere 6,859 **D4**
Bennettsville 8,774 **B8**
Berea 7,500 **B3**
Bishopville 3,429 **C7**
Camden 7,462 **C6**
Cayce 11,701 **D5**
Charleston 69,510 **F8**
Cheraw 5,654 **B8**
Chester 6,820 **B5**
Clemson 8,118 **B2**
Clinton 8,596 **C4**
Columbia 100,385 **C5**
Conway 10,240 **D9**
Cowpens 2,023 **A4**
Darlington 7,989 **C8**
Denmark 4,434 **E5**
Dillon 7,060 **C9**
Easley 14,264 **B2**
Florence 29,176 **C8**
Fort Mill 4,162 **A6**
Fountain Inn 4,226 **B3**
Gaffney 13,453 **A4**
Georgetown 10,144 **E9**
Goose Creek 17,811 **F7**
Greenville 58,242 **B3**
Greenwood 21,613 **C3**
Greer 10,525 **B3**
Hanahan 13,224 **F7**
Hartsville 7,631 **C7**
Hilton Head Island
  11,344 **G6**
Honea Path 4,114 **C3**
James Island 24,124
  k12
Kingstree 4,147 **D8**
Ladson 13,246 **F7**
Lake City 6,731 **D8**
Lancaster 9,703 **B6**
Laurel Bay 5,238 **G6**
Laurens 10,587 **C3**
Manning 4,746 **D7**
Marion 7,700 **C9**
Mauldin 8,143 **B3**
Moncks Corner 3,699
  E7
Mount Pleasant 14,209
  F8
Mullins 6,068 **C9**
Myrtle Beach 18,446
  D10
Newberry 9,866 **C4**
North Augusta 13,593
  D4
North Charleston 62,534
  F8
North Myrtle Beach
  3,960 **D10**
Orangeburg 14,933 **E6**
Rock Hill 35,344 **B5**
St. Andrews 9,908 **F7**
St. Andrews 20,245 **C5**
Seneca 7,436 **B2**
Shannontown 7,900 **D7**
Simpsonville 9,037 **B3**
Spartanburg 43,826 **B4**
Summerville 6,706 **E7**
Sumter 24,890 **D7**
Taylors 12,100 **B3**
Union 10,523 **B4**
Walhalla 3,977 **B1**
West Columbia 10,409
  D5
Williamston 4,310 **B3**
Woodruff 5,171 **B3**
York 6,412 **B5**

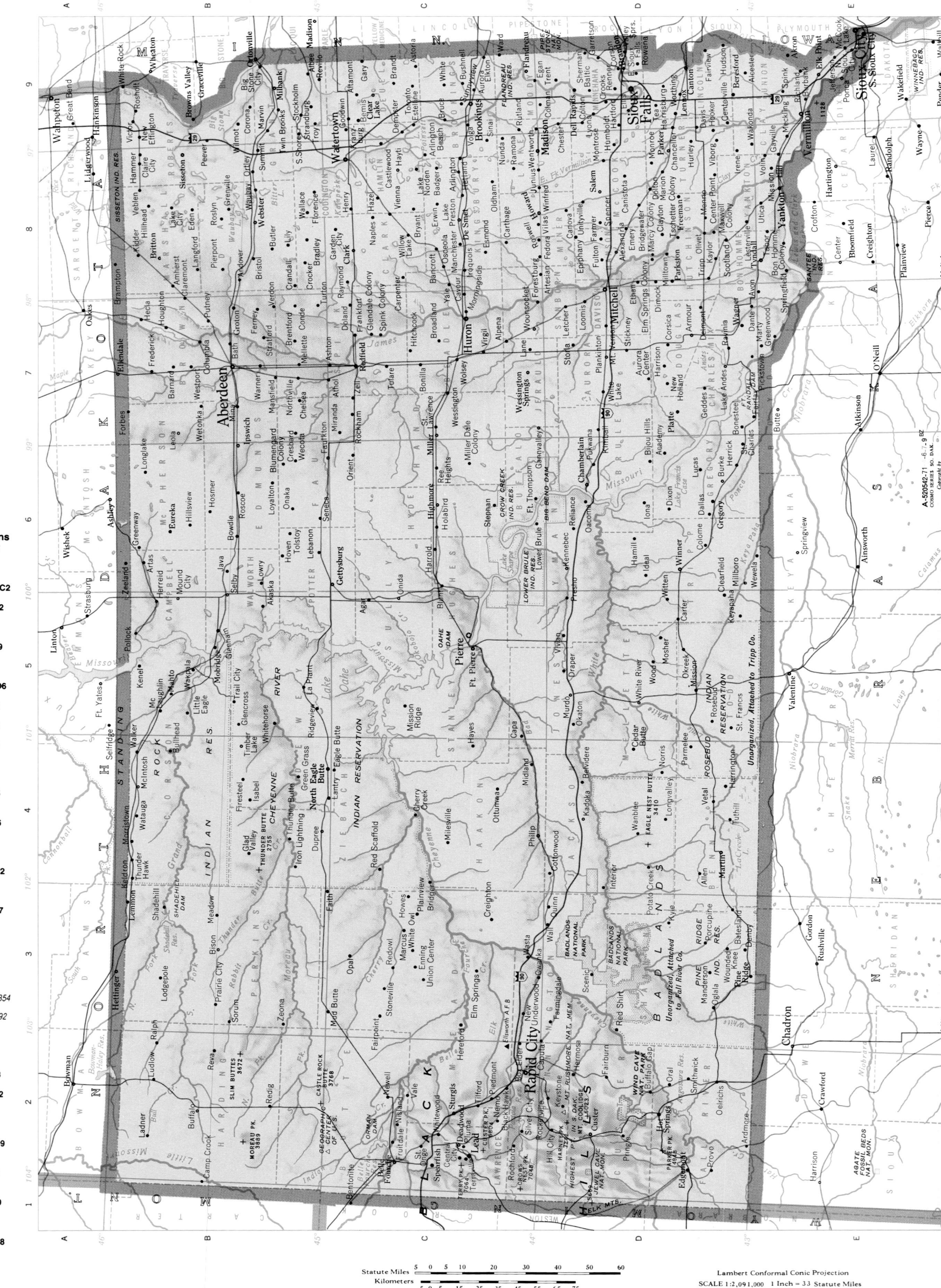

Cities and Towns

Aberdeen 25,851 **B7**
Alcester 885 **D9**
Arlington 991 **C8**
Armour 819 **D7**
Belle Fourche 4,692 **C2**
Beresford 1,865 **D9**
Black Hawk 1,608 **C2**
Box Elder 3,186 **C2**
Brandon 2,589 **D9**
Britton 1,590 **B8**
Brookings 14,951 **C9**
Burke 859 **D6**
Canton 2,886 **D9**
Centerville 892 **D9**
Chamberlain 2,258 **D6**
Clark 1,351 **C8**
Clear Lake 1,310 **C9**
Custer 1,830 **D2**
Deadwood 2,035 **C2**
De Smet 1,237 **C8**
Edgemont 1,468 **D2**
Elk Point 1,661 **E9**
Eureka 1,360 **B6**
Faulkton 981 **B6**
Flandreau 2,114 **C9**
Fort Pierre 1,789 **C5**
Freeman 1,462 **D8**
Garretson 963 **D9**
Gettysburg 1,623 **C6**
Gregory 1,503 **D6**
Groton 1,230 **B7**
Hartford 1,207 **D9**
Highmore 1,055 **C6**
Hot Springs 4,742 **D2**
Howard 1,169 **C8**
Huron 13,000 **C7**
Ipswich 1,153 **B6**
Lake Andes 1,029 **D7**
Lead 4,330 **C2**
Lemmon 1,871 **B3**
Lennox 1,827 **D9**
Martin 1,018 **D4**
Milbank 4,120 **B9**
Miller 1,931 **C7**
Mitchell 13,916 **D7**
Mobridge 4,174 **B5**
North Eagle Butte 1,354 **B4**
North Sioux City 1,992 **E9**
Parker 999 **D8**
Parkston 1,545 **D8**
Philip 1,088 **C4**
Pierre 11,973 **C5**
Pine Ridge 3,059 **D3**
Platte 1,334 **D7**
Rapid City 46,492 **C2**
Redfield 3,027 **C7**
Salem 1,486 **D8**
Scotland 1,022 **D8**
Selby 884 **B5**
Sioux Falls 81,343 **D9**
Sisseton 2,789 **B8**
Spearfish 5,251 **C2**
Springfield 1,377 **E8**
Sturgis 5,184 **C2**
Tyndall 1,253 **E8**
Vermillion 10,136 **E9**
Volga 1,221 **C9**
Wagner 1,453 **D7**
Wall 770 **D3**
Watertown 15,649 **C8**
Webster 2,417 **B8**
Wessington Springs 1,203 **C7**
Winner 3,472 **D6**
Yankton 12,011 **E8**

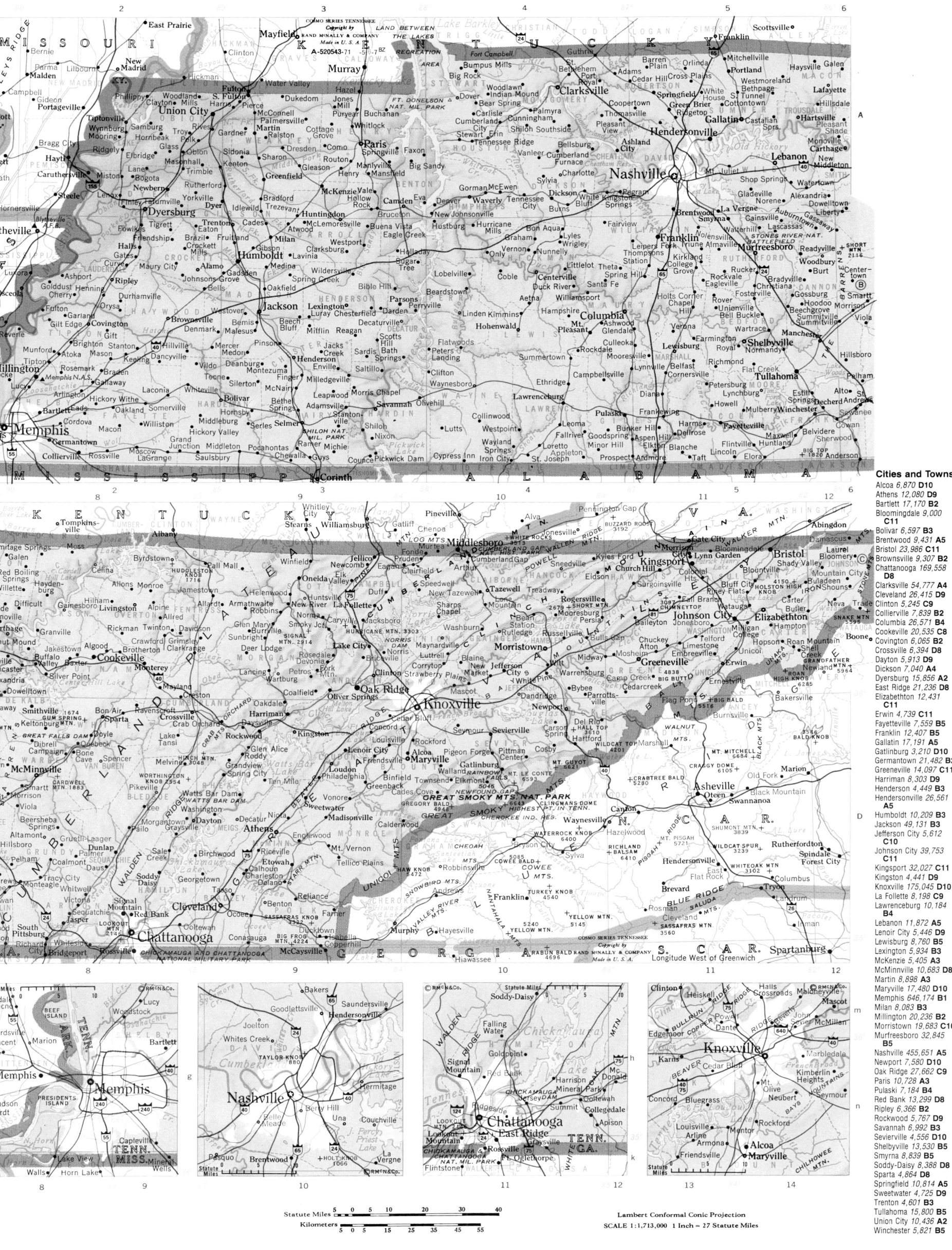

Cities and Towns

Alcoa 6,870 **D10**
Athens 12,080 **D9**
Bartlett 17,170 **B2**
Bloomingdale 9,000 **C11**
Bolivar 6,597 **B3**
Brentwood 9,431 **A5**
Bristol 23,986 **C11**
Brownsville 9,307 **B2**
Chattanooga 169,558 **D8**
Clarksville 54,777 **A4**
Cleveland 26,415 **D9**
Clinton 5,245 **C9**
Collierville 7,839 **B2**
Columbia 26,571 **B4**
Cookeville 20,535 **C8**
Covington 6,065 **B2**
Crossville 6,394 **D8**
Dayton 5,913 **D9**
Dickson 7,040 **A4**
Dyersburg 15,856 **A3**
East Ridge 21,236 **D8**
Elizabethton 12,431 **C11**
Erwin 4,739 **C11**
Fayetteville 7,559 **B5**
Franklin 12,407 **B5**
Gallatin 17,191 **A5**
Gatlinburg 3,210 **D10**
Germantown 21,482 **B2**
Greeneville 14,097 **C11**
Harriman 8,303 **D9**
Henderson 4,449 **B3**
Hendersonville 26,561 **A5**
Humboldt 10,209 **B3**
Jackson 49,131 **B3**
Jefferson City 5,612 **C10**
Johnson City 39,753 **C11**
Kingsport 32,027 **C11**
Kingston 4,441 **D9**
Knoxville 175,045 **D10**
La Follette 8,198 **C9**
Lawrenceburg 10,184 **B4**
Lebanon 11,872 **A5**
Lenoir City 5,446 **D9**
Lewisburg 8,760 **B5**
Lexington 5,934 **B3**
McKenzie 5,405 **A3**
McMinnville 10,683 **D8**
Martin 8,898 **A3**
Maryville 17,480 **D10**
Memphis 646,174 **B1**
Milan 8,083 **B3**
Millington 20,236 **B2**
Morristown 19,683 **C10**
Murfreesboro 32,845 **B5**
Nashville 455,651 **A5**
Newport 7,580 **D10**
Oak Ridge 27,662 **C9**
Paris 10,728 **A3**
Pulaski 7,184 **B4**
Red Bank 13,299 **D8**
Ripley 6,366 **B2**
Rockwood 5,767 **D9**
Savannah 6,992 **B3**
Sevierville 4,556 **D10**
Shelbyville 13,530 **B5**
Smyrna 8,839 **B5**
Soddy-Daisy 8,388 **D8**
Sparta 4,864 **D8**
Springfield 10,814 **A5**
Sweetwater 4,725 **D9**
Trenton 4,601 **B3**
Tullahoma 15,800 **B5**
Union City 10,436 **A2**
Winchester 5,821 **B5**

TEXAS

Cities and Towns

Abilene 98,315 **C3**
Alice 20,961 **F3**
Amarillo 149,230 **B2**
Arlington 160,113 **n9**
Austin 345,496 **D4**
Bay City 17,837 **E5**
Baytown 56,923 **E5**
Beaumont 118,102 **D5**
Beeville 14,574 **E4**
Big Spring 24,804 **C2**
Borger 15,837 **B2**
Brownsville 84,997 **G4**
Brownwood 19,396 **D3**
Bryan 44,337 **D4**
Cleburne 19,218 **C4**
College Station 37,272 **D4**
Conroe 18,034 **D5**
Copperas Cove 19,469 **D4**
Corpus Christi 231,999 **F4**
Corsicana 21,712 **C4**
Dallas 904,078 **C4**
Del Rio 30,034 **E2**
Denison 23,884 **C4**
Denton 48,063 **C4**
Eagle Pass 21,407 **E2**
Edinburg 24,075 **F3**
El Paso 425,259 **o11**
Fort Worth 385,164 **C4**
Galveston 61,902 **E5**
Garland 138,857 **n10**
Grand Prairie 71,462 **n10**
Greenville 22,161 **C4**
Harlingen 43,543 **F4**
Hereford 15,853 **B1**
Houston 1,595,138 **E5**
Huntsville 23,936 **D5**
Irving 109,943 **n10**
Kerrville 15,276 **D3**
Killeen 46,296 **D4**
Kingsville 28,808 **F4**
Lake Jackson 19,102 **E5**
Laredo 91,449 **F3**
Longview 62,762 **C5**
Lubbock 173,979 **C2**
Lufkin 28,562 **D5**
McAllen 66,281 **F3**
Marshall 24,921 **C5**
Mesquite 67,053 **n10**
Midland 70,525 **D1**
Mineral Wells 14,468 **C3**
Nacogdoches 27,149 **D5**
New Braunfels 22,402 **E3**
Odessa 90,027 **D1**
Orange 23,628 **D6**
Palestine 15,948 **D5**
Pampa 21,396 **B2**
Paris 25,498 **C5**
Pasadena 112,560 **r14**
Pecos 12,855 **D1**
Plainview 22,187 **B2**
Port Arthur 61,251 **E6**
Richardson 72,496 **n10**
San Angelo 73,240 **D2**
San Antonio 786,023 **E3**
San Benito 17,988 **F4**
San Marcos 23,420 **E4**
Sherman 30,413 **C4**
Temple 42,354 **D4**
Texarkana 31,271 **C5**
Texas City 41,403 **E5**
Uvalde 14,178 **E3**
Victoria 50,695 **E4**
Waco 101,261 **D4**
Waxahachie 14,264 **C4**
Wichita Falls 94,201 **C3**

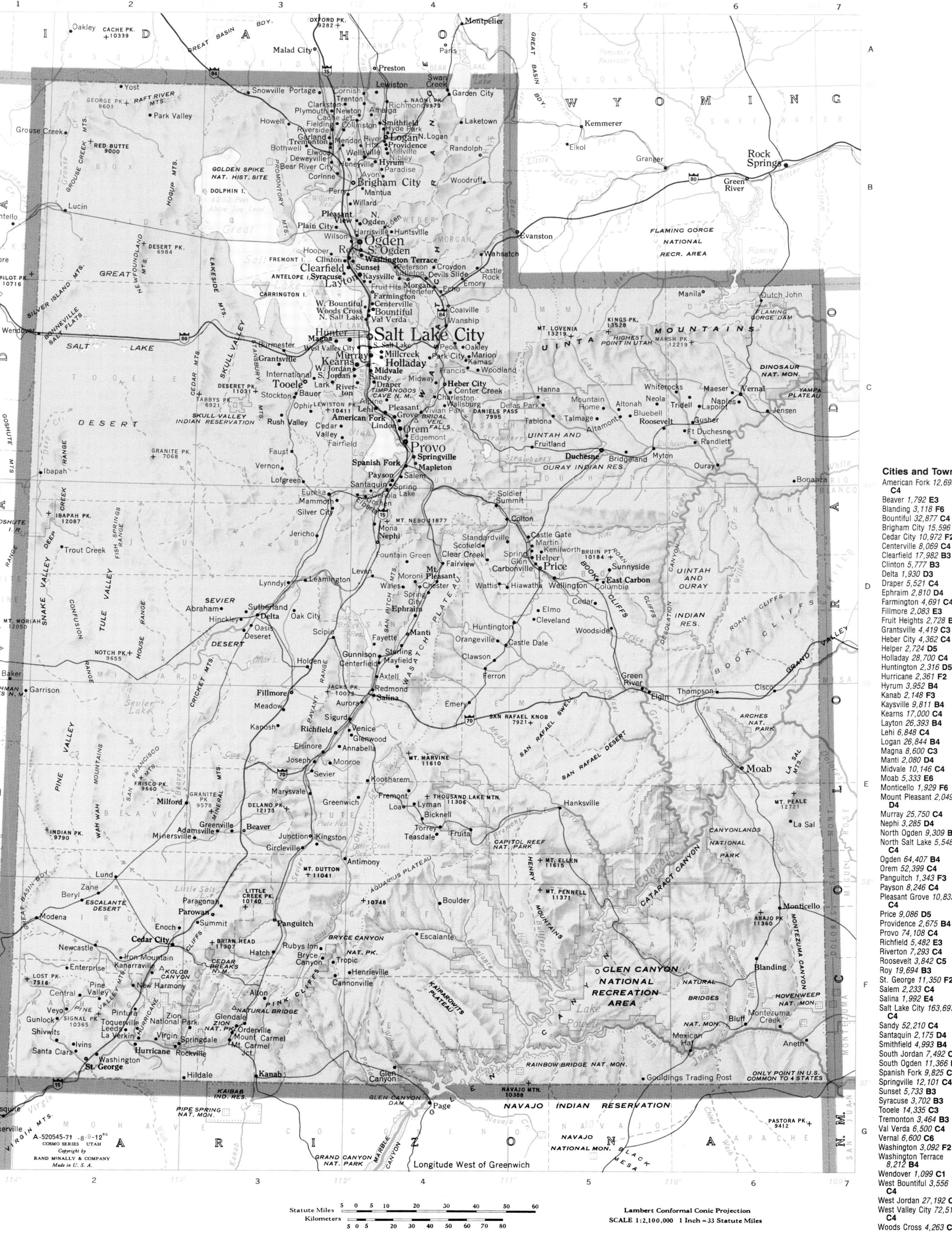

Cities and Towns

American Fork 12,693 **C4**
Beaver 1,792 **E3**
Blanding 3,118 **F6**
Bountiful 32,877 **C4**
Brigham City 15,596 **B3**
Cedar City 10,972 **F2**
Centerville 8,069 **C4**
Clearfield 17,982 **B3**
Clinton 5,777 **B3**
Delta 1,930 **D3**
Draper 5,521 **C4**
Ephraim 2,810 **D4**
Farmington 4,691 **C4**
Fillmore 2,083 **E3**
Fruit Heights 2,728 **B4**
Grantsville 4,419 **C3**
Heber City 4,362 **C4**
Helper 2,724 **D5**
Holladay 28,700 **C4**
Huntington 2,316 **D5**
Hurricane 2,361 **F2**
Hyrum 3,952 **B4**
Kanab 2,148 **F3**
Kaysville 9,811 **B4**
Kearns 17,000 **C4**
Layton 26,393 **B4**
Lehi 6,848 **C4**
Logan 26,844 **B4**
Magna 8,600 **C3**
Manti 2,080 **D4**
Midvale 10,146 **C4**
Moab 5,333 **E6**
Monticello 1,929 **F6**
Mount Pleasant 2,049 **D4**
Murray 25,750 **C4**
Nephi 3,285 **D4**
North Ogden 9,309 **B4**
North Salt Lake 5,548 **C4**
Ogden 64,407 **B4**
Orem 52,399 **C4**
Panguitch 1,343 **F3**
Payson 8,246 **C4**
Pleasant Grove 10,833 **C4**
Price 9,086 **D5**
Providence 2,675 **B4**
Provo 74,108 **C4**
Richfield 5,482 **E3**
Riverton 7,293 **C4**
Roosevelt 3,842 **C5**
Roy 19,694 **B3**
St. George 11,350 **F2**
Salem 2,233 **C4**
Salina 1,992 **E4**
Salt Lake City 163,697 **C4**
Sandy 52,210 **C4**
Santaquin 2,175 **D4**
Smithfield 4,993 **B4**
South Jordan 7,492 **C4**
South Ogden 11,366 **B4**
Spanish Fork 9,825 **C4**
Springville 12,101 **C4**
Sunset 5,733 **B3**
Syracuse 3,702 **B3**
Tooele 14,335 **C3**
Tremonton 3,464 **B3**
Val Verda 6,500 **C4**
Vernal 6,600 **C6**
Washington 3,092 **F2**
Washington Terrace 8,212 **B4**
Wendover 1,099 **C1**
West Bountiful 3,556 **C4**
West Jordan 27,192 **C4**
West Valley City 72,511 **C4**
Woods Cross 4,263 **C4**

VERMONT

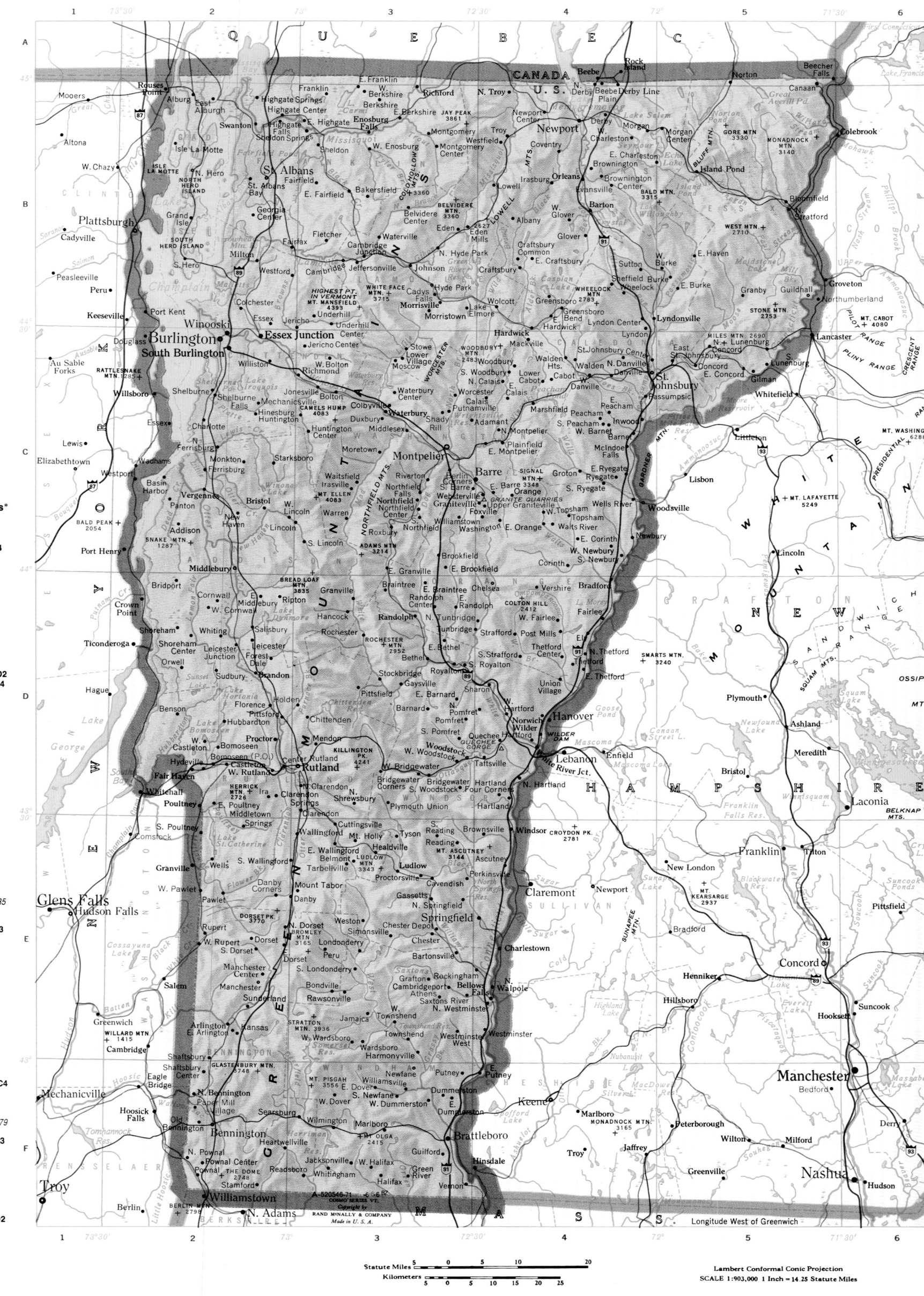

Cities and Towns*

Arlington 800 **E2**
Barre 9,824 **C4**
Barton 1,062 **B4**
Bellows Falls 3,456 **E4**
Bennington 8,600 **F2**
Bethel 900 **D3**
Bradford 831 **D4**
Brandon 1,720 **D2**
Brattleboro 11,886 **F3**
Bristol 1,793 **C2**
Burlington 37,712 **C2**
Castleton 600 **D2**
Derby 598 **B4**
Dorset 550 **E2**
East Arlington 600 **E2**
East Barre 900 **C4**
East Middlebury 550 **D2**
East Montpelier 600 **C4**
Enosburg Falls 1,207
    B3
Essex 800 **B2**
Essex Junction 7,033
    C2
Fair Haven 2,819 **D2**
Gilman 550 **C5**
Graniteville 600 **C4**
Hardwick 1,476 **B4**
Hartford 600 **D4**
Jericho 1,340 **B3**
Johnson 1,393 **B3**
Ludlow 1,352 **E3**
Lyndonville 1,401 **B4**
Manchester 563 **E2**
Manchester Center
    1,060 **E2**
Middlebury 4,000 **C2**
Milton 1,411 **B2**
Montpelier 8,241 **C3**
Morrisville 2,074 **B3**
Newport 4,756 **B4**
North Bennington 1,635
    F2
Northfield 2,033 **C3**
Northfield Falls 600 **C3**
North Springfield 750
    E3
North Troy 717 **B4**
Norwich 1,000 **D4**
Orleans 983 **B4**
Pittsford 666 **D2**
Plainfield 599 **C4**
Poultney 1,554 **D2**
Proctor 1,998 **D2**
Putney 1,100 **F3**
Randolph 2,217 **D3**
Richford 1,471 **B3**
Richmond 865 **C3**
Rutland 18,436 **D3**
St. Albans 7,308 **B2**
St. Johnsbury 6,400 **C4**
Saxtons River 593 **E3**
Shaftsbury 700 **E2**
South Barre 900 **C3**
South Burlington 10,679
    C2
South Royalton 700 **D3**
Springfield 5,632 **E4**
Stowe 531 **C3**
Swanton 2,520 **B2**
Vergennes 2,273 **C2**
Wallingford 800 **E3**
Waterbury 1,892 **C3**
Websterville 600 **C4**
West Rutland 2,351 **D2**
White River Junction
    2,379 **D4**
Wilder 1,328 **D4**
Williamstown 650 **C3**
Wilmington 545 **F3**
Winooski 6,318 **C2**
Woodstock 1,178 **D3**

*Populations are for localities, not incorporated towns.

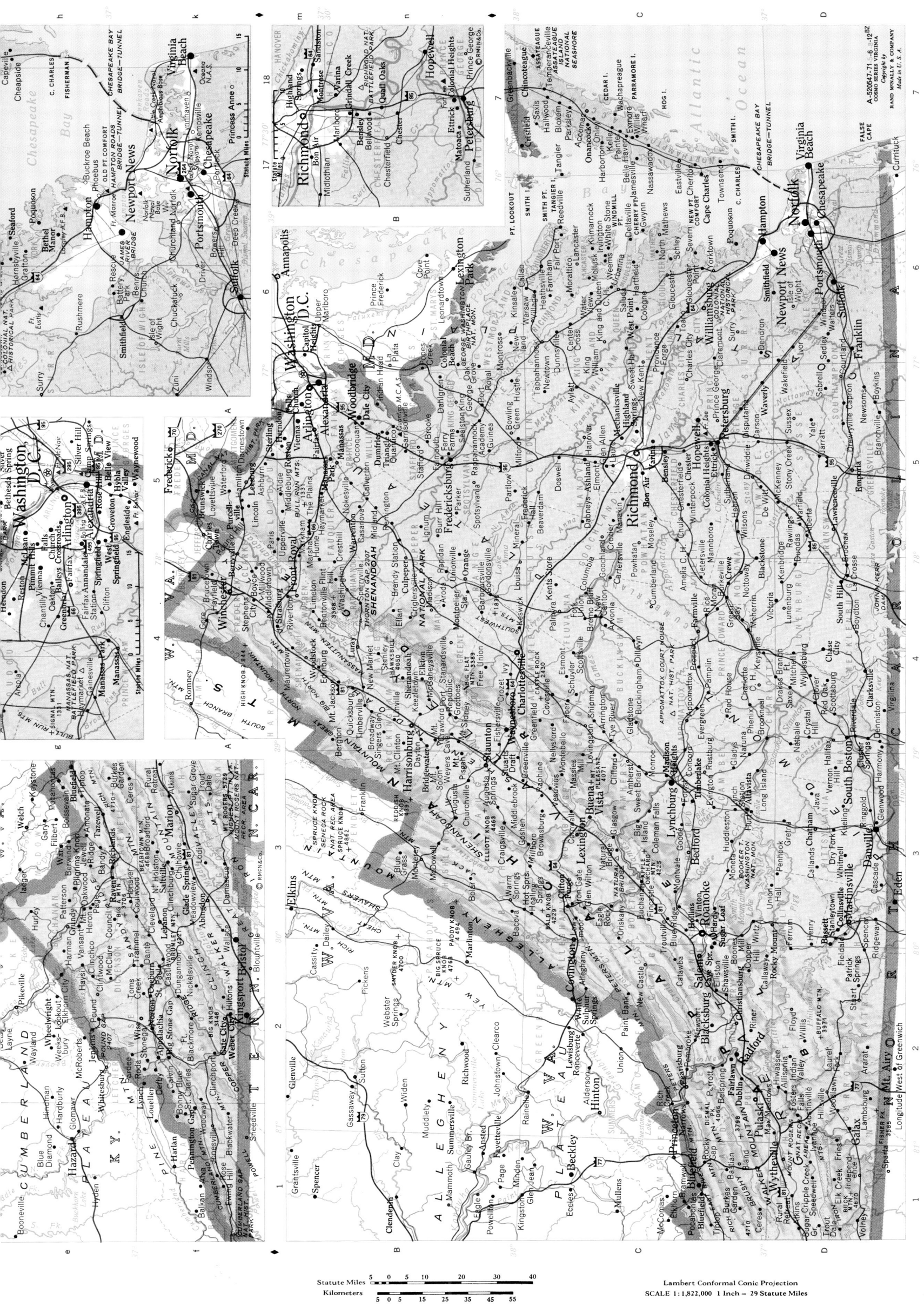

Lambert Conformal Conic Projection
SCALE 1:1,822,000 1 Inch = 29 Statute Miles

Statute Miles
Kilometers

Cities and Towns

Alexandria 103,217 **B5**
Annandale 35,300 **g12**
Appomattox 1,345 **C4**
Arlington 152,700 **B5**
Bedford 5,991 **C3**
Big Stone Gap 4,748 **f9**
Blacksburg 30,638 **C2**
Bluefield 5,946 **C1**
Bon Air 13,000 **C5**
Bristol 19,042 **f9**
Buena Vista 6,717 **C3**
Charlottesville 39,916 **B4**
Chesapeake 114,486 **D6**
Chester 7,000 **C5**
Chincoteague 1,607 **C7**
Christiansburg 10,345 **C2**
Clifton Forge 5,046 **C3**
Collinsville 7,400 **D3**
Colonial Heights 16,509 **C5**
Covington 9,063 **C3**
Culpepper 6,621 **B5**
Dale City 23,000 **B5**
Danville 45,642 **D3**
Emporia 4,840 **D5**
Engleside 21,400 **g12**
Fairfax 19,390 **B5**
Farmville 6,067 **C4**
Franklin 7,308 **D6**
Fredericksburg 15,322 **B5**
Front Royal 11,126 **B4**
Galax 6,524 **D2**
Hampton 122,617 **C6**
Harrisonburg 19,671 **B4**
Herndon 11,449 **B5**
Highland Springs 7,500 **C5**
Hollins 11,000 **C3**
Hopewell 23,397 **C5**
Leesburg 8,357 **A5**
Lexington 7,292 **C3**
Lynchburg 66,743 **C3**
McLean 22,000 **g12**
Manassas 15,438 **B5**
Manassas Park 6,982 **B5**
Marion 7,029 **f10**
Martinsville 18,149 **D3**
Mechanicsville 9,000 **C5**
Newport News 144,903 **D6**
Norfolk 266,979 **D6**
Norton 4,757 **f9**
Petersburg 41,055 **C5**
Poquoson 8,726 **C6**
Portsmouth 104,577 **D6**
Pulaski 10,106 **C2**
Radford 13,225 **C2**
Reston 32,000 **B5**
Richlands 5,796 **e10**
Richmond 219,214 **C5**
Roanoke 100,220 **C3**
Salem 23,958 **C2**
Shenandoah 1,861 **B4**
South Boston 7,093 **D4**
Springfield 12,500 **g12**
Staunton 21,857 **B3**
Sterling 12,000 **A5**
Suffolk 47,621 **D6**
Tazewell 4,468 **e10**
Vienna 15,469 **B5**
Vinton 8,027 **C3**
Virginia Beach 262,199 **D7**
Waynesboro 15,329 **B4**
West Springfield 16,000 **g12**
Williamsburg 9,870 **C6**
Winchester 20,217 **A4**
Woodbridge 35,000 **B5**
Wytheville 7,135 **D1**
Yorktown 390 **C6**

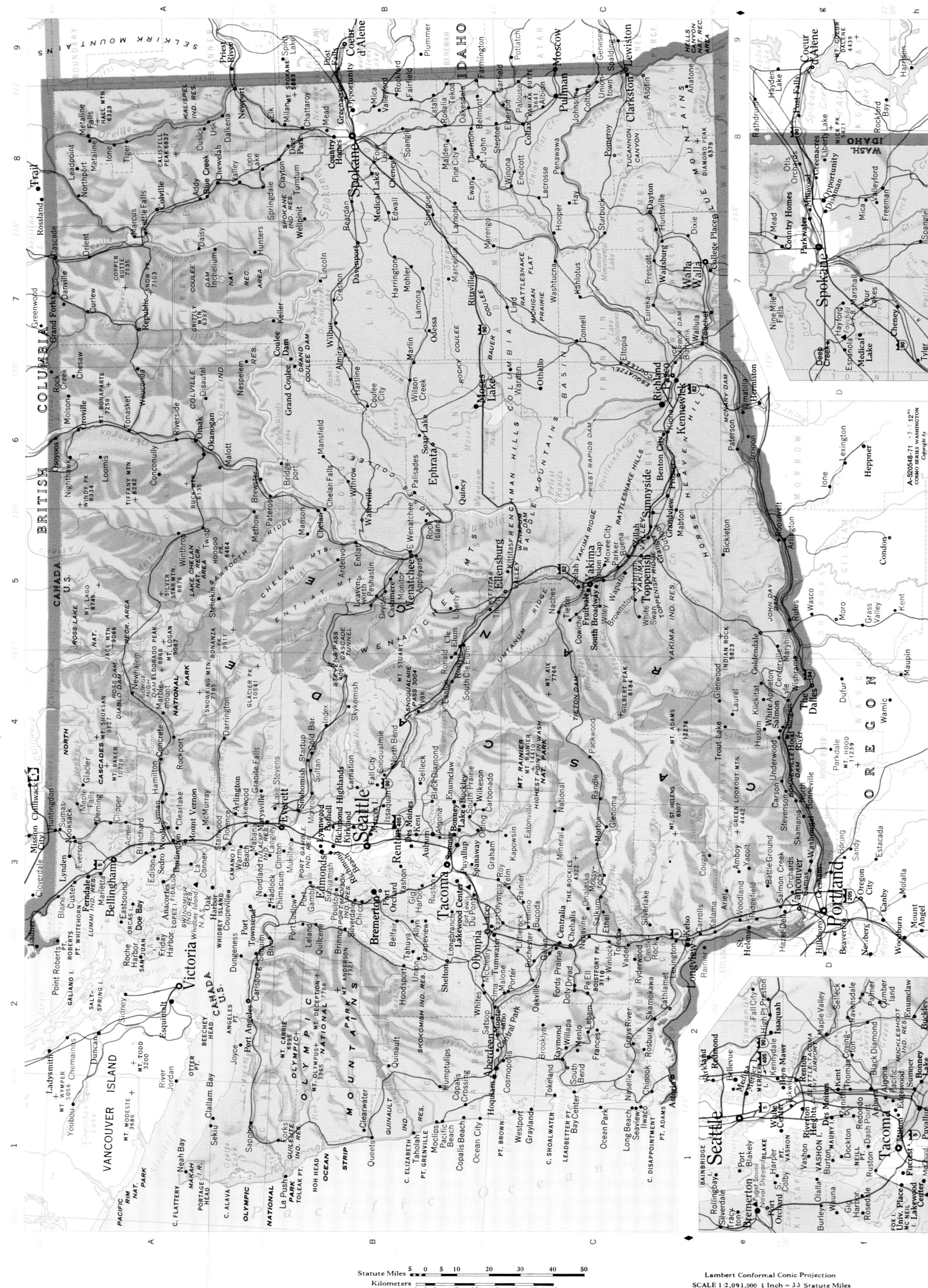

Cities and Towns

Aberdeen 18,739 **C2**
Anacortes 9,013 **A3**
Bellevue 73,903 **e11**
Bellingham 45,794 **A3**
Bonney Lake 5,328 **B3**
Bothell 7,943 **B3**
Bremerton 36,208 **B3**
Camas 5,681 **D3**
Centralia 11,555 **C3**
Chehalis 6,100 **C3**
Chelan 2,802 **B5**
Cheney 7,630 **B8**
Clarkston 6,903 **C8**
Colville 4,510 **A8**
Coulee Dam 1,412 **B7**
Des Moines 7,378 **B3**
Dishman 9,900 **g14**
Edmonds 27,679 **B3**
Ellensburg 11,752 **C5**
Enumclaw 5,427 **B4**
Ephrata 5,359 **B6**
Everett 54,413 **B3**
Ferndale 3,855 **A3**
Forks 3,060 **B1**
Goldendale 3,575 **D5**
Grandview 5,615 **C6**
Hoquiam 9,719 **C2**
Kelso 11,129 **C3**
Kennewick 34,397 **C6**
Kent 23,152 **B3**
Kirkland 18,779 **B3**
Lacey 13,940 **B3**
Lakewood Center
  51,300 **B3**
Longview 31,052 **C3**
Lynden 4,022 **A3**
Lynnwood 22,641 **B3**
Medical Lake 3,600 **B8**
Mercer Island 21,522
  B3
Montesano 3,247 **C2**
Moses Lake 10,629 **B6**
Mount Vernon 13,009
  A3
Oak Harbor 12,271 **A3**
Okanogan 2,302 **A6**
Olympia 27,447 **B3**
Omak 4,007 **A6**
Opportunity 17,600 **B8**
Othello 4,454 **C6**
Parkland 22,300 **f11**
Pasco 18,425 **C6**
Port Angeles 17,311 **A2**
Port Townsend 6,067
  A3
Prosser 3,896 **C6**
Pullman 23,579 **C8**
Puyallup 18,251 **B3**
Quincy 3,525 **B6**
Redmond 23,318 **e11**
Renton 30,612 **B3**
Richland 33,578 **C6**
Richmond Highlands
  20,300 **B3**
Riverton Heights 33,500
  f11
Seattle 493,846 **B3**
Sedro Woolley 6,110
  A3
Shelton 7,629 **B2**
Snohomish 5,294 **B3**
Spokane 171,300 **B8**
Sunnyside 9,225 **C6**
Tacoma 158,501 **B3**
Toppenish 6,517 **C5**
Tumwater 6,705 **B3**
University Place 13,620
  f10
Vancouver 42,834 **D3**
Walla Walla 25,618 **C7**
Wenatchee 17,257 **B5**
White Center 19,700
  e11
Yakima 49,826 **C5**

Statute Miles
Kilometers

Lambert Conformal Conic Projection
SCALE 1:2,091,000 1 Inch = 33 Statute Miles

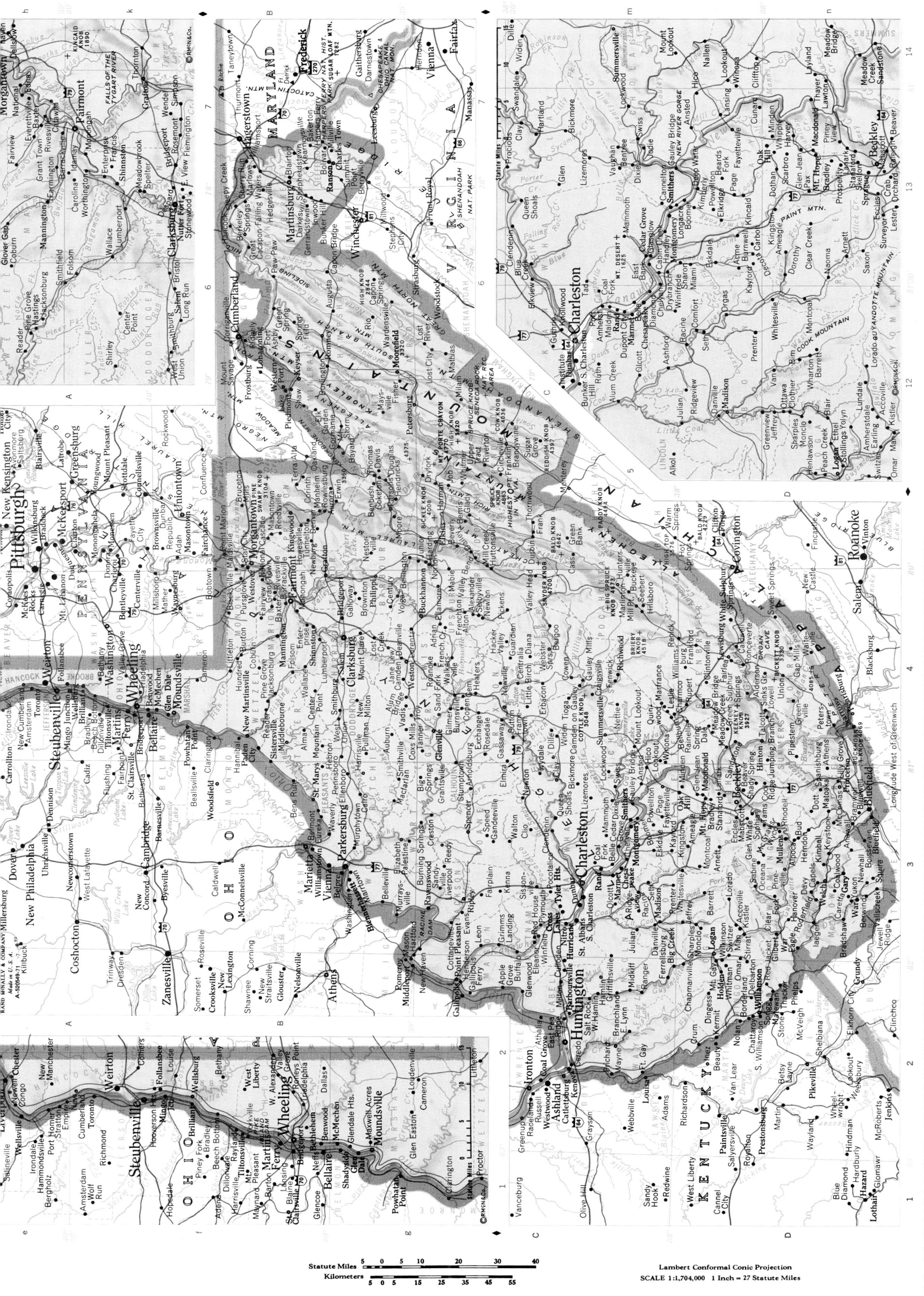

Lambert Conformal Conic Projection
SCALE 1:1,704,000   1 Inch = 27 Statute Miles

Statute Miles 5 0 5 10   20   30   40
Kilometers 5 0 5   15   25   35   45   55

Cities and Towns

Barboursville 2,871 **C2**
Beckley 20,492 **D3**
Bluefield 16,060 **D3**
Bridgeport 6,604 **B4**
Buckhannon 6,820 **C4**
Charleston 63,968 **C3**
Charles Town 2,857 **B7**
Chesapeake 2,364 **C3**
Chester 3,297 **A4**
Clarksburg 22,371 **B4**
Cross Lanes 3,500 **C3**
Dunbar 9,285 **m12**
Elkins 8,536 **C5**
Fairmont 23,863 **B4**
Fayetteville 2,366 **D3**
Follansbee 3,994 **A4**
Gary 2,233 **D3**
Grafton 6,845 **B4**
Harpers Ferry 361 **B7**
Hinton 4,622 **D4**
Huntington 63,684 **C2**
Hurricane 3,751 **C2**
Kenova 4,454 **C2**
Keyser 6,569 **B6**
Kingwood 2,877 **B5**
Lewisburg 3,065 **D4**
Logan 3,029 **D3**
McMechen 2,402 **B4**
Madison 3,228 **C3**
Mannington 3,036 **B4**
Martinsburg 13,063 **B7**
Montgomery 3,104 **C3**
Moorefield 2,257 **B6**
Morgantown 27,605 **B5**
Moundsville 12,419 **B4**
Mullens 2,919 **D3**
New Martinsville 7,109 **B4**
Nitro 8,074 **C3**
Oak Hill 7,120 **C3**
Oceana 2,143 **D3**
Paden City 3,671 **B4**
Parkersburg 39,967 **B3**
Petersburg 2,084 **C5**
Philippi 3,194 **B4**
Point Pleasant 5,682 **C2**
Princeton 7,493 **D3**
Rand 2,500 **C3**
Ranson 2,471 **B7**
Ravenswood 4,126 **C3**
Richwood 3,568 **C4**
Ripley 3,464 **C3**
Romney 2,094 **B6**
Ronceverte 2,312 **D4**
St. Albans 12,402 **C3**
St. Marys 2,219 **B3**
Salem 2,706 **B4**
Shinnston 3,059 **B4**
Sistersville 2,367 **B4**
South Charleston 15,968 **C3**
Spencer 2,799 **C3**
Stonewood 2,058 **k10**
Summersville 2,972 **C4**
Tyler Heights 3,200 **C3**
Vienna 11,618 **B3**
War 2,158 **D3**
Weirton 25,371 **A4**
Welch 3,885 **D3**
Wellsburg 3,963 **A4**
Weston 6,250 **B4**
Westover 4,884 **B5**
Wheeling 43,070 **A4**
White Sulphur Springs 3,371 **D4**
Williamson 5,219 **D2**
Williamstown 3,095 **B3**

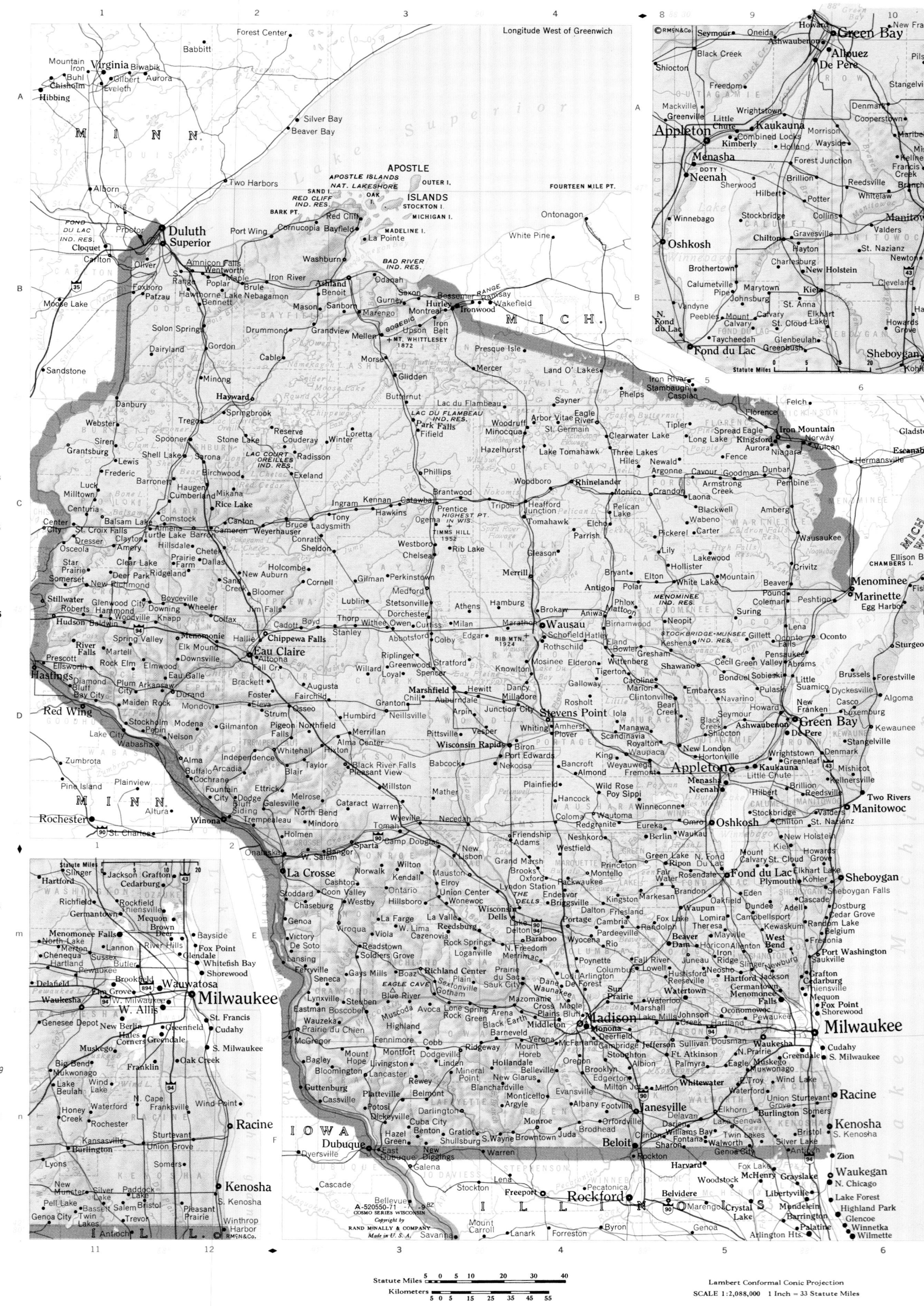

Longitude West of Greenwich

Cities and Towns

Antigo 8,653 **C4**
Appleton 58,913 **D5**
Ashland 9,115 **B3**
Baraboo 8,081 **E4**
Beaver Dam 14,149 **E5**
Beloit 35,207 **F4**
Brookfield 34,035 **m11**
Burlington 8,385 **F5**
Chippewa Falls 12,270 **D2**
Cudahy 19,547 **F6**
De Pere 14,892 **D5**
Eau Claire 51,509 **D2**
Fond du Lac 35,863 **E5**
Fort Atkinson 9,785 **F5**
Franklin 16,871 **n11**
Green Bay 87,899 **D6**
Greendale 16,928 **F5**
Greenfield 31,467 **n11**
Hayward 1,698 **B2**
Hudson 5,434 **D1**
Janesville 51,071 **F4**
Kaukauna 11,310 **D5**
Kenosha 77,685 **F6**
La Crosse 48,347 **E2**
Lake Geneva 5,612 **F5**
Madison 170,616 **E4**
Manitowoc 32,547 **D6**
Marinette 11,965 **C6**
Marshfield 18,290 **D3**
Menasha 14,728 **D5**
Menomonee Falls 27,845 **E5**
Menomonie 12,769 **D2**
Mequon 16,193 **E6**
Merrill 9,578 **C4**
Milwaukee 636,236 **E6**
Monroe 10,027 **F4**
Muskego 15,277 **F5**
Neenah 22,432 **D5**
New Berlin 30,529 **n11**
New London 6,210 **D5**
Oak Creek 16,932 **n12**
Oconomowoc 9,909 **E5**
Oconto 4,505 **D6**
Oshkosh 49,620 **D5**
Park Falls 3,192 **C3**
Platteville 9,580 **F3**
Portage 7,896 **E4**
Port Washington 8,612 **E6**
Prairie du Chien 5,859 **E2**
Racine 85,725 **F6**
Reedsburg 5,038 **E3**
Rhinelander 7,873 **C4**
Rice Lake 7,691 **C2**
River Falls 9,019 **D1**
Shawano 7,013 **D5**
Sheboygan 48,085 **E6**
South Milwaukee 21,069 **F6**
Stevens Point 22,970 **D4**
Stoughton 7,589 **F4**
Sturgeon Bay 8,847 **D6**
Sun Prairie 12,931 **E4**
Superior 29,571 **B1**
Tomah 7,204 **E3**
Two Rivers 13,354 **D6**
Watertown 18,113 **E5**
Waukesha 50,365 **E5**
Waupun 8,132 **E5**
Wausau 32,426 **D4**
Wauwatosa 51,308 **m11**
West Allis 63,982 **m11**
West Bend 21,484 **E5**
Whitefish Bay 14,930 **m12**
Whitewater 11,520 **F5**
Wisconsin Dells 2,521 **E4**
Wisconsin Rapids 17,995 **D4**

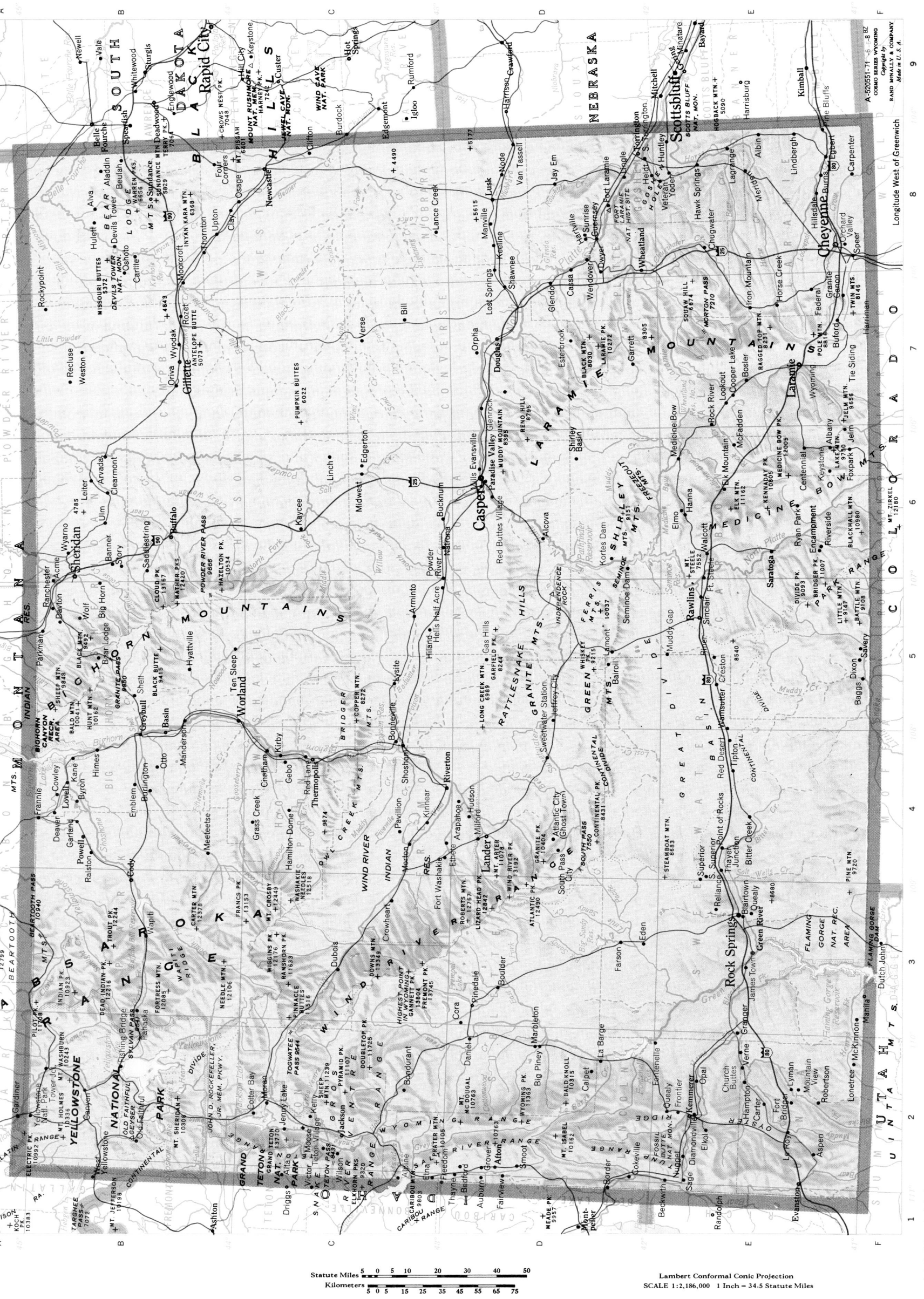

Lambert Conformal Conic Projection
SCALE 1:2,186,000 1 Inch = 34.5 Statute Miles

Statute Miles
5 0 5 10   20   30   40   50
Kilometers
5 0 5 15 25 35 45 55 65 75

Cities and Towns
Afton 1,481 D2
Baggs 433 E5
Basin 1,349 B4
Big Piney 530 D2
Buffalo 3,799 B6
Byron 633 B4
Casper 51,016 D6
Cheyenne 47,283 E8
Cody 6,790 B3
Cokeville 515 D2
Cowley 455 B4
Dayton 701 B5
Devils Tower 40 B8
Diamondville 1,000 E2
Douglas 6,030 D7
Dubois 1,067 C3
Edgerton 510 C6
Encampment 611 E6
Etna 400 C1
Evanston 6,421 E2
Evansville 2,335 D6
Fort Laramie 356 D8
Gillette 12,134 B7
Glenrock 2,736 D7
Green River 12,807 E3
Greybull 2,277 B4
Guernsey 1,512 D8
Hanna 2,288 E6
Hudson 514 D4
Jackson 4,511 C2
Jeffrey City 400 D5
Kemmerer 3,273 E2
Lander 7,867 D4
Laramie 24,410 E7
Lingle 475 D8
Lovell 2,447 B4
Lusk 1,650 D8
Lyman 2,284 E2
Marbleton 537 D2
Medicine Bow 953 E6
Meeteetse 512 B4
Midwest 638 C6
Mills 2,139 D6
Moorcroft 1,014 B8
Mountain View 628 E2
Newcastle 3,596 C8
Orchard Valley 800 E8
Paradise Valley 2,300 D6
Pine Bluffs 1,077 E8
Pinedale 1,066 D3
Powell 5,310 B4
Ranchester 655 B5
Rawlins 11,547 E6
Reliance 500 E3
Riverton 9,247 C4
Rock River 415 E7
Rock Springs 19,458 E3
Saratoga 2,410 E6
Sheridan 15,146 B6
Shirley Basin 450 D6
Shoshoni 879 C4
Sinclair 586 E5
South Superior 586 E4
Story 700 B6
Sundance 1,087 B8
Ten Sleep 407 B5
Teton Village 200 C2
Thermopolis 3,852 C4
Torrington 5,441 D8
Upton 1,193 B8
Wamsutter 681 E5
West Laramie 2,000 E7
Wheatland 5,816 D8
Worland 6,391 B5
Yellowstone National
Park 350 B2

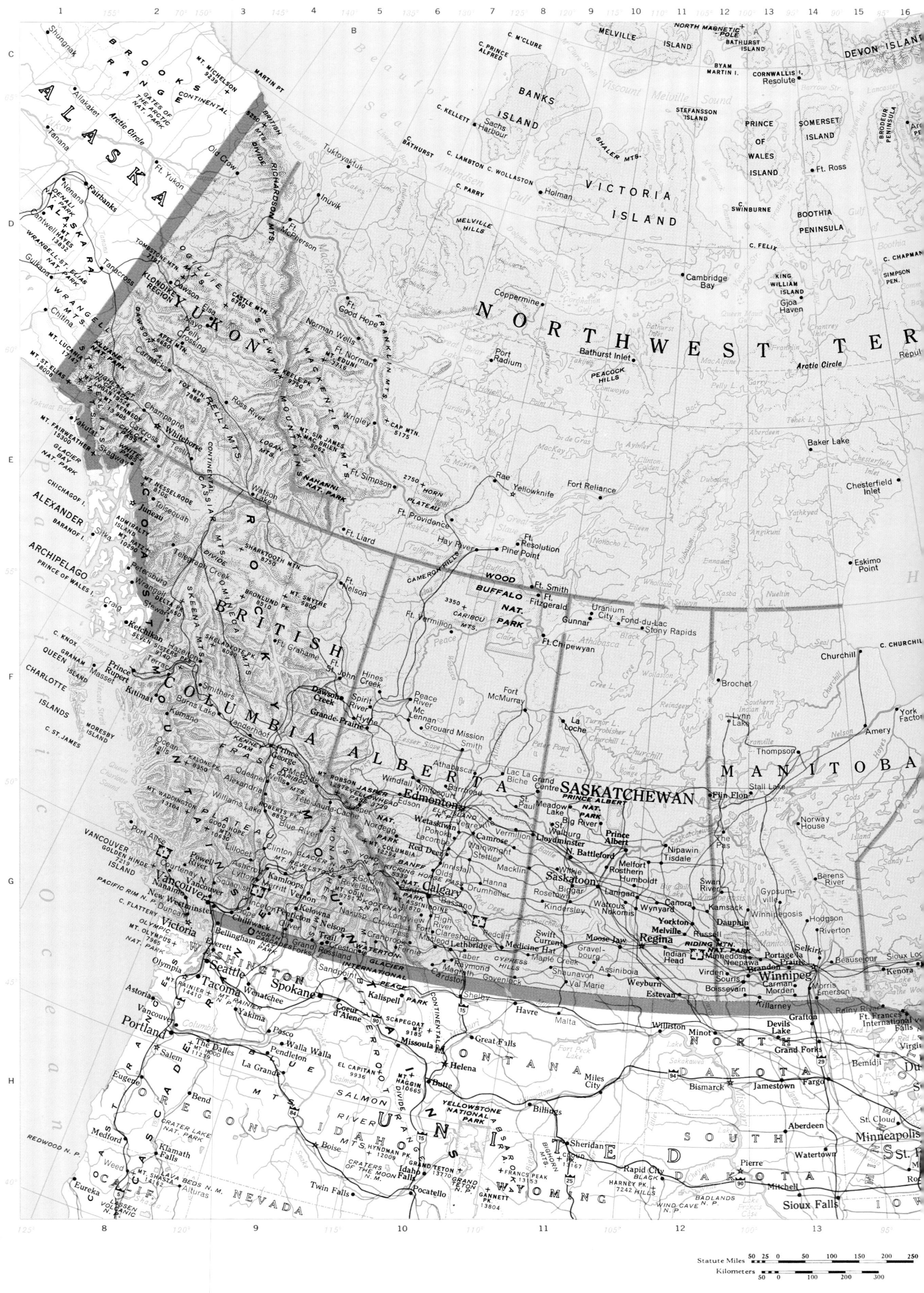

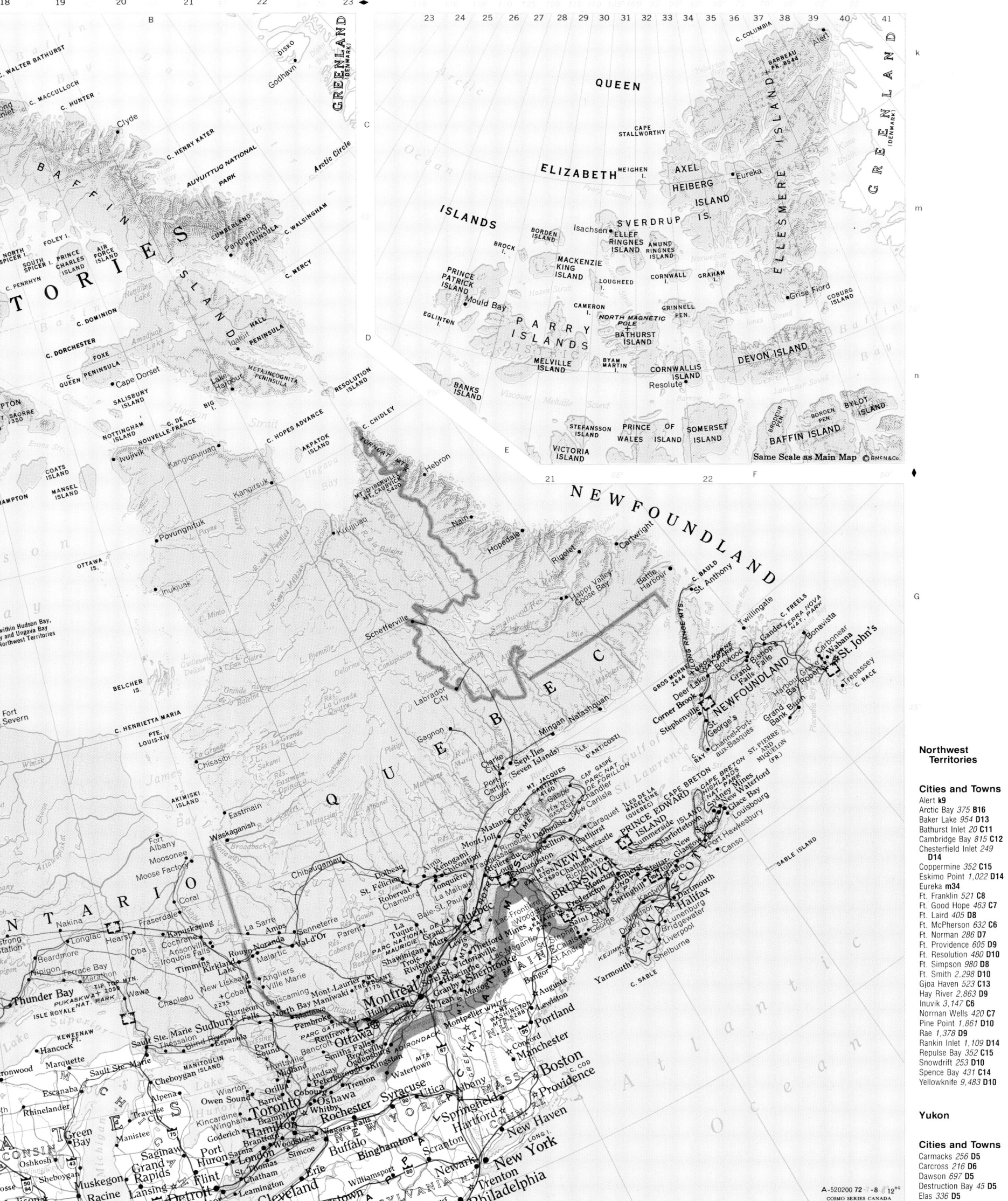

Lambert Conformal Conic Projection
SCALE 1:12,000,000   1 Inch = 189 Statute Miles

A-520200 72 -7 -8 12
COSMO SERIES CANADA
Copyright by
Rand McNally & Company
Made in U.S.A.

Longitude West of Greenwich

Northwest Territories

Cities and Towns
Alert **k9**
Arctic Bay *375* **B16**
Baker Lake *954* **D13**
Bathurst Inlet *20* **C11**
Cambridge Bay *815* **C12**
Chesterfield Inlet *249* **D14**
Coppermine *352* **C15**
Eskimo Point *1,022* **D14**
Eureka **m34**
Ft. Franklin *521* **C8**
Ft. Good Hope *463* **C7**
Ft. Laird *405* **D8**
Ft. McPherson *632* **C6**
Ft. Norman *286* **D7**
Ft. Providence *605* **D9**
Ft. Resolution *480* **D10**
Ft. Simpson *980* **D8**
Ft. Smith *2,298* **D10**
Gjoa Haven *523* **C13**
Hay River *2,863* **D9**
Inuvik *3,147* **C6**
Norman Wells *420* **C7**
Pine Point *1,861* **D10**
Rae *1,378* **D9**
Rankin Inlet *1,109* **D14**
Repulse Bay *352* **C15**
Snowdrift *253* **D10**
Spence Bay *431* **C14**
Yellowknife *9,483* **D10**

Yukon

Cities and Towns
Carmacks *256* **D5**
Carcross *216* **D6**
Dawson *697* **D5**
Destruction Bay *45* **D5**
Elas *336* **D5**
Faro *1,652* **D6**
Haines Junction *366* **D5**
Mayo *398* **D5**
Old Crow *243* **C5**
Pelly Crossing *182* **D5**
Ross River *294* **D6**
Teslin *310* **D6**
Watson Lake *748* **D7**
Whitehorse *14,814* **D6**

Alberta

Cities and Towns

Airdrie 8,414 **D3**
Athabasca 1,731 **B4**
Banff 4,208 **D3**
Barrhead 3,736 **B3**
Bonnyville 4,454 **B5**
Bow Island 1,491 **E5**
Brooks 9,421 **D5**
Calgary 592,743 **D3**
Camrose 12,570 **C4**
Canmore 3,484 **D3**
Cardston 3,267 **E4**
Coaldale 4,579 **E4**
Cochrane 3,544 **D3**
Cold Lake 2,110 **B5**
Coronation 1,309 **C5**
Crowsnest Pass 7,306 **E3**
Devon 3,885 **C4**
Didsbury 3,095 **D3**
Drayton Valley 5,042 **C3**
Drumheller 6,508 **D4**
Edmonton 532,246 **C4**
Edson 5,835 **C2**
Fairview 2,869 **A1**
Fort Chipewyan 944 **f8**
Fort Macleod 3,139 **E4**
Fort McMurray 31,000
  A5
Fort Saskatchewan
  12,169 **C4**
Gibbons 2,276 **C4**
Grand Centre 3,146 **B5**
Grande Cache 4,523 **C1**
Grande Prairie 24,263 **B1**
Grimshaw 2,316 **A2**
Hanna 2,806 **D5**
High Prairie 2,506 **B2**
High River 4,792 **D4**
Hinton 8,342 **C2**
Innisfail 5,247 **C4**
Jasper 3,269 **C1**
Lac La Biche 2,007 **B5**
La Crete 479 **f7**
Lake Louise 355 **D2**
Leduc 12,471 **C4**
Lethbridge 54,072 **E4**
Lloydminster 15,031 **C5**
Magrath 1,576 **E4**
Medicine Hat 40,380 **D5**
Morinville 4,657 **C4**
Nordegg 63 **C2**
Okotoks 3,847 **D4**
Olds 4,813 **D3**
Peace River 5,907 **A2**
Pincher Creek 3,757 **E4**
Ponoka 5,221 **C4**
Raymond 2,837 **E4**
Redcliff 3,876 **D5**
Red Deer 46,393 **C4**
Rocky Mountain House
  4,698 **C3**
St. Albert 31,996 **C4**
St. Paul 4,884 **B5**
Sherwood Park 29,285
  C4
Slave Lake 4,506 **B3**
Smith 216 **B3**
Spruce Grove 10,326 **C4**
Stettler 5,136 **C4**
Stony Plain 4,839 **C3**
Strathmore 2,986 **D4**
Swan Hills 2,497 **B3**
Sylvan Lake 3,779 **C3**
Taber 5,988 **E4**
Valleyview 2,061 **B2**
Vegreville 5,251 **C4**
Vermilion 3,766 **C5**
Vulcan 1,489 **D4**
Wainwright 4,266 **C5**
Westlock 4,424 **B4**
Wetaskiwin 9,597 **C4**
Whitecourt 5,585 **B3**

British Columbia

Cities and Towns

Abbotsford 12,745 **f13**
Armstrong 2,683 **D8**
Burnaby 136,494 **f13**
Burns Lake 1,777 **B5**
Campbell River 15,832 **D5**
Castlegar 6,902 **E9**
Chase 1,777 **D8**
Chetwynd 2,553 **B7**
Chilliwack 40,642 **f14**
Comax 6,607 **E5**
Courtenay 8,992 **E5**
Cranbrook 15,915 **E10**
Creston 4,190 **E9**
Cumberland 1,947 **E5**
Dawson Creek 11,373 **B7**
Duncan 4,228 **g12**
Enderby 1,816 **D8**
Esquimalt 15,870 **h12**
Fernie 5,444 **E10**
Fort Langley 2,326 **f13**
Fort Nelson 3,724 **m18**
Fort St. James 2,284 **B5**
Fort St. John 13,891 **A7**
Fraser Lake 1,543 **B5**
Fruitvale 1,904 **E9**
Gibsons 2,594 **E5**
Golden 3,476 **D9**
Grand Forks 3,486 **E8**
Houston 1,714 **B4**
Invermere 1,969 **D9**
Kamloops 64,048 **D7**
Kelowna 59,196 **E8**
Kimberley 7,375 **E9**
Kitimat 12,814 **B3**
Ladysmith 4,558 **g12**
Lake Cowichan 2,391 **g11**
Langley 15,124 **f13**
Lillooet 1,725 **D7**
Masset 1,569 **C1**
Merritt 6,110 **D7**
Mission 9,948 **f13**
Nanaimo 47,069 **f12**
Nelson 9,143 **E9**
New Westminster 38,550 **f13**
North Vancouver 33,952 **E6**
Oak Bay 16,990 **h12**
100 Mile House 1,925 **D7**
Osoyoos 2,738 **E8**
Parksville 5,216 **E5**
Penticton 23,181 **E8**
Port Alberni 19,892 **E5**
Port Alice 1,668 **D4**
Port Coquitlam 27,535 **f13**
Port Hardy 3,778 **D4**
Powell River 13,423 **E5**
Prince George 67,559 **C6**
Prince Rupert 16,197 **B2**
Qualicum Beach 2,844 **E5**
Quesnel 8,240 **C6**
Revelstoke 5,544 **D8**
Richmond 96,154 **f12**
Salmon Arm 1,946 **D8**
Sidney 7,946 **g12**
Smithers 4,570 **B4**
Squamish 1,590 **E6**
Summerland 7,473 **E8**
Terrace 10,914 **B3**
Trail 9,599 **E9**
Ucluelet 1,593 **E5**
Vancouver 414,281 **f12**
Vanderhoof 2,323 **C5**
Vernon 19,987 **D8**
Victoria 64,379 **h12**
Warfield 1,969 **E9**
White Rock 13,550 **f13**
Williams Lake 8,362 **C6**

Oblique Cylindrical Projection
SCALE 1:4,255,000 1 Inch = 67 Statute Miles

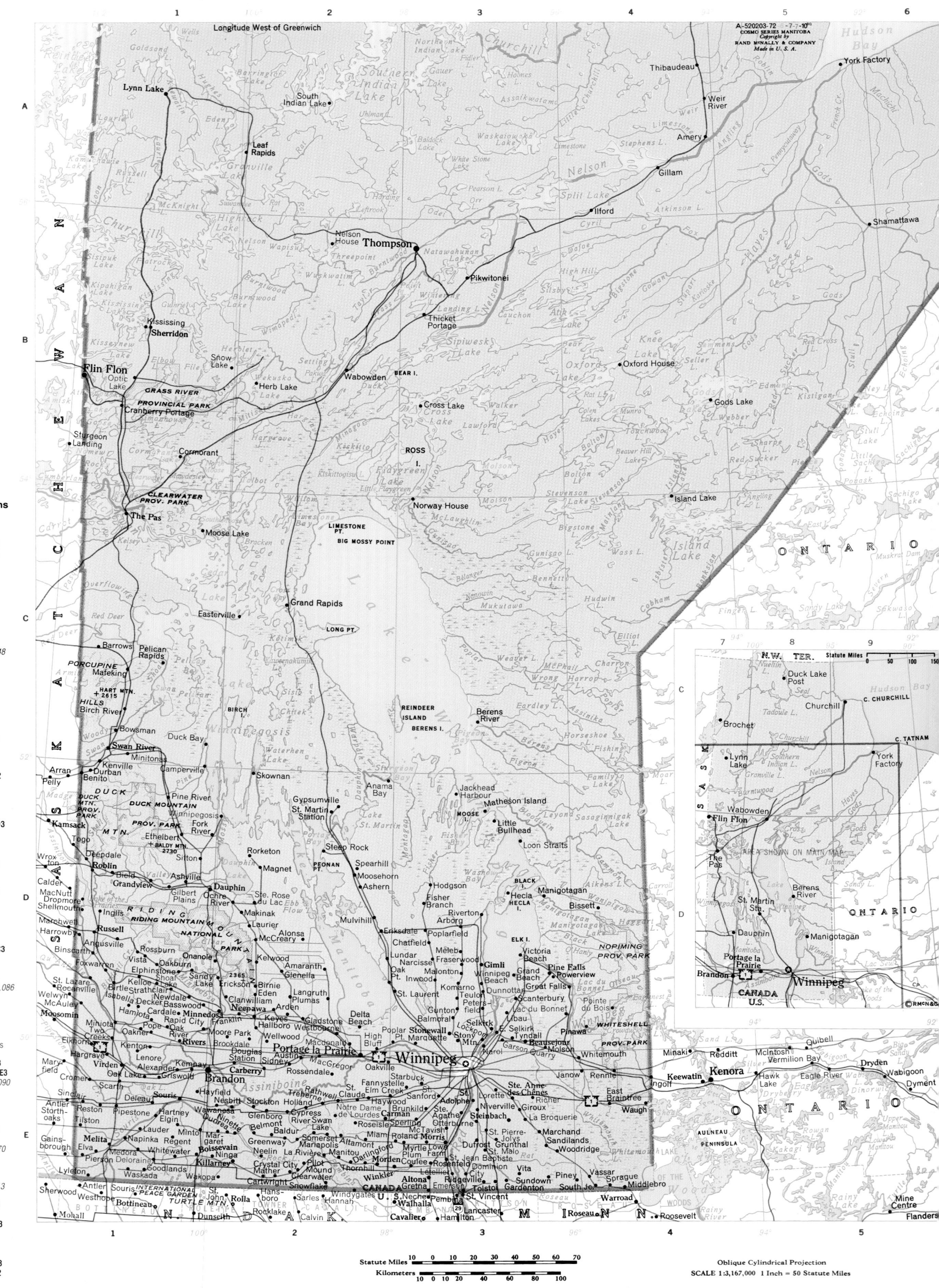

Manitoba

Cities and Towns

Altona *2,757* E3
Arborg *974* D3
Ashern *570* D2
Beausejour *2,462* D3
Berens River *238* C3
Birch River *597* C1
Birtle *887* D1
Boissevain *1,660* E1
Brandon *36,242* E2
Camperville *586* D1
Carberry *1,510* E2
Carman *2,408* E2
Churchill *1,304* f9
Cormorant *445* B1
Cranberry Portage *948*
  B1
Cross Lake *510* B3
Dauphin *8,971* D1
Deloraine *1,136* E1
Duck Bay *594* C1
Easterville *589* C2
Emerson *762* E3
Flin Flon *8,261* B1
Gilbert Plains *812* D1
Gillam *1,427* A4
Gladstone *964* D2
Glenboro *741* E2
Grand Rapids *567* C2
Grandview *1,013* D1
Hamiota *728* D1
Ilford *149* A4
Killarney *2,342* E2
Lac-du-Bonnet *985* D3
Lorette *1,092* E3
Lynn Lake *2,087* A1
MacGregor *795* E2
Manigotagan *216* D3
Manitou *861* E2
Melita *1,156* E1
Minnedosa *2,637* D2
Moose Lake *557* C1
Morden *4,579* E2
Morris *1,570* E3
Neepawa *3,425* D2
Niverville *1,329* E3
Norway House *441* C3
Pilot Mound *838* E2
Pine Falls *885* D3
Plum Coulee *592* E3
Portage-la-Prairie *13,086*
  E2
Rivers *1,107* D1
Roblin *1,953* D1
Rossburn *696* D1
Russell *1,660* D1
Ste. Anne-des-Chênes
  1,338 E3
St. Laurent *1,114* D3
St. Pierre-Jolys *919* E3
Ste. Rose-du-Lac *1,090*
  D2
Selkirk *10,037* D3
Sherridon *138* B1
Shoal Lake *835* D1
Snow Lake *1,853* B1
Souris *1,731* E1
South Indian Lake *770*
  A2
Steinbach *6,676* E3
Stonewall *2,210* D3
Stony Mountain *1,313*
Swan River *3,782* C1
The Pas *6,390* C1
Thompson *14,288* B3
Virden *2,940* E1
Wabowden *655* B2
Winkler *5,046* E3
Winnipeg *564,473* E3
Winnipegosis *855* D2
York Factory *A5*

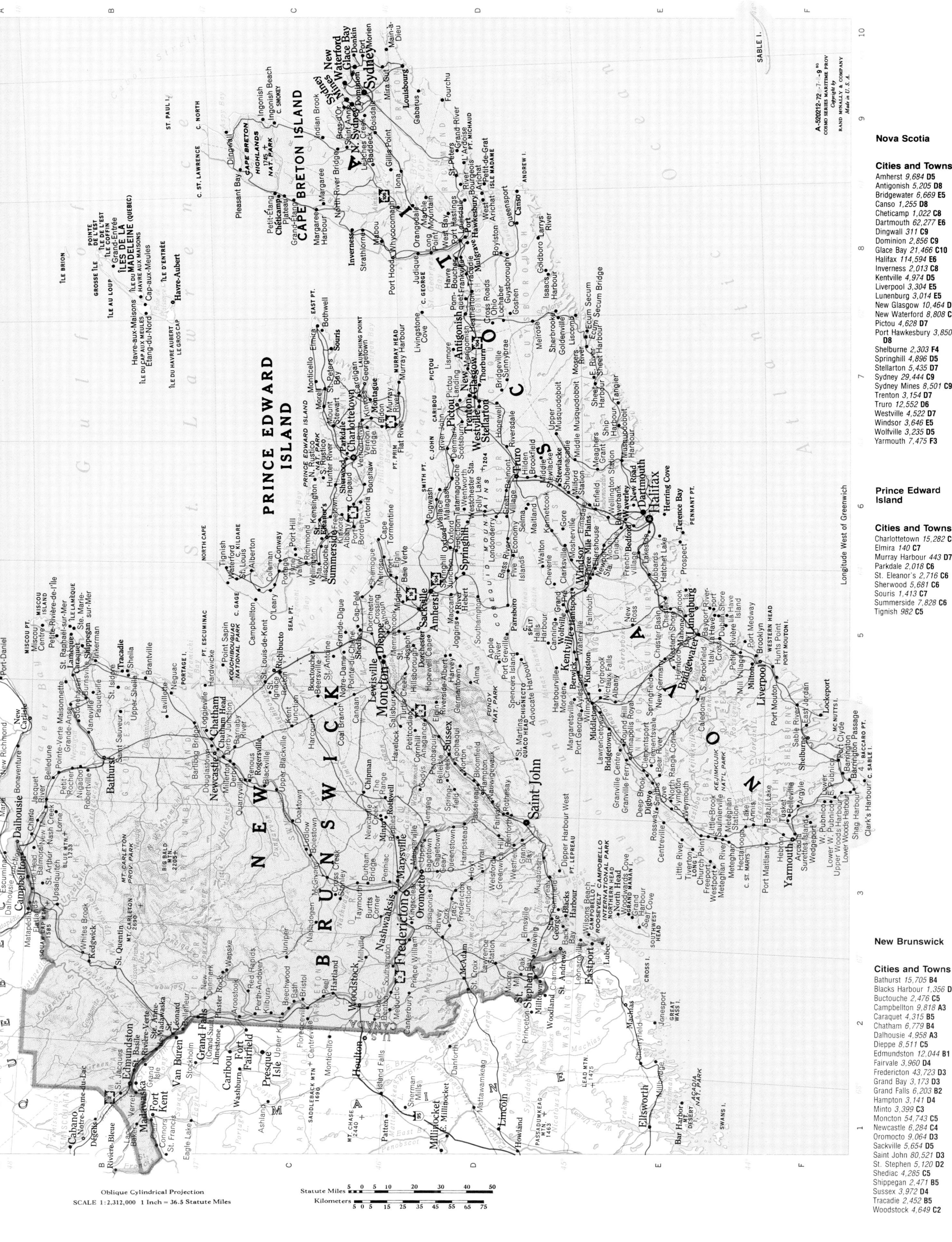

SABLE I.

A-500212-72 -7- -9 80
COSMO SERIES MARITIME PROV
Copyright by
RAND McNALLY & COMPANY
Made in U.S.A.

Nova Scotia

Cities and Towns

Amherst 9,684 **D5**
Antigonish 5,205 **D8**
Bridgewater 6,669 **E5**
Canso 1,255 **D8**
Cheticamp 1,022 **C8**
Dartmouth 62,277 **E6**
Dingwall 311 **C9**
Dominion 2,856 **C9**
Glace Bay 21,466 **C10**
Halifax 114,594 **E6**
Inverness 2,013 **C8**
Kentville 4,974 **D5**
Liverpool 3,304 **E5**
Lunenburg 3,014 **E5**
New Glasgow 10,464 **D7**
New Waterford 8,808 **C9**
Pictou 4,628 **D7**
Port Hawkesbury 3,850 **D8**
Shelburne 2,303 **F4**
Springhill 4,896 **D5**
Stellarton 5,435 **D7**
Sydney 29,444 **C9**
Sydney Mines 8,501 **C9**
Trenton 3,154 **D7**
Truro 12,552 **D6**
Westville 4,522 **D7**
Windsor 3,646 **E5**
Wolfville 3,235 **D5**
Yarmouth 7,475 **F3**

Prince Edward Island

Cities and Towns

Charlottetown 15,282 **C6**
Elmira 140 **C7**
Murray Harbour 443 **D7**
Parkdale 2,018 **C6**
St. Eleanor's 2,716 **C6**
Sherwood 5,681 **C6**
Souris 1,413 **C7**
Summerside 7,828 **C6**
Tignish 982 **C5**

New Brunswick

Cities and Towns

Bathurst 15,705 **B4**
Blacks Harbour 1,356 **D3**
Buctouche 2,476 **C5**
Campbellton 9,818 **A3**
Caraquet 4,315 **B5**
Chatham 6,779 **B4**
Dalhousie 4,958 **A3**
Dieppe 8,511 **C5**
Edmundston 12,044 **B1**
Fairvale 3,960 **D4**
Fredericton 43,723 **D3**
Grand Bay 3,173 **D3**
Grand Falls 6,203 **B2**
Hampton 3,141 **D4**
Minto 3,399 **C3**
Moncton 54,743 **C5**
Newcastle 6,284 **C4**
Oromocto 9,064 **D3**
Sackville 5,654 **D5**
Saint John 80,521 **D3**
St. Stephen 5,120 **D2**
Shediac 4,285 **C5**
Shippegan 2,471 **B5**
Sussex 3,972 **D4**
Tracadie 2,452 **B5**
Woodstock 4,649 **C2**

Oblique Cylindrical Projection
SCALE 1:2,312,000 1 Inch = 36.5 Statute Miles

Statute Miles
Kilometers

NEWFOUNDLAND

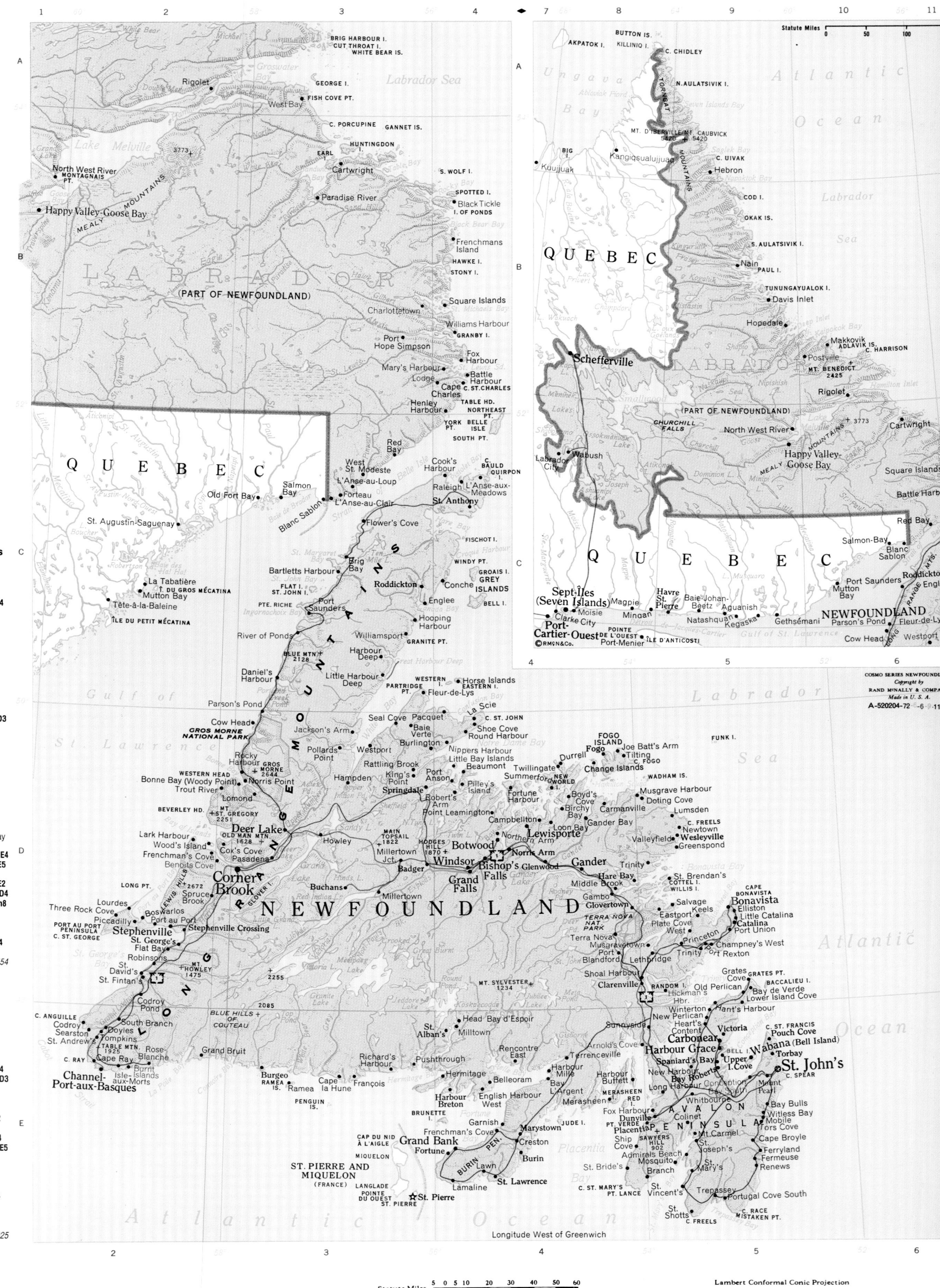

Newfoundland

Cities and Towns

Badger *1,090* **D3**
Baie Verte *2,491* **D3**
Bay Bulls *1,081* **E5**
Bay Roberts *4,512* **E5**
Bishop's Falls *4,395* **D4**
Bonavista *4,460* **D5**
Botwood *4,074* **D4**
Buchans *1,655* **D3**
Burgeo *2,504* **E3**
Burin *2,904* **E4**
Carbonear *5,335* **E5**
Cartwright *658* **D4**
Catalina *1,162* **D5**
Channel-Port-aux-
   Basques *5,988* **E2**
Clarenville *2,878* **D4**
Corner Brook *24,339* **D3**
Deer Lake *4,348* **D3**
Dunville *1,817* **E5**
Durrell *1,145* **D4**
Fogo *1,105* **D4**
Fortune *2,473* **E4**
Gambo *2,932* **D4**
Gander *10,404* **D4**
Glenwood *1,129* **D4**
Glovertown *2,165* **D4**
Grand Bank *3,901* **E4**
Grand Falls *8,765* **D4**
Happy Valley-Goose Bay
   7,103 **B1**
Harbour Breton *2,464* **E4**
Harbour Grace *2,988* **E5**
Hare Bay *1,520* **D4**
Isle-aux-Morts *1,238* **E2**
Joe Batt's Arm *1,155* **D4**
Labrador City *11,538* **h8**
La Scie *1,422* **D4**
Lewisporte *3,963* **D4**
Marystown *6,299* **E4**
Middle Brook *1,083* **D4**
Milltown *1,376* **E4**
Musgrave Harbour *1,554*
   D5
Nain *938* **g9**
Norris Arm *1,216* **D4**
Norris Point *1,033* **D3**
Pasadena *2,685* **D3**
Placentia *2,204* **E5**
Pouch Cove *1,522* **E5**
Ramea *1,386* **E3**
Red Bay *316* **C3**
Rigolet *271* **A2**
Robert's Arm *1,005* **D4**
Rocky Harbour *1,273* **D3**
Roddickton *1,142* **C3**
St. Alban's *1,968* **E4**
St. Anthony *3,107* **C4**
St. George's *1,756* **D2**
St. John's *83,770* **E5**
St. Lawrence *2,012* **E4**
Spaniard's Bay *2,125* **E5**
Springdale *3,501* **D3**
Stephenville *8,876* **D2**
Stephenville Crossing
   2,172 **D2**
Summerford *1,198* **D4**
Torbay *3,394* **E5**
Trepassey *1,473* **E5**
Twillingate *1,506* **D4**
Upper Island Cove *2,025*
   E5
Victoria *1,870* **E5**
Wabana (Bell Island)
   4,254 **E5**
Wabush *3,155* **h8**
Wesleyville *1,225* **D5**
Windsor *5,747* **D4**

♦ **Ontario**

Cities and Towns

Ajax 25,475 D6
Atikokan 4,389 o17
Barrie 38,423 C5
Belleville 34,881 C7
Brampton 149,030 D5
Brantford 74,315 D4
Brockville 19,896 C9
Burlington 114,853 D5
Cambridge 77,183 D4
Chatham 40,952 E2
Cobourg 11,385 D6
Cornwall 46,144 B10
Dryden 6,640 o16
Dundas 19,586 D5
Etobicoke 298,713 D5
Fergus 6,064 D4
Fort Erie 24,096 E6
Gloucester 72,859 h12
Guelph 71,207 D4
Haileybury 4,925 p20
Hamilton 306,434 D5
Hawkesbury 9,877 B10
Kapuskasing 12,014 o19
Kenora 9,817 o16
Kingston 52,616 C8
Kirkland Lake 12,219
  o19
Kitchener 139,734 D4
Lansdowne House 161
  n18
Leamington 12,528 E2
Lindsay 13,596 C6
London 254,280 E3
Markham 77,037 k15
Midland 12,132 C5
Milton 28,067 D5
Mississauga 315,056 D5
Moosonee 1,433 o19
Nakina 936 o18
Nanticoke 19,816 E4
Newcastle 32,229 D6
Newmarket 29,753 C5
Niagara Falls 70,960 D5
Nipigon 2,377 o17
North Bay 51,268 A5
Oakville 75,773 D5
Orillia 23,955 C5
Oshawa 117,519 D6
Ottawa 295,163 h12
Owen Sound 19,883 C4
Pembroke 14,026 B7
Petawawa 5,520 B7
Peterborough 60,620 C6
Port Colborne 19,225 E5
Red Lake 2,065 o16
Richmond Hill 37,778
  k15
St. Catharines 124,018
  D5
Sarnia 50,892 E2
Sault Ste. Marie 82,697
  p18
Scarborough 443,353
  m15
Sioux Lookout 3,074 o17
Smiths Falls 8,831 C8
Stratford 26,262 D3
Sturgeon Falls 6,045 A5
Sudbury 91,829 A4
Tecumseh 6,364 E2
Thunder Bay 112,486
  o17
Timmins 46,114 o19

Toronto 599,217 m15
Trenton 15,085 C7
Vanier (Eastview)
  18,792 h12
Vaughan 29,674 k14
Welland 45,448 E5
Whitby 36,698 D6
Windsor 192,083 E1
Woodstock 26,603 D4
York 134,617 m15

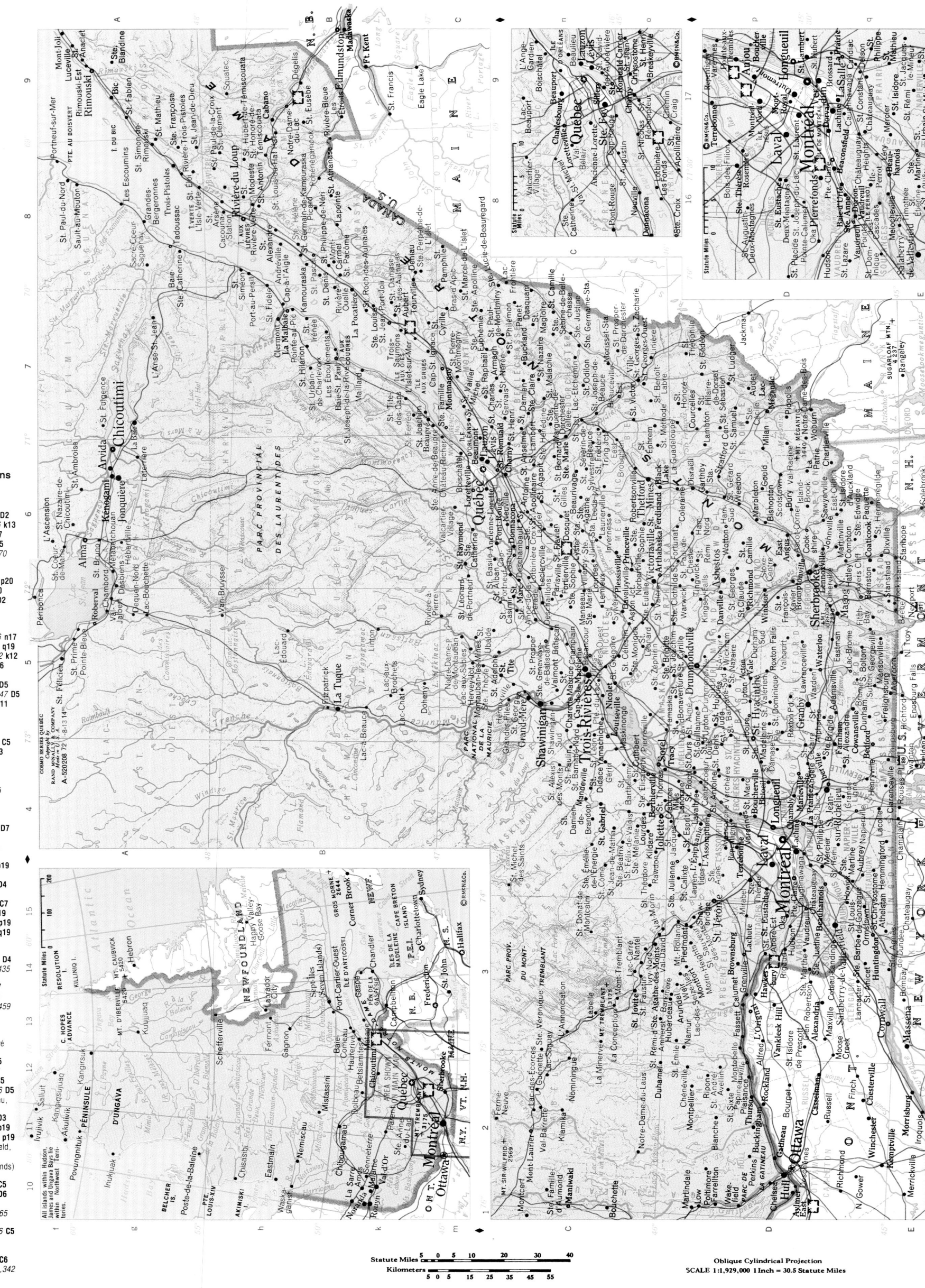

Quebec

Cities and Towns

Alma *26,322* **A6**
Anjou *37,346* **p19**
Asbestos *7,967* **D6**
Aylmer East *26,695* **D2**
Baie-Comeau *12,866* **k13**
Beauport *60,447* **n17**
Bécancour *10,247* **C5**
Bellin (Kangiqsuk) *270* **f12**
Beloeil *17,540* **D4**
Boucherville *29,704* **p20**
Brossard *52,232* **q20**
Buckingham *7,992* **D2**
Cap-de-la-Madeleine *32,626* **C5**
Chambly *12,190* **D4**
Charlesbourg *68,326* **n17**
Châteauguay *36,928* **q19**
Chibougamau *10,732* **k12**
Chicoutimi *60,064* **A6**
Coaticook *6,271* **D6**
Cowansville *12,240* **D5**
Drummondville *27,347* **D5**
Fort-George *2,222* **h11**
Gaspé *17,261* **k14**
Gatineau *74,988* **D2**
Granby *38,069* **D5**
Grand' Mère *15,442* **C5**
Hauterive *13,995* **k13**
Hull *56,225* **D2**
Iberville *8,587* **D4**
Joliette *16,987* **C4**
Jonquière *60,354* **A6**
La Baie *20,935* **A7**
Lachine *37,521* **q19**
Lachute *11,729* **D3**
Lac Mégantic *6,119* **D7**
LaSalle *76,299* **q19**
La Tuque *11,556* **B5**
Laval *268,335* **p19**
Longueuil *124,320* **p19**
Magog *13,604* **D5**
Mascouche *20,345* **D4**
Matane *13,612* **k13**
Montmagny *12,405* **C7**
Montréal *980,354* **q19**
Mont-Royal *19,247* **p19**
Pierrefonds *38,390* **q19**
Pointe-aux-Trembles *36,270* **p20**
Pointe-Claire *24,571* **D4**
Poste-de-la-Baleine *435* **g11**
Québec *166,474* **n17**
Rimouski *29,120* **A9**
Rivière-du-Loup *13,459* **B8**
Roberval *11,429* **A5**
Rouyn *17,224* **k11**
Ste. Anne-de-Beaupré *3,292* **B7**
St. Félicien *9,058* **A5**
Ste. Foy *68,883* **n17**
St. Georges *3,344* **C5**
St. Hyacinthe *38,246* **D5**
St. Jean-sur-Richelieu, *35,640* **D4**
St. Jérôme *25,123* **D3**
St. Laurent *65,900* **p19**
Ste. Thérèse *18,750* **p19**
Salaberry-de-Valleyfield, *29,574* **q18**
Sept-îles (Seven Islands) *29,262* **h13**
Shawinigan *23,011* **C5**
Sherbrooke *74,075* **D6**
Sorel *20,347* **C4**
Thetford Mines *19,965* **C6**
Trois-Rivières *50,466* **C5**
Val-d'Or *21,371* **k11**
Verdun *61,287* **q19**
Victoriaville *21,838* **C6**
Ville St. Georges *10,342* **C7**

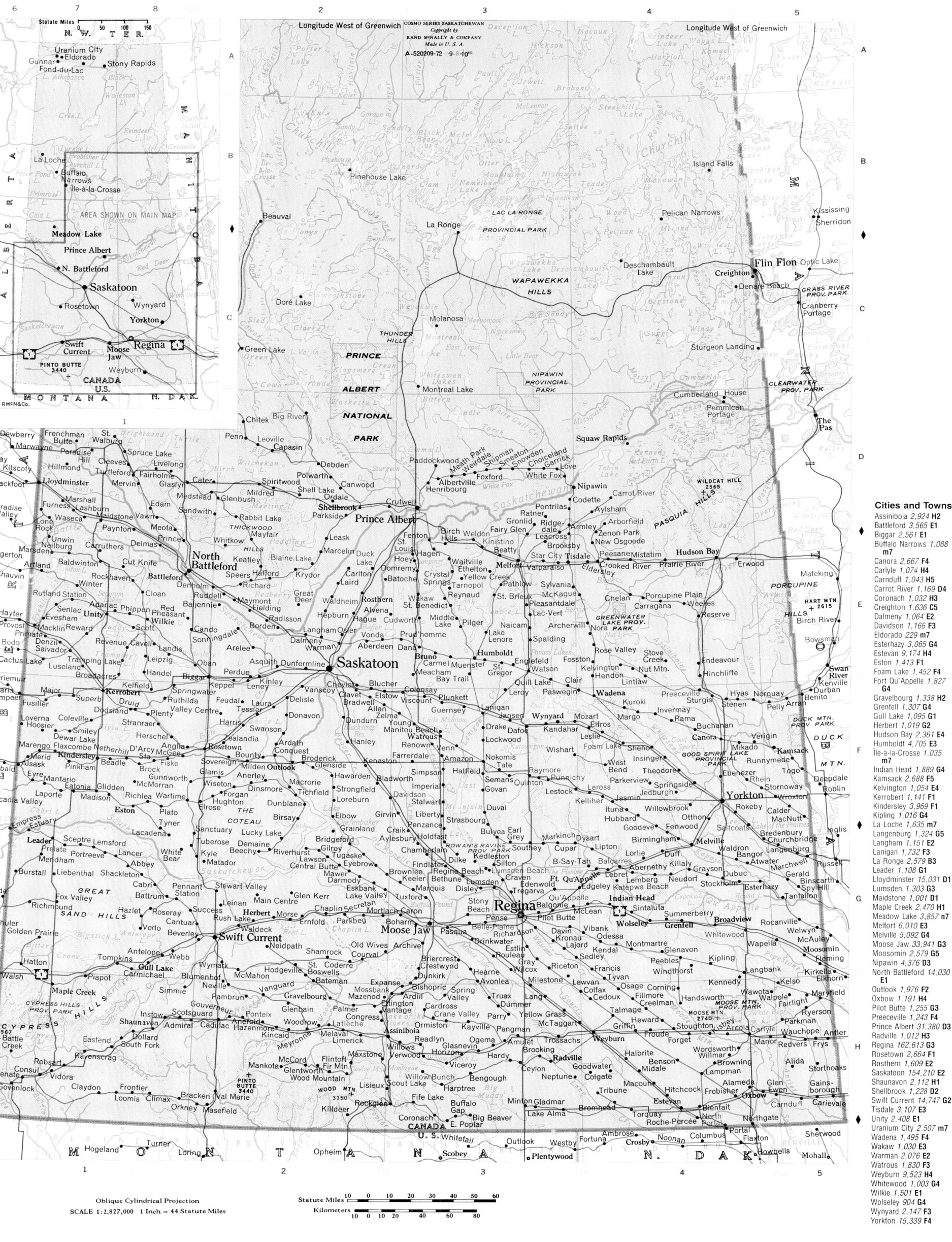

Cities and Towns

Assiniboia 2,924 H2
Battleford 3,565 E1
Biggar 2,561 E1
Buffalo Narrows 1,088 m7
Canora 2,667 F4
Carlyle 1,074 H4
Carnduff 1,043 H5
Carrot River 1,169 D4
Coronach 1,032 H3
Creighton 1,636 C5
Dalmeny 1,064 E2
Davidson 1,166 F3
Eldorado 229 m7
Esterhazy 3,065 G4
Estevan 9,174 H4
Eston 1,413 F1
Foam Lake 1,452 F4
Fort Qu'Appelle 1,827 G4
Gravelbourg 1,338 H2
Grenfell 1,307 G4
Gull Lake 1,095 G1
Herbert 1,019 G2
Hudson Bay 2,361 E4
Humboldt 4,705 E3
Ile-à-la-Crosse 1,035 m7
Indian Head 1,889 G4
Kamsack 2,688 F5
Kelvington 1,054 E4
Kerrobert 1,141 F1
Kindersley 3,969 F1
Kipling 1,016 G4
La Loche 1,635 m7
Langenburg 1,324 G5
Langham 1,151 E2
Lanigan 1,732 F3
La Ronge 2,579 B3
Leader 1,108 G1
Lloydminster 15,031 D1
Lumsden 1,303 G3
Maidstone 1,001 D1
Maple Creek 2,470 H1
Meadow Lake 3,857 m7
Melfort 6,010 E3
Melville 5,092 G4
Moose Jaw 33,941 G3
Moosomin 2,579 G5
Nipawin 4,376 D3
North Battleford 14,030 E1
Outlook 1,976 F2
Oxbow 1,191 H4
Pilot Butte 1,255 G3
Preeceville 1,243 F4
Prince Albert 31,380 D3
Radville 1,012 H3
Regina 162,613 G3
Rosetown 2,664 F1
Rosthern 1,609 E2
Saskatoon 154,210 E2
Shaunavon 2,112 H1
Shellbrook 1,228 D2
Swift Current 14,747 G2
Tisdale 3,107 E3
Unity 2,408 E1
Uranium City 2,507 m7
Wadena 1,495 F4
Wakaw 1,030 E3
Warman 2,076 E2
Watrous 1,830 F3
Weyburn 9,523 H4
Whitewood 1,003 G4
Wilkie 1,501 E1
Wolseley 904 G4
Wynyard 2,147 F3
Yorkton 15,339 F4

The United States and Canada / Facts in Brief

The table below provides a brief description of the United States and Canada. The chief products list includes the top products for each state, province, or territory in three major areas of production. The summary entry for each country indicates the national capital and the country's major products in agriculture, manufacturing, and mining.

The United States

State	Entered Union	Capital	Agriculture	Manufacturing	Mining
				CHIEF PRODUCTS	
Alabama	December 14, 1819, 22nd state	Montgomery	Broilers, beef cattle, soybeans	Metals, paper prod., chemicals	Coal, petroleum, natural gas
Alaska	January 3, 1959, 49th state	Juneau	Greenhouse and nursery prod., milk, potatoes	Food, paper prod., lumber and wood prod.	Petroleum, natural gas, sand and gravel
Arizona	February 14, 1912, 48th state	Phoenix	Beef cattle, cotton, milk	Nonelec. machinery, elec. machinery and equip., trans. equip.	Copper, molybdenum, coal
Arkansas	June 15, 1836, 25th state	Little Rock	Soybeans, broilers, rice	Food, elec. machinery and equip., lumber and wood prod.	Petroleum, bromine, natural gas
California	September 9, 1850, 31st state	Sacramento	Beef cattle, milk, grapes	Trans. equip., elec. machinery and equip., food	Petroleum, cement, natural gas
Colorado	August 1, 1876, 38th state	Denver	Beef cattle, wheat, corn	Food, instruments, nonelec. machinery	Petroleum, molybdenum, coal
Connecticut	January 9, 1788, 5th state	Hartford	Milk, eggs, greenhouse and nursery prod.	Trans. equip., nonelec. machinery, metal prod.	Stone, sand and gravel
Delaware	December 7, 1787, 1st state	Dover	Broilers, soybeans, corn	Chemicals, food, metal prod.	Sand and gravel, magnesium compounds
Florida	March 3, 1845, 27th state	Tallahassee	Oranges, beef cattle, greenhouse and nursery prod.	Food, elec. machinery and equip., trans. equip.	Phosphate rock, petroleum, stone
Georgia	January 2, 1788, 4th state	Atlanta	Broilers, peanuts, eggs	Textiles, food, trans. equip.	Clays, stone, sand and gravel
Hawaii	August 21, 1959, 50th state	Honolulu	Sugar cane, pineapples, milk	Food, printed materials, clothing	Stone, sand and gravel
Idaho	July 3, 1890, 43rd state	Boise	Beef cattle, potatoes, wheat	Lumber and wood prod., food, chemicals	Phosphate rock, silver, lead
Illinois	December 3, 1818, 21st state	Springfield	Corn, soybeans, hogs	Nonelec. machinery, food, elec. machinery and equip.	Coal, petroleum, stone
Indiana	December 11, 1816, 19th state	Indianapolis	Corn, soybeans, hogs	Metals, trans. equip., elec. machinery and equip.	Coal
Iowa	December 28, 1846, 29th state	Des Moines	Beef cattle, hogs, soybeans	Nonelec. machinery, food, elec. machinery and equip.	Stone, sand and gravel
Kansas	January 29, 1861, 34th state	Topeka	Beef cattle, wheat, sorghum grain	Trans. equip., nonelec. machinery, food	Petroleum, natural gas, natural gas liquids
Kentucky	June 1, 1792, 15th state	Frankfort	Tobacco, beef cattle, soybeans	Nonelec. machinery, trans. equip., elec. machinery and equip.	Coal, stone, petroleum
Louisiana	April 30, 1812, 18th state	Baton Rouge	Soybeans, beef cattle, rice	Chemicals, petroleum and coal prod., food	Natural gas, petroleum, natural gas liquids
Maine	March 15, 1820, 23rd state	Augusta	Potatoes, eggs, broilers	Paper prod., leather prod., lumber and wood prod.	Sand and gravel, zinc
Maryland	April 28, 1788, 7th state	Annapolis	Broilers, milk, corn	Food, elec. and electronic equip., metals	Coal, stone, sand and gravel
Massachusetts	February 6, 1788, 6th state	Boston	Milk, greenhouse and nursery prod., eggs	Nonelec. machinery, elec. and electronic equip., instruments	Stone, sand and gravel, lime
Michigan	January 26, 1837, 26th state	Lansing	Milk, beef cattle, corn	Trans. equip., nonelec. machinery, metal prod.	Iron ore, petroleum, natural gas
Minnesota	May 11, 1858, 32nd state	St. Paul	Milk, soybeans, beef cattle	Nonelec. machinery, food, metal prod.	Iron ore, sand and gravel, stone
Mississippi	December 10, 1817, 20th state	Jackson	Soybeans, cotton, beef cattle	Trans. equip., elec. machinery and equip., lumber and wood prod.	Petroleum, natural gas, sand and gravel
Missouri	August 10, 1821, 24th state	Jefferson City	Beef cattle, soybeans, hogs	Trans. equip., food, chemicals	Lead, stone
Montana	November 8, 1889, 41st state	Helena	Beef cattle, wheat, barley	Lumber and wood prod., food, petroleum and coal prod.	Petroleum, coal, copper
Nebraska	March 1, 1867, 37th state	Lincoln	Beef cattle, corn, hogs	Food, nonelec. machinery, elec. and electronic equip.	Petroleum, sand and gravel
Nevada	October 31, 1864, 36th state	Carson City	Beef cattle, milk, hay	Food, printed materials, chemicals	Gold, barite, copper
New Hampshire	June 21, 1788, 9th state	Concord	Milk, eggs, apples	Elec. and electronic equip., nonelec. machinery, instruments	Sand and gravel, stone
New Jersey	December 18, 1787, 3rd state	Trenton	Milk, greenhouse and nursery prod., tomatoes	Chemicals, food, elec. machinery and equip.	Stone, sand and gravel, zinc
New Mexico	January 6, 1912, 47th state	Santa Fe	Beef cattle, cotton, milk	Food, elec. and electronic equip., printed materials	Natural gas, petroleum, natural gas liquids
New York	July 26, 1788, 11th state	Albany	Milk, beef cattle, apples	Printed materials, instruments, nonelec. machinery	Stone, salt, sand and gravel
North Carolina	November 21, 1789, 12th state	Raleigh	Tobacco, broilers, hogs	Textiles, tobacco prod., chemicals	Stone, phosphate rock, sand and gravel
North Dakota	November 2, 1889, 39th state	Bismarck	Wheat, beef cattle, sunflower seeds	Food, nonelec. machinery, printed materials	Petroleum, coal, natural gas
Ohio	March 1, 1803, 17th state	Columbus	Soybeans, corn, milk	Trans. equip., nonelec. machinery, metals	Coal, petroleum, natural gas
Oklahoma	November 16, 1907, 46th state	Oklahoma City	Beef cattle, wheat, milk	Nonelec. machinery, metal prod., petroleum and coal prod.	Petroleum, natural gas, natural gas liquids
Oregon	February 14, 1859, 33rd state	Salem	Beef cattle, wheat, milk	Lumber and wood prod., food, paper prod.	Sand and gravel, stone, nickel
Pennsylvania	December 12, 1787, 2nd state	Harrisburg	Milk, beef cattle, mushrooms	Metals, nonelec. machinery, food	Coal, stone
Rhode Island	May 29, 1790, 13th state	Providence	Greenhouse and nursery prod., milk	Jewelry and silverware, metal prod., nonelec. machinery	Sand and gravel, stone
South Carolina	May 23, 1788, 8th state	Columbia	Soybeans, tobacco, beef cattle	Textiles, chemicals, nonelec. machinery	Stone, clays
South Dakota	November 2, 1889, 40th state	Pierre	Beef cattle, hogs, milk	Food, nonelec. machinery	Gold, stone
Tennessee	June 1, 1796, 16th state	Nashville	Soybeans, beef cattle, milk	Chemicals, food, nonelec. machinery	Coal, stone, zinc
Texas	December 29, 1845, 28th state	Austin	Beef cattle, cotton	Chemicals, nonelec. machinery, petroleum and coal prod.	Petroleum, natural gas, natural gas liquids
Utah	January 4, 1896, 45th state	Salt Lake City	Beef cattle, milk, hay	Metals, nonelec. machinery, trans. equip.	Copper, petroleum, coal
Vermont	March 4, 1791, 14th state	Montpelier	Milk, beef cattle, eggs	Elec. machinery and equip., nonelec. machinery, printed materials	Stone, asbestos
Virginia	June 25, 1788, 10th state	Richmond	Milk, tobacco, beef cattle	Chemicals, food, tobacco prod.	Coal, stone, lime
Washington	November 11, 1889, 42nd state	Olympia	Wheat, beef cattle, milk	Trans. equip., lumber and wood prod., food	Coal, sand and gravel, stone
West Virginia	June 20, 1863, 35th state	Charleston	Beef cattle, milk, apples	Chemicals; metals; stone, clay, glass prod.	Coal, natural gas, petroleum
Wisconsin	May 29, 1848, 30th state	Madison	Milk, beef cattle, hogs	Nonelec. machinery, food, paper prod.	Sand and gravel, stone, iron ore
Wyoming	July 10, 1890, 44th state	Cheyenne	Beef cattle, sheep, sugar beets	Petroleum and coal prod.; chemicals; stone, clay, glass prod.	Petroleum, coal, trona
UNITED STATES	. . .	Washington, D.C.	Beef cattle, milk, corn	Nonelec. machinery, trans. equip., chemicals	Petroleum, natural gas, coal

Canada

Province/Territory	Entered Dominion	Capital	Agriculture	Manufacturing	Mining
				CHIEF PRODUCTS	
Alberta	September 1, 1905, with Saskatchewan, 8th and 9th provinces	Edmonton	Beef cattle, wheat, rye	Food, chemicals, metal prod.	Petroleum, natural gas, natural gas liquids
British Columbia	July 20, 1871, 6th province	Victoria	Milk, hay, beef cattle	Wood prod., paper prod., food	Coal, copper, natural gas
Manitoba	July 15, 1870, 5th province	Winnipeg	Wheat, beef cattle, hogs	Food, machinery, metal prod.	Nickel, copper, petroleum
New Brunswick	July 1, 1867, one of four original provinces	Fredericton	Potatoes, milk, poultry	Paper prod., food, wood prod.	Zinc, silver, lead
Newfoundland	March 31, 1949, 10th province	St. John's	Eggs, poultry, hogs	Food, paper prod., chemicals	Iron ore, zinc, asbestos
Northwest Territories	—	Yellowknife	—	Food, petroleum prod., wood prod.	Zinc, gold, lead
Nova Scotia	July 1, 1867, one of four original provinces	Halifax	Milk, hogs, poultry	Food, paper prod., trans. equip.	Coal, salt, gypsum
Ontario	July 1, 1867, one of four original provinces	Toronto	Beef cattle, milk, hogs	Trans. equip., food, metal prod.	Nickel, uranium, copper
Prince Edward Island	July 1, 1873, 7th province	Charlottetown	Potatoes, hogs, beef cattle	Food, printed materials, wood prod.	—
Québec	July 1, 1867, one of four original provinces	Québec	Milk, hogs, beef cattle	Food, paper prod., metals	Iron ore, gold, asbestos
Saskatchewan	September 1, 1905, with Alberta, 8th and 9th provinces	Regina	Wheat, beef cattle, rapeseed	Food, machinery, printed materials	Petroleum, potash, uranium
Yukon Territory	—	Whitehorse	—	Lumber and wood prod., printed materials, food	Zinc, lead, silver
CANADA	. . .	Ottawa	Beef cattle, wheat, milk	Food, trans. equip., petroleum and coal prod.	Petroleum, natural gas, natural gas liquids

Abbreviations: elec. = electric; equip. = equipment; nonelec. = nonelectric; prod. = products; trans. equip. = transportation equipment

Geographical Information and Maps of the World Index

World Nations and Other Political Units   **290-296**

World Geographical Tables   **297-299**

Populations of Major Cities   **300-301**

Sources   **302-303**

Transliteration Systems   **304**

Geographical Glossary   **305-312**

Maps of the World Index   **313-432**

World Nations and Other Political Units

This table gives the area, population, population density, form of government, capital, and location of all the world's independent nations and other important political units.

Independent nations appear in **boldface type.** Continents are preceded by daggers.

Area figures include inland water.

The populations are either the estimates (E) or census figures (C) given in the 1988 *The World Book Encyclopedia* or, where noted, estimates (E*) made by Rand McNally and Company on the basis of official data, United Nations estimates, and other available information.

Map plate numbers refer to the Maps of the World section of the atlas.

Political unit	Local name	Area sq. miles	km²	Population	Date	Population density per sq. mile	km²	Form of govt./ Political status	Capital	Continent	Map plate
Afghanistan	Afghanistan	251,773	652,089	17,375,000	1988E	69	27	Socialist Republic	Kabul	Asia	23
†Africa	—	11,694,000	30,330,000	600,000,000	1988E	51	20	—	—	Africa	30–31
Alabama, U.S.	Alabama	51,705	133,915	4,021,000	1985E	78	30	State (U.S.)	Montgomery	North America	44
Alaska, U.S.	Alaska	591,004	1,530,700	521,000	1985E	0.9	0.3	State (U.S.)	Juneau	North America	40
Albania	Shqipëri	11,100	28,748	3,248,000	1988E	293	113	Socialist People's Republic	Tiranë	Europe	15
Alberta, Can.	Alberta	251,870	652,330	2,237,724	1981C	9	3	Province (Canada)	Edmonton	North America	42
Algeria	—	919,595	2,381,741	24,316,000	1988E	26	10	Socialist Republic	Algiers	Africa	32
American Samoa	American Samoa	76	197	37,000	—	487	188	U.S. Territory	Pago Pago	Oceania	65
Andaman and Nicobar Islands, India	Andaman and Nicobar	3,185	8,249	188,254	1981C	59	23	Territory of India	Port Blair	Asia	25
Andorra	Valls d'Andorra (Valleys of Andorra)	179	464	44,000	1988E	246	95	Principality; joint Spanish and French rule	Andorra	Europe	13
Angola	Angola	481,354	1,246,700	9,472,000	1988E	20	8	Communist	Luanda	Africa	36
Anguilla	Anguilla	35	91	7,000	—	200	77	British Dependency	The Valley	North America	51
Anhui, China	Anhwei	54,016	139,900	49,665,724	1982C	919	355	Province (China)	Hefei (Ho-fei)	Asia	28
†Antarctica	—	5,100,000	13,209,000	(1)	—	—	—	—	—	Antarctica	66
Antigua and Barbuda	—	171	442	83,000	—	485	188	Constitutional Monarchy	St. John's	North America	51
Arabian Peninsula	—	1,162,000	3,009,600	27,455,000	1988E	24	9	—	—	Asia	23
Argentina	Argentina	1,073,400	2,780,092	31,965,000	1988E	30	11	Republic; under military control	Buenos Aires	South America	56
Arizona, U.S.	Arizona	114,000	295,260	3,187,000	1985E	28	11	State (U.S.)	Phoenix	North America	46
Arkansas, U.S.	Arkansas	53,187	137,754	2,359,000	1985E	44	17	State (U.S.)	Little Rock	North America	45
Armenian Soviet Socialist Republic, U.S.S.R.	Armenia	11,506	29,800	3,267,000	1984E	284	110	Soviet Socialist Republic (U.S.S.R.)	Yerevan	Asia	16
Aruba	Aruba	75	194	67,000	1982E*	893	345	Self-governing	Oranjestad	North America	49
Ascension	Ascension	34	88	about 1,500	—	44	17	Belongs to Great Britain, under administration of St. Helena	Georgetown	Africa	30–31
†Asia	—	16,968,000	43,947,000	3,069,000,000	1988E	181	70	—	—	Asia	21–22
Atlantic Provinces (includes Newfoundland), (Can.)	Atlantic Provinces	208,148	539,101	2,234,032	1981C	11	4	Part of Canada	—	North America	42
†**Australia**	Commonwealth of Australia	2,966,150	7,682,300	16,297,000	1988E	5	2	Constitutional Monarchy	Canberra	Australia	59
Australian Capital Territory (Canberra)	Australian Capital Territory	930	2,400	221,607	1981C	238	92	Territory (Australia)	Canberra	Australia	59
Austria	—	32,374	83,849	7,488,000	1988E	231	89	Federal Republic	Vienna (Wien)	Europe	14
Azerbaijan Soviet Socialist Republic, U.S.S.R.	Azerbaijan	33,436	86,600	6,506,000	1984E	195	75	Soviet Socialist Republic (U.S.S.R.)	Baku	Europe	16
Azores	Açores	905	2,344	about 249,500	—	276	106	Part of Portugal's territory	—	Europe	32
Bahamas	Bahamas	5,380	13,935	246,000	1988E	46	18	Constitutional Monarchy	Nassau	North America	47
Bahrain	Al Baḥrayn	262	678	483,000	1988E	1,843	712	Emirate	Manama	Asia	24
Balearic Islands, Spain	Islas Baleares	1,936	5,014	685,088	1981C	354	137	Province of Spain	Palma	Europe	13
Baltic States, U.S.S.R.	Estonia, Latvia, Lithuania	67,182	174,000	7,644,000	1984E	114	44	Part of U.S.S.R. (3 republics)	—	Europe	8
Bangladesh	Bangladesh	55,598	143,998	109,471,000	1988E	1,969	760	Republic	Dhaka	Asia	25
Barbados	Barbados	166	430	272,000	1988E	1,639	633	Constitutional Monarchy	Bridgetown	North America	51
Beijing (Peking), China	Beijing	6,873	17,800	9,230,687	1982C	1,343	519	Special Municipal District of China	—	Asia	28
Belgium	Belgique (French), België (Flemish)	11,781	30,513	9,886,000	1988E	839	324	Constitutional Monarchy	Brussels	Europe	12
Belize	Belize	8,867	22,965	172,000	1988E	19	7	Constitutional Monarchy	Belmopan	North America	49
Benelux	Belgium, Luxembourg, and Netherlands	27,152	70,325	24,898,000	1988E	917	354	Economic Union	—	Europe	12
Benin	Bénin	43,484	112,622	4,383,000	1988E	101	39	Military Rule	Porto-Novo	Africa	34
Bermuda	Bermuda	21	54	72,000	1988E	3,429	1,333	British Dependency	Hamilton	North America	47
Bhutan	Druk	17,950	46,500	1,507,000	1988E	82	32	Monarchy	Thimphu	Asia	25
Bioko, Equat. Gui.	Bioko	785	2,034	94,000	1982E*	120	46	Territory of Equatorial Guinea	Malabo	Africa	34
Bolivia	Bolivia	424,165	1,098,581	6,918,000	1988E	16	6	Republic	Sucre (official); La Paz (actual)	South America	54
Botswana	Botswana	231,805	600,372	1,202,000	1988E	5	2	Republic	Gaborone	Africa	37
Brazil	Brasil	3,286,487	8,511,965	144,427,000	1988E	44	17	Federal Republic	Brasília	South America	54–56
British Columbia, Can.	British Columbia	365,900	947,800	2,744,467	1981C	7	3	Province (Canada)	Victoria	North America	42
British Honduras, *see* Belize	—	—	—	—	—	—	—	—	—	—	—
British Indian Ocean Territory	British Indian Ocean Territory	30	78	2,000	—	67	26	British Dependency	—	Asia	22
British Solomon Islands, *see* Solomon Islands	—	—	—	—	—	—	—	—	—	—	—
Brunei	Brunei	2,226	5,765	244,000	1988E	110	42	Monarchy	Bandar Seri Begawan	Asia	26
Bulgaria	Balgarija	42,823	110,912	9,328,000	1988E	217	84	People's Republic (Communist Dictatorship)	Sofia	Europe	15
Burkina Faso	Burkina Faso	105,869	274,200	8,604,000	1988E	81	31	Military Rule	Ouagadougou	Africa	34
Burma	Burma	261,218	676,552	39,778,000	1988E	152	59	Socialist Republic	Rangoon	Asia	25
Burundi	Burundi	10,747	27,834	5,025,000	1988E	467	181	Republic	Bujumbura	Africa	36
Byelorussian Soviet Socialist Republic, U.S.S.R.	Byelorussia	80,155	207,600	9,878,000	1984E	123	48	Soviet Socialist Republic (U.S.S.R.)	Minsk	Europe	16
California, U.S.	California	158,706	411,049	26,365,000	1985E	166	64	State (U.S.)	Sacramento	North America	46
Cambodia, *see* Kampuchea	—	—	—	—	—	—	—	—	—	—	—
Cameroon	Cameroun	183,569	475,442	10,374,000	1988E	58	23	Republic	Yaoundé	Africa	34
Canada	Canada	3,849,674	9,970,610	26,489,000	1988E	7	3	Constitutional Monarchy	Ottawa	North America	42

Political unit	Local name	Area sq. miles	km²	Population	Date	Population density per sq. mile	km²	Form of govt./ Political status	Capital	Continent	Map plate
Canary Islands	—	2,796	7,242	1,444,626	1981C	517	199	Part of Spain (2 provinces)	Santa Cruz de Tenerife; Las Palmas de Gran Canaria	Africa	32
Cape Verde	Cabo Verde	1,557	4,033	335,000	1988E	213	83	Republic	Praia	Africa	32
Cayman Islands	Cayman Islands	100	259	18,000	1982E*	180	69	British Dependency	Georgetown	North America	49
Celebes (Indonesia)	Sulawesi	73,057	189,216	10,409,533	1981C	142	55	Part of Indonesia	—	Asia	26
Central African Republic	Centrafrique	240,535	622,984	2,759,000	1988E	11	4	Military Rule	Bangui	Africa	35
Central America	—	201,847	522,781	29,000,000	—	144	55	—	—	North America	49
Ceylon, see Sri Lanka	—	—	—	—	—	—	—	—	—	—	—
Chad	Tchad	495,800	1,284,000	5,395,000	1988E	11	4	Republic/Military Control	N'Djamena	Africa	35
Channel Islands	Channel Islands	75	195	133,000	1982E*	1,773	682	British Crown Dependencies	St. Peter Port; St. Helier	Europe	9
Chile	Chile	292,135	756,626	12,668,000	1988E	43	17	Military Rule	Santiago	South America	56
China	Zhonghua Renmin Gongheguo	3,678,470	9,527,200	1,096,584,000	1988E	298	115	Communist Dictatorship	Beijing (Peking)	Asia	27
Christmas Island (Austl.)	Christmas Island	52	135	3,000	1980E	58	22	External Territory (Australia)	Flying Fish Cove	Oceania	26
Cocos (Keeling) Islands (Austl.)	Cocos (Keeling) Islands	5	13	1,000	1980E	200	77	External Territory (Australia)	—	Oceania	22
Colombia	República de Colombia	439,737	1,138,914	30,577,000	1988E	69	27	Republic	Bogotá	South America	54
Colorado, U.S.	Colorado	104,091	269,595	3,231,000	1985E	31	12	State (U.S.)	Denver	North America	45
Commonwealth of Nations	—	14,314,750	37,075,000	1,253,500,000	1988E	87	34	Association of independent countries & political units	—	—	—
Comoros	Federal and Islamic Republic of the Comoros	838	2,171	500,000	1988E	597	230	Republic	Moroni	Africa	37
Congo	République Populaire du Congo (People's Republic of the Congo)	132,047	342,000	2,130,000	1988E	16	6	Military Rule	Brazzaville	Africa	36
Connecticut, U.S.	Connecticut	5,018	12,997	3,174,000	1985E	633	244	State (U.S.)	Hartford	North America	44
Cook Islands	Cook Islands	91	236	20,000	—	220	85	Self-governing dependency of New Zealand	Avarua	Oceania	61
Corsica	Corse	3,352	8,681	184,000	1982E*	55	21	Part of France (2 departments)	Ajaccio	Europe	11
Costa Rica	República de Costa Ricá (Republic of Costa Rica)	19,575	50,700	2,710,000	1988E	138	53	Republic	San José	North America	49
Cuba	Cuba	42,804	110,861	10,314,000	1988E	241	93	Socialist state and a republic; (actual dictatorship)	Havana (La Habana)	North America	49
Curaçao	Curaçao	171	443	170,000	—	994	383	Largest island of the Netherlands Antilles	Willemstad	North America	49
Cyprus	Kypros (Greek), Kibris (Turkish)	3,572	9,251	688,000	1988E	193	75	Republic	Nicosia	Asia	24
Czechoslovakia	Ceskoslovenská Socialistická	49,370	127,869	15,835,000	1988E	320	124	Socialist Republic (Communist Dictatorship)	Prague (Praha)	Europe	10
Dahomey, see Benin	—	—	—	—	—	—	—	—	—	—	—
Delaware, U.S.	Delaware	2,044	5,295	622,000	1985E	304	117	State (U.S.)	Dover	North America	44
Denmark	Danmark	16,663	43,080	5,144,000	1988E	309	119	Constitutional Monarchy	Copenhagen (København)	Europe	8
Denmark and Possessions	—	857,177	2,220,079	5,246,000	1982E*	6.1	2.4	—	Copenhagen (København)	—	—
District of Columbia (D.C.) [Washington, D.C., U.S.]	District of Columbia	69	179	640,000	1982E*	9,552	3,678	U.S. Federal District	Washington, D.C.	North America	44
Djibouti	Djibouti	8,410	21,783	376,000	1988E	44	17	Republic	Djibouti (city)	Africa	35
Dominica	Dominica	290	751	74,000	1988E	255	99	Republic	Roseau	North America	51
Dominican Republic	República Dominicana	18,816	48,734	6,675,000	1988E	355	137	Republic	Santo Domingo	North America	49
Dutch Guiana, see Suriname	—	—	—	—	—	—	—	—	—	—	—
East Germany	Deutsche Demokratische Republik	41,768	108,178	16,606,000	1988E	398	154	Communist	East Berlin	Europe	10
Ecuador	Ecuador	109,484	283,561	10,013,000	1988E	91	35	Republic	Quito	South America	54
Egypt	Mişr	386,662	1,001,449	50,296,000	1988E	130	50	Republic	Cairo (Al Qahirah)	Africa	33
Ellice Islands, see Tuvalu	—	—	—	—	—	—	—	—	—	—	—
El Salvador	El Salvador	8,124	21,041	6,089,000	1988E	749	289	Republic	San Salvador	North America	49
England	England	50,363	130,439	47,145,000	1988E	936	361	Constitutional Monarchy	London	Europe	9
Equatorial Guinea	Guinea Ecuatorial	10,831	28,051	345,000	1988E	32	14	Military Rule	Malabo on Bioko	Africa	36
Estonian Soviet Socialist Republic, U.S.S.R.	Estonia	17,413	45,100	1,518,000	1984E	87	34	Soviet Socialist Republic (U.S.S.R.)	Tallinn	Europe	8
Ethiopia	Itiopya	471,800	1,221,900	42,403,000	1988E	91	35	Military Rule	Addis Ababa	Africa	35
Eurasia	—	21,034,000	54,478,000	3,761,000,000	1988E	Europe: 170 Asia: 181	Europe: 66 Asia: 70	—	—	—	—
†Europe	—	4,066,000	10,532,000	692,000,000	1988E	170	66	—	—	Europe	5–6
Faeroe Islands	Føroyar (Faeroese) Færøerne (Danish)	540	1,399	45,000	1982E*	83	32	Self-governing Community of Denmark	Tórshavn	Europe	6
Falkland Islands (3) (Islas Malvinas—Argentina)	Falkland Islands	4,618	11,960	1,900	1982E*	.4	.2	British Dependency; [claimed by Argentina]	Stanley	South America	56
Federated States of Micronesia	Federated States of Micronesia	271	702	71,000	1982E*	—	—	Self-governing area associated with U.S.	Kolonia	Oceania	60
Fiji	Fiji	7,056	18,274	717,000	1988E	102	39	Constitutional Monarchy	Suva	Oceania	63
Finland	Suomi (Finnish) Finland (Swedish)	130,559	338,145	4,910,000	1988E	38	15	Republic	Helsinki (Helsingfors)	Europe	7
Florida, U.S.	Florida	58,664	151,939	11,366,000	1985E	194	75	State (U.S.)	Tallahassee	North America	44
France	France	211,208	547,026	55,206,000	1988E	261	101	Republic	Paris	Europe	11
France and Possessions	—	260,661	675,114	55,618,000	1982E*	213	82	—	Paris	—	—
French Guiana	Guyane Française	35,135	91,000	66,000	1982E*	1.9	0.7	Overseas Department (France)	Cayenne	South America	54
French Polynesia	Polynésie Française	1,544	4,000	150,000	1982E*	97	38	Overseas Territory (France)	Papeete	Oceania	61
French West Indies	—	1,112	2,880	620,000	1982E*	558	215	2 overseas departments of France	—	North America	50

Political unit	Local name	Area sq. miles	km²	Population	Date	Population density per sq. mile	km²	Form of govt./ Political status	Capital	Continent	Map plate
Fujian (Fukien), China	Fujian	47,529	123,100	25,931,106	1982C	546	211	Province (China)	Fuzhou (Fu-chóu)	Asia	27
Gabon	Gabon	103,347	267,667	1,232,000	1988E	12	5	Republic	Libreville	Africa	36
Galapagos Islands, Ecuador	Archipiélago de Colón	3,029	7,844	6,200	1982C	2	0.8	Province of Ecuador: (Galapagos Islands)	Baquerizo Moreno	South America	54
Gambia	Gambia	4,361	11,295	733,000	19886E	177	68	Republic	Banjul	Africa	34
Gansu (Kansu), China	Gansu	141,500	366,500	19,569,261	1982C	138	53	Province (China)	Lanzhou (Lan-chou)	Asia	27
Georgia, U.S.	Georgia	58,910	152,576	5,976,000	1985E	101	39	State (U.S.)	Atlanta	North America	44
Georgian Soviet Socialist Republic, U.S.S.R.	Georgia	26,911	69,700	5,167,000	1984E	192	74	Soviet Socialist Republic (U.S.S.R.)	Tbilisi	Asia	16
Germany	Deutschland	137,773	356,829	77,445,000	1988E	562	217	—	—	Europe	10
Ghana	Ghana	92,100	238,537	13,892,000	1988E	151	58	Military Rule	Accra	Africa	34
Gibraltar	Gibraltar	2.3	6.0	30,000	1982E*	13,043	5,000	British Dependency	Gibraltar	Europe	13
Gilbert Islands	Gilbert Islands	105	272	52,000	—	495	191	part of Kiribati	—	Oceania	—
Great Britain	The United Kingdom of Great Britain and Northern Ireland	94,248	244,100	56,672,000	1988E	601	232	Constitutional Monarchy	London	Europe	9
Great Britain and Dependencies	—	113,676	294,415	62,049,000	1982E*	546	211	—	London	—	—
Greece	Ellas	50,944	131,944	10,100,000	1988E	198	77	Republic	Athens (Athinai)	Europe	15
Greenland	Grønland (Danish) Kalaallit Nunaat (Eskimo)	840,004	2,175,600	56,000	1988E	.07	.03	Province of Denmark	Godthåb	North America	41
Grenada	Grenada	133	344	112,000	1982E*	842	326	Parliamentary	St. George's	North America	51
Guadeloupe	Guadeloupe	658	1,704	320,000	1982E*	466	180	Overseas Department (France)	Basse-Terre	North America	51
Guam	Guam	212	549	110,000	1982E*	519	200	Territory of the United States	Agana	Oceania	64
Guangdong (Kwangtung), China	Guangdong	89,340	231,400	59,299,220	1982C	664	256	Province (China)	Guangzhou (Canton)	Asia	27
Guangxi (Kwangsi), China	Guangxi	85,100	220,400	36,420,960	1982C	428	165	Autonomous Region, China	Nanning (Nan-ning)	Asia	27
Guatemala	Guatemala	42,042	108,889	9,150,000	1988E	218	84	Democratic	Guatemala City	North America	49
Guernsey	Guernsey	24	62	55,000	1982E*	1,833	714	British Crown Dependency	St. Peter Port	Europe	9
Guinea	Guinée	94,926	245,857	5,845,000	1988E	62	24	Military Rule	Conakry	Africa	34
Guinea-Bissau	Guiné-Bissau	13,948	36,125	908,000	1988E	64	25	Military Republic	Bissau	Africa	34
Guizhou (Kweichow), China	Guizhou	67,180	174,000	28,552,997	1982C	425	164	Province (China)	Guiyang (Kuei-yang)	Asia	27
Guyana	Guyana	83,000	214,969	1,006,000	1988E	12	5	Republic	Georgetown	South America	54
Haiti	Haïti	10,714	27,750	5,697,000	1988E	532	205	Military Republic	Port-au-Prince	North America	49
Hawaii, U.S.	Hawaii	6,471	16,759	1,054,000	1985E*	163	63	State (U.S.)	Honolulu	Oceania	60
Hebei (Hopeh), China	Hebei	78,260	202,700	53,005,875	1982C	677	261	Province (China)	Shijiazhuang (Shih-chiachuang)	Asia	28
Heilongjiang (Heilungkiang), China	Heilongjiang	179,000	463,600	32,665,546	1982C	182	70	Province (China)	Harbin (Harbin)	Asia	27
Henan (Honan), China	Henan	64,480	167,000	74,422,739	1982C	1,154	446	Province (China)	Zheng-zhou (Cheng-chou)	Asia	27
Hispaniola	La Isla Española	29,418	76,192	12,000,000	—	408	157	—	—	North America	49
Holland, see Netherlands	—	—	—	—	—	—	—	—	—	—	—
Honduras	Honduras	43,277	112,088	4,801,000	1988E	111	43	Republic	Tegucigalpa	North America	49
Hong Kong	Hong Kong	410	1,061	5,375,000	1982E*	13,110	5,066	British Dependency	Victoria	Asia	27
Hubei (Hupeh), China	Hubei	72,394	187,500	47,804,150	1982C	660	255	Province (China)	Wuhan (Wu-han)	Asia	27
Hunan, China	Hunan	81,275	210,500	54,008,851	1982C	665	257	Province (China)	Changsha (C'hang-sha)	Asia	27
Hungary	Magyarország	35,919	93,030	10,827,000	1988E	301	116	People's Republic (Communist Dictatorship)	Budapest	Europe	10
Iceland	Ìsland	39,800	103,000	248,000	1988E	6	2	Republic	Reykjavík	Europe	7
Idaho, U.S.	Idaho	83,564	216,432	1,005,000	1985E	12	4.6-5	State (U.S.)	Boise	North America	46
Illinois, U.S.	Illinois	56,345	145,934	11,535,000	1985E	205	79	State (U.S.)	Springfield	North America	45
India	Bharat	1,269,219	3,287,263	803,975,000	1988E	633	245	Federal Republic	New Delhi	Asia	25
Indiana, U.S.	Indiana	36,185	93,720	5,499,000	1985E	152	59	State (U.S.)	Indianapolis	North America	44
Indonesia	Indonesia	741,101	1,919,443	172,975,000	1988E	233	90	Republic	Jakarta	Asia	26
Indonesian Borneo	Kalimantan	208,287	539,460	6,723,086	1981C	32	12	Part of Indonesia (4 provinces)	—	Asia	26
Inner Mongolia, China	Nei Mongol	454,600	1,177,500	19,274,279	1982C	42	16	Autonomous Region (China)	Hohhot (Hu-ho-hao-t'e)	Asia	27
Iowa, U.S.	Iowa	56,275	145,753	2,884,000	1985E	51	20	State (U.S.)	Des Moines	North America	45
Iran	Īrān	636,300	1,648,000	49,098,000	1988E	77	30	Islamic Republic	Teheran	Asia	23
Iraq	Al'Irāq	169,235	438,317	17,306,000	1988E	102	39	Republic	Baghdad	Asia	24
Ireland	Éire	27,136	70,283	3,716,000	1988E	137	53	Republic	Dublin	Europe	9
Israel	Yisra'el	8,019	20,770	4,284,000	1988E	534	206	Democratic Republic	Jerusalem	Asia	24
Israeli Occupied Areas	Gaza Strip Golan Heights West Bank	2,590	6,728	1,235,000	1982E*	457	176	—	—	Asia	24
Italy	Italia	116,314	301,252	57,240,000	1988E	491	190	Republic	Rome (Roma)	Europe	14
Ivory Coast	Côte d'Ivoire	124,504	322,463	10,826,000	1988E	87	34	Republic	Abidjan	Africa	34
Jamaica	Jamaica	4,244	10,991	2,427,000	1988E	571	221	Constitutional Monarchy	Kingston	North America	49
Jammu and Kashmir	Jammu and Kashmīr	85,806	222,237	9,920,000	1982E*	115	45	In dispute (India and Pakistan)	Srinagar and Jammu	Asia	25
Japan	Nippon	145,834	377,708	121,671,000	1988E	834	322	Constitutional Monarchy	Tokyo	Asia	29
Java (incl. Madura)	Jawa	51,038	132,187	91,269,528	1981C	1,787	690	Part of Indonesia	—	Asia	26
Jersey	Jersey	45	117	78,000	1982E*	1,733	667	British Crown Dependency	St. Helier	Europe	9
Jiangsu (Kiangsu), China	Jiangsu	39,460	102,200	60,521,114	1982C	1,534	592	Province (China)	Nanjing (Nan-ching)	Asia	28
Jiangxi (Kiangsi), China	Jiangxi	63,630	164,800	33,184,827	1982C	522	201	Province (China)	Nanchang (Nan-ch'ang)	Asia	27
Jilin (Kirin), China	Jilin	72,200	187,000	22,560,053	1982C	312	121	Province (China)	Changchun (Ch'ang-ch'un)	Asia	27
Jordan	Al Urdun	37,738	97,740	3,945,000	1988E	105	40	Constitutional Monarchy	Amman	Asia	24

Political unit	Local name	Area sq. miles	km²	Population	Date	Population density per sq. mile	km²	Form of govt./ Political status	Capital	Continent	Map plate
Kampuchea	Kampuchea Prâcheathipâtéyy	69,898	181,035	6,676,000	1988E	96	37	Communist Dictatorship	Phnom Penh	Asia	26
Kansas, U.S.	Kansas	82,277	213,098	2,450,000	1985E	30	11	State (U.S.)	Topeka	North America	45
Kazakh Soviet Socialist Republic, U.S.S.R.	Kazakhstan	1,049,155	2,717,300	15,648,000	1984E	15	6	Soviet Socialist Republic (U.S.S.R.)	Alma-Ata	Asia	19
Kentucky, U.S.	Kentucky	40,409	104,660	3,726,000	1985E	92	36	State (U.S.)	Frankfort	North America	44
Kenya	Kenya	224,961	582,646	23,338,000	1988E	104	40	Republic	Nairobi	Africa	36
Kerguelen Island	Iles Kerguèlen	2,577	6,674	(1)	—	—	—	Part of French Southern and Antarctic Territories	—	Antarctica	30–31
Kirghiz Soviet Socialist Republic, U.S.S.R.	Kirghiz	76,641	198,500	3,886,000	1984E	51	20	Soviet Socialist Republic (U.S.S.R.)	Frunze	Asia	18
Kiribati	Kiribati	281	728	65,000	1988E	231	89	Republic	Tarawa	Oceania	60
Korea	Chosŏn	84,565	219,022	64,099,000	1988E	758	293	—	—	Asia	28
Kuwait	Al Kuwayt	6,880	17,818	1,870,000	1988E	272	105	Emirate	Kuwait	Asia	24
Labrador (Can.)	Labrador	113,641	294,330	31,318	1981C	.3	.1	Part of Newfoundland Province (Canada)	—	North America	42
Laos	Laos	91,431	236,804	3,850,000	1988E	42	16	Socialist Republic (Communist)	Vientiane	Asia	26
Latin America	—	8,000,000	21,000,000	432,000,000	1988E	54	21	—	—	North America, South America	52–53
Latvian Soviet Socialist Republic, U.S.S.R.	Latvia	24,595	63,700	2,587,000	1984E	105	41	Soviet Socialist Republic (U.S.S.R.)	Riga	Europe	8
Lebanon	Lubnăn	4,015	10,400	2,828,000	1988E	704	271	Republic	Beirut	Asia	24
Lesotho	Lesotho	11,720	30,355	1,643,000	1988E	140	54	Military Rule	Maseru	Africa	37
Liaoning (Liaoning), China	Liaoning	58,300	151,000	35,721,693	1982C	613	237	Province (China)	Shenyang (Shen-yang)	Asia	28
Liberia	Liberia	43,000	111,370	2,410,000	1988E	56	22	Republic/Military Rule	Monrovia	Africa	34
Libya	Lībiyă	679,362	1,759,540	4,202,000	1988E	6	2	Socialist Republic/ Military Rule	Tripoli	Africa	33
Liechtenstein	Liechtenstein	62	160	30,000	1988E	484	188	Constitutional Monarchy	Vaduz	Europe	14
Lithuanian Soviet Socialist Republic, U.S.S.R.	Lithuania	25,174	65,200	3,539,000	1984E	141	54	Soviet Socialist Republic (U.S.S.R.)	Vilnius	Europe	8
Louisiana, U.S.	Louisiana	47,752	123,677	4,481,000	1985E	93	36	State (U.S.)	Baton Rouge	North America	45
Luxembourg	Luxembourg	998	2,586	368,000	1988E	369	142	Constitutional Monarchy	Luxembourg	Europe	12
Macao	Macau	6.0	16	275,000	1982E*	45,833	17,188	Portuguese Territory	Macao	Asia	27
Macias Nguema Biyogo, see Bioko	—	—	—	—	—	—	—	—	—	—	—
Madagascar	Madagasikara	226,658	587,041	10,913,000	1988E	48	19	Republic	Antananarivo	Africa	37
Madeira Islands	Arquipélago da Madeira	308	797	258,200	1981C	838	324	District of Portugal	Funchal	Africa	32
Maine, U.S.	Maine	33,265	86,156	1,164,000	1985E	35	14	State (U.S.)	Augusta	North America	44
Malagasy Republic, see Madagascar	—	—	—	—	—	—	—	—	—	—	—
Malawi	Malawi	45,747	118,484	7,752,000	1988E	169	65	Republic	Lilongwe	Africa	36
Malaya	Malaya	50,806	131,588	13,291,200	1988E	262	101	Part of Malaysia	—	Asia	26
Malaysia	Malaysia	127,317	329,749	16,614,000	1988E	130	50	Constitutional Monarchy	Kuala Lumpur	Asia	26
Maldives	Maldives	115	298	197,000	1988E	1,713	661	Republic	Male	Asia	34
Mali	Mali	478,800	1,240,000	8,768,000	1988E	18	7	Republic	Bamako	Africa	34
Malta	Malta	122	316	390,000	1988E	3,197	1,234	Republic	Valletta	Europe	14
Man, Isle of	Isle of Man	227	588	66,000	1982E*	291	112	British Crown Dependency	Douglas	Europe	9
Manitoba, Can.	Manitoba	250,947	649,950	1,026,241	1981C	4	2	Province (Canada)	Winnipeg	North America	42
Marshall Islands	Marshall Islands	70	181	31,000	1982E*	443	171	Self-governing area associated with U.S.	Majaro	Oceania	60
Martinique	Martinique	425	1,102	300,000	1982E*	706	273	Overseas Department (France)	Fort-de-France	North America	51
Maryland, U.S.	Maryland	10,460	27,092	4,392,000	1985E	420	162	State (U.S.)	Annapolis	North America	44
Massachusetts, U.S.	Massachusetts	8,284	21,456	5,822,000	1985E	703	271	State (U.S.)	Boston	North America	44
Mauritania	Mūrītăniyă	397,956	1,030,700	2,069,000	1988E	5	2	Military Rule	Nouakchott	Africa	32
Mauritius	Mauritius	790	2,045	1,075,000	1988E	1,362	526	Constitutional Monarchy	Port Louis	Africa	37
Mayotte	Mayotte	144	374	54,000	1982E*	375	144	French possession— claimed by Comoros	Dzaoudzi	Africa	37
Mexico	México	758,136	1,963,564	84,964,000	1988E	112	43	Republic	Mexico City	North America	48
Michigan, U.S.	Michigan	58,527	151,586	9,088,000	1985E	155	60	State (U.S.)	Lansing	North America	44
Middle America	—	1,050,682	2,721,254	144,964,000	1988E	138	53	—	—	North America	47
Midway Island	Midway Island	2	5	1,500	1982E*	750	288	U.S. Possession	—	Oceania	60
Minnesota, U.S.	Minnesota	84,402	218,601	4,193,000	1985E	50	19	State (U.S.)	St. Paul	North America	45
Mississippi, U.S.	Mississippi	47,689	123,515	2,613,000	1985E	55	21	State (U.S.)	Jackson	North America	45
Missouri, U.S.	Missouri	69,697	180,516	5,029,000	1985E	72	28	State (U.S.)	Jefferson City	North America	45
Moldavian Soviet Socialist Republic, U.S.S.R.	Moldavia	13,012	33,700	4,080,000	1984E	314	121	Soviet Socialist Republic (U.S.S.R.)	Kishinev	Europe	16
Monaco	Monaco	0.73	1.9	29,000	1988E	39,276	15,263	Principality	Monaco	Europe	11
Mongolia	Mongol Ard Uls	604,250	1,565,000	2,052,000	1988E	3	1	People's Democracy (Communist)	Ulan Bator	Asia	27
Montana, U.S.	Montana	147,046	380,848	826,000	1985E	6	2	State (U.S.)	Helena	North America	46
Montserrat	Montserrat	38	98	12,000	1982E*	300	117	British Dependency	Plymouth	North America	51
Morocco	Al Maghrib	177,117	458,730	24,290,000	1988E	137	53	Constitutional Monarchy	Rabat	Africa	32
Mozambique	Moçambique	308,642	799,380	15,330,000	1988E	48	19	Socialist Republic	Maputo	Africa	37
Muscat and Oman, see Oman	—	—	—	—	—	—	—	—	—	—	—
Namibia (5)	Namibia	317,827	823,168	1,070,000	1982E*	3.4	1.3	Under South African administration	Windhoek	Africa	37
Nationalist China see Taiwan	—	—	—	—	—	—	—	—	—	—	—
Nauru	Nauru (English) Naoero (Nauruan)	8	21	9,000	1988E	1,125	429	Republic	—	Oceania	64
Nebraska, U.S.	Nebraska	77,355	200,350	1,606,000	1985E	21	8	State (U.S.)	Lincoln	North America	45
Nepal	Nepal	56,827	147,181	17,649,000	1988E	311	120	Constitutional Monarchy	Kathmandu	Asia	25
Netherlands	Nederland	14,373	37,226	14,644,000	1988E	1,019	393	Constitutional Monarchy	Amsterdam	Europe	12
Netherlands Antilles	Nederlandse Antillen	383	993	260,000	1982E*	679	262	Self-governing; part of Kingdom of the Netherlands	Willemstad	North America	50

Political unit	Local name	Area sq. miles	Area km²	Population	Date	Population density per sq. mile	Population density per km²	Form of govt./ Political status	Capital	Continent	Map plate
Nevada, U.S.	Nevada	110,561	286,352	936,000	1985E	8	3	State (U.S.)	Carson City	North America	46
New Brunswick, Can.	New Brunswick	28,355	73,440	696,403	1981C	25	10	Province (Canada)	Fredericton	North America	42
New Caledonia	Nouvelle-Calédonie	7,375	19,104	140,000	1982E*	19	7.3	Overseas Territory (France)	Nouméa	Oceania	63
New England (U.S.)	New England	66,688	172,681	12,661,000	1985E	190	73	Region of U.S. (6 States)	—	North America	43
Newfoundland, Can.	Newfoundland	156,649	405,720	567,681	1981C	4	2	Province (Canada)	St. John's	North America	42
Newfoundland (island of), (Can.)	Newfoundland	43,008	111,390	536,363	1981C	12	5	Part of Newfoundland Province, Canada	—	North America	42
New Hampshire, U.S.	New Hampshire	9,297	24,032	998,000	1985E	107	42	State (U.S.)	Concord	North America	44
New Hebrides Islands, see Vanuatu	—	—	—	—	—	—	—	—	—	—	—
New Jersey, U.S.	New Jersey	7,787	20,169	7,562,000	1985E	971	375	State (U.S.)	Trenton	North America	44
New Mexico, U.S.	New Mexico	121,593	314,295	1,450,000	1985E	12	5	State (U.S.)	Santa Fe	North America	45
New South Wales, Austl.	New South Wales	309,500	801,600	5,125,683	1981C	17	6	State (Australia)	Sydney	Australia	59
New York, U.S.	New York	49,108	127,189	17,783,000	1985E	362	140	State (U.S.)	Albany	North America	44
New Zealand	New Zealand	103,883	269,057	3,372,000	1988E	32	13	Constitutional Monarchy	Wellington	Oceania	62
Nicaragua	Nicaragua	50,200	130,000	3,662,000	1988E	72	28	Military Republic	Managua	North America	49
Niger	Niger	489,200	1,267,000	6,688,000	1988E	14	5	Military Republic	Niamey	Africa	34
Nigeria	Nigeria	356,669	923,768	105,623,000	1988E	296	114	Military Rule	Lagos	Africa	34
Ningxia (Ningsia), China	Ningxia	25,640	66,400	3,895,578	1982C	152	59	Autonomous Region (China)	Yinchaun	Asia	27
Niue Island	Niue	100	259	3,000	1982E*	29	11	Self-governing area associated with New Zealand	—	Oceania	64
Norfolk Island (Austl.)	Norfolk Island	14	36	2,000	1980C	143	31	External Territory (Australia)	—	Australia	61
†North America	—	9,363,000	24,249,000	418,000,000	1988E	45	17	—	—	North America	38–39
North Borneo, see Sabah	—	—	—	—	—	—	—	—	—	—	—
North Carolina, U.S.	North Carolina	52,669	136,413	6,225,000	1985E	118	46	State (U.S.)	Raleigh	North America	44
North Dakota, U.S.	North Dakota	70,702	183,119	685,000	1985E	10	4	State (U.S.)	Bismarck	North America	45
North Korea	Choson-minjujuui-inmin-konghwaguk	46,540(4)	120,538(4)	21,478,000	1988E	461	178	Republic (Communist rule)	Pyongyang	Asia	28
Northern Ireland	Northern Ireland	5,452	14,121	1,592,000	1988E	292	113	Constitutional monarchy	Belfast	Europe	9
Northern Mariana Islands	Northern Mariana Islands	184	477	18,000	1982E*	98	38	U.S. commonwealth	Saipan	Oceania	60
Northern Territory, Austl.	Northern Territory	519,800	1,346,200	123,333	1981C	0.2	0.09	Territory (Australia)	Darwin	Australia	59
Northwest Territories, Can.	Northwest Territories	1,332,910	3,126,320	45,741	1981C	4	2	Territory (Canada)	Yellowknife	North America	42
Norway	Norge	125,052	323,883	4,174,000	1988E	33	13	Constitutional Monarchy	Oslo	Europe	7
Nova Scotia, Can.	Nova Scotia	21,423	55,490	847,442	1981C	40	15	Province (Canada)	Halifax	North America	42
Ohio, U.S.	Ohio	41,330	107,044	10,744,000	1985E	260	200	State (U.S.)	Columbus	North America	44
Oklahoma, U.S.	Oklahoma	69,956	181,186	3,301,000	1985E	47	18	State (U.S.)	Oklahoma City	North America	45
Oman	'Umān	82,030	212,457	1,350,000	1988E	16	6	Sultanate	Muscat (Masqat)	Asia	23
Ontario, Can.	Ontario	412,581	1,068,580	8,625,107	1981C	21	8	Province (Canada)	Toronto	North America	42
Oregon, U.S.	Oregon	97,073	251,419	2,687,000	1985E	28	11	State (U.S.)	Salem	North America	46
Orkney Islands	Orkney Islands	377	976	19,351	1985E	51	20	Part of Scotland	Kirkwall	Europe	9
Pacific Islands	Oceania	488,297	1,264,450	11,638,860	1988E	24	9	—	—	Oceania	57–58
Pacific Islands, Trust Territory of the	Trust Territory of the Pacific Islands	717	1,857	140,000	1982E*	200	77	Trust Territory administered by the U.S.	Saipan (island)	Oceania	60
Pakistan	Pākistān	310,404	803,943	108,591,000	1988E	350	135	Military Republic	Islamabad	Asia	25
Palau Islands	Palau	192	497	14,000	1982E*	—	—	Part of Trust Territory of the Pacific Islands (U.S. administration)	Koror	Oceania	60
Panama	Panamá	29,762	77,082	2,322,000	1988E	78	30	Republic	Panama City	North America	49
Papua New Guinea	Papua New Guinea	178,704	462,840	3,997,000	1988E	22	9	Constitutional Monarchy	Port Moresby	Oceania	60
Paraguay	Paraguay	157,048	406,752	4,007,000	1988E	25	10	Republic	Asunción	South America	56
Pennsylvania, U.S.	Pennsylvania	45,302	117,348	11,853,000	1985E	262	101	State (U.S.)	Harrisburg	North America	44
Persia, see Iran	—	—	—	—	—	—	—	—	—	—	—
Peru	Peru	496,225	1,285,216	21,254,000	1988E	43	17	Republic	Lima	South America	54
Philippines	Pilipinas	116,000	300,000	58,712,000	1988E	506	196	Republic	Manila	Asia	26
Pitcairn Island	Pitcairn	2	5	65	1982E*	36	14	Part of British Dependency: Pitcairn Islands Group	Adamstown	Oceania	61
Poland	Polska	120,728	312,683	38,462,000	1988E	319	123	People's Republic (Communist Dictatorship)	Warsaw (Warszawa)	Europe	10
Portugal	Portugal	35,553	92,082	10,270,000	1988E	289	112	Republic	Lisbon (Lisboa)	Europe	13
Portuguese Guinea, see Guinea-Bissau	—	—	—	—	—	—	—	—	—	—	—
Prairie Provinces (Can.)	Prairie Provinces	757,985	1,963,172	4,232,278	1981C	6	2	Region of Canada (3 provinces)	—	North America	42
Prince Edward Island, Can.	Prince Edward Island	2,185	5,660	122,506	1981C	56	22	Province (Canada)	Charlottetown	North America	42
Puerto Rico	Puerto Rico	3,515	9,103	3,196,520	1980C	909	351	Commonwealth (U.S. Protection)	San Juan	North America	51
Qatar	Qaṭar	4,416	11,437	332,000	1988E	75	29	Emirate	Doha (Ad Dawhah)	Asia	24
Qinghai (Tsinghai), China	Qinghai	278,400	721,000	3,895,706	1982C	14	5	Province (China)	Xining (Hsi-ning)	Asia	27
Quebec, Can.	Québec	594,860	1,540,680	6,438,403	1981C	11	4	Province (Canada)	Quebec (Quebec City)	North America	42
Queensland, Austl.	Queensland	666,900	1,727,200	2,294,546	1981C	3	1	State (Australia)	Brisbane	Australia	59
Reunion	Réunion	970	2,512	515,314	—	532	205	Overseas Department (France)	Saint-Denis	Africa	37
Rhode Island, U.S.	Rhode Island	1,210	3,140	968,000	1985E	800	308	State (U.S.)	Providence	North America	44
Rhodesia, see Zimbabwe	—	—	—	—	—	—	—	—	—	—	—
Rodrigues	Rodrigues	42	109	32,000	1982E*	762	294	Part of Mauritius	—	Africa	30–31
Romania (Rumania)	România	91,700	237,500	23,560,000	1988E	257	99	Socialist Republic (Communist Dictatorship)	Bucharest (Bucureşti)	Europe	15
Russian Soviet Federative Socialist Republic (R.S.F.S.R.), U.S.S.R.	Rossijskaja S.F.S.R.	6,592,849	17,075,400	142,117,000	1984E	22	8	Soviet Socialist Republic, U.S.S.R.	Moscow	Europe/Asia	19–20
Rwanda	Rwanda	10,169	26,338	6,809,000	1988E	670	259	Republic	Kigali	Africa	36

Political unit	Local name	Area sq. miles	km²	Population	Date	Population density per sq. mile	Population density per km²	Form of govt./ Political status	Capital	Continent	Map plate
Sabah, Malaysia	Sabah	28,460	73,711	915,000	1982E*	31	12	State of Malaysia	Kota Kinabalu	Asia	26
Saint Christopher and Nevis	St. Christopher-Nevis	101	262	44,000	1988E	436	168	Constitutional Monarchy	Basseterre	North America	51
St. Helena	St. Helena	162	419	6,600	1982E*	41	16	British Dependency	Jamestown	Africa	31
Saint Lucia	Saint Lucia	238	616	126,000	1988E	529	204	Constitutional Monarchy	Castries	North America	51
Saint-Pierre and Miquelon	St.-Pierre et Miquelon	93	242	6,700	1982E*	72	28	Territorial collectivity (France)	St.-Pierre	North America	42
Saint Vincent and the Grenadines	St. Vincent	150	388	130,000	1988E	867	335	Constitutional Monarchy	Kingstown	North America	50
Samoa	Samoa Islands	1,173	3,039	189,000	1982E*	161	62	—	—	Oceania	65
San Marino	San Marino	24	61	24,000	1988E	1,000	393	Republic	San Marino	Europe	14
São Tomé and Príncipe	São Tomé e Príncipe	372	964	102,000	1988E	274	106	Republic	São Tomé	Africa	34
Sarawak, Malaysia	Sarawak	48,050	124,450	1,345,000	1982E*	28	11	State of Malaysia	Kuching	Asia	26
Sardinia	Sardegna	9,301	24,090	1,585,959	1981C	171	66	Region of Italy	Cagliari	Europe	14
Saskatchewan, Can.	Saskatchewan	251,866	652,330	983,313	1981C	4	2	Province (Canada)	Regina	North America	42
Saudi Arabia	Al 'Arabīyah as Sa'ūdīyah	830,000	2,149,690	12,566,000	1988E	15	6	Monarchy	Riyadh (Ar Riyad)	Asia	23
Scandinavia	—	315,417	816,927	17,656,000	1988E	56	22	—	—	Europe	7
Scotland	Scotland	30,414	78,772	5,130,000	1988E	169	65	Constitutional Monarchy	Edinburgh	Europe	9
Senegal	Sénégal	75,750	196,192	7,085,000	1988E	94	36	Republic	Dakar	Africa	34
Senegambia	Senegambia	80,111	207,487	7,858,000	1988E	98	38	Confederation	—	Africa	34
Seychelles	Seychelles	175	453	68,000	1988E	389	150	Republic	Victoria	Africa	37
Shaanxi (Shensi), China	Shaanxi	75,599	195,800	28,904,423	1982C	382	148	Province (China)	Xi'an (Sian)	Asia	27
Shandong (Shantung), China	Shandong	59,189	153,300	74,419,054	1982C	1,257	485	Province (China)	Jinan (Tsinan)	Asia	28
Shanghai, China	Shanghai	2,240	5,800	11,859,748	1982C	5,295	2,045	Special Municipality (China)	—	Asia	28
Shanxi (Shansi), China	Shanxi	75,599	195,800	25,291,389	1982C	335	129	Province (China)	Taiyaun (Tai-yaun)	Asia	27
Shetland Islands	Shetland Islands	552	1,430	23,440	1985E	42	16	Region of Scotland; part of Great Britain	Lerwick	Europe	9
Siam, see Thailand	—	—	—	—	—	—	—	—	—	—	—
Sichaun (Szechwan), China	Sichuan	9,926	25,708	4,863,587	1981C	490	189	Region of Italy	Palermo	Europe	14
Sicily	Sicilia	219,700	569,000	99,713,310	1982C	454	175	Province (China)	Chengdu (Ch'eng-tu)	Asia	27
Sierra Leone	Sierra Leone	27,699	71,740	3,678,000	1988E	133	51	Republic (Comm. of Nations)	Freetown	Africa	34
Singapore	Singapore (English) Singapura (Malay)	238	616	2,669,000	1988E	11,167	4,319	Republic	Singapore	Asia	26
Solomon Islands	Solomon Islands	11,500	29,785	304,000	1988E	26	10	Constitutional Monarchy	Honiara	Oceania	63
Somalia	Soomaaliya	246,201	637,657	5,790,000	1988E	24	9	Military (Socialist) Rule	Mogadishu	Africa	35
South Africa (excludes Walvis Bay)	South Africa (English) Suid-Afrika (Afrikaans)	471,445	1,221,037	34,944,000	1988E	74	25	Republic	Cape Town, Pretoria, Bloemfontein	Africa	37
†South America	—	6,886,000	17,835,000	287,000,000	1988E	42	16	—	—	South America	52–53
South Australia, Austl.	South Australia	380,070	984,377	1,284,843	1981C	3	1	State (Australia)	Adelaide	Australia	59
South Carolina, U.S.	South Carolina	31,113	80,582	3,347,000	1985E	108	42	State (U.S.)	Columbia	North America	44
South Dakota, U.S.	South Dakota	77,116	199,730	708,000	1985E	9	4	State (U.S.)	Pierre	North America	45
South Yemen, see Yemen (Aden)	—	—	—	—	—	—	—	—	—	—	—
South Georgia (3)	South Georgia	1,580	4,092	20	1982E*	0.01	.005	Dependency of Falkland Islands (U.K.)	—	South America	56
South Korea	Taehan-Minguk	38,025 (4)	98,484 (4)	42,621,000	1988E	1,121	433	Republic	Seoul	Asia	28
South West Africa, see Namibia	—	—	—	—	—	—	—	—	—	—	—
Soviet Central Asia (or, The Aral-Caspian Lowland)	—	493,090	1,277,100	26,495,000	1982E*	54	21	4 Soviet Socialist Republics: Kirghiz S.S.R.; Tajik S.S.R.; Turkmen S.S.R.; Uzbek S.S.R.	—	Asia	19
Spain	España	194,889	504,759	39,934,000	1988E	205	79	Parliamentary Monarchy	Madrid	Europe	13
Spanish North Africa (2) (Sp.)	Plazas de Soberanía en el Norte de África	12	32	127,000	1982E*	10,583	3,969	Five Possessions (no central government)	—	Africa	13
Spanish Sahara, see Western Sahara	—	—	—	—	—	—	—	—	—	—	—
Sri Lanka	Sri Lanka	25,333	65,610	17,370,000	1988E	686	265	Republic	Colombo	Asia	25
Sudan	As Sūdān	967,500	2,505,813	23,498,000	1988E	24	9	Republic	Khartoum	Africa	35
Sumatra	Sumatera	182,860	473,606	28,016,160	1981C	153	59	Part of Indonesia	—	Asia	26
Suriname	Suríname	63,037	163,265	398,000	1988E	6	2	Authoritarian Rule	Paramaribo	South America	54
Swaziland	Swaziland	6,704	17,363	713,000	1988E	106	41	Monarchy	Mbabane and Lobamba	Africa	37
Sweden	Sverige	173,732	449,964	8,338,000	1988E	48	19	Constitutional Monarchy	Stockholm	Europe	7
Switzerland	Schweiz (German) Suisse (French) Svizzera (Italian)	15,941	41,288	6,551,000	1988E	410	159	Federal Republic	Bern	Europe	14
Syria	Sūrīyah	71,498	185,180	11,857,000	1988E	165	64	Republic	Damascus	Asia	24
Tajik Soviet Socialist Republic, U.S.S.R.	Takjikistan	55,251	143,100	4,365,000	1984E	79	31	Soviet Socialist Republic (U.S.S.R.)	Dushanbe (Stalinabad)	Asia	18
Taiwan	Taiwan	13,900	36,000	20,242,000	1988E	1,456	562	Republic	Taipei	Asia	27
Tanzania	Tanzania	364,900	945,087	25,085,000	1988E	70	27	Republic	Dar es Salaam	Africa	36
Tasmania, Austl.	Tasmania	26,200	67,800	418,956	1981C	16	6	State (Australia)	Hobart	Australia	59
Tennessee, U.S.	Tennessee	42,114	109,152	4,762,000	1985E	113	44	State (U.S.)	Nashville	North America	44
Texas, U.S.	Texas	266,807	691,030	16,370,000	1985E	61	24	State (U.S.)	Austin	North America	45
Thailand	Muang Thai	198,500	514,000	54,345,500	1988E	275	106	Constitutional Monarchy	Bangkok	Asia	26
Tianjin (Tientsin), China	Tianjin	4,250	11,000	7,764,141	1982C	1,827	706	Special Municipality (China)	—	Asia	28
Tibet, China	Xizang	471,662	1,221,600	1,892,393	1982C	4	2	Autonomous Region (China)	Lhasa	Asia	27
Togo	Togo	21,925	56,785	3,307,000	1988E	151	58	Presidential Regime	Lomé	Africa	34
Tokelau (N.Z.)	Tokelau	4	10	1,600	1982E*	410	160	Territory of New Zealand	—	Oceania	61
Tonga	Tonga	289	748	104,000	1988E	360	139	Constitutional Monarchy	Nukualofa	Oceania	61
Transcaucasia (U.S.S.R.)	—	71,853	186,100	14,940,000	1984E	208	80	Part of U.S.S.R. (3 republics)	—	Europe/Asia	16
Trinidad and Tobago	Trinidad and Tobago	1,980	5,128	1,239,000	1988E	626	242	Republic	Port-of-Spain	North America	50
Tristan da Cunha	Tristan da Cunha	40	104	300	1982E*	7.5	2.9	Dependency of St. Helena (U.K.)	Edinburgh	Africa	30–31

Political unit	Local name	Area sq. miles	Area km²	Population	Date	Population density per sq. mile	Population density per km²	Form of govt./ Political status	Capital	Continent	Map plate
Trucial States, *see* United Arab Emirates	—	—	—	—	—	—	—	—	—	—	—
Tunisia	Tūnis	63,170	163,610	7,616,000	1988E	121	47	Republic	Tunis	Africa	32
Turkey	Türkiye	301,382	780,576	53,547,000	1988E	178	69	Republic	Ankara	Europe/Asia	24
Turkey (European)	—	9,121	23,623	5,044,000	1988E	553	214	Part of Turkey	Ankara	Europe	24
Turkmen Soviet Socialist Republic, U.S.S.R.	Turkmenistan	188,456	488,100	3,118,000	1984E	17	6	Soviet Socialist Republic (U.S.S.R.)	Ashkhabad	Asia	19
Turks and Caicos Islands	Turks and Caicos Islands	166	430	7,400	—	45	17	British Dependency	Grand Turk	North America	49
Tuvalu	Tuvalu	10	26	8,000	1988E	800	308	Constitutional Monarchy	Funafuti	Oceania	60
Uganda	Uganda	91,134	236,036	15,908,000	1988E	175	68	Republic	Kampala	Africa	36
Ukrainian Soviet Socialist Republic, U.S.S.R.	Ukraine	233,090	603,700	50,667,000	1984E	217	84	Soviet Socialist Republic (U.S.S.R.)	Kiev	Europe	16
Union of Soviet Socialist Republics U.S.S.R.	Soyuz Sovetskikh Sotsialisticheskikh Respublik	8,649,500	22,402,000	286,230,000	1988E	33	13	Communist Dictatorship	Moscow	Europe/Asia	19–20
Union of Soviet Socialist Republics (European)	—	2,151,000	5,571,000	188,912,000	1988E	88	34	Part of U.S.S.R.	—	Europe	19
United Arab Emirates	Al Imārāt al 'Arabīyah al Muttaḥidah	32,278	83,600	1,465,000	1988E	15	18	Federation	Abu Dhabi	Asia	23
United Arab Republic, *see* Egypt	—	—	—	—	—	—	—	—	—	—	—
United States	United States	3,618,770	9,372,571	245,404,000	1988E	68	26	Republic	Washington, D.C.	North America	43
United States and main outlying areas	United States	3,683,456	9,540,129	234,817,000	1982E*	64	25	—	Washington, D.C.	—	—
Upper Volta, *see* Burkina Faso	—	—	—	—	—	—	—	—	—	—	—
Uruguay	Uruguay	68,037	176,215	2,975,000	1988E	44	17	Republic	Montevideo	South America	55
Utah, U.S.	Utah	84,899	219,889	1,645,000	1985E	25	7	State (U.S.)	Salt Lake City	North America	46
Uzbek Soviet Socialist Republic, U.S.S.R.	Uzbekistan	172,742	447,400	17,498,000	1984E	101	39	Soviet Socialist Republic (U.S.S.R.)	Tashkent	Asia	19
Vanuatu	Vanuatu	5,700	14,763	145,000	1988E	25	10	Republic	Port-Vila	Oceania	63
Vatican City	Città del Vaticano	0.17	0.44	1,000	1988E	5,882	2,273	Independent State	—	Europe	14
Venezuela	Venezuela	352,145	912,050	20,116,000	1988E	57	22	Federal Republic	Caracas	South America	54
Vermont, U.S.	Vermont	9,614	24,900	535,000	1985E	56	21	State (U.S.)	Montpelier	North America	44
Victoria, Austl.	Victoria	87,900	227,600	3,832,100	1981C	44	17	State (Australia)	Melbourne	Australia	59
Vietnam	Viet-nam Dan-chu Cong-hoa	127,242	329,556	62,996,000	1988E	495	191	Communist Dictatorship	Hanoi	Asia	26
Virgin Islands (U.S.)	Virgin Islands	133	344	95,591	1980C	719	278	Self-governing territory of U.S.	Charlotte Amalie	North America	51
Virgin Islands, British	British Virgin Islands	59	153	11,000	1982E*	186	72	British Dependency	Road Town	North America	51
Virginia, U.S.	Virginia	40,767	105,586	5,706,000	1985E	140	54	State (U.S.)	Richmond	North America	44
Wake Island	Wake Island	3	8	200	1982E*	67	26	Unincorporated possession (U.S.)	—	Oceania	60
Wales	Wales	8,018	20,768	2,805,000	1988E	350	135	Constitutional Monarchy	Cardiff	Europe	9
Wallis and Futuna Islands	Iles Wallis-et-Futuna	106	275	11,000	1982E*	112	43	Overseas Territory (France)	Mata-Utu	Oceania	61
Washington, U.S.	Washington	68,139	176,479	4,409,000	1985E	65	25	State (U.S.)	Olympia	North America	46
West Germany	Bundesrepublik Deutschland	96,005	248,651	60,839,000	1988E	635	245	Federal Republic	Bonn	Europe	10
West Indies	West Indies (English) Indias Occidentales (Spanish)	91,973	238,209	29,370,000	1982E*	319	123	—	—	North America	47
West Virginia, U.S.	West Virginia	24,231	62,759	1,936,000	1985E	80	31	State (U.S.)	Charleston	North America	44
Western Australia, Austl.	Western Australia	975,100	2,525,500	1,273,420	1981C	1	0.5	State (Australia)	Perth	Australia	59
Western Sahara	—	102,703	266,000	120,000	1982E*	1.2	0.5	Claimed by Morocco	—	Africa	32
Western Samoa	Samoa i Sisifo	1,097	2,842	167,000	1988E	152	59	Parliamentary	Apia	Oceania	65
White Russia, *see* Byelorussian S.S.R.	—	—	—	—	—	—	—	—	—	—	—
Wisconsin, U.S.	Wisconsin	56,153	145,436	4,775,000	1985E	85	33	State (U.S.)	Madison	North America	45
Wyoming, U.S.	Wyoming	97,809	253,326	509,000	1985E	5	2	State (U.S.)	Cheyenne	North America	46
Xinjiang (Sinkiang), China	Xinjiang	635,833	1,646,800	13,081,681	1982C	21	8	Autonomous Region (China)	Ürümqi (Urumchi)	Asia	27
Yemen	Aljmhoriah Alyemeniah	203,887	528,038	10,479,000	1990E	51	20	Republic	Sana	Asia	23
Yugoslavia	Jugoslavija	98,766	255,804	23,652,000	1988E	238	92	Socialist Republic	Belgrade	Europe	14–15
Yukon Territory, Can.	Yukon Territory	186,661	483,450	23,153	1981C	.12	.05	Territory (Canada)	Whitehorse	North America	42
Yunnan, China	Yunnan	168,420	436,200	32,553,817	1982C	193	75	Province (China)	Kunming (K'un-ming)	Asia	27
Zaire	Zaïre	905,365	2,344,885	33,265,000	1988E	36	14	Presidential regime	Kinshasa	Africa	36
Zambia	Zambia	290,586	752,614	7,834,000	1988E	25	10	Republic	Lusaka	Africa	36
Zanzibar	Zanzibar	1,020	2,642	1,254,250	1988E	1,230	475	Part of Tanzania	Zanzibar	Africa	36
Zhejiang (Chekiang), China	Zhejiang	39,305	101,800	38,884,603	1982C	989	382	Province (China)	Hangzhou (Hang-chou)	Asia	27
Zimbabwe	Zimbabwe	150,804	390,580	9,174,000	1988E	59	23	Republic; Parliamentary	Harare	Africa	37
World	—	57,259,000	148,300,000	5,014,000,000	1988E	87	34	—	—	—	1–2

C = Census; E = Estimate
† Continent
* Rand McNally and Company population estimate as of 1/1/82.
— none, or not applicable.
(1) No permanent population.
(2) Comprises Ceuta, Melilla, and several small islands.
(3) Claimed by Argentina.
(4) The 487 sq. mi. or 1,262 km² of the demilitarized zone are not included in either North or South Korea.
(5) In October 1966 the United Nations terminated the South African mandate over Namibia, a decision which South Africa did not accept.

World Geographical Tables

Earth: Land and Water

	Total area		Area of land			Area of water		
	sq. miles	sq. kilometers	sq. miles	sq. kilometers	per cent	sq. miles	sq. kilometers	per cent
Earth	196,951,000	510,100,000	57,259,000	148,300,000	30%	139,692,000	381,800,000	70%

Continents

Name	Area sq. miles/sq. kilometers	1988 population estimate	Population per sq. mile/sq. kilometer	Highest elevation place/feet/meters	Lowest elevation place/feet/meters (below sea level)	Highest recorded temperature place/°F./°C	Lowest recorded temperature place/°F./°C
Africa	11,694,000/30,330,000	600,000,000	51/20	Kilimanjaro, Tanzania 19,340/5,895	Lake Assal, Djibouti −509/−155	Al Aziziyah, Libya 136°F./58°C	Ifrane, Morocco −11°F./−24°C
Antarctica	5,100,000/13,209,000	(no permanent population)	—	Vinson Massif 16,864/5,140	sea level	Esperanza 58°F./14°C	Vostok Station −127°F./−88°C
Asia	16,968,000/43,947,000	3,069,000,000	181/70	Mount Everest, Nepal-Tibet 29,028/8,848	Dead Sea, Israel-Jordan −1,310/−399	Tirat Zevi, Israel 129°F./54°C	Verkhoyansk, Soviet Union −93°F./−69°C
Australia	2,966,150/7,682,300	16,297,000	5/2	Mount Kosciusko 7,310/2,228	Lake Eyre −52/−16	Cloncurry 128°F./53°C	Charlotte Pass −80°F./−22°C
Europe	4,066,000/10,532,000	692,000,000	170/66	Mount Elbrus 18,481/5,633	Caspian Sea, Soviet Union-Iran −92/−28	Seville, Spain 122°F./50°C	Ust-Ščugor, Soviet Union −67°F./−55°C
North America	9,363,000/24,249,000	418,000,000	45/17	Mount McKinley, U.S. 20,320/6,194	Death Valley, U.S. −282/−86	Death Valley, U.S. 134°F./57°C	Northice, Greenland −87°F./−66°C
South America	6,886,000/17,835,000	287,000,000	42/16	Mount Aconcagua, Argentina 22,831/6,959	Valdés Peninsula, Argentina −131/−40	Rivadavia, Argentina 120°F./49°C	Sarmiento, Argentina −27°F./−33°C
Earth	196,951,000/510,100,000	5,082,297,000	87/34	Mount Everest, Asia 29,028/8,848	Dead Sea, Asia −1,310/−399	Al Aziziyah, Africa 136°F./58°C	Vostok, Antarctica −127°F./−88°C

Historical Population of the World

Area	1650	1750	1800	1850	1900	1914	1920	1939	1950	1982*	1990E
Europe	*100,000,000*	*140,000,000*	*190,000,000*	*265,000,000*	400,000,000	470,000,000	453,000,000	526,000,000	530,000,000	666,400,000	693,000,000
Asia	*335,000,000*	*476,000,000*	*593,000,000*	*754,000,000*	*932,000,000*	1,006,000,000	1,000,000,000	1,247,000,000	1,418,000,000	2,724,900,000	3,172,000,000
Africa	*100,000,000*	*95,000,000*	*90,000,000*	*95,000,000*	*118,000,000*	130,000,000	*140,000,000*	170,000,000	199,000,000	490,300,000	643,000,000
North America	*5,000,000*	*5,000,000*	*13,000,000*	*39,000,000*	106,000,000	141,000,000	147,000,000	186,000,000	219,000,000	379,400,000	427,000,000
South America	*8,000,000*	*7,000,000*	*12,000,000*	*20,000,000*	38,000,000	55,000,000	61,000,000	90,000,000	111,000,000	247,800,000	297,000,000
Oceania, incl. Australia	*2,000,000*	*2,000,000*	*2,000,000*	*2,000,000*	6,000,000	8,000,000	9,000,000	11,000,000	13,000,000	23,200,000	28,000,000
World	*500,000,000*	*725,000,000*	*900,000,000*	*1,175,000,000*	1,600,000,000	1,810,000,000	1,810,000,000	2,230,000,000	2,490,000,000	4,532,000,000	5,260,000,000

*Figures prior to 1982 are rounded to the nearest million.   Figures in italics represent very rough estimates.

Largest Countries: Population

	Name	Population 1988 estimate	Population 1993 estimate
1.	China	1,096,584,000	1,157,692,000
2.	India	803,975,000	871,216,000
3.	Soviet Union	286,230,000	298,271,000
4.	United States	245,404,000	256,726,000
5.	Indonesia	172,975,000	186,896,000
6.	Brazil	144,427,000	158,969,000
7.	Japan	121,671,000	124,122,000
8.	Bangladesh	109,471,000	123,956,000
9.	Pakistan	108,591,000	121,781,000
10.	Nigeria	105,623,000	113,272,000
11.	Mexico	84,964,000	94,905,000
12.	Vietnam	62,996,000	69,088,000
13.	West Germany	60,839,000	60,447,000
14.	Philippines	58,712,000	65,390,000
15.	Italy	57,240,000	60,033,000
16.	Great Britain	56,672,000	57,026,000
17.	France	55,206,000	56,067,000
18.	Thailand	54,345,500	59,068,000
19.	Turkey	53,547,000	59,687,000
20.	Egypt	50,296,000	58,969,000
21.	Iran	49,098,000	55,794,000
22.	South Korea	42,621,000	45,574,000
23.	Ethiopia	42,403,000	42,551,000
24.	Spain	39,934,000	41,424,000
25.	Burma	39,778,000	44,460,000
26.	Poland	38,462,000	39,724,000
27.	South Africa	34,944,000	39,569,000
28.	Zaire	33,265,000	38,378,000
29.	Argentina	31,965,000	34,169,000
30.	Colombia	30,577,000	33,640,000
31.	Canada	26,489,000	27,806,000
32.	Tanzania	25,085,000	30,116,000
33.	Algeria	24,316,000	28,565,000
34.	Morocco	24,290,000	27,972,000
35.	Yugoslavia	23,652,000	24,328,000
36.	Romania	23,560,000	24,408,000
37.	Sudan	23,498,000	27,086,000
38.	Kenya	23,338,000	28,760,000
39.	North Korea	21,478,000	23,929,000
40.	Peru	21,254,000	23,944,000
41.	Taiwan	20,242,000	21,806,000
42.	Venezuela	20,116,000	22,980,000
43.	Nepal	17,649,000	19,840,000
44.	Sri Lanka	17,330,000	18,863,000
45.	Iraq	17,306,000	20,227,000

Smallest Countries: Population

	Name	Population 1988 estimate	Population 1993 estimate
1.	Vatican City	1,000	—
2.	Tuvalu	8,000	—
3.	Nauru	9,000	—
4.	San Marino	24,000	26,000
5.	Monaco	29,000	31,000
6.	Liechtenstein	30,000	33,000
7.	Andorra	44,000	52,000
8.	Saint Christopher and Nevis	44,400	—
9.	Kiribati	65,000	—
10.	Seychelles	68,000	—
11.	Dominica	74,000	—
12.	Antigua and Barbuda	83,000	—
13.	São Tomé and Príncipe	102,000	106,000
14.	Tonga	104,000	114,000
15.	Grenada	119,000	—
16.	Saint Lucia	126,000	—
17.	Saint Vincent and the Grenadines	130,000	—
18.	Vanuatu	145,000	—
19.	Western Samoa	167,000	175,000
20.	Belize	172,000	193,000
21.	Maldives	197,000	223,000
22.	Brunei	244,000	—
23.	Bahamas	246,000	272,000
24.	Iceland	248,000	257,000
25.	Barbados	272,000	287,000
26.	Solomon Islands	304,000	—
27.	Qatar	332,000	386,000
28.	Cape Verde	335,000	355,000
29.	Equatorial Guinea	345,000	390,000
30.	Luxembourg	368,000	370,000
31.	Djibouti	376,000	427,000
32.	Malta	390,000	402,000
33.	Suriname	398,000	436,000
34.	Bahrain	483,000	568,000
35.	Comoros	500,000	582,000
36.	Cyprus	688,000	719,000

Largest Countries: Area

	Name	Area sq. miles	km²
1.	U.S.S.R.	8,649,500	22,402,000
2.	Canada	3,849,674	9,970,610
3.	China	3,678,470	9,527,200
4.	United States	3,618,770	9,372,571
5.	Brazil	3,286,487	8,511,965
6.	Australia	2,966,150	7,682,300
7.	India	1,269,219	3,287,263
8.	Argentina	1,073,400	2,780,092
9.	Sudan	967,500	2,505,813
10.	Algeria	919,595	2,381,741
11.	Zaire	905,365	2,344,885
12.	Saudi Arabia	830,000	2,149,690
13.	Mexico	758,136	1,963,564
14.	Indonesia	741,101	1,919,443
15.	Libya	679,362	1,759,540
16.	Iran	636,300	1,648,000
17.	Mongolia	604,250	1,565,000
18.	Peru	496,225	1,285,216
19.	Chad	495,800	1,284,000
20.	Niger	489,200	1,267,000
21.	Angola	481,354	1,246,700
22.	Mali	478,800	1,240,000
23.	Ethiopia	471,778	1,221,900
24.	South Africa	471,445	1,221,037
25.	Colombia	439,737	1,138,914
26.	Bolivia	424,165	1,098,581
27.	Mauritania	397,956	1,030,700
28.	Egypt	386,662	1,001,449
29.	Tanzania	364,900	945,087
30.	Nigeria	356,669	923,768
31.	Venezuela	352,145	912,050
32.	Pakistan	310,404	803,943
33.	Mozambique	308,642	799,380
34.	Turkey	301,382	780,576
35.	Chile	292,135	756,626
36.	Zambia	290,586	752,614
37.	Burma	261,218	676,552
38.	Afghanistan	251,773	652,089
39.	Somalia	246,201	637,657
40.	Central African Republic	240,535	622,984
41.	Botswana	231,805	600,372
42.	Madagascar	226,658	587,041
43.	Kenya	224,961	582,646
44.	France	211,208	547,026
45.	Thailand	198,500	514,000

Smallest Countries: Area

	Name	Area sq. miles	km²
1.	Vatican City	0.17	0.44
2.	Monaco	0.73	1.9
3.	Nauru	8	21
4.	Tuvalu	10	26
5.	San Marino	24	61
6.	Liechtenstein	62	160
7.	Saint Christopher and Nevis	101	261
8.	Maldives	115	298
9.	Malta	122	316
10.	Grenada	133	344
11.	Saint Vincent and the Grenadines	150	388
12.	Barbados	166	430
13.	Antigua and Barbuda	171	442
14.	Seychelles	175	453
15.	Andorra	179	464
16.	Saint Lucia	238	616
17.	Singapore	238	616
18.	Bahrain	262	678
19.	Kiribati	281	728
20.	Tonga	289	748
21.	Dominica	290	751
22.	São Tomé and Príncipe	372	964
23.	Mauritius	790	2,045
24.	Comoros	838	2,171
25.	Luxembourg	998	2,586
26.	Western Samoa	1,097	2,842
27.	Cape Verde	1,557	4,033
28.	Trinidad and Tobago	1,980	5,128
29.	Brunei	2,226	5,765
30.	Cyprus	3,572	9,251
31.	Lebanon	4,015	10,400
32.	Jamaica	4,244	10,991
33.	Gambia	4,361	11,295
34.	Qatar	4,416	11,437
35.	Bahamas	5,380	13,935
36.	Vanuatu	5,700	14,763
37.	Swaziland	6,704	17,363
38.	Kuwait	6,880	17,818
39.	Fiji	7,056	18,274
40.	Israel	8,019	20,770
41.	El Salvador	8,124	21,041
42.	Djibouti	8,410	21,783
43.	Belize	8,867	22,965
44.	Rwanda	10,169	26,338
45.	Haiti	10,714	27,750

Highest Population Densities

	Country	Population density per sq. mile	km²
1.	Monaco	39,726	15,263
2.	Singapore	11,167	4,319
3.	Vatican City	5,882	2,273
4.	Malta	3,197	1,234
5.	Bangladesh	1,969	760
6.	Bahrain	1,843	712
7.	Maldives	1,713	661
8.	Barbados	1,639	633
9.	Taiwan	1,456	562
10.	Mauritius	1,362	526
11.	Nauru	1,125	429
12.	South Korea	1,121	433
13.	Netherlands	1,019	393
14.	San Marino	1,000	393
15.	Grenada	895	346
16.	St. Vincent and the Grenadines	867	335
17.	Belgium	839	324
18.	Japan	834	322
19.	Tuvalu	800	308
20.	El Salvador	749	289
21.	Lebanon	704	271
22.	Sri Lanka	686	265
23.	West Germany	635	245
24.	India	633	245
25.	Trinidad and Tobago	626	242
26.	Great Britain	601	232
27.	Jamaica	571	221
28.	Saint Lucia	529	205

Lowest Population Densities

	Country	Population density per sq. mile	km²
1.	Mongolia	3	1
2.	Australia	5	2
3.	Botswana	5	2
4.	Mauritania	5	2
5.	Iceland	6	2
6.	Libya	6	2
7.	Suriname	6	2
8.	Canada	7	3
9.	Central African Republic	11	4
10.	Chad	11	4
11.	Gabon	12	5
12.	Guyana	12	5
13.	Niger	14	5
14.	Saudi Arabia	15	6
15.	Bolivia	16	6
16.	Congo	16	6
17.	Oman	16	6
18.	Mali	18	7
19.	Belize	19	7
20.	Angola	20	8
21.	Papua New Guinea	22	9
22.	Somalia	24	9
23.	Sudan	24	9
24.	Paraguay	25	10
25.	Vanuatu	25	10
26.	Zambia	25	10
27.	Algeria	26	10
28.	Solomon Islands	26	10

Principal Rivers

Name	Location	Length miles	km
Nile	Africa	4,145	6,671
Amazon	South America	4,000	6,437
Yangtze (Yangtze Kiang; Chang Jiang)	China	3,915	6,300
Huang He	China	2,903	4,672
Congo	Africa	2,900	4,667
Amur	Soviet Union	2,744	4,416
Lena	Soviet Union	2,734	4,400
Mekong	Asia (Indochinese Peninsula)	2,600	4,180
Niger	Africa	2,600	4,180
Yenisey	Soviet Union	2,543	4,093
Paraná	South America	2,485	3,999
Mississippi	United States	2,348	3,779
Missouri	United States	2,315	3,726
Murray-Darling	Australia	2,310	3,718
Ob	Soviet Union	2,268	3,650
Volga	Soviet Union	2,193	3,530
Purús	Peru-Brazil	2,100	3,380
Madeira	Brazil	2,000	3,200
São Francisco	Brazil	1,988	3,199
Yukon	Canada-United States	1,979	3,185
Rio Grande	United States-Mexico	1,885	3,034
Indus	Tibet-Pakistan	1,800	2,897
Danube	Europe	1,777	2,860
Darling	Australia	1,702	2,739
Euphrates	Asia	1,700	2,736
Zambezi	Africa	1,700	2,736
Brahmaputra	Asia	1,680	2,704
Murray	Australia	1,609	2,589
Paraguay	South America	1,584	2,549
Ural	Soviet Union	1,570	2,527
Amu Darya (Oxus)	Soviet Union-Afghanistan	1,560	2,511
Ganges	India-Bangladesh	1,540	2,478
Salween (Salwin)	Burma-Tibet	1,500	2,414
Arkansas	United States	1,459	2,348
Colorado	United States-Mexico	1,450	2,334
Dnepr (Dnieper)	Soviet Union	1,400	2,200
Orinoco	Venezuela-Colombia	1,284	2,066
Irrawaddy (Irawadi)	Burma	1,250	2,010
Saskatchewan	Canada	1,205	1,939
Mackenzie	Canada	1,071	1,724

Principal Mountains

Name	Height above sea level In feet	In meters	Location
Aconcagua	22,831	6,959	Andes in Argentina
Annapurna	26,504	8,078	Himalaya in Nepal
Ararat	17,011	5,185	Eastern Plateau in Turkey
Chimborazo	20,561	6,267	Andes in Ecuador
Cotopaxi	19,347	5,897	Andes in Ecuador
Ixtacihuatl	17,343	5,286	Plateau of Mexico
Jungfrau	13,642	4,158	Alps in Switzerland
Kilimanjaro	19,340	5,895	Isolated peak in Tanzania
Lassen Peak	10,457	3,187	Cascade in California
Matterhorn	14,692	4,478	Alps on Switzerland-Italy border
Mauna Kea	13,796	4,205	Island of Hawaii
Mauna Loa	13,677	4,169	Island of Hawaii
Mont Blanc	15,771	4,807	Alps on France-Italy-Switzerland border
Mount Cook	12,349	3,764	Southern Alps in New Zealand
Mount Elbrus	18,481	5,633	Caucasus in Soviet Union
Mount Etna	11,122	3,390	Island of Sicily
Mount Everest	29,028	8,848	Himalaya on Nepal-Tibet border
Mount Fuji	12,388	3,776	Island of Honshu in Japan
Mount Godwin Austen, or K2, or Dapsang	28,250*	8,611*	Karakoram, or Mustagh, in Kashmir
Mount Hood	11,239	3,426	Cascade in Oregon
Mount Kanchenjunga, or Kinchinjunga	28,208	8,598	Himalaya on Nepal-India border
Mount Kenya	17,058	5,199	Central Kenya
Mount Kosciusko	7,310	2,228	Australian Alps
Mount Logan	19,524	5,951	St. Elias in Canada
Mount Makalu	27,824	8,481	Himalaya on Nepal-Tibet border
Mount McKinley	20,320	6,194	Alaska Range in Alaska
Mount Rainier	14,410	4,392	Cascade in Washington
Mount Saint Helens	8,364	2,549	Cascade in Washington
Mount Shasta	14,162	4,317	Cascade in California
Mount Whitney	14,491	4,417	Sierra Nevada in California
Olympus	9,570	2,917	Greece
Orizaba, or Citlaltépetl	18,701	5,700	Plateau of Mexico
Pikes Peak	14,110	4,301	Front Range in Colorado
Popocatepetl	17,887	5,452	Plateau of Mexico
Vesuvius	4,190	1,277	Italy

*Traditional measurement.

Major Lakes

Name	Country	Area sq. miles	km²	Depth feet	meters
Caspian Sea	Iran-U.S.S.R.	143,630	372,000	3,363	1,025
Lake Superior	United States-Canada	31,700	82,103	1,333	406
Lake Victoria	Africa	26,828	69,484	270	82
Aral Sea	U.S.S.R.	25,660	66,459	223	68
Lake Huron	United States-Canada	23,050	59,699	750	229
Lake Michigan	United States	22,300	57,757	923	281
Lake Tanganyika	Africa	12,700	32,893	4,708	1,435
Great Bear Lake	Canada	12,275	31,792	1,350	411
Lake Baikal	U.S.S.R.	12,162	31,499	5,315	1,620
Lake Nyasa	Africa	11,100	28,749	2,300	701
Great Slave Lake	Canada	10,980	28,438	2,015	614
Lake Erie	United States-Canada	9,910	25,667	210	64
Lake Winnipeg	Canada	9,398	24,341	70	21
Lake Ontario	United States-Canada	7,550	19,554	802	244
Lake Ladoga	U.S.S.R.	6,835	17,703	738	225
Lake Balkhash	U.S.S.R.	6,670	17,275	85	26
Lake Chad	Africa	6,300	16,300	22	7
Lake Onega	U.S.S.R.	3,820	9,894	393	120
Lake Eyre	Australia	3,700	9,583	52 feet below sea level	16 meters below sea level
Lake Titicaca	Peru-Bolivia	3,200	8,300	900	270
Lake Athabasca	Canada	3,120	8,081	407	124
Lake Nicaragua	Nicaragua	3,060	7,925	141	43
Lake Turkana (Lake Rudolf)	Kenya-Ethiopia	2,473	6,405	200	61
Reindeer Lake	Canada	2,444	6,330	720	219
Lake Torrens	Australia	2,230	5,776	shallow body of water	
Lake Vänern	Sweden	2,156	5,584	328	100
Lake Winnipegosis	Canada	2,013	5,214	38	12

Oceans, Seas, and Gulfs

Name	Area sq. miles	km²	Greatest depth feet	meters
Pacific Ocean	63,800,000	165,200,000	36,198	11,033
Atlantic Ocean	31,530,000	81,662,000	28,374	8,648
Indian Ocean	28,356,300	73,441,700	25,344	7,725
Arctic Ocean	3,662,000	9,485,100	17,880	5,450
Arabian Sea	1,492,000	3,863,000	19,029	5,800
South China Sea	1,300,000	3,370,000	18,241	5,560
Bering Sea	1,140,000	2,952,900	13,422	4,091
Caribbean Sea	1,105,000	2,877,000	24,720	7,535
Mediterranean Sea	969,100	2,510,000	16,302	5,093
Bay of Bengal	839,000	2,172,000	17,251	5,258
Gulf of Mexico	700,000	1,800,000	12,700	3,871
Norwegian Sea	597,000	1,547,000	13,189	4,020
Okhotsk, Sea of	589,800	1,527,600	11,063	3,372
Greenland Sea	465,000	1,205,000	15,899	4,846
Hudson Bay	316,500	819,731	850	259

Principal Islands

Name	Area sq. miles	km²	Highest point name	feet	meters
Greenland	840,004	2,175,600	Mount Gunnbjørn	12,139	3,700
New Guinea	311,737	807,396	Puncak Jaya	16,503	5,030
Borneo	288,151	746,308	Mount Kinabalu	13,455	4,101
Madagascar	226,658	587,041	Maromokotro	9,436	2,876
Baffin Island	195,927	507,449	(unnamed)	7,045	2,147
Sumatra (Sumatera)	182,860	473,606	Kerinci	12,484	3,805
Honshu	87,805	227,414	Mount Fuji	12,388	3,776
Great Britain	84,550	218,980	Ben Nevis	4,406	1,343
Victoria Island (N.W.T., Can.)	83,896	217,290	(unnamed)	2,150	655
Ellesmere Island	75,767	196,236	Barbeau Peak	8,584	2,616
Celebus (Sulawesi)	73,057	189,216	Rantekombola	11,335	3,455
South Island (New Zealand)	58,965	152,719	Mount Cook	12,349	3,764
Java (Djawa)	51,038	132,187	Semeru	12,060	3,676
North Island (New Zealand)	44,244	114,592	Mount Ruapehu	9,175	2,797
(island of) Newfoundland	43,008	111,390	Lewis Hills	2,672	814
Cuba	42,804	110,861	Pico Turquino	6,542	1,994
Luzon (Philippines)	40,420	104,688	Mount Pulog	9,606	2,928
Iceland	39,800	103,000	Hvannadalsh-núkur	6,952	2,119
Mindanao (Philippines)	36,537	94,630	Mount Apo	9,692	2,954
Ireland	32,588	84,404	Carrauntoohill	3,414	1,041
Hokkaido	30,144	78,073	Asahi Mountain	7,513	2,290
Hispaniola	29,418	76,192	Duarte Peak	10,417	3,175
Sakhalin (U.S.S.R.)	29,100	75,369	Lopatina	5,279	1,609
Tasmania	26,200	67,800	Mount Ossa	5,305	1,617
Sri Lanka	25,333	65,610	Pidurutalagala	8,281	2,524
Novaya Zemlya (northern island)	20,000	52,000	(unnamed)	5,075	1,574
Tierra del Fuego	19,280	49,935	Yogan	8,100	2,469
Kyushu	14,114	36,554	Kuju Mountain	5,866	1,788

Waterfalls

Name	Country	River	Height feet	meters
Angel	Venezuela	Churún	3,212	979
Yosemite	United States	Yosemite Creek	2,425	739
Tugela	South Africa	Tugela	2,014	614
Sutherland	New Zealand	Milford Sound	1,904	580
Gavarnie	France	Gave de Pau	1,385	422
Krimml	Austria	Krimml	1,312	400
Takakkaw	Canada	Yoho	1,200	366
Staubbach	Switzerland	Staubbach	984	300
Jog	India	—	830	253
Kaieteur	Guyana	Potaro	741	226

Drainage Basins

Name	Continent	Area sq. miles	km²
Amazon River	South America	2,700,000	7,000,000
Congo River	Africa	1,400,000	3,630,000
Mississippi River	North America	1,247,300	3,230,490
Ob River	Asia	1,125,200	2,914,250
Lena River	Asia	1,000,000	2,600,000
Yenisey River	Asia (Siberia)	1,000,000	2,600,000
Amur River	Asia	770,000	1,990,000
Yangtze River (Yangtze Kiang; Chang Jiang)	Asia	706,000	1,829,000
Mackenzie River system	North America	682,000	1,766,000
Niger River	Africa	580,000	1,500,000
Volga River	Europe	525,000	1,360,000
Saint Lawrence River	North America	498,500	1,291,100

Populations of Major Cities

The largest and most important of the world's major cities are listed in the following table. Also included are some smaller cities because of their regional significance.

Local official names have primarily been used throughout the table. When a commonly used conventional name exists, it has been featured. An alternate name follows in parentheses. A former name is identified in *italics*.

The population of each city has been dated, and is identified as either an official estimate (E) or a census figure (C).

City	Country	City population	Metropolitan area population	Date
Aachen	West Germany	238,587	540,000	1985 E
Abidjan	Ivory Coast	1,850,000	—	1982 E
Acapulco (Acapulco de Juárez)	Mexico	421,088	—	1978 E
Accra	Ghana	964,879	1,420,065	1984 C
Addis Ababa	Ethiopia	1,412,577	—	1984 C
Adelaide	Australia	917,000	—	1986 C
Aden	Yemen	318,000	—	1984 E
Agra	India	723,676	770,352	1981 C
Ahmadabad	India	2,059,725	2,548,057	1981 C
Al Basrah (Basra)	Iraq	370,900	—	1970 E
Aleppo	Syria	961,000	—	1980 E
Alexandria (Al Iskandariyah)	Egypt	2,917,327	—	1986 C
Algiers (Alger)	Algeria	1,721,607	—	1983 E
Allahabad	India	609,232	642,420	1981 C
Alma-Ata	Soviet Union	1,046,000	—	1984 E
Amman	Jordan	900,000	—	1988 E
Amritsar	India	589,229	—	1981 C
Amsterdam	The Netherlands	687,397	945,062	1983 E
Ankara	Turkey	2,235,035	—	1985 C
Anshan (An-shan)	China	1,260,000	—	1984 E
Antananarivo	Madagascar	662,585	—	1985 E
Antwerp (Antwerpen, Anvers)	Belgium	185,021	628,989	1983 E
Asansol	India	187,039	1,050,000	1981 C
Asunción	Paraguay	457,210	655,000	1982 C
Athens (Athinai)	Greece	885,737	3,027,331	1981 C
Atlanta	(Georgia) U.S.	425,022	2,138,231	1980 C
Auckland	New Zealand	820,754	—	1986 C
Augsburg	West Germany	245,193	390,000	1985 E
Austin	(Texas) U.S.	345,890	536,688	1980 C
Baghdad	Iraq	2,969,000	—	1976 E
Baku	Soviet Union	1,084,000	1,661,000	1984 E
Baltimore	(Maryland) U.S.	786,741	2,199,531	1980 C
Bamako	Mali	404,022	—	1976 C
Bandung	Indonesia	1,462,637	1,525,000	1980 C
Bangalore	India	2,476,355	2,921,751	1981 C
Bangkok (Krung Thep)	Thailand	5,153,902	—	1980 C
Barcelona	Spain	1,694,064	—	1986 E
Barranquilla	Colombia	899,781	950,000	1985 C
Basel	Switzerland	174,606	361,809	1986 E
Beijing (Peking)	China	9,470,000	—	1984 E
Beirut	Lebanon	702,000	—	1974 E
Belém	Brazil	758,117	1,000,349	1980 C
Belfast	Northern Ireland	301,600	—	1985 E
Belgrade (Beograd)	Yugoslavia	1,455,046	—	1981 C
Belo Horizonte	Brazil	1,442,483	2,541,788	1980 C
Berlin, East (East Berlin)	East Germany	1,202,895	—	1985 E
Berlin, West (West Berlin)	West Germany	1,860,084	3,775,000	1985 E
Bern (Berne)	Switzerland	138,574	299,221	1986 E
Bhopal	India	672,329	—	1981 C
Bielefeld	West Germany	299,727	525,000	1985 E
Bilbao	Spain	378,221	—	1986 E
Birmingham	England (Great Britain)	1,007,500	2,641,800	1985 E
Birmingham	(Alabama) U.S.	286,799	883,946	1980 C
Bogotá	Colombia	3,982,941	—	1985 C
Bologna	Italy	455,853	—	1981 C
Bombay	India	8,227,332	—	1981 C
Bonn	West Germany	290,769	555,000	1985 E
Bordeaux	France	208,159	650,123	1982 C
Boston	(Massachusetts) U.S.	562,994	2,805,911	1980 C
Brasília	Brazil	411,305	—	1980 C
Brazzaville	Congo	596,200	—	1985 E
Bremen	West Germany	526,377	800,000	1985 E
Bremerhaven	West Germany	133,521	190,000	1985 E
Brisbane	Australia	1,037,815	—	1986 C
Bristol	England (Great Britain)	393,800	—	1985 E
Brussels (Brussel, Bruxelles)	Belgium	137,738	989,877	1983 E
Bucharest (Bucureşti)	Romania	1,961,189	2,227,568	1983 E
Budapest	Hungary	2,075,990	2,600,000	1986 E
Buenos Aires	Argentina	2,908,001	9,927,404	1980 C
Buffalo	(New York) U.S.	357,870	1,015,472	1980 C
Bursa	Turkey	612,510	—	1985 C
Cairo (Al Qahirah)	Egypt	6,052,836	8,500,000	1986 C
Calcutta	India	3,305,006	9,194,018	1981 C
Cali	Colombia	1,350,565	—	1985 C
Canberra	Australia	247,194	—	1986 C
Cape Town	South Africa	789,580	1,490,935	1980 C
Caracas	Venezuela	1,261,116	3,310,236	1988 E
Cardiff	Wales (Great Britain)	278,900	625,000	1985 E
Casablanca	Morocco	2,139,204	—	1982 C
Catania	Italy	378,521	—	1981 C
Cebu	Philippines	490,281	500,000	1980 C
Changchun (Ch'ang-ch'un)	China	1,810,000	—	1984 E
Changsha (Ch'ang-sha)	China	1,210,000	—	1984 E
Charleroi	Belgium	216,144	225,855	1983 E
Chelyabinsk	Soviet Union	1,086,000	—	1984 E
Chengdu (Ch'eng-tu)	China	2,540,000	—	1984 E
Chicago	(Illinois) U.S.	3,005,072	6,060,387	1980 C
Chittagong	Bangladesh	1,391,877	—	1981 C
Chongqing (Chungking, Ch'ung-ch'ing)	China	2,730,000	—	1984 E
Cincinnati	(Ohio) U.S.	385,457	1,401,491	1980 C
Cleveland	(Ohio) U.S.	573,822	1,898,825	1980 C
Cochin	India	513,081	552,408	1981 C
Coimbatore	India	700,923	965,000	1981 C
Cologne (Köln)	West Germany	916,153	1,815,000	1985 E
Colombo	Sri Lanka	616,000	1,540,000	1977 E
Columbus	(Ohio) U.S.	565,032	1,243,833	1980 C
Copenhagen (København)	Denmark	472,729	1,358,540	1985 E
Córdoba	Argentina	968,664	982,018	1980 C
Coventry	England (Great Britain)	312,200	—	1985 E
Curitiba	Brazil	843,733	1,441,743	1980 C
Dakar	Senegal	978,523	—	1979 E
Dallas	(Texas) U.S.	904,078	1,957,378	1980 C
Damascus	Syria	1,200,000	—	1980 E
Dar es Salaam	Tanzania	870,000	—	1978 C
Dayton	(Ohio) U.S.	195,536	942,083	1980 C
Delhi	India	4,884,234	5,729,283	1981 C
Denver	(Colorado) U.S.	492,365	1,428,836	1980 C
Detroit	(Michigan) U.S.	1,203,339	4,488,072	1980 C
Dhaka (Dacca)	Bangladesh	2,365,695	—	1981 C
Dnepropetrovsk	Soviet Union	1,140,000	—	1984 E
Donetsk (Stalino)	Soviet Union	1,064,000	—	1984 E
Dortmund	West Germany	572,094	—	1985 E
Douala	Cameroon	1,000,000	—	1984 E
Dresden	East Germany	519,860	640,000	1985 E
Dublin	Ireland	502,749	983,683	1986 C
Duisburg	West Germany	518,260	—	1985 E
Durban	South Africa	677,760	960,792	1980 C
Düsseldorf	West Germany	561,686	1,225,000	1985 E
Edinburgh	Scotland (Great Britain)	439,672	—	1985 E
Edmonton	(Alberta) Canada	573,982	785,465	1986 C
El Paso	(Texas) U.S.	425,259	479,899	1980 C
Essen	West Germany	619,991	5,125,000	1985 E
Florence (Firenze)	Italy	453,293	—	1981 C
Fortaleza	Brazil	648,815	1,581,588	1980 C
Frankfurt am Main	West Germany	595,348	1,880,000	1985 E
Freetown	Sierra Leone	469,776	—	1985 C
Frunze	Soviet Union	590,000	—	1984 E
Fukuoka	Japan	1,160,402	1,575,000	1985 C
Fushun (Fu-shun)	China	1,220,000	—	1984 E
Gdańsk (German: Danzig)	Poland	468,600	820,000	1985 E
Geneva (Genève, Genf)	Switzerland	159,895	378,274	1986 E
Genoa (Genova)	Italy	760,300	—	1981 C
Ghent (Gent)	Belgium	236,540	—	1983 E
Giza (Al Jizah)	Egypt	1,870,508	—	1986 C
Glasgow	Scotland (Great Britain)	733,794	—	1985 E
Gorki (Gor'kiy)	Soviet Union	1,392,000	—	1984 E
Göteborg (Gothenburg)	Sweden	424,085	698,794	1984 E
Graz	Austria	243,405	—	1981 C
Guadalajara	Mexico	1,725,000	2,856,000	1980 C
Guangzhou (Canton)	China	3,220,000	—	1984 E
Guatemala City	Guatemala	754,243	—	1981 C
Guayaquil	Ecuador	1,199,344	—	1982 C
Guiyang (Kuei-yang)	China	1,360,000	—	1984 E
The Hague ('s Gravenhage)	The Netherlands	449,338	677,962	1983 E
Haifa	Israel	266,100	374,950	1983 E
Hamburg	West Germany	1,579,884	2,260,000	1985 E
Hangzhou (Hang-chou)	China	1,191,582	—	1984 E
Hannover (Hanover)	West Germany	508,298	1,005,000	1985 E
Hanoi	Vietnam	1,443,500	—	1976 C
Harare (Salisbury)	Zimbabwe	656,100	—	1982 C
Harbin	China	2,590,000	—	1984 E
Hartford	(Connecticut) U.S.	136,392	715,923	1980 C
Havana (La Habana)	Cuba	1,924,886	—	1981 C
Helsinki (Helsingfors)	Finland	481,927	932,376	1984 E
Hiroshima	Japan	1,044,129	1,525,000	1985 C
Ho Chi Minh City (Saigon)	Vietnam	3,460,500	—	1979 C
Honolulu	(Hawaii) U.S.	365,048	762,565	1980 C
Houston	(Texas) U.S.	1,595,138	2,735,766	1980 C
Hyderabad	India	2,187,262	2,545,836	1981 C
Hyderabad	Pakistan	751,529	—	1981 C
Ibadan	Nigeria	885,300	—	1977 E
Inchon	South Korea	1,387,491	—	1985 C
Indianapolis	(Indiana) U.S.	700,807	1,166,575	1980 C
Innsbruck	Austria	116,100	—	1981 C
Irkutsk	Soviet Union	589,000	—	1984 E
Istanbul	Turkey	5,475,982	—	1985 C
Izmir (Smyrna)	Turkey	1,489,772	—	1985 C
Jacksonville	(Florida) U.S.	540,920	722,252	1980 C
Jaipur	India	966,677	1,025,000	1981 C
Jakarta	Indonesia	6,503,449	6,700,000	1980 C
Jerusalem	Israel	424,400	—	1983 E
Jidda (Jeddah, Juddah)	Saudi Arabia	1,210,000	—	1986 C
Jinan (Tsinan)	China	1,390,000	—	1984 E
Johannesburg	South Africa	703,980	1,726,073	1980 C
Juárez (Ciudad Juárez)	Mexico	597,096	—	1978 E
Kabul	Afghanistan	1,036,407	—	1982 E
Kananga	Zaire	460,091	—	1984 E
Kano	Nigeria	416,900	—	1977 E
Kanpur	India	1,481,789	1,639,064	1981 C
Kansas City	(Missouri) U.S.	448,033	914,433	1980 C
Kaohsiung	Taiwan	1,172,977	1,480,000	1977 C
Karachi	Pakistan	5,208,170	—	1981 C
Karaganda	Soviet Union	608,000	—	1984 E
Kathmandu	Nepal	150,402	215,000	1971 C
Katowice	Poland	363,300	2,590,000	1985 E
Kawasaki	Japan	1,088,611	—	1985 C
Kazan	Soviet Union	1,039,000	—	1984 E
Khabarovsk	Soviet Union	568,000	—	1984 E
Kharkov	Soviet Union	1,536,000	—	1984 E
Khartoum	Sudan	476,218	817,364	1983 C
Kiel	West Germany	245,682	335,000	1985 E
Kiev	Soviet Union	2,409,000	—	1984 E
Kingston	Jamaica	104,041	524,638	1982 C
Kinshasa	Zaire	2,222,981	—	1984 E
Kishinev	Soviet Union	605,000	—	1984 E
Kitakyushu	Japan	1,056,400	—	1985 C
Kobe	Japan	1,410,843	—	1985 C
Kowloon	Hong Kong	799,123	—	1981 C

City	Country	City population	Metropolitan area population	Date
Kraków	**Poland**	740,100	—	1985 E
Krasnoyarsk	**Soviet Union**	859,000	—	1984 E
Kuala Lumpur	**Malaysia**	937,875	—	1980 C
Kunming (K'un-ming)	**China**	1,480,000	—	1984 E
Kuwait	**Kuwait**	78,116	780,000	1975 C
Kuybyshev	**Soviet Union**	1,250,000	—	1984 E
Kwangju	**South Korea**	906,129	—	1985 C
Kyoto	**Japan**	1,479,125	—	1985 C
Lagos	**Nigeria**	1,149,200	1,476,837	1977 E
Lahore	**Pakistan**	2,952,689	—	1981 C
Lanzhou (Lan-chou)	**China**	1,460,000	—	1984 E
La Paz	**Bolivia**	881,404	—	1982 E
Leeds	**England** (Great Britain)	710,500	2,052,800	1985 E
Leipzig	**East Germany**	554,595	710,000	1985 E
Leningrad	**Soviet Union**	4,295,000	4,827,000	1984 E
León	**Mexico**	589,950	—	1978 E
Liège	**Belgium**	207,496	410,160	1983 E
Lille	**France**	168,424	945,572	1982 C
Lima	**Peru**	4,164,597	4,608,010	1981 C
Linz	**Austria**	197,962	—	1981 C
Lisbon (Lisboa)	**Portugal**	817,627	2,062,200	1981 C
Liverpool	**England** (Great Britain)	491,500	1,481,000	1985 E
Łódź	**Poland**	847,900	1,025,000	1985 E
London	**England** (Great Britain)	6,767,500	—	1985 E
Los Angeles	(California) **U.S.**	2,968,579	7,477,503	1980 C
Louisville	(Kentucky) **U.S.**	298,694	956,756	1980 C
Luanda	**Angola**	1,200,000	—	1988 E
Lubumbashi	**Zaire**	596,297	—	1984 E
Lucknow	**India**	895,947	1,060,000	1981 C
Lüda or **Dalian** (Lüta or Dairen)	**China**	1,590,000	—	1984 E
Ludhiana	**India**	606,250	—	1981 C
Lusaka	**Zambia**	818,994	—	1987 E
Lvov	**Soviet Union**	728,000	—	1984 E
Lyallpur	**Pakistan**	1,104,209	—	1981 C
Lyon	**France**	413,095	1,236,096	1982 C
Madras	**India**	3,276,622	4,289,347	1981 C
Madrid	**Spain**	3,123,713	—	1986 E
Madurai	**India**	817,562	—	1981 C
Managua	**Nicaragua**	677,680	—	1980 E
Manchester	**England** (Great Britain)	451,100	2,582,600	1985 E
Mandalay	**Burma**	472,512	—	1979 E
Manila	**Philippines**	1,630,485	5,926,000	1980 C
Mannheim	**West Germany**	294,984	1,395,000	1985 E
Maputo (*Lourenço Marques*)	**Mozambique**	1,006,765	—	1987 E
Maracaibo	**Venezuela**	1,151,933	—	1988 E
Marseille	**France**	874,436	1,115,697	1982 C
Mecca (Makkah)	**Saudi Arabia**	463,000	—	1986 E
Medan	**Indonesia**	1,378,955	1,450,000	1980 C
Medellín	**Colombia**	1,468,089	—	1985 C
Melbourne	**Australia**	2,645,484	—	1986 C
Memphis	(Tennessee) **U.S.**	646,174	913,472	1980 C
Mexico City	**Mexico**	10,061,000	15,505,000	1982 E
Miami	(Florida) **U.S.**	346,865	1,625,509	1980 C
Milan (Milano)	**Italy**	1,634,638	—	1981 C
Milwaukee	(Wisconsin) **U.S.**	636,297	1,397,143	1980 C
Minneapolis	(Minnesota) **U.S.**	370,951	2,137,133	1980 C
Minsk	**Soviet Union**	1,442,000	—	1984 E
Mombasa	**Kenya**	341,148	—	1979 C
Monrovia	**Liberia**	421,058	—	1984 C
Monterrey	**Mexico**	1,132,000	2,166,000	1980 C
Montevideo	**Uruguay**	1,247,920	—	1985 C
Montreal	(Quebec) **Canada**	1,015,420	2,921,357	1986 C
Moscow	**Soviet Union**	8,275,000	8,537,000	1984 E
Multan	**Pakistan**	736,925	—	1981 C
Munich (München)	**West Germany**	1,266,549	1,940,000	1985 E
Mysore	**India**	439,185	—	1981 C
Nagoya	**Japan**	2,116,350	3,700,000	1985 C
Nagpur	**India**	1,215,425	1,325,000	1981 C
Nairobi	**Kenya**	827,775	—	1979 C
Nanjing (Nan-ching) (Nanking)	**China**	2,210,000	—	1984 E
Nantes	**France**	240,539	474,068	1982 C
Naples (Napoli)	**Italy**	1,210,503	—	1981 C
Nashville	(Tennessee) **U.S.**	455,651	850,505	1980 C
New Delhi	**India**	271,990	—	1981 C
New Kowloon (Linked with Kowloon)	**Hong Kong**	1,651,064	—	1981 C
New Orleans	(Louisiana) **U.S.**	557,927	1,256,256	1980 C
Newcastle upon Tyne (Newcastle)	**England** (Great Britain)	282,200	1,139,900	1985 E
New York City	(New York) **U.S.**	7,071,639	8,274,961	1980 C
Niamey	**Niger**	360,000	—	1981 E
Norfolk	(Virginia) **U.S.**	266,979	1,160,311	1980 C
Nottingham	**England** (Great Britain)	279,400	—	1985 E
Novokuznetsk	**Soviet Union**	572,000	—	1984 E
Novosibirsk	**Soviet Union**	1,384,000	—	1984 E
Nuremberg (Nürnberg)	**West Germany**	465,255	1,025,000	1985 E
Odessa	**Soviet Union**	1,113,000	—	1984 E
Okayama	**Japan**	572,423	—	1985 C
Oklahoma City	(Oklahoma) **U.S.**	403,484	860,969	1980 C
Omaha	(Nebraska) **U.S.**	313,939	585,122	1980 C
Omsk	**Soviet Union**	1,094,000	—	1984 E
Orlando	(Florida) **U.S.**	128,291	700,055	1980 C
Osaka	**Japan**	2,636,260	—	1985 C
Oslo	**Norway**	449,220	541,190	1987 E
Ostrava	**Czechoslovakia**	325,431	745,000	1985 E
Ottawa	(Ontario) **Canada**	300,763	819,263	1986 C
Palermo	**Italy**	699,691	—	1981 C
Panama City	**Panama**	389,172	794,300	1980 C
Paris	**France**	2,176,243	8,706,963	1982 C
Patna	**India**	773,720	—	1981 C
Perm	**Soviet Union**	1,048,000	—	1984 E
Perth	**Australia**	895,710	—	1986 C
Philadelphia	(Pennsylvania) **U.S.**	1,688,210	4,716,818	1980 C
Phnom Penh	**Cambodia**	700,000	—	1985 E
Phoenix	(Arizona) **U.S.**	789,704	1,509,052	1980 C
Pittsburgh	(Pennsylvania) **U.S.**	423,959	2,218,870	1980 C
Port-au-Prince	**Haiti**	738,342	—	1984 E
Portland	(Oregon) **U.S.**	366,383	1,105,699	1980 C
Porto (Oporto)	**Portugal**	330,199	1,550,800	1981 C
Pôrto Alegre	**Brazil**	1,108,883	2,232,370	1980 C
Portsmouth	**England** (Great Britain)	187,900	—	1985 E
Poznań	**Poland**	575,100	610,000	1985 E
Prague (Praha)	**Czechoslovakia**	1,189,828	—	1985 E
Pretoria	**South Africa**	435,100	739,040	1980 C
Providence	(Rhode Island) **U.S.**	156,804	618,514	1980 C
Puebla (Puebla de Zaragoza)	**Mexico**	646,599	—	1980 C
Pune	**India**	1,203,351	1,686,109	1981 C
Pusan	**South Korea**	3,516,807	—	1985 C
Pyongyang	**North Korea**	2,639,448	—	1984 E
Qingdao (Tsingtao)	**China**	1,230,000	—	1984 E
Quebec (Québec)	(Quebec) **Canada**	164,580	603,267	1986 C
Quezon City	**Philippines**	1,165,865	—	1980 C
Quito	**Ecuador**	866,472	—	1982 C
Rabat	**Morocco**	518,616	—	1982 C
Rangoon	**Burma**	1,315,964	2,452,881	1979 E
Rawalpindi	**Pakistan**	794,843	—	1981 C
Recife	**Brazil**	1,184,215	2,348,362	1980 C
Richmond	(Virginia) **U.S.**	219,214	761,311	1980 C
Riga	**Soviet Union**	875,000	—	1984 E
Rio de Janeiro	**Brazil**	5,093,232	9,018,637	1980 C
Riyadh (Ar Riyad)	**Saudi Arabia**	1,380,000	—	1986 E
Rochester	(New York) **U.S.**	241,741	971,230	1980 C
Rome (Roma)	**Italy**	2,830,569	—	1981 C
Rosario	**Argentina**	875,623	954,606	1980 C
Rostov-on-Don	**Soviet Union**	983,000	—	1984 E
Rotterdam	**The Netherlands**	558,832	1,025,580	1983 E
Saarbrücken	**West Germany**	186,229	390,000	1985 E
Sacramento	(California) **U.S.**	275,741	1,099,814	1980 C
Saint Louis	(Missouri) **U.S.**	452,801	1,788,507	1980 C
Saint Paul	(Minnesota) **U.S.**	270,230	—	1980 C
Saint Petersburg	(Florida) **U.S.**	238,647	—	1980 C
Sakai	**Japan**	818,368	—	1985 C
Salonika (Thessaloniki)	**Greece**	406,413	706,180	1981 C
Salt Lake City	(Utah) **U.S.**	163,034	910,222	1980 C
Salvador (Bahia)	**Brazil**	1,496,276	1,772,018	1980 C
Samarkand	**Soviet Union**	515,000	—	1984 E
Sana	**Yemen**	472,185	—	1986 E
San Antonio	(Texas) **U.S.**	786,023	1,071,954	1980 C
San Bernardino	(California) **U.S.**	118,794	1,558,182	1980 C
San Diego	(California) **U.S.**	875,538	1,861,846	1980 C
San Francisco	(California) **U.S.**	678,974	1,488,871	1980 C
San José	**Costa Rica**	241,464	560,000	1984 C
San Juan	**Puerto Rico**	424,600	1,086,376	1980 C
San Justo	**Argentina**	14,135	—	1980 C
San Salvador	**El Salvador**	452,614	—	1984 E
Santiago	**Chile**	4,225,299	—	1984 E
Santo Domingo	**Dominican Rep.**	1,313,172	—	1981 C
Santos	**Brazil**	411,023	—	1980 C
São Paulo	**Brazil**	7,033,529	12,588,439	1980 C
Sapporo	**Japan**	1,542,979	—	1985 C
Saragossa (Zaragoza)	**Spain**	596,080	—	1986 E
Saratov	**Soviet Union**	893,000	—	1984 E
Seattle	(Washington) **U.S.**	493,846	1,607,469	1980 C
Semarang	**Indonesia**	1,026,671	—	1980 C
Sendai	**Japan**	700,248	—	1985 C
Seoul	**South Korea**	9,645,932	—	1985 C
Seville (Sevilla)	**Spain**	668,356	—	1986 E
Shanghai	**China**	12,050,000	—	1984 E
Sheffield	**England** (Great Britain)	538,700	1,303,200	1985 E
Shenyang (Shen-yang)	**China**	4,130,000	—	1984 E
Shijiazhuang (Shih-chia-chuang)	**China**	1,130,000	—	1984 E
Singapore	**Singapore**	2,308,200	2,600,000	1978 E
Sofia	**Bulgaria**	1,056,945	1,142,582	1980 E
Southampton	**England** (Great Britain)	202,300	—	1985 E
Stockholm	**Sweden**	653,455	1,377,560	1984 E
Stuttgart	**West Germany**	561,628	—	1985 E
Suez (As Suways)	**Egypt**	326,820	—	1986 C
Surabaya	**Indonesia**	2,027,913	2,150,000	1980 C
Surat	**India**	775,711	960,000	1981 C
Sverdlovsk	**Soviet Union**	1,286,000	—	1984 E
Sydney	**Australia**	2,989,070	—	1986 C
Taegu	**South Korea**	2,030,672	—	1985 C
Taichung	**Taiwan**	585,205	—	1977 E
Tainan	**Taiwan**	572,590	—	1977 E
Taipei	**Taiwan**	2,220,427	—	1980 C
Taiyuan (T'ai-yuan)	**China**	1,840,000	—	1984 E
Tallinn	**Soviet Union**	458,000	—	1984 E
Tampa	(Florida) **U.S.**	271,523	1,613,603	1980 C
Tashkent	**Soviet Union**	1,986,000	—	1984 E
Tbilisi (Tiflis)	**Soviet Union**	1,140,000	—	1984 E
Tegucigalpa	**Honduras**	571,400	—	1985 E
Teheran (Tehran)	**Iran**	5,734,199	—	1982 E
Tel Aviv-Yafo	**Israel**	325,700	1,350,000	1983 E
Tianjin (Tientsin)	**China**	7,990,000	—	1984 E
Tiranë (Tirana)	**Albania**	260,000	—	1983 E
Tokyo	**Japan**	8,353,674	11,618,281	1985 C
Toledo	(Ohio) **U.S.**	354,635	616,864	1980 C
Toronto	(Ontario) **Canada**	612,289	3,427,168	1986 C
Tripoli (Tarabulus)	**Libya**	990,697	—	1984 C
Tucson	(Arizona) **U.S.**	330,537	531,443	1980 C
Tula	**Soviet Union**	529,000	—	1984 E
Tulsa	(Oklahoma) **U.S.**	360,919	657,173	1980 C
Tunis	**Tunisia**	596,654		1984 C
Turin (Torino)	**Italy**	1,103,520	—	1981 C
Ufa	**Soviet Union**	1,048,000	—	1984 E
Ujung Pandang	**Indonesia**	709,038	—	1980 C
Ulan Bator (Urga)	**Mongolia**	402,900	—	1979 E
Vadodara	**India**	733,656	—	1981 C
Valencia	**Spain**	738,575	—	1986 E
Valparaíso	**Chile**	266,876	—	1984 E
Vancouver	(British Columbia) **Canada**	431,147	1,380,729	1986 C
Varanasi	**India**	708,647	—	1981 C
Venice (Venezia)	**Italy**	332,775	—	1981 C
Victoria	**Hong Kong**	1,183,621	—	1981 C
Vienna (Wien)	**Austria**	1,515,666	—	1981 C
Vladivostok	**Soviet Union**	590,000	—	1984 E
Volgograd (*Stalingrad*)	**Soviet Union**	969,000	—	1984 E
Voronezh	**Soviet Union**	840,000	—	1984 E
Warsaw (Warszawa)	**Poland**	1,659,400	2,080,000	1985 E
Washington, D.C.	**U.S.**	638,432	3,250,822	1980 C
Wellington	**New Zealand**	325,697	—	1986 C
Wiesbaden	**West Germany**	266,623	795,000	1985 E
Winnipeg	(Manitoba) **Canada**	594,551	625,304	1986 C
Wrocław (Breslau)	**Poland**	637,200	—	1985 E
Wuhan (Wu-han)	**China**	3,340,000	—	1984 E
Wuppertal	**West Germany**	376,579	870,000	1985 E
Xi'an (Sian)	**China**	2,280,000	—	1984 E
Xuzhou (Suchow)	**China**	779,289	—	1984 E
Yaoundé	**Cameroon**	313,706	—	1976 C
Yerevan	**Soviet Union**	1,114,000	—	1984 E
Yokohama	**Japan**	2,992,644	—	1985 C
Zagreb	**Yugoslavia**	763,293	—	1981 C
Zaporozhye	**Soviet Union**	844,000	—	1984 E
Zhdanov (Mariupol)	**Soviet Union**	520,000	—	1984 E
Zhengzhou (Cheng-chou)	**China**	1,550,000	—	1984 E
Zurich (Zürich)	**Switzerland**	351,545	834,299	1986 E

C Census
E Official Estimate

Sources

The maps in the Atlas have been compiled from diverse source materials, which are cited in the following lists. The citations are organized by continent and region or country. Within each regional or country group, atlases are listed alphabetically by title and then followed by maps, which are listed according to scale, from the smallest to the largest. Other sources, listed alphabetically by title, follow the map listings.

GENERAL SOURCES

Atlante dei confini sottomarini, *A. Giuffrè Editore, Milano 1979*
Atlante Internazionale del Touring Club Italiano, *TCI, Milano 1977*
Atlas Mira, *G.U.G.K. Moskva 1967*
Atlas Okeanov-Atlantičeski i Indijski Okeany, *Ministerstvo Oborony SSSR-Vojenno-Morskoj Flot, Moskva 1977*
Atlas Okeanov-Tihi Okean, *Ministerstvo Oborony SSSR-Vojenno-Morskoj Flot, Moska 1974*
Atlas of the World, *National Geographic Society (N.G.S.), Washington 1981*
Atlas zur Ozeanographie, *Bibliographisches Institut, Mannheim 1971*
Bertelsmann Atlas International, *C. Bertelsmann Verlag GmbH, München 1963*
Grande Atlante degli Oceani, *Instituto Geografico De Agostini (I.G.D.A.), Novara 1978*
Meyers Neuer Geographischer Handatlas, *Bibliographisches Institut, Mannheim 1966*
The New International Atlas, *Rand McNally & Company, Chicago 1980*
The Odyssey World Atlas, *Western Publishing Company Inc., New York 1966*
The Times Atlas of the World, *John Bartholomew & Son Ltd, Edinburgh 1980*
The World Book Atlas, *World Book Encyclopedia Inc, 1979*
The World Shipping Scene, *Weststadt-Verlag, München 1963*
Weltatlas Erdöl und Erdgas, *George Westermann Verlag, Braunschweig 1976*
Pacific Ocean Floor 1:36,432,000, *N.G.S., Washington 1969*
Atlantic Ocean Floor 1:30,580,000, *N.G.S., Washington 1973*
Indian Ocean 1:25,720,000, *N.G.S. Washington 1967*
Deutsche Meereskarte 1:25,000,000, *Kartographisches Institut Meyer*
Carte générale du Monde 1:10,000,000, *Institut Géographique National (I.G.N.), Paris*
Artic Ocean Floor 1:9,757,000, *N.G.S., Washington 1971*
Carte du Monde 1:5,000,000, *I.G.N., Paris*
Karta Mira 1:2,500,000, *G.U.G.K., Moskva*
Carte Internationale du Monde 1:1,000,000, *Geographical Survey Institute*
Carte Aéronautique du Monde 1:1,000,000, *I.G.N., Paris*
Calendario Atlante, *I.G.D.A., Novara 1982*
Cartactual, *Cartographia, Budapest*
Demographic Yearbook, *United Nations, New York, 1978*
Duden Wörterbuch Geographischer Namen, *Bibliographisches Institut, Mannheim 1966*
Gazetteers (Various), *U.S. Board on Geographical Names, Washington*
Meyers Enzyklopädisches Lexikon, *Bibliographisches Institut, Mannheim 1972–81*
Schtag nach!-Die Staaten der Erde, *Bibliographisches Institut, Mannheim 1977*
Statistical Yearbook, *United Nations, New York, 1978*
Statistik des Auslandes-Länderkurzberichte, *Statistisches Bundesamt, Wiesbaden*
The Columbia Lippincott Gazetteer of the World, *Columbia University Press, New York 1961*
The Europa Year Book 1981, *Europa Publication Ltd., London*
The Statesman's Yearbook 1981–82, *The Macmillan Press Ltd., London*
Webster's New Geographical Dictionary, *G & C Merriam Co, Springfield 1972*

EUROPE

ALBANIA

Shqiperia-Hartë Fizike 1:500,000, *MMS "Hamid Shijaku", Tirana 1970*
Shqiperia Politiko Administrative 1:500,000, *MMS "Hamid Shijaku", Tirana 1969*
Gjeografia e Shqiperise per shkollat e mesme, *Shtëpia Botuese e Librit Shkollor, Tirana 1970*

AUSTRIA

Neuer Schulatlas, *Freytag-Berndt und Artaria KG, Wien 1971*
Generalkarte Österreich 1:200,000, *Mairs Geographischer Verlag, Stuttgart 1974*
Gemeindeverzeichnis von Österreich, *Österreichischen Statistischen Zentralamt, Wien 1970*
Geographisches Namenbuch Österreichs, *Verlag der Österreichischen Akademie der Wissenschaften, Wien 1975*
Statistisches Handbuch für die Republik Österreich, *Österreichischen Statistischen Zentralamt, Wien 1978*

BELGIUM

Atlas de Belgique-Atlas van België, *Comité National de Géographie, Bruxelles 1974*
België, Luxemburg, Belgien 1:350,000, *Pneu. Michelin, Bruxelles 1976*
Belgique, Grand-Duché de Luxembourg, *Pneu. Michelin, Paris 1978*
Lista Alphabetique des Communes-fusion de 1963 à 1977, *Institut National de Statistique, Bruxelles*
Statistique Demographiques 1980, *Institut National de Statistique, Bruxelles*

BULGARIA

Atlas Narodna Republika Bulgarija, *Glavno Upravlenie po Geodezija i Kartografija, Sofija 1973*
Bulgaria 1:1,000,000, *PPWK, Warszawa 1977*
Statističeski Godišnik na Narodna Republika Bălgarija 1973, *Ministerstvo na Informacijata i Săobšenijata, Sofija*

CZECHOSLOVAKIA

Atlas ČSSR, *Kartografie, Praha 1972*
Školní Zeměpisný Atlas Čescoslovenské Socialistické Republiky, *Kartografické* Nakladatelství, Praha 1970
Auto Atlas Č.S.S.R., *Kartografie, Praha 1971*
Č.S.S.R.-Fyzická Mapa 1:500,000, *Ústřední Správa Geodezie a Kartografie, Praha 1963*
Statistická Ročenka Č.S.S.R., *Federální Statistický Úřad, Praha 1980*

DENMARK

Haases Atlas, *P. Haase & Søns Forlag, København 1972*
Opgivne og Tilplantede Landbrugsarealer i Jylland, *Det Kongelige Danske Geografiske Selskab, København 1976*
Danmark 1:300,000, *Geodætisk Institut, København 1972*
Statistisk Årbog Danmark 1980, *Danmarks Statistik, København*

FINLAND

Oppikoulun Kartasto, *Werner Söderström Osakeyhtiö, Porvoo 1972*
Suomi-Finland 1:1,000,000, *Naanmittaushallituksen Kivipaino, Helsinki 1972*
Finland-Suomi 1:1,000,000, *Kümmerly & Frey, Bern 1981*
Suomen Tilastollinen Vuosikirja 1975, *Tilastokeskus, Helsinki*

FRANCE

Atlas Général Larousse, *Librairie Larousse, Paris 1976*
Atlas Général Bordas, *Bordas, Paris 1972*
Atlas Géographique Alpha, *I.G.D.A., Novara 1972*
Atlas Moderne Larousse, *Librairie Larousse-I.G.D.A., Paris 1976*
Carte Administrative de la France 1:1,400,000, *I.G.N., Paris 1977*
Carte de la France 1:1,000,000, *I.G.N., Paris 1971*
France: Routes-Autoroutes 1:1,000,000, *I.G.N., Paris 1978*
Carte Touristique 1:250,000, *I.G.N., Paris 1978*
France 1:200,000, *Pneu. Michelin, Paris*
Carte Touristique 1:100,000, *I.G.N., Paris*
Michelin 1977-France, *Pneu. Michelin, Paris*
Population de la France-Recensement 1975, *Institut National de la Statistique et des Études Économiques, Paris*

GERMAN DEMOCRATIC REPUBLIC

Haack Weltatlas, *V.E.B. Hermann Haack Geographisch-Kartographische Anstalt, Gotha-Leipzig 1972*
Weltatlas-Die Staaten der Erde und ihre Wirtschaft, *V.E.B. Hermann Haack Geographisch-Kartographische Anstalt, Gotha-Leipzig 1972*
Autokarte der D.D.R. 1:600,000, *V.E.B. Landkartenverlag, Berlin 1972*
Statistisches Jahrbuch der Deutschen Demokratischen Republik 1981, *Staatsverlag der D.D.R., Berlin*

GERMANY, FEDERAL REPUBLIC OF

Diercke Weltatlas, *Westermann Verlag, Braunschweig 1977*
Der Grosse Shell Atlas, *Mairs Geographischer Verlag, Stuttgart 1981–82*
Der Neue Weltatlas, *I.G.D.A., Novara 1977*
Deutschland-Strassenkarte 1:1,000,000, *Kümmerly & Frey, Bern 1981*
Bundesrepublik Deutschland-Übersichtskarte 1:500,000, *Institut für Angewandte Geodäsie, Frankfurt 1978*
Topographische Übersichtskarte 1:200,000, *Institut für Angewandte Geodäsie, Frankfurt*
Bevölkerung der Gemeinden, *Statistisches Bundesamt, Wiesbaden 1979*
Statistisches Jahrbuch für die B.R.D. 1980, *Statistisches Bundesamt, Wiesbaden*

GREECE

Greece-Autokarte 1:1,000,000, *Kümmerly & Frey, Bern*
Greece-Autokarte 1:650,000, *Freytag & Berndt, Wien*
Genikos Chartis tis Hellados 1:400,000, *Geografiki Hypiresia Stratoy, Athínai*
Etniki Statistiki Hypiresia tis Hellados 1:200,000, *E.S.Y.E., Athínai*
Statistiki Epetiris tis Hellados 1979, *E.S.Y.E., Athínai*

HUNGARY

Földrajzi Atlas a Középiskolák Számára, *Kartográfiai Vallalat, Budapest 1980*
A Magyar Népköztársaság 1:400,000, *Kartográfiai Vallalat, Budapest 1974*
Magyarorszag Domborzata és Vizei 1:350,000, *Kartogràfiai Vallalat, Budapest 1961*
Megye Terképe, *Cartographia, Budapest 1979–80*
A Magyar Népköztársaság Helységnévtára 1973, *Statisztikai Kiadó Vállalat, Budapest*
Statistical Pocket Book of Hungary 1980, *Statistical Publishing House, Budapest*

ICELAND

Landabréfabok, *Ríkisutgáfa Námsbóka, Reykjavik 1970*
Iceland-Road Guide, *Örn & Örlygur H.F., Reykjavik 1975*

IRELAND

Irish Student's Atlas, *Educational Company of Ireland, Dublin-Cork 1971*
Ireland 1:575,000, *Ordnance Survey Office, Dublin 1979*
Ireland 1:250,000, *Ordnance Survey Office, Dublin 1962*
Census of Population of Ireland 1979, *The Stationery Office, Dublin*

ITALY

Atlante Metodico, *I.G.D.A., Novara 1981*
Atlante Stradale d'Italia 1:200,000, *Touring Club Italiano, Milano*
Carta d'Italia 1:1,250,000, *Instituto Geografico Militare, Firenze 1972*
Carte batimetriche, *Istituto Idrografico della Marina, Genova*
Carta Generale d'Italia 1:500,000, *Touring Club Italiano, Milano 1979*
Carta Generale d'Italia 1:200,000, *I.G.M., Firenze*
Enciclopedia Italiana, *Istituto della Enciclopedia Italiana G. Treccani, Roma*
Il Mare, *I.G.D.A., Novara*
La Montagna, *I.G.D.A., Novara*
XI Censimento Generale della Popolazione 24 ottobre 1971, *Istituto Centrale di Statistica, Roma*
XII Censimento Generale della Popolazione 25 ottobre 1981, *Istituto Centrale di Statistica, Roma*

LUXEMBOURG

Grand-Duché de Luxembourg 1:100,000, *I.G.N., Paris 1970*
Annuaire Statistique-Luxembourg 1981–82, *Service Central de la Statistique et des Études Économiques, Paris*

NETHERLANDS

Atlas van Nederland, *Staatsdrukkerij-en Uitgeverijbedrijf,'s-Gravenhage*
De Grote Vara Gezinsatlas, *Vara Omroepvereniging, Hilversum 1975*
Der Kleine Bosatlas, *Wolter-Noordhoff, Groningen 1974*
Pays-Bas/Nederland 1:400,000, *Pneu. Michelin, Paris 1981*
Gegevens per Gemeente Betreffende de Loop der Bevolking in het Jaar 1980, *Centraal Bureau voor der Statistik, Amsterdam*

NORWAY

Atlas-Større Utgave for Gymnaset, *J. W. Cappelens Forlag A.S., Oslo 1969*
Bilkart Bok Road Atlas, *J. W. Cappelens Forlag A.S., Oslo 1967*
Norge-Bit-Og Turistkart 1:400,000, *J. W. Cappelens Forlag A.S., Oslo 1965*
Folketallet i Kommunene 1972–73, *Statistik Sentralbyraå, Oslo*
Statistisk Årbok 1981, *Statistik Sentralbyrå, Oslo*

POLAND

Atlas Geograficzny, *PPWK, Warszawa 1979*
Narodowy Atlas Polski, *Polska Akademia Nauk, Warszawa 1978*
Polska Kontynenty Świat, *P.P.W.K., Warszawa 1977*
Powszechny Atlas Świat, *P.P.W.K. Warszawa 1981*
Polska Rzeczpospolito. Ludowa-Mapa Administracyjna 1:500,000, *P.P.W.K., Warszawa 1980*
Rocznik Statystyczny 1978, *Glówny Urzad Statystyczny, Warszawa*

PORTUGAL

Portugal 1:1,500,000, *Pneu. Michelin, Paris 1981*
Mapa do Estado das Estradas de Portugal 1:550,000, *Automovel Club de Portugal, Lisboa 1979*
Carto. Corográfica de Portugal 1:400,000, *Instituto Geografico e Cadastral, Lisboa 1968*
Anuário Estatístico-Portugal 1974, *Instituto Nacional de Estatística, Lisboa*

ROMANIA

Atlas Geografic General, *Editura Didactica si Pedagogica, Bucureşti 1974*
Atlasul Republicii Socialiste România, *Institutul de Geologie si Geofizica, Bucureşti*
Rumanien-Bulgarien 1:1,000,000, *Freytag-Berndt und Artaria K.G., Wien*
Anuarul Statistic al Republicii Socialiste România 1980, *Direcţia Centrala de Statistică, Bucureşti*

SPAIN

Atlas Bachillerato Universal y de España, *Aguilar, Madrid 1968*
Atlas Básico Universal, *I.G.D.A. Teide, Novara 1969*
Gran Atlas Aguilar, *Aguilar, Madrid 1969*
Peninsula Iberica, Baleares y Canarias 1:1,000,000, *Instituto Geografico y Catastral, Madrid 1966*
Mapa Militar de España 1:800,000, *Servicio Geografico del Ejercito, Madrid 1971*
España 1:500,000, *Firestone Hispania, Madrid*
España-Mapa Oficial de Carreteras 1:400,000 *Ministerio de Obras Publica, Madrid*
España-Anuario Estadistico 1979, *Instituto Nacional de Estadistica, Madrid*

SWEDEN

Atlas Över Välden, *Generalstabens Litografiska Anstalt, Stockholm 1972*
Atlas Över Välden, *Natur Miljö Befolkning, Stockholm 1974*
Kak Bil Atlas, *Generalstabens Litografiska Anstalt, Stockholm 1973*
Sverige-Bilkarta 1:625,000, *A.B. Kartlitografen, Stockholm 1972*
Statistisk Årsbok 1980, *Statistiska Centralbyrån, Stockholm*

SWITZERLAND

Atlas der Schweiz, *Verlag des Bundesamtes fur Landestopographie, Wabern-Bern*
Schweizerischer Mittelschulatlas, *Konferenz der Kantonalen Erziehungsdirektoren, Zürich 1976*
Switzerland 1:300,000, *Kümmerly & Frey, Bern 1979*
Carte Nazionale de la Suisse 1:200,000, *Service Topographique Federale, Wabern-Bern*

U.S.S.R.

Atlas Avtomobilnyh Dorog, *G.U.G.K., Moskva 1976*
Atlas Obrazovanie i Razvitie Sojuza S.S.R., *G.U.G.K., Moskva 1972*
Malyi Atlas S.S.S.R., *G.U.G.K., Moskva 1973*
SSSR 1:8,000,000, *G.U.G.K., Moskva 1980*
SSSR 1:4,000,000, *G.U.G.K., Moskva 1972*
Latvijskaja SSR 1:600,000, *G.U.G.K., Moskva 1967*
Litovskaja SSR 1:600,000, *G.U.G.K., Moskva 1969*
S.S.S.R. Administrativno-Territorialnoje Delenie Sojuznyh Respublik, *Prezidium Verhovnogo Soveta Sojuza Sovetskih Socialističeskih Respublik Moskva 1971*

UNITED KINGDOM

Philips' Modern School Economic Atlas, *George Philip & Son Ltd, London 1981*
Roads Atlas of Great Britain and Ireland, *George Philip & Son Ltd, London 1971*
The Atlas of Britain and Northern Ireland, *Clarendon Press, Oxford 1963*
Route Planning Map 1:625,000, *Ordnance Survey, Southampton 1973*
Cartes 1:400,000, *Michelin Tyre Co. Ltd., London 1981*

YUGOSLAVIA

Atlas, *Izrađenou u Oour Kartografiji Tlos "Učila", Zagreb 1980*
Jugoslavija-Auto Atlas, *Jugoslavenski Leksikografski Zavod, Zagreb 1972*
Školki Atlas, *Izrađenou u Oour Kartografiji Tlos "Učila", Zagreb 1975*
Jugoslavija 1:1,000,000, *Grafički Zavod Hrvatske, Zagreb 1980*
Statistički Godišnjak Jugoslavije 1975, *Savezni Zavod za Statistiku, Beograd*

ASIA

ARABIAN PENINSULA

The Oxford Map of Saudi Arabia 1:2,600,000, *GEO-projects, Beirut 1981*
Arabian Peninsula 1:2,000,000, *United States Geological Survey, Washington 1963*
Arabische Republik Jemen 1:1,000,000, *Deutsch-Jemenitische Gesellschaft e V, Schwaig 1976*
The United Arab Emirates 1:750,000, *GEO-projects, Beirut 1981*

MIDDLE EAST

Atlas of Iran, *"Sahab" Geographic & Drafting Institute, Tehrán 1971*
Modern Büyük Atlas, *Arkin Kitabevi-I.G.D.A., Istanbul 1981*
The New Israel Atlas-Zev Vilnay, *Israel Universities Press, Yerushalaym 1968*
Iran 1:2,500,000, *Imperial Government of Iran, Tehrān 1968*
Guide Map of Iran 1:2,250,000, *Gita Shenassi Co. Ltd, Tehrān*
Guide Map of Iraq 1:2,000,000, *"Sahab" Geographic & Drafting Institute, Tehrān 1971*
Türkiye 1:2,000,000, *Ravenstein Verlag GmbH, Frankfurt 1975*
Iran 1:1,500,000, *Imperial Government of Iran, Tehrān 1968*
Iraq Tourist Map 1:1,500,000, *Summer Resorts and Tourism Service, Baghdād 1967*
The Oxford Map of Syria 1:1,000,000, *GEO-projects, Beirut 1980*
Turkey-Road Map 1:1,000,000, *Kümmerly & Frey, Bern 1980*
Türkei und Naher Osten 1:800,000, *Reis und Verkehrsverlag, Berlin-Stuttgart 1977*
Israel und Angrenzende Länder-Strassenkarte 1:750,000, *Kümmerly & Frey, Bern 1981*
The Oxford Map of Jordan 1:730,000, *GEO-projects, Beirut 1979*
Map of Israel 1:500,000, *Survey of Israel, Yerushalaym 1979*
The Oxford Map of Kuwait 1:500,000, *GEO-projects, Beirut 1980*
The Oxford Map of Qatar 1:270,000, *GEO-projects, Beirut 1980*
Israel Map of the Cease-Fire Lines 1:250,000, *Survey of Israel, Yerushalaym 1973*
Qatar-Visitor's Map 1:250,000, *Ministry of Information, Doha 1979*
Carte Générale du Liban 1:200,000, *Ministère de la Défense Nationale, Beirut 1967*
Qatar 1:200,000, *Hunting Surveys Ltd., Borchamwood 1975*
Bahrain Islands 1:63,360, *Public Works Department, Al Manāmah 1968*
The Oxford Map of Bahrain 1:57,750, *GEO-projects, Beirut 1980*
Bahrain—A Map for Visitors 1:50,000, *Ministry of Information, Al Manāmah 1976*
Annual Abstract of Statistics 1978, *Central Statistical Organization, Baghdād*
Genel Nüfus Sayımı 12 ekim 1980, *Başbakanlik Devlet İstatistik Enstitüsü, Ankara*
Kuwait—Annual Statistical Abstract, *Central Statistical Office-Ministry of Planning, Al Kuwayt 1976*
List of Localities—Geographical Information and Population 1948–1961–1972–1975, *Central Bureau of Statistics, Yerushalaym*
Recueil de Statistiques Libanaises No. 8-1972, *Direction Centrale de la Statistique, Bayrūt*
Republic of Cyprus—Statistical Abstract 1973, *The Statistics and Research Department, Levkosia*
Statistical Abstract—Syrian Arab Republic 1973, *Central Bureau of Statistics, Dimashq*
Statistical Abstract of Israel 1979, *Central Bureau of Statistics, Yerushalaym*
The Hashemite Kingdom of Jordan, Statistical Yearbook 1976, *Department of Statistics, Ammān*
Türkiye İstatistik Yıllığı 1975, *Başbakanlik Devlet İstatistik Enstitüsü, Ankara*

SOUTH ASIA

National Atlas of India, *National Atlas & Thematic Mapping Organization, Calcutta*
Oxford School Atlas for Pakistan, *Oxford University Press—Pakistan Branch, Karachi 1973*
Tourist Atlas of India, *National Atlas Organization, Calcutta*
Physical Map of India 1:4,500,000, *Survey of India, Calcutta 1974*
Political Map of India 1:4,500,000, *Survey of India, Calcutta 1972*
Railway Map of India 1:3,500,000, *Government of India, Calcutta 1971*
Pākistān 1:3,168,000, *Survey of Pākistān, Rāwalpindi 1966*
Bangladesh 1:2,800,000, *Survey of Bangladesh, Dacca 1979*
Burma 1:2,000,000, *Army Map Service, Washington 1963*
Physical and Political Map of Afghanistan 1:1,500,000, *Afghan Cartographic Institute, Kabul 1968*
Ceylon Physical 1:1,000,000, *Survey Department, Colombo 1973*
New Map of Afghanistan 1:1,000,000, *"Sahab" Geographic & Drafting Institute, Tehrān*
Pākistān 1:1,000,000, *Survey of Pākistān, Rāwalpindi 1968*
Motor Map of Ceylon 1:506,880, *Survey Department, Colombo 1973*
Nepal 1:506,880, *Ministry of Defence, London 1967*
Nepal 1:408,000, *Kümmerly & Frey, Bern 1980*
Bangladesh Population Census Report 1974, *Statistics Division-Ministry of Planning, Dacca*
Geomedical Monograph Series—Afghanistan, *Springer-Verlag, Berlin 1968*
Pakistan Statistical Yearbook 1978, *Statistics Division, Karachi*
Statistical Pocket Book of the Democratic Socialist Republic of Sri Lanka 1979, *Department of Census and Statistics, Colombo*

SOUTHEAST ASIA

Atlas Indonesia, *Yayasan Dwidjendra, Denpasar-Jakarta 1977*
Atlas of Thailand, *Royal Thai Survey Department, Bangkok 1974*
Secondary Atlas for Malaysia and Singapore, *Niugini Press Pty. Ltd., Port Moresby 1975*
Secondary School Atlas for Malaysia, *McGraw-Hill Far Eastern Publishers Ltd., Singapore 1970*
Hành Chính Viet Nam 1:2,500,000, *Hô Chí Minh 1976*
Maluku dan Irian Jaya 1:2,250,000, *Pembina, Jakarta 1975–76*
Bàu-dô Viet Nam 1:2,000,000, *Saigon 1972*
Laos Administratif 1:2,000,000, *Service Géographique National du Laos, Vientiane 1968*
Malaysia 1:2,000,000, *Jabatanarah Pemetaan Negara, 1976*
Map of Thailand and Bangkok 1:2,000,000, *The Shell Company of Thailand Ltd., Bangkok*
Vietnam 1:2,000,000, *G.U.G.K., Moskva 1972*
Kalimantan 1:1,500,000, *Pembina, Jakarta 1975–76*
Philippines 1:1,500,000, *Philippine Coast and Geodetic Survey, Manila 1968*
Cambodia & South Vietnam—Southeast Asia 1:1,250,000, *Army Map Service, Washington 1966*
Carte Générale du Laos, *Service Géographique National du Laos, Vientiane 1968*
Sumatera 1:790,000, *Pembina, Jakarta 1975–76*
Malaysia Barat—West Malaysia 1:760,000, *Jabatanarah Pemetaan Negara, 1968*
Jawa Barat & D.K.I. Jakarta 1:500,000, *Pembina, Jakarta 1974–75*
Jawa Tengah & D.I. Yogyakarta 1:500,000, *Pembina, Jakarta 1974–75*
Jawa Timur 1:500,000, *Pembina, Jakarta 1974–75*

Sabah 1:500,000, *Jabatanarah Pemetaan Negara, 1976*
Nusa Tenggara Barat & Nusa Tenggara Timur 1:330,000, *Pembina, Jakarta 1975*
Jawa Madura 1:225,000, *Pembina, Jakarta 1975–76*
Sulawesi 1:220,000, *Pembina, Jakarta 1975–76*
Gulongan Masharakat-Banchi Pendudok dan Perumahan Malaysia 1970, *Jabatan Perangkaan, Kuala Lumpur*
Sensus Penduluk 1971, *Biro Pusat Statistik, Jakarta*
Statistical Summary of Thailand 1978, *Statistical Reports Division, Bangkok*
Statistik Indonesia 1974–75, *Biro Pusat Statistik, Jakarta*

CHINA, MONGOLIA

Zhonghua Renmin Gongheguo Fen Sheng Dituji, *Ditu Chubanshe, Beijing 1977*
Zhonghua Renmin Gongheguo Ditu 1:6,000,000, *Ditu Chubanshe, Beijing 1980*
China 1:5,500,000, *Cartographia, Budapest 1967*
Zhonghua Renmin Gongheguo Ditu 1:4,000,000, *Ditu Chubanshe, Beijing 1980*
Mongolskaja Narodnaja Respublika 1:3,000,000, *G.U.G.K., Moskva 1972*
Taiwan/Formosa 1:500,000, *Army Map Service, Washington 1964*
China's Changing Map, *Methuen & Co., London 1972*

JAPAN, KOREA

Japan—The Pocket Atlas, *Heibonsha Ltd., Tōkyō 1970*
The National Atlas of Japan, *Geographical Survey Institute, Tōkyō 1977*
Teikoku's Complete Atlas of Japan, *Teikoku Shoin Company Ltd., Tōkyō 1977*
Tourist Map of Japan 1:5,300,000, *Japan National Tourist Organisation, Tōkyō 1974*
Republic of Korea 1:1,000,000, *Chungang Map & Chart Service, Sŏul 1973*
Northern Korea—Road Map of Korea, *Republic of Korea Army Map Service, Sŏul 1971*
Southern Korea 1:700,000, *Republic of Korea Army Map Service, Sŏul 1977*

AFRICA

The Atlas of Africa, *Editions Jeune Afrique, Paris 1973*
Africa 1:14,000,000, *N.G.S., Washington 1980*
Africa 1:9,000,000, *V.E.B. Hermann Haack, Gotha-Leipzig 1977*
Afrique/Africa 1:4,000,000, *Pneu. Michelin, Paris-London*
Africa 1:2,000,000, *Army Map Service, Washington*

NORTH WEST AFRICA

Atlas International de l'Ouest Africain 1:2,500,000, *Organisation de l'Unité Africaine, Dakar 1971*
Mauritanie 1:2,500,000, *I.G.N., Paris 1978*
Algérie-Tunisie 1:1,000,000, *Pneu. Michelin, Paris 1975*
Maroc 1:1,000,000, *Pneu. Michelin, Paris 1975*
Generalkarte Gran Canaria-Tenerife 1:150,000, *Mairs Geographischer Verlag, Stuttgart 1979*
Annuaire Statistique du Maroc, *Direction de la Statistique, Rabat 1976*
Code Géographique National—Code des Communes, *Secretariat d'État au Plan, Alger 1975*
Recensement Général de la Population et des Logements 1975, *Institut National de la Statistique, Tūnis*

NORTH EAST AFRICA

Egypte 1:750,000, *Kummerly & Frey, Bern 1977*
Population Census 1973, *Census and Statistical Department, Tarābulus*

WEST AFRICA

Atlas de Côte d'Ivoire, *Institut de Géographie Tropicale-Université d'Abidjan, Abidjan 1971*
Atlas de Haute-Volta, *Centre Voltaïque de la Recherche Scientifique, Ouagadougou 1969*
Atlas du Cameroun, *Institut de Recherches Scientifiques du Cameroun, Yaoundé*
Atlas for the United Republic of Cameroon, *Collins-Longman, Glasgow 1977*
Ghana Junior Atlas, *E. A. Boateng-Thomas Nelson and Sons Ltd., London 1965*
Liberia in Maps, *Stefan von Gnielinski, Hamburg 1972*
Oxford Atlas for Nigeria, *Oxford University Press, London-Ibadan 1971*
School Atlas for Sierra Leone, *Collins-Longman, Glasgow 1975*
République du Mali 1:2,500,000, *I.G.N., Paris 1971*
Ghana-Administrative 1:2,000,000, *Survey of Ghana, Accra 1968*
Road Map of Nigeria 1:585,000, *Federal Surveys, Lagos 1969*
République Unie du Cameroun 1:1,000,000, *I.G.N., Paris 1972*
République de Haute-Volta-Carte Routière 1:1,000,000, *I.G.N., Paris 1968*
Philips' School Room Map of Ghana 1:1,000,000, *George Philip & Son Ltd., London 1963*
Sénégal 1:1,000,000, *I.G.N., Paris 1974*
Sénégal-Carte Administrative 1:1,000,000, *I.G.N., Paris 1966*
Physical Map of Nigeria 1:1,000,000, *Federal Surveys, Lagos 1965*
République du Côte d'Ivoire 1:1,000,000, *I.G.N., Paris 1970*
Côte d'Ivoire 1:800,000, *Pneu. Michelin, Paris 1978*
Mapa da Guiné 1:650,000, *J. R. Silva, Lisboa 1969*
République du Dahomey-Carte Routière et Touristique 1:500,000, *I.G.N., Paris 1968*
Road Map of Ghana 1:500,000, *Survey of Ghana, Accra 1970*
The Gambia Road Map 1:500,000, *Survey Department The Gambia, Banjul 1973*
Nigeria-Digest of Statistics 1973, *Federal Office of Statistics, Lagos*

EAST AND CENTRAL AFRICA

Atlas Pratique du Tchad, *Institut Tchadien pour les Sciences Humaines, Paris 1972*
Sudan Roads 1:4,000,000, *Sudan Survey Department, Khartoum 1976*
Äthiopie/Ethiopia 1:4,000,000, *Medizinische Länderkunde/Geomedical Monograph Series, Berlin 1972*
Carte de l'Afrique Centrale 1:2,500,000, *I.G.N., Paris 1968*
Highway Map of Ethiopia 1:2,000,000, *Imperial Ethiopian Government, Addis Ababa 1961*
République du Tchad-Carte Routière 1:1,500,000, *I.G.N., Paris 1968*
République Centrafricaine-Carte Routière 1:1,500,000, *I.G.N., Paris 1969*
Territoire Française des Afars et des Issas 1:400,000, *Office Developpement du Tourisme, Djibouti 1970*
Ethiopia-Statistical Abstract 1976, *Central Statistical Office, Addis Ababa*

EQUATORIAL AFRICA

Atlas du Congo, *Office de la Recherche Scientifique et Techique Outre-Mer, Brazzaville 1969*
Atlas for Malawi, *Collins-Longman, Glasgow 1969*
Atlas of Uganda, *Department of Lands and Surveys, Kampala 1967*
Malawi in Maps, *University of London Press Ltd., London 1972*
Tanzania in Maps, *University of London Press, Ltd., London 1975*
The First Kenya Atlas, *George Philip & Son Ltd., London 1973*
Carte de l'Afrique Centrale 1:2,500,000, *I.G.N., Paris 1968*
Carta Rodoviária de Angola 1:2,000,000, *Lello S.A.R.L., Luanda 1974*
Republic of Zambia 1:1,500,000, *Surveyor General, Ministry of Lands and Natural Resources, Lusaka 1972*
Tanzania 1:1,250,000, *Shell & B.P. Tanzania Ltd., Dar es Salaam 1973*
Malawi 1:1,000,000, *Malawi Government, Blantyre 1971*
Road Map of Kenya 1:1,000,000, *George Philip & Son Ltd., London 1972*
République Populaire du Congo 1:1,000,000, *I.G.N., Paris 1973*
Gabon 1:1,000,000, *I.G.N., Paris 1975*
Statistical Abstract 1979, *Central Bureau of Statistics, Nairobi*

SOUTHERN AFRICA

Large Print Atlas for Southern Africa, *George Philip & Son Ltd., London 1976*
Atlas de Madagascar, *Association des Géographes de Madagascar, Antananarivo 1971*
Atlas for Mauritius, *Macmillan Education Ltd., London 1971*
Ontwikkelingsatlas-Development Atlas, *Republic of South Africa-Department of Planning, Pretoria 1966*
Botswana Road Map and Climate Chart 1:6,000,000, *Department of Surveys and Lands, Gaborone 1980*
Madagascar et Comores 1:4,000,000, *I.G.N., Paris 1970*
Suidelike Afrika/Southern Africa 1:2,500,000, *The Government Printer, Pretoria 1973*
Roads of Zimbabwe 1:2,100,000, *Shell Zimbabwe Ltd., Salisbury, 1980*
Carta de Moçambique 1:2,000,000, *Ministerio do Ultramar, Lisboa 1971*
Mapa Rodoviário de Maçambique 1:2,000,000, *J.A.E.M. 1972*
The Black Homelands of South Africa 1:1,900,000, *Perskor Boeke Tekenkantoor, Johannesburg*
Road Map of Zimbabwe 1:1,800,000, *A.A. of Zimbabwe, Salisbury 1980*
Zimbabwe-Mobil 1:1,470,000, *M.O. Collins Ltd., Salisbury 1976*
Rhodesia Relief 1:1,000,000, *Surveyor General, Salisbury 1973*
Lafatsche La Botsvana/Republic of Botswana 1:1,000,000, *Department of Surveys and Lands, Gaborene 1970*
Suid Afrika/South Africa 1:500,000, *The Government Printer, Pretoria*
Lesotho, 1:250,000, *Government Overseas Surveys, Maseru 1969*
Île Maurice-Carte Touristique 1:100,000, *I.G.N., Paris 1978*
La Réunion-Carte Touristique 1:100,000, *I.G.N., Paris 1978*
Annual Statistical Bulletin 1973, *The Bureau of Statistics, Maseru*
Bi-Annual Digest of Statistics 1976, *Central Statistical Office, Port Louis*
Population Census 1970, *Department of Statistics, Pretoria*
Population de Madagascar au Ier Janvier 1972, *Direction Général du Gouvernement, Antananarivo*
South Africa 1980–81-Official Yearbook, *Chris van Rensburg Publications Ltd., Johannesburg*

NORTH AMERICA

CANADA

Atlas Larousse Canadien, *Les Editions Françaises Inc., Québec - Montréal 1971*
Oxford Regional Economic Atlas - United States & Canada, *Clarendon Press, Oxford 1967*
Road Atlas United States - Canada - Mexico, *Rand McNally & Co., Chicago 1981*
The National Atlas of Canada, *Department of Energy, Mines and Resources, Ottawa 1972*
Northwest Territories - Yukon Territory 1:4,000,000, *Department of Energy, Mines and Resources, Ottawa 1974*
Quebec and Newfoundland 1:3,700,000, *N.G.S., Washington 1980*
British Columbia, Alberta and the Yukon Territory 1:3,500,000, *N.G.S., Washington 1978*
Ontario 1:3,000,000, *N.G.S., Washington 1980*
Saskatchewan and Manitoba 1:2,600,000, *N.G.S., Washington 1979*
Canada Year Book 1978-79, *Minister of Industry, Trade and Commerce, Ottawa*

UNITED STATES

Oxford Regional Economic Atlas - United States & Canada, *Clarendon Press, Oxford 1967*
Road Atlas United States - Canada - Mexico, *Rand McNally & Co., Chicago 1981*
Transportation Map of the United States, *U.S. Department of Transportation, Washington 1976*
National Energy Transportation System 7,500,000, *U.S. Geological Survey, Reston, Virginia 1977*
Close-up: Alaska 1:3,295,000, *N.G.S., Washington 1975*
Close-up: The Southwest 1:2,124,000, *N.G.S., Washington 1977*
Close-up: The Northwest 1:2,000,000, *N.G.S., Washington 1973*
Close-up: The Southeast 1:1,780,000, *N.G.S., Washington 1975*
Close-up: California and Nevada 1:1,700,000, *N.G.S., Washington 1978*
Close-up: Florida 1:1,331,000, *N.G.S., Washington 1973*
Close-up: Illinois, Indiana, Ohio and Kentucky 1:1,267,000, *N.G.S., Washington 1977*
Close-up: The Northeast 1:1,215,000, *N.G.S., Washington 1978*
Close-up: The Mid-Atlantic States 1:886,000, *N.G.S., Washington 1973*
Topographic Maps 1:500,000, *U.S. Geological Survey, Washington*
Topographic Maps 1:250,000, *U.S. Geological Survey, Washington*
Togographic Maps 1:24,000, *U.S. Geological Survey, Washington*
Census of Population and Housing 1980, *Bureau of the Census, Washington*

MEXICO

Atlas of Mexico, *Bureau of Business Research, University of Texas, Austin 1975*
Road Atlas United States - Canada - Mexico, *Rand McNally & Co., Chicago 1981*
Mapas de los Estados-Serie Patria, *Libreria Patria S.A., México*
Carta Geografica de México 1:2,500,000, *Asociación Nacional Automovilística, Ciudad de México 1976*
Archeological Map of Middle America 1:2,250,000, *N.G.S., Washington 1968*

CENTRAL AMERICA AND THE CARIBBEAN

Atlas for Barbados, Windwards and Leewards, *Macmillan Education Ltd., London 1974*
Atlas for Guyana & Trinidad & Tobago, *Macmillan Education Ltd, London 1973*
Atlas for the Eastern Caribbean, *Collins-Longman, London 1977*
Atlas Nacional de Cuba, *Academia de Ciencias de Cuba, La Habana 1970*
Atlas of the Commonwealth of the Bahamas, *Kingston Publishers Ltd.-Ministry of Education, Kingston-Nassau 1976*
Jamaica in Maps, *University of London Press Ltd., London 1974*
West Indies and Central Amerika 1:4,500,000, *N.G.S., Washington 1981*
Mapa General-República de Honduras 1:1,000,000, *Instituto Geográfico Nacional, Tegucigalpa 1980*
Mapa Oficial de la República de Panamá 1:1,000,000, *Instituto Geográfico Nacional, Panamá 1979*
Mapa Preliminar de la República de Guatemala 1:1,000,000, *Instituto Geográfico Nacional, Guatemala 1976*
República de Nicaragua 1:1,000,000, *Instituto Geográfico Nacional, Managua 1975*
Belize 1:800,000, *Directorate of Overseas Surveys, London 1974*
Mapa de la República Dominicana 1:600,000, *Instituto Geográfico Universitario, Santo Domingo 1979*
Costa Rica - Mapa Fisico-Politico 1:500,000, *Instituto Geográfico de Costa Rica, San José 1974*
El Salvador 1:500,000, *Ministerio de Obras Públicas, San Salvador 1978*
Mapa Hipsométrico de la República de Guatemala 1:500,000, *Instituto Geográfico Nacional, Guatemala 1979*
Jamaica 1:280,000, *Fairey Surveys Ltd., Maidenhead 1974*
Mapa de Carreteras Estatales de Puerto Rico 1:250,000, *Autoridad de Carreteras Estatales, San Juan 1972*
Nicaragua-Costa Rica 1:250,000, *Instituto Geográfico Nacional, Managua 1972*
Puerto Rico e Islas Limitrofes 1:240,000, *U.S. Geological Survey, Washington 1970*
Turks & Caicos Islands 1:200,000, *Directorate of Overseas Surveys, London 1971*
Cayman Islands 1:150,000, *Directorate of Overseas Surveys, London 1972*
Trinidad 1:150,000, *Director of Surveys-Ministry of Defense, London 1970*
Guadeloupe-Carte Touristique 1:100,000, *I.G.N., Paris 1978*
Martinique-Carte Touristique 1:100,000, *I.G.N., Paris 1977*
Lesser Antilles-Antigua 1:50,000, *Directorate of Overseas Surveys, London 1973*
Tourist Map of Tobago 1:50,000, *Lands & Surveys Department, Port of Spain 1969*
Dominica 1:25,000, *Directorate of Overseas Surveys, London 1978*
Lesser Antilles-Barbuda 1:25,000, *Directorate of Overseas Surveys, London 1970*
Annuario Estadístico de Costa Rica 1977, *Dirección General de Estadística, San José*
Annuario Estadístico de Cuba 1973, *Dirección Central de Estadística, La Habana*
Caribbean Year Book 1978-80, *Caribook Ltd., Toronto*
Fact Sheets on the Commonwealth-Antigua, *British Information Services, London 1974*
Fact Sheets on the Commonwealth-Belize, *British Information Services, London 1976*
Guatemala-III Censo de Habitación 26 de marzo de 1973, *Dirección General de Estadística, Guatemala*
Honduras-Annuario Estadístico 1978, *Dirección General de Estadística, Censos, Tegucigalpa*
Nicaragua-Annuario Estadístico 1975, *Oficina Ejecutiva de Encuestas y Censos, Managua*
Statistical Yearbook for Latin America, *United Nations, New York 1976*
Zentralamerika-Karten zur Bevölkerungs und Wirtschaftsstruktur 1975, *H. Nuhn, P. Krieg & W. Schlick, Hamburg*

SOUTH AMERICA

NORTHERN SOUTH AMERICA

Atlas Basico de Colombia, *Instituto Geográfico Agustin Codazzi, Bogotá 1970*
Atlas de Colombia, *Instituto Geográfico Agustin Codazzi, Bogotá 1979*
Atlas de Venezuela, *Ministerio de Obras Públicas, Caracas 1970*
Atlas for Guyana, Trinidad & Tobago, *Macmillan Education Ltd., London 1973*
Atlas Histórico Geográfico y de Paisajes Peruanos, *Instituto Nacional de Planificación, Lima 1970*
Atlas Nacional do Brasil, *Instituto Brasileiro de Geografia*
Atlas Universal y del Perú, *Thomas Nelson & Sons Ltd., Sunbury on Thames 1968*
Brasil-Didáctico, Rodoviário, Turístico 1:5,000,000, *Gr. Editõra e Publicidade Ltda., Rio de Janeiro*
Mapa de la República de Bolivia 1:4,000,000, *Instituto Geográfico Militar, La Paz 1974*
Mapa Politico del Perú 1:2,400,000, *Editorial "Navarrete", Lima 1975*
Mapa de Carreteras del Perú 1:2,200,000, *Instituto Geográfico Militar, Lima 1979*
Mapa Fisico-Politico 1:2,000,000, *Instituto Geográfico Militar, Lima 1970*
Mapa Fisico de la República de Venezuela 1:2,000,000, *Ministerio de Obras Públicas, Bogotá 1975*
Brasil-Mapa Rodoviário 1:2,000,000, *Ministério dos Transportes, 1971*
Carte de la Guyane Française 1:1,500,000, *I.G.N., Paris 1973*
República de Colombia 1:1,500,000, *Ministerio de Hacienda y Credito Público, Bogotá 1979*
Ecuador 1:1,000,000, *Instituto Geográfico Militar, Quito 1971*
Kaart van Suriname 1:1,000,000, *C. Kersten & Co. N.V., Paramaribo*
Mapa de Bolivia 1:1,000,000, *Instituto Geográfico Militar, La Paz 1973*
Mapa Vial 1:1,000,000, *Ministerio de Obras Públicas, Caracas 1970*
República del Perú-Mapa Fisico-Politico, 1:1,000,000, *Instituto Geográfico Militar, Lima 1978*
Carte de la Guyane Française 1:500,000, *I.G.N., Paris 1976*
Suriname 1:500,000, *Uitgave Centraal Bureau Luchtkartering, 1969*
Guyana 1:500,000, *Ordnance Survey, Georgetown 1972*
Annuário Estatístico do Brasil 1978, *Fundacão Instituto Brasileiro de Geografia e Estatística, Rio de Janeiro*
Boletín Mensual de Estadística-agosto 1977, *D.A.N.E., Bogotá*
Dicionário Geográfico Brasileiro, *Editora Globo, Pôrto Alegre 1972*
Discover Bolivia, *Los Amigos del Libro, La Paz 1972*
Venezuela-Annuário Estadístico 1976, *Oficina Central de Estadística e Informatica, Caracas*

SOUTHERN SOUTH AMERICA

Atlas de la República Argentina, *Instituto Geográfico Militar, Buenos Aires 1972*
Atlas de la República Argentina, *Instituto Geográfico Militar, Santiago 1976*
Atlas de la República de Chile, *Instituto Geográfico Militar, Santiago 1970*
Atlas Escolar de Chile, *Instituto Geográfico Militar, Santiago 1978*
Atlas Universal y de la República Argentina, *Aguilar Argentina S.A. de Ediciones, Buenos Aires 1972*
Mapa de la República Argentina 1:5,000,000, *Instituto Geográfico Militar, Buenos Aires 1973*
Paraguay 1:1,000,000, *Instituto Geográfico Militar, Asuncíon 1974*
República Oriental del Uruguay 1:500,000, *Servicio Geográfico Militar, Montevideo 1961*
Uruguay-Moyennes et Petites Villes 1972, *Institut des Hautes Etudes de l'Amerique Latine, Paris*

AUSTRALIA AND OCEANIA

Atlas of Australian Resources, *Division of National Mapping, Canberra 1980*
New Zealand-Mobil Travel Map, *Mobil Oil New Zealand Ltd., Wellington 1973*
New Zealand Atlas, *A.R. Shearer Government Printer, Wellington 1976*
The Jacaranda Atlas, *Jacaranda Press Pty. Ltd., 1971*
The Jacaranda Atlas For New Zealand, *Jacaranda Press Pty. Ltd., 1971*
Australia-Geographic Map 1:2,500,000, *Minister for National Development, Canberra 1967*
Territory of Papua and New Guinea 1:2,500,000, *Division of National Mapping, Canberra 1970*
Carte de l'Oceanie Française 1:2,000,000, *I.G.N., Paris 1971*
Îles Tuamotu-Îles Marquises 1:2,000,000, *I.G.N., Paris 1969*
New Zealand-Map Guide 1:1,900,000, *New Zealand Tourist and Publicity Department, Wellington 1978*
Mobil New Zealand Road Map, *Mobil Oil New Zealand Ltd., Wellington 1973*
Fiji Islands-World Aeronautical Chart 1:1,000,000, *Ordnance Survey, Southampton 1970*
Close-up: Hawaii 1:675,000, *N.G.S., Washington 1978*
Archipel des Nouvelles-Hébrides 1:500,000, *I.G.N., Paris 1976*
New Zealand 1:500,000, *Department of Lands and Survey, Wellington 1976*
Nouvelle Calédonie 1:500,000, *I.G.N., Paris 1978*
Palau Islands 1:165,000, *Defense Mapping Agency Hydrographic Center, Washington 1973*
General Map of Tokelau Islands 1:100,000, *Department of Lands & Survey, Wellington 1969*
Tahiti-Carte Touristique 1:100,000, *I.G.N., Paris 1977*
Christmas Islands - Gilbert and Ellice Islands Colony 1:50,000, *Directorate of Overseas Survey, London 1970*
Tuvalu, *Government of Tuvalu 1979*
Annual Statistical Abstract-Fiji 1970-71, *Bureau of Statistics, Suva*
Australia - Population and Dwellings in Local Government Areas and Urban Centres 1976, *Australian Bureau of Statistics, Canberra*
Fact Sheet - Pitcairn Islands Group, *British Information Services, London 1974*
Fact Sheet - The Gilbert Islands, *British Information Services, London 1977*
Fact Sheet - The New Hebrides, *British Information Services, London 1976*
Fact Sheet - The Solomon Islands, *British Information Services, London 1976*
Fact Sheet - Tuvalu, *British Information Services, London 1977*
New Zealand Pocket Digest of Statistics 1979, *Department of Statistics, Wellington*
New Zealand Official Yearbook 1978, *Department of Statistics, Wellington*

POLAR REGIONS

Antarctica 1:11,250,000, *U.S. Naval Oceanographic Office, Washington 1965*
Antarctica 1:10,000,000, *American Geographical Society, New York 1970*
Antarctica 1:10,000,000, *Division of National Mapping, Canberra 1979*
Antarctica 1:5,000,000, *American Geographical Society, New York 1970*
Map of the Artic Region 1:5,000,000, *American Geographical Society, New York 1975*

Transliteration Systems

Toponymy: Criteria Used for the Writing of Names on the Maps

The language of geography is a language which defines geographic features in universally recognized terms. In creating this language, toponymy experts and cartographers have confronted complex problems in finding terms which are universally acceptable. So that the reader can fully understand the maps in this atlas, here is a brief explanation of how the toponyms (place-names for geographic features) have been written, particularly those relating to regions or countries where the Roman alphabet is not used. Among these are the Slavic-speaking nations such as the Soviet Union, Yugoslavia and Bulgaria; and China and Japan, which use ideographic characters. Of the European countries, Greece has its own alphabet, which is totally different from the Roman alphabet. Many of the Islamic countries use Arabic, with variations derived from local dialects.

There are two basic systems for Romanizing writing. The first is by phonetic transcription, using combinations of different alphabetical signs for each language when the phonetic sound in other languages should be maintained. For example, the Italian sound "sc" (which must be followed by an "e" or "i" to remain soft) in French is "ch," in English is "sh," and in German is "sch."

The second system is transliteration, in which the words, letters or characters of one language are represented or spelled in the letters or characters of another language.

Chinese, Japanese and Arabic Languages

Various Asian and African countries use non-Roman forms in their writing. For example, the Chinese and Japanese languages use ideographic characters instead of an alphabet, and these ideographic characters are transformed into the Roman alphabet through phonetic transcription. Until recently, one of the methods used for transforming Chinese was the Wade-Giles system, named for its English authors. Used in this atlas is the Pinyin system, which was approved by the Chinese government in 1958 and has been incorporated into the official maps of the People's Republic of China. The Pinyin system also has been adopted by the United States Board on Geographic Names and is used in official United Nations documents. The Pinyin names, however, often are accompanied by the Wade-Giles form, as the latter was widely known.

In Japan, ideographic characters are used, although the Roman alphabet is used in many Japanese scientific works. Japan uses two principal systems for standardizing names. They are the Kunreisiki, used by the government in official publications, and the Hepburn method. Adopted for this atlas is the Hepburn method, the system used in international English-language publications and by the United States Board on Geographic Names.

Romanization of the Arabic alphabet, which is used in many Islamic countries, is by transliteration. Since English and French are still used as an international language in many Arab countries, the name forms proposed by the major English and French sources have been taken into consideration. Generally, the systems proposed by the United States Board on Geographic Names and the Permanent Committee on Geographical Names have been used for most Asian countries and Arab-speaking countries.

Greek, Russian and Other Slavic Languages

Practically all written languages in Europe use the Roman alphabet. The differences in phonetics and grammar are shown by the use of diacritical marks and by groupings of consonants, vocals and syllables which give meaning to the various tones in the language. According to a centuries-old tradition, each written language maintains its formal characters, using the translated form rather than the phonetic transcription when a geographical term must be given in another language. This system, therefore, makes it more a translation than a transliteration.

In the Aegean area, Greek and the Greek alphabet are particularly significant because of historical links to the beginning of European civilization. The 1962 United States Board on Geographic Names and the Permanent Committee on Geographical Names systems, based on modern Greek pronunciation, have been used in transcribing toponyms from official sources for these maps. (The table that follows has an example indicating essential norms for Romanizing the modern Greek alphabet.)

A different situation arises in countries using the Cyrillic alphabet. Six principal Slavic languages using this alphabet are Russian, Byelorussian, Ukrainian, Bulgarian, Serbian, and Macedonian. The Cyrillic alphabet also is used by the non-Slavic people of the central Soviet Union. The nomenclature of these regions has been transliterated in accordance with the system proposed by the International Organization for Standardization, taking into consideration sounds and letters and uses of the diacritical marks normal in Slavic languages. The International Organization for Standardization method is accepted and used in bibliographical works and international documents. (The table which follows gives the relationship between the letters of the Cyrillic and Roman alphabets for the above six languages.) An exception to this transliteration is made by the Soviet Balkan republics of Estonia, Latvia and Lithuania. Here the name forms deriving from the national languages have been adopted, using the Roman alphabet.

Special Cases: Conventional Forms and Multilinguals

Cartographic nomenclature generally derives from the official nomenclature of the sovereign and nonsovereign countries, although a number of cases need an explanation.

In numerous situations, English conventional forms are used along with the local or conventional name in referring to a geographical entity used outside the official language area. For example, Vienna, Prague, Copenhagen and Moscow are English forms for Wien, Praha, København and Moskva, respectively. There have been cases, however, where the conventional or historical form commonly used in English cartography has been applied with the same meaning. Thus, Peking and Nanking are the English conventional forms for Beijing and Nanjing, while Tsinan, Tientsin and Mukden are the former conventional spellings or names for Jinan, Tianjin and Shenyang, respectively. Other examples are Saigon, the former name for Ho Chi Minh, Vietnam; and Bangkok, the name for Krung Thep, which is used in Thailand.

The lack of reliable data for countries, especially ex-colonies without a firm national cartographic tradition, has made it necessary to utilize mapping skills of former colonist nations such as France, the United Kingdom and Belgium. A lack of data has led to the adoption of French and British forms in many areas, as these two languages are widely used for official purposes.

Another special case is that of the multilingual areas. Many countries and areas officially recognize two or more written and spoken languages; therefore, all of the principal written forms appear on the maps. This is true, for example, of Belgium where the official languages are French and Dutch (e.g. Bruxelles/Brussel) and of Italian regions such as Valle d'Aosta and Alto Adige, where French, German and Italian are used (e.g. Aosta/Aoste) (Bolzano/Bozen).

In preparing this atlas, each of these special cases has been taken into full consideration within the limits of the scale, space and readability of the maps.

Transliteration of the Cyrillic Alphabet
(International System—ISO)

Cyrillic Letter		Roman Letter		Cyrillic Letter		Roman Letter	
А	а	a		О	о	o	
Б	б	b		П	п	p	
В	в	v		Р	р	r	
Г	г	g		С	с	s	
Д	д	d		Т	т	t	
Е	е	e	initially, after a vowel or after the mute sign "Ъ", becomes "je"	У	у	u	
				Ф	ф	f	
				Х	х	h	
Ё	ё	ë		Ц	ц	c	
Ж	ж	ž		Ч	ч	č	
З	з	z		Ш	ш	š	
И	и	i		Щ	щ	šč	
Й	й	j	not written if preceded by "И" or "Ы"	Ъ	ъ	—	not written
				Ы	ы	y	
К	к	k		Ь	ь	—	not written
Л	л	l		Э	э	e	
М	м	m		Ю	ю	ju	
Н	н	n		Я	я	ja	

Transcription of Modern Greek
(U. S. B. G. N./P.C.G.N.)

Greek Letter (or combination)		Roman Letter (or combination)		Greek Letter (or combination)		Roman Letter (or combination)	
Α	α	a			μπ	b	beginning a word
	αι	ai				mb	within a word
	αυ	av		Ν	ν	n	
Β	β	v			ντ	d	beginning a word
Γ	γ	g				nd	within a word
	γγ	ng		Ξ	ξ	x	
	γκ	g	beginning a word	Ο	ο	o	
		ng	within a word		οι	oi	
					ου	ou	
Δ	δ	d		Π	π	p	
Ε	ε	e		Ρ	ρ	r	
	ει	i		Σ	σ	s	
	ευ	ev			ς	s	ending a word
Ζ	ζ	z		Τ	τ	t	
Η	η	i			τζ	tz	
	ην	iv		Υ	υ	i	
Θ	θ	th			υι	i	
Ι	ι	i		Φ	φ	f	
Κ	κ	k		Χ	χ	kh	
Λ	λ	l		Ψ	ψ	ps	
Μ	μ	m		Ω	ω	o	

Geographical Glossary

The "Geographical Glossary" lists the principal geographical terms used on the maps. All of these terms, including abbreviations, prefixes and suffixes, appear in the cartographic table as they appear on the maps. Terms are listed in accordance with the English alphabet, without consideration of diacritical marks on letters or of particular groups of letters.

Prefixes and suffixes relating to principal names or forming part of geographical toponyms are followed or preceded by a dash and the language to which they refer: e.g. Chi-/*Dan.* (Chi, a Danish prefix, means large); -bor/*Slvn.* (-bor, a Slovakian suffix, means city). Suffixes can also appear as words in themselves. In this case, the suffix and primary word are coupled together: e.g. Berg, -berg (Berg, which means mountain, can be used alone or as part of another word, such as Hapsberg).

Certain terms are followed or preceded by their abbreviation used on the maps. Both instances are listed: e.g. Fjord, Fj. and Fj., Fjord.

All geographical terms are identified by the language or languages to which each belongs. The language or languages in italics follows the term: e.g. Abbey/*Eng.*; -bad/*Nor., Dut., Swed., Germ.* Each term is translated into a corresponding English term or terms.

Below is a table identifying the abbreviations of various language names used on the maps. Note that certain abbreviations represent a group of languages, instead of one language: e.g. Ural. is the abbreviation for Uralic, a group word for Udmurt, Komi, and Nenets.

Alt. = Altaic (Turkmen, Tatar, Bashkir, Kazakh, Karalpak, Nogai, Kirghiz, Uzbek, Uigur, Altaic, Yakut, Khakass)

Ban. = Bantu (KiSwahili, ChiLuba, Lingala, KiKongo)

Cauc. = Caucasian (Chechen, Ingush, Kalmuck, Georgian)
Iran. = Iranian (Baluchi, Tagus)
Mel. = Melanesian (Fijian, New Caledonian, Micronesian, Nauruan)
Mong. = Mongolian (Buryat, Khalka Mongol)
Poly. = Polynesian (Maori, Samoan, Tongan, Tahitian, Hawaiian)
Sah. = Saharan (Kanuri, Tubu)
Som. = Somalian (Somali, Galla)
Sud. = Sudanese (Peul, Ehoué, Mossi, Yoruba, Ibo)
Ural. = Uralic (Udmurt, Komi, Nenets).

Because of their technical application to geography, some geographical terms may not fully correspond with the meaning given for them in some dictionaries.

Abbreviations of Language Names

Abbreviations in English	English	Abbreviations in English	English	Abbreviations in English	English	Abbreviations in English	English	Abbreviations in English	English	Abbreviations in English	English
Afr.	Afrikaans	Bulg.	Bulgarian	Fr.	French	Khm.	Khmer	Pers.	Persian	Som.	Somalian
A.I.	American Indian	Burm.	Burmese	Gae.	Gaelic	Kor.	Korean	Pol.	Polish	Sp.	Spanish
Alb.	Albanian	Cat.	Catalan	Georg.	Georgian	K.S.	Khoi-San	Poly.	Polynesian	Sud.	Sudanese
Alt.	Altaic	Cauc.	Caucasian	Germ.	German	Laot.	Laotian	Port.	Portuguese	Swa.	Swahili
Amh.	Amharic	Chin.	Chinese	Gr.	Greek	Lapp.	Lappish	Prov.	Provençal	Swed.	Swedish
Ar.	Arabic	Cz.	Czech	Hebr.	Hebrew	Latv.	Latvian	Rmsh.	Romansh	Tam.	Tamil
Arm.	Armenian	Dan.	Danish	Hin.	Hindi	Lith.	Lithuanian	Rom.	Romanian	Thai	Thai
Az.	Azerbaidzhani	Dut.	Dutch	Hung.	Hungarian	Mal.	Malay	Rus.	Russian	Tib.	Tibetan
Ban.	Bantu	Eng.	English	Icel.	Icelandic	Malag.	Malagasy	Sah.	Saharan	Tur.	Turkish
Bas.	Basque	Esk.	Eskimo	Indon.	Indonesian	Mel.	Melanesian	S.C.	Serbo-Croatian	Ural.	Uralic
Beng.	Bengali	Est.	Estonian	Ir.	Irish	Mong.	Mongolian			Urdu	Urdu
Ber.	Berber	Far.	Faroese	Iran.	Iranian	Nep.	Nepalese	Sin.	Sinhalese	Viet.	Vietnamese
Br.	Breton	Finn.	Finnish	It.	Italian	Nor.	Norwegian	Slvk.	Slovak	Wall.	Walloon
		Fle.	Flemish	Jap.	Japanese	Pash.	Pashto	Slvn.	Slovene	Wel.	Welsh

Glossary of Geographical Terms

Local Form	English	Local Form	English	Local Form	English	Local Form	English
A		Ait / *Ar.; Ber.*	sons	Ard- / *Gae.*	high	Badwêynta / *Som.*	ocean
		Aivi, -aivi / *Lapp.*	mountain	Areg / *Ar.*	dune	Badyarada / *Som.*	gulf
		Ak / *Tur.*	white	Areia / *Port.*	beach	Baeg / *Kor.*	white
A- / *Ban.*	people	'Aklé / *Ar.*	dunes	Arena / *Sp.*	beach	Bæk / *Dan.*	brook
A' / *Icel.*	river	Akmeņs / *Latv.*	stone	Argent / *Fr.*	silver	Bælt / *Dan.*	strait
Å / *Dan.; Nor.; Swed.*	stream	Ákra / *Gr.*	point	Arhipelag / *Rus.*	archipelago	Bagni / *It.*	thermal springs
a., an / *Germ.*	on	Akti / *Gr.*	coast	Arkhaios / *Gr.*	old, antique	Baharu / *Mal.*	new
Aa / *Germ.*	stream	Ala / *Malag.*	forest	Arm / *Eng.; Germ.*	branch	Bahia / *Port.*	bay
Aache / *Germ.*	stream	Ala / *Finn.*	low, lower	Arquipélago / *Port.*	archipelago	Bahia / *Sp.*	bay
Aaiún / *Ar.*	springs	Alan / *Tur.*	field	Arr., Arroyo / *Sp.*	stream	Bahir / *Ar.*	river, lake, sea
Aan / *Dut.; Fle.*	on	Alb / *Rom.*	white	Arrecife / *Sp.*	reef	Bahnhof / *Germ.*	railway station
Åb / *Pers.*	stream	Albo / *Sp.*	white	Arroio / *Port.*	stream	Bahr / *Ar.*	wadi
Ābād / *Pers.*	city, town	Albufera / *Sp.*	lagoon	Art / *Tur.*	pass, watershed	Baḥr / *Ar.*	river, lake, sea
Abad, -abad / *Pers.*	city, town	Alcalá / *Sp.*	castle	Aru / *Sin.; Tam.*	river	Baḥrat / *Ar.*	lake
Ābār / *Ar.*	spring	Alcázar / *Sp.*	castle	Ås / *Dan.; Nor.; Swed.*	hills	Bahri / *Ar.*	north, northern
Abbadia / *It.*	abbey	Aldea / *Sp.*	village	Asfar / *Ar.*	yellow	Baḥri / *Ar.*	north
Abbaye / *Fr.*	abbey	Alföld / *Hung.*	lowland	Asif / *Ber.*	river	Bahrïyah / *Ar.*	northern
Abbazia / *It.*	abbey	Ali / *Amh.*	mountain	Asky / *Alt.*	lower	Bai / *Chin.*	white
Abbi / *Amh.*	great	Alia / *Poly.*	stream	Áspros / *Gr.*	white	Băi / *Rom.*	thermal springs
Abd / *Ar.*	servant	Alin / *Mong.*	range	Assa / *Ber.*	wadi	Baia / *Port.*	bay
Abeba / *Amh.*	flower	Alm / *Germ.*	mountain pasture	Atalaya / *Sp.*	frontier	Baie / *Fr.*	bay
Aber / *Br.; Wel.*	estuary			Áth / *Gae.*	ford	Baigne / *Fr.*	seaside resort
Abhang / *Germ.*	slope	Alor / *Mal.*	river	Átha / *Gae.*	ford	Baile / *Gae.*	city, town
Abū / *Ar.*	father, master	Alp / *Germ.*	mountain pasture	Atol / *Port.*	atoll	Bain / *Fr.*	thermal springs
Abyad / *Ar.*	white			Au / *Germ.*	meadow	Bains / *Fr.*	thermal springs
Abyaḍ / *Ar.*	white	Alpe / *Germ.; Fr.; It.*	mountain pasture	Aue / *Germ.*	irrigated field	Baixo / *Port.*	low, lower
Abyār / *Ar.*	well			Aust / *Nor.*	east	Bajan / *Mong.*	rich
Abyss / *Eng.*	ocean depth, deep	Alps / *Eng.*	mountains	Austur / *Icel.*	east	Bajo / *Sp.*	low
Ach / *Germ.*	stream	Alsó / *Hung.*	low, lower	Ava / *Poly.*	canal	Bajrak / *Alb.*	tribe
Achaïf / *Ar.*	dunes	Alt / *Germ.*	old	Aven / *Fr.*	doline, sink	Bakhtïyäri / *Pers.*	western
Ache / *Germ.*	stream	Altin / *Tur.*	lower	Awa / *Poly.*	bay	Bakki / *Icel.*	hill
Achter / *Afr.; Dut.; Fle.*	back	Altiplano / *Sp.*	plateau	Àyios / *Gr.*	saint	Bālā / *Pers.*	high
Acqua / *It.*	water	Alto / *Sp.; It.; Port.*	high	'Ayn / *Ar.*	spring, well	Bald / *Eng.*	peak
Açu / *A.I.*	great	Altopiano / *It.*	plateau	'Ayoún / *Ar.*	springs, wells	Balka / *Rus.*	gorge
Açude / *Port.*	reservoir, dam	Älv / *Swed.*	river	'Ayoún / *Ar.*	spring	Balkan / *Bulg.; Tur.*	mountain range
Ada / *Tur*	island	Am / *Kor.*	mountain, peak	Aza / *Ber.*	wadi	Ballin / *Gae.*	mouth
Adalar / *Tur.*	archipelago	Amane / *Ber.*	water	Azraq / *Ar.*	light blue	Ballon / *Fr.*	dome
Adasr / *Tur.*	island	Amba / *Amh.*	mountain	Azul / *Port.; Sp.*	light blue	Bally / *Gae.*	city, town
Addis / *Amh.*	new	Ambato / *Malag.*	rock	Azur / *Fr.*	light blue	Balta / *Rom.*	marsh
Adi / *Amh.*	village	An / *Gae.*	of			Báltos / *Gr.*	marsh
Adrar / *Ber.*	mount, mountains	An, a. / *Germ.*	on			Ban / *Laot.*	village
		Ana / *Poly.*	grotto	**B**		Bana / *Jap.*	promontory
Aéroport / *Fr.*	airport	Anatolikós / *Gr.*	eastern			Baňa / *Slvk.*	mine
Aeroporto / *It.; Port.*	airport	Äng / *Swed.*	meadow			Bañados / *Sp.*	marsh
Aeropuerto / *Sp.*	airport	Angra / *Port.*	bay, anchorage	B., Bay / *Eng.*	bay	Banc / *Fr.*	bank
Af / *Som.*	mouth, gorge	Ani- / *Malag.*	center	b., bei / *Germ.*	by	Banco / *It.; Sp.*	bank
Afsluitdijk / *Dut.*	dam	Áno / *Gr.*	upper	B., Bucht / *Germ.*	bay	Band / *Pers.*	dam, mountain range
Agadir / *Ber.*	castle	Ānou / *Ber.*	well	Ba / *Sud.*	river		
Agiz / *Tur.*	mouth	Anse / *Fr.*	inlet	Ba- / *Ban.*	people	Bandao / *Chin.*	peninsula
Agro / *Sp.; It.*	plain	Ant- / *Malag.*	center	Ba / *Mel.*	hill, mountain	Bandar / *Ar.; Mal.; Pers.*	port, market
Agua / *Sp.*	water	Ao / *Chin.; Khm.; Thai*	gulf	Baai / *Afr.*	bay	Bang / *Indon.; Mal.*	stream
Aguja / *Sp.*	needle	'Âouâna / *Ar.*	well	Bab / *Ar.*	gate	Bangou / *Sah.*	well
Agulha / *Port.*	needle, promontory	Apă / *Rom.*	water	Bac / *Viet.*	north	Banhado / *Port.*	marsh
		'Aqabat / *Ar.*	pass	Bach / *Germ.*	brook, torrent	Bani / *Ar.*	sons
Ahal / *Georg.*	new	Aqueduc / *Fr.*	aqueduct	Bacino / *It.*	reservoir	Banja / *Bulg.; S.C.; Slvn.*	thermal springs
Aḥmar / *Ar.*	red	Ar / *Mong.*	north	Back / *Eng.*	ridge	Banjaran / *Mal.*	mountain range
Ahrāmāt / *Ar.*	pyramids	Ar / *Sin.; Tam.*	river	Back / *Swed.*	brook	Banka / *Rus.*	sandbank
Ahzar / *Ber.*	wadi	'Arâguîb / *Ar.*	hills	Bäck / *Swed.*	brook	Banke / *Dan.*	bank
Aigialós / *Gr.*	coast	Arba / *Amh.*	mount	Backe / *Swed.*	hill	Baño / *Sp.*	thermal springs
Aigue / *Prov.*	water	Arbore / *Rom.*	tree	Bad, -bad / *Dan.; Germ.; Nor.; Swed.*	thermal springs	Banský / *Cz.*	upper
Aiguille / *Fr.*	needle	Archipiélago / *Sp.*	archipelago			Bánya / *Hung.*	mine
Aigulla / *Port.*	needle	Arcipelago / *It.*	archipelago	Baden, -baden / *Germ.*	thermal springs	Bar / *Gae.*	peak
Aïn / *Ar.*	spring	Arḍ / *Ar.*	region	Bādiyat / *Ar.*	desert	Bar / *Eng.*	sandbar

Local Form	English
Bar / Hin.	great
Bāra / Hin.	great
Bara / S.C.	pond
Barā / Urdu	great
Barajı / Tur.	dam
Barat / Indon.; Mal.	west, western
Barkas / Lith.	castle, city, town
Barlovento / Sp.	windward
Barq / Ar.	hill
Barra / Port.; Sp.	bar, bank
Barrage / Fr.	dam
Barragem / Port.	reservoir
Barranca / Sp.	gorge
Barranco / Port.; Sp.	gorge
Barre / Fr.	bar
Barun / Mong.	western
Bas / Fr.	low
-bas / Rus.	reservoir
Bassa / Port.	flat
Bassejn / Rus.	reservoir
Bassin / Fr.	basin
Bassure / Fr.	flat
Bassurelle / Fr.	flat
Bašta / S.C.	garden
Bataille / Fr.	battle
Batalha / Port.	battle
Batang / Indon.; Mal.	river
Batha / Sah.	stream
Baţin / Ar.	depression
Bāţlāq / Pers.	marsh
Batu / Mal.	rock
Bayan / Mong.	rich
Bayır / Tur.	mountain, slope
Bayou / Fr.	branch, stream
Bayt / Ar.	house
Bazar / Pers.	market
Be / Malag.	great
Beau / Fr.	beautiful
Becken / Germ.	basin
Bed / Eng.	river bed
Beek / Dut.	creek
Be'er / Hebr.	spring
Bei / Chin.	north
Bei, b. / Germ.	by
Beida / Ar.	white
Beinn / Gae.	mount
Bel / Ar.	son
Bel / Bulg.	white
Bel / Tur.	pass
Beled / Ar.	village
Belen / Tur.	mount
Belet / Ar.	village
Beli / S.C.; Slvn.	white
Beli / Tur.	pass
Bellah / Sah.	well
Belogorje / Rus.	mountains
Belt / Dan.; Germ.	strait
Bely / Rus.	white
Bělý / Cz.	white
Ben / Ar.	son
Ben / Gae.	mount
Bender / Pers.	port, market
Bendi / Tur.	dam
Beni / Ar.	son
Beo / S.C.	white
Bereg / Rus.	bank
Berg, -berg / Afr.; Dut.; Fle.; Germ.; Nor.; Swed.	mount
Berge / Afr.	mountain
Bergen / Dut.; Fle.	dunes
Bergland / Germ.	upland
Bermejo / Sp.	red
Besar / Mal.	great
Betsu / Jap.	river
Betta / Tam.	mountain
Bhani / Hin.	community
Bharu / Mal.	new
Bheag / Gae.	little
Bīābān / Pers.	desert
Biały / Pol.	white
Bianco / It.	white
Bien / Viet.	lake
Bight / Eng.	bay
Bijeli / S.C.	white
Bill / Eng.	promontory
Bilo / S.C.	range
Bilý / Cz.	white
Binnen / Dut.; Fle.; Germ.	inner
Biqā' / Ar.	valley
Bir / Ar.	well
Bi'r / Ar.	well
Birkat / Ar.	pond
Bistrica / Bulg.; S.C.; Slvn.	stream
Bjarg / Icel.	rock
Bjerg / Dan.	mount
Bjeshkët / Alb.	mountain pasture
Blaauw / Afr.	blue
Blanc / Fr.	white
Blanco / Sp.	white
Blau / Germ.	blue
Bleu / Fr.	blue
Bluff / Eng.	cliff
Bo- / Ban.	people
Bo / Chin.	white
Bo / Swed.	habitation
Boca / Sp.	gap, mouth
Bôca / Port.	gap, mouth
Bocage / Fr.	forest
Bocca / It.	gap, pass
Bocchetta / It.	gap, pass
Bodden / Germ.	bay, lagoon
Boden / Germ.	soil
Bœng / Khm.	lake, marsh
Bog / Eng.	marsh
Bogaz / Alt.; Az.; Tur.	strait
Bogāzi / Tur.	strait
Bogdo / Mong.	high
Bogen / Nor.	bay
Bois / Fr.	forest
Boka / S.C.	channel
Boloto / Rus.	marsh
Bolšoj / Rus.	great
Bolsón / Sp.	basin
Bom / Port.	good
Bong / Kor.	peak
Bongo / Malag.	upland
Bor / Cz.; Rus.	coniferous forest
Bór / Pol.	forest
-bor / Slvn.	city, town
Bóras / Gr.	north
Börde / Germ.	fertile plain
Bordj / Ar.	fort
Bóreios / Gr.	northern
Borg, -borg / Dan.; Nor.; Swed.	castle
Borgo / It.	village
Born / Germ.	spring
Bory / Pol.	forest
Bosch / Dut.; Fle.	forest
Bosco / It.	wood
Bosque / Sp.	forest
Bosse / Fr.	hill
Botn / Nor.	bay
Bou / Ar.	father, master
Bouche / Fr.	mouth
Boula / Sud.	well
Bourg / Fr.	city, town
Bourne, - bourne / Eng.	frontier
Boven / Afr.	upper
Boz / Tur.	grey
Bozorg / Pers.	great
Brána / Cz.	gate
Braña / Sp.	mountain pasture
Branche / Fr.	branch
Branco / Port.	white
Braţul / Rom.	branch
Bravo / Sp.	wild
Brazo / Sp.	branch
Brdo / Cz.; S.C.	hill
Bre / Nor.	glacier
Bredning / Dan.	bay
Breg / Alb.; Bulg.; S.C.	hill, coast
Brjag / Bulg.	bank
Bro / Dan.; Nor.; Swed.	bridge
Brod / Bulg.; Cz.; Rus.; S.C.; Slvk.; Slvn.	ford
Bród / Pol.	ford
Bron / Afr.	spring
Bronn / Germ.	spring
Bru / Nor.	bridge
Bruch / Germ.	peat-bog
Bruchzone / Germ.	fracture zone
Bruck, -bruck / Germ.	bridge
Brücke / Germ.	bridge
Brug / Dut.; Fle.	bridge
Brugge / Dut.; Fle.	bridge
Bruk / Nor.	factory
Brunn / Swed.	spring
-brunn / Germ.	spring
Brunnen / Germ.	spring
Brygg / Swed.	bridge
Brzeg / Pol.	coast
Bü / Ar.	father, master
Bucht, B. / Germ.	bay
Bugt / Dan.	bay
Buḩayrat / Ar.	lake, lagoon
Bühel / Germ.	hill
Bühl / Germ.	hill
Buhta / Rus.	bay
Bukit / Mal.	mountain, peak
Bukt / Nor.; Swed.	bay
Buku / Indon.	hill, mountain
Bulag / Mong.; Tur.	spring
Bulak / Mong.; Tur.	spring
Būlāq / Tur.	spring
Bult / Afr.	hill
Bulu / Indon.	mountain
Bur / Som.	mount
Bûr / Ar.	port
Burg, - burg / Afr.; Ar.; Dut.; Eng.; Germ.	castle
Burgh / Eng.	city, town
Burgo / Sp.	village
Burha / Hin.	old
Buri / Thai	city, town
Burj / Ar.	village
Burn / Eng.	stream
Burnu / Tur.	promontory
Burqat / Ar.	mount, marsh
Burun / Tur.	cape
Busen / Germ.	bay
Busu / Ban.	land
Bûtat / Ar.	lake, pond
Butte / Eng.; Fr.	flat-topped hill
Büyük / Tur.	great
By / Eng.	near
By, -by / Dan.; Nor.; Swed.	city, town
Bystrica / Cz.; Slvk.	stream
Bystrzyca / Pol.	stream

C

Local Form	English
C., Cap / Cat.; Fr.; Rom.	cape
C., Cape / Eng.	cape
C., Colle / It.	pass
Caatinga / A.I.	forest
Cabeça / Port.	peak
Cabeço / Port.	peak
Cabeza / Sp.	peak
Cabezo / Sp.	peak, mountain
Cabo / Port.; Sp.	cape
Cachoeira / Port.	waterfall, rapids
Cachopo / Port.	reef
Cadena / Sp.	range
Caer / Wel.	castle
Cagan / Cauc.; Mong.	white
Cairn / Gae.	hill
Čāj / Az.; Tur.	river
Cajdam / Mong.	salt marsh
Caka / Chin.	lake
Cala / Sp.; It.	inlet
Calar / Sp.	plateau
Caldas / Sp.; Port.	thermal springs
Caleta / Sp.	inlet
Camp / Cat.; Fr.; Eng.	field
Campagna / It.	plain
Campagne / Fr.	plain
Campo / Sp.; It.; Port.	field
Cañada / Sp.	gorge, ravine
Canale / It.	canal, channel
Caño / Sp.	branch
Cañón / Sp.	gorge
Canyon / Eng.	gorge
Cao / Viet.	mountain
Cap, C. / Cat.; Fr.; Rom.	cape
Car / Gae.	castle
Càrn / Gae.	peak
Carrera / Sp.	road
Carrick / Gae.	rock
Casale / It.	hamlet
Cascada / Sp.	waterfall
Cascata / It.	waterfall
Castel / It.	castle
Castell / Cat.	castle
Castello / It.	castle
Castelo / Port.	castle
Castillo / Sp.	castle
Castro / Sp.; It.	village
Catarata / Sp.	cataract
Catena / It.	mountain range
Catinga / Port.	degraded forest
Cauce / Sp.	river bed
Causse / Fr.	highland
Cava / It.	stone quarry
Çay / Tur.	river
Cay / Eng.	islet, island
Caye / Fr.	island
Cayo / Sp.	islet, island
Ceann / Gae.	promontory
Centralny / Rus.	middle
Čeren / Alb.	black
Černi / Bulg.	black
Černý / Cz.	black
Černy / Rus.	black
Cerrillo / Sp.	hill
Cerrito / Sp.	hill
Cerro / Sp.; Port.	hill, mountain
Cêrro / Port.	hill, mountain
Červen / Bulg.	red
Červony / Rus.	red
Cetate / Rom.	city, town
Chaco / Sp.	scrubland
Chāh / Pers.	well
Chaïf / Ar.	dunes
Chaîne / Fr.	mountain range
Champ / Fr.	field
Chang / Chin.	highland
Chapada / Port.	highland
Chapadão / Port.	highland
Château / Fr.	castle
Châtel / Fr.	castle
Chāy / Tur.	river
Chedo / Kor.	archipelago
Chenal / Fr.	canal
Cheng / Chin.	city, town, wall
Cheon / Kor.	city, river
Chergui / Ar.	eastern
Cherry, -cherry / Hin.; Tam.	city, town
Chew / Amh.	salt mine, salt
Chhāk / Khm.	bay
Chhotla / Hin.	little
Chi- / Ban.	great
Chi / Chin.	marsh, lake
Chi / Kor.	lake, pond
Chi- / Swa.	land
Chiang / Thai	city, town
Chico / Sp.	little
Chine / Eng.	ridge
Ch'on / Kor.	station
Ch'ŏn / Kor.	river
Chŏsuji / Kor.	reservoir
Chott / Ar.	salt marsh
Chu / Chin.; Viet.	mountain, hill
Chuŏr phnum / Khm.	mountain range
Chute / Fr.	waterfall
Chutes / Fr.	waterfalls
Cidade / Port.	city, town
Ciems / Latv.	village
Čierny / Slvk.	black
Cime / Fr.	peak
Cîmp / Rom.	field
Cîmpie / Rom.	plain
Cinco / Sp.; Port.	five
Citeli / Georg.	red
Città / It.	city, town
Ciudad / Sp.	city, town
Ckali / Georg.	water
Ckaro / Georg.	spring
Co / Chin.	lake
Col / Cat.; Fr.	pass
Colina / Port.; Sp.	hill
Coll / Cat.	hill
Collado / Sp.	pass
Colle, C. / It.	pass
Collina / It.	hill
Colline / Fr.	hill
Colonia / Sp.; It.	colony
Coma / Sp.	hill country
Comb / Eng.	basin
Comba / Sp.	basin
Combe / Fr.	basin
Comté / Fr.	county, shire
Con / Viet.	island
Conca / It.	depression
Condado / Sp.	county, shire
Cone / Eng.	volcanic cone
Cône / Fr.	volcanic cone
Contraforte / Port.	front range
Cordal / Sp.	crest
Cordilheira / Port.	mountain range
Cordillera / Sp.	mountain range
Coring / Chin.	lake
Corixa / A.I.	stream
Corno / It.	peak
Cornone / It.	peak
Corrente / It.; Port.	stream
Corriente / Sp.	stream
Costa / Sp.; It.; Port.	coast
Côte / Fr.	coast
Coteau / Fr.	height, slope
Coxilha / Port.	ridge
Craig / Gae.	rock
Cratère / Fr.	crater
Cresta / Sp.; It.	crest
Crêt / Fr.	crest
Crête / Fr.	crest
Crkva / S.C.	church
Crni / S.C.; Slvn.	black
Crven / S.C.	red
Csatorna / Hung.	canal
Cuchilla / Sp.	ridge
Cuenca / Sp.	basin
Cuesta / Sp.	escarpment
Cueva / Sp.	cave
Čuka / Bulg.; S.C.	peak
Çukur / Tur.	well
Cu Lao / Viet.	island
Cumbre / Sp.	peak
Cun / Chin.	village
Cura / A.I.	stone
Curr / Alb.	rock
Cy., City / Eng.	city, town
Czarny / Pol.	black

D

Local Form	English
Da / Chin.	great
Da / Viet.	mountain, peak
Daal / Dut.; Fle.	valley
Daba / Mong.	pass
Daba / Som.	hill
Daban / Chin.; Mong.	pass
Dae / Kor.	great
Dağ / Tur.	mountain
Dağ., Dağı / Tur.	mountain
Dāgh / Pers.; Tur.	mountain
Dağı, Dağ. / Tur.	mountain
Dağları / Tur.	mountain range
Dahar / Ar.	hill
Dahr / Ar.	plateau, escarpment
Dai / Chin.; Jap.	great
Daiet / Ar.	marsh
Dak / Viet.	stream
Dake / Jap.	mountain
Dakhla / Ar.	depression
Dakhlet / Ar.	depression, bay
Dal, -dal / Afr.; Dan.; Dut.; Fle.; Nor.; Swed.	valley
Dala / Alt.	steppe, plain
Dalaj / Mong.	lake, sea
Dalan / Mong.	wall
Dallol / Sud.	valley, torrent
Dalur / Icel.	valley
Damm / Germ.	dam
Dan / Kor.	point

Local Form	English
Danau / Indon.	lake
Danda / Nep.	mountains
Dao / Chin.	island, peninsula
Dao / Viet.	island
Dar / Ar.	house, region
Dar / Swa.	port
Dara / Tur.	torrent, valley
Darb / Ar.	track
Darja / Alt.	river, sea
Darya, Daryā / Pers.	river, sea
Daryācheh / Pers.	lake, sea
Daš / Alt.; Az.	rock
Dasht / Pers.	desert, plain
Dawḥat / Ar.	bay
Dayr / Ar.	convent
De / Sp.; Fr.	of
Deal / Rom.	hill
Dearg / Gae.	red
Debre / Amh.	hill, monastery
Dega / Som.	stone
Deh / Pers.	village
Dēḥ / Som.	stream
Deich / Germ.	dike
Dél / Hung.	south
Delft / Dut.; Fle.	deep
Delger / Mong.	wide, market
-den / Eng.	city, town
Deniz / Tur.	sea
Denizi / Tur.	sea
Dent / Fr.	peak
Deo / Laot.; Viet.	pass
Dépression / Fr.	depression
Depressione / It.	depression
Der / Som.	high
Dera / Hin.; Urdu	temple
Derbent / Tur.	gorge, pass
Dere / Tur.	river, valley
Désert / Fr.	desert
Desfiladero / Sp.	pass
Desh / Hin.	land, country
Desierto / Sp.	desert
Det / Alb.	sea
Détroit / Fr.	strait
Deux / Fr.	two
Dezh / Pers.	castle
Dhar / Ar.	heights, hills
Dhār / Hin.; Urdu	mountain
Dhitikós / Gr.	western
Dien / Khm.; Viet.	rice-field
Diep / Dut.; Fle.	deep, strait
Dijk, -dijk / Dut.; Fle.	dam
Ding / Chin.	mountain, peak
Dique / Sp.	dam
Di Sopra / It.	upper
Di Sotto / It.	lower
Distrito / Sp.; Port.	district
Diu / Hin.	island
Diz / Pers.	castle
Djebel / Ar.	mountain
Dji / Ban.	water
Djup / Swed.	deep
Do / Kor.	Island
Do / S.C.	valley
Dō / Jap.	island, administrative division
Dōho / Som.	valley
Doi / Thai	mountain, peak
Dol / Bulg.; Cz.; Rus.; S.C.	valley
Doł / Pol.	valley
Dolen / Bulg.	low
Dolgi / Rus.	long
Dolina / Bulg.; Cz.; Pol.; Rus.; S.C.; Slvn.	valley
Dolni / Bulg.	low
Dolni / Pol.	lower
Dolny / Pol.	lower
Domb / Hung.	hill
Dôme / Fr.	dome
Dong / Chin.; Viet.	east
Dong / Kor.	city, town
Dong / Thai	mountain
Dong / Viet.	marsh, plain
Donji / S.C.	low, lower
Dorf, -dorf / Germ.	village
Doroga / Rus.	road
Dorp, -dorp / Afr.; Dut.; Fle.	village
Dos / Rom.	ridge
Dos / Sp.	two
Douarn / Br.	land
Dougou / Sud.	settlement
Doukou / Sud.	settlement
Down / Eng.	hill
Drâa / Ar.	dunes, hills
Dracht / Germ.	sandbank
Draw / Eng.	ravine, valley
Drif / Afr.	ford
Drift / Afr.	ford
Droichead / Gae.	bridge
Droûs / Ar.	crest
Dry / Pash.	river
Dubh / Gae.	black
Dugi / S.C.	long
Dugu / Sud.	settlement
Dun / Gae.	castle
Duna / Sp.; It.	dune
Düne / Germ.	dune
Dungar / Hin.	mountain
Düngar / Hin.	mountain
Duong / Viet.	stream
Durchbruch / Germ.	gorge
Ḍurg / Hin.	castle
-durga / Hin.	castle
Duży / Pol.	great
Dvor / Cz.	court
Dvorec / Rus.	castle
Dvúr / Cz.	castle
Dwór / Pol.	court
Dżebel / Bulg.	mountain
Dzong / Tib.	fort, monastery

E

Local Form	English
Ea / Thai	river
Eau / Fr.	water
Ebe / Ban.	forest
Ebene / Germ.	plain
Eck / Germ.	point
Eclusa / Sp.	lock
Écluse / Fr.	lock
Écueil / Fr.	cliff
Edeien / Ber.	sand desert
Edjérir / Ber.	wadi
Egg / Germ.; Nor.	crest, point
Eglab / Ar.	hills
Ehi / Sah.	mountain
Eid / Nor.	isthmus
Eiland / Afr.	island
Eisen / Germ.	iron
Eisenerz / Germ.	iron ore
El / Amh.	well
Elv, -elv / Nor.	river
Embalse / Sp.	reservoir
Embouchure / Fr.	mouth
Emi / Sah.	mountain
En / Fr.	in
Ende / Germ.	end
Enneri / Sah.	stream
Ennis / Gae.	island
Enseada / Port.	Bay, inlet
Ensenada / Sp.	bay, inlet
Ér / Hung.	stream
Erdő / Hung.	forest
Erg / Ar.	sand desert
Erz / Germ.	ore
Espigão / Port.	plateau
Éstān / Pers.	land
Este / Sp.	east
Estero / Sp.	estuary, marsh
Estrecho / Sp.	strait
Estreito / Port.	strait
Estuaire / Fr.	estuary
Estuário / Port.	estuary
Estuario / Sp.; It.	estuary
Észak / Hung.	north
Étang / Fr.	pond
Ewaso / Ban.	river
Ey / Icel.	island
Eyja / Icel.	island
Eyjar / Icel.	islands
Eylandt / Dut.	island
Eżeras / Lith.	lake
Ezers / Latv.	lake

F

Local Form	English
Fa / Mel.	stream
Falaise / Fr.	cliff
Fall, -fall / Germ.; Eng.; Swed.	waterfall
Falls / Eng.	waterfall
Falu / Hung.	village
-falva / Hung.	village
Fan / Sah.	village
Faraglione / It.	cliff
Farallón / Sp.	cliff
Faro / Sp.; It.	lighthouse
Farvand / Dan.	strait
Fehér / Hung.	white
Fehn / Germ.	peat fen, peat-bog
Fekete / Hung.	black
Feld / Dan.; Germ.	field
Fell / Eng.	upland moor
Fell / Icel.	mountain
Fels / Germ.	rock
Fen / Eng.	marsh, peat-bog
Feng / Chin.	mountain, peak
Feste / Germ.	fort
Festung / Germ.	fort
Fier / Rom.	iron
Firn / Germ.	snow-field
Firth / Eng.	estuary, fjord
Fiume / It.	river
Fjäll / Swed.	mountain
Fjärd / Swed.	fjord
Fjell / Nor.	mountain
Fjöll / Icel.	mountain
Fjord, Fj. / Dan.; Nor.; Swed.	fjord
Fjörður / Icel.	fjord, bay
Fleuve / Fr.	river
Fließ / Germ.	torrent
Fljót / Icel.	river
Flói / Icel.	bay, gulf
Floresta / Sp.; Port.	forest
Flow / Eng.	strait
Flughafen / Germ.	airport
Fluß / Germ.	river
Fo / Mel.	stream
Foa / Mel.	stream
Foa / Poly.	cove
Foce / It.	mouth
Föld / Hung.	plain
Fonn / Nor.	glacier
Fontaine / Fr.	fountain
Fonte / It.; Port.	spring
Fontein / Afr.; Dut.	spring
Foort / Afr.; Dut.	ford
Forca / It.	pass
Forcella / It.	defile
Ford / Rus.	fjord
Förde / Germ.	fjord, gulf
Foreland / Eng.	promontory
Foresta / It.	forest
Forêt / Fr.	forest
Fors / Swed.	rapids, waterfall
Forst / Germ.; Dut.	forest
Fortin / It.; Port.	fort
Fortin / Sp.	fort
Fosa / Sp.	trench
Foss / Icel.; Nor.	rapids, waterfall
Fossé / Fr.	trench
Foum / Ar.	pass
Fourche / Fr.	pass
Foz / Sp.; Port.	mouth
Frei / Germ.	free
Fronteira / Port.	frontier
Frontera / Sp.	frontier
Frontón / Sp.	promontory
Fuente / Sp.	spring
Fuerte / Sp.	fort
Fuji / Jap.	mountain
Fülat / Ar.	marsh
Furt / Germ.	ford
Fushë / Alb.	plain

G

Local Form	English
G., Gora / Bulg.; Rus.; S.C.	mountain, hill
G., Gunung / Indon.	mountain
Ga / Jap.	bay
Ga / Mel.	mountain, peak
Gabel / Germ.	pass
Gaissa / Lapp.	mountain
Gala / Sin.; Tam.	mountain
Gam / Hin.; Urdu	village
Gamle / Nor.; Swed.	old
Gana / Sud.	little
Gang / Germ.	passage
Gang / Chin.	port, bay
Gang / Kor.	stream, bay
Gang / Tib.	glacier
Ganga / Hin.	river
Ganj / Hin.; Urdu	market
-gaon / Hin.	city, town
Gaoyuan / Chin.	plateau
Gap / Kor.	point
Gar / Hin.	house
Gara / Bulg.	station
Gara / Ar.	hills, range
Gară / Rom.	station
Garaet / Ar.	marsh, intermittent lake
Garam / Beng.; Hin.; Urdu	village
-gard / Pol.	city, town
Gård, -gård / Dan.; Nor.; Swed.	farmhouse
Gardaneh / Pers.	pass
Gare / Fr.	railway station
Garet / Ar.	hill
Garh, -garh / Hin.; Urdu	castle
Garhi / Hin.; Nep.; Urdu	fort
Garten / Germ.	garden
Gat / Dan.; Fle.; Dut.	strait
Gata / Jap.	bay, lake
Gau, -gau / Germ.	district
Gäu, -gäu / Germ.	district
Gavan / Rus.	port
Gave / Bas.	torrent
Gawa / Jap.	river
Geb., Gebirge / Germ.	mountain range
Gebergte / Afr.; Dut.	mountain range
Gebirge, Geb. / Germ.	mountain range
Geç., Geçit / Tur.	pass
Geçidi / Tur.	pass
Geçit, Geç. / Tur.	pass
Geysir / Icel.	geyser
Ghar / Hin.; Urdu	house
Ghar / Pash.	mountain, mountain range
Gharbīyah / Ar.	western
Ghat / Hin.; Nep.; Urdu	pass
Ghubbat / Ar.	bay
Ghurd / Ar.	dune
Gi / Kor.	peninsula
Giang / Viet.	stream
Giri / Hin.; Urdu	mountain, hill

Local Form	English
Girlo / Rus.	branch
Gjebel / Ar.	mountain
Gji / Alb.	bay
Glace / Fr.	ice
Glaciar / Sp.	glacier
Glacier / Eng.; Fr.	glacier
Glen / Gae.	valley
Gletscher / Germ.	glacier
Gobi / Mong.	desert
Godăr / Pers.	ford
Gok / Kor.	river
Gök / Tur.	blue
Gol / Cauc.; Mong.	river
Göl / Tur.	lake
Gola / It.	gorge
Gold / Germ.; Eng.	gold
Golet / S.C.	mountain
Golf / Germ.	gulf
Golfe / Fr.	gulf
Golfete / Sp.	inlet
Golfo / Sp.; It.; Port.	gulf
Goljam / Bulg.	great
Gölü / Tur.	lake
Gong / Tib.	high
Gonggar / Tib.	mountain
Gongo / Ban.	mountain
Góra / Pol.	mountain
Gora, G. / Bulg.; Rus.; S.C.	mountain, hill
Gorica / S.C.; Slvn.	hill
Gorje / S.C.	mountain range
Gorlo / Rus.	gorge
Gorm / Gae.	blue
Gorni / Bulg.; S.C.; Slvn.	upper
Gornji / S.C.; Slvn.	upper
Górny / Pol.	high
Gorod / Rus.	city, town
Gorodok / Rus.	village
Gorski / Bulg.	upper
Gory / Rus.	mountains
-gou / Chin.	river
Goulbi / Sud.	river, lake
Goulbin / Sud.	wadi
Goulet / Fr.	gap
Gour / Ar.	hills, range
Gourou / Sud.	wadi
Goz / Sah.	dune
Graafschap / Dut.	county, shire
Graben / Germ.	ditch, canal
Gracht / Dut.	canal
Grad, -grad / Bulg.; Rus.; S.C.; Slvn.	city, town, castle
Gradac / S.C.	castle
Gradec / Bulg.	village
Gradec / Slvn.	castle
Græn / Icel.	green
Gran / Sp.; It.	great
Grande / Sp.; It.; Port.	great
Grao / Cat.; Sp.	gap
Grat / Germ.	crest
Grève / Fr.	beach
Grind / Germ.	peak
Grjada / Rus.	range
Gród, -gród / Pol.	castle, city, town
Grön / Icel.	green
Grond / Afr.	soil
Gronden / Dut.; Fle.	flat
Groot / Afr.; Dut.; Fle.	great
Groß / Germ.	great
Grotta / It.	grotto
Grotte / Fr.; Germ.	grotto
Grube / Germ.	mine
Grün / Germ.	green
Grunn / Nor.	ground
Gruppe / Germ.	mountain system
Gruppo / It.	mountain system
Gua / Mal.	cave
Guaçu / A.I.	great
Guan / Chin.	pass
Guazú / A.I.	great
Guba / Rus.	bay
Guchi / Jap.	strait
Guelb / Ar.	hill, mountain
Guelta / Ar.	well
Guic / Br.	village
Güney / Tur.	south, southern
Gunong / Mal.	mountain
Guntō / Jap.	archipelago
Gunung, G. / Indon.	mountain
Guo / Chin.	state, land
Gur / Rom.	mountain
Guri / Jap.	cliff
Gurud / Ar.	hills, dunes
Gyár / Hung.	factory

H

Local Form	English
Haag / Dut.; Fle.	hedge
-håb / Dan.	port
Haḍabat / Ar.	highland
Hadd / Ar.	point
Hadjer / Ar.	hill, mountain
Hae / Kor.	bay, sea
Haehyeop / Kor.	strait

Geographical Glossary

Local Form	English
Haf / *Icel.*	sea
Ḩafar / *Ar.*	well
Hafen / *Germ.*	port
Haff / *Germ.*	lagoon
Hafir / *Ar.*	spring, ditch
Hafnar / *Icel.*	port
Hāfūn / *Som.*	bay
Hage / *Dan.*	point
Hage / *Dut.; Fle.*	hedge
Hågna / *Swed.*	peak
Hai / *Chin.*	sea, lake, bay
Hain / *Germ.*	forest
Haixia / *Chin.*	strait
Ḩajar / *Ar.*	hill, mountain
Hajar / *Ar.*	hill country
Halbinsel / *Germ.*	peninsula
Halma / *Hung.*	hill
Halom / *Hung.*	hill
Halq / *Ar.*	gap
Hals / *Nor.*	peninsula
Halvø / *Dan.*	peninsula
Halvøy / *Nor.*	peninsula
Hama / *Jap.*	beach
Hamāda / *Ar.*	rocky desert
Ḩamādah / *Ar.*	plateau
Ḩamādat / *Ar.*	plateau
Hammam / *Ar.*	thermal springs
Ḩammām / *Ar.*	well
Hamn / *Nor.; Swed.*	port
Hamrā' / *Ar.*	red
Hāmūn / *Jap.*	salt lake
Hana / *Jap.*	cape
Hana / *Poly.*	bay
Hane / *Tur.*	house
Hang / *Kor.*	port
Hank / *Ar.*	escarpment, plateau
Hantō / *Jap.*	peninsula
Har / *Hebr.*	mountain
Hara / *Mong.*	black
Harar / *Swa.*	well
Ḩarrah / *Ar.*	lava field
Ḩarrat / *Ar.*	lava field
Hasi / *Ar.*	well
Ḩasi / *Ar.*	well
Hassi / *Ar.*	well
Ḩasy / *Ar.*	well
Haug / *Nor.*	hill
Haupt- / *Germ.*	principal
Haure / *Lapp.*	lake
Haus / *Germ.*	house
Hausen / *Germ.*	village
Haut / *Fr.*	high
Hauteur / *Fr.*	hill
Hauts Plateaux / *Fr.*	highlands
Hauz / *Pers.*	reservoir
Hav / *Dan.; Nor.; Swed.*	sea, gulf
Haven / *Eng.; Fle.; Dut.*	port
Havn / *Dan.; Nor.*	port
Havre / *Fr.*	port
Hawr / *Ar.*	lake, marsh
Ház / *Hung.*	house
-háza / *Hung.*	house
Hazm / *Ar.*	height, mountain range
He / *Chin.*	river
Head / *Eng.*	headland
Hed / *Dan.; Swed.*	heath
Hegy / *Hung.*	mountain
Hegység / *Hung.*	mountain
Hei / *Nor.*	heath
Heide / *Germ.*	heath
Heijde / *Dut.; Fle.*	heath
Heilig / *Germ.*	saint
Heim, -heim / *Germ.; Nor.*	house
Heiya / *Jap.*	plain
-hely / *Hung.*	locality
Hem / *Swed.*	home
Hen / *Br.*	old
Higashi / *Jap.*	east, eastern
Hima / *Hin.*	ice
Himal / *Nep.*	peak
Hisar / *Tur.*	castle
Ho / *Chin.*	reservoir, river
Ho / *Kor.*	river, reservoir
Hō / *Jap.*	mountain
Hoch / *Germ.*	high, upper
Hochland / *Germ.*	highland
Hochplato / *Afr.*	highland
Hodna / *Ar.*	highland
Hoek / *Dut.; Fle.*	cape
Hof / *Dut.; Germ.*	court
Höfn / *Icel.*	port
Høg / *Nor.*	peak
Hög / *Swed.*	mountain
Hogna / *Nor.*	peak
Höhe / *Germ.*	peak
Høj / *Dan.*	hill
Hoj / *Ural.*	mountain range
Hok / *Jap.*	north
Hoku / *Jap.*	north, northern
Holm / *Dan.; Nor.; Swed.*	island
Holz / *Germ.*	forest
Hon / *Viet.*	island, point
Hong / *Chin.; Viet.*	red
Hono / *Poly.*	bay, anchorage
Hoog / *Afr.; Dut.; Fle.*	high
Hook / *Eng.*	point
Hoorn / *Afr.; Dut.; Fle.*	cape, point
Hora / *Cz.; Slvk.*	point
Horn / *Eng.; Germ.; Icel.; Nor.; Swed.*	point
Horni / *Cz.*	high
Horný / *Slvk.*	upper
Horst / *Germ.*	mountain
Horvot / *Hebr.*	ruins
Hory / *Cz.; Slvk.*	mountain range
Hout / *Dut.; Fle.*	forest
Hovd, -hovd / *Dan.; Nor.*	cape
Ḩowz / *Pers.*	basin
Hrad / *Cz.; Slvk.*	castle, city, town
Hradiště / *Cz.*	citadel
Hřeben / *Cz.*	crest
Hrebet / *Rus.*	mountain range
Hu / *Rmsh.*	lake
Huang / *Chin.*	yellow
Hude / *Germ.*	pasture
Huerta / *Sp.*	market garden
Hügel / *Germ.*	hill
Hügelland / *Germ.*	hill country
Huis, -huis / *Afr.; Dut.; Fle.*	house
Huisie / *Afr.*	house
Huizen, -huizen / *Dut.*	houses
Huk / *Afr.; Dan.; Swed.*	cape
Hum / *S.C.*	hill
Hurst / *Eng.*	grove
Hus / *Dut.; Nor.; Swed.*	house
Huta / *Pol.; Slvk.*	hut
Hütte / *Germ.*	hut
Hver / *Icel.*	crater
Hvit / *Icel.*	white
Hvost / *Rus.*	spit

I

Local Form	English
I., Island / *Eng.*	island
Ierós / *Gr.*	holy
Igarapé / *A.I.*	river
Ighazer / *Ber.*	torrent
Ighil / *Ber.*	hill
Iguidi / *Ber.*	dunes
Ih / *Mong.*	great
Ike / *Jap.*	pond
Ile / *Fr.*	island
Ilha / *Port.*	island
Iller / *Tur.*	administrative division
Ilot / *Fr.*	islet
Imi / *Ar.*	spring
I-n / *Ber.*	well
Inch / *Gae.*	island
Inder / *Dan.; Nor.*	inner
Indre / *Nor.*	inner
Inferiore / *It.*	lower
Inish / *Gae.*	island
Insel / *Germ.*	island
Insulă / *Rom.*	island
Inver / *Gae.*	mouth
Irhazér / *Ber.*	wadi
Irmak / *Tur.*	river
'Irq / *Ar.*	dunes
Is / *Nor.*	glacier
Ís / *Icel.*	ice
Isblink / *Dan.*	glacier
Ishi / *Jap.*	rock
Iske / *Alt.*	old
Isla / *Sp.*	island
Iso / *Finn.*	great
Iso / *Jap.*	cliff
Isola / *It.*	island
Isthmós / *Gr.*	isthmus
Istmo / *Sp.; It.*	isthmus
Ita / *A.I.*	stone
Itä / *Finn.*	east
Itivdleq / *Esk.*	isthmus
Iwa / *Jap.*	rock, cliff
Iztočni / *Bulg.*	eastern
Izvor / *Bulg.; Rom.; S.C.; Slvn.*	spring

J

Local Form	English
J., Jazīrat / *Ar.*	island
J., Jiang / *Chin.*	river
Jabal / *Ar.*	mountain
Jaha / *Ural.*	river
Jam / *Ural.*	lake, river
Jama / *Rus.*	cave
Jan / *Alt.*	great
Janga / *Tur.*	north
Jangi / *Alt.; Iran.*	new
Janūbīyah / *Ar.*	southern
Jar / *Rus.*	bank
Järv / *Est.*	lake
Järve / *Finn.*	lake
Järvi / *Finn.*	lake
Jasirēd / *Som.*	island
Jaun / *Latv.*	new
Jaur / *Lapp.*	lake
Jaure / *Lapp.*	lake
Javr / *Lapp.*	lake
Javrre / *Lapp.*	lake
Jazā'ir / *Ar.*	islands
Jazīrat, J. / *Ar.*	island
Jazovir / *Bulg.*	reservoir
Jbel / *Ar.*	mountain
Jebel / *Ar.*	mountain
Jedid / *Ar.*	new
Jedo / *Kor.*	archipelago
Jezero / *S.C.; Slvn.*	lake
Jezioro / *Pol.*	lake
Jhil / *Hin.; Urdu*	lake
Jian / *Chin.*	mountain
Jiang, J. / *Chin.*	river
Jiao / *Chin.*	cape, cliff
Jibāl / *Ar.*	mountain
Jih / *Cz.*	south
Jima / *Jap.*	island
Jin / *Kor.*	cove
Jing / *Chin.*	spring
Jisr / *Ar.*	bridge
Joch / *Germ.*	pass
Jõgi / *Est.*	river
Jøkel / *Nor.*	glacier
Joki / *Finn.*	river
Jokka / *Lapp.*	river
Jökull / *Icel.*	glacier
Jord, -jord / *Nor.*	earth
Ju / *Ural.*	river
Judeţ / *Rom.*	district
Jugan / *Ural.*	river
Jura / *Lith.*	sea
Jūra / *Latv.*	sea
Jūras Līcis / *Latv.*	bay
Jūrmala / *Latv.*	beach
Jurt / *Cauc.*	village
Južni / *Bulg.; S.C.; Slvn.*	southern
Južny / *Rus.*	southern
Juzur / *Ar.*	islands

K

Local Form	English
Ka / *Poly.*	lake
Kaap / *Afr.*	cape
Kabīr / *Ar.*	great
Kae / *Kor.*	inlet
Kāf / *Ar.*	peak, mountain
Kafr / *Ar.*	village
Kaga / *Ban.*	hills, mountain range
Kahal / *Ar.*	plateau, escarpment
Kai / *Jap.*	sea
Kaikyō / *Jap.*	strait
Kaise / *Lapp.*	mountain
Kal / *Pers.*	stream
Kala / *Az.; Kor.*	fort
Kala / *Finn.*	river
Kala / *Hin.*	black
Kala / *Tur.*	castle
Kalaa / *Ar.*	castle
Kalaki / *Georg.*	city, town
Kale / *Tur.*	castle
Kali / *Hin.*	black
Kali / *Indon.; Mal.*	bay, river
Kallio / *Finn.*	rock
Kaln / *Latv.*	mountain
Kalós / *Gr.*	beautiful, good
Kamen / *Bulg.; Rus.; S.C.; Slvn.*	mountain, peak
Kámen / *Cz.*	rock
Kameň / *Slvk.*	rock
Kami / *Jap.*	upper
Kamień / *Pol.*	rock
Kamm / *Germ.*	crest
Kamp / *Germ.*	field
Kâmpóng / *Khm.*	village
Kámpos / *Gr.*	field
Kampung / *Indon.; Mal.*	village
Kan., Kanal / *Alb.; Dan.; Germ.; Nor.; Rus.; S.C.; Slvn.; Swed.; Tur.*	canal, channel
Kanaal / *Dut.; Fle.*	canal
Kanał / *Pol.*	canal
Kanal, Kan. / *Alb.; Dan.; Germ.; Nor.; Rus.; S.C.; Slvn.; Swed.; Tur.*	canal, channel
Kand, -kand / *Pers.; Tur.*	city, town
Kang / *Chin.; Kor.*	bay, river
Kangas / *Fle.*	heath
Kange / *Esk.*	east
Kangri / *Tib.*	snow-capped mountain
Kantara / *Ar.*	bridge
Kaôh / *Khm.*	island
Kap / *Dan.; Germ.*	cape
Kapija / *S.C.*	gate, gorge
Kapp / *Nor.*	cape
Kar / *Tib.*	white
Kar / *Ural.*	city, town
Kara / *Tur.*	black
Karang / *Indon.; Mal.*	sandbank, cliff
Kari / *Finn.*	cliff
Kariba / *Ban.*	gorge
Kariet / *Ar.*	village
Karki / *Finn.*	peninsula
Kastel / *Germ.*	castle
Kástron / *Gr.*	fort, city, town
Káto / *Gr.*	lower
Kaupstadur / *Icel.*	city, town
Kaupunki / *Finn.*	city, town
Kavīr / *Pers.*	salt desert
Kawa / *Jap.*	river
Kawm / *Ar.*	hill
Kebir / *Ar.*	great
Kedi / *Georg.*	mountain range
Kédia / *Ar.*	mountain, plateau
Kedim / *Ar.*	old
Kef / *Ar.*	mountain
Kefála / *Gr.*	mountain, peak
Kefar / *Hebr.*	village
Kei / *Jap.*	river
Kelet / *Hung.*	east
Ken / *Gae.*	cape
Kent / *Alt.; Iran.; Tur.*	city, town
Kenya / *Swa.*	fog
Kep / *Alb.*	cape
Kep., Kepulauan / *Mal.*	archipelago
Kepulauan, Kep. / *Mal.*	archipelago
Kereszt / *Hung.*	cross
Kerk / *Dut.; Fle.*	church
Keski / *Finn.*	middle
Kette / *Germ.*	mountain range
Keur / *Sud.*	village
Key / *Eng.*	coral island
Kha / *Tib.*	valley
Khal / *Hin.*	canal
Khalīj / *Ar.*	gulf
Khand / *Hin.*	district
Khao / *Thai*	hill, mountain
Kharābeh / *Pers.*	ruins
Khashm / *Ar.*	promontory
Khatt / *Ar.*	wadi
Khawr / *Ar.*	mouth, bay
Khazzān / *Ar.*	dam
Khemis / *Ar.*	fifth
Khersónisos / *Gr.*	peninsula
Khirbat / *Ar.*	ruins
Khlong / *Thai*	stream, mouth
Khokhok / *Thai*	isthmus
Khor / *Ar.*	mouth, bay
Khóra / *Gr.*	land
Khorion / *Gr.*	village
Khowr / *Pers.*	bay
Khrisós / *Gr.*	gold
Ki- / *Ban.*	little
Kibali / *Sud.*	river
Kil / *Gae.*	church
Kilde / *Dan.*	spring
Kilima / *Swa.*	mountain
Kill / *Gae.*	strait
Kilwa / *Ban.*	lake
Kin / *Gae.*	cape
Kinn / *Nor.*	cape, point
Kirche / *Germ.*	church
Kirk / *Eng.*	church
Kis / *Hung.*	little
Kisiwa / *Swa.*	island
Kita / *Jap.*	north, northern
Kızıl / *Tur.*	red
Klein / *Afr.; Dut.; Germ.*	little
Kliff / *Germ.*	cliff
Klint / *Dan.*	reef
Klip / *Afr.; Dut.*	rock, cliff
Klit / *Dan.*	dune
Kloof / *Afr.; Dut.*	gorge
Kloster / *Dan.; Germ.; Nor.; Swed.*	convent
Knob / *Eng.*	mountain
Knock / *Gae.*	mountain, hill
Ko / *Jap.*	bay, lake, little
Ko / *Sud.*	stream
Ko / *Thai*	island, point
Købing / *Dan.*	town
Kogel / *Germ.*	dome
Kōgen / *Jap.*	plateau
Koh / *Hin.; Pers.*	mountain, mountain range
Kol / *Alt.*	river, valley
Kol / *Alt.; Tur.*	lake
Koll / *Nor.*	peak
Kólpos / *Gr.*	gulf
Kong / *Dan.; Nor.; Swed.*	king
Kong / *Indon.; Mal.*	mountain
Kong / *Viet.*	mountain, hill
Konge / *Ban.*	river
König / *Germ.*	king
Koog / *Germ.*	polder
Kop / *Afr.*	hill
Kopec / *Cz.; Slvk.*	hill
Kopf / *Germ.*	peak
Köping / *Swed.*	town
Köprü / *Tur.*	bridge
Körfezi / *Tur.*	gulf
Korfi / *Gr.*	rock
Koro / *Mel.*	mountain, island
Koro / *Sud.*	old
Koru / *Tur.*	forest
Kosa / *Rus.*	spit
Koška / *Rus.*	cliff
Koski / *Finn.*	rapids
Kosui / *Jap.*	lake
Kot / *Urdu*	castle
Kota / *Mal.*	city, town
Kotal / *Pash.; Pers.*	pass
Kotar / *S.C.*	cultivated area
Kotlina / *Pol.*	basin

Local Form	English
Kotlovina / Rus.	basin, plain
Kou / Chin.	mouth, pass
Kourou / Sud.	well
Kowr / Pers.	river
Kowtal / Pers.	pass
Koy / Tur.	bay
Köy / Tur.	village
Kraal / Afr.	village
Kraina / Pol.	land
Kraj / Rus.; S.C.	land
Kraj / Rus.	administrative division
Krajina / S.C.	land
Krak / Ar.	hill, castle
Krans / Afr.	mountain
Kras / S.C.; Slvn.	karst landscape
Krasny / Rus.	red
Kreb / Ar.	hills, mountain range
Kriaž / Ar.	mountain range
Krš / S.C.	karst area, limestone area
Krung / Thai	city, town
Ksar / Ar.	castle
Ksour / Ar.	fortified village
Ku- / Ban.	river branch
Kuala / Mal.	river, mouth
Kubra / Ar.	bridge
Küçük / Tur.	little
Kuduk / Tur.	spring
Küh / Pers.	mountain
Kühhä / Pers.	mountain range
Kul / Alt.; Iran.; Tur.	lake
Kulam, -kulam / Hin.; Tam.	pond
Kulle / Swed.	hill
Kulm / Germ.	peak
Kultuk / Rus.	bay
Kum / Tur.	dunes, sand desert
Kuppe / Germ.	dome, seamount
Kurayb / Ar.	hill
Kurgan / Alt.	hill
Kurgan / Tur.	fort
Kuro / Jap.	black
Kurort / Bulg.; Germ.; Rus.	spa
Kust / Dut.; Fle.	coast
Kust- / Swed.	coast
Küste / Germ.	coast
Kút / Hung.	spring
Kuyu / Tur.	spring
Kvemo / Georg.	low, lower
Kwa / Ban.	village
Kylä / Finn.	village
Kyle / Gae.	strait, channel
Kyō / Jap.	strait
Kyrka / Swed.	church
Kyst / Dan.; Nor.	coast
Kyun / Burm.	island
Kyūryō / Jap.	hills, mountains
Kyzyl / Tur.	red
Kzyl / Tur.	red

L

Local Form	English
L., Lake, Lago / Eng.; It.; Port.; Sp.	lake
La / Tib.	pass
Laagte / Afr.	stream, valley
Labuan / Indon.; Mal.	bay, port
Lac / Fr.	lake
Lach / Som.	stream, wadi
Lacul / Rom.	lake
Lae / Poly.	cape, point
Laem / Thai	bay, port
Låg / Nor.; Swed.	low, lower
Lag / Swed.	stream, wadi
Läge / Swed.	beach
Lagh / Som.	stream, wadi
Lago, L. / It.; Port.; Sp.	lake
Lagoa / Port.	lagoon
Laguna / Alb.; It.; Rus.; Sp.	lagoon, lake
Lagune / Fr.	lagoon
Laht / Est.	bay
Lahti / Finn.	bay, gulf
Laks / Finn.	bay
Lalla / Ar.	saint
Lampi / Finn.	pond
Lande / Fr.	heath
Lang / Afr.; Dut.; Germ.	long
Lang / Viet.	village
Lao / Chin.	old
Lapa / Poly.	mountain range, peak
Largo / Port.; Sp.	basin
Las / Pol.	forest
Las, Lâs / Som.	well
Laut / Mal.	sea
Law / Gae.	hill, mountain
Lázně / Cz.	thermal springs
Lednik / Rus.	glacier
Leite / Germ.	coast
Lekh / Nep.	mountain range

Local Form	English
Les / Bulg.; Cz.; Rus.; Slvk.	forest
Leso / Rus.	forested
Levante / It.; Sp.	eastern
Levkós / Gr.	white
Levy / Rus.	left
Lha / Tib.	temple
Lhari / Hin.; Nep.	mountain
Lho / Tib.	south
Lido / It.	sandbar
Liedao / Chin.	archipelago
Liehtao / Chin.	archipelago
Liels / Latv.	great
Lilla / Swed.	little
Lille / Dan.; Nor.	little
Liman / Alb.; Rus.; Tur.	lagoon, bay
Liman / Tur.	bay, port
Limin / Gr.	port
Limni / Gr.	lake
Ling / Chin.	mountain range, peak
Linna / Finn.	castle
Liqen / Alb.	lake
Lithos / Gr.	stone
Litoral / Port.; Sp.	littoral
Litorale / It.	littoral
Llan / Wel.	church
Llano / Sp.	plain
Llanura / Sp.	plain
Lo- / Ban.	river
Loch / Gae.	lake, inlet
Loch / Germ.	grotto
Loka / Slvn.	forest
Loma / Sp.	hill
Long / Indon.	stream
Loo / Dut.; Fle.	clearing
Lough / Gae.	lake
Loutrá / Gr.	thermal springs
Ložbina / Rus.	depression
Lu- / Ban.	river
Lua / Ban.	river
Lua / Mel.	island, reef
Lua / Poly.	crater
Luang / Thai	yellow
Luch / Germ.	peat-bog
Lücke / Germ.	pass
Lug / Rus.	meadow
Luka / S.C.; Slvn.	port
Lule / Lapp.	east, eastern
Lum / Alb.	river
Lund / Dan.; Swed.	forest
Lung / Rom.	long
Lung / Tib.	valley
Luoto / Finn.	shoal
Lurg / Pers.	salt flat
Lut / Pers.	desert

M

Local Form	English
M., Monte / It.; Port.; Sp.	mountain
Ma / Ar.	water
Ma- / Ban.	people
Maa / Est.; Finn.	island, land
Ma'arrat / Ar.	height
Machi / Jap.	district
Macizo / Sp.	massif
Madhya / Hin.	central
Madinah / Ar.	city, town
Madiq / Ar.	strait
Mado / Swa.	well
Madu / Tam.	pond
Mae / Thai	stream
Mae nam / Thai	stream, mouth
Magh / Gae.	plain
Mägi / Est.	mountain
Măgura / Rom.	height
Mahā / Hin.	great
Mahal / Hin.; Urdu	palace
Mai / Amh.; Ban.	stream
Majdan / S.C.	quarry
Mäki / Finn.	mountain, hill
Makrós / Gr.	long
Mala / Hin.; Tam.	mountain
Malai / Hin.; Tam.	mountain
Malal / A.I.	fence
Malhão / Port.	dome
Mali / Alb.	mountain
Mali / S.C.; Slvn.	little
Malki / Bulg.	little
Malla / Tam.	mountain
Maly / Rus.	little
Malý / Cz.; Slvk.	little
Mały / Pol.	little
Man / Kor.	bay
Manastir / Bulg.; S.C.	monastery
Manche / Fr.	channel
Mar / It.; Port.; Sp.	sea
Mar / Tib.	red
Mar / Ural.	city, town
Marais / Fr.	marsh
Marché / Fr.	market
Mare / Fr.	pond
Mare / It.; Rom.	sea
Mare / Rom.	great
Marea / Rom.	sea
Marécage / Fr.	marsh
Marios / Lith.	reservoir

Local Form	English
Marisma / Sp.	marsh
Mark / Dan.; Nor.; Swed.	land
Markt / Germ.	market
Marsa / Ar.	anchorage, bay
Marsch / Germ.	marsh
Maru / Jap.	mountain
Mas / Prov.	farmhouse
Maşabb / Ar.	mouth
Mashra' / Ar.	landing, pier
Masivul / Rom.	massif
Massiv / Germ.; Rus.	massif
Mata / Poly.	point
Mata / Port.; Sp.	forest
Mata / Som.	waterfall
Mato / Port.; Sp.	forest
Matsu / Jap.	point
Mauna / Poly.	mountain
Mávros / Gr.	black
Mayo / Sud.	river
Maza / Lith.	little
Mazar / Pers.; Tur.	sanctuary
Mazs / Latv.	little
Me / Khm.	river
Me / Mel.	hill, mountain
Me / Thai	great
Medina / Ar.	city, town
Medjez / Ar.	ford
Meer / Dut.; Fle.	lake
Meer / Germ.	lake, sea
Megálos / Gr.	great
Mégas / Gr.	great
Megye / Hung.	district
Mélas / Gr.	black
Melkosopočnik / Rus.	hill country
Mellan / Swed.	central
Men / Chin.	gate, channel
Ménez / Br.	mountain
Menzel / Ar.	bivouac
Meos / Indon.	island
Mer / Fr.	sea
Mercato / It.	market
Merdja / Ar.	lagoon, marsh
Meri / Est.; Finn.	sea
Meridional / Rom.; Sp.	southern
Merín / A.I.	little
Merja / Ar.	lagoon, marsh
Mers / Ar.	port
Mersa / Ar.	port
Mesa / Sp.	mesa, tableland
Meseta / Sp.	plateau
Mésos / Gr.	central
Mesto / Bulg.; S.C.; Slvk.; Slvn.	city, town
Město / Cz.	city, town
Mestre / Port.	principal
Meydan / Tur.	square
Mezad / Hebr.	castle
Mezō / Hung.	field
Mgne., Montagne / Fr.	mountain
Mgnes., Montagnes / Fr.	mountains
Miao / Chin.	temple
Miasto / Pol.	city, town
Mic / Rom.	little
Middel / Afr.; Dut.; Fle.	middle
Midi / Fr.	noon, south
Między / Pol.	central
Miedzyrzecze / Pol.	interfluve
Mierzeja / Pol.	sand spit
Mifraz / Hebr.	bay, gulf
Miftah / Ar.	gorge
Mikrós / Gr.	little
Mina / Port.; Sp.	mine
Minā' / Ar.	port
Minami / Jap.	south, southern
Minamoto / Jap.	spring
Minato / Jap.	port
Mine / Jap.	peak
Mirim / A.I.	little
Misaki / Jap.	cape
Mittel- / Germ.	middle
Mo / Chin.	sand desert
Mo / Nor.; Swed.	heath
Moana / Poly.	lake
Mogila / Bulg.; Rus.	hill
Moku / Poly.	island
Molle / Dan.	mill
Monasterio / Sp.	monastery
Mond / Afr.; Dut.; Fle.	mouth
Mong / Burm.; Thai; Viet.	city, town
Moni / Gr.	monastery
Mont / Cat.; Fr.	mountain
Montagna / It.	mountain
Montagne, Mgne. / Fr.	mountain
Montagnes, Mgnes. / Fr.	mountains
Montaña / Sp.	mountain
Monte, M. / It.; Port.; Sp.	mountain
Monts, Mts. / Fr.	mountains
Moos / Germ.	moor
Mór / Gae.	great
More / Bulg.; Rus.; S.C.	sea
More / Gae.	great
Mori / Jap.	mountain, forest
Morne / Fr.	mountain
Moron / Mong.	river
Morro / Port.; Germ.	hill, peak
Morrón / Sp.	mountain
Morze / Pol.	sea

Local Form	English
Most / Bulg.; Cz.; Pol.; Rus.; S.C.; Slvn.	bridge
Moto / Jap.	spring
Motte / Fr.	hill
Motu / Mel.; Poly.	island, rock
Moutier / Fr.	monastery
Movilă / Rom.	hill
Moyen / Fr.	central
Mta / Georg.	mountain
Mts., Monts, Mountains / Eng.; Fr.	mountains
Muang / Laot.; Thai	city, town, land
Muara / Indon.; Mal.	mouth
Muela / Sp.	mountain
Mühle / Germ.	mill
Mui / Mel.	point
Mui / Viet.	point, cape
Muiden / Dut.; Fle.	mouth
Muir / Gae.	sea
Mukh / Hin.	mouth
Mull / Gae.	promontory
Münde / Germ.	mouth
Mündung / Germ.	mouth
Municipiul / Rom.	commune
Munkhafaḍ / Ar.	depression
Münster / Germ.	monastery
Munte / Rom.	mountain
Muntele / Rom.	mountain
Munţii / Rom.	mountain range
Muren / Mong.	river
Mushāsh / Ar.	spring
Muz / Tur.	ice
Muztagh / Tur.	snow-capped mountain
Mwambo / Ban.	rock, cliff
Myit / Burm.	stream
Mynydd / Wel.	mountain
Myo / Burm.	city, town
Mýri / Icel.	marsh
Mys / Rus.	cape

N

Local Form	English
Na / Cz.; Pol.; Rus.; S.C.; Slvn.	on
Nab / Ar.	spring
Nad / Cz.; Pol.; Rus.	on
Nada / Jap.	bay, sea
Nadi, -nadi / Hin.; Urdu	river
Næs / Dan.	point
Nafūd / Ar.	dunes
Nag / Tib.	black
Nagar, -nagar / Hin.; Tib.	city, town
Nagaram / Hin.; Tam.	city, town
Nagorje / Rus.	plateau, mountains
Nagy / Hung.	great
Nahr / Ar.	river
Naikai / Jap.	sea
Naka / Jap.	central
Nakhon / Thai	city, town
Nam / Burm.; Laot.; Thai	river
Nam / Kor.	south
Namakzar / Pers.	salt desert
Nan / Chin.	south
Narrows / Eng.	strait
Narssaq / Esk.	plain, valley
Näs / Swed.	cape
Nationalpark / Swed.; Germ.	national park
Nau / Lith.	new
Nauja / Lith.	new
Navolok / Rus.	cape, promontory
Ne / Jap.	cliff
Neder / Fle.; Dut.	low
Neem / Est.	cape
Negro / Port.; Sp.	black
Negru / Rom.	black
Nehir / Tur.	river
Nei / Chin.	inner
Nene, -nene / Ban.	great
Néos / Gr.	new
Nero / It.	black
Nes / Icel.; Nor.	cape
Ness / Gae.	promontory
Neu / Germ.	new
Neuf / Fr.	new
Nevado / Sp.	snow-capped mountain
Nez / Fr.	cape
Ngok / Viet.	mountain, peak
Ngolo / Ber.	great
Ni / Kor.	village
Niecka / Pol.	basin
Niemi / Finn.	peninsula
Nieuw / Fle.; Dut.	new
Nij / Dut.	new
Nīl / Hin.	blue
Nishi / Jap.	west
Niski / Pol.	lower
Nisko / S.C.	low
Nisoi / Gr.	islands
Nisos / Gr.	island
Nizina / Pol.	lowland
Nížina / Cz.	depression
Nízký / Cz.	low, lower

Geographical Glossary

Local Form	English
Nizmennost / *Rus.*	lowland, depression
Nižni / *Rus.*	low, lower
Nižný / *Slvk.*	low, lower
No / *Mel.*	stream
Nock / *Gae.*	ridge
Noir / *Fr.*	black
Non / *Thai*	hill
Nong / *Thai*	lake, marsh
Noord / *Afr.; Fle.; Dut.*	north
Noordoost / *Afr.; Fle.; Dut.*	northeast
Nor / *Arm.*	new
Nord / *Fr.; It.; Germ.*	north
Nördlich / *Germ.*	northern
Nørdre / *Dan.; Nor.*	northern
Norra / *Swed.*	northern
Nørre / *Dan.*	northern
Norte / *Sp.*	north
Nos / *Bulg.; Rus.; S.C.; Slvn.*	cape
Nosy / *Malag.*	island
Nótios / *Gr.*	southern
Nou / *Rom.*	new
Novi / *Bulg.; S.C.; Slvn.*	new
Novo / *Port.*	new
Novy / *Rus.*	new
Nový / *Cz.; Slvk.*	new
Now / *Pers.*	new
Nowy / *Pol.*	new
Nudo / *Sp.*	mountain
Nuevo / *Sp.*	new
Nui / *Viet.*	mountain
Numa / *Jap.*	marsh, lake
Nummi / *Finn.*	heath
Nunatak / *Esk.*	peak
Nuovo / *It.*	new
Nur / *Chin.*	lake
Nusa / *Mal.*	island
Nut, -nut / *Nor.*	peak
Nuwara / *Sin.; Tam.*	city, town
Nuwe / *Afr.*	new
Nyanza / *Ban.*	water, river, lake
Nyasa / *Ban.*	lake
Nyeong / *Kor.*	pass
Nyika / *Ban.*	upland
Nyŏng / *Kor.*	mount, pass
Nyugat / *Hung.*	west

O

Local Form	English
Ō / *Jap.*	great
Ó / *Hung.*	old
Ö / *Swed.*	island
Ø, -ø / *Dan.; Nor.*	island
Öar / *Swed.*	islands
Ober / *Germ.*	upper
Oblast / *Rus.*	province
Obo / *Mong.*	mountain, hill
Occidental / *Fr.; Rom.; Sp.*	western
Océan / *Fr.*	ocean
Océano / *Sp.*	ocean
Oceano / *It.; Port.*	ocean
Ocnă / *Rom.*	salt mine
Odde / *Dan.; Nor.*	promontory
Oeste / *Port.; Sp.*	west
Oever / *Fle.; Dut.*	bank
Oewer / *Afr.*	bank
Oie / *Germ.*	islet
Ojos / *Sp.*	spring
Oka / *Jap.*	coast
Oke / *Sud.*	height
Okean / *Rus.*	ocean
Oki / *Jap.*	bay
Okrug / *Rus.*	district
Ola / *Alt.*	city, town
Omuramba / *K.S.*	stream
Onder / *Afr.*	under
Oni / *Malag.*	river
Oos / *Afr.*	east
Oost / *Fle.; Dut.*	east
Oostelijk / *Dut.*	eastern
Opatija / *Slvn.*	abbey
Or / *Fr.*	gold
Oraş / *Rom.*	city, town
Óri / *Gr.*	mountains
Oriental / *Fr.; Port.; Rom.; Sp.*	eastern
Orientale / *It.*	eastern
Orilla / *Sp.*	bank
Órmos / *Gr.*	bay
Óros / *Gr.*	mountain
Ország / *Hung.*	land
Ort / *Germ.*	cape
Orta / *Tur.*	central
Orto / *Alt.*	central
Oseaan / *Afr.*	ocean
Ōshima / *Jap.*	large island
Ost / *Dan.; Germ.*	east
Öst / *Swed.*	east
Ostān, -ostān / *Pers.*	province
Øster / *Dan.; Nor.*	east, eastern
Öster / *Swed.*	east, eastern
Östlich / *Germ.*	eastern
Ostrog / *Rus.*	castle
Ostrov / *Rus.*	island
Ostrovul / *Rom.*	island
Ostrów / *Pol.*	island
Ostrvo / *S.C.*	island
Otok / *S.C.; Slvn.*	island
Otrog / *Rus.*	front range (mountains)
Oua / *Mel.*	stream
Ouar / *Ar.*	rocky desert
Oud / *Fle.; Dut.*	old
Oued / *Ar.*	wadi
Ouest / *Fr.*	west
Ouled / *Ar.*	son
Oum / *Ar.*	mother
Ouro / *Port.*	gold
Outu / *Poly.*	cape
Ova / *Ban.*	people
Ova / *Tur.*	plain
Ovasi / *Tur.*	plain
Øver / *Nor.*	over
Över / *Swed.*	over
Övre / *Swed.*	over
Øy / *Dan.; Nor.*	island
oz., Ozero / *Rus.*	lake
Ozek / *Alt.*	hollow
Ozera / *Rus.*	lakes
Ozero, oz. / *Rus.*	lake

P

Local Form	English
P., Pulau / *Mal.; Indon.*	island
Pää / *Finn.*	principal
Pad / *Rus.*	valley
Padang / *Indon.*	plain
Padiş / *Rom.*	upland
Padół / *Pol.*	valley
Pădure / *Rom.*	forest
Pahorek / *Cz.*	hill
Pahorkatina / *Cz.*	plateau, hills
Pais / *Port.; Sp.*	land, country
Pak / *Thai*	mouth
Pala / *It.*	peak
Palaiós / *Gr.*	old
Palanka / *S.C.*	village
Pali / *Poly.*	cliff
-palli / *Hin.*	village
Pampa / *Sp.*	plain, prairie
Panda / *Swa.*	junction
Panev / *Cz.*	basin
Pantanal / *Sp.*	swamp
Pantano / *Sp.*	swamp, lake
Pao / *Mel.*	hill
Pará / *A.I.*	river
Paramera / *Sp.*	desert highland
Páramo / *Sp.*	moor
Paraná / *A.I.*	river
Parbat / *Hin.; Urdu*	mountain
Parc / *Fr.*	park
Parco / *It.*	park
Parco Nazionale / *It.*	national park
Pardo / *Port.*	grey
Parque / *Sp.*	park
Parque Nacional / *Sp.; Port.*	national park
Pas / *Fr.; Rom.*	pass, strait
Pasaje / *Sp.*	passage
Pasir / *Mal.*	sand, beach
Paso / *Sp.*	pass
Passágem / *Port.*	passage
Passe / *Fr.*	pass
Passo / *It.; Port.*	pass
Pasul / *Rom.*	pass
Patak / *Hung.*	stream
Patam, -patam / *Hin.*	city, town
Patnā / *Hin.*	city, town
Patnam, -patnam / *Hin.*	city, town
Pattinam, -pattinam / *Hin.*	city, town
Pays / *Fr.*	land, country
Pazar / *Tur.*	market
Pea / *Est.*	cape
Pech / *Cat.*	hill
Pedhiás / *Gr.*	plain
Pedra / *Port.*	rock, mountain
Peg., Pegunungan / *Mal.; Indon.*	mountain range
Pegunungan, Peg. / *Mal.; Indon.*	mountain range
Pélagos / *Gr.*	sea
Pele / *Poly.*	peak, hill
Pen / *Br.*	principal
Pen / *Br.; Gae.*	cape, mountain
Peña / *Sp.*	peak
Pendi / *Chin.*	basin
Pendiente / *Sp.*	slope
Penha / *Port.*	peak
Península / *Port.; Sp.*	peninsula
Péninsule / *Fr.*	peninsula
Penisola / *It.*	peninsula
Peñon / *Sp.*	rock, island
Pente / *Fr.*	slope
Perekop / *Rus.*	channel
Pereval / *Rus.*	pass
Perevoz / *Rus.*	ford
Pertuis / *Fr.*	strait
Peščara / *S.C.*	sandy soil
Peski / *Rus.*	sand desert
Petit / *Fr.*	little
Pétra / *Gr.*	rock
Phanom / *Thai; Khm.*	mountain range, mountain
Phau / *Laot.*	mountain
Phnum / *Khm.*	hill, mountain
Phu / *Viet.*	mountain, hill
Phum / *Thai*	forest
Phumĭ / *Khm.*	village
Pi / *Chin.*	cape
Piana, Pianura / *It.*	plain
Piano / *It.*	plain
Piatră / *Rom.*	stone
Pic / *Cat.; Fr.*	peak
Picacho / *Sp.*	peak
Piccolo / *It.*	little
Pico / *Port.; Sp.*	peak
Piedra / *Sp.*	rock, cliff
Pietra / *It.*	stone
Pieve / *It.*	parish
Pik / *Rus.*	peak
Pils / *Latv.*	city, town
Pinar / *Sp.*	pine forest
Pingyuan / *Chin.*	plain
Pioda / *It.*	crest
Pirgos / *Gr.*	tower, peak
Pīsh / *Pers.*	anterior, before
Pitkä / *Finn.*	great
Piton / *Fr.*	mountain, peak
Piz / *Rmsh.*	peak
Pizzo / *It.*	peak
Pjasăci / *Bulg.*	beach
Plaat / *Fle.; Dut.*	sandbank
Plage / *Fr.*	beach
Plaine / *Fr.*	plain
Plan / *Fr.*	plain
Planalto / *Port.*	plateau
Planina / *Bulg.*	mountain
Plano / *Sp.*	plain
Plas / *Dut.; Fle.*	lake, marsh
Plato / *Bulg.; Rus.*	plateau
Platosu / *Tur.*	plateau
Platte / *Germ.*	plain, plateau
Plav / *S.C.*	blue
Plavnja / *Rus.*	marsh
Playa / *Sp.*	beach
Ploskogorje / *Rus.*	plateau
Plou / *Br.*	church
Po / *Kor.*	port
Po / *Chin.*	lake, white
P'o / *Kor.*	bay, lake
Poa / *Mel.*	hill
Poarta / *Rom.*	pass
Poartă / *Rom.*	gate
Pobla / *Cat.*	village
Pobrzeże / *Pol.*	littoral, coast
Poço / *Port.*	well
Poço / *Port.*	point
Pod / *Cz.; Pol.; Rus.; S.C.; Slvn.*	bridge
Podkamenny / *Rus.*	stony
Poggio / *It.*	hill
Pohja / *Finn.*	north, northern
Pohjois- / *Finn.*	north
Pojezierze / *Pol.*	lake region
Pol / *Pers.*	bridge
Pol, -pol / *Rus.*	city, town
Pola / *Port.; Sp.*	village
Polder / *Fle.; Dut.*	reclaimed land
Pole / *Pol.*	field
Pólis / *Gr.*	city, town
Poljana / *Bulg.; Rus.; S.C.; Slvn.*	field, terrace
Poljarny / *Rus.*	polar
Polje / *S.C.; Slvn.*	valley, field, basin
Poluostrov / *Rus.*	peninsula
Pomorije / *Bulg.*	littoral
Pomorze / *Pol.*	littoral
Ponente / *It.*	western
Pont / *Cat.; Fr.*	bridge
Ponta / *Port.*	point
Ponte / *It.; Port.*	bridge
Póntos / *Gr.*	sea
Poort / *Afr.; Fle.; Dut.*	pass
Pore, -pore / *Hin.; Urdu*	city, town
Porog / *Rus.*	rapids
Porte / *Fr.*	gate
Portile / *Rom.*	gorge
Portillo / *Sp.*	pass
Portiţa / *Rom.*	small gate
Porto / *It.*	port
Pôrto / *Port.*	port
Posht / *Pers.*	back, posterior
Potjo / *Indon.*	peak
Potok / *Bulg.; Cz.; Pol.; Rus.; S.C.; Slvn.*	stream
Póvoa / *Port.*	village
Pozo / *Sp.*	well
Pozzo / *It.*	well
Pradesh / *Hin.*	region, state
Prado / *Sp.*	meadow
Praia / *Port.*	beach
Prato / *It.*	meadow
Pré / *Fr.*	meadow
Prealpi / *It.*	prealps
Presa / *Sp.*	reservoir
Presqu'île / *Fr.*	peninsula
Prêto / *Port.*	black
Priehradní nádrž / *Cz.*	reservoir
Pripoljarny / *Rus.*	subpolar
Pristan / *Rus.*	port
Prohod / *Bulg.*	pass
Proliv / *Rus.*	strait
Promontoire / *Fr.*	promontory
Průchod / *Cz.*	pass
Przedgorze / *Pol.*	front range (mountains)
Przełęcz / *Pol.*	pass
Przemysł / *Pol.*	industry
Przylądek / *Pol.*	cape
Pua / *Mel.*	hill
Puebla / *Sp.*	village
Puente / *Sp.*	bridge
Puerto / *Sp.*	port, pass
Puig / *Cat.*	peak
Puits / *Fr.*	well
Pul / *Pash.*	bridge
Pulau, P. / *Mal.; Indon.*	island
Pulau Pulau / *Mal.*	islands
Pulo / *Mal.; Indon.*	island
Puna / *A.I.*	upland
Puncak / *Indon.*	mountain
Punjung / *Mal.; Indon.*	mountain
Punt / *Afr.*	point
Punta / *It.; Sp.*	point
Pur, -pur / *Hin.; Urdu*	city, town
-pura / *Hin.; Urdu*	city, town
Pura / *Indon.*	city, town, temple
Puri, -puri / *Hin.; Urdu*	city, town
Pus / *Alb.*	spring
Pušča / *Rus.*	forest
Pustynja / *Rus.*	desert
Puszcza / *Pol.*	heath
Puszta / *Hung.*	lowland
Put / *Afr.*	well
Put / *Rus.; S.C.*	road
Putra, -putra / *Hin.*	son
Puu / *Poly.*	mountain, volcano
Puy / *Fr.*	peak
Pwell / *Wel.*	pond
Pyeong / *Kor.*	plain
Pyhä / *Finn.*	saint

Q

Local Form	English
Qagan / *Mong.*	white
Qala / *Pash.*	fortified town
Qal'at / *Ar.*	castle
Qalb / *Ar.*	hill
Qalīb / *Ar.*	spring
Qalīq / *Ar.*	spring
Qanāt / *Ar.*	canal
Qantara / *Ar.*	bridge
Qaqortoq / *Esk.*	white
Qar / *Som.*	mountain
Qara / *Pers.*	black
Qarah / *Tur.*	black
Qārat / *Ar.*	height, mountain
Qāret / *Ar.*	village, hill
Qaryah / *Ar.*	village
Qaryat / *Ar.*	village
Qaşr / *Ar.*	castle
Qawz / *Ar.*	dunes
Qeqertarssuaq / *Esk.*	peninsula
Qezel / *Tur.*	red
Qi / *Chin.*	river
Qing / *Chin.*	blue, green
Qiryat / *Hebr.*	city, town
Qolleh / *Pers.*	mountain, peak
Qu / *Chin.*	river, canal
Quan dao / *Viet.*	islands
Quebracho / *Sp.*	stream
Quebrada / *Sp.*	gorge, stream
Quedas / *Port.*	waterfalls
Qulbān / *Ar.*	well
Qundao / *Chin.*	archipelago
Qūr / *Ar.*	height, hill
Qytet / *Alb.*	city, town
Qyteti / *Alb.*	city, town

R

Local Form	English
R., Rio, River / *Eng.; Sp.*	river
Rada / *It.; Sp.*	anchorage
Rade / *Fr.*	anchorage
Rags / *Latv.*	cape
Rahad / *Ar.*	lake, pond
Rajon / *Rus.*	district
Rak / *Fle.; Dut.*	strait
Rakai / *Poly.*	reef
Ramla / *Ar.*	sand
Rancho / *Port.; Sp.*	farm, ranch
Rand / *Afr.; Germ.*	escarpment
Range / *Eng.*	mountain range
Rann / *Urdu*	marsh
Rano / *Malag.*	water
Ranta / *Finn.*	bank, beach
Rapide / *Fr.*	rapids
Ras / *Amh.*	peak
Rās / *Ar.*	point, cape

Local Form	English
Ras, Rás / Ar.	promontory, peak
Rāsiga / Som.	promontory
Rass / Ar.	promontory, peak
Rassa / Lapp.	mountain
Ráth / Gae.	castle
Raunina / Bulg.; Rus.	plain
Raz / Fr.	strait
Razliv / Rus.	flood plain
Récif / Fr.	reef
Recife / Port.	reef
Reede / Germ.; Dut.; Slvn.	anchorage
Reek / Afr.; Gae.	mountain range
Reg / Pash.	dunes
Région / Fr.	region
Rei / Port.	king
Reka / Bulg.; Rus.; S.C.; Slvn.	river
Řeka / Cz.	river
Réma / Gr.	torrent
Renne / Dan.; Nor.	deep
Reprêsa / Port.	dam, reservoir
Represa / Sp.	dam, reservoir
República / Port.; Sp.	republic
République / Fr.	republic
Rés., Réservoir / Fr.	reservoir
Res., Reservoir / Eng.	reservoir
Réservoir, Rés. / Fr.	reservoir
Reshteh / Pers.	mountain range
Respublika / Rus.	republic
Restinga / Port.	cliff, sandbank
Retsugan / Jap.	reef
Rettō / Jap.	archipelago
Rev / Dan.; Nor.; Swed.	reef
Rey / Sp.	king
Ri / Tib.	mountain
Ria / Sp.	estuary
Riacho / Port.	stream
Rialto / It.	plateau
Rialto / It.	rise
Riba / Port.	bank
Ribeira / Port.	river
Ribeirão / Port.	stream
Ribeiro / Port.	stream
Ribera / Sp.	coast
Ribnik / Slvn.	pond
Rid / Bulg.	mountain range
Rif / Icel.	cliff
Riff / Germ.	reef
Rīg / Pash.	dunes
Rijeka / S.C.	river
Rimāl / Ar.	sand desert
Rincón / Sp.	peninsula between two rivers
Ring / Tib.	long
Rinne / Germ.	trench
Rio / Port.	river
Rio, R. / Sp.	river
Riu / Rom.	river
Riva / It.	bank
Rive / Fr.	bank
Rivera / Sp.	brook, stream
Rivier, -rivier / Afr.; Dut.; Fle.	river
Riviera / It.	coast
Rivière / Fr.	river
Roads / Eng.	anchorage
Roc / Fr.	rock
Roca / Port.; Sp.	rock
Rocca / It.	castle
Roche / Fr.	rock
Rocher / Fr.	rock
Rock / Eng.	rock
Rod / Pash.	river
Rode / Germ.	tilled soil
Rodnik / Rus.	spring
Rog / Rus.; S.C.; Slvn.	peak
Roi / Fr.	king
Rojo / Sp.	red
Roque / Sp.	rock
Rot / Germ.	red
Roto / Poly.	lake
Rouge / Fr.	red
Równina / Pol.	plain
Rt / S.C.; Slvn.	cape
Ru / Tib.	mountain
Ruck / Germ.	ridge
Rücken / Germ.	ridge
Rud / Pers.	river
Ruda / Cz.; Slvk.	mine
Ruda / Pol.	ore
Rūdbār / Pers.	river
Rudha / Gae.	point
Rudnik / Rus.; S.C.; Slvn.	mine
Rug / Fle.; Dut.	ridge
Ruggen / Afr.	ridge
Ruina / It.	ruins
Ruine / Fr.; Dut.; Germ.	ruins
Rujm / Ar.	hill
Run / Eng.	stream

S

Local Form	English
S., See / Germ.	lake, sea
Saar / Est.	island

Local Form	English
Saari / Finn.	island
Sabbia / It.	sand
Sabkhat / Ar.	salt flat, salt marsh
Sable / Fr.; Eng.	beach
Sacca / It.	anchorage
Saco / Port.	bay
Sad / Cz.; Slvk.	park
Sad / Pers.	wall
Sadd / Ar.; Pers.	cataract, dam
Safid / Pash.; Urdu; Hin.	white
Şafrā' / Ar.	desert
Sāgar / Hin.	reservoir
Saguia / Ar.	irrigation canal
Sahara / Ar.	desert
Sahel / Ar.	plain, coast
Sahr / Iran.	city, town
Şaḩrā' / Ar.	desert
Said / Ar.	sweet
Saj / Alt.	stream, valley
Saki / Jap.	point
Sala / Latv.; Lith.	island
Saladillo / Sp.	salt desert
Salar / Sp.	salt lake
Sale / Ural.	village
Salina / It.; Sp.	salt flat, salt marsh
Saline / Dut.; Fr.; Germ.	salt flat, salt marsh
Salmi / Finn.	strait
Salseleh-ye Kūh / Pers.	mountain range
Salto / Port.; Sp.	waterfall, rapids
Salz / Germ.	salt
Samudera / Indon.	ocean
Samudra / Hin.	lake
Samut / Thai	sea
San / Jap.; Kor.	mountain
San / It.; Sp.	saint
Sanchi / Jap.	mountain range
Sand / Dan.; Eng.; Nor.; Swed.; Germ.	beach
Šand / Mong.	spring
Sandur / Icel.	sand
Sank / Pers.	rock
Sankt, St. / Germ.; Swed.	saint
Sanmaeg / Kor.	mountain range
Sanmyaku / Jap.	mountain range
Sansanné / Sud.	campsite
Santo / It.; Port.; Sp.	saint
Santuario / It.	sanctuary
São / Port.	saint
Sar / Pers.	cape; peak
Šar / Rus.; Tur.	strait
Saraf / Ar.	well
Sari / Finn.	island
Sari / Tur.	yellow
Sarīr / Ar.	rocky desert
Sary / Tur.	yellow
Sasso / It.	stone
Sat / Rom.	village
Sattel / Germ.	pass
Saurum / Latv.	strait
Schleuse / Germ.	lock
Schloß / Germ.	castle
Schlucht / Germ.	gorge
Schnee / Germ.	snow
Schwarz / Germ.	black
Scoglio / It.	cliff
Se / Jap.	bank, shoal
Sebkha / Ar.	salt flat
Sebkhet / Ar.	salt flat
Sed / Ar.	dam
Seda / Ural.	mountain
See, S. / Germ.	lake, sea
Sefra / Ar.	yellow
Segara / Indon.	lagoon
Şehir / Tur.	city, town
Seki / Jap.	dam
Selat / Mal.; Indon.	strait
Selatan / Indon.	southern
Selkä / Finn.	ridge, lake
Sella / It.	pass
Selo / Bulg.; Rus.; S.C.; Slvn.	village
Selsela Kohe / Pers.	mountain range
Selva / It.; Sp.	forest
Semenanjung / Mal	peninsula
Sen / Jap.	mountain
Seong / Kor.	castle
Sep / Alt.	canal
Serīr / Ar.	rocky desert
Serra / Cat.; Port.	mountain range
Serra / It.	mountain
Serrania / Sp.	mountain range
Sertão / Port.	steppe
Seto / Jap.	strait
Sett., Settentrionale / It.	northern
Settentrionale, Sett. / It.	northern
Seuil / Fr.	sill
Sev / Arm.	black
Sever / Rus.	north
Severny / Rus.	northern
Sfint / Rom.	saint
Sfintu / Rom.	saint
Sgeir / Gae.	cliff
Sha'b / Ar.	cliff
Shahr / Pers.; Hin.	city, town
Sha'ib / Ar.	stream
Shallāl / Ar.	cataract

Local Form	English
Shām / Ar.	north; northern
Shamo / Chin.	sand desert
Shan / Chin.	mountain, mountain range
Shan / Gae.	old
Shand / Mong.	spring
Shankou / Chin.	pass
Shaqq / Ar.	wadi
Sharm / Ar.	bay
Sharqī / Ar.	east, eastern
Sharqīyah / Ar.	eastern
Shatt / Ar.	river, salt lake
Shatt / Ar.	stream
Shēn / Alb.	saint
Sheng / Chin.	province
Shi / Chin.	city, town
Shibīn / Ar.	village
Shih / Chin.	rock
Shima / Jap.	island
Shimo / Jap.	lower
Shin / Jap.	new
Shō / Jap.	island
Shotō / Jap.	archipelago
Shū / Jap.	administrative division
Shui / Chin.	river
Shuiku / Chin.	reservoir
Shur / Pers.	salt
Sidhiros / Gr.	iron
Sīdi / Ar.	master
Sieben / Germ.	seven
Sierra / Sp.	mountain range
Sikt / Ural.	village
Sillon / Fr.	furrow
Šine / Mong.	new
Sink / Eng.	depression
Sinn / Ar.	point
Sint / Dut.; Fle.	saint
Sirt / Tur.	mountain range
Sirtlar / Tur.	mountain range
Sistema / It.; Sp.	mountain system
Sīyāh / Pers.	black
Sjø / Nor.	lake
Sjö / Swed.	lake, sea
Skag / Icel.	peninsula
Skala / Bulg.; Rus.	rock
Skála / Slvk.	rock
Skar / Nor.	pass
Skär / Swed.	cliff
Skeir / Gae.	cliff
Skerry / Gae.	cliff
Skog / Nor.; Swed.	forest
Skóg / Icel.	forest
Skov / Dan.; Nor.	forest
Slatina / S.C.; Slvn.	mineral water
Slätt / Swed.	plain
Slieve / Gae.	mountain
Slot / Dut.; Fle.	castle
Slott / Nor.; Swed.	castle
Slough / Eng.	creek, pond, marsh
Sluis / Dut.; Fle.	sluice
Små / Swed.	little
Sne / Nor.	snow
Sneeuw / Afr.; Dut.	snow
Snežny / Rus.	snowy
Snø / Nor.	snow
So / Kor.	little
Sø / Dan.; Nor.	lake; sea
So / Ural.	passage
Söder / Swed.	south
Södra / Swed.	southern
Solončak / Rus.	salt flat
Sommet / Fr.	peak
Son / Viet.	mountain
Sønder / Dan.; Nor.	southern
Søndre / Dan.	southern
Sone / Jap.	bank
Song / Viet.	river
Sopka / Rus.	volcano
Sopočnik / Rus.	mountain system
Soprana / It.	upper
Šor, Sor / Alt.	salt marsh
Sos / Sp.	upon
Sotavento / Sp.	leeward
Sotoviento / Sp.	leeward
Sottana / It.	lower
Souk / Ar.	market
Souq / Ar.	market
Sour / Ar.	rampart
Source / Eng.; Fr.	spring
Souto / Port.	forest
Spitze / Germ.	peak
Spruit / Afr.	current
Sreden / Bulg.	central
Sredni / Rus.	central
Sredni / Rus.	central
Srednji / S.C.; Slvn.	central
St., Saint, Sankt / Eng.; Fr.; Germ.; Swed.	saint
Stadhur / Icel.	city, town
Stadt, -stadt / Germ.	city, town
Stag / Eng.	city, town
Stagno / It.	pond
-stan / Hin.; Pers.; Urdu	land
Star / Bulg.	old
Stari / S.C.; Slvn.	old

Local Form	English
Stary / Pol.; Rus.	old
Starý / Cz.; Slvk.	old
Stat / Afr.; Dan.; Fle.; Nor.; Dut.; Swed.	city, town
Stathmós / Gr.	railway station
Stausee / Germ.	reservoir
Stavrós / Gr.	cross
Sted / Dan.; Nor.	place
Stedt / Germ.	place
Stein, -stein / Nor.; Germ.	stone
Sten / Nor.; Swed.	stone
Stena / S.C.; Slvn.	rock
Sténa / Cz.	mountain range
Stenón / Gr.	strait, pass
Step / Rus.	steppe
-sthān / Hin.; Pers.; Urdu	land
Stift / Germ.	foundation
Štít / Cz.; Slvk.	peak
Stock / Germ.	massif
Stok / Pol.	slope
Stor / Dan.; Nor.; Swed.	great
Store / Dan.	great
Stræde / Dan.	strait
Strana / Rus.	land
Strand / Germ.; Nor.; Swed.; Afr.; Dan.	beach
Straße / Germ.	street, road
Strath / Gae.	valley
Straum / Nor.; Swed.	stream
Středni / Cz.	central
Středný / Slvk.	central
Strelka / Rus.	spit
Stret / Nor.	strait
Stretto / It.	strait
Strom / Germ.	stream
Strøm / Nor.	stream
Ström / Swed.	stream
Stroom / Dut.	stream
Su / Jap.	sandbank
Su / Tur.	river
Suando / Finn.	pond
Suid / Afr.	south
Suidō / Jap.	strait
Sul / Port.	south
Sund / Dan.; Nor.; Swed.; Germ.	strait
Sungai / Mal.	river
Sunn / Nor.	south
Sūq / Ar.	market
Sur / Fr.	on
Sur / Sp.	south
Surkh / Pers.	red
Suu / Finn.	mouth, river mouth
Suur / Cat.	great
Svart / Nor.; Swed.	black
Sveti / S.C.; Slvn.	saint
Swa / Ban.	great
Swart / Afr.	black
Świety / Pol.	saint
Syrt / Alt.	ridge
Szállás / Hung.	village
Szczyt / Pol.	peak
Szeg / Hung.	bend
Székes / Hung.	residence
Szent / Hung.	saint
Sziget / Hung.	river island

T

Local Form	English
Tadi / Ban.	rock, cliff
Tae / Kor.	great
Tafua / Poly.	mountain
Tag / Alt.; Tur.	mountain
Tahta / Ar.	lower
Tahti / Ar.	lower
Tai / Chin.; Jap.	great
Taipale / Finn.	isthmus
Tajga / Rus.	forest
Take / Jap.	mountain
Tal / Germ.	valley
Tala / Mong.	plain, steppe
Tala / Ber.	spring
Tall / Ar.	hill
Talsperre / Germ.	dam
Tam / Viet.	stream
Tamgout / Ber.	peak
Tan / Chin.; Kor.	sandbank
Tana / Malag.	city, town
Tanana / Malag.	city, town
Tandjung / Mal.	cape, point
Tanezrouft / Ber.	desert
Tang / Tib.	upland
Tangeh / Pers.	strait
Tanjong / Mal.	cape, point
Tanjung, Tg. / Indon.	cape, point
Tanout / Ber.	well
Tao / Chin.	island
Taourirt / Ber.	peak
Targ / Pol.	market
Tärg / Bulg.	market
Tarn / Eng.	glacial lake
Tarso / Sah.	crater
Taš / Alt.	stone

Geographical Glossary

Local Form	English
Tassili / *Ber.*	upland
Tau / *Tur.*	mountain
Taung / *Burm.*	mountain
Ṭawîl / *Ar.*	hill
Tégi / *Sah.*	hill
Teguidda / *Ber.*	well
Tehi / *Ber.*	pass, mountain
Teich / *Germ.*	pond
Tell / *Tur.*	hill
Telok / *Mal.*	bay, port
Teluk / *Mal.*	bay, port
Tempio / *It.*	temple
Ténéré / *Ber.*	rocky desert
Tengah / *Indon.; Mal.*	central
Tepe / *Tur.*	hill
Tepesi / *Tur.*	hill
Termas / *Sp.*	thermal springs
Terme / *It.*	thermal springs
Terra / *It.; Dut.*	land, earth
Terrazzo / *It.*	guyot, tablemount
Terre / *Fr.*	land, earth
Teso / *Cat.*	hill
Téssa / *Ber.*	wadi, depression
Testa / *It.*	point
Tête / *Fr.*	peak
Tetri / *Georg.*	white
Teu / *Poly.*	reef
Teze / *Alt.*	new
Tg., Tanjung / *Indon.*	cape, point
Thaba / *Ban.*	mountain
Thabana / *Ban.*	mountain
Thal / *Germ.*	valley
Thálassa / *Gr.*	sea
Thale / *Thai*	lagoon
Thamad / *Ar.*	well
Theós / *Gr.*	god
Thermes / *Fr.*	thermal springs
Thog / *Tib.*	high, upper
Tian / *Chin.*	field
Tiefe / *Germ.*	deep
Tierra / *Sp.*	land, earth
Timur / *Indon.; Mal.*	eastern
Tind / *Nor.*	mountain
Tinto / *Sp.*	black
Tirg / *Rom.*	market
Tis / *Amh.*	new
Tizgui / *Ber.*	forest
Tizi / *Ber.*	pass
Tjåkko / *Lapp.*	mountain
Tjärn / *Swed.*	tarn, glacial lake
Tji / *Mal.*	stream
To / *Kor.*	island
To / *Mel.*	stream
Tō / *Jap.*	island
Tó / *Hung.*	lake
To / *Ural.*	lake
Tobe / *Tur.*	hill
Toʻfua / *Poly.*	mountain
Tog / *Som.*	valley
Tōge / *Jap.*	pass
Tokoj / *Alt.*	forest
Tônle / *Khm.*	stream, lake
Tope / *Dut.*	peak
Toplice / *S.C.; Slvn.*	thermal springs
Topp / *Nor.*	peak
Tor / *Gae.*	rock
Tor / *Germ.*	gate
Torbat / *Pers.*	tomb
Törl / *Germ.*	pass
Torp / *Swed.*	hut
Torre / *Cat.; It.; Sp.; Port.*	tower
Torrente / *It.; Sp.*	torrent, stream
Tossa / *Cat.*	mountain, peak
Tota / *Sin.*	port
Tour / *Fr.*	tower
Traforo / *It.*	tunnel
Träsk / *Swed.*	lake
Trg / *S.C.*	market
Trog / *Germ.*	trough, trench
Trois / *Fr.*	three
Trung / *Viet.*	central
Tse / *Tib.*	peak, point
Tsi / *Chin.*	pond
Tskali / *Georg.*	river
Tsu / *Jap.*	bay
Tulûl / *Ar.*	hills
Tünel / *Pers.*	tunnel
Tunturi / *Lapp.*	mountain, tundra
Tur'ah / *Ar.*	irrigation canal
Turm / *Germ.*	tower
Turn / *Rom.*	tower
Turó / *Cat.*	dome
Tuz / *Tur.*	salt
Týn / *Cz.*	fortress

U

Local Form	English
U., Unter-, Upon / *Eng.; Germ.*	under, lower
Uaimh / *Gae.*	cave
Uchi / *Jap.*	bay
Udde / *Swed.*	cape
Údolní nádrž / *Cz.*	reservoir
Uebi / *Som.*	river
Új- / *Hung.*	new
Ujście / *Pol.*	mouth
Ujung / *Indon.*	point, cape
Ul / *Chin.; Mong.*	mountain, mountain range
Ula / *Mong.*	mountain range
Ulan / *Mong.*	red
Uls / *Mong.*	state
Umi / *Jap.*	bay
Umm / *Ar.*	mother, spring
Umne / *Mong.*	south
Under / *Mong.*	mountain, peak
Ungur / *Alt.*	cave
Unter-, U. / *Germ.*	under, lower
Upar / *Hin.*	river
ʻUqlat / *Ar.*	well
Ûr / *Tam.*	city, town
Ura / *Jap.*	bay, coast
Ura / *Alt.*	depression
Urd / *Mong.*	south
Uru / *Tam.*	city, town
Ušće / *S.C.*	mouth
Uske / *Alt.*	upper
Ust / *Rus.*	mouth
Ústí / *Cz.*	mouth
Ustup / *Rus.*	terrace
Utan / *Indon.; Mal.*	forest
Utara / *Indon.*	north, northern
Uusi / *Finn.*	new
Uval / *Rus.*	height
Úval / *Cz.*	mountain
ʻUwaynât / *Ar.*	well
Uzboj / *Alt.*	river bed
Uzun / *Tur.*	long
Užūrekis / *Lith.*	gulf

V

Local Form	English
Va / *Alb.*	ford
Va / *Ural.*	water, river
Vaara / *Finn.*	mountain
Väärti / *Finn.*	bay
Vad / *Rom.*	ford
Vær / *Nor.*	port
Våg / *Nor.*	bay
Vähä / *Finn.*	little
Väike / *Est.*	little
Väin / *Est.*	strait
Val / *Fr.; It.*	valley
Val / *Rom.; Rus.*	wall
Valico / *It.*	pass
Vall / *Cat.*	valley
Vall / *Swed.*	pasture
Valle / *It.; Sp.*	valley
Vallée / *Fr.*	valley
Vallei / *Afr.*	valley
Vallo / *It.*	wall
Valta / *Finn.*	cape
Váltos / *Gr.*	marsh
Valul / *Rom.*	wall
Vann / *Dan.; Nor.*	water, lake
Vanua / *Mel.*	land
Vár / *Hung.*	fort
Vara / *Finn.*	mountain
Varoš / *S.C.*	city, town
Város / *Hung.*	city, town
Varre / *Lapp.*	mountain
Vary / *Cz.*	spring
Vas / *S.C.; Slvn.*	village
Vásár / *Hung.*	market
Väst / *Swed.*	west
Väster / *Swed.*	western
Vatn / *Icel.; Nor.*	lake
Vatten / *Swed.*	water, lake
Vatu / *Mel.; Poly.*	island, reef
Vdhr., Vodohranilišče / *Rus.*	reservoir
Vechiu / *Rom.*	old
Vecs / *Latv.*	old
Veen / *Dut.; Fle.*	moor
Vega / *Sp.*	irrigated crops
Veld / *Afr.; Dut.; Fle.*	field
Veli / *S.C.; Slvn.*	great
Velik / *Bulg.*	great
Veliki / *Rus.; S.C.; Slvn.*	great
Veliký / *Cz.*	great
Velký / *Cz.*	great
Vel'ky / *Slvk.*	great
Vella / *Cat.*	old
Ver / *Ural.*	forest
Verde / *It.; Sp.*	green
Verh / *Rus.*	peak
Verhni / *Rus.*	upper
Verk / *Swed.*	factory
Vermelho / *Port.*	red
Vert / *Fr.*	green
Ves / *Cz.*	village
Vesi / *Finn.*	water, lake
Vest / *Dan.; Nor.*	west
Vester / *Dan.; Nor.*	western
Vestur / *Icel.*	west
Vetta / *It.*	summit
Viaduc / *Fr.*	viaduct
Vidda / *Nor.*	upland
Vidde / *Nor.*	upland
Viejo / *Sp.*	old
Vier / *Germ.*	four
Viertel / *Germ.*	quarter
Vieux / *Fr.*	old
Vig / *Dan.*	bay
Vik / *Icel., Nor.; Swed.*	gulf, bay
Vila / *Port.*	city, town
Villa / *Sp.*	city, town
Ville, -ville / *Eng.; Fr.*	city, town
Vinh / *Viet.*	bay
Virful / *Rom.*	peak, mountain
Virta / *Finn.*	river
Višni / *Rus.*	high
Visok / *S.C.*	high
Viz / *Hung.*	water
Viztárolô / *Hung.*	reservoir
Vlakte / *Dut.; Fle.*	plain
Vlei / *Afr.*	pond
Vliet / *Dut.; Fle.*	river
Vloer / *Afr.*	depression
Voda / *Bulg.; Cz.; Rus.; S.C.; Slvn.*	water
Vodny put / *Rus.*	stream, canal
Vodohranilišče, vdhr. / *Rus.*	reservoir
Vodopad / *Rus.*	waterfall
Volcan / *Fr.*	volcano
Volcán / *Sp.*	volcano
Voll / *Nor.*	meadow
Vórios / *Gr.*	northern
Vorota / *Rus.*	gate
Vorrás / *Gr.*	north
Vostočny / *Rus.*	eastern
Vostok / *Rus.*	east
Võtn / *Icel.*	lake, water
Vož / *Ural.*	mouth
Vozvyšennost / *Rus.*	upland
Vpadina / *Rus.*	depression
Vrah / *Bulg.*	peak
Vrata / *Bulg.; S.C.; Slvn.*	pass
Vrch / *Cz.; Slvk.*	mountain
Vrch / *S.C.; Slvn.*	peak
Vrchni- / *Cz.*	upper
Vrchovina / *Cz.*	upland
Vulcan / *Rom.; Rus.*	volcano
Vulcano / *It.*	volcano
Vulkan / *Germ.; Rus.*	volcano
Vuopio / *Lapp.*	bend
Vuori / *Finn.*	rock
Východný / *Cz.*	eastern
Vyšný / *Slvk.*	upper
Vysoki / *Rus.*	high
Vysoky / *Cz.; Slvk.*	high
Vyšši / *Cz.*	high

W

Local Form	English
W., Wâdî / *Ar.*	wadi
Wa / *Ban.*	people
Wabe / *Amh.*	stream
Wad / *Ar.*	wadi
Wad / *Dut.*	tidal flat
Wâdî, W. / *Ar.*	wadi
Wâḥât / *Ar.*	oasis
Wai / *Mel.; Poly.*	stream
Wal / *Afr.*	wall
Wala / *Hin.*	mountain range
Wald / *Germ.*	forest
Wan / *Burm.*	village
Wan / *Chin.; Jap.*	bay
Wand / *Germ.*	bluff
War / *Som.*	pond
Wâr / *Ar.*	desert
-waram / *Hin.; Tam.*	village
Wasser / *Germ.*	water
Wat / *Pol.*	wall
Wat / *Thai*	church
Waterval / *Afr.; Dut.*	waterfall
Watt / *Germ.*	tidal flat
Wâw / *Ar.*	oasis
Weald / *Eng.*	wooded country
Webi / *Som.*	stream
Weg / *Germ.*	way, road
Wei / *Chin.*	cape, point
Weide / *Germ.*	pasture
Weiler / *Germ.*	village
Weiß / *Germ.*	white
Weon / *Kor.*	field
Wer / *Som.*	pond
Werder / *Germ.*	river island
Werk / *Germ.*	factory
Wes / *Afr.*	west
Westlich / *Germ.*	western
Westr- / *Sca.*	western
Wêyn / *Som.*	great
Wêyne / *Som.*	great
Wick / *Eng.*	village
Wiek / *Germ.*	bay
Wielki / *Pol.*	great
Wieś / *Pol.*	village
Wijk / *Dut.; Fle.*	quarter, district
-willer / *Germ.*	village

Local Form	English
Woda / *Pol.*	water
Woestyn / *Afr.*	desert
Wold / *Dut.; Fle.; Eng.*	forest
Wörth / *Germ.*	river island
Woud / *Dut.; Fle.*	forest
Wschodni / *Pol.*	eastern
Wysoczyzna / *Pol.*	upland
Wysoki / *Pol.*	upper
Wyspa / *Pol.*	island
Wyżyna / *Pol.*	highland
Wzgórze / *Pol.*	hill

X

Local Form	English
Xi / *Chin.*	west
Xia / *Chin.*	gorge, strait
Xian / *Chin.*	county, shire
Xiang / *Chin.*	village
Xiao / *Chin.*	little
Xin / *Chin.*	new
Xu / *Chin.*	island

Y

Local Form	English
Yam / *Hebr.*	lake, sea
Yama / *Jap.*	mountain
Yan / *Chin.*	mountain
Yang / *Chin.*	strait, ocean
Yani / *Tur.*	new
Yar / *Tur.*	gorge
Yarimada / *Tur.*	peninsula
Yazı / *Tur.*	plain
Yegge / *Sah.*	well
Yeni / *Tur.*	new
Yeon / *Kor.*	sea
Yeong / *Kor.*	mountain
Yeşil / *Tur.*	green
Ylä / *Finn.*	upper
Yli- / *Finn.*	upper
Yō / *Jap.*	ocean
Yobe / *Sud.*	great
Yŏm / *Kor.*	island
Yoma / *Burm.*	mountain range
Yŏn / *Kor.*	lake, pond
Yŏng / *Kor.*	mountain, peak
Ytter / *Nor.; Swed.*	outer
Yttre / *Swed.*	outer
Yu / *Chin.*	old
Yu / *Chin.*	island
Yu / *Jap.*	thermal spring
Yüan / *Chin.*	spring, river
Yunhe / *Chin.*	canal

Z

Local Form	English
Zâb / *Ar.*	river
Zachodni / *Pol.*	western
Zaki / *Jap.*	cape
Zalew / *Pol.*	gulf
Zaliv / *Bulg.; Rus.; S.C.; Slvn.*	gulf
Zaljev / *Slvn.*	bay
Zámek / *Cz.*	castle
Zan / *Jap.*	mountain
Zand / *Dut.; Fle.*	sand
Zandt / *Dut.; Fle.*	sand
Zangbo / *Chin.*	river
Zapad / *Rus.*	west
Zapaden / *Bulg.*	western
Zapadni / *S.C.; Slvn.*	western
Západní / *Cz.*	western
Zapadny / *Rus.*	western
Zapovednik / *Rus.*	reserve
Zatoka / *Pol.*	gulf
Zavod / *Rus.*	roadstead
Zâwiyat / *Ar.*	monastery
Zdrój / *Pol.*	thermal springs
Ze / *Jap.*	islet
Zee / *Dut.; Fle.*	sea
Zelěny / *Rus.*	green
Žem / *Lith.*	land, country
Zemé / *Cz.; Slvk.*	land, country
Zemlja / *Rus.*	land
Zen / *Jap.*	mountain
Zhan / *Chin.*	mountain
Zhen / *Chin.*	market
Zhong / *Chin.*	central
Zhou / *Chin.*	quarter, district
Zhuang / *Chin.*	village
Ziemia / *Pol.*	land
Zigos / *Gr.*	pass
Ziwa / *Swa.*	marsh
Zizhiqu / *Chin.*	autonomous region
Zlato / *Bulg.*	gold
Zuid / *Dut.; Fle.*	south
Zuidelijk / *Dut.*	southern
Żuława / *Pol.*	marsh
Zun / *Mong.*	east
Zwart / *Dut.*	black
Zwei / *Germ.*	two

Maps of the World Index

All of the toponyms (place-names) which appear on the maps are listed in the Maps of the World Index. Each entry includes the following: Place-name and, where applicable, other forms by which it is written or known; a symbol, where applicable, indicating what kind of feature it is; the page on which the map appears; and the map-reference letters and geographical coordinates indicating its location on the map.

Toponyms

Each toponym, or place-name, is written in full, with accents and diacritical marks. Since many countries have more than one official language, many of these forms are included on the maps. For example, many Belgian place-names are listed as follows: Bruxelles/Brussel; Antwerpen/Anvers, and vice versa, Brussel/Bruxelles; Anvers/Antwerpen. In Italy, certain regions have a special status—they are largely autonomous and officially bilingual. As a result, Index listings appears as follows: Aosta/Aoste; Alto Adige/Sud Tirol, and vice versa. One name, however, may be the only name on the map.

In China, the written forms of commonly used regional languages have been taken into account. These forms are enclosed in parenthesis following the official name: e.g. Xiangshan (Dancheng). However, when the regional is listed first, it is linked to the official name with an→: e.g. Dancheng→Xiangshan. The same style is used for former or historical name forms: e.g. Rhodesia→Zimbabwe and Zimbabwe (Rhodesia).

Place-names for major features (countries, major cities, and large physical features), where applicable, include the English conventional form identified by (EN) and linked in the local name or names with an = sign: e.g. Italia = Italy (EN), and vice versa, Italy (EN) = Italia. Former English names are linked in the Index to the conventional form by an→.

Symbols

The last component with the place-name is a symbol, where applicable, specifying the broad category of the feature named. A table preceding the Index lists all of the symbols used and their meanings; this information also appears as a footnote on each page of the Index. Place names without symbols are cities and towns.

Alphabetization

Place-names are listed in English alphabetical order—26 letters, from A to Z—because of its international usage. Names including two or more words are listed alphabetically according to the first letter of the word: e.g. De Ruyter is listed under D; Le Havre is listed under L. Names with the prefix Mc are listed as if spelled Mac. The generic portion of a name (lake, sierra, mountain, etc.) is placed after the name: e.g. Lake Erie is listed as Erie, Lake; Sierra Morena is listed as Morena, Sierra. In Spanish, "ch" and "ll" groups and the letter "ñ" are included respectively under C, L, and N, without any distinction.

The same place-name sometimes is listed in the Index several times. It may because of the various translations of a name, or it may be that several places have the same name.

Various translations of a name appear as follows:

Danube (EN) = Dunav	Danube (EN) = Donau
Danube (EN) = Dunărea	Danube (EN) = Dunaj

Several places with the same name appear as follows; however, only in these cases is the location—abbreviated and enclosed in brackets—included. A table of these abbreviations precedes the Index.

Abbeville [U.S.]	Aberdeen [Scot.-U.K.]
Abbeville [Fr.]	Aberdeen [N.C.-U.S.]
Aberdeen [S. Afr.]	

Page References

Page references to two-page maps always refer to the left-hand page. If a page contains several maps or insets, a lowercase letter identifies the specific map or inset.

Although a place-name may appear on one or more maps, it is indexed to only one map. Most places are indexed to the regional maps. However, if a place-name appears on either the physical or political continental maps, it is indexed to one of the two types of map. For example, a river or mountain would be indexed to a physical continental map; a city or state would be indexed to a political continental map.

Map-Reference Letters and Geographical Coordinates

The next elements in the Index listing are the map-reference letters and the geographical coordinates, respectively, locating the place on the map.

Map-reference letters consist of a capital and a lowercase letter. Capital letters are across the top and bottom of the maps; lowercase letters are down the sides. The map-reference letters assigned to each place-name refer to the location of the name within the area formed by grid lines connecting the geographical coordinates on either sides of the letters.

Geographical coordinates are the latitude (N for North, S for South) and longitude (E for East, W for West) expressed in degrees and minutes and based on the prime meridian, Greenwich.

Map-reference letters and coordinates for extensive geographical features, such as mountain ranges and countries, are given for the approximate central point of the area. Those for waterways, such as canals and rivers, are given for the mouth of the river, the point where it enters another river or where the feature reaches the map margin. On this page are sample maps showing points to which features are indexed according to map-reference letters and coordinates.

On most maps there is not enough space to place all the names of administrative subdivisions. In these cases the location of the place is shown on the map by a circled letter or number and the place-name and circled letter or number are listed in the map margin. The map-reference numbers and coordinates for these places refer to the location of the circled letter or number on the map.

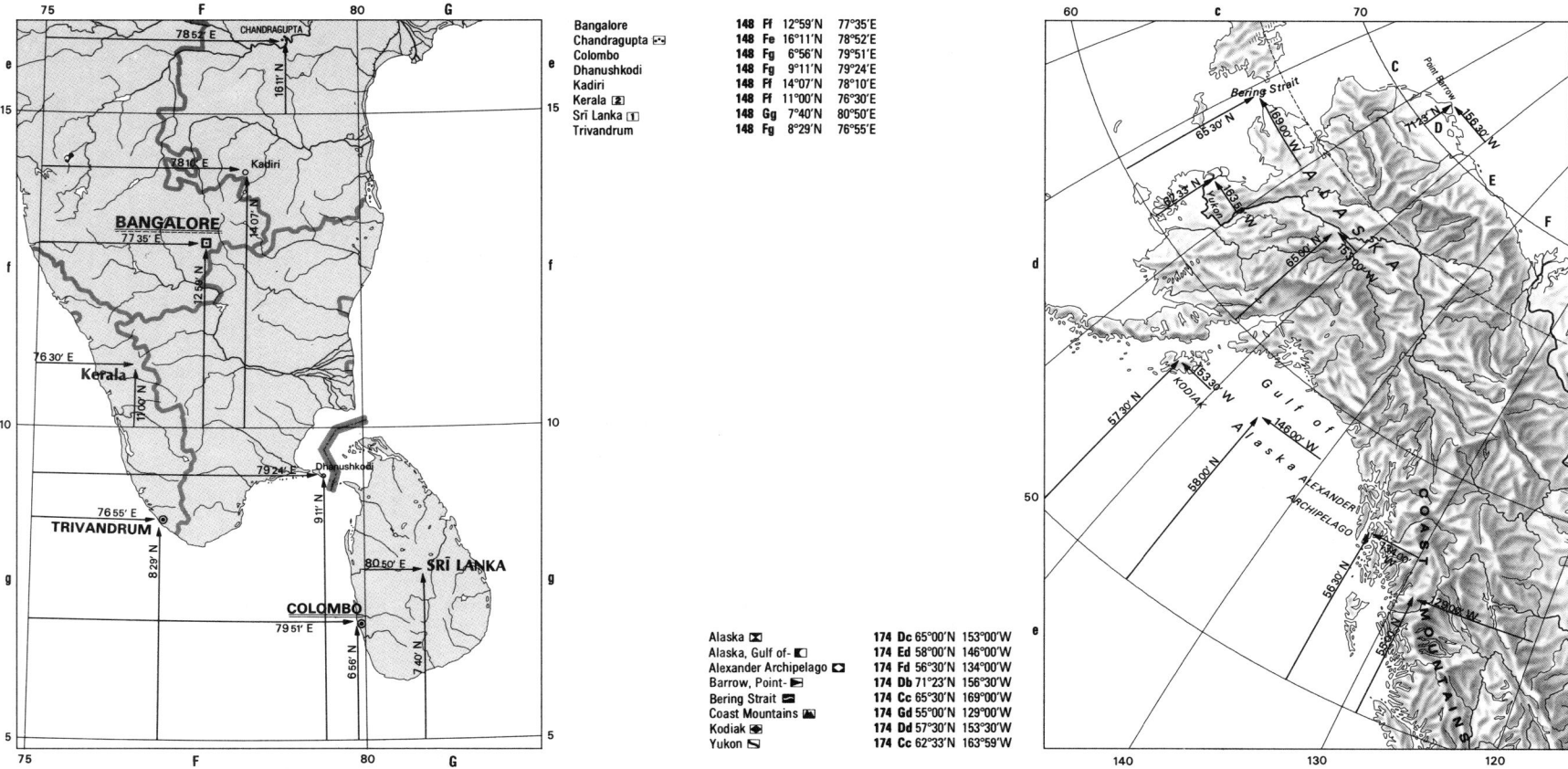

Bangalore	148	Ff	12°59'N	77°35'E
Chandragupta ⊡	148	Fe	16°11'N	78°52'E
Colombo	148	Fg	6°56'N	79°51'E
Dhanushkodi	148	Fg	9°11'N	79°24'E
Kadiri	148	Ff	14°07'N	78°10'E
Kerala ⊡	148	Ff	11°00'N	76°30'E
Sri Lanka ⊡	148	Gg	7°40'N	80°50'E
Trivandrum	148	Fg	8°29'N	76°55'E

Alaska ⊠	174	Dc	65°00'N	153°00'W
Alaska, Gulf of- ◧	174	Ed	58°00'N	146°00'W
Alexander Archipelago ⊡	174	Fd	56°30'N	134°00'W
Barrow, Point- ⊳	174	Db	71°23'N	156°30'W
Bering Strait ⊟	174	Cc	65°30'N	169°00'W
Coast Mountains ⊠	174	Gd	55°00'N	129°00'W
Kodiak ⊞	174	Dd	57°30'N	153°30'W
Yukon ⊠	174	Cc	62°33'N	163°59'W

List of Abbreviations

Abz.-U.S.S.R.   Azerbaijan S.S.R., U.S.S.R.
Afg.   Afghanistan
Afr.   Africa
Agl.   Anguilla
Ak.-U.S.   Alaska, U.S.
Al.-U.S.   Alabama, U.S.
Alb.   Albania
Alg.   Algeria
Alta.-Can.   Alberta, Canada
Am. Sam.   American Samoa
And.   Andorra
Ang.   Angola
Ant.   Antarctica
Ar.-U.S.   Arkansas, U.S.
Arg.   Argentina
Arm.-U.S.S.R.   Armenian S.S.R., U.S.S.R.
Asia   Asia
Atg.   Antigua and Barbuda
Aus.   Austria
Austl.   Australia
Az.-U.S.   Arizona, U.S.
Azr.   Azores
Bah.   Bahamas
Bar.   Barbados
B.A.T.   British Antarctic Territory
B.C.-Can.   British Columbia, Canada
Bel.   Belgium
Ben.   Benin
Ber.   Bermuda
Bhr.   Bahrain
Bhu.   Bhutan
Blz.   Belize
Bnd.   Burundi
Bngl.   Bangladesh
Bol.   Bolivia
Bots.   Botswana
Braz.   Brazil
Bru.   Brunei
Bul.   Bulgaria
Bur.   Burma
Burkina   Burkina Faso
B.V.I.   British Virgin Islands
Bye.-U.S.S.R.   Byelorussian S.S.R., U.S.S.R.
Ca.-U.S.   California, U.S.
Cam.   Cameroon
C. Amer.   Central America
Can.   Canada
Can. Is.   Canary Islands
C.A.R.   Central African Republic
Cay. Is   Cayman Islands
Chad   Chad
Chan. Is.   Channel Islands
Chile   Chile
China   China
Co.-U.S.   Colorado, U.S.
Cocos Is.   Cocos Islands
Col.   Colombia
Con.   Congo
Cook   Cook Islands
Cor. Sea Is.   Coral Sea Islands
C.R.   Costa Rica
Ct.-U.S.   Connecticut, U.S.
Cuba   Cuba
C.V.   Cape Verde
Cyp.   Cyprus
Czech.   Czechoslovakia

D.C.-U.S.   District of Columbia, U.S.
De.-U.S.   Delaware, U.S.
Den.   Denmark
Dji.   Djibouti
Dom.   Dominica
Dom. Rep.   Dominican Republic
Ec.   Ecuador
Eg.   Egypt
El Sal.   El Salvador
Eng.-U.K.   England, U.K.
Eq. Gui.   Equatorial Guinea
Est.-U.S.S.R.   Estonian S.S.R., U.S.S.R.
Eth.   Ethiopia
Eur.   Europe
Falk. Is.   Falkland Islands
Far. Is.   Faeroe Islands
Fiji   Fiji
Fin.   Finland
Fl.-U.S.   Florida, U.S.
Fr.   France
F.R.G.   Federal Republic of Germany
Fr. Gui.   French Guiana
Fr. Poly.   French Polynesia
F.S.M.   Federated States of Micronesia
Ga.-U.S.   Georgia, U.S.
Gabon   Gabon
Gam.   Gambia
G.D.R.   German Democratic Republic
Geo.-U.S.S.R.   Georgian S.S.R., U.S.S.R.
Ghana   Ghana
Gib.   Gibraltar
Grc.   Greece
Gren.   Grenada
Grld.   Greenland
Guad.   Guadeloupe
Guam   Guam
Guat.   Guatemala
Gui.   Guinea
Gui. Bis.   Guinea Bissau
Guy.   Guyana
Haiti   Haiti
Hi.-U.S.   Hawaii, U.S.
H.K.   Hong Kong
Hond.   Honduras
Hun.   Hungary
Ia.-U.S.   Iowa, U.S.
I.C.   Ivory Coast
Ice.   Iceland
Id.-U.S.   Idaho, U.S.
Il.-U.S.   Illinois, U.S.
In.-U.S.   Indiana, U.S.
India   India
Indon.   Indonesia
I. of M.   Isle of Man
Iran   Iran
Iraq   Iraq
Ire.   Ireland
Isr.   Israel
It.   Italy
Jam.   Jamaica
Jap.   Japan
Jor.   Jordan
Kam.   Cambodia
Kaz.-U.S.S.R.   Kazakh S.S.R., U.S.S.R.
Kenya   Kenya

Ker. Is.   Kermadec Islands
Kir.   Kiribati
Kirg.-U.S.S.R.   Kirghiz S.S.R., U.S.S.R.
Ks.-U.S.   Kansas, U.S.
Kuw.   Kuwait
Ky.-U.S.   Kentucky, U.S.
La.-U.S.   Louisiana, U.S.
Laos   Laos
Lat.-U.S.S.R.   Latvian S.S.R., U.S.S.R.
Lbr.   Liberia
Leb.   Lebanon
Les.   Lesotho
Lib.   Libya
Liech.   Liechtenstein
Lith.-U.S.S.R.   Lithuanian S.S.R., U.S.S.R.
Lux.   Luxembourg
Ma.-U.S.   Massachusetts, U.S.
Mac.   Macao
Mad.   Madagascar
Mala.   Malaysia
Mald.   Maldives
Mali   Mali
Malta   Malta
Man.-Can.   Manitoba, Canada
Mar. Is.   Marshall Islands
Mart.   Martinique
Maur.   Mauritius
May.   Mayotte
Mco.   Monaco
Md.-U.S.   Maryland, U.S.
Me.-U.S.   Maine, U.S.
Mex.   Mexico
Mi.-U.S.   Michigan, U.S.
Mid. Is.   Midway Islands
Mn.-U.S.   Minnesota, U.S.
Mo.-U.S.   Missouri, U.S.
Mold.-U.S.S.R.   Moldavian S.S.R., U.S.S.R.
Mong.   Mongolia
Mont.   Montserrat
Mor.   Morocco
Moz.   Mozambique
Ms.-U.S.   Mississippi, U.S.
Mt.-U.S.   Montana, U.S.
Mtna.   Mauritania
Mwi.   Malawi
Nam.   Namibia
N. Amer.   North America
Nauru   Nauru
N.B.-Can.   New Brunswick, Canada
Nb.-U.S.   Nebraska, U.S.
N.C.-U.S.   North Carolina, U.S.
N. Cal.   New Caledonia
N.D.-U.S.   North Dakota, U.S.
Nep.   Nepal
Neth.   Netherlands
Neth. Ant.   Netherlands Antilles
Newf.-Can.   Newfoundland, Canada
N.H.-U.S.   New Hampshire, U.S.
Nic.   Nicaragua
Nig.   Nigeria
Niger   Niger

N. Ire.-U.K.   Northern Ireland, U.K.
N.J.-U.S.   New Jersey, U.S.
N. Kor.   North Korea
N.M.-U.S.   New Mexico, U.S.
N. M. Is.   Northern Mariana Islands
Nor.   Norway
Nor. I.   Norfolk Island
N.S.-Canada   Nova Scotia, Canada
Nv.-U.S.   Nevada, U.S.
N.W.T.-Can.   Northwest Territories, Canada
N.Y.-U.S.   New York, U.S.
N.Z.   New Zealand
Ocn.   Oceania
Oh.-U.S.   Ohio, U.S.
Ok.-U.S.   Oklahoma, U.S.
Oman   Oman
Ont.-Ont.   Ontario, Canada
Or.-U.S.   Oregon, U.S.
Pa.-U.S.   Pennsylvania, U.S.
Pak.   Pakistan
Pal.   Palau
Pan.   Panama
Pap. N. Gui.   Papua New Guinea
Par.   Paraguay
Pas.   Pascua
P.D.R.Y.   Yemen
P.E.I.-Can.   Prince Edward Island, Canada
Peru   Peru
Phil.   Philippines
Pit.   Pitcairn
Pol.   Poland
Port.   Portugal
P.R.   Puerto Rico
Qatar   Qatar
Que.-Can.   Quebec, Canada
Reu.   Reunion
R.I.-U.S.   Rhode Island, U.S.
Rom.   Romania
R.S.F.S.R.-U.S.S.R.   Russian Soviet Federative Socialist Republic, U.S.S.R.
Rwn.   Rwanda
S. Afr.   South Africa
S. Amer.   South America
Sao T.P.   Sao Tome and Principe
Sask.-Can.   Saskatchewan, Canada
Sau. Ar.   Saudi Arabia
S.C.-U.S.   South Carolina, U.S.
Scot.-U.K.   Scotland, U.K.
S.D.-U.S.   South Dakota, U.S.
Sen.   Senegal
Sey.   Seychelles
Sing.   Singapore
S. Kor.   South Korea
S.L.   Sierra Leone
S. Lan.   Sri Lanka
S.M.   San Marino
S.N.A.   Spanish North Africa
Sol. Is.   Solomon Islands
Som.   Somalia
Sp.   Spain
St. C.N.   Saint Christopher-Nevis

St. Hel.   Saint Helena
St. Luc.   Saint Lucia
St. P.M.   Saint Pierre and Miquelon
St. Vin.   Saint Vincent and the Grenadines
Sud.   Sudan
Sur.   Suriname
Sval.   Svalbard
Swe.   Sweden
Switz.   Switzerland
Syr.   Syria
Tad.-U.S.S.R.   Tajik S.S.R., U.S.S.R.
Tai.   Taiwan
Tan.   Tanzania
T.C. Is.   Turks and Caicos Islands
Thai.   Thailand
Tn.-U.S.   Tennessee, U.S.
Togo   Togo
Ton.   Tonga
Trin.   Trinidad and Tobago
T.T.P.I.   Trust Territory of the Pacific Islands
Tun.   Tunisia
Tur.   Turkey
Tur.-U.S.S.R.   Turkmen S.S.R., U.S.S.R.
Tuv.   Tuvalu
Tx.-U.S.   Texas, U.S.
U.A.E.   United Arab Emirates
Ug.   Uganda
U.K.   United Kingdom
Ukr.-U.S.S.R.   Ukrainian S.S.R., U.S.S.R.
Ur.   Uruguay
U.S.   United States
U.S.S.R.   Union of Soviet Socialist Republics
Ut.-U.S.   Utah, U.S.
Uzb.-U.S.S.R.   Uzbek S.S.R., U.S.S.R.
Va.-U.S.   Virginia, U.S.
Van.   Vanuatu
V.C.   Vatican City
Ven.   Venezuela
Viet.   Vietnam
V.I.U.S.   Virgin Islands of the U.S.
Vt.-U.S.   Vermont, U.S.
Wa.-U.S.   Washington, U.S.
Wake   Wake Island
Wales-U.K.   Wales, U.K.
W.F.   Wallis and Futuna
Wi.-U.S.   Wisconsin, U.S.
W. Sah.   Western Sahara
W. Sam.   Western Samoa
W.V.-U.S.   West Virginia, U.S.
Wy.-U.S.   Wyoming, U.S.
Yem.   Yemen
Yugo.   Yugoslavia
Yuk.-Can.   Yukon, Canada
Zaire   Zaire
Zam.   Zambia
Zimb.   Zimbabwe

List of Symbols

Plains and Associated Features
Plain, Basin, Lowland
Delta
Salt Flat

Valleys and Depressions
Valley, Gorge, Ravine, Canyon
Cave, Crater, Quarry
Karst Features
Depression
Polder, Reclaimed Marsh

Vegetational Features
Desert, Dunes
Forest, Woods
Heath, Steppe, Tundra, Moor
Oasis

Political/Administrative Units
1 Independent Nation
2 State, Canton, Region
3 Province, Department, County, Territory, District
4 Municipality
5 Colony, Dependency, Administered Territory

Geographical Regions
Continent
Physical Region
Historical or Cultural Region

Mountain Features
Mount, Mountain, Peak
Volcano
Hill
Mountains, Mountain Range
Hills, Escarpment
Plateau, Highland, Upland
Pass, Gap

Coastal Features
Cape, Point
Coast, Beach
Cliff
Peninsula, Promontory
Isthmus
Sandbank, Tombolo, Sandbar

Islands Rocks, Reefs
Island
Atoll
Rock, Reef
Islands, Archipelago
Rocks, Reefs
Coral Reef

Hydrographic Features
Well, Spring
Geyser, Fumarole
River, Stream, Brook
Waterfall, Rapids, Cataract
River Mouth, Estuary
Lake
Salt Lake
Intermittent Lake, Dry Lake Bed
Reservoir, Artificial Lake
Swamp, Marsh, Pond
Irrigation Canal, Navigable Canal, Ditch, Aqueduct

Ice Features
Glacier, Snowfield
Ice Shelf, Pack Ice

Marine Features
Ocean
Sea
Gulf, Bay
Strait, Fjord, Sea Channel
Lagoon, Anchorage

Submarine Features
Bank, Shoal
Seamount
Rise, Plateau, Tablemount
Seamount Chain, Ridge
Platform, Shelf
Basin, Depression
Escarpment, Slope, Sea Scarp
Fracture
Trench, Abyss, Valley, Canyon

Other Features
National Park, Nature Reserve
Scenic Area, Point of Interest
Recreation Site, Sports Arena
Cave, Cavern
Historic Site, Memorial, Mausoleum, Museum
Ruins
Wall, Walls, Tower, Castle, Fortress
Church, Abbey, Cathedral, Sanctuary
Temple, Synagogue, Mosque
Research or Scientific Station
Railway station
Airport, Heliport
Port, Dock
Military installation
Lighthouse
Mine
Tunnel
Dam, Bridge

A

Å 114 Cc 67.53N 12.59 E
Aa [Eur.] 124 Ic 51.50N 6.25 E
Aa [Fr.] 122 Ic 51.01N 2.06 E
Aa [Fr.] 124 Dd 50.44N 2.18 E
Aa [F.R.G.] 124 Kb 52.07N 8.41 E
Aa [F.R.G.] 124 Jb 52.15N 7.18 E
Aa [Neth.] 124 Hc 51.42N 5.20 E
Aachen 120 Cf 50.46N 6.06 E
Aalen 120 Gh 48.50N 10.06 E
A'âlî an Nîl [3] 168 Ed 9.15N 33.00 E
Aalsmeer 124 Gb 52.15N 4.45 E
Aalst/Alost 122 Kd 50.56N 4.02 E
Aalten 124 Ic 51.55N 6.35 E
Aalter 124 Fc 51.05N 3.27 E
Äänekoski 114 Fe 62.36N 25.44 E
Aa of Weerijs 124 Gc 51.35N 4.46 E
Aar 124 Kd 50.23N 8.00 E
Aarau 128 Cc 47.25N 8.02 E
Aarbergen 124 Kd 50.13N 8.03 E
Aare 128 Cc 47.37N 8.13 E
Aargau [2] 128 Cc 47.30N 8.10 E
Aarlen/Arlon 122 Le 49.41N 5.49 E
Aarschot 122 Kd 50.59N 4.50 E
Aat/Ath 122 Jd 50.38N 3.47 E
Aazanèn 126 Ii 35.06N 3.02W
Āb 146 Md 36.00N 48.05 E
Aba [Nig.] 160 Hh 5.07N 7.22 E
Aba [Zaire] 160 Kh 3.52N 30.14 E
Aba/Ngawa 152 He 32.55N 101.45 E
Abā ad Dūd 146 Ki 27.02N 44.04 E
Abā as Su'ūd 144 Ff 17.28N 44.06 E
Abacaxis, Rio- 202 Gd 3.54S 58.50W
Abaco Island 174 Lg 26.25N 77.10W
Abacou, Pointe l'- 194 Kd 18.03N 73.47W
Abadab, Jabal- 168 Fb 18.53N 35.59 E
Ābādān 142 Gf 30.10N 48.50 E
Ābādeh [Iran] 144 Hc 31.10N 52.37 E
Ābādeh [Iran] 146 Oh 29.08N 52.52 E
Abadiânia 204 Hc 16.06S 48.48W
Abadla 160 Ge 31.01N 2.43W
Abaeté 204 Jd 19.09S 45.27W
Abaeté, Rio- 204 Jd 18.02S 45.12W
Abaetetuba 202 Id 1.42S 48.54W
Abagnar Qi (Xilin Hot) 142 Ne 43.58N 116.08 E
Abag Qi (Xin Hot) 152 Jc 44.01N 114.59 E
Abai 204 Eh 26.01S 55.57W
Abaiang Atoll 208 Id 1.51N 172.58 E
Abaj 136 Hf 49.38N 72.50 E
Abaji 166 Gd 8.28N 6.57 E
Abajo Mountains 188 Kh 37.50N 109.25W
Abakaliki 166 Gd 6.20N 8.03 E
Abakan 142 Ld 53.43N 91.26 E
Abakan 138 Ef 53.43N 91.30 E
Abakwasimbo 170 Eb 0.36N 28.43 E
Abala [Con.] 170 Cc 1.21S 15.30 E
Abala [Niger] 166 Fc 14.56N 3.26 E
Abalak 166 Gb 15.27N 6.17 E
Aban 138 Ee 56.40N 96.10 E
Abancay 202 Df 13.35S 72.55W
Abancourt 124 De 49.42N 1.46 E
Abanga 170 Bb 0.13N 10.28 E
Abano Terme 128 Fe 45.21N 11.47 E
Ābār al Jidd 146 Hf 32.50N 39.50 E
Abarqū 144 Hc 31.08N 53.17 E
Abarqu, Kavīr-e- 146 Og 31.00N 53.50 E
Abashiri 152 Pc 44.01N 144.17 E
Abashiri-Gawa 156a Db 43.56N 144.09 E
Abashiri-Ko 156a Da 44.00N 144.10 E
Abashiri-Wan 156a Db 44.00N 144.35 E
Abasolo 192 Je 24.04N 98.22W
Abatski 136 Hd 56.18N 70.28 E
Abau 214 Dj 10.11S 148.42 E
Abava 114 Eh 57.06N 21.54 E
Abay=Blue Nile (EN) 158 Kg 15.38N 32.31 E
Abaya, Lake- 158 Kh 6.20N 37.55 E
Abaza 138 Ef 52.39N 90.06 E
Abbadia San Salvatore 128 Fh 42.53N 11.41 E
Abbah Quşūr 128 Co 35.57N 8.50 E
Āb Bārīk 146 Oh 29.45N 52.37 E
'Abbāsābād 146 Qd 36.20N 56.25 E
Abbekås 116 Ei 55.24N 13.36 E
Abberton Reservoir 124 Cc 51.50N 0.55 E
Abbeville [Fr.] 122 Hd 50.06N 1.50 E
Abbeville [La.-U.S.] 186 Jl 29.58N 92.08W
Abbeville [S.C.-U.S.] 184 Fh 34.10N 82.23W
Abbey 188 Ka 50.43N 108.45W
Abbeyfeale/Mainistir na Féile 118 Di 52.24N 9.18W
Abbiategrasso 128 Ce 45.24N 8.54 E
Abbot, Mount- 212 Jd 20.03S 147.45 E
Abbot Ice Shelf 222 Pf 72.45S 96.00W
'Abd Al 'Azīz, Jabal- 146 Id 36.25N 40.20 E
'Abd al Kūrī 140 Hh 12.12N 52.13 E
Ābdānān 146 Lf 32.57N 47.26 E
Abdul Ghadir 168 Gc 10.42N 42.59 E
Abdulino 136 Fe 53.42N 53.38 E
Abe, Lake- 168 Gc 11.10N 41.45 E
Abéché 160 Jg 13.49N 20.49 E
Abeek 124 Hc 51.15N 6.00 E
Abe-Gawa 156 Fd 34.55N 138.22 E
Abeløya 179 Pc 79.00N 30.15 E
Abelvær 114 Cd 64.44N 11.11 E
Abemama Atoll 208 Id 0.21N 173.51 E
Abenab 172 Bc 19.12S 18.06 E
Abengourou 160 Gh 6.44N 3.29W
Abengourou [3] 166 Ed 6.35N 3.25W
Åbenrå 114 Bi 55.02N 9.26 E
Åbenrå Fjord 116 Ci 55.05N 9.35 E
Abeokuta 160 Hh 7.09N 3.21 E
Aberaeron 118 Ii 52.15N 4.15W
Aberdare Range 158 Ki 0.25S 36.38 E
Aberdeen [Id.-U.S.] 188 Ie 42.57N 112.50W
Aberdeen [Md.-U.S.] 184 If 39.30N 76.14W
Aberdeen [Ms.-U.S.] 186 Lj 33.49N 88.33W
Aberdeen [N.C.-U.S.] 184 Hh 35.08N 79.26W
Aberdeen [S.Afr.] 172 Cf 32.29S 24.03 E
Aberdeen [Scot.-U.K.] 112 Fd 57.10N 2.04W
Aberdeen [S.D.-U.S.] 176 Je 45.28N 98.29W
Aberdeen [Wa.-U.S.] 182 Cb 46.59N 123.50W
Aberdeen Lake 180 Hd 64.28N 99.00W
Abergavenny 118 Kj 51.50N 3.00W
Aberystwyth 118 Ii 52.25N 4.05W
Abetone 128 Ef 44.08N 10.40 E
Abez 136 Gb 66.32N 61.46 E
Abhā 142 Gh 18.13N 42.30 E
Abhainn an Chláir/Clare 118 Dh 53.20N 9.03W
Abhainn an Lagáin/Lagan 118 Hg 54.37N 5.53W
Abhainn na Bandan/Bandon 118 Ej 51.40N 8.30W
Abhainn na Deirge/Derg 118 Fg 54.40N 7.25W
Abhar 144 Gb 36.09N 49.13 E
Abhar 146 Md 36.02N 49.45 E
Abhazskaja ASSR [3] 136 Eg 43.00N 41.10 E
Abibe, Serranía de- 202 Cb 8.00N 76.30W
Abidjan 160 Gh 5.19N 4.02W
Abidjan [3] 166 Ed 5.30N 4.30W
Abilene [Ks.-U.S.] 186 Hg 38.55N 97.13W
Abilene [Tx.-U.S.] 176 Jf 32.27N 99.44W
Abingdon 118 Lj 51.41N 1.17W
Abinsk 132 Kg 44.52N 38.10 E
Abiquiu 186 Ch 36.12N 106.19W
Abiquiu Reservoir 186 Ch 36.18N 106.32W
Abisko 114 Eb 68.20N 18.51 E
Abitibi 180 Jf 51.04N 80.55W
Abitibi, Lake- 174 Le 48.42N 79.45W
Abiy Adi 168 Fc 13.37N 39.01 E
Abiyata, Lake- 168 Fd 7.38N 38.36 E
Abja-Paluoja 116 Kf 58.02N 25.14 E
Abnūb 164 Fd 27.16N 31.09 E
Åbo/Turku 112 Ic 60.27N 22.17 E
Abo, Massif d'- 168 Ba 21.41N 16.08 E
Abóboras, Serra das- 204 Jc 16.12S 44.35W
Abodo 168 Ed 7.50N 34.25 E
Aboisso 166 Ed 5.28N 3.12W
Aboisso [3] 166 Ed 5.28N 3.02W
Abomey 160 Hh 7.11N 1.59 E
Abong Mbang 166 He 3.59N 13.11 E
Abony 120 Pi 47.11N 20.00 E
Aborigen, pik- 138 Jd 62.05N 149.10 E
Aborlar 150 Ge 9.26N 118.33 E
Aborrebierg 116 Ej 54.59N 12.32 E
Abou Deïa 168 Bc 11.27N 19.17 E
Abou Goulem 168 Cc 13.37N 21.38 E
Abovjan 132 Ni 40.14N 44.37 E
Abraham's Bay 194 Kb 22.21N 72.55W
Abramovski bereg 114 Kc 66.25N 43.05 E
Abrántes 126 De 39.28N 8.12W
Abra Pampa 206 Gb 22.43S 65.42W
Abrego 194 Ki 8.04N 73.14W
Abreojos, Punta- 190 Bc 26.42N 113.35W
Abrets, Les- 122 Li 45.32N 5.35 E
'Abrī 168 Ea 20.48N 30.20 E
Abrolhos, Arquipélago dos- 202 Kg 18.00S 38.40W
Abrud 130 Gc 46.16N 23.04 E
Abruka, ostrov- / Abruka saar 116 Jf 58.08N 22.25 E
Abruka saar / Abruka, ostrov- 116 Jf 58.08N 22.25 E
Abruzzi [2] 128 Hh 42.20N 13.45 E
Absaroka Range 182 Fc 44.45N 109.50W
Abtenau 128 Hc 47.33N 13.21 E
Abū ad Duhūr 146 Ge 35.44N 37.02 E
Abū 'Alī 146 Mi 27.20N 49.33 E
Abū al Khaşīb 146 Lg 30.27N 47.59 E
Abū an Na'am 146 Hj 25.14N 38.49 E
Abū 'Arīsh 144 Ff 16.58N 42.50 E
Abū Ballaş 164 Ee 24.26N 27.39 E
Abū Daghmah 146 Hd 36.25N 38.15 E
Abū Darbah 164 Fd 28.29N 33.20 E
Abu Dhabi (EN)=Abū Ẓaby 142 Hg 24.28N 54.22 E
Abū Ḩād, Wādī- 146 Ei 27.46N 33.30 E
Abū Ḩadrīyah 146 Mi 27.20N 48.58 E
Abū Ḩamad 160 Kg 19.32N 33.19 E
Abū Ḩammād 146 Dg 30.32N 31.40 E
Abū Ḩarbah, Jabal- 146 Ei 27.17N 33.13 E
Abū Ḩashā'ifah, Khalīj- 146 Bg 31.16N 27.25 E
Abuja 160 Hh 9.10N 7.11 E
Abu Jābirah 168 Dc 11.04N 26.51 E
Abū Jifān 146 Lj 24.31N 47.43 E
Abū Kabīr 146 Dg 30.44N 31.40 E
Abū Kamāl 144 Fc 34.27N 40.55 E
Abukuma-Gawa 156 Gb 38.06N 140.52 E
Abukuma-Sanchi 156 Gc 37.20N 140.45 E
Abū Latt 164 Hf 19.58N 40.08 E
Abū Libdah, Khashm- 164 Ie 22.58N 46.13 E
Abū Madd, Ra's- 144 Ee 24.50N 37.12 E
Abū Maţāriq 168 Dc 10.58N 26.17 E
Abu Mendi 168 Fc 11.47N 35.42 E
Abumonbazi 170 Db 3.42N 22.10 E
Abū Muḩarrik, Ghurd- 164 Ed 27.00N 30.00 E
Abū Mūsá 146 Pj 25.52N 55.03 E
Abū Mūsá, Jazīreh-ye- 144 Id 25.52N 55.03 E
Abunã 200 Jf 9.42S 65.23W
Abunã, Rio- 198 Jf 9.41S 65.23W
Abune Yosef 168 Fc 12.09N 39.12 E
Abū Qīr 146 Dg 31.19N 30.04 E
Abū Qīr, Khalīj- 146 Dg 31.20N 30.15 E
Abū Qumayyis, Ra's- 146 Nj 24.34N 51.30 E
Abu Road 148 Ed 24.29N 72.47 E
Abū Sawmah, Ra's- 146 Ei 26.51N 33.59 E
Abū Shanab 168 Dc 13.57N 27.47 E
Abu Simbel (EN) = Abū Sunbul 164 Fe 22.22N 31.38 E
Abū Şukhayr 146 Kg 31.52N 44.27 E
Abū Sunbul = Abu Simbel (EN) 164 Fe 22.22N 31.38 E
Abuta 154 Pc 42.31N 140.46 E
Abut Head 218 De 43.06S 170.15 E
Abū Tij 164 Fd 27.02N 31.19 E
Abū Ţurţūr, Jabal- 146 Cj 25.20N 30.00 E
Abū'Urūq 168 Eb 15.54N 30.27 E
Abuyemeda 168 Fc 10.38N 39.43 E
Abū Zabad 168 Dc 12.21N 29.15 E
Abū Ẓaby=Abu Dhabi (EN) 142 Hg 24.28N 54.22 E
Abū Zanīmah 164 Fd 29.03N 33.06 E
Abwong 168 Ed 9.07N 32.12 E
Åby 116 Gf 58.40N 16.11 E
Abyaḑ 168 Dc 13.46N 26.28 E
Abyaḑ, Al Baḩr al- = White Nile (EN) [3] 168 Ec 12.40N 32.30 E
Abyaḑ, Al Baḩr al- = White Nile (EN) 158 Kg 15.38N 32.31 E
Abyaḑ, Ar Ra's al- 144 Ee 23.32N 38.32 E
Abyaḑ, Jabal- 168 Db 18.55N 28.40 E
Abyaḑ, Ra's al- = Blanc, Cape- (EN) 158 He 37.20N 9.50 E
Abyār Alī 146 Hj 24.25N 39.33 E
Abyār ash Shuwayrif 164 Bd 29.59N 14.16 E
Åbybro 114 Bh 57.09N 9.45 E
Abydos 164 Fd 26.11N 31.55 E
Abyei 168 Dd 9.36N 28.26 E
Åbyek 146 Nd 36.02N 50.31 E
Abymes 197e Ab 16.16N 61.31W
Acacias 202 Dc 3.59N 73.47W
Academy Gletscher 179 Ib 81.45N 33.35W
Acadie 174 Me 46.00N 65.00W
Acaill/Achill 118 Dh 54.00N 10.00W
Acajutla 194 Cg 13.36N 89.50W
Acalayong 166 Ge 1.05N 9.40 E
Acámbaro 190 Dd 20.02N 100.44W
Acandí 202 Cb 8.31N 77.17W
Acaponeta 190 Cd 22.30N 105.22W
Acaponeta, Rio- 192 Gf 22.20N 105.37W
Acapulco de Juárez 176 Jh 16.51N 99.55W
Acará 202 Id 1.57S 48.11W
Acarai, Serra- 202 Gc 1.50N 57.40W
Acaraú 202 Jd 2.53S 40.07W
Acaray, Rio- 204 Eg 25.29S 54.42W
Acari, Rio- [Braz.] 202 Ge 5.18S 59.42W
Acari, Rio- [Braz.] 204 Jb 16.00S 45.03W
Acarigua 202 Eb 9.33N 69.12W
Acatenango, Volcán- 174 Jh 14.30N 91.40W
Acatlán de Osorio 192 Jh 18.12N 98.03W
Acayucan 190 Fe 17.57N 94.55W
Accéglio 128 Af 44.28N 7.00 E
Aččitau, gora- 135 Cc 42.07N 60.31 E
Accomac 184 Jg 37.43N 75.40W
Accra 160 Gh 5.33N 0.13W
Acebal 204 Bk 33.14S 60.50W
Acebuches 192 Hc 28.15N 102.43W
Aceguá [Braz.] 204 Ej 31.52S 54.09W
Aceguá [Ur.] 204 Ej 31.52S 54.12W
Aceh [3] 150 Cf 4.10N 96.50 E
Acerenza 128 Jj 40.48N 15.56 E
Acerra 128 Ij 40.57N 14.22 E
Achacachi 202 Eg 16.03S 68.43W
Achaguas 202 Eb 7.46N 68.14W
Achaïf, 'Erg- 166 Ea 20.49N 4.34W
Achao 206 Ff 42.28S 73.30W
Achar 204 Dk 32.25S 56.10W
Achegour 166 Hb 19.03N 11.53 E
Acheng 152 Mb 45.32N 126.56 E
Acheux-en-Amiénois 124 Ed 50.04N 2.32 E
Achiet-le-Grand 124 Ed 50.08N 2.47 E
Achill/Acaill 118 Dh 54.00N 10.00W
Achilleion 130 Cj 39.34N 19.55 E
Achill Head/Ceann Acla 118 Ch 53.59N 10.13W
Achim 120 Fc 53.02N 9.01 E
Achim 168 Bb 15.53N 19.31 E
Achterwasser 120 Jb 54.00N 13.57 E
Acı Gölü 146 Cd 37.50N 29.54 E
Ačinsk 142 Ld 56.17N 90.30 E
Acıpayam 146 Cd 37.25N 29.22 E
Acireale 128 Jm 37.37N 15.10 E
Aciş 130 Fb 47.32N 22.47 E
Ačisaj 135 Gc 43.33N 68.53 E
Ačit 134 Hh 56.48N 57.54 E
Ačit-Nur 152 Fb 49.30N 90.30 E
Acklins 174 Lg 22.25N 74.00W
Acklins, The Bight of- 194 Jb 22.30N 74.15W
Acle 124 Db 52.38N 1.33 E
Acobamba 202 Df 12.48S 74.34W
Acolin 122 Jh 46.49N 3.23 E
Aconcagua, Cerro- 198 Ji 32.39S 70.00W
Açor, Serra de- 126 Ed 40.13N 7.48W
Açores=Azores (EN) [5] 160 Ee 38.30N 28.00W
Açores, Arquipélago dos-=Azores (EN) 158 Ee 38.30N 28.00W
Acorizal 204 Db 15.12S 56.22W
Acoyapa 194 Eh 11.58N 85.10W
Acquapendente 128 Fh 42.44N 11.52 E
Acquasanta Terme 128 Hh 42.46N 13.24 E
Acquasparta 128 Gh 42.41N 12.33 E
Acquaviva delle Fonti 128 Kj 40.54N 16.50 E
Acqui Terme 128 Cf 44.41N 8.28 E
Acraman, Lake- 212 Hf 32.05S 135.25 E
Acre [2] 202 Ee 9.00S 70.00W
Acre, Rio- 198 Jf 8.45S 67.22W
Acri 128 Kk 39.29N 16.23 E
A Cruña / La Coruña 112 Fg 43.22N 8.23W
Actéon, Groupe- 208 Ng 21.20S 136.30W
Actopan 192 Jg 20.16N 98.56W
Açu 202 Ke 5.34S 36.54W
Acuña 204 Di 29.55S 57.58W
Ada [Ghana] 166 Fd 5.47N 0.38 E
Ada [Ok.-U.S.] 182 He 34.46N 96.41W
Ada [Yugo.] 130 Dd 45.48N 20.08 E
Adaba 168 Fd 7.03N 39.31 E
'Adad 168 Hd 8.23N 46.48 E
'Adāde 168 Gd 9.45N 44.41 E
Adair, Bahía- 192 Cb 31.30N 113.50W
Adair, Cape - 180 Kb 71.31N 71.24W
Adaja 126 Hc 41.32N 4.52W
Adak 178a Cb 51.45N 176.40W
Adalar 130 Mi 40.52N 29.07 E
'Adale 168 He 2.46N 46.20 E
Ådalen 116 Ga 63.20N 17.30 E
Adalselv 116 Dd 60.04N 10.11 E
Adam, Mount- 206 Hh 51.34S 60.04W
Adamantina 204 Ge 21.42S 51.04W
Adamaoua=Adamawa (EN) 158 Ih 7.00N 15.00 E
Adamawa (EN)= Adamaoua 158 Ih 7.00N 15.00 E
Adamello 128 Ed 46.09N 10.30 E
Adamovka 132 Ud 51.32N 59.59 E
Adams 186 Le 43.58N 89.49W
Adams, Mount- 182 Cb 46.12N 121.28W
Adams Lake 188 Fa 51.13N 119.33W
Adams River 180 Ff 50.54N 119.33W
Adam's Rock 220q Ab 25.04S 130.05W
Adamstown 210 Ns 25.04S 130.05W
Adamuz 126 Hf 38.02N 4.31W
Adana 142 Ff 37.01N 35.18 E
Adapazarı 146 Db 40.46N 30.24 E
Adarama 168 Eb 17.05N 34.54 E
Adarān, Jabal- 164 Ig 13.46N 45.08 E
Adare, Cape- 222 Kf 71.17S 170.14 E
Adavale 212 Ie 25.55S 144.36 E
Adda [It.] 110 Gf 45.08N 9.53 E
Adda [Sud.] 168 Cd 9.51N 24.50 E
Ad Ḑab'ah 164 Ec 31.02N 28.26 E
Ad Dabbah 168 Eb 18.03N 30.57 E
Ad Dafīnah 164 He 23.18N 41.58 E
Ad Ḑafrah 146 Ok 23.25N 53.25 E
Ad Dahnā' 140 Gg 24.30N 48.10 E
Addala-Šuhgelmeer, gora- 132 Oh 42.20N 46.15 E
Ad Ḑāli' 164 Hg 13.42N 44.44 E
Ad Damazin 168 Ec 11.49N 34.23 E
Ad 'Dāmir 168 Eb 17.35N 33.58 E
Ad Dammām 142 Hg 26.26N 50.07 E
Ad Dār al Ḩamrā' 144 Ed 27.19N 37.44 E
Ad Dawādimī 146 Kj 24.28N 44.18 E
Ad Dawḩah=Doha (EN) 142 Hg 25.17N 51.32 E
Ad Dawr 146 Je 34.27N 43.47 E
Ad Dayr 164 Fd 25.20N 32.35 E
Ad Dibdibah 146 Lh 28.00N 46.30 E
Ad Ḑiffah 164 Ec 30.30N 25.30 E
Ad Dikākah 168 Ib 19.25N 51.30 E
Ad Dilam 144 Ge 23.59N 47.10 E
Ad Dindar 168 Ec 13.20N 34.05 E
Ad Dir'īyah 146 Lj 24.48N 46.32 E
Addis Ababa (EN) = Adis Abeba 160 Kh 9.01N 38.46 E
Ad Dissān 164 Hf 16.56N 41.41 E
Addis Zemen 168 Fc 12.05N 37.44 E
Ad Dīwānīya 144 Fc 31.59N 44.56 E
Addu Atoll 140 Jj 0.25S 73.10 E
Ad Du'ayn 168 Dc 11.26N 26.09 E
Ad Duwayd 146 Jg 30.13N 42.18 E
Ad Duwaym 168 Ec 14.00N 32.19 E
Adel [Ga.-U.S.] 184 Fj 31.18N 83.25W
Adel [Or.-U.S.] 188 Fe 42.11N 119.54W
Adelaide [Austl.] 210 Eh 34.56S 138.36 E
Adelaide [Bah.] 184 Im 25.00N 77.31W
Adelaide [S.Afr.] 172 Df 32.42S 26.20 E
Adelaide Island 222 Qe 67.15S 68.30W
Adelaide Peninsula 180 Hc 68.05N 97.50W
Adelaide River 210 Ef 13.15S 131.06 E
Adelaye 168 Cd 7.07N 22.49 E
Adelboden 128 Bd 46.30N 7.33 E
Adèle Island 212 Ec 15.30S 123.10 E
Adélie, Terre- 222 Ie 67.00S 139.00 E
Ademuz 126 Kd 40.04N 1.17W
Aden (EN) = Baladīyat 'Adan 142 Gh 12.46N 45.01 E
Aden, Gulf of- 158 Lg 12.00N 48.00 E
Aden, Gulf of- (EN) = 'Admēd, Badyarada- 158 Lg 12.00N 48.00 E
Adenau 124 Id 50.23N 6.56 E
Ader 158 Hg 14.10N 5.05 E
Aderbissinat 166 Gb 15.37N 7.52 E
Adhan, Jabal- 146 Qj 25.27N 56.13 E
Adh Dhahībāt 162 Jc 32.01N 10.42 E
Adh Dhayd 146 Pj 25.17N 55.53 E
Adhélfi 130 Gj 39.08N 23.59 E
Adhelfoi 130 Jm 36.25N 26.37 E
'Adhriyāt, Jibāl- al- 146 Gg 30.25N 36.48 E
Adi, Pulau- 150 Jg 4.18S 133.26 E
Adiaké 166 Ed 5.16N 3.17W
Adi Arkay 168 Fc 13.31N 38.00 E
Adicora 202 Ea 11.57N 69.48W
Adi Dairo 168 Fc 14.21N 38.12 E
Adigala 168 Gc 10.24N 42.18 E
Adige/Etsch 110 Hf 45.10N 12.20 E
Adigrat 168 Fc 14.16N 39.28 E
Adi Keyeh 168 Fc 14.48N 39.23 E
Adi Kwala 168 Fc 14.37N 38.51 E
Ādilābād 148 Fe 19.40N 78.32 E
Adirī 160 If 27.30N 13.16 E
Adirondack Mountains 174 Le 44.00N 74.00W
Adis Abeba = Addis Ababa (EN) 160 Kh 9.01N 38.46 E
Adis Alem 168 Fd 9.03N 38.24 E
Adi Ugri 168 Fc 14.53N 38.49 E
Adiyaman 144 Eb 37.46N 38.17 E
Adjud 130 Kc 46.06N 27.10 E
Adjuntas 197a Bb 18.09N 66.43W
'Admēd, Badyarada- = Aden, Gulf of- (EN) 158 Lg 12.00N 48.00 E
Admer, Erg d'- 162 Ie 24.12N 9.10 E
Admiralty 178 Me 57.50N 134.30W
Admiralty Bay 197n Ba 13.00N 61.16W
Admiralty Gulf 212 Fb 14.20S 125.50 E
Admiralty Inlet 180 Ib 72.30N 86.00W
Admiralty Islands 208 Fe 2.10S 147.00 E
Admiralty Mountains 222 Kf 71.45S 168.30 E
Admont 128 Ic 47.34N 14.27 E
Ado 166 Fd 6.36N 2.56 E
Ado Ekiti 166 Gd 7.38N 5.13 E
Adok 168 Ed 8.11N 30.19 E
Adolfo Gonzales Chaves 204 Bn 38.02S 60.06W
Adolfo López Mateos, Presa- 192 Fe 25.05N 107.20W
Adonara, Pulau- 150 Hh 8.20S 123.10 E
Ādoni 148 Fe 15.38N 77.17 E
Adour 122 Ek 43.32N 1.32W
Adra 126 Ih 36.44N 3.01W
Adrano 128 Im 37.40N 14.50 E
Adrar 160 Gf 27.54N 0.17W
Adrar 158 Hf 25.15N 8.10 E
Adrar 158 Ff 20.30N 13.30W
Adrar [Alg.] [3] 162 Gd 27.00N 1.00W
Adrar [Mtna.] [3] 162 Fe 21.00N 11.00W
Adré 168 Cc 13.28N 22.12 E
Adria 128 Ge 45.03N 12.03 E
Adrian 184 Ee 41.54N 84.02W
Adrianópolis 204 Hg 24.41S 48.50W
Adriatic, Deti-=Adriatic Sea (EN) 110 Hg 43.00N 16.00 E
Adriatico, Mar-=Adriatic Sea (EN) 110 Hg 43.00N 16.00 E
Adriatic Sea (EN)=Adriatic, Deti- 110 Hg 43.00N 16.00 E
Adriatic Sea (EN)= Adriatico, Mar- 110 Hg 43.00N 16.00 E
Adriatic Sea (EN)= Jadransko More 110 Hg 43.00N 16.00 E
Aduard 124 Ia 53.15N 6.25 E
Adula 128 Dd 46.30N 9.05 E
Adulis 168 Fb 15.15N 39.37 E
Adur 124 Bd 50.49N 0.16W
Adusa 170 Eb 1.23N 28.01 E
Adventure Bank (EN) 128 Gm 37.20N 12.10 E
Adwa 160 Kg 14.10N 38.55 E
Adyča 140 Pc 68.13N 135.03 E
Adygalah 138 Jd 62.57N 146.25 E
Adygejskaja avtonomnaja oblast [3] 136 Eg 44.30N 40.05 E
Adžarskaja ASSR [3] 136 Eg 41.40N 42.10 E
Adzopé 166 Ed 6.06N 3.52W
Adzopé [3] 166 Ed 6.15N 3.45W
Adzva 134 Ic 66.36N 59.28 E
Aegean Sea (EN)=Aiyaion Pélagos 110 Ih 39.00N 25.00 E
Aegean Sea (EN)=Ege Denizi 110 Ih 39.00N 25.00 E
Aegina (EN) = Aiyina 130 Gl 37.40N 23.30 E
Aegviidu 116 Ke 59.17N 25.37 E
Aeon Point 220g Bb 1.46N 157.11W
Aerfort na Sionainne/Shannon 118 Ei 52.42N 8.57W
Ærø 116 Dj 54.55N 10.20 E
Ærøskøbing 116 Dj 54.53N 10.25 E
Aerzen 124 Lb 52.02N 9.16 E
Afafi, Massif d'- 166 Ha 22.15N 15.00 E
'Afak 146 Kf 32.04N 45.15 E
Afanasjevo 114 Mg 58.54N 53.16 E
Afareaitu 221e Fc 17.33S 149.47W
Afars and Issas (EN) → Djibouti [1] 160 Lg 11.30N 43.00 E
Aff 122 Dg 47.43N 2.07W
Affollé 158 Fg 16.55N 10.25W
Affrica, Scoglio d'- 128 Eh 42.20N 10.05 E
Afghānistān [1] 142 If 33.00N 65.00 E
Afgōye 168 He 2.09N 45.07 E
'Afīf 144 Fe 23.55N 42.56 E
Afikpo 166 Gd 5.53N 7.55 E
Afipski 132 Kg 44.52N 38.50 E
Aflou 162 Hc 34.07N 2.06 E
Afmadōw 168 Ge 0.29N 42.06 E
Afognak 178 Ie 58.15N 152.30W
Afonso Cláudio 202 Jh 20.05S 41.08W
Afon Teifi 118 Ii 52.06N 4.43W
Afon Tywi 118 Ij 51.40N 4.15W
Afragola 128 Ij 40.55N 14.18 E
Afrērā, Lake- 168 Gc 13.20N 41.03 E
Africa (EN) 106 Eh 10.00N 22.00 E
African Islands 158 Mi 4.53S 53.24 E
Afşin 146 Gc 38.36N 36.55 E
Afsluitdijk 122 La 53.00N 5.15 E
Afton 188 Je 42.44N 110.56W
Afuá 202 Hd 0.10S 50.23W
'Afula 146 Ff 32.36N 35.17 E
Afyonkarahisar 142 Ff 38.45N 30.40 E
Agadem 160 Ig 16.50N 13.17 E
Agadez 160 Hg 16.58N 7.59 E
Agadez [2] 166 Hb 19.45N 10.15 E
Agadez, Irhazer Oua-n- 166 Gb 17.28N 6.26 E
Agadir 160 Ge 30.25N 9.37W
Agadir [3] 162 Fc 30.00N 9.00W
Agadyr 136 Hf 48.17N 72.53 E
Agalega Islands 158 Mj 10.24S 56.30 E
Agalta, Sierra de- 194 Ge 15.00N 85.53W
Agan 136 Hc 61.23N 74.35 E
Agana 210 Fc 13.28N 144.45 E
Agano-Gawa 154 Of 37.57N 139.07 E
Aga Point 220c Bb 13.14N 144.43 E
Agapovka 134 Ij 53.18N 59.10 E
Agaro 168 Fd 7.53N 36.36 E
Agartala 142 Lg 23.49N 91.16 E
Agassiz Pool 186 Ib 48.20N 95.58W
Agat 220c Bb 13.23N 144.39 E
Agat Bay 220c Bb 13.24N 144.39 E
Agats 210 Ee 5.33S 138.08 E
Agattu 178a Ab 52.25N 173.35 E
Agawa Bay 184 Eb 47.22N 84.33W
Agawa Bay 184 Eb 47.20N 84.42W
Agboville 166 Ed 5.56N 4.13W
Agboville [3] 166 Ed 6.00N 4.15W
Agdam 136 Eh 39.58N 46.57 E
Agdaš 132 Oi 40.38N 47.29 E
Agde 122 Jk 43.19N 3.28 E
Agde, Cap d'- 122 Jk 43.16N 3.30 E
Agder 116 Cf 58.25N 8.15 E
Agdz 162 Fc 30.27N 7.56W
Agdžabedi 132 Oi 40.03N 47.28 E
Agematsu 156 Ed 35.47N 137.41 E
Agen 122 Gj 44.12N 0.38 E
Ageo 156 Fd 35.58N 139.35 E
Agepsta, gora- 132 Lh 43.32N 40.30 E
Ager 128 Hb 48.05N 13.51 E
Agere Mariam 168 Fd 5.39N 38.15 E

Index Symbols

- [1] Independent Nation
- [2] State, Region
- [3] District, County
- [4] Municipality
- [5] Colony, Dependency
- Continent
- Physical Region
- Historical or Cultural Region
- Mount, Mountain
- Volcano
- Hill
- Mountains, Mountain Range
- Hills, Escarpment
- Plateau, Upland
- Pass, Gap
- Plain, Lowland
- Delta
- Salt Flat
- Valley, Canyon
- Crater, Cave
- Karst Features
- Depression
- Polder
- Desert, Dunes
- Forest, Woods
- Heath, Steppe
- Oasis
- Cape, Point
- Coast, Beach
- Cliff
- Peninsula
- Isthmus
- Sandbank
- Island
- Atoll
- Rock, Reef
- Islands, Archipelago
- Rocks, Reefs
- Coral Reef
- Well, Spring
- Geyser
- River, Stream
- Waterfall, Rapids
- River Mouth, Estuary
- Lake
- Salt Lake
- Intermittent Lake
- Reservoir
- Swamp, Pond
- Canal
- Glacier
- Ice Shelf, Pack Ice
- Ocean
- Sea
- Gulf, Bay
- Strait, Fjord
- Lagoon
- Bank
- Seamount
- Tablemount
- Ridge
- Shelf
- Basin
- Escarpment, Sea Scarp
- Fracture
- Trench, Abyss
- National Park, Reserve
- Point of Interest
- Recreation Site
- Cave, Cavern
- Historic Site
- Ruins
- Wall, Walls
- Church, Abbey
- Temple
- Scientific Station
- Railway station
- Airport
- Port
- Military installation
- Lighthouse
- Mine
- Tunnel
- Dam, Bridge

Agersø	116	Di	55.10N	11.10 E
Agger	124	Jd	50.48N	7.11 E
Āghā Jārī	144	Gc	30.42N	49.50 E
Aghireşu	130	Gc	46.53N	23.15 E
Agiabampo, Estero de-	192	Ed	26.15N	109.15W
Ağın	146	Hc	38.57N	38.43 E
Aginski Burjatski nacionalny okrug [3]	138	Gf	51.00N	114.30 E
Aginskoje	138	Gf	51.03N	114.33 E
Agnew	212	Ee	28.01 S	120.30 E
Agnibilékrou	166	Ed	7.08N	3.12W
Agnita	130	Hd	45.58N	24.37 E
Agno	128	Fe	45.32N	11.21 E
Agnone	128	Ii	41.48N	14.22 E
Ago	156	Ed	34.19N	136.50 E
Agoare	166	Fd	8.30N	3.25 E
Agogna	128	Ce	45.04N	8.54 E
Agön	116	Gc	61.35N	17.25 E
Agordat	160	Kg	15.32N	37.53 E
Ágordo	128	Gd	46.17N	12.02 E
Agout	122	Hk	43.47N	1.41 E
Āgra	142	Jg	27.11N	78.01 E
Agrahanski poluostrov	132	Oh	43.45N	47.35 E
Agramunt	126	Nc	41.47N	1.06 E
Agreda	126	Kc	41.51N	1.56W
Ağrı	144	Fb	39.44N	43.03 E
Agri	128	Kj	40.13N	16.44 E
Agričaj	132	Oi	41.17N	46.43 E
Ağrı Dağı = Ararat, Mount-(EN)	140	Gf	39.40N	44.24 E
Agrigento	112	Hh	37.19N	13.34 E
Agrihan Island	208	Fc	18.46N	145.40 E
Agrij	130	Gb	47.15N	23.16 E
Agrínion	130	Ek	38.38N	21.25 E
Agropoli	128	Ij	40.21N	14.59 E
Agro Pontino	128	Gi	41.25N	12.55 E
Agryz	114	Mh	56.31N	53.01 E
Agto	179	Ge	67.37N	53.49W
Agua Brava, Laguna-	192	Gf	22.10N	105.32W
Agua Caliente, Cerro-	190	Cc	26.27N	106.12W
Aguachica	202	Db	8.18N	73.38W
Agua Clara	204	Fe	20.27 S	52.52W
Aguada de Pasajeros	194	Gb	22.23N	80.51W
Aguadilla	194	Nd	18.26N	67.09W
Aguadulce	194	Gi	8.15N	80.33W
Agua Fria River	188	Ij	33.23N	112.21W
Agua Limpa, Rio-	204	Gb	14.58 S	51.20W
Aguán, Río-	194	Ef	15.57N	85.44W
Aguanaval, Río-	192	Hf	25.28N	102.53W
Aguapeí	204	Cc	16.12 S	59.43W
Aguapeí, Rio-	204	Cb	15.53 S	58.25W
Aguapei, Rio-	206	Jb	21.03 S	51.47W
Aguapey, Río-	204	Di	29.07 S	56.36W
Agua Prieta	176	If	31.18N	109.34W
Aguaray	206	Hb	22.16 S	63.44W
Aguaray-Guazú, Río- [Par.]	204	Dg	24.05 S	56.40W
Aguaray-Guazú, Río- [Par.]	204	Dg	24.47 S	57.19W
Aguasay	196	Eh	9.25N	63.44W
Aguascalientes	176	Ig	21.53N	102.18W
Aguascalientes [2]	190	Dd	22.00N	102.30W
Aguasvivas	126	Lc	41.20N	0.25W
Água Verde, Rio-	204	Da	13.42 S	56.43W
Agua Vermelha, Represa-	206	Ja	19.53 S	50.17W
Agudo [Braz.]	204	Fi	29.38 S	53.15W
Agudo [Sp.]	126	Hf	38.59N	4.52W
Águeda	126	Dd	40.34N	8.27W
Agueda	126	Fc	41.02N	6.56W
Aguelhok	166	Fb	19.28N	0.51 E
Agüenit	162	Ee	22.11N	13.08W
Aguerguer	158	Ff	23.09N	16.01W
Aguijan Island	208	Fc	14.51N	145.34 E
Aguilar de Campoo	126	Hb	42.48N	4.16W
Aguilar de la Frontera	126	Hg	37.31N	4.39W
Águilas	126	Kg	37.24N	1.35W
Aguililla	192	Hh	18.44N	102.44W
Aguirre, Río-	196	Fh	8.28N	61.02W
Aguja, Cabo de la-	202	Da	11.21N	73.59W
Agujereada, Punta-	197a	Ab	18.31N	67.08W
Agul	138	Ee	55.40N	95.45 E
Agulhas, Cape-(EN) = Agulhas, Kaap-	158	Jl	34.50 S	20.00 E
Agulhas, Kaap- = Agulhas, Cape-(EN)	158	Jl	34.50 S	20.00 E
Agulhas Basin (EN)	106	En	47.00 S	20.00 E
Agulhas Negras, Pico das-	198	Lh	22.23 S	44.38W
Agulhas Plateau (EN)	158	Jm	40.00 S	26.00 E
Agung, Gunung-	150	Gh	8.21 S	115.30 E
Aguni-Shima	152	Mf	26.35N	127.15 E
Ağva	146	Cb	41.05N	29.50 E
Ahaggar	158	Hf	23.10N	5.50 E
Ahaggar, Tassili-oua-n-	158	Hf	20.30N	5.00 E
Aha Hills	172	Cc	19.45 S	21.10 E
Ahalcihe	136	Eg	41.38N	42.59 E
Ahalkalaki	136	Eg	41.25N	43.29 E
Ahangaran	135	Gd	40.57N	69.37 E
Ahar	144	Gb	38.28N	47.04 E
Ahat	130	Mk	38.39N	29.47 E
Ahaus	120	Cd	52.04N	7.00 E
Ahe Atoll	208	Mf	14.30 S	146.18W
Ahenet, Tanezrouft-n-	162	He	22.00N	1.00 E
Ahini	138	Ff	53.18N	105.01 E
Ahipara	218	Ea	35.10 S	173.09 E
Ahja jõgi	116	Lf	58.19N	27.15 E
Ahlat	146	Jc	38.45N	42.29 E
Ahlen	120	De	51.45N	7.55 E
Ahmadābād	142	Jg	23.02N	72.37 E
Aḩmadī	146	Qi	27.56N	56.42 E
Ahmadnagar	148	Ee	19.05N	74.44 E
Ahmadpur East	148	Ec	29.09N	71.16 E
Ahmar	158	Lh	9.23N	41.13 E
Aḩmar, Al Baḩr al- = Red Sea (EN)	158	Kf	25.00N	38.00 E
Ahmeta	132	Nh	42.02N	45.11 E
Ahmetli	130	Kk	38.31N	27.57 E
Ahnet	162	He	24.35N	3.15 E
Ahoa	220h	Ab	13.17 S	176.12W
Ahome	192	Ee	25.55N	109.11W
Ahon, Tarso-	168	Ba	20.23N	18.18 E
Ahr	120	Df	50.33N	7.17 E
Ahram	146	Nh	28.52N	51.16 E
Ahrāmāt al Jīzah	164	Fd	29.55N	31.05 E
Ahrensburg	120	Gc	53.41N	10.15 E
Ahrgebirge	124	Id	50.31N	6.54 E
Ahse	124	Jc	51.42N	7.51 E
Ahsu	132	Pi	40.35N	48.26 E
Ähtäri	114	Ee	62.02N	21.20 E
Ahtärinjarvi	116	Kb	62.40N	24.05 E
Ähtävänjoki	114	Fe	63.38N	22.48 E
Ahtopol	130	Kg	42.06N	27.57 E
Ahtuba	110	Kf	46.42N	48.00 E
Ahtubinsk	112	Kf	48.14N	46.14 E
Ahtyrka	136	De	50.19N	34.55 E
Ahuacapán	194	Cg	13.55N	89.51W
Ahuazotepec	192	Jg	20.03N	98.09W
Ahunui Atoll	208	Mf	19.35 S	140.28W
Åhus	114	Di	55.55N	14.17 E
Ahvāz	142	Gf	31.19N	48.42 E
Ahvenanmaa/Åland [2]	114	Ef	60.15N	20.00 E
Ahvenanmaa/Åland	110	Hc	60.15N	20.00 E
Ahvenanmeri	116	Hd	60.00N	19.30 E
Aḩwar	144	Gg	13.31N	46.42 E
Aibag Gol	154	Ad	41.42N	110.24 E
Aibetsu	156a	Cb	43.55N	142.33 E
Aichach	120	Hh	48.28N	11.08 E
Aichi Ken [2]	154	Ng	35.00N	137.07 E
Aiea	221a	Db	21.23N	157.56W
Aigle	128	Ad	46.20N	6.59 E
Aigle, L'-	122	Gf	48.45N	0.38 E
Aigoual, Mont-	122	Jj	44.07N	3.35 E
Aiguá	204	El	34.12 S	54.45W
Aigues	122	Kj	44.07N	4.43 E
Aigues-Mortes	122	Kk	43.34N	4.11 E
Aiguilles	122	Mj	44.47N	6.52 E
Aiguillon	122	Gj	44.18N	0.21 E
Aigurande	122	Hh	46.26N	1.50 E
Ai He	154	Hd	40.13N	124.30 E
Aihui (Heihe)	142	Od	50.13N	127.26 E
Aikawa	156	Fb	38.02N	138.14 E
Aiken	182	Ke	33.34N	81.44W
Ailao Shan	152	Hg	23.15N	102.20 E
Ailette	124	Fe	49.35N	3.10 E
Ailinginae Atoll	208	Hc	11.08N	166.24 E
Aillte an Mhothair/Moher, Cliffs of-	118	Di	52.58N	9.27W
Ailly-le-Haut-Clocher	124	Dd	50.05N	1.59 E
Ailly-sur-Noye	124	Ee	49.45N	2.22 E
Ailsa Craig	118	Hf	55.16N	5.07W
Ailuk Atoll	208	Hc	10.20N	169.56 E
Aim	138	Ie	58.48N	134.12 E
Aimogasta	206	Gc	28.33 S	66.49W
Aimorés	202	Jg	19.30 S	41.04W
Ain [3]	122	Lh	46.10N	5.20 E
Ain	122	Li	45.48N	5.10 E
Ainaži/Ajnaži	114	Fh	57.52N	24.25 E
Aïn Beïda	162	Ib	35.48N	7.24 E
Aïn Beni Mathar	162	Gc	34.01N	2.01W
Aïn Bessem	126	Ph	36.18N	3.40 E
Aïn Boucif	126	Pi	35.53N	3.09 E
Aïn Defla	126	Nh	36.16N	1.58 E
Aïn el Berd	126	Li	35.21N	0.31W
Aïn el Hammam	126	Qh	36.34N	4.19 E
Aïn el Turck	126	Li	35.44N	0.46W
Aïn Galakka	168	Bb	18.05N	18.31 E
Aínos Óros	130	Dk	38.07N	20.40 E
Aïn Oulmene	126	Ri	35.55N	5.18 E
Aïn Oussera	126	Oi	35.27N	2.54 E
Aïn Sefra	160	Ge	32.45N	0.35W
Ainsworth	186	Ge	42.33N	99.52W
Aïn Taghrout	126	Rh	36.08N	5.05 E
Aïn Tedeles	126	Mh	36.00N	0.18 E
Ain Témouchent	162	Gb	35.18N	1.08W
Aïn Tolba	126	Ki	35.15N	1.15W
Aioi	156	Dd	34.49N	134.28 E
Aiquile	202	Eg	18.10 S	65.10W
Aïr/Azbine	158	Hg	18.00N	8.30 E
Airabu, Pulau-	150	Ef	2.46N	106.14 E
Airai	220a	Bc	7.21N	134.34 E
Airaines	124	De	49.58N	1.57 E
Airão	202	Fd	1.56 S	61.22W
Airbangis	150	Cf	0.12N	99.23 E
Airdrie	188	Ha	51.18N	114.02W
Aire	122	Id	50.38N	2.24 E
Aire [Eng.-U.K.]	118	Mh	53.44N	0.54W
Aire [Fr.]	122	Ke	49.19N	4.49 E
Aire, Canal d'-	122	Id	50.38N	2.25 E
Aire, Isla del-	126	Qe	39.47N	4.16 E
Aire-sur-l'Adour	122	Fk	43.42N	0.16W
Air Force	180	Kc	67.55N	74.05W
Airolo	128	Cd	46.33N	8.35 E
Aïs	219b	Cb	15.26 S	167.15 E
Aisch	120	Hg	49.46N	11.01 E
Aisén del General Carlos Ibáñez del Campo [2]	206	Fg	46.00 S	73.00W
Aishihik	180	Dd	61.34N	137.30W
Ai-Shima	156	Bd	34.30N	131.18 E
Aisne [3]	122	Je	49.30N	3.30 E
Aisne	122	Ie	49.26N	2.50 E
Aisne à la Marne, Canal de l'-	122	Je	49.24N	3.55 E
Aïssa, Djebel-	162	Gc	32.51N	0.30W
Aitana, Pico-	126	Lf	38.39N	0.16W
Aitape	214	Ch	3.08 S	142.21 E
Aitolikón	130	Ek	38.26N	21.21 E
Aitutaki Atoll	208	Lf	18.52 S	159.45W
Ait Youssef ou Ali	126	Ii	35.09N	3.55W
Aiud	130	Gc	46.18N	23.43 E
Aiviekste/Ajviekste	114	Fh	56.36N	25.44 E
Aiwokako Passage	220a	Bb	7.39N	134.33 E
Aix, Ile d'-	122	Eh	46.01N	1.10W
Aix-en-Provence	122	Lk	43.32N	5.26 E
Aixe-sur-Vienne	122	Hi	45.48N	1.08 E
Aix-les-Bains	122	Li	45.42N	5.55 E
Aiyaíon Pélagos = Aegean Sea (EN)	110	Ih	39.00N	25.00 E
Aíyina	130	Gl	37.45N	23.26 E
Aíyina = Aegina (EN)	130	Gl	37.40N	23.30 E
Aiyínion	130	Fi	40.30N	22.33 E
Aíyion	130	Fk	38.15N	22.05 E
Aizawl	148	Id	23.44N	92.43 E
Aizenay	122	Eh	46.44N	1.37W
Aizpute/Ajzpute	114	Eh	56.45N	21.39 E
Aizubange	156	Fc	37.34N	139.49 E
Aizutakada	156	Fc	37.29N	139.48 E
Aizuwakamatsu	154	Of	37.30N	139.56 E
Ajā', Jabal-	146	Ii	27.30N	41.30 E
'Ajab Shīr	146	Kd	37.28N	45.54 E
Ajaccio	112	Gg	41.55N	8.44 E
Ajaccio, Golfe d'-	122a	Ab	41.50N	8.41 E
Ajaguz	142	Ke	47.58N	80.27 E
Ajakli	138	Eb	70.13N	95.55 E
Ajan [R.S.F.S.R.]	138	Fe	59.38N	106.45 E
Ajan [R.S.F.S.R.]	138	Ie	56.27N	138.10 E
Ajanka	138	Ld	63.40N	167.30 E
Ajanta Range	148	Fd	20.30N	76.00 E
Ajat	134	Kj	52.54N	62.50 E
Ajax Peak	188	Id	45.20N	113.40W
Ajdābiyā	160	Je	30.46N	20.14 E
Ajdabul	136	Ge	52.42N	69.01 E
Ajdar	132	Ke	48.42N	39.13 E
Ajdar, Soloncak-	135	Fd	40.50N	66.50 E
Ajdovščina	128	He	45.53N	13.53 E
Ajdyrlinski	134	Ij	52.03N	59.50 E
Ajhal	138	Gc	66.00N	111.32 E
Ajigasawa	154	Pd	40.47N	140.12 E
Aji-Shima	156	Gb	38.15N	141.30 E
Ajjer, Tassili-n-	158	Hf	25.30N	9.00 E
Ajka	120	Ni	47.06N	17.34 E
Ajke, ozero-	132	Vd	50.55N	61.35 E
Ajkino	134	De	62.15N	49.56 E
'Ajlūn	146	Ff	32.20N	35.45 E
'Ajmah, Jabal al-	146	Fh	29.12N	34.02 E
'Ajmān	144	Id	25.25N	55.27 E
Ajmer	142	Jg	26.27N	74.38 E
Ajnaži/Ainaži	114	Fh	57.52N	24.25 E
Ajni	135	Ge	39.23N	68.36 E
Ajo	182	Ee	32.22N	112.52W
Ajo, Cabo de-	126	Ia	43.31N	3.35W
Ajon, ostrov-	140	Sc	69.50N	168.40 E
Ajoupa-Bouillon	197h	Ab	14.50N	61.08W
Ajsary	136	He	53.05N	71.00 E
Ajtos	130	Kg	42.42N	27.15 E
Aju, Kepulauan-	150	Jf	0.28N	131.03 E
'Ajūz, Jabal al-	146	Dj	25.49N	30.43 E
Ajviekste/Aiviekste	114	Fh	56.36N	25.44 E
Ajzpute/Aizpute	114	Eh	56.45N	21.39 E
Akaba	166	Fd	7.57N	1.03 E
Akabira	154	Qc	43.30N	142.04 E
Akabli	162	Hd	26.42N	1.22 E
Akademika Obručeva, hrebet-	138	Ef	51.30N	96.45 E
Akadomari	156	Fc	37.54N	138.24 E
Aka-Gawa	156	Fb	38.54N	139.50 E
Akagi-San	156	Fc	36.33N	139.11 E
Akaishi-Dake	156	Fd	35.27N	138.09 E
Akaishi-Sanmyaku	156	Fd	35.25N	138.10 E
Akajaure	114	Dc	67.42N	17.30 E
Aka-Jima	156b	Ab	26.14N	127.17 E
Akaki	168	Fd	8.51N	38.48 E
Akala	168	Fb	15.38N	36.12 E
Akan	156a	Db	43.08N	144.07 E
Akan-Gawa	156a	Db	43.00N	144.16 E
Akar	146	Dc	38.38N	31.06 E
Akarnaniká Óri	130	Dk	38.45N	21.00 E
Akaroa	216	Dh	43.48 S	172.59 E
Akasaki	156	Cd	35.31N	133.38 E
'Akasha East	168	Ea	21.05N	30.43 E
Akashi	154	Mg	34.38N	134.59 E
Akbaba Tepe	146	Hc	39.32N	39.33 E
Akbajtal, pereval-	136	Hh	38.31N	73.41 E
Akbou	126	Qh	36.28N	4.32 E
Akbulak	136	Fe	51.03N	55.37 E
Akbura	135	Id	40.34N	72.45 E
Akçaabat	146	Hb	40.59N	39.34 E
Akçadağ	146	Gc	38.21N	37.59 E
Akçakale	146	Hd	36.41N	38.56 E
Akçakara Dağı	146	Ic	38.40N	40.52 E
Akçakoca	146	Db	41.05N	31.09 E
Akçaova [Tur.]	130	Mh	41.03N	29.57 E
Akçaova [Tur.]	130	Ll	37.30N	28.02 E
Akčatau	136	Hf	47.59N	74.02 E
Akçay	130	Mm	36.36N	29.45 E
Akçay	130	Ll	37.50N	28.15 E
Akchâr	158	Ff	20.20N	14.28W
Akdağ [Tur.]	146	Gd	37.53N	37.56 E
Ak Dağ [Tur.]	146	Ib	40.35N	41.46 E
Akdağ [Tur.]	146	Fb	40.57N	35.55 E
Akdağ [Tur.]	146	Cc	39.15N	28.49 E
Akdağ [Tur.]	130	Mk	38.18N	29.58 E
Akdağ [Tur.]	130	Ll	37.42N	28.56 E
Akdağ [Tur.]	130	Jk	38.33N	26.30 E
Ak Dağ [Tur.]	144	Cb	36.32N	29.34 E
Ak Dağlar	146	Gc	39.30N	36.00 E
Ak Dağları	146	Ic	38.40N	40.12 E
Akdağmadeni	146	Fc	39.40N	35.54 E
Akdeniz = Mediterranean Sea (EN)	110	Hh	35.00N	20.00 E
Ak-Dovurak	138	Ef	51.10N	90.40 E
Akechi	156	Ed	35.18N	137.22 E
Ake Eze	166	Gd	5.55N	7.40 E
Akelamo	150	If	1.29N	128.39 E
Akera	132	Oj	39.09N	46.48 E
Åkersberga	116	He	59.29N	18.18 E
Akershus [2]	114	Cf	60.00N	11.10 E
Aketi	160	Jh	2.44N	23.46 E
Akharnaí	130	Gk	38.05N	23.44 E
Akhḑar, Al Jabal al-	158	Je	32.30N	21.30 E
Akhḑar, Al Jabal al-	140	Hg	23.30N	57.00 E
Akhḑar, Wādī al-	146	Gh	28.35N	36.35 E
Akhelóös	130	Ej	38.18N	21.10 E
Akhisar	144	Cb	38.55N	27.51 E
Akhmīm	164	Fd	26.34N	31.44 E
Akhtarīn	146	Gd	36.31N	37.20 E
Aki	156	Ce	33.30N	133.53 E
Akiaki Atoll	216	Nc	18.30 S	139.12W
Akiéni	170	Bc	1.11 S	13.53 E
Akimiski	174	Kd	53.00N	81.20W
Akimovka	132	If	46.42N	35.09 E
Aki-Nada	156	Cd	34.05N	132.40 E
Åkirkeby	116	Fi	55.04N	14.56 E
Akita	142	Qf	39.43N	140.07 E
Akita Ken [2]	154	Pe	39.45N	140.20 E
Akjar	132	Ud	51.50N	58.14 E
Akjoujt	160	Fg	19.44N	14.22W
Akka	162	Fd	29.25N	8.15W
Akkanburluk	134	Mj	52.46N	66.35 E
'Akko	144	Ec	32.55N	35.05 E
Akkol	135	Hc	43.25N	70.47 E
Akköy	146	Bd	37.29N	27.15 E
Akkystau	136	Ff	47.17N	51.03 E
Aklavik	180	Dc	68.14N	135.02W
Aklé 'Âouâna	162	Ff	18.09N	5.40W
Aklé Mseïguîlé	166	Eb	16.20N	4.45W
Akmene/Akmenė	116	Jh	56.14N	22.43 E
Akmenė/Akmene	116	Jh	56.14N	22.43 E
Akmeņrags/Akmenrags	116	Ih	56.54N	20.55 E
Akmenrags/Akmeņrags	116	Ih	56.54N	20.55 E
Akmeqit	152	Cd	37.05N	76.55 E
Akniste	116	Kh	56.10N	25.54 E
Akō	156	Dd	34.45N	134.23 E
Akobo	160	Kh	7.47N	33.01 E
Akobo	168	Ed	7.48N	33.03 E
Akola	142	Jg	20.44N	77.00 E
Akonolinga	166	He	3.46N	12.15 E
Akosombo Dam	166	Fd	6.16N	0.03 E
Akpatok	180	Kd	60.24N	68.05W
Akqi	152	Cc	40.50N	78.01 E
Ákra Ámbelos	130	Gj	39.56N	23.56 E
Ákra Kambanós	130	Hl	37.59N	24.45 E
Akranes	114a	Ab	64.19N	22.06W
Ákra Spathí	130	Gl	37.27N	23.31 E
Åkrehamn	114	Ag	59.16N	5.11 E
Akrítas, Ákra- = Akritas, Cape- (EN)	130	Em	36.43N	21.53 E
Akritas Cape- (EN) = Akrítas, Ákra-	130	Em	36.43N	21.53 E
Akron [Co.-U.S.]	186	Ef	40.10N	103.13W
Akron [Oh.-U.S.]	182	Kc	41.04N	81.31W
Akrotiri	146	Ee	34.36N	32.57 E
Akša	138	Gf	50.17N	113.17 E
Aksaj	132	Oh	43.32N	46.55 E
Aksaj [Kaz.-U.S.S.R.]	136	Fe	51.13N	53.01 E
Aksaj [R.S.F.S.R.]	132	Kf	47.15N	39.52 E
Aksakal	130	Li	40.09N	28.07 E
Aksakovo	134	Gi	54.02N	54.09 E
Aksaray	144	Db	38.23N	34.03 E
Aksay	152	Fd	39.28N	94.15 E
Aksayqin Hu	152	Cd	35.12N	79.50 E
Akşehir	144	Db	38.21N	31.25 E
Aksehir Gölü	146	Dc	38.30N	31.28 E
Akseki	146	Dd	37.02N	31.48 E
Aksenovo-Zilovskoje	138	Gf	53.00N	117.35 E
'Aks-e Rostam	146	Ph	28.23N	54.52 E
Aksoran, gora-	136	Hf	48.25N	75.30 E
Akstafa	132	Ni	41.06N	45.28 E
Akstafa	132	Ni	41.13N	45.27 E
Aksu [China]	142	Ke	41.09N	80.15 E
Aksu [Kaz.-U.S.S.R.]	135	Lb	45.34N	79.30 E
Aksu [Kaz.-U.S.S.R.]	136	He	52.28N	71.59 E
Aksu [Kaz.-U.S.S.R.]	136	Hf	46.20N	78.15 E
Aksu [Tur.]	130	Ll	37.56N	28.56 E
Aksu [Tur.]	146	Dd	36.51N	30.54 E
Aksuat	136	If	47.48N	82.50 E
Aksubajevo	114	Mi	54.52N	50.50 E
Aksu He	140	Ke	40.28N	80.52 E
Aksum	168	Fc	14.07N	38.44 E
Ak-Šyjrak	135	Ld	41.49N	78.44 E
Aktag	152	Dd	36.45N	84.40 E
Aktaš [R.S.F.S.R.]	138	Df	50.18N	87.44 E
Aktaš [Uzb.-U.S.S.R.]	136	Gh	39.55N	65.53 E
Aktau	136	He	50.16N	73.07 E
Aktau, gora-	136	Gg	41.45N	64.30 E
Aktjubinsk	112	Le	50.17N	57.10 E
Aktjubinskaja oblast [3]	136	Ff	48.00N	58.00 E
Ak-Tjuz	135	Kc	42.50N	76.07 E
Akto	152	Cd	39.05N	76.02 E
Aktogaj	136	Hf	47.01N	79.40 E
Akula	170	Db	2.22N	20.11 E
Akun	178a	Eb	54.12N	165.35W
Akune	154	Kh	32.01N	130.11 E
Akure	166	Gd	7.15N	5.12 E
Akureyri	112	Eb	65.40N	18.06W
Akuseki-Jima	154	Jj	29.28N	129.33 E
Akutan	178a	Eb	54.08N	165.46W
Akutan	178a	Eb	54.10N	165.55W
Akyab → Sittwe	142	Lg	20.09N	92.54 E
Akyazı	146	Db	40.41N	30.37 E
Akžajkyn, ozero-	135	Fb	44.55N	67.45 E
Akžal	136	If	49.13N	81.30 E
Ål	116	Cd	60.38N	8.34 E
Alà, Monti di-	128	Dj	40.35N	9.16 E
Alabama [2]	182	Je	32.50N	87.30W
Alabama	174	Kf	31.08N	87.57W
Al'Abbāsīyah	168	Ec	12.10N	31.18 E
Alaca	146	Fb	40.10N	34.51 E
Alaçam	146	Fb	41.37N	35.37 E
Alaçam Dağları	130	Lj	39.20N	28.32 E
Alacant / Alicante	112	Fh	38.21N	0.29W
Alacant / Alicante [3]	126	Lf	38.30N	0.30W
Alacant, Golf d'- / Alicante, Golfo de-	126	Lf	38.20N	0.15W
Alaçati	130	Jk	38.16N	26.23 E
Aladağ	146	Jc	43.35N	39.20 E
Ala Dağ [Tur.]	146	Jb	40.11N	42.49 E
Ala Dağ [Tur.]	146	Ed	37.58N	32.04 E
Alādāgh, Kūh-e-	146	Qd	37.13N	57.30 E
Ala Dağları	146	Fd	37.55N	35.13 E
Aladža	132	Rj	39.21N	53.12 E
Aladža Manastir	130	Lf	43.17N	28.01 E
Alagir	132	Nh	43.01N	44.12 E
Alagna Valsesia	128	Be	45.51N	7.56 E
Alagnon	122	Ji	45.27N	3.19 E
Alagoas [2]	202	Ke	9.30 S	36.30W
Alagoas [2]	202	Ke	9.00 S	36.00W
Alagoinhas	200	Mg	12.07 S	38.26W
Alagón	126	Kc	41.46N	1.07W
Alagón	126	Fe	39.44N	6.53W
Ala Gou	152	Ec	42.42N	89.12 E
Alahanpanjang	150	Dg	1.05 S	100.47 E
Alahärmä	114	Fe	63.14N	22.51 E
Al Aḩmadī	146	Mh	29.05N	48.04 E
Alaid, vulkan-	138	Kf	50.50N	155.33 E
Alaior / Alayor	126	Qe	39.56N	4.08 E
Alajärvi	114	Fe	63.00N	23.49 E
Alajku	136	Hg	40.18N	74.29 E
Alajski hrebet	140	Jf	39.45N	72.30 E
Alajuela	190	Hf	10.01N	84.13W
Alajuela [3]	194	Eh	10.30N	84.30W
Alajuela, Lago-	194	Hi	9.05N	79.24W
Alakol, ozero-	140	Ke	46.05N	81.50 E
Alakurtti	114	Hc	66.59N	30.20 E
Alalakeiki Channel	221a	Ec	20.35N	156.30W
Al 'Alamayn	160	Je	30.49N	28.57 E
Alalau, Rio-	202	Fd	0.30 S	61.10W
Al Amādīyah	146	Jd	37.06N	43.29 E
Alamagan Island	208	Fc	17.36N	145.50 E
Al 'Amārah	144	Gc	31.50N	47.09 E
'Alam ar Rūm, Ra's-	146	Bg	31.22N	27.21 E
Alāmarvdasht	146	Oi	27.52N	52.34 E
Alamashindo	168	Ge	4.51N	42.04 E
Alamata	168	Fc	12.25N	39.37 E
Alameda	186	Ci	35.11N	106.37W
Alaminos	150	Gc	16.10N	119.59 E
Al 'Āmirīyah	146	Cg	31.01N	29.48 E
Alamito Creek	186	Dl	29.31N	104.17W
Alamitos, Sierra de los-	192	Hd	26.20N	102.15W
Alamo	188	Hh	37.22N	115.10W
'Alāmo	168	Ge	4.23N	43.09 E
Alamogordo	182	Fe	32.54N	105.57W
Álamos	190	Cc	27.01N	108.56W
Álamos, Sierra-	192	Gc	28.25N	105.00W
Alamosa	182	Fd	37.28N	105.52W
Al Anbār [3]	146	If	34.00N	42.00 E
Åland/Ahvenanmaa [2]	114	Ef	60.15N	20.00 E
Åland/Ahvenanmaa	110	Hc	60.15N	20.00 E
Älandsbro	116	Gb	62.40N	17.50 E
Ålandshav	116	Hd	60.00N	19.30 E
Alange	126	Ff	38.47N	6.15W
Alanje	194	Fi	8.24N	82.33W
Alanya	144	Db	36.33N	32.01 E
Alaotra, Lac-	172	Hc	17.30 S	48.30 E
Alapaha River	184	Fj	30.26N	83.06W
Alapajevsk	136	Gd	57.52N	61.42 E
Alaplı	146	Db	41.08N	31.25 E
Al 'Aqabah = Aqaba (EN)	144	Dd	29.31N	35.00 E
Al 'Aqabah aş Şaghīrah	146	Ej	24.14N	32.53 E
Al 'Arabīyah As-Su'ūdīyah = Saudi Arabia (EN) [1]	142	Gg	25.00N	45.00 E
Alarcón, Embalse de-	126	Je	39.45N	2.20W
Al 'Arīsh	164	Fc	31.08N	33.48 E
Al 'Armah	146	Lj	25.30N	46.30 E
Al Arţāwīyah	146	Ki	26.30N	45.20 E
Alas, Selat-	150	Gh	8.40 S	116.40 E
Al 'Aşab	146	Pk	23.20N	54.10 E
Alaşehir	146	Cc	38.21N	28.32 E
Al Ashkharah	144	Ie	21.47N	59.30 E
Al 'Āshūrīyah	146	Jg	31.02N	43.05 E
Alaska [2]	178	Ic	65.00N	153.00W
Alaska	174	Dc	65.00N	153.00W
Alaska, Gulf of-	174	Ed	58.00N	146.00W
Alaska Peninsula	174	Dd	57.00N	158.00W
Alaska Range	174	Ec	62.30N	150.00W
Alassio	128	Cf	44.00N	8.10 E
Alastaro	116	Jd	60.57N	22.51 E
Alat	135	De	39.26N	63.48 E
Alataw Shan	152	Cb	45.00N	80.00 E
Alataw Shankou = Dzungarian Gate (EN)	140	Ke	45.25N	82.25 E
Al 'Athāmīn	146	Jg	30.35N	43.40 E
Alatri	128	Hi	41.43N	13.21 E
Al 'Aţrun	160	Jg	18.11N	26.36 E
Alatyr	136	Ee	54.50N	46.36 E
Alatyr	114	Li	54.52N	46.36 E
Álava [3]	126	Jb	42.50N	2.45W
Alava, Cape-	188	Cb	48.10N	124.43W
Alaverdi	136	Eg	41.08N	44.37 E
Alavījeh	146	Nf	33.03N	51.05 E
Alavo/Alavus	114	Fe	62.35N	23.37 E
Alavus/Alavo	114	Fe	62.35N	23.37 E
Al 'Awāliq	144	Gg	14.15N	46.30 E
Al 'Awāriq	168	Ha	20.25N	48.40 E
Al 'Awsajīyah	146	Ki	26.04N	44.08 E
'Ālayh	146	Ff	33.48N	35.36 E
Al 'Ayn [Oman]	144	Ie	24.15N	55.45 E
Al 'Ayn [Sau.Ar.]	146	Hj	25.04N	38.06 E
Alayor / Alaior	126	Qe	39.56N	4.08 E
Al 'Ayyōţ	146	Dh	29.37N	31.15 E
Al A'ẓamīyah	146	Kf	33.23N	44.22 E
Alazani	132	Oi	41.03N	46.40 E
Alazeja	138	Kb	70.55N	153.40 E
Al'Azīzīyah	164	Bc	32.32N	13.01 E
Alazores, Puerto de los-	126	Hg	37.05N	4.15W
Alb [F.R.G.]	124	Ke	49.04N	8.20 E
Alb [F.R.G.]	120	Ei	47.35N	8.08 E
Alba	128	Cf	44.42N	8.02 E
Alba [2]	130	Gc	46.08N	23.30 E
Alba Adriatica	128	Hh	42.50N	13.56 E
Al Bāb	146	Gd	36.22N	37.31 E
Albac	130	Fc	46.27N	22.58 E
Albacete	112	Fh	38.59N	1.51W
Albacete [3]	126	Kf	38.50N	2.00W
Al Badārī	164	Fd	26.59N	31.25 E
Alba de Tormes	126	Gd	40.49N	5.31W
Al Bādi	146	Ie	35.56N	41.32 E
Al Badi	164	Ie	22.02N	46.34 E
Ålbæk	116	Dg	57.36N	10.25 E

Index Symbols

[1] Independent Nation · [2] State, Region · [3] District, County · [4] Municipality · [5] Colony, Dependency · Continent · Physical Region · Historical or Cultural Region · Mount, Mountain · Volcano · Hill · Mountains, Mountain Range · Hills, Escarpment · Plateau, Upland · Pass, Gap · Plain, Lowland · Delta · Salt Flat · Valley, Canyon · Crater, Cave · Karst Features · Depression · Polder · Desert, Dunes · Forest, Woods · Heath, Steppe · Oasis · Cape, Point · Coast, Beach · Cliff · Peninsula · Isthmus · Sandbank · Island · Atoll · Rock, Reef · Islands, Archipelago · Rocks, Reefs · Coral Reef · Well, Spring · Geyser · River, Stream · Waterfall, Rapids · River Mouth, Estuary · Lake · Salt Lake · Intermittent Lake · Reservoir · Swamp, Pond · Canal · Glacier · Ice Shelf, Pack Ice · Ocean · Sea · Gulf, Bay · Strait, Fjord · Lagoon · Bank · Seamount · Tablemount · Ridge · Shelf · Basin · Escarpment, Sea Scarp · Fracture · Trench, Abyss · National Park, Reserve · Point of Interest · Recreation Site · Cave, Cavern · Historic Site · Ruins · Wall, Walls · Church, Abbey · Temple · Scientific Station · Railway station · Airport · Port · Military installation · Lighthouse · Mine · Tunnel · Dam, Bridge

Ålbæk Bugt 116 Dg 57.35N 10.30 E
Al Baḥrah 146 Lh 29.40N 47.52 E
Al Baḥr al Aḥmar [3] 168 Fb 19.50N 35.30 E
Al Baḥrayn 140 Hg 26.00N 50.30 E
Al Baḥrayn = Bahrain (EN) 142 Hg 26.00N 50.29 E
Albaida 126 Lf 38.51N 0.31W
Al Bahah 130 Gc 46.04N 23.35 E
Albalate del Arzobispo 126 Lc 41.07N 0.31W
Al Balqā' [3] 146 Ff 31.50N 35.40 E
Al Balyanā 168 Fd 26.14N 32.00 E
Alban 122 Ik 43.54N 2.28 E
Albanel, Lac- 180 Kf 51.05N 73.05W
Albani, Colli- 128 Gi 41.45N 12.45 E
Albania (EN)=Shqiperia [1] 112 Hg 41.00N 20.00 E
Albano, Lago- 128 Gi 41.45N 12.40 E
Albano Laziale 128 Gi 41.44N 12.39 E
Albany 174 Kd 52.17N 81.31W
Albany [Austl.] 210 Ch 35.02S 117.53 E
Albany [Ga.-U.S.] 182 Ke 31.35N 84.10W
Albany [Ky.-U.S.] 182 Je 36.42N 85.08W
Albany [N.Y.-U.S.] 176 Le 42.39N 73.45W
Albany [Or.-U.S.] 182 Cc 44.38N 123.06W
Alba Posse 204 Eh 27.33S 54.42W
Albardón 206 Gd 31.26S 68.32W
Albarracin 126 Kd 40.25N 1.26W
Albarracin, Sierra de- 126 Kd 40.30N 1.30W
Al Başāliyah Qiblī 146 Ej 25.06N 32.47 E
Al Başrah 146 Lg 30.30N 47.27 E
Al Başrah = Basra (EN) 142 Gf 30.30N 47.47 E
Al Batḥā' 146 Kg 31.07N 45.54 E
Al Bāṭin 146 Lh 29.00N 46.35 E
Al Bāṭinah 140 Hg 23.45N 57.20 E
Albatross Bank (EN) 178 Ie 56.10N 152.20W
Albatross Bay 212 Ib 12.45S 141.43 E
Albatross Plateau (EN) 106 Mi 10.00N 103.00W
Albatross Point 218 Fc 38.07S 174.40 E
Al Batrūn 146 Fe 34.15N 35.39 E
Al Bawīṭī 164 Ed 28.21N 28.52 E
Al Bayāḍ 140 Gg 22.00N 47.00 E
Al Bayḍā' 160 Je 32.46N 21.43 E
Al Bayḍā' [3] 164 Dc 32.00N 21.30 E
Al Bayḍā' [Lib.] 164 Cd 28.21N 18.58 E
Al Bayḍā' [Yem.] 164 Ij 13.58N 45.35 E
Albegna 128 Fh 42.30N 11.11 E
Albemarle 184 Gh 35.21N 80.12W
Albemarle Sound 182 Ld 36.03N 76.12W
Albenga 128 Cf 44.03N 8.13 E
Alberche 126 He 39.58N 4.46W
Alberdi 206 Ic 26.10S 58.09W
Albères, Chaîne des- 122 Il 42.28N 2.56 E
Alberes 122 Il 42.28N 2.56 E
Albergaria-a-Velha 126 Dd 40.42N 8.29W
Alberic / Alberique 126 Le 39.07N 0.31W
Alberique / Alberic 126 Le 39.07N 0.31W
Alberobello 128 Lj 40.47N 17.16 E
Albert 122 Id 50.00N 2.39 E
Albert, Canal-/Albert Kanaal =Albert Canal (EN) 122 Lc 51.10N 5.10 E
Albert, Lake- [Afr.] 158 Kh 1.40N 31.00 E
Albert, Lake- [Or.-U.S.] 188 Ee 42.38N 120.13W
Albert, Lake- (EN)=Mobuto Sese Seko, Lac- 158 Kh 1.40N 31.00 E
Alberta [3] 180 Gf 55.00N 115.00W
Albert Canal (EN)=Albert, Canal-/Albert Kanaal 122 Lc 51.10N 5.10 E
Albert Canal (EN)=Albert Kanaal/Albert, Canal- 122 Lc 51.10N 5.10 E
Albert Edward, Mount- 212 Ja 8.23S 147.27 E
Albert Edward Bay 180 Hc 69.35N 103.10W
Alberti 206 He 35.02S 60.16W
Albertirsa 120 Pf 47.15N 19.37 E
Albert Kanaal/Albert, Canal- =Albert Canal (EN) 122 Lc 51.10N 5.10 E
Albert Lea 182 Id 43.39N 93.22W
Albert Nile 158 Kh 3.36N 32.00 E
Albertville [Al.-U.S.] 184 Dh 34.16N 86.12W
Albertville [Fr.] 122 Mi 45.41N 6.23 E
Albestroff 124 If 48.56N 6.51 E
Albi 122 Ik 43.56N 2.09 E
Albia 186 Jf 41.02N 92.48W
Al Bid' 146 Fh 28.28N 35.01 E
Albina 202 Hb 5.30N 54.03W
Albina, Ponta- 158 Ij 15.51S 11.44 E
Albino 128 De 45.46N 9.47 E
Albion [Mi.-U.S.] 184 Gd 42.15N 84.45W
Albion [Nb.-U.S.] 186 Hf 41.42N 98.00W
Albion [N.Y.-U.S.] 184 If 43.15N 78.12W
Al Biqā' [3] 146 Ge 34.00N 36.00 E
Al Biqā' 146 Ge 34.10N 36.10 E
Al Bi'r al Jadīd 146 Hi 26.04N 36.15 E
Al Birk 144 Hi 18.13N 41.33 E
Albis 128 Cc 47.20N 8.30 E
Albo, Monte- 128 Dj 40.32N 9.35 E
Albocàsser / Albocàsser 126 Md 40.21N 0.02 E
Albocàsser / Albocàsser 126 Md 40.21N 0.02 E
Alborán, Isla de- 110 Fh 35.58N 3.02W
Alboran Basin (EN) 128 Ii 36.00N 4.00W
Ålborg 112 Gd 57.03N 9.56 E
Ålborg Bugt 116 Ch 56.45N 10.30 E
Alborz, Reshteh-ye Kūhhā-ye- = Elburz Mountains (EN) 140 Hf 36.00N 53.00 E
Albox 126 Jg 37.23N 2.08W
Albret, Pays d'- 122 Fj 44.10N 0.20W
Ālbū 'Alī 146 He 34.49N 43.35 E
Albufeira 126 Df 37.05N 8.15W
Albū Gharz, Sabkhat- 146 He 34.45N 41.15 E
Al Buhayrat [3] 168 Dd 7.00N 29.30 E
Al Bumbah 164 Dc 32.26N 23.12 E
Albuñol 126 Ih 36.47N 3.12W
Albuquerque [Braz.] 202 Jd 19.23S 57.28W
Albuquerque [N.M.-U.S.] 176 Hf 35.05N 106.40W
Albuquerque, Cayos de- 190 Hf 12.10N 81.50W
Al Buraymī 146 Gc 34.15N 36.46 E
Al Burmah 162 Ic 31.45N 9.02 E

Alburquerque 126 Ee 39.13N 7.00W
Albury [Austl.] 210 Fh 36.05S 146.55 E
Albury [N.Z.] 218 Df 44.14S 170.53 E
Al Buṭanah 158 Kg 15.00N 35.00 E
Al Buṭayn 146 Kj 25.52N 45.50 E
Alby 116 Fb 62.30N 15.28 E
Alcácer do Sal 126 Df 38.22N 8.30W
Alcàcovas 126 Df 38.25N 8.13W
Alcalá de Chivert / Alcalà de Xivert 126 Md 40.18N 0.14 E
Alcalá de Guadaira 126 Gg 37.20N 5.50W
Alcalá de Henares 126 Id 40.29N 3.22W
Alcalá del Júcar 126 Ke 39.12N 1.26W
Alcalá de los Gazules 126 Gh 36.28N 5.44W
Alcalá del Rio 126 Gg 37.31N 5.59W
Alcalá de Xivert / Alcalà de Chivert 126 Md 40.18N 0.14 E
Alcalá la Real 126 Ig 37.28N 3.56W
Alcamo 128 Gm 37.59N 12.58 E
Alcanadre 126 Mc 41.37N 0.12 E
Alcañices 126 Fc 41.42N 6.21W
Alcañiz 126 Lc 41.03N 0.08W
Alcántara 128 Df 37.49N 15.16 E
Alcántara [Braz.] 202 Jd 2.24S 44.24W
Alcántara [Sp.] 126 Fe 39.43N 6.53W
Alcántara, Embalse de- 126 Fe 39.45N 6.48W
Alcantarilla 126 Kg 37.58N 1.13W
Alcaraz 126 Jf 38.40N 2.29W
Alcaraz, Sierra de- 126 Jf 38.35N 2.25W
Alcaudete 126 Hg 37.36N 4.05W
Alcázar de San Juan 126 Ie 39.24N 3.12W
Alcester 219a Ac 9.33S 152.25 E
Alcira/Alzira 126 Le 39.09N 0.26W
Alcobaça [Braz.] 202 Kg 17.30S 39.13W
Alcobaça [Port.] 126 De 39.33N 8.59W
Alcobendas 126 Id 40.32N 3.38W
Alcoi/Alcoy 126 Lf 38.42N 0.28W
Alcolea del Pinar 126 Jc 41.02N 2.28W
Alcorta 204 Bk 33.32S 61.07W
Alcoutim 126 Eg 37.28N 7.28W
Alcoy/Alcoi 126 Lf 38.42N 0.28W
Alcubierre, Sierra de- 126 Lc 41.44N 0.29W
Alcudia/Alcúdia de Mallorca 126 Pe 39.52N 3.07 E
Alcudia, Badia d'-/Alcudia, Bahia de- 126 Pe 39.48N 3.13 E
Alcudia, Bahia de-/Alcúdia, Badia d'- 126 Pe 39.48N 3.13 E
Alcúdia, Sierra de- 126 Hf 38.35N 4.35W
Alcúdia de Mallorca/Alcudia 126 Pe 39.52N 3.07 E
Aldabra Group 172b Ab 9.25S 46.22 E
Aldabra Islands 158 Li 9.25S 46.22 E
Aldama [Mex.] 190 Cc 28.51N 105.54W
Aldama [Mex.] 192 Jf 22.55N 98.04W
Aldan 142 Od 58.37N 125.24 E
Aldan 140 Oc 63.28N 129.35 E
Aldan Plateau (EN) = Aldanskoje nagorje 140 Od 57.30N 127.30 E
Aldanskoje nagorje = Aldan Plateau (EN) 140 Od 57.30N 127.30 E
Aldarhan 152 Gb 47.42N 96.36 E
Alde 124 Db 52.10N 1.32 E
Aldeburgh 118 Oi 52.09N 1.35 E
Aldeia 204 Be 18.12S 55.10W
Aldeia, Serra da- 204 Ic 17.00S 46.50W
Alderney 118 Kl 49.43N 2.12W
Aldershot 124 Bc 51.15N 0.46W
Alderson 188 Jx 50.18N 111.26W
Aledo 186 Kf 41.12N 90.45W
Alegranza 162 Fg 17.03N 13.53W
Alegranza 162 Ed 29.23N 13.30W
Alegre 202 Jh 20.46S 41.32W
Alegre, Rio- 204 Cb 15.14S 59.58W
Alegrete 206 Jc 29.46S 55.46W
Alej 138 Df 52.50N 83.35 E
Alejandra 204 Ci 29.54S 59.50W
Alejandro Selkirk, Isla- 198 Ni 33.45S 80.46W
Alejsk 138 Df 52.28N 82.45 E
Aleksandrija 132 He 48.40N 33.07 E
Aleksandrov 136 Be 56.25N 38.42 E
Aleksandrov Gaj 136 Ee 50.08N 48.32 E
Aleksandrovka 132 Mf 48.59N 32.13 E
Aleksandrovsk 134 Hg 59.10N 57.35 E
Aleksandrovskoje 132 Md 44.39N 43.00 E
Aleksandrovsk-Sahalinsk 142 Qd 50.54N 142.10 E
Aleksandrów Kujawski 120 Od 52.52N 18.42 E
Aleksandrów Łódzki 120 Oe 51.49N 19.19 E
Alem [Arg.] 206 Ic 27.31S 55.15W
Alem [Swe.] 116 Dh 56.57N 16.23 E
Alem Maya 168 Mg 9.27N 41.58 E
Alençon 122 Gf 48.26N 0.05 E
Alenquer 202 Hd 1.56S 54.46W
Alenuihaha Channel 218 Oc 20.26N 156.00W
Alepé 160 Ff 5.30N 3.39W
Aleppo (EN)=Ḩalab 144 Ec 36.14N 37.10 E
Aléria, Plaine d'- 122a Ma 42.06N 9.31 E
Alert 172 Ma 82.30N 62.00W
Alert Bay 188 Ba 50.35N 126.55W
Aleşd 130 Hc 47.04N 22.25 E
Ålestrup 116 Ch 56.42N 9.30 E
Alessandria 128 Ce 44.54N 8.37 E
Ålesund 112 Gc 62.28N 6.09 E
Aleutian Basin (EN) 174 Ad 57.00N 177.00 E
Aleutian Islands 174 Bd 52.00N 176.00W

Aleutian Range 174 Dd 59.00N 155.00W
Aleutian Trench (EN) 106 Je 51.00N 179.00 E
Alexander, Cape- 214 Fi 6.35S 156.30 E
Alexander Archipelago 174 Fd 56.30N 134.00W
Alexanderbaai 172 Be 28.40S 16.30 E
Alexander City 182 Je 32.56N 85.57W
Alexander Island 222 Qe 71.00S 70.00W
Alexandra 216 Ci 45.15S 169.24 E
Alexandra Fiord 180 Ka 79.17N 75.00W
Alexandretta (EN)= İskenderun 142 Ff 36.37N 36.07 E
Alexandretta, Gulf of- (EN) = İskenderun Körfezi 144 Eb 36.30N 35.40 E
Alexandria 172 Fi 40.38N 22.27 E
Alexándria 130 Ff 33.39S 26.24 E
Alexandria [Austl.] 212 He 19.05S 136.40 E
Alexandria [La.-U.S.] 176 Jf 31.18N 92.27W
Alexandria [Mn.-U.S.] 182 Hb 45.53N 95.22W
Alexandria [Rom.] 130 If 43.59N 25.20 E
Alexandria (EN)=Al Iskandariyah [Eg.] 184 If 38.49N 77.06W
Alexandria, Lake- 212 Hg 35.25S 139.10 E
Alexandrita 202 Hg 19.42S 50.27W
Alexandroúpolis 112 Ig 40.51N 25.52 E
Alf 120 Df 50.03N 7.07 E
Alfabia, Sierra de- 126 Od 39.45N 2.48 E
Al Fardah 146 Kd 40.21N 1.07W
Alfaro 126 Kb 42.11N 1.45W
Al Fāshir 160 Jg 13.38N 25.21 E
Al Fashn 168 Ec 28.49N 30.54 E
Alfatar 130 Kf 43.57N 27.17 E
Al Fathah 146 Je 35.04N 43.34 E
Al Fāw 144 Gd 29.58N 48.29 E
Al Fawwārah 146 Ji 26.03N 43.05 E
Al Fayyūm 160 Ke 29.19N 30.58 E
Alfback 124 Ja 50.03N 7.08 E
Al Fifi 168 Dc 10.03N 25.01 E
Alfiós 130 El 37.37N 21.27 E
Alföld 110 If 47.15N 20.05 E
Alfonsine 128 Gf 44.30N 12.03 E
Alford 124 Ca 53.15N 0.11 E
Al Fuḩayḩīl 146 Lg 30.58N 46.45 E
Al Fuhūd 146 Kg 30.58N 46.43 E
Al Fujayrah 144 Id 25.06N 56.21 E
Al Fūlah 168 Kf 11.48N 28.24 E
Al Fuqahā' 164 Cd 27.50N 16.21 E
Al Furāt=Euphrates (EN) 144 Gf 30.00N 47.25 E
Al Fuwayriṭ 146 Ni 26.02N 51.22 E
Alga 136 Ff 49.55N 57.20 E
Algador 126 Ie 39.55N 3.53W
Algarrobo 194 Jh 10.12N 74.04W
Algarve 110 Fh 37.10N 8.15W
Algarve 126 Dg 37.10N 8.15W
Al Ghāb 146 Gb 35.25N 36.25 E
Al Gharbi 162 Dh 34.40N 11.13 E
Al Ghāt 146 Ki 26.00N 45.00 E
Al Ghaydah 144 Hi 16.12N 52.15 E
Al Ghazālah 146 Ie 26.47N 41.23 E
Alghero 128 Cj 40.33N 8.19 E
Alghero, Rada d'- 128 Cj 40.35N 8.20 E
Ålghult 116 Fg 57.01N 15.34 E
Al Ghurāb 146 Dj 25.20N 30.24 E
Al Ghurayfah 168 Hb 25.09N 38.42 E
Al Ghurdaqah 168 Fc 27.14N 33.50 E
Algiers (EN)=Al Jazā'ir 160 He 36.47N 3.03 E
Algiers (EN)=Al Jazā'ir [3] 162 Hb 36.35N 3.00 E
Algoa Bay 158 Jl 33.50S 25.50 E
Algodoeiro, Serra do- 204 Jc 16.30S 44.45W
Algoma 186 Mb 44.36N 87.27W
Algoma Uplands 184 Fb 47.00N 83.35W
Algona 186 Ie 43.04N 94.14W
Algonquin Park 184 Hc 45.50N 78.26W
Algrange 124 Ie 49.21N 6.03 E
Al Habakah 146 Jh 29.51N 42.16 E
Al Hadd 146 Ig 21.31N 59.28 E
Al Hadīdah 144 Ig 21.31N 50.58 E
Al Hadīthah 146 Je 34.07N 42.23 E
Al Hadīthah 146 Fg 30.30N 37.08 E
Al Haḍr 146 Je 35.35N 42.44 E
Al Haffah 146 Gb 35.35N 36.02 E
Al Hā'ir 146 Lj 24.23N 46.50 E
Al Hajar 146 Hb 16.08N 47.50 E
Al Hajarah 146 Jg 30.25N 44.30 E
Al Halfāyeh 146 Kf 31.48N 45.59 E
Alhama 126 Kb 42.11N 1.45W
Al Hamād 144 Ff 32.00N 39.30 E
Alhama de Granada 126 Ih 37.00N 3.59W
Alhama de Murcia 126 Kg 37.51N 1.25W
Alhambra, Sierra- 126 Ih 37.35N 4.13W
Al Hammādah 162 Ic 33.54N 9.48 E
Al Hammām 160 Je 30.50N 29.23 E
Al Hammām [Iraq] 146 Kf 31.08N 44.04 E
Al Hamrā 146 Pj 25.42N 55.47 E
Al Harīq 146 Kj 24.08N 46.27 E
Al Harrah 146 Gg 31.00N 38.00 E
Al Harrah 164 Fd 32.30N 37.45 E
Al Harūj al Aswad 158 If 27.00N 17.10 E
Al Hasā' 146 Lg 30.49N 35.59 E
Al Hasa' 146 Ph 26.35N 48.10 E

Al Hasakah 144 Fb 36.29N 40.45 E
Al Hasan 146 Je 34.39N 43.43 E
Al Hasani 146 Gj 24.58N 37.05 E
Alhaurin el Grande 126 Hh 36.38N 4.41W
Al Hawāmidīyah 146 Dh 29.54N 31.15 E
Al Hawātah 168 Ec 13.25N 34.38 E
Al Hawjā' 146 Hh 28.59N 38.34 E
Al Hawrah 168 Hc 13.49N 47.35 E
Al Hayy 144 Gc 32.10N 46.03 E
Al Hayyāniyah 146 Jh 28.42N 42.18 E
Al Hayz 146 Dd 28.02N 28.39 E
Al Hibāk 144 He 20.20N 53.10 E
Al Hijāz 140 Fg 24.30N 38.30 E
Al Hijāz 144 Eb 36.30N 35.40 E
Al Hillah [Iraq] 130 Fi 40.38N 22.27 E
Al Hillah [Sau.Ar.] 164 Ie 23.50N 46.51 E
Al Hindākīyah 144 Fe 24.51N 40.31 E
Al Hindiyah 146 Kf 32.32N 44.13 E
Al Hinnāh 146 Mi 26.56N 48.45 E
Al Hirmil 146 Ge 34.23N 36.23 E
Al Hoceima 162 Gb 35.15N 3.55W
Al Hoceima [3] 162 Gb 35.00N 4.15W
Alhucemas, Peñon de- 162 Ii 35.13N 3.53W
Al Hudaydah 142 Gh 14.48N 42.57 E
Al Hufrah 164 Cd 29.30N 17.55 E
Al Hufrah 146 Hh 28.49N 38.15 E
Al Hufūf 142 Gg 25.22N 49.34 E
Al Hūj 146 Hh 29.00N 38.25 E
Al Hunayy 144 Fg 13.58N 47.40 E
Al Husayhisah 168 Ec 14.44N 33.18 E
Al Huwayyiṭ 146 Ij 25.36N 40.23 E
'Alī, Sadd al- 164 Ee 23.54N 32.52 E
Aliābād 164 Pd 36.56N 54.50 E
'Alīābād [Iran] 146 Me 36.37N 51.33 E
'Alīābād [Iran] 146 Le 35.04N 46.58 E
'Alīābād, Kūh-e- 144 Id 28.37N 55.51 E
Aliaga 126 Ld 40.40N 0.42W
Aliağa 146 Bc 38.48N 26.59 E
Aliákmon 130 Fi 40.30N 22.47 E
'Alī al Gharbi 146 Lf 32.27N 46.41 E
'Alī ash Sharqī 146 Lf 32.07N 46.44 E
Ali-Bajramly 146 Eh 39.55N 48.57 E
Alibej, ozero- 130 Nd 45.50N 30.00 E
Alibey Adası 130 Jj 39.20N 26.38 E
Alibo 168 Fd 9.53N 37.05 E
Alibunar 130 Fc 45.04N 20.58 E
Alicante/Alacant 112 Fh 38.21N 0.29W
Alicante/Alacant [3] 126 Lf 38.30N 0.30W
Alicante, Golfo de-/Alacant, Golf d'- 126 Lf 38.20N 0.15W
Alice [S.Afr.] 172 Df 32.47S 26.50 E
Alice [Tx.-U.S.] 182 Hf 27.45N 98.04W
Alice, Punta- 128 Ik 39.12N 17.09 E
Alice Springs 210 Eg 23.42S 133.53 E
Aliceville 184 Cc 33.08N 88.09W
Alicudi 128 Il 38.30N 14.20 E
Alīgarh 142 Jg 28.02N 78.17 E
Al Iglim al Janūbiyah = Southern Region (EN) [2] 168 Dd 6.00N 30.00 E
Alīgūdarz 146 Mf 33.24N 49.41 E
Alihe→Oroqen Zizhiqi 152 La 50.35N 123.42 E
Alijó 126 Ec 41.16N 7.28W
Alijos, Rocas- 190 Ad 24.57N 115.44W
'Al Ijūq, Kūh-e- 146 Ng 31.30N 51.45 E
Al Ikhwan 146 Fi 26.19N 34.52 E
Al Ikhwan 140 Hh 12.08N 53.10 E
Alima 158 Ii 1.36S 16.36 E
Al Imārāt al 'Arabīyah al Muttaḩidah = United Arab Emirates (EN) [1] 144 Hg 24.00N 54.00 E
Alimiä 130 Km 36.16N 27.43 E
Alindao 168 Se 5.02N 21.13 E
Alinglapalap Atoll 208 Hd 7.08N 168.16 E
Alingsås 114 Ct 57.56N 12.31 E
Aliquippa 184 Ge 40.38N 80.16W
Al 'Irq→Iraq (EN) [1] 142 Gf 33.00N 44.00 E
Al 'Irqah 144 Gi 13.40N 47.18 E
Ali-Sabjeh 168 Cc 11.08N 42.43 E
'Alī Shāh 'Avaẕ 146 Ne 35.39N 51.04 E
Aliskerovo 138 Le 67.52N 167.40 E
Al Iskandarīyah [Iraq] 164 Fc 30.35N 32.16 E
Al Istiwā'īyah al Gharbīyah 168 Dd 5.20N 28.30 E
Al Istiwā'īyah al Sharkīyah [3] 168 Ed 5.20N 33.50 E
Alistráti 130 Gh 41.04N 23.58 E
Alitak, Cape- 178 Ie 56.51N 154.21W
Alite Reef 219a Ec 8.53S 160.38 E
Alitus/Alytus 136 Ad 54.25N 24.08 E
Alivérion 130 Hk 38.24N 24.02 E
Aliwal North 172 Df 30.44S 26.42 E
Al Jabalayn 168 Ec 12.36N 32.48 E
Al Jadīdah [Eg.] 146 Cj 25.34N 28.51 E
Al Jadīdah [Sau.Ar.] 146 Ig 27.20N 39.32 E
Al Jafr 146 Fg 30.18N 36.15 E
Al Jāfūrah 146 Nj 23.25N 50.17 E
Al Jaghbūb 160 Jf 29.45N 24.31 E
Al Jahrah 146 Lg 31.17N 46.06 E
Al Jalāmīd 146 Hf 31.31N 39.36 E
Al Jamalīyah 146 Ni 25.37N 51.05 E
Al Jamm 162 Jc 35.18N 10.43 E
Al Janā'in 146 Jc 35.18N 10.09 E
Al Janūb [3] 146 Ff 33.20N 35.30 E
Al Jarawī 146 Pj 24.12N 51.31 E
Al Jarrah 146 Lg 30.42N 47.56 E
Al Jawf [Lib.] 160 Jf 24.12N 23.18 E
Al Jawf [Sau.Ar.] 142 Fg 29.45N 39.52 E
Al Jazā'ir→Algeria (EN) [1] 160 Fc 28.00N 3.00 E
Al Jazā'ir→Algiers (EN) 160 He 36.47N 3.03 E
Al Jazā'ir→Algiers (EN) [3] 162 Hb 36.35N 3.00 E
Al Jazā'ir-El Harrach 162 Ph 36.43N 3.08 E

Al Jazīrah [3] 168 Ec 14.40N 33.30 E
Al Jazīrah [Asia] 140 Gf 35.10N 42.00 E
Al Jazīrah [Sud.] 158 Kg 14.25N 33.00 E
Aljezur 126 Gh 36.31N 5.37W
Al Jīfārah 158 Ie 32.30N 11.45 E
Al Jiwā' 144 He 23.00N 54.00 E
Al Jīzah→Giza (EN) 160 Ke 30.01N 31.13 E
Al Jubayl 144 Gd 27.01N 49.40 E
Al Jubaylah 146 Lj 24.54N 46.27 E
Al Junaynah [Sau.Ar.] 146 He 26.17N 42.48 E
Al Junaynah [Sud.] 160 Jg 13.27N 22.27 E
Al Juraid 146 Mi 27.11N 49.52 E
Aljustrel 126 Df 37.52N 8.10W
Al Kaba'ish 146 Lg 30.58N 47.00 E
Al Kāf 162 Ib 36.11N 8.43 E
Al Kāf [3] 162 Ib 36.00N 9.00 E
Alkali Lake 188 Ff 41.42N 119.50W
Al Kāmilīn 168 Eb 15.05N 33.11 E
Al Karak 146 Fg 31.11N 35.42 E
Al Karak [3] 146 Kf 31.11N 35.42 E
Al Karkh 146 Kf 33.20N 44.20 E
Al Karnak 164 Ee 25.43N 32.39 E
Al Kawah 168 Ec 13.44N 32.30 E
Al Kāẓimīyah 146 Kf 33.22N 44.20 E
Alken 124 Kc 50.52N 5.18 E
Al Khabrā' 144 Fe 26.04N 43.33 E
Al Khābūra 144 Ie 23.50N 57.18 E
Al-Khalij al- 'Arabi=Persian Gulf (EN) 140 Hg 27.00N 51.00 E
Al Khalīl 146 Ef 31.32N 35.06 E
Al Khalīl 146 Fe 33.33N 35.05 E
Al Khāliş 146 Kf 33.51N 44.32 E
Al Khandaq 168 Eb 18.36N 30.34 E
Al Khārijah 146 Ee 25.26N 30.33 E
Al Khārijah 146 Lj 24.10N 47.30 E
Al Kharṭūm→Khartoum (EN) [3] 168 Eb 15.50N 33.00 E
Al Kharṭūm→Khartoum (EN) 160 Kg 15.36N 32.32 E
Al Kharṭūm Baḩrī= Khartoum North (EN) 160 Kg 15.38N 32.33 E
Al Khaşab 146 Qi 26.12N 56.15 E
Al Khaṭṭ 146 Qk 25.37N 56.01 E
Al Khawr 144 Ni 25.40N 51.30 E
Al Khidr 146 Kg 31.12N 45.33 E
Al Khubar 146 Be 26.17N 50.12 E
Al Khufayfiyah 144 Fe 24.55N 44.42 E
Al Khums 160 Ie 32.39N 14.16 E
Al Khunn 146 Bc 31.20N 14.10 E
Al Khuwayr 146 Ni 23.18N 49.15 E
Al Kidn 144 Ia 22.30N 54.00 E
Al Kifl 146 Kf 32.14N 44.22 E
Al Kir'ānah 146 Nj 25.00N 51.03 E
Alkmaar 122 Kb 52.37N 4.44 E
Al Kūfah 144 Fc 32.02N 44.24 E
Al Kūfah 146 Lf 32.02N 46.52 E
Al Kuntillah 164 Ge 30.00N 34.41 E
Al Kushḩ 146 Ei 26.14N 32.05 E
Al Kut 144 Gc 32.30N 45.49 E
Al Kuwayt=Kuwait (EN) 142 Gg 29.20N 47.59 E
Al Kuwayt=Kuwait (EN) [1] 142 Gg 29.20N 47.45 E
Al Labbah 146 Ih 29.20N 41.30 E
Al Lādhiqīyah=Latakia (EN) 142 Ff 35.31N 35.07 E
La Lagowa 168 Dc 11.24N 29.08 E
Allagash River 184 Mb 46.35N 69.20W
Allah-Jun 138 Id 61.08N 137.59 E
Allah-Jun 138 Id 60.27N 134.57 E
Allahābād 142 Jg 25.27N 81.51 E
Allahüekber Dağı 146 Jb 40.35N 42.32 E
Allakaket 178 Ic 66.34N 152.41W
Allanmyo 164 Fb 19.22N 95.13 E
Allariz 126 Eb 42.11N 7.48W
All-Awash Island 197b Bb 12.55N 61.10W
Alldays 172 Dd 22.41S 29.06 E
Ålleberg 116 Ef 58.08N 13.36 E
Allegheny Mountains 174 Le 38.30N 80.00W
Allegheny Plateau 184 Lf 41.30N 78.00W
Allegheny Reservoir 184 Hd 41.50N 78.56W
Allegheny River 182 Lc 40.27N 80.00W
Allègre, Pointe- 197b Ab 16.22N 61.45W
Allen 150 Kg 53.20N 124.17 E
Allen, Bog of- 118 Gh 53.20N 7.00W
Allen, Lough-/Loch Aillionn 118 Eg 54.08N 8.08W
Allen 172 Ef 59.00N 81.19W
Allende 190 Dc 28.20N 100.51W
Alleppey 142 Ji 9.29N 76.19 E
Allevard 122 Lj 45.24N 6.05 E
Allevard 130 Jk 39.29N 20.20 E
Allgäu 120 Hh 47.35N 10.10 E
Allgäuer Alpen 120 Hh 47.20N 10.20 E
Alliance [Nb.-U.S.] 182 Gc 42.06N 102.52W
Alliance [Oh.-U.S.] 184 Ge 40.55N 81.06W
Allier 122 Ji 46.30N 3.04 E
Allier 110 Ff 46.57N 3.05 E
Allison 116 Dh 56.59N ...
Alloa 118 Ie 56.07N 3.49W
Allonnes 122 Mj 44.14N 6.38 E
All Saints 197d Bb 17.03N 61.48W
Alm 124 Hb 48.05N 13.55 E
Alma [Ga.-U.S.] 184 Fj 31.33N 82.28W
Alma [Mi.-U.S.] 184 Ed 43.23N 84.39W
Alma [Nb.-U.S.] 186 Gf 40.06N 99.22W

Index Symbols

[1] Independent Nation	Historical or Cultural Region	Pass, Gap
[2] State, Region	Mount, Mountain	Plain, Lowland
[3] District, County	Volcano	Delta
[4] Municipality	Hill	Salt Flat
[5] Colony, Dependency	Mountains, Mountain Range	Valley, Canyon
Continent	Hills, Escarpment	Crater, Cave
Physical Region	Plateau, Upland	Karst Features

Depression	Coast, Beach	Rock, Reef
Polder	Cliff	Islands, Archipelago
Desert, Dunes	Peninsula	Rocks, Reefs
Forest, Woods	Isthmus	Coral Reef
Heath, Steppe	Sandbank	Well, Spring
Oasis	Island	Geyser
Cape, Point	Atoll	River, Stream

Waterfall, Rapids	Canal	Lagoon
River Mouth, Estuary	Glacier	Bank
Lake	Ice Shelf, Pack Ice	Fracture
Salt Lake	Ocean	Seamount
Intermittent Lake	Sea	Ridge
Reservoir	Gulf, Bay	Shelf
Swamp, Pond	Strait, Fjord	Basin

Escarpment, Sea Scarp	Historic Site	Airport
Trench, Abyss	Ruins	Port
National Park, Reserve	Wall, Walls	Military installation
Point of Interest	Church, Abbey	Lighthouse
Recreation Site	Temple	Mine
Scientific Station	Railway station	Tunnel
Cave, Cavern		Dam, Bridge

Name	Page	Grid	Lat	Long
Alma [Que.-Can.]	180	Kg	48.32N	71.40W
Al Ma'āniyah	146	Jg	30.44N	43.00 E
Alma-Ata	142	Je	43.15N	76.57 E
Alma-Atinskaja oblast [3]	136	Hg	44.00N	77.00 E
Almada	126	Cf	38.41N	9.09W
Almadén	126	Hf	38.46N	4.50W
Al Madīnah [Iraq]	146	Lg	30.57N	47.16 E
Al Madīnah [Sau.Ar.] = Medina (EN)	142	Fg	24.28N	39.36 E
Al Madīnah al Fikrīyah	146	Di	27.56N	30.49 E
'Al Madów	168	Hc	10.59N	48.42 E
Al Mafraq	146	Gf	32.21N	36.12 E
Al Maghrib = Morocco (EN)	160	Ge	32.00N	5.50W
Almagro	126	If	38.53N	3.43W
Almagrundet	116	He	59.06N	19.00 E
Al Maḥallah al Kubrá	164	Fc	30.58N	31.10 E
Al Maḥāriq	126		25.37N	30.39 E
Al Mahdīyah	162	Jb	35.30N	11.04 E
Al Mahdīyah [3]	162	Jb	35.30N	11.00 E
Al Maḥfid	164	Ig	14.03N	46.55 E
Al Mahrah	144	Hf	16.56N	52.15 E
Al Maḥras	162	Jc	34.32N	10.30 E
Al Majarr al Kabīr	146	Lg	31.34N	47.10 E
Almajului, Munţii-	130	Fe	44.43N	22.12 E
Al Maks al Qibli	164	Fe	24.35N	30.38 E
Almalyk	136	Gg	40.49N	69.38 E
Al Manādir	146	Pk	23.10N	55.10 E
Al Manāmah=Manama (EN)	142	Ni	26.13N	50.35 E
Al Manāqil	168	Ec	14.15N	32.59 E
Almanor, Lake-	188	Ef	40.15N	121.08W
Almansa	126	Kf	38.52N	1.05W
Almansa, Puerto de-	126	Lf	38.49N	0.58W
Al Manshāh	164	Fd	26.28N	31.48 E
Almansor	126	Df	38.56N	8.54W
Al Manşūrah	164	Fc	31.03N	31.23 E
Al Manzilah	146	Dg	31.09N	31.56 E
Almanzora / Guadalmanzor	126	Kg	37.14N	1.46W
Al Ma'qil	146	Lg	30.33N	47.48 E
Al Maqnah	146	Fh	28.24N	34.45 E
Al Maqţa'	146	Pj	24.25N	54.29 E
Almar	126	Gd	40.54N	5.29W
Al Marāghah	146	Di	26.42N	31.36 E
Al Marsá	128	En	36.53N	10.20 E
Al Mary	160	Je	32.30N	20.54 E
Almaş	130	Gb	47.14N	23.19 E
Almas, Picos das-	198	Lg	13.33S	41.56W
Almas, Rio das-	202	If	14.35S	49.02W
'Al Maskād	168	Hc	11.18N	49.41 E
Almassora / Almazora	126	Le	39.57N	0.03W
Al Maţariyah	164	Fc	31.11N	32.02 E
Al Mawşil = Mosul (EN)	142	Gf	36.20N	43.08 E
Al Mayādin	146	Ie	35.01N	40.27 E
Al Mayyah	146	Ji	27.51N	42.47 E
Almazán	126	Je	41.29N	2.32W
Al Mazār	146	Eg	31.23N	33.23 E
Almazny	138	Gd	62.19N	114.04 E
Almazora / Almassora	126	Le	39.57N	0.03W
Al Mazra'ah	146	Pj	31.16N	35.31 E
Alme, Brilon-	124	Kc	51.27N	8.37 E
Almeida	126	Fc	41.16N	6.04W
Almeirim [Braz.]	202	Id	1.32S	52.34W
Almeirim [Port.]	126	De	39.12N	8.38W
Al Mellem	168	Dd	9.49N	28.45 E
Almelo	122	Mb	52.21N	6.39 E
Almenara, Sierra de la-	126	Kg	37.35N	1.31W
Almendra, Embalse de-	126	Fc	41.13N	6.10W
Almendralejo	126	Ff	38.41N	6.24W
Almería	112	Fh	36.50N	2.27W
Almería	126	Jg	37.10N	2.20W
Almería, Golfo de-	126	Jh	36.46N	2.30W
Almetjevsk	136	Fe	54.54N	52.20 E
Al Metlaoui	162	Ic	34.20N	8.24 E
Älmhult	114	Dh	56.33N	14.08 E
Almijara, Sierra de-	126	Ih	36.55N	3.55W
Almina, Punta-	126	Gi	35.54N	5.17W
Al Minyā [Eg.]	146	Dh	29.45N	31.18 E
Al Minyā [3]	160	Kf	28.06N	30.45 E
Al Miqdādiyah	146	Kf	33.59N	44.56 E
Almirante	194	Fi	9.18N	82.24W
Almirante Brown	222	Gd	64.53S	62.53W
Almirós	130	Fj	39.11N	22.46 E
Almirou, Órmos-	134	Hh	35.23N	24.20 E
Almodóvar	126	Dg	37.31N	8.04W
Almodóvar del Campo	126	Hf	38.43N	4.10W
Almodóvar del Río	126	Gg	37.48N	5.01W
Almonte	126	Fg	37.15N	6.31W
Almonte	126	Fe	39.42N	6.28W
Almoustarat	158	Fb	17.22N	0.07 E
Älmsta	116	Ge	59.58N	18.48 E
Al Mubarraz	144	Gd	25.25N	49.35 E
Al Mudarraj	146	Hj	25.41N	38.40 E
Al Mudawwarah	146	Fh	29.19N	35.59 E
Al Mudhari, Rujm-	146	Hf	32.45N	39.08 E
Al Mughayrā' [Sau.Ar.]	146	Hf	29.17N	37.41 E
Al Mughayrā' [U.A.E.]	146	Oj	24.05N	53.32 E
Al Muglad	168	Ig	11.02N	27.44 E
Al Muharraq	146	Ni	26.16N	50.37 E
Al Mukallā	144	Gh	14.32N	49.08 E
Al Mukhā	144	Fg	13.19N	43.15 E
Al Munastir	162	Jb	35.47N	10.50 E
Al Munastir [3]	162	Jb	35.40N	10.50 E
Almuñécar	126	Ih	36.43N	3.41W
Al Murabba'	146	Kj	25.43N	44.18 E
Almus	146	Gb	40.23N	36.55 E
Al Musannāh	146	Ih	29.02N	47.12 E
Al Mushallah aş Şafrā'	168	Eb	16.25N	33.22 E
Al Musayjid	146	Hj	24.05N	39.06 E
Al Musayyib	146	Kf	32.47N	44.16 E
Al Mustawi	146	Kj	25.55N	44.40 E
Al Muthanna [3]	146	Kg	30.50N	45.20 E
Al Muwayh	164	Ie	22.45N	41.35 E
Al Muwaylih	146	Fi	27.41N	35.28 E
Alnön	116	Gb	62.25N	17.25 E
Alnwick	118	Lf	55.25N	1.42W
Ålö	116	Gf	60.20N	22.15 E
Aloândia	204	Hc	17.43S	49.29W
Alofi	210	Kf	19.03S	169.56W
Alofi, Ile-	208	Jf	14.19S	178.02W
Alofi Bay	220a	Bb	19.01S	169.56W
Aloja	114	Fh	57.44N	24.59 E
Along	148	Ic	28.10N	94.46 E
Alónnisos	130	Fj	39.13N	23.55 E
Alonsa	186	Ga	50.47N	99.00W
Alor, Rio-	204	Ga	24.05S	51.35W
Alor, Kepulauan-	150	Hh	8.15S	124.30 E
Alor, Pulau-	140	Oj	8.15S	124.45 E
Alora	126	Hh	36.48N	4.42W
Alor Setar	142	Mi	6.07N	100.22 E
Alost/Aalst	122	Kd	50.56N	4.02 E
Aloysius, Mount-	212	Fe	26.00S	128.34 E
Alpen = Alps (EN)			46.25N	10.00 E
Alpena	182	Kb	45.04N	83.26W
Alpera	126	Kf	38.58N	1.13W
Alpes = Alps (EN)	110	Gf	46.25N	10.00 E
Alpes Cottiennes	128	Af	44.45N	7.00 E
Alpes-de-Haute-Provence [3]	122	Mj	44.10N	6.10 E
Alpes Grées/Alpi Graie	128	Be	45.30N	7.10 E
Alpes Mancelles	122	Hf	48.25N	0.10W
Alpes-Maritimes	122	Nk	44.00N	7.10 E
Alpes-Maritimes [3]	122	Bf	44.15N	7.10 E
Alpes Pennines/Alpi Pennine	128	Bd	46.05N	7.50 E
Alpes Valaisannes	128	Bd	46.10N	7.30 E
Alpha Cordillera	224	Re	85.30N	125.00W
Alphen aan de Rijn	124	Gb	52.08N	4.42 E
Alphonse Island	158	Mi	7.00S	52.45 E
Alpi = Alps (EN)	110	Gf	46.25N	10.00 E
Alpi Apuane	128	Ef	44.05N	10.20 E
Alpi Aurine	128	Hi	47.00N	11.55 E
Alpi Carniche	128	Ge	46.40N	13.00 E
Alpi Cozie	128	Af	44.45N	7.00 E
Alpi Graie/Alpes Grées	128	Be	45.30N	7.10 E
Alpi Lepontine	128	Cd	46.25N	8.40 E
Alpi Liguri	128	Cf	44.10N	8.05 E
Alpi Marittime	128	Bf	44.15N	7.10 E
Alpi Orobie	128	Dd	46.00N	10.00 E
Alpi Pennine/Alpes Pennines	128	Bd	46.05N	7.50 E
Alpi Retiche=Rhaetian Alps (EN)	128	Dd	46.30N	10.00 E
Alpi Venoste	120	Gj	46.45N	10.55 E
Alprech, Cap d'-	124	Dd	50.42N	1.34 E
Alps (EN) = Alpen	110	Gf	46.25N	10.00 E
Alps (EN) = Alpes	110	Gf	46.25N	10.00 E
Alps (EN) = Alpi	110	Gf	46.25N	10.00 E
Al Qa'āmiyāt	168	Hb	18.50N	48.30 E
Al Qābil	146	Pk	23.56N	55.49 E
Al Qadārif	146	Kg	14.02N	35.24 E
Al Qadimah	144	Ee	22.21N	39.09 E
Al Qadisiya	146	Kg	31.42N	44.28 E
Al Qadmūs	128	Ge	35.05N	36.10 E
Al Qaffay	146	Nj	24.35N	51.44 E
Al Qāhirah=Cairo (EN)	160	Ke	30.03N	31.15 E
Al Qāhirah-Imbabah	164	Fc	30.05N	31.13 E
Al Qāhirah-Mişr al Jadidah	164	Fc	30.06N	31.20 E
Al Qā'iyah	146	Ki	26.27N	45.35 E
Al Qal'ah al Kubrá	128	Eo	35.52N	10.32 E
Al Qalibah	144	Ed	28.24N	37.42 E
Al Qāmishli	146	If	37.02N	41.14 E
Al Qantarah	164	Fc	30.52N	32.19 E
Al Qārah	146	Ih	29.52N	40.15 E
Al Qaryah ash Sharqiyah	164	Bc	30.24N	13.36 E
Al Qaryatayn	146	Ge	34.14N	37.14 E
Al Qaşab	146	Kj	25.18N	45.30 E
Al Qaşabāt	162	Bc	32.35N	14.03 E
Al Qa'şah	146	Ch	28.25N	28.56 E
Al Qaşr	164	Ed	25.42N	28.53 E
Al Qaşrayn	162	Ib	35.11N	8.48 E
Al Qaşrayn [3]	162	Ib	35.15N	9.00 E
Al Qatif	146	Mi	26.33N	50.00 E
Al Qatrāni	146	Gg	31.15N	36.03 E
Al Qatrūn	164	Ce	24.56N	14.38 E
Al Qay'iyah	144	Fe	24.18N	43.30 E
Al Qayrawān	162	Jb	35.41N	10.07 E
Al Qayrawān [3]	162	Jb	35.30N	10.00 E
Al Qayşūmah [Sau.Ar.]	146	Gd	28.16N	46.03 E
Al Qayşūmah [Sau.Ar.]	146	Jh	29.11N	42.58 E
Alqōsh	146	Jf	36.44N	43.06 E
Al Qubayyāt	146	Ge	34.34N	36.17 E
Al Quds [3]	146	Fg	31.45N	35.20 E
Al Qunaytirah	146	Fe	33.07N	35.49 E
Al Qunfudhah	144	Ff	19.08N	41.05 E
Al Qurayyah	146	Gh	28.45N	36.12 E
Al Qurnah	146	Lg	31.00N	47.26 E
Al Quşaymah	164	Fc	30.40N	34.22 E
Al Quşayr [Eg.]	160	Kf	26.06N	34.17 E
Al Quşayr [Syr.]	146	Ge	34.31N	36.35 E
Al Qūşiyah	164	Fd	27.26N	30.49 E
Al Quşūr	128	Co	35.54N	8.53 E
Al Qutayfah	146	Gf	33.44N	36.36 E
Al Quwārah	146	Ji	26.47N	43.28 E
Al Quwayr	146	Jf	36.03N	43.30 E
Al Quzah	146	Hb	15.06N	49.08 E
Als	116	Ci	55.00N	9.55 E
Alsace	122	Nf	48.30N	7.30 E
Alsace, Ballon d'-	122	Mg	47.50N	6.51 E
Alsasua / Altsasu	126	Jb	42.54N	2.10W
Alsdorf	124	Id	50.53N	6.10 E
Alsea River	188	Cd	44.26N	124.05W
Alsenz	124	Je	49.49N	7.51 E
Alsfeld	124	Kd	50.45N	9.16 E
Alsina, Laguna-	204	Am	36.52S	62.07W
Alsten	114	Cd	65.57N	12.36 E
Alsterån	116	Gb	56.55N	16.26 E
Alta	114	Fb	69.58N	23.14 E
Alta	188	Ff	69.58N	23.23 E
Altaelva	114	Fb	69.58N	23.06 E
Altafjorden	114	Fa	70.12N	23.06 E
Altagracia	202	Da	10.07N	71.14W
Alta Gracia	206	Hd	31.40S	64.26W
Altagracia de Orituco	196	Ch	9.52N	66.23W
Altai (EN) = Altay Shan	140	Le	46.30N	93.00 E
Altaj	142	Le	46.20N	96.17 E
Altaj	140	Kd	51.30N	90.00 E
Altajski	138	Df	51.58N	85.30 E
Altajski kraj [3]	138	Df	52.00N	82.30 E
Altamaha River	180	Ke	31.19N	81.17W
Altamira	200	Kf	3.12S	52.12W
Altamira, Cuevas de-	126	Ha	43.23N	4.05W
Altamira, Sierra de-	126	Ge	39.35N	5.10W
Altamirano	192	Mi	16.53N	92.09W
Altamont	188	Fe	42.12N	121.44W
Altamura	128	Kj	40.49N	16.33 E
Altamura, Isla de-	192	Fc	25.00N	108.10W
Altan Bulag	140	Ma	50.12N	106.30 E
Altan-Emel → Xin Barag Youqi				
Altan Xiret → Ejin Horo Qi				
Altar, Desierto de-	174	Hf	31.50N	114.15W
Altar	192	Db	30.39N	111.55W
Altar de los Sacrificios	194	Bc	16.28N	90.32W
Alta Verapaz [3]	194	Be	15.40N	90.00W
Altavista	184	Hg	37.07N	79.18W
Altay = Altai (EN)	142	Le	47.52N	88.07 E
Altay Shan = Altai (EN)	140	Le	46.30N	93.00 E
Altdorf	128	Cd	46.53N	8.40 E
Altea	126	Le	38.36N	0.03W
Altena	124	Jb	52.03N	7.28 E
Altenberge	124	Je	49.33N	7.28 E
Altenburg	120	If	50.59N	12.27 E
Altenglan	124	Je	49.32N	7.39 E
Altenkirchen (Westerwald)	124	Je	50.42N	7.39 E
Alto do Chão	202	Ie	39.12N	7.40W
Altevatnet	114	Eb	68.32N	19.30 E
Altınbaş, Ankara-	146	Ec	39.56N	32.52 E
Altınoluk	130	Jj	39.34N	26.44 E
Altınova	130	Jj	39.13N	26.47 E
Altıntaş	146	Dc	39.04N	30.07 E
Altınyayla	130	Mm	36.59N	29.33 E
Altkirch	122	Ng	47.37N	7.15 E
Altmark	120	Hf	52.40N	11.20 E
Altmühl	120	Hh	48.55N	11.52 E
Alto, Morro-	204	Ib	13.46S	46.50W
Alto, Pico-	126	Ef	38.50N	7.40W
Alto Alentejo [3]	126	Ef	38.50N	7.40W
Alto Araguaia	202	Hf	17.19S	53.12W
Alto Coité	204	Eb	15.47S	54.20W
Alto Garças	202	Hf	16.56S	53.32W
Alto Longá	202	Je	5.15S	42.12W
Alto Molócuè	172	Hc	15.38S	37.42 E
Alto Paraguai	202	Gf	14.30S	56.31W
Alto Paraguay [3]	204	Ce	21.00S	59.00W
Alto Paraíso de Goiás	204	Ib	14.12S	47.38W
Alto Paraná [3]	204	Eg	25.00S	54.50W
Alto Parnaíba	202	Je	9.06S	45.57W
Alto Purús, Rio-	202	Je	9.34S	70.36W
Alto Rio Senguerr	206	Fg	45.02S	70.50W
Altos	202	Jd	5.03S	42.28W
Alto Sucuriú	204	Fd	19.19S	52.47W
Altötting	120	Ih	48.14N	12.41 E
Alto Uruguai, Serra do-	204	Fh	27.35S	53.40W
Altsasu / Alsasua	126	Jb	42.54N	2.10W
Altūn Kūprī	146	Kf	35.45N	44.09 E
Altun Shan	140	Kf	38.00N	88.00 E
Alturas	182	Cc	41.29N	120.32W
Alturitas	196	Cb	9.45N	72.25W
Altynkan	135	Mc	41.03N	70.43 E
Altynkul	135	Bc	43.07N	58.55 E
Alu	219a	Bb	7.05S	155.47 E
Al 'Ubaylah	168	Ja	21.59N	50.57 E
Al Ubayyid	160	Kg	13.11N	30.13 E
Alucra	146	Hb	40.20N	38.46 E
Al 'Udaysāt	164	Ee	25.35N	32.39 E
Al Uqayah	188	Mf	12.03N	28.17 E
Alūksne/Aluksne	114	Gh	57.26N	27.01 E
Alūksne/Aluksne	146	Jh	29.11N	42.58 E
Alūksne ozero	116	Lg	57.22N	27.10 E
Alūksne ozero / Alūksnes ezers	116	Lg	57.22N	27.10 E
Alūksnes ezers / Aluksne ozero	116	Lg	57.22N	27.10 E
'Alūla	168	Ic	11.58N	50.48 E
Al 'Ulá	144	Ed	26.37N	37.52 E
Alunda	116	Ge	60.04N	18.05 E
Alupka	146	Dg	44.24N	34.03 E
Al'Uqaylah	164	Cc	30.16N	19.12 E
Al 'Uqaylāt	146	Ii	28.06N	41.43 E
Al 'Uqayr	144	Gd	25.39N	50.13 E
Al Uqsur = Luxor (EN)	164	Fd	25.39N	32.39 E
Al Urayq	146	Hh	29.00N	39.10 E
Al Urdun = Jordan (EN)	142	Ff	31.00N	36.00 E
Al 'Uruq al Mu'tariḍah	168	Ja	21.00N	54.00 E
Ālūs	168	Ie	34.02N	42.26 E
Alušta	146	Dg	44.42N	34.20 E
Al 'Uthmāniyah	144	Gd	25.15N	49.22 E
Al'Uwaynāt	164	Bd	25.48N	10.33 E
Al 'Uwaynidhiyah	146	Gi	26.38N	36.05 E
Al 'Uwayqilah	146	Jg	30.21N	42.14 E
Al 'Uyūn	144	Fd	24.33N	39.35 E
Al Uzaym	146	Kf	34.12N	44.45 E
Alva	182	Gd	36.48N	98.40W
Alvand, Kūh-e-	146	Me	34.41N	48.28 E
Älvdalen	114	Df	61.14N	14.02 E
Älvdalen	116	Ed	60.30N	13.00 E
Alvear	204	Di	29.06S	56.33W
Alvelos, Serra de-	126	Ee	39.55N	8.01W
Alverca [3]	202	Dd	1.00N	72.00W
Alvesta	114	Df	56.54N	14.33 E
Älvik [Nor.]	114	Bf	60.26N	6.26 E
Alvik [Swe.]	116	Gb	62.25N	17.24 E
Alvin	186	Il	29.25N	95.15W
Älvkarleby	114	Fe	60.34N	17.27 E
Alvord Valley	188	Fe	42.45N	118.25W
Alvey	116	Ae	60.35N	4.50 E
Älvros	116	Fb	62.03N	14.39 E
Älvsborg [2]	114	Ce	58.00N	12.30 E
Älvsbyn	114	Ed	65.40N	21.00 E
Al Wāhidi	144	Gg	14.20N	47.50 E
Al Wajh	142	Fg	26.14N	36.28 E
Al Wannān	146	Mj	25.10N	51.36 E
Alwar	148	Fc	27.34N	76.36 E
Al Warī'ah	146	Li	27.50N	47.29 E
Al Wāsiţah	164	Fd	29.20N	31.12 E
Al Waslātiyah	128	Do	35.51N	9.35 E
Al Watī'ah	164	Bc	32.28N	11.46 E
Al Wazz	168	Eb	15.01N	30.10 E
Al Widyān	140	Gf	31.10N	40.45 E
Alxa Youqi (Ehen Hudag)	152	Hd	39.12N	101.40 E
Alxa Zuoqi (Bayan Hot)	152	Id	38.50N	105.32 E
Alyangula	212	Hb	13.50S	136.25 E
Alygdžer	138	Ef	53.38N	98.16 E
Alymka	138	Se	59.01N	68.40 E
Alytus/Alitus	136	Ce	54.25N	24.08 E
Alz	120	Ih	48.10N	12.48 E
Alzamaj	138	Ee	55.33N	98.39 E
Alzey	120	Kg	49.45N	8.07 E
Alzira/Alcira	126	Le	39.09N	0.26W
Amachachlo Ahzar	166	Fb	15.30N	3.20 E
Amacuro, Rio-	202	Fb	8.32N	60.28W
Amada	164	Fe	22.45N	32.10 E
Amadeus, Lake-	208	Ea	24.50S	130.45 E
Amadi	168	Ed	5.31N	30.20 E
Amadi [Zaire]	170	Eb	3.35N	26.47 E
Amadjuak Lake	180	Kd	64.55N	71.00W
Amadora	126	Cf	38.45N	9.14W
Amadror	162	Id	24.50N	5.21 E
Amadror	162	Id	26.00N	5.21W
Amagasaki	154	Dd	34.42N	135.25 E
Amager	116	Ei	55.35N	12.35 E
Amagi [Jap.]	156b	Bb	27.47N	128.52 E
Amagi [Jap.]	154	Be	33.26N	130.39 E
Amagi-San	156	Fd	34.51N	139.00 E
Amaha	156	Fd	35.13N	139.51 E
Amahai	150	Jg	3.20S	128.55 E
Amain, Monts d'-	122	Gf	48.39N	0.59 E
Amajac, Rio-	192	Jg	21.15N	98.46W
Amakusa-Nada	154	Be	32.25N	129.40 E
Amakusa-Shotō	154	Be	32.20N	130.12 E
Amal [Lib.]	164	Dd	29.25N	21.10 E
Amal [Swe.]	114	Ce	59.03N	12.42 E
Amalfi	128	Jj	40.38N	14.36 E
Amaliás	130	El	37.48N	21.21 E
Amalner	148	Fd	21.03N	75.04 E
Amambai	202	Gh	23.05S	55.13W
Amambai, Rio-	204	Ff	23.22S	53.56W
Amambai, Serra de-	204	Ff	23.10S	55.30W
Amambay [3]	204	Ef	23.00S	56.00W
Amami Ha	194	Ce	17.50N	88.20W
Amami-Ō-Shima	156b	Fb	28.15N	129.20 E
Amami-Shotō=Amami Islands (EN)	140	Og	28.16N	129.21 E
Amami-Shotō	156b	Bb	28.16N	129.21 E
Amami Islands (EN) = Amami-Shotō	140	Og	28.16N	129.21 E
Amān [5]	116	Fc	61.12N	14.45 E
Amana	182	Hc	41.45N	91.51W
Amanã, Lago-	202	Fd	2.35S	64.40W
Amana, Rio-	196	Ig	9.45N	62.39W
Amanab	214	Ch	3.38S	141.16 E
Amanave	221c	Cb	14.19S	170.49W
Amandola	128	Hh	42.59N	13.21 E
Amangeldy	136	Ge	50.10N	65.13 E
Amankaragaj	134	Lg	52.27N	64.08 E
Amantea	128	Kk	39.07N	16.08 E
Amanu Atoll	210	Mf	17.48S	140.46W
Amanzimtoti	172	Fd	30.05S	30.53 E
Amapá	200	Kd	2.03N	50.48W
Amapá, Território do-	202	Hc	1.30N	52.00W
Amapala	194	Dg	13.17N	87.40W
Amara	134	Fe	44.37N	27.19 E
Amara	168	Fc	9.32N	38.45 E
Amara East	168	Ea	20.48N	30.23 E
Amaradia	134	Fe	44.22N	23.43 E
Amarante [Braz.]	202	Je	6.14S	42.50W
Amarante [Port.]	126	De	41.16N	8.05W
Amaranth	186	Ga	50.36N	98.43W
Amargosa	198	Mf	13.01S	39.36W
Amargosa Desert	188	Gg	36.40N	116.30W
Amargosa Range	188	Gg	36.30N	116.40W
Amargosa River	188	Gg	36.13N	116.48W
Amarillo	176	If	35.13N	101.49W
Amárion	134	Dg	35.10N	24.39 E
Amarume	156	Fb	38.51N	139.54 E
Amasra	146	Db	41.45N	32.23 E
Amasya	144	Ea	40.39N	35.51 E
Amathus	146	Df	34.42N	33.08 E
Amatignak Island	178a	Bb	51.16N	179.06W
Amatique, Bahía de-	194	Ce	15.55N	88.45W
Amatlán de Cañas	192	Gg	20.52N	104.27W
Amatrice	128	Hh	42.38N	13.17 E
Amaurilandia	204	Ff	22.10S	52.08W
Amazar	140	Nc	53.50N	120.55 E
Amazon (EN) = Amazonas, Rio- (Solimões)	198	Lf	0.10S	49.00W
Amazon (EN) → Solimões → Amazonas, Rio-	198	Lf	0.10S	49.00W
Amazon, Mouths of the- (EN)	198	Le	0.10S	49.00W
Amazonas [Braz.] [2]	202	Fd	5.00S	63.00W
Amazonas [Col.] [3]	202	Dd	1.00N	72.00W
Amazonas [Peru] [3]	202	Ce	5.00S	77.00W
Amazonas [Ven.] [2]	202	Ec	3.30N	66.00W
Amazonas, Rio- (Solimões) = Amazon (EN)	198	Lf	0.10S	49.00W
Amazon Cone (EN)	198	Le	4.30N	52.00W
Amba Ferit	168	Fc	10.55N	38.55 E
Ambāla	148	Fb	30.21N	76.50 E
Ambalangoda	148	Gg	6.14N	80.03 E
Ambalavao	172	Hd	21.50S	46.57 E
Ambam	166	He	2.23N	11.17 E
Ambanja	172	Hb	13.39S	48.27 E
Ambarčik	142	Sc	69.39N	162.20 E
Ambarès-et-Lagrave	122	Fj	44.55N	0.29W
Ambargasta, Salinas de-	206	Hc	29.20S	64.30W
Ambarny	136	Db	65.54N	33.41 E
Ambasamudram	148	Fg	8.42N	77.28 E
Ambato	200	If	1.15S	78.37W
Ambato-Boéni	172	Hc	16.28S	46.40 E
Ambatofinandrahana	172	Hc	20.33S	46.47 E
Ambatolampy	172	Hc	19.23S	47.25 E
Ambatondrazaka	172	Hc	17.48S	48.26 E
Ambatosoratra	172	Hc	17.36S	48.32 E
Ambelau, Pulau-	150	Hg	3.51S	127.12 E
Amberg	120	Hg	49.27N	11.52 E
Ambergris Cay	194	Dd	18.03N	87.56W
Ambergris Cays	194	Gd	21.18N	71.37W
Ambérieu-en-Bugey	122	Li	45.57N	5.21 E
Amberley [Eng.-U.K.]	124	Bd	50.55N	0.32W
Amberley [N.Z.]	218	Ee	43.09S	172.45 E
Ambert	122	Ji	45.33N	3.45 E
Ambikāpur	148	Gd	23.07N	83.12 E
Ambila	172	Hd	21.58S	47.59 E
Ambilobe	172	Hb	13.11S	49.03 E
Ambitle	219a	Aa	4.05S	153.40 E
Ambjörby	116	Ed	60.30N	13.10 E
Ambla	116	Ke	59.10N	25.44 E
Amblève/Amel	124	Id	50.28N	5.36 E
Amblève/Amel	124	Id	50.21N	6.09 E
Ambo	202	Cf	10.07S	76.10W
Amboasary Sud	172	He	25.01S	46.23 E
Ambodifototra	172	Hc	16.58S	49.52 E
Ambohimahasoa	172	Hd	21.08S	47.12 E
Ambohimanarina	172	Hc	18.49S	47.26 E
Ambohitralanana	172	Hc	15.15S	50.28 E
Amboise	122	Gg	47.25N	0.59 E
Ambon	210	Bb	3.43S	128.12 E
Ambon, Pulau-	150	Ig	3.40S	128.10 E
Amboseli, Lake-	170	Gc	2.37S	37.08 E
Ambositra	172	He	20.30S	47.14 E
Ambre, Cap d'- = Ambre, Cape d'-(EN)	158	Lj	11.57S	49.17 E
Ambre, Cape d'-(EN) = Ambre, Cap d'-	158	Lj	11.57S	49.17 E
Ambre, Montagne d'-	172	Hb	12.30S	49.10 E
Ambriz	160	Ih	7.50S	13.08 E
Ambrolauri	132	Mh	42.31N	43.05 E
Ambrym, Ile-	208	He	16.15S	168.07 E
Ambunti	214	Ch	4.14S	142.50 E
Ambūr	148	Ff	12.47N	78.42 E
Amchitka	178a	Bb	51.30N	179.00 E
Amchitka Pass	178a	Cb	51.30N	179.00 E
Am Dafok	168	Cc	10.28N	23.17 E
Am Dam	168	Cc	12.46N	20.29 E
Amded	162	He	22.10N	3.15 E
Amderma	136	Gb	69.45N	61.39 E
Am Djéména	168	Bc	13.06N	17.19 E
Amdo	152	Fe	32.29N	91.47 E
Ameca	190	Dg	20.41N	105.18W
Ameca, Rio-	192	Gg	20.41N	105.18W
Amel/Amblève	124	Id	50.21N	6.09 E
Ameland	122	La	53.26N	5.48 E
Ameland	124	Ha	53.25N	5.45 E
Ameland-Nes	124	Ha	53.26N	5.48 E
Amelia Island	184	Gj	30.37N	81.27W
Amélie-les-Bains-Palalda	122	Il	42.28N	2.40 E
Amendolara	128	Kk	39.57N	16.35 E
'Āmerī	146	Nh	28.30N	51.05 E
Americana	204	If	22.45S	47.20W
American Falls	188	Ie	42.47N	112.51W
American Falls Reservoir	188	Ie	43.00N	113.00W
American Fork	188	Jf	40.23N	111.48W
American Highland	222	Ff	72.30S	78.00 E
American Samoa [5]	210	Kf	14.50S	170.00W
Americus	182	Ke	32.04N	84.14W
Amersfoort	122	Lb	52.09N	5.24 E
Amery Ice Shelf	222	Fe	69.30S	72.00 E
Ametlla de Mar	126	Md	40.54N	0.48 E
Amfilochía	130	Ej	38.52N	21.10 E
Amfissa	130	Ek	38.32N	22.23 E
Amfreville-la-Campagne	124	Ce	49.13N	0.57 E
Amga	138	El	60.53N	131.50 E
Amga	140	Pc	62.40N	134.59 E
Amgalang → Xin Barag Zuoqi	152	Kb	48.13N	118.14 E
Am Géréda	168	Cc	12.52N	21.10 E
Amgu	154	Nb	45.51N	137.41 E
Amguema	180	Nc	68.03N	177.55W
Amguid	162	Id	26.28N	5.22 E
Amherst	180		26.30N	5.36 E
Amherst, Mount-	212	Fc	18.11S	126.59 E
Amherst Island	184	Ic	44.12N	76.42W
Amiata, Monte-	128	Fg	42.53N	11.37 E
Amiens	112	Gf	49.54N	2.18 E
Āmīj, Wādī-	146	If	33.48N	41.46 E
Amili	148	Jc	28.26N	95.52 E
Amindivi Islands	142	Ji	11.23N	72.23 E
Aminuis	172	Bd	23.43S	19.21 E
'Āmir, Ra's-	158	Je	32.57N	21.43 E

Index Symbols

- [1] Independent Nation
- [2] State, Region
- [3] District, County
- [4] Municipality
- [5] Colony, Dependency
- ■ Continent
- ⬚ Physical Region

- Historical or Cultural Region
- Mount, Mountain
- Volcano
- Hill
- Mountains, Mountain Range
- Hills, Escarpment
- Plateau, Upland

- Pass, Gap
- Plain, Lowland
- Delta
- Salt Flat
- Valley, Canyon
- Crater, Cave
- Karst Features

- Depression
- Polder
- Desert, Dunes
- Forest, Woods
- Heath, Steppe
- Oasis
- Cape, Point

- Coast, Beach
- Cliff
- Peninsula
- Rocks, Reefs
- Coral Reef
- Well, Spring
- Geyser

- Rock, Reef
- Islands, Archipelago
- Isthmus
- Sandbank
- Island
- Atoll
- River, Stream

- Waterfall, Rapids
- River Mouth, Estuary
- Lake
- Salt Lake
- Intermittent Lake
- Sea
- Swamp, Pond

- Canal
- Glacier
- Ice Shelf, Pack Ice
- Ocean
- Ridge
- Gulf, Bay
- Strait, Fjord

- Lagoon
- Bank
- Seamount
- Tablemount
- Shelf
- Basin

- Escarpment, Sea Scarp
- Fracture
- Trench, Abyss
- National Park, Reserve
- Point of Interest
- Recreation Site
- Cave, Cavern

- Historic Site
- Ruins
- Wall, Walls
- Church, Abbey
- Temple
- Scientific Station
- Railway station

- Airport
- Port
- Military installation
- Lighthouse
- Mine
- Tunnel
- Dam, Bridge

Amirante Basin (EN) 158 Mi 7.00S 55.00 E
Amirante Islands 158 Mi 6.00S 53.10 E
Amirante Trench (EN) 172b Bb 6.00S 52.30 E
Amisk Lake 180 Hf 54.35N 102.15W
Amistad, Presa de la- 186 Fl 28.34N 101.15W
Amistad Reservoir 182 Gf 28.34N 101.15W
Amite 186 Kk 30.44N 90.30W
Amlekhganj 148 Gc 27.17N 84.59 E
Amlia 178a Db 52.06N 173.30W
Amlwch 118 Ih 53.25N 4.20W
'Amm Adām 168 Fb 16.22N 36.09 E
'Ammān 142 Ff 31.57N 35.56 E
'Ammān [3] 146 Gg 31.57N 35.56 E
Ammanford 118 Jj 51.48N 3.59W
Ammarnäs 114 Dd 65.58N 16.12 E
Åmmeberg 116 Ff 58.52N 15.00 E
Ammer 120 Hi 47.57N 11.08 E
Ammerån 116 Ga 63.09N 16.13 E
Ammerland 120 Dc 53.15N 8.00 E
Ammersee 120 Hi 48.00N 11.08 E
Ammi-Moussa 126 Ni 35.52N 1.07 E
Ammokhostos → Famagusta (EN) 144 Dc 35.07N 33.57 E
Amnja 134 Me 63.45N 67.07 E
Amnok-kang 152 Ld 39.55N 124.20 E
Āmol 144 Hb 36.23N 52.20 E
Amolar 204 Dd 18.01S 57.30W
Amorgós 130 Im 36.50N 25.53 E
Amorgós 130 Im 36.50N 25.59 E
Amorinópolis 204 Gc 16.36S 51.08W
Amory 186 Lj 33.59N 88.29W
Amos 180 Jg 48.34N 78.07W
Åmot [Nor.] 114 Bg 59.54N 9.54 E
Åmot [Nor.] 116 Be 59.35N 8.00 E
Åmotfors 116 Ee 59.46N 12.22 E
Amoucha 126 Rh 36.23N 5.25 E
Amouliani 130 Gi 40.20N 23.55 E
Amour, Djebel- 162 Hc 33.45N 1.45 E
Amourj 162 Ff 16.10N 7.35W
Amoy (EN) = Xiamen 142 Ng 24.32N 118.06 E
Ampanihy 172 Gd 24.40S 44.45 E
Amparafaravola 172 Hc 17.36S 48.12 E
Amparo 204 If 22.42S 46.47W
Ampato, Nevado de- 198 Ig 15.50S 71.52W
Amper 120 Hh 48.10N 11.50 E
Ampère Seamount (EN) 110 Eh 35.05N 12.13W
Amphitrite Point 188 Cb 48.56N 125.35W
Amposta 126 Md 40.43N 0.35 E
Ampthill 124 Bb 52.02N 0.29W
Ampurdán / Empordà 126 Ob 42.12N 2.45 E
Ampurias / Empúries 126 Pb 42.10N 3.05 E
Amqui 184 Na 48.28N 67.26W
'Amrān 144 Ff 15.41N 43.55 E
Amrāvati 142 Jg 20.56N 77.45 E
Am-Raya 168 Bc 14.05N 16.30 E
Amritsar 142 Jf 31.35N 74.53 E
Amrum 120 Eb 54.40N 8.20 E
Amsaga 162 Ee 20.07N 14.10W
Amsittene, Jebel- 162 Fc 31.11N 9.40W
Amstel 124 Gb 52.22N 4.56 E
Amstelveen 124 Gb 52.18N 4.53 E
Amsterdam 158 Ol 37.57S 77.40 E
Amsterdam [Neth.] 112 Ge 52.22N 4.54 E
Amsterdam [N.Y.-U.S.] 184 Jd 42.56N 74.12W
Amsterdam-Rijnkanaal 124 Hc 51.57N 5.25 E
Amstetten 128 Ib 48.07N 14.52 E
Am Timan 160 Jg 11.02N 20.17 E
Amūd, Jabal al- 144 Ec 30.59N 39.20 E
Āmūdā 146 Id 37.05N 40.54 E
Amu-Darja 135 Ef 37.57N 65.15 E
Amudarja ⇒ Amu Darya (EN) 140 He 43.40N 59.01 E
Āmū Daryā = Amu Darya (EN) 140 He 43.40N 59.01 E
Amu Darya (EN) = Amudarja 140 He 43.40N 59.01 E
Amu Darya (EN) = Āmū Daryā 140 He 43.40N 59.01 E
Amudat 170 Fb 1.58N 34.56 E
Amukta Pass 178a Db 52.25N 172.00W
Amun 219a Ba 5.57S 154.45 E
Amund Ringnes 180 Ha 78.15N 97.00W
Amundsen Bay 222 Ee 66.55S 50.00 E
Amundsen Coast 222 Mg 85.30S 159.00W
Amundsen Glacier 222 Mg 85.35S 159.00W
Amundsen Gulf 174 Gb 71.00N 124.00W
Amundsen-Scott Station 222 Bg 90.00S 0.00
Amundsen Sea (EN) 222 Of 72.30S 112.00W
Amungen 116 Fc 61.10N 15.40 E
Amuntai 142 Nj 2.26S 115.15 E
Amur 140 Qd 52.56N 141.10 E
'Amūr, Wādī- 168 Eb 18.56N 33.34 E
Amurang 150 Hf 1.11N 124.35 E
Amursk 138 If 50.16N 136.55 E
Amurskaja oblast [3] 138 Hf 54.00N 128.00 E
Amurzet 138 Ig 47.41N 131.07 E
Amvrakia, Gulf of- (EN) = Amvrakikós Kólpos 130 Dk 39.00N 21.00 E
Amvrakikós Kólpos = Amvrakia, Gulf of- (EN) 130 Dk 39.00N 21.00 E
Amvrosijevka 132 Kf 47.44N 38.31 E
Am Zoer 168 Cc 14.13N 21.23 E
Anaa Atoll 216 Lc 17.25S 145.30W
Anabar 220e Ba 0.29S 166.57 E
Anabar 140 Nb 73.08N 113.36 E
Anabarskoje ploskogorje 140 Mc 70.00N 108.00 E
An Abhainn Dubh/Blackwater 118 Gh 53.39N 6.43W
An Abhainn Mhór/Blackwater [Ire.] 118 Fj 51.51N 7.50W
An Abhainn Mhór/Blackwater [N.Ire.-U.K.] 118 Gg 54.30N 6.35W
Anabuki 156 Dd 34.02N 134.11 E
Anacasti 206 Gc 28.49S 65.30W
Anaco 202 Fb 9.27N 64.28W
Anaconda 182 Eb 46.08N 112.57W
Anacortes 188 Db 48.30N 122.37W
Anadarko 186 Gi 35.04N 98.15W
Anadolu = Anatolia (EN) 140 Ff 39.00N 35.00 E
Anadyr 142 Tc 64.45N 177.29 E
Anadyr 140 Tc 64.55N 176.05 E
Anadyr Gulf (EN) = Anadyrski zaliv 140 Uc 64.00N 179.00W
Anadyr Range (EN) = Anadyrskoje ploskogorje 140 Tc 67.00N 174.00 E
Anadyrski liman 138 Md 64.30N 178.00 E
Anadyrski zaliv = Anadyr Gulf (EN) 140 Uc 64.00N 179.00W
Anadyrskoje ploskogorje = Anadyr Range (EN) 140 Tc 67.00N 174.00 E
Anáfi 130 Im 36.22N 25.47 E
Anaghit 168 Fb 16.20N 38.39 E
Anagni 128 Hi 41.44N 13.09 E
'Ānah 144 Fc 34.28N 41.56 E
Anaheim 188 Gj 33.51N 117.57W
Anahola 221a Ba 22.09N 159.19W
Anáhuac 192 Id 27.14N 100.09W
Anáhuac, Meseta de- 190 Dd 21.30N 101.00W
An Aird/Ards Peninsula 118 Hg 54.30N 5.30W
Anaj Mudi 140 Jh 10.10N 77.04 E
Anaktuvuk Pass 178 Ic 68.10N 151.50W
Analalava 172 Hb 14.38S 47.45 E
Analavelona 172 Gd 22.37S 44.10 E
Ana María, Golfo de- 194 Hc 21.25N 78.40W
Anambas, Kepulauan- = Anambas Islands (EN) 140 Mi 3.00N 106.00 E
Anambas Islands (EN) = Anambas, Kepulauan- 140 Mi 3.00N 106.00 E
Anambra [2] 166 Gd 6.30N 7.30 E
Anamé 219b De 20.08S 169.49 E
Anamizu 154 Nf 37.14N 136.54 E
Anamur 144 Db 36.06N 32.50 E
Anamur Burun 144 Db 36.03N 32.48 E
Anan [Jap.] 156 Ed 35.19N 137.48 E
Anan [Jap.] 154 Mh 33.55N 134.39 E
Anane, Djebel- 126 Mi 35.12N 0.47 E
Anánes 130 Hm 36.31N 24.08 E
Ananjev 132 Ff 47.43N 29.59 E
Anankwin 148 Je 15.41N 97.59 E
Anantapur 148 Ff 14.41N 77.36 E
Anantnāg (Islāmābād) 148 Fb 33.44N 75.09 E
Anapa 136 Dg 44.53N 37.19 E
Anapo 128 Jm 37.03N 15.16 E
Anápolis 200 Lg 16.20S 48.58W
Anapu, Rio- 202 Hd 2.15S 51.30W
Anār 144 Ic 30.53N 55.18 E
Anārak 144 Hc 33.20N 53.42 E
Anare Station 222 Jd 54.30S 158.55 E
Anaro, Río- 194 Lj 7.48N 70.12W
Añasco 197a Ab 18.17N 67.10W
Anatahan Island 208 Fc 16.22N 145.40 E
Anatolia (EN) = Anadolu 140 Ff 39.00N 35.00 E
Anatolikí Rodhópi 130 Ih 41.44N 25.31 E
Añatuya 206 Hc 28.28S 62.50W
Anauá, Rio- 202 Fc 0.58N 61.21W
Anazah, Jabal- 146 Hf 32.12N 39.18 E
Anazarba 146 Fd 37.15N 35.45 E
An Baile Meánach/Ballymena 118 Gg 54.52N 6.17W
An Bhanna/Bann 118 Gf 55.10N 6.46W
An Bhearú/Barrow 118 Gi 52.10N 7.00W
An Bhinn Bhuí/Benwee Head 118 Dg 54.21N 9.48W
An Bhograch/Boggeragh Mountains 118 Ei 52.05N 9.00W
Ån Bhóinn/Boyne 118 Gh 53.43N 6.15W
An Bhrosnach/Brosna 118 Fh 53.13N 7.58W
An Blascaod Mór/Great Blasket 118 Ci 52.05N 10.32W
Anbyŏn 154 Ie 39.02N 127.32 E
An Cabhán / Cavan 118 Fg 54.00N 7.21W
An Cabhán/Cavan [2] 118 Fh 53.55N 7.30W
An Caisleán Nua/Newcastle 118 Hg 54.12N 5.54W
An Caisleán Nua/Newcastle West 118 Di 52.27N 9.03W
An Caisleán Riabhach/Castlerea 118 Eh 53.46N 8.29W
An Caoláire Rua/Killary Harbour 118 Dh 53.38N 9.55W
Ancares, Sierra de- 126 Fb 42.46N 6.54W
Ancash [3] 202 Ce 9.30S 77.45W
Ancenis 122 Eg 47.22N 1.10W
An Chathair/Caher 118 Fi 52.22N 7.55W
An Cheacha/Caha Mountains 118 Dj 51.45N 9.45W
Anchorage 176 Ec 61.13N 149.53W
An Chorr Chríochach/Cookstown 118 Gg 54.39N 6.45W
Anci (Langfang) 152 Kd 39.29N 116.40 E
An Clár/Clare [2] 118 Ei 52.50N 9.00W
An Cóbh/Cóbh 118 Ej 51.51N 8.17W
Ancohuma, Nevado- 202 Eg 15.51S 68.36W
Ancona 112 Hg 43.38N 13.30 E
Ancón de Sardinas, Bahía de- 202 Cc 1.30N 79.50W
Ancre 122 Ie 49.54N 2.28 E
Ancuabe 172 Fb 12.58S 39.51 E
Ancud 206 Ff 41.52S 73.50W
Ancud, Golfo de- 206 Ff 42.05S 73.00W
Anda 152 Mb 46.24N 125.20 E
Anda (Sartu) 154 Ha 46.35N 125.00 E
Andacollo [Arg.] 206 Fe 37.11S 70.41W
Andacollo [Chile] 206 Fd 30.14S 71.06W
Andahuaylas 202 Df 13.39S 73.23W
An Daingean/Dingle 118 Ci 52.08N 10.15W
Andalgalá 206 Gc 27.36S 66.19W
Åndalsnes 114 Be 62.34N 7.42 E
Andalucía = Andalusia (EN) [2] 126 Hg 37.30N 4.30W
Andalucía = Andalusia (EN) 110 Fh 37.30N 4.30W
Andalusia 182 Je 31.19N 86.29W
Andalusia (EN) = Andalucía [2] 126 Hg 37.30N 4.30W
Andalusia (EN) = Andalucía 110 Fh 37.30N 4.30W
Andaman and Nicobar [3] 148 If 12.30N 92.45 E
Andaman Basin (EN) 140 Lh 10.00N 94.00 E
Andaman Islands 140 Lh 12.30N 92.43 E
Andaman Sea (EN) 140 Lh 10.00N 95.00 E
Andamooka 212 Hf 30.27S 137.12 E
'Andān, Wādī- 144 Ie 21.05N 58.23 E
Andant 204 Am 36.34S 62.07W
Andapa 172 Hb 14.38S 49.33 E
Andara 172 Cc 18.03S 21.27 E
Andelle 124 De 49.19N 1.14 E
Andelys, Les- 122 He 49.15N 1.25 E
Andenes 114 Db 69.19N 16.08 E
Andenne 124 Hd 50.29N 5.06 E
Andenne-Namêche 124 Hd 50.28N 5.00 E
Andéranboukane 166 Fb 15.26N 3.02 E
Anderlecht 124 Gd 50.50N 4.18 E
Anderlues 124 Gd 50.24N 4.16 E
Andermatt 128 Cd 46.38N 8.37 E
Andernach 120 Df 50.26N 7.24 E
Andernos-les-Bains 122 Ej 44.44N 1.06W
Anderson 180 Ec 69.42N 129.01W
Anderson [Ca.-U.S.] 188 Df 40.27N 122.18W
Anderson [In.-U.S.] 182 Jc 40.10N 85.41W
Anderson [S.C.-U.S.] 182 Ke 34.30N 82.39W
Anderstorp 116 Eg 57.17N 13.38 E
Andes (EN) = Andes, Cordillera de los- 198 Jh 20.00S 67.00W
Andes, Cordillera de los- = Andes (EN) 198 Jh 20.00S 67.00W
Andevoranto 172 Hc 18.56S 49.06 E
Andfjorden 114 Db 69.10N 16.20 E
Andhra Pradesh [3] 148 Fe 16.00N 79.00 E
Andía, Sierra de- / Andia, Sierra de- 126 Kb 42.45N 2.00W
Andia, Sierra de- / Andía, Sierra de- 126 Kb 42.45N 2.00W
Andikhásia Ōri 130 Ej 39.47N 21.55 E
Andikíra 130 Fk 38.23N 22.38 E
Andikíthira = Andikithira (EN) 130 Gn 35.52N 23.18 E
Andikithira (EN) = Andikíthira 130 Gn 35.52N 23.18 E
Andikithíron, Stenón- 130 Gn 35.45N 23.25 E
Andilamena 172 Hc 17.01S 48.32 E
Andilanatoby 172 Hc 17.56S 48.14 E
Andīmeshk 146 Mf 32.27N 48.21 E
Andímilos 130 Hm 36.47N 24.14 E
Andíparos 130 Il 37.00N 25.03 E
Andípaxoi 130 Dj 39.08N 20.14 E
Andípsara 130 Ik 38.33N 25.24 E
Andir He 152 Dd 38.00N 83.36 E
Andırın 146 Gd 37.34N 36.20 E
Andirlangar 152 Dd 37.36N 83.50 E
Andírrion 130 Ek 38.20N 21.46 E
Andítilos 130 Km 36.22N 27.28 E
Andižan 142 Je 40.45N 72.22 E
Andižanskaja oblast [3] 136 Hg 40.45N 72.20 E
Andkhvoy 144 Kb 36.56N 65.08 E
Andŏng 152 Md 36.36N 128.44 E
Andorra (Valls d'Andorra) [1] 112 Gg 42.30N 1.30 E
Andorra la Vella 112 Gg 42.31N 1.31 E
Andover 118 Lj 51.13N 1.28W
Andøya 114 Db 69.08N 15.54 E
Andradas 204 If 22.05S 46.35W
Andradina 206 Jb 20.54S 51.23W
Andraitx / Andratx 126 Oe 39.35N 2.25 E
Andratx / Andraitx 126 Oe 39.35N 2.25 E
Andreanof Islands 174 Bd 52.00N 176.00W
Andreapol 114 Hh 56.39N 32.16 E
Andrées Land 179 Jd 73.20N 26.30W
Andrejevka [Kaz.-U.S.S.R.] 136 If 45.47N 80.35 E
Andrejevka [Ukr.-U.S.S.R.] 132 Je 49.32N 36.40 E
Andrejevo-Ivanovka 130 Nb 47.31N 30.21 E
Andrejevsk 138 Ge 58.10N 114.15 E
Andrelândia 204 Je 21.44S 44.18W
Andresito 204 Dk 33.08S 57.09W
Andrespol 120 Pe 51.43N 19.40 E
Andrews 186 Ej 32.19N 102.33W
Andria 128 Ki 41.13N 16.17 E
Andriamena 172 Hc 17.28S 47.29 E
Andriba 172 Hc 17.36S 46.53 E
Andrijevica 130 Cg 42.44N 19.48 E
Andringitra 158 Lk 22.20S 46.55 E
Andrítsaina 130 El 37.29N 21.54 E
Androka 172 Gd 24.59S 44.04 E
Androna, Plateau de l'- 172 Hc 15.30S 48.20 E
Andropov → Rybinsk 112 Jd 58.03N 38.52 E
Ándros 130 Hl 37.50N 24.56 E
Andros 110 Ih 37.50N 24.50 E
Androscoggin River 184 Md 43.55N 69.55W
Andros Island 174 Lg 24.25N 78.00W
Andros Town 190 Id 24.43N 77.47W
Androth Island 148 Ef 10.50N 73.41 E
Androy 158 Lk 25.00S 45.40 E
Andruševka 132 Fe 49.59N 29.01 E
Andrychów 120 Pg 49.52N 19.21 E
Andselv 114 Eb 69.04N 18.30 E
Andudu 170 Eb 2.29N 28.41 E
Andújar 126 Hf 38.03N 4.04W
Andulo 170 Ce 11.28S 16.43 E
Andu Tan 150 Fe 7.35N 114.15 E
Anduze 122 Jj 44.03N 3.59 E
An Ea agail/Errigal 118 Ef 55.02N 8.07W
Aneby 116 Fg 57.50N 14.48 E
Anéfis 166 Fb 18.03N 0.36 E
Anegada 190 Le 18.45N 64.20W
Anegada, Bahía- 206 Hf 40.15S 62.15W
Anegada Passage 190 Le 18.30N 63.40W
Anécho 166 Fd 6.14N 1.36 E
An Éirne/Erne 118 Eg 54.30N 8.15W
An Eithne/Inny 118 Fh 53.35N 7.50W
An Eoghanach/Annalee 118 Fg 54.02N 7.25W
Anet 124 Df 48.51N 1.26 E
Aneto, Pico de- 110 Gg 42.38N 0.40 E
Aney 166 Hb 19.24N 12.56 E
Aneytioum, Ile- 208 Hg 20.12S 169.49 E
An Feabhal / Foyle 118 Ff 55.04N 7.15W
An Fhéil/Feale 118 Di 52.28N 9.40W
An Fheoir/Nore 118 Gi 52.25N 6.58W
Angamos, Punta- [Chile] 206 Fb 23.01S 70.32W
Angamos, Punta- [Pas.] 221d Bb 27.04S 109.17W
Angara 140 Ld 58.06N 93.00 E
Angarsk 142 Md 52.34N 103.54 E
Angarski, pereval- 132 Ig 44.47N 34.25 E
Angarski krjaž 138 Fe 57.30N 103.00 E
Angathonísi 130 Jl 37.28N 27.00 E
Angaur Island 208 Ed 6.54N 134.09 E
Änge [Swe.] 116 Fa 63.27N 14.03 E
Ånge [Swe.] 114 De 62.31N 15.37 E
An Gearrán/Garron Point 118 Hf 55.05N 5.58W
Ángel, Cerro- 192 Hf 22.49N 102.34W
Angelburg 124 Kd 50.47N 8.25 E
Ángel de la Guarda, Isla- 190 Bc 29.20N 113.25W
Angeles 150 Hc 15.09N 120.35 E
Ángeles, Sierra de los- 192 Jf 23.10N 99.20W
Ángel Falls (EN) = Angel, Salto-/Churún Merú 198 Je 5.57N 62.30W
Ángel Falls (EN) = Churún Merú/Angel,Salto- 198 Je 5.57N 62.30W
Ängelholm 114 Ch 56.15N 12.51 E
Angélica 204 Bj 31.33S 61.33W
Angeln 120 Fb 54.40N 9.45 E
Angel Salto-/Churún Merú = Ángel Falls (EN) 198 Je 5.57N 62.30W
Ängelsberg 116 Ge 59.58N 16.02 E
Anger 168 Fd 9.40N 36.06 E
Angereb 168 Fc 13.44N 36.28 E
Ångermanälven 110 Hc 62.48N 17.56 E
Angermünde 120 Jc 53.02N 14.00 E
Angers 112 Ff 47.28N 0.33W
Angikuni Lake 180 Hd 62.10N 99.55W
Angístrion 130 Gl 37.40N 23.20 E
Angkor 148 Kf 13.26N 103.52 E
Anglem, Mount- 218 Bg 46.44S 167.54 E
Anglès 126 Oc 41.57N 2.39 E
Anglesey 110 Fe 53.18N 4.20W
Anglet 122 Ek 43.29N 1.32W
Angleton 186 Il 29.10N 95.26W
Anglin 122 Gh 46.42N 0.52 E
Anglona 128 Cj 40.45N 8.45 E
Anglo-Normandes, Iles- (F) = Channel Islands [5] 118 Kl 49.20N 2.20W
Angmagssalik 224 Mc 65.45N 37.30W
Ango 170 Eb 4.02N 25.52 E
Angoche 160 Kj 16.12S 39.54 E
Angoche, Ilha- 158 Kj 16.20S 39.51 E
Angol 206 Fe 37.48S 72.43W
Angola 184 Ee 41.38N 85.00W
Angola [1] 160 Ij 12.30S 18.30 E
Angola Basin (EN) 106 Ek 15.00S 3.00 E
Angoram 214 Ch 4.04S 144.04 E
Angostura 192 Ee 25.22N 108.11W
Angostura, Presa de la- 192 Mi 16.30N 92.30W
Angostura, Salto- 202 Dc 2.43N 70.57W
Angostura Reservoir 186 Ee 43.18N 103.27W
Angoulême 122 Gi 45.39N 0.09 E
Angoumois 122 Gi 45.30N 0.00
Angra do Héroísmo 160 Ee 38.39N 27.13W
Angra do Heroísmo [3] 162 Bb 38.42N 27.15W
Angra dos Reis 204 Jf 23.00S 44.18W
Angren 136 Hg 41.03N 70.10 E
Angu 170 Db 3.33N 24.28 E
Anguang 154 Gb 45.36N 123.48 E
Anguilla [5] 176 Mh 18.15N 63.05W
Anguilla 174 Mh 18.15N 63.05W
Anguilla, Canal de l'- = Anguilla Channel (EN) 197b Ab 18.09N 63.04W
Anguilla Bank (EN) 197b Ab 18.30N 63.03W
Anguilla Cays 194 Hb 23.31N 78.33W
Anguilla Channel 197b Ab 18.09N 63.04W
Anguilla Channel (EN) = Anguilla, Canal de l'- 197b Ab 18.09N 63.04W
Anguli Nur 154 Cd 41.23N 114.30 E
Anguo 154 Ce 38.25N 115.20 E
Anhanca 170 Cf 16.47S 15.33 E
Anhanguera 204 Hd 18.21S 48.17W
An Hoa 148 Le 15.46N 108.03 E
Anholt 114 Ch 56.40N 11.35 E
Anhua (Dongping) 152 Jf 28.27N 111.15 E
Anhui Sheng (An-hui Sheng) = Anhwei (EN) [2] 152 Ke 32.00N 117.00 E
An-hui Sheng → Anhui Sheng = Anhwei (EN) [2] 152 Ke 32.00N 117.00 E
Anhwei (EN) = Anhui Sheng (An-hui Sheng) [2] 152 Ke 32.00N 117.00 E
Anhwei (EN) = An-hui Sheng → Anhui Sheng [2] 152 Ke 32.00N 117.00 E
Ani 156 Gb 39.59N 140.25 E
Aniak 178 Hd 61.34N 159.30W
An Iarmhí/Westmeath [2] 118 Fh 53.30N 7.30W
Anibare 220e Bb 0.32S 166.57 E
Anibare Bay 220e Bb 0.32S 166.57 E
Aniche 124 Fd 50.20N 3.15 E
Ánidhros 130 Im 36.37N 25.41 E
Anié 166 Fd 7.45N 1.12 E
Anie, Pic d'- 122 Fl 42.57N 0.43W
Aniene 128 Gi 41.56N 12.30 E
Anijangying → Luanping 154 Dd 40.55N 117.19 E
Anikščjaj/Anykščiai 114 Fi 55.31N 25.08 E
Animas Peak 186 Bk 31.35N 108.47W
Anina 130 Ed 45.05N 21.51 E
Anita Garibaldi 204 Gh 27.37S 51.05W
Anittepe 130 Kh 41.21N 27.42 E
Aniva 138 Jg 46.41N 142.35 E
Aniva, mys- 138 Jg 46.00N 143.25 E
Aniva, zaliv- 138 Jg 46.20N 142.40 E
Anivorano Avaratra 172 Hb 12.43S 49.12 E
Anivorano Nord 172 Hb 12.43S 49.12 E
Aniwa, Ile- 208 Hf 19.16S 169.35 E
Anizy-le-Château 124 Fe 49.30N 3.27 E
Anjala 114 Gf 60.41N 26.50 E
Anji 154 Ei 30.39N 119.41 E
Anjiang → Qianyang 152 Jf 27.19N 110.13 E
Anjō 156 Ed 34.57N 137.05 E
Anjou 122 Fg 47.20N 0.30W
Anjou, Val d'- 122 Fg 47.25N 0.15W
Anjouan/Nzwani 158 Lj 12.15S 44.25 E
Anjou Islands (EN) = Anžu, ostrova- 140 Qb 75.30N 143.00 E
Anjozorobe 172 Hc 18.24S 47.52 E
Anju 152 Md 39.37N 125.40 E
Anjuj 138 Ig 49.20N 136.20 E
Anjujski hrebet 138 Lc 67.20N 166.00 E
Anka 166 Gc 12.07N 5.55 E
Ankang (Xing'an) 142 Mf 32.37N 109.03 E
Ankara 142 Ff 39.56N 32.52 E
Ankara-Altındağ 146 Ec 39.56N 32.52 E
Ankara-Çankaya 146 Ec 39.56N 32.52 E
Ankaratra 158 Lj 19.25S 47.12 E
Ankara-Yenimahalle 146 Ec 39.56N 32.52 E
Ankarsrum 114 Dh 57.42N 16.19 E
Ankavandra 172 Hc 18.45S 45.18 E
Ankazoabo 172 Gd 22.16S 44.30 E
Ankazobe 172 Hc 18.17S 47.05 E
Ankeny 186 Jf 41.44N 93.36W
'Ankhor 168 Hc 10.47N 46.18 E
Anklam 120 Jc 53.52N 13.42 E
Ankober 168 Fd 9.40N 39.44 E
Ankoro 170 Ed 6.45S 26.57 E
Ankum 124 Jb 52.33N 7.53 E
An Laoi/Lee 118 Ej 51.55N 8.30W
Anlong 152 If 25.02N 105.30 E
An Longfort / Longford 118 Fh 53.44N 7.47W
An Longfort/Longford [2] 118 Fh 53.40N 7.40W
An Lorgain/Lurgan 118 Gg 54.28N 6.20W
Anlu 152 Je 31.12N 113.46 E
An Mhí/Meath [2] 118 Gh 53.35N 6.40W
An Mhuaidh/Moy 118 Dg 54.12N 9.08W
An Mhuir Cheilteach = Celtic Sea (EN) 110 Fe 51.00N 7.00W
An Muileann gCearr/Mullingar 118 Fh 53.32N 7.20W
An Muirthead/Mullet Peninsula 118 Cg 54.15N 10.04W
Ånn 116 Ea 63.19N 12.33 E
Ånn 114 Ce 63.15N 12.35 E
Ann, Cape- [Ant.] 222 Ee 66.10S 51.22 E
Ann, Cape- [Ma.-U.S.] 184 Ld 42.39N 70.38W
Anna [Il.-U.S.] 186 Lh 37.28N 89.15W
Anna [Nauru] 220e Ba 0.29S 166.56 E
Anna [R.S.F.S.R.] 136 Ee 51.29N 40.26 E
Annaba 160 He 36.54N 7.46 E
Annaba [3] 162 Ib 35.35N 8.00 E
An Nabaṭiyah at Taḥtā 146 Gf 33.23N 35.29 E
Annaberg-Buchholz 120 If 50.34N 13.00 E
An Nabī Şāliḩ 146 Eh 28.38N 33.59 E
An Nabk 144 Ec 34.01N 36.44 E
An Nabk Abū Qaşr 146 Hg 30.21N 38.34 E
An Nafīḑah 128 En 36.08N 10.23 E
An Nafūd 140 Gg 28.30N 41.00 E
An Nāḩiyah 146 Ie 34.26N 41.33 E
An Najaf 142 Gf 31.59N 44.20 E
An Najaf [3] 146 Kg 31.20N 44.07 E
An Nakhl 164 Fd 29.55N 33.45 E
Annalee/An Eoghanach 118 Fg 54.02N 7.25W
Annam (EN) = Trung Phan 140 Mh 15.00N 108.00 E
Annamitique, Chaîne- 148 Le 17.00N 106.00 E
Annan 118 Jg 55.00N 3.16W
Annan 118 Jg 54.59N 3.16W
Anna Paulowna 124 Gb 52.52N 4.52 E
Anna Paulowna-Kleine Sluis 124 Gb 52.52N 4.52 E
Anna Point 220e Ba 0.29S 166.56 E
Annapolis 176 Lf 38.59N 76.30W
Annapolis Royal 184 Oc 44.45N 65.31W
Annapurna 140 Kg 28.34N 83.50 E
Ann Arbor 182 Kc 42.18N 83.45W
Anna Regina 196 Gi 7.16N 58.30W
An Nás/Naas 118 Gh 53.13N 6.39W
An Nashshāsh 146 Pk 23.05N 54.02 E
An Nashwah 146 Lg 30.49N 47.36 E
An Nāşirīyah 144 Gc 31.02N 46.16 E
An Nasser 146 Ej 24.36N 32.58 E
An Nawfalīyah 164 Cc 30.47N 17.50 E
Annecy 122 Mi 45.54N 6.07 E
Annecy, Lac d'- 122 Mi 45.51N 6.11 E
Annemasse 122 Mh 46.12N 6.15 E
Annevoie-Rouillon 124 Gd 50.21N 4.50 E
An Nīl [3] 168 Ea 20.10N 33.00 E
An Nīl al Azraq [3] 168 Ec 12.20N 34.15 E
Anning 152 Hg 24.58N 102.29 E
Anniston 182 Je 33.40N 85.50W
Annobón 158 Hi 1.32S 5.38 E
Annonay 122 Ki 45.14N 4.40 E
Annotto Bay 194 Id 18.16N 76.46W
An Nu'ayrīyah 146 Mi 27.28N 48.27 E
An Nuhūd 160 Jg 12.42N 28.26 E
An Nu' Mān 146 Fi 27.06N 35.46 E
An Nu'mānīyah 146 Kf 32.32N 45.25 E
Annweiler am Trifels 124 Je 49.12N 7.58 E
Anoia/Noya 126 Nc 41.28N 1.56 E
Anoka 186 Jd 45.11N 93.23W
An Omaigh/Omagh 118 Fg 54.36N 7.18W
Anori 202 Fd 3.47S 61.38W
Anosyennes, Chaînes- 172 Hd 24.20S 47.00 E
Áno Viánnos 130 In 35.03N 25.25 E
Anóyia 130 Hn 35.15N 24.54 E
Anping [China] 154 Ce 38.13N 115.32 E
Anping [China] 154 Gd 41.10N 123.25 E
An Pointe/Warrenpoint 118 Gg 54.06N 6.15W
Anpu 152 Ig 21.30N 110.00 E
Anpu Gang 152 Ig 21.25N 109.40 E
Anqing 142 Nf 30.32N 116.59 E
Anqiu 154 Ef 36.25N 119.12 E
An Ráth/Ráth Luirc 118 Ei 52.21N 8.41W
An Ribhéar/Kenmare River 118 Dj 51.50N 9.50W
Anröchte 124 Kc 51.34N 8.20 E
Ans 124 Hd 50.39N 5.32 E
Anşāb 144 Fd 29.11N 44.43 E

Index Symbols

[1] Independent Nation
[2] State, Region
[3] District, County
[4] Municipality
[5] Colony, Dependency
Continent
Physical Region
Historical or Cultural Region
Mount, Mountain
Volcano
Hill
Mountains, Mountain Range
Hills, Escarpment
Plateau, Upland
Pass, Gap
Plain, Lowland
Delta
Salt Flat
Valley, Canyon
Crater, Cave
Karst Features
Depression
Polder
Desert, Dunes
Forest, Woods
Heath, Steppe
Oasis
Cape, Point
Coast, Beach
Cliff
Peninsula
Isthmus
Sandbank
Island
Atoll
Rock, Reef
Islands, Archipelago
Rocks, Reefs
Coral Reef
Well, Spring
Geyser
River, Stream
Waterfall, Rapids
River Mouth, Estuary
Lake
Salt Lake
Intermittent Lake
Reservoir
Swamp, Pond
Canal
Glacier
Ice Shelf, Pack Ice
Ocean
Sea
Gulf, Bay
Strait, Fjord
Lagoon
Bank
Seamount
Tablemount
Ridge
Shelf
Basin
Escarpment, Sea Scarp
Fracture
Trench, Abyss
National Park, Reserve
Point of Interest
Recreation Site
Cave, Cavern
Historic Site
Ruins
Wall, Walls
Church, Abbey
Temple
Scientific Station
Railway station
Airport
Port
Military installation
Lighthouse
Mine
Tunnel
Dam, Bridge

Ansauvillers 124 Ee 49.34N 2.24 E
Ansbach 120 Gg 49.18N 10.35 E
An Sciobairin/Skibbereen 118 Dj 51.33N 9.15W
An Seancheann/Kinsale, Old Head of- 118 Ej 51.36N 8.32W
Anse-à-Veau 194 Kd 18.30N 73.19W
Anse-Bertrand 197e Ab 16.29N 61.31W
Anse-d'Hainault 194 Jd 18.30N 74.27W
Anse la Raye 197k Ab 13.57N 61.03W
Anshan 142 Oe 41.08N 122.59 E
Anshun 142 Mg 26.15N 105.58 E
Ansina 206 Id 31.54S 55.28W
Ansley 186 Gf 41.18N 99.23W
Anson Bay 212 Gb 13.20S 130.05 E
Ansongo 166 Fb 15.40N 0.31 E
An Srath Bán/Strabane 118 Fg 54.49N 7.27W
Anta 202 Df 13.29S 72.09W
Antabamba 202 Df 14.19S 72.55W
Antakya=Antioch (EN) 144 Eb 36.14N 36.07 E
Antalaha 160 Mj 14.55S 50.15 E
Antalya 142 Ff 36.53N 30.42 E
Antalya, Gulf of- (EN)=Antalya Körfezi 144 Db 36.30N 31.00 E
Antalya Körfezi=Antalya, Gulf of- (EN) 144 Db 36.30N 31.00 E
An Tan 148 Le 15.26N 108.39 E
Antananarivo 160 Lj 18.55S 47.30 E
Antananarivo [3] 172 Hc 19.00S 46.40 E
Antanimora 172 Hd 24.48S 45.39 E
An tAonach/Nenagh 118 Ei 52.52N 8.12W
Antarctica (EN) 106 Gr 90.00S 0.00
Antarctic Peninsula (EN) 222 Qe 69.30S 65.00W
Antas, Cachoeira das- 204 Ha 13.06S 48.09W
Antas, Rio das- 204 Gi 29.04S 51.21W
An Teampall Mór/Templemore 118 Fi 52.48N 7.50W
Antela, Laguna de- 126 Eb 42.07N 7.41W
Antelao 128 Gd 46.27N 12.16 E
Antelope Creek 188 Me 43.29N 105.23W
Anten 116 Ef 58.03N 12.30 E
Antequera [Par.] 204 Dg 24.08S 57.07W
Antequera [Sp.] 126 Hg 37.01N 4.33W
Anthony 186 Cj 32.00N 106.34W
Anti-Atlas 158 Ge 30.00N 8.30W
Antibes 122 Nk 43.35N 7.07 E
Antibes, Cap d'- 122 Nk 43.32N 7.07 E
Antica, Isla- 196 Eg 10.24N 62.43W
Anticosti, Ile d'- 174 Me 49.30N 63.00W
Antifer, Cap d'- 122 Ge 49.41N 0.10 E
Antigo 186 Ld 45.09N 89.09W
Antigonish 180 Lg 45.37N 61.58W
Antigua 174 Mh 17.03N 61.48W
Antigua and Barbuda [1] 176 Mh 17.03N 61.48W
Antigua Guatemala 190 Ff 14.34N 90.44W
Antiguo Cauce del Rio Bermejo 206 Hc 25.39S 60.11W
Antiguo Morelos 192 Jf 22.30N 99.05W
Antilla 194 Jc 20.50N 75.45W
Antillas, Mar de las-/Caribe, Mar-=Caribbean Sea (EN) 174 Lh 15.00N 73.00W
Antillas Mayores = Greater Antilles (EN) 174 Lh 20.00N 74.00W
Antillas Menores = Lesser Antilles (EN) 174 Mh 15.00N 61.00W
Antilles, Mer des-/Caraïbe, Mer-=Caribbean Sea (EN) 174 Lh 15.00N 73.00W
An tInbhear Mór/Arklow 118 Gi 52.48N 6.09W
Antioch 188 Eg 38.00N 121.49W
Antioch (EN)=Antakya 144 Eb 36.14N 36.07 E
Antioche, Pertuis d'- 122 Eh 46.05N 1.20W
Antiope Reef 212 Kf 18.18S 168.40W
Antioquia [3] 202 Cb 7.00N 75.30W
Antipajëta 138 Cc 69.09N 77.00 E
Antipodes Islands 208 Ii 49.40S 178.50 E
Antiques, Pointe d'- 197e Ab 16.26N 61.33W
an t-Iúr/Newry 118 Gg 54.11N 6.20W
Antler River 186 Fb 49.08N 101.00W
Antlers 186 Ii 34.14N 95.37W
Antofagasta 200 Ih 23.39S 70.24W
Antofagasta [2] 206 Gb 23.30S 69.00W
Antofagasta de la Sierra 206 Gc 26.04S 67.25W
Antofalla, Salar de- 206 Gc 25.44S 67.45W
Antofalla, Volcán- 206 Gc 25.34S 67.55W
Antoing 124 Fd 50.34N 3.27 E
Antón 194 Gi 8.24N 80.16W
Anton Dohrn Seamount (EN) 118 Cd 57.30N 11.00W
Antongil, Baie d'- 158 Lj 15.45S 49.50 E
Antonina 206 Kc 25.27S 48.43W
Antônio João 204 Ef 23.15S 55.31W
Antonito 186 Dh 37.05N 106.00W
Antón Lizardo, Punta de- 192 Lh 19.03N 95.58W
Antony 124 Ef 48.45N 2.18 E
Antopol 120 Ud 52.12N 24.53 E
Antracit 132 Ke 48.06N 39.06 E
Antreff 124 Ld 50.52N 9.15 E
Antrim/Aontroim 118 Gg 54.43N 6.13W
Antrim Mountains 118 Gf 55.00N 6.10W
Antrodoco 128 Hh 42.25N 13.05 E
Antsakabary 172 Hc 15.03S 48.56 E
Antsalova 172 Gc 18.42S 44.33 E
An tSionainn/Shannon 110 Fe 52.36N 9.41W
Antsirabe 160 Lj 19.51S 47.01 E
Antsiranana 160 Lj 12.17S 49.17 E
Antsiranana [3] 172 Hb 13.40S 49.15 E
An tSiúir/Suir 118 Gi 52.15N 7.00W
Antsla 114 Gh 57.52N 26.33 E
An tSláine/Slaney 118 Gi 52.21N 6.30W
Antsohihy 160 Lj 14.52S 47.58 E
An tSuca/Suck 118 Eh 53.16N 8.03W
Anttola 116 Lc 61.35N 27.39 E
Antu (Songjiang) 154 Jc 42.33N 128.20 E
Antufash, Jazīrat- 164 Hf 15.42N 42.25 E
An Tulach/Tullow 118 Gi 52.48N 6.44W
An Tulach Mhór/Tullamore 118 Fh 53.16N 7.30W
Antwerp (EN)=Antwerpen/Anvers 112 Ge 50.38N 5.34 E
Antwerp (EN)=Anvers/Antwerpen 112 Ge 50.38N 5.34 E
Antwerpen [3] 124 Gc 51.10N 4.30 E
Antwerpen/Anvers=Antwerp (EN) 112 Ge 50.38N 5.34 E
Antwerpen-Ekeren 122 Kc 51.17N 4.25 E
Antwerpen-Hoboken 124 Gc 51.10N 4.21 E
Antwerpen-Merksem 124 Gc 51.15N 4.27 E
Antykan 138 If 54.55N 135.13 E
An Uaimh (Navan) 118 Gh 53.39N 6.41W
Anuradhapura 148 Gg 8.21N 80.23 E
Anuta Island 208 Hf 11.38S 169.50 E
Anvers/Antwerpen=Antwerp (EN) 112 Ge 50.38N 5.34 E
Anvers Island 222 Qe 64.33S 63.35W
Anvik 178 Gd 62.40N 160.12W
Anxi 142 Le 40.30N 96.00 E
Anxiang 152 Jf 29.26N 112.11 E
Anxin 154 Ce 38.55N 115.56 E
Anxious Bay 212 Gf 33.25S 134.35 E
Anyang (Zhangde) 142 Nf 36.01N 114.25 E
A'nyêmaqen Shan 140 Lf 34.30N 100.00 E
Anyi 154 Cj 28.50N 115.31 E
Anykščiai/Anikščiaj 114 Fi 55.31N 25.08 E
Anza 128 Ce 46.00N 8.17 E
Anze 154 Bf 36.09N 112.14 E
Anzegem 124 Fd 50.50N 3.28 E
Anžero-Sudžensk 142 Kd 56.07N 86.00 E
Anzi 170 Dc 0.52S 23.24 E
Anzio 128 Gi 41.27N 12.37 E
Anzoátegui [2] 202 Fb 9.00N 64.30W
Anzob, pereval- 135 Ge 39.07N 68.53 E
Anžu, ostrova- = Anjou Islands (EN) 140 Qb 75.30N 143.00 E
Aoba, Ile- 216 Cc 15.25S 167.50 E
Ao Ban Don 148 Jg 9.20N 99.25 E
Aoga-Shima 152 Oe 32.30N 139.50 E
Aohan Qi (Xinhui) 154 Ec 42.18N 119.53 E
Aoiz 126 Kb 42.47N 1.22W
Aoji 154 Kc 42.31N 130.24 E
Aola 219a Ec 9.32S 160.29 E
Aomen/Macau=Macao (EN) 152 Jg 22.12N 113.33 E
Aomen/Macau=Macao (EN) [5] 142 Ng 22.10N 113.33 E
Aomori 142 Qe 40.49N 140.45 E
Aomori Ken [2] 154 Pd 40.40N 140.40 E
Aono-Yama 156 Bd 34.27N 131.48 E
Aontroim/Antrim 118 Gg 54.43N 6.13W
Aopo 221c Aa 13.29S 172.30W
Aôral, Phnum- 148 Kf 12.02N 104.10 E
Aoré 219b Cb 15.35S 167.10 E
Aosta / Aoste 128 Be 45.44N 7.20 E
Aoste / Aosta 128 Be 45.44N 7.20 E
Aouk, Bahr- 158 Ih 8.51N 18.53 E
Aoukalé 168 Cd 9.10N 20.30 E
Aoukâr [Afr.] 162 Ge 24.00N 2.30W
Aoukâr [Mtna.] 158 Gg 17.30N 9.30W
Aoulef 162 Hd 26.58N 1.05 E
Aoumou 219b Be 21.24S 165.49 E
Aourou 166 Cc 14.28N 11.34W
Aoya 152 Cd 35.32N 133.59 E
Aozou 160 If 21.49N 17.25 E
Apa, Rio- 206 Ib 22.06S 58.00W
Apača 138 Kf 52.50N 157.10 E
Apache 188 Kk 31.44N 109.07W
Apache Junction 188 Jj 33.26N 111.32W
Apahida 130 Gc 46.49N 23.45 E
Apakho 219c Bb 11.25S 166.32 E
Apalachee Bay 174 Kg 29.30N 84.00W
Apalachicola 184 Ek 29.44N 84.59W
Apalachicola River 184 Ek 29.44N 84.59W
Apan 192 Jh 19.43N 98.25W
Apaporis, Rio- 198 Jf 1.23S 69.25W
Aparecida do Taboado 202 Hg 20.05S 51.05W
Aparri 142 Oh 18.22N 121.39 E
Apataki Atoll 208 Mf 15.26S 146.20W
Apatin 130 Bd 45.40N 18.59 E
Apatity 112 Jb 67.34N 33.18 E
Apatzingán de la Constitucion 190 De 19.05N 102.21W
Apaxtla de Castrejón 192 Jh 18.09N 99.52W
Ape 114 Gh 57.32N 26.42 E
Apeldoorn 122 Lb 52.13N 5.58 E
Apeldoorn-Nieuw Milligen 124 Hb 52.14N 5.45 E
Apen 124 Ja 53.13N 7.48 E
Apennines (EN) = Appennini 110 Hg 43.00N 13.00 E
Apere, Rio- 202 Ef 13.44S 65.18W
Aphrodisias 146 Cd 37.45N 28.40 E
Api 170 Eb 3.40N 25.26 E
Api 140 Kf 30.00N 80.57 E
Apia 210 Jf 13.50S 171.44W
Apiacás, Serra dos- 202 Gf 10.15S 57.15W
Apio 219 Ec 9.39S 161.23 E
Apipé Grande, Isla- 204 Di 27.30S 56.54W
Apizaco 192 Jh 19.25N 98.09W
Aplao 202 Dg 16.05S 72.31W
Apo, Mount- 140 Oi 6.59N 125.16 E
Apodi 202 Ke 5.39S 37.48W
Apolda 120 He 51.01N 11.30 E
Apolima 221c Aa 13.49S 172.07W
Apolima Strait 221c Aa 13.50S 172.10W
Apollo Bay 212 Ig 38.45S 143.40 E
Apollonia [Alb.] 130 Ci 40.43N 19.27 E
Apollonia [Lib.] 164 Dc 32.54N 21.58 E
Apolo 202 Ef 14.43S 68.31W
Apón, Rio- 194 Kh 9.50N 72.23W
Apopka, Lake- 184 Gk 28.37N 81.38W
Aporé 204 Fd 18.58S 52.01W
Aporé, Rio- 198 Kg 19.27S 50.57W
Apostle Islands 182 Ib 46.50N 90.30W
Apóstoles 206 Ic 27.55S 55.46W
Apostolovo 132 Hf 47.39N 33.43 E
Apoteri 202 Gc 4.02N 58.34W
Apôtres, Iles des- 222 Ec 45.40S 50.20 E
Appalachia 184 Fg 36.54N 82.48W
Appalachian Mountains 174 Lc 41.00N 77.00W
Äppelbo 116 Ed 60.30N 14.00 E
Appennini = Apennines (EN) 110 Hg 43.00N 13.00 E
Appennino Abruzzese 128 Hh 42.00N 13.55 E
Appennino Calabro 128 Kl 39.00N 16.30 E
Appennino Campano 128 Ii 40.50N 14.45 E
Appennino Ligure 128 Cf 44.30N 9.00 E
Appennino Lucano 128 Jj 40.30N 16.00 E
Appennino Tosco-Emiliano 128 Fg 44.00N 1 830 E
Appennino Umbro-Marchigiano 128 Gg 43.20N 12.55 E
Appenzell 128 Dc 47.20N 9.25 E
Appenzell Ausser-Rhoden [2] 128 Dc 47.20N 9.20 E
Appenzell Inner-Rhoden [2] 128 Dc 47.15N 9.25 E
Appingedam 124 Ia 53.19N 6.52 E
Appleby 118 Kg 54.36N 2.29W
Appleton 182 Jc 44.16N 88.25W
Appomattox 184 Hg 37.21N 78.51W
Apra Harbor 220c Bb 13.27N 144.38 E
Apricena 128 Ji 41.47N 15.27 E
Aprilia 128 Gi 41.36N 12.39 E
Apšeronsk 136 Dg 44.27N 39.44 E
Apšeronski poluostrov = Apsheron Peninsula (EN) 110 Lg 41.00N 50.50 E
Apsheron Peninsula (EN) = Apšeronski poluostrov 110 Lg 41.00N 50.50 E
Apt 122 Lk 43.53N 5.24 E
Apucarana 206 Jb 23.33S 51.29W
Apucarana, Serra da- 204 Gf 23.50S 51.20W
Apuka 138 Ld 60.23N 169.45 E
Apuka 138 Ld 60.25N 169.35 E
Apulia (EN) = Puglia [2] 128 Ki 41.15N 16.15 E
Apurashokoru 220a Ac 7.17N 134.18 E
Apure [2] 202 Eb 7.10N 68.50W
Apure, Rio- 198 Je 7.37N 66.25W
Apurimac [3] 202 Df 14.00S 73.00W
Apurimac, Rio- 198 Ig 12.17S 73.56W
Apurito 196 Bi 7.56N 68.27W
Apuseni, Munţii-=Apuseni Mountains (EN) 110 If 46.30N 22.30 E
Apuseni Mountains (EN)=Apuseni, Munţii- 110 If 46.30N 22.30 E
Āq 146 Kc 38.59N 45.27 E
Āqā 146 Me 35.00N 47.00 E
Aqaba (EN)=Al 'Aqabah 144 Dd 29.31N 35.00 E
Aqaba, Gulf of- (EN)='Aqabah, Khalīj al- 158 Kf 29.00N 34.40 E
Āqā Bāba 146 Md 36.20N 49.46 E
'Aqabah, Khalīj al-=Aqaba, Gulf of- (EN) 158 Kf 29.00N 34.40 E
Āqcheh 144 Kb 36.56N 66.11 E
'Aqdā 146 Of 32.26N 53.37 E
'Aqiq 168 Fb 18.14N 38.12 E
Aqitag 152 Fc 41.49N 90.38 E
Āqotāq 146 Ld 37.10N 47.05 E
Āq Qal'eh 146 Pd 37.01N 54.30 E
Aqqikkol Hu 152 Ed 37.00N 88.20 E
'Aqrah 146 Jd 36.45N 43.54 E
Aqrin, Jabal- 146 Hg 31.32N 38.18 E
Āq Şū 146 Ke 34.35N 44.31 E
Aquidabã, Rio- 204 De 20.58S 57.50W
Aquidabán, Rio- 204 Df 23.11S 57.32W
Aquidauana 202 Gh 20.28S 55.48W
Aquidauana, Rio- 202 Gg 19.44S 56.50W
Aquidauna, Serra de- 204 Ee 20.50S 55.30W
Aquiles Serdán 192 Gc 28.36N 105.53W
Aquin 194 Kd 18.16N 73.24W
Aquitaine, Bassin d'-= Aquitaine Basin (EN) 110 Fg 44.00N 0.10W
Aquitaine Basin (EN)= Aquitaine, Bassin d'- 110 Fg 44.00N 0.10W
Ara 126 Mb 42.25N 0.09 E
'Arab, Bahr al- 158 Jh 9.02N 29.28 E
'Arab, Khalīj al- 164 Ec 30.55N 29.05 E
'Arab, Shatt al- 140 Gf 30.28N 47.59 E
'Arabah, Wādī- 146 Eh 29.07N 32.39 E
'Arabah, Wādī al- 146 Fg 30.58N 32.24 E
Arabatskaja Strelka, kosa- 132 Ig 45.40N 35.05 E
'Arabestān 146 Mg 30.30N 50.00 E
Arabian Basin (EN) 106 Gh 11.30N 65.00 E
Arabian Desert (EN) = Sharqīyah, Aş Şaḥrā' ash- 158 Kf 28.00N 32.00 E
Arabian Peninsula (EN) 140 Gg 25.00N 45.00 E
Arabian Sea (EN) 140 Ih 15.00N 65.00 E
Araç 146 Eb 41.15N 33.21 E
Aracá, Rio- 146 Fd 0.25S 62.55W
Aracaju 200 Mg 10.55S 37.04W
Aracataca 194 Jh 10.35N 74.13W
Aracati 202 Kd 4.34S 37.46W
Araçatuba 200 Kh 21.12S 50.25W
Aracena 126 Fg 37.53N 6.33W
Aracena, Sierra de- 126 Fg 37.56N 6.50W
Aracides, Cape- 219a Ec 8.39S 161.01 E
Aracruz 202 Jg 19.49S 40.16W
Araçuai 202 Jg 16.52S 42.04W
Arad 112 If 46.11N 21.19 E
'Arad 146 Fg 31.15N 35.13 E
Arad [2] 130 Ec 46.11N 21.25 E
Arada 168 Cb 15.01N 20.40 E
'Arādah 168 Ia 22.59N 53.26 E
Arafali 168 Fb 15.04N 39.45 E
Ara Fana 168 Gd 6.01N 41.11 E
Arafune-Yama 156 Fc 36.12N 138.38 E
Arafura, Laut-=Arafura Sea (EN) 208 Ee 9.00S 133.00 E
Arafura Sea (EN) = Arafura, Laut- 208 Ee 9.00S 133.00 E
Aragac, gora- 136 Kg 40.31N 44.10 E
Aragarças 200 Kg 15.55S 52.15W
Aragón [2] 126 Lc 41.00N 1.00W
Aragón [2] 110 Fg 41.00N 1.00W
Aragón 126 Kb 42.13N 1.44W
Aragona 128 Hm 37.24N 13.37 E
Aragua [2] 202 Eb 10.00N 67.10W
Araguacema 202 Ie 8.50S 49.34W
Aragua de Barcelona 196 Dh 9.28N 64.49W
Aragua de Maturin 196 Eh 9.58N 63.29W
Araguaia, Rio- 198 Lf 5.21S 48.41W
Araguaiana 204 Gb 16.49S 53.05W
Araguaia ou Javaes, Braço Menor do- 202 He 9.50S 50.12W
Araguaina 202 Ie 7.12S 48.12W
Araguao, Boca- 202 Fb 9.17N 60.48W
Araguao, Caño- 196 Fh 9.15N 60.50W
Araguapiche, Punta- 196 Fh 9.29N 60.56W
Araguari 202 Ig 18.38S 48.11W
Araguari, Rio- [Braz.] 198 Le 1.15N 49.55W
Araguari, Rio- [Braz.] 204 Hd 18.21S 48.40W
Araguatins 202 Ie 5.38S 48.07W
'Arāguīb 162 Ff 18.50N 7.45W
Aragvi 132 Ni 41.50N 44.43 E
Arai 154 Of 37.09N 138.06 E
Árainn/Inishmore 118 Dh 53.07N 9.45W
Árainn Mhór/Aran Island 118 Ef 55.00N 8.30W
Araioses 202 Jd 2.53S 41.55W
Arāk 142 Gf 34.05N 49.41 E
Arak 162 Hd 25.18N 3.45 E
Arakabesan 220a Ac 7.21N 134.27 E
Arakan [2] 148 Ie 19.00N 94.15 E
Arakan Yoma 140 Lh 19.00N 94.40 E
Arakawa 156 Fb 38.09N 139.25 E
Ara-Kawa [Jap.] 156 Fb 38.09N 139.23 E
Ara-Kawa [Jap.] 156 Fc 37.11N 138.15 E
Arakhthos 130 Ej 39.01N 21.03 E
Araks 130 Gf 39.56N 48.20 E
Aral [China] 152 Dc 40.38N 81.24 E
Aral [Kirg.-U.S.S.R.] 136 Hg 41.48N 74.25 E
Aral Sea (EN) = Aralskoje more 140 He 45.00N 60.00 E
Aralsk 142 Ie 46.48N 61.40 E
Aralskoje more = Aral Sea (EN) 140 He 45.00N 60.00 E
Aralsor, ozero- 132 Pe 49.05N 48.15 E
Aralsulfat 136 Gf 46.50N 61.59 E
Aramac 212 Jd 22.59S 145.14 E
Arambaré 204 Gj 30.55S 51.29W
Ārān 146 Ne 34.03N 51.30 E
Ara Naoimh/Aran Islands 118 Dh 53.07N 9.43W
Aranda de Duero 126 Ic 41.41N 3.41W
Arandelovac 130 De 44.18N 20.35 E
Arandilla 126 Ic 41.40N 3.41W
Aran Island/Árainn Mhór 118 Ef 55.00N 8.30W
Aran Islands/Ara Naoimh 118 Dh 53.07N 9.43W
Aranjuez 126 Id 40.02N 3.36W
Aranos 172 Bd 24.09S 19.09 E
Arañuelo, Campo- 126 Ge 39.55N 5.30W
Aranuka Atoll 208 Id 0.11N 173.36 E
Arao 156 Be 32.59N 130.27 E
Araouane 160 Gg 18.53N 3.35W
Arapahoe 186 Gf 40.18N 99.54W
Arapey Grande, Rio- 204 Dj 30.55S 57.49W
Arapiraca 202 Ke 9.45S 36.39W
Arápis, Ákra- 130 Hi 40.27N 24.00 E
Arapkir 146 Hc 39.03N 38.30 E
Arapoim, Rio- 204 Kb 15.45S 43.39W
Arapongas 206 Jb 23.23S 51.27W
Arapoti 204 Hg 24.08S 49.50W
'Ar'ar 146 Ig 30.59N 41.02 E
'Ar'ar, Wādī 146 Jg 31.23N 42.26 E
Araranguá 206 Kc 28.56S 49.29W
Araraquara 200 Lh 21.47S 48.10W
Araras 204 If 22.22S 47.23W
Araras, Açude- 202 Jd 4.20S 40.30W
Araras, Serra das- 204 Fd 18.45S 53.30W
Ararat [Arm.-U.S.S.R.] 136 Eh 39.50N 44.43 E
Ararat [Austl.] 212 Ig 37.17S 142.56 E
Ararat, Mount- (EN) = Ağrı Dağı 140 Gf 39.40N 44.24 E
Arari 202 Jd 3.28S 44.47W
Arari, Lago- 202 Id 0.37S 49.07W
Aras 140 Gf 39.56N 48.20 E
Aras Dağları 146 Jc 40.00N 43.00 E
Aratika Atoll 208 Mf 15.32S 145.32W
Aratürük/Yiwu 152 Fc 43.15N 94.35 E
Arauca 202 Db 7.03N 70.47W
Arauca [3] 202 Db 6.30N 71.00W
Arauca, Rio- 198 Je 7.24N 66.35W
Arauco 206 Fe 37.15S 73.19W
Araure 196 Bh 9.38N 69.15W
Aravaca, Madrid- 126 Id 40.27N 3.47W
Aravis, Chaîne des- 122 Mi 45.53N 6.28 E
Arawalli Range 140 Jg 25.00N 73.30 E
Araxá 202 Ig 19.35S 46.55W
Áraxos, Ákra- 130 Ek 38.10N 21.23 E
Araya 196 Dg 10.34N 64.15W
Araya, Peninsula de- 202 Fa 10.35N 64.00W
Arba 126 Kc 41.52N 1.18W
Arba'āt 168 Fb 19.50N 37.03 E
Arba'īn, Darb al- 164 Di 26.40N 30.50 E
Arbaj-Here 152 Hb 46.15N 102.48 E
Arba Minch 160 Kh 5.59N 37.38 E
'Arbat 146 Ke 35.25N 45.35 E
Arbatax 128 Dk 39.56N 9.42 E
Arboga 114 Dg 59.24N 15.50 E
Arbogaån 116 Ge 59.26N 16.04 E
Arbois 122 Lh 46.54N 5.46 E
Arboletes 194 Ii 8.52N 76.26W
Arbolito 204 Ek 32.39S 54.15W
Arbon 128 Dc 47.30N 9.25 E
Arbore 130 Ib 47.44N 25.56 E
Arborea 128 Ck 39.46N 8.35 E
Arborea 128 Ck 39.50N 8.50 E
Arborg 186 Ha 50.55N 97.15W
Arbrå 114 Dc 61.29N 16.23 E
Arbresle, L'- 122 Ki 45.50N 4.37 E
Arbroath 118 Ke 56.34N 2.35W
Arbus 128 Ck 39.32N 8.36 E
Arc [Fr.] 122 Mi 45.34N 6.12 E
Arc [Fr.] 122 Lk 43.31N 5.07 E
Arcachon 122 Ej 44.39N 1.10W
Arcachon, Bassin d'- 122 Ej 44.42N 1.09W
Arcadia [Fl.-U.S.] 184 Gl 27.14N 81.52W
Arcadia [La.-U.S.] 186 Jj 32.33N 92.55W
Arcagly-Ajat 134 Jj 53.00N 61.50 E
Arcas, Cayos- 190 Fd 20.12N 91.58W
Arcata 188 Cf 40.52N 124.05W
Arcelia 192 Ih 18.17N 100.16W
Arcen, Arcen en Velden- 124 Ic 51.28N 6.11 E
Arcen en Velden 124 Ic 51.28N 6.11 E
Arcen en Velden - Arcen 124 Ic 51.28N 6.11 E
Arcevia 128 Gg 43.30N 12.56 E
Archangel (EN)=Arhangelsk 112 Kc 64.34N 40.32 E
Archaringa Creek 212 He 28.15S 135.15 E
Archer River 212 Ib 13.28S 141.41 E
Archer's Post 170 Gb 0.39N 37.41 E
Archidona 126 Hg 37.05N 4.23W
Arcidosso 128 Fh 42.52N 11.33 E
Arcipelago Campano 110 Hg 40.30N 13.20 E
Arcis-sur-Aube 122 Kf 48.32N 4.08 E
Arciz 132 Fg 45.59N 29.27 E
Arco [Id.-U.S.] 188 Ie 43.38N 113.18W
Arco [It.] 128 Ee 45.55N 10.53 E
Arconce 122 Kh 46.27N 4.00 E
Arcos 204 Je 20.17S 45.32W
Arcos de Jalón 126 Jc 41.13N 2.16W
Arcos de la Frontera 126 Gh 36.45N 5.48W
Arcos de Valdevez 126 Dc 41.51N 8.25W
Arcoverde 200 Mf 8.25S 37.04W
Arctic Bay 176 Kb 73.02N 85.11W
Arctic Ocean 224 Be 85.00N 170.00 E
Arctic Ocean (EN)= Ishavet 224 Be 85.00N 170.00 E
Arctic Ocean (EN) = Severny Ledovity okean 224 Be 85.00N 170.00 E
Arctic Red River 180 Ec 67.22N 133.30W
Arctic Red River 180 Ec 67.27N 133.45W
Arctic Village 178 Jc 68.08N 145.19W
Arda [Eur.] 130 Jh 41.39N 26.29 E
Arda [It.] 128 Ee 45.02N 10.02 E
Ardabīl 142 Gf 38.15N 48.18 E
Ardahan 146 Jb 41.07N 42.41 E
Ardakāh 146 Hc 32.19N 53.59 E
Ardakān 146 Og 30.16N 52.01 E
Ardal 146 Ng 31.59N 50.39 E
Ardales 126 Hh 36.52N 4.51W
Ardalsfjorden 116 Bc 61.15N 7.30 E
Årdalstangen 114 Bf 61.14N 7.43 E
Ardanuç 146 Jb 41.08N 42.03 E
Ardatov [R.S.F.S.R.] 114 Ki 55.17N 43.12 E
Ardatov [R.S.F.S.R.] 114 Li 54.53N 46.13 E
'Arde 168 Hd 9.58N 46.04 E
Ardèche [3] 122 Kj 44.40N 4.20 E
Ardèche 122 Kj 44.16N 4.39 E
Ardee/Béal Átha Fhirdhia 118 Gh 53.52N 6.33W
Ardencaple Fjord 179 Jd 75.15N 20.10W
Ardenne, Plateau de l'-/Ardennen, Plateau van de- = Ardennes (EN) 110 Ge 50.10N 5.45 E
Ardennen, Plateau van de-/Ardenne, Plateau de l'- = Ardennes (EN) 110 Ge 50.10N 5.45 E
Ardennes [3] 122 Ke 49.40N 4.40 E
Ardennes (EN) = Ardenne, Plateau de l'-/Ardennen, Plateau van de- 110 Ge 50.10N 5.45 E
Ardennes (EN) = Ardennen, Plateau van de- / Ardenne, Plateau de l'- 110 Ge 50.10N 5.45 E
Ardennes, Canal des- 122 Ke 49.26N 4.02 E
Ardennes, Forêt des- 124 Ge 49.48N 4.50 E
Ardentes 122 Hh 46.45N 1.50 E
Ardeşen 146 Ib 41.12N 41.00 E
Ardestān 146 Of 33.22N 52.23 E
Árdhas 130 Jh 41.39N 26.29 E
Ardila 126 Ef 38.12N 7.28W
Ard Mhacha/Armagh 118 Gg 54.21N 6.39W
Ardmore 182 He 34.10N 97.08W
Ardnamurchan, Point of- 118 Ge 56.45N 6.30W
Ardon 132 Nh 43.07N 44.13 E
Ardooie 124 Fd 50.59N 3.12 E
Ardre 124 Fe 49.18N 3.40 E
Ardres 124 Dd 50.51N 1.59 E
Ardrossan 118 If 55.40N 4.55W
Ards Peninsula/An Aird 118 Hg 54.30N 5.30W
Ardud 130 Fb 47.38N 22.53 E
Arebi 170 Eb 2.50N 29.38 E
Arecibo 190 Ke 18.28N 66.43W
Arėgala/Ariogala 116 Ji 55.13N 23.30 E
Areia, Ribeirão da- 204 Jc 16.07S 45.52W
Areia Branca 202 Kd 4.57S 37.08W
Arekalong Peninsula 220a Bb 7.40N 134.38 E
Aremberg 124 Id 50.25N 6.49 E
Arena 150 He 9.14N 120.46 E
Arena, Point- 182 Cd 38.57N 123.44W
Arena, Punta- 190 Cd 23.30N 109.30W
Arena de la Ventana, Punta- 190 Cd 24.04N 109.52W
Arenápolis 202 Gf 14.26S 56.49W
Arenas, Cayo- 190 Fd 22.08N 91.24W
Arenas, Punta de- 206 Gh 53.09S 68.13W
Arenas de San Pedro 126 Gd 40.12N 5.05W
Arenberg 124 Jb 52.42N 7.20 E
Arendal 114 Bg 58.27N 8.48 E
Arendonk 124 Hc 51.19N 5.05 E
Arenys de Mar/Arénys de Mar 126 Oc 41.35N 2.33 E
Arénys de Mar/Arenys de Mar 126 Oc 41.35N 2.33 E
Areópolis 130 Fm 36.40N 22.23 E
Areq, Sebkha Bougg 126 Ji 35.10N 2.45W
Arequipa 200 Ig 16.24S 71.33W
Arequipa [3] 202 Dg 16.00S 72.30W
Arequito 204 Bk 33.09S 61.28W
Arero 168 Fe 4.44N 38.50 E

Index Symbols

[1] Independent Nation
[2] State, Region
[3] District, County
[4] Municipality
[5] Colony, Dependency
Continent
Physical Region
Historical or Cultural Region
Mount, Mountain
Volcano
Hill
Mountains, Mountain Range
Hills, Escarpment
Plateau, Upland
Pass, Gap
Plain, Lowland
Delta
Salt Flat
Valley, Canyon
Crater, Cave
Karst Features
Depression
Polder
Desert, Dunes
Forest, Woods
Heath, Steppe
Oasis
Cape, Point
Coast, Beach
Cliff
Peninsula
Isthmus
Sandbank
Island
Atoll
Rock, Reef
Islands, Archipelago
Rocks, Reefs
Coral Reef
Well, Spring
Geyser
River, Stream
Waterfall, Rapids
River Mouth, Estuary
Lake
Salt Lake
Intermittent Lake
Reservoir
Swamp, Pond
Canal
Glacier
Ice Shelf, Pack Ice
Ocean
Sea
Gulf, Bay
Strait, Fjord
Lagoon
Bank
Seamount
Tablemount
Ridge
Shelf
Basin
Escarpment, Sea Scarp
Fracture
Trench, Abyss
National Park, Reserve
Point of Interest
Recreation Site
Cave, Cavern
Historic Site
Ruins
Wall, Walls
Church, Abbey
Temple
Scientific Station
Railway station
Airport
Port
Military installation
Lighthouse
Mine
Tunnel
Dam, Bridge

Ares, Mola d'- / Ares, Muela de-	126	Ld	40.28N	0.07W
Ares, Muela de- / Ares, Mola d'-	126	Ld	40.28N	0.07W
Åreskutan	114	Ce	63.24N	13.06 E
Åreskutan	114	Ce	63.26N	13.06 E
Arévalo	126	Hc	41.04N	4.43W
Arezzo	128	Fg	43.25N	11.53 E
Arga	126	Kb	42.18N	1.47W
Argajas	134	Ji	55.31N	60.55 E
Argamasilla de Alba	126	Ie	39.07N	3.06W
Argan	152	Ec	40.09N	88.22 E
Arganda	126	Id	40.18N	3.26W
Arga-Sala	138	Gc	68.37N	112.05 E
Argelès-Gazost	122	Fk	43.01N	0.06W
Argelès-sur-Mer	122	Jl	42.33N	3.01 E
Argens	122	Mk	43.24N	6.44 E
Argent, Côte d'-	122	Ej	44.00N	1.30W
Argenta	128	Ff	44.37N	11.50 E
Argentan	122	Ff	48.45N	0.01W
Argentario, Monte-	128	Fh	42.24N	11.09 E
Argentat	122	Hi	45.06N	1.56 E
Argentera	128	Bf	44.10N	7.18 E
Argenteuil	122	If	48.57N	2.15 E
Argentiera, Capo dell'-	128	Cj	40.44N	8.08 E
Argentière-la-Bessée, L'-	122	Mj	44.47N	6.33 E
Argentina	204	Ai	29.33 S	62.17W
Argentina [1]	200	Ji	34.00 S	64.00W
Argentine Basin (EN)	106	Cn	45.00 S	45.00W
Argentino, Lago-	198	Ik	50.13 S	72.25W
Argentino, Mar-	198	Kj	46.00 S	59.40W
Argenton	122	Fg	47.05N	0.13W
Argenton-Château	122	Fh	46.59N	0.27W
Argenton-sur-Creuse	122	Hh	46.35N	1.31 E
Argeş [2]	130	Hd	45.00N	24.50 E
Argeş	130	Je	44.04N	26.37 E
Arghandāb	144	Jc	31.27N	64.23 E
Argo	168	Eb	19.31N	30.25 E
Argolikós Kólpos = Argolis, Gulf of- (EN)	130	Fl	37.20N	22.55 E
Argolis, Gulf of- (EN) = Argolikós Kólpos	130	Fl	37.20N	22.55 E
Argonne	122	Ke	49.30N	5.00 E
Argonne	124	He	49.30N	5.00 E
Árgos	130	Fl	37.38N	22.44 E
Árgos Orestikón	130	Ei	40.30N	21.16 E
Argostólion	130	Dk	38.11N	20.29 E
Arguedas	126	Kb	42.10N	1.36W
Argueil-Fry	124	De	49.37N	1.31 E
Arguello, Point-	188	Ei	34.35N	120.39W
Arguenon	122	Df	48.35N	2.13W
Argun	132	Nh	43.16N	45.52 E
Argun	140	Od	53.20N	121.28 E
Argungu	166	Fc	12.45N	4.31 E
Argyle	197n	Ba	13.10N	61.10W
Argyle, Lake-	208	Df	16.15 S	128.40 E
Argyll	118	Ie	56.20N	5.00W
Arhangelsk = Archangel (EN)	112	Kc	64.34N	40.32 E
Arhangelskaja oblast [3]	136	Ec	63.30N	43.00 E
Arhara	138	Ig	49.30N	130.09 E
Arhavi	146	Ib	41.22N	41.16 E
Arholma	116	He	59.50N	19.05 E
Ar Horqin Qi (Tianshan)	152	Lc	43.55N	120.05 E
Århus	112	Hd	56.09N	10.13 E
Århus [2]	116	Dh	56.10N	10.15 E
Århus Bugt	116	Dh	56.10N	10.20 E
Arhust	152	Ib	47.42N	107.50 E
Ariadnoje	138	Ig	45.08N	134.25 E
Ariake-Kai	154	Kh	32.55N	130.27 E
Ariamsvlei	172	Be	28.08 S	19.50 E
Ariano Irpino	128	Ji	41.09N	15.05 E
Ariari, Río-	202	Dc	2.35N	72.47W
Arias	206	Hd	33.38 S	62.25W
Ari Atoll	148a	Bb	3.30N	72.45 E
Aribinda	166	Ec	14.14N	0.52W
Arica	200	Ig	18.29 S	70.20W
Arica, Golfo de-	198	Ig	18.30 S	70.30W
Arichuna	196	Ci	7.42N	67.08W
Arid, Cape-	212	Ef	34.00 S	123.09 E
Arida	154	Mg	34.05N	135.07 E
Arida-Gawa	156	Dd	34.05N	135.06 E
Aridhaia	130	Fi	40.59N	22.04 E
Ariège [3]	122	Hk	43.00N	1.30 E
Ariège	122	Hk	43.31N	1.25 E
Ariel	204	Cm	36.32 S	59.54W
Aries	130	Gc	46.26N	23.59 E
Ariguani	202	Db	9.50N	74.01W
Ariguani, Río-	194	Ki	9.35N	73.46W
Arīḥā [Jor.]	146	Fg	31.52N	35.27 E
Arīḥā [Syr.]	146	Ge	35.48N	36.36 E
Arikaree River	186	Ff	40.01N	101.56W
Arikawa	156	Ae	32.59N	129.07 E
Arilje	130	Df	43.45N	20.06 E
Arima	202	Fa	10.38N	61.17W
Arinos	204	Ib	15.55 S	46.04W
Arinos, Rio-	198	Kg	10.25 S	58.20W
Arinos Novo, Rio-	204	Db	14.14 S	56.01W
Ariogala/Arėgala	116	Ji	55.13N	23.30 E
Aripuanã	202	Fe	9.10 S	60.38W
Aripuanã, Rio-	198	Jf	5.07 S	60.24W
Ariquemes	202	Fe	9.56 S	63.04W
Arisa	168	Gc	11.11N	41.38 E
'Arish, Wādī al-	146	Eg	31.09N	33.49 E
Arismendi	194	Mi	8.29N	68.22W
Arita	156	Ae	33.11N	129.52 E
Aritzo	128	Dk	39.57N	9.12 E
Arixang/Wenquan	152	Dc	44.59N	81.04 E
Ariza	126	Jc	41.19N	2.03W
Arizaro, Salar de-	206	Gb	24.42 S	67.45W
Arize, Massif de l'-	122	Hl	42.50N	1.30 E
Arizona [2]	182	Ee	34.00N	112.00W
Arizpe	192	Db	30.20N	110.10W
Årjäng	114	Cg	59.23N	12.08 E
Arjeplog	114	Dc	66.03N	17.54 E
Arjo	168	Fd	8.45N	36.30 E
Arjona	202	Ca	10.15N	75.21W
Arkadak	136	Ee	51.58N	43.28 E
Arkadelphia	182	Ie	34.07N	93.04W
Arkalyk	142	Id	50.13N	66.50 E
Arkansas [2]	182	Id	34.50N	93.40W
Arkansas	174	Jf	33.48N	91.04W
Arkansas City	182	Hd	37.04N	97.02W
Arkanū, Jabal-	164	De	22.15N	24.45 E
Arkatag	140	Kf	36.45N	89.10 E
Arkhángelos	130	Lm	36.12N	28.08 E
Árki	130	Jl	37.22N	26.45 E
Arklow/An tInbhear Mór	118	Gi	52.48N	6.09W
Arkona, Kap-	120	Jb	54.41N	13.26 E
Arkonam	148	Ff	13.06N	79.40 E
Arkösund	116	Gf	58.30N	16.56 E
Arkoúdhion	130	Dk	38.33N	20.43 E
Arktičeskoga Instituta, ostrova- = Arkticheski Institut Islands (EN)	138	Da	75.20N	81.50 E
Arkticheski Institut Islands (EN) = Arktičeskoga Instituta, ostrova-	138	Da	75.20N	81.50 E
Arlan, gora-	132	Sj	39.43N	54.40 E
Arlanza	126	Hb	42.06N	4.09W
Arlanzón	126	Ib	42.03N	4.17W
Arlberg	122	Ec	47.08N	10.12 E
Arles	122	Kk	43.40N	4.38 E
Arlington [Or.-U.S.]	188	Ed	45.46N	120.13W
Arlington [Tx.-U.S.]	186	Hj	32.44N	97.07W
Arlington [Va.-U.S.]	182	Ld	38.52N	77.05W
Arlington Heights	186	Me	42.05N	87.59W
Arlit	160	Hg	19.00N	7.38 E
Arlon/Aarlen	122	Le	49.41N	5.49 E
Arlöv	116	Ei	55.39N	13.05 E
Arly	166	Fc	11.35N	1.28 E
Armagh/Ard Mhacha	118	Gg	54.21N	6.39W
Armagnac	122	Gk	43.45N	0.10 E
Armagnac, Collines de l'-	122	Gk	43.30N	0.30 E
Armah, Wādī-	144	Hf	18.12N	51.02 E
Arman	138	Ke	59.43N	150.12 E
Armançon	122	Jg	47.57N	3.30 E
Armandale, Perth-	212	Df	32.09 S	116.00 E
Armant	164	Fd	25.37N	32.32 E
Armáthia	130	Jn	35.26N	26.52 E
Armavir	112	Kf	45.00N	41.08 E
Armenia	200	Ie	4.31N	75.41W
Armenia (EN) = Ermenistan	140	Gf	39.10N	43.00 E
Armenia (EN) = Ermenistan	144	Fb	39.10N	43.00 E
Armenian SSR (EN) = Armjanskaja SSR [2]	136	Eg	40.00N	45.00 E
Armentières	122	Id	50.41N	2.53 E
Armeria	192	Gh	18.56N	103.58W
Armi, Capo dell'-	128	Jm	37.57N	15.41 E
Armidale	210	Gh	30.31 S	151.39 E
Armisvesi	116	Lb	62.30N	26.35 E
Armjansk	132	Hf	46.05N	33.41 E
Armjanskaja Sovetskaja Socialističeskaja Respublika [2]	136	Eg	40.00N	45.00 E
Armjanskaja SSR/Haikakan Sovetakan Socialistakan Respublika [2]	136	Eg	40.00N	45.00 E
Armjanskaja SSR = Armenian SSR (EN) [2]	136	Eg	40.00N	45.00 E
Armoricain, Massif- = Armorican Massif (EN)	110	Ff	48.00N	3.00W
Armorican Massif (EN) = Armoricain, Massif-	110	Ff	48.00N	3.00W
Armour	186	Ge	43.19N	98.21W
Arm River	188	Ma	50.46N	105.00W
Armstrong [Arg.]	204	Bk	32.47 S	61.36W
Armstrong [B.C.-Can.]	188	Fa	50.27N	119.12W
Armstrong [Ont.-Can.]	188	If	50.18N	89.02W
Ārmūdiū	146	Qd	37.15N	56.05 E
Armutçuk Dağ	130	Ki	40.05N	27.23 E
Armutlu	130	Li	40.31N	28.50 E
Armutova	130	Jj	39.23N	26.50 E
Arnaia	130	Gi	40.29N	23.36 E
Arnaud	180	Kd	60.00N	69.55W
Arnautis, Akra-	146	Ee	35.06N	32.17 E
Arnay-le-Duc	122	Kg	47.08N	4.29 E
Arnedo	126	Jb	42.13N	2.06W
Årnes	114	Cf	60.09N	11.28 E
Arnhem	122	Lc	51.59N	5.55 E
Arnhem, Cape-	208	Ef	12.21 S	136.21 E
Arnhem Bay	212	Hb	12.20 S	136.10 E
Arnhem Land	208	Ef	13.10 S	134.30 E
Arno	128	Eg	43.41N	10.17 E
Arno Atoll	208	Id	7.05N	171.41 E
Arnold	124	Aa	53.00N	1.08W
Arnon	122	Ig	47.13N	2.01 E
Arnøy	114	Ea	70.08N	20.36 E
Arnprior	184	Ic	45.26N	76.21W
Arnsberg	124	Ee	51.23N	8.05 E
Arnsberger Wald	124	Kc	51.26N	8.10 E
Arnsberg-Oeventrop	124	Kc	51.24N	8.08 E
Arnsburg	124	Kd	50.29N	8.48 E
Arnstadt	120	Gf	50.50N	10.57 E
Aro, Río-	196	Di	8.01N	64.11W
Aroa	196	Bg	10.26N	68.54W
Aroa, Pointe-	221e	Fc	17.28 S	149.46W
Aroa, Río-	196	Bg	10.41N	68.18W
Aroa, Sierra de-	196	Bg	10.15N	68.55W
Aroab	172	Be	26.47 S	19.40 E
Aroánia Óri	130	Fl	37.57N	22.13 E
Aroche	126	Fg	37.57N	6.57W
Aroche, Pico de-	126	Ff	38.01N	6.56W
Aroeira	204	Ee	21.41 S	54.25W
Arolsen	120	Ff	51.22N	9.01 E
Aroma	168	Fb	15.49N	36.08 E
Aron	122	Jh	46.50N	3.27 E
Arona	128	Ce	45.46N	8.34 E
Aroostook River	184	Nb	46.48N	67.45W
Arorae Island	208	Ie	2.38 S	176.49 E
Arorangi	220p	Bb	21.13 S	159.49W
Aros, Río-	192	Ec	29.30N	109.15W
Arosa	128	Dd	46.47N	9.40 E
Arosa, Ria de- / Arousa, Ria de-	126	Db	42.28N	8.57W
Aros Papigochic, Río-	192	Ec	29.09N	108.35W
Årøsund	116	Ci	55.15N	9.43 E
Arouca	126	Dd	40.56N	8.15W
Arousa, Ria de- / Arosa, Ria de-	126	Db	42.28N	8.57W
Arpaçay	146	Jb	40.45N	43.25 E
Arpajon	122	If	48.35N	2.15 E
Arpino	128	Hi	41.39N	13.36 E
Arquata Scrivia	128	Cf	44.41N	8.53 E
Arque	202	Eg	17.48 S	66.23W
Arques-la-Bataille	124	De	49.53N	1.08 E
Ar Rachidiya	162	Gc	31.55N	4.40W
Ar Rachidiya [3]	162	Gc	31.00N	4.00W
Ar Radīsīyah Baḥrī	164	Fe	24.57N	32.53 E
Arrah	148	Gc	25.34N	84.40 E
Ar Rahad	158	Kg	14.28N	33.31 E
Ar Raḥḥālīyah	146	Jf	32.44N	43.23 E
Arraias	202	If	12.56 S	46.57W
Arraias, Rio- [Braz.]	204	Ia	12.28 S	47.18W
Arraias, Rio- [Braz.]	202	Hf	11.10 S	53.35W
Arraiolos	126	Ef	38.43N	7.59W
Ar Ramādī	144	Fc	33.25N	43.17 E
Ar Ramlah	146	Fh	29.32N	35.57 E
Ar Ramlī al Kabīr	164	Dd	26.30N	22.10 E
Arran, Island of-	118	Hf	55.35N	5.15W
Ar Rank	168	Ec	11.45N	32.48 E
Ar Raqqah	144	Eb	35.56N	39.01 E
Arras	122	Id	50.17N	2.47 E
Ar Rāshidah	146	Cj	25.35N	28.56 E
Ar Rass	146	Jj	25.52N	43.28 E
Ar Rastān	146	Ge	34.55N	36.44 E
Arrats	122	Gj	44.06N	0.52 E
Ar Rawḍah	164	He	21.16N	42.50 E
Ar Rawḍah	164	Ig	14.28N	47.17 E
Ar Rawḍatayn	146	Lh	29.53N	47.44 E
Ar Rayḥānī	146	Pk	23.37N	55.58 E
Arrecife	162	Ed	28.57N	13.32W
Arrecife Alacrán	190	Gd	22.24N	89.42W
Arrecifes	206	Hd	34.03 S	60.07W
Arrecifes, Río-	204	Ck	33.46 S	59.31W
Arrée, Monts d'-	122	Cf	48.26N	3.55W
Arresø	116	Ei	55.55N	12.05 E
Arriaga	192	Mi	16.14N	93.54W
Ar Rifā	144	Hd	26.07N	50.03 E
Ar Rifāʿī	146	Lg	31.43N	46.07 E
Ar Riḥāb	146	Kg	30.52N	45.30 E
Ar Rimāh	146	Lj	25.34N	47.09 E
Ar Rimāl	140	Hg	22.00N	52.50 E
Ar Riyāḍ = Riyadh (EN)	142	Gg	24.38N	46.43 E
Arrochar	118	Ie	56.12N	4.45W
Arroio Grande	204	Fk	32.14 S	53.05W
Arrojado	204	Ja	13.29 S	44.37W
Arrojado, Rio-	204	Ja	13.24 S	44.20W
Arromanches-les-Bains	124	Be	49.20N	0.37W
Arros	122	Gk	43.40N	0.02 E
Arroscia	128	Cg	44.03N	8.11 E
Arroux	122	Jh	46.29N	3.58 E
Arrow, Lough-/Loch Arabhach	118	Eg	54.05N	8.20W
Arrowsmith, Mount-	216	Dh	43.21 S	170.59 E
Arrowtown	218	Cf	44.56 S	168.50 E
Arroyo Barú	204	Cj	31.52 S	58.26W
Arroyo de la Luz	126	Fe	39.29N	6.35W
Arroyo Grande	188	Ei	35.07N	120.34W
Arroyos y Esteros	204	Dg	25.04 S	57.06W
Ar Rub' al Khālī	140	Hg	21.00N	51.00 E
Arruda	204	Db	15.02 S	56.07W
Arrufó	206	Hd	30.15 S	61.45W
Ar Rumaythah	146	Kg	31.32N	45.12 E
Ar Ruq'ī	146	Lh	29.01N	46.33 E
Ar Ruṣāfah	146	He	35.02N	36.17 E
Ar Ruşayriş	160	Kg	11.51N	34.23 E
Ar Rutbah	144	Fc	33.02N	40.17 E
Ar Ruwayḍah	146	Ki	26.23N	44.14 E
Ar Ruways [Qatar]	144	Hd	26.08N	51.13 E
Ar Ruways [U.A.E.]	144	He	24.08N	52.45 E
Ar Ruzayqāt	146	Ej	25.35N	32.28 E
Års	116	Ch	56.48N	9.32 E
Arsenjān	146	Oh	29.56N	53.18 E
Arsenjev	138	Ih	44.12N	133.20 E
Arsi [3]	168	Fd	7.10N	40.00 E
Arsk	114	Lh	56.07N	49.52 E
Årskogen	116	Gb	62.05N	17.20 E
Arslanköy	146	Fd	37.01N	34.17 E
Ars-sur-Moselle	124	Ie	49.05N	6.04 E
Arsuk	179	Hf	61.11N	48.30W
Arsunda	116	Gd	60.32N	16.44 E
Art	219b	Ad	19.43 S	163.39 E
Arta	168	Gc	11.31N	42.50 E
Árta	130	Dj	39.09N	20.59 E
Artá / Artà	126	Pe	39.42N	3.21 E
Artà / Artá	126	Pe	39.42N	3.21 E
Artà, Coves d'- / Artá, Cuevas de-	126	Pe	39.40N	3.24W
Artá, Cuevas de- / Artà, Coves d'-	126	Pe	39.40N	3.24W
Artašat	132	Nj	39.59N	44.33 E
Arteaga	192	Hh	18.28N	102.25W
Artem	138	Ih	43.23N	132.10 E
Artemisa	192	Hd	22.49N	82.46W
Artemón	130	Hm	36.57N	24.43 E
Artem-Ostrov	146	Fg	40.28N	50.18 E
Artemovsk [R.S.F.S.R.]	138	Ef	54.23N	93.30 E
Artemovsk [Ukr.-U.S.S.R.]	132	Ke	48.33N	38.03 E
Artemovski	134	Jh	57.25N	61.58 E
Artesa de Segre	126	Nc	41.54N	1.03 E
Artesia	182	Ge	32.51N	104.24W
Arthur	186	Ff	41.35N	101.31W
Arthur Creek	212	Hd	23.00 S	136.58 E
Arthur River	212	Ih	41.00 S	144.55 E
Arthur's Pass	216	Dh	42.57 S	171.34 E
Arthur's Pass	218	De	42.54 S	171.34 E
Arthur's Town	194	Ja	24.38N	75.32W
Arti	134	Ih	56.26N	58.32 E
Artibonite, Rivière de l'-	194	Kd	19.15N	72.47W
Artigas	206	Id	30.42 S	56.28W
Artigas [3]	204	Dj	30.35 S	57.00W
Artijarvi/Artsjö	116	Ld	60.45N	26.05 E
Artik	132	Mi	40.36N	43.58 E
Artillery Lake	180	Gd	63.08N	107.45W
Artois	122	Id	50.10N	2.30 E
Artois, Collines de l'-	122	Id	50.30N	2.15 E
Artoli	168	Eb	18.19N	33.54 E
Artrutx, Cap d'- / Dartuch, Cabo-	126	Pe	39.56N	3.48 E
Artsjö/Artijarvi	116	Ld	60.45N	26.05 E
Artux	152	Cd	39.40N	76.10 E
Artvin	144	Fa	41.11N	41.49 E
Artyk	138	Jd	64.12N	145.15 E
Aru	170	Fb	2.52N	30.51 E
Aru, Kepulauan- = Aru Islands (EN)	208	Ee	6.00 S	134.30 E
Arua	160	Kh	3.01N	30.55 E
Aruanã	204	Gb	14.54 S	51.05W
Aruba [5]	200	Jd	12.30N	70.00W
Aruba	198	Jd	12.30N	70.00W
Aru Bassin (EN)	150	Jg	5.00 S	134.00 E
Aru Islands (EN) = Aru, Kepulauan-	208	Ee	6.00 S	134.30 E
Arukoron Point	220a	Bb	7.43N	134.38 E
Arun	118	Mk	50.48N	0.33W
Arunāchal Pradesh [3]	148	Ic	27.50N	94.50 E
Arundel	124	Bd	50.51N	0.33W
Arun He	152	Lb	47.36N	124.06 E
Arun Qi	152	Lb	48.09N	123.29 E
Arus, Tanjung-	150	Hf	1.24N	125.06 E
Arusha	160	Ki	3.22 S	36.41 E
Arusha [3]	170	Gc	3.30 S	36.00 E
Arutua Atoll	216	Lc	15.18 S	146.44W
Arutunga	216	Jc	18.52 S	159.46W
Aruwimi	158	Jh	1.13N	23.36 E
Arvada [Co.-U.S.]	186	Dg	39.50N	105.05W
Arvada [Wy.-U.S.]	188	Ld	44.40N	106.03W
Arve	122	Mh	46.12N	6.08 E
Arvert, Presqu'île d'-	122	Ei	45.45N	1.05W
Arvida	180	Kg	48.26N	71.11W
Arvidsjaur	114	Ed	65.35N	19.10 E
Arvika	114	Cg	59.39N	12.36 E
Årviksand	114	Ea	70.12N	20.32 E
Arvin	188	Fi	35.12N	118.50W
Arxan	152	Lb	47.11N	119.58 E
Aryānah	128	En	36.52N	10.11 E
Arys	136	Gg	42.26N	68.48 E
Arys	135	Gc	42.48N	68.15 E
Arys, ozero-	135	Fb	45.50N	66.20 E
Arz	122	Dg	47.39N	2.06W
Arzachena	128	Di	41.05N	9.23 E
Arzamas	136	Ed	55.23N	43.50 E
Arzanah	146	Oj	24.47N	52.34 E
Aržano	128	Kg	43.35N	16.59 E
Arzew	162	Gb	35.51N	0.19W
Arzew, Golfe d'-	126	Li	35.50N	0.10W
Arzew, Salines d'-	126	Li	35.42N	0.18W
Arzfeld	124	Id	50.05N	6.16 E
Arzgir	136	Ef	45.22N	44.13 E
Arzúa	126	Db	42.56N	8.09W
Aš	120	If	50.13N	12.12 E
Ås	116	De	59.40N	10.48 E
As	124	Hc	51.01N	5.35 E
Aša	136	Fd	55.02N	57.18 E
Aså	116	Dg	57.09N	10.25 E
Asab	172	Be	25.29 S	17.59 E
Asaba	166	Gd	6.11N	6.45 E
Asad, Buḥayrat al-	146	He	35.57N	38.10 E
Asadābād [Afg.]	144	Lc	34.52N	71.09 E
Asadābād [Iran]	146	Me	34.47N	48.07 E
Asafik	168	Bc	13.10N	19.26 E
Asahi [Jap.]	156	Gd	35.43N	140.35 E
Asahi [Jap.]	156a	Ca	44.08N	142.35 E
Asahi [Jap.]	156	Fb	38.15N	139.30 E
Asahi [Jap.]	156	Ec	36.57N	137.34 E
Asahi-Dake	156	Fb	38.16N	139.55 E
Asahi-Gawa	156	Cd	34.36N	133.58 E
Asahikawa	142	Qe	43.46N	142.22 E
Asaka-Drainage	156	Gc	37.30N	140.15 E
Asale, Lake-	168	Gc	14.00N	40.20 E
'Asalūyeh	146	Oi	27.28N	52.37 E
Asama-Yama	154	Of	36.27N	138.30 E
Asan-Man	154	If	36.56N	126.51 E
Asansol	142	Kg	23.41N	86.59 E
Asarna	114	De	62.39N	14.21 E
Asarum	116	Fh	56.12N	14.50 E
'Asāyr = Guardafui, Cape- (EN)	158	Mg	11.49N	51.15 E
Asayta	168	Gc	11.33N	41.27 E
Asbest	134	Jh	57.01N	61.31 E
Asbestos	184	Lc	45.46N	71.57W
Asbe Teferi	168	Gd	9.05N	40.51 E
Asbury Park	184	Je	40.14N	74.01W
Ascension	158	Fi	7.57 S	14.22W
Ascensión, Bahía de la-	190	Ge	19.40N	87.30W
Ascensión, Laguna de la-	192	Fb	31.05N	107.55W
Aschaffenburg	120	Fg	49.59N	9.09 E
Ascheberg	124	Jc	51.47N	7.37 E
Aschendorf (Ems), Papenburg-	124	Ja	53.04N	7.22 E
Aschersleben	120	He	51.45N	11.28 E
Ašćikol, ozero-	135	Fb	45.05N	67.20 E
Ašćiozek	132	Pe	49.12N	48.06 E
Ascoli Piceno	128	Hh	42.51N	13.34 E
Ascoli Satriano	128	Ji	41.12N	15.34 E
Ascot	124	Bc	51.24N	0.40W
Aseb	160	Lg	13.00N	42.44 E
Åseda	116	Fh	57.10N	15.20 E
Asedjrad	158	Hf	24.42N	1.40 E
Asekejevo	132	Rc	53.36N	52.51 E
As Ela	168	Gc	11.06N	42.06 E
Asela	160	Kh	7.58N	39.08 E
Åsele	114	Dd	64.10N	17.20 E
Åsen [Nor.]	114	Ce	63.36N	11.03 E
Åsen [Swe.]	114	Cf	61.17N	13.50 E
Asendabo	168	Fd	9.47N	37.36 E
Asendorf	124	Kb	52.46N	9.00 E
Asenovgrad	130	Hg	42.01N	24.52 E
Åsensbruk	116	Ef	58.48N	12.25 E
Åseral	116	Bf	58.37N	7.25 E
Aseri/Azeri	114	Gg	59.29N	26.51 E
Asfeld	124	Ge	49.28N	4.07 E
Aşfūn al Maţā'inah	146	Ej	25.23N	32.32 E
Åsgårdstrand	116	De	59.21N	10.28 E
Ashabad	142	Hf	37.57N	58.23 E
Ashabadskaja oblast [3]	136	Fh	38.30N	59.00 E
Ashanti [3]	166	Ed	6.45N	1.30W
Ashburn	184	Fj	31.43N	83.39W
Ashburton	216	Dh	43.54 S	171.45 E
Ashburton River	208	Cg	21.40 S	114.56 E
Ashdod	146	Fg	31.49N	34.39 E
Ashdown	186	Ij	33.41N	94.08W
Asheboro	184	Hh	35.42N	79.49W
Asheroft	188	Ea	50.43N	121.17W
Asheville	182	Kd	35.34N	82.33W
Ashford	118	Nj	51.09N	0.53 E
Ashford Airport	124	Cc	51.10N	0.59 E
Ash Fork	188	Ii	35.13N	112.29W
Ashibetsu	154	Qc	43.31N	142.11 E
Ashikaga	156	Fc	36.21N	139.27 E
Ashington	118	Lf	55.11N	1.34W
Ashiro	156	Ga	40.06N	141.01 E
Ashiya	156	Be	33.53N	130.40 E
Ashizuri-Misaki	154	Lh	32.44N	133.01 E
Ashkal, Qar'at al-	128	Dm	37.10N	9.40 E
Āshkhāneh	146	Qd	37.28N	57.00 E
Ashland [Ks.-U.S.]	186	Gh	37.11N	99.46W
Ashland [Ky.-U.S.]	182	Kd	38.28N	82.38W
Ashland [Mt.-U.S.]	188	Ld	45.35N	106.16W
Ashland [Oh.-U.S.]	184	Fe	40.52N	82.19W
Ashland [Or.-U.S.]	182	Cc	42.12N	122.42W
Ashland [Wi.-U.S.]	182	Ib	46.35N	90.53W
Ashland, Mount-	188	De	42.05N	122.43W
Ashley	186	Gc	46.02N	99.22W
Ashmore Islands	208	Df	12.15 S	123.05 E
Ashmūn	146	Dg	30.18N	30.58 E
Ashoro	156a	Cb	43.14N	143.31 E
Ashqelon	146	Fg	31.40N	34.35 E
Ash Shabakah	146	Jg	30.49N	43.39 E
Ash Shabb	164	Ee	22.19N	29.46 E
Ash Shā'ib	146	Gh	28.59N	37.07 E
Ash Shallāl	158	Kf	24.03N	32.53 E
Ash Sha'm	146	Id	26.02N	56.05 E
Ash Shamāl [3]	146	Fe	34.30N	36.00 E
Ash Shamālīyah [3]	168	Db	18.40N	30.00 E
Ash 'Shāmīyah	146	Kg	31.57N	44.36 E
Ash Shāmīyah	146	Lg	30.15N	46.55 E
Ash Shaqq	146	Lh	28.20N	47.30 E
Ash Shaqrā'	144	Gd	25.15N	45.15 E
Ash Sha'rā'	146	Kj	24.16N	44.11 E
Ash Sharīqah	144	Id	25.22N	55.23 E
Ash Sharqāţ	144	Fb	35.27N	43.16 E
Ash Sharqī	146	Ge	34.00N	36.30 E
Ash Sharqī	162	Jc	34.45N	11.15 E
Ash Sharqīyah	144	Ie	22.15N	58.30 E
Ash Shatrah	146	Lg	31.25N	46.10 E
Ash Shawbak	146	Fg	30.32N	35.34 E
Ash Shaykh Ḥumayd	146	Fh	28.07N	34.34 E
Ash Shifā	146	Fh	28.30N	35.30 E
Ash Shiḥr	144	Gg	14.44N	49.35 E
Ash Shināfīyah	146	Kg	31.35N	44.39 E
Ash Shu'aybah [Kuw.]	146	Mh	29.03N	48.08 E
Ash Shu'aybah [Sau.Ar.]	146	Ji	27.53N	42.43 E
Ash Shu'bah	146	Kh	28.54N	44.44 E
Ash Shumlūl	146	Li	26.31N	47.20 E
Ash Shuqayq	144	Ff	17.44N	42.01 E
Ash Shurayk	168	Eb	18.48N	33.34 E
Ash Shuwayhāt	146	Oj	24.05N	52.28 E
Ash Shuwaykh	146	Lh	29.21N	47.55 E
Ashtabula	182	Kc	41.53N	80.47W
Ashtabula, Lake-	186	Hc	47.11N	97.58W
Ashtīyān	146	Me	34.30N	49.55 E
Ashton [Id.-U.S.]	188	Jd	44.04N	111.27W
Ashton [St.Vin.]	197n	Bb	12.36N	61.27W
Ashuanipi	180	Kf	52.55N	66.00W
Ashuanipi Lake	180	Kf	52.45N	66.10W
'Āşī, Nahr al- = Orontes (EN)	144	Eb	36.02N	35.58 E
Asia (EN)	106	Ge	40.00N	85.00 E
Asia, Kepulauan-	150	Jf	1.03N	131.18 E
Asiago	128	Fe	45.52N	11.30 E
Asiago, Altopiano di-	128	Fe	45.54N	11.30 E
Asilah	162	Fb	35.28N	6.02W
Asinara	110	Gg	41.04N	8.15 E
Asinara, Golfo dell'-	128	Cj	41.00N	8.35 E
Asino	138	De	56.58N	86.09 E
'Asīr	142	Gh	19.00N	42.00 E
'Asīr	144	Ff	19.00N	42.00 E
Āskadar	134	Hi	53.37N	56.01 E
Aşkale	146	Ic	39.55N	40.42 E
Askanija-Nova	132	Hf	46.27N	33.52 E
Asker	116	De	59.50N	10.26 E
Askersund	114	Dg	58.53N	14.54 E
Askī Al Mawşil	146	Jd	36.34N	42.42 E
Askim [Nor.]	116	De	59.35N	11.10 E
Askim [Swe.]	116	Dg	57.38N	11.56 E
Áskion Óros	130	Ei	40.22N	21.34 E
Askiz	138	Ef	53.08N	90.32 E
Askja	110	Eb	65.03N	16.48W
Askola	116	Kd	60.32N	25.36 E
Asköping	116	Ge	59.09N	16.04 E
Askøy	116	Ad	60.24N	5.11 E
Askøy	116	Ad	60.30N	5.05 E
Askrova	116	Ac	61.30N	4.55 E
Askvoll	114	Af	61.21N	5.04 E
Asl	146	Eh	29.30N	32.43 E
Aslanapa	130	Mj	39.13N	29.52 E
Asmara (EN) = Asmera	160	Kg	15.19N	38.57 E
Asmera = Asmara (EN)	160	Kg	15.19N	38.57 E
Åsnen	116	Fh	56.40N	14.40 E
Asni	162	Fc	31.15N	7.59W
Asnières-sur-Seine	124	Ef	48.55N	2.17 E
Aso	156	Be	32.58N	131.02 E
Aso	128	Hg	43.06N	13.51 E
Asola	128	Ee	45.13N	10.24 E
Asosa	160	Kg	10.02N	34.32 E

Index Symbols

[1] Independent Nation
[2] State, Region
[3] District, County
[4] Municipality
[5] Colony, Dependency
Continent
Physical Region
Historical or Cultural Region
Mount, Mountain
Volcano
Hill
Mountains, Mountain Range
Hills, Escarpment
Plateau, Upland
Pass, Gap
Plain, Lowland
Delta
Salt Flat
Valley, Canyon
Crater, Cave
Karst Features
Depression
Polder
Desert, Dunes
Forest, Woods
Heath, Steppe
Oasis
Cape, Point
Coast, Beach
Cliff
Peninsula
Isthmus
Sandbank
Island
Atoll
Rock, Reef
Islands, Archipelago
Rocks, Reefs
Coral Reef
Well, Spring
Geyser
River, Stream
Waterfall, Rapids
River Mouth, Estuary
Lake
Salt Lake
Intermittent Lake
Reservoir
Swamp, Pond
Canal
Glacier
Ice Shelf, Pack Ice
Ocean
Sea
Gulf, Bay
Strait, Fjord
Lagoon
Bank
Seamount
Tablemount
Ridge
Shelf
Basin
Escarpment, Sea Scarp
Fracture
Trench, Abyss
National Park, Reserve
Point of Interest
Recreation Site
Cave, Cavern
Historic Site
Ruins
Wall, Walls
Church, Abbey
Temple
Scientific Station
Railway station
Airport
Port
Military installation
Lighthouse
Mine
Tunnel
Dam, Bridge

Name	Page	Grid	Lat	Long
Aso-San ▲	156	Be	32.53N	131.06 E
Asoteriba, Jabal- ▲	168	Fa	21.51N	36.30 E
Asouf Mellene ⊾	162	Hd	25.40N	2.08 E
Asō-Wan ◻	156	Ad	34.20N	129.15 E
Äspäs	146	Og	30.40N	52.24 E
Aspe	126	Lf	38.21N	0.46W
Aspen	182	Fd	39.11N	106.49W
Aspermont	186	Fj	33.08N	100.14W
Aspiring, Mount- ▲	216	Ch	44.23S	168.44 E
Aspromonte ▲	128	Jl	38.10N	16.00 E
Assa	162	Fb	28.37N	9.25W
Aş Şadr	144	He	24.40N	54.41 E
Aş Şaff	146	Dh	29.34N	31.17 E
Aş Şāfī	146	Eg	31.02N	35.28 E
As Safirah	146	Gd	36.04N	37.22 E
Aş Şahm	146	Qj	24.10N	56.53 E
Assahoun	166	Fd	6.27N	0.55 E
Aş Şa'īd ⊠	146	Kf	26.00N	32.00 E
Assal, Lac- ⊟	168	Gc	11.40N	42.22 E
As Salamīyah [Sau.Ar.]	144	Ge	24.12N	47.23 E
As Salamīyah [Syr.]	146	Ge	35.01N	37.03 E
Aş Şālihīyah	146	Ie	34.44N	40.45 E
As Sālimīyah	146	Mh	29.20N	48.04 E
As Sallūm	160	Je	31.34N	25.09 E
As Salmān	146	Kg	30.26N	44.30 E
As Salt	146	Ff	32.03N	35.44 E
As Salwá	144	He	24.45N	50.49 E
Assam ⊠	148	Ic	26.00N	93.00 E
Assam ⊠	140	Lg	26.50N	94.00 E
Assamakka	166	Gb	19.21N	5.38 E
As Samawah	144	Gc	31.18N	45.17 E
As Sanām ⊠	168	Ia	22.00N	51.10 E
Assaouas	166	Gb	16.52N	7.27 E
As Sars	128	Dn	36.05N	9.01 E
As Sayl al Kabīr	164	Fe	21.38N	40.25 E
Asse	124	Gd	50.56N	4.12 E
Asse ⊾	122	Lk	43.53N	5.53 E
Assebroek, Brugge-	124	Fc	51.12N	3.16 E
Assekkârai ⊾	166	Fb	15.50N	2.52 E
Assemini	128	Dk	39.17N	9.01 E
Assen	122	Ma	53.00N	6.34 E
Assenede	124	Fc	51.14N	3.45 E
Assens	116	Ci	55.16N	9.55 E
As Sibā'īyah	146	Ej	25.11N	32.41 E
As Sidr	160	Ie	30.39N	18.22 E
As Sidrah = Sirte Desert (EN) ⊠	158	Ie	30.30N	17.30 E
As Sila'	144	He	24.02N	51.46 E
As Sinbillāwayn	146	Dg	30.53N	31.27 E
Assiniboia	180	Gg	49.38N	105.59W
Assiniboine ⊾	174	Je	49.53N	97.08W
Assiniboine, Mount- ▲	174	Hd	50.52N	115.39W
Assis	206	Jb	22.40S	50.25W
Assisi	128	Gg	43.04N	12.37 E
Aßlar	124	Kd	50.36N	8.28 E
Assos ⊠	130	Ji	39.31N	26.20 E
As Subaykhah	128	Eo	35.56N	10.01 E
As Subū' ⊠	146	Fe	22.45N	32.34 E
As Sudd ⊠	160	Jg	15.00N	30.00 E
As Sudd ⊠	158	Kh	8.00N	31.00 E
As Sufāl	168	Hc	14.06N	48.43 E
Aş Şufūf	146	Nk	23.52N	51.45 E
Aş Şukhayrah	162	Jc	34.17N	10.06 E
As Sukhnah	146	He	34.52N	38.52 E
As Sulaymī	146	Ii	26.17N	41.21 E
As Sulayyil	144	Ge	20.27N	45.34 E
Aş Şulb ⊠	146	Mj	25.42N	48.25 E
Aş Şummān ⊾	168	Dg	9.49N	27.39 E
Aş Şummān ⊾	146	Li	27.00N	47.00 E
Assumption Island ⊞	158	Li	9.45S	46.30 E
As Süq	164	Fe	21.54N	42.03 E
Assur ⊠	146	Je	35.25N	43.16 E
Aş Şuwar	146	Ie	35.30N	40.39 E
As Suwaydā'	144	Ec	32.42N	36.34 E
Aş Şuwayrah	146	Kf	32.55N	44.47 E
As Suways = Suez (EN)	146	Kf	29.58N	32.33 E
Astakidha ⊞	130	Jn	35.53N	26.50 E
Astakós	130	Ek	38.32N	21.05 E
Ästäneh [Iran]	146	Md	37.17N	49.59 E
Ästäneh [Iran]	146	Mf	33.53N	49.22 E
Ästärä	144	Mb	38.26N	48.52 E
Astara	112	Kh	38.28N	48.52 E
Aştarak	132	Ni	40.16N	44.18 E
Asten	124	Kc	51.24N	5.45 E
Asti	128	Cf	44.54N	8.12 E
Astico ⊾	128	Fe	45.37N	11.37 E
Astipálaia	130	Jm	36.33N	26.21 E
Astipálaia ⊞	130	Jm	36.35N	26.20 E
Asto, Monte- ▲	122a	Ba	42.30N	9.15 E
Astola Island ⊞	148	Cc	25.07N	63.51 E
Astorga	126	Fb	42.27N	6.03W
Astoria	182	Cb	46.11N	123.50W
Ästorp	116	Eh	56.08N	12.57 E
Astove Island ⊞	158	Lj	10.06S	47.45 E
Astrahan	112	Kf	46.21N	48.03 E
Astrahanskaja oblast ⊠	136	Ef	47.10N	47.30 E
Astrolabe, Cape- ⊾	219a	Ec	8.20S	160.34 E
Astrolabe, Récifs de l'- ⊞	208	Hf	19.49S	165.35 E
Astudillo	126	Ha	42.12N	4.18W
Asturias ⊠	126	Ga	43.20N	6.00W
Asuisui, Cape- ⊾	221c	Aa	13.47S	172.29W
Asunción	200	Kh	25.16S	57.40W
Asunción, Bahía- ◻	192	Bd	27.05N	114.10W
Asunción, Cerro de la- ▲	204	Je	24.15N	99.56W
Asuncion Island ⊞	208	Fc	19.40N	145.24 E
Asunción Mita	194	Cf	14.20N	89.43W
Asunción Nochixtlán	192	Ki	17.28N	97.14W
Åsunden ⊟	116	Eg	57.44N	13.22 E
Åsunden ⊟	116	Fg	58.00N	15.50 E
Aswa ⊾	170	Fb	3.43N	31.55 E
Aswān	160	Kf	24.05N	32.53 E
Aswān, Sadd al- = Aswān High Dam (EN) ⊟	146	Fe	24.01N	32.52 E
Aswān High Dam (EN) = Aswān, Sadd al- ⊟	164	Fe	24.01N	32.52 E
Asyūţ	146	Kf	27.11N	31.11 E
Asyūţī, Wādī al- ⊾	146	Di	27.10N	31.16 E
Aszód	120	Pi	47.39N	19.30 E
'Ata ⊞	221b	Bc	21.03S	174.59W
Atacama ⊠	206	Gc	27.30S	70.00W
Atacama, Desierto de- = Atacama Desert (EN)	198	Jh	22.30S	69.15W
Atacama, Salar de- ⊟	198	Jh	23.30S	68.15W
Atacama Desert (EN) = Atacama, Desierto de-	198	Jh	22.30S	69.15W
Atafu Atoll ⊙	208	Je	8.33S	172.30W
Atakor ▲	158	Hf	23.13N	5.40 E
Atakora ⊠	166	Fc	10.00N	1.35 E
Atakora ▲	166	Fc	10.45N	1.30 E
Atakpamé	160	Hh	7.32N	1.08 E
Atalaia do Norte	202	Dd	4.20S	70.12W
Atalándi	130	Fk	38.39N	23.00 E
Atalaya	202	Df	10.44S	73.45W
Atalayasa / sa Talaiassa ▲	126	Nf	38.55N	1.15 E
Atambua	150	Hh	9.07S	124.54 E
Atami	156	Cd	35.05N	139.02 E
Atangmik	179	Gf	64.53N	52.00W
Aţār	160	Ff	20.30N	13.03W
Atas-Bogdo-Ula ▲	152	Gc	43.20N	96.30 E
Atascadero	188	Ei	35.29N	120.41W
Atasu	136	Hd	48.42N	71.38 E
'Atata ⊞	221b	Ac	21.03S	175.15W
Atatürk Barajı ⊟	146	Ge	37.30N	38.30 E
Atauro, Pulau ⊞	150	Ih	8.13S	125.35 E
Atáviros ▲	130	Km	36.12N	27.52 E
Ataway ⊾	168	Bd	9.59N	18.38 E
Atbara ⊾	168	Eb	17.40N	33.56 E
'Aţbarah	160	Kg	17.42N	33.59 E
'Aţbarah ⊾	158	Kg	17.40N	33.56 E
Atbasar	142	Iă	51.48N	68.20 E
At-Baši	136	Hg	41.08N	75.51 E
Atça	130	Li	37.53N	28.13 E
Atchafalaya Bay ◻	182	If	29.25N	91.20W
Atchison	182	Hd	39.34N	95.07W
Atebubu	166	Ed	7.45N	0.59W
Ateca	126	Kc	41.20N	1.47W
Aterno ⊾	128	Hg	42.11N	13.51 E
Atessa	128	Ih	42.04N	14.27 E
Ath/Aat	122	Jd	50.38N	3.47 E
Athabasca	180	Gf	54.43N	113.17W
Athabasca, Lake- ⊟	174	Hd	59.07N	110.00W
Athabasca, ⊾	174	Hd	58.40N	110.50W
Athamánon, Óri- ▲	130	Ej	39.27N	21.08 E
Athamánon Óri ▲	130	Ej	39.27N	21.08 E
Athens [Al.-U.S.]	184	Dh	34.48N	86.58W
Athens [Ga.-U.S.]	182	Kf	33.57N	83.23W
Athens [Oh.-U.S.]	184	Ff	39.20N	82.06W
Athens [Tn.-U.S.]	184	Eh	35.28N	84.35W
Athens [Tx.-U.S.]	186	Ij	32.12N	95.51W
Athens (EN) = Athínai [Grc.]	112	Ih	37.59N	23.44 E
Athéras ▲	130	Jl	37.38N	26.15 E
Atherton	212	Jc	17.16S	145.29 E
Athínai [Grc.] = Athens (EN)	112	Ih	37.59N	23.44 E
Athi River	170	Gc	1.27S	36.59 E
Athis-de-l'Orne	124	Bf	48.49N	0.30W
Athlone/Baile Átha Luain	118	Fh	53.25N	7.56W
Athol	184	Kd	42.36N	72.14W
Áthos ▲	130	Hi	40.10N	24.20 E
Athos, Mount- (EN) = Áyion Óros ⊠	130	Hi	40.15N	24.15 E
Ath Thamad	146	Fh	29.41N	34.18 E
Ath Thumāmī	146	Ki	27.42N	44.59 E
Athus, Aubange-	124	He	49.34N	5.50 E
Ati	160	Ig	13.13N	18.20 E
Atiak	170	Fb	3.16N	32.07 E
Atiamuri	218	Gc	38.23S	176.02 E
Atibaia, Rio- ⊾	204	If	22.42S	47.17W
Atienza	126	Jc	41.12N	2.52W
Atikokan	180	If	48.45N	91.37W
Atikonak Lake ⊟	180	Lf	52.40N	64.35W
Atimoono ⊙	220n	Bc	10.26S	160.58W
Atitlán, Lago de- ⊟	194	Bf	14.42N	91.12W
Atitlán, Volcán- ▲	190	Ff	14.35N	91.11W
Atiu Island ⊞	208	Lg	20.02S	158.07W
'Atk, Wādī al- ⊾	146	Li	26.03N	46.30 E
'Aţk ⊾	174	Bd	52.15N	174.30W
Atka [Ak.-U.S.]	178a	Db	52.12N	174.12W
Atka [R.S.F.S.R.]	138	Db	60.49N	151.58 E
Atka Iceport ⊟	222	Bf	70.35S	7.45W
Atkarsk	136	Ee	51.52N	44.59 E
Atkasook	178	Hb	70.28N	157.24W
Atkinson	186	Gd	42.32N	98.59W
Atlacomulco de Fabela	192	Jh	19.48N	99.53W
Atlanta [Ga.-U.S.]	176	Kf	33.45N	84.23W
Atlanta [Mi.-U.S.]	184	Ee	45.00N	84.09W
Atlanta [Tx.-U.S.]	186	Ij	33.07N	94.10W
Atlantahavet = Atlantic Ocean (EN)	106	Di	2.00N	25.00W
Atlantic [Ia.-U.S.]	186	If	41.24N	95.01W
Atlantic [N.C.-U.S.]	184	Dh	34.54N	76.20W
Atlantic City	176	Lf	39.27N	74.35W
Atlantic Coastal Plain (EN) ⊠	174	Lf	34.00N	79.00W
Atlantic-Indian Basin (EN) ⊠	222	Ce	60.00S	15.00 E
Atlantic-Indian Ridge (EN) ⊠	106	Eo	52.00S	25.00 E
Atlántico ⊠	202	Da	10.40N	75.00W
Atlántico, Oceano- = Atlantic Ocean (EN)	106	Di	2.00N	25.00W
Atlántico, Océano- ⊞	202	Da	10.40N	75.00W
Atlántico, Océano- = Atlantic Ocean (EN)	106	Di	2.00N	25.00W
Atlantic Ocean (EN) = Atlántico, Oceano- ⊞	106	Di	2.00N	25.00W
Atlantic Ocean (EN) = Atlantiese Oseaan ⊞	106	Di	2.00N	25.00W
Atlantic Ocean (EN) = Atlantique, Océan- ⊞	106	Di	2.00N	25.00W
Atlantic Ocean (EN) =	106	Di	2.00N	25.00W
Atlantic Ocean (EN) = Muhīt, Al Baḥr al-	106	Di	2.00N	25.00W
Atlántida ⊠	194	Df	15.30N	87.00W
Atlantiese Oseaan = Atlantic Ocean (EN)	106	Di	2.00N	25.00W
Atlantique ⊠	166	Fd	6.35N	2.15 E
Atlantique, Océan- = Atlantic Ocean (EN)	106	Di	2.00N	25.00W
Atlantshaf = Atlantic Ocean (EN)	106	Di	2.00N	25.00W
Atlas = Atlas Mountains				
Atlas Mountains (EN) = Atlas ▲	158	Ge	32.00N	2.00W
Atlas ▲	158	Ge	32.00N	2.00W
Atlasova, ostrov- ⊞	138	Kf	50.50N	155.25 E
Atlasovo	138	Jg	46.00N	142.09 E
Atlas Saharien = Saharan Atlas (EN) ▲	158	He	34.00N	2.00 E
Atlas Tellien = Tell Atlas (EN) ▲	158	He	36.00N	2.00 E
Atlin	180	Ec	59.35N	133.42W
Atlin Lake ⊟	180	Ec	59.35N	133.43W
Atlixco	190	Ee	18.54N	98.26W
Atley ⊾	116	Ac	61.20N	4.55 E
Atmore	184	Dj	31.02N	87.29W
Atna Peak ▲	180	Ef	53.57N	128.04W
Atō	156	Bd	34.24N	131.43 E
Atoka	186	Hi	34.23N	96.08W
Átokos ⊞	130	Dk	38.29N	20.49 E
Atotonilco el Alto	192	Hg	20.33N	102.31W
Atoui, Khatt- ⊾	162	De	20.04N	15.58W
Atouila, 'Erg- ⊾	158	Gf	21.15N	3.20W
Atoyac ⊾	192	Ki	16.30N	97.31W
Atoyac de Álvarez	192	Ii	17.12N	100.26W
Atrak ⊾	144	Hf	37.23N	53.57 E
Ätran ⊾	114	Ch	56.53N	12.30 E
Atrato, Rio- ⊾	198	Ie	8.17N	76.58W
Atrek ⊾	140	Hf	37.23N	53.57 E
Atsugi	156	Rc	35.26N	139.20 E
Atsukeshi	154	Db	43.00N	144.51 E
Atsukeshi-Wan ◻	156a	Db	43.00N	144.51 E
Atsumi [Jap.]	156	Ce	38.37N	139.35 E
Atsumi [Jap.]	154	Cd	34.37N	137.05 E
Atsumi-Hantō ⊠	156	Cd	34.40N	137.15 E
Atsumi-Wan ◻	156	Cd	34.45N	137.15 E
Atsuta	156a	Bb	43.24N	141.25 E
Aţ Ţaff ⊠	144	He	23.55N	54.25 E
Aţ Ţafilah	146	Fg	30.50N	35.36 E
Aţ Ţā'if	142	Gg	21.16N	40.25 E
Aţ Tāj	146	Jf	24.13N	23.18 E
Attalla	184	Dh	34.01N	86.05W
Aţ Ţallāb ⊾	164	De	24.01N	23.10 E
Aţ Ta'mīm ⊠	146	Ke	36.00N	44.00 E
Attapu	148	Lf	14.48N	106.50 E
Aţ Ţārmīyah	146	Kf	33.40N	44.24 E
Attawapiskat	176	Kd	52.55N	82.26W
Attawapiskat ⊾	174	Kd	52.57N	82.38W
Attawapiskat Lake ⊟	180	If	52.15N	87.50W
Aţ Ţawīl ▲	146	Hh	29.20N	39.35 E
Aţ Ţaysīyah ⊾	146	Jh	28.00N	44.00 E
Aţ Ţayyārah	168	Dc	13.12N	30.47 E
Attendorn	124	Jc	51.07N	7.54 E
Attersee (Kammersee) ⊟	128	Hc	47.55N	13.33 E
Attert	124	Ie	49.49N	6.05 E
Attert ⊾	124	Ke	49.49N	6.08 E
Attica	184	Dd	40.17N	87.15W
Attichy	124	Fe	49.25N	3.03 E
Attigny	124	Ge	49.29N	4.35 E
At Tih Desert (EN) = Tīh, Şaḥrā' at- ⊾	164	Dc	30.05N	34.00 E
Attikamagen Lake ⊟	180	Ke	55.00N	66.30W
Attleboro	184	Ke	41.56N	71.17W
Attleborough	124	Db	52.31N	1.01 E
Aţ Ţulayhī	146	Kf	27.33N	44.08 E
Aţ Ţurayf	144	Ec	31.44N	38.33 E
At Turbah	168	Gd	12.40N	43.30 E
Aţ Ţuwayshah	168	Dc	12.21N	26.32 E
Atuel, Río- ⊾	198	Ji	36.17S	66.50W
Ätvidaberg	114	Dg	58.12N	16.00 E
Atwater	188	Eh	37.21N	120.36W
Atwood	186	Fe	39.45N	101.03W
Aua Island ⊞	208	Fe	1.27S	143.04 E
Auasbila	194	Ef	14.52N	84.40W
Auatu ▲	168	Gd	7.17N	41.03 E
Auau Channel ⊟	221a	Ec	20.51N	156.45W
Aubagne	122	Lk	43.17N	5.34 E
Aubange	124	Ke	49.35N	5.48 E
Aubange-Athus	124	He	49.34N	5.50 E
Aube ⊠	122	Kf	48.15N	4.05 E
Aube ⊾	124	Jf	48.34N	3.43 E
Aube, Lake- ⊟	122	Jf	50.42N	5.51 E
Aubel	124	Kd	50.42N	5.51 E
Aubenas	122	Kj	44.37N	4.23 E
Aubenton	124	Ff	49.50N	4.12 E
Aubigny-en-Artois	124	Ed	50.21N	2.35 E
Aubigny-sur-Nère	122	Ig	47.29N	2.26 E
Aubin	122	Ij	44.32N	2.15 E
Aubrac, Monts d'- ▲	122	Jj	44.38N	3.00 E
Aubry, Lac- ⊟	184	Ei	67.25N	126.30W
Auburn [Al.-U.S.]	184	Ei	32.36N	85.29W
Auburn [Ca.-U.S.]	188	Ee	41.22N	85.04W
Auburn [In.-U.S.]	184	Ee	41.22N	85.04W
Auburn [Me.-U.S.]	184	Lc	44.06N	70.14W
Auburn [Nb.-U.S.]	186	If	40.23N	95.51W
Auburn [N.Y.-U.S.]	184	Id	42.57N	76.34W
Auburn [Wa.-U.S.]	188	Dc	47.18N	122.13W
Auburn Range ▲	212	Ke	25.10S	150.30 E
Aubusson	122	Ii	45.57N	2.10 E
Aucanquilcha, Cerro- ▲	198	Jh	21.14S	68.28W
Auce	116	Jh	56.28N	22.50 E
Auch	122	Gk	43.39N	0.35 E
Auchel	124	Ed	50.30N	2.28 E
Auchi	166	Gd	7.04N	6.16 E
Auckland	210	Ih	36.52S	174.45 E
Auckland Islands ⊞	208	Ni	50.35S	166.00 E
Auckland Peninsula ⊠	216	Dg	36.15S	174.00 E
Aude ⊠	122	Ik	43.05N	2.30 E
Aude ⊾	122	Ik	43.13N	3.14 E
Auden	186	Ma	50.13N	87.47W
Audenarde/Oudenaarde	122	Jd	50.51N	3.36 E
Audierne	122	Bf	48.01N	4.32W
Audierne, Baie d'- ◻	122	Bg	47.57N	4.28W
Audincourt	122	Mg	47.29N	6.50 E
Audo ▲	168	Gc	6.09N	41.53 E
Audresselles	124	Dd	50.49N	1.35 E
Audru	116	Kf	58.28N	24.19 E
Audruicq	124	Ed	50.53N	2.05 E
Audubon	186	If	41.43N	94.55W
Audun-le-Roman	124	He	49.22N	5.53 E
Audun-le-Tiche	124	He	49.28N	5.57 E
Aue	120	If	50.35N	12.42 E
Aue [F.R.G.] ⊾	120	Fd	52.33N	9.05 E
Aue [F.R.G.] ⊾	124	Lb	52.27N	9.28 E
Auerbach	120	If	50.31N	12.24 E
Auffay	122	De	49.43N	1.06 E
Augathella	210	Fg	25.48S	146.35 E
Augrabies Falls ⊾	158	Jk	28.35S	20.23 E
Augsburg	112	Hf	48.22N	10.53 E
Augusta [Ar.-U.S.]	186	Ki	35.17N	91.22W
Augusta [Austl.]	210	Ch	34.10S	115.10 E
Augusta [Ga.-U.S.]	176	Kf	33.29N	81.57W
Augusta [It.]	128	Jm	37.13N	15.13 E
Augusta [Ks.-U.S.]	186	Hh	37.41N	96.58W
Augusta [Me.-U.S.]	176	Me	44.19N	69.47W
Augusta, Golfo di- ◻	128	Jm	37.10N	15.15 E
Augustów	120	Sc	53.51N	22.59 E
Augustowski, Kanał- ⊟	120	Tc	53.54N	23.26 E
Augustus, Mount- ▲	210	Cf	24.20S	116.50 E
Auki	210	He	8.45S	160.42 E
Auld, Lake- ⊟	212	Ed	22.30S	123.45 E
Aulla	128	Df	44.12N	9.58 E
Aulne ⊾	122	Bf	48.17N	4.16W
Aulneau Peninsula ⊠	186	Ib	49.23N	94.29W
Aulnoye-Aymeries	124	Ge	50.12N	3.50 E
Aulong ⊠	220a	Ac	7.17N	134.17 E
Ault	124	Dd	50.06N	1.27 E
Auluptagel ⊞	220a	Ac	7.19N	134.29 E
Aulus-les-Bains	122	Hl	42.48N	1.20 E
Aumale	122	De	49.46N	1.45 E
Auna	166	Fc	10.11N	4.43 E
Aunay-sur-Odon	124	Be	49.01N	0.38W
Auneau	122	De	48.28N	1.46 E
Auneuil	124	Ee	49.22N	2.00 E
Auning	114	Ch	56.26N	10.23 E
Aunu'u ⊞	221c	Cb	14.17S	170.33W
Auob ⊾	158	Jk	26.27S	20.38 E
Aura	116	Jd	60.36N	22.34 E
Aurangābād	148	Fe	19.53N	75.20 E
Aurari Bay ◻	212	Gb	11.40S	133.40 E
Auray	122	Cg	47.40N	2.59W
Aurdal	114	Bd	60.56N	9.24 E
Aure ⊾	114	Be	63.13N	8.32 E
Aure [Nor.]	116	Bb	62.24N	6.36 E
Aure [Nor.]	114	Be	63.13N	8.32 E
Aurejärvi	116	Jb	62.05N	23.25 E
Aurès, Massif de l'- ▲	158	Mc	35.14N	6.10 E
Aurich	112	Dc	53.28N	7.29 E
Aurillac	122	Ij	44.55N	2.27 E
Aurlandsfjorden ◻	116	Bc	61.05N	7.05 E
Aurlandsvangen	114	Bd	60.54N	7.11 E
Auron ⊾	122	Ig	47.06N	2.24 E
Aurora [Co.-U.S.]	182	Gd	39.44N	104.52W
Aurora [Il.-U.S.]	182	Jc	42.46N	88.19W
Aurora [Mo.-U.S.]	186	Jh	36.58N	93.43W
Aurora [Phil.]	150	He	7.57N	123.36 E
Aurora do Norte	204	Ie	12.38S	46.23W
Aursjøen ⊟	116	Cb	62.20N	8.40 E
Aursunden ⊟	116	Db	62.40N	11.40 E
Aurukun Mission	210	Fb	13.19S	141.45 E
Aurunci, Monti- ▲	128	Hi	41.20N	13.40 E
Aus	158	Ij	26.40S	16.15 E
Au Sable River ⊾	184	Fc	44.25N	83.20W
Ausangate, Nudo- ▲	198	Jg	13.47S	71.13W
Ausiait/Egedesminde	222	Nc	68.50N	52.45W
Ausoni, Monti- ▲	128	Hi	41.25N	13.20 E
Aust-Agder ⊠	116	Bd	58.50N	8.00 E
Austfonna ⊟	179	Oc	79.55N	25.00 E
Austin [Mn.-U.S.]	182	Ic	43.40N	92.59W
Austin [Nv.-U.S.]	182	Ed	39.30N	117.04W
Austin [Tx.-U.S.]	176	Jf	30.16N	97.45W
Austin, Lake- ⊟	212	Df	27.40S	118.00 E
Austral, Chaco- ⊠	198	Jh	25.00S	61.00W
Australes, Îles- → Tubuaï, Îles-	208	Lg	23.00S	150.00W
Australia ⊠	210	Ie	25.00S	135.00 E
Australia ⊠	106	Ii	25.00S	135.00 E
Australian Alps ▲	208	Fh	37.00S	148.00 E
Australian Capital Territory ⊠	212	Jg	35.30S	149.00 E
Australia Occidentale (I) = Western Australia ⊠	212	Ed	25.00S	122.00 E
Österreich ⊡	112	Hf	47.30N	14.00 E
Austvågøy ⊞	114	Db	68.20N	14.36 E
Autazes	202	Gd	3.35S	59.08W
Auteuil-Authouillet	124	De	49.06N	1.17 E
Authie ⊾	122	Hd	50.21N	1.38 E
Autlán de Navarro	190	De	19.46N	104.22W
Autun	122	Kh	46.57N	4.18 E
Auve	124	Ge	49.02N	4.42 E
Auvergne ▣	122	Ii	45.20N	3.00 E
Auvergne, Monts d'- ▲	122	Ii	45.30N	2.45 E
Auvézère ⊾	122	Gi	45.12N	0.50 E
Auvillers-lès-Forges-Mon-Idée	124	Ge	49.52N	4.21 E
Auxerre	122	Jg	47.48N	3.34 E
Auxi-le-Château	122	Id	50.14N	2.07 E
Auxois ⊠	122	Kg	47.20N	4.30 E
Auxonne	122	Lg	47.12N	5.23 E
Auyán-Tepuy ▲	202	Fb	5.55N	62.32W
Auzances	122	Ih	46.01N	2.30 E
Auzoue ⊾	122	Gj	44.03N	0.15 E
Avaavaroa Passage ⊟	220p	Bc	21.16S	159.47W
Avala ▲	130	De	44.42N	20.31 E
Avaldsnes	116	Ae	59.21N	5.16 E
Avallon	122	Jg	47.29N	3.54 E
Avalon Peninsula ⊠	180	Mg	47.30N	53.30W
Avana ⊾	220p	Cb	21.14S	159.41W
Avaré	204	Hf	23.05S	48.55W
Avarua	210	Lg	21.12S	159.46W
Avarua Harbour ◻	220p	Bb	21.11S	159.46W
Avatele	220b	Bb	19.06S	169.55W
Avatele Bay ◻	220b	Bb	19.05S	169.56W
Avatiu	220p	Bb	21.12S	159.47W
Avatiu Harbour ◻	220p	Bb	21.11S	159.47W
Avatolu, Passe- ⊟	220b	Ab	13.19S	176.14W
Avdhira	130	Dc	40.59N	24.57 E
Ave ⊾	126	Dc	41.20N	8.45W
Aveh	146	Me	35.32N	49.09 E
Aveiro [Braz.]	202	Gd	3.15S	55.10W
Aveiro [Port.]	126	Cd	40.38N	8.39W
Aveiro ⊠	126	Cd	40.45N	8.30W
Åvelgem	124	Fd	50.46N	3.26 E
Avellaneda [Arg.]	206	Ic	29.07S	59.40W
Avellaneda [Arg.]	210	Lg	34.39S	58.23W
Avellino	128	Ij	40.54N	14.47 E
Averbode ▲	124	Gc	51.02N	4.59 E
Avereest	124	Lb	52.37N	6.27 E
Avereest-Dedemsvaart	124	Lb	52.37N	6.27 E
Averøya ⊞	114	Be	63.00N	7.35 E
Aversa	128	Ij	40.58N	14.12 E
Avesnes-le-Comte	124	Ed	50.17N	2.32 E
Avesnes-les-Aubert	124	Fd	50.12N	3.23 E
Avesnes-sur-Helpe	124	Gd	50.07N	3.56 E
Aves Ridge (EN) ⊠	190	Lf	14.00N	63.30W
Avesta	114	Df	60.09N	16.12 E
Aveyron ⊠	122	Ij	44.15N	2.30 E
Aveyron ⊾	122	Hj	44.05N	1.16 E
Avezzano	128	Hh	42.02N	13.25 E
Avgan	130	Mk	38.25N	29.24 E
Avgó [Grc.] ⊞	130	In	35.36N	25.34 E
Avgó [Grc.] ⊞	130	Jn	35.55N	26.30 E
Aviemore	118	Jd	57.12N	3.50W
Avigait	179	Gf	62.15N	50.00W
Avigliano	128	Jj	40.44N	15.43 E
Avignon	112	Gg	43.57N	4.49 E
Ávila	126	Gc	40.39N	4.42W
Ávila, Sierra de- ▲	126	Ga	40.35N	5.00W
Avilés	126	Ga	43.33N	5.55W
Avinurme	116	Lf	58.55N	26.52 E
Avioth	124	He	49.34N	5.22 E
Avis	126	De	39.03N	7.53W
Avize	124	Gf	46.07N	4.01 E
Avlaka Burun ⊾	130	Ji	40.07N	25.40 E
Avola [B.C.-Can.]	188	Fa	51.47N	119.19W
Avola [It.]	128	Jn	36.54N	15.08 E
Avon ⊠	118	Kj	51.30N	2.30W
Avon [Eng.-U.K.] ⊾	118	Lk	50.43N	1.46W
Avon [Eng.-U.K.] ⊾	118	Kj	51.30N	2.43W
Avon [Eng.-U.K.] ⊾	118	Kj	51.59N	2.10W
Avon Downs	210	Eg	20.05S	137.30 E
Avon Park	184	Fk	27.36N	81.31W
Avon River ⊾	212	Df	31.40S	116.07 E
Avranches	122	Ef	48.41N	1.22W
Avre [Fr.] ⊾	124	Ee	49.53N	2.20 E
Avre [Fr.] ⊾	122	Hf	48.47N	1.22 E
Avrig	130	Hc	45.43N	24.23 E
Avron ⊾	124	Ki	45.15N	4.50 E
Avşa Adası ⊞	130	Ki	40.30N	27.33 E
Avuavu	219a	Ec	9.50S	160.23 E
Awa ▲	154	Mg	34.35N	135.01 E
Awaji-Shima ⊞	154	Mg	34.35N	134.50 E
'Awālī	146	Ni	26.05N	50.33 E
Awanui	218	Fb	35.03S	173.15 E
Awara Plain ⊾	170	Hb	3.45N	41.07 E
Awasa	168	Fd	7.02N	38.28 E
Awash	168	Gc	8.59N	40.10 E
Awa-Shima ⊞	154	Oe	38.27N	139.14 E
Awaso	166	Ed	6.14N	2.16W
Awat	152	Ec	40.38N	80.22 E
Awatere ⊾	218	Fe	41.36S	174.10 E
Awbārī	164	Bd	26.35N	12.46 E
Awbārī, Şaḥrā' ⊾	164	Bd	26.35N	12.46 E
Awdégle	168	Ge	1.58N	44.51 E
Awe, Loch- ⊟	118	He	56.15N	5.15W
Awjilah	160	Jf	29.06N	21.17 E
Axel Heiberg ⊞	174	Ja	80.30N	92.00W
Axim	166	Ee	4.52N	2.14W
Axió ⊾	130	Fi	40.35N	22.50 E
Axixá	202	Jd	2.51S	44.04W

Index Symbols

[1] Independent Nation	Historical or Cultural Region	Pass, Gap	Depression	Coast, Beach
[2] State, Region	Mount, Mountain	Plain, Lowland	Polder	Cliff
[3] District, County	Volcano	Delta	Desert, Dunes	Peninsula
[4] Municipality	Hill	Salt Flat	Forest, Woods	Isthmus
[5] Colony, Dependency	Mountains, Mountain Range	Valley, Canyon	Heath, Steppe	Sandbank
[6] Continent	Hills, Escarpment	Crater, Cave	Oasis	Island
[7] Physical Region	Plateau, Upland	Karst Features	Cape, Point	Atoll

Rock, Reef	Waterfall, Rapids	Canal	Lagoon	Escarpment, Sea Scarp
Islands, Archipelago	River Mouth, Estuary	Glacier	Bank	Trench, Abyss
Rocks, Reefs	Lake	Ice Shelf, Pack Ice	Seamount	Fracture
Coral Reef	Salt Lake	Sea	Tablemount	National Park, Reserve
Well, Spring	Intermittent Lake	Gulf, Bay	Ridge	Point of Interest
Geyser	Reservoir	Shelf	Basin	Recreation Site
River, Stream	Swamp, Pond	Strait, Fjord		Cave, Cavern

Historic Site	Airport
Ruins	Port
Wall, Walls	Military installation
Church, Abbey	Lighthouse
Temple	Mine
Scientific Station	Tunnel
Railway station	Dam, Bridge

Ax-les-Thermes 122 Hl 42.43N 1.50 E
Ayabaca 202 Cd 4.38S 79.43W
Ayabe 154 Mg 35.18N 135.15 E
Ayachi, Ari n'- 162 Gc 32.30N 4.50W
Ayacucho [3] 202 Df 14.00S 74.00W
Ayacucho [Arg.] 206 Ie 37.09S 58.29W
Ayacucho [Peru] 200 Ig 13.07S 74.13W
Ayakita-Gawa 156 Bf 31.58N 131.23 E
Ayakkum Hu 152 Ed 37.30N 89.20 E
Ayamé 166 Ed 5.37N 3.11W
Ayamonte 126 Eg 37.13N 7.24W
Ayancık 146 Fb 41.57N 34.36 E
Ayangba 166 Gd 7.31N 7.08 E
Ayapel 202 Cb 8.18N 75.08W
Ayas 146 Eb 40.01N 32.21 E
Ayaviri 202 Df 14.52S 70.35W
Äybak 144 Kb 36.16N 68.01 E
Aybastı 146 Gb 40.41N 37.24 E
Aycliffe 118 Lg 54.36N 1.34W
'Aydim, Wādī- 168 Ib 18.08N 53.08 E
Aydın 144 Cb 37.51N 27.51 E
Aydincik 146 Ed 36.08N 33.17 E
Aydın Dağları 146 Bc 38.00N 28.00 E
Aydingkol Hu 152 Ec 42.40N 89.15 E
Aydinkent 146 Dd 37.06N 31.36 E
Aydos Dağı 146 Fd 37.21N 34.22 E
Ayerbe 126 Lb 42.17N 0.41W
Ayer Hitam 150 Df 1.55N 103.11 E
Ayeyarwady 148 Ie 17.00N 95.00 E
Ayeyarwady = Irrawaddy (EN) 140 Lg 15.50N 95.06 E
Ayiá 130 Fj 39.43N 22.46 E
Ayia Marina 130 Jl 37.09N 26.52 E
Ayiásos 130 Jj 39.06N 26.22 E
Ayion Oros=Athos, Mount-(EN) [2] 130 Hi 40.15N 24.15 E
Áyios Evstrátios 130 Ij 39.31N 25.00 E
Áyios Ioánnis, Ákra- 130 In 35.20N 25.46 E
Áyios Kirikos 130 Jl 37.35N 26.14 E
Áyios Minás 130 Jl 37.36N 26.34 E
Áyios Nikólaos 130 In 35.11N 25.43 E
Áyios Theódhoros 130 Gn 35.32N 23.56 E
Áyios Theódōros 146 Fe 35.20N 34.01 E
Áyios Yeóryios 130 Gl 37.28N 23.56 E
Aykota 168 Fb 15.10N 37.03 E
Aylesbury 118 Mj 51.50N 0.50W
Ayllón, Sierra de- 126 Ic 41.15N 3.25W
Aylmer Lake 180 Gd 64.05N 108.30W
Aylsham 124 Db 52.47N 1.15 E
Ayna 126 Jf 38.33N 2.05W
'Aynabo 168 Hd 8.57N 46.30 E
'Ayn ad Darāhim 128 Cn 36.47N 8.42 E
'Ayn al Baydā 146 Ge 34.32N 37.55 E
'Ayn al Ghazāl [Eg.] 146 Dj 25.46N 30.38 E
'Ayn al Ghazāl [Lib.] 160 Jf 21.50N 24.55 E
'Ayn al Shigi 146 Ci 27.01N 28.02 E
'Ayn al Wādī 146 Ci 27.23N 28.13 E
'Ayn Bū Sālim 128 Cn 36.37N 8.59 E
'Ayn Dāllah 164 Ed 27.19N 27.20 E
'Ayn Dār 146 Mj 25.58N 49.14 E
'Ayn Dīwār 146 Jd 37.17N 42.11 E
'Ayn Ilwān 146 Dj 25.44N 30.25 E
'Ayn Khalīfah 146 Bi 26.46N 27.47 E
'Ayn Sifnī 146 Jd 36.42N 43.21 E
'Ayn Sukhnah 164 Fd 29.30N 32.10 E
'Aynūnah 144 Ed 28.05N 35.08 E
Ayod 168 Ed 8.08N 31.24 E
Ayora 126 Ke 39.04N 1.03W
Ayorou 166 Fc 14.44N 0.55 E
'Ayoûn el 'Atroûs 160 Gg 16.38N 9.36W
Ayr 118 If 55.29N 4.28W
Ayr [Austl.] 212 Jc 19.35S 147.24 E
Ayr [Scot.-U.K.] 118 If 55.28N 4.38W
Ayre, Point of- 118 Ig 54.26N 4.22W
Ayrolle, Étang de l'- 122 Jk 43.16N 3.30 E
Aysha 168 Gc 10.45N 42.35 E
Aytré 122 Eh 46.08N 1.06W
Ayutla 192 Gg 20.07N 104.22W
Ayutla de los Libres 192 Ji 16.54N 99.13W
Ayvacık 130 Jj 39.36N 26.24 E
Ayvacık 146 Gb 41.00N 36.45 E
Ayvalık 144 Cb 39.18N 26.41 E
Aywaille 124 Hd 50.28N 5.40 E
Āzādshahr 146 Pd 37.05N 55.08 E
Azahar, Costa del- / Tarongers, Costa dels- 126 Me 39.58N 0.01 E
Azaila 126 Lc 41.17N 0.29W
Azambuja 126 De 39.04N 8.52W
Azamgarh 148 Gc 26.04N 83.11 E
Azángaro 202 Df 14.55S 70.13W
Azannes-et-Soumazannes 124 He 49.18N 5.28 E
Azaouâd=Azaouad (EN) 158 Gg 19.00N 3.00W
Azaouad (EN)=Azaouâd 158 Gg 19.00N 3.00W
Azaouak 158 Hg 13.48N 3.36 E
Azaouak 166 Fb 15.30N 3.18 E
Azaouak, Vallée de l'- 158 Hg 17.30N 3.40 E
Azar 166 Fb 16.02N 4.04 E
Āzarbāijān-e Gharbī [3] 144 Fb 37.00N 45.00 E
Āzarbāijān-e Sharqī [3] 144 Gb 37.00N 47.00 E
Azarbaycan Sovet Socialistik Respublicasy/ Azerbajdžanskaja SSR [2] 136 Eg 40.30N 47.30 E
Azare 166 Hc 11.41N 10.12 E
Āzār Shahr 146 Kd 37.45N 45.59 E
Azay-le-Rideau 122 Gg 47.16N 0.28 E
A'zāz 146 Gd 36.35N 37.03 E
Azazga 126 Qh 36.44N 4.22 E
Azbine/Aïr 158 Hg 18.00N 8.30 E
Azdaak, gora- 132 Ni 40.13N 44.59 E
Azdavay 146 Eb 41.39N 33.18 E
Azefal 158 Ff 21.00N 14.45W
Azeffoun 126 Qh 36.53N 4.25 E
Azemmour 162 Fc 33.17N 8.21W
Azerbaijan SSR (EN) = Azerbajdžanskaja SSR [2] 136 Eg 40.30N 47.30 E
Azerbajdžanskaja Sovetskaja Socialističeskaja Respublika [2] 136 Eg 40.30N 47.30 E
Azerbajdžanskaja SSR/ Azarbaijčan Sovet Socialistik Respublicasy [2] 136 Eg 40.30N 47.30 E
Azerbajdžanskaja SSR = Azerbaijan SSR (EN) [2] 136 Eg 40.30N 47.30 E
Azeri/Aseri 114 Gg 59.29N 26.51 E
Azevedo Sodré 204 Ej 30.04S 54.36W
Azezo 168 Fc 12.33N 37.25 E
Azilal 162 Fc 31.58N 6.35W
Azilal [3] 162 Fc 32.09N 6.05W
Aznā 146 Mf 33.56N 49.24 E
Aznakajevo 114 Mi 54.56N 53.04 E
Azogues 202 Cd 2.44S 78.48W
Azores (EN)=Açores [5] 160 Ee 38.30N 28.00W
Azores (EN)=Açores, Arquipélago dos- 158 Ee 38.30N 28.00W
Azores-Gibraltar Ridge (EN) 106 Df 37.00N 16.00W
Azoum, Bahr- 158 Jg 10.53N 20.15 E
Azov 136 Df 47.05N 39.25 E
Azov, Sea of- (EN) = Azovskoje more 110 Jf 46.00N 36.00 E
Azovskoje more = Azov, Sea of- (EN) 110 Jf 46.00N 36.00 E
Azpeitia 126 Ja 43.11N 2.16W
Azrak, Bahr- 168 Bc 10.50N 19.50 E
Azraq, Baḥr al- = Blue Nile (EN) 158 Kg 15.38N 32.31 E
Azraq ash Shīshān 146 Gg 31.50N 36.49 E
Azrou 162 Fc 33.26N 5.13W
Aztec 186 Ch 36.49N 107.59W
Aztec Ruins 188 Kh 36.51N 108.10W
Azua 194 Ld 18.27N 70.44W
Azuaga 126 Gf 38.16N 5.41W
Azuar 126 Ie 39.08N 3.36W
Azuero, Peninsula de- = Azuero Peninsula (EN) 174 Ki 7.40N 80.30W
Azuero Peninsula (EN)= Azuero, Peninsula de- 174 Ki 7.40N 80.30W
Azul 200 Ki 36.45S 59.50W
Azul, Arroyo del- 204 Cm 36.15S 59.07W
Azul, Cerro- 202a Ab 0.54S 91.21W
Azul, Cordillera- 202 Ce 8.30S 76.00W
Azul, Rio- 192 Oi 17.54N 88.52W
Azul, Serra- 204 Eb 14.50S 54.50W
Azul, Sierras del- 204 Cm 37.02S 59.55W
Azum 168 Cc 10.53N 20.15 E
Azuma-San 156 Gc 37.44N 140.08 E
Azur, Côte d'- 122 Nk 43.30N 7.00 E
Azurduy 202 Fg 19.59S 64.29W
Azzaba 162 Ib 36.44N 7.06 E
Az Zāb al Kabīr 144 Fb 36.00N 43.21 E
Az Zāb aş Şaghīr 144 Fb 35.12N 43.25 E
Az Zabdānī 146 Gf 33.43N 36.05 E
Az Zabū 146 Ch 28.22N 28.56 E
Az Zafīr 144 Ff 19.57N 41.30 E
Az Zaghāwa 168 Cb 15.15N 23.14 E
Az Zāhirah 146 Qk 23.30N 56.15 E
Az Zahrān 146 Ni 26.18N 50.05 E
Az Zallāq 146 Ni 26.03N 50.29 E
Az Zaqāzīq 164 Fc 30.35N 31.31 E
Az Zarqā' 146 Gf 32.05N 36.06 E
Az Zarqā' 146 Oj 24.53N 53.04 E
Az Zāwiyah 164 Bc 32.45N 12.44 E
Az Zāwiyah [3] 164 Bc 32.40N 12.10 E
Az Zaytūn 164 Ed 29.09N 25.47 E
Azzel Matti, Sebkha- 158 Hf 26.00N 0.55 E
Az Zilfī 146 Ki 26.18N 44.48 E
Az Zubayr 146 Lg 30.23N 47.43 E

B

Baa 150 Hi 10.43S 123.03 E
Baaba 219b Ae 20.03S 163.58 E
Ba'ādwēyn 168 Hd 7.12N 47.24 E
Bà an Daingin/Dingle Bay 118 Ci 52.05N 10.15W
Baar 120 Ei 48.00N 8.30 E
Baarle-Hertog 124 Gc 51.27N 4.56 E
Baarn 124 Hb 52.14N 5.17 E
Baas, Bassure de- 124 Dd 50.30N 1.15 E
Bāb 146 Ok 23.55N 53.45 E
Baba 130 Ei 40.55N 21.10 E
Baba 168 Bd 6.25N 17.07 E
Baba Burun [Tur.] 146 Bc 39.29N 26.04 E
Baba Burun [Tur.] 146 Db 41.18N 31.26 E
Babadağ 130 Ll 37.48N 28.52 E
Babadag 130 Le 44.54N 28.43 E
Babadag, gora- 132 Pi 41.01N 48.29 E
Babaeski 146 Bb 41.26N 27.06 E
Bābā-Ḥeydar 146 Nf 32.20N 50.28 E
Babahoyo 202 Cd 1.50S 79.30W
Babajevo 136 Dd 59.24N 35.55 E
Babajtag, gora- 135 Hd 41.13N 70.16 E
Babajurt 132 Oh 43.35N 46.47 E
Bāb al Māndab=Bab el Mandeb (EN) 158 Lg 12.35N 43.25 E
Babanūsah 168 Dc 11.20N 27.48 E
Babao → Qilian 152 Hd 38.14N 100.15 E
Babar, Kepulauan- 150 Ih 7.50S 129.45 E
Babar, Pulau- 208 De 7.55S 129.45 E
Babase 219a Aa 4.01S 153.42 E
Babatag, hrebet- 135 Ge 38.00N 68.10 E
Babati 170 Gc 4.13S 35.45 E
Babbitt 186 Kc 47.43N 91.57W
B'abdā 146 Ff 33.50N 35.32 E
Bab el Mandeb (EN)=Bāb al Māndab 158 Lg 12.35N 43.25 E
Babelthuap Island 208 Ed 7.30N 134.36 E
Babenhausen [F.R.G.] 120 Gh 48.09N 10.15 E
Babenhausen [F.R.G.] 124 Ke 49.58N 8.57 E
Babeni 130 He 44.59N 24.15 E
Baberton 184 Ge 41.02N 81.38W
Bà Bheanntrai/Bantry Bay 118 Dj 51.38N 9.48W
Babian Jiang [Asia] = Black River (EN) 140 Mg 20.17N 106.34 E
Babil [3] 146 Kf 32.40N 44.50 E
Babine Lake 180 Ef 54.45N 126.00W
Babino Polje 128 Lh 42.43N 17.33 E
Babit Point 197b Ab 18.03N 63.02W
Babo 150 Jg 2.33S 133.25 E
Bābol 144 Hb 36.34N 52.42 E
Babol Sar 146 Od 36.43N 52.39 E
Baboquivari Peak 188 Jk 31.46N 111.35W
Babor, Djebel- 126 Rh 36.32N 5.28 E
Baborigame 192 Fd 26.27N 107.16W
Baboua 168 Ad 5.48N 14.49 E
Babozero, ozero- 114 Ic 66.30N 37.25 E
Babu → Hexian 152 Jg 24.28N 111.34 E
Babuna 130 Eh 41.30N 21.40 E
Babuyan 150 Gd 10.01N 118.58 E
Babuyan 150 Hc 19.32N 121.57 E
Babuyan Channel 150 Hc 18.44N 121.40 E
Babuyan Islands 140 Oh 19.15N 121.40 E
Babylon 144 Fc 32.32N 44.25 E
Bač 130 Cd 45.23N 19.14 E
Bacabachi 192 Ed 26.55N 109.24W
Bacabal 200 Lf 4.14S 44.47W
Ba-Cagan 152 Gb 45.40N 99.30 E
Bacajá, Rio- 202 Hd 3.25S 51.50W
Bacalar 192 Oh 18.43N 88.27W
Bacalar, Laguna de- 192 Oh 18.43N 88.22W
Bacalar Chico, Boca- 194 Dd 18.12N 87.53W
Bacan, Kepulauan- 150 Ig 0.35S 127.30 E
Bacan, Pulau- 150 Ig 0.35S 127.30 E
Bacău 112 If 46.34N 26.54 E
Bacău [2] 130 Jc 46.36N 27.00 E
Baccarat 122 Mf 48.27N 6.45 E
Bacchiglione 128 Ge 45.11N 12.14 E
Bacești 130 Kc 46.51N 27.14 E
Bachaquero 194 Li 9.56N 71.08W
Bacharach 124 Jd 50.04N 7.46 E
Bacheli 148 Ge 18.40N 81.15 E
Bachiniva 192 Fc 28.45N 107.15W
Bachu/Maralwexi 152 Cd 39.46N 78.15 E
Bačka 130 Cd 45.50N 19.30 E
Bačka Palanka 130 Cd 45.15N 19.22 E
Bačka Topola 130 Cd 45.49N 19.39 E
Bäckefors 116 Ef 58.48N 12.10 E
Bäckhammar 116 Fe 59.10N 14.11 E
Backnang 120 Fh 48.57N 9.26 E
Bačkovski Manastir 130 Hh 41.56N 24.51 E
Back River 174 Jc 67.15N 95.15W
Bac Lieu 148 Lg 9.17N 105.43 E
Bac Ninh 148 Ld 21.11N 106.03 E
Bacolet 197p Bb 12.02N 61.41W
Bacolod 150 Oh 10.40N 122.57 E
Bac-Phan=Tonkin (EN) 140 Mg 22.00N 105.00 E
Bacqueville, Lac- 180 Ke 58.00N 74.00W
Bacqueville-en Caux 124 Ce 49.47N 1.00 E
Bácsalmás 120 Pj 46.08N 19.20 E
Bács-Kiskun [2] 120 Pj 46.30N 19.25 E
Bacton 124 Db 52.51N 1.28 E
Bād 144 Hc 33.41N 52.01 E
Bada Dağı 130 Mm 36.32N 29.10 E
Badagara 148 Ff 11.36N 75.35 E
Badagri 166 Fd 6.25N 2.53 E
Badain Jaran Shamo 140 Me 40.20N 101.40 E
Badajós, Lago- 202 Fd 3.15S 62.45W
Badajoz 112 Fh 38.53N 6.58W
Badajoz [3] 126 Ff 38.40N 6.10W
Badakhshan [3] 144 Lb 36.45N 72.00 E
Badalona 126 Oc 41.27N 2.15 E
Badanah 144 Fc 30.59N 41.02 E
Badaohao 154 Fd 41.50N 121.59 E
Badas, Kepulauan- 150 Ef 0.35N 107.06 E
Bad Aussee 128 Hc 47.36N 13.47 E
Bad Axe 184 Fd 43.48N 83.00W
Bad Bergzabern 120 Dg 49.06N 8.00 E
Bad Berleburg 124 Kc 51.04N 8.24 E
Bad Bertrich 124 Jd 50.03N 7.02 E
Bad Bramstedt 120 Fc 53.55N 9.53 E
Bad Brückenau 120 Ff 50.18N 9.45 E
Badda 168 Fd 7.55N 39.23 E
Baddo 148 Cc 27.59N 64.21 E
Bad Doberan 120 Hb 54.06N 11.54 E
Bad Driburg 124 Lc 51.44N 9.01 E
Bad Düben 120 Ie 51.36N 12.35 E
Bad Dürkheim 124 Ke 49.28N 8.12 E
Bade 150 Kh 7.10S 139.35 E
Bademli 130 Lk 38.04N 28.04 E
Baden [Aus.] 128 Kb 48.01N 16.14 E
Baden [Switz.] 128 Cc 47.28N 8.18 E
Baden-Baden 120 Eh 48.45N 8.15 E
Badenoch 118 Je 56.50N 4.00W
Baden-Württemberg [2] 120 Eh 48.30N 9.00 E
Bad Essen 124 Kb 52.19N 8.20 E
Bad Freienwalde 120 Kd 52.47N 14.02 E
Badgastein 128 Hc 47.07N 13.08 E
Bādghīsāt [3] 144 Jc 35.00N 63.45 E
Bad Gleichenberg 128 Jd 46.52N 15.54 E
Bad Godesberg, Bonn- 120 Df 50.41N 7.09 E
Bad Hall 128 Ib 48.02N 14.12 E
Bad Harzburg 120 Ge 51.53N 10.34 E
Bad Herrenalb 124 Kf 48.48N 8.25 E
Bad Hersfeld 120 Ff 50.52N 9.42 E
Bad Homburg von der Hoehe 120 Ef 50.13N 8.37 E
Bad Honnef 124 Jd 50.38N 7.12 E
Bà Dhún na nGall/Donegal Bay 110 Fe 54.30N 8.30W
Badhyz 135 Cg 35.50N 62.00 E
Badiraguato 192 Fe 25.22N 107.31W
Bad Ischl 128 Hc 47.43N 13.37 E
Bad Kissingen 120 Gf 50.12N 10.05 E
Bad Kreuznach 120 Dg 49.50N 7.52 E
Badlands 182 Gb 46.45N 103.30W
Bad Langensalza 120 Ge 51.06N 10.39 E
Bad Lauterberg am Harz 120 Ge 51.38N 10.28 E
Bad Liebenwerda 120 Je 51.31N 13.24 E
Bad Liebenzell 124 Kf 48.46N 8.44 E
Bad Mergentheim 120 Fg 49.29N 9.46 E
Bad Mondorf/Mondorf-les-Bains 124 Ie 49.30N 6.17 E
Bad Münster am Stein-Ebernburg 124 Je 49.49N 7.51 E
Bad Münstereifel 124 Id 50.34N 6.45 E
Bad Nauheim 124 Kd 50.22N 8.45 E
Bad Neuenahr-Ahrweiler 120 Df 50.33N 7.08 E
Bad Neustadt an der Saale 120 Gf 50.20N 10.13 E
Bad Oeynhausen 124 Kb 52.12N 8.48 E
Bad Oldesloe 120 Gc 53.49N 10.23 E
Badou [China] 154 Df 36.27N 117.56 E
Badou [Togo] 166 Fd 7.35N 0.36 E
Bad Pyrmont 120 Fe 51.59N 9.15 E
Bad Ragaz 128 Dc 47.00N 9.30 E
Badrah 146 Kf 33.06N 45.58 E
Bad Reichenhall 120 Ii 47.44N 12.53 E
Badr Ḥunayn 144 Ee 23.44N 38.46 E
Bad River 186 Fd 44.22N 100.22W
Bad Salzuflen 124 Kb 52.05N 8.46 E
Bad Salzungen 120 Gf 50.49N 10.14 E
Bad Schwartau 120 Gc 53.55N 10.42 E
Bad Segeberg 120 Gc 53.56N 10.19 E
Bad Tölz 120 Hi 47.46N 11.34 E
Badulla 148 Gg 6.59N 81.03 E
Bad Vilbel 124 Kd 50.11N 8.45 E
Bad Wildungen 120 Fe 51.07N 9.07 E
Bad Wimpfen 120 Fg 49.14N 9.08 E
Baena 126 Hg 37.37N 4.19W
Baeza [Ec.] 202 Cd 0.28S 77.53W
Baeza [Sp.] 126 Ig 37.59N 3.28W
Baf/Paphos 146 Ee 34.50N 32.35 E
Bafa Gölü 146 Bd 37.30N 27.25 E
Bafang 166 Hd 5.09N 10.11 E
Bafatá 160 Fg 12.10N 14.40W
Bafélé 166 Cc 10.09N 10.08W
Baffin 174 Mc 68.00N 70.00W
Baffin Bay [N.Amer.] 174 Mb 73.00N 65.00W
Baffin Bay [Tx.-U.S.] 186 Hm 27.15N 97.30W
Bafia 166 He 4.45N 11.14 E
Bafilo 166 Fd 9.21N 1.16 E
Bafing [Afr.] 158 Fg 13.49N 10.50W
Bafing [I.C.] 166 Dd 7.52N 7.07W
Bafoulabé 166 Cc 13.48N 10.50W
Bafoussam 160 Ih 5.28N 10.25 E
Bāfq 144 Ic 31.35N 55.24 E
Bāfq, Kūh-e- 146 Pg 31.20N 55.10 E
Bafra 144 Ea 41.34N 35.56 E
Bafra Burnu 146 Fb 41.44N 35.58 E
Bāft 146 Qh 29.14N 56.38 E
Bafwaboli 170 Eb 0.39N 26.10 E
Bafwasende 170 Eb 1.05N 27.16 E
Baga 166 Hc 13.06N 13.50 E
Bagaces 194 Eh 10.31N 85.15W
Bagagem, Rio- 204 Ha 13.58S 48.21W
Bagajevski 132 Lf 47.19N 40.25 E
Bāgalkot 148 Fe 16.11N 75.42 E
Bagamoyo 170 Gd 6.26S 38.54 E
Bagansiapi-Api 150 Df 2.09N 100.49 E
Bağarasi 130 Kl 37.42N 27.33 E
Baga Sola 168 Ac 13.32N 14.19 E
Bagata 170 Cc 3.44S 17.57 E
Bagdad 192 Ke 25.57N 97.09W
Bagdarin 138 Gf 54.30N 113.36 E
Bağdere 136 Ic 38.10N 40.45 E
Bagé 200 Ki 31.20S 54.06W
Bages et de Sigean, Étang de- 122 Jk 43.05N 3.01 E
Baggs 188 Lf 41.02N 107.39W
Bàgh Baile na Sgealg/ Ballinskelligs Bay 118 Cj 51.50N 10.15W
Baghdād 142 Gf 33.21N 44.23 E
Baghdād [3] 146 Kf 33.18N 44.36 E
Baghdādī, Ra's- 146 Fj 24.40N 35.06 E
Bāgh-e Chenār 146 Qh 28.11N 56.54 E
Bāgh-e-Malek 146 Mg 31.32N 49.55 E
Bagheria 128 Hl 38.05N 13.30 E
Bāghīn 144 Ic 30.12N 56.48 E
Baghlān 144 Kb 36.13N 68.46 E
Baghlān [3] 144 Kb 35.45N 69.00 E
Bāglung 148 Gc 28.16N 83.36 E
Bagn 116 Cd 60.49N 9.34 E
Bagnara Calabra 128 Jl 38.17N 15.48 E
Bagnères-de-Bigorre 122 Gk 43.04N 0.09 E
Bagnères-de-Luchon 122 Gl 42.47N 0.36 E
Bagni di Lucca 128 Ef 44.01N 10.35 E
Bagno di Romagna 128 Fg 43.50N 11.57 E
Bagnolo Mella 128 Ee 45.26N 10.10 E
Bagnols-sur-Cèze 122 Kj 44.10N 4.37 E
Bago 142 Lh 17.30N 96.30 E
Bagoé 158 Gg 12.36N 6.34W
Bagolino 128 Ee 45.49N 10.28 E
Bagrationovsk 116 Ij 54.23N 20.40 E
Bagrax/Bohu 152 Ec 41.58N 86.29 E
Bagrax Hu/Bosten 140 Ke 42.00N 87.00 E
Bagua 202 Ce 5.40S 78.31W
Baguio 142 Oh 16.25N 120.36 E
Baguirmi 158 Ig 11.40N 16.20 E
Bagzane, Monts- 158 Hg 17.43N 8.45 E
Bahama Islands 174 Lg 24.15N 76.00W
Bahamas [1] 176 Lg 24.15N 76.00W
Bahamas, Canal Viejo de-= Old Bahama Channel (EN) 194 Ib 22.30N 78.05W
Bahār 146 Me 34.54N 48.26 E
Baharampur 148 Hd 24.06N 88.15 E
Baharden 136 Fh 38.28N 57.28 E
Bahardok 136 Fh 38.51N 58.24 E
Bahariya Oasis (EN) = Baḥarīyah, Wāḥāt al- 164 Ed 28.15N 28.57 E
Bahaur 150 Fg 3.20N 114.00 E
Bahāwalnagar 148 Ec 29.59N 73.16 E
Bahāwalpur 142 Jg 29.24N 71.41 E
Bahçe 146 Gd 37.14N 36.34 E
Bahčisaraj 132 Hg 44.45N 33.51 E
Bahi 170 Gd 5.39S 35.19 E
Bahia [2] 202 Jf 12.00S 42.00W
Bahía, Islas de la- 190 Ge 16.20N 86.30W
Bahía Blanca 200 Ji 38.44S 62.16W
Bahía de Caráquez 202 Bd 0.37S 80.25W
Bahía Kino 190 Bc 28.50N 111.55W
Bahía Negra 206 Ib 20.15S 58.12W
Bahías, Cabo dos- 198 Jj 44.55S 65.32W
Bahīj 146 Cg 30.56N 29.35 E
Bahinga 170 Ed 5.57S 27.06 E
Bahi Swamp 170 Gd 6.05S 35.10 E
Bahlui 130 Kb 47.08N 27.44 E
Bahmač 136 De 51.11N 32.50 E
Bahoruco, Sierra de- 194 Ld 18.10N 71.25W
Bahraich 148 Gc 27.35N 81.36 E
Bahrain (EN)=Al Baḥrayn [1] 142 Hg 26.00N 50.29 E
Baḥr al Ghazāl [3] 168 Dd 8.15N 26.50 E
Baḥr ar Ramla al Kabīr 164 Ed 27.00N 26.00 E
Baḥrayn, Khalīj al- 146 Nj 25.45N 50.40 E
Bahr Dar 160 Kg 11.36N 37.22 E
Bahta 138 Dd 62.20N 89.15 E
Bahuşi 130 Jc 46.43N 26.42 E
Baia 130 Le 44.43N 28.40 E
Baia de Aramă 130 Fe 45.00N 22.50 E
Baia de Fier 130 Gd 45.10N 23.46 E
Baia dos Tigres 170 Bf 16.35S 11.43 E
Baia Farta 170 Be 12.37S 13.26 E
Baia Mare 130 Gb 47.40N 23.35 E
Baião 202 Id 2.41S 49.41W
Baia Sprie 130 Gb 47.40N 23.42 E
Baibiene 204 Ci 29.36S 58.10W
Baibokoum 168 Bd 7.45N 15.41 E
Baicheng 142 Oe 45.34N 122.49 E
Baicheng/Bay 152 Dc 41.46N 81.52 E
Băicoi 130 Id 45.02N 25.51 E
Băiculeşti 130 Hd 45.04N 24.42 E
Baidou 168 Cd 5.52N 20.41 E
Baie-Comeau 176 Me 49.13N 68.10W
Baie-Mahault 196 Fd 16.16N 61.35W
Baie-Saint-Paul 180 Kg 47.27N 70.30W
Baie-Trinité 184 Na 49.24N 67.19W
Baie Verte 180 Lg 49.55N 56.11W
Baiguan → Shangyu 154 Fi 30.01N 120.53 E
Baihe 152 Je 32.46N 110.06 E
Bai He [China] 154 Bh 32.10N 112.20 E
Bai He [China] 154 Dd 40.43N 116.33 E
Baikal Lake (EN) = Bajkal, ozero- 140 Md 53.00N 107.40 E
Baikal Range (EN) = Bajkalski hrebet 140 Md 55.00N 108.40 E
Baile an Chaistil/ Ballycastle 118 Gf 55.12N 6.15W
Baile an Róba/Ballinrobe 118 Dh 53.37N 9.13W
Baile Átha Cliath/Dublin 112 Fe 53.20N 6.15W
Baile Átha Cliath/Dublin [2] 118 Gh 53.20N 6.15W
Baile Átha Luain/Athlone 118 Fh 53.25N 7.56W
Baile Átha Troim/Trim 118 Gh 53.34N 6.47W
Baile Borşa 130 Hb 47.41N 24.43 E
Baile Brigin/Balbriggan 118 Gh 53.37N 6.11W
Băile Govora 130 Hd 45.05N 24.11 E
Baile Locha Riach/Loughrea 118 Eh 53.12N 8.34W
Baile Mhistéala/ Mitchelstown 118 Ei 52.16N 8.16W
Bailén 126 If 38.06N 3.46W
Baile na Mainistreach/ Newtownabbey 118 Hg 54.42N 5.54W
Baile Nua na hArda/ Newtownards 118 Hg 54.36N 5.41W
Băile Olăneşti 130 Hd 45.12N 24.14 E
Băileşti 130 Ge 44.01N 23.21 E
Bailleul 124 Ed 50.44N 2.44 E
Bailleul 124 Ce 49.12N 0.26 E
Ba Illi 168 Bc 10.31N 16.29 E
Bailong Jiang 152 Ie 32.42N 105.15 E
Bailundo 170 Ce 12.10S 15.56 E
Baima 152 He 33.05N 100.29 E
Bain 124 Ba 53.04N 0.12W
Bainbridge 182 Ke 30.54N 84.34W
Bain-de-Bretagne 122 Eg 47.50N 1.41W
Baines Drift 172 Dd 22.30S 28.43 E
Baing 150 Hi 10.14S 120.34 E
Baingoin 152 Ee 31.36N 89.48 E
Baiona / Bayona 126 Db 42.07N 8.51W
Baiquan 152 Mb 47.38N 126.04 E
Bā'ir 146 Gg 30.46N 36.41 E
Bā'ir, Wādī- 146 Gg 31.12N 37.31 E
Baird 186 Gj 32.24N 99.24W
Baird Inlet 178 Gd 60.45N 164.00W
Baird Mountains 178 Gc 67.35N 161.30W
Baird Peninsula 180 Jc 69.00N 75.15W
Bairiki 210 Id 1.20N 173.01 E
Bairin Youqi (Daban) 152 Kc 43.30N 118.37 E
Bairin Zuoqi (Lindong) 152 Kc 43.59N 119.22 E
Bairnsdale 210 Fh 37.50S 147.38 E
Bais 150 He 9.35N 123.07 E
Baïse 122 Gj 44.17N 0.18 E
Baisha → Jiande 152 Kf 29.31N 119.17 E
Bai Shan 152 Fc 40.53N 93.48 E
Baisogala/Bajsogala 116 Ji 55.35N 23.44 E
Baitou Shan 140 Oe 42.00N 128.00 E
Baitoushan Tian Chi 154 Jc 42.00N 128.03 E
Baixiang 154 Cf 37.29N 114.44 E
Baixo Alentejo 126 Dg 37.55N 8.10W
Baixo Guandu 202 Jg 19.31S 41.01W
Baixo Longa 170 Cf 15.42S 18.38 E
Baiyanghe 152 Ec 43.12N 88.28 E
Baiyü 152 Ge 31.13N 98.51 E
Baja 120 Oj 46.11N 18.58 E
Baja, Punta- [Mex.] 192 Dc 28.25N 111.45W
Baja, Punta- [Pas.] 221d Ab 27.10S 109.22W
Baja California, Peninsula de- = Lower California (EN) 174 Hg 28.00N 112.00W
Baja California Norte [2] 190 Ac 30.00N 115.00W
Baja California Sur [2] 190 Bd 25.50N 111.50W
Bājah 162 Ib 36.44N 9.11 E
Bājah [3] 162 Ib 36.30N 9.30 E

Index Symbols

[1] Independent Nation
[2] State, Region
[3] District, County
[4] Municipality
[5] Colony, Dependency
Continent
Physical Region
Historical or Cultural Region
Mount, Mountain
Volcano
Hill
Mountains, Mountain Range
Hills, Escarpment
Plateau, Upland
Pass, Gap
Plain, Lowland
Delta
Salt Flat
Valley, Canyon
Crater, Cave
Karst Features
Depression
Polder
Desert, Dunes
Forest, Woods
Heath, Steppe
Oasis
Cape, Point
Coast, Beach
Cliff
Peninsula
Isthmus
Sandbank
Island
Atoll
Rock, Reef
Islands, Archipelago
Rocks, Reefs
Coral Reef
Well, Spring
Geyser
River, Stream
Waterfall, Rapids
River Mouth, Estuary
Lake
Salt Lake
Intermittent Lake
Reservoir
Swamp, Pond
Canal
Glacier
Ice Shelf, Pack Ice
Ocean
Sea
Gulf, Bay
Strait, Fjord
Lagoon
Bank
Seamount
Tablemount
Ridge
Shelf
Basin
Escarpment, Sea Scarp
Fracture
Trench, Abyss
National Park, Reserve
Point of Interest
Recreation Site
Cave, Cavern
Historic Site
Ruins
Wall, Walls
Church, Abbey
Temple
Scientific Station
Railway station
Airport
Port
Military installation
Lighthouse
Mine
Tunnel
Dam, Bridge

Bajalān	146	Md	37.18N	48.47 E
Bajan	152	Jb	49.15N	111.58 E
Bajanaul	136	He	50.47N	75.42 E
Bajandaj	138	Ff	53.04N	105.30 E
Bajan-Delger	152	Jb	45.55N	112.15 E
Bajangol	138	Ff	50.40N	103.25 E
Bajan-Hongor	142	Me	46.20N	100.40 E
Bajan-Ula [Mong.]	152	Jb	49.07N	112.45 E
Bajan-Ula [Mong.]	152	Gb	47.05N	95.15 E
Bajan-Under	152	Gc	44.45N	98.45 E
Baja Verapaz [3]	194	Bf	15.05N	90.20W
Bajawa	150	Hh	8.47 S	120.59 E
Bajčunas	132	Rf	47.17N	53.03 E
Bajdarackaja guba	138	Bc	69.00N	67.30 E
Bajdarata	134	Nb	68.12N	68.18 E
Bajdrag Gol	152	Hb	45.10N	100.45 E
Bājgīrān	146	Rd	37.36N	58.24 E
Baj-Haak	138	Ef	51.07N	94.34 E
Bajiazi	154	Jc	42.41N	129.13 E
Bajina Bašta	130	Cf	43.58N	19.34 E
Bajkal	138	Ff	51.53N	104.47 E
Bajkal, ozero- = Baikal Lake (EN)	140	Md	53.00N	107.40 E
Bajkalovo	134	Kh	57.24N	63.40 E
Bajkalsk	138	Ff	51.30N	104.05 E
Bajkalski hrebet = Baikal Range (EN)	140	Md	55.00N	108.40 E
Bajkit	138	Ed	61.41N	96.25 E
Bajkonur	136	Gf	47.50N	66.07 E
Bajmak	136	Fe	52.36N	58.19 E
Bajmba, Mount-	212	Ke	29.20 S	152.05 E
Bajmok	130	Cd	45.58N	19.26 E
Bajo Baudó	202	Cc	4.58N	77.22W
Bajo Boquete	194	Fi	8.46N	82.26W
Bajo Nuevo	190	Ie	15.50N	78.40W
Bajram-Ali	136	Gh	37.39N	62.12 E
Bajram Curri	130	Dg	42.21N	20.04 E
Bajsogala/Baisogala	116	Ji	55.35N	23.44 E
Bajsun	135	Fe	38.14N	67.12 E
Bajun Islands	158	Li	0.50 S	42.15 E
Bajžansaj	135	Gc	43.13N	69.56 E
Baka	168	Ee	4.33N	30.05 E
Bakacak	130	Ki	40.12N	27.05 E
Bakadžicite	130	Jg	42.25N	26.43 E
Bakal	136	Fe	54.56N	58.48 E
Bakala	168	Cd	6.11N	20.22 E
Bakanas	136	Hg	44.48N	76.15 E
Bakar	128	Ie	45.18N	14.32 E
Bakčar	138	De	57.01N	82.10 E
Bake	150	Dg	3.03 S	100.16 E
Bakel	166	Cc	14.54N	12.27W
Baker [Ca.-U.S.]	188	Gi	35.15N	116.02W
Baker [La.-U.S.]	186	Kk	30.35N	91.10W
Baker [Mt.-U.S.]	182	Gb	46.22N	104.17W
Baker [Or.-U.S.]	182	Dc	44.47N	117.50W
Baker, Mount-	182	Cb	48.47N	121.49W
Baker Island	208	Jd	0.15N	176.27W
Baker Lake	176	Jc	64.10N	95.30W
Baker Lake	174	Jc	64.10N	95.30W
Bakersfield	176	Hf	35.23N	119.01W
Bâ Kêv	148	Lf	13.42N	107.12 E
Bakhma	146	Kd	36.38N	44.17 E
Bakhtarān	142	Gf	34.19N	47.04 E
Bakhtarān [3]	144	Gc	34.15N	47.20 E
Bakhtegān, Daryācheh-ye-	146	Ph	29.20N	54.05 E
Bakhūn, Kūh-e-	144	Id	27.56N	56.18 E
Bakir	146	Bc	38.55N	27.00 E
Bakırköy, İstanbul-	130	Li	40.59N	28.52 E
Bakkaflói	114a	Ca	66.10N	14.45W
Baklan	130	Ml	37.58N	29.36 E
Bako	168	Fd	7.19N	35.08 E
Bako [Eth.]	168	Fd	5.50N	36.37 E
Bako [Eth.]	168	Fd	9.05N	37.07 E
Bakony = Bakony Mountains (EN)	110	Hf	47.15N	17.50 E
Bakony Mountains (EN) = Bakony	110	Hf	47.15N	17.50 E
Bakool [3]	168	Ge	4.10N	43.50 E
Bakouma	168	Cd	5.42N	22.47 E
Bakoye	166	Cc	13.49N	10.50W
Bakpulād	146	Qc	38.10N	57.00 E
Baksan	132	Mh	43.40N	43.28 E
Baksan	132	Nh	43.42N	44.03 E
Baku	112	Kg	40.23N	49.51 E
Bakum	124	Kb	52.44N	8.11 E
Bakungan	150	Cf	2.56N	97.30 E
Bakuriani	132	Mi	41.43N	43.31 E
Bakutis Coast	222	Of	74.45 S	120.00W
Balâ	146	Ec	39.34N	33.08 E
Bala, Cerros de-	202	Ef	14.30 S	67.40W
Balabac	150	Ge	7.59N	117.04 E
Balabac	150	Ge	7.57N	117.01 E
Balabac, Selat- = Balabac Strait (EN)	140	Ni	7.40N	117.00 E
Balabac Strait (EN) = Balabac, Selat-	140	Ni	7.40N	117.00 E
Ba'labakk	146	Ge	34.00N	36.12 E
Balabalangan, Kepulauan-	150	Gg	2.20 S	117.25 E
Balaban Dağı	146	Hb	40.28N	39.15 E
Balabanovo	132	Jb	55.11N	36.40 E
Balabio	219b	Be	20.07 S	164.11 E
Balaci	130	He	44.21N	24.55 E
Balad	146	Ke	34.01N	44.01 E
Bal'ad	168	He	2.22N	45.24 E
Balādīn as Sakrān	146	Kj	25.12N	44.37 E
Baladīyat 'Adan = Aden (EN)	142	Gh	12.46N	45.01 E
Balad Rūz	146	Kf	33.42N	45.05 E
Balagannoje	138	Je	59.43N	149.15 E
Balagansk	138	Ff	53.58N	103.02 E
Bālāghāt	148	Gd	21.48N	80.11 E
Bālāghāt Range	148	Fe	18.45N	76.30 E
Balagna	122a	Aa	42.35N	8.50 E
Balaguer	126	Mc	41.47N	0.49 E
Balahna	136	Ed	56.31N	43.37 E
Balahta	138	Ee	55.24N	91.37 E
Balaka	170	Fe	14.59 S	34.57 E
Balaklava	132	Hg	44.31N	33.34 E
Balakleja	136	Df	49.27N	36.52 E
Balakovo	112	Ke	52.02N	47.45 E
Balama	172	Fb	13.16 S	38.36 E
Balambangam, Pulau-	150	Ge	7.17N	116.55 E
Bālā Morghāb	144	Jb	35.35N	63.20 E
Balan Dağı	130	Lm	36.52N	28.20 E
Balankanche	192	Og	20.45N	88.30W
Balasan	150	Hd	11.28N	123.05 E
Balasore → Bāleshwar	148	Hd	21.30N	86.56 E
Balašov	136	Ee	51.33N	43.10 E
Balassagyarmat	120	Ph	48.05N	19.18 E
Balāţ	164	Ed	25.33N	29.16 E
Balaton	110	Hf	46.50N	17.45 E
Balatonfüred	120	Nj	46.57N	17.53 E
Balatonkeresztúr	120	Nj	46.42N	17.23 E
Balaurin	150	Hh	8.15 S	123.43 E
Bălăuşeri	130	Hc	46.24N	24.41 E
Balayan	150	Hd	13.57N	120.44 E
Balazote	126	Jf	38.53N	2.08W
Balbi, Mount-	214	Ei	5.55 S	154.59 E
Balboa Heights	190	Ig	8.57N	79.33W
Balbriggan/Baile Brigin	118	Gh	53.37N	6.11W
Balcarce	206	Ie	37.50 S	58.15W
Balcarce, Sierras de-	204	Cm	37.50 S	58.40W
Bălceşti	130	Ge	44.37N	23.57 E
Balčik	130	Lf	43.25N	28.10 E
Balclutha	216	Ci	46.14 S	169.44 E
Bald Eagle Mountain	184	Ie	41.00N	77.45W
Bald Head	212	Dg	35.07 S	118.01 E
Bald Knob	186	Ki	35.19N	91.34W
Bald Knob	184	Hg	37.56N	79.51W
Baldo, Monte-	128	Ee	45.40N	10.50 E
Baldock	124	Bc	51.59N	0.11W
Baldone	116	Kh	56.41N	24.22 E
Baldur	186	Gb	49.23N	99.15W
Baldwin	184	Ed	43.54N	85.51W
Baldy Peak	182	Fe	33.55N	109.35W
Bale [3]	168	Gd	6.00N	41.00 E
Baleares / Balears [2]	126	Oe	39.30N	3.00 E
Baleares, Islas-/Balears, Illes- = Balearic Islands (EN)	110	Gh	39.30N	3.00 E
Balearic Islands (EN) = Baleares, Islas-/Balears, Illes-	110	Gh	39.30N	3.00 E
Balearic Islands (EN) = Balears, Illes-/Baleares, Islas-	110	Gh	39.30N	3.00 E
Balears / Baleares [2]	126	Oe	39.30N	3.00 E
Balears, Illes-/Baleares, Islas- = Balearic Islands (EN)	110	Gh	39.30N	3.00 E
Balease, Gunung-	150	Hg	2.24 S	120.33 E
Baleia, Ponta da-	198	Mg	17.40 S	36.07W
Baleine, Rivière à la-	180	Ke	58.15N	67.38W
Balej	138	Gf	51.35N	116.38 E
Balen	124	Hc	51.10N	5.09 E
Baler	150	Hc	15.46N	121.34 E
Bāleshwar	148	Hd	21.30N	86.56 E
Balezino	136	Fd	57.59N	53.02 E
Balfate	194	Df	15.48N	86.25W
Bălgarija = Bulgaria (EN) [1]	112	Ig	43.00N	25.00 E
Balgazyn	138	Ef	50.58N	95.12 E
Balguntay	152	Ec	42.45N	86.18 E
Balḩāf	144	Fg	13.58N	48.11 E
Balhārshāh	148	Fe	19.50N	79.22 E
Balhaš = Balkhash (EN)	142	Je	46.49N	74.59 E
Balhaš, ozero- = Balkhash, Lake- (EN)	140	Je	46.00N	74.00 E
Balho	168	Gc	12.00N	42.10 E
Balholm	114	Bf	61.12N	6.33 E
Bali [3]	150	Gh	8.30 S	115.00 E
Bali, Laut- = Bali Sea (EN)	140	Nj	7.45 S	115.30 E
Bali, Pulau-	140	Nj	8.20 S	115.00 E
Bali, Selat- = Bali Strait (EN)	150	Fh	8.18 S	114.25 E
Baliceaux Island	197n	Bb	12.57N	61.08W
Baliem	150	Kg	4.25 S	138.59 E
Balige	150	Cf	2.20N	99.04 E
Balikesir	144	Cb	39.39N	27.53 E
Balık Gölü	146	Jc	39.45N	43.36 E
Balīkh, Nahr-	146	He	35.53N	39.10 E
Balikpapan	142	Nj	1.17 S	116.50 E
Balimbing	150	Dh	5.55 S	104.34 E
Balimo	214	Ci	8.03 S	142.56 E
Balingen	120	Eh	48.17N	8.51 E
Balinqiao	154	Ec	43.16N	118.38 E
Balintang Channel	150	Hc	19.49N	121.40 E
Bali Sea (EN) = Bali, Laut-	140	Nj	7.45 S	115.30 E
Bali Strait (EN) = Bali, Selat-	150	Fh	8.18 S	114.25 E
Baliza	204	Fc	16.15 S	52.25W
Balk, Gaasterland-	124	Hb	52.54N	5.36 E
Balkan Mountains (EN) = Stara Planina	110	Ig	43.15N	25.00 E
Balkan Peninsula (EN)	110	Ig	41.30N	23.00 E
Balkašino	136	Ge	52.32N	68.46 E
Balkh	144	Kb	36.46N	66.54 E
Balkh [3]	144	Kb	36.30N	67.00 E
Balkhash (EN) = Balhaš	142	Je	46.49N	74.59 E
Balkhash, Lake- (EN) = Balhaš, ozero-	140	Je	46.00N	74.00 E
Balladonia	212	Ef	32.27 S	123.51 E
Ballagen	114	Db	68.20N	16.50 E
Ballaghaderreen/Bealach an Doirín	118	Eh	53.55N	8.35W
Ballantrae	118	If	55.06N	5.00W
Ballantyne Strait	180	Ga	77.30N	115.00W
Ballarat	210	Fh	37.34 S	143.52 E
Ballard, Lake-	212	Ee	29.25 S	120.55 E
Ballé	166	Db	15.20N	8.36W
Ballenas, Bahia-	192	Cd	26.45N	113.25W
Ballenas, Canal de-	192	Cc	29.10N	113.25W
Ballenero, Canal-	206	Fh	54.50 S	71.00W
Ballenita, Punta-	206	Fc	25.46 S	70.44W
Balleny Islands	222	Ke	66.35 S	162.50 E
Balleroy	124	Be	49.11N	0.50W
Balleza	192	Fd	26.57N	106.21W
Balli	130	Ki	40.50N	27.03 E
Ballia	148	Gc	25.45N	84.10 E
Ballina	212	Ke	28.52 S	153.33 E
Ballina/Béal an Átha	118	Dg	54.07N	9.09W
Ballinasloe/Béal Átha na Sluaighe	118	Eh	53.20N	8.13W
Ballinger	186	Gk	31.44N	99.57W
Ballinrobe/Baile an Róba	118	Dh	53.37N	9.13W
Ballinskelligs Bay/Bágh Baile na Sgealg	118	Cj	51.50N	10.15W
Ballshi	130	Ci	40.36N	19.44 E
Ball's Pyramid	208	Gh	31.45 S	159.15 E
Ballycastle/Baile an Chaistil	118	Gf	55.12N	6.15W
Ballyhaunis/Béal Átha hAmhnais	118	Eh	53.46N	8.46W
Ballymena/An Baile Meánach	118	Gg	54.52N	6.17W
Ballyshannon/Béal Átha Seanaidh	118	Eg	54.30N	8.11W
Balmaseda / Valmaseda	126	Ia	43.12N	3.12W
Balmazújváros	120	Ri	47.37N	21.21 E
Balmoral Castle	118	Jd	57.02N	3.15W
Balneario Orense	204	Cn	38.49 S	59.46W
Balneario Oriente	204	Bn	38.55 S	60.32W
Balombo	170	Be	12.21 S	14.43 E
Balonne River	208	Fg	28.47 S	147.56 E
Balota, Vîrful-	130	Gd	45.18N	23.53 E
Balovale	160	Jj	13.33 S	23.07 E
Balrāmpur	148	Gc	27.26N	82.11 E
Balranald	212	If	34.38 S	143.33 E
Balş	130	He	44.21N	24.06 E
Balsas [Braz.]	202	Ie	7.31 S	46.02W
Balsas [Mex.]	192	Jh	18.00N	99.47W
Balsas, Depresión del-	192	Ih	18.00N	100.10W
Balsas, Río- [Mex.]	174	Ih	17.55N	102.10W
Balsas, Río- [Pan.]	194	Ii	8.15N	77.59W
Balsas, Rio das- [Braz.]	202	Ie	9.58 S	47.52W
Balsas, Rio das- [Braz.]	202	Je	7.14 S	44.33W
Bålsta	116	Ge	59.35N	17.30 E
Balsthal	128	Bc	47.19N	7.42 E
Balta	132	Ff	47.57N	29.38 E
Baltanás	126	Hc	41.56N	4.15W
Baltasar Brum	206	Id	30.44 S	57.19W
Baltaţi	130	Kb	47.13N	27.09 E
Baltic Sea (EN) = Baltijas jūra	110	Hd	57.00N	19.00 E
Baltic Sea (EN) = Baltijos jura	110	Hd	57.00N	19.00 E
Baltic Sea (EN) = Baltijskoje more	110	Hd	57.00N	19.00 E
Baltic Sea (EN) = Balti meri	110	Hd	57.00N	19.00 E
Baltic Sea (EN) = Bałtyckie, Morze-	110	Hd	57.00N	19.00 E
Baltic Sea (EN) = Itämeri	110	Hd	57.00N	19.00 E
Baltic Sea (EN) = Östersjön	110	Hd	57.00N	19.00 E
Baltic Sea (EN) = Østersøen	110	Hd	57.00N	19.00 E
Baltic Sea (EN) = Ostsee	110	Hd	57.00N	19.00 E
Baltijas jūra = Baltic Sea (EN)	110	Hd	57.00N	19.00 E
Baltijos jura = Baltic Sea (EN)	110	Hd	57.00N	19.00 E
Baltijsk	136	Be	54.40N	19.58 E
Baltijskaja grjada	114	Fi	55.00N	25.00 E
Baltijskoje more = Baltic Sea (EN)	110	Hd	57.00N	19.00 E
Balţīm	164	Fc	31.33N	31.05 E
Balti meri = Baltic Sea (EN)	110	Hd	57.00N	19.00 E
Baltimore	176	Lf	39.17N	76.37W
Baltit (Hunza)	148	Ea	36.20N	74.40 E
Baltoj Voke	116	Kj	54.24N	25.16 E
Baltrum	120	Dc	53.44N	7.23 E
Bałtyckie, Morze- = Baltic Sea (EN)	110	Hd	57.00N	19.00 E
Baluarte, Río-	192	Ff	22.49N	106.02W
Baluchistān = Baluchistan (EN) [3]	148	Cc	28.00N	63.00 E
Baluchistān = Baluchistan (EN)	140	Ig	28.00N	63.00 E
Baluchistan (EN) = Baluchistān [3]	148	Cc	28.00N	63.00 E
Baluchistan (EN) = Baluchistān	140	Ig	28.00N	63.00 E
Balupe	116	Lh	56.54N	27.02 E
Balurghat	148	Hc	25.13N	88.46 E
Balvard	146	Qh	29.25N	56.06 E
Balve	124	Jc	51.20N	7.52 E
Balver Wald	124	Jc	51.21N	7.51 E
Balvi/Balvy	114	Gh	57.08N	27.20 E
Balvy/Balvi	114	Gh	57.08N	27.20 E
Balya	146	Bc	39.45N	27.35 E
Balygyčan	138	Kd	64.00N	154.10 E
Balykši	132	Qf	47.02N	51.55 E
Bām	146	Qd	36.58N	57.59 E
Bam	144	Id	29.06N	58.21 E
Bama	166	Hc	11.31N	13.41 E
Bamaji Lake	186	Ka	51.09N	91.25W
Bamako	160	Gg	12.38N	8.00W
Bamako [3]	166	Dc	13.00N	8.00W
Bamba	166	Eb	17.02N	1.24W
Bambama	170	Bc	2.32 S	13.33 E
Bambana, Río-	194	Fg	13.27N	83.50W
Bambangando	170	Df	16.59 S	20.57 E
Bambari	160	Jh	5.45N	20.40 E
Bamberg	120	Gg	49.42N	10.52 E
Bambesa	170	Eb	3.28N	25.43 E
Bambesi	168	Ed	9.45N	34.44 E
Bambey	166	Bc	14.42N	16.28W
Bambezi	172	Dc	19.57 S	28.55 E
Bambili	170	Eb	3.39N	26.07 E
Bambio	168	Be	3.54N	16.59 E
Bamboi	166	Ed	8.10N	2.02W
Bambouti	168	Dd	5.24N	27.12 E
Bambouto, Monts-	158	Ih	5.44N	10.04 E
Bambuí	204	Je	20.01 S	45.58W
Bam Co	152	Fe	31.15N	90.32 E
Bamenda	166	Hd	5.56N	10.10 E
Bāmīān	144	Kc	34.50N	67.50 E
Bāmīān [3]	144	Kc	34.45N	67.15 E
Bamiancheng	154	Gc	43.15N	124.00 E
Bamiantong → Muling	154	Kb	44.55N	130.32 E
Bamingui	168	Cd	7.34N	20.11 E
Bamingui	158	Ih	8.33N	19.05 E
Bamingui-Bangoran [3]	168	Cd	7.50N	20.15 E
Bampūr	144	Jd	27.12N	60.27 E
Bampūr	144	Id	27.18N	59.06 E
Banaadir [3]	168	He	2.00N	45.15 E
Banaadir	158	Lh	1.00N	44.00 E
Banaba Island	208	He	0.52 S	169.35 E
Banabuiú, Açude-	202	Ke	5.20 S	39.00W
Banagi	170	Fc	2.16 S	34.51 E
Banalia	170	Eb	1.33N	25.20 E
Banamba	166	Dc	13.32N	7.27W
Bananal, Ilha do- [Braz.]	198	Kg	11.30 S	50.15W
Bananal, Ilha do- [Braz.]	204	Dc	17.05 S	56.25W
Bananga	148	Ig	6.57N	93.54 E
Banarli	130	Kh	41.04N	27.20 E
Banās, Ra's-	158	Kf	23.54N	35.48 E
Banat	110	If	45.30N	21.00 E
Banat	130	Dd	45.30N	21.00 E
Banaz	146	Cc	38.46N	29.46 E
Banaz	146	Cc	38.12N	29.14 E
Banbar	152	Fe	30.48N	94.52 E
Banbridge/Droichead na Banna	118	Gg	54.21N	6.16W
Banbury	118	Li	52.04N	1.20W
Banco, Punta-	194	Fi	8.23N	83.09W
Bancroft	184	Ic	45.03N	77.51W
Bānda	148	Gc	25.29N	80.20 E
Banda, Kepulauan- = Banda Islands (EN)	150	Ig	4.35 S	129.55 E
Banda, Laut- = Banda Sea (EN)	208	De	5.00 S	128.00 E
Banda, Punta-	192	Ab	31.45N	116.45W
Banda Aceh	142	Li	5.34N	95.20 E
Bandai-San	156	Gc	37.38N	140.04 E
Banda Islands (EN) = Banda, Kepulauan-	150	Ig	4.35 S	129.55 E
Bandak	116	Ce	59.25N	8.15 E
Bandar → Machilipatnam	148	Ge	16.10N	81.08 E
Bandar Beheshtī	144	Jd	25.18N	60.37 E
Bandar-e 'Abbās	142	Hg	27.11N	56.17 E
Bandar-e Anzalī	144	Gb	37.28N	49.27 E
Bandar-e Būshehr	142	Hg	28.59N	50.50 E
Bandar-e Chārak	146	Pi	26.43N	54.16 E
Bandar-e Chīrū	146	Oi	26.43N	53.43 E
Bandar-e Deylam	144	Hg	30.05N	50.07 E
Bandar-e-Gaz	146	Od	36.47N	53.59 E
Bandar-e-Khomeynī	146	Mg	30.25N	49.08 E
Bandar-e Lengeh	144	Hd	26.33N	54.53 E
Bandar-e Māh Shahr	144	Gc	30.33N	49.12 E
Bandar-e Maqām	144	Hd	26.56N	53.29 E
Bandar-e Moghūyeh	146	Pi	26.35N	54.31 E
Bandar-e-Rīg	146	Nh	29.29N	50.38 E
Bandar-e Torkeman	144	Hb	36.56N	54.06 E
Bandar Seri Begawan	142	Ni	4.53N	114.56 E
Banda Sea (EN) = Banda, Laut-	208	De	5.00 S	128.00 E
Bande	126	Eb	42.02N	7.58W
Bandeira, Pico da-	198	Lh	20.26 S	41.47W
Bandeirantes	204	Ga	13.41 S	50.48W
Bandeirantes, Ilha dos-	204	Ff	23.22 S	53.50W
Bandera	206	Hc	28.54 S	62.16W
Bandera, Alto-	194	Ld	18.49N	70.37W
Banderas, Bahia de-	190	Cd	20.40N	105.25W
Bandiagara	166	Ec	14.20N	3.37W
Bandiat	122	Gi	45.46N	0.20 E
Bandırma	144	Ca	40.20N	27.58 E
Bandirma Körfezi	130	Ki	40.25N	28.00 E
Bandol	122	Lk	43.08N	5.45 E
Bandon	188	Ce	43.07N	124.25W
Bandon/Abhainn na Bandan	118	Ej	51.40N	8.30W
Bandon/Droichead na Bandan	118	Ej	51.45N	8.45W
Ban Don, Ao-	148	Jg	9.20N	99.25 E
Bandundu	160	Ii	3.18 S	17.20 E
Bandundu [2]	170	Cc	5.00 S	17.00 E
Bandung	142	Mj	6.54 S	107.36 E
Bāneh	146	Ke	35.59N	45.53 E
Banes	190	Id	20.58N	75.43W
Banff [Alta.-Can.]	180	Ff	51.10N	115.34W
Banff [Scot.-U.K.]	118	Kd	57.40N	2.31W
Banfora	166	Ec	10.38N	4.46W
Banga	170	Dd	5.57 S	20.28 E
Bangalore	142	Jh	12.59N	77.35 E
Bangangté	166	Hd	5.09N	10.31 E
Bangar	150	Gf	4.43N	115.04 E
Bangassou	160	Jh	4.44N	22.49 E
Bangeta, Mount-	214	Di	6.16 S	147.04 E
Banggai	150	Hg	1.34 S	123.30 E
Banggai, Kepulauan- = Banggai Archipelago (EN)	208	De	1.30 S	123.15 E
Banggai, Selat-	150	Hg	1.55 S	124.00 E
Banggai Archipelago (EN) = Banggai, Kepulauan-	208	De	1.30 S	123.15 E
Banggi, Pulau-	150	Ge	7.17N	117.12 E
Banghāzī = Benghazi (EN)	160	Je	32.07N	20.04 E
Banghāzī = Benghazi (EN) [3]	164	Dd	27.00N	20.30 E
Bangka, Pulau- [Indon.]	150	If	1.48N	125.09 E
Bangka, Pulau- [Indon.]	140	Mj	2.15 S	106.00 E
Bangka, Selat-	150	Eg	2.30 S	105.40 E
Banğka, Selat- = Bangka Strait (EN)	150	Eg	2.20 S	105.45 E
Bangkalan	150	Fh	7.02 S	112.44 E
Bangka Strait (EN) = Banğka, Selat-	150	Eg	2.20 S	105.45 E
Bangkinang	150	Df	0.21N	101.02 E
Bangko	150	Dg	2.05 S	102.17 E
Bangkok (EN) = Krung Thep	142	Mh	13.45N	100.31 E
Bangladesh [1]	142	Kg	24.00N	90.00 E
Bangli	150	Gh	8.27 S	115.21 E
Bangolo	166	Dd	7.01N	7.09W
Bangong Co	152	Ce	33.45N	79.15 E
Bangor [Me.-U.S.]	182	Nc	44.49N	68.47W
Bangor [Wales-U.K.]	118	Ih	53.13N	4.08W
Bangor/Beannchar	118	Hg	54.40N	5.40W
Bangoran	168	Bd	8.42N	19.06 E
Bangsund	114	Cd	64.24N	11.24 E
Bangu	170	Dd	9.05 S	23.44 E
Bangued	150	Hc	17.36N	120.37 E
Bangui [C.A.R.]	160	Ih	4.22N	18.35 E
Bangui [Phil.]	150	Hc	18.32N	120.46 E
Bangweulu, Lake-	158	Jj	11.05 S	29.45 E
Bangweulu Swamps	170	Fe	11.30 S	30.15 E
Banhā	164	Fc	30.28N	31.11 E
Ban Houayxay	148	Kd	20.18N	100.26 E
Baní	190	Je	18.17N	70.20W
Bani	158	Gg	14.30N	4.12W
Bani, Jbel-	158	Gf	28.30N	9.00W
Bani Bangou	166	Fb	15.03N	2.42 E
Banie	120	Kc	53.08N	14.38 E
Banifing	166	Dc	12.43N	6.25W
Banī Forūr, Jazīreh-ye-	146	Pi	26.07N	54.28 E
Banihal Pass	148	Fb	33.15N	75.09 E
Banija	128	Ke	45.10N	16.10 E
Banikoara	166	Fc	11.18N	2.26 E
Banī ma 'Āriḑ	164	Ie	20.42N	47.42 E
Banī Mazār	164	Fd	28.30N	30.48 E
Banī Muḩammadīyāt	146	Di	27.17N	31.05 E
Banī Suwayf	164	Fd	29.05N	31.05 E
Banī Tonb	146	Pi	26.12N	54.56 E
Banī Walīd	164	Bc	31.46N	13.59 E
Bāniyās	144	Ec	33.15N	35.41 E
Banja	130	Hg	42.33N	24.50 E
Banja Koviljača	130	Ce	44.30N	19.11 E
Banja Luka	128	Lf	44.46N	17.10 E
Banjarmarsin	142	Nj	3.20 S	114.35 E
Banjul	160	Fg	13.27N	16.35W
Bank	132	Pj	39.27N	49.14 E
Bankas	166	Ec	14.05N	3.31W
Bankeryd	116	Fg	57.51N	14.07 E
Banket	172	Ec	17.23 S	30.24 E
Bankhead Lake	184	Di	33.30N	87.15W
Bankilaré	166	Fc	14.35N	0.44 E
Bankja	130	Gg	42.42N	23.08 E
Ban Kongmi	148	Lf	14.31N	106.55 E
Banks [Can.]	174	Gb	73.15N	121.30W
Banks [Can.]	180	Ef	53.25N	130.10W
Banks, Iles- = Banks Islands (EN)	208	Hf	13.50 S	167.35 E
Banks Island	212	Ib	10.10 S	142.15 E
Banks Islands (EN) = Banks, Iles-	208	Hf	13.50 S	167.35 E
Banks Lake	188	Fc	47.45N	119.15W
Banks Peninsula	208	Ii	43.40 S	172.40 E
Banks Strait	212	Jh	40.40 S	148.10 E
Bann/An Bhanna	118	Gf	55.10N	6.46W
Ban Na San	148	Jg	8.53N	99.17 E
Bannerman Town	184	Im	24.09N	76.09W
Banning	188	Gj	33.56N	116.52W
Bannock Range	188	Ie	42.30N	112.20W
Bannu	148	Eb	32.59N	70.36 E
Bañolas / Banyoles	126	Ob	42.07N	2.46 E
Bánovce nad Bebravou	120	Oh	48.44N	18.15 E
Banqiao	152	Hf	25.28N	104.02 E
Banská Bystrica	120	Ph	48.44N	19.09 E
Banská Štiavnica	120	Oh	48.27N	18.55 E
Bansko	130	Gh	41.50N	23.29 E
Bānswāra	148	Ed	23.33N	74.27 E
Banta	168	Ge	1.13N	42.30 E
Bantenan, Tanjung-	150	Fh	8.47 S	114.33 E
Bantry/Beanntraí	118	Dj	51.41N	9.27W
Bantry Bay/Bá Bheanntraí	118	Dj	51.38N	9.48W
Bañuela	126	Hf	38.24N	4.11W
Banyak, Kepulauan- = Banyak Islands (EN)	150	Cf	2.10N	97.15 E
Banyak Islands (EN) = Banyak, Kepulauan-	150	Cf	2.10N	97.15 E
Banyo	166	Hd	6.45N	11.49 E
Banyoles / Bañolas	126	Ob	42.07N	2.46 E
Banyuls-sur-Mer	122	Jl	42.29N	3.08 E
Banyuwangi	142	Nj	8.12 S	114.21 E
Banzare Coast	222	Ie	67.00 S	126.00 E
Banzare Seamounts (EN)	222	Fd	58.50 S	77.44 E
Banzart, Buḩayrat-	128	Dm	37.11N	9.52 E
Bao'an	152	Jg	22.35N	114.10 E
Bao'an → Zhidan	152	Id	36.48N	108.46 E
Baochang → Taibus Qi	152	Kc	41.55N	115.22 E
Baode	152	Jd	38.59N	111.07 E
Baodi	154	De	39.43N	117.18 E
Baoding	142	Nf	38.47N	115.30 E
Baofeng	154	Bh	33.52N	113.04 E
Baoji	142	Mf	34.26N	107.12 E
Baokang	152	Je	31.49N	111.13 E
Baokang → Horqin Zuoyi Zhongqi	152	Lc	44.06N	123.19 E
Bao Loc	148	Lf	11.32N	107.48 E
Baoqing	152	Nb	46.20N	132.11 E
Baoro	168	Bd	5.40N	15.58 E
Baoshan	142	Lg	25.09N	99.12 E
Baotou	142	Me	40.38N	110.00 E
Baoulé [Afr.]	158	Gg	12.35N	6.34W
Baoulé [Mali]	158	Gg	13.33N	9.54W
Baoying	154	Eh	33.15N	119.18 E
Bapaume	122	Id	50.06N	2.51 E
Baqên (Dartang)	152	Fe	31.58N	94.00 E
Bāqerābād	146	Ne	34.56N	50.50 E
Ba'qūbah	144	Fc	33.45N	44.38 E
Baquedano	206	Gb	23.20 S	69.51W
Baquerizo Moreno	202a	Bb	0.54 S	89.37W
Bar	124	Ge	49.42N	4.50 E
Bar [Ukr.-U.S.S.R.]	132	Ee	49.02N	27.40 E
Bar [Yugo.]	130	Cg	42.05N	19.06 E

Index Symbols

- [1] Independent Nation
- [2] State, Region
- [3] District, County
- [4] Municipality
- [5] Colony, Dependency
- Continent
- Physical Region
- Historical or Cultural Region
- Mount, Mountain
- Volcano
- Hill
- Mountains, Mountain Range
- Hills, Escarpment
- Plateau, Upland
- Pass, Gap
- Plain, Lowland
- Delta
- Salt Flat
- Valley, Canyon
- Crater, Cave
- Karst Features
- Depression
- Polder
- Desert, Dunes
- Forest, Woods
- Heath, Steppe
- Oasis
- Cape, Point
- Coast, Beach
- Cliff
- Peninsula
- Isthmus
- Sandbank
- Island
- Atoll
- Rock, Reef
- Islands, Archipelago
- Rocks, Reefs
- Coral Reef
- Well, Spring
- Geyser
- River, Stream
- Waterfall, Rapids
- River Mouth, Estuary
- Lake
- Salt Lake
- Intermittent Lake
- Reservoir
- Swamp, Pond
- Canal
- Glacier
- Ice Shelf, Pack Ice
- Ocean
- Sea
- Gulf, Bay
- Strait, Fjord
- Lagoon
- Bank
- Seamount
- Tablemount
- Ridge
- Shelf
- Basin
- Escarpment, Sea Scarp
- Fracture
- Trench, Abyss
- National Park, Reserve
- Point of Interest
- Recreation Site
- Cave, Cavern
- Historic Site
- Ruins
- Wall, Walls
- Church, Abbey
- Temple
- Scientific Station
- Railway station
- Airport
- Port
- Military installation
- Lighthouse
- Mine
- Tunnel
- Dam, Bridge

Barabai 150 Gg 2.35 S 115.23 E
Barabinsk 142 Jd 55.21 N 78.21 E
Barabinskaja Step 138 Ce 55.00 N 79.00 E
Baraboo 186 Le 43.28 N 89.45 W
Baracaldo 126 Ja 43.18 N 2.59 W
Baracoa 190 Jd 20.21 N 74.30 W
Bărăganului, Cîmpia- 130 Ke 44.55 N 27.15 E
Baragoi 170 Gb 1.47 N 36.47 E
Bārah 168 Ec 13.42 N 30.22 E
Barahona 190 Je 18.12 N 71.06 W
Barak 146 Gd 36.51 N 37.59 E
Baraka 168 Fb 18.13 N 37.35 E
Barakah 168 Fb 18.13 N 37.35 E
Barakāt 168 Ec 14.20 N 33.36 E
Barakī Barak 144 Kc 33.58 N 68.58 E
Baram 150 Ff 4.36 N 113.58 E
Baram 150 Ff 4.36 N 113.59 E
Baramanni 196 Gi 7.50 N 59.13 W
Barama River 196 Gi 7.40 N 59.15 W
Barāmūla 148 Eb 34.12 N 74.21 E
Baran 114 Hi 54.29 N 30.19 E
Bāran 148 Fc 25.06 N 76.31 E
Baraniha 138 Lc 68.31 N 168.25 E
Baranja 128 Me 46.00 N 18.30 E
Baranoa 194 Jh 10.49 N 75.03 W
Baranof 178 Le 57.00 N 135.00 W
Baranoviči 112 Ie 53.08 N 26.02 E
Baranovka 132 Ed 50.18 N 27.41 E
Baranya [2] 120 Oj 46.05 N 18.15 E
Barão de Capanema 204 Da 13.19 S 57.52 W
Barão de Cotegipe 204 Fh 27.37 S 52.23 W
Barão de Grajaú 202 Je 6.45 S 43.01 W
Barão de Melgaço 202 Gg 16.13 S 55.58 W
Baraque de Fraiture 122 Ld 50.16 N 5.45 E
Baratang 148 If 12.13 N 92.45 E
Barataria Bay 186 Ll 29.22 N 89.57 W
Barat Daya, Kepulauan- 140 Oj 7.25 S 128.00 E
Barāwe 160 Lh 1.09 N 44.03 E
Barbacena 200 Lh 21.14 S 43.46 W
Barbacoas [Ven.] 194 Li 9.49 N 70.03 W
Barbacoas [Ven.] 196 Ch 9.29 N 66.58 W
Barbacoas, Bahía de- 194 Jh 10.10 N 75.35 W
Barbado, Rio- 204 Cb 15.12 S 58.58 W
Barbados [1] 176 Nh 13.10 N 59.32 W
Barbados 174 Nh 13.10 N 59.32 W
Barbados Ridge (EN) 196 Gf 12.45 N 59.35 W
Barbagia 128 Dj 40.10 N 9.10 E
Barbar 168 Eb 18.01 N 33.59 E
Bárbara 202 Dd 0.52 S 72.30 W
Barbaria, Cap de- / Berberia, Cabo- 126 Nf 38.38 N 1.23 E
Barbaros 130 Ki 40.54 N 27.27 E
Barbas, Cabo- 162 De 22.18 N 16.41 W
Barbastro 126 Mb 42.02 N 0.08 E
Barbate de Franco 126 Gh 36.12 N 5.55 W
Barbeau Peak 174 La 81.54 N 75.01 W
Barbeton 172 Ee 25.48 S 31.03 E
Barbezieux-Saint-Hilaire 122 Fi 45.28 N 0.09 W
Barbourville 184 Fg 36.52 N 83.53 W
Barboza Ferraz 204 Fg 24.04 S 52.03 W
Barbuda 174 Mh 17.38 N 61.48 W
Barcaldine 210 Fg 23.33 S 145.17 E
Barcarrota 126 Ff 38.31 N 6.51 W
Barcău 130 Ec 46.59 N 21.07 E
Barcellona Pozzo di Gotto 128 Jl 38.09 N 15.13 E
Barcelona [3] 126 Nc 41.40 N 2.00 E
Barcelona [Sp.] 112 Gg 41.23 N 2.11 E
Barcelona [Ven.] 202 Fa 10.08 N 64.42 W
Barcelonnette 122 Mj 44.23 N 6.39 E
Barcelos [Braz.] 202 Fd 0.58 S 62.57 W
Barcelos [Port.] 126 Dc 41.32 N 8.37 W
Barcin 120 Nd 52.52 N 17.57 E
Barcoo River 212 Ie 25.30 S 142.50 E
Barcs 120 Nk 45.58 N 17.28 E
Barda 132 Oi 40.25 N 47.05 E
Bardagé 168 Ba 22.06 N 16.28 E
Bardaï 160 If 21.21 N 16.59 E
Bardār Shāh 146 Ld 36.45 N 47.15 E
Bārdaw 128 En 36.49 N 10.08 E
Barddhamān 148 Hd 23.15 N 87.51 E
Bardejov 120 Rg 49.18 N 21.16 E
Bārḍēre 160 Lh 2.20 N 42.20 E
Bardeskan 146 Qe 35.12 N 57.58 E
Bardīyah 164 Ed 31.46 N 25.06 E
Bardonecchia 128 Ae 45.05 N 6.42 E
Bardsey 118 Ii 52.45 N 4.45 W
Bardstown 184 Eg 37.49 N 85.28 W
Barēda 160 Mg 11.52 N 51.03 E
Bareilly 142 Jg 28.25 N 79.23 E
Barencevo more = Barents Sea (EN) 224 Jd 74.00 N 36.00 E
Barentin 122 Ge 49.33 N 0.57 E
Barentsburg 224 Kd 78.04 N 14.14 E
Barentshavet = Barents Sea (EN) 224 Jd 74.00 N 36.00 E
Barentsøya 179 Oc 78.27 N 21.15 E
Barents Sea (EN) = Barencevo more 224 Jd 74.00 N 36.00 E
Barents Sea (EN) = Barentshavet 224 Jd 74.00 N 36.00 E
Barents Trough (EN) 110 Ia 73.00 N 29.00 E
Barentu 168 Fb 15.06 N 37.36 E
Barfleur 122 Ee 49.40 N 1.15 W
Barfleur, Pointe de- 122 Ee 49.42 N 1.16 W
Barga 142 Kf 30.48 N 81.17 E
Bārgāl 168 Ic 11.18 N 51.07 E
Bargarh 148 Gd 21.20 N 83.37 E
Barguelonne 122 Gj 44.07 N 0.50 E
Barguzin 138 Ff 53.27 N 108.58 E
Barguzinski hrebet 138 Ff 54.30 N 110.00 E
Bar Harbor 184 Mc 44.23 N 68.13 W
Barhi 148 Hd 24.18 N 85.25 E
Bari 112 Hg 41.08 N 16.51 E
Bari [3] 168 Hd 10.00 N 50.00 E
Bari, Terra di- 128 Kj 41.05 N 16.50 E
Ba Ria 148 Lf 10.30 N 107.10 E
Barīdī, Ra's- 146 Gj 24.17 N 37.31 E
Barika 126 Ri 35.22 N 5.05 E
Barīm 164 Hg 12.39 N 43.25 E
Barima, Río- 196 Fh 8.35 N 60.25 W
Barima River 196 Fh 8.35 N 60.25 W
Barinas 202 Db 8.38 N 70.12 W
Barinas [2] 202 Eb 8.10 N 70.00 W
Baring, Cape- 180 Fb 70.01 N 117.28 W
Baringa 170 Db 0.45 N 20.52 E
Barinitas 194 Li 8.45 N 70.25 W
Baripāda 148 Hd 21.56 N 86.43 E
Bariri 204 Hf 22.04 S 48.44 W
Bariri, Reprêsa- 204 Hf 22.21 S 48.39 W
Bārīs 164 Fe 24.40 N 30.36 E
Bari Sādri 148 Ed 24.25 N 74.28 E
Barisāl 148 Id 22.42 N 90.22 E
Barisan, Pegunungan- = Barisan Mountains (EN) 140 Mj 3.00 S 102.15 E
Barisan Mountains (EN) = Barisan, Pegunungan- 140 Mj 3.00 S 102.15 E
Barito 140 Nj 3.32 S 114.29 E
Barjols 122 Lk 43.33 N 6.00 E
Barkā' 144 Ie 23.35 N 57.55 E
Barkam 152 He 31.45 N 102.32 E
Barkan, Ra's-e- 146 Mg 30.01 N 49.35 E
Barkava 116 Lh 56.40 N 26.45 E
Barkley, Lake- 182 Jd 36.40 N 87.55 W
Barkley Sound 188 Cb 48.53 N 125.20 W
Barkly East 172 Df 30.58 S 27.33 E
Barkly Tableland 208 Ef 19.00 S 138.00 E
Barkly West 172 Ce 28.05 S 24.31 E
Barkol 152 Fc 43.35 N 92.51 E
Barkol Hu 152 Fc 43.40 N 92.39 E
Barlavento [3] 162 Cf 16.10 N 24.40 W
Bar-le-Duc 122 Lf 48.47 N 5.10 E
Barlee, Lake- 208 Cg 29.10 S 119.30 E
Barlee Range 212 Dd 23.35 S 116.00 E
Barletta 128 Ki 41.19 N 16.17 E
Barlinek 120 Lc 53.00 N 15.12 E
Barlovento, Islas de- = Windward Islands (EN) 174 Mh 15.00 N 61.00 W
Barma 150 Jg 1.54 S 133.00 E
Barmer 148 Ec 25.45 N 71.23 E
Barmera 212 If 34.15 S 140.28 E
Barmouth 118 Ii 52.43 N 4.03 W
Barnard Castle 118 Lg 54.33 N 1.55 W
Barnaul 142 Kd 53.22 N 83.45 E
Barnes Ice Cap 180 Kc 70.00 N 73.30 W
Barnesville [Ga.-U.S.] 184 Ei 33.04 N 84.09 W
Barnesville [Mn.-U.S.] 186 Hc 46.39 N 96.25 W
Barnet, London- 124 Bc 51.39 N 0.12 W
Barneveld 124 Hb 52.08 N 5.34 E
Barneville-Carteret 122 Ee 49.23 N 1.47 W
Barnim 120 Jd 52.40 N 13.45 E
Barnsley 118 Lh 53.34 N 1.28 W
Barnstaple 118 Ij 51.05 N 4.04 W
Barnstaple (Bideford Bay) 118 Ij 51.05 N 4.20 W
Barnstorf 124 Kb 52.43 N 8.30 E
Barntrup 124 Lc 51.59 N 9.07 E
Barnwell 184 Gi 33.14 N 81.21 W
Baro 158 Kh 8.26 N 33.14 E
Baro [Chad] 168 Bc 12.12 N 18.58 E
Baro [Nig.] 166 Gd 8.36 N 6.25 E
Baroghil Pass 148 Ea 36.54 N 73.22 E
Baronnies 122 Lj 44.15 N 5.30 E
Barora Fa 219a Db 7.30 S 158.20 E
Barora Ite 219a Db 7.36 S 158.24 E
Barotseland 170 Df 15.05 S 24.00 E
Barqah = Cyrenaica (EN) 158 Je 31.00 N 23.00 E
Barqah = Cyrenaica (EN) 164 Dc 31.00 N 22.30 E
Barqah, Jabal al- 146 Ej 24.24 N 32.34 E
Barqah al Bahrīyah = Marmarica (EN) 158 Je 31.40 N 24.30 E
Barqū, Jabal- 128 Dn 36.04 N 9.37 E
Barques, Pointe aux- 184 Fc 44.04 N 82.58 W
Barquisimeto 200 Jd 10.04 N 69.19 W
Barr 122 Nf 48.24 N 7.27 E
Barr, Ra's al- 146 Nj 25.47 N 50.34 E
Barra 200 Lg 11.05 S 43.10 W
Barra 118 Fd 57.00 N 7.30 W
Barra, Ponta da- 158 Kk 23.47 S 35.32 E
Barra, Sound of- 118 Fd 57.10 N 7.20 W
Barraba 212 Kf 30.22 S 150.36 E
Barra Bonita, Reprêsa- 204 Hf 22.38 S 48.20 W
Barra de Navidad 190 De 19.12 N 104.41 W
Barra do Bugres 202 Gg 15.05 S 57.11 W
Barra do Corda 202 Ie 5.30 S 45.15 W
Barra do Cuanza 170 Bd 9.18 S 13.09 E
Barra do Dande 170 Bd 8.28 S 13.22 E
Barra do Garças 202 Hg 15.53 S 52.15 W
Barra Falsa, Ponta da- 158 Kk 22.55 S 35.37 E
Barra Head 118 Fe 56.46 N 7.36 W
Barra Mansa 202 Jh 22.32 S 44.11 W
Barrāmīyah, Wādī al- 146 Ej 25.00 N 33.23 E
Barranca 202 Cd 4.50 S 76.42 W
Barrancabermeja 200 Ie 7.03 N 73.52 W
Barrancas [Col.] 194 Kh 10.57 N 72.50 W
Barrancas [Ven.] 202 Fb 8.42 N 62.11 W
Barrancas, Arroyo- 204 Cj 30.19 S 59.25 W
Barranco 204 Db 15.56 S 57.41 W
Barrancos 126 Ff 38.08 N 6.59 W
Barranqueras 206 Ic 27.29 S 58.56 W
Barranquilla 200 Id 10.59 N 74.48 W
Barranquitas 197a Bb 18.12 N 66.23 W
Barra Patuca 194 Ef 15.50 N 84.17 W
Barras 202 Jd 4.15 S 42.18 W
Barra Velha 204 Hh 26.39 S 48.43 W
Barre 184 Kc 44.12 N 72.30 W
Barreira 204 Db 15.24 S 57.52 W
Barreiras 200 Lg 12.08 S 45.00 W
Barreirinha 202 Gd 2.47 S 57.03 W
Barreirinhas 202 Jd 2.45 S 42.50 W
Barreiro 126 Cf 38.40 N 9.04 W
Barreiro, Rio- 204 Fb 15.43 S 52.45 W
Barreiro Grande 204 Jd 18.12 S 45.10 W
Barreiros 202 Ke 8.49 S 35.12 W
Barren 148 If 12.16 N 93.51 E
Barren, Iles- 172 Gc 18.25 S 43.40 E
Barren Islands 178 Ie 58.55 N 152.15 W
Barretos 206 Kb 20.33 S 48.33 W
Barrie 180 Jh 44.24 N 79.40 W
Barrier Bay 222 Ge 67.45 S 81.10 E
Barrier Islands 219a Db 7.44 S 158.32 E
Barrington Tops 212 Kf 32.00 S 151.28 E
Barro Alto 204 Hb 15.04 S 48.58 W
Barrois, Plateaux du- 122 Kf 48.45 N 5.00 E
Barros, Lagoa dos- 204 Gi 29.56 S 50.23 W
Barros, Tierra de- 126 Ff 38.40 N 6.25 W
Barroso 204 Ke 21.11 S 43.58 W
Barrouallie 197n Ba 13.14 N 61.17 W
Barrow [Ak.-U.S.] 176 Db 71.17 N 156.47 W
Barrow [Arg.] 204 Bn 38.18 S 60.14 W
Barrow/An Bhearú 118 Gi 52.10 N 7.00 W
Barrow, Point- 174 Db 71.23 N 156.30 W
Barrow Creek 210 Eg 21.33 S 133.53 E
Barrow-in-Furness 118 Jg 54.07 N 3.14 W
Barrow Island 208 Cg 20.50 S 115.25 E
Barrow Range 212 Fe 26.05 S 127.30 E
Barrow Strait 174 Jb 74.21 N 94.10 W
Barru 150 Gg 4.25 S 119.37 E
Barry 118 Jj 51.24 N 3.18 W
Barrytown 218 De 42.14 S 171.20 E
Barsakelmes, ostrov- 135 Bb 45.40 N 59.55 E
Barsalogo 166 Ec 13.25 N 1.03 W
Barsatas 136 Hf 48.13 N 78.33 E
Baršć/Forst 120 Ke 51.44 N 14.38 E
Bārsi 148 Fe 18.14 N 75.42 E
Barsinghausen 120 Fd 52.18 N 9.27 E
Barstow 182 De 34.54 N 117.01 W
Bar-sur-Aube 122 Kf 48.14 N 4.43 E
Bar-sur-Seine 122 Kf 48.07 N 4.22 E
Baršyn 136 Gf 49.45 N 69.36 E
Barta/Bārta 116 Ih 56.57 N 20.57 E
Bārta/Barta 116 Ih 56.57 N 20.57 E
Barṭallah 146 Jd 36.23 N 43.25 E
Bartang 135 Hf 37.55 N 71.33 E
Barth 120 Ib 54.22 N 12.44 E
Bartholomew, Bayou- 186 Jj 32.43 N 92.04 W
Bartica 202 Gb 6.24 N 58.37 W
Bartın 146 Eb 41.38 N 32.21 E
Bartle Frere, Mount- 208 Ff 17.23 S 145.49 E
Bartlesville 182 Hd 36.45 N 95.59 W
Bartlett 186 Gf 41.53 N 98.33 W
Bartoszyce 120 Qb 54.16 N 20.49 E
Bartow 184 Gl 27.54 N 81.50 W
Barú, Isla- 194 Jh 10.26 N 75.35 W
Barú, Volcán 190 Hg 8.48 N 82.33 W
Bārūd, Ra's- 146 Ei 26.47 N 33.39 E
Barumini 128 Dk 39.42 N 9.01 E
Barun-Bogdo-Ula 152 Hb 45.00 N 100.20 E
Bāruni 148 Hc 25.29 N 85.59 E
Barun-Šabartuj, gora- 138 Fg 49.43 N 109.58 E
Barun-Urt 152 Jb 46.40 N 113.12 E
Barwice 120 Mc 53.45 N 16.22 E
Barwon River 208 Fg 30.00 S 148.05 E
Barycz 120 Me 51.42 N 16.15 E
Baryš 114 Lj 53.40 N 47.08 E
Baryš 114 Li 54.35 N 46.47 E
Bāsa'īdū 146 Pi 26.39 N 55.17 E
Basail 204 Ch 27.52 S 59.18 W
Basankusu 170 Cb 1.14 N 19.48 E
Basaral, ostrov- 135 Ib 45.25 N 73.45 E
Basauri 126 Ja 43.13 N 2.53 W
Basavilbaso 204 Ck 32.22 S 58.53 W
Bas Champs 124 Dd 50.10 N 1.41 E
Basco 150 Hb 20.27 N 121.58 E
Bascuñán, Cabo- 206 Fc 28.51 S 71.30 W
Basel 112 Gf 47.30 N 7.30 E
Basel-Landschaft [2] 128 Bc 47.30 N 7.45 E
Basel-Stadt [2] 128 Bc 47.35 N 7.40 E
Basentello 128 Kj 40.40 N 16.23 E
Basento 128 Kj 40.20 N 16.49 E
Başeu 130 Kb 47.44 N 27.15 E
Basey 150 Id 11.17 N 125.04 E
Bashi Channel (EN) = Bashi Haixia 152 Lg 22.00 N 121.00 E
Bashi Haixia = Bashi Channel (EN) 152 Lg 22.00 N 121.00 E
Bāsht 146 Ng 30.21 N 51.09 E
Ba Shui 154 Ci 30.25 N 115.02 E
Basilan 140 Oi 6.34 N 122.03 E
Basilan City (Isabela) 142 Oi 6.42 N 121.58 E
Basilan Strait 150 He 6.49 N 122.05 E
Basildon 118 Nj 51.34 N 0.25 E
Basilicata [2] 128 Kj 40.30 N 16.30 E
Basingstoke 118 Lj 51.16 N 1.05 W
Basjanovski 134 Jg 58.19 N 60.44 E
Başkale 146 Jc 38.02 N 44.00 E
Baskatong, Réservoir- 180 Jg 46.47 N 75.50 W
Baškaus 138 Df 51.09 N 87.43 E
Baskil 146 Hc 38.35 N 38.40 E
Baškirskaja ASSR [3] 136 Fe 55.00 N 56.00 E
Baskunčak, ozero- 132 Oe 48.10 N 46.55 E
Bašmakovo 132 Mc 53.12 N 43.03 E
Bāsmenj 146 Ld 37.59 N 46.29 E
Basoko 170 Db 1.14 N 23.36 E
Basongo 170 Dc 4.20 S 20.24 E
Basque Provinces (EN) = Euzkadi / Vascongadas 126 Ja 43.00 N 2.30 W
Basque Provinces (EN) = Vascongadas / Euzkadi 126 Ja 43.00 N 2.30 W
Basra (EN) = Al Başrah 142 Gf 30.30 N 47.47 E
Bas-Rhin [3] 122 Nf 48.35 N 7.40 E
Bass, Ilots de- 208 Mg 27.55 S 143.26 W
Bassano 188 Ia 50.47 N 112.28 W
Bassano del Grappa 128 Fe 45.46 N 11.44 E
Bassar 166 Fd 9.15 N 0.47 E
Bassas da India 158 Lk 21.25 S 39.42 E
Bassein → Pathein 142 Lh 16.47 N 94.44 E
Bassein → Vasai 148 Ee 19.21 N 72.48 E
Basse-Kotto [3] 168 Ce 5.00 N 21.30 E
Basse-Pointe 197h Ab 14.52 N 61.07 W
Basses, Pointe des- 197e Bc 15.52 N 61.17 W
Basse-Sambre 124 Gd 50.27 N 4.37 E
Basse Santa Su 166 Cc 13.19 N 14.13 W
Basse-Terre 190 Le 16.00 N 61.44 W
Basseterre 190 Le 17.18 N 62.43 W
Basse-Terre 196 Fd 16.10 N 61.40 W
Bassett 186 Ge 42.35 N 99.32 W
Bassigny 122 Lf 48.00 N 5.30 E
Bassikounou 162 Ff 15.52 N 5.58 W
Bassila 166 Fd 9.01 N 1.40 E
Bass Islands 219c Ba 9.58 S 167.17 E
Basso, Plateau de- 158 Jg 17.20 N 22.40 E
Bass Strait 208 Fh 39.20 S 145.30 E
Bassum 124 Kb 52.51 N 8.44 E
Basswood Lake 186 Kb 48.05 N 91.35 W
Båstad 114 Ch 56.26 N 12.51 E
Bastak 146 Pi 27.14 N 54.22 E
Bastām 146 Pd 36.29 N 55.04 E
Bastenaken/Bastogne 122 Le 50.00 N 5.43 E
Bastia [Fr.] 112 Gg 42.42 N 9.27 E
Bastia [It.] 128 Gg 43.04 N 12.33 E
Bastogne/Bastenaken 122 Le 50.00 N 5.43 E
Bastrop 186 Kj 32.47 N 91.55 W
Basuo → Dongfang 152 Ih 19.14 N 108.39 E
Basuto 172 Dc 19.52 S 26.32 E
Bas-Zaïre [2] 170 Bd 5.30 S 14.30 E
Bata 160 Hh 1.51 N 9.45 E
Batabanó, Golfo de- 190 Hd 22.15 N 82.30 W
Batagaj 138 Ic 67.38 N 134.38 E
Batagaj-Alyta 138 Ic 67.53 N 130.31 E
Bataguaçu 202 Hh 21.42 S 52.22 W
Bataiporã 204 Ff 22.20 S 53.17 W
Batajnica 130 De 44.54 N 20.17 E
Batajsk 136 Df 47.05 N 39.46 E
Batak 130 Hh 41.57 N 24.13 E
Bataklık Gölü 146 Ed 37.42 N 33.07 E
Batala 148 Fb 31.48 N 75.12 E
Batalha 126 De 39.39 N 8.50 W
Batama 170 Eb 0.56 N 26.39 E
Batamaj 138 Hd 63.30 N 129.25 E
Batamšinski 136 Fe 50.36 N 58.17 E
Batan 150 Hb 20.30 N 121.50 E
Batang [China] 152 Ge 30.02 N 99.10 E
Batang [Indon.] 150 Eh 6.55 S 109.42 E
Batanga 170 Ac 0.21 S 9.18 E
Batangafo 168 Bd 7.18 N 18.18 E
Batangas 142 Oh 13.45 N 121.03 E
Batanghari 140 Mj 1.00 S 104.20 E
Batanghari 150 Mj 1.00 S 104.00 E
Batan Islands 140 Og 20.30 N 121.50 E
Batanta, Pulau- 150 Jg 0.50 S 130.40 E
Bátaszék 120 Oj 46.11 N 18.44 E
Batatais 204 Ie 20.53 S 47.37 W
Batavia 184 Hd 43.00 N 78.11 W
Bat-Cengel 152 Hb 47.47 N 101.58 E
Batchawana 184 Eb 46.58 N 84.34 W
Batchelor 212 Gb 13.04 S 131.01 E
Bătdâmbâng 142 Mh 13.06 N 103.12 E
Batecki 116 Nf 58.38 N 30.31 E
Batéké, Plateaux- 170 Cc 3.30 S 15.45 E
Batel, Esteros del- 204 Ci 28.30 S 58.20 W
Batemans Bay 212 Kg 35.43 S 150.11 E
Batesburg 184 Gi 33.56 N 81.33 W
Batesville [Ar.-U.S.] 186 Ki 35.46 N 91.39 W
Batesville [Ms.-U.S.] 186 Li 34.18 N 90.00 W
Bath [Eng.-U.K.] 118 Kj 51.23 N 2.22 W
Bath [Me.-U.S.] 184 Md 43.55 N 69.49 W
Bath [N.B.-Can.] 184 Nb 46.32 N 67.33 W
Bath [St.C.N.] 197c Ab 17.08 N 62.37 W
Batha 168 Bc 14.00 N 19.00 E
Bathinda 148 Fb 30.12 N 74.57 E
Bá Thrá Lí/Tralee Bay 118 Di 52.15 N 9.59 W
Bathsheba 196 Gf 13.13 N 59.31 W
Bá Thuath Reanna/ Liscannor Bay 118 Di 52.55 N 9.25 W
Bathurst 174 Ib 76.00 N 100.30 W
Bathurst [Austl.] 212 Jf 33.25 S 149.35 E
Bathurst [N.B.-Can.] 176 Me 47.36 N 65.39 W
Bathurst, Cape- 174 Gb 70.35 N 128.00 W
Bathurst Inlet 176 Ic 66.50 N 108.01 W
Bathurst Inlet 174 Ic 68.10 N 108.50 W
Bathurst Island 208 Ef 11.35 S 130.25 E
Bati 168 Gc 11.13 N 40.01 E
Batié 166 Ed 9.53 N 2.55 W
Bāṭin, Wādī al- 144 Gc 30.25 N 47.35 E
Batman 144 Fb 37.52 N 41.07 E
Batman 146 Id 37.45 N 41.00 E
Batna 160 He 35.34 N 6.11 E
Batna [3] 162 Ib 35.10 N 6.00 E
Ba To 148 Lf 14.46 N 108.44 E
Bato Bato 150 Ge 5.06 N 119.50 E
Batoka 170 Ef 16.47 S 27.15 E
Baton Rouge 176 Jf 30.23 N 91.11 W
Batopilas 192 Fd 27.01 N 107.44 W
Batouri 166 He 4.26 N 14.22 E
Batovi 204 Fb 15.53 S 53.24 W
Batovi, Coxilha de- 204 Ej 30.33 S 54.27 W
Båtsfjord 114 Ga 70.38 N 29.44 E
Bat-Sumber 152 Ib 48.25 N 106.42 E
Batticaloa 148 Gg 7.43 N 81.42 E
Batti Maly 148 Ig 8.50 N 92.51 E
Battipaglia 128 Ij 40.37 N 14.58 E
Battle 124 Cd 50.55 N 0.30 E
Battle 180 Gf 52.42 N 108.15 W
Battle Creek 182 Jc 42.19 N 85.11 W
Battle Creek 188 Kb 48.36 N 109.11 W
Battle Harbour 176 Nd 52.17 N 55.35 W
Battle Mountain 182 Dc 40.38 N 116.56 W
Battonya 120 Rj 46.17 N 21.01 E
Battowia Island 197n Bb 12.58 N 61.09 W
Batu 168 Fd 6.59 N 39.37 E
Batu, Kepulauan- = Batu Islands (EN) 140 Lj 0.18 S 98.28 E
Batuasa 150 Jg 3.32 S 130.08 E
Batuata, Pulau- 150 Hh 6.12 S 122.42 E
Batudaka, Pulau- 150 Hg 0.28 S 121.48 E
Batui 150 Hg 1.17 S 122.33 E
Batu Islands (EN) = Batu, Kepulauan- 140 Lj 0.18 S 98.28 E
Batumi 112 Kg 41.38 N 41.38 E
Batu Pahat 150 Df 1.51 N 102.56 E
Baturaja 150 Dg 4.08 S 104.10 E
Baturino 138 De 57.45 N 85.12 E
Baturité 202 Kd 4.20 S 38.53 W
Batz, Ile de- 122 Bf 48.45 N 4.01 W
Bau 150 Ff 1.25 N 110.09 E
Baubau 142 Oj 5.28 S 122.38 E
Baucau 150 Ih 8.27 S 126.27 E
Bauchi 160 Hg 10.19 N 9.50 E
Bauchi [2] 166 Hc 10.40 N 10.00 E
Bauchi Plateau 166 Gc 10.00 N 9.30 E
Baud 122 Cg 47.52 N 3.01 W
Baudette 186 Ib 48.43 N 94.36 W
Baudo, Serrania de- 202 Cb 6.00 N 77.05 W
Baudour, Saint-Ghislain- 124 Fd 50.29 N 3.49 E
Baugé 122 Fg 47.33 N 0.06 W
Bauges 122 Mi 45.38 N 6.10 E
Baúl, Cerro- 192 Ii 17.38 N 100.19 W
Baula 150 Hg 4.09 S 121.41 E
Bauld, Cape- 174 Nd 51.38 N 55.25 W
Baule-Escoublac, La- 122 Dg 47.17 N 2.24 W
Bauman Fiord 180 Ia 77.45 N 86.00 W
Baume-les-Dames 122 Mg 47.21 N 6.22 E
Baunach 120 Gg 49.59 N 10.51 E
Baunani 219a Ec 9.08 S 160.51 E
Baunei 128 Dj 40.02 N 9.40 E
Baures 202 Ff 13.35 S 63.35 W
Bauru 200 Lh 22.19 S 49.04 W
Baús 204 Fd 18.19 S 53.10 W
Baús, Serra dos- 204 Fd 18.20 S 53.25 W
Bauska 114 Fh 56.24 N 24.13 E
Bautzen/Budyšin 120 Ke 51.11 N 14.26 E
Baux-de-Provence, Les- 122 Kk 43.45 N 4.48 E
Bavaria (EN) = Bayern [2] 120 Hg 49.00 N 11.30 E
Bavaria (EN) = Bayern 110 Hf 49.00 N 11.30 E
Bavarian Forest (EN) = Bayerischer Wald 120 Ig 49.00 N 12.55 E
Bavay 124 Fd 50.18 N 3.47 E
Båven 116 Ge 59.00 N 16.55 E
Bavispe 192 Eb 30.24 N 108.50 W
Bavispe, Río de- 192 Ec 29.15 N 109.11 W
Bavly 114 Mi 54.26 N 53.18 E
Bawah, Pulau- 150 Ef 2.31 N 106.03 E
Bawal, Pulau- 150 Fg 2.44 S 110.06 E
Bawe 210 Ee 2.59 S 134.43 E
Bawean, Pulau- 150 Fh 5.46 S 112.40 E
Bawku 166 Ec 11.03 N 0.15 W
Baxian 152 Kd 39.03 N 116.24 E
Baxol 152 Ge 30.07 N 96.56 E
Bay [3] 168 Ge 2.50 N 43.30 E
Bay/Baicheng 152 Dc 41.46 N 81.52 E
Bayamo 190 Id 20.23 N 76.39 W
Bayamón 194 Nd 18.24 N 66.09 W
Bayan 154 Ia 46.05 N 127.24 E
Bayanbulak 152 Dc 43.05 N 84.05 E
Bayanga 168 Be 2.53 N 16.19 E
Bayan Gol 152 Gd 37.18 N 96.50 E
Bayan Gol → Dengkou 142 Me 40.25 N 106.59 E
Bayan Har Shan 140 Lf 34.20 N 97.00 E
Bayan Har Shankou 152 Ge 34.06 N 97.38 E
Bayan Hot → Alxa Zuoqi 152 Id 38.50 N 105.32 E
Bayan Hure → Chen Barag Qi 152 Kb 49.21 N 119.25 E
Bayan Huxu → Horqin Youyi Zhongqi 152 Lb 45.04 N 121.27 E
Bayano, Lago de- 194 Hi 9.00 N 78.30 W
Bayan Obo 152 Ic 41.50 N 109.58 E
Bayan Qagan 154 Ga 46.11 N 123.59 E
Bayan Qagan → Qahar Youyi Houqi 154 Bd 41.28 N 113.10 E
Bayan Ul Hot → Xi Ujimqin Qi 152 Kc 44.31 N 117.33 E
Bayas 192 Gf 23.32 N 104.50 W
Bayat 146 Fb 40.39 N 34.15 E
Bayauca 204 Bl 34.51 S 61.18 W
Bayawan 150 He 9.20 N 123.00 E
Bayāẓ 146 Pg 30.42 N 55.28 E
Bayāzeh 146 Pf 30.42 N 55.28 E
Baybay 150 Hd 10.41 N 124.48 E
Bayburt 144 Fa 40.16 N 40.15 E
Bay City [Mi.-U.S.] 182 Kc 43.36 N 83.53 W
Bay City [Tx.-U.S.] 182 Hf 29.09 N 95.39 W
Bayerische Alpen 120 Hi 47.30 N 11.30 E
Bayerischer Wald = Bavarian Forest (EN) 120 Ig 49.00 N 12.55 E
Bayern = Bavaria (EN) [2] 120 Hg 49.00 N 11.30 E
Bayern = Bavaria (EN) 110 Hf 49.00 N 11.30 E
Bayes, Cap- 219b Be 20.57 S 165.25 E
Bayeux 122 Fe 49.16 N 0.42 W
Bayfield 186 Kc 46.49 N 90.49 W
Bay Fiord 180 Ja 79.00 N 84.00 W
Baygorria 204 Dk 32.52 S 56.44 W
Baygorria, Lago Artificial de- 204 Dk 33.05 S 57.00 W
Bayḩān al Qişāb 164 Ig 14.48 N 45.44 E
Bayındır 146 Bc 38.13 N 27.40 E
Bayjī 146 Je 34.56 N 43.29 E
Bay Minette 184 Dj 30.53 N 87.47 W
Baynūnah 146 Ok 23.50 N 52.50 E
Bayombong 150 Hc 16.29 N 121.09 E
Bayona / Baiona 126 Db 42.07 N 8.51 W
Bayonnaise Seamount (EN) 208 Jf 12.00 S 179.30 W
Bayonne 112 Fg 43.29 N 1.29 W
Bayou Bodcau Lake 186 Jj 32.58 N 93.30 W
Bayou D'Arbonne Lake 186 Jj 32.45 N 92.27 W
Bayramiç 130 Jj 39.48 N 26.37 E
Bayreuth 120 Hg 49.57 N 11.35 E
Bayrūt [3] 146 Ff 33.56 N 35.30 E
Bayrūt = Beirut (EN) 142 Ff 33.53 N 35.30 E
Bay Saint Louis 186 Lk 30.19 N 89.20 W
Bay Springs 186 Lk 31.59 N 89.17 W
Bayt al Faqīh 144 Fg 14.31 N 43.17 E
Baytik Shan 152 Fb 45.15 N 90.50 E
Bayt Laḩm = Bethlehem (EN) 146 Fg 31.43 N 35.12 E
Baytown 182 If 29.44 N 94.58 W
Bayuda Desert (EN) = Bayyūḑah, Şaḩrā'- 158 Kg 18.00 N 33.00 E
Bayunglencir 150 Dg 2.03 S 103.41 E
Bayview 188 Gc 48.00 N 116.30 W
Bay View 218 Gc 39.26 S 176.52 E
Bayy al Kabīr 164 Cc 31.11 N 15.53 E

Index Symbols

[1] Independent Nation
[2] State, Region
[3] District, County
[4] Municipality
[5] Colony, Dependency
Continent
Physical Region
Historical or Cultural Region
Mount, Mountain
Volcano
Hill
Mountains, Mountain Range
Hills, Escarpment
Plateau, Upland
Pass, Gap
Plain, Lowland
Delta
Salt Flat
Valley, Canyon
Crater, Cave
Karst Features
Depression
Polder
Desert, Dunes
Forest, Woods
Heath, Steppe
Oasis
Cape, Point
Coast, Beach
Cliff
Peninsula
Isthmus
Sandbank
Island
Atoll
Rock, Reef
Islands, Archipelago
Rocks, Reefs
Coral Reef
Well, Spring
Geyser
River, Stream
Waterfall, Rapids
River Mouth, Estuary
Lake
Salt Lake
Intermittent Lake
Reservoir
Swamp, Pond
Canal
Glacier
Ice Shelf, Pack Ice
Ocean
Sea
Gulf, Bay
Strait, Fjord
Lagoon
Bank
Seamount
Tablemount
Ridge
Shelf
Basin
Escarpment, Sea Scarp
Fracture
Trench, Abyss
National Park, Reserve
Point of Interest
Recreation Site
Cave, Cavern
Historic Site
Ruins
Wall, Walls
Church, Abbey
Temple
Scientific Station
Railway station
Airport
Port
Military installation
Lighthouse
Mine
Tunnel
Dam, Bridge

Bayyūḍah, Ṣaḥrā'- = Bayuda Desert (EN) 158 Kg 18.00N 33.00 E
Baza 126 Jg 37.29N 2.46W
Baza, Sierra de- 126 Jg 37.15N 2.45W
Bazardjuzju, gora- 110 Kg 41.13N 47.51 E
Bazaruto, Ilha do- 172 Fd 21.40S 35.25 E
Bazas 122 Fj 44.26N 0.13W
Bazhong 152 Ie 31.54N 106.42 E
Bazoches-sur-Vesle 124 Fe 49.19N 3.37 E
Baztan / Baztán 126 Ka 43.09N 1.31 E
Baztán / Baztan 126 Ka 43.09N 1.31 E
Beach 182 Gb 46.55N 103.52W
Beachy Head 118 Nk 50.44N 0.16 E
Beacon 184 Ke 41.31N 73.59W
Beaconsfield [Austl.] 212 Jh 41.12S 146.48 E
Beaconsfield [Eng.-U.K.] 124 Bc 51.36N 0.38W
Beagle, Canal- 206 Gh 54.53S 68.10W
Beagle Gulf 212 Gb 12.00S 130.20 E
Bealach an Doirin/Ballaghaderreen 118 Eh 53.55N 8.35W
Béalanana 172 Hb 14.33S 48.44 E
Béal an Átha/Ballina 118 Dg 54.07N 9.09W
Béal an Bheara/Gweebarra Bay 118 Eg 54.52N 8.20W
Béal Átha Fhirdhia/Ardee 118 Gh 53.52N 6.33W
Béal Átha hAmhnais/Ballyhaunis 118 Eh 53.46N 8.46W
Béal Átha na Muice/Swinford 118 Eh 53.57N 8.57W
Béal Átha na Sluaighe/Ballinasloe 118 Eh 53.20N 8.13W
Béal Átha Seanaidh/Ballyshannon 118 Eg 54.30N 8.11W
Beale, Cape- 188 Cb 48.44N 125.20W
Béal Easa/Foxford 118 Dh 53.59N 9.07W
Béal Feirste/Belfast 112 Fe 54.35N 5.55W
Beal Range 212 Ie 25.30S 141.30 E
Béal Tairbirt/Belturbet 118 Fg 54.06N 7.26W
Beanna Boirche/Mourne Mountains 118 Gg 54.10N 6.04W
Beannchar/Bangor 118 Hg 54.40N 5.40W
Beanntrai/Bantry 118 Dj 51.41N 9.27W
Bear Bay 180 Ia 75.45N 86.30W
Beardmore 186 Mb 49.36N 87.57W
Beardstown 186 Kg 39.59N 90.26W
Bear Island (EN) = Bjørnøya 110 Ha 74.30N 19.00 E
Bear Islands (EN) = Medveži, ostrova- 140 Sb 70.52N 161.26 E
Bear Lake 182 Ec 42.00N 111.20W
Bear Lodge Mountains 186 Dd 44.35N 104.15W
Béarn 122 Fk 43.20N 0.45W
Bearpaw Mountains 188 Kb 48.15N 109.30W
Bear Peninsula 222 Of 74.36S 110.50W
Bear River 188 If 41.30N 112.08W
Bearskin Lake 180 If 53.57N 90.59W
Beās 148 Eb 31.10N 74.59 E
Beas de Segura 126 Jf 38.15N 2.53W
Beata, Cabo- 190 Je 17.36N 71.25W
Beata, Isla- 194 Le 17.35N 71.31W
Beata Ridge (EN) 190 Je 16.00N 72.30W
Beatrice 182 Hc 40.16N 96.44W
Beatrice, Cape- 212 Hb 14.15S 137.00 E
Beatton 180 Fe 56.06N 120.22W
Beatton River 180 Fe 56.10N 120.25W
Beatty 182 Dd 36.54N 116.46W
Beattyville 184 Ia 48.52N 77.10W
Beatys Butte 182 Fe 42.23N 119.20W
Beau-Bassin 172a Bb 20.13S 57.27 E
Beaucaire 122 Kk 43.48N 4.38 E
Beaucamps-le-Vieux 124 De 49.50N 1.47 E
Beaucanton 184 Ia 49.05N 79.15W
Beauce 122 Hf 48.22N 1.50 E
Beaudesert 212 Ke 27.59S 153.00 E
Beaufort [Mala.] 150 Ge 5.20N 115.45 E
Beaufort [S.C.-U.S.] 184 Gi 32.26N 80.40W
Beaufort/Befort 124 Ie 49.50N 6.18 E
Beaufort, Massif de- 122 Mi 45.50N 6.40 E
Beaufort Island 222 Kf 76.57S 166.56 E
Beaufort Sea 224 Ad 73.00N 140.00W
Beaufort West 160 Jl 32.20S 22.33 E
Beaugency 122 Hg 47.47N 1.38 E
Beaujolais, Monts du- 122 Kh 46.00N 4.22 E
Beauly 118 Id 57.29N 4.29W
Beaumesnil 124 Ce 49.01N 0.43 E
Beaumetz-lès-Loges 124 Ed 50.14N 2.39 E
Beaumont [Bel.] 124 Gd 50.14N 4.14 E
Beaumont [Fr.] 122 Gj 44.46N 0.46 E
Beaumont [Fr.] 122 Ee 49.40N 1.51W
Beaumont [Fr.] 124 Hf 48.51N 5.47 E
Beaumont [Ms.-U.S.] 186 Lk 31.11N 88.55W
Beaumont [N.Z.] 218 Cf 45.49S 169.32 E
Beaumont [Tx.-U.S.] 176 Jf 30.05N 94.06W
Beaumont-de-Lomagne 122 Gk 43.53N 0.59 E
Beaumont-en-Argonne 124 He 49.32N 5.03 E
Beaumont-le-Roger 124 Ce 49.05N 0.47 E
Beaumont-sur-Oise 124 Ee 49.08N 2.17 E
Beaumont-sur-Sarthe 122 Gf 48.13N 0.08 E
Beaune 122 Kg 47.02N 4.50 E
Beaupré 184 Lb 47.03N 70.53W
Beauraing 124 Gd 50.07N 4.48 E
Beaurepaire 122 Li 45.20N 5.03 E
Beausejour 180 Hf 50.04N 96.33W
Beautemps Beaupré 219b Ce 20.25S 166.08 E
Beauvais 122 Ie 49.26N 2.05 E
Beauval 124 Ed 50.06N 2.20 E
Beauvoir-sur-Mer 122 Dh 46.55N 2.03W
Beaver [Ak.-U.S.] 178 Jc 66.22N 147.24W
Beaver [Ok.-U.S.] 186 Fh 36.48N 100.30W
Beaver [Ut.-U.S.] 182 Ed 38.17N 112.38W
Beaver Creek [Co.-U.S.] 186 Ef 40.20N 103.33W
Beaver Creek [U.S.] 186 Gf 40.04N 99.20W
Beaver Creek [U.S.] 186 Ec 47.20N 103.39W
Beaver Creek [U.S.] 186 Gh 43.25N 103.59W
Beaver Dam 186 Le 43.28N 88.50W
Beaver Falls 184 Ge 40.45N 80.21W
Beaverhead Mountains 188 Id 45.00N 113.20W
Beaver Island 184 Ec 45.40N 85.31W
Beaver Lake 186 Jh 36.20N 93.55W
Beaver River [U.S.] 186 Gh 36.10N 98.45W
Beaver River [Ut.-U.S.] 188 Ig 39.10N 112.57W
Beaverton 188 Dd 45.29N 122.48W
Beāwar 148 Ec 26.06N 74.19 E
Bebedouro 206 Kb 20.56S 48.28W
Becan 192 Oh 18.37N 89.35W
Becanchén 192 Oh 19.50N 89.22W
Beccles 118 Oi 52.28N 1.34 E
Bečej 130 Dd 45.37N 20.03 E
Beceni 130 Jd 45.23N 26.47 E
Becerreá 126 Eb 42.51N 7.10W
Becerro, Cayos- 194 Ff 15.57N 83.17W
Béchar 160 Ge 31.37N 2.13W
Béchar 162 Gd 30.00N 2.00W
Becharof Lake 178 He 58.00N 156.30W
Bechet 130 Gf 43.46N 23.57 E
Bechevin Bay 178 Ge 55.00N 163.27W
Bechyně 120 Kg 49.18N 14.28 E
Beckingen 124 Ie 49.24N 6.42 E
Beckley 182 Kd 37.46N 81.12W
Beckum 120 Ee 51.45N 8.02 E
Beckumer Berge 124 Kc 51.43N 8.10 E
Beclean 130 Hb 47.11N 24.11 E
Bédarieux 122 Jk 43.37N 3.09 E
Bedburg-Hau 124 Ic 51.46N 6.11 E
Bedele 168 Fd 8.27N 36.22 E
Bedesa 168 Gd 8.53N 40.46 E
Bedford 118 Mi 52.10N 0.50W
Bedford [Eng.-U.K.] 118 Mi 52.08N 0.29W
Bedford [In.-U.S.] 184 Df 38.52N 86.29W
Bedford [Pa.-U.S.] 184 He 40.00N 78.31W
Bedford [Va.-U.S.] 184 Hg 37.20N 79.31W
Bedford Level 118 Ni 52.30N 0.05 E
Bedford Point 197b Bb 12.13N 61.36W
Bedfordshire 118 Mi 52.05N 0.20W
Bednja 128 Kd 46.18N 16.45 E
Bednodemjanovsk 132 Mc 53.55N 43.12 E
Bedourie 212 Hd 24.21S 139.28 E
Bedum 124 Ia 53.18N 6.39 E
Beech Grove 184 Df 39.43N 86.03W
Beecroft Head 212 Kg 35.01S 150.50 E
Beef Island 197a Db 18.27N 64.31W
Beelitz 120 Id 52.14N 12.58 E
Beemster 124 Gb 52.34N 4.56 E
Beerfelden 124 Ke 49.34N 8.59 E
Beernem 124 Fc 51.09N 3.20 E
Beerse 124 Gc 51.19N 4.52 E
Beersel 124 Gd 50.46N 4.18 E
Beersheba (EN) = Be'er Sheva' 144 Dc 31.14N 34.47 E
Be'er Sheva' = Beersheba (EN) 144 Dc 31.14N 34.47 E
Beerze 124 Hc 51.36N 5.19 E
Beeskow 120 Kd 52.10N 14.14 E
Beestekraal 172 De 25.23S 27.38 E
Beeston 118 Li 52.56N 1.12W
Beethoven Peninsula 222 Qf 71.40S 73.45W
Beetsterzwaag, Opsterland- 124 Ia 53.03N 6.04 E
Beeville 182 Hf 28.24N 97.45W
Befale 170 Db 0.28N 20.58 E
Befandriana Avaratra 172 Hc 15.15S 48.32 E
Befandriana Nord 172 Hc 15.15S 48.32 E
Befandriana Sud 172 Gd 22.06S 43.54 E
Befori 170 Db 0.06N 22.17 E
Befort/Beaufort 124 Ie 49.50N 6.18 E
Bega 210 Fh 36.40S 149.50 E
Bega 130 Dd 45.13N 20.19 E
Bégard 122 Cf 48.38N 3.18W
Begejski kanal 130 Dd 45.27N 20.27 E
Beggars Point 197d Bb 17.10N 61.48W
Bègles 122 Fj 44.48N 0.32W
Begna 114 Bf 60.35N 10.00 E
Begoml 116 Mj 54.46N 28.14 E
Begunicy 116 Me 59.31N 29.30 E
Behābād 146 Pg 31.52N 55.57 E
Behbehān 144 Hc 30.35N 50.14 E
Behring Point 194 Ia 24.27N 77.43W
Behshahr 144 Hb 36.43N 53.34 E
Bei'an 152 Oe 48.16N 126.29 E
Beibu Wan = Tonkin, Gulf of- (EN) 140 Mh 20.00N 108.00 E
Beida He 152 Gc 40.18N 99.01 E
Beihai 142 Mg 21.31N 109.07 E
Bei Hulsan Hu 152 Gd 36.55N 95.55 E
Bei Jiang 152 Jg 23.02N 112.58 E
Beijing = Peking (EN) 142 Nf 39.55N 116.23 E
Beijing Shi (Pei-ching Shih) 152 Kc 40.15N 116.30 E
Beila 162 Df 18.10N 15.53W
Beilen 124 Ib 52.52N 6.32 E
Beilerstroom 124 Ib 52.41N 6.12 E
Beiliutang He 154 Eg 34.12N 119.33 E
Beilsteim 124 Jd 50.07N 7.15 E
Beilu He 152 Fe 34.34N 94.00 E
Beinamar 168 Bd 8.40N 15.23 E
Beine-Nauroy 124 Ge 49.15N 4.13 E
Beipiao 152 Lc 41.49N 120.45 E
Beira 160 Kj 19.50S 34.52 E
Beira Alta 126 Ed 40.40N 7.35W
Beira Baixa 126 Ee 39.55N 7.30W
Beira Litoral 126 Dd 40.15N 8.25W
Beiru He 154 Bh 33.40N 113.35 E
Beirut (EN) = Bayrūt 142 Ff 33.53N 35.30 E
Bei Shan 140 Le 41.30N 96.00 E
Beitstad 114 Cd 64.05N 11.22 E
Beiuş 130 Fc 46.40N 22.21 E
Beiwei Tan 152 Kg 21.10N 116.10 E
Beizhen [China] 152 Kd 37.24N 117.59 E
Beizhen [China] 154 Fd 41.36N 121.47 E
Beja 126 Ef 38.01N 7.52W
Beja 126 Eg 37.58N 7.50W
Bejaia 160 He 36.45N 5.05 E
Bejaia 162 Ib 36.40N 5.10 E
Bejaia, Golfe de- 126 Rh 36.45N 5.20 E
Béjar 126 Gd 40.23N 5.46W
Beji 148 Dc 29.47N 67.58 E
Bejneu 136 Ff 45.15N 55.05 E
Bejsug 132 Kf 46.02N 38.35 E
Bejsugski liman 132 Kf 46.05N 38.25 E
Bekabad 136 Gg 40.13N 69.14 E
Bekasi 150 Eh 6.14S 106.59 E
Bekdaš 136 Fg 41.31N 52.40 E
Békés 120 Rj 46.46N 21.08 E
Békés 120 Qj 46.45N 21.00 E
Békéscsaba 120 Rj 46.41N 21.06 E
Bekilli 130 Mk 38.14N 29.26 E
Bekily 172 Hd 24.12S 45.18 E
Bekkai 156a Db 43.25N 145.07 E
Bekoji 168 Fd 7.32N 39.15 E
Bekopaka 172 Gc 19.08S 44.45 E
Bekovo 132 Mc 52.29N 43.45 E
Bela [India] 148 Gc 25.56N 81.59 E
Bela [Pak.] 148 Dc 26.14N 66.19 E
Bélabo 166 He 4.52N 13.10 E
Bela Crkva 130 Ee 44.54N 21.26 E
Bela Dila 148 Ge 18.40N 80.55 E
Bela Floresta 204 Ge 20.36S 51.16W
Belaga 150 Ff 2.42N 113.47 E
Belaja [R.S.F.S.R.] 110 Ld 56.00N 54.32 E
Belaja [R.S.F.S.R.] 132 Kg 45.03N 39.25 E
Belaja [R.S.F.S.R.] 138 Mc 65.30N 173.15 E
Belaja Cerkov 112 Jf 49.49N 30.07 E
Belaja Gora 138 Jc 68.30N 146.15 E
Belaja Holunica 136 Fd 58.53N 50.50 E
Belaja Kalitva 136 Ef 48.09N 40.49 E
Bela Krajina 128 Je 45.35N 15.15 E
Bela Lorena 204 Ib 15.13S 46.01W
Belang 150 Hf 0.57N 124.47 E
Bela Palanka 130 Ff 43.13N 22.19 E
Belarbi 126 Li 35.09N 0.27W
Belaruskaja Sovetskaja Socialistyčnaja Respublika /Belorusskaja SSR 136 Ce 53.50N 28.00 E
Belau = Palau (EN) 128 Di 41.11N 9.23 E
Bela Vista [Braz.] 204 Dc 17.37S 57.01W
Bela Vista [Braz.] 202 Gh 22.06S 56.31W
Bela Vista [Moz.] 172 Ee 26.20S 32.40 E
Belawan 150 Cf 3.47N 98.41 E
Běła Woda/Weißwasser 120 Ke 51.31N 14.38 E
Belayan 150 Gg 0.14S 116.36 E
Belbo 128 Cf 44.54N 8.31 E
Bełchatów 120 Pe 51.22N 19.21 E
Belcher Channel 180 Ia 77.20N 94.30W
Belcher Islands 174 Ld 56.20N 79.30W
Belchite 126 Lc 41.18N 0.45W
Belcy 136 Cf 47.46N 27.55 E
Bełczyna 120 Ne 51.25N 17.50 E
Belebej 136 Fe 54.10N 54.07 E
Belecke, Warstein- 124 Kc 51.29N 8.20 E
Beled 120 Ni 47.28N 17.06 E
Beled Wëyne 160 Lh 4.47N 45.12 E
Bélel 166 Hd 7.03N 14.26 E
Belém [Braz.] 200 Lf 1.27S 48.29W
Belem [Mex.] 192 Dd 27.45N 110.27W
Belém [Moz.] 172 Fb 14.08S 35.58 E
Belém de São Francisco 202 Ke 8.46S 38.58W
Belen 182 Fe 34.40N 106.46W
Belén [Arg.] 206 Gc 27.39S 67.02W
Belén [Nic.] 194 Eh 11.30N 85.53W
Belén [Par.] 204 Df 23.30S 57.06W
Belén [Ur.] 204 Dj 30.47S 57.47W
Belén, Cuchilla de- 204 Dj 30.55S 56.30W
Belén de Escobar 204 Cl 34.21S 58.47W
Belene 130 If 43.39N 25.07 E
Bélep, Iles- 208 Hf 19.45S 163.40 E
Beles 168 Fc 10.55N 35.10 E
Belev 132 Jc 53.50N 36.10 E
Beleye 168 Fc 11.24N 36.10 E
Belfast [Me.-U.S.] 184 Mc 44.27N 69.01W
Belfast [S.Afr.] 172 Ee 25.43S 30.03 E
Belfast/Béal Feirste 112 Fe 54.35N 5.55W
Belfast Lough/Loch Lao 118 Hg 54.40N 5.50W
Belfield 186 Ec 46.53N 103.12W
Belford 118 Lf 55.36N 1.49W
Belfort 122 Mg 47.45N 7.00 E
Belgaum 142 Jh 15.52N 74.30 E
Belgica Bank (EN) 224 Ld 78.28N 15.00W
Belgicafjella 222 Df 72.35S 31.10 E
België/Belgique = Belgium (EN) 112 Ge 50.30N 4.30 E
Belgique/België = Belgium (EN) 112 Ge 50.30N 4.30 E
Belgium (EN) = België/Belgique 112 Ge 50.30N 4.30 E
Belgium (EN) = Belgique/België 112 Ge 50.30N 4.30 E
Belgorod 112 Je 50.36N 36.35 E
Belgorod-Dnestrovski 136 Df 46.12N 30.17 E
Belgorodskaja oblast 136 De 50.45N 37.30 E
Belgrade (EN) = Beograd 112 Ig 44.50N 20.30 E
Bel Hairane 162 Ic 31.17N 6.20 E
Beli 166 Hd 7.52N 10.58 E
Belice 128 Gm 37.35N 12.52 E
Beli Drim 130 Dg 42.05N 20.20 E
Belidži 132 Pi 41.53N 48.20 E
Beli Lom 130 If 43.41N 26.00 E
Beli Manastir 128 Me 45.46N 18.37 E
Belimbegovo 130 Eh 42.00N 21.35 E
Belin-Béliet 122 Fj 44.30N 0.47W
Belinga 170 Bb 1.04N 13.12 E
Belinski 132 Mc 52.58N 43.29 E
Belinyu 150 Eg 1.38S 105.46 E
Beliş 130 Gc 46.39N 23.02 E
Beli Timok 130 Ff 43.55N 22.18 E
Belitung, Pulau- 140 Mj 2.50S 107.55 E
Belize 194 Ce 17.35N 88.35W
Belize (British Honduras) 176 Kh 17.15N 88.45W
Belize City 176 Kh 17.30N 88.12W
Belize River 194 Ce 17.32N 88.14W
Beljajevka 132 Gf 46.29N 30.14 E
Beljanica 130 Ee 44.07N 21.43 E
Belka 116 Mg 57.40N 29.47 E
Belkovski, ostrov- 138 Ia 75.30N 136.00 E
Bellac 122 Hh 46.07N 1.03 E
Bella Coola 180 Ef 52.22N 126.46W
Bellagio 128 De 45.59N 9.15 E
Bellaire [Oh.-U.S.] 184 Ge 40.02N 80.46W
Bellaire [Tx.-U.S.] 186 Il 29.43N 95.28W
Bellaria-Igea Marina 128 Gf 44.09N 12.28 E
Bellary 142 Jh 15.09N 76.56 E
Bella Unión 204 Dj 30.15S 57.35W
Bella Vista [Arg.] 206 Ic 28.30S 59.03W
Bella Vista [Par.] 204 Df 22.08S 56.31W
Bellavista, Capo- 128 Dk 39.56N 9.43 E
Bell Bay 180 Jb 71.10N 84.55W
Belle-Anse 194 Kd 18.14N 72.04W
Belledonne 122 Mi 45.18N 6.08 E
Bellefontaine [Mart.] 197h Ab 14.40N 61.10W
Bellefontaine [Oh.-U.S.] 184 Fe 40.22N 83.45W
Belle Fourche 182 Gc 44.40N 103.51W
Belle Fourche River 186 Ed 44.26N 102.19W
Bellegarde 122 Ig 47.59N 2.26 E
Bellegarde-sur-Valserine 122 Lh 46.06N 5.49 E
Belle Glade 184 Gl 26.41N 80.40W
Belle Ile 110 Ff 47.19N 3.11W
Belle Isle 180 Lf 51.55N 55.20W
Belle Isle, Strait of- 174 Nd 51.35N 56.30W
Bellencombre 124 De 49.42N 1.14 E
Belleplaine 197q Ab 13.15N 59.34W
Belleville [Fr.] 122 Kh 46.06N 4.45 E
Belleville [Il.-U.S.] 186 Lg 38.31N 90.00W
Belleville [Ks.-U.S.] 186 Hg 39.49N 97.38W
Belleville [Ont.-Can.] 180 Jh 44.10N 77.23W
Bellevue [Nb.-U.S.] 186 If 41.09N 95.54W
Bellevue [Wa.-U.S.] 188 Dc 47.37N 122.12W
Belley 122 Li 45.46N 5.41 E
Bellheim 124 Ke 49.12N 8.17 E
Bellingham [Eng.-U.K.] 118 Kf 55.09N 2.16W
Bellingham [Wa.-U.S.] 176 Ge 48.46N 122.29W
Bellingsfors 116 Ef 58.59N 12.15 E
Bellingshausen 222 Re 62.12S 58.56W
Bellingshausen Ice Shelf 222 Ce 71.00S 89.00W
Bellingshausen Sea (EN) 222 Pf 71.00S 85.00W
Bellinzona 128 Dd 46.11N 9.02 E
Bello 202 Cb 6.19N 75.34W
Bellocq 204 Bl 35.55S 61.32W
Bellona, Récifs- 208 Gg 21.00S 159.00 E
Bellona Island 214 Fj 11.17S 159.47 E
Bellot Strait 180 Ib 72.00N 94.30W
Bellow Falls 184 Kd 43.08N 72.28W
Bell Peninsula 180 Jd 63.45N 81.30W
Bell River 180 Jg 49.49N 77.39W
Bell Rock → Inchcape 118 Ke 56.26N 2.24W
Bellsund 179 Nc 77.39N 14.15 E
Belluno 128 Gd 46.09N 12.13 E
Bellville 172 Bf 33.53S 18.36 E
Bell Ville 206 Hd 32.37S 62.42W
Belmond 186 Je 42.51N 93.37W
Belmont 184 Hd 42.14N 78.02W
Belmonte [Braz.] 202 Kg 15.51S 38.54W
Belmonte [Port.] 126 Ed 40.21N 7.21W
Belmonte [Sp.] 126 Je 39.34N 2.42W
Belmopan 176 Kh 17.15N 88.46W
Belo 172 Gd 20.44S 44.00 E
Beloeil 124 Fd 50.35N 3.43 E
Belogorsk [R.S.F.S.R.] 142 Od 50.57N 128.25 E
Belogorsk [R.S.F.S.R.] 138 De 55.02N 88.28 E
Belogorsk [Ukr.-U.S.S.R.] 132 Ig 45.01N 34.33 E
Belogradčik 130 Ff 43.38N 22.41 E
Belogradčiški prohod 130 Ff 43.38N 22.28 E
Belo Horizonte 200 Lg 19.55S 43.56W
Beloit [Ks.-U.S.] 186 Gg 39.28N 98.06W
Beloit [Wi.-U.S.] 182 Jc 42.31N 89.02W
Belojarovo 138 Hf 51.35N 128.55 E
Belojarski 136 Gc 63.40N 66.45 E
Beloje more = White Sea (EN) 110 Kb 66.00N 44.00 E
Beloje ozero = White Lake (EN) 110 Jc 60.11N 37.35 E
Belokany 132 Oi 41.43N 46.28 E
Belomorsk 112 Jc 64.29N 34.43 E
Belomorsko-Baltijski kanal = White Sea-Baltic Canal (EN) 110 Jc 63.30N 34.48 E
Belomorsko-Kulojskoje plato 114 Jd 65.20N 41.50 E
Beloozersk 132 Dc 52.28N 25.13 E
Belopolje 136 De 51.09N 34.18 E
Belorečensk 132 Kg 44.43N 39.52 E
Beloreck 136 Fe 53.58N 58.24 E
Belorusskaja grjada 132 Ec 53.50N 27.00 E
Belorusskaja Sovetskaja Socialističeskaja Respublika 136 Ce 53.50N 28.00 E
Belorusskaja SSR/Belaruskaja Sovetskaja Socialistyčnaja Respublika 136 Ce 53.50N 28.00 E
Belorusskaja SSR = Byelorussian SSR (EN) 136 Ce 53.50N 28.00 E
Belo-sur-Mer 172 Gd 20.44S 44.00 E
Belo-sur-Tsiribihina 172 Gc 19.39S 44.32 E
Belot, Lac- 180 Ec 66.50N 126.20W
Belo-Tsiribihina 172 Gc 19.39S 44.32 E
Beloveżskaja Pušča, zapovednik- 120 Ud 52.45N 24.15 E
Belovo 138 Df 54.25N 86.18 E
Belovodsk 132 Ke 49.10N 39.33 E
Belovodskoe 135 Jc 42.47N 74.13 E
Belozersk 136 Dd 60.03N 37.48 E
Belper 124 Aa 53.02N 1.28W
Belted Range 188 Gh 37.25N 116.10W
Belton [Mo.-U.S.] 186 Ig 38.49N 94.32W
Belton [Tx.-U.S.] 186 Hk 31.04N 97.28W
Belton Lake 186 Hk 31.08N 97.32W
Belturbet/Béal Tairbirt 118 Fg 54.06N 7.26W
Beluha, gora- 140 Ke 49.48N 86.35 E
Belvedere Marittimo 128 Jk 39.37N 15.52 E
Belvidere 186 Le 42.15N 88.50W
Bely 114 Hi 55.50N 32.58 E
Bely, Island (EN) = Bely, ostrov- 140 Jb 73.10N 70.45 E
Bely, ostrov- = Bely, Island (EN) 140 Jb 73.10N 70.45 E
Belyando River 212 Jd 21.38S 146.50 E
Bely Čeremoš 130 Ia 48.06N 25.04 E
Bely Jar 138 De 58.26N 85.03 E
Belyje Berega 132 Ic 53.12N 34.42 E
Belz 132 Dd 50.23N 24.03 E
Bełżec 120 Tf 50.24N 23.26 E
Belzoni 186 Kj 33.11N 90.29W
Bełżyce 120 Se 51.11N 22.18 E
Bemaraha, Plateau de- 158 Lj 19.00S 45.15 E
Bembe 170 Bd 7.02S 14.18 E
Bembéréké 166 Fc 10.13N 2.40 E
Bembézar 126 Gg 37.45N 5.13W
Bembridge 124 Ad 50.41N 1.05W
Bemidji 182 Ib 47.29N 94.53W
Ben 146 Nf 32.32N 50.45 E
Benāb 144 Gb 37.18N 46.05 E
Benabarre / Benavarri 126 Mb 42.07N 0.29 E
Benaco → Garda, Lago di- 110 Hf 45.35N 10.35 E
Bena Dibele 170 Dc 4.07S 22.50 E
Benaize 122 Hh 46.34N 1.04 E
Benalla 212 Jg 36.33S 145.59 E
Benares → Vārānasi 142 Kg 25.20N 83.00 E
Benasc/Benasque 126 Mb 42.36N 0.32 E
Benasque/Benasc 126 Mb 42.36N 0.32 E
Benavarri / Benabarre 126 Mb 42.07N 0.29 E
Benavente 126 Gc 42.00N 5.41W
Benbecula 118 Fd 57.27N 7.20W
Bencheng → Luannan 154 Ee 39.30N 118.42 E
Ben-Chicao, Col de- 126 Oh 36.12N 2.51 E
Bend 182 Cc 44.03N 121.19W
Bendaja 166 Cd 7.10N 11.15W
Bendel 166 Gd 6.00N 5.50 E
Bendela 170 Cc 3.18S 17.36 E
Bender Bäyla 160 Mh 9.30N 50.30 E
Bendersiyada 168 Hc 11.14N 48.57 E
Bendery 136 Cf 46.48N 29.22 E
Bendigo 210 Fh 36.46S 144.17 E
Bendorf 124 Jd 50.26N 7.34 E
Bēne/Bene 116 Jh 56.28N 23.01 E
Bene/Bēne 116 Jh 56.28N 23.01 E
Bénéna 166 Ec 13.06N 4.22W
Benepú, Rada- 221d Ac 27.10S 109.25W
Benešov 120 Kg 49.47N 14.40 E
Benevento 128 Ii 41.08N 14.45 E
Bengal 140 Kg 24.00N 90.00 E
Bengal, Bay of- (EN) 140 Kh 15.00N 90.00 E
Bengamisa 170 Eb 0.57N 25.10 E
Bengbis 166 He 3.27N 12.27 E
Bengbu 142 Nf 32.47N 117.23 E
Benghazi (EN) = Banghāzī 160 Je 32.07N 20.04 E
Benghazi (EN) = Banghāzī 164 Dd 27.00N 20.30 E
Beng He 154 Eg 35.04N 118.22 E
Benghisa Point 128 Io 35.50N 14.35 E
Bengkalis 150 Df 1.28N 102.08 E
Bengkulu 142 Mj 3.48S 102.16 E
Bengkulu 150 Dg 3.48S 102.16 E
Bengo 170 Bd 8.30S 13.40 E
Bengo, Baia do- 158 Ii 8.43S 13.21 E
Bengough 188 Mb 49.24N 105.08W
Bengtsfors 114 Cg 59.02N 12.13 E
Benguela 160 Ij 12.35S 13.26 E
Benguela 170 Be 12.00S 15.00 E
Benguerir 162 Fc 32.14N 7.57W
Benguérua, Ilha- 172 Fd 21.53S 35.26 E
Bengue Viejo 194 Ce 17.05N 89.08W
Bengut, Cap- 162 Hb 36.55N 3.54 E
Beni 160 Jh 0.30N 29.28 E
Beni 202 Ef 14.00S 65.30W
Beni, Rio- 198 Jg 10.23S 65.24W
Beni Abbes 162 Gc 30.08N 2.10W
Beni Baufrah 126 Hi 35.05N 4.18W
Benicarló 126 Md 40.25N 0.26 E
Benicasim / Benicàssim 126 Md 40.03N 0.04 E
Benicàssim / Benicasim 126 Md 40.03N 0.04 E
Beni Chougran, Monts des- 126 Mi 35.30N 0.15 E
Benidorm 126 Lf 38.32N 0.08W
Beni Enzar 126 Ji 35.14N 2.57W
Beni Haoua 126 Nh 36.32N 1.34 E
Beni Mellal 160 Ge 32.20N 6.21W
Beni Mellal 162 Fc 32.30N 6.30W
Benin 166 Gd 5.45N 5.04 E
Bénin (Dahomey) 160 Hh 9.30N 2.15 E
Benin, Bight of- 158 Hh 5.30N 4.00 E
Benin City 160 Hh 6.20N 5.38 E
Beni Ounif 162 Gc 32.03N 1.15W
Benisa / Benissa 126 Mf 38.43N 0.03 E
Beni Saf 126 Ki 35.19N 1.23W
Benisheikh 166 Hc 11.48N 12.29 E
Benissa / Benisa 126 Mf 38.43N 0.03 E
Benito Juárez 192 Mi 17.50N 92.32W
Benito Juárez, Presa- 192 Li 16.27N 95.30W
Benjamen Island 172b Bb 5.27S 53.21 E
Benjamin 186 Gj 33.35N 99.48W
Benjamin Aceval 204 Dg 24.58S 57.34W
Benjamin Constant 200 If 4.22S 70.02W
Benjamin Hill 192 Db 30.10N 111.10W
Benkei-Misaki 156a Bb 42.50N 140.11 E
Benkelman 186 Ff 40.03N 101.32W
Benkovac 128 Jf 44.02N 15.37 E
Ben Mehidi 128 Bn 36.46N 7.54 E
Bennett, Lake- 212 Gd 23.50S 131.00 E
Bennetta, ostrov- 138 Ja 76.45N 149.00 E
Benneydale 218 Fc 38.31S 175.21 E
Bennichab 162 Df 19.26N 15.21W
Bennington 184 Kd 42.53N 73.12W
Benom 150 Df 3.50N 102.06 E
Benoni 160 Jk 26.19S 28.27 E
Bénoué = Benue (EN) 158 Hh 7.48N 6.46 E
Benoy 168 Bd 8.59N 16.19 E
Benrath 124 Ic 51.10N 6.52 E
Bensekrane 126 Ki 35.04N 1.13W
Bensheim 120 Eg 49.41N 8.37 E
Ben Slimane 162 Fc 33.37N 7.07W
Benson [Az.-U.S.] 188 Jk 31.58N 110.18W

Index Symbols

1 Independent Nation
2 State, Region
3 District, County
4 Municipality
5 Colony, Dependency
Continent
Physical Region
Historical or Cultural Region
Mount, Mountain
Volcano
Hill
Mountains, Mountain Range
Hills, Escarpment
Plateau, Upland
Pass, Gap
Plain, Lowland
Delta
Salt Flat
Valley, Canyon
Crater, Cave
Karst Features
Depression
Polder
Desert, Dunes
Forest, Woods
Heath, Steppe
Oasis
Cape, Point
Coast, Beach
Cliff
Peninsula
Isthmus
Sandbank
Island
Atoll
Rock, Reef
Islands, Archipelago
Rocks, Reefs
Coral Reef
Well, Spring
Geyser
River, Stream
Waterfall, Rapids
River Mouth, Estuary
Lake
Salt Lake
Intermittent Lake
Reservoir
Swamp, Pond
Canal
Glacier
Ice Shelf, Pack Ice
Ocean
Sea
Gulf, Bay
Strait, Fjord
Lagoon
Bank
Seamount
Tablemount
Ridge
Shelf
Basin
Escarpment, Sea Scarp
Fracture
Trench, Abyss
National Park, Reserve
Point of Interest
Recreation Site
Cave, Cavern
Historic Site
Ruins
Wall, Walls
Church, Abbey
Temple
Scientific Station
Railway station
Airport
Port
Military installation
Lighthouse
Mine
Tunnel
Dam, Bridge

Benson [Mn.-U.S.]	186	Id	45.19N	95.36W
Benson Point	220g	Ab	1.56N	157.30W
Bent	144	Id	26.17N	59.31 E
Benteng [Indon.]	150	Hg	0.24S	121.59 E
Benteng [Indon.]	150	Hh	6.08N	120.27 E
Bentheim	120	Dd	52.19N	7.10 E
Bentiaba	170	Be	14.15S	12.24 E
Bentiaba	170	Be	14.29S	12.50 E
Bentinck	148	Jf	11.45N	98.03 E
Bentinck Island	212	Hc	17.05S	139.30 E
Bentiu	168	Dd	9.14N	29.50 E
Bento Conçalves	206	Jc	29.10S	51.31W
Bento Gomes, Rio-	204	Dc	16.40S	57.12W
Benton [Ar.-U.S.]	186	Ji	34.34N	92.35W
Benton [Il.-U.S.]	186	Lg	38.01N	88.55W
Bentong	150	Df	3.32N	101.55 E
Benton Harbor	184	Dd	42.07N	86.27W
Bentonville	186	Ih	36.22N	94.13W
Ben Tre	148	Lf	10.14N	106.23 E
Benue [2]	166	Gd	7.15N	8.20 E
Benue	158	Hh	7.48N	6.46 E
Benue (EN)=Bénoué	158	Hh	7.48N	6.46 E
Benwee Head/An Bhinn Bhuí	118	Dg	54.21N	9.48W
Benxi	142	Oe	41.16N	123.48 E
Bény-Bocage, Le-	124	Bf	48.56N	0.50W
Beo	150	If	4.15N	126.48 E
Beograd = Belgrade (EN)	112	Ig	44.50N	20.30 E
Beograd-Krnjača	130	De	44.52N	20.28 E
Beograd-Zemun	130	De	44.53N	20.25 E
Béoumi	166	Dd	7.40N	5.34W
Beppu	152	Ne	33.17N	131.30 E
Beppu-Wan	156	Be	33.20N	131.35 E
Bequia Head	197n	Ba	13.03N	61.12W
Bequia Island	196	Ff	13.01N	61.13W
Berabevú	204	Bk	33.20S	61.52W
Beraketa	172	Hd	24.11S	45.42 E
Berati	130	Ci	40.42N	19.57 E
Beratus, Gunung-	150	Gg	1.02S	116.20 E
Berau, Teluk- = McCluer Gulf (EN)	150	Jg	2.30S	132.30 E
Berberá	160	Lg	10.25N	45.02 E
Berbérati	160	Ih	4.16N	15.47 E
Berberia, Cabo- / Barbaria, Cap de-	126	Nf	38.38N	1.23 E
Berbice River	202	Gb	6.17N	57.32W
Berca	130	Jd	45.17N	26.41 E
Berchères-sur-Vesgre	124	Df	48.51N	1.33 E
Berchtesgaden	120	Ii	47.38N	13.00 E
Berck	122	Hd	50.24N	1.36 E
Berck-Berck-Plage	124	Dd	50.24N	1.34 E
Berda	132	Jf	46.47N	36.52 E
Berdâle	168	Hd	7.04N	47.51 E
Berdičev	136	Cf	49.53N	28.36 E
Berdigestjah	138	Hd	62.03N	126.50 E
Berdjansk	136	Df	46.43N	36.48 E
Berdsk	138	Df	54.47N	83.05 E
Beregomet	130	Ia	48.10N	25.24 E
Beregovo	136	Cf	48.13N	22.41 E
Bereku	170	Gc	4.27S	35.44 E
Berekua	196	Fe	15.14N	61.19W
Berekum	166	Ed	7.27N	2.35W
Berens	180	Hf	52.21N	97.01W
Berens River	180	Hf	52.22N	97.02W
Beresford	186	He	43.05N	96.47W
Berestečko	120	Vf	50.16N	25.14 E
Bereşti	130	Kc	46.06N	27.53 E
Berettyó	130	Ec	46.59N	21.07 E
Berettyóújfalu	120	Ri	47.13N	21.33 E
Bereza	136	Ce	52.33N	24.58 E
Berezan	132	Gd	50.19N	31.31 E
Berežany	132	De	49.29N	25.00 E
Berezina [Bye.-U.S.S.R.]	132	Dc	53.48N	25.59 E
Berezina [U.S.S.R.]	110	Je	52.33N	30.14 E
Berezino [Bye.-U.S.S.R.]	132	Fc	53.51N	29.00 E
Berezino [Bye.-U.S.S.R.]	116	Mj	54.55N	28.16 E
Berezino [Ukr.-U.S.S.R.]	130	Mc	46.16N	29.11 E
Bereznegovatoje	132	Hf	47.20N	32.49 E
Bereznik	136	Ec	62.53N	42.42 E
Berezniki	112	Ld	59.24N	56.46 E
Berezno	132	Ed	51.01N	26.45 E
Berezovka [Bye.-U.S.S.R.]	120	Vc	53.40N	25.37 E
Berezovka [R.S.F.S.R.]	134	Hd	64.59N	56.29 E
Berezovka [Ukr.-U.S.S.R.]	136	Df	47.12N	30.56 E
Berezovka Višerka	134	Hf	60.55N	56.50 E
Berezovo	136	Gc	63.58N	65.00 E
Berezovski [R.S.F.S.R.]	138	De	55.39N	86.16 E
Berezovski [R.S.F.S.R.]	134	Jh	56.55N	60.50 E
Berezovy	138	If	51.41N	135.52 E
Berga [Sp.]	126	Nb	42.06N	1.51 E
Berga [Swe.]	116	Gg	57.13N	16.02 E
Bergama	144	Cb	39.07N	27.10 E
Bergamo	128	De	45.41N	9.43 E
Bergantiños	126	Da	43.20N	8.45W
Bergara / Vergara	126	Ja	43.07N	2.25W
Bergby	114	Df	60.56N	17.02 E
Bergen [G.D.R.]	120	Jb	54.25N	13.26 E
Bergen [Neth.]	124	Gb	52.40N	4.42 E
Bergen [Nor.]	112	Gc	60.23N	5.20 E
Bergen/Mons	122	Jd	50.27N	3.56 E
Bergen aan Zee, Bergen-	124	Gb	52.40N	4.38 E
Bergen-Bergen aan Zee	124	Gb	52.40N	4.38 E
Bergen op Zoom	124	Kc	51.30N	4.17 E
Bergerac	122	Gj	44.51N	0.29 E
Bergeyk	124	Hc	51.19N	5.22 E
Bergh	124	Ic	51.53N	6.16 E
Bergheim	120	Cf	50.58N	6.39 E
Bergh-'s Heerenberg	124	Ic	51.53N	6.16 E
Bergisches Land	120	De	51.15N	7.10 E
Bergisch Gladbach	120	Df	50.59N	7.08 E
Bergkvara	116	Gh	56.23N	16.05 E
Bergneustadt	124	Jc	51.02N	7.39 E
Bergö	116	Ib	62.55N	21.10 E
Bergsjö	114	Df	61.59N	17.04 E
Bergslagen	116	Fd	60.05N	14.30 E
Bergstraße	124	Ke	49.40N	8.40 E
Bergues	124	Ed	50.58N	2.26 E
Bergum, Tietjerksteradeel-	124	Ha	53.12N	6.00 E
Bergviken	116	Gc	61.10N	16.45 E
Bergville	172	De	28.52S	29.18 E
Berh	152	Jb	47.45N	111.07 E
Berhala, Selat-	150	Dg	0.48S	104.25 E
Berici, Monti-	128	Fe	45.26N	11.31 E
Berīkān	146	Nh	28.17N	51.14 E
Berikulski	138	De	55.32N	88.08 E
Beringa, ostrov- = Bering Island (EN)	138	Lf	55.00N	166.10 E
Beringen	124	Hc	51.03N	5.13 E
Bering Glacier	178	Kd	60.15N	143.30W
Bering Island (EN) = Beringa, ostrov-	138	Lf	55.00N	166.10 E
Beringovo more = Bering Sea (EN)	174	Bd	60.00N	175.00W
Beringovski	142	Tc	63.07N	179.19 E
Bering proliv = Bering Strait (EN)	174	Cc	65.30N	169.00W
Bering Sea	174	Bd	60.00N	175.00W
Bering Sea (EN) = Beringovo more	174	Bd	60.00N	175.00W
Bering Strait	174	Cc	65.30N	169.00W
Bering Strait (EN) = Bering proliv	174	Cc	65.30N	169.00W
Berislav	132	Hf	46.51N	33.29 E
Berisso	204	Dl	34.52S	57.53W
Berit Dağı	146	Gc	38.01N	36.52 E
Berīzak	146	Qi	26.06N	57.15 E
Berja	126	Jh	36.51N	2.57W
Berkåk	114	Be	62.50N	10.00 E
Berkane	162	Gc	34.56N	2.20W
Berkel	120	Cd	52.09N	6.12 E
Berkeley	182	Cd	37.57N	122.18W
Berkhamsted	124	Bc	51.45N	0.33W
Berkner Island	222	Rf	79.30S	49.30W
Berkovica	130	Gf	43.14N	23.07 E
Berks	118	Lj	51.15N	1.20W
Berkshire [3]	118	Lj	51.30N	1.10W
Berkshire Downs	118	Lj	51.35N	1.25W
Berkshire Hills	184	Kd	42.20N	73.10W
Berlaimont	124	Fd	50.12N	3.49 E
Berlanga de Duero	126	Jc	41.28N	2.51W
Berlengas, Ilhas-	126	Ce	39.25N	9.30W
Berlevåg	114	Ga	70.51N	29.06 E
Berlin	182	Mc	44.29N	71.10W
Berlin (Ost) = East Berlin (EN)	112	He	52.31N	13.24 E
Berlin (Ost) = East Berlin (EN) [2]	120	Jd	52.30N	13.25 E
Berlin (West) = West Berlin (EN)	112	He	52.31N	13.24 E
Berlin-Pankow	120	Jd	52.34N	13.24 E
Bermeja, Sierra-	126	Gh	36.30N	5.15W
Bermejillo	190	Dc	25.53N	103.37W
Bermejito, Rio-	204	Bg	25.39S	60.11W
Bermejo, Isla-	204	An	39.01S	62.01W
Bermejo, Paso del-	198	Ii	32.50S	70.05W
Bermejo, Rio- [Arg.]	198	Ji	31.52S	67.22W
Bermejo, Rio- [S.Amer.]	198	Kh	26.52S	58.23W
Bermen, Lac-	180	Kf	53.35N	68.55W
Bermeo	126	Ja	43.26N	2.43W
Bermillo de Sayago	126	Fc	41.22N	6.06W
Bermuda [5]	176	Mf	32.20N	64.45W
Bermuda Islands	174	Mf	32.20N	64.45W
Bermuda Rise (EN)	174	Mf	32.30N	65.00W
Bern/Berne	112	Gf	46.55N	7.30 E
Bern / Berne [2]	128	Bd	46.55N	7.40 E
Bernalda	128	Kj	40.24N	16.41 E
Bernalillo	186	Ci	35.18N	106.33W
Bernard Islands	220d	Bb	7.18N	151.32 E
Bernardo de Irigoyen	204	Bk	32.10S	61.09W
Bernardo do Irigoyen	206	Jc	26.15S	53.39W
Bernasconi	206	He	37.54S	63.43W
Bernau bei Berlin	120	Jd	52.40N	13.35 E
Bernaville	124	Ed	50.08N	2.10 E
Bernay	122	Ge	49.06N	0.36 E
Bernburg	120	He	51.48N	11.44 E
Berndorf	128	Kc	47.57N	16.06 E
Berne [F.R.G.]	124	Ka	53.11N	8.29 E
Berne [In.-U.S.]	184	Ee	40.39N	84.57W
Berne/Bern	112	Gf	46.55N	7.30 E
Berne / Bern [2]	128	Bd	46.55N	7.40 E
Berner Alpen = Bernese Alps (EN)	128	Bd	46.25N	7.30 E
Berneray	118	Fd	57.43N	7.15W
Bernese Alps (EN) = Berner Alpen	128	Bd	46.25N	7.30 E
Bernesga	126	Gb	42.28N	5.31W
Bernesq	124	Be	49.16N	0.56W
Bernier Bay	180	Ib	71.08N	88.00W
Bernier Island	212	Cd	24.50S	113.10 E
Bernina	128	Dd	46.23N	9.54 E
Bernina	128	Ed	46.25N	10.01 E
Bernina, Piz-	128	Dd	46.23N	9.54 E
Berninapaß	128	Ed	46.25N	10.01 E
Bernissart	124	Fd	50.28N	3.38 E
Bernkastel-Kues	120	Dg	49.55N	7.04 E
Bernstorffs Isfjord	179	Hf	63.10N	40.45W
Berón de Astrada	204	Dh	27.33S	57.32W
Beroroha	172	Hd	21.39S	45.10 E
Béroubouay	166	Fc	10.32N	2.44 E
Beroun	120	Kg	49.58N	14.04 E
Berounka	120	Kg	50.00N	14.24 E
Berovo	130	Fh	41.43N	22.51 E
Berre, Étang de-	122	Lk	43.27N	5.08 E
Berriane	162	Hc	32.50N	3.46 E
Berrouaghia	126	Oh	36.08N	2.55 E
Berry	122	Hh	47.00N	2.00 E
Berry-au-Bac	124	Fe	49.24N	3.54 E
Berryessa, Lake-	188	Dg	38.37N	122.16W
Berry Head	118	Jk	50.24N	3.29W
Berry Islands	190	Ic	25.34N	77.45W
Berry River	188	Ja	50.50N	111.36W
Beršad	136	Cf	48.23N	29.33 E
Berseba	172	Be	26.01S	17.41 E
Bersenbrück	124	Jb	52.33N	7.56 E
Berthierville	184	Kb	46.05N	73.11W
Bertincourt	124	Ed	50.05N	2.59 E
Bertogne	124	Hd	50.05N	5.40 E
Bertolinia	202	Je	7.38S	43.57W
Bertoua	160	Ih	4.35N	13.41 E
Bertraghboy Bay	118	Dh	53.23N	9.50W
Bertrix	124	He	49.51N	5.15 E
Beru Island	208	Ie	1.20S	176.00 E
Berwick-upon-Tweed	118	Lf	55.46N	2.00W
Berwyn	118	Ji	52.53N	3.24W
Besalampy	172	Gc	16.44S	44.24 E
Besançon	112	Gf	47.15N	6.02 E
Besar, Gunung-	150	Gg	1.25S	115.39 E
Besbre	122	Jh	46.33N	3.44 E
Besed	132	Gc	52.38N	31.11 E
Besikama	150	Hh	9.36S	124.57 E
Beskid Mountains (EN)	110	Hf	49.40N	20.00 E
Beskid Niski	120	Rg	49.20N	21.30 E
Beskid Średni	120	Pg	49.45N	19.20 E
Beskid Wysoki	120	Pg	49.30N	20.00 E
Beskidy Wschodnie	120	Sg	49.20N	22.30 E
Beskidy Zachodnie	120	Pg	49.30N	19.30 E
Beskol	135	Ma	46.06N	81.01 E
Beslan	136	Eg	43.10N	44.35 E
Besna Kobila	130	Fg	42.32N	22.14 E
Besni	146	Gd	37.41N	37.52 E
Besparmak Dağ	130	Kl	37.30N	27.35 E
Bessao	168	Bd	7.53N	15.59 E
Bessarabia (EN) = Bessarabija	130	Lb	47.00N	28.30 E
Bessarabija = Bessarabia (EN)	130	Lb	47.00N	28.30 E
Bessarabka	132	Ff	46.20N	28.59 E
Bességes	122	Kj	44.17N	4.06 E
Bessemer	182	Je	33.25N	86.57W
Bessin	122	Fe	49.10N	1.00W
Bessines-sur-Gartempe	122	Hh	46.06N	1.22 E
Besšoki, gora-	132	Rh	43.57N	52.30 E
Best	124	Hc	51.30N	5.24 E
Bestjah [R.S.F.S.R.]	138	Hc	66.00N	123.35 E
Bestjah [R.S.F.S.R.]	138	Hd	61.17N	128.50 E
Bestobe	136	He	52.30N	73.05 E
Bestwig	124	Kc	51.22N	8.24 E
Betafo	172	Hc	19.49S	46.50 E
Betanzos [Bol.]	202	Eg	19.34S	65.27W
Betanzos [Sp.]	126	Da	43.17N	8.12W
Betanzos, Ria de-	126	Da	43.23N	8.15W
Bétaré Oya	166	Hd	5.36N	14.05 E
Bétérou	166	Fd	9.12N	2.16 E
Beteta	126	Jd	40.34N	2.04W
Bethal	172	De	26.27S	29.28 E
Bethanien	160	Ik	26.32S	17.11 E
Bethanien [3]	172	Be	26.30S	17.00 E
Bethany [Mo.-U.S.]	186	If	40.16N	94.02W
Bethany [Ok.-U.S.]	186	Hi	35.31N	97.38W
Bethel	176	Cc	60.48N	161.46W
Bétheniville	124	Ge	49.18N	4.22 E
Bethlehem [Pa.-U.S.]	184	Je	40.36N	75.22W
Bethlehem [S.Afr.]	160	Jk	28.15S	28.15 E
Bethlehem (EN) = Bayt Laḥm	146	Fg	31.43N	35.12 E
Bethulie	172	Df	30.32S	25.59 E
Béthune	122	Id	50.32N	2.38 E
Béthune	122	He	49.53N	1.09 E
Béticas, Cordilleras-	110	Fh	37.35N	3.30W
Betioky	172	Gd	23.42S	44.22 E
Betong [Mala.]	150	Ff	1.26N	111.30 E
Betong [Thai.]	148	Kg	5.45N	101.05 E
Betor	168	Fc	11.37N	39.00 E
Bétou	170	Cb	3.03N	18.31 E
Betpak-Dala	140	Ie	46.00N	70.00 E
Betroka	172	Hd	23.15S	46.05 E
Bet She'an	146	Ff	32.30N	35.30 E
Betsiamites, Rivière-	180	Kg	48.56N	68.38W
Betsiboka	158	Lj	16.03S	46.36 E
Bette, Picco-	158	If	22.00N	19.12 E
Bettembourg/Bettemburg	124	Ie	49.31N	6.06 E
Bettemburg/Bettembourg	124	Ie	49.31N	6.06 E
Bettendorf	186	Kf	41.32N	90.30W
Bettles Field	178	Ic	66.53N	151.51W
Bettna	116	Gf	58.55N	16.38 E
Bettola	128	Df	44.47N	9.36 E
Betūl	148	Fd	21.55N	77.54 E
Betuwe	122	Lc	51.55N	5.30 E
Betwa	148	Hc	25.55N	80.12 E
Betz	124	Ee	49.09N	2.57 E
Betzdorf	120	Df	50.47N	7.53 E
Beulah	184	Dc	44.38N	86.06W
Beult	124	Cc	51.13N	0.26 E
Beuvron	122	Hg	47.29N	1.15 E
Beuzeville	124	Ce	49.20N	0.21 E
Beveland	124	Fc	51.30N	3.40 E
Beveren	124	Gc	51.13N	4.15 E
Beveridge Reef	208	Kg	20.00S	168.00W
Beverley [Austl.]	212	Df	32.06S	116.56 E
Beverley [Eng.-U.K.]	118	Mh	53.51N	0.26W
Beverwijk	122	Kb	52.28N	4.40 E
Bewsher, Mount-	222	Ff	70.54S	65.28 E
Bexhill	118	Nk	50.50N	0.29 E
Bexley, London-	124	Cc	51.26N	0.09 E
Beyağaç	130	Ll	37.13N	28.57 E
Beyānlū	146	Ld	36.02N	47.53 E
Bey Dağı	146	Hc	38.15N	38.22 E
Bey Dağları	144	Db	36.40N	30.15 E
Beykoz	146	Cb	41.08N	29.05 E
Beyla	166	Dd	8.41N	8.38W
Beyoğlu, İstanbul-	130	Lh	41.02N	28.59 E
Beyoneisu-Retsugan	152	Oe	31.55N	139.55 E
Beypazari	146	Db	40.10N	31.55 E
Beyra	168	Hd	6.57N	47.19 E
Beyram	146	Oi	27.26N	53.31 E
Beyşehir	146	Dd	37.41N	31.43 E
Beyşehir Gölü	144	Db	37.40N	31.30 E
Bezaha	172	Gd	23.29S	44.30 E
Bežanickaja vozvyšennost	114	Gh	56.45N	29.30 E
Bežanicy	114	Gh	56.58N	29.57 E
Bezdan	130	Bd	45.51N	18.56 E
Bezdež	120	Vd	52.18N	25.20 E
Bezdéz	120	Kf	50.32N	14.43 E
Bežeck	136	Dd	57.50N	36.41 E
Bezenčuk	114	Lj	53.01N	49.24 E
Bezerra, Rio-	204	Ia	13.16S	47.31W
Bezerros	202	Ke	8.14S	35.45W
Béziers	122	Jk	43.21N	3.15 E
Bezmein	136	Fh	38.05N	58.12 E
Bežta	136	Eg	42.08N	46.08 E
Bhadrak	148	Hd	21.04N	86.30 E
Bhadrāvati	148	Ff	13.52N	75.43 E
Bhāgalpur	142	Kg	25.15N	87.00 E
Bhaironghati	148	Fb	31.01N	78.53 E
Bhakkar	148	Eb	31.38N	71.04 E
Bhamo	148	Jd	24.16N	97.14 E
Bhandāra	148	Fd	21.10N	79.39 E
Bhanjan	148	Gc	25.47N	83.36 E
Bhārat Juktarashtra = India (EN) [1]	142	Jh	20.00N	77.00 E
Bharatpur	148	Fc	27.13N	77.29 E
Bharūch	148	Ed	21.46N	72.54 E
Bhatinda → Bathinda	148	Eb	30.12N	74.57 E
Bhātpāra	148	Hd	22.52N	88.24 E
Bhavnagar	142	Jg	21.46N	72.09 E
Bhera	148	Eb	32.29N	72.55 E
Bheri	148	Gc	28.44N	81.16 E
Bhikhna-Thori	148	Gc	27.20N	84.38 E
Bhīlwāra	148	Ec	25.21N	74.38 E
Bhīma	140	Jh	16.25N	77.17 E
Bhind	148	Fc	26.34N	78.48 E
Bhiwāni	148	Fc	28.47N	76.08 E
Bhopāl	142	Jg	23.16N	77.24 E
Bhubaneshwar	142	Kg	20.14N	85.50 E
Bhuj	148	Dd	23.16N	69.40 E
Bhusāwal	148	Fd	21.03N	75.46 E
Bhutan (Druk-Yul) [1]	142	Lg	27.30N	90.30 E
Bia	166	Ed	5.21N	3.11W
Bia, Phou-	140	Mh	18.36N	103.01 E
Biá, Rio-	202	Ed	3.28S	67.23W
Bīābān, Kūh-e-	146	Qi	26.30N	57.25 E
Biabou	197n	Ba	13.12N	61.09W
Biafra	158	Hh	5.00N	7.30 E
Biafra, Bight of-	158	Hh	3.20N	9.20 E
Biak	150	Kg	1.10S	136.06 E
Biak, Pulau-	208	Ee	1.00S	136.00 E
Biała Piska	120	Sc	53.37N	22.04 E
Biała Podlaska	120	Td	52.02N	23.06 E
Biała Podlaska [2]	120	Td	52.00N	23.05 E
Białobrzegi	120	Qe	51.40N	20.57 E
Białogard	120	Lb	54.01N	16.00 E
Białostocka, Wysoczyzna-	120	Tc	53.23N	23.10 E
Białowieża	120	Td	52.41N	23.50 E
Białystok	112	Ie	53.09N	23.09 E
Białystok [2]	120	Tc	53.10N	23.10 E
Biancavilla	128	Im	37.38N	14.52 E
Bianco	128	Kl	38.05N	16.09 E
Bianco, Monte- / Blanc, Mont-	110	Gf	45.50N	6.52 E
Biankouma	166	Dd	7.44N	7.37W
Biankouma [3]	166	Dd	7.43N	7.40W
Bianzhuang → Cangshan	154	Eg	34.51N	118.03 E
Biaro, Pulau-	150	If	2.05N	125.20 E
Biarritz	122	Ek	43.29N	1.34W
Biasca	128	Cd	46.22N	8.57 E
Bibā	164	Fd	28.55N	30.59 E
Bibai	152	Pc	43.19N	141.52 E
Bibala	170	Be	14.50S	13.30 E
Biban, Chaine des-	126	Qh	36.12N	4.25 E
Bibbiena	128	Fg	43.42N	11.49 E
Biberach an der Riß	120	Fh	48.06N	9.48 E
Bibiani	166	Ed	6.28N	2.20W
Bic	184	Ma	48.22N	68.42W
Bicaj	130	Dh	41.59N	20.25 E
Bicas	204	Ke	21.43S	43.04W
Bicaz	130	Jc	46.55N	26.04 E
Bicaz, Pasul-	130	Ic	46.49N	25.52 E
Bičenekski, pereval-	132	Nj	39.33N	45.48 E
Bicester	118	Lj	51.54N	1.09W
Bichena	168	Fc	10.21N	38.14 E
Bickerton Island	212	Hb	13.45S	136.10 E
Bicske	120	Oi	47.29N	18.38 E
Bičura	138	Ff	50.36N	107.35 E
Bid	146	Qd	36.33N	57.35 E
Bida	160	Hh	9.05N	6.01 E
Bīdar	148	Fe	17.54N	77.33 E
Bidasoa	126	Ka	43.22N	1.47W
Biddeford	182	Mc	43.30N	70.26W
Bideford	118	Ij	51.01N	4.13W
Bideford Bay → Barnstaple	118	Ij	51.05N	4.20W
Bidon V/Poste Maurice Cortier	162	He	22.18N	1.05 E
Bié [3]	170	Ce	13.00S	17.30 E
Bié, Planalto do-	158	Ij	13.30S	17.02 E
Biebrza	120	Sc	53.13N	22.28 E
Biecz	120	Rg	49.44N	21.14 E
Biedenkopf	120	Ef	50.55N	8.32 E
Biei	156a	Cb	43.35N	142.28 E
Biel/Bienne	128	Bc	47.10N	7.15 E
Bielefeld	120	Ed	52.02N	8.32 E
Bielefeld-Brackwede	124	Kc	51.59N	8.31 E
Bielefeld-Sennestadt	124	Kc	51.57N	8.35 E
Biella	128	Ce	45.34N	8.03 E
Bielsk	120	Pd	52.40N	19.49 E
Bielska, Wysoczyzna-	120	Sd	52.35N	23.00 E
Bielsko [2]	120	Og	49.50N	19.00 E
Bielsko-Biała	120	Pg	49.49N	19.02 E
Bielsk Podlaski	120	Td	52.47N	23.12 E
Bien Dong = South China Sea (EN)	140	Ni	10.00N	113.00 E
Bien Hoa	148	Lf	10.57N	106.49 E
Bienne	122	Lh	46.20N	5.38 E
Bienne/Biel	128	Bc	47.10N	7.15 E
Bienvenida	126	Jd	40.30N	2.23W
Bienville, Lac-	180	Ke	55.20N	72.40W
Bierbeek	124	Gd	50.50N	4.46 E
Bieszczady	120	Sg	49.10N	22.35 E
Bièvre	124	Hc	49.56N	5.01 E
Biferno	128	Ji	41.59N	15.02 E
Bifoum	170	Bc	0.20S	10.23 E
Bifuka	154	Qb	44.29N	142.21 E
Biga	146	Bb	40.13N	27.14 E
Bigadiç	146	Cc	39.23N	28.08 E
Big Bald Mountain	184	Nb	47.37N	66.38W
Big Baldy Mountain	188	Jc	46.58N	110.37W
Big Bay [Mi.-U.S.]	184	Db	46.49N	87.44W
Big Bay [Van.]	219b	Cb	15.05S	166.54 E
Big Beaver House	180	If	52.58N	89.57W
Big Belt Mountains	188	Jc	46.40N	111.25W
Big Black River	186	Kj	32.00N	91.05W
Big Blue River	182	Hd	39.11N	96.32W
Big Creek Peak	188	Id	44.28N	113.32W
Big Dry Creek	188	Lc	47.30N	106.19W
Big Falls	186	Jb	48.11N	93.46W
Biggar	180	Gf	52.04N	108.00W
Biggenden	212	Ke	25.30S	152.00 E
Biggleswade	118	Mi	52.05N	0.17W
Big Hatchet Peak	186	Bk	31.37N	108.20W
Big Hole River	188	Id	45.34N	112.20W
Bighorn Basin	182	Fc	44.15N	108.10W
Bighorn Lake	188	Kd	45.08N	108.10W
Bighorn Mountains	174	Ie	44.00N	107.30W
Bighorn River	182	Fb	46.09N	107.28W
Bight, Head of-	212	Gf	31.30S	131.10 E
Big Island	180	Kd	62.43N	70.40W
Big Lake	186	Fk	31.12N	101.28W
Big Lake	184	Nc	45.10N	67.40W
Big Lost River	188	Ie	43.50N	112.44W
Big Muddy Creek	188	Mb	48.08N	104.36W
Big Muddy Lake	188	Mb	49.08N	104.54W
Bignona	166	Bc	12.49N	16.14W
Bigorre	122	Gk	43.06N	0.05 E
Big Porcupine Creek	188	Lc	46.17N	106.47W
Big Quill Lake	180	Hf	51.51N	104.18W
Big Rapids	184	Ed	43.42N	85.29W
Big River	180	Gf	53.50N	107.01W
Big River	180	Fb	72.50N	125.00W
Big Sand Lake	180	He	57.45N	99.45W
Big Sandy	188	Jb	48.11N	110.07W
Big Sandy Creek	186	Eg	38.06N	102.29W
Big Sandy River [Az.-U.S.]	188	Ii	34.19N	113.31W
Big Sandy River [Wy.-U.S.]	188	Kf	41.50N	109.48W
Big Sheep Mountains	188	Mc	47.03N	105.43W
Big Sioux River	182	Hc	42.30N	96.25W
Big Smoky Valley	182	Dd	38.30N	117.15W
Big Snowy Mountains	188	Kc	46.50N	109.30W
Big Spring	176	If	32.15N	101.28W
Big Spruce Knob	184	Gf	38.16N	80.12W
Big Stone Lake	186	Hd	45.25N	96.40W
Big Timber	188	Kd	45.50N	109.57W
Big Trout Lake	180	If	53.45N	90.00W
Biguglia, Étang de-	122a	Ba	42.36N	9.29 E
Big Wood Cay	194	Ia	24.21N	77.44W
Big Wood River	188	He	42.52N	114.55W
Bihać	128	Jf	44.49N	15.52 E
Bihār	148	Hc	25.11N	85.31 E
Bihār [3]	148	Hd	25.00N	86.00 E
Biharamulo	170	Fc	2.38S	31.20 E
Bihor [2]	130	Fc	47.00N	22.00 E
Bihoro	152	Pc	43.49N	144.07 E
Bihorului, Munții-	130	Fc	46.40N	22.45 E
Bija	140	Kd	52.25N	85.05 E
Bijagós, Arquipélago dos- = Bijagos Islands (EN)	158	Fg	11.15N	16.05W
Bijagós Islands (EN) = Bijagós, Arquipélago dos-	158	Fg	11.15N	16.05W
Bijapur	148	Fe	16.50N	75.42 E
Bijār	144	Gb	35.52N	47.36 E
Bijeljina	128	Nf	44.45N	19.13 E
Bijelo Polje	130	Cf	43.02N	19.45 E
Bijiang (Zhiziluo)	152	Gf	26.39N	99.00 E
Bijie	152	If	27.15N	105.16 E
Bijlikol, ozero-	135	Hc	43.05N	70.40 E
Bijou Creek	186	Ef	40.17N	103.52W
Bijoutier Island	172b	Bb	7.04S	52.45 E
Bijsk	142	Kd	52.34N	85.15 E
Bikāner	142	Jg	28.01N	73.18 E
Bikar Atoll	208	Ic	12.15N	170.06 E
Bikeqi	154	Ad	40.45N	111.17 E
Bikin	138	Ig	46.51N	134.02 E
Bikin	138	Ig	46.43N	134.02 E
Bikini Atoll	208	Hc	11.35N	165.23 E
Bikoro	160	Ii	0.45S	18.07 E
Bilād Ghāmid	164	Hf	19.58N	41.38 E
Bilād Zahrān	164	He	20.15N	41.15 E
Bilāspur	142	Kg	22.03N	82.10 E
Bilate	168	Fd	6.34N	38.01 E
Bilauktaung Range	140	Lh	13.00N	99.00 E
Bilbao	112	Fg	43.15N	2.58W
Bilbays	164	Fc	30.25N	31.34 E
Bileća	128	Mh	42.53N	18.26 E
Bilecik	144	Ca	40.09N	29.59 E
Bilehsavār	146	Mc	39.28N	48.20 E
Bílé Karpaty = White Carpathians (EN)	120	Nh	48.55N	17.50 E
Bilesha Plain	170	Hb	0.35N	40.45 E
Biłgoraj	120	Sf	50.34N	22.43 E
Bili	170	Eb	4.09N	25.10 E
Bili	170	Db	4.50N	22.29 E
Bilibino	142	Sc	68.03N	166.20 E
Biliran	150	Hd	11.35N	124.28 E
Bilishti	130	Di	40.37N	20.59 E
Biliu He	154	Ge	39.30N	122.36 E
Bill Baileys Bank (EN)	118	Ca	60.40N	10.20W
Billerbeck	124	Jc	51.58N	7.18 E
Billericay	124	Cc	51.37N	0.35 E
Billingen	116	Ef	58.24N	13.45 E
Billings	176	Ie	45.47N	108.27W
Billings, Represa-	204	If	23.45S	46.40W
Billingshurst	124	Bc	51.01N	0.27W
Bill Williams River	188	Hi	34.17N	114.03W
Billy Chinook, Lake-	188	Ed	44.33N	121.20W
Bilma	160	Ig	18.41N	12.56 E

Index Symbols

[1] Independent Nation; [2] State, Region; [3] District, County; [4] Municipality; [5] Colony, Dependency; Continent; Physical Region; Historical or Cultural Region; Mount, Mountain; Volcano; Hill; Mountains, Mountain Range; Hills, Escarpment; Plateau, Upland; Pass, Gap; Plain, Lowland; Delta; Salt Flat; Valley, Canyon; Crater, Cave; Karst Features; Depression; Polder; Desert, Dunes; Forest, Woods; Heath, Steppe; Oasis; Cape, Point; Coast, Beach; Cliff; Peninsula; Isthmus; Sandbank; Island; Atoll; Rock, Reef; Islands, Archipelago; Rocks, Reefs; Coral Reef; Well, Spring; Geyser; River, Stream; Waterfall, Rapids; River Mouth, Estuary; Lake; Salt Lake; Intermittent Lake; Reservoir; Swamp, Pond; Canal; Glacier; Ice Shelf, Pack Ice; Ocean; Sea; Gulf, Bay; Strait, Fjord; Lagoon; Bank; Seamount; Tablemount; Ridge; Shelf; Basin; Escarpment, Sea Scarp; Fracture; Trench, Abyss; National Park, Reserve; Point of Interest; Recreation Site; Cave, Cavern; Historic Site; Ruins; Wall, Walls; Church, Abbey; Temple; Scientific Station; Railway station; Airport; Port; Military installation; Lighthouse; Mine; Tunnel; Dam, Bridge

Bil-Bod

Biloela 212 Kd 24.24S 150.30 E
Bilo Gora 128 Le 45.50N 17.10 E
Biloku 202 Gc 1.46N 58.33W
Biloxi 182 Je 30.24N 88.53W
Bilqās Qism Awwal 146 Dg 31.13N 31.21 E
Bilteni 130 Ge 44.52N 23.17 E
Biltine 168 Cc 14.32N 20.55 E
Biltine [3] 168 Cc 15.00N 21.00 E
Bilzen 124 Hd 50.51N 5.31 E
Bima 170 Eb 3.23N 25.09 E
Bimbān 146 Ej 24.26N 32.53 E
Bimberi Peak 212 Jg 35.40S 148.47 E
Bimbila 166 Fd 8.51N 0.04 E
Bimbo 168 Be 4.18N 18.33 E
Bimini Islands 190 Ic 25.44N 79.15W
Bināb 146 Md 36.35N 48.41 E
Binačka Morava 130 Eg 42.27N 21.47 E
Binaiya, Gunung- 150 Ig 3.11S 129.26 E
Binatang 150 Ff 2.10N 111.38 E
Binboga Daği 146 Gc 38.21N 36.32 E
Binche 124 Gd 50.24N 4.10 E
Binder 152 Jb 48.35N 110.36 E
Bindura 160 Kj 17.17S 31.20 E
Bine el Ouidane 162 Fc 32.08N 6.28W
Binéfar 126 Mc 41.51N 0.18 E
Binem 168 Bb 18.43N 19.40 E
Binga [Zaire] 170 Db 2.23N 20.30 E
Binga [Zimb.] 172 Dc 17.37S 27.20 E
Bingen 120 Dg 49.58N 7.54 E
Bingham [Me.-U.S.] 184 Mc 45.03N 69.53W
Bingham [N.M.-U.S.] 186 Cj 33.56N 106.17W
Binghamton 182 Lc 42.06N 75.55W
Bin Ghunaymah, Jabal- 158 If 25.00N 15.30 E
Bing Inlet 184 Gc 45.13N 80.30W
Bingöl 144 Fb 38.53N 40.29 E
Bingöl Dağları 146 Ic 39.20N 41.20 E
Binhai (Dongkan) 152 Ke 34.00N 119.52 E
Binjai 150 Cf 3.36N 98.30 E
Binkiliç 130 Lh 41.25N 28.11 E
Binongko, Pulau- 150 Hh 5.57S 124.02 E
Bin Qirdān 162 Jc 33.08N 11.13 E
Bintan, Pulau- 150 Df 1.05N 104.30 E
Bintuhan 150 Dg 4.48S 103.22 E
Bintulu 150 Ff 3.10N 113.02 E
Bin Walīd, Jabal- 128 En 36.52N 10.47 E
Binxian 154 Df 37.22N 117.57 E
Binxian (Binzhou) [China] 152 Mb 45.45N 127.27 E
Binxian (Binzhou) [China] 152 Id 35.02N 108.06 E
Binzhou → Binxian [China] 152 Id 35.02N 108.06 E
Binzhou → Binxian [China] 152 Mb 45.45N 127.27 E
Bioara 148 Fd 23.58N 76.55 E
Biobío [2] 206 Fe 37.45S 72.00W
Biobío 206 Fe 36.49S 73.10W
Biograd na Moru 128 Jg 43.57N 15.27 E
Bioko [3] 166 Ge 3.00N 8.40 E
Bioko 158 Hh 4.30N 9.30 E
Biokovo 128 Lg 43.18N 17.02 E
Biorra/Birr 118 Fh 53.05N 7.54W
Bippen 124 Jb 52.35N 7.44 E
Bir 148 Fe 18.59N 75.46 E
Bira 138 Ig 49.03N 132.27 E
Bi'r Abraq 164 Fe 23.35N 34.48 E
Bi'r Abū al Ḥuṣayn 164 Ee 22.53N 29.55 E
Bi'r Abū Gharādiq 146 Cg 30.06N 28.06 E
Bi'r Abū Hashim 164 Fe 23.42N 34.08 E
Bi'r Abū Minqat 164 Ed 26.30N 27.35 E
Birah Kaprah 164 Kd 36.52N 44.01 E
Birāk 164 Bd 27.39N 14.17 E
Birakan 138 Ig 49.02N 131.40 E
Bi'r al 'Abd 146 Eg 31.22N 32.58 E
Bi'r al Ghuzaylah 164 Bd 28.50N 10.45 E
Bi'r al Ḥakīm 164 Dc 31.36N 23.29 E
Bi'r al Hasa 168 Fa 22.58N 35.40 E
Bi'r al Khamsah 164 Ec 30.57N 25.46 E
Bi'r 'Allāq 164 Bc 31.10N 11.55 E
Bi'r al Mushayqīq 162 Jc 30.53N 10.18 E
Bi'r al Qurayyah 146 Ei 26.22N 33.01 E
Bi'r al Uzam 164 Dc 31.46N 23.59 E
Bi'r al Wa'r 160 If 22.39N 14.10 E
Bi'r al Washkah 164 Cd 28.52N 15.35 E
Birao 160 Jg 10.17N 22.47 E
Bi'r 'Arjā' 146 Ij 25.17N 40.58 E
Bi'r ar Rāh 146 If 33.27N 40.25 E
Bi'r ar Rūmān 162 Ic 32.31N 8.21 E
Birātnagar 148 Hc 26.29N 87.17 E
Biratori 154 Qc 42.35N 142.12 E
Bi'r Baylī 164 Ec 30.32N 25.08 E
Bi'r Bayzaḥ 146 Fj 25.10N 34.05 E
Bi'r Bū Ḥawsh 164 Dd 24.34N 22.07 E
Bi'r Bū Zurayyq 164 Dd 24.32N 22.38 E
Birca 130 Gf 43.58N 23.37 E
Birch 180 Ge 58.28N 112.17W
Birch Mountains 180 Ge 57.20N 112.55W
Bird 180 Ie 56.30N 94.14W
Bi'r Dibs 164 Ee 22.12N 29.32 E
Bird Island [Gren.] 197p Bb 12.12N 61.33W
Bird Island [Sey.] 172b Ca 3.43S 55.12 E
Birdsville 212 He 25.54S 139.22 E
Birdum 212 Gc 15.39S 133.13 E
Birecik 146 Gd 37.02N 37.58 E
Bir El Ater 162 Ic 34.44N 8.03 E
Bir el Mrabba'ab 146 He 34.30N 39.07 E
Bir Enzarān 162 Ee 23.53N 14.32W
Bireuen 150 Ce 5.12N 96.41 E
Bi'r Fajr 146 Gh 28.54N 37.54 E
Bi'r Fu'ād 164 Ec 30.27N 26.27 E
Bir Gandūs 162 De 21.36N 16.30W
Birganj 148 Gc 27.00N 84.52 E
Bir Gara 168 Bc 13.11N 15.58 E
Bir-Ghbalou 126 Ph 36.16N 3.35 E
Birgi 130 Lk 38.15N 28.05 E
Bi'r Ḥasanah 146 Eg 30.28N 33.47 E
Bi'r Ḥaymir 146 Hj 24.41N 38.04 E
Bi'r Ḥulayyī 146 Fj 24.06N 34.32 E
Birigui 204 Ge 21.18S 50.19W
Biriliussy 138 Ee 57.07N 90.42 E
Birīn 146 Ge 35.01N 36.40 E
Birine 126 Pi 35.37N 3.13 E
Birjand 142 Hf 32.53N 59.13 E
Birjusa 140 Ld 57.43N 95.24 E
Birjusinsk 138 Ee 55.55N 97.55 E
Bi'r Karawayn 146 Ci 27.06N 28.32 E
Birkeland 114 Bg 58.20N 8.14 E
Birkenfeld 120 Dg 49.39N 7.11 E
Birkenhead 118 Jh 53.24N 3.02W
Birkerød 116 Ei 55.50N 12.26 E
Bi'r Khālidah 146 Bg 30.50N 27.15 E
Birksgate Range 212 Fe 27.10S 129.45 E
Bîrlad 130 Kc 46.14N 27.40 E
Bîrlad 130 Kc 45.36N 27.31 E
Bir Lehlú 162 Fd 26.21N 9.34W
Bi'r Ma'sūr 146 Fj 24.31N 34.12 E
Birmingham [Al.-U.S.] 176 Kf 33.31N 86.49W
Birmingham [Eng.-U.K.] 112 Fe 52.30N 1.50W
Bi'r Misāḥah 164 Ee 22.12N 27.57 E
Bi'r Murr 164 Fe 23.21N 30.05 E
Bi'r Murrah 164 Fe 22.32N 33.54 E
Bi'r Nāhid 164 Ec 30.13N 28.52 E
Bi'r Naṣīf 144 Ee 24.51N 39.11 E
Birnie Atoll 208 Je 3.35S 171.31W
Birnin Gaouré 166 Fc 13.05N 2.54 E
Birnin Gwari 166 Gc 11.02N 6.47 E
Birnin Kebbi 166 Fc 12.28N 4.12 E
Birni Nkonni 160 Hg 13.48N 5.15 E
Birnin Kudu 166 Gc 11.27N 9.30 E
Birni Yauri 166 Fc 10.47N 4.49 E
Bi'r Nukhaylah 146 Dj 24.01N 30.52 E
Birobidžan 142 Pe 48.48N 132.57 E
Birr/Biorra 118 Fh 53.05N 7.54W
Birs 128 Bc 47.26N 7.33 E
Bi'r Safājah 164 Fd 26.50N 34.54 E
Bi'r Sayyālah 146 Ei 26.07N 33.56 E
Bi'r Shalatayn 164 Ge 23.08N 35.36 E
Birsk 136 Fd 55.25N 55.32 E
Birštonas 116 Kj 54.33N 24.07 E
Bi'r Ṭarfāwī 164 Ee 22.55N 28.53 E
Biru 152 Fe 31.30N 93.50 E
Bi'r Umm al 'Abbās 146 Ei 26.57N 32.34 E
Bi'r Umm Fawākhīr 146 Ei 26.01N 33.38 E
Bi'r Umm Sa'īd 146 Eh 29.40N 33.34 E
Bi'r Umm Ṭunayḍibah 146 Ej 25.16N 33.06 E
Biruni 136 Gg 41.42N 60.45 E
Biržai/Biržaj 136 Cd 56.12N 24.48 E
Biržaj/Biržai 136 Cd 56.12N 24.48 E
Bîrzava 130 Ec 46.07N 21.59 E
Bîrzava 130 Dd 45.16N 20.49 E
Birzebbuga 128 Io 35.49N 14.32 E
Bisa, Pulau- 150 Ig 1.15S 127.28 E
Bisaccia 128 Ji 41.01N 15.22 E
Bisacquino 128 Hm 37.42N 13.15 E
Bisan Shotō 156 Cd 34.24N 134.00 E
Bisbee 182 Fe 31.27N 109.55W
Biscarrosse et de Parentis, Étang de- 122 Ej 44.21N 1.10W
Biscay, Bay of- (EN) = Gascogne, Golfe de- 110 Fg 44.00N 4.00W
Biscay, Bay of- (EN) = Gascogne, Golfe de- 110 Fg 43.50N 2.30W
Biscay, Bay of- (EN) = Vizcaya, Golfo de- 110 Fg 43.50N 2.30W
Bisceglie 128 Ki 41.14N 16.30 E
Bischofshofen 128 Hc 47.25N 13.13 E
Bischofswerda/Biskopicy 120 Ke 51.07N 14.11 E
Biscoe Islands 222 Qe 66.00S 66.30W
Biscotasi Lake 184 Fb 47.20N 82.05W
Biscucuy 196 Bh 9.22N 69.59W
Bisert 136 Fd 56.52N 59.03 E
Bisert 134 Hh 56.39N 57.59 E
Biševo 128 Kh 42.59N 16.01 E
Biševski kanal 128 Kg 43.00N 16.03 E
Bisha 168 Fb 15.28N 37.33 E
Bishārah 164 De 22.58N 22.39 E
Bishārīyīn, Barq al- 168 Eb 19.26N 32.22 E
Bishnupur 148 Hd 23.05N 87.19 E
Bishop 182 Dd 37.22N 118.24W
Bishop Auckland 118 Lg 54.40N 1.40W
Bishop Rock 118 Gl 49.53N 6.25W
Bishop's Falls 180 Lg 49.01N 55.30W
Bishop's Stortford 118 Nj 51.53N 0.09 E
Bishop's Waltham 124 Ad 50.57N 1.13W
Bishri, Jabal- 146 He 35.20N 39.20 E
Bishui 152 La 52.07N 123.43 E
Biskopicy/Bischofswerda 120 Ke 51.07N 14.11 E
Biskra 160 He 34.51N 5.44 E
Biskra [3] 162 Ic 34.40N 6.00 E
Biskupiec 120 Qc 53.52N 20.27 E
Bislig 150 Ie 8.13N 126.19 E
Bismarck 176 Ie 46.48N 100.47W
Bismarck, Kap- 179 Kc 76.40N 18.40W
Bismarck Archipelago 208 Fe 5.00S 150.00 E
Bismarck Sea 214 Dh 4.00S 147.30 E
Bismarck Range 214 Ci 5.30S 144.45 E
Bismil 146 Id 37.51N 40.40 E
Bison 186 Fd 45.31N 102.28W
Bisotūn 146 Le 34.23N 47.26 E
Bispfors 116 Ga 63.02N 16.37 E
Bissau 160 Fg 11.51N 15.35W
Bissaula 166 Hd 7.01N 10.27 E
Bisseca, Lach- 168 Ge 0.45N 41.33 E
Bissett 184 Hb 46.13N 78.02W
Bisson, Banc du- 172 Hb 12.00S 46.25 E
Bistcho Lake 180 Fe 59.45N 118.50W
Bistineau, Lake- 186 Jj 32.25N 93.22W
Bistra 130 Dh 41.37N 20.44 E
Bistra 130 Fd 45.29N 22.11 E
Bistreţ 130 Gf 43.54N 23.30 E
Bistrica 130 Cf 43.28N 19.42 E
Bistrica 130 Dg 42.09N 20.59 E
Bistriţa 130 Hb 47.08N 24.29 E
Bistriţa [Rom.] 130 Hb 47.04N 24.25 E
Bistriţa [Rom.] 130 Jc 46.30N 26.57 E
Bistriţa-Năsăud [2] 130 Hb 47.05N 24.35 E
Bitam 170 Bb 2.05N 11.29 E
Bitam 126 Ri 35.15N 5.11 E
Bitburg 120 Cg 49.58N 6.32 E
Bitche 122 Ne 49.03N 7.26 E
Bitéa 168 Cc 13.11N 20.10 E
Bithia 128 Cl 38.55N 8.52 E
Bithynia 130 Mi 40.20N 29.30 E
Bitjug 132 Kd 50.37N 39.55 E
Bitkine 168 Bc 11.59N 18.13 E
Bitlis 144 Fb 38.22N 42.06 E
Bitola 112 Ig 41.02N 21.20 E
Bitonto 128 Ki 41.06N 16.41 E
Bitterfeld 120 Ie 51.37N 12.19 E
Bitterfontein 160 Il 31.00S 18.32 E
Bitterroot Range 174 He 47.06N 115.10W
Bitterroot River 188 Hc 46.52N 114.06W
Bitti 128 Dj 40.29N 9.23 E
Bitung 150 If 1.27N 125.11 E
Biu 160 Ig 10.37N 12.12 E
Bivolari 130 Kb 47.32N 27.26 E
Bivolu, Vîrful- 130 Ib 47.15N 25.56 E
Bivona 128 Hm 37.37N 13.26 E
Biwa-Ko 154 Ng 35.13N 136.05 E
Bixad [Rom.] 130 Ic 46.06N 25.52 E
Bixad [Rom.] 130 Gb 47.56N 23.24 E
Bixby 186 Ii 35.57N 95.53W
Biyalā 146 Dg 31.10N 31.13 E
Biyang 152 Je 32.40N 113.21 E
Biyārjomand 146 Pd 36.06N 55.53 E
Bizbuljak 134 Gj 53.43N 54.16 E
Biže 135 Kb 45.10N 77.58 E
Bizen 154 Mg 34.44N 134.09 E
Bizerte 160 He 37.17N 9.52 E
Bizerte [3] 162 Ib 37.00N 9.30 E
Bizkaia / Vizcaya [3] 126 Ja 43.15N 2.55W
Bjala 130 If 43.27N 25.44 E
Bjala Slatina 130 Gf 43.28N 23.56 E
Bjargtangar 110 Db 65.30N 24.32W
Bjärnå/Perniö 114 Ff 60.12N 23.08 E
Bjärnum 116 Eh 56.17N 13.42 E
Bjästa 116 Ha 63.12N 18.30 E
Bjelašnica [Yugo.] 128 Mh 42.51N 18.09 E
Bjelašnica [Yugo.] 128 Mg 43.09N 18.23 E
Bjelašnica [Yugo.] 128 Mg 43.43N 18.09 E
Bjelolasica 128 Ie 45.16N 14.58 E
Bjelovar 128 Ke 45.54N 16.51 E
Bjerkvik 114 Db 68.33N 17.34 E
Bjerringbro 116 Ch 56.23N 9.40 E
Bjervamoen 116 Ce 59.25N 9.04 E
Bjeshkët e Nemuna 130 Cg 42.30N 19.50 E
Björbo 116 Fd 60.28N 14.42 E
Bjørkelangen 116 De 59.53N 11.34 E
Björkfors 116 Ff 58.01N 15.54 E
Björklinge 116 Gd 60.02N 17.33 E
Björkö 114 Eg 59.55N 19.00 E
Björna 114 Ee 63.34N 18.33 E
Bjørnafjorden 116 Ad 60.05N 5.20 E
Björneborg 116 Fe 59.15N 14.15 E
Björneborg/Pori 112 Ic 61.29N 21.47 E
Bjorne Peninsula 180 Ia 77.30N 87.00W
Bjørnesfjorden 116 Bd 60.10N 7.40 E
Bjørnevatn 114 Gb 69.40N 30.00 E
Bjørnøya = Bear Island (EN) 110 Ha 74.30N 19.00 E
Bjurholm 114 Ee 63.56N 19.13 E
Bjuröklubb 114 Ed 64.28N 21.35 E
Bjuv 116 Eh 56.05N 12.54 E
Bla 166 Dc 12.56N 5.45W
Blace 130 Ef 43.18N 21.18 E
Blackall 210 Fg 24.25S 145.28 E
Black Bank (EN) = Zwarte Bank 124 Fa 53.15N 3.55 E
Black Bay 186 Lb 48.40N 88.30W
Blackburn 118 Kh 53.45N 2.29W
Blackburn, Mount- 174 Ec 61.44N 143.26W
Black Butte Lake 188 Dg 39.45N 122.20W
Black Coast 222 Qf 71.45S 62.00W
Black Down Hills 118 Jk 50.57N 3.09W
Blackduck 186 Ic 47.44N 94.33W
Blackfoot 182 Ec 43.11N 112.20W
Blackfoot Reservoir 188 Je 42.55N 111.35W
Black Forest (EN) = Schwarzwald 110 Gf 48.05N 8.15 E
Black Head 118 Hk 50.01N 5.03W
Black Hills 174 Ie 44.00N 104.00W
Black Isle 118 Id 57.35N 4.20W
Black Lake 180 Ge 59.11N 105.20W
Blackman's 197q Ab 13.11N 59.32W
Black Mesa 188 Jh 36.35N 110.20W
Blackmoor 118 Ik 50.23N 4.50W
Black Mountain 182 Kd 36.54N 82.54W
Black Mountains [U.S.] 188 Hi 35.30N 114.30W
Black Mountains [Wales-U.K.] 118 Jj 51.57N 3.08W
Blackpool 118 Jh 53.50N 3.03W
Black Range 182 Fe 33.20N 107.50W
Black River 192 Id 18.01N 77.51W
Black River [Az.-U.S.] 188 Jj 33.44N 110.13W
Black River [Mi.-U.S.] 184 Fd 43.00N 82.25W
Black River [N.Y.-U.S.] 184 Id 43.59N 76.04W
Black River [U.S.] 186 Ki 35.38N 91.19W
Black River [Wi.-U.S.] 186 Ke 43.57N 91.22W
Black River (EN) = Babian Jiang [Asia] 140 Mg 20.17N 106.34 E
Black River (EN) = Đà, Sông- [Asia] 140 Mg 20.17N 106.34 E
Black River Falls 186 Kd 44.16N 90.52W
Black Rock 206 Lh 53.39S 41.48W
Black Rock [Ire.] 118 Cg 54.05N 10.20W
Black Rock [Phil.] 150 Ge 8.48N 119.50 E
Black Rock Desert 182 Dc 41.10N 119.00W
Blacksburg 184 Gg 37.15N 80.25W
Black Sea (EN) = Černoje more 110 Jg 43.00N 35.00 E
Black Sea (EN) = Černo More 110 Jg 43.00N 35.00 E
Black Sea (EN) = Karadeniz 110 Jg 43.00N 35.00 E
Black Sea (EN) = Neagră, Marea- 110 Jg 43.00N 35.00 E
Blacksod Bay 118 Dg 54.08N 10.00W
Blacksod Bay/Cuan an Fhóid Duibh 118 Dg 54.08N 10.00W
Blackstairs Mountains/Na Staighri Dubha 118 Ki 52.33N 6.49W
Blackstone 184 Hg 37.04N 78.01W
Blackville 184 Ob 46.47N 65.54W
Black Volta 158 Gh 8.38N 1.30W
Black Volta (EN) = Volta Noire [3] 166 Ec 12.30N 4.00W
Black Volta (EN) = Volta Noire 158 Gh 8.38N 1.30W
Blackwater 124 Cc 51.43N 0.28 E
Blackwater/An Abhainn Dubh 118 Gh 53.39N 6.43W
Blackwater/An Abhainn Mhór [Ire.] 118 Fj 51.51N 7.50W
Blackwater/An Abhainn Mhór [N.Ire.-U.K.] 118 Gg 54.30N 6.35W
Blackwell 186 Hh 36.48N 97.17W
Blackwood River 212 Df 34.35S 115.02 E
Blagnac 122 Hk 43.38N 1.24 E
Blagodarny 132 Mg 45.04N 43.24 E
Blagoevgrad 130 Gg 42.01N 23.06 E
Blagoevgrad [2] 130 Gh 41.45N 23.25 E
Blagoveščenka 138 Cf 52.50N 79.55 E
Blagoveščensk [R.S.F.S.R.] 136 Fd 55.01N 55.59 E
Blagoveščensk [R.S.F.S.R.] 142 Od 50.17N 127.32 E
Blåhø 116 Cb 62.45N 9.19 E
Blain 122 Eg 47.29N 1.45W
Blaine [Mn.-U.S.] 186 Jd 45.11N 93.14W
Blaine [Wa.-U.S.] 188 Db 48.59N 122.44W
Blair 186 Hf 41.33N 96.08W
Blair Athol 212 Jd 22.42S 147.33 E
Blairgowrie 118 Je 56.36N 3.21W
Blairmore 188 Hb 49.36N 114.26W
Blaise 122 Kf 48.38N 4.43 E
Blaj 130 Gc 46.11N 23.55 E
Blake Basin (EN) 182 Mf 29.00N 76.00W
Blakely 184 Ej 31.23N 84.56W
Blakeney Point 118 Ni 52.59N 1.00 E
Blake Plateau (EN) 174 Lf 31.00N 79.00W
Blakstad 114 Bg 58.30N 8.39 E
Blanc, Cap- / Blanco, Cabo- 126 Oe 39.22N 2.46 E
Blanc, Cape- (EN) = Abyaḍ, Ra's al- 158 He 37.20N 9.50 E
Blanc, Cape- (EN) = Nouâdhibou, Râs- 158 Ff 20.46N 17.03W
Blanc, Lac- 184 Kb 47.45N 73.12W
Blanc, Le- 122 Hh 46.38N 1.04 E
Blanc, Mont- / Bianco, Monte- 110 Gf 45.50N 6.52 E
Blanca, Bahía- 198 Ji 38.55S 62.10W
Blanca, Cerro- 194 Gi 8.40N 80.35W
Blanca, Cordillera- 202 Ce 9.10S 77.35W
Blanca, Costa- 126 Lg 37.38N 0.40W
Blanca, Isla- 192 Pj 21.24N 86.50W
Blanca, Punta- 192 Bc 29.05N 114.45W
Blancagrande 204 Bm 36.32S 60.53W
Blanca Peak 174 If 37.35N 105.29W
Blanche, Lake- [Austl.] 212 Ed 22.25S 123.15 E
Blanche, Lake- [Austl.] 212 He 29.15S 139.40 E
Blanche, Point- 197b Ac 18.00N 63.03W
Blanche Channel 219a Cc 8.30S 157.30 E
Blanc-Nez, Cap- 124 Dd 50.56N 1.42 E
Blanco, Cabo- 190 Gh 9.33N 85.06W
Blanco, Cabo- / Blanc, Cap- 126 Oe 39.22N 2.46 E
Blanco, Cape- 182 Cc 42.50N 124.34W
Blanco, Cerro- 192 Fe 25.43N 107.39W
Blanco, Río- 202 Ff 12.30S 64.18W
Blanco del Sur, Cayo- 194 Gb 22.02N 81.24W
Blanda 114a Bb 65.39N 20.18W
Blanding 188 Kh 37.37N 109.29W
Blanes 126 Oc 41.41N 2.48 E
Blangy-le-Château 124 Ce 49.14N 0.17 E
Blangy-sur-Bresle 122 He 49.56N 1.38 E
Blanice [Czech.] 120 Kg 49.48N 14.58 E
Blanice [Czech.] 120 Kg 49.17N 14.09 E
Blankaholm 116 Gg 57.35N 16.31 E
Blankenberge 122 Jc 51.19N 3.08 E
Blankenheim 124 Id 50.26N 6.39 E
Blanquilla, Isla- 202 Fa 11.51N 64.37W
Blanquillo 204 Ek 32.55S 55.40W
Blansko 120 Mg 49.22N 16.39 E
Blantyre 160 Ki 15.47S 35.00 E
Blantyre-Limbe 170 Gf 15.49S 35.03 E
Blåskavlen 116 Bd 60.58N 7.18 E
Błaszki 120 Oe 51.39N 18.27 E
Blatná 120 Jg 49.26N 13.53 E
Blato 128 Kh 42.56N 16.48 E
Blåvands Huk 110 Gd 55.33N 8.05 E
Blavet 122 Cg 47.46N 3.18W
Blaye 122 Fi 45.08N 0.40W
Blaye-les-Mines 122 Ij 44.01N 2.08 E
Bled 128 Id 46.22N 14.08 E
Blefjell 116 Ce 59.48N 9.10 E
Bleialf 124 Id 50.14N 6.17 E
Blekinge [2] 114 Dh 56.20N 15.20 E
Blekinge 116 Fh 56.20N 15.05 E
Blenheim 210 Ii 41.31S 173.57 E
Bletchley 118 Mj 52.00N 0.46W
Bleus, Monts- 170 Fb 1.30N 30.30 E
Blida 160 He 36.34N 2.55 E
Blida [3] 162 Hb 36.35N 2.30 E
Blidö 116 He 59.35N 18.55 E
Blidsberg 116 Eg 57.56N 13.29 E
Blies 124 Je 49.07N 7.04 E
Blieskastel 124 Je 49.14N 7.15 E
Bligh Water 219d Ab 17.00S 178.00 E
Blind River 180 Jg 46.10N 82.58W
Blitar 150 Fh 8.06S 112.09 E
Blitta 166 Fd 8.19N 0.59 E
Block Island 184 Le 41.11N 71.35W
Bloemfontein 160 Jk 29.12S 26.07 E
Bloemhof 172 De 27.38S 25.32 E
Blois 122 Hg 47.35N 1.20 E
Blokhus 116 Cg 57.15N 9.35 E
Blomberg 124 Lc 51.56N 9.05 E
Blönduós 114a Bb 65.40N 20.18W
Bloody Foreland/Cnoc Fola 118 Ef 55.09N 8.17W
Bloomfield [Ia.-U.S.] 186 Jf 40.45N 92.25W
Bloomfield [In.-U.S.] 184 Df 39.01N 86.56W
Bloomington [Il.-U.S.] 182 Jc 40.29N 88.59W
Bloomington [In.-U.S.] 182 Jd 39.10N 86.32W
Bloomington [Mn.-U.S.] 186 Jd 44.50N 93.17W
Bloomsburg 184 Ie 41.01N 76.27W
Blosseville Kyst 179 Je 68.45N 27.25W
Blötberget 116 Fd 60.07N 15.04 E
Blountstown 184 Ej 30.29N 85.03W
Bludenz 128 Dc 47.09N 9.49 E
Blue Earth 186 Ie 43.38N 94.06W
Bluefield 182 Kd 37.14N 81.17W
Bluefields 176 Kh 12.00N 83.45W
Bluefields, Bahía de- 194 Fg 12.02N 83.44W
Blue Mesa Reservoir 186 Cg 38.28N 107.15W
Blue Mountain 184 Ie 40.15N 77.30W
Blue Mountain [Or.-U.S.] 188 Ge 42.25N 117.50W
Blue Mountain [U.S.] 186 Ii 34.41N 94.03W
Blue Mountain Lake 184 Jd 43.53N 74.26W
Blue Mountain Pass 188 Ge 42.18N 117.45W
Blue Mountain Peak 190 Ie 18.03N 76.35W
Blue Mountains [Austl.] 212 Kf 33.35S 150.15 E
Blue Mountains [U.S.] 182 Ec 44.35N 118.25W
Blue Mud Bay 212 Hb 13.25S 135.55 E
Blue Nile (EN) = Abay 158 Kg 15.38N 32.31 E
Blue Nile (EN) = Azraq, Baḥr al- 158 Kg 15.38N 32.31 E
Bluenose Lake 180 Fc 68.00N 121.00W
Blue Ridge 184 Eh 34.52N 84.20W
Blue Ridge 174 Kf 37.00N 82.00W
Blue Stack/Na Cruacha 118 Eg 54.45N 8.06W
Bluestone Lake 184 Gg 37.30N 80.50W
Bluff [N.Z.] 216 Ci 46.36S 168.21 E
Bluff [Ut.-U.S.] 188 Kh 37.17N 109.33W
Bluff Point 212 Ce 27.50S 114.05 E
Bluffton 184 Ee 40.44N 85.11W
Blumberg 120 Ei 47.50N 8.32 E
Blumenau 206 Kc 26.56S 49.03W
Blyth 118 Lf 55.07N 1.30W
Blyth 124 Db 52.19N 1.41 E
Blythe 182 Ee 33.37N 114.36W
Blytheville 182 Jd 35.56N 89.55W
Bø [Nor.] 114 Bg 59.25N 9.04 E
Bo [S.L.] 160 Fh 7.58N 11.45W
Boa 166 Dd 8.26N 7.10W
Boac 150 Hd 12.28N 122.28 E
Boaco 194 Eg 12.28N 85.40W
Boaco [3] 194 Eg 12.35N 85.25W
Boa Esperança 204 Je 21.05S 45.34W
Boa Esperança, Represâ- 202 Je 6.50S 44.00W
Boa Esperançao, Serra da- 204 Je 20.57S 45.40W
Bo'ai 154 Bg 35.10N 113.03 E
Boal 126 Fa 43.26N 6.49W
Boali 168 Be 4.48N 18.07 E
Boano, Pulau- 150 Ig 2.56S 127.56 E
Boardman 188 Fd 45.51N 119.43W
Boa Sentença, Serra da- 204 Ed 19.13S 57.33W
Boa Vista 158 Eg 16.05N 22.50W
Boa Vista [Braz.] 204 Ec 17.51S 54.13W
Boa Vista [Braz.] 200 Je 2.49N 60.40W
Boa Vista [Braz.] 204 Ia 12.40S 46.51W
Bobai 152 Ig 22.15N 109.58 E
Bobalí, Cerros de- 194 Ki 8.53N 73.28W
Bobbio 128 Df 44.46N 9.23 E
Bobigny 122 If 48.54N 2.27 E
Böblingen 120 Fh 48.41N 9.01 E
Bobo Dioulasso 160 Gg 11.12N 4.18W
Bobojod, gora- 135 Hd 40.50N 70.20 E
Bobolice 120 Mc 53.57N 16.36 E
Bobonong 172 Dd 21.58S 28.25 E
Bobovdol 130 Gg 42.22N 23.00 E
Bóbr 120 Ld 52.04N 15.04 E
Bobrik 132 Ec 52.08N 26.48 E
Bobrinec 132 He 48.04N 32.09 E
Bobrka 120 Ug 49.34N 24.20 E
Bobrov 136 Ee 51.06N 40.01 E
Bobrovica 132 Gd 50.43N 31.28 E
Bobrowniki 120 Tc 53.08N 23.50 E
Bobrujsk 112 Ie 53.09N 29.15 E
Bobures 202 Db 9.15N 71.11W
Boby, Pic- 172 Hd 22.12S 46.55 E
Boca del Río 192 Ee 25.20N 108.25W
Boca de Pozo 196 Dg 11.00N 64.23W
Boca do Acre 200 Jf 8.45S 67.23W
Bocage, Cap- 219b Be 21.12S 165.37 E
Bocâina 204 Db 15.16S 56.45W
Bocaiúva 204 Kc 17.07S 43.49W
Bocajá 204 Ef 22.45S 55.13W
Bocaranga 168 Bd 6.59N 15.39 E
Boca Raton 182 Kf 26.21N 80.05W
Bocas del Toro 190 Hg 9.20N 82.15W
Bocas del Toro [3] 194 Fi 8.50N 82.10W
Bocas del Toro, Archipiélago de- 194 Fi 9.20N 82.10W
Bocay 194 Ef 14.19N 85.10W
Bochaine 122 Lj 44.20N 5.50 E
Bochnia 120 Qg 49.58N 20.26 E
Bocholt [Bel.] 124 Hc 51.10N 5.35 E
Bocholt [F.R.G.] 120 Ce 51.50N 6.36 E
Bochum 120 De 51.29N 7.13 E
Bocognano 122a Ba 42.05N 9.04 E
Bocoio 170 Be 12.28S 14.08 E
Boconó 194 Li 9.15N 70.16W
Bocşa 130 Ed 45.23N 21.47 E
Boda 168 Be 4.19N 17.28 E
Boda 116 Fc 61.01N 15.13 E
Böda 116 Gg 57.15N 17.03 E
Bodafors 116 Fg 57.30N 14.42 E
Bodajbo 142 Nd 57.51N 114.10 E
Bodalangi 170 Db 3.14N 22.14 E
Bode 120 Hd 52.01N 11.12 E
Bödefeld-Freiheit, Schmallenberg- 124 Kc 51.15N 8.24 E

Index Symbols

- [1] Independent Nation
- [2] State, Region
- [3] District, County
- [4] Municipality
- [5] Colony, Dependency
- Continent
- Physical Region
- Historical or Cultural Region
- Mount, Mountain
- Volcano
- Hill
- Mountains, Mountain Range
- Hills, Escarpment
- Plateau, Upland
- Pass, Gap
- Plain, Lowland
- Delta
- Salt Flat
- Valley, Canyon
- Crater, Cave
- Karst Features
- Depression
- Polder
- Desert, Dunes
- Forest, Woods
- Heath, Steppe
- Oasis
- Cape, Point
- Coast, Beach
- Cliff
- Peninsula
- Isthmus
- Sandbank
- Island
- Atoll
- Rock, Reef
- Islands, Archipelago
- Rocks, Reefs
- Coral Reef
- Well, Spring
- Geyser
- River, Stream
- Waterfall, Rapids
- River Mouth, Estuary
- Lake
- Salt Lake
- Intermittent Lake
- Reservoir
- Swamp, Pond
- Canal
- Glacier
- Ice Shelf, Pack Ice
- Ocean
- Sea
- Gulf, Bay
- Strait, Fjord
- Lagoon
- Bank
- Seamount
- Tablemount
- Ridge
- Shelf
- Basin
- Escarpment, Sea Scarp
- Fracture
- Trench, Abyss
- National Park, Reserve
- Point of Interest
- Recreation Site
- Cave, Cavern
- Historic Site
- Ruins
- Wall, Walls
- Church, Abbey
- Temple
- Scientific Station
- Railway station
- Airport
- Port
- Military installation
- Lighthouse
- Mine
- Tunnel
- Dam, Bridge

Name	Page	Grid	Lat	Long
Bodegraven	124	Gb	52.06N	4.44 E
Bodélé ⊡	158	Ig	16.30N	17.30 E
Boden	112	Ib	65.50N	21.42 E
Bodenheim	124	Ke	49.56N	8.18 E
Bodensee = Constance, Lake- (EN) ☒	110	Gf	47.35N	9.25 E
Bodmin	118	Ik	50.29N	4.43W
Bodmin Moor ▲	118	Ik	50.35N	4.40W
Bodø	112	Hb	67.17N	14.23 E
Bodoquena	204	De	20.12S	56.48W
Bodoquena, Serra da- ▲	202	Gh	21.00S	56.50W
Bodrog ◣	120	Rh	48.07N	21.25 E
Bodrogköz ⊡	120	Rh	48.15N	21.45 E
Bodrum	144	Cb	37.02N	27.06 E
Bodrum Yarımadası ◪	130	Kl	37.05N	27.30 E
Bodva ◣	120	Qh	48.12N	20.47 E
Boën	122	Ji	45.44N	4.00 E
Boende	160	Ji	0.13S	20.52 E
Boeo, Capo- (Lilibeo, Capo-) ◪	128	Gm	37.34N	12.41 E
Boerne	186	Gl	29.47N	98.44W
Boesmanland = Bushmanland (EN) ⊡	172	Be	29.30S	19.00 E
Boffa	166	Cc	10.10N	14.02W
Boga	130	Cg	42.24N	19.38 E
Bogale	148	Je	16.17N	95.24 E
Bogalusa	186	Lk	30.47N	89.52W
Bogandé	166	Ec	12.59N	0.08W
Bogangolo	168	Bd	5.34N	18.15 E
Bogatić	130	Ce	44.51N	19.29 E
Bogatynia	120	Kf	50.55N	14.59 E
Boğazkale	146	Fc	40.01N	34.35 E
Boğazlıyan	146	Fc	39.12N	35.15 E
Bogbonga	170	Cb	1.35N	19.25 E
Bogcang Zangbo ◣	152	Ee	31.56N	87.24 E
Bogda Feng ▲	152	Ec	43.45N	88.32 E
Bogdan ◪	130	Hg	42.37N	24.28 E
Bogdanovka	132	Mi	41.15N	43.36 E
Bogda Shan ▲	140	Ke	43.35N	90.00 E
Bogen	114	Db	68.32N	17.00 E
Bogenfels	172	Be	27.23S	15.22 E
Bogense	116	Di	55.34N	10.06 E
Boggeragh Mountains/An Bhograch ▲	118	Ei	52.05N	9.00W
Boggy Peak ▲	197d	Bb	17.03N	61.51W
Boghar	126	Oi	35.55N	2.43 E
Boghni	126	Ph	36.32N	3.57 E
Bogia	214	Ch	4.16S	144.58 E
Bognor Regis	124	Bd	50.47N	0.39W
Bogny-sur-Meuse	122	Ge	49.54N	4.43 E
Bogoduhov	132	Id	50.12N	35.31 E
Bogomila	130	Eh	41.36N	21.28 E
Bogor	142	My	6.35S	106.47 E
Bogoridick	136	De	53.50N	38.08 E
Bogorodčany	120	Uh	48.45N	24.40 E
Bogorodsk	114	Kh	56.09N	43.32 E
Bogorodskoje [R.S.F.S.R.]	114	Mh	57.51N	50.48 E
Bogorodskoje [R.S.F.S.R.]	138	Jf	52.22N	140.30 E
Bogotá	200	Ie	4.36N	74.05W
Bogotá ③	202	Dc	4.20N	74.10W
Bogotol	138	De	56.17N	89.43 E
Bogey	114	Dc	67.54N	15.11 E
Bogra	148	Hd	24.51N	89.22 E
Boguçany	138	Ee	58.23N	97.39 E
Boguçar	132	Le	49.57N	40.33 E
Bogué	162	Ef	16.36N	14.15W
Boguševsk	114	Hi	54.50N	30.13 E
Boguslav	136	Df	49.33N	30.54 E
Bo Hai = Chihli, Gulf of- (EN) ☒	150	Nf	38.30N	120.00 E
Bohai Haixia ☒	152	Ld	38.00N	121.30 E
Bohain-en-Vermandois	124	Fe	49.59N	3.27 E
Bohemia (EN) = Čechy ⊡	110	Hf	50.00N	14.30 E
Bohemia (EN) = Čechy ⊡	120	Kf	50.00N	14.30 E
Bohemian Forest (EN) = Böhmerwald ▲	110	Hf	49.00N	13.30 E
Bohemian Forest (EN) = Šumava ▲	110	Hf	49.00N	13.30 E
Bohicon	166	Fd	7.12N	2.04 E
Böhmerwald = Bohemian Forest (EN) ▲	110	Hf	49.00N	13.30 E
Bohmte	124	Kb	52.22N	8.19 E
Bohodoyou	166	Dd	9.46N	9.04W
Bohol	140	Oi	9.50N	124.10 E
Böhönye	120	Nj	46.24N	17.24 E
Bohor ▲	128	Jd	46.04N	15.26 E
Bohu/Bagrax	152	Ec	41.58N	86.29 E
Bohus	116	Eg	57.51N	12.01 E
Bohuslän ⊡	116	Df	58.15N	11.50 E
Boiano	202	Ig	0.27S	61.46W
Boiano	128	Ii	41.29N	14.29 E
Boina ☒	158	Lj	16.00S	46.30 E
Bois, Lac des - ☒	180	Eg	66.50N	125.15W
Bois, Rio dos- [Braz.] ◣	204	Gd	18.35S	50.02W
Bois, Rio dos- [Braz.] ◣	204	Ha	13.55S	49.51W
Bois Blanc Island ◪	184	Gc	45.45N	84.28W
Boischaut ⊡	122	Hh	46.40N	1.45 E
Boise	176	Hd	43.37N	116.13W
Boise City	186	Eh	36.44N	102.31W
Boise River ◣	188	Gd	43.49N	117.01W
Boissay	124	De	49.31N	1.21 E
Boissevain	180	Mg	49.14N	100.03W
Boizenburg	120	Gc	53.23N	10.43 E
Bojador, Cabo-►	158	Ff	26.08N	14.30W
Bojana ◣	130	Dg	41.52N	19.22 E
Bojanowo	120	Me	51.42N	16.44 E
Bojarka	136	De	50.19N	30.18 E
Bojčinovci	130	Gf	43.28N	23.20 E
Bojnürd	144	Ib	37.28N	57.19 E
Bojonegoro	150	Fh	7.09S	111.52 E
Bojuru	204	Gj	31.38S	51.26W
Bokatola	170	Cc	0.38S	18.46 E
Boké	166	Cc	10.56N	14.18W
Bokhara River ◣	212	Ja	29.55S	146.42 E
Bokn ◪	116	Ae	59.15N	5.25 E
Boknafjorden ☒	110	Gb	59.10N	5.35 E
Boko	170	Bc	4.47S	14.38 E
Bokol Mayo	168	Ge	4.31N	41.32 E
Bokoro	168	Bc	12.23N	17.03 E
Bokote	170	Dc	0.05S	20.08 E
Bokpyin	148	Jf	11.16N	98.46 E
Boksitogorsk	136	Dd	59.29N	33.52 E
Bokungu	170	Dc	0.41S	22.19 E
Bol [Chad]	168	Ac	13.30N	14.41 E
Bol [Yugo.]	128	Kg	43.16N	16.40 E
Bola, Bahr- ◣	168	Bd	9.50N	18.59 E
Bolama	166	Bc	11.35N	15.28W
Bolands	197d	Bb	17.02N	61.53W
Bolaños, Rio- ◣	192	Gg	21.14N	104.08W
Bolaños de Calatrava	126	If	38.54N	3.40W
Bolattau, gora- ▲	135	Ha	46.44N	71.54 E
Bolayir	130	Ji	40.31N	26.45 E
Bolbec	122	Ge	49.34N	0.29 E
Bolda ◣	132	Pg	45.58N	48.35 E
Bole [Eth.]	168	Fd	6.37N	37.22 E
Bole [Ghana]	166	Ed	9.02N	2.29W
Bole/Bortala	152	Dc	44.59N	81.57 E
Bolehov	132	Ce	49.03N	23.50 E
Bolesławiec	120	Le	51.16N	15.34 E
Bolgatanga	160	Dg	10.47N	0.51W
Bolgrad	132	Fg	45.40N	28.38 E
Bolhov	136	De	53.30N	36.01 E
Boli	152	Nb	45.46N	130.31 E
Bolia	170	Cc	1.36S	18.23 E
Boliden	114	Ed	64.52N	20.23 E
Bolinao, Cape-►	150	Gc	16.22N	119.50 E
Bolintin Vale	130	Ie	44.27N	25.46 E
Bolívar ②	202	Fb	6.20N	63.30W
Bolívar ③	202	Db	9.00N	74.40W
Bolívar [Mo.-U.S.]	186	Jg	37.37N	93.25W
Bolívar [Tn.-U.S.]	184	Ch	35.15N	88.59W
Bolívar, Cerro- ▲	202	Fb	7.28N	63.25W
Bolívar, Pico- ▲	198	Ie	8.30N	71.02W
Bolivia ③	200	Jg	17.00S	65.00W
Bolivia, Altiplano de- ◪	198	Jg	18.00S	68.00W
Boljevac	130	Ef	43.50N	21.58 E
Bollendorf	124	Ie	49.51N	6.22 E
Bollène	122	Kj	44.17N	4.45 E
Bollnäs	114	Df	61.21N	16.25 E
Bollon	212	Je	28.02S	147.28 E
Bollstabruk	116	Ga	63.00N	17.41 E
Bollullos par del Condado	126	Fg	37.20N	6.32W
Bolmen ☒	114	Ch	56.55N	13.40 E
Bolnisi	132	Ni	41.28N	44.31 E
Bolobo	170	Cc	2.10S	16.14 E
Bolodek	138	Jf	53.43N	133.09 E
Bologna	112	Hg	44.29N	11.20 E
Bolognesi	202	Df	10.01S	74.05W
Bologoje	112	Jd	57.54N	34.02 E
Bolohovo	132	Jb	54.05N	37.52 E
Bolomba	170	Cb	0.29N	19.12 E
Bolon	170	Dc	3.59S	21.22 E
Bolotnoje	138	Ig	55.41N	84.33 E
Bolovens, Plateau des- ☒	148	Le	15.20N	106.20 E
Bolşaja Balahnja ◣	138	Fb	73.37N	107.05 E
Bolşaja Berestovica	120	Uc	53.09N	24.02 E
Bolşaja Černigovka	114	Mj	52.08N	50.48 E
Bolşaja Glušica	114	Mj	52.24N	50.29 E
Bolşaja Ižora	116	Me	59.55N	29.40 E
Bolşaja Kinel ◣	114	Mj	53.14N	50.30 E
Bolşaja Koksaga ◣	114	Lh	56.07N	47.48 E
Bolşaja Kuonamka ◣	138	Gb	70.50N	113.20 E
Bolşaja Oju ◣	134	Jb	69.42N	60.42 E
Bolşaja Rogovaja ◣	134	Jc	66.30N	60.40 E
Bolşaja Synja ◣	134	Id	65.58N	58.01 E
Bolşaja Tap ◣	134	Lg	59.55N	65.42 E
Bolşaja Ussurka ◣	138	Jg	46.09N	133.30 E
Bolşaja Vladimirovka	136	He	50.53N	79.30 E
Bolşakovo	116	Ij	54.50N	21.36 E
Bolsena	128	Fh	42.39N	11.59 E
Bolsena, Lago di- ☒	128	Fh	42.35N	11.55 E
Bolşereck	136	Kf	52.22N	156.24 E
Bolşeustikinskoje	134	Li	55.57N	58.20 E
Bolşevik	134	Jd	62.40N	147.30 E
Bolşevik, ostrov-	138	Mb	78.40N	102.30 E
Bolshevik Island (EN) ◪	140	Mb	78.40N	102.30 E
Bolşezemelskaja tundra ☒	134	Hc	67.30N	58.30 E
Bolshevik Island (EN) = Bolşevik, ostrov- ◪	140	Mb	78.40N	102.30 E
Bolşije Uki	136	Hd	56.57N	72.37 E
Bolşoj Anjuj ◣	138	Lc	68.30N	160.50 E
Bolşoj Begičev, ostrov- ◪	138	Gb	74.20N	112.30 E
Bolşoj Berezovy, ostrov- ◪	116	Md	60.15N	28.35 E
Bolşoj Boktybaj, gora- ▲	136	Ff	48.30N	58.20 E
Bolşoj Bolvanski Nos, mys-►	134	Ia	70.27N	59.05 E
Bolşoj Čeremšan ◣	114	Li	54.12N	49.40 E
Bolşoje Muraškino	114	Ki	55.47N	44.46 E
Bolşoje Vlasjevo	138	Jf	53.25N	140.55 E
Bolşoje Zagorje	116	Mg	57.47N	28.58 E
Bolşoj Gašun ◣	132	Mf	47.22N	42.42 E
Bolşoj Ik ◣	114	Hj	51.47N	56.20 E
Bolşoj Irgiz ◣	136	Ee	52.01N	47.24 E
Bolşoj Jenisej ◣	138	Ef	51.40N	94.26 E
Bolşoj Jugan ◣	136	Hc	60.55N	73.40 E
Bolşoj Kamen	138	Jh	43.08N	132.28 E
Bolşoj Klimecki, ostrov- ◪	116	Lc	62.00N	35.15 E
Bolşoj Kujalnik ◣	132	Gf	46.46N	30.38 E
Bolşoj Kumak ◣	132	Ud	51.22N	58.55 E
Bolşoj Ljahovski, ostrov- = Great Lyakhov (EN) ◪	138	Jb	73.35N	142.00 E
Bolşoj Murta	138	Ee	56.55N	93.10 E
Bolşoj Nimnyr	138	He	58.08N	125.45 E
Bolşoj Pit ◣	138	Ee	59.02N	91.40 E
Bolşoj Tjuters, ostrov- ◪	116	Le	59.50N	27.10 E
Bolşoj Uluj	136	Dd	56.45N	90.46 E
Bolşoj Uvat, ozero- ☒	136	Hd	58.20N	71.30 E
Bolşoj Uzen ◣	114	Kf	48.50N	49.40 E
Bolşón, Cerro del- ▲	198	Jh	27.13S	66.06W
Bolşovcy	120	Uh	49.08N	24.47 E
Bolsward	124	Ha	53.04N	5.30 E
Boltaña	126	Mb	42.27N	0.04 E
Bolton	118	Kh	53.35N	2.26W
Bolu	144	Da	40.44N	31.37 E
Bolu Dağları ▲	146	Eb	41.05N	32.05 E
Bolungarvik	114a	Aa	66.09N	23.15W
Boluntay	152	Fd	36.29N	92.18 E
Bolva ◣	132	Ic	53.17N	34.20 E
Bolvadin	146	Dc	38.42N	31.04 E
Bolzano/Bozen	112	Hf	46.31N	11.22 E
Bom, Rio- ◣	128	Gf	23.56S	51.44W
Boma	160	Ii	5.51S	13.03 E
Bomassa	170	Cb	2.12N	16.12 E
Bombala	212	Jg	36.54S	149.14 E
Bombarral	126	Ce	39.16N	9.09W
Bombay	142	Jh	18.58N	72.50 E
Bomberai, Jazirah- ◪	150	Jg	3.00S	133.00 E
Bombo	170	Fb	0.35N	32.32 E
Bomboma	170	Cb	2.26N	18.57 E
Bom Comércio	202	Ee	9.45S	65.54W
Bom Conselho	202	Ke	9.10S	36.41W
Bom Despacho	202	Ig	19.43S	45.15W
Bomdila	148	Ic	27.16N	92.23 E
Bomi/Bowo	152	Se	30.02N	95.39 E
Bomi Hills	160	Fd	6.52N	10.45W
Bomili	170	Eb	1.40N	27.01 E
Bom Jardim de Goiás	204	Fc	16.17S	52.07W
Bom Jardim de Minas	204	Je	21.57S	44.11W
Bom Jesus	204	Gi	28.42S	50.24W
Bom Jesus da Lapa	200	Lg	13.15S	43.25W
Bom Jesus de Goiás	204	Hd	18.12S	49.37W
Bømlafjorden ☒	116	Ae	59.40N	5.20 E
Bømlo ◪	114	Ag	59.45N	5.10 E
Bomokandi ◣	170	Eb	3.30N	26.08 E
Bomongo	170	Cb	1.22N	18.21 E
Bom Retiro	204	Hh	27.48S	49.31W
Bom Sucesso	204	Je	21.02S	44.46W
Bomu ◣	158	Jh	4.08N	22.26 E
Bomu (EN) = Mbomou ◣	168	Cd	5.30N	23.30 E
Bon, Cape- (EN) = Ṭib Ra's at-►	158	Ie	37.05N	11.03 E
Bona, Mount- ▲	178	Kd	61.20N	141.50W
Bonaire ◪	202	Ea	12.10N	68.15W
Bonaire Basin (EN) ☒	196	Cg	11.25N	67.30W
Bonampak ⚏	192	Ni	16.43N	91.05W
Bonanza	194	Ef	14.01N	84.35W
Bonanza Peak ▲	188	Eb	48.14N	120.52W
Bonao	194	Ld	18.56N	70.25W
Bonaparte, Mount- ▲	188	Fb	48.45N	119.08W
Bonaparte Archipelago ◪	208	Df	14.20S	125.20 E
Bonaparte Rocks ◪	188	Ea	51.16N	120.35W
Bonasse	197p	Cb	12.24N	61.30W
Bonavista	196	Fg	10.05N	61.52W
Bonavista Bay ☒	180	Mg	48.39N	53.07W
Bon-Cagan-Nur ☒	152	Gb	49.00N	103.20 E
Bonda	170	Bc	0.29N	19.12 E
Bondeno	128	Ff	44.53N	11.25 E
Bondo	166	Ed	8.02N	2.48W
Bondoukou	166	Ed	8.02N	2.48W
Bondoukou ③	166	Ed	8.20N	2.55W
Bone, Gulf of- (EN) = Bone, Teluk- ☒	140	Oj	4.00S	120.40 E
Bone, Teluk- = Bone, Gulf of- (EN) ☒	140	Oj	4.00S	120.40 E
Bone Bay	197a	Db	18.45N	64.22W
Bonelohe	150	Hh	5.48S	120.27 E
Bönen	124	Jc	51.36N	7.46 E
Bone Rate, Kepulauan- ◪	150	Hh	7.00S	121.00 E
Bone Rate, Pulau- ◪	150	Hh	7.22S	121.08 E
Bonete, Cerro- ▲	206	Gc	27.51S	68.47W
Bong	152	Ce	6.49N	10.19W
Bong ③	166	Dd	7.00N	9.40W
Bonga	168	Fd	7.16N	36.14 E
Bongabong	150	Hd	12.45N	121.29 E
Bongandanga	170	Db	1.30N	21.03 E
Bongo, Massif des- ▲	158	Jh	8.40N	22.25 E
Bongolava ▲	158	Lk	18.35S	45.20 E
Bongor	160	Ig	10.17N	15.22 E
Bongouanou	166	Ed	6.39N	4.12W
Bongouanou ③	166	Ed	6.43N	4.12W
Bong Son	148	Lf	14.26N	109.01 E
Bonham	186	Hj	33.35N	96.11W
Bonheiden	124	Gc	51.02N	4.32 E
Bonhomme, Pic- ▲	194	Kd	19.05N	72.15W
Bonifacio	122a	Bb	41.23N	9.09 E
Bonifacio, Bocche di- = Bonifacio, Strait of- (EN) ☒	110	Gg	41.18N	9.15 E
Bonifacio, Bouches de- = Bonifacio, Strait of- (EN) ☒	110	Gg	41.18N	9.15 E
Bonifacio, Strait of- (EN) = Bonifacio, Bocche di- ☒	110	Gg	41.18N	9.15 E
Bonifacio, Bouches de- ☒	110	Gg	41.18N	9.15 E
Bonifati, Capo-►	128	Jk	39.33N	15.52 E
Bonin Basin (EN) ☒	214	Bb	29.00N	137.00 E
Bonin Islands (EN) = Ogasawara-Shotō ☒	140	Qg	27.00N	142.10 E
Bonin Trench (EN) ☒	106	If	30.00N	145.00 E
Bonita Springs	186	Ce	26.21N	81.47W
Bonito [Braz.]	204	De	21.08S	56.28W
Bonito [Braz.]	204	Jb	15.20S	44.58W
Bonito, Pico- ▲	190	Ge	15.38N	86.55W
Bonito, Rio- [Braz.] ◣	204	Ga	13.38S	50.17W
Bonito, Rio- [Braz.] ◣	204	Jb	16.31S	51.23W
Bonn	112	Gf	50.44N	7.06 E
Bonn-Bad Godesberg	120	Df	50.41N	7.09 E
Bonnebosq	124	Ce	49.12N	0.05 E
Bonnechère River ◣	184	Ic	45.31N	76.33W
Bonners Ferry	188	Ga	48.41N	116.18W
Bonnet, Lac du- ☒	186	Ga	50.20N	95.55W
Bonnétable	122	Gf	48.11N	0.26 E
Bonnet Plume ◣	180	Dd	65.53N	134.58W
Bonneval	122	Hf	48.11N	1.24 E
Bonneville	122	Mh	46.05N	6.25 E
Bonneville Salt Flats ☒	188	If	40.45N	113.50W
Bonnières-sur-Seine	124	De	49.02N	1.35 E
Bonningues-lès-Ardres	124	Ed	50.47N	2.01 E
Bonny	166	Ge	4.25N	7.10 E
Bonny	128	Dj	40.25N	9.02 E
Bō-no-Misaki ►	154	Bf	31.15N	130.13 E
Bonorva	128	Cj	40.25N	8.46 E
Bonthain	150	Gh	5.32S	119.56 E
Bonthe	166	Cf	7.32N	12.30W
Bontoc	150	Hc	17.05N	120.58 E
Bonyhád	120	Oj	46.18N	18.32 E
Boo, Kepulauan- ◪	150	Ig	1.12S	129.24 E
Boola	166	Dd	8.22N	8.43W
Booligal	212	If	33.52S	144.53 E
Boone [Ia.-U.S.]	186	Je	42.04N	93.53W
Boone [N.C.-U.S.]	184	Db	36.13N	81.41W
Booneville [Ar.-U.S.]	186	Ji	35.08N	93.55W
Booneville [Ms.-U.S.]	186	Li	34.39N	88.34W
Boon Point►	197d	Bb	17.10N	61.50W
Boonville [In.-U.S.]	184	Df	38.03N	87.16W
Boonville [Mo.-U.S.]	186	Jg	38.58N	92.44W
Boos	124	De	49.23N	1.12 E
Boothia, Gulf of- ☒	174	Jb	71.00N	91.00W
Boothia Peninsula ◪	174	Jb	70.30N	95.00W
Boot Reefs ◪	214	Cj	10.00S	144.35 E
Booué	160	Ii	0.06S	11.56 E
Bophuthatswana ⊡	158	Jk	26.00S	25.30 E
Bopolu	166	Cd	7.04N	10.29W
Boppard	124	Jd	50.14N	7.36 E
Boquerón	116	Ae	59.40N	5.20 E
Boquerón ③	114	Ag	59.45N	5.10 E
Boquilla, Presa de la- ☒	192	Gd	27.30N	105.30W
Boquillas del Carmen	192	Hc	29.17N	102.53W
Bor [Czech.]	120	Ig	49.43N	12.47 E
Bor [R.S.F.S.R.]	136	Kd	56.23N	44.07 E
Bor [Sud.]	160	Kh	6.12N	31.33 E
Bor [Swe.]	116	Fg	57.07N	14.10 E
Bor [Tur.]	130	Fe	37.54N	34.34 E
Bor [Yugo.]	130	Fe	44.06N	22.06 E
Bora-Bora, Ile- ◪	208	Lf	16.30S	151.45W
Boraha, Nosy- ◪	158	Lj	16.50S	49.55 E
Borah Peak ▲	174	He	44.08N	113.14W
Boraldaj ◣	135	Gc	42.30N	69.05 E
Böramo	168	Gd	9.58N	43.07 E
Borås	114	Ch	57.43N	12.55 E
Borazjān	144	Nh	29.16N	51.12 E
Borba [Braz.]	202	Ad	4.24S	59.35W
Borba [Port.]	126	Ef	38.48N	7.27W
Borborema, Planalto da- ☒	198	Mf	7.00S	37.30W
Borca	130	Ke	44.20N	27.45 E
Borcea, Braţul- ◣	130	Ke	44.40N	27.53 E
Borchgrevink Coast ☒	222	Kf	73.00S	171.00 E
Borça	146	Ji	41.22N	41.40 E
Borculo	124	Ib	52.07N	6.31 E
Borda da Mata, Serra- ▲	204	Je	21.18S	47.06W
Bordeaux	112	Gg	44.50N	0.34W
Borden ◪	180	Ga	78.30N	110.30W
Borden Peninsula ◪	174	Kb	73.00N	83.00W
Borders ③	118	Kf	55.35N	3.00W
Bordertown	210	Fh	36.19S	140.47 E
Bordighera	128	Bg	43.46N	7.39 E
Bordj Bou Arreridj	162	Hb	36.04N	4.46 E
Bordj el Emir Abdelkader	126	Oi	35.52N	2.16 E
Bordj Fly Sainte Marie	162	Ph	36.44N	3.43 E
Bordj Menaiel	126	Ph	36.44N	3.43 E
Bordj Messouda	162	Jc	30.12N	9.25 E
Bordj Moktar	160	Hf	21.20N	0.56 E
Bordj Omar Driss	158	Hf	28.09N	6.49 E
Bord Khûn-e Now	146	Nh	28.03N	51.28 E
Bordon Camp	124	Bc	51.07N	0.51W
Boreal, Chaco- ⊡	198	Jh	20.30S	60.00W
Boren ☒	116	Ff	58.35N	15.10 E
Borensberg	116	Ff	58.34N	15.17 E
Borgå/Porvoo	114	Ff	60.24N	25.40 E
Borgarnes	114a	Bb	64.32N	21.55W
Borgefjell ▲	114a	Cd	65.23N	13.50 E
Borgentreich	124	Kc	51.34N	9.15 E
Borger [Neth.]	124	Ib	52.55N	6.48 E
Borger [Tx.-U.S.]	182	Gd	35.39N	101.24W
Borgholm	114	Di	56.53N	16.39 E
Borghorst, Steinfurt-	124	Jb	52.08N	7.22 E
Borgia	128	Kl	38.49N	16.30 E
Borgloon	124	Hd	50.48N	5.20 E
Borgomanero	128	Ce	45.42N	8.28 E
Borgorose	128	Hh	42.11N	13.15 E
Borgo San Dalmazzo	128	Bf	44.20N	7.30 E
Borgo San Lorenzo	128	Fg	43.57N	11.23 E
Borgosesia	128	Ce	45.43N	8.16 E
Borgo Val di Taro	128	Df	44.29N	9.46 E
Borgo Valsugana	128	Fd	46.03N	11.27 E
Borgu ⊡	158	Ig	11.30N	3.40 E
Borgworm/Waremme	122	Kc	50.42N	5.15 E
Bori	166	Ge	4.42N	7.21 E
Borinquen, Punta-►	197a	Ab	18.30N	67.10W
Borislav	132	Ce	49.18N	23.27 E
Borisoglebsk	112	Kd	51.23N	42.06 E
Borisov	136	Cd	54.15N	28.30 E
Borisovka	132	Id	50.36N	36.00 E
Borispol	136	Df	50.20N	30.59 E
Bo River ◣	168	Cd	6.48N	27.55 E
Borja [Peru]	202	Ce	4.28S	77.33W
Borja [Sp.]	126	Kc	41.50N	1.32W
Borjas Blancas / les Borges Blanques	126	Mc	41.31N	0.52 E
Borken	124	Ic	51.51N	6.52 E
Borkou ⊡	158	Jf	18.15N	18.50 E
Borkou-Ennedi-Tibesti ③	160	Jf	18.00N	19.00 E
Borkovići	130	Cf	43.04N	18.34 E
Borkum	120	Cc	53.35N	6.41 E
Borlänge	114	Df	60.29N	15.25 E
Borlu	130	Lk	38.44N	28.27 E
Bormida ◣	128	Cf	44.17N	8.44 E
Bormio	128	Ed	46.28N	10.22 E
Born ☒	124	Ke	49.58N	8.19 E
Born ⊡	122	Ej	44.05N	1.15W
Borna	120	If	51.07N	12.30 E
Borndiep ☒	124	Ha	53.25N	5.35 E
Borne	124	Ib	52.18N	6.45 E
Borneo/Kalimantan ◪	140	Ni	1.00N	114.00 E
Bornheim	124	Id	50.46N	7.00 E
Bornholm ②	116	Fi	55.10N	15.00 E
Bornholm ◪	110	Hd	55.10N	15.00 E
Bornos	126	Gh	36.48N	5.44W
Bornova, İzmir-	146	Bc	38.27N	27.14 E
Bornu ②	166	Hc	12.30N	12.40 E
Bornu ⊡	158	Ig	12.30N	13.00 E
Boro ◣	158	Jh	8.52N	26.11 E
Borodino [R.S.F.S.R.]	114	Ii	55.32N	35.49 E
Borodino [R.S.F.S.R.]	138	Ee	55.57N	95.03 E
Borodinskoje	116	Md	61.00N	29.29 E
Borogoncy	138	Id	62.39N	131.08 E
Borohoro Shan ▲	140	Ke	42.00N	85.00 E
Boromo	166	Ec	11.45N	2.56W
Borongan	150	Id	11.37N	125.26 E
Borotou	166	Dd	8.44N	7.30W
Borovan	130	Gf	43.26N	23.45 E
Borovec	130	Gg	42.16S	23.53 E
Boroviči	130	Dd	58.24N	33.56 E
Borovici	116	Mg	57.58N	29.47 E
Borovljanka	138	Df	52.38N	84.35 E
Borovo	128	Me	45.24N	18.59 E
Borovski	136	Gd	57.03N	65.44 E
Borovskoj	135	Ga	53.48N	64.17 E
Borrachas, Islas- ◪	196	Dg	10.18N	64.44W
Borrān	168	Hc	10.11N	48.53 E
Borrby	116	Fi	55.27N	14.10 E
Borriana / Burriana	126	Le	39.53N	0.05W
Borroloola	210	Ef	16.04S	136.17 E
Borş	130	Eb	47.07N	21.49 E
Borşa	130	Hb	47.39N	24.40 E
Borščovočny hrebet = Borshchovochny Range (EN) ▲	138	Gf	52.00N	118.30 E
Borsec	130	Ic	46.57N	25.34 E
Borshchovochny Range (EN) = Borščovočny hrebet ▲	138	Gf	52.00N	118.30 E
Borsod-Abaúj-Zemplén ②	120	Qh	48.15N	21.00 E
Bortala He ◣	152	Dc	44.53N	82.45 E
Bort-les-Orgues	122	Ii	45.24N	2.30 E
Borüjen	146	Ng	31.59N	51.18 E
Borüjerd	144	Nf	33.54N	48.46 E
Borzia	142	Nd	50.24N	116.31 E
Borzna	132	Hd	51.15N	32.29 E
Boržomi	132	Mi	41.50N	43.25 E
Borzsöny ▲	120	Oi	47.55N	19.00 E
Bosa	128	Cj	40.18N	8.30 E
Bosanska Dubica	128	Ke	45.11N	16.48 E
Bosanska Gradiška	128	Le	45.09N	17.15 E
Bosanska Krupa	128	Kf	44.53N	16.10 E
Bosanski Brod	128	Me	45.08N	18.01 E
Bosanski Novi	128	Ke	45.03N	16.22 E
Bosanski Petrovac	128	Kf	44.34N	16.21 E
Bosanski Šamac	128	Me	45.04N	18.28 E
Bosansko Grahovo	128	Kf	44.11N	16.22 E
Bösaso	160	Lg	11.13N	49.08 E
Bosavi, Mount- ▲	212	Ia	6.35S	142.50 E
Bosbeek ◣	124	Hc	51.06N	5.48 E
Bose	142	Mg	24.01N	106.32 E
Boshan	152	Kd	36.30N	117.50 E
Boshrüyeh	146	Qf	33.53N	57.26 E
Bosilegrad	130	Fg	42.30N	22.28 E
Bosingfeld, Extertal-	124	Lb	52.04N	9.07 E
Bosna ◣	128	Me	45.04N	18.28 E
Bosna = Bosnia (EN) ⊡	110	Hg	44.00N	18.00 E
Bosnia = Bosnia (EN) ⊡	128	Lf	44.00N	18.00 E
Bosnia-Hercegovina (EN) ②	128	Lf	44.15N	17.50 E
Bosnia (EN) = Bosna ⊡	128	Lf	44.00N	18.00 E
Bosnia = Bosna ⊡	110	Hg	44.00N	18.00 E
Bosnia i Hercegovina ②	128	Lf	44.15N	17.50 E
Bosnik	150	Kg	1.10S	136.14 E
Bošnjakovo	138	Jf	49.41N	142.10 E
Bosobolo	170	Cb	4.11N	19.54 E
Böso-Hantö ◪	154	Pg	35.20N	140.10 E
Bosporus (EN) = İstanbul Boğazı ☒	110	Ig	41.00N	29.00 E
Bosque Bonito	192	Gb	30.42N	105.06W
Bossangoa	160	Ih	6.29N	17.27 E
Bosse Bangou	166	Fc	13.21N	1.18 E
Bossembélé	168	Bd	5.16N	17.39 E
Bossembélé II	168	Bd	5.41N	16.38 E
Bossier City	182	Ie	32.31N	93.43W
Bosso	160	Hg	13.42N	13.19 E
Bossut, Cape-►	212	Ec	18.43S	121.38 E
Bostān	148	Db	30.26N	67.02 E
Bostānābād	146	Me	37.50N	46.50 E
Bosten/Bagrax Hu ☒	140	Ke	42.00N	87.00 E
Boston [Eng.-U.K.]	118	Mi	52.59N	0.01W
Boston [Ma.-U.S.]	176	Lc	42.21N	71.04W
Boston Bar	188	Fa	49.52N	121.26W
Boston Mountains ▲	182	Id	35.50N	93.20W
Botan ◣	146	Jd	37.44N	41.48 E
Botas, Ribeirão das- ◣	204	Fe	20.26S	53.43W
Botesdale	204	Db	12.10S	47.30W
Botev ▲	110	Ja	42.43N	24.55 E
Botevgrad	130	Gg	42.54N	23.47 E
Bothnia, Gulf of- (EN) = Pohjanlahti ☒	110	Hc	63.00N	20.00 E
Bothnia, Gulf of- (EN) = Bottniska viken ☒	110	Hc	63.00N	20.00 E
Boticas	126	Ec	41.41N	7.40W
Botletle ◣	172	Cd	21.07S	24.42 E
Botlih	132	Oh	42.40N	46.13 E
Botna ◣	130	Mc	46.50N	29.30 E
Botoşani	120	Jb	47.40N	26.40 E
Botoşani ②	130	Jb	47.45N	26.43 E
Botrange ▲	122	Md	50.30N	6.08 E
Botswana ①	160	Jk	22.00S	24.00 E

Index Symbols

	① Independent Nation; ② State, Region; ③ District, County; ④ Municipality; ⑤ Colony, Dependency; ■ Continent; ■ Physical Region
	▪ Historical or Cultural Region; ▲ Mount, Mountain; ▲ Volcano; ▲ Hill; ▲ Mountains, Mountain Range; ▲ Hills, Escarpment; ▲ Plateau, Upland
	)(Pass, Gap; ☒ Plain, Lowland; ▼ Delta; ☒ Salt Flat; ☒ Valley, Canyon; ☒ Crater, Cave; ☒ Karst Features
	☒ Depression; ▼ Polder; ☒ Desert, Dunes; ☒ Forest, Woods; ☒ Heath, Steppe; ☒ Oasis; ► Cape, Point
	☒ Coast, Beach; ☒ Cliff; ☒ Peninsula; ☒ Isthmus; ☒ Sandbank; ◪ Island; ◉ Atoll
	☒ Rock, Reef; ☒ Islands, Archipelago; ☒ Rocks, Reefs; ☒ Coral Reef; ☒ Well, Spring; ☒ Geyser; ◣ River, Stream
	☒ Waterfall, Rapids; ☒ River Mouth, Estuary; ☒ Lake; ☒ Salt Lake; ☒ Intermittent Lake; ☒ Reservoir; ☒ Swamp, Pond
	☒ Canal; ☒ Glacier; ☒ Ice Shelf, Pack Ice; ☒ Ocean; ☒ Sea; ☒ Shelf; ☒ Gulf, Bay; ☒ Strait, Fjord; ☒ Basin
	☒ Lagoon; ☒ Bank; ☒ Fracture; ☒ Seamount; ☒ Tablemount; ☒ Trench, Abyss; ☒ Ridge; ☒ Point of Interest; ☒ Cave, Cavern
	☒ Escarpment, Sea Scarp; ☒ Ruins; ☒ Wall, Walls; ☒ Church, Abbey; ☒ Temple; ☒ Recreation Site; ☒ Scientific Station; ☒ Railway station
	☒ Historic Site; ☒ Airport; ☒ Port; ☒ Military installation; ☒ Lighthouse; ☒ Mine; ☒ Tunnel; ☒ Dam, Bridge

Botte Donato 128 Kk 39.17N 16.27 E
Bottineau 182 Gb 48.50N 100.27W
Bottniska viken=Bothnia, Gulf of- (EN) 110 Hc 63.00N 20.00 E
Bottrop 120 Ce 51.31N 6.55 E
Botucatu 206 Kb 22.52S 48.26W
Botucatu, Serra de- 204 Hf 23.00S 48.20W
Botwood 180 Lg 49.08N 55.21W
Bouaflé 166 Dd 6.59N 5.45W
Bouaflé [3] 166 Dd 7.03N 5.48W
Bouaké 160 Gh 7.41N 5.02W
Bouaké [3] 166 Dd 7.45N 5.02W
Bou Anane 162 Gc 32.02N 3.03W
Bouar 160 Ih 5.57N 15.36 E
Bou Arfa 162 Gc 32.32N 1.57W
Boubin 120 Jh 48.58N 13.50 E
Bouca 160 Ih 6.30N 18.17 E
Bouchain 124 Fd 50.17N 3.19 E
Bouchegouf 128 Bn 36.28N 7.44 E
Bouche Island 197k Bb 13.57N 60.53W
Bouches-du-Rhône [3] 122 Kk 43.30N 5.00 E
Boudenib 162 Gc 31.57N 3.36W
Boudeuse Cay 172b Bb 6.05S 52.51 E
Boû Djébéha 166 Eb 18.33N 2.45W
Bouenza [3] 170 Bc 3.00S 13.00 E
Boufarik 126 Oh 36.36N 2.54 E
Bougaa 126 Rh 36.20N 5.05 E
Bougainville Island 208 Ge 6.00S 155.00 E
Bougainville Reef 212 Jc 15.30S 147.05 E
Bougainville Strait [Ocn.] 219a Cb 6.40S 156.10 E
Bougainville Strait [Van.] 219b Cb 15.50S 167.10 E
Bougouni 160 Gg 11.25N 7.28W
Bougtob 162 Hc 34.02N 0.05 E
Bouguenais 122 Eg 47.11N 1.37W
Bouguirat 126 Mi 35.45N 0.15 E
Bougzoul 126 Oi 35.42N 2.51 E
Bou Hadjar 128 Cn 36.30N 8.06 E
Bouhalla, Jbel- 126 Gi 35.06N 5.07W
Bou Hamed 126 Hi 35.19N 4.58W
Bouillante 197e Ab 16.08N 61.46W
Bouillon 122 Le 49.48N 5.04 E
Bouira 162 Hb 36.23N 3.54 E
Bouira [3] 162 Hb 36.15N 4.10 E
Bou Ismaïl 126 Oh 36.38N 2.41 E
Bou Izakarn 162 Fd 29.10N 9.44W
Bou Kadir 126 Nh 36.04N 1.07 E
Boukombé 166 Fc 10.11N 1.06 E
Boû Lanouâr 162 De 21.16N 16.30W
Boulay-Moselle 124 Ie 49.11N 6.30 E
Boulder [Co.-U.S.] 176 Ie 40.01N 105.17W
Boulder [Mt.-U.S.] 188 Ic 46.14N 112.07W
Boulder City 188 Hi 35.59N 114.50W
Boulemane 162 Gc 33.22N 4.45W
Boulemane [3] 162 Gc 33.02N 4.04W
Boulevard Atlántico 204 Dn 38.19S 57.59W
Boulia 212 Hd 22.54S 139.54 E
Bouligny 122 Le 49.17N 5.45 E
Boulogne 122 Eg 47.05N 1.40W
Boulogne-Billancourt 122 If 48.50N 2.15 E
Boulogne-sur-Mer 122 Hd 50.43N 1.37 E
Boulonnais 122 Hd 50.42N 1.40 E
Boulou, Le- 122 Il 42.31N 2.50 E
Bouloupari 219b Ce 21.52S 166.03 E
Boulsa 166 Ec 12.39N 0.34W
Boultoum 166 Hc 14.40N 10.18 E
Bou Maad, Djebel- 126 Oh 36.26N 2.08 E
Boumba 166 Ie 2.02N 15.12 E
Boumdeid 162 Ef 17.26N 11.21W
Boum Kabir 166 Bc 10.11N 19.24 E
Boumort 126 Nb 42.14N 1.08 E
Bouna 160 Gh 9.16N 3.00W
Bouna [3] 166 Ed 9.15N 3.20W
Boû Nâga 162 Ef 19.00N 13.13W
Bou Nasser, Adrar- 162 Gc 33.35N 3.53W
Boundary Peak 188 Fh 37.51N 118.21W
Boundiali 166 Dd 9.31N 6.29W
Boundiali [3] 166 Dd 9.23N 6.32W
Boundji 170 Cc 1.03S 15.22 E
Boungou 168 Cd 6.45N 22.06 E
Bountiful 182 Ec 40.53N 111.53W
Bounty Bay 220q Ab 25.03S 130.05W
Bounty Islands 208 Ii 47.45S 179.05 E
Bounty Trough (EN) 106 Jn 46.00S 178.00 E
Bourail 216 Cd 21.34S 165.30 E
Bourbon-Lancy 122 Jh 46.37N 3.47 E
Bourbonnais 122 Ih 46.30N 3.00 E
Bourbonne-les-Bains 122 Lg 47.57N 5.45 E
Bourbourg 124 Ed 50.57N 2.12 E
Bourbre 122 Li 45.47N 5.11 E
Bourem 166 Eb 16.58N 0.21W
Bouressa 166 Fa 20.01N 2.18 E
Bourg-Achard 124 Ce 49.21N 0.49 E
Bourganeuf 122 Hi 45.57N 1.45 E
Bourgar'oûn, Cap- 162 Ib 37.06N 6.28 E
Bourg-de-Péage 122 Li 45.02N 5.03 E
Bourg-en-Bresse 122 Lh 46.12N 5.13 E
Bourges 112 Gf 47.05N 2.24 E
Bourget, Lac du- 122 Li 45.44N 5.52 E
Bourgneuf, Baie de- 122 Dg 47.05N 2.13W
Bourgogne 124 Ge 49.21N 4.04 E
Bourgogne=Burgundy (EN) 110 Gf 47.00N 4.30 E
Bourgogne=Burgundy (EN) 122 Kg 47.00N 4.30 E
Bourgogne, Canal de- 122 Jg 47.58N 3.30 E
Bourgogne, Porte de- 122 Mg 47.38N 6.52 E
Bourgoin-Jallieu 122 Li 45.35N 5.17 E
Bourgtheroulde-Infreville 124 Ce 49.18N 0.53 E
Bourguébus 124 Be 49.07N 0.18W
Boû Rjeimat 162 Df 19.04N 15.08W
Bourke 210 Fh 30.05S 145.56 E
Bourne 124 Bb 52.46N 0.23W
Bournemouth 118 Lk 50.43N 1.54W
Bourtanger Moor 124 Jb 52.50N 7.06 E
Bourth 124 Cf 48.46N 0.49 E
Bou Saâda 162 Hb 35.12N 4.11 E
Bou Sellam 126 Qh 36.26N 4.34 E
Boussac 122 Ih 46.21N 2.13 E
Boussé 166 Ec 12.39N 1.53W
Boussens 122 Gk 43.11N 0.58 E
Bousso 168 Bc 10.29N 16.43 E
Bouthaleb, Djebel- 126 Ri 35.48N 5.12 E
Boutilimit 162 Ef 17.33N 14.42W
Bou Tlelis 126 Li 35.34N 0.54W
Boutonne 122 Fi 45.55N 0.49W
Bouvet Øy 222 Cd 54.26S 3.24 E
Bouxwiller 124 Jf 48.49N 7.29 E
Bouza 166 Gc 14.25N 6.02 E
Bouzanne 122 Hh 46.38N 1.28 E
Bouzghaia 126 Nh 36.20N 1.15 E
Bouzonville 124 Ie 49.18N 6.32 E
Bovalino 128 Kl 38.09N 16.11 E
Bova Marina 128 Jm 37.56N 15.55 E
Bovec 128 Hd 46.20N 13.33 E
Bovenkarspel 128 Hb 52.42N 5.17 E
Boves 124 Ee 49.51N 2.23 E
Bovino 128 Ji 41.15N 15.20 E
Bovril 204 Cj 31.21S 59.26W
Bowa → Muli 152 Hf 27.55N 101.13 E
Bowen [Arg.] 206 Ge 35.02S 67.31W
Bowen [Austl.] 210 Fg 20.01S 148.15 E
Bowers Bank (EN) 178a Bb 54.00N 180.00
Bowers Ridge (EN) 178a Bb 54.30N 180.00
Bowie 186 Hj 33.34N 97.51W
Bowkān 146 Ld 36.31N 46.12 E
Bowland, Forest of- 118 Kh 54.00N 2.35W
Bowling Green [Ky.-U.S.] 182 Jd 37.00N 86.27W
Bowling Green [Oh.-U.S.] 184 Fe 41.22N 83.40W
Bowman 182 Gb 46.11N 103.24W
Bowman Bay 180 Kc 65.33N 73.40W
Bowman Island 222 He 65.17S 103.08 E
Bowman, Mount- 188 Ea 51.10N 121.55W
Bowo/Bomi 152 Ge 30.02N 95.39 E
Bowokan, Kepulauan- 150 Hg 2.05S 123.35 E
Bowral 212 Kf 34.28S 150.25 E
Bow River 160 Gg 49.56N 111.42W
Box Elder Creek 188 Kc 46.57N 108.04W
Boxelder Creek 188 Nd 45.59N 103.57W
Boxholm 114 Dg 58.12N 15.03 E
Boxian 152 Ke 33.46N 115.44 E
Boxing 152 Kd 37.07N 118.04 E
Boxmeer 124 Hc 51.39N 5.57 E
Boxtel 122 Lc 51.35N 5.20 E
Boyabat 146 Fb 41.28N 34.46 E
Boyabo 170 Cb 3.43N 18.46 E
Boyacá [3] 202 Db 5.30N 72.50W
Boyang 152 Kf 29.00N 116.41 E
Boyer, Cap- 219b De 21.37S 168.07 E
Boyer Ahmadī-e Kohkīlūyeh [3] 144 Hc 31.00N 50.30 E
Boyle/Mainistir na Búille 118 Eh 53.58N 8.18W
Boyne/An Bhóinn 118 Gh 53.43N 6.15W
Boyne City 184 Ec 45.13N 85.01W
Boynes, Iles de- 158 Nm 49.58S 69.59 E
Boynton Beach 184 Gl 26.32N 80.03W
Boysen Reservoir 188 Ke 43.19N 108.11W
Boz, Kūh-e- 146 Pi 27.46N 55.54 E
Bozburun 130 Lm 36.41N 28.04 E
Bozburun 130 Li 40.32N 28.46 E
Bozburun Dağı 146 Dd 37.18N 31.03 E
Bozcaada 146 Bc 39.50N 26.04 E
Bozcaada 146 Bc 39.49N 26.03 E
Bozdağ 130 Lk 38.20N 28.06 E
Boz Dağı [Tur.] 146 Cd 37.18N 29.12 E
Boz Dağı [Tur.] 146 Cc 38.19N 28.08 E
Boz Dağları 130 Kj 38.20N 27.45 E
Bozdoğan 130 Ll 37.40N 28.19 E
Bozeman 176 He 45.41N 111.02W
Bozen / Bolzano 112 Hf 46.31N 11.22 E
Bozene 170 Cb 2.56N 19.12 E
Bozhen 154 De 38.04N 116.34 E
Bozkol, zaliv- 135 Cb 45.20N 61.45 E
Bozkurt 146 Fb 41.57N 34.01 E
Bozok Platosu 146 Fc 39.05N 35.05 E
Bozouls 122 Ij 44.28N 2.43 E
Bozoum 160 Ih 6.19N 16.23 E
Bozova 146 Hd 37.22N 38.31 E
Bozovici 130 Fe 44.56N 22.00 E
Bozqūsh, Kūh-e- 146 Ld 37.45N 47.40 E
Bozüyük 146 Dc 39.54N 30.03 E
Bra 128 Bf 44.42N 7.51 E
Braås 116 Fg 57.04N 15.03 E
Braathen, Cape- 222 Pf 71.48S 96.05W
Brabant [3] 124 Gd 50.45N 4.30 E
Brabant 122 Lc 51.10N 5.05 E
Brabant-les-Villers 124 Gf 48.51N 4.59 E
Brâbich 166 Eb 17.30N 3.00W
Brač 128 Kg 43.19N 16.40 E
Bracadale, Loch- 118 Gd 57.20N 6.35W
Bracciano 128 Gh 42.06N 12.40 E
Bracciano, Lago di- 128 Gh 42.05N 12.15 E
Bräcke 114 De 62.43N 15.27 E
Brackettville 186 Fl 29.19N 100.24W
Brački kanal 128 Kg 43.24N 16.40 E
Brackley 124 Ab 52.02N 1.09W
Bracknell 118 Mj 51.26N 0.46W
Brackwede, Bielefeld- 124 Kc 51.59N 8.31 E
Brad 130 Fc 46.08N 22.47 E
Bradano 128 Kj 40.23N 16.51 E
Bradenton 182 Kf 27.29N 82.34W
Bradford [Eng.-U.K.] 118 Lh 53.48N 1.45W
Bradford [Pa.-U.S.] 184 He 41.57N 78.39W
Bradley Reef 214 Gi 6.52S 160.48 E
Brady 182 He 31.08N 99.20W
Brady Mountains 186 Gk 31.20N 99.40W
Brædstrup 116 Ci 55.58N 9.37 E
Braemar 118 Jd 57.01N 3.24W
Braga 112 Fg 41.33N 8.26W
Braga [2] 126 Dc 41.35N 8.25W
Bragadiru 130 If 43.46N 25.31 E
Bragado 206 He 35.08S 60.30W
Bragança [2] 126 Fc 41.30N 6.45W
Bragança [Braz.] 200 Lf 1.03S 46.46W
Bragança [Port.] 126 Fc 41.49N 6.45W
Bragança Paulista 204 If 22.57S 46.34W
Brahestad/Raahe 114 Fd 64.41N 24.29 E
Brāhmanbāria 148 Id 23.59N 91.07 E
Brahmapur 142 Kh 19.19N 84.47 E
Brahmaputra 140 Lg 24.02N 90.59 E
Brăila 112 If 45.16N 27.59 E
Brăila [2] 130 Kd 45.13N 27.48 E
Brăilei, Balta- 130 Ke 45.00N 28.00 E
Braine 124 Fe 49.20N 3.32 E
Braine-l'Alleud/Eigenbrakel 124 Gd 50.41N 4.22 E
Brainerd 182 Ib 46.21N 94.12W
Braintree 124 Cc 51.53N 0.34 E
Braithwaite Point 212 Gb 11.58S 134.00 E
Brake (Unterweser) 120 Ec 53.20N 8.29 E
Brakel [Bel.] 124 Fd 50.47N 3.45 E
Brakel [F.R.G.] 124 Lc 51.43N 9.11 E
Brakna [3] 162 Ef 17.30N 13.30W
Brålanda 116 Ef 58.34N 12.22 E
Bralorne 188 Da 50.47N 122.49W
Bramming 116 Ci 55.28N 8.42 E
Brämön 116 Gb 62.10N 17.40 E
Brampton 184 Hd 43.41N 79.46W
Bramsche 120 Dd 52.24N 7.59 E
Bran, Pasul- 130 Id 45.26N 25.17 E
Branco 162 Cf 16.39N 24.41W
Branco, Cabo- 198 Mf 7.09S 34.47W
Branco, Rio- [Braz.] 198 Jf 1.24S 61.51W
Branco, Rio- [Braz.] 204 De 21.00S 57.48W
Branco ou Cabixi, Rio- 204 Ba 13.55S 60.10W
Brandberg 158 Ik 21.08S 14.35 E
Brandbu 114 Cf 60.26N 10.28 E
Brande 114 Bi 55.57N 9.07 E
Brandenburg 120 Id 52.25N 12.33 E
Brandenburg 120 Jd 52.10N 13.30 E
Brändö 116 Id 60.25N 21.05 E
Brandon [Eng.-U.K.] 124 Cb 52.27N 0.37 E
Brandon [Fl.-U.S.] 184 Fl 27.56N 82.17W
Brandon [Man.-Can.] 176 Je 49.50N 99.57W
Brandon [Vt.-U.S.] 184 Kd 43.47N 73.05W
Brandon Head/Na Machairí 118 Ci 52.16N 10.15W
Brandon Mount/Cnoc Bréanainn 118 Ci 52.14N 10.15W
Brandval 116 Ed 60.19N 12.02 E
Brandvlei 172 Cf 30.25S 20.30 E
Brandýs nad Labem-Stará Boleslav 120 Kf 50.11N 14.40 E
Brănești 130 Je 44.27N 26.20 E
Braniewo 120 Pb 54.24N 19.50 E
Bransby Point 197c Bc 16.43N 62.14W
Bransfield Strait 222 Re 63.00S 59.00W
Brańsk 120 Sd 52.45N 22.51 E
Branson 186 Jh 36.39N 93.13W
Brantevik 116 Fi 55.31N 14.21 E
Brantford 180 Jh 43.08N 80.16W
Brantôme 122 Gi 45.22N 0.39 E
Bras d'Or Lake 180 Lg 45.50N 60.50W
Brasil=Brazil (EN) [1] 200 Kf 9.00S 53.00W
Brasil, Planalto do- = Brazilian Highlands (EN) 198 Lg 17.00S 45.00W
Brasiléia 202 Ef 11.00S 68.44W
Brasília 200 Lg 15.47S 47.55W
Brasilia de Minas 204 Jc 16.12S 44.26W
Brasla 116 Kg 57.08N 24.50 E
Braslav 114 Gi 55.37N 27.05 E
Brașov 112 If 45.38N 25.35 E
Brașov [2] 130 Id 45.40N 25.10 E
Brass 166 Ge 4.19N 6.14 E
Brassac 122 Ik 43.38N 2.30 E
Brasschaat 124 Gc 51.17N 4.27 E
Brasstown Bald 184 Fh 34.52N 83.48W
Brastavățu 130 Hf 43.55N 24.24 E
Brataj 130 Ci 40.16N 19.40 E
Bratca 130 Fc 46.56N 22.37 E
Bråte 116 De 59.43N 11.27 E
Bratislava 112 Hf 48.09N 17.07 E
Bratsk 142 Md 56.05N 101.48 E
Bratskoje vodohranilišče = Bratsk Reservoir (EN) 138 Fe 56.30N 102.00 E
Bratsk Reservoir (EN) = Bratskoje vodohranilišče 138 Fe 56.30N 102.00 E
Brattleboro 182 Mc 42.51N 72.36W
Brattvåg 116 Bb 62.36N 6.27 E
Braubach 124 Jd 50.17N 7.40 E
Braunau am Inn 128 Hb 48.16N 13.02 E
Braunschweig 120 Gd 52.16N 10.32 E
Brava 158 Eg 14.52N 24.43W
Brava, Costa- 126 Pc 41.45N 3.04 E
Bråviken 116 Gf 58.40N 16.30 E
Bravo del Norte, Rio- = Grande, Rio- (EN) 174 Jg 25.57N 97.09W
Brawley 182 De 32.59N 115.34W
Bray 172 Ce 25.26S 23.38 E
Bray 180 Jc 69.20N 77.00W
Bray/Brè 118 Gh 53.12N 6.06W
Bray, Pays de- 122 He 49.46N 1.26 E
Bray-Dunes 124 Ec 51.05N 2.31 E
Braye 122 Gg 47.45N 0.42 E
Bray Head 118 Cj 51.53N 10.25W
Bray-sur-Somme 124 Ee 49.56N 2.43 E
Brazi 130 Je 44.52N 26.01 E
Brazil 184 Df 39.32N 87.08W
Brazil (EN)=Brasil [1] 200 Kf 9.00S 53.00W
Brazil Basin (EN) 106 Dk 15.00S 25.00W
Brazilian Highlands (EN) = Brasil, Planalto do- 198 Lg 17.00S 45.00W
Brazos 174 Jg 28.53N 95.23W
Brazos Santiago Pass 186 Hm 26.05N 97.16W
Brazzaville 160 Ii 4.16S 15.17 E
Brčko 128 Mf 44.52N 18.49 E
Brda 120 Oc 53.07N 18.08 E
Brdy 120 Jg 49.35N 13.50 E
Bré/Bray 118 Gh 53.12N 6.06W
Brea, Punta- 197a Bc 17.56N 66.55W
Breaden, Lake- 212 Fe 25.45S 125.40 E
Breaksea Sound 218 Bf 45.35S 166.40 E
Breaza [Rom.] 130 Id 45.11N 25.40 E
Breaza [Rom.] 130 Ib 47.37N 25.20 E
Breaza, Virful- 130 Hb 47.22N 24.02 E
Brebes 150 Eh 6.53S 109.03 E
Brèche 124 Ee 49.16N 2.30 E
Brechin 118 Ke 56.44N 2.40W
Brecht 124 Gc 51.21N 4.38 E
Brechte 124 Jb 52.15N 7.10 E
Breckenridge [Mn.-U.S.] 186 Hc 46.16N 96.35W
Breckenridge [Tx.-U.S.] 186 Gj 32.45N 98.54W
Breckland 118 Ni 52.30N 0.35 E
Břeclav 120 Mh 48.46N 16.54 E
Brecon 118 Jj 51.57N 3.24W
Brecon Beacons 118 Jj 51.53N 3.31W
Breda 122 Kc 51.35N 4.46 E
Bredaryd 116 Eg 57.10N 13.44 E
Bredasdorp 160 Jl 34.32S 20.02 E
Brede 124 Cd 50.55N 0.43 E
Bredene 124 Ec 51.14N 2.58 E
Bredstedt 120 Eb 54.37N 8.59 E
Bredy 136 Ge 52.26N 60.21 E
Bree 124 Hc 51.08N 5.36 E
Breg 120 Ei 47.57N 8.31 E
Bregalnica 130 Eh 41.36N 21.56 E
Bregenz 128 Dc 47.30N 9.46 E
Bréhat, Ile de- 122 Df 48.51N 3.00W
Breiðafjörður 110 Db 65.15N 23.15W
Breidvika 120 Df 70.15S 24.15 E
Breimsvatnet 116 Bc 61.40N 6.25 E
Breisach am Rhein 120 Dh 48.02N 7.35 E
Breisgau 120 Di 47.50N 7.42 E
Breisund 116 Ab 62.30N 6.00 E
Breit Bridge 172 Dd 22.12S 29.59 E
Breivikbotn 114 Fa 70.37N 22.29 E
Brejão 204 Ia 12.59S 46.28W
Brekken 114 Ce 62.39N 11.53 E
Brekstad 114 Be 63.41N 9.41 E
Bremangerlandet 114 Af 61.50N 5.00 E
Brembana, Val- 128 De 45.55N 9.40 E
Brembo 128 De 45.35N 9.32 E
Bremen [2] 120 Ec 53.05N 8.50 E
Bremen [F.R.G.] 112 Ge 53.05N 8.48 E
Bremen [In.-U.S.] 184 De 41.27N 86.09W
Bremerhaven 112 Ge 53.33N 8.35 E
Bremerton 182 Cb 47.34N 122.38W
Bremervörde 120 Fc 53.29N 9.08 E
Brendel 188 Kg 38.57N 109.50W
Brenham 186 Hk 30.10N 96.24W
Brenne 122 Hh 46.44N 1.14 E
Brennero, Passo del- = Brenner Pass (EN) 110 Hf 47.00N 11.30 E
Brennerpaß=Brenner Pass (EN) 110 Hf 47.00N 11.30 E
Brenner Pass (EN) = Brennero, Passo del- 110 Hf 47.00N 11.30 E
Brenner Pass (EN) = Brennerpaß 110 Hf 47.00N 11.30 E
Brenta 128 Ge 45.11N 12.18 E
Brentwood 118 Nj 51.38N 0.18 E
Brescia 112 Hf 45.33N 10.15 E
Breskens 124 Fc 51.24N 3.33 E
Breslau (EN) = Wrocław 112 He 51.06N 17.00 E
Bresle 122 Hd 50.04N 1.22 E
Bressanone / Brixen 128 Fd 46.43N 11.39 E
Bressay 118 La 60.08N 1.05W
Bresse 122 Lh 46.30N 5.15 E
Bressuire 122 Fh 46.51N 0.29W
Brest [Bye.-U.S.S.R.] 112 Ie 52.06N 23.42 E
Brest [Fr.] 112 Ff 48.24N 4.29W
Brestova 128 Ie 45.08N 14.14 E
Brestskaja oblast [3] 136 Ce 52.20N 25.30 E
Bretagne=Brittany (EN) 110 Ff 48.00N 3.00W
Bretagne=Brittany (EN) 122 Df 48.00N 3.00W
Brețcu 130 Jc 46.03N 26.18 E
Breteuil [Fr.] 124 Cf 48.50N 0.55 E
Breteuil [Fr.] 124 Ee 49.38N 2.18 E
Breton, Marais- 122 Eh 46.56N 2.00W
Breton, Pertuis- 122 Eh 46.16N 1.22W
Breton Sound 186 Ll 29.30N 89.30W
Brett 124 Cc 51.58N 0.57 E
Brett, Cape- 218 Fa 35.10S 174.20 E
Bretten 124 Ke 49.03N 8.42 E
Bretteville-sur-Laize 124 Be 49.03N 0.20W
Breueh, Pulau- 150 Be 5.41N 95.05 E
Breuil-Cervinia 128 Be 45.56N 7.38 E
Breukelen 124 Db 52.10N 5.01 E
Breuna 124 Lc 51.25N 9.11 E
Breves 202 Hd 1.40S 50.29W
Brevik 114 Bg 59.04N 9.42 E
Brevoort 180 Ld 63.30N 64.20W
Brewarrina 212 Je 29.57S 146.52 E
Brewerville 166 Cd 6.25N 10.47W
Brewster 188 Fb 48.06N 119.47W
Brewster, Kap- 224 Md 70.10N 21.30W
Brewton 182 Je 31.07N 87.04W
Brezice 128 Je 45.54N 15.35 E
Brézina 162 Hc 33.05N 1.16 E
Březnice 120 Jg 49.33N 13.57 E
Breznik 130 Fg 42.44N 22.54 E
Brezno 120 Ph 48.49N 19.39 E
Brezoi 130 Hd 45.21N 24.15 E
Brezolles 124 Df 48.41N 1.04 E
Brezovo 130 Ig 42.21N 25.05 E
Bria 160 Jh 6.32N 21.59 E
Briance 122 Hi 45.47N 1.12 E
Briançon 122 Mj 44.54N 6.39 E
Brianza 128 De 45.45N 9.15 E
Briare, Canal de- 122 If 48.02N 2.43 E
Bribie Island 212 Ke 27.00S 153.05 E
Bričany 130 Ka 48.18N 27.04 E
Bride 118 Fi 52.05N 7.50W
Bridgend 118 Jj 51.31N 3.35W
Bridgeport [Ca.-U.S.] 188 Fg 38.10N 119.13W
Bridgeport [Ct.-U.S.] 182 Mc 41.11N 73.11W
Bridgeport [Nb.-U.S.] 186 Ef 41.40N 103.06W
Bridge River 188 Ea 50.45N 121.55W
Bridger Peak 188 Lf 41.12N 107.02W
Bridges Point 220g Bb 1.58N 157.28W
Bridgeton 184 Jf 39.26N 75.14W
Bridgetown [Austl.] 212 Df 33.57S 116.08 E
Bridgetown [Bar.] 176 Nh 13.06N 59.37W
Bridgewater 180 Lh 44.23N 64.31W
Bridgwater 118 Kj 51.08N 3.00W
Bridgwater Bay 118 Jj 51.16N 3.12W
Bridlington 118 Mg 54.05N 0.12W
Bridlington Bay 118 Mg 54.04N 0.08W
Bridport 118 Kk 50.44N 2.46W
Brie 122 Jf 48.40N 3.30 E
Brielle 124 Gc 51.54N 4.10 E
Brienzer See 128 Bd 46.45N 7.55 E
Briey 122 Le 49.15N 5.56 E
Brig 128 Bd 46.20N 8.00 E
Brigach 120 Ei 47.58N 8.30 E
Brigham City 182 Ec 41.31N 112.01W
Brighstone 124 Ad 50.38N 1.23W
Bright 212 Jg 36.44S 146.58 E
Brightlingsea 124 Dc 51.48N 1.02 E
Brighton [Co.-U.S.] 186 Dg 39.59N 104.49W
Brighton [Eng.-U.K.] 112 Fe 50.50N 0.10W
Brignoles 122 Mk 43.24N 6.04 E
Brihuega 126 Jd 40.45N 2.52W
Brijuni 128 Hf 44.55N 13.46 E
Brikama 166 Bc 13.16N 16.39W
Brilhante, Rio- 202 Hh 21.58S 54.18W
Brilon 124 Kc 51.24N 8.35 E
Brilon-Alme 124 Kc 51.27N 8.37 E
Brimstone Hill 197c Ab 17.21N 62.49W
Brindisi 112 Hg 40.38N 17.56 E
Brinkley 186 Ki 34.53N 91.12W
Brinkmann 204 Aj 30.52S 62.02W
Brionne 124 Ce 49.12N 0.43 E
Brioude 122 Ji 45.18N 3.24 E
Brisbane 210 Gg 27.28S 153.02 E
Brisighella 128 Ff 44.13N 11.46 E
Bristol 222 Ad 59.02S 26.31W
Bristol [Eng.-U.K.] 112 Fe 51.27N 2.35W
Bristol [Tn.-U.S.] 184 Fg 36.36N 82.11W
Bristol Bay 174 Dd 58.00N 159.00W
Bristol Channel 110 Fe 51.20N 4.00W
Bristol Lake 188 Hi 34.28N 115.41W
Bristow 186 Hi 35.50N 96.23W
Britannia Range 222 Jf 80.00S 158.00 E
British Columbia [2] 180 Fe 55.00N 125.00W
British Honduras → Belize [1] 176 Kh 17.15N 88.45W
British Indian Ocean Territory (EN) [5] 142 Jj 7.00S 72.00 E
British Isles 110 Fd 54.00N 4.00W
British Mountains 178 Kc 69.20N 140.20W
British Solomon Islands → Solomon Islands [1] 210 Ge 8.00S 159.00 E
British Virgin Islands [5] 176 Mh 18.20N 64.50W
Brits 172 Ce 25.40S 27.46 E
Britstown 172 Cf 30.37S 23.30 E
Britt 186 Ie 43.06N 93.48W
Brittany (EN)=Bretagne 110 Ff 48.00N 3.00W
Brittany (EN)=Bretagne 122 Df 48.00N 3.00W
Britton 186 Hd 45.48N 97.45W
Brive-la-Gaillarde 122 Hi 45.09N 1.32 E
Briviesca 126 Ib 42.33N 3.19W
Brixen / Bressanone 128 Fd 46.43N 11.39 E
Brixham, Torbay- 118 Jk 50.24N 3.30W
Brjansk 112 Je 53.15N 34.22 E
Brjanskaja oblast [3] 136 De 52.50N 33.20 E
Brjuhoveckaja 132 Kg 45.46N 39.01 E
Brjukoviči 120 Tg 49.52N 24.00 E
Brno 112 Hf 49.12N 16.37 E
Broa, Ensenada de la- 194 Fb 22.35N 82.00W
Broadback 180 Jf 51.21N 78.53W
Broad Bay 118 Gc 58.15N 6.15W
Broadford 118 Hd 57.14N 5.54W
Broad Sound 212 Jd 22.10S 149.45 E
Broadstairs 124 Dc 51.22N 1.27 E
Broadus 182 Fb 45.27N 105.25W
Brocēni/Broceny 116 Jh 56.41N 22.30 E
Broceny/Brocēni 116 Jh 56.41N 22.30 E
Brochet 180 He 57.53N 101.40W
Brochu, Lac- 184 Ja 48.26N 74.15W
Brock 180 Ga 77.55N 114.30W
Brocken 120 Ge 51.48N 10.36 E
Brockman, Mount- 212 Dd 22.28S 117.18 E
Brockton 184 Ld 42.05N 71.01W
Brockville 180 Jh 44.35N 75.41W
Brod 130 Eh 41.31N 21.14 E
Brodarevo 130 Cf 43.14N 19.43 E
Broderick Falls 170 Fb 0.37N 34.46 E
Brodeur Peninsula 174 Kb 73.00N 88.00W
Brodick 118 Hf 55.35N 5.09W
Brodnica 120 Pc 53.16N 19.23 E
Brody 132 Dd 50.04N 25.12 E
Broglie 124 Ce 49.01N 0.32 E
Brok 120 Rd 52.43N 21.52 E
Brok 120 Rd 52.38N 21.55 E
Broken Arrow 186 Ih 36.03N 95.48W
Broken Bow 186 Gf 41.24N 99.38W
Broken Bow Lake 186 Ii 34.10N 94.40W
Broken Hill 210 Fh 31.57S 141.27 E
Broken Ridge (EN) 106 Hm 31.30S 95.00 E
Brokind 116 Ff 58.13N 15.40 E
Brokopondo 202 Hb 5.04N 55.00W
Bromary 116 Je 59.55N 23.00 E
Bromley, London- 124 Cc 51.25N 0.01 E
Bromölla 114 Dh 56.04N 14.28 E
Brønderslev 116 Cg 57.16N 9.58 E
Brong-Ahafo [3] 166 Ed 7.45N 1.30W
Bronnikovo 134 Ng 58.59N 69.27 E
Brønnøysund 114 Cd 65.28N 12.13 E
Bronte 128 Im 37.47N 14.50 E
Brooke's Point 150 Ge 8.47N 117.50 E
Brookfield 186 Jg 39.47N 93.04W
Brookhaven 186 Kk 31.35N 90.26W
Brookings [Or.-U.S.] 182 Cc 42.03N 124.17W
Brookings [S.D.-U.S.] 182 Hc 44.19N 96.48W
Brooks 180 Gf 50.35N 111.53W
Brooks Banks (EN) 214 Mc 24.05N 166.50W
Brooks Range 174 Dc 68.00N 154.00W
Brookston 186 Jc 46.50N 92.32W

Index Symbols

[1] Independent Nation
[2] State, Region
[3] District, County
[4] Municipality
[5] Colony, Dependency
Continent
Physical Region
Historical or Cultural Region
Mount, Mountain
Volcano
Hill
Mountains, Mountain Range
Hills, Escarpment
Plateau, Upland
Pass, Gap
Plain, Lowland
Delta
Salt Flat
Valley, Canyon
Crater, Cave
Karst Features
Depression
Polder
Desert, Dunes
Forest, Woods
Heath, Steppe
Oasis
Cape, Point
Coast, Beach
Cliff
Peninsula
Isthmus
Sandbank
Island
Atoll
Rock, Reef
Islands, Archipelago
Rocks, Reefs
Coral Reef
Well, Spring
Geyser
River, Stream
Waterfall, Rapids
River Mouth, Estuary
Lake
Salt Lake
Intermittent Lake
Reservoir
Swamp, Pond
Canal
Glacier
Ice Shelf, Pack Ice
Ocean
Sea
Gulf, Bay
Strait, Fjord
Lagoon
Bank
Seamount
Tablemount
Ridge
Shelf
Basin
Escarpment, Sea Scarp
Fracture
Trench, Abyss
National Park, Reserve
Point of Interest
Recreation Site
Cave, Cavern
Historic Site
Ruins
Wall, Walls
Church, Abbey
Temple
Scientific Station
Railway station
Airport
Port
Military installation
Lighthouse
Mine
Tunnel
Dam, Bridge

Brooksville 184 Fk 28.33N 82.23W
Brookton 212 Df 32.22S 117.01 E
Brookville [In.-U.S.] 184 Ef 39.25N 85.01W
Brookville [Pa.-U.S.] 184 He 41.10N 79.06W
Broom 118 Hd 57.45N 5.05W
Broom, Loch- 118 Hd 57.55N 5.15W
Broome 210 Df 17.58S 122.14 E
Brora 118 Jc 58.01N 3.51W
Brora 118 Jc 58.00N 3.50W
Brosna/An Bhrosnach 118 Fh 53.13N 7.58W
Broşteni 130 Ib 47.14N 25.42 E
Brou 122 Hf 48.13N 1.11 E
Brough 118 Kg 54.32N 2.19W
Broughton Island 176 Mc 67.35N 63.50W
Broussard 186 Kk 30.09N 91.58W
Brovary 132 Gd 50.32N 30.48 E
Brovst 116 Cg 57.06N 9.32 E
Brown Bank (EN)=Bruine Bank 124 Fb 52.35N 3.20 E
Brownfield 182 Ge 33.11N 102.16W
Browning 188 Ib 48.34N 113.01W
Browns Bank (EN) 180 Kh 42.40N 66.05W
Brownsville [Tn.-U.S.] 184 Ch 35.36N 89.15W
Brownsville [Tx.-U.S.] 176 Jg 25.54N 97.30W
Brownwood 182 He 31.43N 98.59W
Browse Island 212 Eb 14.05S 123.35 E
Bruay-en-Artois 122 Id 50.29N 2.33 E
Bruay-sur-l'Escaut 124 Fd 50.23N 3.32 E
Bruce 186 Lj 33.59N 89.21W
Bruce, Mount- 208 Cg 22.36S 118.08 E
Bruce Crossing 184 Cb 46.32N 89.10W
Bruce Peninsula 180 Jh 44.59N 81.20W
Bruce Rock 212 Df 31.53S 118.09 E
Bruche 122 Nf 48.34N 7.43 E
Bruchhausen-Vilsen 124 Lb 52.50N 9.01 E
Bruchmühlbach-Miesau 124 Je 49.23N 7.28 E
Bruchsal 120 Eg 49.08N 8.36 E
Bruck an der Leitha 128 Kb 48.01N 16.46 E
Bruck an der Mur 128 Jc 47.25N 15.17 E
Brue 118 Kj 51.13N 3.00W
Bruges/Brugge 122 Jc 51.13N 3.14 E
Brugg 128 Cc 47.29N 8.12 E
Brugge/Bruges 122 Jc 51.13N 3.14 E
Brugge-Assebroek 124 Fc 51.12N 3.16 E
Brüggen 124 Ic 51.15N 6.11 E
Brugge-Sint-Andries 124 Fc 51.12N 3.10 E
Brühl [F.R.G.] 124 Ke 49.24N 8.32 E
Brühl [F.R.G.] 124 Id 50.50N 6.54 E
Bruine Bank=Brown Bank (EN) 124 Fb 52.35N 3.20 E
Bruin Point 182 Ed 39.39N 110.22W
Brule River 184 Cc 45.57N 88.12W
Brumado 202 Jf 14.13S 41.40W
Brummen 124 Ib 52.06N 6.10 E
Brummo 116 Ef 58.50N 13.40 E
Brumunddal 114 Cf 60.53N 10.56 E
Bruna 128 Eh 42.45N 10.53 E
Brune 124 Fe 49.45N 3.47 E
Bruneau 188 He 42.53N 115.48W
Bruneau River 188 He 42.57N 115.58W
Bruneck / Brunico 128 Fd 46.48N 11.56 E
Brunehamel 124 Ge 49.46N 4.11 E
Brunei [1] 142 Ni 4.30N 114.40 E
Brunei, Teluk- 140 Ni 5.05N 115.18 E
Brunette Downs 212 Hc 18.38S 135.57 E
Brunflo 114 Fa 63.05N 14.49 E
Brunico / Bruneck 128 Fd 46.48N 11.56 E
Brunna 116 Ge 59.52N 17.25 E
Brunner 218 De 42.26S 171.19 E
Brunner, Lake- 218 De 42.35S 171.25 E
Brunnsberg 116 Ec 61.17N 13.55 E
Brunsbüttel 120 Fc 53.54N 9.07 E
Brunssum 124 Hd 50.57N 5.57 E
Brunswick [Ga.-U.S.] 182 Ke 31.10N 81.29W
Brunswick [Me.-U.S.] 182 Nc 43.55N 69.58W
Brunswick, Peninsula- 198 Ik 53.30S 71.25W
Brunswick Lake 184 Fa 49.00N 83.23W
Bruntál 120 Ng 49.59N 17.28 E
Bruny Island 212 Jh 43.30S 147.05 E
Brus 130 Ef 43.23N 21.02 E
Brus, Laguna de- 194 Ef 15.50N 84.35W
Brush 182 Gc 40.15N 103.37W
Brus Laguna 194 Ef 15.47N 84.35W
Brusque 206 Kc 27.06S 48.56W
Brussel/Bruxelles=Brussels (EN) 112 Ge 50.50N 4.20 E
Brussels (EN)=Brussel/Bruxelles 112 Ge 50.50N 4.20 E
Brussels (EN)=Bruxelles/Brussel 112 Ge 50.50N 4.20 E
Brusset, 'Erg- 166 Hb 18.55N 10.30 E
Brusturi 130 Fb 47.09N 22.15 E
Brusy 120 Nc 53.53N 17.45 E
Bruxelles/Brussel=Brussels (EN) 112 Ge 50.50N 4.20 E
Bruzual 196 Bh 8.03N 69.19W
Bryan [Oh.-U.S.] 184 Ee 41.30N 84.34W
Bryan [Tx.-U.S.] 182 He 30.40N 96.22W
Bryan Coast 222 Pf 73.35S 84.00W
Bryne 114 Ag 58.44N 5.39 E
Brza Palanka 130 Fe 44.28N 22.27 E
Brzava kanal 130 Dd 45.16N 20.49 E
Brzeg 120 Nf 50.52N 17.27 E
Brzeg Dolny 120 Me 51.15N 16.40 E
Brzeziny 120 Pe 51.48N 19.46 E
Brzozów 120 Sg 49.42N 22.02 E
Bsharrī 146 Ge 34.15N 36.01 E
Bû 124 Df 48.48N 1.30 E
Bua 116 Eg 57.14N 12.07 E
Buada Lagoon 220e Ab 0.32S 166.54 E
Buala 210 Ge 8.10S 159.35 E
Bū al Ḩidān, Wādī- 164 Cd 27.25N 19.22 E
Buapinang 150 Hg 4.46S 121.34 E
Buatan 150 Df 0.44N 101.51 E
Bū aţ Tifl 164 Dd 28.54N 22.30 E
Bua Yai 148 Ke 15.34N 102.24 E
Bu'ayrāt al Ḩasūn 164 Cc 31.24N 15.44 E
Bubanza 170 Ec 3.06S 29.23 E
Bubaque 166 Bc 11.17N 15.50W
Būbīyan 146 Mh 29.45N 48.15 E
Bubu 170 Gd 6.03S 35.19 E
Bubye 172 Ed 22.20S 31.07 E
Buca 130 Kk 38.22N 27.11 E
Bučač 132 De 49.04N 25.23 E
Bucačača 138 Gf 52.59N 116.55 E
Bucak 146 Dd 37.28N 30.36 E
Bucaramanga 200 Ie 7.08N 73.09W
Bucas Grande 150 Ie 9.40N 125.58 E
Buccament Bay 197n Ba 13.12N 61.17W
Buccaneer Archipelago 212 Ec 16.17S 123.20 E
Bucecea 130 Jb 47.46N 26.26 E
Buchanan 160 Fh 5.53N 10.03W
Buchanan, Lake- [Austl.] 212 Jd 21.30S 145.50 E
Buchanan, Lake- [Tx.-U.S.] 186 Gk 30.48N 98.25W
Buchanan Bay 180 Ka 78.55N 75.00W
Buchan Gulf 180 Kb 71.48N 74.06W
Buchardo 206 Hd 34.43S 63.31W
Bucharest (EN)=Bucureşti 112 Ig 44.26N 26.06 E
Buchen 120 Fg 49.31N 9.20 E
Buchholz in der Nordheide 120 Fc 53.20N 9.52 E
Buchon, Point- 188 Ei 35.15N 120.54W
Buchs 128 Dc 47.10N 9.30 E
Buchy 124 De 49.35N 1.22 E
Bückeburg 124 Lb 52.16N 9.03 E
Buckeye 188 Ij 33.22N 112.35W
Buckhaven 118 Je 56.11N 3.03W
Buckie 118 Kd 57.40N 2.58W
Buckingham [Eng.-U.K.] 124 Bb 52.00N 0.59W
Buckingham [Que.-Can.] 184 Jc 45.35N 75.25W
Buckingham Bay 212 Hb 12.10S 135.46 E
Buckinghamshire [3] 118 Mj 51.50N 0.55W
Buckland 178 Gc 66.16N 161.20W
Buckle Island 222 Ke 66.47S 163.14 E
Buckley Bay 222 Je 68.16S 148.12 E
Bucks 118 Mj 51.50N 0.55W
Bucksport 184 Mc 44.34N 68.48W
Buco Zau 170 Bc 4.50S 12.33 E
Bu Craa 162 Ed 26.17N 12.46W
Bucureşti [2] 130 Je 44.30N 26.05 E
Bucureşti=Bucharest (EN) 112 Ig 44.26N 26.06 E
Bucy-lès-Pierrepont 124 Fe 49.39N 3.54 E
Bucyrus 184 Fe 40.47N 82.57W
Bud 114 Be 62.55N 6.55 E
Budacu, Vîrful- 130 Ib 47.07N 25.41 E
Buda-Košelevo 132 Gc 52.43N 30.39 E
Budapest 112 Hf 47.30N 19.05 E
Budapest [2] 120 Pi 47.30N 19.05 E
Búðardalur 114a Bb 65.07N 21.46W
Budaun 148 Fc 28.03N 79.07 E
Budbud 168 He 4.13N 46.31 E
Budd Coast 222 He 66.30S 113.00 E
Buddusò 128 Dj 40.35N 9.15 E
Bude [Eng.-U.K.] 118 Ik 50.50N 4.33W
Bude [Ms.-U.S.] 186 Kk 31.28N 90.51W
Bude Bay 118 Ik 50.50N 4.37W
Budel 124 Hc 51.16N 5.30 E
Budennovsk 136 Eg 44.45N 44.08 E
Budeşti 130 Je 44.14N 26.27 E
Budia 126 Jd 40.38N 2.45W
Büdingen 120 Ff 50.18N 9.07 E
Búdir 114a Cb 64.56N 14.01W
Budjala 170 Cb 2.39N 19.42 E
Budkowiczanka 120 Nf 50.52N 17.33 E
Budogošč 114 Hg 59.19N 32.29 E
Budrio 128 Ff 44.32N 11.32 E
Budslav 116 Lj 54.49N 27.32 E
Budva 130 Bg 42.17N 18.51 E
Budyšin/Bautzen 120 Ke 51.11N 14.26 E
Budžjak 130 Lc 46.15N 28.45 E
Buea 166 Ge 4.09N 9.14 E
Buëch 122 Lj 44.12N 5.57 E
Buenaventura [Col.] 200 Ie 3.53N 77.04W
Buenaventura [Mex.] 190 Cc 29.51N 107.29W
Buenaventura, Bahía de- 202 Cc 3.45N 77.15W
Buena Vista 202 Bb 31.10N 115.40W
Buenavista 192 Ef 23.39N 109.42W
Buena Vista [Co.-U.S.] 186 Cg 38.50N 106.08W
Buena Vista [Mex.] 192 Mi 16.05N 93.00W
Buena Vista [Ven.] 196 Eh 9.02N 63.49W
Buena Vista, Bahia de- 194 Hb 22.30N 79.08W
Buendia, Embalse de- 126 Jd 40.25N 2.43W
Buenópolis 204 Jc 17.54S 44.11W
Buenos Aires [2] 206 Ie 36.00S 60.00W
Buenos Aires [Arg.] 200 Ki 34.36S 58.27W
Buenos Aires [C.R.] 194 Fi 10.04N 84.26W
Buenos Aires, Lago- 198 Ij 46.30S 72.00W
Buffalo 180 Fe 60.52N 115.03W
Buffalo [N.Y.-U.S.] 176 Le 42.54N 78.53W
Buffalo [Ok.-U.S.] 186 Gh 36.50N 99.38W
Buffalo [S.D.-U.S.] 186 Gb 45.35N 103.33W
Buffalo [Tx.-U.S.] 186 Hk 31.28N 96.04W
Buffalo [Wy.-U.S.] 182 Fc 44.21N 106.42W
Buffalo Bill Reservoir 188 Kd 44.29N 109.13W
Buffalo Lake 180 Fd 60.12N 115.25W
Buffalo Narrows 180 Ge 55.51N 108.30W
Buffalo Pound Lake 188 Ma 50.38N 105.20W
Buffels 172 Be 29.41S 17.04 E
Bū Fishah 128 En 36.18N 10.28 E
Buford 184 Fh 34.07N 84.00W
Buftea 130 Ie 44.34N 25.57 E
Bug 110 Ie 52.31N 21.05 E
Buga 202 Cc 3.55N 76.18W
Bugarach, Pech de- 122 Il 42.52N 2.23 E
Bugeat 122 Hi 45.36N 1.56 E
Bugene 170 Fc 1.35S 31.08 E
Bugey 122 Li 45.48N 5.30 E
Bugojno 128 Lf 44.03N 17.27 E
Bugøynes 114 Gb 69.58N 29.39 E
Bugrino 134 Db 68.48N 49.09 E
Bugsuk 150 Ge 8.15N 117.18 E
Bugt 152 Lb 48.47N 121.55 E
Bugulma 136 Fe 54.33N 52.48 E
Bugun 136 Hc 43.22N 70.10 E
Bugun 135 Gc 42.56N 68.36 E
Bügür/Luntai 152 Dc 41.46N 84.10 E
Buguruslan 136 Fe 53.39N 52.30 E
Buhara 142 If 39.48N 64.25 E
Buharskaja oblast [3] 136 Gg 41.20N 64.20 E
Bū Ḩaşā' 146 Ok 23.20N 53.20 E
Buhera 172 Ec 19.18S 31.29 E
Buh He 152 Gd 36.58N 99.48 E
Buhl 188 He 42.36N 114.46W
Bühl 120 Eh 48.42N 8.09 E
Bùhōdle 168 Hd 8.15N 46.20 E
Buhtarminskoje vodohranilišče 136 If 49.10N 84.00 E
Bui Dam 166 Ed 8.22N 2.10W
Builth Wells 118 Ji 52.09N 3.24W
Buin [Chile] 206 Fd 33.44S 70.44W
Buin [Pap.N.Gui.] 214 Fi 6.50S 155.44 E
Buinsk 136 Ee 54.59N 48.17 E
Buir Nur 152 Kb 47.48N 117.42 E
Buitrago del Lozoya 126 Id 41.00N 3.38W
Buj 136 Ed 58.29N 41.31 E
Buj 134 Gh 56.15N 54.12 E
Bujalance 126 Hg 37.54N 4.22W
Bujanovac 130 Eg 42.28N 21.47 E
Bujaraloz 126 Lc 41.30N 0.09W
Buje 128 He 45.24N 13.40 E
Bujnaksk 136 Eg 42.49N 47.07 E
Bujukly 138 Jg 49.33N 142.55 E
Bujumbura 160 Ji 3.23S 29.22 E
Bujunda 138 Kd 62.00N 153.30 E
Bük 120 Mi 47.23N 16.45 E
Buk 120 Md 52.22N 16.31 E
Buka Island 208 Ge 5.15S 154.35 E
Bukakata 170 Fc 0.18S 32.02 E
Bukama 160 Ji 9.12S 25.51 E
Buka Passage 219a Ba 5.25S 154.41 E
Bukavu 160 Ji 2.30S 28.52 E
Bukene 170 Fc 4.14S 32.53 E
Bukhā 146 Qi 26.10N 56.09 E
Bukit Besi 150 Df 4.46N 103.12 E
Bukit Mertajam 150 De 5.22N 100.28 E
Bukittinggi 142 Mj 0.19S 100.22 E
Bükk 120 Qh 48.05N 20.30 E
Bukoba 160 Ki 1.20S 31.49 E
Bukovina 130 Ia 48.00N 25.30 E
Bukowiec 120 Ld 52.23N 15.20 E
Bukuru 166 Gd 9.48N 8.52 E
Būl, Kūh-e- 144 Hc 30.48N 52.45 E
Bulajevo 136 He 54.53N 70.26 E
Bulan 150 Hd 12.40N 123.52 E
Bulanaš 134 Kh 57.16N 62.02 E
Bulancak 146 Hb 40.57N 38.14 E
Bulanık 146 Jc 39.05N 42.15 E
Būlāq 164 Fd 25.12N 30.32 E
Bulawayo 160 Jk 20.09S 28.34 E
Buldan 146 Cc 38.03N 28.51 E
Buldir 178a Bb 52.21N 175.54 E
Bulgan [Mong.] 152 Fb 46.05N 91.34 E
Bulgan [Mong.] 152 Hb 48.45N 103.34 E
Bulgan [Mong.] 152 Hc 44.05N 103.32 E
Bulgaria (EN)=Bălgarija [1] 112 Ig 43.00N 25.00 E
Buli 150 If 0.53N 128.18 E
Buli, Teluk- 150 If 0.45N 128.30 E
Bululuyan, Cape- 150 Ge 8.20N 117.11 E
Bulki 168 Fd 6.01N 36.36 E
Bullahār 168 Gc 10.23N 44.27 E
Bullange/Büllingen 124 Id 50.25N 6.16 E
Bullaque 126 Hf 38.59N 4.17W
Bulla Regia 128 Cn 36.33N 8.45 E
Bullas 126 Kf 38.03N 1.40W
Bulle 128 Bd 46.37N 7.04 E
Buller 218 Dd 41.44S 171.35 E
Bullfinch 212 Df 30.59S 119.06 E
Büllingen/Bullange 124 Id 50.25N 6.16 E
Bullion Mountains 188 Hi 34.25N 116.00W
Bulloo River 208 Fg 28.43S 142.30 E
Bull Point [Eng.-U.K.] 118 Ij 51.12N 4.10W
Bull Point [Falk.Is.] 206 Ih 52.19S 59.18W
Bulls 218 Fd 40.10S 175.23 E
Bulls Bay 184 Hi 32.59N 79.33W
Bull Shoals Lake 186 Jh 36.30N 92.50W
Bully Choop Mountain 188 Df 40.35N 122.45W
Bully-les-Mines 124 Ed 50.26N 2.43 E
Bulo Berde 168 He 3.52N 45.40 E
Bulolo 214 Di 7.12S 146.39 E
Bulqiza 130 Dh 41.30N 20.21 E
Bulter 186 Ig 38.16N 94.20W
Bultfontein 172 De 28.20S 26.05 E
Bulukumba 150 Hh 5.33S 120.11 E
Bulungu [Zaire] 170 Cc 4.33S 18.36 E
Bulungu [Zaire] 170 Dd 6.04S 21.54 E
Bumba 160 Jh 2.11N 22.28 E
Bumbah, Khalīj al- 164 Dc 32.25N 23.06 E
Buna 170 Gb 2.47N 39.31 E
Buna 130 Ch 41.52N 19.22 E
Bunbury 210 Ch 33.19S 115.38 E
Buncrana/Bun Cranncha 118 Ff 55.08N 7.27W
Bun Cranncha/Buncrana 118 Ff 55.08N 7.27W
Bunda 170 Fc 2.03S 33.52 E
Bundaberg 210 Gg 24.52S 152.21 E
Bünde 120 Ed 52.12N 8.35 E
Bundesrepublik Deutschland =Germany, Federal Republic of- (EN) [1] 112 Ge 51.00N 9.00 E
Bun Dobhráin/Bundoran 118 Eg 54.28N 8.17W
Bundoran/Bun Dobhráin 118 Eg 54.28N 8.17W
Bungay 124 Db 52.27N 1.27 E
Bungku 150 Hg 2.33S 121.58 E
Bungo 170 Cd 7.26S 15.24 E
Bungo Strait (EN)=Bungo-Suidō 154 Lh 32.40N 132.18 E
Bungo-Suidō=Bungo Strait (EN) 154 Lh 32.40N 132.18 E
Bungotakada 156 Be 33.33N 131.27 E
Bungsberg 120 Gb 54.12N 10.43 E
Buni 166 Hc 11.12N 12.02 E
Bunja 160 Kh 1.34N 30.15 E
Bunji 148 Ea 35.40N 74.36 E
Bunker 186 Kh 37.27N 91.13W
Bunker Group 212 Kd 23.50S 152.20 E
Bunkeya 170 Ee 10.24S 26.58 E
Bunkie 186 Jk 30.57N 92.11W
Bunnerfjällen 116 Ea 63.10N 12.34 E
Buñol 126 Le 39.25N 0.47W
Bunschoten 124 Hb 52.14N 5.24 E
Buntingford 124 Bc 51.57N 0.01W
Buntok 150 Fg 1.42S 114.48 E
Bünyan 146 Fc 38.51N 35.52 E
Bunyu, Pulau- 150 Gf 3.30N 117.50 E
Buon Me Thuot 148 Lf 12.40N 108.03 E
Buor-Haja, guba- 138 Ib 71.00N 131.00 E
Buotama 138 Hd 61.17N 128.55 E
Buqayq 144 Gd 25.56N 49.40 E
Buqda Kōsār 168 Ge 4.31N 44.49 E
Buqūm, Ḩarrat 164 Hd 20.54N 42.00 E
Bur 138 Hb 71.40N 123.40 E
Bura 170 Gc 1.06S 39.57 E
Buram 160 Jg 10.49N 25.10 E
Buran 136 If 48.04N 85.15 E
Burang 152 De 30.18N 81.08 E
Burāq 146 Gf 33.10N 36.29 E
Buras 186 Ll 29.21N 89.32W
Buraydah 142 Gg 26.20N 43.59 E
Burbach 124 Kd 50.43N 8.03 E
Burdab 168 Hd 9.05N 46.30 E
Burdekin River 212 Jc 19.39S 147.30 E
Burdêre 168 He 3.30N 45.37 E
Burdur 144 Db 37.43N 30.17 E
Burdur Gölü 146 Dd 37.44N 30.12 E
Burdwood Bank (EN) 206 Ih 54.15S 59.00W
Bure 124 Db 52.38N 1.45 E
Bure [Eth.] 168 Fd 8.20N 35.08 E
Bure [Eth.] 168 Fc 10.43N 37.03 E
Bureå 114 Ed 64.37N 21.12 E
Bureinski hrebet = Bureya Range (EN) 140 Pd 50.40N 134.00 E
Bureja 138 Hg 49.43N 129.51 E
Bureja 140 Oe 49.25N 129.35 E
Büren 120 Ee 51.33N 8.34 E
Buren-Cogt 152 Jb 46.45N 111.30 E
Bureya Range (EN) = Bureinski hrebet 140 Pd 50.40N 134.00 E
Burfjord 114 Fb 69.56N 22.03 E
Būr Gābo 168 Gf 1.10S 41.50 E
Burgas 112 Ig 42.30N 27.28 E
Burgas [2] 130 Kg 42.30N 27.20 E
Burgas, Gulf of- (EN)=Burgaski Zaliv 130 Kg 42.30N 27.33 E
Burgaski Zaliv=Burgas, Gulf of- (EN) 130 Kg 42.30N 27.33 E
Burg auf Fehmarn 120 Hb 54.26N 11.12 E
Burg auf Fehmarn-Puttgarden 120 Hb 54.30N 11.13 E
Burgaw 184 Ih 34.33N 77.56W
Burgaz Dağı 130 Mk 38.25N 29.46 E
Burg bei Magdeburg 120 Hd 52.16N 11.51 E
Burgdorf [F.R.G.] 120 Gd 52.27N 10.01 E
Burgdorf [Switz.] 128 Bc 47.04N 7.37 E
Burgenland [2] 128 Kc 47.30N 16.25 E
Burgersdorp 172 Df 31.00S 26.20 E
Burgess Hill 124 Bd 50.58N 0.08W
Burgfjället 114 Dd 64.56N 15.03 E
Burghausen 120 Ih 48.10N 12.50 E
Burghūth, Sabkhat al- 146 Ie 34.58N 41.06 E
Burglengenfeld 120 Ig 49.12N 12.02 E
Burgos [3] 126 Ib 42.20N 3.40W
Burgos [Mex.] 192 Je 24.57N 98.57W
Burgos [Sp.] 112 Fg 42.21N 3.42W
Burg-Reuland 124 Id 50.12N 6.09 E
Burgsvik 114 Eh 57.03N 18.16 E
Burgundy (EN)=Bourgogne 110 Gf 47.00N 4.30 E
Burgundy (EN)=Bourgogne 122 Kg 47.00N 4.30 E
Burgwald 124 Kd 50.57N 8.48 E
Būr Hakkaba 168 Ge 2.43N 44.10 E
Burhaniye 146 Bc 39.30N 26.58 E
Burhānpur 142 Jg 21.18N 76.14 E
Burias 150 Hd 12.57N 123.08 E
Buribaj 134 Ik 51.57N 58.11 E
Burica, Punta- 190 Hg 8.03N 82.53W
Burien 188 Dc 47.27N 122.21W
Burin Peninsula 180 Lg 47.00N 55.40W
Buriram 148 Kf 14.59N 103.08 E
Buriti, Rio- 204 Ca 12.50S 58.28W
Buriti Alegre 204 Hd 18.09S 49.03W
Buriti Bravo 202 Je 5.50S 43.50W
Buriti dos Lopes 202 Jd 3.10S 41.52W
Buritis 204 Ib 15.37S 46.26W
Burj al Ḩaţţābah 162 Ic 30.20N 9.30 E
Burjasot / Burjassot 126 Le 39.31N 0.25W
Burjassot / Burjasot 126 Le 39.31N 0.25W
Burjatskaja ASSR [3] 138 Ff 53.00N 110.00 E
Burj Şāfitā 146 Ge 34.49N 36.07 E
Burkandja 138 Jd 63.27N 147.27 E
Burkburnett 186 Gi 34.06N 98.34W
Burke 186 Ge 43.11N 99.18W
Burke, Mount- 188 Ha 50.18N 114.30W
Burke Island 222 Of 73.08S 105.06W
Burke River 212 Hd 23.12S 139.33 E
Burkesville 184 Eg 36.48N 85.22W
Burketown 210 Ef 17.44S 139.22 E
Burkina Faso (Upper Volta) [1] 160 Gg 13.00N 2.00W
Burley 182 Ec 42.32N 113.48W
Burli 132 Rd 51.28N 52.44 E
Burlingame 186 Ig 38.45N 95.50W
Burlington [Co.-U.S.] 182 Gd 39.18N 102.16W
Burlington [Ia.-U.S.] 182 Ic 40.49N 91.07W
Burlington [Ks.-U.S.] 186 Ig 38.12N 95.45W
Burlington [N.C.-U.S.] 184 Hg 36.06N 79.26W
Burlington [Ont.-Can.] 184 Hd 43.19N 79.43W
Burlington [Vt.-U.S.] 182 Mc 44.28N 73.14W
Burlington [Wi.-U.S.] 186 Le 42.41N 88.17W
Burma (Myanmar-Nainggan-Daw) [1] 142 Lg 22.00N 98.00 E
Burnazului, Cîmpia- 130 Ie 44.10N 25.50 E
Burnett River 212 Kd 24.46S 152.25 E
Burney 188 Ef 40.53N 121.40W
Burnham Market 124 Cb 52.57N 0.44 E
Burnham-on-Crouch 124 Cc 51.37N 0.50 E
Burnie 212 Jh 41.04S 145.54 E
Burnley 118 Kh 53.48N 2.14W
Burns 182 Dc 43.35N 119.03W
Burnside 180 Gc 66.55N 108.04W
Burnside, Lake- 212 Ee 25.20S 123.10 E
Burns Lake 180 Ef 54.14N 125.46W
Burnsville 184 Fh 35.55N 82.18W
Burnt Lava Flow 188 Ef 41.35N 121.35W
Burnt River 184 Hc 44.35N 78.46W
Burntwood 180 He 56.08N 96.33W
Bur'o 160 Lh 9.30N 45.34 E
Burqin 152 Eb 47.43N 86.53 E
Burqin He 152 Eb 47.42N 86.50 E
Burra 212 Hf 33.40S 138.56 E
Burragorang Lake 212 Kf 34.00S 150.25 E
Burreli 130 Ch 41.37N 20.00 E
Burrendong Reservoir 212 Jf 32.40S 149.10 E
Burriana / Borriana 126 Le 39.53N 0.05W
Burro, Serranias del- 192 Ic 28.50N 101.35W
Burrow Head 118 Ig 54.41N 4.24W
Bursa 142 Ee 40.11N 29.04 E
Būr Sa'īd = Port Said (EN) 160 Ke 31.16N 32.18 E
Burscheid 124 Jc 51.06N 7.07 E
Bürstadt 124 Ke 49.38N 8.27 E
Burštyn 132 De 49.16N 24.37 E
Būr Sūdān=Port Sudan (EN) 160 Kg 19.37N 37.14 E
Burt Lake 184 Ec 45.27N 84.40W
Burtnieku, ozero- / Burtnieku ezers 116 Kg 57.35N 25.10 E
Burtnieku ezers / Burtnieku, ozero- 116 Kg 57.35N 25.10 E
Burton 184 Fd 43.02N 83.36W
Burton Latimer 124 Bb 52.21N 0.40W
Burton upon Trent 118 Li 52.49N 1.36W
Burträsk 114 Ed 64.31N 20.39 E
Buru, Pulau- 208 De 3.24S 126.40 E
Burullus, Buḩayrat al- 146 Dg 31.30N 30.50 E
Burultokay/Fuhai 152 Eb 47.06N 87.23 E
Burum Gana 166 Hc 13.00N 11.57 E
Burūn, Ra's- 146 Eg 31.14N 33.04 E
Burundaj 136 Hg 43.20N 76.49 E
Burundi [1] 160 Ki 3.15S 30.00 E
Bururi 170 Ec 3.57S 29.37 E
Burutu 166 Gd 5.21N 5.31 E
Bury 118 Kh 53.36N 2.17W
Burylbajtal 136 Ib 44.56N 73.59 E
Buryn 132 Hd 51.13N 33.48 E
Bury Saint Edmunds 118 Ni 52.15N 0.43 E
Burzil Pass 148 Fb 34.54N 75.06 E
Busalla 128 Cf 44.34N 8.57 E
Busanga [Zaire] 170 Ee 10.12S 25.23 E
Busanga [Zaire] 170 Dc 0.51S 22.04 E
Busanga Swamp 170 Ee 14.10S 25.50 E
Buşayrah 146 Ie 35.09N 40.26 E
Būsh 146 Dh 29.09N 31.08 E
Būshehr [3] 144 Hd 28.00N 52.00 E
Būshgān 146 Nh 28.48N 51.42 E
Bushimaie 158 Ji 6.02S 23.45 E
Bushmanland (EN) = Boesmanland 172 Be 29.30S 19.00 E
Busia 170 Fb 0.28N 34.06 E
Busigny 124 Fd 50.02N 3.28 E
Businga 170 Db 3.20N 20.53 E
Busira 158 Ii 0.15S 18.59 E
Busk 132 Dd 50.01N 24.37 E
Buskerud [2] 114 Bf 60.30N 9.10 E
Busko-Zdrój 120 Qf 50.28N 20.44 E
Busoga [3] 170 Fb 0.45N 33.30 E
Buşrá ash Shām 146 Gf 32.31N 36.29 E
Busselton 212 Df 33.39S 115.20 E
Bussum 122 Lb 52.16N 5.10 E
Bustamante, Bahía- 206 Gg 45.07S 66.27W
Buşteni 130 Id 45.24N 25.32 E
Busto Arsizio 128 Ce 45.37N 8.51 E
Buštyna 120 Th 48.03N 23.28 E
Busuanga 150 Hd 12.05N 120.05 E
Busu-Djanoa 170 Db 1.43N 21.23 E
Büsum 120 Eb 54.08N 8.51 E
Buta 160 Jh 2.48N 24.44 E
Butajira 168 Fd 8.08N 38.27 E
Buta Ranquil 206 Ge 37.03S 69.50W
Butare 170 Ec 2.36S 29.44 E
Butaritari Atoll 208 Id 3.03N 172.49 E
Bute, Island of- 118 Hf 55.50N 5.05W
Bute Inlet 188 Ca 50.37N 124.53W
Butembo 160 Jh 0.09N 29.17 E
Butera 128 Im 37.11N 14.11 E
Butere 170 Fb 0.13N 34.30 E
Butha Qi (Zalantum) 152 Lb 48.02N 122.42 E
Buthidaung 148 Id 20.52N 92.32 E
Butiá 206 Jd 30.07S 51.58W
Butler 184 He 40.51N 79.55W
Butser Hill 124 Bd 50.57N 0.59W
Butte 176 He 46.00N 112.32W
Butterworth [Mala.] 150 Df 5.25N 100.24 E
Butterworth [S.Afr.] 172 Df 32.23S 28.04 E
Button Bay 180 Ie 58.45N 94.25W
Butuan 142 Oi 8.57N 125.33 E
Butung, Palau- 140 Oj 5.00S 122.55 E
Buturlinovka 132 Ld 50.48N 40.45 E
Butzbach 124 Kd 50.26N 8.41 E
Bützow 120 Hc 53.50N 11.59 E
Buxtehude 120 Fc 53.28N 9.42 E
Buxton [Eng.-U.K.] 118 Lh 53.15N 1.55W
Buxton [N.C.-U.S.] 184 Jh 35.16N 75.32W
Buyo 166 Dd 6.16N 7.03W
Büyükanafarta 130 Ji 40.17N 26.22 E
Büyükçekmece 130 Lh 41.01N 28.34 E
Büyükkarıştıran 130 Kh 41.18N 27.32 E
Büyük Kemikli Burun 130 Ji 40.18N 26.14 E
Büyük Mahya 130 Kh 41.47N 27.36 E

Index Symbols

[1] Independent Nation
[2] State, Region
[3] District, County
[4] Municipality
[5] Colony, Dependency
Continent
Physical Region
Historical or Cultural Region
Mount, Mountain
Volcano
Hill
Mountains, Mountain Range
Hills, Escarpment
Plateau, Upland
Pass, Gap
Plain, Lowland
Delta
Salt Flat
Valley, Canyon
Crater, Cave
Karst Features
Depression
Polder
Desert, Dunes
Forest, Woods
Heath, Steppe
Oasis
Cape, Point
Coast, Beach
Cliff
Peninsula
Isthmus
Sandbank
Island
Atoll
Rock, Reef
Islands, Archipelago
Rocks, Reefs
Coral Reef
Well, Spring
Geyser
River, Stream
Waterfall, Rapids
River Mouth, Estuary
Lake
Salt Lake
Intermittent Lake
Reservoir
Swamp, Pond
Canal
Glacier
Ice Shelf, Pack Ice
Ocean
Sea
Gulf, Bay
Strait, Fjord
Lagoon
Bank
Seamount
Tablemount
Ridge
Shelf
Basin
Escarpment, Sea Scarp
Fracture
Trench, Abyss
National Park, Reserve
Point of Interest
Recreation Site
Cave, Cavern
Historic Site
Ruins
Wall, Walls
Church, Abbey
Temple
Scientific Station
Railway station
Airport
Port
Military installation
Lighthouse
Mine
Tunnel
Dam, Bridge

Büyük Menderes ⌇ 144 Cb 37.57N 28.58 E
Büyükorhan 130 Lj 39.45N 28.55 E
Buyun Shan 152 Lc 40.06N 122.42 E
Buzači, poluostrov- 110 Lf 45.00N 52.00 E
Buzan ⌇ 132 Pf 46.18N 49.06 E
Buzançais 122 Hh 46.53N 1.25 E
Buzancy 124 Ge 49.25N 4.57 E
Buzău 130 Jd 45.09N 26.50 E
Buzău [2] 130 Jd 45.09N 26.50 E
Buzău ⌇ 130 Kd 45.26N 27.44 E
Buzaymah 164 De 24.55N 22.02 E
Buzen 156 Be 33.37N 131.08 E
Buzet 128 He 45.24N 13.59 E
Búzhăn 146 Le 34.09N 47.05 E
Búzi 172 Ec 19.51 S 34.30 E
Búzi ⌇ 172 Ec 19.52 S 34.46 E
Buziaş 130 Hd 45.39N 21.36 E
Búzios, Ilha dos- 204 Jf 23.48S 45.08W
Bužora, gora- 120 Th 48.24N 23.15 E
Buzuluk 132 Rc 52.46N 52.17 E
Buzuluk [R.S.F.S.R.] 132 Rc 52.47N 52.16 E
Buzuluk [R.S.F.S.R.] ⌇ 132 Md 50.13N 42.12 E
Buzzards Bay 184 Le 41.33N 70.47W
Bwagaoia 219a Ad 10.42S 152.50 E
Byälven ⌇ 116 Ee 59.06N 12.54 E
Byam Martin 180 Ha 75.15N 104.15W
Byam Martin Channel 180 Ha 76.00N 105.00W
Bychava 120 Se 51.01N 22.32 E
Byczyna 120 Pf 51.07N 18.11 E
Bydgoszcz 112 He 53.08N 18.00 E
Bydgoszcz [2] 120 Nc 53.10N 18.00 E
Byelorussian SSR (EN)= Belorusskaja SSR [2] 132 Ce 53.50N 28.00 E
Bygdin 116 Cc 61.20N 8.35 E
Bygland 114 Bg 58.51N 7.51 E
Byglandsfjord 116 Bf 58.41N 7.48 E
Byglandsfjorden 116 Bf 58.50N 7.50 E
Byhov 136 De 53.31N 30.15 E
Byk ⌇ 130 Mc 46.55N 29.25 E
Bykovec 130 Lb 47.12N 28.18 E
Bykovo 132 Ne 49.47N 45.25 E
Bykovski 138 Mb 71.56N 129.05 E
Bylot 174 Lb 73.13N 78.34W
Byrd, Cape- 222 Qe 69.38S 76.07W
Byrdbreen 222 Df 71.35S 26.00 E
Byrd Glacier 222 Jg 80.15S 160.20 E
Byron, Cape- 208 Gg 28.39S 153.38 E
Byron Bay 212 Ke 28.39S 153.37 E
Byron Bay 180 Gc 68.55N 108.25W
Byrranga, gory- = Byrranga Mountains (EN) 140 Mb 75.00N 104.00 E
Byrranga Mountains (EN) = Byrranga, gory- 140 Mb 75.00N 104.00 E
Bystraja 138 Kf 52.40N 156.10 E
Bystrica 120 Se 51.40N 22.33 E
Bystřice 120 Lf 50.11N 15.30 E
Bystrovka 135 Jc 42.45N 75.43 E
Bystrzyca [Pol.] ⌇ 120 Se 51.16N 22.45 E
Bystrzyca [Pol.] ⌇ 120 Me 51.16N 16.54 E
Bystrzyca Kłodzka 120 Mf 50.19N 16.39 E
Bytantaj ⌇ 138 Ic 68.40N 134.50 E
Bytča 120 Vd 49.14N 18.35 E
Byten 120 Vd 52.49N 25.33 E
Bytom 120 So 50.22N 18.54 E
Bytów 120 Nb 54.11N 17.30 E
Byumba 170 Fc 1.35S 30.04 E
Byxelkrok 114 Dh 57.20N 17.00 E
Bzura ⌇ 120 Qd 52.23N 20.09 E
Bzyb ⌇ 132 Lh 43.12N 40.15 E

C

Cà, Sông- ⌇ 148 Le 18.40N 105.40 E
Caacupé 206 Ic 25.23S 57.09W
Čaadajevka 132 Nc 53.09N 45.56 E
Caaguazú 206 Ic 25.26S 56.02W
Caaguazú [3] 204 Eg 25.00S 55.45W
Caála 170 Ce 12.55S 15.35 E
Caapucú 204 Dh 26.13S 57.12W
Caarapó 204 Ef 22.38S 54.48W
Caatinga 202 Ig 17.10S 45.53W
Caatinga 198 Lf 9.00S 42.00W
Caatinga, Rio- ⌇ 204 Jc 17.10S 45.52W
Caazapá 206 Ic 26.09S 56.24W
Caazapá [3] 204 Dh 26.10S 56.00W
Cabaçal, Rio- ⌇ 204 Bb 16.00S 57.42W
Cabadbaran 150 Ie 9.10N 125.38 E
Cabaiguán 174 Hb 22.05N 79.30W
Caballeria, Cabo de- / Cavalleria, Cap de- 126 Qd 40.05N 4.05 E
Caballo Cocha 206 Dd 3.54S 70.32W
Caballo Reservoir 186 Cj 32.58N 107.18W
Cabañas 126 Jg 37.40N 3.00W
Cabanatuan 142 Oh 15.29N 120.58 E
Cabano 184 Mb 47.41N 68.54W
Čabar 128 Ie 45.36N 14.39 E
Cabeceira do Apa 204 Ef 22.01S 55.46W
Cabeceiras 204 Ib 15.48S 46.59W
Cabeceiras de Basto 126 Ec 41.31N 7.59W
Cabedelo 192 Lh 19.04N 95.50W
Cabeza, Arrecife- 192 Lh 19.04N 95.50W
Cabeza de Buey 126 Gf 38.43N 5.13W
Cabildo 126 Bn 38.29S 61.54W
Cabimas 200 Id 10.23N 71.28W
Cabinda 160 li 5.35S 12.13 E
Cabinda [3] 170 Bd 5.00S 12.30 E
Cabinet Mountains 186 Hb 48.08N 115.46W
Cabixi, Rio- → Branco, Rio- ⌇ 206 Ba 13.55S 60.10W
Cabo Bojador 162 Ed 26.08N 14.30W
Cabo Frio 200 Le 22.53S 42.01W
Cabo Gracias a Dios 194 Fd 14.59N 83.10W
Cabonga, Réservoir- 180 Jg 47.20N 76.35W
Caboolture 212 Ke 27.05S 152.50 E
Cabora Bassa, Dique de- 172 Ec 15.34S 32.42 E

Cabora Bassa, Lago de- = Cabora Bassa, Lake- (EN) 158 Kj 15.40S 31.40 E
Cabora Bassa, Lake- = Cabora Bassa, Lago de- 158 Kj 15.40S 31.40 E
Caborca 190 Bb 30.37N 112.06W
Cabot Strait 174 Ne 47.20N 59.30W
Cabourg 122 Fe 49.17N 0.08W
Cabo Verde=Cape Verde (EN) 160 Eg 16.00N 24.00W
Cabo Verde, Ilhas do=Cape Verde Islands (EN) 160 Eg 16.00N 24.10W
Cabra 126 Hg 37.28N 4.27W
Cabral, Serra do- 204 Jc 17.45S 44.22W
Cabras 128 Ck 39.56N 8.32 E
Cabras, Stagno di- 128 Ck 39.55N 8.30 E
Cabreira 126 Ec 41.39N 8.04W
Cabrera ⌇ 194 Md 19.38N 69.54W
Cabrera, Illa- / Cabrera, Isla- 126 Oe 39.09N 2.56 E
Cabrera, Isla- / Cabrera, Illa- 126 Oe 39.09N 2.56 E
Cabrera, Sierra de- 126 Fb 42.10N 6.25W
Cabrejas, Puerto de- 126 Jd 40.08N 2.25W
Cabri 188 Ka 50.37N 108.28W
Cabriel ⌇ 126 Ke 39.14N 1.03W
Cabrits, Capo- 197bc 15.53N 61.36W
Cabrits, Îlet- 197bc 14.23N 60.52W
Cabrón, Cabo- 194 Md 19.22N 69.54W
Čabulja 128 Lg 43.30N 17.35 E
Cabure 194 Mh 11.08N 69.38W
Cacacas, Islas- 196 Dg 10.22N 64.26W
Caçador 206 Jc 26.47S 51.00W
Čačak 130 Df 43.54N 20.21 E
Caçapava dó Sul 204 Jd 30.30S 53.30W
Caccamo 128 Hm 37.56N 13.40 E
Caccia, Capo- 128 Cj 40.34N 8.09 E
Cacequi 204 Ei 29.53S 54.49W
Cáceres [3] 126 Ge 39.40N 6.00W
Cáceres [Braz.] 200 Kg 16.04S 57.41W
Cáceres [Sp.] 126 Fe 39.29N 6.22W
Cáceres, Laguna- 204 Dd 18.56S 57.48W
Cachari 206 le 36.24S 59.32W
Cache Peak 188 le 42.11N 113.40W
Cacheu 166 Bc 12.10N 16.21W
Cachimbo 200 Kf 9.08S 55.10W
Cachimbo, Serra do- 198 Kf 8.30S 55.50W
Cachimo 170 Bd 8.20S 21.21 E
Cáchira 194 Kj 7.46N 73.03W
Cáchira, Rio- ⌇ 194 Kj 7.52N 73.40W
Cachoeira 202 Kf 12.36S 38.58W
Cachoeira Alta 204 Gd 18.48S 50.58W
Cachoeira de Goiás 204 Gc 16.44S 50.38W
Cachoeira do Arari 202 Id 1.01S 48.58W
Cachoeira do Sul 206 Jc 29.58S 52.54W
Cachoeira Dourada, Represa de- 202 Ig 18.30S 49.00W
Cachoeirinha 204 Gc 29.57S 51.05W
Cachoeiro de Itapemirim 202 Jh 20.51S 41.06W
Cacin ⌇ 204 Ee 21.50S 55.43W
Cacinbinho 130 Ce 44.38N 26.10 E
Cáciulaţi 170 Ce 10.08S 19.18 E
Cacolo 170 Ce 13.45S 15.05 E
Caconda 170 Bd 8.47S 13.21 E
Cacuaco 170 Be 14.29S 14.10 E
Caculé 202 Jf 14.30S 42.13W
Caculuvar ⌇ 170 Bf 16.46S 14.56 E
Cacuso 170 Cd 9.26S 15.45 E
Čadan 138 Ef 51.17N 91.40 E
Cadaqués 126 Pb 42.17N 3.17 E
Cadca 120 Og 49.26N 18.48 E
Caddo Lake 186 Ij 32.42N 94.01W
Cadereyta Jiménez 192 le 25.36N 100.00W
Cadi, Serra de- / Cadí, Sierra del- 126 Nb 42.17N 1.42 E
Cadí, Sierra del- / Cadi, Serra de- 126 Nb 42.17N 1.42 E
Cadibarrawirracanna, Lake- 212 He 28.50S 135.25 E
Cadibona, Colle di- 128 Cf 44.20N 8.22 E
Cadillac [Fr.] 122 Fj 44.38N 0.19W
Cadillac [Mi.-U.S.] 184 Cc 44.15N 85.24W
Cádiz 126 Fh 36.32N 6.18W
Cádiz [3] 126 Gh 36.52N 5.45W
Cádiz [Ca.-U.S.] 188 Gh 36.30N 5.45W
Cádiz [Ph.] 150 Hd 10.57N 123.18 E
Cádiz, Bahía de- 126 Fh 36.30N 6.16W
Cádiz, Golfo de- 110 Fh 36.50N 7.10W
Cadiz Lake 188 Hi 34.18N 115.24W
Cadore 128 Gd 46.30N 12.20 E
Cadwell 182 Dc 46.30N 116.41W
Čadyr-Lunga 132 Ff 46.04N 28.52 E
Caen 122 Ff 49.11N 0.21W
Caen, Campagne de- 122 Ff 49.05N 0.20W
Caernarfon 118 Ih 53.08N 4.16W
Caernarfon Bay 118 Ih 53.05N 4.30W
Caerphilly 118 Jj 51.35N 3.14W
Caetité 202 Jf 14.04S 42.29W
Cafayate 206 Fc 26.05S 65.58W
Cafelândia [Braz.] 204 Fc 16.40S 53.25W
Cafelândia [Braz.] 204 He 21.49S 49.35W
Cafundó, Serra do- 204 Hd 14.40S 48.23W
Čagan 136 Ne 50.30N 79.10 E
Cagan-Aman 132 Ne 47.32N 46.43 E
Cagan-Nur [Mong.] 152 Ea 49.40N 89.55 E
Cagan-Nur [Mong.] 152 la 50.25N 105.15 E
Cagan-Ula 152 Gb 49.35N 98.25 E
Cagatá, Arroyo- 204 Df 23.26S 56.36W
Cagayan de Oro 142 Oh 8.29N 124.39 E
Cagayan Islands 150 Ge 9.40N 121.16 E
Cagayan Sulu 150 Ge 7.01N 118.30 E
Čagda 138 Ie 58.42N 130.37 E
Cageri 132 Mh 42.39N 42.42 E

Çağiş 130 Lj 39.30N 28.01 E
Cagli 128 Gg 43.33N 12.39 E
Cagliari 112 Dh 39.13N 9.07 E
Cagliari, Golfo di- 128 Dk 39.10N 9.10 E
Cagliari, Stagno di- 128 Dk 39.15N 9.05 E
Cagnes-sur-Mer 122 Nk 43.40N 7.09 E
Čagoda 114 Ig 59.12N 35.13 E
Čagodošča ⌇ 114 Ig 58.58N 36.37 E
Caguas 190 Ke 18.14N 66.02W
Çagyl 170 Bf 40.43N 55.25 E
Cahama 170 Bf 16.16S 14.17 E
Caha Mountains/An Cheacha 118 Dj 51.45N 9.45W
Caher/An Chathair 118 Fi 52.22N 7.55W
Cahersiveen/Cathair Saidhbhín 118 Cj 51.57N 10.13W
Cahore Point/Rinn Chathóir 118 Gi 52.34N 6.11W
Cahors 122 Hj 44.26N 1.26 E
Cai, Rio- ⌇ 204 Gi 29.56S 51.16W
Caia 172 Fc 17.49S 35.20 E
Caia ⌇ 126 Ef 38.50N 7.05W
Caiabis, Serra dos- 202 Ef 11.40S 56.30W
Caiapó, Rio- ⌇ 204 Gb 15.49S 51.53W
Caiapó, Serra do- 198 Kg 17.00S 52.00W
Caiapônia 204 Gc 16.57S 51.49W
Caibarién 190 Id 22.31N 79.28W
Caiçara 204 Gc 15.34S 50.12W
Caicara 202 Eb 7.37N 66.10W
Caicara de Maturin 196 Fn 9.49N 63.36W
Caicó 202 Ke 6.27S 37.06W
Caicos Bank (EN) 190 Jd 21.35N 71.55W
Caicos Islands 174 Lg 21.45N 71.35W
Caicos Passage 190 Jd 21.35N 72.30W
Caille Island 197p Bb 12.17N 61.35W
Caimanera 194 Jd 19.59N 75.09W
Caine, Rio- ⌇ 202 Bg 18.23S 65.21W
Cai Nuoc 148 Lg 8.56N 105.01 E
Caird Coast 222 Af 76.00S 24.30W
Cairngorm Mountains 118 Jd 57.06N 3.30W
Cairns 210 Ff 16.55S 145.46 E
Cairo [Ga.-U.S.] 182 lg 30.53N 84.12W
Cairo [Il.-U.S.] 182 Jf 37.00N 89.11W
Cairo (EN)=Al Qāhirah 160 Ke 30.03N 31.15 E
Cairo Montenotte 128 Cf 44.24N 8.16 E
Caiseal/Cashel 118 Fi 52.31N 7.53W
Caisleán an Bharraigh/ Castlebar 118 Dh 53.52N 9.17W
Caister-on-Sea 124 Db 52.40N 1.45 E
Caiundo 170 Cf 15.42S 17.27 E
Caiúva, Lagoa- 204 Ba 32.24S 52.30W
Caiyuanzhen → Shengsi 154 Gi 30.42N 122.29 E
Caizi Hu 154 Di 30.48N 117.05 E
Čaja ⌇ 138 De 58.17N 92.43 E
Cajabamba 202 Cd 7.58S 77.59W
Cajamarca 202 Ce 7.10S 78.31W
Cajamarca [3] 204 Ce 6.15S 78.50W
Cajapió 202 Id 2.58S 44.48W
Cajatambo 202 Cf 10.29S 77.02W
Cajkovski 136 Fd 56.47N 54.09 E
Çakırgöl Dağı 146 Hb 40.34N 39.42 E
Cakmak 146 Fd 37.37N 34.19 E
Çakmak Dağı 146 Jc 39.46N 42.12 E
Čakor 130 Df 42.40N 20.02 E
Čakovec 128 Kd 46.23N 16.26 E
Cakrani 130 Cd 40.36N 19.37 E
Çal 146 Cc 38.05N 29.24 E
Cal, Rio de la- ⌇ 204 Cc 17.27S 58.15W
Calabar 160 Hh 4.57N 8.19 E
Calabozo 202 Eb 8.56N 67.26W
Calabozo, Ensenada de- 194 Lh 11.30N 71.45W
Calabria [2] 128 Kl 39.00N 16.30 E
Calaburras, Punta de- 126 Hh 36.30N 4.38W
Calacoto 202 Eg 17.18S 68.39W
Calacuccia 122a Ba 42.20N 9.01 E
Calaf 126 Nc 41.44N 1.31 E
Calafat 130 Ff 43.59N 22.56 E
Calafate 206 Ik 50.20S 72.16W
Cala Figuera, Cabo de- / Cala Figuera Cap de- 126 Oe 39.22N 2.46 E
Cala Figuera, Cap de- / Cala Figuera, Cabo de- 126 Oe 39.22N 2.46 E
Calagua Islands 150 Hd 14.27N 122.55 E
Calahorra 126 Kb 42.18N 1.58W
Calai 170 Cf 17.50S 19.20 E
Calais [Fr.] 112 Ge 50.57N 1.51 E
Calais [Me.-U.S.] 184 Nb 45.11N 67.17W
Calais, Pas de-=Dover, Strait of- (EN) 110 Ge 51.00N 1.30 E
Calakmul 192 Oh 18.05N 89.55W
Calalaste, Sierra de- 206 Gc 25.30S 67.30W
Calama 200 Ih 22.28S 68.56W
Calamar 194 Ih 10.14N 74.56W
Calamian Group 150 Nh 12.00N 120.00 E
Calamocha 126 Kd 40.55N 1.18W
Cälan 130 Fd 45.44N 22.59 E
Calanda 126 Ld 40.56N 0.14W
Calandula 160 li 9.06S 15.58 E
Calang 150 Cf 4.30N 95.40 E
Calangiánus 128 Dj 40.56N 9.11 E
Calapan 142 Oh 13.25N 121.10 E
Calar Alto 126 Jg 37.13N 2.25W
Cälärasi 130 Ke 44.12N 27.20 E
Cälärasi [2] 130 Ke 44.15N 27.00 E
Cala Ratjada 126 Pe 39.42N 3.25 E
Cala del Mundo 128 Gm 38.31N 2.28W
Calatafimi 128 Gm 37.55N 12.52 E
Calatañazor 126 Jc 41.42N 2.49W
Calatayud 126 Kc 41.21N 1.38W
Calatrava, Campo de- 126 If 38.50N 4.15W
Calavà, Capo- 128 Il 38.10N 14.55 E
Calavon ⌇ 122 Lk 43.53N 5.25 E
Calayan 150 Hc 19.20N 121.27 E
Calbayog 142 Oh 12.04N 124.36 E
Ca Mau, Mui = Ca Mau Point (EN) 140 Mi 8.38N 104.44 E

Calçoene 202 Hc 2.30N 50.57W
Calcutta 142 Kg 22.32N 88.22 E
Caldaro / Kaltern 128 Fd 46.25N 11.14 E
Caldas [3] 202 Dk 5.15N 75.30W
Caldas da Rainha 126 Ce 39.24N 9.08W
Caldas Novas 204 Hc 17.45S 48.38W
Calder ⌇ 118 Lh 53.44N 1.21W
Caldera 206 Fc 27.04S 70.50W
Calderina, Sierra de la- 126 le 39.19N 3.48W
Caldes de Montbui 126 Oc 41.38N 2.10 E
Caldwell 182 Gf 39.44N 81.32W
Câleanu, Vîrful- 130 Fd 45.19N 22.32 E
Caledon 172 Bf 34.12S 19.23 E
Caledon ⌇ 158 Jl 30.32S 26.05 E
Caledonia [Blz.] 194 Cd 18.14N 88.29W
Caledonia [Mn.-U.S.] 186 Ke 43.38N 91.29W
Caledonian Canal 118 Id 57.20N 4.30W
Calella 126 Oc 41.37N 2.40 E
Caleta Olivia 206 Gg 46.26S 67.32W
Calexico 188 Hj 32.40N 115.30W
Çalgal Dağı 146 Mc 39.06N 38.05 E
Calgary 176 Hd 51.03N 114.05W
Calhoun 184 Eh 34.30N 84.57W
Cali 200 le 3.27N 76.31W
Calicut (Kozhikode) 142 Jh 11.19N 75.46 E
Caliente 188 Gg 37.37N 114.31W
California [2] 182 Dd 37.30N 119.30W
California, Gulf of- (EN) 174 Hg 28.00N 112.00W
California, Gulf of- (EN)= California, Golfo de- 174 Hg 28.00N 112.00W
Cälimän, Munţii- 130 Ib 47.07N 25.03 E
Cälimänesti 130 Hd 45.14N 24.20 E
Calimere, Point- 148 Ff 10.18N 79.52 E
Calingasta 206 Gd 31.19S 69.25W
Calipatria 188 Gb 33.08N 115.31W
Calispell Peak 188 Gb 48.26N 117.30W
Calitri 128 Jj 40.54N 15.26 E
Calitzdorp 172 Df 33.33S 21.42 E
Caliviny 197p Bb 12.01N 61.43W
Calixtlahuaca 192 Jh 19.15N 99.45W
Calka 132 Mi 41.35N 44.05 E
Calkini 192 Ng 20.22N 90.03W
Callabonna, Lake- 212 le 29.45S 140.05 E
Callaghan, Mount- 188 Gg 39.42N 116.57W
Callain/Callan 118 Fi 52.33N 7.23W
Callan/Callainn 118 Fi 52.33N 7.23W
Callander [Ont.-Can.] 184 Ha 46.13N 79.23W
Callander [Scot.-U.K.] 118 le 56.15N 4.13W
Callao 200 lg 12.02S 77.05W
Callao [3] 202 Cf 2.04S 77.09W
Calliaqua 197n Ba 13.08N 61.12W
Callosa de Ensariá / Callosa d'eu Sarriá 126 Lf 38.39N 0.07W
Callosa de Segura 126 Lf 38.08N 0.52W
Callosa d'eu Sarriá / Callosa de Ensariá 126 Lf 38.39N 0.07W
Calmalli 192 Cc 28.14N 113.33W
Câlmäţui [Rom.] ⌇ 130 Kd 44.50N 27.50 E
Câlmäţui [Rom.] ⌇ 130 If 43.46N 25.10 E
Calonne ⌇ 124 Ce 49.17N 0.12 E
Calore ⌇ 128 li 41.11N 14.28 E
Čalovo 126 Ni 47.52N 17.47 E
Calp / Calpe 126 Mf 38.39N 0.03 E
Calpe / Calp 126 Mf 38.39N 0.03 E
Caltabellotta 128 Hm 37.34N 13.13 E
Caltagirone 128 Im 37.14N 14.31 E
Caltanissetta 128 Im 37.29N 14.04 E
Caltilibük 130 Lj 39.57N 28.36 E
Čaltyr 132 Le 47.17N 39.29 E
Caluago 170 Cd 8.21S 19.40 E
Calucinga 170 Ce 11.19S 16.13 E
Câlugareni 130 le 44.11N 25.59 E
Calulo 170 Bd 9.59S 14.54 E
Caluquembe 170 Be 13.46S 14.41 E
Calvados [2] 122 Fe 49.10N 0.30W
Calvados, Côte du- 122 Fe 49.22N 0.30W
Calvert Island 180 Ee 51.35N 128.00W
Calvert River ⌇ 212 Hc 16.17S 137.44 E
Calvi 122a Aa 42.34N 8.45 E
Calvillo 192 Hg 21.51N 102.43W
Calvinia 160 ll 31.25S 19.45 E
Calvitero 126 Gd 40.20N 5.43W
Cam ⌇ 118 Ni 52.21N 0.15 E
Camabatela 170 Cd 8.13S 15.23 E
Camacá 202 Kg 15.24S 39.30W
Camacupa 170 Ce 12.01S 17.22 E
Camaguán 196 Ch 8.06N 67.36W
Camagüey 176 Kg 21.23N 77.55W
Camagüey [3] 194 Ic 21.30N 78.00W
Camagüey, Archipiélago de- 190 Id 22.18N 78.00W
Camaiore 128 Eg 43.56N 10.18 E
Camajuani 194 Hb 22.26N 79.45W
Camamu 202 Kf 13.57S 39.07W
Camaná 202 Dg 16.37S 72.42W
Camanongue 170 Ce 11.27S 20.22 E
Camapuã 204 Fb 19.30S 54.05W
Camapuã, Sertão de- 198 Kg 19.00S 53.30W
Camaquã 204 Gj 30.51S 51.49W
Camaquã, Rio- ⌇ 204 Gj 31.17S 51.47W
Camarat, Cap- 122 Mk 43.12N 6.41 E
Camargo [Bol.] 206 Gb 20.39S 65.13W
Camargo [Sp.] 126 la 43.24N 3.54W
Camargos, Represa- 204 Je 21.20S 44.30W
Camargue 122 Kk 43.31N 4.34 E
Camariñas 126 Ca 43.07N 9.10W
Camarón, Cabo- 190 Ge 16.00N 85.04W
Camarones 206 Gf 44.48S 65.42W
Camarones, Bahia- 206 Gf 44.45S 65.34W
Camas [Wa.-U.S.] 188 Dd 45.35N 122.24W
Camas [Wa.-U.S.] 148 Lg 9.11N 105.08 E
Ca Mau 148 Lg 9.11N 105.08 E
Ca Mau, Mui = Ca Mau Point (EN) 140 Mi 8.38N 104.44 E

Ca Mau Point (EN)=Ca Mau, Mui- 140 Mi 8.38N 104.44 E
Cambados 126 Db 42.30N 8.48W
Camberg 124 Bc 50.18N 8.16 E
Camberley 124 Bc 51.21N 0.44W
Cambo 170 Cg 7.40S 17.17 E
Cambodia (EN) = Kampuchea 142 Mh 13.00N 105.00 E
Camboriú 206 Ek 27.04S 48.37W
Cambo-les-Bains 122 Ek 43.22N 1.24 E
Camboriú, Ponta- 204 lg 25.10S 47.55W
Cambrai 122 Jd 50.10N 3.14 E
Cambremer 124 Ce 49.09N 0.03 E
Cambrésis 124 Fd 50.15N 3.05 E
Cambrian Mountains 110 Fe 52.35N 3.35W
Cambridge 118 Ni 52.25N 0.05W
Cambridge [Eng.-U.K.] 118 Ni 52.12N 0.07 E
Cambridge [Blz.] 194 Cd 18.14N 88.29W
Cambridge [Ma.-U.S.] 184 Ld 42.22N 71.06W
Cambridge [Md.-U.S.] 184 If 38.34N 76.04W
Cambridge [Mn.-U.S.] 186 Jd 45.31N 93.14W
Cambridge [N.Z.] 218 Fj 37.53S 175.28 E
Cambridge [Oh.-U.S.] 184 Ge 40.02N 81.36W
Cambridge Airport 126 Ce 52.10N 0.08 E
Cambridge Bay 176 Ic 69.03N 105.05W
Cambridge Gulf 212 Fb 14.55S 128.15 E
Cambridgeshire [3] 118 Mi 52.25N 0.05W
Cambutal, Cerro- 194 Gj 7.16N 80.36W
Camden [Al.-U.S.] 182 Fg 32.00N 87.17W
Camden [Ar.-U.S.] 182 le 33.35N 92.50W
Camden [N.J.-U.S.] 184 Jf 39.57N 75.07W
Camden [S.C.-U.S.] 184 Gh 34.16N 80.36W
Camden [Tn.-U.S.] 184 Ca 36.04N 88.06W
Camden Bay 178 Kb 70.00N 145.00W
Camdenton 182 Jf 38.00N 92.45W
Camel ⌇ 118 Ik 50.33N 4.55W
Çameli 146 Cd 37.05N 29.20 E
Camerino 128 Hg 43.08N 13.04 E
Cameron 180 Ha 76.15N 104.00W
Cameron [Az.-U.S.] 188 Jl 35.51N 111.25W
Cameron [La.-U.S.] 182 Jl 29.48N 93.19W
Cameron [Mo.-U.S.] 186 lg 39.44N 94.14W
Cameron [Tx.-U.S.] 186 Hk 30.51N 96.59W
Cameron [Wi.-U.S.] 186 Kd 45.25N 91.44W
Cameron Hills 180 Fe 60.00N 118.00W
Cameron Mountains 218 Bf 46.00S 166.55 E
Cameroon [1] 160 lh 6.00N 12.00 E
Cameroon Mountain 158 Hh 4.12N 9.11 E
Camerota 128 Jj 40.02N 15.22 E
Cameroun = Cameroon (EN) 160 lh 6.00N 12.00 E
Cametá 202 Id 2.15S 49.30W
Camiguin [Phil.] 150 He 9.11N 124.42 E
Camiguin [Phil.] 150 Hc 18.56N 121.55 E
Camiling 150 Hc 15.42N 120.24 E
Camilla 184 Ej 31.14N 84.12W
Caminha 126 Dc 41.52N 8.50W
Camiranga 202 Id 1.48S 46.17W
Camissombo 170 Bd 8.10S 20.39 E
Camoapa 194 Eg 12.23N 85.31W
Camocim 200 Lf 2.54S 40.50W
Camonica, Val- 128 Ed 46.00N 10.20 E
Camooweal 212 Hc 19.55S 138.07 E
Camopi 202 Hc 3.13N 52.20W
Camorta 148 lg 8.08N 93.30 E
Camotes Islands 150 Hd 11.00N 124.45 E
Campagne-lès-Hesdin 124 Dd 50.24N 1.52 E
Campana 204 Cl 34.10S 58.57W
Campana, Isla- 206 Eg 48.20S 75.15W
Campanário 126 Gf 38.52N 5.37W
Campania [2] 128 li 41.00N 14.30 E
Campaniquiz, Cerros- 202 Cd 4.30S 77.40W
Campbell, Cape- 218 Ee 41.44S 174.16 E
Campbell Island 218 Cc 52.30S 169.10 E
Campbell Plateau (EN) 208 lj 51.00S 170.00 E
Campbell River 180 Ef 50.01N 125.15W
Campbellsville 184 Eg 37.21N 85.20W
Campbellton 180 Kg 48.00N 66.40W
Campbelltown, Sydney- 212 Kf 34.04S 150.49 E
Campbeltown 118 Hf 55.26N 5.36W
Campeche 176 Jh 19.51N 90.32W
Campeche [2] 190 Fe 19.00N 90.30W
Campeche, Bahía de- = Campeche, Gulf of- (EN) 174 Jg 20.00N 94.00W
Campeche, Gulf of- (EN) = Campeche, Bahía de- 174 Jg 20.00N 94.00W
Campeche Bank (EN) 190 Fd 22.00N 90.00W
Campechuela 194 Ic 20.14N 77.17W
Camperdown 212 le 38.14S 143.09 E
Campidano 128 Ck 39.30N 8.45 E
Campina Grande 200 Mf 7.13S 35.53W
Campinas 198 Lh 22.54S 47.05W
Campina Verde 204 Hd 19.31S 49.28W
Campine/Kempen 124 Lc 51.10N 5.20 E
Campinorte 204 Hb 14.20S 49.08W
Campione d'Italia 128 Ce 45.59N 8.59 E
Campo 166 Ge 2.22N 9.49 E
Campo Alegre 196 Bh 9.15N 68.25W
Campo Alegre de Goiás 204 lc 17.36S 47.46W
Campobasso 128 li 41.34N 14.39 E
Campo Belo 204 Je 20.53S 45.16W
Campo de Criptana 126 Je 39.24N 3.07W
Campo de la Cruz 194 Jh 10.23N 74.52W
Campo del Cielo 206 Hc 27.53S 61.49W
Campo Florido 204 Hd 19.46S 48.34W
Campo Formoso 202 Jf 10.31S 40.20W
Campo Gallo 206 Hc 26.35S 62.50W
Campo Garay 204 Hi 29.41S 61.37W
Campo Grande [Arg.] 204 Eh 27.13S 54.58W
Campo Grande [Braz.] 200 Kh 20.27S 54.37W
Campo Largo [Arg.] 206 Hc 26.48S 60.50W
Campo Largo [Braz.] 204 Hf 25.26S 49.32W
Campo Maior [Braz.] 202 Jd 4.49S 42.10W
Campo Maior [Port.] 126 Ee 39.01N 7.04W
Campomarino 128 Jh 41.57N 15.02 E
Campo Mourão 206 Jb 24.03S 52.22W

Index Symbols

[1] Independent Nation	Historical or Cultural Region	Pass, Gap
[2] State, Region	Mount, Mountain	Plain, Lowland
[3] District, County	Volcano	Delta
[4] Municipality	Hill	Salt Flat
[5] Colony, Dependency	Mountains, Mountain Range	Valley, Canyon
Continent	Hills, Escarpment	Crater, Cave
Physical Region	Plateau, Upland	Karst Features

Depression	Coast, Beach	Rock, Reef
Polder	Cliff	Islands, Archipelago
Desert, Dunes	Peninsula	Rocks, Reefs
Forest, Woods	Isthmus	Coral Reef
Heath, Steppe	Sandbank	Well, Spring
Oasis	Island	Geyser
Cape, Point	Atoll	River, Stream

Waterfall, Rapids	Canal	Lagoon
River Mouth, Estuary	Glacier	Bank
Lake	Ice Shelf, Pack Ice	Seamount
Salt Lake	Ocean	Tablemount
Intermittent Lake	Sea	Ridge
Reservoir	Gulf, Bay	Shelf
Swamp, Pond	Strait, Fjord	Basin

Escarpment, Sea Scarp	Historic Site	Airport
Fracture	Ruins	Port
Trench, Abyss	Wall, Walls	Military installation
National Park, Reserve	Church, Abbey	Lighthouse
Point of Interest	Temple	Mine
Recreation Site	Scientific Station	Tunnel
Cave, Cavern	Railway station	Dam, Bridge

Campos	200	Lh	21.45S	41.18W
Campos [Braz.]	198	Kh	21.00S	51.00W
Campos [Braz.]	198	Lg	15.00S	44.30W
Campos, Laguna-	204	Be	20.50S	61.31W
Campos, Tierra de-	126	Hb	42.10N	4.50W
Campos Altos	204	Id	19.41S	46.10W
Campos Belos	204	Ia	13.03S	46.53W
Campos do Jordão	204	Jf	22.44S	45.35W
Campos Novos	204	Gh	27.24S	51.12W
Campos Sales	202	Je	7.04S	40.23W
Campo Tures / Sand in Taufers	128	Fd	46.55N	11.57 E
Camp Verde	182	Ee	34.34N	111.51W
Cam Ranh	148	Lf	11.54N	109.13 E
Camrose	180	Gf	53.01N	112.50W
Camseil	180	Fc	65.40N	118.07W
Camsell Portage	180	Ge	59.38N	109.42W
Çan	146	Bb	40.02N	27.03 E
Canaan [Ct.-U.S.]	184	Kd	42.02N	73.20W
Canaan [Trin.]	196	Fg	11.09N	60.49W
Canaan Mountain	188	Jh	37.45N	111.51W
Cana Brava, Ribeirão-	204	Ic	16.35S	46.34W
Cana Brava, Rio- [Braz.]	204	Ib	14.40S	47.07W
Cana Brava, Rio- [Braz.]	204	Ha	12.12S	48.40W
Cana Brava, Rio- [Braz.]	204	Ha	13.11S	48.11W
Canada	176	Jc	60.00N	95.00W
Cañada	126	Fb	42.50N	6.05W
Canada Basin (EN)	224	Ad	80.00N	145.00W
Cañada de Gómez	206	Hd	32.49S	61.24W
Canadian	186	Fi	35.55N	100.23W
Canadian River	174	Jf	35.27N	95.03W
Canaguá, Rio-	194	Mj	7.57N	69.36W
Canaima	202	Fb	6.07N	62.55W
Canakkale bogazı = Dardanelles (EN)	110	Ig	40.15N	26.25 E
Canala	219b	Be	21.32S	165.57 E
Canandaigua	184	Id	42.53N	77.19W
Cananea	190	Bb	30.57N	110.18W
Cananéia	204	Ig	25.01S	47.57W
Canapolis	204	Hd	18.44S	49.13W
Canarias, Islas-=Canary Islands (EN)	160	Ff	28.00N	15.30W
Canarias, Islas-=Canary Islands (EN)	158	Ff	28.00N	15.30W
Canaries	197k	Ab	13.55N	61.04W
Canaronero, Laguna-	192	Ff	23.00N	106.15W
Canarreos, Archipiélago de los-	190	Hd	21.50N	82.30W
Canary Basin (EN)	106	Dg	30.00N	25.00W
Canary Islands (EN)= Canarias, Islas-	160	Ff	28.00N	15.30W
Canary Islands (EN)= Canarias, Islas-	158	Ff	28.00N	15.30W
Cañas [C.R.]	194	Eh	10.25N	85.07W
Cañas [Pan.]	194	Gj	7.27N	80.16W
Canastra, Serra da-	204	Ie	20.00S	46.20W
Canatlán	192	Ge	24.31N	104.47W
Cañaveral	126	Fe	39.47N	6.23W
Canaveral, Cape-	174	Kg	28.30N	80.35W
Canavese	128	Be	45.20N	7.40 E
Canavieiras	202	Kg	15.39S	38.57W
Canazei	128	Fd	46.28N	11.46 E
Canberra	210	Fh	35.17S	149.08 E
Canby [Mn.-U.S.]	186	Hd	44.43N	96.16W
Canby [Or.-U.S.]	188	Dd	45.16N	122.42W
Cance	122	Ki	45.12N	4.48 E
Canche	122	Hd	50.31N	1.39 E
Cancon	122	Gj	44.32N	0.37 E
Cancún	190	Gd	21.05N	86.46W
Cancún, Isla-	192	Pg	21.05N	86.46W
Çandarli	130	Jk	38.56N	26.56 E
Çandarli Körfezi	130	Jk	38.52N	26.55 E
Candé	122	Eg	47.34N	1.02W
Candela	192	Id	26.50N	100.40W
Candelaria	192	Nh	18.18N	91.21W
Candelaria, Cerro-	192	Hf	23.25N	103.43W
Candelaria, Rio- [Bol.]	204	Cc	17.17S	58.39W
Candelaria, Rio- [Mex.]	192	Nh	18.38N	91.15W
Candelaro	128	Ji	41.34N	15.53 E
Cândido de Abreu	204	Gg	24.35S	51.20W
Cândido Mendes	202	Id	1.27S	45.43W
Candlemas Islands	222	Ad	57.03S	26.40W
Candói	204	Fg	25.43S	52.11W
Çandyr	132	Sj	38.13N	55.44 E
Canela	206	Jc	29.22S	50.50W
Canelli	128	Cf	44.43N	8.17 E
Canelones	204	Dl	34.32S	56.17W
Canelones	204	El	34.35S	56.00W
Canendiyu	204	Eg	24.20S	55.00W
Cañete [Chile]	206	Fe	37.48S	73.24W
Cañete [Sp.]	126	Kd	40.03N	1.39W
Cangallo	204	Cm	37.13S	58.42W
Cangamba	170	Ce	13.44S	19.53 E
Cangas	126	Db	42.16N	8.47W
Cangas de Narcea	126	Fa	43.11N	6.33W
Cangas de Onís	126	Ga	43.21N	5.07W
Cangola	170	Cd	7.58S	15.53 E
Cangombe	170	Ce	14.24S	19.59 E
Cangshan (Bianzhuang)	154	Eg	34.51N	118.03 E
Canguçu	204	Fj	31.24S	52.41W
Canguçu, Serra do-	204	Fj	31.20S	52.40W
Canguinha	204	Eb	14.42S	55.40W
Cangumbe	170	Ce	12.00S	19.09 E
Cangyuan	152	Gg	23.10N	99.15 E
Cangzhou	152	Kd	38.14N	116.58 E
Cani, Iles-	128	Em	37.21N	10.07 E
Caniapiscau	174	Md	57.40N	69.30W
Caniapiscau, Lac-	180	Kf	54.00N	70.10W
Canicatti	128	Hm	37.21N	13.51 E
Canigou	122	Il	42.31N	2.27 E
Canik Dağlari	146	Gb	40.50N	37.10 E
Canim Lake	188	Ea	51.52N	120.45W
Canindé	202	Kd	4.22S	39.19W
Canindé, Rio-	202	Je	6.15S	42.52W
Cañitas de Felipe Pescador	192	Hf	23.36N	102.43W
Çankaya, Ankara-	146	Ec	39.56N	32.52 E
Çankırı	144	Da	40.36N	33.37 E
Canna	118	Gd	57.03N	6.33W
Cannac	219a	Ac	9.15S	153.29 E
Çannakale	144	Ca	40.09N	26.24 E
Cannanore	148	Ff	11.51N	75.22 E
Cannanore Islands	148	Ef	10.05N	72.10 E
Cannes	122	Nk	43.33N	7.01 E
Cannich	118	Id	57.20N	4.45W
Canning Basin	212	Ed	20.10S	123.00 E
Cannobio	128	Cd	46.04N	8.42 E
Cannock	118	Ki	52.42N	2.01W
Cannonball River	186	Fc	46.26N	100.38W
Cann River	212	Jg	37.34S	149.10 E
Caño, Isla del-	194	Fi	8.44N	83.53W
Canoas	206	Jc	29.56S	51.11W
Canoas, Punta-	192	Bc	29.25N	115.10W
Canoas, Rio-	206	Jc	27.36S	51.25W
Canoeiros	202	Ig	18.02S	45.31W
Canoinhas	204	Gh	26.10S	50.24W
Canoinhas, Rio-	204	Gh	26.07S	50.22W
Cañoles / Cànyoles	126	Le	39.02N	0.29W
Canon City	182	Fd	38.27N	105.14W
Canon Fiord	180	Ja	80.15N	83.00W
Canonnier, Pointe du-	197b	Ab	18.04N	63.10W
Canora	180	Hf	51.37N	102.26W
Canosa di Puglia	128	Ki	41.13N	16.04 E
Canouan Island	196	Ff	12.43N	61.20W
Canourgue, La-	122	Jj	44.25N	3.13 E
Canso, Strait of -	180	Lg	45.35N	61.23W
Canta	202	Cf	11.25S	76.38W
Cantabria	126	Ha	43.15N	4.00W
Cantabrian Mountains (EN) =Cantábrica, Cordillera-	110	Fg	43.00N	5.00W
Cantábrica, Cordillera-= Cantabrian Mountains (EN)	110	Fg	43.00N	5.00W
Cantábrico, Mar-	126	Ha	44.00N	4.00W
Cantal	122	Ii	45.05N	2.40 E
Cantal	110	Gf	45.10N	2.50 E
Cantalejo	126	Ic	41.15N	3.55W
Cantanhede	126	Dd	40.21N	8.36W
Cantaura	202	Fb	9.19N	64.21W
Cantavieja	126	Ld	40.32N	0.24W
Cantavir	130	Cd	45.55N	19.46 E
Canterbury	118	Oj	51.17N	1.05 E
Canterbury	218	De	43.30S	171.50 E
Canterbury Bight	208	Ii	44.10S	172.00 E
Can Tho	142	Mi	10.02N	105.47 E
Cantiles, Cayo-	194	Fc	21.36N	82.02W
Canto do Buriti	202	Je	8.07S	42.58W
Canton [Il.-U.S.]	186	Kf	40.33N	90.02W
Canton [Mo.-U.S.]	186	Kf	40.08N	91.32W
Canton [Ms.-U.S.]	186	Kj	32.37N	90.02W
Canton [N.Y.-U.S.]	184	Jc	44.37N	75.11W
Canton [Oh.-U.S.]	182	Kc	40.48N	81.23W
Canton [S.D.-U.S.]	186	He	43.18N	96.35W
Canton (EN)=Guangzhou	142	Ng	23.07N	113.18 E
Canton Atoll	208	Je	2.50S	171.41W
Cantù	128	De	45.44N	9.08 E
Cantwell	178	Jd	63.23N	148.57W
Cañuelas	204	Cl	35.03S	58.44W
Canumã, Rio-	198	Kf	3.55S	59.10W
Canutama	202	Fe	6.32S	64.20W
Canvey Island	124	Cc	51.31N	0.36 E
Čany	138	Ce	55.19N	76.56 E
Čany, ozero-	140	Jd	54.50N	77.30 E
Cany-Barville	124	Ce	49.47N	0.38 E
Cànyoles / Cañoles	126	Le	39.02N	0.29W
Canyon [Mn.-U.S.]	186	Jc	47.02N	92.29W
Canyon [Tx.-U.S.]	182	Ge	34.59N	101.55W
Canyon [Wy.-U.S.]	188	Jd	44.44N	110.30W
Canyon Lake	186	Gl	29.52N	98.16W
Canzar	170	Dd	7.36S	21.33 E
Cao Bang	148	Ld	22.40N	106.15 E
Caojiahe → Qichun	154	Ci	30.15N	115.26 E
Caojian	152	Gf	25.38N	99.07 E
Caombo	170	Cd	8.42S	16.33 E
Caorle	128	Ge	45.36N	12.53 E
Caoxian	154	Cg	34.49N	115.33 E
Caozhou → Heze	152	Kd	35.14N	115.28 E
Capaccio	128	Jj	40.25N	15.05 E
Čapajev	136	Fe	50.14N	51.08 E
Čapajevsk	136	Ee	53.01N	49.36 E
Capanaparo, Rio-	202	Eb	7.01N	67.07W
Capanema [Braz.]	204	Fg	25.40S	53.48W
Capanema [Braz.]	202	Id	1.12S	47.11W
Capanema, Serra do-	204	Fh	26.05S	53.16W
Capão Alto	204	Gh	27.56S	50.30W
Capão Bonito	204	Hf	24.01S	48.20W
Capão Doce, Morro do-	204	Gh	26.43S	51.25W
Caparo, Rio-	194	Lj	7.46N	70.23W
Capatárida	194	Lh	11.11N	70.37W
Capbreton	122	Ek	43.38N	1.26W
Cap Breton Canyon (EN)	122	Ek	43.40N	1.50W
Čapčama, pereval-	135	Hd	41.34N	70.50 E
Cap-Chat	184	Na	49.06N	66.42W
Capcir	122	Il	42.45N	2.10 E
Cap-de-la-Madeleine	180	Kg	46.22N	72.32W
Capdenac-Gare	122	Ij	44.34N	2.05 E
Cape Barren Island	212	Jh	40.25S	148.10 E
Cape Basin (EN)	106	Em	37.00S	7.00 E
Cape Breton Island	174	Me	46.00N	60.30W
Cape Charles	184	Jg	37.17N	76.00W
Cape Coast	160	Gh	5.06N	1.15W
Cape Cod Bay	184	Le	41.52N	70.22W
Cape Coral	184	Gl	26.33N	81.58W
Cape Dorset	176	Lc	64.14N	76.32W
Cape Dyer	176	Mc	66.30N	61.18W
Cape Fear River	184	Ii	33.53N	78.00W
Cape Girardeau	182	Jd	37.19N	89.32W
Cape Johnson Tablemount (EN)	208	Jc	17.08N	177.15W
Capel	124	Bc	51.08N	0.19W
Cape Lisburne	178	Fc	68.52N	166.05W
Capelka	116	Mf	58.02N	29.07 E
Capella	150	Lg	4.58S	141.06 E
Capelongo	170	Ce	14.54S	15.05 E
Capem	204	Ea	13.14S	55.14W
Cape May	184	Jf	38.56N	74.54W
Cape Mount	166	Cd	7.05N	10.50W
Cape Province/ Kaapprovinsie	172	Cf	32.00S	22.00 E
Cape Rise (EN)	106	En	42.00S	15.00 E
Cape Smith	180	Jd	60.44N	78.29W
Capesterre	197e	Bc	15.54N	61.13W
Capesterre-Belle-Eau	196	Fd	16.03N	61.34W
Cape Town / Kaapstad	160	Il	33.55S	18.22 E
Cape Verde (EN)=Cabo Verde	160	Eg	16.00N	24.00W
Cape Verde (EN)=Cap Vert	166	Bc	14.45N	17.20W
Cape Verde Basin (EN)	106	Ch	15.00N	30.00W
Cape Verde Islands (EN)= Cabo Verde, Ilhas do-	158	Eg	16.00N	24.10W
Cape Verde Terrace (EN)	162	Cf	18.00N	20.00W
Cape Yakataga	178	Kd	60.04N	142.26W
Cape York Peninsula	208	Ff	14.00S	142.30 E
Cap-Haïtien	176	Lh	19.45N	72.15W
Capiibary, Arroyo-	204	Dg	24.06S	56.26W
Capiibary, Rio-	204	Eg	25.30S	55.33W
Capim, Rio-	198	Lf	1.40S	47.47W
Capinópolis	204	Hd	18.41S	49.35W
Capira	194	Hi	8.45N	79.53W
Capital Federal	206	Id	34.36S	58.27W
Capitán Arturo Prat	222	Re	62.29S	59.39W
Capitán Bado	206	Ib	23.16S	55.32W
Capitán Bermúdez	204	Bk	32.49S	60.43W
Capitán Sarmiento	204	Cl	34.10S	59.48W
Capitão Noronha, Rio-	204	Ea	13.19S	54.36W
Capivara, Represa da-	204	Gf	22.40S	50.57W
Capivari, Rio-	204	Dd	19.16S	57.10W
Capivarita	204	Fj	30.18S	52.19W
Cap Lopez, Baie du-	170	Ac	0.40S	9.00 E
Čaplygin	132	Kc	53.17N	39.59 E
Cappelle, La-	122	Je	49.58N	3.55 E
Cappeln (Oldenburg)	124	Kb	52.49N	8.07 E
Cap Point	196	Fe	14.07N	60.57W
Capraia	128	Dg	43.05N	9.50 E
Caprara, Punta-	128	Ci	41.07N	8.19 E
Capreol	184	Gb	46.43N	80.56W
Caprera	128	Di	41.10N	9.30 E
Capri	128	Ij	40.33N	14.14 E
Capri	128	Ij	40.35N	14.15 E
Capricorn, Cape-	212	Kd	23.30S	151.15 E
Capricorn Channel	212	Kd	22.15S	151.30 E
Capricorn Group	208	Gg	23.30S	152.00 E
Caprivi Strip (EN) = Caprivizipfel	158	Jj	18.00S	23.00 E
Caprivizipfel = Caprivi Strip (EN)	158	Jj	18.00S	23.00 E
Captain Cook	221a	Fd	19.30N	155.55W
Captains Flat	212	Jg	35.35S	149.27 E
Captieux	122	Fj	44.17N	0.15W
Capua	128	Ii	41.06N	14.12 E
Capuchin, Cape-	197g	Ba	15.38N	61.28W
Capunda	170	Ce	10.41S	17.23 E
Cap Vert=Cape Verde (EN)	166	Bc	14.45N	17.20W
Caquetá	202	Dc	1.00N	74.00W
Caquetá, Rio-	198	Jf	3.08S	64.46W
Čara	140	Oc	60.17N	120.40 E
Čara [R.S.F.S.R.]	138	Ge	58.54N	118.12 E
Čara [R.S.F.S.R.]	138	Ge	56.58N	118.17 E
Carabobo	202	Ea	10.10N	68.05W
Caracal	130	He	44.07N	24.21 E
Caracarai	202	Fc	1.50N	61.08W
Caracas	200	Jd	10.30N	66.56W
Caracas	202	Ea	10.15N	66.25W
Carache	194	Li	9.38N	70.14W
Caracol	204	De	21.59S	57.02W
Caracol, Rio-	204	Df	22.13S	57.03W
Caracollo	202	Eg	17.39S	67.10W
Caraguatá, Cuchilla-	204	Ek	32.05S	54.54W
Caraguatatuba	204	Jf	23.37S	45.25W
Caraïbe, Mer-/Antilles, Mer des-=Caribbean Sea (EN)	174	Lh	15.00N	73.00W
Carajas, Serra dos-	202	He	6.00S	51.20W
Caramoan Peninsula	150	Hd	13.48N	123.40 E
Caramulo, Serra do-	126	Dd	40.34N	8.11W
Caraná, Rio-	204	Ca	13.20S	59.17W
Carandaí	204	Ke	20.57S	43.48W
Carandazal	204	Dd	19.50S	57.09W
Caransebeş	130	Fd	45.25N	22.13 E
Carapá, Rio-	204	Eg	24.30S	54.20W
Carapelle	128	Ji	41.30N	15.55 E
Caraquet	184	Ob	47.47N	64.57W
Caraş	130	Ee	44.49N	21.20 E
Caraş Severin	130	Ed	45.20N	22.00 E
Caratasca, Cayo-	194	Fe	16.02N	83.20W
Caratasca, Laguna de-	190	He	15.20N	83.50W
Caratinga	202	Jg	19.47S	42.08W
Carauari	202	Ed	4.52S	66.54W
Caraúbas	202	Ke	5.47S	37.34W
Caravaca	126	Kf	38.06N	1.51W
Caravelas	200	Mg	17.45S	39.15W
Caraveli	202	Dg	15.46S	73.22W
Caravelle, Presqu'île de la-	197h	Bb	14.45N	60.55W
Caravelle, Rocher de la-	197h	Bb	14.48N	60.53W
Carázinho	206	Jc	28.18S	52.48W
Carazo	194	Dh	11.45N	86.15W
Carballino	126	Db	42.26N	8.04W
Carballo	126	Da	43.13N	8.41W
Carberry	186	Gb	49.52N	99.20W
Carbet, Pitons du-	197h	Ab	14.42N	61.07W
Carbon, Cap- [Alg.]	126	Li	35.54N	0.20W
Carbon, Cap- [Alg.]	126	Rh	36.47N	5.06 E
Carbonara, Capo-	128	Dk	39.06N	9.31 E
Carbondale [Il.-U.S.]	182	Jd	37.44N	89.13W
Carbondale [Pa.-U.S.]	184	Je	41.35N	75.31W
Carbonera, Cuchilla de la-	204	El	34.10S	54.00W
Carboneras	126	Kh	36.59N	1.54W
Carboneras, Cerro-	192	Ih	18.10N	101.10W
Carbones	126	Gg	37.36N	5.39W
Carbonia	128	Ck	39.10N	8.31 E
Carcans, Étang de-	122	Ei	45.06N	1.07W
Carcar	150	Hd	10.06N	123.38 E
Carcarañá, Rio-	204	Bk	32.27S	60.48W
Carcassonne	122	Ik	43.13N	2.21 E
Carcross	180	Ed	60.10N	134.42W
Çardak [Tur.]	130	Ji	40.22N	26.43 E
Çardak [Tur.]	146	Cd	37.48N	29.40 E
Čardara	136	Gg	41.15N	68.01 E
Čardarinskoje vodohranilišče	135	Gd	41.05N	68.15 E
Cárdenas [Cuba]	190	Hd	23.02N	81.12W
Cárdenas [Mex.]	192	Mi	17.59N	93.22W
Cárdenas [Mex.]	190	Ed	22.00N	99.40W
Cárdenas, Bahía de-	194	Gb	23.05N	81.10W
Cardener/Cardoner	126	Nc	41.41N	1.51 E
Cardiel, Lago-	206	Fg	48.55S	71.15W
Cardiff	112	Fe	51.30N	3.13W
Cardigan	118	Ii	52.06N	4.40W
Cardigan Bay	110	Fe	52.30N	4.20W
Cardona [Sp.]	126	Nc	41.55N	1.41 E
Cardona [Ur.]	204	Dk	33.54S	57.22W
Cardoner/Cardener	126	Nc	41.41N	1.51 E
Cardozo	204	Dk	32.38S	56.21W
Cardston	180	Gg	49.12N	113.18W
Čardžou	142	If	39.06N	63.34 E
Čardžouskaja oblast	136	Gh	39.00N	63.00 E
Carei	130	Fb	47.41N	22.28 E
Careiro	202	Gd	3.12S	59.45W
Carentan	122	Ee	49.18N	1.14W
Carey	188	Ie	43.20N	113.58W
Carey, Lake-	208	Dg	29.05S	122.15 E
Cargados Carajos Islands	158	Mj	16.35S	59.40 E
Cargèse	122a	Aa	42.08N	8.35 E
Carhaix-Plouguer	122	Cf	48.17N	3.35W
Cari	128	Hi	41.23N	13.50 E
Caria	130	Ll	37.30N	29.00 E
Cariacica	202	Jh	20.16S	40.25W
Cariaco	196	Eg	10.29N	63.33W
Cariaco, Golfo de-	196	Eg	10.30N	64.00W
Cariaco Basin (EN)	196	Dg	10.37N	65.10W
Cariati	128	Kk	39.30N	16.57 E
Caribana, Punta-	194	Ii	8.37N	76.52W
Caribbean Sea	174	Lh	15.00N	73.00W
Caribbean Sea (EN)= Antillas, Mar de las-/ Caribe, Mar-	174	Lh	15.00N	73.00W
Caribbean Sea (EN)= Antilles, Mer des-/Caraïbe, Mer-	174	Lh	15.00N	73.00W
Caribbean Sea (EN)= Caraibe, Mer-/Antilles, Mer des-	174	Lh	15.00N	73.00W
Caribbean Sea (EN)= Caribe, Mar-/Antillas, Mar de las-	174	Lh	15.00N	73.00W
Caribe, Mar-/Antillas, Mar de las-=Caribbean Sea (EN)	174	Lh	15.00N	73.00W
Cariboo Mountains	180	Ff	53.00N	121.00W
Caribou	184	Mb	46.52N	68.01W
Caribou	180	Ie	59.20N	94.45W
Caribou Island	184	Eb	47.27N	85.52W
Caribou Lake	186	La	50.25N	89.00W
Caribou Mountains	174	Hd	59.12N	115.40W
Caribou Range	188	Je	43.05N	111.15W
Caričin Grad	130	Eg	42.57N	21.45 E
Carignan	122	Le	49.38N	5.10 E
Carignano	128	Bf	44.55N	7.40 E
Cariñena	126	Kc	41.20N	1.13W
Carinhanha	202	Jf	14.18S	43.47W
Carinhanha, Rio-	204	Kb	14.20S	43.47W
Carini	128	Hl	38.08N	13.11 E
Carinola	128	Hi	41.11N	13.58 E
Carinthia (EN) = Kärnten	128	Hd	46.45N	14.00 E
Carinthia (EN) = Kärnten	128	Hd	46.45N	14.00 E
Caripe	196	Eg	10.21N	63.29W
Caripito	202	Fa	10.08N	63.06W
Caris, Rio-	196	Eh	8.09N	63.46W
Carlet	126	Le	39.14N	0.31W
Carleton Place	184	Ic	45.07N	76.08W
Carletonville	172	De	26.23S	27.22 E
Carlin	188	Gf	40.43N	116.07W
Carling	122	Ie	49.10N	6.43 E
Carlingford Lough/Loch Cairlinn	118	Gg	54.05N	6.14W
Carlinville	186	Lg	39.17N	89.53W
Carlisle [Eng.-U.K.]	112	Fe	54.54N	2.55W
Carlisle [Pa.-U.S.]	184	Ie	40.12N	77.12W
Carlisle Bay	197q	Ab	13.05N	59.37W
Carloforte	128	Ck	39.08N	8.18 E
Carlos Beguerie	204	Cl	35.29S	59.06W
Carlos Casares	206	He	35.38S	61.21W
Carlos Chagas	202	Jg	17.43S	40.45W
Carlos Reyles	204	Dk	33.03S	56.29W
Carlos Tejedor	204	Al	35.23S	62.25W
Carlow/Ceatharlach	118	Gi	52.50N	6.55W
Carlow/Ceatharlach	118	Gi	52.50N	7.00W
Carloway	118	Gc	58.17N	6.47W
Carlsbad [Ca.-U.S.]	188	Gj	33.10N	117.21W
Carlsbad [N.M.-U.S.]	176	If	32.25N	104.14W
Carlyle	180	Hg	49.38N	102.16W
Carlyle Lake	186	Lg	38.40N	89.18W
Carmacks	180	Dd	62.05N	136.18W
Carmagnola	128	Bf	44.51N	7.43 E
Carmarthen	118	Ij	51.52N	4.19W
Carmarthen Bay	118	Ij	51.40N	4.30W
Carmaux	122	Ij	44.03N	2.09 E
Carmel Head	118	Ih	53.24N	4.34W
Carmelita	194	Be	17.21N	90.10W
Carmelo	206	Id	34.00S	58.17W
Carmen	204	Dk	33.15S	56.01W
Carmen, Isla-	190	Bc	25.57N	111.12W
Carmen, Isla del-	192	Nh	18.42N	91.40W
Carmen, Laguna del-	192	Mh	18.15N	93.50W
Carmen, Rio del-	192	Fb	30.42N	106.29W
Carmen, Sierra del-	192	Hc	29.00N	102.30W
Carmen de Patagones	206	Hf	40.48S	62.59W
Carmensa	206	Ge	35.08S	67.38W
Carmi	186	Lg	38.07N	88.10W
Carmichael	188	Eg	38.38N	121.19W
Carmo de Minas	204	Jf	22.07S	45.08W
Carmo do Paranaiba	204	Id	18.59S	46.21W
Carmona	126	Gg	37.28N	5.38W
Carnac	122	Cg	47.35N	3.05W
Carnamah	212	De	29.42S	115.53 E
Carnarvon [Austl.]	210	Cg	24.53S	113.40 E
Carnarvon [S.Afr.]	160	Jl	30.56S	22.08 E
Carnarvon Range	212	Ee	25.10S	121.00 E
Carnatic (EN)	140	Jh	10.30N	79.00 E
Carnegie, Lake-	208	Dg	26.10S	122.30 E
Carnegie Ridge (EN)	106	Nj	1.00S	85.00W
Carn Eige	118	Hd	57.30N	5.05W
Carney Island	222	Nf	73.57S	121.00W
Carnia	128	Gd	46.25N	13.00 E
Car Nicobar	148	Ig	9.10N	92.47 E
Carnot	168	Be	4.56N	16.03 E
Carnoustie	118	Ke	56.30N	2.44W
Carnsore Point/Ceann an Chairn	118	Gi	52.10N	6.22W
Carn Ui Néid/Mizen Head	110	Fe	51.27N	9.49W
Caro	184	Fd	43.29N	83.24W
Carol City	184	Gm	25.56N	80.16W
Carolina [Braz.]	200	Lf	7.20S	47.28W
Carolina [P.R.]	197a	Cb	18.24N	65.57W
Carolina [S.Afr.]	172	Ee	26.05S	30.06 E
Carolina Beach	184	Ih	34.02N	77.54W
Carolinas, Puntan-	220b	Bb	14.54N	145.38 E
Caroline Atoll	208	Le	9.58S	150.13W
Caroline Islands	208	Fd	8.00N	147.00 E
Carondelet Reef	208	Je	5.34S	173.51W
Caroni, Rio-	198	Je	8.21N	62.43W
Caronie → Nebrodi	128	Im	37.55N	14.35 E
Carora	202	Da	10.11N	70.05W
Carpathian Mountains (EN)	110	If	48.00N	24.00 E
Carpathian Mountains (EN) = Carpații Occidentali	130	Fc	46.30N	22.10 E
Carpathian Mountains (EN) =Carpații Orientali	130	Ib	47.30N	25.30 E
Carpații Meridionali= Transylvanian Alps (EN)	110	If	45.30N	24.15 E
Carpații Occidentali = Carpathian Mountains (EN)	130	Fc	46.30N	22.10 E
Carpații Orientali= Carpathian Mountains (EN)	130	Ib	47.30N	25.30 E
Carpen	130	Ge	44.20N	23.15 E
Carpentaria, Gulf of-	208	Ef	14.00S	139.00 E
Carpentras	122	Lj	44.03N	5.03 E
Carpi	128	Ef	44.47N	10.53 E
Carpina	202	Ke	7.51S	35.15W
Carr, Cape-	222	Ie	66.07S	130.51 E
Carraig Fhearghais/ Carrickfergus	118	Hg	54.43N	5.44W
Carraig na Siúire / Carrick on Suir	118	Fi	52.21N	7.25W
Carrara	128	Ef	44.05N	10.06 E
Carrauntoohil	110	Fe	5200N	9.45W
Carreiro, Rio-	204	Gi	29.07S	51.43W
Carreño	126	Ga	43.35N	5.46W
Carreta, Punta-	202	Cf	14.13S	76.18W
Carretero, Puerto-	126	Ig	37.28N	3.40W
Carriacou	196	Ff	12.30N	61.27W
Carrick	118	If	55.15N	4.40W
Carrickfergus/Carraig Fhearghais	118	Hg	54.43N	5.44W
Carrick on Shannon / Cora Droma Rúisc	118	Eh	53.57N	8.05W
Carrick on Suir / Carraig na Siúire	118	Fi	52.21N	7.25W
Carrington	182	Hb	47.27N	99.08W
Carrión	126	Hc	41.53N	4.32W
Carrión de los Condes	126	Hb	42.20N	4.36W
Carrizal	194	Kh	11.58N	72.12W
Carrizo Peak	186	Dj	33.20N	105.38W
Carrizos	192	Gc	29.58N	105.16W
Carrizo Springs	186	Gl	28.31N	99.52W
Carrizo Wash	188	Ki	34.36N	109.26W
Carrizozo	186	Dj	33.38N	105.53W
Carroll	186	Ie	42.04N	94.52W
Carroll Inlet	222	Qf	73.18S	78.30W
Carrollton [Ga.-U.S.]	184	Ei	33.35N	85.05W
Carrollton [Il.-U.S.]	186	Kg	39.18N	90.24W
Carrollton [Ky.-U.S.]	184	Ef	38.41N	85.11W
Carrollton [Mo.-U.S.]	186	Jg	39.22N	93.30W
Carron, Loch-	118	Hd	57.30N	5.40W
Carrot	180	Hf	53.50N	101.18W
Carrowmore Lough	118	Dg	54.12N	9.47W
Çarşamba	146	Gb	41.12N	36.44 E
Çarşamba	146	Ed	37.53N	32.37 E
Čaršanga	136	Gh	37.31N	66.03 E
Čarsk	136	If	49.35N	81.05 E
Carson	188	Ed	45.44N	121.49W
Carson City	176	Hf	39.10N	119.46W
Carson Lake	188	Fg	39.19N	118.43W
Carson Sink	188	Fg	39.45N	118.30W
Cartagena [Col.]	200	Id	10.25N	75.32W
Cartagena [Sp.]	112	Fh	37.36N	0.59W
Cartago	194	Fi	9.50N	83.45W
Cartago [Col.]	202	Cc	4.46N	75.56W
Cartago [C.R.]	190	Hg	9.52N	83.55W
Cartaxo	126	De	39.09N	8.47W
Carter, Mount-	212	Ib	13.05S	143.15 E
Cartersville	184	Eh	34.10N	85.05W
Carterton	218	Fd	41.01S	175.31 E
Carthage [Mo.-U.S.]	186	Ih	37.11N	94.19W
Carthage [Tx.-U.S.]	186	Ij	32.09N	94.20W
Cartier	184	Gb	46.42N	81.32W
Cartier Island	210	Df	12.30S	123.30 E
Cartwright	176	Nd	53.50N	56.45W
Caruaru	200	Mf	8.17S	35.58W

Index Symbols

1 Independent Nation; 2 State, Region; 3 District, County; 4 Municipality; 5 Colony, Dependency; Continent; Physical Region; Historical or Cultural Region; Mount, Mountain; Volcano; Hill; Mountains, Mountain Range; Hills, Escarpment; Plateau, Upland; Pass, Gap; Plain, Lowland; Delta; Salt Flat; Valley, Canyon; Crater, Cave; Karst Features; Depression; Polder; Desert, Dunes; Forest, Woods; Heath, Steppe; Oasis; Cape, Point; Coast, Beach; Cliff; Peninsula; Isthmus; Sandbank; Island; Atoll; Rock, Reef; Islands, Archipelago; Rocks, Reefs; Coral Reef; Well, Spring; Geyser; River, Stream; Waterfall, Rapids; River Mouth, Estuary; Lake; Salt Lake; Intermittent Lake; Reservoir; Swamp, Pond; Canal; Glacier; Ice Shelf, Pack Ice; Ocean; Sea; Gulf, Bay; Strait, Fjord; Lagoon; Bank; Seamount; Tablemount; Ridge; Shelf; Basin; Escarpment, Sea Scarp; Fracture; Trench, Abyss; National Park, Reserve; Point of Interest; Recreation Site; Cave, Cavern; Historic Site; Ruins; Wall, Walls; Church, Abbey; Temple; Scientific Station; Railway station; Airport; Port; Military installation; Lighthouse; Mine; Tunnel; Dam, Bridge

Name	Pg	Grid	Lat	Long
Carúpano	202	Fa	10.40N	63.14W
Carutapera	202	Id	1.13S	46.01W
Čarvak	135	Gd	41.38N	69.56 E
Carvin	124	Ed	50.29N	2.58 E
Carvoeiro, Cabo-	126	Ce	39.21N	9.24W
Čaryn	135	Lc	43.50N	79.12 E
Čaryš	138	Df	52.22N	83.45 E
Casablanca	160	Ga	33.36N	7.37W
Casablanca [2]	162	Fc	33.37N	7.35W
Casa Branca	204	Ie	21.46S	47.05W
Casa Grande	182	Ee	32.53N	111.45W
Casalbordino	128	Ih	42.09N	14.35 E
Casale Monferrato	128	Ce	45.08N	8.27 E
Casalmaggiore	128	Ff	44.59N	10.26 E
Casalvasco	204	Cb	15.19S	59.59W
Casal Velino	128	Jj	40.11N	15.06 E
Casamance [3]	166	Bc	12.50N	15.00W
Casamance [3]	166	Bc	12.50N	16.46W
Casanare [3]	202	Db	5.20N	72.00W
Casanare, Rio-	202	Eb	6.02N	69.51W
Casanay	196	Eg	10.30N	63.25W
Casa Nova	202	Je	9.25S	41.08W
Casarano	128	Mj	40.00N	18.10 E
Casas Grandes, Rio-	192	Eb	30.22N	107.31W
Casas-Ibáñez	126	Ke	39.17N	1.28W
Casca, Rio da-	204	Eb	14.52S	55.52W
Cascade	188	Hd	44.31N	115.59W
Cascade Point	218	Cf	44.01S	168.22 E
Cascade Range	174	Ge	45.00N	121.30W
Cascais	126	Cf	38.42N	9.25W
Cascavel [Braz.]	202	Ff	4.07S	38.14W
Cascavel [Braz.]	206	Jb	24.57S	53.28W
Cáscia	128	Hg	42.43N	13.01 E
Casciana Terme	128	Eg	43.32N	10.38 E
Cascina	128	Eg	43.41N	10.33 E
Casentino	128	Fg	43.40N	11.50 E
Case-Pilote	197h	Ab	14.38N	61.08W
Caserta	128	Ii	41.04N	14.20 E
Casey	222	He	66.17S	110.32 E
Casey Bay	222	Ee	67.00S	48.00 E
Cashel/Caiseal	118	Fi	52.31N	7.53W
Casigua	194	Ki	8.46N	72.30W
Casilda	206	Hd	33.03S	61.10W
Casimcea	130	Le	44.24N	28.33 E
Casino	212	Ke	28.52S	153.03 E
Casiquiare, Brazo-	202	Ec	2.01N	67.07W
Čáslav	120	Lg	49.55N	15.25 E
Casma	202	Ce	9.28S	78.19W
Časnačorr, gora-	114	Hc	67.45N	33.29 E
Čašniki	114	Gi	54.52N	29.08 E
Casoli	128	Ih	42.07N	14.18 E
Casoria	128	Ii	40.54N	14.17 E
Caspe	126	Lc	41.14N	0.02W
Casper	176	Ie	42.51N	106.19W
Caspian Depression (EN) = Prikaspijskaja nizmennost	110	Lf	48.00N	52.00 E
Caspian Sea (EN) = Kaspijskoje more	110	Lg	42.00N	50.30 E
Caspian Sea (EN) = Mäzandarän, Daryä-ye-	110	Lg	42.00N	50.30 E
Cassai	158	Ii	3.02S	16.57 E
Cassamba	170	De	13.04S	20.25 E
Cassange, Rio-	204	Dc	17.06S	57.23W
Cassano allo Ionio	128	Kk	39.47N	16.19 E
Cassano allo Ionio-Sibari	128	Kk	39.45N	16.27 E
Cass City	184	Fd	43.36N	83.10W
Cassel	124	Jc	50.47N	2.29 E
Casselton	186	Hc	46.54N	97.13W
Cássia	204	Ie	20.36S	46.56W
Cassiar	180	Ee	59.16N	129.40W
Cassiar Mountains	174	Gd	59.00N	129.00W
Cassilândia	202	Hg	19.09S	51.45W
Cassinga	170	Cf	15.06S	16.06 E
Cassino [Braz.]	204	Fk	32.11S	52.10W
Cassino [It.]	128	Hi	41.30N	13.49 E
Cassis	122	Lk	43.13N	5.32 E
Cass Lake	186	Ic	47.23N	94.36W
Cass River-	184	Fd	43.23N	83.59W
Cassununga	204	Fc	16.03S	53.38W
Castagneto Carducci	128	Eg	43.10N	10.36 E
Castagniccia	122a	Ba	42.25N	9.30 E
Castañar, Sierra del-	126	He	39.35N	4.10W
Castanhal	202	Id	1.18S	47.55W
Castaños	192	Id	26.47N	101.25W
Castelbuono	128	Jm	37.56N	14.05 E
Castel di Sangro	128	Ii	41.47N	14.06 E
Castelfidardo	128	Hg	43.28N	13.33 E
Castelfranco Veneto	128	Fe	45.40N	11.55 E
Casteljaloux	122	Gj	44.19N	0.06 E
Castellabate	128	Ij	40.17N	14.57 E
Castellammare, Golfo di-	128	Gl	38.10N	12.55 E
Castellammare del Golfo	128	Gl	38.01N	12.53 E
Castellammare di Stabia	128	Ij	40.42N	14.29 E
Castellana Grotte	128	Lj	40.53N	17.10 E
Castellane	122	Mk	43.51N	6.31 E
Castellaneta	128	Kj	40.38N	16.56 E
Castelldefels	126	Nc	41.17N	1.58 E
Castelli [Arg.]	206	Hc	25.57S	60.37W
Castelli [Arg.]	204	Dm	36.06S	57.47W
Castelló de la Plana / Castellón [2]	126	Ld	40.10N	
Castelló de la Plana/ Castellón de la Plana	112	Fh	39.59N	0.02W
Castellón / Castelló de la Plana	126	Ld	40.10N	0.10W
Castellón de la Plana / Castelló de la Plana	112	Fh	39.59N	0.02W
Castellón de la Plana-El Grao	126	Me	39.58N	0.01 E
Castellote	126	Ld	40.10N	0.19W
Castelnaudary	122	Hk	43.19N	1.57 E
Castelnau-de-Médoc	122	Fi	45.02N	0.48W
Castelnovo ne' Monti	128	Ef	44.26N	10.24 E
Castelo Branco	126	Ee	39.49N	7.30W
Castelo Branco [2]	126	Ee	40.00N	7.30W
Castelo de Vide	126	Ee	39.25N	7.27W
Castelo do Piauí	202	Je	5.20S	41.33W
Castel San Giovanni	128	De	45.04N	9.26 E
Castelsardo	128	Cj	40.55N	8.43 E
Castelsarrasin	122	Hj	44.02N	1.06 E
Casteltermini	128	Hm	37.32N	13.39 E
Castelvetrano	128	Gm	37.41N	12.47 E
Castets	122	Ek	43.53N	1.09W
Castiglione del Lago	128	Gg	43.07N	12.03 E
Castiglione della Pescaia	128	Fg	42.46N	10.53 E
Castiglion Fiorentino	128	Fg	43.20N	11.55 E
Castilla-La Mancha [2]	126	Ie	39.30N	3.30W
Castilla la Nueva = New Castile (EN)	126	Id	40.00N	3.45W
Castilla la Vieja = Old Castile (EN)	126	Ic	41.30N	4.00W
Castilla-León [2]	126	Hc	41.30N	4.30W
Castillejo	126	Gc	41.14N	5.30W
Castillon-la-Bataille	122	Fj	44.51N	0.02W
Castillonnès	122	Gj	44.39N	0.36 E
Castillos	206	Jd	34.12S	53.50W
Castillos, Laguna de-	204	Fl	34.20S	53.54W
Castlebar/Caisleán an Bharraigh	118	Dh	53.52N	9.17W
Castle Bruce	197b	Bb	15.26N	61.16W
Castle Dome Peak	188	Hj	33.05N	114.08W
Castle Douglas	118	Gg	54.57N	3.56W
Castlegar	180	Fg	49.19N	117.40W
Castleisland/Oileán Ciarraí	118	Di	52.14N	9.27W
Castlemaine	212	Ig	37.04S	144.13 E
Castle Peak	188	Hd	44.03N	114.32W
Castlepoint	218	Gd	40.55S	176.13 E
Castlepollard	118	Fh	53.41N	7.17W
Castlerea/An Caisleán Riabhach	118	Eh	53.46N	8.29W
Castlereagh Bay	212	Hb	12.10S	135.10 E
Castle Rock Butte	186	Ed	45.00N	103.27W
Castle Rock Lake	186	Le	43.56N	89.58W
Častoozerje	134	Mi	55.34N	67.53 E
Castor	188	Ja	52.13N	111.53W
Castres	122	Ik	43.36N	2.15 E
Castricum	124	Gb	52.33N	4.42 E
Castries	176	Ma	14.01N	61.00W
Castrignano del Capo	128	Mk	39.50N	18.20 E
Castrignano del Capo-Marina di Leuca	128	Mk	39.48N	18.21 E
Castro [Braz.]	206	Jb	24.47S	50.03W
Castro [Chile]	206	Ff	42.29S	73.46W
Castro Alves	202	Kf	12.45S	39.26W
Castrocaro Terme e Terra del Sole	128	Ff	44.10N	11.57 E
Castro Daire	126	Ed	40.54N	7.56W
Castro del Rio	126	Hf	37.41N	4.28W
Castrojeriz	126	Hb	42.17N	4.08W
Castropol	126	Ea	43.32N	7.02W
Castrop-Rauxel	124	Jc	51.33N	7.19 E
Castro-Urdiales	126	Ia	43.23N	3.13W
Castro Verde	126	Dg	37.42N	8.05W
Castrovillari	128	Kk	39.49N	16.12 E
Castrovirreyna	202	Cf	13.16S	75.19W
Castuera	126	Gf	38.43N	5.33W
Častyje	134	Lg	57.19N	54.59 E
Casupá	204	El	34.09S	55.38W
Caswell Sound	218	Bf	45.00S	167.10 E
Çat	146	Jc	39.40N	41.03 E
Čata	120	Oi	47.58N	18.40 E
Catacamas	194	Ef	14.54N	85.56W
Catahoula Lake	186	Jk	31.30N	92.06W
Çatak	146	Jd	38.01N	43.07 E
Çatak	146	Jd	37.53N	42.39 E
Catalan Coastal Range (EN) = Costero Catalana, Cadena- / Mediterrani Català, Sistema- / Costero	110	Gg	41.35N	1.40 E
Catalão	202	Ig	18.10S	47.57W
Çatal Balkan	130	Jg	42.46N	27.00 E
Çatalca	130	Lh	41.09N	28.27 E
Çatal Dağ	130	Lj	39.51N	28.20 E
Catalina	206	Gc	25.13S	69.43W
Catalina, Isla-	194	Md	18.21N	69.00W
Catalina, Punta-	206	Gg	52.32S	68.47W
Catalonia (EN) = Cataluña/ Catalunya [2]	126	Nc	42.00N	2.00 E
Catalonia (EN) = Catalunya/ Cataluña	110	Gg	42.00N	2.00 E
Cataluña/Catalunya = Catalonia (EN) [2]	126	Nc	42.00N	2.00 E
Cataluña/Catalunya = Catalonia (EN)	110	Gg	42.00N	2.00 E
Catalunya/Cataluña = Catalonia (EN) [2]	126	Nc	42.00N	2.00 E
Catalunya/Cataluña = Catalonia (EN)	110	Gg	42.00N	2.00 E
Çatalzeytin	146	Fb	41.57N	34.13 E
Catamarca [2]	206	Gc	28.28S	67.00W
Catanduanes	140	Oh	13.45N	124.15 E
Catanduva	206	Jb	21.08S	48.58W
Catanduvas	204	Gj	25.12S	53.08W
Catánia	112	Ih	37.30N	15.06 E
Catánia, Golfo di-	128	Jm	37.25N	15.10 E
Catánia, Piana di-	128	Im	37.25N	14.50 E
Catanzaro	112	Kh	38.54N	16.35 E
Catanzaro-Marina di Catanzaro	128	Kl	38.49N	16.36 E
Catarman	150	Hd	12.30N	124.38 E
Catastrophe, Cape-	208	Dd	35.00S	136.00 E
Catatumbo, Rio-	194	Li	9.21N	71.45W
Catemaco, Lago-	192	Ih	18.25N	95.05W
Catete	170	Bd	9.07S	13.41 E
Cathair na Mart/Westport	118	Dh	53.48N	9.32W
Cathair Saidhbhin/ Cahersiveen	118	Cj	51.57N	10.13W
Cathcart	172	Df	32.18S	27.09 E
Catherine, Mount-	160	Jh	28.31N	33.57 E
Catholic Island	187	Nb	12.40N	61.24W
Catio	166	Bc	11.17N	15.15W
Cat Island	194	Ib	24.30N	75.30W
Çatkal	135	Hd	41.36N	70.05 E
Çatkalski hrebet	136	Kg	41.30N	70.50 E
Cat Lake	180	If	51.40N	91.52W
Catoche, Cabo-	174	Kg	21.36N	87.07W
Cato Island	208	Gg	23.15S	155.35 E
Catolé do Rocha	202	Ke	6.21S	37.45W
Catoute	126	Fb	42.45N	6.20W
Catria	128	Gg	43.28N	12.42 E
Catriló	206	He	36.26S	63.24W
Catrimani, Rio-	202	Fc	0.28N	61.44W
Catskill Mountains	184	Jd	42.10N	74.30W
Cattenom	124	Le	49.25N	6.15 E
Cattólica	128	Gf	43.58N	12.44 E
Catu	202	Kf	12.21S	38.23W
Catuane	172	Ee	26.48S	32.14 E
Catumbela	170	Be	12.27S	13.29 E
Catur	172	Dc	13.45S	35.37 E
Cauca [2]	202	Cc	2.30N	77.00W
Cauca, Rio-	198	Ie	8.54N	74.28W
Cauca [2]	202	Cb	7.59N	75.13W
Caucasus (EN) = Kavkaz, Bolšoj-	110	Kg	42.30N	45.00 E
Caucete	206	Gd	31.38S	68.16W
Caudebec-en-Caux	124	Ce	49.32N	0.44 E
Caudete	126	Lf	38.42N	0.59W
Caudry	122	Jd	50.08N	3.25 E
Caumont-l'Eventé	124	Be	49.05N	0.48W
Caungula	160	Ii	8.26S	18.37 E
Čaunskaja guba	138	Lc	69.30N	170.00 E
Caupolicán	202	Ef	13.30S	68.30W
Cauquenes	206	Fe	35.58S	72.21W
Caura, Rio-	196	Fe	7.38N	64.53W
Causapscal	184	Na	48.22N	67.14W
Caussade	122	Hj	44.10N	1.32 E
Čausy	132	Gc	53.50N	30.59 E
Cauterets	122	Fl	42.53N	0.07W
Cauto, Rio-	194	Ic	20.33N	77.15W
Cauvery	140	Jh	11.09N	78.52 E
Caux, Pays de-	122	Gg	49.40N	0.40 E
Cávado	126	Dc	41.32N	8.48W
Cavaillon	126	Lk	43.50N	5.02 E
Cavalaire-sur-Mer	122	Mk	43.10N	6.32 E
Cavalcante	202	Ia	13.48S	47.30W
Cavalese	128	Fd	46.17N	11.27 E
Cavalleria, Cap de-/ Caballeria, Cabo de-	126	Qd	40.05N	4.05 E
Cavalli Islands	218	Ea	35.00S	173.55 E
Cavallo, Isola-	122a	Bb	41.22N	9.16 E
Cavallo Pass	186	Hl	28.25N	96.26W
Cavally	158	Ac	4.22N	7.32W
Cavan/An Cabhán	118	Fg	54.00N	7.21W
Cavan/An Cabhán [2]	118	Fh	53.55N	7.30W
Cavarzere	128	Ge	45.08N	12.05 E
Çavdarhisar	130	Mj	39.12N	29.37 E
Çavdir	130	Mk	37.09N	29.42 E
Caviana, Ilha-	202	Hc	0.10N	50.05W
Cavili	150	Ge	9.17N	120.50 E
Cavour, Canale-	128	Be	45.11N	7.54 E
Cavtat	128	Mh	42.35N	18.13 E
Caxambu	204	Ie	21.59S	44.56W
Caxias	200	Lf	4.50S	43.21W
Caxias do Sul	206	Kb	29.10S	51.11W
Caxito	170	Bd	8.34S	13.40 E
Çay	146	Dc	38.35N	31.02 E
Cayambe	202	Cc	0.05N	78.08W
Cayambe, Volcán-	198	Ie	0.02N	77.59W
Cayastá	206	Hd	31.12S	60.10W
Cayce	184	Gi	33.59N	81.04W
Çaycuma	146	Eb	41.25N	32.05 E
Çayeli	146	Ib	41.05N	40.44 E
Cayenne	200	Ke	4.56N	52.20W
Cayeux-sur-Mer	124	Dd	50.11N	1.29 E
Cayman Brac	190	Ie	19.43N	79.49W
Cayman Islands [5]	176	Kh	19.30N	80.30W
Cayman Islands	194	Ic	19.30N	80.30W
Cayman Ridge	190	Ie	19.30N	80.30W
Cayman Trench (EN)	106	Bh	19.00N	80.00W
Cayo [3]	194	Ce	17.00N	88.50W
Cayon	197c	Ab	17.21N	62.43W
Cayones, Cayos-	194	Fe	16.05N	83.12W
Cay Sal Bank	190	Hd	23.45N	80.00W
Cayuga Lake	184	Id	42.45N	76.45W
Cazalla de la Sierra	126	Gg	37.56N	5.45W
Caza Pava	204	Dh	28.17S	56.07W
Cazaux et de Sanguinet, Étang de-	122	Ej	44.29N	1.10W
Cazombo	160	Jj	11.54S	22.53 E
Cazorla	126	Jg	37.55N	3.00W
Cazorla, Sierra de-	126	Jf	37.55N	2.55W
Cea	126	Gb	42.45N	5.36W
Ceahlău	130	Ib	47.03N	25.58 E
Ceanannas Mór/Kells	118	Gh	53.44N	6.53W
Ceann Caillighe/Hags Head	118	Di	52.57N	9.28W
Ceann Acla/Achill Head	118	Ch	53.59N	10.13W
Ceann an Chairn/Carnsore Point	118	Gi	52.10N	6.22W
Ceann Chill Mhantáin/ Wicklow Head	118	Hi	52.58N	6.00W
Ceann Iorrais/Erris Head	110	Te	54.19N	10.00W
Ceann Léime/Loop Head	118	Di	52.34N	9.56W
Ceann Ros Eoghain/Rossan Point	118	Eg	54.42N	8.48W
Ceann Sléibhe/Slea Head	118	Ci	52.06N	10.27W
Ceann Toirc/Kanturk	118	Ei	52.10N	8.55W
Ceará [2]	202	Kd	5.00S	39.30W
Ceará-Mirim	202	Ke	5.38S	35.26W
Ceatharlach/Carlow	118	Gi	52.50N	6.55W
Ceatharlach/Carlow [2]	118	Gi	52.50N	7.00W
Cebaco, Isla-	194	Gj	7.32N	81.09W
Ceballos	192	Hd	26.32N	104.09W
Čebarkul	134	Ji	54.58N	60.25 E
Čeboksary	112	Kd	56.09N	47.15 E
Cebollati	204	Fk	33.16S	53.47W
Cebollati, Rio-	204	Fk	33.09S	53.38W
Cebollera, La-	126	Ic	41.10N	3.32W
Cebollera, Sierra-	126	Jc	42.00N	2.40W
Ceborucco, Volcán-	192	Gg	21.09N	104.30W
Cebreros	126	Hc	40.27N	4.28W
Cebrikovo	130	Nb	47.09N	30.02 E
Cebu	142	Oh	10.18N	123.54 E
Cebu	140	Oh	10.20N	123.45 E
Cece	120	Oj	46.46N	18.39 E
Čečen, ostrov-	132	Od	44.00N	47.45 E
Čečeno-Inguškaja ASSR [3]	136	Eg	43.15N	45.30 E
Cecerleg	142	Me	47.30N	101.27 E
Čečersk	132	Gc	52.30N	30.58 E
Cecina	128	Eg	43.19N	10.31 E
Cecina	128	Eg	43.18N	10.29 E
Čečuisk	138	Fe	58.07N	108.32 E
Cedar City	176	Hf	37.41N	113.04W
Cedar Creek	186	Fc	46.07N	101.18W
Cedar Creek Reservoir	186	Ij	32.20N	96.10W
Cedar Falls	182	Ic	42.32N	92.27W
Cedar Grove	197d	Bb	17.10N	61.49W
Cedar Lake	180	Hf	53.25N	100.00W
Cedar Rapids	176	Ic	41.59N	91.40W
Cedar River [Nb.-U.S.]	186	Hf	41.22N	97.57W
Cedar River [U.S.]	182	Ic	41.17N	91.20W
Cedartown	184	Eh	34.01N	85.15W
Cedar-Tree Point	197d	Ba	17.42N	61.53W
Cedeira	126	Da	43.39N	8.03W
Cedral	192	If	23.48N	100.44W
Cedrino	128	Dj	40.23N	9.44 E
Cedro	202	Ke	6.36S	39.03W
Cedrón	126	Ie	39.48N	3.33W
Cedros, Isla- = Cedros Island (EN)	174	Hg	28.10N	115.15W
Cedros Island (EN) = Cedros, Isla-	174	Hg	28.10N	115.15W
Cedros Trench (EN)	190	Ac	27.45N	115.45W
Ceduna	212	Gf	32.07S	133.40 E
Cedynia	120	Kd	52.50N	14.14 E
Cefalú	128	Il	38.02N	14.01 E
Cega	126	Hc	41.33N	4.46W
Čegdomyn	142	Pd	51.07N	133.05 E
Čegem	136	Db	43.36N	43.48 E
Cegléd	120	Pi	47.10N	19.48 E
Ceglie Messápico	128	Lj	40.39N	17.31 E
Cehegín	126	Kf	38.06N	1.48W
Cehotina	128	Bf	43.31N	18.45 E
Čehov [R.S.F.S.R.]	114	Ii	55.11N	37.29 E
Čehov [R.S.F.S.R.]	138	Jg	47.24N	142.05 E
Ceica	130	Fc	46.51N	22.11 E
Çekerek	146	Fb	40.04N	35.31 E
Çekerek	146	Fb	40.34N	35.46 E
Čekmaguš	134	Gi	54.50N	54.40 E
Celano	128	Hh	42.05N	13.33 E
Celaya	190	Dd	20.31N	100.37W
Celebes/Sulawesi	140	Og	2.00S	121.10 E
Celebes Basin (EN)	150	Hf	4.00N	123.00 E
Celebes Sea (EN) = Sulawesi, Laut-	140	Oi	3.00N	122.00 E
Celeken	136	Fh	39.27N	53.10 E
Čeleken, poluostrov-	132	Rj	39.25N	53.35 E
Celendín	202	Ce	6.52S	78.09W
Celerain, Punta-	192	Pg	20.16N	86.59W
Celeste	204	El	34.25S	57.30W
Celestún	192	Ng	20.52N	90.24W
Celinograd	142	Jd	51.10N	71.30 E
Celinogradskaja oblast [3]	136	Jd	51.00N	70.00 E
Čeljabinsk	142	Id	55.10N	61.24 E
Čeljabinskaja oblast [3]	136	Ie	54.00N	61.00 E
Celje	128	Id	46.14N	15.16 E
Čeljuskin, mys-	140	Mb	77.45N	104.20 E
Celldömölk	120	Ni	47.15N	17.09 E
Celle	120	Ge	52.37N	10.05 E
Celles	124	Fd	50.43N	3.27 E
Celles, Houyet-	124	Hd	50.19N	5.01 E
Cellina	128	Gd	46.02N	12.47 E
Celone	128	Ji	41.36N	15.41 E
Celorico da Beira	126	Ed	40.38N	7.23W
Celtic Sea	118	Fi	51.00N	7.00W
Celtic Sea (EN) = An Mhuir Cheilteach	118	Fi	51.00N	7.00W
Cemaes Head	118	Ii	52.07N	4.44W
Čemal	138	Df	51.25N	86.05 E
Čembar	136	Dd	53.10N	43.22 E
Čemdalsk	138	Ed	59.45N	103.18 E
Çemernica	128	Lf	44.30N	17.15 E
Çemerno	128	Mf	43.36N	20.28 E
Çemişkezek	146	Hc	39.04N	38.55 E
Cenajo, Embalse de-	126	Kf	38.20N	1.55W
Cenderawasih, Teluk-	208	Da	2.25S	135.10 E
Cengel	152	Eb	48.56N	89.10 E
Cengel Geçidi	146	Kc	39.45N	44.02 E
Ceno	128	Ee	44.41N	10.05 E
Centenary	172	Ec	16.44S	31.07 E
Centennial	188	Lf	41.51N	106.07W
Centennial Lake	184	Ic	45.15N	77.00W
Centennial Mountains	188	Jd	44.35N	111.55W
Center	186	Ik	31.48N	94.11W
Center Hill Lake	184	Eg	36.00N	85.45W
Centerville	186	Hf	40.43N	92.52W
Centinela, Farallón-	196	Cg	10.49N	66.05W
Centinela, Picacho del-	190	Dc	29.07N	102.27W
Cento	128	Ff	44.43N	11.17 E
Centola-Palinuro	128	Jj	40.02N	15.17 E
Centrafrique = Central African Republic (EN) [1]	160	Jh	7.00N	21.00 E
Central [Bots.] [3]	172	Dd	21.30S	26.00 E
Central [Ghana] [3]	166	Ed	5.30N	1.00W
Central [Kenya] [3]	170	Gc	0.45S	37.00 E
Central [Mwi.] [3]	170	Fe	13.30S	34.00 E
Central [Par.] [3]	204	Dg	25.30S	57.30W
Central [Scot.-U.K.] [3]	118	Ie	56.15N	4.10W
Central [Ug.] [3]	170	Fb	0.10N	32.05 E
Central [Zam.] [3]	170	Ee	14.30S	29.00 E
Central, Chaco-	198	Kh	25.00S	59.45W
Central, Cordillera- [Col.]	198	Ie	5.00N	75.20W
Central, Cordillera- [Dom.Rep.]	190	Ke	18.45N	70.30W
Central, Cordillera- [P.R.]	194	Nd	18.10N	66.35W
Central, Massif-	110	Gf	45.00N	3.10 E
Central, Meseta-	174	Jg	23.00N	103.00W
Central, Sistema-	110	Fg	40.30N	5.00W
Central African Republic (EN) = Centrafrique [1]	160	Jh	7.00N	21.00 E
Central America (EN)	106	Bh	20.00N	100.00W
Central Auckland [3]	218	Fb	36.45S	174.40 E
Central Brâhui Range	148	Dc	29.20N	66.55 E
Central City	186	Hf	41.07N	98.00W
Centralia [Il.-U.S.]	186	Lg	38.31N	89.08W
Centralia [Wa.-U.S.]	182	Cb	46.43N	122.58W
Central Makrän Range	140	Jc	26.40N	64.30 E
Centralno Tungusskoje plato	138	Fd	61.15N	102.00 E
Centralny-Kospašski	134	Kg	59.03N	57.50 E
Central Pacific Basin (EN)	106	Ki	5.00N	175.00W
Central Plains	174	Ke	40.20N	90.00W
Central Plateau	220e	Bb	0.32S	166.56 E
Central Point	188	De	42.23N	122.57W
Central Range	208	Fe	5.00S	142.30 E
Central Russian Uplands (EN) = Srednerusskaja vozvyšennost	110	Je	52.00N	38.00 E
Central Siberian Uplands (EN) = Srednesibirskoje ploskogorje	140	Mc	65.00N	105.00 E
Central Urals (EN) = Sredni Ural	110	Ld	58.00N	59.00 E
Centre [Burkina] [3]	166	Ec	12.00N	1.00W
Centre [Togo] [3]	166	Fd	9.15N	1.00 E
Centre, Canal du-	122	Jh	46.28N	3.59 E
Centre-Est [3]	166	Ec	11.30N	0.20W
Centre-Nord [3]	166	Ec	13.20N	0.55W
Centre-Ouest [3]	166	Ec	12.00N	2.30W
Centre-Sud [3]	166	He	3.30N	11.50 E
Centro, Cayo-	192	Ph	18.35N	87.20W
Centúripe	128	Im	37.37N	14.44 E
Čepca	136	Fc	58.35N	50.05 E
Čepelare	130	Hh	41.44N	24.41 E
Cephalonia (EN) = Kefallinia	110	Ih	38.15N	20.35 E
Čepin	128	Me	45.32N	18.34 E
Ceplenita	130	Ib	47.23N	26.58 E
Cepu	150	Fh	7.09S	111.35 E
Ceram Sea (EN) = Seram, Laut-	208	Da	2.30S	128.00 E
Cerbatana, Serrania de la-	202	Eb	6.50N	66.15W
Cercal	126	Dg	37.47N	8.42W
Cercal [3]	122a	Bb	41.33N	9.22 E
Čerčerov [2]	132	Rg	49.10N	21.05 E
Čerdakly	114	Sc	54.23N	48.51 E
Čerdyn	134	Hf	60.25N	56.29 E
Cère	122	Hj	44.55N	1.49 E
Čereha	114	Gh	57.47N	28.22 E
Čeremhovo	142	Md	53.09N	103.05 E
Čeremuhovo	134	Jf	60.20N	60.00 E
Čerepanovo	138	Df	54.13N	83.32 E
Čerepovec	112	Jd	59.08N	37.54 E
Ceres [Arg.]	206	Hc	29.53S	61.57W
Ceres [Braz.]	202	Ig	15.17S	49.35W
Ceres [S.Afr.]	172	Df	33.21S	19.18 E
Ceresio → Lugano, Lago di-	128	Cd	46.00N	9.00 E
Céret	122	Il	42.29N	2.45 E
Cerf Island	202	Dc	8.53S	75.47W
Cerfontaine	124	Gd	50.10N	4.25 E
Cergy	124	Ee	49.02N	2.04 E
Cerignola	128	Ji	41.16N	15.54 E
Čerikov	132	Gc	53.35N	31.25 E
Cérilly	122	Ih	46.37N	2.50 E
Čerkasskaja oblast [3]	136	Df	49.15N	31.15 E
Čerkassy	112	Gf	49.26N	32.04 E
Çerkeş	146	Eb	40.50N	32.54 E
Čerkessk	136	Db	44.14N	42.04 E
Çerkezköy	130	Kh	41.17N	28.00 E
Čerlak	138	He	54.09N	74.58 E
Čerlakski	134	Lh	53.47N	74.31 E
Čermasan	134	Gi	55.10N	55.20 E
Čermei	130	Dh	46.33N	21.51 E
Čermenika	130	Dh	41.03N	20.20 E
Čermoz	134	Hg	58.47N	56.10 E
Cerna [Rom.]	130	Fe	44.53N	22.50 E
Cerna [Rom.]	130	Fd	44.42N	22.25 E
Cerna [Rom.]	130	Hc	46.23N	23.57 E
Čërnaja [R.S.F.S.R.]	134	Mb	47.39N	29.11 E
Čërnaja [Ukr.-U.S.S.R.]	130	Mb	47.39N	29.11 E
Černa Skala, prohod-	130	Kh	41.53N	24.33 E
Černatica	130	Gg	42.35N	23.15 E
Černavčicy	120	Td	52.11N	23.47 E
Černavoda	130	Le	44.22N	28.01 E
Cernay	122	Ng	47.49N	7.10 E
Cernay-en-Dormois	124	Ge	49.13N	4.46 E
Černevo	116	Mf	58.35N	28.23 E
Černigovskaja oblast [3]	136	De	51.30N	31.18 E
Černi Lom	130	If	43.33N	25.57 E
Černi vrăh	130	Gg	42.35N	23.15 E

Index Symbols

[1] Independent Nation	Historical or Cultural Region	Pass, Gap	Depression	Coast, Beach	Rock, Reef	Waterfall, Rapids	Canal	Lagoon	Escarpment, Sea Scarp	Historic Site	Airport
[2] State, Region	Mount, Mountain	Plain, Lowland	Polder	Cliff	Islands, Archipelago	River Mouth, Estuary	Glacier	Bank	Fracture	Ruins	Port
[3] District, County	Volcano	Delta	Desert, Dunes	Peninsula	Rocks, Reefs	Lake	Ice Shelf, Pack Ice	Seamount	Trench, Abyss	Wall, Walls	Military installation
[4] Municipality	Hill	Salt Flat	Forest, Woods	Isthmus	Coral Reef	Salt Lake	Sea	Tablemount	National Park, Reserve	Church, Abbey	Lighthouse
[5] Colony, Dependency	Mountains, Mountain Range	Valley, Canyon	Heath, Steppe	Sandbank	Well, Spring	Intermittent Lake	Ridge	Point of Interest	Temple	Mine
Continent	Hills, Escarpment	Crater, Cave	Oasis	Island	Geyser	Reservoir	Shelf	Recreation Site	Scientific Station	Tunnel
Physical Region	Plateau, Upland	Karst Features	Cape, Point	Atoll	River, Stream	Swamp, Pond	Gulf, Bay	Basin	Strait, Fjord	Cave, Cavern	Railway station	Dam, Bridge

Černjahovsk 136 Ce 54.38N 21.48 E
Černjanka 132 Jd 50.55N 37.49 E
Černobyl 136 De 51.17N 30.13 E
Černogorsk 138 Ef 53.45N 91.18 E
Černoje more = Black Sea (EN) ▦ 110 Jg 43.00N 35.00 E
Černo More = Black Sea (EN) ▦ 110 Jg 43.00N 35.00 E
Černomorskoje 132 Hg 45.31N 32.42 E
Černovcy 112 If 48.18N 25.56 E
Černovickaja oblast 3 136 Cf 48.20N 26.10 E
Černuška 132 Nf 56.31N 56.03 E
Černy Jar 132 Oe 48.03N 46.05 E
Černyje Zemli ▦ 132 Nf 45.55N 46.00 E
Černyševa, grjada- ▦ 134 Ic 66.20N 59.45 E
Černyševa, zaliv- ◧ 138 Mb 45.50N 59.10 E
Černyševsk 138 Gf 52.35N 117.02 E
Černyševski 138 Gd 62.58N 112.15 E
Černyškovski 132 Me 48.27N 42.14 E
Cérou ◲ 122 Hj 44.08N 1.52 E
Cerralvo 192 Kg 26.06N 99.37W
Cerralvo, Isla- ▦ 190 Cd 24.15N 109.55W
Cerredo, Torre de- ▦ 126 Ha 43.13N 4.50W
Cerriku 130 Ch 41.02N 19.57 E
Cerrito [Col.] 202 Db 6.51N 72.42W
Cerrito [Par.] 204 Dh 27.19S 57.40W
Cerritos 190 Dd 22.26N 100.17W
Cerro Azul 206 Mb 24.50S 49.15W
Cerro Azul 192 Kg 21.12N 97.44W
Cerro Chato 204 Ek 33.06S 55.08W
Cerro Colorado 204 Ek 33.52S 55.33W
Cerro de las Mesas ▦ 192 Kh 18.47N 96.05W
Cerro de Pasco 200 Ig 10.41S 76.16W
Cerro Grande 204 Gj 30.36S 51.45W
Cerro Largo 206 Jc 28.09S 54.45W
Cerro Largo 3 204 Ek 32.20S 54.20W
Cerrón, Cerro- ▦ 194 Lh 10.19N 70.39W
Cerro San Valentín ▦ 198 Ij 46.36S 73.20W
Cerros Colorados, Embalse- ◧ 206 Ge 38.35S 68.40W
Cerro Vera 204 Dk 33.11S 57.28W
Cerrudo Cué 204 Dh 27.34S 57.57W
Čerski 142 Sc 68.45N 161.45 E
Čerskogo, hrebet- [R.S.F.S.R.] ▦ 138 Gf 52.00N 114.00 E
Čerskogo, hrebet- [R.S.F.S.R.] = Cherski Mountains (EN) ▦ 140 Qc 65.00N 145.00 E
Certaldo 128 Fg 43.33N 11.02 E
Čertkovo 132 Ke 49.20N 40.12 E
Cervaro ◲ 128 Ji 41.30N 15.52 E
Cervati ◲ 128 Jj 40.17N 15.29 E
Červen [Bul.] 130 Jf 43.37N 26.02 E
Červen [Bye.-U.S.S.R.] 132 Fc 53.43N 28.29 E
Červen brjag 130 Hf 43.16N 24.06 E
Cervera 126 Nc 41.40N 1.17 E
Cervera del Rio Alhama 126 Kg 42.01N 1.57W
Cervera de Pisuerga 126 Hb 42.52N 4.30W
Cerveteri 128 Gh 42.00N 12.06 E
Cervia 128 Gf 44.15N 12.22 E
Cervin/Cervino ▦ 128 Be 45.58N 7.39 E
Cervin/Cervin ▦ 128 Be 45.58N 7.39 E
Cervione 122a Ba 42.20N 9.29 E
Cervonoarmejsk 120 Vf 50.03N 25.18 E
Cervonoarmejskoje 130 Ld 45.50N 28.38 E
Cervonograd 136 Ce 50.24N 24.12 E
Cesano ◲ 128 Hg 43.45N 13.10 E
Cesar, Rio- ◲ 202 Db 9.50N 73.30W
Cesar, Rio- ◲ 194 Ki 9.00N 73.58W
Cesena 128 Gf 44.08N 12.15 E
Cesenatico 128 Gf 44.12N 12.24 E
Cēsis/Cesis 136 Cd 57.18N 25.18 E
Cēsis/Cēsis 136 Cd 57.18N 25.18 E
Česká Lipa 120 Kf 50.42N 14.32 E
Česká Třebová 120 Mg 49.54N 16.27 E
České Budějovice 120 Kh 48.58N 14.29 E
České středohoří ▦ 120 Jf 50.35N 14.00 E
České země 3 120 Kg 49.45N 15.00 E
Českomoravská Vrchovina = Moravian Upland (EN) ▦ 110 Hf 49.20N 15.30 E
Československá Socialistická Republika (ČSSR) 1 112 Hf 49.30N 17.00 E
Československo = Czechoslovakia (EN) 1 112 Hf 49.30N 17.00 E
Český Krumlov 120 Kh 48.49N 14.19 E
Český Les = North Bohemian Forest (EN) ▦ 120 Ig 49.50N 12.30 E
Česma 134 Jj 53.50N 60.40 E
Česma ◲ 128 Ke 45.35N 16.29 E
Çeşme 146 Bc 38.18N 26.19 E
Çeşme Yarımadası ▦ 146 Bc 38.30N 26.30 E
Češskaja guba = Chesha Bay (EN) ◧ 134 Kb 67.20N 46.30 E
Cessnock 212 Kf 32.50S 151.21 E
Cestos ◲ 158 Gh 5.27N 9.35W
Cesvaine/Cesvaine 116 Lb 56.55N 26.20 E
Cesvaine/Cesvaine 116 Lb 56.55N 26.20 E
Cetate 138 Ge 44.06N 23.03 E
Cetina ◲ 128 Kg 43.27N 16.42 E
Cetinje 130 Bg 42.24N 18.55 E
Çetinkaya 146 Gc 39.15N 37.38 E
Cetraro 128 Jk 39.31N 15.56 E
Cetynia ◲ 120 Sd 52.33N 22.26 E
Ceuta 5 160 Ge 35.53N 5.19W
Ceva-i-Ra (Conway Reef) ▦ 208 Eg 21.45S 174.35 E
Cevedale/Zufallspitze ▦ 128 Ed 46.27N 10.37 E
Cévennes ▦ 122 Jj 44.40N 4.00 E
Ceyhan 144 Eb 37.04N 35.47 E
Ceyhan ◲ 146 Fd 36.55N 35.42 E
Ceylanpınar 146 Id 36.51N 40.02 E
Ceylon → Sri Lanka 1 142 Ki 7.40N 80.50 E
Cèze ◲ 122 Kj 44.06N 4.42 E
Chaalis, Abbaye de- ▦ 122 Kj 49.08N 2.40 E
Cha-am 148 Jf 12.48N 99.58 E
Chabanais 122 Gi 45.52N 0.43 E
Chabjuwardoo Bay ◧ 212 Cd 22.55S 113.50 E

Chablais ▦ 122 Mh 46.20N 6.30 E
Chábóksar 146 Nd 36.58N 50.34 E
Chabówka 120 Pg 49.34N 19.58 E
Chacabuco 206 Hd 34.38S 60.29W
Chachani, Nevado- ▦ 202 Ce 16.12S 71.33W
Chachapoyas 202 Ce 6.13S 77.51W
Chachoengsao 148 Kf 13.41N 101.03 E
Chaco 3 206 Hc 26.00S 60.30W
Chaco 3 204 Bd 20.00S 60.30W
Chaco Mesa ▦ 186 Ci 35.50N 107.35W
Chaco River ◲ 186 Bh 36.46N 108.39W
Chad (EN) = Tchad 1 160 Ig 15.00N 19.00 E
Chad, Lake- (EN) = Tchad, Lac- ◧ 158 Ig 13.20N 14.00 E
Chadegán 146 Nf 32.46N 50.38 E
Chadileuvú, Rio- ◲ 206 Ge 38.49S 64.57W
Chadron 182 Gc 42.50N 103.02W
Chaeryŏng 154 Mh 38.24N 125.37 E
Chafarinas, Islas- ◲ 126 Ji 35.11N 2.26W
Chagai Hills ▦ 140 Jg 29.30N 64.15 E
Chagang-Do 2 154 Ie 40.50N 126.30 E
Chaghcharán 142 If 34.31N 65.15 E
Chagny 122 Kh 46.55N 4.45 E
Chagos Archipelago ▦ 140 Jj 6.00S 72.00 E
Chagos-Laccadive Plateau (EN) ▦ 106 Gi 3.00N 73.00 E
Chagu, Serra do- ▦ 196 Ch 9.20N 66.16W
Chahár Borjak 144 Jc 30.17N 62.03 E
Chahbounia 126 Jk 35.33N 2.46 E
Ch'aho 154 Jd 40.12N 128.38 E
Chai Badan 148 Kf 15.05N 101.04 E
Chaibāsa 148 Hd 22.34N 85.49 E
Chaigoubu → Huai'an 154 Cd 40.40N 114.25 E
Chai He ◲ 154 Gc 42.20N 123.51 E
Chaillu, Massif du- ▦ 158 Ii 2.32S 11.10 E
Chainat 148 Ke 15.10N 100.10 E
Chaiyaphum 148 Ke 16.09N 102.02 E
Chajul 194 Bf 15.30N 91.02W
Chakari 172 Dc 18.09S 29.52 E
Chak Chak 168 Bd 8.40N 26.54 E
Chake Chake 160 Ki 5.15S 39.46 E
Chakhānsür 144 Jc 31.10N 62.04 E
Chala 202 Dg 15.52S 74.16W
Chalais 122 Gi 45.17N 0.02 E
Chalatenango 194 Cf 14.03N 88.56W
Chalan Kanoa 220b Ba 15.08N 145.43 E
Chalbi Desert ▦ 158 Kh 3.00N 37.20 E
Chalchuapa 194 Cg 13.59N 89.41W
Chalcidice (EN) = Khalkidhikí ▦ 110 Ig 40.25N 23.25 E
Chālesbán 146 Ne 35.18N 50.03 E
Chaleur Bay ◧ 180 Kg 47.50N 65.30W
Chalhuanca 202 Df 14.17S 73.15W
Chaling 152 Jf 26.47N 113.32 E
Chalky Inlet ◧ 218 Bg 46.05S 166.30 E
Challans 122 Eh 46.51N 1.53W
Challapata 202 Eg 18.54S 66.47W
Challis 188 Hd 44.30N 114.14W
Chalmette 186 Ll 29.56N 89.58W
Châlons-sur-Marne 122 Kf 48.57N 4.22 E
Châlon-sur-Saône 122 Kh 46.47N 4.51 E
Chalosse ▦ 122 Fk 43.45N 0.30W
Chaltubo 132 Mh 42.19N 42.34 E
Chālūs 144 Nd 36.38N 51.26 E
Chālūs ◲ 144 Nd 36.39N 51.26 E
Cham 120 Ig 49.13N 12.40 E
Chama 170 Fe 11.12S 33.10 E
Chama, Rio- ◲ 194 Li 9.03N 71.37W
Chama, Rio- ◲ 186 Bh 36.03N 106.05W
Chaman 148 Db 30.55N 66.27 E
Chaman Bid 146 Qd 37.25N 56.38 E
Chamba [India] 148 Fb 32.34N 76.08 E
Chamba [Tan.] 170 Gd 11.35S 36.58 E
Chambal ◲ 148 Jg 26.29N 79.15 E
Chambaran, Plateau de- ▦ 122 Li 45.10N 5.20 E
Chambas 186 Bd 22.12N 78.55W
Chamberlain 186 Ge 43.49N 99.20W
Chamberlain Lake ◧ 184 Mb 46.17N 69.20W
Chamberlain River ◲ 212 Fc 15.35S 127.51 E
Chambersburg 184 If 39.57N 77.40W
Chambéry 122 Li 45.34N 5.56 E
Chambeshi ◲ 170 Fe 11.53S 29.48 E
Chambley-Bussières 124 Je 49.03N 5.54 E
Chambly 124 Ee 49.10N 2.15 E
Chambois 124 Cf 48.48N 0.07 E
Chambon, Lac de- ◧ 122 Hh 46.25N 1.35 E
Chambord 122 Hg 47.37N 1.31 E
Chamchamal 146 Kg 35.32N 44.50 E
Chame, Punta- ▦ 194 Hi 8.39N 79.42W
Chamela 192 Hh 19.30N 105.05W
Chamela, Bahia- ◧ 192 Hh 19.30N 105.05W
Chamelecón, Rio- ◲ 194 Cf 15.51N 87.49W
Chamical 206 Gc 30.21S 66.19W
Chamiss Bay ◧ 180 Ba 50.07N 127.22W
Chamoli 148 Gb 30.24N 79.21 E
Chamonix-Mont-Blanc 122 Mi 45.55N 6.52 E
Chamouchouane, Rivière- ◲ 184 La 48.40N 72.20W
Champagne 110 Gf 49.00N 4.30 E
Champagne ▦ 122 Lf 49.00N 4.30 E
Champagne Berrichonne ▦ 122 Hh 47.00N 2.00 E
Champagne Humide ▦ 122 Lf 48.30N 4.30 E
Champagne Pouilleuse ▦ 122 Kf 49.00N 4.30 E
Champaign 182 Jc 40.07N 88.14W
Champaqui, Cerro- ▦ 198 Ji 31.59S 64.56W
Champasak 148 Le 14.53N 105.52 E
Champaubert 124 Lf 48.53N 3.47 E
Champdóré, Lac- ◧ 180 Ne 55.55N 65.45W
Champdu Feu, Le- ▦ 124 Nf 48.24N 7.15 E
Champeigne ▦ 122 Gh 47.15N 0.50 E
Champerico 194 Bf 14.18N 91.55W

Champlain, Lake- ◧ 182 Mc 44.45N 73.15W
Champlite 122 Lg 47.37N 5.31 E
Champotón 190 Fe 19.21N 90.43W
Champsaur ▦ 122 Mj 44.45N 6.10 E
Chāmrājnagar 148 Ff 11.55N 76.57 E
Chañaral 206 Fc 26.21S 70.37W
Chança ◲ 126 Eg 37.33N 7.31W
Chan Chan ▣ 202 Ce 8.07S 79.02W
Chanco 206 Fe 35.44S 72.32W
Chandalar 178 Jc 67.30N 148.30W
Chandalar ◲ 178 Jc 66.36N 145.48W
Chandausi 148 Fc 28.27N 78.46 E
Chandeleur Islands ◲ 182 Jf 29.48N 88.51W
Chandeleur Sound ◧ 186 Ll 29.55N 89.10W
Chandigarh 142 Jf 30.44N 76.55 E
Chandler 180 Lg 48.21N 64.41W
Chandless, Rio- ◲ 202 Ee 9.08S 69.51W
Chāndpur 148 Id 23.13N 90.39 E
Chandrapur 148 Fe 16.11N 78.52 E
Chandragupta ▣ 148 If 19.57N 79.18 E
Chang, Ko- ▦ 148 Kf 12.00N 102.23 E
Changajn Nuruu = Khangai Mountains (EN) ▦ 140 Le 47.30N 100.00 E
Chang'an → Rong'an 152 If 25.16N 109.23 E
Changane ◲ 158 Kk 24.43S 33.32 E
Changbai 154 Id 41.25N 128.11 E
Changbai Shan ▦ 140 Oe 42.00N 128.00 E
Changchun 142 Ng 43.51N 125.20 E
Changdao(Sihou) 154 Ff 37.56N 120.42 E
Changde 142 Ng 29.04N 111.42 E
Ch'angdo 154 Ie 38.30N 127.45 E
Changfeng (Shuijiahu) 154 Dh 32.29N 117.10 E
Changge 154 Bg 34.12N 113.45 E
Changhang 154 If 36.01N 126.42 E
Chang He ◲ 154 If 31.21N 118.21 E
Changhowŏn 154 If 37.07N 127.38 E
Changhua 152 La 24.05N 120.32 E
Changhŭng 154 Ig 34.40N 126.54 E
Changji 152 Ec 44.01N 87.16 E
Chang Jiang ◲ 152 Dj 28.59N 116.42 E
Changjiang (Shiliu) 152 Ih 19.20N 109.03 E
Chang Jiang (Yangtze Kiang) ◲ 140 Of 31.48N 121.10 E
Changjiang Kou ◧ 152 Le 31.24N 121.59 E
Changjin-gang ◲ 154 Id 40.30N 127.12 E
Changjin-ho ◧ 154 Id 40.30N 127.12 E
Changjin-ŭp 152 Mc 40.23N 127.15 E
Changli 154 Ee 39.43N 119.10 E
Changling 152 Lc 44.15N 123.58 E
Changlung 148 Ga 34.56N 77.29 E
Changning 154 Dd 40.14N 116.13 E
Changsha 142 Ng 28.12N 113.02 E
Changshan 154 Ej 28.55N 118.31 E
Changshan Qundao ◲ 158 Mc 39.10N 122.34 E
Changshu 154 Fi 31.38N 120.44 E
Changsŏng 154 Ig 35.00N 126.43 E
Changsong ◲ 154 Id 40.30N 127.12 E
Changting 154 Jb 44.27N 128.50 E
Changtu 154 Kc 42.47N 124.08 E
Changuillo 202 Cf 14.40S 75.12W
Changuinola 194 Fi 9.26N 82.31W
Changwu 154 Ei 31.01N 119.55 E
Changxing 154 Ei 31.01N 119.55 E
Changxing Dao ▦ 154 Fe 39.35N 121.42 E
Changyi 154 Ef 36.52N 119.25 E
Changyŏn 152 Md 38.15N 125.05 E
Changyuan 154 Cg 35.12N 114.40 E
Changzhi 152 Jd 36.07N 113.10 E
Changzhou 154 Ei 31.46N 119.56 E
Channel Islands [Chan.Is.] ◲ 110 Ff 49.20N 2.20W
Channel Islands [U.S.] ◲ 174 Mf 34.00N 120.00W
Channel Islands = Anglo-Normandes Îles- (F) ◲ 111 Kl 49.20N 2.20W
Channel Port-aux-Basques 176 Ne 47.35N 59.11W
Channel Rock ▦ 186 Ib 23.00N 77.55W
Channing 186 Sl 35.41N 102.20W
Chantada 126 Eb 42.37N 7.46W
Chantengo, Laguna- ◧ 192 Ji 16.35N 99.10W
Chanthaburi 148 Kf 12.35N 102.06 E
Chantilly 122 Je 49.12N 2.28 E
Chantonnay 122 Eh 46.41N 1.03W
Chantrey Inlet ◧ 176 Jc 67.48N 96.20W
Chanute 186 Id 37.33N 95.27W
Chao'an (Chaozhou) 152 Kg 23.41N 116.37 E
Chaobai Xinhe ◲ 154 Dd 39.07N 117.41 E
Chao He ◲ 154 Dd 40.36N 117.08 E
Chao Hu ◧ 154 Di 31.31N 117.33 E
Chao Phraya ◲ 148 Kf 13.32N 100.36 E
Chaor He ◲ 152 Kb 46.49N 123.45 E
Chaoxian 154 Di 31.37N 117.49 E
Chaoyang [China] 154 Kc 42.41N 120.26 E
Chaoyang [China] 152 Kg 23.17N 116.37 E
Chaoyang → Huinan 154 Ic 42.41N 126.03 E
Chaoyang → Jiayin 152 Nb 48.53N 130.21 E
Chaoyangchuan 154 Jc 42.53S 129.23 E
Chaoyangcun 154 La 50.01N 124.22 E
Chaozhong 154 La 50.53N 123.23 E
Chaozhou → Chao'an 152 Kg 23.41N 116.37 E
Chapada dos Guimarães 202 Gg 15.26S 55.45W
Chapadinha 200 Jd 3.44S 43.21W
Chapais 184 Ja 49.47N 74.56W
Chapala 192 Jg 20.18N 103.12W
Chapala, Lago de- ◧ 174 Jg 20.15N 103.00W
Chaparral 202 Cc 3.43N 75.28W
Chapecó 204 Fh 27.06S 52.36W
Chapecó, Rio- ◲ 204 Fh 27.06S 53.01W
Chapel Hill 184 Hh 35.55N 79.04W
Chapicuy 204 Dj 31.40S 57.55W
Chapleau 176 Kg 47.50N 83.24W
Chaplin Lake ◧ 188 Ld 50.28N 106.40W
Chāpra 148 Gc 25.46N 84.45 E
Chapman, Cape- ▦ 180 Ic 69.55N 89.27W
Chappell 188 Mf 41.06N 102.28W
Chapultepec 192 Hf 23.27N 103.04W
Chaqui 202 Eg 19.36S 65.32W

Char 162 Ee 21.31N 12.51W
Charadai 204 Ch 27.38S 59.54W
Charagua 202 Fg 19.48S 63.13W
Charam 146 Ng 30.45N 50.44 E
Charaña 202 If 17.36S 69.28W
Charcas 192 If 23.08N 101.07W
Charco de la Aguja 192 Gc 28.25N 104.01W
Charcot Island ◈ 228 Qe 69.45S 75.15W
Chard [Alta.-Can.] 180 Ge 55.48N 111.10W
Chard [Eng.-U.K.] 118 Kk 50.53N 2.58W
Chardávol 146 Lf 33.45N 46.38 E
Chardonnières 194 Jd 18.16N 74.10W
Charente 3 122 Gi 45.40N 0.05 E
Charente ◲ 122 Ei 45.57N 1.05W
Charente-Maritime 3 122 Fi 45.30N 0.45W
Charentonne ◲ 124 Ce 49.07N 0.44 E
Chari ◲ 158 Ig 12.58N 14.31 E
Chari-Baguirmi 3 168 Bc 12.00N 17.00 E
Chārīkār 144 Kb 35.01N 69.11 E
Charing 124 Cc 51.12N 0.48 E
Charité-sur-Loire, La- 122 Jg 47.11N 3.01 E
Chariton 186 Jf 41.00N 93.19W
Chariton River ◲ 186 Jf 39.19N 92.57W
Charity 202 Gb 7.24N 58.36W
Charleroi 122 Kd 50.25N 4.26 E
Charleroi-Jumet 122 Kd 50.27N 4.26 E
Charleroi-Marcinelle 122 Kd 50.25N 4.28 E
Charles ◲ 180 Kd 62.38N 74.15W
Charles, Cape- [Can.] ▦ 174 Nd 52.13N 55.40W
Charles, Cape- [Va.-U.S.] 182 Ld 37.08N 75.58W
Charles, Peak- ▦ 212 Ef 32.52S 121.11 E
Charlesbourg 184 Lb 46.52N 71.16W
Charles City 182 Ic 43.04N 92.40W
Charles de Gaulle, Aéroport- = Charles de Gaulle, Airport- (EN) ▦ 124 Ee 49.02N 2.35 E
Charles de Gaulle, Airport- (EN) = Charles de Gaulle, Aéroport- ▦ 124 Ee 49.02N 2.35 E
Charleston [Ill.-U.S.] 186 Lg 39.30N 88.10W
Charleston [Mo.-U.S.] 186 Lh 36.55N 89.21W
Charleston [Ms.-U.S.] 186 Ka 34.01N 90.04W
Charleston [N.Z.] 218 Dd 41.54S 171.27 E
Charleston [S.C.-U.S.] 176 Lf 32.48N 79.57W
Charleston [W.V.-U.S.] 176 Kf 38.21N 81.38W
Charleston Peak ▦ 182 Dd 36.16N 115.42W
Charles Town 184 If 39.18N 77.52W
Charlestown 196 Ed 17.12N 62.35W
Charleval 124 De 49.22N 1.23 E
Charleville 210 Fg 26.24S 146.15 E
Charleville-Mézières 122 Ke 49.46N 4.43 E
Charleville Mézières-Mohon 124 Md 49.46N 4.43 E
Charlevoix 184 Ec 45.19N 85.16W
Charlieu 122 Kh 46.09N 4.11 E
Charlotte [Mi.-U.S.] 184 Ed 42.36N 84.50W
Charlotte [N.C.-U.S.] 176 Kf 35.13N 80.50W
Charlotte Amalie 196 De 18.21N 64.56W
Charlotte Bank (EN) ◲ 208 If 11.47S 173.13 E
Charlotte Harbor ◧ 184 Fl 26.45N 82.12W
Charlottenberg 116 Ee 59.53N 12.17 E
Charlottesville 182 Ld 38.02N 78.29W
Charlottetown 176 Me 46.14N 63.08W
Charlton 212 Ig 36.16S 143.21 E
Charlton ◲ 180 Jf 52.00N 79.26W
Charly 124 Lf 48.58N 3.17 E
Charmes 122 Mf 48.22N 6.17 E
Charnley River ◲ 212 Ec 16.20S 124.53 E
Charny-sur-Meuse 124 Me 49.12N 5.22 E
Charolais ▦ 122 Kh 46.26N 4.16 E
Charouine 162 Gd 29.01N 0.16W
Charroux 122 Gi 46.09N 0.24 E
Chārsadda 148 Ea 34.09N 71.44 E
Charters Towers 210 Fg 20.05S 146.16 E
Chartres 122 Hf 48.27N 1.30 E
Charzykowskie, Jezioro- ◧ 120 Nc 53.47N 17.30 E
Chascomús 206 Je 35.34S 58.01W
Chase 188 Fa 50.49N 119.41W
Chasŏng 154 Id 41.25N 126.35 E
Chassagne 170 Ce 10.26S 18.32 E
Chassezac ◲ 122 Kj 44.26N 4.19 E
Chassiron, Pointe de- ▦ 122 Eh 46.03N 1.24W
Chat 146 Pd 37.59N 55.16 E
Châtaigneraie ▦ 122 Hi 44.45N 2.20 E
Châtál 146 Pd 37.40N 55.06 E
Château-Arnoux 122 Lj 44.06N 6.00 E
Chateaubelair 197n Ba 13.17N 61.15W
Château-Chinon 122 Jg 47.04N 3.56 E
Château-d'Oléron, Le- 122 Ei 45.54N 1.12W
Château-du-Loir 122 Gg 47.42N 0.25 E
Châteaudun 122 Hf 48.05N 1.20 E
Château-Gontier 122 Fg 47.50N 0.42W
Châteaulin 122 Bf 48.12N 4.05W
Châteaulin, Bassin de- ◲ 122 Bf 48.18N 3.50W
Châteaumeillant 122 Ih 46.34N 2.12 E
Châteauneuf-de-Randon 122 Jj 44.39N 3.40 E
Châteauneuf-sur-Cher 122 Ih 46.52N 2.19 E
Châteauneuf-sur-Loire 122 If 47.52N 2.14 E
Château-Porcien 124 Md 49.32N 4.15 E
Châteaurenard 122 Kk 43.53N 4.51 E
Château-Renault 122 Gg 47.35N 0.55 E
Châteauroux 122 Hh 46.49N 1.42 E
Château-Salins 122 Mf 48.49N 6.30 E
Château-Thierry 122 Je 49.03N 3.24 E
Châteaux, Pointe des- ▦ 197n Bb 16.15N 61.11W
Châtelaillon-Plage 122 Ei 46.04N 1.05W
Châtelet 124 Kd 50.24N 4.31 E
Châtellerault 122 Gh 46.48N 0.32 E
Chatham [Eng.-U.K.] 118 Nj 51.23N 0.32 E
Chatham [N.B.-Can.] 180 Kg 47.02N 65.26W
Chatham [Ont.-Can.] 184 Ed 42.24N 82.11W
Chatham [Ala.-U.S.] 184 Dj 34.40N 79.26W
Chatham Island ◲ 208 Ii 44.00S 176.30W
Chatham Islands 208 Ii 44.00S 176.30W
Chatham Rise (EN) ▦ 208 Ii 43.30S 180.00 E
Chatham Strait ◧ 178 Me 57.30N 134.45W

Châtillon-en-Bazois 122 Jg 47.03N 3.40 E
Châtillon-sur-Indre 122 Hh 46.59N 1.10 E
Châtillon-sur-Marne 124 Fe 49.06N 3.45 E
Châtillon-sur-Seine 122 Kg 47.51N 4.33 E
Chatom 184 Cj 31.28N 88.16W
Châtre, La- 122 Hh 46.35N 1.59 E
Chatsworth 172 Ec 19.38S 30.50 E
Chattahoochee 184 Ej 30.42N 84.51W
Chattahoochee ◲ 174 Kf 30.52N 84.57W
Chattanooga 176 Kf 35.03N 85.19W
Chatteris 124 Cb 52.27N 0.03 E
Chaucas 204 Cc 16.46S 58.44W
Chaudfontaine 124 Md 50.35N 5.38 E
Chaudière, Rivière- ◲ 184 Lb 46.43N 71.17W
Chau Doc 148 Lf 10.42N 105.07 E
Chauk 148 Ig 20.53N 94.49 E
Chaulnes 124 Ee 49.49N 2.48 E
Chaumont 122 Lf 48.07N 5.08 E
Chaumont-en-Vexin 124 De 49.16N 1.53 E
Chaumont-Gistoux 124 Gd 50.41N 4.44 E
Chaumont-Porcien 124 Md 49.39N 4.15 E
Chaumont-sur-Aire 124 Hf 48.56N 5.15 E
Chaumont-sur-Loire 122 Hg 47.29N 1.11 E
Chauny 122 Je 49.37N 3.13 E
Chausey, Iles- ◲ 122 Ef 48.53N 1.50W
Chauvigny 122 Gh 46.34N 0.39 E
Chavantina 202 Hf 14.40S 52.21W
Chavarria 204 Ci 28.57S 58.35W
Chaves [Braz.] 202 Id 0.10S 49.55W
Chaves [Port.] 126 Ec 41.44N 7.28W
Chavuma 170 De 13.05S 22.42 E
Chayia 146 If 32.09N 40.58 E
Chazelles-sur-Lyon 122 Ki 45.38N 4.23 E
Chbar 148 Lf 12.46N 107.10 E
Cheaha Mountain ▦ 184 Ei 33.30N 85.47W
Cheat River ◲ 184 Hf 39.45N 79.55W
Cheb 120 If 50.04N 12.23 E
Cheboygan 182 Kb 45.39N 84.29W
Chech, 'Erg- ▦ 158 Gf 25.00N 3.00W
Chechaouene 162 Fb 35.10N 5.16W
Chechaouene 3 162 Fb 35.00N 5.00W
Checheng 152 Lg 22.05N 120.42 E
Che-Chiang Sheng → Zhejiang 3 152 Kf 29.00N 120.00 E
Chech'ŏn 154 Jf 37.08N 128.12 E
Chęciny 120 Qf 50.48N 20.28 E
Cheddar Gorge ◲ 118 Kj 51.13N 2.47W
Cheduba ◲ 148 Ie 18.48N 93.38 E
Cheektowaga 184 Hd 42.57N 78.38W
Chefu 172 Ed 22.27S 32.45 E
Chegga 160 Gf 25.22N 5.49W
Cheghelvandí 146 Mf 33.42N 48.25 E
Chegutu 172 Ec 18.07S 30.08 E
Chehel Päyeh 146 Qg 31.54N 57.14 E
Cheju 152 Me 33.31N 126.32 E
Cheju-Do 2 154 Ih 33.25N 126.30 E
Cheju-Do 2 140 Of 33.25N 126.30 E
Cheju-Haehyŏp ◧ 154 Ih 33.40N 126.28 E
Chela, Serra da- ▦ 158 Ij 16.00S 13.10 E
Chelan 188 Fc 47.51N 120.01W
Chelan, Lake- ◧ 188 Eb 48.05N 120.30W
Chelforó, Arroyo- ◲ 204 Cm 36.55S 58.12W
Cheliff ◲ 158 Gd 36.10N 1.20 E
Cheliff, Plaine du- ▦ 126 Mi 35.57N 0.45 E
Chellalat el Adhaouara 126 Pi 35.56N 3.25 E
Chelleh Kháneh, Küh-e- ▦ 146 Md 36.52N 48.36 E
Chełm 120 Te 51.10N 23.28 E
Chełm 2 120 Te 51.10N 23.30 E
Chelmer ◲ 124 Cc 51.44N 0.42 E
Chełmińskie, Pojezierze- ◲ 120 Oc 53.20N 19.00 E
Chełmno 120 Oc 53.22N 18.26 E
Chelmsford 118 Nj 51.44N 0.28 E
Chełmża 120 Oc 53.12N 18.37 E
Cheltenham 118 Kj 51.54N 2.04W
Chelva 126 Ke 39.45N 0.59W
Chemainus 188 Db 48.55N 123.43W
Chemama ▦ 162 Ef 16.50N 14.00 E
Chembe 172 Ec 17.09S 34.53 E
Chembe 170 Ee 11.58S 28.45 E
Chemillé 122 Fg 47.13N 0.43W
Chemnitz → Karl-Marx-Stadt 112 He 50.50N 12.55 E
Chemult 188 Ee 43.13N 121.47W
Chenab ◲ 140 Jf 29.13N 70.49 E
Chenachane 162 Gd 26.00N 4.15W
Chenachane ◲ 158 Ge 25.17N 3.10W
Chenärbäshi 146 Lf 33.20N 46.20 E
Chen Barag Qi (Bayan Hure) 168 Kb 49.21N 119.25 E
Chencha 168 Cd 6.15N 37.34 E
Chencoyi 192 Nh 19.48N 90.14W
Cheney 188 Gc 47.29N 117.34W
Cheney Reservoir ◧ 186 Hd 37.45N 97.50W
Cheng'an 154 Cf 36.27N 114.41 E
Chengde 152 Kc 41.00N 117.57 E
Chengdu 142 Mf 30.45N 104.04 E
Chengkou 152 Ie 31.58N 108.37 E
Chengmai 152 Ih 19.50N 109.59 E
Chengshan Jiao ▦ 154 Gf 37.25N 122.42 E
Chengxian 152 Id 33.44N 105.42 E
Chengzitan 154 Fe 39.31N 122.12 E
Cheniscikali ◲ 132 Mh 42.06N 42.16 E
Chenjiagang 154 Eh 34.22N 119.45 E
Chenonceaux 122 Hg 47.20N 1.04 E
Chenxi 152 If 28.01N 110.12 E
Chenxian 152 Jf 25.47N 113.04 E
Chenying → Wannian 154 Dj 28.42N 117.04 E
Cheo Reo 219b Ce 20.47S 167.09 E
Chepén 202 Ce 7.14S 79.26W
Chepes 206 Gc 31.21S 66.36W
Chepo 194 Hi 9.10N 79.06W
Cher 3 122 Ig 47.00N 2.30 E
Cher ◲ 110 Gf 47.21N 0.29 E

Index Symbols

1 Independent Nation	▦ Historical or Cultural Region	▦ Pass, Gap	▦ Depression	▦ Coast, Beach	▦ Rock, Reef
2 State, Region	▦ Mount, Mountain	▦ Plain, Lowland	▦ Polder	▦ Cliff	▦ Islands, Archipelago
3 District, County	▦ Volcano	▦ Delta	▦ Desert, Dunes	▦ Peninsula	▦ Rocks, Reefs
4 Municipality	▦ Hill	▦ Salt Flat	▦ Forest, Woods	▦ Isthmus	▦ Coral Reef
5 Colony, Dependency	▦ Mountains, Mountain Range	▦ Valley, Canyon	▦ Heath, Steppe	▦ Sandbank	▦ Well, Spring
▦ Continent	▦ Hills, Escarpment	▦ Crater, Cave	▦ Oasis	▦ Island	▦ Geyser
▦ Physical Region	▦ Plateau, Upland	▦ Karst Features	▦ Cape, Point	▦ Atoll	▦ River, Stream

▦ Waterfall, Rapids	▦ Canal	▦ Lagoon	▦ Escarpment, Sea Scarp	▦ Historic Site	▦ Airport
▦ River Mouth, Estuary	▦ Glacier	▦ Bank	▦ Fracture	▦ Ruins	▦ Port
▦ Lake	▦ Ice Shelf, Pack Ice	▦ Seamount	▦ Trench, Abyss	▦ Wall, Walls	▦ Military installation
▦ Salt Lake	▦ Ocean	▦ Tablemount	▦ National Park, Reserve	▦ Church, Abbey	▦ Lighthouse
▦ Intermittent Lake	▦ Sea	▦ Ridge	▦ Point of Interest	▦ Temple	▦ Mine
▦ Reservoir	▦ Gulf, Bay	▦ Shelf	▦ Recreation Site	▦ Scientific Station	▦ Tunnel
▦ Swamp, Pond	▦ Strait, Fjord	▦ Basin	▦ Cave, Cavern	▦ Railway station	▦ Dam, Bridge

Cheradi, Isole-→ Coradi, Isole- 128 Lj 40.27N 17.09 E
Cherangany Hills 170 Gb 1.15N 35.27 E
Cheraw 184 Hh 34.42N 79.53W
Cherbaniani Reef 148 Ef 12.18N 71.53 E
Cherbourg 112 Ff 49.39N 1.39W
Cherchell 162 Hb 36.36N 2.12 E
Chère 122 Eg 47.42N 1.50W
Chergui, Chott Ech- 158 He 34.21N 0.30 E
Chéri 166 Hc 13.26N 11.21 E
Cherlen → Kerulen 140 Ne 48.48N 117.00 E
Cherokee 186 le 42.45N 95.33W
Cherokees, Lake O' the- 186 Ih 36.39N 94.49W
Cherski Mountains (EN) = Čerskogo, hrebet- [R.S.F.S.R.] 140 Qc 65.00N 145.00 E
Chertsey 124 Bc 51.23N 0.30W
Cherwell 118 Lj 51.44N 1.15W
Chesapeake 184 Lg 36.45N 76.15W
Chesapeake Bay 174 Lf 38.40N 76.25W
Chesapeake Bay Bridge-Tunnel 184 Ig 37.00N 76.02W
Chesha Bay (EN) = Češskaja guba 110 Kb 67.20N 46.30 E
Chesham 124 Bc 51.42N 0.36W
Cheshire [3] 118 Kj 53.15N 2.30W
Cheshire Plain 118 Kh 53.20N 2.40W
Cheshunt 124 Bc 51.42N 0.02W
Chesne, Le- 122 Ke 49.31N 4.46 E
Chester 118 Kh 53.10N 2.55W
Chester [Eng.-U.K.] 118 Kh 53.12N 2.54W
Chester [Il.-U.S.] 186 Lh 37.55N 89.49W
Chester [Mt.-U.S.] 188 Jb 48.31N 110.58W
Chester [Pa.-U.S.] 184 Jf 39.50N 75.23W
Chester [S.C.-U.S.] 184 Gh 34.40N 81.12W
Chesterfield 118 Lj 53.15N 1.25W
Chesterfield, Ile- 172 Gc 16.20S 43.58 E
Chesterfield, Récifs et Iles- =Chesterfield Reefs and Islands (EN) 208 Gf 20.00S 159.00 E
Chesterfield Inlet 176 Jc 63.21N 90.42W
Chesterfield Inlet 174 Jc 63.25N 90.45W
Chesterfield Reefs and Islands (EN)=Chesterfield, Récifs et Iles- 208 Gf 20.00S 159.00 E
Chesterton Range 212 Je 25.30S 147.30 E
Chestnut Ridge 184 He 40.10N 79.25W
Chesuncook Lake 184 Mb 46.00N 69.20W
Chetaibi 162 Ib 37.04N 7.23 E
Chetumal 176 Fe 18.35N 88.07W
Chetumal, Bahia de- 190 Ge 18.20N 88.05W
Cheviot 218 Ke 42.49S 173.16 E
Chew Bahir→Stefanie, Lake- (EN) 158 Kh 4.38N 36.50 E
Chewelah 188 Gb 48.17N 117.43W
Cheyenne [Ok.-U.S.] 186 Gg 35.37N 99.40W
Cheyenne [Wy.-U.S.] 176 le 41.08N 104.49W
Cheyenne 182 Gc 44.40N 101.15W
Cheyenne Wells 186 Gg 38.51N 102.11W
Cheylard, Le- 122 Kj 44.54N 4.25 E
Cheyne Bay 212 Df 34.35S 118.50 E
Chhatarpur 148 Ef 24.54N 79.36 E
Chhindwāra 148 Ff 22.04N 78.56 E
Chi 148 Ke 15.11N 104.43 E
Chiamboni, Rās- 168 Gf 1.38S 41.36 E
Chiana, Val di- 128 Fg 43.15N 11.50 E
Chianciano Terme 128 Fg 43.02N 11.49 E
Chiange 106 lj 15.45S 13.54 E
Chiang-hsi Sheng → Jiangxi Sheng [2] 152 Kf 28.00N 116.00 E
Chiang Mai 148 Lh 18.46N 98.58 E
Chiang Rai 148 Lh 19.54N 99.50 E
Chiang-su Sheng → Jiangsu Sheng = Kiangsu (EN) [2] 152 Ke 33.00N 120.00 E
Chiani 128 Gg 42.44N 12.07 E
Chianti 128 Fg 43.30N 11.25 E
Chiapa, Rio- 192 Mj 16.30N 93.10W
Chiapas [2] 176 Fe 16.30N 92.30W
Chiapas, Meseta de- 190 Fe 16.30N 92.00W
Chiaramonte Gulfi 128 Im 37.02N 14.42 E
Chiaravalle 128 Gf 43.36N 13.19 E
Chiaromonte 128 Kj 40.07N 16.13 E
Chiautla de Tapia 192 Jb 18.17N 98.36W
Chiavari 128 Df 44.19N 9.19 E
Chiavenna 128 De 46.19N 9.24 E
Chiayi 152 Lg 23.29N 120.27 E
Chiba 152 Pd 35.36N 140.07 E
Chiba Ken [2] 154 Gg 35.40N 140.20 E
Chibemba 170 Bf 15.45S 14.06 E
Chibia 170 Bf 15.11S 13.41 E
Chibougamau 176 Le 49.53N 74.21W
Chibougamau, Lac- 184 Ja 49.50N 74.15W
Chibougamau, Rivière- 184 Ja 49.50N 74.25W
Chiburi-Jima 154 Lf 36.01N 133.02 E
Chicago 176 Kf 41.53N 87.38W
Chicago Heights 186 Mf 41.30N 87.38W
Chicala 170 Ce 11.59S 19.30 E
Chicapa 170 Ji 6.25S 20.48 E
Chic-Chocs, Monts- 184 Na 48.55N 66.45W
Chicha 168 Bb 16.52N 18.33 E
Chichagof 178 Kf 57.30N 135.30W
Chichancanab, Laguna de- 192 Oh 19.54N 88.46W
Chichaoua 162 Fc 31.32N 8.46W
Chichas, Cordillera de- 202 Be 20.30S 66.30W
Chicheng 152 Kc 40.55N 115.47 E
Chichén Itzá 176 Gd 20.40N 88.35W
Chichester 118 Mk 50.50N 0.48W
Chichester Range 212 Cd 22.20S 119.20 E
Chichibu 154 Gg 35.59N 139.05 E
Chichijima-Rettō 214 Cb 27.06N 142.12 E
Chichilla de Monte Aragón 126 Kf 38.55N 1.43W
Chichiriviche 196 Mh 10.56N 68.45W
Chickasawhay River 186 Lk 31.00N 88.45W
Chickasha 182 Hd 35.02N 97.58W
Chicken 178 Kd 64.04N 141.56W

Chiclana de la Frontera 126 Fh 36.25N 6.08W
Chiclayo 200 If 6.46S 79.50W
Chico 182 Cd 39.44N 121.50W
Chico, Rio- [Arg.] 198 Jj 49.56S 68.32W
Chico, Rio- [Arg.] 198 Jj 43.48S 66.25W
Chicoana 206 Gc 25.06S 65.03W
Chicomo 172 Ed 24.31S 34.17 E
Chiconono 172 Fb 12.57S 35.45 E
Chicopee 184 Kd 42.10N 72.36W
Chicote 170 Df 16.01S 21.48 E
Chicoutimi 176 Le 48.26N 71.04W
Chicoutimi Nord 184 La 48.29N 71.02W
Chicualacuala 172 Ed 22.05S 31.42 E
Chidenguele 172 Ed 24.55S 34.10 E
Chidley, Cape- 174 Mc 60.25N 64.30W
Chiemsee 120 li 47.54N 12.29 E
Chiengi 170 Ed 8.39S 29.10 E
Chienti 128 Gg 43.18N 13.45 E
Chiers 122 Ke 49.39N 5.00 E
Chiese 128 Ee 45.08N 10.25 E
Chieti 128 Ih 42.21N 14.10 E
Chièvres 122 Id 50.35N 3.48 E
Chifeng/Ulanhad 152 Kc 42.16N 118.57 E
Chifumage 170 De 12.10S 22.30 E
Chifwefwe 170 Fe 13.35S 29.35 E
Chigasaki 154 Gg 35.19N 139.24 E
Chignik 178 Me 56.18N 158.23W
Chigombe 172 Ed 23.26S 33.19 E
Chigorodó 194 lj 7.41N 76.41W
Chigubo 172 Ed 22.50S 33.31 E
Chigu Co 152 Ff 28.40N 91.50 E
Chi He 154 Db 32.51N 117.59 E
Chihli, Gulf of- (EN) = Bo Hai 140 Nf 38.30N 120.00 E
Chihuahua 176 lg 28.38N 106.05W
Chihuahua [2] 190 Cc 28.30N 106.00W
Chii-san 154 lg 35.20N 127.44 E
Chikaskia River 186 Hh 36.37N 97.15W
Chikugo 156 Be 33.13N 130.30 E
Chikugo-Gawa 156 Be 33.10N 130.21 E
Chikuma-Gawa 156 Fc 37.00N 138.35 E
Chikwana 170 Ff 16.03S 34.48 E
Chilapa de Álvarez 192 Ji 17.36N 99.10W
Chilas 148 Ea 35.26N 74.05 E
Chilaw 148 Fg 7.34N 79.47 E
Chilcotin 180 Ff 51.46N 122.22W
Childers 212 Ke 25.14S 152.17 E
Childress 182 Ge 34.25N 100.13W
Chile 200 li 30.00S 71.00W
Chile Basin (EN) 106 Mm 33.00S 90.00W
Chile Chico 206 Gc 46.33S 71.44W
Chilecito [Arg.] 206 Gc 29.10S 67.30W
Chilecito [Arg.] 206 Gd 33.53S 69.03W
Chile Rise (EN) 106 Mm 40.00S 90.00W
Chilia, Brațul- 130 Mc 45.13N 29.43 E
Chililabombwe 170 Ee 12.22S 27.50 E
Chi-lin Sheng → Jilin Sheng = Kirin (EN) [2] 152 Mc 43.00N 126.00 E
Chilko Lake 188 Ca 51.20N 124.05W
Chilko River 188 Da 52.00N 123.40W
Chillán 200 li 36.36S 72.07W
Chillar 206 Je 37.18S 59.59W
Chillicothe [Il.-U.S.] 186 Lf 40.55N 89.29W
Chillicothe [Mo.-U.S.] 186 Kg 39.48N 93.33W
Chillicothe [Oh.-U.S.] 182 Kd 39.20N 82.59W
Chilliwack 188 Db 49.10N 121.57W
Chiloé, Isla de- 198 lj 42.30S 73.55W
Chilón 192 Mi 17.14N 92.25W
Chiloquin 188 Cd 42.35N 121.52W
Chilpancingo de los Bravos 190 Ee 17.33N 99.30W
Chiltern Hills 118 Mj 51.42N 0.48W
Chilton 186 Ld 44.02N 88.10W
Chiluage 170 Dd 9.31S 21.46 E
Chilumba 170 Fe 10.27S 34.16 E
Chilwa, Lake- 170 Gf 15.12S 35.50 E
Chimala 170 Ff 8.51S 34.01 E
Chimaltenango 194 Bf 14.39N 90.49W
Chimaltenango [3] 194 Bf 14.40N 90.55W
Chimán 194 Hi 8.42N 78.37W
Chimanas, Islas- 196 Dg 10.17N 64.38W
Chimanimani 172 Ec 19.48S 32.50 E
Chimay 124 Ga 50.03N 4.19 E
Chimbas 206 Ff 31.28S 68.30W
Chimborazo, Volcán- 198 If 1.28S 78.48W
Chimbote 200 If 9.05S 78.36W
Chimichagua 196 Ki 9.16S 73.49W
Chimoio 172 Ec 19.06S 33.23 E
Chimorra 126 He 38.18N 4.53W
Chin [2] 148 Id 22.00N 93.30 E
China [Jap.] 156b Bb 27.20N 128.19 E
China [Mex.] 192 Je 25.42N 99.14W
China (EN) = Zhōngguó 140 Mg 35.00N 105.00 E
China → Zhonghua Renmin Gongheguo [1] 142 Mf 35.00N 105.00 E
Chinacates 192 Gf 25.00N 105.13W
China Lake 188 Gi 35.46N 117.39W
Chinandega 190 Gf 12.37N 87.09W
Chinandega [3] 194 Dg 12.45N 87.05W
Chinati Peak 186 Dl 29.57N 104.29W
Chincha Alta 200 Cf 13.27S 76.08W
Chinchaga 180 Fe 58.52N 118.19W
Chinchilla 212 Ke 26.45S 150.38 E
Chinchón 126 Id 40.08N 3.25W
Chinchorro, Banco- 190 Ge 18.35N 87.20W
Chincoteague 184 Lf 37.55N 75.23W
Chinde 160 Kj 18.34S 36.27 E
Chin-Do 154 Ig 34.25N 126.15 E
Chindu 152 Ge 33.30N 96.31 E
Chindwin 140 Lg 21.26N 95.15 E

Chinhoyi 160 Kj 17.22S 30.12 E
Chiniot 148 Eb 31.43N 72.59 E
Chinipas 192 Ed 27.23N 108.32W
Chinju 152 Md 35.11N 128.05 E
Chinko 158 Jh 4.50N 23.53 E
Chinle 188 Kh 36.09N 109.33W
Chinle Creek 188 Kh 37.12N 109.43W
Chinmen = Quemoy (EN) 152 Kg 24.25N 118.25 E
Chino 156 Fd 36.00N 138.09 E
Chinon 122 Gg 47.10N 0.15 E
Chinook 188 Kb 48.35N 109.14W
Chinquila 192 Pg 21.30N 87.25W
Chinsali 170 Fe 10.33S 32.04 E
Chinteche 170 Fe 11.50S 34.10 E
Chinú 202 Cb 9.06N 75.24W
Chinvali 154 He 49.44N 5.20 E
Chinyŏng 154 Jg 35.18N 128.44 E
Chioco 172 Ec 16.25S 32.50 E
Chioggia 128 Ge 45.13N 12.17 E
Chios (EN) = Khios 110 Ih 38.22N 26.00 E
Chipata 160 Kj 13.39S 32.40 E
Chipepo 170 Ef 16.49S 27.50 E
Chipindo 170 Ce 13.48S 15.48 E
Chiping 154 Df 36.35N 116.16 E
Chipinge 172 Ec 20.12S 32.38 E
Chipman 184 Ob 46.11N 65.53W
Chippawa, Lake- 186 Kc 45.56N 91.13W
Chippewa Falls 182 Ic 44.56N 91.24W
Chippewa River [Mn.-U.S.] 186 Id 44.56N 95.44W
Chippewa River [Wi.-U.S.] 186 Jd 44.25N 92.10W
Chipping Ongar 124 Cc 51.42N 0.15 E
Chiputneticook Lakes 184 Mc 45.45N 68.45W
Chiquián 202 Cf 10.09S 77.11W
Chiquimula 194 Cf 14.48N 89.33W
Chiquimula [3] 194 Cf 14.40N 89.25W
Chiquimulilla 194 Bf 14.05N 90.23W
Chiquinquirá 202 Db 5.37N 73.50W
Chiquitos, Llanos de- 202 Fg 18.00S 61.30W
Chirāla 148 Ge 15.49N 80.21 E
Chiran 156 Bf 31.22N 130.27 E
Chiredzi 160 Kk 21.03S 31.45 E
Chirfa 166 Ha 20.57N 12.21 E
Chirgua, Rio- 196 Bh 8.30N 68.01W
Chiricahua Peak 188 Jj 31.52N 109.20W
Chiriguaná 194 Ki 9.22N 73.37W
Chirikof 178 Me 55.50N 155.35W
Chiriqui [3] 194 Fi 8.30N 82.00W
Chiriqui, Golfo de- 194 Fi 8.00N 82.20W
Chiriqui, Laguna de- 190 Hg 9.03N 82.00W
Chiriqui Grande 194 Fi 8.57N 82.07W
Chirnogi 194 Je 44.07N 26.34 E
Chiromo 170 Ff 16.33S 35.08 E
Chirripó, Cerro- 174 Hi 9.29N 83.29W
Chirripó, Rio- [C.R.] 194 Fh 10.41N 83.41W
Chirripó, Rio- [C.R.] 194 Fh 10.03N 83.16W
Chirundu 170 Ef 15.59S 28.54 E
Chisamba 170 Ee 14.59S 28.23 E
Chisăpăni Garhi 148 Hc 27.34N 85.08 E
Chisasibi 176 Ld 53.50N 79.00W
Chisenga 170 Fd 9.56S 33.26 E
Chishui 152 Hf 28.30N 105.44 E
Chişineu Criş 130 Ec 46.32N 21.31 E
Chisone 128 Bf 44.49N 7.25 E
Chitado 170 Bf 17.18S 13.54 E
Chita-Hantō 156 Ee 34.50N 136.50 E
Chitati 168 Ac 14.40N 14.30 E
Chitato 160 Ji 7.22S 20.49 E
Chitembo 170 Ce 13.31S 16.45 E
Chitina 178 Kd 61.31N 144.27W
Chitina 178 Kd 61.30N 144.28W
Chitipa 170 Fd 9.43S 33.16 E
Chitorgarh 148 Ee 24.53N 74.38 E
Chitose 154 Pc 42.49N 141.39 E
Chitradurga 148 Ff 14.14N 76.24 E
Chitrāl 148 Ea 35.51N 71.47 E
Chitré 190 Hi 7.58N 80.26W
Chittagong 148 Lg 22.20N 91.50 E
Chittoor 148 Ff 13.12N 79.07 E
Chiumbe 170 Ji 6.59S 21.12 E
Chiume 170 Df 15.08S 21.12 E
Chiusi 128 Fg 43.01N 11.57 E
Chiusi, Lago di- 128 Fg 43.05N 12.00 E
Chiva 126 Le 39.28N 0.43W
Chivacoa 196 Bg 10.10N 68.54W
Chivapuri, Rio- 196 Ci 6.25N 66.23W
Chivasso 128 Be 45.11N 7.53 E
Chivay 202 Dg 15.38S 71.36W
Chivhu 172 Ec 19.01S 30.53 E
Chivilcoy 206 Hd 34.53S 60.01W
Chizu 156 Dd 35.15N 134.14 E
Chŏăm Khsant 148 Kf 14.13N 104.56 E
Choapa, Rio- 206 Fd 31.38S 71.34W
Chobe [3] 172 Cc 18.30S 25.00 E
Chobe 172 Cc 17.47S 25.00 E
Choch'iwŏn 154 If 36.37N 127.18 E
Chocó [2] 202 Cb 6.00N 77.00W
Chocolate Mountains 188 Hj 33.25N 114.10W
Chodecz 120 Pd 52.24N 19.01 E
Chodov 120 la 50.15N 12.45 E
Chodzież 120 Lc 52.59N 16.55 E
Choele-Choel 206 Gf 39.16S 65.41W
Choiceland 180 le 53.29N 104.29W
Choique 206 Ge 38.19S 64.23W
Choiseul 208 Ec 7.00S 157.00 E
Choiseul Island 197a Kb 13.47N 61.03W
Choix 192 Ee 26.43N 108.17W
Chojna 120 Jc 52.58N 14.28 E
Chojnice 120 Nc 53.42N 17.34 E
Chojnów 120 Kd 51.16N 15.56 E
Chōkai-San 140 Qf 39.10N 140.02 E
Choke 158 Kg 10.45N 37.35 E

Chókué 172 Ed 24.27S 32.55 E
Cho La 152 Ge 31.52N 98.51 E
Cholet 122 Fg 47.04N 0.53W
Chŏlla-Namdo [2] 154 Ig 34.45N 127.00 E
Chŏlla-Pukto [2] 154 Ig 35.45N 127.15 E
Cholo 170 Gf 16.04S 35.08 E
Cholula 192 Jb 19.04N 98.18W
Choluteca 190 Gf 13.18N 87.12W
Choluteca [3] 194 Dg 13.20N 87.10W
Choluteca, Rio- 194 Dg 13.07N 87.19W
Choma 160 Jj 16.49S 26.59 E
Chomo/Yadong 152 Ff 27.38N 89.03 E
Chomo Lhari 152 Ff 27.50N 89.16 E
Chomutov 120 Ja 50.28N 13.25 E
Ch'ŏnan 152 Md 36.48N 127.09 E
Chon Buri 148 Kf 13.22N 100.59 E
Chone 202 Bd 0.42S 80.07W
Ch'ŏngch'ŏn-gang 154 He 39.35N 125.28 E
Ch'ŏngjin 154 Oe 41.46N 129.49 E
Ch'ŏngju Si [2] 154 Jf 41.45N 129.45 E
Ch'ŏngju 152 Md 36.38N 127.30 E
Chŏngp'yŏng 154 Ig 35.34N 126.51 E
Chongyang 152 Cj 29.32N 114.02 E
Chongzuo 152 Hg 22.29N 107.22 E
Chŏnju 154 Md 35.49N 127.09 E
Chonos, Archipiélago de los- 198 Ij 45.00S 74.00W
Chontaleña, Cordillera- 194 Eh 11.50N 85.00W
Chontales [3] 194 Eg 12.05N 85.10W
Chopim 204 Fg 25.35S 53.05W
Chopinzinho 204 Fg 25.51S 52.30W
Chorito, Sierra del- 126 le 39.25N 4.25W
Choroszcz 120 Sc 53.09N 22.59 E
Chorreras, Cerro- 192 Fd 26.02N 106.21W
Ch'ŏrwŏn 154 Ig 38.15N 127.13 E
Chorzele 120 Qc 53.16N 20.55 E
Chorzów 120 Of 50.19N 18.57 E
Ch'osan 154 Hd 40.45N 125.50 E
Chosébuz/Cottbus 120 Ke 51.46N 14.20 E
Chōshi 154 Pg 35.44N 140.50 E
Chos Malal 206 Fe 37.23S 70.16W
Chosŏn M.I.K. = North Korea (Chosŏn M.I.K.)=Chosŏn Minjujuŭi-Inmin-Konghwaguk (EN) [1] 142 Oe 40.00N 127.30 E
Chosŏn Minjujuŭi-Inmin-Konghwaguk [1] 142 Oe 40.00N 127.30 E
Choszczno 120 Lc 53.10N 15.26 E
Chota 202 Ce 6.33S 78.39W
Chotanāgpur Plateau 140 Kg 22.00N 86.00 E
Choteau 188 Ic 47.49N 112.11W
Chotla, Cerro de- 192 Ih 17.55N 101.31W
Choukhot, Djebel- 126 Qh 36.01N 4.11 E
Choum 166 Ec 21.18N 12.59W
Chovd → Kobdo 152 Fb 48.06N 92.11 E
Chövsgöl Nuur → Hubsugul Nur 140 Md 51.00N 100.30 E
Chowchilla 188 Eh 37.07N 120.16W
Chowra 148 Ig 8.27N 93.02 E
Chréa 126 Oh 36.25N 2.53 E
Chřiby 120 Ng 49.10N 17.20 E
Christchurch 210 li 43.32S 172.37 E
Christian, Cape- 180 Kb 70.32N 68.18W
Christian, Point- 220a Ab 25.04S 130.07W
Christiana 172 De 27.52S 25.08 E
Christian IV Gletscher 179 le 68.40N 30.20W
Christiansburg 184 Ha 37.07N 80.26W
Christiansfeld 116 Ce 55.21N 9.29 E
Christianshåb/Qasigiánguit 179 Gd 68.45N 51.30W
Christiansø 116 Fi 55.20N 15.10 E
Christian Sound 178 Le 55.56N 134.40W
Christiansted 197a Dc 17.46N 64.42W
Christiansted Harbor 197a Dc 17.46N 64.42W
Christie Bay 180 Gd 62.45N 110.15W
Christmas → Kiritimati Atoll 208 Lg 1.52N 157.20W
Christmas Creek 212 Fc 18.53S 125.55 E
Christmas Island 212 Fc 18.29S 125.23 E
Christmas Island 106 Ki 10.30S 105.40 E
Christmas Ridge (EN) 106 Ki 10.00N 165.00W
Chrudim 120 Lf 49.57N 15.47 E
Chrzanów 120 Pf 50.09N 19.24 E
Chrząstowa 120 Nc 53.35N 16.58 E
Chuanshan 154 Jg 31.11N 121.42 E
Chúbar 146 Mc 38.11N 48.51 E
Chubut [2] 206 Gf 44.00S 69.00W
Chubut, Rio- 198 Jj 43.20S 65.03W
Chucunaque, Rio- 194 lj 8.09N 77.44W
Chuginadak 178 Ef 52.49N 169.50W
Chŭgoku-Sanchi 154 Pf 35.15N 133.30 E
Chu Lai 148 Le 15.25N 108.48 E
Chuhuichupa 192 Ec 29.38N 108.22W
Chui 204 Fk 33.41S 53.27W
Chuka 170 Gc 0.20S 37.39 E
Chukai 150 Df 4.15N 103.25 E
Chukchi Peninsula (EN) = Čukotski poluostrov 140 Uc 66.00N 175.00 E
Chukchi Plateau 224 Bd 78.00N 165.00W
Chukchi Sea 224 Bd 69.00N 171.00W
Chukchi Sea (EN) = Čukotskoje more 69.00N 171.00W
Chula Vista 188 Gj 32.39N 117.05W
Chulitna 178 Jd 62.55N 139.29W
Chullo 154 Jg 37.10N 127.12 E
Chulucanas 202 Be 5.06S 80.10W
Chumbicha 206 Gc 28.50S 66.14W
Chumikan 140 Se 54.42N 135.18 E
Chumphon 148 Jf 10.32N 99.13 E
Chuna 138 Fd 57.53N 128.49 E
Chunan 154 Jg 35.08N 127.44 E
Ch'unch'ŏn 152 Md 37.52N 127.44 E
Chunga 170 Ef 15.03S 26.00 E
Ch'ungch'ŏng-Namdo [2] 154 If 36.30N 127.00 E

Ch'ungch'ŏng-Pukto [2] 154 Jf 36.45N 128.00 E
Ch'ungju 152 Md 36.58N 127.56 E
Chungking → Chongqing 142 Mg 29.34N 106.27 E
Ch'ungmu 154 Jg 34.51N 128.26 E
Chunya 170 Fd 8.32S 33.25 E
Chuŏr Phnum Krâvanh 140 Mh 12.00N 103.15 E
Chuquibamba 202 Dg 15.50S 72.39W
Chuquibambilla 202 Df 14.07S 72.43W
Chuquicamata 206 Gb 22.19S 68.56W
Chuquisaca [3] 202 Eg 20.00S 64.20W
Chur/Cuera 128 Dd 46.50N 9.35 E
Churchill 176 Jd 58.46N 94.10W
Churchill [Can.] 174 Md 53.30N 60.10W
Churchill [Can.] 174 Jd 58.47N 94.12W
Churchill, Cape - 180 le 58.46N 93.12W
Churchill Falls 180 Lf 53.30N 64.10W
Churchill Lake 180 Le 56.05N 108.15W
Churchill Peak 180 Ee 58.20N 125.02W
Churchill Range 222 Eg 81.30S 158.30 E
Chūru 148 Ec 28.18N 74.57 E
Churuguara 202 Ea 10.49N 69.32W
Churún Merú/Angel, Salto- = Ángel Falls (EN) 198 Je 5.57N 62.30W
Chuska Mountains 188 Kh 36.15N 108.50W
Chute-des-Passes 180 Kg 49.50N 71.00W
Chuxian 152 Ke 32.16N 118.15 E
Chuxiong 152 Hf 25.02N 101.32 E
Chuy 204 Fk 33.41S 53.27W
Ciamis 150 Eh 7.20S 108.21 E
Ciarraí/Kerry [2] 118 Di 52.10N 9.30W
Ciatura 132 Mh 42.17N 43.17 E
Cibuta, Cerro- 192 Db 31.02N 110.58W
Ćićarija 128 He 45.28N 13.54 E
Ćićevac 130 Nb 43.43N 21.27 E
Cicicleja 130 Nb 47.23N 30.50 E
Cicolano 128 Hh 45.15N 13.10 E
Cidacos 126 Kb 42.19N 1.55W
Cide 146 Ea 41.54N 33.00 E
Cidlina 120 Lf 50.09N 15.12 E
Ciechanów 120 Qd 52.53N 20.38 E
Ciechanów [2] 120 Qd 52.55N 20.40 E
Ciechanowiec 120 Sd 52.42N 22.31 E
Ciechanowska, Wysoczyzna- 120 Qc 53.10N 20.30 E
Ciego de Ávila 190 Jd 21.51N 78.46W
Ciego de Ávila [3] 194 Hb 22.00N 78.40W
Ciénaga 202 Da 11.00N 74.14W
Ciénaga de Flores 192 le 25.57N 100.11W
Ciénaga de Oro 194 Ji 8.53N 75.38W
Cieneguita 192 Fd 27.57N 106.59W
Cienfuegos 176 Kg 22.09N 80.27W
Cienfuegos [3] 194 Gb 22.15N 80.30W
Cies, Islas- 126 Db 42.13N 8.54W
Cieszanów 120 Tf 50.16N 23.08 E
Cieza 126 Kf 38.14N 1.25W
Çiftehan 146 Dc 39.22N 31.03 E
Cifuentes 126 Jd 40.47N 2.37W
Çiğanak 146 Mf 45.05N 73.58 E
Čigirin 132 He 49.03N 32.42 E
Cigüela 126 le 39.08N 3.44W
Cihanbeyli 146 Ec 38.40N 32.56 E
Cihanbeyli Platosu 146 Ec 38.40N 32.45 E
Cihareşi 132 Mf 42.47N 43.02 E
Cihuatlán 192 Gh 19.14N 104.35W
Čiily 146 Me 44.13N 66.46 E
Cijara, Embalse de- 126 He 39.18N 4.52W
Cijulang 150 Eh 7.44S 108.27 E
Čik 130 Dd 45.42N 20.04 E
Cikorija 138 Ff 51.02N 106.39 E
Cikura 126 Qh 36.01N 4.25 E
Cilacap 150 Eh 7.44S 109.00 E
Čikurački, vulkan- 138 Kf 50.15N 155.29 E
Cilalci 140 If 52.03N 9.30W
Cill Airne/Killarney 118 Di 52.03N 9.30W
Cill Chainnigh/Kilkenny 118 Fi 52.39N 7.15W
Cill Chainnigh/Kilkenny [2] 118 Fi 52.40N 7.15W
Cill Chaoi/Kilkee 118 Di 52.41N 9.38W
Cill Dara/Kildare 118 Gh 53.10N 6.55W
Cill Dara/Kildare [2] 118 Gh 53.10N 6.45W
Cill Mhantáin/Wicklow 118 Hi 52.59N 6.03W
Cill Mhantáin/Wicklow [2] 118 Hi 52.59N 6.30W
Cill Mocheallóg/Kilmallock 118 Ei 52.25N 8.35W
Cill Rois/Kilrush 118 Di 52.39N 9.29W
Cilma 134 Fd 65.25N 52.05 E
Cilo Dağı 146 Kd 37.30N 44.00 E
Cimaltepec, Sierra- 190 Ee 16.00N 96.40W
Cimarron 186 Gh 36.31N 104.55W
Cimarron, Rio- 174 Jf 36.10N 96.17W
Cîmini, Monti- 128 Gg 42.24N 12.12 E
Cimišlija 132 Ff 46.32N 28.46 E
Çimkent 142 le 42.18N 69.36 E
Čimkentskaja oblast [3] 136 Gd 68.40 E
Cimljansk 132 Le 47.37N 42.04 E
Cimljanskoje vodohranilišče = Tsimlyansk Reservoir (EN) 110 Kf 48.00N 43.00 E
Cimone 110 Kf 44.12N 10.40 E
Cîmpeni 130 Gc 46.22N 23.03 E
Cîmpia Turzii 130 Id 46.33N 23.53 E
Cîmpina 130 Jd 45.08N 25.44 E
Cîmpulung 130 Id 45.16N 25.03 E
Cîmpulung Moldovenesc 130 Ib 47.32N 25.34 E
Cîntang, gora- 136 Id 45.00N 80.25 E
Cina, Tanjung- 150 Dh 5.55S 104.35 E
Çinar 146 Jd 37.39N 40.08 E
Cinaruco, Rio- 196 Ci 6.41N 67.07W
Çinarcik 146 Mi 40.39N 29.06 E
Cinca 126 Mc 41.26N 0.21 E
Cincar 128 Lg 43.54N 17.04 E
Cincinnati 176 Kf 39.06N 84.31W

Index Symbols

[1] Independent Nation	Historical or Cultural Region	Pass, Gap	Depression
[2] State, Region	Mount, Mountain	Plain, Lowland	Polder
[3] District, County	Volcano	Delta	Desert, Dunes
[4] Municipality	Hill	Salt Flat	Forest, Woods
[5] Colony, Dependency	Mountains, Mountain Range	Valley, Canyon	Heath, Steppe
Continent	Hills, Escarpment	Crater, Cave	Oasis
Physical Region	Plateau, Upland	Karst Features	Island

Coast, Beach	Rock, Reef	Waterfall, Rapids	Canal
Cliff	Islands, Archipelago	River Mouth, Estuary	Glacier
Peninsula	Rocks, Reefs	Ice Shelf, Pack Ice	Ocean
Rocks, Reefs	Coral Reef	Intermittent Lake	Sea
Well, Spring	Salt Lake	Reservoir	Ridge
Geyser	Island	Gulf, Bay	Shelf
River, Stream	Cape, Point	Strait, Fjord	Basin

Lagoon	Escarpment, Sea Scarp	Historic Site	Airport
Bank	Fracture	Ruins	Port
Seamount	Trench, Abyss	Wall, Walls	Military installation
Tablemount	National Park, Reserve	Church, Abbey	Lighthouse
Point of Interest	Temple	Mine	
Recreation Site	Scientific Station	Tunnel	
Cave, Cavern	Railway station	Dam, Bridge	

Cinco Irmãos, Serra dos- 204 Ff 22.55S 52.50W
Cinco Saltos 206 Ge 38.49S 68.04W
Cindrelu, Vîrful- 130 Gd 45.35N 23.48 E
Çine 146 Cd 37.36N 28.04 E
Çine 130 Kl 37.46N 27.49 E
Ciney 122 Ld 50.18N 5.06 E
Cingirlau 136 Fe 51.07N 54.05 E
Cingoli 128 Hg 43.22N 13.13 E
Cintalapa de Figueroa 192 Mi 16.44N 93.43W
Cinto, Monte- 110 Gg 42.23N 8.56 E
Cintra, Golfo de- 162 De 23.00N 16.15W
Cinzas, Rio das- 204 Gf 22.56S 50.32W
Ciociaria 128 Hi 41.45N 13.15 E
Cionn Mhálanna/Malin Head 110 Fd 55.23N 7.24W
Cionn tSáile/Kinsale 118 Ej 51.42N 8.32W
Ciorani 130 Je 44.49N 26.25 E
Ciotat, La- 122 Lk 43.10N 5.36 E
Čiovo 128 Kg 43.30N 16.18 E
Cipa 138 Ge 55.20N 115.55 E
Cipikan 138 Gf 54.58N 113.21 E
Cipó 202 Kf 11.06S 38.31W
Cipolletti 206 Ge 38.56S 67.59W
Čiprovci 130 Ff 43.23N 22.53 E
Čir 132 Me 48.35N 42.55 E
Circeo, Capo- 128 Hi 41.14N 13.03 E
Čirčik 136 Gg 41.28N 69.35 E
Circle [Ak.-U.S.] 178 Kc 65.50N 144.04W
Circle [Mt.-U.S.] 188 Mc 47.25N 105.35W
Circleville 184 Ff 39.36N 82.57W
Cirebon 142 Mj 6.44S 108.34 E
Cirencester 118 Lj 51.44N 1.59W
Cirié 128 Be 45.14N 7.36 E
Čirinda 138 Fc 67.30N 100.35 E
Čirip, vulkan- 138 Jg 45.20N 147.58 E
Čirka-Kem 136 Hd 64.45N 32.10 E
Cirò 128 Lk 39.23N 17.04 E
Cirò Marina 128 Lk 39.22N 17.08 E
Ciron 122 Fj 44.36N 0.18W
Čirpan 130 Ig 42.12N 25.20 E
Cirque Mountain 180 Le 58.55N 63.33W
Cisa, Passo della- 128 Df 44.28N 9.55 E
Ciscaucasia (EN) 110 Kf 45.00N 43.00 E
Cisco 186 Gj 32.23N 98.59W
Ciskei 172 Df 31.30S 26.40 E
Čišmy 136 Fe 54.35N 55.25 E
Cisnădie 130 Hd 45.43N 24.09 E
Cisne, Islas del- 190 He 17.22N 83.51W
Cistern Point 194 Ib 24.40N 77.45W
Cistierna 126 Gb 42.48N 5.07W
Čistoozernoje 138 Cf 54.43N 76.43 E
Čistopol 136 Fd 55.23N 50.39 E
Čita 142 Nd 52.03N 113.30 E
Çitak 130 Mk 38.08N 29.39 E
Citeli-Ckaro 132 Oi 41.28N 46.06 E
Čitinskaya oblast 138 Gf 52.30N 117.30 E
Citlaltépetl, Volcán- → Orizaba, Pico de- 174 Jh 19.01N 97.16W
Citrusdale 172 Bf 32.36S 19.00 E
Città del Vaticano = Vatican City (EN) [1] 112 Hg 41.54N 12.27 E
Città di Castello 128 Gg 43.27N 12.14 E
Cittanova 128 Kl 38.21N 16.05 E
Ciucaşu, Vîrful- 130 Id 45.31N 25.55 E
Ciucea 130 Fc 46.57N 22.49 E
Ciudad 192 Gf 23.44N 105.44W
Ciudad Acuña 190 Dc 29.18N 100.55W
Ciudad Altamirano 192 Ih 18.20N 100.40W
Ciudad Bolívar 200 Je 8.08N 63.33W
Ciudad Bolivia 202 Db 8.21N 70.34W
Ciudad Camargo [Mex.] 190 Cc 27.40N 105.10W
Ciudad Camargo [Mex.] 190 Ec 26.19N 98.50W
Ciudad Cuauhtémoc 192 Mj 15.37N 92.00W
Ciudad Dario 192 Dg 12.43N 86.08W
Ciudad de Areco 204 Cl 34.18S 59.46W
Ciudad de la Habana [3] 194 Fb 23.10N 82.10W
Ciudad del Carmen 190 Fe 18.38N 91.50W
Ciudad del Maiz 192 Jf 22.24N 99.36W
Ciudad de México=Mexico City (EN) 176 Jh 19.24N 99.09W
Ciudad de Nutrias 202 Eb 8.07N 69.19W
Ciudad de Rio Grande 190 Dd 23.50N 103.02W
Ciudadela/Ciutadella 126 Pd 40.02N 3.50 E
Ciudad Guayana 200 Je 8.22N 62.40W
Ciudad Guerrero 190 Cc 28.33N 107.30W
Ciudad Guzmán 190 De 19.41N 103.29W
Ciudad Hidalgo [Mex.] 192 Ih 19.41N 100.34W
Ciudad Hidalgo [Mex.] 192 Mj 14.41N 92.09W
Ciudad Juárez 176 If 31.44N 106.29W
Ciudad Lerdo 190 Dc 25.32N 103.32W
Ciudad Madero 176 Jg 22.16N 97.50W
Ciudad Mante 190 Ed 22.44N 98.57W
Ciudad Mendoza 192 Kh 18.48N 97.11W
Ciudad Obregón 176 Ig 27.59N 109.56W
Ciudad Ojeda 202 Da 10.12N 71.19W
Ciudad Piar 202 Fb 7.27N 63.19W
Ciudad Real 126 If 38.59N 3.56W
Ciudad Real [3] 126 If 39.00N 4.00W
Ciudad Rio Bravo 190 Ec 25.59N 98.06W
Ciudad-Rodrigo 126 Fd 40.36N 6.32W
Ciudad Valles 190 Ed 21.59N 99.01W
Ciudad Victoria 176 Jg 23.44N 99.08W
Ciutadella/Ciudadela 126 Pd 40.02N 3.50 E
Civa Burnu 146 Gb 41.22N 36.35 E
Cividale del Friuli 128 Hd 46.06N 13.25 E
Civilsk 114 Li 55.53N 47.29 E
Civita Castellana 128 Gh 42.17N 12.25 E
Civitanova Marche 128 Hg 43.18N 13.44 E
Civitavecchia 128 Fh 42.06N 11.48 E
Civitella del Tronto 128 Hh 42.46N 13.40 E
Çivril 146 Cc 38.56N 35.29 E
Cixerri 128 Ck 39.17N 8.59 E
Cixi (Hushan) 154 Fi 30.10N 121.14 E
Cixian 154 Cf 36.22N 114.22 E
Čiža 136 Eb 67.06N 44.19 E
Cizre 144 Fb 37.20N 42.12 E
Cjurupinsk 132 Hf 46.37N 32.43 E
Čkalovsk 114 Kh 56.47N 43.17 E
Clacton-on-Sea 118 Oj 51.48N 1.09 E
Clain 122 Gh 46.47N 0.33 E
Claire, Côte- 222 Ie 66.30S 133.00 E
Claire, Lake- 180 Ge 58.30N 112.00W
Clair Engle Lake 188 Df 40.52N 122.43W
Claise 122 Gh 46.56N 0.42 E
Clamecy 122 Jg 47.27N 3.31 E
Clan Alpine Mountains 188 Gg 39.40N 117.55W
Clanton 184 Di 32.50N 86.38W
Clanwilliam 172 Bf 32.11S 18.54 E
Claraz 204 Cm 37.54S 59.17W
Clár Chlainne Mhuiris/Claremorris 118 Eh 53.44N 9.00W
Clare [Austl.] 212 Hf 33.50S 138.36 E
Clare [Mi.-U.S.] 184 Ed 43.49N 84.46W
Clare/Abhainn an Chláir 118 Dh 53.20N 9.03W
Clare/An Clár [2] 118 Ei 52.50N 9.00W
Clare/Cliara 118 Dh 53.49N 10.00W
Claremont 184 Kd 43.23N 72.21W
Claremore 186 Ih 36.19N 95.36W
Claremorris/Clár Chlainne Mhuiris 118 Eh 53.44N 9.00W
Clarence 218 Ee 42.10S 173.56 E
Clarence 218 Ee 42.10S 173.57 E
Clarence, Cape- 180 Ib 73.55N 90.12W
Clarence Cannon Reservoir 186 Kg 39.31N 91.45W
Clarence Island 222 Re 61.12S 54.05W
Clarence River 212 Ke 29.25S 153.22 E
Clarence Strait [Ak.-U.S.] 178 Me 55.25N 132.00W
Clarence Strait [Austl.] 212 Gb 12.00S 131.00 E
Clarence Town 194 Jb 23.06N 74.59W
Clarendon 186 Fi 34.56N 100.53W
Clarenville 180 Mg 48.09N 53.58W
Claresholm 180 Gf 50.02N 113.35W
Clarinda 184 If 40.44N 95.02W
Clarines 196 Dh 9.56N 65.10W
Clarión, Isla- 190 Be 18.22N 114.44W
Clarion Fracture Zone (EN) 106 Lh 18.00N 130.00W
Clarion River 184 He 41.07N 79.41W
Clark 186 Hd 44.53N 97.44W
Clark, Lake- 178 Id 60.15N 154.15W
Clark, Mount - 180 Fd 64.25N 124.14W
Clarkdale 188 Ii 34.46N 112.03W
Clarke Range 212 Jd 20.50S 148.35 E
Clark Fork 174 He 48.09N 116.15W
Clark Hill Lake 184 Fi 33.50N 82.20W
Clark Mountain 188 Hi 35.32N 115.35W
Clarksburg 182 Kd 39.17N 80.21W
Clarksdale 182 Ie 34.12N 90.34W
Clarks Fork 188 Kd 45.39N 108.43W
Clark's Harbour 184 Od 43.26N 65.38W
Clarkston 188 Gc 46.30N 117.03W
Clarksville [Ar.-U.S.] 186 Ji 35.28N 93.28W
Clarksville [Tn.-U.S.] 182 Jd 36.32N 87.21W
Clarksville [Tx.-U.S.] 186 Ij 33.37N 95.03W
Claro, Rio- [Braz.] 202 Hg 15.28S 51.45W
Claro, Rio- [Braz.] 202 Hg 19.08S 50.40W
Clary 124 Fd 50.00N 3.24 E
Claude 186 Fi 35.07N 101.22W
Claustra / Klosters 128 Dd 46.52N 9.52 E
Clavering 179 Jd 74.20N 21.10W
Claxton 184 Gi 32.10N 81.55W
Clay Center 186 Hg 39.23N 96.08W
Clay Cross 124 Aa 53.09N 1.25W
Claye-Souilly 124 Ef 48.57N 2.42 E
Clayton 182 Gd 36.27N 103.11W
Clear, Cape- 118 Dj 51.26N 9.31W
Clear Boggy Creek 186 Ii 34.03N 95.47W
Clear Creek [Az.-U.S.] 188 Ji 34.59N 110.38W
Clear Creek [Wy.-U.S.] 188 Ld 44.53N 106.04W
Clearfield [Pa.-U.S.] 184 He 41.02N 78.27W
Clearfield [Ut.-U.S.] 188 If 41.07N 112.01W
Clear Fork Brazos 186 Gj 33.01N 98.40W
Clear Lake 182 Cd 39.02N 122.50W
Clear Lake [Ia.-U.S.] 186 Je 43.08N 93.23W
Clear Lake [S.D.-U.S.] 186 Hd 44.45N 96.41W
Clear Lake Reservoir 188 Ef 41.52N 121.08W
Clearwater 182 Kf 27.58N 82.48W
Clearwater 180 Ge 56.45N 111.22W
Clearwater Mountains 182 Db 46.00N 115.30W
Clearwater River [Alta.-Can.] 188 Ha 52.23N 114.50W
Clearwater River [U.S.] 188 Gc 46.25N 117.02W
Cleburne 182 He 32.21N 97.23W
Clécy 124 Bf 48.55N 0.29W
Clee Hills 118 Ki 52.25N 2.35W
Cleethorpes 118 Mh 53.34N 0.02W
Clères 124 De 49.36N 1.07 E
Clerf/Clervaux 124 Id 50.03N 6.02 E
Clermont [Austl.] 212 Jd 22.49S 147.39 E
Clermont [Fr.] 122 Ie 49.23N 2.24 E
Clermont-en-Argonne 124 He 49.06N 5.04 E
Clermont-Ferrand 112 Gf 45.47N 3.05 E
Clermont-l'Hérault 122 Jk 43.37N 3.26 E
Clervaux/Clerf 124 Id 50.03N 6.02 E
Clervé 124 Ie 49.57N 6.01 E
Cles 128 Fd 46.22N 11.02 E
Clevedon 118 Kj 51.27N 2.51W
Cleveland [3] 118 Mg 54.40N 1.00W
Cleveland 118 Lg 54.25N 1.05W
Cleveland [Ms.-U.S.] 186 Kj 33.45N 90.50W
Cleveland [Oh.-U.S.] 176 Ke 41.30N 81.41W
Cleveland [Tn.-U.S.] 182 Kd 35.10N 84.53W
Cleveland [Tx.-U.S.] 186 Ik 30.21N 95.05W
Cleveland, Mount- 182 Eb 48.56N 113.51W
Cleveland Heights 184 Ge 41.30N 81.34W
Clevelândia 204 Fh 26.24S 52.21W
Cleveland Mountain 188 Ic 46.37N 113.47W
Clew Bay/Cuan Mó 118 Dh 53.50N 9.50W
Cliara/Clare 118 Dh 53.49N 10.00W
Cliff 186 Bj 32.59N 108.36W
Clifton [Az.-U.S.] 182 Fe 33.03N 109.18W
Clifton [St.Vin.] 197n Bb 12.36N 61.26W
Clifton [Tx.-U.S.] 186 Hk 31.47N 97.35W
Clinch River 184 Eh 35.53N 84.29W
Cline, Mount- 188 Ga 52.10N 116.40W
Clines Corners 186 Di 35.01N 105.34W
Clingmans Dome 184 Fh 35.35N 83.30W
Clinton [Ar.-U.S.] 186 Ji 35.36N 92.28W
Clinton [B.C.-Can.] 180 Ff 51.05N 121.35W
Clinton [Ia.-U.S.] 182 Ic 41.51N 90.12W
Clinton [Il.-U.S.] 186 Lf 40.09N 88.57W
Clinton [Mo.-U.S.] 186 Jg 38.22N 93.46W
Clinton [Ms.-U.S.] 186 Kj 32.20N 90.20W
Clinton [N.C.-U.S.] 184 Hh 34.59N 78.20W
Clinton [N.Z.] 218 Cg 46.13S 169.23 E
Clinton [Ok.-U.S.] 182 Hd 35.31N 98.59W
Clinton-Colden Lake 180 Gd 63.55N 107.30W
Clintonville 186 Ld 44.37N 88.46W
Clipperton, Ile- 174 Ih 10.17N 109.13W
Clipperton Fracture Zone (EN) 106 Li 10.00N 115.00W
Clisson 122 Eg 47.05N 1.17W
Cloates, Point- 212 Cd 22.45S 113.40 E
Clochán an Aifir/Giant's Causeway 118 Gf 55.15N 6.35W
Clodomira 206 Hc 27.35S 64.08W
Cloich na Coillte/Clonakilty 118 Ej 51.37N 8.54W
Clonakilty/Cloich na Coillte 118 Ej 51.37N 8.54W
Cloncurry 210 Fg 20.42S 140.30 E
Clones/Cluain Eois 118 Fg 54.11N 7.14W
Clonmel/Cluain Meala 118 Fi 52.21N 7.42W
Cloppenburg 120 Ed 52.51N 8.02 E
Cloquet 182 Ib 46.43N 92.28W
Clorinda 200 Kh 25.20S 57.40W
Cloud Peak 182 Fc 44.25N 107.10W
Clouère 122 Gh 46.26N 0.17 E
Cloverdale 188 Dg 38.48N 123.01W
Clovis [Ca.-U.S.] 188 Fh 36.49N 119.42W
Clovis [N.M.-U.S.] 176 If 34.24N 103.12W
Cluain Meala/Clonmel 118 Fi 52.21N 7.42W
Cluain Eois/Clones 118 Fg 54.11N 7.14W
Cluj [2] 130 Gc 46.49N 23.35 E
Cluj Napoca 112 If 46.46N 23.36 E
Cluny 122 Kh 46.26N 4.39 E
Cluses 122 Mh 46.04N 6.36 E
Clusone 128 De 45.53N 9.57 E
Clutha 218 Cg 46.21S 169.48 E
Clwyd [3] 118 Jh 53.10N 3.15W
Clwyd 118 Jh 53.20N 3.30W
Clyde 118 If 55.56N 4.29W
Clyde [N.W.T.-Can.] 176 Mb 70.25N 68.30W
Clyde [N.Z.] 218 Cf 45.11S 169.19 E
Clyde, Firth of- 118 If 55.42N 5.00W
Clyde Inlet 180 Kb 70.20N 68.20W
Cna 110 Ke 54.32N 42.05 E
Cnoc Bréanainn/Brandon Mount 118 Ci 52.14N 10.15W
Cnoc Fola/Bloody Foreland 118 Ef 55.09N 8.17W
Cnoc Mhaoldonn/Knockmealdown Mountains 118 Fi 52.15N 8.00W
Cnori 132 Ni 41.35N 45.59 E
Cnossus (EN) = Knosós 130 In 35.18N 25.10 E
Côa 126 Ec 41.05N 7.06W
Coachella Canal 188 Hj 33.34N 116.00W
Coahuayana 192 Hh 18.44N 103.41W
Coahuila [2] 190 Dc 27.20N 102.00W
Coalcomán, Sierra de- 192 Hh 18.30N 102.55W
Coalcomán de Matamoros 192 Hh 18.47N 103.09W
Coaldale 188 Ib 49.43N 112.37W
Coalgate 186 Hi 34.32N 96.13W
Coalinga 188 Eh 36.09N 120.21W
Coalville 118 Li 52.44N 1.20W
Coamo 194 Nd 18.05N 66.22W
Coari 202 Fd 4.05S 63.08W
Coari, Lago de- 202 Fd 4.15S 63.25W
Coari, Rio- 198 Jf 4.30S 63.33W
Coast [3] 170 Gc 3.00S 39.30 E
Coast Mountains 174 Gd 55.00N 129.00W
Coast Plain (EN)= Kustvlakte 122 Ic 51.00N 2.30 E
Coast Plain (EN) = Maritime, Plaine- 122 Ic 51.00N 2.30 E
Coast Ranges 174 Ge 41.00N 123.30W
Coatbridge 118 If 55.52N 4.01W
Coatepec 192 Kh 19.27N 96.58W
Coatepel, Cerro- 192 Kh 18.25N 97.35W
Coatepeque 194 Bf 14.42N 91.52W
Coats 174 Kc 62.30N 83.00W
Coats Land (EN) 222 Af 77.00S 28.00W
Coatzacoalcos 176 Jh 18.09N 94.25W
Coatzacoalcos, Bahia- 192 Lh 18.10N 94.27W
Coatzacoalcos, Rio- 192 Lh 18.09N 94.24W
Coba 190 Gd 20.36N 87.35W
Cobadin 130 Le 44.05N 28.13 E
Cobalt 180 Jg 47.24N 79.41W
Cobán 190 Fe 15.29N 90.19W
Cobar 212 Jf 31.30S 145.49 E
Cobb, Mount- 188 Dg 38.45N 122.40W
Cobb Seamount (EN) 174 Fe 46.46N 130.43W
Cóbh/An Cóbh 118 Ej 51.51N 8.17W
Cobija 202 Ef 11.02S 68.44W
Cobo 204 Dm 37.48S 57.38W
Cobourg 180 Jh 43.58N 78.10W
Cobourg Peninsula 212 Gb 11.20S 132.15 E
Cöbué 172 Eb 12.07S 34.52 E
Coburg 120 Gf 50.15N 10.58 E
Coburg 180 Ja 75.57N 79.00W
Coburn Mountain 184 Lc 45.28N 70.06W
Coca, Pizzo di- 128 Ed 46.04N 10.01 E
Cocalinho 204 Gb 14.22S 51.00W
Cocentaina 126 Lf 38.45N 0.26W
Cochabamba 200 Jg 17.24S 66.09W
Cochabamba [3] 202 Eg 17.30S 65.40W
Coche, Isla- 196 Eg 10.47N 63.56W
Cochem 120 Df 50.08N 7.09 E
Cochin 142 Ji 9.58N 76.14 E
Cochin China (EN)=Nam Phan 140 Mg 11.00N 107.00 E
Cochinos, Bahia de-=Pigs, Bay of- (EN) 194 Gb 22.07N 81.10W
Cochons, Ile aux- 222 Ec 46.05S 50.08 E
Cochran 184 Fj 32.23N 83.21W
Cochrane 180 He 57.55N 101.32W
Cochrane [Alta.-Can.] 188 Ha 51.11N 114.28W
Cochrane [Ont.-Can.] 176 Ke 49.04N 81.01W
Cockburn, Canal- 206 Fh 54.20S 71.30W
Cockburn, Mount- 212 Gd 22.46S 130.36 E
Cockburn Bank 118 El 49.40N 8.50W
Cockburn Island 184 Fc 45.55N 83.22W
Cockburn Town 194 Ja 24.02N 74.31W
Cockermouth 118 Jg 54.40N 3.21W
Coclé [3] 194 Gi 8.30N 80.15W
Coco, Cayo- 194 Hb 22.30N 78.28W
Coco, Ile- 197b Bc 17.52N 62.49W
Coco, Isla del- 174 Ki 5.32N 87.04W
Cocoa 182 Kf 28.21N 80.44W
Cocoa Beach 184 Gk 28.19N 80.36W
Cocoa Point 197d Ba 17.33N 61.46W
Cocobeach 170 Ab 0.59N 9.36 E
Coco Channel 148 If 14.00N 93.00 E
Coco Islands 148 If 14.05N 93.18 E
Coconino Plateau 188 Ii 35.50N 112.30W
Coco o Segovia, Rio- 174 Kh 15.00N 83.08W
Cocorocuma, Cayos- 194 Ff 15.45N 83.00W
Cócos 204 Jb 14.10S 44.33W
Cocos 220c Bb 13.14N 144.39 E
Cocos Islands (Keeling Islands) [5] 142 Lk 12.10S 96.55 E
Cocos Islands (Keeling Islands) 140 Lk 12.10S 96.55 E
Cocos Ridge (EN) 106 Ni 5.30N 86.00W
Cocula 192 Hg 20.23N 103.50W
Cocuzzo 128 Kk 39.13N 16.08 E
Cod, Cape- 174 Le 41.42N 70.15W
Cod, Cape- 184 Me 41.50N 70.00W
Coda Cavallo, Capo- 128 Dj 40.51N 9.43 E
Codaeşti 130 Kc 46.52N 27.45 E
Codajás 202 Fd 3.50S 62.05W
Codera, Cabo- 196 Cg 10.35N 66.04W
Codfish Island 218 Bg 46.45S 167.40 E
Codigoro 128 Gf 44.49N 12.08 E
Codlea 130 Id 45.42N 25.27 E
Codó 202 Jd 4.29S 43.53W
Codogno 128 De 45.09N 9.42 E
Codrington 196 Fd 17.38N 61.50W
Codrington Lagoon 197d Ba 17.39N 61.51W
Codrului, Munţii- 130 Fc 46.35N 22.10 E
Cody 182 Fc 44.32N 109.05W
Coen 210 Ff 13.56S 143.12 E
Coesfeld 120 De 51.56N 7.09 E
Coetivy Island 158 Mi 7.08S 56.16 E
Coeur d'Alene 182 Db 47.41N 116.46W
Coevorden 122 Mb 52.40N 6.45 E
Coëvrons, Les- 122 Ff 48.12N 0.10W
Coffeyville 186 Ih 37.02N 95.37W
Coffs Harbour 210 Gh 30.18S 153.08 E
Cofre de Perote, Cerro- (Nauhcampatépetl) 192 Kh 19.29N 97.08W
Cofrentes 126 Ke 39.14N 1.04W
Coggeshall 124 Cc 51.52N 0.41 E
Coghinas 128 Cj 40.56N 8.48 E
Coghinas, Lago del- 128 Dj 40.45N 9.05 E
Coglians 128 Gd 46.37N 12.53 E
Cognac 122 Fi 45.42N 0.20W
Cogne 128 Be 45.37N 7.21 E
Cogolludo 126 Id 40.57N 3.05W
Čograjskoje vodohranilišče 132 Ng 45.30N 44.30 E
Coiba, Isla de- 190 Hg 7.27N 81.45W
Coig, Rio- (Coyle) 206 Gh 50.58S 69.11W
Coihaique 206 Fg 45.34S 72.04W
Coimbatore 142 Jh 11.00N 76.58 E
Coimbra [2] 126 Dd 40.12N 8.25W
Coimbra [Braz.] 204 Dd 19.55S 57.47W
Coimbra [Port.] 112 Fg 40.12N 8.25W
Coin 126 Hh 36.40N 4.45W
Coipasa, Salar de- 202 Eg 19.30S 68.10W
Čojbalsan 142 Ne 48.04N 114.30 E
Cojedes 196 Bh 9.37N 68.55W
Cojedes [2] 202 Eb 9.20N 68.20W
Cojedes, Rio- 196 Bh 8.44N 68.15W
Cojutepeque 194 Cg 13.43N 88.56W
Čoka 130 Dd 45.56N 20.09 E
Cokeville 188 Je 42.05N 110.55W
Cokover River 212 Ed 20.40S 120.45 E
Čokurdah 138 Jb 70.38N 147.55 E
Colac [Austl.] 212 Ig 38.20S 143.35 E
Colac [N.Z.] 218 Bg 46.22S 167.53 E
Colatina 200 Lg 19.32S 40.37W
Colbeck, Cape- 222 Mf 77.06S 157.48W
Colbitz-Letzlinger Heide 120 Hd 52.27N 11.35 E
Colby 186 Fg 39.24N 101.03W
Colchester 118 Nj 51.54N 0.54 E
Cold Bay 178 Ge 55.11N 162.30W
Cold Lake 180 Gf 54.27N 110.10W
Coldstream 118 Kf 55.39N 2.15W
Coldwater [Ks.-U.S.] 186 Gh 37.16N 99.19W
Coldwater [Mi.-U.S.] 184 Ee 41.57N 85.00W
Colebrook 184 Lc 44.53N 71.30W
Coleman 186 Gk 31.50N 99.26W
Coleman River 212 Ic 15.06S 141.38 E
Coleraine/Cúil Raithin 118 Gf 55.08N 6.40W
Coleridge, Lake- 218 De 43.20S 171.30 E
Coles, Punta- 202 Dg 17.42S 71.23W
Colesberg 172 Df 30.45S 25.05 E
Colfax [La.-U.S.] 186 Jk 31.31N 92.42W
Colfax [Wa.-U.S.] 188 Gc 46.53N 117.22W
Colfontaine 124 Fd 50.25N 3.50 E
Colhué Huapi, Lago- 206 Gg 45.30S 68.48W
Colibaşi 130 He 44.56N 24.54 E
Colibris, Pointe des- 197e Bb 16.17N 61.06W
Colima 176 Ih 19.14N 103.43W
Colima [2] 190 De 19.10N 104.00W
Colima, Nevado de- 174 Ih 19.33N 103.38W
Colinas 204 Hb 14.12S 48.03W
Coll 118 Ge 56.40N 6.35W
Collado Bajo 126 Kd 40.14N 1.50W
Collarada 126 Lb 42.43N 0.29W
Colle di Val d'Elsa 128 Fg 43.25N 11.07 E
Colleferro 128 Gi 41.44N 12.59 E
College 178 Jd 64.51N 147.47W
College Place 188 Fc 46.03N 118.23W
College Station 186 Hk 30.37N 96.21W
Collegno 128 Be 45.05N 7.34 E
Collie 212 Df 33.21S 116.09 E
Collier Bay 212 Ec 16.10S 124.15 E
Collierville 184 Ch 35.03N 89.40W
Collingwood [N.Z.] 216 Dh 40.41S 172.41 E
Collingwood [Ont.-Can.] 184 Gc 44.29N 80.13W
Collinson Peninsula 180 Hb 70.00N 101.10W
Collinsville 212 Jd 20.34S 147.51 E
Collmberg 120 Je 51.15N 13.02 E
Colmar 122 Nf 48.05N 7.22 E
Colmena 204 Bi 28.45S 60.06W
Colmenar 126 Hh 36.54N 4.20W
Colmenar Viejo 126 Id 40.40N 3.46W
Colne 124 Cc 51.51N 0.59 E
Colne Point 124 Dc 51.46N 1.03 E
Colnett, Punta- 192 Ab 31.00N 116.20W
Cologne (EN)=Köln 112 Ge 50.56N 6.57 E
Colombia 204 He 20.10S 48.40W
Colombia [1] 200 Ie 4.00N 72.00W
Colombian Basin (EN) 174 Lh 13.00N 76.00W
Colombier, Pointe à- 197b Bc 17.55N 62.53W
Colombo 142 Ji 6.56N 79.51 E
Colón [Arg.] 206 Hd 33.53S 61.07W
Colón [Arg.] 206 Id 32.13S 58.08W
Colón [Cuba] 190 Hd 22.43N 80.54W
Colón [Hond.] [3] 194 Ef 15.20N 84.30W
Colón [Pan.] 176 Li 9.22N 79.54W
Colón [Pan.] [3] 194 Hi 9.30N 79.15W
Colón [Ur.] 204 Ek 33.53S 54.43W
Colon, Archipiélago de-/Galápagos, Islas-= Galapagos Islands (EN) 198 Gf 0.30S 90.30W
Colón, Montañas de- 194 Ef 14.55N 84.45W
Colona 212 Gf 31.38S 132.05 E
Colonarie 197n Ba 13.14N 61.08W
Colonarie 197n Ba 13.14N 61.08W
Colonel Hill 194 Jb 22.52N 74.15W
Colonia 214 Bf 9.31N 138.08 E
Colonia [2] 204 Dl 34.10S 57.30W
Colonia agricola de Turén 196 Bh 9.15N 69.05W
Colonia Carlos Pellegrini 204 Di 28.32S 57.10W
Colonia del Sacramento 206 Id 34.28S 57.51W
Colonia Elisa 204 Ch 26.56S 59.32W
Colonia Juárez 192 Eb 30.19N 108.05W
Colonia Las Heras 206 Gg 46.33S 68.57W
Colonia Lavalleja 206 Id 31.06S 57.01W
Colonial Heights 184 Ig 37.15N 77.25W
Colonia Morelos 192 Eb 30.50N 109.10W
Colonne, Capo- 128 Lk 39.02N 17.12 E
Colonsay 118 Ge 56.05N 6.10W
Colorado 194 Fh 10.46N 83.35W
Colorado [2] 182 Fd 39.30N 105.30W
Colorado, Cerro- 192 Bb 31.31N 115.31W
Colorado, Rio- [Arg.] 198 Ji 39.50S 62.08W
Colorado, Rio- [N.Amer.] 174 Hf 31.45N 114.40W
Colorado City 186 Fj 32.24N 100.52W
Colorado Plateau 174 Hf 36.30N 118.00W
Colorado River [N.Amer.] 174 Hf 31.45N 114.40W
Colorado River [U.S.] 174 Jg 28.36N 95.58W
Colorados, Archipiélago de los- 194 Eb 22.36N 84.20W
Colorado Springs 176 If 38.50N 104.49W
Colotlán 192 Hf 22.03N 103.16W
Colpon-Ata 135 Kc 42.39N 77.06 E
Coltishall 124 Db 52.44N 1.22 E
Colui 170 Cf 15.10S 16.40 E
Columbia 174 Ge 46.15N 124.05W
Columbia [Ky.-U.S.] 184 Eg 37.06N 85.18W
Columbia [Mo.-U.S.] 182 Id 38.57N 92.20W
Columbia [Ms.-U.S.] 186 Lk 31.15N 89.56W
Columbia [Pa.-U.S.] 184 Ie 40.02N 76.30W
Columbia [S.C.-U.S.] 176 Kf 34.00N 81.03W
Columbia [Tn.-U.S.] 184 Dh 35.37N 87.02W
Columbia, Cape- 174 La 83.08N 70.35W
Columbia, Mount- 174 Hd 57.00N 117.00W
Columbia Basin 182 Db 46.45N 119.05W
Columbia Falls 188 Hb 48.23N 114.11W
Columbia Mountains 174 Hd 52.00N 119.00W
Columbia Plateau 174 He 44.00N 117.30W
Columbia Seamount (EN) 202 Lh 20.40S 31.30W
Columbine, Cape- 158 Il 32.49S 17.51 E
Columbretes, Islas-/Columbretes, Els- 126 Me 39.52N 0.40 E
Columbretes, Els-/Columbretes, Islas- 126 Me 39.52N 0.40 E
Columbus [Ga.-U.S.] 176 Kf 32.29N 84.59W
Columbus [In.-U.S.] 182 Jd 39.13N 85.55W
Columbus [Ks.-U.S.] 186 Ih 37.10N 94.50W
Columbus [Ms.-U.S.] 182 Je 33.30N 88.25W
Columbus [Mt.-U.S.] 188 Kd 45.38N 109.15W
Columbus [Nb.-U.S.] 182 Hc 41.25N 97.22W
Columbus [N.M.-U.S.] 186 Ck 31.50N 107.38W
Columbus [Oh.-U.S.] 176 Kf 39.57N 83.00W
Columbus [Tx.-U.S.] 186 Hl 29.42N 96.33W
Columbus Point 194 Ja 24.08N 75.16W
Colville 176 Dc 70.25N 150.30W
Colville, Cape- 218 Fb 36.28S 175.21 E
Colville Channel 218 Fb 36.25S 175.30 E
Colville Lake 180 Ec 67.06N 126.00W
Colville Lake 180 Ec 67.10N 126.00W
Col Visentin 128 Gd 46.05N 12.20 E
Colwyn Bay 118 Jh 53.18N 3.43W
Coma 168 Fd 8.27N 36.55 E
Comacchio 128 Gf 44.42N 12.11 E
Comacchio, Valli di- 128 Gf 44.40N 12.05 E
Comai (Damxoi) 152 Ff 28.26N 91.32 E
Comala 192 Hh 19.19N 103.45W
Comalcalco 190 Fe 18.16N 93.13W
Coman, Mount- 222 Qf 73.49S 64.18W
Comanche [Mt.-U.S.] 188 Kc 46.02N 108.54W
Comanche [Tx.-U.S.] 186 Gk 31.54N 98.36W
Comandante Fontana 204 Cg 25.20S 59.41W

Index Symbols

[1] Independent Nation
[2] State, Region
[3] District, County
[4] Municipality
[5] Colony, Dependency
Continent
Physical Region
Historical or Cultural Region
Mount, Mountain
Volcano
Hill
Mountains, Mountain Range
Hills, Escarpment
Plateau, Upland
Pass, Gap
Plain, Lowland
Delta
Salt Flat
Valley, Canyon
Crater, Cave
Karst Features
Depression
Polder
Desert, Dunes
Forest, Woods
Heath, Steppe
Oasis
Cape, Point
Coast, Beach
Cliff
Peninsula
Isthmus
Sandbank
Island
Atoll
Rock, Reef
Islands, Archipelago
Rocks, Reefs
Coral Reef
Well, Spring
Geyser
River, Stream
Waterfall, Rapids
River Mouth, Estuary
Lake
Salt Lake
Intermittent Lake
Reservoir
Swamp, Pond
Canal
Glacier
Ice Shelf, Pack Ice
Ocean
Sea
Gulf, Bay
Strait, Fjord
Lagoon
Bank
Seamount
Tablemount
Ridge
Shelf
Basin
Escarpment, Sea Scarp
Fracture
Trench, Abyss
National Park, Reserve
Point of Interest
Recreation Site
Cave, Cavern
Historic Site
Ruins
Wall, Walls
Church, Abbey
Temple
Scientific Station
Railway station
Airport
Port
Military installation
Lighthouse
Mine
Tunnel
Dam, Bridge

Name	Page	Grid	Lat	Long
Comandău	130	Jd	45.46N	26.16 E
Comăneşti	130	Jc	46.25N	26.26 E
Comayagua	190	Gf	14.25N	87.37W
Comayagua [3]	194	Df	14.30N	87.40W
Combarbala	206	Fd	31.11 S	71.02W
Combeaufontaine	124	Gf	47.43N	5.53 E
Combermere Bay [C]	148	Ie	19.37N	93.34 E
Comblain-au-Pont	124	Hd	50.28N	5.35 E
Combles	124	Ed	50.01N	2.52 E
Combourg	122	Ef	48.25N	1.45W
Combraille [X]	122	Jh	46.30N	3.10 E
Combrailles [X]	122	Ih	46.15N	2.10 E
Comedero	192	Fe	24.37N	106.46W
Comendador	194	Ld	18.53N	71.42W
Comeragh Mountains/Na Comaraigh [A]	118	Fi	52.13N	7.35W
Comerio	197a Bb		18.13N	66.16W
Comilla	148	Id	23.27N	91.12 E
Comines	124	Fd	50.46N	3.01 E
Comines/Komen	124	Ed	50.46N	2.59 E
Comino [S]	128	In	36.00N	14.20 E
Comino, Capo- [P]	128	Dj	40.32N	9.49 E
Comiso	128	In	36.56N	14.36 E
Comitán de Domínguez	190	Fe	16.15N	92.08W
Commentry	122	Ih	46.17N	2.45 E
Commerce	186	Ij	33.15N	95.54W
Commercy	122	Lf	48.45N	5.35 E
Comminges [X]	122	Gk	43.15N	0.45 E
Committee Bay [C]	174	Kc	68.30N	86.30W
Commonwealth Bay [C]	222	Je	66.54 S	142.40 E
Communism Peak (EN) = Kommunizma, pik- [A]	140	Jf	38.57N	72.08 E
Como	128	De	45.47N	9.05 E
Como, Lago di- (Lario) [S]	128	De	46.00N	9.15 E
Comodoro Rivadavia	200	Jj	45.50 S	67.30W
Comondú	190	Bc	26.03N	111.46W
Comores/Comoros [1]	160	Lj	12.10 S	44.10 E
Comores, Archipel des- = Comoro Islands (EN)	158	Lj	12.10 S	44.15 E
Comorin, Cape-	140	Ji	8.04N	77.34 E
Comoro Islands (EN) = Comores, Archipel des-	158	Lj	12.10 S	44.15 E
Comoros/Comoros [1]	158	Lj	12.10 S	44.10 E
Comox	188	Cb	49.40N	124.55W
Compiègne	122	Ie	49.25N	2.50 E
Compostela	190	Dd	21.14N	104.55W
Comprida, Ilha- [P]	204	Ig	24.50 S	47.42W
Compton	188	Fj	33.54N	118.13W
Comstock	186	Fl	29.41N	101.11W
Comtal, Causse du- [A]	122	Ij	44.26N	2.38 E
Cona	152	Ff	28.01N	91.57 E
Čona [S]	140	Mc	62.00N	110.00 E
Co Nag [S]	152	Fe	32.00N	91.25 E
Conakry	160	Fh	9.31N	13.43W
Conara Junction	212	Jh	41.50 S	147.26 E
Concarneau	122	Cg	47.52N	3.55W
Conceição da Barra	202	Kg	18.35 S	39.45W
Conceição do Araguaia	202	Ie	8.15 S	49.17W
Conceição do Mato Dentro	204	Hd	19.01 S	43.25W
Concepción [3]	204	Df	23.00 S	57.00W
Concepción [Arg.]	206	Di	28.23 S	57.53W
Concepción [Arg.]	206	Gc	27.20 S	65.35W
Concepción [Bol.]	202	Fg	16.15 S	62.04W
Concepción [Chile]	200	Ii	36.50 S	73.03W
Concepción [Par.]	200	Kh	23.25 S	57.17W
Concepción [Peru]	202	Cf	11.55 S	75.17W
Concepción del Uruguay	206	Id	32.29 S	58.14W
Concepción, Bahía- [C]	192	Dd	26.40N	111.48W
Concepción, Laguna- [S]	202	Fg	17.30 S	61.25W
Concepción, Punta- [P]	192	Dd	26.50N	111.50W
Concepción, Río- [S]	204	Ab	15.46 S	62.10W
Concepción del Bermejo	206	Bh	26.36 S	60.57W
Concepción del Oro	190	Dc	24.38N	101.25W
Conception, Point- [P]	174	Gf	34.27N	120.27W
Conception Bay [C]	180	Mg	48.00N	53.00W
Conception Island [C]	194	Jb	23.52N	75.03W
Concha	194	Li	9.02N	71.45W
Conchas	204	Hf	23.01 S	48.00W
Conchas Dam	186	Di	35.22N	104.11W
Conchas Lake [S]	186	Di	35.20N	104.14W
Conches-en-Ouche	122	Gf	48.58N	0.56 E
Concho River [S]	186	Gk	31.32N	99.43W
Conchos, Río- [Mex.] [S]	174	Ig	25.35N	104.25W
Conchos, Río- [Mex.] [S]	192	Fc	29.35N	105.00W
Concord [Ca.-U.S.]	188	Eh	37.59N	122.00W
Concord [N.H.-U.S.]	176	Le	43.01N	71.32W
Concordia [Arg.]	200	Ki	31.24 S	58.02W
Concordia [Braz.]	204	Fh	27.14 S	52.01W
Concordia [Ks.-U.S.]	186	Hg	39.34N	97.39W
Concordia [Mex.]	192	Ff	23.17N	106.04W
Concordia Baai [C]	197c Aa		17.31N	62.58W
Con Cuong	148	Ke	19.02N	104.54 E
Conda	170	Bc	11.06 S	14.20 E
Condamine River [S]	212	Je	27.00 S	149.50 E
Condat	122	Ii	45.22N	2.46 E
Conde	202	Kf	11.49 S	37.37W
Condé-en-Brie	124	Fe	49.01N	3.33 E
Condega	194	Dg	13.21N	86.24W
Condé-sur-l'Escaut	124	Fd	50.27N	3.35 E
Condé-sur-Marne	124	Ge	49.03N	4.11 E
Condé-sur-Noireau	122	Ff	48.51N	0.33W
Condobolin	212	Jf	33.05 S	147.09 E
Condom	122	Gj	43.58N	0.22 E
Condon	188	Ed	45.14N	120.11W
Cóndor, Cordillera del- [A]	202	Cd	4.20 S	78.30W
Condroz/Condruzisch Plateau [X]	122	Kd	50.25N	5.00 E
Condruzisch Plateau/ Condroz [X]	122	Kd	50.25N	5.00 E
Conecuh River [S]	180	Je	31.00N	87.14W
Conegliano	128	Ge	45.53N	12.18 E
Conejera, Isla- / Conills, Illa des- [P]	126	Oe	39.11N	2.57 E
Conejo	192	De	24.05N	111.00W
Conejo, Cerro- [A]	192	Jg	21.24N	99.06W
Conero [A]	128	Hg	43.33N	13.36 E
Conesa	204	Bk	33.36 S	60.21W
Conference Island [A]	197p Bb		12.09N	61.35W
Conflans-en-Jarnisy	124	He	49.10N	5.51 E
Conflans-Sainte-Honorine	124	Ef	48.59N	2.06 E
Confolens	122	Gh	46.01N	0.40 E
Confuso, Rio- [S]	204	Dg	25.09 S	57.34W
Conghua	152	Jg	23.31N	113.30 E
Congo [1]	158	Ii	1.00 S	15.00 E
Congo [S]	158	Ii	6.04 S	12.24 E
Congo, Democratic Republic of the- → Zaire [1]	160	Ji	1.00 S	25.00 E
Congo Basin (EN) [S]	158	Ih	0.00	17.00 E
Congonhas	204	Ke	20.30 S	43.52W
Conil de la Frontera	126	Fh	36.16N	6.05W
Conills, Illa des- / Conejera, Isla- [P]	126	Oe	39.11N	2.57 E
Coniston	184	Gb	46.29N	80.51W
Conn, Lough-/Loch Con [S]	118	Dg	54.04N	9.20W
Connacht/Connaught [S]	118	Eh	53.30N	9.00W
Connaught/Connacht [S]	118	Eh	53.30N	9.00W
Conneaut	184	Ge	41.58N	80.34W
Connecticut [2]	182	Mc	41.45N	72.45W
Connecticut River [S]	182	Mc	41.17N	72.21W
Connell	188	Fc	46.40N	118.52W
Connellsville	184	He	40.02N	79.38W
Connemara, Mountains of- [A]	118	Dh	53.30N	9.45W
Connersville	184	Ef	39.39N	85.08W
Conn Lake [S]	180	Kb	70.30N	73.30W
Connors Range [A]	212	Jd	21.40 S	149.10 E
Conon [S]	118	Id	57.35N	4.30W
Conquista	204	Ic	19.56 S	47.33W
Conrad	188	Jb	48.10N	111.57W
Conroe	186	Ik	30.19N	95.27W
Conroe Lake [S]	186	Ik	30.26N	95.37W
Conscripto Bernardi	204	Cj	31.03 S	59.05W
Conselheiro Lafaiete	202	Jh	20.40 S	43.48W
Conselice	128	Ff	44.31N	11.49 E
Consett	118	Kf	54.51N	1.49W
Consolación del Sur	194	Fb	22.30N	83.31W
Con Son [S]	148	Lg	8.43N	106.36 E
Constance, Lake- (EN) = Bodensee [S]	110	Gf	47.35N	9.25 E
Constância	112	Hg	44.11N	28.39 E
Constanța	130	Le	44.30N	28.30 E
Constantina	126	Gg	37.52N	5.37W
Constantine	160	He	36.22N	6.37 E
Constantine [2]	162	Ib	36.20N	6.35 E
Constantine, Cape- [P]	178	Ke	58.25N	158.50W
Constitución [Chile]	206	Fe	35.20 S	72.25W
Constitución [Ur.]	204	Dj	31.05 S	57.50W
Consuegra	126	Ie	39.28N	3.36W
Consuelo Peak [A]	208	Fg	24.58 S	148.10 E
Contamana	202	De	7.15 S	74.54W
Contas, Rio de- [S]	198	Mg	14.17 S	39.01W
Contoy, Isla- [P]	192	Jg	21.30N	86.48W
Contraforte Central, Serra do- [A]	204	Ic	17.15 S	47.50W
Contramaestre	194	Ic	20.18N	76.15W
Contravesía, Sierra- [A]	126	Ik	36.50N	3.10W
Contreras, Embalse de- [S]	126	Ke	39.32N	1.30W
Contreras, Islas- [C]	194	Gj	7.50N	81.47W
Contreras, Puerto de- [V]	126	Ke	39.32N	1.30W
Contres	122	Hg	47.25N	1.26 E
Contumazá	202	Ce	7.22 S	78.49W
Contwig	124	Je	49.13N	7.26 E
Contwoyto Lake [S]	180	Gc	65.40N	110.40W
Conty	124	Ee	49.44N	2.09 E
Convención	202	Db	8.28N	73.20W
Conversano	128	Lj	40.58N	17.07 E
Conway [Ar.-U.S.]	182	Id	35.05N	92.26W
Conway [N.H.-U.S.]	184	Ld	43.58N	71.07W
Conway [S.C.-U.S.]	184	Hi	33.51N	79.04W
Conway, Mount- [A]	212	Gd	23.45 S	133.25 E
Conway Reef / Ceva-i-Ra [S]	208	Ig	21.45 S	174.35 E
Conwy [S]	118	Jh	53.17N	3.50W
Conwy	118	Jh	53.17N	3.50W
Conyers	184	Fi	33.40N	84.00W
Conza, Sella di-	128	Ji	40.50N	15.18 E
Coober Pedy	212	Gf	29.01 S	134.43 E
Cooch Behär → Koch Bihär	148	Hc	26.19N	89.26 E
Cook	212	Gf	30.37 S	130.25 E
Cook [S]	222	Ad	59.27 S	27.10W
Cook, Bahía- [C]	206	Fi	55.10 S	70.10W
Cook, Cap- [P]	219b Dd		19.32 S	169.28 E
Cook, Cape- [P]	188	Ba	50.08N	127.55W
Cook, Mount- [A]	208	Hi	43.36 S	170.09 E
Cook, Récif de- [C]	219b Ad		19.25 S	163.50 E
Cook, Mount- [A]	212	Df	32.25 S	116.18 E
Cookes Peak [A]	186	Cj	32.32N	107.44W
Cookeville	184	Fg	36.10N	85.31W
Cook Ice Shelf [S]	222	Je	68.40 S	152.30 E
Cook Inlet [C]	174	Dc	60.30N	152.00W
Cook Island [S]	220g Bb		1.57N	157.28W
Cook Islands [5]	210	Lf	20.00 S	158.00W
Cook Islands [S]	208	Lf	20.00 S	158.00W
Cookstown/An Chorr Chríochach	118	Gg	54.39N	6.45W
Cook Strait [S]	208	Ii	41.20 S	174.25 E
Cooktown	210	Fi	15.28 S	145.15 E
Coolangatta [V]	122	Ef	50.57N	3.35 E
Coolgardie	212	Ef	30.57 S	121.10 E
Coolidge [Az.-U.S.]	186	Ee	33.00N	111.31W
Coolidge [Ks.-U.S.]	186	Fg	38.03N	101.59W
Coolidge Dam [A]	188	Jj	33.11N	110.32W
Cooma	212	Jg	36.14 S	149.08 E
Coonabarabran	212	Jf	31.16 S	149.17 E
Coonamble	212	Jf	30.57 S	148.23 E
Coonoor	148	Ff	11.21N	76.49 E
Coon Rapids	186	Jd	45.09N	93.18W
Cooper	186	Ij	33.23N	95.35W
Cooper, Mount- [A]	186	Ga	50.13N	117.12W
Cooper Creek [S]	208	Eg	28.29 S	137.46 E
Cooper's Town	194	Ii	26.51N	77.31W
Cooperstown [N.D.-U.S.]	186	Hc	47.27N	98.07W
Cooperstown [N.Y.-U.S.]	184	Jd	42.43N	74.56W
Coosa River [S]	180	Je	32.30N	86.16W
Coos Bay	182	Cc	43.22N	124.13W
Coos Bay [C]	188	Ce	43.23N	124.16W
Cootamundra	212	Jf	34.39 S	148.02 E
Čop	132	Ce	48.26N	22.14 E
Copainalá	192	Mi	17.05N	93.12W
Copán	194	Cf	14.50N	89.12W
Copán [3]	194	Cf	14.50N	89.09W
Copán [S]	176	Kh	14.50N	89.09W
Copenhagen (EN) = København	112	Hi	55.40N	12.35 E
Copertino	128	Mj	40.16N	18.03 E
Copetonas	204	Bn	38.43N	60.27W
Copiapó	200	Ih	27.22 S	70.20W
Copiapó, Rio- [S]	206	Fc	27.19 S	70.56W
Çöpköy	130	Jf	41.13N	26.49 E
Coporito	196	Fh	8.56N	62.00W
Coporolo [S]	170	Be	12.56 S	13.00 E
Copparo	128	Ff	44.54N	11.49 E
Copper [S]	178	Kd	60.30N	144.50W
Copperbelt [3]	170	Ee	13.00 S	28.00 E
Copper Center	178	Kd	61.58N	145.19W
Copper Cliff	180	Jg	46.28N	81.04W
Copper Harbor	184	Cc	47.27N	87.53W
Coppermine	174	Hc	67.50N	115.05W
Coppermine [S]	174	Hc	67.49N	115.04W
Coppermine Point [P]	184	Eb	46.59N	84.47W
Copper Queen	172	Dc	17.31 S	29.20 E
Coqên (Maindong)	152	Ee	31.15N	85.13 E
Coquet [S]	118	Lf	55.22N	1.37W
Coquille	188	Ce	43.11N	124.11W
Coquimbo	200	Ih	29.58 S	71.21W
Coquimbo [2]	206	Fd	31.00 S	71.00W
Corabia	112	If	43.47N	24.30 E
Coração de Jesus	204	Jc	16.42 S	44.22W
Coradi o Cheradi, Isole- [C]	128	Lj	40.27N	17.09 E
Cora Droma Rúisc / Carrick on Shannon	118	Eh	53.57N	8.05W
Corail	194	Kd	18.34N	73.53W
Corail, Mer de- = Coral Sea [S]	208	Gf	20.00 S	158.00 E
Coral, Cabeza de- [S]	192	Ph	18.47N	87.19W
Coral Gables	182	Kf	25.45N	80.16W
Coral Harbour	176	Kc	64.08N	83.10W
Coral Sea (EN) = Corail, Mer de- [S]	208	Gf	20.00 S	158.00 E
Coral Sea Basin (EN) [S]	208	Gf	14.00 S	152.00 E
Coral Sea Islands Territory [5]	212	Lc	18.00 S	158.00 E
Coralville	186	Kf	41.40N	91.35W
Coralville Lake [S]	186	Kf	41.47N	91.48W
Corantijn River [S]	198	Ke	5.55N	57.05W
Corato	128	Ki	41.09N	16.25 E
Corbara, Lago di- [S]	128	Gg	42.45N	12.15 E
Corbeil-Essones	122	If	48.36N	2.29 E
Corbières [X]	122	Ik	42.55N	2.38 E
Corbigny	122	Jg	47.15N	3.40 E
Corby	118	Mi	52.29N	0.40W
Corcaigh/Cork	112	Ce	51.54N	8.28W
Corcaigh/Cork [2]	118	Ej	52.00N	8.30W
Corcoran	188	Fh	36.06N	119.33W
Corcovado, Cerro- [A]	192	Bb	30.40N	114.55W
Corcovado, Golfo- [C]	198	Ij	43.30 S	73.30W
Corcovado, Volcán- [A]	198	Ij	43.12 S	72.48W
Corcubión	126	Cb	42.57N	9.11W
Corcubión, Ría de- [C]	126	Cb	42.54N	9.09W
Cordes	122	Hj	44.04N	1.57 E
Cordevole [S]	128	Gd	46.05N	12.04 E
Cordilheiras, Serra das- [A]	202	Ie	7.30 S	48.30W
Cordillera [3]	204	Dg	25.15 S	57.00W
Cordillera Central [Phil.] [A]	150	Hc	17.20N	120.57 E
Cordillera Central [S.Amer.] [A]	198	If	8.00 S	77.00W
Cordillera Occidental [S.Amer.] [A]	198	Ig	14.00 S	74.00W
Cordillera Oriental [S.Amer.] [A]	198	If	7.00 S	76.00W
Córdoba [Arg.]	206	Hd	32.00 S	64.00W
Córdoba [Arg.]	200	Ji	31.25 S	64.10W
Córdoba [Col.] [3]	202	Cb	8.20N	75.40W
Córdoba [Mex.]	190	Ee	18.53N	96.56W
Córdoba [Sp.]	112	Ef	37.53N	4.46W
Córdoba [Sp.]	126	Hg	38.00N	4.50W
Córdoba, Sierras de- [A]	198	Ji	31.15 S	64.00W
Cordova	176	Ec	60.33N	145.46W
Corfu (EN) = Kérkira	110	Hh	39.40N	19.45 E
Corfu, Strait of- (EN) = Kerkíras, Stenón- [S]	130	Dj	39.35N	20.05 E
Coria	126	Fe	39.59N	6.32W
Coria del Río	126	Fg	37.16N	6.03W
Coribe	204	Ja	13.50 S	44.28W
Coricudgy, Mount- [A]	212	Kf	32.50 S	150.22 E
Corigliano Calabro	128	Kk	39.36N	16.31 E
Coringa Islets [C]	212	Jc	17.00 S	150.00 E
Corinth (EN) = Kórinthos [S]	130	Fl	37.55N	22.53 E
Corinth, Gulf of- (EN) = Korinthiakós Kólpos [C]	110	Ih	38.12N	22.30 E
Corinth Canal (EN) = Korínthou, Dhiórix- [S]	130	Fl	37.57N	22.58 E
Corinto [Braz.]	202	Jg	18.21 S	44.27W
Corinto [Nic.]	194	Dg	12.29N	87.10W
Corisco [S]	166	Ge	0.55N	9.19 E
Cork/Corcaigh	112	Ce	51.54N	8.28W
Cork/Corcaigh [2]	118	Ej	52.00N	8.30W
Cork Harbour [C]	118	Ej	51.45N	8.15W
Corleone	128	Im	37.49N	13.18 E
Çorlu	144	Ca	41.09N	27.48 E
Çorlu [S]	130	Je	41.01N	28.00 E
Cormeilles	124	Ce	49.15N	0.23 E
Cormoran Reef [C]	220a Bb		7.50N	134.32 E
Cornelio	192	Di	30.05N	111.08W
Cornélio Procópio	206	Jb	23.08 S	50.39W
Cornelius Grinnel Bay [C]	180	Ld	63.20N	64.50W
Corner Brook	176	Ne	48.57N	57.57W
Corner Seamounts (EN) [S]	174	Nf	35.30N	51.30W
Cornia [S]	128	Eg	42.57N	10.33 E
Corning [Ar.-U.S.]	186	Kh	36.24N	90.35W
Corning [Ca.-U.S.]	188	Dg	39.56N	122.11W
Corning [N.Y.-U.S.]	184	Id	42.10N	77.04W
Corno Grande [A]	128	Hh	42.28N	13.34 E
Cornouaille [X]	122	Cg	48.00N	4.00W
Cornwall [3]	118	Ik	50.30N	4.40W
Cornwall [S]	110	Fe	50.30N	4.40W
Cornwall [S]	118	Hk	50.20N	5.05W
Cornwall [V]	180	Ia	73.30N	95.00W
Cornwall, Cape- [P]	118	Hk	50.08N	5.43W
Cornwallis [S]	180	Ia	75.15N	95.00W
Coro	200	Jh	11.25N	69.41W
Coro, Golfete de- [C]	194	Mh	11.34N	69.53W
Corocoro	202	Eg	17.12 S	68.28W
Corocoro, Isla- [S]	196	Fh	8.31N	60.60W
Corod	130	Kd	45.54N	27.37 E
Coroico	202	Eg	16.10 S	67.44W
Coromandel [Braz.]	204	He	18.28 S	47.13W
Coromandel [N.Z.]	218	Fb	36.46 S	175.30 E
Coromandel Coast [A]	140	Kh	14.00N	80.10 E
Coromandel Peninsula [A]	216	Eb	36.50 S	175.35 E
Coromandel Range [A]	218	Fb	37.00 S	175.40 E
Coron	150	He	12.05N	120.12 E
Corona	186	Di	34.15N	105.36W
Corona Bank (EN) [S]	212	Dc	12.20 S	118.30 E
Coronado, Bahía de- [C]	174	Kk	9.00N	83.50W
Coronado, Isla- [S]	192	Aa	32.25N	117.15W
Coronados, Isla- [P]	192	Dd	26.07N	111.17W
Coronation	188	Ja	52.05N	111.27W
Coronation [S]	222	Re	60.37 S	45.35W
Coronation, Cap- [P]	219b Cf		22.15 S	167.02 E
Coronation Gulf [C]	174	Ic	68.25N	110.00W
Coronda	204	Bj	31.58 S	60.55W
Coronda, Laguna- [S]	204	Bk	32.06 S	60.52W
Coronel	206	Fe	37.01 S	73.08W
Coronel Bogado	206	Ic	27.11 S	56.18W
Coronel Dorrego	206	He	38.42 S	61.17W
Coronel du Graty	204	Bh	27.40 S	60.56W
Coronel Fabriciano	202	Jg	19.31 S	42.38W
Coronel Oviedo	206	Ic	25.25 S	56.27W
Coronel Ponce	204	Eb	15.34 S	55.01W
Coronel Pringles	206	He	37.58 S	61.22W
Coronel Rodolfo Bunge	204	Bm	35.40 S	60.08W
Coronel Suárez	206	He	37.28 S	61.55W
Coronel Vidal	204	Dm	37.27 S	57.43W
Coronel Vivida	204	Fg	25.58 S	52.34W
Coropuna, Nudo- [A]	198	Ig	15.30 S	72.41W
Čorovoda	130	Di	40.30N	20.13 E
Corozal [Blz.]	194	Cd	18.24N	88.24W
Corozal [Col.]	194	Ji	9.18N	75.17W
Corpus Christi	176	Ig	27.48N	97.24W
Corpus Christi, Lake- [S]	186	Hl	28.10N	97.53W
Corpus Christi Bay [C]	186	Hm	27.48N	97.15W
Corque	202	Eg	18.21 S	67.42W
Corral de Bustos	204	Ak	33.17 S	62.12W
Correggio	128	Ef	44.46N	10.47 E
Córrego do Ouro	204	Gc	16.18 S	50.32W
Corrente	202	If	10.27 S	45.10W
Corrente, Rio- [Braz.] [S]	202	Jg	19.19 S	50.50W
Corrente, Rio- [Braz.] [S]	204	Ia	13.08 S	43.28W
Corrente, Rio- [Braz.] [S]	204	Ib	14.14 S	46.58W
Correntes	204	Ec	17.37 S	54.56W
Correntes, Rio- [S]	204	Ec	17.38 S	55.08W
Correnti, Capo delle- [P]	110	Hh	36.40N	15.05 E
Correnti, Isola delle- [S]	128	Jn	36.38N	15.05 E
Correntina	202	Jf	13.20 S	44.39W
Correntina, Rio- → Éguas, Rio das- [S]	204	Ja	13.26 S	41.14W
Corrèze [3]	122	Hi	45.15N	1.50 E
Corrèze [S]	122	Hi	45.10N	1.28 E
Corrib, Lough-/Loch Coirib [S]	118	Dh	53.05N	9.10W
Corrientes	200	Kh	27.30 S	58.50W
Corrientes [3]	206	Ic	29.00 S	58.00W
Corrientes, Cabo- [Arg.] [P]	204	Dm	38.01 S	57.32W
Corrientes, Cabo- [Col.] [P]	202	Cb	5.30N	77.34W
Corrientes, Cabo- [Cuba] [P]	194	Fc	21.45N	84.31W
Corrientes, Cabo- [Mex.] [P]	174	Ig	20.25N	105.42W
Corrientes, Ensenada de- [C]	194	Ec	21.45N	84.30W
Corrientes, Rio- [Braz.] [S]	204	Cj	30.21 S	59.33W
Corrientes, Rio- [Peru] [S]	202	Dd	3.43 S	74.40W
Corrieyairack Pass [X]	118	Ie	57.05N	4.40W
Corrigan	186	Ik	31.00N	94.50W
Corrigin	212	Df	32.21 S	117.52 E
Corry	184	He	41.56N	79.39W
Corryong	212	Jg	36.12 S	147.54 E
Corse = Corsica (EN) [S]	110	Gg	42.00N	9.00 E
Corse, Cap- [P]	110	Gg	43.00N	9.23 E
Corse-du-Sud [3]	122a Ak		41.50N	9.00 E
Corsewall Point [P]	118	Hf	55.02N	5.05W
Corsica (EN) = Corse [S]	110	Gg	42.00N	9.00 E
Corsica, Canale di- [S]	128	Dh	42.45N	9.45 E
Corsicana	182	Id	32.06N	96.28W
Cort Adelaer, Kap- [P]	179	Hf	61.45N	42.00W
Corte	122a Bb		42.19N	9.09 E
Cortegana	126	Fg	37.55N	6.49W
Cortes	126	Kc	41.55N	1.25W
Cortés	194	Cf	15.30N	88.00W
Cortez	182	Ff	37.21N	108.35W
Cortina d'Ampezzo	128	Gd	46.32N	12.08 E
Čortkov	132	De	49.02N	25.50 E
Cortland	184	Id	42.36N	76.10W
Cortona	128	Fg	43.16N	11.59 E
Corubal [S]	166	Bc	11.57N	15.06W
Coruche	126	Df	38.57N	8.31W
Çoruh [S]	144	Ca	41.36N	41.35 E
Çorum	146	Fb	40.29N	35.36 E
Corumbá	200	Kg	19.01 S	57.39W
Corumbá, Rio- [S]	202	Ig	18.19 S	48.55W
Corumbá de Goiás	204	Hb	15.55 S	48.48W
Corumbáiba	204	Hd	18.09 S	48.34W
Corumo, Rio- [S]	196	Fi	6.49N	60.52W
Corvallis	182	Cc	44.34N	123.16W
Corvo [S]	158	De	39.42N	31.06W
Corzuela	204	Bh	26.57 S	60.58W
Cosalá	192	Fe	24.23N	106.41W
Cosamaloapan	192	Lh	18.22N	95.48W
Cosenza	112	Hh	39.18N	16.15 E
Coshocton	184	Ge	40.16N	81.53W
Cosigüina, Punta- [P]	194	Dg	12.54N	87.41W
Cosmoledo Group [C]	158	Li	9.43 S	47.35 E
Cosne-Cours-sur-Loire	122	Ig	47.24N	2.55 E
Cossato	128	Ce	45.34N	8.10 E
Costa, Cordillera de la- [A]	198	Ki	9.50N	66.00W
Costa Rica [1]	190	Hf	10.00N	84.00W
Costa Verde [X]	126	Ga	43.40N	5.40W
Costeşti	130	He	44.40N	24.53 E
Costiera, Catena- [A]	128	Kk	39.25N	16.10 E
Coswig	120	Ie	51.08N	13.35 E
Cotabato	150	He	7.13N	124.15 E
Cotagaita	202	Eh	20.50 S	65.41W
Cotahuasi	202	Dg	15.12 S	72.56W
Côte-d'Ivoire = Ivory Coast (EN) [1]	160	Gh	8.00N	5.00W
Côte-d'Or [3]	122	Kg	47.30N	4.50 E
Côte d'Or [A]	122	Kg	47.10N	4.50 E
Cotentin [X]	110	Ff	49.30N	1.30W
Côtes-du-Nord [3]	122	Df	48.25N	2.40W
Cotiella [A]	126	Mb	42.31N	0.19 E
Cotmeana	130	He	44.58N	24.37 E
Cotmeana [S]	130	He	44.24N	24.45 E
Cotonou	160	Hh	6.21N	2.26 E
Cotopaxi, Volcán- [A]	198	If	0.40 S	78.26W
Cotswold Hills [A]	118	Kj	51.45N	2.10W
Cottage Grove	188	De	43.48N	123.03W
Cottbus [2]	120	Je	51.45N	14.00 E
Cottbus/Chóśebuz	124	Cb	52.17N	0.08 E
Cottenham	124	Cb	52.17N	0.08 E
Cottondale	184	Ej	30.48N	85.23W
Cottonwood Wash [S]	188	Ji	35.05N	110.22W
Cotui	194	Ld	19.03N	70.09W
Cotulla	186	Gl	28.26N	99.14W
Coubre, Pointe de la- [P]	122	Eh	45.42N	1.14W
Coucy-le-Château-Auffrique	124	Ee	49.31N	3.19 E
Coudekerque-Branche	124	Ec	51.02N	2.24 E
Coudersport	184	He	41.46N	78.01W
Couesnon [S]	122	Ef	48.37N	1.31W
Couhé	122	Gh	46.18N	0.11 E
Couilly-Pont-aux-Dames	124	Ef	48.53N	2.52 E
Coulee Dam	188	Fb	48.00N	118.59W
Coulihaut	197g Bb		15.29N	61.27W
Coulman Island [S]	222	Kf	73.28 S	169.45 E
Coulogne	124	Dd	50.55N	1.53 E
Coulommiers	122	If	48.49N	3.05 E
Coulonge, Rivière- [S]	184	Ic	45.51N	76.40W
Coulounieix-Chamiers	122	Gi	45.10N	0.42 E
Council	188	Gd	44.44N	116.26W
Council Bluffs	182	If	41.16N	95.52W
Courcelles	124	Gd	50.28N	4.22 E
Courcelles-Chaussy	124	Ke	49.07N	6.24 E
Courland (EN) = Kurzeme [X]	110	Id	56.50N	22.00 E
Couronne, La-	122	Gi	45.37N	0.06 E
Courseulles-sur-Mer	124	Be	49.20N	0.27W
Courtenay	180	Dg	49.41N	125.00W
Courtine-le-Trucq, La-	122	Ii	45.42N	2.16 E
Courtisols	124	Ge	48.58N	4.31 E
Courtrai/Kortrijk	122	Jd	50.50N	3.16 E
Coushatta	186	Jk	32.00N	93.21W
Cousin [S]	122	Kh	46.58N	4.15 E
Coutances	122	Ee	49.03N	1.26W
Couto de Magalhães, Rio- [S]	204	Fa	13.37 S	53.09W
Coutras	122	Fi	45.02N	0.08W
Couture, Lac- [S]	180	Jd	60.05N	75.20W
Couvin	122	Kd	50.03N	4.29 E
Couvin-Mariembourg	124	Gd	50.06N	4.31 E
Covarrubias	126	Ib	42.04N	3.31W
Covasna	130	Jd	45.51N	26.11 E
Coventry	118	Li	52.25N	1.30W
Coveñas	194	Ji	9.25N	75.42W
Covilhã	112	Ee	40.17N	7.30W
Covington [Ga.-U.S.]	184	Fi	33.37N	83.51W
Covington [Ky.-U.S.]	182	Kc	39.05N	84.30W
Covington [Tn.-U.S.]	184	Cg	35.34N	89.39W
Covington [Va.-U.S.]	184	Hf	37.48N	79.59W
Covurlui [S]	130	Kd	45.46N	28.02 E
Cowal, Lake- [S]	212	Jf	33.36 S	147.25 E
Cowan, Lake- [S]	212	Ef	31.50 S	121.50 E
Cowansville	184	Kc	45.13N	72.45W
Cowcowing Lakes [S]	212	Df	30.58 S	117.15 E
Cowell	212	Hf	33.41 S	136.55 E
Cowes	118	Lk	50.46N	1.18W
Cowichan Lake	188	Cb	48.54N	124.20W
Cowra	212	Jf	33.50 S	148.41 E
Coxim	200	Kg	18.30 S	54.45W
Coxim, Rio- [S]	204	Eb	18.34 S	54.46W
Cox's Bāzār	148	Id	21.26N	91.59 E
Coyah	166	Cd	9.43N	13.23W
Coyame	192	Gb	29.28N	105.06W
Coyanosa Draw [S]	186	Ek	31.18N	103.06W
Coycoyan, Sierra de- [A]	192	Ji	17.30N	98.20W
Coyle, Rio- → Coig, Rio- [S]	206	Gb	50.58 S	69.11W
Coyote [S]	186	Cj	30.48N	112.35W
Coyotitán	192	Fe	23.46N	...
Coyuca, Laguna de- [S]	192	Ii	16.57N	100.05W

Index Symbols

- [1] Independent Nation
- [2] State, Region
- [3] District, County
- [4] Municipality
- [5] Colony, Dependency
- Continent
- Physical Region
- Historical or Cultural Region
- Mount, Mountain
- Volcano
- Hill
- Mountains, Mountain Range
- Hills, Escarpment
- Plateau, Upland
- Pass, Gap
- Plain, Lowland
- Delta
- Salt Flat
- Valley, Canyon
- Crater, Cave
- Karst Features
- Depression
- Polder
- Desert, Dunes
- Forest, Woods
- Heath, Steppe
- Oasis
- Cape, Point
- Coast, Beach
- Cliff
- Peninsula
- Isthmus
- Sandbank
- Island
- Atoll
- Rock, Reef
- Islands, Archipelago
- Rocks, Reefs
- Coral Reef
- Well, Spring
- Geyser
- River, Stream
- Waterfall, Rapids
- River Mouth, Estuary
- Lake
- Salt Lake
- Intermittent Lake
- Reservoir, Pond
- Swamp, Pond
- Canal
- Glacier
- Ice Shelf, Pack Ice
- Ocean
- Sea
- Gulf, Bay
- Strait, Fjord
- Lagoon
- Bank
- Seamount
- Tablemount
- Ridge
- Shelf
- Basin
- Escarpment, Sea Scarp
- Fracture
- Trench, Abyss
- National Park, Reserve
- Point of Interest
- Recreation Site
- Cave, Cavern
- Historic Site
- Ruins
- Wall, Walls
- Church, Abbey
- Temple
- Scientific Station
- Railway station
- Airport
- Port
- Military installation
- Lighthouse
- Mine
- Tunnel
- Dam, Bridge

Cradock	160	Jl	32.08S	25.36 E
Craig [Ak.-U.S.]	178	Me	55.29N	133.09W
Craig [Co.-U.S.]	182	Fc	40.31N	107.33W
Craigmont	188	Gc	46.15N	116.28W
Craigs Range	212	Ke	26.40S	151.30 E
Crailsheim	120	Gg	49.09N	10.05 E
Craiova	112	Ig	44.19N	23.48 E
Cranbrook [Austl.]	212	Df	34.18S	117.32 E
Cranbrook [B.C.-Can.]	180	Fg	49.31N	115.46W
Cranbrook [Eng.-U.K.]	124	Cc	51.05N	0.32 E
Crandon	186	Ld	45.34N	88.54W
Crane [Or.-U.S.]	188	Fe	43.25N	118.35W
Crane [Tx.-U.S.]	186	Ek	31.24N	102.21W
Crane Lake	186	Jb	48.16N	92.28W
Crane Lake	188	Ka	50.06N	109.06W
Cranleigh	124	Bc	51.08N	0.29W
Craon	122	Fg	47.51N	0.57W
Craonne	124	Fe	49.26N	3.47 E
Crapaud, Puy-	122	Fh	46.40N	0.40W
Crary Mountains	222	Of	76.48S	117.40W
Crasna	130	Fa	48.09N	22.20 E
Crasna [Rom.]	130	Fb	47.10N	22.54 E
Crasna [Rom.]	130	Kc	46.31N	27.51 E
Crater Lake [Or.-U.S.]	182	Cc	42.56N	122.06W
Crater Lake [St.Vin.]	197n	Ba	13.19N	61.11W
Crateús	200	Lf	5.10S	40.40W
Crati	128	Kk	39.43N	16.31 E
Crato [Braz.]	202	Ke	7.14S	39.23W
Crato [Port.]	126	Ee	39.17N	7.39W
Crau	122	Kk	43.36N	4.50 E
Crauford, Cape-	180	Jb	73.44N	84.51W
Cravo Norte	202	Db	6.17N	70.12W
Crawford	186	Ee	42.41N	103.25W
Crawfordsville	184	De	40.02N	86.54W
Crawley	118	Mj	51.07N	0.12W
Crazy Mountains	188	Jc	46.08N	110.20W
Crazy Peak	182	Eb	46.01N	110.16W
Creciente, Isla-	192	De	24.23N	111.37W
Crécy-en-Ponthieu	124	Dd	50.15N	1.53 E
Crécy-la-Chapelle	124	Ef	48.51N	2.55 E
Crécy-sur-Serre	124	Fe	49.42N	3.37 E
Crediton	118	Jk	50.47N	3.39W
Cree [Sask.-Can.]	180	Ge	58.50N	105.40W
Cree [Scot.-U.K.]	118	Ig	54.52N	4.20W
Creede	186	Ch	37.51N	106.56W
Creel	190	Cc	27.45N	107.38W
Cree Lake	180	Ge	57.30N	106.30W
Creglingen	120	Gg	49.28N	10.02 E
Creil	122	Ie	49.16N	2.29 E
Crema	128	De	45.22N	9.41 E
Cremenea, Bratul-	130	Ke	44.57N	27.54 E
Crémieu, Plateau de-	122	Li	45.40N	5.30 E
Cremona	128	Ee	45.07N	10.02 E
Crepaja	130	Dd	45.01N	20.39 E
Crepori, Rio-	202	Ge	5.42S	57.08W
Crépy-en-Valois	122	Ie	49.14N	2.54 E
Cres	128	If	44.58N	14.24 E
Cres	128	If	44.40N	14.25 E
Crescent	188	Ee	43.29N	121.41W
Crescent City	182	Cc	41.45N	124.12W
Crescent Lake	184	Gk	29.28N	81.30W
Crespo	204	Bk	32.02S	60.19W
Crest	122	Lj	44.44N	5.02 E
Crested Butte	186	Cg	38.52N	106.59W
Creston [B.C.-Can.]	188	Gb	49.06N	116.31W
Creston [Ia.-U.S.]	182	Ic	41.04N	94.22W
Crestone Peak	186	Dh	37.58N	105.36W
Crestview	182	Je	30.46N	86.34W
Creswell	184	Ih	35.52N	76.23W
Creswell Bay	180	Ib	72.40N	93.30W
Creswell Creek	212	Hc	18.10S	135.11 E
Crete	186	Hf	40.38N	96.58W
Crete (EN) = Kriti [2]	130	Hn	35.35N	25.00 E
Crete (EN) = Kriti	110	Ih	35.15N	24.45 E
Crete, Sea of- (EN) = Kritikón Pélagos	130	Hn	36.00N	25.00 E
Créteil	122	If	48.47N	2.28 E
Cretin, Cape-	214	Di	6.40S	147.52 E
Creus, Cabo de-/Creus, Cap de-	110	Gg	42.19N	3.19 E
Creus, Cap de-/Creus, Cabo de-	110	Gg	42.19N	3.19 E
Creuse [3]	122	Hh	46.05N	2.00 E
Creuse	122	Gh	47.00N	0.34 E
Creusot, Le-	122	Kh	46.48N	4.26 E
Creutzwald	122	Me	49.12N	6.41 E
Crèvecoeur-en-Auge	124	Ce	49.07N	0.01 E
Crèvecoeur-le-Grand	124	Ee	49.36N	2.05 E
Crevillent / Crevillente	126	Lf	38.15N	0.48W
Crevillente / Crevillent	126	Lf	38.15N	0.48W
Crewe	118	Kh	53.05N	2.27W
Crézancy	124	Fe	49.03N	3.30 E
Criciúma	200	Lh	28.40S	49.23W
Cricket Mountains	188	Ig	38.50N	113.00W
Crieff	118	Je	56.23N	3.52W
Criel-sur-Mer	124	Dd	50.01N	1.19 E
Criel-sur-Mer-Mesnil-Val	124	Dd	50.03N	1.20 E
Crikvenica	128	Ie	45.11N	14.42 E
Crillon	124	De	49.31N	1.56 E
Crimea (EN) = Krymski poluostrov	110	Jf	45.00N	34.00 E
Crimean Mountains (EN) = Krymskije gory	110	Jg	44.45N	34.30 E
Crimmitschau	120	If	50.49N	12.23 E
Criquetot-l'Esneval	124	Ce	49.39N	0.16 E
Crissolo	128	Bf	44.42N	7.09 E
Cristal, Monts de-	170	Bb	0.30N	10.30 E
Cristal, Sierra del-	194	Jc	20.33N	75.31W
Cristalândia	202	If	10.36S	49.11W
Cristalina	202	Ig	16.45S	47.36W
Cristalino, Rio-	202	Hf	12.40S	50.40W
Cristallo	128	Gd	46.34N	12.12 E
Cristóbal Colón, Pico-	198	Id	10.50N	73.45W
Cristuru Secuiesc	130	Ic	46.17N	25.02 E
Crişu Alb	130	Ec	46.42N	21.16 E
Crişu Negru	130	Ec	46.42N	21.16 E
Crişu Repede	130	Dc	46.55N	20.59 E
Crixás	204	Hb	14.27S	49.58W
Crixás-Açu, Rio-	202	Hf	13.19S	50.36W
Crixás Mirim, Rio-	204	Ga	13.28S	50.36W
Crkvena Planina	130	Fg	42.48N	22.22 E
Crna Gora	130	Eg	42.16N	21.35 E
Crna Gora	130	Ce	44.05N	19.50 E
Crna Gora = Montenegro (EN) [2]	130	Cg	42.30N	19.18 E
Crna Gora=Montenegro (EN)	130	Cg	42.30N	19.18 E
Crna Reka	130	Ef	43.50N	21.55 E
Crna reka	130	Eh	41.33N	21.59 E
Crni Drim	130	Dg	42.05N	20.23 E
Crni Timok	130	Ff	43.55N	22.18 E
Črni vrh	128	Jd	46.29N	15.14 E
Crni vrh	128	Kf	44.36N	16.30 E
Črnomelj	128	Je	45.34N	15.12 E
Croatia (EN) = Hrvatska [2]	128	Jf	45.00N	15.30 E
Croatia (EN) = Hrvatska	110	Hf	45.00N	15.30 E
Croatia (EN) = Hrvatska	128	Je	45.00N	15.30 E
Crocker, Banjaran-	150	Ge	5.40N	116.20 E
Crockett	186	Ik	31.19N	95.28W
Crocq	122	Ii	45.52N	2.22 E
Crocus Bay	197b	Ab	18.13N	63.05W
Croisette, Cap-	122	Lk	43.13N	5.20 E
Croisic, Le-	122	Dg	47.18N	2.30W
Croisic, Pointe du-	122	Dg	47.17N	2.33W
Croisilles	124	Ed	50.12N	2.53 E
Croissy-sur-Celle	124	Ee	49.42N	2.11 E
Croix, Lac la-	186	Jb	48.21N	92.05W
Croix-Haute, Col de la-	122	Lj	44.43N	5.40 E
Croker, Cape-	212	Gb	10.58S	132.35 E
Croker Bay	180	Jb	74.38N	83.15W
Croker Island	212	Gb	11.10S	132.30 E
Cromarty	118	Id	57.40N	4.02W
Cromer	118	Oi	52.56N	1.18 E
Cromwell	218	Cf	45.03S	169.14 E
Crooked Island	190	Jd	22.45N	74.13W
Crooked Island Passage	190	Jd	22.55N	74.35W
Crooked River	188	Ed	44.34N	121.16W
Crookston	182	Hb	47.47N	96.37W
Crosby [Mn.-U.S.]	186	Jc	46.28N	93.57W
Crosby [N.D.-U.S.]	186	Eb	48.55N	103.18W
Cross	166	Ge	4.55N	8.15 E
Cross City	184	Fk	29.32N	83.07W
Crossett	186	Kj	33.08N	91.58W
Cross Fell	118	Kg	54.42N	2.29W
Cross Lake	180	Hf	54.47N	97.22W
Crossman Peak	188	Hi	34.32N	114.07W
Cross River [2]	166	Gd	5.40N	8.10 E
Cross Sound	178	Le	58.10N	136.30W
Crotone	128	Lk	39.05N	17.08 E
Crotto	204	Bm	36.35S	60.10W
Crouch	124	Cc	51.37N	0.53 E
Crow Agency	188	Ld	45.36N	107.27W
Crowborough	124	Cc	51.03N	0.09 E
Crow Creek	186	Df	40.23N	104.29W
Crowell	186	Gj	33.59N	99.43W
Crow Lake	186	Jb	49.12N	93.57W
Crowley	186	Jk	30.13N	92.22W
Crowley, Lake-	188	Fh	37.37N	118.44W
Crowley Ridge	186	Ki	35.45N	90.45W
Crownpoint	186	Bi	35.42N	108.07W
Crown Prince Frederik	180	Ic	70.05N	86.40W
Crowsnest Pass	180	Gg	49.00N	114.30W
Crows Nest Peak	186	Ed	44.03N	103.58W
CroLdon	212	Ic	18.12S	142.14 E
Croydon, London-	118	Mj	51.23N	0.07W
Crozet, Iles- = Crozet Islands (EN)	222	Ec	46.30S	51.00 E
Crozet Basin (EN)	106	Gm	39.00S	60.00 E
Crozet Islands (EN) = Crozet, Iles-	222	Ec	46.30S	51.00 E
Crozet Ridge (EN)	106	Fn	45.00S	45.00 E
Crozon	122	Bf	48.15N	4.29W
Crozon, Presqu'île de-	122	Bf	48.15N	4.25W
Crucero, Cerro-	192	Gg	21.41N	104.25W
Cruces	194	Gb	22.21N	80.16W
Crump Lake	188	Fe	42.17N	119.50W
Crumpton Point	197g	Ba	15.35N	61.19W
Cruz, Cabo-	190	Ie	19.51N	77.44W
Cruz Alta [Arg.]	204	Bk	33.01S	61.49W
Cruz Alta [Braz.]	200	Kh	28.39S	53.36W
Cruz del Eje	206	Hd	30.44S	64.48W
Cruzeiro do Oeste	206	Jb	23.46S	53.04W
Cruzeiro do Sul	200	If	7.38S	72.36W
Cruzen Island	222	Mf	74.47S	140.42W
Cruz Grande	192	Ji	16.44N	99.08W
Crvanj	128	Mg	43.25N	18.11 E
Crvenka	130	Cd	45.39N	19.28 E
Crystal Brook	212	Hf	33.21S	138.13 E
Crystal City [Man.-Can.]	186	Gb	49.08N	98.57W
Crystal City [Tx.-U.S.]	186	Gl	28.41N	99.50W
Crystal Falls	184	Cb	46.06N	88.20W
Crystal Springs	186	Kk	31.59N	90.21W
Csákvár	120	Oi	47.24N	18.27 E
Cserhát	120	Pi	47.55N	19.30 E
Csongrád	120	Qj	46.42N	20.09 E
Csongrád [2]	120	Qj	46.25N	20.15 E
Csorna	120	Ni	47.37N	17.15 E
CSSR → Ceskoslovenská Socialistická Republika [1]	112	Hf	49.30N	17.00 E
Csurgó	120	Nj	46.16N	17.06 E
Ctesiphon	146	Kf	33.05N	44.35 E
Ču	142	Je	43.33N	73.45 E
Ču	140	Ie	45.00N	67.44 E
Cuajinicuilapa	192	Ji	16.28N	98.25W
Cuale	170	Cd	7.40S	17.01 E
Cualiacán, Río-	192	Fe	24.31N	107.41W
Cuamba	160	Kj	14.49S	36.33 E
Cuan an Fhóid Duibh	118	Dg	54.08N	10.00W
Cuan an Fhóid Duibh/Blacksod Bay	118	Dg	54.08N	10.00W
Cuanavale	170	Cf	15.07S	19.14 E
Cuan Bhaile Átha Cliath/Dublin Bay	118	Gh	53.20N	6.06W
Cuan Chill Ala/Killala Bay	118	Dg	54.15N	9.10W
Cuan Dhun Dealgan/Dundalk Bay	118	Gh	53.57N	6.17W
Cuan Dhún Droma/Dundrum Bay	118	Hg	54.13N	5.45W
Cuando	158	Jj	18.27S	23.32 E
Cuando-Cubango [3]	170	Df	16.00S	20.30 E
Cuan Eochaille/Youghal Harbour	118	Fj	51.52N	7.50W
Cuangar	170	Cf	17.36S	18.37 E
Cuango	158	Ii	3.14S	17.22 E
Cuango [Ang.]	170	Cd	9.07S	18.05 E
Cuango [Ang.]	170	Cd	6.17S	16.41 E
Cuan Loch Garman/Wexford Harbour	118	Gi	52.20N	6.25W
Cuan Mó/Clew Bay	118	Dh	53.50N	9.50W
Cuan na Gaillimhe/Galway Bay	110	Fe	53.10N	9.15W
Cuan na gCaorach/Sheep Haven	118	Ff	55.10N	7.52W
Cuan Phort Láirge/Waterford Harbour	118	Gi	52.10N	6.57W
Cuan Shligigh/Sligo Bay	118	Eg	54.20N	8.40W
Cuanza	158	Ii	9.19S	13.08 E
Cuanza Norte [3]	170	Bd	8.50S	14.30 E
Cuanza Sul [3]	170	Be	10.50S	14.50 E
Cuareim, Arroyo-	204	Dj	30.12S	57.36W
Cuaró	204	Dj	30.37S	56.54W
Cuaró Grande, Arroyo-	204	Dj	30.18S	57.12W
Cuarto, Rio-	206	Hd	33.25S	63.02W
Cuatir	170	Cf	17.01S	18.09 E
Cuatro Ciénegas de Carranza	192	Hd	26.59N	102.05W
Cuauhtémoc	190	Cc	28.25N	106.52W
Cuautitlán	192	Jh	19.40N	99.11W
Cuay Grande	204	Di	28.40S	56.17W
Cuba [1]	176	Lg	21.30N	80.00W
Cuba	174	Lg	21.30N	80.00W
Cuba [Mo.-U.S.]	186	Kg	38.04N	91.24W
Cuba [N.M.-U.S.]	186	Ch	36.01N	107.04W
Cuba [Port.]	126	Ef	38.10N	7.53W
Cubabi, Cerro-	192	Cb	31.42N	112.46W
Cubagua, Isla-	196	Dg	10.49N	64.11W
Cubal	170	Be	13.03S	14.15 E
Cubal [Ang.]	170	Be	11.19S	13.48 E
Cubal [Ang.]	170	Bf	15.22S	12.39 E
Cubango	158	Jj	18.53S	22.24 E
Çubuk	146	Eb	40.59N	32.05 E
Čubukulah, gora-	138	Kc	66.23N	153.59 E
Cucalón, Sierra de-	126	Kd	40.59N	1.10W
Cuchi	170	Ce	14.40S	16.52 E
Cuchi	158	Ij	15.28S	17.21 E
Cuchibi	170	De	15.00S	20.45 E
Cuchilla Águila, Cerro-	192	Ig	21.27N	101.03W
Cuchivero, Río-	196	Di	7.40N	65.57W
Cuchumatanes, Sierra de los-	194	Bf	15.35N	91.25W
Cuckfield	124	Bc	51.01N	0.08W
Cuckmere	124	Cd	50.45N	0.09 E
Cucui	202	Ec	1.12N	66.50W
Cucumbi	170	Ce	10.17S	19.03 E
Cucurpe	192	Db	30.20N	110.43W
Cúcuta	200	Ie	7.54N	72.31W
Cudahy	186	Me	42.57N	87.52W
Cudalbi	130	Kd	45.47N	27.42 E
Cuddalore	142	Jh	11.45N	79.45 E
Cuddapah	148	Ff	14.28N	78.49 E
Čudovo	136	Dd	59.08N	31.41 E
Čudskoje ozero = Peipus, Lake- (EN)	110	Id	58.45N	27.30 E
Cue	212	De	27.25S	117.54 E
Cuebe	170	Cf	15.48S	17.30 E
Cuelei	170	Cf	15.33S	17.21 E
Cuéllar	126	Hc	41.29N	4.19W
Cuemba	170	Ce	12.09S	18.07 E
Cuenca [3]	126	Ke	40.00N	2.00W
Cuenca [Ec.]	200	If	2.53S	78.59W
Cuenca [Sp.]	126	Jd	40.04N	2.08W
Cuenca, Serrania de-	110	Fg	40.10N	1.55W
Cuencamé de Ceniceros	192	He	24.53N	103.42W
Cuera/Chur	128	Dd	46.50N	9.35 E
Cuerda del Pozo, Embalse de la-	126	Jc	41.51N	2.44W
Cuernavaca	176	Jh	18.55N	99.15W
Cuero	186	Hl	29.06N	97.18W
Cuevas del Almanzora	126	Kg	37.18N	1.53W
Cugir	130	Gd	45.50N	23.22 E
Cugo	170	Cd	7.22S	17.06 E
Čugujev	132	Je	49.50N	36.41 E
Čugujevka	154	Mb	44.08N	133.53 E
Čuhloma	136	Ed	58.47N	42.41 E
Cuiabá	200	Kg	15.35S	56.05W
Cuiabá, Rio-	198	Kg	17.05S	56.36W
Cuiabá Mirim, Rio-	204	Ec	16.20S	55.55W
Cuidado, Punta-	221d	Bb	27.08S	109.19W
Cuijk, Cuijk en Sint Agatha-	124	Hc	51.44N	5.52 E
Cuijk en Sint Agatha-Cuijk	124	Hc	51.44N	5.52 E
Cuilapa	194	Bf	14.17N	90.18W
Cuillin Hills	118	Gd	57.14N	6.15W
Cuilo [Afr.]	158	Ii	3.22S	17.22 E
Cuilo [Ang.]	170	Cd	5.52S	16.35 E
Cúil Raithin/Coleraine	118	Gf	55.08N	6.40W
Cuiluan	152	Mb	47.39N	128.34 E
Cuima	170	Ce	13.14S	15.38 E
Cuito	158	Ij	18.01S	20.48 E
Cuito Cuanavale	160	Ij	15.13S	19.08 E
Cuitzeo, Lago de-	192	Ih	19.55N	101.05W
Cuiuni, Rio-	202	Fd	0.45S	63.07W
Cujmir	130	Fe	44.13N	22.56 E
Čukata	130	Ih	41.50N	25.15 E
Čukotski nacionalny okrug [3]	138	Mc	66.00N	172.30 E
Čukotski poluostrov = Chukchi Peninsula (EN)	140	Uc	66.00N	175.00W
Čukotskoje more = Chukchi Sea (EN)	224	Bd	69.00N	171.00W
Çukurca	146	Jd	37.15N	43.37 E
Çukurdağı	130	Ll	37.58N	28.44 E
Čulakkurgan	136	Gg	43.48N	69.12 E
Culan	122	Ih	46.33N	2.21 E
Cu Lao, Hon-	148	Lf	10.30N	109.13 E
Culasi	150	Hd	11.26N	122.03 E
Culbertson	188	Mb	48.09N	104.31W
Culebra, Isla de-	194	Od	18.19N	65.17W
Culebra, Sierra de la-	126	Fc	41.55N	6.20W
Culebra Peak	186	Dh	37.06N	105.10W
Culemborg	124	Hc	51.57N	5.14 E
Culiacán Rosales	176	Ig	24.48N	107.24W
Culion	150	Hd	11.53N	120.01 E
Culion	150	Gd	11.50N	119.55 E
Culiseu, Rio-	202	Hf	12.14S	53.17W
Cullera	126	Le	39.10N	0.15W
Cullman	182	Je	34.11N	86.51W
Čulman	142	Od	56.52N	124.52 E
Culpeper	184	Hf	38.28N	78.01W
Culuene, Rio-	198	Kg	12.56S	52.51W
Culukidze	132	Mh	42.18N	42.25 E
Culver, Point-	212	Ef	32.54S	124.43 E
Culverden	218	Ee	42.46S	172.51 E
Čulym	138	De	55.06N	80.58 E
Čulym	140	Kd	57.40N	83.50 E
Čulyšman	138	Df	51.20N	87.45 E
Cuma	170	Ce	12.52S	15.04 E
Cumaná	200	Jd	10.28N	64.10W
Cumanacoa	196	Eg	10.15N	63.55W
Cumaovasi	130	Kk	38.15N	27.09 E
Cumbal, Volcán-	202	Cc	0.57N	77.52W
Cumberland	118	Kg	54.40N	2.50W
Cumberland	174	Kf	37.09N	88.25W
Cumberland [B.C.-Can.]	188	Cb	49.37N	125.01W
Cumberland [Md.-U.S.]	182	Ld	39.39N	78.46W
Cumberland [Va.-U.S.]	184	Hg	37.31N	78.16W
Cumberland, Cap-	219b	Cb	14.39S	166.37 E
Cumberland, Lake-	184	Eg	36.57N	84.55W
Cumberland Bay	197n	Ba	13.16N	61.17W
Cumberland Island	184	Gj	30.51N	81.27W
Cumberland Islands	212	Jd	20.40S	149.10 E
Cumberland Lake	180	Hf	54.00N	102.20W
Cumberland Peninsula	174	Mc	66.50N	64.00W
Cumberland Plateau	174	Kf	36.00N	85.00W
Cumberland Sound	174	Mc	65.10N	65.30W
Cumbernauld	118	Jf	55.58N	3.59W
Cumbria [3]	118	Kg	54.35N	2.45W
Cumbrian Mountains	118	Jg	54.30N	3.05W
Čumerna	130	Ig	42.47N	25.58 E
Čumikan	138	If	54.42N	135.19 E
Cummins	212	Hf	34.16S	135.44 E
Cumnock	118	If	55.27N	4.16W
Cumpas	192	Eb	30.02N	109.48W
Çumra	146	Ed	37.34N	32.48 E
Čumyš	138	Df	53.30N	83.10 E
Čuna	140	Ld	57.42N	95.35 E
Cunagua	194	Hb	22.05N	78.20W
Cuñapirú	204	Ej	31.32S	55.35W
Cuñapirú, Arroyo-	204	Ej	31.12S	55.31W
Cuñapirú, Cuchilla de-	204	Ej	31.12S	55.36W
Cunaviche, Río-	196	Ci	7.19N	67.11W
Cunderdin	212	Df	31.39S	117.15 E
Cundinamarca [3]	202	Db	5.00N	74.00W
Čundža	136	Hg	43.32N	79.28 E
Cunene [3]	170	Cf	16.30S	15.00 E
Cunene=Kunene (EN)	158	Ij	17.20S	11.50 E
Cuneo	128	Bf	44.23N	7.32 E
Cunhinga	170	Ce	12.14S	16.48 E
Cunillera, Isla- / Sa Conillera, Illa-	126	Nf	38.59N	1.12 E
Čunja	140	Lc	61.30N	96.20 E
Cunnamulla	210	Fg	28.04S	145.41 E
Čunski [R.S.F.S.R.]	138	Ee	57.23N	97.40 E
Čunski [R.S.F.S.R.]	138	Ee	56.03N	99.48 E
Cuorgnè	128	Be	45.23N	7.39 E
Čupa	136	Db	66.17N	33.01 E
Cupar	118	Je	56.19N	3.01W
Cupica, Golfo de-	202	Cb	6.35N	77.30W
Ćuprija	130	Ef	43.56N	21.22 E
Cúpula, Pico-	192	De	24.47N	110.50W
Čur	114	Mh	57.11N	53.01 E
Curaçá	202	Ke	8.59S	39.54W
Curaçao	198	Jd	12.11N	69.00W
Curacautin	206	Fe	38.26S	71.53W
Cura Malal, Sierra de-	204	Am	37.44S	62.16W
Curanilahue	206	Fe	37.28S	73.21W
Čurapča	138	Id	61.56N	132.18 E
Curaray, Rio-	202	Dd	2.20S	74.05W
Curdimurka	210	Eg	29.30S	137.10 E
Curé	204	De	21.25S	56.25W
Cure	122	Jg	47.40N	3.41 E
Curepipe	172a	Bb	20.19S	57.31 E
Curepto	206	Fe	35.05S	72.01W
Cureski prohod (Vitinja)	130	Gg	42.47N	23.45 E
Curiapo	202	Fb	8.33N	61.00W
Curicó	200	Ii	34.59S	71.14W
Curicuriari, Rio-	202	Ed	0.14S	66.48W
Curitabanos	206	Jc	27.18S	50.36W
Curitiba	200	Lh	25.25S	49.15W
Curoca	170	Bf	15.43S	11.55 E
Currais Novos	202	Ke	6.15S	36.31W
Curralinho	202	Id	1.48S	49.47W
Curral-Velho	162	Cf	15.59N	22.48W
Current	184	Im	25.27S	76.45W
Current River	186	Kh	36.15N	90.57W
Currie	212	Ig	39.56S	143.52 E
Curtea de Argeş	130	Hd	45.08N	24.41 E
Curtici	130	Ec	46.21N	21.18 E
Curtis	186	Ff	40.38N	100.31W
Curtis Channel	212	Kd	23.55S	152.05 E
Curtis Island [Austl.]	212	Kd	23.40S	151.10 E
Curtis Island [Ker.Is.]	208	Jh	30.35S	178.36W
Curuá, Rio- [Braz.]	198	Kf	5.23S	54.22W
Curuá, Rio- [Braz.]	204	Ga	13.26S	51.24W
Curuá, Rio- [Braz.]	202	Gd	1.55S	55.07W
Curuçá	202	Id	0.43S	47.50W
Curuçá, Rio-	202	Dd	4.27S	71.23W
Curuguaty	206	Ib	24.31S	55.42W
Curuguaty, Arroyo-	204	Dg	24.06S	56.02W
Curup	150	Dg	3.28S	102.32 E
Curupira, Sierra de-	202	Fc	1.25N	64.30W
Cururupu	202	Jd	1.50S	44.52W
Curuzú Cuatiá	206	Ic	29.47S	58.03W
Curvelo	202	Jg	18.45S	44.25W
Cushing	186	Hi	35.59N	96.46W
Cushing, Mount-	180	Ee	57.36N	126.51W
Cusio → Orta, Lago d'-	128	Ce	45.50N	8.25 E
Čusovaja	110	Ld	58.13N	56.30 E
Čusovoj	136	Fd	58.17N	57.50 E
Cusset	122	Jh	46.08N	3.28 E
Cusseta	184	Ei	32.18N	84.47W
Čust	135	Hd	41.00N	71.15 E
Custer	186	Ee	43.46N	103.36W
Cutato	170	Ce	10.33S	16.48 E
Cut Bank	182	Eb	48.38N	112.20W
Cutervo	202	Ce	6.22S	78.51W
Cuthbert	184	Ej	31.46N	84.48W
Cutral Có	206	Ge	38.56S	69.14W
Cutro	128	Kk	39.02N	16.59 E
Cuttack	142	Kg	20.30N	85.50 E
Čuvašskaja ASSR [3]	136	Ed	55.30N	47.10 E
Cuvelai	170	Cf	15.40S	15.47 E
Cuvette [3]	170	Cc	0.10S	15.30 E
Cuvier Basin (EN)	212	Cd	22.00S	111.00 E
Cuvier Island	218	Fb	36.25S	175.45 E
Cuvo ou Queve	158	Ij	10.50S	13.47 E
Cuxhaven	120	Ec	53.53N	8.42 E
Cuya	206	Fa	19.07S	70.08W
Cuyahoga Falls	184	Ge	41.08N	81.55W
Cuyo Islands	150	Hd	11.04N	120.57 E
Cuyubini, Rio-	196	Fh	8.20N	60.20W
Cuyuni, Rio-	198	Ke	6.23N	58.41W
Cuyuni River	198	Kf	6.23N	58.41W
Cuyutlán, Laguna-	192	Gh	19.00N	104.10W
Cuzco	200	Ig	13.31S	71.59W
Cuzco [3]	202	Df	12.30S	72.30W
Cuzna	126	Hf	38.04N	4.41W
Cvikov	120	Kf	50.48N	14.40 E
Čvrsnica	128	Lg	43.35N	17.35 E
Cyangugu	170	Ec	2.29S	28.54 E
Cybinka	120	Kd	52.12N	14.48 E
Cyclades (EN) = Kikládhes	110	Ih	37.00N	25.10 E
Čyjyrčyk, pereval-	135	Id	40.15N	73.20 E
Cypress Hills	174	Ie	49.40N	109.30W
Cypress Lake	188	Kb	49.28N	109.29W
Cyprus (EN)=Kıbrıs/Kypros [1]	142	Ff	35.00N	33.00 E
Cyprus (EN)=Kıbrıs/Kypros	140	Ff	35.00N	33.00 E
Cyprus (EN)=Kypros/Kıbrıs [1]	142	Ff	35.00N	33.00 E
Cyprus (EN)=Kypros/Kıbrıs	140	Ff	35.00N	33.00 E
Cyrenaica (EN)=Barqah	158	Je	31.00N	23.00 E
Cyrenaica (EN)=Barqah	164	Dc	31.00N	22.30 E
Cyrene	164	Dc	32.48N	21.59 E
Cyrus Field Bay	180	Ld	62.50N	65.00W
Cysoing	124	Fd	50.34N	3.13 E
Cythera (EN)=Kithira	130	Fm	36.09N	23.00 E
Czaplinek	120	Mc	53.34N	16.14 E
Czarna [Pol.]	120	Rf	50.30N	21.15 E
Czarna [Pol.]	120	Pe	51.12N	19.53 E
Czarna Białostocka	120	Tc	53.18N	23.19 E
Czarna Dąbrówka	120	Nb	54.20N	17.32 E
Czarna Hańcza	120	Tc	53.50N	23.47 E
Czarnków	120	Md	52.55N	16.34 E
Czchów	120	Qg	49.50N	20.39 E
Czechoslovakia (EN)= Československo [1]	112	Hf	49.30N	17.00 E
Czechowice-Dziedzice	120	Og	49.54N	19.00 E
Czeremcha	120	Td	52.32N	23.15 E
Czersk	120	Nc	53.48N	18.00 E
Częstochowa	112	He	50.49N	19.06 E
Częstochowa [2]	120	Pf	50.50N	19.05 E
Człopa	120	Mc	53.06N	16.08 E
Człuchów	120	Nc	53.41N	17.21 E

D

Đà, Sông- [Asia] = Black River (EN)	140	Mg	20.17N	106.34 E
Da'an (Dalai)	152	Lb	45.35N	124.16 E
Dabaga	170	Gd	8.07S	35.55 E
Dabakala	166	Ed	8.22N	4.26W
Dabakala [3]	166	Ed	8.27N	4.28W
Daban → Bairin Youqi	152	Kc	43.30N	118.37 E
Dabas	120	Pi	47.11N	19.19 E
Daba Shan	140	Mf	32.15N	109.00 E
Dabat	168	Fc	12.58N	37.45 E
Dabay Sima	168	Gc	12.43N	42.17 E
Dabba/Daocheng	152	Hf	29.01N	100.26 E
Dabbāgh, Jabal-	144	Ed	27.52N	35.45 E
Dabeiba	202	Cb	7.02N	76.16W
Dąbie	120	Od	52.06N	18.49 E
Dąbie, Jezioro-	120	Kc	53.29N	14.40 E
Dabie Shan	140	Nf	31.15N	115.00 E
Dabl, Wādī-	146	Gh	29.05N	36.14 E
Dabnou	166	Gc	14.09N	5.22 E
Dabola	166	Cc	10.45N	11.07W
Daborow	168	Hd	6.11N	48.22 E
Dabou	166	Ed	5.19N	4.23W
Dabqig → Uxin Qi	152	Id	38.27N	109.08 E
Dabraš	130	Gh	41.40N	23.50 E
Dąbrowa Białostocka	120	Tc	53.40N	23.20 E
Dąbrowa Górnicza	120	Pf	50.20N	19.11 E
Dąbrowa Tarnowska	120	Qf	50.11N	21.00 E
Dabsan Hu	152	Fd	36.58N	95.00 E
Dăbuleni	130	Hf	43.48N	24.05 E
Dabus	168	Fc	10.38N	35.10 E
Dacata	168	Gd	7.16N	42.15 E
Dacca → Dhaka	142	Lg	23.43N	90.25 E
Dachangzhen	154	Eh	32.13N	118.44 E
Dachau	120	Hh	48.16N	11.26 E
Dachen Dao	154	Fj	28.29N	121.53 E
Dachstein	128	Hc	47.30N	13.36 E
Dacia Seamount (EN)	110	Ei	31.10N	13.42W

Index Symbols

[1] Independent Nation
[2] State, Region
[3] District, County
[4] Municipality
[5] Colony, Dependency
Continent
Physical Region
Historical or Cultural Region
Mount, Mountain
Volcano
Hill
Mountains, Mountain Range
Hills, Escarpment
Plateau, Upland
Pass, Gap
Plain, Lowland
Delta
Salt Flat
Valley, Canyon
Crater, Cave
Karst Features
Depression
Polder
Desert, Dunes
Forest, Woods
Heath, Steppe
Oasis
Cape, Point
Coast, Beach
Cliff
Peninsula
Isthmus
Sandbank
Island
Atoll
Rock, Reef
Islands, Archipelago
Rocks, Reefs
Coral Reef
Well, Spring
Geyser
River, Stream
Waterfall, Rapids
River Mouth, Estuary
Lake
Salt Lake
Intermittent Lake
Reservoir
Swamp, Pond
Canal
Glacier
Ice Shelf, Pack Ice
Ocean
Sea
Gulf, Bay
Strait, Fjord
Lagoon
Bank
Seamount
Tablemount
Ridge
Shelf
Basin
Escarpment, Sea Scarp
Fracture
Trench, Abyss
National Park, Reserve
Point of Interest
Recreation Site
Cave, Cavern
Historic Site
Ruins
Wall, Walls
Church, Abbey
Temple
Scientific Station
Railway station
Airport
Port
Military installation
Lighthouse
Mine
Tunnel
Dam, Bridge

Dačice 120 Lg 49.05N 15.26 E
Dac Lac, Caonguyen- 148 Lf 12.50N 108.05 E
Dadali 219a Dc 8.07 S 159.06 E
Dadanawa 202 Gc 2.50N 59.30W
Daday 146 Eb 41.28N 33.28 E
Dade City 184 Fk 28.22N 82.12W
Dadou 122 Hk 43.44N 1.49 E
Dādra and Nagar Haveli 148 Ed 20.20N 72.50 E
Dadu 148 Dc 26.44N 67.47 E
Dadu He 140 Mg 29.32N 103.44 E
Dadukou 154 Di 30.30N 117.03 E
Dăeni 130 Le 44.50N 28.07 E
Daet 150 Hd 14.05N 122.55 E
Dafang 152 If 27.06N 105.32 E
Dafeng (Dazhongji) 154 Fh 33.11N 120.27 E
Dagana 166 Bb 16.31N 15.30W
Dagana 168 Bc 13.05N 16.00 E
Daga Post 168 Ed 9.13N 33.58 E
Dağardi 130 Lj 39.26N 29.00 E
Dagash 168 Eb 19.22N 33.24 E
Dagda 116 Lh 56.04N 27.36 E
Dagdan-Daba 152 Gb 48.20N 96.50 E
Dagéla 168 Bc 10.40N 18.26 E
Dagestanskaja ASSR 136 Eg 43.00N 47.00 E
Dagestanskije Ogni 136 Eg 42.06N 48.12 E
Dagezhen → Fengning 154 Dd 41.12N 116.39 E
Dagu 154 Ed 38.58N 117.40 E
Daguan 152 Hf 27.48N 103.54 E
Dagu He 154 Ff 37.34N 121.17 E
Daguokui Shan 154 Jb 45.19N 129.50 E
Dagupan 150 Hc 16.03N 120.20 E
Dagxoi → Yidun 152 Ge 30.25N 99.28 E
Dagzê 152 Ff 29.41N 91.24 E
Dagzê Co 152 Ee 31.54N 87.29 E
Daheiding Shan 152 Mb 47.58N 129.10 E
Dahei He 154 Ad 40.34N 111.05 E
Da Hinggan Ling = Greater Khingan Range (EN) 140 Oe 49.00N 122.00 E
Dahlak Archipelago 158 Lg 15.40N 40.30 E
Dahlak Kebir 168 Gb 15.38N 40.11 E
Daḩl al Furayy 146 Li 26.45N 47.03 E
Dahlem 124 Id 50.23N 6.33 E
Dahlonega Plateau 184 Fh 34.30N 83.45W
Dahm, Ramlat- 164 If 16.25N 45.45 E
Dahme 120 Je 51.52N 13.26 E
Dahmouni 126 Ni 35.25N 1.29 E
Dahn 124 Je 49.09N 7.47 E
Dahomey → Bénin 160 Hh 9.30N 2.15 E
Dahongliutan 152 Cd 36.00N 79.12 E
Dahra 126 Mh 36.18N 0.55 E
Dahra [Lib.] 164 Cd 29.40N 17.40 E
Dahra [Sen.] 166 Bb 15.21N 15.29W
Dahra, Massif de- 126 Oh 36.30N 2.05 E
Dahūk 146 Jd 36.52N 43.00 E
Dahūk 146 Jd 36.57N 43.00 E
Dahushan 154 Gd 41.37N 122.09 E
Daḩy, Nafūd ad- 164 Ie 22.00N 45.25 E
Dai 219a Eb 7.53 S 160.37 E
Daia 130 If 44.00N 25.59 E
Daïa, Région des- 162 Hc 33.30N 3.25 E
Daicheng 154 De 38.42N 116.37 E
Daigo 154 Pf 36.46N 140.21 E
Dai Hai 154 Bd 40.31N 112.43 E
Dailekh 148 Gc 28.50N 81.44 E
Daimanji-San 156 Cc 36.15N 133.19 E
Daimiel 126 Ie 39.04N 3.37W
Dainanji-San 156 Ec 36.36N 137.42 E
Dainichi-San 156 Ec 36.09N 136.30 E
Dainkog 152 Ge 32.31N 97.59 E
Daiō-Zaki 156 Eg 34.22N 136.53 E
Dairbhre/Valentia 118 Cj 51.55N 10.20W
Daireaux 204 Bm 36.36S 61.45W
Dairen → Dalian 142 Of 38.55N 121.39 E
Dai-Sen 156 Cd 35.24N 133.34 E
Daisengen-Dake 156a Bc 41.35N 140.09 E
Daishan (Gaotingzhen) 154 Gi 30.15N 122.13 E
Daitō [Jap.] 156 Cd 35.19N 132.58 E
Daitō [Jap.] 156 Gb 39.02N 141.22 E
Daitō Islands (EN) = Daitō-Shotō 140 Pg 25.00N 131.15 E
Daitō-Shotō = Daito Islands (EN) 140 Pg 25.00N 131.15 E
Daitō-Zaki 156 Gd 35.18N 140.24 E
Daixian 154 Be 39.03N 112.57 E
Daiyue → Shanyin 154 Be 39.30N 112.48 E
Dajabón 194 Ld 19.33N 71.42W
Dajarra 210 Eg 21.42S 139.31 E
Dajitit, Mali i- 130 Ch 41.22N 19.55 E
Daka 166 Ed 8.19N 0.13W
Dakar 160 Fg 14.40N 17.26W
Dākhilah, Wāḩāt ad- = Dakhla Oasis (EN) 158 Jf 25.30N 29.10 E
Dakhla 160 Ff 23.42N 15.56W
Dakhlet Nouâdhibou 162 De 20.30N 16.00W
Dakla Oasis (EN) = Dākhilah, Wāḩāt ad- 158 Jf 25.30N 29.10 E
Dakoro 166 Gc 14.30N 6.25 E
Đakovica 130 Dg 42.23N 20.26 E
Đakovo 128 Me 45.19N 18.25 E
Dakski 116 Kg 57.38N 25.32 E
Dak To 148 Lf 14.42N 107.51 E
Dal 116 Dd 60.15N 11.12 E
Dal, Jökulsá á- 114a Cb 65.40N 14.20W
Đala 130 Dc 46.09N 20.07 E
Dala [Ang.] 170 De 11.03S 20.17 E
Dala [Sol.Is.] 219a Ec 8.36S 160.41 E
Dalaba 166 Cc 10.42N 12.15W
Dalai → Da'an 152 Lb 45.35N 124.16 E
Dalai Nur 152 Kc 43.18N 116.15 E
Dala-Järna 116 Fd 60.33N 14.21 E
Dālaki 146 Nh 29.19N 51.06 E
Dalälven 110 Hc 60.38N 17.27 E
Dalaman 130 Ln 36.44N 28.49 E
Dalaman 146 Cd 36.41N 28.45 E
Dalāmī 168 Ec 11.52N 30.28 E
Dalan-Dzadgad 142 Me 43.47N 104.29 E
Dalane 116 Bf 58.35N 6.20 E
Dalarna 116 Fd 61.00N 14.05 E
Dalarö 116 He 59.08N 18.24 E
Da Lat 142 Mh 11.56N 108.25 E
Dălbandin 148 Cc 28.53N 64.25 E
Dalbosjön 116 Ef 58.45N 12.50 E
Dalboslätten 116 Ef 58.35N 12.25 E
Dalby [Austl.] 212 Ke 27.11 S 151.16 E
Dalby [Swe.] 116 Ei 55.40N 13.20 E
Dale [Nor.] 114 Af 60.35N 5.49 E
Dale [Nor.] 114 Af 61.22N 5.25 E
Dale Hollow Lake 184 Eg 36.36N 85.19W
Dalen 114 Bg 59.27N 8.00 E
Dalfsen 124 Ib 52.30N 6.14 E
Dalgaranger, Mount- 212 De 27.51 S 117.06 E
Dălgopol 130 Kf 43.03N 27.21 E
Dalhart 182 Gd 36.04N 102.31W
Dalhousie 180 Kg 48.04N 66.23W
Dalhousie, Cape - 180 Eb 70.15N 129.41W
Dali [China] 152 Ie 34.55N 110.00 E
Dali [China] 142 Mg 25.43N 100.07 E
Dalian 142 Of 38.55N 121.39 E
Dalias 126 Jh 36.49N 2.52W
Dalizi 152 Mc 41.45N 126.50 E
Dalj 128 Me 45.29N 18.59 E
Daljā' 164 Fd 27.39N 30.42 E
Dalkowskie, Wzgórza- 120 Le 51.35N 15.50 E
Dall [Ak.-U.S.] 178 Mf 54.50N 132.55W
Dall [Can.] 178 Mf 55.00N 133.00W
Dallas [Or.-U.S.] 188 Dd 44.55N 123.19W
Dallas [Tx.-U.S.] 176 Jf 32.47N 96.48W
Dalmā' 146 Oj 24.30N 52.20 E
Dalmā', Qārat- 164 Dd 25.32N 23.57 E
Dalmacija = Dalmatia (EN) 110 Hg 43.00N 17.00 E
Dalmacija = Dalmatia (EN) 128 Kg 43.00N 17.00 E
Dalmaj, Hawr- 146 Kf 32.20N 45.28 E
Dalmally 118 Ie 56.24N 4.58W
Dalmatia (EN) = Dalmacija 110 Hg 43.00N 17.00 E
Dalmatia (EN) = Dalmacija 128 Kg 43.00N 17.00 E
Dalmatovo 134 Kh 56.16N 63.00 E
Dalnegorsk 142 Pe 44.31N 135.31 E
Dalnerečensk 142 Pe 45.55N 133.45 E
Dalni [R.S.F.S.R.] 138 Kf 53.15N 157.30 E
Dalni [R.S.F.S.R.] 138 Ih 44.57N 135.03 E
Dalnjaja, gora- 138 Mc 68.08N 179.53 E
Daloa 160 Gh 6.53N 6.27W
Daloa 166 Dd 6.58N 6.23W
Dalou Shan 140 Mg 28.00N 106.40 E
Dalqān 146 Kj 24.15N 45.47 E
Dalqū 168 Ea 20.07N 30.35 E
Dalrymple, Mount- 208 Fg 21.02S 148.38 E
Dalsbruk/Taalintendas 116 Jd 60.02N 22.31 E
Dalsfjorden 116 Ac 61.20N 5.05 E
Dalsjöfors 116 Eg 57.43N 13.05 E
Dalsland 116 Ef 58.35N 12.55 E
Dalslands kanal 116 Ef 58.50N 12.25 E
Dals Långed 114 Cg 58.55N 12.18 E
Dalton 184 Eh 34.47N 84.58W
Daltonganj 148 Gd 24.02N 84.04 E
Dalul 168 Gc 14.22N 40.21 E
Daluo 152 Hg 21.38N 100.15 E
Dalupiri 150 Hc 19.05N 121.12 E
Dalvík 114a Bb 65.58N 18.32W
Dalwallinu 212 Df 30.17S 116.40 E
Dalyan 130 Lm 36.50N 28.39 E
Daly Bay 180 Id 64.00N 89.40W
Daly City 188 Dh 37.42N 122.29W
Daly River 208 Ef 13.20S 130.19 E
Daly Waters 212 Gc 16.15S 133.22 E
Damā, Wādī- 146 Fi 27.09N 35.47 E
Damagarim 166 Gc 13.42N 9.00 E
Damān 148 Ed 20.10N 73.00 E
Damān 148 Ed 20.10N 73.00 E
Damanhūr 164 Fc 31.02N 30.28 E
Damar, Pulau- 150 Ih 7.09S 128.40 E
Damara 168 Be 4.58N 18.42 E
Damaraland 170 Bd 21.00S 17.30 E
Damas Cays 194 Hb 23.58N 79.55W
Damascus (EN) = Dimashq 142 Ff 33.30N 36.15 E
Dāmash 146 Md 36.46N 49.46 E
Damaturu 166 Hc 11.45N 11.58 E
Damāvand 146 Oe 35.56N 52.08 E
Damāvand, Qolleh-ye- 140 Hf 35.59N 52.08 E
Damba 170 Cd 6.50S 15.07 E
Dambaslar 130 Kh 41.13N 27.14 E
Dame Marie, Cap- 190 Je 18.36N 74.26W
Damergou 166 Hg 15.00N 9.00 E
Dāmghān 146 Pd 36.09N 54.22 E
Damianópolis 204 Ib 14.33S 46.10W
Damiao 152 He 30.52N 104.38 E
Damietta (EN) = Dumyāţ 160 Ke 31.25N 31.48 E
Daming 154 Cf 36.17N 115.09 E
Daming Shan 152 Ig 23.23N 108.30 E
Damīr Qābū 146 Id 36.54N 41.47 E
Dammartin-en-Goële 124 Ee 49.03N 2.41 E
Dammastock 128 Cd 46.38N 8.25 E
Damme [Bel.] 124 Fc 51.15N 3.17 E
Damme [F.R.G.] 124 Kb 52.31N 8.12 E
Dammer Berge 124 Kb 52.35N 8.17 E
Damoh 148 Fd 23.50N 79.27 E
Damongo 166 Ed 9.05N 1.49W
Damous 126 Nh 36.33N 1.42 E
Dampier 210 Cg 20.39S 116.45 E
Dampier, Selat- = Dampier Strait (EN) 150 Jg 0.40S 130.40 E
Dampier Archipelago 212 Dd 20.35S 116.35 E
Dampier Land 212 Ec 17.30S 122.55 E
Dampierre 124 Df 48.42N 1.59 E
Dampier Strait 212 Ja 5.36S 148.12 E
Dampier Strait (EN) = Dampier, Selat- 150 Jg 0.40S 130.40 E
Damqawt 144 Hf 16.34N 52.50 E
Damqog Kanbab/Maquan He 152 Df 29.36N 84.09 E
Dam Qu 152 Fe 33.56N 92.41 E
Damville 124 Df 48.52N 1.04 E
Damvillers 124 He 49.20N 5.24 E
Damwoude, Dantumadeel- 124 Ha 53.18N 5.59 E
Damxoi → Comai 152 Ff 28.26N 91.32 E
Damxung 152 Fe 30.34N 91.16 E
Danakil = Danakil Plain (EN) 158 Lg 12.25N 40.30 E
Danakil Plain (EN) = Danakil 158 Lg 12.25N 40.30 E
Danané 166 Dd 7.16N 8.09W
Danané 166 Dd 7.25N 8.10W
Da Nang 142 Mh 16.04N 108.13 E
Danba/Rongzhag 152 He 30.48N 101.54 E
Danbury 184 Ke 41.23N 73.27W
Danby Lake 188 Hi 34.14N 115.07W
Dancheng 154 Ch 33.36N 115.14 E
Dancheng → Xiangshan 152 Lf 29.29N 121.52 E
Dandarah 164 Fd 26.10N 32.39 E
Dandeldhura 148 Gc 29.18N 80.35 E
Dandenong, Melbourne- 212 Jg 37.59S 145.12 E
Dandong 142 Oe 40.10N 124.15 E
Daneborg 179 Jd 74.25N 20.10W
Danells Fjord 179 Hf 60.45N 42.45W
Daneţi 130 Hf 43.59N 24.03 E
Danfeng (Longjuzhai) 152 Je 33.44N 110.22 E
Danforth Hills 186 Cf 40.15N 108.00W
Danfu 219a Aa 4.12S 153.04 E
Dangara 136 Gh 38.09N 69.22 E
Dangchengwan → Subei 152 Fd 39.36N 94.58 E
Dange 170 Cd 7.56S 15.03 E
Dang He 152 Fc 40.30N 94.42 E
Dangjin Shankou 140 Lf 39.15N 94.30 E
Dangla 168 Fc 11.16N 36.50 E
Dangla Shan → Tanggula Shan 140 Lf 33.00N 92.00 E
Dangoura, Mont- 168 Dd 6.12N 26.27 E
Dangrek Range (EN) = Dong Rak, Phanom- 140 Mh 14.25N 104.30 E
Dangshan 152 Ke 34.22N 116.21 E
Dangtu 154 Ei 31.33N 118.30 E
Dangu 124 De 49.15N 1.42 E
Dangyang 154 Ai 30.49N 111.47 E
Dan He 154 Bg 35.05N 112.59 E
Daniel 188 Je 42.52N 110.04W
Daniel, Serra- 204 Ea 13.40S 54.55W
Danielskuil 172 Ce 28.11S 23.33 E
Danilov 136 Ed 58.12N 40.13 E
Danilovgrad 130 Cg 42.33N 19.07 E
Danilovka 132 Nd 50.21N 44.06 E
Daning 152 Jd 36.31N 110.45 E
Danjiang → Junxian 152 Je 32.31N 111.32 E
Danjiangkou Shuiku 152 Je 32.37N 111.30 E
Danjo-Guntō 152 Me 32.00N 128.20 E
Đank 146 Qk 23.33N 56.16 E
Dankov 132 Kc 53.16N 39.07 E
Dankova, Pik- 135 Kd 41.00N 77.37 E
Danli 194 Df 14.00N 86.35W
Danmark = Denmark (EN) 112 Gd 56.00N 10.00 E
Danmark Fjord 224 Me 81.10N 23.20W
Danmarks Havn 224 Ld 76.50N 18.30W
Danmarksstrædet = Denmark Strait (EN) 110 Dc 67.00N 25.00W
Dannemora 114 Df 60.11N 17.49 E
Dannenberg (Elbe) 120 Hc 53.06N 11.06 E
Dannevirke 218 Gd 40.12S 176.06 E
Danot 168 Hd 7.33N 45.17 E
Dantumadeel 124 Ha 53.18N 5.59 E
Dantumadeel-Damwoude 124 Ha 53.18N 5.59 E
Danube (EN) = Donau 110 If 45.20N 29.40 E
Danube (EN) = Duna 110 If 45.20N 29.40 E
Danube (EN) = Dunaj 110 If 45.20N 29.40 E
Danube (EN) = Dunărea 110 If 45.20N 29.40 E
Danube (EN) = Dunav 110 If 45.20N 29.40 E
Danube, Mouths of the- (EN) = Dunării, Delta- 110 If 45.30N 29.45 E
Danville [Ar.-U.S.] 186 Ji 35.03N 93.24W
Danville [Il.-U.S.] 182 Jc 40.08N 87.37W
Danville [Ky.-U.S.] 182 Kd 37.39N 84.46W
Danville [Va.-U.S.] 182 Ld 36.34N 79.25W
Danxian (Nada) 152 Ih 19.38N 109.32 E
Danyang 154 Eh 32.00N 119.33 E
Danzig → Gdánsk 112 He 54.23N 18.40 E
Dao 150 Hd 10.31N 121.57 E
Dāo 126 Dd 40.20N 8.11W
Daocheng/Dabba 152 Hf 29.01N 100.26 E
Daokou → Huaxian 154 Cg 35.33N 114.30 E
Daosa 148 Fc 26.53N 76.20 E
Dao Shui 154 Ci 30.42N 114.40 E
Dao Timni 166 Ha 20.38N 13.39 E
Daoura 162 Gd 29.03N 4.33W
Dao Xian 152 Jf 25.37N 111.36 E
Dapaong 166 Fc 10.52N 0.12 E
Dapchi 166 Hc 12.29N 11.29 E
Da Qaidam 142 Lf 37.50N 95.18 E
Daqing Shan 154 Ad 41.00N 111.00 E
Daqin Tal → Naiman Qi 152 Lc 42.49N 120.38 E
Daquing Shan 154 Ed 40.30N 119.38 E
Dar'ā 144 Fc 32.37N 36.06 E
Dārāb 146 Ph 28.45N 54.34 E
Darabani 130 Ja 48.11N 26.35 E
Daraçya Yarımadası 130 Lm 36.40N 28.10 E
Darāfisah 168 Ec 13.23N 31.59 E
Dār al 'Umayrah 168 Gc 12.39N 44.07 E
Dārān 146 Nf 32.59N 50.24 E
Darasun 138 Gf 51.39N 113.59 E
Đaravica 130 Dg 42.32N 20.08 E
Daraw 146 Ej 24.25N 32.56 E
Darazo 166 Hc 11.00N 10.25 E
Darband 144 Ic 31.38N 57.02 E
Darband, Kūh-e- 146 Qg 31.34N 57.08 E
Darbandī Khān, Sad ad- 146 Ke 35.07N 45.50 E
Darbėnai/Darbenaj 116 Ih 56.02N 21.08 E
Darbenaj/Darbėnai 116 Ih 56.02N 21.08 E
Dar Ben Karriche el Bahri 126 Gi 35.51N 5.21W
Darbhanga 148 Hc 26.10N 85.54 E
Dārboruk 168 Gd 9.44N 44.31 E
Darby 188 He 46.01N 114.11W
Darchan → Darhan 142 Me 49.33N 106.21 E
Darda 128 Me 45.38N 18.42 E
Dardanelle Lake 186 Ji 35.25N 93.20W
Dardanelles (EN) = Çanakkale boğazı 110 Ig 40.15N 26.25 E
Dardo/Kangding 152 He 30.01N 101.58 E
Dar el Kouti 158 Jh 8.50N 21.50 E
Darende 146 Gc 38.34N 37.30 E
Dar es Salaam 160 Ki 6.48S 39.17 E
Dar es Salaam 170 Gd 6.50S 39.02 E
Darfield 218 Ee 43.29S 172.07 E
Darfo Boario Terme 128 Ee 45.53N 10.11 E
Dārfūr 158 Jg 13.30N 24.00 E
Dārfūr al Janūbīyah 168 Dc 11.30N 25.10 E
Dārfūr ash Shamālīyah 168 Db 16.00N 25.30 E
Dargan-Ata 136 Gg 40.29N 62.12 E
Dargaville 216 Dg 35.56S 173.52 E
Darhan (Darchan) 142 Me 49.33N 106.21 E
Darhan Muminggan Lianheqi 152 Jc 41.45N 110.24 E
Darica [Tur.] 130 Mi 40.45N 29.23 E
Darica [Tur.] 130 Kj 40.00N 27.50 E
Darien 184 Gj 31.22N 81.26W
Darién 194 Ii 8.10N 77.45W
Darién 190 Ig 8.30N 77.30W
Darién, Golfo de- 198 Ie 8.25N 76.53W
Darién, Serranía de- 190 Ig 8.30N 77.30W
Dariense, Cordillera- 194 Eg 12.55N 85.30W
Darja 135 Ee 38.13N 65.46 E
Darjeeling → Dārjiling 148 Hc 27.02N 88.16 E
Dārjiling 148 Hc 27.02N 88.16 E
Dar-Kebdani 126 Ii 35.07N 3.21W
Dark Head 197n Ba 13.17N 61.17W
Dārkhovīn 146 Mg 30.45N 48.25 E
Darlag 152 Ge 33.49N 99.08 E
Darling 172 Bf 33.23S 18.23 E
Darling Downs 212 Ke 27.30S 150.30 E
Darling Range 208 Ch 32.00S 116.30 E
Darling River 208 Fh 34.07S 141.55 E
Darlington [Eng.-U.K.] 118 Lg 54.31N 1.34W
Darlington [S.C.-U.S.] 184 Hh 34.19N 79.53W
Darłowo 120 Mb 54.26N 16.23 E
Darmouth 118 Jk 50.21N 3.35W
Darmstadt 120 Eg 49.52N 8.39 E
Darnah 160 Je 32.46N 22.39 E
Darnah 164 Dc 31.00N 23.40 E
Darnétal 124 De 49.27N 1.09 E
Darney 122 Mf 48.05N 6.03 E
Darnley, Cape- 222 Fe 67.43S 69.30 E
Darnley Bay 180 Fc 69.45N 123.45W
Daroca 126 Kc 41.07N 1.25W
Darou Khoudos 166 Bb 15.06N 16.50W
Darovskoj 114 Kg 58.47N 47.59 E
Darrah, Mount- 188 Hb 49.28N 114.35W
Darregueira 206 He 37.42S 63.10W
Darreh Gaz 144 Ib 37.27N 59.07 E
Darrehshahr 146 Lf 33.10N 47.18 E
D'Arros Island 172b Bb 5.24S 53.18 E
Dar Rounga 158 Jg 9.45N 22.20 E
Dar Sila 168 Cc 12.11N 21.21 E
Darß 120 Ib 54.25N 12.31 E
Darßer Ort 120 Ib 54.29N 12.31 E
Dart 118 Jk 50.20N 3.33W
Dart, Cape- 222 Nf 73.06S 126.20W
D'Artagnan Bank (EN) 212 Eb 13.00S 121.00 E
Dartang → Baqên 152 Fe 31.58N 94.00 E
Dartford 124 Cc 51.27N 0.13 E
Dartmoor 118 Jk 50.35N 4.00W
Dartmouth 180 Lh 44.40N 63.34W
Dartuch, Cabo- / Artrutx, Cap d'- 126 Pe 39.56N 3.48 E
Daru 214 Ci 9.04S 143.12 E
Daruneh 146 Qe 35.10N 57.18 E
Daruvar 128 Le 45.35N 17.14 E
Darvaza 136 Fg 40.12N 58.24 E
Darvel, Teluk- 150 Gf 4.50N 118.30 E
Darwin 210 Ef 12.28S 130.50 E
Darwin, Bahía- 206 Fg 45.27S 74.40W
Darwin, Isla- 202a Aa 1.39N 92.00W
Darwin, Port- 212 Gb 12.20S 130.40 E
Daryā-ye Panj 144 Kb 37.06N 68.20 E
Dar Zagaoua 168 Cb 15.15N 23.14 E
Dar Zebada 168 Bc 13.45N 18.50 E
Dās 146 Oj 25.09N 52.53 E
Dašava 120 Ug 49.13N 24.05 E
Daš-Balbar 152 Jb 49.31N 114.21 E
Dasha He 154 Ce 38.27N 114.39 E
Dashengtang Shan 154 Dc 42.07N 117.12 E
Dashennongjia 152 Je 31.26N 110.18 E
Dashiqiao → Yingkou 154 Gd 40.39N 122.31 E
Dashitou 154 Jc 43.18N 128.29 E
Dasht 146 Qd 37.17N 56.04 E
Dasht Āb 146 Qh 28.59N 56.32 E
Dashtak 146 Qi 30.23N 52.30 E
Dasht-e-Āzādegan 146 Mg 31.32N 48.10 E
Daškesan 132 Oi 40.30N 46.03 E
Dasseneiland 172 Bf 33.26S 18.05 E
Dastgardān 146 Qe 34.19N 56.51 E
Dastjerd-e Qaddādeh 146 Nf 32.44N 51.32 E
Datça 146 Bd 36.45N 27.40 E
Date 154 Pc 42.27N 140.51 E
Dāth, Sha'īb ad- 146 Jj 25.45N 43.10 E
Datia 148 Fc 25.40N 78.28 E
Datian Ding 152 Jg 22.17N 111.13 E
Datil 186 Ci 34.09N 107.47W
Datong [China] 142 Ne 40.09N 113.17 E
Datong [China] 152 Hd 36.56N 101.40 E
Datteln 124 Jc 51.40N 7.23 E
Datteln-Hamm-Kanal 124 Jc 51.39N 7.21 E
Datu 140 Mi 2.05N 109.39 E
Datu, Teluk- 140 Ni 2.00N 111.00 E
Datu Plang 150 He 6.58N 124.40 E
Dāūd Khel 148 Eb 32.53N 71.34 E
Daudzeva 116 Kh 56.28N 25.18 E
Daugaard-Jensen Land 179 Fb 80.10N 63.30W
Daugaj/Daugai 116 Kj 54.20N 24.28 E
Daugai/Daugaj 116 Kj 54.20N 24.28 E
Daugava = Western Dvina (EN) 136 Cd 57.04N 24.03 E
Daugavpils 112 Id 55.53N 26.32 E
Daule 202 Cd 1.50S 79.57W
Daun 120 Cf 50.12N 6.50 E
Daung Kyun 148 Jf 12.14N 98.05 E
Daunia, Monti della- 128 Ji 41.25N 15.05 E
Dauphin 180 Hf 51.09N 100.03W
Dauphiné 122 Lj 44.50N 6.00 E
Dauphin Lake 180 Hf 51.15N 99.45W
Daura 166 Gc 13.02N 8.18 E
Daurada, Costa- / Dorada, Costa- 126 Nc 41.08N 1.10 E
Dautphetal 124 Kd 50.52N 8.33 E
Dāvangere 148 Ff 14.28N 75.55 E
Davao 142 Oi 7.04N 125.36 E
Davao Gulf 140 Oi 6.40N 125.55 E
Dāvarān, Kūh-e- 146 Qg 30.40N 56.15 E
Dāvar Panāh 144 Jd 27.21N 62.21 E
Dāvarzan 146 Qd 36.23N 56.50 E
Đavat 130 Eh 41.04N 21.06 E
Davenport [Ia.-U.S.] 176 Je 41.32N 90.41W
Davenport [Wa.-U.S.] 188 Fc 47.39N 118.09W
Davenport Range 212 Gd 20.45S 134.50 E
Daventry 124 Ab 52.15N 1.10W
Davert 124 Jc 51.51N 7.36 E
Davey, Port- 212 Jh 43.20S 145.55 E
David 176 Ki 8.25N 82.27W
David City 186 Hf 41.15N 97.08W
David-Gorodok 132 Ec 52.03N 27.13 E
David Point 197p Bb 12.14N 61.39W
Davidson 178 Ma 51.18N 105.59W
Davidson Mountains 178 Kc 68.45N 142.10W
Davies, Mount- 212 Fe 26.14S 129.16 E
Davis 182 Cd 38.33N 121.44W
Davis 222 Fe 68.35S 77.58 E
Davis, Cape- 222 Ee 66.24S 56.50 E
Davis, Mount- 184 Hf 39.47N 79.10W
Davis Bay 222 Ie 66.08S 134.05 E
Davis Inlet 180 Le 56.00N 61.30W
Davis Mountains 186 Ek 30.35N 104.00W
Davis Sea (EN) 222 Ge 66.00S 92.00 E
Davisstrædet = Davis Strait (EN) 174 Nc 68.00N 58.00W
Davis Strait 174 Nc 68.00N 58.00W
Davis Strait (EN) = Davisstrædet 174 Nc 68.00N 58.00W
Davlekanovo 136 Fe 54.13N 55.03 E
Davo 166 Dd 5.00N 6.08W
Davos/Tavau 128 Dd 46.47N 9.50 E
Davutlar 130 Kl 37.43N 27.17 E
Dawa 154 Gd 40.58N 122.01 E
Dawanlê 168 Gd 11.06N 42.38 E
Dawei 142 Lh 14.05N 98.12 E
Dawen He 154 Dg 35.37N 116.23 E
Dawes Range 212 Kd 24.30S 151.10 E
Dawḩarab 164 Hf 16.17N 41.57 E
Dawlatābād 144 Jb 36.30N 64.51 E
Dawson [Ga.-U.S.] 184 Ej 31.47N 84.26W
Dawson [Yuk.-Can.] 176 Fc 64.04N 139.25W
Dawson, Mount- 188 Ga 51.09N 117.25W
Dawson Creek 176 Gd 55.45N 120.07W
Dawson-Lambton Glacier 222 Af 76.15S 27.30W
Dawson Range 180 Ed 65.15N 137.45W
Dawson River 212 Jd 23.38S 149.46 E
Dawu 152 He 30.45N 101.11 E
Dawu (Erlangdian) 154 Ci 31.33N 114.07 E
Dawu → Maqên 152 He 34.29N 100.01 E
Dawukou → Shizuishan 152 Id 39.03N 106.24 E
Dax 122 Ek 43.43N 1.03W
Da Xi 152 Lf 28.10N 120.14 E
Daxian 152 Ie 31.15N 107.28 E
Daxin 152 Ig 22.52N 107.14 E
Daxing 154 De 39.45N 116.19 E
Daxinggou 154 Jc 43.23N 129.39 E
Daxue Shan 140 Mf 30.30N 101.30 E
Dayan → Lijiang 142 Mg 26.56N 100.15 E
Dayang He 154 Ge 39.52N 123.40 E
Dayao 152 Hf 25.49N 101.18 E
Daye 154 Ci 30.05N 114.58 E
Dayishan → Guanyun 154 Eg 34.18N 119.14 E
Daymān, Cuchilla del- 204 Dj 31.38S 57.10W
Daymán, Río- 204 Dj 31.40S 58.02W
Daym Zubayr 168 Dd 7.43N 26.13 E
Dayong 152 Jf 29.09N 110.30 E
Dayr, Jabal ad- 168 Ec 12.27N 30.45 E
Dayr az Zawr 142 Gf 35.20N 40.09 E
Dayr Hāfir 146 Gd 36.09N 37.42 E
Dayr Mawās 146 Di 27.38N 30.51 E
Dayrūţ 164 Fd 27.33N 30.49 E
Dayton [Oh.-U.S.] 176 Kf 39.45N 84.15W
Dayton [Wa.-U.S.] 188 Gc 46.19N 117.59W
Daytona Beach 176 Kg 29.12N 80.59W
Dayu 152 Jf 25.29N 114.22 E
Da Yunhe = Grand Canal (EN) 140 Nf 39.54N 116.44 E
Dayville 188 Fd 44.28N 119.32W
Dayyinah 146 Oj 24.57N 52.24 E
Dazhongji → Dafeng 154 Fh 33.11N 120.27 E
Dazhu 152 Ie 30.42N 107.12 E
Dazjā 146 Pe 35.50N 55.46 E
Dazkırı 154 Cd 37.54N 29.42 E
De Aar 160 Jl 30.39S 24.00 E
Dead 118 Ei 52.40N 8.30W
Deadhorse 178 Jb 70.11N 148.27W
Deadmans Cay 194 Jb 23.14N 75.14W
Dead Sea (EN) = Mayyit, Al Baḩr al- 140 Ff 31.30N 35.30 E
Deadwood 186 Ed 44.23N 103.44W
Deal 118 Oj 51.13N 1.24 E
Dealu Mare 130 Jb 47.27N 26.40 E
De'an 154 Cj 29.18N 115.46 E
Deán Funes 206 Hd 30.26S 64.21W
Dearborn 184 Fd 42.18N 83.10W
Dearg, Beinn- 118 Id 57.48N 4.57W
Deary 188 Gc 46.52N 116.31W
Dease 180 Ee 59.55N 128.29W
Dease Arm 180 Fc 66.50N 120.00W
Dease Lake 176 Fd 58.35N 130.02W
Dease Strait 180 Gc 69.00N 107.00W

Index Symbols

1 Independent Nation
2 State, Region
3 District, County
4 Municipality
5 Colony, Dependency
Continent
Physical Region
Historical or Cultural Region
Mount, Mountain
Volcano
Hill
Mountains, Mountain Range
Hills, Escarpment
Plateau, Upland
Pass, Gap
Plain, Lowland
Delta
Salt Flat
Valley, Canyon
Crater, Cave
Karst Features
Depression
Polder
Desert, Dunes
Forest, Woods
Heath, Steppe
Oasis
Cape, Point
Coast, Beach
Cliff
Peninsula
Isthmus
Sandbank
Island
Atoll
Rock, Reef
Islands, Archipelago
Rocks, Reefs
Coral Reef
Well, Spring
Geyser
River, Stream
Waterfall, Rapids
River Mouth, Estuary
Lake
Salt Lake
Intermittent Lake
Reservoir
Swamp, Pond
Canal
Glacier
Ice Shelf, Pack Ice
Ocean
Sea
Gulf, Bay
Strait, Fjord
Lagoon
Bank
Seamount
Tablemount
Ridge
Shelf
Basin
Escarpment, Sea Scarp
Fracture
Trench, Abyss
National Park, Reserve
Point of Interest
Recreation Site
Cave, Cavern
Historic Site
Ruins
Wall, Walls
Church, Abbey
Temple
Scientific Station
Railway station
Airport
Port
Military installation
Lighthouse
Mine
Tunnel
Dam, Bridge

Death Valley	188	Gh	36.20N	116.50W
Death Valley	174	Hf	36.30N	117.00W
Deauville	122	Ge	49.22N	0.04 E
Debak	150	Ff	1.34N	111.25 E
Debalcevo	132	Ke	48.20N	38.29 E
Debao	152	Ig	23.17N	106.21 E
Debar	130	Dh	41.32N	20.32 E
Debark	168	Fc	13.08N	37.53 E
Debdou	162	Gc	33.59N	3.03W
Debed	132	Ni	41.22N	44.58 E
Deben	124	Db	52.01N	1.22 E
De Beque	186	Bg	39.20N	108.13W
Dębica	120	Rf	50.04N	21.24 E
De Bilt	124	Hb	52.06N	5.11 E
Debin	138	Kd	62.18N	150.47 E
Dęblin	120	Re	51.35N	21.50 E
Dębno	120	Kd	52.45N	14.40 E
Débo, Lac-	166	Eb	15.18N	4.09W
Deborah East, Lake-	212	Df	30.45S	119.10 E
Deborah West, Lake-	212	Df	30.45S	119.05 E
Deboyne Islands	208	Gf	10.43S	152.22 E
Debrc	130	Ce	44.37N	19.54 E
Debre Berhan	168	Fd	9.41N	39.33 E
Debrecen	112	If	47.32N	21.38 E
Debrecen [2]	120	Ri	47.31N	21.40 E
Debre Libanos	168	Fd	9.43N	38.52 E
Debre Markos	160	Kg	10.20N	37.44 E
Debre Sina	168	Fd	9.51N	39.46 E
Debre Tabor	168	Fc	11.51N	38.00 E
Debre Zeyt	160	Kh	8.47N	39.00 E
De-Buka, Glacier-	222	Nf	76.00S	131.00W
Decatur [Al.-U.S.]	182	Je	34.36N	86.59W
Decatur [Ga.-U.S.]	184	Ei	33.46N	84.18W
Decatur [Il.-U.S.]	182	Jd	39.51N	89.32W
Decatur [In.-U.S.]	184	Ee	40.50N	84.56W
Decatur [Tx.-U.S.]	186	Hj	33.14N	97.35W
Decazeville	122	Ij	44.33N	2.15 E
Deccan	140	Jh	14.00N	77.00 E
Decelles, Reservoir-	184	Hb	47.40N	78.08W
Deception Bay	212	Ia	7.07S	144.05 E
Dechang	152	Hf	27.22N	102.12 E
Děčín	120	Kf	50.47N	14.13 E
Decize	122	Jh	46.50N	3.28 E
Decorah	186	Ke	43.18N	91.48W
Deda	130	Hc	46.56N	24.54 E
Dededo	220c	Ba	13.31N	144.49 E
Dedegöl Dağı	146	Dd	37.39N	31.17 E
Dedemsvaart, Avereest-	124	Ib	52.37N	6.27 E
Dédougou	166	Ec	12.28N	3.28W
Dedoviči	114	Gh	57.33N	29.58 E
Dedza	170	Fe	14.22S	34.20 E
Dee [Eng.-U.K.]	118	Jh	53.19N	3.11W
Dee [Scot.-U.K.]	118	Ig	54.50N	4.03W
Dee [Scot.-U.K.]	118	Kd	57.08N	2.04W
Deep Creek Range	188	If	40.00N	113.57W
Deering	178	Gc	66.05N	162.43W
Deer Isle	184	Mc	44.13N	68.41W
Deer Lake [Newf.-Can.]	180	Lg	49.10N	57.25W
Deer Lake [Ont.-Can.]	180	If	52.40N	94.30W
Deer Lodge	188	Ic	46.25N	112.43W
Deer Park	188	Gc	47.57N	117.28W
Defiance	184	Ee	41.17N	84.21W
Defla	126	Qi	35.14N	4.26 E
De Funiak Springs	184	Dj	30.43N	86.07W
Dega Ahmedo	168	Gd	7.50N	42.53 E
Dêgê	152	Ge	31.52N	98.36 E
Degebe	126	Ef	38.13N	7.29W
Degeberga	116	Fi	55.50N	14.05 E
Degeh Bur	168	Gd	8.13N	43.34 E
Degema	166	Ge	4.45N	6.46 E
Degerby	116	Id	60.02N	20.23 E
Degerfors	114	Dg	59.14N	14.26 E
Degerhamn	114	Dh	56.21N	16.24 E
Deggendorf	120	Ih	48.50N	12.58 E
Değirmendere	130	Kk	38.06N	27.09 E
De Gray Lake	186	Ji	34.15N	93.15W
De Grey River	212	Dd	20.12S	119.11 E
Degtarsk	134	Jh	56.42N	60.06 E
De Haan	124	Fc	51.16N	3.02 E
Dehaj	146	Pg	30.42N	54.53 E
Dehaq	146	Nf	32.55N	50.57 E
Deh Bārez	146	Qi	27.26N	57.12 E
Deh Bīd	146	Og	30.38N	53.13 E
Deh Dasht	146	Ng	30.47N	50.34 E
Dehdez	146	Ng	31.43N	50.17 E
Deh-e-Namak	146	Oe	35.25N	52.50 E
Deh-e Shīr	146	Og	31.29N	53.45 E
Deh-e Ziyār	146	Qg	30.40N	57.00 E
Dehgolān	146	Le	35.17N	47.25 E
Dehiwala-Mount Lavinia	148	Fg	6.50N	79.52 E
Dehlorān	146	Lf	32.41N	47.16 E
Deh Now	146	Qf	33.01N	57.41 E
Dehra Dūn	148	Fb	30.19N	78.02 E
Dehui	152	Mc	44.33N	125.38 E
Deinze	122	Jd	50.59N	3.32 E
Dej	130	Gb	47.09N	23.52 E
Deje	116	Ee	59.36N	13.28 E
Dejen	168	Fc	10.05N	38.11 E
Dejës, Mali i-	130	Dh	41.42N	20.10 E
Dejnau	136	Gh	39.18N	63.11 E
De Jongs, Tanjung-	150	Kh	6.56S	138.32 E
De Kalb	186	Lf	41.56N	88.45W
Dekar	172	Cd	21.30S	21.58 E
Dekese	160	Ji	3.27S	21.24 E
Dekina	166	Gd	7.42N	7.01 E
Dékoa	168	Bd	6.19N	19.04 E
De Koog, Texel-	124	Ga	53.07N	4.46 E
De La Garma	204	Bm	37.58S	60.25W
De Land	184	Gk	29.02N	81.18W
Delano	188	Dd	35.41N	119.15W
Delano Peak	182	Ed	38.22N	112.23W
Delārām	144	Jc	32.11N	63.25 E
Delarof Islands	178a	Cb	51.30N	178.45W
Delaware	184	Fe	40.18N	83.06W
Delaware [2]	182	Ld	39.10N	75.30W
Delaware	186	Ek	32.00N	104.00W
Delaware Bay	174	Lf	39.05N	75.15W
Delaware River	182	Ld	39.20N	75.25W
Delbrück	124	Kc	51.46N	8.34 E
Del Carril	204	Cl	35.31S	59.30W
Delčevo	130	Fh	41.58N	22.47 E
Del City	186	Hi	35.27N	97.27W
Delegate	212	Jg	37.03S	148.58 E
Delémont/Delsberg	128	Bc	47.22N	7.21 E
Delet/Teili	116	Id	60.15N	20.35 E
Delfinópolis	204	Ie	20.20S	46.51W
Delft	122	Kb	52.00N	4.21 E
Delfzijl	122	Ma	53.19N	6.56 E
Delgada, Punta-	198	Jj	42.46S	63.38W
Delgado, Cabo-=Delgado, Cape-(EN) [3]	172	Fb	12.30S	39.00 E
Delgado, Cabo-=Delgado, Cape-(EN)	158	Lj	10.40S	40.38 E
Delgado, Cape-(EN)= Delgado, Cabo- [3]	172	Fb	12.30S	39.00 E
Delgado, Cape-(EN)= Delgado, Cabo-	158	Lj	10.40S	40.38 E
Delger Muren	152	Hb	49.17N	100.40 E
Delhi [Co.-U.S.]	186	Eh	37.42N	103.58W
Delhi [India]	148	Jg	28.40N	77.13 E
Delhi [N.Y.-U.S.]	184	Jd	42.17N	74.57W
Deliblatska Peščara	130	Dd	45.00N	21.00 E
Delice	146	Fc	39.58N	34.02 E
Deliceirmak	146	Fb	40.28N	34.10 E
Delicias [Cuba]	194	Ic	21.11N	76.34W
Delicias [Mex.]	190	Cc	28.13N	105.28W
Delijān	146	Nf	33.59N	50.40 E
Delingha	152	Gd	37.26N	97.25 E
Dēliņkalns/Delinkalns, gora-	116	Lg	57.30N	27.02 E
Delinkalns, gora-/ Dēliņkalns	116	Lg	57.30N	27.02 E
Delitzsch	120	Ie	51.32N	12.21 E
Deljatin	130	Ha	48.29N	24.45 E
Delle	122	Mg	47.30N	7.00 E
Dell Rapids	186	He	43.50N	96.43W
Dellys	126	Hb	36.55N	3.55 E
Delmarva Peninsula	174	Lf	38.50N	75.30W
Delme	124	If	48.53N	6.24 E
Delme	124	Ka	53.05N	8.40 E
Delmenhorst	120	Ec	53.03N	8.37 E
Delnice	128	Ie	45.24N	14.48 E
Delo	168	Fd	5.49N	37.57 E
De-Longa, ostrova- = De Long Islands (EN)	140	Rb	76.30N	153.00 E
De Long Islands (EN) = De-Longa, ostrova-	140	Rb	76.30N	153.00 E
De Long Mountains	178	Gc	68.20N	162.00W
De Long Strait (EN) = Longa, proliv-	140	Tb	70.20N	178.00 E
Deloraine	212	Jh	41.31S	146.39 E
Delorme, Lac-	180	Kf	54.35N	69.55W
Delphi (EN) = Dhelfoi	130	Fk	38.29N	22.30 E
Del Rio	182	Gf	29.22N	100.54W
Delsberg/Delémont	128	Bc	47.22N	7.21 E
Delsbo	114	Dc	61.48N	16.35 E
Delta [Co.-U.S.]	182	Fd	38.44N	108.04W
Delta [Ut.-U.S.]	182	Ed	39.21N	112.35W
Delta Amacuro [2]	202	Fb	8.30N	61.30W
Delta Junction	178	Jd	64.02N	145.41W
Delvāda	148	Ed	20.46N	71.02 E
Del Valle	204	Bl	35.54S	60.43W
Delvina	130	Dj	39.57N	20.06 E
Dëma	134	Gi	54.42N	55.58 E
Demanda, Sierra de la-	126	Ib	42.15N	3.05W
Demba	170	Dd	5.30S	22.16 E
Dembi	168	Fd	8.05N	36.28 E
Dembia	168	Cd	5.07N	24.25 E
Dembi Dolo	168	Ed	8.32N	34.49 E
Demer	122	Kd	50.58N	4.45 E
Demerara Plateau (EN)	198	Le	4.30N	44.00W
Demerara River	202	Gb	6.48N	58.10W
Demidov	132	Gb	55.15N	31.29 E
Demidovka	120	Vf	50.20N	25.27 E
Deming	182	Fe	32.16N	107.45W
Demini, Rio-	202	Fd	0.46S	62.56W
Demirci	146	Cc	39.03N	28.40 E
Demir Kapija	130	Fh	41.25N	22.15 E
Demirköy	130	Kh	41.49N	27.45 E
Demirtaş	130	Mi	40.16N	29.06 E
Demjanka	136	Gd	59.34N	69.20 E
Demjansk	114	Hh	57.38N	32.29 E
Demjanskoje	136	Gd	59.36N	69.18 E
Demmin	120	Jc	53.54N	13.02 E
Demopolis	184	Di	32.31N	87.50W
Dempo, Gunung-	140	Mj	4.02S	103.09 E
Demta	150	Lg	2.20S	140.08 E
Denain	122	Jd	50.20N	3.23 E
Denan	168	Gd	6.30N	43.30 E
Denau	136	Gh	38.18N	67.55 E
Den Bosch/'s-Hertogenbosch	122	Lc	51.41N	5.19 E
Den Burg, Texel-	124	Ga	53.03N	4.47 E
Den Chai	148	Ke	17.59N	100.04 E
Dendang	150	Eg	3.05S	107.54 E
Dender/Dendre	122	Kc	51.02N	4.06 E
Dendermonde/Termonde	124	Gc	51.02N	4.07 E
Dendre/Dender	122	Kc	51.02N	4.06 E
Dendtler Island	222	Pf	72.58S	89.57W
Denekamp	124	Jb	52.23N	7.00 E
Deneżkin Kamen, gora-	136	Fc	60.25N	59.31 E
Dengarh	148	Hd	23.50N	81.42 E
Dêngkagoin → Têwo	152	He	34.03N	103.21 E
Dengkou (Bayan Gol)	142	Me	40.25N	106.59 E
Dêngqên	152	Ge	31.29N	95.32 E
Dengzhou → Penglai	152	Ld	37.44N	120.45 E
Den Haag/'s-Gravenhage= The Hague (EN)	112	Ge	52.06N	4.18 E
Den Ham	124	Ib	52.28N	6.32 E
Denham → Shark Bay	212	Ce	25.55S	113.32 E
Denham, Mount-	194	Id	18.13N	77.32W
Denham Range	212	Jd	21.55S	147.45 E
Denham Sound	212	Ce	25.40S	113.15 E
Den Helder	122	Kb	52.54N	4.45 E
Denia / Dénia	126	Mf	38.51N	0.07 E
Dénia / Denia	126	Mf	38.51N	0.07 E
Deniliquin	212	Ig	35.32S	144.58 E
Denio	188	Ff	41.59N	118.39W
Denis Island	172b	Ca	3.48S	55.40 E
Denison [Ia.-U.S.]	182	Hc	42.01N	95.20W
Denison [Tx.-U.S.]	182	He	33.45N	96.33W
Denison, Mount-	178	Ie	58.25N	154.27W
Denizli	144	Cb	37.46N	29.06 E
Denklingen, Reichshof-	124	Jd	50.55N	7.39 E
Denman Glacier	222	Ge	66.45S	99.25 E
Denmark [Austl.]	212	Df	34.57S	117.21 E
Denmark [S.C.-U.S.]	184	Gi	33.19N	81.09W
Denmark (EN)=Danmark [1]	112	Gd	56.00N	10.00 E
Denmark Strait (EN) = Danmarksstrædet	110	Dc	67.00N	25.00W
Dennery	197k	Bb	13.55N	60.54W
Den Oever, Wieringen-	124	Hb	52.56N	5.02 E
Denpasar	142	Nj	8.39S	115.13 E
Denton	182	He	33.13N	97.08W
D'Entrecasteaux, Point-	212	Df	34.50S	116.00 E
D'Entrecasteaux Islands	208	Ge	9.35S	150.40 E
D'Entrecasteaux Reefs (EN) = Entrecasteaux, Récifs d'-	208	Hf	18.20S	163.00 E
Denver	176	If	39.43N	105.01W
Deoghar	148	Hd	24.29N	86.42 E
Deolāli	148	Ee	19.54N	73.50 E
De Panne/La Panne	124	Ec	51.06N	2.35 E
Dependencias Federales [2]	202	Fa	11.45N	64.25W
De Pere	186	Ld	44.27N	88.04W
Deputatski	138	Ic	69.13N	139.55 E
Dêqên	152	Gf	28.32N	98.50 E
Deqing	152	Jg	23.14N	111.42 E
De Queen	186	Ii	34.02N	94.21W
De Quincy	186	Jk	30.27N	93.26W
Dequing	154	Fi	30.34N	120.05 E
Dera, Lach-	168	Ge	0.15N	42.17 E
Dera, Lagh-	158	Lh	0.15N	42.17 E
Dera Bugti	148	Dc	29.02N	69.09 E
Dera Ghāzi Khan	142	Jf	30.03N	70.38 E
Dera Ismāīl Khan	148	Eb	31.50N	70.54 E
Derbent [R.S.F.S.R.]	112	Kg	42.00N	48.18 E
Derbent [Tur.]	130	Lk	38.11N	28.33 E
Derby	118	Lh	53.05N	1.40W
Derby [Austl.]	210	Df	17.18S	123.38 E
Derby [Eng.-U.K.]	118	Li	52.55N	1.30W
Derby [Ks.-U.S.]	186	Hh	37.33N	97.16W
Derbyshire [3]	118	Lh	53.10N	1.35W
Đerdap	130	Fe	44.41N	22.10 E
Derecske	120	Ri	47.21N	21.34 E
Dereköy	130	Kh	41.56N	27.21 E
Dereli	146	Hb	40.45N	38.27 E
Derg/Abhainn na Deirge	118	Fg	54.40N	7.25W
Derg, Lough-/Loch Deirgeirt	118	Ei	53.00N	8.20W
Dergači [R.S.F.S.R.]	132	Pd	51.13N	48.46 E
Dergači [Ukr.-U.S.S.R.]	132	Jd	50.09N	36.09 E
Der Grabow	120	Ib	54.23N	12.50 E
De Ridder	186	Jk	30.51N	93.17W
Derik	146	Id	37.22N	40.17 E
Derkul	132	Qd	51.17N	51.15 E
Dermott	186	Kj	33.32N	91.26W
Dernieres, Isles-	186	Kl	29.02N	90.47W
Derong	152	Gf	28.44N	99.18 E
De Rose Hill	212	Ge	26.25S	133.15 E
Déroute, Passage de la-	122	Ee	49.12N	1.51W
Derry / Londonderry	112	Fd	55.00N	7.19W
Dersa, Eglab-	162	Gd	26.45N	4.26W
Dersca	130	Jb	47.59N	26.12 E
Dersingham	124	Cb	52.51N	0.30 E
Derudeb	168	Fb	17.32N	36.06 E
Derventa	128	Lf	44.59N	17.55 E
Derwent [Eng.-U.K.]	118	Mg	53.42N	0.40W
Derwent [Eng.-U.K.]	124	Ab	52.53N	1.17W
Derwent River	212	Jh	43.03S	147.22 E
Deržavinsk	136	Ge	51.03N	66.19 E
Desaguadero, Rio-	198	Ji	34.13S	66.47W
Désappointement, Iles du-	208	Mf	14.10S	141.20W
Des Arc	186	Ki	34.58N	91.30W
Desborough	124	Bb	52.26N	0.49W
Descalvado	204	Ie	21.54S	47.37W
Descartes	122	Gh	46.58N	0.45 E
Deschambault Lake	180	Hf	54.50N	103.30W
Deschutes River	182	Cb	45.38N	120.54W
Descoberto, Rio-	204	Hc	16.20S	48.19W
Dese	160	Kg	11.07N	39.38 E
Deseado, Rio-	198	Jj	47.45S	65.54W
Desecheo, Isla-	197a	Ab	18.25N	67.28W
Desengaño, Punta-	206	Gg	49.15S	67.37W
Desenzano del Garda	128	Ee	45.28N	10.32 E
Desertas, Ilhas-	162	Dc	32.30N	16.30W
Desert Center	188	Hj	33.42N	115.26W
Desert Peak	188	If	40.28N	112.38W
Deshaies	197e	Ab	16.18N	61.47W
Desiderio, Rio-	204	Ja	12.20S	44.50W
Desmaraisville	184	Ia	49.31N	76.10W
De Smet	186	Hd	44.23N	97.33W
Desmochado	204	Ch	27.07S	58.06W
Des Moines	174	Je	40.22N	91.26W
Des Moines [Ia.-U.S.]	176	Je	41.35N	93.37W
Des Moines [N.M.-U.S.]	186	Eh	36.46N	103.50W
Desmoronado, Cerro-	190	Dd	20.21N	105.01W
Desna	110	Je	50.33N	30.32 E
Desnățui	130	Ge	43.53N	23.35 E
Des Noeuf, Ile-	172b	Bb	6.14S	53.03 E
Desolación, Isla-	198	Ik	53.00S	74.10W
De Soto	186	Kg	38.08N	90.33W
Despeñaperros, Desfiladero de-	126	If	38.24N	3.30W
Des Roches, Ile-	172b	Bb	5.41S	53.41 E
Dessau	120	Ie	51.50N	12.15 E
Destruction Bay	180	Dd	61.20N	139.00W
Desvres	122	Hd	50.40N	1.50 E
Deta	130	Ed	45.24N	21.14 E
Dete	172	Dc	18.37S	26.51 E
Detmold	120	Ee	51.56N	8.53 E
Detour, Point-	184	Dc	45.36N	86.37W
Detroit [Mi.-U.S.]	176	Ke	42.20N	83.03W
Detroit [Or.-U.S.]	188	Dd	44.42N	122.10W
Detroit Lakes	186	Ic	46.49N	95.51W
Dettifoss	114a	Cb	65.49N	16.24W
Detva	120	Ph	48.34N	19.25 E
Deûle	124	Ed	50.44N	2.56 E
Deurdeur	126	Oh	36.14N	2.16 E
Deurne	124	Hc	51.28N	5.48 E
Deutsche Bucht	120	Db	54.30N	7.30 E
Deutsche Demokratische Republik=German Democratic Republic (EN) [1]	112	He	52.00N	12.30 E
Deutschlandsberg	128	Jd	46.49N	15.13 E
Deux-Bassins, Col des-	126	Ph	36.27N	3.18 E
Deux-Sèvres [3]	122	Fh	46.30N	0.15W
Deva	130	Fd	45.53N	22.54 E
Dévaványa	120	Qi	47.02N	20.58 E
Deveci Dağları	146	Gb	40.05N	36.00 E
Devecser	120	Ni	47.06N	17.26 E
Develi	146	Fc	38.22N	35.06 E
Deventer	122	Mb	52.15N	6.10 E
Deverd, Cap-	219b	Be	20.46S	164.22 E
Deveron	118	Kd	57.40N	2.30W
Devès, Monts du-	122	Jj	44.57N	3.46 E
Devetak	128	Mg	43.58N	19.00 E
Devil River Peak	218	Ed	40.58S	172.39 E
Devil's Hole	118	Ne	56.38N	0.40 E
Devil's Island (EN)=Diable, Ile du-	202	Hb	5.17N	52.35W
Devils Lake	182	Hb	48.07N	98.59W
Devils Lake	186	Gb	48.01N	98.52W
Devils Paw	178	Me	58.44N	133.50W
Devils River	186	Fl	29.39N	100.58W
Devils Tower	188	Md	44.31N	104.57W
Devin	130	Hh	41.45N	24.24 E
Devizes	118	Lj	51.22N	1.59W
Devnja	130	Kf	43.13N	27.33 E
Devodi Munda	148	Ge	17.37N	82.57 E
De Volet Point	197n	Ba	13.22N	61.13W
Devolli	130	Di	40.30N	20.50 E
Devolli	130	Ci	40.49N	19.51 E
Dévoluy	122	Lj	44.39N	5.53 E
Devon [3]	118	Jk	50.50N	3.50W
Devon	118	Jk	50.50N	4.00W
Devon	174	Kb	75.00N	87.00W
Devon	124	Ba	53.04N	0.49W
Devonport	210	Fi	41.11S	146.21 E
Devoto	204	Aj	31.24S	62.19W
Devrek	146	Db	41.13N	31.57 E
Devrez	146	Fb	41.06N	34.25 E
Dewa	158	Lh	4.11N	42.06 E
Dewar Lakes	180	Kc	68.00N	73.00W
Dewās	148	Fd	22.58N	76.04 E
Dewa-Sanchi	156	Gb	39.30N	140.15 E
Dewey	186	Ih	36.48N	95.56W
De Witt	186	Ki	34.18N	91.20W
Dexemhare	168	Fb	15.04N	39.03 E
Dexing	154	Dj	28.55N	117.33 E
Dexter	186	Lh	36.48N	89.57W
Deyang	152	He	31.07N	104.25 E
Dey-Dey, Lake-	212	Ge	29.15S	131.05 E
Deyhūk	146	Qf	33.17N	57.30 E
Deyyer	144	Hd	27.50N	51.55 E
Dez	146	Mg	31.39N	48.52 E
Dezfūl	142	Gf	32.23N	48.24 E
Dez Gerd	146	Ng	30.45N	51.57 E
Dezhou	152	Kd	37.28N	116.18 E
Dežneva, mys-	140	Uc	66.06N	169.45W
Dháfni	130	Fl	37.48N	22.02 E
Dhahab	164	Fd	28.29N	34.32 E
Dhaka (Dacca)	142	Lg	23.43N	90.25 E
Dhamār	144	Fg	14.37N	44.23 E
Dhamtari	148	Gd	20.41N	81.34 E
Dhānbād	148	Hd	23.48N	86.27 E
Dhanghar	148	Gc	28.42N	80.36 E
Dhanushkodi	148	Fg	9.11N	79.24 E
Dhaulagiri	140	Kg	28.44N	83.25 E
Dhekeleia	146	Ee	35.03N	33.40 E
Dhelfoi = Delphi (EN)	130	Fk	38.29N	22.30 E
Dhelvinákion	130	Dj	39.56N	20.28 E
Dhenkanal	148	Hd	20.40N	85.36 E
Dheskáti	130	Ej	39.55N	21.49 E
Dhespotikó	130	Hm	36.58N	25.00 E
Dhiapóndioi Nisoi	130	Cj	39.50N	19.25 E
Dhībān	146	Fg	31.30N	35.47 E
Dhidhimótikhon	130	Jh	41.21N	26.30 E
Dhikti Óros	130	In	35.15N	25.30 E
Dhílos	130	Il	37.24N	25.16 E
Dhimitsána	130	Fl	37.36N	22.03 E
Dhionisiádhes, Nísoi-	130	Jn	35.21N	26.10 E
Dhiórix Potidhaia	130	Gi	40.10N	23.20 E
Dhī-Qār [3]	146	Lg	31.10N	46.10 E
Dhirfis Óros	130	Gk	38.38N	23.50 E
Dhisoron Óros	130	Fh	41.11N	22.57 E
Dhivounia	130	Jn	35.50N	26.28 E
Dhodhekánisos = Dodecanese (EN)	130	Jm	36.20N	27.00 E
Dhodhóni = Dodona (EN)	130	Dj	39.33N	20.46 E
Dholpur	148	Fc	26.42N	77.54 E
Dhomokós	130	Fj	39.08N	22.18 E
Dhone	148	Fe	15.25N	77.53 E
Dhonoúsa	130	Il	37.10N	25.50 E
Dhorāji	148	Ed	21.44N	70.27 E
Dhoxáton	130	Hh	41.06N	24.14 E
Dhragónisos	130	Il	37.27N	25.29 E
Dhuburi	148	Hc	26.02N	89.58 E
Dhule	142	Jg	20.54N	74.47 E
Dhuliān	148	Hd	24.41N	87.58 E
Dia	130	In	35.27N	25.13 E
Diable, Ile du-=Devil's Island (EN)	202	Hb	5.17N	52.35W
Diable, Morne au-	197g	Ba	15.37N	61.27W
Diable, Pointe du- [Mart.]	197h	Bb	14.47N	60.54W
Diable, Pointe du- [Van.]	219b	Dc	16.01S	168.12 E
Diablo, Punta del-	204	Fl	34.22S	53.46W
Diablo, Puntan-	220b	Ba	15.00N	145.34 E
Diablo Range	188	Eh	36.45N	121.20W
Diafarabé	166	Ec	14.10N	5.00W
Dialafara	166	Cc	13.27N	11.23W
Diamant, Pointe du-	197h	Ac	14.27N	61.04W
Diamant, Rocher du-	197h	Ac	14.27N	61.03W
Diamante [Arg.]	206	Hd	32.04S	60.39W
Diamante [It.]	128	Jk	39.41N	15.49 E
Diamante, Punta del-	192	Ji	16.47N	99.52W
Diamantina	202	Jg	18.15S	43.36W
Diamantina, Chapada-	198	Lg	11.30S	41.10W
Diamantina, Rio-	204	Fc	16.42S	52.45W
Diamantina Depth (EN)	106	Hm	33.30S	102.00 E
Diamantina Lakes	212	Id	23.46S	141.09 E
Diamantina River	208	Eg	26.45S	139.10 E
Diamantina Trench (EN)	106	Hm	36.00S	104.00 E
Diamantino	200	Kg	14.25S	56.27W
Diamantino, Rio-	204	Fc	16.08S	52.28W
Diamond Harbour	148	Hd	22.12N	88.12 E
Diamond Island	197p	Bb	12.20N	61.35W
Diamond Jenness Peninsula	180	Fb	71.00N	117.00W
Diamond Peak [Nv.-U.S.]	188	Hg	39.40N	115.48W
Diamond Peak [Or.-U.S.]	188	De	43.33N	122.09W
Diamond Peak [U.S.]	188	Id	44.09N	113.05W
Diamond Peak [U.S.]	188	Gc	46.07N	117.32W
Diamou	166	Cc	14.05N	11.16W
Diana, Baie-	180	Kd	61.00N	70.00W
Dianbai	152	Jg	21.33N	110.58 E
Dianbu → Feidong	154	Di	31.53N	117.29 E
Diancang Shan	152	Hf	25.42N	100.02 E
Dian Chi	152	Hg	24.50N	102.45 E
Diane, Étang de-	122a	Ba	42.07N	9.32 E
Dianjiang	152	Ie	30.19N	107.25 E
Diano Marina	128	Cg	43.54N	8.05 E
Dianópolis	202	If	11.38S	46.50W
Dianra	166	Dd	8.45N	6.18W
Diapaga	166	Fc	12.04N	1.47 E
Diaz	204	Bk	32.22S	61.05W
Dibā	144	Id	25.39N	56.15 E
Dibā, Dawḩat-	146	Qk	25.38N	56.18 E
Dībagah	146	Je	35.52N	43.49 E
Dibang	148	Jc	27.50N	95.32 E
Dibaya	170	Dd	6.30S	22.57 E
Dibaya-Lubue	170	Cc	4.09S	19.52 E
Dibella	170	Hb	17.31N	12.59 E
Dibrugarh	142	Lg	27.29N	94.54 E
Dibs	146	Ke	35.40N	44.04 E
Dibsī Afnān	146	Ee	35.55N	38.16 E
Dickens	186	Fj	33.37N	100.50W
Dickinson	182	Gb	46.53N	102.47W
Dickins Seamount (EN)	178	Lf	54.30N	137.00W
Dickson	184	Dg	36.05N	87.23W
Dicle	146	Ic	38.22N	40.04 E
Dicle=Tigris (EN)	140	Gf	31.00N	47.25 E
Didam	124	Ic	51.56N	6.09 E
Didao	154	Kb	45.22N	130.48 E
Didcot	124	Ac	51.36N	1.15W
Didesa	168	Fd	9.30N	35.32 E
Didiéni	166	Dc	13.23N	8.05W
Didyma	130	Kl	37.21N	27.13 E
Die	122	Lj	44.45N	5.22 E
Dieburg	120	Eg	49.54N	8.51 E
Diecinueve de Abril	204	El	34.22S	54.04W
Dieciocho de Julio	204	Fk	33.41S	53.33W
Diefenbaker Lake	180	Gf	51.00N	107.00W
Diège	122	Ii	45.36N	2.16 E
Diego Garcia	140	Jj	6.20S	72.20 E
Diego Ramirez, Islas-	206	Hi	56.30S	68.44W
Diekirch	122	Me	49.53N	6.10 E
Die Lewitz	120	Hc	53.30N	11.30 E
Diéma	166	Dc	14.33N	9.11W
Diemel	120	Fe	51.39N	9.27 E
Diemelsee	124	Kc	51.19N	8.43 E
Diemelstadt	124	Lc	51.27N	9.01 E
Dien Bien Phu	148	Kd	21.23N	103.01 E
Diepenbeek	124	Hd	50.54N	5.24 E
Diepholz	120	Ed	52.36N	8.22 E
Dieppe	122	He	49.56N	1.05 E
Dieppe Bay Town	197c	Ab	17.25N	62.48W
Dierdorf	124	Jd	50.33N	7.40 E
Dieren, Rheden-	124	Ib	52.03N	6.08 E
Di'er Songhua Jiang	152	Lc	45.26N	124.39 E
Diest	124	Hd	50.59N	5.03 E
Dieulefit	122	Lj	44.31N	5.04 E
Dieulouard	124	If	48.51N	6.04 E
Dieuze	122	Mf	48.49N	6.43 E
Dieveniškes	116	Kj	54.10N	25.44 E
Die Ville	124	Id	50.40N	6.55 E
Diez	124	Kd	50.22N	8.01 E
Dif	170	Hb	0.59N	40.57 E
Diffa	166	Hc	13.19N	12.37 E
Diffa [2]	166	Hb	16.00N	13.30 E
Differdange/Differdingen	122	Le	49.32N	5.52 E
Differdingen/Differdange	122	Le	49.32N	5.52 E
Difuntos, Laguna de los- → Negra, Laguna-	204	Fl	34.03S	53.40W
Digby	180	Kh	44.40N	65.50W
Dighton	186	Fg	38.29N	100.28W
Digne	122	Mj	44.06N	6.14 E
Digoin	122	Jh	46.29N	3.59 E
Digora	132	Nh	43.07N	44.06 E
Digos	150	Ie	6.45N	125.20 E
Digranes	114a	Ca	66.02N	14.45W
Digul	150	Kh	7.07S	138.42 E
Dihāng	148	Jc	27.48N	95.30 E
Dijar	132	Tf	46.33N	56.05 E
Dijlah=Tigris (EN)	140	Gf	31.00N	47.25 E
Dijle	122	Kd	50.53N	4.42 E
Dijon	112	Gf	47.19N	5.01 E
Dik	168	Bd	9.58N	17.31 E
Dikanäs	114	Dd	65.14N	16.00 E
Dikhil	168	Gc	11.06N	42.22 E
Dikili	146	Bc	39.04N	26.53 E
Dikli	116	Kg	57.30N	25.00 E
Diksmuide/Dixmude	122	Ic	51.02N	2.52 E
Dikson	142	Kb	73.30N	80.35 E
Dikwa	166	Hc	12.02N	13.55 E

Index Symbols

[1] Independent Nation
[2] State, Region
[3] District, County
[4] Municipality
[5] Colony, Dependency
Continent
Physical Region
Historical or Cultural Region
Mount, Mountain
Volcano
Hill
Mountains, Mountain Range
Hills, Escarpment
Plateau, Upland
Pass, Gap
Plain, Lowland
Delta
Salt Flat
Valley, Canyon
Crater, Cave
Karst Features
Depression
Polder
Desert, Dunes
Forest, Woods
Heath, Steppe
Oasis
Cape, Point
Coast, Beach
Cliff
Peninsula
Isthmus
Sandbank
Island
Atoll
Rock, Reef
Islands, Archipelago
Rocks, Reefs
Coral Reef
Well, Spring
Geyser
River, Stream
Waterfall, Rapids
River Mouth, Estuary
Lake
Salt Lake
Intermittent Lake
Reservoir
Swamp, Pond
Canal
Glacier
Ice Shelf, Pack Ice
Ocean
Sea
Gulf, Bay
Strait, Fjord
Lagoon
Bank
Seamount
Tablemount
Ridge
Shelf
Basin
Escarpment, Sea Scarp
Fracture
Trench, Abyss
National Park, Reserve
Point of Interest
Recreation Site
Cave, Cavern
Historic Site
Ruins
Wall, Walls
Church, Abbey
Temple
Scientific Station
Railway station
Airport
Port
Military installation
Lighthouse
Mine
Tunnel
Dam, Bridge

Dila 168 Fd 6.23N 38.19 E
Dilbeek 124 Gd 50.51N 4.16 E
Dili 142 Oj 8.33S 125.34 E
Di Linh 148 Lf 11.35N 108.04 E
Diližan 132 Ni 40.46N 44.55 E
Dilj 128 Me 45.16N 18.01 E
Dill 124 Kd 50.33N 8.29 E
Dillenburg 120 Ef 50.44N 8.17 E
Dillia 158 Ig 14.09N 12.50 E
Dilling 160 Jg 12.03N 29.39 E
Dillingen (Saar) 124 Ie 49.21N 6.44 E
Dillingham 176 Dd 59.02N 158.29W
Dillon [Mt.-U.S.] 182 Eb 45.13N 112.38W
Dillon [S.C.-U.S.] 184 Hh 34.25N 79.22W
Dilly 166 Dc 14.57N 7.43W
Dilolo 160 Jj 10.42S 22.20 E
Dilsen 124 Hc 51.02N 5.44 E
Dimashq=Damascus (EN) 142 Ff 33.30N 36.15 E
Dimbelenge 170 Dd 5.30S 23.53 E
Dimbokro 166 Ed 6.39N 4.42W
Dimbokro [3] 166 Ed 6.50N 4.45W
Dimboola 212 Ig 36.27S 142.02 E
Dimbovița [2] 130 Ie 44.55N 25.30 E
Dimbovița 130 Je 44.14N 26.27 E
Dimbovnic 130 Ie 44.20N 25.40 E
Dimitrovgrad [Bul.] 130 Ig 42.03N 25.36 E
Dimitrovgrad [R.S.F.S.R.] 136 Ee 54.14N 49.42 E
Dimitrovgrad [Yugo.] 130 Fg 43.01N 22.47 E
Dimmitt 186 Ei 34.33N 102.19W
Dimona 146 Fg 31.04N 35.02 E
Dimovo 130 Ff 43.44N 22.44 E
Dinagat 150 Id 10.12N 125.35 E
Dinājpur 148 Hc 25.38N 88.38 E
Dinan 122 Df 48.27N 2.02W
Dinangourou 166 Ec 14.27N 2.14W
Dinant 122 Kd 50.16N 4.55 E
Dinar 146 Dc 38.04N 30.10 E
Dinar, Kūh-e- 146 Ng 30.50N 51.35 E
Dinara 128 Kf 44.04N 16.23 E
Dinara=Dinaric Alps (EN) 110 Hg 43.50N 16.35 E
Dinard 122 Df 48.38N 2.04W
Dinaric Alps (EN)= Dinara 110 Hg 43.50N 16.35 E
Dindar, Nahr ad- 168 Ec 14.06N 33.40 E
Dinder 168 Ec 14.06N 33.40 E
Dindigul 148 Ff 10.21N 77.57 E
Dindima 166 Hc 10.14N 10.09 E
Dinga 170 Cd 5.19S 16.34 E
Dingbian 152 Id 37.35N 107.37 E
Dingden, Hamminkeln- 124 Ic 51.46N 6.37 E
Dinggyê 152 Ef 28.25N 87.45 E
Dinghai 152 Le 30.05N 122.07 E
Dingle 116 Df 58.32N 11.34 E
Dingle/An Daingean 118 Ci 52.08N 10.15W
Dingle Bay/Bá an Daingin 118 Ci 52.05N 10.15W
Dingolfing 120 Ih 48.38N 12.30 E
Dingshuzhen 154 Ei 31.16N 119.50 E
Dingtao 154 Cg 35.04N 115.35 E
Dinguiraye 166 Cc 11.18N 10.43W
Dingwall 118 Id 57.35N 4.26W
Dingxi 152 Hd 35.33N 104.32 E
Dingxian 152 Jd 39.29N 115.00 E
Dingxiang 154 Be 38.32N 112.59 E
Dingxing 152 Kd 39.11N 115.48 E
Dingyuan 154 Dh 32.32N 117.41 E
Dingzi Gang 154 Ff 36.33N 120.59 E
Dinh, Mui- 140 Mh 11.22N 109.01 E
Dinkel 124 Ib 52.30N 6.58 E
Dinosaur 186 Bf 40.15N 109.01W
Dinskaja 132 Kg 45.09N 39.12 E
Dinslaken 124 Ic 51.34N 6.44 E
Ḑinsōr 168 Ge 2.23N 42.58 E
Dintel 124 Gc 51.39N 4.24 E
Dinuba 188 Fh 36.36N 119.27W
Dinwiddie 184 Ig 37.05N 77.35W
Dioila 166 Dc 12.28N 6.47W
Diois, Massif du- 122 Lj 44.35N 5.20 E
Diomede Islands 178 Fc 65.33N 169.00W
Dion 166 Dc 10.12N 8.39W
Diorama 204 Gc 16.21S 51.14W
Dios 219a Ba 5.33S 154.58 E
Diosig 130 Eb 47.18N 22.00 E
Dioura 166 Dc 14.51N 5.15W
Diourbel 166 Bc 14.40N 16.15W
Diourbel [3] 166 Bc 14.45N 16.10W
Dipkarpas 146 Fe 35.36N 34.23 E
Dipolog 142 Oi 8.35N 123.20 E
Dir 148 Ea 35.12N 71.53 E
Dira, Djebel- 126 Ph 36.05N 3.38 E
Diré 166 Eb 16.15N 3.24W
Dire Dawa 168 Gd 9.35N 41.53 E
Diriamba 194 Dh 11.51N 86.14W
Dirico 170 Df 17.58S 20.45 E
Dirj 164 Bc 30.09N 10.26 E
Dirk Hartog Island 212 Ce 25.45S 113.00 E
Dirkou 166 Hb 19.01N 12.53 E
Dirranbandi 210 Fg 28.35S 148.14 E
Dirty Devil River 188 Jh 37.53N 110.24W
Disappointment, Cape- [B.A.T.] 206 Mh 54.53S 36.07W
Disappointment, Cape- [U.S.] 188 Cc 46.18N 124.03W
Disappointment, Lake- 208 Dg 23.30S 122.50 E
Discovery Tablemount (EN) 158 Hm 42.00S 0.10 E
Dishna 164 Fd 26.07N 32.28 E
Disko Bay (EN)=Disko Bugt 224 Nc 69.15N 52.30W
Disko Bugt=Disko Bay (EN) 224 Nc 69.15N 52.30W
Diskofjord 179 Ge 69.39N 53.45W
Disko Ø 224 Nc 69.50N 53.30W
Disna 114 Gi 55.33N 28.12 E
Disna 114 Gi 55.34N 28.12 E
Disnaj, ozero- / Dysnų ežeras 114 Gi 55.35N 26.32 E
Dispur 148 Ic 26.07N 91.48 E
Diss 124 Db 52.23N 1.07 E
District of Columbia, [2] 182 Ld 38.54N 77.01W
Distrito Federal [Braz.] [2] 202 Ig 15.45S 47.45W
Distrito Federal [Mex.] [2] 190 Ee 19.15N 99.10W
Disūq 146 Dg 31.08N 30.39 E
Dithmarschen 120 Fb 54.10N 9.15 E
Ditrău 130 Ic 46.49N 25.31 E
Dittaino 128 Im 37.25N 15.00 E
Diu 148 Ed 20.42N 70.59 E
Dīvāndarreh 146 Le 35.55N 47.02 E
Divénié 170 Bc 2.41S 12.05 E
Divenskaja 116 Ne 59.09N 30.09 E
Dives [Fr.] 122 Fg 47.11N 0.05W
Dives [Fr.] 122 Fe 49.19N 0.05W
Dives-sur-Mer 124 Be 49.17N 0.06W
Diviaka 130 Ci 41.00N 19.32 E
Diviči 132 Pi 42.10N 49.01 E
Divin 120 Ue 51.57N 24.09 E
Divinópolis 200 Lh 20.09S 44.54W
Divion 124 Ed 50.28N 2.30 E
Divisões ou de Santa Marta, Serra das- 202 Hg 16.40S 50.50W
Divisor, Sierra de- 202 De 8.00S 73.50W
Divnogorsk 138 Ee 55.58N 92.32 E
Divnoje 136 Ef 45.53N 43.22 E
Divo 166 Dd 5.50N 5.22W
Divo [3] 166 Dd 5.57N 5.15W
Divoká Orlice 120 Mf 50.09N 16.06 E
Divor 126 Df 38.59N 8.29W
Divriği 146 Hc 39.23N 38.07 E
Dīvrūd 146 Nd 36.52N 49.34 E
Dixmude/Diksmuide 122 Ic 51.02N 2.52 E
Dixon [Il.-U.S.] 186 Lf 41.50N 89.29W
Dixon [N.M.-U.S.] 186 Dh 36.11N 105.53W
Dixon Entrance 174 Fd 54.25N 132.30W
Diyālā [3] 146 Kf 34.00N 45.00 E
Diyālā 140 Gf 33.14N 44.31 E
Diyarbakır 144 Fb 37.55N 40.14 E
Dizy 124 Fe 49.04N 3.58 E
Dizy-le-Gros 124 Ge 49.38N 4.01 E
Dja 158 Ih 2.02N 15.12 E
Djado 160 If 21.01N 12.18 E
Djado, Plateau du- 158 If 21.45N 12.50 E
Djakarta → Jakarta 142 Mj 6.10S 106.46 E
Djakovo 120 Th 48.03N 23.01 E
Djamaa 162 Ic 33.32N 6.00 E
Djambala 160 Ii 2.33S 14.45 E
Djanet 160 Hf 24.34N 9.29 E
Djaret 162 Hd 26.35N 1.38 E
Djatkovo 136 De 53.36N 34.20 E
Djatlovo 132 Dc 53.31N 25.24 E
Djaul Island 214 Eh 2.56S 150.55 E
Djebel Ṭāriq, El Bōghāz-= Gibraltar, Strait of- (EN) 110 Fh 35.57N 5.36W
Djédaa 168 Bc 13.31N 18.34 E
Djedi 158 He 34.39N 5.55 E
Djedoug, Djebel- 126 Qi 35.53N 4.20 E
Djelfa 160 He 34.40N 3.15 E
Djelfa [3] 162 Hc 34.15N 3.30 E
Djéma 160 Jh 6.03N 25.19 E
Djember 168 Bc 10.25N 17.50 E
Djemila 162 Ib 36.19N 5.44 E
Djenane 126 Pi 35.43N 3.59 E
Djenné 166 Ec 13.55N 4.33W
Djerem 166 Hd 5.20N 13.24 E
Dji 168 Cd 6.47N 22.14 E
Djibo 166 Ec 14.06N 1.38W
Djibouti 160 Lg 11.35N 43.08 E
Djibouti (Afars and Issas) [1] 160 Lg 11.30N 43.00 E
Djokupunda 170 Dd 5.27S 20.58 E
Djolu 160 Jh 0.37N 22.21 E
Djoua 170 Bb 1.13N 13.12 E
Djougou 166 Fd 9.42N 1.40 E
Djoum 166 He 2.40N 12.40 E
Djourab, Erg du- 168 Bb 16.40N 18.50 E
Djugu 170 Fb 1.55N 30.30 E
Djultydag, gora- 132 Oi 41.58N 46.56 E
Djup 116 Bd 60.50N 8.00 E
Djúpi vogur 114a Cb 64.39N 14.17W
Djurbeldžin 135 Jd 41.10N 74.59 E
Djurdjura, Djebel- 126 Qh 36.27N 4.15 E
Djurmo 116 Fd 60.33N 15.10 E
Djurö 116 Ef 58.50N 13.30 E
Djursholm 116 He 59.24N 18.05 E
Djursland 116 Dh 56.20N 10.45 E
Djurtjuli 136 Fd 55.29N 54.55 E
Dmitrija Lapteva, proliv- = Dmitri Laptev Strait (EN) 140 Qb 73.00N 142.00 E
Dmitrijev-Lgovski 132 Ic 52.08N 35.05 E
Dmitri Laptev Strait (EN) = Dmitrija Lapteva, proliv- 140 Qb 73.00N 142.00 E
Dmitrov 114 Ih 56.26N 37.31 E
Dmitrovsk-Orlovski 132 Ic 52.31N 35.09 E
Dnepr 110 Jf 46.30N 32.18 E
Dneprodzeržinsk 136 Df 48.30N 34.37 E
Dneprodzeržinskoje vodohranilišče 132 Ie 48.45N 34.10 E
Dnepropetrovsk 112 Jf 48.27N 34.59 E
Dnepropetrovskaja oblast [3] 136 Df 48.15N 35.00 E
Dneprorudnoje 132 If 47.23N 35.01 E
Dneprovski liman 132 Gf 46.35N 31.55 E
Dneprovsko-Bugski kanal 132 Dc 52.03N 25.10 E
Dnepr Upland (EN) = Pridneprovskaja vozvyšennost 110 Jf 49.00N 32.00 E
Dnestr 110 Jf 46.18N 30.17 E
Dnestrovsk 130 Mc 46.39N 29.48 E
Dnestrovski liman 132 Gf 46.15N 30.15 E
Dno 136 Cd 57.49N 29.59 E
Doany 172 Hb 14.22S 49.30 E
Doba 168 Bd 8.39N 16.51 E
Dobbiaco / Toblach 128 Gd 46.44N 12.14 E
Dobele 114 Fh 56.39N 23.16 E
Döbeln 120 Je 51.07N 13.07 E
Doberai, Jazirah- 150 Jg 1.30S 132.30 E
Dobo 150 Jh 5.46S 134.13 E
Doboj 128 Mf 44.44N 18.05 E
Dobra 120 Oe 51.54N 18.37 E
Dobre Miasto 120 Qc 53.59N 20.25 E
Dobreta Turnu Severin 112 Ig 44.38N 22.40 E
Dobrinka 132 Lc 52.08N 40.29 E
Dobříš 120 Kg 49.47N 14.10 E
Dobrjanka 136 Fd 58.29N 56.29 E
Dobrodzień 120 Of 50.44N 18.27 E
Dobrogea = Dobruja (EN) 110 Ig 44.00N 28.00 E
Dobrogea=Dobruja (EN) 130 Ke 44.00N 28.00 E
Dobrogean, Masivul- 130 Le 44.50N 28.30 E
Dobromil 120 Sg 49.34N 22.49 E
Dobropolje 132 Je 48.28N 37.02 E
Dobrotești 130 He 44.17N 24.53 E
Dobrotvor 120 Uf 50.10N 24.27 E
Dobrudžansko Plato 130 Kf 43.32N 27.50 E
Dobruja (EN) = Dobrogea 110 Ig 44.00N 28.00 E
Dobruja (EN)=Dobrogea 130 Ke 44.00N 28.00 E
Dobruš 132 Gc 52.26N 31.19 E
Dobruška 120 Mf 50.18N 16.10 E
Dobrzyń nad Wisłą 120 Pd 52.38N 19.20 E
Dobrzyńskie, Pojezierze- 120 Pc 53.00N 19.20 E
Dobšiná 120 Qh 48.49N 20.22 E
Doce, Rio- [Braz.] 204 Gd 18.28S 51.05W
Doce, Rio- [Braz.] 198 Mg 19.37S 39.49W
Doce Leguas, Cayos de las- 194 Hc 20.55N 79.05W
Doce Leguas, Laberinto de las- 194 Hc 20.39N 78.35W
Docker River 212 Fd 24.58S 129.03 E
Docksta 116 Ha 63.03N 18.20 E
Doctor Arroyo 192 If 23.40N 100.11W
Doctor Cecilio Báez 204 Dg 25.03S 56.19W
Doctor Pedro P. Peña 206 Hb 22.26S 62.22W
Doctor Petru Groza 130 Fc 46.37N 22.25 E
Doda 148 Fb 33.08N 75.34 E
Doda Betta 148 Ff 11.24N 76.44 E
Dodecanese (EN) = Dhodhekánisos 130 Jm 36.20N 27.00 E
Dodecanese (EN) = Nótioi Sporádhes 110 Ih 36.00N 27.00 E
Dodge City 182 Gd 37.45N 100.00W
Dodgeville 186 Ke 42.58N 90.08W
Dodman Point 118 Ik 50.13N 4.48W
Dodoma 160 Ki 6.11S 35.45 E
Dodoma [3] 170 Gd 6.00S 36.00 E
Dodona (EN) = Dhodhóni 130 Dj 39.33N 20.46 E
Dodurga 130 Mj 39.48N 29.55 E
Doesburg 124 Ib 52.01N 6.08 E
Doetinchem 122 Mc 51.58N 6.17 E
Dofa 150 Ig 1.47S 125.22 E
Dogai Coring 152 Ee 34.30N 89.10 E
Doğanbey 130 Jk 38.04N 26.53 E
Doğanşehir 146 Gc 38.06N 37.53 E
Dog Creek 188 Da 51.35N 122.15W
Dogger Bank 110 Ge 55.00N 3.00 E
Dog Island 196 Ec 18.15N 63.13W
Dog Lake [Man.-Can.] 186 Ga 51.02N 98.30W
Dog Lake [Ont.-Can.] 186 Lb 48.46N 89.32W
Dog Lake [Ont.-Can.] 184 Ea 48.18N 84.10W
Dogliani 128 Bf 44.32N 7.56 E
Dōgo 154 Lf 36.15N 133.17 E
Dogonbadān 144 Hc 30.21N 50.48 E
Dogondoutchi 166 Fc 13.38N 4.02 E
Dōgo-San 156 Cd 35.04N 133.14 E
Dog Rocks 194 Ha 24.05N 79.51W
Doğubayazıt 146 Kc 39.32N 44.08 E
Doğu Karadeniz Dağları 144 Ea 40.40N 40.00 E
Dogwood Point 197c Ab 17.06N 62.38W
Doha (EN)=Ad Dawḩah 142 Hg 25.17N 51.32 E
Dohad 148 Ed 22.50N 74.16 E
Dohāzāri 148 Id 22.10N 92.04 E
Doi Luang Chinag Dao 148 Je 19.23N 98.54 E
Doilungdêqên 152 Ff 29.47N 90.49 E
Doire Baltée/Dora Baltea 128 Ce 45.11N 8.03 E
Doische 124 Gd 50.08N 4.45 E
Dojransko jezero 130 Fh 41.13N 22.44 E
Doka 168 Fc 13.31N 35.46 E
Dokhara, Dunes de- 162 Ic 32.50N 6.00 E
Dokka 114 Cf 60.50N 10.05 E
Dokka 116 Dd 60.49N 10.05 E
Dokkum 122 La 53.19N 6.00 E
Dokšicy 114 Gi 54.56N 27.46 E
Doksy 120 Kf 50.34N 14.40 E
Dokučajevsk 132 Jf 47.43N 37.47 E
Dolak, Pulau- 208 Ee 7.50S 138.30 E
Dolbeau 180 Kg 48.52N 72.14W
Dol-de-Bretagne 122 Ef 48.33N 1.45W
Dôle 122 Lg 47.06N 5.30 E
Doleib Hill 168 Ed 9.22N 31.36 E
Dolenjsko 128 Je 45.50N 15.10 E
Dolgaja, kosa- 132 Jf 46.40N 37.45 E
Dolgellau 118 Ji 52.44N 3.53W
Dolgi, ostrov- 134 Ib 69.15N 59.05 E
Dolgi Most 138 Ee 56.45N 96.58 E
Dolianova 128 Dk 39.22N 9.10 E
Dolina 132 De 48.58N 24.01 E
Dolinsk 138 Jg 47.20N 142.50 E
Dolinskaja 136 Df 48.07N 32.44 E
Dolinskoje 130 Mb 47.33N 29.50 E
Dolj [2] 130 Ge 44.10N 23.40 E
Dollart 122 Na 53.17N 7.10 E
Dolly Cays 194 Ib 23.39N 77.22W
Dolní Dăbnik 130 Hf 43.24N 24.26 E
Dolní Dvořiště 120 Kh 48.39N 14.27 E
Dolnomoravský úval 120 Nh 49.00N 17.15 E
Dolnośląskie, Bory- 120 Le 51.25N 15.20 E
Dolný Kubín 120 Pg 49.12N 19.17 E
Dolo 160 Lh 4.11N 42.05 E
Dolomiten/Dolomiti = Dolomites (EN) 110 Hf 46.23N 11.51 E
Dolomites (EN) = Dolomiten/Dolomiti 110 Hf 46.23N 11.51 E
Dolomites (EN) = Dolomiti/ Dolomiten 110 Hf 46.23N 11.51 E
Dolomiti/Dolomiten = Dolomites (EN) 110 Hf 46.23N 11.51 E
Dolon, pereval- 135 Jd 41.48N 75.45 E
Dolonnur/Duolun 152 Kc 42.10N 116.30 E
Dolores [Arg.] 206 Ie 36.20S 57.40W
Dolores [Guat.] 194 Ce 16.31N 89.25W
Dolores [Ur.] 206 Id 33.33S 58.13W
Dolores Hidalgo 192 Ig 21.10N 100.56W
Dolores River 188 Kg 38.49N 109.17W
Dolphin, Cape- 206 Ih 51.15S 58.58W
Dolphin and Union Strait 180 Gc 69.00N 115.00W
Dom, Kūh-e- 146 Of 33.52N 53.00 E
Domačevo 120 Te 51.46N 23.37 E
Domaniç 146 Cc 39.48N 29.37 E
Domantai/Domantaj 116 Ji 55.57N 23.19 E
Domantaj/Domantai 116 Ji 55.57N 23.19 E
Domart-en-Ponthieu 124 Ed 50.04N 2.07 E
Domaša, údolná nadrž- 120 Rg 49.05N 21.47 E
Domažlice 120 Ig 49.27N 12.56 E
Dombaj-Ulgen, gora- 132 Lh 43.14N 41.46 E
Dombarovski 136 Fe 50.47N 59.34 E
Dombås 112 Kc 62.05N 9.08 E
Dombe Grande 170 Be 12.56S 13.07 E
Dombes 122 Lh 46.00N 5.03 E
Dombóvár 120 Oj 46.23N 18.07 E
Dombrád 120 Rh 48.14N 21.56 E
Domburg 124 Fc 51.34N 3.30 E
Dôme, Monts- 122 Ii 45.45N 2.55 E
Dôme, Puy de- 122 Ii 45.47N 2.58 E
Domérat 122 Ih 46.21N 2.32 E
Domeyko, Cordillera- 198 Jh 24.30S 69.00W
Domfront 122 Ff 48.36N 0.39W
Domingo M. Irala 204 Eg 25.54S 54.43W
Domingos Martins 202 Jh 20.22S 40.40W
Dominica [1] 176 Mh 15.30N 61.20W
Dominica 174 Mh 15.30N 61.20W
Dominical 194 Fi 9.13N 83.51W
Dominicana, República-= Dominican Republic (EN) [1] 176 Lh 19.00N 70.40W
Dominican Republic (EN)= Dominicana, República- [1] 176 Lh 19.00N 70.40W
Dominica Passage 196 Fe 15.10N 61.15W
Dominica Passage (EN)= Dominique, Canal de la- 196 Fe 15.10N 61.15W
Dominion, Cape 180 Kc 66.10N 74.30W
Dominique, Canal de la-= Dominica Passage (EN) 196 Fe 15.10N 61.15W
Domino 180 Lf 53.28N 55.46W
Domiongo 170 Dc 4.37S 21.15 E
Dommartin-Varimont 124 Gf 48.59N 4.46 E
Domme 122 Hj 44.48N 1.13 E
Dommel 122 Lc 51.40N 5.20 E
Domnești 130 Hd 45.12N 24.50 E
Domo 168 Hd 7.57N 46.51 E
Domodedovo 114 Ii 55.27N 37.47 E
Domodossola 128 Cd 46.07N 8.17 E
Domont 124 Ee 49.02N 2.20 E
Dom Pedrito 206 Jd 30.59S 54.40W
Dom Pedro 202 Jd 5.00S 44.27W
Dompierre-sur-Besbre 122 Jh 46.31N 3.41 E
Dompu 150 Gh 8.32S 118.28 E
Domusnovas 128 Ck 39.19N 8.39 E
Domuyo, Volcán- 198 Ii 36.38S 70.26W
Don 192 Ed 26.26N 109.02W
Don [Eng.-U.K.] 118 Mh 53.39N 0.59W
Don [Fr.] 122 Eg 47.40N 1.56W
Don [R.S.F.S.R.] 110 Jf 47.04N 39.18 E
Don [Scot.-U.K.] 118 Kd 57.10N 2.04W
Donaldsonville 186 Kk 30.06N 90.59W
Donau=Danube (EN) 110 If 45.20N 29.40 E
Donaueschingen 120 Ei 47.57N 8.30 E
Donaumoos 120 Hh 48.40N 11.15 E
Donauried 120 Gh 48.35N 10.40 E
Donauwörth 120 Gh 48.42N 10.48 E
Don Benito 126 Gf 38.57N 5.52W
Doncaster 118 Lh 53.32N 1.07W
Dondjušany 130 Ka 48.11N 27.31 E
Dondo [Ang.] 160 Ii 9.40S 14.26 E
Dondo [Moz.] 172 Ec 19.36S 34.44 E
Dondra Head 140 Ki 5.55N 80.35 E
Donec 110 Kf 47.40N 40.50 E
Doneck [R.S.F.S.R.] 132 Ke 48.21N 39.59 E
Doneck [Ukr.-U.S.S.R.] 112 Jf 48.00N 37.48 E
Doneckaja oblast [3] 136 Df 48.00N 37.45 E
Donecki krjaž = Donec Ridge (EN) 110 Jf 48.15N 38.45 E
Donec Ridge (EN) = Donecki krjaž 110 Jf 48.15N 38.45 E
Donegal/Dún na nGall 118 Eg 54.39N 8.06W
Donegal/Dún na nGall [2] 118 Fg 54.50N 8.00W
Donegal Bay/Bá Dhún na nGall 118 Fe 54.30N 8.30W
Donegal Mountains 118 Eg 54.50N 8.10W
Donga 166 Hd 8.19N 10.01 E
Dongara 212 Ce 29.15S 114.56 E
Dongbei Pingyuan 154 Gc 44.00N 124.00 E
Dongchuan (Tangdan) 152 Hf 26.07N 103.05 E
Dongcun → Lanxian 154 Ae 38.17N 111.38 E
Dong Dao 154 Cl 16.45N 113.00 E
Donge 124 Gc 51.41N 4.49 E
Dong'e (Tongcheng) 154 Df 36.19N 116.14 E
Dongen 124 Gc 51.37N 4.57 E
Donges 122 Dg 47.18N 2.04W
Dongfang (Basuo) 152 Ih 19.14N 108.39 E
Dongfanghong 154 La 46.15N 133.07 E
Dongfeng 154 Hc 42.41N 125.33 E
Donggala 150 Gg 0.40S 119.44 E
Donggou 152 Ld 39.55N 124.08 E
Dongguang 154 Df 37.54N 116.32 E
Dong Hai=East China Sea (EN) 140 Og 29.00N 125.00 E
Donghai Dao 152 Jg 21.00N 110.25 E
Dong He 152 Hc 42.12N 101.10 E
Dong Hoi 148 Le 17.29N 106.36 E
Dong Jang 140 Ng 23.02N 113.31 E
Dongkala 150 Hh 5.18S 122.03 E
Dongkan → Binhai 152 Ke 34.00N 119.52 E
Donglan 152 Ig 24.35N 107.22 E
Dongliao He 154 Gc 43.24N 123.42 E
Dongming 154 Cg 35.17N 115.04 E
Dongnan Qiuling 152 Jg 24.00N 113.00 E
Dongning 152 Nc 44.02N 131.06 E
Dongo 170 Ce 14.36S 15.43 E
Dongola (EN)=Dunqulah 160 Kg 19.10N 30.29 E
Dongou 170 Cb 2.02N 18.04 E
Dongoun → Haiyang 154 Ff 36.46N 121.09 E
Dongping 152 Kd 35.51N 116.15 E
Dongping → Anhua 152 Jf 28.27N 111.15 E
Dong Rak, Phanom-= Dangrek Range (EN) 140 Mh 14.25N 104.30 E
Dongsha Dao 152 Kg 20.45N 116.45 E
Dongsha Qundao 140 Ng 20.42N 116.43 E
Dongsheng 152 Id 39.48N 110.00 E
Dongtai 152 Le 32.47N 120.18 E
Dong Taijnar Hu 152 Fd 37.25N 94.00 E
Dongtin Hu 140 Ng 29.18N 112.45 E
Dong Ujimqin Qi (Uliastai) 152 Kc 45.31N 116.58 E
Dongwe 170 De 13.56S 23.53 E
Dongxiang 152 Kf 28.15N 116.38 E
Dongyang 154 Fj 29.16N 120.14 E
Dongying 152 Kd 37.30N 118.30 E
Dongzhi (Yaodu) 154 Di 30.06N 117.01 E
Donington 124 Bb 52.54N 0.12W
Doniphan 186 Kh 36.37N 90.50W
Donja Brela 128 Kg 43.23N 16.55 E
Donji Miholjac 128 Me 45.45N 18.10 E
Donji Vakuf 128 Lf 44.08N 17.24 E
Donjon, Le- 122 Jh 46.21N 3.48 E
Donna 114 Cc 66.06N 12.35 E
Donnacona 184 Lb 46.40N 71.47W
Donner Pass 182 Cd 39.19N 120.20W
Donnersberg 124 Je 49.38N 7.55 E
Donner und Blitzen River 188 Fe 43.17N 118.49W
Donnybrook 212 Df 33.35S 115.49 E
Donostia / San Sebastián 112 Fg 43.19N 1.59W
Donskaja grjada = Don Upland (EN) 110 Kf 49.10N 42.00 E
Donskoj 132 Kb 54.01N 38.20 E
Don Upland (EN) = Donskaja grjada 110 Kf 49.10N 42.00 E
Donuzlav, ozero- 132 Hg 45.25N 33.10 E
Doolette Bay 222 Je 67.55S 147.00 E
Doon 118 If 55.26N 4.38W
Doonerak, Mount- 178 Ic 67.56N 150.37W
Doorn 124 Hb 52.02N 5.19 E
Doornik/Tournai 122 Jd 50.36N 3.23 E
Door Peninsula 186 Md 44.55N 87.20W
Do Qu 152 He 31.48N 102.09 E
Dora, Lake- 212 Ed 22.05S 122.56 E
Dora Baltea/Doire Baltée 128 Ce 45.11N 8.03 E
Dorada, Costa- / Daurada, Costa- 126 Nc 41.08N 1.10 E
Dora Riparia 128 Be 45.05N 7.44 E
Dorat, Le- 122 Hh 46.13N 1.05 E
Dorbiljin/Emin 152 Db 46.32N 83.39 E
Dorchester 118 Kk 50.43N 2.26W
Dorchester, Cape - 180 Jc 65.28N 77.30W
Dordabis 172 Bd 22.52S 17.38 E
Dordogne [3] 122 Gi 45.10N 0.50 E
Dordogne 110 Ff 45.02N 0.35W
Dordrecht [Neth.] 122 Kc 51.49N 4.40 E
Dordrecht [S.Afr.] 172 Df 31.20S 27.03 E
Dore 122 Ji 46.00N 3.28 E
Dore, Monts- 110 Gf 45.30N 2.45 E
Doré Lake 180 Gf 54.45N 107.20W
Dores do Indaiá 202 Ig 19.27S 45.36W
Dorgali 128 Dj 40.17N 9.35 E
Dori 160 Gg 14.02N 0.02W
Doring 158 Il 31.52S 18.39 E
Dorking 124 Bc 51.13N 0.20W
Dormagen 124 Ic 51.06N 6.50 E
Dormans 122 Je 49.04N 3.38 E
Dormidontovka 138 Ig 47.45N 134.58 E
Dornbirn 128 Dc 47.25N 9.44 E
Dornoch 118 Id 57.52N 4.02W
Dornoch Firth 118 Id 57.52N 4.02W
Doro 166 Eb 16.09N 0.51W
Dorog 120 Oi 47.43N 18.44 E
Dorogobuž 132 Hb 54.56N 33.15 E
Dorohoi 130 Jb 47.57N 26.24 E
Dorotea 114 Dd 64.16N 16.24 E
Dorre Island 212 Ce 25.10S 113.05 E
Dorrigo 212 Kf 30.20S 152.45 E
Dorset [3] 118 Kk 50.50N 2.10W
Dorset 118 Kk 50.55N 2.15W
Dorsten 120 Ce 51.40N 6.58 E
Dortmund 112 Ge 51.31N 7.27 E
Dortmund-Ems-Kanal 120 De 51.42N 7.27 E
Dörtyol 146 Gd 36.52N 36.12 E
Do Rūd 144 Gc 33.29N 49.04 E
Doruma 170 Eb 4.44N 27.42 E
Dörverden 124 Lb 52.51N 9.14 E
Doséo, Bahr- 168 Bd 9.01N 19.38 E
Dos Hermanas 126 Gg 37.17N 5.55W
Dos Lagunas 194 Ce 17.42N 89.36W
Dospat 130 Hh 41.39N 24.10 E
Dospat 130 Hh 41.23N 24.05 E
Dos Picachos, Cerro- 192 Bc 29.25N 114.10W
Dosse 120 Ic 53.13N 12.20 E
Dosso 160 Hg 13.03N 3.12 E
Dosso [2] 166 Fc 13.30N 3.30 E
Dossor 136 Ff 47.32N 53.01 E
Dostluk 135 Ff 37.45N 65.22 E
Dothan 182 Je 31.13N 85.24W
Dotnuva 116 Ji 55.18N 23.55 E
Douai 122 Jd 50.22N 3.04 E
Douala 160 Hh 4.03N 9.42 E
Douaouir 166 Ea 20.45N 2.30W
Douarnenez 122 Bf 48.06N 4.20W
Douarnenez, Baie de- 122 Bf 48.10N 4.25W
Double Mountain Fork Brazos 186 Gj 33.15N 100.00W
Doubrava 120 Lf 50.03N 15.20 E

Index Symbols

[1] Independent Nation
[2] State, Region
[3] District, County
[4] Municipality
[5] Colony, Dependency
Continent
Physical Region
Historical or Cultural Region
Mount, Mountain
Volcano
Hill
Mountains, Mountain Range
Hills, Escarpment
Plateau, Upland
Pass, Gap
Plain, Lowland
Delta
Salt Flat
Valley, Canyon
Crater, Cave
Karst Features
Depression
Polder
Desert, Dunes
Forest, Woods
Heath, Steppe
Oasis
Cape, Point
Coast, Beach
Cliff
Peninsula
Isthmus
Sandbank
Island
Atoll
Rock, Reef
Islands, Archipelago
Rocks, Reefs
Coral Reef
Well, Spring
Geyser
River, Stream
Waterfall, Rapids
River Mouth, Estuary
Lake
Salt Lake
Intermittent Lake
Reservoir
Swamp, Pond
Canal
Glacier
Ice Shelf, Pack Ice
Ocean
Sea
Gulf, Bay
Strait, Fjord
Lagoon
Bank
Seamount
Tablemount
Ridge
Shelf
Basin
Escarpment, Sea Scarp
Fracture
Trench, Abyss
National Park, Reserve
Point of Interest
Recreation Site
Cave, Cavern
Historic Site
Ruins
Wall, Walls
Church, Abbey
Temple
Scientific Station
Railway station
Airport
Port
Military installation
Lighthouse
Mine
Tunnel
Dam, Bridge

Name	Page	Grid	Lat	Long
Doubs [3]	122	Mg	47.10N	6.25 E
Doubs	122	Lh	46.54N	5.02 E
Doubtful Sound	218	Bf	45.15S	166.50 E
Doubtless Bay	218	Ea	34.55S	173.25 E
Douchy-les-Mines	124	Fd	50.18N	3.23 E
Doudeville	124	Ce	49.43N	0.48 E
Doué-la-Fontaine	122	Fg	47.12N	0.17W
Douentza	166	Eb	15.03N	2.57W
Douera	126	Oh	36.40N	2.57 E
Dougga	162	Ib	36.24N	9.13 E
Douglas [Ak.-U.S.]	178	Me	58.16N	134.26W
Douglas [Az.-U.S.]	182	Fe	31.21N	109.33W
Douglas [Ga.-U.S.]	184	Fj	31.31N	82.51W
Douglas [I. of M.]	118	Ig	54.09N	4.28W
Douglas [S.Afr.]	172	Ce	29.04S	23.46 E
Douglas [Wy.-U.S.]	182	Fc	42.45N	105.24W
Douglas Lake	184	Fh	36.00N	83.22W
Douglas Range	222	Qf	70.00S	69.35W
Doullens	122	Id	50.09N	2.21 E
Doumé	166	He	4.14N	13.27 E
Douna	166	Ec	14.39N	1.43W
Doupovské hory	120	Jf	50.13N	13.08 E
Dour	124	Fd	50.24N	3.47 E
Dourada, Serra- [Braz.]	204	Gb	16.00S	50.05W
Dourada, Serra- [Braz.]	204	Ha	13.10S	48.45W
Dourados	200	Kh	22.13S	54.48W
Dourados, Rio- [Braz.]	204	Ee	21.58S	54.18W
Dourados, Rio- [Braz.]	204	Id	18.17S	47.36W
Dourbali	168	Bc	11.49N	15.52 E
Dourdan	122	If	48.32N	2.01 E
Douro	110	Fg	41.08N	8.40W
Douro Litoral	126	Dc	41.05N	8.20W
Doushi → Gong'an	152	Je	30.05N	112.12 E
Douve	122	Ee	49.19N	1.44W
Douvres-la-Delivrande	124	Be	49.17N	0.23W
Douze	122	Fk	43.54N	0.30W
Douzy	124	He	49.40N	5.03 E
Dove	118	Li	52.50N	1.35W
Dove Bugt	179	Jc	76.25N	21.00W
Dove Creek	186	Bh	37.46N	108.54W
Dover [De.-U.S.]	176	Lf	39.10N	75.32W
Dover [Eng.-U.K.]	112	Ge	51.08N	1.19 E
Dover [N.H.-U.S.]	184	Ld	43.12N	70.55W
Dover [Oh.-U.S.]	184	Ge	40.32N	81.30W
Dover, Strait of-	110	Ge	51.00N	1.30 E
Dover, Strait of- (EN) = Calais, Pas de-	110	Ge	51.00N	1.30 E
Dover Foxcroft	184	Mc	45.11N	69.13W
Dovey	118	Ji	52.34N	3.59W
Dovre	116	Cc	61.59N	9.15 E
Dovrefjell	110	Gc	62.10N	9.25 E
Dowa	170	Fe	13.39S	33.56 E
Dowagiac	184	De	41.59N	86.06W
Dowlatābād	146	Qh	28.20N	57.13 E
Downey	188	Ie	42.26N	112.07W
Downham Market	124	Sc	52.36N	0.22 E
Downieville	188	Eg	39.34N	120.50W
Downpatrick/Dún Pádraig	118	Hg	54.20N	5.43W
Dow Sar	146	Me	35.06N	48.02 E
Dözen	156	Cc	36.05N	132.59 E
Dozois, Reservoir-	184	Ib	47.30N	77.00W
Dozulé	124	Be	49.14N	0.03W
Drâa	158	Ff	28.40N	11.07W
Drâa, Cap-	162	Ed	28.44N	11.05W
Drâa, Hamada du-	158	Gf	28.30N	7.30W
Draá Ben Khedda	126	Ph	36.44N	3.57 E
Draa el Baguel	162	Ic	30.17N	6.25 E
Draa el Mizan	126	Ph	36.32N	3.50 E
Drac	122	Li	45.13N	5.41 E
Drac, Cuevas del-	126	Pe	39.32N	3.15 E
Dracena	204	Ge	21.32S	51.29W
Dragalina	130	Ke	44.26N	27.19 E
Dragan	114	Dd	64.00N	15.21 E
Drăgănești-Olt	130	He	44.09N	24.42 E
Drăgănești-Vlașca	130	Ie	44.06N	25.36 E
Drăgășani	130	He	44.39N	24.16 E
Dragobia	130	Cg	42.26N	19.59 E
Dragón, Bocas del-/Dragon's Mouths	202	Fa	10.45N	61.46W
Dragonera, Isla- / Sa Dragonera, Illa-	126	Oe	39.35N	2.19 E
Dragon's Mouths/Dragón, Bocas del-	202	Fa	10.45N	61.46W
Drager	116	Ei	55.36N	12.41 E
Draguignan	122	Mk	43.32N	6.28 E
Drahanská vrchovina	120	Mg	49.30N	16.45 E
Drain	188	De	43.40N	123.19W
Drake	186	Fc	47.55N	100.23W
Drake, Paso- = Drake Passage (EN)	198	Jk	58.00S	70.00W
Drakensberg	158	Jk	29.00S	29.00 E
Drake Passage (EN) = Drake, Paso-	198	Jk	58.00S	70.00W
Dráma	130	Hh	41.09N	24.09 E
Drammen	112	Hd	59.44N	10.15 E
Dramselva	116	De	59.44N	10.14 E
Drangajökull	114a	Aa	66.09N	22.15W
Dranse	122	Mh	46.24N	6.30 E
Drau=Drava (EN)	110	Hf	45.33N	18.55 E
Drava	110	Hf	45.33N	18.55 E
Dráva=Drava (EN)	110	Hf	45.33N	18.55 E
Drava (EN)=Drau	110	Hf	45.33N	18.55 E
Drava (EN)=Dráva	110	Hf	45.33N	18.55 E
Dravograd	128	Jd	46.35N	15.01 E
Drawa	120	Lc	53.13N	15.45 E
Drawno	120	Lc	53.13N	15.45 E
Drawsko, Jezioro-	120	Mc	53.33N	16.10 E
Drawsko Pomorskie	120	Lc	53.33N	15.49 E
Drayton Valley	180	Gf	53.13N	115.00W
Drean	128	Be	36.41N	7.45 E
Dreieich	124	Ke	50.01N	8.43 E
Drenovci	128	Mf	44.55N	18.55 E
Drenthe [3]	124	Be	52.45N	6.30 E
Dresden	112	He	51.03N	13.45 E
Dresden [2]	184	He	51.03N	13.45 E
Dreux	122	Hf	48.44N	1.22 E
Drevsjø	114	Cf	61.54N	12.02 E
Drezdenko	120	Lc	52.51N	15.50 E
Dricëni/Driceni	116	Lh	56.39N	27.11 E
Driceni/Dricëni	116	Lh	56.39N	27.11 E
Driffield	118	Mg	54.01N	0.26W
Driggs	188	Je	43.44N	111.14W
Drina	110	Hg	44.53N	19.21 E
Drincea	130	Fe	44.07N	22.59 E
Drin Gulf (EN)=Drinit, Gjiri i-	130	Ch	41.45N	19.28 E
Drini	110	Hg	41.45N	19.34 E
Drini i Zi	130	Dg	42.05N	20.23 E
Drinit, Gjiri i-=Drin Gulf (EN)	130	Ch	41.45N	19.28 E
Drinjača	128	Nf	44.17N	19.10 E
Drinosi	130	Di	40.17N	20.02 E
Drissa	114	Gi	55.47N	27.57 E
Drisvjaty, ozero- / Drūkšiu ežeras	116	Li	55.37N	26.45 E
Driva	116	Cb	62.40N	8.34 E
Drjanovo	130	Ig	42.58N	25.28 E
Drniš	128	Kg	43.52N	16.09 E
Drøbak	114	Cg	59.39N	10.39 E
Drocea, Vîrful-	130	Fc	46.12N	22.14 E
Drogheda/Droichead Átha	118	Gh	53.43N	6.21W
Drogičin	132	Dc	52.13N	25.10 E
Drogobyč	132	Cg	49.22N	23.33 E
Drohiczyn	120	Sd	52.24N	22.41 E
Droichead Átha/Drogheda	118	Gh	53.43N	6.21W
Droichead na Bandan/Bandon	118	Ej	51.45N	8.45W
Droichead na Banna/Banbridge	118	Gg	54.21N	6.16W
Drokija	132	Ee	48.01N	27.53 E
Drôme [3]	122	Lj	44.35N	5.10 E
Drôme	124	Be	49.19N	0.45W
Drömling	120	Hd	52.29N	11.04 E
Dronero	128	Bf	44.28N	7.22 E
Dronne	122	Fi	45.02N	0.09W
Dronning Fabiolafjella	222	Df	71.30S	35.40 E
Dronning Louise Land	179	Jc	76.45N	24.00W
Dronten	122	Lj	52.31N	5.42 E
Dropt	122	Fi	44.35N	0.06W
Drovjanoj	138	Cb	72.25N	72.45 E
Drowning River	186	Na	50.55N	84.35W
Druja	116	Li	55.47N	27.29 E
Drūkšiu ežeras / Drisvjaty, ozero-	116	Li	55.37N	26.45 E
Druk-Yul = Bhutan [1]	142	Lg	27.30N	90.30 E
Drulingen	124	Jf	48.52N	7.11 E
Drumheller	180	Gf	51.28N	112.42W
Drummond [Mt.-U.S.]	188	Ic	46.40N	113.09W
Drummond [Wi.-U.S.]	186	Kc	46.20N	91.15W
Drummond Island	184	Fb	46.00N	83.40W
Drummond Range	212	Jd	23.30S	147.15 E
Drummondville	180	Kg	45.50N	72.20W
Drummore	118	Ig	54.42N	4.54W
Drumochter, Pass of-	118	Ie	56.50N	4.12W
Drunen	124	Hc	51.41N	5.10 E
Druskininkai/Druskininkaj	114	Fi	54.04N	24.06 E
Druskininkaj/Druskininkai	114	Fi	54.04N	24.06 E
Drut	132	Gc	53.04N	30.35 E
Druten	124	Hc	51.54N	5.38 E
Družba [Kaz.-U.S.S.R.]	136	If	45.18N	82.29 E
Družba [Ukr.-U.S.S.R.]	132	Hc	52.02N	33.59 E
Družkovka	132	Je	48.36N	37.33 E
Družnaja Gorka	116	Ne	59.11N	30.10 E
Družnino	134	Hh	56.48N	59.29 E
Družno, Jezioro-	120	Pb	54.08N	19.30 E
Drvar	128	Kf	44.22N	16.23 E
Drvenik	128	Lg	43.09N	17.15 E
Dryden	180	Jg	49.47N	92.50W
Dry Fork	188	Me	43.30N	105.24W
Drygalski Ice Tongue	222	Kf	75.24S	163.30 E
Drygalski Island	222	Ge	65.45S	92.30 E
Drysdale River	212	Fb	13.59S	126.51 E
Dry Tortugas	182	Ka	24.38N	82.55W
Drzewica	120	Qe	51.27N	20.28 E
Drzewiczka	120	Qe	51.28N	20.35 E
Dschang	166	Hd	5.27N	10.04 E
Dua	170	Db	3.20N	20.53 E
Duaca	202	Ea	10.18N	69.10W
Duancun → Wuxiang	154	Bf	36.50N	112.51 E
Duarte, Pico-	174	Lh	19.00N	71.00W
Duartina	204	Hf	22.24S	49.25W
Dubawnt	180	Hd	64.30N	100.06W
Dubawnt Lake	174	Ic	63.08N	101.30W
Dubayy, Ra's-	146	Pj	24.20N	54.09 E
Dubayy	142	Hg	25.15N	55.18 E
Dubbo	210	Fh	32.15S	148.36 E
Dübener Heide	120	Ie	51.40N	12.40 E
Dubenski	132	Td	51.29N	56.38 E
Dubh Artach	118	Ge	56.08N	6.39W
Dubica	128	Ke	45.13N	16.48 E
Dublin	182	Fj	32.32N	82.54W
Dublin/Baile Átha Cliath	112	Ce	53.20N	6.15W
Dublin/Baile Átha Cliath [2]	118	Gh	53.20N	6.15W
Dublin Bay/Cuan Bhaile Átha Cliath	118	Gh	53.20N	6.06W
Dubljany	120	Tf	49.50N	23.16 E
Dublon	220d	Db	7.23N	151.53 E
Dubna	136	Dd	56.47N	37.10 E
Dubnica nad Váhom	120	Oh	48.58N	18.10 E
Dubno	132	Dd	50.29N	25.46 E
Du Bois	184	Hf	41.06N	78.46W
Dubois [Id.-U.S.]	188	Id	44.10N	112.14W
Dubois [Wy.-U.S.]	188	Je	43.33N	109.38W
Dubossary	130	Mc	47.17N	29.10 E
Dubovka	136	Ee	49.03N	44.50 E
Dubovoje	128	Cd	9.48N	13.31 W
Dubreka	166	Cd	9.48N	13.31W
Dubrovica	132	Ed	51.34N	26.34 E
Dubrovnik	112	Hg	42.39N	18.07 E
Dubrovno	114	Hi	54.33N	30.41 E
Dubrovnoje	136	Gd	57.58N	69.25 E
Dubuque	182	Ic	42.30N	90.41W
Dubysa	116	Ji	55.02N	23.27 E
Duc de Gloucester, Iles du- = Duke of Gloucester, Islands (En)	208	Mg	20.38S	143.20W
Duchang	154	Dj	29.16N	116.11 E
Duchesne	188	Jf	40.10N	110.24W
Duchess	212	Hd	21.22S	139.52 E
Ducie Atoll	208	Og	24.40S	124.47W
Duck River	184	Dg	36.02N	87.52W
Duckwater Peak	188	Hg	38.58N	115.26W
Duclair	124	Ce	49.29N	0.53 E
Duc Lap	148	Lf	12.27N	107.38 E
Ducos	197h	Bb	14.34N	60.58W
Dudelange/Düdelingen	124	Ie	49.28N	6.06 E
Düdelingen/Dudelange	124	Ie	49.28N	6.06 E
Duderstadt	120	Gd	51.31N	10.16 E
Dudinka	142	Kc	69.25N	86.15 E
Dudley	118	Ki	52.30N	2.05W
Düdo	168	Id	9.20N	50.14 E
Dudub	168	Hd	6.55N	46.42 E
Dudune	219b	Ce	21.21S	167.44 E
Dudweiler, Saarbrücken-	124	Je	49.17N	7.02 E
Düdweyn	168	Gd	9.19N	44.53 E
Dudypta	138	Db	70.55N	89.50 E
Duékoué	166	Dd	6.45N	7.21W
Dueodde	116	Fj	54.59N	15.05 E
Duerna	126	Gb	42.19N	5.54W
Duero	110	Fg	41.08N	8.40W
Dufek Coast	222	Lg	84.30S	179.00W
Duffer Peak	188	Ff	41.40N	118.44W
Duff Islands	208	He	9.50S	167.10 E
Dugi Otok	128	Ig	44.00N	15.00 E
Dugo Selo	128	Ke	45.48N	16.15 E
Du Gué, Rivière-	180	Ke	57.20N	70.46W
Duhovnickoje	132	Pc	52.29N	48.15 E
Duijan Yan	152	Hi	31.01N	103.28 E
Duisburg	120	Ce	51.26N	6.45 E
Duitama	202	Db	5.50N	73.02W
Dujuma	168	Ge	1.14N	42.34 E
Dukagjini	130	Cg	42.18N	19.45 E
Dūkān	146	Nf	35.56N	44.58 E
Dūkān, Sad ad-	146	Kd	36.10N	44.56 E
Dukat	130	Fg	42.26N	22.21 E
Duke of Gloucester Islands (EN)=Duc de Gloucester, Iles du-	208	Mg	20.38S	143.20W
Duke of York	219a	Aa	10.15S	152.28 E
Duke of York Bay	180	Jc	65.25N	84.50W
Duk Faiwil	168	Ed	7.45N	31.25 E
Duk Faiwil	168	Ed	7.30N	31.29 E
Dukhān	144	Hd	25.25N	50.48 E
Dukielska, Przełęcz-	120	Rg	49.25N	21.42 E
Dukku	166	Hc	10.49N	10.46 E
Dukla	120	Rg	49.34N	21.41 E
Dukou	142	Mg	26.31N	101.44 E
Dūkštas/Dūkštas	116	Li	55.32N	26.28 E
Dūkštas/Dūkštas	116	Li	55.32N	26.28 E
Dulan (Qagan Us)	142	Lf	36.29N	98.29 E
Dulce, Bahía-	192	Ji	16.30N	98.50W
Dulce, Golfo-	190	Bg	8.36N	83.15W
Dulce, Río-	200	Jj	30.31N	62.32W
Dulce Nombre de Culmí	194	Ef	15.09N	85.37W
Duldurga	138	Gf	50.38N	113.35 E
Dulgalah	140	Pc	67.30N	133.20 E
Dulia	170	Db	2.57N	24.08 E
Dülmen	120	Db	51.50N	7.18 E
Dulovka	116	Mg	57.27N	28.29 E
Dulovo	130	Kf	43.49N	27.09 E
Duluth	176	Je	46.47N	92.06W
Dūmā	146	Gf	33.35N	36.24 E
Dumaguete	150	He	9.18N	123.18 E
Dumai	150	Df	1.41N	101.27 E
Dumaran	150	Gd	10.33N	119.51 E
Dumaresq River	212	Je	28.40S	150.28 E
Dumas [Ar.-U.S.]	186	Kj	33.53N	91.29W
Dumas [Tx.-U.S.]	186	Fj	35.52N	101.58W
Dumayr	146	Gf	33.38N	36.40 E
Dumbarton	118	If	55.57N	4.35W
Dumbéa	219b	Cf	22.09S	166.27 E
Dumbrăveni [Rom.]	130	Kd	45.31N	27.09 E
Dumbrăveni [Rom.]	130	Hc	46.14N	24.34 E
Dumbrăveni [Rom.]	130	Jd	46.39N	26.25 E
Dumfries	118	Jf	55.04N	3.37W
Dumfries and Galloway [3]	118	Jf	55.00N	3.35W
Dumka	148	Ld	24.16N	87.15 E
Dümmer	120	Ee	52.30N	8.19 E
Dumoine, Lac-	184	Ib	46.52N	77.52W
Dumoine, Rivière-	184	Ib	46.13N	77.50W
Dumont d'Urville	222	Je	66.40S	140.01 E
Dumont D'Urville Sea (EN)	222	Je	63.00S	140.00 E
Dumpu	210	Fe	5.52S	145.46 E
Dümrek	130	Kk	39.55N	30.56 E
Dumuhe	154	Gb	46.13N	133.33 E
Dumyât=Damietta (EN)	160	Ke	31.25N	31.48 E
Dumyât, Maşabb-	146	Cg	31.29N	31.51 E
Duna=Danube (EN)	110	If	45.20N	29.40 E
Dunaföldvár	120	Pi	46.48N	18.56 E
Dunaharaszti	120	Pi	47.21N	19.05 E
Dunaj=Danube (EN)	110	If	45.20N	29.40 E
Dunajec	120	Qf	50.15N	20.44 E
Dunajevcy	132	Ee	48.53N	26.51 E
Dunajská Streda	120	Ni	47.01N	17.38 E
Dunakeszi	120	Pi	47.38N	19.08 E
Dunántúl	110	Hf	47.00N	18.00 E
Dunărea=Danube (EN)	110	If	45.20N	29.40 E
Dunărea Veche	130	Le	45.17N	28.02 E
Dunării, Delta-= Danube, Mouths of the (EN)	130	Me	45.05N	29.45 E
Duna-Tisza Köze	120	Pj	46.30N	19.30 E
Dunaváros	120	Pj	46.40N	19.00 E
Dunav=Danube (EN)	110	If	45.20N	29.40 E
Dunavăţu de Jos	130	Me	44.59N	29.13 E
Dunav-Tisa-Dunav kanal	218	Df	45.23S	170.38 E
Dunback	118	Kf	56.00N	2.31W
Dunbar	188	Kj	32.43N	109.06W
Duncan [Az.-U.S.]	188	Kj	32.43N	109.06W
Duncan [B.C.-Can.]	188	Db	48.47N	123.42W
Duncan [Ok.-U.S.]	182	He	34.30N	97.57W
Duncan Passage	148	If	11.00N	92.00 E
Duncansby Head	110	Fd	58.39N	3.01W
Dundaga	116	Jg	57.31N	22.14 E
Dundalk	184	If	39.15N	76.31W
Dundalk/Dún Dealgan	118	Gg	54.01N	6.25W
Dundalk Bay/Cuan Dhun Dealgan	118	Gh	53.57N	6.17W
Dundas	172	Ee	28.12S	30.16 E
Dundas (Thule Air Base)	179	Fc	76.30N	69.00W
Dundas, Lake-	212	Ef	32.35S	121.50 E
Dundas Peninsula	180	Gb	74.40N	113.00W
Dundas Strait	212	Gb	11.20S	131.35 E
Dún Dealgan/Dundalk	118	Gg	54.01N	6.25W
Dundee [S.Afr.]	172	Ee	28.12S	30.16 E
Dundee [Scot.-U.K.]	112	Fd	56.28N	3.00W
Dund Hot → Zhenglan Qi	154	Cc	42.14N	115.59 E
Dundrum Bay/Cuan Dhún Droma	118	Hg	54.13N	5.45W
Dunedin [Fl.-U.S.]	184	Fk	28.02N	82.47W
Dunedin [N.Z.]	210	Ii	45.53S	170.31 E
Dunfanaghy	118	Ff	55.11N	7.59W
Dunfermline	118	Je	56.04N	3.29W
Dungannon/Dún Geanainn	118	Fg	54.31N	6.46W
Dún Garbhán/Dungarvan	118	Fi	52.05N	7.37W
Düngarpur	148	Ed	23.50N	73.43 E
Dungarvan/Dún Garbhán	118	Fi	52.05N	7.37W
Dungas	166	Gc	13.04N	9.20 E
Dungau	120	Ih	48.45N	12.30 E
Dungeness	118	Nk	50.55N	0.58 E
Dungu	170	Eb	3.42N	28.40 E
Dungu	170	Eb	3.37N	28.34 E
Dunhua	152	Mc	43.22N	128.12 E
Dunhuang	152	Fc	40.10N	94.50 E
Dunkerque	122	Jj	51.03N	2.22 E
Dunkery Beacon	118	Jj	51.11N	3.35W
Dunkirk	182	Lc	42.29N	79.21W
Dunkwa	166	Ed	5.58N	1.47W
Dún Laoghaire	118	Gh	53.17N	6.08W
Dún Mànmhai/Dunmanway	118	Dj	51.43N	9.07W
Dunmanway/Dún Mànmhai	118	Dj	51.43N	9.07W
Dún na nGall/Donegal	118	Ff	54.39N	8.06W
Dún na nGall/Donegal [2]	118	Ff	54.50N	8.00W
Dunnellon	184	Fk	29.03N	82.28W
Dunnet Head	110	Fd	58.40N	3.23W
Dunning	186	Ff	41.50N	100.06W
Dunqulah=Dongola (EN)	160	Kg	19.10N	30.29 E
Dunqulah al Qadīmah	168	Dc	18.13N	30.45 E
Dunqunāb	168	Ea	21.06N	37.05 E
Dunqunāb, Khalīj-	168	Ea	21.06N	37.08 E
Dunrankin	184	Fb	48.39N	83.04W
Duns	118	Kf	55.47N	2.20W
Dünsberg	124	Kd	50.39N	8.35 E
Dunsmuir	188	Df	41.13N	122.16W
Dunstable	124	Bc	51.53N	0.31W
Dunstan Mountains	218	Cf	44.55S	169.30 E
Dun-sur-Auron	122	Ih	46.53N	2.34 E
Dun-sur-Meuse	124	He	49.23N	5.11 E
Duntroon	218	Df	44.51S	170.41 E
Dunvegan	118	Gd	57.26N	6.35W
Duobukur	152	La	50.19N	124.57 E
Duolun/Dolonnor	152	Kc	42.10N	116.30 E
Dupree	186	Fd	45.03N	101.36W
Duqm	142	Hf	19.41N	57.32 E
Duque de Bragança, Quedas-	158	Ii	9.05S	16.10 E
Duque de Caxias	202	Jh	22.47S	43.18W
Duque de York, Isla-	206	Bf	50.40S	75.20W
Du Quoin	184	Cf	38.01N	89.14W
Durack Range	212	Fc	17.00S	128.00 E
Durack River	212	Fc	15.33S	127.52 E
Durağan	146	Ed	41.25N	35.04 E
Durance	110	Gg	43.55N	4.44 E
Durand	186	Kd	44.38N	91.58W
Durand, Récif-	219b	Df	22.02S	168.39 E
Durango [Co.-U.S.]	176	If	37.16N	107.53W
Durango [Sp.]	126	Ja	43.10N	2.37W
Durañona	204	Bm	37.55N	60.31W
Durant	182	He	33.59N	96.23W
Duras	122	Fi	44.41N	0.11 E
Duratón	126	Hb	41.37N	4.07W
Durazno	200	Kf	33.22N	56.31W
Durazno [2]	204	Dk	33.05N	56.05W
Durazno, Cuchilla Grande del-	204	Dk	33.00N	56.15W
Durazzo (EN)=Durrësi	130	Ch	41.19N	19.26 E
Durban	172	Ee	29.55S	30.56 E
Durbe	116	Je	56.39N	21.14 E
Durbet-Daba, pereval-	152	Gb	49.37N	89.25 E
Durbuy	124	Hd	50.21N	5.28 E
Đurđevac	128	Le	46.02N	17.04 E
Düren	120	Cf	50.48N	6.29 E
Durg	148	If	21.11N	81.17 E
Durgāpur	148	Ld	23.30N	87.20 E
Durgen-Nur	152	Fb	47.40N	93.30 E
Durham [S.Afr.]	172	Dd	26.42S	27.40 E
Durham [2]	118	Le	54.45N	1.40W
Durham [Eng.-U.K.]	112	Fd	54.47N	1.34W
Durham [N.C.-U.S.]	182	Gd	36.00N	78.54W
Durkee	188	Ge	44.36N	117.28W
Durlas/Thurles	118	Fi	52.41N	7.49W
Ďurmä	144	Ge	24.37N	46.08 E
Durmersheim	124	Kf	48.56N	8.19 E
Durmitor	110	Hg	43.09N	19.02 E
Durnford, Punta-	162	Dd	23.41N	16.00W
Durrësi=Durazzo (EN)	130	Ch	41.19N	19.26 E
Durrësi, Gjiri-	130	Ch	41.16N	19.28 E
Dursey/Oiléan Baoi	118	Cj	51.36N	10.12W
Dursunbey	146	Ce	39.35N	28.38 E
Durtal	122	Fg	47.40N	0.15W
Duru → Wuchuan	152	Jf	28.28N	107.57 E
Duruksi	168	Hd	8.29N	45.38 E
Durusu Gölü	130	Lh	41.20N	28.38 E
Durüz, Jabal ad-	146	Gf	32.40N	36.44 E
D'Urville Island	216	Dh	40.50S	173.50 E
Dušak	135	Cf	37.15N	60.01 E
Dusa Mareb	168	Hd	5.31N	46.24 E
Dušanbe	142	If	38.35N	68.48 E
Dušeti	132	Nh	42.05N	44.42 E
Dusetos	116	Li	55.42N	26.02 E
Dushan	142	Mg	25.55N	107.36 E
Dushan Hu	154	Dg	35.06N	116.48 E
Dusky Sound	218	Bf	45.45S	166.30 E
Düsseldorf	112	Ge	51.13N	6.46 E
Dusti	135	Gf	37.22N	68.43 E
Dutch Harbor	178a	Eb	53.53N	166.32W
Dutlwe	172	Cd	23.58S	23.54 E
Dutton, Mount-	188	Ih	38.01N	112.13W
Duved	116	Ea	63.24N	12.52 E
Duvergé	194	Ld	18.22N	71.31W
Düvertepe	130	Lj	39.14N	28.27 E
Duvno	128	Lg	43.43N	17.14 E
Duwayhin	144	He	24.16N	51.20 E
Duwayhin, Khawr-	146	Nj	24.20N	51.25 E
Duyfken Point	212	Ib	12.35S	141.40 E
Duyun	142	Mg	26.20N	107.28 E
Düz	162	Ic	33.28N	9.01 E
Düzce	144	Da	40.50N	31.10 E
Dve Mogili	130	If	43.36N	25.52 E
Dvina Gulf (EN) = Dvinskaja guba	110	Jb	65.00N	39.45 E
Dvinskaja guba = Dvina Gulf (EN)	110	Jb	65.00N	39.45 E
Dvor	128	Ke	45.04N	16.23 E
Dvuh Cirkov, gora-	138	Lc	67.30N	168.20 E
Dvůr Králové nad Labem	120	Lf	50.26N	15.48 E
Dwārka	148	Dd	22.14N	68.58 E
Dworshak Reservoir	188	Hc	46.45N	116.00W
Dyer, Cape-	174	Mc	66.37N	61.18W
Dyero	166	Dc	12.50N	6.30W
Dyer Plateau	222	Qf	70.45S	65.30W
Dyersburg	182	Jd	36.03N	89.23W
Dyfed [3]	118	Ji	52.05N	4.00W
Dyhmau, gora-	132	Mh	43.05N	43.12 E
Dyje	120	Mh	48.37N	16.56 E
Dyjsko-Svratecký úval	120	Mh	48.56N	16.25 E
Dyle	124	Gd	50.57N	4.40 E
Dylewska Góra	120	Pc	53.34N	19.57 E
Dynów	120	Sg	49.49N	22.14 E
Dyr, Djebel-	128	Cn	36.13N	8.46 E
Dyrhólaey	110	Ec	63.24N	19.08W
Dysná ežeras / Disnaj, ozero-	116	Gi	55.35N	26.32 E
Dytike Rodhópi [3]	130	Hh	41.45N	24.05 E
Dzabhan	140	Ke	48.54N	93.23 E
Dżagdy, hrebet-	138	If	53.40N	131.00 E
Dżalagaš	135	Gf	45.05N	64.40 E
Dżalal-Abad	135	Id	40.56N	73.05 E
Dżalilabad	136	Eh	39.12N	48.31 E
Dżalinda	138	Hc	53.31N	123.59 E
Dżambejty	132	Rd	50.14N	52.38 E
Dżambul [Kaz.-U.S.S.R.]	142	Hf	42.54N	71.22 E
Dżambul [Kaz.-U.S.S.R.]	142	Jb	42.54N	71.22 E
Dżambulskaja oblast [3]	135	Jb	43.50N	71.00 E
Dzamyn-Ud	152	Jb	43.50N	111.45 E
Dżanakoj	132	Hf	45.42N	34.22 E
Dżansugurov	136	If	45.35N	79.29 E
Dżanybek	132	Qe	49.24N	46.50 E
Dzaoudzi	160	Lj	12.47S	45.17 E
Dżardżan	138	Hc	68.43N	124.05 E
Dżargalant [Mong.]	152	Gb	47.20N	99.35 E
Dżargalant [Mong.]	152	Ib	48.35N	105.50 E
Dżarkurgan	135	Hf	37.29N	67.25 E
Dżebariki-Haja	138	Id	62.23N	135.50 E
Dżebel [Bul.]	130	Ih	41.30N	25.18 E
Dżebel [Tur.-U.S.S.R.]	132	Sj	39.37N	54.18 E
Dżerbail	132	Oj	39.23N	47.01 E
Dzereg	152	Gb	47.08N	92.50 E
Dżergalan	135	Lc	42.33N	79.02 E
Dzermuk	132	Nj	39.50N	45.39 E
Dzerżinsk [Bye.-U.S.S.R.]	132	Ec	53.44N	27.08 E
Dzerżinsk [R.S.F.S.R.]	136	Ee	56.16N	43.32 E
Dzerżinsk [Ukr.-U.S.S.R.]	132	Je	48.22N	37.50 E
Dzerżinskaja, gora-	116	Lk	53.53N	27.10 E
Dzerżinskoje	136	Je	56.49N	95.18 E
Dżetygara	142	Hd	52.11N	61.12 E
Dżetysaj	135	Gd	40.49N	68.20 E
Dżezkazgan [Kaz.-U.S.S.R.]	135	Lc	47.47N	67.46 E
Dżezkazgan [Kaz.-U.S.S.R.]	135	Gf	47.53N	67.27 E
Dżezkazganskaja oblast [3]	135	Gf	47.30N	70.00 E
Dzhugdzur Range (EN) = Dżugdżur, hrebet-	140	Pd	58.00N	136.00 E
Działdówka	120	Qc	52.58N	20.05 E
Działoszyce	120	Qf	50.22N	20.21 E
Dzibalchén	192	Oh	19.31N	89.45W
Dzibilchaltún	192	Og	21.05N	89.36W
Dzierzgoń	120	Pc	53.56N	19.21 E
Dzierżoniów	112	Mf	50.44N	16.39 E
Dżirgatal	135	Ie	39.13N	71.12 E
Dzizak	135	Hd	40.07N	67.52 E
Dżugdżur, hrebet-=Dzhugdzur Range (EN)	140	Pd	58.00N	136.00 E

Index Symbols

[1] Independent Nation	Pass, Gap	Coast, Beach	Lagoon
[2] State, Region	Plain, Lowland	Cliff	Bank
[3] District, County	Delta	Peninsula	Seamount
[4] Municipality	Salt Flat	Isthmus	Tablemount
[5] Colony, Dependency	Valley, Canyon	Sandbank	Ridge
Continent	Crater, Cave	Island	Shelf
Physical Region	Karst Features	Islands, Archipelago	Basin
Historical or Cultural Region	Depression	Rock, Reef	Escarpment, Sea Scarp
Mount, Mountain	Polder	Rocks, Reefs	Fracture
Volcano	Desert, Dunes	Coral Reef	Trench, Abyss
Hill	Forest, Woods	Well, Spring	National Park, Reserve
Mountains, Mountain Range	Heath, Steppe	Geyser	Point of Interest
Hills, Escarpment	Oasis	River, Stream	Recreation Site
Plateau, Upland	Cape, Point	Waterfall, Rapids	Cave, Cavern
		River Mouth, Estuary	Historic Site
		Lake	Ruins
		Salt Lake	Wall, Walls
		Intermittent Lake	Church, Abbey
		Reservoir	Temple
		Swamp, Pond	Scientific Station
		Canal	Railway station
		Glacier	Airport
		Ice Shelf, Pack Ice	Port
		Ocean	Military installation
		Sea	Lighthouse
		Gulf, Bay	Mine
		Strait, Fjord	Tunnel
			Dam, Bridge

Dzungarian Gate (EN)= Alataw Shankou	140	Ke	45.25N	82.25 E
Dzungarian Gate (EN) = Džungarskije vorota	140	Ke	45.25N	82.25 E
Džungarski Alatau, hrebet-	140	Ke	45.00N	81.00 E
Džungarskije vorota = Dzungarian Gate (EN)	140	Ke	45.25N	82.25 E
Dzun-Hara	152	Ib	48.40N	106.40 E
Dzun-Mod	152	Ib	47.50N	106.57 E
Džurak-Sal	132	Mf	47.18N	43.36 E
Džusaly	136	Gf	45.29N	64.05 E
Džvari	132	Mh	42.42N	42.02 E

E

Éadan Doire/Edenderry	118	Fh	53.21N	7.03W
Eads	186	Eg	38.29N	102.47W
Eagle	178	Kd	64.46N	141.16W
Eagle	180	Lf	53.35N	57.25W
Eagle Creek	188	La	52.22N	107.24W
Eagle Lake	184	Mb	47.02N	68.36W
Eagle Lake [Ca.-U.S.]	188	Ef	40.39N	120.44W
Eagle Lake [Me.-U.S.]	184	Mb	46.20N	69.20W
Eagle Lake [Ont.-Can.]	186	Jb	49.42N	93.13W
Eagle Mountain	186	Kc	47.54N	90.33W
Eagle Nest	186	Dh	36.35N	105.14W
Eagle Pass	186	Gf	28.43N	100.30W
Eagle Peak [Ca.-U.S.]	182	Cc	41.17N	120.12W
Eagle Peak [Tx.-U.S.]	186	Dk	30.56N	105.01W
Eagle River [Ak.-U.S.]	178	Jd	61.19N	149.34W
Eagle River [Wi.-U.S.]	186	Ld	45.55N	89.15W
Eagle Summit	178	Jc	65.30N	145.38W
Ealing, London-	124	Bc	51.30N	0.19W
Ear Falls	186	Ja	50.38N	93.13W
Earn	118	Je	56.25N	3.30W
Earn, Loch-	118	Ie	56.28N	4.10W
Earnslaw, Mount-	218	Cf	44.37S	168.25 E
Easley	184	Fh	34.50N	82.36W
East Alligator River	212	Gb	12.08S	132.42 E
East Anglia	118	Ni	52.25N	1.00 E
East Angus	184	Lc	45.29N	71.40W
East Bay [Can.]	180	Jd	64.05N	81.30W
East Bay [U.S.]	186	Ll	29.05N	89.15W
East Berlin (EN)=Berlin (Ost)	112	He	52.31N	13.24 E
East Berlin (EN)=Berlin (Ost) [2]	120	Jd	52.30N	13.25 E
Eastbourne [Eng.-U.K.]	118	Nk	50.46N	0.17 E
Eastbourne [N.Z.]	218	Fd	41.17S	174.54 E
East Caicos	194	Lc	21.41N	71.30W
East Cape [Fl.-U.S.]	184	Gm	25.07N	81.05W
East Cape [N.Z.]	208	Ih	37.41S	178.33 E
East Caroline Basin (EN)	106	Ii	4.00N	146.45 E
East Chicago	184	De	41.38N	87.27W
East China Sea (EN)=Dong Hai	140	Og	29.00N	125.00 E
East China Sea (EN)= Higashi-Shina-Kai	140	Og	29.00N	125.00 E
East Coast [2]	218	Gc	38.20S	177.50 E
East Dereham	118	Ni	52.41N	0.56 E
Eastend	188	Kb	49.31N	108.48W
East Entrance	220a	Bb	7.50N	134.40 E
Easter Island (EN) = Pascua, Isla de- / Rapa Nui	208	Qg	27.07S	109.22W
Easter Island (EN) = Rapa Nui / Pascua, Isla de-	208	Qg	27.07S	109.22W
Eastern [Ghana] [3]	166	Ed	6.30N	0.30W
Eastern [Kenya] [3]	170	Gb	0.05N	38.00 E
Eastern [S.L.] [3]	166	Cd	8.15N	11.00W
Eastern [Ug.] [3]	170	Fb	1.30N	33.50 E
Eastern [Zam.] [3]	170	Fe	13.00S	32.15 E
Eastern Fields	214	Dj	10.03S	145.22 E
Eastern Ghats	140	Jh	14.00N	78.50 E
Eastern Point	197b	Ab	18.07N	63.01W
Eastern Sayans (EN)= Vostočny Sajan	140	Ld	53.00N	97.00 E
Eastern Siberia (EN)	140	Rc	65.00N	155.00 E
Eastern Sierra Madre (EN)= Madre Oriental, Sierra-	174	Jg	22.00N	99.30W
Eastern Turkistan (EN)	140	Jf	40.00N	80.00 E
East Falkland/Soledad, Isla-	198	Kk	51.45S	58.50W
East Fork	186	Ie	42.41N	94.12W
East Friesland (EN)= Ostfriesland	120	Dc	53.20N	7.40 E
East Frisian Islands (EN)= Ostfriesische Inseln	120	Dc	53.45N	7.25 E
East Grand Forks	186	Hc	47.56N	97.01W
East Grand Rapids	184	Ed	42.56N	85.35W
East Greenland (EN)= Østgrønland [2]	179	Id	72.00N	35.00W
East Grinstead	118	Mj	51.08N	0.01W
East Ilsley	124	Ac	51.32N	1.17W
East Kilbride	118	If	55.46N	4.10W
East Lansing	184	Ed	42.44N	84.29W
East Las Vegas	188	Hh	36.07N	115.01W
Eastleigh	118	Lk	50.58N	1.22W
East London	160	Jl	33.00S	27.55 E
East Lynn Lake	184	Ff	38.05N	82.20W
Eastmain	180	Jf	52.14N	78.31W
Eastmain	180	Jf	52.15N	78.34W
Eastman	184	Fi	32.12N	83.11W
East Mariana Basin (EN)	106	Jh	12.00N	153.00 E
East Midlands Airport	124	Ab	52.50N	1.20W
East Novaya Zemlya Trough (EN)	136	Fa	73.30N	61.00 E
Easton	184	Je	40.41N	75.13W
East Pacific Rise (EN)	106	Ml	20.00S	110.00W
East Point	184	Ei	33.40N	84.27W
East Point [B.V.I.]	197a	Db	18.43N	64.16W
East Point [V.I.U.S.]	197a	Dc	17.46N	64.33W
Eastport	184	Nc	44.54N	67.00W
East Pryor Mountain	188	Kd	45.14N	108.30W
East Retford	118	Mh	53.19N	0.56W
East Road	124	Cd	51.00N	1.02 E
East Schelde (EN)= Oosterschelde	122	Jc	51.30N	4.00 E
East Scotia Basin (EN)	198	Mk	57.00S	35.00W
East Siberian Sea (EN) = Vostočno Sibirskoje more	224	Cd	74.00N	166.00 E
East St. Louis	182	Id	38.38N	90.05W
East Sussex [3]	118	Nk	50.55N	0.15 E
East Tavaputs Plateau	188	Kg	39.45N	109.30W
East Wear Bay	124	Dc	51.08N	1.18 E
Eaton	184	Ef	39.44N	84.37W
Eatonia	188	Ka	51.13N	109.23W
Eatonton	184	Fi	33.20N	83.23W
Eatonville	188	Dc	46.51N	122.17W
Eau Claire	182	Ic	44.49N	91.31W
Eau-Claire, Lac à l' -	180	Ke	56.20N	74.00W
Eauripik Atoll	208	Fd	6.42N	143.03 E
Eauripik Ridge (EN)	214	Cg	3.00N	142.00 E
Eauze	122	Gk	43.52N	0.06 E
Ébano	192	Jf	22.13N	98.24W
Ebbegebirge	124	De	51.10N	7.45 E
Ebbw Vale	118	Jj	51.47N	3.12W
Ebebiyin	166	He	2.09N	11.20 E
Ebeltoft	116	Dh	56.12N	10.41 E
Ebensburg	184	He	40.28N	78.44W
Ebensee	128	Hc	47.48N	13.46 E
Eberbach	120	Eg	49.28N	8.59 E
Eber Gölü	146	Dc	38.38N	31.12 E
Ebersbach	128	Ke	51.01N	14.35 E
Eberswalde	120	Jd	52.50N	13.50 E
Ebetsu	154	Pc	43.07N	141.34 E
Ebino	154	Kh	32.02N	130.47 E
Ebinur Hu	140	Ke	44.55N	82.55 E
Ebla	144	Eb	35.42N	36.50 E
Ebo	170	Ce	11.02S	14.40 E
Ebola	170	Db	3.20N	20.57 E
Eboli	128	Jj	40.36N	15.04 E
Ebolowa	160	Ih	2.54N	11.09 E
Ebombo	170	Ed	5.42S	26.07 E
Ebon Atoll	208	Hd	4.38N	168.43 E
Ebre/Ebro	110	Gg	40.43N	0.54 E
Ebre, Delta de l'-/Ebro, Delta del- = Ebro, Delta of the- (EN)	126	Md	40.43N	0.54 E
Ebril, Récif-	216	Od	22.40S	133.30W
Ebro/Ebre	110	Gg	40.43N	0.54 E
Ebro, Delta del-/Ebre, Delta de l'- = Ebro, Delta of the- (EN)	126	Md	40.43N	0.54 E
Ebro, Delta of the- (EN) = Ebre, Delta de l'-/Ebro, Delta del-	126	Md	40.43N	0.54 E
Ebro, Delta of the- (EN) = Ebro, Delta del-/Ebre, Delta de l'-	126	Md	40.43N	0.54 E
Ebro, Embalse del-	126	Ia	43.00N	3.58W
Ebschloh	120	Ef	50.58N	8.15 E
Ecaussines	124	Gd	50.34N	4.10 E
Ecbatana	146	Me	34.48N	48.30 E
Eceabat	130	Ji	40.11N	26.21 E
Echdeiria	162	Ed	27.14N	10.27W
Echegarate, Puerto de-	126	Jb	42.57N	2.14W
Echeng [China]	152	Kd	36.10N	116.03 E
Echeng [China]	154	Ci	30.24N	114.52 E
Echez	122	Gk	43.28N	0.02 E
Echigo-Sanmyaku	156	Fc	37.30N	139.15 E
Echizen-Misaki	156	Dd	35.59N	135.57 E
Echo Bay	176	Hc	66.04N	118.00W
Echo Seamount (EN)	162	Dd	25.23N	19.25W
Echt	124	Hc	51.06N	5.52 E
Echternach	124	Ie	49.49N	6.25 E
Echuca	212	Ig	36.10S	144.45 E
Echzell	124	Kd	50.23N	8.52 E
Écija	126	Gg	37.32N	5.05W
Eckernförde	120	Fb	54.28N	9.50 E
Eckerö	114	Ef	60.15N	19.35 E
Eclipse Sound	180	Jb	72.40N	79.30W
Ečmiadzin	132	Nh	40.09N	44.18 E
Écommoy	122	Gg	47.50N	0.16 E
Ecos	124	De	49.10N	1.39 E
Ecouis	124	De	49.19N	1.26 E
Écouves, Forêt d'-	122	Gf	48.32N	0.04 E
Ecrins, Barre des-	122	Mj	44.55N	6.22 E
Ecuador [1]	200	If	2.00S	77.30W
Ecury-sur-Coole	124	Gf	48.54N	4.20 E
Ed [Eth.]	168	Gc	13.56N	41.40 E
Ed [Swe.]	114	Cg	58.54N	11.56 E
Edam-Volendam	124	Hb	52.30N	5.03 E
Edane	116	Ee	59.38N	12.49 E
Eday	118	Kb	59.11N	2.47W
Edchera	162	Ed	27.02N	13.04W
Eddrachillis Bay	118	Hc	58.19N	5.15W
Eddystone Point	212	Jh	41.00S	148.20 E
Eddystone Rocks	118	Ik	50.15N	4.10W
Eddyville	184	Cg	37.03N	88.04W
Ede [Neth.]	122	Lb	52.03N	5.40 E
Ede [Nig.]	166	Fd	7.44N	4.26 E
Edéa	160	Ih	3.48N	10.08 E
Edefors	114	Ec	66.13N	20.54 E
Edéia	204	Hc	17.18S	49.55W
Edelény	120	Qh	48.18N	20.44 E
Eden	118	Jg	54.57N	3.01W
Eden [Austl.]	212	Jg	37.04S	149.54 E
Eden [Tx.-U.S.]	186	Gk	31.13N	99.51W
Edenburg	172	De	29.45S	25.56 E
Edenderry/Éadan Doire	118	Fh	53.21N	7.03W
Edenkoben	124	Ke	49.17N	8.09 E
Edenton	184	Ig	36.04N	76.39W
Eder	120	Fe	51.13N	9.27 E
Edersee	120	Fe	51.11N	9.03 E
Edertal	124	Lc	51.09N	9.09 E
Edewecht	124	Ja	53.08N	7.59 E
Edgar Ranges	212	Ec	18.43S	123.25 E
Edgartown	184	Le	41.23N	70.31W
Edgecumbe	218	Gb	37.58S	176.50 E
Edgeley	186	Gc	46.22N	98.43W
Edgell	180	Ld	61.50N	65.00W
Edgemont	186	Ee	43.18N	103.50W
Edgeøya	224	Jd	77.45N	22.30 E
Édhessa	130	Fi	40.48N	22.03 E
Edina	186	Jd	44.55N	93.20W
Edinburg	182	Hf	26.18N	98.10W
Edinburgh	112	Fd	55.57N	3.13W
Edinburgh, Arrecife-	194	Ff	14.50N	82.39W
Edincik	146	Bb	40.20N	27.51 E
Edingen/Enghien	124	Gd	50.42N	4.02 E
Edirne	146	Bb	41.40N	26.34 E
Edisto Island	184	Gi	32.35N	80.10W
Edisto River	184	Gi	32.39N	80.24W
Edith, Mount-	188	Jc	46.26N	111.11W
Edith Ronne Land (EN)	222	Rg	81.40S	50.00W
Edjeleh	162	Id	27.42N	9.53 E
Edjereh	162	He	24.35N	4.30 E
Édjérir	166	Fb	18.06N	0.50 E
Edmond	186	Hi	35.39N	97.29W
Edmonds	188	Dc	47.48N	122.22W
Edmonton	176	Hd	53.33N	113.28W
Edmundston	180	Kg	47.22N	68.20W
Edna	186	Hl	28.42N	96.39W
Edremit	144	Cb	39.35N	27.01 E
Edremit, Gulf of- (EN)= Edremit Körfezi	146	Bc	39.30N	26.45 E
Edremit Körfezi=Edremit, Gulf of- (EN)	146	Bc	39.30N	26.45 E
Edsbro	114	Eg	59.54N	18.29 E
Edsbruk	116	Gf	58.02N	16.28 E
Edsbyn	116	Fc	61.23N	15.49 E
Edson	180	Ff	53.35N	116.26W
Edsvalla	116	Ee	59.26N	13.13 E
Eduardo Castex	206	He	35.54S	64.18W
Eduni, Mount-	180	Ed	64.08N	128.10W
Edward, Lake-	158	Ji	0.25S	29.30 E
Edward, Lake- (EN)= Rutanzige, Lac-	158	Ji	0.25S	29.30 E
Edwards Creek	212	He	28.21S	135.51 E
Edwards Plateau	174	If	31.20N	101.00W
Edward VIII Bay	222	Ee	66.50S	57.00 E
Edward VII Peninsula	222	Mf	77.40S	155.00W
Edzo	180	Fd	62.47N	116.08W
Eeklo	122	Jc	51.11N	3.34 E
Eelde	124	Ia	53.08N	6.33 E
Eel River	182	Cc	40.40N	124.20W
Eem	124	Hb	52.16N	5.20 E
Eems	124	Ja	53.19N	7.03 E
Eemskanaal	124	Ia	53.19N	6.57 E
Eenrum	124	Ia	53.23N	6.25 E
Eersel	124	Hc	51.22N	5.19 E
Eesti Nõukogude Socialistik Vabarijk/Estonskaja SSR [2]	136	Cd	59.00N	26.00 E
Eesti NSV=Estonian SSR (EN) [2]	136	Cd	59.00N	26.00 E
Efaté, Ile-	208	Hf	17.40S	168.25 E
Eferding	128	Ib	48.19N	14.01 E
Efes = Ephesus (EN)	130	Kl	37.55N	27.20 E
Effingham	186	Lg	39.07N	88.33W
Eflâni	146	Eb	41.26N	32.57 E
Eforie	130	Le	44.01N	28.38 E
Ega	126	Kb	42.19N	1.55W
Egadi, Isole-=Egadi Islands (EN)	110	Hh	38.00N	12.15 E
Egadi Islands (EN)=Egadi, Isole-	110	Hh	38.00N	12.15 E
Egan Range	188	Hg	39.00N	115.00W
Eganville	184	Ic	47.33N	77.06W
Egbe	166	Gd	8.13N	5.31 E
Ege Denizi=Aegean Sea (EN)	110	Ih	39.00N	25.00 E
Egedesminde/Ausiait	224	Nc	68.50N	52.45W
Egegik	178	He	58.13N	157.22W
Egentliga Finland/Varsinais-Suomi	116	Jd	60.40N	22.30 E
Eger	120	Qi	47.54N	20.23 E
Eger	120	Kf	50.32N	14.08 E
Egersund	114	Ag	58.27N	6.00 E
Egerton, Mount-	212	Dd	24.45S	117.45 E
Egeskov	116	Di	55.10N	10.30 E
Eggegebirge	120	Ee	51.40N	8.55 E
Eggenfelden	120	Ih	48.24N	12.46 E
Eggenstein-Leopoldshafen	124	Ke	49.05N	8.23 E
Eggum	114	Cb	68.19N	13.42 E
Eghezée	124	Gd	50.36N	4.56 E
Egijn-Gol	152	Ha	49.24N	103.36 E
Égletons	122	Ii	45.24N	2.03 E
Eglinton	180	Fa	75.45N	118.50W
Egmont, Cape-	216	Dg	39.17S	173.45 E
Egmont, Mount-	218	Fc	39.18S	174.04 E
Egnazia	128	Lj	40.50N	17.25 E
Eğridir	146	Dd	37.52N	30.51 E
Eğridir Gölü	144	Db	38.02N	30.53 E
Eğrigöz Dağ	130	Mj	39.21N	29.07 E
Egtved	116	Ci	55.37N	9.18 E
Éguas ou Correntina, Rio das-	204	Ja	13.26S	44.14W
Eguey	158	Ig	16.10N	16.10 E
Egvekinot	142	Uc	66.19N	179.10W
Egypt (EN)=Mişr [1]	160	Jf	27.00N	30.00 E
Eha Amufu	166	Gd	6.40N	7.46 E
Ehen Hudag → Alxa Youqi	152	Hd	39.12N	101.40 E
Ehime Ken [2]	154	Lh	33.35N	132.40 E
Ehingen (Donau)	120	Fh	48.17N	9.44 E
Ehrang, Trier-	124	Ie	49.49N	6.41 E
Ehrwald	128	Ec	47.24N	10.55 E
Ei	156	Bf	31.13N	130.30 E
Eiao, Ile-	208	Me	8.00S	140.40W
Eibar	126	Ja	43.11N	2.28W
Eibergen	124	Ib	52.07N	6.40 E
Eichsfeld	120	Ge	51.25N	10.20 E
Eichstätt	120	Hh	48.53N	11.11 E
Eickelborn, Lippetal-	124	Kc	51.39N	8.13 E
Eide	116	Bb	62.55N	7.26 E
Eider	120	Eb	54.19N	8.58 E
Eiderstedt	120	Eb	54.22N	8.50 E
Eidet	114	Cd	64.27N	13.37 E
Eidfjord	114	Bf	60.28N	7.05 E
Eidfjorden	116	Bd	60.25N	6.45 E
Eidslandet	116	Ad	60.44N	5.45 E
Eidsvåg	114	Be	62.47N	8.03 E
Eidsvoll	114	Cf	60.19N	11.14 E
Eidsvollfjellet	179	Nc	79.00N	13.00 E
Eierlandse Gat	124	Ga	53.12N	4.52 E
Eifel	120	Cf	50.15N	6.45 E
Eiffel Flats	172	Dc	18.13S	29.48 E
Eigat, Jabal-	168	Fa	22.00N	35.01 E
Eigenbrakel/Braine-l'Alleud	124	Gd	50.41N	4.22 E
Eigerøya	116	Af	58.25N	5.55 E
Eigg	118	Ge	56.54N	6.10W
Eight Degree Channel	140	Ji	8.00N	73.00 E
Eights Coast	222	Pf	73.30S	96.00W
Eighty Mile Beach	212	Ec	19.45S	121.00 E
Eigrim, Jabal-	168	Fb	19.22N	35.18 E
Eijsden	124	Hd	50.46N	5.42 E
Eikeren	116	Ce	59.40N	10.00 E
Eikesdalsvatnet	116	Cb	62.35N	8.10 E
'Eilai	168	Eb	16.33N	30.54 E
Eildon, Lake-	212	Jg	37.10S	145.50 E
Eilenburg	120	Ie	51.28N	12.37 E
Eiler Rasmussen, Kap-	179	Kb	82.40N	20.00W
Eil Malk	220a	Ac	7.09N	134.22 E
Eina	116	Dd	60.38N	10.36 E
Einasleigh	212	Ic	18.31S	144.05 E
Einasleigh River	212	Ic	17.30S	142.17 E
Einbeck	120	Fe	51.49N	9.52 E
Eindhoven	122	Lc	51.26N	5.28 E
Einsiedeln	128	Cc	47.08N	8.45 E
Éire/Ireland [1]	112	Fe	53.00N	8.00W
Eiríksjökull	114a	Bb	64.46N	20.24W
Eirunepé	200	Jf	6.40S	69.52W
Eisack/Isarco	128	Fd	46.27N	11.18 E
Eisacktal/Isarco, Valle-	128	Fd	46.45N	11.35 E
Eisenach	120	Gf	50.59N	10.19 E
Eisenberg	120	Hf	50.58N	11.54 E
Eisenberg	124	Kc	51.15N	8.50 E
Eisenberg (Pfalz)	124	Ke	49.33N	8.06 E
Eisenerz	128	Ic	47.32N	14.53 E
Eisenerzer Alpen	128	Ic	47.30N	14.40 E
Eisenhüttenstadt	120	Kd	52.10N	14.42 E
Eisenstadt	128	Kc	47.51N	16.31 E
Eisenwurzen	128	Jc	47.56N	15.02 E
Eišiškės/Ejšiškes	114	Fi	54.14N	25.02 E
Eisleben	120	He	51.32N	11.33 E
Eitorf	124	Jd	50.46N	7.27 E
Eivissa/Ibiza=Iviza (EN)	110	Gh	39.00N	1.25 E
Eje, Sierra del-	126	Fb	42.20N	6.55W
Ejea de los Caballeros	126	Kb	42.08N	1.08W
Ejeda	172	Gd	24.19S	44.21 E
Ejido	202	Db	8.33N	71.14W
Ejido Insurgentes	192	De	25.12N	111.45W
Ejin Horo Qi (Altan Xiret)	152	Id	39.31N	109.45 E
Ejin Qi	142	Me	41.50N	100.50 E
Ejšiškes/Eišiškės	114	Fi	54.14N	25.02 E
Ejura	166	Ed	7.23N	1.22W
Ejutla de Crespo	190	Ee	16.34N	96.44W
Ekalaka	188	Md	45.53N	104.33W
Ekecek Dağı	146	Fc	38.39N	34.03 E
Ekenäs/Tammisaari	114	Fg	59.58N	23.26 E
Ekeren, Antwerpen-	122	Kc	51.17N	4.25 E
Eket	166	Ge	4.39N	7.56 E
Eketahuna	218	Fd	40.39S	175.44 E
Ekhinádhes Nisoi	130	Ek	38.25N	21.02 E
Ekiatapski hrebet	138	Mc	68.40N	177.50 E
Ekibastuz	136	He	51.42N	75.22 E
Ekimčan	138	If	53.07N	133.02 E
Ekoli	170	Dc	0.23S	24.16 E
Ekoln	116	Ge	59.45N	17.35 E
Ekombe	170	Db	1.16N	21.36 E
Ekonda	138	Fc	65.47N	105.17 E
Eksjö	114	Dh	57.40N	14.57 E
Ekuma	172	Bc	18.10S	15.47 E
Ekwan	180	Jf	53.12N	82.15W
El Aaiún	160	Ff	27.10N	13.12W
El Aargub	162	De	23.37N	15.52W
El Aatf	162	De	23.30N	15.30W
El Abadia	126	Nh	36.13N	1.40 E
El Abd	126	Mi	35.29N	0.42 E
El Abiodh Sidi Cheikh	162	Hc	32.53N	0.34 E
El 'Aqâba [3]	162	Ef	16.30N	12.00W
El 'Aqâba	162	Ef	16.49N	12.05W
El Adeb Larache	162	Id	27.22N	8.52 E
El Affroun	126	Oh	36.28N	2.37 E
Elafonisos Channel (EN)= Elafonisou, Stenon-	130	Fm	36.25N	23.00 E
Elafónisos	130	Fm	36.29N	22.58 E
Elafonisou Stenón-= Elafónisi Channel (EN)	130	Fm	36.25N	23.00 E
El Agreb	162	Ic	30.48N	5.30 E
El Aguilar	206	Gb	32.12S	65.42W
El Álamo	192	Ab	31.34N	116.02W
El Alia	162	Ic	32.42N	5.26 E
El Amria	126	Ki	35.32N	1.01W
Elan	130	Lc	46.06N	28.04 E
El Andévalo	126	Fg	37.40N	7.00W
El Aouinet	128	Bo	35.52N	7.54 E
El Arahal	126	Gg	37.16N	5.33W
El Aricha	162	Gc	34.13N	1.16W
Elása	130	Jn	35.17N	26.20 E
Elassón	130	Fj	39.54N	22.11 E
Elat	142	Fg	29.33N	34.57 E
Eláti	130	Dk	38.43N	20.39 E
Elato Atoll	208	Fd	7.28N	146.10 E
El Attaf	126	Nh	36.13N	1.40 E
Elâzığ	144	Eb	38.41N	39.14 E
El Azúcar, Presa de-	192	Jd	26.15N	99.00W
Elba	184	Dj	31.25N	86.04W
Elba	110	Hg	42.45N	10.15 E
Elban	138	If	50.05N	136.30 E
El Banco	202	Db	9.01N	73.58W
El Barco de Ávila	126	Gd	40.21N	5.31W
El Barco de Valdeorras	126	Fb	42.25N	6.59W
Elbasani	130	Dh	41.06N	20.05 E
El Baúl	202	Eb	8.57N	68.17W
El Bayadh	162	Hc	33.41N	1.01 E
Elbe	126	Ge	53.50N	9.00 E
Elbe (EN)=Labe	110	Ge	53.50N	9.00 E
Elbe-Lübeck-Kanal	120	Gc	53.50N	10.36 E
Elbert, Mount-	174	If	39.07N	106.27W
Elberton	184	Fh	34.07N	82.52W
Elbe-Seitenkanal	120	Gd	52.22N	10.34 E
Elbeuf	122	Ge	49.17N	1.00 E
Elbeyl	144	Eb	36.41N	37.26 E
El Bierzo	126	Fb	42.40N	6.50W
Elbistan	146	Gc	38.13N	37.12 E
Elblag	112	He	54.10N	19.25 E
Elbląg [2]	120	Pb	54.10N	19.25 E
Elbląski, Kanał-	120	Pc	53.43N	19.53 E
El Bolsón	206	Ff	41.58S	71.31W
El Bonillo	126	Jf	38.57N	2.32W
Elbow	188	La	51.07N	106.35W
Elbow Cays	194	Gb	23.57N	80.29W
Elbow Lake	186	Id	46.00N	95.58W
Elbrus	110	Kg	43.21N	42.26 E
Elbsandsteingebirge	120	Kf	50.50N	14.12 E
'Ēlbūr	168	He	4.40N	46.40 E
Elburg	122	Lb	52.26N	5.50 E
El Burgo de Osma	126	Ic	41.35N	3.04W
Elburgon	170	Gc	0.18S	35.49 E
El Burro	192	Ic	29.16N	101.55W
Elburz Mountains (EN)= Alborz, Reshteh-ye Kūhhā-ye-	140	Hf	36.00N	53.00 E
El Cajon	182	De	32.48N	116.58W
El Callao	202	Fb	7.21N	61.49W
El Calvario	196	Ch	8.59N	67.00W
El Campo	186	Hl	29.12N	96.16W
El Canelo	192	Ie	24.19N	100.23W
El Cármen	204	Cd	18.49S	58.33W
El Carmen de Bolívar	202	Cb	9.43N	75.07W
El Casco	192	Ge	25.34N	104.35W
El Castillo	194	Eh	11.01N	84.24W
El Centro	182	De	32.48N	115.34W
El Cerro	202	Fg	17.31S	61.34W
El Chaparro	196	Dh	9.10N	65.01W
Elche / Elx	126	Lf	38.15N	0.42W
Elcho Island	212	Hb	11.55S	135.45 E
El Cuy	206	Ge	39.56S	68.20W
Elda	126	Lf	38.29N	0.47W
Ēldab	168	Hd	8.58N	46.38 E
Elde	120	Ic	53.17N	12.40 E
'Ēl Dēre	160	Lh	3.55N	47.10 E
El Dere	168	Gd	5.07N	43.12 E
El Descanso	192	Aa	32.12N	116.55W
El Desemboque	190	Bb	30.30N	112.59W
El Difícil	194	Ji	9.51N	74.14W
Eldikan	138	Id	60.38N	135.07 E
El Djouf	158	Gf	21.25N	6.40W
El Doncello	202	Cc	1.43N	75.17W
Eldorado	186	Fk	30.52N	100.36W
El Dorado	190	Cd	24.17N	107.31W
Eldorado	206	Jc	26.24S	54.38W
El Dorado [Ar.-U.S.]	182	Ie	33.13N	92.40W
El Dorado [Ks.-U.S.]	182	Hd	37.49N	96.52W
El Dorado [Ven.]	200	Je	6.44N	61.38W
Eldorado Paulista	204	Hg	24.32S	48.06W
El Dorado Springs	186	Ih	37.52N	94.01W
Eldoret	170	Gb	0.31N	35.17 E
Eldsberga	116	Eh	56.36N	12.59 E
'Ēl Đubbo	168	Ge	3.52N	44.45 E
Eldžik	135	De	39.25N	63.01 E
Elefantes, Rio dos-	172	Ed	24.03S	32.40 E
El Eglab	158	Gf	26.30N	5.00W
Eleja/Elėja	114	Fh	56.28N	23.41 E
Elėja/Eleja	114	Fh	56.28N	23.41 E
Elektrėnai/Elektrenaj	116	Kj	54.46N	24.47 E
Elektrenaj/Elektrėnai	116	Kj	54.46N	24.47 E
Elektrostal	136	Dd	55.48N	38.29 E
Elele	166	Gd	5.06N	6.49 E
Elena	130	Ig	42.56N	25.53 E
El Encanto [Bol.]	204	Cc	16.57S	59.24W
El Encanto [Col.]	202	Dd	1.37S	73.13W
Elephant Butte Reservoir	186	Cj	33.19N	107.10W
Elephant Island	222	Re	61.10S	55.14W
Elephant Mountain	186	Ek	30.02N	103.30W
Elesbão Veloso	202	Je	6.13S	42.08W
El Escorial	126	Hd	40.35N	4.10W
Eleşkirt	146	Jc	39.49N	42.40 E
El Estor	194	Cf	15.32N	89.21W
Eleuthera	174	Lg	25.15N	76.20W
Elevsis	130	Gk	38.02N	23.32 E
Elevtheroúpolis	130	Hi	40.55N	24.15 E
El Fendek	126	Gi	35.34N	5.35W
El Ferrol	126	Da	43.29N	8.14W
El Fud	168	Gd	7.15N	42.51 E
El Fuerte [Mex.]	192	Hf	23.50N	103.06W
El Fuerte [Mex.]	190	Cc	26.25N	108.39W
Elgåhogna	116	Eb	62.09N	12.04 E
'Ēl Gāl	168	Ic	11.23N	50.23 E
El Galhak	168	Ec	11.03N	32.42 E
El Gassi	162	Ic	30.55N	5.50 E
Elgen	138	Kd	62.45N	150.40 E
Elgepiggen	114	Ce	62.10N	11.22 E
El Ghomri	126	Mi	35.41N	0.12 E
Elgi	138	Jd	64.20N	142.05 E
Elgin [Il.-U.S.]	182	Jc	42.02N	88.17W
Elgin [N.D.-U.S.]	186	Fc	46.24N	101.51W
Elgin [Or.-U.S.]	188	Gd	45.34N	117.55W
Elgin [Scot.-U.K.]	118	Jd	57.39N	3.20W
Elginski	138	Jd	64.48N	141.50 E
Elgjaij	138	Gd	62.28N	117.37 E
El Goléa	160	He	30.34N	2.53 E
Elgon, Mont-	158	Kh	1.08N	34.33 E
Elgoran	168	Gd	5.04N	44.22 E
El Grao, Castellón de la Plana-	126	Me	39.58N	0.01 E
El Grao, Valencia-	126	Le	39.27N	0.20W
El Grao de Gandia, Gandia-	126	Lf	38.59N	0.09W
El Guapo	196	Dg	10.09N	65.58W
El Guayabo	194	Ki	8.37N	72.20W
El Hadjar	128	Bn	36.48N	7.45 E
El Hajeb	162	Fc	33.42N	5.22W
El Ham	126	Qi	35.42N	4.52 E
El Hammam	126	Li	35.50N	0.15W

Index Symbols

- [1] Independent Nation
- [2] State, Region
- [3] District, County
- [4] Municipality
- [5] Colony, Dependency
- Continent
- Physical Region
- Historical or Cultural Region
- Mount, Mountain
- Volcano
- Hill
- Mountains, Mountain Range
- Hills, Escarpment
- Plateau, Upland
- Pass, Gap
- Plain, Lowland
- Delta
- Salt Flat
- Valley, Canyon
- Crater, Cave
- Karst Features
- Depression
- Polder
- Desert, Dunes
- Forest, Woods
- Heath, Steppe
- Oasis
- Cape, Point
- Coast, Beach
- Cliff
- Peninsula
- Isthmus
- Sandbank
- Island
- Atoll
- Rock, Reef
- Islands, Archipelago
- Rocks, Reefs
- Coral Reef
- Well, Spring
- Geyser
- River, Stream
- Waterfall, Rapids
- River Mouth, Estuary
- Lake
- Salt Lake
- Intermittent Lake
- Reservoir
- Swamp, Pond
- Canal
- Glacier
- Ice Shelf, Pack Ice
- Ocean
- Sea
- Gulf, Bay
- Strait, Fjord
- Lagoon
- Bank
- Seamount
- Tablemount
- Ridge
- Shelf
- Basin
- Escarpment, Sea Scarp
- Fracture
- Trench, Abyss
- National Park, Reserve
- Point of Interest
- Recreation Site
- Cave, Cavern
- Historic Site
- Ruins
- Wall, Walls
- Church, Abbey
- Temple
- Scientific Station
- Railway station
- Airport
- Port
- Military installation
- Lighthouse
- Mine
- Tunnel
- Dam, Bridge

'Ēl Ḩamurre 168 Hd 7.11N 48.55 E
El Hank 158 Gf 24.00N 6.30W
El Harrach, Al Jazā'ir- 126 Ph 36.43N 3.08 E
Elhotovo 132 Nh 43.20N 44.13 E
Elhovo 130 Jg 42.10N 26.34 E
El Huecú 206 Fe 37.37S 70.36W
Elida 186 Ej 33.57N 103.39W
Éliki, Vallée d'- 166 Gc 14.45N 7.15 E
Elila 170 Ec 2.43S 25.53 E
Elila 158 Ji 2.45S 25.53 E
Elimäki 116 Ld 60.43N 26.28 E
Elin Pelin 130 Gg 42.40N 23.36 E
Elisejna 130 Gf 43.05N 23.29 E
Elisenvaara 116 Mc 61.19N 29.47 E
Elista 112 Kf 46.16N 44.14 E
Elizabeth [Austl.] 210 Eh 34.45S 138.39 E
Elizabeth [N.J.-U.S.] 184 Je 40.40N 74.13W
Elizabeth, Cape- 188 Cc 47.22N 124.22W
Elizabeth City 182 Ld 36.18N 76.14W
Elizabeth Reef 208 Gg 29.55S 159.05 E
Elizabethton 184 Fg 36.21N 82.13W
Elizabethtown [Ky.-U.S.] 184 Eg 37.42N 85.52W
Elizabethtown [N.C.-U.S.] 184 Hh 34.38N 78.37W
El Jadida 160 Ge 33.15N 8.30W
El Jadida [3] 162 Fc 32.54N 8.30W
El Jicaro 194 Dg 13.43N 86.08W
'Ēl Jilib 168 He 3.48N 47.07 E
Elk 120 Sc 53.50N 22.22 E
Ełk 120 Sc 53.32N 22.47 E
El Kala 162 Ib 36.54N 8.27 E
El Kantara 162 Ib 35.13N 5.43 E
El Karimia 126 Nh 36.07N 1.33 E
Elk City [Id.-U.S.] 182 Hd 45.51N 115.29W
Elk City [Ok.-U.S.] 186 Gi 35.25N 99.25W
El Kelaa des Srarhna 162 Fc 32.03N 7.24W
El Kelaa des Srarhna [3] 162 Fc 32.03N 7.30W
El Kere 168 Gd 5.51N 42.06 E
Elkhart [In.-U.S.] 182 Jc 41.41N 85.58W
Elkhart [Ks.-U.S.] 186 Fh 37.00N 101.54W
El Khatt 162 Ef 19.00N 12.25W
Elkhead Mountains 186 Cf 40.50N 107.05W
El Khnâchîch 166 Ea 21.20N 3.45W
Elkhorn River 186 Hf 41.07N 96.19W
Elkins 184 Hf 38.56N 79.53W
Elk Lake 184 Gb 47.42N 80.11W
Elk Mountain 188 Lf 41.38N 106.32W
Elk Mountains 186 Cg 38.55N 106.50W
Elko 176 He 40.50N 115.46W
Elk Peak 188 Jc 46.27N 110.46W
Elk River 186 Jd 45.18N 93.35W
Elk River 184 Gf 38.21N 81.38W
Elku kalns 116 Kg 57.04N 25.23 E
Ell, Lake- 212 Fe 29.15S 127.45 E
Ellás=Greece (EN) [1] 112 Ih 39.00N 22.00 E
Ellé 122 Cg 47.52N 3.32W
Ellef Ringneu 174 Ib 78.30N 104.00W
Ellen, Mount- 182 Ed 38.07N 110.49W
Ellendale 182 Hb 46.06N 98.32W
Ellensburg 182 Cb 46.40N 120.32W
Ellenville 184 Je 41.43N 74.23W
Ellesmere 174 Kb 79.00N 82.00W
Ellesmere, Lake- 218 Ee 43.45S 172.30 E
Ellice 180 Hc 68.02N 103.25W
Ellice Islands → Tuvalu [1] 210 Ie 8.00S 178.00 E
Elliot [Austl.] 212 Gc 17.35S 133.35 E
Elliot [S.Afr.] 172 Df 31.18S 27.50 E
Elliot, Mount- 212 Jc 19.29S 146.58 E
Elliot Lake 180 Jg 46.23N 82.39W
Ellisras 172 Dd 23.40S 27.46 E
Elliston 212 Gf 33.39S 134.55 E
Ellisville 186 Lk 31.36N 89.12W
Ellmau 128 Gc 47.31N 12.18 E
Ellös 114 Cg 58.11N 11.27 E
Ellsworth [Ks.-U.S.] 186 Gg 38.44N 98.14W
Ellsworth [Me.-U.S.] 184 Mc 44.33N 68.26W
Ellsworth [Nb.-U.S.] 186 Ee 42.04N 102.15W
Ellsworth, Lake- 186 Gi 34.48N 98.20W
Ellsworth Land (EN) 222 Pf 75.30S 80.00W
Ellsworth Mountains 222 Pf 78.30S 85.00W
Ellwangen (Jagst) 120 Gh 48.57N 10.08 E
Elm 120 Gd 52.09N 10.53 E
El Macao 194 Md 18.46N 68.33W
Elmadağ 146 Ec 39.55N 33.15 E
Elma Dağı 130 Mk 38.46N 29.32 E
El Maestrat/El Maestrazgo 126 Ld 40.30N 0.10W
El Maestrazgo/El Maestrat 126 Ld 40.30N 0.10W
El Mahia 166 Ea 22.30N 2.30W
El Maitén 206 Ff 42.03S 71.10W
Elmaki 166 Gb 17.55N 8.20 E
El Malah 126 Ph 36.18N 3.14 E
Elmali 146 Cd 36.44N 29.56 E
Elmalı 146 Ic 39.25N 40.35 E
El Manteco 196 Ei 7.27N 62.32W
El Marfil 204 Bb 15.35S 60.19W
El Marsa 126 Mh 36.24N 0.55 E
El Medo 168 Gd 5.41N 41.46 E
El Meghaïer 162 Ic 33.57N 5.56 E
Elmhurst 186 Mf 41.53N 87.56W
El Milagro 206 Gd 31.01S 65.59W
Elmira 182 Lc 42.06N 76.50W
El Mrâyer 162 Fe 21.30N 8.10W
El Mreiti 162 Fe 23.29N 7.52W
El Mreyyé 158 Gg 19.30N 7.00W
Elmshorn 120 Fc 53.45N 9.39 E
Elmstein 124 Je 49.22N 7.56 E
Elne 122 Il 42.36N 2.58 E
El Nevado, Cerro- 206 Ge 35.35S 68.30W
El Niabo 168 Fe 4.33N 39.59 E
El Nihuil 206 Gd 34.58S 68.40W
El Novillo 192 Ec 28.40N 109.30W
El Novillo, Presa- 192 Ec 29.05N 109.45W
El Ochenta y Uno 192 Kg 21.35N 97.57W
Elorn 122 Bf 48.27N 4.16W
Elortondo 204 Bk 33.42S 61.37W
Elorza 202 Eb 7.03N 69.31W
Elota, Rio- 192 Ff 23.52N 106.56W
El Oued 162 Ic 33.20N 6.53 E
Eloy 188 Jj 32.45N 111.33W
El Palmar 196 Fh 8.01N 61.53W
El Palmito 192 Ge 25.40N 104.59W
El Panadés/El Penedès 126 Nc 41.25N 1.30 E
El Pao [Ven.] 196 Eh 8.06N 62.33W
El Pao [Ven.] 196 Bh 9.38N 68.08W
El Paraiso 194 Dg 13.51N 86.34W
El Paraiso [3] 194 Df 14.10N 86.30W
El Páramo 126 Gb 42.25N 5.45W
El Pardo, Madrid- 126 Id 40.32N 3.46W
El Paso [Il.-U.S.] 186 Lf 40.44N 89.01W
El Paso [Tx.-U.S.] 176 If 31.45N 106.29W
El Penedès/El Panadés 126 Nc 41.25N 1.30 E
El Perú 196 Fi 7.19N 61.49W
El Pico 202 Fg 15.57S 64.42W
El Pilar 196 Eg 10.32N 63.09W
El Pintado 206 Hb 24.38S 61.27W
El Port / Puerto de Sóller 126 Oe 39.48N 2.41 E
El Porvenir [Hond.] 194 Df 14.41N 87.11W
El Porvenir [Pan.] 194 Hi 9.12N 80.08W
El Porvenir [Ven.] 196 Bi 6.55N 68.42W
El Potosí 192 Ie 24.51N 100.19W
el Prat de Llobregat / Prat de Llobregat 126 Oc 41.20N 2.06 E
El Priorat/El Priorato 126 Mc 41.10N 1.00 E
El Priorato/El Priorat 126 Mc 41.10N 1.00 E
El Progreso [3] 194 Cf 14.50N 90.00W
El Progreso [Guat.] 194 Bf 14.51N 90.04W
El Progreso [Hond.] 190 Ge 15.21N 87.49W
El Puente del Arzobispo 126 Ge 39.48N 5.10W
El Puerto 192 Dc 28.45N 111.20W
El Puerto de Santa María 126 Fh 36.36N 6.13W
El Rastro 196 Ch 9.03N 67.27W
El Real de Santa María 194 Ii 8.08N 77.43W
El Reno 182 Hd 35.32N 97.57W
El Ribeiro 126 Db 42.25N 8.10W
Elrose 188 Ka 51.13N 108.01W
El Saler 126 Le 39.23N 0.20W
El Salto 190 Cd 23.47N 105.23W
El Salvador [1] 176 Kh 13.50N 88.55W
El Samán de Apure 196 Bi 7.55N 68.44W
El Sauce [Mex.] 192 De 24.34N 111.29W
El Sauce [Nic.] 194 Dg 12.53N 86.32W
El Sauz 192 Fc 29.03N 106.15W
Elsberry 186 Kg 39.10N 90.47W
Elsdorf 124 Id 50.56N 6.34 E
Else 124 Kb 52.12N 8.40 E
El Seibo 194 Md 18.46N 68.52W
Elsen, Paderborn- 124 Kc 51.44N 8.41 E
Elsen Nur 152 Fd 35.08N 92.20 E
'Ēl Shāma 168 Ge 2.46N 41.03 E
El Socorro 196 Dh 8.59N 65.44W
El Sombrero 202 Eb 9.23N 67.03W
Elst 126 Hc 51.55N 5.52 E
Elsterwerda 120 Je 51.27N 13.32 E
El Sueco 190 Cc 29.54N 106.24W
El Taht 126 Mi 35.27N 0.46 E
El Tala 206 Gc 26.07S 65.17W
Eltanin Bay 222 Pf 73.40S 82.00W
Eltham 218 Fc 39.26S 174.18 E
El Tigre 200 Je 8.55N 64.15W
El Tigre, Isla- 194 Dg 13.16N 87.38W
El Toboso 126 Je 39.31N 3.00W
El Tocuyo 202 Eb 9.47N 69.48W
Elton 136 Oe 49.08N 46.50 E
Elton, ozero- 136 Ef 49.10N 46.40 E
El Torcal 126 Hh 36.55N 4.35W
El Toro / Toro, Monte- 126 Qe 39.59N 4.07 E
El Trébol 204 Bk 32.12S 61.42W
El Trigo 206 Cl 35.52S 59.24W
El Triunfo [Hond.] 194 Dg 13.06N 87.00W
El Triunfo [Mex.] 192 Df 23.47N 110.08W
El Tuito 192 Gg 20.19N 105.22W
El Turbio 206 Fh 51.41S 72.05W
Eltville am Rhein 124 Kd 50.02N 8.07 E
Eltz 124 Jd 50.12N 7.18 E
Elūru 148 Ge 17.05N 82.15 E
Elva 114 Gg 58.13N 26.25 E
El Valle 194 Gi 8.31N 80.08W
El Vallés / El Vallès 126 Oc 41.35N 2.15 E
Elvas 126 Ef 38.53N 7.10W
El Vejo, Cerro- 202 Db 7.30N 73.05W
El Venado, Isla- 194 Fh 11.57N 83.44W
Elverum 114 Cf 60.53N 11.34 E
El Viejo 194 Dg 12.40N 87.10W
El Viejo, Volcán- 174 Kh 12.38N 87.11W
El Vigía 194 Li 8.38N 71.39W
El Vigía, Cerro- 192 Gg 21.25N 104.00W
El Wak 170 Hb 2.49N 40.56 E
Elwell, Lake- 188 Jb 48.22N 111.17W
Elwood 184 Ee 40.17N 85.50W
Elx / Elche 126 Lf 38.15N 0.42W
Ely [Eng.-U.K.] 118 Ni 52.24N 0.16 E
Ely [Mn.-U.S.] 182 Ib 47.54N 91.51W
Ely [Nv.-U.S.] 176 Hf 39.15N 114.53W
Elyria 184 Fe 41.22N 82.06W
El Yunque 197a Cb 18.18N 65.47W
Elz 124 Kd 50.25N 8.02 E
Elzbach 124 Jd 50.12N 7.22 E
Emaé 219b Dc 17.04S 168.22 E
Ema jõgi / Emajygi 116 Lf 58.20N 27.15 E
Emajygi / Ema jõgi 116 Lf 58.20N 27.15 E
Emali 170 Gc 2.05S 37.28 E
Emāmshahr [Iran] 144 Hb 36.50N 54.29 E
Emāmshahr [Iran] 146 Ib 36.25N 55.01 E
Emāmzādeh 'Abbās 146 Lf 32.25N 47.55 E
Emān 114 Dh 57.08N 16.30 E
Emba 174 Ff 48.50N 58.10 E
Emba 110 Lf 46.38N 53.04 E
Embarcaí, Rio- 204 Ff 23.27S 53.58W
Embarcación 206 Hb 23.13S 64.06W
Embarras Portage 180 Ge 58.25N 111.28W
Embarras River 186 Mg 38.39N 87.37W
Embrun 122 Mj 44.34N 6.30 E
Embu 170 Gc 0.32S 37.27 E
Emden 120 Dc 53.22N 7.13 E
Emeldžak 138 He 58.27N 126.57 E
Emerald 210 Fg 23.32S 148.10 E
Emerald 180 Ga 76.50N 114.00W
Emerson 186 Hb 49.00N 97.12W
Emet 146 Cc 39.20N 29.15 E
Emi Koussi 158 Ig 19.55N 18.30 E
Emiliano Zapata 192 Ni 17.45N 91.46W
Emilia-Romagna [2] 128 Ef 44.45N 11.00 E
Emilio R. Coni 204 Cj 30.04S 58.16W
Emily Rocu 198 Hh 29.40S 87.25W
Emin/Dorbiljin 152 Db 46.32N 83.39 E
Emine, Nos- 130 Kg 42.42N 27.54 E
Emirau Island 214 Dh 1.40S 150.00 E
Emirdağ 146 Dc 39.01N 31.10 E
Emisu, Tarso- 158 If 21.13N 18.32 E
Emlichheim 120 Cd 52.37N 6.51 E
Emmaboda 114 Dh 56.38N 15.32 E
Emmaste 114 Fg 58.43N 22.36 E
Emme 128 Bd 47.10N 7.35 E
Emmeloord, Noordoostpolder- 124 Hb 52.42N 5.44 E
Emmelshausen 124 Jd 50.09N 7.34 E
Emmen 122 Mb 52.47N 6.55 E
Emmendingen 120 Dh 48.08N 7.51 E
Emmen-Emmer-Compascuum 124 Jb 52.49N 7.03 E
Emmen-Klazienaveen 124 Jb 52.44N 7.01 E
Emmen-Nieuw-Weerdinge 124 Jb 52.52N 7.01 E
Emmental 128 Bd 46.55N 7.45 E
Emmen-Weerdinge 124 Ib 52.49N 6.57 E
Emmer 124 Lb 52.03N 9.23 E
Emmer-Compascuum, Emmen- 124 Jb 52.49N 7.03 E
Emmerich 120 Ce 51.50N 6.15 E
Emmet 212 Id 24.40S 144.28 E
Emmetsburg 186 Ie 43.07N 94.41W
Emmett 188 Ge 43.52N 116.30W
Emmonak 178 Gd 62.46N 164.30W
Emőd 120 Qi 47.56N 20.49 E
Emory 188 Jf 41.05N 111.16W
Emory Peak 182 Gf 29.13N 103.17W
Empalme 190 Bc 27.58N 110.51W
Empangeni 172 Ee 28.50S 31.48 E
Empedrado 206 Ii 27.57S 58.48W
Emperor Seamounts (EN) 106 Je 40.00N 171.00 E
Empoli 128 Eg 43.43N 10.57 E
Empordà / Ampurdán 126 Ob 42.12N 2.45 E
Emporia [Ks.-U.S.] 182 Hd 38.24N 96.11W
Emporia [Va.-U.S.] 184 Ig 36.42N 77.33W
Emporium 184 Hd 41.31N 78.14W
Empress Augusta Bay 219a Bb 6.25S 155.05 E
Empress Mine 172 Dc 18.27S 29.27 E
Empúries / Ampurias 126 Pb 42.10N 3.05 E
Ems 122 Na 53.19N 7.03 E
Emsbach 124 Kd 50.24N 8.06 E
Emsdetten 120 Dd 52.11N 7.32 E
Ems-Jade-Kanal 120 Dc 53.30N 7.30 E
Emsland 120 Dd 52.50N 7.20 E
Emstek 124 Kb 52.50N 8.09 E
Emumägi/Emumjagi 116 Lf 58.54N 26.23 E
Emumjagi/Emumägi 116 Lf 58.54N 26.23 E
Ena 156 Ed 35.27N 137.24 E
Enånger 114 Df 61.32N 17.00 E
Enaratoli 150 Kg 3.55S 136.21 E
Enard Bay 118 Hc 58.06N 5.20W
Ena-San 156 Ed 35.26N 137.36 E
Enbetsu 154 Pb 44.44N 141.47 E
Encantada, Cerro de la- 174 Hf 31.00N 115.23W
Encantada, Sierra de la- 192 Hc 28.30N 102.20W
Encantadas, Serra das- 204 Fj 30.40S 53.00W
Encantado, Cerro- 190 Bc 27.03N 112.30W
Encarnación 200 Kh 27.20S 55.54W
Encarnación de Díaz 192 Hg 21.31N 102.14W
Enchi 166 Ed 5.49N 2.49W
Encinal 186 Gl 28.02N 99.21W
Encinasola 126 Ff 38.08N 6.52W
Encontrados 202 Db 8.46N 72.30W
Encounter Bay 212 Hg 35.35S 138.45 E
Encrucijada 194 Hb 22.37N 79.52W
Encruzilhada do Sul 204 Fj 30.32S 52.31W
Encs 120 Rh 48.20N 21.08 E
Ende 142 Oj 8.50S 121.39 E
Endeavour Strait 212 Ib 10.50S 142.15 E
Endelave 116 Di 55.45N 10.15 E
Enderbury Atoll 208 Je 3.08S 171.05W
Enderby 188 Fa 50.33N 119.08W
Enderby Land 222 Ee 67.30S 53.00 E
Endicott Mountains 178 Ic 67.50N 152.00W
Ené, Rio- 202 Df 11.09S 74.19W
Energetik 136 Fe 51.44N 58.48 E
Enewetak Atoll 208 Hc 11.30N 162.15 E
Enez 146 Bb 40.44N 26.04 E
Enez Körfezi 130 Ii 40.45N 26.00 E
Enfer, Pointe d'- 197h Bc 14.24N 60.52W
Enfer, Portes d'- 170 Ed 5.05S 27.30 E
Enfield 184 Ig 36.11N 77.47W
Enfield, London- 124 Bc 51.40N 0.04W
Engadin/Engiadin'ota/Engadina 128 Dd 46.35N 10.00 E
Engadina/Engadin/Engiadin'ota 128 Dd 46.35N 10.00 E
Engaño, Cabo- 190 Ke 18.37N 68.20W
Engaru 154 Qb 44.03N 143.31 E
Engelberg 128 Cd 46.50N 8.24 E
Engelhard 184 Jh 35.31N 76.00W
Engels 112 Ke 51.30N 46.07 E
Engelskirchen 124 Jd 50.59N 7.24 E
Engenho 204 Db 15.10S 56.25W
Enger 124 Kb 52.08N 8.34 E
Engeren 116 Ec 61.35N 12.05 E
Engershatu 168 Fb 16.34N 38.15 E
Enggano, Pulau- 140 Mj 5.24S 102.16 E
Enghien/Edingen 124 Gd 50.42N 4.02 E
Engiadin'ota/Engadina/Engadin 128 Dd 46.35N 10.00 E
England [2] 118 Li 52.30N 1.30W
England 110 Fe 52.30N 1.30W
Englehart 180 Jg 47.49N 79.52W
Englewood 186 Dg 39.39N 104.59W
English 184 Df 38.20N 86.28W
English Channel 110 Fe 50.20N 1.00W
English Channel (EN)=La Manche 110 Fe 50.20N 1.00W
English Coast 222 Qf 73.30S 73.00W
English River 186 Kb 49.13N 90.58W
English River 186 Ia 50.12N 95.00W
Engozero, ozero- 114 Hd 65.45N 33.30 E
Énguera 126 Lf 38.59N 0.41W
Engure/Engures 116 Jg 57.09N 23.06 E
Engures/Engure 116 Jg 57.09N 23.06 E
Engures, ozero- / Engures ezers 116 Jg 57.15N 23.10 E
Engures ezers / Engures, ozero- 116 Jg 57.15N 23.10 E
Enh-Gajvan 152 Gb 48.05N 97.35 E
Enid 176 Jf 36.19N 97.48W
Enid Lake 186 Li 34.10N 89.50W
Eniwa 154 Pc 42.53N 141.14 E
Eniwa-Dake 156a Bb 42.47N 141.17 E
Enkenbach-Alsenborn 124 Je 49.29N 7.53 E
Enkhuizen 122 Lb 52.42N 5.17 E
Enklinge 116 Id 60.20N 20.45 E
Enköping 114 Dg 59.38N 17.04 E
Enna 128 Im 37.34N 14.16 E
Ennadai 180 Hd 61.10N 101.00W
Ennadai Lake 180 Hd 60.55N 101.20W
Enné 168 Bc 14.24N 18.45 E
Ennedi 158 Jg 17.15N 22.00 E
Ennell, Lough-/Loch Ainninn 118 Fh 53.28N 7.24W
Ennepetal 124 Jc 51.18N 7.21 E
Ennigerloh 124 Kc 51.50N 8.01 E
Enning 186 Ed 44.37N 102.31W
Ennis [Mt.-U.S.] 188 Jd 45.21N 111.44W
Ennis [Tx.-U.S.] 186 Hj 32.20N 96.38W
Ennis/Inis 118 Ei 52.50N 8.59W
Enniscorthy/Inis Córthaidh 118 Gi 52.30N 6.34W
Enniskillen/Inis Ceithleann 118 Fg 54.21N 7.38W
Ennistimon / Inis Diomáin 118 Di 52.57N 9.13W
Enns 128 Ib 48.12N 14.28 E
Enns 110 Hf 48.14N 14.30 E
Enstaler Alpen 128 Ic 47.37N 14.35 E
Eno 114 He 62.48N 30.09 E
Enontekiö 114 Fb 68.23N 23.38 E
Enonvesi [Fin.] 116 Lc 61.20N 26.30 E
Enonvesi [Fin.] 116 Mb 62.10N 28.55 E
Enozero, ozero- 114 Jb 68.10N 38.00 E
Enrekang 150 Gg 3.34S 119.47 E
Enrique Carbó 204 Ck 33.08S 59.14W
Enriquillo 194 Le 17.54N 71.14W
Enriquillo, Lago- 190 Je 18.27N 71.39W
Enschede 122 Mb 52.12N 6.53 E
Ensenada [Arg.] 204 Dl 34.51S 57.55W
Ensenada [Mex.] 176 Hf 31.52N 116.37W
Enshi 152 Ie 30.16N 109.26 E
Enshū-Nada 156 Ed 34.30N 138.00 E
Entebbe 160 Kh 0.04N 32.28 E
Entenbühl 120 Ig 49.46N 12.24 E
Enterprise [Al.-U.S.] 184 Ej 31.19N 85.51W
Enterprise [N.W.T.-Can.] 180 Fd 60.39N 116.08W
Enterprise [Or.-U.S.] 188 Gd 45.25N 117.17W
Entinas, Punta- 126 Jh 36.41N 2.46W
Entrada, Punta- 190 Ab 30.22N 115.59W
Entraygues-sur-Truyère 122 Ij 44.39N 2.34 E
Entrecasteaux, Récifs d'- = D'Entrecasteaux Reefs (EN) 208 Hf 18.20S 163.00 E
Entrepeñas, Embalse de- 126 Jd 40.34N 2.42W
Entre Rios 202 Fh 21.32S 64.12W
Entre Rios [2] 206 Id 32.00S 59.00W
Entre Rios de Minas 204 Je 20.41S 44.04W
Entrevaux 122 Mk 43.57N 6.49 E
Entroncamento 126 De 39.28N 8.28W
Enugu 160 Hh 6.26N 7.29 E
Enugu Ezike 166 Gd 6.59N 7.27 E
Envermeu 124 De 49.54N 1.16 E
Envigado 202 Cb 6.08N 75.39W
Envira 202 De 7.18S 70.13W
Envira, Rio- 202 De 7.19S 70.15W
Enyamba 170 Dc 3.40S 24.58 E
Enyélé 170 Cb 2.49N 18.06 E
Enz 120 Fh 49.00N 9.10 E
Enza 128 Ef 44.54N 10.31 E
Enzan 154 Og 34.52N 138.44 E
Enzgau 124 Kf 48.48N 8.37 E
Eo 126 Ea 43.28N 7.03W
Eochaill/Youghal 118 Fj 51.57N 7.50W
Eolie o Lipari, Isole-=Lipari Islands (EN) 110 Hh 38.35N 14.55 E
Epanomi 130 Fi 40.26N 22.56 E
Epazote, Cerro- 190 Cd 24.35N 105.07W
Epe [Neth.] 124 Hb 52.21N 5.59 E
Epe [Nig.] 166 Fd 6.35N 3.59 E
Epéna 170 Cb 1.22N 17.29 E
Épernay 122 Je 49.03N 3.57 E
Epe-Vaassen 124 Hb 52.17N 5.58 E
Ephesus (EN)=Efes 130 Kl 37.55N 27.20 E
Ephraim 188 Jg 39.22N 111.35W
Ephrata 188 Fc 47.19N 119.33W
Epi, Ile- 208 Hf 16.43S 168.15 E
Epidamnus 130 Ch 41.19N 19.26 E
Epidaurus (EN) = Epidhavros 130 Gl 37.38N 23.09 E
Epidhavros = Epidaurus (EN) 130 Gl 37.38N 23.09 E
Épila 126 Kc 41.36N 1.17W
Épinal 122 Mf 48.11N 6.27 E
Epirus (EN)=Ipiros 110 Ih 39.30N 20.40 E
Epirus (EN)=Ipiros 130 Dj 39.30N 20.40 E
Episkopi 146 Ee 34.40N 32.54 E
Eppelheim 124 Ke 49.24N 8.38 E
Epping 124 Cc 51.42N 0.07 E
Eppingen 124 Ke 49.08N 8.54 E
Epsom 118 Mj 51.20N 0.16W
Epte 122 He 49.04N 1.31 E
Epukiro 172 Bd 21.41S 19.08 E
Epukiro 172 Bd 21.28S 19.59 E
Epulu 170 Eb 1.15N 28.21 E
Eqlīd 144 Hc 30.55N 52.39 E
Équateur = Equator (EN) 170 Eb 1.00N 20.00 E
Equator (EN)=Équateur [2] 170 Eb 1.00N 20.00 E
Equatorial Guinea (EN)= Guinea Ecuatorial [1] 160 Hh 2.00N 9.00 E
Equinox Mountain 184 Kd 43.15N 73.10W
Era [It.] 128 Eg 43.40N 10.38 E
Era [Sud.] 168 Dd 5.30N 29.50 E
Eraclea 128 Kj 40.15N 16.40 E
Eraclea Minoa 128 Hm 37.25N 13.18 E
Eradaka 219b Dc 17.39S 168.08 E
Eräjärvi 116 Kc 61.35N 24.34 E
Eratini 130 Fk 38.22N 22.14 E
Erbaa 146 Kb 40.42N 36.36 E
Erbach 120 Eg 49.39N 9.00 E
Erbeskopf 120 Dg 49.44N 7.05 E
Erbil 142 Gf 36.11N 44.01 E
Erbil [3] 146 Je 36.10N 44.00 E
Ercek 146 Jc 38.39N 43.36 E
Erçek Gölü 146 Jc 38.39N 43.32 E
Erciş 146 Jc 39.00N 43.19 E
Erciyas Dağı 140 Ff 38.32N 35.28 E
Ercolano 128 Ij 40.48N 14.21 E
Ercsi 120 Oi 47.15N 18.54 E
Érd 120 Oi 47.22N 18.56 E
Erdaobaihe 152 Mc 42.28N 128.05 E
Erdao Jiang 154 Ic 42.35N 127.10 E
Erdek 146 Bb 40.24N 27.48 E
Erdek Körfezi 146 Bb 40.25N 27.45 E
Erdemli 146 Fd 36.37N 34.18 E
Erdene-Cagan 152 Kb 45.55N 115.30 E
Erdene-Dalaj 152 Hb 46.02N 104.55 E
Erdene-Mandal 152 Hb 48.30N 101.21 E
Erdi 158 Jg 19.05N 22.40 E
Erdi Ma 168 Cb 18.35N 23.30 E
Erding 120 Hh 48.18N 11.56 E
Erdinger Moos 120 Hh 48.20N 11.50 E
Erdre 122 Eg 47.13N 1.32W
Erebus, Mount- 222 Kf 77.32S 167.09 E
Erechim 206 Jc 27.38S 52.17W
Ereğli [Tur.] 144 Db 37.31N 34.04 E
Ereğli [Tur.] 144 Da 41.17N 31.25 E
Erei, Monti- 128 Im 37.35N 14.20 E
Ereke 150 Hg 4.45S 123.10 E
Eren 146 Dd 37.25N 30.05 E
Erenhot 142 Ne 43.35N 112.00 E
Erepecu, Lago do- 202 Gd 1.20S 56.35W
Eresma 126 Hc 41.26N 4.45W
Erétria 130 Gk 38.25N 23.48 E
Erfelek 146 Fb 41.55N 34.57 E
Erfengshan 154 Ag 35.50N 111.47 E
Erfoud 162 Gc 31.26N 4.14W
Erft 120 Ce 51.11N 6.44 E
Erftstadt 124 Id 50.48N 6.49 E
Erfurt 112 He 50.59N 11.02 E
Erfurt [2] 120 Gf 51.00N 11.00 E
Ergani 146 Hc 38.17N 39.46 E
Ergene 146 Bb 41.01N 26.22 E
Erges 126 Ee 39.40N 7.01W
Ergig, Bahr- 168 Bc 11.22N 15.24 E
Ergli/Ērgļi 114 Fh 56.55N 25.41 E
Ērgļi/Ergli 114 Fh 56.55N 25.41 E
Ergun He 140 Od 53.20N 121.28 E
Ergun Youqi (Labudalin) 152 La 50.16N 120.09 E
Ergun Zuoqi (Genhe) 142 Od 50.47N 121.32 E
Er Hai 152 Ff 25.45N 100.10 E
Eria 126 Gb 42.03N 5.44W
Eriba 168 Fb 16.37N 36.04 E
Eriboll, Loch- 118 Ic 58.30N 4.40W
Eric 180 Kf 51.52N 65.45W
Erice 128 Gl 38.02N 12.35 E
Ericeira 126 Cf 38.59N 9.25W
Erichsen Lake 180 Jb 70.38N 80.20W
Ericht, Loch- 118 Ie 56.50N 4.25W
Erick 186 Gi 35.13N 99.52W
Eridu 146 Lg 36.00N 44.00 E
Erie 176 Ke 42.08N 80.04W
Erie, Lake- 174 Ke 42.15N 81.00W
'Erigābo 168 Hc 10.37N 47.24 E
Erîgât 158 Gg 19.40N 4.50W
Erikoússa 130 Cj 39.53N 19.35 E
Eriksdale 186 Ga 50.52N 98.06W
Eriksenstretet 179 Oc 79.00N 26.00 E
Erikub Atoll 208 Id 9.08N 170.02 E
Erimanthos Óros 130 El 37.58N 21.48 E
Erimo-Misaki 152 Pc 41.55N 143.15 E
Eriskay 118 Fd 57.04N 7.13W
Eritrea [3] 168 Fb 15.00N 39.00 E
Eritrea 158 Kg 15.00N 40.00 E
Eritrea 168 Fb 15.00N 40.00 E
Erjas 126 Ee 39.40N 7.01W
Erkelenz 124 Ic 51.05N 6.19 E
Erken 116 He 59.50N 18.35 E
Erkowit 168 Fb 18.46N 37.07 E
Erlangdian → Dawu 154 Ci 31.33N 114.07 E
Erlangen 120 Hg 49.36N 11.01 E
Erlang Shan 152 Hf 29.58N 102.20 E
Erlauf 128 Jb 48.12N 15.11 E
Erldunda 212 Ge 25.14S 133.12 E
Erlenbach 124 Ke 49.07N 8.11 E
Erlong Shan 152 Mc 43.30N 128.44 E
Ermelo [Neth.] 124 Hb 52.19N 5.37 E
Ermelo [S.Afr.] 172 De 26.34S 29.58 E
Ermenek 146 Ed 36.38N 32.54 E
Ermenistan=Armenia (EN) 140 Gf 39.10N 43.00 E
Ermenistan=Armenia (EN) 144 Fb 39.10N 43.00 E
Ermenonville 124 Ee 49.08N 2.42 E
Ermesinde 126 Dc 41.13N 8.33W
Ermoúpolis 130 Hl 37.27N 24.56 E
Erndtebrück 124 Kd 50.59N 8.16 E
Erne/An Éirne 118 Eg 54.30N 8.15W
Ernée 122 Ff 48.18N 0.56W
Ernest Legouvé Reef 208 Lh 35.12S 150.35W

Index Symbols

[1] Independent Nation
[2] State, Region
[3] District, County
[4] Municipality
[5] Colony, Dependency
Continent
Physical Region
Historical or Cultural Region
Mount, Mountain
Volcano
Hill
Mountains, Mountain Range
Hills, Escarpment
Plateau, Upland
Pass, Gap
Plain, Lowland
Delta
Salt Flat
Valley, Canyon
Crater, Cave
Karst Features
Depression
Polder
Desert, Dunes
Forest, Woods
Heath, Steppe
Oasis
Cape, Point
Coast, Beach
Cliff
Peninsula
Isthmus
Sandbank
Island
Atoll
Rock, Reef
Islands, Archipelago
Rocks, Reefs
Coral Reef
Well, Spring
Geyser
River, Stream
Waterfall, Rapids
River Mouth, Estuary
Lake
Salt Lake
Intermittent Lake
Reservoir
Swamp, Pond
Canal
Glacier
Ice Shelf, Pack Ice
Ocean
Sea
Gulf, Bay
Strait, Fjord
Lagoon
Bank
Seamount
Tablemount
Ridge
Shelf
Basin
Escarpment, Sea Scarp
Fracture
Trench, Abyss
National Park, Reserve
Point of Interest
Recreation Site
Cave, Cavern
Historic Site
Ruins
Wall, Walls
Church, Abbey
Temple
Scientific Station
Railway station
Airport
Port
Military installation
Lighthouse
Mine
Tunnel
Dam, Bridge

Ernici, Monti- 128 Hi 41.50N 13.20 E
Erode 148 Ff 11.21N 77.44 E
Eromanga 212 Ie 26.40S 143.16 E
Erongoberg 172 Bd 21.40S 15.40 E
Erpengdianzi 154 Hd 41.12N 125.29 E
Errego 172 Fc 16.02S 37.10 E
Errigal/An Ea agail 118 Ef 55.02N 8.07W
Erris Head/Ceann Iorrais 110 Fe 54.19N 10.00W
Erromango, Ile- 208 Hf 18.48S 169.05 E
Erseka 130 Di 40.20N 20.41 E
Erstein 122 Nf 48.26N 7.40 E
Ertai 152 Fb 46.02N 90.10 E
Ertil 136 Ee 51.50N 40.51 E
Ertix He 140 Ke 47.52N 84.16 E
Erts 172 De 25.08S 29.55 E
Ertvågøy 116 Ca 63.15N 8.25 E
Eruh 146 Jd 37.46N 42.15 E
Erval, Serra do- 204 Fk 30.25S 51.55W
Ervânia 204 Ee 21.43S 55.32W
Erve 122 Fg 47.50N 0.20W
Ervy-le-Châtel 122 Jf 48.02N 3.55 E
Erwin 184 Fg 36.09N 82.25W
Erwitte 124 Kc 51.37N 8.21 E
Eryuan 152 Gf 26.09N 99.56 E
Erzeni 130 Ch 41.26N 19.27 E
Erzgebirge=Ore Mountains (EN) 110 He 50.30N 13.15 E
Erzin 138 Ef 50.17N 95.10 E
Erzincan 144 Eb 39.44N 39.29 E
Erzurum 142 Gf 39.55N 41.17 E
Esan-Misaki 154 Pd 41.48N 141.12 E
Esashi [Jap.] 154 Pd 41.52N 140.07 E
Esashi [Jap.] 154 Qb 44.56N 142.35 E
Esashi [Jap.] 154 Pe 39.12N 141.09 E
Esbjerg 112 Gd 55.28N 8.27 E
Esbo/Espoo 114 Ff 60.13N 24.40 E
Escalante 188 Jh 37.47N 111.36W
Escalante Desert 188 Ih 37.50N 113.30W
Escalante River 188 Jh 37.17N 110.53W
Escalaplano 128 Dk 39.37N 9.21 E
Escalón 190 Dc 26.45N 104.20W
Escalona 126 Hd 40.10N 4.24W
Escanaba 176 Ke 45.45N 87.04W
Escanaba River 184 Dc 45.47N 87.04W
Escandón, Puerto de- 126 Ld 40.17N 1.00W
Escandorgue 122 Jk 43.46N 3.14 E
Escarpada Point 140 Oh 18.31N 122.13 E
Escarpé, Cap- 219b Ce 20.41S 167.13 E
Escatrón 126 Lc 41.17N 0.19W
Escaut=Schelde (EN) 122 Kc 51.22N 4.15 E
Esch an der Alzette/Esch-sur-Alzette 122 Le 49.30N 5.59 E
Eschkopf 124 Je 49.19N 7.51 E
Esch-sur-Alzette/Esch an der Alzette 122 Le 49.30N 5.59 E
Eschwege 120 Ge 51.11N 10.04 E
Eschweiler 120 Cf 50.49N 6.17 E
Escocesa, Bahía- 194 Md 19.25N 69.45W
Escondida, Punta- 192 Kj 15.49N 97.03W
Escondido 188 Gj 33.07N 117.05W
Escondido, Río- 194 Fg 12.04N 83.45W
Escravos 166 Gd 5.36N 5.11 E
Escudo, Puerto del- 126 Ia 43.05N 3.50W
Escudo de Veraguas, Isla- 194 Gi 9.06N 81.33W
Escuinapa de Hidalgo 190 Cd 22.51N 105.48W
Escuintla [3] 194 Bf 14.10N 91.00W
Escuintla [Guat.] 190 Ff 14.18N 90.47W
Escuintla [Mex.] 192 Mj 15.20N 92.38W
Escuro, Rio- [Braz.] 204 Ha 12.50S 49.28W
Escuro, Rio- [Braz.] 204 Ic 17.31S 46.39W
Ese 170 Eb 4.04N 26.40 E
Ese-Hajja 138 Ic 67.35N 134.55 E
Eséka 166 He 3.39N 10.46 E
Eşen 146 Cd 36.27N 29.16 E
Esendere 146 Kd 37.46N 44.40 E
Ésera / Éssera 126 Mb 42.06N 0.15 E
Eşfahān [3] 146 Nc 32.50N 51.50 E
Eşfahān=Isfahan (EN) 142 Hf 32.40N 51.38 E
Esfandārān 146 Og 31.52N 52.32 E
Esfarāyen, Reshteh-ye- 146 Oc 36.46N 57.10 E
Esgueva 126 Hc 41.40N 4.43W
Eshowe 172 Ee 28.58S 31.29 E
Eshtehārd 146 Ne 35.44N 50.23 E
Esigodini 172 Dd 20.18S 28.56 E
Esino 128 Hg 43.39N 13.22 E
Esk 118 Jg 54.58N 3.04W
Eskifjörður 114a Cb 65.04N 14.01W
Eskilstuna 114 Dg 59.22N 16.30 E
Eskimo Point 176 Jc 61.07N 94.03W
Eskişehir 142 Ff 39.46N 30.32 E
Esla 126 Fc 41.29N 6.03W
Eslāmābād 144 Gc 34.11N 46.35 E
Eşler Daği 130 Ml 37.24N 29.43 E
Eslohe (Sauerland) 124 Kc 51.15N 8.10 E
Eslöv 114 Ci 55.50N 13.20 E
Eşme 146 Cc 38.24N 28.59 E
Esmeralda [Braz.] 204 Gi 28.03S 51.12W
Esmeralda [Cuba] 194 Hc 21.51N 78.07W
Esmeralda, Isla- 206 Eg 48.57S 75.25W
Esmeralda Bank (EN) 220b Ab 14.57N 145.15 E
Esmeraldas 200 Ie 0.59N 79.42W
Es Mercadal / Mercadal 126 Qe 39.59N 4.05 E
Esnagami Lake 186 Ma 50.21N 86.48W
Esneux 124 Hd 50.32N 5.34 E
Espada, Punta- 194 Lg 12.05N 71.07W
Espagnol Point 197n Ba 13.22N 61.09W
Espalion 122 Ij 44.31N 2.46 E
Espalmador, Isla- / s'Espalmador, Illa- 126 Nf 38.47N 1.26 E
España=Spain (EN) [1] 112 Fg 40.00N 4.00W
Espanola [N.M.-U.S.] 186 Ch 36.06N 106.02W
Espanola [Ont.-Can.] 184 Gb 46.15N 81.46W
Española, Isla- 202a Bb 1.25S 89.42W
Espardell, Isla- / s'Espardell, Illa- 126 Nf 38.47N 1.27 E
Esparta 194 Ei 9.59N 84.40W
Espeland 116 Ad 60.23N 5.28 E
Espelkamp 120 Ed 52.25N 8.37 E
Esperance 210 Dh 33.51S 121.53 E
Esperance, Cape- 219a Dc 9.15S 159.43 E
Esperance Bay 212 Ef 33.50S 121.55 E
Esperance Harbour 197k Ba 14.04N 60.55W
Esperancita 204 Bc 16.55S 60.06W
Esperantina 202 Jd 3.54S 42.14W
Esperanza 222 Re 63.26S 57.00W
Esperanza [Arg.] 206 Hd 31.27S 60.56W
Esperanza [Mex.] 192 Ed 27.35N 109.56W
Esperanza [P.R.] 197a Cb 18.06N 65.29W
Esperanza, Sierra la- 194 Ef 15.40N 85.45W
Espevær 114 Ag 59.36N 5.10 E
Espichel, Cabo- 126 Cf 38.25N 9.13W
Espiel 126 Gf 38.12N 5.01W
Espigão, Serra do- 204 Gh 26.55S 50.25W
Espinal [Bol.] 204 Cc 17.13S 58.43W
Espinal [Col.] 202 Dc 4.10N 74.54W
Espinazo del Diablo, Sierra- 192 Ff 24.00N 106.00W
Espinhaço, Serra do- 198 Lg 17.30S 43.30W
Espinho 126 Dc 41.01N 8.38W
Espinilho, Serra do- 204 Ei 28.30S 55.06W
Espinillo 204 Cg 24.58S 58.34W
Espino 196 Dh 8.34N 66.01W
Espinosa 202 Jf 14.56S 42.50W
Espinouse, Monts de l'- 122 Ik 43.32N 2.46 E
Espírito Santo [2] 202 Jg 20.00S 40.30W
Espiritu Santo, Bahía del- 192 Ph 19.20N 87.35W
Espiritu Santo, Isla- 192 De 24.30N 110.22W
Espita 192 Og 21.01N 88.19W
Esplanada 202 Kf 11.47S 37.57W
Espoo/Esbo 114 Ff 60.13N 24.40 E
Espoo-Tapiola 116 Kd 60.11N 24.49 E
Esposende 126 Dc 41.32N 8.47W
Espumoso 204 Fi 28.44S 52.51W
Espuña, Sierra de- 126 Kg 37.52N 1.34W
Espungabera 172 Ed 20.28S 32.46 E
Esquel 200 Ij 42.55S 71.20W
Esquina 206 Id 30.01S 59.32W
Esquipular 194 Cf 14.34N 89.21W
Essandsjøen 116 Da 63.05N 12.00 E
Essaouira 160 Ge 31.31N 9.46W
Essaouira [3] 162 Fc 31.04N 9.03W
Essen [Bel.] 124 Gc 51.28N 4.28 E
Essen [F.R.G.] 112 Ge 51.27N 7.01 E
Essen (Oldenburg) 124 Jb 52.42N 7.55 E
Essendon, Mount- 212 Ed 24.59S 120.28 E
Essequibo River 198 Ke 6.50N 58.30W
Éssera / Ésera 126 Mb 42.06N 0.15 E
Essex 188 Hi 34.42N 115.12W
Essex [3] 118 Nj 51.50N 0.35 E
Essex 118 Nj 51.50N 0.30 E
Essex Mountain 188 Ke 42.02N 109.13W
Esslingen am Neckar 120 Fh 48.45N 9.18 E
Esso 138 Ke 55.55N 158.40 E
Essonne [3] 122 If 48.36N 2.20 E
Essonne 122 If 48.37N 2.29 E
Est [Burkina] [3] 166 Fc 12.00N 1.00 E
Est [Cam.] [3] 166 He 4.00N 14.00 E
Est, Canal de l'- 122 Lf 48.45N 5.35 E
Est, Cap- 172 Ic 15.16S 50.29 E
Est, Ile de l'- 222 Ec 46.15S 52.05 E
Est, Pointe de l'- 180 Lg 49.08N 61.41W
Estaca de Bares, Punta de la- / Estaca de Vares, Punta de la- 110 Fg 43.46N 7.42W
Estaca de Vares, Punta de la- / Estaca de Bares, Punta de la- 110 Fg 43.46N 7.42W
Estados, Isla de los-=Staten Island (EN) 198 Jk 54.47S 64.15W
Estados Unidos Mexicanos [1] 176 Ig 23.00N 102.00W
Estahbān 146 Ph 29.08N 54.04 E
Estaimpuis 124 Fd 50.42N 3.15 E
Estância 202 Kf 11.16S 37.26W
Estancias, Sierra de las- 126 Jg 37.35N 2.20W
Estanislao del Campo 204 Bg 25.03S 60.06W
Estarreja 126 Dd 40.45N 8.34W
Estats, Pica d'-/Estats, Pico d'- 122 Hl 42.40N 1.24 E
Estats, Pic d'- 122 Hl 42.40N 1.24 E
Estats, Pico d'-/Estats, Pica d'- 122 Hl 42.40N 1.24 E
Estcourt 172 De 29.01S 29.52 E
Este 128 Fe 45.14N 11.39 E
Este, Punta- 197a Cb 18.08N 65.16W
Este, Punta del- 206 Jd 34.59S 54.57W
Esteban Rams 204 Bi 29.47S 61.29W
Esteli 190 Gf 13.05N 86.23W
Esteli [3] 194 Dg 13.10N 86.20W
Estella 126 Jb 42.40N 2.02W
Estepa 126 Hg 37.18N 4.54W
Estepona 126 Gh 36.26N 5.08W
Esterel 122 Mk 43.30N 6.50 E
Esternay 124 Ff 48.44N 3.34 E
Esterri d'Àneu/Esterri de Aneu 126 Nb 42.38N 1.08 E
Esterri de Aneu / Esterri d'Àneu 126 Nb 42.38N 1.08 E
Esterwegen 124 Jb 52.59N 7.37 E
Estes Park 186 Df 40.23N 105.31W
Este Sudeste, Cayos del- 190 Hf 12.26N 81.27W
Estevan 180 Hg 49.07N 103.05W
Estherville 186 Ie 43.24N 94.50W
Estissac 122 Jf 48.16N 3.49 E
Eston 188 Ka 51.10N 108.46W
Estonia (EN) 110 Id 59.00N 26.00 E
Estonian SSR (EN)=Eesti NSV [2] 136 Cd 59.00N 26.00 E
Estonskaja Sovetskaja Socialističeskaja Respublika [2] 136 Cd 59.00N 26.00 E
Estonskaja SSR/Eesti Nõukogude Socialistlik Vabariijk [2] 136 Cd 59.00N 26.00 E
Estoril 126 Cf 38.42N 9.24W
Estrées-Saint-Denis 124 Ee 49.26N 2.39 E
Estreito 204 Gj 31.50S 51.44W
Estreito, Represa do- 204 Ie 20.15S 47.09W
Estrêla [Braz.] 204 Gj 31.15S 51.45W
Estrêla [Braz.] 204 Gi 29.29S 51.58W
Estrela, Arroyo- 204 Df 22.05S 56.25W
Estrêla, Serra da- 204 Fc 16.27S 53.24W
Estrêla, Serra da- 110 Fg 40.20N 7.38W
Estrêla do Sul 204 Id 18.21S 47.49W
Estrella 126 If 38.28N 3.35W
Estrella, Punta- 192 Bb 30.55N 114.40W
Estrema, Serra da- 204 Jc 16.50S 45.07W
Estremadura 126 Ce 39.15N 9.10W
Estremoz 126 Ef 38.51N 7.35W
Estrondo, Serra do- 202 Ie 9.00S 48.45W
Estry 124 Bf 48.54N 0.44W
Estuaire [3] 170 Ab 0.10N 10.00 E
Es Vedrà, Illa- / Vedrá, Isla- 126 Nf 38.52N 1.12 E
Esztergom 120 Oi 47.48N 18.45 E
Etah 179 Ec 78.19N 72.38W
Étain 122 Le 49.13N 5.38 E
Etajima 156 Cd 34.15N 132.29 E
Étalle 124 He 49.41N 5.36 E
Étampes 122 If 48.26N 2.09 E
Étaples 122 Hd 50.31N 1.39 E
Etāwah 148 Fc 26.46N 79.02 E
Ethe, Virton- 124 He 49.35N 5.35 E
Ethel Reefs 219d Ab 16.56S 177.13 E
Ethiopia (EN)=Itiopya [1] 160 Kh 9.00N 39.00 E
Ethiopian Plateau (EN) 158 Kg 10.00N 38.10 E
Etive, Loch- 118 He 56.35N 5.15W
Etna 110 Hh 37.50N 14.55 E
Etna 116 Dd 60.50N 10.03 E
Etna (Mongibello) 110 Hh 37.50N 14.55 E
Etne 116 Ae 59.40N 5.56 E
Etoile Cay 172b Bb 5.53S 53.01 E
Etolin Island 178 Me 56.08N 132.26W
Etolin Strait 178 Fd 60.20N 165.15W
Etomo-Misaki 156a Bb 42.20N 140.55 E
Etorofu Tō / Iturup, ostrov- 140 Qe 44.54N 147.30 E
Etosha Pan 158 Ij 18.50S 16.20 E
Etoumbi 170 Bb 0.01N 14.57 E
Etrépagny 124 De 49.18N 1.37 E
Étretat 122 Ge 49.42N 0.12 E
Etropole 130 Gg 42.50N 24.00 E
Etruria 206 Hd 32.56S 63.15W
Etsch/Adige 110 Hf 45.10N 12.20 E
Ettelbrüch/Ettelbruck 124 Ie 49.51N 6.07 E
Ettelbruck/Ettelbrüch 124 Ie 49.51N 6.07 E
Etten-Leur 124 Gc 51.35N 4.39 E
Ettersberg 120 He 51.03N 11.15 E
Ettlingen 124 Kf 48.57N 8.24 E
Etzna Tixmucuy 192 Nh 19.35N 90.13W
Eu 122 Hd 50.03N 1.25 E
'Eua Iki 221b Bc 21.07S 174.59W
Eua Island 216 Gd 21.22S 174.56W
Euboea (EN)=Évvoia 110 Ih 38.30N 24.00 E
Eucla 210 Dh 31.43S 128.52 E
Euclid 184 Ge 41.34N 81.33W
Euclides da Cunha 202 Kf 10.31S 39.01W
Eucumbene, Lake- 212 Jg 36.05S 148.45 E
Eudora 186 Kj 33.07N 91.16W
Eufaula 184 Ej 31.54N 85.09W
Eufaula Lake 186 Ii 35.17N 95.31W
Euganei, Colli- 128 Fe 45.19N 11.40 E
Eugene 176 Ge 44.02N 123.05W
Eugenia, Punta- 174 Hg 27.50N 115.03W
Eugênio Penzo 204 Ef 22.13S 55.53W
Eugmo 114 Fe 63.49N 22.45 E
Eume 126 Da 43.25N 8.08W
Eunice [La.-U.S.] 186 Jk 30.30N 92.26W
Eunice [N.M.-U.S.] 186 Ej 32.26N 103.09W
Eupen 122 Md 50.38N 6.02 E
Euphrates (EN)=Al Furāt 140 Gf 30.00N 47.25 E
Euphrates (EN)=Firat 140 Gf 30.00N 47.25 E
Eupora 186 Lj 33.32N 89.16W
Eura 114 Ff 61.08N 22.08 E
Eurajoki 116 Ic 61.12N 21.44 E
Eurasia Basin (EN) 224 Ge 87.00N 80.00 E
Eure [3] 122 Ge 49.10N 1.00 E
Eure 122 He 49.18N 1.12 E
Eure-et-Loir [3] 122 Hf 48.30N 1.30 E
Eureka [Ca.-U.S.] 176 Ge 40.47N 124.09W
Eureka [Ks.-U.S.] 186 Hh 37.49N 96.17W
Eureka [Mt.-U.S.] 188 Hb 48.53N 115.03W
Eureka [Nv.-U.S.] 182 Dd 39.31N 115.58W
Eureka [N.W.T.-Can.] 180 Ia 80.00N 85.59W
Eureka [S.D.-U.S.] 186 Gd 45.46N 99.38W
Eureka [Ut.-U.S.] 188 Ig 39.57N 112.07W
Eureka Sound 180 Ia 79.00N 87.00W
Europa, Ile d'- 158 Lk 22.20S 40.22 E
Europa, Picos de- 110 Fg 43.12N 4.48W
Europa, Punta de- 126 Gh 36.10N 5.22W
Europe (EN) 106 Fd 50.00N 20.00 E
Europoort 122 Jc 51.58N 4.00 E
Euskal Mendiak / Vascos, Montes- 126 Jb 42.50N 2.10W
Euskirchen 120 Cf 50.40N 6.47 E
Eustis 184 Gk 28.51N 81.41W
Eutaw 184 Di 32.50N 87.53W
Eutin 120 Gb 54.08N 10.37 E
Euzkadi / Vascongadas = Basque Provinces (EN) 126 Ja 43.00N 2.30W
Evale 170 Cf 16.33S 15.44 E
Evans, Lac- 180 Jf 50.50N 77.00W
Evans, Mount- 188 Ic 46.05N 113.07W
Evans Strait 180 Jd 63.20N 82.00W
Evanston [Il.-U.S.] 186 Me 42.03N 87.42W
Evanston [Wy.-U.S.] 182 Ec 41.16N 110.58W
Evansville 176 Kf 37.58N 87.35W
Evant 186 Gk 31.29N 98.09W
Evart 184 Ed 43.54N 85.14W
Évaux-les-Bains 122 Ih 46.10N 2.29 E
Evaz 146 Oi 27.46N 53.59 E
Evciler [Tur.] 130 Mk 38.03N 29.54 E
Evciler [Tur.] 130 Jj 39.46N 26.46 E
Evelyn, Mount- 212 Gb 13.36S 132.53 E
Evenkijski nacionalny okrug [3] 138 Ed 65.00N 98.00 E
Evensk 142 Rc 61.57N 159.14 E
Everard, Lake- 212 Hf 31.25S 135.05 E
Everard Ranges 212 Ge 27.05S 132.30 E
Everest, Mount- (EN)=Qomolangma Feng 140 Kg 27.59N 86.56 E
Everest, Mount- (EN)=Saragmatha 140 Kg 27.59N 86.56 E
Everett 182 Cb 47.59N 122.13W
Everett Mountains 180 Kd 62.45N 67.10W
Evergem 124 Fc 51.07N 3.42 E
Evergem-Sleidinge 124 Fc 51.08N 3.41 E
Everglades City 184 Gm 25.52N 81.23W
Evergreen 184 Dj 31.26N 86.57W
Evertsberg 116 Ec 61.08N 13.57 E
Evesham 118 Li 52.05N 1.56W
Evesham, Vale of- 118 Li 52.05N 1.50W
Évian-les-Bains 122 Mh 46.23N 6.35 E
Evijärvi 114 Fe 63.22N 23.29 E
Evinayong 166 He 1.27N 10.34 E
Évinos 130 Ek 38.19N 21.32 E
Evje 114 Bg 58.36N 7.51 E
Évora 112 Fh 38.34N 7.54W
Évora [2] 126 Ef 38.35N 7.50W
Evoron 138 If 51.23N 136.23 E
Evowghlī 146 Kc 38.43N 45.13 E
Evre 122 Eg 47.22N 1.02W
Evrecy 124 Be 49.06N 0.30W
Évreux 122 He 49.01N 1.09 E
Évron 122 Ff 48.10N 0.24W
Evros 130 Ji 40.52N 26.12 E
Evrótas 130 Fm 36.48N 22.41 E
Évry 122 If 48.38N 2.27 E
Évvoia=Euboea (EN) 110 Ih 38.30N 24.00 E
Évvoia, Gulf of- (EN)=Vórios Evvoïkós Kólpos 130 Gk 38.45N 23.10 E
Evzonoi 130 Fh 41.06N 22.33 E
Ewa Beach 221a Cb 21.19N 158.00W
Ewing Seamount (EN) 158 Hk 23.20S 8.45 E
Ewo 170 Bc 0.55S 14.49 E
Excelsior Mountain 188 Fg 38.02N 119.18W
Excelsior Mountains 188 Fg 38.10N 118.30W
Excelsior Springs 186 Ig 39.20N 94.13W
Exe 118 Jk 50.37N 3.25W
Executive Committee Range 222 Nf 76.50S 126.00W
Exeter [Eng.-U.K.] 112 Fe 50.43N 3.31W
Exeter [N.H.-U.S.] 184 Ld 42.59N 70.56W
Exeter Sound 180 Lc 66.10N 62.00W
Exmoor 118 Jj 51.10N 3.45W
Exmouth [Austl.] 212 Cd 21.55S 114.07 E
Exmouth [Eng.-U.K.] 118 Jk 50.37N 3.25W
Exmouth Gulf 208 Cg 22.00S 114.20 E
Exmouth Plateau (EN) 212 Cc 16.00S 114.00 E
Expedition Range 212 Jd 24.30S 149.05 E
Explorer Tablemount (EN) 190 He 16.55N 83.15W
Externsteine 124 Kc 51.52N 8.55 E
Extertal 124 Lb 52.04N 9.07 E
Extertal-Bösingfeld 124 Lb 52.04N 9.07 E
Extremadura [2] 126 Ge 39.00N 6.00W
Exuma Cays 190 Id 24.00N 76.20W
Exuma Sound 190 Id 24.15N 76.00W
Eyasi, Lake- 158 Ki 3.40S 35.05 E
Eydehavn 116 Cf 58.31N 8.53 E
Eye 124 Db 52.19N 1.09 E
Eyemouth 118 Kf 55.52N 2.06W
Eye Peninsula 118 Gc 58.13N 6.05W
Eygurande 122 Ii 45.40N 2.28 E
Eyjafjallajökull 114a Bc 63.38N 19.36W
Éyl 160 Lh 8.00N 49.51 E
Eymoutiers 122 Hi 45.44N 1.44 E
Eyneuil 146 Hb 41.03N 39.08 E
Eyrarbakki 114a Bc 63.52N 21.09W
Eyre 212 Ff 32.15S 126.18 E
Eyre, Lake- 208 Eg 28.43S 137.11 E
Eyre Creek 208 Eg 26.40S 139.00 E
Eyre Mountains 218 Cf 45.20S 168.20 E
Eyre North, Lake- 212 He 28.40S 137.10 E
Eyre Peninsula 208 Ef 34.00S 135.45 E
Eyre South, Lake- 212 He 29.30S 137.20 E
Eyrieux 122 Kj 44.48N 4.48 E
Eystrup 124 Lb 52.47N 9.13 E
Eythorne 124 Dc 51.11N 1.17 E
Eyvānaki 146 Oe 35.24N 51.56 E
Eyzies-de-Tayac, Les- 122 Hj 44.56N 1.01 E
Ezequiel Ramos Mexia, Embalse- 206 Ge 39.30S 69.00W
Ezere 116 Jh 56.27N 22.17 E
Ežerelis 116 Ji 54.50N 23.38 E
Ezine 146 Bc 39.47N 26.20 E
Eznas/Jieznas 116 Kj 54.34N 24.17 E
Ežva 134 Ef 61.47N 50.40 E

F

Faaa 221e Fc 17.33S 149.36W
Faaite Atoll 216 Lc 16.45S 145.14W
Fabens 186 Ck 31.30N 106.10W
Fåberg 116 Dc 61.10N 10.24 E
Faber Lake 180 Fd 63.55N 117.15W
Fåborg 114 Ci 55.06N 10.15 E
Fabriano 128 Gg 43.20N 12.54 E
Făcăeni 130 Ke 44.34N 27.54 E
Facatativá 202 Dc 4.49N 74.22W
Facha 164 Cd 29.30N 17.20 E
Fachi 160 Ig 18.06N 11.34 E
Facpi Point 220c Bb 13.20N 144.38 E
Fada 160 Jg 17.14N 21.33 E
Fada N'Gourma 160 Hg 12.04N 0.21 E
Faddeja, zaliv- 138 Fa 76.30N 107.30 E
Faddejevski, ostrov- 138 Ja 75.30N 144.00 E
Fadiffolu Atoll 148a Ba 5.25N 73.30 E
Fādilī 146 Mi 26.58N 49.15 E
Faeara, Pointe- 221e Fc 17.52S 149.11W
Faenza 128 Ff 44.17N 11.53 E
Faeroe-Iceland Ridge (EN) 110 Fc 64.00N 10.00W
Faeroe Islands (EN) = Færøerne/Föroyar [5] 112 Fc 62.00N 7.00W
Faeroe Islands (EN) = Færøerne/Föroyar 110 Fc 62.00N 7.00W
Faeroe Islands (EN) = Föroyar/Færøerne [5] 112 Fc 62.00N 7.00W
Faeroe Islands (EN) = Föroyar/Færøerne 110 Fc 62.00N 7.00W
Færøerne/Föroyar=Faeroe Islands (EN) [5] 112 Fc 62.00N 7.00W
Færøerne/Föroyar=Faeroe Islands (EN) 110 Fc 62.00N 7.00W
Fafa 168 Bd 7.18N 18.16 E
Fafe 126 Dc 41.27N 8.10W
Fafen 158 Lh 5.47N 44.11 E
Faga 166 Fc 13.45N 0.58 E
Fagaloa Bay 221c Ba 13.54S 171.28W
Fagamalo 221c Aa 13.25S 172.21W
Făgăraş 130 Hd 45.51N 24.58 E
Făgăraşului, Munţii- 130 Hd 45.35N 25.00 E
Fagataufa Atoll 208 Ng 22.14S 138.45W
Fågelmara 116 Fh 56.15N 15.57 E
Fagerhult 116 Fg 57.09N 15.40 E
Fagernes 114 Bf 60.59N 9.15 E
Fagersta 114 Df 60.00N 15.47 E
Fäget 130 Fd 45.51N 22.11 E
Fagita 150 Jg 1.48S 130.25 E
Fagnano, Lago- 206 Gh 54.38S 68.00W
Fagne 122 Kd 50.10N 4.25 E
Faguibine, Lac- 158 Gg 16.45N 3.54W
Fahlián 146 Ng 30.12N 51.28 E
Fahner Höhe 120 Ge 51.10N 10.45 E
Faial 158 Ee 38.34N 28.42W
Fā'id 146 Eg 30.19N 32.19 E
Faioa 220h Bc 13.23S 176.08W
Fairbairn Reservoir 212 Jd 23.40S 148.00 E
Fairbanks 176 Ec 64.51N 147.43W
Fairborn 184 Ef 39.48N 84.03W
Fairbury 182 Hc 40.08N 97.11W
Fairchild 186 Kd 44.36N 90.58W
Fairfield [Al.-U.S.] 184 Di 33.29N 86.55W
Fairfield [Ca.-U.S.] 188 Dg 38.15N 122.01W
Fairfield [Ia.-U.S.] 186 Kf 40.59N 91.57W
Fairfield [Id.-U.S.] 188 He 43.21N 114.48W
Fairfield [Il.-U.S.] 186 Lg 38.23N 88.22W
Fair Isle 118 Lb 59.30N 1.40W
Fairlie 218 Df 44.06S 170.50 E
Fairmont [Mn.-U.S.] 182 Ic 43.39N 94.28W
Fairmont [W.V.-U.S.] 182 Ld 39.28N 80.08W
Fair Ness 180 Kd 63.24N 72.05W
Fairview [Mt.-U.S.] 188 Mc 47.51N 104.03W
Fairview [Ok.-U.S.] 186 Gh 36.16N 98.29W
Fairview Peak 188 De 43.35N 122.39W
Fairweather, Mount- 174 Fd 58.54N 137.32W
Faisalabad (Lyallpur) 142 Jf 31.25N 73.05 E
Fais Island 208 Fd 9.46N 140.31 E
Faistós = Phaistos (EN) 130 Hn 35.03N 24.48 E
Faith 182 Gb 45.02N 102.02W
Faizābād 148 Gc 26.47N 82.08 E
Fajardo 194 Od 18.20N 65.39W
Fajou, Ilet à- 197e Ab 16.21N 61.35W
Fakahina Atoll 208 Mf 15.59S 140.08W
Fakaofo Atoll 208 Je 9.22S 171.14W
Fakarava Atoll 208 Mf 16.20S 145.37W
Fakaura 156 Fa 40.38N 139.55 E
Fakel 114 Mh 57.40N 53.05 E
Fakenham 124 Cb 52.50N 0.50 E
Fakfak 150 Jg 2.55S 132.18 E
Fakhr 146 Pg 31.25N 54.01 E
Fakse Bugt 116 Ei 55.10N 12.15 E
Faksefjell 116 Ec 61.20N 12.52 E
Fakse Ladeplads 116 Ei 55.15N 12.08 E
Faku 154 Gc 42.30N 123.24 E
Falaba 166 Cd 9.51N 11.19W
Fala-Beguets 220d Bb 7.21N 151.40 E
Falaise 122 Ff 48.54N 0.12W
Falaise de Tiguidit 166 Gb 16.22N 7.45 E
Falakrón Óros 130 Gh 41.19N 24.00 E
Falalu 220d Ba 7.38N 151.41 E
Falam 148 Id 22.55N 93.41 E
Falas 220d Ba 7.32N 151.46 E
Fălciu 130 Lc 46.18N 28.08 E
Falcón [2] 202 Ea 11.00N 69.50W
Falcon, Cap- 126 Li 35.46N 0.48W
Falcon, Presa- 186 Gm 26.37N 99.11W
Falconara Marittima 128 Hg 43.37N 13.24 E
Falcone, Punta- 128 Cj 40.58N 8.12 E
Falcon Reservoir 182 Hf 26.37N 99.11W
Faléa 166 Cc 12.16N 11.15W
Faleallej Pass 220d Bb 7.26N 151.34 E
Falealupo 221c Aa 13.30S 172.48W
Falelima 221c Aa 13.32S 172.41W
Falémé 158 Fg 14.46N 12.14W
Falenki 114 Mg 58.23N 51.36 E
Falerum 116 Gf 58.09N 16.13 E
Falešty 132 Ef 47.35N 27.44 E
Falevai 221c Ba 13.55S 171.59W
Falfurrias 182 Hf 27.14N 98.09W
Falkenberg 114 Ch 56.54N 12.28 E
Falkensee 120 Jd 52.34N 13.05 E
Falkirk 118 Jf 56.00N 3.48W
Falkland Islands/Malvinas, Islas- [5] 200 Kk 51.45S 59.00W
Falkland Islands/Malvinas, Islas- 198 Kk 51.45S 59.00W
Falkland Plateau (EN) 198 Lk 51.00S 50.00W
Falkland Sound 206 Ih 51.45S 59.25W
Falkonéra 130 Gm 36.50N 23.53 E
Falköping 114 Cg 58.10N 13.31 E
Fallingbostel 120 Fd 52.52N 9.42 E
Fallon [Mt.-U.S.] 188 Mc 46.48N 105.00W
Fallon [Nv.-U.S.] 188 Fg 39.28N 118.47W

Index Symbols

[1] Independent Nation
[2] State, Region
[3] District, County
[4] Municipality
[5] Colony, Dependency
Continent
Physical Region
Historical or Cultural Region
Mount, Mountain
Volcano
Hill
Mountains, Mountain Range
Hills, Escarpment
Plateau, Upland
Pass, Gap
Plain, Lowland
Delta
Salt Flat
Valley, Canyon
Crater, Cave
Karst Features
Depression
Polder
Desert, Dunes
Forest, Woods
Heath, Steppe
Oasis
Cape, Point
Coast, Beach
Cliff
Peninsula
Isthmus
Sandbank
Island
Atoll
Rock, Reef
Islands, Archipelago
Rocks, Reefs
Coral Reef
Well, Spring
Geyser
River, Stream
Waterfall, Rapids
River Mouth, Estuary
Lake
Salt Lake
Intermittent Lake
Reservoir
Swamp, Pond
Canal
Glacier
Ice Shelf, Pack Ice
Ocean
Sea
Gulf, Bay
Strait, Fjord
Lagoon
Bank
Seamount
Tablemount
Ridge
Shelf
Basin
Escarpment, Sea Scarp
Fracture
Trench, Abyss
National Park, Reserve
Point of Interest
Recreation Site
Cave, Cavern
Historic Site
Ruins
Wall, Walls
Church, Abbey
Temple
Scientific Station
Railway station
Airport
Port
Military installation
Lighthouse
Mine
Tunnel
Dam, Bridge

Fall River 182 Mc 41.43N 71.08W
Falls City 182 Hc 40.03N 95.36W
Falmouth [Atg.] 197d Bb 17.01N 61.46W
Falmouth [Eng.-U.K.] 118 Hk 50.08N 5.04W
Falmouth [Jam.] 194 Id 18.30N 77.39W
Falmouth [Ky.-U.S.] 184 Ef 38.40N 84.20W
Falmouth Bay 118 Hk 50.10N 5.05W
Falmouth Harbour 197d Bb 17.01N 61.46W
Falo 220d Bb 7.29N 151.53 E
False Bay 158 Il 34.15S 18.35 E
False Pass 178 Gf 54.52N 163.24W
Falset 126 Mc 41.08N 0.49 E
Faluo, Cabo- [Dom.Rep.] 194 Le 17.47N 71.41W
Falso, Cabo- [Hond.] 194 Ff 15.12N 83.20W
Falso, Cabo- [Mex.] 190 Cd 22.52N 109.58W
Falso Cabo de Hornos 206 Gi 55.43S 68.05W
Falster 114 Ci 54.50N 12.00 E
Falsterbo 116 Ei 55.24N 12.50 E
Falterona 128 Fg 43.52N 11.42 E
Fălticeni 130 Jb 47.27N 26.18 E
Falun 112 Hc 60.36N 15.38 E
Fama 168 Cb 15.22N 20.34 E
Famagusta (EN)=
Gazimağusa 144 Dc 35.07N 33.57 E
Famatina,
Nevados de- 206 Gc 29.00S 67.51W
Famenne 122 Ld 50.15N 5.15 E
Fana 166 Dc 12.45N 6.57W
Fanan 220d Bb 7.11N 151.59 E
Fanchang 152 Ke 31.00N 118.11 E
Fancy 197n Ba 13.22N 61.12W
Fandriana 172 Hd 20.13S 47.20 E
Fangak 168 Ed 9.04N 30.53 E
Fangatau Atoll 208 Mf 15.50S 140.52W
Fangcheng 152 Je 33.09N 113.05 E
Fangliao 152 Lg 22.22N 120.25 E
Fangshan 154 Ce 39.43N 115.58 E
Fangxian 152 Je 32.03N 110.41 E
Fangzheng 152 Mb 45.50N 128.49 E
Fangzi 154 Ef 36.36N 119.08 E
Fanjiatun 154 Hc 43.42N 125.05 E
Fanjing Shan 152 If 27.57N 108.50 E
Fannaråken 116 Bc 61.31N 7.55 E
Fanning → Tabuaeran
Atoll 208 Ld 3.52N 159.20W
Fano 128 Hg 43.50N 13.01 E
Fanø 116 Ci 55.25N 8.25 E
Fanø Bugt 116 Ci 55.25N 8.10 E
Fanshi 154 Be 39.11N 113.16 E
Fan Si Pan 140 Mg 22.15N 103.50 E
Fanuatapu 221c Ba 13.59S 171.20W
Fanxian 154 Cg 35.53N 115.29 E
Fāqūs 146 Dg 30.44N 31.48 E
Farab 135 De 39.12N 63.38 E
Faraba 166 Cc 12.52N 11.23W
Faraday 222 Qe 65.15S 64.15W
Faraday Seamounts (EN) 110 Df 49.30N 28.30W
Faradje 170 Eb 3.44N 29.43 E
Faradofay 160 Lk 25.01S 46.59 E
Farafangana 172 Hd 22.48S 47.50 E
Farāfirah, Wāḥāt al- =
Farafra Oasis (EN) 158 Jf 27.15N 28.10 E
Farafra Oasis (EN)=
Farāfirah, Wāḥāt al- 158 Jf 27.15N 28.10 E
Farāh 142 If 32.22N 62.07 E
Farāh [3] 144 Jc 33.00N 62.30 E
Farāh 140 If 31.29N 61.24 E
Far'ah, Wādī al- 146 Hj 24.02N 38.09 E
Farahābād 146 Od 36.47N 53.06 E
Faranah 166 Cc 10.02N 10.44W
Farasān, Jazā'ir- 144 Ff 16.48N 41.54 E
Farasān al Kabīr 164 Hf 16.42N 42.00 E
Faraulep Atoll 208 Fd 8.36N 144.33 E
Farcău, Virful- 130 Hb 47.55N 24.27 E
Farciennes 124 Gd 50.26N 4.33 E
Fardes 126 Jg 37.35N 3.00W
Fare 221e Db 16.42S 151.01W
Fareham 118 Lk 50.51N 1.10W
Farewell, Cape- 208 Ii 40.30S 172.43 E
Farewell Spit 218 Ed 40.30S 172.50 E
Färgelanda 116 Df 58.34N 11.59 E
Fargo 176 Je 46.52N 96.48W
Faribault 186 Jd 44.18N 93.16W
Faribault, Lac- 180 Ke 58.00N 72.00W
Farīd, Qarāt al- 146 Ch 28.43N 28.21 E
Faridpur 148 Hd 23.36N 89.50 E
Fārila 114 Df 61.48N 15.51 E
Farilhões, Ilhas- 126 Ce 39.28N 9.34W
Farim 166 Bc 12.29N 15.13W
Farini d'Olmo 128 Df 44.43N 9.34 E
Fariš 135 Fd 40.33N 66.52 E
Fāris 146 Ej 24.37N 32.54 E
Fāris 168 Ia 20.11N 50.56 E
Faris Seamount (EN) 178 Jf 54.30N 147.15W
Färjestaden 114 Dh 56.39N 16.27 E
Farkadhón 130 Fj 39.36N 22.04 E
Farmahīn 146 Me 34.30N 49.41 E
Farmakonisi 130 Kl 37.18N 27.08 E
Farmerville 186 Jj 32.47N 92.24W
Farmington [Me.-U.S.] 184 Lc 44.40N 70.09W
Farmington [Mo.-U.S.] 186 Kh 37.47N 90.25W
Farmington
[N.M.-U.S.] 182 Fd 36.44N 108.12W
Farmville 184 Hg 37.17N 78.25W
Färnäs 116 Fc 61.00N 14.38 E
Farnborough 124 Bc 51.16N 0.44W
Farne Deep 118 Mf 55.30N 0.50W
Farne Islands 118 Lf 55.38N 1.38W
Farnham [Eng.-U.K.] 124 Bc 51.12N 0.48W
Farnham [Que.-Can.] 184 Kc 45.17N 72.59W
Farnham, Mount- 184 Ga 50.29N 116.30W
Faro 112 Fh 37.01N 7.56W
Faro [2] 126 Dg 37.12N 8.10W
Fårö 114 Eh 57.55N 19.10 E
Faro 166 Hd 9.21N 12.55 E
Faro, Punta- 194 Jh 11.07N 74.51W
Faro, Punta del- → Peloro,
Capo- 128 Jl 38.16N 15.39 E
Faro, Sierra del- 126 Eb 42.37N 7.55W
Faro de Avión 126 Db 42.18N 8.16W
Faro de Chantada 126 Eb 42.37N 7.55W
Farofa, Serra da- 204 Gh 28.00S 50.10W
Fårösund 114 Eh 57.52N 19.03 E
Farosund 116 Hg 57.55N 19.05 E
Farquhar, Cape- 212 Cd 23.35S 113.35 E
Farquhar Group 158 Mj 10.10S 51.10 E
Farrar 118 Id 57.27N 4.35W
Farrāshband 146 Oh 28.53N 52.06 E
Farris 116 Ce 59.05N 10.00 E
Farruch, Cabo- / Ferrutx,
Cap de- 126 Pe 39.47N 3.21 E
Farrukhābād 148 Fc 27.24N 79.34 E
Fārs [3] 144 Hd 29.00N 53.00 E
Fārs 146 Hg 29.00N 53.00 E
Fārs, Khalīj-e- = Persian
Gulf (EN) 140 Hg 27.00N 51.00 E
Fārsābād 146 Mc 39.30N 48.05 E
Fársala 130 Fj 39.18N 22.23 E
Farshūṭ 146 Ei 26.03N 32.09 E
Farsø 116 Ch 56.47N 9.21 E
Farsund 114 Bg 58.05N 6.48 E
Fartak, Ra's- 144 Hf 15.38N 52.15 E
Fartura, Rio- 204 Gc 16.29S 50.33W
Fartura, Serra da- [Braz.] 204 Hf 23.20S 49.25W
Fartura, Serra da- [Braz.] 204 Fh 26.21S 52.52W
Fārūj 146 Rd 37.14N 58.14 E
Farvel, Kap-/
Ūmánarssuaq 224 Nb 59.50N 43.50W
Farwell Island 222 Pf 72.49S 91.10W
Fāryāb [3] 144 Jb 36.00N 65.00 E
Fasā 146 Oh 28.56N 53.42 E
Fasano 128 Lj 40.50N 17.22 E
Fastnet Rock 118 Dj 51.24N 9.35W
Fastov 136 Ce 50.06N 30.01 E
Fataka Island 208 If 11.55S 170.12 E
Fatala 166 Cc 10.13N 14.00W
Fatehpur 148 Ec 28.01N 74.58 E
Fatež 132 Ic 52.06N 35.52 E
Father Lake 184 Ja 49.24N 75.18W
Fatick 166 Bc 14.20N 16.25W
Fátima 126 De 39.37N 8.39W
Faṭīrah, Wādī- 146 Ei 26.39N 32.58 E
Fatsa 146 Gb 40.59N 37.24 E
Fatu Hiva, Ile- 208 Nf 10.28S 138.38W
Fatu Hutu, Ile- 208 Ne 9.00S 138.50W
Fatumanini, Passe- 220h Ab 13.14S 176.13W
Fatunda 170 Cc 4.08S 17.13 E
Fauabu 219a Ec 8.34S 160.43 E
Faucigny 122 Mh 46.05N 6.35 E
Faucille, Col de la- 122 Mh 46.22N 6.02 E
Faulkton 186 Gd 45.02N 99.08W
Faulquemont 124 Ie 49.03N 6.36 E
Fauquembergues 124 Ed 50.36N 2.05 E
Făurei 130 Kd 45.04N 27.14 E
Fauro 219a Cb 6.55S 156.07 E
Fauske 114 Dc 67.15N 15.24 E
Fauville-en-Caux 124 Ce 49.39N 0.35 E
Faux-Lap 172 He 25.32S 45.30 E
Fåvang 116 Dc 61.26N 10.13 E
Favara 128 Hm 37.19N 13.39 E
Faversham 124 Cc 51.19N 0.54 E
Favignana 128 Gm 37.56N 12.20 E
Favignana 128 Gm 37.55N 12.19 E
Favorite 124 Kf 48.49N 8.16 E
Fawley 124 Ad 50.49N 1.21W
Fawn 180 Ie 55.22N 88.20W
Fa'w Qiblī 146 Ei 26.07N 32.24 E
Faxaflói 110 Dc 64.24N 23.00W
Faxinal 204 Gf 23.59S 51.22W
Faya-Largeau 168 Ig 17.55N 19.07 E
Fayaoué 219b Ce 20.39S 166.32 E
Fayd 146 Ji 27.07N 42.31 E
Fayette [Al.-U.S.] 184 Di 33.42N 87.50W
Fayette [Oh.-U.S.] 184 Ee 41.41N 84.20W
Fayetteville [Ar.-U.S.] 182 Id 36.04N 94.10W
Fayetteville [N.C.-U.S.] 176 Lf 35.03N 78.54W
Fayetteville [Tn.-U.S.] 184 Dh 35.09N 86.35W
Faylakah, Jazīrat- 146 Mh 29.27N 48.20 E
Faysh Khābūr 146 Jd 37.04N 42.23 E
Fayu Island 208 Gd 8.35N 151.22 E
Fazenda de Cima 204 Db 15.56S 56.37W
Fazenda Nova 204 Gc 16.11S 50.48W
Fāzilka 148 Eb 30.24N 74.02 E
Fazrān 146 Mi 26.13N 49.12 E
Fazzān=Fezzan (E) 164 Bd 25.30N 14.00 E
Fazzān=Fezzan (EN) 158 If 26.00N 14.00 E
Fdérick 160 Ff 22.39N 12.43W
Feale/An Fhéil 118 Di 52.28N 9.40W
Fear, Cape- 182 Le 33.50N 77.58W
Featherston 218 Fd 41.07S 175.19 E
Feathertop, Mount- 212 Jg 36.54S 147.08 E
Fécamp 122 Ge 49.45N 0.22 E
Fecht 122 Nf 48.11N 7.26 E
Federación 206 Id 31.00S 57.54W
Federal 206 Id 30.55S 58.45W
Federovka [Kaz.-U.S.S.R.] 136 Ge 53.38N 62.42 E
Federovka [R.S.F.S.R.] 134 Gj 53.10N 55.10 E
Federsee 120 Fh 48.05N 9.38 E
Fedje 114 Af 60.47N 4.42 E
Fedorovka 132 Qd 51.16N 52.00 E
Fefan 220d Bb 7.21N 151.51 E
Fegen 116 Eg 57.06N 13.02 E
Fegen 116 Eg 57.11N 13.09 E
Fehérgyarmat 130 Si 47.59N 22.31 E
Fehmarn 120 Hb 54.30N 11.10 E
Fehmarnbelt 116 Dj 54.35N 11.15 E
Fehrbellin 120 Id 52.48N 12.46 E
Feicheng 154 Df 36.15N 116.46 E
Feidong (Dianbu) 154 Di 31.53N 117.29 E
Fei Huang He 154 Fg 34.15N 120.17 E
Feijó 202 De 8.09S 70.21W
Feilding 216 Eh 40.12S 175.35 E
Feira 170 Ff 15.37S 30.25 E
Feira de Santana 200 Mg 12.15S 38.57W
Feiran Oasis 146 Eh 28.42N 33.38 E
Feistritz 128 Ke 47.01N 16.08 E
Feixi (Shangpaihe) 154 Di 31.42N 117.09 E
Feixian 154 Dg 35.16N 117.59 E
Feixiang 154 Cf 36.32N 114.47 E
Fejão Prêto ou Furtado, Rio-
204 Dc 17.33S 57.23W
Fejér [2] 120 Oi 47.10N 18.35 E
Fejø 116 Dj 54.55N 11.25 E
Feke 146 Fd 37.53N 35.58 E
Feuete-víz 120 Ok 45.47N 18.13 E
Felanitx 126 Pe 39.28N 3.08 E
Feldbach 128 Jd 46.57N 15.53 E
Feldberg 120 Di 47.52N 7.59 E
Feldioara 130 Id 45.49N 25.36 E
Feldkirch 128 Dc 47.14N 9.36 E
Feliciano, Arroyo- 204 Cj 31.06S 59.54W
Felidu Atoll 148a Bb 3.30N 73.30 E
Felipe Carrillo Puerto 190 Ge 19.35N 88.03W
Felix, Cape - 180 Hc 69.55N 97.47W
Felixlândia 204 Jd 18.47S 44.55W
Felixstowe 118 Oj 51.58N 1.20 E
Felletin 122 Ii 45.53N 2.11 E
Feltre 128 Fd 46.01N 11.54 E
Femer Bælt 116 Dj 54.35N 11.15 E
Femø 116 Dj 54.55N 11.35 E
Femund 114 Ce 62.15N 11.50 E
Fena Valley Reservoir 220c Bb 13.20N 144.45 E
Fener Burnu 146 Hb 41.07N 39.25 E
Fénérive 172 Hc 17.22S 49.25 E
Fenerwa 168 Fc 13.05N 39.01 E
Fénétrange 124 Jf 48.51N 7.01 E
Fengcheng [China] 152 Lc 40.28N 124.01 E
Fengcheng [China] 152 Cj 28.11N 115.47 E
Fengdu 152 If 29.58N 107.39 E
Fenghua 154 Fj 29.40N 121.24 E
Fengjie 152 Ie 31.06N 109.30 E
Fenglingdu 152 Je 34.40N 110.19 E
Fengnan (Xugezhuang) 154 Ee 39.34N 118.05 E
Fengning (Dagezhen) 154 Dd 41.12N 116.39 E
Fengqing 152 Gg 24.41N 99.53 E
Fengqiu 152 Cg 35.02N 114.24 E
Fengrun 154 Ee 39.50N 118.09 E
Fengshui Shan 154 La 52.15N 123.30 E
Fengtai [China] 154 De 39.51N 116.17 E
Fengtai [China] 154 Dh 32.43N 116.43 E
Fengweiba → Zhenkang 152 Gg 23.54N 99.00 E
Fengxian 154 Dg 34.42N 116.35 E
Fengxian (Nanqiao) 154 Fi 30.55N 121.27 E
Fengxiang 152 Ie 34.32N 107.34 E
Fengxiang → Luobei 152 Nb 47.36N 130.58 E
Fengxin 154 Cj 28.42N 115.23 E
Fengyang 154 Dh 32.53N 117.33 E
Fengzhen 152 Jc 40.28N 113.09 E
Fen He 152 Jd 35.36N 110.42 E
Feni Islands 208 Ge 4.05S 153.42 E
Fennimore 186 Ke 42.59N 90.39W
Fens, The- 118 Mi 52.40N 0.00
Fensfjorden 116 Ad 60.50N 4.50 E
Fenshui Guan 152 Kf 27.56N 117.50 E
Fenton 184 Fd 42.48N 83.42W
Fenua Fu 220h Ac 13.23S 176.11W
Fenualoa 219c Bb 10.16S 166.15 E
Fenyang 152 Jd 37.17N 111.45 E
Feodosija 136 Df 45.02N 35.23 E
Fer, Cap de- 162 Ib 37.05N 7.10 E
Fer, Point au- 186 Kl 29.20N 91.21W
Feragen 116 Db 62.30N 11.55 E
Férai 130 Ji 40.54N 26.10 E
Ferdows 144 Ic 34.00N 58.09 E
Fère-Champenoise 122 Jf 48.45N 3.59 E
Fère-en-Tardenois 124 Fe 49.12N 3.31 E
Ferentino 128 Hi 41.42N 13.15 E
Ferfer 168 Hd 5.06N 45.09 E
Fergana 136 Hg 40.23N 71.46 E
Fergana 140 Je 40.30N 71.00 E
Ferganskaja oblast [3] 136 Hg 40.30N 71.20 E
Ferganski hrebet 136 Hg 41.00N 74.00 E
Fergus Falls 182 Hb 46.17N 96.04W
Ferguson Lake 180 Hc 69.00N 105.00W
Fergusson Island 208 Ge 9.30S 150.40 E
Ferkéssédougou 166 Dd 9.36N 5.12W
Ferkéssédougou [3] 166 Ed 9.20N 4.55W
Ferlo 158 Fg 15.00N 14.00W
Ferlo 158 Fg 15.42N 15.30W
Fermo 128 Hg 43.09N 13.43 E
Fermoselle 126 Fc 41.19N 6.23W
Fermoy/Mainistir Fhear Mai 118 Ei 52.08N 8.16W
Fernandina, Isla- 198 Gf 0.25S 91.30W
Fernandina Beach 184 Gj 30.40N 81.27W
Fernando de Noronha, Ilha-
198 Mf 3.51S 32.25W
Fernando de Noronha,
Território de- [2] 202 Ld 3.50S 33.00W
Fernandópolis 206 Kb 20.16S 50.00W
Fernán-Núñez 126 Hg 37.40N 4.43W
Fernelmont 124 Hd 50.35N 5.02 E
Fernie 188 Hb 49.30N 115.03W
Ferrandina 128 Kj 40.29N 16.27 E
Ferrara 128 Ff 44.50N 11.35 E
Ferrat, Cap- 126 Li 35.54N 0.23W
Ferrato, Capo- 128 Dk 39.18N 9.38 E
Ferré 204 Bl 34.08S 61.08W
Ferré, Cap- 197b Bc 14.28N 60.49W
Ferreira do Alentejo 126 Df 38.03N 8.07W
Ferreñafe 202 Ce 6.38S 79.48W
Ferret, Cap- 122 Ej 44.37N 1.15W
Ferriday 186 Kk 31.38N 91.33W
Ferrières 124 Hd 50.24N 5.36 E
Ferro, Capo- 128 Di 41.09N 9.31 E
Ferro, Rio- 204 Ea 12.27S 54.31W
Ferro, Monte- 128 Cj 40.08N 8.36 E
Ferrutx, Cap de- / Farruch,
Cabo- 126 Pe 39.47N 3.21 E
Ferry, Pointe- 197e Ab 16.17N 61.49W
Ferté-Bernard, La- 122 Gf 48.11N 0.40 E
Ferté-Macé, La- 122 Ff 48.36N 0.22W
Ferté-Saint-Aubin, La- 122 Hg 47.43N 1.56 E
Ferté-sous-Jouarre, La- 122 Jf 48.57N 3.08 E
Fertilia 128 Cj 40.36N 8.17 E
Fertő 120 Mi 47.50N 16.45 E
Fès 160 Ge 34.02N 4.59W
Fès [3] 162 Gc 34.00N 5.00W
Feshi 170 Cd 6.07S 18.10 E
Fessenden 186 Gc 47.39N 99.38W
Festieux 124 Fe 49.31N 3.45 E
Festus 186 Kg 38.13N 90.24W
Fetești 130 Ke 44.23N 27.50 E
Fethiye 144 Cb 36.37N 29.07 E
Fethiye Körfezi 146 Cd 36.40N 29.00 E
Fetlar 118 Ma 60.37N 0.52W
Fetsund 114 Cg 59.56N 11.10 E
Feuchtwangen 120 Gg 49.10N 10.20 E
Feuilles, Baie-aux- 180 Ke 58.55N 69.15W
Feuilles, Rivière-aux- 180 Ke 58.46N 70.05W
Feurs 122 Ki 45.45N 4.14 E
Fevik 116 Cf 58.23N 8.42 E
Feyzābād 142 Jf 37.06N 70.34 E
Fezzan (EN)=Fazzān 158 If 26.00N 14.00 E
Fezzan (EN)=Fazzān 164 Bd 25.30N 14.00 E
Fezzane, Emi- 164 Ha 21.42N 14.15 E
Ffestiniog 118 Ji 52.58N 3.55W
Fiambalá 206 Gc 27.41S 67.38W
Fianarantsoa 160 Lk 21.28S 47.05 E
Fianarantsoa [3] 172 Hd 21.30S 47.05 E
Fianga 168 Bd 9.55N 15.09 E
Fiche 168 Fd 9.48N 38.44 E
Fichtelgebirge 110 He 50.00N 12.00 E
Ficksburg 172 De 28.57S 27.50 E
Fidenza 128 Ef 44.52N 10.03 E
Fieni 130 Id 45.08N 25.25 E
Fier 122 Li 45.56N 5.50 E
Fieri 130 Ci 40.43N 19.34 E
Fife [3] 118 Je 56.05N 3.15W
Fife Ness 118 Ke 56.17N 2.36W
Fiffa 166 Dc 11.27N 9.52W
Fifth Cataract (EN)=
Khāmis, Ash Shallāl al- 158 Kg 18.23N 33.47 E
Figalo, Cap- 126 Ki 35.35N 1.12W
Figeac 122 Ij 44.36N 2.02 E
Figeholm 116 Gg 57.22N 16.33 E
Figtree 172 Dd 20.22S 28.20 E
Figueira, Baía da- 204 Dc 16.33S 57.25W
Figueira da Foz 126 Dd 40.09N 8.52W
Figueira de Castelo Rodrigo 126 Fd 40.54N 6.58W
Figueras/Figueres 126 Ob 42.16N 2.58 E
Figueres/Figueras 126 Ob 42.16N 2.58 E
Figuig 160 Ge 32.06N 1.14W
Figuig [3] 162 Gc 33.00N 2.01W
Fiherenana 172 Gd 23.19S 43.37 E
Fijāj, Shaṭṭ al- 162 Ic 33.55N 9.10 E
Fiji [1] 210 If 18.00S 178.00 E
Fiji Islands 208 If 18.00S 178.00 E
Fik 168 Gd 8.08N 42.18 E
Filabres, Sierra de los- 126 Jg 37.15N 2.20W
Filabusi 172 Dd 20.32S 29.16 E
Filadélfia 202 Ie 7.21S 47.30W
Filadelfia [C.R.] 194 Eh 10.26N 85.34W
Filadelfia [It.] 128 Kl 38.47N 16.17 E
Filakara 219b Ac 16.49S 168.24 E
Fil'akovo 120 Ph 48.16N 19.50 E
Filamana 166 Dc 10.30N 7.57W
Filatova Gora 116 Mg 57.39N 28.21 E
Filchner Ice Shelf 222 Af 79.00S 40.00W
Filey 118 Mg 54.12N 0.17W
Filiași 130 Ge 44.33N 23.31 E
Filiátai 130 Dj 39.36N 20.49 E
Filiatrá 130 El 37.09N 21.35 E
Filicudi 128 Il 38.35N 14.35 E
Filingué 166 Fc 14.21N 3.19 E
Filiouri 130 Ii 40.57N 25.20 E
Filippiás 130 Dj 39.12N 20.53 E
Filippoi 130 Hh 41.02N 24.20 E
Filippoi = Philippi (EN) 130 Hh 41.02N 24.18 E
Filipstad 114 Dg 59.43N 14.10 E
Fillefjell 116 Cc 61.09N 8.15 E
Filliévres 124 Ed 50.19N 2.10 E
Fillmore 188 Ig 38.58N 112.20W
Fils 120 Fh 48.35N 9.20 E
Filtu 168 Gd 5.06N 40.40 E
Fimaina 130 Jl 37.35N 26.26 E
Fimi 158 Ii 3.01S 16.58 E
Fin [Iran] 146 Pi 27.38N 55.55 E
Fin [Iran] 146 Nf 33.57N 51.24 E
Finale Emilia 128 Ff 44.50N 11.17 E
Finale Ligure 128 Cf 44.10N 8.20 E
Findhorn 118 Jd 57.41N 3.32W
Findik 146 Jd 37.31N 41.58 E
Findikli 146 Ib 41.17N 41.09 E
Findlay 182 Kc 41.02N 83.40W
Findlay, Mount- 188 Ga 50.04N 116.28W
Findlay Group 180 Ha 77.15N 104.00W
Fineveke 220h Ab 13.19S 176.12W
Fingoé 172 Ec 15.10S 31.53 E
Finike 146 Dd 36.18N 30.09 E
Finistère [3] 122 Bf 48.20N 4.00W
Finisterre, Cabo de- 110 Fg 42.53N 9.16W
Finisterre Range 212 Ja 5.50S 146.05 E
Finke 210 Eg 25.34S 134.35 E
Finke, Mount- 212 Gf 30.55S 134.02 E
Finke River 208 Eg 27.00S 136.10 E
Finland/Suomi [1] 112 Ic 64.00N 26.00 E
Finland, Gulf of- (EN) =
Finski zaliv 110 Ic 60.00N 27.00 E
Finland, Gulf of- (EN)=
Soomenlaht 110 Ic 60.00N 27.00 E
Finland, Gulf of- (EN)=
Suomenlahti 110 Ic 60.00N 27.00 E
Finlay 180 Fe 55.59N 123.50W
Finlay Mountains 186 Dk 31.30N 105.35W
Finne 120 He 51.13N 11.19 E
Finngrunden 116 Hc 61.00N 18.19 E
Finnigan, Mount- 212 Jc 15.50S 145.20 E
Finniss, Cape- 212 Gf 33.38S 134.51 E
Finnmark [3] 114 Fb 69.50N 24.10 E
Finnmark 116 Fc 61.40N 14.45 E
Finnmarksvidda 110 Ib 69.30N 24.20 E
Finnøy 116 Ae 59.10N 5.50 E
Finnskogen 116 Ed 60.40N 12.40 E
Finnsnes 114 Eb 69.14N 18.02 E
Finnveden 116 Eh 56.50N 13.40 E
Finote Selam 168 Fc 10.42N 37.12 E
Finschhafen 212 Ja 6.35S 147.50 E
Finse 116 Bd 60.36N 7.30 E
Finski zaliv = Finland, Gulf
of- (EN) 110 Ic 60.00N 27.00 E
Finspång 114 Dg 58.43N 15.47 E
Finstadåa 116 Dc 61.47N 11.10 E
Finsteraarhorn 128 Cd 46.32N 8.08 E
Finsterwalde 120 Je 51.38N 13.43 E
Finström 116 Hd 60.16N 19.50 E
Fiora 128 Fh 42.20N 11.34 E
Fiorenzuola d'Arda 128 Df 44.56N 9.55 E
Firat=Euphrates (EN) 140 Gf 30.00N 47.25 E
Firenze = Florence (EN) 112 Hg 43.46N 11.15 E
Firenzuola 128 Ff 44.07N 11.23 E
Firmat 204 Bk 33.27S 61.29W
Firminópolis 204 Gc 16.40S 50.19W
Firminy 122 Ki 45.23N 4.18 E
Fīrozābād 148 Fc 27.09N 78.25 E
Firozpur 148 Eb 30.55N 74.36 E
Fīrūzābād 146 Oh 28.50N 52.36 E
Fīrūzābād [Iran] 146 Le 34.09N 46.25 E
Fīrūzābād [Iran] 146 Pg 31.59N 54.20 E
Fīrūz Kūh 146 Oe 35.45N 52.47 E
Fischbach 124 Je 49.44N 7.24 E
Fischbacher Alpen 128 Jc 47.26N 15.30 E
Fischland 120 Ib 54.22N 12.25 E
Fisher Glacier 222 Ef 73.15S 66.00 E
Fisher Peak 184 Gg 36.33N 80.50W
Fisher Strait 180 Jd 63.00N 84.00W
Fishguard 112 Fe 51.59N 4.59W
Fish River 172 Cf 31.14S 20.15 E
Fish River' Canyon 172 Be 27.35S 17.35 E
Fiskárdhon 130 Dk 38.28N 20.35 E
Fiskenæs Bank (EN) 179 Gf 63.18N 52.10W
Fiskenæsset 179 Gf 63.10N 50.45W
Fismes 122 Je 49.18N 3.41 E
Fišt, gora- 136 Dg 43.57N 39.55 E
Fitchburg 184 Ld 42.35N 71.48W
Fitjar 116 Ag 59.55N 5.20 E
Fito, Mount- 221c Ba 13.55S 171.44W
Fitri, Lac- 168 Bc 12.50N 17.28 E
Fitzcarrald 202 Df 11.49S 71.48W
Fitzgerald [Alta.-Can.] 180 Ge 59.52N 111.40W
Fitzgerald [Ga.-U.S.] 184 Fj 31.43N 83.15W
Fitzroy Crossing 212 Fc 18.11S 125.35 E
Fitzroy River [Austl.] 208 Df 17.31S 123.35 E
Fitzroy River [Austl.] 212 Kd 23.32S 150.52 E
Fitzwilliam Island 184 Gc 45.30N 81.45W
Fiuggi 128 Hi 41.48N 13.13 E
Fiumicino 128 Gi 41.46N 12.14 E
Five Island Harbour 197d Bb 17.06N 61.54W
Fivizzano 128 Ef 44.14N 10.08 E
Fizi 160 Ji 4.18S 28.57 E
Fizuli 136 Eh 39.35N 47.11 E
Fjærlandsfjorden 116 Bc 61.15N 6.40 E
Fjällbacka 116 Df 58.36N 11.17 E
Fjärås 114 Ch 57.26N 12.09 E
Fjerritslev 116 Cg 57.05N 9.16 E
Fjöllum, Jökulsá á- 114a Ca 66.02N 16.27W
Fjugesta 116 Fe 59.10N 14.52 E
Flacq 172a Bb 20.12S 57.43 E
Flade Isblink 179 Kb 81.25N 16.00W
Fladen 116 Dg 57.07N 11.35 E
Flagler 186 Eg 39.18N 103.04W
Flagstaff 176 Hf 35.12N 111.39W
Flåm 114 Bf 60.50N 7.07 E
Flamborough Head 118 Mg 54.07N 0.04W
Fläming 120 Ie 52.00N 13.00 E
Flaming Gorge Reservoir 188 Kf 41.15N 109.30W
Flamingo 184 Gm 25.09N 80.56W
Flamingo, Teluk- 150 Kh 5.33S 138.00 E
Flanders (EN)=Flandres/
Vlaanderen 110 Ge 51.00N 3.20 E
Flanders (EN)=Flandres/
Vlaanderen 122 Jc 51.00N 3.20 E
Flanderu (EN)=Vlaanderen/
Flandres 110 Ge 51.00N 3.20 E
Flanders (EN)=Vlaanderen/
Flandres 122 Jc 51.00N 3.20 E
Flanders, East- (EN) =
Oost-Vlaanderen [3] 124 Fc 51.00N 3.40 E
Flanders, West- (EN) =
West-Vlaanderen [3] 124 Ec 51.00N 3.00 E
Flanders Plain (EN) =
Flandres, Plaine des- 122 Id 50.40N 2.50 E
Flanders Plain (EN) =
Vlaamse Vlakte 122 Id 50.40N 2.50 E
Flandreau 186 Hd 44.03N 96.36W
Flandres/Vlaanderen=
Flanders (EN) 110 Ge 51.00N 3.20 E
Flandres/Vlaanderen=
Flanders (EN) 122 Jc 51.00N 3.20 E
Flandres, Plaine des- =
Flanders Plain (EN) 122 Id 50.40N 2.50 E
Flannan Islands 118 Fc 58.20N 7.35W
Flåren 116 Fh 57.00N 14.05 E
Flasher 186 Fc 46.27N 101.14W
Fläsjön 114 Dd 64.06N 15.51 E
Flat 178 Hd 62.27N 158.01W
Flatey 114a Ab 65.22N 22.56W
Flateyri 114a Aa 66.03N 23.31W
Flathead Lake 182 Eb 47.52N 114.08W
Flathead Range 188 Ib 48.05N 113.28W
Flathead River 188 Hc 47.22N 114.47W
Flat Point 197b Ab 18.15N 63.05W
Flat River 186 Kh 37.51N 90.31W
Flattery, Cape- 174 Ge 48.23N 124.43W
Flåvatnet 116 Ce 59.20N 8.50 E
Flaxton 186 Eb 48.54N 102.24W
Flaygreen Lake 180 Hf 53.50N 97.20W
Flèche, La- 122 Fg 47.42N 0.05W
Fleckenstein 124 Je 49.05N 7.48 E
Fleet 124 Bc 51.17N 0.50W
Fleetwood 118 Jh 53.56N 3.01W

Index Symbols

[1] Independent Nation
[2] State, Region
[3] District, County
[4] Municipality
[5] Colony, Dependency
Continent
Physical Region
Historical or Cultural Region
Mount, Mountain
Volcano
Hill
Mountains, Mountain Range
Hills, Escarpment
Plateau, Upland
Pass, Gap
Plain, Lowland
Delta
Salt Flat
Valley, Canyon
Crater, Cave
Karst Features
Depression
Polder
Desert, Dunes
Forest, Woods
Heath, Steppe
Oasis
Cape, Point
Coast, Beach
Cliff
Peninsula
Isthmus
Sandbank
Island
Atoll
Rock, Reef
Islands, Archipelago
Rocks, Reefs
Coral Reef
Well, Spring
Geyser
River, Stream
Waterfall, Rapids
River Mouth, Estuary
Lake
Salt Lake
Intermittent Lake
Reservoir
Swamp, Pond
Canal
Glacier
Ice Shelf, Pack Ice
Ocean
Sea
Gulf, Bay
Strait, Fjord
Lagoon
Bank
Seamount
Tablemount
Ridge
Shelf
Basin
Escarpment, Sea Scarp
Fracture
Trench, Abyss
National Park, Reserve
Point of Interest
Recreation Site
Cave, Cavern
Historic Site
Ruins
Wall, Walls
Church, Abbey
Temple
Scientific Station
Railway station
Airport
Port
Military installation
Lighthouse
Mine
Tunnel
Dam, Bridge

Flekkefjord 114 Bg 58.17N 6.41 E
Flémalle 124 Hd 50.36N 5.29 E
Flemish Bight [C] 122 Ib 51.44N 2.30 E
Flemish Cap (EN) 174 Oe 47.00N 45.00W
Flemsøya [I] 116 Bb 62.40N 6.20 E
Flen 116 Dg 59.04N 16.35 E
Flensburg Fjord [C] 116 Cj 54.50N 9.45 E
Flensburg 112 Ge 54.47N 9.26 E
Flensburger Förde [C] 116 Cj 54.50N 9.45 E
Flers 122 Ff 48.45N 0.34W
Flesberg 116 Ce 59.51N 9.27 E
Fleurance 122 Gk 43.50N 0.40 E
Fleury-sur-Andelle 122 De 49.22N 1.21 E
Fleuve [3] 166 Cb 16.00N 13.50W
Flevoland [X] 122 Lb 52.25N 5.30 E
Flian [N] 114 Ef 58.27N 13.05 E
Flims 128 Dd 46.50N 9.16 E
Flinders Bay [C] 212 Df 34.25S 115.19 E
Flinders Island [I] 208 Fi 40.00S 148.00 E
Flinders Passage 212 Jc 18.50S 149.00 E
Flinders Ranges [A] 208 Eh 31.25S 138.45 E
Flinders Reefs [I] 208 Ff 17.40S 148.30 E
Flinders River [N] 208 Ff 17.36S 140.36 E
Flin Flon 176 Id 54.56N 101.53W
Flint [Mi.-U.S.] 176 Ke 43.01N 83.41W
Flint [Wales-U.K.] 118 Jh 53.15N 3.07W
Flint Hills [A] 186 Hh 37.20N 96.35W
Flint Island [I] 208 Lf 11.26S 151.48W
Flint River [N] 182 Ke 30.52N 84.38W
Flisa 116 Cf 60.37N 12.04 E
Flisa [N] 116 Ed 60.36N 12.01 E
Flisegga [A] 116 Be 59.55N 7.50 E
Flitwick 124 Bb 52.00N 0.29W
Flix 126 Mc 41.14N 0.33 E
Flixecourt 124 Ed 50.01N 2.05 E
Flize 124 Ge 49.42N 4.46 E
Flobecq/Vloesberg 124 Gd 50.44N 3.44 E
Floby 116 Ef 58.08N 13.20 E
Floda [Swe.] 116 Fd 60.26N 14.49 E
Floda [Swe.] 116 Eg 57.48N 12.22 E
Flood Range [A] 222 Nf 76.03S 134.00W
Flora [Il.-U.S.] 186 Lg 38.40N 88.29W
Flora [Nor.] 114 Af 61.36N 5.00 E
Florac 122 Jj 44.19N 3.36 E
Florala 184 Dj 31.00N 86.20W
Florange 124 Ie 49.20N 6.07 E
Florence [Al.-U.S.] 182 Je 34.49N 87.40W
Florence [Ks.-U.S.] 186 Hg 38.15N 96.56W
Florence [Or.-U.S.] 188 Cd 44.01N 124.07W
Florence [S.C.-U.S.] 182 Le 34.12N 79.44W
Florence (EN) = Firenze 112 Hg 43.46N 11.15 E
Florencia [Arg.] 204 Ci 28.02S 59.15W
Florencia [Col.] 200 Ie 1.36N 75.36W
Florencio Sánchez 204 Dk 33.53S 57.24W
Florennes 124 Gd 50.15N 4.37 E
Florentino Ameghino, Embalse- [<] 206 Gf 43.48S 66.25W
Florenville 122 Le 49.42N 5.18 E
Flores 190 Ge 16.58N 89.50W
Flores [I] 204 Dk 33.35S 56.50W
Flores [I] 158 Se 39.26N 31.13W
Flores, Arroyo de las- [N] 204 Cl 35.36S 59.01W
Flores, Laut- = Flores Sea (EN) 140 Oj 8.00S 121.00 E
Flores, Pulau- [I] 140 Oj 8.30S 121.00 E
Flores Island [I] 188 Bb 49.20N 126.10W
Flores Sea (EN) = Flores, Laut- 140 Oj 8.00S 121.00 E
Florešty 132 Ff 47.55N 28.18 E
Floriano 200 Lf 6.47S 43.01W
Florianópolis 200 Lh 27.35S 48.34W
Florida [Braz.] 204 Ei 29.15S 54.36W
Florida [Cuba] 190 Jd 21.32N 78.14W
Florida [Fl.-U.S.] [2] 182 Kf 28.00N 82.00W
Florida [Ur.] 206 Md 34.06S 56.13W
Florida [Ur.] [2] 204 Ek 33.50S 55.55W
Florida, Estrecho de- = Florida, Straits of- (EN) 174 Kg 24.00N 81.00W
Florida, Straits of- (EN) 174 Kg 24.00N 81.00W
Florida, Straits of- (EN) = Florida, Estrecho de- 174 Kg 24.00N 81.00W
Florida Bay [C] 184 Gm 25.00N 80.45W
Floridablanca 202 Db 7.04N 73.06W
Florida City 184 Gm 25.27N 80.29W
Florida Islands [I] 214 Gi 9.00S 160.10 E
Florida Keys [I] 182 Kg 24.45N 81.00W
Floridia 128 Jm 37.05N 15.09 E
Florido, Río- [N] 192 Gd 27.43N 105.10W
Flórina 130 Ei 40.47N 21.24 E
Florø 114 Ab 61.36N 5.00 E
Flotte, Cap de- [I] 219bc Ej 21.11S 167.24 E
Floydada 186 Fj 33.59N 101.20W
Fluessen [I] 122 Lb 52.57N 5.30 E
Flumen [N] 126 Lc 41.43N 0.09W
Flumendosa [N] 128 Dk 39.26N 9.37 E
Fluminimaggiore 128 Ck 39.26N 8.30 E
Flumini Mannu [N] 128 Ck 39.16N 9.00 E
Flums 128 Dc 47.05N 9.20 E
Fluvià / Fluviá [N] 126 Pb 42.12N 3.07 E
Fluvià / Fluviá [N] 126 Pb 42.12N 3.07 E
Flying Fish, Cape- [I] 222 Of 72.06S 102.29W
Flying Fish Cove 150 Ei 10.25S 105.43 E
Fly River [N] 208 Fe 8.00S 142.21 E
Fnideq 134 Ab 35.50N 5.22W
Fnjóská [N] 114a Bb 65.54N 18.07W
Foa [I] 221bBa 19.45S 174.18W
Foam Lake 188 Na 51.39N 103.33W
Foča 130 Ib 43.31N 18.47 E
Foça 130 Jk 38.39N 26.46 E
Fochi 168 Bb 18.56N 15.57 E
Fochi [X] 168 Bb 18.25N 15.40 E
Focşani 130 Kd 45.42N 27.11 E
Fodda [N] 126 Nh 36.14N 1.33 E
Fodé 168 Cd 5.29N 23.18 E
Færingehavn 179 Gf 63.45N 51.28W
Foga, Dallol- [N] 166 Fc 12.05N 3.32 E
Foggaret ez Zoua 162 Hd 27.22N 2.50 E
Foggia 128 Hg 41.27N 15.34 E

Foggo 166 Gc 11.23N 9.57 E
Foglia [N] 128 Gg 43.55N 12.54 E
Föglö [I] 116 Ie 60.00N 20.25 E
Fogo [Can.] [I] 174 Oe 49.40N 54.10W
Fogo [C.V.] [I] 158 Eg 14.55N 24.25W
Fohnsdorf 128 Ic 47.12N 14.41 E
Föhr [I] 120 Ca 54.45N 8.30 E
Föhren 124 Ie 49.51N 6.46 E
Foix 122 Hl 42.58N 1.36 E
Fojnica 128 Lg 43.58N 17.54 E
Fokino 132 Ic 53.27N 34.26 E
Folda [N] 114 Dc 67.36N 14.50 E
Folégandros [I] 130 Hm 36.38N 24.54 E
Foley 180 Kc 68.30N 75.00W
Foleyet 180 Jg 48.16N 82.30W
Folgefonni [A] 114 Bf 60.00N 6.20 E
Foligno 128 Gh 42.57N 12.42 E
Folkestone 118 Oj 51.05N 1.11 E
Folkingham 124 Bb 52.52N 0.24W
Folkston 184 Fj 30.50N 82.01W
Folldals verk 114 Be 62.08N 10.00 E
Follebu 114 Cf 61.14N 10.17 E
Follina 116 De 63.40N 14.37 E
Follo [X] 116 De 59.55N 10.55 E
Follonica 128 Eh 42.55N 10.45 E
Follonica, Golfo di- [C] 128 Eh 42.55N 10.40 E
Folschviller 124 Ie 49.04N 6.41 E
Fomboni 172 Gb 12.16S 43.45 E
Fomento 194 Hb 22.06N 79.43W
Fond d'Or Bay [C] 197k Bb 13.56N 60.54W
Fond-du-Lac 180 Gc 59.19N 107.10W
Fond du Lac 182 Jc 43.47N 88.27W
Fond-du-Lac [N] 180 Gc 59.17N 106.00W
Fondi 128 Hi 41.21N 13.25 E
Fongen [A] 116 De 63.11N 11.38 E
Fongoro [X] 168 Cc 11.30N 22.25 E
Fonni 128 Dj 40.07N 9.15 E
Fonoifua [I] 221bBb 20.17S 174.38W
Fonsagrada 126 Ea 43.08N 7.04W
Fonsea a 202 Da 10.53N 72.50W
Fonseca, Golfo de- [C] 174 Kh 13.08N 87.40W
Fontaine-Bellenger 124 De 49.11N 1.16 E
Fontainebleau 122 Jf 48.24N 2.42 E
Fontaine-Henry, Château de- [A] 124 Be 49.17N 0.27W
Fontaine-le-Dun 124 De 49.49N 0.51 E
Fontaine-l'Evêque 124 Gd 50.25N 4.19 E
Fontas 180 Fc 58.17N 121.46W
Fonte Boa 202 Ed 2.32S 66.01W
Fontenay-le-Comte 122 Fh 46.28N 0.49W
Fontenay-Trésigny 124 Ef 48.42N 2.52 E
Fontenelle Reservoir [<] 188 Je 42.05N 110.06W
Fontevraud-l'Abbaye 122 Gg 47.11N 0.03 E
Fontur [I] 110 Eb 66.23N 14.32W
Fonuafo'ou Falcon [I] 216 Fb 20.19S 175.25W
Fonualei Island [I] 208 Jf 18.01S 174.19W
Fonyód 120 Nj 46.44N 17.33 E
Foraker, Mount- [A] 178 Id 62.56N 151.26W
Forbach 122 Me 49.11N 6.54 E
Forbes 212 Ji 33.23S 148.01 E
Forbes, Mount- [A] 188 Ga 51.52N 116.56W
Forcados 166 Gd 5.21N 5.25 E
Forcados [N] 166 Gd 5.23N 5.19 E
Forcalquier 122 Lk 43.58N 5.47 E
Forchheim 120 Hg 49.43N 11.04 E
Ford City 188 Fi 35.09N 119.27W
Førde 116 Ac 61.27N 5.52 E
Ford Ranges [A] 222 Mf 77.00S 145.00W
Fordyce 186 Ij 33.49N 92.25W
Forécariah 166 Cg 9.26N 13.06W
Forel, Mont- [A] 224 Mc 67.05N 36.55W
Forelshogna [A] 116 Db 62.41N 10.47 E
Forest 184 Ei 32.22N 89.28W
Forest Park 184 Ei 33.37N 84.22W
Forestville 184 Ma 48.45N 69.06W
Forez, Monts du- [A] 122 Ji 45.35N 3.48 E
Forez, Plaine du- [X] 122 Ki 45.45N 4.10 E
Forfar 118 Ke 56.38N 2.54W
Forges-les-Eaux 124 He 49.37N 1.33 E
Forggensee [<] 120 Hi 47.36N 10.44 E
Forks 188 Cc 47.57N 124.23W
Forli 128 Gf 44.13N 12.03 E
Forli, Bocca di- [A] 128 Li 41.45N 14.10 E
Formazza 128 Cd 46.22N 8.26 E
Formby Point [I] 118 Jg 53.33N 3.06W
Formentera [I] 126 Nf 38.42N 1.28 E
Formentor, Cabo de- [I] / Formentor, Cap de- [I] 126 Pe 39.58N 3.12 E
Formentor, Cap de- / Formentor, Cabo de- [I] 126 Pe 39.58N 3.12 E
Formerie 124 He 49.39N 1.44 E
Formia 128 Hi 41.15N 13.37 E
Formiga 128 Cb 37.16N 24.47W
Formigas [I] 206 Cb 25.00S 60.00W
Formosa [2] 204 Cb 25.00S 60.00W
Formosa [Arg.] 204 Ch 26.10S 58.11W
Formosa [Braz.] 202 Ig 15.32S 47.20W
Formosa → Taiwan [I] 142 Qg 23.30N 121.00 E
Formosa, Serra- [A] 198 Kg 12.00S 55.00W
Formoso [Braz.] 202 Ih 20.27S 45.25W
Formoso [Braz.] 206 Cb 37.16N 24.47W
Formoso, Rio- [Braz.] [N] 202 Ja 13.26S 44.14W
Formoso, Rio- [Braz.] [N] 204 Ed 18.25S 52.28W
Fornæs [I] 116 Cc 56.27N 10.58 E
Fornovo di Taro 128 Ef 44.42N 10.06 E
Føroyar/Færøerne = Faeroe Islands (EN) [5] 112 Fc 62.00N 7.00W
Føroyar/Færøerne = Faeroe Islands (EN) [5] 110 Fc 62.00N 7.00W
Forres 118 Jd 57.37N 3.38W
Forrest 212 Fh 30.51S 128.06 E
Forrest City 186 Ki 35.01N 90.47W

Forrester Island [I] 222 Nf 74.06S 132.00W
Forsayth 212 Ic 18.35S 143.36 E
Forserum 116 Fg 57.42N 14.28 E
Forshaga 116 Ec 59.32N 13.28 E
Forsnäs 114 Ec 66.14N 18.39 E
Forssa 116 Ff 60.49N 23.38 E
Forst/Baršć 120 Ke 51.44N 14.38 E
Forsyth 188 Lc 46.16N 106.41W
Fort Albany 180 Kd 52.15N 81.37W
Fortaleza 200 Mf 3.43S 38.30W
Fortaleza, Ribeirão- [N] 204 Fd 19.50S 53.25W
Fort Augustus 118 Id 57.09N 4.41W
Fort Beaufort 172 Df 32.46S 26.40 E
Fort Benton 188 Eb 47.49N 110.40W
Fort Bragg 182 Cd 39.26N 123.48W
Fort Bridger 188 Jf 41.19N 110.23W
Fort-Carnot [Mad.] 172 Hd 21.53S 48.26 E
Fort Chipewyan 180 Gc 58.42N 111.08W
Fort Cobb Reservoir [<] 186 Gi 35.12N 98.29W
Fort Collins 182 Fc 40.35N 105.05W
Fort Collinson 180 Fb 71.37N 117.57W
Fort Coulonge 184 Lc 45.51N 76.44W
Fort Davis 186 Ek 30.35N 103.54W
Fort-de-France 190 Mh 14.36N 61.05W
Fort-de-France, Baie de- [C] 197h Ab 14.34N 61.04W
Fort Dodge 182 Ic 42.30N 94.10W
Forte 204 Ib 14.16S 47.17W
Forte dei Marmi 128 Eg 43.57N 10.10 E
Fortescue River [N] 208 Cg 21.00S 116.06 E
Fort Frances 176 Je 48.36N 93.24W
Fort Franklin 180 Fc 65.12N 123.26W
Fort Garland 186 Dh 37.26N 105.26W
Fort Gibson Lake [<] 186 Ih 36.00N 95.18W
Fort Good Hope 176 Gc 66.15N 128.38W
Forth 118 Je 56.04N 3.42W
Forth, Firth of- [C] 110 Fd 56.05N 2.55W
Fort Hall 180 If 51.32N 88.00W
Fort Hope 180 If 51.32N 88.00W
Fortín Avalos Sánchez 204 Bf 23.28S 60.07W
Fortín Boquerón 204 Bf 22.47S 59.57W
Fortín Buenos Aires 204 Bf 22.57S 61.51W
Fortín Cadete Pastor Pando 204 Ca 24.20S 58.54W
Fortín Capitán Figari 204 Cf 23.12S 59.32W
Fortín Carlos A. López 204 Ce 21.19S 59.44W
Fortín Comandante Nowak 204 Ce 24.51S 58.15W
Fortín Coronel Bogado 204 Ce 20.46S 59.09W
Fortín Coronel Hermosa 204 Bf 22.33S 60.01W
Fortín Coronel Martínez 204 Cf 22.15S 59.09W
Fortín Florida 204 Cd 20.45S 59.17W
Fortín Galpón 204 Cd 19.51S 58.16W
Fortín Gaspar Rodríguez de Francia 204 Cf 23.01S 59.57W
Fortín General Caballero 204 Cg 24.08S 59.30W
Fortín General Delgado 204 Cg 24.28S 59.15W
Fortín General Díaz 206 Hb 23.31S 60.34W
Fortín Guaraní 204 Cg 22.44S 59.30W
Fortín Hernandarias 204 Be 21.58S 61.30W
Fortín José M. López 204 Be 20.07S 60.15W
Fortín Lagerenza 204 Be 20.06S 61.03W
Fortín Madrejón 204 Ce 20.38S 59.52W
Fortín Mariscal López 204 Ce 23.39S 59.44W
Fortín Max Paredes 204 Cd 19.16S 59.58W
Fortín May Alberto Gardel 204 Af 22.46S 62.12W
Fortín Mayor Long 204 Ae 20.33S 62.01W
Fortín Mayor R. Santacruz 204 Be 20.15S 60.37W
Fortín Nueva Asunción 204 Be 20.42S 61.55W
Fortín Pikyrenda 204 Bf 20.20S 61.48W
Fortín Pilcomayo [Arg.] 204 Bf 23.52S 60.53W
Fortín Pilcomayo [Par.] 204 Bf 23.44S 60.51W
Fortín Pratts Gill 204 Bf 22.41S 61.33W
Fortín Presidente Ayala 204 Cf 23.30S 59.46W
Fortín Ravelo 204 Bf 19.18S 60.35W
Fortín Suárez Arana 204 Be 18.40S 60.09W
Fortín Teniente 1 Alfredo Stroessner 204 Cg 22.45S 61.32W
Fortín Teniente 1 H. Mendoza 204 Cd 19.54S 59.47W
Fortín Teniente 1 M. Cabello 204 Bf 23.28S 61.19W
Fortín Teniente 1 Ramiro Espínola 204 Be 21.28S 61.18W
Fortín Teniente Acosta 204 Bf 22.41S 60.32W
Fortín Teniente Agripino Enciso 204 Be 21.12S 61.34W
Fortín Teniente Américo Picco 204 Be 19.35S 59.43W
Fortín Teniente Aristigueta 204 Bf 22.21S 60.38W
Fortín Teniente E. Ochoa 204 Bf 21.42S 61.02W
Fortín Teniente Esteban Martínez 204 Cg 24.02S 59.51W
Fortín Teniente Juan E. López 204 Be 21.48S 61.48W
Fortín Teniente Montania 204 Cf 22.04S 59.57W
Fortín Teniente R. Rueda 204 Be 21.49S 60.49W
Fortín Toledo 204 Bf 22.20S 60.21W
Fortín Torres 204 Ce 21.01S 59.30W
Fortín Vanguardia 204 Cd 19.39S 58.16W
Fortín Vitiones 204 Cf 21.01S 59.30W
Fortín Zenteno 204 Cg 20.13S 59.59W
Fort Jeudey, Point of- [I] 197p Bb 12.00N 61.42W
Fort Kent 184 Mb 47.15N 68.36W
Fort Knox [I] 184 Fh 37.53N 85.55W
Fort-Lamy → N'Djamena 160 Ig 12.07N 15.03 E
Fort Lauderdale 182 Kf 26.07N 80.08W
Fort Liard 176 Hc 60.15N 123.28W
Fort-Liberté 194 Ld 19.38N 71.57W
Fort MacKay 180 Gc 57.08N 111.42W
Fort Macleod 180 Gd 49.43N 113.25W
Fort Mac Mahon 162 Hd 29.46N 1.37 E
Fort Madison 186 Kf 40.38N 91.21W
Fort-Mahon-Plage 124 Dd 50.21N 1.34 E
Fort McMurray 176 Hd 56.44N 111.23W
Fort McPherson 176 Hc 67.27N 134.53W
Fort Miribel 162 Hd 29.26N 3.00 E
Fort Morgan 186 Ef 40.15N 103.48W
Fort Myers 176 Kg 26.37N 81.54W
Fort Myers Beach 184 Gl 26.27N 81.57W

Fort Nelson 176 Gd 58.49N 122.39W
Fort Nelson [N] 180 Fe 59.33N 124.01W
Fort Norman 180 Ed 64.56N 125.22W
Fortore [N] 128 Ji 41.55N 15.17 E
Fort Payne 184 Eh 34.27N 85.43W
Fort Peck 188 Lb 48.01N 106.27W
Fort Peck Lake [<] 182 Kf 47.45N 106.50W
Fort Pierce 182 Kf 27.27N 80.20W
Fort Pierre 200 Mf 44.21N 100.22W
Fort Portal 170 Fb 0.39N 30.17 E
Fort Providence 176 Hc 61.21N 117.39W
Fort Qu'Appelle 188 Na 50.56N 103.09W
Fort Resolution 180 Gd 61.10N 113.40W
Fortress 218 Gg 46.34S 168.48 E
Fort Saint James 180 Ff 54.26N 124.15W
Fort Saint John 180 Fe 56.15N 120.51W
Fort Sandeman 148 Db 31.20N 69.27 E
Fort Saskatchewan 180 Gd 53.43N 113.13W
Fort Scott 186 Ih 37.50N 94.42W
Fort-Ševčenko 136 Fg 44.30N 50.14 E
Fort Severn 176 Kd 56.00N 87.38W
Fort Simpson 176 Gc 61.52N 121.23W
Fort Smith [Ar.-U.S.] 176 Jf 35.23N 94.25W
Fort Smith [N.W.T.-Can.] 176 Hd 60.00N 111.53W
Fort Stockton 182 Ge 30.53N 102.53W
Fort Sumner 186 Di 34.28N 104.15W
Fortuna 188 Cf 40.36N 124.09W
Fortuna, Rio de la- [N] 204 Cc 16.36S 58.46W
Fortune Bay [C] 180 Lg 47.15N 55.40W
Fortuneswell 118 Kk 50.33N 2.27W
Fort Vermilion 180 Fe 58.24N 116.00W
Fort Walton Beach 182 Je 30.25N 86.36W
Fort Washakie 188 Ke 43.00N 108.53W
Fort Wayne 176 Ke 41.04N 85.09W
Fort William 118 He 56.49N 5.07W
Fort Worth 176 Jf 32.45N 97.20W
Fort Yates 186 Fc 46.05N 100.38W
Fort Yukon 176 Fc 66.34N 145.17W
Forūr, Jazīreh-ye- [I] 146 Pi 26.17N 54.32 E
Foshan 142 Ng 22.59N 113.05 E
Fosheim Peninsula [I] 180 Ja 80.00N 84.30W
Fosnavåg 116 Ab 62.21N 5.39 E
Fosney 116 Ad 60.45N 4.55 E
Fossacesia 128 Ih 42.15N 14.29 E
Fossa Magna (EN) [X] 156 Fc 36.00N 138.08 E
Fossano 128 Bf 44.33N 7.43 E
Fossato, Colle di- [A] 128 Gg 43.20N 12.49 E
Fossberg 116 Cc 61.50N 8.34 E
Fossil 188 Ed 44.59N 120.13W
Fossil Bluff [I] 222 Qf 71.20S 68.17W
Fossombrone 128 Gg 43.41N 12.48 E
Fosston 186 Ic 47.35N 95.45W
Fos-sur-Mer 122 Kk 43.26N 4.57 E
Foster 212 Jg 38.39S 146.12 E
Foster, Mount- [A] 178 Le 59.48N 135.29W
Foster Bugt [C] 179 Jd 73.40N 21.40W
Fotadrevo 172 Fe 24.04S 64.23 E
Fotuha'a [I] 221bBa 19.49S 174.44W
Foucarmont 124 De 49.51N 1.34 E
Fougamou 170 Bc 1.13S 10.36 E
Fougères 122 Ef 48.21N 1.12W
Foul, Khalij- [C] 164 Ge 23.30N 35.40 E
Foula [I] 118 Ka 60.10N 2.05W
Foul Bay [C] 197q Bb 13.06N 59.27W
Fouligny 124 Ie 49.06N 6.33 E
Foulness Island [I] 118 Nj 51.36N 0.55 E
Foulness Point [I] 124 Cc 51.37N 0.57 E
Foulwind, Cape- [I] 218 Dd 41.45S 171.28 E
Fouman 146 Nd 5.43N 10.55 E
Foumban 166 Gd 5.43N 10.55 E
Foumbouni 172 Gb 11.50S 43.30 E
Foum Zguid 162 Fc 30.05N 6.52W
Foundation Ice Stream [N] 222 Rg 83.15S 60.00W
Fountains Abbey [I] 118 Lg 54.07N 1.34W
Fouquet Island [I] 172bBb 5.25S 53.20 E
Fourchambault 122 Jg 47.01N 3.05 E
Fourchue, Ile- [I] 197hBc 17.57N 62.55W
Fourmies 122 Kd 50.01N 4.03 E
Four Mountains, Islands of the- [I] 178a Db 52.50N 170.00W
Fournaise [A] 130 Jf 37.34N 26.30 E
Fouron/Voeren 124 Hd 50.45N 5.48 E
Fours 122 Jh 46.49N 3.43 E
Fourth Cataract (EN) = Rabī', Ash Shallāl ar- [N] 158 Kg 18.47N 32.03 E
Fous, Pointe des- [I] 197g Bb 15.12N 61.20W
Fouta [X] 166 Cg 11.30N 12.30W
Fouta Djalon [X] 158 Fg 11.30N 12.30W
Foutouna, Ile- [I] 208 If 19.32S 170.13 E
Foux, Cap-à- [I] 194 Kd 19.45N 73.27W
Fouzon [N] 122 Hg 47.16N 1.27 E
Foveaux Strait [I] 208 If 46.40S 168.10 E
Fowey 118 Hk 50.20N 4.38W
Fowler [Co.-U.S.] 186 Eg 38.08N 104.00W
Fowler [In.-U.S.] 184 De 40.37N 87.19W
Fowlers Bay [C] 212 Gf 32.00S 132.25 E
Fowman 146 Nc 37.13N 49.19 E
Fox Basin [C] 174 Lc 68.25N 77.00W
Foxe Channel [I] 176 Lc 64.30N 80.00W
Foxen [<] 116 De 59.25N 11.55 E
Fox Peninsula [I] 180 Lc 65.00N 76.00W
Foxford/Béal Easa 118 Dh 53.59N 9.07W
Fox Glacier 218 Ch 43.28S 170.00 E
Fox Islands [I] 174 Cd 54.00N 168.00W
Fox Peak [A] 218 Dd 43.50S 170.47 E
Fox River [N] 186 Lf 41.21N 88.50W
Foxton 218 Ge 40.28S 175.17 E
Fox Valley 188 Ma 50.29N 109.28W
Foyle / An Feabhal [N] 118 Gg 55.04N 7.15W
Foyle, Lough-/Loch Feabhail [C] 118 Ff 55.05N 7.10W
Foynes 118 Di 52.37N 9.06W
Foz do Cunene 170 Bf 17.15S 11.48 E
Foz do Iguaçu 200 Kh 25.33S 54.35W
Fraga 126 Mc 41.31N 0.21 E
Fragoso, Cayo [I] 194 Hb 22.44N 79.30W
Fraire, Walcourt- 124 Gd 50.16N 4.30 E
Fram 204 Gd 27.06S 55.58W
Fram Basin [I] 224 He 88.00N 80.00 E
Framlingham 124 Db 52.13N 1.20 E

Franca 206 Kb 20.32S 47.24W
Français, Récif des- [I] 216 Bc 19.30S 163.45 E
Franca-Josifa, zemlja- = Franz Joseph Land (EN) [I] 140 Ha 81.00N 55.00 E
Francavilla al Mare 128 Ih 42.25N 14.17 E
Francavilla Fontana 128 Lj 40.32N 17.35 E
France [I] 112 Gf 46.00N 2.00 E
Frances 180 Ed 60.16N 129.11W
Francés, Punta- [I] 194 Fc 21.38N 83.12W
Francesi, Punta di li- [I] 128 Di 41.08N 9.02 E
Francés Viejo, Cabo- [I] 194 Md 19.39N 69.55W
Franceville 160 Ii 1.38S 13.35 E
Franche-Comté [I] 122 Lh 47.00N 6.00 E
Franches Montagnes [A] 128 Ac 47.15N 7.00 E
Francia 204 Dk 32.34S 36.38W
Francis Case, Lake- [<] 174 Je 43.15N 99.00W
Francisco Beltrão 206 Jc 26.05S 53.04W
Francisco Escárcega 192 Nh 18.37N 90.43W
Francisco I. Madero 192 Ge 24.32N 104.22W
Francisco Madero 204 Al 35.52S 62.03W
Francisco Morazán [3] 194 Df 14.15N 87.15W
Francisco Sá 202 Ig 16.28S 43.40W
Franciscus Bay [C] 172 Ge 25.00S 14.50 E
Francistown 160 Jk 21.09S 27.31 E
Francofonte 128 Im 37.14N 14.53 E
Franconian Jura (EN) = Fränkische Alb [A] 110 Hf 49.00N 11.30 E
Francs Peak [A] 182 Gc 43.58N 109.20W
Franeker 122 La 53.11N 5.32 E
Frankenau 124 Kc 51.06N 8.56 E
Frankenberg (Eder) 120 Ee 51.04N 8.40 E
Frankenhöhe [A] 120 Gg 49.15N 10.15 E
Frankenthal (Pfalz) 124 Ke 49.32N 8.21 E
Frankenwald [A] 120 Hf 50.18N 11.36 E
Frankfort [In.-U.S.] 184 De 40.17N 86.31W
Frankfort [Ky.-U.S.] 176 Kf 38.12N 84.52W
Frankfort [Mi.-U.S.] 184 Dc 44.38N 86.14W
Frankfort (EN) = Frankfurt [2] 120 Kd 52.20N 14.30
Frankfort on the Main (EN) = Frankfurt am Main 112 Ge 50.07N 8.41 E
Frankfort on the Oder (EN) = Frankfurt (Oder) 120 Kd 52.21N 14.33 E
[2] 120 Kd 52.20N 14.30
Frankfurt (Oder) = Frankfort on the Oder (EN) 120 Kd 52.21N 14.33 E
Frankfurt am Main = Frankfurt on the Main (EN) 112 Ge 50.07N 8.41 E
Fränkische Alb = Franconian Jura (EN) [A] 110 Hf 49.00N 11.30
Fränkische Saale [N] 120 Ff 50.03N 9.42 E
Fränkische Schweiz [A] 120 Hg 49.45N 11.20 E
Franklin [In.-U.S.] 184 Df 39.29N 86.03W
Franklin [Ky.-U.S.] 184 Dg 36.43N 86.35W
Franklin [La.-U.S.] 176 Kl 29.48N 91.30W
Franklin [N.C.-U.S.] 184 Fh 35.11N 83.23W
Franklin [N.H.-U.S.] 184 Ld 43.27N 71.39W
Franklin [Pa.-U.S.] 184 He 41.24N 79.49W
Franklin [Tn.-U.S.] 184 Dh 35.55N 86.52W
Franklin Bay [C] 174 Gc 68.45N 125.35W
Franklin Delano Roosevelt Lake [<] 182 Db 48.20N 118.10W
Franklin Island [I] 222 Kf 76.05S 168.11 E
Franklin Lake [Nv.-U.S.] [<] 188 Ha 40.24N 115.12W
Franklin Lake [N.W.T.-Can.] [<] 180 Hb 66.55N 96.00W
Franklin Mountains [A] 174 Gc 63.15N 123.30W
Franklin Strait [I] 180 Hb 71.30N 96.30W
Fransfontein 172 Hc 20.12S 15.01 E
Fränsta 116 Gb 62.30N 16.09 E
Franz Josef Glacier 218 Ch 43.23S 170.11 E
Franz Joseph Land (EN) = Franca-Josifa, zemlja- [I] 140 Ha 81.00N 55.00 E
Frascati 128 Gi 41.48N 12.41 E
Fraser [Can.] [N] 174 Ge 49.09N 123.12W
Fraser [Newf.-Can.] [N] 180 Le 56.39N 63.08W
Fraserburg 172 Cf 31.55S 21.30 E
Fraserburgh 118 Ld 57.42N 2.00W
Fraserdale 180 Jg 49.51N 81.38W
Fraser Plateau [A] 208 Gg 25.15S 153.10 E
Fraser Range 212 Gl 31.30S 122.50 E
Frasertown 218 Gc 38.58S 177.24 E
Frasnes-les-Anvaing 124 Fd 50.40N 3.36 E
Frauenfeld 128 Cc 47.35N 8.54 E
Fray Bentos 206 Mc 33.08S 58.18W
Frechen 124 Id 50.55N 6.49 E
Frechilla 126 Hb 42.08N 4.50W
Fredericia 114 Bi 55.35N 9.46 E
Frederick [Md.-U.S.] 184 If 39.25N 77.25W
Frederick [Ok.-U.S.] 186 Gi 34.23N 99.01W
Frederick E. Hyde Fjord [C] 179 Jb 82.40S 22.00W
Frederick Reef [I] 208 Gg 21.00S 154.25 E
Fredericksburg [Tx.-U.S.] 186 Gk 30.17N 98.52W
Fredericksburg [Va.-U.S.] 184 If 38.18N 77.30W
Fredericktown 186 Kh 37.33N 90.18W
Frederico Westphalen 204 Fh 27.22S 53.24W
Fredericton 176 Me 45.58N 66.39W
Frederiksberg [2] 116 Ei 55.55N 12.15 E
Frederiksdal 178 Dh 53.59N 9.07W
Frederikshåb/Pâmiut 179 Hf 62.00N 49.45W
Frederikshåbs Bank (EN) [I] 179 Gf 62.16N 49.45W
Frederikshavn 112 Hd 57.26N 10.32 E
Frederikssund 116 Ei 55.50N 12.04 E
Frederiksted 196 Di 17.42N 64.48W
Frederiksværk 116 Ei 55.58N 12.02 E
Fredonia 188 Ed 36.57N 112.32W
Fredrika 114 Ed 64.05N 18.24 E
Fredrikshamn/Hamina 114 Gf 60.34N 27.12 E
Fredrikstad 114 Cg 59.13N 10.57 E
Fredvang 114 Cb 68.05N 13.10 E
Freeling Heights [A] 210 Hf 30.10S 139.25 E
Freels, Cape- [I] 180 Mf 49.15N 53.29W
Freeport [Bah.] 190 Ic 26.30N 78.45W
Freeport [Il.-U.S.] 182 Jc 42.17N 89.36W

Index Symbols

[1] Independent Nation
[2] State, Region
[3] District, County
[4] Municipality
[5] Colony, Dependency
■ Continent
[X] Physical Region

Historical or Cultural Region
Mount, Mountain
Volcano
Hill
Mountains, Mountain Range
Hills, Escarpment
Plateau, Upland

Pass, Gap
Plain, Lowland
Delta
Salt Flat
Valley, Canyon
Crater, Cave
Karst Features

Depression
Polder
Cliff
Desert, Dunes
Forest, Woods
Heath, Steppe
Cape, Point

Coast, Beach
Isthmus
Peninsula
Coral Reef
Well, Spring
Oasis
Island

Rock, Reef
Islands, Archipelago
Rocks, Reefs
Lake
Salt Lake
Intermittent Lake
River, Stream

Waterfall, Rapids
River Mouth, Estuary
Glacier
Ice Shelf, Pack Ice
Ocean
Ridge
Swamp, Pond

Canal
Bank
Seamount
Tablemount
Shelf
Basin
Strait, Fjord

Lagoon
Bank
Trench, Abyss
National Park, Reserve
Point of Interest
Recreation Site
Cave, Cavern

Escarpment, Sea Scarp
Fracture
Trench, Abyss
Wall, Walls
Church, Abbey
Temple
Scientific Station

Historic Site
Ruins
Church, Abbey
Mine
Lighthouse
Railway station

Airport
Port
Military installation
Lighthouse
Mine
Tunnel
Dam, Bridge

Freeport [N.Y.-U.S.] 184 Ke 40.40N 73.35W
Freeport [Tx.-U.S.] 182 Hf 28.55N 95.22W
Freer 186 Gm 27.53N 98.37W
Freetown [Atg.] 197d Bb 17.03N 61.42W
Freetown [S.L.] 160 Fh 8.30N 13.15W
Fregenal de la Sierra 126 Ff 38.10N 6.39W
Fregene 128 Gi 41.51N 12.12 E
Fréhel, Cap- 122 Df 48.42N 2.19W
Frei 116 Ba 63.01N 7.48 E
Freiberg 120 Jf 50.55N 13.22 E
Freiberger Mulde 120 Ie 51.10N 12.48 E
Freiburg/Fribourg 128 Bd 46.50N 7.10 E
Freiburg/Fribourg [2] 128 Bd 46.40N 7.10 E
Freiburg im Breisgau 112 Gf 48.00N 7.51 E
Freilassing 120 Ii 47.51N 12.59 E
Freirina 206 Fc 28.30S 71.06W
Freisen 124 Je 49.33N 7.15 E
Freising 120 Hh 48.24N 11.44 E
Freistadt 128 Ib 48.30N 14.30 E
Freital 120 Je 51.01N 13.39 E
Fréjus 122 Mk 43.26N 6.44 E
Fréjus, Col de- 122 Mi 45.07N 6.40 E
Fréjus, Colle del- 122 Mi 45.07N 6.40 E
Fremantle, Perth- 212 Df 32.03S 115.45 E
Fremont [Ca.-U.S.] 182 Cd 37.34N 122.01W
Fremont [Nb.-U.S.] 182 Hc 41.26N 96.30W
Fremont [Oh.-U.S.] 184 Fe 41.21N 83.08W
Fremont River 188 Jg 38.24N 110.42W
French Frigate Shoals 208 Kb 23.45N 166.10W
French Guiana (EN) =
Guyane Française [5] 200 Ke 4.00N 53.00W
French Lick 184 Df 38.33N 86.37W
Frenchman Creek 186 Ff 40.13N 100.50W
Frenchman River 182 Fb 48.24N 107.05W
French Pass 218 Ed 40.55S 173.50 E
French Plain (EN) 110 Gf 47.00N 1.00 E
French Polynesia (EN) =
Polynésie Française [5] 210 Mf 16.00S 145.00W
French River 184 Gc 45.56N 80.54W
Frenda 162 Hb 35.04N 1.02 E
Frentani, Monti dei- 128 Ii 41.55N 14.30 E
Freren 124 Jb 52.29N 7.33 E
Fresco 166 Dd 5.05N 5.34W
Fresco, Rio- 202 He 6.39S 52.00W
Freshfield, Cape- 222 Je 68.22S 151.05 E
Fresnes-en-Woëvre 124 He 49.06N 5.37 E
Fresnillo de González
Echevarría 190 Dd 23.10N 102.53W
Fresno 176 Hf 36.45N 119.45W
Fresno River 188 Eh 37.05N 120.33W
Fresquel 122 Ik 43.14N 2.24 E
Fresvikbreen 116 Bc 61.02N 6.45 E
Freu, Cabo- / Freu, Cap des-
126 Pe 39.45N 3.27 E
Freu, Cap des- / Freu, Cabo-
126 Pe 39.45N 3.27 E
Freudenberg 124 Jd 50.54N 7.52 E
Freudenstadt 120 Eh 48.26N 8.25 E
Frévent 122 Id 50.16N 2.17 E
Freycinet Estuary 212 Ce 26.25S 113.45 E
Freycinet Peninsula 212 Jh 42.15S 148.20 E
Freyming-Merlebach 124 Ie 49.09N 6.47 E
Freyre 204 Aj 31.10S 62.02W
Freyung 120 Jh 48.48N 13.33 E
Fri 130 Jn 35.25N 26.56 E
Fria 166 Cc 10.27N 13.32W
Fria, Cape- 158 Ij 18.27S 12.01 E
Frias 206 Gc 28.39S 65.09W
Fribourg/Freiburg 128 Bd 46.50N 7.10 E
Fribourg/Freiburg [2] 128 Bd 46.40N 7.10 E
Fridtjof Nansen, Mount- 222 Lg 85.21S 167.33W
Friedberg 128 Kc 47.26N 16.03 E
Friedberg (Hessen) 120 Ef 50.21N 8.46 E
Friedrichshafen 120 Fi 47.39N 9.29 E
Friedrichsthal 124 Je 49.19N 7.06 E
Friesach 128 Id 46.57N 14.24 E
Friese Gat 124 Ia 53.30N 6.05 E
Friese Wad 124 Ha 53.24N 5.45 E
Friesische Inseln/
Waddeneilanden = Frisian
Islands (EN) 110 Hc 54.00N 6.00 E
Friesland [3] 124 Ha 53.03N 5.45 E
Friesland 110 Ge 53.05N 6.00 E
Friesland 122 La 53.05N 6.00 E
Friesoythe 120 Dc 53.01N 7.51 E
Frigate Island 197p Cb 12.25N 61.29W
Friggesund 116 Gc 61.54N 16.32 E
Frignano 128 Ef 44.20N 10.50 E
Frindsbury Reef 219a Da 5.00S 159.07 E
Frinnaryd 116 Fg 57.56N 14.49 E
Frinton-on-Sea 124 Dc 51.50N 1.15 E
Frio, Cabo- 198 Lh 22.53S 42.00W
Frio, Rio- 194 Eh 11.08N 84.46W
Frio Draw 186 Ei 34.50N 102.08W
Friona 186 Ei 34.38N 102.43W
Frio River 186 Gl 28.30N 98.10W
Frisco Peak 188 Ig 38.31N 113.14W
Frisian Islands (EN) =
Friesische Inseln/
Waddeneilanden 110 Hc 54.00N 6.00 E
Frisian Islands (EN) =
Waddeneilanden/
Friesische Inseln 110 Hc 54.00N 6.00 E
Fristad 116 Eg 57.50N 13.01 E
Fritsla 116 Eg 57.33N 12.47 E
Fritzlar 120 Fe 51.08N 9.17 E
Friuli 128 Ge 46.00N 13.00 E
Friuli-Venezia
Giulia 128 Gd 46.00N 13.00 E
Frobisher Bay 174 Mc 62.30N 66.00W
Frobisher Lake 180 Ge 56.20N 108.20W
Froidchapelle 124 Gd 50.09N 4.20 E
Froissy 124 Ee 49.34N 2.13 E
Frolovo 136 Ef 49.45N 43.39 E
Fromberg 188 Kd 45.23N 108.54W
Frombork 120 Pb 54.22N 19.41 E
Frome 118 Kj 51.14N 2.20W
Frome, Lake- 208 Eh 30.50S 139.50 E
Fröndenberg 124 Jc 51.28N 7.46 E
Fronteira 126 Ee 39.03N 7.39W
Fronteiras 202 Je 7.05S 40.37W
Frontera 192 Mh 18.32N 92.38W
Frontera, Punta- 192 Mh 19.36N 92.42W
Fronteras 192 Eb 30.56N 109.31W
Frontignan 122 Jk 43.27N 3.45 E
Frontino, Páramo- 202 Cb 6.28N 76.04W
Front Range 174 If 39.45N 105.45W
Front Royal 184 Hf 38.56N 78.13W
Frosinone 128 Hi 41.38N 13.19 E
Frösö 116 Fa 63.11N 14.32 E
Frostburg 184 Hf 39.39N 78.56W
Frost Glacier 222 Ie 67.05S 129.00 E
Frövi 116 Fe 59.28N 15.22 E
Frøya 114 Be 63.43N 8.42 E
Frøysjøen 116 Ac 61.50N 5.05 E
Frozen Strait 180 Jc 65.50N 84.30W
Fruges 122 Id 50.31N 2.08 E
Frunze [Kirg.-U.S.S.R.] 142 Je 42.54N 74.36 E
Frunze [Kirg.-U.S.S.R.] 135 Hd 40.06N 71.45 E
Frunzovka 130 Mb 47.20N 29.37 E
Fruška Gora 130 Cd 45.10N 19.35 E
Frutal 202 Ih 20.02S 48.55W
Frutigen 128 Bd 46.35N 7.40 E
Fry Canyon 188 Jh 37.38N 110.08W
Frýdek Místek 120 Og 49.41N 18.22 E
Frylinckspan 172 Ce 26.46S 22.28 E
Ftéri 130 Ej 39.09N 21.33 E
Fua'amotu 221b Ac 21.15S 175.08W
Fua Mulaku Island 148a Bc 0.15S 73.30 E
Fu'an 152 Kf 27.10N 119.44 E
Fu-chien Sheng → Fujian
Sheng = Fukien (EN) [2] 152 Kf 26.00N 118.00 E
Fuchskauten 120 Ef 50.40N 8.05 E
Fuchū [Jap.] 156 Cd 34.34N 133.14 E
Fuchū [Jap.] 156 Fd 35.41N 139.28 E
Fuchun-Jiang 154 Fi 30.15N 120.15 E
Fuchunjiang-Shuiku 154 Ej 29.29N 119.31 E
Fucino, Conca del- 128 Hh 42.01N 13.31 E
Fudai 156 Ga 40.01N 141.52 E
Fuding 152 Lf 27.19N 120.08 E
Fuengirola 126 Hh 36.32N 4.37W
Fuente de Cantos 126 Ff 38.15N 6.18W
Fuente del Maestre 126 Ff 38.32N 6.27W
Fuente Obejuna 126 Gf 38.16N 5.25W
Fuentesaúco 126 Gc 41.14N 5.30W
Fuentes de Andalucía 126 Gg 37.28N 5.21W
Fuerte 190 Cc 25.54N 109.22W
Fuerte, Isla- 194 Ii 9.23N 76.11W
Fuerte, Sierra del- 192 Hd 27.30N 102.45W
Fuerte Olimpo 206 Ib 21.02S 57.54W
Fuerteventura 158 Ff 28.20N 14.00W
Fuga 150 Hc 18.52N 121.22 E
Fugong 152 Gf 27.03N 98.57 E
Fugou 154 Cg 34.04N 114.23 E
Fugu 152 Jd 39.02N 111.03 E
Fuguo → Zhanhua 154 Ef 37.42N 118.08 E
Fuhai/Burultokay 152 Eb 47.06N 87.23 E
Fuhayrī, Wādī- 144 Hf 16.04N 52.11 E
Fu He 154 Dj 28.36N 116.04 E
Fuji 154 Og 35.09N 138.38 E
Fujian Sheng (Fu-chien
Sheng) = Fukien (EN) [2] 152 Kf 26.00N 118.00 E
Fujieda 156 Fd 34.51N 138.15 E
Fuji-Gawa 156 Fd 35.07N 138.38 E
Fujin 152 Nb 47.15N 132.01 E
Fujinomiya 156 Fd 35.12N 138.38 E
Fujioka 156 Fc 36.15N 139.03 E
Fuji-San 140 Pf 35.26N 138.43 E
Fujisawa 156 Fd 35.21N 139.27 E
Fujiyoshida 156 Fd 35.29N 138.47 E
Fukagawa 152 Pc 43.43N 142.03 E
Fūkah 146 Bg 31.04N 27.55 E
Fukang 152 Ec 44.10N 87.59 E
Fuka-Shima 156 Be 32.43N 131.56 E
Fukiage 156 Bf 31.30N 130.20 E
Fukien (EN) = Fu-chien
Sheng → Fujian Sheng [2] 152 Kf 26.00N 118.00 E
Fukien (EN) = Fujian Sheng
(Fu-chien Sheng) [2] 152 Kf 26.00N 118.00 E
Fukuchiyama 154 Mg 35.18N 135.07 E
Fukue 154 Jh 32.41N 128.50 E
Fukueichiao 152 Lf 25.19N 121.34 E
Fukue-Jima 154 Jh 32.41N 128.48 E
Fukui 152 Od 36.04N 136.13 E
Fukui Ken [2] 154 Ng 36.00N 136.20 E
Fukuma 156 Be 33.47N 130.28 E
Fukuoka 142 Pf 33.35N 130.24 E
Fukuoka Ken [2] 154 Kh 33.28N 130.45 E
Fukuroi 156 Ed 34.45N 137.54 E
Fukushima [Jap.] 152 Pd 37.45N 140.28 E
Fukushima [Jap.] 152 Pc 41.29N 140.15 E
Fukushima Ken [2] 154 Pf 37.25N 140.10 E
Fukuyama 152 Ne 34.29N 133.22 E
Fukuyama-Matsunaga 156 Cd 34.27N 133.16 E
Fūlādī, Kūh-e- 144 Kc 34.38N 67.32 E
Fūlād Mahalleh 146 Od 36.02N 53.44 E
Fulanga 219d Cc 19.08S 178.34W
Fulda 120 Ff 50.33N 9.40 E
Fulda 110 Ge 51.25N 9.39 E
Fuliji 154 Dh 33.47N 116.59 E
Fulin → Hanyuan 152 Hf 29.25N 102.12 E
Fuling 152 If 29.40N 107.21 E
Fullerton 186 Hf 41.22N 97.58W
Fulton [Arg.] 204 Cm 37.25S 58.48W
Fulton [Il.-U.S.] 186 Kf 41.52N 90.11W
Fulton [Ky.-U.S.] 184 Cg 36.30N 88.53W
Fulton [Mo.-U.S.] 186 Kg 38.52N 91.57W
Fulton [N.Y.-U.S.] 184 Id 43.20N 76.26W
Fulufjället 116 Ec 61.33N 12.43 E
Fumaiolo 128 Gg 43.47N 12.04 E
Fumay 122 Kd 50.00N 4.42 E
Fumel 122 Gj 44.30N 0.58 E
Funabashi 154 Og 35.42N 139.59 E
Funabiki 156 Gc 37.26N 140.35 E
Funafuti 210 Ie 8.01S 178.00 E
Funafuti Atoll 208 Ie 8.31S 179.08 E
Funagata 156 Gb 38.42N 140.18 E
Funagata-Yama 156 Gb 38.27N 140.37 E
Funakoshi-Wan 156 Hb 39.25N 142.00 E
Funan 154 Ch 32.38N 115.35 E
Funäsdalen 114 Ce 62.32N 12.33 E
Funchal 160 Fe 32.38N 16.54W
Fundación 202 Da 10.29N 74.12W
Fundão 126 Ed 40.08N 7.30W
Fundy, Bay of- 174 Me 45.00N 66.00W
Funeral Peak 188 Gh 36.08N 116.37W
Fungalei 220h Bb 13.17S 176.07W
Funhalouro 172 Ed 23.05S 34.24 E
Funing [China] 152 Ig 23.39N 105.33 E
Funing [China] 154 Eh 33.48N 119.47 E
Funing [China] 154 Ee 39.56N 119.15 E
Funiu Shan 152 Je 33.40N 112.10 E
Funtua 166 Gc 11.32N 7.19 E
Fuping 154 Ce 38.49N 114.15 E
Fuqing 152 Kf 25.47N 119.24 E
Furancungo 172 Eb 14.54S 33.37 E
Furano 154 Qc 43.21N 142.23 E
Fūren 156a Ca 44.17N 142.25 E
Furenai 156a Cb 42.43N 142.15 E
Fūren-Ko 156a Db 43.20N 145.20 E
Fūrg 146 Ph 28.18N 55.13 E
Fur Jiang 154 Hc 42.37N 125.33 E
Furmanov 114 Jh 57.16N 41.07 E
Furnas, Represa de- 202 Ih 21.20S 45.50W
Furnas, Serra das- 204 Fb 15.45S 53.20W
Furneaux Group 208 Fi 40.10S 148.05 E
Furnes/Veurne 122 Ic 51.04N 2.40 E
Furqlus 146 Ge 34.36N 37.05 E
Furrīyānah 162 Ic 34.57N 8.34 E
Fürstenau 124 Jb 52.31N 7.43 E
Fürstenauer Berge 124 Jb 52.35N 7.45 E
Fürstenfeld 128 Kc 47.03N 16.05 E
Fürstenfeldbruck 120 Hh 48.11N 11.15 E
Fürstenlager 124 Ke 49.42N 8.38 E
Fürstenwalde 120 Kd 52.22N 14.04 E
Furtado, Rio- → Feijão
Prêto, Rio- 204 Dc 17.33S 57.23W
Fürth [F.R.G.] 120 Gg 49.28N 11.00 E
Fürth [F.R.G.] 124 Ke 49.39N 8.47 E
Furth im Wald 120 Ig 49.18N 12.51 E
Furubira 156a Bb 43.16N 140.39 E
Furudal 114 Df 61.10N 15.08 E
Furukawa 152 Pd 38.34N 140.58 E
Furusund 116 He 59.40N 18.55 E
Fury and Hecla Strait 180 Jc 69.55N 84.00W
Fushan [China] 154 Ag 35.58N 111.51 E
Fushan [China] 154 Ff 37.30N 121.15 E
Fushë-Arëzi 130 Dg 42.04N 20.02 E
Fushë-Lura 130 Dh 41.48N 20.13 E
Fu Shui 154 Cj 29.52N 115.26 E
Fushun 142 Oe 41.46N 123.56 E
Fusong 152 Mc 42.20N 127.17 E
Füsselberg 124 Je 49.32N 7.14 E
Füssen 120 Gi 47.34N 10.42 E
Futa, Passo della- 128 Ff 44.05N 11.17 E
Futago-Yama 156 Be 33.35N 131.38 E
Futaoi-Jima 156 Bd 34.06N 130.47 E
Futog 130 Cd 45.15N 19.42 E
Futuna, Ile- 208 Jf 14.17S 178.09W
Fuwah 146 Dg 31.12N 30.33 E
Fuxian (Wafangdian) 152 Ld 39.38N 121.59 E
Fuxian Hu 152 Hg 24.30N 102.55 E
Fuxin 142 Oe 41.59N 121.38 E
Fuxin Monggolzu Zizhixian 154 Fc 42.06N 121.46 E
Fuyang 152 Ke 32.47N 115.46 E
Fuyang He 154 Dg 38.14N 116.05 E
Fuyang Zhan 154 Ch 32.56N 115.53 E
Fuyu [China] 152 Lb 45.10N 124.52 E
Fuyu [China] 152 Lb 47.48N 124.26 E
Fuyuan [China] 152 Nb 48.21N 134.18 E
Fuyuan [China] 152 Lc 42.44N 124.57 E
Fuyuan [China] 152 Hf 25.43N 104.20 E
Fuyun/Koktokay 142 Ke 47.13N 89.39 E
Füzesabony 120 Qi 47.45N 20.25 E
Fuzhou [China] 142 Ng 26.10N 119.20 E
Fuzhou [China] 152 Kf 27.58N 116.20 E
Fuzhou He 154 Fe 39.36N 121.35 E
Fyllas Bank (EN) 179 Gf 64.00N 53.00W
Fyn [2] 116 Di 55.20N 10.30 E
Fyn 110 Hd 55.20N 10.30 E
Fyne, Loch- 118 He 56.10N 5.20W
Fyresdal 114 Bg 59.11N 8.06 E
Fyresvatn 116 Ce 59.05N 8.10 E
Fzâra, Gara'et- 128 Bn 36.47N 7.30 E

G

Gaasbeek 124 Gd 50.48N 4.10 E
Gaasterland 124 Hb 52.54N 5.36 E
Gaasterland 124 Hb 52.53N 5.35 E
Gaasterland-Balk 124 Hb 52.54N 5.36 E
Gabaru Reef 220a Bb 7.53N 134.31 E
Gabas 122 Fk 43.46N 0.42W
Gabba' 168 Id 8.02N 50.08 E
Gabbs 188 Gg 38.52N 117.55W
Gabela 160 Ij 10.52S 14.23 E
Gabès, Gulf of-(EN) = Qābis,
Khalīj- 158 Ie 34.00N 10.25 E
Gabon [1] 160 Ii 1.00S 11.45 E
Gabon 170 Ab 0.25N 9.20 E
Gaborone 160 Jk 24.40S 25.55 E
Gabras 168 Dc 10.16N 26.14 E
Gabriel Strait 180 Kd 61.50N 65.40W
Gabriel y Galán, Embalse
de- 126 Fd 40.15N 6.15W
Gabrovo 130 Ig 42.52N 25.19 E
Gabrovo [2] 130 Ig 42.52N 25.19 E
Gacé 122 Gf 48.48N 0.18 E
Gachsārān 146 Ng 30.12N 50.47 E
Gackle 186 Gc 46.38N 99.09W
Gacko 128 Mg 43.10N 18.32 E
Gadag 148 Fe 15.25N 75.37 E
Gäddede 114 Dd 64.30N 14.09 E
Gadê 152 Ge 34.13N 99.29 E
Gadjač 132 Id 50.22N 34.01 E
Gádor, Sierra de- 126 Jh 36.55N 2.45W
Gadsden 182 Je 34.02N 86.02W
Gadūk, Gardaneh-ye- 146 Oe 35.55N 52.55 E
Gadzi 168 Be 4.47N 16.42 E
Gael Hamkes Bugt 179 Jd 74.00N 22.00W
Găeşti 130 Ie 44.43N 25.19 E
Gaeta 128 Hi 41.12N 13.35 E
Gaeta, Golfo di- 128 Hi 41.05N 13.30 E
Gaferut Island 208 Fd 9.14N 145.23 E
Gaffney 184 Gh 35.05N 81.39W
Gag, Pulau- 150 Ig 0.25S 129.53 E
Gagan 219a Ba 5.14S 154.37 E
Gagarin [R.S.F.S.R.] 136 Dd 55.35N 35.01 E
Gagarin [Uzb.-U.S.S.R.] 135 Gd 40.40N 68.05 E
Gagévésouva, Pointe- 219b Ca 13.04S 166.32 E
Gaggenau 124 Kf 48.48N 8.20 E
Gagnef 114 Df 60.35N 15.04 E
Gagnoa 160 Gh 6.08N 5.56W
Gagnoa [3] 166 Dd 6.03N 6.00W
Gagnon 180 Kf 51.55N 68.10W
Gagra 136 Eg 43.17N 40.15 E
Gahkom 146 Ph 28.12N 55.50 E
Gahkom, Kūh-e- 146 Ph 28.10N 55.57 E
Gaíba, Laguna- 204 Dc 17.45S 57.43W
Gail 128 Hd 46.36N 13.53 E
Gaillac 122 Hk 43.54N 1.55 E
Gaillefontaine 124 De 49.39N 1.37 E
Gaillimh/Galway 112 Fe 53.16N 9.03W
Gaillimh/Galway [2] 118 Eh 53.20N 9.00W
Gaillon 124 De 49.10N 1.20 E
Gailtaler Alpen 128 Gd 46.40N 13.00 E
Gaiman 206 Gf 43.17S 65.29W
Găineşti 130 Ib 47.25N 25.55 E
Gainesville [Fl.-U.S.] 176 Kg 29.40N 82.20W
Gainesville [Ga.-U.S.] 182 Ke 34.18N 83.50W
Gainesville [Mo.-U.S.] 186 Jh 36.36N 92.26W
Gainesville [Tx.-U.S.] 182 He 33.37N 97.08W
Gainsborough 118 Mh 53.24N 0.46W
Gairdner, Lake- 208 Eh 31.35S 136.00 E
Gairloch 118 Hd 57.43N 5.40W
Gai Xian 152 Lc 40.24N 122.17 E
Gaiziņa kalns /
Gajzinkalns 116 Kh 56.50N 25.59 E
Gaj 136 Fe 51.31N 58.30 E
Gajny 136 Fc 60.20N 54.15 E
Gajsin 136 Cf 48.50N 29.27 E
Gajvoron 132 Fe 48.22N 29.52 E
Gajzinkalns / Gaiziņa
kalns 116 Kh 56.50N 25.59 E
Galaasija 135 Ee 39.52N 64.27 E
Gălăbovo 130 Ig 42.08N 25.51 E
Gala Gölü 130 Ji 40.45N 26.12 E
Galaico, Macizo- 126 Eb 42.30N 7.20W
Galán, Cerro- 206 Gc 25.55S 66.52W
Galana 158 Li 3.09S 40.08 E
Galanta 120 Nh 48.12N 17.44 E
Galap 220a Bb 7.38N 134.39 E
Galápagos, Islas-/Colón,
Archipiélago de- =
Galapagos Islands (EN) 198 Gf 0.30S 90.30W
Galapagos Fracture Zone
(EN) 106 Mi 0.00 100.00W
Galapagos Islands (EN) =
Colon, Archipiélago de-/
Galápagos, Islas- 198 Gf 0.30S 90.30W
Galapagos Islands (EN) =
Galápagos, Islas-/Colón,
Archipiélago de- 198 Gf 0.30S 90.30W
Galarza 204 Di 28.06S 56.41W
Galashiels 118 Kf 55.37N 2.49W
Galaţi 112 If 45.27N 28.03 E
Galaţi [2] 130 Kd 45.33N 27.56 E
Galatina 128 Mj 40.10N 18.10 E
Galatone 128 Mj 40.09N 18.04 E
Galatzó 126 Oe 39.38N 2.29 E
Galdar 162 Dd 28.09N 15.39W
Galdhøpiggen 114 Bf 61.37N 8.17 E
Galeana [Mex.] 192 Fb 30.07N 107.38W
Galeana [Mex.] 192 Ie 24.50N 100.04W
Galeh Dār 146 Oi 27.38N 52.42 E
Galela 150 If 1.50N 127.50 E
Galena [Ak.-U.S.] 178 Hd 64.44N 156.57W
Galena [Il.-U.S.] 186 Ke 42.25N 90.26W
Galeota Point 196 Fg 10.08N 60.59W
Galera, Punta- 206 Fe 39.59S 73.43W
Galera, Rio- 204 Bb 14.25S 60.07W
Galera Point 196 Fg 10.49N 60.55W
Galesburg 182 Ic 40.57N 90.22W
Galga 120 Pi 47.33N 19.43 E
Gal Gaduud [3] 168 Hd 5.00N 47.00 E
Galheirão, Rio- 204 Ja 12.23S 45.05W
Galheiros 204 Ia 13.18S 46.25W
Gali 132 Lh 42.36N 41.42 E
Galič [R.S.F.S.R.] 136 Ed 58.23N 42.21 E
Galič [Ukr.-U.S.S.R.] 132 De 49.06N 24.43 E
Galicea Mare 130 Ge 44.06N 23.18 E
Galicia 110 Fg 43.00N 8.00W
Galicia / Galiza [2] 126 Eb 43.00N 8.00W
Galicia (EN) = Galicija 110 If 49.50N 21.00 E
Galicia (EN) = Galicija [Eur.]
120 Qg 49.50N 21.00 E
Galicia (EN) = Galicja 110 If 49.50N 21.00 E
Galicia (EN) = Galicja 120 Qg 49.50N 21.00 E
Galicija [Eur.] = Galicia (EN)
120 Qg 49.50N 21.00 E
Galicija [Ukr.-U.S.S.R.] 120 Tg 49.00N 24.00 E
Galicija = Galicia (EN) 110 If 49.50N 21.00 E
Galicja = Galicia (EN) 110 If 49.50N 21.00 E
Galicja = Galicia (EN) 120 Qg 49.50N 21.00 E
Galilee, Lake- 212 Jd 22.20S 145.55 E
Galimy 138 Kd 62.19N 156.00 E
Galina Point 194 Id 18.24N 76.53W
Galion 184 Fe 40.44N 82.46W
Galion, Baie du- 197h Bb 14.44N 60.57W
Galiton 128 Cm 37.30N 8.52 E
Galiuro Mountains 188 Jj 32.40N 110.20W
Galiza / Galicia [2] 126 Eb 43.00N 8.00W
Gālka'yo 160 Lh 6.49N 47.23 E
Galkino 134 Ki 55.40N 62.55 E
Gallarate 128 Ce 45.40N 8.47 E
Gallatin 184 Dg 36.24N 86.27W
Gallatin Range 188 Jd 45.15N 111.05W
Gallatin River 188 Jd 45.56N 111.29W
Galle 142 Ki 6.02N 80.13 E
Gállego 126 Lc 41.39N 0.51W
Gallegos, Rio- 198 Jk 51.36S 68.59W
Gallinas, Punta- 198 Id 12.25N 71.40W
Gallinas Peak 186 Di 34.15N 105.45W
Gallipoli 128 Lj 40.03N 17.58 E
Gallipoli Peninsula (EN) =
Gelibolu Yarımadası 130 Ji 40.20N 26.30 E
Gallipolis 184 Ff 38.49N 82.14W
Gällivare 112 Ib 67.08N 20.42 E
Galljaaral 135 Fd 40.02N 67.35 E
Gällö 114 De 62.55N 15.14 E
Gallo 126 Jd 40.48N 2.09W
Gallo, Capo- 128 Hl 38.15N 13.19 E
Gallo Mountains 186 Bi 34.00N 108.15W
Galloway 118 If 55.00N 4.25W
Galloway, Mull of- 118 Ig 54.38N 4.50W
Gallup 176 If 35.32N 108.44W
Gallur 126 Kc 41.52N 1.19W
Gallura 128 Dj 41.00N 9.15 E
Galmaarden/Gammerages 124 Fd 50.45N 3.58 E
Galole 170 Hc 1.30S 40.02 E
Galt 184 Gd 43.22N 80.19W
Gal Tardo 168 He 3.37N 45.58 E
Galtasen 116 Eg 57.48N 13.30 E
Galty Mountains/Na
Gaibhlte 118 Ei 52.23N 8.11W
Galut 152 Hb 46.43N 100.08 E
Galveston 176 Jg 29.18N 94.48W
Galveston Bay 174 Jg 29.36N 94.57W
Galveston Island 186 Il 29.13N 94.55W
Gálvez 206 Hd 32.02S 61.13W
Galway/Gaillimh 112 Fe 53.16N 9.03W
Galway/Gaillimh [2] 118 Eh 53.20N 9.00W
Galway Bay/Cuan na
Gaillimhe 110 Fe 53.10N 9.15W
Gamaches 124 De 49.59N 1.33 E
Gamagōri 156 Ed 34.49N 137.13 E
Gamarra 202 Db 8.19N 73.44W
Gamba [China] 152 Ef 28.17N 88.31 E
Gamba [Gabon] 170 Ac 2.37S 10.00 E
Gambaga 166 Ec 10.32N 0.26W
Gambela 160 Kh 8.15N 34.36 E
Gambell 178 Ed 63.46N 171.46W
Gambia [1] 160 Fg 13.25N 16.00W
Gambia 158 Fg 13.28N 16.34W
Gambia (EN) = Gambie 166 Bc 13.28N 16.34W
Gambie = Gambia (EN) 166 Bc 13.28N 16.34W
Gambier, Iles- = Gambier
Islands (EN) 208 Ng 23.09S 134.58W
Gambier Islands (EN) =
Gambier, Iles- 208 Ng 23.09S 134.58W
Gambo 168 Ce 4.39N 22.16 E
Gamboma 170 Cc 1.53S 15.51 E
Gamboula 168 Be 4.08N 15.09 E
Gamda → Zamtang 152 He 32.23N 101.05 E
Gamelão 204 Db 15.29S 57.50W
Gamkonora, Gunung- 150 If 1.21N 127.31 E
Gamlakarleby/Kokkola 112 Ic 63.50N 23.07 E
Gamla Uppsala 116 Ge 59.54N 17.38 E
Gamleby 114 Dh 57.54N 16.24 E
Gammerages/Galmaarden 124 Fd 50.45N 3.58 E
Gamo Gofa [3] 168 Fd 5.45N 37.20 E
Gamua 220h Bb 13.15S 176.08W
Gamud 168 Fe 4.05N 38.06 E
Gamvik 114 Ga 71.03N 28.14 E
Ganāne, Webi- = Juba (EN)
158 Lh 0.15S 42.38 E
Gananoque 184 Ic 44.20N 76.10W
Ganāveh 146 Nh 29.32N 50.31 E
Gancedo 204 Bh 27.30S 61.42W
Gancevići 132 Ec 52.45N 26.29 E
Gand/Gent = Ghent (EN) 122 Jc 51.03N 3.43 E
Ganda 170 Be 12.59S 14.40 E
Gandadiwata, Bulu- 150 Gg 2.42S 119.27 E
Gandajika 170 Dd 6.45S 23.57 E
Gandak 148 Hc 25.39N 85.13 E
Gander 176 Ne 48.57N 54.34W
Ganderkesee 124 Ka 53.04N 8.33 E
Gandesa 126 Mi 41.03N 0.26 E
Gandhinagar 142 Jg 23.21N 72.40 E
Gāndhi Sāgar 148 Fd 24.30N 75.30 E
Gandia / Gandia 126 Lf 38.58N 0.11W
Gandia / Gandia 126 Lf 38.58N 0.11W
Gandia-El Grao de Gandia 126 Lf 38.59N 0.09W
Gandu 202 Kf 13.45S 39.30W
Ganetti 168 Eb 17.58N 31.13 E
Ganga = Ganges (EN) 140 Lg 23.20N 90.30 E
Gangaw 148 Id 22.10N 94.08 E
Gangca (Shaliuhe) 152 Hd 37.30N 100.14 E
Gangdisê Shan 140 Kf 31.00N 83.00 E
Ganges 122 Jk 43.56N 3.42 E
Ganges (EN) = Ganga 140 Lg 23.20N 90.30 E
Ganges, Mouths of the- (EN)
140 Lg 23.20N 90.30 E
Gangi 128 Im 37.48N 14.12 E
Gango 170 Cd 9.48S 15.40 E
Gangtok 142 Kg 27.20N 88.37 E
Gangu 152 Ie 34.45N 105.12 E
Gangziyao 154 Cf 36.17N 114.06 E
Ganhe 152 La 50.43N 123.00 E
Gan He 152 Mb 49.12N 125.14 E
Gani 150 Ig 0.47S 128.13 E
Ganjgah 146 Md 37.42N 48.16 E
Gan Jiang 140 Ng 29.12N 116.00 E
Ganjig → Horqin Zuoyi Houqi 152 Lc 42.57N 122.14 E
Gannan 152 Lb 47.53N 123.26 E
Gannat 122 Jh 46.06N 3.12 E
Gannett Peak 174 Ie 43.10N 109.40W
Gansbaai 172 Bf 34.35S 19.22 E

Index Symbols

- [1] Independent Nation
- [2] State, Region
- [3] District, County
- [4] Municipality
- [5] Colony, Dependency
- Continent
- Physical Region
- Historical or Cultural Region
- Mount, Mountain
- Volcano
- Hill
- Mountains, Mountain Range
- Hills, Escarpment
- Plateau, Upland
- Pass, Gap
- Plain, Lowland
- Delta
- Salt Flat
- Valley, Canyon
- Crater, Cave
- Karst Features
- Depression
- Polder
- Desert, Dunes
- Forest, Woods
- Heath, Steppe
- Oasis
- Cape, Point
- Coast, Beach
- Cliff
- Peninsula
- Isthmus
- Sandbank
- Island
- Atoll
- Rock, Reef
- Islands, Archipelago
- Rocks, Reefs
- Coral Reef
- Well, Spring
- Geyser
- River, Stream
- Waterfall, Rapids
- River Mouth, Estuary
- Lake
- Salt Lake
- Intermittent Lake
- Reservoir
- Swamp, Pond
- Canal
- Glacier
- Ice Shelf, Pack Ice
- Ocean
- Sea
- Gulf, Bay
- Strait, Fjord
- Lagoon
- Bank
- Seamount
- Tablemount
- Ridge
- Shelf
- Basin
- Escarpment, Sea Scarp
- Fracture
- Trench, Abyss
- National Park, Reserve
- Point of Interest
- Recreation Site
- Cave, Cavern
- Historic Site
- Ruins
- Wall, Walls
- Church, Abbey
- Temple
- Scientific Station
- Railway station
- Airport
- Port
- Military installation
- Lighthouse
- Mine
- Tunnel
- Dam, Bridge

Gansu Sheng (Kan-su Sheng) = Kansu (EN) [2] 152 Hd 38.00N 102.00 E
Ganta 166 Dd 7.14N 8.59W
Gantang → Taiping 154 Ei 30.18N 118.07 E
Ganyu (Qingkou) 154 Eg 34.50N 119.07 E
Ganzhou 142 Ng 25.49N 114.56 E
Gao [3] 166 Eb 18.15N 1.00W
Gao [Mali] 160 Hg 16.15N 0.01 E
Gao [Niger] 166 Gb 15.25N 5.45 E
Gao'an 152 Kf 28.27N 115.24 E
Gaobeidian → Xincheng 154 Ce 39.20N 115.50 E
Gaocheng 154 Ce 38.02N 114.50 E
Gaolan (Shidongsi) 152 Hd 36.23N 103.55 E
Gaoliangjian → Hongze 152 Ke 33.10N 119.58 E
Gaoligong Shan 152 Gf 25.45N 98.45 E
Gaolou Ling 152 Ig 24.47N 106.48 E
Gaomi 154 Ef 36.23N 119.45 E
Gaoping 152 Jd 35.46N 112.55 E
Gaoqing (Tianzhen) 154 Df 37.10N 117.50 E
Gaotai 152 Gd 39.20N 99.58 E
Gaotingzhen → Daishan 154 Gi 30.15N 122.13 E
Gaoua 166 Ec 10.20N 3.11W
Gaoual 166 Cc 11.45N 13.12W
Gaoyang 154 Ce 38.42N 115.47 E
Gaoyi 154 Cf 37.37N 114.37 E
Gaoyou 154 Eh 32.46N 119.27 E
Gaoyou Hu 152 Ke 32.50N 119.15 E
Gaozhou 152 Jg 21.56N 110.47 E
Gap 122 Mj 44.34N 6.05 E
Gar 152 Ce 32.12N 79.57 E
Gara, Lough-/Loch Uí Ghadra 118 Eh 53.55N 8.30W
Gara'ad 168 Hd 6.54N 49.20 E
Garabato 204 Bi 28.56S 60.09W
Garachiné 194 Hi 8.04N 78.22W
Garachiné, Punta- 194 Hi 8.06N 78.25W
Gara Dragoman 130 Fg 42.55N 22.56 E
Ga'raet el Oubeïra 128 Cn 36.50N 8.23 E
Gara Kostenec 130 Gg 42.18N 23.52 E
Garalo 166 Dc 11.00N 7.26W
Gara Muleta 168 Gd 9.05N 41.43 E
Garanhuns 200 Mf 8.54S 36.29W
Garapan 220b Ba 15.12N 145.43 E
Garapuava 204 Ic 16.06S 46.33W
Garavutı 135 Gf 37.36N 68.29 E
Garba 168 Cd 9.12N 20.30 E
GarbahärreL 168 Ge 3.20N 42.17 E
Garberville 188 Df 40.06N 123.48W
Gārbosh, Kūh-e- 146 Nf 32.36N 50.04 E
Garça 204 Hf 22.14S 49.37W
Garças, Rio das- 204 Fb 15.54S 52.16W
Garcias 204 Fe 20.34S 52.13W
Gard [3] 122 Jj 44.00N 4.00 E
Garda 128 Ee 45.34N 10.42 E
Garda, Lago di- (Benaco) = Garda Lake- (EN) 110 Hf 45.35N 10.35 E
Garda, Lake- (EN) = Garda, Lago di- (Benaco) 110 Hf 45.35N 10.35 E
Gardabani 132 Ni 41.29N 45.05 E
Garde, Cap de- 128 Bn 36.58N 7.47 E
Gardelegen 120 Hd 52.32N 11.22 E
Garden City [Ga.-U.S.] 184 Gi 32.06N 81.09W
Garden City [Ks.-U.S.] 182 Gd 37.58N 100.53W
Garden Grove 188 Gj 33.46N 117.57W
Garden Peninsula 184 Dc 45.40N 86.35W
Gardermoen 116 Dd 60.13N 11.06 E
Gardey 204 Cm 37.17S 59.21W
Gardēz 144 Kc 33.37N 69.07 E
Gardiner 188 Jd 45.02N 110.42W
Gardiner Range 212 Fc 19.15S 128.50 E
Gardner → Nikumaroro Atoll 208 Je 4.40S 174.32W
Gardner Pinnacles 208 Kb 25.00N 167.55W
Gardno, Jezioro- 120 Nb 54.43N 17.05 E
Gardon → Gard 122 Kk 43.51N 4.37 E
Gardone Riviera 128 Ee 45.37N 10.34 E
Gard ou Gardon 122 Kk 43.51N 4.37 E
Gareloi 178a Cb 51.47N 178.48W
Garessio 128 Cf 44.12N 8.02 E
Garfagnana 128 Ef 44.05N 10.30 E
Gargaliánoi 130 El 37.04N 21.38 E
Gargano 110 Hg 41.50N 16.00 E
Gargano, Testa del- 128 Ki 41.35N 16.12 E
Gargantua, Cape- 184 Eb 47.36N 85.02W
Gargždai/Gargždaj 114 Ei 55.43N 21.24 E
Gargždaj/Gargždai 114 Ei 55.43N 21.24 E
Gari 136 Gd 59.28N 62.25 E
Garibaldi 204 Gi 29.15S 51.32W
Garibaldi, Mount- 188 Db 49.51N 123.01W
Garies 172 Bf 30.30S 18.00 E
Garigliano 128 Hi 41.13N 13.45 E
Garimpo 204 Ed 18.41S 54.50W
Garissa 160 Ki 0.28S 39.38 E
Garkida 166 Hc 10.25N 12.34 E
Garland 186 Hj 32.54N 96.39W
Garlasco 128 Ce 45.12N 8.55 E
Garliava/Garljava 116 Jj 54.46N 23.55 E
Garljava/Garliava 116 Jj 54.46N 23.55 E
Garm 135 He 39.02N 70.18 E
Garmisch-Partenkirchen 120 Hi 47.30N 11.06 E
Garmsar 146 Oe 35.20N 52.13 E
Garnet Bank (EN) 204 Hk 33.05S 49.25W
Garnet Range 188 Ic 46.45N 113.15W
Garnett 186 Ig 38.17N 95.14W
Garonne 110 Ff 45.02N 0.36W
Garonne, Canal latéral à la- 122 Fj 44.34N 0.09W
Garopába 204 Hi 28.04S 48.40W
Garoua 160 Ih 9.18N 13.24 E
Garoua Boulaï 168 Ad 5.53N 14.33 E
Garōwe 160 Lh 8.25N 48.33 E
Garpenberg 116 Gd 60.19N 16.12 E
Garphyttan 116 Fe 59.19N 14.56 E
Garrel 124 Kb 52.57N 8.01 E
Garreru 220a Bc 7.20N 134.33 E
Garri, Kūh-e- 146 Mf 33.59N 48.25 E
Garrigues 122 Kj 44.10N 4.30 E
Garrison 186 Fc 47.40N 101.25W
Garron Point/An Gearrán 118 Hf 55.05N 5.58W
Garrovillas 126 Fe 39.43N 6.33W
Garruchos 204 Ei 28.11S 55.39W
Garry 118 Je 56.45N 3.45W
Garry Bay 180 Ic 69.00N 85.10W
Garry Lake 174 Jc 66.00N 100.00W
Garsen 170 Hc 2.16S 40.07 E
Gartar/Qianning 152 He 30.27N 101.29 E
Gartempe 122 Gh 46.47N 0.50 E
Gartog → Markam 152 Gf 29.32N 98.33 E
Garut 150 Eh 7.13S 107.54 E
Garuva 204 Hh 26.01S 48.51W
Garvie Mountains 218 Cf 45.30S 168.50 E
Garwa 148 Gd 24.11N 83.49 E
Garwolin 120 Re 51.54N 21.37 E
Gary 182 Jc 41.36N 87.20W
Garyarsa 152 De 31.40N 80.26 E
Garzê 152 Ge 31.42N 99.58 E
Garzón [Col.] 202 Cc 2.13N 75.38W
Garzón [Ur.] 206 Jd 34.36S 54.33W
Gasan-Kuli 136 Fh 37.29N 53.59 E
Gascogne = Gascony (EN) 122 Gk 43.30N 0.10 E
Gascogne, Golfe de- = Biscay, Bay of- (EN) 110 Fg 43.50N 2.30W
Gasconade River 186 Kg 38.40N 91.33W
Gascony (EN) = Gascogne 122 Gk 43.30N 0.10 E
Gascoyne Junction 212 De 25.03S 115.12 E
Gascoyne River 208 Cg 24.52S 113.37 E
Gasefjord 179 Je 70.00N 27.30W
Gaseland 179 Jd 70.20N 29.00W
Gash 158 Kg 16.48N 35.51 E
Gas Hu 152 Fd 38.08N 90.45 E
Gashua 160 Ig 12.52N 11.03 E
Gaspar Strait (EN) = Kelasa, Selat- 150 Eg 2.40S 107.15 E
Gaspé 176 Me 48.50N 64.29W
Gaspé, Cap de - 180 Lg 48.45N 64.10W
Gaspé, Péninsule de- = Gaspé Peninsula (EN) 174 Me 48.30N 65.00W
Gaspé Peninsula (EN) = Gaspé, Péninsule de- 174 Me 48.30N 65.00W
Gassan 156 Gb 38.34N 140.01 E
Gassol 166 Hd 8.32N 10.28 E
Gaston, Lake- 184 Ig 36.35N 78.00W
Gastonia 182 Kd 35.16N 81.11W
Gastoúni 130 El 37.51N 21.15 E
Gastre 206 Gf 42.17S 69.14W
Gästrikland 116 Gd 60.30N 16.30 E
Gata, Akra- 146 Ee 34.34N 33.02 E
Gata, Cabo de- 110 Fh 36.43N 2.12W
Gata, Sierra de- 126 Fd 40.15N 6.45W
Gătaia 130 Ed 45.26N 21.26 E
Gatčina 136 Dd 59.34N 30.09 E
Gate 186 Fh 36.51N 100.01W
Gate City 184 Fg 36.38N 82.37W
Gateshead 118 Lg 54.58N 1.37W
Gateshead 180 Hb 70.35N 100.15W
Gathemo 124 Bf 48.46N 0.58W
Gâtinais 122 If 48.00N 2.20 E
Gâtine, Hauteurs de- 122 Fh 46.38N 0.38W
Gatineau, Rivière- 180 Jg 45.27N 75.42W
Gatlinburg 184 Fh 35.43N 83.31W
Gato, Cumbres del- 192 Fd 27.00N 106.35W
Gattinara 128 Ce 45.37N 8.22 E
Gatún 194 Hi 9.16N 79.55W
Gatún, Lago- = Gatun Lake (EN) 190 Ig 9.12N 79.55W
Gatun Lake (EN) = Gatún, Lago- 190 Ig 9.12N 79.55W
Gatvand 146 Mf 32.15N 48.50 E
Gatwich Airport 124 Bc 51.08N 0.12W
Gaucín 126 Gh 36.31N 5.19W
Gauhati → Guwāhāti 142 Lg 26.11N 91.44 E
Gauiena/Gaujiena 116 Lg 57.25N 26.28 E
Gauja 114 Fh 57.10N 24.16 E
Gaujiena/Gauiena 116 Lg 57.25N 26.28 E
Gaula [Nor.] 116 Da 63.21N 10.14 E
Gaula [Nor.] 116 Ac 61.22N 5.41 E
Gauldalen 116 Db 63.00N 11.00 E
Gauley River 184 Gf 38.10N 81.12W
Gau-Odernheim 124 Ke 49.46N 8.12 E
Gaurdak 136 Gh 37.49N 66.01 E
Gauri Phanta 148 Gc 28.41N 80.33 E
Gausdal 116 Cc 61.20N 9.55 E
Gausta 114 Bg 59.50N 8.39 E
Gāvbandī 146 Oi 27.12N 53.04 E
Gāvbūs, Kūh-e- 146 Oi 27.10N 54.00 E
Gavdhopoúla 130 Go 34.56N 24.00 E
Gávdhos 110 Ii 34.50N 24.05 E
Gāveh 146 Le 35.00N 46.58 E
Gavere 124 Fd 50.56N 3.40 E
Gavkhūnī, Bātlāq-e- 146 Of 32.06N 52.52 E
Gāv Kosh 146 Le 34.00N 48.00 E
Gävle 112 Hc 60.40N 17.10 E
Gävleborg [2] 114 Df 61.30N 16.15 E
Gävlebukten 116 Gd 60.40N 17.20 E
Gavorrano 128 Eh 42.55N 10.54 E
Gavri 116 Lh 56.49N 27.58 E
Gavrilov-Jam 114 Jh 57.19N 39.51 E
Gavrilov Posad 132 La 56.33N 40.07 E
Gāw Koshi 144 Id 28.38N 57.12 E
Gawler 212 Hf 34.37S 138.44 E
Gawler Ranges 208 Eh 32.30S 136.00 E
Gaxun Nur 140 Me 42.25N 101.00 E
Gaya [India] 142 Kg 24.47N 85.00 E
Gaya [Niger] 166 Fc 11.53N 3.27 E
Gaya He 154 Jc 42.58N 129.52 E
Gaylord 184 Ec 45.02N 84.40W
Gayndah 212 Ke 25.37S 151.36 E
Gaz 146 Nf 32.48N 51.37 E
Gaza [3] 172 Ed 23.30S 33.00 E
Gaza (EN) = Ghazzah 144 Dc 31.30N 34.28 E
Gaz-Ačak 136 Gg 41.11N 61.27 E
Gazalkent 135 Gd 41.33N 69.46 E
Gazaoua 166 Gc 13.32N 7.55 E
Gazelle, Récif de la- 219b Be 20.11S 165.27 E
Gaziantep 142 Ff 37.05N 37.22 E
Gaziemir 130 Kk 38.19N 27.10 E
Gazimağusa = Famagusta (EN) 144 Dc 35.07N 33.57 E
Gazimur 138 Hf 52.57N 120.22 E
Gazipaşa 146 Ed 36.17N 32.20 E
Gazli 136 Gg 40.09N 63.23 E
Gbarnga 160 Gh 7.00N 9.29W
Gboko 166 Gd 7.21N 8.58 E
Gbon 166 Dd 9.50N 6.27W
Gdańsk [2] 120 Ob 54.25N 18.40 E
Gdánsk (Danzig) 112 He 54.23N 18.40 E
Gdansk, Gulf of- (EN) = Gdańska, Zatoka- 110 He 54.40N 19.15 E
Gdov 114 Gg 58.47N 27.54 E
Gdynia 112 He 54.32N 18.33 E
Gearhart Mountain 188 Ee 42.30N 120.53W
Gêba 166 Bc 11.58N 15.00W
Gebe, Pulau- 150 Ig 0.05S 129.20 E
Gebze 146 Cb 40.48N 29.25 E
Gecha 168 Fd 7.29N 35.25 E
Geçitkale 148 Ee 35.15N 33.45 E
Gedinne 124 Ge 49.59N 4.56 E
Gediz 146 Cc 39.02N 29.25 E
Gediz 144 Cb 38.39N 26.45 E
Gedo 168 Fd 9.00N 37.29 E
Gedo [3] 168 Ge 3.00N 42.00 E
Gedo 168 Ge 2.20N 41.20 E
Gedser, Sydfalster- 114 Ci 54.35N 11.57 E
Gedser Odde 116 Dj 54.34N 11.59 E
Geel 122 Kc 51.10N 5.00 E
Geelong 210 Fh 38.08S 144.21 E
Geelvink Channel 212 Ce 28.30S 114.10 E
Geer 124 Hd 50.51N 5.42 E
Geeste 124 Jb 52.36N 7.16 E
Geesthacht 120 Gc 53.26N 10.22 E
Gê'gyai 152 De 32.29N 80.52 E
Ge Hu 154 Ei 31.36N 119.51 E
Geidam 166 Hc 12.53N 11.56 E
Geigar 168 Ec 11.59N 32.46 E
Geihoku 156 Cd 34.44N 132.17 E
Geikie 180 He 57.48N 103.46W
Geilo 114 Bf 60.31N 8.12 E
Geiranger 116 Bb 62.06N 7.12 E
Geisenheim 124 Je 49.59N 7.58 E
Geislingen an der Steige 120 Fh 48.37N 9.51 E
Geita 170 Fc 2.52S 32.10 E
Geithus 114 Bg 59.57N 9.59 E
Geiyo-Shotō 156 Cd 34.15N 132.45 E
Gejiu 142 Mg 23.22N 103.14 E
Gel [Sud.] 158 Jh 7.46N 29.36 E
Gel [Sud.] 168 Ed 6.08N 31.17 E
Gela 128 Im 37.04N 14.15 E
Gela, Golfo di- 128 Im 37.05N 14.10 E
Geladi 168 Hd 6.57N 46.25 E
Geldenaken/Jodoigne 124 Gd 50.43N 4.52 E
Gelderland [3] 124 Hb 52.10N 5.50 E
Geldermalsen 124 Hc 51.53N 5.19 E
Geldern 120 Ce 51.31N 6.20 E
Geldrop 124 Hc 51.25N 5.33 E
Geleen 122 Ld 50.58N 5.52 E
Gelembé 130 Kj 39.10N 27.50 E
Gelemso 168 Gd 8.48N 40.32 E
Gelendžik 136 Dg 44.33N 38.06 E
Gélengdeng 168 Bc 10.56N 15.32 E
Gelgaudiškis 116 Ji 55.02N 22.58 E
Gelibolu 146 Bb 40.24N 26.40 E
Gelibolu Yarımadası = Gallipoli Peninsula (EN) 130 Ji 40.20N 26.30 E
Gélise 122 Gj 44.11N 0.17 E
Gellinsōr 168 Hd 6.24N 46.46 E
Gelnhausen 120 Ff 50.12N 9.11 E
Gelsenkirken 120 De 51.31N 7.06 E
Gemena 160 Ih 3.15N 19.46 E
Gemerek 146 Gc 39.11N 36.05 E
Gemert 124 Hc 51.33N 5.41 E
Gemi, Jabal- 168 Ed 9.01N 34.09 E
Gemlik 146 Cb 40.26N 29.09 E
Gemlik Körfezi 146 Cb 40.25N 28.55 E
Gemona del Friuli 128 Hd 46.16N 13.09 E
Gemünden (Felda) 124 Ld 50.42N 9.03 E
Gemünden (Wohra) 124 Kd 50.58N 8.58 E
Gemünden am Main 120 Ff 50.03N 9.42 E
Genale 158 Lh 0.15S 42.38 E
Genç 146 Ic 38.46N 40.35 E
Gendringen 124 Ic 51.52N 6.23 E
Gendringen-Ulft 124 Ic 51.54N 6.24 E
Genemuiden 124 Ib 52.37N 6.02 E
General Acha 206 He 37.23S 64.36W
General Alvear [Arg.] 206 Gd 34.58S 67.42W
General Alvear [Arg.] 206 He 36.03S 60.01W
General Arenales 204 Bl 34.18S 61.18W
General Artigas 204 Dh 26.53S 56.17W
General Belgrano 206 Ie 35.46S 58.30W
General Belgrano Station 222 Af 77.50S 38.00W
General Bernardo O'Higgins 222 Re 63.19S 57.54W
General Bravo 192 Je 25.48N 99.10W
General Cabrera 206 Hd 32.48S 63.52W
General Capdevila 204 Bh 27.26S 61.28W
General Carneiro 204 Gh 26.28S 51.25W
General Carrera, Lago- 198 Ij 46.30S 72.00W
General Cepeda 192 Ie 25.23N 101.27W
General Conesa [Arg.] 204 Dm 36.30S 57.20W
General Conesa [Arg.] 206 Hf 40.06S 64.26W
General Enrique Martínez 204 Fk 33.12S 53.50W
General Eugenio A. Garay 206 Hb 20.31S 62.08W
General Galarza 204 Ck 32.43S 59.24W
General Güemes 206 Hb 24.40S 65.00W
General Guido 206 Ie 36.40S 57.46W
General José de San Martín 204 Ch 26.33S 59.21W
General Juan Madariaga 206 Ie 37.00S 57.09W
General Lamadrid 206 He 37.16S 61.17W
General Lavalle 206 Ie 36.24S 56.58W
General Manuel Belgrano, Cerro- 198 Jh 29.01S 67.49W
General O'Brien 204 Bl 34.54S 60.45W
General Pico 206 He 35.40S 63.44W
General Pinedo 206 Hc 27.19S 61.17W
General Pinto 204 Bl 34.46S 61.53W
General Pirán 204 Dm 37.16S 57.45W
General Roca 206 Ge 39.02S 67.35W
General Salgado 204 Ge 20.39S 50.22W
General Santos 142 Oi 6.05N 125.10 E
General Sarmiento 204 Cl 34.33S 58.43W
General Terán 192 Je 25.16N 99.41W
General-Toševo 130 Lf 43.42N 28.02 E
General Treviño 192 Jd 26.14N 99.29W
General Trias 192 Fc 28.21N 106.22W
General Vargas 204 Ei 29.42S 54.40W
General Viamonte 204 Bl 35.01S 61.01W
General Villegas 206 He 35.02S 63.01W
Genesee River 184 Id 43.16N 77.36W
Geneseo 184 Id 42.46N 77.49W
Geneva [Al.-U.S.] 184 Ej 31.02N 85.52W
Geneva [Nb.-U.S.] 186 Hf 40.32N 97.36W
Geneva [N.Y.-U.S.] 184 Id 42.53N 76.59W
Geneva (EN) = Genève 112 Gf 46.10N 6.10 E
Geneva, Lake- (EN) = Léman, Lac- 110 Gf 46.25N 6.30 E
Genève [2] 128 Ad 46.10N 6.15 E
Genève = Geneva (EN) 112 Gf 46.10N 6.10 E
Genevois 122 Mh 46.00N 6.10 E
Genhe → Ergun Zuoqi 142 Od 50.47N 121.32 E
Geni 168 Ed 8.31N 33.10 E
Geničesk 136 Df 46.12N 34.48 E
Genil 126 Gg 37.42N 5.19W
Genk 122 Ld 50.58N 5.30 E
Genkai-Nada 156 Ae 33.45N 130.00 E
Gennargentu 110 Gg 40.00N 9.20 E
Gennep 124 Hc 51.42N 5.59 E
Genoa (EN) = Genova 112 Gg 44.25N 8.57 E
Genoa, Gulf of- (EN) = Genova, Golfo di- 110 Gg 44.10N 8.55 E
Genova = Genoa (EN) 112 Gg 44.25N 8.57 E
Genova, Golfo di- = Genoa, Gulf of- (EN) 110 Gg 44.10N 8.55 E
Genova-Nervi 128 Df 44.23N 9.02 E
Genova-Voltri 128 Cf 44.26N 8.45 E
Genovesa, Isla- 202a Ba 0.20N 89.58W
Genrietty, ostrov- 138 Ka 77.00N 157.00 E
Gent/Gand = Ghent (EN) 122 Jc 51.03N 3.43 E
Gentbrugge, Gent- 124 Fc 51.03N 3.45 E
Gent-Gentbrugge 124 Fc 51.03N 3.45 E
Genthin 120 Id 52.24N 12.10 E
Gent-Sint-Amandsberg 124 Fc 51.04N 3.45 E
Genū, Kūhhā-ye- 144 Id 27.25N 56.09 E
Genyem 150 Lg 2.46S 140.12 E
Genzano di Lucania 128 Kj 40.51N 16.02 E
Genzano di Roma 128 Fi 41.42N 11.41 E
Geographe Bay 208 Ch 33.35S 115.15 E
Geographe Channel 212 Cd 24.40S 113.20 E
Geographical Society Øer 179 Jd 72.40N 22.20W
Geokčaj 132 Oi 40.40N 47.42 E
Geok-Tepe 136 Fh 38.10N 57.58 E
Geomagnetic Pole (1975) (EN) 222 Hf 78.40S 109.33 E
Georga, zemlja- 140 Ga 80.30N 49.00 E
George 172 Cf 33.58S 22.24 E
George 174 Md 58.30N 66.00W
George, Lake- [Austl.] 212 Jg 35.05S 149.25 E
George, Lake- [Fl.-U.S.] 184 Gk 29.17N 81.36W
George, Lake- [Ug.] 170 Fc 0.00 30.12 E
George, Lake- [U.S.] 184 Kd 43.35N 73.35W
George Gill Range 212 Gd 24.15S 131.35 E
Georges Bank (EN) 182 Nc 41.15N 67.30W
George Sound 218 Bf 44.50S 167.20 E
George Town [Austl.] 210 Fi 41.06S 146.50 E
Georgetown [Austl.] 210 Ff 18.18S 143.33 E
Georgetown [Bah.] 194 Jb 23.30N 75.46W
George Town [Cay.Is.] 190 He 19.18N 81.23W
Georgetown [De.-U.S.] 184 Jf 38.42N 75.23W
Georgetown [Gam.] 160 Fg 13.32N 14.46W
Georgetown [Guy.] 200 Ke 6.48N 58.10W
Georgetown [Ky.-U.S.] 184 Ef 38.13N 84.33W
Georgetown [Oh.-U.S.] 184 Ff 38.52N 83.54W
Georgetown [S.C.-U.S.] 182 Le 33.23N 79.18W
Georgetown [St.Hel.] 160 Fi 7.56S 14.25W
Georgetown [St.Vin.] 196 Ff 13.16N 61.08W
Georgetown [Tx.-U.S.] 186 Hk 30.38N 97.41W
George Town (Pinang) 142 Mi 5.25N 100.20 E
George V Coast 222 Je 68.30S 147.30 E
George VI Sound 222 Qf 71.00S 68.00W
George West 186 Gl 28.20N 98.07W
Georgia [2] 182 Ke 32.50N 83.15W
Georgia (EN) 110 Kg 42.00N 44.00 E
Georgia, Strait of - 180 Fg 49.00N 123.20W
Georgia del Sur/South Georgia 222 Ad 54.15S 36.45W
Georgian Bay 174 Ke 45.15N 80.50W
Georgian SSR (EN) = Gruzinskaja SSR [2] 136 Eg 42.00N 44.00 E
Georgijevka [Kaz.-U.S.S.R.] 136 Hg 43.02N 74.43 E
Georgijevka [Kaz.-U.S.S.R.] 136 If 49.19N 81.35 E
Georgijevsk 132 Mg 44.09N 43.28 E
Georgina River 208 Eg 23.30S 139.47 E
Georgsmarienhütte 120 Ed 52.16N 8.02 E
Gera 120 If 50.52N 12.05 E
Gera [2] 120 Hf 50.45N 11.55 E
Gera 120 Ge 51.08N 10.56 E
Geraardsbergen/Grammont 124 Fd 50.46N 3.52 E
Gerais, Chapadão dos- 204 Jc 17.40S 45.35W
Geral, Serra- [Braz.] 204 Gi 29.10S 50.15W
Geral, Serra- [Braz.] 204 Gf 23.54S 50.46W
Geral, Serra- [Braz.] 198 Kh 26.30S 50.30W
Geral da Serra, Coxilha- 204 Ej 30.20S 55.15W
Geral de Goiás, Serra- 198 Lg 13.00S 46.15W
Geraldine 218 Df 44.05S 171.15 E
Geral do Paraná, Serra- 204 Ib 14.45S 47.30W
Geraldton [Austl.] 210 Cg 28.46S 114.36 E
Geraldton [Ont.-Can.] 180 Ig 49.44N 86.57W
Gérardmer 122 Mf 48.04N 6.53 E
Gerāsh 146 Pi 27.40N 54.06 E
Gerbiči, gora- 138 Fc 66.39N 105.02 E
Gerca 130 Ja 48.10N 26.17 E
Gercüş 146 Id 37.34N 41.23 E
Gerecse 120 Oi 47.41N 18.29 E
Gerede 146 Eb 40.48N 32.12 E
Gerede 146 Eb 40.52N 32.39 E
Gerês, Serra do- 126 Ec 41.48N 8.00W
Gereshk 144 Jc 31.48N 64.34 E
Gérgal 126 Jg 37.07N 2.33W
Gering 186 Ef 41.50N 103.40W
Gerlachovský štít 120 Qg 49.12N 20.09 E
Gerlogubi 168 Hd 6.56N 45.03 E
Gerlovo 130 Jf 43.03N 26.35 E
German Democratic Republic (EN) = Deutsche Demokratische Republik [1] 112 He 52.00N 12.30 E
Germania 204 Al 34.34S 62.03W
Germania Land 179 Kc 76.50N 20.00W
Germany, Federal Republic of- (EN) = Bundesrepublik Deutschland [1] 112 Ge 51.00N 9.00 E
Germencik 130 Kl 37.51N 27.37 E
Germersheim 124 Ke 49.13N 8.22 E
Germī 144 Hc 33.32N 54.58 E
Germi 146 Mc 39.01N 48.03 E
Germiuton 172 De 26.15S 28.05 E
Gernika-Lumo / Guernica y Luno 126 Ja 43.19N 2.41W
Gernsbach 124 Kf 48.46N 8.19 E
Gernsheim 124 Ke 49.45N 8.29 E
Gero 154 Ng 35.48N 137.14 E
Gerolstein 124 Id 50.13N 6.40 E
Gerona/Girona 126 Oc 41.59N 2.49 E
Gerona / Girona [3] 126 Ob 42.10N 2.40 E
Gerpinnes 124 Gd 50.20N 4.31 E
Gers [3] 122 Gk 43.40N 0.30 E
Gers 122 Gj 44.09N 0.39 E
Gersprenz 124 Le 49.59N 9.04 E
Gerze 146 Fb 41.48N 35.12 E
Gêrzê 152 De 32.20N 84.04 E
Gescher 124 Jc 51.57N 7.00 E
Geseke 124 Kc 51.39N 8.31 E
Geser 150 Jg 3.53S 130.54 E
Gesunda 116 Fd 60.54N 14.32 E
Gesunden 116 Fa 63.10N 15.55 E
Geta 114 Ef 60.23N 19.50 E
Getafe 126 Id 40.18N 3.43W
Gete 122 Ld 50.55N 5.08 E
Getinge 114 Ch 56.49N 12.44 E
Gettysburg 186 Gd 45.01N 99.57W
Gettysburg Seamount (EN) 162 Eb 36.32N 11.37W
Getúlio Vargas 204 Fh 27.50S 52.16W
Getz Ice Shelf 222 Nf 74.15S 125.00W
Geul 124 Hd 50.40N 5.43 E
Gevaş 146 Jc 38.16N 43.05 E
Gévaudan 122 Jj 44.27N 3.30 E
Gevelsberg 124 Jc 51.19N 7.20 E
Gevgelija 130 Fh 41.08N 22.31 E
Gévora 126 Ff 38.53N 6.57W
Gevsjön 116 Ea 63.25N 12.40 E
Gewane 168 Gc 10.10N 40.39 E
Gex 122 Mh 46.20N 6.04 E
Gexianzhuang → Qinghe 154 Cf 37.03N 115.39 E
Geyersberg 120 Fg 49.50N 9.30 E
Geyik Dağı 146 Ed 36.54N 32.10 E
Geyikli 130 Jj 39.48N 26.12 E
Geyser, Banc du- 172 Hb 12.25S 46.25 E
Geysir 110 Dc 64.19N 20.18W
Geyve 146 Db 40.30N 30.18 E
Ghabāri, Darb al- 146 Cj 25.10N 29.50 E
Ghadāmis 160 He 30.08N 9.30 E
Ghadduwah 164 Bd 26.26N 14.18 E
Ghaghara 140 Kg 24.52N 84.55 E
Ghaghe 219a Db 7.23S 158.12 E
Ghallah, Wādī al- 158 Jg 10.25N 27.32 E
Ghamrah, Wādī al- 146 Hj 25.47N 38.45 E
Ghana [1] 160 Gh 8.00N 2.00W
Ghanzi 160 Jk 21.42S 21.38 E
Ghanzi [3] 172 Cd 22.00S 23.00 E
Ghār ad Dimā' 128 Cn 36.27N 8.26 E
Gharaqābād 146 Me 35.06N 49.50 E
Gharbī, Al Hajar al- 146 Qj 24.10N 56.15 E
Gharbīyah, Aş Şaḩrā' al- = Western Desert (EN) 158 Jf 27.30N 28.00 E
Ghardaïa 160 He 32.29N 3.40 E
Ghārib, Jabal- 164 Fd 28.07N 32.54 E
Gharrāf, Shaţţ al- 146 Kf 32.30N 45.48 E
Gharsah, Shaţţ al- 162 Ic 34.06N 7.50 E
Gharyān 164 Bc 32.10N 13.01 E
Gharyān [3] 164 Bc 30.35N 12.00 E
Ghāt 160 If 24.58N 10.11 E
Ghatere 219a Db 7.58S 159.01 E
Ghaţţī 146 Gg 31.16N 37.31 E
Ghazāl, Baḩr al- 168 Ed 9.31N 30.25 E
Ghazal, Bahr el- 168 Bc 14.00N 16.30 E
Ghazal, Bahr el- 158 Ig 13.01N 15.28 E
Ghazaouet 162 Gb 35.06N 1.51W
Ghazipur 148 Gc 25.35N 83.34 E
Ghaznī 142 If 33.33N 68.26 E
Ghāznī [3] 144 Kc 33.00N 68.00 E
Ghazzah = Gaza (EN) 144 Dc 31.30N 34.28 E
Ghent (EN) = Gand/Gent 122 Jc 51.03N 3.43 E
Ghent (EN) = Gent/Gand 122 Jc 51.03N 3.43 E
Gheorghe Gheorghiu-Dej 130 Jc 46.12N 26.46 E
Gheorghieni 130 Ic 46.43N 25.37 E
Gheorghiu-Dej 136 De 51.00N 39.31 E
Gherla 130 Gb 47.02N 23.55 E
Ghidigeni 130 Kc 46.03N 27.30 E
Ghidole (EN) = Gidole 168 Fd 5.37N 37.29 E
Ghilarza 128 Cj 40.07N 8.50 E
Ghimeş, Pasul- 130 Jc 46.33N 26.07 E
Ghisonaccia 122a Ba 42.00N 9.24 E
Ghizunabeana Islands 219a Db 7.33S 158.45 E
Ghowr [3] 144 Jc 34.00N 65.00 E
Ghriss 126 Mi 35.15N 0.10 E
Ghubbat al Qamar 140 Hh 16.00N 52.30 E
Ghudāf, Wādī al- 146 Jf 32.56N 43.30 E
Ghurāb, Jabal al- 146 Hf 34.00N 38.42 E
Ghurayrah 164 Hf 18.37N 42.41 E
Ghūrīān 144 Jc 34.21N 61.30 E

Index Symbols

[1] Independent Nation
[2] State, Region
[3] District, County
[4] Municipality
[5] Colony, Dependency
Continent
Physical Region
Historical or Cultural Region
Mount, Mountain
Volcano
Hill
Mountains, Mountain Range
Hills, Escarpment
Plateau, Upland
Pass, Gap
Plain, Lowland
Delta
Salt Flat
Valley, Canyon
Crater, Cave
Karst Features
Depression
Polder
Desert, Dunes
Forest, Woods
Heath, Steppe
Oasis
Cape, Point
Coast, Beach
Cliff
Peninsula
Isthmus
Sandbank
Island
Atoll
Rock, Reef
Islands, Archipelago
Rocks, Reefs
Coral Reef
Well, Spring
Geyser
River, Stream
Waterfall, Rapids
River Mouth, Estuary
Lake
Salt Lake
Intermittent Lake
Reservoir
Swamp, Pond
Canal
Glacier
Ice Shelf, Pack Ice
Ocean
Sea
Gulf, Bay
Strait, Fjord
Lagoon
Bank
Seamount
Tablemount
Ridge
Shelf
Basin
Escarpment, Sea Scarp
Fracture
Trench, Abyss
National Park, Reserve
Point of Interest
Recreation Site
Cave, Cavern
Historic Site
Ruins
Wall, Walls
Church, Abbey
Temple
Scientific Station
Railway station
Airport
Port
Military installation
Lighthouse
Mine
Tunnel
Dam, Bridge

Ghurraḥ, Jabal al- 128 Cn 36.36N 8.23 E
Ghuzayyil, Sabkhat- 164 Dd 29.50N 19.45 E
Giaginskaja 132 Lg 44.47N 40.10 E
Giala, Jabal- 146 Ei 27.20N 32.57 E
Gialo Oasis (EN)=Jālū, Wāḥāt- 158 Jf 29.00N 21.20 E
Gia Nghia 148 Lf 11.59N 107.42 E
Giannutri 128 Fh 42.15N 11.05 E
Giant's Causeway/Clochán an Aifir 118 Gf 55.15N 6.35W
Giarre 128 Jm 37.43N 15.11 E
Gibara 194 Ic 21.07N 76.08W
Gibbon Point 197b Bb 18.14N 63.00W
Gibb River 212 Fc 16.25S 126.25 E
Gibbs Islands 222 Re 61.30S 55.31W
Gibellina 128 Gm 37.47N 12.58 E
Gibeon 172 Be 25.09S 17.43 E
Gibeon [3] 172 Bd 25.00S 18.30 E
Gibostad 114 Db 69.21N 18.00 E
Gibraleón 126 Fg 37.23N 6.58W
Gibraltar 112 Fh 36.11N 5.22W
Gibraltar [5] 112 Fh 36.11N 5.22W
Gibraltar, Estrecho de- = Gibraltar, Strait of- (EN) 110 Fh 35.57N 5.36W
Gibraltar, Strait of- (EN) = Djebel Ṭāriq, El Bōghāz- 110 Fh 35.57N 5.36W
Gibraltar, Strait of- (EN) = Gibraltar, Estrecho de- 110 Fh 35.57N 5.36W
Gibson Desert 208 Dg 24.30S 126.00 E
Gidami 168 Fd 8.58N 34.40 E
Giddings 186 Hk 30.11N 96.56W
Gidigič 130 Lb 47.04N 28.38 E
Gidole=Ghidole (EN) 168 Fd 5.37N 37.29 E
Gien 122 Ig 47.42N 2.38 E
Giens, Presqu'île de- 122 Mk 43.02N 6.08 E
Gier 122 Ki 45.35N 4.46 E
Gießen 120 Ef 50.35N 8.39 E
Gieten 124 Ia 53.01N 6.48 E
Giethoorn 124 Ib 52.43N 6.07 E
Gifford 180 Jb 70.21N 83.05W
Gifford Seamount (EN) 198 Ii 39.00S 82.00W
Gifhorn 120 Gd 52.29N 10.33 E
Gift Lake 180 Fe 55.49N 115.57W
Gifu 142 Pf 35.25N 136.45 E
Gifu Ken [2] 154 Ng 35.50N 137.00 E
Gigant 132 Lf 46.29N 41.20 E
Giganta, Cerro- 190 Bc 26.07N 111.36W
Giganta, Sierra de la- 190 Bc 26.18N 111.39W
Gigante 202 Cc 2.24N 75.34W
Gigen 130 Hf 43.42N 24.29 E
Gigha 118 Hf 55.41N 5.44W
Giglio 128 Eh 42.20N 10.55 E
Gijón 112 Fg 43.32N 5.40W
Gikongoro 170 Ec 2.30S 29.35 E
Gila Bend 188 Ij 32.57N 112.43W
Gila Bend Mountains 188 Ij 33.10N 113.10W
Gīlān [3] 144 Gb 37.00N 49.50 E
Gīlān-e-Gharb 146 Ke 34.08N 45.55 E
Gila River 182 Ee 32.43N 114.33W
Gilbert, Mount- 188 Ca 50.51N 124.20W
Gilbert River 212 Ic 16.35S 141.15 E
Gilbert Seamount (EN) 178 If 52.50N 150.10W
Gilbués 202 Ie 9.50S 45.21W
Gilé 172 Fc 16.09S 38.19 E
Giles Meterological Station 212 Fc 25.02S 128.18 E
Gilford Island 188 Ba 50.45N 126.25W
Gilgandra 212 Jf 31.42S 148.39 E
Gilğau 130 Gb 47.17N 23.43 E
Gilgil 170 Gc 0.30S 36.19 E
Gilgit 142 Jf 35.55N 74.18 E
Gilgit 148 Ea 35.44N 74.38 E
Giljuj 138 Hf 54.17N 127.05 E
Gillam 180 Ie 56.21N 94.43W
Gilleleje 116 Eh 56.07N 12.19 E
Gillen, Lake- 212 Ee 26.10S 124.40 E
Gillenfeld 124 Id 50.07N 6.54 E
Gillette 182 Fc 44.18N 105.30W
Gillian, Lake - 180 Jc 69.30N 75.30W
Gillingham 118 Nj 51.24N 0.33 E
Gilo 168 Ed 8.10N 33.15 E
Gilort 128 Ge 44.36N 23.27 E
Gilroy 188 Eh 37.00N 121.34W
Giluwe, Mount- 214 Ci 6.04S 143.53 E
Gilvān 146 Md 36.47N 49.08 E
Gimån 116 Gb 62.28N 16.20 E
Gimbi 168 Fd 9.10N 35.51 E
Gimie, Mount- 196 Ff 13.52N 61.01W
Gimli 180 Hf 50.39N 97.00W
Gimo 116 Hd 60.11N 18.11 E
Gimolskoje, ozero- 114 He 63.00N 32.15 E
Gimone 122 Hk 44.00N 1.06 E
Ginda 168 Fb 15.27N 39.06 E
Ginetu 219a Ac 9.30S 152.43 E
Gingin 212 Df 31.21S 115.42 E
Gin Gin 212 Kd 25.00S 151.58 E
Gingoog 150 Ie 8.50N 125.07 E
Ginir 168 Gd 7.08N 40.43 E
Ginosa 128 Kj 40.35N 16.45 E
Ginowan 156b Ab 26.17N 127.45 E
Giofra Oasis (EN)=Jufrah, Wāḥāt al- 158 If 29.10N 16.00 E
Gioia, Golfo di- 128 Jl 38.30N 15.45 E
Gioia del Colle 128 Kj 40.48N 16.55 E
Gioia Tauro 128 Jl 38.25N 15.54 E
Gion 168 Fd 8.24N 37.55 E
Gióna Óros 130 Fk 38.35N 22.15 E
Giovi, Passo dei- 128 Cf 44.33N 8.57 E
Giraltovce 120 Rg 49.07N 21.31 E
Girardot 202 Dc 4.18N 74.49W
Girdle Ness 118 Kd 57.08N 2.02W
Giresun 144 Ea 40.55N 38.24 E
Giresun Dağları 146 Hb 40.40N 38.10 E
Giri 170 Cb 0.28N 17.59 E
Giridih 148 Hd 24.11N 86.18 E
Giriftu 170 Gb 2.00N 39.45 E
Girne 146 Ee 35.20N 33.19 E
Girón 202 Cd 3.10S 79.09W
Girona/Gerona 126 Oc 41.59N 2.49 E
Girona / Gerona [3] 126 Ob 42.10N 2.40 E
Gironde [3] 122 Fj 44.55N 0.30W
Gironde 110 Ff 45.35N 1.03W
Gironella 126 Nb 42.02N 1.53 E
Girou 122 Hk 43.46N 1.23 E
Girvan 118 If 55.15N 4.51W
Girvas 114 He 62.31N 33.44 E
Gisborne 210 Ih 38.39S 178.01 E
Gisenyi 170 Ec 1.42S 29.15 E
Gislaved 116 Eg 57.18N 13.32 E
Gisors 122 He 49.17N 1.47 E
Gissar 136 Ge 38.31N 68.36 E
Gissarski hrebet 135 Ge 39.00N 68.40 E
Gistad 116 Ff 58.27N 15.55 E
Gistel 124 Ec 51.10N 2.57 E
Gistral 126 Ea 43.28N 7.35W
Gitarama 170 Ec 2.05S 29.16 E
Gitega 170 Ec 3.26S 29.56 E
Gitu 146 Me 35.20N 48.05 E
Giudicarie, Valli- 128 Ed 46.00N 10.40 E
Giulianova 128 Hh 42.45N 13.57 E
Giumalău, Vîrful- 130 Ib 47.26N 25.29 E
Giurgeni 130 Ke 44.35N 27.48 E
Giurgiu 130 If 43.53N 25.58 E
Giurgiu [2] 130 Ie 44.13N 26.00 E
Give 116 Ci 55.51N 9.15 E
Givet 122 Kd 50.08N 4.50W
Givors 122 Ki 45.35N 4.46 E
Givry-en-Argonne 124 Gf 48.57N 4.53 E
Givry Island 220d Bb 7.07N 151.53 E
Giwa 166 Gc 11.18N 7.27 E
Giza (EN)=Al Jīzah 160 Ke 30.01N 31.13 E
Gižduvan 136 Gg 40.06N 64.40 E
Gižiga 138 Ld 62.03N 160.30 E
Gižiginskaja guba 138 Kd 61.10N 158.30 E
Gizo 214 Fi 8.06S 156.51 E
Gizo 219a Cc 8.07S 156.50 E
Giżycko 120 Rb 54.03N 21.47 E
Gjalicës, Mali i- 130 Dg 42.01N 20.28 E
Gjamyš, gora- 132 Oi 40.20N 46.25 E
Gjende 116 Cc 61.30N 8.35 E
Gjerstad 116 Cf 58.52N 9.00 E
Gjevilvatn 116 Cb 62.40N 9.25 E
Gjirokastra 130 Di 40.05N 20.10 E
Gjoa Haven 176 Jc 68.38N 95.57W
Gjøvik 112 Hc 60.48N 10.42 E
Gjuhës, Kep i- 130 Ci 40.25N 19.18 E
Glace Bay 180 Lg 46.12N 59.57W
Glacier Bay 178 Ie 58.40N 136.00W
Glacier Peak 182 Cb 48.07N 121.07W
Glacier Strait 180 Ja 76.15N 79.00W
Gladbeck 124 Ic 51.34N 6.59 E
Gladenbach 124 Kd 50.46N 8.34 E
Gladewater 186 Ij 32.33N 94.56W
Gladstone [Austl.] 210 Gg 23.51S 151.16 E
Gladstone [Man.-Can.] 186 Ga 50.15N 98.50W
Gladstone [Mi.-U.S.] 184 Dc 45.51N 87.03W
Gladstone [Mo.-U.S.] 186 Ig 39.13N 94.34W
Glafsfjorden 116 Ee 59.35N 12.35 E
Gláma 114a Ab 65.48N 23.00W
Glåma 110 Hd 59.12N 10.57 E
Glamis Castle 118 Ke 56.37N 3.00W
Glamoč 128 Kf 44.03N 16.51 E
Glan 114 Dg 58.35N 15.55 E
Glan [Aus.] 128 Id 46.36N 14.25 E
Glan [F.R.G.] 120 Dg 49.47N 7.43 E
Glan-Münchweiler 124 Je 49.28N 7.26 E
Glarner Alpen 128 Cd 46.55N 9.00 E
Glärnisch 128 Cd 47.00N 9.00 E
Glarus 128 Dc 47.03N 9.04 E
Glarus [2] 128 Dd 46.55N 9.05 E
Glasgow [Ky.-U.S.] 184 Eg 37.00N 85.55W
Glasgow [Mt.-U.S.] 182 Fb 48.12N 106.38W
Glasgow [Scot.-U.K.] 112 Fd 55.53N 4.15W
Glashütte 120 Jf 50.51N 13.47 E
Glass 118 Id 57.25N 4.30W
Glassboro 184 Jf 39.42N 75.07W
Glass Mountains 186 Ek 30.25N 103.15W
Glastonbury 118 Kj 51.09N 2.43W
Glauchau 120 If 50.49N 12.32 E
Glava 116 Ee 59.33N 12.34 E
Glazov 112 Ld 58.09N 52.40 E
Gleann Dá Loch/Glendalough 118 Gh 53.00N 6.20W
Gledićske Planine 130 Df 43.49N 20.55 E
Gleinalpe 128 Jc 47.10N 15.05 E
Gleisdorf 128 Jc 47.06N 15.43 E
Glen 124 Bb 52.50N 0.07W
Glénan, Iles de- 122 Cg 47.43N 4.00W
Glen Arbor 184 Ec 44.53N 85.58W
Glenavy 218 Df 44.55S 171.06 E
Glen Canyon 188 Jh 37.05N 111.41W
Glencoe [Mn.-U.S.] 186 Id 44.46N 94.09W
Glencoe [S.Afr.] 172 Ee 28.12S 30.07 E
Glendale [Az.-U.S.] 182 Ee 33.32N 112.11W
Glendale [Ca.-U.S.] 182 De 34.10N 118.17W
Glendalough/Gleann Dá Loch 118 Gh 53.00N 6.20W
Glendive 182 Gb 47.06N 104.43W
Glendo Reservoir 188 Me 42.31N 104.58W
Glenhope 216 Dh 41.39S 172.39 E
Glen Innes 210 Gg 29.44S 151.44 E
Glennallen 178 Jd 62.07N 145.33W
Glenner 128 Dd 46.46N 9.12 E
Glenns Ferry 188 He 42.57N 115.18W
Glenorchy 218 Cf 44.52S 168.24 E
Glenrock 188 Me 42.52N 105.52W
Glen Rose 186 Hj 32.14N 97.45W
Glenrothes 118 Je 56.12N 3.05W
Glens Falls 184 Kd 43.17N 73.41W
Glenville 186 Gf 38.57N 80.51W
Glenwood [Ia.-U.S.] 186 If 41.03N 95.45W
Glenwood [Mn.-U.S.] 186 Id 45.39N 95.23W
Glenwood Springs 182 Fd 39.32N 107.19W
Glibokaja 130 Ja 48.05N 26.00 E
Glina 128 Ke 45.20N 16.06 E
Glinjany 120 Ug 49.46N 24.33 E
Glittertinden 110 Gc 61.39N 8.33 E
Gliwice 120 Of 50.17N 18.40 E
Globe 182 Ee 33.24N 110.47W
Globino 132 He 49.24N 33.18 E
Głogów 120 Me 51.40N 16.05 E
Glomfjord 114 Cc 66.49N 13.58 E
Glommersträsk 114 Ed 65.16N 19.38 E
Glonn 120 Hh 48.11N 11.45 E
Glorieuses, Iles- 158 Lj 11.30S 47.20 E
Glottof, Mount- 178 Ie 57.30N 153.30W
Gloucester 118 Kj 51.53N 2.15W
Gloucester [Eng.-U.K.] 118 Kj 51.53N 2.14W
Gloucester [Ma.-U.S.] 184 Ld 42.41N 70.39W
Gloucester, Cape- 214 Di 5.27S 148.25 E
Gloucestershire [3] 118 Lj 51.50N 1.55W
Glover Island 197p Bb 11.59N 61.47W
Glover's Reef 194 De 16.49N 87.48W
Gloversville 184 Jd 43.03N 74.21W
Głowno 120 Pe 51.58N 19.44 E
Głubczyce 120 Nf 50.13N 17.49 E
Glubokoje [Bye.-U.S.S.R.] 136 Cd 55.08N 27.41 E
Glubokoje [Kaz.-U.S.S.R.] 136 Ie 50.06N 82.19 E
Glubokoje, ozero- 116 Md 60.30N 29.25 E
Głuchołazy 120 Nf 50.20N 17.22 E
Glücksburg 120 Fb 54.50N 9.33 E
Glückstadt 120 Fc 53.47N 9.25 E
Gluhov 136 De 51.43N 33.57 E
Gluša 132 Fc 53.06N 28.52 E
Glyngøre 116 Ch 56.46N 8.52 E
Gmünd [Aus.] 128 Hb 48.46N 14.59 E
Gmünd [Aus.] 128 Hd 46.54N 13.32 E
Gmunden 128 Hc 47.55N 13.48 E
Gnarp 114 Dc 62.03N 17.16 E
Gnesta 114 Dg 59.03N 17.18 E
Gniben 116 Dh 56.01N 11.18 E
Gniew 120 Oc 53.51N 18.49 E
Gniewkowo 120 Od 52.54N 18.25 E
Gniezno 120 Nd 52.31N 17.37 E
Gnjilane 130 Eg 42.28N 21.29 E
Gnosjö 114 Ch 57.22N 13.44 E
Gnowangerup 212 Df 33.56S 117.50 E
Goa, Damān and Diu [3] 148 Ee 15.35N 74.00 E
Goageb 172 Be 26.44S 17.15 E
Goālpāra 148 Ic 26.10N 90.37 E
Goat 219b Dd 18.42S 169.17 E
Goat Island 197d Ba 17.44N 61.51W
Goat Point 197d Ba 17.44N 61.51W
Goba 160 Kh 7.01N 39.59 E
Gobabis 160 Ik 22.30S 18.58 E
Gobabis [3] 172 Bd 22.00S 19.00 E
Göbel 130 Lj 40.00N 28.09 E
Gober 166 Gc 13.48N 6.51 E
Gobernador Gregores 206 Fg 48.46S 70.15W
Gobernador Ingeniero Valentin Virasoro 206 Ic 28.03S 56.02W
Gobernador Mansilla 204 Ck 32.33S 59.22W
Gobi Altai (EN) = Gov'altajn Nuruu 140 Me 44.00N 102.00 E
Gobi Desert (EN) = Gov' 140 Me 43.00N 106.00 E
Gobō 154 Mh 33.53N 135.10 E
Göçbeyli 130 Kj 39.13N 27.25 E
Goceano 128 Dj 40.30N 9.15 E
Goce Delčev 130 Gh 41.33N 23.42 E
Goch 120 Ce 51.40N 6.10 E
Gochas 172 Bd 24.55S 18.55 E
Goczałkowickie, Jezioro- 120 Og 49.53N 18.50 E
Göd 120 Pi 47.42N 19.08 E
Godafoss 114a Cb 65.41N 17.33W
Godalming 124 Bc 51.11N 0.36W
Godār 146 Qh 29.45N 57.30 E
Godār-e Shah 146 Me 34.45N 48.10 E
Godāvari 140 Kh 17.00N 81.45 E
Godbout, Rivière- 184 Na 49.21N 67.42W
Gode 168 Gd 5.55N 43.40 E
Godeč 130 Gf 43.01N 23.03 E
Godelbukta 222 Df 70.00S 20.58 E
Goderich 184 Gd 43.45N 81.43W
Goderville 124 Ce 49.39N 0.22 E
Godhavn/Qeqertarssuaq 224 Nc 69.20N 53.35W
Godhra 148 Ed 22.45N 73.38 E
Godinlabe 168 Hd 5.54N 46.40 E
Gödöllő 120 Pi 47.36N 19.22 E
Godoy Cruz 206 Gd 32.55S 68.50W
Gods Lake 180 If 54.40N 94.09W
Gods Lake 180 If 54.40N 94.20W
Gods Mercy, Bay of - 180 Id 63.30N 86.10W
Gods River 180 Ie 56.22N 92.52W
Godthåb/Nūk 224 Nc 64.15N 51.40W
Godthåbfjord 179 Gf 64.20N 51.30W
Godwin Austen (EN) = Qogir Feng 140 Jf 35.53N 76.30 E
Godwin Austen → K2 140 Jf 35.53N 76.30 E
Goedereede 124 Fc 51.49N 3.58 E
Goéland, Lac au- 184 Ig 49.45N 76.50W
Goélands, Lac aux- 180 Le 55.30N 64.30W
Goële 124 Ee 49.10N 2.40 E
Goelette Island 172b Bc 10.13S 51.08 E
Goeree 122 Jc 51.50N 3.55 E
Goes 122 Jc 51.30N 3.54 E
Gogama 184 Gb 47.40N 81.43W
Gō-Gawa 156 Cd 35.01N 132.13 E
Gogebic Range 184 Cb 46.45N 89.25W
Gogland, ostrov- 114 Gf 60.05N 27.00 E
Gog Magog Hills 124 Cb 52.09N 0.11 E
Gogounou 166 Fc 10.50N 2.50 E
Gogrial 168 Dd 8.32N 28.07 E
Gogu, Vîrful- 130 Fd 45.12N 22.30 E
Gogui 166 Db 15.39N 9.21W
Gohelle 124 Ed 50.28N 2.45 E
Goiandira 202 Ig 18.08S 48.06W
Goianésia 202 Ig 15.19S 49.04W
Goiânia 200 Ig 16.40S 49.16W
Goianinha 202 Ke 6.16S 35.12W
Goiás 202 Hg 15.56S 50.08W
Goiás [2] 202 If 12.00S 48.00W
Goiatuba 202 Ig 18.01S 49.22W
Goikul 220a Bc 7.22N 134.36 E
Göinge 116 Eh 56.20N 13.50 E
Goio-Erê 206 Jb 24.12S 53.01W
Goioxim 204 Gg 25.14S 52.01W
Goirle 124 Hc 51.34N 5.05 E
Góis 126 Dd 40.09N 8.07W
Goito 128 Ee 45.15N 10.40 E
Gojam [3] 168 Fc 10.33N 37.35 E
Gojō 156 Dd 34.21N 135.42 E
Gojōme 156 Gb 39.56N 140.07 E
Gojra 148 Eb 31.09N 72.41 E
Gojthski, pereval- 132 Kg 44.15N 39.18 E
Gokase-Gawa 156 Be 32.35N 131.42 E
Gokasho-Wan 156 Ed 34.20N 136.40 E
Gökbel Dağı 130 Kl 37.28N 28.00 E
Gökçay 146 Ed 36.36N 33.23 E
Gökçeada 144 Ca 40.10N 25.50 E
Gökçeören 130 Lk 38.35N 28.32 E
Gökçeyazı 130 Kj 39.38N 27.39 E
Gökdere 146 Ed 36.39N 33.35 E
Gökırmak 146 Fb 41.24N 35.08 E
Göksu [Tur.] 146 Fd 37.37N 35.35 E
Göksu [Tur.] 146 Fd 36.20N 34.05 E
Göksu [Tur.] 130 Mi 40.23N 29.58 E
Göksun 146 Gc 38.03N 36.30 E
Göktepe 146 Ed 37.16N 32.46 E
Gök Tepe 130 Mm 36.53N 29.17 E
Gokwe 172 Dc 18.13S 28.55 E
Gol 114 Bf 60.42N 8.57 E
Golāghāt 148 Ic 26.31N 93.58 E
Golaja Pristan 132 Hf 46.29N 32.31 E
Gołańcz 120 Nd 52.57N 17.18 E
Golconda [Il.-U.S.] 186 Lh 37.22N 88.29W
Golconda [Nv.-U.S.] 188 Gf 40.57N 117.30W
Gölcük 146 Cb 40.44N 29.44 E
Golčův Jenikov 120 Lg 49.49N 15.30 E
Gołdap 120 Sb 54.19N 22.19 E
Gold Beach 188 Ce 42.25N 124.25W
Gold Coast 210 Gg 27.58S 153.25 E
Gold Coast 158 Gh 5.20N 0.45W
Golden [B.C.-Can.] 180 Ff 51.18N 116.58W
Golden [Co.-U.S.] 186 Dg 39.46N 105.13W
Golden Bay 218 Ed 40.50S 172.50 E
Goldendale 188 Ed 45.49N 120.50W
Goldene Aue 120 Ge 51.25N 11.00 E
Golden Gate 188 Dh 37.49N 122.29W
Golden Hinde 188 Bb 49.39N 125.45W
Golden Meadow 186 Kl 29.23N 90.16W
Golden Vale/Machaire na Mumhan 118 Fi 52.30N 8.00W
Goldfield 188 Gh 37.42N 117.14W
Gold River 188 Bb 49.41N 126.08W
Goldsboro 182 Ld 35.23N 77.59W
Goldsworthy 212 Dd 20.20S 119.30 E
Göle 146 Jb 40.48N 42.36 E
Golegã 126 De 39.24N 8.29W
Goleniów 120 Kc 53.36N 14.50 E
Golešnica 130 Eh 41.42N 21.33 E
Goleta, Cerro- 192 Ih 18.38N 100.04W
Golfito 190 Hg 8.38N 83.11W
Golfo Aranci 128 Dj 41.00N 9.37 E
Gölgeli Dağları 130 Ml 37.15N 29.06 E
Gölhisar 130 Ml 37.08N 29.30 E
Goliad 186 Hl 28.40N 97.23W
Golija [Yugo.] 130 Df 43.19N 20.18 E
Golija [Yugo.] 130 Bf 43.02N 18.47 E
Goljak 130 Eg 42.44N 21.31 E
Goljama Kamčija 130 Kf 43.03N 27.29 E
Goljama Sjutkja 130 Hh 41.54N 24.01 E
Goljamo Konare 130 Hg 42.16N 24.33 E
Goljam Perelik 130 Hh 41.36N 24.34 E
Goljam Persenk 130 Hh 41.49N 24.33 E
Gölköy 146 Gb 40.15N 37.26 E
Gölkük 130 Kj 39.19N 27.59 E
Göllheim 124 Ke 49.35N 8.03 E
Gölmarmara 130 Kk 38.42N 27.56 E
Golmud 142 Lf 36.22N 94.55 E
Golmud He 152 Gd 36.54N 95.11 E
Golo 122a Ba 42.31N 9.32 E
Goloby 120 Ve 51.06N 25.06 E
Gologory 120 Ug 49.35N 24.30 E
Gololcha 168 Gd 8.12N 40.05 E
Golovin 178 Gd 64.33N 163.02W
Golovnin Seamount (EN) 138 Kg 46.50N 157.00 E
Golpāyegan 144 Hc 33.27N 50.18 E
Gölpazarı 146 Db 40.17N 30.19 E
Golšanka 120 Zb 54.00N 26.16 E
Golspie 118 Jd 57.58N 3.58W
Gol Tappeh 146 Kd 36.35N 45.45 E
Golubac 130 Ee 44.39N 21.38 E
Golub-Dobrzyń 120 Pc 53.08N 19.02 E
Golungo Alto 170 Bd 9.08S 14.47 E
Golyšmanovo 136 Gd 56.23N 68.23 E
Goma 160 Ji 1.37S 29.12 E
Gómara 126 Jc 41.37N 2.13W
Gombe 160 Ig 10.17N 11.10 E
Gombi 166 Hc 10.10N 12.44 E
Gomel 112 Je 52.25N 31.00 E
Gomelskaja oblast [3] 136 Ce 52.20N 29.40 E
Gomera 158 Ff 28.06N 17.08W
Gómez Farías 192 Ie 24.57N 101.02W
Gómez Palacio 190 Dc 25.34N 103.30W
Gomo 152 Ee 33.26N 85.21 E
Gomo Co 152 Ee 33.45N 85.35 E
Goms 128 Cd 46.25N 8.10 E
Gonābād 144 Ic 34.20N 58.42 E
Gonaïves 190 Je 19.27N 72.43W
Gonam 138 Ie 57.18N 131.20 E
Gonâve, Golfe de la- 190 Je 19.00N 73.30W
Gonâve, Ile de la- 190 Je 18.51N 73.03W
Gonbad-e Qābūs 144 Ib 37.15N 55.09 E
Gonda 148 Gc 27.08N 81.56 E
Gonder 160 Kg 12.38N 37.27 E
Gonder [3] 168 Fc 12.00N 38.00 E
Gondia 148 Gd 21.27N 80.12 E
Gondo 158 Gg 14.20N 3.10W
Gondomar 126 Dc 41.09N 8.32W
Gondwana 140 Kg 23.00N 81.00 E
Gönen 146 Bb 40.06N 27.39 E
Gönen 146 Bb 40.06N 27.36 E
Gonfreville-l'Orcher 124 Ce 49.30N 0.14 E
Gong'an (Doushi) 152 Je 30.05N 112.12 E
Gongbo'gyamda 152 Ff 29.59N 93.25 E
Gonggar 152 Ff 29.17N 90.50 E
Gongga Shan 140 Mg 29.34N 101.53 E
Gonghe 152 Hd 36.21N 100.47 E
Gongliu/Tokkuztara 152 Dc 43.30N 82.15 E
Gongola [2] 166 Hd 8.40N 11.20 E
Gongola 158 Ih 9.30N 12.04 E
Gongpoquan 152 Gc 41.50N 97.00 E
Gongshan 152 Gf 27.39N 98.35 E
Gongxian (Xiaoyi) 154 Bg 34.46N 112.57 E
Gongzhuling → Huaide 152 Lc 43.30N 124.52 E
Goñi 204 Dk 33.31S 56.24W
Goniądz 120 Sc 53.30N 22.45 E
Gonīshān 146 Pd 37.04N 54.06 E
Gonjo 152 Ge 30.52N 98.20 E
Gonohe 156 Ga 40.31N 141.19 E
Go-no-ura 156 Ae 33.45N 129.41 E
Gönuk 146 Ic 39.00N 40.41 E
Gonzales 186 Hl 29.30N 97.27W
Gonzáles, Riacho- 204 Df 22.48S 57.54W
González 192 Jf 22.50N 98.27W
Goodenough, Cape- 222 Ie 66.16S 126.10 E
Goodenough Bay 212 Ja 9.55S 150.00 E
Goodenough Island 214 Ei 9.22S 150.16 E
Good Hope, Cape of- / Groeie Hoop, Kaap die- 158 Il 34.21S 18.28 E
Goodhouse 172 Be 28.57S 18.13 E
Gooding 188 He 42.56N 114.43W
Goodland 182 Gd 39.21N 101.43W
Goodnews Bay 178 Ge 59.07N 161.35W
Goodsir, Mount- 188 Ga 51.12N 116.20W
Good Spirit Lake 188 Na 51.34N 102.40W
Goodwin Sands 124 Dc 51.15N 1.35 E
Goodyear 188 Ij 33.26N 112.21W
Goole 118 Mh 53.42N 0.52W
Goomalling 212 Df 31.19S 116.49 E
Goondiwindi 210 Gg 28.32S 150.19 E
Goonyella 212 Jd 21.43S 147.58 E
Goor 124 Ib 52.14N 6.37 E
Goose Lake 182 Cc 41.57N 120.25W
Goose River 186 Hc 47.28N 96.52W
Gopło, Jezioro- 120 Od 52.35N 18.20 E
Göppingen 120 Fh 48.42N 9.40 E
Góra 120 Me 51.40N 16.33 E
Gora 130 Di 40.40N 20.30 E
Góra Kalwaria 120 Re 51.59N 21.12 E
Gorakhpur 142 Kg 26.45N 83.22 E
Goransko 130 Bf 43.07N 18.50 E
Gorata 130 Ih 41.45N 25.55 E
Goražde 128 Mg 43.40N 18.59 E
Gorda 188 Ei 35.55N 121.27W
Gorda, Cayo- 194 Ff 15.55N 82.15W
Gorda, Punta- [Ca.-U.S.] 188 Cf 40.16N 124.20W
Gorda, Punta- [Cuba] 194 Fb 22.24N 82.10W
Gorda, Punta- [Nic.] 194 Ff 14.21N 83.12W
Gördes 130 Lk 38.54N 28.18 E
Gördes 130 Kj 38.46N 27.58 E
Gordil 168 Cd 9.44N 21.35 E
Gordior 146 Ec 39.37N 32.00 E
Gordon [Nb.-U.S.] 186 Ee 42.48N 102.12W
Gordon [Wi.-U.S.] 186 Kc 46.15N 91.47W
Gordon, Lake- 212 Jh 43.05S 146.05 E
Gordon Horne Peak 188 Fa 51.46N 118.50W
Gordonvale 212 Jc 17.05S 145.47 E
Goré 168 Bd 7.55N 16.38 E
Gore 168 Fd 8.09N 35.34 E
Gore 218 Cg 46.06S 168.56 E
Görele 146 Hb 41.02N 39.00 E
Görenez Dağı 130 Lk 39.00N 28.01 E
Gorenjsko 128 Id 46.20N 14.10 E
Gorey/Guaire 118 Gi 52.40N 6.18W
Gorgān 146 Hf 36.50N 54.29 E
Gorgān 146 Pd 36.59N 54.05 E
Gorgān, Khalīj-e- 146 Od 36.40N 53.50 E
Gorgany 120 Uh 48.30N 24.15 E
Gorgin 146 Ld 36.15N 47.55 E
Gorgin 146 Ld 36.16N 47.52 E
Gorgol [3] 162 Ef 15.45N 13.00W
Gorgol el Abiod 162 Ef 16.14N 12.58W
Gorgona 128 Dg 43.25N 9.55 E
Gorgona, Isla- 202 Cc 2.59N 78.12W
Gorgora 168 Fc 12.14N 37.17 E
Gorham 184 Lc 44.23N 71.11W
Gori 136 Eg 42.00N 44.02 E
Gorinchem 122 Kc 51.50N 5.00 E
Goring 124 Ac 51.31N 1.08W
Goris 132 Oj 39.31N 46.22 E
Gorizia 128 He 45.57N 13.38 E
Gorj [2] 130 Gd 45.00N 23.20 E
Gorjačegorsk 138 De 55.24N 88.55 E
Gorjači Kljuc 132 Kg 44.36N 39.07 E
Gorjanci 128 Je 45.45N 15.20 E
Gorki [Bye.-U.S.S.R.] 132 Gb 54.17N 31.00 E
Gorki [R.S.F.S.R.] 112 Kd 57.38N 45.05 E
Gorki [R.S.F.S.R.] 138 Bc 65.05N 65.15 E
Gorko-Solenoje, ozero- 132 Oe 49.20N 46.05 E
Gorkovskaja oblast [3] 136 Ed 56.15N 44.45 E
Gorkovskoje vodohranilišče = Gorky Reservoir (EN) 110 Kd 57.00N 43.10 E
Gorkum 120 Hf 50.10N 11.08 E
Gorky Reservoir (EN) = Gorkovskoje vodohranilišče 110 Kd 57.00N 43.10 E
Gørlev 116 Di 55.32N 11.14 E
Gorlice 120 Rg 49.40N 21.10 E
Görlitz 120 Ke 51.10N 15.00 E
Gorlovka 112 Jf 48.18N 38.03 E
Gornalunga 128 Jm 37.24N 15.03 E
Gorna Orjahovica 130 If 43.07N 25.41 E
Gornjak [R.S.F.S.R.] 138 Df 51.00N 81.29 E
Gornjak [Ukr.-U.S.S.R.] 120 Uf 50.16N 24.13 E
Gornji Milanovac 130 De 44.02N 20.27 E
Gornji Vakuf 128 Lg 43.56N 17.36 E

Index Symbols

[1] Independent Nation
[2] State, Region
[3] District, County
[4] Municipality
[5] Colony, Dependency
Continent
Physical Region
Historical or Cultural Region
Mount, Mountain
Volcano
Hill
Mountains, Mountain Range
Hills, Escarpment
Plateau, Upland
Pass, Gap
Plain, Lowland
Delta
Salt Flat
Valley, Canyon
Crater, Cave
Karst Features
Depression
Polder
Desert, Dunes
Forest, Woods
Heath, Steppe
Oasis
Cape, Point
Coast, Beach
Cliff
Peninsula
Isthmus
Sandbank
Island
Atoll
Rock, Reef
Islands, Archipelago
Rocks, Reefs
Coral Reef
Well, Spring
Geyser
River, Stream
Waterfall, Rapids
River Mouth, Estuary
Lake
Salt Lake
Intermittent Lake
Reservoir
Swamp, Pond
Canal
Glacier
Ice Shelf, Pack Ice
Ocean
Sea
Gulf, Bay
Strait, Fjord
Lagoon
Bank
Seamount
Tablemount
Ridge
Shelf
Basin
Escarpment, Sea Scarp
Fracture
Trench, Abyss
National Park, Reserve
Point of Interest
Recreation Site
Cave, Cavern
Historic Site
Ruins
Wall, Walls
Church, Abbey
Temple
Scientific Station
Railway station
Airport
Port
Military installation
Lighthouse
Mine
Tunnel
Dam, Bridge

Name	Page	Grid	Lat.	Long.
Gorno-Altajsk	142	Kd	51.58N	85.58 E
Gorno-Altajskaja avtonomnaja oblast [3]	138	Df	51.00N	87.00 E
Gorno-Badahšanskaja avtonomnaja oblast [3]	136	Hh	38.15N	73.00 E
Gorno-Čujski	138	Ge	57.40N	111.40 E
Gornozavodsk [R.S.F.S.R.]	134	Ig	58.25N	58.20 E
Gornozavodsk [R.S.F.S.R.]	138	Jg	46.30N	141.55 E
Gorny [R.S.F.S.R.]	138	Ih	44.50N	133.56 E
Gorny [R.S.F.S.R.]	138	If	50.48N	136.26 E
Gorny [R.S.F.S.R.]	132	Pd	51.45N	48.34 E
Gornyje Ključi	154	Lb	45.15N	133.30 E
Gorochan	168	Fd	9.26N	37.05 E
Gorodec [R.S.F.S.R.]	136	Ed	56.40N	43.30 E
Gorodec [R.S.F.S.R.]	116	Mf	58.30N	29.55 E
Gorodenka	132	De	48.42N	25.32 E
Gorodišče [Bye.-U.S.S.R.]	120	Vc	53.16N	26.03 E
Gorodišče [R.S.F.S.R.]	132	Nc	53.16N	45.42 E
Gorodišče [Ukr.-U.S.S.R.]	132	Ge	49.17N	31.27 E
Gorodnica	132	Ed	50.49N	27.22 E
Gorodnja	132	Gd	51.55N	31.31 E
Gorodok [Bye.-U.S.S.R.]	136	Cd	55.26N	29.59 E
Gorodok [Ukr.-U.S.S.R.]	132	Ce	49.47N	23.39 E
Gorodok [Ukr.-U.S.S.R.]	132	Ee	49.10N	26.31 E
Gorodovikovsm	136	Ef	46.05N	41.59 E
Gorohov	120	Uf	50.28N	24.47 E
Gorohovec	114	Kh	56.12N	42.42 E
Goroka	210	Ec	6.02S	145.22 E
Gorom Gorom	166	Ec	14.26N	0.14W
Gorong, Kepulauan-	150	Jg	4.05S	131.20 E
Gorongosa, Serra da-	172	Ec	18.24S	34.06 E
Gorontalo	142	Oi	0.33N	123.03 E
Goroual	166	Fc	14.42N	0.53 E
Goroubi	166	Fc	13.07N	2.18 E
Górowo Iławeckie	120	Qb	54.17N	20.30 E
Gorron	122	Ff	48.25N	0.49W
Goršečnoje	132	Kd	51.33N	38.09 E
Gorski Kotar	128	Ib	45.26N	14.40 E
Gorssel	128	Ib	52.12N	6.13 E
Gort	118	Eh	53.04N	8.50W
Goru, Vîrful-	130	Jd	45.48N	26.25 E
Görükle	130	Li	40.14N	28.50 E
Goryn	136	Ce	52.09N	27.17 E
Gorzów [2]	120	Ld	54.25N	15.15 E
Gorzów Wielkopolski	120	Ld	52.44N	15.15 E
Goschen Strait	212	Kb	10.09S	150.56 E
Gosen	154	Of	37.44N	139.11 E
Gosford	212	Kf	33.26S	151.21 E
Goshen	184	Ee	41.35N	85.50W
Goshogawara	154	Pd	40.48N	140.27 E
Gosier	197e	Bb	16.12N	61.30W
Goslar	120	Ge	51.54N	10.26 E
Gospić	128	Jf	44.33N	15.23 E
Gosport	118	Lk	50.48N	1.08W
Gossen	116	Bb	62.50N	6.55 E
Gossi	166	Eb	15.49N	1.15W
Gossinga	168	Dd	8.39N	25.59 E
Gostivar	130	Dh	41.48N	20.54 E
Gostyń	120	Me	51.53N	17.00 E
Gostynin	120	Pd	52.26N	19.29 E
Gota älv	110	Hd	57.42N	11.52 E
Göta Kanal	110	Hd	58.50N	13.58 E
Götaland	110	Hd	57.30N	14.30 E
Götaland	114	Dh	57.30N	14.30 E
Göteborg	112	Hd	57.43N	11.58 E
Göteborg och Bohus [2]	114	Cg	58.30N	11.30 E
Gotel Mountains	158	Ih	7.00N	11.40 E
Gotemba	156	Fd	35.18N	138.56 E
Götene	114	Cg	58.32N	13.29 E
Gotha	120	Gf	50.57N	10.43 E
Gothenburg	186	Ff	40.56N	100.09W
Gothèye	166	Fc	13.52N	1.34 E
Gotland [2]	114	Ef	57.30N	18.30 E
Gotland	110	Hd	57.30N	18.30 E
Gotō-Nada	156	Ae	32.45N	129.30 E
Gotō-Rettō	152	Me	32.50N	129.00 E
Gotowasi	150	If	0.38N	128.26 E
Gotska Sandön	114	Eg	58.25N	19.15 E
Gōtsu	154	Lg	35.00N	132.14 E
Göttingen	120	Fe	51.32N	9.56 E
Gottwaldov	120	Ng	49.13N	17.39 E
Goubangzi	154	Fd	41.23N	121.48 E
Gouda	122	Kc	52.01N	4.43 E
Goudiri	166	Cc	14.11N	12.43W
Gouet	122	Df	48.32N	2.45W
Gough Island	158	Gm	40.20S	10.00W
Gough Lake	180	Le	52.02N	112.28W
Gouin, Réservoir-	180	Kg	48.35N	74.50W
Goulbin Kaba	166	Gc	13.42N	6.19 E
Goulburn	210	Fh	34.45S	149.43 E
Goulburn Islands	212	Gb	11.50S	133.30 E
Gould Bay	222	Rf	78.10S	44.00W
Gould Coast	222	Mg	84.30S	150.00W
Goulia	166	Dc	10.01N	7.11W
Goulimine	162	Ed	28.59N	10.04W
Gouménissa	130	Fi	40.57N	22.27 E
Gouna	168	Hd	8.32N	13.34 E
Gounda	168	Cd	9.22N	20.57 E
Goundam	166	Eb	16.24N	3.38W
Goundi	168	Bd	9.22N	17.22 E
Goundoumaria	168	Hc	13.42N	11.10 E
Gounou Gaya	168	Bd	9.38N	15.31 E
Gourara	162	Hd	29.00N	0.40 E
Gouraya	126	Nh	36.34N	1.55 E
Gourcy	166	Ec	13.13N	2.21W
Gourdon	122	Hj	44.44N	1.23 E
Gouré	160	Ig	13.58N	10.18 E
Gourin	122	Cf	48.08N	3.36W
Gourma [Burkina]	166	Fc	12.20N	1.30 E
Gourma [Mali]	166	Eb	15.45N	2.00W
Gourma-Rharous	166	Eb	16.52N	1.55W
Gournay-en-Bray	122	He	49.29N	1.44 E
Gournià	158	Ik	35.06N	25.48 E
Gouro	168	Bb	19.40N	19.28 E
Gourrama	162	Gc	32.20N	4.05W
Goussainville	124	Fd	49.01N	2.28 E
Gouyave	197p	Bb	12.10N	61.44W
Gouzeaucourt	124	Fd	50.03N	3.07 E
Gouzon	122	Ih	46.11N	2.14 E
Gov' = Gobi Desert (EN)	140	Me	43.00N	106.00 E
Gov'altajn Nuruu = Gobi Altai (EN)	140	Me	44.00N	102.00 E
Govena, mys-	138	Le	59.47N	166.02 E
Gove Peninsula	212	Hb	12.05S	136.50 E
Governador Valadares	200	La	18.51S	41.56W
Governor's Harbour	190	Ic	25.10N	76.14W
Gowanda	184	Hd	42.28N	78.57W
Gower	118	Ij	51.36N	4.10W
Gowganda	184	Gb	47.38N	80.46W
Goya	200	Kh	29.10S	59.20W
Goyave	197e	Ab	16.08N	61.34W
Goyaves, Ilets à-	197e	Ab	16.10N	61.40W
Goyder River	212	Hb	12.38S	135.05 E
Goyōmai-Kaikyō	156a	Db	43.24N	145.50 E
Goz Arian	168	Bc	14.35N	20.00 E
Goz Beida	168	Cc	12.13N	21.25 E
Gozha Co	152	De	34.59N	81.06 E
Gözlü Baba Dağı	130	Lk	38.15N	28.28 E
Gozo	110	Hh	36.05N	14.15 E
Graaff-Reinet	172	Cf	32.14S	24.32 E
Graafschap	122	Mb	52.05N	6.30 E
Graben Neudorf	124	Ke	49.10N	8.28 E
Grabia	120	Oe	51.26N	18.56 E
Grabière Point	197	Bb	15.30N	61.29W
Grabo	166	De	4.55N	7.30W
Grabowa	120	Mb	54.26N	16.20 E
Gračac	128	Jf	44.18N	15.51 E
Gračanica	128	Mf	44.42N	18.18 E
Gračanica, Manastir-	130	Eg	42.36N	21.12 E
Gracias	194	Cf	14.35N	88.35W
Gracias a Dios [3]	194	Ef	15.20N	84.20W
Gracias a Dios, Cabo-	174	Kh	15.00N	83.08W
Graciosa [Azr.]	158	Ee	39.04N	28.00W
Graciosa [Can.Is.]	162	Dd	29.15N	13.30W
Gradačac	128	Mf	44.53N	18.26 E
Gradaús, Serra dos-	198	Kf	8.00S	50.45W
Gradec [It.]	128	He	45.40N	13.23 E
Grado [Sp.]	126	Fa	43.23N	6.04W
Grænalon	114a	Cb	64.10N	17.24W
Grænlandshaf = Greenland Sea (EN)	224	Ld	77.00N	1.00W
Grafenau	120	Jh	48.51N	13.24 E
Grafham Water	118	Lh	52.19N	0.10W
Grafing bei München	120	Hh	48.03N	11.58 E
Grafschaft Bentheim	124	Cc	52.30N	7.05 E
Grafton [Austl.]	212	Ke	29.41S	152.56 E
Grafton [N.D.-U.S.]	182	Hb	48.25N	97.25W
Grafton [W.V.-U.S.]	184	Hf	39.21N	80.00W
Grafton, Mount-	188	Vg	38.40N	114.45W
Graham [Can.]	180	Ef	53.40N	132.30W
Graham [N.C.-U.S.]	184	Hg	36.05N	79.25W
Graham [N.W.T.-Can.]	180	Ia	77.17N	90.50W
Graham [Tx.-U.S.]	186	Gj	33.06N	98.35W
Graham, Mount-	182	Ek	32.42N	109.52W
Graham Land (EN)	222	Qe	66.00S	63.30W
Graham Moore, Cape -	180	Je	72.51N	76.05W
Grahamstown	160	Jl	33.19S	26.31 E
Grain Coast	158	Gh	5.00N	9.00W
Graisivaudan	122	Li	45.15N	5.50 E
Grajaú	202	Ie	5.49S	46.08W
Grajaú, Rio-	202	Jd	3.41S	44.48W
Grajewo	120	Sc	53.39N	22.27 E
Gram	116	Ci	55.17N	9.04 E
Gramalote	202	Kk	7.54N	72.48W
Gramat	122	Hj	44.48N	1.43 E
Gramat, Causse de-	122	Hj	44.40N	1.50 E
Graminha, Represa da-	204	le	21.33S	46.38W
Grammichele	110	Hh	37.13N	14.38 E
Grammont/Geraardsbergen	124	Fd	50.46N	3.52 E
Grámmos Óros	130	Di	40.20N	20.45 E
Grampian [3]	118	Kf	57.25N	2.35W
Grampian Mountains	110	Fd	56.45N	4.00W
Gramshi	130	Di	40.52N	20.11 E
Gran	116	Dd	60.22N	10.34 E
Granada [Col.]	202	Dc	3.33N	73.44W
Granada [Nic.]	190	Gf	11.56N	85.57W
Granada [Nic.]	194	En	11.50N	86.00W
Granada [Sp.]	112	Ff	37.13N	3.41W
Granada [Sp.] [3]	126	Ig	37.15N	3.15W
Granada, Vega de-	126	Ig	37.15N	4.00W
Granard/Gránard	118	Hh	53.47N	7.30W
Gránard/Granard	118	Hh	53.47N	7.30W
Granby	180	Kg	45.24N	72.43W
Gran Canaria	158	Ff	28.00N	15.36W
Gran Chaco	198	Ih	23.00S	61.00W
Grand Anse Bay	197p	Bb	12.01N	61.45W
Grand Bahama	174	Lg	26.40N	78.20W
Grand Ballon	122	Ng	47.55N	7.08 E
Grand Bank	180	Lg	47.06N	55.47W
Grand Banks (EN)	174	Oe	45.00N	50.00W
Grand Bassa	166	Dd	6.10N	9.40W
Grand-Bassam	166	Eb	5.12N	3.44W
Grand Bay	197p	Cb	12.29N	61.23W
Grand Bay	197p	Bb	15.14N	61.19W
Grand-Béréby	166	De	4.38N	6.55W
Grand-Bourg	196	Fe	15.53N	61.19W
Grand Caille Point	197k	Ab	13.50N	61.05W
Grandcamp-Maisy	124	Ae	49.23N	1.02W
Grand Canal	118	Gh	53.21N	6.14W
Grand Canal (EN) = Da Yunhe	140	Nf	39.54N	116.44 E
Grand Canyon	182	Ed	36.03N	112.09W
Grand Canyon	174	Hf	36.10N	112.45W
Grand' Case	197b	Ab	18.06N	63.03W
Grand Cayman	190	Id	19.20N	81.15W
Grand Cess	166	De	4.24N	8.13W
Grand Colombier	122	Li	45.54N	5.46 E
Grand-Combe, La-	122	Kj	44.13N	4.02 E
Grand Coulee	188	Fc	47.56N	119.00W
Grand-Couronne	124	De	49.21N	1.01 E
Grandcourt	124	De	49.55N	1.30 E
Grand Cul de Sac Bay	197k	Ab	13.59N	61.02W
Grand Cul-de-Sac Marin	197e	Ab	16.20N	61.35W
Grande, Arroyo-	204	Dm	37.32S	57.34W
Grande, Bahía-	198	Jk	50.45S	68.45W
Grande, Boca-	202	Fb	8.45N	60.35W
Grande, Cerro-	204	Gb	15.37S	51.48W
Grande, Cerro-	192	If	23.40N	100.40W
Grande, Ciénaga-	194	Ji	9.13N	75.46W
Grande, Corixa-	204	Cc	17.10S	58.20W
Grande, Cuchilla- [Arg.]	204	Cj	31.45S	58.35W
Grande, Cuchilla- [Ur.]	198	Ki	33.15S	55.07W
Grande, Ile-	122	Cf	48.48N	3.35W
Grande, Ilha-	202	Jh	23.10S	44.10W
Grande, Río-	202	Fb	8.39N	60.59W
Grande, Río-	174	Jg	25.57N	97.09W
Grande, Río-	174	Jg	25.57N	97.09W
Grande, Río- [Braz.]	198	Kh	20.06S	51.04W
Grande, Río- (EN) = Bravo del Norte, Río-	174	Jg	25.57N	97.09W
Grande, Río- o Guapay, Río-	198	Jg	15.51S	64.39W
Grande, Serra-	198	Lf	6.00S	40.52W
Grande, Sierra-	192	Gc	29.40N	104.55W
Grande Anse	197k	Ba	14.40N	61.11W
Grande-Anse	197e	Bb	16.18N	61.04W
Grande Cache	180	Ff	53.14N	119.00W
Grande Casse, Pointe de la-	122	Mi	45.24N	6.50 E
Grande Cayemite	194	Kd	18.37N	73.45W
Grande Chartreuse	122	Li	45.22N	5.50 E
Grande Comore/Njazidja	158	Lj	11.35S	43.20 E
Grande de Santa Marta, Ciénaga-	194	Jh	10.50N	74.25W
Grande de Santiago, Río-	174	Ig	21.36N	105.26W
Grande Inferior, Cuchilla-	204	Dk	33.50S	56.10W
Grande Kabylie	126	Mh	36.45N	4.00 E
Grande-Motte, La-	122	Kk	43.34N	4.07 E
Grande ou Sete Quedas, Ilha-	204	Ef	23.45S	54.03W
Grande Pointe [Guad.]	197e	Ac	15.59N	61.38W
Grande Pointe [Guad.]	197b	Bc	17.50N	62.50W
Grande Prairie	176	Md	55.10N	118.48W
Grand Erg de Bilma	158	Ie	18.30N	13.50 E
Grand Erg Occidental	158	He	30.20N	0.01 E
Grand Erg Oriental	158	Ie	30.00N	7.00 E
Grande Rivière à Goyaves	197e	Ab	16.18N	61.37W
Grande Rivière de la Baleine	174	Ld	55.15N	77.45W
Grande Rivière du Nord	194	Kd	19.35N	72.11W
Grande Ronde River	188	Gc	46.05N	116.59W
Grandes, Salinas-	198	Ji	30.00S	65.05W
Grande Sebkha d'Oran	126	Li	35.32N	0.48W
Grandes Rousses, Les-	122	Mi	45.06N	6.07 E
Grande-Synthe	124	Ec	51.01N	2.17 E
Grande Terre	196	Fe	16.20N	61.25W
Grande Vigie, Pointe de la-	197e	Ba	16.31N	61.28W
Grand Falls [N.B.-Can.]	180	Kg	47.03N	67.44W
Grand Falls [Newf.-Can.]	176	Ne	48.56N	55.40W
Grand Forks [B.C.-Can.]	188	Hb	49.02N	118.27W
Grand Forks [N.D.-U.S.]	176	Je	47.55N	97.03W
Grand Found, Anse du-	197b	Bc	17.53N	62.49W
Grand Gedeh [3]	166	Dd	5.45N	8.05W
Grand Haven	184	Dd	43.04N	86.10W
Grand Ilet	197e	Ac	15.50N	61.36W
Grand Island	176	Je	40.55N	98.21W
Grand Junction	176	If	39.05N	108.33W
Grand-Lahou	166	Dd	5.08N	5.01W
Grand Lake [La.-U.S.]	186	Kl	29.55N	91.35W
Grand Lake [La.-U.S.]	186	Jl	29.55N	92.47W
Grand Lake [N.B.-Can.]	184	Nc	45.42N	66.05W
Grand Lake [Newf.-Can.]	180	Lf	49.00N	57.20W
Grand Lake [Oh.-U.S.]	184	Ee	40.30N	84.32W
Grand Lake Victoria	180	Jf	47.35N	77.33W
Grand Manan Channel	184	Nc	44.40N	66.52W
Grand Manan Island	180	Kh	44.40N	66.50W
Grand Marais [Mi.-U.S.]	184	Eb	46.40N	85.59W
Grand Marais [Mn.-U.S.]	186	Kb	47.45N	90.20W
Grand-Mère	184	Kb	46.37N	72.41W
Grand Morin	122	If	48.54N	2.50 E
Grândola	126	Df	38.10N	8.34W
Grândola, Serra de-	126	Df	38.08N	8.34W
Grand Passage	219b	Ad	18.45S	163.10 E
Grand-Popo	166	Fd	6.17N	1.50 E
Grand Portage	186	Lc	47.58N	89.41W
Grand Prairie	186	He	32.45N	96.59W
Grandpré	124	Gd	49.20N	4.52 E
Grand Rapids [Man.-Can.]	180	Hf	53.10N	99.17W
Grand Rapids [Mi.-U.S.]	176	Ke	42.58N	85.40W
Grand Rapids [Mn.-U.S.]	182	Ib	47.14N	93.31W
Grand Récif Sud	216	Cd	22.38S	167.00 E
Grand River [Mo.-U.S.]	186	Jf	39.23N	93.06W
Grand River [Mo.-U.S.]	186	Jf	40.22N	93.57W
Grand River [Ont.-Can.]	184	Hd	42.51N	79.34W
Grand River [S.D.-U.S.]	186	Fc	45.40N	100.32W
Grand'Rivière	197k	Ba	14.52N	61.11W
Grand Roy	197p	Bb	12.07N	61.45W
Grand Saint Bernard, Col du-	122	Be	45.50N	7.10 E
Grand-Sans-Toucher	197e	Ab	16.06N	61.41W
Grand Teton	182	Dc	43.44N	110.48W
Grand Traverse Bay	184	Ec	45.02N	85.30W
Grand Turk	190	Jd	21.28N	71.09W
Grand Turk	174	Lh	21.00N	71.10W
Grand Union Canal	124	Bc	51.30N	0.02W
Grand Valley	182	Ed	39.27N	108.03W
Grand Veymont, Le-	122	Li	44.52N	5.32 E
Grandview [Man.-Can.]	186	Fa	51.10N	100.45W
Grandview	158	Db	38.53N	94.32W
Grandvilliers	124	De	49.40N	1.56 E
Grand Wash Cliffs	188	Ih	35.45N	113.45W
Granger	188	Je	41.21N	120.11W
Grängesberg	116	Fd	60.05N	14.59 E
Grangeville	176	He	45.56N	116.07W
Gran Guardia	206	Ic	25.52S	58.53W
Granite City	186	Kg	38.42N	90.09W
Granite Falls	186	Id	44.49N	95.33W
Granite Pass	188	Ld	44.38N	107.30W
Granite Peak [Nv.-U.S.]	182	Dc	41.40N	117.35W
Granite Peak [U.S.]	186	Gb	45.10N	109.48W
Granite Range	188	Ff	41.00N	119.35W
Granitola, Punta-	128	Gm	37.34N	12.41 E
Grankulla/Kauniainen	116	Kd	60.13N	24.45 E
Granma [3]	194	Ic	20.30N	77.00W
Gran Malvina, Isla-/West Falkland	198	Kk	51.40S	60.00W
Gran Morelos [Mex.]	192	Fc	28.15N	106.30W
Gran Morelos [Mex.]	192	Eb	30.40N	108.35W
Gränna	116	Ff	58.01N	14.28 E
Granollers/Granollérs	126	Oc	41.37N	2.18 E
Granollers/Granollérs	126	Oc	41.37N	2.18 E
Gran Paradiso/Gran Paradis	128	Be	45.32N	7.16 E
Gran Paradiso/Gran Paradis	128	Be	45.32N	7.16 E
Gran Pilastro/Hochfeiler	128	Fd	46.58N	11.44 E
Gran San Bernardo, Colle del-	128	Be	45.50N	7.10 E
Gran Sasso d'Italia	110	Hg	42.25N	13.40 E
Grant	186	Ff	40.50N	101.56W
Grant, Mount-	188	Fg	38.34N	118.48W
Gran Tarajal	162	Ed	28.12N	14.01W
Grantham	118	Mi	52.54N	0.38W
Grant Island	222	Nf	74.24S	131.20W
Grantown-on-Spey	118	Jd	57.20N	3.38W
Grant Range	188	Hg	38.25N	115.30W
Grants	186	Eh	35.09N	107.52W
Grantsburg	186	Jd	45.47N	92.41W
Grants Pass	182	Cc	42.26N	123.19W
Granville	122	Ef	48.50N	1.36W
Granville Lake	180	He	56.00N	100.20W
Granvin	116	Bd	60.33N	6.43 E
Grao de Sagunto, Sagunto-	126	Le	39.40N	0.16W
Grappa, Monte-	128	Fe	45.52N	11.48 E
Grappler Bank (EN)	197a	Cc	17.48N	65.55W
Graskop	172	Ed	24.58S	30.49 E
Gräsmark	116	Ee	59.57N	12.55 E
Gräsö	114	Ef	60.25N	18.25 E
Grasse	122	Mk	43.40N	6.55 E
Grasset,Lac-	184	Ha	49.58N	78.10W
Grassrange	188	Kc	47.01N	108.48W
Grästen	114	Bi	54.55N	9.36 E
Grästorp	116	Ef	58.20N	12.40 E
Graubünden / Grigioni / Grischun [2]	128	Dd	46.35N	9.35 E
Grau-du-Roi, Le-	122	Kk	43.32N	4.08 E
Graulhet	122	Hk	43.46N	2.00 E
Graus	126	Mb	42.11N	0.20 E
Grave	122	Mc	51.45N	5.45 E
Grave, Pointe de-	122	Ei	45.34N	1.04W
Gravedona	128	Dd	46.09N	9.18 E
Gravelbourg	180	Gg	49.53N	106.34W
Gravelines	122	Id	50.59N	2.07 E
Gravenhage, 's- /Den Haag = The Hague (EN)	112	Ge	52.06N	4.18 E
Gravenhage-Scheveningen, 's-	122	Kb	52.06N	4.18 E
Gravenhurst	184	Hc	44.55N	79.22W
Gravenor Bay	197d	Ba	17.33N	61.45W
Graves	122	Fj	44.35N	0.30W
Gravesend	118	Nj	51.27N	0.24 E
Gravesend-Tilbury	118	Nj	51.28N	0.23 E
Gravina in Puglia	128	Kj	40.49N	16.25 E
Gravone	122a	Ab	41.55N	8.47 E
Gray	122	Lg	47.27N	5.35 E
Gray Feather Bank (EN)	214	Df	40.00N	84.43W
Grayling	184	Ec	44.40N	84.43W
Grays	118	Nj	51.28N	0.20 E
Grays Harbor	182	Cc	46.56N	124.05W
Grayson	184	Fd	38.20N	82.57W
Grays Peak [U.S.]	182	Fd	39.37N	105.45W
Graz	112	Hf	47.04N	15.27 E
Grazalema	126	Gh	36.46N	5.22W
Grdelica	130	Fg	42.54N	22.04 E
Greåker	116	De	59.16N	11.02 E
Great Artesian Basin	208	Gg	25.00S	143.00 E
Great Astrolabe Reef	219c	Bc	18.52S	178.31 E
Great Australian Bight	208	Eh	35.00S	130.00 E
Great Bacolet Point	197p	Bb	12.05N	61.37W
Great Bahama Bank (EN)	174	Lg	23.15N	78.00W
Great Bardfield	124	Cc	51.56N	0.29 E
Great Barrier Island	208	Ih	36.10S	175.25 E
Great Barrier Reef	208	Gb	19.10S	149.00 E
Great Basin	174	Hf	40.00N	117.00W
Great Bear	180	Hd	66.00N	120.00W
Great Bear Lake	174	Hc	66.00N	120.00W
Great Belt (EN) = Store Bælt	110	Hd	55.30N	11.00 E
Great Bend	186	Hd	38.22N	98.46W
Great Blasket/An Blascaod Mór	118	Ci	52.05N	10.32W
Great Britain	110	Fd	54.00N	3.00W
Great Central Lake	188	Cb	49.27N	125.12W
Great Channel	140	Li	6.00N	94.00 E
Great Chesterford	124	Cb	52.04N	0.12 E
Great Dismal Swamp	184	Hg	36.30N	76.30W
Great Dividing Range	208	Fg	25.00S	147.00 E
Great Dunmow	124	Cc	51.53N	0.22 E
Greater Accra [3]	166	Fd	5.45N	0.10 E
Greater Antilles (EN) = Antillas Mayores	174	Lh	20.00N	74.00W
Greater Khingan Range (EN) = Da Hinggan Ling	140	Oe	49.00N	122.00 E
Greater Manchester [3]	118	Kh	53.35N	2.10W
Greater Sunda Islands (EN)	140	Nj	3.52S	111.20 E
Great Exhibition Bay	216	Df	34.40S	173.00 E
Great Exuma Island	190	Id	23.32N	75.50W
Great Falls	176	He	47.30N	111.17W
Great Fisher Bank (EN) = Storefiskbank	118	Qe	56.50N	4.00 E
Great Fish River	158	Ik	17.11S	28.08 E
Great Guana Cay	194	Ia	24.00N	76.20W
Great Harbour Cay	184	Im	25.45N	77.52W
Great Inagua	174	Lg	21.02N	73.20W
Great Indian Desert/Thar	140	Jg	27.00N	70.00 E
Groot-Karasberge	158	Ik	27.20S	18.45 E
Great Karroo (EN) = Groot Karoo	158	Jl	33.00S	22.00 E
Great Lake	212	Jh	41.52S	146.45 E
Great Lakes (EN) = Bolšoj Ljahovski, ostrov-	138	Jb	73.35N	142.00 E
Great Namaland/Groot Namaland	172	Be	26.00S	17.00 E
Great Nicobar	140	Li	7.00N	94.00 E
Great North East Channel	212	Ja	9.30S	143.25 E
Great Ormes Head	118	Jh	53.21N	3.52W
Great Ouse	118	Ni	52.44N	0.23 E
Great Plain of the Koukdjuak	180	Kc	66.25N	72.50W
Great Plains	174	Je	42.00N	100.00W
Great Reef	219c	Bb	10.14S	166.02 E
Great Ruaha	158	Ki	7.56S	37.52 E
Great Sacandaga Lake	184	Jd	43.08N	74.10W
Great Sale Cay	184	Hl	27.00N	78.12W
Great Salt Lake	174	He	41.10N	112.30W
Great Salt Lake Desert	182	Ec	40.40N	113.30W
Great Salt Plains Lake	186	Gh	36.44N	98.12W
Great Salt Pond	197c	Ab	17.15N	62.38W
Great Sandy Desert [Austl.]	208	Dg	21.30S	125.00 E
Great Sandy Desert [U.S.]	182	Cc	43.35N	120.15W
Great Sea Reef	219d	Bb	16.15S	178.33 E
Great Shelford	124	Cb	52.07N	0.08 E
Great Sitkin	178a	Cb	52.03N	176.07W
Great Slave Lake	174	Hc	61.30N	114.00W
Great Smoky Mountains	184	Fh	35.35N	83.30W
Great Stour	118	Oj	51.19N	1.15 E
Great Valley [U.S.]	184	Ie	40.15N	76.50W
Great Valley [U.S.]	182	Kd	36.30N	82.00W
Great Victoria Desert	208	Dg	28.30S	127.45 E
Great Yarmouth	118	Oi	52.37N	1.44 E
Grebbestad	114	Cg	58.42N	11.15 E
Grebenka	132	Hd	50.07N	32.25 E
Gréboun, Mont-	166	Gb	20.00N	8.35 E
Greci	130	Ld	45.11N	28.14 E
Gredos, Sierra de-	126	Gd	40.20N	5.05W
Greece (EN) = Ellás	112	Ih	39.00N	22.00 E
Greeley [Co.-U.S.]	182	Fd	40.25N	104.42W
Greeley [Nb.-U.S.]	186	Gf	41.33N	98.32W
Greely Ford	180	Ja	80.40N	85.00W
Green-Bell, ostrov-	140	Ia	81.10N	64.00 E
Green	188	Ie	43.07N	123.28W
Green Bay	176	Ke	44.30N	88.01W
Green Bay	182	Jb	45.00N	87.30W
Greencastle	184	Df	39.38N	86.52W
Green Cay	194	Ia	24.02N	77.11W
Greeneville	184	Fg	36.10N	82.50W
Greenfield [In.-U.S.]	184	Ef	39.47N	85.46W
Greenfield [Ma.-U.S.]	184	Kd	42.36N	72.36W
Greenhorn Mountain	186	Gf	37.57N	105.00W
Green Island	218	Df	45.54S	170.26 E
Green Island [Atg.]	197d	Bb	17.05N	61.40W
Green Island [Gren.]	197p	Bb	12.14N	61.35W
Green Islands	208	Ic	4.30S	154.10 E
Greenland	197q	Ab	59.37S	59.34W
Greenland (EN) = Grønland/Kalaallit Nunaat	224	Nd	70.00N	40.00W
Greenland (EN) = Grønland/Kalaallit Nunaat	174	Pb	70.00N	40.00W
Greenland (EN) = Kalaallit Nunaat/Grønland [3]	174	Pb	70.00N	40.00W
Greenland Basin (EN)	224	Ld	77.00N	0.00
Greenland Sea (EN) = Grønlandshaf	224	Ld	77.00N	1.00W
Greenland Sea (EN) = Grønlandshavet	224	Ld	77.00N	1.00W
Green Lookout Mountain	188	Dd	45.52N	122.08W
Green Mountains	174	Le	43.45N	72.45W
Greenock	118	If	55.57N	4.45W
Greenough River	212	Ce	28.51S	114.38 E
Green Peter Lake	188	Dd	44.28N	122.30W
Green River [U.S.]	174	Hf	37.55N	87.30W
Green River [U.S.]	174	If	38.11N	109.53W
Green River [Ut.-U.S.]	182	Ed	38.59N	110.10W
Green River Lake	184	Fg	37.15N	85.15W
Greensboro	176	Lf	36.04N	79.47W
Greensburg [In.-U.S.]	184	Ef	39.20N	85.29W
Greensburg [Ks.-U.S.]	186	Gg	37.36N	99.18W
Greensburg [Pa.-U.S.]	184	Hf	40.18N	79.33W
Greenstone Point	118	Hd	57.55N	5.40W
Greenvale	212	Jc	18.55S	145.05 E
Greenville [Al.-U.S.]	184	Dj	31.50N	86.38W
Greenville [II.-U.S.]	186	Ke	38.53N	89.25W
Greenville [Lbr.]	160	Gh	4.59N	9.02W
Greenville [Me.-U.S.]	184	Mc	45.28N	69.35W
Greenville [Ms.-U.S.]	176	Kf	33.25N	91.05W
Greenville [N.C.-U.S.]	184	If	35.37N	77.25W
Greenville [Oh.-U.S.]	184	Ee	40.06N	84.37W
Greenville [Pa.-U.S.]	184	Ge	41.24N	80.22W
Greenville [S.C.-U.S.]	176	Lf	34.51N	82.23W
Greenville [Tx.-U.S.]	186	He	33.08N	96.07W
Greenwich	118	Mj	51.28N	0.00
Greenwich, Antich-	124	Mj	51.28N	0.00
Greenwood [In.-U.S.]	184	Ef	39.37N	86.07W
Greenwood [Ms.-U.S.]	184	Gh	34.55N	82.00W
Greenwood, Lake-	184	Fh	34.11N	82.10W
Greer	184	Gh	34.55N	82.14W
Greers Ferry Lake	186	Ji	35.30N	92.10W
Greeson, Lake-	186	Ji	34.10N	93.45W

Index Symbols

[1] Independent Nation	Historical or Cultural Region	Pass, Gap	Depression	Coast, Beach	Rock, Reef
[2] State, Region	Mount, Mountain	Plain, Lowland	Polder	Isthmus	Islands, Archipelago
[3] District, County	Volcano	Delta	Cliff	Peninsula	Rocks, Reefs
[4] Municipality	Hill	Salt Flat	Desert, Dunes	Sandbank	Coral Reef
[5] Colony, Dependency	Mountains, Mountain Range	Valley, Canyon	Forest, Woods	Island	Well, Spring
Continent	Hills, Escarpment	Crater, Cave	Heath, Steppe		Geyser
Physical Region	Plateau, Upland	Karst Features	Oasis	Atoll	River, Stream

Cape, Point	Waterfall, Rapids	Canal	Lagoon	Escarpment, Sea Scarp	Historic Site
	River Mouth, Estuary	Glacier	Bank	Fracture	Ruins
	Lake	Ice Shelf, Pack Ice	Seamount	Trench, Abyss	Wall, Walls
	Salt Lake	Ocean	Tablemount	National Park, Reserve	Church, Abbey
	Intermittent Lake	Sea	Ridge	Point of Interest	Temple
	Reservoir	Gulf, Bay	Shelf	Recreation Site	Scientific Station
	Swamp, Pond	Strait, Fjord	Basin	Cave, Cavern	Railway station

Airport
Port
Military installation
Lighthouse
Mine
Tunnel
Dam, Bridge

Name	Page	Grid	Lat.	Long.
Grefrath	124	Ic	51.18N	6.19 E
Gregoria Pérez de Denis	204	Bi	28.14S	61.32W
Gregorio, Rio-	202	De	6.50S	70.46W
Gregório, Rio-	204	Ha	13.42S	49.58W
Gregory, Lake-	212	He	28.55S	139.00 E
Gregory Lake	212	Fd	20.10S	127.20 E
Gregory Range	208	Ff	19.00S	143.00 E
Gregory River	212	Hc	17.53S	139.17 E
Greifenburg	128	Hd	46.45N	13.11 E
Greifswald	120	Jb	54.06N	13.23 E
Greifswalder Bodden	120	Jb	54.15N	13.35 E
Greifswalder Oie	120	Jb	54.14N	13.55 E
Grein	128	Ib	48.13N	14.51 E
Greiz	120	If	50.39N	12.12 E
Grěko, Akra-	184	Fe	34.56N	34.05 E
Gremiha	112	Jb	68.03N	39.29 E
Gremjačinsk	134	Hg	58.34N	57.51 E
Grenå	114	Ch	56.25N	10.53 E
Grenada	186	Lj	33.47N	89.55W
Grenada [1]	176	Mh	12.07N	61.40W
Grenada	174	Mh	12.07N	61.40W
Grenada Basin (EN)	190	Lf	13.30N	62.00W
Grenada Lake	186	Lj	33.50N	89.40W
Grenadines	190	Lf	12.40N	61.15W
Grenchen	128	Bc	47.11N	7.25 E
Grenen	110	Hd	57.44N	10.40 E
Grenfell	186	Ea	50.25N	102.56W
Grenoble	112	Gf	45.10N	5.43 E
Grenora	186	Eb	48.37N	103.56W
Grense-Jakobselv	114	Hb	69.47N	30.50 E
Grenville	196	Ff	12.07N	61.37W
Grenville, Cape-	212	Ib	12.00S	143.15 E
Gréoux-les-Bains	122	Lk	43.45N	5.53 E
Gresham	188	Dd	45.30N	122.26W
Gresik	150	Fh	7.09S	112.38 E
Gressoney-la-Trinité	128	Be	45.50N	7.49 E
Gretas klackar	116	Gc	61.34N	17.50 E
Gretna	186	Kl	29.55N	90.03W
Grevelingen	124	Fc	51.45N	4.00 E
Greven	120	Dd	52.06N	7.37 E
Grevená	130	Ei	40.05N	21.25 E
Grevenbroich	120	Ce	51.05N	6.35 E
Grevenbrück, Lennestadt-	124	Kc	51.08N	8.01 E
Grevenmacher	124	Ie	49.41N	6.27 E
Grevesmühlen	120	Hc	53.52N	11.11 E
Grey	218	De	42.26S	171.11 E
Greybull	188	Kd	44.30N	108.03W
Greybull River	188	Kd	44.28N	108.03W
Grey Islands	190	Lf	50.50N	55.35W
Greymouth	216	Dh	42.27S	171.12 E
Grey Range	208	Fg	27.00S	143.35 E
Greystones/Ná Clocha Liatha	118	Gh	53.09N	6.04W
Greytow	172	Ee	29.07S	30.30 E
Greytown	218	Fd	41.05S	175.28 E
Gribanovski	132	Ld	51.29N	41.58 E
Gribb Bank (EN)	222	Ge	63.00S	90.30 E
Gribës, Mali i-	130	Ci	40.34N	19.34 E
Gribingui [3]	168	Bd	7.00N	19.30 E
Gribingui	168	Bd	8.33N	19.05 E
Griend	124	Ha	53.15N	5.20 E
Griesheim	124	Ke	49.52N	8.33 E
Grieskirchen	128	Hb	48.14N	13.50 E
Griffin	182	Ke	33.15N	84.16W
Griffith	212	Jf	34.17S	146.03 E
Grigioni / Grischun / Graubünden [2]	128	Dd	46.35N	9.35 E
Grigoriopol	130	Mb	47.09N	29.13 E
Grijalva	174	Jh	18.36N	92.39W
Grijalva, Rio-	192	Mh	18.36N	92.38W
Grim, Cape-	212	Ih	40.41S	144.41 E
Grimari	168	Cd	5.44N	20.03 E
Grimbergen	124	Gd	50.56N	4.23 E
Grimma	120	Ie	51.14N	12.43 E
Grimmen	120	Jb	54.06N	13.03 E
Grimsby	118	Mh	53.35N	0.05W
Grimsey	114a	Ca	66.33N	18.00W
Grimsstadir	114a	Cb	65.39N	16.07W
Grimstad	114	Bg	58.20N	8.36 E
Grimsvötn	114a	Cb	64.24N	17.22W
Grindavík	114a	Ac	63.50N	22.30W
Grindelwald	128	Cd	46.38N	8.03 E
Grindsted	114	Bi	55.45N	8.56 E
Grinnell	186	Jf	41.45N	92.43W
Grinnel Peninsula	180	Ia	76.40N	95.00W
Grintavec	128	Id	46.22N	14.32 E
Griquatown	172	Ce	28.49S	23.15 E
Grischun / Graubünden / Grigioni [2]	128	Dd	46.35N	9.35 E
Grise Fiord	176	Kb	76.10N	83.15W
Gris-Nez, Cap-	122	Hd	50.52N	1.35 E
Grisslehamn	116	Hd	60.06N	18.50 E
Grjazi	136	De	52.29N	39.57 E
Grjazovec	136	Ed	58.53N	40.15 E
Grmeč	128	Kf	44.43N	16.15 E
Grobiņa/Grobinja	114	Eh	56.33N	21.11 E
Grobinja/Grobiņa	114	Eh	56.33N	21.11 E
Groblersdal	172	De	25.15S	29.25 E
Grocka	130	De	44.41N	20.43 E
Grodk/Spremberg	120	Ke	51.33N	14.22 E
Grodków	120	Nf	50.43N	17.22 E
Grodnenskaja oblast [3]	136	Ce	53.45N	25.10 E
Grodno	112	Ie	53.42N	23.50 E
Grodzisk Mazowiecki	120	Qd	52.07N	20.37 E
Grodzjanka	132	Fc	53.34N	28.48 E
Groeie Hoop, Kaap die- / Good Hope, Cape of-	158	Il	34.21S	18.28 E
Groenlo	124	Ib	52.04N	6.39 E
Groesbeek	124	Hc	51.47N	5.56 E
Grofa, gora-	130	Ha	48.34N	24.03 E
Groix	122	Cg	47.38N	3.28W
Groix, Ile de-	122	Cg	47.38N	3.28W
Grójec	120	Qe	51.52N	20.52 E
Gröll Seamount (EN)	202	Lf	14.00S	32.00W
Gromnik	120	Nf	50.42N	17.07 E
Gronau (Westfalen)	120	Dd	52.12N	7.02 E
Grong	114	Cd	64.30N	12.27 E
Groningen [3]	124	Ia	53.13N	6.33 E
Groningen [Neth.]	112	Ge	53.13N	6.33 E
Groningen [Sur.]	202	Gb	5.48N	55.28W
Groningerwad	124	Ia	53.27N	6.25 E
Grønland/Kalaallit Nunaat = Greenland (EN) [5]	224	Nd	70.00N	40.00W
Grønland/Kalaallit Nunaat = Greenland (EN)	174	Pb	70.00N	40.00W
Grønlandshavet = Greenland Sea (EN)	224	Ld	77.00N	1.00W
Grønnedal	179	Hf	61.20N	47.45W
Grönskara	116	Fg	57.05N	15.44 E
Groot	158	Jl	33.45S	24.58 E
Groot Baai	197b	Ab	18.01N	63.04W
Groote Eylandt	208	Ef	14.00S	136.40 E
Grootfontein	160	Ij	19.32S	18.05 E
Grootfontein [3]	172	Bc	19.00S	19.00 E
Groot-Karasberge = Great Karasberg (EN)	158	Ik	27.20S	18.45 E
Groot Karoo = Great Karroo (EN)	158	Jl	33.00S	22.00 E
Grootlaagte	172	Cd	20.55S	21.27 E
Groot Namaland/Great Namaland	172	Be	26.00S	17.00 E
Grootvloer	172	Ce	30.00S	20.40 E
Gropeni	130	Kd	45.05N	27.54 E
Gros Caps, Pointe des-	197e	Bb	16.28N	61.25W
Gros Islet Bay	197k	Ba	14.05N	60.58W
Gros Islets	197k	Ba	14.05N	60.58W
Gros-Morne	197h	Ab	14.43N	61.01W
Gros-Morne	180	Lg	49.00N	57.22W
Grosne	122	Kh	46.42N	4.56 E
Gros Piton	197k	Ab	13.49N	61.04W
Große Aa	124	Jb	52.25N	7.23 E
Große Aue	124	Kb	52.30N	8.38 E
Großefehn	124	Ja	53.24N	7.33 E
Große Laaber	120	Ih	48.50N	12.30 E
Großenhain	120	Je	51.17N	13.33 E
Großenkneten	124	Kb	52.57N	8.16 E
Grosse Pointe	197e	Bb	16.01N	61.17W
Großer Arber	120	Jg	49.07N	13.07 E
Großer Feldberg	124	Kd	50.13N	8.28 E
Großer Gleichberg	120	Gf	50.23N	10.35 E
Großer Inselsberg	120	Gf	50.52N	10.28 E
Grosseto	128	Fh	42.46N	11.08 E
Grosseto, Formiche di-	128	Eh	42.40N	10.55 E
Groß-Gerau	120	Eg	49.55N	8.29 E
Großglockner	110	Hf	47.04N	12.42 E
Großräschen	120	Je	51.35N	14.00 E
Groß-Umstadt	124	Ke	49.52N	8.56 E
Großvenediger	128	Gc	47.06N	12.21 E
Grostenquin	124	If	48.59N	6.44 E
Gros Ventre Range	188	Je	43.30N	110.15W
Groswater Bay	174	Nd	54.20N	57.30W
Grøtavær	114	Db	68.58N	16.16 E
Grote Nete	124	Gc	51.07N	4.34 E
Grotli	114	Be	62.01N	7.40 E
Grottaglie	128	Lj	40.32N	17.26 E
Grottammare	128	Hh	42.59N	13.52 E
Groumania	166	Ed	7.55N	4.00W
Groundhog River	184	Ga	49.43N	81.58W
Grouse Creek Mountains	188	If	41.55N	113.50W
Grove Mountains	222	Ff	72.53S	74.53 E
Groves	186	Jl	29.57N	93.55W
Grovfjord	114	Db	68.41N	17.09 E
Grow, Idaarderadeel-	124	Ha	53.06N	5.50 E
Grozny	112	Kg	43.20N	45.42 E
Grubišno Polje	128	Le	45.42N	17.10 E
Grudovo	130	Kg	42.21N	27.10 E
Grudziądz	120	Oc	53.29N	18.45 E
Grumento Nova	128	Jj	40.17N	15.53 E
Grumo Appula	128	Ki	41.01N	16.42 E
Grums	116	Ee	59.21N	13.06 E
Grünau	172	Be	27.47S	18.23 E
Grünberg	124	Kd	50.36N	8.57 E
Gründau	124	Ld	50.14N	9.05 E
Grundkallegrund	116	Hd	60.40N	18.45 E
Grundy	184	Fg	37.17N	82.06W
Gruñidera	192	Ie	24.15N	101.58W
Grünstadt	124	Ke	49.34N	8.10 E
Gruppo di Brenta	128	Ed	46.10N	10.55 E
Gruyère	128	Bd	46.40N	7.10 E
Gruža	130	Df	43.54N	20.47 E
Gruzinskaja Sovetskaja Socialističeskaja Respublika [2]	136	Eg	42.00N	44.00 E
Gruzinskaja SSR/Sakartvelos Sabčata Socialisturi Respublica [2]	136	Eg	42.00N	44.00 E
Gruzinskaja SSR = Georgian SSR (EN) [2]	136	Eg	42.00N	44.00 E
Grybów	120	Qg	49.38N	20.56 E
Grycksbo	116	Fd	60.41N	15.28 E
Gryfice	120	Lc	53.56N	15.12 E
Gryfino	120	Kc	53.15N	14.30 E
Grythyttan	116	Fe	59.42N	14.32 E
Grytviken	222	Ad	54.17S	36.31W
Gstaad, Saanen-	128	Bd	46.28N	7.17 E
Guacanayabo, Golfo de-	190	Id	20.28N	77.30W
Guacara	196	Cg	10.14N	67.53W
Guaçu	204	Ef	22.11S	54.31W
Guadaira	126	Fg	37.20N	6.01W
Guadajoz	126	Hg	37.50N	4.51W
Guadalajara [3]	126	Jd	40.50N	2.30W
Guadalajara [Mex.]	176	Ig	20.40N	103.20W
Guadalajara [Sp.]	126	Id	40.38N	3.10W
Guadalaviar	126	Kd	40.21N	1.08W
Guadalbullón	126	Ig	37.59N	3.47W
Guadalcanal	126	Gf	38.06N	5.49W
Guadalcanal Island	208	He	9.32S	160.12 E
Guadalén	126	If	38.05N	3.32W
Guadalentín o Sangonera	126	Kg	37.59N	1.04W
Guadalete	126	Fh	36.35N	6.13W
Guadalfeo	126	Ih	36.43N	3.35W
Guadalimar	126	Ig	37.59N	3.44W
Guadalmanzor / Almanzora	126	Kg	37.14N	1.46W
Guadalmena	126	Jf	38.20N	2.55W
Guadalmez	126	Gf	38.46N	5.04W
Guadalop / Guadalope	126	Lc	41.15N	0.03W
Guadalope / Guadalop	126	Lc	41.15N	0.03W
Guadalquivir	110	Fh	36.47N	6.22W
Guadalupe [Mex.]	190	Dc	25.41N	100.15W
Guadalupe [Mex.]	192	Hf	22.45N	102.31W
Guadalupe [Mex.]	192	Id	26.12N	101.23W
Guadalupe [Sp.]	126	Ge	39.27N	5.19W
Guadalupe, Isla de-	174	Hg	29.00N	118.16W
Guadalupe, Laguna de- → Setúbal	204	Bj	21.33S	60.35W
Guadalupe, Sierra de-	126	Ge	39.25N	5.25W
Guadalupe Bravos	192	Fb	31.23N	106.07W
Guadalupe Mountains	186	Dj	32.20N	105.00W
Guadalupe Peak	182	Ge	31.50N	104.52W
Guadalupe River	186	Hl	28.30N	96.53W
Guadalupe Victoria, Presa-	192	Gf	23.50N	104.55W
Guadalupe y Calvo	192	Fd	26.06N	106.58W
Guadarrama	126	He	39.53N	4.10W
Guadarrama, Puerto de-	126	Hd	40.43N	4.10W
Guadarrama, Sierra de-	126	Id	40.55N	4.00W
Guadazaón	126	Ke	39.42N	1.36W
Guadeloupe [5]	176	Mh	16.15N	61.35W
Guadeloupe	174	Mh	16.15N	61.35W
Guadeloupe, Canal de la- = Guadeloupe Passage (EN)	190	Le	16.40N	61.50W
Guadeloupe Passage	196	Fd	16.40N	61.50W
Guadeloupe Passage (EN) = Guadeloupe, Canal de la-	190	Le	16.40N	61.50W
Guadiana	110	Fh	37.14N	7.22W
Guadiana, Canal del-	126	Ie	39.20N	3.20W
Guadiana, Ojos del-	126	Ie	39.08N	3.31W
Guadiana Menor	126	Ig	37.56N	3.15W
Guadiaro	126	Gh	36.17N	5.17W
Guadiela	126	Jd	40.22N	2.49W
Guadix	126	Ig	37.18N	3.08W
Guafo, Boca del-	206	Ff	43.40S	74.15W
Guafo, Isla-	206	Ff	43.36S	74.43W
Guaíba	206	Jd	30.06S	51.19W
Guaíba, Rio-	204	Gj	30.15S	51.12W
Guaimaca	194	Df	14.52N	86.51W
Guaimorato, Laguna de-	194	Ef	15.58N	85.55W
Guainía [3]	202	Ec	2.30N	69.00W
Guainía, Rio-	198	Je	2.01N	67.07W
Guaiquinima, Cerro-	202	Fb	5.49N	63.40W
Guaíra [3]	204	Dg	25.45S	56.30W
Guaíra [Braz.]	206	Jb	24.04S	54.15W
Guaíra [Braz.]	204	He	20.19S	48.18W
Guaíra Falls (EN) = Sete Quedas, Saltos das-	206	Jb	24.02S	54.16W
Guairas	204	Ja	12.39S	44.16W
Guaire/Gorey	118	Gi	52.40N	6.18W
Guaitecas, Islas-	206	Ff	43.57S	73.50W
Guajaba, Cayo-	196	Ic	21.50N	77.30W
Guajará Mirim	200	Jg	10.48S	65.22W
Guajira, Peninsula de la-	198	Id	12.00N	71.30W
Guajolotes, Sierra del-	192	Ge	26.00N	105.15W
Guakolak, Tanjung-	150	Eh	6.50S	105.14 E
Gualaco	194	Df	15.06N	86.07W
Gualán	194	Cf	15.08N	89.22W
Gualdo Tadino	128	Gg	43.14N	12.47 E
Gualeguay	204	Ck	33.09S	59.20W
Gualeguay, Rio-	204	Ck	33.19S	59.39W
Gualeguaychu	206	Id	33.01S	58.31W
Gualeguaychú, Rio-	204	Ck	33.05S	58.25W
Gualicho, Salina del-	206	Gf	40.24S	65.15W
Guam [5]	210	Fc	13.28N	144.47 E
Guam	208	Fc	13.28N	144.47 E
Guamini	206	He	37.02S	62.25W
Guampi, Sierra de-	202	Eb	6.00N	65.35W
Guamuchil	190	Cc	25.22N	108.22W
Gua Musang	150	Df	4.53N	101.58 E
Gu'an	154	De	39.24N	116.10 E
Guanabacoa	194	Fb	23.07N	82.18W
Guanabara, Baia de-	204	Kf	22.50S	43.10W
Guanacaste [3]	194	Eh	10.30N	85.15W
Guanacaste, Cordillera de-	194	Eh	10.45N	85.05W
Guanacevi	192	Ge	25.56N	105.57W
Guanahacabibes, Golfo de-	194	Eb	22.08N	84.35W
Guanahacabibes, Peninsula de-	194	Ec	21.57N	84.35W
Guana Island	197a	Db	18.29N	64.34W
Guanaja	194	Ee	16.27N	85.54W
Guanaja, Isla de-	194	Ee	16.30N	85.55W
Guanajay	194	Fb	22.55N	82.42W
Guanajibo	197a	Ab	18.10N	67.09W
Guanajibo, Punta-	197a	Ab	18.12N	67.10W
Guanajuato	190	Dd	21.01N	101.15W
Guanajuato [2]	190	Dd	21.00N	101.00W
Guanambi	202	Jf	14.13S	42.47W
Guanare	202	Eb	9.03N	69.45W
Guanare, Rio-	196	Ch	8.13N	67.46W
Guanare Viejo, Rio-	194	Mi	8.19N	68.10W
Guanarito	196	Bh	8.42N	69.12W
Guandacol	206	Gc	29.31S	68.32W
Guandi Shan	152	Jd	38.09N	111.27 E
Guane	190	Hd	22.12N	84.05W
Guangde	152	Ke	30.51N	119.26 E
Guangdong Sheng (Kuang-tung Sheng) = Kwangtung (EN) [2]	152	Jg	23.00N	113.00 E
Guangfeng	154	Ej	28.27N	118.12 E
Guanghua	152	Je	32.18N	111.45 E
Guangji (Wuxue)	152	Kf	29.58N	115.32 E
Guangling	154	Ce	39.46N	114.16 E
Guangmao Shan	152	Hf	26.48N	100.56 E
Guangming Ding	154	Ei	30.09N	118.11 E
Guangnan	152	Ig	24.02N	105.04 E
Guangrao	154	Ef	37.03N	118.25 E
Guangshan	154	Ci	32.02N	114.53 E
Guangshui	154	Ci	31.37N	114.01 E
Guangxi Zhuangzu Zizhiqu (Kuang-hsi-chuang-tsu Tzu-chih-ch'ü) = Kwangsi Chuang (EN) [2]	152	Ig	24.00N	109.00 E
Guangyuan	142	Mf	32.27N	105.55 E
Guangzhou = Canton (EN)	142	Ng	23.07N	113.18 E
Guan He	154	Ch	32.18N	115.44 E
Guánica	197a	Bc	17.59N	66.56W
Guanipa, Rio-	196	Eh	9.56N	62.26W
Guannan (Xin'anzhen)	154	Eg	34.04N	119.21 E
Guantánamo	176	Lg	20.08N	75.12W
Guantánamo [3]	194	Jc	20.10N	75.00W
Guantánamo, Bahia de-	194	Jd	20.00N	75.10W
Guantánamo Bay	190	Id	20.00N	75.10W
Guantánamo Bay Naval Station	194	Jd	20.00N	75.08W
Guantao (Nanguantao)	154	Cf	36.33N	115.18 E
Guanting Shuiku	154	Cd	40.13N	115.36 E
Guanxian	142	Mf	31.00N	103.38 E
Guanyun (Dayishan)	154	Eg	34.18N	119.14 E
Guapay, Rio- → Grande, Rio-	198	Jg	15.51S	64.39W
Guapé	204	Je	20.47S	45.55W
Guapi	202	Cc	2.35N	77.55W
Guápiles	194	Fh	10.13N	83.46W
Guapó	204	Hc	16.51S	49.33W
Guaporé	206	Jc	28.51S	51.54W
Guaporé	204	Gi	29.10S	51.54W
Guaporé, Rio-	198	Jg	11.55S	65.04W
Guaqui	202	Eg	16.35S	68.51W
Guará	204	Gg	25.23S	51.17W
Guara, Sierra de-	126	Lb	42.17N	0.10W
Guarabira	202	Ke	6.51S	35.29W
Guaranda	202	Cd	1.35S	78.59W
Guaraniaçu	206	Jc	25.06S	52.52W
Guarani de Goiás	204	Ia	13.57S	46.28W
Guarapiche, Rio-	196	Eh	9.57N	62.52W
Guarapuava	206	Jc	25.23S	51.27W
Guaraqueçaba	204	Hg	25.17S	48.21W
Guararapes	204	Ge	21.15S	50.38W
Guaratinguetá	204	Jf	22.49S	45.13W
Guaratuba	204	Hg	25.54S	48.34W
Guarayos, Rio-	204	Bb	14.38S	62.11W
Guarda	126	Ed	40.32N	7.16W
Guarda [2]	126	Ed	40.40N	7.10W
Guardafui, Cape- (EN) = 'Asāyr	158	Mg	11.49N	51.15 E
Guardal	126	Jg	37.36N	2.45W
Guarda-Mor	204	Ic	17.47S	47.06W
Guardiagrele	128	Ih	42.11N	14.13 E
Guardian Seamount (EN)	174	Ki	9.32N	87.40W
Guardo	126	Hb	42.47N	4.50W
Guardunha, Serra da-	126	Ed	40.05N	7.31W
Guareí, Rio-	204	Ff	22.40S	53.34W
Guareña	126	Gc	41.29N	5.23W
Guarenas	196	Cg	10.28N	66.37W
Guaribas, Rio-	204	Jc	16.22S	45.03W
Guaribe, Rio-	196	Dh	9.53N	65.11W
Guárico [2]	202	Eb	8.40N	66.35W
Guárico, Embalse del-	196	Ch	9.00N	67.20W
Guárico, Rio-	202	Eb	7.55N	67.23W
Guariquito, Rio-	196	Cl	7.40N	66.18W
Guarita, Rio-	204	Fh	27.11S	53.44W
Guaritico, Caño-	196	Bi	7.52N	68.53W
Guaritire, Rio-	204	Ba	13.43S	60.38W
Guarujá	204	If	24.00S	46.16W
Guarulhos	206	Kb	23.28S	46.32W
Guasave	190	Cc	25.34N	108.27W
Guasdualito	202	Db	7.15N	70.44W
Guasipati	202	Fb	7.28N	61.54W
Guasopa	219a	Ac	9.14S	152.55 E
Guastalla	128	Ef	44.55N	10.39 E
Guatemala	176	Jh	14.38N	90.31W
Guatemala [1]	176	Jh	14.38N	90.31W
Guatemala [3]	194	Bf	14.40N	90.30W
Guatemala Basin (EN)	106	Mh	11.00N	95.00W
Guateque	202	Db	5.05N	73.30W
Guatimozin	204	Ak	33.27S	62.27W
Guatisimiña	202	Fc	4.33N	63.57W
Guatraché	206	He	37.40S	63.32W
Guaviare [2]	202	Dc	2.00N	72.00W
Guaviare, Rio-	198	Je	4.03N	67.44W
Guaviravi	204	Di	29.22S	56.50W
Guaxupé	204	Ie	21.18S	46.42W
Guayabal [Cuba]	194	Ic	20.42N	77.36W
Guayabal [Ven.]	196	Ci	8.00N	67.24W
Guayabero, Rio-	202	Ec	4.03N	67.44W
Guayalejo, Rio-	192	Kf	22.13N	97.52W
Guayama	194	Ne	17.59N	66.07W
Guayana, Macizo de la- = Guaiana Highlands (EN)	198	Ke	5.00N	60.00W
Guayana Basin (EN)	106	Ci	10.00N	52.00W
Guayaneco, Archipiélago-	206	Eg	47.45S	75.10W
Guayanés, Punta-	197a	Cb	18.04N	65.48W
Guayanilla	197a	Bb	18.02N	66.47W
Guayanilla, Bahía de-	197a	Bc	17.58N	66.45W
Guayape, Rio-	194	Df	14.26N	86.02W
Guayaquil	200	If	2.10S	79.50W
Guayaquil, Golfo de-	198	Hf	3.00S	80.30W
Guaycurú, Rio-	204	Ch	27.19S	58.45W
Guaymas	176	Hg	27.56N	110.54W
Guayquiraró, Rio-	204	Cj	30.10S	58.34W
Guba [Eth.]	168	Fc	11.15N	35.20 E
Guba [Zaire]	170	Ee	10.38S	26.25 E
Guba Dolgaja	136	Fa	70.19N	58.45 E
Gubaha	136	Fd	58.52N	57.36 E
Guban	158	Lg	10.15N	44.26 E
Gubbio	128	Gg	43.21N	12.35 E
Gubdor	134	Hf	60.15N	56.35 E
Guber	120	Rb	54.13N	21.02 E
Gubin	120	Ke	51.56N	14.45 E
Gubio	166	Hc	12.30N	12.47 E
Gubkin	136	De	51.17N	37.33 E
Gúdar, Sierra de-	126	Ld	40.27N	0.42W
Gudara	136	Hh	38.23N	72.42 E
Gudauta	132	Lh	43.07N	40.37 E
Gudbrandsdalen	114	Bf	61.30N	10.00 E
Gudenå	116	Dh	56.29N	10.13 E
Gudermes	136	Eg	43.22N	46.08 E
Gudivāda	148	Ge	16.27N	80.59 E
Gudiyāttam	148	Ff	12.57N	78.52 E
Gudou Shan	152	Jg	22.12N	112.57 E
Güdül	146	Eb	40.13N	32.15 E
Güdür	148	Ff	14.08N	79.51 E
Gudvangen	116	Bd	60.52N	6.50 E
Guebwiller	122	Ng	47.55N	7.12 E
Guéckédou	166	Cd	8.33N	10.09W
Guelma	162	Ib	36.28N	7.26 E
Guelma [3]	162	Ib	36.15N	7.30 E
Guelph	180	Jh	43.33N	80.15W
Guelta Zemmur	162	Ed	25.08N	12.22W
Guemar	162	Ic	33.29N	6.48 E
Guémené-Penfao	122	Eg	47.38N	1.50W
Guénange	124	Ie	49.18N	6.11 E
Guéné	166	Fc	11.44N	3.13 E
Guer	122	Dg	47.54N	2.07W
Güera	162	De	20.52N	17.03W
Guéra [3]	168	Bc	11.30N	18.30 E
Guéra, Massif de-	158	Ig	11.55N	18.12 E
Guérande	122	Dg	47.20N	2.26W
Guerara	162	Hc	32.48N	4.30 E
Guerche-sur-l'Aubois, La-	122	Ih	46.57N	2.57 E
Guercif	162	Gc	34.14N	3.22W
Guerdjoumane, Djebel-	126	Oh	36.25N	2.51 E
Güere, Rio-	196	Dh	9.50N	65.08W
Guéréda	168	Cc	14.31N	22.05 E
Guéret	122	Hh	46.10N	1.52 E
Guérin-Kouka	166	Fd	9.41N	0.37 E
Guernica y Luno / Gernika-Lumo	126	Ja	43.19N	2.41W
Guernsey	118	Kl	49.27N	2.35W
Guerrero	192	Ic	28.20N	100.26W
Guerrero [2]	190	De	17.40N	100.00W
Guessou-Sud	166	Fc	10.03N	2.38 E
Guest Peninsula	222	Mf	76.18S	148.00W
Guge	168	Fd	6.12N	37.30 E
Gügerd, Kūh-e-	146	Oe	34.50N	53.00 E
Guglionesi	128	Ii	41.55N	14.55 E
Guguan Island	208	Fc	17.19N	145.51 E
Guia	204	Db	15.22S	56.14W
Guia Lopes da Laguna	204	De	21.26S	56.07W
Guiana (EN) = Guyana [1]	200	Ke	5.00N	59.00W
Guiana Highlands (EN) = Guayana, Macizo de la-	198	Ke	5.00N	60.00W
Guiana Island	197d	Bb	17.06N	61.44W
Guichi (Chizhou)	152	Ke	30.38N	117.30 E
Guichón	204	Dk	32.21S	57.12W
Guide	152	Hd	36.00N	101.30 E
Guider	166	Hd	9.56N	13.57 E
Guidimaka [3]	162	Ef	15.30N	12.00W
Guidimouni	166	Gc	13.42N	9.30 E
Guiding	152	If	26.33N	107.16 E
Guidong	152	Jf	26.11N	113.58 E
Guiers	122	Li	45.37N	5.37 E
Guiglo	166	Dd	6.33N	7.29W
Guiglo [3]	166	Dd	6.30N	7.40W
Guijá	172	Ed	24.29S	33.00 E
Güija, Lago de-	184	Cf	14.13N	89.34W
Gui Jiang	140	Ng	23.28N	111.18 E
Guijk en Sint Agatha	124	Hc	51.44N	5.52 E
Guijuelo	126	Gd	40.33N	5.40W
Guil	122	Mj	44.40N	6.36 E
Guildford	118	Mj	51.14N	0.35W
Guiler Gol	154	Ga	46.03N	122.06 E
Guilin	142	Ng	25.21N	110.15 E
Guillaume Delisle, Lac-	180	Je	56.25N	76.00W
Guillestre	122	Mj	44.40N	6.39 E
Guilvinec	122	Bg	47.47N	4.17W
Guimarães [Braz.]	202	Jd	2.08S	44.36W
Guimarães [Port.]	126	Dc	41.27N	8.18W
Guimaras	150	Hd	10.35N	122.37 E
Guinchos Cay	194	Hb	22.45N	78.06W
Guinea (EN) = Guinée [1]	160	Fg	11.00N	10.00W
Guinea, Gulf of-	158	Hh	2.00N	2.30 E
Guinea, Gulf of- (EN) = Guinée, Golfe de-	158	Hh	2.00N	2.30 E
Guinea Basin (EN)	106	Di	0.00	5.00W
Guinea-Bissau (EN) = Guiné-Bissau [1]	160	Fg	12.00N	15.00W
Guinea Ecuatorial = Equatorial Guinea (EN) [1]	160	Hh	2.00N	9.00 E
Guinea Rise (EN)	106	Dj	4.00S	0.00
Guiné-Bissau = Guinea-Bissau (EN) [1]	160	Fg	12.00N	15.00W
Guinée = Guinea (EN) [1]	160	Fg	11.00N	10.00W
Guinée, Kolfe de- = Guinea, Gulf of- (EN)	158	Hh	2.00N	2.30 E
Guinée Forestière [3]	166	Dd	8.40N	9.50W
Guinée Maritime [3]	166	Cc	10.00N	14.00W
Güines	190	Hd	22.50N	82.02W
Guînes	124	Dd	50.52N	1.52 E
Guingamp	122	Cf	48.33N	3.09W
Guinguinéo	166	Bc	14.16N	15.57W
Guiones, Punta-	194	Ei	9.54N	85.41W
Guiping	152	Ig	23.23N	110.00 E
Guipúzcoa [3]	126	Ja	43.10N	2.10W
Guir	162	Gc	30.29N	2.18W
Guir, Hamada du-	158	Ge	31.00N	3.20W
Güira de Melena	194	Fb	22.48N	82.30W
Guiratinga	202	Hg	16.21S	53.45W
Güiria	202	Fa	10.34N	62.18W
Guiscard	124	Fe	49.39N	3.03 E
Guise	122	Je	49.54N	3.38 E
Guitiriz	126	Ea	43.11N	7.54W
Guiuan	150	Id	11.02N	125.43 E
Guixi	152	Kf	28.18N	117.15 E
Guixian	152	Ig	23.10N	109.35 E
Guiyang	142	Mg	26.38N	106.43 E
Guizhou Sheng (Kuei-chou Sheng) = Kweichow (EN) [2]	152	If	27.00N	107.00 E
Gujan-Mestras	122	Ej	44.38N	1.04W
Gujarāt [3]	148	Ed	22.51N	71.30 E
Gujarāt	140	Jg	22.51N	71.30 E
Gujrānwāla	142	Jf	32.09N	74.11 E

Index Symbols

- [1] Independent Nation
- [2] State, Region
- [3] District, County
- [4] Municipality
- [5] Colony, Dependency
- Continent
- Physical Region
- Historical or Cultural Region
- Mount, Mountain
- Volcano
- Hill
- Mountains, Mountain Range
- Hills, Escarpment
- Plateau, Upland
- Pass, Gap
- Plain, Lowland
- Delta
- Salt Flat
- Valley, Canyon
- Crater, Cave
- Karst Features
- Depression
- Polder
- Desert, Dunes
- Forest, Woods
- Heath, Steppe
- Oasis
- Cape, Point
- Coast, Beach
- Cliff
- Peninsula
- Isthmus
- Sandbank
- Island
- Atoll
- Rock, Reef
- Islands, Archipelago
- Rocks, Reefs
- Coral Reef
- Well, Spring
- Geyser
- River, Stream
- Waterfall, Rapids
- River Mouth, Estuary
- Lake
- Salt Lake
- Intermittent Lake
- Reservoir
- Swamp, Pond
- Canal
- Glacier
- Ice Shelf, Pack Ice
- Ocean
- Sea
- Gulf, Bay
- Strait, Fjord
- Lagoon
- Bank
- Seamount
- Tablemount
- Ridge
- Shelf
- Basin
- Escarpment, Sea Scarp
- Fracture
- Trench, Abyss
- National Park, Reserve
- Point of Interest
- Recreation Site
- Cave, Cavern
- Historic Site
- Ruins
- Wall, Walls
- Church, Abbey
- Temple
- Scientific Station
- Railway station
- Airport
- Port
- Military installation
- Lighthouse
- Mine
- Tunnel
- Dam, Bridge

Gujrāt 148 Eb 32.34N 74.05 E
Gukovo 132 Ke 48.04N 39.58 E
Gulang 152 Hd 37.30N 102.54 E
Gulbarga 142 Jh 17.20N 76.50 E
Gulbene 136 Cd 57.12N 26.49 E
Gulča 136 Hg 40.19N 73.33 E
Gulf 204 Ad 19.08S 62.01W
Gulf Breeze 184 Dj 30.22N 87.07W
Gulf Coastal Plain (EN) 174 Jf 31.00N 92.00W
Gulfport 182 Je 30.22N 89.06W
Gulian 152 La 52.58N 122.09 E
Gulin 152 If 28.02N 105.47 E
Gulistan 136 Gg 40.30N 68.45 E
Guliya Shan 152 Lb 49.48N 122.25 E
Gulja 138 Hf 54.43N 121.03 E
Gulja/Yining 152 Dc 43.54N 81.21 E
Guljajpole 132 Jf 47.37N 36.18 E
Gulkana 178 Jd 62.16N 145.23W
Gulkeviči 132 Lg 45.19N 40.44 E
Gull Bay 186 Lb 49.47N 89.02W
Gulleråsen 116 Fc 61.04N 15.11 E
Gullfoss 114a Bb 64.20N 20.08W
Gullkronafjärd 116 Jd 60.05N 22.15 E
Gull Lake 180 Gf 50.08N 108.27W
Gullringen 116 Fg 57.48N 15.42 E
Gull River 186 Lb 49.50N 89.04W
Gullspång 116 Ff 58.59N 14.06 E
Güllü 130 Mk 38.16N 29.07 E
Güllük 146 Bd 37.14N 27.36 E
Gülpinar 130 Jj 39.32N 26.07 E
Gülşehir 146 Fc 38.45N 34.38 E
Gulstav 116 Dj 54.43N 10.41 E
Gulu 160 Kh 2.47N 32.18 E
Guma /Pishan 152 Cd 37.38N 78.19 E
Gumbiri, Jabal- 168 Ee 4.18N 30.57 E
Gumel 166 Gc 12.38N 9.23 E
Gummersbach 120 De 51.02N 7.33 E
Gummi 166 Gc 12.09N 5.07 E
Gümüşçey 130 Ki 40.17N 27.17 E
Gümüşhacıköy 146 Fb 40.53N 35.14 E
Gümüşhane 144 Ea 40.27N 39.29 E
Gümüşsu 130 Nk 38.14N 30.01 E
Guna 148 Fd 24.19N 77.19 E
Guna 168 Fc 11.44N 38.15 E
Gundagai 212 Jg 35.04S 148.07 E
Gundji 170 Db 2.05N 21.27 E
Gündoğdu 130 Ki 40.15N 27.07 E
Gündoğmuş 146 Ed 36.48N 32.01 E
Güney 130 Mk 38.09N 29.05 E
Güney Doğu Toroslar 140 Gf 38.30N 41.00 E
Gungu 170 Cd 5.44S 19.19 E
Gunma Ken 154 Of 36.20N 139.05 E
Gunnar 180 Ge 59.23N 108.53W
Gunnbjørns Fjeld 224 Mc 68.55N 29.20W
Gunnedah 212 Kf 30.59S 150.15 E
Gunnison 182 Fd 38.33N 106.56W
Gunnison River 186 Bg 39.04N 108.33W
Gunt 135 Hf 37.30N 71.03 E
Guntakal 148 Fe 15.10N 77.23 E
Guntersville 184 Dh 34.21N 86.18W
Guntersville Lake 184 Dh 34.45N 86.03W
Guntūr 142 Kh 16.18N 80.27 E
Gunungapi, Pulau- 150 Ih 6.38S 126.40 E
Gunungsitoli 150 Cf 1.17N 97.37 E
Günz 120 Gh 48.27N 10.16 E
Günzburg 120 Gh 48.27N 10.16 E
Gunzenhausen 120 Gg 49.06N 10.45 E
Guo He 154 Dh 32.58N 117.13 E
Guojiadian 154 Hc 43.20N 124.37 E
Guoyang 154 Dh 33.31N 116.12 E
Guozhen 154 Bj 29.24N 113.09 E
Gurahonț 130 Fc 46.16N 22.21 E
Gura Humorului 130 Ib 47.33N 25.54 E
Gurban Obo 152 Jc 43.06N 112.28 E
Gurbantünggüt Shamo 152 Eb 45.30N 87.30 E
Gurdžaani 132 Ni 41.43N 45.48 E
Güre 130 Mk 38.39N 29.10 E
Gurgei, Jabal- 168 Cc 13.50N 24.19 E
Gurghiului, Munții- 130 Ic 46.41N 25.12 E
Gurgueia, Rio- 198 Lf 6.50S 43.24W
Guri → Raúl Leoni, Represa- 202 Fb 7.30N 63.00W
Gurjev 112 Lf 47.07N 51.56 E
Gurjevsk 138 Df 54.20N 86.00 E
Gurjevskaja oblast 136 Ff 47.30N 52.00 E
Gurk 128 Id 46.52N 14.18 E
Gurk 128 Id 46.36N 14.31 E
Gurktaler Alpen 128 Hd 46.55N 14.00 E
Guro 172 Ec 17.26S 33.20 E
Gürpınar 146 Jc 38.18N 43.25 E
Gurskoje 138 If 50.20N 138.05 E
Gurskøy 114 Ae 62.15N 5.40 E
Gürsu 130 Mi 40.13N 29.12 E
Gurué 172 Fc 15.28S 36.59 E
Gurumeti 170 Fc 2.05S 33.57 E
Gürün 146 Gc 38.43N 37.17 E
Gurupá 202 Hd 1.25S 51.39W
Gurupá, Ilha Grande do- 202 Hd 1.00S 51.30W
Gurupi 200 Lg 11.43S 49.04W
Gurupi, Rio- 198 Lf 1.13S 46.06W
Gurupi, Serra do- 202 Id 5.00S 47.30W
Guru Sikhar 148 Ed 24.39N 72.46 E
Gus 114 Ji 55.00N 41.12 E
Gusau 160 Hg 12.10N 6.40 E
Gusev 136 Ce 54.37N 22.12 E
Gushan 154 Ge 39.54N 123.36 E
Gushi 152 Ke 32.02N 115.39 E
Gushikawa 156b Ab 26.21N 127.52 E
Gūshk 146 Ph 28.13N 55.52 E
Gus-Hrustalny 114 Ji 55.38N 40.40 E
Gusinaja, guba- 138 Kb 72.00N 150.00 E
Gusinaja Zemlja, poluostrov- 136 Fa 71.50N 52.00 E
Gusinje 130 Cg 42.34N 19.50 E
Gusinoozersk 138 Ff 51.17N 106.30 E
Guspini 128 Ck 39.32N 8.37 E
Güssing 128 Kc 47.04N 16.20 E
Gustav Holm, Kap- 179 Ie 66.45N 34.00W
Gustavia 197b Bc 17.54N 62.52W
Gustavs/Kustavi 116 Id 60.33N 21.21 E
Gustavs/Kustavi 116 Id 60.30N 21.25 E
Gustavsfors 116 Ee 59.12N 12.06 E
Gustavus 178 Le 58.25N 135.44W
Güstrow 120 Ic 53.48N 12.10 E
Gusum 116 Gf 58.16N 16.29 E
Gütersloh 120 Ee 51.54N 8.23 E
Guthrie [Ok.-U.S.] 186 Hi 35.53N 97.25W
Guthrie [Tx.-U.S.] 186 Fj 33.37N 100.19W
Gutian 152 Kf 26.40N 118.42 E
Gutiérrez Zamora 192 Kg 20.27N 97.05W
Gutii, Vîrful- 130 Gb 47.42N 23.52 E
Guting → Yutai 154 Dg 35.00N 116.40 E
Gutu 172 Ec 19.39S 31.10 E
Guwāhāti 142 Lg 26.11N 91.44 E
Guyana = Guiana (EN) 200 Ke 5.00N 59.00W
Guyane Française = French Guiana (EN) 200 Ke 4.00N 53.00W
Guyang 152 Jc 41.02N 110.04 E
Guyenne 122 Gj 44.35N 1.00 E
Guymon 182 Gd 36.41N 101.29W
Guyonneau, Anse- 197e Ab 16.14N 61.47W
Guyuan 152 Id 36.01N 106.17 E
Guyuan (Pingdingbu) 154 Cd 41.40N 115.41 E
Guzar 135 Fe 38.37N 66.18 E
Güzelyurt 146 Ee 35.12N 32.59 E
Güzelyurt Körfezi 146 Ee 35.15N 32.50 E
Gūzhān 146 Le 34.20N 46.57 E
Guzhen 154 Dh 33.20N 117.19 E
Guzhou → Rongjiang 152 If 25.58N 108.30 E
Guzmán, Laguna de- 192 Fb 31.20N 107.30W
Gvardejsk 114 Ei 54.40N 21.03 E
Gvardejskoje 132 Hg 45.06N 33.59 E
Gvary 116 Ce 59.23N 9.09 E
Gwa 148 Ie 17.36N 94.35 E
Gwadabawa 166 Gc 13.22N 5.14 E
Gwādar 142 Ig 25.07N 62.19 E
Gwai 172 Dc 19.17S 27.39 E
Gwai 158 Jj 17.59S 26.52 E
Gwalior 142 Jg 26.13N 78.10 E
Gwanda 172 Dd 20.56S 29.00 E
Gwane 170 Eb 4.43N 25.50 E
Gwda 120 Mc 53.04N 16.44 E
Gweebarra Bay/Béal an Bheara 118 Eg 54.52N 8.20W
Gwent 118 Kj 51.45N 2.55W
Gweru 160 Jj 19.27S 29.49 E
Gweta 172 Dd 20.13S 25.14 E
Gwydir River 212 Je 29.27S 149.48 E
Gwynedd 118 Ji 52.50N 3.50W
Gyaca 152 Ff 29.09N 92.38 E
Gya'gya → Saga 152 Ef 29.22N 85.15 E
Gyai Qu 152 Fe 31.30N 94.40 E
Gyaisi/Jiulong 152 Hf 28.58N 101.33 E
Gya La 152 Df 28.42N 84.35 E
Gyala Shankou 152 Df 28.42N 84.35 E
Gyangzê 152 Ef 29.00N 89.38 E
Gyaring Co 152 Ee 31.10N 88.15 E
Gyaring Hu 152 Ge 34.55N 98.00 E
Gyda 138 Cb 70.52N 78.30 E
Gydanskaja guba 138 Cb 71.20N 76.30 E
Gydanski poluostrov = Gyda Peninsula (EN) 140 Jb 70.50N 79.00 E
Gyda Peninsula (EN) = Gydanski poluostrov 140 Jb 70.50N 79.00 E
Gyigang → Zayü 152 Gf 28.43N 97.25 E
Gyirong (Zongga) 152 Ef 28.57N 85.12 E
Gyldenløves Fjord 179 Hf 64.10N 40.30W
Gyldenløves Høj 116 Di 55.33N 11.52 E
Gympie 210 Gg 26.11S 152.40 E
Gyoma 120 Qj 46.56N 20.50 E
Gyöngyös 120 Pi 47.47N 19.56 E
Győr 112 Hf 47.41N 17.38 E
Győr 120 Ni 47.40N 17.39 E
Győr-Sopron 120 Ni 47.40N 17.15 E
Gypsumville 180 Hf 51.45N 98.35W
Gysinge 116 Gd 60.17N 16.53 E
Gyttorp 116 Fe 59.31N 14.58 E
Gyula 120 Rj 46.39N 21.17 E

H

Haacht 124 Gd 50.59N 4.38 E
Häädemeeste/Hjademeste 116 Kf 58.00N 24.28 E
Ha'afeva 221b Ba 19.57S 174.43W
Haafusia 220h Bb 13.18S 176.09W
Haag, Mount- 222 Qf 77.40S 79.00W
Haaksbergen 124 Ib 52.09N 6.45 E
Haamstede, Westerschouwen- 124 Fc 51.42N 3.45 E
Haanja Kõrgustik 116 Lg 57.30N 27.30 E
Ha'ano 221b Ba 19.40S 174.17W
Ha'apai Group 208 Jf 19.47S 174.27W
Haapajärvi 114 Fe 63.45N 25.20 E
Haapamäki 116 Kb 62.15N 24.28 E
Haapasaari 116 Ld 60.15N 27.10 E
Haapaselkä [Fin.] 116 Mb 62.10N 28.10 E
Haapaselkä [Fin.] 116 Mc 61.35N 28.15 E
Haapiti 221e Fc 17.34S 149.52W
Haapsalu 136 Cd 58.57N 23.32 E
Ha'arava 146 Fg 30.58N 32.24 E
Haardt 120 Dg 49.15N 8.00 E
Haardtkopf 124 Je 49.51N 7.04 E
Haaren, Wünnenberg- 124 Kc 51.34N 8.44 E
Haarlem 122 Kb 52.23N 4.38 E
Haarlemmermeer 124 Gb 52.20N 4.41 E
Haarlerberg 124 Ib 52.20N 6.25 E
Haarstrang 124 Kc 51.30N 8.20 E
Haast 210 Hi 43.52S 169.01 E
Haast Pass 218 Cf 44.06S 169.21 E
Habahe/Kaba 152 Eb 47.53N 86.12 E
Habarovsk 142 Pe 48.27N 135.06 E
Habarovski kraj 138 If 53.00N 137.00 E
Ḩabarūt 144 Hf 17.22N 52.42 E
Ḩabashīyah, Jabal- 168 Ib 16.45N 50.05 E
Habaswein 170 Gb 1.01N 39.29 E
Habay [Alta.-Can.] 180 Fe 58.52N 118.45W
Habay [Bel.] 124 He 49.45N 5.38 E
Habay [Som.] 168 Ge 1.08N 43.46 E
Ḩabbān 168 Hc 14.21N 47.05 E
Ḩabbānīyah 146 Jf 33.22N 43.35 E
Ḩabbānīyah, Hawr al- 146 Jf 33.17N 43.29 E
Habbārīyah, Bi'r al- 146 Jf 32.17N 42.12 E
Habibas, Iles- 126 Ki 35.44N 1.08W
Habichtswald 120 Fe 51.20N 9.25 E
Habo 116 Fg 57.55N 14.04 E
Haboro 152 Pc 44.22N 141.42 E
Ḩabshān 146 Ok 23.50N 53.37 E
Hache 120 Ec 53.05N 8.50 E
Hachenburg 124 Jd 50.39N 7.50 E
Hachijō 156 Fe 35.15N 139.45 E
Hachijō-Fuji 156 Fe 33.08N 139.46 E
Hachijō-Jima 152 Oe 33.05N 139.50 E
Hachiman 156 Ed 35.46N 136.57 E
Hachimori 156 Fa 40.22N 140.00 E
Hachinohe 142 Qe 40.30N 141.29 E
Hachiōji 156 Fd 35.39N 139.18 E
Hachiro-Gata 156 Fa 40.00N 140.00 E
Hacibey De 146 Kd 36.58N 44.18 E
Hackås 114 De 62.55N 14.31 E
Håckren 116 Ea 63.10N 13.35 E
Hačmas 136 Eg 41.25N 48.52 E
Hadagang 154 Kb 45.24N 131.12 E
Hadamar 124 Kd 50.27N 8.03 E
Ḩaḑan, Ḩarrat- 164 He 21.30N 41.23 E
Hadano 156 Fd 35.22N 139.14 E
Ḩadāribah, Ra's al- 168 Fa 22.04N 36.54 E
HaDarom 146 Fg 30.40N 34.50 E
Hadd, Ra's al- 140 Hg 22.32N 59.59 E
Haddad 158 Ig 14.40N 18.46 E
Ḩadded 168 Hc 10.10N 48.28 E
Haddington 118 Kf 55.58N 2.47W
Haddummati Atoll 148a Bb 1.45N 73.30 E
Hadejia 166 Hc 12.27N 10.03 E
Hadejia 166 Hc 12.50N 10.51 E
Hadeland 116 Dd 60.25N 10.35 E
Hadeln 120 Ec 53.45N 8.45 E
Hadera 146 Ff 32.26N 34.55 E
Haderslev 114 Bi 55.15N 9.30 E
Hadīboh 144 Hg 12.39N 54.02 E
Hadım 146 Ed 36.59N 32.28 E
Hadimköy 146 Cb 41.09N 28.37 E
Ḩadīyah 144 Ed 25.34N 38.41 E
Hadjer el Hamis 168 Ac 12.51N 14.50 E
Hadjout 126 Oh 36.31N 2.25 E
Hadleigh 124 Cb 52.03N 0.56 E
Hadley Bay 180 Gb 72.30N 108.30W
Ha Dong 148 Ld 20.58N 105.46 E
Ḩaḑramawt 140 Gh 15.00N 50.00 E
Hadrian's Wall 118 Kg 54.59N 2.26W
Hadsten 116 Dh 56.20N 10.03 E
Hadsund 116 Dh 56.43N 10.07 E
Hadytajaha 134 Nc 66.57N 69.12 E
Hadyžensk 132 Kg 44.25N 39.31 E
Hadzibeisui liman 130 Nc 46.40N 30.30 E
Haedo, Cuchilla de- 204 Dj 31.40S 56.18W
Haeju 154 He 38.02N 125.42 E
Haena 214 Oc 22.13N 159.34W
Ḩafar al 'Atk 146 Lj 25.56N 46.47 E
Ḩafar al Bāṭin 144 Gd 28.27N 46.00 E
Haffner Bjerg 179 Fc 76.30N 63.00W
Ḩaffūz 128 Do 35.38N 9.40 E
Hafik 146 Gc 39.52N 37.24 E
Ḩafīrat al 'Aydā 144 Ed 26.26N 39.12 E
Ḩafīt 146 Pk 23.59N 55.49 E
Ḩafīt, Jabal- 146 Pj 24.03N 55.46 E
Hafnarfjörður 114a Bb 64.04N 21.57W
Haft Gel 146 Mg 31.27N 49.27 E
Hāfūn 168 Ic 10.10N 51.05 E
Hāfūn, Rās- = Hafun, Ras- (EN) 158 Mg 10.27N 51.24 E
Hafun, Ras- (EN) = Hāfūn, Rās- 158 Mg 10.27N 51.24 E
Hāfūn Bay North 168 Ic 10.37N 51.15 E
Hāfūn Bay South 168 Ic 10.15N 51.05 E
Hagadera 170 Hb 0.02N 40.17 E
Hagby 116 Gh 56.33N 16.10 E
Hageland 124 Gd 50.55N 4.45 E
Hagemeister 178 Ge 58.40N 161.00W
Hagen 120 De 51.21N 7.28 E
Hagenow 120 Hc 53.26N 11.12 E
Hagere Hiywet 168 Fd 8.58N 37.53 E
Hagerman 188 He 42.49N 114.54W
Hagerstown 182 Ld 39.39N 77.43W
Hagetmau 122 Fk 43.40N 0.35W
Hagfors 114 Cf 60.02N 13.42 E
Häggenås 116 Fa 63.24N 14.55 E
Hagi 154 Kg 34.24N 131.25 E
Ha Giang 148 Kd 22.50N 104.59 E
Hagman, Puntan- 220b Ba 15.09N 145.48 E
Hagondange 122 Me 49.15N 6.10 E
Hags Head/Ceanna Cailligh 118 Di 52.57N 9.28W
Hague, Cap de la- 110 Ff 49.43N 1.57W
Haguenau 122 Nf 48.49N 7.47 E
Hagunía 162 Ed 27.26N 12.24W
Hahajima-Rettō 214 Cb 26.37N 142.10 E
Hahns Peak 186 Cf 40.56N 107.01W
Hahót 120 Mj 46.38N 16.56 E
Hai'an 154 Fh 32.33N 120.26 E
Haicheng 152 Lc 40.51N 122.43 E
Haidenaab 120 Ig 49.35N 12.08 E
Hai Duong 148 Ld 20.56N 106.19 E
Haifa (EN) = Ḩefa 142 Ff 32.50N 35.00 E
Haifeng 152 Kg 22.58N 115.21 E
Haiger 124 Kd 50.45N 8.13 E
Hai He 154 De 38.57N 117.43 E
Haikakan Sovetakan Socialistakan Respublika/Armjanskaja SSR 136 Eg 40.00N 45.00 E
Haikang (Leizhou) 152 Jg 20.56N 110.06 E
Haikou 142 Ng 20.05N 110.20 E
Ḩā'il 142 Gg 27.33N 41.42 E
Hailang He 154 Jb 44.33N 129.33 E
Hailar 142 Ne 49.14N 119.42 E
Hailar He 140 Ne 49.30N 117.50 E
Hailin 152 Mc 44.35N 129.22 E
Hailong (Meihekou) 152 Mc 42.32N 125.37 E
Hailsham 124 Cd 50.52N 0.16 E
Hailun 152 Mb 47.29N 126.55 E
Hailuoto/Karlö 110 Ib 65.02N 24.42 E
Haima Tan 150 Gd 10.52N 116.53 E
Haimen [China] 154 Fi 31.53N 121.10 E
Haimen [China] 154 Fj 28.40N 121.27 E
Haina 124 Kc 51.03N 8.56 E
Hainan Dao 140 Mh 19.00N 109.00 E
Hainaut 124 Fd 50.30N 4.00 E
Hainaut 122 Jd 50.20N 3.50 E
Hainburg an der Donau 128 Kb 48.09N 16.56 E
Haines 176 Fd 59.14N 135.27W
Haines Junction 180 Dd 60.45N 137.30W
Hainich 120 Ge 51.05N 10.27 E
Hainleite 120 Ge 51.20N 10.48 E
Hai Phong 142 Mg 20.52N 106.41 E
Haïti = Haiti (EN) 176 Lh 19.00N 72.25W
Haiti (EN) = Haïti 176 Lh 19.00N 72.25W
Haixing (Suji) 154 De 38.10N 117.29 E
Haixin Shan 152 Hd 37.00N 100.03 E
Haiyan (Sanjiaocheng) 152 Hd 36.58N 100.50 E
Haiyan (Wuyuanzhen) 154 Fi 30.31N 120.56 E
Haiyang (Dongoun) 154 Ff 36.46N 121.09 E
Haiyang Dao 154 Ge 39.03N 123.12 E
Haiyou → Sanmen 152 Lf 29.08N 121.22 E
Haiyuan 152 Id 36.35N 105.40 E
Haizhou 154 Eg 34.34N 119.08 E
Haizhou Wan 140 Nf 35.00N 119.30 E
Ḩajar Banga 168 Cc 11.30N 23.00 E
Hajdarken 136 Hh 39.55N 71.24 E
Hajdú-Bihar 120 Ri 47.25N 21.30 E
Hajdúböszörmény 120 Ri 47.40N 21.31 E
Hajdúdorog 120 Ri 47.49N 21.30 E
Hajdúhadház 120 Ri 47.41N 21.40 E
Hajdúnánás 120 Ri 47.51N 21.26 E
Hajdúság 120 Ri 47.35N 21.30 E
Hajdúszoboszló 120 Ri 47.27N 21.24 E
Hajihi-Zaki 156 Fb 38.19N 138.31 E
Ḩājjīābād [Iran] 146 Ph 28.21N 54.27 E
Ḩājjīābād [Iran] 146 Ph 28.19N 55.55 E
Ḩājjīabād-e Māsīleh 146 Ne 34.49N 51.13 E
Hajla 130 Dg 42.43N 20.10 E
Hajnówka 120 Td 52.45N 23.36 E
Hajós 120 Pj 46.24N 19.07 E
Hajpudyrskaja guba 134 Ib 68.40N 59.30 E
Hakase-Yama 156 Fc 37.22N 139.43 E
Hakasskaja avtonomnaja oblast 138 Df 53.30N 90.00 E
Hakata-Wan 156 Be 33.40N 130.20 E
Hakefjord 116 Dg 57.41N 11.44 E
Hakha 148 Id 22.39N 93.37 E
Hakkâri 144 Fb 37.34N 43.45 E
Hakken-Zan 156 Dd 34.10N 135.54 E
Hakkōda San 156 Ga 40.40N 140.53 E
Hako-Dake 156a Ca 44.40N 142.25 E
Hakodate 142 Qe 41.45N 140.43 E
Hakone-Yama 156 Fd 35.13N 139.00 E
Hakui 154 Nf 36.53N 136.47 E
Hakupu 220k Bb 19.06S 169.50W
Haku-San 156 Ec 36.09N 136.45 E
Hal/Halle 122 Kd 50.44N 4.14 E
Halab 146 Md 36.17N 48.03 E
Ḩalab = Aleppo (EN) 142 Ff 36.12N 37.10 E
Ḩalabjah 146 Ke 35.10N 45.59 E
Halač 136 Gh 39.04N 64.53 E
Halachó 192 Ng 20.29N 90.05W
Halahei 154 Ga 46.11N 122.46 E
Ḩalā'ib 160 Kf 22.13N 36.38 E
Halalii Lake 221a Ab 21.52N 160.11W
Halangingie Point 220k Bb 19.03S 169.58W
Hålaveden 116 Ff 58.05N 14.45 E
Halawa 221a Eb 21.10N 156.44W
Halawa, Cape- 221a Eb 21.10N 156.43W
Ḩalbā 146 Ge 34.33N 36.05 E
Halberstadt 120 He 51.54N 11.03 E
Halcon, Mount- 150 Hd 13.16N 121.00 E
Haldean-Sogotyn-Daba 152 Gb 49.05N 97.55 E
Halden 114 Cg 59.09N 11.23 E
Haldensleben 120 Hd 52.18N 11.25 E
Haldia 148 Hd 22.08N 88.05 E
Haldwani 148 Fc 29.13N 79.31 E
Hale, Mount- 212 De 26.00S 117.10 E
Haleakala Crater 221a Ec 20.43N 156.12W
Haleiwa 221a Cb 21.36N 158.06W
Halemaumau 221a Fd 19.24N 155.17W
Hale River 212 Hd 24.56S 135.53 E
Halesworth 124 Db 52.21N 1.30 E
Haleyville 184 Dh 34.14N 87.37W
Ḩalfā al Gadida 160 Kg 15.19N 35.34 E
Half Assini 166 Ed 5.03N 2.53W
Halfeti 146 Gd 37.15N 37.52 E
Halfway 180 Fe 56.13N 121.26W
Halh-Gol 152 Kb 48.01N 118.10 E
Ḩalī 168 Gb 18.38N 41.22 E
Haliburton 184 Hc 45.03N 78.33W
Halifax 176 Me 44.39N 63.36W
Halifax, Mount- 212 Jc 19.05S 146.20 E
Halifax Bay 212 Jc 18.50S 146.30 E
Hālil 144 Id 27.28N 58.44 E
Halīleh, Ra's-e- 146 Nh 28.46N 50.56 E
Halilovo 132 Ud 51.27N 58.10 E
Ḩalin 168 Hd 9.08N 48.47 E
Haliut → Urad Zhonghou Lianheqi 152 Ic 41.34N 108.32 E
Haljala 116 Le 59.22N 26.09 E
Haljasavej 138 Cd 63.20N 78.30 E
Hall 178 Ed 60.40N 173.05W
Halladale 118 Jc 58.30N 3.50W
Hallam Peak 188 Fa 52.11N 118.46W
Halland 114 Ch 56.45N 13.00 E
Halland 116 Eh 57.00N 12.45 E
Hallandsås 116 Eh 56.23N 13.00 E
Halla-san 154 Ih 33.22N 126.32 E
Ḩallat 'Ammār 146 Gh 29.08N 36.02 E
Hall Beach 180 Jc 68.10N 81.56W
Halle 120 He 51.30N 12.00 E
Halle 120 He 51.30N 11.50 E
Halle/Hal 122 Kd 50.44N 4.14 E
Halle (Westfalen) 124 Kb 52.05N 8.22 E
Halleberg 116 Ef 58.23N 12.25 E
Hällefors 116 Fe 59.47N 14.30 E
Hälleforsnäs 116 Ge 59.10N 16.30 E
Hallein 128 Hc 47.41N 13.06 E
Hällekis 116 Ef 58.38N 13.25 E
Hallen 114 De 63.11N 14.05 E
Hallenberg 124 Kc 51.07N 8.38 E
Hallencourt 124 De 49.59N 1.53 E
Halle-Neustadt 120 He 51.31N 11.53 E
Hallertau 120 Hh 48.35N 11.50 E
Hällestad 116 Ff 58.44N 15.34 E
Hallettsville 186 Hl 29.27N 96.57W
Halley Bay 222 Af 75.31S 26.38W
Halli 116 Kc 61.52N 24.50 E
Hallie-Jackson Bank (EN) 219c Ba 9.45S 166.10 E
Halligen 120 Eb 54.35N 8.35 E
Hallingdal 114 Bf 60.40N 9.15 E
Hallingdalselva 116 Cd 60.23N 9.35 E
Hallingskarvet 110 Gc 60.37N 7.45 E
Hall in Tirol (Solbad Hall in Tirol) 128 Fc 47.17N 11.31 E
Hall Islands 208 Gd 8.37N 152.00 E
Halliste jõgi 116 Kf 58.23N 24.25 E
Hall Lake 180 Jc 68.40N 82.20W
Hall Land 179 Fb 81.12N 61.10W
Hallock 186 Hb 48.47N 96.57W
Hall Peninsula 174 Mc 63.30N 66.00W
Hallsberg 114 Dg 59.04N 15.07 E
Halls Creek 210 Df 18.13S 127.40 E
Hallstahammar 114 Dg 59.37N 16.13 E
Hallstatt 128 Hc 47.33N 13.39 E
Hallstavik 114 Ef 60.03N 18.36 E
Halluin 124 Fd 50.47N 3.08 E
Halmahera 208 Dd 1.00N 128.00 E
Halmahera, Laut- = Halmahera Sea (EN) 208 De 1.00S 129.00 E
Halmahera Sea (EN) = Halmahera, Laut- 208 De 1.00S 129.00 E
Halmer-Ju 136 Gb 67.58N 64.40 E
Halmeu 130 Gb 47.58N 23.01 E
Halmstad 112 Hd 56.39N 12.50 E
Haloze 128 Jd 46.20N 15.50 E
Ḩalq al Wādī 162 Jb 36.49N 10.18 E
Hals 114 Ch 57.00N 10.19 E
Hälsingland 116 Gc 61.30N 17.00 E
Halsön 116 Ib 62.50N 21.10 E
Halstead 124 Cc 51.57N 0.38 E
Halsteren 124 Gc 51.32N 4.16 E
Haltang He 152 Fd 39.00N 94.40 E
Halten Bank (EN) 114 Bd 64.45N 8.45 E
Haltern 124 Jc 51.44N 7.11 E
Haltiatunturi 114 Eb 69.18N 21.16 E
Haltom City 186 Hj 32.48N 97.16W
Halturin 136 Ed 58.35N 48.55 E
Hālūl 146 Oj 25.40N 52.25 E
Halver 124 Jc 51.12N 7.29 E
Ham 122 Je 49.45N 3.04 E
Ham, Roches de- 124 Ae 49.02N 1.02W
Hamada 156 Cd 34.53N 132.03 E
Hamadān 142 Gf 34.48N 48.30 E
Hamadān 144 Gb 35.00N 48.40 E
Hamadia 126 Ni 35.28N 1.52 E
Hamaguir 162 Gc 30.54N 3.02W
Ḩamāh 144 Eb 35.08N 36.45 E
Hamakita 156 Ed 34.49N 137.45 E
Hamamasu 156a Bb 43.36N 141.21 E
Hamamatsu 152 Oe 34.42N 137.44 E
Hamanaka 156a Db 43.05N 145.05 E
Hamanaka-Wan 156a Db 43.07N 145.10 E
Hamana-Ko 156 Ed 34.45N 137.34 E
Hamanen, Oued el- 162 Hd 25.52N 1.26 E
Hamaoka 156 Fd 34.39N 138.07 E
Hamar 112 Hc 60.48N 11.06 E
Hamar-Daban, hrebet- 138 Ff 51.10N 105.00 E
Hamasaka 156 Dd 35.38N 134.27 E
Ḩamāṭah, Jabal- 164 Ge 24.12N 35.00 E
Hamatonbetsu 154 Qb 45.07N 142.23 E
Hambantota 148 Gg 6.10N 81.07 E
Hambre, Cayos del- 194 Fb 22.15N 82.47W
Hamburg 120 Fc 53.35N 10.00 E
Hamburg [F.R.G.] 112 Ge 53.33N 10.00 E
Hamburg [S.Afr.] 172 Df 33.18S 27.28 E
Hamburg-Altona 120 Fc 53.33N 9.57 E
Hamburg-Harburg 120 Fc 53.28N 10.00 E
Hamburgsund 116 Df 58.33N 11.16 E
Ḩamḑ, Wādī al- 140 Fg 25.58N 36.42 E
Ḩamḑah 164 Hf 19.02N 43.36 E
Häme 114 Ff 61.30N 24.30 E
Häme 116 Kc 61.30N 25.30 E
Hämeenkangas 116 Jc 61.45N 22.40 E
Hämeenlinna/Tavastehus 114 Ff 61.00N 24.27 E
Hämeenselkä 116 Kb 62.30N 25.00 E
Hamelin Pool 212 Ce 26.15S 114.05 E
Hameln 120 Fd 52.06N 9.21 E
HaMerkaz 146 Fg 32.05N 34.55 E
Hamero Hadad 168 Gd 7.28N 42.13 E
Hamersley Range 212 Dd 21.55S 116.45 E
Hamgyŏng-Namdo 154 Id 40.00N 127.30 E
Hamgyŏng-Pukto 154 Jd 41.45N 129.50 E
Hamgyŏng-Sanmaek 154 Jd 41.00N 128.45 E
Hamhŭng 142 Of 39.54N 127.32 E
Hami/Kumul 142 Le 42.48N 93.27 E
Ḩamīdīyeh 146 Mg 31.29N 48.26 E
Hamilton [Austl.] 212 Ig 37.45S 142.02 E
Hamilton [Ber.] 176 Mf 32.17N 64.46W
Hamilton [Mt.-U.S.] 182 Eb 46.15N 114.09W
Hamilton [N.Z.] 210 Ih 37.47S 175.17 E
Hamilton [Oh.-U.S.] 182 Kd 39.23N 84.33W
Hamilton [Ont.-Can.] 176 Le 43.15N 79.51W
Hamilton [Scot.-U.K.] 118 If 55.47N 4.03W
Hamilton [Tx.-U.S.] 186 Gk 31.42N 98.07W

Index Symbols

1 Independent Nation
2 State, Region
3 District, County
4 Municipality
5 Colony, Dependency
Continent
Physical Region
Historical or Cultural Region
Mount, Mountain
Volcano
Hill
Mountains, Mountain Range
Hills, Escarpment
Plateau, Upland
Pass, Gap
Plain, Lowland
Delta
Salt Flat
Valley, Canyon
Crater, Cave
Karst Features
Depression
Polder
Desert, Dunes
Forest, Woods
Heath, Steppe
Oasis
Cape, Point
Coast, Beach
Cliff
Peninsula
Isthmus
Sandbank
Island
Atoll
Rock, Reef
Islands, Archipelago
Rocks, Reefs
Coral Reef
Well, Spring
Geyser
River, Stream
Waterfall, Rapids
River Mouth, Estuary
Lake
Salt Lake
Intermittent Lake
Reservoir
Swamp, Pond
Canal
Glacier
Ice Shelf, Pack Ice
Ocean
Sea
Gulf, Bay
Strait, Fjord
Lagoon
Bank
Seamount
Tablemount
Ridge
Shelf
Basin
Escarpment, Sea Scarp
Fracture
Trench, Abyss
National Park, Reserve
Point of Interest
Recreation Site
Cave, Cavern
Historic Site
Ruins
Wall, Walls
Church, Abbey
Temple
Scientific Station
Railway station
Airport
Port
Military installation
Lighthouse
Mine
Tunnel
Dam, Bridge

Hamilton, Lake-	186	Ji	34.30N	93.05W
Hamilton, Mount-	188	Hg	39.14N	115.32W
Hamilton River	212	Hd	23.30S	139.47 E
Hamīn, Wādī al-	164	Dc	30.28N	22.00 E
Hamina/Fredrikshamn	114	Gf	60.34N	27.12 E
Hamm	120	De	51.41N	7.48 E
Ḩammām al 'Alīl	146	Jd	36.10N	43.16 E
Ḩammām al Anf	162	Jb	36.44N	10.20 E
Ḩammāmāt	162	Jb	36.24N	10.37 E
Ḩammāmāt, Khalīj-	162	Jb	36.05N	10.40 E
Hammam Bou Hadjar	126	Li	35.23N	0.58W
Hammami	158	Ff	23.03N	11.30W
Hammam Righa	126	Oh	36.23N	2.24 E
Ḩammār, Hawr al-	144	Gc	30.50N	47.10 E
Hammarstrand	116	Ga	63.06N	16.21 E
Hamme	124	Gc	51.06N	4.08 E
Hammelburg	120	Ff	50.07N	9.54 E
Hammerdal	116	Ff	63.36N	15.21 E
Hammeren	116	Fi	55.18N	14.47 E
Hammerfest	112	Ia	70.40N	23.45 E
Hamminkeln	124	Ic	51.44N	6.35 E
Hamminkeln-Dingden	124	Ic	51.46N	6.37 E
Hammond [In.-U.S.]	184	De	41.36N	87.30W
Hammond [La.-U.S.]	182	Ie	30.30N	90.28W
Hammonton	184	Jf	39.38N	74.48W
Hamont, Hamont-Achel-	124	Hc	51.15N	5.33 E
Hamont-Achel	124	Hc	51.15N	5.33 E
Hamont-Achel-Hamont	124	Hc	51.15N	5.33 E
Hamoyet, Jabal-	158	Kg	17.33N	38.02 E
Hampden	218	Df	45.20S	170.49 E
Hampshire [3]	118	Lk	51.00N	1.10W
Hampshire Downs	118	Lj	51.15N	1.15W
Hampton [Ia.-U.S.]	186	Je	42.45N	93.12W
Hampton [Va.-U.S.]	184	Ig	37.02N	76.23W
Hampton Butte	188	Ee	43.46N	120.17W
Hamp'yong	154	Ig	35.04N	126.31 E
Ḩamrā'	168	Dc	10.54N	29.54 E
Hamra [R.S.F.S.R.]	138	Gd	60.17N	114.10 E
Hamra [Swe.]	116	Fc	61.39N	15.00 E
Ḩamrā', Al Ḩamādah al-	158	If	29.30N	12.00 E
Hamra, Saguia el-	158	Ff	27.24N	13.43W
Hamrān	146	Kd	36.22N	45.44 E
Ḩamrat ash Shaykh	168	Dc	14.35N	27.58 E
Ḩamrīn, Jabal-	146	Ke	34.30N	44.30 E
Hāmūn-e Hīrmand, Daryācheh-ye-	144	Jc	31.30N	61.20 E
Han	166	Ec	10.41N	2.27W
Hana	214	Oc	20.45N	155.59W
Hanahan	184	Hi	32.55N	80.00W
Hanaizumi	156	Gb	38.51N	141.12 E
Ḩanak	144	Ed	25.33N	36.56 E
Hanalei	221a	Ba	22.13N	159.30W
Hanamaki	154	Pe	39.23N	141.07 E
Hanang	158	Ki	4.26S	35.24 E
Hanaoka	156	Ga	40.21N	140.34 E
Hanapepe	221a	Bb	21.55N	159.35W
Hanau	120	Ef	50.08N	8.55 E
Han-Bogdo	152	Ic	43.12N	107.10 E
Hanceville	180	Ff	51.55N	123.02W
Hancheng	152	Jd	35.30N	110.25 E
Hanchuan	154	Bi	30.39N	113.46 E
Hancock	184	Cb	47.07N	88.35W
Handa	156	Ed	34.53N	136.56 E
Handan	142	Nf	36.35N	114.28 E
Handen	116	He	59.10N	18.08 E
Handeni	170	Gd	5.26S	38.01 E
Handlová	120	Oh	48.44N	18.46 E
Handöl	116	Ea	63.16N	12.26 E
Handyga	142	Pc	62.40N	135.36 E
Ḩanegev=Negev Desert (EN)	146	Fg	30.30N	34.55 E
Hanford	188	Fh	36.20N	119.39W
Han-gang	152	Md	37.45N	126.11 E
Hanga Roa	221d	Ab	27.09S	109.26W
Hang'bu He	154	Di	31.33N	117.05 E
Hanggin Houqi (Xamba)	152	Ic	40.59N	107.07 E
Hanggin Qi (Xin Zhen)	152	Id	39.54N	108.55 E
Hangö/Hanko	114	Fg	59.50N	22.57 E
Hangöudde/Hankoniemi	116	Je	59.50N	23.10 E
Hangu	154	De	39.16N	117.50 E
Hangzhou	142	Of	30.18N	120.11 E
Hangzhou Wan	154	Fj	30.25N	121.00 E
Ḩanīsh	164	Hg	13.45N	42.45 E
Ḩanīsh al Kabīr, Jazīrat al-	164	Hg	13.43N	42.45 E
Hanja, vozvyšennost-	116	Lg	57.30N	27.30 E
Ḩanjūrah, Ra's-	146	Pj	24.44N	54.39 E
Hanka, ozero- = Khanka, Lake- (EN)	140	Pe	45.00N	132.24 E
Hankasalmi	116	Lb	62.23N	26.26 E
Hankensbüttel	120	Gd	52.44N	10.36 E
Hanko/Hangö	114	Fg	59.50N	22.57 E
Hankoniemi/Hangöudde	116	Je	59.50N	23.10 E
Hankou, Wuhan-	154	Ci	30.35N	114.16 E
Hanksville	188	Jg	38.25N	110.10W
Hanlar	132	Oi	40.34N	46.20 E
Hanmej, gora-	134	Lc	67.08N	66.00 E
Hanmer Springs	218	Ee	42.31S	172.50 E
Hann, Mount-	212	Fc	15.50S	125.50 E
Hanna [Alta.-Can.]	180	Gf	51.38N	111.54W
Hanna [Wy.-U.S.]	186	Lf	41.52N	106.34W
Hannah Bay	180	Jf	51.15N	79.50W
Hannibal	182	Id	39.42N	91.22W
Hanningfield Reservoir	124	Cc	51.37N	0.28 E
Hannō	156	Fd	35.53N	139.17 E
Hannover	112	Ge	52.22N	9.43 E
Hann River	212	Fc	17.10S	126.10 E
Hannuit/Hannut	124	Hd	50.40N	5.05 E
Hannut/Hannuit	124	Hd	50.40N	5.05 E
Hanö	116	Fi	56.00N	14.50 E
Hanöbukten	116	Fi	55.45N	14.30 E
Ha Noi	142	Mg	21.02N	105.51 E
Hanover [N.H.-U.S.]	184	Kd	43.42N	72.17W
Hanover [Ont.-Can.]	184	Gc	44.09N	81.02W
Hanover [Pa.-U.S.]	184	If	39.47N	76.59W
Hanover [S.Afr.]	172	Cf	31.04S	24.29 E
Hanover, Isla-	206	Fh	51.00S	74.40W
Hanpan, Cape-	212	Ka	5.01S	154.37 E
Han Pijesak	128	Mf	44.05N	18.57 E
Hansen Mountains	222	Ee	68.16S	58.47 E
Hanshan	154	Ei	31.43N	118.07 E
Hanshou	154	Aj	28.55N	111.58 E
Han Shui	140	Nf	30.34N	114.17 E
Hanstholm	116	Cg	57.07N	8.38 E
Han Sum	154	Eb	44.33N	119.58 E
Han-sur-Lesse, Rochefort-	124	Hd	50.08N	5.11 E
Han-sur-Nied	124	If	48.59N	6.26 E
Hantau	136	Hg	44.13N	73.48 E
Hantengri Feng	152	Dc	42.03N	80.11 E
Hants	118	Lj	51.10N	1.10W
Hanty-Mansijsk	142	Ic	61.00N	69.06 E
Hanty-Mansijski nacionalny okrug [3]	136	Hc	62.00N	72.30 E
Hantzsch	180	Kc	67.32N	72.26W
Hanušovice	120	Mf	50.05N	16.55 E
Hanwang	152	He	31.25N	104.13 E
Hanyang	154	Ci	30.33N	114.01 E
Hanyang, Wuhan-	154	Ci	30.33N	114.16 E
Hanyū	156	Fc	36.11N	139.32 E
Hanyuan (Fulin)	152	Hf	29.25N	102.12 E
Hanzhong	142	Mf	32.59N	107.11 E
Hanzhuang	154	Dg	34.38N	117.23 E
Hao Atoll	208	Mf	18.15S	140.54W
Hāora	142	Kg	22.35N	88.20 E
Haoud el Hamra	162	Ic	31.58N	5.59 E
Hao Xi	154	Ej	28.28N	119.56 E
Haoxue	154	Bi	30.02N	112.25 E
Haparanda	114	Fd	65.50N	24.10 E
Hapčeranga	138	Kg	49.42N	112.20 E
Happy Valley-Goose Bay	176	Md	53.19N	60.24W
Hapsu	154	Jd	41.13N	128.51 E
Ḩaql	146	Fh	29.18N	34.57 E
Ḩaql al Burqān	146	Lh	28.55N	47.57 E
Ḩaql al Manāqīsh	146	Lh	29.02N	47.32 E
Ḩaql as Şābirīyah	146	Lh	29.48N	47.50 E
Hara, zaliv-/Hara laht	116	Ke	59.35N	25.30 E
Hara-Ajrag	152	Ib	45.50N	109.20 E
Harabali	136	Ef	47.25N	47.16 E
Ḩaraḑ	144	Ge	24.14N	49.11 E
Haraiki Atoll	208	Mf	17.28S	143.27W
Hara laht/Hara, zaliv-	116	Ke	59.35N	25.30 E
Haramachi	154	Pf	37.38N	140.58 E
Haram Dāgh	144	Gb	37.35N	46.43 E
Harami, pereval-	132	Oh	42.48N	46.12 E
Harand	146	Of	32.34N	52.26 E
Harani'ia Point	219a	Ed	10.21S	161.16 E
Hara Nur	152	Fb	48.05N	93.12 E
Ḩarardêre	168	He	4.32N	47.53 E
Harare	160	Kj	17.50S	31.10 E
Harat	168	Fb	16.05N	39.28 E
Hara-Tas, krjaž-	138	Fb	72.00N	107.00 E
Haratini	220n	Bc	10.28S	160.58W
Ḩarat Zuwayyah	160	Jf	24.14N	21.59 E
Hara-Us-Nur	152	Fb	48.00N	92.10 E
Haraz	168	Bc	13.57N	19.26 E
Harāz	146	Od	36.40N	52.43 E
Harāzah, Jabal-	168	Eb	15.03N	30.27 E
Haraze	168	Cd	9.55N	20.48 E
Harbel	166	Cd	6.16N	10.21W
Harbin	142	Oe	45.45N	126.37 E
Harbor Beach	184	Fd	43.51N	82.39W
Harbour Breton	180	Lg	47.29N	55.50W
Harbour Grace	180	Mg	47.41N	53.15W
Harburg, Hamburg-	120	Fc	53.28N	10.00 E
Harcourt	184	Ob	46.30N	65.15W
Harcuvar Mountains	188	Ii	34.00N	113.30W
Harcyzsk	132	Kf	47.59N	38.11 E
Hardanger	116	Bd	60.20N	6.30 E
Hardangerfjorden	110	Gc	60.10N	6.00 E
Hardangerjøkulen	116	Bd	60.35N	7.25 E
Hardangervidda	114	Bf	60.20N	7.30 E
Hardelot Plage, Neufchâtel Hardelot-	124	Dd	50.38N	1.35 E
Hardenberg	124	Ib	52.34N	6.37 E
Harderwijk	122	Lb	52.21N	5.36 E
Hardin	182	Fb	45.44N	107.37W
Harding	172	Df	30.34S	29.58 E
Hardinsburg	182	Dg	37.47N	86.28W
Härdler	124	Kc	51.06N	8.14 E
Hardoi	148	Gc	27.25N	80.07 E
Hardwār	148	Fc	29.58N	78.10 E
Hardy, Peninsula-	206	Gi	55.25S	68.30W
Hareid	116	Bb	62.22N	6.02 E
Hareidlandet	116	Ae	62.20N	5.55 E
Hare Indian	180	Ec	66.18N	128.38W
Harelbeke	124	Fd	50.51N	3.18 E
Haren	124	Ia	53.11N	6.38 E
Haren (Ems)	124	Jb	52.47N	7.14 E
Harer	160	Lh	9.18N	42.08 E
Harerge [3]	168	Gd	9.00N	41.30 E
Harēri Mālinwarfā	168	He	4.34N	47.21 E
Harewa	168	Gd	9.54N	41.58 E
Harfleur	124	Ce	49.30N	0.12 E
Harg	116	Hd	60.11N	18.24 E
Hargeysa	160	Lh	9.30N	44.03 E
Harghita [2]	130	Ic	46.25N	25.45 E
Harghita, Munţii-	130	Ic	46.31N	25.33 E
Harghita, Vîrful-	130	Ic	46.27N	25.35 E
Hargla	116	Lg	57.31N	26.25 E
Harhorin	152	Hb	47.13N	102.50 E
Har Hu	152	Gd	38.15N	97.40 E
Ḩarīb	144	Gg	14.56N	45.30 E
Haridwār	148	Fc	29.58N	78.10 E
Harihari	218	De	43.09S	170.34 E
Hari kurk	116	Je	59.00N	22.50 E
Harim	146	Gd	36.12N	36.31 E
Ḩarīm, Jabal al-	146	Qj	25.58N	56.14 E
Harima-Nada	156	Dd	34.30N	134.35 E
Haringey, London-	124	Bc	51.36N	0.06W
Haringvliet	124	Gc	51.49N	4.12 E
Harīrūd	140	If	37.24N	60.38 E
Härjångsfjället	116	Ea	63.01N	12.35 E
Harjavalta	114	Ff	61.19N	22.08 E
Härjedalen	116	Eb	62.20N	13.05 E
Härjehågna	116	Ec	61.44N	12.08 E
Hårkan	116	Fa	63.20N	14.55 E
Harkov	112	Je	50.00N	36.15 E
Harkovskaja oblast [3]	136	Df	49.40N	36.30 E
Harlan [Ia.-U.S.]	186	If	41.39N	95.19W
Harlan [Ky.-U.S.]	184	Fg	36.51N	83.19W
Harlan County Lake	186	Gf	40.04N	99.16W
Harlech Castle	118	Ii	52.52N	4.07W
Harlem	188	Kb	48.32N	108.47W
Harleston	124	Db	52.24N	1.18 E
Harlingen [Neth.]	122	La	53.10N	5.24 E
Harlingen [Tx.-U.S.]	182	Hf	26.11N	97.42W
Harlovka	114	Ib	68.47N	37.15 E
Harlovka	114	Ib	68.47N	37.20 E
Harlow	118	Nj	51.47N	0.08 E
Harlowton	188	Kc	46.26N	109.50W
Harlu	114	Hf	61.51N	30.54 E
Härman	130	Id	45.43N	25.41 E
Harmancık	146	Cc	39.41N	29.10 E
Harmånger	114	Df	61.56N	17.13 E
Harmanli	130	Ih	41.56N	25.54 E
Harmil	168	Gb	16.30N	40.12 E
Harmony	186	Ke	43.33N	91.59W
Harnai	148	Ee	17.48N	73.06 E
Harney Basin	174	Ge	43.15N	120.40W
Harney Lake	182	Dc	43.14N	119.07W
Harney Peak	182	Gc	44.00N	103.30W
Härnön	116	Gb	62.35N	18.00 E
Härnösand	112	Hc	62.38N	17.56 E
Haro	126	Jb	42.35N	2.51W
Haro, Cabo-	192	Dd	27.50N	110.52W
Harovsk	132	Ed	59.59N	40.11 E
Harøya	116	Bb	62.45N	6.25 E
Harøyfjorden	116	Bb	62.45N	6.35 E
Harpenden	124	Bc	51.48N	0.21W
Harper [Ks.-U.S.]	186	Gh	37.17N	98.01W
Harper [Lbr.]	160	Gh	4.22N	7.43W
Harper, Mount-	178	Kd	64.14N	143.50W
Harper Pass	218	De	42.44S	171.53 E
Harplinge	116	Eh	56.45N	12.43 E
Harqin Qi (Jinshan)	154	Ed	41.57N	118.40 E
Harqin Zuoyi Monggolzu Zizhixian	154	Ed	41.05N	119.40 E
Ḩarrat al 'Uwayrid	144	Ed	27.00N	37.30 E
Harricana	180	Jf	51.10N	79.47W
Harricana, Rivière-	184	Ha	51.10N	79.45W
Harrington-Harbour	180	Lf	50.26N	59.30W
Harris	197c	Bc	16.28N	62.10W
Harris	118	Gd	57.53N	6.55W
Harris, Lake-	184	Gk	28.46N	81.49W
Harris, Sound of-	118	Fd	57.45N	7.08W
Harrisburg	176	Le	40.16N	76.52W
Harrismith	172	De	28.18S	29.03 E
Harrison [Ar.-U.S.]	186	Jh	36.14N	93.07W
Harrison [Mi.-U.S.]	184	Ec	44.01N	84.48W
Harrison [Nb.-U.S.]	186	Ee	42.41N	103.53W
Harrison, Cape-	180	Lf	54.56N	57.55W
Harrison Bay	178	Ib	70.30N	151.30W
Harrisonburg	184	Hf	38.27N	78.54W
Harrison Lake	188	Eb	49.31N	121.59W
Harrison Point	197q	Ab	13.18N	59.38W
Harrisonville	186	Ig	38.39N	94.21W
Harrisville [Mi.-U.S.]	184	Fc	44.39N	83.17W
Harrisville [W.V.-U.S.]	184	Gf	39.13N	81.04W
Harrodsburg	184	Eg	37.46N	84.51W
Harrogate	118	Lh	54.00N	1.33W
Harrow, London-	124	Bc	51.36N	0.20W
Harry S. Truman Reservoir	186	Jg	38.00N	93.45W
Har Sai Shan	152	Gd	35.26N	97.41 E
Harsewinkel	124	Kc	51.58N	8.14 E
Harshō	166	Hc	11.17N	47.30 E
Harsim	146	Lf	33.48N	46.50 E
Harsin	146	Le	34.16N	47.35 E
Harstad	114	Db	68.47N	16.30 E
Harsvik	114	Cd	64.03N	10.02 E
Hart	184	Dd	43.42N	86.22W
Hart	180	Dc	65.51N	136.22W
Hartao	154	Gc	42.30N	122.08 E
Hartbees	158	Jk	28.45S	20.33 E
Hartberg	128	Jc	47.17N	15.58 E
Hårteigen	116	Bd	60.12N	7.04 E
Hartford [Ct.-U.S.]	176	Le	41.46N	72.41W
Hartford [Ky.-U.S.]	184	Dg	37.27N	86.55W
Hartford City	184	Ee	40.29N	85.23W
Hartington	186	He	42.37N	97.16W
Hartland	186	Nb	46.18N	67.32W
Hartland Point	118	Ij	51.02N	4.31W
Hartlepool	118	Lg	54.42N	1.11W
Hartmannberge	172	Ac	17.30S	12.23 E
Hartola	116	Lc	61.35N	26.01 E
Harts	158	Jk	28.24S	24.18 E
Hartselle	184	Dh	34.27N	86.56W
Harts Range	212	Gd	23.05S	134.55 E
Hartsville	184	Gh	34.23N	80.04W
Hartwell	184	Fh	34.21N	82.56W
Hartwell Lake	184	Fh	34.30N	82.55W
Harun, Bukit-	150	Gf	4.06N	115.46 E
Haruno	156	Ce	33.30N	133.30 E
Harves Bank (EN)	197c	Ac	16.52N	62.35W
Harvey [Austl.]	212	Df	33.05S	115.54 E
Harvey [N.D.-U.S.]	182	Hb	47.47N	99.56W
Harvey Bay	212	Kd	25.00S	153.00 E
Harwich	118	Oj	51.57N	1.17 E
Haryana [3]	148	Fc	29.30N	76.30 E
Harz	116	He	51.45N	10.30 E
Hasaki	156	Gd	35.44N	140.48 E
Hasama	156	Gb	38.42N	141.13 E
Hasan	138	Ih	42.26N	130.39 E
Ḩasanābād [Iran]	146	Ph	28.47N	54.19 E
Ḩasanābād [Iran]	146	Nd	36.28N	50.17 E
Hasan Dağı	144	Db	38.08N	34.12 E
Hasan Langī	146	Qi	27.22N	56.52 E
Hasavjurt	130	Oh	43.16N	46.35 E
Ḩasb, Sha'īb-	146	Kg	31.45N	44.17 E
Hāsbayyā	146	Ff	33.43N	33.52 E
Hasdo	148	Hd	21.44N	82.44 E
Hase	120	Db	52.41N	7.18 E
Hasekijata	130	Kg	42.08N	27.30 E
Hasenkamp	204	Cj	31.31S	59.51W
Hashaf-Rūd	144	Jb	35.58N	61.07 E
Hashimoto	156	Dd	34.19N	135.37 E
Hashtpar	146	Md	37.48N	48.55 E
Hasi Hausert	162	Ee	22.35N	14.18W
Haskell	182	He	33.10N	99.44W
Haskerland	124	Hb	52.58N	5.47 E
Haskerland-Joure	124	Hb	52.58N	5.47 E
Haskovo	130	Ih	41.56N	25.33 E
Haskovo [2]	130	Ih	41.50N	25.55 E
Hasle	116	Fi	55.11N	14.43 E
Haslemere	118	Mj	51.06N	0.43W
Haslev	116	Di	55.20N	11.58 E
Hăşmaşu Mare, Vîrful-	130	Ic	46.30N	25.50 E
Haspengouws Plateau/ Hesbaye	122	Ld	50.35N	5.10 E
Haspres	124	Fd	50.15N	3.25 E
Hassa	146	Gd	36.50N	36.29 E
Hassan	148	Ff	13.00N	76.05 E
Hassberge	120	Gf	50.12N	10.29 E
Hassela	116	De	62.07N	16.42 E
Hassel Sound	180	Ha	78.30N	99.00W
Hasselt	122	Ld	50.56N	5.20 E
Hassi Bel Guebbour	162	Id	28.30N	6.41 E
Hassi el Ghella	126	Ki	35.27N	1.03W
Hassi Mameche	126	Mi	35.51N	0.04 E
Hassi Messaoud	160	He	31.43N	6.03 E
Hassi R'mel	162	Hc	32.55N	3.16 E
Hassi Serouenout	162	Ie	24.00N	7.50 E
Hässleholm	114	Ch	56.09N	13.46 E
Hasslö	116	Fh	56.05N	15.25 E
Haßloch	124	Ke	49.23N	8.16 E
Hastière	124	Gd	50.13N	4.50 E
Hastière-Hastière par-delà	124	Gd	50.13N	4.50 E
Hastière-par-delà, Hastière	124	Gd	50.13N	4.50 E
Hastings [Bar.]	197q	Ab	13.04N	59.35W
Hastings [Eng.-U.K.]	118	Nk	50.51N	0.36 E
Hastings [Mi.-U.S.]	184	Ed	42.39N	85.17W
Hastings [Mn.-U.S.]	186	Jd	44.44N	92.51W
Hastings [Nb.-U.S.]	186	Hc	40.35N	98.23W
Hastings [N.Z.]	216	Eg	39.38S	176.50 E
Hästveda	116	Eh	56.16N	13.56 E
Hašuri	132	Mi	41.59N	43.33 E
Hasvik	114	Fa	70.29N	22.09 E
Ḩasy al Qaţţār	164	Ec	30.14N	27.11 E
Ḩasy Hague	164	Bd	26.17N	10.31 E
Hat'ae-Do	154	Hg	34.23N	125.17 E
Hatanga	142	Mb	71.58N	102.30 E
Hatanga	140	Mb	72.55N	106.00 E
Hatch	186	Cj	32.40N	107.09W
Hatches Creek	212	Hd	20.56S	135.12 E
Haţeg	130	Fd	45.37N	22.57 E
Hatgal	152	Ha	50.26N	100.09 E
Ḩaţībah, Ra's-	144	Ee	21.59N	38.55 E
Ha Tien	148	Kf	10.23N	104.29 E
Ha Tinh	148	Le	18.20N	105.54 E
Hato Mayor	194	Md	18.46N	69.15W
Ḩattā, Jabal-	146	Qj	24.45N	56.04 E
Hattem	124	Ib	52.28N	6.06 E
Hatten	124	Ka	53.03N	8.23 E
Hatteras, Cape-	174	Lf	35.13N	75.32W
Hatteras Inlet	184	Jh	35.00N	75.40W
Hatteras Island	182	Ld	35.25N	75.30W
Hattfjelldal	114	Cd	65.36N	14.00 E
Hattiesburg	182	Je	31.19N	89.16W
Hattingen	124	Jc	51.24N	7.10 E
Hatu Iti, Ile-	216	Ma	8.42S	140.43W
Hatutaa, Ile-	208	Me	7.30S	140.38W
Hatvan	120	Pi	47.40N	19.41 E
Hat Yai	148	Kg	7.01N	100.27 E
Hatyrka	138	Md	62.03N	175.05 E
Haubourdin	124	Ed	50.36N	2.59 E
Hauge	114	Bg	58.21N	6.17 E
Haugesund	112	Gd	59.25N	5.18 E
Hauho	116	Kc	61.10N	24.33 E
Hauhungaroa Range	218	Fc	38.40S	175.35 E
Haukeligrend	114	Bg	59.51N	7.11 E
Haukipudas	114	Fd	65.15N	25.28 E
Haukivesi	110	Ic	62.05N	28.30 E
Haukivuori	116	Lb	62.01N	27.13 E
Hauraha	219a	Ed	10.49S	161.57 E
Hauraki Gulf	216	Eg	36.35S	175.00 E
Hauroko, Lake-	218	Bf	45.55S	167.20 E
Hausa	162	Ed	27.06N	11.01W
Hausruck	128	Hb	48.07N	13.35 E
Haut, Isle au-	184	Mc	44.03N	68.38W
Haut Atlas=High Atlas (EN)	158	Ge	32.00N	6.00W
Haute-Champagne	124	Ge	49.18N	4.15 E
Haute-Corse [3]	122a	Aa	42.30N	9.00 E
Haute-Garonne [3]	122	Hk	43.25N	1.30 E
Haute-Guinée [3]	166	Dc	11.30N	10.00W
Haute-Kotto [3]	168	Cd	7.00N	23.00 E
Haute-Loire [3]	122	Ji	45.05N	3.50 E
Haute-Marne [3]	122	Lf	48.05N	5.10 E
Hauterive	184	Ma	49.11N	68.16W
Hautes-Alpes [3]	122	Mj	44.40N	6.30 E
Haute-Sangha [3]	168	Be	4.30N	16.00 E
Haute-Saône [3]	122	Mg	47.40N	6.10 E
Haute-Saône, Plateau de-	122	Lg	47.50N	6.00 E
Haute-Savoie [3]	122	Mi	46.00N	6.20 E
Hautes Fagnes/Hoge Venen	120	Bf	50.30N	6.00 E
Hautes-Pyrénées [3]	122	Gk	43.00N	0.10 E
Haute-Vienne [3]	122	Hi	45.50N	1.10 E
Haut-Mbomou [3]	168	Dd	6.00N	26.00 E
Hautmont	122	Jd	50.15N	3.56 E
Haut-Ogooué [3]	170	Bc	2.00S	14.00 E
Haut-Rhin [3]	122	Ng	48.00N	7.20 E
Hauts-Bassins [3]	166	Ec	12.30N	4.30W
Hauts-de-Seine [3]	122	If	48.50N	2.11 E
Hauts Plateaux	158	He	34.00N	0.01 E
Haut-Zaïre [2]	170	Eb	2.30N	25.30 E
Hauula	221a	Db	21.36N	157.54W
Hauz-Han	135	Cf	37.16N	61.15 E
Hauz-Hanskoje vodohranilišče	135	Cf	37.10N	61.20 E
Havana	186	Kf	40.18N	90.04W
Havana (EN)=La Habana	176	Kg	23.08N	82.22W
Havant and Waterloo	118	Mk	50.51N	0.59W
Havast	135	Gd	40.16N	68.51 E
Havasu, Lake-	188	Hi	34.30N	114.20W
Havel	120	Hd	52.53N	11.58 E
Havelange	124	Hd	50.23N	5.14 E
Havelange-Méan	124	Hd	50.22N	5.20 E
Havelberg	120	Id	52.49N	12.05 E
Havelland	120	Id	52.25N	12.45 E
Havelländisches Luch	120	Id	52.40N	12.40 E
Havelock [N.C.-U.S.]	184	Ih	34.53N	76.54W
Havelock [N.Z.]	218	Ed	41.17S	173.46 E
Havelock North	218	Gc	39.40S	176.53 E
Havelte	124	Ib	52.46N	6.16 E
Haverfordwest	118	Ij	51.49N	4.58W
Haverhill [Eng.-U.K.]	118	Ni	52.05N	0.26 E
Haverhill [Ma.-U.S.]	184	Ld	42.47N	71.05W
Havering, London-	124	Cc	51.36N	0.11 E
Havířov	120	Og	49.48N	18.27 E
Havlíčkův Brod	120	Lg	49.36N	15.34 E
Havøysund	114	Fa	71.03N	24.40 E
Havran	146	Bc	39.33N	27.06 E
Havre	176	Ie	48.33N	109.41W
Havre, Le-	112	Gf	49.30N	0.08 E
Havre-Saint-Pierre	176	Md	50.15N	63.36W
Havsa	130	Jh	41.33N	26.49 E
Havza	146	Fb	41.05N	35.45 E
Hawaii [2]	210	Kb	24.00N	167.00W
Hawaiian Islands	208	Kb	24.00N	167.00W
Hawaiian Ridge (EN)	106	Kg	24.00N	165.00W
Hawaii Island	208	Lc	19.30N	155.30W
Ḩawallī	144	Gd	29.19N	48.02 E
Ḩawār	146	Nj	25.40N	50.45 E
Hawarden	218	Ee	42.56S	172.39 E
Ḩawashīyah, Wādī-	146	Eh	28.31N	32.58 E
Hawaymī, Sha'īb al-	146	Kg	30.58N	44.15 E
Hawd	158	Lh	7.40N	47.43 E
Ḩawḑ Al Waqf	146	Ei	26.03N	32.22 E
Hawea, Lake-	218	Cf	44.30S	169.20 E
Hawera	218	Dg	39.35S	174.17 E
Hawi	210	Lb	20.14N	155.50W
Hawick	118	Kf	55.25N	2.47W
Ḩawīzah, Hawr al-	146	Lg	31.35N	47.38 E
Hawkdun Range	218	Cf	44.50S	170.00 E
Hawke Bay	216	Eg	39.25S	177.20 E
Hawke Harbour	180	Lf	53.01N	55.50W
Hawker	212	Hf	31.53S	138.25 E
Hawkes, Mount-	222	Rg	83.55S	56.05W
Hawke's Bay [2]	218	Gc	39.30S	176.40 E
Hawkesbury	184	Jc	45.36N	74.37W
Hawkhurst	124	Cc	51.02N	0.30 E
Hawkinsville	184	Fi	32.17N	83.28W
Hawksbill	184	Hf	38.33N	78.23W
Hawk Springs	186	Mf	41.48N	104.09W
Ḩawmat as Sūq	162	Jc	33.53N	10.51 E
Hawng Tuk	148	Jd	20.28N	99.56 E
Ḩawrā'	168	Hb	15.43N	48.18 E
Ḩawrān, Wādī-	144	Fc	33.58N	42.34 E
Ḩawsh 'Isá	146	Dg	30.55N	30.17 E
Hawthorne	182	Dd	38.32N	118.38W
Hawthorne, Mount-	222	Pf	72.10S	98.39W
Haxtun	186	Ef	40.39N	102.38W
Hay	210	Fh	34.30S	144.51 E
Hay	174	Hc	60.51N	115.44W
Hayachine-San	156	Gb	39.34N	141.29 E
Hayakita	156a	Bb	42.45N	141.48 E
Hayange	122	Me	49.20N	6.03 E
Hayasaki-Seto	156	Be	32.34N	130.10 E
Hayasui-no-Seto	154	Kh	33.20N	132.00 E
Hayato	156	Bf	31.45N	130.43 E
Haybān	168	Ec	11.13N	30.31 E
Haybān, Jabal-	168	Ec	11.15N	30.31 E
Hayden	188	Jj	33.00N	110.47W
Hayes [Man.-Can.]	180	Ie	57.00N	92.15W
Hayes [N.W.T.-Can.]	180	Hc	67.20N	95.02W
Hayes, Mount-	178	Jd	63.37N	146.43W
Hayes Halvø=Hayes Peninsula (EN)	224	Od	77.40N	64.30W
Hayes Peninsula (EN)= Hayes Halvø	224	Od	77.40N	64.30W
Ḩayl	146	Qj	24.33N	56.06 E
Hayl, Wādī al-	146	He	34.47N	39.18 E
Hayling Island	124	Bd	50.48N	0.58W
Haymana	146	Ec	39.27N	32.30 E
Haymana Platosu	146	Ec	39.25N	32.45 E
Hayrabolu	146	Bb	41.12N	27.06 E
Ḩayrān	164	Hf	16.02N	42.49 E
Hay River	176	Hc	60.51N	115.40W
Hay River	212	Hd	25.00S	138.00 E
Hayrūt	168	Ib	15.59N	52.09 E
Hays	182	Hd	38.53N	99.20W
Hay Springs	186	Ee	42.41N	102.41W
Haystack Peak	188	Ig	39.50N	113.55W
Hayward [Ca.-U.S.]	188	Dh	37.40N	122.05W
Hayward [Wi.-U.S.]	186	Kc	46.01N	91.29W
Haywards Heath	124	Bc	51.00N	0.06W
HaZafon [3]	146	Ff	32.50N	35.20 E
Hazar, Wādī-	168	Hb	17.50N	49.07 E
Hazarasp	135	Cd	41.19N	61.08 E
Hazard	184	Fg	37.15N	83.12W
Hazar Gölü	146	Hc	38.30N	39.25 E
Hazārībāgh	148	Hd	23.59N	85.21 E
Hazebrouck	122	Id	50.43N	2.32 E
Hazelton	180	Ee	55.15N	127.40W
Hazen	186	Fc	47.18N	101.38W
Hazen Strait	180	Ga	77.15N	110.00W
Ḩazeva	146	Fg	30.48N	35.15 E
Hazlehurst [Ga.-U.S.]	184	Fj	31.52N	82.36W
Hazlehurst [Ms.-U.S.]	186	Kk	31.52N	90.24W
Hazleton	184	Je	40.58N	76.00W
Hazlett, Lake-	212	Fd	21.30S	128.50 E
Hazrah, Ra's al-	146	Nj	24.22N	51.36 E
Hazro	146	Ic	38.15N	40.47 E
Heacham	124	Cb	52.55N	0.29 E
Headley	124	Bc	51.07N	0.49W
Healdsburg	188	Dg	38.37N	122.52W
Heanor	124	Aa	53.00N	1.18W
Heard Island	186	Ff	53.00S	73.35 E

Index Symbols

[1] Independent Nation
[2] State, Region
[3] District, County
[4] Municipality
[5] Colony, Dependency
Continent
Physical Region
Historical or Cultural Region
Mount, Mountain
Volcano
Hill
Mountains, Mountain Range
Hills, Escarpment
Plateau, Upland
Pass, Gap
Plain, Lowland
Delta
Salt Flat
Valley, Canyon
Crater, Cave
Karst Features
Depression
Polder
Desert, Dunes
Forest, Woods
Heath, Steppe
Oasis
Cape, Point
Coast, Beach
Cliff
Peninsula
Isthmus
Sandbank
Island
Atoll
Rock, Reef
Islands, Archipelago
Rocks, Reefs
Coral Reef
Well, Spring
Geyser
River, Stream
Waterfall, Rapids
River Mouth, Estuary
Lake
Salt Lake
Intermittent Lake
Reservoir
Swamp, Pond
Canal
Glacier
Ice Shelf, Pack Ice
Ocean
Sea
Gulf, Bay
Strait, Fjord
Lagoon
Bank
Seamount
Tablemount
Ridge
Shelf
Basin
Escarpment, Sea Scarp
Fracture
Trench, Abyss
National Park, Reserve
Point of Interest
Recreation Site
Cave, Cavern
Historic Site
Ruins
Wall, Walls
Church, Abbey
Temple
Scientific Station
Railway station
Airport
Port
Military installation
Lighthouse
Mine
Tunnel
Dam, Bridge

Hearne 186 Hk 30.53N 96.36W
Hearst 180 Jg 49.41N 83.40W
Heart River 186 Fc 46.47N 100.51W
Heathrow Airport London 124 Bc 51.28N 0.30W
Hebbronville 186 Gm 27.18N 98.41W
Hebei Sheng (Ho-pei Sheng) =Hopeh (EN) [2] 152 Kd 39.00N 116.00 E
Heber City 188 Jf 40.30N 111.25W
Hebi 152 Jd 35.53N 114.09 E
Hebian 152 Jd 38.35N 113.06 E
Hebiji 154 Cf 36.00N 114.08 E
Hebrides 110 Fd 57.00N 6.30W
Hebrides, Sea of the- 118 Ge 57.00N 7.00W
Hebron [N.D.-U.S.] 186 Ec 46.54N 102.03W
Hebron [Newf.-Can.] 180 Le 58.15N 62.35W
Heby 116 Ge 59.56N 16.53 E
Hecate Strait 180 Ef 53.20N 131.00W
Hecelchakán 192 Ng 20.10N 90.08W
Hechi (Jnchengjiang) 152 Ig 24.44N 108.02 E
Hechingen 120 Eh 48.21N 8.59 E
Hechuan 152 Ie 30.07N 106.15 E
Hecla 186 Gd 45.43N 98.09W
Hecla and Griper Bay 180 Ga 76.00N 111.30W
Hecla Island 186 Ha 51.08N 96.45W
Heddalsvatnet 116 Ce 59.30N 9.15 E
Hede 114 Ce 62.25N 13.30 E
Hede → Sheyang 154 Fh 33.47N 120.15 E
Hedemarken 116 Dd 60.50N 11.20 E
Hedemora 114 Df 60.17N 15.59 E
Hedensted 116 Ci 55.46N 9.42 E
Hedesunda 114 Df 60.25N 17.00 E
Hedesunda fjärdarna 116 Gd 60.20N 17.00 E
Hedmark [2] 114 Cf 61.30N 11.45 E
Hedo-Misaki 156b Bb 26.52N 128.16 E
Heemskerk 124 Gb 52.30N 4.42 E
Heemstede 124 Gb 52.21N 4.37 E
Heerenberg, Bergh 's- 124 Ic 51.53N 6.16 E
Heerenveen 122 Lb 52.57N 5.55 E
Heerhugowaard 124 Gb 52.40N 4.50 E
Heerlen 122 Ld 50.54N 5.59 E
Ḥefa [3] 146 Ff 32.35N 35.00 E
Ḥefa = Haifa (EN) 142 Ff 32.50N 35.00 E
Hefei 142 Nf 31.47N 117.15 E
Hefeng 152 Jf 29.49N 110.01 E
Hegang 142 Pe 47.20N 130.12 E
Hegau 120 Ei 47.50N 8.45 E
Hegura Jima 152 Od 37.50N 136.55 E
Heide 120 Fb 54.12N 9.06 E
Heidelberg 120 Eg 49.25N 8.42 E
Heidenheim an der Brenz 120 Gh 48.41N 10.09 E
Heidenreichstein 128 Jb 48.52N 15.07 E
Hei-Gawa 156 Gb 39.38N 141.58 E
Heigun-Tō 156 Ce 33.47N 132.15 E
Hei He 152 Hd 38.15N 100.15 E
Heihe → Aihui 142 Od 50.13N 127.26 E
Heilbron 172 De 27.21S 27.58 E
Heilbronn 120 Fg 49.08N 9.13 E
Heiligenblut 128 Gd 47.02N 12.50 E
Heiligenhafen 120 Gb 54.22N 10.59 E
Heiligenhaus 124 Ic 51.19N 6.58 E
Heiligenstadt 120 Ge 51.23N 10.08 E
Heilinzi 154 Ib 44.33N 126.41 E
Heilong Jiang 140 Qd 52.56N 141.10 E
Heilongjiang Sheng (Hei-lung-chiang Sheng)= Heilungkiang (EN) [2] 152 Mb 48.00N 128.00 E
Heiloo 124 Gb 52.36N 4.43 E
Hei-lung-chiang Sheng → Heilongjiang Sheng=Heilungkiang (EN) [2] 152 Mb 48.00N 128.00 E
Heilungkiang (EN)= Heilongjiang Sheng (Hei-lung-chiang Sheng) [2] 152 Mb 48.00N 128.00 E
Heilungkiang (EN)=Hei-lung-chiang Sheng → Heilongjiang Sheng [2] 152 Mb 48.00N 128.00 E
Heimæy 114a Bc 63.26N 20.17W
Heimbach 124 Id 50.38N 6.29 E
Heimdal 114 Ce 63.21N 10.22 E
Heimsheim 124 Kf 48.48N 8.51 E
Heinävesi 114 Ge 62.26N 28.36 E
Heinola 114 Gf 61.13N 26.02 E
Heinsberg 124 Ic 51.04N 6.05 E
Heishan 154 Gd 41.42N 122.07 E
Heishan Xia 152 Hd 37.18N 104.39 E
Heishui [China] 154 Ec 42.06N 119.22 E
Heishui [China] 152 He 32.03N 103.05 E
Heist, Knokke- 122 Jc 51.21N 3.15 E
Heist-op-den-Berg 124 Gc 51.05N 4.43 E
Hei-Zaki 156 Hb 39.39N 142.00 E
Hejgijaha 154 Pd 65.27N 72.50 E
Hejian 154 De 38.27N 116.05 E
Hejing 152 Ec 42.18N 86.18 E
Hejjaha 134 Kb 68.18N 62.32 E
Hekimhan 146 Gc 38.49N 37.56 E
Hekinan 156 Ed 34.52N 136.58 E
Hekla 110 Ec 64.00N 19.40W
Hekou 154 Ci 31.20N 114.25 E
Hekou → Yanshan 154 Dj 28.18N 117.41 E
Hel 120 Ob 54.37N 18.48 E
Helagsfjället 114 Ce 62.55N 12.27 E
Helan 152 Id 38.35N 106.16 E
Helan Shan 152 Id 39.00N 106.00 E
Helden's Point 197c Ab 17.24N 62.50W
Helena [Ar.-U.S.] 182 Ie 34.32N 90.35W
Helena [Guy.] 202 Gb 6.41N 57.55W
Helena [Mt.-U.S.] 176 He 46.36N 112.01W
Helen Glacier 222 Ge 66.40S 93.55 E
Helen Reef 208 Ed 2.53N 131.47 E
Helensburgh 118 Ie 56.01N 4.44W
Helensville 218 Fb 36.40S 174.27 E
Helgaå 116 Fi 55.53N 14.08 E
Helgasjön 116 Fh 56.55N 14.45 E
Helgeland [2] 114 Cd 66.15N 13.05 E
Helgoland 120 Db 54.12N 7.53 E
Helgoländer Bucht 120 Eb 54.10N 8.04 E
Helikón Óros 130 Fk 38.20N 22.50 E
Helixi 154 Ei 30.39N 119.01 E
Heljulja 116 Nc 61.37N 30.38 E
Hella 114a Bc 63.50N 20.24W
Hellberge 120 Hd 52.34N 11.17 E
Hèlleh 146 Nh 29.10N 50.40 E
Hellendoorn 122 Mb 52.24N 6.26 E
Hellendoorn-Nijverdal 124 Ib 52.22N 6.27 E
Hellenic Trough (EN) 110 Ii 35.00N 24.00 E
Hellental 124 Id 50.29N 6.26 E
Hellesylt 114 Be 62.05N 6.54 E
Hellin 126 Kf 38.31N 1.41W
Hells Canyon 182 Db 45.20N 116.45W
Hellweg 124 Kc 51.40N 8.00 E
Helmand [3] 144 Jc 31.00N 64.00 E
Helmand 140 If 31.12N 61.34 E
Helme 120 He 51.20N 11.20 E
Helmeringhausen 172 Be 25.54S 16.57 E
Helmond 122 Lc 51.29N 5.40 E
Helmsdale 118 Jc 58.07N 3.40W
Helmsdale 118 Jc 58.10N 3.40W
Helmstedt 120 Hd 52.14N 11.02 E
Helong 152 Mc 42.32N 129.00 E
Helpe Majeure 124 Fd 50.11N 3.47 E
Helpringham 124 Bb 52.56N 0.18W
Helpter Berge 120 Jc 53.30N 13.36 E
Helsingborg 112 Hd 56.03N 12.42 E
Helsinge 116 Eh 56.01N 12.12 E
Helsingfors/Helsinki 112 Ic 60.10N 24.58 E
Helsingør 114 Ch 56.02N 12.37 E
Helsinki/Helsingfors 112 Ic 60.10N 24.58 E
Helska, Mierzeja- 120 Ob 54.45N 18.39 E
Helston 118 Hk 50.05N 5.16W
Helvecia 204 Bj 31.06S 60.05W
Helwân (EN)=Ḥulwān 164 Fd 29.51N 31.20 E
Ḥemār 146 Qg 31.42N 57.31 E
Hemčik 138 Ef 51.40N 92.10 E
Hemel Hempstead 118 Mj 51.46N 0.28W
Hemer 124 Jc 51.23N 7.46 E
Hemnesberget 114 Cc 66.14N 13.38 E
Hemsby 124 Db 52.41N 1.42 E
Hemse 116 Hg 57.14N 18.22 E
Hemsedal 116 Cd 60.50N 8.40 E
Hemsö 116 Ee 62.45N 18.05 E
Hen 116 Dd 60.13N 10.14 E
Henan 152 He 34.33N 101.55 E
Hen and Chickens Islands 218 Fa 35.55S 174.45 E
Henan Sheng (Ho-nan Sheng)=Honan (EN) [2] 152 Je 34.00N 114.00 E
Henares 126 Id 40.24N 3.30W
Henashi-Zaki 156 Fa 40.37N 139.51 E
Henbury 212 Gd 24.35S 133.15 E
Hendaye 122 Ek 43.22N 1.47W
Hendek 146 Db 40.48N 30.45 E
Henderson [Arg.] 204 Bm 36.18S 61.43W
Henderson [Ky.-U.S.] 184 Dg 37.50N 87.35W
Henderson [N.C.-U.S.] 184 Hg 36.20N 78.25W
Henderson [Nv.-U.S.] 182 Dd 36.02N 115.01W
Henderson [Tx.-U.S.] 186 Ij 32.09N 94.48W
Henderson Island 208 Og 24.22S 128.19W
Henderson Seamount (EN) 182 Df 25.34N 119.33W
Hendersonville [N.C.-U.S.] 184 Fh 35.19N 82.28W
Hendersonville [Tn.-U.S.] 184 Dg 36.18N 86.37W
Hendījān 146 Mg 30.14N 49.43 E
Hendorābī, Jazīreh-ye- 146 Oi 26.40N 53.37 E
Hendrik Verwoerddam 172 Df 30.45S 25.33 E
Hengām, Jazīreh-ye- 146 Pi 26.39N 55.53 E
Hengduan Shan 140 Lg 27.30N 99.00 E
Hengelo 122 Mb 52.15N 6.45 E
Hengshan [China] 152 Id 37.51N 109.20 E
Hengshan [China] 152 Jf 27.16N 112.51 E
Hengshan [China] 154 Kb 45.24N 131.01 E
Heng Shan [China] 152 Jf 27.18N 112.41 E
Heng Shan [China] 152 Jd 39.42N 113.45 E
Hengshui 152 Kd 37.39N 115.46 E
Hengxian 152 Ig 22.46N 109.15 E
Hengyang 142 Ng 26.56N 112.35 E
Henik Lakes 180 Hd 61.05N 97.20W
Hénin-Liétard 122 Id 50.25N 2.56 E
Henley-on-Thames 124 Bc 51.32N 0.54W
Hennan 114 De 62.02N 15.54 E
Hennan 116 Fb 62.05N 15.45 E
Hennebont 122 Cg 47.48N 3.17W
Hennef (Sieg) 124 Jd 50.47N 7.17 E
Hennigsdorf bei Berlin 120 Jd 52.38N 13.12 E
Henrietta Maria, Cape - 180 Je 55.09N 82.19W
Henry, Mount- 188 Hb 48.53N 115.31W
Henry Bay 222 Ie 66.40S 120.40 E
Henryetta 186 Ii 35.27N 95.59W
Henry Kater Peninsula 180 Kc 69.15N 67.30W
Henry Mountains 188 Jh 37.55N 110.50W
Henrys Fork River 188 Je 43.25N 111.56W
Henslow, Cape- 219a Ec 9.56S 160.38 E
Hentej 140 Me 48.50N 109.00 E
Hentiesbaai 172 Ad 22.08S 14.18 E
Henzada 142 Lh 17.38N 95.28 E
Heping → Yanhe 152 If 28.31N 108.28 E
Heppenheim (Bergstraße) 124 Ke 49.38N 8.39 E
Heppner 188 Fd 45.21N 119.33W
Hepu (Lianzhou) 152 Ig 21.40N 109.12 E
Hequ 152 Jd 39.22N 111.15 E
Herakol Daği 146 Id 37.45N 42.35 E
Heralds Cays 212 Jc 16.55S 149.10 E
Herāt 142 If 34.20N 62.12 E
Herāt [3] 144 Jc 34.30N 62.00 E
Hérault [3] 122 Jk 43.40N 3.30 E
Hérault 122 Jk 43.17N 3.26 E
Herbert [N.Z.] 218 Df 45.13S 170.46 E
Herbert [Sask.-Can.] 188 La 50.26N 107.12W
Herberton 212 Jc 17.23S 145.23 E
Herbert River 212 Jc 18.32S 146.17 E
Herbiers, Les- 122 Eh 46.52N 1.01W
Herborn 120 Ef 50.41N 8.19 E
Herby 120 Of 50.45N 18.40 E
Hercegnovi 130 Bg 42.27N 18.32 E
Hercegovina 110 Hg 43.00N 17.50 E
Hercegovina 128 Lg 43.00N 17.50 E
Herdubreid 114a Cb 65.11N 16.21W
Heredia 190 Hf 10.00N 84.07W
Heredia [3] 194 Fh 10.30N 84.00W
Hereford 118 Ki 52.15N 2.50W
Hereford [Eng.-U.K.] 118 Ki 52.04N 2.43W
Hereford [Tx.-U.S.] 182 Ge 34.49N 102.24W
Hereford and Worcester [3] 118 Ki 52.10N 2.35W
Hereheretue Atoll 208 Mf 19.54S 144.58W
Hereke 130 Mi 40.48N 29.39 E
Herekino 218 Ea 35.16S 173.13 E
Herent 124 Gd 50.54N 4.40 E
Herentals 124 Gc 51.11N 4.50 E
Herfølge 116 Ei 55.25N 12.10 E
Herford 120 Ed 52.08N 8.41 E
Héricourt 122 Mg 47.35N 6.45 E
Herington 186 Hg 38.40N 96.57W
Heriot 216 Ci 45.51S 169.16 E
Heris 146 Lc 38.14N 47.07 E
Herisau 128 Dc 47.24N 9.16 E
Herk 124 Hd 50.58N 5.07 E
Herk-de-Stad 124 Hd 50.56N 5.10 E
Herkimer 184 Jd 43.02N 74.59W
Herlen He 152 Kb 48.48N 117.00 E
Hermagor 128 Hd 46.37N 13.22 E
Hermanas 192 Id 27.14N 101.14W
Herma Ness 118 Ma 60.50N 0.54W
Hermano Peak 186 Bh 37.17N 108.48W
Hermansverk 116 Bc 61.11N 6.51 E
Hermanus 172 Bf 34.25S 19.16 E
Hermeskeil 124 Ie 49.39N 6.57 E
Hermiston 188 Fd 45.51N 119.17W
Hermitage 218 De 43.44S 170.05 E
Hermit Islands 208 Fe 1.32S 145.05 E
Hermosa de Santa Rosa, Sierra- 192 Id 28.00N 101.45W
Hermosillo 176 Hg 29.04N 110.58W
Hermoso Campo 204 Bh 27.36S 61.21W
Hernád 120 Qh 48.00N 20.58 E
Hernandarias 206 Jc 25.22S 54.45W
Hernández [Arg.] 204 Bk 32.21S 60.02W
Hernández [Mex.] 192 Hf 23.02N 102.02W
Hernani 126 Ka 43.16N 1.58W
Herne 120 De 51.33N 7.13 E
Herne Bay 118 Oj 51.23N 1.08 E
Herning 112 Gd 56.08N 8.59 E
Heroica Alvarado 192 Lh 18.46N 95.46W
Heroica Tlapacoyan 192 Kh 19.58N 97.13W
Heroica Zitácuaro 192 Ih 19.24N 100.22W
Hérouville-Saint-Clair 124 Be 49.12N 0.19W
Herowābād 146 Md 37.37N 48.32 E
Herradura 204 Ch 26.29S 58.18W
Herre 116 Ce 59.06N 9.34 E
Herrera 204 Ck 32.26S 58.38W
Herrera [3] 194 Gj 7.54N 80.38W
Herrera del Duque 126 Ge 39.10N 5.03W
Herrera de Pisuerga 126 Hb 42.36N 4.20W
Herrero, Punta- 192 Ph 19.10N 87.30W
Herrljunga 116 Ef 58.05N 13.02 E
Hers 122 Hk 43.18N 1.33 E
Herschel 180 Dc 69.35N 139.05W
Herselt 124 Gc 51.03N 4.53 E
Herserange 124 He 49.31N 5.47 E
Hershey 184 Ie 40.17N 76.39W
Hersilia 204 Bj 30.00S 61.51W
Herson 112 Jf 46.38N 32.35 E
Hersonesski, mys- 132 Hg 44.33N 33.25 E
Hersonskaja oblast [3] 136 Df 46.40N 33.30 E
Herstal 120 Cf 50.40N 5.38 E
Herten 124 Jc 51.36N 7.08 E
Hertford 118 Mj 51.48N 0.05W
Hertford 118 Mj 51.50N 0.05W
Hertfordshire [3] 118 Mj 51.45N 0.20W
Hertogenbosch, 's- /Den Bosch 122 Lc 51.41N 5.19 E
Hertugen Af Orleans Land 179 Jc 78.15N 21.12W
Hervás 126 Gd 40.16N 5.51W
Herve 124 Hd 50.38N 5.48 E
Herve, Plateau van-/Herveland 124 Hd 50.40N 5.50 E
Herveland/Herve, Plateau van- 124 Hd 50.40N 5.50 E
Hervey Bay 212 Ke 25.15S 152.50 E
Herzberg 120 Je 51.41N 13.14 E
Herzberg am Harz 120 Ge 51.39N 10.20 E
Herzebrock 124 Kc 51.53N 8.15 E
Herzele 124 Fd 50.53N 3.53 E
Herzliyya 146 Ff 32.10N 34.51 E
Herzogenrath 124 Id 50.52N 6.06 E
Herzog-Ernst-Bucht (Vahsel Bay) 222 Af 77.48S 34.39W
Hesāmābād 146 Me 35.52N 48.25 E
Hesbaye/Haspengouws Plateau 122 Ld 50.35N 5.10 E
Hesdin 122 Id 50.22N 2.02 E
Hesel 124 Ja 53.18N 7.36 E
Heshi 146 Md 37.30N 48.15 E
Heshun 152 Jd 37.18N 113.32 E
Hesse (EN)=Hessen [2] 120 Ff 50.30N 9.15 E
Hesselberg 120 Gg 49.05N 10.35 E
Hesselø 116 Dh 56.10N 11.45 E
Hessen=Hesse (EN) [2] 120 Ff 50.30N 9.15 E
Hess Tablemount (EN) 208 Jc 17.50N 174.15W
Heta 138 Eb 71.35N 99.45 E
Heta 140 Mb 71.54N 102.00 E
Hettange-Grande 124 Ie 49.24N 6.09 E
Hettinger 186 Ec 46.00N 102.39W
Heuberg 120 Eh 48.06N 8.55 E
Heuchin 124 Ed 50.28N 2.16 E
Heuru 219a Ed 10.12S 161.25 E
Hève, Cap de la- 122 Ge 49.30N 0.04 E
Heves 120 Qi 47.36N 20.17 E
Heves [2] 120 Qi 47.50N 20.15 E
Hexham 118 Kg 54.58N 2.06W
Hexi 152 Hf 27.44N 102.09 E
Hexian 154 Ei 31.43N 118.22 E
Hexian (Babu) 152 Jg 24.28N 111.34 E
Hexigten Qi (Jingfeng) 152 Kc 43.15N 117.31 E
Heydarābād 146 Kd 37.06N 45.27 E
Heysham 118 Kg 54.02N 2.54W
Heyuan 152 Jg 23.41N 114.43 E
Heywood 212 Ig 38.08S 141.38 E
Heze (Caozhou) 152 Kd 35.14N 115.28 E
Hezuo 152 Hd 35.02N 102.57 E
Hialeah 184 Gm 25.49N 80.17W
Hiawatha 186 Ig 39.51N 95.32W
Hibara-Ko 156 Gc 37.42N 140.03 E
Hibbing 182 Ib 47.25N 92.56W
Hibernia Reef 212 Eb 12.00S 123.25 E
Hibiki-Nada 156 Bd 34.15N 130.45 E
Hibiny 114 Hc 67.40N 33.35 E
Hiburi-Jima 156 Ce 33.10N 132.18 E
Hickman 184 Cg 36.34N 89.11W
Hickory 184 Gh 35.44N 81.21W
Hick's Cay 194 Ce 17.39N 88.08W
Hida-Gawa 156 Ed 35.25N 137.03 E
Hidaka [Jap.] 154 Qc 42.53N 142.28 E
Hidaka [Jap.] 156 Dd 35.28N 134.47 E
Hidaka-Gawa 156 De 33.53N 135.08 E
Hidaka Sanmyaku 154 Qc 42.25N 142.50 E
Hidalgo [2] 190 Ed 20.30N 99.00W
Hidalgo [Mex.] 190 Ed 24.15N 99.26W
Hidalgo [Mex.] 192 Jd 27.47N 99.52W
Hidalgo del Parral 176 Ig 26.56N 105.40W
Hida-Sanchi 156 Ec 36.20N 137.00 E
Hida-Sanmyaku 154 Nf 36.10N 137.30 E
Hiddensee 120 Jb 54.33N 13.07 E
Hidra 116 Bf 58.15N 6.35 E
Hidrolândia 204 Hc 16.58S 49.16W
Hidrolina 204 Hb 14.37S 49.25W
Hieflau 128 Ic 47.36N 14.44 E
Hiei-Zan 156 Dd 35.05N 135.50 E
Hienghène 216 Cd 20.35S 164.56 E
Hierro 158 Ff 27.45N 18.00W
Higashi 156b Bb 26.38N 128.08 E
Higashihiroshima 156 Cd 34.25N 132.43 E
Higashi-izu 156 Fd 34.48N 139.02 E
Higashi-matsuyama 156 Fc 36.02N 139.22 E
Higashimuroran 156a Bb 42.21N 141.02 E
Higashine 154 Pe 38.26N 140.24 E
Higashiōsaka 156 Dd 34.40N 135.37 E
Higashi Rishiri 156a Ba 45.16N 141.15 E
Higashi-Shina-Kai=East China Sea (EN) 140 Og 29.00N 125.00 E
Higgins 186 Fh 36.07N 100.02W
Higham Ferrers 124 Bb 52.18N 0.35W
High Atlas (EN)=Haut Atlas 158 Ge 32.00N 6.00W
Highland [3] 118 Id 57.30N 5.00W
Highland Park 186 Me 42.11N 87.48W
High Level 180 Fe 58.30N 117.05W
Highmore 186 Gd 44.31N 99.27W
High Plains 174 If 38.30N 103.00W
High Point 182 Ld 35.58N 79.59W
High Prairie 180 Fe 55.27N 116.30W
High River 180 Gf 50.35N 113.52W
Highrock Lake 180 He 55.49N 100.23W
High Springs 184 Fk 29.50N 82.36W
High Tatra (EN)=Vysoké Tatry 120 Pg 49.10N 20.00 E
High Willhays 118 Jk 50.41N 3.59W
Highwood Mountains 188 Jc 47.25N 110.30W
High Wycombe 118 Mj 51.38N 0.46W
Higuera de Zaragoza 192 Ee 25.59N 109.16W
Higüero, Punta- 194 Nd 18.22N 67.16W
Higuerote 196 Cg 10.29N 66.06W
Higüey 194 Md 18.37N 68.43W
Hiidenvesi 116 Kd 60.20N 24.10 E
Hii-Gawa 156 Cd 35.26N 132.52 E
Hiiraan [3] 168 He 4.00N 45.30 E
Hiitola 114 Gf 61.16N 29.42 E
Hiiumaa/Hiuma 110 Id 58.50N 22.40 E
Hijar 126 Lc 41.10N 0.27W
Hijāz, Jabal al- 164 Hf 19.45N 41.55 E
Hiji 156 Be 33.22N 131.32 E
Hiji-Gawa 156 Ce 33.36N 132.29 E
Hikami 156 Dd 35.11N 135.02 E
Hikari 154 Kh 33.58N 131.56 E
Hiketa 156 Dd 34.13N 134.24 E
Hikiā 116 Kd 60.45N 24.55 E
Hiki-Gawa 156 De 33.35N 135.26 E
Ḥikmah, Ra's al- 146 Bg 31.17N 27.44 E
Hikone 154 Ng 35.15N 136.15 E
Hiko-San 156 Be 33.29N 130.56 E
Hikueru Atoll 216 Mc 17.36S 142.37W
Hikurangi 218 Fa 35.36S 174.17 E
Hikurangi 218 Hb 37.55S 178.04 E
Hila 150 Ih 7.35S 127.24 E
Hilāl, Ra's al- 164 Dc 32.55N 22.11 E
Hiland 188 Le 43.08N 107.18W
Hilchenbach 124 Kc 51.00N 8.06 E
Hildburghausen 120 Gf 50.25N 10.45 E
Hilden 124 Ic 51.10N 6.56 E
Hildesheim 120 Fd 52.09N 9.58 E
Hillaby, Mount- 196 Gf 13.12N 59.35W
Hillared 116 Eg 57.38N 13.09 E
Hillary Coast 222 Kf 79.00S 161.00 E
Hill Bank 194 Ce 17.35N 88.42W
Hill City 186 Gg 39.22N 99.51W
Hillcrest Center 188 Fi 35.23N 118.57W
Hille 124 Kb 52.20N 8.45 E
Hillegom 124 Gb 52.18N 4.35 E
Hillekrog 116 Dj 54.36N 11.30 E
Hillerød 116 Ei 55.56N 12.19 E
Hillerstorp 116 Eg 57.19N 13.52 E
Hillesheim 124 Id 50.19N 6.41 E
Hillingdon, London- 124 Bc 51.31N 0.27W
Hillsboro [Il.-U.S.] 184 Cf 39.09N 89.29W
Hillsboro [N.D.-U.S.] 186 Hc 47.26N 97.03W
Hillsboro [Oh.-U.S.] 184 Ff 39.12N 83.37W
Hillsboro [Or.-U.S.] 188 Dd 45.31N 122.59W
Hillsboro [Tx.-U.S.] 186 Hj 32.01N 97.08W
Hillsborough 197p Cb 12.29N 61.26W
Hillsdale 184 Ee 41.55N 84.38W
Hillsville 184 Gg 36.46N 80.44W
Hillswich 118 La 60.28N 1.30W
Hilo 210 Lc 19.44N 155.05W
Hilo Bay 221a Fd 19.44N 155.05W
Hilok 138 Gf 51.22N 110.30 E
Hilok 140 Md 51.19N 106.59 E
Hilton Head Island 184 Gi 32.12N 80.45W
Hiltrup, Münster- 124 Jc 51.54N 7.38 E
Hilvan 146 Hd 37.30N 38.58 E
Hilvarenbeek 124 Hc 51.29N 5.08 E
Hilversum 122 Lb 52.14N 5.10 E
Himāchal Prādesh [3] 148 Fb 31.00N 78.00 E
Himalaya=Himalayas (EN) 140 Kg 29.00N 83.00 E
Himalayas (EN)=Himalaya 140 Kg 29.00N 83.00 E
Himara 130 Ci 40.07N 19.44 E
Himeji 152 Ne 34.49N 134.42 E
Hime-Jima 156 Be 33.43N 131.40 E
Hime-Kawa 156 Ec 37.02N 137.50 E
Hime-Shima 156 Ae 32.49N 128.41 E
Hime-Zaki 156 Fb 38.05N 138.34 E
Himi 154 Nf 36.51N 136.59 E
Himki 114 Ii 55.56N 37.28 E
Himmelbjerget 116 Ch 56.06N 9.42 E
Himmerfjärden 116 Ge 59.00N 17.43 E
Himmerland 116 Ch 56.50N 9.45 E
Himo 170 Gc 3.23S 37.33 E
Ḥimṣ=Homs (E) 142 Ff 34.44N 36.43 E
Hims, Bahrat- 146 Ge 34.39N 36.34 E
Hinai 156 Ga 40.13N 140.35 E
Ḥināķiyah, Wādī al- 146 Ij 24.30N 40.30 E
Hinca Renancó 206 Hd 34.50S 64.23W
Hinche 194 Kd 19.09N 72.01W
Hinchinbrook 178 Jd 60.22N 146.30W
Hinchinbrook Island 212 Jc 18.25S 146.15 E
Hinckley 124 Ab 52.32N 1.22W
Hindås 116 Eg 57.42N 12.27 E
Hindhead 124 Bc 51.06N 0.44W
Ḥindī, Badwēynta-=Indian Ocean (EN) 106 Gl 21.00S 82.00 E
Hindmarsh, Lake- 212 Ig 36.05S 141.55 E
Hinds 218 Df 44.00S 171.34 E
Hindsholm 116 Di 55.30N 10.40 E
Hindukush 140 Jf 35.00N 71.00 E
Hindustan 140 Jg 25.00N 79.00 E
Hinesville 184 Gj 31.51N 81.36W
Hinganghāt 148 Fd 20.34N 78.50 E
Hınıs 146 Ic 39.22N 41.44 E
Hınıs 146 Jc 39.18N 42.12 E
Hinlopenstretet 179 Oc 79.15N 21.00 E
Hinnøya 110 Hb 68.30N 16.00 E
Hino-Gawa 156 Cd 35.27N 133.22 E
Hinojosa del Duque 126 Gf 38.30N 5.09W
Hinokage 156 Be 32.39N 131.24 E
Hi-no-Misaki 156 Cd 35.26N 132.38 E
Hino-Misaki 156 De 33.53N 135.04 E
Hinterrhein 128 Dd 46.49N 9.25 E
Hinton 180 Ff 53.25N 117.34W
Hi-Numa 156 Gc 36.16N 140.30 E
Hınzır Burun 146 Fb 36.22N 35.45 E
Hiou 219b Ca 13.08S 166.33 E
Hipólito 192 Ie 25.41N 101.26W
Hippolytushoef, Wieringen- 124 Gb 52.54N 4.59 E
Hippone 128 Bn 36.52N 7.44 E
Hirado 154 Jh 33.22N 129.33 E
Hirado-Shima 154 Jh 33.19N 129.32 E
Hiraka 156 Gb 39.16N 140.29 E
Hirakata 156 Dd 34.48N 135.38 E
Hīrākud 148 Gd 21.15N 84.15 E
Hiraman 170 Ge 1.07S 39.55 E
Hiranai 156a Bc 40.54N 140.57 E
Hirara 152 Mg 24.48N 125.17 E
Hira-Shima 156 Ae 33.01N 129.15 E
Hirata 156 Cd 35.26N 132.49 E
Hiratsuka 156 Fd 35.19N 139.19 E
Hirfanlı barajı Gölü 146 Ec 39.10N 33.32 E
Hirgis 152 Fb 49.32N 93.48 E
Hirgis-Nur 140 Le 49.12N 93.24 E
Hirhafok 162 Ie 23.29N 5.45 E
Hîrlău 130 Jb 47.26N 26.54 E
Hiromi 156 Ce 33.15N 132.38 E
Hiroo 152 Pc 42.17N 143.19 E
Hirosaki 152 Pc 40.35N 140.28 E
Hiroshima 142 Pf 34.24N 132.27 E
Hiroshima Ken [2] 154 Lg 34.35N 132.50 E
Hiroshima-Wan 156 Cd 34.10N 132.20 E
Hirschhorn (Neckar) 124 Ke 49.27N 8.54 E
Hirson 122 Ke 49.55N 4.05 E
Hîrşova 130 Ke 44.41N 27.56 E
Hirtibaciu 130 Hd 45.44N 24.14 E
Hirtshals 114 Bh 57.35N 9.58 E
Hirvensalmi 116 Lc 61.38N 26.48 E
His 168 Hc 10.50N 46.54 E
Hisai 156 Ed 34.40N 136.28 E
Hisaka-Shima 156 Ae 32.48N 128.52 E
Hisar 148 Fc 29.10N 75.43 E
Hisar 130 Jg 42.35N 27.00 E
Hisarcik 130 Mj 39.15N 29.15 E
Hisarja 130 Hg 42.30N 24.42 E
Ḥismā 146 Fh 28.30N 35.50 E
Ḥişn al 'Abr 164 If 16.08N 47.14 E
Ḥişn aş Şaḩābī 164 Dc 30.01N 20.48 E
Hispaniola (EN)=La Española 174 Lh 19.00N 71.00W
Histon 124 Cb 52.15N 0.06 E
Histria 130 Le 44.30N 28.45 E
Hīt 146 Jf 33.38N 42.49 E
Hita 154 Kh 33.19N 130.56 E
Hitachi 154 Pf 36.36N 140.39 E
Hitachi-ōta 156 Gc 36.32N 140.31 E
Hitchin 124 Bc 51.57N 0.16W
Hitiaa 221e Fc 17.36S 149.18W
Hitotsuse-Gawa 156 Be 32.03N 131.31 E
Hitoyoshi 154 Kh 32.15N 130.45 E
Hitra 110 Gc 63.30N 8.45 E
Hiuchi-ga-Take 156 Fc 36.57N 139.17 E
Hiuchi-Nada 156 Cd 34.05N 133.15 E
Hiuma/Hiiumaa 110 Id 58.50N 22.40 E

Index Symbols

[1] Independent Nation
[2] State, Region
[3] District, County
[4] Municipality
[5] Colony, Dependency
Continent
Physical Region
Historical or Cultural Region
Mount, Mountain
Volcano
Hill
Mountains, Mountain Range
Hills, Escarpment
Plateau, Upland
Pass, Gap
Plain, Lowland
Delta
Salt Flat
Valley, Canyon
Crater, Cave
Karst Features
Depression
Polder
Desert, Dunes
Forest, Woods
Heath, Steppe
Oasis
Cape, Point
Coast, Beach
Cliff
Peninsula
Isthmus
Sandbank
Island
Atoll
Rock, Reef
Islands, Archipelago
Rocks, Reefs
Coral Reef
Well, Spring
Geyser
River, Stream
Waterfall, Rapids
River Mouth, Estuary
Lake
Salt Lake
Intermittent Lake
Reservoir
Swamp, Pond
Canal
Glacier
Ice Shelf, Pack Ice
Ocean
Sea
Gulf, Bay
Strait, Fjord
Lagoon
Bank
Seamount
Tablemount
Ridge
Shelf
Basin
Escarpment, Sea Scarp
Fracture
Trench, Abyss
National Park, Reserve
Point of Interest
Recreation Site
Cave, Cavern
Historic Site
Ruins
Wall, Walls
Church, Abbey
Temple
Scientific Station
Railway station
Airport
Port
Military installation
Lighthouse
Mine
Tunnel
Dam, Bridge

Hiv 132 Oi 41.46N 47.57 E
Hiva 136 Gg 41.25N 60.23 E
Hiva Oa, Ile- 208 Ne 9.45S 139.00W
Hiw 146 Ei 26.01N 32.16 E
Hjädemeste/Häädemeeste 116 Kf 58.00N 24.28 E
Hjallerup 116 Dg 57.10N 10.09 E
Hjälmare kanal 116 Fe 59.25N 15.55 E
Hjälmaren 110 Hd 59.15N 15.45 E
Hjelm 116 Dh 56.10N 10.50 E
Hjelmelandsvågen 114 Bg 59.15N 6.10 E
Hjelmsøya 114 Fa 71.05N 24.43 E
Hjeltefjorden 116 Ad 60.40N 4.55 E
Hjerkinn 116 Cb 62.13N 9.32 E
Hjo 114 Dg 58.18N 14.17 E
Hjørring 114 Bh 57.28N 9.59 E
Hlatikulu 172 Ee 26.58S 31.19 E
Hlavni město Praha [3] 120 Kf 50.05N 14.25 E
Hlavni město SSR Bratislava [3] 120 Nh 48.10N 17.10 E
Hlinsko 120 Lg 49.46N 15.54 E
Hlohovec 120 Nh 48.25N 17.48 E
Hluhluwe 172 Ee 28.02S 32.17 E
Hmelnickaja oblast [3] 136 Cf 49.30N 27.00 E
Hmelnicki 136 Cf 49.24N 26.57 E
Hmelnik 136 Cf 49.33N 27.59 E
Hnilec 120 Rh 48.53N 21.01 E
Ho 166 Fd 6.36N 0.28 E
Hoa Binh 148 Ld 20.50N 105.20 E
Hoanib 172 Ac 19.23S 13.06 E
Hoare Bay 176 Lc 65.30N 63.10W
Hoback Peak 188 Je 43.10N 110.33W
Hobart [Austl.] 210 Fi 42.53S 147.19 E
Hobart [Ok.-U.S.] 186 Gi 35.01N 99.06W
Hobbs 182 Ge 32.42N 103.08W
Hobbs Coast 222 Nf 74.50S 131.00W
Hobda 132 Sd 50.55N 54.38 E
Hoboken, Antwerpen- 124 Gc 51.10N 4.21 E
Hoboksar 152 Eb 46.47N 85.43 E
Hobq Shamo 152 Ic 40.30N 108.00 E
Hobro 114 Bh 56.38N 9.48 E
Hoburgen 114 Eh 56.55N 18.07 E
Hobyā 160 Lh 5.20N 48.38 E
Hocalar 130 Mk 38.37N 29.57 E
Hochalmspitze 128 Hc 47.01N 13.19 E
Hochfeiler/Gran Pilastro 128 Fd 46.58N 11.44 E
Hochgolling 128 Hc 47.16N 13.45 E
Hochschwab 128 Jc 47.36N 15.05 E
Höchstadt an der Aisch 120 Gg 49.42N 10.44 E
Hochstetters Forland 179 Kc 75.45N 20.00W
Höchst im Odenwald 124 Ke 49.48N 9.00 E
Hochtor 128 Gc 47.05N 12.48 E
Hockenheim 124 Ke 49.19N 8.33 E
Hodaka-Dake 156 Ec 36.17N 137.39 E
Hodda 168 Ic 11.30N 50.45 E
Hoddesdon 124 Cc 51.45N 0.00
Hodgenville 184 Eg 37.34N 85.44W
Hodh 158 Gg 16.10N 8.40W
Hodh ech Chargui [3] 162 Ff 17.00N 7.15W
Hodh el Gharbi [3] 162 Ff 16.30N 10.00W
Hódmezővásárhely 120 Qj 46.25N 20.20 E
Hodna, Chott el- 162 Hb 35.25N 4.45 E
Hodna, Monts du- 162 Hb 35.50N 4.50 E
Hodna, Plaine du- 126 Qi 35.35N 4.35 E
Hodonin 120 Nh 48.52N 17.08 E
Hodorov 132 De 49.25N 24.18 E
Hodžambas 135 Ee 38.06N 65.01 E
Hodža-Pirjah, gora- 135 Fe 38.47N 67.35 E
Hodžejli 136 Fg 42.23N 59.20 E
Hœdic, Ile de- 122 Dg 47.20N 2.52W
Hoegaarden 124 Gd 50.47N 4.53 E
Hoei/Huy 122 Ld 50.31N 5.14 E
Hoë Karoo 158 Jl 30.00S 21.30 E
Hoekse Waard 124 Gc 51.45N 4.25 E
Hoek van Holland 122 Kc 51.59N 4.09 E
Hoeselt 124 Hd 50.51N 5.29 E
Hof 120 Hf 50.19N 11.55 E
Höfdakaupstadur 114a Bb 65.50N 20.19W
Hofgeismar 120 Fe 51.29N 9.24 E
Hofheim 124 Kd 50.05N 8.27 E
Hofmeyr 172 Df 31.39S 25.50 E
Höfn 114a Cb 64.15N 15.13W
Hofors 114 Df 60.33N 16.17 E
Hofsjökull 110 Ec 64.49N 18.48W
Hōfu 154 Kg 34.03N 131.34 E
Höganäs 116 Eh 56.12N 12.33 E
Hogarth, Mount- 212 Hd 21.48S 136.58 E
Hogback Mountain 188 Id 44.54N 112.07W
Hog Cliffs 197d Ba 17.38N 61.44W
Hoge Venen/Hautes Fagnes 120 Bf 50.30N 6.00 E
Högfors/Karkkila 114 Ff 60.32N 24.11 E
Hog Island 197b Bb 12.00N 61.44W
Hogne, Somme-Leuze- 124 Hd 50.15N 5.17 E
Hog Point 197d Ba 17.43N 61.48W
Högsby 114 Dh 57.10N 16.02 E
Høgste Breakulen 116 Bc 61.41N 7.02 E
Høgstegia 116 Db 62.23N 10.08 E
Hogsty Reef 194 Kc 21.41N 73.49W
Hŏhang-nyŏng 154 Jd 41.48N 128.20 E
Hohe Acht 120 Cf 50.23N 7.03 E
Hohe Eifel 124 Id 50.16N 6.50 E
Hohenau 204 Eh 27.05S 55.45W
Hohenems 128 Dc 47.22N 9.41 E
Hohenloher Ebene 120 Fg 49.20N 9.40 E
Hohes Venn 120 Bf 50.30N 6.00 E
Hohe Tauern 128 Gc 47.10N 12.30 E
Hohhot 142 Ne 40.51N 111.38 E
Hohneck, Le- 122 Nf 48.02N 7.01 E
Hōhoku 156 Bd 34.17N 130.57 E
Höhr-Grenzhausen 124 Jd 50.26N 7.40 E
Höhtiäinen 116 Mb 62.50N 29.40 E
Hoh Xil Hu 152 Fd 35.35N 91.06 E
Hoh Xil Shan 140 Lf 35.20N 91.00 E
Hoi An 148 Le 15.52N 108.19 E
Hoima 170 Fb 1.26N 31.21 E
Hoisington 186 Gg 38.31N 98.47W
Hoj, vozvyšennost- 134 Ob 68.50N 71.30 E
Højer 116 Cj 54.58N 8.43 E
Hojniki 136 Ce 51.54N 29.56 E
Hōjō 154 Lh 33.58N 132.46 E
Hökensås 116 Ff 58.11N 14.08 E
Hokianga Harbour 218 Ea 35.30S 173.20 E
Hokitika 210 Ii 42.43S 170.58 E
Hok-Kai = Okhotsk, Sea of- (EN) 140 Qd 53.00N 150.00 E
Hokkaidō 140 Qe 43.00N 143.00 E
Hokkaidō Ken [2] 154 Qc 43.00N 143.00 E
Hokksund 114 Bg 59.47N 9.59 E
Hokmābād 146 Qd 36.37N 57.36 E
Hokota 156 Gc 36.10N 140.30 E
Hol 116 Cd 60.36N 8.22 E
Holap 220d Ba 7.39N 151.54 E
Holbæk 116 Di 55.43N 11.43 E
Holbeach 124 Cb 52.48N 0.01 E
Holbeach Marsh 124 Cb 52.52N 0.02 E
Holbox, Isla- 192 Pg 21.33N 87.15W
Holbrook 182 Ee 34.54N 110.10W
Holdenville 186 Hi 35.05N 96.24W
Holderness 118 Mh 53.47N 0.10W
Holdrege 186 Gf 40.26N 99.22W
Hold With Hope 179 Jd 73.40N 21.45W
Hole in the Wall 184 Im 25.51N 77.12W
Hølen 116 De 59.32N 10.45 E
Holešov 120 Ng 49.20N 17.33 E
Holetown 197q Ab 13.11N 59.39W
Holguín 176 Lg 20.53N 76.15W
Holguín [3] 194 Jc 20.40N 75.50W
Hol-Hol 168 Gc 11.20N 42.50 E
Holitna 178 Hd 61.40N 157.12W
Höljes 114 Cf 60.54N 12.36 E
Hollabrunn 128 Kb 48.33N 16.05 E
Holland 184 Dd 42.47N 86.07W
Holland [Eng.-U.K.] 124 Bb 52.52N 0.10W
Holland [Neth.] 110 Ge 52.20N 4.45 E
Hollandale 186 Kj 33.10N 90.58W
Hollandsbird Island 172 Ad 24.45S 14.34 E
Hollands Diep 124 Gc 51.40N 4.30 E
Hollesley Bay 124 Db 52.04N 1.33 E
Hollick-Kenyon Plateau 222 Pf 79.00S 97.00W
Hollis 186 Gi 34.41N 99.55W
Hollister [Ca.-U.S.] 188 Eh 36.51N 121.24W
Hollister [Id.-U.S.] 188 He 42.23N 114.35W
Hollola 116 Kc 61.03N 25.26 E
Höllviksnäs 116 Ei 55.25N 12.57 E
Holly Springs 186 Li 34.41N 89.26W
Hollywood 182 Kf 26.00N 80.09W
Holm 114 Hh 57.09N 31.12 E
Holma 166 Hd 9.54N 13.03 E
Holman Island 180 Fb 70.40N 117.35W
Hólmavík 114a Bb 65.43N 21.41W
Holmes Reefs 208 Ff 16.30S 148.00 E
Holmestrand 116 De 59.29N 10.18 E
Holm Land 179 Kb 80.16N 18.20W
Holms 179 Gd 74.30N 57.00W
Holmsjö 116 Fh 56.25N 15.32 E
Holmsjön [Swe.] 114 De 62.25N 15.20 E
Holmsjön [Swe.] 116 Gb 62.40N 16.35 E
Holmsk 138 Jg 47.00N 142.03 E
Holmski 132 Kg 44.50N 38.24 E
Holmsland Klit 116 Ch 56.00N 8.10 E
Holmsund 114 Ee 63.42N 20.21 E
Holmsveden 116 Gc 61.07N 16.43 E
Holmudden 116 Hg 57.57N 19.21 E
Holod 130 Fc 46.47N 22.08 E
Holohit, Punta- 192 Og 21.37N 88.08W
Holothuria Banks (EN) 212 Fb 13.25S 126.00 E
Holsnøy 116 Ad 60.35N 5.05 E
Holstebro 114 Bh 56.21N 8.38 E
Holsted 116 Ci 55.30N 8.55 E
Holstein 186 Ie 42.29N 95.33W
Holsteinsborg/Sisimiut 224 Nc 67.05N 53.45W
Holt 124 Db 52.54N 1.05 E
Holten 124 Ib 52.17N 6.27 E
Holton 186 Ig 39.28N 95.44W
Holtoson 138 Ff 50.18N 103.20 E
Holtyn-Daba 152 Ib 47.40N 107.20 E
Holwerd, Westdongeradeel- 124 Ha 53.22N 5.54 E
Holy Cross 178 Hd 62.12N 159.47W
Holyhead 118 Ih 53.20N 4.38W
Holy Island [Eng.-U.K.] 118 Lf 55.41N 1.48W
Holy Island [Wales-U.K.] 118 Ih 53.18N 4.37W
Holyoke [Co.-U.S.] 186 Ef 40.35N 102.18W
Holyoke [Ma.-U.S.] 184 Kd 42.12N 72.37W
Holýšov 120 Jg 49.36N 13.07 E
Homa Bay 170 Fc 0.31S 34.27 E
Homalin 148 Id 24.52N 94.55 E
Homathko River 188 Ca 50.55N 124.50W
Homberg (Ohm) 124 Kd 50.44N 8.59 E
Hombori 166 Eb 15.17N 1.42W
Hombre Muerto, Salar del- 206 Gc 25.23S 67.06W
Homburg 120 Dg 49.19N 7.20 E
Home Bay 174 Mc 68.45N 67.10W
Homécourt 124 He 49.14N 5.59 E
Home Hill 212 Jc 19.40S 147.25 E
Homer [Ak.-U.S.] 176 Dd 59.39N 151.33W
Homer [La.-U.S.] 186 Jj 32.48N 93.04W
Homert 124 Kc 51.16N 8.06 E
Homerville 184 Fj 31.02N 82.45W
Homestead 184 Gm 25.29N 80.29W
Homewood 184 Di 33.29N 86.48W
Hommelstø 114 Cd 65.25N 12.30 E
Hommersåk 116 Af 58.55N 5.50 E
Homoine 172 Fd 23.52S 35.08 E
Homoljske Planina 130 Ee 44.20N 21.45 E
Homonhon 150 Id 10.44N 125.43 E
Homosassa 184 Fk 28.47N 82.37W
Homs (EN) = Ḥimṣ 142 Ff 34.44N 36.43 E
Honan (EN) = Henan Sheng (Ho-nan Sheng) [2] 152 Je 34.00N 114.00 E
Honan (EN) = Ho-nan Sheng → Henan Sheng [2] 152 Je 34.00N 114.00 E
Ho-nan Sheng → Henan Sheng = Honan (EN) [2] 152 Je 34.00N 114.00 E
Honaz 130 Ml 37.45N 29.17 E
Honaz Dağı 130 Ml 37.41N 29.18 E
Honbetsu 154 Qc 43.18N 143.33 E
Honda 202 Db 5.13N 74.45W
Honda, Bahia- 194 Lg 12.21N 71.47W
Hondeklipbaai 172 Bf 30.20S 17.18 E
Hòn Diên, Núi- 148 Lf 11.33N 108.38 E
Hondo 190 Ge 18.29N 88.19W
Hondo [Jap.] 154 Kh 32.27N 130.12 E
Hondo [N.M.-U.S.] 186 Dj 33.23N 105.16W
Hondo [Tx.-U.S.] 186 Gl 29.21N 99.09W
Hondo, Rio- 186 Dj 33.22N 104.24W
Hondschoote 124 Ed 50.59N 2.35 E
Hondsrug 122 Mb 52.50N 6.50 E
Honduras 176 Kh 15.00N 86.30W
Honduras, Cabo de- 194 De 16.01N 86.01W
Honduras, Golfo de- = Honduras, Gulf of- (EN) 174 Kh 16.10N 87.50W
Honduras, Gulf of- 174 Kh 16.10N 87.50W
Honduras, Gulf of- (EN) = Honduras, Golfo de- 174 Kh 16.10N 87.50W
Hønefoss 114 Cf 60.10N 10.18 E
Honey Lake 188 Ef 40.16N 120.19W
Honfleur 122 Ge 49.25N 0.14 E
Hông, Sông- [Asia] = Red River (EN) 140 Mg 20.17N 106.34 E
Hong'an (Huang'an) 154 Ci 31.17N 114.37 E
Hongch'ŏn 154 If 37.41N 127.52 E
Hong-Do 154 Hg 34.41N 125.13 E
Hong He 154 Ch 32.24N 115.32 E
Honghton Lake 184 Ec 44.22N 84.43W
Hong Hu 152 Je 30.00N 113.25 E
Honghu (Xindi) 154 Bj 29.50N 113.28 E
Honghui 152 Id 36.46N 105.05 E
Hong Kong/Xianggang [5] 142 Ng 22.15N 114.10 E
Hongliuyuan 152 Gc 41.02N 95.24 E
Hongluoxian 154 Fd 41.01N 120.52 E
Hongning → Wulian 154 Eg 35.45N 119.13 E
Hongor 154 Bb 45.48N 112.45 E
Hongqizhen 152 Ih 18.48N 109.30 E
Hongshui He 140 Mg 23.47N 109.33 E
Hongsŏng 154 If 36.36N 126.40 E
Hongtong 154 Af 36.15N 111.41 E
Hongū 156 De 33.50N 135.46 E
Honguedo, Détroit d'- 180 Lg 49.30N 64.00W
Hongwansi → Sunan 152 Gd 38.59N 99.25 E
Hongwŏn 154 Id 40.02N 127.58 E
Hongyuan (Hurama) 152 He 32.45N 102.38 E
Hongze (Gaoliangjian) 152 Ke 33.10N 119.58 E
Hongze Hu 152 Ke 33.20N 118.40 E
Honiara 210 Ge 9.27S 159.57 E
Honikulu, Passe- 220h Ac 13.23S 176.11W
Honiton 118 Jk 50.48N 3.13W
Honjō 154 Pe 39.23N 140.03 E
Honkajoki 116 Jb 61.59N 22.16 E
Hon-kawane 156 Fd 35.07N 138.06 E
Honningsvåg 114 Ga 70.59N 26.01 E
Hönö 116 Dg 57.42N 11.39 E
Honokaa 221a Fc 20.05N 155.28W
Honokohau 221a Eb 21.01N 156.37W
Honolulu 210 Lb 21.19N 157.52W
Honomu 221a Fd 19.52N 155.07W
Honrubia 126 Je 39.37N 2.16W
Honshū 140 Pf 36.00N 136.00 E
Hontenisse 124 Gc 51.23N 4.00 E
Hontenisse-Kloosterzande 124 Gc 51.23N 4.00 E
Honuapo Bay 221a Fd 19.05N 155.33W
Honuu 138 Jc 66.27N 143.06 E
Honyō 156 Fc 36.14N 139.10 E
Hood 180 Gc 67.25N 108.53W
Hood, Mount- 174 Ge 45.23N 121.41W
Hood Point 212 Df 34.23S 119.34 E
Hood River 188 Ed 45.43N 121.31W
Hoogeveen 122 Mb 52.43N 6.29 E
Hoogezand-Sappemeer 124 Ia 53.09N 6.48 E
Hooglede 124 Fd 50.59N 3.05 E
Hoogstraten 124 Gc 51.24N 4.46 E
Hooker 186 Fh 36.52N 101.13W
Hooker, Cape- 222 Kf 70.38S 166.45 E
Hook Head/Rinn Duáin 118 Gi 52.07N 6.55W
Hook Island 212 Jc 20.10S 148.55 E
Hoolehua 221a Db 21.10N 157.05W
Hoonah 178 Le 58.07N 135.26W
Hooper, Cape- 180 Kc 68.24N 66.43W
Hooper Bay 178 Fd 61.31N 166.06W
Hoopeston 186 Mf 40.28N 87.40W
Höör 116 Ei 55.56N 13.32 E
Hoorn 122 Lb 52.38N 5.04 E
Hoornaar 124 Gc 51.53N 4.57 E
Hoover Dam 188 Hi 36.00N 114.27W
Hopa 146 Ib 41.25N 41.24 E
Hope [Ar.-U.S.] 186 Jj 33.40N 93.36W
Hope [Az.-U.S.] 188 Ij 33.44N 113.42W
Hope [B.C.-Can.] 188 Eb 49.23N 121.26W
Hope, Ben- 118 Ic 58.24N 4.36W
Hope, Lake- 212 Ef 32.50S 121.40 E
Hope, Point- 174 Cc 68.21N 166.50W
Hopedale 180 Le 55.50N 60.10W
Hopefield 172 Bf 33.04S 18.21 E
Hopeh (EN) = Hebei Sheng (Ho-pei Sheng) [2] 152 Kd 39.00N 116.00 E
Hopeh (EN) = Ho-pei Sheng → Hebei Sheng [2] 152 Kd 39.00N 116.00 E
Hopeh (EN) = Hu-pei Sheng → Hubei Sheng [2] 152 Je 31.00N 112.00 E
Ho-pei Sheng → Hebei Sheng = Hopeh (EN) [2] 152 Kd 39.00N 116.00 E
Hopelchén 192 Oh 19.46N 89.51W
Hopen 179 Oc 76.35N 25.10 E
Hopër 110 Kf 49.36N 42.19 E
Hopes Advance, Cap- 180 Kd 61.05N 69.33W
Hopetoun [Austl.] 212 Ig 35.44S 142.22 E
Hopetoun [Austl.] 210 Dh 33.57S 120.07 E
Hopetown 172 Ce 29.34S 24.03 E
Hopewell 184 Ig 37.17N 77.19W
Hopewell Islands 180 Je 58.20N 78.10W
Hopin 148 Jd 24.59N 96.31 E
Hopkins, Lake- 212 Fd 24.15S 128.50 E
Hopkinsville 182 Jd 36.52N 87.29W
Hopsten 124 Jb 52.23N 7.37 E
Hoptrup 116 Ci 55.11N 9.28 E
Hoquiam 182 Cb 46.59N 123.53W
Hor 138 Ig 47.55N 135.01 E
Hor 138 Ig 47.48N 134.43 E
Hōrai 156 Ed 34.55N 137.34 E
Hōrai-San 156 Dd 35.13N 135.53 E
Horasan 146 Jb 40.03N 42.11 E
Horaždovice 120 Jg 49.20N 13.42 E
Horb am Neckar 120 Eh 48.26N 8.41 E
Hörby 116 Ei 55.51N 13.39 E
Horconcitos 194 Fi 8.19N 82.10W
Hordaland [2] 114 Bf 60.15N 6.30 E
Hordogoj 138 Gd 62.32N 115.38 E
Horezmskaja oblast [3] 136 Gg 41.30N 60.40 E
Horezu 130 Hd 45.09N 24.01 E
Horgen 128 Cc 47.15N 8.36 E
Horgoš 130 Cc 46.09N 19.58 E
Horgos 136 Ig 44.10N 80.20 E
Hořice 120 Lf 50.22N 15.38 E
Horinger 154 Ad 40.24N 111.46 E
Horizon Tablemount (EN) 208 Kc 19.40N 168.30W
Horizontina 204 Eh 27.37S 54.19W
Horley 124 Bc 51.10N 0.10W
Horlick Mountains 222 Og 85.23S 121.00W
Hormigas 192 Gc 29.12N 105.45W
Hormoz 144 Id 27.06N 56.28 E
Hormoz, Kūh-e- 144 Id 27.27N 55.10 E
Hormoz, Tangeh-ye- = Hormuz, Strait of- (EN) 140 Hg 26.34N 56.15 E
Hormozgān [3] 144 Id 27.30N 56.00 E
Hormūd-e Bāgh 146 Pi 27.30N 54.18 E
Hormuz, Strait of- (EN) = Hormoz, Tangeh-ye- 140 Hg 26.34N 56.15 E
Horn 110 Db 66.28N 22.30W
Horn 180 Fd 61.30N 118.00W
Horn [Aus.] 128 Jb 48.39N 15.39 E
Horn [Swe.] 116 Fg 57.54N 15.50 E
Horn, Cape- (EN) = Hornos, Cabo de- 198 Jk 55.59S 67.16W
Hornád 120 Qh 48.00N 20.58 E
Hornaday 180 Fc 69.22N 123.56W
Hornavan 114 Dc 66.14N 17.30 E
Hornbach 124 Je 49.12N 7.22 E
Horn-Bad Meinberg 124 Kc 51.54N 8.57 E
Hornby Bay 180 Fc 66.35N 117.50W
Horncastle 118 Mh 53.13N 0.07W
Horndal 116 Gd 60.18N 16.25 E
Horndean 124 Bd 50.55N 0.59W
Horne, Iles de- = Horn Islands (EN) 208 Jf 14.19S 178.05W
Hörnefors 114 Ee 63.38N 19.54 E
Hornell 184 Id 42.19N 77.39W
Hornepayne 180 Jg 49.13N 84.47W
Hornindalsvatn 116 Bc 61.55N 6.25 E
Hornisgrinde 120 Eh 48.36N 8.12 E
Horn Islands (EN) = Horne, Iles de- 208 Jf 14.19S 178.05W
Hörnli 128 Cc 47.23N 8.56 E
Hornomoravský úval 120 Ng 49.25N 17.20 E
Hornos, Cabo de- = Horn, Cape- (EN) 198 Jk 55.59S 67.16W
Hornoy-le-Bourg 124 De 49.51N 1.54 E
Horn Plateau 180 Fd 62.10N 119.30W
Hornsea 118 Mh 53.55N 0.10W
Hornslandet 116 Gc 61.40N 17.30 E
Horns Rev 116 Bi 55.30N 7.45 E
Hornsund 179 Nc 76.58N 15.28 E
Hornsundtind 179 Nc 76.55N 16.10 E
Horog 142 Jf 37.31N 71.33 E
Horoizumi 156a Cb 42.01N 143.07 E
Horokanai 156a Ca 44.02N 142.09 E
Horol 132 He 49.29N 33.49 E
Horol [R.S.F.S.R.] 154 Lb 44.30N 132.03 E
Horol [Ukr.-U.S.S.R.] 132 He 49.47N 33.16 E
Horonobe 154 Pb 45.00N 141.51 E
Hořovice 120 Jg 49.50N 13.54 E
Horqin Youyi Qianqi (Ulan Hot) 142 Oe 46.04N 122.00 E
Horqin Youyi Zhongqi (Bayan Huxu) 152 Lb 45.04N 121.27 E
Horqin Zuoyi Houqi (Ganjig) 152 Lc 42.57N 122.14 E
Horqin Zuoyi Zhongqi (Baokang) 152 Lc 44.06N 123.19 E
Horqueta 206 Ib 23.24S 56.53W
Horred 116 Eg 57.21N 12.28 E
Horse Creek [Co.-U.S.] 186 Eg 38.05N 103.19W
Horse Creek [U.S.] 188 Nf 41.57N 103.58W
Horsehead Lake 186 Gc 47.02N 99.47W
Horsens 114 Bi 55.52N 9.52 E
Horsham [Austl.] 210 Fh 36.43S 142.13 E
Horsham [Eng.-U.K.] 118 Mj 51.04N 0.21W
Hørsholm 116 Ei 55.53N 12.30 E
Horšovský Týn 120 Ig 49.32N 12.57 E
Horst 124 Ic 51.28N 6.03 E
Horst 124 Gd 50.56N 4.47 E
Hörstel 124 Jb 52.19N 7.35 E
Horstmar 124 Jb 52.05N 7.19 E
Horsunlu 130 Ll 37.55N 28.36 E
Horta 162 Bb 38.32N 28.28W
Horta [3] 162 Bb 38.35N 28.40W
Horta, Cap de l'- / Huertas, Cabo de- 126 Lf 38.21N 0.24W
Horten 116 De 59.25N 10.30 E
Horton 180 Ec 70.01N 126.42W
Hörvik 116 Fh 56.03N 14.46 E
Ḥorvot 'Avedat 146 Fg 30.48N 34.46 E
Ḥorvot Meẓada 146 Fg 31.19N 35.21 E
Horwood Lake 184 Fa 48.03N 82.20W
Hosaina 168 Fd 7.33N 37.52 E
Hose Mountains 150 Ff 2.00N 114.10 E
Hosenofu 164 De 23.34N 21.15 E
Hoseynābād [Iran] 146 Ne 34.30N 50.59 E
Hoseynābād [Iran] 146 Le 35.33N 47.08 E
Hoseynīyeh 146 Mg 32.42N 48.14 E
Hoshāb 148 Cc 26.01N 63.56 E
Hosingen 124 Id 50.01N 6.05 E
Hoskins 214 Ei 5.30S 150.32 E
Hospet 148 Fe 15.16N 76.24 E
Hospital, Cuchilla del- 204 Ej 31.40S 54.53W
Hospitalet del Infante / l'Hospitalet de l'Infant 126 Md 40.59N 0.56 E
Hospitalet de Llobregat 126 Oc 41.22N 2.08 E
Hoste, Isla- 198 Jk 55.15S 69.00W
Hot 148 Je 18.06N 98.35 E
Hotagen 114 De 63.55N 14.29 E
Hotaka 156 Ec 36.20N 137.53 E
Hotan 142 Jf 37.07N 79.55 E
Hotan He 140 Ke 40.30N 80.48 E
Hotazel 172 Ce 27.15S 23.00 E
Hotin 132 Ee 48.29N 26.29 E
Hoting 114 Dd 64.07N 16.10 E
Hotkovo 114 Ih 56.18N 38.00 E
Hotont 152 Hb 47.23N 102.30 E
Hot Springs 182 Gc 43.26N 103.29W
Hot Springs → Truth or Consequences 182 Fe 33.08N 107.15W
Hot Springs National Park 176 Jf 34.30N 93.03W
Hot Springs Peak 188 Gf 41.22N 117.26W
Hotspur Seamount (EN) 202 Kg 18.00S 36.00W
Hottah Lake 180 Fc 65.05N 118.36W
Hottentot Bay 172 Ae 26.07S 14.57 E
Hotton 124 Hd 50.16N 5.27 E
Hottstedt 120 He 51.39N 11.30 E
Houailou 216 Cd 21.17S 165.38 E
Houat, Ile de- 122 Dg 47.24N 2.58W
Houdan 122 Hf 48.47N 1.36 E
Houeillès 122 Gj 44.12N 0.02 E
Houffalize 124 Hd 50.08N 5.47 E
Houghton 182 Jb 47.06N 88.34W
Houillères, Canal des- 124 If 48.42N 6.55 E
Houji → Liangshan 154 Dg 35.48N 116.07 E
Houlgate 124 Be 49.18N 0.04W
Houlton 182 Nb 46.08N 67.51W
Houma [China] 152 Jd 35.36N 111.23 E
Houma [La.-U.S.] 182 If 29.36N 90.43W
Houndé 166 Ec 11.30N 3.31W
Hourn, Loch- 118 Hd 57.10N 5.40W
Hourtin, Étang d'- 122 Ei 45.10N 1.06W
House Range 188 Ig 39.30N 113.15W
Houston [Mo.-U.S.] 186 Kh 37.22N 91.58W
Houston [Tx.-U.S.] 176 Jg 29.46N 95.22W
Houthalen-Helchteren 124 Hc 51.02N 5.22 E
Houthulst 124 Ed 50.59N 2.57 E
Houthulst-Merkem 124 Ed 50.57N 2.51 E
Houtman Abrolhos 212 Ce 28.40S 113.50 E
Houtskär/Houtskari 116 Id 60.15N 21.20 E
Houtskari/Houtskär 116 Id 60.15N 21.20 E
Houyet 124 Hd 50.11N 5.01 E
Houyet-Celles 124 Hd 50.19N 5.01 E
Hov 116 Di 55.55N 10.16 E
Hova 116 Ff 58.52N 14.13 E
Hovden 116 Be 59.32N 7.21 E
Hovden 116 Ac 61.40N 4.50 E
Hove 118 Mk 50.49N 0.10W
Hovgaard 179 Kc 80.00N 18.45W
Hovmantorp 116 Fh 56.47N 15.08 E
Hovu-Aksy 138 Ef 51.01N 93.43 E
Howa 168 Db 17.30N 27.08 E
Howar 158 Jg 17.30N 27.08 E
Howard 186 Hd 44.01N 97.32W
Howe, Cape- 208 Fh 37.31S 149.59 E
Howell 184 Fd 42.36N 83.55W
Howick [N.Z.] 218 Fb 36.54S 174.56 E
Howick [S.Afr.] 172 Ee 29.28S 30.14 E
Howland 184 Mc 45.14N 68.40W
Howland Island 208 Jd 0.48N 176.38W
Howrah → Hāora 142 Kg 22.35N 88.20 E
Howth 118 Gh 53.23N 6.04W
Ḥowẓ Soltān 146 Ne 35.06N 51.06 E
Hoxie 186 Fg 39.21N 100.26W
Höxter 120 Fe 51.46N 9.23 E
Hoxud 152 Ec 42.16N 86.51 E
Hoy 118 Jc 58.52N 3.18W
Hoya 124 Lb 52.48N 9.09 E
Høyanger 114 Bf 61.13N 6.05 E
Hoyerswerda/Wojerecy 120 Ke 51.26N 14.15 E
Hoyos 126 Fd 40.10N 6.43W
Hōyo-Shotō 156 Ce 33.50N 132.30 E
Hoytiäinen 114 Ge 62.48N 29.39 E
Hozat 146 Hc 39.07N 39.14 E
Hpunhpu 148 Jc 26.42N 97.17 E
Hradec Králové 120 Lf 50.13N 15.50 E
Hradiště 120 Jf 50.13N 13.08 E
Hrami 132 Ni 41.20N 45.07 E
Hrastnik 128 Jd 46.09N 15.06 E
Hřebeny 120 Kg 49.50N 14.10 E
Hristinovka 132 Fe 48.53N 29.56 E
Hroma 138 Jb 71.30N 144.49 E
Hromtau 136 Fe 50.18N 58.35 E
Hron 120 Oi 47.49N 18.45 E
Hrubieszów 120 Tf 50.49N 23.55 E
Hrubý-Jeseník 120 Nf 50.05N 17.10 E
Hrustalny 138 Ih 44.24N 135.06 E
Hrvatska = Croatia (EN) [2] 128 Jf 45.00N 15.30 E
Hrvatska = Croatia (EN) [2] 110 Hf 45.00N 15.30 E
Hrvatska = Croatia (EN) 128 Je 45.00N 15.30 E
Ḥrvot Shivta 146 Fg 30.53N 34.38 E
Hsin-chiang-wei-wu-erh Tzu-chih-ch'ü → Xinjiang Uygur Zizhiqu [2] 152 Ec 42.00N 86.00 E
Hsinchu 152 Lg 24.48N 120.58 E
Hsinying 152 Lg 23.25N 120.20 E
Hsipaw 148 Jd 22.37N 97.18 E
Hsi-tsang Tzu-chih-ch'ü → Xizang Zizhiqu [2] 152 Ee 32.00N 90.00 E
Hsuphāng 148 Jd 20.18N 98.42 E
Huab 172 Ad 20.49S 13.24 E
Huabei Pingyuan 140 Nf 37.00N 117.00 E
Huachacalla 202 Eg 18.45S 68.17W
Huachinera 192 Eb 30.15N 108.50W
Huacho 202 Cf 11.07S 77.37W
Huaco 206 Gd 30.09S 68.31W
Huacrachuco 202 Ce 8.39S 77.05W
Huade 152 Jc 41.50N 114.00 E
Huadian 152 Mc 42.59N 126.38 E

Index Symbols

[1] Independent Nation
[2] State, Region
[3] District, County
[4] Municipality
[5] Colony, Dependency
Continent
Physical Region
Historical or Cultural Region
Mount, Mountain
Volcano
Hill
Mountains, Mountain Range
Hills, Escarpment
Plateau, Upland
Pass, Gap
Plain, Lowland
Delta
Salt Flat
Valley, Canyon
Crater, Cave
Karst Features
Depression
Polder
Desert, Dunes
Forest, Woods
Heath, Steppe
Oasis
Cape, Point
Coast, Beach
Cliff
Peninsula
Isthmus
Sandbank
Island
Atoll
Rock, Reef
Islands, Archipelago
Rocks, Reefs
Coral Reef
Well, Spring
Geyser
River, Stream
Waterfall, Rapids
River Mouth, Estuary
Lake
Salt Lake
Intermittent Lake
Reservoir
Swamp, Pond
Canal
Glacier
Ice Shelf, Pack Ice
Ocean
Sea
Gulf, Bay
Strait, Fjord
Lagoon
Bank
Seamount
Tablemount
Ridge
Shelf
Basin
Escarpment, Sea Scarp
Fracture
Trench, Abyss
National Park, Reserve
Point of Interest
Recreation Site
Cave, Cavern
Historic Site
Ruins
Wall, Walls
Church, Abbey
Temple
Scientific Station
Railway station
Airport
Port
Military installation
Lighthouse
Mine
Tunnel
Dam, Bridge

Hua Hin 148 Jf 12.34N 99.58 E
Huahine, Iles- 208 Lf 16.45S 151.00W
Huahine Iti 221e Eb 16.45S 151.00W
Huahine Nui 221e Eb 16.43S 151.00W
Huahuapán 192 Ge 24.31N 105.57W
Huai'an 154 Eh 33.30N 119.08 E
Huai'an (Chaigoubu) 154 Cd 40.40N 114.25 E
Huaibei 152 Ke 33.56N 116.48 E
Huaibin (Wulongji) 154 Ci 32.27N 115.23 E
Huaide (Gongzhuling) 152 Lc 43.30N 124.52 E
Huaidian → Shenqiu 152 Ke 33.27N 115.05 E
Huai He 140 Nf 33.12N 118.33 E
Huaiji 152 Jg 23.57N 112.12 E
Huailai (Shacheng) 152 Kc 40.29N 115.30 E
Huainan 142 Nf 32.32N 116.59 E
Huaining (Shipai) 154 Di 30.25N 116.39 E
Huairen 152 Jd 39.50N 113.07 E
Huairou 154 Dd 40.20N 116.37 E
Huaiyang 154 Ch 33.44N 114.52 E
Huaiyin (Wangying) 154 Eh 33.35N 119.02 E
Huaiyuan 154 Dh 32.58N 117.10 E
Huajuapán de León 190 Ee 17.48N 97.46W
Hualalai 221a Fd 19.41N 155.52W
Hualapai Mountains 188 Ii 34.40N 113.45W
Hualien 152 Lg 23.58N 121.36 E
Huallaga, Rio- 198 If 5.07S 75.30W
Huallanca 202 Ce 8.49S 77.52W
Huamachuco 202 Ce 7.48S 78.04W
Huamahuaca 206 Gb 23.13S 65.23W
Huambo 160 Ij 12.47S 15.43 E
Huambo [3] 170 Ce 12.30S 15.40 E
Huanan 152 Nb 46.14N 130.33 E
Huancabamba [Peru] 202 Ce 5.14S 79.28W
Huancabamba [Peru] 202 Cf 10.21S 75.32W
Huancané 202 Eg 15.12S 69.46W
Huancapi 202 Df 13.41S 74.04W
Huancavelica 200 Ig 12.46S 75.02W
Huancavelica [3] 202 Df 13.00S 75.00W
Huancayo 200 Ig 12.04S 75.14W
Huanchaca, Serrania- 204 Bb 14.30S 60.39W
Huang'an → Hong'an 154 Ci 31.17N 114.37 E
Huangcaoba → Xingyi 152 Hf 25.03N 104.55 E
Huangchuan 152 Ke 32.00N 115.02 E
Huanggang 154 Ci 30.27N 114.53 E
Huangangliang 152 Kc 43.33N 117.32 E
Huanggang Shan 152 Kf 27.50N 117.47 E
Huanggi Hai 154 Bd 40.51N 113.17 E
Huang Hai = Yellow Sea (EN) 140 Of 36.00N 124.00 E
Huang He = Yellow River (EN) 140 Nf 37.32N 118.19 E
Huanghe Kou 154 Ef 37.54N 118.48 E
Huangheyan → Madoi 142 Lf 35.00N 98.56 E
Huanghua 154 De 38.23N 117.21 E
Huanghuashi 154 Bj 28.14N 113.11 E
Huangliu 152 Ih 18.41N 108.46 E
Huangmao Jian 152 Kf 27.55N 119.11 E
Huangmei 154 Ci 30.05N 115.56 E
Huangnihe 154 Ic 43.33N 127.28 E
Huangpi 154 Ci 30.53N 114.22 E
Huangpu 152 Jg 23.05N 113.25 E
Huang Shan 152 Ke 30.10N 118.10 E
Huangshi 142 Nf 30.12N 115.00 E
Huang Shui 152 Hd 36.05N 103.20 E
Huangtu Gaoyuan 140 Mf 37.00N 108.00 E
Huanguelén 204 Bm 37.02S 61.57W
Huangxian 152 Ld 37.32N 120.30 E
Huangyan 152 Lf 28.39N 121.17 E
Huangyan Dao 150 Gc 15.05N 117.45 E
Huangyuan 152 Hd 36.40N 101.12 E
Huangzhai → Yangqu 154 Be 38.05N 112.37 E
Huangzhong 152 Hd 36.30N 101.30 E
Huanren 152 Mc 41.16N 125.22 E
Huan Shui 154 Ci 30.40N 114.21 E
Huanta 202 Df 12.56S 74.15W
Huantai (Suozhen) 154 Ef 36.57N 118.05 E
Huánuco 200 If 9.55S 76.14W
Huánuco [3] 202 Ce 9.30S 75.50W
Huanxian 152 Id 36.36N 107.06 E
Huaraz 200 If 9.32S 77.32W
Huarmey 202 Cf 10.04S 78.10W
Huarong 154 Bj 29.31N 112.33 E
Huascarán, Nevado- 198 If 9.07S 77.37W
Huasco 206 Fc 28.28S 71.14W
Hua Shan 152 Je 34.27N 110.05 E
Huatabampo 190 Cc 26.50N 109.38W
Huatong 154 Fd 40.03N 121.56 E
Huatusco de Chicuéllar 192 Kh 19.09N 96.57W
Huauchinango 192 Jg 20.11N 98.03W
Huautla de Jiménez 192 Kh 18.08N 96.51W
Huaxian (Daokou) 154 Cg 35.33N 114.30 E
Huayllay 202 Cf 11.01S 76.21W
Huaynamota, Rio- 192 Gg 21.51N 104.42W
Huaytará 202 Cf 13.36S 75.22W
Hubbard Creek Lake 186 Gj 32.45N 99.00W
Hubbard Lake 184 Fc 44.49N 83.34W
Hubei Sheng (Hu-pei Sheng) = Hupeh (EN) 152 Je 31.00N 112.00 E
Hubli-Dhārwār 142 Jh 15.21N 75.10 E
Hubsugul Nur (Chövsgöl Nuur) [2] 140 Md 51.00N 100.30 E
Hückelhoven 124 Ic 51.03N 6.13 E
Hückeswagen 124 Jc 51.09N 7.21 E
Hucknall 118 Lh 53.02N 1.11W
Hucqueliers 124 Dd 55.03N 1.54 E
Huczwa 120 Tf 50.49N 23.59 E
Hudat [Abz.-U.S.S.R.] 132 Pi 41.34N 48.43 E
Hudat [Eth.] 168 Fe 4.45N 39.27 E
Huddersfield 118 Lh 53.39N 1.47W
Huddinge 116 Ge 59.14N 17.59 E
Ḥuddun 168 Hd 9.08N 47.32 E
Huddur Hadama 168 Ge 4.07N 43.55 E
Hude (Oldenburg) 124 Ka 53.07N 8.28 E
Huder 152 Lb 49.59N 121.30 E
Hudiksvall 112 Hc 61.44N 17.07 E
Hudson 174 Le 40.42N 74.02W
Hudson [Fl.-U.S.] 184 Fk 28.22N 82.42W
Hudson [N.Y.-U.S.] 184 Kd 42.15N 73.47W
Hudson, Lake- 186 Ih 36.20N 95.05W
Hudson Bay 180 Hf 52.52N 102.23W
Hudson Bay 174 Kd 60.00N 86.00W
Hudson Canyon (EN) 184 Kf 39.27N 72.12W
Hudson Hope 180 Fe 56.02N 121.55W
Hudson Land 179 Jd 73.45N 22.30W
Hudson Mountains 222 Pf 74.32S 99.20W
Hudson Strait 174 Li 62.30N 72.00W
Hudžirt 152 Hb 47.05N 102.45 E
Hue 142 Mh 16.28N 107.36 E
Huebra 126 Fc 41.02N 6.48W
Huechucuicui, Punta- 206 Ff 41.47S 74.02W
Hueco Montains 186 Dj 32.05N 105.55W
Huedin 130 Gc 46.52N 23.03 E
Huehuetenango 190 Fe 15.20N 91.28W
Huehuetenango [3] 194 Bf 15.40N 91.35W
Huejutla de Reyes 192 Jg 21.08N 98.25W
Huelgoat 122 Cf 48.22N 3.45W
Huelma 126 Ig 37.39N 3.27W
Huelva 112 Fh 37.16N 6.57W
Huelva [3] 126 Fg 37.40N 7.00W
Huelva, Ribera de- 126 Gg 37.27N 6.00W
Huércal-Overa 126 Kg 37.23N 1.57W
Huerfano Mountain 186 Bh 36.30N 108.10W
Huertas, Cabo de- / Horta, Cap de l'- 126 Lf 38.21N 0.24W
Huerva 126 Lc 41.39N 0.52W
Huesca 126 Lb 42.08N 0.05W
Huesca [3] 126 Lb 42.10N 0.10W
Huéscar 126 Jg 37.49N 2.32W
Hueso, Sierra del- 192 Gb 30.15N 105.20W
Huesos, Arroyo de los- 204 Cm 36.30S 59.09W
Huetamo de Núñez 192 Ih 18.35N 100.53W
Huete 126 Jd 40.08N 2.41W
Huez 122 Mi 45.06N 6.04 E
Ḥufrat an Naḥās 168 Cd 9.45N 24.19 E
Huftarøy 116 Ad 60.05N 5.15 E
Hugh Butler Lake 186 Ff 40.22N 100.42W
Hughenden 210 Fg 20.51S 144.12 E
Hughes 178 Ic 66.03N 154.16W
Hughes Range 188 Hb 49.55N 115.28W
Hugo 186 Ii 34.01N 95.31W
Huguan 154 Bf 36.05N 113.12 E
Huhur He 154 Fc 43.55N 120.47 E
Hui'an 152 Kf 25.07N 118.47 E
Huiarau Range 218 Gc 38.35S 177.10 E
Huib-Hochplato 172 Be 27.10S 16.50 E
Huichang 152 Kf 25.33N 115.45 E
Huicheng → Shexian 154 Ej 29.53N 118.27 E
Huicholes, Sierra de los- 192 Gf 22.00N 104.00W
Huich'ŏn 152 Mc 40.10N 126.17 E
Huifa He 152 Ic 43.06N 126.53 E
Hui He [China] 154 Be 39.21N 112.37 E
Hui He [China] 152 Kb 48.51N 119.12 E
Huiji He 154 Ch 33.53N 115.37 E
Huila [3] 202 Cc 2.30N 75.45W
Huila [3] 170 Ce 15.00S 15.00 E
Huila, Nevado del- 198 Ie 3.00N 76.00W
Huilai 152 Kg 23.05N 116.18 E
Huili 152 Hf 26.37N 102.19 E
Huimanguillo 192 Mi 17.51N 93.23W
Huimin 152 Kd 37.29N 117.30 E
Huinan (Chaoyang) 154 Ic 42.41N 126.03 E
Huisne 122 Gg 47.59N 0.11 E
Huissen 124 Hc 51.56N 5.55 E
Huiten Nur 152 Fd 35.30N 91.55 E
Huittinen 116 Jc 61.11N 22.42 E
Huivuilay, Isla de- 192 Dd 27.03N 110.01W
Huixian [China] 152 Ie 33.46N 106.06 E
Huixian [China] 154 Bg 35.27N 113.47 E
Huixtla 190 Fe 15.09N 92.28W
Huize 152 Hf 26.28N 103.18 E
Huizen 124 Hb 52.18N 5.16 E
Huizhou 152 Jg 23.02N 114.28 E
Hukou 154 Dj 29.44N 116.14 E
Hu Kou 152 Jd 36.09N 110.20 E
Hüksan-Chedo 152 Me 34.30N 125.20 E
Hukuntsi 172 Cd 23.59S 21.44 E
Hulah Lake 186 Hh 36.58N 96.10W
Hulan 152 Mb 46.03N 126.36 E
Hulan He 152 Mb 45.54N 126.42 E
Ḥulayfā' 144 Fd 26.00N 40.47 E
Hulett 188 Md 44.41N 104.36W
Hulga 134 Jd 64.15N 60.58 E
Hulin 152 Nb 45.52N 132.58 E
Hulin He 154 Hb 45.19N 124.06 E
Hull 180 Jg 45.26N 75.43W
Hull → Kingston upon Hull 112 Fe 53.45N 0.20W
Hull → Orona Atoll 208 Je 4.29S 172.10W
Hull Bay 222 Nf 74.55S 137.40W
Hull Glacier 222 Nf 75.05S 137.15W
Hull Mountain 188 Dg 39.31N 122.59W
Hüls, Krefeld- 124 Ic 51.22N 6.31 E
Hulst 124 Gc 51.17N 4.04 E
Hultsfred 114 Dh 57.29N 15.50 E
Huludao 152 Lc 40.44N 120.59 E
Hulun Nur 140 Ne 49.00N 117.30 E
Ḥulwān = Helwān (EN) 164 Fd 29.51N 31.20 E
Hulwāt, Qūr al- 146 Hh 28.49N 38.50 E
Huma [China] 152 Ma 51.44N 126.36 E
Huma [Ton.] 221b Bc 21.19S 174.56W
Humacao 194 Od 18.09N 65.50W
Huma He 152 Ma 51.42N 126.42 E
Humaitá [Braz.] 200 Jf 7.31S 63.02W
Humaitá [Par.] 206 Ic 27.03S 58.33W
Humansdorp 172 Cf 34.02S 24.46 E
Humbe 170 Bf 16.42S 14.54 E
Humber 170 Fe 53.40N 0.10W
Humberside [3] 118 Mh 53.55N 0.30W
Humberto de Campos 202 Jd 2.37S 43.27W
Humboldt 216 Cd 21.53S 166.25 E
Humboldt [Ia.-U.S.] 124 Ia 42.43N 94.13W
Humboldt [Nb.-U.S.] 186 Ie 40.10N 95.57W
Humboldt [Sask.-Can.] 180 Gf 52.12N 105.07W
Humboldt [Tn.-U.S.] 184 Ch 35.49N 88.55W
Humboldt Gletscher 174 Fc 79.40N 63.45W
Humboldt Range 188 Ff 40.15N 118.10W
Humboldt River 174 He 40.02N 118.31W
Hume, Lake- 212 Jg 36.05S 147.05 E
Humenné 120 Rh 48.56N 21.55 E
Hummelfjell 116 Db 62.27N 11.17 E
Hümmling, Der- 120 Dd 52.52N 7.31 E
Humphreys Peak 174 Hf 35.20N 111.40W
Humppila 114 Ff 60.56N 23.22 E
Humuya, Rio- 194 Df 15.13N 87.57W
Hūn 160 If 29.07N 15.56 E
Húnaflói 110 Db 65.50N 20.50W
Hunan Sheng (Hu-nan Sheng) [3] 152 Jf 28.00N 112.00 E
Hu-nan Sheng → Hunan Sheng [3] 152 Jf 28.00N 112.00 E
Hunchun 154 Kc 42.52N 130.21 E
Hundested 116 Di 55.58N 11.52 E
Hunedoara 130 Fd 45.45N 22.54 E
Hunedoara [2] 130 Fd 45.45N 22.52 E
Hünfeld 120 Ff 50.40N 9.46 E
Hünfelden 124 Kd 50.19N 8.11 E
Hunga Ha'apai 221b Ab 20.33S 175.24W
Hungary (EN) = Magyarország [1] 112 Hf 47.00N 20.00 E
Hunga Tonga 221b Ab 20.32S 175.23W
Hungen 124 Kd 50.28N 8.54 E
Hŭngnam 152 Md 39.50N 127.38 E
Hungry Horse Reservoir 188 Ib 48.15N 113.50W
Hun He [China] 154 Gd 40.41N 122.12 E
Hun He [China] 154 Be 39.47N 113.15 E
Hunish, Rubha- 118 Gd 57.43N 6.20W
Hunjiang 152 Mc 41.55N 126.27 E
Hun Jiang 154 Hd 40.52N 125.42 E
Hunneberg 116 Ef 58.20N 12.27 E
Hunnebostrand 116 Df 58.27N 11.18 E
Hunsrück 120 Dg 49.50N 7.10 E
Hunstanton 118 Ni 52.57N 0.30 E
Hunte 120 Ec 53.14N 8.20 E
Hunter, Ile- 208 Ig 22.24S 172.03 E
Hunter Island 212 Ih 40.30S 144.45 E
Hunter Ridge (EN) 2 208 Ig 21.30S 174.30 E
Hunter River 212 Kf 32.30S 151.42 E
Hunterville 218 Fc 39.56S 175.34 E
Huntingdon 118 Mi 52.30N 0.10W
Huntingdon [Eng.-U.K.] 118 Mi 52.20N 0.12W
Huntingdon [Pa.-U.S.] 184 He 40.31N 78.02W
Huntingdon [Que.-Can.] 184 Jc 45.05N 74.08W
Huntington [In.-U.S.] 184 Ee 40.53N 85.30W
Huntington [W.V.-U.S.] 182 Kd 38.24N 82.26W
Huntly [N.Z.] 218 Fb 37.33S 175.10 E
Huntly [Scot.-U.K.] 118 Kd 57.27N 2.47W
Huntsville [Al.-U.S.] 176 Kf 34.44N 86.35W
Huntsville [Ont.-Can.] 180 Jg 45.20N 79.13W
Huntsville [Tx.-U.S.] 176 Ht 30.43N 95.33W
Hunucmá 192 Og 21.01N 89.52W
Hünxe 124 Ic 51.39N 6.47 E
Hunyani 172 Ec 15.37S 30.39 E
Hunyuan 152 Jd 39.38N 113.42 E
Hunza → Baltit 148 Ea 36.20N 74.40 E
Hunze 122 Ma 53.13N 6.40 E
Huocheng (Shuiding) 152 Dc 44.03N 80.49 E
Huojia 154 Bg 35.16N 113.39 E
Huolongmen 152 Mb 49.49N 125.49 E
Huolu 154 Ce 38.05N 114.18 E
Huon, Ile- 208 Hf 18.01S 162.57 E
Huon Gulf 212 Ja 7.10S 147.25 E
Huon Peninsula 214 Di 6.25S 147.30 E
Huonville 212 Jh 43.01S 147.02 E
Huoqin 154 Dh 32.21N 116.17 E
Huoshan 152 Ke 31.19N 116.20 E
Huo Shan [China] 152 Ke 31.06N 116.12 E
Huo Shan [China] 152 Jd 37.00N 111.52 E
Huoxian 152 Jd 36.39N 111.47 E
Hupeh (EN) = Hubei Sheng (Hu-pei Sheng) [2] 152 Je 31.00N 112.00 E
Hu-pei Sheng → Hubei Sheng = Hopeh (EN) [2] 152 Je 31.00N 112.00 E
Hür 146 Qg 30.50N 57.07 E
Hurama → Hongyuan 152 He 32.45N 102.38 E
Huränd 146 Lc 38.40N 47.20 E
Hurd, Cape- 184 Gc 45.13N 81.44W
Hurdalssjøen 116 Dd 60.20N 11.05 E
Hurd Deep = La Grande Trench (EN) 118 Kl 49.40N 3.00W
Hurdiyo 168 Ic 10.32N 51.08 E
Hurepoix 122 If 48.30N 2.10 E
Hure Qi 154 Fc 42.44N 121.44 E
Hurkett 186 Lb 48.50N 88.29W
Hurmuli 18 Il 51.01N 136.56 E
Huron 182 Hc 44.22N 98.13W
Huron, Lake- 174 Ke 44.30N 82.15W
Huron Mountains 184 Db 46.45N 87.45W
Hurricane 188 Ih 37.11N 113.17W
Hurricane Cliffs 188 Ih 37.00N 113.05W
Hurrungane 116 Bc 61.27N 7.51 E
Hursley 126 Ac 51.01N 1.24W
Hurst 186 Hj 32.49N 97.09W
Hurstpierpoint 124 Bd 50.55N 0.10W
Hürth 120 Cf 50.52N 6.52 E
Hurum 116 De 59.35N 10.35 E
Hurunui 218 Ee 42.54S 173.18 E
Hurup 116 Ch 56.45N 8.25 E
Húsavík 114a Cb 66.03N 17.21W
Hushan → Cixi 154 Fi 30.10N 121.14 E
Huşi 130 Lc 46.41N 28.04 E
Huskvarna 116 Fg 57.48N 14.16 E
Huslia 178 Hc 65.42N 156.24W
Husnes 116 Ae 59.52N 5.46 E
Husnesfjorden 116 Ae 59.50N 5.35 E
Hussigny-Godbrange 124 He 49.29N 5.52 E
Hust 132 Ce 48.10N 23.27 E
Hustadvika 116 Ba 63.00N 7.05 E
Husum [F.R.G.] 120 Fb 54.28N 9.03 E
Husum [Swe.] 114 Ee 63.20N 19.10 E
Hutag 152 Hb 49.23N 102.43 E
Hutchinson [Ks.-U.S.] 182 Hd 38.05N 97.56W
Hutchinson [Mn.-U.S.] 186 Id 44.54N 94.22W
Hutch Mountain 188 Ji 34.47N 111.22W
Ḥūth 164 Hf 16.14N 43.58 E
Hutou 152 Nb 46.00N 133.36 E
Hutte Sauvage, Lac de la- 180 Ke 55.57N 65.45W
Hutton, Mount- 212 Je 25.51S 148.20 E
Hutubi 152 Ec 44.07N 86.57 E
Hutuiti, Caleta- 221d Bb 27.07S 109.17W
Hutuo He 154 De 38.14N 116.05 E
Huvhojtun, gora- 138 Le 57.44N 160.45 E
Huxley, Mount- 218 Cf 44.04S 169.41 E
Huy 120 Ge 51.55N 10.55 E
Huy/Hoei 122 Ld 50.31N 5.14 E
Huzgan 146 Mg 31.27N 48.04 E
Huzhou → Wuxing 152 Le 30.47N 120.07 E
Hvaler 116 De 59.05N 11.00 E
Hvalynsk 136 Ee 52.30N 48.07 E
Hvammstangi 114a Bb 65.24N 20.57W
Hvannadalshnúkur 110 Ec 64.01N 16.41W
Hvar 128 Kg 43.11N 16.27 E
Hvar 128 Kg 43.07N 16.45 E
Hvarski kanal 128 Kg 43.15N 16.37 E
Hvatovka 132 Oc 52.21N 46.36 E
Hveragerdi 114a Bb 64.00N 21.12W
Hveravellir 114a Bb 64.54N 19.35W
Hvide Sande 116 Ci 55.59N 8.08 E
Hvítá [Ice.] 114a Bb 64.35N 21.46W
Hvítá [Ice.] 114a Bb 64.00N 20.58W
Hvittingfoss 116 De 59.29N 10.01 E
Hvojnaja 114 Ig 58.56N 34.31 E
Hwach'on-ni 154 Ie 38.58N 126.02 E
Hwange 160 Jj 18.21S 26.30 E
Hwang-Hae = Yellow Sea (EN) 140 Of 36.00N 124.00 E
Hwanghae-Namdo [2] 154 He 38.15N 125.30 E
Hwanghae-Pukto [2] 154 He 38.30N 126.25 E
Hwangju 154 He 38.40N 125.45 E
Hyannis [Ma.-U.S.] 184 Le 41.39N 70.17W
Hyannis [Nb.-U.S.] 186 Ff 42.00N 101.44W
Hybo 116 Gc 61.48N 16.12 E
Hyde Park 196 Gi 6.30N 58.16W
Hyderābād [India] 142 Jh 17.23N 78.28 E
Hyderābād [Pak.] 142 Ig 25.22N 68.22 E
Hyères 122 Mk 43.07N 6.07 E
Hyères, Iles d'- 122 Ml 43.00N 6.20 E
Hyesan 152 Mc 41.24N 128.10 E
Hyltebruk 114 Ch 57.00N 13.14 E
Hyndman Peak 188 He 43.50N 114.10W
Hyōgo Ken [2] 154 Mg 34.50N 134.48 E
Hyrov 120 Sg 49.32N 22.48 E
Hyrum 188 Jf 41.38N 111.51W
Hyrylä 116 Kd 60.24N 25.02 E
Hyrynsalmi 114 Gd 64.40N 28.32 E
Hysham 188 Lc 46.18N 107.14W
Hythe [Eng.-U.K.] 124 Ad 50.52N 1.24W
Hythe [Eng.-U.K.] 118 Oj 51.05N 1.05 E
Hyūga 154 Kh 32.25N 131.38 E
Hyūga-Nada 156 Be 32.25N 131.45 E
Hyvinge/Hyvinkää 114 Ff 60.38N 24.52 E
Hyvinkää/Hyvinge 114 Ff 60.38N 24.52 E

I

Iaco, Rio- 202 Ee 9.03S 68.35W
Iacobeni 130 Ib 47.26N 25.19 E
Iakora 172 Hd 23.08S 46.38 E
Ialomiţa [2] 130 Ke 44.30N 27.30 E
Ialomiţa 130 Ke 44.42N 27.51 E
Ialomiţei, Balta- 130 Ke 44.30N 28.00 E
Iapó, Rio- 204 Gg 24.30S 50.24W
Iaşi 112 If 47.10N 27.36 E
Iaşi [2] 130 Kb 47.07N 27.39 E
Iba 150 Gc 15.20N 119.58 E
Ibadan 160 Hh 7.23N 3.54 E
Ibagué 200 Ie 4.27N 75.14W
Ibaiti 206 Jb 23.50S 50.10W
Iballja 130 Cg 42.11N 20.00 E
Ibañeta, Puerto de- → Roncesvalles, Puerto de- 126 Ka 43.01N 1.19W
Ibans, Laguna de- 194 Ef 15.53N 84.52W
Ibar 130 Df 43.44N 20.45 E
Ibara 156 Cd 34.36N 133.28 E
Ibaraki 156 Dd 34.49N 135.34 E
Ibaraki Ken [2] 154 Pf 36.25N 140.30 E
Ibaré 204 Ej 30.49S 54.16W
Ibarra 200 Ie 0.21N 78.07W
Ibarreta 206 Ic 25.13S 59.51W
Ibb 142 Gh 13.58N 44.11 E
Ibba 174 Ke 4.48N 29.06 E
Ibba 168 Dd 7.09N 28.41 E
Ibbenbüren 120 Dd 52.16N 7.44 E
Ibdekkene 166 Fb 18.28N 0.38 E
Ibembo 170 Db 2.38N 23.37 E
Ibenga 170 Cb 2.20N 18.08 E
Iberá, Esteros del- 204 Di 28.05S 57.05W
Iberá, Laguna- 204 Di 28.30S 57.09W
Iberian Basin (EN) 106 De 40.00N 16.00W
Iberian Mountains (EN) = Ibérica, Cordillera- 110 Fg 41.30N 2.30W
Iberian Peninsula (EN) = Peninsula Ibérica 110 Fg 40.00N 4.00W
Ibérica, Cordillera- = Iberian Mountains (EN) 110 Fg 41.30N 2.30W
Iberville, Lac d'- 180 Ke 56.00N 73.10W
Ibestad 114 Db 68.48N 17.08 E
Ibi [Nig.] 166 Gd 8.11N 9.45 E
Ibi [Sp.] 126 Lf 38.38N 0.34W
Ibiá 202 Ig 19.29S 46.32W
Ibiagui 204 Ja 13.03S 44.12W
Ibiaí 204 Jc 16.51S 44.55W
Ibibobo 204 Ff 21.35S 62.58W
Ibicaraí 202 Kf 14.51S 39.36W
Ibicuí, Rio- 198 Kh 29.25S 56.47W
Ibicui da Armada, Rio- 204 Ej 30.16S 54.54W
Ibicuy 204 Ck 33.44S 59.10W
Ibicuy, Rio- 204 Ck 33.48S 59.10W
Ibigawa 156 Ed 35.29N 136.34 E
Ibipetuba 202 Jf 11.00S 44.32W
Ibiraiaras 204 Gi 28.22S 51.39W
Ibirama 204 Hh 27.04S 49.31W
Ibirapuitã, Rio- 204 Ei 29.22S 55.57W
Ibirocai, Arroio- 204 Di 29.26S 56.43W
Ibiruba 204 Fi 28.38S 53.06W
Ibitinga 204 He 21.45S 48.49W
Ibitinga, Represa- 204 He 21.41S 49.05W
Ibity 172 Hd 20.10S 46.58 E
Ibiza/Eivissa = Iviza (EN) 110 Gh 39.00N 1.25 E
Ibiza / La Vila d'Eivissa 126 Nf 38.54N 1.26 E
Iblei, Monti- 128 Im 37.10N 14.55 E
Ibn Hāni', Ra's- 146 Fe 35.35N 35.43 E
Ibn Qawrah 168 Ib 15.43N 50.32 E
Ibo 172 Gb 12.22S 40.36 E
Ibo-Gawa 156 Dd 34.46N 134.35 E
Iboundji, Mont- 170 Bc 1.08S 11.48 E
Ibrā' 144 Ie 22.38N 58.40 E
Ibrah 168 Dc 10.36N 25.20 E
Ibrāhīm, Jabal- 140 Gg 20.27N 41.09 E
Ibresi 114 Li 55.18N 47.05 E
'Ibrī 144 Ie 23.16N 56.32 E
Ibrim 164 Fe 22.39N 32.05 E
Ibshawāy 146 Dh 29.22N 30.41 E
Ibuki-Sanchi 156 Ed 35.35N 136.25 E
Ibuki-Yama 156 Ed 35.25N 136.24 E
Ibusuki 154 Ki 31.16N 130.39 E
Iča 138 Ke 55.28N 155.58 E
Ica 200 Ig 14.04S 75.42W
Ica [3] 202 Cf 14.20S 75.30W
Iça, Rio- 198 Jf 3.07S 67.58W
Icaiché 192 Oh 18.05N 89.10W
Içamaquã, Rio- 204 Ei 28.34S 56.00W
Içana, Rio- 202 Ec 0.26N 67.19W
Icara 204 Hi 28.42S 49.18W
Icaraíma 204 Ff 23.23S 53.41W
İçel 144 Db 36.48N 34.38 E
Iceland (EN) = Island 110 Eb 65.00N 18.00W
Iceland Basin (EN) 110 Dc 60.00N 20.00W
Ichalkaranji 148 Ee 16.42N 74.28 E
Ichibusa-Yama 156 Be 32.19N 131.06 E
Ichihara 154 Pg 35.31N 140.05 E
Ichikawa 156 Fd 35.44N 139.55 E
Ichi-Kawa 156 Dd 34.46N 134.43 E
Ichinohe 154 Pd 40.13N 141.17 E
Ichinomiya 154 Ng 35.18N 136.48 E
Ichinoseki 154 Pe 38.55N 141.08 E
Ich'ŏn [N.Kor.] 154 Ie 38.29N 126.53 E
Ich'ŏn [S.Kor.] 154 If 37.17N 127.27 E
Ichtegem 124 Fc 51.06N 3.00 E
Ičigemski hrebet 138 Ld 63.30N 164.00 E
Ičinskaja Sopka, vulkan- 140 Rd 55.39N 157.40 E
Ičnja 136 De 50.52N 32.25 E
Icó 202 Ke 6.24S 38.51W
Icy Cape 178 Gb 70.20N 161.52W
Idaarderadeel 124 Ha 53.06N 5.50 E
Idaarderadeel-Grow 124 Ha 53.06N 5.50 E
Idabel 186 Ij 33.54N 94.50W
Idah 166 Gd 7.06N 6.44 E
Idaho [2] 182 Ec 45.00N 115.00W
Idaho Falls 176 He 43.30N 112.02W
Idalia 186 Eg 39.43N 102.14W
Idān 168 Hd 6.03N 49.01 E
Idanha-a-Nova 126 Ee 39.55N 7.14W
Idar-Oberstein 120 Dg 49.42N 7.18 E
Idarwald 124 Je 49.50N 7.13 E
Idel 114 Id 64.08N 34.12 E
Ideles 162 Ie 23.49N 5.55 E
Ider 152 Hb 49.16N 100.41 E
Idfū 164 Fe 24.58N 32.52 E
Idhi Óros 110 Ih 35.15N 24.45 E
Idhra 130 Gl 37.21N 23.28 E
Idhra 130 Gl 37.20N 23.30 E
Idhras, Kólpos- 130 Gl 37.22N 23.22 E
Idice 128 Ff 44.35N 11.49 E
Idil 146 Id 37.21N 41.54 E
Idíni 162 Df 17.58N 15.40W
Idiofa 170 Cc 4.59S 19.36 E
Idjil, Kédia d'- 162 Ee 22.38N 12.33W
Idkerberget 116 Fd 60.23N 15.14 E
Idle 118 Mh 53.27N 0.48W
Idlib 144 Eb 35.55N 36.38 E
Idokogo 170 Ab 0.35N 9.19 E
Idolo, Isla del- 192 Kg 21.25N 97.27W
Idre 116 Ec 61.52N 12.43 E
Idrica 116 Mh 56.18N 28.55 E
Idrija 128 Id 46.00N 14.02 E
Idro, Lago d'- 128 Ee 45.47N 10.30 E
Idstein 120 Ef 50.14N 8.16 E
Idževan 132 Ni 40.52N 45.04 E
Iecava 130 Kh 56.33N 24.11 E
Iecava 130 Jh 56.40N 23.40 E
Iepê 204 Gf 22.40S 51.05W
Ieper/Ypres 122 Id 50.51N 2.53 E
Ierápetra 130 In 35.01N 25.45 E
Ierisós 130 Gi 40.24N 23.53 E
Ierisoú, Kólpos- 130 Gi 40.26N 23.55 E
Iernut 130 Hc 46.27N 24.15 E
Ie-Shima 156b Ab 26.43N 127.47 E
Ieshima-Shotō 156 Dd 34.40N 134.30 E
Iesolo 128 Ge 45.32N 12.38 E
Iezerul, Virful- 130 Hd 45.28N 24.57 E
Ifakara 170 Gd 8.08S 36.41 E
Ifaki 166 Gd 7.48N 5.14 E
'Ifāl, Wādī al- 146 Fh 28.07N 35.02 E
Ifalik Atoll 208 Fd 7.15N 144.27 E
Ifanadiana 172 Hd 21.17S 47.35 E
Ife 166 Fd 7.28N 4.34 E
Iferouâne 160 Hg 19.04N 8.24 E
Ifetesene 162 Hd 25.30N 4.33 E
Ifni 162 Ed 29.15N 10.08W
Ifon 166 Gd 6.58N 5.55 E
Iforas, Adrar des- 158 Hg 19.00N 2.00 E
Iga 156 Ed 34.49N 136.12 E
Igal 120 Nj 46.32N 17.57 E
Iganga 170 Fb 0.37N 33.29 E
Igara Paraná, Rio- 202 Dd 2.09S 71.47W

Index Symbols

- Independent Nation
- State, Region
- District, County
- Municipality
- Colony, Dependency
- Continent
- Physical Region
- Historical or Cultural Region
- Mount, Mountain
- Volcano
- Hill
- Mountains, Mountain Range
- Hills, Escarpment
- Plateau, Upland
- Pass, Gap
- Plain, Lowland
- Delta
- Salt Flat
- Valley, Canyon
- Crater, Cave
- Karst Features
- Depression
- Polder
- Desert, Dunes
- Forest, Woods
- Heath, Steppe
- Oasis
- Cape, Point
- Coast, Beach
- Cliff
- Peninsula
- Isthmus
- Sandbank
- Island
- Atoll
- Rock, Reef
- Islands, Archipelago
- Rocks, Reefs
- Coral Reef
- Well, Spring
- Geyser
- River, Stream
- Waterfall, Rapids
- River Mouth, Estuary
- Lake
- Salt Lake
- Intermittent Lake
- Reservoir
- Swamp, Pond
- Canal
- Glacier
- Ice Shelf, Pack Ice
- Ocean
- Sea
- Gulf, Bay
- Strait, Fjord
- Lagoon
- Bank
- Seamount
- Tablemount
- Ridge
- Shelf
- Basin
- Escarpment, Sea Scarp
- Fracture
- Trench, Abyss
- National Park, Reserve
- Point of Interest
- Recreation Site
- Cave, Cavern
- Historic Site
- Ruins
- Wall, Walls
- Church, Abbey
- Temple
- Scientific Station
- Railway station
- Airport
- Port
- Military installation
- Lighthouse
- Mine
- Tunnel
- Dam, Bridge

Igarapava 204 Ie 20.03S 47.47W
Igarapé-Açu 202 Id 1.07S 47.37W
Igarapé-Miri 202 Id 1.59S 48.58W
Igarka 142 Kc 67.28N 86.35 E
Igatimí 206 Ib 24.05S 55.30W
Igawa 170 Fd 8.46S 34.23 E
Igbetti 166 Fd 8.45N 4.08 E
Iğdır 146 Kc 39.56N 44.02 E
Iggesund 114 Df 61.38N 17.04 E
Iglesias 128 Ck 39.19N 8.32 E
Iglesiente 128 Ck 39.20N 8.40 E
Igli 162 Gc 30.27N 2.18W
Iglino 134 Hi 54.50N 56.28 E
Igloolik 176 Kc 69.24N 81.49W
Ignace 180 Ig 49.26N 91.41W
Ignalina 114 Gi 55.22N 26.13 E
Ignatovo 114 If 60.49N 37.48 E
Iğneada 146 Bb 41.50N 27.58 E
Iğneada Burun 130 Lh 41.54N 28.03 E
Igombe 170 Fc 4.25S 31.58 E
Igoumenítsa 130 Dj 39.30N 20.16 E
Igra 136 Fd 57.33N 53.10 E
Igreja, Morro de- 204 Hi 28.08S 49.30W
Igren 132 Ie 48.29N 35.13 E
Igrim 136 Gc 63.12N 64.29 E
Iguaçu, Rio- 198 Kh 25.36S 54.36W
Igualada 126 Nc 41.35N 1.38 E
Iguala de la Independencia 190 Ee 18.21N 99.32W
Iguana, Sierra de la- 192 Id 26.30N 100.15W
Iguape 204 Ig 24.43S 47.33W
Iguariaça, Serra do- 204 Ei 29.03S 55.15W
Iguassu Falls (EN)=Iguazú, Cataratas del- 198 Kh 25.41S 54.26W
Iguatemi 202 Hh 23.35S 54.30W
Iguatemi, Rio- 204 Ef 23.55S 54.10W
Iguatu 200 Mf 6.22S 39.18W
Iguazú, Cataratas del- = Iguassu Falls (EN) 198 Kh 25.41S 54.26W
Iguéla 170 Ac 1.55S 9.19 E
Iguidi, 'Erg- 158 Gf 27.00N 6.00W
Iharagna 172 Ib 13.22S 50.00 E
Ihavandiffulu Atoll 148a Ba 7.00N 72.55 E
Iheya-Jima 156b Ab 27.03N 127.57 E
Ih-Hajrhan 152 Ib 46.56N 105.56 E
Ihiala 166 Gd 5.51N 6.51 E
Ihirene 162 He 20.28N 4.37 E
Ihnāsiyat al Madīnah 146 Dh 29.05N 30.56 E
Ih-Obo-Ula 152 Gc 44.55N 95.20 E
Ihosy 160 Lk 22.25S 46.07 E
Ihotry, Lac- 172 Gd 21.56S 43.41 E
Ihrhove, Westoverledingen- 124 Ja 53.10N 7.27 E
Ihsaniye 146 Dc 36.55N 34.46 E
Ihtiman 130 Gg 42.26N 23.49 E
Ih-Ula 152 Hb 49.27N 101.27 E
Ii 114 Fd 65.19N 25.27 E
Iida 154 Ng 35.31N 137.50 E
Iide-San 156 Fc 37.52N 139.41 E
Iijoki 114 Fd 65.20N 25.17 E
Iisaku/Isaku 116 Le 59.14N 27.41 E
Iisalmi 114 Ge 63.34N 27.11 E
Iisvesi 116 Lb 62.45N 26.50 E
Iittala 116 Kc 61.04N 24.10 E
Iivaara 114 Gd 65.47N 29.40 E
Iiyama 156 Fc 36.52N 138.20 E
Iizuka 156 Be 33.38N 130.41 E
Ija 138 Fe 55.02N 101.00 E
Ijebu Ode 166 Fd 6.49N 3.56 E
IJmuiden, Velsen- 124 Gb 52.28N 4.35 E
Ijoubbâne, 'Erg- 166 Da 22.30N 6.00W
IJssel 122 Lb 52.30N 5.50 E
IJsselmeer 122 Lb 52.45N 5.25 E
IJsselmuiden 124 Hb 52.34N 5.56 E
IJsselstein 124 Hb 52.01N 5.02 E
Ijuí 206 Jc 28.23S 53.55W
Ijuí, Rio- 204 Eh 27.58S 55.20W
Ijūin 156 Bf 31.37N 130.24 E
Ijuízinho, Rio- 204 Ei 28.20S 54.28W
Ijuw 220e Bb 0.31S 166.57 E
Ijzendijke 124 Fc 51.20N 3.37 E
IJzer 122 Ic 51.09N 2.43 E
Ik 110 Ld 55.55N 52.36 E
Ikaalinen 114 Ff 61.46N 23.03 E
Ikalamavony 172 Hd 21.10S 46.32 E
Ikamatua 218 De 42.17S 171.42 E
Ikaría 130 Jl 37.35N 26.10 E
Ikaríon Pélagos 130 Jl 37.30N 26.35 E
Ikast 116 Ch 56.08N 9.10 E
Ikatski hrebet 138 Gf 54.00N 111.15 E
Ikawa 156 Fd 35.13N 138.14 E
Ikeda [Jap.] 156 Cd 34.01N 133.48 E
Ikeda [Jap.] 152 Pc 42.55N 143.27 E
Ikeda-Ko 156 Bf 31.14N 130.34 E
Ikej 138 Ff 54.12N 100.04 E
Ikeja 166 Fd 6.36N 3.21 E
Ikela 160 Ji 1.11S 23.16 E
Ikelemba 170 Cb 0.07N 18.17 E
Ikerre 166 Gd 7.30N 5.14 E
Ikerssuaq 179 Ie 65.10N 39.45W
Iki 156 Ae 33.45N 129.45 E
Iki-Kàikyō 154 Jh 33.45N 129.50 E
Ikitsuki-Shima 156 Ae 33.25N 129.25 E
İkizdere 146 Ib 40.47N 40.33 E
Ikom 166 Gd 5.58N 8.42 E
Ikongo [Mad.] 172 Hd 21.53S 48.26 E
Ikongo [Tan.] 170 Gd 9.04S 36.51 E
Ikopa 172 Hc 16.50S 46.50 E
Ikot Ekpene 166 Gd 5.10N 7.43 E
Ikuno 156 Dd 35.10N 134.48 E
Ikurangi, Mount- 220p Bb 21.12S 159.45W
Ila 166 Fd 7.40N 4.40 E
Ilaferh 162 He 21.50N 1.20 E
Ilagan 142 Oh 17.10N 121.54 E
Ilām [3] 144 Gc 33.00N 47.00 E
Ilām [Iran] 144 Gc 33.38N 46.26 E
Ilām [Nep.] 148 Hc 26.54N 87.56 E
Ilan 152 Lg 24.45N 121.44 E
Ilanski 138 Ee 56.10N 96.03 E
Ilaro 166 Fd 6.53N 3.01 E
Iława 120 Pc 53.37N 19.33 E
Ilbengja 138 Hd 62.55N 124.10 E
Ile-à-la-Crosse 180 Ge 55.27N 107.53W
Ilebo 160 Ji 4.44S 20.33 E
Ile-de-France 122 Ie 49.00N 2.20 E
Ile de France 179 Kc 77.45N 27.45W
Ile-de-France, Côte de l'- 122 Jf 48.55N 3.50 E
Ilek 136 Fe 51.32N 53.27 E
Ilek 110 Le 51.30N 53.20 E
Ileksa 114 Ie 62.30N 36.57 E
Ilerh 162 He 21.40N 2.22 E
Ile Rousse, L'- 122a Aa 42.38N 8.56 E
Ileša 114 Le 62.37N 46.35 E
Ilesha [Nig.] 166 Fd 8.55N 3.25 E
Ilesha [Nig.] 166 Fd 7.37N 4.44 E
Ilet 114 Li 55.57N 48.14 E
Ilfracombe 118 Ij 51.13N 4.08W
Ilgaz 146 Eb 40.56N 33.38 E
Ilgaz Dağları 146 Eb 41.00N 33.35 E
Ilgın 146 Dc 38.17N 31.55 E
Ilha Grande 202 Ed 0.27S 65.02W
Ilha Grande, Baía da- 204 Jf 23.09S 44.30W
Ílhavo 126 Dd 40.36N 8.40W
Ilhéus 200 Mg 14.49S 39.02W
Ili 140 Je 45.24N 74.08 E
Ilia 130 Fd 45.56N 22.39 E
Iliamna 178 Ie 59.45N 154.54W
Iliamna Lake 178 He 59.30N 155.00W
Ilič 135 Gd 40.55N 68.29 E
İliç 146 Hc 39.28N 38.34 E
Ilica 130 Kj 39.52N 27.46 E
Iličevsk [Abz.-U.S.S.R.] 132 Nj 39.33N 44.59 E
Iličevsk [Ukr.-U.S.S.R.] 136 Df 46.18N 30.37 E
Ilidža 128 Mg 43.50N 18.19 E
Iligan 142 Oi 8.14N 124.14 E
Iligan Bay 150 He 8.25N 124.05 E
Ilim 138 Fe 56.50N 103.25 E
Ilimskoje vodohranilišče 138 Fe 57.20N 102.30 E
Ilinski [R.S.F.S.R.] 138 Jg 47.59N 142.21 E
Ilinski [R.S.F.S.R.] 114 Hf 61.02N 32.42 E
Ilinski [R.S.F.S.R.] 134 Gg 58.35N 55.41 E
Ilion 184 Jd 43.01N 75.04W
Ilio Point 221a Db 21.13N 157.16W
Ilir 138 Fe 55.13N 100.45 E
Ilirska Bistrica 128 Ie 45.34N 14.16 E
Iljaly 135 Bd 41.53N 59.40 E
Ilkal 148 Fe 15.58N 76.08 E
Ilkeston 124 Ab 52.58N 1.18W
Ill 122 Nf 48.40N 7.53 E
Illampu, Nevado del- 202 Eg 15.50S 68.34W
Illana Bay 150 He 7.25N 123.45 E
Illapel 206 Fd 31.38S 71.10W
Illa Sa Conillera / Isla Cunillera 126 Nf 38.59N 1.12 E
Illbillee, Mount- 212 Ge 27.02S 132.30 E
Ille 122 Ef 48.08N 1.40W
Ille-et-Vilaine [3] 122 Ef 48.10N 1.30W
Illéla 166 Gc 14.28N 5.15 E
Iller 120 Fh 48.23N 9.58 E
Illescas 126 Id 40.07N 3.50W
Ille-sur-Têt 122 Il 42.40N 2.37 E
Illi, Ba- 168 Bc 10.44N 16.21 E
Illimani, Nevado del- 198 Jg 16.39S 67.48W
Illingen 124 Je 49.22N 7.03 E
Illinois [2] 182 Jd 40.00N 89.00W
Illinois 174 Jf 38.58N 90.27W
Illinois Peak 188 Hc 47.02N 115.04W
Illizi 160 Hf 26.29N 8.28 E
Ilm 120 He 51.07N 11.40 E
Ilmajoki 116 Jb 62.44N 22.34 E
Ilmen, ozero- 110 Jd 58.20N 31.20 E
Ilmenau 120 Gf 50.41N 10.54 E
Ilmenau 120 Gc 53.23N 10.10 E
Il Montello 128 Ge 45.49N 12.07 E
Ilo 202 Dg 17.38S 71.20W
Iloilo 142 Oh 10.42N 122.34 E
Ilok 128 Ne 45.13N 19.23 E
Ilomantsi 114 He 62.40N 30.55 E
Ilorin 160 Hh 8.30N 4.33 E
Iloron, Cerro- 192 Gg 20.57N 104.22W
Ilova 128 Ke 45.25N 16.45 E
Ilovik 128 If 44.27N 14.33 E
Ilovlja 132 Ne 49.18N 44.01 E
Ilovlja 132 Me 49.14N 43.54 E
Ilpyrski 138 Le 59.52N 164.12 E
Ilski 132 Kg 44.51N 38.32 E
Iltin 138 Nc 67.52N 178.48W
Ilubabor [3] 168 Ed 7.50N 35.00 E
Ilukste/Ilūkste 116 Li 55.58N 26.26 E
Ilūkste/Iluuste 116 Li 55.58N 26.26 E
Ilulissat/Jakobshavn 224 Nc 69.20N 50.50W
Ilwaki 150 Ih 7.56S 126.26 E
Ilyč 134 He 62.32N 56.40 E
Ilz 120 Jh 48.35N 13.30 E
Iłżanka 120 Re 51.14N 21.47 E
Imabari 154 Lg 34.03N 133.00 E
Imagane 154 Pc 42.26N 140.01 E
Imaichi 154 Of 36.43N 139.41 E
Imán, Sierra del- 204 Eh 27.42S 55.28W
Imanburluk 134 Mj 53.40N 67.15 E
Imandra, ozero- 110 Jb 67.30N 33.00 E
Imano-Yama 156 Ce 32.51N 132.49 E
Imari 154 Jh 33.16N 129.53 E
Imaruí 204 Hi 28.21S 48.49W
Imataca, Serranía de- 196 Fi 7.45N 61.00W
Imatra 114 Gf 61.10N 28.46 E
Imazu 156 Ed 35.24N 136.01 E
Imbabah, Al Qāhirah- 164 Fc 30.05N 31.13 E
Imbert 194 Ld 19.45N 70.50W
Imbituba 206 Kc 28.14S 48.40W
Imeni 26 Bakinskih Komissarov [Abz.-U.S.S.R.] 136 Eh 39.19N 49.12 E
Imeni 26 Bakinskih Komissarov [Tur.-U.S.S.R.] 136 Fh 39.21N 54.12 E
İmeni Gastello 138 Jd 61.35N 147.59 E
Imeni Karla Liebknechta 132 Id 51.38N 35.29 E
İmeni Mariny Raskovoj 138 Jd 62.05N 146.30 E
İmeni Poliny Osipenko 138 If 52.23N 136.25 E
Imi 160 Lh 6.28N 42.11 E
Imilili 162 De 22.50N 15.54W
Imi n'Tanout 162 Fc 31.03N 8.08W
Imišli 136 Eh 39.53N 48.03 E
Imjin-gang 154 If 37.47N 126.40 E
Imlay 188 Ff 40.42N 118.07W
Immenstadt im Allgäu 120 Gi 47.34N 10.13 E
Imo [2] 166 Gd 5.30N 7.20 E
Imola 128 Ff 44.21N 11.42 E
Imotski 128 Lg 43.27N 17.13 E
Imperatriz 200 Lf 5.32S 47.29W
Imperia 128 Cg 43.53N 8.03 E
Imperial 186 Ff 40.31N 101.39W
Imperial de Aragón, Canal- 126 Kb 42.02N 1.33W
Imperial Valley 188 Hj 32.50N 115.30W
Impfondo 160 Ih 1.37N 18.04 E
Imphāl 142 Lg 24.49N 93.57 E
Imphy 122 Jh 46.56N 3.15 E
Impilanti 114 Hf 61.41N 31.12 E
Imrali Adasi 130 Li 40.32N 28.32 E
İmroz 146 Ab 40.11N 25.55 E
Imst 128 Ec 47.14N 10.44 E
Imtan 146 Gf 32.24N 36.49 E
Imuris 192 Db 30.47N 110.52W
Im-Zouren 126 Ii 35.04N 3.50W
Ina 154 Ng 35.50N 137.57 E
Ina 120 Kc 53.32N 14.38 E
I-n-Abanrherit 166 Gb 17.58N 6.05 E
Inabu 156 Ed 35.13N 137.30 E
Inaccessible Island 158 Fl 37.17S 12.45W
Inaccessible Islands 222 Re 60.34S 46.44W
I-n-Afaleleh 162 Ie 23.34N 9.12 E
I Naftan, Puntan- 220b Ba 15.05N 145.45 E
Ina-Gawa 156 Fc 37.23N 139.18 E
I-n-Amenas 160 Hf 28.03N 9.33 E
Inami 156 De 33.48N 135.12 E
Inanba-Jima 156 Fe 33.39N 139.18 E
Inangahua Junction 218 Dd 41.52S 171.56 E
Inanwatan 150 Jg 2.08S 132.10 E
Iñapari 202 Ef 10.57S 69.35W
Inarajan 220c Bb 13.16N 144.45 E
I-n-Arhâta 166 Ea 21.09N 0.18W
Inari 112 Ib 68.54N 27.01 E
Inari, Lake- (EN)= Inarijärvi 110 Ib 69.00N 28.00 E
Inarijärvi=Inari, Lake- (EN) 110 Ib 69.00N 28.00 E
Inawashiro 156 Gc 37.34N 140.05 E
Inawashiro-Ko 154 Pf 37.30N 140.03 E
I-n-Azaoua 166 Ga 20.54N 7.28 E
I-n Azaoua 166 Ga 20.47N 7.31 E
Inazawa 156 Ed 35.15N 136.47 E
Inca 126 Oe 39.43N 2.54 E
Inca de Oro 206 Gc 26.45S 69.54W
Incaguasi 206 Fc 29.13S 71.03W
İnce Burun [Tur.] 130 Ki 40.28N 27.16 E
İnce Burun [Tur.] 140 Fe 42.07N 34.56 E
İncekum Burun 146 Ed 36.13N 33.58 E
Inceler 130 Ml 37.42N 29.35 E
I-n-Chaouâg 166 Fb 16.23N 0.10 E
Inchcape (Bell Rock) 118 Ke 56.26N 2.24W
Inchiri [3] 162 Df 20.00N 15.00W
Inch'ŏn 142 Of 37.28N 126.38 E
Incirliova 130 Kl 37.50N 27.43 E
Incudine, Monte- 122a Bb 41.51N 9.12 E
Indaiá, Rio- 204 Jd 18.27S 45.22W
Indaia Grande, Ribeirão- 204 Fd 19.31S 52.29W
Indaiatuba 204 If 23.05S 47.14W
Indal 116 Gb 62.34N 17.06 E
Indalsälven 114 De 62.31N 17.27 E
Inda Selase 168 Fc 14.06N 38.17 E
Indawgyi 148 Jc 25.08N 96.20 E
Indefatigable Banks 118 Ph 53.35N 2.20 E
Independence [Ca.-U.S.] 188 Fh 36.48N 118.12W
Independence [Ia.-U.S.] 186 Ke 42.28N 91.54W
Independence [Ks.-U.S.] 182 Hd 37.13N 95.42W
Independence [Mo.-U.S.] 186 Ig 39.05N 94.04W
Independence [Va.-U.S.] 184 Gg 36.38N 81.11W
Independence Fjord 224 Me 82.00N 30.25W
Independence Mountains 188 Gf 41.15N 116.05W
Independência [Braz.] 204 Fa 13.34S 53.57W
Independência [Braz.] 202 Je 5.23S 40.19W
Independenta 130 Kd 45.29N 27.45 E
Inder → Jalaid Qi 152 Lb 46.41N 122.52 E
Inder, ozero- 132 Qe 48.25N 51.55 E
Inderborski 112 Lf 48.32N 51.47 E
India (EN) 140 Jh 20.00N 77.00 E
India (EN)=Bhārat Juktarashtra [1] 142 Jh 20.00N 77.00 E
India Muerta, Arroyo de la- 204 Fk 33.40S 54.04W
Indiana 184 He 40.39N 79.11W
Indiana [2] 182 Jc 40.00N 86.15W
Indianapolis 176 Kf 39.46N 86.09W
Indian Church 194 Ce 17.45N 88.40W
Indian Creek Point 197d Bb 17.00N 61.43W
Indian Harbour 180 Lf 54.27N 57.13W
Indian Head 180 Hf 50.32N 103.40W
Indian Ocean 106 Gl 21.00S 82.00 E
Indian Ocean (EN)=Ḥindi, Badwēynta- 106 Gl 21.00S 82.00 E
Indian Ocean (EN)=Indico, Oceano- 106 Gl 21.00S 82.00 E
Indian Ocean (EN)= Indien,Océan- 106 Gl 21.00S 82.00 E
Indian Ocean (EN) = Indiese Oseaan 106 Gl 21.00S 82.00 E
Indian Ocean (EN)= Indonesia, Samudera- 106 Gl 21.00S 82.00 E
Indianola 186 Kj 33.27N 90.39W
Indianópolis 204 Id 19.02S 47.55W
Indian Peak 188 Ig 38.16N 113.53W
Indian Rock 188 Ec 46.01N 120.49W
Indian Springs 182 Dd 36.34N 115.40W
Indiantown 184 Gl 27.01N 80.28W
Indian Town Point 197d Bb 17.06N 61.40W
Indiapora 204 Gd 19.57S 50.17W
Indias Occidentales=West Indies (EN) 190 Je 19.00N 70.00W
Indico, Oceano-=Indian Ocean (EN) 106 Gl 21.00S 82.00 E
Indien,Océan-=Indian Ocean (EN) 106 Gl 21.00S 82.00 E
Indiese Oseaan = Indian Ocean (EN) 106 Gl 21.00S 82.00 E
Indiga 136 Eb 67.41N 49.00 E
Indigirka 140 Qb 70.48N 148.54 E
Indigskaja guba 134 Dc 67.45N 48.20 E
Inđija 130 Dd 45.03N 20.05 E
Indio 182 De 33.43N 116.13W
Indio, Río- 194 Fh 10.57N 83.44W
Indio Rico 204 Bn 38.19S 60.53W
Indispensable Reefs 208 Hf 12.40S 160.25 E
Indispensable Strait 219a Ec 9.00S 160.30 E
Indochina (EN) 140 Mh 16.00N 107.00 E
Indonesia [1] 142 Nj 5.00S 120.00 E
Indonesia, Samudera-= Indian Ocean (EN) 106 Gl 21.00S 82.00 E
Indore 142 Jg 22.43N 75.50 E
Indra 116 Li 55.53N 27.40 E
Indragiri 150 Dg 0.22S 103.26 E
Indramayu 150 Eh 6.20S 108.19 E
Indrāvati 148 Ge 18.44N 80.16 E
Indre [3] 122 Hh 46.50N 1.40 E
Indre 122 Gg 47.14N 0.11 E
Indre Arna 116 Ad 60.26N 5.30 E
Indre-et-Loire [3] 122 Gg 47.15N 0.45 E
Indus 140 Ig 24.20N 67.47 E
İnebolu 144 Da 41.58N 33.46 E
Inece 130 Kh 41.41N 27.04 E
Inecik 130 Ki 40.56N 27.16 E
İnegöl 144 Ca 40.05N 29.31 E
Inés Indart 204 Bl 34.24S 60.33W
Ineu 130 Ec 46.26N 21.51 E
Ineu, Vîrful- 130 Hb 47.32N 24.53 E
Inezgane 162 Fc 30.21N 9.32W
I-n-Ezzane 162 Je 23.29N 11.15 E
Inferior, Laguna- 192 Li 16.15N 94.45W
Infiernillo, Presa del- 190 De 18.35N 101.45W
Infiesto 126 Ga 43.21N 5.22W
Infreschi, Punta degli- 128 Jk 39.59N 15.25 E
Ingá 202 Ke 7.17S 35.36W
Inga 170 Bd 5.39S 13.39 E
Ingå/Inkoo 114 Ff 60.03N 24.01 E
Ingabu 148 Je 17.49N 95.16 E
Ingai, Rio- 204 Je 21.10S 44.52W
I-n Gall 166 Gb 16.47N 6.56 E
Ingarö 116 He 59.15N 18.30 E
Ingavi 204 Bb 15.02S 60.29W
Ingelheim am Rhein 124 Ke 49.59N 8.02 E
Ingelmunster 124 Fd 50.55N 3.15 E
Ingelstad 116 Fh 56.45N 14.55 E
Ingende 170 Cc 0.15S 18.57 E
Ingeniero Guillermo N. Juárez 206 Hb 23.54S 61.51W
Ingeniero Jacobacci 206 Gf 41.18S 69.35W
Ingeniero Luiggi 206 He 35.25S 64.29W
Ingenio Santa Ana 206 Gc 27.28S 65.41W
Ingermanland (EN) 110 Id 59.00N 30.00 E
Ingham 210 Ff 18.39S 146.10 E
Ingička 135 Ee 39.47N 65.58 E
Inglefield Bredning 179 Fc 77.40N 65.00W
Inglefield Land 179 Fc 78.44N 68.20W
Inglewood [Austl.] 212 Ke 28.25S 151.05 E
Inglewood [Ca.-U.S.] 188 Fj 33.58N 118.21W
Inglewood [N.Z.] 218 Fc 39.09S 174.12 E
Ingoda 138 Gf 52.03N 113.30 E
Ingolf Fjord 179 Kb 80.35N 17.35W
Ingólfshödi 114a Cc 63.48N 16.39W
Ingolsladt 120 Hh 48.46N 11.26 E
Ingrāj Bāzār 148 Hc 25.00N 88.09 E
I-n-Guezzâm 160 Hg 19.32N 5.42 E
Ingul 132 Gf 47.02N 31.59 E
Ingulec 136 Df 47.43N 33.10 E
Ingulec 132 Hf 46.41N 32.48 E
Inguri 132 Lh 42.24N 41.32 E
Inhaca, Ilha da- 158 Kk 26.02S 32.58 E
Inhambane 160 Kk 23.52S 35.23 E
Inhambane [3] 172 Ed 23.00S 34.30 E
Inhambane, Baía de- 172 Fd 23.50S 35.20 E
Inhaminga 172 Fc 18.25S 35.01 E
Inhanduí-Guaçu, Rio- 204 Fe 21.37S 52.59W
Inhanduízinho, Rio- 204 Fe 21.34S 53.36W
Inharrime 172 Fd 24.28S 35.01 E
Inhassoro 172 Fd 21.32S 35.12 E
Inhaúma 204 Ja 13.01S 44.39W
I-n-Hihaou 162 He 23.00N 2.00 E
Inhobi, Rio- 204 Ef 23.45S 54.40W
Inhumas 202 Ig 16.22S 49.30W
Iniö 116 Id 60.25N 21.25 E
Inírida, Río- 198 Je 3.55N 67.52W
Inis/Ennis 118 Ei 52.50N 8.59W
Inis Airc/Inishark 118 Ch 53.37N 10.16W
Inis Bó Finne/Inishbofin 118 Ch 53.38N 10.12W
Inis Ceithleann/Enniskillen 118 Fg 54.21N 7.38W
Inis Córthaidh/Enniscorthy 118 Gi 52.30N 6.34W
Inis Díomáin / Ennistimon 118 Di 52.57N 9.13W
Inis Eoghain/Inishowen Peninsula 118 Ff 55.15N 7.20W
Inishark/Inis Airc 118 Ch 53.37N 10.16W
Inishbofin/Iniu Bó Finne 118 Ch 53.38N 10.12W
Inisheer/Inis Oírr 118 Dh 53.03N 9.31W
Inishkea 118 Cg 54.08N 10.11W
Inishmaan/Inis Meáin 118 Dh 53.05N 9.35W
Inishmore/Árainn 118 Dh 53.07N 9.45W
Inishmurray/Inis Muirigh 118 Eg 54.26N 8.40W
Inishowen Peninsula/Inis Eoghain 118 Ff 55.15N 7.20W
Inishtranull 118 Ff 55.27N 7.14W
Inishturk/Inis Toirc 118 Ch 53.43N 10.05W
Inis Meáin/Inishmaan 118 Dh 53.05N 9.35W
Inis Muirigh/Inishmurray 118 Eg 54.26N 8.40W
Inis Oírr/Inisheer 118 Dh 53.03N 9.31W
Inis Toirc/Inishturk 118 Ch 53.43N 10.05W
Inja 138 Je 59.22N 144.50 E
Inja [R.S.F.S.R.] 138 Df 50.27N 86.42 E
Inja [R.S.F.S.R.] 138 Je 59.30N 144.48 E
Injeŭp 154 Je 38.04N 128.10 E
Injibara 168 Fc 10.55N 36.58 E
Injune 212 Je 25.51S 148.34 E
I-n-Kak 166 Fb 16.20N 0.17 E
Inkisi 170 Bc 4.46S 14.52 E
Inkoo/Ingå 114 Ff 60.03N 24.01 E
Inland Kaikoura Range 218 Ee 42.00S 173.35 E
Inland Sea (EN)= Setonaikai 140 Pf 34.10N 133.00 E
Inn 110 Hf 48.35N 13.28 E
Innamincka 212 Ie 27.45S 140.44 E
Inner Hebrides 118 Ge 57.00N 6.45W
Inner Mongolia (EN)=Nei Monggol Zizhiqu (Nei-meng-ku Tzu-chih-ch'ü) [2] 152 Jc 44.00N 112.00 E
Inner Silver Pit 118 Nh 53.30N 0.40 E
Inner Sound 118 Hd 57.30N 5.55W
Innerste 120 Fd 52.15N 9.50 E
Innisfail [Alta.-Can.] 188 Ia 52.02N 113.57W
Innisfail [Austl.] 212 Jc 17.32S 146.02 E
Innokentjevka 138 Ig 49.42N 136.55 E
Innokentjevski 138 Jg 48.38N 140.12 E
Innoko 178 Hd 62.14N 159.45W
In'noshima 156 Cd 34.19N 133.10 E
Innsbruck 112 Hf 47.16N 11.24 E
Innuksuac 180 Je 58.27N 78.08W
Innviertel 128 Hb 48.15N 13.15 E
Innvikfjorden 116 Bc 61.50N 6.35 E
Inny/An Eithne 118 Fh 53.35N 7.50W
Ino 156 Ce 33.33N 133.26 E
Inobonto 150 Hf 0.52N 123.57 E
Inongo 160 Ii 1.57S 18.16 E
Inoni 170 Cc 3.04S 15.39 E
Inönü 130 Nj 39.48N 30.09 E
I-n-Ouagar 166 Gb 16.12N 6.54 E
I-n-Ouzzal 162 He 21.34N 1.59 E
Inowrocław 120 Od 52.48N 18.15 E
I-n-Salah 160 Hf 27.13N 2.28 E
Insar 114 Kj 53.52N 44.23 E
Insar 114 Ki 54.42N 45.18 E
Inscription, Cape- 208 Cg 25.30S 112.59 E
Insjön 116 Fd 60.41N 15.05 E
Ińsko 120 Lc 53.27N 15.33 E
Instanbul Boğazi = Bosporus (EN) 110 Ig 41.00N 29.00 E
Instruč 116 Ij 54.39N 21.48 E
Insurăţei 130 Ke 44.55N 27.36 E
Inta 112 Mb 66.05N 60.08 E
I-n-Tabezas 166 Fb 17.54N 1.50 E
I-n-Tallak 166 Fb 16.19N 3.15 E
Intepe 130 Ji 40.00N 26.20 E
Interlaken 128 Bd 46.41N 7.52 E
International Falls 182 Ib 48.36N 93.25W
Interview 148 If 12.55N 92.43 E
Inthanon, Doi- 148 Je 18.35N 98.29 E
Intibucá [3] 194 Cf 14.20N 88.15W
Intiyaco 206 Hc 28.39S 60.05W
Intorsura Buzaului 130 Jd 45.41N 26.02 E
Intracoastal Waterway 186 Im 28.45N 95.40W
Inubō-Zaki 156 Gd 35.42N 140.52 E
Inukjuak 176 Ld 58.30N 78.15W
Inútil, Bahia- 206 Fh 52.45S 71.24W
Inuvik 176 Fc 68.25N 133.30W
Inuyama 156 Ed 35.23N 136.56 E
Inva 134 Gg 58.59N 55.40 E
Inveraray 118 He 56.13N 5.05W
Invercargill 210 Hi 46.25S 168.21 E
Inverell 212 Ke 29.47S 151.07 E
Inverness 112 Fd 57.27N 4.15W
Inverurie 118 Kd 57.17N 2.23W
Investigator Group 208 Eh 33.45S 134.30 E
Investigator Strait 212 Hg 35.25S 137.10 E
Inyangani 172 Ec 18.13S 32.46 E
Inyangani 158 Kj 18.18S 32.51 E
Inyati 172 Dc 19.40S 28.51 E
Inyazura 172 Ec 18.43S 32.10 E
Inyo Mountains 188 Gh 36.50N 117.45W
Inza 136 Ee 53.53N 46.28 E
Inzá 202 Cc 2.33N 76.04W
Inžavino 132 Mc 52.19N 42.31 E
Inzer 134 Hi 54.14N 57.34 E
Inzer 134 Hi 54.30N 56.28 E
Inzia 170 Cc 3.45S 17.57 E
Iō/Kazan-Rettō=Volcano Islands (EN) 140 Qg 25.00N 141.00 E
Ioánnina 112 Ih 39.40N 20.50 E
Ioanninon, Límni- 130 Dj 39.40N 20.53 E
Iokanga 114 Jb 68.03N 39.40 E
Iola 186 Ih 37.55N 95.24W
Iolotan 136 Gh 37.18N 62.21 E
Iona 170 Bf 16.52S 12.34 E
Iona 118 Ge 56.19N 6.25W
Ionava/Jonava 114 Fi 55.05N 24.17 E
Ion Corvin 130 Ke 44.07N 27.48 E
Ione 188 Eg 38.21N 120.56W
Ionia 184 Ed 42.59N 85.04W
Ionian Basin (EN) 110 Hh 36.00N 20.00 E
Ionian Islands (EN)=Iónioi Nísoi 110 Ih 38.30N 20.30 E
Ionian Sea (EN)=Ionio, Mar- 110 Hh 39.00N 19.00 E
Ionian Sea (EN)=Iónion Pélagos 110 Hh 39.00N 19.00 E
Ionio, Mar-=Ionian Sea (EN) 110 Hh 39.00N 19.00 E
Iónioi Nísoi [2] 130 Dk 38.40N 20.10 E
Iónioi Nísoi=Ionian Islands (EN) 110 Ih 38.30N 20.30 E
Iónion Pélagos=Ionian Sea (EN) 110 Hh 39.00N 19.00 E
Ioniškelis/Joniškėlis 116 Ki 56.00N 24.14 E
Ioniškis/Joniškis 114 Fh 56.16N 23.37 E
Iony, ostrov- 138 Je 56.15N 143.20 E
Iori 132 Oi 41.03N 46.27 E
Ios 130 Im 36.44N 25.18 E

Index Symbols

[1] Independent Nation; [2] State, Region; [3] District, County; [4] Municipality; [5] Colony, Dependency; Continent; Physical Region; Historical or Cultural Region; Mount, Mountain; Volcano; Hill; Mountains, Mountain Range; Hills, Escarpment; Plateau, Upland; Pass, Gap; Plain, Lowland; Delta; Salt Flat; Valley, Canyon; Crater, Cave; Karst Features; Depression; Polder; Desert, Dunes; Forest, Woods; Heath, Steppe; Oasis; Cape, Point; Coast, Beach; Cliff; Peninsula; Isthmus; Sandbank; Island; Atoll; Rock, Reef; Islands, Archipelago; Rocks, Reefs; Coral Reef; Well, Spring; Geyser; River, Stream; Waterfall, Rapids; River Mouth, Estuary; Lake; Salt Lake; Intermittent Lake; Reservoir; Swamp, Pond; Canal; Glacier; Ice Shelf, Pack Ice; Ocean; Sea; Gulf, Bay; Strait, Fjord; Lagoon; Bank; Seamount; Tablemount; Ridge; Shelf; Basin; Escarpment, Sea Scarp; Fracture; Trench, Abyss; National Park, Reserve; Point of Interest; Recreation Site; Cave, Cavern; Historic Site; Ruins; Wall, Walls; Church, Abbey; Temple; Scientific Station; Railway station; Airport; Port; Military installation; Lighthouse; Mine; Tunnel; Dam, Bridge

Ios	130	Im	36.42N	25.20 E
Iō-Shima	154	Ki	31.51N	130.13 E
Iowa [2]	182	Ic	42.15N	93.15W
Iowa City	182	Ic	41.40N	91.32W
Iowa Falls	186	Je	42.31N	93.16W
Iowa Park	186	Gj	33.57N	98.40W
Iowa River	186	Kf	41.10N	91.02W
Iō-Yama	156a	Da	44.10N	145.10 E
Ipa	132	Fc	52.07N	29.12 E
Ipameri	202	Ig	17.43S	48.09W
Ipatovo	136	Ef	45.43N	42.53 E
Ipaumirim	202	Ke	6.47S	38.43W
Ipel'	120	Oi	47.49N	18.52 E
Ipiales	202	Cc	0.50N	77.37W
Ipiaú	202	Kf	14.08S	39.44W
Ipiranga	204	Gg	25.01S	50.35W
Ipiros [2]	130	Dj	39.30N	20.40 E
Ipiros=Epirus (EN)	110	Ih	39.30N	20.40 E
Ipiros=Epirus (EN)	130	Dj	39.30N	20.40 E
Ipixuma, Rio-	202	Fe	5.50S	63.00W
Ipixuna	202	De	7.34S	72.36W
Ipoh	142	Mi	4.35N	101.05 E
Ipoly	120	Oi	47.49N	18.52 E
Iporá	202	Hg	16.28S	51.07W
Iporā	204	Ff	23.59S	53.37W
Ippy	168	Cd	6.15N	21.12 E
Ipsala	146	Bb	40.55N	26.23 E
Ipsízonos Óros	130	Gi	40.28N	23.34 E
Ipswich [Austl.]	210	Gg	27.36S	152.46 E
Ipswich [Eng.-U.K.]	112	Ge	52.04N	1.10 E
Ipswich [S.D.-U.S.]	186	Gd	45.27N	99.02W
Ipu	202	Jd	4.20S	40.42W
Iqaluit	176	Mc	63.44N	68.28W
Iqe	152	Fd	38.04N	94.24 E
Iquique	200	Ih	20.13S	70.10W
Iquitos	200	If	3.50S	73.15W
Iraan	186	Fk	30.54N	101.54W
Ira Banda	168	Cd	5.57N	22.06 E
Irabu-Jima	152	Mg	24.50N	125.10 E
Iracoubo	202	Hb	5.29N	53.13W
Iraël	134	Gd	64.27N	55.08 E
Irago-Suidō	156	Ed	34.35N	136.55 E
Irago-Zaki	156	Ed	34.35N	137.01 E
Iráklia	130	Gh	41.10N	23.16 E
Iráklia	130	Im	36.50N	25.26 E
Iráklion	112	Ih	35.20N	25.08 E
Irān=Iran (EN) [1]	142	Hf	32.00N	53.00 E
Iran (EN)=Irān [1]	142	Hf	32.00N	53.00 E
Iran, Pegunungan-=Iran Mountains (EN)	140	Ni	2.05N	114.55 E
Iran, Plateau of- (EN)	140	Hf	32.00N	56.00 E
Irani, Serra do-	204	Fh	27.00S	52.12W
Iran Mountains (EN)=Iran, Pegunungan-	140	Ni	2.05N	114.55 E
Irānshahr	142	Ig	27.13N	60.41 E
Irapa	196	Eg	10.34N	62.35W
Irapuá, Arroio-	204	Fj	30.15S	53.10W
Irapuato	176	Ig	20.41N	101.28W
Iraq (EN) = Al 'Irāq [1]	142	Gf	33.00N	44.00 E
'Irāq al 'Arabi	146	Kg	31.50N	45.50 E
Irati	206	Jc	25.27S	50.39W
Irati	126	Kb	42.35N	1.16W
Irazú, Volcán	174	Ki	9.59N	83.51W
Irbeni Väin	116	Ig	57.48N	22.05 E
Irbid	144	Ec	32.33N	35.51 E
Irbid [3]	146	Gf	32.27N	35.51 E
Irbiktepe	130	Jh	41.00N	26.30 E
Irbit	136	Gd	57.41N	63.03 E
Irbit	134	Kh	57.42N	63.07 E
Irebu	170	Cc	0.37S	17.45 E
Irecê	202	Jf	11.18S	41.52W
Iregua	126	Jb	42.27N	2.24W
Ireland	110	Fe	53.00N	8.00W
Ireland/Éire [1]	112	Fe	53.00N	8.00W
Ireland Trough (EN)	110	Ed	55.00N	12.40W
Iren	134	Hh	57.27N	56.59 E
Ireng River	202	Gc	3.33N	59.51W
Irês Corações	202	Ih	21.42S	45.16W
Iretama	204	Fg	24.27S	52.02W
Irgiz	136	Gf	48.36N	61.16 E
Irgiz	136	Gf	48.13N	62.08 E
Irharrhar [Alg.]	162	Ie	21.01N	6.01 E
Irharrhar [Alg.]	158	Hf	28.00N	6.15 E
Irherm	162	Fc	30.04N	8.26W
Iri	154	Ig	35.56N	126.57 E
Irian Jaya [3]	150	Kg	3.55S	138.00 E
Iriba	160	Jg	15.07N	22.15 E
Irîgui	158	Gg	16.43N	5.30W
Iriklinski	132	Ud	51.39N	58.38 E
Iriklinskoje vodohranilišče	132	Ud	51.45N	58.45 E
Iringa	160	Ki	7.46S	35.42 E
Iringa [3]	170	Gd	8.00S	35.30 E
Irinja, gora-	138	Fe	58.20N	104.30 E
Iriomote Jima	152	Lg	24.20N	123.50 E
Iriona	194	Ef	15.57N	85.11W
Iriri, Rio-	198	Kf	3.52S	52.37W
Irish Sea	110	Fe	53.30N	5.20W
Irish Sea (EN)=Muir Eireann	110	Fe	53.30N	5.20W
Irituia	202	Id	1.46S	47.26W
Irkeštam	135	Ie	39.38N	73.55 E
Irkutsk	142	Md	52.16N	104.20 E
Irkutskaja oblast [3]	138	Fe	56.00N	104.00 E
Irlir, gora-	135	Dc	42.40N	63.30 E
Irminio	128	In	36.46N	14.36 E
Irnijärvi	114	Gd	65.36N	29.05 E
Iro, Lac-	168	Bc	10.06N	19.25 E
Iroise, Mer d'-	122	Bf	48.15N	4.55W
Iron Gate (EN) = Portile de Fier	110	Ig	44.41N	22.31 E
Iron Knob	212	Hf	32.44S	137.08 E
Iron Mountain	182	Jb	45.49N	88.04W
Iron Mountains	118	Fg	54.15N	7.50W
Iron River [Mi.-U.S.]	182	Jb	46.05N	88.39W
Iron River [Wi.-U.S.]	186	Kc	46.34N	91.24W
Ironside Mountain	188	Fd	44.15N	118.08W
Ironton [Mo.-U.S.]	186	Kh	37.36N	90.38W
Ironton [Oh.-U.S.]	184	Ff	38.32N	82.40W
Ironwood	182	Ib	46.27N	90.10W
Iroquois Falls	180	Jg	48.46N	80.41W
Irō-Zaki	154	Og	34.35N	138.55 E
Irpen	136	De	50.31N	30.16 E
Irpinia	128	Ij	40.55N	15.00 E
Irrawaddy → Ayeyarwady	148	Ie	17.00N	95.00 E
Irrawaddy (EN) = Ayeyarwady	140	Lg	15.50N	95.06 E
Irrel	124	Ie	49.51N	6.28 E
Irsāva	120	Th	48.15N	23.05 E
Irsina	128	Kj	40.45N	16.14 E
Irtek	132	Rd	51.29N	52.42 E
Irthlingborough	124	Bb	52.19N	0.36W
Irtyš	140	Ic	61.04N	68.52 E
Irtyšsk	136	He	53.21N	75.27 E
Irumu	170	Eb	1.27N	29.52 E
Irún	126	Ka	43.21N	1.47W
Irurzun	126	Kb	42.55N	1.50W
Irves šaurums	116	Ig	57.48N	22.05 E
Irvine	118	If	55.37N	4.40W
Irving	186	Hj	32.49N	96.56W
Is, Jabal-	168	Fa	21.49N	35.39 E
Isa, Ra's-	164	Hf	15.11N	42.39 E
Isabel	186	Fd	45.24N	101.26W
Isabel, Bahía-	202a	Ab	0.38S	91.25W
Isabela	197	Ab	18.31N	67.07W
Isabela → Basilan City	150	He	6.42N	121.58 E
Isabela, Cabo-	194	Ld	19.56N	71.01W
Isabela, Isla- [Ec.]	198	Gf	0.30S	91.06W
Isabela, Isla- [Mex.]	192	Gg	21.51N	105.55W
Isabella, Cordillera-	190	Gf	13.30N	85.30W
Isabel Segunda	194	Od	18.09N	65.27W
Isabey	130	Ml	38.00N	29.24 E
Isaccea	130	Ld	45.16N	28.28 E
Isachsen	176	Ib	78.50N	103.30W
Isafjörður	112	Db	66.03N	23.09W
Isahaya	154	Jh	32.50N	130.03 E
Isakov, Seamount (EN)	208	Ga	31.35N	151.07 E
Isana, Río-	202	Ec	0.26N	67.19W
Isandja	170	Dc	2.59S	22.00 E
Isanga	170	Dc	1.26S	22.18 E
Isangi	170	Db	0.46N	24.15 E
Isanlu Makutu	166	Gd	8.16N	5.48 E
Isaouane-n-Irarraren	162	Id	27.15N	8.00 E
Isaouane-n-Tifernine	162	Id	27.00N	7.30 E
Isar	120	Ih	48.49N	12.58 E
Isarco/Eisack	128	Fd	46.27N	11.18 E
Isarco, Valle-/Eisacktal	128	Fd	46.45N	11.35 E
Isbergues	124	Ed	50.37N	2.27 E
Iscayachi	202	Eh	21.31S	65.03W
Ischgl	128	Ec	47.01N	10.17 E
Ischia	128	Hj	40.44N	13.57 E
Ischia	128	Hj	40.45N	13.55 E
Ise	152	Oe	34.29N	136.42 E
Isefjord	116	Di	55.50N	11.50 E
Išejevka	114	Li	54.28N	48.17 E
Isen	120	Ih	48.20N	12.45 E
Isenach	124	Ke	49.38N	8.28 E
Isen-Zaki	156b	Bb	27.39N	128.55 E
Iseo, Lago d'- (Sebino)	128	Ee	45.45N	10.05 E
Iseran, Col de l'-	122	Ni	45.25N	7.02 E
Isère [3]	122	Li	45.10N	5.50 E
Isère	122	Kj	44.59N	4.51 E
Išerit, gora-	134	If	61.08N	59.10 E
Iserlohn	120	De	51.22N	7.42 E
Isernia	128	Ii	41.36N	14.14 E
Isesaki	156	Fc	36.19N	139.12 E
Iset	140	Id	56.36N	66.24 E
Isetskoje	134	Lh	56.29N	65.21 E
Ise-Wan	154	Ng	34.40N	136.42 E
Iseyin	166	Fd	7.58N	3.36 E
Isfahan (EN) = Eşfahān	142	Hf	32.40N	51.38 E
Isfana	135	Ge	39.51N	69.32 E
Isfara	135	Hd	40.07N	70.38 E
Isfendiyar Dağları	144	Da	41.45N	34.10 E
Isfjorden	179	Nc	78.15N	15.00 E
Isha Baydabo	160	Lh	3.04N	43.48 E
Ishasha River	170	Ec	0.50S	29.40 E
Ishavet=Arctic Ocean (EN)	224	Be	85.00N	170.00 E
Isherton	202	Gc	2.19N	59.22W
Ishigaki	152	Lg	24.20N	124.09 E
Ishikari	156a	Bb	43.13N	141.18 E
Ishikari-Dake	156a	Cb	43.33N	143.00 E
Ishikari-Gawa	156a	Bb	43.15N	141.20 E
Ishikari-Heiya	156a	Bb	43.00N	141.40 E
Ishikari-Wan	152	Pc	43.25N	141.00 E
Ishikawa [Jap.]	152	Mf	26.27N	127.50 E
Ishikawa [Jap.]	156	Gc	37.09N	140.27 E
Ishikawa Ken [2]	154	Nf	36.35N	136.40 E
Ishim Steppe (EN) = Išimskaja step	140	Id	55.00N	67.30 E
Ishinomaki	152	Pd	38.25N	141.18 E
Ishinomaki-Wan	156	Gb	38.20N	141.15 E
Ishioka	154	Pf	36.11N	140.16 E
Ishitate-San	156	De	33.44N	134.03 E
Ishizuchi-Yama	156	Ce	33.45N	133.05 E
Ishodnaja, gora-	138	Nd	64.50N	173.26W
Ishpeming	184	Db	46.30N	87.40W
Isidro Alves	204	Ee	20.09S	55.12W
Isigny-sur-Mer	122	Ee	49.19N	1.06W
Isii	156	Dd	34.04N	134.26 E
Işıklar Dağı	146	Bb	40.50N	27.05 E
Işikli	130	Mk	38.19N	29.51 E
Isikli Göl	130	Mk	38.14N	29.55 E
Isili	128	Dk	39.44N	9.06 E
Isilkul	136	He	54.55N	71.16 E
Išim	142	Id	56.09N	69.27 E
Išim	140	Jd	57.45N	71.12 E
Išimbaj	136	Fe	53.28N	56.02 E
Išimskaja step = Ishim Steppe (EN)	140	Id	55.00N	67.30 E
Isinga	138	Gf	52.55N	112.00 E
Isiolo	170	Gb	0.21N	37.35 E
Isiro	160	Jh	2.48N	27.41 E
Isisford	212	Id	24.16S	144.26 E
Isjangulovo	134	Hj	52.12N	56.36 E
Iskandar	135	Gd	41.35N	69.43 E
Iskăr	130	Hf	43.44N	24.27 E
Iskăr, Jazovir-	130	Gg	42.25N	23.35 E
Iškašim	136	Hh	36.44N	71.39 E
İskenderun=Alexandretta (EN)	142	Ff	36.37N	36.07 E
İskenderun Körfezi=Alexandretta, Gulf of- (EN)	144	Eb	36.30N	35.40 E
İskilip	146	Fb	40.45N	34.29 E
Iski-Naukat	135	Id	40.14N	72.41 E
Iskininski	132	Rf	47.13N	52.36 E
Iskitim	138	Df	54.38N	83.18 E
Iskushuban	168	Ic	10.13N	50.14 E
Iskut	180	Ee	56.45N	131.48W
Isla Cristina	126	Eg	37.12N	7.19W
İslâhiye	146	Gd	37.26N	36.41 E
Islāmābād	142	Jf	33.42N	73.10 E
Islāmābād → Anantnāg	148	Fb	33.44N	75.09 E
Isla Mujeres	192	Pg	21.12N	86.43W
Island=Iceland (EN) [1]	112	Eb	65.00N	18.00W
Island=Iceland (EN)	110	Eb	65.00N	18.00W
Island Harbour	197b	Ab	18.16N	63.02W
Island Lagoon	212	Hf	31.30S	136.40 E
Island Lake	180	If	53.58N	94.46W
Island Lake	180	If	53.45N	94.30W
Island Pond	184	Lc	44.50N	71.53W
Islands, Bay of - [Can.]	180	Lg	49.10N	58.15W
Islands, Bay of- [N.Z.]	218	Fa	35.10S	174.10 E
Islao, Massif de l'-	158	Lk	22.30S	45.20 E
Islas de la Bahía [3]	194	De	16.20N	86.30W
Islay	110	Fd	55.46N	6.10W
Islaz	130	Hf	43.44N	24.45 E
Isle	122	Fj	44.55N	0.15W
Isle-Jourdain, L'-	122	Hk	43.37N	1.05 E
Isle of Man [5]	118	Ig	54.15N	4.30W
Isle of Wight [3]	118	Lk	50.40N	1.15W
Isle-sur-la-Sorgue, L'-	122	Lk	43.55N	5.03 E
Isleta	186	Ci	34.55N	106.42W
Isle-Verte	184	Ma	48.01N	69.22W
Isloč	116	Lj	53.55N	26.13 E
Ismael Cortinas	204	Dk	33.56S	57.08W
Ismailia (EN)=Al Ismā'īlīyah	164	Fc	30.35N	32.16 E
Ismailly	132	Pi	40.47N	48.13 E
Ismantorps Borg	116	Gh	56.45N	16.40 E
Isnā	160	Kf	25.18N	32.33 E
Isny im Allgäu	120	Gi	47.42N	10.02 E
Isojärvi	116	Ic	61.45N	21.45 E
Isojoki/Storå	114	Ee	62.07N	21.58 E
Isoka	170	Fe	10.08S	32.38 E
Isola del Liri	128	Hi	41.41N	13.34 E
Isola di Capo Rizzuto	128	Ll	38.58N	17.05 E
Isonzo	128	He	45.43N	13.33 E
Isonzo (EN)=Soča	128	He	45.43N	13.33 E
Isosyöte	114	Gd	65.37N	27.35 E
Isparta	144	Db	37.46N	30.33 E
Isperih	130	Jf	43.43N	26.50 E
Ispica	128	In	36.47N	14.55 E
İspir	146	Ib	40.29N	41.00 E
Ispiriz Dağı	146	Jc	38.03N	43.55 E
Israel (EN)=Yisra'el [1]	142	Ff	31.30N	35.00 E
Isratu	168	Fb	16.20N	39.55 E
Issa	116	Mh	56.55N	28.50 E
Issano	202	Gb	5.49N	59.25W
Issaran, Ra's-	146	Eh	28.50N	32.56 E
Issel	120	Cd	52.00N	6.10 E
Isser	126	Ph	36.51N	3.40 E
Issia	166	Dd	6.29N	6.35W
Issia [3]	166	Dd	6.30N	6.35W
Issoire	122	Ji	45.33N	3.15 E
Issoudun	122	Hh	46.57N	2.00 E
Issyk	135	Kc	43.20N	77.28 E
Issyk-Kul, ozero-	140	Je	42.25N	77.15 E
Issyk-Kulskaja oblast [3]	136	Hg	42.10N	78.00 E
Ist	128	If	44.17N	14.47 E
İstanbul	142	Ee	41.01N	28.58 E
İstanbul-Bakırköy	130	Li	40.59N	28.52 E
İstanbul-Beyoğlu	130	Lh	41.02N	28.59 E
İstanbul-Kadıköy	130	Mi	40.59N	29.01 E
İstanbul-Üsküdar	146	Cb	41.01N	29.03 E
Isteren	116	Db	62.00N	11.50 E
Istgāh-e Eqbālīyeh	146	Ne	35.50N	50.45 E
Isthilart	204	Dj	31.11S	57.58W
Istiaia	130	Gk	38.57N	23.09 E
Istisu	132	Nj	39.57N	46.00 E
Istmina	202	Cb	5.09N	76.42W
Isto, Mount-	174	Ec	69.12N	143.48W
Istok	130	Dg	42.47N	20.29 E
Istokpoga, Lake-	184	Gl	27.22N	81.17W
Istra = Istria (EN)	110	Hf	45.00N	14.00 E
Istres	122	Kk	43.31N	4.59 E
Istria	130	Le	44.34N	28.43 E
Istria (EN) = Istra	110	Hf	45.00N	14.00 E
Isulan	150	He	7.02N	124.29 E
Itabaiana	202	Kf	10.41S	37.26W
Itabaianinha	202	Kf	11.16S	37.47W
Itaberá	204	Hf	23.51S	49.09W
Itaberaba	202	Jf	12.32S	40.18W
Itaberaí	202	Ig	16.02S	49.48W
Itabira	202	Jg	19.37S	43.13W
Itabirito	204	Ke	20.15S	43.48W
Itabuna	200	Mg	14.48S	39.16W
Itacaiúna, Rio-	202	Ie	5.21S	49.08W
Itacarambi	204	Jb	15.01S	44.03W
Itacoatiara	200	Kf	3.08S	58.25W
Itacolomi, Pico do-	204	Ke	20.26S	43.29W
Itacuai, Rio-	202	Dd	4.20S	70.12W
Itacumbi	204	Ei	28.44S	55.08W
Itacurubi del Rosario	204	Dg	24.29S	56.41W
Itaguari, Rio-	204	Jb	14.11S	44.40W
Itaguaru	204	Hb	15.44S	49.37W
Itagüi	202	Cb	6.12N	75.40W
Itaimbèzinho	204	Gi	28.38S	50.34W
Itaituba	200	Kf	4.17S	55.59W
Itajaí	200	Lh	26.53S	48.39W
Itajai Açu, Rio-	204	Hh	26.54S	48.33W
Itajubá	202	Ih	22.26S	45.27W
Itajuípe	202	Kf	14.41S	39.22W
Itaka	138	Gf	53.54N	118.42 E
Italia = Italy (EN) [1]	112	Hg	42.50N	12.50 E
Italiana, Penisola-	110	Hg	42.50N	12.50 E
Itálica	126	Fg	37.25N	6.05W
Italy (EN) = Italia [1]	112	Hg	42.50N	12.50 E
Itambacuri	202	Jg	18.01S	41.42W
Itambé, Pico de-	198	Lg	18.23S	43.21W
Itämeri = Baltic Sea (EN)	110	Hd	57.00N	19.00 E
Itampolo	172	Gd	24.41S	43.57 E
Itanagar	148	Ic	26.57N	93.15 E
Itanará, Rio-	204	Eg	24.00S	55.53W
Itanhaém	206	Kb	24.11S	46.47W
Itano	156	Dd	34.09N	134.28 E
Itapaci	204	Hb	14.57S	49.34W
Itapagé	202	Kd	3.41S	39.34W
Itapajipe	204	Hd	19.54S	49.22W
Itaparaná, Rio-	202	Fe	5.47S	63.03W
Itapebi	202	Kg	15.56S	39.32W
Itapecerica	204	Je	20.28S	45.07W
Itapecuru-Mirim	202	Jd	3.24S	44.20W
Itapemirim	202	Jh	21.01S	40.50W
Itaperina, Pointe-	158	Lk	24.59S	47.06 E
Itaperuna	202	Jh	21.12S	41.54W
Itapetinga	202	Jg	15.15S	40.15W
Itapetininga	206	Kb	23.36S	48.03W
Itapetininga, Rio-	204	Hf	23.35S	48.27W
Itapeva	204	Hf	23.58S	48.52W
Itapeva, Lagoa-	204	Hi	29.30S	49.55W
Itapicuru, Rio- [Braz.]	202	Kf	11.47S	37.32W
Itapicuru, Rio- [Braz.]	198	Lf	2.52S	44.12W
Itapipoca	202	Kd	3.31S	39.33W
Itapiranga [Braz.]	202	Gd	2.45S	58.01W
Itapiranga [Braz.]	204	Fh	27.08S	53.43W
Itapirapuã, Pico-	204	Hg	24.17S	49.12W
Itápolis	204	He	21.35S	48.46W
Itaporã	204	Ef	22.01S	54.54W
Itaporanga [Braz.]	204	Hf	23.42S	49.29W
Itaporanga [Braz.]	202	Ke	7.18S	38.10W
Itapuã	204	Gj	30.16S	51.01W
Itapúa [3]	204	Eh	26.50S	55.50W
Itapuranga	202	Ig	15.35S	49.59W
Itaqui	206	Ic	29.08S	56.33W
Itaquyry	204	Eg	24.56S	55.13W
Itararé	204	Hg	24.07S	49.20W
Itararé, Rio-	204	Hf	23.10S	49.42W
Itārsi	148	Fd	22.37N	77.45 E
Itarumã	204	Gd	18.42S	51.25W
Itati	204	Ch	27.16S	58.15W
Itatinga	204	Hf	23.07S	48.36W
Itatski	138	De	56.07N	89.20 E
Itaum	204	Ef	22.00S	55.20W
Itaúna	202	Jh	20.04S	44.34W
Itaya-Tōge	156	Gc	37.50N	140.13 E
Itbāy	158	Kf	22.00N	35.30 E
Itbayat	150	Hb	20.46N	121.50 E
Itchen	124	Ad	50.57N	1.22W
Ite	202	Dg	17.50S	70.58W
Itéa	130	Fk	38.26N	22.25 E
Ithaca	182	Lc	42.26N	76.30W
Ithaca (EN)=Itháki	130	Dk	38.24N	20.40 E
Itháki	130	Dk	38.22N	20.43 E
Itháki = Ithaca (EN)	130	Dk	38.24N	20.40 E
Ith Hils	120	Fd	52.05N	9.35 E
Ithnayn, Harrat-	146	Ii	26.40N	40.10 E
Itigi	170	Fd	5.42S	34.29 E
Itimbiri	158	Jh	2.02N	22.44 E
Itiopya=Ethiopia (EN) [1]	160	Kh	9.00N	39.00 E
Itiquira	202	Hg	17.05S	54.56W
Itiquira, Rio-	198	Kg	17.18S	56.44W
Itirapina	204	If	22.15S	47.49W
Itiúba	202	Kf	10.43S	39.51W
Itivdleq	179	Ge	66.38N	53.51W
Itō	154	Og	34.58N	139.05 E
Itoigawa	154	Nf	37.02N	137.51 E
Itoko	170	Dc	1.00S	21.45 E
Itoman	156b	Ab	26.07N	127.40 E
Iton	122	Hf	49.09N	1.12 E
Itremo, Massif de l'-	172	Hd	20.45S	46.30 E
Iţsā	146	Dh	29.15N	30.48 E
Itsukaichi	156	Cd	34.22N	132.22 E
Itsuki	156	Be	32.24N	130.50 E
Ittiri	128	Cj	40.36N	8.34 E
Itu [Braz.]	204	If	23.16S	47.19W
Itu [Nig.]	166	Gd	5.12N	7.59 E
Itu, Rio-	204	Ei	29.25S	55.51W
Ituí, Rio-	202	Dd	4.38S	70.19W
Ituiutaba	202	Ig	18.58S	49.28W
Itula	170	Ec	3.29S	27.52 E
Itumbiara	202	Ig	18.25S	49.13W
Itumkale	132	Nh	42.43N	45.35 E
Ituna	188	Na	51.10N	103.30W
Itungi Port	170	Fd	9.35S	33.56 E
Itupiranga	202	Ie	5.09S	49.20W
Iturama	204	Gd	19.44S	50.11W
Itúrbide	192	Oh	19.40N	89.37W
Ituri	158	Jh	1.40N	27.01 E
Iturregui	204	Bm	36.50S	61.08W
Iturup, ostrov- / Etorofu Tō	140	Qe	44.54N	147.30 E
Itutinga	204	Je	21.18S	44.40W
Ituverava	206	Kb	20.20S	47.47W
Ituxi, Rio-	198	Jf	7.18S	64.51W
Ituzaingó	204	Dh	27.36S	56.41W
Itz	120	Gg	49.58N	10.52 E
Itzehoe	120	Fc	53.55N	9.31 E
Ivaceviči	132	Dc	52.43N	25.21 E
Ivaí	204	Gg	25.01S	50.52W
Ivaí, Rio- [Braz.]	204	Fi	29.08S	53.16W
Ivaí, Rio- [Braz.]	198	Kh	23.18S	53.42W
Ivaíporã	204	Gg	24.15S	51.45W
Ivajlovgrad	130	Jh	41.32N	26.08 E
Ivakoany, Massif de l'-	172	Hd	23.50S	46.25 E
Ivalojoki	114	Gc	68.43N	27.36 E
Ivančice	120	Mg	49.06N	16.22 E
Ivangorod	114	Gg	59.23N	28.20 E
Ivangrad	130	Cg	42.51N	19.52 E
Ivanhoe	210	Fh	32.54S	144.18 E
Ivanić-Grad	128	Ke	45.42N	16.24 E
Ivaniči	120	Uf	50.38N	24.24 E
Ivanjica	130	Df	43.35N	20.14 E
Ivanjska	128	Lf	44.55N	17.04 E
Ivankov	132	Fd	50.57N	29.58 E
Ivano-Frankovo	120	Tg	49.52N	23.46 E
Ivano-Frankovsk	112	If	48.55N	24.43 E
Ivano-Frankovskaja oblast [3]	136	Cf	48.40N	24.40 E
Ivanovka [R.S.F.S.R.]	138	Hf	50.18N	127.59 E
Ivanovka [Ukr.-U.S.S.R.]	132	Gf	46.57N	30.28 E
Ivanovo [Bye.-U.S.S.R.]	132	Dc	52.10N	25.32 E
Ivanovo [R.S.F.S.R.]	112	Kd	57.00N	40.59 E
Ivanovskaja oblast [3]	136	Ed	57.00N	41.50 E
Ivanovskoje	116	Me	59.12N	28.59 E
Ivanščica	128	Kd	46.11N	16.10 E
Ivdel	136	Gc	60.42N	60.28 E
Ivenec	116	Lk	53.55N	26.49 E
Ivigtut	179	Hf	61.15N	48.00W
Ivindo	158	Ii	0.09S	12.09 E
Ivinheima	204	Ff	22.10S	53.37W
Ivinheima, Rio-	202	Hh	23.14S	53.42W
Ivinski razliv	114	If	61.10N	35.00 E
Iviza (EN)=Eivissa/Ibiza	110	Gh	39.00N	1.25 E
Iviza (EN)=Ibiza/Eivissa	110	Gh	39.00N	1.25 E
Ivje	120	Vc	53.55N	25.51 E
Ivohibe	172	Hd	22.29S	46.52 E
Ivoire, Côte d'-=Ivory Coast (EN)	158	Gh	5.00N	5.00W
Ivolândia	204	Gc	16.34S	50.51W
Ivory Coast (EN) = Côte-d'Ivoire [1]	160	Gh	8.00N	5.00W
Ivory Coast (EN)=Ivoire, Côte d'-	158	Gh	5.00N	5.00W
Ivösjön	116	Fh	56.05N	14.25 E
Ivrea	128	Be	45.28N	7.52 E
Ivrindi	130	Kj	39.34N	27.29 E
Ivry-la-Bataille	124	Df	48.53N	1.28 E
Ivry-sur-Seine	124	Ef	48.49N	2.23 E
Ivujivik	176	Lc	62.25N	77.54W
Iwai-Jima	156	Be	33.47N	131.58 E
Iwaizumi	154	Pe	39.50N	141.48 E
Iwaki	142	Qf	36.55N	140.48 E
Iwaki-Gawa	156	Ga	41.01N	140.22 E
Iwaki-Hisanohama	156	Gc	37.09N	140.59 E
Iwaki-Jōban	156	Gc	37.02N	140.50 E
Iwaki-Kawamae	156	Gc	37.12N	140.45 E
Iwaki-Miwa	156	Gc	37.09N	140.42 E
Iwaki-Nakoso	156	Gc	36.56N	140.48 E
Iwaki-Onahama	156	Gc	36.57N	140.53 E
Iwaki-San	156	Ga	40.40N	140.20 E
Iwaki-Taira	156	Gc	37.05N	140.55 E
Iwaki-Uchigō	156	Gc	37.04N	140.50 E
Iwaki-Yoshima	156	Gc	37.05N	140.50 E
Iwaki-Yotsukura	156	Gc	37.07N	140.58 E
Iwakuni	152	Ne	34.09N	132.11 E
Iwami	156	Dd	35.35N	134.20 E
Iwami-Kōgen	156	Cd	35.00N	132.30 E
Iwamizawa	152	Pc	43.12N	141.46 E
Iwanai	154	Pc	42.58N	140.30 E
Iwanuma	156	Gb	38.07N	140.52 E
Iwase	156	Gc	36.21N	140.06 E
Iwasuge-Yama	156	Fc	36.44N	138.32 E
Iwata	156	Ed	34.42N	137.48 E
Iwate	154	Pe	39.30N	141.30 E
Iwate Ken [2]	154	Pe	39.30N	141.15 E
Iwate San	154	Pe	39.49N	141.26 E
Iwo	166	Fd	7.38N	4.11 E
Iwŏn	152	Mc	40.19N	128.37 E
Iwuy	124	Fd	50.14N	3.19 E
Ixiamas	202	Ef	13.45S	68.09W
Ixmiquilpan	192	Jg	20.29N	99.14W
Ixopo	172	Ef	30.08S	30.00 E
Ixtapa, Punta-	192	Ii	17.39N	101.40W
Ixtepec	190	Ee	16.34N	95.06W
Ixtlahuacán del Río	192	Hg	20.52N	103.15W
Ixtlán del Río	190	Dd	21.02N	104.22W
Iyaḥ	168	Hd	9.00N	49.38 E
Iyo	154	Lh	33.46N	132.42 E
Iyo-mishima	156	Ce	33.58N	133.33 E
Iyo-Nada	156	Ce	33.40N	132.15 E
Iž	128	Jf	44.03N	15.06 E
Iž	114	Mh	56.00N	52.41 E
Izabal [3]	194	Cf	15.30N	89.00W
Izabal, Lago de-	190	Ge	15.30N	89.10W
Izad Khvāst	146	Og	31.31N	52.07 E
Izamal	192	Og	20.56N	89.01W
Izamal	190	Gd	20.56N	89.01W
Izapa	190	Ff	14.55N	92.10W
'Izbat al Jājah	146	Dj	24.48N	30.35 E
'Izbat Dush	146	Dj	24.34N	30.42 E
Izberbaš	136	Eg	42.33N	47.52 E
Izbiceni	130	Hf	43.50N	24.39 E
Izborsk	116	Mg	57.39N	28.01 E
Izegem	124	Fd	50.55N	3.12 E
Izeh	146	Mg	31.50N	49.50 E
Izena-Shima	156b	Ab	26.56N	127.56 E
Iževsk	112	Ld	56.51N	53.14 E
Izjaslav	132	Ed	50.09N	26.51 E
Izjum	136	Df	49.12N	37.17 E
Izkī	144	Ie	22.57N	57.49 E
Ižma	134	Fd	65.02N	53.55 E
Ižma	110	Lb	65.19N	52.54 E
Izmail	112	If	45.21N	28.50 E
İzmir (Smyrna)	142	Ef	38.25N	27.09 E
Izmir, Gulf of- (EN)=İzmir Körfezi	146	Bc	38.30N	26.50 E
İzmir-Bornova	146	Bc	38.27N	27.14 E
İzmir Körfezi=Izmir, Gulf of- (EN)	146	Bc	38.30N	26.50 E
İzmit	142	Ee	40.46N	29.55 E
İzmit Körfezi	146	Cb	40.45N	29.35 E
Iznajar, Embalse de-	126	Hg	37.15N	4.30W
Iznalloz	126	Ig	37.23N	3.31W
İznik	146	Cb	40.26N	29.43 E
İznik Gölü	146	Cb	40.26N	29.30 E

Index Symbols

[1] Independent Nation
[2] State, Region
[3] District, County
[4] Municipality
[5] Colony, Dependency
Continent
Physical Region
Historical or Cultural Region
Mount, Mountain
Volcano
Hill
Mountains, Mountain Range
Hills, Escarpment
Plateau, Upland
Pass, Gap
Plain, Lowland
Delta
Salt Flat
Valley, Canyon
Crater, Cave
Karst Features
Depression
Polder
Desert, Dunes
Forest, Woods
Heath, Steppe
Oasis
Cape, Point
Coast, Beach
Cliff
Peninsula
Isthmus
Sandbank
Island
Atoll
Rock, Reef
Islands, Archipelago
Rocks, Reefs
Coral Reef
Well, Spring
Geyser
River, Stream
Waterfall, Rapids
River Mouth, Estuary
Lake
Salt Lake
Intermittent Lake
Reservoir
Swamp, Pond
Canal
Glacier
Ice Shelf, Pack Ice
Ocean
Sea
Gulf, Bay
Strait, Fjord
Lagoon
Bank
Seamount
Tablemount
Ridge
Shelf
Basin
Escarpment, Sea Scarp
Fracture
Trench, Abyss
National Park, Reserve
Point of Interest
Recreation Site
Cave, Cavern
Historic Site
Ruins
Wall, Walls
Church, Abbey
Temple
Scientific Station
Railway station
Airport
Port
Military installation
Lighthouse
Mine
Tunnel
Dam, Bridge

Izobilny 132 Lg 45.19N 41.42 E
Izola 128 He 45.32N 13.40 E
Ižorskaja vozvyšennost ⬛ 116 Me 59.35N 29.30 E
Izozog, Bañados del- ⬛ 202 Fg 18.50 S 52.10W
Izra' 146 Gf 32.51N 36.15 E
Izsák 120 Pj 46.48N 19.22 E
Iztočni Rodopi ⬛ 130 Ih 41.44N 25.31 E
Izúcar de Matamoros 192 Jh 18.36N 98.28W
Izu-Hantŏ ⬛ 154 Og 34.55N 138.55 E
Izuhara 154 Jg 34.12N 129.17 E
Izu Islands (EN) = Izu-
  Shotŏ 🞄 140 Pf 32.00N 140.00 E
Izumi [Jap.] 154 Kh 32.05N 130.22 E
Izumi [Jap.] 156 Gb 38.19N 140.51 E
Izumi [Jap.] 156 Dd 34.29N 135.26 E
Izumi-sano 156 Dd 34.24N 135.18 E
Izumo 154 Lg 35.22N 132.46 E
Izu-Shotŏ = Izu Islands (EN)
  🞄 140 Pf 32.00N 140.00 E
Izvesti CIK, ostrova- =
  Izvestiya Tsik Islands (EN)
  🞄 138 Da 75.55N 82.30 E
Izvestiya Tsik Islands (EN)
  = Izvesti CIK, ostrova- 🞄 138 Da 75.55N 82.30 E

J

Jaala 116 Lc 61.03N 26.29 E
Jaama/Jama 116 Lf 58.59N 27.45 E
Jääsjärvi ⬛ 116 Lc 61.35N 26.05 E
Jaba ⬛ 146 Qe 35.55N 56.35 E
Jabal, Baḥr al- = Mountain
  Nile (EN) ⬛ 158 Kh 9.30N 30.30 E
Jabal Abū Rujmayn ⬛ 146 Ge 34.50N 37.56 E
Jabal al Awliyā' 168 Eb 15.14N 32.30 E
Jabal az̧ Z̧annah 146 Oj 24.11N 52.38 E
Jabalón ⬛ 126 Hf 38.53N 4.05W
Jabalpur 142 Jg 23.10N 79.57 E
Jabal Şabāyā ⬛ 164 Hf 18.35N 41.03 E
Jabālyah 146 Fg 31.32N 34.29 E
Jabal Zuqar, Jazīrat- ⬛ 164 Hg 14.00N 42.45 E
Jabbārah ⬛ 164 Hf 19.27N 40.03 E
Jabbeke 124 Fc 51.11N 3.05 E
Jabjabah, Wādī- ⬛ 168 Ea 22.37N 33.17 E
Jablah 146 Fe 35.21N 35.55 E
Jablanac 128 If 44.43N 14.53 E
Jablanica ⬛ 130 Dh 41.15N 20.30 E
Jablanica [Bul.] 130 Hf 43.01N 24.06 E
Jablanica [Yugo.] 128 Lg 43.39N 17.45 E
Jabločny 138 Jg 47.09N 142.03 E
Jablonec nad Nisou 120 Lf 50.44N 15.10 E
Jablonovo 120 Gf 51.51N 112.50 E
Jablonovy hrebet =
  Yablonovy Range (EN) ⬛ 140 Nd 53.30N 115.00 E
Jablunkovský průsmyk ⬛ 120 Og 49.31N 18.45 E
Jaboatão 202 Ke 8.07 S 35.01W
Jaboti 204 De 20.48 S 56.23W
Jaboticabal 206 Kb 21.16 S 48.19W
Jabrīn ⬛ 146 Ni 27.51N 51.26 E
Jabuka ⬛ 128 Jg 43.05N 15.28 E
Jabung, Tanjung- ⬛ 150 Dg 1.01 S 104.22 E
Jabuticatubas 204 Kd 19.30 S 43.45W
Jaca 126 La 42.34N 0.33W
Jacaltenango 194 Bf 15.40N 91.44W
Jacaré, Rio- ⬛ 204 Je 21.03 S 45.16W
Jacarei 204 Jf 23.19 S 45.58W
Jacarezinho 206 Kb 23.09 S 49.59W
Jáchal, Rio- ⬛ 198 Jc 30.44 S 68.08W
Jaciara [Braz.] 204 Ib 14.12 S 46.41W
Jaciara [Braz.] 204 Eb 15.51 S 54.57W
Jackman 184 Lc 45.38N 70.16W
Jack Mountain ⬛ 188 Eb 48.47N 120.57W
Jackpot 188 Hf 41.59N 114.09W
Jacksboro 186 Gj 33.13N 98.10W
Jacks Mountain ⬛ 184 Ie 40.45N 77.30W
Jackson [Al.-U.S.] 184 Dj 31.31N 87.53W
Jackson [Bar.] 197q Ab 10.33N 59.43W
Jackson [Ky.-U.S.] 184 Fg 37.33N 83.23W
Jackson [Mi.-U.S.] 182 Kc 42.15N 84.24W
Jackson [Mn.-U.S.] 186 Ie 43.37N 94.59W
Jackson [Mo.-U.S.] 186 Lh 37.23N 89.40W
Jackson [Ms.-U.S.] 176 Jf 32.18N 90.12W
Jackson [Oh.-U.S.] 184 Ff 39.03N 82.40W
Jackson [Tn.-U.S.] 182 Jd 35.37N 88.49W
Jackson [Wy.-U.S.] 188 Je 43.29N 110.38W
Jackson, Cape- ⬛ 218 Md 40.59 S 174.19 E
Jackson, Mount- [Ant.] ⬛ 222 Qf 71.23 S 63.22W
Jackson, Mount- [Austl.] ⬛ 212 Df 30.15 S 119.16 E
Jackson Bay ⬛ 218 Ce 43.55 S 168.40 E
Jackson Head ⬛ 218 Ce 43.58 S 168.37 E
Jackson Lake ⬛ 188 Je 43.55N 110.40W
Jacksonville [Ar.-U.S.] 186 Ji 34.52N 92.07W
Jacksonville [Fl.-U.S.] 176 Kf 30.20N 81.40W
Jacksonville [Il.-U.S.] 186 Kg 39.44N 90.14W
Jacksonville [N.C.-U.S.] 182 Le 34.45N 77.26W
Jacksonville [Tx.-U.S.] 186 Hi 31.58N 95.17W
Jacksonville Beach 182 Ke 30.18N 81.24W
Jacmel 190 Je 18.14N 72.32W
Jacobābād 148 De 28.17N 68.26 E
Jacobina 202 Jf 11.11 S 40.31W
Jacob Lake 188 Ih 36.45N 112.13W
Jacobs 186 La 50.15N 89.46W
Jacona de Plancarte 192 Mh 19.57N 102.16W
Jacques-Cartier, Détroit de - ⬛
  180 Lg 50.00N 63.30W
Jacques-Cartier, Mont - ⬛ 180 Kg 48.58N 65.57W
Jacuba, Rio- ⬛ 204 Ea 18.25 S 52.28W
Jacui, Rio- ⬛ 198 Ki 30.02 S 51.15W
Jacuí-Mirim, Rio- ⬛ 204 Fi 28.51 S 53.07W
Jacundá 202 Id 4.33 S 49.28W
Jacundá, Rio- ⬛ 202 Hd 1.57 S 50.26W
Jacupiranga 206 Kb 24.42 S 48.00W
Jada 166 Ha 8.46N 12.09 E
Jadal ⬛ 166 Fb 18.37N 5.00 E
Jadar ⬛ 128 Nf 44.38N 19.16 E
Jaddi, Rās- ⬛ 148 Cc 25.14N 63.31 E
Jade ⬛ 120 Ec 53.25N 8.05 E
Jadebusen ⬛ 120 Ec 53.30N 8.10 E
Jadīd Ra's al Fil 168 Dc 12.40N 25.43 E
Jadito Wash ⬛ 188 Ji 35.22N 110.50W
J.A.D. Jensens
  Nunatakker ⬛ 179 Hf 62.45N 48.20W
Jädraås 116 Gd 60.51N 16.28 E
Jadransko More = Adriatic
  Sea (EN) ⬛ 110 Hg 43.00N 16.00 E
Jadrin 114 Li 55.57N 46.11 E
Jádú 164 Bc 31.57N 12.01 E
Ja'el 168 Ic 10.56N 51.09 E
Jaén 126 Ig 37.46N 3.47W
Jaén [3] 126 If 38.00N 3.30W
Jæren ⬛ 116 Af 58.45N 5.45 E
Jærens rev ⬛ 116 Af 58.45N 5.29 E
Jaffa, Cape- ⬛ 212 Hg 36.58 S 139.40 E
Jaffna 142 Ji 9.40N 80.00 E
Jafr, Qā' al- ⬛ 146 Gg 30.17N 36.20 E
Jāgala jögi ⬛ 116 Ke 59.28N 25.04 E
Jagdalpur 142 Kh 19.04N 82.02 E
Jagdaqi 152 La 50.26N 124.02 E
Jagersfontein 172 Fg 29.45 S 25.29 E
Jaghbūb, Wāḩāt al- =
  Jarabub Oasis (EN) ⬛ 158 Jf 29.41N 24.43 E
Jagotin 132 Gd 50.17N 31.47 E
Jagst ⬛ 120 Fg 49.14N 9.11 E
Jaguapitã 204 Ib 23.07 S 51.33W
Jaguaquara 202 Kf 13.32 S 39.58W
Jaguarão 206 Jd 32.34 S 53.23W
Jaguarão, Rio- ⬛ 204 Fk 32.39 S 53.12W
Jaguarari 202 Jf 10.16 S 40.12W
Jaguari 204 Ei 29.30 S 54.41W
Jaguari, Rio- [Braz.] ⬛ 204 Ei 29.42 S 55.07W
Jaguari, Rio- [Braz.] ⬛ 204 If 22.41 S 47.17W
Jaguariaíva 206 Kb 24.15 S 49.42W
Jaguaribe 202 Ke 5.53 S 38.37W
Jaguaribe, Rio- ⬛ 198 Mf 4.25 S 37.45W
Jaguaruana 202 Kd 4.50 S 37.47W
Jaguey Grande 194 Gb 22.32N 81.08W
Jahadyjaha ⬛ 134 Pc 67.03N 72.01 E
Jahām, 'Irq- ⬛ 146 Li 26.12N 47.00 E
Jahorina ⬛ 128 Mg 43.42N 18.35 E
Jahrom 144 Md 28.31N 53.33 E
Jahroma 114 Ih 56.20N 37.29 E
Jaice 128 Lf 44.21N 17.17 E
Jaicoa, Cordillera- ⬛ 197a Ab 18.25N 67.05W
Jaicós 202 Je 7.21 S 41.08W
Jailolo 150 If 1.05N 127.30 E
Jailolo, Selat- ⬛ 150 If 0.05N 129.05 E
Jaina, Isla de- ⬛ 192 Ng 20.14N 90.40W
Jaipur 142 Jg 26.55N 75.49 E
Jaisalmer 148 Ec 26.55N 70.54 E
Jaja 138 De 56.12N 86.26 E
Jajarm 146 Qd 36.58N 56.27 E
Jajce 128 Lf 44.21N 17.17 E
Jajere 166 Hc 11.59N 11.26 E
Jajpan 135 Md 40.23N 70.50 E
Jajsan 132 Td 50.51N 56.14 E
Jajva 136 Fd 59.20N 57.16 E
Jajva ⬛ 134 Hg 59.16N 56.42 E
Jakarta (Djakarta) 142 Mj 6.10 S 106.46 E
Jakobshavn/Ilulissat 224 Nc 69.50N 50.50W
Jakobstad/Pietarsaari 114 Fe 63.40N 22.42 E
Jakoruda 130 Gg 42.02N 23.40 E
Jakupica ⬛ 130 Eh 41.43N 21.26 E
Jakutsk 142 Nc 62.13N 129.49 E
Jakutskaja ASSR [3] 138 Hc 67.00N 130.00 E
Jal 186 Gj 32.07N 103.12W
Jalaid Qi (Inder) 152 Lb 46.41N 122.52 E
Jalājil 146 Kj 25.41N 45.28 E
Jalālābād 144 Lc 34.26N 70.28 E
Jalālah al Baḩrīyah, Jabal
  al- ⬛ 146 Eh 29.20N 32.20 E
Jalālah al Qiblīyah, Jabal al-
  146 Eh 28.42N 32.22 E
Jalán, Rio- ⬛ 194 Df 15.43N 87.34W
Jalandhar 142 Jf 31.19N 75.34 E
Jalapa [3] 194 Cf 14.35N 89.55W
Jalapa [Guat.] 190 Gf 14.38N 89.59W
Jalapa [Mex.] 192 Mh 17.43N 92.49W
Jalapa [Nic.] 190 Gf 13.55N 86.08W
Jalapa Enriquez 176 Jh 19.32N 96.55W
Jalasjarvi 114 Fe 62.30N 22.45 E
Jales 204 Ge 20.16 S 50.33W
Jálgaon 148 Fd 21.01N 75.34 E
Jalhay 124 Ie 50.34N 5.58 E
Jalib Shahab 146 Jb 30.23N 46.09 E
Jalingo 166 Hd 8.53N 11.22 E
Jalisco [2] 190 Dd 20.20N 103.40W
Jālīṭah = La Galite (EN) ⬛ 158 Hf 37.32N 8.56 E
Jālīṭah, Canal de- ⬛ 128 Cm 37.30N 9.00 E
Jalkot 148 Ea 35.15N 73.17 E
Jallas ⬛ 126 Cb 42.54N 9.08W
Jālna 148 Fe 19.50N 75.53 E
Jalón ⬛ 126 Kc 41.47N 1.04W
Jalostotitlán 192 Hj 21.12N 102.28W
Jalpa 192 Hj 21.14N 102.58W
Jalpaiguri 148 Nc 26.31N 88.44 E
Jalpan 192 Jg 21.14N 99.29W
Jalpug, ozero- ⬛ 132 Fg 45.25N 28.40 E
Jalta 136 Gg 44.30N 34.10 E
Jaltepec, Rio- ⬛ 192 Li 17.26N 94.59W
Jālū 164 Dd 28.30N 21.05 E
Jālū, Wāḩāt- = Gialo Oasis
  (EN) ⬛ 158 Jf 29.00N 21.20 E
Jaluit Atoll ⬛ 208 Hd 6.00N 169.35 E
Jalutorovsk 136 Ld 56.40N 66.18 E
Jam [Iran] 146 Qe 35.45N 55.02 E
Jam [Iran] 146 Oi 27.50N 52.22 E
Jama/Jaama 116 Lf 58.59N 27.45 E
Jamaari 158 Ig 12.06N 10.14 E
Jamaica 194 Jc 17.35N 78.00W [approx]
Jamaica [1] 176 Db 18.15N 77.30W
Jamaica [2] 176 Db 18.15N 77.30W
Jamaica ⬛ 194 Ja 18.15N 77.30W
Jamaica Channel 190 Jf 18.00N 75.30W
Jamaica Channel (EN) =
  Jamaïque, Canal de- ⬛ 194 Jd 18.00N 75.30W
Jamaïque, Canal de- =
  Jamaica Channel (EN) ⬛ 194 Jd 18.00N 75.30W
Jamal, poluostrov- = Yamal
  Peninsula (EN) ⬛ 140 Ib 70.00N 70.00 E
Jamalo-Nenecki nacionalny
  okrug [3] 138 Cc 67.00N 75.00 E
Jamālpur 148 Hd 24.55N 89.56 E
Jamāme 160 Lh 0.04N 42.46 E
Jamantau, gora- ⬛ 110 Le 54.15N 58.06 E
Jamanxim, Rio- ⬛ 198 Kf 4.43 S 56.18W
Jamari, Rio- ⬛ 202 Fe 8.27 S 63.30W
Jamarovka 138 Gf 50.38N 110.16 E
Jambi 142 Mj 1.38 S 103.42 E
Jambi [3] 150 Dg 1.36 S 103.37 E
Jambol 130 Jg 42.29N 26.30 E
Jambol [2] 130 Jg 42.15N 26.35 E
Jambongan, Pulau- ⬛ 150 Ge 6.41N 117.25 E
Jambuair, Tanjung- ⬛ 150 Ce 5.16N 97.30 E
Jambusar 148 Ed 22.03N 72.48 E
James Bay ⬛ 174 Kd 51.00N 80.30W
Jameson Land ⬛ 179 Jd 70.45N 23.45W
James River [U.S.] ⬛ 174 Je 42.52N 97.18W
James River [U.S.] ⬛ 184 Ig 36.56N 76.27W
James Ross ⬛ 222 Re 64.15 S 57.45W
James Ross Strait ⬛ 180 Hc 69.50N 96.30W
Jamestown [Austl.] 212 Hf 33.12 S 138.36 E
Jamestown [N.D.-U.S.] 182 Hb 46.54N 98.42W
Jamestown [N.Y.-U.S.] 182 Lc 42.05N 79.15W
Jamestown [St.Hel.] 160 Gj 15.56 S 5.43W
Jamestown Reservoir ⬛ 186 Gc 47.15N 98.40W
Jamm 116 Mf 58.24N 28.15 E
Jammer Bugt ⬛ 114 Bh 57.20N 9.30 E
Jammu 142 Jf 32.44N 74.52 E
Jammu and Kashmir [3] 148 Fb 34.00N 76.00 E
Jämnagar 142 Jg 22.28N 70.04 E
Jamno, Jezioro- ⬛ 120 Mb 54.15N 16.10 E
Jampol 132 Fe 48.16N 28.17 E
Jämsä 114 Ff 61.52N 25.12 E
Jamsah 146 Ei 27.38N 33.35 E
Jämsänkoski 116 Kc 61.55N 25.11 E
Jamshedpur 142 Kg 22.48N 86.11 E
Jamsk 138 Ke 59.37N 154.10 E
Jämtland [2] 114 De 63.00N 14.40 E
Jämtland ⬛ 116 Fa 63.25N 14.05 E
Janà ⬛ 146 Mi 27.22N 49.54 E
Jana ⬛ 140 Pb 71.31N 136.32 E
Janakpur 148 Hc 26.42N 85.55 E
Janaucu, Ilha- ⬛ 202 Hc 0.30N 50.10W
Janaul 134 Gh 56.16N 54.59 E
Janda, Laguna de la- ⬛ 126 Hg 36.15N 5.51W
Jandaia 204 Gc 17.06 S 50.07W
Jandaq 146 Pe 34.02N 54.26 E
Jandiatuba, Rio- ⬛ 202 Ed 3.28 S 68.42W
Jandowae 212 Ke 26.47 S 151.06 E
Jandula ⬛ 126 Hf 38.03N 4.06W
Jane Peak ⬛ 218 Cf 45.20 S 168.19 E
Janesville 182 Jc 42.41N 89.01W
Jangada 204 Db 15.14 S 56.29W
Jangada, Rio- ⬛ 204 Db 15.12 S 56.24W
Jangao Shan ⬛ 152 Gf 25.31N 98.08 E
Jangijer 135 Gd 40.18N 68.50 E
Jangijul 136 Ga 41.07N 69.03 E
Jangirabad 135 Ed 40.03N 65.59 E
Jango 204 De 20.27 S 55.29W
Jangy-Bazar 135 Hd 41.40N 70.52 E
Janikowo 120 Od 52.45N 18.07 E
Janīn 146 Ff 32.28N 35.18 E
Janisjarvi, ozero- ⬛ 114 Ne 62.00N 31.00 E
Janja 128 Nf 44.40N 19.19 E
Jan Mayen ⬛ 110 Fa 71.00N 8.30W
Jan Mayen Ridge (EN) ⬛ 110 Fb 69.00N 8.00W
Jano-Indigirskaja
  nizmennost ⬛ 138 Ib 71.00N 139.30 E
Janos 190 Cb 30.56N 108.08W
Jánoshalma 120 Pj 46.18N 19.20 E
Jánosháza 120 Ni 47.07N 17.10 E
Janów Lubelski 120 Sf 50.43N 22.24 E
Janów Podlaski 120 Td 52.11N 23.11 E
Jansenville 172 Ff 32.56 S 24.40 E
Janski zaliv ⬛ 140 Pb 72.00N 136.00 E
Jantarny 116 Hj 54.53N 19.55 E
Jantra ⬛ 130 If 43.38N 25.34 E
Januária 202 Jg 15.29 S 44.22W
Janūbīyah, Aş Şaḩrā' al-=
  Southern Desert (EN) ⬛ 158 Jf 24.00N 30.00 E
Janykurgan 136 Kg 43.55N 67.14 E
Janzhong Ansha ⬛ 150 Ge 9.30N 116.54 E
Japan (EN) = Nippon [1] 140 Pf 35.00N 135.00 E
Japan (EN) = Nippon [1] 140 Pf 38.00N 137.00 E
Japan, Sea of- (EN) =
  Japonskoje more ⬛ 140 Pf 40.00N 134.00 E
Japan, Sea of- (EN) =
  Nippon-Kai ⬛ 140 Pf 40.00N 134.00 E
Japan, Sea of- (EN) = Tong-
  Hae ⬛ 140 Pf 40.00N 134.00 E
Japan Basin (EN) ⬛ 152 Nc 40.00N 135.00 E
Japan Trench (EN) ⬛ 106 If 37.00N 143.00 E
Japiim 202 Dc 8.30 S 72.54W
Japonskoje more = Japan,
  Sea of- (EN) ⬛ 140 Pf 40.00N 134.00 E
Jäppilä 116 Lg 62.23N 27.26 E
Japtiksale 134 Pb 69.25N 72.29 E
Japurá 202 Ed 1.24 S 69.25W
Japurá, Rio- ⬛ 198 Jf 3.08 S 64.46W
Jaqué 194 Hj 7.31N 78.10W
Jaquet, Point- ⬛ 197g Ba 15.38N 61.26W
Jaquirana 202 Dc 8.58 S 50.23W
Jar 114 Mg 58.17N 52.06 E
Jarabub Oasis (EN) =
  Jaghbūb, Wāḩāt al- ⬛ 158 Jf 29.41N 24.43 E
Jaraguá [Braz.] 204 Hc 15.45 S 49.20W
Jaraguá [Braz.] 202 If 26.29 S 49.04W
Jaraguá, Serra do- ⬛ 204 Hb 26.40 S 49.15W
Jaraguari 204 Ea 20.09 S 54.25W
Jaraiz de la Vera 126 Gd 40.04N 5.45W
Jarama ⬛ 126 Id 40.02N 3.39W
Jaramillo 206 Gg 47.11 S 67.09W
Jarandilla 126 Gd 40.08N 5.39W
Jaransk 136 Ed 57.18N 47.55 E
Jarash 146 Ff 32.17N 35.54 E
Jarau, Cêrro do- ⬛ 204 Dj 30.18 S 56.32W
Jarbah ⬛ 158 Ie 33.48N 10.54 E
Järbo 116 Gd 60.43N 16.36 E
Jarcevo [R.S.F.S.R.] 132 Hb 55.05N 32.45 E
Jarcevo [R.S.F.S.R.] 138 Ed 60.15N 90.10 E
Jardānwīyah 146 Jj 25.24N 42.42 E
Jardim 202 Gh 21.28 S 56.09W
Jardine River ⬛ 212 Ib 11.10 S 142.30 E
Jardines de la Reina,
  Archipiélago de los- 190 Id 20.50N 78.55W
Jardinópolis 204 Ie 21.02 S 47.46W
Jarega 134 Fe 63.27N 53.31 E
Jaremča 132 De 48.31N 24.33 E
Jarenga 114 Le 62.08N 49.03 E
Järfälla 116 Ge 59.24N 17.50 E
Jargava 130 Lc 46.27N 28.27 E
Jari, Rio- ⬛ 198 Kf 1.09 S 51.54W
Jarīd, Shaṭṭ al- ⬛ 158 He 33.42N 8.26 E
Jarīr, Wādī- ⬛ 146 Jj 25.38N 42.30 E
Jarjis 162 Jc 33.30N 11.07 E
Jarkovo 134 Mh 57.26N 67.05 E
Jarmah 164 Bd 26.32N 13.04 E
Järna 116 Ge 59.06N 17.34 E
Jarnac 122 Fi 45.41N 0.10W
Järnlunden ⬛ 116 Ff 58.10N 15.40 E
Jarny 122 Le 49.09N 5.53 E
Jarocin 120 Ne 51.59N 17.31 E
Jaroměřice nad Rokytnou 120 Lg 49.06N 15.54 E
Jaroměř 120 Lf 50.21N 15.55 E
Jaroslavl 112 Jd 57.37N 39.52 E
Jaroslavskaja oblast [3] 136 Dd 57.45N 39.15 E
Jaroslavski 154 Lb 44.10N 132.13 E
Järosław 120 Sf 50.02N 22.42 E
Järpen 116 Ea 63.21N 13.29 E
Jarrähi ⬛ 146 Mg 30.44N 48.46 E
Jarroto, ozero- ⬛ 134 Oc 67.55N 71.40 E
Jar-Sale 138 Cc 66.50N 70.50 E
Jartai 152 Ia 39.45N 105.46 E
Jartai Yanchi 152 Ia 39.45N 105.40 E
Jarudej ⬛ 134 Od 65.50N 71.50 E
Jarud Qi (Lubei) 152 Lc 44.30N 120.55 E
Järva-Jaani/Jarva-Jani 116 Ke 59.00N 25.49 E
Jarva-Jani/Järva-Jaani 116 Ke 59.00N 25.49 E
Järvakandi/Jarvakandi 116 Kf 58.45N 24.44 E
Jarvakandi/Järvakandi 116 Kf 58.45N 24.44 E
Järvenpää 116 Ff 60.28N 25.06 E
Jarvis Island ⬛ 208 Ke 0.23 S 160.01W
Järvsö 114 Df 61.43N 16.10 E
Jaščera 116 Ne 59.05N 30.00 E
Jaselda ⬛ 132 Ec 52.20N 26.29 E
Jasień 120 Le 51.46N 15.01 E
Jasikan 166 Fd 7.24N 0.28 E
Jasinja 130 Uh 48.14N 24.31 E
Jasinovataja 132 Je 48.05N 37.57 E
Jasiołka ⬛ 120 Rg 49.47N 21.30 E
Jasīra 168 Ic 1.57N 45.16 E
Jasīred Mayd ⬛ 168 Hc 11.12N 47.13 E
Jāsk 144 Ne 25.38N 57.46 E
Jaškul 132 Nf 46.11N 45.17 E
Jaśkul 132 Nf 46.17N 45.10 E
Jaslo 120 Rg 49.45N 21.29 E
Jasmund ⬛ 120 Jb 54.32N 13.35 E
Jasnogorsk 132 Jb 54.29N 37.42 E
Jasny [R.S.F.S.R.] 136 Fe 51.01N 59.59 E
Jasny [R.S.F.S.R.] 138 Hf 53.18N 128.05 E
Jason Islands ⬛ 206 Hh 51.00 S 61.00W
Jasper [Alta.-Can.] 176 Kd 52.53N 118.05W
Jasper [Al.-U.S.] 182 Id 33.50N 87.17W
Jasper [Fl.-U.S.] 184 Ej 30.31N 82.57W
Jasper [In.-U.S.] 184 Df 38.24N 86.56W
Jasper [Tn.-U.S.] 184 Eh 35.04N 85.38W
Jasper [Tx.-U.S.] 186 Jj 30.55N 93.60W
Jasper Seamount (EN) ⬛ 174 Gf 30.32N 122.42W
Jaşşān 146 Kc 32.36N 45.59 E
Jastrowie 120 Mc 53.26N 16.49 E
Jastrzebie Zdrój 120 Og 49.58N 18.34 E
Jászapáti 120 Qi 47.31N 20.09 E
Jászberény 120 Pi 47.30N 19.55 E
Jászárokszállás 120 Pi 47.38N 19.59 E
Jászság [2] 120 Pi 47.25N 20.00 E
Jat, Uad el- ⬛ 158 Ff 26.47N 13.03W
Jatai 200 Kg 17.53 S 51.43W
Jatapu, Rio- ⬛ 202 Gd 2.30 S 58.17W
Jatátí, Rio- ⬛ 204 Je 23.35 S 45.10W [approx]
Jatobá, Rio- ⬛ 202 If 9.11 S 38.09W [approx]
Jaú 206 Kb 22.18 S 48.33W
Jaú, Rio- ⬛ 202 Fd 1.55 S 61.25W
Jaua, Cerro- ⬛ 197 Jf 4.48N 64.26W
Jauaperi, Rio- ⬛ 202 Fd 1.26 S 61.35W
Jauja 202 Cf 11.48 S 75.30W
Jaumave 192 Jg 23.25N 99.23W
Jaunanna 116 Lg 57.13N 27.01 E
Jaunelgava/Jaunjelgava 114 Ph 56.37N 25.06 E
Jaunfeld ⬛ 128 Ic 46.36N 14.45 E
Jaungulbene 116 Lh 57.00N 26.42 E
Jaunjelgava/Jaunelgava 114 Ph 56.37N 25.06 E
Jaunpiebalga 116 Lg 57.05N 26.03 E
Jaunpur 148 Gd 25.44N 82.41 E
Jauru 204 Da 16.12 S 54.17W
Jauru, Rio- [Braz.] ⬛ 204 Dc 16.22 S 57.46W
Jauru, Rio- [Braz.] ⬛ 202 Gg 18.40 S 54.36W
Java → Araguaia, Braço
  Menor do- ⬛ 202 He 9.50 S 50.12W
Javaés → Araguaia, Braço
  Menor do- ⬛ 202 He 9.50 S 50.12W
Javalambre 126 Ld 40.05N 1.10W
Javalambre, Sierra de- ⬛ 126 Kd 40.05N 1.00W
Javan 135 Ge 38.19N 69.01 E
Jávänrüd 146 Lc 34.48N 46.30 E
Javari, Rio- ⬛ 198 If 4.21 S 70.02W
Jarash 146 Ff ...
Java = Jawa (EN) ⬛ 140 Mj 7.20 S 110.00 E
Java Sea (EN) = Jawa, Laut-
  140 Mj 5.00 S 110.00 E [approx]
Java Trench (EN) ⬛ 106 Hk 10.30 S 110.00 E
Jávea / Xàbia 126 Mf 38.47N 0.10 E
Javier / Xavier 126 Kb 42.36N 1.13W
Javor 128 Mf 44.07N 18.59 E
Javorie ⬛ 120 Ph 48.27N 19.18 E
Javornik ⬛ 120 Jg 49.08N 13.35 E
Javorniky ⬛ 120 Og 49.20N 18.20 E
Javorov 132 Cd 50.00N 23.27 E
Javorová skála ⬛ 120 Kg 49.31N 14.30 E
Jävre 114 Ed 65.09N 21.29 E
Jawa = Java (EN) ⬛ 140 Mj 7.20 S 110.00 E
Jawa, Laut- = Java Sea (EN)
  140 Mj 5.00 S 110.00 E
Jawa Barat [3] 150 Eh 7.00 S 107.00 E
Jawa Tengah [3] 150 Eh 7.00 S 110.00 E
Jawa Timur [3] 150 Fh 8.00 S 113.00 E
Jawf, Wādī- ⬛ 164 If 15.50N 45.30 E
Jawor 120 Me 51.03N 16.11 E
Jaworzno 120 Pf 50.13N 19.15 E
Jaya, Puncak- ⬛ 208 Ee 4.10 S 137.00 E
Jayapura 210 Fe 2.32 S 140.42 E
Jayawijaya, Pegunungan- 150 Kg 4.30 S 139.30 E
Jāyezān 146 Mg 30.50N 49.52 E
Jaypur 148 He 18.51N 82.35 E
Jazā'ir Siyāl ⬛ 168 Fa 23.00N 36.02 E
Jaz Mūriān, Hāmūn-e- ⬛ 144 Id 27.20N 58.55 E
Jazva ⬛ 134 Hf 60.23N 56.50 E
Jazvän 146 Md 36.58N 48.40 E
Jazykovo 114 Li 54.20N 47.22 E
Jazzīn 146 Ff 33.32N 35.34 E
Jdiouia 126 Mi 35.56N 1.06 E
Jean-Rabel 194 Kd 19.52N 73.11W
Jebala ⬛ 126 Gi 35.25N 5.30W
Jebal Bārez, Kūh-e- ⬛ 144 Id 28.30N 58.20 E
Jebba 166 Fd 9.08N 4.50 E
Jebel 130 Ed 45.33N 21.14 E
Jebha 126 Hi 35.13N 4.40W
Jedincy 132 Ee 48.06N 27.19 E
Jedisa 132 Nh 42.45N 44.14 E
Jędrzejów 120 Qf 50.39N 20.18 E
Jeetze ⬛ 120 Hc 53.09N 11.04 E
Jefferson 186 Ie 42.01N 94.23W
Jefferson, Mount- [Nv.-U.S.]
  ⬛ 182 Dd 38.46N 116.55W
Jefferson, Mount- [Or.-U.S.]
  ⬛ 188 Ed 44.40N 121.47W
Jefferson City 176 Jf 38.34N 92.10W
Jefferson River ⬛ 188 Jd 45.56N 111.30W
Jeffersonville 184 Ef 38.17N 85.44W
Jef-Jef el Kebir ⬛ 168 Ca 20.30N 21.25 E
Jefremov 136 De 53.11N 38.07 E
Jega 166 Fc 12.13N 4.23 E
Jegorjevsk 114 Ji 55.25N 39.07 E
Jegorlyk ⬛ 132 Lf 46.32N 41.52 E
Jegorlykskaja 132 Lf 46.34N 40.44 E
Jehegnadzor 132 Nj 39.47N 45.18 E
Jeja ⬛ 132 Kf 46.39N 38.36 E
Jejsk 136 Df 46.40N 38.15 E
Jejuí Guazú, Rio- ⬛ 204 Dg 24.13 S 57.09W
Jēkabpils/Jekabpils 136 Cd 56.30N 25.59 E
Jekabpils/Jēkabpils 136 Cd 56.30N 25.59 E
Jekaterinovka 132 Nc 52.04N 44.30 E
Jekkevarre ⬛ 114 Eb 69.48N 20.00 E
Jelabuga 136 Fd 55.48N 52.05 E
Jelai ⬛ 150 Fg 2.59 S 110.45 E
Jelan 132 Md 50.57N 43.43 E
Jelancy 138 Ff 52.44N 106.27 E
Jelanec 132 Gf 47.42N 31.50 E
Jelcz 120 Ne 51.01N 17.18 E
Jelec 112 Je 52.37N 38.30 E
Jelec 134 Lf 67.03N 64.15 E
Jelenia Góra 120 Lf 50.55N 15.46 E
Jelenia Góra [2] 120 Le 50.55N 15.45 E
Jelgava 136 Cd 56.39N 23.41 E
Jelica ⬛ 130 Df 43.47N 20.20 E
Jelin vrh ⬛ 130 Df 43.49N 19.27 E
Jelizavety, mys- ⬛ 140 Qd 54.30N 142.40 E
Jelizovo [Bye.-U.S.S.R.] 132 Fc 53.24N 29.00 E
Jelizovo [R.S.F.S.R.] 138 Kf 53.06N 158.20 E
Jelling 116 Ci 55.45N 9.26 E
Jelnja 132 Hb 54.35N 33.11 E
Jelogui 138 Dd 63.10N 87.45 E
Jelow Gir 146 Lf 32.58N 47.48 E
Jelšava 120 Qg 48.38N 20.14 E
Jelva ⬛ 136 Ed 61.49N 50.50 E
Jemaja, Pulau- ⬛ 150 Ef 2.55N 105.45 E
Jemanželinsk 136 Je 54.45N 61.20 E
Jember 142 Nj 8.10 S 113.42 E
Jemca 136 Ec 63.04N 40.18 E
Jemca ⬛ 136 Ec 63.32N 41.56 E
Jemeppe-sur-Sambre 124 Gd 50.28N 4.40 E
Jeminay 152 Eb 47.28N 85.48 E
Jemnice 120 Lg 49.01N 15.35 E
Jena 120 Hf 50.56N 11.35 E
Jenakijevo 132 Ke 48.13N 38.18 E
Jenašimski Polkan, gora- ⬛ 138 Ee 59.50N 93.00 E
Jendyr ⬛ 134 Mf 61.38N 67.20 E
Jeneponto 150 Gh 5.41 S 119.42 E
Jenisej = Yenisey (EN) ⬛ 140 Kb 71.50N 82.40 E
Jenisejsk 138 Ee 58.27N 92.10 E
Jenisejski krjaž = Yenisey
  Ridge (EN) ⬛ 140 Ld 59.00N 92.30 E
Jenisejski zaliv = Yenisey
  Bay (EN) ⬛ 138 Db 72.00N 81.00 E
Jennersdorf 128 Kc 46.56N 16.08 E
Jennings 186 Jk 30.13N 92.39W
Jenny Lind ⬛ 180 Hc 68.50N 101.30W
Jenny Point ⬛ 197g Bf 15.46N 61.17W
Jensen 188 Kf 40.22N 109.17W
Jens Munk ⬛ 180 Jc 69.40N 79.40W
Jequitái 200 La 15.55 S 44.05W
Jequitaí ⬛ 204 Jc 17.15 S 44.28W
Jequitaí, Rio- ⬛ 204 Jc 17.04 S 44.50W [approx]
Jequitinhonha, Rio- ⬛ 198 Mg 15.51 S 38.53W
Jerada 162 Gc 34.19N 2.09W
Jeraliiev 136 Fg 43.01 S [approx]
Jerbogačen 138 Fd 61.15N 107.57 E
Jérémie 190 Je 18.39N 74.08W
Jeremoabo 202 Kf 10.04 S 38.21W

Jerer 168 Gd 7.40N 43.48 E
Jerevan 112 Kg 40.11N 44.30 E
Jerez, Punta- 192 Kf 22.54N 97.46W
Jerez de García Salinas 190 Dd 22.39N 103.00W
Jerez de la Frontera 126 Fh 36.41N 6.08W
Jerez de los Caballeros 126 Ff 38.19N 6.46W
Jergeni 110 Kf 47.00N 44.00 E
Jericho 212 Jd 23.36S 146.08 E
Jermak 136 He 52.02N 76.55 E
Jermakovskoje 138 Ef 53.16N 92.24 E
Jermentau 136 He 51.38N 73.10 E
Jermolajevo 134 Gj 52.43N 55.48 E
Jeroaquara 204 Gb 15.23S 50.25W
Jerofej Pavlovič 138 Hf 53.58N 121.57 E
Jerome 188 He 42.43N 114.31W
Jersa 134 Fc 66.19N 52.32 E
Jersey 118 Kl 49.15N 2.10W
Jersey City 182 Mc 40.44N 74.04W
Jerseyville 186 Kg 39.07N 90.20W
Jeršov 136 Ee 51.20N 48.17 E
Jertarski 134 Lh 56.47N 64.25 E
Jerte 126 Fe 39.58N 6.17W
Jerusalem (EN)=
Yerushalayim 142 Ff 31.46N 35.14 E
Jeruslan 132 Od 50.20N 46.25 E
Jervis Bay 212 Kg 35.05S 150.44 E
Jerzu 128 Dk 39.47N 9.31 E
Jesberg 124 Lc 51.00N 9.09 E
Jesenice [Yugo.] 128 Jf 44.14N 15.34 E
Jesenice [Yugo.] 128 Id 46.27N 14.04 E
Jeseník 120 Nf 50.14N 17.12 E
Jesi 128 Hg 43.31N 13.14 E
Jesil 136 Ge 51.58N 66.24 E
Jeskianhor, kanal- 135 Fe 39.15N 66.00 E
Jessej 138 Fc 68.29N 102.10 E
Jessentuki 132 Mg 44.03N 42.51 E
Jessheim 114 Cf 60.09N 11.11 E
Jessore 148 Hd 23.10N 89.13 E
Ještěd 120 Kf 50.42N 14.59 E
Jestro, Wabe- 158 Lh 4.11N 42.09 E
Jesup 182 Ke 31.36N 81.53W
Jesús Carranza 192 Li 17.26N 95.02W
Jesús María 206 Hd 30.59S 64.06W
Jesús María, Boca de- 192 Ke 24.29N 97.40W
Jesús María, Río- 192 Gg 21.55N 104.30W
Jetmore 186 Gg 38.03N 99.54W
Jeumont 124 Gd 50.18N 4.06 E
Jever 120 Dc 53.35N 7.54 E
Jevgenjevka 135 Kc 43.27N 77.40 E
Jevišovka 120 Mh 48.52N 16.36 E
Jevlah 136 Eg 40.35N 47.10 E
Jevnaker 114 Cf 60.15N 10.28 E
Jevpatorija 136 Df 45.12N 33.18 E
Jevrejskaja avtonomnaja
oblast 138 Ig 48.30N 132.00 E
Jeyḩūn 146 Pi 27.16N 55.12 E
Jeypore → Jaypur 148 He 18.51N 82.35 E
Jezercës 110 Hg 42.26N 19.49 E
Jezero 128 Lf 44.21N 17.10 E
Jeziorak, Jezioro- 120 Pc 53.50N 19.35 E
Jeziorany 120 Qc 53.58N 20.46 E
Jeziorka 120 Rd 52.10N 21.06 E
Jhang Sadar 148 Eb 31.16N 72.19 E
Jhānsi 142 Jg 25.26N 78.35 E
Jhelum 148 Eb 32.56N 73.44 E
Jhelum 140 Jf 31.12N 72.08 E
Jiaji → Qionghai 152 Jh 19.25N 110.28 E
Jialing Jiang 140 Mg 29.34N 106.35 E
Jialu He 154 Ch 33.40N 115.01 E
Jiamusi 142 Pe 46.49N 130.21 E
Ji'an [China] 152 Mc 41.08N 126.10 E
Ji'an [China] 142 Ng 27.12N 114.59 E
Jianchang 154 Ed 40.49N 119.46 E
Jianchuan 152 Gf 26.32N 99.53 E
Jiande (Baisha) 152 Kf 29.31N 119.17 E
Jiang'an 152 If 28.40N 105.07 E
Jiangbiancun 152 Kf 27.13N 115.57 E
Jiangcheng 152 Hg 22.37N 101.48 E
Jiangdu (Xiannümiao) 154 Eh 32.30N 119.33 E
Jiange 152 Ie 31.59N 105.28 E
Jianghua (Shuikou) 152 Jg 24.58N 111.56 E
Jiangjin 152 If 29.15N 106.18 E
Jiangle 152 Kf 26.48N 117.29 E
Jiangling (Jingzhou) 152 Je 30.21N 112.10 E
Jiangmen 152 Jg 22.35N 113.02 E
Jiangpu 154 Eh 32.03N 118.37 E
Jiangshan 154 Ej 28.45N 118.37 E
Jiangsu Sheng (Chiang-su
Sheng)=Kiangsu (EN) [2] 152 Ke 33.00N 120.00 E
Jiangxi Sheng (Chiang-hsi
Sheng) = Kiangsi (EN) [2] 152 Kf 28.00N 116.00 E
Jiangyou (Zhongba) 152 He 31.48N 104.39 E
Jianhu 154 Eh 33.28N 119.47 E
Jianli 152 Jf 29.50N 112.55 E
Jian'ou 152 Kf 27.08N 118.20 E
Jianping 154 Ed 41.27N 119.37 E
Jianping (Yebaishou) 152 Kc 41.55N 119.37 E
Jianshi 152 Ie 30.32N 109.43 E
Jianshui 152 Hg 23.39N 102.46 E
Jianyang 152 Kf 27.23N 118.03 E
Jiaocheng 152 Jd 37.32N 112.09 E
Jiaoding Shan 152 Lc 41.11N 120.01 E
Jiaohe [China] 152 Mc 43.43N 127.20 E
Jiaohe [China] 154 De 38.01N 116.17 E
Jiaolai He [China] 154 Ef 37.07N 119.35 E
Jiaolai He [China] 154 Fc 43.02N 120.48 E
Jiaoliu He 154 Gb 45.21N 122.48 E
Jiaonan (Wanggezhuang) 154 Eg 35.53N 119.58 E
Jiaoxian 152 Kd 36.20N 120.00 E
Jiaozhou-Wan 154 Ff 36.10N 120.15 E
Jiaozuo 142 Nf 35.15N 113.18 E
Jiashan 154 Fi 30.51N 120.54 E
Jiashan (Mingguang) 154 Dh 32.47N 118.00 E
Jiashi/Payzawat 152 Cd 39.29N 76.39 E
Jiawang 154 Dg 34.27N 117.26 E
Jiaxian 154 Bh 33.58N 113.13 E
Jiaxing 152 Le 30.44N 120.46 E
Jiayin (Chaoyang) 152 Nb 48.52N 130.21 E
Jiayu 152 Jf 30.00N 113.57 E
Jiayuguan 152 Gd 39.49N 98.18 E
Jibalei 168 Ic 10.07N 50.47 E
Jibão, Serra do- 204 Jb 14.48S 45.15W
Jibiya 166 Gc 13.06N 7.14 E
Jibou 130 Gb 47.16N 23.15 E
Jicarón, Isla- 194 Gj 7.16N 81.47W
Jičín 120 Lf 50.26N 15.22 E
Jiddah 142 Fg 21.29N 39.12 E
Jiddat al Ḩarāsīs 144 Ie 20.05N 56.00 E
Jiehu → Yinan 154 Eg 35.33N 118.27 E
Jieshou 154 Ch 33.17N 115.22 E
Jiesjjavrre 114 Fb 69.40N 24.12 E
Jiexiu 152 Jd 37.00N 112.00 E
Jieyang 152 Kg 23.32N 116.25 E
Jieznas/Eznas 116 Kj 54.34N 24.17 E
Jifn, Wādī al- 146 Jj 25.48N 42.15 E
Jiftūn, Jazā'ir- 146 Ei 27.13N 33.56 E
Jīgley 168 He 4.25N 45.22 E
Jiguaní 194 Ic 20.22N 76.26W
Jigüey, Bahía de- 194 Hb 22.08N 78.05W
Jigzhi 152 He 33.28N 101.29 E
Jihlava 120 Lg 49.24N 15.34 E
Jihlava 120 Mh 48.55N 16.37 E
Jihlavské vrchy 120 Lg 49.15N 15.20 E
Jihočeský kraj [3] 120 Kg 49.05N 14.30 E
Jihomoravský kraj [3] 120 Mg 49.10N 16.40 E
Jijel 162 Ib 36.48N 5.46 E
Jijel [3] 162 Ib 36.45N 5.45 E
Jijia 130 Lc 46.54N 28.05 E
Jijiga 168 Gd 9.21N 42.48 E
Jijona / Xixona 126 Lf 38.32N 0.30W
Jikharrah 164 Dd 29.17N 21.38 E
Jilava 130 Je 44.20N 26.05 E
Jilf al Kabīr, Haḑabat al- 164 Ee 23.30N 26.00 E
Jilib 160 Lh 0.29N 42.47 E
Jilin 142 Oe 43.51N 126.33 E
Jilin Sheng (Chi-lin Sheng)
=Kirin (EN) [2] 152 Mc 43.00N 126.00 E
Jiliu He 152 La 52.02N 120.41 E
Jiloca 126 Kc 41.21N 1.39W
Jima=Jimma (EN) 160 Kh 7.39N 36.49 E
Jimāl, Wādī- 146 Fj 24.40N 35.06 E
Jimaní 194 Ld 18.28N 71.51W
Jimbe 170 De 11.05S 24.00 E
Jimbolia 130 Dd 45.48N 20.43 E
Jimena 126 Ig 37.50N 3.28W
Jimena de la Frontera 126 Gh 36.26N 5.27W
Jiménez 190 Dc 27.08N 104.55W
Jiménez de Teúl 192 Gf 23.10N 104.05W
Jimma (EN)=Jima 160 Kh 7.39N 36.49 E
Jimo 154 Ff 36.24N 120.27 E
Jimsar 152 Ec 43.59N 89.04 E
Jimulco 192 He 25.20N 103.10W
Jināh 146 Dj 25.20N 30.31 E
Jinan (Tsinan) 142 Nf 36.35N 117.00 E
Jincheng [China] 152 Jd 35.32N 112.53 E
Jincheng [China] 154 Fd 41.12N 121.25 E
Jinchuan /Quqên 152 He 31.02N 102.02 E
Jind 148 Fc 29.19N 76.19 E
Jindřichův Hradec 120 Kg 49.09N 15.00 E
Jinfo Shan 152 If 29.01N 107.14 E
Jing/Jinghe 152 Dc 44.39N 82.50 E
Jing'an 154 Cj 28.51N 115.21 E
Jingbian (Zhangjiapan) 152 Id 37.32N 108.45 E
Jingde 154 Ei 30.18N 118.30 E
Jingdezhen 142 Ng 29.18N 117.18 E
Jingfeng → Hexigten Qi 152 Kc 43.15N 117.31 E
Jinggang Shan 152 Jf 26.42N 114.07 E
Jinggu 152 Hg 23.28N 100.39 E
Jinghai 154 De 38.57N 116.56 E
Jinghe/Jing 152 Dc 44.39N 82.50 E
Jinghong (Yunjinghong) 152 Hg 21.59N 100.48 E
Jinghong Dao 150 Fe 9.45N 114.28 E
Jingjiang 154 Fh 32.01N 120.15 E
Jingle 154 Ae 38.22N 111.56 E
Jingmen 152 Je 31.00N 112.11 E
Jingning 152 Id 35.30N 105.45 E
Jingping → Pinglu 154 Be 39.32N 112.14 E
Jingpo Hu 154 Jc 43.50N 128.53 E
Jingshan 154 Bi 31.04N 113.08 E
Jingtai 152 Hd 37.10N 104.08 E
Jingxian [China] 152 If 26.40N 109.37 E
Jingxian [China] 152 Ke 30.41N 118.29 E
Jingxing (Weishui) 154 Ce 38.03N 114.09 E
Jingyu 154 Ic 42.25N 126.48 E
Jingyuan 152 Hd 36.35N 104.40 E
Jingzhi 154 Ef 36.18N 119.22 E
Jingzhou → Jiangling 152 Je 30.21N 112.10 E
Jinhu (Licheng) 154 Eh 33.01N 119.01 E
Jinhua 152 Kf 29.09N 119.38 E
Jining [China] 142 Nf 35.26N 116.36 E
Jining [China] 142 Ne 41.02N 113.07 E
Jinja 160 Kh 0.26N 33.13 E
Jin Jiang 154 Cj 28.23N 115.48 E
Jinkou 154 Ci 30.20N 114.07 E
Jinotega 190 Gf 13.06N 86.00W
Jinotega [3] 194 Eg 14.00N 85.25W
Jinotepe 190 Gf 11.51N 86.12W
Jinping 152 Hg 22.45N 103.15 E
Jinsha 152 If 27.18N 106.16 E
Jinsha → Nantong 154 Fh 32.06N 120.52 E
Jinsha Jiang 140 Mg 28.46N 104.38 E
Jinshan 154 Fi 30.54N 121.09 E
Jinshan → Harqin Qi 154 Ed 41.57N 118.40 E
Jinshi 154 Aj 29.03N 111.52 E
Jinta 152 Gc 40.00N 99.00 E
Jintan 154 Ei 31.45N 119.34 E
Jinxi 152 Lc 40.46N 120.50 E
Jinxian [China] 152 Ld 39.06N 121.44 E
Jinxian [China] 154 Dj 28.21N 116.16 E
Jinxiang 154 Dg 35.04N 116.19 E
Jinyang 152 Hf 27.39N 103.12 E
Jinyun 154 Fj 28.39N 120.05 E
Jinzhai (Meishan) 154 Ci 31.40N 115.52 E
Jinzhou 142 Oe 41.09N 121.08 E
Jinzū-Gawa 156 Ec 36.45N 137.13 E
Jiparaná, Rio- 198 Jf 8.03S 62.52W
Jipijapa 202 Bd 1.22S 80.34W
Jiquilisco 194 Cg 13.19N 88.35W
Jiquilisco, Bahía de- 194 Cg 13.10N 88.28W
Jirjā 164 Fd 26.20N 31.53 E
Jishou 152 If 28.18N 109.43 E
Jishu 154 Ib 44.16N 126.50 E
Jisr ash Shughur 146 Ge 35.48N 36.19 E
Jiu 130 Gf 43.47N 23.48 E
Jiucai Ling 152 Jf 25.33N 111.18 E
Jiucheng → Wucheng 154 Df 37.12N 116.04 E
Jiuding Shan 152 He 31.30N 104.00 E
Jiujiang 142 Ng 29.39N 116.00 E
Jiuling Shan 152 Jf 28.55N 114.50 E
Jiulong/Gyaisi 152 Hf 28.58N 101.33 E
Jiuquan (Suzhou) 142 Lf 39.46N 98.34 E
Jiurongcheng 154 Gf 37.22N 122.33 E
Jiutai 152 Mc 44.10N 125.50 E
Jīwani, Rās- 148 Cc 25.01N 61.44 E
Jixi [China] 142 Pe 45.15N 130.55 E
Jixi [China] 154 Ei 30.04N 118.36 E
Jixian [China] 154 Cg 35.23N 114.04 E
Jixian [China] 154 Dd 40.03N 117.24 E
Jixian [China] 154 Cf 37.34N 115.34 E
Jiyang 154 Df 36.59N 117.11 E
Jiyuan 154 Bg 35.06N 112.35 E
Jiyun He 154 De 39.05N 117.45 E
Jiz, Wādī al- 168 Ib 16.12N 52.14 E
Jīzān 142 Gh 16.54N 42.32 E
Jize 154 Cf 36.54N 114.52 E
Jizera 120 Kf 50.10N 14.43 E
Jizerské Hory 120 Lf 50.50N 15.13 E
Jizl, Wādī al- 146 Hj 25.39N 38.25 E
Jizō-Zaki 154 Lg 35.33N 133.18 E
Jmbe 170 De 10.20S 16.40 E
Jnchengjiang → Hechi 152 Ig 24.44N 108.02 E
Joaçaba 204 Gh 27.10S 51.30W
Joal-Fadiout 166 Bc 14.10N 16.51W
João Câmara 202 Ke 5.32S 35.48W
João Monlevade 204 Kd 19.50S 43.08W
João Pessoa 200 Mf 7.07S 34.52W
João Pinheiro 202 Ig 17.45S 46.10W
Joaquín V. González 206 Hb 25.00S 64.11W
Jobado 194 Ic 20.54N 77.17W
Jódar 126 Ig 37.50N 3.21W
Jodhpur 142 Jg 26.17N 73.02 E
Jodoigne/Geldenaken 124 Gd 50.43N 4.52 E
Joensuu 112 Ic 62.36N 29.46 E
Joerg Plateau 222 Qf 75.00S 69.30W
Joes Hill 220g Bb 1.48N 157.19W
Jōetsu 152 Od 37.06N 138.15 E
Joeuf 124 Ie 49.14N 6.01 E
Jôf di Montasio 128 Hd 46.26N 13.26 E
Joffre, Mount- 188 Ha 50.32N 115.13W
Jogbani 148 Hc 26.25N 87.15 E
Jõgeva/Jygeva 114 Gg 58.46N 26.26 E
Joghatāy 146 Qd 36.36N 57.01 E
Joghatāy, Kūh-e- 146 Qd 36.30N 57.00 E
Jōhana 156 Ec 36.31N 136.54 E
Johannesburg 160 Jk 26.15S 28.00 E
Jōhen 156 Ce 32.57N 132.35 E
John Day 188 Fd 44.25N 118.57W
John Day River 182 Cb 45.44N 120.39W
John H. Kerr Reservoir 184 Hg 36.31N 78.18W
John Martin Reservoir 186 Eg 38.05N 103.02W
John o' Groat's 118 Jc 58.38N 3.05W
Johnson 186 Fh 37.34N 101.45W
Johnson, Pico de- 192 Cc 29.13N 112.07W
Johnson City [Tn.-U.S.] 182 Kd 36.19N 82.21W
Johnson City [Tx.-U.S.] 186 Gk 30.17N 98.25W
Johnsons Crossing 180 Ed 60.29N 133.17W
Johnsons Point 197d Bb 17.02N 61.53W
Johnston Atoll [5] 210 Kc 17.00N 168.30W
Johnston Atoll 208 Kc 17.00N 168.30W
Johnstone, Lake- 212 Ef 32.20S 120.40 E
Johnstone Strait 188 Ca 50.25N 126.00W
Johnstown [N.Y.-U.S.] 184 Jd 43.01N 74.22W
Johnstown [Pa.-U.S.] 182 Lc 40.20N 78.56W
Johor [2] 150 Df 2.00N 103.30 E
Johor Baharu 142 Mi 1.28N 103.45 E
Joia 204 Ei 28.39S 54.08W
Joigny 122 Jg 47.59N 3.24 E
Joinvile 200 Lh 26.18S 48.50W
Joinville 122 Lf 48.27N 5.08 E
Joinville Island 222 Re 63.15S 55.45W
Jokau 168 Ed 8.24N 33.49 E
Jokela 116 Kd 60.33N 24.59 E
Jokelbugten 179 Kc 78.25N 19.00W
Jokioinen 116 Jd 60.49N 23.28 E
Jokkmokk 114 Ec 66.36N 19.51 E
Jøkuleggi 116 Cc 61.03N 8.12 E
Jolfā 146 Kc 38.57N 45.38 E
Joliet 182 Jc 41.32N 88.05W
Joliette 180 Kg 46.01N 73.26W
Jolo 150 He 6.00N 121.00 E
Jolo Group 140 Oi 6.00N 121.09 E
Jølstravatnet 116 Bc 61.30N 6.15 E
Jomala 116 Hd 60.09N 19.58 E
Jombang 150 Fh 7.33S 112.14 E
Jomda 152 Ge 31.37N 98.20 E
Jönåker 116 Gf 58.44N 16.40 E
Jonava/Ionava 114 Fi 55.05N 24.17 E
Jonê 152 He 34.35N 103.32 E
Jones Bank 118 Fl 49.50N 8.00W
Jonesboro [Ar.-U.S.] 182 Id 35.50N 90.42W
Jonesboro [La.-U.S.] 186 Jj 32.15N 92.43W
Jones Mountains 222 Pf 73.32S 94.00W
Jones Sound 174 Kb 76.00N 85.00W
Jonesville 184 Fg 36.41N 83.06W
Jonglei 168 Ed 6.50N 31.18 E
Jonglei [3] 168 Ed 7.20N 32.00 E
Jonglei, Tur'ah-=Jonglei
Canal (EN) 168 Ed 9.22N 31.30 E
Jonglei Canal (EN)=Jonglei,
Tur'ah- 168 Ed 9.22N 31.30 E
Joniškėlis/Ioniškelis 116 Ki 56.00N 24.14 E
Joniškis/Ioniškis 114 Fh 56.16N 23.37 E
Jönköping 112 Hd 57.47N 14.11 E
Jönköping [2] 114 Dh 57.30N 14.30 E
Jonquière 180 Kg 48.25N 71.15W
Jonuta 192 Mh 18.05N 92.08W
Jonzac 122 Fi 45.27N 0.26W
Joplin 176 Jf 37.06N 94.31W
Jordan 182 Fb 47.19N 106.55W
Jordan 144 Ec 31.46N 35.33 E
Jordan (EN)=Al Urdun [1] 142 Ff 31.00N 36.00 E
Jordan Valley 188 Ge 42.58N 117.03W
Jordão, Rio- 204 Fg 25.46S 52.07W
Jorhāt 142 Lg 26.45N 94.13 E
Jörn 114 Ed 65.04N 20.02 E
Joroinen 114 Ge 62.11N 27.50 E
Jørpeland 114 Bg 59.01N 6.03 E
Jos 160 Hh 9.55N 8.54 E
José A. Guisasola 204 Bn 38.40S 61.05W
José Battle y Ordóñez 204 Ek 33.28S 55.07W
José Bonifácio 204 He 21.03S 49.41W
José de San Martín 206 Ff 44.02S 70.29W
Joselandia 204 Dc 16.32S 56.12W
José Otávio 204 Ej 31.17S 54.07W
José Pedro Varela 204 Ek 33.27S 54.32W
Joseph, Lake- 184 Hc 45.14N 79.45W
Joseph Bonaparte Gulf 208 Df 14.55S 128.15 E
Josephine Seamount (EN) 110 Eh 36.52N 14.20W
Joseph Lake 180 Kf 52.48N 65.17W
Joshimath 148 Fb 30.34N 79.34 E
Joškar-Ola 112 Kd 56.40N 47.55 E
Jos Plateau 158 Hh 10.00N 9.30 E
Josselin 122 Dg 47.57N 2.33W
Jostedalen 116 Bc 61.35N 7.20 E
Jostedalsbreen 114 Bf 61.40N 7.00 E
Jostefonn 116 Bc 61.26N 6.33 E
Jost Van Dyke 197a Db 18.28N 64.45W
Jotunheimen 110 Gc 61.40N 8.20 E
Joubertberge 172 Ac 18.45S 13.55 E
Joué-lès-Tours 122 Gg 47.21N 0.40 E
Jouquara, Rio- 204 Db 15.06S 57.06W
Joure, Haskerland- 124 Hb 52.58N 5.47 E
Joutsa 114 Gf 61.44N 26.07 E
Joutseno 114 Gf 61.06N 28.30 E
Jovan, Deli- 130 Fe 44.15N 22.13 E
Jovellanos 194 Gb 22.48N 81.12W
Joviânia 204 Hc 17.49S 49.30W
Jowhar 160 Lh 2.46N 45.32 E
Jow Kār 146 Me 34.26N 48.42 E
Jowzjān [3] 144 Kb 36.30N 66.00 E
Joya, Laguna de la- 192 Mj 15.55N 93.40W
Jreïda 162 Df 18.19N 16.03W
Juan Aldama 190 Dd 24.19N 103.21W
Juana Ramírez, Isla- 192 Kg 21.50N 97.40W
Juan Blanquier 204 Cl 35.46S 59.18W
Juancheng 154 Cg 35.33N 115.30 E
Juan de Fuca, Strait of- 174 Ge 48.20N 124.00W
Juan de Nova, Ile- 158 Lj 17.03S 42.45 E
Juan E. Barra 204 Bm 37.48S 60.29W
Juan
Fernández,Archipiélago-=
Juan Fernández Islands
(EN) 198 Ii 33.00S 80.00W
Juan Fernández Islands (EN)
=Juan
Fernández,Archipiélago- 198 Ii 33.00S 80.00W
Juan G. Bazán 204 Bg 24.33S 60.50W
Juangriego 196 Eg 11.05N 63.57W
Juanjuí 202 Ce 7.11S 76.45W
Juan L. Lacaze 204 Dl 34.26S 57.27W
Juárez [Arg.] 206 Ie 37.40S 59.48W
Juárez [Mex.] 192 Id 27.37N 100.44W
Juárez, Sierra de- 192 Bb 32.00N 115.50W
Juarzohn 166 Dd 5.20N 8.58W
Juàzeirinho 202 Ke 7.04S 36.35W
Juàzeiro 200 Lf 9.25S 40.30W
Juàzeiro do Norte 200 Mf 7.12S 39.20W
Jūbā 160 Kh 4.51N 31.37 E
Juba (EN) = Ganāne, Webi- 158 Lh 0.15S 42.38 E
Juba, Rio- 204 Db 14.59S 57.44W
Jūbāl, Maḑīq- 146 Ei 27.40N 33.55 E
Jubaland (EN) 158 Lh 1.00N 42.00 E
Jubayl [Eg.] 146 Eh 28.12N 33.38 E
Jubayl [Leb.] 146 Fe 34.07N 35.39 E
Jubayt [Sud.] 168 Fb 18.57N 36.50 E
Jubayt [Sud.] 168 Fa 20.59N 36.18 E
Jubbada Dhexe [3] 168 Ge 1.15N 42.30 E
Jubbada Hoose [3] 168 Gf 0.30S 42.00 E
Jubbah 146 Ih 28.02N 40.56 E
Jubilee Lake 212 Fe 29.10S 126.40 E
Juby, Cap- 158 Ff 27.57N 12.55W
Júcar/Xúquer 110 Fh 39.09N 0.14W
Juçara 204 Gb 15.53S 50.51W
Jucaro 194 Hc 21.37N 78.51W
Jüchen 124 Ic 51.06N 6.30 E
Juchipila 192 Hg 21.25N 103.07W
Juchipila, Río- 192 Hg 21.03N 103.25W
Juchitán de Zaragoza 176 Jh 16.26N 95.01W
Jučjugej 138 Jd 63.20N 142.15 E
Judas, Punta- 194 Ei 9.31N 84.32W
Judayyidat 'Ar'ar 144 Fc 31.22N 41.26 E
Judenburg 128 Ic 47.10N 14.40 E
Judith Mountains 188 Kc 47.12N 109.15W
Judith River 188 Kc 47.44N 109.38W
Judoma 138 Ie 59.08N 135.03 E
Judomski hrebet 138 Jd 61.05N 141.30 E
Juegang → Rudong 154 Fh 32.19N 121.11 E
Juelsminde 116 Di 55.43N 10.01 E
Jufrah, Wāḩāt al- = Giofra
Oasis (EN) 158 If 29.10N 16.00 E
Jug 134 Hh 57.43N 56.12 E
Jug 110 Kc 60.45N 46.20 E
Jugo-Osetinskaja
avtonomnaja oblast [3] 136 Eg 42.20N 44.05 E
Jugorski poluostrov 134 Kb 69.30N 62.30 E
Jugorski Šar, proliv- 136 Gb 69.45N 60.35 E
Jugoslavija = Yugoslavia
(EN) [1] 112 Hg 44.00N 19.00 E
Jugo-Tala 138 Kc 66.03N 151.05 E
Jugydjan 134 Gf 61.42N 54.58 E
Juhaym 146 Kh 29.36N 45.24 E
Juhnov 132 Ib 54.43N 35.12 E
Juhor 130 Ef 43.50N 21.15 E
Juhoslovenská nižina 120 Ph 48.10N 19.40 E
Juhua Dao 154 Fd 40.32N 120.48 E
Juigalpa 194 Eg 12.05N 85.24W
Juina, Rio- 204 Ca 12.36S 58.57W
Juine 122 If 48.32N 2.23 E
Juininha, Rio- 204 Ca 12.55S 59.13W
Juist 120 Cc 53.40N 7.00 E
Juiz de Fora 200 Lh 21.45S 43.20W
Jujuy [2] 206 Gb 23.00S 66.00W
Jukagirskoje ploskogorje 138 Kc 66.00N 155.30 E
Jukonda 134 Mg 59.38N 67.20 E
Juksejevo 134 Gg 59.52N 54.16 E
Jula 114 Ke 63.48N 44.44 E
Juldybajevo 134 Hj 52.20N 57.52 E
Julesburg 186 Ef 40.59N 102.16W
Juli 202 Eg 16.13S 69.27W
Juliaca 202 Dg 15.30S 70.08W
Julia Creek 212 Id 20.39S 141.45 E
Julian Alps (EN)=Julijske
Alpe 128 Hd 46.20N 13.45 E
Juliana Top 202 Gc 3.41N 56.32W
Julianehåb/Qaqortoq 224 Nc 60.50N 46.10W
Jülich 120 Cf 50.56N 6.22 E
Jülicher Borde 124 Id 50.50N 6.30 E
Julijske Alpe=Julian Alps
(EN) 128 Hd 46.20N 13.45 E
Julimes 192 Gc 28.25N 105.27W
Júlio de Castilhos 204 Fi 29.14S 53.41W
Jullundur → Jalandhar 142 Jf 31.19N 75.34 E
Julong/New Kowloon 142 Ng 22.20N 114.09 E
Julu 154 Cf 37.13N 115.02 E
Juma 114 Hd 65.05N 33.13 E
Juma He 154 De 39.31N 116.08 E
Jumaymah, Birkat al- 146 Jh 29.36N 43.36 E
Jumentos Cays 194 Jb 23.00N 75.50W
Jumet, Charleroi- 122 Kd 50.27N 4.26 E
Jumièges 124 Ce 49.26N 0.49 E
Jumilla 126 Kf 38.29N 1.17W
Jümme 124 Ja 53.13N 7.31 E
Junāgadh 148 Ed 21.31N 70.28 E
Junan (Shizilu) 154 Eg 35.10N 118.50 E
Junaynah, Ra's al- 146 Eh 29.01N 33.58 E
Juncal 192 De 24.50N 111.47W
Juncos 197a Cb 18.13N 65.55W
Junction [Tx.-U.S.] 186 Gk 30.29N 99.46W
Junction [Ut.-U.S.] 188 Ig 38.14N 112.13W
Junction City 182 Hd 39.02N 96.50W
Jundiaí 206 Kb 23.11S 46.52W
Jundiaí do Sul 204 Gf 23.27S 50.17W
Jundūbah 162 Ib 36.30N 8.45 E
Jundūbah [3] 162 Ib 36.28N 8.41 E
Juneau 176 Fd 57.20N 134.27W
Junee 212 Jf 34.52S 147.35 E
Jungar Qi (Shagedu) 152 Jd 39.37N 110.58 E
Jungfrau 128 Bd 46.32N 7.58 E
Junggar Pendi=Dzungarian
Basin (EN) 140 Ke 45.00N 88.00 E
Junín [3] 202 Df 11.30S 75.00W
Junín [Arg.] 200 Ji 34.35S 60.57W
Junín [Peru] 202 Cf 11.10S 76.00W
Junín, Lago de- 202 Cf 11.02S 76.05W
Junín de los Andes 206 Fe 39.56S 71.05W
Juniville 124 Ge 49.24N 4.23 E
Jūniyah 146 Ff 33.59N 35.38 E
Junjaha 134 Jc 66.25N 62.00 E
Junlian 152 Hf 28.12N 104.34 E
Junsele 114 De 63.41N 16.54 E
Juntura 188 Fe 43.45N 118.05W
Junxian (Danjiang) 152 Je 32.31N 111.32 E
Juodupė 116 Kh 56.03N 25.44 E
Juojärvi 116 Mb 62.45N 28.35 E
Juoksengi 114 Fc 66.34N 23.51 E
Jupiá, Represa de- 206 Jb 20.47S 51.39W
Juquiá 204 Ig 24.19S 47.38W
Juquiá, Rio- 204 Ig 24.22S 47.49W
Juquiá, Serra do- 204 Gg 25.10S 52.00W
Jur 138 Ie 59.48N 137.29 E
Jur 158 Jh 8.39N 29.18 E
Jura [2] 128 Ac 47.25N 6.15 E
Jura [3] 122 Lh 46.50N 5.50 E
Jura 110 Gf 46.45N 6.30 E
Jura 118 Hf 56.00N 5.50W
Jūra/Jura 114 Fi 55.03N 22.10 E
Jura/Jūra 114 Fi 55.03N 22.10 E
Jura, Sound of- 118 Hf 55.55N 5.22W
Juradó 202 Cb 7.07N 77.46W
Juratiški 116 Kj 54.02N 26.00 E
Juraybÿ'āt 146 Kh 29.08N 45.30 E
Jurbarkas 114 Fi 55.08N 22.47 E
Jurdī, Wādī- 146 Ei 26.33N 32.44 E
Jurga 138 De 55.42N 84.55 E
Jurgamyš 134 Li 55.25N 64.28 E
Juribej 134 Nb 68.55N 69.05 E
Jurien Bay 212 Cf 30.15S 115.00 E
Jurigue, Rio- 204 Ec 16.29S 54.37W
Jurilovca 130 Le 44.46N 28.52 E
Jurja 114 Lg 59.03N 49.20 E
Jurjaha 134 Gc 66.42N 56.00 E
Jurjevec 114 Kh 57.22N 43.06 E
Jurjev-Polski 114 Jh 56.31N 39.44 E
Jurjuzan 134 Ii 54.52N 58.28 E
Jurjuzan 134 Hi 55.43N 56.57 E
Jurla 134 Gg 59.20N 54.16 E
Jūrmala/Jurmala 136 Cd 56.59N 23.38 E
Jurmala/Jūrmala 136 Cd 56.59N 23.38 E
Jurmo 116 Ie 59.50N 21.35 E
Jurong 154 Ei 31.56N 119.10 E
Juruá 202 Ed 3.27S 66.03W
Juruá, Rio- 198 Jf 2.37S 65.44W
Juruena, Rio- 198 Kf 7.20S 58.03W
Jurumirim, Represa de- 206 Kb 23.20S 49.00W
Juruti 202 Gd 2.09S 56.04W
Jurva 116 Ib 62.41N 21.59 E
Jusan-Kō 156a Bc 41.00N 140.20 E
Jusayrah 146 Nj 25.53N 50.36 E

Index Symbols

[1] Independent Nation
[2] State, Region
[3] District, County
[4] Municipality
[5] Colony, Dependency
Continent
Physical Region
Historical or Cultural Region
Mount, Mountain
Volcano
Hill
Mountains, Mountain Range
Hills, Escarpment
Plateau, Upland
Pass, Gap
Plain, Lowland
Delta
Salt Flat
Valley, Canyon
Crater, Cave
Karst Features
Depression
Polder
Desert, Dunes
Forest, Woods
Heath, Steppe
Oasis
Cape, Point
Coast, Beach
Cliff
Peninsula
Isthmus
Sandbank
Island
Atoll
Rock, Reef
Islands, Archipelago
Rocks, Reefs
Coral Reef
Well, Spring
Geyser
River, Stream
Waterfall, Rapids
River Mouth, Estuary
Lake
Salt Lake
Intermittent Lake
Reservoir
Swamp, Pond
Canal
Glacier
Ice Shelf, Pack Ice
Ocean
Sea
Gulf, Bay
Strait, Fjord
Lagoon
Bank
Seamount
Tablemount
Ridge
Shelf
Basin
Escarpment, Sea Scarp
Fracture
Trench, Abyss
National Park, Reserve
Point of Interest
Recreation Site
Cave, Cavern
Historic Site
Ruins
Wall, Walls
Church, Abbey
Temple
Scientific Station
Railway station
Airport
Port
Military installation
Lighthouse
Mine
Tunnel
Dam, Bridge

Jusheng 152 Mb 48.44N 126.37 E
Ju Shui 154 Ci 31.09N 114.52 E
Juškozero 136 Dc 64.45N 32.08 E
Jussarö 116 Je 59.50N 23.35 E
Justo Daract 206 Gd 33.52S 65.11W
Jusva 134 Gg 58.59N 54.57 E
Jutai 202 Ee 5.11S 68.54W
Jutai, Rio- 198 Jf 2.43S 66.57W
Jüterbog 120 Je 51.59N 13.05 E
Juti 204 Ef 22.52S 54.37W
Jutiapa [3] 194 Bf 14.10N 89.50W
Jutiapa [Guat.] 190 Gf 14.17N 89.54W
Jutiapa [Hond.] 194 Df 15.46N 86.34W
Juticalpa 190 Gf 14.42N 86.15W
Jutland (EN)=Jylland 110 Gd 56.00N 9.15 E
Juuka 114 Ge 63.14N 29.15 E
Juva 114 Gf 61.54N 27.51 E
Juventud, Isla de la-=Pines, Isle of- (EN) 174 Kg 21.40N 82.50W
Juxian 152 Kd 35.33N 118.45 E
Jūybār 146 Od 36.38N 52.53 E
Juye 154 Dg 35.23N 116.05 E
Jūyom 146 Oh 28.10N 54.02 E
Juža 114 Kh 56.36N 42.01 E
Južnaja Keltma 134 Gf 60.30N 55.40 E
Južna Morava 130 Ef 43.41N 21.24 E
Južni Rodopi 130 Ih 41.15N 25.30 E
Južnoje 138 Jg 46.13N 143.27 E
Južno-Jenisejski 138 Ee 58.48N 94.45 E
Južno-Kurilsk 138 Jh 44.05N 145.52 E
Južno-Sahalinsk 142 Qe 46.58N 142.42 E
Južno-Uralsk 136 Ge 54.26N 61.15 E
Južny, mys- 138 Ke 57.42N 156.55 E
Južny Bug 110 Jf 46.59N 31.58 E
Južny Ural=Southern Urals (EN) 110 Le 54.00N 58.30 E
Jygeva/Jõgeva 114 Gg 58.46N 26.26 E
Jylland=Jutland (EN) 110 Gd 56.00N 9.15 E
Jylland Bank 116 Bh 56.55N 7.20 E
Jyske Ås 116 Dg 57.15N 10.14 E
Jyväskylä 112 Ic 62.14N 25.44 E

K

K2 (Godwin Austen) 140 Jf 35.53N 76.30 E
Ka 166 Fc 11.39N 4.11 E
Kaabong 170 Fb 3.31N 34.09 E
Kaahka 136 Fh 37.21N 59.38 E
Kaala 221a Cb 21.31N 158.09W
Kaala-Gomén 219b Be 20.40S 164.24 E
Kaalualu Bay 221a Fe 18.58N 155.37W
Kaamanen 114 Gb 69.06N 27.12 E
Kaap Kruis 172 Ad 21.46S 13.58 E
Kaap Plateau (EN)= Kaapplato 158 Jk 27.30S 23.45 E
Kaapplato=Kaap Plateau (EN) 158 Jk 27.30S 23.45 E
Kaapprovinsie/Cape Province [2] 172 Cf 32.00S 22.00 E
Kaapstad / Cape Town 160 Il 33.55S 18.22 E
Kaarst 124 Ic 51.15N 6.37 E
Kaarta 166 Cc 14.35N 10.00W
Kaba/Habahe 152 Eb 47.53N 86.12 E
Kabaena, Pulau- 150 Hh 5.15S 121.55 E
Kabah 192 Og 20.07N 89.29W
Kabala 166 Cd 9.35N 11.33W
Kabale 170 Ec 1.15S 29.59 E
Kabalega Falls (Murchison Falls) 170 Fb 2.17N 31.41 E
Kabalo 160 Ji 6.03S 26.55 E
Kabaman 219a Aa 4.38S 152.42 E
Kabambare 170 Ec 4.16S 27.07 E
Kabamet 170 Gb 0.30N 35.45 E
Kabanjahe 150 Cf 3.06N 98.30 E
Kabardino-Balkarskaja ASSR [3] 136 Eg 43.30N 43.30 E
Kabare 170 Ec 2.29S 28.48 E
Kabasalan 150 He 7.48N 122.45 E
Kaba-Shima [Jap.] 156 Ae 32.34N 129.47 E
Kaba-Shima [Jap.] 156 Ae 32.45N 129.00 E
Kabba 166 Gd 7.50N 6.04 E
Kåbdalis 114 Ec 66.09N 20.00 E
Kaberamaido 170 Fb 1.45N 33.10 E
Kabetogama Lake 186 Jb 48.28N 92.59W
Kabhegy 120 Ni 47.03N 17.39 E
Kabinakagami Lake 184 Ea 48.58N 84.25W
Kabinda 160 Ji 6.08S 24.29 E
Kabīr, Wādī al- 128 Dn 36.23N 9.52 E
Kabīr Kūh 146 Lf 33.25N 46.45 E
Kabkābīyah 168 Cc 13.39N 24.05 E
Kableškovo 130 Kg 42.39N 27.34 E
Kabna 168 Eb 19.10N 32.41 E
Kabo 168 Bd 7.35N 18.38 E
Kābol [3] 144 Kc 34.30N 69.00 E
Kābol (Kabūl) 142 If 34.31N 69.12 E
Kabompo 170 De 13.36S 24.12 E
Kabompo 158 Jj 14.11S 23.11 E
Kabondo Dianda 170 Ed 8.53S 25.40 E
Kabongo 170 Ed 7.19S 25.35 E
Kabou 166 Fd 9.27N 0.49 E
Kabūdiyāh, Ra's- 162 Jb 35.14N 11.10 E
Kabūd Rāhang 146 Me 35.12N 48.44 E
Kābul 140 Jf 33.55N 72.14 E
Kabūl → Kābol 142 If 34.31N 69.12 E
Kabunda 170 Ee 12.13S 29.23 E
Kabunga 170 Ec 1.42S 28.08 E
Kaburuang, Pulau- 150 If 3.48N 126.48 E
Kabwe 160 Jj 14.27S 28.27 E
Kača 132 Hg 44.44N 33.32 E
Kačanik 130 Eg 42.14N 21.15 E
Kačanovo 116 Lg 57.24N 27.53 E
Kačergine 116 Jj 54.53N 23.49 E
Kachchh, Gulf of 140 Ig 22.36N 69.30 E
Kachchh, Rann of 148 Dd 23.51N 70.30 E
Kachia 166 Gd 9.52E 7.57 E
Kachikau 172 Cc 18.09S 24.29 E
Kachin [2] 148 Jc 26.00N 97.30 E
Kačiry 136 He 53.04N 76.07 E
Kačkanar 136 Fd 58.42N 59.35 E
Kaçkar Dağı 144 Fa 41.10N 40.50 E
Kačug 138 Ff 54.00N 105.52 E
Kaczawa 120 Me 51.18N 16.27 E
Kadada 132 Oc 53.09N 46.01 E
Kadaň 120 Jf 50.23N 13.16 E
Kadan Kyun 148 Jf 12.30N 98.22 E
Kadei 158 Ih 3.31N 16.03 E
Kadijevka 136 Df 48.32N 38.40 E
Kadıköy 146 Bb 40.51N 26.50 E
Kadıköy, İstanbul- 130 Mi 40.59N 29.01 E
Kadina 212 Hf 33.58S 137.43 E
Kadınhanı 146 Ec 38.15N 32.14 E
Kadiolo 166 Dc 10.34N 5.45W
Kadiri 148 Ff 14.07N 78.10 E
Kadirli 144 Eb 37.23N 36.05 E
Kadja 168 Cc 12.02N 22.28 E
Kadmat Island 148 Ef 11.14N 72.47 E
Kadnikov 114 Jg 59.30N 40.24 E
Kadoka 186 Fe 43.50N 101.31W
Kadoma 160 Jj 18.21S 29.55 E
Kaduj 114 Ig 59.14N 37.09 E
Kaduna 160 Hg 10.31N 7.26 E
Kaduna [2] 166 Gc 11.00N 7.30 E
Kaduna 158 Hh 8.45N 5.48 E
Kāduqlī 160 Jg 11.01N 29.43 E
Kadykčan 138 Jd 63.05N 146.58 E
Kadžaran 132 Oj 39.11N 46.10 E
Kadžerom 134 Gd 64.41N 55.54 E
Kadži-Saj 135 Kc 42.08N 77.10 E
Kaech'ŏn 154 He 39.42N 125.53 E
Kaédi 160 Fg 16.08N 13.31W
Kaélé 166 Hc 10.07N 14.27 E
Kaena Point 221a Cb 21.35N 158.17W
Kaeo 218 Ea 35.06S 173.47 E
Kaesŏng 142 Of 37.58N 126.33 E
Kaesŏng Si [2] 154 Ie 38.05N 126.30 E
Kāf 146 Gg 31.24N 37.29 E
Kafakumba 170 Dd 9.41S 23.44 E
Kafan 136 Eh 39.12N 46.28 E
Kafanchan 166 Gd 9.35N 8.18 E
Kaffrine 166 Bc 14.06N 15.33W
Kafia Kingi 168 Cd 9.16N 24.25 E
Kafiréos, Dhiékplous- 130 Hl 38.00N 24.40 E
Kafirévs, Ákra- 130 Hk 38.10N 24.35 E
Kafr ad Dawwār 146 Dg 31.08N 30.07 E
Kafr ash Shaykh 164 Fc 31.07N 30.56 E
Kafta 168 Fc 13.54N 37.11 E
Kafu 170 Fb 1.39N 32.05 E
Kafue 160 Jj 15.47S 28.11 E
Kafue 158 Jj 15.56S 28.55 E
Kafue Dam 170 Ef 15.45S 28.28 E
Kafue Flats 170 Ef 15.40S 26.25 E
Kafufu 170 Fd 7.12S 31.31 E
Kaga 154 Nf 36.18N 136.18 E
Kaga Bandoro 168 Bd 7.02N 19.13 E
Kagalaska 178a Cb 51.47N 176.23W
Kagalnik 132 Kf 47.04N 39.18 E
Kagami 156 Be 32.34N 130.40 E
Kagan 136 Gh 39.43N 64.32 E
Kagarlyk 132 Ge 49.53N 30.56 E
Kagawa Ken [2] 154 Mg 34.15N 134.15 E
Kagera 158 Ki 0.57S 31.47 E
Kağızman 146 Jb 40.09N 43.07 E
Kagoshima 142 Pf 31.36N 130.33 E
Kagoshima Bay (EN)= Kagoshima-Wan 154 Ki 31.27N 130.40 E
Kagoshima Ken [2] 154 Ki 31.45N 130.40 E
Kagoshima-Taniyama 156 Bf 31.31N 130.31 E
Kagoshima-Wan= Kagoshima Bay (EN) 154 Ki 31.27N 130.40 E
Kagul 136 Cf 45.53N 28.14 E
Kagul 130 Ld 45.32N 28.27 E
Kahal Tabelbala 162 Gd 28.45N 2.15W
Kahama 170 Fc 3.50S 32.36 E
Kahemba 160 Ii 7.17S 19.00 E
Kahi 132 Oi 41.23N 46.59 E
Kahiu Point 221a Eb 21.13N 156.58W
Kahler Asten 120 Ee 51.11N 8.29 E
Kahnūj 146 Qi 27.58N 57.47 E
Kahoku 156 Gb 38.30N 141.20 E
Kahoku-Gata 156 Ec 36.40N 136.40 E
Kahoolawe Island 208 Lb 20.33N 156.35W
Kahouanne, Ilet à- 197e Ab 16.22N 61.47W
Kahovka 136 Df 46.47N 33.32 E
Kahovskoje vodohranilišče = Kakhovua Reservoir (EN) 110 Jf 47.25N 34.10 E
Kahramanmaraş 144 Eb 37.36N 36.55 E
Kahrūyeh 146 Ng 31.43N 51.48 E
Kâhta 146 Hd 37.46N 38.36 E
Kahuku 221a Db 21.41N 157.57W
Kahuku Point 221a Db 21.43N 157.59W
Kahului 221a Ec 20.53N 156.27W
Kahului Bay 221a Ec 20.55N 156.30W
Kahurangi Point 218 Ed 40.46S 172.13 E
Kahurestan 144 Id 27.10N 55.45 E
Kai, Kepulauan- 208 Ee 5.35S 132.45 E
Kaiama 166 Fd 9.36N 3.57 E
Kaiapoi 218 Ee 43.23S 172.39 E
Kaibab Plateau 188 Ih 36.30N 112.15W
Kai Beuar 150 Jh 5.35S 133.00 E
Kaidu He/Karaxabar He 152 Ec 41.55N 86.38 E
Kaieteur Falls 202 Gc 5.10N 59.28W
Kaifeng 142 Nf 34.45N 114.25 E
Kaihua 154 Ej 29.10N 118.24 E
Kai Kecil 150 Jh 5.45S 132.40 E
Kaikohe 218 Ea 35.24S 173.48 E
Kaikoura 216 Dh 42.25S 173.41 E
Kaili 152 If 26.35N 107.59 E
Kailu 152 Lc 43.37N 121.19 E
Kailua [Hi.-U.S.] 221a Db 21.23N 157.44W
Kailua [Hi.-U.S.] 221a Fd 19.39N 155.59W
Kaimana 150 Jg 3.39S 133.45 E
Kaimanawa Mountains 218 Fc 39.15S 176.00 E
Kaimon-Dake 156 Bf 31.10N 130.32 E
Kain, Tournai- 124 Fd 50.38N 3.22 E
Kainach 128 Jd 46.54N 15.31 E
Kainan [Jap.] 156 De 33.36N 134.22 E
Kainan [Jap.] 156 Dd 34.09N 135.12 E
Kainantu 214 Di 6.15S 145.53 E
Kainji Dam 166 Fd 9.55N 4.40 E
Kainji Reservoir 166 Fc 10.30N 4.35 E
Kaipara Harbour 218 Fb 36.25S 174.15 E
Kaiparowits Plateau 188 Jh 37.20N 111.15W
Kaiser Franz Josephs Fjord 179 Jd 73.30N 24.00W
Kaisersesch 124 Jd 50.14N 7.09 E
Kaiserslautern 120 Dg 49.27N 7.45 E
Kaiserstuhl 120 Dh 48.06N 7.40 E
Kaishantun 152 Mc 42.43N 129.37 E
Kaišiadorys/Kajšjadoris 114 Fi 54.53N 24.31 E
Kaita 156 Cd 34.20N 132.32 E
Kaitaia 218 Ea 35.07S 173.14 E
Kaitangata 218 Cg 46.17S 169.51 E
Kaithal 148 Fc 29.48N 76.23 E
Kaitong → Tongyu 152 Lc 44.47N 123.05 E
Kaituma River 196 Gh 8.11N 59.41W
Kaiwaka 216 Dg 36.10S 174.26 E
Kaiwi Channel 214 Oc 21.13N 157.30W
Kaixian 152 Ie 31.10N 108.25 E
Kaiyuan [China] 152 Hg 23.47N 103.15 E
Kaiyuan [China] 152 Lc 42.33N 124.04 E
Kaiyuh Mountains 178 Hd 64.00N 158.00W
Kaja 158 Jg 12.02N 22.28 E
Kajaani 112 Ic 64.14N 27.41 E
Kajaapu 150 Dh 5.26S 102.24 E
Kajabbi 210 Fg 20.02S 140.02 E
Kajak 138 Fb 71.30N 103.15 E
Kajang 150 Df 2.59N 101.47 E
Kajdak, sor- 132 Rg 44.40N 53.30 E
Kajerkan 138 Dc 69.25N 87.30 E
Kajiado 170 Gc 1.51S 36.47 E
Kajiki 156 Bf 31.44N 130.40 E
Kajmakčalan 130 Ei 40.58N 21.48 E
Kajnar 130 Lb 47.50N 28.06 E
Kajo Kaji 168 Ee 3.53N 31.40 E
Kajrakkumskoje vodohranilišče 135 Hd 40.20N 70.05 E
Kajrakty 136 Hf 48.31N 73.14 E
Kajšjadoris/Kaišiadorys 114 Fi 54.53N 24.31 E
Kajuru 166 Gc 10.19N 7.41 E
Kākā 168 Ec 10.36N 32.11 E
Kaka 168 Fd 7.28N 39.06 E
Kakagi Lake 186 Jb 49.13N 93.52W
Kakamas 172 Ce 28.45S 20.33 E
Kakamega 170 Fb 0.17N 34.45 E
Kakamigahara 156 Ed 35.25N 136.50 E
Kakanj 128 Mf 44.08N 18.05 E
Kaka Point 221a Ec 20.32N 156.33W
Kakata 166 Cd 6.32N 10.21W
Kake 156 Cd 34.36N 132.19 E
Kakegawa 156 Ed 34.46N 138.00 E
Kakenge 170 Dc 4.51S 21.55 E
Kakeroma-Jima 156b Ba 28.08N 129.15 E
Kakhovka Reservoir (EN) = Kahovskoje vodohranilišče 110 Jf 47.25N 34.10 E
Kākī 146 Nh 28.19N 51.34 E
Kākināda 142 Kh 16.56N 82.13 E
Kakisa Lake 180 Fd 60.55N 117.40W
Kakizaki 156 Fc 37.16N 138.22 E
Kaklkan 146 Cd 36.15N 29.24 E
Kakogawa 156 Dd 34.46N 134.51 E
Kakpin 166 Ed 8.39N 3.48W
Kaktovik 178 Kb 70.08N 143.37W
Kakuda 156 Gc 37.58N 140.47 E
Kakuma 170 Fb 3.43N 34.52 E
Kakunodate 154 Pe 39.40N 140.32 E
Kakva 134 Jg 59.37N 60.50 E
Kakya 170 Gc 1.36S 39.02 E
Kalaa 126 Mi 35.35N 0.20 E
Kalaa Khasba 128 Co 35.38N 8.36 E
Kalaallit Nunaat/Grønland= Greenland (EN) [5] 224 Nd 70.00N 40.00W
Kalaallit Nunaat/Grønland= Kreenland (EN) 174 Pb 70.00N 40.00W
Kalabahi 150 Hh 8.13S 124.31 E
Kalabáka 130 Ej 39.42N 21.38 E
Kalabera 220b Ba 15.14N 145.48 E
Kalabo 170 De 14.58S 22.41 E
Kalâbsha 164 Fe 23.33N 32.50 E
Kalač 136 Ee 50.23N 41.01 E
Kalačinsk 136 Hd 55.03N 74.34 E
Kalač-na-Donu 136 Ef 48.43N 43.32 E
Kaladan 148 Id 20.09N 92.57 E
Ka Lae 214 Od 18.55N 155.41W
Kalahari Desert 158 Jk 23.00S 22.00 E
Kalaheo 221a Bb 21.56N 159.32W
Kalai-Mor 136 Gh 35.37N 62.31 E
Kalaj Humo 135 He 38.25N 70.47 E
Kalajoki 114 Fd 64.15N 23.57 E
Kalakan 138 Ge 55.10N 116.45 E
Kalaldi 166 Hd 6.30N 14.04 E
Kalāleh 146 Pd 37.25N 55.40 E
Kalámai 112 Ih 37.02N 22.07 E
Kalamákion 130 Gl 37.55N 23.43 E
Kalamazoo 182 Jc 42.17N 85.32W
Kalambo Falls 170 Fd 8.36S 31.14 E
Kalamitski zaliv 132 Hg 45.00N 33.25 E
Kálamos 130 Dk 38.37N 20.55 E
Kalamunda, Perth- 212 Df 31.57S 116.03 E
Kalan 144 Eb 39.07N 39.32 E
Kalanshiyū, Sarīr- 158 Jf 27.00N 21.30 E
Kalao, Pulau- 150 Hh 7.18S 120.58 E
Kalaotoa, Pulau- 150 Hh 7.22S 121.47 E
Kalapana 221a Gd 19.21N 154.59W
Kalaraš 132 Ff 47.16N 28.16 E
Kälarne 116 Gb 62.59N 16.05 E
Kalarski hrebet 138 Ge 56.30N 118.50 E
Kalasin [Indon.] 150 Ff 0.12N 114.16 E
Kalasin [Thai.] 148 Ke 16.29N 103.31 E
Kalāt 148 Dc 29.02N 66.35 E
Kalāteh 146 Pd 36.29N 54.10 E
Kalau 221b Bc 21.28S 174.57W
Kalaupapa 221a Eb 21.12N 156.59W
Kalaus 132 Ng 45.43N 44.07 E
Kalavárdha 130 Km 36.20N 27.57 E
Kálavrita 130 Fk 38.02N 22.07 E
Kalbā' 146 Qj 25.03N 56.21 E
Kalbīyah, Sabkhat al- 128 Eo 35.51N 10.17 E
Kaldbakur 114a Ab 65.49N 23.39W
Kaldygajty 132 Re 49.20N 52.38 E
Kale [Tur.] 146 Cd 36.14N 29.59 E
Kale [Tur.] 146 Cd 37.26N 28.51 E
Kalecik 146 Eb 40.06N 33.25 E
Kalehe 170 Ec 2.06S 28.55 E
Kalemie 160 Ji 5.56S 29.12 E
Kāl-e Shur 144 Jb 35.05N 60.59 E
Kalevala 136 Db 65.12N 31.10 E
Kalewa 148 Id 23.12N 94.18 E
Kaleybar 146 Lc 38.47N 47.02 E
Kalgoorlie 210 Dh 30.45S 121.28 E
Kaliakoúdha 130 Ek 38.48N 21.46 E
Kaliakra, Nos- 130 Lf 43.18N 28.30 E
Kalibo 150 Hd 11.43N 122.22 E
Kalí Límni 130 Kn 35.35N 27.08 E
Kalima 160 Ji 2.34S 26.37 E
Kalimantan/Borneo 140 Ni 1.00N 114.00 E
Kalimantan Barat [3] 150 Ff 0.01N 110.30 E
Kalimantan Selatan [3] 150 Gg 2.30S 115.30 E
Kalimantan Tengah [3] 150 Fg 2.00S 113.30 E
Kalimantan Timur [3] 150 Gf 1.30N 116.30 E
Kálimnos 130 Jm 36.57N 26.59 E
Kálimnos 130 Jl 37.00N 27.00 E
Kalinin [R.S.F.S.R.] 112 Jd 56.52N 35.55 E
Kalinin [Tur.-U.S.S.R.] 136 Fg 42.07N 59.40 E
Kalininabad 135 Gf 37.53N 68.57 E
Kaliningrad [R.S.F.S.R.] 112 Ie 54.43N 20.30 E
Kaliningrad [R.S.F.S.R.] 114 Ii 55.55N 37.57 E
Kaliningradskaja oblast [3] 136 Ce 54.45N 21.20 E
Kalinino [Arm.-U.S.S.R.] 132 Ni 41.08N 44.14 E
Kalinino [R.S.F.S.R.] 132 Kg 45.05N 38.59 E
Kalininsk [Mold.-U.S.S.R.] 130 Ka 48.07N 27.16 E
Kalininsk [R.S.F.S.R.] 132 Nd 51.30N 44.30 E
Kalininskaja oblast [3] 136 Dd 57.20N 34.40 E
Kalinkoviči 136 Ce 52.07N 29.23 E
Kalino 134 Hg 58.15N 57.35 E
Kalinovik 128 Mg 43.31N 18.26 E
Kalinovka 132 Fe 49.29N 28.32 E
Kaliro 170 Fb 0.54N 33.30 E
Kalispell 176 He 48.12N 114.19W
Kalisz 120 Oe 51.46N 18.06 E
Kalisz [2] 120 Of 51.45N 18.05 E
Kalisz Pomorski 120 Lc 53.19N 15.54 E
Kalitva 132 Le 48.10N 40.46 E
Kaliua 170 Fd 5.04S 31.48 E
Kalix 114 Fd 65.51N 23.08 E
Kalixälven 114 Fd 65.47N 23.13 E
Kalja 134 Jf 60.20N 60.01 E
Kaljazin 136 Dd 57.15N 37.55 E
Kalkandere 146 Ib 40.55N 40.28 E
Kalkar 124 Ic 51.44N 6.18 E
Kalkaska 184 Ec 44.44N 85.11W
Kalkfeld 172 Bd 20.53S 16.11 E
Kalkfontein 172 Cd 22.07S 20.54 E
Kalkim 130 Kj 39.48N 27.13 E
Kalkrand 172 Bd 24.03S 17.33 E
Kall 114 Ce 63.28N 13.15 E
Kållands Halvö 116 Ef 58.35N 13.05 E
Kållandsö 116 Ef 58.40N 13.10 E
Kallaste 114 Gg 58.41N 27.08 E
Kallavesi 110 Ic 62.50N 27.45 E
Kalletal 124 Kb 52.08N 8.57 E
Kallhäll 116 Ge 59.27N 17.48 E
Kallídhromon Óros 130 Fk 38.44N 22.34 E
Kallinge 114 Dh 56.14N 15.17 E
Kallonís, Kolpos- 130 Jj 39.07N 26.08 E
Kallsjön 114 Ce 63.35N 13.00 E
Kalmakkyrgan 135 Fa 46.58N 64.30 E
Kalmar 112 Hd 56.40N 16.22 E
Kalmar [2] 114 Dh 57.20N 16.00 E
Kalmarsund 114 Dh 56.40N 16.25 E
Kalmit 124 Ke 49.19N 8.05 E
Kalmius 132 Jf 47.03N 37.34 E
Kalmthout 124 Gc 51.23N 4.28 E
Kalmyckaja ASSR [3] 136 Ef 46.30N 45.30 E
Kalmykovo 132 Qe 49.05N 51.47 E
Kalnciems 116 Jh 56.48N 23.34 E
Kalnik 128 Kd 46.10N 16.30 E
Kalocsa 120 Oj 46.32N 19.00 E
Kalofer 130 Hg 42.37N 24.59 E
Kalohi Channel 221a Ec 21.00N 156.56W
Kaloko 170 Ed 6.47S 25.47 E
Kalole 170 Ec 3.42S 27.22 E
Kaloli Point 221a Gd 19.37N 154.57W
Kalomo 170 Ef 17.02S 26.30 E
Kalpa 148 Fb 31.37N 78.10 E
Kalpákion 130 Dj 39.53N 20.35 E
Kalpeni Island 148 Ef 10.05N 73.38 E
Kalpin 152 Cc 40.31N 79.03 E
Kalsūbai 140 Jh 19.36N 73.43 E
Kaltern/Caldaro 128 Fd 46.25N 11.14 E
Kaltungo 166 Hd 9.49N 11.19 E
Kaluga 112 Je 54.31N 36.16 E
Kalulushi 170 Ee 12.50S 28.05 E
Kalumburu Mission 212 Fb 14.18S 126.39 E
Kalundborg 114 Ci 55.41N 11.06 E
Kaluš 136 Cf 49.03N 24.23 E
Kałuszyn 120 Rd 52.13N 21.49 E
Kalužskaja oblast [3] 136 De 54.20N 35.30 E
Kalvåg 114 Af 61.46N 4.53 E
Kalvarija 114 Fi 54.27N 23.14 E
Kalya 170 Fd 6.28S 30.03 E
Kalyān 148 Ee 19.15N 73.09 E
Kám 120 Mi 47.06N 16.53 E
Kama 170 Ec 3.32S 27.07 E
Kama [R.S.F.S.R.] 134 Nf 60.27N 69.00 E
Kama [U.S.S.R.] 110 Ld 55.45N 52.00 E
Kamae 156 Be 32.48N 131.56 E
Kamaï 168 Ba 21.12N 17.30 E
Kamaing 148 Jc 25.31N 96.44 E
Kamaishi 154 Pe 39.16N 141.53 E
Kamakou 221a Eb 21.07N 156.52W
Kamakura 156 Fd 35.19N 139.32 E
Kamālia 148 Eb 30.44N 72.39 E
Kamalo 221a Eb 21.03N 156.53W
Kaman 146 Ec 39.25N 33.45 E
Kamand, Āb-e- 146 Mf 33.28N 49.04 E
Kamanjab 172 Ac 19.35S 14.51 E
Kamanyola 170 Ec 2.46S 29.00 E
Kamarān 144 Ff 15.12N 42.35 E
Kamarang 202 Fb 5.53N 60.35W
Kama Reservoir (EN) = Kamskoje vodohralinišče 110 Ld 58.50N 56.15 E
Kamaši 136 Gh 38.48N 66.29 E
Kamativi 172 Dc 18.19S 27.03 E
Kambalda 212 Ef 31.10S 121.37 E
Kambalnaja Sopka, vulkan- 138 Kf 51.17N 156.57 E
Kambara 156 Fd 35.07N 138.36 E
Kambara 219d Cc 18.57S 178.57W
Kambarka 114 Nh 56.18N 54.14 E
Kambia 166 Cd 9.07N 12.55W
Kambja 116 Lf 58.11N 26.43 E
Kambove 170 Ee 10.52S 26.35 E
Kamčatka 138 Le 56.10N 162.30 E
Kamčatka, poluostrov- = Kamchatka Peninsula (EN) 140 Rd 56.00N 160.00 E
Kamčatskaja oblast [3] 138 Kf 54.50N 159.00 E
Kamčatski zaliv 138 Le 55.30N 163.00 E
Kamchatka Peninsula (EN) = Kamčatka, poluostrov- 140 Rd 56.00N 160.00 E
Kamčija 130 Kf 43.02N 27.53 E
Kamčijska Plato 130 Kg 42.56N 27.32 E
Kameda [Jap.] 156a Bc 41.49N 140.46 E
Kameda [Jap.] 156 Fc 37.52N 139.06 E
Kameda-Hantō 156a Bc 41.45N 141.00 E
Kámeiros 130 Km 36.18N 27.56 E
Kamelik 132 Pc 52.06N 49.30 E
Kamen 124 Jc 51.36N 7.40 E
Kaménai 130 Im 36.25N 25.25 E
Kamende 170 Dd 6.28S 24.33 E
Kamenec 120 Td 52.23N 23.49 E
Kamenec-Podolski 136 Cf 48.39N 26.33 E
Kamenjam Rt- 128 Hf 44.46N 13.56 E
Kamenka [Kaz.-U.S.S.R.] 132 Qd 51.07N 50.20 E
Kamenka [Mold.-U.S.S.R.] 132 Fe 48.03N 28.45 E
Kamenka [R.S.F.S.R.] 136 Ee 53.13N 44.03 E
Kamenka [R.S.F.S.R.] 132 Kd 50.43N 39.25 E
Kamenka [R.S.F.S.R.] 154 Nb 44.28N 136.01 E
Kamenka [R.S.F.S.R.] 114 Kd 65.54N 44.04 E
Kamenka [Ukr.-U.S.S.R.] 136 Df 49.03N 32.06 E
Kamenka-Bugskaja 120 Uf 50.01N 24.25 E
Kamenka-Dneprovskaja 132 If 47.29N 34.29 E
Kamen-Kaširski 132 Dd 51.36N 24.59 E
Kamen-na-Obi 138 Df 53.47N 81.20 E
Kamennogorsk 114 Gf 60.59N 29.12 E
Kamennoje, ozero- 114 Hd 64.30N 30.15 E
Kamennomostski 132 Lg 44.17N 40.12 E
Kamen-Rybolov 154 Kb 44.45N 132.04 E
Kamenskoje 138 Ld 62.30N 166.12 E
Kamensk-Šahtinski 132 Le 48.18N 40.16 E
Kamensk-Uralski 142 Id 56.28N 61.54 E
Kamenz/Kamjenc 120 Ke 51.16N 14.06 E
Kameoka 156 Dd 35.00N 135.35 E
Kameškovo 114 Jh 56.22N 41.01 E
Kamet 148 Fb 30.55N 79.35 E
Kameyama 156 Ed 34.51N 136.27 E
Kami-Agata 156 Ad 34.38N 129.25 E
Kamiah 188 Gc 46.14N 116.02W
Kamicharo 156a Cb 43.11N 143.52 E
Kamienna 120 Re 51.06N 21.47 E
Kamienna Góra 120 Mf 50.47N 16.01 E
Kamień Pomorski 120 Kc 53.58N 14.46 E
Kamiénsk 120 Pe 51.12N 19.30 E
Kamieskroon 172 Bf 30.09S 17.56 E
Kami-furano 156a Cb 43.29N 142.27 E
Kamiiso 154 Pd 41.49N 140.39 E
Kamiita 156 Dd 34.08N 134.24 E
Kamiji 170 Dd 6.39S 23.17 E
Kamikawa 156a Cb 43.50N 142.47 E
Kami-Koshiki-Jima 156 Af 31.50N 129.55 E
Kamina 160 Ji 8.44S 24.59 E
Kaminak Lake 180 Id 62.13N 95.00W
Kaminokuni 156a Bc 41.48N 140.05 E
Kamino-Shima 156 Ad 34.30N 129.25 E
Kaminoyama 154 Pe 38.09N 140.17 E
Kaminuriak Lake 180 Hd 63.00N 95.45W
Kamioka 154 Nf 36.16N 137.18 E
Kami-shihoro 156a Cb 43.13N 143.16 E
Kamisunagawa 156a Bb 43.28N 141.58 E
Kamitsushima 156 Ad 34.39N 129.28 E
Kamituga 170 Ec 3.04S 28.11 E
Kamiyama 156 De 33.58N 134.21 E
Kami-yūbetsu 156a Ca 44.11N 143.34 E
Kamjenc/Kamenz 120 Ke 51.16N 14.06 E
Kamloops 176 Gd 50.40N 120.20W
Kamloops Plateau 188 Ea 50.10N 120.35W
Kammersee → Attersee 128 Hc 47.55N 13.33 E
Kamnik 128 Id 46.14N 14.37 E
Kamo [Arm.-U.S.S.R.] 132 Ni 40.22N 45.05 E
Kamo [Jap.] 156 Fc 37.39N 139.03 E
Kamo [N.Z.] 218 Fa 35.41S 174.17 E
Kamōda-Misaki 156 De 33.50N 134.45 E
Kamogawa 156 Gd 35.06N 140.05 E
Kamp 128 Jb 48.23N 15.48 E
Kampala 160 Kh 0.19N 32.35 E
Kampar 150 Df 4.18N 101.09 E
Kampar 150 Mi 0.32N 103.08 E
Kampen 122 Lb 52.33N 5.54 E
Kampene 170 Ec 3.36S 26.40 E
Kamphaeng Phet 148 Je 16.26N 99.33 E
Kamp-Lintorf 124 Ic 51.30N 6.32 E
Kamp'o 154 Jg 35.48N 129.30 E
Kâmpóng Cham 142 Mh 12.00N 105.27 E
Kâmpóng Chhnâng 148 Kf 12.15N 104.40 E

Index Symbols

[1] Independent Nation
[2] State, Region
[3] District, County
[4] Municipality
[5] Colony, Dependency
Continent
Physical Region
Historical or Cultural Region
Mount, Mountain
Volcano
Hill
Mountains, Mountain Range
Hills, Escarpment
Plateau, Upland
Pass, Gap
Plain, Lowland
Delta
Salt Flat
Valley, Canyon
Crater, Cave
Karst Features
Depression
Polder
Desert, Dunes
Forest, Woods
Heath, Steppe
Oasis
Cape, Point
Coast, Beach
Cliff
Peninsula
Isthmus
Sandbank
Island
Atoll
Rock, Reef
Islands, Archipelago
Rocks, Reefs
Coral Reef
Well, Spring
Geyser
River, Stream
Waterfall, Rapids
River Mouth, Estuary
Lake
Salt Lake
Intermittent Lake
Reservoir
Swamp, Pond
Canal
Glacier
Ice Shelf, Pack Ice
Ocean
Sea
Gulf, Bay
Strait, Fjord
Lagoon
Bank
Seamount
Tablemount
Ridge
Shelf
Basin
Escarpment, Sea Scarp
Fracture
Trench, Abyss
National Park, Reserve
Point of Interest
Recreation Site
Cave, Cavern
Historic Site
Ruins
Wall, Walls
Church, Abbey
Temple
Scientific Station
Railway station
Airport
Port
Military installation
Lighthouse
Mine
Tunnel
Dam, Bridge

Name	Page	Grid	Lat.	Long.
Kâmpóng Saôm	142	Mh	10.38N	103.30 E
Kâmpóng Saôm, Chhâk-	148	Kf	10.50N	103.32 E
Kâmpóng Thum	148	Kf	12.42N	104.54 E
Kâmpôt	148	Kf	10.37N	104.11 E
Kampti	166	Ec	10.08N	3.27W
Kampuchea → Cambodia	142	Mh	13.00N	105.00 E
Kamrau, Teluk-	150	Jg	3.32S	133.37 E
Kamsack	180	Hf	51.34N	101.54W
Kamsar	166	Cc	10.40N	14.36W
Kamskoje Ustje	114	Li	55.14N	49.16 E
Kamskoje vodohranilišče = Kama Reservoir (EN)	110	Ld	58.50N	56.15 E
Kam Summa	168	Ge	0.21N	42.44 E
Kamuenai	156a	Bb	43.08N	140.26 E
Kamui-Dake	156a	Cb	42.25N	142.52 E
Kamui-Misaki	152	Pc	43.20N	140.20 E
Kámuk, Cerro-	194	Fi	9.17N	83.04W
Kamvoúnia Óri	130	Ei	40.00N	21.52 E
Kāmyārān	146	Le	34.47N	46.56 E
Kamyšin	112	Ke	50.06N	45.24 E
Kamyšlov	136	Gd	56.52N	62.43 E
Kamyšovaja Buhta	132	Hg	44.31N	33.33 E
Kamysty-Ajat	134	Jj	53.01N	61.35 E
Kamyzjak	136	Ef	46.06N	48.05 E
Kan	146	Ne	35.45N	51.16 E
Kan	138	Ee	56.31N	93.47 E
Kana	172	Dc	18.32S	27.24 E
Kanaaupscow	180	Jf	54.01N	76.32W
Kanaaupscow	180	Jf	53.40N	77.08W
Kanab	182	Ed	37.03N	112.32W
Kanab Creek	188	Ih	36.24N	112.38W
Kanaga	178a	Cb	51.45N	177.10W
Kanagawa Ken	154	Og	35.30N	139.10 E
Kanaliasem	150	Dg	1.44S	103.35 E
Kanami-Zaki	156b	Bb	27.53N	128.58 E
Kananga	160	Ji	5.54S	22.25 E
Kanariktok	180	Le	55.03N	60.10W
Kanaš	114	Li	55.31N	47.31 E
Kanathea	219d	Cb	17.16S	179.09W
Kanaya	156	Fd	34.48N	138.07 E
Kanayama	156	Ed	35.39N	137.09 E
Kanazawa	142	Pf	36.34N	136.39 E
Kanbalu	148	Jd	23.12N	95.31 E
Kanbe	148	Je	16.42N	96.01 E
Kanchanaburi	148	Jf	14.02N	99.33 E
Kānchenjunga	140	Kg	27.42N	88.08 E
Kānchipuram	148	Ff	12.50N	79.43 E
Kandalakša	112	Jb	67.09N	32.21 E
Kandalaksha, Gulf of- (EN) = Kandalakšski zaliv	110	Jb	66.35N	32.45 E
Kandalakšski zaliv = Kandalaksha, Gulf of- (EN)	110	Jb	66.35N	32.45 E
Kandangan	150	Gg	2.47S	115.16 E
Kándanos	130	Gn	35.20N	23.44 E
Kandava	114	Fh	57.03N	22.46 E
Kandavu Island	208	If	19.00S	178.13 E
Kandavu Passage	219d	Ac	18.45S	178.00 E
Kandel	124	Ke	49.05N	8.12 E
Kandel	120	Eh	48.04N	8.01 E
Kandhelioúsa	130	Jm	36.30N	26.58 E
Kandi	160	Hg	11.08N	2.56 E
Kandıra	146	Db	41.04N	30.09 E
Kandla	148	Ed	23.02N	70.14 E
Kandrian	214	Di	6.13S	149.33 E
Kandry	134	Gi	54.34N	54.10 E
Kandy	142	Ki	7.18N	80.38 E
Kane	184	He	41.40N	78.48W
Kane Basin	224	Od	79.35N	67.00W
Kaneh	146	Pi	27.04N	54.18 E
Kanem	168	Bc	15.00N	16.00 E
Kanem	158	Ig	14.45N	15.30 E
Kaneohe	214	Oc	21.25N	157.48W
Kaneohe Bay	221a	Db	21.28N	157.48W
Kánestron, Ákra-	130	Gj	39.56N	23.45 E
Kanev	132	Ge	49.42N	31.29 E
Kanevskaja	136	Df	46.06N	38.58 E
Kaneyama	156	Fc	37.27N	139.30 E
Kang	172	Cd	23.44S	22.50 E
Kangaba	166	Dc	11.56N	8.25W
Kangal	146	Gc	39.15N	37.24 E
Kangalassy	138	Hd	62.17N	129.58 E
Kangâmiut	179	Ge	65.39N	53.55W
Kangān [Iran]	146	Oi	27.50N	52.03 E
Kangān [Iran]	146	Qj	25.48N	57.28 E
Kangar	150	De	6.26N	100.12 E
Kangaré	166	Dc	11.37N	8.08W
Kangaroo Island	208	Eh	35.50S	137.05 E
Kangasala	116	Kc	61.28N	24.05 E
Kangasniemi	114	Gf	61.59N	26.38 E
Kangâtsiaq	179	Ge	68.20N	53.18W
Kangāvar	146	Le	34.30N	47.58 E
Kangbao	154	Cd	41.51N	114.37 E
Kangding/Dardo	152	He	30.01N	101.58 E
Kangean, Kepulauan- = Kangean Islands (EN)	150	Gh	6.55S	115.30 E
Kangean, Pulau-	150	Gh	6.54S	115.20 E
Kangean Islands (EN) = Kangean, Kepulauan-	150	Gh	6.55S	115.30 E
Kangeeak Point	180	Lc	68.01N	64.45W
Kangen	158	Kh	6.47N	33.09 E
Kangerdlugssuaq	179	Ie	68.20N	31.40W
Kangetet	170	Gb	1.58N	36.06 E
Kanggup'o	154	Id	41.07N	127.31 E
Kanggye	152	Mc	40.58N	126.36 E
Kangi	168	Dd	8.10N	27.39 E
Kangjin	154	Ig	34.38N	126.46 E
Kangiqsujuaq	180	Kd	61.36N	71.57W
Kangirsuk	176	Lc	60.00N	70.01W
Kangmar	152	Ef	28.32N	89.43 E
Kangnŭng	152	Md	37.44N	128.54 E
Kango	170	Bb	0.09N	10.08 E
Kangondu	170	Gc	1.06S	37.42 E
Kangping	154	Gc	42.45N	123.20 E
Kangrinboqê Feng	152	De	31.04N	81.30 E
Kangto	148	Ic	27.52N	92.30 E
Kangwŏn-Do [N.Kor.]	154	Ie	38.45N	127.35 E
Kangwŏn-Do [S.Kor.]	154	Jf	37.45N	128.15 E
Kani	166	Dd	8.29N	6.36W
Kaniama	170	Dd	7.31S	24.11 E
Kanibadam	135	Hd	40.17N	70.25 E
Kaniet Islands	208	Fe	0.53S	145.30 E
Kanija	130	Lc	46.16N	28.13 E
Kanimeh	135	Ed	40.18N	65.09 E
Kanin, poluostrov- = Kanin Peninsula (EN)	110	Kb	68.00N	45.00 E
Kanina	130	Ci	40.26N	19.31 E
Kanin Kamen	134	Bb	68.15N	45.15 E
Kanin Nos	136	Eb	68.39N	43.14 E
Kanin Nos, mys-	110	Kb	68.39N	43.16 E
Kanin Peninsula (EN) = Kanin, poluostrov-	110	Kb	68.00N	45.00 E
Kanioumé	166	Eb	15.46N	3.09W
Kanita	156a	Bc	41.02N	140.38 E
Kanjiža	130	Dc	46.04N	20.03 E
Kankaanpää	114	Ff	61.48N	22.25 E
Kankakee	182	Jc	41.07N	87.52W
Kankakee River	186	Lf	41.23N	88.16W
Kankalabé	166	Cc	11.00N	12.00W
Kankan	160	Gg	10.23N	9.18W
Kanker	148	Gd	20.17N	81.29 E
Kankesanturai	148	Gg	9.49N	80.02 E
Kankossa	162	Ef	15.55N	11.31W
Kankunski	138	He	57.39N	126.25 E
Kanla	120	Hf	50.48N	11.35 E
Kanmav Kyun	148	Jf	11.40N	98.28 E
Kanmon-Kaikyō	156	Bd	33.56N	130.57 E
Kanmuri-Yama	156	Cd	34.28N	132.05 E
Kannapolis	182	Kd	35.30N	80.37W
Kannone-Jima	154	Jj	28.51N	128.58 E
Kannonkoski	116	Kb	62.58N	25.15 E
Kannus	114	Fe	63.54N	23.54 E
Kano	160	Hg	12.00N	8.31 E
Kano	166	Gc	12.00N	9.00 E
Kanona	170	Fe	13.04S	30.38 E
Kan'onji	154	Lg	34.07N	133.39 E
Kanoya	154	Ki	31.23N	130.51 E
Kanozero, ozero-	114	Ic	67.00N	34.05 E
Kānpur	142	Kg	26.28N	80.21 E
Kansas	182	Hd	38.45N	98.15W
Kansas	174	Jf	39.07N	94.36W
Kansas City [Ks.-U.S.]	176	Jf	39.07N	94.39W
Kansas City [Mo.-U.S.]	176	Jf	39.05N	94.35W
Kanshi	152	Kg	24.57N	116.52 E
Kansk	142	Ld	56.13N	95.41 E
Kansŏng	154	Je	38.22N	128.28 E
Kansu (EN) = Gansu Sheng (Kan-su Sheng)	152	Hd	38.00N	102.00 E
Kansu (EN) = Kan-su Sheng → Gansu Sheng	152	Hd	38.00N	102.00 E
Kan-su Sheng → Gansu Sheng = Kansu (EN)	152	Hd	38.00N	102.00 E
Kansyat	150	Kg	2.15S	138.51 E
Kant	135	Jc	42.52N	74.50 E
Kantang	148	Jg	7.23N	99.32 E
Kantchari	166	Fc	12.29N	1.31 E
Kanté	166	Fd	9.57N	1.03 E
Kantemirovka	136	Df	49.45N	39.53 E
Kantō-Heiya	156	Fc	36.00N	139.30 E
Kantō-Sanchi	156	Fc	36.00N	138.45 E
Kantubek	135	Bb	45.06N	59.16 E
Kanturk/Ceann Toirc	118	Ei	52.10N	8.55W
Kanuma	156	Fc	36.34N	139.45 E
Kanye	160	Jk	24.58S	25.21 E
Kanyu	172	Cd	20.04S	24.36 E
Kanzenze	170	Ee	10.31S	25.12 E
Kao	221b	Aa	19.40S	175.01W
Kaohsiung	142	Og	22.38N	120.17 E
Kaôk Nhêk	148	Lf	13.05N	107.04 E
Kaoko Otavi	172	Ac	18.15S	13.37 E
Kaokoveld	172	Ac	18.00S	13.00 E
Kaokoveld	158	Ij	19.30S	13.30 E
Kaolack	160	Fg	14.09N	16.04W
Kao Neua, Col de-	148	Le	18.23N	105.10 E
Kaouadja	168	Cd	8.00N	23.14 E
Kaouar	166	Hb	19.05N	12.52 E
Kapaa	221a	Ba	22.05N	159.19W
Kapanga	160	Ji	8.21S	22.35 E
Kapar	146	Ld	36.32N	47.30 E
Kapčagaj	136	Hg	43.52N	77.03 E
Kapčagajskoje vodohranilišče	136	Hg	43.45N	78.00 E
Kapchorwa	170	Fb	1.24N	34.27 E
Kap Dan	179	Ie	65.32N	37.30W
Kapelle	124	Fc	51.39N	3.57 E
Kapellskär	116	He	59.43N	19.04 E
Kapena	170	Ee	10.47S	28.20 E
Kapenguria	170	Gb	1.14N	35.07 E
Kapfenberg	128	Jc	47.26N	15.18 E
Kapıdağı Yarımadası	130	Ki	40.28N	27.50 E
Kapingamarangi Atoll	208	Gd	1.04N	154.46 E
Kapingamarangi Rise (EN)	208	Gd	1.00N	157.00 E
Kapiri Mposhi	170	Ee	13.58S	28.41 E
Kāpīsā	144	Kc	34.45N	69.30 E
Kapiskau	180	Jf	52.45N	81.58W
Kapit	150	Ff	2.01N	112.56 E
Kapiti Island	218	Fd	40.50S	174.55 E
Kapka, Massif du-	168	Cb	15.07N	21.45 E
Kapoeta	160	Kh	4.47N	33.35 E
Kapona	170	Ed	7.11S	29.09 E
Kapos	120	Oj	46.44N	18.29 E
Kaposvár	120	Nj	46.22N	17.48 E
Kapp	116	Dd	60.42N	10.52 E
Kappeln	120	Fb	54.40N	9.56 E
Kapša	114	Hg	59.52N	33.45 E
Kapsan	154	Jd	41.05N	128.18 E
Kapsukas	114	Fi	54.33N	23.23 E
Kapuas [Indon.]	140	Mj	0.25S	109.40 E
Kapuas [Indon.]	150	Fg	3.01S	114.20 E
Kapuas Hulu, Pegunungan- = Kapuas Mountains (EN)	150	Ff	1.25N	113.15 E
Kapuas Mountains (EN) = Kapuas Hulu, Pegunungan	150	Ff	1.25N	113.15 E
Kapugargin	130	Lm	36.40N	28.50 E
Kapušany	120	Rg	49.03N	21.21 E
Kapuskasing	176	Ke	49.25N	82.26W
Kapustin Jar	132	Ne	48.35N	45.45 E
Kapustoje	114	Ic	67.17N	34.12 E
Kaputdžuh, gora-	132	Oj	39.12N	46.01 E
Kapuvár	120	Ni	47.36N	17.02 E
Kara	166	Fd	9.33N	1.12 E
Kara	166	Fd	9.35N	1.05 E
Kara	134	Lb	69.10N	64.45 E
Kara Ada [Tur.]	130	Jk	38.25N	26.20 E
Kara Ada [Tur.]	130	Km	36.58N	27.28 E
Kara-Balta	136	Hg	42.49N	73.57 E
Karabas	136	Hf	49.30N	73.00 E
Karabaš	134	Ji	55.29N	60.13 E
Karabekaul	136	Gh	38.28N	64.10 E
Karabiga	130	Ki	40.24N	27.18 E
Karabil, vozvyšennost-	135	Df	36.20N	63.30 E
Kara-Bogaz-Gol	136	Fg	41.01N	52.59 E
Kara-Bogaz-Gol, proliv-	132	Ri	41.04N	52.59 E
Kara-Bogaz-Gol, zaliv-	110	Lg	41.00N	53.15 E
Karabuk	144	Da	41.12N	32.37 E
Karabulak [Kaz.-U.S.S.R.]	135	Lb	44.54N	78.29 E
Karabulak [Kaz.-U.S.S.R.]	136	Gg	42.31N	69.47 E
Kara Burun	130	Km	36.32N	27.58 E
Karaburun [Tur.]	146	Cb	41.21N	28.40 E
Karaburun [Tur.]	146	Bc	38.37N	26.31 E
Karabutak	136	Gf	49.57N	60.08 E
Karacabey	146	Cb	40.13N	28.21 E
Karaca Dağ	146	Hd	37.40N	39.50 E
Karačajevo-Čerkessakaja avtonomnaja oblast	136	Eg	43.45N	41.45 E
Karačajevsk	132	Lh	43.44N	41.58 E
Karacaköy	146	Cb	41.22N	28.30 E
Karacaoğlan	130	Kh	41.32N	27.04 E
Karacasu	146	Cd	37.43N	28.37 E
Karačev	136	De	53.04N	34.59 E
Karāchi	142	Ig	24.52N	67.03 E
Kara Dağ [Tur.]	146	Ed	37.23N	33.10 E
Kara Dağ [Tur.]	146	Jd	37.40N	43.42 E
Karadah	132	Oh	42.29N	46.54 E
Karadeniz = Black Sea (EN)	110	Jg	43.00N	35.00 E
Kara Dong	152	Dd	38.26N	81.50 E
Karagajly	136	Hf	49.20N	75.48 E
Karaganda	142	Je	49.50N	73.10 E
Karagandinskaja oblast	136	Hf	50.00N	74.00 E
Karaginski, ostrov-	140	Sd	58.48N	164.05 E
Karaginski zaliv	140	Sd	58.50N	164.00 E
Kara Gölü	130	Mm	36.42N	29.50 E
Karagoš, gora-	138	Df	51.44N	89.24 E
Karahalli	130	Mk	38.20N	29.32 E
Karaidelski	134	Hi	55.49N	57.05 E
Kara-Irtyš	140	Ke	47.52N	84.16 E
Karaisali	146	Fd	37.16N	35.03 E
Karaj	146	Ne	35.48N	50.59 E
Karaj	146	Ne	35.07N	51.35 E
Karak, gora-	136	Gg	44.59N	63.05 E
Kara-Kala	136	Fh	38.28N	56.18 E
Karakalpak ASSR (EN) = Karakalpakskaja ASSR	136	Fg	43.30N	59.00 E
Karakalpakskaja ASSR = Karakalpak ASSR (EN)	136	Fg	43.30N	59.00 E
Karakax/Moyu	152	Cd	37.17N	79.42 E
Karakax He	152	Dd	38.06N	80.24 E
Karakaya Barajı	146	Hc	38.25N	38.45 E
Karakeçi	146	Hd	37.26N	39.26 E
Karakelong, Pulau-	150	If	4.15N	126.48 E
Karakoçan	146	Ic	38.02N	40.07 E
Karakoin, ozero-	135	Ga	46.10N	68.40 E
Karakojsu	132	Oh	42.30N	47.05 E
Karakolka	135	Kd	41.29N	77.24 E
Karakoram	140	Jf	34.00N	78.00 E
Karakoram Pass	140	Jf	35.30N	77.50 E
Karakore	168	Gc	10.25N	40.01 E
Karakoro	166	Cc	14.43N	12.03 E
Karakorum Shan	152	Cd	36.00N	76.00 E
Karakorum Shankou	135	Kg	35.30N	77.50 E
Karaköy	146	Ic	39.04N	41.42 E
Kara-Kul	135	Id	41.34N	72.47 E
Karakul, ozero-	136	Hh	39.05N	73.25 E
Karakumski kanal imeni V.I. Lenina	136	Gh	37.42N	64.20 E
Karakumy	140	Hf	39.00N	60.00 E
Karakuwisa	172	Bc	18.56S	19.40 E
Karam	138	Fe	55.09N	107.37 E
Karama	150	Gg	2.18S	119.06 E
Karaman	144	Db	37.11N	33.14 E
Karamanli	130	Ml	37.22N	29.49 E
Karamay	142	Ke	45.30N	84.55 E
Karamea	216	Dh	41.15S	172.06 E
Karamea Bight	218	Dd	41.25S	171.50 E
Karamet-Nijaz	136	Gh	37.43N	64.31 E
Karamiran He	152	Dd	37.50N	84.35 E
Karamiran Shankou	152	Ed	36.15N	87.05 E
Karamiševo	116	Mg	57.44N	28.50 E
Karamoja	170	Fb	2.45N	34.15 E
Karamürsel	130	Mi	40.42N	29.36 E
Kara-myk	136	Hh	39.30N	71.51 E
Karamyš	132	Nd	51.18N	45.00 E
Karān	146	Mi	27.43N	49.49 E
Karaova	130	Kl	37.05N	27.40 E
Karapınar	146	Ed	37.43N	33.33 E
Kara-Saki	156	Ad	34.40N	129.29 E
Kara-Sal	132	Mf	47.18N	43.36 E
Karasay	152	Dd	36.48N	83.48 E
Karasburg	160	Ik	28.00S	18.43 E
Kara Sea (EN) = Karskoje more	224	Hd	76.00N	70.00 E
Karašica	128	Me	45.36N	18.36 E
Karasjok	114	Fb	69.27N	25.30 E
Kara Strait (EN) = Karskije Vorota, proliv-	140	Hb	70.30N	58.00 E
Karasu	146	Db	41.04N	30.47 E
Karasu [Tur.]	146	Jc	38.32N	43.10 E
Karasu [Tur.]	146	Ic	38.49N	41.28 E
Karasu [Tur.]	140	Ff	38.52N	38.48 E
Karasu Dağları	146	Ic	39.30N	40.45 E
Karasuk	138	Cf	53.44N	78.08 E
Karasuk	138	Cf	53.35N	77.30 E
Karasuyama	156	Gc	36.39N	140.08 E
Karatá, Laguna-	194	Fg	13.56N	83.30W
Karatal	136	Hf	46.26N	77.10 E
Karataş [Tur.]	146	Fd	36.36N	35.21 E
Karataş [Tur.]	130	Lk	38.34N	28.17 E
Karataş Burun	146	Fb	36.35N	35.22 E
Karatau	136	Hg	43.10N	70.29 E
Karatau, hrebet-	140	Ie	43.40N	69.00 E
Karatj	114	Ec	66.43N	18.33 E
Karatobe	132	Re	49.42N	53.33 E
Karaton	136	Ff	46.25N	53.34 E
Karatsu	154	Jh	33.26N	130.00 E
Karatsu-Wan	156	Be	33.30N	130.00 E
Kara-Turgaj	140	Ie	48.01N	62.45 E
Karaul [Kaz.-U.S.S.R.]	136	Hf	49.00N	79.20 E
Karaul [R.S.F.S.R.]	138	Db	70.10N	83.08 E
Karaulbazar	135	Ee	39.29N	64.47 E
Karaulkala	135	Bc	42.18N	58.41 E
Karáva	130	Ej	39.19N	21.36 E
Karavanke	128	Id	46.25N	14.25 E
Karavastase, Laguna e-	130	Ci	40.55N	19.30 E
Karávi	130	Gm	36.45N	23.35 E
Karavonísia	130	Jn	35.59N	26.26 E
Karawa	170	Db	3.20N	20.18 E
Karaxabar He/Kaidu He	152	Ec	41.55N	86.38 E
Karažal	136	Hf	47.59N	70.53 E
Karbalā'	142	Gf	32.36N	44.02 E
Karbalā	146	Jf	32.30N	43.45 E
Kårbole	114	Df	61.59N	15.19 E
Karcag	120	Qi	47.19N	20.56 E
Karčenski proliv	110	Jf	45.22N	36.38 E
Kardhámaina	130	Km	36.47N	27.09 E
Kardhámila	130	Jk	38.31N	26.06 E
Kardhiotissa	130	Im	36.38N	25.01 E
Kardhítsa	130	Ej	39.22N	21.55 E
Kärdla/Kjardla	114	Fg	59.01N	22.42 E
Kărdžali	130	Ih	41.39N	25.22 E
Kărdžali	130	Ih	41.30N	25.30 E
Kareha, Jbel-	126	Gi	35.15N	5.30W
Karelia (EN)	110	Jc	64.00N	32.00 E
Karelskaja ASSR	136	Dc	63.30N	33.30 E
Karema	170	Fd	6.49S	30.26 E
Karen → Kayin	148	Je	17.30N	97.45 E
Karen	148	If	12.51E	92.53 E
Karesuando	114	Fb	68.27N	22.29 E
Karêt	158	Gf	24.00N	7.30W
Kärevere/Kjarevere	116	Lf	58.23N	26.30 E
Kargala	132	Sd	51.59N	55.10 E
Kargapazari Dağı	146	Ib	40.07N	41.35 E
Kargapolje	134	Li	55.57N	64.27 E
Kargasok	138	De	59.07N	81.01 E
Kargat	138	De	55.10N	80.17 E
Kargı	146	Fb	41.08N	34.30 E
Kargil	148	Fb	34.34N	76.06 E
Kargilik/Yecheng	142	Jf	37.54N	77.26 E
Kargopol	136	Dc	61.32N	38.58 E
Karhula	114	Gf	60.31N	26.57 E
Kari	166	Hc	11.14N	10.34 E
Kariaí	112	Ig	40.15N	24.15 E
Kariba	160	Jj	16.30S	28.45 E
Kariba, Lake-	158	Jj	17.00S	28.00 E
Kariba-Dake	156a	Ab	42.37N	139.56 E
Kariba Dam	172	Dc	16.30S	28.50 E
Karibib	160	Ik	21.58S	15.51 E
Karibib	172	Bd	22.00S	16.00 E
Kariet-Arkmane	126	Ji	35.06N	2.45W
Karigasniemi	114	Fb	69.24N	25.50 E
Karijärvi	116	Jc	61.35N	22.30 E
Karikachi Tōge	156a	Cb	43.10N	142.40 E
Kārikāl	148	Ff	10.55N	79.50 E
Karikari, Cape-	218	Ea	34.47S	173.24 E
Karima (EN) = Kuraymah	160	Kg	18.33N	31.51 E
Karimama	166	Fc	12.04N	3.11 E
Karimata, Kepulauan- = Karimata Islands (EN)	150	Eg	1.25S	109.05 E
Karimata, Pulau-	150	Eg	1.36S	108.55 E
Karimata, Selat- = Karimata Strait (EN)	140	Mj	2.05S	108.40 E
Karimata Islands (EN) = Karimata, Kepulauan-	150	Eg	1.25S	109.05 E
Karimata Strait (EN) = Karimata, Selat-	140	Mj	2.05S	108.40 E
Karīmganj	148	Id	24.42N	92.33 E
Karīmnagar	148	Fe	18.26N	79.09 E
Karimunjawa, Kepulauan- = Karimunjawa Islands (EN)	150	Fh	5.50S	110.25 E
Karimunjawa Islands (EN) = Karimunjawa, Kepulauan-	150	Fh	5.50S	110.25 E
Karin [Som.]	168	Hc	10.51N	45.45 E
Karin [Som.]	168	Hc	10.59N	49.13 E
Karis/Karjaa	114	Ff	60.05N	23.40 E
Karisimbi	158	Ji	1.30S	29.27 E
Káristos	130	Hk	38.01N	24.25 E
Karjaa/Karis	114	Ff	60.05N	23.40 E
Karkār	168	Hd	9.57N	49.20 E
Karkaralinsk	136	Hf	49.23N	75.31 E
Karkar Island	208	Fe	4.40S	146.00 E
Karkas, Kūh-e	146	Nf	33.27N	51.48 E
Karkheh	144	Gc	31.31N	47.55 E
Karkinitski zaliv	110	Jf	45.55N	33.00 E
Karkkila/Högfors	114	Ff	60.32N	24.11 E
Karkku	116	Jc	61.25N	23.01 E
Kärkölä	116	Kd	60.55N	25.15 E
Kärla/Kjarla	116	Jf	58.16N	22.05 E
Karlholm	116	Gd	60.31N	17.37 E
Karlik Shan	140	Le	43.00N	94.30 E
Karlino	120	Lb	54.03N	15.51 E
Karliova	146	Ic	39.18N	41.01 E
Karl Marx, pik-	136	Hh	37.08N	72.29 E
Karl-Marx-Stadt	120	If	50.45N	12.50 E
Karl-Marx-Stadt (Chemnitz)	112	He	50.50N	12.55 E
Karlö/Hailuoto	110	Ib	65.02N	24.42 E
Karlobag	128	Jf	44.32N	15.05 E
Karlovac	128	Je	45.29N	15.33 E
Karlovka	132	Ie	49.28N	35.08 E
Karlovo	130	Hg	42.38N	24.48 E
Karlovy Vary	120	If	50.14N	12.52 E
Karlsbad	124	Kf	48.55N	8.35 E
Karlsborg	114	Df	58.32N	14.31 E
Karlshamn	114	Dh	56.10N	14.51 E
Karlskoga	114	Dg	59.20N	14.31 E
Karlskrona	112	Hd	56.10N	15.35 E
Karlsöarna	116	Gg	57.15N	18.00 E
Karlsruhe	120	Eg	49.01N	8.24 E
Karlstad [Mn.-U.S.]	186	Hb	48.35N	96.31W
Karlstad [Swe.]	112	Hd	59.22N	13.30 E
Karluk	178	Ie	57.34N	154.28W
Karmah = Kerma (EN)	168	Eb	19.38N	30.25 E
Karmana	135	Ed	40.09N	65.15 E
Karmøy	114	Ag	59.15N	5.15 E
Karnāli	148	Gc	28.45N	81.16 E
Karnataka (Mysore)	148	Ff	13.30N	76.00 E
Karnobat	130	Jg	42.39N	26.59 E
Kärnten = Carinthia (EN)	128	Hd	46.45N	14.00 E
Kärnten = Carinthia (EN)	128	Hd	46.45N	14.00 E
Karoi	172	Dc	16.50S	29.40 E
Karonga	160	Ki	9.56S	33.56 E
Karora	168	Fb	17.39N	38.22 E
Káros	130	Im	36.53N	25.39 E
Kárpathos	130	Kn	35.30N	27.14 E
Kárpathos = Karpathos (EN)	110	Ih	35.40N	27.10 E
Karpathos (EN) = Kárpathos	110	Ih	35.40N	27.10 E
Karpáthou, Stenón-	130	Kn	35.50N	27.30 E
Karpenísion	130	Ek	38.55N	21.47 E
Karpinsk	134	Jg	59.45N	60.01 E
Karpuzlu	130	Kl	37.33N	27.50 E
Kars	144	Fa	40.37N	43.05 E
Karsakpaj	136	Gf	47.48N	66.45 E
Kärsämäki	114	Fe	64.00N	25.46 E
Karsava/Kārsava	114	Gh	56.47N	27.42 E
Kārsava/Karsava	114	Gh	56.47N	27.42 E
Karši	142	If	38.53N	65.48 E
Karşiyaka	130	Ki	40.26N	28.00 E
Karsiyaka	130	Kk	38.27N	27.07 E
Karskije Vorota, proliv- = Kara Strait (EN)	140	Hb	70.30N	58.00 E
Karskoje more = Kara Sea (EN)	224	Hd	76.00N	70.00 E
Kars Platosu	146	Jb	40.40N	43.07 E
Karst (EN) = Kras	110	Hf	45.48N	14.00 E
Kårsta	116	He	59.39N	18.14 E
Karstula	114	Fe	62.52N	24.47 E
Kartal	146	Cb	40.53N	29.10 E
Kartaly	136	Ge	53.03N	60.40 E
Kartaly-Ajat	134	Jj	53.01N	61.50 E
Karttula	116	Lb	62.53N	26.58 E
Kartuzy	120	Ob	54.20N	18.12 E
Karumai	156	Ga	40.20N	141.28 E
Karumba	212	Ic	17.29S	140.50 E
Kārūn	140	Gf	30.25N	48.12 E
Karungi	114	Fc	66.03N	23.57 E
Karungu	170	Fc	0.51S	34.09 E
Karunki	114	Fc	66.02N	24.01 E
Karūr	148	Ff	10.57N	78.05 E
Karvia	114	Fe	62.08N	22.34 E
Karviná	120	Og	49.51N	18.32 E
Kārwār	148	Ef	14.48N	74.08 E
Karwendelgebirge	128	Fc	47.28N	11.20 E
Karymskoje	138	Gf	51.37N	114.21 E
Kaş	146	Cd	36.12N	29.38 E
Kas	168	Cc	12.34N	24.14 E
Kas	136	Jd	59.58N	90.42 E
Kasaba [Tur.]	130	Mm	36.18N	29.44 E
Kasaba [Zam.]	170	Ee	10.44S	29.43 E
Kasado-Shima	156	Be	33.57N	131.50 E
Kasah	132	Mi	40.03N	43.52 E
Kasai	156	Dd	34.56N	134.49 E
Kasai	158	Ii	3.02S	16.57 E
Kasai Occidental	170	Dc	5.00S	21.30 E
Kasai Oriental	170	Dc	3.00S	23.00 E
Kasaji	170	De	10.22S	23.27 E
Kasaku	170	Ec	1.55S	25.50 E
Kasama [Jap.]	156	Gc	36.22N	140.16 E
Kasama [Zam.]	160	Kj	10.13S	31.12 E
Kasan	135	Ee	39.01N	65.35 E
Kasane	160	Jj	17.48S	25.09 E
Kasanga	170	Fd	8.28S	31.09 E
Kasangulu	170	Bc	4.36S	15.10 E
Kasansaj	135	Hd	41.10N	71.32 E
Kasaoka	156	Cd	34.30N	133.29 E
Kāsaragod	148	Ef	12.30N	75.00 E
Kasari	156b	Ba	28.27N	129.41 E
Kasari-Zaki	156b	Ba	28.31N	129.42 E
Kašary	132	Le	49.02N	41.03 E
Kasatori-Yama	156	Ce	33.33N	132.55 E
Kasba Lake	180	Hd	60.20N	102.10W
Kasba Tatla	162	Fc	32.36N	6.16W
Kaseda	154	Ki	31.25N	130.19 E
Kasempa	170	Ee	13.27S	25.50 E
Kasenga	160	Jj	10.22S	28.37 E
Kasenye	170	Fb	1.24N	30.26 E
Kasese [Ug.]	170	Fb	0.10N	30.05 E
Kasese [Zaire]	170	Ec	1.38S	27.07 E
Kashaf-Rūd	144	Jb	35.58N	61.07 E
Kāshān	142	Hf	33.59N	51.29 E
Kashi	142	Jf	39.29N	75.58 E
Kashihara	156	Dd	34.31N	135.47 E
Kashima [Jap.]	156	Cd	35.31N	132.59 E
Kashima [Jap.]	156	Be	33.07N	130.07 E
Kashima [Jap.]	156	Gd	35.58N	140.38 E
Kashima-Nada	156	Gc	36.30N	140.45 E
Kashiobwe	170	Ed	9.39S	28.37 E
Kashiwazaki	154	Of	37.25N	138.30 E
Kashkū'īyeh	146	Qh	28.58N	56.37 E
Kāshmar	144	Ib	35.12N	58.27 E
Kashmīr	140	Jf	34.00N	76.00 E
Kashmor	148	Dc	28.26N	69.35 E
Kasimov	136	Ee	54.59N	41.28 E
Kašin	136	Dd	57.23N	37.37 E
Kasindi	170	Eb	0.02N	29.43 E

Index Symbols

1 Independent Nation · 2 State, Region · 3 District, County · 4 Municipality · 5 Colony, Dependency · Continent · Physical Region

Historical or Cultural Region · Mount, Mountain · Volcano · Hill · Mountains, Mountain Range · Hills, Escarpment · Plateau, Upland

Pass, Gap · Plain, Lowland · Delta · Salt Flat · Valley, Canyon · Crater, Cave · Karst Features

Depression · Polder · Desert, Dunes · Forest, Woods · Heath, Steppe · Oasis · Cape, Point

Coast, Beach · Cliff · Peninsula · Isthmus · Sandbank · Island · Atoll

Rock, Reef · Islands, Archipelago · Rocks, Reefs · Coral Reef · Well, Spring · Geyser · River, Stream

Waterfall, Rapids · River Mouth, Estuary · Lake · Salt Lake · Intermittent Lake · Reservoir · Swamp, Pond

Canal · Glacier · Ice Shelf, Pack Ice · Ocean · Sea · Gulf, Bay · Strait, Fjord

Lagoon · Bank · Seamount · Tablemount · Ridge · Shelf · Basin

Escarpment, Sea Scarp · Fracture · Trench, Abyss · National Park, Reserve · Point of Interest · Recreation Site · Cave, Cavern

Historic Site · Ruins · Wall, Walls · Church, Abbey · Temple · Scientific Station · Railway station

Airport · Port · Military installation · Lighthouse · Mine · Tunnel · Dam, Bridge

Kašira	114 Ji	54.52N	38.11 E
Kasiruta, Pulau-	150 Ig	0.25S	127.12 E
Kasisty	138 Fb	73.40N	109.45 E
Kaškadarinskaja oblast	136 Gh	38.50N	66.10 E
Kaškadarja	135 Ee	39.35N	64.38 E
Kaskaskia River	186 Lh	37.59N	89.56W
Kaskelen	136 Hg	43.09N	76.37 E
Kaskinen/Kaskö	114 Ee	62.23N	21.13 E
Kaskö/Kaskinen	114 Ee	62.23N	21.13 E
Kasli	134 Ji	55.53N	60.48 E
Kaslo	188 Gb	49.55N	116.55W
Kasongo	160 Ji	4.27S	26.40 E
Kasongo-Lunda	170 Cd	6.28S	16.49 E
Kásos	130 Jn	35.25N	26.55 E
Kásou, Stenón-	130 Jn	35.25N	26.35 E
Kaspi	132 Ni	41.58N	44.25 E
Kaspičan	130 Kf	43.18N	27.11 E
Kaspijsk	136 Fg	42.57N	47.35 E
Kaspijski	136 Ef	45.25N	47.22 E
Kaspijskoje more = Caspian Sea (EN)	110 Lg	42.00N	50.30 E
Kasplja	132 Gb	55.24N	30.43 E
Kasr, Ra's-	168 Fb	18.04N	38.33 E
Kassaar/Kassar	116 Jf	58.47N	22.40 E
Kassalá	160 Kg	15.28N	36.24 E
Kassalá [3]	168 Fc	14.40N	35.30 E
Kassándra	130 Gi	40.00N	23.30 E
Kassándras, Ákra-	130 Gj	39.57N	23.21 E
Kassándras, Kólpos- = Kassandra, Gulf of- (EN)	130 Gi	40.05N	23.30 E
Kassel	120 Fe	51.19N	9.30 E
Kassiópi	130 Cj	39.47N	19.55 E
Kastamonu	144 Da	41.22N	33.47 E
Kastanéai	130 Jh	41.39N	26.28 E
Kastellaun	124 Jd	50.04N	7.27 E
Kastéllion [Grc.]	130 Gn	35.30N	23.39 E
Kastéllion [Grc.]	130 In	35.12N	25.20 E
Kastéllos, Ákra-	130 Kn	35.23N	27.09 E
Kasterlee	124 Gc	51.15N	4.57 E
Kastløsa	116 Gh	56.28N	16.25 E
Kastoria	130 Ei	40.31N	21.16 E
Kastorías, Límni-	130 Ei	40.31N	21.18 E
Kastornoje	132 Kd	51.51N	38.07 E
Kastós	130 Dk	38.35N	20.55 E
Kasuga	156 Be	33.32N	130.27 E
Kasugai	156 Ed	35.14N	136.58 E
Kasulu	170 Fc	4.34S	30.06 E
Kasumbalesa	170 Ee	12.13S	27.48 E
Kasumi	156 Dd	35.38N	134.38 E
Kasumi-ga-Ura	154 Pf	36.00N	140.25 E
Kasumkent	132 Pi	41.42N	48.10 E
Kasungan	150 Pg	1.58S	113.24 E
Kasungu	170 Fe	13.02S	33.29 E
Kasupe	170 Gf	15.10S	35.18 E
Kaszuby	148 Bb	31.07N	74.27 E
Kataba	120 Ob	54.10N	18.15 E
Katahdin, Mount-	160 Jj	16.05S	25.57 E
Katajsk	182 Nb	45.55N	68.55W
Katako-Kombe	134 Kh	56.18N	62.35 E
Katanga	170 Bc	3.24S	24.25 E
Katanga	170 Ed	10.00S	25.30 E
Katanga	138 Fd	60.10N	102.10 E
Katangli	138 Jf	51.43N	143.16 E
Katanning	212 Df	33.42S	117.33 E
Katav-Ivanovsk	134 Ii	54.47N	58.15 E
Katchall	148 Ig	7.57N	93.22 E
Katchi	162 Ef	17.00N	13.55W
Katchiungo	170 Ce	12.33S	16.14 E
Katende, Chutes de-	170 Dd	6.30S	22.10 E
Katérini	130 Fi	40.16N	22.30 E
Katesh	170 Gc	4.31S	35.23 E
Katete	170 Fe	14.06S	32.05 E
Katha	148 Jd	24.11N	96.21 E
Katherine	210 Ef	14.28S	132.16 E
Katherine River	212 Gb	14.39S	131.42 E
Käthiäwär	140 Jg	21.58N	70.30 E
Kāthmāndāi = Kathmandu (EN)	142 Kg	27.43N	85.19 E
Kathmandu → Kāthmāndāu	142 Kg	27.43N	85.19 E
Kathua	170 Gc	1.17S	39.03 E
Kati	166 Dc	12.43N	8.05W
Katihär	148 Hc	25.32N	87.35 E
Katima Mulilo	170 Df	17.28S	24.14 E
Katiola	166 Dd	8.08N	5.06W
Katiola	166 Dd	8.13N	5.02W
Katiu Atoll	216 Mc	16.26S	144.22W
Katla	114a Bc	63.36N	18.58W
Katlabuh, ozero-	130 Ld	45.25N	29.00 E
Katlanovo	130 Eh	41.54N	21.41 E
Katmai, Mount-	178 Ie	58.17N	154.56W
Káto Akhaïa	130 Ek	38.09N	21.33 E
Katofio	166 Ee	11 02S	28.01 E
Katompi	170 Ed	6.11S	26.20 E
Katonga	170 Fb	0.10N	30.40 E
Katon-Karagaj	136 If	49.11N	85.37 E
Káto Ólimbos	130 Fj	39.55N	22.28 E
Katoomba	212 Kf	33.42S	150.18 E
Katopasa, Gunung-	150 Hg	1.14S	121.25 E
Katowice	112 He	50.16N	19.00 E
Katowice [2]	120 Of	50.15N	19.00 E
Katrancık Dağı	146 Dd	37.27N	30.25 E
Kātrīnā, Dayr- = Saint Catherine, Monastery of- (EN)	164 Fd	28.31N	33.57 E
Kātrīnā, Jabal-	158 Kf	28.31N	33.57 E
Katrineholm	114 Dg	59.00N	16.12 E
Katsina	160 Hg	13.00N	7.36 E
Katsina Ala	166 Gd	7.48N	8.52 E
Katsumoto	154 Jh	33.51N	129.42 E
Katsuta	154 Pf	36.24N	140.32 E
Katsuura	154 Pg	35.08N	140.18 E
Katsuyama [Jap.]	154 Nf	36.03N	136.30 E
Katsuyama [Jap.]	154 Cd	35.06N	133.41 E
Kattakurgan	136 Gh	39.55N	66.15 E
Kattawa	130 Kh	35.57N	27.46 E

Kattegat	110 Hd	57.00N	11.00 E
Katthammarsvik	116 Hg	57.26N	18.50 E
Katulo, Lagh-	170 Hb	2.08N	40.56 E
Katumbi	170 Fe	10.49S	33.32 E
Katun	140 Kd	52.25N	85.05 E
Katwijk aan Zee	122 Kb	52.13N	4.24 E
Katwijk aan Zee, Katwijk-	124 Gb	52.12N	4.25 E
Katzenelnbogen	124 Jd	50.17N	7.57 E
Kau	150 If	1.11N	127.54 E
Kauai Channel	214 Oc	21.45N	158.50W
Kauai Island	208 Lb	22.03N	159.30W
Kaub	124 Jd	50.05N	7.46 E
Kauehi Atoll	216 Lc	15.51S	145.09W
Kaufbeuren	120 Gi	47.53N	10.37 E
Kauhajoki	114 Fe	62.26N	22.11 E
Kauhava	114 Fe	63.06N	23.05 E
Kauiki Head	214 Oc	20.46N	155.59W
Kaukauna	186 Gd	44.17N	88.17W
Kaukauveld	158 Jk	20.00S	21.50 E
Kaukonen	114 Fc	67.29N	24.54 E
Kaukura Atoll	208 Mf	15.45S	146.42W
Kaula Island	208 Kb	21.40N	160.32W
Kaulakahi Channel	221a Ba	22.02N	159.53W
Kaumalapau	221a Ec	20.47N	156.59W
Kaunakakai	214 Oc	21.05N	157.02W
Kaunas	112 Ie	54.54N	23.54 E
Kaunasskoje vodohranilišče / Kauno marios	116 Kj	54.50N	24.15 E
Kauniainen/Grankulla	116 Kd	60.13N	24.45 E
Kauno marios / Kaunasskoje vodohranilišče	116 Kj	54.50N	24.15 E
Kaunos	130 Lm	36.50N	28.35 E
Kaupanger	114 Bf	61.11N	7.14 E
Kau Paulatmada, Gunung-	150 Ig	3.15S	126.09 E
Kaura Namoda	166 Gc	12.36N	6.35 E
Kauriäla Ghät	148 Gc	28.27N	80.59 E
Kaušany	132 Ff	46.39N	29.25 E
Kaustinen	114 Fe	63.33N	23.42 E
Kautokeino	114 Fb	68.59N	23.08 E
Kavacık	130 Lj	39.40N	28.30 E
Kavadarci	130 Fh	41.26N	22.01 E
Kavaja	130 Ch	41.11N	19.33 E
Kavak [Tur.]	130 Ji	40.36N	26.54 E
Kavak [Tur.]	146 Gb	41.05N	36.03 E
Kavaklidere	130 Ll	37.26N	28.22 E
Kavála	112 Ig	40.56N	24.25 E
Kaválas, Kólpos-	130 Hi	40.52N	24.25 E
Kavalerovo	138 Ih	44.19N	135.05 E
Kavali	148 Ff	14.55N	79.59 E
Kavär	146 Oh	29.11N	52.44 E
Kavaratti	142 Jh	10.33N	72.38 E
Kavaratti Island	148 Ef	10.33N	72.38 E
Kavarna	130 Lf	43.25N	28.20 E
Kavarskas/Kovarskas	116 Kj	55.24N	25.03 E
Kavendou, Mont-	158 Fg	10.41N	12.12W
Kavieng	214 Bb	2.34S	150.48 E
Kavīr, Dasht-e-	140 Hf	34.40N	54.30 E
Kavkaz	132 Jg	45.21N	36.12 E
Kavkaz, Bolšoj- = Caucasus (EN)	110 Kg	42.30N	45.00 E
Kävlinge	116 Ei	55.48N	13.06 E
Kävlingeån	116 Ei	55.47N	13.06 E
Kawa	168 Eb	19.10N	30.39 E
Kawabe	156 Bb	39.39N	140.15 E
Kawachi-nagano	156 Dd	34.27N	135.34 E
Kawagoe	156 Fd	35.55N	139.28 E
Kawaguchi	156 Fd	34.27N	135.35 E
Kawaihae Bay	221a Fc	20.02N	155.51W
Kawaihoa Point	221a Ab	21.47N	160.12W
Kawakawa	218 Fa	35.23S	174.04 E
Kawalusu, Pulau-	150 If	4.15N	125.19 E
Kawamata	156 Gc	37.40N	140.36 E
Kawambwa	170 Dd	9.47S	29.05 E
Kawaminami	156 Be	32.12N	131.32 E
Kawamoto	156 Cd	34.59N	132.29 E
Kawanishi	156 Gc	37.59N	140.03 E
Kawanoe	156 Cd	34.01N	133.34 E
Kawartha Lakes	184 Hc	44.32N	78.30W
Kawasaki [Jap.]	156 Gb	38.10N	140.38 E
Kawasaki [Jap.]	154 Og	35.32N	139.43 E
Kawashiri-Misaki	156 Bd	34.26N	130.58 E
Kawauchi	156a Bc	41.12N	141.00 E
Kawau Island	218 Fb	36.25S	174.50 E
Kawaura	156 Be	32.21N	130.05 E
Kawhia	218 Fc	38.04S	174.49 E
Kawich Range	188 Dh	37.40N	116.30W
Kawio, Kepulauan-	150 If	4.30N	125.30 E
Kawkareik	148 Je	16.33N	98.14 E
Kawm Umbū	164 Fe	24.28N	32.57 E
Kawthaung	148 Jg	9.59N	98.33 E
Kaxgar He	140 Jf	39.46N	78.15 E
Kax He	152 Dc	43.37N	81.48 E
Kaya	166 Ec	13.05N	1.05W
Kayah [2]	148 Je	19.15N	97.30 E
Kayak [3]	178 Ke	59.52N	144.30W
Kayalı Dağı	130 Jj	39.58N	26.38 E
Kayan	140 Ni	2.55N	117.35 E
Kayanga	166 Cc	11.58N	15.00W
Kayangel Islands	208 Bd	8.04N	134.43 E
Kayangel Passage	220a Ba	8.01N	134.42 E
Kaycee	188 Le	43.43N	106.38W
Kayenta	188 Jh	36.44N	110.17W
Kayes	160 Fg	14.26N	11.27W
Kayin [2]	148 Je	17.30N	97.45 E
Kayoa, Pulau-	150 Ig	0.05S	127.25 E
Kayin	142 Pf	38.43N	35.30 E
Kayseri	150 Ef	31.30N	104.50 E
Kayuagung	150 Ef	1.31N	106.26 E
Kayu Ara, Pulau-	150 Ef	0.05S	104.50 E
Kazačje	138 Ib	70.40N	136.13 E
Kazah	132 Ni	41.05N	45.22 E
Kazahskaja Sovetskaja Socialističeskaja Respublika [2]	136 Gf	48.00N	68.00 E

Kazahskaja SSR/Kazak Sovettik Socialistik Respublikasy [2]	136 Gf	48.00N	68.00 E
Kazahskaja SSR = Kazakh SSR (EN) [2]	136 Gf	48.00N	68.00 E
Kazahski melkosopočnik = Kazakh Hills (EN) [2]	140 Je	49.00N	73.00 E
Kazahski zaliv	132 Rh	42.40N	52.25 E
Kazakh Hills (EN) = Kazahski melkosopočnik	140 Je	49.00N	73.00 E
Kazakh SSR (EN) = Kazahskaja SSR [2]	136 Gf	48.00N	68.00 E
Kazakhstan (EN) [2]	140 Hd	51.11N	52.52 E
Kazaklija	130 Lc	46.05N	28.38 E
Kazak Sovettik Socialistik Respublikasy [2]	136 Gf	48.00N	68.00 E
Kazalak	130 Ke	44.03N	27.24 E
Kazalinsk	136 Ef	45.46N	62.07 E
Kazan	112 Kd	55.45N	49.08 E
Kazan	174 Jc	64.02N	95.30W
Kazandžik	136 Fh	39.17N	55.34 E
Kazanka	132 Hf	47.50N	32.49 E
Kazanka	114 Li	55.48N	49.05 E
Kazanlâk	130 Ig	42.37N	25.24 E
Kazan-Rettō/Iō = Volcano Islands (EN)	140 Qg	25.00N	141.00 E
Kazanskoje	136 Gd	55.38N	69.14 E
Kazarman	136 Hg	41.20N	74.02 E
Kazatin	136 Cf	49.43N	28.50 E
Kazbegi	132 Nh	42.39N	44.39 E
Kazbek, gora-	110 Kg	42.42N	44.31 E
Kaz Dağı [Tur.]	130 Mk	38.35N	29.15 E
Kaz Dağı [Tur.]	144 Cb	39.42N	26.50 E
Kâzerûn	144 Hd	29.37N	51.38 E
Kažim	134 Ef	60.20N	51.32 E
Kazi-Magomed	132 Pi	40.03N	48.56 E
Kazimierza Wielka	120 Qf	50.16N	20.30 E
Kâzimkarabekir	146 Ed	37.14N	32.59 E
Kazincbarcika	120 Qh	48.15N	20.38 E
Kazinga Channel	170 Ec	0.13S	29.53 E
Kazly-Rūda/Kazlu-Ruda	116 Jj	54.42N	23.32 E
Kazlu-Ruda/Kazly-Rūda	116 Jj	54.42N	23.32 E
Kazo	156 Fc	36.08N	139.36 E
Kaztalovka	132 Pe	49.46N	48.44 E
Kazumba	170 Dd	6.25S	22.02 E
Kazuno	154 Pd	40.14N	140.48 E
Kazym	136 Gc	63.54N	65.50 E
Kazyr	138 Ef	53.50N	92.53 E
Kcynia	120 Nd	53.00N	17.30 E
Kdyně	120 Jg	49.24N	13.02 E
Ké	168 Bb	18.32N	17.55 E
Kéa	130 Hl	37.39N	24.20 E
Kéa	130 Hl	37.37N	24.20 E
Keaau	221a Fd	19.37N	155.03W
Keahole Point	221a Ed	19.44N	156.04W
Kealaikahiki Channel	221a Ec	20.35N	156.42W
Kealaikahiki Point	221a Ec	20.32N	156.42W
Kealakekua Bay	221a Fd	19.28N	155.56W
Keams Canyon	188 Ji	35.49N	110.12W
Keanae	221a Ec	20.52N	156.09W
Keanapapa Point	221a Dc	20.54N	156.56W
Kearney	182 Hc	40.42N	99.05W
Kearns	188 Jf	40.39N	111.59W
Kéas, Stenón-	130 Hl	37.40N	24.12 E
Keats Bank (EN)	208 Ib	3.23N	173.28 E
Keb	116 Mg	57.44N	28.38 E
Keban Baraji	146 Hc	38.53N	39.00 E
Kébémér	166 Bb	15.22N	16.27W
Kebir, Oued el-	128 Bn	36.51N	7.57 E
Kebnekaise	110 Hb	67.53N	18.33 E
Kebri Dehar	160 Lh	6.45N	44.17 E
Kebumen	150 Eh	7.40S	109.39 E
Kecel	120 Pj	46.32N	19.16 E
Kechika	180 Ee	59.38N	127.09W
Kecskemét	120 Pj	46.54N	19.42 E
Kedah [2]	150 De	6.00N	100.40 E
Kédainiai/Kedajnjaj	114 Fi	55.18N	23.59 E
Kedajnjaj/Kédainiai	114 Fi	55.18N	23.59 E
Kedgwick	184 Nb	47.39N	67.21W
Kediri	142 Nj	7.49S	112.01 E
Kédougou	166 Cc	12.33N	12.11W
Kedva	134 Fd	64.14N	53.30 E
Kędzierzyn-Koźle	120 Of	50.20N	18.10 E
Keele	180 Fd	64.24N	124.47W
Keele Peak	174 Fd	63.26N	130.19W
Keeling Islands → Cocos Islands	142 Lk	12.10S	96.55 E
Keeling Islands → Cocos Islands	140 Lk	12.10S	96.55 E
Keelung	142 Og	25.08N	121.44 E
Keene	184 Kd	42.55N	72.17W
Keer-Weer, Cape-	212 Ib	13.58S	141.30 E
Keetmanshoop	160 Ik	26.36S	18.08 E
Keetmanshoop [3]	172 Be	26.30S	18.00 E
Keewatin	180 Ig	49.46N	94.34W
Kefa [3]	168 Fd	7.00N	36.00 E
Kefallinía = Cephalonia (EN)	110 Ih	38.15N	20.35 E
Kefamenanu	150 Hh	9.27S	124.29 E
Kefar Sava	146 Ff	32.10N	34.54 E
Keffi	166 Gd	8.51N	7.52 E
Keflavik	114a Ab	64.01N	22.34W
Kegen	136 Hg	42.58N	79.12 E
Kegums	116 Kh	56.41N	24.44 E
Kehdingen	124 Ka	53.45N	9.20 E
Kehl	124 Jg	48.34N	7.49 E
Kehra	116 Lf	59.19N	25.18 E
Keighley	118 La	53.52N	1.54W
Keila/Kejla	116 Le	59.19N	24.27 E
Keila jõgi / Kejla	116 Le	59.24N	24.17 E
Keimoes	172 Ce	28.41S	21.00 E
Keipel Bank (EN)	212 Le	25.15S	159.30 E
Keita	160 Hg	14.46N	5.46 E
Keïta, Bahr-	168 Bd	9.14N	18.21 E
Keitele	112 Ic	62.55N	26.00 E
Keith [Austl.]	212 Ig	36.06S	140.21 E

Keith [Scot.-U.K.]	118 Kd	57.32N	2.57W
Keith Arm	180 Fc	65.20N	122.00W
Keiyasi	219d Ab	17.53S	177.45 E
Kejla/Keila	114 Fg	59.19N	24.27 E
Kejla / Keila jõgi	116 Ke	59.25N	24.15 E
Kejvy	114 Ic	67.30N	37.45 E
Kekaha	221a Bb	21.58N	159.43W
Kekerengu	218 Ee	42.00S	174.00 E
Kékes	120 Qi	47.52N	20.01 E
Keklau	220a Bb	7.35N	134.39 E
Kelafo	168 Gd	5.37N	44.13 E
Kelakam	166 Hc	13.35N	11.44 E
Kela Met	168 Fb	15.50N	38.23 E
Kelan	152 Jd	38.44N	111.34 E
Kelang	142 Mi	3.02N	101.27 E
Kelantan [2]	150 De	5.20N	102.00 E
Kelasa, Selat- = Gaspar Strait (EN)	150 Eg	2.40S	107.15 E
Kelberg	124 Id	50.18N	6.55 E
Kelçyra	130 Di	40.19N	20.11 E
Kelefesia	221b Bb	20.30S	174.44W
Kelekçi	130 Ml	37.14N	29.28 E
Kelem	168 Fe	4.49N	35.59 E
Keles	130 Mj	39.55N	29.14 E
Keles	135 Gd	41.02N	68.37 E
Kelheim	120 Hh	48.55N	11.52 E
Kelifely, Causse du-	172 Hc	17.15S	45.30 E
Kelifski uzboj	135 Ef	37.45N	64.40 E
Keli Hâji Ibrâhim	146 Kd	36.42N	45.00 E
Kelkheim	124 Kd	50.08N	8.27 E
Kelkit	146 Hb	40.08N	39.27 E
Kelkit	144 Ea	36.32N	40.46 E
Kellé	170 Bc	0.06S	14.33 E
Kellerberrin	212 Df	31.38S	117.43 E
Kellerwald	120 Fe	51.03N	9.10 E
Kellett, Cape -	180 Eb	72.57N	125.27W
Kellett Strait	180 Fa	75.50N	117.40W
Kellog	138 Dd	62.27N	86.35 E
Kellogg	182 Db	47.32N	116.07W
Kelloselkä	114 Gc	66.56N	29.00 E
Kells/Ceanannas Mór	118 Gh	53.44N	6.53W
Kelmé/Kelme	114 Fi	55.39N	22.58 E
Kelme/Kelmé	114 Fi	55.39N	22.58 E
Kelmency	130 Ja	48.27N	26.47 E
Kelmis/La Calamine	124 Hd	50.43N	6.00 E
Kélo	168 Bd	9.15N	15.48 E
Kelowna	176 He	49.53N	119.29W
Kelsey	180 He	56.00N	97.00W
Kelsey Bay	180 Gf	50.24N	125.57W
Kelso	188 Dc	46.09N	122.54W
Kelso Bank (EN)	212 Ld	24.10S	159.30 E
Kel Tepe [Tur.]	146 Eb	41.05N	32.27 E
Kel Tepe [Tur.]	130 Ni	40.39N	30.06 E
Keltie, Mount-	222 Jf	79.15S	159.00 E
Keluang	150 Df	2.02N	103.19 E
Kelvin Seamount (EN)	182 Od	38.50N	64.00W
Kelyehēd	168 Hd	8.44N	49.10 E
Kem	136 Dc	64.57N	34.31 E
Kema	114 If	64.57N	37.15 E
Ké Macina	166 Dc	13.57N	5.23W
Kemah	146 Hc	39.36N	39.02 E
Kemaliye	146 Hc	39.16N	38.29 E
Kemalpaşa	130 Kk	38.25N	27.26 E
Kemalpaşa	146 Cc	40.00N	28.43 E
Kembé	168 Ce	4.36N	21.54 E
Kemer [Tur.]	146 De	36.36N	30.34 E
Kemer [Tur.]	130 Mm	36.36N	29.21 E
Kemer Baraji	130 Ll	37.30N	28.35 E
Kemeri/Ķemeri	116 Jh	56.56N	23.25 E
Ķemeri/Kemeri	116 Jh	56.56N	23.25 E
Kemerovo	142 Kd	55.20N	86.05 E
Kemerovskaja oblast [3]	138 Dc	55.00N	87.00 E
Kemi	112 Ib	65.44N	24.34 E
Kemi, Lake- (EN) = Kemijärvi	114 Gc	66.36N	27.24 E
Kemijärvi	114 Gc	66.40N	27.25 E
Kemijärvi = Kemi, Lake- (EN)	114 Gc	66.36N	27.24 E
Kemijoki	110 Ib	65.47N	24.30 E
Kemió/Kimito	116 Jd	60.10N	22.40 E
Kemlja	114 Ki	54.43N	45.15 E
Kemmerer	188 Jf	41.48N	110.32W
Kémo-Gribingui [3]	168 Bd	6.00N	19.00 E
Kemp, Lake-	186 Gj	33.45N	99.13W
Kempaž	134 Ef	64.03N	61.02 E
Kempele	114 Fd	64.55N	25.30 E
Kempen	124 Ic	51.22N	6.25 E
Kempen/Campine	122 Ic	51.10N	5.20 E
Kempenich	124 Id	50.25N	7.08 E
Kemp Land	222 Ee	67.10S	58.00 E
Kemps Bay	194 Db	24.02N	77.33W
Kempsey	212 Kf	31.05S	152.50 E
Kempston	124 Bb	52.06N	0.29W
Kempt, Lac-	180 Kg	47.25N	74.15W
Kempten/Allgäu	120 Gi	47.43N	10.19 E
Ken	148 Hc	25.46N	80.31 E
Ken, Loch-	118 If	55.02N	4.02W
Kena	114 Ic	62.60N	39.05 E
Kenadsa	162 Gc	31.34N	2.26W
Kenai	176 Dc	60.33N	151.15W
Kenai Mountains	174 Dd	60.00N	150.00W
Kenai Peninsula	174 Dd	60.24N	150.00W
Kendal	118 Kg	54.20N	2.45W
Kendall	184 Gm	25.41N	80.19W
Kendall, Cape-	180 Jd	63.36N	87.13W
Kendari	142 Ni	3.57S	122.35 E
Kendawangan	150 Fg	2.32S	110.12 E
Kendégué	168 Ad	10.46N	17.13 E
Kenduang	148 Fb	31.30N	82.30 E
Kenema	160 Fh	7.52N	11.12W
Kenge	170 Cc	4.52S	16.59 E
Kengere	170 Ee	11.10S	25.28 E
Keng Tung	148 Jd	21.17N	99.36 E
Kéniéba	166 Cc	12.50N	11.14W
Keningau	150 Gf	5.20N	116.10 E
Kenitra	160 Gb	34.16N	6.36W
Kenitra	162 Gb	34.00N	6.00W

Kenli (Xishuanghe)	154 Ef	37.35N	118.30 E
Kenmare	182 Gb	48.40N	102.05W
Kenmare/Neidin	118 Dj	51.53N	9.35W
Kenmare River/An Ribhéar	118 Dj	51.50N	9.50W
Kennebunk	184 Ld	43.23N	70.33W
Kennedy Peak	148 Id	23.19N	93.46 E
Kennedy Range	212 Cd	24.30S	115.00 E
Kenner	186 Ki	29.59N	90.15W
Kennet	118 Mj	51.28N	0.57W
Kennett	186 Kh	36.14N	90.03W
Kennewick	188 Fc	46.12N	119.07W
Kennington	124 Cc	51.09N	0.53 E
Kenn Reef	208 Gg	21.10S	155.50 E
Kénogami	184 La	48.26N	71.14W
Kénogami, Lac-	184 La	48.21N	71.28W
Kenogami River	180 Jf	50.26N	84.29W
Keno Hill	180 Dd	63.54N	135.18W
Kenora	176 Je	49.47N	94.29W
Kenosha	182 Jc	42.35N	87.49W
Kent [3]	118 Nj	51.20N	0.55 E
Kent	118 Nj	51.10N	0.55 E
Kent [S.L.]	166 Cd	8.10N	13.10W
Kent [Wa.-U.S.]	188 Dc	47.23N	122.14W
Kent, Vale of-	118 Nj	51.10N	0.30 E
Kentau	136 Gg	43.32N	68.33 E
Kent Group	212 Jg	39.30S	147.20 E
Kenton	184 Fe	40.38N	83.38W
Kent Peninsula	180 Gc	68.30N	107.00W
Kentucky [2]	182 Jd	37.30N	85.15W
Kentucky Lake	182 Jd	36.25N	88.05W
Kentucky River	184 Ef	38.41N	85.11W
Kenya [1]	160 Kh	1.00N	38.00 E
Kenya, Mount-/Kirinyaga	160 Kh	0.10S	37.20 E
Keokea	221a Ec	20.42N	156.21W
Keokuk	182 Ic	40.24N	91.24W
Keonjhargarh	148 Hd	21.38N	85.35 E
Keowee, Lake-	184 Fh	34.55N	82.50W
Kepe	114 Hd	65.09N	32.08 E
Kepi	150 Nk	6.32S	139.19 E
Kepno	120 Ne	51.17N	17.59 E
Kepsut	146 Cc	39.41N	28.09 E
Kerala [3]	148 Ff	11.00N	76.30 E
Kerama-Rettō	156b Ab	26.10N	127.15 E
Kerang	158 Jg	35.44S	143.55 E
Keratéa	130 Gl	37.48N	23.59 E
Kerava/Kervo	116 Kd	60.24N	25.07 E
Kerč	112 Jf	45.22N	36.27 E
Kerčenski poluostrov	132 Ig	45.15N	36.00 E
Kerdhílion Óros	130 Gi	40.47N	23.39 E
Kerema	214 Di	7.58S	145.46 E
Keren	168 Fb	15.46N	38.27 E
Keret, ozero-	114 Hd	66.50N	32.50 E
Kerewan	166 Bc	13.29N	16.06W
Kerguelen	158 Nm	49.20S	69.30 E
Kerguelen, Îles-	158 Nm	49.15S	69.10 E
Kerguelen Plateau (EN)	106 Go	55.00S	75.00 E
Kericho	170 Gc	0.22S	35.17 E
Keri Kera	168 Ec	12.21N	32.46 E
Kerimäki	116 Mc	61.55N	29.17 E
Kerinci, Gunung-	140 Mj	1.42S	101.16 E
Kerio	158 Km	3.59N	36.07 E
Kerion	130 Dl	37.40N	20.49 E
Keriya/Yutian	142 Kf	36.52N	81.42 E
Keriya He	152 Dd	38.30N	82.10 E
Keriya Shankou	152 Dd	35.12N	81.44 E
Kerka	120 Mj	46.29N	16.36 E
Kerken	124 Ic	51.27N	6.26 E
Kerkennah Islands (EN) = Qarqannah, Juzur-	158 Le	34.44N	11.12 E
Kerketevs Óros	130 Jl	37.44N	26.38 E
Kerki	136 Gh	37.50N	65.13 E
Kerkini Óros	130 Fh	41.21N	22.50 E
Kérkira	130 Cj	39.36N	19.55 E
Kérkira=Corfu (EN)	110 Hh	39.39N	19.45 E
Kerkiras, Stenón- = Corfu, Strait of- (EN)	130 Dj	39.35N	20.05 E
Kerkrade	124 Id	50.52N	6.04 E
Kerma (EN) = Karmah	168 Eb	19.38N	30.25 E
Kermadec Islands	208 Ij	30.00S	178.30W
Kermadec Ridge (EN)	208 Ij	30.00S	178.30W
Kermadec Trench (EN)	106 Mm	30.00S	177.00W
Kermajärvi	116 Mb	62.28N	28.40 E
Kermân	142 Hf	30.17N	57.05 E
Kermän [3]	144 Ic	30.50N	57.50 E
Kermânshâhân	146 Pg	31.17N	54.55 E
Kerme	130 Kl	37.20N	28.00 E
Kerme Körfezi	130 Kl	36.50N	28.00 E
Kermit	186 Ek	31.51N	103.06W
Kern River	188 Fi	35.13N	119.17W
Kérouané	166 Dd	9.16N	9.01W
Kerpen	124 Id	50.52N	6.41 E
Kerrobert	180 Gf	51.55N	109.08W
Kerrville	182 He	30.03N	99.08W
Kerry/Ciarraí [2]	118 Di	52.10N	9.30W
Kerry, Mountains of-	118 Dj	51.55N	9.50W
Kertamulya	150 Fg	0.23N	109.09 E
Kerteh	150 De	4.31N	103.27 E
Kerteminde	116 Ci	55.27N	10.40 E
Kerulen (Cherlen)	154 Ne	48.48N	117.00 E
Kervo/Kerava	116 Kd	60.24N	25.07 E
Kerzaz	162 Gd	29.27N	1.25W
Kerženec	114 Ki	56.04N	45.01 E
Kesagami Lake	180 Jf	50.23N	80.10W
Kesälahti	116 Mc	61.54N	29.50 E
Keşan	130 Jh	40.51N	26.37 E
Kesap	146 Hb	40.55N	38.31 E
Kesen'numa	154 Pe	38.54N	141.35 E
Kesen'numa-Wan	156 Gb	38.50N	141.35 E
Keshan	152 Mb	48.04N	125.51 E
Keskastel	124 Ie	48.58N	7.02 E
Keskin	146 Ec	39.41N	33.37 E
Keski-Suomi [2]	114 Fe	62.30N	25.30 E
Kestenga	114 Hd	65.53N	31.45 E
Keswick	118 Jg	54.37N	3.08W
Keszthely	120 Mj	46.46N	17.15 E
Ket	136 Kd	58.55N	81.32 E
Kéta	166 Fd	5.55N	0.59 E

Keta, ozero-	138	Dc	68.45N	90.00 E
Ketanda	138	Jd	60.38N	141.30 E
Ketapang	142	Mj	1.52S	109.59 E
Ketchikan	176	Fd	55.21N	131.35W
Ketchum	182	Ec	43.41N	114.22W
Ketchum Mountain	186	Fk	31.15N	101.00W
Kete Krachi	166	Ed	7.46N	0.03W
Ketelmeer	124	Hb	52.35N	5.45 E
Ketli, Jbel-	126	Gi	35.22N	5.17W
Ketmen, hrebet-	135	Lc	43.20N	80.00 E
Kétou	166	Fd	7.22N	2.36 E
Kętrzyn	120	Rb	54.06N	21.23 E
Kettering [Eng.-U.K.]	118	Mi	52.24N	0.44W
Kettering [Oh.-U.S.]	184	Ef	39.41N	84.10W
Kettle River	188	Fb	48.42N	118.07W
Kettle River Range	188	Fb	48.30N	118.40W
Keuka Lake	184	Id	42.27N	77.10W
Keur Massène	162	Df	16.33N	16.14W
Keuruu	114	Fe	62.16N	24.42 E
Keuruunselkä	116	Kb	62.10N	24.40 E
Kevelaer	124	Ic	51.35N	6.15 E
Kew	194	Kc	21.54N	72.02W
Kewanee	182	Jc	41.14N	89.56W
Keweenaw Bay	184	Cb	46.56N	88.23W
Keweenaw Peninsula	182	Jb	47.12N	88.25W
Key, Lough-/Loch Cé	118	Eg	54.00N	8.15W
Keya Paha River	186	Gb	42.54N	99.00W
Keyhole Reservoir	188	Md	44.21N	104.51W
Key Largo	184	Gm	25.04N	80.28W
Keystone Lake	186	Hh	36.15N	96.25W
Key West	176	Kg	24.33N	81.48W
Kez	114	Mh	57.56N	53.43 E
Kezi	172	Dd	20.55S	28.29 E
Kežma	138	Fe	59.02N	101.09 E
Kežmarok	120	Qg	49.08N	20.25 E
Kgalagadi [3]	172	Ce	25.00S	22.00 E
Kgatleng [3]	172	Dd	24.28S	26.05 E
Kghoti	172	Cd	24.55S	21.59 E
Khabr, Kūh-e-	144	Id	28.50N	56.26 E
Khābūr, Nahr al-	146	Ie	35.08N	40.26 E
Khadari, Wādī al-	168	Dc	10.29N	27.00 E
Khādim, Shūshat al-	146	Bh	28.35N	27.43 E
Khadki (Kirkee)	148	Ee	18.34N	73.52 E
Khadra	126	Mh	36.15N	0.35 E
Khafs Banbān	146	Lj	25.31N	46.27 E
Khairónia	130	Fk	38.30N	22.51 E
Khairpur	148	Dc	27.32N	68.46 E
Khāīz, Kūh-e-	146	Ng	30.27N	50.55 E
Khakhea	172	Cd	24.42S	23.30 E
Khalatse	148	Fb	34.20N	76.49 E
Khálki	130	Km	36.13N	27.37 E
Khálki	130	Km	36.14N	27.36 E
Khalkidhiki = Chalcidice (EN)	110	Ig	40.25N	23.25 E
Khalkís	130	Gk	38.28N	23.36 E
Khaluf	146	Ie	20.29N	57.59 E
Khambhāt	148	Ed	22.18N	72.37 E
Khambhāt, Gulf of-	140	Jg	21.00N	72.30 E
Khāmgaon	148	Fd	20.41N	76.34 E
Khamili	130	Jn	35.52N	26.14 E
Khamir	144	Ff	15.59N	43.57 E
Khāmis, Ash Shallāl al- = Fifth Cataract (EN)	158	Kg	18.23N	33.47 E
Khamīs Mushayṭ	144	Ff	18.18N	42.44 E
Khammam	148	Ge	17.15N	80.09 E
Khamseh	146	Md	36.40N	48.50 E
Khān	146	Qj	24.13N	56.20 E
Khan	172	Ad	22.42S	14.54 E
Khānābād	144	Kb	36.41N	69.07 E
Khān al Baghdādī	146	Jf	33.51N	42.33 E
Khān al Hammād	146	Kf	32.19N	44.17 E
Khānaqīn	146	Gc	34.21N	45.22 E
Khān az Zabīb	146	Gg	31.28N	36.06 E
Khandwa	148	Fd	21.50N	76.20 E
Khāneh Sorkh, Gardaneh-ye-	146	Qh	29.49N	56.06 E
Khānewāl	148	Eb	30.18N	71.56 E
Khangai Mountains (EN) = Changajn Nuruu	140	Le	47.30N	100.00 E
Khánia	112	Ih	35.31N	24.02 E
Khanion, Kólpos-	130	Gn	35.35N	23.50 E
Khanka, Lake- (EN) = Hanka, ozero-	140	Pe	45.00N	132.24 E
Khanka Lake (EN) = Xingkai Hu	140	Pe	45.00N	132.24 E
Khānpur	148	Ec	28.39N	70.39 E
Khān Shaykhūn	146	Ge	35.26N	36.38 E
Khan Takhtī	146	Lc	38.09N	44.55 E
Khān Yūnus	146	Fg	31.21N	34.19 E
Khānzīr, Rās-	168	Hc	10.50N	45.50 E
Khao Laem	148	Kf	14.19N	101.11 E
Khao Miang	148	Ke	17.42N	101.01 E
Khao Mokochu	148	Je	15.56N	99.06 E
Khao Saming	148	Kf	12.16N	102.26 E
Khar	146	Me	35.53N	48.55 E
Kharagpur	148	Kg	22.20N	87.20 E
Khárakas	130	In	35.01N	25.07 E
Khārān	146	Qh	28.55N	57.09 E
Kharānaq	146	Pf	32.20N	54.39 E
Kharānaq, Kūh-e-	146	Pf	32.10N	54.39 E
Kharga Oasis (EN) = Khārijah, Wāḥāt al-	158	Kf	25.20N	30.35 E
Khārijah, Wāḥāt al- = Kharga Oasis (EN)	158	Kf	25.20N	30.35 E
Kharīt, Wādī al-	146	Ej	24.26N	33.03 E
Kharīṭah, Shiqqat al-	164	If	17.10N	47.50 E
Khārk	146	Nh	29.15N	50.20 E
Khārk, Jazīreh-ye-	146	Nh	29.15N	50.20 E
Khār Kūh	146	Og	31.39N	53.46 E
Kharmān, Kūh-e-	144	Hd	29.13N	53.35 E
Kharshah, Qārat al-	146	Bg	30.35N	27.25 E
Khartoum (EN) = Al Kharṭūm	160	Kg	15.36N	32.32 E
Khartoum (EN) = Al Kharṭūm [3]	168	Eb	15.50N	33.00 E
Khartoum North (EN) Al Kharṭūm Bahrī	160	Kg	15.38N	32.33 E
Khāsh	144	Jc	31.31N	62.52 E
Khāsh	144	Jc	31.11N	62.05 E
Khashm al Qirbah	168	Fc	14.58N	35.55 E
Khāsi Jaintia	140	Lg	25.35N	91.38 E
Khatikhon, Yam- = Mediterranean Sea (EN)	110	Hh	35.00N	20.00 E
Khaṭṭ	164	Dd	28.40N	22.40 E
Khātūn, Kūh-e-	146	Og	30.25N	53.38 E
Khawr al Fakkān	146	Qk	25.21N	56.22 E
Khawr al Juḥaysh	168	Ia	20.36N	50.59 E
Khawr al Mufattaḥ	146	Mh	28.40N	48.25 E
Khawr Umm Qasr	146	Lg	30.02N	47.56 E
Khay'	144	Ff	18.45N	41.24 E
Khaybar	144	Ed	25.42N	39.31 E
Khaybar, Ḩarrat-	146	Hj	25.30N	39.45 E
Khazzī, Qārat-	158	Jf	21.26N	24.30 E
Khemis	126	Qh	36.10N	4.04 E
Khemis Anjra	126	Gi	35.41N	5.32W
Khémis Beni Arouss	126	Gi	35.19N	5.38W
Khémis Miliana	162	Hb	36.16N	2.13 E
Khemisset	162	Fc	33.49N	6.04W
Khemisset [3]	162	Fc	33.49N	6.00W
Khemmarat	148	Ke	16.03N	105.11 E
Khenchela	162	Ib	35.26N	7.08 E
Khenifra	162	Fc	32.56N	5.40W
Khenifra [3]	162	Fc	33.00N	5.08W
Kherāmeh	146	Oh	29.32N	53.21 E
Khersan	146	Ng	31.33N	50.22 E
Khersónisos Akrotíri	130	Hn	35.35N	24.10 E
Kheyrābād [Iran]	146	Ph	29.26N	55.19 E
Kheyrābād [Iran]	146	Mg	31.49N	48.23 E
Khionótripa	130	Hh	41.18N	24.05 E
Khios	130	Jk	38.22N	26.08 E
Khios = Chios (EN)	110	Ih	38.22N	26.00 E
Khirbat Isrīyah	146	Ge	35.21N	37.46 E
Khirr, Nahr al-	146	Kf	33.17N	44.21 E
Khlomón Óros	130	Fk	38.36N	23.00 E
Khlong Yai	148	Kf	11.46N	102.53 E
Khokhropār	148	Ec	25.42N	70.12 E
Khok Kloi	148	Jg	8.17N	98.19 E
Khok Samrong	148	Ke	15.03N	100.44 E
Kholm	144	Kb	36.42N	67.41 E
Khomām	146	Md	37.22N	49.40 E
Khomas Highland (EN) = Khomas Hochland	158	Ik	22.40S	16.20 E
Khomas Hochland = Khomas Highland (EN)	158	Ik	22.40S	16.20 E
Khomeyn	146	Nf	33.38N	50.04 E
Khomeynīshahr	146	Nf	32.42N	51.27 E
Khonj	146	Oi	27.52N	53.27 E
Khon Kaen	148	Ke	16.26N	102.50 E
Khonsār	146	Nf	33.21N	50.19 E
Khóra	130	El	37.03N	21.43 E
Khor Anghar	168	Gc	12.27N	43.18 E
Khorāsān [3]	144	Ic	35.00N	58.00 E
Khorāsān	140	Hf	34.00N	56.00 E
Khorāsānī, Godār-e	146	Qg	30.44N	57.03 E
Khóra Sfakíon	130	Hn	35.12N	24.09 E
Khorat Plateau	140	Mh	15.30N	102.50 E
Khormūj, Kūh-e-	144	Hd	28.43N	51.22 E
Khorof Harar	170	Hb	2.14N	40.44 E
Khorramābād	144	Gc	33.30N	48.20 E
Khorramshahr	144	Gc	30.25N	48.11 E
Khorsābād	146	Jd	36.38N	43.17 E
Khoshyeylāq	146	Pd	36.53N	55.15 E
Khosrowābād	146	Mg	30.00N	48.25 E
Khosrowshah	146	Ld	37.57N	46.03 E
Khouribga	162	Fc	32.53N	6.54W
Khouribga [3]	162	Fc	32.56N	6.36W
Khowst	146	Kb	33.22N	69.57 E
Khrisí	130	Io	34.52N	25.42 E
Khrisoúpolis	130	Hi	40.59N	24.42 E
Khristianá	130	Im	36.14N	25.13 E
Khu Dağı	146	Jc	38.35N	43.40 E
Khuff [Lib.]	164	Cd	28.17N	18.20 E
Khuff [Sau.Ar.]	144	Ed	25.20N	37.20 E
Khulna	142	Kg	22.48N	89.33 E
Khūrān	146	Pi	26.50N	55.40 E
Khurayṣ	144	Gd	25.05N	48.02 E
Khurayt	168	Dc	13.57N	26.02 E
Khurīyā Murīyā, Jazā'ir- = Kuria Muria Islands (EN)	140	Hh	17.30N	56.00 E
Khurr, Wādī al-	146	Jg	30.52N	42.10 E
Khursanīyah	146	Mi	27.18N	49.16 E
Khūshābar	146	Md	37.59N	48.54 E
Khutse	172	Cd	23.20S	24.34 E
Khuwayy	168	Dc	13.05N	29.14 E
Khuzdār	148	Dc	27.48N	66.37 E
Khūzestān [3]	144	Gc	32.00N	48.30 E
Khūzestān	140	Gf	30.33N	50.00 E
Khvojeh Lāk, Kūh-e-	146	Le	35.43N	46.29 E
Khvor	146	Pf	33.47N	55.03 E
Khvorāsgān	146	Nf	32.39N	51.45 E
Khvormūj	146	Nh	28.39N	51.23 E
Khvoshkūh	146	Qi	27.37N	56.41 E
Khvoy	146	Kc	38.33N	44.58 E
Khyber Pass	148	Eb	34.05N	71.10 E
Kia	219a	Db	7.32S	158.26 E
Kia	219d	Bb	16.14S	179.05 E
Kiamba	150	He	5.59N	124.37 E
Kiambi	170	Ed	7.20S	28.01 E
Kiamichi River	186	Ij	33.57N	95.14W
Kiangarow, Mount-	212	Ke	26.49S	151.33 E
Kiangsi (EN) = Jiangxi Sheng (Chiang-hsi Sheng) [2]	152	Kf	28.00N	116.00 E
Kiangsu (EN) = Chiang-su Sheng → Jiangsu Sheng [2]	152	Ke	33.00N	120.00 E
Kiangsu (EN) = Jiangsu Sheng (Chiang-su Sheng) [2]	152	Ke	33.00N	120.00 E
Kiantajärvi	112	Gd	65.03N	29.07 E
Kiáton	130	Fk	38.01N	22.45 E
Kibali	170	Eb	3.37N	28.34 E
Kibangou	170	Bc	3.27S	12.21 E
Kibartaj/Kybartai	116	Jj	54.38N	22.44 E
Kibasira Swamp	170	Gd	8.20S	36.18 E
Kibau	170	Gd	8.35S	35.17 E
Kibaya	170	Gd	5.18S	36.34 E
Kibbish	168	Fe	4.40N	35.53 E
Kiberg	114	Ha	70.17N	31.00 E
Kibikogen	156	Cd	34.45N	133.15 E
Kiboko	170	Gc	2.15S	37.42 E
Kibombo	170	Ec	3.54S	25.55 E
Kibondo	170	Fc	3.35S	30.42 E
Kibre Mengist	168	Fd	5.58N	39.00 E
Kıbrıs/Kypros = Cyprus (EN) [1]	142	Ff	35.00N	33.00 E
Kıbrıs/Kypros = Cyprus (EN)	140	Ff	35.00N	33.00 E
Kibungo	170	Fc	2.10S	30.32 E
Kibuye	170	Ec	2.03S	29.21 E
Kibwezi	170	Gc	2.25S	37.58 E
Kičevo	130	Dh	41.31N	20.58 E
Kichi Kichi	168	Bb	17.36N	17.19 E
Kicking Horse Pass	180	Ff	51.50N	116.30W
Kidal	160	Hg	18.26N	1.24 E
Kidapawan	150	Ie	7.01N	125.03 E
Kidatu	170	Gd	7.42S	36.57 E
Kidira	166	Cc	14.28N	12.13W
Kidnappers, Cape-	218	Gc	39.38S	177.06 E
Kiekie	221a	Ab	21.53N	160.13W
Kiel	112	He	54.20N	10.08 E
Kiel Canal (EN) = Nord-Ostsee-Kanal	110	Ge	53.53N	9.08 E
Kielce	112	Ie	50.52N	20.37 E
Kielce [2]	120	Qf	50.50N	20.35 E
Kieler Bucht	120	Gb	54.35N	10.35 E
Kienge	170	Ee	10.33S	27.33 E
Kierspe	124	Jc	51.08N	7.35 E
Kieta	210	Ge	6.15S	155.37 E
Kietrz	120	Of	50.05N	18.01 E
Kiev (EN) = Kijev	112	Je	50.26N	30.31 E
Kiev Reservoir (EN) = Kijevskoje vodohranilišče	110	Je	51.00N	30.25 E
Kiffa	160	Fg	16.36N	11.23W
Kifisiá	130	Gk	38.04N	23.49 E
Kifisós	130	Gk	38.26N	23.15 E
Kifrī	146	Ke	34.42N	44.58 E
Kigač	136	Pf	46.28N	49.08 E
Kigali	160	Ki	1.57S	30.04 E
Kiğı	146	Ic	39.19N	40.21 E
Kigille	168	Ed	8.40N	34.02 E
Kigoma	160	Ji	4.52S	29.38 E
Kigoma [3]	170	Fc	4.50S	30.05 E
Kigosi	170	Fc	4.40S	31.27 E
Kihelkonna	116	If	58.20N	21.54 E
Kihniö	116	Jb	62.12N	23.11 E
Kihnu	114	Fg	58.10N	24.00 E
Kiholo	221a	Fd	19.51N	155.55W
Kiholo Bay	221a	Fd	19.52N	155.56W
Kihti/Skiftet	116	Id	60.15N	21.05 E
Kii-Hantō	152	Oe	34.00N	135.45 E
Kiikka	116	Jc	61.20N	22.46 E
Kiil	132	Se	49.27N	54.50 E
Kiiminki	114	Fd	65.08N	25.44 E
Kii-Sanchi	156	Dd	34.15N	135.50 E
Kii-Suido	154	Mh	34.00N	134.55 E
Kija	138	De	56.52N	86.40 E
Kijev = Kiev (EN)	112	Je	50.26N	30.31 E
Kijevka	136	He	50.16N	71.34 E
Kijevskaja oblast [3]	136	De	50.20N	30.45 E
Kijevskoje vodohranilišče = Kiev Reservoir (EN)	110	Je	51.00N	30.25 E
Kijma	136	Ge	51.35N	67.34 E
Kikai-Jima	152	Mf	28.15N	130.00 E
Kikerino	116	Me	59.23N	29.38 E
Kikinda	130	Dd	45.50N	20.29 E
Kikládhes = Cyclades (EN)	110	Ih	37.00N	25.10 E
Kikonai	154	Pd	41.40N	140.26 E
Kikori	210	Fe	7.25S	144.13 E
Kikori River	208	Fe	7.23S	144.16 E
Kikuchi	156	Be	32.59N	130.49 E
Kikuma	156	Cd	34.03N	132.51 E
Kikvidze	132	Md	50.44N	43.03 E
Kikwit	160	Ii	5.02S	18.49 E
Kil [Nor.]	116	Cf	58.52N	9.19 E
Kil [Swe.]	114	Cg	59.30N	13.19 E
Kilafors	114	Df	61.15N	16.33 E
Kilambé, Cerro-	194	Eg	13.34N	85.42W
Kilauea	221a	Ba	22.13N	159.25W
Kilauea Crater	221a	Fd	19.24N	155.17W
Kilauea Point	221a	Ba	22.14N	159.24W
Kilbrannan Sound	118	Hf	55.40N	5.25W
Kilbuck Mountains	178	Hd	60.30N	159.45W
Kilchu	152	Mc	40.58N	129.20 E
Kilcoy	212	Ke	26.57S	152.33 E
Kildare/Cill Dara	118	Gh	53.10N	6.55W
Kildare/Cill Dara [2]	118	Gh	53.15N	6.45W
Kildin, ostrov-	114	Ib	69.20N	34.10 E
Kilembe	170	Cd	5.42S	19.55 E
Kilgore	186	Ij	32.23N	94.53W
Kilgoris	170	Fc	1.00S	34.53 E
Kiliç	130	Mi	40.40N	29.23 E
Kilifi	170	Gc	3.38S	39.51 E
Kili Island	208	Hd	5.39N	169.04 E
Kilija	136	Cf	45.27N	29.14 E
Kilijskoje girlo	130	Md	45.13N	29.43 E
Kilimanjaro [3]	170	Gc	4.00S	37.40 E
Kilimanjaro, Mount-	158	Ki	3.04S	37.22 E
Kilimli	146	Db	41.29N	31.50 E
Kilinailau Islands	214	Fh	4.45S	155.20 E
Kilindoni	160	Ki	7.55S	39.39 E
Kilingi-Nõmme/Kilingi-Nymme	114	Fg	58.08N	24.59 E
Kilingi-Nymme/Kilingi-Nõmme	114	Fg	58.08N	24.59 E
Kilis	146	Gd	36.44N	37.05 E
Kilitbahir	146	Bb	40.12N	26.20 E
Kilkee/Cill Chaoi	118	Di	52.41N	9.38W
Kilkenny/Cill Chainnigh	118	Fi	52.39N	7.15W
Kilkenny/Cill Chainnigh [2]	118	Fi	52.40N	7.20W
Kilkieran Bay	118	Dh	53.15N	9.45W
Kilkis	130	Fi	41.00N	22.52 E
Killala Bay/Cuan Chill Ala	118	Dg	54.15N	9.10W
Killarney/Cill Airne	118	Di	52.03N	9.30W
Killary Harbour/An Caoláire Rua	118	Dh	53.38N	9.55W
Killdeer	186	Ec	47.22N	102.45W
Killeen	182	He	31.08N	97.44W
Killinek	180	Ld	60.25N	64.40W
Killini	130	El	37.56N	21.09 E
Killini Óros	130	Fl	37.55N	22.26 E
Kilmallock/Cill Mocheallóg	118	Ei	52.25N	8.35W
Kilmarnock	118	If	55.37N	4.30W
Kilmez	114	Mh	57.03N	51.24 E
Kilmez	114	Mh	56.58N	50.29 E
Kilmore	212	Ig	37.18S	144.57 E
Kilombero	170	Gd	8.31S	37.22 E
Kilosa	160	Ki	6.50S	36.59 E
Kilpisjärvi	114	Eb	69.03N	20.48 E
Kilp-Javr	114	Hb	69.07N	32.28 E
Kilrush/Cill Rois	118	Di	52.39N	9.29W
Kilsbergen	116	Fe	59.20N	14.45 E
Kiltān Island	148	Ef	11.29N	73.00 E
Kilwa	170	Ed	9.17S	28.20 E
Kilwa Kisiwani	160	Ki	8.58S	39.30 E
Kilwa Kivinje	170	Gd	8.45S	39.24 E
Kilwa Masoko	170	Gd	8.56S	39.31 E
Kilyos → Kumköy	130	Mh	41.15N	29.02 E
Kim	186	Eh	37.15N	103.21W
Kimamba	170	Gd	6.47S	37.08 E
Kimba	212	Hf	33.09S	136.25 E
Kimball [Nb.-U.S.]	186	Ef	41.14N	103.40W
Kimball [S.D.-U.S.]	186	Ge	43.45N	98.57W
Kimball, Mount-	178	Kd	63.14N	144.39W
Kimbe	212	Ka	5.31S	150.12 E
Kimbe Bay	214	Ei	5.30S	150.30 E
Kimberley	208	Df	16.00S	126.00 E
Kimberley [B.C.-Can.]	180	Fg	49.41N	115.59W
Kimberley [S.Afr.]	160	Jk	28.43S	24.46 E
Kimberley Plateau	212	Fc	17.00S	127.00 E
Kimch'aek (Sŏngjin)	152	Mc	40.41N	129.12 E
Kimch'ŏn	152	Md	36.07N	128.07 E
Kimhandu	158	Ki	7.05S	37.35 E
Kimi	130	Hk	38.38N	24.06 E
Kimito/Kemiö	116	Jd	60.10N	22.40 E
Kimje	154	Ih	35.48N	126.53 E
Kimobetsu	156a	Bb	42.47N	140.56 E
Kimolos	130	Hm	36.48N	24.34 E
Kimongo	170	Bc	4.29S	12.58 E
Kimovsk	136	De	54.01N	38.36 E
Kimpu-San	156	Fd	35.52N	138.37 E
Kimry	136	Dd	56.52N	37.24 E
Kimvula	170	Cd	5.44S	15.58 E
Kinabalu, Gunong-	140	Ni	6.05N	116.33 E
Kinabatangan	150	Ge	5.42N	118.23 E
Kinango	170	Gc	4.08S	39.19 E
Kinaros	130	Jm	36.59N	26.17 E
Kincardine	180	Jh	44.11N	81.38W
Kind	116	Eg	57.35N	13.25 E
Kinda	170	Ed	9.18S	25.04 E
Kinda	116	Ff	58.05N	15.40 E
Kindamba	170	Bc	3.44S	14.31 E
Kinder	186	Jk	30.29N	92.51W
Kinder Scout	118	Lh	53.23N	1.52W
Kindersley	180	Gf	51.27N	109.10W
Kindi	166	Ec	12.26N	2.01W
Kindia	160	Fg	10.04N	12.51W
Kindu	160	Ji	2.57S	25.56 E
Kinel	114	Mj	53.14N	50.40 E
Kinesi	170	Fc	1.28S	33.52 E
Kinešma	136	Ed	57.28N	42.16 E
King	219a	Aa	4.24S	152.43 E
King, Cayos-	194	Fg	12.45N	83.20W
Kingaroy	212	Ke	26.33S	151.50 E
King Christian	180	Ha	77.45N	102.00W
King Christian IX Land (EN) = Kong Christian IX Land	224	Mc	68.00N	36.30W
King Christian X Land (EN) = Kong Christian X Land	224	Md	72.20N	32.30W
King City	182	Cd	36.13N	121.08W
King Edward River	212	Fb	14.14S	126.35 E
Kingfisher	186	Hi	35.52N	97.56W
King Frederik VI Coast (EN) = Kong Frederik VI Kyst	224	Nc	63.00N	43.30W
King Frederik VIII Land (EN) = Kong Frederik VIII Land	224	Md	78.30N	28.00W
King George Island	222	Re	62.00S	58.15W
King George Islands	180	Je	57.15N	78.30W
King George Sound	212	Dg	35.10S	118.10 E
Kingisepp	114	Gg	59.23N	28.37 E
Kingisepp/Kingissepp	136	Cd	58.17N	22.29 E
King Island	208	Fh	39.50S	144.00 E
Kingissepp/Kingisepp	136	Cd	58.17N	22.29 E
King Lear Peak	188	Ff	41.12N	118.34W
King Leopold Ranges	212	Fc	17.30S	125.45 E
Kingman [Az.-U.S.]	182	Ed	35.12N	114.04W
Kingman [Ks.-U.S.]	186	Gh	37.39N	98.07W
Kingman Reef	208	Kd	6.19N	162.28W
Kingombe [Zaire]	170	Ec	2.52S	26.35 E
Kingombe [Zaire]	170	Ec	2.35S	26.37 E
Kingoome Inlet	188	Ba	50.49N	126.13W
Kingoonya	210	Eh	30.54S	135.18 E
King Peninsula	222	Of	73.12S	101.00W
Kingsclere	124	Ac	51.19N	1.15W
Kingscote	212	Hg	35.40S	137.38 E
King's Lynn	118	Ni	52.45N	0.24 E
King Sound	208	Df	17.00S	123.30 E
Kings Peak [Ca.-U.S.]	188	Cf	40.10N	124.08W
Kings Peak [U.S.]	174	He	40.46N	110.22W
Kingsport	182	Kd	36.32N	82.33W
Kings River	188	Fh	36.03N	119.49W
Kingston [Jam.]	176	Lh	18.00N	76.50W
Kingston [Nor.I.]	210	Hg	29.04S	167.58 E
Kingston [N.Y.-U.S.]	182	Mc	41.55N	74.00W
Kingston [N.Z.]	216	Ci	45.20S	168.43 E
Kingston [Ont.-Can.]	176	Le	44.14N	76.30W
Kingston Peak	188	Hi	35.42N	115.52W
Kingston South East	210	Eh	36.50S	139.51 E
Kingston upon Hull (Hull)	112	Fe	53.45N	0.20W
Kingston-upon-Thames, London-	118	Mj	51.28N	0.19W
Kingstown	176	Mh	13.09N	61.14W
Kingsville	182	Hf	27.31N	97.52W
Kings Worthy	124	Ac	51.05N	1.18W
Kingussie	118	Id	57.05N	4.04W
King William	174	Jc	69.00N	97.30W
King William's Town	160	Jl	32.51S	27.22 E
Kiniama	170	Ee	11.26S	28.19 E
Kınık	146	Bc	39.05N	27.23 E
Kinkala	170	Bc	4.22S	14.46 E
Kinlochleven	118	Ie	56.43N	4.58W
Kinna	116	Eg	57.30N	12.41 E
Kinnairds Head	118	Ld	57.42N	2.00W
Kinnared	116	Eg	57.02N	13.06 E
Kinnekulle	116	Ef	58.35N	13.23 E
Kinneret, Yam-	146	Ff	32.48N	35.35 E
Kino-Kawa	156	Dd	34.13N	135.08 E
Kinomoto	156	Ed	35.31N	136.13 E
Kinoosao	180	He	57.06N	102.01W
Kinós Kefalaí	130	Fj	39.25N	22.34 E
Kinross	118	Je	56.13N	3.27W
Kinsale / Cionn tSáile	118	Ej	51.42N	8.32W
Kinsale, Old Head of-/An Seancheann	118	Ej	51.36N	8.32W
Kinsangire	170	Gd	7.26S	38.35 E
Kinsarvik	114	Bf	60.23N	6.43 E
Kinshasa [2]	170	Cc	4.00S	16.00 E
Kinshasa (Leopoldville)	160	Ii	4.18S	15.18 E
Kinsley	186	Gh	37.55N	99.25W
Kinston	182	Ld	35.16N	77.35W
Kintampo	166	Ed	8.03N	1.43W
Kintap	150	Gg	3.51S	115.13 E
Kintyre	118	Hf	55.32N	5.35W
Kin-Wan	156b	Ab	26.25N	127.54 E
Kinyan	166	Dc	11.51N	6.01W
Kinyeti	158	Kh	3.57N	32.54 E
Kinzig [Eur.]	120	Dh	48.37N	7.49 E
Kinzig [F.R.G.]	120	Ef	50.08N	8.54 E
Kioa	219d	Bb	16.39S	179.55 E
Kipaka	170	Ec	4.09S	26.30 E
Kiparissia	130	El	37.15N	21.40 E
Kiparissia, Gulf of- (EN) = Kiparissiakós Kólpos	130	El	37.30N	21.25 E
Kiparissiakós Kólpos = Kiparissia, Gulf of- (EN)	130	El	37.30N	21.25 E
Kipawa, Lac-	180	Jg	46.55N	79.00W
Kipembawe	170	Fd	7.39S	33.24 E
Kipengere Range	158	Ki	9.10S	34.15 E
Kiperčeny	130	Lb	47.32N	28.40 E
Kipili	170	Fd	7.26S	30.36 E
Kipini	170	Hc	2.32S	40.31 E
Kipling	186	Ea	50.10N	102.38W
Kippure	118	Gh	53.11N	6.20W
Kiprarenukk, mys- / Undva neem	116	If	58.25N	21.45 E
Kípros = Cyprus (EN)	144	Db	35.01N	33.00 E
Kipushi	170	Ee	11.46S	27.14 E
Kirakira	210	Hf	10.27S	161.56 E
Kiraz	146	Cc	39.21N	27.25 E
Kirazlı	146	Bb	40.01N	26.40 E
Kirbla	116	Jf	58.42N	23.49 E
Kircasalih	130	Jh	41.23N	26.48 E
Kirchberg (Hunsrück)	124	Je	49.57N	7.24 E
Kirchhain	124	Kd	50.49N	8.58 E
Kirchheimbolanden	124	Ke	49.40N	8.01 E
Kirchheim unter Teck	120	Fh	48.39N	9.27 E
Kirchhundem	124	Kc	51.06N	8.06 E
Kirchhundem-Rahrbach	124	Jc	51.02N	7.59 E
Kirchlengern	124	Kb	52.12N	8.38 E
Kirdimi	168	Bb	18.11N	18.38 E
Kireç	130	Lj	39.33N	28.22 E
Kirenga	140	Md	57.47N	107.59 E
Kirensk	142	Md	57.46N	108.08 E
Kirghiz SSR (EN) = Kirgizskaja SSR [2]	136	Hg	41.30N	75.00 E
Kirghiz Steppe (EN)	110	Lf	49.30N	50.30 E
Kirgizskaja Sovetskaja Socialističeskaja Respublika [2]	136	Hg	41.30N	75.00 E
Kirgizskaja SSR/Kyrgyz Sovetik Soi ialistik Respublikasy [2]	136	Hg	41.30N	75.00 E
Kirgizskaja SSR = Kirghiz SSR (EN) [2]	136	Hg	41.30N	75.00 E
Kirgizski hrebet	136	Hg	42.30N	74.00 E
Kiri	170	Cc	1.27S	19.00 E
Kiribati [1]	210	Je	0.01S	174.00W
Kirikhan	146	Gd	36.32N	36.19 E
Kırıkkale	144	Db	39.50N	33.31 E
Kirillov	114	Jg	59.54N	38.27 E
Kirillovskoje	116	Md	60.28N	29.28 E
Kirin (EN) = Chi-lin Sheng → Jilin Sheng [2]	152	Mc	43.00N	126.00 E
Kirin (EN) = Jilin Sheng (Chi-lin Sheng) [2]	152	Mc	43.00N	126.00 E
Kirinyaga/Kenya, Mount-	158	Ki	0.10S	37.20 E
Kirishima-Yama	156	Bf	31.56N	130.52 E
Kiriši	136	Dd	59.27N	32.02 E
Kiritimati Atoll (Christmas)	208	Ld	1.52N	157.20W
Kirja	114	Li	55.05N	46.52 E
Kirkağaç	146	Bc	39.06N	27.40 E
Kirkby Lonsdale	118	Kg	54.13N	2.36W
Kirkcaldy	118	Je	56.07N	3.10W
Kirkcudbright	118	Ig	54.50N	4.03W
Kirkee → Khadki	148	Ee	18.34N	73.52 E
Kirkenær	116	Cf	60.28N	12.03 E
Kirkenes	112	Jb	69.43N	30.03 E
Kirkjubæjarklaustur	114a	Bc	63.47N	18.04W
Kirkkonummi/Kyrkslätt	116	Kd	60.07N	24.26 E
Kirkland	188	Dc	47.41N	122.12W
Kirkland Lake	176	Ke	48.09N	80.02W

Index Symbols

- [1] Independent Nation
- [2] State, Region
- [3] District, County
- [4] Municipality
- [5] Colony, Dependency
- Continent
- Physical Region
- Historical or Cultural Region
- Mount, Mountain
- Volcano
- Hill
- Mountains, Mountain Range
- Hills, Escarpment
- Plateau, Upland
- Pass, Gap
- Plain, Lowland
- Delta
- Salt Flat
- Valley, Canyon
- Crater, Cave
- Karst Features
- Depression
- Polder
- Desert, Dunes
- Forest, Woods
- Heath, Steppe
- Oasis
- Cape, Point
- Coast, Beach
- Cliff
- Peninsula
- Isthmus
- Sandbank
- Island
- Atoll
- Rock, Reef
- Islands, Archipelago
- Rocks, Reefs
- Coral Reef
- Well, Spring
- Geyser
- River, Stream
- Waterfall, Rapids
- River Mouth, Estuary
- Lake
- Salt Lake
- Intermittent Lake
- Reservoir
- Swamp, Pond
- Canal
- Glacier
- Ice Shelf, Pack Ice
- Ocean
- Sea
- Gulf, Bay
- Strait, Fjord
- Lagoon
- Bank
- Seamount
- Tablemount
- Ridge
- Shelf
- Basin
- Escarpment, Sea Scarp
- Fracture
- Trench, Abyss
- National Park, Reserve
- Point of Interest
- Recreation Site
- Cave, Cavern
- Historic Site
- Ruins
- Wall, Walls
- Church, Abbey
- Temple
- Scientific Station
- Railway station
- Airport
- Port
- Military installation
- Lighthouse
- Mine
- Tunnel
- Dam, Bridge

Kırklareli 144 Ca 41.44N 27.12 E
Kirkpatrick, Mount- 222 Kg 84.20 S 166.19 E
Kırkpınar Dağı 146 Fd 37.14N 34.15 E
Kirksville 182 Ic 40.12N 92.35W
Kirkük 142 Gf 35.28N 44.23 E
Kirkwall 118 Kc 58.59N 2.58W
Kirkwood [Mo.-U.S.] 186 Kg 38.35N 90.24W
Kirkwood [S.Afr.] 172 Df 33.22 S 25.15 E
Kırlangıç Burun 146 Dd 36.13N 30.25 E
Kirn 120 Dg 49.47N 7.27 E
Kirobasi 146 Ed 36.43N 33.52 E
Kirov [R.S.F.S.R.] 136 De 54.03N 34.21 E
Kirov [R.S.F.S.R.] 112 Kd 58.33N 49.42 E
Kirova, zaliv- 132 Pj 39.05N 49.05 E
Kirovabad 112 Kg 40.40N 46.22 E
Kirovakan 136 Eg 40.48N 44.28 E
Kirovgrad 134 Jh 57.26N 60.04 E
Kirovo 135 Hd 40.28N 70.34 E
Kirovo-Čepeck 136 Fd 58.35N 50.03 E
Kirovograd 112 Jf 48.30N 32.18 E
Kirovogradskaja oblast ③ 136 Df 48.20N 31.50 E
Kirovsk [R.S.F.S.R.] 136 Db 67.37N 33.37 E
Kirovsk [R.S.F.S.R.] 114 Hg 59.53N 31.01 E
Kirovsk [Tur.-U.S.S.R.] 135 Cf 37.43N 60.24 E
Kirovskaja oblast ③ 136 Ed 58.30N 50.00 E
Kirovski [Kaz.-U.S.S.R.] 136 Hg 44.53N 78.12 E
Kirovski [R.S.F.S.R.] 132 Pg 45.48N 48.08 E
Kirovski [R.S.F.S.R.] 138 Kf 54.25N 155.37 E
Kirovski [R.S.F.S.R.] 138 Kf 54.26N 127.00 E
Kirovski [R.S.F.S.R.] 138 Ig 45.05N 133.27 E
Kirovskoje 135 Hc 42.39N 71.35 E
Kirpilski liman 132 Kg 45.50N 38.05 E
Kirriemuir 118 Je 56.41N 3.01W
Kirs 136 Fd 59.21N 52.18 E
Kirsanov 132 Mc 52.41N 42.45 E
Kırşehir 144 Dd 39.09N 34.10 E
Kırthar Range 140 Ig 27.00N 67.20 E
Kirton 124 Bb 52.55N 0.03W
Kiruna 112 Ib 67.51N 20.13 E
Kirundu 170 Ec 0.44 S 25.32 E
Kiryū 156 Fc 36.25N 139.20 E
Kiržač 114 Jh 56.11N 38.53 E
Kisa 114 Dh 57.59N 15.37 E
Kisabi 170 Ed 8.03 S 29.11 E
Kisač 130 Cd 45.21N 19.44 E
Kisakata 156 Fb 39.14N 139.54 E
Kisaki 170 Gd 7.28 S 37.36 E
Kisalföld 120 Mi 47.30N 17.00 E
Kisangani 160 Jh 0.25N 25.12 E
Kisarazu 156 Fd 35.23N 139.55 E
Kisbér 120 Oi 47.30N 18.02 E
Kiselevsk 138 Df 54.03N 86.49 E
Kiserawe 170 Gd 6.54 S 39.05 E
Kishangarh 148 Ec 26.34N 74.52 E
Kishb, Harraṭ al- 164 He 22.47N 41.30 E
Kishi 166 Fd 9.05N 3.51 E
Kishiwada 154 Mg 34.28N 135.22 E
Kisii 170 Fc 0.41 S 34.46 E
Kisiju 170 Gd 7.24 S 39.20 E
Kišinev 112 If 46.59N 28.52 E
Kısır Dağı 146 Jb 40.58N 43.04 E
Kiska 178a Bb 52.00N 177.30 E
Kiska Volcano 178a Bb 52.07N 177.36 E
Kiskőrei Víztároló 120 Qi 47.44N 20.40 E
Kiskőrös 120 Pj 46.37N 19.18 E
Kiskunfélegyháza 120 Pj 46.33N 19.51 E
Kiskunhalas 120 Pj 46.26N 19.30 E
Kiskunmajsa 120 Pj 46.29N 19.45 E
Kiskunság 120 Pj 46.35N 19.15 E
Kislovodsk 136 Eg 43.54N 42.42 E
Kismanyo 160 Li 0.22 S 42.32 E
Kisofukushima 156 Ed 35.51N 137.41 E
Kiso-Gawa 154 Ng 35.05N 136.45 E
Kisoro 170 Ec 1.17 S 29.41 E
Kiso-Sanmyaku 156 Ed 35.45N 137.45 E
Kisria, Daiet el- 126 Oi 35.44N 2.47 E
Kissámou, Kólpos- 130 Gn 35.35N 23.40 E
Kissidougou 166 Cd 9.11N 10.06W
Kissimmee 184 Gk 28.18N 81.24W
Kissimmee, Lake- 184 Gl 27.55N 81.16W
Kissü, Jabal- 168 Da 21.35N 25.09 E
Kistelek 120 Pj 46.28N 19.59 E
Kisterenye 120 Ph 48.01N 19.50 E
Kisújszállás 120 Qi 47.13N 20.46 E
Kisuki 156 Cd 35.17N 132.54 E
Kisumu 160 Ki 0.06 S 34.45 E
Kisvárda 120 Sh 48.13N 22.05 E
Kita 160 Gg 13.03N 9.30W
Kitab 136 Jh 39.08N 66.54 E
Kita-Daitō-Jima 152 Nf 25.55N 131.20 E
Kitaibaraki 156 Pf 36.48N 140.45 E
Kita-Iō-Jima 214 Cb 25.26N 141.17 E
Kitaj, ozero- 130 Md 45.35N 29.15 E
Kitakami 156 Pg 39.30N 141.10 E
Kitakami-Gawa 156 Gb 38.25N 141.19 E
Kitakami-Sanchi 156 Gb 39.30N 141.30 E
Kitakata 154 Of 37.39N 139.52 E
Kitakyushu 156 Pf 33.53N 130.50 E
Kitale 160 Kh 1.01N 35.00 E
Kitami 152 Pc 43.48N 143.54 E
Kitamiaioi 156a Cb 43.43N 143.57 E
Kitami-Fuji 156a Cb 43.42N 143.14 E
Kitami-Sanchi 152 Qb 44.30N 142.30 E
Kitami Tōge 156a Cb 43.55N 142.55 E
Kitan-Kaikyō 156 Dd 34.15N 135.00 E
Kita-Taiheyō = Pacific Ocean (EN) 214 Ch 22.00N 179.00 E
Kita-Ura 156 Gc 36.00N 140.34 E
Kit Carson 186 Gc 38.46N 102.48W
Kitchener 180 Jh 43.27N 80.29W
Kitee 114 He 62.06N 30.09 E
Kitessa 168 Dd 5.22N 25.22 E
Kitgum 170 Fb 3.19N 32.53 E
Kithira = Cythera (EN) 130 Fm 36.09N 23.00 E
Kithira = Kythera (EN) 130 Ih 36.15N 23.00 E
Kithira Channel (EN) = Kithiron, Dhiékplous- 130 Fm 36.00N 23.00 E

Kithiron, Dhiékplous- = Kithira Channel (EN) 130 Fm 36.00N 23.00 E
Kithnos 130 Hl 37.25N 24.26 E
Kithnos 130 Hl 37.23N 24.25 E
Kithnou, Stenón- 130 Hl 37.25N 24.30 E
Kitimat 176 Gd 54.05N 128.38W
Kitimat Ranges 180 Ef 53.58N 128.39W
Kitoushi-Yama 156a Cb 43.27N 143.25 E
Kitriani 130 Hm 36.54N 24.44 E
Kitridge Point 197q Bb 13.09N 59.25W
Kitros 130 Fi 40.22N 22.35 E
Kitsuki 156 Be 33.25N 131.37 E
Kittanning 184 He 40.49N 79.31W
Kittery 184 Ld 43.05N 70.45W
Kittilä 114 Fc 67.40N 24.54 E
Kitui 160 Ki 1.22 S 38.01 E
Kitunda 170 Fd 6.48 S 33.13 E
Kitutu 170 Ec 3.17 S 28.05 E
Kitwe-Nkana 160 Jj 12.49 S 28.13 E
Kitzbühel 128 Gc 47.27N 12.23 E
Kitzbüheler Alpen 128 Gc 47.20N 12.20 E
Kitzingen 120 Gg 49.44N 10.10 E
Kiunga [Kenya] 170 Hc 1.45 S 41.29 E
Kiunga [Pap.N.Gui.] 214 Ci 6.07 S 141.18 E
Kiuruvesi 114 Ge 63.39N 26.37 E
Kivalina 178 Gc 67.59N 164.33W
Kivercy 132 Dd 50.50N 25.31 E
Kiviõli/Kiviyli 114 Fe 63.10N 25.09 E
Kiviyli/Kiviõli 116 Ld 60.55N 27.40 E
Kivik 114 Di 55.41N 14.15 E
Kivu, Lac- = Kivu, Lake- (EN) 170 Ec 2.30 S 27.30 E
Kivu, Lake- (EN) = Kivu, Lac-
Kiwai Island 214 Ci 8.30 S 143.25 E
Kıyıkamaki Dāgh 146 Kc 38.47N 45.51 E
Kiyıköy 146 Cb 41.25N 28.01 E
Kiyosato 156a Db 43.51N 144.35 E
Kizel 136 Fd 59.03N 57.40 E
Kizema 114 Kf 61.09N 44.46 E
Kizilcabölük 130 Ml 37.37N 29.01 E
Kızılca Dağı 146 Cd 36.55N 29.52 E
Kızılcahaman 146 Dc 40.28N 32.39 E
Kızıl Dağ 146 Ed 36.25N 32.42 E
Kizilhisar 130 Ml 37.33N 29.18 E
Kızılırmak 146 Ed 40.22N 33.59 E
Kızılırmak 140 Fe 41.45N 35.59 E
KizilJurt 132 Oh 43.13N 46.55 E
Kizilskoje 134 Ij 52.44N 58.54 E
Kızıltepe 146 Id 37.12N 40.36 E
Kizimen, vulkan- 138 Le 55.03N 160.27 E
Kizinga 138 Ef 51.51N 109.55 E
Kizir 138 Ef 54.10N 93.30 E
Kizljar 138 Eg 43.50N 46.42 E
Kizljarski zaliv 132 Og 44.35N 46.55 E
Kizukuri 156a Bc 40.48N 140.22 E
Kizyl-Arvat 136 Fh 38.00N 56.20 E
Kizyl-Atrek 136 Fh 37.38N 54.47 E
Kizyl-Su 136 Fh 39.46N 53.01 E
Kjahta 138 Ff 50.26N 106.25 E
Kjalvaz 132 Pj 38.38N 48.20 E
Kjardla/Kärdla 114 Fg 59.01N 22.42 E
Kjarevere/Kärevere 116 Lf 58.23N 26.30 E
Kjarla/Kärla 116 Jf 58.16N 22.05 E
Kjellerup 124 Ch 56.17N 9.26 E
Kjøllefjord 114 Ga 70.56N 27.27 E
Kjølur 114a Bb 64.50N 19.25W
Kløpsvik 114 Db 68.06N 16.21 E
Kjubjume 138 Jd 63.28N 140.30 E
Kjurdamir 136 Eg 40.20N 48.07 E
Kjusjur 138 Hb 70.35N 127.45 E
Kjustendil 130 Fg 42.17N 22.41 E
Kjustendil ② 130 Fg 42.17N 22.41 E
Kjyosumi-Yama 156 Gd 35.10N 140.09 E
Klabat, Gunung- 150 If 1.28N 125.02 E
Kladanj 130 Cd 44.14N 18.42 E
Kladno 120 Kf 50.09N 14.07 E
Kladovo 130 Ee 44.37N 22.37 E
Klagenfurt 112 He 46.38N 14.18 E
Klaipeda/Klajpeda 112 Id 55.43N 21.07 E
Klajpeda/Klaipeda 112 Id 55.43N 21.07 E
Klamath 188 Cf 41.32N 124.02W
Klamath Falls 176 Ke 42.13N 121.46W
Klamath Mountains 182 Cc 41.40N 123.20W
Klamath River 188 Cf 41.33N 124.04W
Klamono 150 Jg 1.08 S 131.30 E
Klaralven 114 Hf 59.23N 13.32 E
Klaten 150 Fh 7.42 S 110.35 E
Klatovy 120 Jg 49.24N 13.19 E
Klawer 172 Bf 31.44 S 18.36 E
Klazienaveen, Emmen- 120 Ec 52.44N 7.01 E
Kleck 132 Ec 53.03N 26.40 E
Klecko 120 Nd 52.38N 17.26 E
Kleinblittersdorf 124 Je 49.09N 7.02 E
Kleine Nete 124 Gc 51.08N 4.34 E
Kleine Sluis, Anna Paulowna- 124 Gb 52.52N 4.52 E
Klein-Karoo = Little Karroo (EN) 172 Cf 33.42 S 21.20 E
Klerksdorp 172 Cf 26.58 S 26.39 E
Kletnja 136 De 53.27N 33.17 E
Kletski 132 Ne 49.19N 43.04 E
Kleve 120 De 51.47N 6.09 E
Klibreck, Ben- 118 Ic 58.15N 4.30W
Klička 138 Gf 50.24N 118.01 E
Klimovići 136 De 53.37N 32.01 E
Klimovo 132 Hc 52.23N 32.16 E
Klin 136 Dd 56.20N 36.42 E
Klina 130 Dg 42.37N 20.35 E
Klincy 136 De 52.46N 32.17 E

Klingbach 124 Ke 49.11N 8.24 E
Klingenthal 120 If 50.22N 12.28 E
Klinovec 120 If 50.24N 12.58 E
Klintehamn 114 Eh 57.24N 18.12 E
Klippan 116 Fe 56.08N 13.06 E
Klipplaat 172 Cf 33.02 S 24.21 E
Kliševcy 130 Aa 48.23N 26.13 E
Klisura 130 Hg 42.42N 24.27 E
Klitmøller 116 Cg 57.02N 8.31 E
Kljazma 116 Kd 56.10N 42.58 E
Ključevskaja Sopka, vulkan- 140 Sd 56.04N 160.38 E
Kljuci 138 Le 56.14N 160.58 E
Klobuck 120 Of 50.55N 18.57 E
Klodawa 120 Of 52.16N 18.55 E
Kłodzka, Kotlina- 120 Mf 50.30N 16.35 E
Kłodzko 120 Mf 50.28N 16.40 E
Kløfta 116 Dd 60.04N 11.09 E
Kłomnice 120 Pf 50.56N 19.21 E
Klondike Plateau 180 Dd 63.10N 139.55W
Klondike River 180 Dd 64.03N 139.26W
Klooga/Kloga 116 Ke 59.24N 24.10 E
Kloosteezande, Hontenisse- 124 Gc 51.23N 4.00 E
Klosi 130 Dh 41.29N 20.06 E
Klosterneuburg 128 Kb 48.18N 16.19 E
Klosters / Claustra 128 Eb 46.52N 9.52 E
Kloten 128 Cc 47.27N 8.35 E
Klotz, Lac- 180 Kd 60.40N 73.00W
Kluane Lake 180 Dd 61.15N 138.40W
Kluczbork 120 Of 50.59N 18.13 E
Knaben 116 Bf 58.39N 7.04 E
Knäred 116 Eh 56.32N 13.19 E
Knared 184 Hf 43.30N 24.05 E
Knife River 186 Fc 47.20N 101.23W
Knin 128 Kf 44.02N 16.12 E
Knislinge 116 Fh 56.11N 14.05 E
Knittelfeld 128 Ic 47.13N 14.49 E
Knivskjellodden 114 Fa 71.11N 25.40 E
Knivsta 116 Ge 59.43N 17.48 E
Knjaževac 130 Ff 43.34N 22.15 E
Knobly Mountain 184 Hf 39.15N 79.05W
Knockmealdown Mountains/ Cnoc Mhaoldonn 118 Fi 52.15N 8.00W
Knokke-Heist 122 Jc 51.21N 3.15 E
Knokke-Westkapelle 124 Fc 51.19N 3.18 E
Knolls grund 116 Gg 57.30N 17.30 E
Knøsen 116 Bd 62.30N 10.18 E
Knosós = Cnossus (EN) 130 In 35.18N 25.10 E
Knox, Cape - 180 Ef 54.11N 133.05W
Knox Coast 222 Ne 66.30 S 105.00 E
Knoxville [Ia.-U.S.] 186 Jf 41.19N 93.06W
Knoxville [Tn.-U.S.] 176 Kf 35.58N 83.56W
Knud Rasmussen Land 224 Nd 80.00N 55.00W
Knüllgebirge 120 Ff 50.50N 9.30 E
Knutsholstind 116 Cc 61.26N 8.34 E
Knysna 160 Jl 34.02 S 23.02 E
Koartac 148 Kd 60.50N 69.30W
Koba 150 Eg 2.29 S 106.24 E
Koba, Pulau- 150 Jh 6.25 S 134.28 E
Kobar Sink 168 Gc 14.00N 40.30 E
Kobayashi 154 Kj 31.59N 130.59 E
Kobdo 142 Le 48.01N 91.38 E
Kobdo (Chvod) 152 Pb 48.06N 92.11 E
Kōbe 142 Pf 34.41N 135.10 E
Kobeljaki 132 Ie 49.08N 34.12 E
Kobenhavn ② 116 Ei 55.40N 12.10 E
København = Copenhagen (EN) 112 Hi 55.40N 12.35 E
Kobenni 150 Ff 15.55N 9.05W
Kobern-Gondorf 124 Jd 50.19N 7.28 E
Kobjaj 138 Hd 63.30N 126.26 E
Koblenz 120 Df 50.21N 7.36 E
Kobo 168 Fc 12.09N 39.39 E
Koboldo 138 Jf 52.58N 132.42 E
Kobra 114 Mg 59.10N 50.54 E
Kobrin 136 Ce 52.13N 24.23 E
Kobrinskoje 116 Ne 59.22N 30.14 E
Kobroor, Pulau- 150 Jh 6.12 S 134.32 E
Kobuk 174 Cc 66.45N 161.00W
Kobuleti 132 Li 41.49N 41.45 E
Koca 146 Eb 41.41N 32.15 E
Kocabaş 146 Bb 40.08N 27.57 E
Koca Çay 146 Cd 36.17N 29.16 E
Koca Çay [Tur.] 130 Lj 38.43N 28.30 E
Koca Çay [Tur.] 130 Lj 39.56N 28.32 E
Koca Çay/Orhaneli 146 Cc 40.13N 28.58 E
Kočani 130 Kl 41.55N 22.25 E
Koçarli 130 Kl 37.45N 27.42 E
Kocasu 130 Mj 39.42N 29.31 E
Kočečum 138 Ee 64.17N 100.10 E
Kočetovka 132 Lc 53.01N 40.31 E
Kočevje 128 Je 45.39N 14.51 E
Kočevski Rog 128 Je 45.41N 15.00 E
Koch'ang 156 Jc 35.41N 127.55 E
Ko Chang 148 Kf 12.00N 102.23 E
Koch Bihār 148 Hc 26.19N 89.26 E
Kochi 152 Nf 33.33N 133.33 E
Kōchi Ken ② 154 Lh 33.20N 133.30 E
Kōchisar Ovası 146 Se 51.39N 33.27 E
Kock 120 Se 51.39N 22.27 E
Kočkorka 138 De 42.11N 75.45 E
Kočmar 130 Kf 43.41N 27.28 E
Koçubeyi 136 Eg 44.23N 46.31 E
Koçubejevskoje 128 Kf 44.26N 16.31 E
Kodiak 166 Dc 11.40N 5.40W
Kodiak 174 Df 58.46N 153.23W
Kodino 114 Je 63.06N 39.40 E
Kodomari 156a Bc 41.08N 140.18 E
Kodok 168 Ed 9.53N 32.07 E
Kodry 128 Jg 45.11N 10.18 E
Kodža Balkan 130 Jf 42.50N 27.00 E
Koekenaap 172 Bf 31.29 S 18.19 E
Koes 172 Bc 25.59 S 19.08 E
Kofa Mountains 188 Ij 33.20N 114.00W
Kofçaz 146 Bb 41.58N 27.12 E

Koffiefontein 172 Ce 29.30 S 25.00 E
Kofiau, Pulau- 150 Ig 1.11 S 129.50 E
Köflach 128 Jc 47.04N 15.05 E
Koforidua 160 Gh 6.05N 0.15W
Köfu [Jap.] 156 Fc 35.18N 138.33 E
Kōfu [Jap.] 152 Od 35.39N 138.35 E
Koga 156 Fc 36.12N 139.42 E
Kogaluc 180 Je 59.38N 77.30W
Koganei 156 Dd 35.24N 134.15 E
Køge 114 Ci 55.27N 12.11 E
Køge Bugt 116 Ei 55.30N 12.20 E
Kogel 134 He 62.38N 57.07 E
Kogilnik (Kunduk) 130 Md 45.51N 29.38 E
Kogon 166 Cc 11.09N 14.42W
Kogota 156 Gb 38.32N 141.01 E
Kohala Mountains 221a Fc 20.05N 155.43W
Kohāt 148 Eb 33.35N 71.26 E
Kohila 116 Ke 59.11N 24.46 E
Kohima 148 Ic 25.40N 94.07 E
Koh-i Mārān 148 Dc 29.05N 66.50 E
Kohinggo 219a Ec 8.13 S 157.10 E
Kohma 114 Jh 56.57N 41.07 E
Kohtla-Järve/Kohtla-Järve 136 Cd 59.25N 27.14 E
Kohtla-Järve/Kohtla-Järve 136 Cd 59.25N 27.14 E
Kohu Daği 130 Mm 36.30N 29.50 E
Kohunlich 192 Oh 18.30N 88.55W
Koide 156 Fc 37.14N 138.57 E
Koigi/Kojgi 116 Kf 58.49N 73.49 E
Koin 166 Ee 6.30N 51.15 E
Koindu 166 Cd 8.28N 10.20W
Koitere 114 He 62.58N 30.45 E
Kojā 144 Jh 25.34N 61.13 E
Kojandytau 135 Lb 44.20N 78.45 E
Kojda 114 Kc 66.23N 42.31 E
Koje-Do 156 Jc 34.52N 128.37 E
Kojetin 120 Ng 49.21N 17.20 E
Koigi/Kojgi 116 Kf 58.49N 25.40 E
Ko-Jima [Jap.] 156 Ea 33.07N 139.40 E
Ko-Jima [Jap.] 154 Od 41.22N 139.47 E
Kojō 156 Md 38.57N 127.52 E
Kojonup 212 Df 33.50 S 117.09 E
Kojtaš 135 If 37.29N 67.22 E
Kojtezek, pereval- 135 If 37.29N 72.45 E
Kojur 146 Mc 36.23N 51.43 E
Kojva 134 Ig 58.15N 58.14 E
Kokai-Gawa 168 Cc 10.03N 22.04 E
Kokand 142 Ie 40.33N 70.57 E
Kōkar 114 Eg 59.55N 20.55 E
Kōkarsfjärden 116 Ie 59.55N 20.45 E
Kokas 150 Jg 2.42 S 132.26 E
Kokava nad Rimavicou 120 Ph 48.34N 19.50 E
Kokčetav 156 Dd 34.17N 135.26 E
Kokčetavskaja oblast ③ 136 Ne 53.30N 70.00 E
Kokemäenjoki 116 Ic 61.33N 21.42 E
Kokemäki/Kumo 116 If 61.15N 22.21 E
Kok-Jangak 136 Hg 40.59N 73.15 E
Kokkina 156 Ee 35.10N 32.36 E
Kokkola/Gamlakarleby 112 Ic 63.50N 23.07 E
Koko [Eth.] 168 Fc 10.20N 36.04 E
Koko [Nig.] 166 Fc 11.26N 4.30 E
Kokomo 182 Jf 40.29N 86.08W
Kokonau 150 Kg 4.43 S 136.26 E
Kokong 172 Cd 24.27 S 23.03 E
Koko Nor (EN) = Qinghai Hu 140 Mf 37.00N 100.20 E
Kokpekty 136 If 48.45N 82.24 E
Koksaal-Tau, hrebet- 136 Hg 41.00N 78.00 E
Kökşenga 114 Kf 61.27N 42.38 E
Koksijde 124 Ec 51.06N 2.39 E
Koksoak 180 Ke 58.31N 68.11W
Kokstad 160 Jl 30.32 S 29.29 E
Koktal 142 Ke 44.05N 79.44 E
Koktokay/Fuyun 142 Ke 47.13N 89.39 E
Kokubu 154 Kj 31.44N 130.46 E
Kola 136 Db 68.53N 33.01 E
Kola, Pulau- 150 Jh 5.30 S 134.35 E
Kolahun 166 Cd 8.17N 10.05W
Kolaka 150 Gg 4.03 S 121.36 E
Kolamadulu Atoll 148a Bb 2.25N 73.10 E
Kola Peninsula (EN) = Kolski poluostrov
Kolār Gold Fields 148 Ff 12.55N 78.17 E
Kolari 114 Fc 67.20N 23.48 E
Kolárovo 120 Ni 47.55N 18.00 E
Kolback 116 Ge 59.34N 16.15 E
Kolbäcksån 116 Ge 59.34N 16.16 E
Kolbio 170 Hc 1.09 S 41.12 E
Kolbuszowa 120 Rf 50.15N 21.47 E
Kolby 116 Di 55.48N 10.33 E
Kolčugino 114 Jh 56.16N 39.23 E
Kolda 160 Gg 12.53N 14.57W
Kolding 112 Gd 55.31N 9.29 E
Kole [Zaire] 170 Dc 3.28 S 16.55 E
Kole [Zaire] 170 Ec 2.07 S 25.26 E
Koléa 126 Oh 36.38N 2.46 E
Kolendo 138 Jf 53.43N 142.57 E
Kolente 166 Cd 9.25N 13.08W
Kolesnoje 130 Mc 46.04N 29.45 E
Kolga 116 Ke 59.28N 25.29 E
Kolga, zaliv-/Kolga laht 116 Ke 59.35N 25.15 E
Kolga laht/Kolga, zaliv- 116 Ke 59.30N 25.15 E
Kolguev, ostrov- 110 Me 69.05N 49.15 E
Kolhapur 142 Hg 16.42N 74.13 E
Kolhozabad 135 If 37.35N 68.33 E
Kolhozbentskoje, vodohranilišče- 135 Df 37.10N 62.30 E
Koli 114 Kc 63.06N 29.53 E
Kolimbiné 166 Ce 14.45N 11.00 E
Kolin 120 Lf 50.02N 15.13 E
Kolino 168 Fd 9.53N 32.07 E
Koljučinskaja guba 138 Nc 66.50N 174.30W
Kolka 116 Jg 57.44N 22.27 E
Kolkasrags 114 Fh 57.46N 22.37 E
Kolki 130 Dl 51.07N 25.42 E
Kollinai 130 Fl 37.17N 22.22 E

Kollumüli 114a Cb 65.47N 14.21W
Kolmården 116 Gf 58.41N 16.35 E
Köln = Cologne (EN) 112 Ge 50.56N 6.57 E
Köln-Lövenich 124 Id 50.57N 6.50 E
Kolno 120 Rc 53.25N 21.56 E
Köln-Porz 120 Df 50.53N 7.03 E
Koło 120 Od 52.12N 18.38 E
Koloa 221a Bb 21.54N 159.28W
Kołobrzeg 112 Lb 54.12N 15.33 E
Kolodnja 132 Hb 54.49N 32.11 E
Kologriv 114 Kg 58.51N 44.17 E
Kolokani 116 Dc 13.34N 8.03W
Koloko 166 Dc 11.05N 5.19W
Kolokolkova guba 134 Fb 68.30N 52.30 E
Kololo 168 Gd 7.27N 41.59 E
Kolombangara Island 214 Fi 8.00 S 157.05 E
Kolomna 136 De 55.05N 38.49 E
Kolomyja 136 Cf 48.32N 25.01 E
Kolondiéba 166 Dc 11.06N 6.53W
Kolonga 221b Ac 21.08 S 175.04W
Kolonodale 150 Hg 2.00 S 121.19 E
Kolosovka 136 Ne 56.28N 73.36 E
Kolossa 166 Dc 13.52N 7.35W
Kolovai 221b Ac 21.06 S 175.20W
Kolozero, ozero- 114 Hb 68.15N 33.15 E
Kolp 116 Je 59.20N 36.50 E
Kolpaševo 142 Kd 58.20N 82.50 E
Kolpino 114 Ng 59.45N 30.33 E
Kolpny 132 Kc 52.16N 37.00 E
Kolski poluostrov = Kola Peninsula (EN) 110 Jb 67.30N 37.00 E
Koltubanovski 132 Re 52.57N 52.02 E
Kolubara 130 Dd 44.40N 20.15 E
Koluszki 120 Pe 51.44N 19.49 E
Koluton 136 Ge 51.42N 69.25 E
Kolva [R.S.F.S.R.] 134 Hf 60.22N 56.33 E
Kolva [R.S.F.S.R.] 136 Fb 65.55N 57.20 E
Kolvickoje, ozero- 114 Hc 67.05N 33.30 E
Kölvrå 116 Ch 56.18N 9.08 E
Kolwezi 160 Jj 10.43 S 25.28 E
Kolyma 140 Sc 69.30N 161.00 E
Kolyma Plain (EN) = Kolymskaja nizmennost 140 Rc 68.30N 154.00 E
Kolyma Range (EN) = Kolymskoje nagorje 140 Rc 62.30N 155.00 E
Kolymskaja nizmennost = Kolyma Plain (EN) 140 Rc 68.30N 154.00 E
Kolymskoje nagorje = Kolyma Range (EN) 140 Rc 62.30N 155.00 E
Kolyšlej 132 Nc 52.40N 44.31 E
Kolžat 136 Jg 43.29N 80.37 E
Kom 170 Gb 1.05N 38.02 E
Kom 130 Gf 43.10N 23.03 E
Komádi 120 Rj 47.00N 21.30 E
Komadugu Gana 166 Hc 13.05N 12.24 E
Komadugu Yobe 158 Ig 13.42N 13.24 E
Komagane 156 Ed 35.43N 137.54 E
Koma-ga-Take [Jap.] 156 Fc 35.53N 138.13 E
Koma-ga-Take [Jap.] 156 Gb 39.47N 140.50 E
Koma-ga-Take [Jap.] 156a Bb 42.04N 140.40 E
Komandorski Islands (EN) = Komandorskije ostrova- 140 Sd 55.00N 167.00 E
Komandorskije ostrova = Komandorski Islands (EN) 140 Sd 55.00N 167.00 E
Komandorskije Basin (EN) 140 Sd 55.00N 167.00 E
Komarin 138 Le 57.00N 168.00 E
Komárno 132 Gc 51.27N 30.32 E
Komárom 120 Oi 47.46N 18.09 E
Komárom ② 120 Oi 47.44N 18.07 E
Komárom ② 120 Oi 48.15N 18.15 E
Komatipoort 172 Ee 25.25 S 31.55 E
Komatsu 152 Od 36.24N 136.37 E
Komatsujima 154 Mh 34.01N 134.35 E
Komba, Pulau- 150 Hh 7.47 S 123.35 E
Kombissiri 166 Ec 12.04N 1.20W
Kombolcha 168 Fc 11.05N 39.45 E
Komebail Lagoon 220a Ac 7.24N 134.27 E
Komen/Comines 124 Ec 50.46N 2.59 E
Komi ASSR ③ 110 Kc 64.00N 55.00 E
Komi-Permjacki nacionalny okrug ③ 136 Fd 60.00N 54.30 E
Komló 120 Oj 46.12N 18.16 E
Kommunarsk 136 Jf 48.27N 38.52 E
Kommunary 116 Ne 60.55N 30.10 E
Kommunizma, pik- = Communism Peak (EN) 142 Jf 38.57N 72.08 E
Komodo, Pulau- 150 Hh 8.36 S 119.30 E
Komoé 166 Ee 10.25N 4.20W
Komono 170 Bc 5.12N 3.44W
Komono 158 De 3.15 S 13.14 E
Komoran, Pulau- 150 Kh 8.18 S 138.45 E
Komoro 156 Fc 36.19N 138.24 E
Komotini 130 Ih 41.07N 25.24 E
Komovi 130 Ih 42.41N 19.39 E
Kompasberg 158 Jl 31.46 S 24.32 E
Komrat 132 Ff 46.17N 28.38 E
Komsa 138 Ee 61.40N 89.25 E
Komsomolec 134 Kj 53.45N 62.02 E
Komsomolec, ostrov- 140 Ma 80.00N 95.00 E
Komsomolec, zaliv- 132 Pg 46.30N 52.45 E
Komsomol [R.S.F.S.R.] 136 Me 57.25N 86.02 E
Komsomol [Kaz.-U.S.S.R.] 136 Gf 53.44N 62.02 E
Komsomolsk [R.S.F.S.R.] 114 Ki 54.27N 45.45 E
Komsomolsk [R.S.F.S.R.] 132 Kf 61.20N 63.15 E
Komsomolsk [R.S.F.S.R.] 138 Mc 69.12N 172.55 E
Komsomolsk-na-Amure 138 Jf 50.36N 137.02 E
Komsomolskoje [Ukr.-U.S.S.R.] 132 Je 49.36N 36.33 E
Komsomolskoje [Ukr.-U.S.S.R.] 132 Kf 47.37N 38.05 E

Index Symbols

① Independent Nation	Historical or Cultural Region
② State, Region	Mount, Mountain
③ District, County	Volcano
④ Municipality	Hill
⑤ Colony, Dependency	Mountains, Mountain Range
Continent	Hills, Escarpment
Physical Region	Plateau, Upland

Pass, Gap	Depression
Plain, Lowland	Polder
Delta	Desert, Dunes
Salt Flat	Forest, Woods
Valley, Canyon	Heath, Steppe
Crater, Cave	Oasis
Karst Features	Cape, Point

Coast, Beach	Rock, Reef
Cliff	Islands, Archipelago
Peninsula	Rocks, Reefs
Isthmus	Coral Reef
Sandbank	Well, Spring
Island	Geyser
Atoll	River, Stream

Waterfall, Rapids	Canal
River Mouth, Estuary	Glacier
Lake	Ice Shelf, Pack Ice
Salt Lake	Ocean
Intermittent Lake	Sea
Reservoir	Gulf, Bay
Swamp, Pond	Strait, Fjord

Lagoon	Escarpment, Sea Scarp
Bank	Fracture
Seamount	Trench, Abyss
Tablemount	National Park, Reserve
Ridge	Point of Interest
Shelf	Recreation Site
Basin	Cave, Cavern

Historic Site	Airport
Ruins	Port
Wall, Walls	Military installation
Church, Abbey	Lighthouse
Temple	Mine
Scientific Station	Tunnel
Railway station	Dam, Bridge

Komsomolskoj Pravdy, ostrova- 138 Fa 77.15N 107.30 E
Kömün-Do 154 Ig 34.02N 127.19 E
Kömür Burun 130 Jk 38.39N 26.25 E
Komusan 152 Mc 42.07N 129.42 E
Kona 166 Ec 14.57N 3.53W
Kona Coast 221a Fd 19.35N 155.56W
Konakovo 136 Dd 56.42N 36.46 E
Konar 144 Lc 34.25N 70.32 E
Konārak 148 Hh 19.54N 86.07 E
Konarha [3] 144 Lb 35.15N 71.00 E
Konda 136 Gc 60.40N 69.46 E
Kondagaon 148 Ge 19.36N 81.40 E
Kondinin 212 Df 32.30S 118.16 E
Kondinskoje 134 Mg 59.40N 67.25 E
Kondoa 160 Ki 4.54S 35.47 E
Kondopoga 112 Jc 62.13N 34.17 E
Kondratjevo 116 Md 60.36N 28.02 E
Kondrovo 136 De 54.49N 35.55 E
Kondurča 114 Mj 53.31N 50.24 E
Koné 216 Bd 21.04S 164.52 E
Konečnaja 136 He 50.45N 78.27 E
Konevic, ostrov- 116 Nd 60.50N 30.45 E
Kong 166 Ed 9.09N 4.37W
Kōng 148 Lf 13.32N 105.58 E
Kōng, Kaôh- 148 Kf 11.20N 103.00 E
Konga/Koonga 116 Jf 58.34N 24.00 E
Kongauru 220a Ac 7.04N 134.17 E
Kong Christian IX Land = King Christian IX Land (EN) 224 Mc 68.00N 36.30W
Kong Christian X Land = King Christian X Land (EN) 224 Md 72.20N 32.30W
Kongeå 116 Ci 55.23N 8.39 E
Kong Frederik VIII Land = King Frederik VIII Land (EN) 224 Md 78.30N 28.00W
Kong Frederik VI Kyst = King Frederik VI Coast (EN) 224 Nc 63.00N 43.30W
Konginkangas 116 Kb 62.46N 25.48 E
Kongju 154 If 36.27N 127.08 E
Kong Karls Land 179 Oc 78.50N 28.00 E
Kong Kong 168 Ed 7.26N 33.14 E
Kongolo 160 Ji 5.23S 27.00 E
Kongor 168 Ed 7.10N 31.21 E
Kong Oscars Fjord 224 Md 72.20N 23.00W
Kongoussi 166 Ec 13.19N 1.32W
Kongsberg 114 Bg 59.39N 9.39 E
Kongsøya 179 Oc 78.55N 28.40 E
Kongsvinger 114 Cf 60.12N 12.00 E
Kongur Shan 140 Jf 38.40N 75.21 E
Kongwa 170 Gd 6.12S 36.25 E
Kong Wilhelms Land 179 Jc 75.48N 23.15W
Koniecpol 120 Pf 50.48N 19.41 E
Königslutter am Elm 120 Gd 52.15N 10.49 E
Königswinter 124 Jd 50.41N 7.11 E
Königs Wusterhausen 120 Jd 52.17N 13.37 E
Konin 120 Od 52.13N 18.16 E
Konin [2] 120 Od 52.15N 18.15 E
Konispoli 130 Dj 39.39N 20.10 E
Kónitsa 130 Di 40.03N 20.45 E
Konj 128 Kg 43.43N 16.55 E
Konjed Jān 146 Nf 33.30N 50.27 E
Konjic 128 Lg 43.39N 17.58 E
Konjuh 128 Mf 44.18N 18.33 E
Konkan 148 Ee 18.05N 73.25 E
Konkiep 172 Be 28.00S 17.23 E
Konko 170 Ed 10.12S 27.27 E
Konkouré 166 Cd 9.58N 13.42W
Konnevesi 116 Lb 62.37N 26.19 E
Konnevesi 116 Lb 62.40N 26.35 E
Konnivesi 116 Lc 61.10N 26.10 E
Konoša 112 Kc 60.58N 40.15 E
Kōnosu 156 Fc 36.04N 139.30 E
Konotop 112 Je 51.14N 33.12 E
Konqi He 140 Ke 41.48N 86.47 E
Konrei 220a Bb 7.43N 134.37 E
Konsei-Tōge 156 Fc 36.52N 139.22 E
Konsen-Daichi 156a Db 43.20N 144.50 E
Końskie 120 Qe 51.12N 20.26 E
Konstantinovka 126 Je 48.29N 37.43 E
Konstantinovsk 132 Lf 47.35N 41.05 E
Konstanz 120 Fi 47.40N 9.11 E
Kontagora 160 Hg 10.24N 5.29 E
Kontcha 166 Hd 7.58N 12.14 E
Kontich 124 Gc 51.08N 4.27 E
Kontiolahti 114 Ge 62.46N 29.51 E
Kontiomäki 114 Gd 64.21N 28.09 E
Kontum 148 Lf 14.21N 108.00 E
Kontum, Plateau de- 148 Lf 13.55N 108.05 E
Konušin, mys- 114 Kc 67.10N 43.50 E
Konušinski bereg 134 Bc 66.45N 44.40 E
Konya 142 Ff 37.52N 32.31 E
Konya Ovası 146 Ed 37.30N 33.20 E
Konz 124 Ie 49.42N 6.35 E
Konza 170 Gc 1.45S 37.07 E
Konžakovski Kamen, gora- 110 Ld 59.38N 59.08 E
Koocanusa, Lake- 188 Hb 48.45N 115.15W
Kook, Punta- 221d Ab 27.08S 109.26W
Koolau Range 221a Db 21.21N 157.47W
Koonga/Konga 116 Jf 58.34N 24.00 E
Koorda 212 Df 30.50S 117.29 E
Koosa 116 Lf 58.33N 27.07 E
Kootenay Lake 188 Gb 49.35N 116.50W
Kootenay River 174 He 49.15N 117.39W
Kopa 135 Jc 43.31N 75.48 E
Kopaonik 130 Df 43.15N 20.50 E
Kópasker 114a Ca 66.18N 16.27W
Kópavogur 114a Bb 64.06N 21.55W
Kopejsk 136 Gd 55.08N 61.39 E
Koper 128 He 45.33N 13.44 E
Kopervik 114 Ag 59.17N 5.18 E
Kopetdag, hrebet- 144 Hf 37.45N 58.15 E
Kop Geçidi 146 Ib 40.01N 40.28 E
Ko Phangan 148 Jg 9.45N 100.00 E
Köping 114 Dg 59.31N 16.00 E
Köpingsvik 116 Gh 56.53N 16.43 E
Kopjevo 138 Df 54.59N 89.55 E
Kopliku 130 Cg 42.13N 19.26 E
Köpmanholmen 114 Ee 63.10N 18.34 E
Koporje 116 Me 59.40N 29.08 E
Koporski zaliv 116 Me 59.45N 28.45 E
Koppal 148 Fe 15.21N 76.09 E
Koppang 114 Cf 61.34N 11.04 E
Koppány 120 Oj 46.35N 18.26 E
Kopparberg 116 Fe 59.52N 14.59 E
Kopparberg [2] 114 Df 61.00N 14.30 E
Kopparstenarna 116 Hf 58.32N 19.20 E
Koppom 116 Ee 59.43N 12.09 E
Koprivnica 128 Kd 46.10N 16.50 E
Kopru 146 Dd 36.49N 31.10 E
Köprüören 130 Mj 39.30N 29.47 E
Kor 144 Hd 29.36N 53.18 E
Korab 110 Ig 41.44N 20.32 E
Korablino 114 Jj 53.57N 40.00 E
Korahe 168 Gd 6.36N 44.16 E
Korak 220a Bc 7.21N 134.34 E
Koralpe 128 Id 46.45N 15.00 E
Koramlik 152 Ed 37.32N 85.42 E
Korana 128 Je 45.30N 15.35 E
Korangi 148 Dd 24.47N 67.08 E
Koraput 148 Ge 18.49N 82.43 E
Korba 148 Gd 22.21N 82.41 E
Korbach 120 Ee 51.17N 8.52 E
Korça 130 Di 40.37N 20.46 E
Korčula 128 Lh 42.58N 17.08 E
Korčula 128 Kh 42.57N 16.55 E
Korčulanski kanal 128 Kg 43.03N 16.40 E
Kordān 146 Ne 35.56N 50.50 E
Kordel 124 Ie 49.50N 6.38 E
Kordestān [3] 144 Gb 35.30N 47.00 E
Kord Küy 144 Hb 36.48N 54.07 E
Kordun 128 Je 45.10N 15.35 E
Korea Bay (EN) = Sŏjosŏn-man 140 Of 39.15N 125.00 E
Korean Peninsula (EN) 140 Of 35.30N 125.30 E
Korea Strait (EN) = Taehan-Haehyŏp 140 Of 34.40N 129.00 E
Korea Strait (EN) = Tsushima-Kaikyō 140 Of 34.40N 129.00 E
Korec 132 Ed 50.37N 27.10 E
Korem 168 Fc 12.30N 39.32 E
Korenovsk 136 Df 45.28N 39.28 E
Korf 138 Ld 60.18N 166.01 E
Korfovski 138 Ig 48.11N 135.04 E
Korgen 114 Cc 66.05N 13.50 E
Kõrgesaare/Kyrgesare 116 Jf 59.00N 22.25 E
Korhogo 160 Gh 9.27N 5.38W
Korhogo [3] 166 Dd 9.35N 5.55W
Koribundu 166 Cd 7.43N 11.42W
Korienzé 166 Eb 15.24N 3.47W
Korinthiakós Kólpos = Corinth, Gulf of- (EN) 110 Ih 38.12N 22.30 E
Kórinthos 130 Fl 37.55N 22.53 E
Kórinthos = Corinth (EN) [3] 130 Fl 37.55N 22.53 E
Korinthou, Dhiórix- = Corinth Canal (EN) 130 Fl 37.57N 22.58 E
Koriolei 160 Lh 1.48N 44.30 E
Kőrishegy 120 Ni 47.12N 17.49 E
Koritnik 130 Dg 42.05N 20.34 E
Kōriyama 152 Pd 37.24N 140.23 E
Korjakskaja Sopka, vulkan- 140 Rd 53.20N 158.47 E
Korjakski nacionalny okrug [3] 138 Le 60.00N 163.00 E
Korjakskoje nagorje = Koryak Range (EN) 140 Tc 62.30N 172.00 E
Korjažma 136 Ec 61.18N 47.07 E
Korjukovka 136 Hd 51.47N 32.17 E
Korkino 134 Ji 54.54N 61.25 E
Korkodon 138 Kd 64.43N 154.05 E
Korkuteli 146 Dd 37.04N 30.13 E
Korla 142 Ke 41.44N 86.09 E
Körmend 120 Mi 47.01N 16.36 E
Kormy, gora- 138 Fd 62.15N 106.08 E
Kornati 128 Jg 43.49N 15.20 E
Kornejevka 134 Ni 54.01N 68.27 E
Kornešty 130 Kb 47.23N 28.00 E
Korneuburg 128 Kb 48.21N 16.20 E
Kórnik 120 Nd 52.17N 17.04 E
Kornsjø 114 Cg 58.57N 11.39 E
Koro 166 Ec 14.05N 3.04W
Koroba 212 Ia 5.40S 142.45 E
Koroča 132 Jd 50.50N 37.13 E
Köroğlu Dağları 144 Da 40.40N 32.35 E
Köroğlu Tepe 146 Db 40.31N 31.53 E
Korogwe 170 Gd 5.09S 38.29 E
Koro Island 208 If 17.32S 179.42 E
Koroit 212 Ig 38.17S 142.22 E
Korolevo 120 Th 48.08N 23.07 E
Korolevu 219d Ac 18.12S 177.53 E
Korom, Bahr 168 Bc 10.35N 19.45 E
Koromiri 220p Cc 21.15S 159.43W
Koronadal 150 He 6.12N 125.01 E
Korónia, Límni- 130 Gi 40.40N 23.10 E
Koronowo 120 Nc 53.19N 17.57 E
Koronowski e, Jezioro- 120 Nc 53.22N 17.55 E
Koror 210 Ed 7.20N 134.29 E
Koror 208 Ed 7.20N 134.30 E
Körös 120 Qj 46.43N 20.12 E
Koro Sea 216 Ec 18.00S 180.00
Korosten 112 Ie 50.57N 28.39 E
Korostyšev 132 Fd 50.18N 29.05 E
Korotaiha 134 Jb 68.55N 60.55 E
Koro Toro 160 Ig 16.05N 18.30 E
Korovin Volcano 178a Db 52.22N 174.10W
Korpijärvi 116 Lc 61.15N 27.10 E
Korpilahti 114 Fe 62.01N 25.33 E
Korpo/Korppoo 116 Id 60.10N 21.35 E
Korppoo/Korpo 116 Id 60.10N 21.35 E
Korsakov 138 Jg 46.37N 142.51 E
Korshäs 114 Ee 62.47N 21.12 E
Korsholm/Mustasaari 116 Ia 63.05N 21.43 E
Korso 116 Kd 60.21N 25.06 E
Korsør 114 Ci 55.20N 11.09 E
Korsun-Ševčenkovski 132 Ge 49.26N 31.18 E
Korsze 120 Rb 54.10N 21.09 E
Kortemark 124 Fc 51.02N 3.02 E
Kortrijk/Courtrai 122 Jd 50.50N 3.16 E
Korucu 130 Kj 39.28N 27.22 E
Koru Dağ 130 Ji 40.42N 26.45 E
Koryak Range (EN) = Korjakskoje nagorje 140 Tc 62.30N 172.00 E
Korzybie 120 Mb 54.18N 16.50 E
Kos 130 Km 36.53N 27.18 E
Kos 130 Km 36.50N 27.10 E
Kosa 134 Gg 59.56N 55.01 E
Kosa 134 Gf 60.11N 55.10 E
Kosai 156 Ed 34.43N 137.30 E
Kosaja Gora 132 Jb 54.09N 37.31 E
Kosaka 156 Ga 40.20N 140.44 E
Kō-Saki 156 Ad 34.05N 129.13 E
Ko Samui 148 Jg 9.30N 99.58 E
Kosan-ŭp 152 Md 38.51N 127.25 E
Koščagyl 132 Rf 46.52N 53.47 E
Kościan 120 Md 52.06N 16.38 E
Kościerzyna 120 Nb 54.08N 18.00 E
Kosciusko 186 Lj 32.58N 89.35W
Kosciusko, Mount- 208 Fh 36.27S 148.16 E
Kose/Koze 116 Ke 59.11N 25.05 E
Köse Dağ 146 Gb 40.06N 37.58 E
Kosha 168 Ea 20.49N 30.32 E
Koshigaya 156 Fd 35.55N 139.45 E
Koshiji 156 Fc 37.24N 138.45 E
Koshiki-Kaikyō 156 Bf 31.45N 130.05 E
Koshiki Rettō 152 Me 31.45N 129.45 E
Koshimizu 156a Db 43.51N 144.25 E
Kōshoku 154 Of 36.38N 138.06 E
Kōshyū Seamount (EN) 156 Df 31.35N 135.50 E
Košice 112 If 48.43N 21.15 E
Kosjerić 130 Cf 44.00N 19.55 E
Kosju 134 Id 65.38N 58.59 E
Kosju 134 Ic 66.18N 59.53 E
Koşk 130 Ll 37.51N 28.03 E
Koski 116 Jd 60.39N 23.09 E
Koskolovo 116 Me 59.34N 28.30 E
Koslan 136 Ec 63.29N 48.52 E
Kosma 134 Dd 65.43N 49.50 E
Kosmaj 130 De 44.28N 20.33 E
Kosŏng 152 Md 38.40N 128.19 E
Kosov 130 Ia 48.15N 25.08 E
Kosovo [3] 130 Dg 42.35N 21.00 E
Kosovo 130 Eg 42.40N 21.05 E
Kosovska Mitrovica 130 Dg 42.53N 20.52 E
Kosrae (Kusaie) 208 Hd 5.19N 162.59 E
Kossol Passage 220a Bb 7.52N 134.36 E
Kossol Reef 220a Bb 7.57N 134.41 E
Kossou, Barrage de- 166 Dd 7.01N 5.29W
Kossovo 132 Dc 52.47N 25.10 E
Kostajnica 128 Ke 45.13N 16.33 E
Kostenec 130 Gg 42.16N 23.49 E
Koster 172 De 25.57S 26.42 E
Kosteröarna 116 Df 58.55N 11.05 E
Kostjukoviči 132 Hc 53.23N 32.06 E
Kostjukovka 132 Gc 52.32N 30.58 E
Kostolac 130 Ee 44.44N 21.12 E
Kostopol 132 Ed 50.53N 26.29 E
Kostriževka 130 Ia 48.31N 25.45 E
Kostroma 112 Kd 57.47N 40.59 E
Kostromskaja oblast [3] 136 Ed 58.30N 44.00 E
Kostrzyń 120 Nd 52.25N 17.14 E
Kostrzyn 120 Kd 52.37N 14.39 E
Kosva 134 Hg 58.50N 56.45 E
Koszalin 120 Mb 54.12N 16.09 E
Koszalin [2] 120 Mb 54.10N 16.10 E
Kőszeg 120 Mi 47.23N 16.33 E
Kota 142 Jg 25.16N 75.55 E
Kotaagung 150 Dh 5.30S 104.38 E
Kota Baharu 142 Mi 6.08N 102.15 E
Kotabaru 150 Gg 3.14S 116.13 E
Kotabumi 152 Mj 4.50S 104.54 E
Kotadabok 150 Dg 0.30S 104.33 E
Kota Kinabalu 142 Ni 5.59N 116.04 E
Kotamobagu 150 Hf 0.46N 124.19 E
Ko Tao 148 Jf 10.05N 99.52 E
Kotari 128 Jf 44.05N 15.30 E
Ko Tarutau 148 Jg 6.35N 99.40 E
Kota Tinggi 150 Df 1.44N 103.54 E
Kotel 130 Jg 42.53N 26.27 E
Kotelnič 136 Ed 58.20N 48.20 E
Kotelnikovo 132 Mf 47.38N 43.09 E
Kotelny, ostrov- 140 Pb 75.45N 138.44 E
Kotelva 132 Id 50.03N 34.45 E
Köthen 120 He 51.45N 11.58 E
Kotido 170 Fb 3.00N 34.09 E
Kotjužany 136 Gb 47.50N 28.27 E
Kotka 114 Gf 60.28N 26.55 E
Kot Kapūra 148 Eb 30.35N 74.54 E
Kotlas 112 Kc 61.16N 46.35 E
Kotlenik 130 Df 43.51N 20.42 E
Kotlenski prohod 130 Jg 42.53N 26.27 E
Kotlik 178 Gd 63.02N 163.33W
Kotlin, ostrov- 116 Md 60.00N 29.45 E
Kotly 116 Me 59.30N 28.48 E
Kotobi 166 Ed 6.42N 4.08W
Kotohira 156 Cd 34.11N 133.48 E
Koton Karifi 166 Gd 8.06N 6.48 E
Kotor 130 Bg 42.25N 18.46 E
Kotorosl 114 Jh 57.38N 39.57 E
Kotorska, Boka- 130 Bg 42.25N 18.40 E
Kotor Varoš 128 Lf 44.37N 17.22 E
Kotouba 166 Ed 8.41N 3.12W
Kotovo 136 Ee 50.18N 44.48 E
Kotovsk [Mold.-U.S.S.R.] 132 Ff 46.49N 28.33 E
Kotovsk [R.S.F.S.R.] 136 Ee 52.35N 41.32 E
Kotovsk [Ukr.-U.S.S.R.] 136 Cf 47.43N 29.33 E
Kotra 120 Uc 53.32N 24.17 E
Kotri 148 Dc 25.22N 68.18 E
Kötschach 128 Gd 46.40N 13.00 E
Kottayam 148 Fg 9.35N 76.31 E
Kotto 158 Jh 4.14N 22.02 E
Kotton 168 Id 9.37N 50.32 E
Kotu 221b Ba 19.57S 174.48W
Kotu Group 208 Jg 20.00S 174.45W
Kotuj 140 Mb 71.55N 102.05 E
Kotujkan 138 Fb 70.40N 103.25 E
Koturdepe 132 Rj 39.26N 53.40 E
Kotzebue 176 Cc 66.53N 162.39W
Kotzebue Sound 174 Cc 66.20N 163.00W
Kouandé 166 Fc 10.20N 1.42 E
Kouango 168 Be 4.58N 19.59 E
Kouba Modounga 168 Bb 15.40N 18.15 E
Koudougou 160 Gg 11.44N 4.31W
Kouéré 166 Ec 10.27N 3.59W
Koufália 130 Fi 40.47N 22.35 E
Koufonisi [Grc.] 130 Jo 34.56N 26.10 E
Koufonision [Grc.] 130 Im 36.55N 25.35 E
Koufonisiou, Stenón- 130 Jo 35.00N 26.10 E
Kouilou [3] 170 Bc 4.00S 12.00 E
Kouilou 158 Ii 4.28S 11.41 E
Koukdjuak 180 Kc 66.47N 73.10W
Kouki 168 Bd 7.10N 17.18 E
Koukourou 168 Cd 7.12N 20.02 E
Koulamoutou 170 Bc 1.08S 12.29 E
Koulikoro 166 Dc 12.51N 7.34W
Koulountou 166 Cc 13.15N 13.37W
Koumac 210 Hg 20.30S 164.12 E
Koumac, Grand Récif de- 219b Be 20.32S 164.04 E
Koumbi-Saleh 162 Ff 15.47N 7.58W
Koumi 156 Fc 36.05N 138.28 E
Koumpentoum 166 Cc 13.59N 14.34W
Koumra 168 Bd 8.55N 17.33 E
Koundara 160 Fg 12.29N 13.18W
Koundian 166 Cc 13.08N 10.42W
Kounoúpoi 130 Jm 36.32N 26.27 E
Kounradski 136 Hf 46.57N 75.01 E
Kounta 166 Eb 17.30N 0.40W
Koupéla 166 Ec 12.11N 0.21W
Kouqian → Yongji 154 Ic 43.40N 126.30 E
Kourou 202 Hb 5.09N 52.39W
Kouroussa 166 Dc 10.39N 9.53W
Koury 166 Ec 12.10N 4.48W
Koussané 166 Cc 14.52N 11.15W
Koussèri 166 Ic 12.05N 15.02 E
Koutiala 160 Gg 12.23N 5.27W
Koutoumo 219b Cf 22.40S 167.32 E
Koutous 166 Hc 14.30N 10.00 E
Kouvola 114 Gf 60.52N 26.42 E
Kouyou 170 Cc 0.45S 16.38 E
Kova 138 Fe 58.20N 100.20 E
Kovač 130 Cf 43.31N 19.07 E
Kovačica 130 Dd 45.06N 20.38 E
Koval 120 Pd 52.31N 19.10 E
Kovalevka 130 Nc 46.42N 30.31 E
Kovarskas/Kavarskas 116 Ki 55.24N 25.03 E
Kovdor 136 Db 67.33N 30.25 E
Kovdozero, ozero- 114 Hc 66.47N 32.00 E
Kovel 136 Ce 51.13N 24.43 E
Kovenskaja 134 Mf 61.24N 67.39 E
Kovinskaja grjada 138 Fe 57.15N 101.00 E
Kovozero, ozero- 114 Ic 67.50N 35.10 E
Kovrov 136 Ed 56.24N 41.20 E
Kovylkino 114 Ki 54.02N 43.58 E
Kowfi Kosh, Gardaneh-ye- 146 Og 30.47N 53.12 E
Kowŏn 152 Md 39.26N 127.15 E
Kowtal-e Do Rāh 144 Lb 36.07N 71.15 E
Kowt-e 'Ashrow 144 Kc 34.27N 68.48 E
Kōyama 156 Bf 31.19N 130.57 E
Kōya-San 156 Dd 34.13N 135.35 E
Köyceğiz 146 Cd 36.55N 28.43 E
Köycegiz Gölü 130 Lm 36.55N 28.40 E
Koyoshi-Gawa 156 Gb 39.24N 140.01 E
Koyuk 178 Gd 64.56N 161.08W
Koyukuk 174 Dc 64.56N 157.30W
Kozaklı 146 Fc 39.13N 34.49 E
Kozan 146 Fd 37.27N 35.49 E
Kozáni 130 Ei 40.18N 21.47 E
Kozara 128 Ke 45.00N 16.55 E
Kozawa 156a Bb 42.58N 140.40 E
Koze/Kose 116 Ke 59.11N 25.05 E
Kozelsk 136 De 54.01N 35.46 E
Koževnikovo 136 Hd 56.18N 84.00 E
Kozhikode → Calicut 142 Jh 11.19N 75.46 E
Kozienice 120 Re 51.35N 21.33 E
Kožim 134 Id 65.43N 59.31 E
Kožim 134 Id 65.45N 59.15 E
Kozjak 130 Eh 41.06N 21.54 E
Kozloduj 130 Gf 43.47N 23.44 E
Kozlovka 114 Li 55.52N 48.13 E
Kozlovščina 120 Vc 53.14N 25.20 E
Kozlu 146 Db 41.25N 31.44 E
Kozluk 146 Ic 38.11N 41.29 E
Koźmin 120 Ne 51.50N 17.28 E
Kozmodemjansk 114 Lh 56.20N 46.36 E
Kožozero, ozero- 114 Je 63.05N 38.05 E
Kożuchów 120 Le 51.45N 15.35 E
Kožuf 130 Fh 41.09N 22.10 E
Kōzu-Shima 156 Fd 34.15N 139.10 E
Kožva 134 Hd 65.07N 56.57 E
Kožva 134 Hd 65.10N 57.00 E
Kozyrevsk 138 Ke 55.59N 159.59 E
Kpalimé 166 Fd 6.54N 0.38 E
Kpandu 166 Fd 7.00N 0.18 E
Kpessi 166 Fd 8.04N 1.16 E
Kra, Isthmus of- (EN) = Kra, Khokhok- 140 Lh 10.20N 99.00 E
Kra, Khokhok- = Kra, Isthmus of- (EN) 140 Lh 10.20N 99.00 E
Kraba 130 Ch 41.12N 19.59 E
Krabbfjärden 116 Gf 58.45N 17.40 E
Krabi 148 Jg 8.05N 98.53 E
Krabit, Mali i- 130 Cg 42.07N 19.59 E
Kra Buri 148 Jf 10.24N 98.47 E
Krâchéh 142 Mh 12.29N 106.01 E
Kragerø 114 Bg 58.52N 9.25 E
Kragujevac 130 De 44.01N 20.55 E
Kraichbach 124 Ke 49.22N 8.31 E
Kraichgau 120 Eg 49.10N 8.50 E
Kraichtal 124 Ke 49.07N 8.46 E
Krajina 130 Fe 44.10N 22.30 E
Krajište 130 Fg 42.35N 22.25 E
Krajnovka 132 Oh 43.57N 47.24 E
Krakatau, Gunung- 140 Mj 6.07S 105.24 E
Krak des Chevaliers 146 Ge 34.46N 36.19 E
Krakovec 120 Tg 49.56N 23.13 E
Kraków 112 He 50.03N 19.58 E
Kraków [2] 120 Pf 50.05N 20.00 E
Kraków-Nowa Huta 120 Qf 50.04N 20.05 E
Krakowsko-Częstochowska, Wyżyna- 120 Pf 50.50N 19.15 E
Kralendijk 196 Bf 12.10N 68.16W
Kraljevica 128 Ie 45.16N 14.34 E
Kraljevo 130 Df 43.44N 20.43 E
Kralupy nad Vltavou 120 Kf 50.14N 14.19 E
Kramatorsk 132 Je 48.43N 37.32 E
Kramfors 114 De 62.56N 17.47 E
Krammer 124 Gc 51.38N 4.15 E
Kranenburg 124 Ic 51.47N 6.01 E
Kranidhion 130 Gl 37.23N 23.09 E
Kranj 128 Id 46.14N 14.22 E
Krapina 128 Jd 46.10N 15.53 E
Krapkowice 120 Nf 50.29N 17.56 E
Kras=Karst (EN) 110 Hf 45.48N 14.00 E
Krasavino 136 Ec 60.59N 46.28 E
Krasiczyn 120 Sg 49.48N 22.39 E
Krasilov 120 Ee 49.37N 26.59 E
Kraskino 154 Kc 42.44N 130.48 E
Krāslava/Kraslava 114 Gi 55.54N 27.10 E
Kraslava/Krāslava 114 Gi 55.54N 27.10 E
Krasnaja Poljana 132 Lh 43.40N 40.12 E
Kraśnik 120 Sf 50.56N 22.13 E
Kraśnik Fabryczny, Kraśnik- 120 Sf 50.58N 22.12 E
Kraśnik-Kraśnik Fabryczny 120 Sf 50.58N 22.12 E
Krasnoarmejsk [Kaz.-U.S.S.R.] 136 Ge 53.57N 69.43 E
Krasnoarmejsk [R.S.F.S.R.] 136 Ee 51.02N 45.42 E
Krasnoarmejsk [Ukr.-U.S.S.R.] 132 Je 48.11N 37.12 E
Krasnoarmejski 138 Mc 69.37N 172.02 E
Krasnodar 112 Jf 45.02N 39.00 E
Krasnodarski kraj [3] 136 Df 45.20N 39.30 E
Krasnodon 132 Ke 48.17N 39.44 E
Krasnogorodskoje 116 Mh 56.47N 28.18 E
Krasnogorsk [R.S.F.S.R.] 138 Jg 48.26N 142.10 E
Krasnogorsk [R.S.F.S.R.] 114 Ii 55.51N 37.20 E
Krasnogorski 134 Ji 54.36N 61.15 E
Krasnograd 136 Df 49.22N 35.27 E
Krasnogvardejsk 135 Fe 39.45N 67.16 E
Krasnogvardejskoje 132 Lg 45.49N 41.31 E
Krasnoholmski 134 Gh 56.02N 55.05 E
Krasnoilsk 130 Ia 48.02N 25.48 E
Krasnojarsk 142 Ld 56.01N 92.50 E
Krasnojarski 134 Ik 51.58N 59.57 E
Krasnojarski kraj [3] 138 Ee 57.30N 95.00 E
Krasnojarskoje vodohranilišče 138 Ee 55.05N 91.30 E
Krasnoje 120 Ug 49.49N 24.39 E
Krasnoje Selo 114 Hg 59.43N 30.03 E
Krasnoje Znamja 136 Df 36.50N 62.29 E
Krasnokamensk 138 Gf 50.00N 118.05 E
Krasnokamsk 136 Fd 58.04N 55.45 E
Krasnokutsk 136 He 52.59N 75.59 E
Krasnolesje 116 Ij 54.23N 22.25 E
Krasnolesny 132 Kd 51.52N 39.35 E
Krasnooktjabrski [Kirg.-U.S.S.R.] 135 Jc 42.45N 74.20 E
Krasnooktjabrski [R.S.F.S.R.] 114 Lh 56.43N 47.37 E
Krasnooskolskoje vodohranilišče 132 Je 49.25N 37.35 E
Krasnoostrovski 116 Md 60.12N 28.39 E
Krasnoperekopsk 136 Df 45.57N 33.47 E
Krasnorečenski 154 Mb 44.38N 135.15 E
Krasnoščelje 114 Ic 67.23N 37.02 E
Krasnoselki 120 Uc 53.14N 24.30 E
Krasnoselkup 136 Dc 65.41N 82.28 E
Krasnoslobodsk [R.S.F.S.R.] 114 Ki 54.27N 43.47 E
Krasnoslobodsk [R.S.F.S.R.] 132 Ne 48.40N 44.31 E
Krasnoturinsk 136 Gd 59.46N 60.18 E
Krasnoufimsk 136 Fd 56.37N 57.46 E
Krasnouralsk 136 Gd 58.24N 60.03 E
Krasnousolski 136 Fe 53.54N 56.29 E
Krasnovišersk 136 Fc 60.23N 57.03 E
Krasnovodskaja oblast [3] 136 Fh 39.50N 55.00 E
Krasnovodsk 142 He 40.00N 53.00 E
Krasnovodski poluostrov 110 Lg 40.30N 53.15 E
Krasnovodski zaliv 132 Rj 39.50N 53.15 E
Krasnozatonski 136 Fc 61.41N 51.01 E
Krasnozavodsk 114 Jh 56.29N 38.13 E
Krasnoznamensk [Kaz.-U.S.S.R.] 136 Ge 51.03N 69.30 E
Krasnoznamensk [R.S.F.S.R.] 116 Jj 54.52N 22.27 E
Krasny Čikoj 138 Ff 50.25N 108.45 E
Krasny Holm 114 Ig 58.04N 37.09 E
Krasny Jar [R.S.F.S.R.] 136 De 57.07N 84.40 E
Krasny Jar [R.S.F.S.R.] 136 Hd 55.14N 72.56 E
Krasnyje Barrikady 132 Of 46.13N 47.50 E
Krasnyje Okny 130 Mb 47.34N 29.23 E
Krasny Kut 136 Ee 50.58N 46.58 E
Krasny Liman 132 Je 48.59N 37.47 E
Krasny Luč 132 Ke 48.09N 38.57 E
Krasny Oktjabr 136 Gd 55.37N 64.48 E
Krasny Profintern 114 Jh 57.47N 40.29 E
Krasnystaw 120 Tf 50.59N 23.10 E
Krasny Sulin 132 Lf 47.53N 40.09 E
Kratovo 130 Fg 42.05N 22.12 E
Kraulshavn 179 Gd 74.10N 57.00W
Krawang 150 Eh 6.19S 107.17 E
Krefeld 120 Ce 51.20N 6.34 E
Krefeld-Hüls 124 Ic 51.22N 6.31 E
Kremastá, Límni- 130 Ek 38.50N 21.30 E

Index Symbols

[1] Independent Nation
[2] State, Region
[3] District, County
[4] Municipality
[5] Colony, Dependency
Continent
Physical Region
Historical or Cultural Region
Mount, Mountain
Volcano
Hill
Mountains, Mountain Range
Hills, Escarpment
Plateau, Upland
Pass, Gap
Plain, Lowland
Delta
Salt Flat
Valley, Canyon
Crater, Cave
Karst Features
Depression
Polder
Desert, Dunes
Forest, Woods
Heath, Steppe
Oasis
Cape, Point
Coast, Beach
Cliff
Peninsula
Isthmus
Sandbank
Island
Atoll
Rock, Reef
Islands, Archipelago
Rocks, Reefs
Coral Reef
Well, Spring
Geyser
River, Stream
Waterfall, Rapids
River Mouth, Estuary
Lake
Salt Lake
Intermittent Lake
Reservoir
Swamp, Pond
Canal
Glacier
Ice Shelf, Pack Ice
Ocean
Sea
Gulf, Bay
Strait, Fjord
Lagoon
Bank
Seamount
Tablemount
Ridge
Shelf
Basin
Escarpment, Sea Scarp
Fracture
Trench, Abyss
National Park, Reserve
Point of Interest
Recreation Site
Cave, Cavern
Historic Site
Ruins
Wall, Walls
Church, Abbey
Temple
Scientific Station
Railway station
Airport
Port
Military installation
Lighthouse
Mine
Tunnel
Dam, Bridge

Kremenchug Reservoir (EN) = Kremenčugskoje vodohranilišče 110 Jf 49.20N 32.30 E
Kremenčug 112 Jf 49.04N 33.25 E
Kremenčugskoje vodohranilišče = Kremenchug Reservoir (EN) 110 Jf 49.20N 32.30 E
Kremenec 132 Dd 50.06N 25.43 E
Kremennaja 132 Ke 49.03N 38.14 E
Kremmling 186 Cf 40.03N 106.24W
Krems 128 Jb 48.25N 15.36 E
Krems an der Donau 128 Jb 48.25N 15.36 E
Kremsmünster 128 Ib 48.03N 14.08 E
Krenitzin Islands 178a Eb 54.08N 166.00W
Kresta, zaliv- 138 Nc 65.30N 179.00W
Krestcy 114 Hg 58.15N 32.31 E
Krestovy, pereval- 132 Nh 42.32N 44.30 E
Kretek 150 Fh 7.59S 110.19 E
Kretinga 114 Ei 55.55N 21.17 E
Kreuzau 124 Id 50.45N 6.29 E
Kreuzberg 120 Ff 50.22N 9.58 E
Kreuzlingen 128 Dc 47.39N 9.10 E
Kreuztal 120 Df 50.58N 7.59 E
Kria Vrisi 130 Fi 40.41N 22.18 E
Kribi 160 Hh 2.57N 9.55 E
Kričev 136 De 53.43N 31.43 E
Kričim 130 Hg 42.08N 24.31 E
Krim 128 Ie 45.56N 14.28 E
Krimml 128 Gc 47.13N 12.11 E
Krimpen aan den IJssel 124 Gc 51.55N 4.35 E
Kriós, Ákra- 110 Ih 35.14N 23.35 E
Krishna 140 Kh 15.57N 80.59 E
Krishnanagar 148 Hd 23.24N 88.30 E
Kristdala 116 Gg 57.24N 16.11 E
Kristiansand 112 Gd 58.10N 8.00 E
Kristianstad 114 Dh 56.02N 14.08 E
Kristianstad [2] 114 Ch 56.15N 14.00 E
Kristiansund 112 Gc 63.07N 7.45 E
Kristiinankaupunki/Kristinestad 114 Ee 62.17N 21.23 E
Kristineberg 114 Ed 65.04N 18.35 E
Kristinehamn 114 Dg 59.20N 14.07 E
Kristinestad/Kristiinankaupunki 114 Ee 62.17N 21.23 E
Kriti = Crete (EN) [2] 130 Hn 35.35N 25.00 E
Kriti = Crete (EN) 110 Ih 35.15N 24.45 E
Kritikón Pélagos = Crete, Sea of- (EN) 130 Hn 36.00N 25.00 E
Krivaja 128 Mf 44.27N 18.10 E
Kriva Palanka 130 Fg 42.12N 22.21 E
Kriviči 116 Ij 54.44N 27.20 E
Krivodol 130 Gf 43.23N 23.29 E
Krivoje Ozero 132 Gf 47.57N 30.21 E
Krivoj Rog 112 Jf 47.54N 33.21 E
Križevci 128 Kd 46.02N 16.32 E
Krk 128 Ie 45.02N 14.35 E
Krk 128 Ie 45.05N 14.35 E
Krka [Yugo.] 128 Je 45.53N 15.36 E
Krka [Yugo.] 128 Jg 43.43N 15.51 E
Krkonoše 120 Lf 50.46N 15.35 E
Krn 128 Hd 46.16N 13.40 E
Krndija 128 Le 45.27N 17.55 E
Krnjača, Beograd- 130 De 44.52N 20.28 E
Krnov 120 Nf 50.05N 17.41 E
Krobia 120 Me 51.47N 16.58 E
Krøderen 116 Cd 60.15N 9.40 E
Krokeai 130 Fm 36.53N 22.33 E
Krokek 116 Gf 58.40N 16.24 E
Kroken 114 Dd 65.22N 14.16 E
Krokom 114 De 63.20N 14.28 E
Krolevec 132 Hd 51.32N 33.30 E
Kroměříž 120 Ng 49.18N 17.22 E
Krompachy 120 Qh 48.56N 20.52 E
Kronach 120 Hf 50.14N 11.19 E
Kröng Kaôh Kŏng 148 Kf 11.37N 102.59 E
Kronoberg [2] 114 Dh 56.40N 14.40 E
Kronockaja Sopka, vulkan- 138 Lf 54.47N 160.35 E
Kronocki, mys- 138 Lf 54.43N 162.07 E
Kronocki zaliv 138 Lf 54.00N 161.00 E
Kronoki 138 Lf 54.33N 161.14 E
Kronprins Christian Land 179 Jb 80.45N 22.00W
Kronprinsesse Mærtha Kyst 222 Bf 72.00S 7.30W
Kronprins Frederiks Bjerge 179 Ie 67.20N 34.00W
Kronprins Olav Kyst 222 Ee 68.30S 42.30 E
Kronštadt 136 Cc 60.01N 29.44 E
Kroonstad 160 Jk 27.46S 27.12 E
Kropotkin [R.S.F.S.R.] 136 Ef 45.26N 40.34 E
Kropotkin [R.S.F.S.R.] 138 Ge 58.36N 115.27 E
Kroppefjäll 116 Ef 58.40N 12.13 E
Krośniewice 120 Pd 52.16N 19.10 E
Krosno 120 Rg 49.42N 21.46 E
Krosno [2] 120 Rg 49.40N 21.45 E
Krosno Odrzańskie 120 Ld 52.04N 15.05 E
Krossfjorden 116 Ad 60.10N 5.05 E
Krotoszyn 120 Ne 51.42N 17.26 E
Kroviga, gora- 120 Ed 60.40N 91.30 E
Krško 128 Je 45.58N 15.28 E
Krstača 130 Dg 42.58N 20.08 E
Krugersdorp 160 Jk 26.05S 27.35 E
Krui 150 Dh 5.11S 103.56 E
Kruibeke 124 Gc 51.10N 4.19 E
Kruiningen 124 Gc 51.27N 4.02 E
Kruja 130 Ch 41.30N 19.48 E
Krulevščina 116 Li 55.03N 27.52 E
Krumbach 120 Gh 48.15N 10.22 E
Krumovgrad 130 Ih 41.28N 25.39 E
Krung Thep = Bangkok (EN) 142 Mh 13.45N 100.31 E
Krupanj 130 Ce 44.22N 19.22 E
Krupinica 120 Oh 48.05N 18.54 E
Krupinská vrchovina 120 Ph 48.20N 19.15 E
Kruså 116 Cj 54.50N 9.25 E
Krušedol 130 Cd 45.07N 19.57 E
Kruševac 130 Ef 43.35N 21.20 E
Kruševo 130 Eh 41.22N 21.15 E
Krušné Hory = Ore Mountains (EN) 110 He 50.30N 13.15 E
Krustpils 116 Lh 56.29N 26.00 E
Kruzof 178 Le 57.10N 135.40W
Krym 132 Jg 45.23N 36.36 E
Krymsk 136 Dg 44.54N 37.57 E
Krymskaja oblast [3] 136 Dg 45.15N 34.20 E
Krymskije gory = Crimean Mountains (EN) 110 Jg 44.45N 34.30 E
Krymski poluostrov = Crimea (EN) 110 Jf 45.00N 34.00 E
Krynica 120 Qg 49.25N 20.56 E
Krzemieniucha 120 Sb 54.12N 22.54 E
Krzepice 120 Of 50.58N 18.44 E
Krzna 120 Td 52.08N 23.31 E
Krzywiń 120 Me 51.58N 16.49 E
Krzyż 120 Md 52.53N 16.01 E
Ksar el Boukhari 162 Hb 35.53N 2.45 E
Ksar el Kebir 162 Fc 35.00N 5.59W
Ksar es Srhir 126 Gi 35.51N 5.34W
Ksenjevka 138 Gf 53.34N 118.44 E
Kšenski 132 Jd 51.52N 37.44 E
Ksour, Monts des- 162 Gc 32.45N 0.10W
Kstovo 114 Kh 56.12N 44.11 E
Kū', Wādī al- 168 Dc 12.18N 25.43 E
Kuai He 154 Dh 33.09N 117.32 E
Kuala Belait 150 Ff 4.35N 114.11 E
Kuala Dungun 150 Df 4.47N 103.26 E
Kuala Kangsar 150 Df 4.46N 100.56 E
Kualakapuas 150 Fg 3.01S 114.21 E
Kuala Kerai 150 De 5.32N 102.12 E
Kualakurun 150 Fg 1.07S 113.53 E
Kualalangsa 150 Cf 4.32N 98.01 E
Kuala Lipis 150 Df 4.11N 102.03 E
Kuala Lumpur 142 Mi 3.10N 101.42 E
Kuala Lumpur [2] 150 Df 3.14N 101.40 E
Kuala Pilah 150 Df 2.44N 102.15 E
Kuala Rompin 150 Df 2.49N 103.29 E
Kuala Terengganu 142 Mi 5.20N 103.08 E
Kuancheng 154 Ed 40.37N 118.31 E
Kuandang 150 Hf 0.52N 122.55 E
Kuandian 152 Lc 40.45N 124.48 E
Kuang-hsi-chuang-tsu Tzu-chih-ch'ü → Guangxi Zhuangzu Zizhiqu [2] 152 Ig 24.00N 109.00 E
Kuang-tung Sheng → Guangdong Sheng [2] 152 Jg 23.00N 113.00 E
Kuantan 150 Df 3.48N 103.20 E
Kuba 136 Eg 41.20N 48.35 E
Kuban 110 Jf 45.20N 37.30 E
Kuba-Shima 156b Ab 26.10N 127.15 E
Kubaysah 146 Jf 33.35N 42.37 E
Kubbum 168 Cc 11.47N 23.47 E
Kubena 114 Jg 59.37N 39.48 E
Kubenskoje, ozero- 114 Jg 59.40N 39.30 E
Kubnja 114 Li 55.32N 48.28 E
Kubokawa 154 Lh 33.12N 133.08 E
Kubolta 130 Lb 47.48N 28.03 E
Kubrat 130 Jf 43.48N 26.30 E
Kubumesaai 150 Gf 1.31N 115.06 E
Kučaj 130 Ef 43.53N 21.44 E
Kučevo 130 Ee 44.29N 21.41 E
Kuching 142 Ni 1.33N 110.20 E
Kuchinoerabu-Shima 154 Ki 30.28N 130.10 E
Kuchinotsu 156 Be 32.36N 130.12 E
Küçükçekmece 130 Li 40.59N 28.46 E
Küçükerenköy 146 Ee 35.22N 33.45 E
Küçükkuyu 130 Jj 39.32N 26.36 E
Küçuk Menderes 130 Kl 37.57N 27.16 E
Kučurgan 130 Mc 46.35N 29.55 E
Kudaka-Jima 156b Ab 26.10N 127.54 E
Kudamatsu 156 Bd 34.01N 131.53 E
Kudat 150 Ge 6.53N 116.50 E
Kudeb 116 Mg 57.30N 28.16 E
Kudirkos-Naumestis 116 Jj 54.43N 22.49 E
Kudowa Zdrój 120 Mf 50.27N 16.20 E
Kudremukh 148 Ff 13.08N 75.16 E
Kudus 150 Fh 6.48S 110.50 E
Kudymkar 136 Fd 59.01N 54.37 E
Kuee Ruins 221a Fd 19.12N 155.23W
Kuei-chou Sheng → Guizhou Sheng = Kweichow (EN) [2] 152 If 27.00N 107.00 E
Kufi 146 Cc 38.10N 29.43 E
Kufrah, Wāḥāt al- = Kufra Oasis (EN) 158 Jf 24.10N 23.15 E
Kufra Oasis (EN) = Kufrah, Wāḥāt al- 158 Jf 24.10N 23.15 E
Kufstein 128 Gc 47.35N 12.10 E
Kuganavolok 114 Ie 62.16N 36.55 E
Kugmallit Bay 180 Ec 69.30N 133.20W
Kugojeja 132 Kf 46.33N 39.38 E
Kūh, Ra's al- 144 Id 25.48N 57.19 E
Kuḥaylī 168 Eb 19.29N 32.49 E
Kūhbonān 146 Qg 31.23N 56.19 E
Kūhdasht 146 Lf 33.32N 47.36 E
Kūh-e Būrh 146 Pi 27.22N 54.40 E
Kūh-e Gāvbūs 146 Oi 27.10N 54.00 E
Kūh-e Karkas 146 Nf 33.27N 51.48 E
Kūh-e Kārūn 146 Ng 31.27N 50.18 E
Kūhestak 146 Qi 26.47N 57.02 E
Kūhīn, Gardaneh-ye- 146 Md 36.23N 49.37 E
Kühlungsborn 120 Hb 54.09N 11.43 E
Kuhmo 114 Gd 64.08N 29.31 E
Kuhmoinen 116 Kc 61.34N 25.11 E
Kuhn 179 Kd 74.45N 19.45W
Kūhpāyeh 144 Ic 30.35N 57.15 E
Kūhpāyeh [Iran] 146 Qg 30.43N 57.30 E
Kūhpāyeh [Iran] 146 Of 32.43N 52.26 E
Kūhrān, Kūh-e- 144 Id 26.46N 58.12 E
Kuhtuj 138 Je 59.23N 143.10 E
Kuhva 116 Mg 57.17N 28.17 E
Kuiseb 172 Ad 23.00S 14.33 E
Kuishan Ding 152 Ig 22.32N 109.52 E
Kuito 160 Ij 12.23S 16.56 E
Kuiu 178 Me 57.45N 134.10W
Kuivaniemi 114 Fd 65.35N 25.11 E
Kujang 152 Md 39.52N 126.01 E
Kujawy 120 Od 52.45N 18.30 E
Kujbyšev [R.S.F.S.R.] 114 Li 55.01N 49.06 E
Kujbyšev [R.S.F.S.R.] 112 Le 53.12N 50.09 E
Kujbyšev [R.S.F.S.R.] 138 Ce 55.27N 78.29 E
Kujbyševskaja oblast [3] 136 Fe 53.20N 50.30 E
Kujbyševski [Kaz.-U.S.S.R.] 136 Ge 53.15N 66.51 E
Kujbyševski [Taj.-U.S.S.R.] 135 Gf 37.53N 68.44 E
Kujbyševskoje vodohranilišče = Kuybyshev Resevoir (EN) 110 Ke 53.50N 49.00 E
Kujeda 134 Gh 56.26N 55.35 E
Kujgan 136 Hf 45.22N 74.10 E
Kuji 154 Pd 40.11N 141.46 E
Kuji-Gawa 156 Gi 36.30N 140.37 E
Kujtun 138 Ff 54.21N 101.35 E
Kujūkuri-Hama 156 Gd 35.40N 140.30 E
Kujū-San 154 Kh 33.09N 131.15 E
Kūkalār, Kūh-e- 146 Ng 31.50N 50.53 E
Kukalaya, Rio- 194 Fg 13.39N 83.37W
Kukësi 130 Dg 42.05N 20.24 E
Kukkia 116 Kc 61.20N 24.40 E
Kukmor 114 Mh 56.13N 50.52 E
Kükürt Tepe 146 Ib 41.07N 41.27 E
Kül 144 Id 27.15N 55.52 E
Kula [Bul.] 130 Ff 43.53N 22.31 E
Kula [Tur.] 146 Cc 38.30N 28.40 E
Kula [Yugo.] 130 Cd 45.37N 19.32 E
Kulai 150 Df 1.40N 103.36 E
Kulanak 135 Jd 41.18N 75.34 E
Kulandy 136 Ff 46.08N 59.31 E
Kular 138 Ib 70.32N 134.26 E
Kular, hrebet- 138 Ic 69.00N 133.30 E
Kulata 130 Gh 41.23N 23.22 E
Kulautuva 116 Jj 54.55N 23.43 E
Kulbus 168 Cc 14.24N 22.31 E
Kuldiga/Kuldīga 136 Cd 56.59N 21.59 E
Kuldīga/Kuldiga 136 Cd 56.59N 21.59 E
Kuldur 138 Ig 49.10N 131.40 E
Kulebaki 114 Ki 55.26N 42.32 E
Kulenjin 146 Me 35.40N 49.30 E
Kulen Vakuf 128 Kf 44.33N 16.06 E
Kulgera 210 Eg 25.50S 133.18 E
Kulikov 120 Ug 49.55N 24.06 E
Kulim 150 De 5.22N 100.34 E
Kuljab 136 Gh 37.55N 69.47 E
Kuljabskaja oblast [3] 136 Gh 38.00N 69.40 E
Kullaa 116 Jc 61.28N 22.10 E
Kullen 114 Ch 56.18N 12.26 E
Kulmasa 166 Ed 9.35N 2.27W
Kulmbach 120 Hf 50.06N 11.27 E
Kuloj 114 Kf 61.03N 42.30 E
Kuloj [R.S.F.S.R.] 136 Eb 66.00N 43.30 E
Kuloj [R.S.F.S.R.] 114 Kf 61.01N 42.12 E
Kulp 146 Ic 38.30N 41.02 E
Kulsary 136 Ff 46.57N 54.02 E
Kultuk 136 Ff 51.44N 103.42 E
Kulu 138 Jd 62.15N 147.45 E
Kulu [India] 148 Fb 31.58N 77.06 E
Kulu [Tur.] 146 Ei 39.06N 33.05 E
Kulumadau 219a Ac 9.03S 152.43 E
Kulunda 138 Cf 52.35N 78.57 E
Kulundinskaja step 138 Cf 52.45N 79.00 E
Kulundinskoje, ozero- 138 Cf 53.00N 79.30 E
Kum 146 Bc 38.38N 27.32 E
Kum, Kūh-e- 146 Oh 29.55N 53.45 E
Kuma 156 Ce 33.39N 132.54 E
Kuma [R.S.F.S.R.] 114 Hc 66.15N 31.02 E
Kuma [R.S.F.S.R.] 134 Mg 59.33N 66.40 E
Kuma [U.S.S.R.] 110 Kg 44.56N 47.00 E
Kumagaya 154 Of 36.08N 139.23 E
Kumai [Indon.] 150 Fg 3.23S 112.33 E
Kumai [Indon.] 150 Fg 2.44S 111.43 E
Kumaishi 156a Ab 42.08N 139.59 E
Kumak 132 Vd 51.13N 60.08 E
Kumamoto 142 Pf 32.48N 130.43 E
Kumamoto Ken [2] 154 Kh 32.30N 130.50 E
Kumano 154 Nh 33.54N 136.05 E
Kumano-Gawa 156 De 33.45N 135.59 E
Kumano-Nada 156 Ee 34.00N 136.30 E
Kumanovo 130 Eg 42.08N 21.43 E
Kumara [N.Z.] 218 De 42.38S 171.11 E
Kumara [R.S.F.S.R.] 138 Hf 51.35N 126.45 E
Kumasi 160 Gh 6.41N 1.37W
Kumba 166 Ge 4.38N 9.25 E
Kumbakonam 148 Ff 10.58N 79.23 E
Kumbe 150 Lh 8.21S 140.13 E
Kumbo 166 Hd 6.12N 10.40 E
Kumboro Cape 219a Cb 7.18S 157.32 E
Kŭmch'ŏn 154 Ie 38.10N 126.30 E
Kum-Dag 136 Fh 39.13N 54.40 E
Kumdah 164 Ie 20.23N 45.05 E
Kume-Jima 152 Mf 26.20N 126.45 E
Kumertau 136 Fe 52.46N 55.47 E
Kumhwa 154 Ie 38.17N 127.28 E
Kumihama 156 Dd 35.36N 134.54 E
Kuminski 136 Gd 58.40N 65.55 E
Kumköy (Kilyos) 130 Mh 41.15N 29.02 E
Kumkuduk 152 Fc 40.15N 91.55 E
Kumkurgan 135 Ff 37.50N 67.35 E
Kumla 114 Dg 59.08N 15.08 E
Kumlinge 116 Id 60.15N 20.45 E
Kumluca 146 Dd 36.22N 30.18 E
Kummerower See 120 Ic 53.49N 12.52 E
Kumo/Kokemäki 114 Ff 61.15N 22.21 E
Kumola 135 Fa 46.58N 64.30 E
Kumo-Manyčski kanal 132 Ng 45.27N 44.38 E
Kumon Taung 140 Lg 26.30N 96.50 E
Kumora 138 Ge 55.56N 111.13 E
Kumru 146 Gb 40.53N 37.17 E
Kumu 170 Eb 3.04N 25.09 E
Kumuh 132 Oh 42.11N 47.07 E
Kumukahi, Cape- 214 Od 19.31N 154.49W
Kumul/Hami 142 Le 42.48N 93.27 E
Kümüx 152 Ec 42.15N 88.10 E
Kumzār 146 Qj 26.20N 56.25 E
Kunashiri-Tō / Kunašir, ostrov- 140 Qe 44.05N 145.51 E
Kunašir, ostrov- / Kunashiri-Tō 140 Qe 44.05N 145.51 E
Kunaširski proliv = Nemuro Strait (EN) 138 Jh 43.50N 145.30 E
Kunchaung 148 Jd 23.50N 96.35 E
Kunda 114 Gg 59.30N 26.30 E
Kunda jõgi 116 Le 59.25N 26.27 E
Kundelungu, Monts- 170 Ed 9.30S 28.00 E
Kundiawa 212 Ia 6.00S 145.00 E
Kunduchi 170 Gd 6.40S 39.13 E
Kunduk → Kogilnik 130 Md 45.51N 29.38 E
Kunduk → Sasyk, ozero- 132 Fg 45.45N 29.40 E
Kunene 158 Ij 17.20S 11.50 E
Kunene (EN) = Cunene 158 Ij 17.20S 11.50 E
Künes/Xinyuan 152 Dc 43.24N 83.18 E
Künes He 152 Dc 43.32N 82.29 E
Kungälv 114 Ch 57.52N 11.58 E
Kungej-Alatau, hrebet- 136 Hg 42.50N 77.15 E
Kùngmiut 179 Ie 65.50N 36.45W
Kungrad 136 Fg 43.06N 58.54 E
Kungsbacka 114 Ch 57.29N 12.04 E
Kungsbackafjorden 116 Eg 57.25N 12.04 E
Kungshamn 116 Df 58.21N 11.15 E
Kungsör 116 Ge 59.25N 16.05 E
Kungu 170 Cb 2.47N 19.12 E
Kungur 136 Fd 57.25N 56.57 E
Kunhegyes 120 Qi 47.22N 20.38 E
Kunhing 148 Jd 21.18N 98.26 E
Kunigami-Misaki 156b Bb 27.26N 128.43 E
Kunimi-Dake 156 Be 32.33N 131.01 E
Kunisaki 156 Be 33.34N 131.45 E
Kunisaki-Hantō 156 Be 33.30N 131.40 E
Kunja 114 Hh 57.09N 31.10 E
Kunja-Urgenč 136 Fg 42.20N 59.12 E
Kunlong 148 Jd 23.25N 98.39 E
Kunlun Guan 152 Ig 23.06N 108.40 E
Kunlun Shan 140 Kf 36.00N 84.00 E
Kunlun Shankou 152 Fd 35.40N 94.03 E
Kunming 142 Mg 25.08N 102.43 E
Kunnui 156a Bb 42.26N 140.19 E
Kunovat 134 Ld 64.59N 65.35 E
Kunsan 152 Md 35.59N 126.43 E
Kunshan 154 Fi 31.22N 120.57 E
Kuntaur 166 Cc 13.40N 14.53W
Kununurra 212 Fc 15.47S 128.44 E
Kunyao 170 Gb 1.47N 35.03 E
Kunyu Shan 154 Ff 37.15N 121.46 E
Künzelsau 120 Fg 49.17N 9.41 E
Kuohijärvi 116 Kc 61.15N 24.55 E
Kuolimo 116 Lc 61.15N 27.35 E
Kuop Atoll 208 Gd 7.03N 151.56 E
Kuopio 112 Ic 62.54N 27.41 E
Kuopio [2] 114 Ge 63.20N 27.35 E
Kuorboaivi 114 Gb 69.41N 27.45 E
Kuortane 116 Jb 62.48N 23.30 E
Kupa 128 Ke 45.28N 16.24 E
Kupang 142 Ok 10.10S 123.35 E
Kupiano 214 Dj 10.10S 148.02 E
Kupičev 120 Uf 50.58N 24.52 E
Kupino 138 Cf 54.22N 77.18 E
Kupiškis 114 Fi 55.49N 25.01 E
Kupjansk 136 Df 49.42N 37.37 E
Kupjansk-Uzlovoj 132 Je 49.39N 37.45 E
Küplü [Tur.] 130 Jh 41.07N 26.21 E
Küplü [Tur.] 130 Mi 40.06N 30.00 E
Kuppenheim 124 Kf 48.50N 8.15 E
Kupreanof 178 Me 56.50N 133.30W
Kuqa 142 Ke 41.43N 82.57 E
Kura [R.S.F.S.R.] 132 Mh 44.05N 44.45 E
Kura [U.S.S.R.] 110 Kh 39.20N 49.25 E
Kuragaty 135 Ic 43.55N 73.34 E
Kuragino 138 Ef 53.53N 92.40 E
Kurahashi-Jima 156 Cd 34.08N 132.31 E
Kuraminski hrebet 135 Hd 40.50N 70.30 E
Kurashiki 154 Lg 34.35N 133.46 E
Kurashiki-Kojima 156 Cd 34.28N 133.48 E
Kurashiki-Tamashima 156 Cd 34.33N 133.40 E
Kura-Take 156 Be 32.27N 130.20 E
Kuraymah = Karima (EN) 160 Kg 18.33N 31.51 E
Kurayoshi 154 Lg 35.28N 133.49 E
Kurbneshi 130 Dh 41.47N 20.05 E
Kurčatov 132 Id 51.41N 35.42 E
Kurdaj 135 Jc 43.18N 74.59 E
Kurdistan 140 Gf 37.00N 44.00 E
Kurdistan 144 Fb 37.00N 44.00 E
Kurdufān 158 Jg 13.00N 30.00 E
Kurdufān al Janūbīyah [3] 168 Dc 11.00N 29.30 E
Kurdufān ash Shamālīyah [3] 168 Dc 14.50N 29.40 E
Kure 154 Lg 34.14N 132.34 E
Küre 146 Eb 41.48N 33.43 E
Kure Island 208 Jb 28.25N 178.25W
Kurejka 140 Kc 66.25N 87.12 E
Kurgaldžinski 136 He 50.30N 70.03 E
Kurgalski, mys- 116 Me 59.39N 28.03 E
Kurgan 142 Id 55.26N 65.18 E
Kurganinsk 132 Lg 44.57N 40.35 E
Kurganskaja oblast [3] 136 Gd 55.30N 65.00 E
Kurgan-Tjube 136 Gh 37.51N 68.46 E
Kurgan-Tjubinskaja oblast [3] 136 Gh 37.30N 68.30 E
Kuria Island 208 Id 0.14N 173.25 E
Kuria Muria Islands (EN) = Khurīyā Murīyā, Jazā'ir 140 Hh 17.30N 56.00 E
Kuri Bay 212 Ec 15.35S 124.50 E
Kurikka 114 Fe 62.37N 22.25 E
Kurikoma 156 Gb 38.50N 140.59 E
Kurikoma-Yama 156 Gb 38.57N 140.47 E
Kuril Basin (EN) 138 Jg 47.00N 150.00 E
Kuril Islands (EN) = Kurilskije ostrova 140 Re 46.10N 152.00 E
Kurilo 130 Gg 42.49N 23.21 E
Kurilsk 138 Jg 45.16N 147.58 E
Kurilskije ostrova = Kuril Islands (EN) 140 Re 46.10N 152.00 E
Kuril Trench (EN) 106 Je 47.00N 155.00 E
Kuring Kuru 172 Bc 17.38S 18.33 E
Kurino 156 Bf 31.57N 130.43 E
Kurinskaja kosa 132 Pj 39.05N 49.10 E
Kurinwás, Rio- 194 Fg 12.49N 83.41W
Kuriyama 156a Bb 43.03N 141.45 E
Kürkhūd, Kūh-e- 146 Qd 37.15N 56.30 E
Kurkosa 132 Pj 38.59N 49.08 E
Kurkūmā, Ra's- 146 Gj 25.51N 36.39 E
Kurkur 146 Ek 23.54N 32.19 E
Kurlovski 114 Ji 55.29N 40.39 E
Kurmuk 168 Ec 10.33N 34.17 E
Kurnool 142 Jh 15.50N 78.03 E
Kurobe 154 Nf 36.51N 137.26 E
Kurobe-Gawa 156 Ec 36.55N 137.26 E
Kurogi 156 Be 33.14N 130.40 E
Kuroishi 154 Pd 40.38N 140.36 E
Kuroiso 154 Pf 36.58N 140.03 E
Kuromatsunai 154 Pc 42.43N 140.20 E
Kurono-Seto 156 Be 32.05N 130.10 E
Kurort Družba 130 Kf 43.12N 28.00 E
Kurort Slănčev brjag 130 Kg 42.40N 27.42 E
Kurort Zlatni pjasăci 130 Lf 43.16N 28.02 E
Kuro-Shima 154 Ji 31.52N 129.58 E
Kurovskoje 114 Ji 55.35N 38.59 E
Kurów 120 Se 51.25N 22.10 E
Kurow 216 Dh 44.44S 170.28 E
Kurpiowska, Puszcza- 120 Rc 53.20N 21.30 E
Kuršėnai/Kuršenaj 136 Cd 56.03N 22.58 E
Kuršenaj/Kuršėnai 136 Cd 56.03N 22.58 E
Kuršiu užurekis 116 Ii 55.05N 21.00 E
Kursk 112 Je 51.42N 36.12 E
Kurskaja kosa 114 Ei 55.18N 21.00 E
Kurskaja oblast [3] 136 De 51.45N 36.15 E
Kurski zaliv 114 Ei 55.05N 21.00 E
Kuršumlija 130 Ef 43.09N 21.16 E
Kurtalan 146 Id 37.57N 41.42 E
Kurtamyš 136 Ge 54.55N 64.27 E
Kürti 160 Kg 18.07N 31.33 E
Kurtistown 221 Fd 19.36N 155.04W
Kurty 135 Kb 44.19N 76.42 E
Kuru 168 Dd 9.08N 26.57 E
Kurucaşile 146 Eb 41.51N 32.43 E
Kuruktag 152 Ec 41.30N 89.00 E
Kuruman 160 Jk 27.28S 23.28 E
Kuruman 158 Jk 26.56S 20.39 E
Kurume 154 Kh 33.19N 130.31 E
Kurunegala 148 Gg 7.29N 80.22 E
Kurur, Jabal- 168 Ea 20.31N 31.32 E
Kurzeme = Courland (EN) 110 Id 56.50N 22.00 E
Kurzemes Augstiene / Kurzemskaja vozvyšennost 116 Jh 56.45N 22.15 E
Kurzemskaja vozvyšennost / Kurzemes Augstiene 116 Jh 56.45N 22.15 E
Kusa 134 Ii 55.20N 59.29 E
Kuşada Körfezi 130 Kl 37.50N 27.08 E
Kuşadasi 146 Bd 37.51N 27.15 E
Kusagaki-Guntō 152 Me 31.00N 129.00 E
Kusaie → Kosrae 208 Hd 5.19N 162.59 E
Kusalu/Kuusalu 116 Ke 59.23N 25.25 E
Kusary 132 Pi 41.24N 48.29 E
Kusatsu [Jap.] 156 Fc 36.37N 138.35 E
Kusatsu [Jap.] 156 Dd 35.03N 135.59 E
Kuščevskaja 132 Kf 46.33N 39.37 E
Kuščinski 132 Oi 40.33N 46.06 E
Kusel 124 Je 49.33N 7.24 E
Kuş Gölü 146 Bb 40.10N 27.59 E
Kushida-Gawa 156 Ed 34.36N 136.34 E
Kushikino 154 Ki 31.44N 130.16 E
Kushima 154 Ki 31.29N 131.14 E
Kushimoto 154 Mh 33.28N 135.47 E
Kushiro 142 Qe 42.58N 144.23 E
Kushiro-Gawa 156a Db 42.59N 144.23 E
Kushtia 148 Hd 23.55N 89.07 E
Kuška 135 Dg 35.16N 62.18 E
Kuskokwim 174 Cc 60.17N 162.27W
Kuskokwim Bay 174 Cd 59.45N 162.25W
Kuskokwim Mountains 174 Dc 62.30N 156.00W
Kušmurun 136 Ge 52.27N 64.40 E
Kušmurun, ozero- 136 Ge 52.40N 64.45 E
Kušnarenkovo 134 Gi 55.06N 55.22 E
Kušnica 136 Ce 48.29N 23.20 E
Kusŏng 152 Md 39.59N 125.16 E
Kussharo Ko 154 Rc 43.35N 144.15 E
Kustanaj 142 Id 53.10N 63.35 E
Kustanajskaja oblast [3] 136 Ge 53.00N 64.00 E
Kustavi/Gustavs 116 Id 60.33N 21.21 E
Kustavi/Gustavs 116 Id 60.30N 21.25 E
Küstenkanal 120 Dc 53.08N 7.40 E
Kūstī 160 Kg 13.10N 32.40 E
Kustvlakte = Coast Plain (EN) 122 Ic 51.00N 2.30 E
Kusu 156 Be 33.16N 131.09 E
Kušum 132 Qd 51.06N 51.18 E
Kušva 136 Fd 58.18N 59.45 E
Kut, Ko- 148 Kf 11.40N 102.35 E
Kut, Ko- 148 Kf 11.40N 102.35 E
Kūt 'Abdollāh 146 Mg 31.13N 48.39 E
Kutacane 150 Cf 3.30N 97.48 E
Kutahya 144 Cb 39.25N 29.59 E
Kutaisi 112 Kg 42.15N 42.40 E
Kutch, Gulf of- → Kachchh, Gulf of 140 Ig 22.36N 60.30 E
Kutch, Rann of- 148 Ed 24.05N 70.10 E
Kutchan 154 Pc 42.54N 140.45 E
Kutcharo-Ko 156a Ca 45.10N 142.20 E
Kutina 128 Ke 45.29N 16.47 E
Kutkai 148 Jd 23.27N 97.56 E
Kutkašen 132 Oi 40.58N 47.52 E
Kutná Hora 120 Lg 49.57N 15.16 E
Kutno 120 Pd 52.15N 19.23 E
Kutse, gora- / Kuutse Mägi 116 Lg 57.58N 26.24 E
Kuttara-Ko 156a Bb 42.30N 141.10 E
Kutu 160 Ii 2.44S 18.09 E
Kutum 168 Cc 14.12N 24.40 E
Kúty 120 Nh 48.40N 17.01 E
Kuty 130 Ia 48.13N 25.15 E
Kuujjuaq 176 Md 58.10N 68.30W
Kuuli-Majak 136 Fg 40.16N 52.45 E

Index Symbols

1 Independent Nation
2 State, Region
3 District, County
4 Municipality
5 Colony, Dependency
Continent
Physical Region
Historical or Cultural Region
Mount, Mountain
Volcano
Hill
Mountains, Mountain Range
Hills, Escarpment
Plateau, Upland
Pass, Gap
Plain, Lowland
Delta
Salt Flat
Valley, Canyon
Crater, Cave
Karst Features
Depression
Polder
Desert, Dunes
Forest, Woods
Heath, Steppe
Oasis
Cape, Point
Coast, Beach
Cliff
Peninsula
Isthmus
Sandbank
Island
Atoll
Rock, Reef
Islands, Archipelago
Rocks, Reefs
Coral Reef
Well, Spring
Geyser
River, Stream
Waterfall, Rapids
River Mouth, Estuary
Lake
Salt Lake
Intermittent Lake
Reservoir
Swamp, Pond
Canal
Glacier
Ice Shelf, Pack Ice
Ocean
Sea
Gulf, Bay
Strait, Fjord
Lagoon
Bank
Seamount
Tablemount
Ridge
Shelf
Basin
Escarpment, Sea Scarp
Fracture
Trench, Abyss
National Park, Reserve
Point of Interest
Recreation Site
Cave, Cavern
Historic Site
Ruins
Wall, Walls
Church, Abbey
Temple
Scientific Station
Railway station
Airport
Port
Military installation
Lighthouse
Mine
Tunnel
Dam, Bridge

Kuurne	124	Fd	50.51N	3.17 E
Kuusalu/Kusalu	116	Ke	59.23N	25.25 E
Kuusamo	112	Ib	66.00N	29.11 E
Kuusankoski	116	Ld	60.54N	26.38 E
Kuutse Mägi / Kutse, gora-	116	Lg	57.58N	26.24 E
Kuvandyk	132	Td	51.29N	57.28 E
Kuvango	160	Ij	14.29S	16.18 E
Kuvdlorssuaq	179	Gd	74.38N	56.40W
Kuvšinovo	114	Ih	57.03N	34.13 E
Kuwait (EN) = Al Kuwayt	142	Gg	29.20N	47.59 E
Kuwait (EN) = Al Kuwayt [1]	142	Gg	29.30N	47.45 E
Kuwana	156	Ed	35.04N	136.39 E
Kuybychev Reservoir (EN) = Kujbyševskoje vodohranilišče	110	Ke	53.50N	49.00 E
Kuytun	152	Kc	44.25N	84.58 E
Kuyucak	130	Li	37.55N	28.28 E
Kuzey Kibris = North Cyprus (EN)	144	Db	35.15N	33.40 E
Kuzneck	136	Ee	53.07N	46.36 E
Kuznecki Alatau	140	Kd	54.45N	88.00 E
Kuznečnoje	116	Mc	61.04N	29.58 E
Kuźnia Raciborska	120	Of	50.11N	18.15 E
Kuzomen	136	Db	66.18N	36.49 E
Kuzovatovo	114	Lj	53.33N	47.41 E
Kuzumaki	156	Ga	40.02N	141.26 E
Kuzuryū-Gawa	156	Ec	36.13N	136.08 E
Kvænangen	114	Za	70.05N	21.13 E
Kvaløy	114	Eb	69.40N	18.30 E
Kvaløya	114	Fa	70.37N	23.52 E
Kvalsund	114	Fa	70.30N	24.00 E
Kvau	116	Cc	61.40N	9.42 E
Kvareli	132	Ni	41.57N	45.47 E
Kvarkeno	134	Lj	52.05N	59.40 E
Kvarnbergsvattnet	114	Dd	64.36N	14.03 E
Kvarner	128	If	44.45N	14.15 E
Kvarnerić	128	If	44.45N	14.58 E
Kvemo-Kedi	132	Oi	41.22N	46.31 E
Kvenna	116	Bd	60.01N	7.56 E
Kvichak	178	He	59.10N	156.40W
Kvichak Bay	178	He	58.48N	157.30W
Kvikkjokk	114	Dc	66.57N	17.47 E
Kvina	116	Bf	58.17N	6.56 E
Kvinesdal	116	Bf	58.19N	6.57 E
Kvissleby	116	Gb	62.17N	17.21 E
Kviteggia	116	Bb	62.05N	6.40 E
Kviteseid	116	Ce	59.24N	8.30 E
Kvitøya	224	Je	80.08N	32.35 E
Kwa	158	Ii	3.10S	16.11 E
Kwahu Plateau	166	Ed	6.30N	0.30W
Kwailibesi	219a	Ec	8.20S	160.40 E
Kwajalein Atoll	208	Hd	9.05N	167.20 E
Kwakoegron	202	Gb	5.15N	55.20W
Kwale [Kenya]	170	Gc	4.11S	39.27 E
Kwale [Nig.]	166	Gd	5.45N	6.25 E
Kwamouth	170	Cc	3.10S	16.12 E
Kwa Mtoro	170	Gd	5.14S	35.26 E
Kwando	170	Df	18.27S	23.32 E
Kwangdae-ri	152	Mc	40.34N	127.33 E
Kwangju	142	Of	35.09N	126.55 E
Kwango	158	Ii	3.14S	17.22 E
Kwangsi Chuang (EN) = Guangxi Zhuangzu Zizhiqu (Kuang-hsi-chuang-tsu Tzu-chih-ch'ü) [2]	152	Ig	24.00N	109.00 E
Kwangtung (EN) = Guangdong Sheng (Kuang-tung Sheng) [2]	152	Jg	23.00N	113.00 E
Kwanmo-bong	154	Jd	41.42N	129.13 E
Kwara [2]	166	Fd	8.30N	5.00 E
Kweichow (EN) = Guizhou Sheng (Kuei-chou Sheng) [2]	152	If	27.00N	107.00 E
Kweichow (EN) = Kuei-chou Sheng → Guizhou Sheng	152	If	27.00N	107.00 E
Kwekwe	172	Jj	18.55S	29.49 E
Kweneng [3]	172	Cd	24.00S	24.00 E
Kwenge	158	Ii	4.50S	18.44 E
Kwethluk	178	Kd	60.49N	161.27W
Kwidzyn	120	Oc	53.45N	18.56 E
Kwigillingok	178	Ke	59.51N	163.08W
Kwilu	158	Ii	3.22S	17.22 E
Kwisa	120	Le	51.33N	15.23 E
Kwoka, Gunung-	150	Jg	0.31S	132.27 E
Kyabé	160	Ih	9.27N	18.57 E
Kyabram	212	Jg	36.19S	145.03 E
Kyaikkami	148	Je	16.04N	97.34 E
Kyaikto	148	Je	17.18N	97.01 E
Kyaka	170	Fc	1.16S	31.25 E
Kyancutta	210	Eh	33.08S	135.34 E
Kyan-Zaki	156b	Ab	26.05N	127.40 E
Kyaukpyu	148	Id	20.51N	92.58 E
Kyaukse	148	Jd	21.36N	96.08 E
Kybartai/Kibartai	116	Jj	54.38N	22.44 E
Kyeintali	148	Ie	18.00N	94.29 E
Kyelang	148	Fb	32.35N	77.02 E
Kyfhauser	120	He	51.25N	11.08 E
Kyjov	120	Ng	49.01N	17.08 E
Kyle, Lake-	172	Ed	20.12S	31.00 E
Kyle of Lochalsh	118	Fd	57.17N	5.43W
Kyll	120	Gg	49.48N	6.42 E
Kyllburg	124	Id	50.02N	6.35 E
Kyma	114	Ld	64.48N	47.31 E
Kymi [2]	114	Gf	61.00N	28.00 E
Kymijoki	116	Ld	60.30N	26.52 E
Kyn	134	Ib	57.52N	58.32 E
Kynnefjäll	116	Df	58.42N	11.41 E
Kynsivesi	116	Lb	62.25N	26.10 E
Kyoga, Lake-	158	Kh	1.30N	33.00 E
Kyōga-Dake	156	Be	33.00N	130.05 E
Kyōga-Misaki	156	Ec	35.45N	135.11 E
Kyonan	156	Fd	35.07N	139.49 E
Kyŏnggi-Do [2]	154	If	37.30N	127.15 E
Kyŏnggi-man	154	Hf	37.25N	126.00 E
Kyŏngju	152	Md	35.50N	129.13 E
Kyŏngsang-Namdo [2]	154	Jg	35.15N	128.30 E
Kyŏngsang-Pukto [2]	154	Jf	36.20N	128.40 E
Kyŏngsŏng	154	Jd	41.40N	129.40 E
Kyōto	142	Pf	35.00N	135.45 E
Kyōto Fu	154	Mg	35.25N	135.15 E
Kypros → Kipros = Cyprus (EN)	144	Db	35.01N	33.00 E
Kyra	138	Gg	49.36N	111.58 E
Kyren	138	Ff	51.41N	102.10 E
Kyrenia	146	Ee	35.20N	33.19 E
Kyrgesara/ Kõrgesaare	116	Je	59.00N	22.25 E
Kyrgyz Sovetik Socialistik Respublikasy/Kirgizskaja SSR [2]	136	Hg	41.30N	75.00 E
Kyritz	120	Id	52.57N	12.24 E
Kyrkheden	116	Ed	60.10N	13.29 E
Kyrksæterora	114	Be	63.17N	9.06 E
Kyrkslätt/Kirkkonummi	116	Kd	60.07N	24.26 E
Kyrö	116	Kd	60.42N	22.45 E
Kyrönjoki	116	Ia	63.14N	21.45 E
Kyrösjärvi	116	Jc	61.45N	23.10 E
Kyröskoski	116	Jc	61.40N	23.11 E
Kyštym	136	Gd	55.42N	60.34 E
Kysucké Nové Mesto	120	Og	49.18N	18.48 E
Kythera (EN) = Kíthira	146	Ee	36.15N	23.00 E
Kythraia	146	Ee	35.15N	33.29 E
Kyuquot Sound	188	Bb	49.55N	127.25W
Kyūshū	140	Pf	32.50N	131.00 E
Kyushu-Palau Ridge (EN)	106	Ih	20.00N	136.00 E
Kyūshū-Sanchi	156	Be	32.40N	131.10 E
Kyyjärvi	116	Kb	63.02N	24.34 E
Kyyvesi	116	Lc	61.55N	27.05 E
Kyzikos	146	Bb	40.28N	27.47 E
Kyzyl	142	Lc	51.42N	94.27 E
Kyzylart, pereval-	136	Hh	39.22N	73.20 E
Kyzyl-Kija	136	Hg	40.14N	72.12 E
Kyzylkum	140	Ie	42.00N	64.00 E
Kyzylrabot	136	Ih	37.28N	74.45 E
Kyzylsu [U.S.S.R.]	135	Gf	37.22N	69.22 E
Kyzylsu [U.S.S.R.]	135	He	39.17N	71.25 E
Kyzylžar	136	Gf	48.17N	69.49 E
Kzyl-Orda	142	Ie	44.48N	65.28 E
Kzyl-Ordinskaja oblast [3]	136	Gf	45.00N	65.00 E
Kzyltu	136	He	53.41N	72.15 E

L

Laa an der Thaya	128	Kb	48.43N	16.23 E
Laakdal	124	Gc	51.05N	4.59 E
La Alberca	126	Fd	40.29N	6.06W
La Alcarria	126	Jd	40.31N	2.45W
La Almunia de Doña Godina	126	Kc	41.29N	1.22W
La Araucania [2]	206	Fe	37.50S	73.15W
La Ardilla, Cerro-	192	Hf	22.15N	102.40W
La Armuña	126	Gc	41.05N	5.35W
Laasphe	124	Kd	50.56N	8.24 E
La Asunción	202	Fa	11.02N	63.53W
Laau Point	221a	Bb	21.06N	157.16W
Laayoune	126	Ni	35.42N	2.00 E
Lab	130	Kg	42.45N	21.01 E
Laba	132	Kg	45.10N	39.40 E
La Babia	192	He	28.34N	102.04W
Labaddey	168	Ge	0.32N	42.45 E
Labadie Bank	118	Ek	50.30N	8.15W
La Banda	206	Hc	27.44S	64.15W
La Bañeza	126	Gb	42.18N	5.54W
La Barca	192	Hg	20.17N	102.34W
Labardén	204	Dm	36.57S	58.06W
La Barge	188	Je	42.16N	110.12W
La Barra, Punta-	194	Lh	11.30N	70.10W
La-Barre-en-Ouche	124	Cf	48.57N	0.40 E
Labbezanga	166	Fc	14.59N	0.43 E
Labé	160	Gd	11.19N	12.17W
Labe = Elbe (EN)	110	Ge	53.50N	9.00 E
Labelle	184	Ma	46.17N	74.44W
La Belle	184	Gl	26.46N	81.26W
La Berzosa	126	Ha	43.35N	3.30W
Labin	128	Ie	45.05N	14.08 E
Labinsk	136	Eg	44.35N	40.44 E
Labis	150	Df	2.23N	103.02 E
La Bisbal / la Bisbal d'Empordà	126	Pc	41.57N	3.03 E
la Bisbal d'Empordà/La Bisbal	126	Pc	41.57N	3.03 E
La Blanca, Laguna-	204	Bj	30.14S	60.38W
Laboe	120	Gb	54.24N	10.13 E
Laborec	120	Rf	48.31N	21.54 E
Laborie	197k	Bb	13.45N	61.00W
Labota	150	Hg	2.52S	122.01 E
Labouheyre	122	Fj	44.13N	0.55W
Laboulaye	206	Hd	34.07S	63.24W
Labra, Peña-	126	Ha	43.05N	4.26W
Labrador	174	Md	55.00N	70.00W
Labrador Basin (EN)	174	Od	53.00N	48.00W
Labrador City	176	Md	52.57N	66.54W
Labrador Sea	174	Nd	57.00N	53.00W
Labrang → Xiahe	152	Hd	35.18N	102.30 E
Labrieville	184	Ma	49.19N	69.34W
Labrit	122	Fj	44.06N	0.33W
La Broye	128	Ac	46.55N	7.02 E
Labuan, Pulau-	150	Ge	5.19N	115.13 E
Labudalin → Ergun Youqi	152	La	50.16N	120.09 E
Labuha	150	Ig	0.37S	127.29 E
Labuhan	150	Eh	6.22S	105.50 E
Labuhanbajo	150	Gh	8.30S	119.54 E
Labuhanbilik	150	Df	2.31N	100.10 E
Labuk, Teluk-	150	Ge	6.10N	117.50 E
La Bureba	126	Ib	42.36N	3.24W
Labutta	148	Ie	16.09N	94.46 E
Labytnangi	134	Ic	66.39N	66.21 E
Lac [3]	168	Ac	13.30N	14.20 E
Lača, ozero-	114	Jf	61.20N	38.50 E
La Cadena	192	He	25.53N	104.12W
La Calamine/Kelmis	124	Hd	50.43N	6.00 E
La Calandria	204	Cj	30.48S	58.39W
Lac Allard	180	Lf	50.30N	63.30W
La Campiña	126	Hg	37.45N	4.45W
Lacanau	122	Ej	44.59N	1.05W
Lacanau, Étang de-	122	Ej	44.58N	1.07W
Lacanau-Lacanau-Océan	122	Ej	45.00N	1.12W
Lacanau-Océan, Lacanau-	122	Ei	45.00N	1.12W
Lacantún, Rio-	192	Ni	16.36N	90.39W
Lácaram	130	Ce	45.00N	19.34 E
La Carlota [Arg.]	206	Hd	33.26S	63.18W
La Carlota [Phil.]	150	Hd	10.25N	122.55 E
La Carlota [Sp.]	126	Hg	37.40N	4.56W
La Carolina	126	If	38.15N	3.37W
Lacaune	122	Ik	43.43N	2.42 E
Lacaune, Monts de-	122	Ik	43.40N	2.36 E
Lac du Bonnet	186	Ha	50.35N	96.05W
La Ceiba [Hond.]	178	Kh	15.47N	86.50W
La Ceiba [Ven.]	194	Li	9.28N	71.04W
Lacepede Bay	212	Hg	36.45S	139.45 E
Lacepede Islands	212	Ec	16.50S	122.10 E
La Cerdaña/La Cerdanya	126	Nb	42.24N	1.40 E
La Cerdanya/La Cerdaña	126	Nb	42.24N	1.40 E
Lacey	188	Dc	47.07N	122.49W
La Chaux-de-Fonds	128	Ac	47.06N	6.50 E
Lachay, Punta-	204	Cf	11.18S	77.39W
La China, Sierra-	204	Bm	36.47S	60.34W
Lachine	184	Kc	45.26N	73.40W
Lachlan River	208	Hc	34.21S	143.57 E
La Chorrera [Col.]	202	Dd	0.45S	73.00W
La Chorrera [Pan.]	190	Ig	8.53N	79.47W
Laçi	130	Ch	41.38N	19.43 E
Lačin	132	Oj	39.39N	46.33 E
La Ciutat de Mallorca / Palma	112	Gb	39.34N	2.39 E
Lackawanna	184	Hd	42.49N	78.49W
Lac La Biche	180	Gf	54.46N	111.58W
Lac la Martre	180	Fd	63.21N	117.00W
Lac Mégantic	184	Kg	45.35N	70.53W
La Colina	204	Bm	37.20S	61.32W
La Coloma	194	Fb	22.15N	83.34W
La Colorada	192	Dc	28.41N	110.25W
Lacombe	180	Gf	52.28N	113.44W
Lacon	184	Fj	41.02N	89.24W
La Concepción [Pan.]	194	Fi	8.31N	82.37W
La Concepción [Ven.]	194	Lh	10.48N	71.46W
La Concha	192	Gg	21.46N	105.29W
Laconi	128	Dk	39.51N	9.03 E
Laconia	182	Mc	43.32N	71.29W
Laconia, Gulf of- (EN) = Lakonikós Kólpos	130	Fm	36.35N	22.40 E
La Coronilla	204	Fk	33.44S	53.31W
La Coruña [3]	126	Da	43.10N	8.25W
La Coruña / A Coruña	112	Fg	43.22N	8.23W
La Côte-Saint-André	122	Li	45.23N	5.15 E
Lacq	122	Fk	43.25N	0.37W
Lacroix-sur-Meuse	124	Hf	48.58N	5.31 E
La Crosse [Ks.-U.S.]	186	Gg	38.32N	99.18W
La Crosse [Wi.-U.S.]	176	Je	43.49N	91.15W
La Cruz [Arg.]	206	Ic	29.10S	56.38W
La Cruz [C.R.]	194	Eh	11.04N	85.39W
La Cruz [Mex.]	190	Cd	23.55N	106.54W
La Cruz [Ur.]	206	Id	33.56S	56.15W
La Cruz de Rio Grande	194	Eg	13.06N	84.10W
La Cruz de Taratara	194	Mh	11.03N	69.44W
La Cuesta	192	Hd	28.45N	102.25W
La Cumbre	206	Hd	30.58S	64.30W
Lac Yora	168	Cb	19.08N	18.21 E
Ladário	204	Dc	19.01S	57.35W
Ladbergen	124	Jc	52.08N	7.45 E
Ladek-Zdrój	120	Mf	50.21N	16.50 E
Ladenburg	124	Ke	49.28N	8.37 E
La Désirade	196	Fc	16.19N	61.03W
La Digue Island	172b	Ca	4.21S	55.50 E
Ladik	146	Fb	40.36N	36.45 E
Ladispoli	128	Gh	41.56N	12.05 E
Lado, Jabal-	168	Ed	5.06N	31.35 E
Ladoga, Lake- (EN) = Ladožskoje ozero	110	Jc	61.00N	31.00 E
Ladong	152	Ig	24.49N	109.34 E
La Dorada	202	Db	5.22N	74.42W
Ladožskoje ozero = Ladoga, Lake- (EN)	110	Jc	61.00N	31.00 E
Ladrones, Islas-	194	Fj	7.52S	82.26W
Lādūškin	116	Fc	54.35N	20.10 E
Ladva-Vetka	114	If	61.20N	34.29 E
Lady Ann Strait	180	Ja	75.45N	80.00W
Ladybrand	172	De	29.19S	27.25 E
Lady Evelyn Lake	184	Gb	47.20N	80.10W
Lady Newnes Ice Shelf	222	Kf	73.40S	167.30 E
Ladysmith [B.C.-Can.]	180	Dh	48.58N	123.49W
Ladysmith [S.Afr.]	160	Jk	28.34S	29.45 E
Ladysmith [Wi.-U.S.]	182	Ib	45.28N	91.07W
Ladyžin	132	Fe	48.40N	29.13 E
Lae	210	Ic	6.43S	147.01 E
Lae Atoll	208	Hd	8.56N	166.14 E
La Eduvigis	204	Bg	22.44S	59.05W
Laem, Khao-	148	Kf	14.19N	101.11 E
Laer [F.R.G.]	124	Jc	52.04N	7.21 E
Laer [F.R.G.]	124	Kb	52.06N	7.58 E
Lærdalsøyri	114	Bf	61.06N	7.29 E
Læsø	116	Dh	57.15N	11.00 E
Læsø Rende	116	Dg	57.15N	10.45 E
La Española = Hispaniola (EN)	174	Lh	19.00N	71.00W
La Esperanza [Bol.]	202	Ff	14.34S	62.10W
La Esperanza [Hond.]	194	Dg	14.19N	88.10W
La Estrada	126	Db	42.41N	8.29W
Lafayette [Al.-U.S.]	184	Ei	32.54N	85.24W
Lafayette [In.-U.S.]	176	Kf	40.25N	86.53W
Lafayette [La.-U.S.]	176	Jf	30.14N	92.01W
La Fère	124	Ge	49.40N	3.22 E
La Ferté-sur-Risle	124	Cf	48.59N	0.48 E
La Ferté-Frênel	124	Cf	48.50N	0.30 E
La Ferté-Milon	124	Fe	49.10N	3.07 E
Laffān, Ra's-	146	Nj	25.54N	51.35 E
Lafia	166	Gd	8.29N	8.31 E
Lafiagi	166	Gd	8.52N	5.15 E
La Foa	219b	Be	21.43S	165.49 E
La Follette	184	Eg	36.23N	84.07W
La Fria	194	Ki	8.13N	72.15W
Laft	146	Pi	26.54N	55.46 E
La Fuente de San Esteban	126	Fd	40.48N	6.15W
Laga, Monti della-	128	Hh	42.45N	13.35 E
La Galite (EN) = Jāliṯah	158	He	37.32N	8.56 E
La Gallareta	204	Bi	29.34S	60.23W
Lagamar	204	Id	18.13S	46.48W
Lagan	116	Eh	56.55N	13.59 E
Lagan	116	Eh	56.33N	12.56 E
Lagan/Abhainn an Lagáin	118	Hg	54.37N	5.53W
Lagarina, Val-	128	Fe	45.50N	11.10 E
La Garita Mountains	186	Dh	38.00N	106.40W
Lagarto	202	Kf	10.54S	37.41W
Lagash	146	Lg	31.27N	46.13 E
Lagawe	150	Hc	16.49N	121.06 E
Lage	124	Kc	51.59N	8.48 E
*Lågen [Nor.]	116	De	59.03N	10.05 E
Lågen [Nor.]	116	Cf	61.08N	10.25 E
Lagh Bogal	170	Gb	0.42N	40.55 E
Laghmān [3]	144	Lb	35.00N	70.15 E
Laghouat	158	Hc	33.48N	2.53 E
Laghouat [3]	162	Hc	33.30N	3.15 E
La Gloria	194	Kh	8.53N	73.48W
Lagôa	182	Dg	37.08N	8.27W
Lagoa da Prata	204	Je	20.01S	45.33W
Lagoa Vermelha	206	Jc	28.13S	51.32W
Lagodehi	132	Oi	41.50N	46.14 E
La Gomera	194	Bf	14.05N	91.03W
Lagonegro	128	Ij	40.07N	15.46 E
Lagonoy Gulf	150	Hd	13.35N	123.25 E
Lágos [Sp.]	130	Ih	41.01N	25.07 E
Lagos [2]	166	Fd	6.30N	3.30 E
Lagos [Nig.]	160	Hh	6.27N	3.23 E
Lagos [Port.]	126	Dg	37.06N	8.40W
Lagos, Baía de-	126	Dg	37.06N	8.39W
Lagos de Moreno	190	Dc	21.21N	101.55W
La Grande	182	Db	45.20N	118.05W
La Grande Fosse	118	Kl	49.40N	3.00W
La Grande Rivière	174	Ld	53.50N	79.00W
La Grande Trench (EN) = Hurd Deep	118	Kl	49.40N	3.00W
Lagrange	184	Ef	41.39N	85.25W
La Grange [Ky.-U.S.]	182	Ef	38.24N	85.23W
La Grange [Ga.-U.S.]	182	Jd	33.02N	85.02W
La Grange [Tx.-U.S.]	186	Hl	29.54N	96.52W
La Granja = San Ildefonso	126	Id	40.54N	4.00W
La Gran Sabana	202	Fb	5.30N	61.30W
La Grita	194	Ki	8.08N	71.59W
La Guaira	202	Db	11.30N	72.30W
La Guajira	202	Da	11.30N	72.30W
Lagua Lichan, Puntan-	220b	Ba	15.16N	145.50 E
Laguardia	126	Jb	42.33N	2.35W
La Guardia [Sp.]	126	Dc	41.54N	8.53W
La Guardia [Sp.]	126	Ie	39.47N	3.29W
La Guasima	192	Fe	21.06N	97.49W
Laguiole	122	Ij	44.41N	2.51 E
Laguna Alsina	204	Am	36.49S	62.13W
Laguna Beach	188	Gj	33.33N	117.51W
Laguna Blanca	204	Cg	25.08S	58.15W
Laguna de Bay	150	Hd	14.23N	121.15 E
Laguna Limpia	204	Ch	26.29S	59.41W
Laguna Mountains	188	Gj	32.55N	116.25W
Laguna Paiva	206	Id	31.19S	60.39W
Laguna Superior	190	Fe	16.20N	94.25W
Laguna Veneta	128	Ge	45.25N	12.22 E
Laguna Yema	204	Bg	24.15S	61.15W
Lagunas [Bol.]	202	Fg	19.38S	63.43W
Lagunas [Mex.]	190	Fe	17.50N	101.04W
Lagunillas [Mex.]	192	Ji	17.50N	101.04W
Lagunillas [Ven.]	194	Lh	10.08N	71.16W
Laha	152	Lb	48.13N	124.36 E
La Habana [3]	194	Fb	23.00N	82.20W
La Habana = Havana (EN)	176	Kg	23.08N	82.22W
Lahad Datu	150	Ge	5.02N	118.19 E
Laham	150	Fc	14.54N	4.25 E
Lahat	150	Dg	3.48S	103.32 E
Lai	160	Ih	9.24N	16.18 E
Laiagam	214	Ci	5.33S	143.31 E
Lai'an	154	Hh	32.28N	118.26 E
Lai Chau	148	Kd	22.02N	103.10 E
Laichow'Moray	118	Gd	57.40N	3.30W
Laidley	212	Kf	27.38S	152.24 E
Laifeng	152	If	29.31N	109.23 E
Laighean/Leinster	118	Gh	53.00N	7.00W
Laignes	124	Gg	47.50N	4.22 E
Laihia	114	Kg	62.58N	22.01 E
Lainioälven	114	Ec	67.50N	22.40 E
Lairg	118	Gc	58.01N	4.25W
Lairi, Batha de-	168	Bc	10.49N	17.06 E
Lais	150	Dg	3.32S	102.03 E
La Isabela	194	Bg	22.57N	80.01W
La Ferrière-sur-Risle	124	Cf	48.59N	0.48 E
Laiševo	114	Li	55.26N	49.32 E
Laishui	154	Ce	39.23N	115.42 E
Laisvall	114	Dc	66.08N	17.10 E
Laitila	114	Ef	60.53N	21.41 E
Laiwu	154	Df	36.12N	117.40 E
Laiwui	150	Ig	1.22S	127.40 E
Laixi (Shuiji)	154	Ff	36.52N	120.31 E
Laiyang	152	Ld	36.59N	120.39 E
Laiyuan	152	Jd	39.19N	114.43 E
Laizhou Wan	154	Ef	37.30N	119.30 E
Laja	206	Fe	37.16S	72.42W
Laja	134	Hc	66.20N	56.16 E
La Jara	126	He	39.40N	4.55W
Lajeado	204	Gi	29.27S	51.58W
Lajedo, Serra do-	204	Hd	19.08S	49.56W
Lajes [Braz.]	200	Kh	27.48S	50.19W
Lajes [Braz.]	202	Ke	5.41S	36.14W
Lajes do Pico	162	Bb	38.23N	28.16W
Lajosmizse	120	Pi	47.01N	19.33 E
La Junta [Co.-U.S.]	186	Fh	37.59N	103.33W
La Junta [Mex.]	192	Fc	28.28N	107.20W
Lak Bor	170	Hb	1.18N	40.40 E
Lake Cargelligo	212	Jf	33.18S	146.23 E
Lake Charles	176	Jf	30.12N	93.12W
Lake City	182	Ke	30.12N	82.38W
Lake District	118	Jg	54.30N	3.10W
Lake Fork Creek	188	Jf	40.13N	110.07W
Lake Geneva	184	Fc	42.36N	88.26W
Lake George	184	Kd	43.25N	73.45W
Lake Grace	212	Df	33.06S	118.28 E
Lake Harbour	180	Kd	62.51N	69.53W
Lake Havasu City	188	Hi	34.27N	114.22W
Lake Itasca	186	Ic	46.51N	95.13W
Lake Jackson	186	Il	29.02N	95.27W
Lake King	212	Df	33.05S	119.42 E
Lakeland	182	Kf	28.03N	81.57W
Lake Louise	188	Ga	51.26N	116.11W
Lakemba	219d	Cc	17.53S	178.32W
Lakemba Passage	219d	Cb	17.53S	178.32W
Lake Mills	186	Je	43.25N	93.32W
Lake Minchumina	178	Lc	63.53N	152.19W
Lake Murray	214	Ci	6.54S	141.28 E
Lake Oswego	188	Dc	45.26N	122.39W
Lake Placid	184	Kc	44.18N	73.59W
Lake Providence	186	Kj	32.48N	91.11W
Lake Pukaki	218	Cf	44.11S	170.08 E
Lake Range	188	Ff	40.15N	119.25W
Lake River	180	Jf	54.28N	82.30W
Lakes Entrance	212	Jg	37.53S	147.59 E
Lakeside	188	If	41.13N	112.57W
Lake Tekapo	218	Df	44.00S	170.29 E
Lakeview	182	Cc	42.11N	120.21W
Lakeville	184	Ge	44.39N	93.14W
Lakewood [Co.-U.S.]	186	Eg	39.44N	105.06W
Lakewood [Oh.-U.S.]	184	Ge	41.29N	81.50W
Lake Worth	184	Gl	26.37N	80.03W
Lakhdar, Chergui Kef-	126	Pi	35.57N	3.16 E
Lakhdaria	126	Ph	36.34N	3.35 E
Lāki	116	Hh	41.50N	24.50 E
Lakin	186	Fh	37.58N	101.15W
Lakinsk	114	Jh	56.04N	39.58 E
Lákmos Óros	130	Ej	39.40N	21.07 E
Lakonía	208	Hf	14.17S	167.30 E
Laconia, Gulf of- (EN)	130	Fm	36.35N	22.40 E
Lakonikós Kólpos = Laconia, Gulf of- (EN)	130	Fm	36.35N	22.42 E
Lakota [3]	166	Dd	5.53N	5.41W
Lakota [I.C.]	166	Dd	5.51N	5.41W
Lakselv	114	Ga	70.03N	25.01 E
Laksefjorden	114	Ga	70.58N	27.00 E
Lakshadweep [3]	148	Ef	11.00N	72.00 E
Lakshadweep [3]	140	Jh	11.00N	72.00 E
La Laguna	200	Bb	14.30S	61.06W
Lalanna	172	Hd	23.28S	45.05 E
Lalapaga	120	Jh	41.50N	26.44 E
Lâleh Zâr, Kûh-e-	140	Hg	29.24N	56.46 E
La Leonesa	204	Ch	27.03S	58.43W
Lāli	146	Mf	32.21N	49.06 E
Lalibela	168	Fc	12.00N	39.04 E
La Libertad [3]	194	Ce	16.47N	90.07W
La Libertad [El Sal.]	190	Gf	13.29N	89.16W
La Libertad [Guat.]	194	Bf	16.47N	90.07W
La Libertad [Guat.]	194	Ce	17.10N	89.20W
La Libertad [Hond.]	194	Df	14.44N	87.40W
La Ligua	206	Fd	32.27S	71.14W
Lalin	126	Db	42.39N	8.07W
La Línea	126	Gh	36.10N	5.21W
Lalin He	154	Hb	45.28N	125.43 E
Lalitpur	148	Gd	24.41N	78.25 E
Lalla Khedidja	126	Qh	36.27N	4.14 E
Lālmanir Hāt	148	Hc	25.54N	89.27 E
La Loche	180	Ge	56.29N	109.27W
La Louvière	122	Kd	50.29N	4.11 E
La Lucila	204	Bj	30.25S	61.01W
Lalzit, Gjiri i-	130	Ch	41.31N	19.29 E
La Maddalena	128	Di	41.13N	9.24 E
La Maiella	128	Hh	42.05N	14.07 E
La Maladeta/Malditos, Montes-	126	Mb	42.40N	0.50 E
La Malbaie	180	Kg	47.39N	70.10W
La Mancha	110	Fh	39.05N	3.00W
La Manche = English Channel (EN)	110	Fg	50.00N	0.00
Lamap	216	Cc	16.26S	167.43 E
Lamar	186	Fh	38.05N	102.37W
La Maragateria	126	Fb	42.20N	6.15W
La Marina	126	Lf	38.35N	0.05W
La Marmora	128	Dk	39.59N	9.20 E
La Marque	186	Il	29.22N	94.58W
Lamas	202	Cf	6.25S	76.32W
Lamastre	122	Kj	44.59N	4.35 E
Lamawan	154	Ad	40.05N	111.25 E
Lamballe	122	Df	48.28N	2.31W
Lambarené	160	Ii	0.42S	10.13 E

Index Symbols

[1] Independent Nation	Historical or Cultural Region	Pass, Gap	Depression	Coast, Beach	Rock, Reef	Waterfall, Rapids	Canal	Lagoon	Escarpment, Sea Scarp	Historic Site	Airport
[2] State, Region	Mount, Mountain	Plain, Lowland	Polder	Cliff	Islands, Archipelago	River Mouth, Estuary	Bank	Seamount	Ruins	Port
[3] District, County	Volcano	Delta	Desert, Dunes	Peninsula	Rocks, Reef	Glacier	Ice Shelf, Pack Ice	Trench, Abyss	Wall, Walls	Military installation
[4] Municipality	Hill	Salt Flat	Forest, Woods	Isthmus	Coral Reef	Lake	Ocean	Tablemount	National Park, Reserve	Lighthouse
[5] Colony, Dependency	Mountains, Mountain Range	Valley, Canyon	Heath, Steppe	Sandbank	Well, Spring	Salt Lake	Sea	Ridge	Point of Interest	Mine
Continent	Hills, Escarpment	Crater, Cave	Oasis	Island	Geyser	Intermittent Lake	Gulf, Bay	Shelf	Recreation Site	Scientific Station	Tunnel
Physical Region	Plateau, Upland	Karst Features	Cape, Point	Atoll	River, Stream	Reservoir	Strait, Fjord	Basin	Cave, Cavern	Railway station	Dam, Bridge

Lambari	204	Je	21.58S	45.21W
Lambasa	216	Ec	16.26S	179.24 E
Lambay/Reachrainn	118	Gh	53.29N	6.01W
Lambayeque	202	Ce	6.42S	79.55W
Lambayeque [3]	202	Ce	6.20S	80.00W
Lambert Glacier	222	Ff	71.00S	70.00 E
Lambert Land	179	Jc	79.10N	21.00W
Lamberts Bay	160	Il	32.05S	18.17 E
Lambro	128	De	45.08N	9.32 E
Lambsheim	124	Ke	49.31N	8.17 E
Lambton, Cape -	180	Fb	71.04N	123.08W
Lamé	168	Ad	9.15N	14.32 E
Lame Deer	188	Ld	45.37N	106.40W
Lamego	126	Ec	41.06N	7.49W
Lamentin	197e	Ab	16.16N	61.38W
La Mesa	188	Gj	32.46N	117.01W
Lamesa	182	Ge	32.44N	101.57W
La Meta	128	Hi	41.41N	13.56 E
Lamezia Terme	128	Kl	38.59N	16.17 E
Lamezia Terme - Nicastro	128	Kl	38.59N	16.19 E
Lamezia Terme - Sambiase	128	Kl	38.58N	16.17 E
Lamezia Terme - Sant'Eufemia Lamezia	128	Kl	38.55N	16.15 E
Lamía	130	Fk	38.54N	22.26 E
Lamina	204	De	20.34S	56.14W
Lamlam, Mount-	220c	Bb	13.20N	144.40 E
Lammermuir Hills	118	Kf	55.52N	2.40W
Lammhult	116	Fg	57.10N	14.35 E
Lammi	114	Ff	61.05N	25.01 E
Lamoil	220d	Ba	7.39N	151.41 E
Lamon Bay	140	Oh	14.25N	122.00 E
Lamone	128	Gf	44.29N	12.08 E
Lamoni	186	Jf	40.37N	93.56W
Lamont	184	Fj	30.21N	83.50W
La Montaña	198	If	10.00S	72.50W
La Moraña	126	Hd	40.45N	4.55W
La Mosquitia	194	Ef	15.00N	84.20W
Lamotrek Atoll	208	Fd	7.30N	146.20 E
Lamotte-Beuvron	122	Ig	47.36N	2.01 E
La Moure	186	Gc	46.21N	98.18W
Lampang	148	Je	18.16N	99.34 E
Lampasas	186	Gk	31.03N	98.12W
Lampazos de Naranjo	192	Id	27.01N	100.31W
Lampedusa	128	Go	35.30N	12.35 E
Lampertheim	120	Eg	49.36N	8.28 E
Lampeter	118	Ii	52.07N	4.05W
Lamphun	148	Je	18.35N	99.00 E
Lampione	128	Go	35.35N	12.20 E
Lampung [3]	150	Dg	5.00S	105.00 E
Lamu	160	Li	2.16S	40.54 E
Lamud	202	Ce	6.09S	77.55W
Lan	132	Ec	52.09N	27.18 E
Lana	128	Fd	46.37N	11.09 E
Lana, Río de la-	192	Li	17.49N	95.09W
Lanai City	221a	Ec	20.50N	156.55W
Lanaihale	221a	Ec	20.49N	156.52W
Lanai Island	208	Lb	20.50N	156.55W
Lanaken	124	Hd	50.53N	5.39 E
Lanao, Lake-	150	He	7.50N	124.15 E
Lanark	118	Jf	55.41N	3.48W
Lanbi Kyun	148	Jf	10.50N	98.15 E
Lancang (Menglangba)	152	Gg	22.37N	99.57 E
Lancang Jiang=Mekong (EN)	140	Mh	10.15N	105.55 E
Lancashire [3]	118	Kh	53.55N	2.40W
Lancashire Plain	118	Kh	53.40N	2.45W
Lancaster	118	Kh	53.45N	2.50W
Lancaster [Ca.-U.S.]	182	De	34.42N	118.08W
Lancaster [Eng.-U.K.]	118	Kg	54.03N	2.48W
Lancaster [Mo.-U.S.]	186	Jf	40.31N	92.32W
Lancaster [N.H.-U.S.]	184	Lc	44.29N	71.34W
Lancaster [Oh.-U.S.]	184	Ff	39.43N	82.37W
Lancaster [Ont.-Can.]	184	Jc	45.12N	74.30W
Lancaster [Pa.-U.S.]	182	Lc	40.01N	76.19W
Lancaster [S.C.-U.S.]	184	Gh	34.43N	80.47W
Lancaster Sound	174	Kb	74.13N	84.00W
Lançeiro	204	Fe	20.59S	53.43W
Lancelin	212	Df	31.01S	115.19 E
Lanciano	128	Ih	42.14N	14.23 E
Lančin	130	Ha	48.31N	24.49 E
Lancun	154	Ff	36.25N	120.11 E
Łańcut	120	Sf	50.05N	22.13 E
Land	116	Cd	60.45N	10.00 E
Lândana	170	Bd	5.15S	12.10 E
Landau an der Isar	120	Ih	48.41N	12.41 E
Landau in der Pfalz	120	Eg	49.12N	8.07 E
Land Bay	222	Mf	75.25S	141.45W
Landeck	128	Ec	47.08N	10.34 E
Landen	124	Hd	50.45N	5.05 E
Lander	182	Fc	42.50N	108.44W
Landerneau	122	Bf	48.27N	4.15W
Lander River	212	Gd	20.25S	132.00 E
Landeryd	116	Eg	57.05N	13.16 E
Landes [3]	122	Fj	44.00N	0.50W
Landes	122	Fj	44.15N	1.00W
Landesbergen	124	Lb	52.34N	9.08 E
Landeta	204	Ak	32.01S	62.04W
Landete	126	Ke	39.54N	1.22W
Landfallis	148	If	13.40N	93.02 E
Land Glacier	222	Mf	75.40S	141.45W
Landi Kotal	148	Eb	34.06N	71.09 E
Landless Corner	170	Ee	14.53S	28.04 E
Landrecies	124	Fd	50.08N	3.42 E
Landsberg am Lech	120	Gh	48.03N	10.52 E
Landsbro	116	Fg	57.22N	14.54 E
Land's End	110	Fe	50.03N	5.44W
Lands End	180	Fa	76.25N	122.45W
Landshut	120	Ih	48.32N	12.09 E
Landskrona	114	Ci	55.52N	12.50 E
Landsort	116	Gf	58.45N	17.50 E
Landsortsdjupet	116	Hf	58.40N	18.30 E
Landstuhl	124	Je	49.25N	7.34 E
Landusky	188	Kc	47.54N	108.37W
La Neuve-Lyre	124	Cf	48.54N	0.45 E
Lanfeng → Lankao	154	Cg	34.49N	114.48 E
Lang	188	Mb	49.56N	104.23W
La'nga Co	152	De	30.41N	81.17 E
Langadhás	130	Gi	40.45N	23.04 E
Langádhia	130	Fl	37.39N	22.03 E
Långan	114	De	63.19N	14.44 E
Langano, Lake-	168	Fd	7.36N	38.43 E
Langara	150	Hg	4.02S	123.00 E
Langarfoss	114a	Cb	65.35N	14.15W
Langasian	150	Ie	8.16N	125.39 E
Langdon	186	Gb	48.46N	98.22W
Langeac	122	Ji	45.06N	3.29 E
Langeais	122	Gg	47.20N	0.24 E
Langeb	168	Fb	17.46N	36.41 E
Langebaan	172	Bf	33.06S	18.02 E
Langeberg	172	Cf	33.56S	20.45 E
Langedijk	124	Gb	52.42N	4.48 E
Langeland	114	Ci	55.00N	10.50 E
Langelands Bælt	116	Dj	54.50N	10.55 E
Längelmävesi	116	Kc	61.30N	24.20 E
Langen	124	Ke	49.59N	8.40 E
Langenberg	124	Kc	51.17N	8.34 E
Langenburg	186	Fa	50.50N	101.43W
Langenfeld (Rheinland)	124	Ic	51.06N	6.57 E
Langenhagen	120	Fd	52.27N	9.45 E
Langenselbold	124	Ld	50.11N	9.02 E
Langenthal	128	Bc	47.13N	7.49 E
Langeoog	120	Dc	53.46N	7.32 E
Langeri	138	Jf	50.08N	143.20 E
Langesund	116	Ce	59.00N	9.45 E
Langesundsfjorden	116	Cf	59.00N	9.48 E
Langevåg	116	Bb	62.27N	6.12 E
Langfang → Anci	152	Kd	39.29N	116.40 E
Långfjället	116	Eb	62.10N	12.20 E
Langfjorden	116	Bb	62.45N	7.30 E
Langhe	128	Bf	44.30N	8.00 E
Langholm	118	Kf	55.09N	3.00W
Langjökull	110	Ec	64.39N	20.00W
Langkawi, Pulau-	150	Ce	6.22N	99.48 E
Langkon	150	Ge	6.32N	116.42 E
Langlade	184	Ja	48.12N	75.57W
Langnau im Emmental	128	Bd	46.56N	7.46 E
Langogne	122	Jj	44.43N	3.51 E
Langon	122	Fj	44.33N	0.15W
Langorūd	146	Nd	37.11N	50.10 E
Langøya	114	Db	68.44N	14.50 E
Langreo	126	Ga	43.18N	5.41W
Langres	122	Lg	47.52N	5.20 E
Langres, Plateau de-	110	Gf	47.41N	5.03 E
Langrune-sur-Mer	124	Be	49.19N	0.22W
Langsa	142	Li	4.28N	97.58 E
Långsele	116	Ga	63.11N	17.04 E
Långshyttan	116	Gd	60.27N	16.01 E
Lang Son	148	Ld	21.50N	106.44 E
Lang Suan	148	Jg	9.55N	99.07 E
Languedoc	110	Gg	44.00N	4.00 E
Languedoc	122	Jj	44.00N	4.00 E
Langueyú, Arroyo-	204	Cm	36.39S	58.27W
Langwedel	124	Lb	52.58N	9.13 E
Langxi	154	Ei	31.08N	119.11 E
Langzhong	152	Ie	31.40N	106.04 E
Lan Hsu	152	Lg	22.00N	121.30 E
Laniel	184	Hb	47.06N	79.15W
Lanin, Volcán-	198	Ii	39.38S	71.30W
Lankao (Lanfeng)	154	Cg	34.49N	114.48 E
Länkipohja	116	Kc	61.44N	24.48 E
Lannemezan	122	Gk	43.08N	0.23 E
Lannemezan, Plateau de-	122	Gk	43.09N	0.27 E
Lannion	122	Cf	48.44N	3.28W
Lannion, Baie de-	122	Cf	48.43N	3.34W
La Noria	206	Gb	20.23S	69.53W
Lansdowne House	180	If	52.13N	87.53W
L'Anse	184	Cb	46.45N	88.27W
Lansing [Ia.-U.S.]	186	Ke	43.22N	91.13W
Lansing [Mi.-U.S.]	176	Ke	42.43N	84.34W
Lansjärv	114	Fc	66.39N	22.12 E
Łańskie, Jezioro-	120	Qc	53.33N	20.30 E
Lantar	138	Ie	56.05N	137.35 E
Lanta Yai, Ko-	148	Jg	7.35N	99.03 E
Lanteri	204	Ci	28.50S	59.39W
Lanterne	122	Mg	47.44N	6.03 E
Lanús	204	Cl	34.43S	58.24W
Lanusei	128	Dk	39.53N	9.32 E
Lanvaux, Landes de-	122	Dg	47.47N	2.36W
Lanxi [China]	154	Ej	29.13N	119.28 E
Lanxi [China]	154	Ha	46.15N	126.16 E
Lanxian (Dongcun)	154	Ae	38.17N	111.38 E
Lanyi He	154	Ae	38.40N	110.53 E
Lanzarote	158	Ff	29.00N	13.40W
Lanzhou	142	Mf	36.03N	103.41 E
Lanzo Torinese	128	Be	45.16N	7.28 E
Lao	128	Jk	39.47N	15.48 E
Laoag	142	Oh	18.12N	120.36 E
Laoang	150	Id	12.34N	125.00 E
Lao Cai	142	Mg	22.30N	103.57 E
Laocheng	154	Hc	42.37N	124.04 E
Laoha He	152	Lc	43.24N	120.39 E
Lao He	154	Cj	29.02N	115.47 E
Laohuanghe Kou	154	Ef	37.39N	119.02 E
Laois [2]	118	Fi	53.00N	7.30W
Laojunmiao → Yumen	142	Lf	39.50N	97.44 E
Laojun Shan	152	Je	33.45N	111.38 E
Lao Ling	154	Id	41.24N	126.10 E
Laon	122	Je	49.34N	3.37 E
Laona	186	Ld	45.34N	88.40W
Laonnois	124	Fe	49.35N	3.40 E
La Orchila, Isla-	202	Ea	11.48N	66.10W
La Oroya	200	Ig	11.32S	75.57W
Laos [1]	142	Mh	18.00N	105.00 E
Laoshan (Licun)	154	Ff	36.10N	120.25 E
Laotougou	154	Jc	42.54N	129.09 E
Laou	126	Gi	35.26N	5.05W
Laoye Ling	154	Kb	44.50N	130.10 E
Lapa	206	Kc	25.45S	49.42W
Lapai	166	Gd	9.03N	6.43 E
Lapalisse	122	Jh	46.15N	3.38 E
La Palma	158	Ff	28.40N	17.52W
La Palma [El Sal.]	194	Cf	14.19N	89.11W
La Palma [Pan.]	190	Ig	8.25N	78.09W
La Palma del Condado	126	Fg	37.23N	6.33W
La Paloma	204	El	34.40S	54.10W
La Pampa [2]	206	Ge	37.00S	66.00W
La Panne/De Panne	124	Ec	51.06N	2.35 E
La Paragua	202	Fb	6.50N	63.20W
La Partida, Isla-	192	De	24.30N	110.25W
La Paz [Arg.]	206	Gd	33.28S	67.33W
La Paz [Arg.]	206	Id	30.45S	59.39W
La Paz [Bol.]	200	Jg	16.30S	68.09W
La Paz [Bol.] [3]	202	Eg	15.00S	68.00W
La Paz [Col.]	194	Kh	10.23N	73.10W
La Paz [Hond.]	190	Gf	14.16N	87.40W
La Paz [Hond.] [3]	194	Df	14.15N	87.50W
La Paz [Mex.]	176	Hg	24.10N	110.18W
La Paz [Ur.]	204	Dl	34.46S	56.13W
La Paz [Ven.]	194	Lh	10.41N	72.00W
La Paz, Bahía de-	190	Bd	24.09N	110.25W
La Paz, Llano de-	192	De	24.00N	110.30W
La Paz Centro	194	Dg	12.20N	86.41W
La Pedrera	202	Ed	1.18S	69.40W
Lapeer	184	Fd	43.03N	83.19W
La Pelada	204	Bj	30.52S	60.59W
La Pérouse, Bahía-	221d	Bb	27.04S	109.18W
La Perouse Strait (EN) = Laperuza, proliv-	140	Qe	45.30N	142.00 E
La Perouse Strait (EN)= Sōya-Kaikyō	140	Qe	45.30N	142.00 E
Laperuza, proliv- = La Perouse Strait (EN)	140	Qe	45.30N	142.00 E
La Pesca	190	Ed	23.47N	97.47W
La Petite-Pierre	124	Jf	48.52N	7.19 E
La Picasa, Laguna-	204	Al	34.20S	62.14W
La Piedad Cavadas	192	Hg	20.21N	102.00W
La Pine	188	Ee	43.40N	121.30W
Lapinjärvi/ Lappträsk	116	Ld	60.36N	26.09 E
Lapinlahti	114	Ge	63.22N	27.30 E
La Plaine	197g	Bb	15.20N	61.15W
La Plana	126	Ld	40.00N	0.05W
Lapland (EN)=Lappi	110	Ib	66.50N	22.00 E
Lapland (EN)=Lappland	110	Ib	66.50N	22.00 E
La Plant	186	Fd	45.10N	100.38W
La Plata	200	Ki	34.55S	57.57W
la Pobla de Lillet	126	Nb	42.15N	1.59 E
la Pobla de Segur / Pobla de Segur	126	Mb	42.15N	0.58 E
La Pocatièr	184	Lb	47.21N	70.02W
La Porte	184	De	41.36N	86.43W
Lapovo	130	Ee	44.11N	21.06 E
Lappajärvi	114	Fe	63.08N	23.40 E
Lappeenranta/Villmanstrand	112	Ic	61.04N	28.11 E
Lappfjärd/Lapväärtti	116	Ib	62.15N	21.32 E
Lappi	116	Ic	61.06N	21.50 E
Lappi [2]	114	Gc	67.40N	26.30 E
Lappi=Lapland (EN)	110	Ib	66.50N	22.00 E
Lappo/Lapua	114	Fe	62.57N	23.00 E
Lappträsk/Lapinjärvi	116	Ld	60.36N	26.09 E
Lapri	138	He	55.45N	124.59 E
Laprida	206	He	37.33S	60.49W
Lâpseki	146	Bb	40.20N	26.31 E
Lapta	146	Ee	35.20N	33.10 E
Laptev Sea (EN) = Laptevyh, more-	224	Fd	76.00N	126.00 E
Laptevyh, more- = Laptev Sea (EN)	224	Fd	76.00N	126.00 E
Lapua/Lappo	114	Fe	62.57N	23.00 E
La Puebla / Sa Pobla	126	Pe	39.46N	3.01 E
La Puebla de Cazalla	126	Gg	37.14N	5.19W
Lapuna	204	Ba	13.19S	60.28W
La Puntilla	198	Hf	2.11S	81.01W
La Purísima	192	Cd	26.10N	112.04W
Lăpuş	130	Hb	47.30N	24.01 E
Lăpuş	130	Gb	47.39N	23.24 E
La Push	188	Cc	47.55N	124.38W
Lapväärtti/Lappfjärd	116	Ib	62.15N	21.32 E
Łapy	120	Sd	53.00N	22.53 E
Laqīyat al Arba'in	168	Da	20.03N	28.02 E
La Quemada	192	Hf	22.27N	102.45W
La Quiaca	206	Gb	22.06S	65.37W
L'Aquila	112	Hg	42.22N	13.22 E
Lar	144	Hd	27.41N	54.17 E
Lara [2]	202	Ea	10.10N	69.50W
La Rábida, Monasterio de-	126	Fg	37.12N	6.55W
Larache	162	Fb	35.12N	6.09W
Laragne-Montéglin	122	Lj	44.19N	5.49 E
Lārak	144	Id	26.52N	56.22 E
La Rambla	126	Hg	37.36N	4.44W
Laramie	176	Ie	41.19N	105.35W
Laramie Mountains	182	Fc	42.00N	105.40W
Laramie Peak	188	Me	42.17N	105.27W
Laramie River	188	Me	42.12N	104.32W
Laranjal, Rio-	204	Ff	23.12S	53.45W
Laranjeiras do Sul	206	Jc	25.25S	52.25W
Larantuka	150	Hh	8.21S	122.59 E
Larat	150	Jh	7.09S	131.45 E
Larat, Pulau-	150	Jh	7.10S	131.50 E
La Raya	194	Ji	8.20N	74.34W
L'Arba	126	Ph	36.34N	3.09 E
L'Arbaa Naït Irathen	126	Qh	36.38N	4.12 E
Lärbro	114	Eh	57.47N	18.47 E
Larche, Col de-	122	Mj	44.25N	6.53 E
Larde	172	Fc	16.28S	39.43 E
Larderello	128	Eg	43.14N	10.53 E
Laredo [Sp.]	126	Ia	43.24N	3.25W
Laredo [Tx.-U.S.]	176	Jg	27.31N	99.30W
Laren	124	Hb	52.16N	5.16 E
Lārestān	140	Hg	27.00N	55.30 E
Lārestān	144	Id	27.00N	55.30 E
Large Island	197p	Cb	12.24N	61.30W
Largentière	122	Kj	44.32N	4.18 E
Largo, Cayo-	194	Gc	21.38N	81.28W
Largs	118	If	55.48N	4.52W
La Ribera	126	Kb	42.30N	2.00W
Larimore	186	Hc	47.54N	97.38W
Larino	128	Ii	41.48N	14.54 E
Lario → Como, Lago di-	128	Dd	46.00N	9.15 E
La Rioja	200	Jh	29.25S	66.50W
La Rioja	126	Jb	42.20N	2.20W
La Rioja [Arg.] [2]	206	Gc	30.00S	67.30W
La Rioja [Sp.] [2]	126	Jb	42.15N	2.30W
Lárisa	112	Ih	39.38N	22.25 E
La Rivière-Thibouville, Nassandres-	124	Ce	49.07N	0.44 E
Lārkāna	148	Dc	27.33N	68.13 E
Larmor-Plage	122	Cg	47.42N	3.23W
Larnaka/Lárnax	144	Dc	34.55N	33.38 E
Lárnax/Larnaka	144	Dc	34.55N	33.38 E
Larne/Latharna	118	Hg	54.51N	5.49W
Larned	186	Gg	38.11N	99.06W
La Robla	126	Gb	42.48N	5.37W
La Roche	219b	De	21.28S	168.02 E
La Roche-en-Ardenne	122	Ld	50.11N	5.35 E
La Rochefoucauld	122	Gi	45.44N	0.23 E
La Roche-Guyon	124	De	49.05N	1.38 E
La Roda	126	Je	39.13N	2.09W
La Romana	190	Ke	18.25N	68.58W
La Ronge	180	Ge	55.06N	105.17W
La Ronge, Lac-	174	Id	55.05N	104.59W
Larose	186	Kl	29.35N	90.23W
La Rosita	192	Ic	28.24N	101.43W
Larouco	126	Ec	41.56N	7.40W
Larreynaga	194	Dg	12.40N	86.34W
Larrey Point	212	Dc	20.00S	119.10 E
Larrimah	210	Ef	15.35S	133.12 E
Larsa	146	Kg	31.16N	45.49 E
Lars Christensen Kyst	222	Fe	69.30S	68.00 E
Larsen, Mount-	222	Kf	74.51S	162.12 E
Larsen Ice Shelf	222	Qe	68.30S	62.30W
La Rumorosa	192	Aa	32.34N	116.06W
Laruns	122	Fk	43.00N	0.25W
Larvik	114	Bg	59.04N	10.00 E
Larzac, Causse du-	122	Jk	43.57N	3.11 E
La Sabana [Arg.]	204	Ch	27.52S	59.57W
La Sabana [Col.]	202	Ec	2.20N	68.32W
Las Adjuntas, Presa de-	192	Jf	23.55N	98.45W
La Sagra	126	Jg	37.57N	2.34W
La Sagra	126	Id	40.05N	4.00W
La Salle	186	Lf	41.20N	89.06W
La Salle, Pic-	190	Je	18.22N	71.59W
La Sal Mountains	188	Kg	38.30N	109.10W
Las Alpujarras	126	Ih	36.50N	3.25W
La Sanabria	126	Fb	42.08N	6.30W
Las Animas	186	Eg	38.04N	103.13W
Lās 'ānōd	168	Hd	8.26N	47.24 E
La Sarre	180	Jg	48.48N	79.12W
Las Aves, Islas-	202	Ea	11.58N	67.33W
Las Avispas	204	Bi	29.53S	61.18W
Las Bardenas	126	Kb	42.10N	1.25W
Las Bonitas	196	Di	7.52N	65.40W
Las Breñas	206	Hc	27.05S	61.05W
Las Cabezas de San Juan	126	Gh	36.59N	5.56W
Lascahobas	194	Ld	18.50N	71.56W
Lascano	204	Ek	33.40S	54.12W
Las Casitas, Cerro-	190	Cd	23.31N	109.53W
Lascaux, Grotte de-	122	Hi	45.03N	1.11 E
Las Cejas	206	Hc	26.53S	64.44W
Las Chilcas, Arroyo-	204	Cm	37.16S	58.26W
Las Choapas	190	Fe	17.55N	94.05W
Las Cinco Villas	126	Kb	42.05N	1.07W
Las Cruces	182	Fe	32.23N	106.29W
Lāsdāred	168	Hc	10.10N	46.01 E
Lās Dawa'o	168	Hc	10.22N	49.03 E
La Segarra	126	Nc	41.30N	1.10 E
La Selva	126	Oc	41.40N	2.50 E
La Serena	200	Ih	29.54S	71.16W
La Serena	126	Gf	38.45N	5.30W
la Seu d'Urgell / Seo de Urgel	126	Nb	42.21N	1.28 E
Las Flores	206	Ie	36.03S	59.07W
Lāsh-e Joveyn	144	Jc	31.43N	61.37 E
Las Heras	206	Gd	32.51S	68.49W
Lashio	142	Lg	22.58N	97.48 E
Lashkar Gāh	142	If	31.35N	64.21 E
Las Hurdes	126	Fd	40.20N	6.20W
La Sila	110	Hh	39.15N	16.30 E
Łasin	120	Pc	53.32N	19.05 E
Lāsjerd	146	Oe	35.24N	53.04 E
Łask	120	Pe	51.36N	19.07 E
Las Lajas	206	Fe	38.31S	70.22W
Las Lomitas	206	Hb	24.42S	60.36W
Las Margaritas	192	Ni	16.19N	91.59W
Las Mariñas	126	Da	43.20N	8.15W
Las Marismas	126	Fg	37.00N	6.15W
Las Mercedes	202	Eb	9.07N	66.24W
Las Mesteñas	192	Gc	28.13N	104.35W
Las Minas, Cerro-	190	Gf	14.33N	88.39W
Las Minas, Sierra de-	190	Ge	15.05N	90.00W
Las Mixtecas, Sierra de-	192	Ki	17.45N	97.15W
La Sola, Isla-	202	Fa	11.20N	63.34W
La Solana	126	If	38.56N	3.14W
Lasolo	150	Hg	3.29S	122.04 E
La Sorcière	197k	Bb	13.59N	60.56W
Las Palmas [3]	162	Ed	28.20N	14.20W
Las Palmas de Gran Canaria	160	Ff	28.06N	15.24W
Las Palomas	192	Fb	33.03N	107.19W
Las Petas	204	Cc	16.23S	59.11W
La Spezia	112	Gg	44.07N	9.50 E
Las Piedras	206	Id	34.45S	56.13W
Las Plumas	200	Jj	43.40S	67.15W
Lās Qoray	168	Hc	11.15N	48.22 E
Las Rosas	204	Bk	32.28S	61.34W
Lassen Peak	182	Cc	40.29N	121.31W
Lassigny	124	Ee	49.35N	2.51 E
Laßnitz	128	Jd	46.46N	15.32 E
Lasso	220b	Ba	15.02N	145.38 E
Las Tablas	194	Gj	7.46N	80.17W
Last Mountain Lake	180	Gf	51.10N	105.15W
Las Toscas	204	Ci	28.21S	59.17W
Lastovo	128	Kh	42.46N	16.55 E
Lastovo	128	Kh	42.45N	16.50 E
Lastovski kanal	128	Kh	42.50N	16.59 E
Las Tres Virgenes, Volcán-	190	Bc	27.27N	112.34W
Las Tunas [3]	194	Ic	21.00N	77.00W
Las Tunas, Punta-	197a	Bb	18.30N	66.37W
Las Varillas	206	Hd	31.52S	62.43W
Las Vegas [N.M.-U.S.]	182	Fd	35.36N	105.13W
Las Vegas [Nv.-U.S.]	176	Hf	36.11N	115.08W
Las Villuercas	126	Ge	39.33N	5.27W
Łaszczów	120	Tf	50.32N	23.40 E
Lata	221c	Db	14.14S	169.29W
Latacunga	202	Cd	0.55S	78.37W
La Tagua	202	Dd	0.03S	74.40W
Latakia (EN)=Al Lādhiqīyah	142	Ff	35.31N	35.07 E
Late Island	216	Gc	18.48S	174.39W
Laterza	128	Kj	40.37N	16.48 E
Latgale	116	Lh	56.45N	27.30 E
Latgales Augstiene / Latgalskaja vozvyšennost	116	Lh	56.10N	27.30 E
Latgalskaja vozvyšennost / Latgales Augstiene	116	Lh	56.10N	27.30 E
Latharna/Larne	118	Hg	54.51N	5.49W
Lathen	124	Jb	52.52N	7.19 E
La Tigra	204	Bh	27.06S	60.34W
Latina	128	Gi	41.28N	12.52 E
Latisana	128	Ge	45.47N	13.00 E
Latium (EN) = Lazio [2]	128	Gh	42.02N	12.23 E
La Toja	126	Db	42.27N	8.50W
La Toma	206	Gd	33.03S	65.37W
La Tontouta	219b	Ce	22.00S	166.15 E
Latorica	120	Rh	48.28N	21.50 E
La Tortuga, Isla-	202	Ea	10.56N	65.20W
La Trinidad	194	Dg	12.58N	86.14W
La Trinidad de Orichuna	196	Bi	7.07N	69.45W
La Trinité	196	Fe	14.44N	60.58W
Latronico	128	Kj	40.05N	16.01 E
Lattari, Monti-	128	Ij	40.40N	14.30 E
La Tuque	180	Kg	47.27N	72.47W
Lātūr	148	Fe	18.24N	76.35 E
Latvian SSR (EN)=Latvijas PSR [2]	136	Cd	57.00N	25.00 E
Latvijas Padomju Socialistiska Respublika / Latvijskaja SSR [2]	136	Cd	57.00N	25.00 E
Latvijas PSR=Latvian SSR (EN) [2]	136	Cd	57.00N	25.00 E
Latvijskaja Sovetskaja Socialističeskaja Respublika [2]	136	Cd	57.00N	25.00 E
Latvijskaja SSR/Latvijas Padomju Socialistiska Respublika [2]	136	Cd	57.00N	25.00 E
Lau	158	Kh	6.56N	30.16 E
Laubach	124	Kd	50.33N	8.59 E
Lauchert	120	Fh	48.05N	9.15 E
Lauchhammer	120	Je	51.30N	13.48 E
Lauenburg	120	Gc	53.22N	10.34 E
Lauf an der Pegnitz	120	Hg	49.31N	11.17 E
Laughlan Islands	219a	Ac	9.15S	153.40 E
Laughlin Peak	186	Dh	36.38N	104.12W
Lau Group	208	Jf	18.20S	178.30W
Lauhanvuori	116	Jb	62.10N	22.10 E
Laujar de Andarax	126	Jh	36.59N	2.51W
Laukaa	114	Fe	62.25N	25.57 E
Laukuva	116	Ji	55.35N	22.08 E
Laulau, Bahia-	220b	Ba	15.08N	145.46 E
Launceston [Austl.]	210	Fi	41.26S	147.08 E
Launceston [Eng.-U.K.]	118	Ik	50.38N	4.21W
La Unión [Bol.]	204	Bb	15.18S	61.05W
La Unión [Chile]	206	Ff	40.17S	73.05W
La Unión [Col.]	202	Cc	1.37N	77.08W
La Unión [El Sal.]	190	Gf	13.20N	87.51W
La Unión [Mex.]	192	Ii	17.58N	101.49W
La Unión [Peru]	202	Ce	9.46S	76.48W
La Unión [Sp.]	126	Lg	37.37N	0.52W
La Unión [Ven.]	194	Ni	8.13N	67.46W
Laura	212	Ic	15.34S	144.28 E
La Urbana	196	Ci	7.08N	66.56W
Laurel [Ms.-U.S.]	182	Je	31.42N	89.08W
Laurel [Mt.-U.S.]	182	Fb	45.40N	108.46W
Laureles	204	Ej	31.23S	55.52W
Laurel Hill	184	He	40.02N	79.17W
Laurel Mountain	184	Hf	39.20N	79.50W
Laurens	184	Fh	34.30N	82.01W
Laurentian Plateau (EN)= Laurentien, Plateau-	174	Md	50.00N	70.00W
Laurentian Scarp	184	Ic	45.50N	76.15W
Laurentide Scarp	184	Kb	46.38N	73.00W
Laurentien, Plateau-= Laurentian Plateau (EN)	174	Md	50.00N	70.00W
Lauria	128	Jj	40.02N	15.50 E
Lau Ridge (EN)	106	Kl	25.00S	179.00 E
Laurie River	180	He	56.00N	100.58W
Laurinburg	184	Hh	34.47N	79.27W
Laurium	184	Cb	47.14N	88.26W
Lauro Muller	204	Hi	28.24S	49.23W
Lausanne	112	Gf	46.30N	6.40 E
Lausitzer Gebirge	120	Kf	50.48N	14.40 E
Lausitzer Neiße	120	Kd	52.04N	14.46 E
Laut, Pulau-	150	Ef	4.43N	107.59 E
Laut, Pulau-	140	Nj	3.40S	116.10 E
Lautaret, Col du-	122	Mi	45.02N	6.24 E
Lautaro	206	Fe	38.31S	72.27W
Lautém	150	Ih	8.22S	126.54 E
Lauter	120	Eg	48.58N	8.11 E
Lauterbach	120	Ff	50.38N	9.24 E
Lauterbourg	124	Kf	48.59N	8.11 E
Lauterecken	124	Je	49.39N	7.36 E
Lauthala	219d	Cb	16.45S	179.41W
Laut Kecil, Kepulauan-	150	Gg	4.50S	115.45 E
Lautoka	216	Ec	17.37S	177.27 E
Lauvergne Island	220d	Cb	7.00N	152.00 E
Lauwersmeer	124	Ia	53.25N	6.15 E
Lauzerte	122	Hj	44.15N	1.08 E
Lauzon	184	Lb	46.50N	71.10W
Lava	120	Rb	54.37N	21.14 E
Lava, Nosy- [Mad.]	172	Hb	14.33S	47.36 E
Lava, Nosy- [Mad.]	172	Hb	12.49S	48.41 E
Lavaca River	186	Hl	28.50N	96.36W
Lava Flow	186	Bi	34.45N	108.20W
Laval	122	Ff	48.04N	0.46W
La Vall d'Uxó / Vall de Uxó	126	Le	39.49N	0.14W
Lavalle	204	Ci	29.01S	59.11W
Lavalleja [2]	204	El	34.00S	55.00W
Lāvān, Jazīreh-ye-	144	Hd	26.48N	53.00 E

Index Symbols

- [1] Independent Nation
- [2] State, Region
- [3] District, County
- [4] Municipality
- [5] Colony, Dependency
- Continent
- Physical Region
- Historical or Cultural Region
- Mount, Mountain
- Volcano
- Hill
- Mountains, Mountain Range
- Hills, Escarpment
- Plateau, Upland
- Pass, Gap
- Plain, Lowland
- Delta
- Salt Flat
- Valley, Canyon
- Crater, Cave
- Karst Features
- Depression
- Polder
- Desert, Dunes
- Forest, Woods
- Heath, Steppe
- Oasis
- Cape, Point
- Coast, Beach
- Cliff
- Peninsula
- Isthmus
- Sandbank
- Island
- Atoll
- Rock, Reef
- Islands, Archipelago
- Rocks, Reefs
- Coral Reef
- Well, Spring
- Geyser
- River, Stream
- Waterfall, Rapids
- River Mouth, Estuary
- Lake
- Salt Lake
- Intermittent Lake
- Reservoir
- Swamp, Pond
- Canal
- Glacier
- Ice Shelf, Pack Ice
- Ocean
- Sea
- Gulf, Bay
- Strait, Fjord
- Lagoon
- Bank
- Seamount
- Tablemount
- Ridge
- Shelf
- Basin
- Escarpment, Sea Scarp
- Fracture
- Trench, Abyss
- National Park, Reserve
- Point of Interest
- Recreation Site
- Cave, Cavern
- Historic Site
- Ruins
- Wall, Walls
- Church, Abbey
- Temple
- Scientific Station
- Railway station
- Airport
- Port
- Military installation
- Lighthouse
- Mine
- Tunnel
- Dam, Bridge

Name	Page	Grid	Lat	Long
Lavandou, Le-	122	Mk	43.08N	6.22 E
Lavanggu	219a	Ed	11.37S	160.15 E
Lavant	128	Id	46.38N	14.56 E
Lavapié, Punta-	198	Ii	37.09S	73.35W
Lävar Meydän	146	Pg	30.20N	54.30 E
Lavassaare	116	Kf	58.29N	24.16 E
Lavaur	122	Hk	43.42N	1.49 E
La Vecilla	126	Gb	42.51N	5.24W
La Vega	190	Je	19.13N	70.31W
La Vela de Coro	194	Mh	11.27N	69.34W
Lavelanet	122	Hl	42.56N	1.51 E
Lavello	128	Ji	41.03N	15.48 E
La Venta	190	Fe	18.08N	94.03W
Laventie	124	Ed	50.38N	2.46 E
La Ventura	192	Ie	24.37N	100.54W
La Vera	126	Gd	40.05N	5.30W
L'Averdy, Cape-	219a	Ba	5.33S	155.04 E
Laverton	212	Ee	28.38S	122.25 E
Lavia	114	Ff	61.36N	22.36 E
La Victoria	202	Ea	10.14N	67.20W
La Vila d'Eivissa / Ibiza	126	Nf	38.54N	1.26 E
La Vila Joiosa / Villajoyosa	126	Lf	38.30N	0.14W
La Villita, Presa-	192	Hh	18.05N	102.05W
La Viña	202	Ce	6.54S	79.28W
Lavoisier Island	222	Qe	66.12S	66.44W
Lavougba	168	Cd	5.37N	23.19 E
Lavouras	204	Db	14.59S	56.47W
Lavras	202	Jh	21.14S	45.00W
Lavras do Sul	204	Fj	30.49S	53.59W
Lavrentija	138	Nc	65.33N	171.02W
Lávrion	130	Hl	37.43N	24.03 E
Lavumisa	172	Ee	27.15S	31.55 E
Lawas	150	Gf	4.51N	115.24 E
Lawdar	144	Gg	13.53N	45.52 E
Lawe	124	Ed	50.38N	2.42 E
Lawers, Ben-	124	Be	56.33N	4.15W
Lawit, Gunong-	150	Ff	1.23N	112.55 E
Lawqah	146	Jh	29.49N	42.45 E
Lawra	166	Ec	10.39N	2.52W
Lawrence [Ks.-U.S.]	182	Hd	38.58N	95.14W
Lawrence [Ma.-U.S.]	182	Mc	42.42N	71.09W
Lawrence [N.Z.]	218	Cf	45.55S	169.42 E
Lawrenceburg [Ky.-U.S.]	184	Ef	38.02N	84.54W
Lawrenceburg [Tn.-U.S.]	184	Dh	35.15N	87.20W
Lawson, Mount-	212	Ja	7.44S	146.37 E
Lawton	184	Dg	34.37N	98.25W
Lawu, Gunong-	140	Nj	7.38S	111.11 E
Lawz, Jabal al-	146	Fh	28.41N	35.18 E
Laxå	114	Dg	58.59N	14.37 E
Lay	122	Eh	46.18N	1.17W
Laylá	122	Gg	22.17N	46.45 E
Layon	122	Fg	47.20N	0.45W
Layou	197n	Ba	13.12N	61.17W
Layou	197c	Bb	15.23N	61.26W
Laysan Island	208	Jb	25.50N	171.50W
Layton	188	Jf	41.04N	111.58W
La Zarca	192	Ge	25.50N	104.44W
Lazarev	138	Jf	52.13N	141.35 E
Lazarevac	128	De	44.23N	20.16 E
Lázaro Cárdenas, Presa-	192	Ge	25.35N	105.05W
Lazdijai/Lazdijaj	114	Fi	54.13N	23.33 E
Lazdijaj/Lazdijai	114	Fi	54.13N	23.33 E
Lazeh	146	Oi	26.48N	53.22 E
Lazio = Latium (EN)	128	Gh	42.02N	12.23 E
Lazo	154	Mc	43.25N	134.01 E
Lazovsk	132	Ff	47.38N	28.12 E
Lazy	120	Pf	50.27N	19.26 E
Lea	118	Si	51.30N	0.01 E
Lead	182	Gc	44.21N	103.46W
Leader	188	Ka	50.53N	109.31W
Lead Hill	186	Jh	37.06N	92.38W
Leadville	186	Ef	39.15N	106.20W
Leaf River	186	Lk	31.00N	88.45W
League City	186	Il	29.31N	95.05W
Leamington	184	Fd	42.03N	82.36W
Leandro N. Alem	204	Bl	34.30S	61.24W
Leane, Lough-/Loch Léin	118	Di	52.05N	9.35W
Le'an Jiang	154	Dj	28.58N	116.41 E
Learmonth	212	Cd	22.13S	114.04 E
Leavenworth [Ks.-U.S.]	186	Ig	39.19N	94.55W
Leavenworth [Wa.-U.S.]	188	Ec	47.36N	120.40W
Łeba	120	Nb	54.47N	17.33 E
Łeba	120	Nb	54.47N	17.25 E
Lebach	124	Ie	49.24N	6.55 E
Lébamba	170	Bc	2.12S	11.30 E
Lebanon [In.-U.S.]	184	De	40.03N	86.28W
Lebanon [Ky.-U.S.]	184	Eg	37.34N	85.15W
Lebanon [Mo.-U.S.]	186	Jh	37.41N	92.40W
Lebanon [N.H.-U.S.]	184	Kd	43.38N	72.15W
Lebanon [Or.-U.S.]	188	Dd	44.32N	122.54W
Lebanon [Pa.-U.S.]	184	Hf	40.21N	76.25W
Lebanon [Tn.-U.S.]	184	Dg	36.12N	86.18W
Lebanon = Lubnän	142	Ff	33.50N	35.50 E
Lebanon Mountains (EN) = Lubnän, Jabal-	144	Ec	34.00N	36.30 E
Lebap	135	Gd	41.02N	61.54 E
Le Bec-Hellouin	124	Ce	49.14N	0.43 E
Lebedin	136	De	50.36N	34.30 E
Lebedinyj	138	He	58.25N	125.58 E
Lebedjan	138	He	53.02N	39.07 E
Lebjažje [Kaz.-U.S.S.R.]	138	He	51.28N	77.46 E
Lebjažje [R.S.F.S.R.]	134	Mi	55.16N	66.29 E
Lebo	170	Db	4.29N	23.57 E
Lebomboberge	158	Kk	26.15S	32.00 E
Lebombo Mountains	172	Ee	26.15S	32.00 E
Lębork	120	Nb	54.33N	17.44 E
Le Bourget	124	Ef	48.56N	2.25 E
Lebrija	126	Ff	36.55N	6.04W
Łebsko, Jezioro-	120	Nb	54.44N	17.24 E
Lebu	206	Fe	37.37S	73.39W
Le Carbet	197h	Ab	14.43N	61.11W
Le Cateau	124	Fd	50.06N	3.33 E
Le Catelet	124	Fd	50.01N	3.15 E
Lecce	128	Kh	40.23N	18.11 E
Lecco	128	De	45.51N	9.23 E
Lech	128	Ec	47.12N	10.09 E
Lech	128	Ec	48.44N	10.56 E
Lechang	152	Jf	25.15N	113.25 E
Lechfeld	120	Gh	48.10N	10.50 E
Lechiguiri, Cerro-	192	Li	16.43N	95.30W
Lechtaler Alpen	128	Ec	47.15N	10.30 E
Léconi	170	Bc	1.35S	14.14 E
Léconi	170	Bc	1.11S	13.16 E
Le Cornate	128	Eg	43.10N	10.58 E
Le Coudray-Saint-Germer	124	De	49.25N	1.50 E
Le Crotoy	124	De	50.13N	1.37 E
Łęczna	120	Se	51.19N	22.52 E
Łęczyca	120	Pd	52.04N	19.13 E
Led	114	Ke	62.20N	43.00 E
Lede	124	Fd	50.57N	3.59 E
Ledesma	126	Gc	41.05N	6.00W
Le Diamant	197h	Ac	14.29N	61.02W
Ledjanaja, gora-	140	Tc	61.45N	171.15 E
Lednik Entuziastov	222	Cf	70.30S	16.00 E
Lednik Mušketova	222	Cf	72.00S	14.00 E
Ledo, Cabo-	170	Bd	9.41S	13.12 E
Ledolom Tajmyrski	222	Ff	66.00S	83.00 E
Lędyczek	120	Mc	53.33N	16.58 E
Lee/An Laoi	118	Ej	51.55N	8.30W
Leech Lake	182	Ib	47.09N	94.23W
Leeds [Al.-U.S.]	184	Di	33.33N	86.33W
Leeds [Eng.-U.K.]	112	Fe	53.50N	1.35W
Leeds [N.D.-U.S.]	186	Gb	48.17N	99.27W
Leek	124	Ia	53.10N	6.24 E
Leer (Ostfriesland)	124	Ha	53.14N	7.26 E
Leerdam	124	Hc	51.53N	5.06 E
Lées	122	Fk	43.38N	0.14W
Leesburg	182	Kf	29.49N	81.53W
Leeste, Weyhe-	124	Kb	52.59N	8.50 E
Leesville	186	Jk	31.08N	93.16W
Leeuwarden	122	La	53.12N	5.46 E
Leeuwarderadeel	124	Ha	53.16N	5.46 E
Leeuwarderadeel-Stiens	124	Ha	53.16N	5.46 E
Leeuwin, Cape-	212	Cf	34.25S	115.00 E
Leeward Islands	190	Le	17.00N	63.00W
Leeward Islands (EN) = Sous le Vent, Iles-	208	Lf	16.38S	151.30W
Léfini	170	Cc	2.57S	16.10 E
Lefka	130	Jh	41.52N	26.16 E
Lefke	146	Ee	35.07N	32.51 E
Lefkoşa/Levkosía = Nicosia (EN)	142	Ff	35.10N	33.22 E
Le François	197h	Ab	14.37N	60.54W
Lefroy, Lake-	212	Ef	31.15S	121.40 E
Łęg	120	Rf	50.38N	21.49 E
Leganés	126	Id	40.19N	3.45W
Legazpi	142	Oh	13.09N	123.44 E
Legden	124	Jb	52.02N	7.06 E
Legé	124	Eg	46.53N	1.36W
Legges Tor	212	Jh	41.32S	147.40 E
Leghorn (EN) = Livorno	128	Fg	43.33N	10.19 E
Legionowo	120	Qd	52.25N	20.56 E
Léglise	124	Ge	49.48N	5.32 E
Legnago	128	Fe	45.11N	11.18 E
Legnano	124	Cf	45.36N	8.54 E
Legnica	120	Me	51.13N	16.09 E
Legnica	120	Me	51.15N	16.10 E
Le Grand-Quevilly	124	De	49.25N	1.02 E
Le Grand-Wintersberg	122	Mf	48.59N	7.37 E
Léguer	122	Cf	48.44N	3.32W
Leh	148	Fb	34.10N	77.35 E
Lehi	188	Jf	40.24N	111.51W
Lehmann	204	Bj	31.08S	61.27W
Le Houlme	124	De	49.31N	1.02 E
Lehrte	120	Fd	52.23N	9.58 E
Lehtimäki	116	Jb	62.47N	23.55 E
Lehua Island	221a	Aa	22.01N	160.06W
Lehututu	172	Cd	23.53S	21.49 E
Leibnitz	128	Jd	46.46N	15.32 E
Leibo	152	Hf	28.13N	103.34 E
Leicester	112	Fe	52.38N	1.05W
Leicester	118	Mi	52.40N	1.00W
Leicestershire	118	Mi	52.38N	1.00W
Leichhardt Range	212	Jd	20.40S	147.05 E
Leichhardt River	212	Hc	17.35S	139.48 E
Leiden	122	Kc	52.09N	4.30 E
Leidschendam	124	Gc	52.05N	4.26 E
Leie	124	Ec	51.03N	3.43 E
Leifear/Lifford	118	Fg	54.50N	7.29W
Leigh Creek	212	Hf	30.28S	138.25 E
Leighton Buzzard	124	Bc	51.55N	0.39W
Leigong Shan	152	If	26.23N	108.15 E
Leikanger	114	Ae	62.07N	5.20 E
Léim an Mhadaidh / Limavady	118	Gf	55.03N	6.57W
Leimen	124	Ke	49.21N	8.41 E
Leimus	194	Ef	14.44N	84.07W
Leine	120	Fd	52.40N	9.40 E
Leinster/Laighean	118	Gh	53.00N	7.00W
Leipzig	120	Hf	51.18N	12.20 E
Leipzig	120	Ie	51.20N	12.20 E
Leira	116	Cd	60.58N	9.18 E
Leiria	126	Cd	39.45N	8.48W
Leiria	126	De	39.40N	8.30W
Leirvik	114	Ag	59.47N	5.30 E
Leisi/Lejsi	116	Jf	58.33N	22.30 E
Leisler, Mount-	212	Fd	23.30S	129.20 E
Leiston	124	Db	52.12N	1.34 E
Leitariegos, Puerto de-	126	Fa	43.00N	6.25W
Leitha	128	Lc	47.52N	17.18 E
Leithagebirge	128	Kc	47.58N	16.40 E
Leitir Ceanainn/Letterkenny	118	Fg	54.57N	7.44W
Leitrim/Liatroim	118	Fg	54.57N	8.20W
Leiva, Cerro-	202	Dc	2.54N	74.48W
Leiyang	152	Jf	26.25N	112.55 E
Leizhou Bandao	140	Ng	20.40N	110.05 E
Lejasciems	116	Lg	57.08N	26.36 E
Lejsi/Leisi	116	Jf	58.33N	22.30 E
Lek	122	Lc	51.54N	4.36 E
Lékana	170	Cc	2.19S	14.36 E
Leketi, Monts de la-	158	Ii	2.34S	14.17 E
Lekhainá	130	El	37.56N	21.16 E
Lekhal	126	Ph	36.20N	3.51 E
Lekitobi	150	Hg	1.58S	124.33 E
Lekmi Lagoon	166	Fd	6.30N	4.07 E
Leknes	114	Cb	68.10N	13.42 E
Łęknica	120	Ke	51.32N	14.48 E
Lékoumou	170	Bc	3.00S	13.50 E
Leksand	114	Df	60.44N	15.01 E
Leksozero, ozero-	114	He	63.45N	31.00 E
Leksula	150	Ig	3.46S	126.31 E
Leksvik	114	Ce	63.40N	10.37 E
Le Lamentin	196	Fe	14.37N	61.01W
Leland	186	Kj	33.24N	90.54W
Lélång	116	Ee	59.10N	12.10 E
Lelčicy	136	Kj	51.49N	28.21 E
Leleiwi Point	221a	Gd	19.44N	155.00W
Lelepa	219b	Dc	17.36S	168.13 E
Leleque	206	Ff	42.23S	71.03W
Leli → Tianlin	152	Ig	24.22N	106.11 E
Lelija	128	Mg	43.26N	18.29 E
Leling	154	Df	37.44N	117.13 E
Léliogat	219b	Ce	21.18S	167.35 E
Le Locle	124	Ac	47.05N	6.45 E
Le Lorrain	197h	Ab	14.50N	61.04W
Lelystad	122	Lb	52.31N	5.27 E
Le Madonie	128	Hm	37.50N	14.00 E
Le Maire, Estrecho de-	206	Hm	54.50S	65.00W
Léman, Lac- = Geneva, Lake- (EN)	122	Gf	46.25N	6.30 E
Leman Bank	118	Oh	53.10N	1.58 E
Lemankoa	219a	Ba	5.03S	154.34 E
Le Marin	197h	Bc	14.28N	60.52W
Le Mars	186	He	42.47N	96.10W
Lembeck	124	Ic	51.44N	6.59 E
Lemberg	124	Je	49.00N	7.23 E
Lembolovskaja vozvyšennost	116	Md	60.50N	30.15 E
Lembruch	124	Kb	52.32N	8.21 E
Leme	204	If	22.12S	47.24W
Lemelerberg	124	Ib	52.29N	6.23 E
Lemesós/Limassol	144	Dc	34.40N	33.02 E
Lemgo	120	Ed	52.02N	8.54 E
Lemhi Range	188	Hd	44.30N	113.25 E
Lemieux Islands	180	Ld	64.00N	64.20W
Lemju	134	He	63.50N	56.57 E
Lemland	116	Id	60.05N	20.10 E
Lemmer, Lemsterland-	124	Hb	52.51N	5.42 E
Lemmon	182	Gb	45.56N	102.10W
Lemnos, Mount-	188	Jj	32.26N	110.47W
Lemnos (EN) = Límnos	110	Ih	39.55N	25.15 E
Le Morne Rouge	197h	Ab	14.46N	61.08W
Lemotol Bay	220d	Bb	7.21N	151.35 E
Le Moyne, Lac-	180	Ke	57.00N	68.00W
Lempa, Rio-	190	Gf	13.14N	88.49W
Lempäälä	116	Jc	61.19N	23.45 E
Lempira	194	Cf	14.20N	88.40W
Lemro	148	Jd	20.25N	93.20 E
Le Portel	124	Dd	50.42N	1.34 E
Lemsterland	124	Hb	52.51N	5.42 E
Lemsterland-Lemmer	122	Lb	52.51N	5.42 E
Le Murge	128	Ji	40.50N	16.40 E
Lemvig	110	Hg	56.32N	8.18 E
Lemya	134	Jc	66.30N	62.00 E
Lena	138	Gd	72.25N	126.40 E
Lena, Mount-	188	Jf	40.50N	109.27W
Lena Mountains (EN) = Prilenskoje plato	140	Oc	60.45N	125.00 E
Lena Tablemount (EN)	158	Ln	53.00S	45.00 E
Lençóis Paulista	204	Hf	22.36S	48.47W
Lendava	128	Kd	46.34N	16.27 E
Lendery	114	Ch	63.26N	31.12 E
Le Neubourg	124	Ce	49.09N	0.55 E
Lenger	136	Gg	42.10N	69.55 E
Lengerich	122	Gb	52.11N	7.52 E
Lenghu	142	Lf	38.50N	93.30 E
Lengoué	170	Cb	0.49N	15.47 E
Lengshuijiang	152	Jf	27.41N	111.28 E
Lengua de Vaca, Punta-	206	Fd	30.14S	71.38W
Lengulu	170	Dh	3.15N	26.30 E
Lenhovda	114	Dh	57.00N	15.17 E
Lenina, pik- = Lenin Peak (EN)	140	Jf	39.19N	73.01 E
Leninabad	142	Ld	40.17N	69.37 E
Leninabadskaja oblast	136	Mk	40.00N	69.10 E
Lenin Canal (EN) = Volgo-Donskoj sudohodny kanal imeni V. I. Lenina	110	Kf	48.40N	43.37 E
Leningrad	112	Jc	59.55N	30.15 E
Leningradskaja	222	Kf	69.30S	159.23 E
Leningradskaja oblast	136	Dd	60.00N	31.00 E
Leningradski [R.S.F.S.R.]	138	Mc	69.17N	178.10 E
Leningradski [Taj.-U.S.S.R.]	136	Ll	37.32N	68.40 E
Lenino	132	Gf	45.17N	35.44 E
Leninogorsk [Kaz.-U.S.S.R.]	142	Kd	50.27N	83.32 E
Leninogorsk [R.S.F.S.R.]	134	Fe	54.38N	52.30 E
Lenin Peak = Lenina, pik-	140	Jf	39.19N	73.01 E
Leninsk [R.S.F.S.R.]	136	Ne	48.42N	45.11 E
Leninsk [Tur.-U.S.S.R.]	135	Bc	42.04N	59.24 E
Leninsk [Uzb.-U.S.S.R.]	135	Id	40.38N	72.15 E
Leninsk-Kuznecki	140	Lc	54.38N	86.10 E
Leninskoje [R.S.F.S.R.]	138	Lg	47.59N	132.38 E
Leninskoje [R.S.F.S.R.]	134	Fd	58.21N	47.07 E
Leninváros	120	Ri	47.55N	21.05 E
Lenkoran	112	Kg	38.44N	48.50 E
Lenmalu	150	Jg	1.58S	130.00 E
Lenne	124	Jc	51.15N	7.50 E
Lenne	120	Fe	51.25N	7.30 E
Lennestadt	124	Kc	51.08N	8.03 E
Lennestadt-Grevenbrück	124	Kc	51.08N	8.01 E
Lennox	206	Gi	55.19S	67.00W
Lennox Hills	118	Ie	56.05N	4.10W
Leno-Angarskoje plato	138	Fe	55.00N	104.30 E
Lenoir	184	Gh	35.55N	81.32W
Lens	122	Id	50.26N	2.50 E
Lensk	142	Nc	61.00N	114.50 E
Lenti	128	Mi	46.37N	16.33 E
Lentiira	114	Gd	64.21N	29.50 E
Lentini	128	Jm	37.17N	15.01 E
Lentua	116	Gd	64.14N	29.36 E
Lentvaris	116	Kj	54.38N	25.13 E
Léo	166	Ec	11.06N	2.06W
Leoben	128	Jc	47.23N	15.06 E
Léogâne	194	Kd	18.31N	72.38W
Leok	150	Hf	1.11N	121.26 E
Leola	186	Gb	45.43N	98.56W
Leominster	118	Ki	52.14N	2.45W
Léon	122	Ek	43.53N	1.18W
León	112	Fg	42.36N	5.34W
León	126	Gc	42.40N	6.00W
León [Mex.]	176	Ig	21.10N	101.42W
León [Nic.]	176	Kh	12.26N	86.54W
León [Sp.]	126	Gb	42.40N	6.00W
León, Montes de-	126	Fb	42.30N	6.20W
León, Puerto del-	126	Hh	36.50N	4.21W
Leonardville	172	Bd	23.29S	18.49 E
Leonberg	124	Kf	48.48N	9.01 E
Leone, Monte-	124	Cd	46.15N	8.10 E
Leones	204	Ak	32.39S	62.18W
Leonessa	128	Gg	42.34N	12.58 E
Leonforte	128	Im	37.38N	14.23 E
Leónidhion	130	Fl	37.10N	22.52 E
Leonora	212	Ee	28.53S	121.20 E
Leopold and Astrid Coast	222	Gd	67.10S	84.10 E
Leopoldina	202	Jh	21.32S	42.38W
Leopold McClintock, Cape-	180	Fa	77.38N	116.20W
Leopoldsburg	124	Hc	51.07N	5.15 E
Leopoldville → Kinshasa	160	Ii	4.18S	15.18 E
Leovo	132	Ff	46.29N	28.15 E
Lepa	221c	Bb	14.01S	171.28W
Lepar, Pulau-	150	Eg	2.57S	106.50 E
Le Parcq	124	Ed	50.23N	2.06 E
Lepaterique	194	Df	14.02N	87.27W
Lepe	126	Ee	37.15N	7.12W
Lepel	136	Ce	54.53N	28.46 E
Lepenica	128	Ce	44.10N	21.08 E
Leping	152	Kf	28.59N	117.07 E
Lepini, Monti-	128	Gi	41.35N	13.00 E
Le Plessis-Belleville	124	Ee	49.06N	2.46 E
Leppävirta	116	Lb	62.29N	27.47 E
Le Prêcheur	197h	Ab	14.48N	61.14W
Lepsy	135	Je	46.18N	78.20 E
Leptis Magna	164	Bc	32.38N	14.18 E
Leqemt/Nekemt = Nekemt	160	Kh	9.05N	36.33 E
Lercara Friddi	128	Hm	37.45N	13.36 E
Lerchenfeld Glacier	222	Ff	77.50S	34.50W
Lere	166	Ic	10.23N	8.35 E
Léré	168	Ad	9.39N	14.13 E
Lérida	202	Dd	0.06N	70.43W
Lérida / Lleida	126	Nc	41.37N	0.37 E
Lerma	126	Hb	42.02N	3.45W
Lerma, Rio-	192	Hg	20.13N	102.46W
Le Robert	197h	Ab	14.41N	60.57W
Léros	130	Ik	37.08N	26.50 E
Lerum	114	Ch	57.46N	12.16 E
Lerwick	118	La	60.09N	1.09W
Léry	197h	Bb	14.34N	60.57W
Les Alberes/Albères, Montes-	122	Il	42.28N	2.56 E
Les Allobroges	219b	Dc	16.47S	168.09 E
Les Anses-d'Arlets	197h	Ac	14.29N	61.05W
les Borges Blanques / Borjas Blancas	126	Mc	41.31N	0.52 E
Les Cayes	190	Je	18.12N	73.45W
Les Escoumins	184	Ma	48.25N	69.29W
Les Falaises	124	Ce	49.44N	0.21 E
Leshan	152	Hf	29.34N	103.45 E
Lesina, Lago di-	128	Ji	41.55N	15.25 E
Lesja	116	Cb	62.07N	8.52 E
Lesjöfors	114	Dg	59.59N	14.11 E
Leskino	138	Cc	72.25N	79.40 E
Lesko	120	Sg	49.29N	22.21 E
Leskov	222	Ad	56.40S	28.10W
Leskoviku	130	Di	40.09N	20.35 E
Les Mangles	197e	Ab	16.23N	61.27W
Lesneven	122	Bf	48.34N	4.19W
Lešnica	130	Ce	44.39N	19.19 E
Lesnoj [R.S.F.S.R.]	116	Mc	61.01N	28.51 E
Lesnoj [R.S.F.S.R.]	134	Ge	59.49N	52.10 E
Lesogorski	116	Mc	61.01N	28.51 E
Lesosibirsk	142	Ld	58.15N	92.30 E
Lesotho	160	Jk	29.30S	28.30 E
Lesozavodsk	138	Ig	45.26N	133.25 E
Lesozavodski	114	Hc	66.45N	32.50 E
Lesparre-Médoc	122	Fi	45.18N	0.56W
L'Espérance Rock	208	Jh	31.26S	178.54W
Les Ponts-de-Cé	122	Fg	47.25N	0.31W
Lessay	122	Ee	49.13N	1.32W
Lesse	122	Kd	50.14N	4.54 E
Lessebo	114	Dh	56.45N	15.16 E
Lessen/Lessines	124	Fd	50.43N	3.50 E
Lesser Antilles (EN) = Antillas Menores	174	Mh	15.00N	61.00W
Lesser Caucasus (EN) = Maly Kavkaz	110	Kg	41.00N	44.35 E
Lesser Khingan Range (EN) = Xiao Hinggan Ling	140	Oe	48.45N	127.00 E
Lesser Slave Lake	174	Kd	55.25N	115.30W
Lesser Sunda Islands (EN)	140	Oj	9.13S	121.12 E
Lessines/Lessen	124	Fd	50.43N	3.50 E
Lessini	128	Fe	45.41N	11.13 E
Les Tantes	197p	Bb	12.19N	61.33W
Lésvos = Lesbos (EN)	110	Ih	39.10N	26.32 E
Leszno	120	Me	51.51N	16.35 E
Leszno	120	Qd	51.50N	16.35 E
Letälven	116	Fe	59.05N	14.20 E
Letchworth	124	Bc	51.58N	0.13W
Letea, Ostrovul-	130	Md	45.30N	29.20 E
Letenye	120	Mj	46.26N	16.44 E
Lethbridge	176	Kd	49.42N	110.50W
Lethem	200	Ke	3.20N	59.50W
Leti, Kepulauan- = Leti Islands (EN)	150	Ih	8.13S	127.50 E
Letiahau	158	Jk	21.04S	24.25 E
Leticia	200	Jf	4.09S	69.57W
Leti Islands (EN) = Leti, Kepulauan-	150	Ih	8.13S	127.50 E
Leting	154	Ee	39.25N	118.55 E
Letka	134	Mg	58.59N	50.14 E
Letlhakane	172	Di	21.25S	25.36 E
Letnerečenski	114	Id	64.19N	34.25 E
Letni bereg	134	Id	64.50N	38.20 E
Letohrad	120	Mf	50.03N	16.31 E
Letovice	120	Mg	49.33N	16.36 E
Letpadan	148	Je	17.47N	95.45 E
Le Translay	124	De	49.58N	1.41 E
Letsôk-aw Kyun	148	Je	11.37N	98.15 E
Letterkenny/Leitir Ceanainn	118	Fg	54.57N	7.44W
Leu	130	Ge	44.11N	24.00 E
Leucas (EN) = Levkás	130	Dk	38.43N	20.38 E
Leucate	122	Il	42.55N	3.02 E
Leucate ou de Salses, Étang de-	122	Il	42.51N	3.00 E
Leuk	124	Bd	46.20N	7.38 E
Leukónoikon	146	Ee	35.17N	33.42 E
Leulumoega	221c	Ba	13.49S	171.55W
Leuna	120	Ie	51.19N	12.01 E
Leušeny	132	Fe	46.51N	28.11 E
Leuser, Gunung-	148	Li	3.45N	97.11 E
Leutkirch im Allgäu	120	Gi	47.50N	10.02 E
Leuven/Louvain	122	Kd	50.53N	4.42 E
Leuze-en-Hainaut	124	Fd	50.36N	3.36 E
Levádheia	130	Fk	38.26N	22.53 E
Levaja Hetta	138	Cc	65.15N	73.20 E
Levanger	114	Ce	63.45N	11.18 E
Levante, Riviera di-	128	Df	44.15N	9.30 E
Levanzo	128	Hm	38.00N	12.20 E
Lévêque, Cape-	212	Ec	16.25S	122.55 E
Leverkusen-Opladen	120	Ce	51.04N	7.01 E
Lévezou, Plateau du-	122	Ij	44.09N	2.53 E
Levice	120	Oh	48.13N	18.37 E
Levico Terme	128	Fd	46.01N	11.18 E
Levin	216	Eh	40.37S	175.17 E
Levis	180	Kg	46.48N	71.10W
Levisa Fork	184	Fg	38.06N	82.37W
Levitha	130	Jm	37.00N	26.28 E
Levittown	184	Ie	40.09N	74.50W
Levká Óri	130	Gn	35.20N	24.00 E
Levkás = Leucas (EN)	130	Dk	38.43N	20.38 E
Levkosía / Lefkosa = Nicosia (EN)	142	Ff	35.10N	33.22 E
Levoča	120	Qg	49.02N	20.35 E
Levroux	122	Hh	46.59N	1.37 E
Levski	130	If	43.22N	25.08 E
Lev Tolstoj	132	Kc	53.12N	39.25 E
Levuka	219a	Bb	17.41S	178.50 E
Lévuo/Lévuo	116	Kh	56.02N	24.28 E
Lewes [De.-U.S.]	184	Jf	38.47N	75.08W
Lewes [Eng.-U.K.]	118	Nk	50.52N	0.01 E
Lewin Brzeski	120	Nf	50.46N	17.37 E
Lewis, Butt of-	118	Gc	58.31N	6.15W
Lewis and Clark Lake	186	Hf	42.50N	97.45W
Lewis Range	178	Hb	48.30N	113.15W
Lewis River	188	Dd	46.05N	122.48W
Lewis Smith Lake	184	Dh	34.00N	87.07W
Lewisburg	184	Gg	37.47N	80.27W
Lewisporte	180	Mf	49.15N	55.03W
Lewiston [Id.-U.S.]	176	Hf	46.25N	117.01W
Lewiston [Me.-U.S.]	182	Mc	44.06N	70.13W
Lewistown [Mt.-U.S.]	182	Fb	47.04N	109.26W
Lewistown [Pa.-U.S.]	184	Ie	40.37N	77.36W
Lexington [Ky.-U.S.]	176	Kf	38.03N	84.30W
Lexington [Mo.-U.S.]	186	Ig	39.11N	93.53W
Lexington [N.C.-U.S.]	184	Gh	35.49N	80.15W
Lexington [Ok.-U.S.]	186	Hi	35.01N	97.20W
Lexington [Va.-U.S.]	184	Gg	37.47N	79.27W
Leygues, Iles-	222	Fc	48.45S	69.30 E

Index Symbols

- [1] Independent Nation
- [2] State, Region
- [3] District, County
- [4] Municipality
- [5] Colony, Dependency
- Continent
- Physical Region
- Historical or Cultural Region
- Mount, Mountain
- Volcano
- Hill
- Mountains, Mountain Range
- Hills, Escarpment
- Plateau, Upland
- Pass, Gap
- Plain, Lowland
- Delta
- Salt Flat
- Valley, Canyon
- Crater, Cave
- Karst Features
- Depression
- Polder
- Desert, Dunes
- Forest, Woods
- Heath, Steppe
- Oasis
- Cape, Point
- Coast, Beach
- Cliff
- Peninsula
- Isthmus
- Sandbank
- Island
- Atoll
- Rock, Reef
- Islands, Archipelago
- Rocks, Reefs
- Coral Reef
- Well, Spring
- Geyser
- River, Stream
- Waterfall, Rapids
- River Mouth, Estuary
- Lake
- Salt Lake
- Intermittent Lake
- Reservoir
- Swamp, Pond
- Canal
- Lagoon
- Bank
- Seamount
- Ridge
- Shelf
- Basin
- Glacier
- Ice Shelf, Pack Ice
- Ocean
- Sea
- Gulf, Bay
- Strait, Fjord
- Escarpment, Sea Scarp
- Fracture
- Trench, Abyss
- Tablemount
- National Park, Reserve
- Point of Interest
- Recreation Site
- Cave, Cavern
- Historic Site
- Ruins
- Wall, Walls
- Church, Abbey
- Temple
- Scientific Station
- Railway station
- Airport
- Port
- Military installation
- Lighthouse
- Tunnel
- Dam, Bridge

Leyre 122 Ej 44.39N 1.01W
Leysdown-on-Sea 124 Cc 51.23N 0.55 E
Leyte 140 Oh 10.50N 124.50 E
Lez 122 Kj 44.13N 4.43 E
Leżajsk 120 Sf 50.16N 22.24 E
Lézard, Pointe à- 197e Ab 16.08N 61.47W
Lézarde, Rivière- 197h Ab 14.36N 61.01W
Lezha 130 Ch 41.47N 19.39 E
Lézignan-Corbières 122 Ik 43.12N 2.46 E
Lgov 136 De 51.41N 35.17 E
Lhari 152 Fe 30.48N 93.25 E
Lhaua 142 Lg 29.42N 91.07 E
Lhazê 152 Ef 29.13N 87.44 E
Lhazhong 152 Ee 31.28N 86.36 E
Lhokseumawe 150 Ce 5.10N 97.08 E
Lhoksukon 150 Ce 5.03N 97.19 E
L'Hôpital 124 Ie 49.10N 6.44 E
Lhorong 152 Ge 30.45N 95.48 E
l'Hospitalet de l'Infant / Hospitalet del Infante 126 Md 40.59N 0.56 E
Lhozhag 152 Ff 28.18N 90.51 E
Lhünzhub (Poindo) 152 Fe 30.17N 91.20 E
Liádhi 130 Jm 36.55N 26.10 E
Liákoura 130 Fk 38.32N 22.37 E
Liamone 122a Aa 42.04N 8.43 E
Liancheng 152 Kf 25.48N 116.48 E
Liancourt 124 Ee 49.20N 2.28 E
Liane 124 Dd 50.43N 1.36 E
Liangcheng 154 Bd 40.32N 112.28 E
Liangpran, Gunung- 150 Ff 1.04N 114.23 E
Liangshan (Houji) 154 Dg 35.48N 116.07 E
Liangzhou → Wuwei 142 Mf 37.58N 102.48 E
Liangzi Hu 152 Je 30.15N 114.32 E
Lianjiang 152 Jg 21.42N 110.14 E
Lianshui 154 Eh 33.47N 119.16 E
Lianxian 152 Jg 24.48N 112.26 E
Lianyin 152 La 53.26N 123.50 E
Lianyungang 154 Ke 34.38N 119.27 E
Lianyungang (Xinpu) 142 Nf 34.34N 119.15 E
Lianzhou → Hepu 152 Ig 21.40N 109.12 E
Lianzhushan 154 Kb 45.28N 131.45 E
Liaocheng 152 Kd 36.27N 115.58 E
Liaodong Bandao=Liaotung Peninsula (EN) 140 Of 40.00N 122.20 E
Liaodong Wan=Liaotung, Gulf of- (EN) 152 Lc 40.00N 121.30 E
Liao He 140 Oe 40.39N 122.12 E
Liaoning Sheng (Liao-ning Sheng) [2] 152 Lc 41.00N 123.00 E
Liao-ning Sheng → Liaoning Sheng [2] 152 Lc 41.00N 123.00 E
Liaotung, Gulf of- (EN)= Liaodong Wan 152 Lc 40.00N 121.30 E
Liaotung Peninsula (EN)= Liaodong Bandao 140 Of 40.00N 122.20 E
Liaoyang 152 Lc 41.16N 123.10 E
Liaoyuan 142 Oe 42.55N 125.09 E
Liaozhong 154 Gd 41.30N 122.42 E
Liard 174 Gc 61.52N 121.18W
Liard River 180 Ee 59.15N 126.09W
Liat, Pulau- 150 Eg 2.53S 107.05 E
Liatorp 116 Fh 56.40N 14.16 E
Liatroim/Leitrim [2] 118 Eg 54.20N 8.20W
Liban 158 Lh 5.05N 40.05 E
Libano 204 Bm 37.32S 61.18W
Libby 188 Hb 48.23N 115.33W
Libenge 160 Ih 3.39N 18.38 E
Liberal 182 Gd 37.02N 100.55W
Liberec 120 Lf 50.46N 15.03 E
Liberia 190 Gf 10.38N 85.27W
Liberia [1] 160 Fh 6.00N 10.00W
Libertad [Ur.] 204 Dl 34.38S 56.39W
Libertad [Ven.] 202 Eb 8.20N 69.37W
Libertad [Ven.] 194 Li 8.08N 71.28W
Libertade, Rio- 202 He 9.35S 52.17W
Libertador General Bernardo O'Higgins [2] 206 Fd 33.35S 70.45W
Libertador General San Martin 206 Hb 23.48S 64.48W
Libertador General San Martin, Cumbre del- 198 Jh 24.55S 66.40W
Liberty [Mo.-U.S.] 186 Ig 39.15N 94.25W
Liberty [Tx.-U.S.] 186 Ik 30.03N 94.47W
Lībīyā=Libya (EN) [1] 160 If 27.00N 17.00 E
Lībīyah, Aş Şaḩrā' al-= Libyan Desert (EN) 158 Jf 24.00N 25.00 E
Libo 152 If 25.28N 107.52 E
Libobo, Tanjung- 150 Ig 0.54S 128.28 E
Liboi 170 Hb 0.24N 40.57 E
Libourne 122 Fj 44.55N 0.14W
Libramont-Chevigny 124 He 49.55N 5.23 E
Librazhdi 130 Dh 41.11N 20.19 E
Libreville 160 Hh 0.23N 9.27 E
Libro Point 150 Gd 11.26N 119.29 E
Libya (EN)=Lībīyā [1] 160 If 27.00N 17.00 E
Libyan Desert (EN)= Lībīyah, Aş Şaḩrā' al- 158 Jf 24.00N 25.00 E
Licantén 206 Fe 34.59S 72.00W
Licata 128 Hm 37.06N 13.56 E
Lice 146 Ic 38.28N 40.39 E
Licenciado Matienzo 204 Cm 37.55S 58.54W
Lich 124 Kd 50.31N 8.50 E
Licheng → Jinhu 154 Eh 33.01N 119.01 E
Lichfield 118 Li 52.42N 1.48W
Lichinga 160 Kj 13.20S 35.20 E
Lichtenau 124 Kc 51.37N 8.54 E
Lichtenburg 172 De 26.08S 26.08 E
Lichtenfels 120 Hf 50.09N 11.04 E
Lichtenvoorde 124 Ic 51.59N 6.34 E
Licking River 184 Ef 39.06N 84.30W
Licosa, Punta- 128 Ij 40.15N 14.54 E
Licuare 172 Fc 17.54S 36.49 E
Licun → Laoshan 154 Ff 36.10N 120.25 E
Licungo 172 Fc 17.40S 37.22 E
Lida 136 Ce 53.56N 25.18 E
Lidan 116 Ef 58.31N 13.09 E
Liddel 118 Kf 55.04N 2.57W
Liddon Gulf 180 Gb 75.00N 113.30W
Liden 114 De 62.42N 16.48 E
Lidhorikion 130 Fk 38.32N 22.12 E
Lidhult 116 Eh 56.50N 13.26 E
Lidingö 116 Eg 59.22N 18.08 E
Lidköping 114 Cg 58.30N 13.10 E
Lido 166 Fc 12.54N 3.44 E
Lido, Venezia- 128 Ge 45.25N 12.22 E
Lido di Ostia 128 Gi 41.44N 12.16 E
Lidzbark 120 Pc 53.17N 19.49 E
Lidzbark Warmiński 120 Qb 54.09N 20.35 E
Lié 122 Df 48.00N 2.40W
Liebenau 124 Lb 52.36N 9.06 E
Liebig, Mount- 212 Gd 23.15S 131.20 E
Liechtenstein [1] 112 Gf 47.10N 9.30 E
Liège [3] 124 Hd 50.30N 5.40 E
Liège/Luik 112 Ge 50.38N 5.34 E
Lieksa 114 He 63.19N 30.01 E
Lielupe 114 Fh 57.03N 23.56 E
Lielvarde/Lielvārde 116 Kh 56.40N 24.49 E
Lielvārde/Lielvarde 116 Kh 56.40N 24.49 E
Lienen 124 Jb 52.09N 7.59 E
Lienz 128 Gd 46.50N 12.47 E
Liepāja/Liepaja 112 Id 56.35N 21.01 E
Liepaja/Liepāja 112 Id 56.35N 21.01 E
Liepajas, ozero- / Liepājas ezers 116 Ih 56.35N 20.35 E
Liepājas ezers / Liepajas, ozero- 116 Ih 56.35N 20.35 E
Liepna 116 Lg 57.16N 27.35 E
Liepupe 116 Kg 57.22N 24.22 E
Lier/Lierre 122 Kc 51.08N 4.34 E
Lierbyen 116 De 59.47N 10.14 E
Lierneux 124 Hd 50.17N 5.48 E
Lierre/Lier 122 Kc 51.08N 4.34 E
Liesborn, Wadersloh- 124 Kc 51.43N 8.16 E
Lieser 120 Dg 49.55N 7.01 E
Liesing 128 Jc 47.20N 15.02 E
Liestal 128 Bc 47.29N 7.44 E
Liești 130 Kd 45.37N 27.31 E
Lieto 116 Jd 60.30N 22.27 E
Lietuvos Tarybu Socialistine Respublika/Litovskaja SSR [2] 136 Cd 56.00N 24.00 E
Lietuvos TSR=Lithuanian SSR (EN) [2] 136 Cd 56.00N 24.00 E
Lietvesi 116 Lc 61.30N 28.00 E
Lieurey 124 Ce 49.14N 0.29 E
Lieuvin 122 Ge 49.10N 0.30 E
Lievestuoreenjärvi 116 Lb 62.20N 26.10 E
Liévin 122 Id 50.25N 2.46 E
Lievre, Rivière du- 184 Jc 45.35N 75.25W
Liezen 128 Ic 47.34N 14.14 E
Lifford/Leifear 118 Fg 54.50N 7.29W
Li Fiord 180 Ia 80.17N 94.35W
Lifjell 116 Ce 59.30N 8.52 E
Lifou, Ile- 208 Hg 20.53S 167.13 E
Lifuka 221b Ba 19.48S 174.21W
Ligatne/Līgatne 116 Kg 57.07N 25.00 E
Līgatne/Ligatne 116 Kg 57.07N 25.00 E
Lighthouse Reef 194 De 17.20N 87.32W
Lignano Sabbiadoro 128 He 45.42N 13.09 E
Lignières 122 Ih 46.45N 2.10 E
Lignon 122 Ki 45.15N 4.08 E
Ligny-en-Barrois 122 Lf 48.41N 5.20 E
Ligonha 172 Fc 16.51S 39.09 E
Ligure, Mar-=Ligurian Sea (EN) 110 Gg 43.30N 9.00 E
Liguria [2] 128 Cf 44.30N 8.50 E
Ligurian Sea (EN)=Ligure, Mar- 110 Gg 43.30N 9.00 E
Lihir Group 208 Ge 3.05S 152.40 E
Lihme 116 Ch 56.36N 8.44 E
Lihoslavl 116 Jh 57.09N 35.29 E
Lihou Reefs and Cays 208 Gf 17.25S 151.40 E
Lihue 216 Oc 21.59N 159.22W
Lihula 114 Fg 58.44N 23.49 E
Liinahamari 114 Hb 69.40N 31.22 E
Lijiang (Dayan) 142 Mg 26.56N 100.15 E
Lijin 154 Ef 37.29N 118.15 E
Lika 128 Jf 44.30N 15.30 E
Lika 128 Jf 44.46N 15.10 E
Likasi 160 Jj 10.59S 26.43 E
Likati 170 Db 3.21N 23.53 E
Likati 170 Db 2.53N 24.03 E
Likénai/Likenaj 116 Kh 56.11N 24.42 E
Likenaj/Likénai 116 Kh 56.11N 24.42 E
Likenäs 116 Ed 60.37N 13.02 E
Likhapani 148 Jc 27.19N 95.54 E
Likiep Atoll 208 Hc 9.53N 169.09 E
Likoma Islands 170 Fe 12.04S 34.44 E
Likoto 170 Dc 1.10S 24.45 E
Likouala [3] 170 Cb 2.00N 17.30 E
Likouala 170 Cc 1.13S 16.48 E
Likouala aux Herbes 170 Cc 0.50S 17.11 E
Liku 220k Bb 19.02S 169.47W
Lilibeo, Capo- → Boeo, Capo- 128 Gm 37.34N 12.41 E
Lilienfeld 128 Jb 48.01N 15.36 E
Lilienthal 124 Ka 53.08N 8.55 E
Lilla Edet 114 Cg 58.08N 12.08 E
Lille [Bel.] 124 Gc 51.14N 4.50 E
Lille [Fr.] 112 Ge 50.38N 3.04 E
Lille Bælt=Little Belt (EN) 110 Gd 55.20N 9.45 E
Lillebonne 122 Ge 49.31N 0.33 E
Lillehammer 114 Cf 61.08N 10.30 E
Lille Hellefiske Bank (EN) 178 Ge 65.05N 54.00W
Lillers 122 Id 50.34N 2.29 E
Lillesand 114 Bg 58.15N 8.24 E
Lillestrøm 116 De 59.57N 11.05 E
Lillhärdal 114 Df 61.51N 14.04 E
Lillie Glacier 222 Kf 70.45S 163.55 E
Lillo 126 Ie 39.43N 3.18W
Lillooet 180 Ff 50.42N 121.56W
Lillooet Range 188 Eb 50.00N 121.45W
Lillooet River 180 Fg 49.45N 122.10W
Lilongwe 160 Kj 13.59S 33.47 E
Liloy 150 He 8.08N 122.40 E
Lim [Afr.] 168 Bd 7.54N 15.46 E
Lim [Yugo.] 128 Ng 43.45N 19.13 E
Lima [3] 202 Cf 12.00S 76.35W
Lima 126 Dc 41.41N 8.50W
Lima [Mt.-U.S.] 188 Id 44.38N 112.36W
Lima [Oh.-U.S.] 182 Kc 40.43N 84.06W
Lima [Par.] 204 Df 23.54S 56.20W
Lima [Peru] 200 Ig 12.03S 77.03W
Lima [Swe.] 116 Ed 60.56N 13.21 E
Lima, Pulau-Pulau- 150 Gg 3.03S 107.24 E
Limagne 122 Jh 46.00N 3.20 E
Limah 146 Qj 25.56N 56.25 E
Liman [R.S.F.S.R.] 132 Og 45.45N 47.14 E
Liman [Ukr.-U.S.S.R.] 130 Md 45.42N 29.46 E
Limanskoje 130 Mc 46.38N 29.54 E
Limari, Rio- 206 Fd 30.44S 71.43W
Limassol/Lemesós 144 Dc 34.40N 33.02 E
Limavady/Léim an Mhadaidh 118 Gf 55.03N 6.57W
Limay 124 Df 48.59N 1.44 E
Limay, Rio- 198 Ji 38.59S 68.00W
Limbara 128 Dj 40.51N 9.10 E
Limbaži 114 Fh 57.31N 24.47 E
Limbé 194 Kd 19.42N 72.24W
Limbe, Blantyre- 170 Gf 15.49S 35.03 E
Limbot 219b Cb 14.12S 167.34 E
Limboto 150 Hf 0.37N 122.57 E
Limbourg 124 Hd 50.37N 5.56 E
Limbourg/Limburg 122 Lc 51.05N 5.40 E
Limburg [Bel.] [3] 124 Hc 51.00N 5.30 E
Limburg [Neth.] [3] 124 Hc 51.14N 5.50 E
Limburg/Limbourg 122 Lc 51.05N 5.40 E
Limburg an der Lahn 120 Ef 50.23N 8.03 E
Limedsforsen 116 Ed 60.54N 13.23 E
Limeira 206 Kb 22.34S 47.24W
Limerick/Luimneach 112 Fe 52.40N 8.38W
Limerick/Luimneach [2] 118 Ei 52.30N 9.00W
Limestone, Haḑabat- 164 Fe 24.50N 32.00 E
Limfjorden 110 Gd 56.55N 9.10 E
Limia 126 Dc 41.41N 8.50W
Limingen 114 Cd 64.47N 13.36 E
Liminka 114 Fd 64.49N 25.29 E
Limmat 128 Cc 47.30N 8.15 E
Limmen Bight 212 Hb 14.45S 135.40 E
Limmen Bight River 212 Hc 15.15S 135.30 E
Limni 130 Gk 38.46N 23.19 E
Límnos=Lemnos (EN) 110 Ih 39.55N 25.15 E
Limoeiro 202 Ke 7.52S 35.27W
Limoges 112 Gf 45.51N 1.15 E
Limogne, Causse de- 122 Hj 44.20N 1.55 E
Limon 182 Gd 39.16N 103.41W
Limón [3] 194 Fi 10.00N 83.15W
Limón [C.R.] 176 Kh 10.00N 83.02W
Limón [Hond.] 194 Ef 15.52N 85.33W
Limone Piemonte 128 Bf 44.12N 7.34 E
Limousin 122 Hi 45.30N 1.50 E
Limousin, Plateaux du- 122 Hi 45.50N 1.10 E
Limoux 122 Ik 43.04N 2.14 E
Limpopo 158 Jk 25.12S 33.32 E
Limu Ling 152 Ie 19.02N 109.43 E
Limuru 170 Gc 1.06S 36.39 E
Līnah 146 Jh 28.42N 43.48 E
Lin'an 152 Ke 30.14N 119.39 E
Linapacan 150 Gd 11.27N 119.49 E
Linares [Chile] 200 Ii 35.51S 71.36W
Linares [Mex.] 190 Ed 24.52N 99.34W
Linares [Sp.] 126 If 38.05N 3.38W
Linares Viejo 204 Bf 23.09S 61.46W
Linaro, Capo- 128 Fh 42.02N 11.50 E
Lincang 142 Mg 23.48N 100.04 E
Lincheng 154 Cf 37.26N 114.34 E
Lincheng → Xuecheng 154 Dg 34.48N 117.14 E
Lincoln 118 Mh 53.20N 0.30W
Lincoln [Arg.] 206 Hd 34.52S 61.32W
Lincoln [Eng.-U.K.] 118 Mh 53.14N 0.33W
Lincoln [Il.-U.S.] 186 Lf 40.09N 89.22W
Lincoln [Nb.-U.S.] 176 Je 40.48N 96.42W
Lincoln [N.Z.] 218 Ee 43.38S 172.29 E
Lincoln, Mount- 186 Cg 39.21N 106.07W
Lincoln City 188 Cd 44.59N 124.01W
Lincoln Sea 224 Ne 83.00N 56.00W
Lincolnshire [3] 118 Mh 53.00N 0.10W
Lincoln Wolds 118 Mh 53.20N 0.10W
Lindashalvøya 116 Ad 60.40N 5.15 E
Lindau 120 Fi 47.33N 9.41 E
Linde [Neth.] 124 Hb 52.49N 5.52 E
Linde [R.S.F.S.R.] 138 Hd 64.59N 124.36 E
Linden [Guy.] 202 Gb 6.00N 58.18W
Linden [Tn.-U.S.] 184 Dh 35.37N 87.50W
Lindenows Fjord 179 Hf 60.25N 43.00W
Linderödsåsen 116 Ei 55.53N 13.56 E
Lindesberg 114 Dg 59.35N 15.15 E
Lindesnes 110 Gd 58.00N 7.02 E
Lindhorst 124 Lb 52.22N 9.17 E
Lindhos 130 Lm 36.06N 28.04 E
Lindi 160 Ki 10.00S 39.43 E
Lindi [3] 170 Gd 9.30S 38.20 E
Lindi 158 Jh 0.33N 25.05 E
Lindis Pass 218 Cf 44.35S 169.39 E
Lindlar 124 Jc 51.01N 7.23 E
Lindome 116 Eg 57.34N 12.05 E
Lindong → Bairin Zuoqi 152 Kc 43.59N 119.22 E
Lindsay [Ca.-U.S.] 188 Fh 36.12N 119.05W
Lindsay [Ont.-Can.] 184 Hc 44.21N 78.44W
Lindsdal 116 Gh 56.44N 16.18 E
Line Islands 208 Le 0.01S 157.00W
Linfen 152 Jd 36.03N 111.32 E
Lingayen 142 Oh 16.01N 120.14 E
Lingayen Gulf 150 Hc 16.15N 120.14 E
Lingbi 154 Dh 33.33N 117.33 E
Lingbo 114 Df 61.03N 16.41 E
Lingchuan 154 Bg 35.46N 113.16 E
Lingen (Ems) 120 Dd 52.31N 7.19 E
Lingfield 124 Bc 51.10N 0.01W
Lingga, Kepulauan-=Lingga Archipelago (EN) 140 Mj 0.02S 104.35 E
Lingga, Pulau- 150 Dg 0.12S 104.35 E
Lingga Archipelago (EN)= Lingga, Kepulauan- 140 Mj 0.02S 104.35 E
Linghed 116 Fd 60.47N 15.51 E
Lingling 152 Jf 26.24N 111.41 E
Lingomo 170 Db 0.38N 21.59 E
Lingqiu 154 Ce 39.26N 114.06 E
Lingshan 152 Ig 22.30N 109.17 E
Lingshan Dao 154 Fg 35.45N 120.10 E
Lingshi 154 Af 36.50N 111.46 E
Lingshou 154 Ce 38.18N 114.22 E
Linguère 160 Fg 15.24N 15.07W
Lingwu 152 Id 38.05N 106.20 E
Lingxian 154 Df 37.20N 116.35 E
Lingyuan 154 Ed 41.15N 119.23 E
Linh, Ngoc- 140 Mh 15.04N 107.59 E
Linhai 152 La 51.36N 124.22 E
Linhai (Taizhou) 152 Lf 28.52N 121.08 E
Linhares 202 Jg 19.25S 40.04W
Linhe 152 Ic 40.49N 107.28 E
Linhuaiguan 154 Dh 32.54N 117.39 E
Linjiang 154 Il 41.49N 126.55 E
Linköping 112 Hd 58.25N 15.37 E
Linkou 152 Nb 45.18N 130.18 E
Linkuva 116 Jh 56.02N 23.58 E
Linlü Shan 154 Bf 36.02N 113.42 E
Linmingguan → Yongnian 154 Cf 36.47N 114.30 E
Linn, Mount- 188 Df 40.03N 122.48W
Linneryd 116 Fh 56.40N 15.07 E
Linnhe, Loch- 118 He 56.37N 5.25W
Linnich 124 Id 50.59N 6.16 E
Linosa 128 Go 35.50N 12.50 E
Linovo 120 Ud 52.28N 24.35 E
Linqing 152 Kd 36.48N 115.49 E
Linqu 154 Ef 36.31N 118.32 E
Linquan 154 Ch 33.04N 115.16 E
Linru 154 Bg 34.10N 112.51 E
Lins 206 Kb 21.40S 49.45W
Linsell 116 Eb 62.09N 13.53 E
Linshu (Xiazhuang) 154 Eg 34.56N 118.38 E
Linslade 124 Bc 51.55N 0.40W
Linta 172 Ge 25.02S 44.05 E
Lintao 152 Hd 35.20N 104.00 E
Linthal 128 Cd 46.55N 9.00 E
Linton [Eng.-U.K.] 124 Cb 52.06N 0.16 E
Linton [N.D.-U.S.] 186 Fc 46.16N 100.14W
Linxi [China] 154 Ee 39.42N 118.26 E
Linxi [China] 142 Ne 43.36N 118.02 E
Linxia 142 Mf 35.36N 103.59 E
Linxian 152 Jd 37.57N 111.00 E
Linxiang 154 Bj 29.29N 113.28 E
Linyi [China] 154 Df 37.11N 116.51 E
Linyi [China] 152 Kd 35.09N 118.15 E
Linz 112 Hf 48.18N 14.18 E
Linze (Shahezhen) 152 Hd 39.10N 100.21 E
Lion, Golfe du-=Lion, Gulf of- (EN) 110 Gg 43.00N 4.00 E
Lion, Gulf of- (EN)=Lion, Golfe du- 110 Gg 43.00N 4.00 E
Lions Den 172 Ec 17.16S 30.02 E
Lion-sur-Mer 124 Be 49.18N 0.19W
Lioppa 150 Ih 7.40S 126.00 E
Lios Mór/Lismore 118 Fi 52.08N 7.55W
Lios na gCearrbhach/ Lisburn 118 Gg 54.31N 6.03W
Lios Tuathail/Listovel 118 Di 52.27N 9.29W
Liouesso 170 Cb 1.02N 15.43 E
Lipa 150 Hd 13.57N 121.10 E
Lipany 120 Qg 49.10N 20.58 E
Lipari 128 Il 38.28N 14.57 E
Lipari 128 Il 38.30N 14.55 E
Lipari, Isole → Eolie, Isole- 110 Hh 38.35N 14.55 E
Lipari Islands (EN)=Eolie o Lipari, Isole- 110 Hh 38.35N 14.55 E
Lipeck 112 Je 52.37N 39.35 E
Lipeckaja oblast [3] 136 De 52.45N 39.10 E
Lipenská přehradní nádrž 120 Kh 48.45N 14.05 E
Liperi 114 Ge 62.32N 29.22 E
Lipez, Cordillera de- 202 Eh 22.00S 66.45W
Liphook 124 Bc 51.04N 0.48W
Lipkani 130 Ja 48.13N 26.48 E
Lipljan 130 Eg 42.32N 21.08 E
Lipno 120 Pd 52.51N 19.10 E
Lipova 130 Ec 46.05N 21.42 E
Lipovcy 138 Ih 44.15N 131.45 E
Lippborg, Lippetal- 124 Kc 51.40N 8.02 E
Lippe 124 Cc 51.39N 6.38 E
Lipper Bergland 124 Kb 52.05N 8.57 E
Lippetal 124 Kc 51.40N 8.13 E
Lippetal-Eickelborn 124 Kc 51.39N 8.13 E
Lippetal-Lippborg 124 Kc 51.40N 8.02 E
Lippischer Wald 124 Kc 51.56N 8.45 E
Lippstadt 120 Ee 51.40N 8.21 E
Lipsko 120 Re 51.09N 21.39 E
Lipsoi 130 Jl 37.20N 26.45 E
Liptako 158 Hg 14.15N 0.02 E
Liptovský Mikuláš 120 Pg 49.05N 19.38 E
Lira 170 Fb 2.15N 32.54 E
Liranga 170 Cc 0.40S 17.36 E
Liri 128 Hi 41.25N 13.52 E
Liria / Llíria 126 Le 39.38N 0.36W
Lis 126 De 39.53N 8.58W
Lisa 130 Cf 43.08N 19.42 E
Lisac 130 Eg 42.45N 21.56 E
Lisakovsk 136 Ge 52.33N 62.28 E
Lisala 160 Jh 2.09N 21.31 E
Lisboa [2] 126 Ce 39.00N 9.08W
Lisboa=Lisbon (EN) 112 Fh 38.43N 9.08W
Lisbon 186 Hc 46.27N 97.41W
Lisbon (EN)=Lisboa 112 Fh 38.43N 9.08W
Lisbon Canyon (EN) 126 Cf 38.20N 9.20W
Lisburn/Lios na gCearrbhach 118 Gg 54.31N 6.03W
Lisburne, Cape- 178 Fc 68.52N 166.14W
Liscannor Bay/Bá Thuath Reanna 118 Di 52.55N 9.25W
Lisec 120 Uh 48.48N 24.45 E
Li Shan 154 Ag 35.25N 111.58 E
Lishi 152 Jd 37.29N 111.08 E
Lishu 154 Hc 43.19N 124.20 E
Lishui 152 Kf 28.30N 119.55 E
Lisianski Island 208 Jb 26.02N 174.00W
Lisičansk 136 Df 48.53N 38.28 E
Lisieux 122 Ge 49.09N 0.14 E
Liska 130 Dh 41.19N 20.58 E
L'Isle-Adam 124 Ee 49.07N 2.14 E
Lismore 210 Gg 28.48S 153.17 E
Lismore/Lios Mór 118 Fi 52.08N 7.55W
Liss 124 Bc 51.02N 0.54W
Liss 146 Hg 31.14N 38.31 E
List 120 Ea 55.01N 8.26 E
Lista 116 Bf 58.10N 6.40 E
Listafjorden 116 Bf 58.10N 6.35 E
Lister, Mount- 222 Kf 78.04S 162.41 E
Lištica 128 Lg 43.23N 17.39 E
Listovel/Lios Tuathail 118 Di 52.27N 9.29W
Listowel 184 Gd 43.44N 80.57W
Liswarta 120 Pe 51.06N 19.01 E
Lit 116 Fa 63.19N 14.49 E
Litang [China] 152 Ig 23.12N 109.05 E
Litang [China] 152 He 30.02N 100.18 E
Litani Rivier 202 Hc 3.18N 54.06W
Litchfield 186 Id 45.08N 94.31W
Lithgow 210 Gh 33.29S 150.09 E
Lithinon, Ákra- 130 Ho 34.55N 24.44 E
Lithuania (EN) 110 Id 56.00N 24.00 E
Lithuanian SSR (EN)= Lietuvos TSR [2] 136 Cd 56.00N 24.00 E
Litókhoron 130 Fi 40.06N 22.30 E
Litoměřice 120 Kf 50.32N 14.08 E
Litovel 120 Ng 49.43N 17.05 E
Litovko 138 Ig 49.17N 135.10 E
Litovskaja Sovetskaja Socialističeskaja Respublika [2] 136 Cd 56.00N 24.00 E
Litovskaja SSR/Lietuvos Tarybu Socialistine Respublika [2] 136 Cd 56.00N 24.00 E
Little Abaco Island 190 Ic 26.53N 77.43W
Little Abitibi River 184 Ha 49.29N 79.32W
Little Aden 144 Fg 12.45N 44.52 E
Little America 188 Kf 41.32N 109.47W
Little Andaman 140 Lh 10.45N 92.30 E
Little Bahama Bank (EN) 190 Ic 26.30N 78.00W
Little Barrier Island 218 Fb 36.10S 175.05 E
Little Beaver Creek 186 Ec 46.17N 103.56W
Little Belt (EN)=Lille Bælt 110 Gd 55.20N 9.45 E
Little Belt Mountains 188 Jc 46.45N 110.35W
Little Blue River 186 Hg 39.41N 96.40W
Little Bow River 188 Ib 49.53N 112.29W
Little Carpathians (EN) = Malé Karpaty 120 Nh 48.30N 17.20 E
Little Cayman 190 He 19.41N 80.03W
Little Colorado River 174 Hf 36.11N 111.48W
Little Current 180 Jg 45.58N 81.56W
Little Current 180 Jf 50.57N 84.36W
Little Dry Creek 188 Lc 47.21N 106.22W
Little Exuma Island 194 Jb 23.27N 75.37W
Little Falls 182 Ib 45.59N 94.21W
Littlefield 186 Ej 33.55N 102.20W
Little Fort 188 Ea 51.25N 120.12W
Little Grand Rapids 180 Hf 52.02N 95.25W
Little Halibut Bank 118 Lc 58.20N 1.15W
Littlehampton 124 Bd 50.48N 0.32W
Little Inagua Island 190 Jd 21.30N 73.00W
Little Karroo (EN)=Klein-Karoo 172 Cf 33.42S 21.20 E
Little Missouri 174 Ie 47.30N 102.25W
Little Namaland (EN)= Namakwaland 172 Be 29.00S 17.00 E
Little Nicobar 148 Ig 7.20N 93.40 E
Little Ouse 118 Ni 52.30N 0.22 E
Littleport 124 Cb 52.27N 0.18 E
Little Powder River 188 Md 45.28N 105.20W
Little Quill Lake 188 Ma 51.55N 104.05W
Little River 218 Ee 43.46S 172.47 E
Little Rock 176 Jf 34.44N 92.15W
Little Rocky Mountains 188 Kb 48.00N 108.45W
Little Scarcies 166 Cd 8.51N 13.09W
Little Sioux River 186 Hf 41.49N 96.04W
Little Sitkin 178a Bb 51.55N 178.30 E
Little Smoky 180 Fe 55.39N 117.37W
Little Snake River 186 Bf 40.27N 108.26W
Littleton [Co.-U.S.] 186 Dg 39.37N 105.01W
Littleton [N.H.-U.S.] 184 Lc 44.18N 71.46W
Little White River [Ont.-Can.] 184 Fb 46.15N 83.00W
Little White River [S.D.-U.S.] 186 Fe 43.44N 100.40W
Littoral [3] 166 He 4.30N 10.00 E
Litvinov 120 Jf 50.36N 13.36 E
Liuhe 152 Mc 42.16N 125.45 E
Liu He [China] 152 Lc 42.46N 126.13 E
Liu He [China] 154 Gd 41.48N 122.43 E
Liuheng Dao 154 Gj 29.43N 122.08 E
Liujia Xia 152 Hd 35.50N 103.00 E
Liukang Tenggaja, Kepulauan- 150 Gh 6.45S 118.50 E
Liupai → Tian'e 152 If 25.05N 107.12 E
Liupan Shan 152 Id 35.40N 106.15 E
Liuqu He 154 Fd 40.10N 120.15 E
Liuwa Plain 170 De 14.27S 22.25 E
Liuyang 154 Bj 28.09N 113.38 E
Liuzhangzhen → Yuanqu 152 Jd 35.19N 111.44 E
Liuzhou 142 Mg 24.22N 109.20 E
Līvāni/Livany 114 Gh 56.22N 26.12 E
Livanjsko Polje 128 Kg 43.51N 16.50 E
Livany/Līvāni 114 Gh 56.22N 26.12 E
Livarot 124 Ce 49.01N 0.09 E
Livengood 178 Jc 65.32N 148.33W
Livenza 128 Ge 45.35N 12.51 E
Live Oak 184 Fj 30.18N 82.59W
Livermore 188 Eh 37.41N 121.46W
Livermore, Mount- 186 Dk 30.37N 104.08W
Liverpool [Eng.-U.K.] 112 Fe 53.25N 2.55W

Index Symbols

[1] Independent Nation
[2] State, Region
[3] District, County
[4] Municipality
[5] Colony, Dependency
Continent
Physical Region
Historical or Cultural Region
Mount, Mountain
Volcano
Hill
Mountains, Mountain Range
Hills, Escarpment
Plateau, Upland
Pass, Gap
Plain, Lowland
Delta
Salt Flat
Valley, Canyon
Crater, Cave
Karst Features
Depression
Polder
Desert, Dunes
Forest, Woods
Heath, Steppe
Oasis
Cape, Point
Coast, Beach
Cliff
Peninsula
Isthmus
Sandbank
Island
Atoll
Rock, Reef
Islands, Archipelago
Rocks, Reefs
Coral Reef
Well, Spring
Geyser
River, Stream
Waterfall, Rapids
River Mouth, Estuary
Lake
Salt Lake
Intermittent Lake
Reservoir
Swamp, Pond
Canal
Glacier
Ice Shelf, Pack Ice
Ocean
Sea
Gulf, Bay
Strait, Fjord
Lagoon
Bank
Seamount
Tablemount
Ridge
Shelf
Basin
Escarpment, Sea Scarp
Fracture
Trench, Abyss
National Park, Reserve
Point of Interest
Recreation Site
Cave, Cavern
Historic Site
Ruins
Wall, Walls
Church, Abbey
Temple
Scientific Station
Railway station
Airport
Port
Military installation
Lighthouse
Mine
Tunnel
Dam, Bridge

Liverpool [N.S.-Can.] 180 Lh 44.02N 64.43W
Liverpool, Cape - 180 Jb 73.38N 78.05W
Liverpool Bay [Can.] 180 Ec 70.00N 129.00W
Liverpool Bay [Eng.-U.K.] 118 Jh 53.30N 3.16W
Liverpool Range 212 Kf 31.40S 150.30 E
Liverpool River 212 Gb 12.00S 134.00 E
Livezi 130 Ge 44.14N 23.47 E
Livigno 128 Ed 46.32N 10.04 E
Livingston [Guat.] 194 Cf 15.50N 88.45W
Livingston [Mt.-U.S.] 182 Eb 45.40N 110.34W
Livingston [Newf.-Can.] 180 Kf 53.40N 66.10W
Livingston [Tn.-U.S.] 184 Eg 36.23N 85.19W
Livingston [Tx.-U.S.] 186 Ik 30.43N 94.56W
Livingston, Lake- 186 Ik 30.45N 95.15W
Livingstone, Chutes de-= Livingstone Falls (EN) 158 Ii 4.50S 14.30 E
Livingstone Falls (EN)= Livingstone, Chutes de- 158 Ii 4.50S 14.30 E
Livingstone Memorial 170 Fe 12.19S 30.18 E
Livingstone Mountains 170 Fd 9.45S 34.20 E
Livingstonia 170 Fe 10.36S 34.07 E
Livingston Island 222 Qe 62.36S 60.30W
Livno 128 Lg 43.50N 17.01 E
Livny 136 De 52.28N 37.37 E
Livonia 184 Fd 42.25N 83.23W
Livonia (EN)=Livonija 110 Id 57.30N 25.30 E
Livonija=Livonia (EN) 110 Id 57.30N 25.30 E
Livorno=Leghorn (EN) 112 Hg 43.33N 10.19 E
Livradois, Montu du- 122 Ji 45.30N 3.33 E
Livramento do Brumado 202 Jf 13.39S 41.50W
Livron-sur-Drôme 122 Kj 44.46N 4.51 E
Liwale 170 Gd 9.46S 37.56 E
Liwiec 120 Rd 52.35N 21.33 E
Liwonde 170 Gf 15.01S 35.13 E
Lixi 152 Hf 26.21N 102.03 E
Lixian [China] 152 Jf 29.40N 111.45 E
Lixian [China] 152 Ie 34.11N 105.02 E
Lixian [China] 154 Ce 38.29N 115.34 E
Lixin 154 Dh 33.09N 116.12 E
Lixoúrion 130 Dk 38.12N 20.26 E
Liyang 154 Ei 31.26N 119.29 E
Lizard 118 Hl 49.57N 5.13W
Lizard Point 110 Ff 49.56N 5.13W
Lizhu 154 Fj 29.58N 120.26 E
Lizy sur Ourcq 124 Fe 49.01N 3.02 E
Ljady 116 Mf 58.35N 28.55 E
Ljahoviči 132 Ec 53.04N 26.15 E
Ljahovskije ostrova = Lyakhov Islands (EN) 140 Qb 73.30N 141.00 E
Ljalja 134 Jg 59.10N 61.30 E
Ljamin 134 Of 61.18N 71.45 E
Ljangar 135 Ed 40.23N 65.59 E
Ljangasovo 114 Lg 58.33N 49.29 E
Ljapin 134 Je 63.38N 61.58 E
Ljaskelja 116 Nc 61.39N 31.03 E
Ljaskovec 130 If 43.06N 25.43 E
Ljig 130 De 44.14N 20.15 E
Ljuban [Bye.-U.S.S.R.] 132 Ec 52.48N 27.59 E
Ljuban [R.S.F.S.R.] 114 Hg 59.22N 31.13 E
Ljubar 132 Ee 49.55N 27.44 E
Ljubaščevka 130 Nb 47.50N 30.07 E
Ljubeli 128 Id 46.26N 14.16 E
Ljubercy 136 Dd 55.40N 37.55 E
Ljubešöv 120 Ve 51.45N 25.37 E
Ljubim 114 Jg 58.22N 40.41 E
Ljubimec 130 Jh 41.50N 26.05 E
Ljubinje 128 Mh 42.57N 18.06 E
Ljubišnja 130 Cf 43.20N 19.07 E
Ljubljana 112 Hf 46.02N 14.30 E
Ljuboml 132 Cd 51.15N 23.59 E
Ljubotin 132 Ie 49.59N 35.55 E
Ljubovija 130 Ce 44.12N 19.22 E
Ljubuški 128 Lg 43.12N 17.33 E
Ljubytino 114 Hg 58.50N 33.25 E
Ljudinovo 136 De 53.51N 34.28 E
Ljugarn 114 Eh 57.19N 18.42 E
Ljungan 110 Hc 62.19N 17.23 E
Ljungaverk 116 Gb 62.29N 16.03 E
Ljungby 114 Ch 56.50N 13.56 E
Ljungbyholm 116 Gh 56.38N 16.10 E
Ljungdalen 114 Ce 62.51N 12.47 E
Ljungsbro 116 Ff 58.31N 15.30 E
Ljungskile 116 Df 58.14N 11.55 E
Ljusdal 114 Df 61.50N 16.05 E
Ljusnan 116 Hc 61.12N 17.08 E
Ljusne 114 Df 61.13N 17.08 E
Ljusterö 116 Fe 59.30N 18.35 E
Ljuta 116 Mf 58.33N 28.45 E
Llandilo 118 Jj 51.53N 3.59W
Llandovery 118 Jj 51.59N 3.48W
Llandrindod Wellu 118 Ji 52.15N 3.23W
Llandudno 118 Jh 53.19N 3.49W
Llanelli 118 Ij 51.42N 4.10W
Llanes 128 Ha 43.25N 4.45W
Llangefni 118 Ih 53.16N 4.18W
Llangollen 118 Ji 52.58N 3.10W
Llano 186 Gk 30.45N 98.41W
Llano Estacado 174 If 33.30N 102.40W
Llano River 186 Gk 30.35N 98.25W
Llanos 198 Je 5.00N 70.00W
Llanos de Sonora 190 Bc 28.20N 111.00W
Llanquihue, Lago- 206 Ff 41.08S 72.48W
Llata 202 Ce 9.25S 76.47W
Lleida/Lérida 126 Mc 41.37N 0.37 E
Lleida / Lérida 126 Nc 42.00N 1.10 E
Llerena 126 Ff 38.14N 6.01W
Lleyn 118 Ii 52.54N 4.30W
Llica 202 Eg 19.52S 68.16W
Llíria / Liria 126 Le 39.38N 0.36W
Llívia 126 Nb 42.28N 1.59 E
Llobregat 126 Oc 41.19N 2.09 E
Lloret de Mar 126 Oc 41.42N 2.51 E
Llorona, Punta- 194 Fi 8.37N 83.44W
Llorri / Orri, Pic de l'- 126 Nb 42.23N 1.12 E
Lloydminster 180 Gf 53.17N 110.00W
Llucena / Lucena del Cid 126 Ld 40.08N 0.17W
Lluchmayor/Llucmajor 126 Oe 39.29N 2.54 E
Llucmajor/Lluchmayor 126 Oe 39.29N 2.54 E
Llullaillaco, Volcán- 198 Jh 24.43S 68.33W
Lo 219b Ca 13.21S 166.38 E
Loa 188 Jg 38.24N 111.38W
Loa, Río- 206 Fb 21.26S 70.04W
Loanatit, Pointe- 219b Dd 19.21S 169.14 E
Loange 158 Ji 4.17S 20.02 E
Loango 170 Bc 4.39S 11.48 E
Loano 128 Cf 44.08N 8.15 E
Loban 114 Mh 56.59N 51.12 E
Lobatse 160 Jk 25.13S 25.41 E
Löbau/Lubij 120 Ke 51.06N 14.40 E
Lobaye [3] 168 Be 4.00N 17.40 E
Lobaye 158 Ih 3.41N 18.35 E
Lobenstein 120 Hf 50.27N 11.39 E
Loberia 206 Ie 38.09S 58.47W
Łobez 120 Lc 53.39N 15.36 E
Lobito 160 Ij 12.22S 13.34 E
Lobo 150 Jg 3.45S 134.05 E
Lobo 166 Dd 6.02N 6.47W
Lobos 206 Ie 35.11S 59.06W
Lobos 162 Ed 28.45N 13.49W
Lobos, Cabo- 192 Cc 29.55N 112.45W
Lobos, Cay- 194 Ib 22.24N 77.32W
Lobos, Cayo- 192 Ph 18.22N 87.24W
Lobos, Isla- 192 Dd 27.20N 110.36W
Lobos, Islas de- 192 Kg 21.27N 97.15W
Lobos de Afuera, Islas- 202 Be 6.57S 80.42W
Lobos de Tierra, Isla- 202 Be 6.27S 80.52W
Lobva 136 Gd 59.12N 60.30 E
Łobżonka 120 Nc 53.07N 17.18 E
Locana 128 Be 45.25N 7.27 E
Locarno 128 Cd 46.10N 8.48 E
Loch Aillionn/Allen, Lough- 118 Eg 54.08N 8.08W
Loch Ainninn 118 Fh 53.28N 7.24W
Loch Ainninn/Ennell, Lough- 118 Fh 53.28N 7.24W
Loch Arabhach/Arrow, Lough- 118 Eg 54.05N 8.20W
Lochboisdale 118 Fd 57.09N 7.19W
Loch Cairlinn/Carlingford Lough 118 Gg 54.05N 6.14W
Loch Ce/Key, Lough- 118 Eg 54.00N 8.15W
Loch Coirib/Corrib, Lough- 118 Dh 53.05N 9.10W
Loch Con/Conn, Lough- 118 Dg 54.04N 9.20W
Loch Cuan/Strangford Lough 118 Hg 54.26N 5.36W
Loch Deirgeirt/Derg, Lough- 118 Ei 53.00N 8.20W
Lochearnhead 118 Ie 56.23N 4.18W
Loch Éirne Íochtair/Lower Lough Erne 118 Fg 54.30N 7.50W
Loch Éirne Uachtair/Upper Lough Erne 118 Fg 54.20N 7.30W
Lochem 124 Ib 52.10N 6.25 E
Loches 122 Gg 47.08N 1.00 E
Loch Feabhail/Foyle, Lough- 118 Ff 55.05N 7.10W
Loch Garman/Wexford 118 Fe 52.20N 6.27W
Loch Garman/Wexford [2] 118 Gi 52.20N 6.40W
Lochgilphead 118 He 56.03N 5.26W
Lochinver 118 Hc 58.09N 5.15W
Loch Katrine 118 Ie 56.18N 4.30W
Loch Lao/Belfast Lough 118 Hg 54.40N 5.50W
Loch Léin/Leane, Lough- 118 Di 52.05N 9.35W
Loch Leven 118 Je 56.13N 3.10W
Lochmaddy 118 Fd 57.36N 7.10W
Loch Measca/Mask, Lough- 118 Dh 53.35N 9.20W
Lochnagar 118 Je 56.55N 3.10W
Loch nEathach/Neagh, Lough- 110 Fe 54.38N 6.24W
Loch Ness 118 Id 57.15N 4.30W
Łochów 120 Rd 52.32N 21.48 E
Loch Pholl an Phúca / Poulaphouca Reservoir 118 Gh 53.10N 6.30W
Loch Rí/Ree, Lough- 118 Fh 53.35N 8.00W
Lochsa River 188 Hc 46.08N 115.36W
Loch Sileann/Sheelin, Lough- 118 Fh 53.48N 7.20W
Loch Suili/Swilly, Lough- 118 Ff 55.10N 7.38W
Loch Ui Ghadra/Gara, Lough- 118 Eh 53.55N 8.30W
Lochy 118 He 56.49N 5.06W
Lochy, Loch- 118 Ie 56.55N 4.55W
Lockerbie 118 Jf 55.07N 3.22W
Lockhart 186 Hl 29.53N 97.41W
Lock Haven 184 Ie 41.09N 77.28W
Löcknitz 120 Hc 53.07N 11.16 E
Lockport 184 Hd 43.11N 78.39W
Locminé 122 Dg 47.53N 2.50W
Locri 128 Kl 38.14N 16.16 E
Lod 146 Fg 31.58N 34.54 E
Lodalskåpa 114 Bf 61.47N 7.12 E
Loddon 124 Db 52.32N 1.29 E
Loddon River 212 Ig 36.41S 143.55 E
Lodejnoje Pole 136 Dc 60.44N 33.33 E
Lodève 122 Jk 43.43N 3.19 E
Lodi [Ca.-U.S.] 188 Eg 38.08N 121.16W
Lodi [It.] 128 De 45.19N 9.30 E
Lødingen 114 Db 68.25N 16.00 E
Lodja 160 Ji 3.29S 23.26 E
Lodosa 126 Jb 42.25N 2.05W
Lödöse 116 Ef 58.02N 12.08 E
Lodwar 160 Kh 3.07N 35.36 E
Łódź 112 He 51.46N 19.30 E
Łódź [2] 120 Pe 51.45N 19.30 E
Loei 148 Ke 17.32N 101.34 E
Loeriesfontein 172 Bf 30.56S 19.26 E
Lofanga 221b Ba 19.50S 174.33W
Loffa [3] 166 Dd 7.45N 10.00W
Loffa 158 Fh 6.36N 11.05W
Lofoten 110 Hb 68.30N 15.00 E
Lofoten Basin (EN) 110 Ga 70.00N 4.00 E
Lofsdalen 116 Eb 62.07N 13.16 E
Loftahammar 116 Gg 57.52N 16.40 E
Loga 166 Fc 13.37N 3.14 E
Logan [N.M.-U.S.] 186 Ei 35.22N 103.25W
Logan [Oh.-U.S.] 184 Ff 39.32N 82.24W
Logan [Ut.-U.S.] 182 Ec 41.44N 111.50W
Logan [W.V.-U.S.] 184 Gg 37.52N 81.58W
Logan, Mount- [Can.] 174 Ec 60.34N 140.24W
Logan, Mount- [Wa.-U.S.] 188 Eb 48.32N 120.57W
Logan Martin Lake 184 Di 33.40N 86.15W
Logan Mountains 180 Ed 61.00N 128.00W
Logansport 184 De 40.45N 86.21W
Loge 158 Ii 7.49S 13.06 E
Logojsk 116 Lj 54.12N 27.57 E
Logone 158 Ig 12.06N 15.02 E
Logone Birni 166 Ic 11.47N 15.06 E
Logone Occidental [3] 168 Bd 8.40N 16.00 E
Logone Occidental 168 Bd 9.07N 16.26 E
Logone Oriental [3] 168 Bd 8.20N 16.30 E
Logone Oriental 168 Bd 8.07N 16.26 E
Logroño [Arg.] 204 Bi 29.30S 61.42W
Logroño [Sp.] 126 Jb 42.28N 2.27W
Logrosán 126 Ge 39.20N 5.29W
Løgstør 114 Bh 56.58N 9.15 E
Logudoro 128 Cj 40.35N 8.40 E
Løgumkloster 116 Ci 55.03N 8.57 E
Lögurinn 114a Cb 65.15N 14.30W
Lohja/Lojo 114 Ff 60.15N 24.05 E
Lohjanjärvi 116 Jd 60.15N 23.55 E
Lohjanselkä/Lojo åsen 116 Kd 60.15N 24.10 E
Löhme 124 Kc 51.41N 8.42 E
Löhne 120 Ed 52.11N 8.41 E
Lohne (Oldenburg) 124 Kb 52.40N 8.14 E
Lohra 124 Kd 50.44N 8.38 E
Lohr am Main 120 Ff 49.59N 9.35 E
Lohusuu/Lokusu 116 Lf 58.53N 27.01 E
Lohvica 132 Hd 50.22N 33.15 E
Loi, Phou- 148 Kd 20.16N 103.12 E
Loiblpaß 128 Id 46.26N 14.16 E
Loi-Kaw 148 Je 19.41N 97.13 E
Loile 170 Dc 0.52S 20.12 E
Loimaa 114 Ff 60.51N 23.03 E
Loimijoki 116 Jc 61.13N 22.38 E
Loing 122 If 48.23N 2.48 E
Loir 122 Fg 47.33N 0.32W
Loire [3] 122 Ji 45.30N 4.00 E
Loire 110 Ff 47.16N 2.11W
Loire, Canal latéral à la- 122 Jh 46.29N 3.59 E
Loire, Val de- 122 Hg 47.40N 1.35 E
Loire-Atlantique [3] 122 Eg 47.15N 1.50W
Loiret [3] 122 Ig 47.55N 2.20 E
Loir-et-Cher [3] 122 Hg 47.30N 1.30 E
Loisach 124 Hi 47.56N 11.27 E
Loison 124 Hs 49.30N 5.17 E
Loja [Ec.] 200 If 4.00S 79.13W
Loja [Sp.] 126 Hg 37.10N 4.09W
Lojo/Lohja 114 Ff 60.15N 24.05 E
Lojo åsen/Lohjanselkä 116 Kd 60.15N 24.10 E
Loka 168 Ee 4.16N 31.01 E
Lokači 120 Uf 50.43N 24.44 E
Lokalahti 116 Id 60.41N 21.28 E
Lokandu 170 Ec 2.31S 25.47 E
Lokantekojärvi 114 Gc 68.56N 27.40 E
Lokbatan 132 Pi 40.21N 49.42 E
Lokčim 134 Ef 61.48N 51.45 E
Løken 116 De 59.48N 11.29 E
Lokeren 122 Jc 51.06N 4.00 E
Lokichar 170 Gb 2.23N 35.39 E
Lokichokio 170 Fb 4.12N 34.21 E
Lokitaung 170 Gb 4.16N 35.45 E
Løkken [Den.] 116 Cg 57.22N 9.43 E
Løkken [Nor.] 116 Ba 63.05N 9.36 E
Loknja 114 Hh 56.49N 30.09 E
Loko 166 Gd 8.00N 7.50 E
Lokoja 166 Gd 7.48N 6.44 E
Lokolo 170 Cc 0.43S 19.40 E
Lokomo 166 Ie 2.41N 15.19 E
Lokoro 170 Cc 1.43S 18.23 E
Lokossa 166 Fd 6.38N 1.43 E
Lokot 132 Ic 52.33N 34.31 E
Lokoti 166 Hd 6.22N 14.20 E
Loksa 116 Fg 59.34N 25.44 E
Loks Land 180 Ld 62.27N 64.30W
Lokuru 219a Cc 8.35S 157.20 E
Lokusu/Lohusuu 116 Lf 58.53N 27.01 E
Lokwa Kangole 170 Gb 3.32N 35.54 E
Lol 158 Jh 9.13N 28.59 E
Lola 166 Dd 7.48N 8.32W
Lolimi 168 Ee 4.35N 33.59 E
Loliondo 170 Gc 2.03S 35.37 E
Lolland 110 He 54.45N 11.30 E
Lollar 124 Kd 50.38N 8.42 E
Lolo 170 Db 2.13N 23.00 E
Lolo 170 Bc 0.40S 12.28 E
Lolodorf 166 He 3.14N 10.44 E
Lolo Pass 182 Db 46.40N 114.33W
Loloway 219b Cb 15.17S 167.58 E
Lom 130 Gf 43.49N 23.14 E
Lom [Afr.] 166 Hd 5.20N 13.24 E
Lom [Bul.] 130 Gf 43.50N 23.15 E
Loma Bonita 192 Lh 18.07N 95.53W
Lomaloma 219d Cb 17.17S 178.59W
Lomami 170 Db 0.46N 24.16 E
Loma Mountains 158 Fh 9.10N 11.07W
Lomas de Vallejos 204 Dh 27.44S 57.56W
Loma Verde 204 Cl 35.16S 58.24W
Lomba 170 Df 15.36S 21.32 E
Lombarda, Serra- 202 Hc 2.50N 51.50W
Lombarde, Prealpi- 128 De 46.00N 9.30 E
Lombardia = Lombardy (EN) [2] 128 De 45.40N 9.30 E
Lombardy (EN) = Lombardia [2] 128 De 45.40N 9.30 E
Lomblen, Pulau- 140 Oj 8.25S 123.30 E
Lombok, Pulau- 140 Nj 8.45S 116.30 E
Lombok, Selat- 150 Gh 8.30S 115.50 E
Lomé 160 Hh 6.08N 1.13 E
Lomela 160 Ji 2.18S 23.17 E
Lomela 158 Ji 0.14S 20.42 E
Lomellina 128 Ce 45.15N 8.45 E
Loméméti 219b Dd 19.30S 169.27 E
Lomié 166 He 3.10N 13.37 E
Lomlom 219c Bb 10.19S 166.16 E
Lomma 116 Ei 55.41N 13.05 E
Lomme 124 Hd 50.08N 5.10 E
Lommel 122 Lc 51.14N 5.18 E
Lomnica 120 Ug 49.02N 24.47 E
Lomond, Loch- 118 Ie 56.08N 4.38W
Lomonosov 136 Cd 59.55N 29.40 E
Lomonosovki 136 Ge 52.50N 66.28 E
Lomonosov Ridge (EN) 224 De 88.00N 140.00 E
Lomont 122 Mg 47.21N 6.36 E
Lompobatang, Gunung- 150 Gh 5.20S 119.55 E
Lompoc 182 Ce 34.38N 120.27W
Lomsegga 116 Cc 61.49N 8.22 E
Łomża 120 Sc 53.11N 22.05 E
Łomża [2] 120 Sc 53.10N 22.05 E
Lønahorg 116 Bd 60.42N 6.25 E
Loncoche 206 Fe 39.22S 72.38W
Londa 148 Ee 15.28N 74.31 E
Londerzeel 124 Gc 51.01N 4.18 E
Londiani 170 Gc 0.10S 35.36 E
Londinières 124 De 49.50N 1.24 E
London [Eng.-U.K.] 112 Fe 51.30N 0.10W
London [Kir.] 220g Bb 1.58N 157.29W
London [Ky.-U.S.] 184 Eg 37.08N 84.05W
London [Ont.-Can.] 176 Ke 42.59N 81.14W
London-Barnet 124 Bc 51.39N 0.12W
London-Bexley 124 Cc 51.26N 0.09 E
London Bridge 197p Bb 12.17N 61.35W
London-Bromley 124 Cc 51.25N 0.01 E
London-Croydon 118 Mj 51.23N 0.07W
Londonderry / Derry 112 Fd 55.00N 7.19W
Londonderry, Cape- 212 Fb 13.45S 126.55 E
London-Ealing 124 Bc 51.30N 0.19W
London-Enfield 124 Bc 51.40N 0.04W
London-Greenwich 118 Mj 51.28N 0.00
London-Haringey 124 Bc 51.36N 0.06W
London-Harrow 124 Bc 51.36N 0.20W
London-Havering 124 Cc 51.36N 0.11 E
London-Hillingdon 124 Bc 51.31N 0.27W
London-Kingston-upon-Thames 118 Mj 51.28N 0.19W
London-Redbridge 124 Cc 51.35N 0.08 E
London-Sutton 124 Bc 51.21N 0.12W
London-Wandsworth 124 Bc 51.27N 0.12W
London-Westminster 124 Bc 51.30N 0.07W
Londrina 200 Kh 23.18S 51.09W
Londuimbali 170 Ce 12.15S 15.19 E
Lone Pine 188 Fh 36.36N 118.04W
Long, Loch- 118 Ie 56.04N 4.50W
Longa 170 Ce 14.41S 18.29 E
Longa [Ang.] 170 Be 10.15S 13.30 E
Longa [Ang.] 170 Cf 16.25S 19.04 E
Longa, proliv- = De Long Strait (EN) 140 Tb 70.20N 178.00 E
Longá, Rio- 202 Jd 3.09S 41.56W
Long Akah 150 Ff 3.19N 114.47 E
Longarone 128 Gd 46.16N 12.18 E
Longbangun 150 Gf 0.36N 115.11 E
Long Bay [Bar.] 197q Bb 13.04N 59.29W
Long Bay [S.C.-U.S.] 182 Le 33.35N 78.45W
Long Beach [Ca.-U.S.] 176 Hf 33.46N 118.11W
Long Beach [N.Y.-U.S.] 184 Ke 40.35N 73.40W
Long Beach [Wa.-U.S.] 188 Cc 46.21N 124.03W
Long Branch 182 Mc 40.17N 73.59W
Long Buckby 124 Ab 52.18N 1.04W
Long Cay 194 Jb 22.37N 74.20W
Longchuan 152 Kg 24.10N 115.17 E
Long Creek 188 Nb 49.07N 103.00W
Long Eaton 124 Ab 52.54N 1.16W
Longfeng 154 Ha 46.31N 125.02 E
Longford / An Longfort 118 Fh 53.44N 7.47W
Longford / An Longfort [2] 118 Fh 53.40N 7.40W
Long Forties 118 Nd 57.10N 0.05 E
Long Hu 154 Dj 29.37N 116.12 E
Longhua 154 Dd 41.18N 117.44 E
Longido 170 Gc 2.44S 36.41 E
Long Island [Atg.] 197d Bb 17.08N 61.45W
Long Island [Bah.] 174 Lg 23.10N 75.10W
Long Island [Can.] 180 Jf 54.50N 79.20W
Long Island [Can.] 184 Nc 44.20N 66.15W
Long Island [Pap.N.Gui.] 208 Fe 5.20S 147.05 E
Long Island [U.S.] 174 Le 40.50N 73.00W
Long Island Sound 184 Ke 41.05N 72.58W
Longjiang 152 Lb 47.20N 123.09 E
Longjuzhai → Danfeng 152 Je 33.44N 110.22 E
Longkou 152 Ld 37.39N 120.20 E
Longlac 180 Ig 49.50N 86.32W
Long Lake [N.D.-U.S.] 186 Fc 46.43N 100.07W
Long Lake [Ont.-Can.] 186 Mb 49.32N 86.45W
Longmalinau 150 Gf 3.30N 116.31 E
Long Men 152 Je 34.40N 110.30 E
Longmont 186 Df 40.10N 105.06W
Longnan 152 Jg 24.54N 114.48 E
Longobucco 128 Kk 39.27N 16.37 E
Longoz 130 Kf 43.02N 27.41 E
Longping → Luodian 152 If 25.26N 106.47 E
Long Point 184 Gd 42.34N 80.15W
Long Point Bay 184 Gd 42.40N 80.14W
Longpujungan 150 Gf 2.34N 115.40 E
Longquan 152 Kf 28.06N 119.05 E
Long Range Mountains 180 Lg 48.00N 58.30W
Longreach 210 Fg 23.26S 144.15 E
Longs Sand 124 Dc 51.37N 1.10 E
Longs Peak 174 Ie 40.15N 105.37W
Long Sutton 124 Cb 52.47N 0.08 E
Longtan 154 Eh 32.10N 119.03 E
Longtown 118 Kf 55.01N 2.58W
Longueau 124 Ee 49.52N 2.21 E
Longué-Jumelles 122 Fg 47.23N 0.07W
Longueville-sur-Scie 124 De 49.48N 1.06 E
Longuyon 122 Le 49.26N 5.36 E
Long Valley 188 Jl 34.37N 111.30W
Longview [Tx.-U.S.] 176 Jf 32.30N 94.44W
Longview [Wa.-U.S.] 182 Cb 46.08N 122.57W
Longwu 152 Hg 24.07N 102.18 E
Longwy 122 Le 49.31N 5.46 E
Longxi 152 Hd 35.01N 104.38 E
Longxian 152 Id 35.00N 106.53 E
Longxian → Wengyuan 152 Jg 24.21N 114.13 E
Longxi Shan 152 Kf 26.35N 117.17 E
Long Xuyen 148 Lf 10.23N 105.25 E
Longyan 152 Kf 25.06N 117.01 E
Longyao 154 Cf 37.21N 114.46 E
Longyearbyen 224 Kd 78.13N 15.38 E
Longyou 154 Ej 29.01N 119.10 E
Longzhou 152 Ig 22.23N 106.49 E
Lonigo 128 Fe 45.23N 11.23 E
Löningen 120 Dd 52.44N 7.46 E
Lonja 128 Ke 45.27N 16.41 E
Lonjsko Polje 128 Ke 45.24N 16.42 E
Lönsboda 116 Fh 56.24N 14.19 E
Lons-le-Saunier 122 Lh 46.40N 5.33 E
Lontra, Ribeirão- 204 Fe 21.28S 53.37W
Lookout, Cape- [N.C.-U.S.] 182 Le 34.35N 76.32W
Lookout, Cape- [Or.-U.S.] 188 Dd 45.20N 124.00W
Lookout Mountain 184 Eh 34.40N 85.20W
Lookout Pass 182 Db 47.27N 115.42W
Loolmalasin 170 Gc 3.03S 35.49 E
Loop Head/Ceann Léime 118 Di 52.34N 9.56W
Loosdrechtse Plassen 124 Hb 52.10N 5.08 E
Lop 152 Dd 37.01N 80.16 E
Lopatina, gora- 140 Qd 50.52N 143.10 E
Lopatino 132 Nc 52.37N 45.47 E
Lopatka, mys- 140 Rd 50.52N 156.40 E
Lop Buri 148 Kf 14.48N 100.37 E
Lopča 138 He 55.44N 122.45 E
Lopévi 219b Dc 16.30S 168.21 E
Lopez, Cap-=Lopez, Cape- (EN) 158 Hi 0.37S 8.43 E
Lopez, Cape-(EN)=Lopez, Cap- 158 Hi 0.37S 8.43 E
Lop Nur 140 Le 40.30N 90.30 E
Lopnur/Yuli 152 Ec 41.22N 86.09 E
Lopori 158 Ih 1.14N 19.49 E
Loppersum 124 Ia 53.19N 6.45 E
Lopphavet 114 Ea 70.25N 22.00 E
Loppi 116 Kd 60.43N 24.27 E
Lopud 128 Lh 42.41N 17.57 E
Łopuszno 120 Qf 50.57N 20.15 E
Lora del Rio 126 Gg 37.39N 5.32W
Lorain 182 Kc 41.28N 82.11W
Lorán, Boca- 196 Fh 9.00N 60.45W
Lorca 126 Kg 37.40N 1.42W
Lorch 124 Jd 50.03N 7.49 E
Lord Howe Island 208 Gh 31.35S 159.05 E
Lord Howe Rise (EN) 106 Jm 32.00S 162.00 E
Lord Mayor Bay 180 Ic 69.45N 92.00W
Lordsburg 186 Bj 32.21N 108.43W
Loreley 124 Jd 50.08N 7.43 E
Lorena 204 Jf 22.44S 45.08W
Lorengau 214 Dh 2.01S 147.17 E
Lorestān [3] 144 Gc 33.30N 48.40 E
Loreto 202 Dd 5.00S 75.00W
Loreto [Arg.] 204 Dh 27.46S 57.17W
Loreto [Bol.] 202 Fg 15.13S 64.40W
Loreto [Braz.] 202 Ie 7.05S 45.09W
Loreto [It.] 128 Hg 43.26N 13.36 E
Loreto [Mex.] 192 If 22.16N 101.58W
Loreto [Mex.] 190 Bc 26.01N 111.21W
Loreto [Par.] 206 Ib 23.16S 57.11W
Loreto Aprutino 128 Hh 42.26N 13.59 E
Lorica 202 Cb 9.14N 75.49W
Lorient 112 Ff 47.45N 3.22W
Lőrinci 120 Pi 47.44N 19.41 E
Lorn, Firth of- 118 He 56.20N 5.40W
Lorne 212 Ig 38.33S 143.59 E
Lörrach 120 Di 47.37N 7.40 E
Lorrain, Plateau- 122 Me 49.00N 6.30 E
Lorrain, Rivière du- 197h Ab 14.50N 61.03W
Lorraine 122 Lf 49.00N 6.00 E
Lorraine, Plaine- 122 Lf 48.10N 5.50 E
Lorsch 124 Ke 49.39N 8.34 E
Los 114 Df 61.44N 15.10 E
Los, Iles de-=Los Islands (EN) 166 Cd 9.30N 13.48W
Los Alamos 176 If 35.53N 106.19W
Los Amates 194 Cf 15.16N 89.06W
Los Amores 204 Ci 28.06S 59.59W
Los Ángeles 200 Ii 37.28S 72.21W
Los Angeles 176 Hf 34.03N 118.15W
Los Angeles Aqueduct 188 Fi 35.22N 118.05W
Losap Atoll 218 Gd 6.54N 152.44 E
Los Banos 188 Eh 37.04N 120.51W
Los Blancos 206 Hb 23.36S 62.36W
Los Charrúas 204 Cj 31.10S 58.11W
Los Chiles 194 Eh 11.02N 84.43W
Los Conquistadores 204 Cj 30.36S 58.28W
Los Frailes, Islas- 196 Eg 11.12N 63.45W
Los Frentones 204 Bh 26.25S 61.25W
Los Gatos 188 Eh 37.14N 121.59W
Losheim 124 Ie 49.31N 6.45 E
Los Hermanos, Islas- 202 Fa 11.45N 64.25W
Łosice 120 Sd 52.14N 22.43 E
Lošinj 128 If 44.35N 14.28 E
Los Islands (EN)=Los, Iles de- 166 Cd 9.30N 13.48W
Los Juries 204 Ai 28.28S 62.06W
Los Lagos 206 Fe 39.51S 72.50W
Los Lagos [2] 206 Ff 41.20S 73.00W
Los Llanos de Aridane 162 Dd 28.39N 17.54W
Los Médanos, Istmo de- 194 Mh 11.35N 69.45W
Los Mochis 176 Ig 25.45N 108.53W
Los Monegros 126 Lc 41.29N 0.03W
Los Monjes, Islas- 202 Da 12.25N 70.55W
Los Navalmorales 126 He 39.43N 4.38W
Loso 170 Ec 1.10S 27.10 E
Los Palacios 194 Fb 22.35N 83.15W
Los Palacios y Villafranca 126 Gg 37.10N 5.56W
Los Pedroches 126 Hf 38.27N 4.45W
Los Pirpintos 204 Ah 26.08S 62.05W
Los Remedios, Rio de- 204 Fe 24.41N 106.28W
Los Reyes de Salgado 192 Hh 19.35N 102.29W
Los Roques, Islas- 202 Ea 11.50N 66.45W

Index Symbols

[1] Independent Nation
[2] State, Region
[3] District, County
[4] Municipality
[5] Colony, Dependency
Continent
Physical Region
Historical or Cultural Region
Mount, Mountain
Volcano
Hill
Mountains, Mountain Range
Hills, Escarpment
Plateau, Upland
Pass, Gap
Plain, Lowland
Delta
Salt Flat
Valley, Canyon
Crater, Cave
Karst Features
Depression
Polder
Desert, Dunes
Forest, Woods
Heath, Steppe
Oasis
Cape, Point
Coast, Beach
Cliff
Peninsula
Isthmus
Sandbank
Island
Atoll
Rock, Reef
Islands, Archipelago
Rocks, Reefs
Coral Reef
Well, Spring
Geyser
River, Stream
Waterfall, Rapids
River Mouth, Estuary
Lake
Salt Lake
Intermittent Lake
Reservoir
Swamp, Pond
Canal
Glacier
Ice Shelf, Pack Ice
Ocean
Sea
Gulf, Bay
Strait, Fjord
Lagoon
Bank
Seamount
Tablemount
Ridge
Shelf
Basin
Escarpment, Sea Scarp
Fracture
Trench, Abyss
National Park, Reserve
Point of Interest
Recreation Site
Cave, Cavern
Historic Site
Ruins
Wall, Walls
Church, Abbey
Temple
Scientific Station
Railway station
Airport
Port
Military installation
Lighthouse
Mine
Tunnel
Dam, Bridge

Los Roques Basin (EN) 196 Cf 12.20N 67.40W
Los Santos 194 Gj 7.56N 80.25W
Los Santos [3] 194 Gj 7.45N 80.30W
Losser 124 Jb 52.16N 7.01 E
Lossiemouth 118 Jd 57.43N 3.18W
Lossnen 116 Eb 62.30N 12.50 E
Los Taques 194 Lh 11.50N 70.16W
Los Telares 206 Hc 28.59S 63.26W
Los Teques 202 Ea 10.21N 67.02W
Los Testigos, Islas- 202 Fa 11.23N 63.06W
Lost River 188 Ef 41.56N 121.30W
Lost River Range 188 Id 44.10N 113.35W
Lost Trail Pass 182 Eb 45.41N 113.57W
Los Vilos 206 Fd 31.55S 71.31W
Lot [3] 122 Hj 44.30N 1.30 E
Lot 110 Gg 44.18N 0.20 E
Lota 206 Fe 37.05S 73.10W
Lotagipi Swamp 168 Ee 4.36N 34.55 E
Løten 116 Dd 60.49N 11.19 E
Lot-et-Garonne [3] 122 Gj 44.20N 0.30 E
Lothair 172 Ee 26.26S 30.27 E
Lothian [3] 118 Jf 55.55N 3.30W
Lothian 118 Jf 55.55N 3.05W
Loto 170 Dc 2.47S 22.30 E
Lotofaga 221c Ba 13.59S 171.50W
Lotoi 170 Cc 1.35S 18.30 E
Lotru 130 Hd 45.20N 24.16 E
Lotrului, Munţii- 130 Gd 45.30N 23.52 E
Lotta 114 Hb 68.39N 30.20 E
Lottefors 116 Gc 61.25N 16.24 E
Löttorp 116 Gg 57.10N 16.59 E
Lotuke, Jabal- 168 Ee 4.07N 33.48 E
Louang Namtha 148 Kd 20.57N 101.25 E
Louangphrabang 142 Mh 19.52N 102.08 E
Loubomo 160 Ii 4.12S 12.41 E
Loučná 120 Lf 50.06N 15.48 E
Loudéac 122 Df 48.10N 2.45W
Loudima 170 Bc 4.07S 13.04 E
Loudon 184 Eh 35.44N 84.20W
Loudun 122 Gh 47.00N 0.04 E
Loué 122 Fg 48.00N 0.09W
Loue 122 Lg 47.01N 5.27 E
Loufan 154 Ae 38.04N 111.47 E
Louga 166 Bb 15.37N 16.13W
Louga [3] 166 Bb 15.00N 15.30W
Louge 122 Hk 43.27N 1.20 E
Loughborough 118 Li 52.47N 1.11W
Lougheed 180 Ha 77.30N 105.00W
Loughrea/Baile Locha Riach 118 Eh 53.12N 8.34W
Louhans 122 Lh 46.38N 5.13 E
Louhi 136 Db 66.04N 33.01 E
Louisa 184 Ff 38.07N 82.36W
Louiseville 184 Kb 46.16N 72.57W
Louisiade Archipelago 208 Kf 11.00S 153.00 E
Louisiana 186 Kg 39.27N 91.03W
Louisiana [2] 182 Ie 31.15N 92.15W
Louis Trichardt 172 Dd 23.01S 29.43 E
Louisville [Ky.-U.S.] 176 Kf 38.16N 85.45W
Louisville [Ms.-U.S.] 186 Lj 33.07N 89.03W
Louis-XIV, Pointe- 180 Jf 54.50N 79.30W
Loukoléla 170 Cc 1.02S 17.07 E
Loulan Yiji 152 Ec 40.32N 89.50 E
Loulé 126 Dg 37.08N 8.02W
Loum 166 Ge 4.43N 9.44 E
Lount Lake 186 Ia 50.10N 94.20W
Louny 120 Jf 50.22N 13.49 E
Loup City 186 Gf 41.17N 98.58W
Loupe, La- 122 Hf 48.28N 1.01 E
Loup River 182 Hc 41.24N 97.19W
Loups Marins, Lacs des- 180 Ke 56.40N 74.00W
Lourdes 122 Fk 43.06N 0.03W
Lourenço Marques → Maputo 160 Kk 25.58S 32.34 E
Lousa, Serra da- 126 Dd 40.04N 8.13W
Loushan Guan 152 If 28.02N 106.51 E
Louštín 120 Jf 50.12N 13.48 E
Louth [Austl.] 212 Jf 30.32S 145.07 E
Louth [Eng.-U.K.] 118 Mh 53.22N 0.01W
Louth/Lú [2] 118 Gh 53.55N 6.30W
Loutrá Aidhipsoú 130 Gk 38.51N 23.03 E
Loutrá Killínis 130 El 37.52N 21.07 E
Loutrákion 130 Fl 37.59N 23.00 E
Louvain/Leuven 122 Kd 50.53N 4.42 E
Louvet Point 197k Bb 13.58N 60.53W
Louviers 122 He 49.13N 1.10 E
Lövånger 114 Ed 64.22N 21.18 E
Lovászi 120 Mj 46.33N 16.34 E
Lovat 110 Jd 58.14N 31.28 E
Lovćen 130 Bg 42.24N 18.49 E
Loveč 130 Hf 43.08N 24.43 E
Loveč [2] 130 Hf 43.08N 24.43 E
Loveland 186 Df 40.24N 105.05W
Lovell 182 Fc 44.50N 108.24W
Lovelock 182 Dc 40.11N 118.28W
Lövenich, Köln- 124 Id 50.57N 6.50 E
Lovere 128 Ee 45.49N 10.04 E
Loviisa/Lovisa 114 Gf 60.27N 26.14 E
Loving 186 Dj 32.17N 104.06W
Lovington 182 Ge 33.27N 103.21W
Lovisa/Loviisa 114 Gf 60.27N 26.14 E
Lovoi 170 Ed 8.05S 26.40 E
Lovosice 120 Kf 50.31N 14.03 E
Lovozero 114 Ib 68.01N 35.01 E
Lövstabruk 116 Gd 60.24N 17.53 E
Lövstabukten 116 Gd 60.35N 17.45 E
Lovua 170 De 11.31S 23.35 E
Lovua 170 Dd 6.07S 20.35 E
Low, Cape- 180 Id 63.06N 85.18W
Lowa 158 Ji 1.24S 25.52 E
Lowell 182 Mc 42.39N 71.18W
Löwenberg/Mark 120 Jd 52.53N 13.09 E
Lower Arrow Lake 188 Fb 49.40N 118.08W
Lower Austria (EN) = Niederösterreich [2] 128 Jb 48.30N 15.45 E
Lower California (EN) = Baja California, Peninsula de- 174 Hg 28.00N 112.00W
Lower Hutt 218 Fd 41.13S 174.55 E
Lower Lake 188 Dg 38.55N 122.36W
Lower Lake 188 Ef 41.15N 120.02W
Lower Lough Erne/Loch Éirne Íochtair 118 Fg 54.30N 7.50W
Lower Post 180 Ee 59.55N 128.30W
Lower Red Lake 186 Ic 48.00N 94.50W
Lower Rhine (EN) = Neder-Rijn 122 Mc 51.59N 6.20 E
Lower Saxony (EN) = Niedersachsen [2] 120 Fd 52.00N 10.00 E
Lower Trajan's Wall (EN) = Nižni Trajanov val 130 Ld 45.45N 28.30 E
Lower Tunguska (EN) = Nižnjaja Tunguska 140 Kc 65.48N 88.04 E
Lowestoft 118 Oi 52.29N 1.45 E
Lowestoft Ness 118 Oi 52.28N 1.44 E
Lowgar [3] 144 Kc 33.50N 69.00 E
Łowicz 120 Pd 52.07N 19.56 E
Lowlands 118 Jf 56.00N 4.00W
Lowrah 140 If 31.33N 66.33 E
Lowshān 146 Md 36.39N 49.32 E
Low Tatra (EN) = Nizke Tatry 120 Ph 48.54N 19.40 E
Lowther 180 Hb 74.35N 97.40W
Lowville 184 Jd 43.47N 75.30W
Loxton [Austl.] 212 If 34.27S 140.35 E
Loxton [S.Afr.] 172 Cf 31.30S 22.22 E
Loyalty Islands (EN) = Loyauté, Iles- 208 Hg 21.00S 167.00 E
Loyauté, Iles- = Loyalty Islands (EN) 208 Hg 21.00S 167.00 E
Loyoro 170 Fb 3.21N 34.17 E
Lozère [3] 122 Jj 44.30N 3.30 E
Lozère, Mont- 122 Jj 44.25N 3.46 E
Loznica 130 Ce 44.32N 19.13 E
Lozovaja 136 Df 48.53N 36.15 E
Lozva 136 Gd 59.36N 62.20 E
Lú/Louth [2] 118 Gh 53.55N 6.30W
Lua 170 Cb 2.46N 18.26 E
Luacano 170 De 11.16S 21.38 E
Luachimo 170 Dd 6.33S 20.59 E
Luaha-Sibuha 150 Cg 0.31S 98.28 E
Luahoko 221b Ba 19.40S 174.24W
Luala 172 Fc 17.57S 36.30 E
Lualaba 158 Jh 0.26N 25.20 E
Luama 170 Ec 4.46S 26.53 E
Lua Makika 221a Ec 20.35N 156.34W
Luampa 170 De 14.32S 24.10 E
Lu'an 152 Ke 31.44N 116.30 E
Luanda 160 Ii 8.48S 13.14 E
Luanda [3] 170 Bd 9.00S 13.15 E
Luando 158 Ij 10.19S 16.40 E
Luang, Khao- 148 Jg 8.31N 99.47 E
Luang, Thale- 148 Kg 7.30N 100.15 E
Luang Chiang Dao, Doi- 148 Je 19.23N 98.54 E
Luanginga 158 Jj 15.11S 22.55 E
Luang Prabang Range 148 Ke 18.30N 101.15 E
Luangue 170 Dc 4.17S 20.01 E
Luangwa 158 Kj 15.36S 30.25 E
Luan He 140 Nf 39.20N 119.10 E
Luaniva 220h Bb 13.16S 176.07W
Luannan (Bencheng) 154 Ee 39.30N 118.42 E
Luanping (Anijangying) 154 Dd 40.55N 117.19 E
Luanshya 160 Jj 13.08S 28.25 E
Luanxian 152 Kd 39.45N 118.44 E
Luanza 170 Ed 8.40S 28.40 E
Luapula [3] 170 Ee 10.40S 29.15 E
Luapula 158 Ji 9.26S 28.33 E
Luarca 126 Fa 43.32N 6.32W
Luashi 170 De 10.56S 23.37 E
Luau 170 De 10.42S 22.12 E
Luba 166 Ge 3.28N 8.40 E
Lubaantum 194 Ce 16.17N 88.58W
Lubaczów 120 Tf 50.10N 23.07 E
Lubaczówka 120 Sf 50.08N 22.35 E
Lubalo 170 Cd 9.07S 19.15 E
Lubalo 170 Cd 7.22S 19.20 E
Lubamba 170 Ed 5.14S 26.02 E
Lubań 120 Le 51.08N 15.18 E
Lubana/Lubāna 116 Lh 56.49N 26.49 E
Lubāna/Lubana 116 Lh 56.49N 26.49 E
Lubānas, ozero- / Lubānas ezers 116 Lh 56.40N 27.00 E
Lubānas ezers / Lubānas, ozero- 116 Lh 56.40N 27.00 E
Lubang Islands 150 Hd 13.45N 120.15 E
Lubango 160 Ij 14.55S 13.28 E
Lubao 160 Ji 5.22S 25.45 E
Lubartów 120 Se 51.28N 22.46 E
Lubawa 120 Pc 53.30N 19.45 E
Lübbecke 120 Ed 52.18N 8.37 E
Lubbeek 124 Gd 50.53N 4.50 E
Lübben (Spreewald)/Lubin 120 Je 51.57N 13.54 E
Lübbenau/Lubnjow 120 Je 51.52N 13.58 E
Lubbock 176 If 33.35N 101.51W
Lübeck 112 He 53.52N 10.42 E
Lübecker Bucht 120 Gb 54.00N 10.55 E
Lübeck-Travemünde 120 Gc 53.57N 10.52 E
Lubefu 170 Dc 4.43S 24.25 E
Lubefu 170 Dc 4.10S 23.00 E
Lubei → Jarud Qi 152 Lc 44.30N 120.55 E
Lubelska, Wyżyna- 120 Sf 51.00N 23.00 E
Lubenec 120 Jf 50.08N 13.20 E
Lubenka 132 Sd 50.28N 54.06 E
Lubero 170 Ec 0.06S 29.06 E
Lubéron, Montagne du- 122 Lk 43.48N 5.22 E
Lubi 170 Dc 4.59S 23.26 E
Lubie, Jezioro- 120 Lc 53.30N 15.50 E
Lubień Kujawski 120 Pd 52.25N 19.10 E
Lubij/Löbau 120 Ke 51.06N 14.40 E
Lubilash 158 Ji 6.02S 23.45 E
Lubin 120 Me 51.24N 16.13 E
Lubin/Lübben (Spreewald) 120 Je 51.57N 13.54 E
Lublin 112 Ie 51.15N 22.35 E
Lublin [2] 120 Se 51.15N 22.35 E
Lubliniec 120 Of 50.40N 18.41 E
Lubnān = Lebanon (EN) [1] 142 Ff 33.50N 35.50 E
Lubnān, Jabal- = Lebanon Mountains (EN) 144 Ec 34.00N 36.30 E
Lubnjow/Lübbenau 120 Je 51.52N 13.58 E
Lubny 136 De 50.01N 33.00 E
Luboń 120 Md 52.23N 16.54 E
Lubraniec 120 Od 52.33N 18.50 E
Lubsko 120 Ke 51.46N 14.59 E
Lubsza 120 Ke 51.55N 14.45 E
Lubudi 170 Ed 9.57S 25.58 E
Lubudi 158 Ji 9.13S 25.38 E
Lubue 170 Cc 4.10S 19.53 E
Lubuklinggau 150 Dg 3.10S 102.52 E
Lubuksikaping 150 Df 0.08N 100.10 E
Lubumba 170 Ec 3.58S 29.06 E
Lubumbashi 160 Jj 11.40S 27.30 E
Lubuskie, Pojezierze- 120 Ld 52.18N 15.20 E
Lubutu 160 Ji 0.44S 26.35 E
Lucala 170 Cd 9.16S 15.16 E
Lucala 170 Bd 6.38S 12.34 E
Lucania, Mount- 180 Dd 61.01N 140.29W
Lucas 204 Ea 13.05S 55.56W
Lucca 128 Eg 43.50N 10.29 E
Lucea 194 Hd 18.27N 78.10W
Luce Bay 118 Ig 54.47N 4.50W
Lucedale 186 Lk 30.55N 88.35W
Lučegorsk 138 Ig 46.25N 134.20 E
Lucélia 204 Ge 21.44S 51.01W
Lucena [Phil.] 150 Hd 13.56N 121.37 E
Lucena [Sp.] 126 Hg 37.24N 4.29W
Lucena del Cid / Llucena 126 Ld 40.08N 0.17W
Luc-en-Diois 122 Lj 44.37N 5.27 E
Lučenec 120 Ph 48.20N 19.41 E
Lucera 128 Ji 41.30N 15.20 E
Lucerne (EN) = Luzern 128 Cc 47.05N 8.20 E
Lucerne, Lake- (EN) = Vierwaldstätter See 128 Cc 47.00N 8.30 E
Lucero 192 Fb 30.49N 106.30W
Lucheng 154 Bf 36.18N 113.15 E
Lucheringo 172 Fb 11.43S 36.15 E
Lucheux 124 Ed 50.12N 2.25 E
Luchico 170 Cd 6.12S 19.42 E
Lüchow 120 Hd 52.58N 11.09 E
Lüchun 152 Hg 23.02N 102.19 E
Lucipara, Kepulauan- 150 Ih 5.30S 127.33 E
Lucira 170 Be 13.52S 12.32 E
Luck 136 Ce 50.47N 25.20 E
Luckau 120 Je 51.51N 13.43 E
Luckenwalde 120 Jd 52.05N 13.10 E
Lucknow 142 Kg 26.51N 80.55 E
Luçon 122 Eh 46.27N 1.10W
Lucrecia, Cabo- 194 Jc 21.04N 75.37W
Luc-sur-Mer 124 Be 49.18N 0.21W
Lucunga 170 Bd 6.49S 14.35 E
Lucusse 170 De 12.33S 20.51 E
Lüda → Dalian 142 Of 38.55N 121.39 E
Luda Kamčija 130 Kg 43.03N 27.29 E
Ludbreg 128 Kd 46.15N 16.37 E
Lüdenscheid 120 De 51.13N 7.37 E
Lüderitz 160 Ik 26.38S 15.10 E
Lüderitz [3] 172 Be 26.00S 15.00 E
Lüderitz Bay 172 Be 26.35S 15.10 E
Ludhiāna 142 Jf 30.54N 75.51 E
Lüdinghausen 120 De 51.46N 7.28 E
Ludington 182 Jc 43.57N 86.27W
Ludlow 118 Ki 52.22N 2.43W
Ludogorije 130 Jf 43.46N 26.56 E
Ludogorsko Plato 130 Kf 43.36N 27.03 E
Luduş 130 Hc 46.29N 24.06 E
Ludvika 114 Df 60.09N 15.11 E
Ludwigsburg 120 Fh 48.54N 9.11 E
Ludwigshafen am Rhein 120 Eg 49.29N 8.27 E
Ludwigslust 120 Hc 53.19N 11.30 E
Ludza 114 Gh 56.32N 27.45 E
Luebo 160 Ji 5.21S 21.25 E
Lueki 170 Ec 3.22S 25.51 E
Lueki 170 Ec 3.24S 25.57 E
Luele 170 Dd 7.55S 20.00 E
Luembe 170 Dd 6.37S 21.06 E
Luembé 170 Dd 6.37S 21.05 E
Luena [Ang.] 160 Ij 11.48S 19.55 E
Luena [Ang.] 170 De 12.31S 22.34 E
Luena [Zaire] 170 Ed 9.27S 25.47 E
Luena [Zam.] 170 Df 15.20S 23.30 E
Luengué 170 Df 16.54S 21.52 E
Luenha 172 Ec 16.24S 33.48 E
Luera Peak 186 Cj 33.47N 107.49W
Lueta 170 Dd 7.04S 21.40 E
Lueyang 152 Ie 33.25N 106.14 E
Lufeng 152 Kg 22.57N 115.41 E
Lufico 170 Bd 6.22S 13.30 E
Lufira 158 Ji 8.16S 26.27 E
Lufira, Chutes de la- 170 Ed 9.50S 27.30 E
Lufkin 182 Ie 31.20N 94.44W
Lug 130 De 44.23N 20.45 E
Luga 136 Cd 58.44N 29.50 E
Luga 136 Cd 59.43N 28.18 E
Lugano 128 Cd 46.00N 8.57 E
Lugano, Lago di- (Ceresio) 128 Cd 46.00N 9.00 E
Luganville 210 Hf 15.32S 167.10 E
Lugards Falls 158 Ki 3.03S 38.42 E
Lügde 124 Lc 51.57N 9.15 E
Lugela 172 Fc 16.26S 36.39 E
Lugenda 158 Kj 11.26S 38.33 E
Lugnaquillia 110 Fe 52.58N 6.27W
Lugo [3] 126 Eb 43.00N 7.30W
Lugo [It.] 128 Ff 44.25N 11.54 E
Lugo [Sp.] 126 Ea 43.00N 7.34W
Lugoj 130 Ed 45.41N 21.55 E
Lugovoj [Kaz.-U.S.S.R.] 136 Hg 42.55N 72.47 E
Lugovoj [R.S.F.S.R.] 136 Gd 59.44N 65.55 E
Lugovski 138 Ge 58.05N 112.55 E
Lugulu 170 Ec 2.17S 26.32 E
Luh 114 Kh 56.14N 42.28 E
Luhe 154 Eh 32.21N 118.50 E
Luhe 120 Gc 53.18N 10.11 E
Luhin Sum 152 Kb 46.41N 118.38 E
Luhit 148 Jc 27.48N 95.28 E
Luhovicy 114 Ji 54.59N 39.02 E
Luhuo 152 He 31.21N 100.40 E
Lui 170 Cd 8.41S 17.58 E
Luia 170 Dd 8.26S 21.45 E
Luiana 170 Df 17.22S 22.59 E
Luiana 158 Jj 17.27S 23.14 E
Luie 170 Cc 4.33S 17.41 E
Luik/Liège 112 Ge 50.38N 5.34 E
Luilaka 158 Ji 0.52S 20.12 E
Luilu 170 Dd 6.22S 23.50 E
Luimneach/Limerick 112 Fe 52.40N 8.38W
Luimneach/Limerick [2] 118 Ei 52.30N 9.00W
Luing 118 He 56.13N 5.39W
Luino 128 Cd 46.00N 8.44 E
Luio 170 De 13.15S 21.39 E
Lui Pătru, Vîrful- 130 Gd 45.30N 23.30 E
Luis Correia 202 Jd 2.53S 41.40W
Luishia 170 Ee 11.13S 27.07 E
Luitpold Coast 222 Af 78.30S 32.00W
Luiza 170 Dd 7.12S 22.25 E
Luján [Arg.] 206 Gd 32.22S 65.57W
Luján [Arg.] 206 Id 34.34S 59.07W
Lujiang 154 Di 31.15N 117.17 E
Lukafu 170 Ee 10.30S 27.33 E
Lukanga Swamp 170 Ee 14.25S 27.45 E
Lukavac 128 Mf 44.33N 18.32 E
Lukengo 170 Ed 5.46S 29.06 E
Lukenie 158 Ii 2.44S 18.09 E
Lukeville 188 Ik 31.57N 112.50W
Lukojanov 136 Ed 55.02N 44.30 E
Lukolela 170 Cc 1.03S 17.12 E
Lukonzolwa 170 Ed 8.47S 28.39 E
Lukov 120 Ue 51.14N 24.25 E
Lukovit 130 Hf 43.12N 24.10 E
Łuków 120 Se 51.56N 22.23 E
Lukuga 158 Ji 5.40S 26.55 E
Lukula 170 Bd 5.23S 12.57 E
Lukulu 170 De 14.23S 23.15 E
Lukusashi 170 Fe 14.38S 30.00 E
Luleå 112 Ib 65.34N 22.10 E
Luleälven 110 Ib 65.35N 22.03 E
Lüleburgaz 144 Ca 41.24N 27.21 E
Lüliang Shan 140 Nf 37.45N 111.25 E
Lulimba 170 Ec 4.42S 28.38 E
Luling 186 Hl 29.41N 97.39W
Lulong 154 Ee 39.53N 118.52 E
Lulonga 170 Cb 0.37N 18.23 E
Lulonga 158 Ih 0.43N 18.23 E
Lulua 158 Ji 5.02S 21.07 E
Lulu Fakahega, Mount- 220h Bb 13.16S 176.10W
Luma 221c Db 14.14S 169.32W
Lumajang 150 Fh 8.08S 113.13 E
Lumajangdong Co 152 De 34.00N 81.37 E
Lumbala Kaquengue 160 Jj 14.06S 21.25 E
Lumbala N'guimbo 170 De 12.39S 22.32 E
Lumberton 182 Le 34.37N 79.00W
Lumbo 172 Gc 15.00S 40.44 E
Lumbrales 126 Fd 40.56N 6.43W
Lumbres 124 Ed 50.42N 2.08 E
Lumby 188 Fa 50.15N 118.58W
Lumding 148 Ic 25.45N 93.10 E
Lumege 170 De 11.34S 20.48 E
Lumesule 170 Ge 11.14S 38.06 E
Lumi 214 Ch 3.29S 142.03 E
Lummen 124 Hd 50.59N 5.15 E
Lumparland 116 Id 60.10N 20.15 E
Lumphăt 148 Lf 13.30N 106.59 E
Lumsden [N.Z.] 218 Cf 45.44S 168.26 E
Lumsden [Sask.-Can.] 188 Ma 50.34N 104.53W
Lumuna 170 Ec 3.46S 26.24 E
Lumut 150 Df 4.14N 100.38 E
Luna 126 Gb 42.40N 5.49W
Luna, Laguna de- 204 Di 28.06S 56.46W
Lunan Shan 152 Hf 27.00N 102.30 E
Lunayyir, Harrat- 146 Gj 25.10N 37.50 E
Lunca Ilvei 130 Hb 47.22N 24.59 E
Lund 114 Ci 55.42N 13.11 E
Lunda [3] 170 Cd 9.30S 20.00 E
Lundazi 160 Kj 12.19S 33.13 E
Lunde 116 Gb 62.53N 17.51 E
Lundevatn 116 Bf 58.20N 6.35 E
Lundi 158 Kk 21.19S 32.24 E
Lundu 150 Ef 1.40N 109.51 E
Lundy Island 118 Ij 51.10N 4.40W
Lüneburg 120 Gc 53.15N 10.24 E
Lüneburger Heide 120 Gc 53.10N 10.20 E
Lunel 122 Kk 43.41N 4.08 E
Lünen 120 De 51.37N 7.31 E
Lunéville 122 Mf 48.36N 6.30 E
Lunga 158 Jj 14.34S 26.26 E
Lungué-Bungo 158 Jj 14.19S 23.14 E
Lungwebungu 170 De 14.19S 23.14 E
Lüni 148 Ec 26.00N 73.00 E
Lüni 148 Ed 24.41N 71.14 E
Lunigiana 128 Df 44.20N 9.55 E
Luninec 136 Ce 52.16N 26.50 E
Lunino 132 Nc 53.35N 45.14 E
Lunsemfwa 170 Fe 14.54S 30.12 E
Luntai/Bügür 152 Dc 41.46N 84.10 E
Luobei (Fengxiang) 152 Nb 47.36N 130.58 E
Luobuzhuang 152 Ed 39.30N 88.15 E
Luocheng 152 Ig 24.51N 108.53 E
Luodian (Longping) 152 If 25.26N 106.47 E
Luoding 152 Jg 22.43N 111.33 E
Luohe 152 Je 33.30N 114.08 E
Luo He 152 Id 32.18N 109.12 E
Luoma Hu 154 Eg 34.10N 118.12 E
Luonteri 116 Lc 61.35N 27.45 E
Luoping 152 Hg 24.58N 104.19 E
Luopioinen 116 Kc 61.22N 24.40 E
Luoshan 154 Ch 32.13N 114.32 E
Luotian 154 Ci 30.48N 115.23 E
Luoxiao Shan 152 Jf 26.35N 114.00 E
Luoyang 142 Nf 34.41N 112.25 E
Luoyuan 152 Kf 26.31N 119.32 E
Luozi 170 Bc 4.57S 14.08 E
Lupa 170 Fd 8.39S 33.12 E
Lupane 172 Dc 18.56S 27.48 E
Łupawa 120 Nb 54.42N 17.07 E
Lupeni 130 Gd 45.21N 23.14 E
Luperón 194 Ld 19.54N 70.57W
Łupków 120 Sg 49.12N 22.06 E
Luputa 170 Dd 7.10S 23.42 E
Lūq 160 Lh 3.56N 42.32 E
Luqiao 154 Fj 28.39N 120.05 E
Luqu 152 He 34.36N 102.30 E
Luque 206 Ic 25.16S 57.34W
Luquillo 197a Cb 18.22N 65.43W
Luray 184 Hf 38.40N 78.28W
Lure 122 Mg 47.41N 6.30 E
Lure, Montagne de- 122 Lj 44.07N 5.47 E
Luremo 170 Cd 8.30S 17.51 E
Lurgan/An Lorgain 118 Gg 54.28N 6.20W
Lurín 202 Cf 12.17S 76.52W
Lúrio 172 Gb 13.32S 40.30 E
Lúrio 158 Lj 13.31S 40.42 E
Lusaka 160 Jj 15.25S 28.17 E
Lusambo 160 Ji 4.58S 23.27 E
Lusanga 170 Cc 4.44S 18.58 E
Lusangi 170 Ec 4.37S 27.08 E
Lu Shan 152 Kf 29.30N 115.55 E
Lushan [China] 154 Cj 29.33N 115.58 E
Lushan [China] 154 Bh 33.44N 112.54 E
Lushi 152 Je 34.04N 111.02 E
Lushiko 170 Cd 6.12S 19.42 E
Lushnja 130 Ci 40.56N 19.42 E
Lushoto 170 Gc 4.47S 38.17 E
Lu Shui 154 Bj 29.54N 113.39 E
Lushui (Luzhangjie) 152 Gf 26.00N 98.50 E
Lüshun (Port Arthur) [China] 152 Ld 38.50N 121.13 E
Lusignan 122 Gh 46.26N 0.07 E
Lusk 182 Gc 42.46N 104.27W
Lussac-les-Châteaux 122 Gh 46.24N 0.43 E
Lustrafjorden 116 Bc 61.20N 7.20 E
Lūt, Dasht-e- = Lut, Dasht-i- (EN) 140 Hf 33.00N 57.00 E
Lut, Dasht-i- (EN) = Lūt, Dasht-e- 140 Hf 33.00N 57.00 E
Lu Tao 152 Lg 22.35N 121.30 E
Lutembo 170 De 13.28S 21.22 E
Luti 219a Cb 7.14S 157.00 E
Lütjenburg 120 Gb 54.17N 10.35 E
Luton 118 Mj 51.53N 0.25W
Luton Airport 124 Bc 51.50N 0.22W
Lutong 150 Ff 4.28N 114.00 E
Lutshima 170 Cd 5.22S 18.59 E
Lutshima 170 Cd 5.22S 18.59 E
Lutterworth 124 Ab 52.27N 1.12W
Lutuai 170 De 12.40S 20.12 E
Lutugino 132 Ke 48.23N 39.13 E
Lützow-Holmbukta 222 De 69.10S 37.30 E
Lutzputs 172 Ce 28.22S 20.37 E
Luuk 150 He 5.58N 121.18 E
Luverne 186 He 43.39N 96.13W
Luvidjo 170 Ed 6.26S 26.59 E
Luvua 158 Ji 6.46S 26.58 E
Luvuei 170 De 13.06S 21.12 E
Luwegu 158 Ki 8.31S 37.23 E
Luwingu 170 Ee 10.16S 29.54 E
Luwuk 150 Hg 0.56S 122.47 E
Luxembourg [3] 124 He 50.00N 5.30 E
Luxembourg/Luxemburg 112 Gf 49.45N 6.05 E
Luxembourg/Luxemburg [1] 112 Gf 49.45N 6.05 E
Luxemburg/Luxembourg 112 Gf 49.45N 6.05 E
Luxemburg/Luxembourg [1] 112 Gf 49.45N 6.05 E
Luxeuil-les-Bains 122 Mg 47.49N 6.23 E
Luxi 152 Hg 24.34N 103.44 E
Luxi (Mangshi) 142 Lg 24.29N 98.40 E
Luxor (EN) = Al Uqşur 164 Fd 25.41N 32.39 E
Luy 122 Ek 43.39N 1.08W
Luy de Béarn 122 Fk 43.39N 0.47W
Luy de France 122 Fk 43.38N 0.47W
Luyi 154 Ch 33.51N 115.28 E
Luz 204 Jd 19.48S 45.41W
Luz, Costa de la- 126 Fh 36.40N 6.20W
Luza 136 Ec 60.39N 47.15 E
Luza 110 Kc 60.40N 46.25 E
Luzarches 124 Ee 49.07N 2.25 E
Luzern [2] 128 Cc 47.05N 8.10 E
Luzern = Lucerne (EN) 128 Cc 47.05N 8.20 E
Luzhai 152 Ig 24.31N 109.46 E
Luzhangjie → Lushui 152 Gf 26.00N 98.50 E
Luzhou 142 Mg 28.55N 105.20 E
Luziânia 202 Ig 16.15S 47.56W
Lužická Nisa 120 Kd 52.04N 14.46 E
Lužické Hory 120 Kf 50.48N 14.40 E
Luzilândia 202 Jd 3.28S 42.22W
Lužnice 120 Kg 49.16N 14.25 E
Luzon 140 Oh 16.00N 121.00 E
Luzon Strait (EN) 140 Og 21.00N 122.00 E
Luz-Saint-Sauveur 122 Gl 42.52N 0.01 E
Lužskaja guba 116 Me 59.35N 28.25 E
Lužskaja vozvyšennost 116 Mf 58.15N 28.45 E
Luzy 122 Jh 46.47N 3.58 E
Łużyca 120 Oe 51.33N 18.15 E
Lvov 112 If 49.50N 24.00 E
Lvovskaja oblast [3] 136 Cf 49.45N 24.00 E
Lwowa 214 Hj 10.44S 165.45 E
Lwówek 120 Md 52.28N 16.10 E
Lwówek Śląski 120 Le 51.07N 15.35 E
Lyakhov Islands (EN) = Ljahovskije ostrova 140 Qb 73.30N 141.00 E
Lyall, Mount- 218 Bf 45.17S 167.33 E
Lyallpur → Faisalabad 142 Jf 31.25N 73.05 E
Lychsele 114 Ed 64.36N 18.40 E
Lycia 130 Mm 36.30N 29.30 E
Lyckeby 116 Fh 56.12N 15.39 E
Lyckebyån 116 Fh 56.11N 15.40 E
Lyčkovo 114 Hh 57.57N 32.24 E
Lydd 118 Nk 50.57N 0.55 E
Lydd Airport 124 Cd 50.58N 0.56 E
Lydenburg 172 Ee 25.10S 30.29 E
Lydia 130 Lk 38.35N 28.30 E
Lygna 116 Bf 58.10N 7.02 E
Lygnern 116 Eg 57.29N 12.20 E

Index Symbols

[1] Independent Nation
[2] State, Region
[3] District, County
[4] Municipality
[5] Colony, Dependency
Continent
Physical Region
Historical or Cultural Region
Mount, Mountain
Volcano
Hill
Mountains, Mountain Range
Hills, Escarpment
Plateau, Upland
Pass, Gap
Plain, Lowland
Delta
Salt Flat
Valley, Canyon
Crater, Cave
Karst Features
Depression
Polder
Desert, Dunes
Forest, Woods
Heath, Steppe
Oasis
Cape, Point
Coast, Beach
Cliff
Peninsula
Isthmus
Sandbank
Island
Atoll
Rock, Reef
Islands, Archipelago
Rocks, Reefs
Coral Reef
Well, Spring
Geyser
River, Stream
Waterfall, Rapids
River Mouth, Estuary
Lake
Salt Lake
Intermittent Lake
Reservoir
Swamp, Pond
Canal
Glacier
Ice Shelf, Pack Ice
Ocean
Sea
Gulf, Bay
Strait, Fjord
Lagoon
Bank
Seamount
Tablemount
Ridge
Shelf
Basin
Escarpment, Sea Scarp
Fracture
Trench, Abyss
National Park, Reserve
Point of Interest
Recreation Site
Cave, Cavern
Historic Site
Ruins
Wall, Walls
Church, Abbey
Temple
Scientific Station
Railway station
Airport
Port
Military installation
Lighthouse
Mine
Tunnel
Dam, Bridge

Lyme Bay 118 Kk 50.38N 3.00W
Lyminge 124 Dc 51.07N 1.05 E
Lymington 118 Lk 50.46N 1.33W
Łyna 120 Rb 54.37N 21.14 E
Lynchburg 182 Ld 37.24N 79.09W
Lynd 210 Ff 18.56S 144.30 E
Lynden 188 Db 48.57N 122.27W
Lyndon River 212 Cd 23.29S 114.06 E
Lyngdal 114 Bg 58.08N 7.05 E
Lyngen 114 Eb 69.58N 20.30 E
Lyngør 116 Cf 58.38N 9.10 E
Lyngseidet 114 Eb 69.35N 20.13 E
Lynn 184 Ld 42.28N 70.57W
Lynnaj, gora- 138 Ld 62.55N 163.58 E
Lynn Canal 178 Le 58.50N 135.15W
Lynn Deeps 124 Cb 52.58N 0.20 E
Lynn Lake 176 Id 56.51N 101.03W
Lyntupy 116 Li 55.02N 26.27 E
Lynx Lake 180 Gd 62.25N 106.20W
Lyon 112 Gf 45.45N 4.51 E
Lyon Inlet 180 Jc 66.20N 83.40W
Lyonnais, Monts du- 122 Ki 45.40N 4.30 E
Lyon River 212 De 25.00S 115.20 E
Lyons [Ga.-U.S.] 184 Fi 32.12N 82.19W
Lyons [Ks.-U.S.] 186 Gg 38.21N 98.12W
Lyons, Forêt de- 124 De 49.25N 1.30 E
Lyons-la-Forêt 124 De 49.24N 1.28 E
Lyra Reef 214 Eh 1.50S 153.35 E
Lys 122 Jc 51.03N 3.43 E
Łysa Góra 120 Nd 52.07N 17.33 E
Lysaja, gora- 116 Lj 54.12N 27.40 E
Lysá nad Labem 120 Kf 50.12N 14.50 E
Lysefjorden 116 Be 59.00N 6.14 E
Lysekil 114 Cf 58.16N 11.26 E
Lyskovo 136 Ed 56.03N 45.03 E
Lyss 128 Bc 47.04N 7.19 E
Lysva 136 Fd 58.07N 57.47 E
Lytham Saint Anne's 118 Jh 53.45N 3.01W
Lyttelton 218 Ee 43.36S 172.43 E
Lytton 188 Ea 50.14N 121.34W
Lyža 134 Hd 65.42N 56.40 E

M

Ma, Oued el- 162 Fe 24.03N 9.10W
Ma, Song 148 Le 19.45N 105.55 E
Maâdis, Djebel- 126 Qi 35.52N 4.44 E
Maalaea Bay 221a Ec 20.47N 156.29W
Ma'āmīr 146 Mg 30.04N 48.20 E
Ma'ān 144 Ec 30.12N 35.44 E
Ma'Ān [3] 146 Gg 30.20N 35.35 E
Maanselka 114 Ge 63.54N 28.30 E
Maanselkä 110 Ib 68.07N 28.29 E
Ma'anshan 152 Ke 31.38N 118.30 E
Maardu 116 Ke 59.28N 24.56 E
Maarianhamina/Mariehamn 114 Ef 60.06N 19.57 E
Ma 'arrat an Nu 'mān 146 Ge 35.38N 36.40 E
Maarssen 124 Hb 52.08N 5.03 E
Maas=Meuse (EN) 110 Ge 51.49N 5.01 E
Maaseik 122 Lc 51.06N 5.48 E
Maaseik-Neeroeteren 124 Hc 51.05N 5.42 E
Maasin 150 Hd 10.08N 124.50 E
Maasmechelen/Mechelen 124 Hd 50.57N 5.40 E
Maassluis 124 Gc 51.55N 4.17 E
Maastricht 122 Ld 50.52N 5.43 E
Maasupa 219a Ec 9.18S 161.15 E
Ma'āzah, Al Haḑabat al- 164 Fd 27.44N 31.44 E
Mabalane 172 Ed 23.38S 32.31 E
Mabaruma 196 Gh 8.12N 59.47W
Mabechi-Gawa 156 Ga 40.31N 141.31 E
Mabella 186 Lb 48.37N 89.58W
Mabel Lake 188 Fa 50.35N 118.44W
Mablethorpe 118 Nh 53.21N 0.15 E
Mabote 172 Ed 22.03S 34.08 E
Ma'būs Yūsuf 160 Jf 25.45N 21.00 E
Maçaão 126 Ee 39.33N 8.00W
McAdam 180 Kg 45.36N 67.20W
Macaé 202 Jh 22.23S 41.47W
Macajai, Rio- 202 Fc 2.25N 60.50W
McAlester 182 He 34.56N 95.46W
McAllen 182 Hf 26.12N 98.15W
Macaloge 172 Fb 12.25S 35.25 E
Mac Alpine Lake 180 Hc 66.40N 102.50W
Macambará 204 Di 29.08S 56.03W
Macamic 184 Ha 48.48N 79.01W
Macamic, Lac- 184 Ha 48.46N 79.00W
Macao (EN)=Aomen/Macau 152 Jg 22.12N 113.33 E
Macao (EN)=Aomen/Macau [5] 142 Ng 22.10N 113.33 E
Macao (EN)=Macau/Aomen 152 Jg 22.12N 113.33 E
Macao (EN)=Macau/Aomen [5] 142 Ng 22.10N 113.33 E
Macapá 200 Ke 0.02N 51.03W
Macará 202 Cd 4.21S 79.56W
Macaracas 194 Gj 7.44N 80.33W
Macareo, Caño- 202 Fb 9.47N 61.36W
McArthur 184 Ff 39.14N 82.29W
Mc Arthur River 212 Hc 15.54S 136.40 E
Macas 202 Cd 2.18S 78.06W
Maçãs 126 Fc 41.29N 6.39W
Macatete, Sierra de- 192 Dd 28.00N 110.05W
Macau 200 Mf 5.07S 36.38W
Macau/Aomen=Macao (EN) 152 Jg 22.12N 113.33 E
Macau/Aomen=Macao (EN) [5] 142 Ng 22.10N 113.33 E
Macaúbas 202 Jf 13.02S 42.42W
Macauley Island 208 Ih 30.13S 178.33W
Macaya, Pic de- 190 Je 18.23N 74.02W
McBeth Fiord 180 Kc 69.43N 69.20W
McCamey 186 Ek 31.08N 102.13W
McCammon 188 Ie 42.39N 112.12W
Mc Carthy 178 Kd 61.26N 142.55W
McClellanville 184 Hi 33.06N 79.28W
MacClenny 184 Fj 30.18N 82.07W
Macclesfield 118 Kh 53.16N 2.07W
Macclesfield Bank (EN) 150 Fc 15.50N 114.20 E
McClintock 180 Ie 57.48N 94.12W
McClintock, Mount- 222 Jg 80.13S 157.26 E
McClintock Channel 174 Ib 71.00N 101.00W
McCluer Gulf (EN)=Berau, Teluk- 150 Jg 2.30S 132.30 E
McClure Strait 174 Hb 74.30N 116.00W
McClusky 186 Fc 47.29N 100.27W
McComb 182 Ie 31.14N 90.27W
McConaughy, Lake- 186 Ff 41.18N 101.46W
McConnelsville 184 Gf 39.39N 81.51W
McCook 186 Gc 40.12N 100.38W
McCormick 184 Fi 33.55N 82.19W
McDame 180 Ee 59.13N 129.14W
McDermitt 188 Gf 41.59N 117.36W
Macdhui, Ben- 118 Jd 57.04N 3.40W
Macdonald, Lake- 212 Fd 23.30S 129.00 E
Mc Donald Islands 222 Fd 52.59S 72.50 E
McDonald Peak [Ca.-U.S.] 188 Ef 40.58N 120.26W
McDonald Peak [Mt.-U.S.] 188 Ic 47.29N 113.46W
Macdonald Range 188 Hb 49.12N 114.46W
Macdonnell Ranges 208 Eg 23.45S 132.20 E
McDouglas Sound 180 Hd 75.13N 97.30W
Macduff 118 Kd 57.40N 2.29W
Macedo de Cavaleiros 126 Fc 41.32N 6.58W
Macedonia (EN)= Makedhonia 110 Ig 41.00N 23.00 E
Macedonia (EN)= Makedhonia 130 Fh 41.00N 23.00 E
Macedonia (EN) = Makedonija [2] 130 Eh 41.50N 22.00 E
Macedonia (EN)= Makedonija 110 Ig 41.00N 23.00 E
Macedonia (EN)= Makedonija 130 Fh 41.00N 23.00 E
Maceió 200 Mf 9.40S 35.43W
Macenta 166 Dd 8.33N 9.28W
Macerata 128 Hg 43.18N 13.27 E
McGehee 186 Kj 33.38N 91.24W
McGill 188 Hg 39.23N 114.47W
Macgillycuddy's Reeks/Na Cruacha Dubha 118 Di 52.00N 9.50W
McGrath 178 Hd 62.58N 155.38W
MacGregor 186 Gb 49.57N 98.49W
McGregor 186 Jc 46.36N 93.19W
McGregor Lake 188 Ia 50.31N 112.53W
Mc Gregor Range 212 Ie 26.40S 142.45 E
McGuire, Mount- 188 Hd 45.10N 114.36W
Machachi 202 Cd 0.30S 78.34W
Machado 204 Je 21.41S 45.56W
Machagai 206 Hc 26.56S 60.03W
Machaila 172 Ed 22.15S 32.58 E
Machaire na Mumhan/Golden Vale 118 Fi 52.30N 8.00W
Machaire Rátha/Maghera 118 Gg 54.51N 6.40W
Machakos 170 Gc 1.31S 37.16 E
Machala 202 Cd 3.16S 79.58W
Machaneng 172 Dd 23.12S 27.30 E
Machareti 202 Fh 20.49S 63.24W
Machar Marshes 168 Ed 9.20N 33.10 E
Machattie, Lake- 212 Hd 24.50S 139.48 E
Machault 124 Ge 49.21N 4.30 E
Macheke 172 Ec 18.05S 31.51 E
Macheng 152 Je 31.10N 115.00 E
Machias 184 Nc 44.43N 67.28W
Machida 156 Fd 35.32N 139.27 E
Machilipatnam (Bandar) 148 Ge 16.10N 81.08 E
Machine, La- 122 Jh 46.53N 3.28 E
Machiques 202 Da 10.04N 72.34W
Machmi, Al- 146 Jg 31.32N 42.28 E
Machona, Laguna- 192 Mh 18.20N 93.40W
Machów 120 Rf 50.34N 21.40 E
Machupicchu 200 Ig 13.07S 72.34W
Macia 172 Ef 25.02S 33.06 E
Mc Ilwraith Range 212 Ib 13.45S 143.20 E
Mâcin 130 Ld 45.15N 28.09 E
Macina 158 Gg 14.30N 5.00W
McIntosh 186 Fd 45.55N 101.21W
Macintyre River 212 Je 29.25S 148.45 E
Maçka 146 Hb 40.50N 39.38 E
Mackay [Austl.] 210 Fg 21.09S 149.11 E
Mackay [Id.-U.S.] 188 Ie 43.55N 113.37W
Mackay, Lake- 208 Dg 22.30S 129.00 E
McKay Lake 186 Mb 49.35N 86.22W
McKean Atoll 208 Je 3.36S 174.08W
McKeand 180 Kd 63.00N 65.05W
McKeesport 184 He 40.21N 79.52W
McKenzie 184 Cg 36.08N 88.31W
Mackenzie 174 Fc 69.15N 134.08W
Mackenzie Bay [Ant.] 222 Fe 68.20S 71.15 E
Mackenzie Bay [Can.] 174 Fc 69.00N 136.30W
McKenzie Island 180 If 51.05N 93.48W
Mackenzie King 174 Hb 77.45N 111.00W
Mackenzie Mountains 174 Gc 64.00N 130.00W
McKenzie River 188 Dd 44.07N 123.06W
Mackenzie River 212 Jd 23.38S 149.46 E
McKerrow, Lake- 218 Cf 44.30S 168.05 E
Mackinac, Straits of- 184 Eb 45.49N 84.45W
Mackinaw City 184 Ec 45.47N 84.44W
McKinley, Mount- 174 Dc 63.30N 151.00W
McKinley Park 178 Jd 63.44N 148.54W
McKinney 186 Hj 33.12N 96.37W
Mackinnon Road 170 Gc 3.44S 39.03 E
McLaughlin 186 Fd 45.49N 100.49W
McLean 186 Fi 35.14N 100.36W
McLeans Town 184 Ii 26.39N 77.59W
Maclean Strait 180 Ha 77.30N 103.10W
Maclear 172 Df 31.02S 28.23 E
Macleay River 212 Kf 30.52S 153.01 E
Mc Leod, Lake- 208 Cg 24.10S 113.35 E
McLeod Bay 180 Gd 62.53N 110.15W
McLeod Lake 180 Ff 54.59N 123.02W
McLoughlin, Mount- 188 De 42.27N 122.19W
McLure 188 Ea 51.03N 120.14W
Macmillan 180 Dd 62.52N 135.55W
McMillan, Lake- 186 Dj 32.40N 104.20W
Macmillan Pass 180 Ed 63.00N 130.00W
McMinnville [Or.-U.S.] 188 Dd 45.13N 123.12W
McMinnville [Tn.-U.S.] 184 Eh 35.41N 85.46W
McMurdo 222 Kf 77.51S 166.37 E
McNaughton Lake 180 Ff 52.40N 117.50W
Macomb 186 Kf 40.27N 90.40W
Macomer 128 Cj 40.16N 8.47 E
Macomia 172 Gb 12.15S 40.08 E
Mâcon 122 Kh 46.18N 4.50 E
Macon 176 Kf 32.50N 83.38W
Macon [Mo.-U.S.] 186 Jg 39.44N 92.28W
Macon [Ms.-U.S.] 186 Lj 33.07N 88.34W
Macondo 170 De 12.36S 23.43 E
Mâconnais, Monts du- 122 Kh 46.18N 4.45 E
Macoris, Cabo- 194 Ld 19.47N 70.28W
Macouba 197h Ab 14.52N 61.09W
McPherson 182 Hd 38.22N 97.40W
Mc Pherson Range 212 Ke 28.20S 153.00 E
Macquarie 222 Jd 54.30S 158.30 E
Macquarie Harbour 212 Jh 42.20S 145.25 E
Macquarie Ridge (EN) 106 Jo 57.00S 159.00 E
Macquarie River 208 Fh 30.07S 147.24 E
Mac Robertson Land 222 Fe 70.00S 65.00 E
Macroom/Maigh Chromtha 118 Ej 51.54N 8.57W
Macugnaga 128 Be 45.58N 7.58 E
Macujer 202 Dc 0.24N 73.07W
Macuro 196 Fg 10.39N 61.56W
Macusani 202 Df 14.05S 70.26W
Macuspana 192 Mi 17.48N 92.36W
Mačva 130 Ce 44.49N 19.30 E
McVicar Arm 180 Fc 65.10N 120.30W
Ma'dabā 146 Fg 31.43N 35.48 E
Madagali 166 Hc 10.53N 13.38 E
Madagascar 158 Lj 20.00S 47.00 E
Madagascar (EN)= Madagasikara [1] 160 Lj 19.00S 46.00 E
Madagascar Basin (EN) 106 Fl 27.00S 53.00 E
Madagascar Plateau (EN) 106 Fm 30.00S 45.00 E
Madagasikara=Madagascar (EN) [1] 160 Lj 19.00S 46.00 E
Madā'in Şāliḩ 146 Gi 26.48N 37.53 E
Madalai 220a Ac 7.20N 134.28 E
Madama 166 Ha 21.58N 13.39 E
Madan 130 Hh 41.30N 24.57 E
Madang 210 Fe 5.13S 145.48 E
Madaniyīn 160 Ie 33.21N 10.30 E
Madaniyīn [3] 162 Jc 33.00N 10.45 E
Madaoua 166 Gc 14.05N 5.58 E
Madara 130 Kf 43.17N 27.06 E
Madara-Shima 156 Ae 33.35N 129.45 E
Madaroumfa 166 Gc 13.18N 7.09 E
Madau 219a Ac 9.00S 152.26 E
Madawaska Highlands 184 Hc 45.20N 78.15W
Maddalena 128 Di 41.15N 9.25 E
Maddalena, Colle della- 122 Mj 44.25N 6.53 E
Maddaloni 128 Ii 41.02N 14.23 E
Made, Made en Drimmelen- 124 Gc 51.41N 4.48 E
Made en Drimmelen 124 Gc 51.41N 4.48 E
Made en Drimmelen-Made 124 Gc 51.41N 4.48 E
Madeir 168 Dd 7.50N 29.12 E
Madeira [5] 160 Fe 32.40N 16.45W
Madeira 158 Fe 32.44N 17.00W
Madeira, Arquipélago da-= Madeira Islands (EN) 158 Fe 32.40N 16.45W
Madeira, Rio- 198 Kf 3.22S 58.45W
Madeira Islands (EN)= Madeira, Arquipélago da- 158 Fe 32.40N 16.45W
Madeleine, Ile de la - 180 Lg 47.26N 61.44W
Madeleine, Monts de la- 122 Jh 46.03N 3.50 E
Maden 146 Hc 38.23N 39.40 E
Madenassa Veld 158 Jj 19.00N 25.30 E
Madera [Ca.-U.S.] 188 Eh 36.57N 120.03W
Madera [Mex.] 190 Cc 29.12N 108.07W
Mader-Chih 126 Ri 35.26N 5.07 E
Madero, Puerto del- 126 Jc 41.48N 2.05W
Madesimo 128 Dd 46.26N 9.21 E
Madgaon 148 Ee 15.22N 73.49 E
Madhya Pradesh [3] 148 Fd 22.00N 79.00 E
Madimba 170 Cc 4.58S 15.08 E
Madina do Boé 166 Cc 11.45N 14.13W
Madinani 166 Dd 9.37N 6.57W
Madīnat al Abyār 164 Dc 32.11N 20.36 E
Madīnat ash Sha'b 142 Gh 12.50N 44.56 E
Madingo-Kayes 170 Bc 4.10S 12.18 E
Madingou 170 Bc 4.09S 13.34 E
Madirovalo 172 Hc 16.29S 46.30 E
Madison [Fl.-U.S.] 184 Fj 30.28N 83.25W
Madison [In.-U.S.] 184 Ef 38.44N 85.23W
Madison [Mn.-U.S.] 186 Hd 45.01N 96.11W
Madison [S.D.-U.S.] 186 He 44.00N 97.07W
Madison [Wi.-U.S.] 176 Ke 43.05N 89.22W
Madison [W.V.-U.S.] 184 Gf 38.03N 81.50W
Madison Range 188 Jd 45.15N 111.20W
Madison River 188 Jd 45.56N 111.30W
Madisonville 182 Jd 37.20N 87.30W
Madiun 150 Fh 7.37S 111.31 E
Mado Gashi 170 Gb 0.44N 39.10 E
Madoi (Huangheyan) 142 Lf 35.00N 98.56 E
Madon 122 Mf 48.36N 6.06 E
Madona 114 Gh 56.53N 26.20 E
Madra Dağı 130 Kj 39.23N 27.12 E
Madrakah, Ra's al- 144 If 18.59N 57.45 E
Madranbaba Dağı 130 Ll 37.38N 28.12 E
Madras [India] 142 Kh 13.05N 80.17 E
Madras [Or.-U.S.] 188 Ed 44.38N 121.08W
Madre, Laguna- [Mex.] 190 Ed 25.00N 97.40W
Madre, Laguna- [Tx.-U.S.] 182 Hf 27.00N 97.35W
Madre, Sierra- [N.Amer.] 174 Jh 15.20N 92.20W
Madre, Sierra- [Phil.] 140 Oh 16.20N 122.00 E
Madre de Dios 202 Df 12.36S 69.59W
Madre de Dios [3] 202 Df 12.00S 70.15W
Madre de Dios, Isla- 198 Ik 50.15S 75.05W
Madre de Dios, Rio- 198 Jg 10.59S 66.08W
Madre del Sur, Sierra-= Southern Sierra Madre (EN) 174 Jj 17.00N 100.00W
Madre de Oaxaca, Sierra- 192 Ki 17.30N 96.30W
Madre Occidental, Sierra-= Western Sierra Madre (EN) 174 Ig 25.00N 105.00W
Madre Oriental, Sierra-= Eastern Sierra Madre (EN) 174 Jg 22.00N 99.30W
Madrid 112 Fg 40.24N 3.41W
Madrid [2] 126 Id 40.30N 3.40W
Madrid-Aravaca 126 Id 40.27N 3.47W
Madridejos 126 Ie 39.28N 3.32W
Madrid-El Pardo 126 Id 40.32N 3.46W
Madrid-Vallecas 126 Id 40.23N 3.37W
Madrid-Villaverde 126 Id 40.21N 3.42W
Madrigal de las Altas Torres 126 Hc 41.05N 5.00W
Mad River 188 Cf 40.57N 124.07W
Madriz [3] 194 Dg 13.30N 86.30W
Madrona, Sierra- 126 Hf 38.25N 4.10W
Madula 170 Eb 0.28N 25.23 E
Madura, Palau- 140 Nj 7.00S 113.20 E
Madurai 142 Ji 9.56N 78.07 E
Madvār, Kūh-e- 144 Hc 30.36N 54.52 E
Madwin 164 Cd 28.42N 17.31 E
Madyan 140 Fg 27.40N 35.35 E
Madžalis 132 Oh 42.08N 47.50 E
Maebara 156 Be 33.34N 130.13 E
Maebashi 152 Od 36.23N 139.04 E
Mae Hong Son 148 Je 19.16N 97.56 E
Mæl 116 Ce 59.56N 8.48 E
Mae Nam Khong=Mekong (EN) 140 Mh 10.15N 105.55 E
Maesawa 156 Gb 39.03N 141.07 E
Mae Sot 148 Je 16.40N 98.35 E
Maestra, Sierra- 174 Lh 20.00N 76.45W
Maevatanana 172 Hc 16.56S 46.49 E
Maéwo, Ile- 208 Hf 15.10S 168.10 E
Mafeteng 172 De 29.45S 27.18 E
Mafia Channel 170 Gd 7.50S 39.35 E
Mafia Island 158 Ki 7.50S 39.50 E
Mafikeng 160 Jk 25.53S 25.39 E
Mafra [Braz.] 206 Kc 26.07S 49.49W
Mafra [Port.] 126 Cf 38.56N 9.20W
Magadan 142 Rd 59.34N 150.48 E
Magadanskaja oblast [3] 138 Kd 62.30N 154.00 E
Magadi 170 Gc 1.54S 36.17 E
Magallanes, Estrecho de- = Magellan, Strait of- (EN) 198 Ik 54.00S 71.00W
Magallanes y Antártica Chilena [2] 206 Fh 51.30S 73.30W
Magangué 202 Db 9.14N 74.46W
Maganik 130 Cg 42.44N 19.16 E
Maganoy 150 He 6.51N 124.31 E
Magaria 166 Gc 12.59N 8.50 E
Magazine Mountain 186 Ji 35.10N 93.38W
Magdagači 136 Hf 53.29N 125.55 E
Magdala 204 Bm 36.06S 61.43W
Magdalena [3] 200 Db 10.00N 74.15W
Magdalena [Arg.] 204 Dl 35.04S 57.32W
Magdalena [Bol.] 202 Ff 13.20S 64.08W
Magdalena [Mex.] 190 Bb 30.38N 110.57W
Magdalena [N.M.-U.S.] 186 Ci 34.07N 107.14W
Magdalena, Bahía- 192 Ce 24.35N 112.00W
Magdalena, Isla- 190 Bd 24.55N 112.15W
Magdalena, Llano de la- 190 Bd 24.30N 111.40W
Magdalena, Rio- [Col.] 198 Id 11.06N 74.51W
Magdalena, Rio- [Mex.] 192 Cb 30.48N 112.32W
Magda Plateau 180 Jb 72.18N 82.55W
Magdeburg 112 He 52.10N 11.40 E
Magdeburg [2] 120 Hd 52.15N 11.35 E
Magdeburger Börde 120 Hd 52.00N 11.30 E
Magdelaine Cays 208 Gf 16.35S 150.15 E
Magee 186 Lk 31.52N 89.44W
Magelang 150 Fh 7.28S 110.13 E
Magellan, Strait of- (EN) = Magallanes, Estrecho de- 198 Ik 54.00S 71.00W
Magellan Seamounts (EN) 208 Gc 17.30N 152.00 E
Magenta 128 Ce 45.28N 8.53 E
Magerøya 114 Fa 71.03N 25.45 E
Magetan 150 Fh 7.39S 111.20 E
Maggiorasca 128 Df 44.33N 9.29 E
Maggiore, Lago- (Verbano) 128 Ce 45.55N 8.40 E
Maghāghah 164 Fd 28.39N 30.50 E
Maghama 162 Ef 15.31N 12.50W
Maghera/Machaire Rátha 118 Gg 54.51N 6.40W
Maghnia 162 Gc 34.51N 1.44W
Magic Reservoir 188 He 43.20N 114.18W
Mágina, Sierra de- 126 Ig 37.45N 3.30W
Magistralny 138 Fe 56.03N 107.35 E
Maglaj 128 Mf 44.33N 18.06 E
Măglenik 130 Ih 41.20N 25.45 E
Maglie 128 Mj 40.07N 18.18 E
Măgliž 130 Ig 42.36N 25.33 E
Magnetawan River 184 Gc 45.46N 80.37W
Magnetic Island 212 Jc 19.10S 146.50 E
Magnitka 134 Ii 55.21N 59.43 E
Magnitnaja, gora- 134 Ij 53.10N 59.10 E
Magnitogorsk 112 Le 53.27N 59.04 E
Magnolia 186 Jj 33.16N 93.14W
Magnor 114 Cg 59.57N 12.12 E
Magny-en-Vexin 122 He 49.09N 1.47 E
Mago 138 Jf 53.18N 140.20 E
Magoé 172 Ec 15.48S 31.43 E
Magoebaskloof 172 Ed 23.51S 30.02 E
Magog 184 Kc 45.16N 72.09W
Magosa/Ammokhostos= Famagusta (EN) 144 Dc 35.07N 33.57 E
Magra [Alg.] 126 Qi 35.29N 4.58 E
Magra [It.] 128 Df 44.03N 9.58 E
Magtá Lahjar 162 Ef 17.50N 13.20W
Maguarinho, Cabo- 202 Id 0.20S 48.20W
Magude 172 Ee 25.02S 32.40 E
Magumeri 166 Hc 12.07N 12.49 E
Magura, gora- 120 Th 48.50N 23.44 E
Magway 148 Jd 20.00N 95.00 E
Magway 142 Lg 20.09N 94.55 E
Magyarország = Hungary (EN) [1] 112 Hf 47.00N 20.00 E
Mahābād 144 Gb 36.45N 45.53 E
Mahabalipuram 148 Gf 12.37N 80.12 E
Mahabe 172 Hc 17.05S 45.20 E
Mahabo 172 Gd 20.21S 44.39 E
Mahačkala 112 Kg 42.58N 47.30 E
Mahadday Wēyne 168 He 3.00N 45.32 E
Mahādeo Range 148 Ee 17.50N 74.15 E
Mahafaly, Plateau- 172 Gd 24.30S 44.00 E
Mahagi 170 Fb 2.18N 30.59 E
Mahajamba 172 Hc 15.33S 47.08 E
Mahājan 148 Ec 28.47N 73.50 E
Mahajanga 160 Lj 15.17S 46.43 E
Mahajanga [3] 172 Hc 16.30S 47.00 E
Mahajilo 172 Hc 19.42S 45.22 E
Mahakam 140 Nj 0.35S 117.17 E
Mahalapye 172 Dd 23.07S 26.46 E
Mahalevona 172 Hc 15.26S 49.55 E
Mahallāt 146 Nf 33.55N 50.27 E
Mahamid 168 Cb 15.09N 20.25 E
Māhān 146 Qg 30.05N 57.19 E
Mahānadi 140 Kg 20.19N 86.45 E
Mahanoro 172 Hc 19.53S 48.49 E
Maharadze 136 Eg 41.53N 42.01 E
Mahārāshtra [3] 148 Ee 18.00N 75.00 E
Mahārlū, Daryācheh-ye- 146 Oh 29.25N 52.50 E
Maḩās 168 He 4.24N 46.07 E
Maha Sarakham 148 Ke 16.12N 103.16 E
Mahavavy 158 Lj 15.57S 45.54 E
Mahbés 162 Fd 27.10N 9.50W
Maḩḑah 146 Pj 24.24N 55.59 E
Mahdia 202 Gb 5.16N 59.09W
Mahe 148 Ff 11.42N 75.32 E
Mahébourg 172a Bb 20.24S 57.42 E
Mahé Island 158 Mi 4.40S 55.28 E
Mahendra Giri 148 Ge 18.58N 84.21 E
Mahenge 160 Ki 8.41S 36.43W
Maheno 218 Df 45.10S 170.50 E
Mahesāna 148 Ed 23.36N 72.24 E
Mahi 148 Ed 22.16N 72.58 E
Mahia Peninsula 216 Eg 39.10S 177.55 E
Mahmūdābād 146 Od 36.38N 52.15 E
Mahmudābād 146 Lc 39.25N 47.15 E
Mahmūd-e 'Erāqī 144 Kb 35.01N 69.20 E
Mahmudiye 146 Dc 39.30N 31.00 E
Mahmutşevketpaşa 130 Mh 41.09N 29.11 E
Māhneshān 146 Ld 36.45N 47.38 E
Mahnevo 134 Jg 58.27N 61.42 E
Mahnomen 186 Ic 47.19N 95.59W
Mahón/Maó 126 Qe 39.53N 4.15 E
Mahoré/Mayotte 158 Lj 12.50S 45.10 E
Mahrāt, Jabal- 168 Ib 17.00N 52.00 E
Mahuan Dao 150 Gd 10.52N 115.47 E
Mahua Point 219a Fd 10.28S 162.05 E
Maiana Atoll 208 Id 0.55N 173.00 E
Maiao, Ile- (Tubai-Manu) 208 Lf 17.34S 150.35W
Maicao 202 Da 11.23N 72.15W
Maicasagi, Lac- 184 Ia 49.52N 76.48W
Maîche 122 Mg 47.15N 6.48 E
Maicuru, Rio- 202 Hd 2.10S 54.17W
Maidenhead 124 Bc 51.31N 0.42W
Maidstone 118 Nj 51.17N 0.32 E
Maiduguri 160 Ig 11.51N 13.09 E
Măieruş 130 Id 45.54N 25.32 E
Maigh Chromtha/Macroom 118 Ej 51.54N 8.57W
Maigudo 168 Fd 7.26N 37.10 E
Maihara 156 Ed 35.20N 136.18 E
Maikala Range 148 Gd 22.30N 81.30 E
Maiko 170 Eb 0.14N 25.33 E
Maikona 170 Gb 2.56N 37.38 E
Maikoor, Pulau- 150 Jh 6.15S 134.15 E
Main 120 Ef 50.00N 8.18 E
Mainalon Óros 130 Fl 37.40N 22.15 E
Main Barrier Range 212 If 31.25S 141.25 E
Mainburg 120 Hh 48.39N 11.47 E
Main Camp 220g Ba 2.01N 157.25W
Main Channel 184 Gc 45.22N 81.50W
Mai-Ndombe, Lac- 158 Ii 2.10S 18.15 E
Main-Donau-Kanal 120 Gg 49.55N 10.50 E
Maindong → Coqên 152 Ee 31.15N 85.13 E
Maine [2] 182 Nb 45.15N 69.15W
Maine 122 Ff 48.15N 0.10W
Maine [Fr.] 122 Eg 47.09N 1.27W
Maine [Fr.] 122 Fg 47.25N 0.37W
Maine, Gulf of- 174 Me 43.00N 68.00W
Maine-et-Loire [3] 122 Fg 47.30N 0.20W
Mainé-Soroa 166 Hc 13.18N 12.02 E
Mainistir Fhear Mai/Fermoy 118 Ei 52.08N 8.16W
Mainistir na Búille/Boyle 118 Eh 53.58N 8.18W
Mainistir na Corann/Midleton 118 Ej 51.55N 8.10W
Mainistir na Féile/Abbeyfeale 118 Di 52.24N 9.18W
Mainit, Lake- 150 Ie 9.26N 125.32 E
Mainland [Scot.-U.K.] 110 Fd 59.00N 3.10W
Mainland [Scot.-U.K.] 110 Fc 60.20N 1.22W
Maintal 124 Kd 50.08N 8.51 E
Maintenon 122 Hf 48.35N 1.35 E
Maintirano 160 Lj 18.03S 44.03 E
Mainz 120 Eg 50.00N 8.15 E
Maio 162 Cf 23.10N 15.10W
Maio 158 Eg 15.15N 23.10W
Maipo, Volcán- 198 Ji 34.10S 69.50W
Maipú 206 Ie 36.52S 57.52W
Maiquetía 202 Ea 10.36N 66.57W
Maira 128 Bf 44.49N 7.38 E
Mairi 202 Jf 11.43S 40.08W
Mairipotaba 204 Hc 17.21S 49.31W
Maisān [3] 146 Lg 32.00N 47.00 E
Maisí, Punta- 190 Jd 20.15N 74.09W
Maišiagala/Maišjagala 116 Kj 54.51N 25.14 E
Maišjagala/Maišiagala 116 Kj 54.51N 25.14 E
Maiter 126 Qi 35.23N 4.17 E

Index Symbols

[1] Independent Nation
[2] State, Region
[3] District, County
[4] Municipality
[5] Colony, Dependency
Continent
Physical Region
Historical or Cultural Region
Mount, Mountain
Volcano
Hill
Mountains, Mountain Range
Hills, Escarpment
Plateau, Upland
Pass, Gap
Plain, Lowland
Delta
Salt Flat
Valley, Canyon
Crater, Cave
Karst Features
Depression
Polder
Desert, Dunes
Forest, Woods
Heath, Steppe
Oasis
Cape, Point
Coast, Beach
Cliff
Peninsula
Isthmus
Sandbank
Island
Atoll
Rock, Reef
Islands, Archipelago
Rocks, Reefs
Coral Reef
Well, Spring
Geyser
River, Stream
Waterfall, Rapids
River Mouth, Estuary
Lake
Salt Lake
Intermittent Lake
Reservoir
Swamp, Pond
Canal
Glacier
Ice Shelf, Pack Ice
Ocean
Sea
Gulf, Bay
Strait, Fjord
Lagoon
Bank
Seamount
Tablemount
Ridge
Shelf
Basin
Escarpment, Sea Scarp
Fracture
Trench, Abyss
National Park, Reserve
Point of Interest
Recreation Site
Cave, Cavern
Historic Site
Ruins
Wall, Walls
Church, Abbey
Temple
Scientific Station
Railway station
Airport
Port
Military installation
Lighthouse
Mine
Tunnel
Dam, Bridge

Maitland [Austl.] 212 Hf 34.22 S 137.40 E
Maitland [Austl.] 210 Gh 32.44 S 151.33 E
Maíz, Isla Grande del- 194 Fg 12.10N 83.03W
Maíz, Isla Pequeña del- 194 Fg 12.18N 82.59W
Maíz, Islas del- 190 Hf 12.15N 83.00W
Maizhokunggar 152 Ff 29.50N 91.40 E
Maizières-lès-Metz 124 Ie 49.13N 6.09 E
Maizuru 154 Mg 35.27N 135.20 E
Maizuru-Nishimaizuru 156 Dd 35.28N 135.19 E
Maizuru-Wan 156 Dd 35.30N 135.20 E
Maja [R.S.F.S.R.] 140 Pg 60.17N 134.41 E
Maja [R.S.F.S.R.] 138 If 54.37N 134.50 E
Majagual 194 Ji 8.35N 74.37W
Majakovski 132 Mh 42.02N 42.47 E
Majangat 152 Fb 48.20N 91.58 E
Majardah, Wādī- 128 Em 37.07N 10.13 E
Majdanpek 128 Dn 36.39N 9.37 E
Majdanpek 130 Ee 44.25N 21.56 E
Majene 142 Nj 3.33 S 118.57 E
Majërtën=Mijirtein (EN) 168 Lh 9.00N 50.00 E
Majevica 128 Mf 44.40N 18.40 E
Maji 168 Fd 6.10N 35.35 E
Majia He 152 Kd 38.09N 117.53 E
Majja 138 Id 61.38N 130.25 E
Majkain 136 He 51.27N 75.52 E
Majkamys 135 Ka 46.34N 77.37 E
Majkop 112 Kg 44.35N 40.07 E
Majli-Saj 135 Id 41.15N 72.30 E
Majma'ah 146 Kj 25.54N 45.20 E
Majmak 136 Hg 42.40N 71.14 E
Majmakan 138 Ie 57.30N 135.23 E
Majmeča 138 Fb 71.20N 104.15 E
Majn 138 Mc 65.03N 172.10 E
Majna [R.S.F.S.R.] 114 Li 54.09N 47.37 E
Majna [R.S.F.S.R.] 138 Ef 53.00N 91.28 E
Major, Puig-/Mayor, Puig- 126 Oe 39.48N 2.48 E
Majorca (EN)=Mallorca 110 Gh 39.30N 3.00 E
Majrur 168 Db 16.40N 26.53 E
Majski [R.S.F.S.R.] 138 Hf 52.18N 129.38 E
Majski [R.S.F.S.R.] 132 Nh 43.36N 44.03 E
Maju, Pulau- 150 If 1.20N 126.25 E
Majuro Atoll 160 Ii 7.09N 171.12 E
Makabana 160 Ii 3.28 S 12.36 E
Makaha 221a Cb 21.29N 158.13W
Makahuena Point 221a Bb 21.52N 159.27W
Makalamabedi 172 Cd 20.20 S 23.51 E
Makale 150 Gg 3.06 S 119.51 E
Makallé 206 Ic 27.13 S 59.17W
Makalondi 166 Fc 12.50N 1.41 E
Makamby, Nosy- 172 Hc 15.42 S 45.54 E
Makanči 136 If 46.51N 81.57 E
Makanza 170 Cb 1.36N 19.07 E
Makapala 221a Fc 20.13N 155.45W
Makapu Point 220k Ba 18.59 S 169.55W
Makapuu Head 221a Db 21.18N 157.39W
Makara, prohod- 130 Ih 41.16N 25.26 E
Makarene, Irhazer- 166 Gb 18.07N 7.35 E
Mákares 130 Il 37.05N 25.42 E
Makarfi 166 Gc 11.23N 7.53 E
Makari 166 Hc 12.35N 14.28 E
Makari Mountains 170 Ed 6.05 S 29.50 E
Makarjev 114 Kh 57.57N 43.49 E
Makarov 138 Jg 48.39N 142.51 E
Makarov Basin (EN) 224 Ce 87.00N 170.00 E
Makarov Seamount (EN) 208 Gb 29.30N 153.30 E
Makarska 128 La 43.18N 17.02 E
Makā Rúd 146 Nd 36.21N 51.16 E
Makasar → Ujung Pandang 142 Nj 5.07 S 119.24 E
Makasar, Selat-=Makassar Strait (EN) 140 Nj 2.00 S 117.30 E
Makassar Strait (EN)= Makasar, Selat- 140 Nj 2.00 S 117.30 E
Makat 112 Lf 47.40N 53.28 E
Makatea, Ile- 208 Mf 15.50 S 148.15W
Makaw 148 Jc 26.27N 96.42 E
Makawao 221a Ec 20.51N 156.19W
Makay, Massif du- 172 Hd 21.15 S 45.15 E
Makedhonía 130 Fi 40.40N 22.30 E
Makedhonía=Macedonia (EN) 110 Ig 41.00N 23.00 E
Makedhonía=Macedonia (EN) 130 Fh 41.00N 23.00 E
Makedonija = Macedonia (EN) 130 Eh 41.50N 22.00 E
Makedonija=Macedonia (EN) 110 Ig 41.00N 23.00 E
Makedonija=Macedonia (EN) 130 Eh 41.50N 22.00 E
Makejevka 132 Jf 48.00N 37.58 E
Makelulu, Mount- 220a Bb 7.34N 134.35 E
Makemo Atoll 208 Mf 16.35 S 143.40W
Makeni 160 Fh 8.53N 12.03W
Makgadikgadi Pans 158 Jk 20.50 S 25.30 E
Makhfar al Buşayyah 146 Ji 30.08N 46.07 E
Makhfar al Hammām 146 He 35.51N 38.45 E
Makhyah, Wādī- 144 Gf 17.40N 49.01 E
Maki 158 Fc 45.38N 138.52 E
Makian, Pulau- 150 If 0.20N 127.25 E
Makikihi 218 Df 44.38 S 171.09 E
Makinsk 138 Df 52.37N 70.26 E
Makkah=Mecca (EN) 142 Fg 21.27N 39.49 E
Makkovik 180 Le 55.05N 59.11W
Maknassy 128 Sa 34.37N 9.36 E
Makó 120 Qj 46.13N 20.29 E
Makokou 160 Ih 0.34N 12.52 E
Makongai 219d Bb 17.27 S 178.58 E
Makongolosi 170 Eb 8.24 S 33.09 E
Makorako 218 Gi 39.09 S 176.03 E
Mauoura 219b Dc 17.08 S 168.26 E
Makov 120 Qg 49.22N 18.29 E
Maków Mazowiecki 120 Rd 52.52N 21.06 E
Makrá 130 Im 36.16N 25.53 E
Makrän 140 Hg 26.00N 60.00 E

Makrónisos 130 Hl 37.42N 24.07 E
Maksatiha 114 Ih 57.48N 35.55 E
Makteir 158 Ff 21.50N 11.40W
Makthar 162 Ib 35.51N 9.12 E
Makthar 128 Do 35.50N 9.13 E
Mākū 146 Kc 39.17N 44.31 E
Makū 144 Hd 27.52N 52.26 E
Makubetsu 156a Cb 42.54N 143.19 E
Makumbato 170 Fd 8.51 S 34.50 E
Makumbi 170 Fd 5.51 S 20.41 E
Makunduchi 170 Gd 6.25 S 39.33 E
Makung 152 Kg 23.35N 119.35 E
Makurazaki 154 Ki 31.16N 139.19 E
Makurdi 160 Hh 7.44N 8.32 E
Makushin Volcano 178a Eb 53.53N 166.50W
Makušino 136 Gd 55.13N 67.13 E
Makuyuni 170 Gc 3.33 S 36.06 E
Malá 114 Ed 65.11N 18.44 E
Mala, Punta- 118 Ei 52.08N 8.39W
Malabang 190 Ig 7.28N 80.00 E
Malabar Coast 150 He 7.38N 124.03 E
Malabo 140 Jh 10.00N 76.15 E
Malabrigo 160 Hh 3.45N 8.47 E
204 Ci 29.20 S 59.58W
Malacca, Strait of- (EN)= Melaka, Selat- 140 Mi 2.30N 101.20 E
Malacky 120 Nh 48.27N 17.01 E
Malad City 188 Ie 42.12N 112.15W
Maladeta / Malditos, Montes- 126 Mb 42.40N 0.50 E
Malá Fatra 120 Og 49.08N 18.50 E
Málaga [Col.] 202 Db 6.42N 72.44W
Málaga [Sp.] 112 Fh 36.43N 4.25W
Malagarasi 158 Ji 5.12 S 29.47 E
Malagón 126 Ie 39.10N 3.51W
Malaimbandy 172 Hd 20.20 S 45.36 E
Malaita Island 208 He 9.00 S 161.00 E
Malaja Kuonamka 138 Gb 70.50N 113.20 E
Malaja Ob 138 Bc 66.08N 65.50 E
Malaja Sosva 136 Gc 63.10N 64.22 E
Malaja Višera 138 Dd 58.52N 32.14 E
Malaja Viska 132 Ge 48.39N 31.38 E
Malakāl 160 Kh 9.31N 31.39 E
Malakal Harbor 220a Ac 7.20N 134.26 E
Malakal Pass 220a Ac 7.17N 134.28 E
Mala Kapela 128 Jf 44.55N 15.28 E
Malakobi 219a Db 7.19 S 158.07 E
Malang 142 Nj 7.59 S 112.37 E
Malangen 114 Eb 69.30N 18.20 E
Malanje 160 Ii 9.33 S 16.22 E
Malanje 170 Cd 9.30 S 16.18 E
Malanville 166 Fc 11.52N 3.23 E
Malao 219b Cb 15.10 S 166.51 E
Mała Panew 120 Nf 50.44N 17.52 E
Mälaren 110 Hd 59.30N 17.15 E
Malargüe 206 Ge 35.28 S 69.35W
Malartic, Lac- 184 Ha 48.15N 78.05W
Malaspina Glacier 178a Ke 59.50N 140.30W
Malatya 142 Ff 38.21N 38.19 E
Malāvi 146 Lf 33.10N 47.50 E
Malawi 160 Kj 13.30 S 34.00 E
Malawi, Lake- 158 Kj 12.00 S 34.30 E
Malaya 150 Df 4.00N 102.00 E
Malaybalay 150 Ie 8.09N 125.05 E
Malaÿer 144 Gc 34.17N 48.50 E
Malaÿer 144 Me 34.16N 48.12 E
Malay Peninsula (EN) 140 Mi 6.00N 102.00 E
Malay Peninsula (EN)= Malaysia, Semenanjung- 150 Df 4.00N 102.00 E
Malaysia 142 Mi 2.00N 112.00 E
Malaysia, Semenanjung-= Malay Peninsula (EN) 150 Df 4.00N 102.00 E
Malazgirt 146 Jc 39.09N 42.31 E
Malberg 118 Id 50.03N 6.35 E
Mālbor 146 Og 30.45N 52.05 E
Malbork 120 Pb 54.02N 19.01 E
Malbrán 206 Hc 29.21 S 62.27W
Malchin 124 Ic 53.44N 12.47 E
Maldegem 124 Ic 51.13N 3.27 E
Malden 118 Kh 36.34N 89.57W
Malden Island 208 Le 4.03 S 154.59W
Malditos, Montes- / Maladeta 126 Mb 42.40N 0.50 E
Maldive Islands 140 Ji 3.15N 73.00 E
Mal di Ventre 128 Ck 40.00N 8.20 E
Maldives 142 Ji 3.15N 73.00 E
Maldonado 206 Jd 34.54 S 54.57W
Maldonado 204 Ei 34.40 S 54.55W
Maldonado, Punta- 192 Jj 16.20N 98.35W
Male 128 Ed 46.21N 10.55 E
Māle, Lac du- 184 Ja 48.30N 75.30W
Malea, Cape- (EN) = Maléas, Ákra- 130 Gm 36.26N 23.12 E
Maléas, Ákra- = Malea, Cape- (EN) 130 Gm 36.26N 23.12 E
Male Atoll 140 Ji 4.29N 73.30 E
Malebo, Pool- 158 Ii 4.17 S 15.20 E
Malégaon 148 Hd 20.33N 74.32 E
Maléha 166 Dc 11.48N 9.43W
Malek 168 Db 6.04N 31.36 E
Malé Karpaty = Little Carpathians (EN) 120 Nh 48.30N 17.20 E
Malek Kandī 146 Kd 37.09N 46.06 E
Malékoula, Ile- 208 Hf 16.15 S 167.30 E
Malema 172 Fb 14.57 S 37.25 E
Malemba Nkulu 170 Ed 8.02 S 26.48 E
Malenga 114 Ie 63.50N 36.25 E
Malesherbes 122 If 48.18N 2.25 E
Malgomaj 114 Cd 64.47N 16.12 E
Malhada 204 Kb 14.21 S 43.47W
Malhanski hrebet 138 Ff 50.30N 109.00 E
Malhão da Estrêla 126 Ed 40.19N 7.37W
Malha Wells 168 Db 15.08N 26.12 E

Malheur Lake 182 Dc 43.20N 118.45W
Malheur River 188 Gd 44.03N 116.59W
Mali 166 Cc 12.05N 12.18W
Mali 160 Gg 17.00N 4.00W
Mali 219a Bb 16.20 S 179.21 E
Mali 148 Jc 25.42N 97.30 E
Mália 130 In 35.17N 25.28 E
Maliakós Kólpos 130 Fk 38.52N 22.38 E
Malik, Wādī al- 158 Kg 18.02N 30.58 E
Mali kanal 130 Cd 45.42N 19.19 E
Malik Siah, Kūh-i- 144 Jd 29.51N 60.52 E
Malili 150 Pg 2.38 S 121.06 E
Mālilla 116 Fg 57.23N 15.48 E
Mali Lošinj 128 If 44.32N 14.28 E
Malimba, Monts- 170 Ed 7.32 S 29.30 E
Malin 132 Jh 50.46N 29.14 E
Malinalco 192 Jh 18.57N 99.30W
Malinaltepec 192 Ji 17.03N 98.40W
Malindi 160 Li 3.13 S 40.07 E
Malines/Mechelen 122 Kc 51.02N 4.29 E
Mhàlanna 110 Fd 55.23N 7.24W
Malino, Bukit- 150 Hf 0.45N 120.47 E
Malinovoje Ozero 138 Cf 51.40N 79.55 E
Malinyi 170 Gd 8.56 S 36.08 E
Malipo 152 Hg 23.07N 104.42 E
Maliqi 130 Di 40.43N 20.41 E
Malita 150 Ie 6.25N 125.36 E
Maljen 130 De 44.07N 20.03 E
Maljovica 130 Gg 42.11N 23.22 E
Malka 132 Mh 43.44N 44.15 E
Malkara 146 Bb 40.53N 26.54 E
Malki Lom 130 Ih 43.39N 26.04 E
Malko Tãrnovo 130 Kh 41.59N 27.32 E
Mallacoota 212 Jg 37.30 S 149.50 E
Mallaig 118 Hd 57.00N 5.50W
Mallamalla Range 148 Fe 16.17N 79.29 E
Mallãq, Wãdî- 128 Cn 36.32N 8.51 E
Mallawī 164 Fd 27.44N 30.50 E
Mallery Lake 180 Hd 64.00N 98.00W
Malles Venosta / Mals in Vinschgau 128 Ed 46.41N 10.32 E
Mallet 204 Gg 25.55 S 50.50W
Mallnitz 128 Hd 46.59N 13.10 E
Mallorca=Majorca (EN) 110 Gh 39.30N 3.00 E
Mallow/Mala 118 Ei 52.08N 8.39W
Malm 128 Gd 64.04N 11.13 E
Malmbäck 116 Fg 57.35N 14.28 E
Malmberget 114 Ec 67.10N 20.40 E
Malmédy 122 Md 50.26N 6.02 E
Malmesbury 172 Bf 33.28 S 18.44 E
Malmö 116 Ci 55.36N 13.00 E
Malmöhus 114 Ci 55.45N 13.30 E
Malmön 136 Df 58.21N 11.20 E
Malmslätt 116 Ff 58.25N 15.30 E
Malmyž 136 Cd 56.30N 50.41 E
Maloarhangelsk 219b Cb 15.41 S 167.10 E
Maloelap 132 Jc 52.26N 36.29 E
Maloggia/Malojapaß 208 Id 8.45N 171.03 E
Malojapaß/Maloggia 128 Dd 46.24N 9.41 E
Malojaroslavec 128 Dd 46.24N 9.41 E
Maloje Polesje 132 Ss 55.02N 36.28 E
Malolo 120 Uf 50.10N 24.30 E
Malolos 150 Ha 14.51N 120.49 E
Malombe, Lake- 219b Ab 17.45 S 177.10 E
Malone 170 Fd 14.38 S 35.12 E
Malonga 184 Jc 44.52N 74.19W
Małopolska 120 De 10.24 S 23.10 E
Malorita 120 Pf 50.45N 20.08 E
Malošujka 132 Dd 51.48N 24.05 E
Maløy 114 Ie 63.47N 37.22 E
Malpaso 114 Af 61.56N 5.07 E
Malpelo, Isla de- 192 Mi 17.20N 93.30W
Malprabha 198 Re 3.59N 81.35W
Malsch 148 Fe 16.12N 76.03 E
Malše 124 Kh 48.59N 14.29 E
Mals in Vinschgau / Malles Venosta 120 Kh 48.59N 14.29 E
Malta 128 Ed 46.41N 10.32 E
Malta 112 Hh 35.50N 14.30 E
Malta 110 Hh 35.54N 14.31 E
Malta [Lat.-U.S.S.R.] 116 Ln 56.18N 27.15 E
Malta [Mt.-U.S.] 182 Fb 48.21N 107.52W
Malta, Canale di-=Malta Channel (EN) 128 In 36.30N 14.30 E
Malta Channel (EN)=Malta, Canale di- 128 In 36.30N 14.30 E
Maltahöhe 160 Ik 24.50 S 17.00 E
Maltahöhe 172 Bd 24.50 S 16.59 E
Maltepe 130 Mi 40.56N 29.08 E
Malton 118 Mg 54.08N 0.48W
Maltsch 150 Ig 4.10N 73.30 E
Maluku, Kepulauan-= Moluccas (EN) 150 Ig 4.10N 73.30 E
Maluku, Laut-=Molucca Sea (EN) 140 Oj 0.05 S 125.00 E
Malumfashi 166 Gc 11.48N 7.37 E
Malunda 150 Gg 3.00 S 118.50 E
Malung 114 Cf 60.40N 13.44 E
Malungsfors 166 Ec 10.26N 32.12 E
Malūṭ 219a Ec 8.21 S 160.38 E
Maluu 186 Ji 34.22N 92.49W
Malvern [Ar.-U.S.] 118 Kj 52.07N 2.19W
Malvern [Eng.-U.K.] 204 Ci 29.37 S 58.59W
Malvinas, Islas-/Falkland Islands 200 Kk 51.45 S 59.00W
Malvinas, Islas-/Falkland Islands 198 Kk 51.45 S 59.00W
Maly, ostrov- 116 Ld 60.02N 27.58 E
Malya 170 Fc 68.35N 161.03W
Maly Anjuj 114 Mi 34.05N 33.31 E
Maly Čeremšan 146 Kb 40.50N 100.14 E
Maly Dunaj 198 Cb 73.00N 70.30 E
Malygina, proliv- 138 Cb 73.00N 70.30 E
Maly Jenisej 138 Ef 51.40N 94.26 E

Maly Kavkaz=Lesser Caucasus (EN) 110 Kg 41.00N 44.35 E
Maly Ljahovski, ostrov- 138 Jb 74.07N 140.36 E
Maly Tajmyr, ostrov- 138 Fa 78.08N 107.08 E
Maly Tjuters, ostrov- 116 Le 59.45N 26.53 E
Maly Uzen 110 Kf 48.50N 49.38 E
Mama 138 Ge 58.20N 112.54 E
Mamadyš 114 Mi 55.45N 51.24 E
Mamagota 219a Bb 6.46 S 155.24 E
Mamaia 130 Le 44.17N 28.37 E
Mamakan 138 Ge 57.48N 114.05 E
Mamantel 192 Nh 18.33N 91.05W
Mamanuca Group 219d Ab 17.34 S 177.04 E
Mamaqān 146 Kd 37.51N 45.59 E
Mambaj 204 Ib 14.28 S 46.07W
Mambajao 150 He 9.15N 124.43 E
Mambasa 170 Eb 1.21N 29.03 E
Mambéré 168 Bc 3.31N 16.03 E
Mambili 170 Cb 0.07N 16.08 E
Mamborê 204 Fg 24.18 S 52.32W
Mambova 170 Ef 17.44 S 25.11 E
Mambrui 170 Hc 3.07 S 40.09 E
Mamedkala 132 Ph 42.12N 48.06 E
Mamer 124 Ie 49.38N 6.02 E
Mamers 122 Gf 48.21N 0.23 E
Mamfe 166 Gg 5.46N 9.17 E
Mamiá, Lago- 202 Fd 4.15 S 63.05W
Mamisonski, pereval- 132 Mh 42.43N 43.45 E
Mamljutka 136 Ga 54.57N 68.35 E
Mammoth Cave 184 Dg 37.10N 86.08W
Mammoth Hot Springs 188 Id 44.59N 110.43W
Mamonovo 120 Pb 54.28N 19.57 E
Mamoré, Río- 198 Gg 10.23 S 65.53W
Mamou 160 Fg 10.23N 12.05W
Mamoutzou 172 Hb 12.47 S 45.14 E
Mampikony 172 Hc 16.05 S 47.37 E
Mampodre, Picos de- 126 Ga 43.02N 5.12W
Mampong 166 Ed 7.04N 1.24W
Mamry, Jezioro- 120 Rb 54.08N 21.42 E
Mamuju 150 Gg 2.41 S 118.54 E
Mamuno 172 Cd 22.17 S 20.02 E
Ma'mūrah, Ra's al- 128 En 36.27N 10.49 E
Mamurokawa 156 Gb 38.54N 140.15 E
Man 160 Gh 7.24N 7.33W
Man 166 Dd 7.13N 7.41W
Man, Calf of- 118 Ig 54.03N 4.48W
Man, Isle of- 118 Ig 54.15N 4.30W
Mana 214 Oc 22.02N 159.46W
Mana 138 Ge 55.57N 92.28 E
Manacapuru 202 Fd 3.18 S 60.37W
Manacor 126 Pe 39.34N 3.13 E
Manado 142 Oi 1.29N 124.51 E
Managua 176 Kh 12.09N 86.17W
Managua 194 Dg 12.20N 86.20W
Managua, Lago de- 190 Gf 12.20N 86.20W
Manakara 172 He 22.07 S 48.00 E
Manam 208 Fe 4.05 S 145.03 E
Manamo, Caño- 202 Fb 9.55N 62.16W
Manananara 172 Hc 16.10 S 49.45 E
Mananara 172 Hd 23.21 S 47.42 E
Mananjary 172 He 21.14 S 48.17 E
Manankoro 166 Dc 10.28N 7.25W
Manantenina 172 Hd 24.17 S 47.18 E
Manaoba 219a Ec 8.06 S 160.49 E
Manapire, Río- 196 Ci 7.42N 66.07W
Manapouri, Lake- 218 Bf 45.30 S 167.30 E
Manāşir 144 Fe 24.10N 53.40 E
Manār, Jabal- 144 Fg 14.10N 44.17 E
Manas 142 Ff 44.18N 86.13 E
Manas, gora- 135 Id 42.18N 71.06 E
Manas Hu 152 Fb 45.38N 85.12 E
Manasi 142 Ed 44.10N 86.40 E
Manasquan 184 Je 40.08N 74.03W
Manati 194 Ic 21.19N 76.56W
Manatí 218 Ea 34.59 S 173.32 E
Manatuto 150 Hj 8.30 S 126.01 E
Manaure 194 Kh 11.46N 72.28W
Manaus 200 Jf 3.08 S 60.01W
Manavgat 146 Dd 36.47N 31.26 E
Manbij [Syr.] 146 Gd 36.31N 37.57 E
Manbij [Syr.] 148 Fe 16.44N 77.59 E
Mancelona 184 Dc 44.54N 85.04W
Mancha Real 126 Ig 37.47N 3.37W
Manche 122 Ee 49.00N 1.10W
Mancheng 154 Ic 38.57N 115.19 E
Manchester [Ct.-U.S.] 184 Ke 41.47N 72.31W
Manchester [Eng.-U.K.] 110 Ge 53.30N 2.15W
Manchester [Ia.-U.S.] 186 Ke 42.29N 91.27W
Manchester [Ky.-U.S.] 184 Dg 37.09N 83.46W
Manchester [N.H.-U.S.] 176 Mc 42.59N 71.28W
Manchester [Tn.-U.S.] 184 Ch 35.29N 86.05W
Manchok 166 Gd 9.06N 8.31 E
Manchuria (EN) 140 Oe 47.00N 125.00 E
Manciano 128 Fg 42.35N 11.31 E
Mand 144 Gd 28.11N 51.17 E
Manda [Chad] 168 Bb 9.11N 18.13 E
Manda [Tan.] 170 Fe 10.30 S 34.35 E
Manda, Jabal- 168 Cc 8.39N 24.27 E
Mandabe 172 Gd 21.02 S 44.55 E
Mandaguari 204 Fg 23.32 S 51.42W
Manda Island 170 Hc 2.17 S 40.57 E
Mandal 114 Ag 58.02N 7.27 E
Mandalay 140 Lg 22.00N 96.06 E
Mandal-Gobi 142 Me 45.45N 106.12 E
Mandalī 146 Je 33.45N 45.33 E
Mandalselva 116 Bf 58.02N 7.28 E
Mandan 182 Gb 46.50N 100.54W
Mandal → Sonid Zuoqi 152 Ib 43.50N 113.45 E
Mandar 150 Gg 3.30 S 119.00 E
Mandara, Monts- = Mandara Mountains (EN) 166 Hc 10.45N 13.40 E

Mandara Mountains (EN) = Mandara, Monts- 166 Hc 10.45N 13.40 E
Mandas 128 Dk 39.38N 9.07 E
Mandasor 148 Fd 24.04N 75.04 E
Mandera 148 Lh 3.56N 41.52 E
Manderscheid 124 Id 50.06N 6.49 E
Mandi 194 Id 18.02N 77.30W
Mandi 148 Fb 31.43N 76.55 E
Mandiana 166 Dc 10.38N 8.41W
Mandimba 172 Fb 14.21 S 35.39 E
Mandingues, Monts- 166 Cc 13.00N 11.00W
Mandioli, Pulau- 150 Ig 0.44 S 127.14 E
Mandioré, Laguna- 204 Dd 18.08 S 57.33W
Mandritsa 204 Rq 25.46 S 49.19W
Mandø 116 Ci 55.15N 8.35 E
Mandoudhíon 130 Gk 38.48N 23.29 E
Mandrákion 130 Km 36.36N 27.08 E
Mandritsara 172 Hc 15.49 S 48.48 E
Mandurah 212 Df 32.32 S 115.43 E
Manduria 128 Lj 40.24N 17.38 E
Māndvi 148 Dd 22.50N 69.22 E
Mandya 148 Ff 12.33N 76.54 E
Māne 116 Ce 59.56N 8.48 E
Mãneciu Ungureni 130 Id 45.19N 25.59 E
Manendragarh 148 Gd 23.10N 82.35 E
Maneromango 170 Gd 7.16 S 38.46 E
Manevici 132 Dd 51.19N 25.33 E
Manfalūṭ 164 Fd 27.19N 30.58 E
Manfredonia 128 Ji 41.38N 15.55 E
Manfredonia, Golfo di- 128 Ki 41.35N 16.05 E
Manga [Afr.] 158 Ig 15.00N 14.00 E
Manga [Braz.] 202 Jf 14.46 S 43.56W
Mangabeiras, Chapada das- 198 Lg 10.00 S 46.30W
Mangai 170 Cc 4.03 S 19.35 E
Mangaia Island 208 Lg 21.55 S 157.55W
Mangakino 218 Fc 38.22 S 175.46 E
Mangalia 130 If 43.48N 28.35 E
Mangalmé 168 Bc 12.21N 19.37 E
Mangalore 142 Jh 12.52N 74.53 E
Mangareva, Ile- 208 Ng 23.07 S 134.57W
Mangfall 120 Li 47.51N 12.08 E
Manggar 150 Fg 2.53 S 108.16 E
Manggawitu 219a Dd 11.30 S 159.59 E
Mangin Yoma 148 Jd 24.20N 95.42 E
Mangistau 132 Qg 44.03N 51.57 E
Mangit 136 Gg 42.07N 60.01 E
Mangkalihat, Tanjung- 150 Gf 1.02N 118.59 E
Manglares, Cabo- 202 Cc 1.36N 79.02W
Mangnai 152 Fd 37.48N 91.55 E
Mangniu He 154 Ib 45.10N 126.58 E
Mango [Fiji] 219d Cb 17.27 S 179.09W
Mango [Ton.] 221b Bb 20.20 S 174.43W
Mangoche 170 Fe 14.28 S 35.16 E
Mangoky [Mad.] 158 Lk 21.29 S 43.41 E
Mangoky [Mad.] 172 Hd 23.27 S 45.13 E
Mangole, Pulau- 150 Ig 1.53 S 125.50 E
Mangonui 218 Ea 34.59 S 173.32 E
Mangrove Cay 194 Ia 24.51N 76.14W
Mangrullo, Cuchilla- 204 Fk 32.27 S 53.50W
Mangshi → Luxi 142 Lg 24.29N 98.40 E
Mangualde 126 Ed 40.36N 7.46W
Mangueira, Lagoa- 206 Jd 33.06 S 52.48W
Mangueni, Plateau de- 158 Hf 22.35N 12.40 E
Mangula 172 Hd 24.17 S 47.18 E
Mangum 152 Le 52.03N 122.09 E
Mangyšlak 172 Ec 16.52 S 30.08 E
Mangum 186 Gi 34.53N 99.30W
Manguredjipa 170 Eb 0.21N 28.44 E
Mangyšlak 136 Fg 43.40N 51.15 E
Mangyšlak, plato- 136 Fg 43.25N 53.00 E
Mangyšlakskaja oblast 136 Fg 44.00N 53.00 E
Mangyšlakski zaliv 132 Qg 44.45N 51.00 E
Manhattan 182 Hd 39.11N 96.35W
Manhica 156 Js 25.24 S 32.48 E
Mani 170 Ed 6.27 S 25.20 E
Mani 202 Dc 4.49N 72.17W
Māni', Wādī al- 146 Ge 34.16N 41.02 E
Mania 172 Hd 19.42 S 45.22 E
Maniago 128 Gd 46.10N 12.43 E
Manica 172 Ee 18.56 S 32.53 E
Manicoré 202 Gd 5.49 S 61.17W
Manicoré, Rio- 202 Fe 5.51 S 61.19W
Manicouagan 180 Kf 51.00N 68.20W
Manicouagan 174 Hd 51.00N 68.15W
Manicouagan, Réservoir- 176 Mc 51.30N 68.19W
Manigotagan 186 Ha 51.06N 96.18W
Manihi Atoll 208 Mf 14.24 S 145.56W
Manihiki Anchorage 221a Bb 10.24 S 161.01W
Manihiki Atoll 208 Le 10.24 S 161.01W
Manika, Plateau de la- 170 Ed 10.00 S 26.00W
Manila [Phil.] 142 Oh 14.35N 121.00 E
Manila [Ut.-U.S.] 188 Jf 40.59N 109.43W
Manila Bay 150 Ha 14.30N 120.45 E
Manilaid/Manilaijd 116 Kf 58.08N 24.03 E
Manilaijd/Manilaid 116 Kf 58.08N 24.03 E
Manily 138 Ld 62.30N 165.20 E
Maningrida Settlement 212 Gb 12.05 S 134.10 E
Maniouro, Pointe- 219b Dc 17.41 S 168.26 E
Manipa, Selat- 150 Ig 3.20 S 127.23 E
Manipur 148 Jd 24.00N 94.00 E
Manisa 142 Cf 38.36N 27.26 E
Manisa Daği 146 Cc 38.33N 27.28 E
Manises 126 Ke 39.29N 0.27W
Manissauá-Missu, Rio- 202 Hf 10.34 S 53.23W
Manistee 184 Cc 44.15N 86.19W
Manistee River 184 Cc 44.15N 86.21W
Manistique 184 Cb 45.57N 86.15W
Manito Lake 180 Fe 52.43N 109.43W
Manitoba 174 Gc 55.00N 97.00W
Manitoba 180 Ge 50.00N 98.00W
Manitoba, Lake- 174 Gd 51.00N 98.45W
Manitou Islands 184 Cc 45.05N 86.00W
Manitou Lake 184 Gc 45.50N 82.00W
Manitoulin Island 180 Jg 45.45N 82.30W

Index Symbols

- Independent Nation
- State, Region
- District, County
- Municipality
- Colony, Dependency
- Continent
- Physical Region
- Historical or Cultural Region
- Mount, Mountain
- Volcano
- Hill
- Mountains, Mountain Range
- Hills, Escarpment
- Plateau, Upland
- Pass, Gap
- Plain, Lowland
- Delta
- Salt Flat
- Valley, Canyon
- Crater, Cave
- Karst Features
- Depression
- Polder
- Desert, Dunes
- Forest, Woods
- Heath, Steppe
- Oasis
- Cape, Point
- Coast, Beach
- Cliff
- Peninsula
- Sandbank
- Island
- Rock, Reef
- Islands, Archipelago
- Rocks, Reefs
- Coral Reef
- Well, Spring
- Geyser
- River, Stream
- Waterfall, Rapids
- River Mouth, Estuary
- Lake
- Salt Lake
- Intermittent Lake
- Reservoir
- Swamp, Pond
- Canal
- Glacier
- Ice Shelf, Pack Ice
- Ocean
- Sea
- Gulf, Bay
- Strait, Fjord
- Lagoon
- Bank
- Seamount
- Tablemount
- Ridge
- Shelf
- Basin
- Escarpment, Sea Scarp
- Fracture
- Trench, Abyss
- National Park, Reserve
- Point of Interest
- Recreation Site
- Cave, Cavern
- Historic Site
- Ruins
- Wall, Walls
- Church, Abbey
- Temple
- Scientific Station
- Railway station
- Airport
- Port
- Lighthouse
- Mine
- Tunnel
- Dam, Bridge

Manitou Springs 186 Dg 38.52N 104.55W
Manitouwadge 186 Nb 49.08N 85.47W
Manitowoc 182 Jc 44.06N 87.40W
Manitsoq/Sukkertoppen 186 Md 65.25N 53.00W
Maniwaki 180 Jg 46.23N 75.58W
Manizales 200 Ie 5.05N 75.32W
Manja 172 Gd 21.23S 44.20 E
Manja 134 Jd 64.23N 60.50 E
Manjača 128 Lf 44.35N 17.05 E
Manjacaze 172 Ed 24.42S 33.33 E
Manjakandriana 172 Hc 18.55S 47.47 E
Manji 156a Bb 43.09N 141.59 E
Manjīl 144 Gb 36.44N 49.24 E
Manjimup 212 Df 34.14S 116.09 E
Mānjra 148 Fe 18.49N 77.52 E
Mān Kāt 148 Jd 22.05N 98.01 E
Mankato [Ks.-U.S.] 186 Gg 39.47N 98.12W
Mankato [Mn.-U.S.] 182 Ic 44.10N 94.01W
Mankono 166 Dd 8.04N 6.12W
Mankono [3] 166 Dd 7.58N 6.02W
Mankoya 160 Jj 14.50S 25.00 E
Manley Hot Springs 178 Ic 65.00N 150.37W
Manlleu 126 Ob 42.00N 2.17 E
Manmād 148 Ed 20.15N 74.27 E
Manmanoc, Mount- 150 Hc 17.40N 121.06 E
Manna 150 Dh 4.27S 102.55 E
Mannahill 212 Hf 32.26S 139.59 E
Mannar 148 Fg 8.59N 79.54 E
Mannar, Gulf of- 140 Ji 8.30N 79.00 E
Mannheim 112 Gf 49.29N 8.28 E
Manning [Alta.-Can.] 180 Fe 56.55N 117.33W
Manning [S.C.-U.S.] 184 Gi 33.42N 80.12W
Manning, Cape- 220g Ba 2.02N 157.26W
Manning Strait 219a Db 7.24S 158.04 E
Manningtree 124 Dc 51.57N 1.04 E
Mann Ranges 212 Fe 26.00S 129.30 E
Mann River 212 Gb 12.20S 134.07 E
Mannu, Capo- 128 Cj 40.02N 8.22 E
Mannu, Rio- [It.] 128 Cj 40.50N 8.23 E
Mannu, Rio- [It.] 128 Cj 40.41N 8.59 E
Mano 166 Cd 6.56N 11.31W
Mano [Jap.] 156 Fc 37.58N 138.20 E
Mano [S.L.] 166 Cd 7.55N 12.00W
Manoa 202 Ee 9.40S 65.27W
Man of War, Cayos- 194 Fg 13.02N 83.22W
Manokwari 210 Ee 2.30S 134.36 E
Manombo 172 Gd 22.55S 43.28 E
Manompana 172 Hc 16.41S 49.45 E
Manonga 170 Fc 4.08S 34.12 E
Manono 160 Ji 7.18S 27.25 E
Manono 221c Aa 13.50S 172.05W
Manosque 122 Lk 43.50N 5.47 E
Manouane, Lac- 180 Kf 50.40N 70.45W
Mano-Wan 156 Fc 37.55N 138.15 E
Manp'ojin 154 Id 41.09N 126.17 E
Manra Atoll (Sydney) 208 Je 4.27S 171.15W
Manresa 126 Nc 41.44N 1.50 E
Mans, Le- 112 Gf 48.00N 0.12 E
Mansa 160 Jj 11.12S 28.53 E
Mansa Konko 166 Bc 13.28N 15.33W
Mansel 174 Lc 62.00N 79.50W
Mansfield [Austl.] 212 Jg 37.03S 146.05 E
Mansfield [Eng.-U.K.] 118 Lh 53.09N 1.11W
Mansfield [La.-U.S.] 186 Jj 32.02N 93.43W
Mansfield [Oh.-U.S.] 182 Kc 40.46N 82.31W
Mansfield [Pa.-U.S.] 184 Ie 41.47N 77.05W
Mansfield, Mount- 184 Kc 44.33N 72.49W
Mansle 122 Gi 45.52N 0.11 E
Manso, Rio- 204 Db 14.42S 56.16W
Manso, Rio- ou Mortes, Rio das- 198 Kg 11.45S 50.44W
Mansôa 166 Bc 12.04N 15.19W
Mansourah 126 Qh 36.04N 4.28 E
Mansourah, Djebel- 126 Qh 36.02N 4.28 E
Manta 202 Bd 0.57S 80.42W
Manta, Bahia de- 202 Bd 0.50S 80.40W
Mantalingajan, Mount- 150 Ge 8.48N 117.40 E
Manteca 188 Eh 37.48N 121.13W
Mantecal [Ven.] 196 Bi 7.33N 69.09W
Mantecal [Ven.] 196 Di 6.52N 65.38W
Manteigas 126 Ed 40.24N 7.32W
Manteo 184 Jh 35.55N 75.40W
Mantes-la-Jolie 122 Hf 48.59N 1.43 E
Manti 188 Jg 39.16N 111.38W
Mantiqueira, Serra da- 198 Lh 22.00S 44.45W
Manto 194 Df 14.55N 86.23W
Manton 184 Ec 44.24N 85.24W
Mantova 128 Ee 45.09N 10.48 E
Mäntsälä 116 Kd 60.38N 25.20 E
Mänttä 114 Fe 62.02N 24.38 E
Mantua 194 Eb 22.17N 84.17W
Manturovo 136 Ed 58.22N 44.44 E
Mäntyharju 114 Gf 61.25N 26.53 E
Mäntyluoto 116 Ic 61.35N 21.29 E
Manu 202 Df 12.15S 70.50W
Manuae Atoll [Cook] 208 Lf 19.21S 158.56W
Manuae Atoll [Fr.Poly.] 208 Lf 16.32S 154.38W
Manua Islands 208 Kf 14.13S 169.35W
Manuangi Atoll 208 Mf 19.12S 141.16W
Manūbah 128 En 36.48N 10.06 E
Manuel 192 Jf 22.44N 98.19W
Manuel Alves, Rio- 202 If 11.19S 48.28W
Manuel Benavides 192 Hc 29.05N 103.55W
Manuel Derqui 204 Ch 27.50S 58.48W
Manuel J. Cobo 204 Dl 35.49S 57.54W
Manuel Ocampo 204 Bk 33.46S 60.39W
Manuga Reefs 219a Ad 11.00S 153.21 E
Manui, Pulau- 150 Hg 3.35S 123.08 E
Manujān 146 Qi 27.24N 57.32 E
Mānūk, Tell- 146 Hf 33.10N 38.50 E
Manukau 210 Ih 36.56S 174.56 E
Manulu Lagoon 220g Bb 1.56N 157.20W
Manus Island 208 Fe 2.05S 147.00 E
Many 186 Jk 31.34N 93.29W
Manyara, Lake- 170 Gc 3.35S 35.50 E
Manyas 146 Bb 40.02N 27.58 E
Manyč 110 Kf 47.15N 40.00 E
Manyč-Gudilo, ozero- 110 Kf 46.25N 42.35 E
Manyoni 170 Fd 5.45S 34.50 E
Manzanal, Puerto del- 126 Fb 42.32N 6.10W
Manzanares 126 Ie 39.00N 3.22W
Manzaneda, Cabeza de- 126 Eb 42.20N 7.15W
Manzanilla 126 Fg 37.23N 6.25W
Manzanillo [Cuba] 176 Lg 20.21N 77.07W
Manzanillo [Mex.] 176 Ih 19.03N 104.20W
Manzanillo, Bahía de- [Dom.Rep.] 194 Ld 19.45N 71.46W
Manzanillo, Bahía de- [Mex.] 192 Gh 19.04N 104.25W
Manzanillo, Punta- 194 Hi 9.38N 79.32W
Manzano Mountains 186 Ci 34.45N 106.20W
Manzhouli 142 Ne 49.33N 117.28 E
Manzilah, Buḩayrat al- 146 Eg 31.15N 32.00 E
Manzil Bū Ruqaybah 162 Ib 37.10N 9.48 E
Manzil bū Zalafah 128 En 36.41N 10.35 E
Manzil Tamīn 128 En 36.47N 10.59 E
Manzini 172 Ee 26.29S 31.22 E
Mao 219b Dc 17.29S 168.29 E
Mao [Chad] 160 Ig 14.07N 15.19 E
Mao [Dom.Rep.] 190 Je 19.34N 71.05W
Maó / Mahón 126 Qe 39.53N 4.15 E
Maoke, Pegunungan- 150 Kg 4.00S 138.00 E
Maomao Shan 152 Hd 37.12N 103.10 E
Maoming 142 Ng 21.41N 110.52 E
Maoniu Shan 152 He 32.50N 104.12 E
Maotou Shan 152 Hg 24.31N 100.38 E
Maouri, Dallol- 166 Fc 12.05N 3.32 E
Mapai 172 Ed 22.51S 31.58 E
Mapanda 170 Dd 9.32S 24.16 E
Mapati 170 Bc 3.38S 13.21 E
Mapi 210 Ee 7.07S 139.23 E
Mapi 150 Kh 7.00S 139.16 E
Mapia, Kepulauan- 208 Ed 0.50N 134.20 E
Mapimí, Bolsón de- 174 Ig 27.30N 103.15W
Mapinhane 172 Fd 22.15S 35.07 E
Mapire 196 Di 7.45N 64.42W
Mapiri 202 Eg 15.15S 68.10W
Maple Creek 180 Gg 49.55N 109.27W
Maprik 214 Ch 3.38S 143.03 E
Mapuera, Rio- 202 Gd 1.05S 57.02W
Maputo [3] 172 Ee 26.00S 32.30 E
Maputo (Lourenço Marques) 160 Kk 25.58S 32.34 E
Maputo, Baía de- 158 Kk 26.05S 33.00 E
Maqèn (Dawu) 152 He 34.29N 100.01 E
Maqran, Wādī al- 164 Ie 20.55N 47.12 E
Maqu 152 He 34.05N 101.45 E
Maquan He/Damqog Kanbab 152 Df 29.36N 84.09 E
Maquela do Zombo 160 Ii 6.03S 15.08 E
Maquinchao 206 Gf 41.15S 68.44W
Maquoketa 186 Ke 42.04N 90.40W
Mar, Serra do- 198 Lh 25.00S 48.00W
Mara [3] 170 Fc 2.30S 34.00 E
Mara 170 Fc 1.31S 33.56 E
Maraã 202 Ed 1.50S 65.22W
Marab 168 Fc 14.54N 37.55 E
Marabá 202 Ie 5.21S 49.07W
Marabahan 150 Fg 3.00S 114.45 E
Marabá Paulista 204 Gf 22.06S 51.56W
Maracá, Ilha de- 202 Hc 2.05N 50.25W
Maracaibo 200 Id 10.40N 71.37W
Maracaibo, Lago de- = Maracaibo, Lake- (EN) 198 Ie 9.50N 71.30W
Maracaibo, Lake- (EN) = Maracaibo, Lago de- 198 Ie 9.50N 71.30W
Maracaju 202 Gh 21.38S 55.09W
Maracaju, Serra de- [Braz.] 198 Kh 21.00S 55.00W
Maracaju, Serra de- [S.Amer.] 204 Ef 23.57S 55.01W
Maracanã 202 Id 0.46S 47.27W
Maracás 202 Jf 13.26S 40.27W
Maracay 200 Jd 10.15N 67.36W
Marādah 164 Cd 29.14N 19.13 E
Maradi 160 Hg 13.29N 7.06 E
Maradi [2] 166 Gc 14.15N 7.15 E
Marāgheh 144 Gb 37.23N 46.40 E
Marāh 144 Gd 25.04N 45.28 E
Maraho 168 Bb 18.21N 17.28 E
Marahuaca, Cerro- 198 Je 3.34N 65.27W
Marajó, Baía de- 198 Lf 1.00S 48.30W
Marajó, Ilha de- 198 Lf 1.00S 49.30W
Marakei Atoll 208 Id 1.58N 173.25 E
Maralal 170 Gb 1.06N 36.42 E
Maralinga 212 Gf 30.13S 131.35 E
Maralwexi/Bachu 152 Cd 39.46N 78.15 E
Maramag 150 He 7.46N 125.00 E
Maramasike Island 214 Gi 9.30S 161.25 E
Maramba 160 Jj 17.51S 25.52 E
Marampa 166 Cd 8.41N 12.28W
Maramureş [2] 130 Gb 47.40N 24.00 E
Maranchón 126 Jc 41.03N 2.12W
Marānd 144 Gb 38.26N 45.46 E
Marandellas 172 Ec 18.10S 31.36 E
Marang 150 De 5.12N 103.13 E
Maranhão [2] 202 Je 5.00S 45.00W
Maranhão, Rio- 202 If 14.34S 49.02W
Marano, Laguna di- 128 He 45.44N 13.10 E
Maranoa River 212 Je 27.50S 148.37 E
Marañón, Río- 198 If 4.30S 73.35W
Marans 122 Fh 46.18N 1.00W
Marão 172 Ed 24.18S 34.07 E
Marão, Serra do- 126 Ec 41.15N 7.55W
Maraoué 166 Dd 6.54N 5.31W
Marapanim 202 Id 0.42S 47.42W
Marapi, Gunung- 150 Dg 0.23S 100.28 E
Marargiu, Capo- 128 Cj 40.20N 8.23 E
Marari, Serra do- 204 Gh 27.30S 51.00W
Mara Rosa 204 Ha 13.58S 49.09W
Mărăşeşti 130 Kd 45.53N 27.14 E
Maratea 128 Jk 39.59N 15.43 E
Marathon 180 Ig 48.46N 86.26W
Marathon 186 Ek 30.12N 103.15W
Marathón 130 Gk 38.09N 23.58 E
Maratua, Pulau- 150 Gf 2.15N 118.36 E
Marau 204 Fi 28.27S 52.12W
Maravari 219a Cb 7.54S 156.44 E
Marāveh Tappeh 146 Pd 37.55N 55.57 E
Maravilha 204 Fh 26.47S 53.09W
Maravillas Creek 186 El 29.34N 102.47W
Maravovo 219a Dc 9.17S 159.38 E
Marāwah 164 Dc 32.29N 21.25 E
Marawi 150 He 8.13N 124.15 E
Marawī 168 Eb 18.29N 31.49 E
Marāwiḩ 146 Oj 24.18N 53.18 E
Marayes 206 Gd 31.29S 67.20W
Marbella 126 Hh 36.31N 4.53W
Marble Bar 212 Dd 21.11S 119.44 E
Marble Canyon 188 Jh 36.30N 111.50W
Marble Falls 186 Gk 30.34N 98.17W
Marble Hall 172 Dd 24.57S 29.13 E
Marburg 120 Ef 50.49N 8.46 E
Marca, Ponta da- 158 Ij 16.31S 11.42 E
Marcal 120 Ni 47.38N 17.32 E
Marcala 194 Df 14.07N 88.00W
Marçal Dağları 130 Kl 37.09N 28.00 E
Marcali 120 Nj 46.35N 17.25 E
March 118 Ni 52.33N 0.06 E
March 120 Mh 48.10N 16.59 E
Marche 122 Hh 46.10N 1.30 E
Marche = Marches (EN) [2] 128 Hh 43.30N 13.15 E
Marche, Plateau de la- 122 Hh 46.16N 1.30 E
Marche-en-Famenne 122 Ld 50.14N 5.20 E
Marchena 126 Gg 37.20N 5.24W
Marchena, Isla- 202a Aa 0.20N 90.30W
Marches (EN) = Marche [2] 128 Hh 43.30N 13.15 E
Marchesato 128 Kk 39.05N 17.00 E
Marchfeld 128 Kb 48.15N 16.40 E
Mar Chiquita, Laguna- 204 Dm 37.37S 57.24W
Mar Chiquita, Laguna- 198 Ji 30.42S 62.36W
Marciana Marina 128 Eh 42.48N 10.12 E
Marcigny 122 Kh 46.16N 4.02 E
Marcilly-sur-Eure 124 Df 48.49N 1.21 E
Marcinelle, Charleroi- 124 Gd 50.25N 4.28 E
Marck 124 Dd 50.57N 1.57 E
Marcoing 124 Fd 50.07N 3.11 E
Marcos Juaréz 206 Hd 32.42S 62.06W
Marcus Baker, Mount- 178 Jd 61.26N 147.45W
Marcus Island (EN) = Minami-Tori-Shima 208 Gb 26.32N 142.09 E
Marcy, Mount- 182 Mc 44.07N 73.56W
Mardakert 132 Oi 40.12N 46.52 E
Mardakjan 132 Qi 40.29N 50.12 E
Mardān 148 Eb 34.09N 71.52 E
Mardarovka 130 Mb 47.30N 29.40 E
Mar del Plata 200 Ki 38.01S 57.35W
Marden 124 Cc 51.10N 0.30 E
Mardin 144 Fb 37.18N 40.44 E
Mardın Dağları 146 Id 37.20N 41.00 E
Maré, Ile- 208 Hg 21.30S 168.00 E
Mare, Muntele- 130 Gc 46.29N 23.14 E
Marechal Cândido Rondon 204 Eg 24.34S 54.04W
Maree, Loch- 118 Hd 57.40N 5.30W
Mareeba 212 Jc 17.00S 145.26 E
Mārēg 168 He 3.47N 47.18 E
Maremma 128 Fh 42.30N 11.30 E
Marennes 122 Ei 45.49N 1.07W
Marettimo 128 Gm 37.56N 12.05 E
Mareuil-en-Brie 124 Ff 48.57N 3.45 E
Marfa 182 Ge 30.18N 104.01W
Marfil, Laguna- 204 Bb 15.30S 60.20W
Margai Caka 152 Ed 35.10N 86.55 E
Marganec 136 Df 47.38N 34.40 E
Margaret River 212 Df 33.57S 115.04 E
Margarida 204 De 21.41S 56.44W
Margarita, Isla- 202 Fa 11.00N 64.00W
Margarita Belén 204 Ch 27.16S 58.58W
Margarítion 130 Dj 39.21N 20.26 E
Margate [Eng.-U.K.] 118 Oj 51.24N 1.24 E
Margate [S.Afr.] 172 Ef 30.55S 30.15 E
Margeride, Monts de la- 122 Jj 44.50N 3.25 E
Marghera, Venezia- 128 Ge 45.28N 12.44 E
Margherita di Savoia 128 Ki 41.22N 16.09 E
Margherita Peak 158 Kh 0.22N 29.51 E
Marghine, Catena del- 128 Cj 40.20N 8.50 E
Marghita 130 Fb 47.21N 22.20 E
Marghūb, Kūh-e- 146 Qf 33.06N 57.30 E
Margilan 136 Hg 40.28N 71.46 E
Margina 130 Fd 45.51N 22.16 E
Marguerite Bay 222 Qe 68.30S 68.30W
Margut 124 He 49.35N 5.16 E
Marha 138 Hd 60.35N 123.10 E
Marha 140 Nc 63.20N 118.50 E
Mari 146 Ee 34.44N 33.18 E
Mari 146 Ie 34.39N 40.53 E
Maria Atoll [Fr.Poly.] 208 Ng 22.00S 136.10W
Maria Atoll [Fr.Poly.] 208 Lg 21.48S 154.41W
Maria Cleofas, Isla- 192 Fg 21.16N 106.14W
Maria Elena 206 Gb 22.21S 69.40W
Mariager 116 Ch 56.39N 10.00 E
Mariager Fjord 116 Dh 56.40N 10.20 E
María Grande, Arroyo- 204 Ci 29.21S 58.45W
María Ignacia 204 Cm 37.24S 59.30W
Maria Island [Austl.] 212 Jh 42.40S 148.05 E
Maria Island [Austl.] 212 Hb 14.55S 135.40 E
Maria Island [St.Luc.] 197k Bb 13.44N 60.56W
Mariakani 170 Gc 3.52S 39.28 E
Maria Laach 124 Jd 50.25N 7.15 E
María Madre, Isla- 192 Fg 21.35N 106.33W
María Magdalena, Isla- 192 Fg 21.25N 106.25W
Mariana Islands 208 Fc 16.00N 145.30 E
Marianao 190 Hd 23.05N 82.26W
Mariana Trench (EN) 106 Ih 14.00N 147.30 E
Marianna [Ar.-U.S.] 186 Ki 34.46N 90.46W
Marianna [Fl.-U.S.] 184 Ej 30.47N 85.14W
Mariannelund 116 Fg 57.37N 15.34 E
Mariano I. Loza 204 Ci 29.22S 58.12W
Mariánské Lázně 120 Ig 49.58N 12.43 E
Marías, Islas- 174 Ig 21.25N 106.28W
Marias Pass 188 Ib 48.19N 113.21W
Marias River 182 Eb 47.56N 110.30W
Maria Theresa Reef 208 Lh 36.58S 151.23W
Mariato, Punta- 190 Hg 7.13N 80.53W
Maria van Diemen, Cape- 218 Ea 34.29S 172.39 E
Mariazell 128 Jc 47.46N 15.19 E
Ma'rib 144 Gf 15.30N 45.21 E
Maribo 116 Dj 54.46N 11.31 E
Maribor 128 Jd 46.33N 15.39 E
Marica 130 Ig 42.02N 25.50 E
Marica 110 Ig 40.52N 26.12 E
Maricao 197a Bb 18.10N 66.58W
Maricopa 188 Ij 33.04N 112.03W
Marīdī 168 De 4.55N 29.28 E
Marīdī 168 Dd 6.05N 29.24 E
Marié, Rio- 202 Ed 0.25S 66.26W
Marie Byrd Land (EN) 222 Nf 80.00S 120.00W
Mariec 114 Lh 56.31N 49.51 E
Marie Galante 190 Le 15.56N 61.16W
Marie-Galante, Canal de- 197e Bc 15.55N 61.25W
Mariehamn/Maarianhamina 114 Ef 60.06N 19.57 E
Marie Louise Island 172b Bb 6.11S 53.09 E
Mariembourg, Couvin- 124 Gd 50.06N 4.31 E
Marienburg 124 Jd 50.04N 7.08 E
Marienmünster 124 Lc 51.50N 9.13 E
Marienstatt 124 Jd 50.40N 7.49 E
Mariental 160 Ik 24.36S 17.59 E
Mariestad 114 Cg 58.43N 13.51 E
Marietta [Ga.-U.S.] 182 Ke 33.57N 84.33W
Marietta [Oh.-U.S.] 184 Gf 39.26N 81.27W
Mariga 166 Gd 9.36N 5.57 E
Marignac 122 Gl 42.55N 0.39 E
Marignane 122 Lk 43.25N 5.13 E
Marigot [Dom.] 196 Fe 15.32N 61.18W
Marigot [Guad.] 196 Ec 18.04N 63.06W
Marigot [Haiti] 194 Kd 18.14N 72.19W
Marigot [Mart.] 197h Ab 14.49N 61.02W
Marigot [St.Luc.] 197k Ab 13.58N 61.02W
Mariinsk 138 De 56.13N 87.45 E
Mariinski Posad 114 Lh 56.08N 47.48 E
Mariinskoje 138 Jf 51.43N 140.19 E
Marijovo 130 Eh 41.04N 21.45 E
Marijskaja ASSR [3] 136 Ed 56.40N 48.00 E
Marília 206 Jb 22.13S 50.01W
Mariluz 204 Fg 24.02S 53.13W
Marimba 170 Cd 8.22S 17.02 E
Marimbondo, Cachoeira do- 204 He 20.18S 49.10W
Marín 126 Db 42.23N 8.42W
Marin, Cul-de-Sac du- 197h Bc 14.27N 60.53W
Marina di Catanzaro, Catanzaro- 128 Kl 38.49N 16.36 E
Marina di Gioiosa Ionica 128 Kl 38.18N 16.20 E
Marina di Leuca, Castrignano del Capo- 128 Mk 39.48N 18.21 E
Marina di Pisa 128 Eg 43.40N 10.16 E
Marina di Ravenna 128 Gf 44.29N 12.17 E
Marina Gorka 136 Ce 53.31N 28.12 E
Marinduque 150 Hd 13.24N 121.58 E
Marineland 184 Gk 29.43N 81.12W
Marines 124 De 49.09N 1.59 E
Marinette 182 Jb 45.06N 87.38W
Maringá 200 Kh 23.25S 51.55W
Maringa 158 Ih 1.14N 19.48 E
Marinha Grande 126 De 39.45N 8.56W
Marino [It.] 128 Gi 41.46N 12.39 E
Marino [Van.] 219b Db 14.59S 168.03 E
Marins, Pico dos- 204 Jf 22.27S 45.10W
Marinsko 116 Mf 58.46N 28.39 E
Marion 158 Km 46.36S 37.55 E
Marion [Al.-U.S.] 184 Di 32.32N 87.26W
Marion [Ia.-U.S.] 186 Ke 42.02N 91.36W
Marion [Il.-U.S.] 186 Lh 37.44N 88.56W
Marion [In.-U.S.] 184 Ee 40.33N 85.40W
Marion [Oh.-U.S.] 182 Kc 40.35N 83.08W
Marion [S.C.-U.S.] 184 Hh 34.11N 79.23W
Marion [Va.-U.S.] 184 Gg 36.51N 81.30W
Marion, Lake- 184 Gi 33.30N 80.25W
Marion Reefs 208 Gf 19.10S 152.20 E
Maripa 202 Eb 7.26N 65.09W
Mariposa 188 Fh 37.29N 119.58W
Mariquita, Cerro- 192 Jf 23.13N 98.22W
Marisa 150 Hf 0.28N 121.56 E
Mariscala 204 El 34.03S 54.47W
Mariscal Estigarribia 206 Hb 22.02S 60.38W
Marismas, Puerto de las- 126 Ff 38.02N 6.12W
Maritime 166 Fd 6.30N 1.20 E
Mariupol' 112 Jf 47.06N 37.33 E
Mariusa, Caño 196 Fh 9.43N 61.26W
Mariusa, Isla- 196 Fh 9.39N 61.19W
Marīvan 146 Le 35.31N 46.10 E
Marjamaa/Märjamaa 116 Kf 58.54N 24.21 E
Märjamaa/Marjamaa 116 Kf 58.54N 24.21 E
Marjanovka [R.S.F.S.R.] 136 He 54.58N 72.38 E
Marjanovka [Ukr.-U.S.S.R.] 120 Uf 50.23N 24.55 E
Mark 124 Gc 51.39N 4.39 E
Mark [F.R.G.] 124 Jc 51.13N 7.36 E
Mark [Swe.] 116 Eg 57.35N 12.35 E
Marka 160 Lh 1.43N 44.46 E
Markako, ozero- 136 If 48.45N 85.50 E
Markala 166 Dc 13.39N 6.05W
Markam (Gartog) 152 Gf 29.32N 98.33 E
Markaryd 114 Ch 56.26N 13.36 E
Markazi [3] 144 Hb 35.30N 51.30 E
Marken 124 Hb 52.27N 5.05 E
Markerwaard 124 Hb 52.31N 5.15 E
Market Deeping 124 Bb 52.40N 0.18W
Market Harborough 118 Mi 52.29N 0.55W
Markham, Mount- 222 Kg 82.51S 161.21 E
Markham Bay 180 Kd 63.30N 71.40W
Markham River 212 Ja 6.35S 146.25 E
Marki 120 Rd 52.20N 21.07 E
Märkische Schweiz 120 Jd 52.35N 14.00 E
Markit 152 Cd 38.53N 77.35 E
Markounda 168 Bd 7.37N 16.59 E
Markovac 130 Ee 44.14N 21.06 E
Markovka 132 Ke 49.31N 39.32 E
Markovo 142 Tc 64.40N 170.25 E
Markoye 166 Fc 14.39N 0.02 E
Marksburg 124 Jd 50.16N 7.40 E
Marksville 186 Jk 31.08N 92.04W
Marktoberdorf 120 Gi 47.47N 10.37 E
Marktredwitz 120 If 50.00N 12.05 E
Markulešty 130 Lb 47.51N 28.07 E
Marl 120 De 51.39N 7.05 E
Marlagne 124 Gd 50.25N 4.40 E
Marlborough [2] 218 Ed 41.50S 173.40 E
Marlborough [Austl.] 212 Jd 22.49S 149.53 E
Marlborough [Guy.] 196 Gi 7.29N 58.38W
Marle 122 Je 49.44N 3.46 E
Marlin 186 Hk 31.18N 96.53W
Marlinton 184 Gf 38.14N 80.06W
Marlow [Eng.-U.K.] 124 Bc 51.34N 0.46W
Marlow [Ok.-U.S.] 186 Hi 34.39N 97.57W
Marmande 122 Gj 44.30N 0.10 E
Marmara 146 Bb 40.35N 27.33 E
Marmara, Sea of- (EN) = Marmara Denizi 110 Ig 40.40N 28.15 E
Marmara Adası 146 Bb 40.38N 27.37 E
Marmara Denizi = Marmara, Sea of- (EN) 110 Ig 40.40N 28.15 E
Marmara Ereğlisi 130 Ki 40.58N 27.57 E
Marmara Gölü 130 Lk 38.37N 28.02 E
Marmarica (EN) = Barqah al Bahrīyah 158 Je 31.40N 24.30 E
Marmaris 144 Cb 36.51N 28.16 E
Marmelos, Rio dos- 202 Fe 6.08S 61.47W
Marmion Lake 186 Kb 48.54N 91.30W
Marmolada 128 Fd 46.26N 11.51 E
Marmora 184 Ic 44.29N 77.41W
Marmore, Cascata delle- 128 Gh 42.35N 12.45 E
Marne 120 Ec 53.57N 9.00 E
Marne [3] 122 Kf 48.55N 4.10 E
Marne 110 Gf 48.49N 2.24 E
Marne à la Saône, Canal de la- 122 Kf 48.44N 4.36 E
Marne au Rhin, Canal de la- 122 Nf 48.35N 7.47 E
Mårnes 114 Dc 67.09N 14.06 E
Marneuli 132 Ni 41.29N 44.45 E
Maro 168 Bd 8.25N 18.46 E
Maro 168 Bb 19.23N 16.38 E
Maroa 202 Ec 2.43N 67.33W
Maroantsetra 160 Lj 15.27S 49.44 E
Marokau Atoll 216 Mc 18.02S 142.17W
Marolambo 172 Hd 20.04S 48.08 E
Maromandia 172 Hb 14.11S 48.06 E
Maromme 122 He 49.28N 1.02 E
Maromokotro 172 Hb 14.01S 48.58 E
Maroni, Fleuve- 198 Ke 5.45N 53.58W
Marónia 130 Ii 40.55N 25.31 E
Maronne 122 Hi 45.04N 1.56 E
Maroochydore 212 Ke 26.39S 153.06 E
Maro Reef 208 Jb 25.25N 170.35W
Maros 150 Gg 5.00S 119.34 E
Maros 130 Dc 46.15N 20.12 E
Maroua 160 Ig 10.36N 14.20 E
Marovoay 172 Hc 16.06S 46.37 E
Marowijne River 202 Hb 5.45N 53.58W
Marqādah 146 Ie 35.44N 40.46 E
Mar Qu 152 He 31.58N 101.54 E
Marquard 172 De 28.54S 27.28 E
Marquenterre 124 Dd 50.20N 1.41 E
Marquesas Islands (EN) = Marquises, Iles- 208 Ne 9.00S 139.30W
Marquette 182 Jb 46.33N 87.24W
Marquion 124 Fd 50.13N 3.05 E
Marquis [Gren.] 197p Bb 12.06N 61.37W
Marquis [St.Luc.] 197k Ba 14.02N 60.55W
Marquis, Cape- 197k Ba 14.03N 60.54W
Marquise 124 Dd 50.49N 1.42 E
Marquises, Iles- = Marquesas Islands (EN) 208 Ne 9.00S 139.30W
Marracuene 172 Ee 25.44S 32.41 E
Marradi 128 Ff 44.04N 11.37 E
Marrah, Jabal- 158 Jg 13.04N 24.21 E
Marrak 164 Hf 16.26N 41.54 E
Marrakech 160 Ge 31.38N 8.00W
Marrakech [3] 162 Fc 32.00N 8.00W
Marrawah 212 Ih 40.56S 144.41 E
Marree 210 Eg 29.39S 138.04 E
Marreh, Kūh-e- 146 Oh 29.15N 52.20 E
Marrero 186 Kl 29.54N 90.07W
Marresalja 134 Mb 69.44N 66.59 E
Marresalskije Koški, ostrova- 134 Mb 69.30N 67.10 E
Marromeu 172 Fc 18.17S 35.56 E
Marrti 114 Gc 67.28N 28.22 E
Marrupa 172 Fb 13.12S 37.30 E
Marsá al 'Alam 164 Fd 25.05N 34.54 E
Marsá al Burayqah 164 Cc 30.25N 19.35 E
Marsá al Uwayjah 164 Cc 30.55N 17.52 E
Marsa Ben Mehidi 126 Ji 35.05N 2.11W
Marsabit 160 Kh 2.20N 37.59 E
Marsala 128 Gm 37.48N 12.26 E
Marsā Maţrūh 160 Je 31.21N 27.14 E
Marsá Sha'b 168 Fa 22.52N 35.47 E
Marsá Umm Ghayj 146 Fj 25.38N 34.30 E
Marsberg 120 Ee 51.27N 8.51 E
Marsciano 128 Gh 42.54N 12.20 E
Marsdiep 124 Gb 52.58N 4.45 E
Marseille = Marseilles (EN) 112 Gg 43.18N 5.24 E
Marseille-en-Beauvaisis 122 He 49.35N 1.57 E
Marseilles (EN) = Marseille 112 Gg 43.18N 5.24 E
Marshall [Ak.-U.S.] 178 Gd 61.52N 162.04W
Marshall [Ar.-U.S.] 186 Ji 35.55N 92.38W
Marshall [Il.-U.S.] 186 Mg 39.23N 87.42W
Marshall [Lbr.] 166 Cd 6.09N 10.23W
Marshall [Mn.-U.S.] 182 Hc 44.27N 95.47W
Marshall [Mo.-U.S.] 186 Jg 39.07N 93.12W
Marshall [Tx.-U.S.] 182 Ie 32.33N 94.23W
Marshall Islands [5] 210 Hd 9.00N 168.00 E
Marshall Islands 208 Hd 9.00N 168.00 E
Marshall River 212 Hd 22.59S 136.59 E
Marshalltown 182 Ic 42.03N 92.54W
Marshfield 186 Kd 44.40N 90.10W
Marsh Harbour 190 Ic 26.33N 77.03W
Mārshinān, Kūh-e- 146 Of 32.53N 52.24 E
Marsh Island 186 Kl 29.35N 91.53W

Index Symbols

[1] Independent Nation
[2] State, Region
[3] District, County
[4] Municipality
[5] Colony, Dependency
Continent
Physical Region
Historical or Cultural Region
Mount, Mountain
Volcano
Hill
Mountains, Mountain Range
Hills, Escarpment
Plateau, Upland
Pass, Gap
Plain, Lowland
Delta
Salt Flat
Valley, Canyon
Crater, Cave
Karst Features
Depression
Polder
Desert, Dunes
Forest, Woods
Heath, Steppe
Oasis
Cape, Point
Coast, Beach
Cliff
Peninsula
Isthmus
Sandbank
Island
Atoll
Rock, Reef
Islands, Archipelago
Rocks, Reefs
Coral Reef
Well, Spring
Geyser
River, Stream
Waterfall, Rapids
River Mouth, Estuary
Lake
Salt Lake
Intermittent Lake
Reservoir
Swamp, Pond
Canal
Glacier
Ice Shelf, Pack Ice
Ocean
Sea
Gulf, Bay
Strait, Fjord
Lagoon
Bank
Seamount
Tablemount
Ridge
Shelf
Basin
Escarpment, Sea Scarp
Fracture
Trench, Abyss
National Park, Reserve
Point of Interest
Recreation Site
Cave, Cavern
Historic Site
Ruins
Wall, Walls
Church, Abbey
Temple
Scientific Station
Railway station
Airport
Port
Military installation
Lighthouse
Mine
Tunnel
Dam, Bridge

Marsica	128	Hi	41.55N	13.35 E
Marsico Nuovo	128	Jj	40.25N	15.44 E
Marsjaty	134	Jf	60.05N	60.29 E
Marsland	186	Ee	42.29N	103.16W
Mars-la-Tour	124	He	49.06N	5.54 E
Marson	124	Gf	48.55N	4.32 E
Märsta	116	Ge	59.37N	17.51 E
Marstal	116	Dj	54.51N	10.31 E
Marstrand	116	Dg	57.53N	11.35 E
Marta	128	Fh	42.14N	11.42 E
Martaban	148	Je	16.32N	97.37 E
Martaban, Gulf of- (EN)	140	Lh	16.30N	97.00 E
Martap	166	Hd	6.54N	13.03 E
Martapura [Indon.]	150	Dg	4.19S	104.22 E
Martapura [Indon.]	150	Fg	3.25S	114.51 E
Martelange/Martelingen	124	He	49.50N	5.44 E
Martelingen/Martelange	124	He	49.50N	5.44 E
Martés, Sierra de-	126	Le	39.20N	0.57W
Martha's Vineyard	182	Mc	41.25N	70.40W
Martigny	128	Bd	46.06N	7.05 E
Martigues	122	Lk	43.24N	5.03 E
Martil	126	Gi	35.37N	5.17W
Martim Vaz, Ilhas-	198	Nh	20.30S	28.51W
Martin	126	Lc	41.18N	0.19W
Martin [Czech.]	120	Og	49.04N	18.55 E
Martin [S.D.-U.S.]	182	Gc	43.10N	101.44W
Martin [Tn.-U.S.]	184	Cg	36.21N	88.51W
Martina Franca	128	Lj	40.42N	17.20 E
Martinez de Hoz	204	Bl	35.19S	61.37W
Martinez de la Torre	192	Kg	20.04N	97.03W
Martin Garcia, Isla-	204	Cl	34.11S	58.15W
Martin Hills	222	Pg	82.04S	88.01W
Martinho Campos	204	Jd	19.20S	45.13W
Martinique [5]	176	Mh	14.40N	61.00W
Martinique	174	Mh	14.40N	61.00W
Martinique, Canal de la-= Martinique Passage (EN)	190	Le	15.10N	61.20W
Martinique Passage	196	Fe	15.10N	61.20W
Martinique Passage (EN)= Martinique, Canal de la-	190	Le	15.10N	61.20W
Martin Lake	184	Ei	32.50N	85.55W
Martin Peninsula	222	Of	74.25S	114.10W
Martinsburg	184	If	39.28N	77.59W
Martins Ferry	184	Ge	40.07N	80.45W
Martinsville [In.-U.S.]	184	Df	39.26N	86.25W
Martinsville [Va.-U.S.]	182	Ld	36.43N	79.53W
Marton	218	Fd	40.05S	175.23 E
Martos	126	Ig	37.43N	3.58W
Martre, Lac la-	180	Fd	63.20N	118.00W
Martuk	136	Fe	50.47N	56.31 E
Martuni	132	Ni	40.06N	45.18 E
Maru	166	Gc	12.21N	6.24 E
Marud	148	Ee	18.19N	72.58 E
Marudi	150	Ff	4.11N	114.19 E
Marudu, Teluk-	150	Ge	6.45N	116.55 E
Marugame	156	Cd	34.18N	133.47 E
Maruko	156	Fc	36.19N	138.15 E
Märün	146	Mg	31.02N	49.36 E
Marungu, Monts-	158	Ji	7.42S	30.00 E
Maruoka	156	Ec	36.09N	136.16 E
Maruseppu	156a	Ca	44.01N	143.19 E
Marutea Atoll [Fr.Poly.]	208	Ng	21.30S	135.34W
Marutea Atoll [Fr.Poly.]	208	Mf	17.00S	143.10W
Maruyama-Gawa	156	Dd	35.40N	134.50 E
Marvão	126	Ee	39.24N	7.23W
Marvast	146	Pg	30.30N	54.15 E
Marvast, Kavīr-e-	146	Pg	30.20N	54.25 E
Mårvatn	116	Cd	60.10N	8.15 E
Marv-Dasht	144	Hd	29.50N	52.40 E
Marvejols	122	Jj	44.33N	3.17 E
Marvine, Mount-	188	Jg	38.40N	111.39W
Marx	132	Od	51.42N	46.46 E
Mary	142	If	37.36N	61.50 E
Maryborough [Austl.]	210	Gg	25.32S	152.42 E
Maryborough [Austl.]	212	Ig	37.03S	143.45 E
Marydale	172	Ce	29.23S	22.05 E
Maryjskaja oblast [3]	136	Gh	37.15N	62.30 E
Maryland [2]	182	Ld	39.00N	76.45W
Maryland [3]	166	De	4.45N	8.00W
Maryport	118	Jg	54.43N	3.30W
Mary River	212	Gb	12.53S	131.38 E
Marysville [Ca.-U.S.]	188	Eg	39.09N	121.35W
Marysville [Ks.-U.S.]	186	Hg	39.51N	96.39W
Marysville [N.B.-Can.]	184	Nc	45.59N	66.35W
Marysville [Oh.-U.S.]	184	Fe	40.13N	83.22W
Marysville [Wa.-U.S.]	188	Db	48.03N	122.11W
Maryville [Mo.-U.S.]	182	Ic	40.21N	94.52W
Maryville [Tn.-U.S.]	184	Fh	35.46N	83.58W
Marzūq	160	If	25.55N	13.55 E
Marzūq, Ḥamādat-	164	Bd	26.00N	12.30 E
Marzūq, Ṣaḥrā'-	158	If	24.30N	13.00 E
Masachapa	194	Dh	11.47N	86.31W
Masāhim, Kūh-e-	146	Pg	30.21N	55.20 E
Masai Steppe	158	Ki	4.45S	37.00 E
Masaka	170	Fc	0.20S	31.44 E
Masākin	162	Jb	35.44N	10.35 E
Masalembo, Kepulauan-	150	Fh	5.30S	114.26 E
Masally	136	Eh	39.01N	48.40 E
Masalog, Puntan-	220b	Ba	15.01N	145.41 E
Masamba	150	Hg	2.33S	120.20 E
Masan	152	Md	35.11N	128.24 E
Masasi	160	Kj	10.43S	38.48 E
Masaya	190	Gf	11.58N	86.06W
Masaya [3]	194	Dh	12.00N	86.10W
Masbate	150	Hd	12.10N	123.35 E
Masbate	140	Oh	12.15N	123.30 E
Mascara	162	Hb	35.24N	0.08 E
Mascara [3]	162	Hb	35.30N	0.15 E
Mascareignes, Iles-/ Mascarene Islands	158	Mk	21.00S	57.00 E
Mascarene Basin (EN)	106	Fk	15.00S	56.00 E
Mascarene Islands/ Mascareignes, Iles-	158	Mk	21.00S	57.00 E
Mascarene Plateau (EN)	106	Gk	10.00S	60.00 E
Mascota	192	Gg	20.32N	104.49W
Mas-d'Azil, Le-	122	Hk	43.05N	1.22 E
Masee, Island-/Oiléan Mhic Aodha	118	Hg	54.50N	5.50W
Masela, Pulau-	150	Ih	8.09S	129.50 E
Maseru	160	Jk	29.28S	27.29 E
Maşfūţ	146	Qk	24.48N	56.06 E
Mashābih	146	Gj	25.37N	36.32 E
Mashan	154	Kb	45.12N	130.32 E
Mashava	172	Ed	20.02S	30.29 E
Mashhad	142	Hf	36.18N	59.36 E
Mashike	154	Pc	43.51N	141.31 E
Mashiki	156	Be	32.47N	130.50 E
Mashīz	146	Qh	29.56N	56.37 E
Mashkel	144	Jd	28.02N	63.25 E
Mashonaland North [3]	172	Ec	17.00S	31.00 E
Mashonaland South [3]	172	Ec	18.00S	31.00 E
Mashra' ar Raqq	168	Dd	8.25N	29.16 E
Mashū-Ko	156a	Db	43.35N	144.30 E
Masiaca	192	Ed	26.45N	109.18W
Masīlah, Wādī al-	140	Hh	15.10N	51.08 E
Masi-Manimba	170	Cc	4.46S	17.55 E
Masindi	170	Fb	1.42N	31.43 E
Maşīrah, Jazīrat-	140	Hg	20.29N	58.33 E
Maşīrah, Khalīj-	140	Hg	20.15N	57.40 E
Masisi	170	Ec	1.24S	28.49 E
Masjed-Soleymān	144	Gc	31.58N	49.18 E
Mask, Lough-/Loch Measca	118	Dh	53.35N	9.20W
Maskanah	146	Hd	36.01N	38.05 E
Maskelynes, Iles-	219b	Cc	16.32S	167.49 E
Maşloc	130	Ed	46.00N	21.27 E
Maslovare	128	Lf	44.34N	17.33 E
Masoala, Cap-	158	Mj	15.59S	50.13 E
Masoala, Presqu'île de-	172	Ic	15.40S	50.12 E
Mason	186	Gk	30.45N	99.14W
Mason Bay	218	Bg	46.55S	167.45 E
Mason City	176	Je	43.09N	93.12W
Masovia (EN)= Mazowsze	110	Ie	52.40N	20.20 E
Masparro, Rio-	194	Mi	8.04N	69.26W
Masqat=Muscat (EN)	142	Hg	23.29N	58.33 E
Massa	128	Ef	44.01N	10.09 E
Massachusetts [2]	182	Mc	42.15N	71.50W
Massachusetts Bay	184	Ld	42.20N	70.50W
Massaciuccoli, Lago di-	128	Eg	43.50N	10.20 E
Massafra	128	Lj	40.35N	17.07 E
Massaguet	168	Bc	12.28N	15.26 E
Massakori	168	Bc	13.00N	15.44 E
Massa Marittima	128	Eg	43.03N	10.53 E
Massangano	170	Bd	9.37S	14.17 E
Massangena	172	Ed	21.32S	32.57 E
Massapê	202	Jd	3.31S	40.19W
Massawa (EN)=Mitsiwa	160	Kg	15.37N	39.39 E
Massena	182	Mc	44.56N	74.57W
Massénya	168	Bc	11.24N	16.10 E
Masset	180	Ef	54.02N	132.09W
Masseube	122	Gk	43.26N	0.35 E
Massey Sound	180	Ia	78.00N	94.00W
Massiac	122	Ji	45.15N	3.13 E
Massiaru	116	Kg	57.52N	24.27 E
Massillon	184	Ge	40.48N	81.32W
Massinga	172	Fd	23.20S	35.22 E
Masson Island	222	Ge	66.08S	96.34 E
Massuma	170	De	14.05S	22.00 E
Mastābah	164	Ge	20.49N	39.26 E
Maštaga	132	Pi	40.32N	49.59 E
Masterton	216	Eh	40.57S	175.39 E
Mastūrah	164	Ge	23.06N	38.50 E
Masuda	152	Ne	34.40N	131.51 E
Māsūleh	146	Md	37.10N	48.59 E
Masurai, Gunung-	150	Dg	2.30S	101.51 E
Masuria (EN)	110	Ie	53.50N	21.30 E
Masurian Lakes (EN)	110	Ie	53.45N	21.45 E
Masvingo	160	Kk	20.05S	30.50 E
Masvingo [3]	172	Ed	21.00S	31.00 E
Maşyāf	146	Ge	35.03N	36.21 E
Maszewo	120	Lc	53.29N	15.02 E
Matabaé, Cap-	219b	Cb	15.38S	166.46 E
Matabeleland North [3]	172	Dc	19.00S	27.30 E
Matabeleland South [3]	172	Dd	21.00S	29.30 E
Matachel	126	Ff	38.50N	6.17W
Matachewan	180	Jg	47.56N	80.39W
Matacu	204	Bc	17.21S	61.28W
Matadi	160	Ii	5.49S	13.27 E
Matador	186	Fi	34.01N	100.49W
Matagalpa	176	Kh	12.53N	85.57W
Matagalpa [3]	194	Eg	13.00N	85.30W
Matagami	180	Jg	49.45N	77.35W
Matagami, Lac-	184	Ia	49.54N	77.32W
Mata Gassile	168	Ge	6.30N	42.16 E
Matagorda Bay	186	Hl	28.35N	96.20W
Matagorda Island	182	Hf	28.15N	96.30W
Matagorda Peninsula	186	Hl	28.32N	96.07W
Mataiea	221e	Fc	17.46S	149.25W
Mataiva Atoll	208	Mf	14.53S	148.40W
Mataj	136	Hf	45.51N	78.43 E
Matak, Pulau-	150	Ef	3.18N	106.16 E
Matakana Island	218	Kh	37.35S	176.05 E
Matala	170	Ce	14.43S	15.02 E
Matalaa, Pointe-	220h	Bc	13.20S	176.08W
Matale	148	Gg	7.28N	80.37 E
Mataliele	172	Df	30.24S	28.43 E
Matam	166	Cb	15.40N	13.15W
Matamey	166	Gc	13.26N	8.28 E
Matamoros [Mex.]	176	Jg	25.53N	97.30W
Matamoros [Mex.]	190	Dc	25.32N	103.15W
Matana, Danau-	150	Hg	2.28S	121.20 E
Ma'ṭan as Sarra	164	De	21.41N	21.52 E
Matancita	192	De	25.09N	111.59W
Matane	180	Kg	48.51N	67.32W
Matankari	166	Fc	13.46N	4.01 E
Matanza	204	Cl	34.33S	58.35W
Matanzas	176	Kg	23.03N	81.35W
Matanzas [3]	194	Gb	22.40N	81.10W
Matão	204	He	21.35S	48.22W
Matapalo, Cabo-	194	Fi	8.23N	83.19W
Matapan, Cape- (EN)= Tainaron, Ákra-	110	Ih	36.23N	22.29 E
Matape, Rio-	192	Dc	28.17N	110.41W
Mata Point	220k	Bb	19.07S	169.50W
Matara	148	Gg	5.56N	80.33 E
Matara	168	Fc	14.35N	39.28 E
Mataram	142	Nj	8.35S	116.07 E
Mataranka	212	Gb	14.56S	133.07 E
Mataró	126	Oc	41.32N	2.27 E
Matarraña/Matarranya	126	Mc	41.14N	0.22 E
Matarranya/Matarraña	126	Mc	41.14N	0.22 E
Mataso	219b	Dc	17.15S	168.25 E
Matatula, Cape-	221c	Cb	14.15S	170.34W
Mataura	218	Cg	46.12S	168.52 E
Mataura	218	Cg	46.34S	168.44 E
Mata-Utu	210	Jf	13.17S	176.08W
Mata-Utu, Baie de-	220h	Bb	13.19S	176.07W
Matavai	216	Gb	13.28S	172.35W
Matavera	220p	Cb	21.13S	159.44W
Mataverj	221d	Ab	27.10S	109.27W
Matawai	218	Gc	38.21S	177.32 E
Matawin, Réservoir-	184	Kb	46.45N	73.50W
Matawin, Rivière-	184	Kb	46.55N	72.55W
Maṭāy	146	Dh	28.25N	30.46 E
Maṭbakhayn	164	Hf	17.29N	41.48 E
Matca	130	Kd	45.51N	27.32 E
Matehuala	190	Dd	23.39N	100.39W
Matemo, Ilha-	172	Gb	12.13S	40.36 E
Matera	128	Kj	40.40N	16.36 E
Matese	128	Ii	41.25N	14.20 E
Mátészalka	120	Si	47.57N	22.20 E
Matfors	114	De	62.21N	17.02 E
Matha	122	Fi	45.52N	0.19W
Mathematicians Seamounts (EN)	190	Be	15.30N	111.00W
Matheson	184	Ga	48.32N	80.28W
Mathis	186	Hl	28.06N	97.50W
Mathrákion	130	Cj	39.46N	19.31 E
Mathura	148	Fc	27.30N	77.41 E
Mati	150	Ie	6.57N	126.13 E
Mati	130	Ch	41.39N	19.34 E
Matias Cardoso	204	Kb	14.52S	43.56W
Matias Romero	190	Ee	16.53N	95.02W
Maticora, Rio-	194	Lh	11.01N	71.09W
Matina	194	Fh	10.05N	83.17W
Matinha	202	Id	3.06S	45.02W
Māṭir	162	Ib	37.03N	9.40 E
Matiyure, Rio-	196	Ci	7.36N	67.39W
Matkaselkja	116	Nc	61.57N	30.33 E
Mātmāṭah	162	Ic	33.33N	9.58 E
Matnog	150	Hd	12.35N	124.05 E
Mato, Cerro-	196	Di	7.15N	65.14W
Mato, Rio-	196	Di	7.09N	65.07W
Matočkin Šar, proliv-	136	Fa	73.30N	54.55 E
Mato Grosso [2]	202	Gf	14.00S	56.00W
Mato Grosso [Braz.]	204	Dd	18.18S	57.20W
Mato Grosso [Braz.]	200	Kg	15.00S	59.57W
Mato Grosso, Planalto do- = Mato Grosso, Plateau of- (EN)	198	Kg	15.30S	56.00W
Mato Grosso, Plateau of- (EN) = Mato Grosso, Planalto do-	198	Kg	15.30S	56.00W
Mato Grosso do Sul [2]	202	Hg	20.00S	55.00W
Matos Costa	204	Gh	26.27S	51.09W
Matosinhos	126	Dc	41.11N	8.42W
Matou	154	Cj	29.50N	115.32 E
Matou → Qiuxian	154	Cf	36.50N	115.10 E
Mátra	110	If	47.53N	19.57 E
Maṭraḥ	144	Ie	23.29N	58.31 E
Matrei in Osttirol	128	Gc	47.00N	12.32 E
Matsiatra	172	Hd	21.25S	45.33 E
Matsudo	154	Qg	35.48N	139.55 E
Matsue	152	Nd	35.28N	133.04 E
Matsukawa [Jap.]	156	Ed	35.36N	137.53 E
Matsukawa [Jap.]	156	Gc	37.40N	140.28 E
Matsu Liehtao	152	Kf	26.05N	119.56 E
Matsumae	156a	Bc	41.26N	140.07 E
Matsumae-Hantō	156a	Bc	41.40N	140.15 E
Matsumoto	152	Od	36.14N	137.58 E
Matsunaga, Fukuyama-	156	Cd	34.27N	133.16 E
Matsuo	156	Gb	39.58N	141.02 E
Matsu-Ōminato	156a	Bc	41.16N	141.09 E
Matsusaka	154	Ng	34.34N	136.32 E
Matsushima	156	Gb	38.22N	141.04 E
Matsutō	156	Ec	36.31N	136.33 E
Matsuura	156	Ae	33.22N	129.42 E
Matsuyama	142	Pf	33.50N	132.45 E
Matsuzaki	156	Fd	34.44N	138.45 E
Mattagami Lake	184	Gb	47.57N	81.35W
Mattagami River	180	Jf	50.43N	81.30W
Mattawa	180	Jg	46.19N	78.42W
Matterhorn [Eur.]	128	Be	45.58N	7.39 E
Matterhorn [Nv.-U.S.]	188	Hf	41.49N	115.23W
Matthew, Ile-	208	Ig	22.20S	171.20 E
Matthews Ridge	202	Fb	7.30N	60.10W
Matthew Town	190	Jd	20.57N	73.40W
Maṭṭī, Sabkhat-	168	Ia	23.30N	52.00 E
Mattighofen	128	Hb	48.06N	13.09 E
Mattoon	186	Lg	39.29N	88.22W
Matua, ostrov-	138	Kg	48.00N	153.10 E
Matucana	202	Cf	11.51S	76.24W
Matuku Island	216	Ec	19.10S	179.46 E
Matundu	170	Db	4.21N	23.40 E
Matundu	170	Gd	8.50S	39.30 E
Maturin	200	Je	9.45N	63.11W
Matvejev Kurgan	132	Kf	47.34N	38.55 E
Maúa	172	Fb	13.52S	37.09 E
Maubeuge	122	Jd	50.17N	3.58 E
Ma-ubin	148	Je	16.44N	95.39 E
Maudheimvidda	222	Bf	74.00S	8.00W
Maud Seamount (EN)	222	Ce	65.00S	2.35 E
Maués	202	Gd	3.24S	57.42W
Maués, Rio-	202	Gd	3.22S	57.44W
Mau Escarpment	170	Gc	0.40S	36.02 E
Mauges, Les-	122	Fg	47.10N	1.00W
Maug Islands	208	Fb	20.01N	145.13 E
Maui Island	208	Lb	20.45N	156.20W
Mauke Island	208	Lg	20.09S	157.23W
Mau Kyun	148	Jf	12.45N	98.20 E
Mauldre	124	Df	48.59N	1.49 E
Maule [2]	206	Fe	35.45S	72.15W
Mauléon	122	Fh	46.55N	0.45W
Mauléon-Licharre	122	Fk	43.14N	0.53W
Maullín	206	Ff	41.38S	73.37W
Maumee	184	Fe	41.34N	83.39W
Maumere	150	Hh	8.37S	122.14 E
Maun	160	Jj	19.58S	23.26 E
Maun	128	If	44.26N	14.55 E
Mauna Kea	208	Lc	19.50N	155.28W
Maunaloa	221a	Db	21.08N	157.13W
Mauna Loa	221a	Fd	19.28N	155.36W
Maunath	148	Gc	25.40N	82.38 E
Maunawili	221a	Db	21.21N	157.47W
Maunga Roa	220p	Bb	21.13S	159.48W
Maungdaw	148	Id	20.49N	92.22 E
Maunoir, Lac-	180	Fc	67.30N	125.00W
Maupihaa Atoll (Mopelia, Atoll-)	208	Lf	16.50S	153.55W
Maupin	188	Ed	45.11N	121.05W
Maupiti, Ile-	208	Lf	16.27S	152.15W
Maurepas, Lake-	186	Kk	30.15N	90.30W
Maures, Massif des-	122	Mk	43.16N	6.23 E
Mauriac	122	Ii	45.13N	2.20 E
Maurice, Lake-	212	Ge	29.30S	131.00 E
Maurienne	122	Mi	45.13N	6.30 E
Mauritania (EN)= Mūrītāniyā [1]	160	Fg	20.00N	12.00W
Mauriti	202	Ke	7.23S	38.46W
Mauritius [1]	160	Mj	18.00S	57.40 E
Mauritius	158	Mk	20.17S	57.33 E
Mauron	122	Df	48.05N	2.18W
Maurs	122	Ij	44.43N	2.12 E
Mauston	186	Ke	43.48N	90.05W
Mauthausen	128	Ib	48.14N	14.31 E
Mauzé-sur-le-Mignon	122	Fh	46.12N	0.40W
Mavinga	170	Df	15.47S	20.24 E
Mavita	172	Ec	19.32S	33.09 E
Mavrovoúni [Grc.]	130	Fj	39.37N	22.47 E
Mavrovoúni [Grc.]	130	Gh	41.07N	23.08 E
Mawchi	148	Je	18.49N	97.09 E
Mawei	152	Kf	26.02N	119.30 E
Mawlaik	148	Id	23.38N	94.25 E
Mawlamyine	142	Le	16.30N	97.38 E
Mawqaq	146	Ii	27.25N	41.08 E
Mawson	222	Fe	67.36S	62.53 E
Mawson Coast	222	Fe	67.40S	63.30 E
Mawson Escarpment	222	Ff	73.05S	68.10 E
Maxcanú	190	Fd	20.35N	90.01W
Maxixe	172	Fd	23.51S	35.21 E
Maxwell Bay	180	Ib	74.32N	89.00W
May, Isle of-	118	Ke	56.10N	2.30W
Maya, Pulau-	150	Eg	1.10S	109.35 E
Mayaguana Island	190	Jd	22.23N	72.57W
Mayaguana Passage	194	Kb	22.32N	73.15W
Mayagüez	190	Ke	18.12N	67.09W
Mayahi	166	Gc	13.58N	7.40 E
Mayama	170	Bc	3.51S	14.54 E
Mayāmey	146	Pd	36.24N	55.42 E
Maya Mountains	190	Ge	16.40N	88.50W
Mayapán	190	Gd	20.38N	89.27W
Mayari	194	Jc	20.40N	75.41W
Maybell	186	Bf	40.31N	108.05W
Maychew	168	Fc	12.46N	39.34 E
Mayd	168	Hc	10.57N	47.06 E
Maydān	146	Ke	34.55N	45.37 E
Maydena	212	Jh	42.55S	146.30 E
Maydī	144	Ff	16.18N	42.48 E
Mayen	120	Df	50.20N	7.13 E
Mayenne	122	Ff	48.18N	0.37W
Mayenne [3]	122	Ff	48.05N	0.40W
Mayenne	122	Fg	47.30N	0.32W
Mayfa'ah	168	Hc	14.16N	47.35 E
Mayfield	184	Cg	36.44N	88.38W
May Glacier	222	Ie	67.00S	130.00 E
Mayi He	154	Jb	45.52N	128.46 E
Maymyo	148	Jd	22.02N	96.28 E
Maynas	202	Dd	3.00S	75.00W
Mayo	176	Fc	63.35N	135.54W
Mayo/Muigheo [2]	118	Dh	53.50N	9.30W
Mayo, Mountains of-	118	Dg	54.05N	9.30W
Mayo, Rio-	192	Ed	26.45N	109.47W
Mayo Darlé	166	Hd	6.30N	11.55 E
Mayo-Kébbi [3]	168	Bd	10.00N	15.30 E
Mayo-Kébbi	168	Ad	9.18N	13.33 E
Mayoko	170	Bc	2.18S	12.49 E
Mayon, Mount-	140	Oh	13.15N	123.41 E
Mayor, Puig-/Major, Puig-	126	Oe	39.48N	2.48 E
Mayor Island	218	Gb	37.15S	176.15 E
Mayor Pablo Lagerenza	206	Ha	19.58S	60.45W
Mayotte [5]	160	Lj	12.50S	45.10 E
Mayotte/Mahoré	158	Lj	12.50S	45.10 E
May Pen	190	Ie	17.58N	77.14W
Mayraira Point	150	Hc	18.39N	120.51 E
Mayran, Laguna de-	192	He	25.40N	102.45W
Mayreau Island	197n	Bb	12.39N	61.23W
May-sur-Orne	124	Be	49.06N	0.22W
Maysville	184	Ff	38.39N	83.46W
Mayumba [Gabon]	160	Ii	3.25S	10.39 E
Mayumba [Zaire]	170	Ed	7.16S	27.03 E
Mayum La	152	De	30.35N	82.27 E
Mayville	184	Hd	42.15N	79.32W
Mayyit, Al Baḥr al-=Dead Sea (EN)	140	Ff	31.30N	35.30 E
Mazabuka	170	Ef	15.51S	27.46 E
Mazagão	202	Hd	0.07S	51.17W
Mazamet	122	Ik	43.30N	2.24 E
Māzandarān [3]	144	Hb	36.00N	54.00 E
Māzandarān, Daryā-ye-= Caspian Sea (EN)	110	Lg	42.00N	50.30 E
Mazar	152	Cd	36.27N	77.03 E
Mazara del Vallo	128	Gm	37.39N	12.35 E
Mazār-e Sharīf	142	If	36.42N	67.06 E
Mazarrón, Golfo de-	126	Kg	37.30N	1.18W
Mazartag	152	Dd	38.29N	80.50 E
Mazaruni River	202	Gb	6.25N	58.38W
Mazatenango	190	Ff	14.32N	91.30W
Mazatlán	176	Ig	23.13N	106.25W
Mažeikiai/Mažejkjaj	114	Fh	56.20N	22.22 E
Mažejkjaj/Mažeikiai	114	Fh	56.20N	22.22 E
Mazhafah, Jabal-	146	Fh	28.48N	34.57 E
Mazhūr, 'Irq al-	146	Ji	27.25N	43.55 E
Mazinga	197c	Ab	17.29N	62.58W
Mazirbe	116	Jg	57.40N	22.10 E
Mazoe	172	Ec	17.30S	30.58 E
Mazoe	158	Kj	16.32S	33.25 E
Mazomeno	170	Ec	4.55S	27.13 E
Mazong Shan	152	Gc	41.33N	97.10 E
Mazowsze	120	Qd	52.40N	20.20 E
Mazowsze=Masovia (EN)	110	Ie	52.40N	20.20 E
Mazsalaca	116	Kg	57.45N	24.59 E
Mazunga	172	Dd	21.44S	29.52 E
Mazurskie, Pojezierze-	120	Qc	53.40N	21.00 E
Mazzarino	128	Im	37.18N	14.13 E
Mba	219d	Ab	17.32S	177.42 E
Mbabane	160	Kk	26.18S	31.07 E
Mbabo, Tchabal-	166	Hd	7.16N	12.09 E
Mbacké	166	Bc	14.48N	15.55W
Mbaéré	168	Be	3.47N	17.31 E
Mbaïki	160	Ih	3.53N	18.00 E
Mbakaou	166	Hd	6.19N	12.49 E
Mbakaou, Barrage de-	166	Hd	6.25N	13.00 E
Mbala	160	Ki	8.50S	31.22 E
Mbalam	166	He	2.13N	13.49 E
Mbale	160	Kh	1.05N	34.10 E
Mbali	168	Be	4.27N	18.20 E
Mbalmayo	166	He	3.31N	11.30 E
Mbam	158	Ih	4.24N	11.17 E
Mbamba Bay	170	Fe	11.17S	34.46 E
Mbandaka	160	Ih	0.04N	18.16 E
Mbanga	166	Ge	4.30N	9.34 E
Mbanika	219a	Dc	9.05S	159.12 E
M'banza Congo	170	Bd	6.16S	14.15 E
Mbanza-Ngungu	160	Ii	5.35S	14.47 E
Mbarangandu	170	Gd	8.57S	37.24 E
Mbarara	170	Fc	0.36S	30.38 E
Mbari	168	Ce	4.34N	22.43 E
Mbatiki	219d	Bb	17.46S	179.08 E
Mbava	219a	Cb	7.49S	156.37 E
Mbé	166	Hd	7.51N	13.36 E
Mbengga	219d	Bc	18.23S	178.08 E
Mbengwi	166	Hd	6.01N	10.00 E
Mbéré	168	Bd	9.07N	16.26 E
Mbeya	160	Ki	8.54S	33.27 E
Mbeya [3]	170	Fd	8.00S	33.30 E
Mbi	168	Be	4.28N	18.07 E
Mbigou	170	Bc	1.53S	11.56 E
Mbinda	160	Ii	2.07S	12.52 E
Mbinga	170	Ge	10.56S	35.01 E
Mbingué	166	Dc	10.00N	5.54W
Mbini	166	Ge	1.34N	9.37 E
Mbini [3]	166	He	1.30N	10.00 E
Mbini	158	Ih	1.30N	10.30 E
Mbini	166	He	1.40N	9.45 E
Mboki	168	Dd	5.19N	25.58 E
Mbokonimbeti	219a	Ec	8.57S	160.05 E
Mbomo	170	Bb	0.24N	14.44 E
Mbomou=Bomu (EN) [3]	168	Cd	5.30N	23.30 E
Mbomou=Bomu (EN)	158	Jh	4.08N	22.26 E
Mborokua	219a	Dc	9.02S	158.44 E
Mbour	166	Bc	14.24N	16.58W
Mbout	162	Ef	16.01N	12.35W
Mbozi	170	Fd	9.02S	32.56 E
Mbrés	168	Bd	6.40N	19.48 E
M'Bridge	170	Bd	7.14S	12.52 E
Mbua	219d	Bb	16.48S	178.37 E
Mbuji-Mayi	160	Ji	6.09S	23.33 E
Mbulo	219a	Dc	8.46S	158.21 E
Mbulu	170	Gc	3.51S	35.32 E
Mburucuyá	204	Ci	28.03S	58.14W
Mbutha	219d	Bb	16.39S	179.51 E
Mbuyuni	170	Gd	7.23S	36.32 E
Mbwemburu	170	Gd	9.29S	39.39 E
Mcensk	136	Dd	53.17N	36.32 E
M'Chedallah	126	Qh	36.22N	4.16 E
Mcherrah	162	Gd	27.00N	4.30W
Mchinga	170	Gd	9.44S	39.42 E
Mchinji	170	Fe	13.48S	32.54 E
Mdandu	170	Fd	9.09S	34.42 E
M'Daourouch	128	Bn	36.05N	7.49 E
Mdennah	162	Gd	25.00N	4.50W
Mdiq	126	Gi	35.41N	5.19W
Mead	184	Fa	49.29N	83.50W
Mead, Lake-	182	Ed	36.05N	114.25W
Meade	186	Ff	37.17N	100.20W
Meade	178	Hb	70.50N	156.25W
Meade Peak	188	Je	42.30N	111.15W
Meadow Lake	180	Gf	54.07N	108.20W
Meadville	184	Ge	41.38N	80.10W
Me-akan-Dake	156a	Cb	43.23N	143.59 E
Mealhada	126	Dd	40.22N	8.27W
Mealy Mountains	180	Lf	53.20N	59.30W
Meama	221b	Ba	19.45S	174.34W
Méan, Havelange-	124	Hd	50.22N	5.20 E
Meander Reef	150	Ge	8.09N	119.14 E
Meander River	180	Fe	59.02N	117.42W
Meanguera, Isla-	194	Dg	13.12N	87.43W
Mearim, Rio-	198	Lf	3.04S	44.35W
Meath/An Mhí [2]	118	Gh	53.35N	6.40W
Meaux	122	If	48.57N	2.52 E
Mecca (EN)=Makkah	142	Fg	21.27N	39.49 E
Mechara	168	Gd	8.34N	40.28 E
Mechelen/Maasmechelen	124	Hd	50.57N	5.40 E
Mechelen/Malines	122	Kc	51.02N	4.29 E
Mecheraa-Asfa	126	Ni	35.24N	1.03 E
Mecheria	162	Gc	33.33N	0.17W
Mechernich	124	Id	50.36N	6.39 E
Mechongué	204	Cn	38.09S	58.13W
Mecidiye	130	Ji	40.38N	26.32 E
Mecitözü	146	Fb	40.31N	35.19 E
Mecklemburgischer Höhenrücken	120	Ic	53.40N	12.10 E
Mecklenburg	120	Hc	53.30N	12.00 E
Mecklenburger Bucht	120	Hb	54.20N	11.40 E
Mecklenburger Schweiz	120	Ic	53.45N	12.35 E

Index Symbols

[1] Independent Nation; [2] State, Region; [3] District, County; [4] Municipality; [5] Colony, Dependency; Continent; Physical Region; Historical or Cultural Region; Mount, Mountain; Volcano; Hill; Mountains, Mountain Range; Hills, Escarpment; Plateau, Upland; Pass, Gap; Plain, Lowland; Delta; Salt Flat; Valley, Canyon; Crater, Cave; Karst Features; Depression; Polder; Desert, Dunes; Forest, Woods; Heath, Steppe; Oasis; Cape, Point; Coast, Beach; Cliff; Peninsula; Isthmus; Sandbank; Island; Atoll; Rock, Reef; Islands, Archipelago; Rocks, Reefs; Coral Reef; Well, Spring; Geyser; River, Stream; Waterfall, Rapids; River Mouth, Estuary; Lake; Salt Lake; Intermittent Lake; Reservoir; Swamp, Pond; Canal; Glacier; Ice Shelf, Pack Ice; Ocean; Sea; Gulf, Bay; Strait, Fjord; Lagoon; Bank; Seamount; Tablemount; Ridge; Shelf; Basin; Escarpment, Sea Scarp; Fracture; Trench, Abyss; National Park, Reserve; Point of Interest; Recreation Site; Cave, Cavern; Historic Site; Ruins; Wall, Walls; Church, Abbey; Temple; Scientific Station; Railway station; Airport; Port; Military installation; Lighthouse; Mine; Tunnel; Dam, Bridge

Name	Page	Grid	Lat	Long
Mecoacán, Laguna-	192	Mh	18.20N	93.10W
Meconta	172	Fb	14.59S	39.50 E
Mecsek	120	Oj	46.10N	18.18 E
Mecúbúri	172	Gb	14.10S	40.31 E
Mecúfi	172	Gb	13.17S	40.33 E
Mecula	172	Fb	12.05S	37.39 E
Médala	162	Ff	15.30N	5.37W
Medan	142	Li	3.35N	98.40 E
Médanos [Arg.]	204	Ck	33.24S	59.05W
Médanos [Arg.]	206	He	38.50S	62.41W
Medanosa, Punta-	206	Gg	48.06S	65.55W
Mede	128	Ce	45.06N	8.44 E
Médéa	162	Hb	36.16N	2.45 E
Médéa [3]	162	Hb	36.20N	3.25 E
Medebach	124	Kc	51.12N	8.43 E
Medellin	150	Hd	11.08N	123.58 E
Medellin	200	Ie	6.15N	75.35W
Medelpad	116	Gb	62.35N	16.15 E
Medemblik	124	Hb	52.46N	5.06 E
Medenica	120	Tg	49.21N	23.45 E
Mederdra	162	Df	16.54N	15.40W
Medetziz	128	Tf	37.25N	34.40 E
Medford [Or.-U.S.]	176	Ge	42.19N	122.52W
Medford [Wi.-U.S.]	186	Kd	45.09N	90.20W
Medgidia	130	Le	44.15N	28.17 E
Medi	168	Ed	5.06N	30.44 E
Media Luna, Arrecife de la-	194	Ff	15.13N	82.36W
Medianeira	204	Eg	25.17S	54.05W
Mediaş	130	Hc	46.10N	24.21 E
Medical Lake	188	Gc	47.34N	117.41W
Medicine Bow	188	Lf	41.54N	106.12W
Medicine Bow Mountains	188	Lf	41.10N	106.25W
Medicine Butte	188	Jf	41.29N	110.48W
Medicine Hat	176	Md	50.03N	110.40W
Medicine Lake	188	Mb	48.28N	104.24W
Medicine Lodge	186	Jf	37.17N	98.35W
Međimurje	128	Kd	46.25N	16.30 E
Medina (EN) = Al Madīnah [Sau.Ar.]	142	Fg	24.28N	39.36 E
Medina Az-Zahra	126	Hg	37.52N	4.50W
Medinaceli	126	Jc	41.10N	2.26W
Medina del Campo	126	Hc	41.18N	4.55W
Medina de Rioseco	126	Gc	41.53N	5.02W
Medina-Sidonia	126	Gh	36.27N	5.55W
Medinilla, Farallon de-	208	Fc	16.01N	146.04 E
Medininkai/Medininkaj	116	Kj	54.32N	25.46 E
Medinīpur	148	Hd	22.26N	87.20 E
Medio, Arroyo del-	204	Bk	33.16S	
Mediterranean Sea (EN) = Akdeniz	110	Hh	35.00N	20.00 E
Mediterranean Sea (EN) = Khalīkhon, Yam-	110	Hh	35.00N	20.00 E
Méditerranée, Mer-	110	Hh	35.00N	20.00 E
Mediterráneo, Mar-	110	Hh	35.00N	20.00 E
Mediterraneo, Mar-	110	Hh	35.00N	20.00 E
Mediterraneo, Mar-	110	Hh	35.00N	20.00 E
Mesoyéios Thálassa	110	Hh	35.00N	20.00 E
Mediterranean Sea (EN) = Mutawassit, Al Baḥr al-	110	Hh	35.00N	20.00 E
Méditerranée, Mer- = Mediterranean Sea (EN)	110	Hh	35.00N	20.00 E
Mediterráneo, Mar- = Mediterranean Sea (EN)	110	Hh	35.00N	20.00 E
Mediterráneo, Mar- = Mediterranean Sea (EN)	110	Hh	35.00N	20.00 E
Mediterrani Català, Sistema- / Costeras Catalanas, Cordilleras- = Catalan Coastal Range (EN)	110	Gg	41.35N	1.40 E
Medje	170	Eb	2.25N	27.18 E
Medjerda, Monts de la-	162	Hb	36.35N	8.15 E
Mednogorsk	136	Fe	51.26N	57.40 E
Medny, ostrov-	138	Lf	54.40N	167.50 E
Médoc	122	Fi	45.00N	1.00W
Médog	152	Gf	29.18N	95.27 E
Médouneu	170	Bb	1.01N	10.48 E
Medveđa	130	Fg	42.51N	21.36 E
Medvedica [R.S.F.S.R.]	114	Mh	57.05N	37.31 E
Medvedica [R.S.F.S.R.]	110	Kf	49.35N	42.41 E
Medvednica	128	Je	45.55N	15.58 E
Medvedok	114	Mh	57.24N	50.06 E
Medvenka	132	Jd	51.27N	36.08 E
Medveži, ostrova- = Bear Islands	140	Sb	70.52N	161.26 E
Medvežjegorsk	136	Cc	62.56N	34.29 E
Medway	124	Cc	51.23N	0.31 E
Medzilaborce	120	Rg	49.16N	21.55 E
Meekatharra	210	Cg	26.36S	118.29 E
Meeker	186	Cf	40.02N	107.55W
Meerane	120	If	50.51N	12.23 E
Meerbusch	124	Ic	51.16N	6.40 E
Meerut	148	Fc	28.59N	77.42 E
Meeteetse	188	Kd	44.09N	108.52W
Mefarlane, Lake-	212	Hd	32.00S	136.40 E
Mega [Eth.]	160	Kh	4.03N	38.20 E
Mega [Indon.]	150	Jg	0.41S	131.53 E
Mega, Pulau-	150	Dg	4.00S	101.02 E
Megalo	168	Gd	6.52N	40.47 E
Megalópolis	130	Fl	37.24N	22.08 E
Megálo Sofráno	130	Jm	36.04N	26.25 E
Meganision	130	Dk	38.38N	20.43 E
Meganom, mys-	132	Hg	44.48N	35.05 E
Mégara	130	Gk	38.00N	23.21 E
Megéve	122	Mi	45.52N	6.37 E
Meghalaya [3]	148	Ic	26.00N	91.00 E
Megid	164	Dd	28.35N	22.10 E
Megion	136	Hc	61.00N	76.15 E
Megiscane, Lac-	184	Ic	48.30N	76.04W
Megri	130	Oj	38.30N	46.15 E
Mehadia	130	Fe	44.54N	22.22 E
Mehaigne	124	Hd	50.32N	5.13 E
Meharry, Mount-	212	Dd	23.00S	118.35 E
Mehdia	126	Ni	35.25N	1.45 E
Mehdīshahr	146	Oe	35.44N	53.22 E
Mehedinti [2]	130	Fe	44.30N	23.00 E
Mehetia, Île-	216	Lc	17.52S	148.03W
Mehrabān	146	Je	38.05N	47.08 E
Mehrān	146	Lf	33.07N	46.10 E
Mehrān	146	Pi	26.52N	55.24 E
Mehrenga	114	Je	63.17N	41.20 E
Mehrīz	146	Pg	31.35N	54.28 E
Mehun-sur-Yèvre	122	Ig	47.09N	2.13 E
Meia Meia	170	Gd	5.49S	35.48 E
Meia Ponte, Rio-	202	Ig	18.32S	49.36W
Meiganga	166	Hd	6.31N	14.18 E
Meighen	180	Ha	79.55N	99.00W
Meihekou → Hailong	152	Mc	42.32N	125.37 E
Meiktila	148	Ib	20.52N	95.52 E
Meilü → Wuchuan	152	Jg	21.28N	110.44 E
Meinerzhagen	124	Jc	51.07N	7.39 E
Meiningen	120	Gf	50.33N	10.25 E
Meishan [China]	152	Eh	30.05N	103.48 E
Meishan [China]	154	Ei	31.06N	119.43 E
Meishan → Jinzhai	154	Ci	31.40N	115.52 E
Meißen	120	Je	51.09N	13.29 E
Meißner	120	Fe	51.12N	9.50 E
Meitan (Yiquan)	152	If	27.48N	107.32 E
Meixian	152	Ka	24.21N	116.07 E
Meixiyukou	154	Bd	40.01N	113.08 E
Méjean, Causse-	122	Jj	44.16N	3.22 E
Mejillones	206	Fb	23.06S	70.27W
Mékambo	170	Bb	1.01N	13.56 E
Mekdela	168	Fc	11.28N	39.20 E
Mekele = Meqele (EN)	160	Kg	13.30N	39.28 E
Mékhé	162	Bb	15.07N	16.38W
Mekherrhane, Sebkha-	158	Hf	26.22N	1.20 E
Meknès	160	Ge	33.54N	5.32W
Meknès [3]	162	Fc	33.00N	5.30W
Mekong (EN) = Lancang Jiang	140	Mh	10.15N	105.55 E
Mekong (EN) = Mae Nam Khong	140	Mh	10.15N	105.55 E
Mekong (EN) = Mékôngk	140	Mh	10.15N	105.55 E
Mekong (EN) = Mènam Khong	140	Mh	10.15N	105.55 E
Mekong Delta (EN)	140	Mi	10.20N	106.40 E
Mekongga, Gunung-	150	Hg	3.35S	121.15 E
Mékôngk = Mekong (EN)	140	Mh	10.15N	105.55 E
Mekoryuk	178	Fg	60.23N	166.12W
Mékrou	166	Fc	12.24N	2.49 E
Mel, Ilha do-	204	Hg	25.31S	48.20W
Melaab	126	Ni	35.43N	1.20 E
Mēlādén	168	Hc	10.25N	49.52 E
Melaka	142	Mi	2.12N	102.15 E
Melaka [2]	150	Df	2.15N	102.15 E
Melaka, Selat- = Malacca, Strait of- (EN)	140	Mi	2.30N	101.20 E
Melamo, Cabo-	158	Lj	14.24S	40.49 E
Melanesia	208	Hf	13.00S	164.00 E
Melanesian Basin (EN)	106	Jj	0.05S	160.35 E
Melawi	150	Ff	0.05N	111.29 E
Melbourne [Ar.-U.S.]	186	Kh	36.04N	91.54W
Melbourne [Austl.]	210	Fh	37.49S	144.58 E
Melbourne [Eng.-U.K.]	124	Bb	52.49N	1.26W
Melbourne [Fl.-U.S.]	182	Kf	28.05N	80.37W
Melbourne-Dandenong	182	Gf	37.59S	145.12 E
Melchor Múzquiz	190	Dc	27.53N	101.31W
Melchor Ocampo	192	Hi	17.59N	102.11W
Meldorf	120	Fb	54.05N	9.05 E
Mele, Capo-	128	Cg	43.57N	8.10 E
Melekeiok	220a	Bc	7.29N	134.38 E
Melela	172	Fc	17.04S	38.36 E
Melenci	130	Dd	45.31N	20.19 E
Melenki	136	Ed	55.23N	41.42 E
Meleto Dağı	146	Ic	38.35N	41.32 E
Meleuz	136	Fd	52.58N	55.59 E
Mélèzes, Rivière aux-	180	Ke	57.00N	69.00W
Melfa	128	Hi	41.30N	13.35 E
Melfi [Chad]	168	Bc	11.04N	17.56 E
Melfi [It.]	128	Jj	41.00N	15.39 E
Melfort	180	Hf	52.52N	104.36W
Melgaço	202	Hi	1.47S	50.44W
Melilla [5]	160	Ge	35.19N	2.58W
Melincué, Laguna-	204	Bk	33.42S	61.28W
Melinești	130	Ge	44.34N	23.43 E
Melipilla	206	Fd	33.42S	71.13W
Melita	186	Fb	49.16N	101.00W
Meliti	130	Ei	40.50N	21.35 E
Melito di Porto Salvo	128	Jm	37.55N	15.47 E
Melito di Porto Salvo, Punta di-	128	Jm	37.57N	15.45 E
Melitopol	132	Jf	46.50N	35.22 E
Melk	120	Jg	48.13N	15.19 E
Mellakou	126	Ni	35.13N	10.13 E
Melle [Fr.]	122	Fh	46.13N	0.08W
Melle [F.R.G.]	124	Kb	52.12N	8.21 E
Mellen	186	Kc	46.20N	90.40W
Mellerud	118	Ef	58.42N	12.28 E
Mellid	126	Fb	42.55N	8.01W
Mellish Reef	212	Lc	17.25S	155.50 E
Mellish Seamount (EN)	208	Ia	34.00N	178.15 E
Mellit	168	Dc	14.08N	25.33 E
Melluco	172	Fb	12.33S	39.37 E
Meluli	172	Fc	16.28S	39.44 E
Melun	122	If	48.32N	2.40 E
Melville	188	Na	50.55N	102.48W
Melville, Cape-	212	Ia	14.10S	144.30 E
Melville, Lake-	180	Lf	53.42N	59.30W
Melville Bay	212	Hb	12.05S	136.45 E
Melville Bay (EN) = Melville Bugt	224	Od	75.35N	62.30W
Melville Bugt = Melville Bay (EN)	224	Od	75.35N	62.30W
Melville Hills	180	Fc	69.20N	123.00W
Melville Island	208	Ef	11.40S	131.00 E
Melville Peninsula	174	Kc	68.00N	84.00W
Melville Sound	180	Gc	68.05N	107.30W
Melvin, Lough-	118	Eg	54.25N	8.10W
Mélykút	120	Pj	46.13N	19.23 E
Memaliaj	130	Ci	40.20N	19.58 E
Memambetsu	154	Db	43.55N	144.11 E
Memba	172	Gb	14.10S	40.30 E
Memba, Baia de-	172	Gb	14.11S	40.35 E
Memberamo	150	Kg	1.28S	137.52 E
Memboro	150	Gh	9.22S	119.32 E
Memmert	124	Ja	53.39N	6.53 E
Memmingen	120	Gg	47.59N	10.10 E
Mempawah	150	Ef	0.22N	108.58 E
Memphis	164	Fd	29.52N	31.15 E
Memphis [Mo.-U.S.]	186	Jf	40.28N	92.10W
Memphis [Tn.-U.S.]	176	Jf	35.08N	90.03W
Memphis [Tx.-U.S.]	186	Fi	34.44N	100.32W
Memuro	154	Qc	42.55N	143.03 E
Memuro-Dake	154a	Cb	42.52N	142.45 E
Mena	168	Gd	5.30N	41.06 E
Mena [Ar.-U.S.]	186	Ii	34.35N	94.15W
Mena [Ukr.-U.S.S.R.]	136	Cd	51.33N	32.14 E
Menabe	158	Lk	20.00S	44.40 E
Menai Strait	118	Ih	53.12N	4.12W
Ménaka	160	Hc	15.55N	2.26 E
Mènam Khong = Mekong (EN)	140	Mh	10.15N	105.55 E
Menangalaku	150	Gh	9.36S	119.01 E
Menard	186	Gk	30.55N	99.47W
Menawashei	168	Dc	12.40N	25.01 E
Menčul, gora-	120	Th	48.16N	23.49 E
Mendala, Puncak-	150	Lg	4.44S	140.20 E
Mendanau, Pulau-	150	Eg	2.51S	107.26 E
Mendanha	202	Kg	18.06S	43.30W
Mende	122	Jj	44.31N	3.30 E
Mendebo	168	Fd	6.50N	39.40 E
Mendelejevsk	114	Ni	55.57N	52.22 E
Menden (Sauerland)	120	De	51.26N	7.48 E
Mendes	126	Mi	35.39N	0.52 E
Méndez	192	Je	25.07N	98.34W
Mendi [Eth.]	168	Fd	9.48N	35.05 E
Mendi [Pap.N.Gui.]	214	Ci	6.10S	143.40 E
Mendig	120	Jf	50.22N	7.16 E
Mendip Hills	118	Kj	51.15N	2.40W
Mendocino, Cape-	188	Dg	39.19N	123.48W
Mendocino Fracture Zone	96	Af	40.25N	124.25W
Mendota [Ca.-U.S.]	188	Eh	36.45N	120.23W
Mendota [Il.-U.S.]	186	Lf	41.33N	89.07W
Mendoza	200	Ji	32.54S	68.50W
Mendoza [2]	206	Gd	33.30S	68.30W
Mené, Landes du-	122	Df	48.15N	2.32W
Mene de Mauroa	194	Lh	10.43N	71.01W
Mene Grande	202	Db	9.49S	70.56W
Menemen	146	Bc	38.36N	27.04 E
Menen/Menin	122	Jd	50.48N	3.07 E
Meneng Point	220e	Bb	0.33S	166.57 E
Meneses	204	Dj	30.53S	56.30W
Ménez-Hom	122	Bf	48.13N	4.16W
Menfi	128	Gm	37.36N	12.58 E
Mengcheng	152	Ke	33.11N	116.30 E
Mengdingjie	152	Gg	23.31N	99.07 E
Menggala	150	Eg	4.28S	105.17 E
Mengibar	126	Ig	37.58N	3.48W
Mengjin	154	Bg	34.50N	112.26 E
Mengla	152	Hg	21.30N	101.35 E
Menglangba → Lancang	152	Gg	22.37N	99.57 E
Menglian	152	Gg	22.20N	99.27 E
Mengoun Huizu Zizhixian	152	Dh	38.04N	117.06 E
Mengyin	152	Df	35.42N	117.56 E
Mengzi	142	Mg	23.23N	103.24 E
Menihek Lakes	180	Kf	54.00N	66.30W
Menin/Menen	122	Jd	50.48N	3.07 E
Menindee	212	If	32.24S	142.26 E
Menindee Lake	212	If	32.20S	142.23 E
Meningie	212	Hg	35.42S	139.20 E
Menjapa, Gunung-	150	Gf	1.05N	116.05 E
Menno	186	Hd	43.14N	97.34W
Menoikion Óros	130	Gh	41.11N	23.48 E
Menominee	186	Lc	45.07N	87.39W
Menongue	160	Ij	14.40S	17.41 E
Menor, Mar-	126	Lg	37.43N	0.48W
Menorca = Minorca (EN)	110	Gg	40.00N	4.00 E
Mentasta Lake	178	Kd	62.55N	143.45W
Mentawai, Kepulauan- = Mentawai Islands (EN)	140	Lj	2.00S	99.30 E
Mentawai Islands (EN) = Mentawai, Kepulauan-	140	Lj	2.00S	99.30 E
Menton	122	Nk	43.47N	7.30 E
Mentougou	154	Dd	39.56N	116.02 E
Menyuan	152	Hf	37.30N	101.35 E
Menzelinsk	114	Mi	55.45N	53.09 E
Menzies	210	Ee	29.41S	121.02 E
Menzies, Mount-	222	Ff	73.30S	61.50 E
Meon	204	Dk	31.25S	57.55W
Meoqui	190	Cc	28.17N	105.29W
Meponda	172	Eb	13.25S	34.52 E
Meppel	120	Mb	52.42N	6.11 E
Meppen	120	Dc	52.41N	7.19 E
Mé Qu	152	He	33.58N	102.10 E
Mequinensa, Pantà de- / Mequinenza, Embalse de-	126	Lc	41.15N	0.02W
Mequinenza, Embalse de- / Mequinensa, Pantà de-	126	Lc	41.15N	0.02W
Merabello, Gulf of- (EN) = Merabéllou, Kólpos-	130	In	35.14N	25.47 E
Merabéllou, Kólpos- = Merabello, Gulf of- (EN)	130	In	35.14N	25.47 E
Merak	150	Eh	5.56S	106.00 E
Meråker	114	Gc	63.26N	11.45 E
Méraláb	219b	Db	14.27S	168.03 E
Meramangye, Lake-	212	Ge	28.25S	132.15 E
Meran / Merano	128	Fd	46.40N	11.09 E
Merano / Meran	128	Fd	46.40N	11.09 E
Meratus, Pegunungan-	150	Gg	2.45S	115.40 E
Merauke	210	Fa	8.28S	140.20 E
Mercadal / Es Mercadal	126	Qe	39.59N	4.05 E
Mercato Saraceno	128	Gg	43.57N	12.12 E
Merced	182	Cd	37.18N	120.29W
Mercedario, Cerro-	198	Ii	31.59S	70.14W
Mercedes [Arg.]	206	Ic	34.39S	59.27W
Mercedes [Arg.]	206	Ic	29.12S	58.05W
Mercedes [Arg.]	200	Ji	33.40S	65.30W
Mercedes [Ur.]	200	Ki	33.16S	58.01W
Merchants Bay	180	Lc	67.10N	62.50W
Merchtem	124	Gd	50.58N	4.14 E
Mercury Islands	218	Fb	36.35S	175.50 E
Mercy, Cape-	180	Ld	64.56N	63.40W
Mercy Bay	180	Fb	74.15N	118.10W
Meredith, Cape-	206	Hm	52.12S	60.38W
Meredith, Lake-	186	Fi	35.36N	101.42W
Meredoua	162	Hd	25.20N	2.05 E
Merefa	136	Df	49.51N	36.00 E
Merelbeke	124	Fd	51.00N	3.45 E
Merenga	138	Kd	61.43N	156.05 E
Mergui	142	Lf	12.26N	98.36 E
Mergui Archipelago	140	Lf	12.00N	98.00 E
Méri	166	Hc	10.47N	14.06 E
Meriç	130	Ji	41.11N	26.25 E
Meriç	146	Bb	40.52N	26.12 E
Mérida [Mex.]	176	Kg	20.58N	89.37W
Mérida [Sp.]	126	Ff	38.55N	6.20W
Mérida [Ven.]	200	Ie	8.36N	71.08W
Mérida, Cordillera de-	198	Ie	8.40N	71.00W
Meridian	176	Kf	32.22N	88.42W
Mérignac	122	Fj	44.50N	0.38W
Merikarvia	114	Ef	61.51N	21.30 E
Merin, Laguna-	206	Jd	32.45S	52.50W
Meringur	212	If	34.24S	141.29 E
Merir Island	208	Ed	4.19N	132.19 E
Merizo	220b	Bb	13.16N	144.40 E
Merke	135	Ic	42.52N	73.12 E
Merkem, Houthulst-	124	Ed	50.57N	2.51 E
Merkine/Merkinė	116	Kj	54.07N	24.20 E
Merkinė/Merkine	116	Kj	54.07N	24.20 E
Merkis/Merkys	114	Fi	54.10N	24.11 E
Merksem, Antwerpen-	124	Gc	51.15N	4.27 E
Merksplas	124	Gc	51.22N	4.52 E
Merkys/Merkis	114	Fi	54.10N	24.11 E
Meroe	168	Eb	16.05N	33.55 E
Meroe	168	Eb	16.56N	33.59 E
Merouane, Chott-	162	Ic	34.00N	6.02 E
Merredin	212	Df	31.29S	118.16 E
Merrick	118	If	55.08N	4.29W
Merrill	182	Jb	45.11N	89.41W
Merriman	186	Fe	42.55N	101.42W
Merritt	180	Ff	50.07N	120.47W
Merritt Island	182	Kf	28.21N	80.42W
Merritt Reservoir	186	Fe	42.35N	100.55W
Mersa Fatma	168	Gc	14.53N	40.19 E
Mersa Teklay	168	Fb	17.25N	38.45 E
Mersea Island	124	Cc	51.47N	0.57 E
Merseburg	120	He	51.22N	12.00 E
Mers el Kebir	126	Li	35.44N	0.43W
Mersey	118	Kh	53.25N	3.00W
Merseyside [3]	118	Kh	53.30N	3.00W
Mersin → İçel	142	Fd	36.48N	34.38 E
Mersing	150	Df	2.26N	103.50 E
Mers-les-Bains	124	Bd	50.04N	1.23 E
Mersrags/Mērsrags	116	Jg	57.19N	23.01 E
Mērsrags/Mersrags	116	Jg	57.19N	23.01 E
Merta	148	Ec	26.39N	74.02 E
Merta Road	124	Ec	26.43N	73.55 E
Merthyr Tydfil	118	Jj	51.46N	3.23W
Merti	170	Gb	1.04N	38.40 E
Mértola	126	Fg	37.38N	7.40W
Mertule Maryam	168	Fc	10.50N	38.15 E
Mertvyj Kultuk, sor-	132	Ng	45.30N	53.30 E
Mertz Glacier	222	Je	67.40S	144.45 E
Meru	170	Gb	0.03N	37.39 E
Meru [Fr.]	124	Be	49.14N	2.08 E
Meru, Mount-	170	Gc	3.14S	36.45 E
Merure	204	Fb	15.33S	53.05W
Merville	124	Ed	50.38N	2.38 E
Merzifon	144	Ca	40.53N	35.29 E
Merzig	120	Cg	49.27N	6.38 E
Meša	114	Li	55.34N	49.24 E
Mesa [Az.-U.S.]	176	Hf	33.25N	111.50W
Mesa [Co.-U.S.]	186	Dg	39.14N	108.08W
Mesabi Range	186	Jc	47.30N	92.50W
Mesagne	128	Lj	40.33N	17.48 E
Mescalero	186	Dj	33.09N	105.46W
Meščera = Moscow Basin (EN)	110	Kd	55.00N	40.30 E
Meschede	120	Se	51.21N	8.17 E
Mescit Dağı	146	Ib	40.22N	41.11 E
Meščovsk	114	Jj	54.19N	35.18 E
Mesegon	220b	Bb	7.09N	151.55 E
Meseta Meridional	110	Fh	39.30N	3.30W
Meseta Septentrional	110	Fh		
Meskiana	128	Bo	35.38N	7.40 E
Meskiana, Oued-	128	Bo	35.48N	7.53 E
Meslo	168	Fd	6.22N	39.50 E
Mesnil-Val, Criel-sur-Mer-	124	Bd	50.03N	1.20 E
Mesola	128	Gf	44.55N	12.14 E
Mesolóngion	130	Ek	38.22N	21.26 E
Mesopotamia	144	Fc	34.00N	44.00 E
Mesopotamia [Arg.]	198	Ms	30.00S	59.00W
Mesopotamia [Asia]	140	Gf	34.00N	44.00 E
Mediterranean Sea (EN)	110	Hh	35.00N	20.00 E
Mesquite [Nv.-U.S.]	188	Hh	36.48N	114.04W
Mesquite [Tx.-U.S.]	186	Hj	32.46N	96.36W
Mesra	126	Mi	35.50N	0.10 E
Messaad	210	Hc	34.10N	3.30 E
Messalo	158	Lj	11.40S	40.46 E
Messaré, Órmos-	130	No	35.00N	24.40 E
Messina [It.]	112	Mh	38.11N	15.34 E
Messina [S.Afr.]	160	Kk	22.23S	30.00 E
Messina, Strait of- (EN) = Messina, Stretto di-	110	Hh	38.15N	15.35 E
Messina, Stretto di- = Messina, Strait of- (EN)	110	Hh	38.15N	15.35 E
Messini	130	Fl	37.03N	22.01 E
Messíni	130	El	37.15N	21.50 E
Messiniakós Kólpos	130	Fm	36.45N	22.10 E
Messoyéios Thálassa =	138	Cc	67.52N	77.27 E
Mesta	130	Hi	40.51N	24.44 E
Mestecăniş, Pasul-	130	Ib	47.28N	25.20 E
Mesters Vig	179	Jd	72.15N	24.20W
Mestia	162	Mb	43.03N	42.43 E
Mestre, Espigão-	202	If	12.30S	46.00W
Mestre, Venezia-	128	Ge	45.29N	12.14 E
Mesuji	150	Eg	4.08S	105.52 E
Meta	198	Je	6.12N	67.28W
Meta Incognita Peninsula	174	Mc	62.40N	68.00W
Metairie	186	Kl	29.59N	90.09W
Metaliferi, Munţii-	130	Fc	46.10N	22.50 E
Metallifere, Colline-	128	Eg	43.10N	10.55 E
Metán	206	Hc	25.29S	64.57W
Metangula	172	Eb	12.43S	34.49 E
Metaponto	128	Kj	40.20N	16.50 E
Metauro	128	Gg	43.50N	13.03 E
Metautu	221c	Ba	13.57S	171.54W
Meteghan	184	Nc	44.11N	66.10W
Metelen	124	Ic	52.09N	7.12 E
Meteóra	130	Ej	39.43N	21.40 E
Meteor Seamount (EN)	158	Hm	48.00S	8.30 E
Meteor Trench (EN)	106	Do	56.30S	27.40W
Méthana	130	Gl	37.35N	23.23 E
Methánon, Khersónisos-	130	Gl	37.36N	23.22 E
Methven	218	De	43.38S	171.38 E
Methwold	124	Cb	52.31N	0.33 E
Metković	124	Lg	43.03N	17.39 E
Metlakatla	178	Me	55.08N	131.35W
Metlika	128	Je	45.39N	15.19 E
Metlili Chaamba	162	Hc	32.16N	3.38 E
Metmárfag	162	Ed	26.26N	13.26W
Metohija	130	Dg	42.40N	20.27 E
Metro	150	Eh	5.05S	105.20 E
Metropolis	186	Lh	37.09N	88.44W
Métsovon	130	Ej	39.46N	21.11 E
Métsovon, Zigós- = Métsovon Pass (EN)	130	Ej	39.47N	21.15 E
Métsovon Pass (EN) = Métsovon, Zigós-	130	Ej	39.47N	21.15 E
Mettet	124	Gd	50.19N	4.40 E
Mettingen	124	Jb	52.19N	7.47 E
Mettlach	124	Gf	49.30N	6.36 E
Mettmann	124	Ic	51.15N	6.58 E
Metu	160	Kh	8.20N	35.38 E
Metuje	120	Kf	50.20N	16.05 E
Metz	112	Gf	49.08N	6.10 E
Metzervisse	124	Hd	49.19N	6.17 E
Meu	122	Cf	48.02N	1.47W
Meulaboh	142	Lh	4.09N	96.08 E
Meulan	124	De	49.01N	1.54 E
Meulebeke	124	Fd	50.57N	3.17 E
Meureudu	150	Ce	5.16N	96.16 E
Meurthe	122	Mf	48.47N	6.09 E
Meurthe-et-Moselle [3]	122	Lf	49.00N	6.10 E
Meuse [3]	122	Lf	49.00N	5.30 E
Meuse, Côtes de-	122	Le	49.15N	5.22 E
Meuse (EN) = Maas	110	Ge	51.49N	5.01 E
Meuzenti	168	Bb	18.14N	17.06 E
Mexia	186	Hk	31.41N	96.29W
Mexiana, Ilha-	202	Ic	0.00	49.35W
Mexicali	176	Hf	32.40N	115.29W
Mexican Hat	188	Kh	37.09N	109.52W
Mexicanos, Laguna de los-	192	Fc	28.09N	106.57W
Mexico	186	Je	39.10N	91.53W
México [1]	176	Jg	19.00N	99.00W
México [2]	190	Ee	19.20N	99.30W
Mexico, Golfo de- = Mexico, Gulf of- (EN)	174	Kg	25.00N	90.00W
Mexico, Gulf of-	174	Kg	25.00N	90.00W
Mexico, Gulf of- (EN) = México, Golfo de-	174	Kg	25.00N	90.00W
Mexicana, Altiplanicie- = Mexican Plateau (EN)	174	Ig	25.30N	104.00W
Mexico Basin (EN)	106	Bg	25.00N	90.00W
Mexico City (EN) = Ciudad de México	176	Jg	19.24N	99.09W
Meybod	146	Pf	32.16N	53.59 E
Meydán-e Gel	146	Ph	29.04N	54.50 E
Meydāni, Ra's-e	146	Rj	25.24N	59.27 E
Meyeti	168	Gd	6.37N	42.20 E —	
Meyisti	130	Mm	36.09N	29.34 E
Meymac	122	Ii	45.32N	2.09 E
Meymaneh	146	Ue	35.55N	64.47 E
Meymeh	146	Of	33.27N	51.10 E
Meymeh	146	Lf	32.05N	47.16 E
Meza	114	Hi	55.43N	31.30 E
Mezcala	192	Ji	17.56N	99.37W

Index Symbols

- [1] Independent Nation
- [2] State, Region
- [3] District, County
- [4] Municipality
- [5] Colony, Dependency
- Continent
- Physical Region
- Historical or Cultural Region
- Mount, Mountain
- Volcano
- Hill
- Mountains, Mountain Range
- Hills, Escarpment
- Plateau, Upland
- Pass, Gap
- Plain, Lowland
- Delta
- Salt Flat
- Valley, Canyon
- Crater, Cave
- Karst Features
- Depression
- Polder
- Desert, Dunes
- Forest, Woods
- Heath, Steppe
- Cape, Point
- Coast, Beach
- Cliff
- Peninsula
- Isthmus
- Sandbank
- Island
- Atoll
- Rock, Reef
- Islands, Archipelago
- Rocks, Reefs
- Coral Reef
- Well, Spring
- Geyser
- River, Stream
- Waterfall, Rapids
- River Mouth, Estuary
- Lake
- Salt Lake
- Intermittent Lake
- Reservoir
- Swamp, Pond
- Canal
- Glacier
- Ice Shelf, Pack Ice
- Ocean
- Sea
- Gulf, Bay
- Strait, Fjord
- Lagoon
- Bank
- Fracture
- Seamount
- Tablemount
- Ridge
- Shelf
- Basin
- Escarpment, Sea Scarp
- Trench, Abyss
- National Park, Reserve
- Point of Interest
- Recreation Site
- Cave, Cavern
- Historic Site
- Ruins
- Wall, Walls
- Church, Abbey
- Temple
- Scientific Station
- Railway station
- Airport
- Port
- Military installation
- Lighthouse
- Mine
- Tunnel
- Dam, Bridge

Mezcalapa, Río- 192 Mh 18.36N 92.39W
Mezdra 130 Gf 43.09N 23.42 E
Meždurečenski 136 Gd 59.36N 65.53 E
Meždušarski, ostrov- 136 Fa 71.20N 53.00 E
Mèze 122 Jk 43.25N 3.36 E
Mezen 112 Kb 65.50N 44.13 E
Mezen 110 Kb 66.00N 43.59 E
Mézenc, Mont- 122 Kj 44.55N 4.11 E
Meženin 120 Sc 53.07N 22.29 E
Mezenskaja guba 110 Kb 66.40N 43.45 E
Mezenskaja Pižma 114 Ld 64.30N 48.32 E
Mežgorje 120 Th 48.30N 23.37 E
Mežica 128 Id 46.31N 14.52 E
Mézidon-Canon 124 Be 49.05N 0.04W
Mézin 122 Gj 44.03N 0.16 E
Mezőberény 120 Rj 46.49N 21.02 E
Mezőcsát 120 Qi 47.49N 20.55 E
Mezőföld 120 Oj 46.55N 18.35 E
Mezőkovácsháza 120 Qj 46.24N 20.55 E
Mezőkövesd 120 Qi 47.49N 20.35 E
Mezőtúr 120 Qi 47.00N 20.38 E
Mežozerny 134 Ii 54.10N 59.25 E
Mežpjanje 114 Ki 55.25N 45.00 E
Mezquital 192 Gf 23.29N 104.23W
Mezquital, Río- 192 Gf 22.55N 104.54W
Mezquitic 192 Hf 22.23N 103.41W
Mgači 138 Jf 51.02N 142.18 E
Mglin 132 Hc 53.04N 32.53 E
Mhow 148 Fd 22.33N 75.46 E
Miahuatlán de Porfirio Diaz 192 Ki 16.20N 96.36W
Miajadas 126 Ge 39.09N 5.54W
Miaméré 168 Bd 9.02N 19.55 E
Miami [Az.-U.S.] 188 Jj 33.24N 110.52W
Miami [Fl.-U.S.] 176 Kg 25.46N 80.12W
Miami [Ok.-U.S.] 182 Id 36.53N 94.53W
Miami Beach 182 Kf 25.47N 80.08W
Miānābād 146 Qd 37.02N 57.27 E
Miāndowāb 144 Gb 36.58N 46.06 E
Miandrivazo 172 Hc 19.30S 45.28 E
Mianduhe 152 Lb 49.12N 121.09 E
Miāneh 144 Gb 37.26N 47.42 E
Miang, Khao- 148 Ke 17.42N 101.01 E
Miangas, Pulau- 150 Ie 5.35N 126.35 E
Mianning 152 Hf 28.31N 102.10 E
Miānwāli 148 Eb 32.35N 71.33 E
Mianyang 152 He 31.23N 104.49 E
Mianyang (Xiantaozhen) 154 Bi 30.22N 113.27 E
Miaodao Qundao 152 Ld 38.10N 120.45 E
Miao'er Shan 152 Jf 25.50N 110.22 E
Miao Ling 152 If 26.05N 108.00 E
Miarinarivo 172 Hc 18.56S 46.54 E
Miass 136 Gd 55.01N 60.06 E
Miass 136 Gd 56.06N 64.30 E
Miasskoje 134 Ji 55.15N 61.55 E
Miasteczko Krajeńskie 120 Nc 53.06N 17.01 E
Miastko 120 Mb 54.01N 17.00 E
Michael, Mount- 212 Ja 6.25S 145.20 E
Michajlova Island 222 Ge 66.30S 85.00 E
Michalovce 120 Rh 48.46N 21.55 E
Michelstadt 124 Le 49.41N 9.01 E
Miches 194 Md 18.59N 69.03W
Michigan [2] 182 Jc 44.00N 85.00W
Michigan, Lake- 174 Ke 44.00N 87.00W
Michigan City 182 Jc 41.43N 86.54W
Michipicoten Bay 184 Eb 47.55N 84.56W
Michipicoten Island 180 Ig 47.45N 85.45W
Michoacán [2] 190 De 19.10N 101.50W
Michów 120 Se 51.32N 22.19 E
Mico, Río- 194 Eg 12.11N 84.16W
Micoud 197k Bb 13.50N 60.54W
Micronesia 208 Gc 11.00N 159.00 E
Micronesia,Federated States of- [5] 210 Gd 6.30N 152.00 E
Mičurin 130 Kg 42.10N 27.51 E
Mičurinsk 112 Ke 52.54N 40.31 E
Midai, Pulau- 150 Ef 3.00N 107.47 E
Midar 162 Gc 34.57N 3.32W
Mid-Atlantic Ridge (EN) 106 Di 0.00 20.00W
Middelburg [Neth.] 122 Jc 51.30N 3.37 E
Middelburg [S.Afr.] 172 Cf 31.30S 25.00 E
Middelburg [S.Afr.] 172 De 25.47S 29.28 E
Middelfart 114 Bi 55.30N 9.45 E
Middelharnis 124 Gc 51.45N 4.12 E
Middelkerke 124 Ec 51.11N 2.49 E
Middelkerke-Westende 124 Ec 51.10N 2.46 E
Middle Alkali Lake 188 Ef 41.28N 120.04W
Middle America Trench (EN) 106 Mh 15.00N 95.00W
Middle Andaman 148 If 12.30N 92.50 E
Middle Atlas (EN)=Moyen Atlas 158 Ge 33.30N 4.30W
Middlebury 184 Kc 44.01N 73.10W
Middle Caicos 194 Lc 21.47N 71.43W
Middle Fork Feather River 188 Eg 38.47N 121.36W
Middle Island 172b Ab 9.22S 46.21 E
Middle Loup River 186 Gf 41.17N 98.23W
Middlemarch 218 Df 45.30S 170.07 E
Middle Reef 219a Ee 12.35S 160.30 E
Middlesboro 182 Kd 36.36N 83.43W
Middlesbrough 112 Fe 54.35N 1.14W
Middlesex 194 Ce 17.02N 88.31W
Middlesex 124 Bc 51.35N 0.10W
Middlesex 118 Mj 51.30N 0.05W
Middleton 178 Je 59.25N 146.25W
Middleton Reef 208 Gg 29.30S 159.10 E
Middletown [Ct.-U.S.] 184 Ke 41.33N 72.39W
Middletown [N.Y.-U.S.] 184 Je 41.26N 74.26W
Middletown [Oh.-U.S.] 184 Ef 39.31N 84.25W
Midelt 162 Gc 32.41N 4.45W
Mid Glamorgan [3] 118 Jj 51.35N 3.35W
Midhordland 116 Ad 60.15N 5.55 E
Midhurst 124 Bd 50.59N 0.44W
Midi, Canal du- 110 Gg 43.36N 1.25 E
Midi de Bigorre, Pic du- 122 Gl 42.56N 0.08 E
Midi d'Ossau, Pic du- 122 Fl 42.51N 0.26W
Mid-Indian Basin (EN) 106 Gj 10.00S 80.00 E
Mid-Indian Ridge (EN) 106 Gj 3.00S 75.00 E
Midland [Mi.-U.S.] 184 Ed 43.37N 84.14W
Midland [Ont.-Can.] 180 Jh 44.45N 79.53W
Midland [S.D.-U.S.] 186 Fd 44.04N 101.10W
Midland [Tx.-U.S.] 182 Ge 32.00N 102.05W
Midlands [3] 172 Dc 19.00S 30.00 E
Midlands 118 Li 52.40N 1.50W
Midleton/Mainistir na Corann 118 Ej 51.55N 8.10W
Midnapore → Medinīpur 148 Hd 22.26N 87.20 E
Midongy du Sud 172 Hd 23.34S 47.01 E
Midou 122 Fk 43.54N 0.30W
Midouze 122 Fk 43.48N 0.51W
Mid-Pacific Mountains (EN) 106 Jg 20.00N 170.00 E
Midway Islands [5] 210 Jb 28.13N 177.22W
Midway Islands 208 Jb 28.13N 177.22W
Midwest 188 Le 43.25N 106.16W
Midwest City 186 Hi 35.27N 97.24W
Midyat 146 Id 37.25N 41.23 E
Midžor 110 Ig 43.24N 22.40 E
Miechów 120 Qf 50.23N 20.01 E
Miedwie, Jezioro- 120 Kc 53.15N 14.55 E
Międzychód 120 Ld 52.36N 15.53 E
Międzylesie 120 Mf 50.10N 16.40 E
Międzyrzec Podlaski 120 Se 52.00N 22.47 E
Międzyrzecz 120 Ld 52.27N 15.34 E
Międzyrzecze Łomżyńskie 120 Rd 52.45N 21.45 E
Miehikkälä 116 Ld 60.40N 27.42 E
Mie Ken [2] 154 Ng 34.35N 136.25 E
Miekojärvi 114 Fc 66.36N 24.23 E
Miélan 122 Gk 43.26N 0.19 E
Mielec 120 Rf 50.18N 21.25 E
Mielno 120 Mb 54.16N 16.01 E
Mien 116 Fh 56.25N 14.50 E
Mier 192 Jd 26.26N 99.09W
Miercurea Ciuc 130 Ic 46.21N 25.48 E
Mieres 126 Ga 43.15N 5.46W
Miersig 130 Ec 46.53N 21.51 E
Mier y Noriega 192 If 23.25N 100.07W
Miesbach 120 Hi 47.47N 11.50 E
Mieso 168 Gd 9.15N 40.45 E
Mifune 156 Be 32.43N 130.48 E
Migang Shan 152 Id 35.32N 106.13 E
Miguel Alamán, Presa- 192 Kh 18.13N 96.32W
Miguel Auza 192 He 24.18N 103.25W
Miguel Hidalgo, Presa- 192 Ed 26.40N 108.45W
Miha Chakaja 136 Eg 42.17N 42.02 E
Mihăilesti 130 Ie 44.20N 25.54 E
Mihail Kogălniceanu 130 Le 44.22N 28.27 E
Mihajlov 136 De 54.16N 39.03 E
Mihajlovgrad 130 Gf 43.25N 23.13 E
Mihajlovgrad [2] 130 Gf 43.25N 23.13 E
Mihajlovka [Kaz.-U.S.S.R.] 135 Hc 43.01N 71.31 E
Mihajlovka [R.S.F.S.R.] 136 Ee 50.05N 43.15 E
Mihajlovsk 134 Ih 56.29N 59.07 E
Mihalıççık 146 Dc 39.52N 31.30 E
Mihara 156 Cd 34.24N 133.05 E
Mihara-Yama 156 Fd 34.43N 139.23 E
Mi He 154 Ef 37.12N 119.10 E
Mihonoseki 156 Cd 35.34N 133.18 E
Miho-Wan 156 Cd 35.30N 133.20 E
Miiraku 156 Ae 32.45N 128.40 E
Mijaly 132 Re 48.54N 53.50 E
Mijares/Millars 126 Le 39.55N 0.01W
Mijdaḥah 168 Hc 14.00N 48.26 E
Mijdrecht 124 Gb 52.12N 4.52 E
Mijirtein (EN)=Majërtën 158 Lh 9.00N 50.00 E
Mikasa 154 Pc 43.20N 141.40 E
Mikata 156 Dd 35.34N 135.54 E
Miki 156 Dd 34.47N 134.07 E
Mikinai = Mycenae (EN) 130 Fl 37.43N 22.45 E
Mikindani 170 Ge 10.17S 40.07 E
Mikkeli [2] 114 Ge 62.00N 27.30 E
Mikkeli/Sankt Michel 112 Ic 61.41N 27.15 E
Mikomoto-Jima 156 Fd 34.34N 138.56 E
Mikonos 130 Il 37.27N 25.20 E
Mikonos 130 Il 37.27N 25.23 E
Mikonou, Stenón- 130 Il 37.30N 25.20 E
Mikrá Préspa, Límni- 130 Ei 40.45N 21.06 E
Mikre 130 Hf 43.02N 24.31 E
Mikró Sofráno 130 Jm 36.05N 26.24 E
Mikulkin, mys- 134 Cc 67.48N 46.40 E
Mikulov 120 Mh 48.49N 16.39 E
Mikumi 170 Gd 7.24S 36.59 E
Mikun 136 Fc 62.21N 50.05 E
Mikuni 156 Ec 36.13N 136.09 E
Mikuni-Sanmyaku 154 Of 36.50N 138.40 E
Mikuni-Tōge 156 Fc 36.46N 138.50 E
Mikuni-Yama 156 Dd 35.21N 134.01 E
Mikura-Jima 152 Oe 33.50N 139.35 E
Milaca 186 Jd 45.45N 93.39W
Miladummadulu Atoll 148a Ba 6.15N 73.15 E
Milagro 202 Cd 2.07S 79.36W
Milājerd 146 Me 34.37N 49.12 E
Milan [Mo.-U.S.] 186 Jf 40.12N 93.07W
Milan [Tn.-U.S.] 184 Ch 35.55N 88.46W
Milan (EN) = Milano 112 Gf 45.28N 9.12 E
Milange 172 Fc 16.05S 35.47 E
Milano = Milan (EN) 112 Gf 45.28N 9.12 E
Milâs 146 Bd 37.19N 27.47 E
Milazzo 128 Jl 38.13N 15.14 E
Milazzo, Capo di- 128 Jl 38.16N 15.14 E
Milazzo, Golfo di- 128 Jl 38.15N 15.20 E
Milbank 182 Hb 45.13N 96.38W
Mildenhall 124 Cb 52.21N 0.31 E
Mildura 210 Fh 34.12S 142.09 E
Mile 152 Hg 24.28N 103.26 E
Mile 168 Gc 11.08N 40.55 E
Miléai 130 Gj 39.20N 23.09 E
Miles 210 Gg 26.40S 150.11 E
Miles City 182 Fb 46.25N 105.51W
Milet = Miletus (EN) 130 Kl 37.30N 27.16 E
Miletus (EN) = Milet 130 Kl 37.30N 27.16 E
Milevec 130 Fg 42.34N 22.27 E
Milevsko 120 Kg 49.27N 14.22 E
Milford 188 Ig 38.24N 113.01W
Milford Haven 118 Hj 51.44N 5.02W
Milford Lake 186 Hg 39.15N 97.00W
Milford Sound 216 Ch 44.40S 167.55 E
Milford Sound 218 Bf 44.35S 167.50 E
Milgis 170 Gb 1.48N 38.06 E
Milḥ, Baḥr al- 144 Fc 32.40N 43.35 E
Milḥ, Ra's al- 164 Ec 31.55N 25.02 E
Miliana 126 Oh 36.17N 2.14 E
Mili Atoll 208 Id 6.08N 171.55 E
Milicz 120 Ne 51.32N 17.17 E
Milkovo 138 Kf 54.43N 158.43 E
Milk River 188 Ib 49.09N 112.05W
Milk River 182 Eb 49.09N 112.05W
Milkūh 144 Jc 32.45N 61.55 E
Mill 180 Jd 63.57N 78.00W
Millars/Mijares 126 Le 39.55N 0.01W
Millau 122 Jj 44.06N 3.05 E
Milledgeville 184 Fi 33.04N 83.14W
Mille Lacs, Lac des - 180 Ig 48.50N 90.30W
Mille Lacs Lake 182 Ib 46.15N 93.40W
Millen 184 Gi 32.48N 81.57W
Miller [Nb.-U.S.] 186 Gf 40.57N 99.26W
Miller [S.D.-U.S.] 186 Gd 44.31N 98.59W
Millerovo 136 Ef 48.52N 40.25 E
Miller Seamount (EN) 178 Kf 53.30N 144.20W
Millerton 218 Dd 41.38S 171.52 E
Millevaches, Plateau de- 122 Ii 45.45N 2.11 E
Millicent 212 Ig 37.36S 140.22 E
Millington 184 Ch 35.20N 89.54W
Millinocket 184 Mc 45.39N 68.43W
Mill Island 222 He 65.30S 100.40 E
Millmerran 212 Ke 27.52S 151.16 E
Mills Lake 180 Fd 61.28N 118.15W
Millstatt 128 Hd 46.48N 13.35 E
Millville 184 Jf 39.24N 75.02W
Millwood Lake 186 Jj 33.45N 94.00W
Milne Land 179 Jd 71.20N 27.30W
Milo 158 Gg 11.04N 9.14W
Milolii 221a Fd 19.11N 155.55W
Milos 130 Hm 36.45N 24.26 E
Milos = Milos (EN) 130 Hm 36.41N 24.25 E
Milos (EN) = Milos 130 Hm 36.41N 24.25 E
Milparinka 212 Ie 29.44S 141.53 E
Miltenberg 120 Fg 49.42N 9.15 E
Milton [Fl.-U.S.] 184 Dj 30.38N 87.03W
Milton [N.Z.] 218 Cg 46.07S 169.58 E
Milton-Freewater 188 Fd 45.56N 118.23W
Milton Keynes 118 Mi 52.03N 0.42W
Miltou 168 Bc 10.14N 17.26 E
Milumbe, Monts- 170 Ed 8.00S 27.30 E
Miluo 154 Bj 28.51N 113.05 E
Miluo Jiang 152 Jf 28.51N 112.59 E
Milwaukee 176 Ke 43.02N 87.55W
Milwaukee Depth (EN) 106 Bh 19.30N 67.45W
Milwaukee Seamounts (EN) 208 Ia 32.18N 171.55 E
Milwaukie 188 Dd 45.27N 122.38W
Mimi-Gawa 156 Be 32.20N 131.37 E
Mimizan 122 Ej 44.12N 1.14W
Mimoň 120 Kf 50.40N 14.44 E
Mimongo 170 Bc 1.38S 11.39 E
Mimoso 204 Hb 15.10S 48.05W
Min 152 Kf 26.05N 119.32 E
Mīna 126 Mi 35.58N 0.31 E
Mina [Mex.] 192 Id 26.01N 100.32W
Mina [Nv.-U.S.] 188 Fg 38.24N 118.07W
Mina, Cerro- 194 Ki 8.21N 73.10W
Mīnā' Abd Allāh 146 Mh 29.01N 48.10 E
Mīnā' al Aḥmadī 146 Mh 29.04N 48.09 E
Mīnāb 146 Qi 27.09N 57.05 E
Mīnāb 146 Qi 27.01N 56.53 E
Mīnā' Barānīs 164 Ge 23.55N 35.28 E
Minahassa=Minahassa Peninsula (EN) 140 Oi 1.00N 124.35 E
Minahassa Peninsula (EN)= Minahassa 140 Oi 1.00N 124.35 E
Minakuchi 156 Ed 34.59N 136.11 E
Minamata 154 Kh 32.13N 130.24 E
Minami-Daitō-Jima 152 Nf 25.50N 131.15 E
Minami-furano 156a Cb 43.10N 142.32 E
Minami-Iō-Jima 214 Cc 24.14N 141.28 E
Minami-kayabe 156a Bc 41.53N 141.01 E
Minami-Tori-Shima=Marcus Island (EN) 208 Gb 26.32N 142.09 E
Minas [Cuba] 194 Ic 21.29N 77.37W
Minas [Indon.] 150 Df 0.50N 101.29 E
Minas [Ur.] 200 Ki 34.23S 55.14W
Minas de Riotinto 126 Fg 37.42N 6.35W
Minas Gerais [2] 202 Jg 18.00S 44.30W
Mīnā' Su'ūd 146 Mh 28.44N 48.24 E
Minatitlán [Mex.] 190 Fe 17.59N 94.31W
Minatitlán [Mex.] 192 Gh 19.22N 104.04W
Minaya 126 Je 39.17N 2.19W
Minbu 148 Id 20.11N 94.53 E
Minbya 148 Id 20.22N 93.16 E
Minchinmávida, Volcán- 206 Ff 42.49S 72.28W
Mincio 128 Ee 45.04N 10.59 E
Mindanao 140 Oi 8.00N 125.00 E
Mindanao Sea 140 Oi 9.15N 123.40 E
Mindel 120 Gh 48.31N 10.23 E
Mindelheim 120 Gh 48.03N 10.29 E
Mindelo 160 Eg 16.53N 25.00W
Minden [F.R.G.] 120 Ed 52.17N 8.55 E
Minden [La.-U.S.] 186 Jj 32.37N 93.17W
Minden [Nb.-U.S.] 186 Gf 40.30N 98.57W
Mindif 166 Hc 10.24N 14.26 E
Mindoro 140 Oh 12.50N 121.05 E
Mindoro Strait 150 Hd 12.20N 120.40 E
Mindouli 170 Bc 4.17S 14.21 E
Mindszent 120 Qj 46.32N 20.12 E
Mine 156 Bd 34.12N 131.11 E
Minehead 118 Jj 51.13N 3.29W
Mine Head 118 Fj 52.00N 7.35W
Mineiros 202 Hg 17.34S 52.34W
Mineral del Monte 192 Jg 20.08N 98.40W
Mineral'nyje Vody 136 Eg 44.12N 43.08 E
Mineral Wells 182 He 32.48N 98.07W
Minerva Reefs 208 Jg 23.50S 179.00W
Minervino Murge 128 Ki 41.05N 16.05 E
Minervois 122 Ik 43.25N 2.45 E
Minfeng/Niya 152 Dd 37.04N 82.46 E
Minga 170 Ee 11.08S 27.56 E
Mingala 168 Cd 5.06N 21.49 E
Mingan 180 Lf 50.18N 64.01W
Mingečaur 132 Oi 40.46N 47.02 E
Mingečaurskoje vodohranilišče 132 Oi 40.55N 46.45 E
Mingenew 212 De 29.11S 115.26 E
Minggang 154 Ch 32.27N 114.02 E
Mingguang → Jiashan 154 Dh 32.47N 118.00 E
Ming He 154 Cf 37.14N 114.47 E
Minglanilla 126 Ke 39.32N 1.36W
Mingoyo 170 Ge 10.06S 39.38 E
Mingshui 152 Mb 47.15N 125.53 E
Mingshui → Zhangqiu 154 Df 36.44N 117.33 E
Mingteke 152 Bd 37.09N 74.58 E
Mingteke Daban 152 Bd 37.00N 74.50 E
Minguez, Puerto- 126 Ld 40.50N 0.59W
Mingulay 118 Fe 56.50N 7.40W
Mingyuegou 154 Jc 43.08N 128.55 E
Minhe 152 Hd 36.20N 102.50 E
Minho 126 Dc 41.40N 8.30W
Minho 126 Dc 41.52N 8.51W
Minicoy Island 140 Ji 8.17N 73.02 E
Minigwal, Lake- 212 Ee 29.35S 123.10 E
Minija 116 Ii 55.20N 21.12 E
Minilya 212 Cd 23.51S 113.58 E
Minilya River 212 Cd 23.56S 113.51 E
Minipi Lake 180 Lf 52.28N 60.50W
Ministra, Sierra- 126 Jc 41.07N 2.30W
Minjar 134 Hi 55.04N 57.33 E
Min Jiang 140 Mg 28.46N 104.38 E
Minmaya 154 Pd 41.10N 140.28 E
Minna 160 Hh 9.37N 6.33 E
Minna Bluff 222 Kf 78.32S 166.30 E
Minneapolis [Ks.-U.S.] 186 Hg 39.08N 97.42W
Minneapolis [Mn.-U.S.] 176 Je 44.59N 93.13W
Minnedosa 180 Hf 50.14N 99.51W
Minnedosa River 186 Fb 49.53N 100.08W
Minnesota [2] 182 Ib 46.00N 94.15W
Minnesota River 182 Ic 44.54N 93.10W
Mino 156 Ed 35.32N 136.54 E
Miño 110 Fg 41.52N 8.51W
Minobu 156 Fd 35.22N 138.26 E
Minobu-Sanchi 156 Fd 35.15N 138.20 E
Minokamo 156 Ed 35.26N 137.00 E
Mino-Mikawa-Kōgen 156 Ed 35.10N 137.25 E
Minorca (EN)=Menorca 110 Gg 40.00N 4.00 E
Minot 176 Ie 48.14N 101.18W
Minqin 152 Hd 38.42N 103.11 E
Minqing 152 Kf 26.15N 118.52 E
Minquan 154 Cg 34.39N 115.08 E
Minquiers, les- 118 Km 48.58N 2.08W
Min Shan 152 He 33.35N 103.00 E
Minsk 112 Ie 53.54N 27.34 E
Minskaja oblat [3] 136 Ce 53.50N 27.40 E
Minskaja vozvyšennost 116 Lj 54.00N 27.10 E
Mińsk Mazowiecki 120 Rd 52.11N 21.34 E
Minta 166 He 4.35N 12.48 E
Minto, Lac - 180 Ke 57.15N 74.50W
Minto, Mount- 222 Kf 71.47S 168.45 E
Minto Inlet 180 Fb 71.19N 117.00W
Minto Reef 208 Gd 8.08N 154.17 E
Minturn 186 Cg 39.35N 106.26W
Mīnūdasht 146 Pd 37.10N 55.25 E
Minuf 146 Dg 30.28N 30.56 E
Minusinsk 138 Ef 53.43N 91.48 E
Minvoul 170 Bb 2.09N 12.08 E
Minwakh 168 Hb 16.48N 48.06 E
Minxian 152 He 34.26N 104.02 E
Miory 114 Gi 55.39N 27.41 E
Mios Num 150 Kg 1.30S 135.10 E
Miquan 152 Ec 44.05N 87.33 E
Miquelon 180 Jg 49.00N 76.00W
Miquelon 174 Ne 47.03N 56.20W
Mira 126 Dg 37.43N 8.47W
Mira [It.] 128 Ge 45.26N 12.08 E
Mira [Port.] 126 Dd 40.26N 8.44W
Mira, Peña- 126 Fc 41.55N 6.28W
Mirābād 144 Jc 30.25N 61.50 E
Mirabela 204 Ic 16.15S 44.11W
Miracatu 204 Ig 24.17S 47.28W
Miracema 202 Jh 21.25S 42.11W
Mirador, Serra do- 204 Hh 26.45S 49.50W
Miraflores [Col.] 202 Dc 1.30N 72.16W
Miraflores [Col.] 202 Db 5.12N 73.12W
Mirah, Wādī al- 146 If 32.26N 41.42 E
Miraj 148 Ee 16.50N 74.38 E
Miramar 206 Ie 38.16S 57.51W
Miramar, Laguna- 192 Ni 16.20N 91.20W
Miramas 122 Lk 43.35N 5.00 E
Mirambeau 122 Fi 45.22N 0.34W
Miramichi Bay 180 Kg 47.07N 65.10W
Miramont-de-Guyenne 122 Gj 44.36N 0.22 E
Miran 152 Ed 39.15N 88.50 E
Miranda [2] 202 Ea 10.15N 66.25W
Miranda [Arg.] 204 Cm 36.32S 59.09W
Miranda [Braz.] 202 Gh 20.14S 56.22W
Miranda de Corvo 126 Dd 40.06N 8.20W
Miranda de Ebro 126 Jb 42.41N 2.57W
Miranda do Douro 126 Fc 41.30N 6.16W
Mirande 122 Gk 43.31N 0.25 E
Mirandela 126 Ec 41.29N 7.11W
Mirandola 128 Ff 44.53N 11.04 E
Mirandópolis 204 Ge 21.09S 51.06W
Mirante do Paranapanema 204 Gf 22.17S 51.54W
Mira Por Vos 194 Jb 22.04N 74.38W
Mirapuxi, Rio- 204 Ga 13.06S 51.10W
Mirassol 204 He 20.46S 49.28W
Miravalles 126 Fb 42.45N 6.53W
Miravalles, Volcán- 174 Kh 10.45N 85.10W
Miravete, Puerto de- 126 Ge 39.43N 5.43W
Mir-Bašir 132 Oi 40.19N 46.58 E
Mirbāṭ 144 Hf 16.58N 54.50 E
Mirdita 130 Ch 41.49N 19.56 E
Mirebalais 194 Kd 18.50N 72.06W
Mirebeau 122 Gh 46.47N 0.11 E
Mirecourt 122 Mf 48.18N 6.08 E
Mirepoix 122 Hk 43.05N 1.53 E
Mirgorod 136 Df 50.00N 33.40 E
Miri 142 Ni 4.23N 113.59 E
Miria 166 Gc 13.43N 9.07 E
Mirim, Lagoa- 198 Ki 32.45S 52.50W
Mirina 130 Ij 39.52N 25.04 E
Miriñay, Esteros del- 204 Di 28.49S 57.10W
Miriñay, Río- 204 Dj 30.10S 57.39W
Mirny 142 Nc 62.33N 113.53 E
Mirny 222 Ge 66.33S 93.01 E
Mironovka 132 Ge 49.40N 31.01 E
Mirosławiec 120 Mc 53.21N 16.05 E
Mirpur 148 Eb 33.11N 73.46 E
Mīrpur Khās 142 Ig 25.32N 69.00 E
Mirqah Sūr 146 Kd 36.50N 44.19 E
Mīrsāle 168 Hd 5.58N 47.54 E
Mirşani 130 He 44.01N 24.01 E
Mirtöön Pélagos 130 Gm 37.00N 24.00 E
Miryang 154 Jg 35.29N 128.45 E
Mirzāpur 148 Gc 25.09N 82.35 E
Misaki 156 Ce 33.23N 132.07 E
Misawa 154 Pd 40.41N 141.24 E
Misery, Mount- 197c Ab 17.22N 62.48W
Mishan 152 Nb 45.34N 131.50 E
Mishawaka 184 De 41.40N 86.11W
Mishima 156 Fd 35.07N 138.54 E
Mi-Shima 154 Kg 34.47N 131.10 E
Mishraq, Khashm- 146 Lj 24.13N 46.18 E
Misilmeri 128 Hl 38.02N 13.27 E
Misima Island 214 Ej 10.40S 152.45 E
Misiones [2] 206 Jc 27.00S 55.00W
Misiones [3] 204 Dh 27.00S 57.00W
Misiones, Sierra de- 204 Eh 26.45S 54.20W
Miskah 146 Jj 24.53N 42.58 E
Miski, Enneri- 168 Bb 18.10N 17.45 E
Miškino 134 Ki 55.20N 63.55 E
Miskitos, Cayos- 190 Hf 14.23N 82.46W
Miskolc 112 If 48.06N 20.47 E
Miskolc [2] 120 Qh 48.06N 20.43 E
Mismār 168 Fb 18.13N 35.38 E
Misool, Pulau- 208 Ee 1.52S 130.10 E
Misquah Hills 182 Ib 47.17N 92.00W
Mişr=Egypt (EN) [1] 160 Jf 27.00N 30.00 E
Mişr al Jadīdah, Al Qāhirah- 164 Fc 30.06N 31.20 E
Mişrātah 160 Ie 32.23N 15.06 E
Mişrātah [3] 164 Cd 29.00N 16.00 E
Mişrātah, Ra's- 158 Ie 32.25N 15.05 E
Misserghin 126 Li 35.37N 0.44W
Missinaibi 180 Jf 50.44N 81.30W
Missinaibi Lake 184 Fa 48.23N 83.40W
Missinipe 180 He 55.36N 104.45W
Mission [S.D.-U.S.] 186 Fe 43.18N 100.40W
Mission [Tx.-U.S.] 186 Gm 26.13N 98.20W
Mission 188 Db 49.08N 122.18W
Mission Range 188 Ic 47.30N 113.55W
Mississippi [2] 182 Je 32.50N 89.30W
Mississippi 174 Kg 29.00N 89.15W
Mississippi Delta 174 Kg 29.10N 89.15W
Mississippi Fan (EN) 182 Jf 26.45N 88.30W
Mississippi River 184 Ic 45.26N 76.16W
Mississippi Sound 186 Lk 30.15N 89.00W
Misso 116 Lg 57.33N 27.23 E
Missoula 176 He 46.52N 114.01W
Missour 162 Gc 33.03N 3.59W
Missouri [2] 182 Id 38.30N 93.30W
Missouri 174 Jf 38.50N 90.08W
Missouri, Coteau du- 186 Gc 46.00N 99.30W
Missouri Valley 186 If 41.33N 95.53W
Mistassini 180 Kf 50.30N 74.00W
Mistassini 184 Ka 48.58N 72.40W
Mistassini, Lac- 174 Ld 51.00N 75.00W
Mistassini, Rivière- 180 Kg 48.42N 72.20W
Mistelbach an der Zaya 128 Kb 48.34N 16.34 E
Misterhult 116 Gg 57.28N 16.33 E
Mistrás 130 Fl 37.04N 22.22 E
Mistretta 128 Im 37.56N 14.22 E
Misugi 156 Ed 34.33N 136.15 E
Misumi [Jap.] 156 Bd 34.46N 131.58 E
Misumi [Jap.] 156 Be 32.37N 130.29 E
Mita, Punta- 192 Gg 32.04N 105.33W
Mitare, Río- 194 Mh 11.28N 69.56W
Mitchell [Austl.] 212 Je 26.29S 147.58 E
Mitchell [Or.-U.S.] 188 Ed 44.34N 120.09W
Mitchell [S.D.-U.S.] 182 Hc 43.40N 98.01W
Mitchell, Mount- 174 Kf 35.46N 82.16W
Mitchell Range 212 Hb 12.50S 135.35 E
Mitchell River 208 Ff 15.12S 141.35 E
Mitchell River Mission 212 Ic 15.28S 141.44 E
Mitchelstown/Baile Mhistéala 118 Ei 52.16N 8.16W
Mithimna 130 Jj 39.22N 26.10 E
Mitiaro Island 208 Lf 19.49S 157.43W
Mitidja, Plaine de la- 126 Oh 36.36N 3.00 E
Mitilini 130 Jj 39.06N 26.33 E
Mitilinis, Stenón- 130 Jj 39.10N 26.35 E
Mitla 190 Ee 16.55N 96.17W
Mitla, Laguna- 192 Ii 17.03N 100.25W
Mito 152 Pd 36.22N 140.28 E
Mitomoni 170 Ge 10.54S 35.19 E
Mitsamiouli 172 Gb 11.23S 43.18 E
Mitsinjo 172 Hc 16.00S 45.52 E
Mitsio, Nosy- 172 Hb 12.54S 48.36 E
Mitsiwa=Massawa (EN) 160 Kg 15.37N 39.39 E
Mitsiwa Channel 168 Fb 15.30N 40.00 E
Mitsuishi 156a Cb 42.15N 142.33 E
Mitsukaido 156 Fc 36.01N 139.59 E
Mitsuke 156 Fc 37.32N 138.56 E
Mitsushima 156 Ad 34.16N 129.20 E
Mittelfranken [3] 120 Gg 49.20N 10.40 E
Mittelland 128 Bd 46.50N 7.05 E
Mittellandkanal 110 He 52.16N 11.41 E
Mittelmark 120 Jd 52.20N 13.20 E
Mittenwald 120 Hi 47.27N 11.15 E
Mittersheim 124 If 48.52N 6.56 E
Mittersill 128 Gc 47.16N 12.29 E
Mittweida 120 If 50.59N 12.59 E
Mitú 200 Ie 1.08N 70.03W

Index Symbols

[1] Independent Nation
[2] State, Region
[3] District, County
[4] Municipality
[5] Colony, Dependency
Continent
Physical Region
Historical or Cultural Region
Mount, Mountain
Volcano
Hill
Mountains, Mountain Range
Hills, Escarpment
Plateau, Upland
Pass, Gap
Plain, Lowland
Delta
Salt Flat
Valley, Canyon
Crater, Cave
Karst Features
Depression
Polder
Desert, Dunes
Forest, Woods
Heath, Steppe
Oasis
Cape, Point
Coast, Beach
Cliff
Peninsula
Isthmus
Sandbank
Island
Atoll
Rock, Reef
Islands, Archipelago
Rocks, Reefs
Coral Reef
Well, Spring
Geyser
River, Stream
Waterfall, Rapids
River Mouth, Estuary
Lake
Salt Lake
Intermittent Lake
Reservoir
Swamp, Pond
Canal
Glacier
Ice Shelf, Pack Ice
Ocean
Sea
Gulf, Bay
Strait, Fjord
Lagoon
Bank
Seamount
Tablemount
Ridge
Shelf
Basin
Escarpment, Sea Scarp
Fracture
Trench, Abyss
National Park, Reserve
Point of Interest
Recreation Site
Cave, Cavern
Historic Site
Ruins
Wall, Walls
Church, Abbey
Temple
Scientific Station
Railway station
Airport
Port
Military installation
Lighthouse
Mine
Tunnel
Dam, Bridge

Mitumba, Monts-=Mitumba Range (EN) 158 Ji 6.00S 29.00 E
Mitumba Range (EN)= Mitumba, Monts- 158 Ji 6.00S 29.00 E
Mituva 116 Jj 55.00N 22.45 E
Mitwaba 170 Ed 8.38S 27.20 E
Mitzic 170 Bb 0.47N 11.34 E
Miura 156 Fd 35.08N 139.37 E
Miura-Hantō 156 Fd 35.15N 139.40 E
Mixco Viejo 194 Bf 14.52N 90.40W
Mixian 154 Bg 34.31N 113.22 E
Mixteco, Rio- 192 Jh 18.11N 98.30W
Miya-Gawa 156 Ed 34.32N 136.42 E
Miyagi Ken 154 Pe 38.30N 140.50 E
Miyagusuku-Jima 156b Ab 26.22N 127.59 E
Miyāh, Wādī al- 146 Gi 26.06N 36.31 E
Miyāh, Wādī al- [Eg.] 146 Ej 25.00N 33.23 E
Miyāh, Wādī al- [Syr.] 146 He 34.44N 39.57 E
Miyake-Jima 152 Oe 34.05N 139.30 E
Miyako 152 Pd 39.38N 141.57 E
Miyako-Jima 152 Mg 24.45N 125.20 E
Miyakonojō 154 Ki 31.44N 131.04 E
Miyako-Rettō 152 Lg 24.25N 125.00 E
Miyako-Wan 156 Hb 39.40N 142.00 E
Miyama 156 Dd 35.17N 135.34 E
Miyanojō 156 Bf 31.54N 130.27 E
Miyanoura-Dake 154 Ki 30.20N 130.29 E
Miyata 156 Be 33.45N 130.45 E
Miyazaki 152 Ne 31.54N 131.26 E
Miyazaki Ken 154 Kh 32.05N 131.20 E
Miyazu 154 Mg 35.32N 135.11 E
Miyazuka-Yama 156 Fd 34.24N 139.16 E
Miyazu-Wan 156 Dd 35.35N 135.13 E
Miyoshi 154 Lg 34.48N 132.51 E
Miyun 152 Kc 40.22N 116.53 E
Miyun Shuiku 154 Dd 40.31N 116.58 E
Mizan Teferi 168 Fd 6.53N 35.28 E
Mizdah 164 Bc 31.26N 12.59 E
Mizen Head/Carn Ui Néid 110 Fe 51.27N 9.49W
Mizhi 152 Jd 37.50N 110.03 E
Mizija 130 Gf 43.43N 23.51 E
Mizil 130 Je 45.01N 26.27 E
Mizorām 148 Id 23.00N 93.00 E
Mizque 202 Eg 17.56S 65.19W
Mizuho 156 Cd 34.50N 132.29 E
Mizuho 222 Ef 70.43S 40.20 E
Mizunami 156 Ed 35.22N 137.15 E
Mizusawa 154 Pe 39.08N 141.08 E
Mjadel 116 Lj 54.54N 27.03 E
Mjakiševo 116 Mh 56.30N 28.54 E
Mjakit 138 Kd 61.23N 152.10 E
Mjällom 116 Ha 62.59N 18.26 E
Mjaundža 138 Jd 63.02N 147.13 E
Mjölby 114 Dg 58.19N 15.08 E
Mjøndalen 116 De 59.45N 10.01 E
Mjorn 116 Eg 57.54N 12.25 E
Mjøsa 110 Hc 60.40N 11.00 E
Mkoani 170 Gd 5.22S 39.39 E
Mkokotoni 170 Gd 5.52S 39.15 E
Mkushi Bona 170 Ee 13.37S 29.23 E
Mkushi River 170 Ee 13.33S 29.40 E
Mkuze 172 Ee 27.10S 32.00 E
Mladá Boleslav 120 Kf 50.21N 14.54 E
Mladenovac 130 De 44.26N 20.42 E
Mlava 130 Ee 44.45N 21.14 E
Mława 120 Qc 53.06N 20.23 E
Mljet 128 Lh 42.45N 17.30 E
Mljetski kanal 128 Lh 42.48N 17.35 E
Mmadinare 172 Dd 21.53S 27.45 E
Mnichovo Hradiště 120 Kf 50.32N 14.59 E
Mnogoveršinny 138 If 53.55N 139.50 E
Moa 194 Jc 20.40N 74.56W
Moa 166 Cd 6.59N 11.36W
Moa, Pulau- 150 Ih 8.10S 127.56 E
Moab 182 Fd 38.35N 109.33W
Moabi 170 Bc 2.24S 10.59 E
Moala 219d Bc 18.36S 179.53 E
Moamba 172 Ee 25.36S 32.15 E
Moanda [Gabon] 170 Bc 1.34S 13.11 E
Moanda [Zaire] 170 Bd 5.56S 12.21 E
Moatize 172 Ec 16.10S 33.46 E
Moba 160 Ji 7.03S 29.47 E
Mobara 156 Gd 35.25N 140.17 E
Mobārakeh 146 Nf 32.20N 51.30 E
Mobaye 160 Jh 4.19N 21.11 E
Mobayi-Mbongo 170 Db 4.18N 21.11 E
Mobeka 170 Cb 1.53N 19.46 E
Moberly 182 Id 39.25N 92.26W
Mobile 176 Kf 30.42N 88.05W
Mobile Bay 182 Je 30.25N 88.00W
Mobridge 182 Gb 45.32N 100.26W
Mobuto Sese Seko, Lac-= Albert, Lake- (EN) 158 Kh 1.40N 31.00 E
Moca 194 Ld 19.24N 70.31W
Moçambique=Mozambique (EN) 160 Lj 15.03S 40.45 E
Moçambique=Mozambique (EN) 160 Kj 18.15S 35.00 E
Moçambique, Canal de-= Mozambique Channel (EN) 158 Lk 20.00S 43.00 E
Mocapra, Rio- 196 Ci 7.56N 66.46W
Mocha, Isla- 206 Fe 38.22S 73.56W
Moc Hoa 148 Lf 10.46N 105.56 E
Mochudi 172 Dd 24.23S 26.08 E
Mocimboa da Praia 160 Lj 11.20S 40.21 E
Möckeln 116 Fh 56.40N 14.10 E
Mockfjärd 116 Fd 60.30N 14.58 E
Môco, Serra- 158 Ij 12.28S 15.10 E
Mocoa 202 Cc 1.09N 76.38W
Mococa 204 Ie 21.28S 47.01W
Mocovi 204 Ci 28.24S 59.42W
Moctezuma [Mex.] 192 If 22.45N 101.05W
Moctezuma [Mex.] 192 Fb 30.12N 106.26W
Moctezuma [Mex.] 190 Cc 29.48N 109.42W
Moctezuma, Rio- [Mex.] 192 Jg 21.59N 98.34W
Moctezuma, Rio- [Mex.] 192 Ec 29.09N 109.40W
Mocuba 160 Kj 16.51S 36.56 E
Mocubúri 172 Fb 14.39S 38.54 E
Močurica 130 Jg 42.31N 26.32 E
Modane 122 Mi 45.12N 6.40 E
Modderrivier 172 Ce 29.02S 24.37 E
Modena [It.] 128 Ef 44.40N 10.55 E
Modena [Ut.-U.S.] 188 Ih 37.49N 113.55W
Moder 122 Of 48.49N 8.06 E
Modesto 182 Cd 37.39N 120.59W
Modica 128 In 36.52N 14.46 E
Modjamboli 170 Db 2.28N 22.06 E
Modjigo 166 Hb 17.09N 13.12 E
Mödling 128 Kb 48.05N 16.28 E
Modriča 128 Mf 44.58N 18.18 E
Modum 116 Ce 59.55N 10.00 E
Moe 212 Jg 38.10S 146.15 E
Moelv 114 Cf 60.56N 10.42 E
Moen 220d Bb 7.26N 151.52 E
Moengo 202 Hb 5.37N 54.24W
Moen-jo-Daro 148 Dc 27.19N 68.07 E
Moenkopi Wash 188 Ji 35.54N 111.26W
Moerbeke 124 Fc 51.10N 3.56 E
Moers 120 Ce 51.27N 6.39 E
Moeskroen/Mouscron 122 Jd 50.44N 3.13 E
Moffat 118 Jf 55.20N 3.27W
Moga 170 Ec 2.21S 26.49 E
Mogadishu (EN)=Muqdisho 160 Lh 2.03N 45.22 E
Mogadouro 126 Fc 41.20N 6.43W
Mogadouro, Serra do- 126 Fc 41.19N 6.40W
Mogāl 146 Nd 36.35N 50.35 E
Mogalakwena 172 Dd 22.27S 28.55 E
Mogami 156 Gb 38.45N 140.30 E
Mogami-Gawa 156 Oe 38.54N 139.50 E
Mogami Trench (EN) 156 Fb 39.00N 139.00 E
Mogaung 156 Jc 25.18N 96.56 E
Mogho 168 Ge 4.49N 40.19 E
Mogielnica 120 Qe 51.42N 20.43 E
Mogilev 112 Je 53.56N 30.18 E
Mogilev-Podolskij 132 Ee 48.27N 27.48 E
Mogilevskaja oblast 136 De 53.45N 30.30 E
Mogilno 120 Nd 52.40N 17.58 E
Mogincual 172 Gc 15.34S 40.24 E
Mogoča 142 Nd 53.44N 119.44 E
Mogočin 138 De 57.43N 83.40 E
Mogogh 168 Ed 8.26N 31.19 E
Mogojto 138 Gf 54.25N 110.27 E
Mogojtuj 138 Gf 51.15N 114.58 E
Mogok 148 Jd 22.55N 96.30 E
Mogollon Rim 182 Ee 34.20N 111.00W
Mogotes, Punta- 204 Dn 38.06S 57.33W
Mogotón, Pico- 194 Dg 13.45N 86.23W
Mogrein 160 Ff 25.13N 11.34W
Mogroum 168 Bc 11.06N 15.25 E
Moguer 126 Fg 37.16N 6.50W
Mogzon 138 Gf 51.42N 111.59 E
Mohács 120 Ok 45.59N 18.42 E
Mohaka 218 Gc 39.07S 177.12 E
Mohaka 218 Gc 39.07S 177.12 E
Mohales Hoek 172 Df 30.15S 27.25 E
Mohall 186 Fb 48.46N 101.31W
Mohammadābād 146 Pg 31.47N 54.27 E
Mohammadia 126 Mi 35.35N 0.04 E
Mohammedia 162 Fc 33.42N 7.24W
Mohanganj 148 Id 24.54N 90.59 E
Mohang-ni 154 If 36.46N 126.08 E
Mohave, Lake- 182 Ed 35.25N 114.38W
Mohawk Mountains 188 Ij 32.25N 113.25W
Mohe 142 Od 53.27N 122.18 E
Moheda 116 Fh 57.00N 14.34 E
Mohéli/Mwali 158 Lj 12.15S 43.45 E
Moher, Cliffs of-/Aillte an Mhothair 118 Di 52.58N 9.27W
Mohican, Cape- 178 Fd 60.12N 167.28W
Mohinora 174 Ig 26.06N 107.04W
Möhne 120 Ee 51.27N 8.00 E
Möhnesee 124 Ke 51.29N 8.05 E
Mohns Ridge (EN) 110 Ga 73.00N 5.00 E
Moholm 116 Ff 58.37N 14.02 E
Mohon, Charleville-Mézières- 124 Ge 49.46N 4.43 E
Mohon Peak 188 Ii 34.57N 113.15W
Mohoro 170 Gd 8.08S 39.10 E
Mohotani, Ile- 216 Na 9.59S 138.49W
Mohovaja 138 Kf 53.01N 158.38 E
Moi 116 Bf 58.28N 6.32 E
Moikovac 130 Cg 42.58N 19.35 E
Moimenta da Beira 126 Ed 40.59N 7.37W
Moindou 219b Be 21.42S 165.41 E
Moinești 130 Jc 46.28N 26.29 E
Moirai 130 Hn 35.03N 24.52 E
Mo i Rana 112 Hb 66.18N 14.08 E
Mõisaküla/Myjzakjula 116 Fg 58.07N 25.10 E
Moisés Ville 204 Bj 30.43S 61.29W
Moisie 180 Kf 50.11N 66.06W
Moisie 180 Kf 50.13N 66.06W
Moissac 122 Hj 44.06N 1.05 E
Moïssala 168 Bd 8.21N 17.46 E
Moitaco 196 Dh 8.01N 61.21W
Möja 116 He 59.25N 18.55 E
Mojácar 126 Kg 37.08N 1.51W
Mojada, Sierra- 192 Hd 27.15N 103.45W
Mojana, Caño- 194 Ji 9.02N 74.46W
Mojave 182 Dd 35.03N 118.10W
Mojave Desert 174 Hf 35.00N 117.00W
Mojiguaçu, Rio- 206 He 20.53S 48.10W
Moji Mirim 204 If 22.26S 46.57W
Mojjero 138 Fc 68.44N 103.30 E
Mojo 168 Fd 8.36N 39.09 E
Mojo 168 Gd 8.00N 41.50 E
Mojos, Llanos de- 198 Jg 15.00S 65.00W
Moju, Rio- 202 Id 1.40S 48.25W
Mojynty 136 Hf 47.10N 73.18 E
Mokambo 170 Ee 12.25S 28.21 E
Mokapu Peninsula 221a Db 21.26N 157.45W
Mokau 216 Dg 38.41S 174.37 E
Mokau 218 Fc 38.42S 174.37 E
Mokhotlong 172 De 29.17S 29.05 E
Mokil Atoll 208 Gd 6.40N 159.47 E
Moklakan 138 Gf 54.48N 118.56 E
Möklinta 116 Gd 60.05N 16.32 E
Mokochu, Khao- 148 Je 15.56N 99.06 E
Mokohinau Islands 218 Fa 35.55S 175.05 E
Mokolo 166 Hc 10.45N 13.48 E
Mokp'o 142 Of 34.47N 126.23 E
Mokra Gora 130 Dg 42.50N 20.25 E
Mokrany 130 Ue 51.48N 24.23 E
Mokrin 130 Dd 45.56N 20.25 E
Mokša 110 Ke 54.44N 41.53 E
Mokwa 166 Gd 9.17N 5.03 E
Mol 122 Lc 51.11N 5.07 E
Mola di Bari 128 Li 41.04N 17.05 E
Molango 192 Jg 20.47N 98.43W
Moláoi 130 Fm 36.48N 22.51 E
Molara 128 Dj 40.50N 9.45 E
Molas, Punta- 192 Pg 20.35N 86.44W
Molat 128 If 44.13N 14.50 E
Molatón 126 Kf 38.59N 1.24W
Molay-Littry, Le- 124 Be 49.15N 0.53W
Moldau (EN)=Vltava 110 He 50.21N 14.30 E
Moldava nad Bodvou 120 Qh 48.37N 21.00 E
Moldavia (EN)=Moldova 110 If 46.30N 27.00 E
Moldavia (EN) = Moldova 130 Jc 46.30N 27.00 E
Moldavian SSR (EN)= Moldavskaja SSR 136 Cf 47.00N 29.00 E
Moldavskaja Sovetskaja Socialističeskaja Respublika 136 Cf 47.00N 29.00 E
Moldavskaja SSR/ Respublika Sovetike Sočialiste Moldovenjaske 136 Cf 47.00N 29.00 E
Moldavskaja SSR= Moldavian SSR (EN) 136 Cf 47.00N 29.00 E
Molde 112 Gc 62.44N 7.11 E
Moldefjorden 116 Bb 62.45N 7.05 E
Moldotau, hrebet- 135 Jd 40.00N 74.50 E
Moldova 130 Jc 46.54N 26.58 E
Moldova = Moldavia (EN) 110 If 46.30N 27.00 E
Moldova = Moldavia (EN) 130 Jc 46.30N 27.00 E
Moldova Nouă 130 Ee 44.44N 21.41 E
Moldoveanu, Vîrful- 110 If 45.36N 24.44 E
Moldoviţa 130 Ib 47.41N 25.32 E
Mole 124 Bc 51.24N 0.20W
Moléne, Ile de- 122 Bf 48.24N 4.58W
Molens van Kinderdijk 124 Gc 51.52N 4.40 E
Molepolole 160 Jk 24.25S 25.30 E
Môle Saint-Nicolas 194 Kd 19.47N 73.22W
Molĕtai / Moletaj 116 Ki 55.13N 25.36 E
Moletaj / Molĕtai 116 Ki 55.13N 25.36 E
Molfetta 128 Ki 41.12N 16.36 E
Molihong Shan 154 Hc 42.11N 124.43 E
Molina, Parameras de- 126 Jd 40.55N 2.01W
Molina de Aragón 126 Kd 40.51N 1.53W
Molina de Segura 126 Kf 38.03N 1.12W
Moline 186 Kf 41.30N 90.31W
Moliniere Point 197p Bb 12.05N 61.45W
Molise 128 Ii 41.40N 14.30 E
Molkābād 146 Oe 34.32N 52.35 E
Molkom 116 Ee 59.36N 13.43 E
Moll 204 Cl 35.04S 59.39W
Möll 128 Hd 46.50N 13.26 E
Mollafeneri 130 Mi 40.54N 29.30 E
Mölle 116 Eh 56.17N 12.29 E
Mollendo 200 Ig 17.02S 72.01W
Molliens-Dreuil 124 Ee 49.52N 2.01 E
Mölln 120 Gc 53.38N 10.41 E
Möllösund 116 Df 58.04N 11.28 E
Mölndal 114 Ch 57.39N 12.01 E
Mölnlycke 116 Eg 57.39N 12.09 E
Moločansk 132 If 47.10N 35.36 E
Moločny, liman- 132 If 46.30N 35.20 E
Molócuè 172 Fc 17.03S 38.52 E
Molodečno 136 Ce 54.19N 26.53 E
Molodežnaja 222 Ee 67.40S 45.51 E
Molodi 116 Mf 58.00N 28.52 E
Molodogvardejskoje 136 He 54.07N 70.50 E
Mologa 110 Jd 58.50N 37.11 E
Molokai Island 208 Lb 21.08N 157.00W
Moloma 114 Lg 58.20N 48.28 E
Molong 212 Jf 33.06S 148.52 E
Molopo 158 Jk 28.31S 20.13 E
Moloundou 166 Ie 2.02N 15.13 E
Molteno 172 Df 31.24S 26.22 E
Molu, Pulau- 150 Jh 6.45S 131.33 E
Moluccas (EN)=Maluku, Kepulauan- 208 De 2.00S 128.00 E
Molucca Sea (EN)=Maluku, Laut- 140 Oj 0.05S 125.00 E
Molygino 138 Ee 58.11N 94.45 E
Moma 172 Fc 16.44S 39.14 E
Moma 138 Jc 66.20N 143.06 E
Mombaça 202 Ke 5.45S 39.28W
Mombasa 160 Ki 4.03S 39.40 E
Mombo 170 Gc 4.53S 38.17 E
Mombōyo 170 Cc 0.16S 19.00 E
Mombuca, Serra da- 204 Fd 18.15S 52.26W
Momčilgrad 130 Ih 41.32N 25.25 E
Mömling 124 Le 49.50N 9.09 E
Momotombo, Volcán- 194 Dg 12.26N 86.33W
Mompono 170 Db 0.04N 21.48 E
Mompós 202 Db 9.14N 74.27W
Momski hrebet 138 Jc 66.00N 145.00 E
Mon 148 Je 17.22N 97.20 E
Møn 114 Ci 55.00N 12.20 E
Mona, Canal de la-=Mona Passage (EN) 174 Mh 18.30N 67.45W
Mona, Isla- 190 Ke 18.05N 67.54W
Mona, Punta- 194 Fi 9.38N 82.37W
Monach Islands 118 Fd 57.32N 7.40W
Monaco 112 Gg 43.42N 7.23 E
Monadhliath Mountains 118 Id 57.15N 4.10W
Monagas 202 Fb 9.20N 63.00W
Monaghan/Muineachán 118 Gg 54.15N 6.58W
Monaghan/Muineachán 118 Gg 54.10N 7.00W
Monahans 186 Ek 31.36N 102.54W
Mona Passage (EN)=Mona, Canal de la- 174 Mh 18.30N 67.45W
Monapo 172 Gb 14.55S 40.18 E
Monarch Mountain 180 Ef 51.54N 125.54W
Monashee Mountains 180 Ff 51.00N 118.43W
Monastyrščina 132 Gb 54.19N 31.48 E
Monatélé 166 He 4.16N 11.12 E
Monbetsu [Jap.] 154 Qc 42.28N 142.07 E
Monbetsu [Jap.] 152 Pc 44.21N 143.22 E
Monbetsu-Shokotsu 156a Ca 44.23N 143.16 E
Moncalieri 128 Be 45.00N 7.41 E
Moncalvo 128 Ce 45.03N 8.16 E
Monção [Braz.] 202 Id 3.30S 45.15W
Monção [Port.] 126 Db 42.05N 8.29W
Moncayo 126 Kc 41.46N 1.50W
Moncayo, Sierra del- 126 Kc 41.45N 1.50W
Mončegorsk 136 Db 67.56N 32.58 E
Mönchengladbach 120 Ce 51.12N 6.26 E
Mönchengladbach-Rheydt 124 Ic 51.10N 6.27 E
Mönchengladbach-Wickrath 124 Ic 51.08N 6.25 E
Mönchgut 120 Jb 54.20N 13.40 E
Monchique 126 Dg 37.19N 8.33W
Monchique, Serra de- 126 Dg 37.19N 8.36W
Monclova 176 Ig 26.54N 101.25W
Moncton 176 Me 46.06N 64.07W
Mondai 204 Fh 27.05S 53.25W
Mondego 126 Dd 40.09N 8.52W
Mondego, Cabo- 126 Dd 40.11N 8.55W
Mondeville 124 Be 49.10N 0.19W
Mondjoko 170 Dc 1.41S 21.12 E
Mondo 168 Bc 13.43N 15.32 E
Mondoñedo 126 Ea 43.26N 7.22W
Mondorf-les-Bains/Bad Mondorf 124 Ie 49.30N 6.17 E
Mondoubleau 122 Gg 47.59N 0.54 E
Mondovi 128 Bf 44.23N 7.49 E
Mondragone 128 Hi 41.07N 13.53 E
Mondy 138 Ff 51.40N 100.59 E
Monédières, Les- 122 Hi 45.30N 1.52 E
Monemvasia 130 Gm 36.41N 23.03 E
Monessen 184 He 40.09N 79.53W
Monett 186 Jh 36.55N 93.55W
Monfalcone 128 He 45.49N 13.32 E
Monferrato 128 Cf 44.55N 8.05 E
Monforte 126 Ee 39.03N 7.26W
Monforte de Lemos 126 Eb 42.31N 7.30W
Monga 170 Db 4.12N 22.49 E
Mongala 170 Cb 1.53N 19.46 E
Mongalla 168 Ed 5.12N 31.46 E
Mongbwalu 170 Fb 1.58N 30.02 E
Mong Cai 148 Ld 21.32N 107.58 E
Monger, Lake- 212 De 29.15S 117.05 E
Mongga 219a Cb 7.57S 156.59 E
Mongolküre/Zhaosu 152 Dc 43.10N 81.07 E
Monghyr → Munger 148 Hc 25.23N 86.28 E
Mongibello 110 Hh 37.50N 14.55 E
Mongibello → Etna 110 Hh 37.50N 14.55 E
Monginevro, Colle del- 122 Mj 44.56N 6.44 E
Mongo 160 Ig 12.11N 18.42 E
Mongo 166 Cd 9.34N 12.11W
Mongol Altajn Nuruu = Mongolian Altai (EN) 140 Le 46.30N 93.00 E
Mongol Ard Uls = Mongolia (EN) 142 Me 47.00N 104.00 E
Mongolia (EN) = Mongol Ard Uls 142 Me 47.00N 104.00 E
Mongolian Altai (EN) = Mongol Altajn Nuruu 140 Le 46.30N 93.00 E
Mongonu 166 Hc 12.41N 13.36 E
Mongororo 166 Cc 12.01N 22.28 E
Mongoumba 168 Be 3.38N 18.36 E
Möng Pan 148 Jd 20.19N 98.22 E
Mongrove, Punta- 192 Hi 17.56N 102.11W
Mongu 160 Jj 15.17S 23.08 E
Monguel 162 Ef 16.25N 13.08W
Möng Yai 148 Jd 22.25N 98.02 E
Monheim 124 Ic 51.05N 6.53 E
Mönichkirchen 128 Kc 47.30N 16.02 E
Mon Idée, Auvillers-lès-Forges- 124 Ge 49.52N 4.21 E
Monigotes 204 Bj 30.30S 61.39W
Moni Hosiou Loukâ 130 Fk 38.24N 22.49 E
Monistrol-sur-Loire 122 Ki 45.17N 4.10 E
Monito, Isla- 197a Ab 18.09N 67.56W
Monitor Peak 188 Gg 38.50N 116.32W
Monitor Range 188 Gg 38.45N 116.40W
Monjolos 204 Jd 18.18S 44.05W
Monkayo 150 Ie 7.50N 126.00 E
Monkey Bay 170 Fe 14.05S 34.55 E
Monkey Point 194 Fg 11.36N 83.39W
Monkey River 194 Ce 16.22N 88.29W
Mońki 120 Sc 53.24N 22.49 E
Monkoto 170 Dc 1.38S 20.39 E
Monmouth 118 Kj 51.45N 3.00W
Monmouth [Il.-U.S.] 186 Kf 40.55N 90.39W
Monmouth [Or.-U.S.] 188 Dd 44.51N 123.14W
Monmouth [Wales-U.K.] 118 Kj 51.50N 2.43W
Monmouth Mountain 188 Da 51.00N 123.47W
Mönne 120 De 51.28N 7.30 E
Monnikendam 124 Hb 52.27N 5.02 E
Monnow 118 Kj 51.48N 2.42W
Mono 166 Fd 6.45N 1.50 E
Mono 219a Bb 7.20S 155.35 E
Monobe-Gawa 156 Ce 33.32N 133.42 E
Mono Lake 182 Dd 38.00N 119.00W
Monólithos 130 Km 36.07N 27.45 E
Monopoli 128 Lj 40.57N 17.18 E
Monor 120 Pi 47.21N 19.27 E
Monou 168 Cb 16.24N 22.11 E
Monóvar / Monòver 126 Lf 38.26N 0.50W
Monòver / Monóvar 126 Lf 38.26N 0.50W
Monowai, Lake- 218 Bf 45.55S 167.25 E
Monreal del Campo 126 Kd 40.47N 1.21W
Monreale 128 Hl 38.05N 13.17 E
Monroe [Ga.-U.S.] 184 Fi 33.47N 83.43W
Monroe [La.-U.S.] 176 Jf 32.33N 92.07W
Monroe [Mi.-U.S.] 184 Fe 41.55N 83.24W
Monroe [N.C.-U.S.] 184 Gh 34.59N 80.33W
Monroe [Or.-U.S.] 188 Dd 44.19N 123.18W
Monroe [Wi.-U.S.] 186 Le 42.36N 89.38W
Monroe, Lake- 184 Df 39.05N 86.25W
Monroe City 186 Kg 39.39N 91.44W
Monroeville 184 Dj 31.31N 87.20W
Monrovia 160 Fh 6.19N 10.48W
Mons/Bergen 122 Jd 50.27N 3.56 E
Monsanto 126 Ed 40.02N 7.07W
Monschau 120 Cf 50.33N 6.15 E
Monselice 128 Fe 45.14N 11.45 E
Monserrate, Isla- 192 De 25.41N 111.05W
Monsheim 124 Ke 49.38N 8.12 E
Møns Klint 116 Ej 54.58N 12.33 E
Mönsterås 114 Dh 57.02N 16.26 E
Montabaur 120 Df 50.26N 7.50 E
Montagna Grande 128 Gm 37.56N 12.44 E
Montagne 122 Jh 46.10N 3.40 E
Montagu 222 Ad 58.25S 26.20W
Montague 178 Je 60.00N 147.30W
Montague, Isla- 192 Bb 31.45N 114.48W
Montaigu 122 Eh 46.59N 1.19W
Montalbán 126 Ld 40.50N 0.48W
Montalbano Ionico 128 Kj 40.17N 16.34 E
Montalcino 128 Fg 43.03N 11.29 E
Montalegre 126 Ec 41.49N 7.48W
Montalto di Castro 128 Fh 42.21N 11.37 E
Montalto Uffugo 128 Kk 39.24N 16.09 E
Montalvânia 204 Jb 14.28S 44.32W
Montana 126 Bd 46.18N 7.30 E
Montana 182 Eb 47.00N 110.00W
Montana-Vermala 128 Bd 46.18N 7.30 E
Montánchez 126 Fe 39.13N 6.09W
Montánchez, Sierra de- 126 Ge 39.15N 5.55W
Montargis 122 Ig 48.00N 2.45 E
Montataire 124 Ee 49.16N 2.26 E
Montauban [Fr.] 122 Df 48.12N 2.03W
Montauban [Fr.] 122 Hj 44.01N 1.21 E
Montauk Point 184 Le 41.04N 71.52W
Montbard 122 Kg 47.37N 4.20 E
Montbéliard 122 Mg 47.31N 6.48 E
Montblanc 126 Nc 41.22N 1.10 E
Montbrison 122 Ki 45.36N 4.03 E
Montceau-les-Mines 122 Kh 46.40N 4.22 E
Mont Cenis, Col du- 110 Gf 45.15N 6.54 E
Montchanin 122 Kh 46.45N 4.27 E
Mont Darwin 172 Ec 16.46S 31.35 E
Mont-de-Marsan 122 Fk 43.53N 0.30W
Montdidier 122 Ie 49.39N 2.34 E
Mont-Dore [Fr.] 122 Ii 45.34N 2.49 E
Mont-Dore [N.Cal.] 219b Cf 22.17S 166.35 E
Monte, Laguna del- 204 Am 37.00S 62.28W
Monteagudo 202 Fg 19.49S 63.59W
Monte Albán 176 Jh 17.02N 96.45W
Monte Alegre 202 Hd 2.01S 54.04W
Monte Alegre, Rio- 204 Gc 17.16S 50.41W
Monte Alegre de Goiás 204 Ia 13.14S 47.10W
Montealegre del Castillo 126 Kf 38.47N 1.19W
Monte Alegre de Minas 204 Hd 18.52S 48.52W
Monte Azul 202 Jg 15.09S 42.53W
Montebello 184 Jc 45.39N 74.56W
Monte Bello Islands 212 Dd 20.25S 115.30 E
Monte-Carlo 122 Nk 43.44N 7.25 E
Montecarlo 204 Eh 26.34S 54.47W
Monte Carmelo 204 Id 18.43S 47.29W
Monte Caseros 204 Id 30.15S 57.39W
Montecatini Terme 128 Eg 43.53N 10.46 E
Montecchio Maggiore 128 Fe 45.30N 11.24 E
Monte Comán 206 Gd 34.36S 67.54W
Montecristi 194 Ld 19.52N 71.39W
Monte Cristo 204 Bb 14.43S 61.14W
Montecristo 128 Eh 42.20N 10.20 E
Monte Ermoso 204 Bn 38.55S 61.33W
Monte Escobedo 192 Hf 22.18N 103.35W
Montefalco 128 Gh 42.52N 12.39 E
Montefeltro 128 Gg 43.55N 12.15 E
Montefiascone 128 Gh 42.32N 12.02 E
Montefrio 126 Hg 37.19N 4.01W
Montego Bay 176 Lh 18.30N 77.55W
Monteiro 202 Ke 7.53S 37.07W
Montelíbano 194 Ji 8.02N 75.29W
Montélimar 122 Kj 44.34N 4.45 E
Monte Lindo, Arroyo- 204 Cg 25.28S 59.25W
Monte Lindo, Rio- 206 Ib 23.56S 57.12W
Monte Lindo Chico, Riacho- 204 Dg 25.53S 57.53W
Monte Lindo Grande, Riacho- 204 Cg 25.45S 58.06W
Montello [Nv.-U.S.] 188 Hf 41.16N 114.12W
Montello [Wi.-U.S.] 186 Le 43.48N 89.20W
Montemorelos 190 Ec 25.12N 99.49W
Montemor-o-Novo 126 Df 38.39N 8.13W
Montemor-o-Velho 126 Dd 40.10N 8.41W
Montemuro, Serra de- 126 Dc 40.58N 8.01W
Montenegro 206 Jc 29.42S 51.28W
Montenegro (EN) = Crna Gora 130 Cg 42.30N 19.18 E
Montenegro (EN)=Crna Gora 130 Cg 42.30N 19.18 E
Monte Plata 194 Md 18.48N 69.47W
Montepuez 172 Fb 13.07S 39.00 E
Montepuez 172 Gb 12.32S 40.27 E
Montepulciano 128 Fg 43.05N 11.47 E
Monte Quemado 206 Hc 25.48S 62.52W
Monte Real 126 Dn 39.51N 8.52W
Montereale, Passo di- 128 Hh 42.31N 13.13 E
Montereau-faut-Yonne 122 If 48.23N 2.57 E
Monterey 182 Cd 36.37N 121.55W
Monterey Bay 182 Cd 36.45N 121.55W
Montería 200 Ie 8.46N 75.53W
Montero 202 Fg 17.20S 63.15W
Monteros 206 Gc 27.10S 65.30W
Monterotondo 128 Gh 42.03N 12.37 E
Monterrey 176 Ig 25.40N 100.19W
Montesano 188 Dc 46.59N 123.36W
Monte San Savino 128 Fg 43.20N 11.43 E
Monte Sant'Angelo 128 Ji 41.42N 15.57 E
Monte Santu, Capo di- 128 Dj 45.05N 9.44 E

Index Symbols

1 Independent Nation
2 State, Region
3 District, County
4 Municipality
5 Colony, Dependency
Continent
Physical Region
Historical or Cultural Region
Mount, Mountain
Volcano
Hill
Mountains, Mountain Range
Hills, Escarpment
Plateau, Upland
Pass, Gap
Plain, Lowland
Delta
Salt Flat
Valley, Canyon
Crater, Cave
Karst Features
Depression
Polder
Desert, Dunes
Forest, Woods
Heath, Steppe
Oasis
Cape, Point
Coast, Beach
Cliff
Peninsula
Isthmus
Sandbank
Island
Atoll
Rock, Reef
Islands, Archipelago
Rocks, Reefs
Coral Reef
Well, Spring
Geyser
River, Stream
Waterfall, Rapids
River Mouth, Estuary
Lake
Salt Lake
Intermittent Lake
Reservoir
Swamp, Pond
Canal
Glacier
Ice Shelf, Pack Ice
Ocean
Sea
Gulf, Bay
Strait, Fjord
Lagoon
Bank
Seamount
Tablemount
Ridge
Shelf
Basin
Escarpment, Sea Scarp
Fracture
Trench, Abyss
National Park, Reserve
Point of Interest
Recreation Site
Cave, Cavern
Historic Site
Ruins
Wall, Walls
Church, Abbey
Temple
Scientific Station
Railway station
Airport
Port
Military installation
Lighthouse
Mine
Tunnel
Dam, Bridge

Montes Claros 200 Lg 16.43 S 43.52 W
Montes Claros de Goiás 204 Gb 15.54 S 51.13 W
Montesilvano 128 Ih 42.31 N 14.09 E
Montevarchi 128 Fg 43.31 N 11.34 E
Montevideo [2] 204 Dl 34.50 S 56.10 W
Montevideo [Mn.-U.S.] 186 Id 44.57 N 95.43 W
Montevideo [Ur.] 200 Ki 34.53 S 56.11 W
Monte Vista 186 Ch 37.35 N 106.09 W
Montfaucon 124 He 49.17 N 5.08 E
Montfort-l'Amaury 124 Df 48.47 N 1.49 E
Montfort-sur-Risle 124 Ce 49.18 N 0.40 E
Montgenèvre, Col de- 122 Mj 44.56 N 6.44 E
Montgomery 176 Kf 32.23 N 86.18 W
Montgomery Pass 188 Fh 38.00 N 118.20 W
Montguyon 122 Fi 45.13 N 0.11 W
Monthermé 124 Ge 49.53 N 4.44 E
Monthey 128 Ad 46.15 N 6.56 E
Monthois 124 Ge 49.19 N 4.43 E
Monticello [Ar.-U.S.] 186 Kj 33.38 N 91.47 W
Monticello [Fl.-U.S.] 184 Fj 30.33 N 83.52 W
Monticello [Ia.-U.S.] 186 Ke 42.15 N 91.12 W
Monticello [In.-U.S.] 184 De 40.45 N 86.46 W
Monticello [Ky.-U.S.] 184 Eg 36.50 N 84.51 W
Monticello [N.Y.-U.S.] 184 Je 41.39 N 74.41 W
Monticello [Ut.-U.S.] 182 Fd 37.52 N 109.21 W
Montiel 126 Jf 38.42 N 2.52 W
Montiel, Campo de- 126 Jf 38.46 N 2.44 W
Montiel, Cuchilla de- 204 Cj 31.05 S 59.10 W
Montignac 122 Hi 45.04 N 1.10 E
Montigny-le-Roi 122 Lf 48.00 N 5.30 E
Montigny-lès-Metz 122 Me 49.06 N 6.09 E
Montigny-le-Tilleul 124 Gd 50.23 N 4.22 E
Montijo [Pan.] 194 Gj 7.59 N 81.03 W
Montijo [Port.] 126 Df 38.42 N 8.58 W
Montijo [Sp.] 126 Ff 38.55 N 6.37 W
Montijo, Golfo de- 194 Gj 7.40 N 81.07 W
Montilla 126 Hg 37.35 N 4.38 W
Montividiu 204 Gc 17.24 S 51.14 W
Montivilliers 122 Ge 49.33 N 0.12 E
Mont Joli 180 Kg 48.35 N 68.11 W
Mont-Laurier 180 Jg 46.33 N 75.30 W
Mont-Louis 122 Il 42.31 N 2.07 E
Mont Louis 184 Oa 49.15 N 65.43 W
Montluçon 122 Ih 46.20 N 2.36 E
Montmagny 180 Kg 46.59 N 70.33 W
Montmarault 122 Ih 46.19 N 2.57 E
Montmédy 122 Le 49.31 N 5.22 E
Montmirail 122 Jf 48.52 N 3.32 E
Montmorency 124 Ef 49.00 N 2.20 E
Montmorillon 122 Gh 46.26 N 0.52 E
Montmort-Lucy 124 Ff 48.55 N 3.49 E
Monto 212 Kd 24.52 S 151.07 E
Montoire-sur-le-Loir 122 Gg 47.45 N 0.52 E
Montone 128 Gg 44.24 N 12.14 E
Montoro 126 Hf 38.01 N 4.23 W
Montpelier [Id.-U.S.] 182 Ec 42.19 N 111.18 W
Montpelier [Vt.-U.S.] 176 Le 44.16 N 72.35 W
Montpellier 112 Gg 43.36 N 3.53 E
Montpon-Ménestérol 122 Gi 45.01 N 0.10 E
Montréal 176 Le 45.31 N 73.34 W
Montreal Lake 180 Gf 54.20 N 105.40 W
Montreal River 184 Hb 47.08 N 79.27 W
Montréjeau 122 Gk 43.05 N 0.35 E
Montreuil [Fr.] 124 Ef 48.52 N 2.26 E
Montreuil [Fr.] 122 Hd 50.28 N 1.46 E
Montreuil-l'Argillé 124 Cf 48.56 N 0.29 E
Montreux 128 Ad 46.26 N 6.55 E
Montrose [Co.-U.S.] 182 Fd 38.29 N 107.53 W
Montrose [Scot.-U.K.] 118 Ke 56.43 N 2.29 W
Monts, Pointe des- 184 Na 49.19 N 67.23 W
Mont-Saint-Aignan 124 De 49.28 N 1.05 E
Mont-Saint-Michel, Baie du- 122 Ef 48.40 N 1.40 W
Mont-Saint-Michel, Le- 122 Ef 48.38 N 1.30 W
Montsalvy 122 Ij 44.42 N 2.30 E
Montsant, Serra del-/ Montsant, Sierra de- 126 Mc 41.17 N 0.50 E
Montsant, Sierra de-/ Montsant, Serra del- 126 Mc 41.17 N 0.50 E
Montsec, Serra del-/ Montsech, Sierra del- 126 Mb 42.02 N 0.50 E
Montsech, Sierra del-/ Montsec, Serra del- 126 Mb 42.02 N 0.50 E
Montsent de Pallars/ Montseny 126 Nb 42.29 N 1.02 E
Montseny/Pallars, Montsent de- 126 Nb 42.29 N 1.02 E
Montseny, Macizo del- 126 Oc 41.48 N 2.24 E
Montserrado [3] 166 Cd 6.35 N 10.35 W
Montserrat [5] 176 Mh 16.45 N 62.12 W
Montserrat, Monasterio de- / Montserrat, Monestir de- 126 Nc 41.35 N 1.49 E
Montserrat, Monestir de- / Montserrat, Monasterio de- 126 Nc 41.35 N 1.49 E
Montuosa, Isla- 194 Fj 7.28 N 82.14 W
Montville 124 De 49.33 N 1.07 E
Monument Peak 188 He 42.07 N 114.14 W
Monument Valley 188 Jh 36.50 N 110.20 W
Monveda 170 Db 2.57 N 21.27 E
Monviso 110 Gg 44.40 N 7.07 E
Monywa 148 Jd 22.07 N 95.08 E
Monza 128 De 45.35 N 9.16 E
Monze 170 Ef 16.16 S 27.29 E
Monzen 156 Ec 37.17 N 136.46 E
Monzón 126 Mc 41.55 N 0.12 E
Mo'oka 156 Fc 36.27 N 139.59 E
Moonbeam 184 Fa 49.25 N 82.11 W
Moonie 212 Ke 27.40 S 150.19 E
Moonie River 212 Je 29.19 S 148.43 E
Moonta 212 Hf 34.04 S 137.35 E
Moora 210 Ch 30.39 S 116.00 E
Moorcroft 188 Md 44.16 N 104.57 W
Moore 186 Hi 35.20 N 97.29 W
Moore, Lake- 208 Cg 29.50 S 117.35 E
Moorea, Ile- 208 Mf 17.32 S 149.50 W
Moore's Island 184 Il 26.18 N 77.33 W
Moorhead 182 Hb 46.53 N 96.45 W
Moormerland 124 Ja 53.18 N 7.26 E
Moormerland-Neermoor 124 Ja 53.18 N 7.26 E
Moorreesburg 172 Bf 33.09 S 18.40 E
Moosburg an der Isar 120 Hh 48.28 N 11.56 E
Moose 174 Kd 50.48 N 81.18 W
Moosehead Lake 182 Nb 45.40 N 69.40 W
Moose Jaw 176 Id 50.23 N 105.32 W
Moose Jaw River 188 Ma 50.34 N 105.17 W
Moose Lake 186 Jc 46.25 N 92.45 W
Mooselookmeguntic Lake 184 Lc 44.53 N 70.48 W
Moose Mountain 186 Eb 49.45 N 102.37 W
Moose Mountain Creek 186 Eb 49.12 N 102.10 W
Moosomin 180 Hf 50.09 N 101.40 W
Moosonee 176 Kd 51.17 N 80.39 W
Mopeia 172 Fc 17.59 S 35.43 E
Mopelia, Atoll- → Maupihaa Atoll 208 Lf 16.50 S 153.55 W
Mopti 160 Gg 14.30 N 4.12 W
Mopti [3] 166 Ec 14.40 N 4.15 W
Moqokorei 168 He 4.04 N 46.08 E
Moquegua 202 Dg 17.12 S 70.56 W
Moquegua [3] 202 Dg 16.50 S 70.55 W
Mór 120 Oi 47.23 N 18.12 E
Mor, Glen- 118 Id 57.10 N 4.40 W
Mora [Cam.] 166 Hc 11.03 N 14.09 E
Mora [Port.] 126 Df 38.56 N 8.10 W
Mora [Sp.] 126 Ie 39.41 N 3.46 W
Mora [Swe.] 114 Df 61.00 N 14.33 E
Morača 130 Cg 42.16 N 19.09 E
Morača, Manastir- 130 Cg 42.46 N 19.24 E
Morādābād 142 Jg 28.50 N 78.47 E
Morada Nova de Minas 204 Jd 18.25 S 45.22 W
Móra d'Ebre/Mora de Ebro 126 Mc 41.05 N 0.38 E
Mora de Ebro/Móra d'Ebre 126 Mc 41.05 N 0.38 E
Mora de Rubielos 126 Ld 40.15 N 0.45 W
Morafenobe 172 Gc 17.49 S 44.55 E
Moraģ 120 Pc 53.56 N 19.56 E
Mórahalom 120 Pj 46.13 N 19.53 E
Moraleda, Canal- 206 Ff 44.30 S 73.30 W
Moraleja 126 Fd 40.04 N 6.39 W
Morales [Col.] 194 Ki 8.17 N 73.52 W
Morales [Guat.] 192 Cf 15.29 N 88.49 W
Morales, Laguna- 192 Kf 23.35 N 97.45 W
Moramanga 172 Hc 18.57 S 48.11 E
Moran 188 Je 43.50 N 110.28 W
Morane Atoll 208 Ng 23.10 S 137.07 W
Morangas, Ribeirão- 204 Fd 19.59 S 52.19 W
Morant Bay 194 Ie 17.53 N 76.25 W
Morant Cays 190 Ie 17.24 N 75.59 W
Morant Point 194 Ie 17.55 N 76.10 W
Morar, Loch- 118 He 56.58 N 5.45 W
Moraramo 172 Hc 17.46 S 48.10 E
Mora River 186 Di 35.44 N 104.23 W
Moraska, Góra- 120 Md 52.30 N 16.52 E
Morata, Puerto de- 126 Kc 41.29 N 1.31 W
Moratalla 126 Kf 38.12 N 1.53 W
Moratuwa 148 Fg 6.46 N 79.53 E
Morava 110 Hf 48.10 N 16.59 E
Morava = Moravia (EN) 110 Hf 49.30 N 17.00 E
Morava = Moravia (EN) 120 Mg 49.30 N 17.00 E
Moravia (EN) = Morava 110 Hf 49.30 N 17.00 E
Moravia (EN) = Morava 120 Mg 49.30 N 17.00 E
Moravian Gate (EN) = Moravská brána 110 Hf 49.33 N 17.42 E
Moravian Upland (EN) = Českomoravská Vrchovina 110 Hf 49.20 N 15.30 E
Moravica 130 Df 43.51 N 20.05 E
Moravská brána = Moravian Gate (EN) 110 Hf 49.33 N 17.42 E
Moravské Budějovice 120 Lg 49.03 N 15.49 E
Morawa 212 De 29.13 S 116.00 E
Morawhanna 202 Gb 8.16 N 59.45 W
Moray Firth 118 Fd 57.50 N 3.30 W
Morbach 124 Je 49.49 N 7.07 E
Morbihan [3] 122 Dg 47.55 N 2.50 W
Morbihan 122 Dg 47.35 N 2.48 W
Morbylånga 114 Dh 56.31 N 16.23 E
Morcenx 122 Fj 44.02 N 0.55 W
Mordāb 146 Md 37.26 N 49.25 E
Mordaga 154 Ja 51.14 N 120.43 E
Morden 180 Hg 49.11 N 98.05 W
Mordovo 132 Lc 52.05 N 40.46 E
Mordovskaja ASSR [3] 136 Ee 54.20 N 44.30 E
Møre 116 Fh 56.25 N 15.55 E
More, Ben- 118 Ie 56.23 N 4.31 W
Morea 172 Bd 22.41 S 15.54 E
More Assynt, Ben- 118 Ic 58.07 N 4.51 W
Moreau River 182 Gb 45.18 N 100.43 W
Morecambe 118 Kg 54.04 N 2.53 W
Morecambe Bay 118 Kg 54.07 N 3.00 W
Moree 210 Fg 29.28 S 149.51 E
Morehead [Ky.-U.S.] 184 Ff 38.11 N 83.25 W
Morehead [Pap.N.Gui.] 214 Ci 8.50 S 141.57 E
Morehead City 174 Lf 34.43 N 76.43 W
Moreiz, gora- 136 Gb 69.30 N 62.05 E
Moreju 134 Ib 68.20 N 59.45 E
Morelia 176 Ih 19.42 N 101.07 W
Morella 126 Ld 40.37 N 0.06 W
Morelos 192 Ic 28.25 N 100.53 W
Morelos [2] 190 Ee 18.45 N 99.00 W
Morena, Sierra- 110 Fh 38.00 N 5.00 W
Moreni 130 Ie 44.59 N 25.39 E
Møre og Romsdal [2] 114 Be 62.40 N 7.50 E
Moresby 118 Ef 52.45 N 131.50 W
Moreton Bay 212 Ke 27.20 S 153.15 E
Moreton Island 212 Ke 27.10 S 153.25 E
Moret-sur-Loing 122 If 48.22 N 2.49 E
Moreuil 122 Ie 49.46 N 2.29 E
Morez 122 Mh 46.31 N 6.02 E
Mörfelden 124 Ke 49.59 N 8.34 E
Morgan City 186 Kl 29.42 N 91.12 W
Morganfield 184 Dg 37.41 N 87.55 W
Morganton 184 Gh 35.45 N 81.41 W
Morgantown [Ky.-U.S.] 184 Dg 37.14 N 86.41 W
Morgantown [W.V.-U.S.] 184 Hf 39.38 N 79.57 W
Morges 128 Ad 46.31 N 6.30 E
Morghāb 144 Jb 38.18 N 61.12 E
Morhange 122 Mf 48.55 N 6.38 E
Mori [China] 152 Fc 43.49 N 90.11 E
Mori [Jap.] 154 Pc 42.06 N 140.35 E
Moriarty 186 Ci 34.59 N 106.03 W
Morichal Largo, Río- 196 Eh 9.27 N 62.25 W
Moriguchi 156 Dd 34.44 N 135.34 E
Morin Dawa (Nirji) 152 Lb 48.30 N 124.28 E
Morioka 142 Qf 39.42 N 141.09 E
Moriyoshi 156 Ga 40.07 N 140.22 E
Moriyoshi-Yama 156 Gb 39.59 N 140.33 E
Morjärv 114 Fc 66.04 N 22.43 E
Morki 114 Lh 56.28 N 49.00 E
Morko 116 Gf 59.00 N 17.40 E
Morkoka 138 Gc 65.03 N 115.40 E
Mørkøv 116 Di 55.40 N 11.32 E
Morlaix 122 Cf 48.35 N 3.50 W
Morlanwelz 124 Gd 50.27 N 4.14 E
Mörlunda 116 Fg 57.19 N 15.51 E
Mormanno 128 Jk 39.53 N 15.59 E
Morne-à-l'Eau 196 Fd 16.21 N 61.31 W
Morne Diablotin 190 Le 15.30 N 61.24 W
Mornington, Isla- 206 Eg 49.45 S 75.23 W
Mornington Island 212 Hc 16.35 S 139.24 E
Moro 188 Ed 45.29 N 120.44 W
Moro Almanzor, Plaza del- 126 Gd 40.15 N 5.18 W
Morobe 210 Fe 7.45 S 147.37 E
Morocco (EN) = Al Maghrib [1] 160 Ge 32.00 N 5.50 W
Morogoro 160 Ki 6.49 S 37.40 E
Morogoro [3] 170 Gd 8.20 S 37.00 E
Moro Gulf 150 He 6.51 N 123.00 E
Moroleón 192 Ig 20.08 N 101.12 W
Morombe 160 Lk 21.44 S 43.23 E
Morón [Arg.] 204 Cl 34.39 S 58.37 W
Morón [Cuba] 190 Id 22.06 N 78.38 W
Morón [Ven.] 202 Ea 10.29 N 68.11 W
Morona, Río- 202 Cd 4.45 S 77.04 W
Morondava 160 Lk 20.15 S 44.17 E
Morón de la Frontera 126 Gg 37.08 N 5.27 W
Morones, Sierra- 192 Hg 21.55 N 103.05 W
Moroni 160 Lj 11.41 S 43.16 E
Moron Us He 140 Lf 34.42 N 95.00 E
Morotai, Pulau- 208 Dd 2.20 N 128.25 E
Moroto 160 Kh 2.32 N 34.39 E
Morovița 130 Ed 45.16 N 21.16 E
Morozov 130 Ig 42.30 N 25.10 E
Morozovsk 136 Ef 48.20 N 41.50 E
Morpeth 118 Lf 55.10 N 1.41 W
Morphou → Güzelyurt 146 Ee 35.12 N 32.59 E
Morrilton 186 Ji 35.09 N 92.45 W
Morrinhos 202 Ig 17.44 S 49.07 W
Morrinsville 218 Fb 37.39 S 175.32 E
Morris [Il.-U.S.] 184 Cf 41.22 N 88.26 W
Morris [Man.-Can.] 180 Hg 49.21 N 97.22 W
Morris [Mn.-U.S.] 186 Id 45.35 N 95.55 W
Morris, Mount- 212 Ge 26.09 S 131.04 E
Morrisburg 184 Jc 44.54 N 75.11 W
Morris Jesup, Kap- 224 Me 83.45 N 35.50 W
Morrison Dennis Cays 194 Ff 14.28 N 82.53 W
Morristown 184 Fg 36.13 N 83.18 W
Morrito 194 Eh 11.37 N 85.05 W
Morro, Punta del- 192 Kh 19.51 N 96.27 W
Morro Bay 182 Cd 35.22 N 120.51 W
Morro do Chapéu 202 Jf 11.33 S 41.09 W
Morrosquillo, Golfo de- 194 Ji 9.35 N 75.40 W
Morro Vermelho, Serra do- 204 Jc 17.45 S 45.20 W
Mörrum 116 Fh 56.11 N 14.45 E
Morrumbala 172 Fc 17.20 S 35.35 E
Morrumbene 172 Fd 23.39 S 35.20 E
Mörrumsån 116 Fh 56.09 N 14.44 E
Mors 116 Ch 56.50 N 8.45 E
Moršansk 136 Ee 53.26 N 41.49 E
Morsbach 124 Jd 50.52 N 7.45 E
Morsberg 124 Ke 49.43 N 8.54 E
Mörsil 114 Ce 63.19 N 13.38 E
Mörskom/Myrskylä 116 Kd 60.40 N 25.51 E
Morsott 128 Co 35.40 N 8.01 E
Mortagne 122 Mf 48.33 N 6.27 E
Mortagne-au-Perche 122 Gf 48.31 N 0.33 E
Mortagne-sur-Sèvre 122 Fg 47.00 N 0.57 W
Mortain 122 Ff 48.39 N 0.56 W
Mortara 128 Ce 45.15 N 8.44 E
Mortcha 158 Jg 16.00 N 21.10 E
Morteau 122 Mg 47.04 N 6.37 E
Morteaux-Couliboeuf 124 Bf 48.56 N 0.04 W
Morteros 206 Hd 30.42 S 62.00 W
Mortes, Rio das- 204 Je 21.09 S 44.53 W
Mortes, Rio das- → Manso, Rio- 198 Kg 11.45 S 50.44 W
Mortesoro 168 Ec 10.12 N 34.09 E
Mortlock Islands 208 Gd 5.27 N 153.40 E
Morton 188 Dc 46.33 N 122.17 W
Mortsel 124 Gc 51.10 N 4.28 E
Morumbi 204 Ef 23.46 S 54.06 W
Morvan 122 Jg 47.05 N 4.00 E
Morven 212 Je 26.25 S 147.07 E
Morvern 118 He 56.35 N 5.50 W
Morvi 148 Ed 22.49 N 70.50 E
Morwell 210 Fh 38.14 S 146.24 E
Morzine 122 Mh 46.11 N 6.43 E
Moržovec, ostrov- 114 Kc 66.45 N 42.35 E
Moša 114 Je 62.25 N 39.48 E
Mosbach 120 Fg 49.21 N 9.09 E
Mosby 116 Bf 58.14 N 7.54 E
Mosčny, ostrov- 114 Gg 60.00 N 27.50 E
Mosconi 204 Bl 35.44 S 60.34 W
Moscos Islands 148 Jf 14.00 N 97.45 E
Moscow [Id.-U.S.] 182 Db 46.44 N 116.59 W
Moscow (EN) = Moskva 110 Jd 55.08 N 38.50 E
Moscow (EN) = Moskva [R.S.F.S.R.] 112 Jd 55.45 N 37.35 E
Moscow Basin (EN) = Meščera 110 Kd 55.00 N 40.30 E
Moscow Canal (EN) = Moskvy, kanal imeni- 110 Jd 56.43 N 37.08 E
Moscow Upland (EN) = Moskovskaja vozvyšennost 110 Jd 56.30 N 37.30 E
Mosel = Moselle (EN) 110 Ge 50.22 N 7.36 E
Moselberge 124 Ie 49.57 N 6.56 E
Moselle [3] 122 Me 49.00 N 6.30 E
Moselle 110 Ge 50.22 N 7.36 E
Moselle (EN) = Mosel 110 Ge 50.22 N 7.36 E
Moses Lake 182 Db 47.08 N 119.17 W
Mosgiel 216 Di 45.53 S 170.22 E
Moshi 160 Ki 3.21 S 37.20 E
Mosina 120 Md 52.16 N 16.51 E
Mosjøen 114 Cd 65.50 N 13.12 E
Moskalvo 138 Jf 53.39 N 142.37 E
Moskenesøy 114 Cc 67.59 N 13.00 E
Moskovskaja oblast [3] 136 Dd 55.45 N 37.45 E
Moskovskaja vozvyšennost = Moscow Upland (EN) 110 Jd 56.30 N 37.30 E
Moskovski 135 Gf 37.40 N 69.39 E
Moskva [R.S.F.S.R.] = Moscow (EN) 112 Jd 55.45 N 37.35 E
Moskva [Tur.-U.S.S.R.] 135 Ee 38.27 N 64.24 E
Moskva = Moscow (EN) 110 Jd 55.08 N 38.50 E
Moskva, pik- 135 He 38.55 N 71.52 E
Moskvy, kanal imeni- = Moscow Canal (EN) 110 Jd 56.43 N 37.08 E
Moslavačka Gora 128 Ke 45.38 N 16.42 E
Moso 219b Dc 17.32 S 168.15 E
Mosomane 172 Dd 24.01 S 26.19 E
Mosoni-Duna 120 Ni 47.44 N 17.47 E
Mosonmagyaróvár 120 Ni 47.52 N 17.17 E
Mosquero 186 Ei 35.47 N 103.58 W
Mosquito, Baie - 180 Jd 60.40 N 78.00 W
Mosquito, Riacho- 204 Cf 22.12 S 57.57 W
Mosquito Coast (EN) = Mosquitos, Costa de los- 174 Kh 13.00 N 83.45 W
Mosquitos, Costa de los- = Mosquito Coast (E) 174 Kh 13.00 N 83.45 W
Mosquitos, Golfo de los- 174 Ki 9.00 N 81.20 W
Moss 112 Hd 59.26 N 10.42 E
Mossaka 170 Cc 1.13 S 16.48 E
Mossâmedes 204 Gc 16.07 S 50.11 W
Mossbank 188 Mb 49.55 N 105.59 W
Mossburn 216 Ci 45.41 S 168.15 E
Mosselbaai 160 Jl 34.11 S 22.08 E
Mossendjo 170 Bc 2.57 S 12.44 E
Mossman 210 Ff 16.28 S 145.22 E
Mossø 116 Ch 56.05 N 9.50 E
Mossoró 200 Mf 5.11 S 37.20 W
Moss Point 186 Lk 30.25 N 88.29 W
Mossuril 172 Gb 14.58 S 40.40 E
Most 120 Jf 50.32 N 13.39 E
Mostaganem 160 He 35.56 N 0.05 E
Mostaganem [3] 162 Hb 35.40 N 0.30 E
Mostar 128 Lg 43.21 N 17.49 E
Mostardas 204 Gj 31.06 S 50.57 W
Møsting, Kap- 178 Hf 63.45 N 41.00 W
Mostiska 132 Ce 49.48 N 23.09 E
Mostiștea 130 Je 44.15 N 26.54 E
Mostovskoj 132 Lg 44.22 N 40.48 E
Mosty 136 Ce 53.27 N 24.33 E
Mosul (EN) = Al Mawșil 142 Gf 36.20 N 43.08 E
Møsvatn 114 Bg 59.50 N 8.05 E
Mota 168 Fc 11.05 N 37.53 E
Mota 219b Ca 13.40 S 167.42 E
Motaba 170 Cb 2.03 N 18.03 E
Motacusito 204 Bc 17.35 S 61.31 W
Mota del Marqués 126 Gc 41.38 N 5.10 W
Motagua 174 Kh 15.44 N 88.14 W
Motajica 128 Le 45.04 N 17.40 E
Motala 114 Dg 58.33 N 15.03 E
Motala ström 116 Gf 58.38 N 16.10 E
Motatán 194 Li 9.24 N 70.36 W
Motatán, Río- 194 Li 9.32 N 71.02 W
Motegi 156 Gc 36.32 N 140.10 E
Mothe 219d Cc 18.40 S 178.30 W
Mothe-Achard, La- 122 Eh 46.37 N 1.40 W
Motherwell 118 Jf 55.48 N 4.00 W
Motīhāri 148 Gc 26.39 N 84.55 E
Motilla del Palancar 126 Ke 39.34 N 1.53 W
Motiti Island 218 Gb 37.40 S 176.25 E
Motlav 219b Ca 13.40 S 167.40 E
Motobu 156b Ab 26.40 N 127.55 E
Motol 120 Vd 52.17 N 25.40 E
Motovski zaliv 114 Hb 69.30 N 32.30 E
Motoyoshi 156 Gb 38.48 N 141.31 E
Motozintla de Mendoza 192 Mj 15.22 N 92.14 W
Motril 126 Ih 36.45 N 3.31 W
Motru 130 Fe 44.48 N 23.00 E
Motru 130 Ge 44.33 N 23.27 E
Motsuta-Misaki 156a Ab 42.36 N 139.49 E
Mott 186 Ec 46.22 N 102.20 W
Motteville 124 Ce 49.38 N 0.51 E
Motu 218 Gb 37.51 S 177.35 E
Motueka 218 Ed 41.07 S 173.01 E
Motuhora Island 218 Gb 37.50 S 177.00 E
Motu-Iti 221d Ac 27.11 S 109.27 W
Motu-Iti → Tupai Atoll 216 Kc 16.17 S 151.50 W
Motul 190 Gd 21.06 N 89.17 W
Motu-Nui 221d Ac 27.12 S 109.28 W
Motu One Atoll 208 Lf 15.48 S 154.33 W
Motupae 220n Ac 10.27 S 161.02 W
Motupena Point 219a Bb 6.32 S 155.09 E
Moturiki 219d Bb 17.46 S 178.45 E
Motutapu 220p Cb 21.14 S 159.43 W
Motu Tautara 221d Ab 27.05 S 109.26 W
Motutunga Atoll 208 Mf 17.06 S 144.22 W
Moubray Bay 222 Kf 72.11 S 170.15 E
Mouchard 122 Lh 46.58 N 5.48 E
Mouchoir Bank (EN) 190 Jd 20.57 N 70.42 W
Mouchoir Passage 194 Lc 21.10 N 71.00 W
Moudjéria 162 Ef 17.52 N 12.20 W
Mouila 160 Ii 1.52 S 11.01 E
Mouka 168 Cd 7.16 N 21.52 E
Moul 166 Hb 15.03 N 13.18 E
Mould Bay 176 Hb 76.15 N 119.30 W
Moule 196 Fd 16.20 N 61.21 W
Moule à Chique, Cap- 197k Bb 13.43 N 60.57 W
Moulins 122 Jh 46.34 N 3.20 E
Moulmein → Mawlamyine 142 Le 16.30 N 97.38 E
Moulouya 158 Ge 35.06 N 2.20 W
Moult 124 Be 49.07 N 0.10 W
Moultrie 184 Fj 31.11 N 83.47 W
Moultrie, Lake- 184 Gi 33.20 N 80.05 W
Mouly, Pointe de- 219b Ce 20.43 S 166.23 E
Mounda, Ákra- 130 Dk 38.03 N 20.47 E
Moundou 160 Ih 8.34 N 16.05 E
Moundsville 184 Gf 39.54 N 80.44 W
Mo'unga'one 221b Ba 19.38 S 174.29 W
Moungoudou 170 Bc 2.40 S 12.41 E
Mountainair 186 Ci 34.31 N 106.15 W
Mountain Grove 186 Jh 37.08 N 92.16 W
Mountain Home [Ar.-U.S.] 186 Jh 36.21 N 92.23 W
Mountain Home [Id.-U.S.] 182 Dc 43.08 N 115.41 W
Mountain Nile (EN) = Jabal, Baḩr al- 158 Kh 9.30 N 30.30 E
Mountain Village 178 Gd 62.05 N 163.44 W
Mount Airy 184 Gg 36.31 N 80.37 W
Mount Barker 212 Df 34.38 S 117.40 E
Mount Carmel 186 Mg 38.25 N 87.46 W
Mount Desert Island 184 Mc 44.20 N 68.20 W
Mount Douglas 210 Fg 21.30 S 146.50 E
Mount Eba 212 Hf 30.12 S 135.40 E
Mount Forest 184 Gd 43.59 N 80.44 W
Mount Frere 172 Df 31.00 S 28.58 E
Mount Gambier 210 Fh 37.50 S 140.46 E
Mount Hagen 214 Ci 5.52 S 144.13 E
Mount Hope 212 Hf 34.07 S 135.23 E
Mount Isa 210 Eg 20.44 S 139.30 E
Mountlake Terrace 188 Dc 47.47 N 122.18 W
Mount Lebanon 184 Ge 40.23 N 80.03 W
Mount Lofty Ranges 212 Hg 35.15 S 138.50 E
Mount Magnet 210 Cg 28.04 S 117.49 E
Mount Maunganui 216 Eg 37.38 S 176.12 E
Mount Morgan 212 Kd 23.39 S 150.23 E
Mountnorris Bay 212 Gb 11.20 S 132.45 E
Mount Peck 188 Ha 50.10 N 115.02 W
Mount Pleasant [Ia.-U.S.] 186 Kf 40.58 N 91.33 W
Mount Pleasant [Mi.-U.S.] 184 Ed 43.35 N 84.47 W
Mount Pleasant [S.C.-U.S.] 184 Hi 32.47 N 79.52 W
Mount Pleasant [Tx.-U.S.] 186 Ij 33.09 N 94.58 W
Mount Pleasant [Ut.-U.S.] 188 Jg 39.33 N 111.27 W
Mount's Bay 118 Hk 50.03 N 5.25 W
Mount Somers 218 De 43.42 S 171.25 E
Mount Sterling [Il.-U.S.] 186 Kg 39.59 N 90.45 W
Mount Sterling [Ky.-U.S.] 184 Ff 38.04 N 83.56 W
Mount Vancouver 180 Dd 60.20 N 139.41 W
Mount Vernon [Al.-U.S.] 184 Cj 31.05 N 88.01 W
Mount Vernon [Austl.] 212 Dd 24.13 S 118.14 E
Mount Vernon [Il.-U.S.] 182 Jd 38.19 N 88.55 W
Mount Vernon [In.-U.S.] 184 Dg 37.56 N 87.54 W
Mount Vernon [Ky.-U.S.] 184 Eg 37.21 N 84.20 W
Mount Vernon [Oh.-U.S.] 184 Fe 40.23 N 82.30 W
Mount Vernon [Wa.-U.S.] 182 Cb 48.25 N 122.20 W
Moura [Austl.] 212 Jd 24.35 S 150.00 E
Moura [Port.] 126 Ef 38.08 N 7.27 W
Mourão 126 Ef 38.23 N 7.21 W
Mourdi 168 Cb 17.50 N 22.25 E
Mourdi, Dépression du- = Mourdi Depression (EN) 158 Jg 18.10 N 23.00 E
Mourdiah 166 Dc 14.26 N 7.31 W
Mourdi Depression (EN) = Mourdi, Dépression du- 158 Jg 18.10 N 23.00 E
Mourmelon-le-Grand 124 Ge 49.08 N 4.22 E
Mourne Mountains/Beanna Boirche 118 Gg 54.10 N 6.04 W
Mouscron/Moeskroen 122 Jd 50.44 N 3.13 E
Moussoro 160 Ig 13.39 N 16.29 E
Moustiers-Sainte-Marie 122 Mk 43.51 N 6.13 E
Moutier/Münster 128 Bc 47.16 N 7.22 E
Moutiers 122 Mi 45.29 N 6.32 E
Moutong 150 Hf 0.28 N 121.13 E
Mouy 124 Ee 49.19 N 2.19 E
Mouydir 158 Hf 25.00 N 4.10 E
Mouyondzi 170 Bc 3.58 S 13.57 E
Mouzaia 126 Oh 36.28 N 2.41 E
Mouzon 124 He 49.36 N 5.05 E
Movas 192 Ec 28.10 N 109.25 W
Moxico 170 De 11.51 S 20.01 E
Moxico [3] 170 De 12.00 S 20.00 E
Moy/An Mhuaidh 118 Dg 54.12 N 9.08 W
Moyahua 192 Hg 21.16 N 103.10 W
Moyale [Eth.] 160 Kh 3.32 N 39.04 E
Moyale [Kenya] 168 Gb 3.32 N 39.03 E
Moyamba 166 Cd 8.10 N 12.26 W
Moÿ-de-l'Aisne 124 Fe 49.45 N 3.22 E
Moyen Atlas = Middle Atlas (EN) 158 Ge 33.30 N 4.30 W
Moyen-Chari [3] 168 Bd 9.00 N 18.00 E
Moyenne Guinée [3] 166 Cc 11.15 N 12.30 W
Moyenneville 124 Dd 50.04 N 1.45 E
Moyen-Ogooué [3] 170 Bc 0.30 S 10.30 E
Moyeuvre-Grande 124 Ie 49.15 N 6.02 E
Moyo 170 Fb 3.40 N 31.43 E
Moyo, Pulau- 150 Gh 8.15 S 117.34 E
Moyobamba 200 If 6.02 S 76.58 W
Moyowosi 170 Fc 4.50 S 31.24 E
Moyto 168 Bc 12.35 N 16.33 E
Moyu/Karakax 152 Cd 37.17 N 79.42 E
Možajsk 114 Ii 55.32 N 36.02 E
Mozambique (EN) = Moçambique 160 Lj 15.03 S 40.45 E
Mozambique (EN) = Moçambique [1] 160 Kj 18.15 S 35.00 E
Mozambique, Canal de- = Mozambique Channel (EN) 158 Lk 20.00 S 43.00 E
Mozambique Channel (EN) = Moçambique, Canal de- 158 Lk 20.00 S 43.00 E

Index Symbols

[1] Independent Nation
[2] State, Region
[3] District, County
[4] Municipality
[5] Colony, Dependency
Continent
Physical Region
Historical or Cultural Region
Mount, Mountain
Volcano
Hill
Mountains, Mountain Range
Hills, Escarpment
Plateau, Upland
Pass, Gap
Plain, Lowland
Delta
Salt Flat
Valley, Canyon
Crater, Cave
Karst Features
Depression
Polder
Desert, Dunes
Forest, Woods
Heath, Steppe
Oasis
Cape, Point
Coast, Beach
Cliff
Peninsula
Isthmus
Sandbank
Island
Atoll
Rock, Reef
Islands, Archipelago
Rocks, Reefs
Coral Reef
Well, Spring
Geyser
River, Stream
Waterfall, Rapids
River Mouth, Estuary
Lake
Salt Lake
Intermittent Lake
Reservoir
Swamp, Pond
Canal
Glacier
Ice Shelf, Pack Ice
Ocean
Sea
Gulf, Bay
Strait, Fjord
Lagoon
Bank
Seamount
Tablemount
Ridge
Shelf
Basin
Escarpment, Sea Scarp
Fracture
Trench, Abyss
National Park, Reserve
Point of Interest
Recreation Site
Cave, Cavern
Historic Site
Ruins
Wall, Walls
Church, Abbey
Temple
Scientific Station
Railway station
Airport
Port
Military installation
Lighthouse
Mine
Tunnel
Dam, Bridge

Mozambique Channel (EN) =Mozambique, Canal de- 158 Lk 20.00S 43.00E
Mozambique Plateau (EN) 158 Kl 32.00S 35.00E
Mozdok 136 Eg 43.44N 44.38E
Možga 136 Fd 56.28N 52.13E
Mozuli 116 Mh 56.32N 28.14E
Mozyr 136 Ce 52.02N 29.16E
Mpala 170 Ed 6.45S 29.31E
Mpanda 160 Ki 6.22S 31.02E
Mpigi 170 Fb 0.15N 32.20E
Mpika 160 Kj 11.50S 31.27E
Mpoko 168 Be 4.19N 18.33E
Mporokoso 170 Fd 9.23S 30.08E
Mpouia 170 Cc 2.37S 16.13E
Mpui 170 Fd 8.21S 31.50E
Mpulungu 170 Fd 8.46S 31.07E
Mpwapwa 170 Gd 6.21S 36.29E
Mrągowo 120 Rc 53.52N 21.19E
Mrakovo 134 Hj 52.43N 56.38E
Mrkonjić Grad 128 Lf 44.25N 17.06E
Mrocza 120 Nc 53.14N 17.36E
Mroga 120 Pd 52.09N 19.42E
Msangesi 170 Ge 11.40S 36.45E
Msid, Djebel- 128 Cn 36.25N 8.04E
Msif 126 Qi 35.23N 4.45E
M'Sila 162 Hb 35.42N 4.33E
M'Sila [3] 162 Hb 35.00N 4.30E
M'Sila 126 Qi 35.31N 4.30E
Mšinskaja 116 Nf 58.55N 30.03E
Msta 110 Jd 58.25N 31.20E
Mstislavl 132 Gc 53.59N 31.45E
Mszana Dolna 120 Qg 49.42N 20.05E
Mtakuja 170 Fd 7.22S 30.37E
Mtama 170 Ge 10.18S 39.22E
Mtelo 170 Gb 1.39N 35.23E
Mtera Reservoir 170 Gd 7.01S 35.55E
Mtito Andei 170 Gc 2.41S 38.10E
Mtubatuba 172 Ee 28.30S 32.08E
Mtwara 160 Lj 10.16S 40.11E
Mtwara [3] 170 Ge 10.40S 39.00E
Mu, Cerro- 194 Ki 9.29N 73.07W
Mua 220h Ac 13.21S 176.10W
Mu'a 221b Ac 21.11S 175.07W
Mua, Baie de- 220h Bc 13.23S 176.09W
Muaná 202 Id 1.32S 49.13W
Muang Huon 148 Kd 20.09N 101.27E
Muang Khammouan 148 Ke 17.24N 104.48E
Muang Không 148 Lf 14.07N 105.51E
Muang Khôngxédôn 148 Le 15.34N 105.49E
Muang Khoua 148 Kd 21.05N 102.31E
Muang Pak Lay 148 Ke 18.12N 101.25E
Muang Pakxan 148 Ke 18.22N 103.39E
Muang Pakxong 148 Le 15.11N 106.14E
Muang Sing 148 Kd 21.11N 101.09E
Muang Tahoi 148 Ld 16.10N 106.38E
Muang Thai=Thailand (EN) [1] 142 Mh 15.00N 100.00E
Muang Vangviang 148 Ke 18.56N 102.27E
Muang Xaignabouri 148 Ke 19.15N 101.45E
Muang Xay 148 Kd 20.42N 101.59E
Muang Xépôn 148 Le 16.41N 106.14E
Muanzanza 170 Dd 6.32S 20.51E
Muar 150 Df 2.02N 102.34E
Muaraaman 150 Dg 3.07S 102.12E
Muarabungo 150 Dg 1.28S 102.07E
Muaraenim 150 Dg 3.39S 103.48E
Muaralasan 150 Gf 1.48N 117.12E
Muarapajang 150 Gg 1.32S 115.48E
Muarasiberut 150 Cg 1.36S 99.11E
Muarasiram 150 Gg 0.46S 116.11E
Muaratebo 150 Dg 1.30S 102.26E
Muaratewe 150 Fg 0.57S 114.53E
Muarawahau 150 Gf 1.02N 116.52E
Mubarek 136 Ee 39.16N 65.07E
Mubende 170 Fb 0.35N 31.23E
Mubi 160 Ig 10.16N 13.16E
Much 124 Jd 50.55N 7.24E
Muchinga Escarpment 170 Fe 13.40S 30.00E
Muchinga Mountains 170 Fe 12.00S 31.45E
Muck 118 Ge 56.50N 6.14W
Mücke 124 Ld 50.37N 9.02E
Mucojo 172 Gb 12.04S 40.28E
Muconda 170 De 10.34S 21.20E
Mucua 172 Ec 18.09S 34.58E
Mucubela 172 Fc 16.54S 37.49E
Mucuchíes 194 Li 8.45N 70.55W
Mucumbura 172 Ec 16.10S 31.42E
Mucur 146 Fc 39.04N 34.23E
Mucusso 170 Df 18.00S 21.25E
Mudanjiang 142 Oe 44.35N 129.34E
Mudan Jiang 140 Oe 46.18N 129.31E
Mudanya 146 Cb 40.22N 28.52E
Muddy Gap 188 Le 42.22N 107.27W
Mudgee 212 Jf 32.36S 149.35E
Mud Lake 188 Ie 43.53N 112.24W
Mud Lake 188 Gh 37.55N 117.05W
Mudon 148 Je 16.15N 97.44E
Mudug [3] 168 Hd 6.30N 48.00E
Mudug 168 Hd 6.20N 47.00E
Mudurnu 146 Db 40.28N 31.13E
Muecate 172 Fb 14.53S 39.38E
Mueda 172 Fb 11.39S 39.33E
Muerto, Cayo- 194 Ff 14.34N 82.44W
Muerto, Mar- 192 Li 16.10N 94.10W
Mufulira 160 Jj 12.33S 28.14E
Mufu Shan 152 Jf 29.00N 113.50E
Mufu Shan 152 Jf 29.15N 114.20E
Mugello 128 Fg 43.55N 11.25E
Múggia 128 He 45.36N 13.46E
Mughshin, Wādī- 168 Ib 19.44N 55.00E
Mugi 156 De 33.40N 134.25E
Mu Gia, Deo- 148 Le 17.40N 105.47E
Mugila, Monts- 170 Ed 6.49S 29.08E
Muğla 144 Cb 37.12N 28.22E
Mugodžary 140 He 49.00N 58.40E
Mugur an Na'ām 146 Ig 31.56N 40.30E
Muhaiwir 146 If 33.28N 40.59E
Muḥammad, Ra's- 146 Fd 27.42N 34.13E
Muḥammad Qawl 168 Fa 20.54N 37.05E
Muhen 138 Ig 48.10N 136.08E
Muheza 170 Gd 5.10S 38.47E
Muhīt, Al Baḥr al-=Atlantic Ocean (EN) 106 Di 2.00N 25.00W
Mühlacher 120 Eh 48.57N 8.50E
Mühldorf am Inn 120 Ih 48.15N 12.32E
Mühlhausen in Thüringen 120 Ge 51.13N 10.27E
Mühlig-Hofmann Gebirge 222 Cf 72.00S 5.20E
Mühlviertel 128 Ib 48.30N 14.10E
Muhoršibir 138 Ff 51.01N 107.50E
Muhos 114 Gd 64.50N 26.01E
Muhu 116 Jf 58.37N 23.05E
Muhu 114 Fg 58.35N 23.15E
Muhu, Proliv- / Muhu Väin 116 Jf 58.45N 23.15E
Muhulu 170 Ec 1.03S 27.17E
Muhu Väin / Muhu, Proliv- 116 Jf 58.45N 23.15E
Muhuwesi 170 Ge 11.16S 37.58E
Muiderslot 124 Hb 52.20N 5.06E
Muigheo/Mayo [2] 118 Dh 53.50N 9.30W
Muikamachi 154 Of 37.04N 138.53E
Muineachán/Monaghan 118 Gg 54.15N 6.58W
Muineachán/Monaghan [2] 118 Gg 54.10N 7.00W
Muine Bheag 118 Gi 52.42N 6.57W
Muir Bhreatan=Saint George's Channel (EN) 110 Fe 52.00N 6.00W
Muir Eireann=Irish Sea (EN) 110 Fe 53.30N 5.20W
Muiron Islands 212 Cd 21.35S 114.20E
Muir Seamount (EN) 174 Mf 33.41N 63.32W
Muite 172 Fb 14.02S 39.02E
Mujeres, Isla- 192 Pg 21.13N 86.43W
Mujezerski 114 He 63.57N 32.01E
Muji 152 Cd 37.27N 78.33E
Mujnak 136 Fg 43.44N 59.02E
Mujnakski zaliv 135 Bc 43.50N 58.40E
Mujunkum, peski- 140 Je 44.00N 70.30E
Mukačevo 136 Cf 48.26N 22.45E
Mukah 150 Ff 2.54N 112.06E
Mukawa 156a Bb 42.35N 141.55E
Mu-Kawa 156a Bb 42.33N 141.53E
Mukawwar 168 Fa 20.48N 37.13E
Mukdahan 148 Ke 16.31N 104.42E
Mukeru 220a Bc 7.25N 134.30E
Mukho 154 Jf 37.33N 129.07E
Mukinbudin 212 Df 30.54S 118.13E
Mukojima-Rettō 214 Cb 27.37N 142.10E
Mukomuko 150 Dg 2.35S 101.07E
Muksu 135 He 39.17N 71.25E
Mula 126 Kf 38.03N 1.30W
Mula 148 Dc 27.57N 67.36E
Mulainagiri 148 Ff 13.24N 75.43E
Mulaku Atoll 148a Bb 2.57N 73.34E
Mulaly 136 Hf 45.27N 78.20E
Mulan 152 Mb 46.00N 128.02E
Mulanje 170 Gf 16.02S 35.30E
Mulanje 158 Kj 16.03S 35.31E
Mulatre, Point- 197g Bb 15.17N 61.15W
Mulatupo Sasardí 194 Ii 8.57N 77.45W
Mulchatna 178 Hd 59.39N 157.08W
Mulchén 206 Fe 37.34S 72.14W
Mulda 134 Kc 67.28N 63.34E
Mulde 120 Ie 51.48N 12.10E
Mulebreen 222 Ee 67.28S 59.21E
Mulegé 190 Bc 26.53N 112.01W
Mulegé, Sierra de- 190 Bc 37.30N 112.40W
Mulenda 170 Dc 4.18S 24.58E
Muleshoe 186 Ei 34.13N 102.43W
Mulgrave Island 212 Ib 10.05S 142.10E
Mulhacén 110 Fh 37.03N 3.19W
Mülheim an der Ruhr 124 Ic 51.26N 6.53E
Mülheim-Kärlich 124 Jd 50.23N 7.30E
Mulhouse 112 Gf 47.45N 7.20E
Muli (Bowa) 152 Hf 27.55N 101.13E
Mulifanua 221c Aa 13.50S 172.02W
Muling 154 Kb 44.34N 130.12E
Muling (Bamiantong) 154 Kb 44.55N 130.32E
Muling Guan 154 Ef 36.10N 118.46E
Muling He 154 Lb 45.53N 133.30E
Mull, Island of- 110 Fd 56.27N 6.00W
Mull, Sound of- 118 He 56.35N 5.50W
Mullen 186 Fe 42.03N 101.01W
Mullens 184 Gg 37.35N 81.25W
Muller, Pegunungan- 150 Ff 0.40N 113.50E
Mullet Peninsula/An Muirthead 118 Cg 54.15N 10.04W
Mullett Lake 184 Ec 45.30N 84.30W
Mullewa 212 De 28.33S 115.31E
Müllheim 120 Di 47.48N 7.38E
Mullingar/An Muileann gCearr 118 Fh 53.32N 7.20W
Mullsjö 116 Eg 57.55N 13.53E
Mulobezi 170 Ef 16.47S 25.10E
Mulock Glacier 222 Jf 79.03S 159.10E
Mulongo 170 Ed 7.50S 26.57E
Multān 142 Jf 30.11N 71.29E
Multé 192 Ni 17.41N 91.24W
Multia 116 Kb 62.25N 24.47E
Multien 124 Ee 49.05N 2.55E
Mulu, Gunong- 150 Ff 4.03N 114.56E
Mulvane 186 Hh 37.29N 97.14W
Mulymja 134 Lf 60.12N 64.32E
Mumbué 170 Ce 13.53S 17.19E
Mumbwa 170 Ee 14.59S 27.04E
Mumhan/Munster 118 Ei 52.30N 9.00W
Mumra 132 Og 45.43N 47.41E
Mun 140 Mh 15.19N 105.30E
Muna 192 Og 20.29N 89.43W
Muna 140 Oc 67.52N 123.10E
Muna, Pulau- 150 Hg 5.00S 122.30E
Munābāo 148 Ec 25.45N 70.17E
Munamägi/Munamjagi 116 Lg 57.38N 27.10E
Munamjagi/Munamägi 116 Lg 57.38N 27.10E
Munaybarah, Sharm- 146 Gi 26.04N 36.38E
Muncar 150 Fh 8.29S 114.21E
Münchberg 120 Hf 50.12N 11.47E
München=Munich (EN) 112 Hf 48.09N 11.35E
Münchhausen 124 Kd 50.57N 8.43E
Muncho Lake 180 Ee 58.56N 125.46W
Munch'ŏn 154 Ie 39.14N 127.22E
Muncie 182 Jc 40.11N 85.23W
Munda 219a Cc 8.19S 157.15E
Mundaring, Perth- 212 Df 31.54S 116.10E
Munday 186 Gj 33.27N 99.38W
Mundemba 166 Ge 4.59N 8.40E
Münden 120 Fe 51.25N 9.41E
Mundesley 124 Db 52.52N 1.25E
Mundford 124 Cb 52.30N 0.39E
Mundiwindi 210 Dg 23.52S 120.09E
Mundo 126 Kf 38.19N 1.40W
Mundo Novo 202 Jf 11.52S 40.28W
Munellës, Mali i- 130 Dh 41.58N 20.06E
Munera 126 Je 39.02N 2.28W
Mungana 212 Ic 17.07S 144.24E
Mungbere 160 Jh 2.38N 28.30E
Munger 148 Hc 25.23N 86.28E
Mungindi 212 Je 28.58S 148.59E
Munhango 170 Ce 12.10S 18.34E
Munh-Hajrhan-Ula 140 Le 46.40N 91.30E
Munich (EN)=München 112 Hf 48.09N 11.35E
Muniesa 126 Lc 41.02N 0.48W
Munīfah 144 Gd 27.38N 49.00E
Munising 184 Db 46.25N 86.40W
Munkedal 114 Cg 58.29N 11.41E
Munkfors 114 Cg 59.50N 13.32E
Munku-Sardyk, gora- 140 Md 51.45N 100.20E
Muñoz Gamero, Península- 206 Fh 52.30S 73.10W
Munsan 154 If 37.55N 126.22E
Münsingen 120 Fh 48.25N 9.30E
Munster 122 Nf 48.03N 7.08E
Münster [F.R.G.] 120 De 51.58N 7.38E
Münster [F.R.G.] 124 Ke 49.55N 8.52E
Münster/Moutier 128 Bc 47.16N 7.22E
Munster/Mumhan 118 Ei 52.30N 9.00W
Münster-Hiltrup 124 Jc 51.54N 7.38E
Münsterland [F.R.G.] 120 De 52.00N 7.30E
Münsterland [F.R.G.] 124 Kb 52.45N 8.10E
Münstermaifeld 124 Jd 50.15N 7.22E
Muntenia 130 Ie 44.00N 26.00E
Munteni Buzău 130 Je 44.38N 26.59E
Muntok 150 Eg 2.04S 105.11E
Munzur Dağları 146 Hc 39.30N 39.10E
Muong Sen 148 Ke 19.24N 104.08E
Muonio 112 Ib 67.57N 23.42E
Muonioälven 110 Ib 67.11N 23.34E
Muonionjoki 110 Ib 67.11N 23.34E
Muping 154 Ff 37.23N 121.36E
Muqaddam 168 Eb 18.04N 31.30E
Muqayshiṭ 146 Oj 24.10N 53.45E
Muqdisho=Mogadishu (EN) 160 Lh 2.03N 45.22E
Mur 110 Hf 46.18N 16.55E
Mura 110 Hf 46.18N 16.55E
Muradiye [Tur.] 146 Jc 39.00N 43.43E
Muradiye [Tur.] 130 Kk 38.39N 27.24E
Murafa 132 Fe 48.13N 28.14E
Murakami 154 Oe 38.14N 139.29E
Murallón, Cerro- 198 Ij 49.48S 73.25W
Murán 120 Qh 48.45N 20.02E
Mur'anyo 168 Ic 11.41N 50.27E
Muraši 136 Ed 59.24N 48.59E
Murat 122 Ii 45.07N 2.52E
Murat 140 Ff 38.52N 38.48E
Murat Dağı 146 Cb 38.55N 29.43E
Muratlı [Tur.] 146 Ib 41.29N 41.41E
Muratlı [Tur.] 130 Kh 41.10N 27.30E
Murau 128 Ic 47.06N 14.10E
Muravera 128 Dk 39.25N 9.34E
Murayama 156 Gb 38.29N 140.23E
Mürchen Khvort 146 Nf 33.06N 51.30E
Murchison 218 Ed 41.48S 172.20E
Murchison, Mount- [Austl.] 212 De 26.46S 116.25E
Murchison, Mount- [N.Z.] 218 De 43.01S 171.17E
Murchison Falls → Kabalega Falls 170 Fb 2.17N 31.41E
Murchison River 208 Cg 27.50S 114.00E
Murcia 112 Fh 37.59N 1.07W
Murcia [2] 126 Kg 38.00N 1.30W
Mur-de-Barrez 122 Ij 44.51N 2.39E
Murdo 186 Fe 43.53N 100.43W
Mure, La- 122 Lj 44.54N 5.47E
Mureaux, Les- 124 Df 49.00N 1.55E
Mürefte 130 Ki 40.40N 27.14E
Muren 142 Me 49.38N 100.10E
Mureş [2] 130 Hc 46.30N 24.40E
Mureş 110 If 46.15N 20.12E
Muret 122 Hk 43.28N 1.21E
Murewa 172 Ec 17.39S 31.47E
Murfreesboro 182 Jd 35.51N 86.23W
Murg 120 Eh 48.55N 8.10E
Murgab 140 If 38.18N 61.12E
Murgab [Taj.-U.S.S.R.] 136 Hh 38.10N 73.59E
Murgab [Tur.-U.S.S.R.] 135 Df 37.32N 62.01E
Murgaš 130 Gg 42.50N 23.40E
Murgeni 130 Lc 46.12N 28.01E
Murgon 212 Ke 26.15S 151.57E
Muri 220p Cc 21.15S 159.43W
Muriaé 202 Jh 21.08S 42.22W
Murici 202 Ke 9.19S 35.56W
Muriege 170 Dd 9.53S 21.13E
Murihiti 220n Ab 10.23S 161.02W
Murilo Atoll 208 Gd 8.40N 152.11E
Mūrītānīyā=Mauritania (EN) [1] 160 Fg 20.00N 12.00W
Müritz 120 Ic 53.25N 12.43E
Murkong Selek 148 Jc 27.44N 95.18E
Murmansk 112 Jb 68.58N 33.05E
Murmanskaja oblast [3] 136 Db 68.00N 35.30E
Murmaši 136 Db 68.49N 32.49E
Murnau 120 Hi 47.41N 11.12E
Muro / Muro de Mallorca 126 Pe 39.44N 3.03E
Muro, Capo di- 122a Ab 41.44N 8.40E
Muro de Mallorca / Muro 126 Pe 39.44N 3.03E
Muro Lucano 128 Jj 40.45N 15.29E
Murom 112 Kd 55.34N 42.02E
Muromcevo 136 Hd 56.23N 75.14E
Muroran 142 Qe 42.18N 140.59E
Muros 126 Cb 42.47N 9.02W
Muros y Noya, Ría de- 126 Db 42.45N 9.00W
Muroto 152 Ne 33.18N 134.09E
Muroto Zaki 154 Mh 33.16N 134.10E
Murowana Goślina 120 Nd 52.35N 17.01E
Murphy [Id.-U.S.] 188 Ge 43.13N 116.33W
Murphy [N.C.-U.S.] 184 Eh 35.05N 84.01W
Murphysboro 186 Lh 37.46N 89.20W
Murrah al Kubrá, Al Buḥayrah al- 146 Eg 30.20N 32.23E
Murray [Ky.-U.S.] 184 Cg 36.37N 88.19W
Murray [Ut.-U.S.] 188 Jf 40.40N 111.53W
Murray, Lake- [Pap.N.Gui.] 214 Ci 7.00S 141.30E
Murray, Lake- [S.C.-U.S.] 184 Gh 34.04N 81.23W
Murray Bridge 212 Hg 35.07S 139.17E
Murray Fracture zone (EN) 106 Lf 34.00N 135.00W
Murray Islands 212 Ia 9.55S 144.05E
Murray Ridge (EN) 106 Gg 21.00N 61.50E
Murray River 208 Eh 35.22S 139.22E
Murraysburg 172 Cf 31.58S 23.47E
Murro di Porco, Capo- 128 Jm 37.00N 15.20E
Murrumbidgee River 208 Fh 34.43S 143.12E
Murrupula 172 Fc 15.27S 38.47E
Murska Sobota 128 Kd 46.40N 16.10E
Murten 128 Bd 46.56N 7.08E
Murter 128 Jg 43.47N 15.37E
Murtle Lake 188 Fa 52.08N 119.38W
Murud, Gunong- 150 Gf 3.52N 115.30E
Murupara 218 Gc 38.27S 176.42E
Mururoa Atoll 208 Ng 21.52S 138.55W
Murwāra 148 Gd 23.51N 80.24E
Murwillumbah 212 Ke 28.19S 153.24E
Mürz 128 Jc 47.24N 15.17E
Mürzzuschlag 128 Jc 47.36N 15.41E
Muş 144 Fb 38.44N 41.30E
Muša/Mūša 114 Fh 56.24N 24.12E
Mūša/Muša 114 Fh 56.24N 24.12E
Mūsa, Jabal-=Sinai, Mount- (EN) 146 Eh 28.32N 33.59E
Musa Ali 168 Gc 12.30N 42.27E
Musāfi 146 Qk 25.18N 56.10E
Musā'id 146 Ed 31.36N 25.03E
Musala 110 Ig 42.11N 23.34E
Musallam 146 Lg 31.53N 46.56E
Musan 152 Mc 42.14N 129.13E
Musandam Peninsula 146 Qi 26.18N 56.24E
Musay'īd 146 Nj 25.00N 51.33E
Musaymir 164 Hg 13.27N 44.37E
Muscat (EN)=Masqaṭ 142 Hg 23.29N 58.33E
Muscat and Oman (EN) → Oman (EN) [1] 142 Hg 21.00N 57.00E
Muscatine 186 Kf 41.25N 91.03W
Musgrave 212 Ib 14.47S 143.30E
Musgrave Ranges 208 Eg 26.10S 131.50E
Mūshā 146 Di 27.07N 31.14E
Mus-Haja, gora- 140 Qc 62.35N 140.50E
Mushāsh al 'Ashāwī 146 Mj 24.12N 48.50E
Mushāsh Ramlān 146 Mj 24.25N 49.15E
Mushayrib, Ra's- 146 Nj 24.18N 51.44E
Mushie 170 Cc 3.01S 16.54E
Mūsi 146 Ge 15.20N 80.06E
Musi 140 Mj 2.20S 104.56E
Mūsiān 146 Lf 32.28N 47.26E
Musicians Seamounts (EN) 208 Kb 29.00N 162.00W
Muskegon 182 Jc 43.14N 86.16W
Muskegon Heights 184 Dd 43.12N 86.12W
Muskegon River 184 Dd 43.14N 86.20W
Muskö 116 He 59.00N 18.05E
Muskogee 182 Hd 35.45N 95.22W
Muskoka, Lake- 184 Hc 45.00N 79.25W
Musoma 160 Ki 1.30S 33.48E
Musone 128 Hg 43.28N 13.38E
Mussaṭṭaḥah, Al Jazīrah al- 128 Em 37.11N 10.20E
Mussau Island 214 Dh 1.25S 149.38E
Musselkanaal, Stadskanaal- 124 Jb 52.56N 7.02E
Musselshell River 182 Fb 47.21N 107.58W
Mussende 170 Ce 10.31S 16.02E
Mussidan 122 Gi 45.02N 0.22E
Mussomeli 128 Hm 37.35N 13.45E
Must 152 Fb 46.40N 92.40E
Muṣṭafā, Ra's- 128 Fn 36.50N 11.07E
Mustafakemalpaşa 146 Cb 40.02N 28.24E
Mustahil 168 Gd 5.15N 44.44E
Mustang 148 Gc 29.11N 83.58E
Mustang Draw 186 Fj 32.00N 101.40W
Mustang Island 186 Hm 28.00N 96.55W
Mustasaari/Korsholm 116 Ia 63.05N 21.43E
Musters, Lago- 206 Gg 45.27S 69.13W
Mustique Island 196 Ff 12.39N 61.15W
Mustjala 116 Jf 58.25N 22.04E
Mustla 114 Fg 58.14N 25.52E
Mustvee 114 Gg 58.52N 26.59E
Musu-dan 154 Jd 40.50N 129.43E
Muswellbrook 212 Kf 32.16S 150.53E
Muszyna 120 Qg 49.21N 20.54E
Mūṭ 164 Ed 25.29N 28.59E
Mut 146 Ed 36.39N 33.27E
Mūtaf, Ra's al- 144 Hd 27.41N 51.27E
Mutalau 220k Ba 18.56S 169.50W
Mutarara 160 Kj 17.27S 35.04E
Mutare 160 Kj 18.58S 32.40E
Mutatá 202 Cb 7.16N 76.32W
Mutawassiṭ, Al Baḥr al-=Mediterranean Sea (EN) 110 Hh 35.00N 20.00E
Mutha 170 Gc 1.48S 38.26E
Muting 150 Lh 7.23S 140.20E
Mutis, Gunung- 150 Hh 9.34S 124.14E
Mutoko 172 Ec 17.24S 32.13E
Mutoraj 138 Fd 61.20N 100.20E
Mutsamudu 160 Lj 12.09S 44.25E
Mutshatsha 170 De 10.39S 24.27E
Mutsu 152 Pc 41.05N 140.55E
Mutsu-Wan 154 Pd 41.10N 140.55E
Muttaburra 212 Id 22.36S 144.33E
Mutterstadt 124 Ke 49.27N 8.21E
Mutton/Oiléan Coarach 118 Di 52.49N 9.31W
Mutton Bird Islands 218 Bg 47.15S 167.25E
Mutuali 172 Fb 14.53S 37.00E
Mutún 204 Dd 19.10S 57.54W
Mutunópolis 204 Ha 13.40S 49.15W
Mutusjärvi 114 Gb 69.31N 26.57E
Muurame 116 Kb 62.08N 25.40E
Mu Us Shamo=Ordos Desert (EN) 140 Mf 38.45N 109.10E
Muxima 170 Bd 9.32S 13.57E
Muy, Le- 122 Mk 43.28N 6.33E
Muyinga 170 Fc 2.51S 30.20E
Muy Muy 194 Eg 12.46N 85.38W
Muzaffarābād 148 Eb 34.22N 73.28E
Muzaffargarh 148 Eb 30.04N 71.12E
Muzaffarnagar 148 Fc 29.28N 77.41E
Muzaffarpur 148 Hc 26.07N 85.24E
Muzambinho 204 Ie 21.22S 46.32W
Muzat He 152 Dc 41.15N 83.27E
Muži 138 Bc 65.27N 64.40E
Muzillac 122 Dg 47.33N 2.29W
Mužlja 130 Dd 45.21N 20.25E
Muztag [China] 140 Kf 36.25N 87.25E
Muztag [China] 140 Kf 35.55N 80.20E
Muztagata 152 Cd 38.17N 75.07E
Mvolo 168 Dd 6.03N 29.56E
Mvomero 170 Gd 6.20S 37.25E
Mvoung 170 Bb 0.04N 12.18E
Mwadingusha 170 Ee 10.45S 27.15E
Mwali/Mohéli 158 Lj 12.15S 43.45E
Mwanza [3] 170 Fc 2.30S 32.30E
Mwanza [Mwi.] 170 Ff 15.37S 34.31E
Mwanza [Tan.] 160 Ki 2.31S 32.54E
Mwanza [Zaire] 170 Ed 7.54S 26.45E
Mwatate 170 Gc 3.30S 38.23E
Mweelrea 118 Dh 53.38N 9.50W
Mweka 160 Ji 4.51S 21.34E
Mwene Ditu 160 Ji 7.03S 23.27E
Mwenezi 172 Ed 21.22S 30.45E
Mwenga 170 Ec 3.02S 28.26E
Mweru, Lake- 158 Ji 9.00S 28.45E
Mweru Wantipa, Lake- 170 Ed 8.42S 29.46E
Mwimbi 170 Fd 8.39S 31.40E
Mwinilunga 170 De 11.44S 24.26E
Mya 158 He 31.40N 5.15E
Myaing 148 Id 21.37N 94.51E
Myanaung 148 Je 18.17N 95.19E
Myanmar-Nainggan-Daw→Burma [1] 142 Lg 22.00N 98.00E
Myaungmya 148 Ie 16.36N 94.56E
Mycenae (EN) = Mikinai 130 Fl 37.43N 22.45E
Myebon 148 Id 20.03N 93.22E
Myingyan 142 Lg 21.28N 95.23E
Myinmoletkat Taung 148 Jf 13.28N 98.48E
Myitta 148 Jf 14.10N 98.31E
Myjava 120 Mh 48.33N 16.58E
Myjzakjula/Mõisaküla 114 Fg 58.07N 25.10E
Mylius Erichsens Land 179 Jb 81.40N 24.00W
Myitkyinā 142 Lg 25.23N 97.24E
Mymensingh 148 Id 24.45N 90.24E
Mynämäki 114 Ef 60.40N 22.00E
Mynaral 136 Hf 45.22N 73.39E
Myōkō-Zan 156 Fc 36.52N 138.06E
Mýrdalsjökull 114a Bc 63.40N 19.06W
Myre 114 Db 68.51N 15.05E
Myrskylä/Mörskom 116 Kd 60.40N 25.51E
Myrtle Beach 182 Le 33.42N 78.54W
Myrtle Point 188 Ce 43.04N 124.08W
Mysen 116 Cg 59.33N 11.20E
Mysia 130 Kj 39.30N 28.00E
Myśla 120 Kd 52.40N 14.29E
Myślenice 120 Pg 49.51N 19.56E
Myślibórz 120 Kd 52.55N 14.52E
Mysore 142 Jh 12.18N 76.39E
Mysore → Karnataka [3] 148 Ff 13.30N 76.00E
Mys Šmidta 138 Nc 68.45N 178.40W
Myszków 120 Pf 50.36N 19.20E
Myszyniec 120 Rc 53.24N 21.21E
My Tho 142 Mh 10.21N 106.21E
Mytišči 114 Ii 55.56N 37.46E
Mývatn 114a Cb 65.36N 17.00W
Myzeqeja 130 Ci 41.01N 19.36E
M'Zab 162 Hc 32.35N 3.20E
Mže 120 Jg 49.46N 13.24E
Mziha 170 Gd 5.54S 37.47E
Mzimba 170 Fe 11.54S 33.36E
Mzuzu 160 Kj 11.27S 33.55E

N

Naab 120 Ig 49.01N 12.02E
Naaldwijk 124 Gc 51.59N 4.12E
Naalehu 214 Od 19.04N 155.35W
Naantali/Nådendal 114 Ff 60.27N 22.02E
Naarden 124 Hb 52.18N 5.10E
Naas/An Nás 118 Gh 53.13N 6.39W
Nabadid 168 Gd 9.38N 43.29E
Nabão 126 De 39.31N 8.21W
Nabari 156 Ed 34.37N 136.05E
Naberera 170 Gc 4.12S 36.56E
Naberežnyje Čelny 112 Ld 55.42N 52.19E
Nābha 148 Fb 30.22N 76.09E
Nabire 210 Ee 3.22S 135.29E
Nabī Shu'ayb, Jabal an- 140 Gh 15.17N 43.59E
Nabq 146 Fh 28.04N 34.25E
Nābul 160 Ie 36.27N 10.44E
Nābul [3] 162 Jb 36.45N 10.45E
Nābulus 146 Ff 32.13N 35.16E
Nābulus [3] 146 Ff 32.18N 35.17E

Index Symbols

[1] Independent Nation
[2] State, Region
[3] District, County
[4] Municipality
[5] Colony, Dependency
Continent
Physical Region
Historical or Cultural Region
Mount, Mountain
Volcano
Hill
Mountains, Mountain Range
Hills, Escarpment
Plateau, Upland
Pass, Gap
Plain, Lowland
Delta
Salt Flat
Valley, Canyon
Crater, Cave
Karst Features
Depression
Polder
Desert, Dunes
Forest, Woods
Heath, Steppe
Oasis
Cape, Point
Coast, Beach
Cliff
Peninsula
Isthmus
Sandbank
Island
Atoll
Rock, Reef
Islands, Archipelago
Rocks, Reefs
Coral Reef
Well, Spring
Geyser
River, Stream
Waterfall, Rapids
River Mouth, Estuary
Lake
Salt Lake
Intermittent Lake
Reservoir
Swamp, Pond
Canal
Glacier
Ice Shelf, Pack Ice
Ocean
Sea
Gulf, Bay
Strait, Fjord
Lagoon
Bank
Seamount
Tablemount
Ridge
Shelf
Basin
Escarpment, Sea Scarp
Fracture
Trench, Abyss
National Park, Reserve
Point of Interest
Recreation Site
Cave, Cavern
Historic Site
Ruins
Wall, Walls
Church, Abbey
Temple
Scientific Station
Railway station
Airport
Port
Military installation
Lighthouse
Mine
Tunnel
Dam, Bridge

Nabusanke 170 Fb 0.01N 32.03 E
Nacala 172 Gb 14.33S 40.40 E
Nacala-a-Velha 160 Lj 14.33S 40.36 E
Nacaome 194 Dg 13.31N 87.30W
Nacaroa 172 Fb 14.23S 39.55 E
Nacereddine 126 Ph 36.08N 3.26 E
Nachikatsuura 156 De 33.39N 135.55 E
Nachingwea 170 Ge 10.23S 38.46 E
Nachi-San 156 De 33.42N 135.51 E
Náchod 120 Mf 50.26N 16.10 E
Nachuge 148 If 10.35N 92.28 E
Nachvak Fiord 180 Le 59.03N 63.45W
Nacimiento Reservoir 188 Ei 35.43N 121.00W
Nacka 114 Ee 59.18N 18.10 E
Ná Clocha Liatha/ Greystones 118 Gh 53.09N 6.04W
Nacogdoches 186 Ik 31.36N 94.39W
Na Comaraigh/Comeragh Mountains 118 Fi 52.13N 7.35W
Nacori, Sierra- 192 Ec 29.50N 108.50W
Nacozari, Rio- 192 Ec 29.48N 109.42W
Nacozari de García 190 Cb 30.24N 109.39W
Na Cruacha/Blue Stack 118 Eg 54.45N 8.06W
Na Cruacha Dubha 118 Di 52.00N 9.50W
Na Cruacha Dubha/ Macgillycuddy's Reeks 118 Di 52.00N 9.50W
Nacunday, Rio- 204 Eh 26.03S 54.45W
Nada → Danxian 152 Ih 19.38N 109.32 E
Nådendal/Naantali 114 Ff 60.27N 22.02 E
Nadiād 148 Ed 22.42N 72.52 E
Nădlac 130 Dc 46.10N 20.45 E
Nador 162 Gb 35.11N 2.56W
Nador [3] 162 Gb 35.00N 3.00W
Nădusa 130 Fi 40.38N 22.04 E
Nadvoicy 136 Dc 63.52N 34.20 E
Nadvornaja 132 De 48.38N 24.34 E
Nadym 142 Jc 65.35N 72.42 E
Nadym 138 Cc 66.20N 72.30 E
Naeba-San 156 Fc 36.51N 138.41 E
Nærbø 116 Af 58.40N 5.39 E
Næstved 114 Ci 55.14N 11.46 E
Nafada 166 Hc 11.06N 11.20 E
Nafarroa / Navarra [2] 126 Kb 42.45N 1.40W
Näfels 128 Dc 47.06N 9.04 E
Naftah 128 Dn 36.57N 9.04 E
Naftan Rock 220b Bb 14.50N 145.32 E
Naft-e-Safid 146 Mg 31.40N 49.17 E
Naft-e-Shāh 146 Kf 33.59N 45.30 E
Naft Khāneh 146 Ke 34.02N 45.28 E
Nafūsah, Jabal- 158 Ie 31.50N 12.00 E
Năg 148 Dc 27.24N 65.08 E
Naga 142 Oh 13.28N 123.39 E
Năga, Kreb en- 162 Fe 24.00N 6.00W
Nagagami Lake 184 Ea 49.28N 85.02W
Nagagami River 186 Na 50.25N 84.20W
Nagahama [Jap.] 156 Ed 35.23N 136.16 E
Nagahama [Jap.] 156 Ce 33.36N 132.29 E
Nagai 156 Gb 38.06N 140.02 E
Nagai 178 Ge 55.11N 159.55W
Na Gaibhlte/Galty Mountains 118 Ei 52.23N 8.11W
Nāgāland [3] 148 Ic 26.30N 94.00 E
Nagano 142 Pf 36.39N 138.11 E
Nagano Ken [2] 154 Nf 36.10N 138.00 E
Nagano-Matsushiro 156 Fc 36.34N 138.10 E
Nagano-Shinonoi 156 Fc 36.35N 138.06 E
Nagaoka 152 Od 37.27N 138.51 E
Nāgappattinam 148 Ff 10.46N 79.50 E
Nagara-Gawa 156 Ed 35.02N 136.43 E
Nagarote 194 Dg 12.16N 86.34W
Nagarzê 152 Ff 28.59N 90.28 E
Nagasaki 142 Of 32.47N 129.56 E
Nagasaki-Hantō 156 Ae 32.40N 129.45 E
Nagasaki Ken [2] 154 Jh 33.00N 129.50 E
Nagashima 156 Ed 34.12N 136.19 E
Naga-Shima 156 Ce 33.50N 132.05 E
Nagashima 156 Be 32.10N 130.10 E
Naga-Shima-Kaikyō 156 Be 32.15N 130.10 E
Nagato 154 Kg 34.21N 131.10 E
Nagayo 156 Ae 32.50N 129.52 E
Nāgda 148 Fd 23.27N 75.25 E
Nāgercoil 148 Fg 8.10N 77.26 E
Naghora Point 214 Gj 10.50S 162.24 E
Nagichot 168 Ee 4.16N 33.34 E
Nagi-San 156 Dd 35.10N 134.10 E
Nagiso 156 Ed 35.36N 137.36 E
Nago 152 Mf 26.35N 128.01 E
Nagold 120 Eh 48.33N 8.43 E
Nagold 120 Eh 48.33N 8.43 E
Nagorno-Karabahskaja avtonomnaja oblast [3] 136 Eh 39.55N 46.45 E
Nagorny [R.S.F.S.R.] 138 Md 63.10N 179.05 E
Nagorny [R.S.F.S.R.] 138 He 55.45N 124.58 E
Nagorsk 114 Mg 59.21N 50.48 E
Nago-Wan 156b Ab 26.35N 127.55 E
Nagoya 142 Pf 35.10N 136.55 E
Nāgpur 142 Jg 21.09N 79.06 E
Nagqu 142 Lf 31.30N 92.00 E
Nag's Head 197c Ab 17.13N 62.38W
Nagua 194 Md 19.23N 69.50W
Naguabo 197a Cb 18.13N 65.44W
Nagyatád 120 Nj 46.13N 17.22 E
Nagybajom 120 Mj 46.23N 16.31 E
Nagyecsed 120 Si 47.52N 22.24 E
Nagyhalász 120 Rh 48.08N 21.46 E
Nagykálló 120 Ri 47.53N 21.51 E
Nagykanizsa 120 Mj 46.27N 16.59 E
Nagykáta 120 Pi 47.25N 19.45 E
Nagykőrös 120 Pi 47.02N 19.47 E
Nagykunság 120 Qj 46.55N 20.15 E
Nagy-Milic 120 Rh 48.35N 21.28 E
Naha 142 Og 26.13N 127.40 E
Nahanni Butte 180 Fd 61.04N 123.24W
Nahari 156 De 33.25N 134.01 E
Nahariyya 146 Ff 33.00N 35.05 E
Nahāvand 144 Gc 34.12N 48.22 E
Nahe 120 Dg 49.58N 7.57 E
Nahičevan 112 Kh 39.13N 45.27 E
Nahičevanskaja ASSR [3] 136 Eh 39.15N 45.35 E
Na'hīmābād 146 Qg 30.51N 56.31 E
Nahodka 142 Pe 42.48N 132.52 E
Nahr al Qāsh 168 Fb 16.48N 35.51 E
Nahr Ar Rahad 168 Ec 12.43N 30.39 E
Nahr Ouassel 126 Oi 35.45N 2.46 E
Nahuala, Laguna- 192 Ji 16.50N 99.40W
Nahuel Huapí, Lago- 206 Ff 40.58S 71.30W
Nahunta 184 Gj 31.12N 81.59W
Naie 156a Bb 43.24N 141.52 E
Naiguatá, Pico- 202 Ea 10.33N 66.46W
Naila 120 Hf 50.19N 11.42 E
Na'īmābād 146 Pd 36.14N 54.39 E
Naiman Qi (Daqin Tal) 152 Lc 42.49N 120.38 E
Nā'īn 146 Of 32.52N 53.05 E
Nain 176 Md 57.00N 61.40W
Nairai 219d Bb 17.49S 179.24 E
Nairn 118 Jd 57.35N 3.53W
Nairobi 160 Ki 1.17S 36.49 E
Nairobi [3] 170 Gc 1.17S 36.50 E
Naissaar/Najssar 116 Ke 59.35N 24.25 E
Naitamba 219d Cb 17.01S 179.17W
Naizishan 154 Ic 43.41N 127.27 E
Najafābād 144 Hc 32.37N 51.21 E
Najd 140 Gg 25.00N 44.30 E
Najd 144 Fe 25.00N 44.30 E
Nájera 126 Jb 42.25N 2.44W
Najerilla 126 Jb 42.31N 2.42W
Naj' Ḥammādī 164 Fd 26.03N 32.15 E
Najibābād 148 Fc 29.38N 78.20 E
Najin 152 Nc 42.15N 130.18 E
Najō 156 Ec 35.47N 136.12 E
Najrān 164 Hf 17.30N 44.10 E
Najrān 164 Hf 17.30N 44.10 E
Najssar/Naissaar 116 Ke 59.35N 24.25 E
Najstenjarvi 116 He 62.18N 32.42 E
Naju 154 Ig 35.02N 126.43 E
Najzataš, pereval- 135 If 37.52N 73.46 E
Nakadōri-Jima 154 Jh 32.58N 129.05 E
Nakagawa 156a Ca 44.47N 142.05 E
Naka-Gawa [Jap.] 156 De 33.56N 134.42 E
Naka-Gawa [Jap.] 156 Gc 36.20N 140.36 E
Nakagusuku-Wan 156b Ab 26.15N 127.50 E
Nakahechi 156 De 33.47N 135.29 E
Naka-lō-Jima 214 Cc 24.47N 141.20 E
Naka-Jima 156 Ce 33.58N 132.37 E
Nakajō 156 Oe 38.03N 139.24 E
Naka-Koshiki-Jima 156 Af 31.48N 129.50 E
Nakalele Point 221a Eb 21.02N 156.35W
Nakama 156 Be 33.50N 130.43 E
Nakaminato 156 Gc 36.22N 140.36 E
Nakamura 154 Lh 32.59N 132.56 E
Nakanai Mountains 212 Ka 5.35S 151.10 E
Nakano 156 Fc 36.45N 138.22 E
Naka-no-Dake 156 Fc 37.04N 139.06 E
Nakanojō 156 Fc 36.35N 138.51 E
Naka-no-Shima [Jap.] 154 Lf 36.05N 133.04 E
Naka-no-Shima [Jap.] 152 Mf 29.50N 129.50 E
Nakasato 156a Bc 40.58N 140.26 E
Naka-satsunai 156a Cb 42.42N 143.08 E
Nakashibetsu 154 Rc 43.36N 145.00 E
Nakasongola 170 Fb 1.19N 32.28 E
Nakatonbetsu 156a Ca 44.58N 142.17 E
Nakatsu 154 Kh 33.34N 131.13 E
Nakatsugawa 154 Ng 35.29N 137.30 E
Nakfa 168 Fb 16.40N 38.30 E
Nakhon Pathom 148 Kf 13.49N 100.06 E
Nakhon Phanom 148 Ke 17.22N 104.46 E
Nakhon Ratchasima 142 Mh 14.57N 102.09 E
Nakhon Sawan 142 Mh 15.42N 100.06 E
Nakhon Si Thammarat 142 Li 8.26N 99.58 E
Nakijin 156b Ab 26.42N 127.59 E
Nakina 176 Kd 50.10N 86.42W
Nakkila 116 Ic 61.22N 22.00 E
Nakło nad Notecią 120 Nc 53.08N 17.35 E
Naknek 178 He 58.44N 157.02W
Nakonde 170 Fd 9.19S 32.46 E
Nakskov 114 Ci 54.50N 11.09 E
Näkten 116 Fb 62.50N 14.40 E
Naktong-gang 154 Jg 35.07N 128.57 E
Nakuru 160 Ki 0.20S 35.56 E
Nakusp 188 Ga 50.15N 117.48W
Nāl 148 Dc 26.02N 65.29 E
Nalajch → Nalajha 152 Ib 47.45N 107.16 E
Nalajha (Nalajch) 152 Ib 47.45N 107.16 E
Nalčik 112 Kg 43.29N 43.37 E
Nallıhan 146 Db 40.11N 31.21 E
Nalón 126 Fa 43.32N 6.04W
Nālūt 160 Ie 31.52N 10.59 E
Nalwasha 170 Gc 0.43S 36.26 E
Na Machairi/Brandon Head 118 Ci 52.16N 10.15W
Namacurra 172 Fc 17.29S 37.01 E
Namai Bay 220a Bb 7.32N 134.39 E
Namak, Daryācheh-ye- = Namak Lake (EN) 140 Hf 34.45N 51.36 E
Namak, Kavīr-e- 144 Ic 34.30N 57.40 E
Namakan Lake 186 Jb 48.27N 92.35W
Namak-e Mīghān, Kavīr-e- 146 Me 34.13N 49.49 E
Namaki 146 Pg 31.16N 55.29 E
Namakia 172 Hc 15.56S 45.48 E
Namak Lake (EN) = Namak, Daryācheh-ye- 140 Hf 34.45N 51.36 E
Namakwaland = Little Namaland (EN) 172 Be 29.00S 17.00 E
Namanga 170 Gc 2.33S 36.47 E
Namangan 142 Je 41.00N 71.40 E
Namanganskaja oblast [3] 136 Hg 41.00N 71.20 E
Namanyere 170 Fd 7.31S 31.03 E
Namapa 172 Fb 13.43S 39.50 E
Namaqua Seamount (EN) 172 Af 31.30S 11.20 E
Namarrói 172 Fc 15.57S 36.51 E
Namasagali 170 Fb 1.01N 32.57 E
Namasale 170 Fb 1.30N 32.37 E
Namatanai 214 Eh 3.40S 152.27 E
Namathu 219d Bb 17.21S 179.26 E
Nambavatu 219d Bb 16.36S 178.55 E
Namber 150 Jg 1.04S 134.49 E
Nambour 212 Ke 26.38S 152.58 E
Nambouwalu 216 Ec 16.59S 178.42 E
Nam Can 148 Kg 8.46N 104.59 E
Namcha Barwa 140 Lg 29.38N 95.04 E
Namche Bazar 148 Hc 27.49N 86.43 E
Nam Co 140 Lf 30.45N 90.35 E
Namčy 138 Hd 62.35N 129.40 E
Namdalen 114 Cd 64.38N 12.35 E
Nam Dinh 142 Mg 20.25N 106.10 E
Nämdö 116 He 59.10N 18.40 E
Nam Du, Quan Dao- 148 Kg 9.42N 104.22 E
Namêche, Andenne- 124 Hd 50.28N 5.00 E
Namelaki Passage 220a Bc 7.24N 134.38 E
Namen/Namur 122 Kd 50.28N 4.52 E
Namerikawa 156 Ec 36.45N 137.20 E
Náměšt nad Oslavou 120 Mg 49.12N 16.09 E
Nametil 172 Fc 15.43S 39.21 E
Namib Desert/ Namibwoestyn 158 Ik 23.00S 15.00 E
Namibe 160 Ij 15.12S 12.10 E
Namibe [3] 170 Bf 15.20S 12.30 E
Namibia (South West Africa) [1] 160 Ik 22.00S 17.00 E
Namibwoestyn/Namib Desert 158 Ik 23.00S 15.00 E
Namie 154 Pf 37.29N 140.59 E
Namīn 146 Mc 38.25N 48.30 E
Namioka 156 Ga 40.42N 140.35 E
Namiquipa 192 Fc 29.15N 107.40W
Namiranga 172 Gb 10.33S 40.30 E
Namja La 152 Df 29.58N 82.34 E
Namkham 148 Jd 23.50N 97.41 E
Namlea 150 Ig 3.18S 127.06 E
Namling 152 Ef 29.44N 89.05 E
Namnoi, Khao- 148 Jf 10.36N 98.38 E
Namoi River 212 Je 30.00S 148.07 E
Namoluk Island 208 Gd 5.55N 153.08 E
Namonuito Atoll 208 Gd 8.46N 150.02 E
Namorik Atoll 208 Hd 5.36N 168.07 E
Namous 162 Gc 30.28N 0.14W
Nampa 182 Dc 43.34N 116.34W
Nampala 166 Db 15.17N 5.33W
Nam Phan = Cochin China (EN) 140 Mg 11.00N 107.00 E
Nam Phong 148 Ke 16.45N 102.52 E
Nampi 154 De 38.02N 116.42 E
Namp'o 152 Md 38.44N 125.25 E
Nampula 160 Kj 15.07S 39.15 E
Nampula [3] 172 Fb 15.00S 39.30 E
Namsê Shankou 152 Df 29.58N 82.34 E
Namsos 112 Hc 64.30N 11.30 E
Namtu 148 Jd 23.05N 97.24 E
Namu 188 Ba 51.49N 127.52W
Namu Atoll 208 Hd 8.00N 168.10 E
Namuka-I-Lau 219d Cc 18.51S 178.38W
Namūli, Serra- 158 Kj 15.21S 37.00 E
Namuno 172 Fb 13.37S 38.48 E
Namur [3] 124 Gd 50.20N 4.50 E
Namur/Namen 122 Kd 50.28N 4.52 E
Namur-Saint Servais 124 Gd 50.28N 4.50 E
Namuruputh 170 Gb 4.34N 35.57 E
Namur-Wépion 124 Gd 50.25N 4.52 E
Namutoni 172 Bc 18.30S 17.55 E
Namwala 170 Ef 15.45S 26.26 E
Namwŏn 154 Ig 35.24N 127.23 E
Namysłów 120 Ne 51.05N 17.42 E
Nan 148 Ke 18.48N 100.46 E
Nan 140 Mh 15.42N 100.09 E
Nana 168 Bd 5.00N 15.50 E
Nana Barya 168 Bd 7.59N 17.43 E
Nanae 156a Bc 41.53N 140.41 E
Nanaimo 180 Fg 49.10N 123.56W
Nanakuli 221a Cb 21.23N 158.08W
Nanam 154 Jd 41.44N 129.40 E
Nana-Mambéré [3] 168 Bd 6.00N 16.00 E
Nanango 212 Ke 26.40S 152.00 E
Nanao 152 Od 37.03N 136.58 E
Nanao-Wan 156 Ec 37.10N 137.00 E
Nanatsu-Shima 156 Ec 37.35N 136.50 E
Nancha 152 Mb 47.08N 129.09 E
Nanchang 142 Ng 28.40N 115.58 E
Nancheng 152 Kf 27.32N 116.36 E
Nanchong 142 Mf 30.47N 106.03 E
Nancowry 148 Ig 7.59N 93.32 E
Nancy 112 Gf 48.41N 6.12 E
Nanda Devi 140 Jf 30.23N 79.59 E
Nandaime 194 Dh 11.46N 86.03W
Nandan [China] 152 Ig 24.59N 107.31 E
Nandan [Jap.] 154 Mg 34.15N 134.43 E
Nandaran → Qingyuan 154 Ce 38.46N 115.29 E
Nanded 142 Jh 19.09N 77.20 E
Nandewar Range 212 Kf 30.40S 151.10 E
Nandi 216 Ec 17.48S 177.25 E
Nandu Jiang 152 Jg 20.04N 110.22 E
Nanduri 219d Bb 16.27S 179.09 E
Nandyāl 148 Fe 15.29N 78.29 E
Nanfen 154 Gd 41.06N 123.45 E
Nanfeng 152 Kf 27.15N 116.30 E
Nanga-Eboko 166 He 4.41N 12.22 E
Nanga Parbat 140 Jf 35.15N 74.36 E
Nangapinoh 150 Fg 0.20S 111.44 E
Nangarhār [3] 144 Lc 34.15N 70.30 E
Nangatayap 150 Fg 1.32S 110.34 E
Nangis 122 If 48.33N 3.00 E
Nangnim-san 154 Id 40.21N 126.55 E
Nangnim-Sanmaek 154 Id 40.30N 127.00 E
Nangong 152 Kd 37.22N 115.23 E
Nangqên 152 Ge 32.15N 96.13 E
Nanguan 154 Af 36.42N 111.41 E
Nanguantao → Guantao 154 Cf 36.33N 115.18 E
Nangweshi 170 Df 16.26S 23.20 E
Nang Xian 152 Ff 29.02N 93.05 E
Nan Hai = South China Sea (EN) 140 Ni 10.00N 113.00 E
Nanhaoqian → Shangyi 154 Bd 41.06N 113.58 E
Nanhe 154 Cf 36.58N 114.41 E
Nanhua 152 Hf 25.16N 101.18 E
Nanhui 154 Fi 31.03N 121.46 E
Nan Hulsan Hu 152 Gd 36.45N 95.45 E
Nanjian 152 Hf 25.05N 100.32 E
Nanjiang 152 Ie 32.22N 106.45 E
Nanjing (Nanking) 142 Nf 31.59N 118.51 E
Nankai Trough (EN) 152 Ne 32.00N 135.00 E
Nanking → Nanjing 142 Nf 31.59N 118.51 E
Nankoku 154 Lh 33.39N 133.44 E
Nanle 154 Cf 36.06N 115.12 E
Nanling 154 Ei 30.55N 118.19 E
Nan Ling 140 Ng 25.00N 112.00 E
Nanlou Shan 154 Ic 43.24N 126.40 E
Nanma → Yiyuan 154 Ef 36.11N 118.10 E
Nanning 142 Mg 22.50N 108.18 E
Nannup 212 Df 33.59S 115.45 E
Nanortalik 179 Hf 60.32N 45.45W
Nanpan Jiang 152 Ig 24.56N 106.12 E
Nänpära 148 Gc 27.52N 81.30 E
Nanping [China] 142 Ng 26.42N 118.09 E
Nanping [China] 152 He 33.15N 104.13 E
Nanpu 154 Ee 39.16N 118.12 E
Nanqiao → Fengxian 154 Fi 30.55N 121.27 E
Nansei-Shotō = Ryukyu Islands (EN) 140 Og 26.30N 128.00 E
Nansen Cordillera (EN) 224 Ge 87.00N 90.00 E
Nansen Land 179 Hb 83.20N 46.00W
Nanshan Islands (EN) = Nansha Qundao 140 Ni 9.40N 113.30 E
Nansha Qundao = Nanshan Islands (EN) 140 Ni 9.40N 113.30 E
Nansio 170 Fc 2.08S 33.03 E
Nant 122 Jj 44.01N 3.18 E
Nantais, Lac - 180 Kd 61.00N 73.50W
Nantai-San 156 Fc 36.46N 139.29 E
Nanterre 122 If 48.54N 2.12 E
Nantes 112 Ff 47.13N 1.33W
Nantes à Brest, Canal de- 122 Bf 48.12N 4.06W
Nanteuil-le-Haudouin 124 Ee 49.08N 2.48 E
Nanticoke 184 Je 41.13N 76.00W
Nantō 156 Ed 34.17N 136.29 E
Nantong 152 Le 32.00N 120.52 E
Nantong (Jinsha) 154 Fh 32.06N 120.52 E
Nantou 152 Lg 23.54N 120.51 E
Nantua 122 Lh 46.09N 5.37 E
Nantucket 184 Le 41.17N 70.06W
Nantucket Island 182 Mc 41.16N 70.03W
Nantucket Sound 184 Le 41.30N 70.15W
Nanuku Passage 219d Cb 16.45S 179.15W
Nanuku Reef 219d Cb 16.40S 179.26W
Nanumanga Island 208 Ie 6.18S 176.20 E
Nanumea Atoll 208 Ie 5.43S 176.00 E
Nanuque 202 Jg 17.50S 40.21W
Nanusa, Pulau-Pulau- 150 If 4.42N 127.06 E
Nanwan Shuiku 154 Bh 32.02N 113.57 E
Nanwei Dao = Spratly (EN) 150 Fe 8.42N 111.42 E
Nanwei Tan 152 Kg 21.00N 116.00 E
Nanweng He 152 Ma 51.10N 125.59 E
Nanxian 154 Bj 29.22N 112.25 E
Nanxiang 154 Fi 31.18N 121.17 E
Nanxiong 152 Jf 25.13N 114.18 E
Nanxun 154 Fi 30.53N 120.26 E
Nanyandang Shan 152 Lf 27.37N 120.06 E
Nanyang 142 Nf 32.56N 112.32 E
Nanyang Hu 154 Dg 35.15N 116.39 E
Nanyō 154 Pe 38.03N 140.10 E
Nanyuki 160 Kh 0.01N 37.04 E
Nanzhang 152 Je 31.45N 111.53 E
Nanzhao 152 Je 33.28N 112.29 E
Nao, Cabo de la-/Nau, Cap de la- 110 Gh 38.44N 0.14 E
Naococane, Lac- 180 Kf 52.50N 70.40W
Naoero / Nauru [1] 210 Nh 0.31S 166.56 E
Naoetsu 156 Fc 37.11N 138.14 E
Não-me-Toque 204 Fi 28.28S 52.49W
Naours, Souterrains de- 124 Ed 50.05N 2.17 E
Napa 188 Dg 38.18N 122.17W
Napanee 184 Ic 44.15N 76.57W
Napassoq 179 Ge 65.45N 52.38W
Napata 168 Eb 18.29N 31.51 E
Na-Peng 148 Jd 23.10N 98.26 E
Napf 128 Bc 47.01N 7.57 E
Napier 210 Ih 39.30S 176.54 E
Napier, Mount- 212 Fc 17.32S 129.10 E
Napier Mountains 222 Ee 66.30S 53.40 E
Naples [Fl.-U.S.] 182 Kf 26.08N 81.48W
Naples [Id.-U.S.] 188 Gb 48.34N 116.24W
Naples (EN) = Napoli 112 Hg 40.50N 14.15 E
Naples, Gulf of- (EN) = Napoli, Golfo di- 128 Ij 40.45N 14.10 E
Napo 152 Ig 23.25N 105.49 E
Napo, Rio- 198 If 3.20S 72.40W
Napoleon 186 Gc 46.30N 99.46W
Napoli = Naples (EN) 112 Hg 40.50N 14.15 E
Napoli, Golfo di- = Naples, Gulf of- (EN) 128 Ij 40.45N 14.10 E
Napostá 204 An 38.26S 62.15W
Napuka, Ile- 208 Mf 14.12S 141.15W
Naqa 168 Eb 16.16N 33.17 E
Naqadeh 144 Gb 36.57N 45.23 E
Naqsh-e-Rostam 146 Og 30.01N 52.50 E
Nar 118 Ni 52.45N 0.24 E
Nāra 148 Dc 24.07N 69.07 E
Nara [Jap.] 152 Oe 34.41N 135.50 E
Nara [Mali] 166 Db 15.11N 7.15W
Naračenskibani 130 Hh 41.54N 24.45 E
Naracoorte 212 Ig 36.58S 140.44 E
Nara-Ken [2] 154 Mg 34.20N 135.55 E
Naran 154 Bb 45.20N 113.41 E
Naranjo 192 Ee 25.48N 108.31W
Naranjos [Bol.] 204 Cd 18.38S 59.09W
Naranjos [Mex.] 192 Kg 21.21N 97.41W
Narao 156 Ae 32.52N 129.04 E
Narathiwat 148 Kg 6.25N 101.48 E
Nārāyanganj 148 Id 23.37N 90.30 E
Narbonne 122 Ik 43.11N 3.00 E
Narca, Ponta da- 170 Bd 6.07S 12.16 E
Narcea 126 Fa 43.28N 6.06W
Narcondam 148 If 13.15N 94.30 E
Nardò 128 Mj 40.11N 18.02 E
Naré 204 Bj 30.58S 60.28W
Nares Land 179 Hb 82.25N 47.30W
Nares Strait 174 Lb 78.50N 73.00W
Narew 120 Td 52.55N 23.29 E
Narew 120 Qd 52.26N 20.42 E
Narian, Pointe- 219b Be 20.05S 164.00 E
Narin Gol 152 Fd 36.54N 92.51 E
Nariño [3] 202 Cc 1.30N 78.00W
Narita 156 Gd 35.47N 140.18 E
Narjan-Mar 112 Lb 67.39N 53.00 E
Närke 116 Ff 59.05N 15.05 E
Narlı 146 Gd 37.27N 37.09 E
Narmada 140 Jg 21.38N 72.36 E
Narman 146 Ib 40.21N 41.52 E
Närnaul 148 Fc 28.03N 76.06 E
Narni 128 Gh 42.31N 12.31 E
Naroč 116 Lj 54.57N 26.49 E
Naroč 116 Lj 54.27N 26.45 E
Naroč, ozero- 132 Eb 54.50N 26.45 E
Naroda 134 Jd 64.15N 60.09 E
Narodnaja, gora- 110 Mb 65.04N 60.09 E
Naro-Fominsk 136 Dd 55.24N 36.43 E
Narok 170 Gc 1.05S 35.52 E
Narovlja 132 Fd 51.48N 29.31 E
Närpes/Närpio 116 Ib 62.28N 21.20 E
Närpio/Närpes 116 Ib 62.28N 21.20 E
Narrabri 212 Jf 30.19S 149.47 E
Narrandera 212 Jf 34.45S 146.33 E
Narrogin 212 Df 32.56S 117.10 E
Narromine 212 Jf 32.14S 148.15 E
Narrows, The- 197c Ab 17.12N 62.38W
Narryer, Mount- 212 De 26.30S 116.25 E
Narsimhapur 148 Fd 22.57N 79.12 E
Narssalik 179 Hf 61.42N 49.11W
Narssaq [Grld.] 179 Gf 64.00N 51.33W
Narssaq [Grld.] 179 Hf 61.00N 46.00W
Narssarssuaq 179 Hf 61.10N 45.15W
Narthákion 130 Fj 39.14N 22.22 E
Nartkala 132 Mh 43.32N 43.47 E
Narubis 172 Be 26.55S 18.35 E
Narugo 156 Gb 38.44N 140.43 E
Năruja 130 Jd 45.50N 26.47 E
Naru-Shima 156 Ae 32.50N 128.56 E
Naruto 154 Mg 34.11N 134.37 E
Naruto-Kaikyō 156 Dd 34.15N 134.40 E
Narva 112 Id 59.23N 28.11 E
Narva 114 Gg 59.29N 28.02 E
Narva Jõesuu/Narva-Jyesuu 116 Me 59.21N 28.04 E
Narva-Jyesuu / Narva-Jõesuu 116 Me 59.21N 28.04 E
Narva laht 114 Gg 59.30N 27.40 E
Narvik 112 Hb 68.26N 17.25 E
Narvski zaliv 114 Gg 59.30N 27.40 E
Narvskoje vodohranilišče 116 Me 59.10N 28.30 E
Narym 138 De 58.58N 81.40 E
Naryn 142 Je 41.26N 75.59 E
Naryn 140 Je 40.54N 71.45 E
Naryncol 136 Ig 42.43N 80.08 E
Narynskaja oblast [3] 136 Hg 41.20N 75.40 E
Nås 114 Df 60.27N 14.29 E
Na Sailti/Saltee Islands 118 Gi 52.07N 6.36W
Nasåker 114 De 63.23N 16.54 E
Nasarawa 166 Gd 8.32N 7.43 E
Năsăud 130 Hb 47.17N 24.24 E
Nasawa 219b Bb 15.12S 168.06 E
Nasbinals 122 Jj 44.40N 3.03 E
Na Sceiri/Skerries 118 Gh 53.35N 6.07W
Nāshik 142 Jg 20.05N 73.48 E
Nash Point 118 Jj 51.24N 3.27W
Nashtārud 146 Nd 36.45N 51.02 E
Nashua 184 Ld 42.44N 71.28W
Nashville [Ar.-U.S.] 186 Jj 33.57N 93.51W
Nashville [Ga.-U.S.] 184 Fj 31.12N 83.15W
Nashville [Il.-U.S.] 186 Lg 38.21N 89.23W
Nashville [In.-U.S.] 184 Df 39.12N 86.15W
Nashville [Tn.-U.S.] 176 Kf 36.09N 86.48W
Nashville Seamount (EN) 174 Nf 35.00N 57.20W
Našice 128 Me 45.30N 18.06 E
Nasielsk 120 Qd 52.36N 20.48 E
Näsijärvi 110 Ic 61.35N 23.40 E
Nāşir 168 Ed 8.36N 33.04 E
Naskaupi 180 Lf 53.45N 60.51W
Nasorolevu 219d Bb 16.38S 179.24 E
Naşr 164 Dd 28.59N 31.13 E
Naşr 146 Dg 30.36N 30.23 E
Naşrābād 146 Of 32.09N 52.08 E
Nass 180 Ee 55.00N 129.50W
Nassandres 124 Ce 49.07N 0.44 E
Nassandres-La Rivière Thibouville 124 Ce 49.07N 0.44 E
Nassau [Bah.] 176 Lg 25.05N 77.21W
Nassau [F.R.G.] 124 Jd 50.19N 7.48 E
Nassau, Bahia- 206 Gi 55.25S 67.40W
Nassau Island 208 Kf 11.33S 165.25W
Nassau River 212 Ic 15.58S 141.30 E
Nasser, Birkat- = Nasser, Lake- (EN) 158 Kf 22.40N 32.00 E
Nasser, Lake- (EN) = Nasser, Birkat- 158 Kf 22.40N 32.00 E
Nassian 166 Ed 9.24N 4.29W
Nässjö 114 Dh 57.39N 14.41 E
Nassogne 124 Hd 50.08N 5.21 E
Na Staighri Dubha/ Blackstairs Mountains 118 Gi 52.33N 6.49W
Nastapoka Islands 180 Je 56.50N 76.50W
Nastätten 124 Jd 50.12N 7.52 E
Nastola 116 Kd 60.57N 25.56 E
Nasu 156 Gc 37.02N 140.06 E
Nasu-Dake 156 Fc 37.07N 139.58 E
Näsviken 116 Gc 61.45N 16.52 E
Natá 194 Gi 8.20N 80.31W
Nata 172 Dd 20.13S 26.11 E
Nata 158 Jk 20.13S 26.10 E
Natal [2] 172 Ee 29.00S 30.00 E

Index Symbols

[1] Independent Nation
[2] State, Region
[3] District, County
[4] Municipality
[5] Colony, Dependency
Continent
Physical Region
Historical or Cultural Region
Mount, Mountain
Volcano
Hill
Mountains, Mountain Range
Hills, Escarpment
Plateau, Upland
Pass, Gap
Plain, Lowland
Delta
Salt Flat
Valley, Canyon
Crater, Cave
Karst Features
Depression
Polder
Desert, Dunes
Forest, Woods
Heath, Steppe
Oasis
Cape, Point
Coast, Beach
Cliff
Peninsula
Isthmus
Sandbank
Island
Atoll
Rock, Reef
Islands, Archipelago
Rocks, Reefs
Coral Reef
Well, Spring
Geyser
River, Stream
Waterfall, Rapids
River Mouth, Estuary
Lake
Salt Lake
Intermittent Lake
Reservoir
Swamp, Pond
Canal
Glacier
Ice Shelf, Pack Ice
Ocean
Sea
Gulf, Bay
Strait, Fjord
Lagoon
Bank
Seamount
Tablemount
Ridge
Shelf
Basin
Escarpment, Sea Scarp
Fracture
Trench, Abyss
National Park, Reserve
Point of Interest
Recreation Site
Cave, Cavern
Historic Site
Ruins
Wall, Walls
Church, Abbey
Temple
Scientific Station
Railway station
Airport
Port
Military installation
Lighthouse
Mine
Tunnel
Dam, Bridge

Natal [B.C.-Can.]	188	Hb	49.44N	114.50W
Natal [Braz.]	200	Mf	5.47S	35.13W
Natal [Indon.]	150	Cf	0.33N	99.07 E
Natal Basin (EN)	106	Fm	30.00S	40.00 E
Natanz	146	Nf	33.31N	51.54 E
Natashquan	180	Lf	50.11N	61.49W
Natashquan	180	Lf	50.09N	61.37W
Natchez	182	Ie	31.34N	91.23W
Natchitoches	182	Ie	31.46N	93.05W
Natewa Bay	219d	Bb	16.35S	179.40 E
Nathorsts Land	179	Jd	72.20N	27.00W
Nathula	219d	Ab	16.53S	177.25 E
Natitingou	160	Hg	10.19N	1.22 E
Natityāy, Jabal-	164	Fe	23.01N	34.22 E
Natividad, Isla-	192	Bd	27.55N	115.10W
Natividade	202	If	11.43S	47.47W
Natori	154	Pe	38.11N	140.58 E
Natron, Lake-	158	Ki	2.25S	36.00 E
Naţrūn, Wādī an-	146	Dg	30.25N	30.13 E
Natsudomari-Zaki	156a	Bc	41.00N	140.53 E
Nåttarö	116	Hf	58.50N	18.10 E
Nättraby	116	Fh	56.12N	15.31 E
Natuna, Kepulauan- = Natuna Islands (EN)	140	Mi	2.45N	109.00 E
Natuna Besar, Pulau-	150	Ef	4.00N	108.15 E
Natuna Islands (EN) = Natuna, Kepulauan-	140	Mi	2.45N	109.00 E
Naturaliste, Cape-	208	Ch	33.32S	115.01 E
Naturaliste Channel	212	Ce	25.25S	113.00 E
Naturita	186	Bg	38.14N	108.34W
Naturno / Naturns	128	Ed	46.39N	11.00 E
Naturns / Naturno	128	Ed	46.39N	11.00 E
Nau	135	Gd	40.09N	69.22 E
Nau, Cap de la-/Nao, Cabo de la-	110	Gh	38.44N	0.14 E
Naucelle	122	Ij	44.12N	2.21 E
Nauëji-Akmjane/Naujoji-Akmenė	114	Fh	56.21N	22.50 E
Naugo/Nauvo	116	Id	60.10N	21.50 E
Nauhcampatépetl → Cofre de Perote, Cerro-	192	Kh	19.29N	97.08W
Nauja Bay	180	Kc	68.58N	75.00W
Naujamestis/Naujamiestis	116	Ki	55.41N	24.09 E
Naujamiestis/Naujamestis	116	Ki	55.41N	24.09 E
Naujoji-Akmenė/Nauëji-Akmjane	114	Fh	56.21N	22.50 E
Naukluft	172	Bd	24.10S	16.10 E
Naumburg [F.R.G.]	124	Lc	51.15N	9.10 E
Naumburg [G.D.R.]	120	He	51.09N	11.49 E
Nā'ūr	146	Fg	31.53N	35.50 E
Nauru	208	He	0.31S	166.56 E
Nauru / Naoero [1]	210	He	0.31S	166.56 E
Nauški	138	Ff	50.28N	106.07 E
Nausori	216	Ec	18.02S	178.32 E
Nauta	202	Dd	4.32S	73.33W
Nautanwa	148	Gc	27.26N	83.25 E
Nautla	192	Kg	20.13N	96.47W
Nauvo/Naugo	116	Id	60.10N	21.50 E
Nava	192	Ic	28.25N	100.45W
Navacerrada, Puerto de-	126	Id	40.47N	4.00W
Nava del Rey	126	Gc	41.20N	5.05W
Navahermosa	126	He	39.38N	4.28W
Navajo Mountain	188	Jh	37.02N	110.52W
Navajo Reservoir	186	Ch	36.55N	107.30W
Navalmoral de la Mata	126	Ge	39.54N	5.32W
Navan → An Uaimh	118	Gh	53.39N	6.41W
Navarin, mys-	140	Tc	62.16N	179.10 E
Navarino, Isla-	198	Jk	55.05S	67.40W
Navarra / Nafarroa [2]	126	Kb	42.45N	1.40W
Navarro	204	Cl	35.01S	59.16W
Navarro Mills Lake	186	Hk	31.56N	96.45W
Navašino	114	Ki	55.33N	42.12 E
Navasota	186	Hk	30.23N	96.05W
Navasota River	186	Hk	30.20N	96.09W
Navassa	190	Ie	18.24N	75.01W
Navaste jõgi / Navesti	116	Kf	58.56N	24.58 E
Nävekvarn	116	Gf	58.38N	16.49 E
Naver	118	Ic	58.30N	4.15W
Navesti / Navaste jõgi	116	Kf	58.56N	24.58 E
Navia	126	Fa	43.32N	6.43W
Navia	126	Fa	43.33N	6.44W
Navidad, Bahía de-	192	Gh	19.10N	104.45W
Navidad Bank (EN)	194	Mc	20.00N	68.50W
Naviti	219d	Ab	17.07S	177.15 E
Navlja	136	De	52.50N	34.31 E
Navlja	132	Ic	52.42N	34.03 E
Năvodari	130	Le	44.19N	28.36 E
Navoi	136	Gg	40.10N	65.15 E
Navoja	190	Cc	27.06N	109.26W
Navolato	192	Fe	24.47N	107.42W
Navoloki	114	Jh	57.28N	41.59 E
Návpaktos	130	Ek	38.24N	21.50 E
Návplion	130	Fl	37.34N	22.48 E
Navrongo	166	Ec	10.54N	1.06W
Navsāri	148	Ed	20.55N	72.55 E
Navtílos	130	Gn	35.57N	23.13 E
Navua	219d	Bc	18.13S	178.10 E
Navy Board Inlet	180	Jb	73.30N	81.00W
Nawa	146	Gf	32.53N	36.03 E
Nawābshāh	148	Dc	26.15N	68.25 E
Nawāşīf, Ḩarrat-	164	He	21.20N	42.10 E
Naws, Ra's-	144	If	17.18N	55.16 E
Náxos	130	Il	37.06N	25.23 E
Naxos	128	Jm	37.49N	15.15 E
Náxos = Naxos (EN)	110	Ih	37.02N	25.35 E
Naxos (EN) = Náxos	110	Ih	37.02N	25.35 E
Nayarit [2]	190	Cd	22.00N	105.00W
Nayarit, Sierra de-	190	Dd	22.00N	103.50W
Nayau	219d	Cb	17.58S	179.03W
Nāy Band [Iran]	146	Oi	27.23N	52.38 E
Nāy Band [Iran]	146	Qf	32.20N	57.34 E
Nāy Band, Kūh-e-	144	Ic	32.27N	57.23 E
Nāy Band, Ra's-e-	146	Oi	27.23N	52.34 E
Nayoro	152	Pc	44.21N	142.28 E
Nayyāl, Wādī-	146	Gh	28.58N	37.50 E
Nazaré [Braz.]	202	Kf	13.02S	39.00W
Nazaré [Port.]	126	Ce	39.36N	9.04W
Nazareth (EN) = Naẕerat	146	Ff	32.42N	35.18 E
Nazarovo	138	Ee	56.01N	90.36 E
Nazas	192	Ge	25.14N	104.08W
Nazas, Río-	174	Ig	25.35N	105.00W
Nazca	200	Ig	14.50S	74.55W
Nazca Ridge (EN)	106	Nl	22.00S	82.00W
Naze	152	Mf	28.23N	129.30 E
Naẕerat = Nazareth (EN)	146	Ff	32.42N	35.18 E
Nazik Gölü	146	Jc	38.48N	42.15 E
Nazilli	144	Cb	37.55N	28.21 E
Nazimiye	146	Hc	39.11N	39.50 E
Nazimovo	138	Ee	59.30N	90.58 E
Nazino	138	Cd	60.15N	78.58 E
Nazlū	146	Kd	37.42N	45.16 E
Nazran	132	Nh	43.15N	44.46 E
Nazret	168	Fd	8.34N	39.18 E
Nazw'a	144	Ie	22.54N	57.31 E
Nazym	134	Nf	61.12N	68.57 E
Nazyvajevsk	136	Hd	55.34N	71.21 E
Nbâk	162	Ef	17.15N	14.59W
Nchanga	170	Ee	12.31S	27.52 E
Ncheu	170	Fe	14.49S	34.38 E
Ndala	170	Fc	4.46S	33.16 E
N'dalatando	170	Bd	9.18S	14.54 E
Ndali	166	Fd	9.51N	2.43 E
Ndélé	160	Jh	8.24N	20.39 E
Ndélélé	166	He	4.02N	14.56 E
Ndendé	170	Bc	2.23S	11.23 E
Ndindi	170	Bc	3.46S	11.09 E
N'Djamena (Fort-Lamy)	160	Ig	12.07N	15.03 E
Ndola	160	Jj	12.58S	28.38 E
Ndouana, Pointe-	219b	Dc	16.35S	168.09 E
Ndrhamcha, Sebkha de-	162	Df	18.45N	15.48W
Ndui Ndui	219b	Cb	15.24S	167.46 E
Nduindui	214	Fi	9.48S	159.58 E
Né	122	Fi	45.40N	0.23W
Nea	219c	Ab	10.51S	165.47 E
Nea	114	Ce	63.13N	11.02 E
Néa Alikarnassós	130	In	35.20N	25.09 E
Néa Artáki	130	Gk	38.31N	23.38 E
Neagari	156	Ec	36.26N	136.26 E
Neagh, Lough-/Loch nEathach	110	Fe	54.38N	6.24W
Neagră, Marea- = Black Sea (EN)	110	Jg	43.00N	35.00 E
Neah Bay	188	Cb	48.22N	124.37W
Néa Ionía	130	Fj	39.23N	22.56 E
Neajlov	130	Je	44.11N	26.12 E
Neale, Lake-	212	Fd	24.20S	130.00 E
Neamţ [2]	130	Jb	47.00N	26.20 E
Neápolis [Grc.]	130	Gm	36.31N	23.04 E
Neápolis [Grc.]	130	Ei	40.19N	21.23 E
Neápolis [Grc.]	130	In	35.15N	25.37 E
Near Islands	174	Bd	52.40N	173.30W
Neath	118	Jj	51.40N	3.48W
Neath	118	Jj	51.37N	3.50W
Néa Zíkhni	130	Gh	41.02N	23.50 E
Néba	219b	Ae	20.09S	163.55 E
Nebaj	194	Bf	15.24N	91.08W
Nebbou	166	Ec	11.18N	1.53W
Nebesnaja, Gora-	135	Mc	43.15N	80.45 E
Nebit-Dag	142	Hf	39.30N	54.22 E
Neblina, Cerro de la-	198	Je	1.08N	66.10W
Nebo	212	Jd	21.40S	148.39 E
Nebo, Mount-	188	Jg	39.49N	111.46W
Nebolči	114	Hg	59.08N	33.21 E
Nebraska [2]	182	Gc	41.30N	100.00W
Nebraska City	182	Hc	40.41N	95.52W
Nebrodi (Caronie)	128	Im	37.55N	14.35 E
Necedah	186	Kd	44.02N	90.03W
Nechako	180	Ff	53.55N	122.44W
Nechako Reservoir	180	Ef	53.00N	126.10W
Nechar, Djebel-	126	Qi	35.52N	4.59 E
Neches River	186	Jl	29.55N	93.52W
Nechí	194	Ji	8.07N	74.46W
Nechí, Río-	194	Ji	8.08N	74.46W
Neckako Plateau	180	Ff	53.25N	124.40W
Neckar	120	Eg	49.31N	8.26 E
Neckargemünd	124	Ke	49.29N	8.50 E
Neckarsteinach	124	Ke	49.25N	8.50 E
Neckarsulm	120	Fg	49.11N	9.14 E
Necker Island	208	Kb	23.35N	164.42W
Necochea	200	Ki	38.34S	58.45W
Necy	124	Bf	48.50N	0.07W
Nedeley	168	Bb	15.34N	18.10 E
Nederland	186	Jl	29.58N	93.59W
Nederland = Netherlands (EN) [1]	112	Ge	52.15N	5.30 E
Nederlandse Antillen [Neth.Ant.] = Netherlands Antilles (EN) [5]	200	Jd	12.15N	69.00W
Nederlandse Antillen [Neth.Ant.] = Netherlands Antilles (EN) [5]	200	Jd	18.06N	63.10W
Neder-Rijn = Lower Rhine (EN)	122	Mc	51.59N	6.20 E
Nêdong	142	Lg	29.14N	91.46 E
Nedstrand	116	Ae	59.21N	5.51 E
Nedstrandefjorden	116	Ae	59.20N	5.50 E
Neede	124	Ib	52.08N	6.37 E
Needham Market	124	Db	52.09N	1.02 E
Needham's Point	197q	Ab	13.05N	59.36W
Needles	182	Ee	34.51N	114.37W
Neembucú [3]	204	Dh	27.00S	58.00W
Neenah	186	Ld	44.11N	88.28W
Neepawa	186	Ga	50.13N	99.29W
Neermoor, Moormerland-	124	Ja	53.18N	7.26 E
Neeroeteren, Maaseik-	124	Hc	51.05N	5.42 E
Neerpelt	124	Hc	51.13N	5.25 E
Nefasit	168	Fb	15.18N	39.04 E
Nefedova	136	Hd	58.48N	72.34 E
Né Finn/Nephin	118	Dg	54.01N	9.22W
Neftah	162	Ic	33.52N	7.53 E
Neftečala	132	Pj	39.19N	49.13 E
Neftegorsk [R.S.F.S.R.]	136	Fe	52.45N	51.13 E
Neftegorsk [R.S.F.S.R.]	132	Kg	44.22N	39.42 E
Neftegorsk [R.S.F.S.R.]	138	Jf	53.00N	143.00 E
Neftejugansk	136	Hc	61.05N	72.45 E
Neftekamsk	136	Fd	56.06N	54.17 E
Neftekumsk	136	Eg	44.43N	44.59 E
Neftjanyje Kamin	132	Qi	40.15N	50.49 E
Negage	170	Cd	7.46S	15.18 E
Negara	150	Fh	8.22S	114.37 E
Negele = Neghelle (EN)	160	Kh	5.20N	39.37 E
Negeri Sembilan [2]	150	Df	2.45N	102.10 E
Negev Desert (EN) = Ḥanegev	146	Fg	30.30N	34.55 E
Neghelle (EN) = Negele	160	Kh	5.20N	39.37 E
Negla, Arroyo-	204	Df	22.52S	56.41W
Negola	170	Be	14.10S	14.30 E
Negomano	172	Fb	11.26S	38.33 E
Negombo	148	Fg	7.13N	79.50 E
Negonego Atoll	208	Mf	18.47S	141.48W
Negotin	130	Fe	44.13N	22.32 E
Negra, Cordillera-	202	Ce	9.25S	77.40W
Negra, Coxilha-	204	Ej	31.02S	55.45W
Negra, Peña-	126	Fb	42.11N	6.30W
Negra, Ponta-	204	Jf	23.21S	44.36W
Negra, Punta-	198	Hf	6.06S	81.10W
Negra, Serra-	204	Fc	16.30S	52.10W
Negra o de los Difuntos, Laguna-	204	Fl	34.03S	53.40W
Negreira	126	Db	42.54N	8.44W
Negreni	130	He	44.34N	24.36 E
Negreşti	130	Gb	47.52N	23.26 E
Negrine	162	Ic	34.29N	7.31 E
Negrinho, Rio-	204	Ed	19.20S	55.05W
Negro, Cabo-	126	Gi	35.41N	5.17W
Negro, Río- [Arg.]	198	Jj	41.02S	62.47W
Negro, Río- [Arg.]	204	Ch	27.27S	58.54W
Negro, Río- [Bol.]	202	Ff	14.11S	63.07W
Negro, Rio- [Braz.]	206	Jc	26.01S	50.30W
Negro, Rio- [Braz.]	202	Gg	19.13S	57.17W
Negro, Río- [Par.]	206	Ib	24.23S	57.11W
Negro, Río- [S.Amer.]	204	Ce	20.11S	58.10W
Negro, Río- [S.Amer.]	198	Kf	3.08S	59.55W
Negro, Río- [Ur.]	198	Ki	33.24S	58.22W
Negro, Río → Chixoy, Río-	194	Be	16.28N	90.33W
Negros	140	Oi	10.00N	123.00 E
Negru, Rîu-	130	Id	45.45N	25.46 E
Negru Vodă	130	Lf	43.49N	28.12 E
Nehajevski	132	Ld	50.27N	41.46 E
Nehalem River	188	Dd	45.40N	123.56W
Nehāvand	146	Me	35.56N	49.31 E
Nehe	152	Lb	48.28N	124.53 E
Nehoiu	130	Jd	45.26N	26.17 E
Néhoué, Baie de-	219b	Be	20.21S	164.09 E
Neiba	194	Ld	18.28N	71.25W
Neiba, Bahía de-	194	Ld	18.15N	71.02W
Neidín/Kenmare	118	Dj	51.53N	9.35W
Neige, Crêt de la-	122	Lh	46.16N	5.56 E
Neiges, Piton des-	158	Mk	21.05S	55.29 E
Neijiang	142	Mg	29.38N	104.58 E
Neilton	188	Dc	47.25N	123.52W
Nei-meng-ku Tzu-chih-ch'ü → Nei Monggol Zizhiqu [2]	152	Jc	44.00N	112.00 E
Nei Monggol Gaoyuan	140	Ne	42.00N	111.00 E
Nei Monggol Zizhiqu (Nei-meng-ku Tzu-chih-ch'ü) = Inner Mongolia (EN) [2]	152	Jc	44.00N	112.00 E
Neiqiu	154	Cf	37.17N	114.30 E
Neiva	200	Ie	2.56N	75.18W
Neja	136	Ed	58.19N	43.52 E
Nejanilini Lake	180	He	59.30N	97.50W
Nejdek	120	If	50.19N	12.44 E
Nejo	168	Fd	9.30N	35.32 E
Nejva	134	Kh	57.54N	62.18 E
Nekemt = Leqemt (EN)	160	Kh	9.05N	36.33 E
Neksø	116	Fi	55.04N	15.09 E
Nelemnoje	138	Kc	65.23N	151.08 E
Nelgese	138	Ic	66.40N	136.30 E
Nelichu	168	Ed	6.08N	34.25 E
Nelidovo	136	Dd	56.13N	32.50 E
Neligh	186	Ge	42.08N	98.02W
Neljaty	138	Ge	56.29N	115.50 E
Nelkan	138	Jd	64.15N	143.03 E
Nellore	142	Jh	12.56N	79.08 E
Nelma	138	Ig	47.40N	139.08 E
Nelson [2]	218	Ed	41.45S	172.30 E
Nelson	174	Jd	57.04N	92.30W
Nelson [B.C.-Can.]	180	Fg	49.29N	117.17W
Nelson [N.Z.]	210	Ii	41.16S	173.15 E
Nelson, Cape- [Austl.]	208	Fh	38.26S	141.33 E
Nelson, Cape- [Pap.N.Gui.]	212	Ja	9.00S	149.15 E
Nelson Island	178	Gd	60.35N	164.45W
Nelson's Dockyard	197d	Bb	17.00N	61.46W
Nelspruit	160	Kk	25.30S	30.58 E
Néma	160	Gg	16.36N	7.15W
Néma, Dahr-	162	Ff	16.14N	7.30W
Neman	114	Fi	55.03N	22.01 E
Neman	110	Id	55.18N	21.23 E
Nembrala	150	Hi	10.53S	122.50 E
Nemda	114	Kh	57.31N	43.15 E
Neméa	130	Fl	37.49N	22.39 E
Neméa	130	Fl	37.49N	22.40 E
Nemenčinė	116	Kj	54.50N	25.39 E
Nëmërçkes, Mali i-	130	Di	40.08N	20.24 E
Nemira, Vîrful-	130	Jc	46.15N	26.19 E
Nemirov [Ukr.-U.S.S.R.]	132	Fe	48.59N	28.50 E
Nemirov [Ukr.-U.S.S.R.]	120	Tf	50.08N	23.28 E
Némiscau	180	Jf	51.30N	77.00W
Nemjuga	114	Kd	65.29N	43.40 E
Nemours	122	If	48.16N	2.42 E
Nemrut Dağı	146	Jc	38.40N	42.12 E
Nemunas	110	Id	55.18N	21.23 E
Nemunėlis	116	Kh	56.24N	24.10 E
Nemuro	152	Qc	43.20N	145.35 E
Nemuro-Hantō	156a	Db	43.20N	145.35 E
Nemuro-Kaikyō = Nemuro Strait (EN)	138	Jh	43.50N	145.30 E
Nemuro Strait (EN) = Kunaširski proliv	138	Jh	43.50N	145.30 E
Nemuro Strait (EN) = Nemuro-Kaikyō	138	Jh	43.50N	145.30 E
Nemuro-Wan	156a	Db	43.25N	145.25 E
Nenagh/An tAonach	118	Ei	52.52N	8.12W
Nenana	178	Jd	64.34N	149.07W
Nenana	178	Jd	64.30N	149.00W
Nendo Island	208	Hf	10.40S	165.54 E
Nene	118	Ni	52.48N	0.13 E
Nenecki nacionalny okrug [3]	136	Fb	67.30N	54.00 E
Nenjiang	142	Oe	49.10N	125.12 E
Nen Jiang	140	Oe	45.26N	124.39 E
Neo	156	Ed	35.38N	136.37 E
Neodesha	186	Ih	37.25N	95.41W
Néon Karlovásion	130	Jl	37.47N	26.42 E
Neosho	186	Ih	36.52N	94.22W
Neosho River	186	Ih	35.48N	95.18W
Néouvielle, Massif de-	122	Gl	42.51N	0.07 E
Nepal [1]	142	Kg	28.00N	84.00 E
Nepalganj	148	Gc	28.03N	81.37 E
Nephi	182	Ed	39.43N	111.50W
Nephin/Né Finn	118	Dg	54.01N	9.22W
Nepisiguit River	184	Ob	47.37N	65.38W
Nepoko	158	Jh	1.40N	27.01 E
Nepomuk	120	Jg	49.29N	13.34 E
Ner	120	Od	52.10N	18.40 E
Nera [It.]	128	Gh	42.26N	12.24 E
Nera [Rom.]	130	Ee	44.49N	21.22 E
Nérac	122	Gj	44.08N	0.21 E
Neratovice	120	Kf	50.16N	14.31 E
Nerău	130	Dd	45.58N	20.34 E
Nerbio / Nervión	126	Ja	43.14N	2.53W
Nerča	138	Gf	51.54N	116.30 E
Nerčinsk	138	Gf	51.58N	116.35 E
Nerčinski Zavod	138	Gf	51.17N	119.30 E
Nerehta	136	Ed	57.28N	40.34 E
Nereju	130	Jd	45.42N	26.43 E
Nereta	116	Kh	56.12N	25.24 E
Neretva	128	Lg	43.02N	17.27 E
Neretvanski kanal	128	Lg	43.03N	17.11 E
Nerica	134	Fd	65.20N	52.45 E
Neringa	114	Ei	55.24N	21.05 E
Neringa	114	Ei	55.18N	21.00 E
Neringa-Joudkrante/Neringa-Juodkrantė	116	Ii	55.35N	21.01 E
Neringa-Juodkrantė/Neringa-Juodkrante	116	Ii	55.35N	21.01 E
Neringa-Nida	116	Ii	55.18N	20.53 E
Neringa-Preila/Neringa-Prejla	116	Ii	55.20N	20.59 E
Neringa-Prejla/Neringa-Preila	116	Ii	55.20N	20.59 E
Neriquinha	170	Df	15.45S	21.33 E
Neris/Njaris	116	Kj	54.55N	25.45 E
Nerja	126	Ih	36.44N	3.52W
Nerjungri	138	He	56.40N	124.47 E
Nerl [R.S.F.S.R.]	114	Ih	57.07N	37.39 E
Nerl [R.S.F.S.R.]	114	Jh	56.11N	40.34 E
Nerpio	126	Jf	38.09N	2.18W
Nerussa	132	Hc	52.33N	33.47 E
Nerva	126	Fg	37.42N	6.32W
Nervi, Genova-	128	Df	44.23N	9.02 E
Nervión / Nerbio	126	Ja	43.14N	2.53W
Nes	116	Cd	60.34N	9.59 E
Nes, Ameland-	124	Ha	53.26N	5.48 E
Nesbyen	114	Bf	60.34N	9.06 E
Nesebăr	130	Kg	42.39N	27.44 E
Nesjøen	116	Db	63.00N	12.00 E
Neskaupstaður	114a	Db	65.09N	13.42W
Nesle	124	Ee	49.46N	2.45 E
Nesna	114	Cc	66.12N	13.02 E
Ness City	186	Gg	38.27N	99.54W
Nesterov [R.S.F.S.R.]	114	Fi	54.42N	22.34 E
Nesterov [Ukr.-U.S.S.R.]	132	Cd	50.03N	24.00 E
Néstos	130	Hi	40.51N	24.44 E
Nesttun	116	Ad	60.19N	5.20 E
Nesviž	132	Ec	53.13N	26.39 E
Netanya	146	Ff	32.20N	34.51 E
Netcong	184	Je	40.54N	74.43W
Nete	122	Kc	51.10N	4.15 E
Nethe	124	Lc	51.44N	9.23 E
Netherdale	212	Jd	21.08S	148.32 E
Netherlands (EN) = Nederland [1]	112	Ge	52.15N	5.30 E
Netherlands Antilles (EN) = Nederlandse Antillen [Neth.Ant.] [5]	200	Jd	12.15N	69.00W
Netherlands Antilles (EN) = Nederlandse Antillen [Neth.Ant.] [5]	200	Jd	18.06N	63.10W
Neto	128	Lk	39.12N	17.09 E
Netphen	124	Kd	50.55N	8.06 E
Nettebach	124	Jd	50.26N	7.28 E
Nettersheim	124	Id	50.30N	6.38 E
Nettetal	124	Ic	51.18N	6.12 E
Nettiling Lake	174	Lc	66.30N	70.40W
Nettuno	128	Gi	41.27N	12.39 E
Netzahualcóyotl, Presa-	192	Mi	17.00N	93.30W
Neubourg, Campagne du-	122	Ge	49.08N	1.00 E
Neubrandenburg	120	Jc	53.34N	13.16 E
Neubrandenburg [2]	120	Jc	53.35N	13.15 E
Neuburg an der Donau	120	Hh	48.44N	11.11 E
Neuchâtel [2]	128	Ac	47.05N	6.50 E
Neuchâtel/Neuenburg	128	Ad	46.59N	6.56 E
Neuchâtel, Lac de-	128	Ad	46.55N	6.55 E
Neuenbürg	124	Kf	48.50N	8.35 E
Neuenburg/Neuchâtel	128	Ad	46.59N	6.56 E
Neuenhaus	124	Ib	52.30N	6.58 E
Neuenkirchen	124	Jb	52.15N	7.22 E
Neuerburg	124	Id	50.01N	6.18 E
Neufchâteau [Bel.]	122	Le	49.51N	5.26 E
Neufchâteau [Fr.]	122	Lf	48.21N	5.42 E
Neufchâtel-en-Bray	122	He	49.44N	1.27 E
Neufchâtel-Hardelot	124	Dd	50.37N	1.38 E
Neufchâtel Hardelot-Hardelot Plage	124	Dd	50.38N	1.35 E
Neufchâtel-sur-Aisne	124	Ge	49.26N	4.02 E
Neuffossé, Canal de-	124	Ed	50.45N	2.15 E
Neuhaus am Rennweg	120	Hf	50.31N	11.09 E
Neuilly-en-Thelle	124	Ee	49.13N	2.17 E
Neuilly-Saint-Front	124	Fe	49.10N	3.16 E
Neu-Isenburg	124	Kd	50.03N	8.42 E
Neukirchen-Vluyn	124	Ic	51.27N	6.35 E
Neum	128	Lh	42.55N	17.38 E
Neumagen-Dhron	124	Ie	49.51N	6.54 E
Neumarkter Sattel	128	Id	47.06N	14.22 E
Neumarkt in der Oberpfalz	120	Hg	49.17N	11.28 E
Neumünster	120	Fb	54.04N	9.59 E
Neunkirchen [Aus.]	128	Kc	47.43N	16.05 E
Neunkirchen [F.R.G.]	120	Dg	49.21N	7.11 E
Neunkirchen [F.R.G.]	124	Kd	50.48N	8.00 E
Neunkirchen [F.R.G.]	124	Jd	50.51N	7.20 E
Neuquén	200	Ji	39.00S	68.05W
Neuquén [2]	206	Ge	39.00S	70.00W
Neuquén, Río-	198	Ji	38.59S	68.00W
Neuruppin	120	Id	52.56N	12.48 E
Neuse River	184	Ih	35.06N	76.30W
Neusiedl am See	128	Kc	47.56N	16.50 E
Neusiedler See	120	Mi	47.50N	16.45 E
Neuss	120	Ce	51.12N	6.42 E
Neustadt (Hessen)	124	Ld	50.51N	9.07 E
Neustadt am Rübenberge	120	Fd	52.30N	9.28 E
Neustadt an der Aisch	120	Gg	49.35N	10.36 E
Neustadt an der Orla	120	Hf	50.44N	11.45 E
Neustadt an der Weinstraße	120	Eg	49.21N	8.09 E
Neustadt bei Coburg	120	Hf	50.19N	11.07 E
Neustadt in Holstein	120	Gb	54.06N	10.49 E
Neustrelitz	120	Jc	53.22N	13.05 E
Neu-Ulm	120	Gh	48.24N	10.01 E
Neuville-les-Dieppe	124	De	49.55N	1.06 E
Neuville-sur-Saône	122	Ki	45.52N	4.51 E
Neuwerk	120	Ec	53.55N	8.30 E
Neuwied	120	Df	50.26N	7.28 E
Neva	110	Jd	59.55N	30.15 E
Nevada [2]	182	Dd	39.00N	117.00W
Nevada [Ia.-U.S.]	186	Je	42.01N	93.27W
Nevada [Mo.-U.S.]	182	Id	37.51N	94.22W
Nevada, Sierra- [Sp.]	110	Fh	37.05N	3.10W
Nevada, Sierra- [U.S.]	174	Hf	38.00N	119.15W
Nevada del Cocuy, Sierra-	198	Ie	6.10N	72.15W
Nevada de Santa Marta, Sierra-	198	Id	10.50N	73.40W
Nevado, Cerro-	198	Ie	3.59N	74.04W
Neve, Serra da-	158	Ij	13.52S	13.26 E
Nevel	136	Cd	56.02N	29.55 E
Nevele	124	Fc	51.02N	3.33 E
Nevelsk	138	Jg	46.37N	141.57 E
Neverkino	132	Oc	52.47N	46.48 E
Nevers	122	Jg	46.59N	3.10 E
Nevesinje	128	Mg	43.16N	18.07 E
Nevinnomyssk	136	Eg	44.38N	41.58 E
Nevis	190	Le	17.10N	62.34W
Nevis, Ben-	110	Fd	56.48N	5.01W
Nevis Peak	197c	Ab	17.10N	62.34W
Nevjansk	136	Gd	57.32N	60.13 E
Nevşehir	144	Db	38.38N	34.43 E
Nevskoje	154	Lb	45.42N	133.40 E
Newala	170	Ge	10.56S	39.18 E
New Albany [In.-U.S.]	182	Jd	38.18N	85.49W
New Albany [Ms.-U.S.]	186	Li	34.29N	89.00W
New Alresford	124	Ac	51.05N	1.10W
New Amsterdam	200	Ke	6.17N	57.36W
Newark [De.-U.S.]	184	Jf	39.41N	75.45W
Newark [N.J.-U.S.]	182	Mc	40.44N	74.11W
Newark [N.Y.-U.S.]	184	Id	43.03N	77.06W
Newark [Oh.-U.S.]	182	Kc	40.03N	82.25W
Newark-on-Trent	118	Mh	53.05N	0.49W
New Bedford	182	Mc	41.38N	70.56W
New Bern	182	Ld	35.07N	77.03W
Newberry [Mi.-U.S.]	184	Eb	46.21N	85.30W
Newberry [S.C.-U.S.]	184	Gh	34.17N	81.37W
New Braunfels	182	Hf	29.42N	98.08W
New Britain	184	Ke	41.40N	72.47W
New Britain Island	208	Ge	5.40S	151.00 E
New Britain Trench (EN)	214	Ei	6.00S	153.00 E
New Brunswick	184	Je	40.29N	74.27W
New Brunswick [2]	180	Kg	46.30N	66.45W
New Buckenham	124	Db	52.28N	1.05 E
New Buffalo	184	De	41.47N	86.45W
Newburgh	182	Mc	41.30N	74.00W
Newbury	118	Lj	51.25N	1.20W
New Caledonia (EN) = Nouvelle-Calédonie [5]	210	Hg	21.30S	165.30 E
New Caledonia (EN) = Nouvelle-Calédonie	208	Hg	21.30S	165.30 E
New Caledonia Basin (EN)	208	Hg	30.00S	165.00 E
New Carlisle	184	Oa	48.01N	65.20W
New Castile (EN) = Castilla la Nueva	126	Id	40.00N	3.45W
Newcastle [Austl.]	210	Gh	32.56S	151.46 E
New Castle [In.-U.S.]	184	Ef	39.55N	85.22W
Newcastle [N.B.-Can.]	180	Kg	47.00N	65.34W
New Castle [Pa.-U.S.]	182	Kc	41.00N	80.22W
Newcastle [S.Afr.]	172	De	27.49S	29.55 E
Newcastle [St.C.N.]	197c	Ab	17.13N	62.34W
Newcastle [Wy.-U.S.]	182	Gc	43.50N	104.11W
Newcastle/An Caisleán Nua	118	Hg	54.12N	5.54W
Newcastle Creek	212	Gc	17.20S	133.23 E
Newcastle-under-Lyme	118	Kh	53.00N	2.14W
Newcastle-upon-Tyne	112	Fd	54.59N	1.35W
Newcastle Waters	210	Ef	17.24S	133.24 E
Newcastle West/An Caisleán Nua	118	Di	52.27N	9.03W
New Delhi	142	Jg	28.36N	77.12 E
New Denver	188	Ga	50.00N	117.22W
Newell	186	Ed	44.43N	103.25W
Newell, Lake-	188	Ja	50.25N	111.56W
New England	174	Le	44.00N	71.20W
New England Range	208	Gh	30.00S	151.50 E
New England Seamounts (EN)	174	Mf	38.00N	61.00W
Newenham, Cape-	178	Ge	58.37N	162.12W
New Forest	118	Lk	50.55N	1.35W

Index Symbols

[1] Independent Nation · [2] State, Region · [3] District, County · [4] Municipality · [5] Colony, Dependency · Continent · Physical Region · Historical or Cultural Region · Mount, Mountain · Volcano · Hill · Mountains, Mountain Range · Hills, Escarpment · Plateau, Upland · Pass, Gap · Plain, Lowland · Delta · Salt Flat · Valley, Canyon · Crater, Cave · Karst Features · Depression · Polder · Desert, Dunes · Forest, Woods · Heath, Steppe · Oasis · Cape, Point · Coast, Beach · Cliff · Peninsula · Isthmus · Sandbank · Island · Atoll · Rock, Reef · Islands, Archipelago · Rocks, Reefs · Coral Reef · Well, Spring · Geyser · River, Stream · Waterfall, Rapids · River Mouth, Estuary · Lake · Salt Lake · Intermittent Lake · Reservoir · Swamp, Pond · Canal · Glacier · Ice Shelf, Pack Ice · Ocean · Sea · Gulf, Bay · Strait, Fjord · Lagoon · Bank · Seamount · Tablemount · Ridge · Shelf · Basin · Escarpment, Sea Scarp · Fracture · Trench, Abyss · National Park, Reserve · Point of Interest · Recreation Site · Cave, Cavern · Historic Site · Ruins · Wall, Walls · Church, Abbey · Temple · Scientific Station · Railway station · Airport · Port · Military installation · Lighthouse · Mine · Tunnel · Dam, Bridge

Newfoundland [2]	180	Lf	52.00N	56.00W
Newfoundland	174	Ne	48.30N	56.00W
Newfoundland Basin (EN)	106	De	45.00N	40.00W
New Galloway	118	If	55.05N	4.10W
New Georgia	208	Ge	8.30S	157.20 E
New Georgia Island	214	Fi	8.15S	157.30 E
New Georgia Sound (The Slot)	214	Fi	8.00S	158.10 E
New Glasgow	180	Lg	45.35N	62.39W
New Guinea/Pulau Irian	208	Fe	5.00S	140.00 E
New Guinea Trench (EN)	208	Ee	0.05N	135.50 E
New Hampshire [2]	182	Mc	43.35N	71.40W
New Hampton	186	Je	43.03N	92.19W
New Hanover Island	208	Ge	2.30S	150.15 E
New Harmony	184	Df	38.08N	87.56W
New Haven	176	Le	41.18N	72.56W
Newhaven	118	Nk	50.47N	0.03 E
New Hebrides / Nouvelles-Hébrides	208	Hf	16.01S	167.01 E
New Hebrides Trench (EN)	106	Jl	20.00S	168.00 E
New Iberia	182	If	30.00N	91.49W
New Ireland Island	208	Ge	3.20S	152.00 E
New Jersey [2]	182	Mc	40.15N	74.30W
New Kowloon/Julong	142	Ng	22.20N	114.09 E
New Liskeard	180	Jg	47.30N	79.40W
New London	182	Mc	41.21N	72.07W
New Madrid	186	Lh	36.36N	89.32W
Newman	212	Dd	23.15S	119.35 E
Newmarket [Eng.-U.K.]	118	Ni	52.15N	0.25 E
Newmarket [Ont.-Can.]	184	Hc	44.03N	79.28W
New Martinsville	184	Gf	39.39N	80.52W
New Meadows	188	Gd	44.58N	116.32W
New Mexico [2]	182	Fe	34.30N	106.00W
Newnan	184	Ei	33.23N	84.48W
New Norfolk	212	Jh	42.47S	147.03 E
New Orleans	176	Jg	29.58N	90.07W
New Philadelphia	184	Ge	40.30N	81.27W
New Pine Creek	188	Ee	42.01N	120.18W
New-Plymouth	210	Ih	39.04S	174.04 E
Newport [Ar.-U.S.]	186	Ki	35.37N	91.17W
Newport [Eng.-U.K.]	124	Cc	51.59N	0.15 E
Newport [Eng.-U.K.]	118	Lk	50.42N	1.18W
Newport [Fl.-U.S.]	184	Ej	30.14N	84.12W
Newport [Or.-U.S.]	182	Cc	44.38N	124.03W
Newport [R.I.-U.S.]	184	Le	41.30N	71.19W
Newport [Tn.-U.S.]	184	Fh	35.58N	83.11W
Newport [Vt.-U.S.]	184	Kc	44.56N	72.13W
Newport [Wales-U.K.]	118	Kj	51.35N	3.00W
Newport [Wa.-U.S.]	188	Gb	48.11N	117.03W
Newport Beach	182	De	33.37N	117.54W
Newport News	176	Lf	37.04N	76.28W
Newport Pagnell	124	Bb	52.05N	0.43W
New Providence Island	190	Ic	25.02N	77.24W
Newquay	118	Hk	50.25N	5.05W
New Quebec Crater (EN) = Nouveau-Québec, Cratère du-	180	Kd	61.30N	73.55W
New Richmond [Oh.-U.S.]	184	Ef	38.57N	84.16W
New Richmond [Que.-Can.]	184	Oa	48.10N	65.52W
New River [Blz.]	194	Cd	18.22N	88.24W
New River [Guy.]	202	Gc	3.23N	57.36W
New River [U.S.]	184	Ff	38.50N	82.06W
New Rockford	186	Gc	47.41N	99.15W
New Romney	124	Cd	50.59N	0.56 E
New Ross / Ros Mhic Thriúin	118	Gi	52.24N	6.56W
Newry/an t-Iúr	118	Gg	54.11N	6.20W
New Salem	186	Fc	46.51N	101.25W
New Sandy Bay	197n	Ba	13.20N	61.08W
New Schwabenland (EN)	222	Cf	72.30S	1.00 E
New Siberia (EN) = Novaja Sibir, ostrov-	140	Qb	75.00N	149.00 E
New Siberian Islands (EN) = Novosibirskije ostrova	140	Qb	75.00N	142.00 E
New Smyrna Beach	184	Gk	29.02N	80.56W
New South Wales [2]	212	Jf	33.00S	146.00 E
Newton [Ia.-U.S.]	186	Jf	41.42N	93.03W
Newton [Il.-U.S.]	186	Lg	38.59N	88.10W
Newton [Ks.-U.S.]	182	Hd	38.03N	97.21W
Newton [Ma.-U.S.]	184	Ld	42.21N	71.13W
Newton [Ms.-U.S.]	186	Lj	32.19N	89.10W
Newton [N.J.-U.S.]	184	Je	41.03N	74.45W
Newton Abbot	118	Jk	50.32N	3.36W
Newton Stewart	118	Ig	54.57N	4.29W
Newtontoppen	224	Kd	72.02N	17.30 E
Newtown	118	Ji	52.32N	3.19W
New Town	186	Ec	47.59N	102.30W
Newtownabbey/Baile na Mainistreach	118	Hg	54.42N	5.54W
Newtownards/Baile Nua na hArda	118	Hg	54.36N	5.41W
New Ulm	182	Ic	44.19N	94.28W
New Westminster	180	Fg	49.12N	122.55W
New York	176	Le	40.43N	74.01W
New York [2]	182	Lc	43.00N	75.00W
New York State Barge Canal	184	Hd	43.05N	78.43W
New Zealand [1]	210	Ii	41.00S	174.00 E
New Zealand	208	Ii	41.00S	174.00 E
Nexpa, Río-	192	Hh	18.05N	102.46W
Neyagawa	156	Dd	34.46N	135.36 E
Neyrīz	146	Ph	29.12N	54.19 E
Neyshābūr	144	Ib	36.12N	58.50 E
Nežárka	120	Kg	49.11N	14.43 E
Nežin	136	De	51.02N	31.57 E
Ngabé	170	Cc	3.12S	16.11 E
Ngahere	218	De	42.24S	171.26 E
Ngajangel.	220a	Ba	8.05N	134.43 E
Ngala	166	Hc	12.20N	14.11 E
Ngaliema, Chutes-	158	Jh	0.30N	25.30 E
Ngamegei Passage	220a	Bb	7.44N	134.34 E
Ngami, Lake-	172	Cd	20.37S	22.40 E
Ngamiland [3]	172	Cc	19.09S	22.47 E
Ngamring	152	Ef	29.14N	87.12 E
Ngangala	168	Ee	4.42N	31.55 E
Ngangerabeli Plain	170	Hc	1.30S	40.15 E
Ngangla Ringco	152	De	31.40N	83.00 E
Nganglong Kangri	152	De	32.45N	81.12 E
Nganglong Kangri	140	Kf	32.00N	83.00 E
Ngangzê Co	152	Ee	31.00N	86.55 E
Ngao	148	Je	18.45N	99.59 E
Ngaoundéré	160	Ih	7.19N	13.35 E
Ngapara	218	Df	44.57S	170.45 E
Ngara	170	Fc	2.28S	30.39 E
Ngardmau	220a	Bb	7.37N	134.35 E
Ngardmau Bay	220a	Bb	7.39N	134.35 E
Ngardololok	220a	Ac	7.00N	134.16 E
Ngaregur	220a	Bb	7.45N	134.38 E
Ngarekeukl	220a	Ac	7.00N	134.14 E
Ngariungs	220a	Ba	8.03N	134.43 E
Ngaruangl	220a	Ba	8.10N	134.39 E
Ngaruangl Passage	220a	Ba	8.07N	134.40 E
Ngaruawahia	218	Fb	37.40S	175.09 E
Ngaruroro	218	Gc	39.34S	176.55 E
Ngatangiia	220p	Cb	21.14S	159.43W
Ngatangiia Harbour	220p	Cb	21.14S	159.43W
Ngateguil, Point-	220a	Bc	7.26N	134.37 E
Ngatik Atoll	208	Gd	5.51N	157.16 E
Ngatpang	220a	Bc	7.28N	134.32 E
Ngau Island	219d	Bc	18.02S	179.18 E
Ngauruhoe	218	Fc	39.09S	175.38 E
Ngawa/Aba	152	He	32.55N	101.45 E
Ngayu	170	Eb	1.35N	27.13 E
Ngemelis Islands	220a	Ac	7.07N	134.15 E
Ngeregong	220a	Ac	7.07N	134.22 E
Ngergoi	220a	Ac	7.05N	134.17 E
Ngesebus	220a	Ac	7.03N	134.16 E
Nggamea	219d	Cb	16.46S	179.46W
Nggatokae	219a	Dc	8.46S	158.11 E
Nggela Pile	219a	Ec	9.08S	160.20 E
Nggela Sule	219a	Ec	9.03S	160.12 E
Nggelelevu	219d	Cb	16.05S	179.09W
Ngidinga	170	Cd	5.37S	15.17 E
Ngiro, Ewaso-	170	Gb	0.28N	39.55 E
Ngo	170	Cc	2.29S	15.45 E
Ngoangoa	168	Dd	5.58N	25.10 E
Ngobasangel	220a	Ac	7.16N	134.20 E
Ngoko	170	Cb	1.40N	16.03 E
Ngola Shankou	152	Gd	35.30N	99.36 E
Ngoma	170	Ef	15.58S	25.56 E
Ngoring Hu	152	Gd	35.00N	97.30 E
Ngorongoro Crater	158	Ki	3.10S	35.35 E
Ngoui	166	Cb	16.09N	13.55W
Ngouna	219b	Dc	17.26S	168.21 E
Ngounié [3]	170	Bc	2.00S	11.00 E
Ngounié	170	Bc	0.37S	10.18 E
Ngoura	168	Bc	12.52N	16.27 E
Ngouri	168	Bc	13.38N	15.22 E
Ngourti	166	Hb	15.19N	13.12 E
Ngousouboot, Pointe-	219b	Ca	13.58S	167.27 E
Ngudu	170	Fc	2.58S	33.20 E
Nguigmi	160	Ig	14.15N	13.07 E
Ngulu Atoll	208	Ed	8.18N	137.29 E
Nguni	170	Gc	0.50S	38.20 E
Nguru	160	Ig	12.53N	10.28 E
Nhachengue	172	Fd	22.51S	35.11 E
Nhamundá	202	Gd	2.14S	56.43W
Nhamundá, Rio-	202	Gd	2.12S	56.41W
Nhandeara	204	Ge	20.40S	50.02W
Nhandutiba	204	Jb	14.37S	44.12W
Nharea	170	Ce	11.28S	16.53 E
Nha Trang	142	Mh	12.15N	109.11 E
Nhecolândia	204	Dd	19.16S	57.04W
Nhia	170	Be	10.15S	14.12 E
Nhulunbuy	210	Ef	12.00S	135.58 E
Niafounké	166	Eb	15.56N	4.00W
Niagara Escarpment	184	Gc	44.30N	80.35W
Niagara Falls	174	Le	43.05N	79.04W
Niagara Falls [N.Y.-U.S.]	182	Lc	43.06N	79.02W
Niagara Falls [Ont.-Can.]	180	Jh	43.06N	79.04W
Niagara River	184	Hd	43.15N	79.04W
Niagassola	166	Dc	12.19N	9.07W
Niah	150	Ff	3.52N	113.44 E
Niakaramandougou	166	Dd	8.40N	5.17W
Niamey	160	Hg	13.31N	2.07 E
Niamey [2]	166	Fc	14.00N	2.00 E
Niandan	166	Dc	10.35N	9.45W
Niangara	160	Jh	3.42N	27.52 E
Niangay, Lac-	166	Eb	15.50N	3.00W
Niangoloko	166	Ec	10.17N	4.55W
Nia-Nia	170	Eb	1.24N	27.36 E
Nianzishan	152	Lb	47.31N	122.50 E
Niao Dao	152	Gd	37.20N	99.50 E
Niaoshu Shan	152	He	34.54N	104.04 E
Niari [3]	170	Bc	4.30S	13.00 E
Niari	170	Bc	3.56S	12.12 E
Nias, Palau-	140	Li	1.05N	97.35 E
Niassa [3]	172	Fb	13.00S	36.00 E
Niassa, Lago-=Nyasa, Lake- (EN)	158	Kj	12.00S	34.30 E
Niau, Ile-	208	Mf	16.09S	146.21W
Nibāk	146	Nj	24.24N	50.50 E
Nibe	116	Ch	56.59N	9.38 E
Nica	134	Lh	57.29N	64.33 E
Nica/Nīca	116	Ih	56.25N	20.56 E
Nīca/Nica	116	Ih	56.25N	20.56 E
Nicanor Olivera	204	Cn	38.17S	59.12W
Nicaragua [1]	176	Kh	13.00N	85.00W
Nicaragua, Lago de-= Nicaragua, Lake- (EN)	174	Kh	11.35N	85.25W
Nicaragua, Lake- (EN)= Nicaragua, Lago de-	174	Kh	11.35N	85.25W
Nicastro, Lamezia Terme-	128	Kl	38.59N	16.19 E
Nice	112	Gg	43.42N	7.15 E
Niceville	184	Dj	30.31N	86.29W
Nichicum, Lac-	180	Kf	53.08N	70.55W
Nichinan [Jap.]	156	Cd	35.10N	133.16 E
Nichinan [Jap.]	154	Ki	31.36N	131.23 E
Nicholas Channel	194	Gb	23.25N	80.05W
Nicholas Channel (EN)= Nicolás, Canal-	190	Hd	23.25N	80.05W
Nicholasville	184	Eg	37.53N	84.34W
Nicholls Town	194	Ia	25.08N	78.00W
Nicholson Range	212	De	27.15S	116.45 E
Nicholson River	208	Ef	17.31S	139.36 E
Nickerson Ice Shelf	222	Mf	75.45S	145.00W
Nickol Bay	212	Dd	20.40S	116.50 E
Nicobar Islands	140	Li	8.00N	93.30 E
Nicoclí	194	Ii	8.26N	76.48W
Nicolajevka	130	Nb	47.33N	30.41 E
Nicola River	188	Ea	50.25N	121.18W
Nicolás, Canal-=Nicholas Channel (EN)	190	Hd	23.25N	80.05W
Nicolet	184	Kb	46.14N	72.37W
Nicopolis (EN) = Nikópolis	130	Dj	39.00N	20.45 E
Nicosia	128	Im	37.45N	14.24 E
Nicosia (EN) = Lefkosa / Levkosia	142	Ff	35.10N	33.22 E
Nicosia (EN) = Levkosia / Lefkosa	142	Ff	35.10N	33.22 E
Nicotera	128	Jl	38.33N	15.56 E
Nicoya	190	Gf	10.09N	85.27W
Nicoya, Golfo de-	190	Hg	9.47N	84.48W
Nicoya, Península de-= Nicoya Peninsula (EN)	174	Ki	10.00N	85.25W
Nicoya Peninsula (EN)= Nicoya, Península de-	174	Ki	10.00N	85.25W
Nicuadala	172	Fc	17.37S	36.50 E
Niculiţel	130	Ld	45.11N	28.29 E
Nida	120	Qf	50.18N	20.52 E
Nidda	124	Ld	50.25N	9.00 E
Nidda	120	Ef	50.06N	8.34 E
Nidder	124	Kd	50.12N	8.47 E
Nideggen	124	Id	50.42N	6.29 E
Nidelva [Nor.]	116	Da	63.26N	10.25 E
Nidelva [Nor.]	116	Cf	58.24N	8.48 E
Nido, Sierra del-	192	Fc	29.30N	106.45W
Nidže	130	Ei	41.00N	21.50 E
Nidzica	120	Qc	53.22N	20.26 E
Nidzica	120	Qf	50.12N	20.40 E
Nidzkie, Jezioro-	120	Rc	53.37N	21.30 E
Niebüll	120	Eb	54.48N	8.50 E
Nied	124	Ie	49.23N	6.40 E
Nieddu	128	Dj	40.44N	9.34 E
Niederbayern	120	Ih	48.35N	12.30 E
Niederbronn-les-Bains	122	Nf	48.58N	7.38 E
Niedere Tauern	128	Hc	47.20N	14.00 E
Niederlausitz	120	Ke	51.40N	14.15 E
Nieder-Olm	124	Ke	49.54N	8.13 E
Niederösterreich = Lower Austria (EN) [2]	128	Jb	48.30N	15.45 E
Niedersachsen=Lower Saxony (EN) [2]	120	Fd	52.00N	10.00 E
Niederwald	120	Df	50.10N	8.00 E
Niederzier	124	Id	50.53N	6.28 E
Niefang	166	He	1.50N	10.14 E
Niegocin, Jezioro-	120	Rb	54.00N	21.50 E
Niel	124	Gc	51.07N	4.20 E
Nielfa, Puerto de-	126	Hf	38.32N	4.23W
Niéllé	166	Dc	10.12N	5.38W
Niellim	168	Bd	9.42N	17.49 E
Niemba	170	Ed	5.57S	28.26 E
Niemba	170	Ed	5.57S	28.26 E
Niemodlin	120	Nf	50.39N	17.37 E
Niéna	166	Dc	11.25N	6.20W
Nienburg (Weser)	120	Fd	52.38N	9.13 E
Niepołomice	120	Qf	50.03N	20.13 E
Niermalak, Pointe-	219b	Cb	14.21S	167.24 E
Niers	120	Be	51.43N	5.57 E
Nierstein	124	Ke	49.53N	8.20 E
Niesky/Niska	120	Ke	51.18N	14.49 E
Nieszawa	120	Od	52.50N	18.55 E
Nieuport/Nieuwpoort	122	Ic	51.08N	2.45 E
Nieuw Amsterdam	202	Gb	5.53N	55.05W
Nieuwe Pekelj	124	Ia	53.04N	6.59 E
Nieuweschans	124	Ja	53.11N	7.15 E
Nieuw Milligen, Apeldoorn-	124	Hb	52.14N	5.45 E
Nieuw Nickerie	200	Ke	5.57N	56.59W
Nieuwolda	124	Ia	53.14N	6.59 E
Nieuwoudtville	172	Bf	31.22S	19.06 E
Nieuwpoort/Nieuport	122	Ic	51.08N	2.45 E
Nieuw-Weerdinge, Emmen-	124	Jb	52.52N	7.01 E
Nieves	192	He	24.00N	103.01W
Nièvre [3]	122	Jg	47.05N	3.30 E
Nièvre	122	Jh	46.59N	3.10 E
Nigata	154	Lg	34.13N	132.29 E
Niğde	144	Db	37.59N	34.42 E
Nigenān	146	Qe	34.13N	57.19 E
Niger [1]	160	Hg	16.00N	8.00 E
Niger [2]	166	Gd	9.40N	6.00 E
Niger	158	Hh	5.33N	6.33 E
Niger Basin (EN)	158	Gg	15.00N	2.00 E
Niger Delta	158	Hh	4.50N	6.00 E
Nigeria [1]	160	Hh	10.00N	8.00 E
Night Hawk Lake	184	Ga	48.28N	81.00W
Nightingale Island	158	Fi	37.24S	12.28W
Nigríta	130	Gi	40.54N	23.30 E
Nihiru Atoll	208	Mf	16.42S	142.50W
Nihoa Island	208	Kb	23.06N	161.58W
Nihonmatsu	154	Pf	37.35N	140.26 E
Nihuil, Embalse del-	206	Ge	35.05S	68.45W
Niigata	142	Pf	37.55N	139.03 E
Niigata Ken [2]	154	Of	37.30N	138.50 E
Niihama	154	Lh	33.58N	133.16 E
Niihau Island	208	Kb	21.55N	160.10W
Nii-Jima	152	Oe	34.20N	139.15 E
Niikappu-Gawa	156a	Cb	42.22N	142.16 E
Niimi	154	Lg	34.59N	133.28 E
Niisato	156	Gb	39.36N	141.49 E
Niitsu	154	Of	37.48N	139.07 E
Níjar	126	Jh	36.58N	2.12W
Nijkerk	124	Hb	52.14N	5.29 E
Nijlen	124	Gc	51.10N	4.39 E
Nijmegen	122	Lc	51.50N	5.50 E
Nijvel/Nivelles	122	Kd	50.36N	4.20 E
Nijverdal, Hellendoorn-	124	Ib	52.22N	6.27 E
Nikel	136	Db	69.24N	30:13 E
Níki	130	Ei	40.55N	21.25 E
Nikitin Seamount (EN)	140	Kj	3.00S	83.00 E
Nikki	166	Fd	9.56N	3.12 E
Nikkō	156	Fc	36.44N	139.35 E
Nikolajev [Ukr.-U.S.S.R.]	112	Jf	46.58N	32.00 E
Nikolajev [Ukr.-U.S.S.R.]	132	Ce	49.32N	23.58 E
Nikolajevka	135	Kc	43.37N	77.01 E
Nikolajevo	116	Mf	58.14N	29.32 E
Nikolajevsk	136	Ee	50.02N	45.31 E
Nikolajevskaja oblast [3]	136	Df	47.20N	32.00 E
Nikolajevski	138	Hf	54.50N	129.25 E
Nikolajevsk-na-Amure	142	Qd	53.08N	140.44 E
Nikolsk [R.S.F.S.R.]	136	Ed	59.33N	45.31 E
Nikolsk [R.S.F.S.R.]	136	Ee	53.42N	46.03 E
Nikolski [Ak.-U.S.]	178a	Eb	53.15N	168.22W
Nikolski [Kaz.-U.S.S.R.]	136	Gf	47.55N	67.33 E
Nikonga	170	Fc	4.40S	31.28 E
Nikopol [Bul.]	130	Hf	43.42N	24.54 E
Nikopol [Ukr.-U.S.S.R.]	136	Df	47.35N	34.25 E
Nikópolis = Nicopolis (EN)	130	Dj	39.00N	20.45 E
Nīkpey	146	Md	36.50N	48.10 E
Niksar	146	Gb	40.36N	36.58 E
Nikšić	130	Bg	42.46N	18.58 E
Nikumaroro Atoll (Gardner)	208	Je	4.40S	174.32W
Nikunau Island	208	Ie	1.23S	176.26 E
Nīl, Kūh-e-	146	Ng	30.52N	50.49 E
Nīl, Nahr an-=Nile (EN)	158	Ke	30.10N	31.06 E
Nila, Pulau-	150	Ih	6.44S	129.31 E
Nilakka	114	Ge	63.07N	26.33 E
Niland	188	Hj	33.14N	115.31W
Nilandu Atoll	148a	Bb	3.00N	72.55 E
Nile [3]	170	Fb	3.00N	31.30 E
Nile (EN)=Nīl, Nahr an-	158	Ke	30.10N	31.06 E
Nile Delta (EN)	158	Ke	31.20N	31.00 E
Nīleh, Kūh-e-	146	Nf	32.59N	50.32 E
Niles	184	De	41.50N	86.15W
Nilka	152	Dc	43.47N	82.20 E
Nīl Kowtal	144	Kc	34.48N	67.22 E
Nilsiä	114	Ge	63.12N	28.05 E
Nilüfer	130	Li	40.18N	28.27 E
Nimba [3]	166	Dd	6.45N	8.45W
Nimba, Monts-=Nimba Mountains (EN)	158	Gh	7.35N	8.28W
Nimba Mountains (EN)= Nimba, Monts-	158	Gh	7.35N	8.28W
Nîmes	112	Gg	43.50N	4.21 E
Nimjad	162	Df	17.25N	15.41W
Nimmitabel	212	Jg	36.31S	149.16 E
Nimpkish River	188	Ba	50.32N	126.59W
Nimrod Glacier	222	Kg	82.27S	161.00 E
Nimrud	146	Jd	36.06N	43.20 E
Nīmrūz [3]	144	Jc	30.30N	62.00 E
Nims	124	Ie	49.51N	6.28 E
Nimule	160	Kh	3.36N	32.03 E
Nimún, Punta-	192	Ng	20.46N	90.25W
Nin	128	Jf	44.14N	15.11 E
Nina	172	Bd	22.57S	18.14 E
Nīnawā [3]	146	Je	35.45N	42.45 E
Nīnawā=Nineveh (EN)	144	Fb	36.22N	43.09 E
Nine Degree Channel	140	Ji	9.00N	73.00 E
Ninetyeast Ridge (EN)	106	Gj	10.00S	90.00 E
Ninety Mile Beach [Austl.]	212	Jg	38.15S	147.25 E
Ninety Mile Beach [N.Z.]	218	Ea	34.45S	173.00 E
Nineveh (EN)=Nīnawā	144	Fb	36.22N	43.09 E
Ning'an	152	Mc	44.22N	129.23 E
Ningbo	142	Og	29.55N	121.28 E
Ningcheng (Tianyi)	152	Kc	41.34N	119.25 E
Ningde	152	Kf	26.44N	119.29 E
Ningdu	152	Kf	26.31N	115.59 E
Ningguo	154	Ei	30.39N	119.00 E
Ninghai	154	Fj	29.19N	121.26 E
Ning-hsia-hui-tsu Tzu-chih-ch'ü → Ningxia Huizu Zizhiqu [2]	152	Id	37.00N	106.00 E
Ningjin [China]	154	Cf	37.37N	114.55 E
Ningjin [China]	154	Df	37.39N	116.48 E
Ningjing Shan	152	Ge	31.45N	97.15 E
Ninglang	152	Hf	27.17N	100.52 E
Ningling	154	Cg	34.27N	115.18 E
Ningnan	152	Hf	27.05N	102.44 E
Ningqiang	152	Ie	32.48N	106.15 E
Ningsia Hui (EN) = Ningxia Huizu Zizhiqu (Ning-hsia-hui-tsu Tzu-chih-ch'ü) [2]	152	Id	37.00N	106.00 E
Ningwu	152	Jd	38.59N	112.14 E
Ningxia Huizu Zizhiqu (Ning-hsia-hui-tsu Tzu-chih-ch'ü) = Ningsia Hui (EN) [2]	152	Id	37.00N	106.00 E
Ningxian	152	Id	35.27N	107.50 E
Ningxiang	154	Bj	28.16N	112.33 E
Ningyang	154	Dg	35.45N	116.48 E
Ningyō-Tōge	156	Cd	35.19N	133.56 E
Ninh Binh	148	Ld	20.15N	105.59 E
Ninh Hoa	148	Lf	12.29N	109.08 E
Ninigo Group	208	Fe	1.15S	144.15 E
Niniva	221b	Ba	19.46S	174.38W
Ninnis Glacier	222	Je	68.12S	147.12 E
Ninohe	152	Pc	40.16N	141.18 E
Ninove	124	Fd	50.50N	4.00 E
Nioaque	202	Gh	21.08S	55.48W
Niobrara	186	He	42.25N	98.00W
Niobrara	174	Je	42.45N	98.00W
Nioghalvfjerdsfjorden	179	Kc	79.30N	18.45W
Nioki	170	Cc	2.43S	17.41 E
Niono	166	Dc	14.15N	6.00W
Nioro du Rip	166	Bc	13.45N	15.48W
Nioro du Sahel	160	Gg	15.14N	9.37W
Niort	122	Fh	46.19N	0.28W
Nipawin	180	Hf	53.22N	104.00W
Nipe, Bahía de-	194	Jc	20.47N	75.42W
Nipesotsu-Yama	156a	Cb	43.27N	143.02 E
Nipigon	176	Ke	49.01N	88.16W
Nipigon, Lake-	174	Ke	49.50N	88.30W
Nipigon Bay	186	Mb	48.53N	87.50W
Nipissing, Lake-	174	Le	46.17N	80.00W
Nippon=Japan (EN) [1]	142	Pf	38.00N	137.00 E
Nippon-Kai=Japan, Sea of- (EN)	140	Pf	40.00N	134.00 E
Nippur	146	Kf	32.10N	45.10 E
Niquelândia	202	If	14.27S	48.27W
Niquero	194	Ic	20.03N	77.35W
Niquitao, Teta de-	194	Li	9.07N	70.30W
Niquivil	206	Gd	30.25S	68.42W
Nīr	146	Lc	38.02N	47.59 E
Niraj	130	Hc	46.29N	24.28 E
Nirasaki	156	Fd	35.43N	138.27 E
Nirji → Morin Dawa	152	Lb	48.30N	124.28 E
Nirmal	148	Fe	19.06N	78.21 E
Niš	112	Ig	43.19N	21.54 E
Nisa	126	Ee	39.31N	7.39W
Nişāb	144	Gg	14.24N	46.38 E
Nisāh, Sha'īb-	146	Lj	24.11N	47.11 E
Nišava	130	Ef	43.22N	21.46 E
Niscemi	128	Im	37.09N	14.23 E
Nishibetsu-Gawa	156a	Db	43.23N	145.17 E
Nishikawa	156	Gb	38.26N	140.08 E
Nishiki	156	Bd	34.16N	131.57 E
Nishinomiya	156	Dd	34.43N	135.20 E
Nishino'omote	152	Ne	30.44N	131.00 E
Nishi-No-Shima	154	Lf	36.06N	133.00 E
Nishino-Shima	214	Cb	27.30N	140.53 E
Nishiokoppe	156a	Ca	44.20N	142.57 E
Nishi-Sonogi-Hantō	156	Ae	32.55N	129.45 E
Nishiwaki	156	Dd	34.59N	134.58 E
Nísiros	130	Km	36.35N	27.10 E
Niska/Niesky	120	Ke	51.18N	14.49 E
Niška Banja	130	Ff	43.18N	22.01 E
Nisko	120	Sf	50.31N	22.09 E
Nismes, Viroinval-	124	Gd	50.05N	4.33 E
Nísoi Aiyaíou [2]	130	Il	37.40N	25.40 E
Nisporeny	132	Ff	47.06N	28.10 E
Nissan	219a	Ba	4.30S	154.14 E
Nissan	116	Eh	56.40N	12.51 E
Nisser	116	Ce	59.10N	8.30 E
Nissum Bredning	116	Ch	56.40N	8.20 E
Nissum Fjord	116	Ch	56.20N	8.15 E
Nita	156	Cd	35.12N	133.00 E
Nitchequon	180	Kf	53.15N	70.44W
Niterói	200	Lh	22.53S	43.07W
Nith	118	Jf	55.00N	3.35W
Nitra	120	Oh	48.19N	18.05 E
Nitra	120	Oi	47.46N	18.10 E
Niuafo'ou Island	208	Jf	15.35S	175.38W
Niuato Putapu Island	208	Jf	15.57S	173.45W
Niue [5]	210	Kf	19.02S	169.55W
Niue Island	208	Kf	19.02S	169.55W
Niu'erhe	152	La	51.30N	121.40 E
Niufu	156a	Ca	44.35N	142.35 E
Niulakita Island	208	If	10.45S	179.30 E
Niutaca, Corrente-	204	De	20.42S	57.37W
Niutao Island	208	Ie	6.06S	177.16 E
Niutg, Gunung-	150	Ef	1.00N	109.55 E
Niutoushan	152	Ke	31.00N	119.35 E
Niuzhuang	154	Gd	40.57N	122.30 E
Nivala	114	Fe	63.58N	25.01 E
Nive	122	Ek	43.30N	1.29W
Nivelles/Nijvel	122	Kd	50.36N	4.20 E
Nivernais	122	Jg	47.00N	3.30 E
Nivernais, Canal du-	122	Jg	47.40N	3.40 E
Nivernais, Collines du-	122	Jg	47.10N	3.30 E
Nivillers	124	Ee	49.28N	2.10 E
Nixon	186	Hl	29.16N	97.46W
Niya/Minfeng	152	Dd	37.04N	82.46 E
Nīyābād	146	Le	35.12N	46.20 E
Niyodo-Gawa	156	Ce	33.28N	133.29 E
Nīza	146	Ph	28.25N	55.55 E
Nizāmābad	148	Fe	18.40N	78.07 E
Nižankoviči	120	Sg	49.40N	22.48 E
Nizip	144	Eb	37.01N	37.46 E
Nízke Tatry = Low Tatra (EN)	120	Ph	48.54N	19.40 E
Nízký-Jeseník	120	Ng	49.50N	17.30 E
Nižná	120	Pg	49.19N	19.32 E
Nižneangarsk	142	Md	55.47N	109.33 E
Nižnegorski	132	Ig	45.27N	34.44 E
Nižnejansk	138	Ib	71.24N	136.00 E
Nižnekamsk	136	Fd	55.38N	51.49 E
Nižnekolymsk	138	Lc	68.38N	160.56 E
Nižnetroicki	134	Fi	54.20N	53.41 E
Nižneudinsk	138	Ef	54.54N	99.03 E
Nižnevartovsk	142	Jc	61.00N	77.00 E
Nižni Baskunčak	136	Ef	48.13N	46.50 E
Nižni Bestjah	138	Hd	61.48N	129.55 E
Nižni Casučej	138	Gf	50.27N	115.08 E
Nižnije Sergi	134	Ih	56.40N	59.19 E
Nižnije Serogozy	132	If	46.49N	34.24 E
Nižni Kuranah	138	He	58.40N	125.48 E
Nižni Lomov	136	Ee	53.32N	43.41 E
Nižni Odes	134	Ge	63.40N	54.52 E
Nižni Oseredok, ostrov-	132	Pg	45.45N	48.35 E
Nižni Tagil	112	Ld	57.55N	59.57 E
Nižni Trajanov val = Lower Trajan's Wall (EN)	130	Ld	45.45N	28.30 E
Nižnjaja Omra	134	Ge	62.46N	55.46 E
Nižnjaja Peša	136	Eb	66.43N	47.36 E
Nižnjaja Pojma	138	Ee	56.08N	97.18 E
Nižnjaja Salda	134	Jg	58.05N	60.48 E
Nižnjaja Tavda	136	Gd	57.40N	66.12 E
Nižnjaja Tojma	114	Ke	62.22N	44.15 E
Nižnjaja Tunguska=Lower Tunguska (EN)	140	Kc	65.48N	88.04 E
Nižnjaja Tura	134	Ig	58.37N	59.49 E
Nižnjaja Zolotica	114	Jd	65.41N	40.13 E
Nižny Pjandž	135	Gf	37.14N	68.35 E
Nizza Monferrato	128	Cf	44.46N	8.21 E
Njajs	134	Je	62.25N	60.47 E
Njamunas	110	Id	55.18N	21.23 E
Njandoma	136	Ec	61.43N	40.12 E
Njaris/Neris	116	Kj	54.55N	25.45 E
Njazepetrovsk	134	Ih	56.03N	59.38 E
Njazidja/Grande Comore	158	Lj	11.35S	43.20 E
Njegoš	130	Bg	42.53N	18.45 E
Njinjo	170	Gd	8.48S	38.54 E
Njombe	160	Ki	9.20S	34.46 E

Index Symbols

[1] Independent Nation
[2] State, Region
[3] District, County
[4] Municipality
[5] Colony, Dependency
Continent
Physical Region
Historical or Cultural Region
Mount, Mountain
Volcano
Hill
Mountains, Mountain Range
Hills, Escarpment
Plateau, Upland
Pass, Gap
Plain, Lowland
Delta
Salt Flat
Valley, Canyon
Crater, Cave
Karst Features
Depression
Polder
Desert, Dunes
Forest, Woods
Heath, Steppe
Oasis
Cape, Point
Coast, Beach
Cliff
Peninsula
Isthmus
Sandbank
Island
Atoll
Rock, Reef
Islands, Archipelago
Rocks, Reefs
Coral Reef
Well, Spring
Geyser
River, Stream
Waterfall, Rapids
River Mouth, Estuary
Lake
Salt Lake
Intermittent Lake
Reservoir
Swamp, Pond
Canal
Glacier
Ice Shelf, Pack Ice
Ocean
Sea
Gulf, Bay
Strait, Fjord
Lagoon
Bank
Seamount
Tablemount
Ridge
Shelf
Basin
Escarpment, Sea Scarp
Fracture
Trench, Abyss
National Park, Reserve
Point of Interest
Recreation Site
Cave, Cavern
Historic Site
Ruins
Wall, Walls
Church, Abbey
Temple
Scientific Station
Railway station
Airport
Port
Military installation
Lighthouse
Mine
Tunnel
Dam, Bridge

Njombe 158 Ki 6.56S 35.06 E
Njudung 116 Fg 57.25N 14.50 E
Njuja 138 Gd 60.32N 116.25 E
Njuk, ozero- 114 Hd 64.25N 31.45 E
Njuksenica 114 Kf 60.28N 44.15 E
Njukža 138 He 56.30N 121.40 E
Njunes 114 Eb 68.45N 19.30 E
Njurba 142 Nc 63.17N 118.20 E
Njurundabommen 114 De 62.16N 17.22 E
Njutånger 116 Gc 61.37N 17.03 E
Njuvčim 134 Ef 61.22N 50.42 E
Nkambe 166 Hd 6.38N 10.40 E
Nkawkaw 166 Ed 6.33N 0.46W
Nkayi [Con.] 160 Ii 4.05S 13.18 E
Nkayi [Zimb.] 172 Dc 19.00S 28.54 E
Nkhata Bay 170 Fe 11.36S 34.18 E
Nkongsamba 160 Hh 4.57N 9.56 E
Nkota Kota 160 Kj 12.55S 34.18 E
Nkululu 170 Fd 6.26S 32.49 E
Nkusi 170 Fb 1.07N 30.40 E
Nkwalini 172 Ee 28.45S 31.30 E
'Nmai 148 Jc 25.42N 97.30 E
Nnewi 166 Gd 6.01N 6.55 E
Nö 156 Ec 37.05N 137.59 E
Noailles 124 Ee 49.20N 2.12 E
Noākhāli 148 Id 22.49N 91.06 E
Noatak 178 Gc 67.34N 162.59W
Nobel 184 Gc 45.25N 80.06W
Nobeoka 152 Ne 32.35N 131.40 E
Noblesville 184 Ee 40.03N 86.00W
Noboribetsu 154 Pc 42.25N 141.11 E
Noce 128 Fd 46.09N 11.04 E
Nodaway River 186 Ig 39.54N 94.58W
Noën 152 Hc 43.15N 102.20 E
Noeux-les-Mines 124 Ed 50.29N 2.40 E
Nogajskaja step 132 Ng 44.15N 46.00 E
Nogales [Az.-U.S.] 182 Ee 31.21N 110.55W
Nogales [Mex.] 176 Hf 31.20N 110.56W
Nogaro 122 Fk 43.46N 0.02W
Nogat 120 Pb 54.11N 19.15 E
Nōgata 156 Be 33.44N 130.44 E
Nogent-le-Rotrou 122 Gf 48.19N 0.50 E
Nogent-sur-Marne 124 Ef 48.50N 2.29 E
Nogent-sur-Oise 124 Ee 49.16N 2.28 E
Nogent-sur-Seine 122 Jf 48.29N 3.30 E
Noginsk [R.S.F.S.R.] 136 Dd 55.54N 38.28 E
Noginsk [R.S.F.S.R.] 138 Ed 64.25N 91.10 E
Nogliki 138 Jf 51.45N 143.15 E
Nōgo-Hakusan 156 Ed 35.46N 136.31 E
Nogoyá 206 Id 32.24S 59.48W
Nogoya, Arroyo- 204 Ck 32.55S 59.59W
Nógrád 120 Ph 48.00N 19.35 E
Nogueira, Serra da- 126 Fc 41.42N 6.52W
Noguera Pallaresa 126 Mb 42.15N 0.54 E
Noguera Ribagorçana/ Noguera Ribagorzana 126 Mc 41.40N 0.43 E
Noguera Ribagorzana/ Noguera Ribagorçana 126 Mc 41.40N 0.43 E
Noh, Laguna- 192 Nh 18.40N 90.20W
Nohain 122 Ig 47.24N 2.55 E
Noheji 154 Pd 40.52N 141.08 E
Nohfelden 124 Je 49.35N 7.09 E
Noia / Noya 126 Db 42.47N 8.53W
Noidore, Rio- 204 Fb 14.50S 52.34W
Noir, Causse- 122 Jj 44.09N 3.15 E
Noire, Montagne- 122 Ik 43.28N 2.18 E
Noires, Montagnes- 122 Cf 48.09N 3.40W
Noirétable 122 Ji 45.49N 3.46 E
Noirmoutier, Ile de- 122 Dh 46.58N 2.12W
Noirmoutier-en-l'Ile 122 Dg 47.00N 2.15W
Nojima-Zaki 156 Fd 34.54N 139.50 E
Nojiri-Ko 156 Fc 36.49N 138.13 E
Noka 219b Cc 10.40S 166.03 E
Nokaneng 172 Cc 19.40S 22.12 E
Nokia 114 Ff 61.28N 23.30 E
Nok Kundi 148 Cc 28.48N 62.46 E
Nokomis 188 Ma 51.30N 105.00W
Nokou 168 Ac 14.35N 14.47 E
Nokra 168 Fb 15.42N 39.56 E
Nol 116 Eg 57.55N 12.03 E
Nola 168 Be 3.32N 16.04 E
Nolin Lake 184 Dg 37.20N 86.10W
Nolinsk 136 Ed 57.33N 50.00 E
Nomad 210 Fe 6.21S 142.12 E
Noma Omuramba 172 Cc 19.10S 22.16 E
Noma-Zaki 156 Bf 31.25N 130.06 E
Nombre de Dios 192 Gf 23.51N 104.14W
Nome 176 Cc 64.30N 165.24W
Nomeny 124 If 48.54N 6.14 E
Nomozaki 156 Ae 32.35N 129.45 E
Nomo-Zaki 156 Ae 32.35N 129.45 E
Nomuka 221b Bb 20.15S 174.48W
Nomuka Group 208 Jg 20.20S 174.45W
Nomuka Iki 221b Bb 20.17S 174.49W
Nomwin Atoll 208 Gd 8.32N 151.47 E
Nonacho Lake 180 Gd 62.40N 109.30W
Nonancourt 124 Df 48.46N 1.12 E
Nonette 124 Ee 49.12N 2.24 E
Nong'an 152 Mc 44.24N 125.08 E
Nong Han 148 Ke 17.21N 103.06 E
Nong Khai 142 Mh 17.52N 102.45 E
Nongoma 172 Ee 27.53S 31.38 E
Nonoava 192 Fd 27.28N 106.44W
Nonouti Atoll 208 Ie 0.40S 174.21 E
Nonsan 154 If 36.12N 127.05 E
Nonsuch Bay 197d Bb 17.03N 61.42W
Nontron 122 Gi 45.32N 0.40 E
Noord-Beveland 124 Fc 51.35N 3.45 E
Noord-Brabant 124 Gc 51.30N 5.00 E
Noord-Holland 124 Gb 52.40N 4.50 E
Noordhollandskanaal 122 Kb 52.55N 4.50 E
Noordoewer 172 Be 28.45S 17.37 E
Noordoostpolder 124 Hb 52.42N 5.44 E
Noordoostpolder 122 Lb 52.42N 5.44 E
Noordoostpolder-Emmeloord 124 Hb 52.42N 5.44 E
Noordwijk aan Zee 122 Kb 52.14N 4.26 E
Noordwijk aan Zee, Noordwijk- 124 Gb 52.14N 4.26 E
Noordwijk-Noordwijk aan Zee 124 Gb 52.14N 4.26 E
Noordzee = North Sea (EN) 110 Gd 55.20N 3.00 E
Noordzeekanaal 122 Kb 52.30N 4.35 E
Noormarkku/Norrmark 116 Ic 61.35N 21.52 E
Noorvik 178 Gc 66.50N 161.12W
Nootka Island 188 Bb 49.32N 126.42W
Nootka Sound 188 Bb 49.33N 126.38W
Nóqui 170 Bd 5.50S 13.27 E
Nora 114 Dg 59.31N 15.02 E
Nora 168 Fc 15.40N 39.55 E
Nora 128 Dk 39.00N 9.02 E
Noranda 180 Jg 48.15N 79.01W
Noraskog 116 Fe 59.40N 14.50 E
Norberg 116 Fd 60.04N 15.56 E
Norcia 128 Hh 42.48N 13.05 E
Nord 179 Kb 81.45N 17.30W
Nord [Burkina] 166 Ec 13.40N 2.50W
Nord [Cam.] 166 Hd 9.00N 13.50 E
Nord [Fr.] 122 Jd 50.30N 3.10 E
Nord, Canal du- 122 Id 49.57N 2.55 E
Nord, Mer du- = North Sea (EN) 110 Gd 55.20N 3.00 E
Nordausques 124 Ed 50.49N 2.05 E
Nordaustlandet 224 Jd 79.48N 22.24 E
Nordborg 116 Ci 55.03N 9.45 E
Nordby 116 Ci 55.27N 8.25 E
Norddeutsches Tiefland = North German Plain (EN) 110 He 53.00N 11.00 E
Norden 120 Dc 53.36N 7.12 E
Nordenham 120 Ec 53.39N 8.29 E
Nordenskiöld Archipelago (EN) = Nordenskjölda, ostrova- 138 Ea 76.50N 96.00 E
Nordenskjölda, ostrova- = Nordenskiöld Archipelago (EN) 138 Ea 76.50N 96.00 E
Norderney 120 Dc 53.42N 7.10 E
Norderstedt 120 Fc 53.41N 9.58 E
Nordfjord 116 Bc 61.50N 6.15 E
Nordfjord 114 Af 61.55N 5.10 E
Nordfjordeid 114 Af 61.54N 6.00 E
Nordfold 114 Dc 67.46N 15.12 E
Nordfriesische Inseln = North Frisian Islands (EN) 120 Ea 54.50N 8.30 E
Nordfriesland = North Friesland (EN) 120 Eb 54.40N 8.55 E
Nordgau 120 Hg 49.15N 11.50 E
Nordgrønland = North Greenland (EN) 179 Gc 79.30N 50.00W
Nordhausen 120 Ge 51.31N 10.48 E
Nordhordland 116 Ad 60.50N 5.50 E
Nordhorn 120 Dd 52.26N 7.05 E
Nord-Jylland 116 Cg 57.15N 10.00 E
Nordkapp [Nor.] = North Cape (EN) 110 Ia 71.11N 25.48 E
Nordkapp [Sval.] 179 Nb 80.31N 20.00 E
Nordkinn 110 Ia 71.08N 27.39 E
Nordkinnhalvøya 114 Ga 70.55N 27.45 E
Nord-Kvaløy 114 Ea 70.10N 19.11 E
Nordland 114 Cc 67.06N 13.20 E
Nördlingen 120 Gh 48.51N 10.30 E
Nordloher Tief 124 Ja 53.10N 7.45 E
Nordmark 116 Fe 59.50N 14.06 E
Nordmøre 116 Ca 63.00N 8.30 E
Nordostrundingen 224 Le 81.30N 11.00W
Nord-Ostsee-Kanal = Kiel Canal (EN) 110 Ge 53.53N 9.08 E
Nord-Ouest 166 Hd 6.30N 10.30 E
Nordøyane 116 Bb 62.40N 6.15 E
Nordreisa 114 Eb 69.46N 21.03 E
Nordre Rønner 116 Dg 57.22N 10.56 E
Nordrhein-Westfalen = North Rhine-Westphalia (EN) 120 De 51.30N 7.30 E
Nordsee = North Sea (EN) 110 Gd 55.20N 3.00 E
Nordsjøen = North Sea (EN) 110 Gd 55.20N 3.00 E
Nordskjobotn 114 Eb 69.13N 19.34 E
Nordsøen = North Sea (EN) 110 Gd 55.20N 3.00 E
Nord Strand 120 Eb 54.30N 8.55 E
Nordtiroler Kalkalpen 120 Hi 47.30N 11.30 E
Nord-Trøndelag 114 Cd 64.25N 12.00 E
Nordwestfjord 179 Jd 71.30N 26.30W
Nore/An Fheoir 118 Gi 52.25N 6.58W
Norefjell 116 Cd 60.16N 9.29 E
Norefjorden 116 Cd 60.10N 9.00 E
Norfolk 118 Ni 52.45N 0.40 E
Norfolk 118 Oi 52.40N 1.05 E
Norfolk [Nb.-U.S.] 182 Hc 42.02N 97.25W
Norfolk [Va.-U.S.] 176 Lf 38.40N 76.14W
Norfolk Island 210 Hg 29.05S 167.59 E
Norfolk Island 208 Hg 29.05S 167.59 E
Norfolk Ridge (EN) 208 Hg 29.00S 168.00 E
Norfork Lake 186 Jh 36.25N 92.10W
Norg 124 Ia 53.04N 6.32 E
Norge = Norway (EN) 112 Gc 62.00N 10.00 E
Norheimsund 114 Bf 60.22N 6.08 E
Norikura-Dake 156 Ec 36.06N 137.33 E
Norilsk 142 Kc 69.20N 88.06 E
Normal 186 Lf 40.31N 88.59W
Norman 182 Hd 35.15N 97.26W
Norman, Lake- 184 Gh 35.35N 81.00W
Normanby Island 214 Ej 10.00S 151.00 E
Normanby River 212 Ib 14.25S 144.08 E
Normand, Bocage- 122 Ef 49.00N 1.10W
Normandie = Normandy (EN) 110 Gf 49.00N 0.10 E
Normandie = Normandy (EN) 122 Gf 49.00N 0.10 E
Normandie, Collines de- = Normandy Hills (EN) 110 Ff 48.50N 0.40W
Normandin 184 Ka 48.52N 72.30W
Normandy (EN) = Normandie 110 Gf 49.00N 0.10 E
Normandy (EN) = Normandie 122 Gf 49.00N 0.10 E
Normandy Hills (EN) = Normandie, Collines de- 110 Ff 48.50N 0.40W
Norman Island 197a Db 18.20N 64.37W
Norman River 212 Ic 17.28S 140.39 E
Normanton 210 Ff 17.40S 141.05 E
Norman Wells 176 Gc 65.17N 126.51W
Norquinco 206 Ff 41.51S 70.54W
Norra Dellen 116 Gc 61.55N 16.40 E
Norrahammar 116 Fg 57.42N 14.06 E
Norrala 116 Gc 61.22N 16.59 E
Norra Midsjöbanken 116 Gh 56.10N 17.30 E
Norra Ny 114 Cf 60.24N 13.15 E
Norra Storfjället 114 Dd 65.53N 15.14 E
Norrbotten 114 Ec 67.26N 19.35 E
Nørre Åby 116 Ci 55.27N 9.54 E
Nørre Alslev 116 Dj 54.54N 11.54 E
Nørre-Nebel 116 Ci 55.47N 8.18 E
Norrent-Fontes 124 Ed 50.35N 2.24 E
Nørresundby 114 Bh 57.04N 9.55 E
Norrhult 114 Dh 57.08N 15.10 E
Norris Lake 184 Fg 36.20N 83.55W
Norristown 184 Je 40.07N 75.20W
Norrköping 112 Hd 58.36N 16.11 E
Norrland 110 Hc 64.27N 17.20 E
Norrland 114 Dd 65.00N 18.00 E
Norrmark/Noormarkku 116 Ic 61.35N 21.52 E
Norrsundet 116 Gd 60.56N 17.08 E
Norrtälje 114 Eg 59.46N 18.42 E
Norseman 210 Dh 32.12S 121.46 E
Norsewood 218 Gd 40.04S 176.13 E
Norsjö 114 Ed 64.55N 19.29 E
Norsjø 116 Ce 59.20N 9.20 E
Norsk 138 Hf 52.20N 129.59 E
Norske Havet = Norwegian Sea (EN) 110 Gc 70.00N 2.00 E
Norske Øer 179 Kc 79.00N 18.00W
Norsup 219b Cc 16.04S 167.23 E
Norte, Baia- 204 Hh 27.30S 48.35W
Norte, Cabo- [Braz.] 202 Ic 1.40N 50.00W
Norte, Cabo- [Pas.] 221d Ab 27.03S 109.24W
Norte, Canal do- 202 Hc 0.30N 50.30W
Norte, Punta- 206 Hf 42.04S 63.45W
Norte, Serra do- 202 Gf 11.00S 59.00W
Norte del Cabo San Antonio, Punta- 206 Ie 36.17S 56.47W
Norte de Santander 202 Db 8.00N 73.00W
Nortelândia 202 Gf 14.25S 56.48W
North, Cape - 180 Lg 47.02N 60.25W
North Adams 184 Kd 42.42N 73.02W
Northallerton 118 Lg 54.20N 1.26W
Northam [Austl.] 210 Ch 31.39S 116.40 E
Northam [S.Afr.] 172 Dd 24.58S 27.11 E
North America (EN) 106 Me 40.00N 95.00W
North American Basin (EN) 106 Bf 30.00N 60.00W
Northampton 118 Mi 52.30N 1.00W
Northampton [Austl.] 212 Ce 28.21S 114.37 E
Northampton [Eng.-U.K.] 118 Mi 52.14N 0.54W
Northampton [Ma.-U.S.] 184 Kd 42.19N 72.38W
Northampton Seamounts (EN) 208 Jb 25.20N 172.04W
Northamptonshire 118 Mi 52.25N 0.55W
North Andaman 148 If 13.15N 92.55 E
North Arm 180 Gd 62.00N 114.30W
North Astrolabe Reef 219d Bc 18.39S 178.32 E
North Augusta 184 Gi 33.30N 81.58W
North Aulatsivik 180 Le 59.45N 64.04W
North Australian Basin (EN) 106 Hk 14.30S 116.30 E
North Battleford 176 Id 52.47N 108.17W
North Bay 176 Le 46.19N 79.28W
North Belcher Islands 180 Je 56.45N 79.45W
North Berwick 118 Ke 56.04N 2.44W
North Bohemian Forest (EN) = Český Les 120 Ig 49.50N 12.30 E
North Bohemian Forest (EN) = Oberpfälzer Wald 120 Ig 49.50N 12.30 E
North Buganda 170 Fb 0.50N 32.10 E
North Caicos 194 Lc 21.56N 71.59W
North Canadian River 186 Hd 35.17N 95.31W
North Cape 208 Ih 34.25S 173.03 E
North Cape (EN) = Nordkapp [Nor.] 110 Ia 71.11N 25.48 E
North Caribou Lake 180 If 52.48N 90.45W
North Carolina 180 Ll 35.30N 80.00W
North Channel 180 Jg 46.02N 82.50W
North Channel/Sruth na Maoile 110 Fd 55.10N 5.40W
Northchapel 124 Bc 51.03N 0.38W
North Charleston 184 Hi 32.53N 80.00W
North Chicago 186 Me 42.20N 87.51W
North Cove 188 Cc 46.47N 124.06W
North Cyprus 142 Ff 35.15N 33.40 E
North Dakota 182 Gb 47.30N 100.15W
North Downs 118 Nj 51.20N 0.10 E
North East 184 Hd 42.13N 79.51W
North-East 172 Dd 21.00S 27.30 E
Northeast Cape 178 Fd 63.18N 168.42W
North-Eastern 170 Hb 1.00N 40.15 E
Northeast Islands 220d Ba 7.36N 151.57 E
Northeast Pacific Basin (EN) 106 Lg 20.00N 140.00W
North East Point 220g Bb 1.57N 157.16W
Northeast Point [Bah.] 194 Kc 21.18N 72.54W
Northeast Point [Bah.] 194 Kb 22.43N 73.50W
Northeast Providence Channel 190 Ic 25.40N 77.09W
Northeim 120 Fe 51.42N 10.00 E
North Entrance 220a Bb 7.59N 134.37 E
Northern [Ghana] 166 Ed 9.30N 1.00W
Northern [Mwi.] 170 Fe 11.00S 34.00 E
Northern [S.L.] 166 Cd 9.15N 11.45W
Northern [Ug.] 170 Fb 2.45N 32.45 E
Northern [Zam.] 170 Fe 11.00S 31.00 E
Northern Cay 194 De 17.27N 87.28W
Northern Cook Islands 208 Kf 10.00S 161.00W
Northern Dvina (EN) = Severnaja Dvina 110 Kc 64.32N 40.30 E
Northern Guinea (EN) 158 Gh 8.30N 1.00W
Northern Indian Lake 180 He 57.20N 97.17W
Northern Ireland 118 Gg 54.40N 6.45W
Northern Mariana Islands 210 Fc 16.00N 145.30 E
Northern Sporades (EN) = Vórioi Sporádhes, Nisoi- 110 Ih 39.15N 23.55 E
Northern Territory 212 Gc 20.00S 134.00 E
Northern Urals (EN) = Severny Ural 110 Lc 62.00N 59.00 E
Northern Uvals (EN) = Severnyje Uvaly 110 Kd 59.30N 49.00 E
North Esk 118 Ke 56.45N 2.30W
Northfield 186 Jd 44.27N 93.09W
North Fiji Basin (EN) 106 Jk 16.00S 174.00 E
North Foreland 118 Oj 51.23N 1.27 E
North Fork Grand River 186 Ed 45.47N 102.16W
North Fork John Day River 188 Fd 44.45N 119.38W
North Fork Moreau River 186 Ed 45.09N 102.50W
North Fork Pass 180 Dd 64.00N 138.00W
North Fork Powder River 188 Le 43.40N 106.30W
North Fork Red 186 Gi 34.25N 99.14W
North Fort Myers 184 Gl 26.40N 81.54W
North Friesland (EN) = Nordfriesland 120 Eb 54.40N 8.55 E
North Frisian Islands (EN) = Nordfriesische Inseln 120 Ea 54.50N 8.30 E
North German Plain (EN) = Norddeutsches Tiefland 110 He 53.00N 11.00 E
North Greenland (EN) = Nordgrønland 179 Gc 79.30N 50.00W
North Highlands 188 Eg 38.40N 121.23W
North Horr 170 Gb 3.19N 37.04 E
North Island [N.Z.] 208 Ih 39.00S 176.00 E
North Island [Sey.] 172b Bc 10.07S 51.11 E
North Kent 180 Ia 76.40N 90.15W
North Korea (EN) = Chosŏn M.I.K. 142 Oe 40.00N 127.30 E
North Lakhimpur 148 Ic 27.14N 94.07 E
Northland 218 Ea 35.30S 173.40 E
North Las Vegas 188 Hh 36.12N 115.07W
North Lincoln Land 180 Ja 76.15N 80.00W
North Little Rock 182 Ie 34.46N 92.14W
North Loup River 186 Gf 41.17N 98.23W
North Magnetic Pole (1980) (EN) 224 Qd 77.03N 101.08W
North Malosmadulu Atoll 148a Ba 5.35N 72.55 E
North Mamm Peak 188 Cg 39.23N 107.52W
North Mayreau Channel 197n Bb 12.41N 61.20W
North Miami 184 Gm 25.56N 80.09W
North Minch 118 Fd 58.05N 5.55W
North Palisade 188 Fh 37.10N 118.38W
North Pass [F.S.M.] 220d Ba 7.41N 151.48 E
North Pass [U.S.] 186 Ll 29.10N 89.15W
North Platte 182 Gc 41.08N 100.46W
North Platte 174 Ie 41.15N 100.45W
North Point [Bar.] 197q Ab 13.20N 59.36W
North Point [Cook] 220n Ab 10.22S 161.02W
North Pole (EN) 224 Ge 90.00N 0.00
Northport 184 Di 33.14N 87.35W
North Powder 188 Gd 45.03N 117.55W
North Raccoon River 186 Jf 41.35N 93.31W
North Reef 219a Ee 12.13S 160.04 E
North Rhine-Westphalia (EN) = Nordrhein-Westfalen 120 De 51.30N 7.30 E
North Rim 188 Ih 36.12N 112.03W
North River 180 Ie 58.53N 94.42W
North Rona 118 Hb 59.10N 5.40W
North Ronaldsay 118 Kb 59.25N 2.30W
North Saskatchewan River 174 Id 53.15N 105.06W
North Sea 110 Gd 55.20N 3.00 E
North Sea (EN) = Noordzee 110 Gd 55.20N 3.00 E
North Sea (EN) = Nord, Mer du- 110 Gd 55.20N 3.00 E
North Sea (EN) = Nordsee 110 Gd 55.20N 3.00 E
North Sea (EN) = Nordsjøen 110 Gd 55.20N 3.00 E
North Sea (EN) = Nordsøen 110 Gd 55.20N 3.00 E
North Sentinel 148 If 11.33N 92.15 E
North Shoshone Peak 188 Gg 39.10N 117.29W
North Siberian Plain (EN) = Severo-Sibirskaja nizmennost 140 Mb 72.00N 104.00 E
North Sound 194 Gd 19.25N 81.26W
North Sound 197d Bb 17.07N 61.45W
North Stradbroke Island 212 Ke 27.35S 153.30 E
North Taranaki Bight 218 Fc 38.50S 174.25 E
North Thompson 188 Ff 50.41N 120.11W
North Tokelau Trough (EN) 106 Kj 3.00S 165.00W
North Tonawanda 184 Hd 43.02N 78.54W
North Trap 218 Bg 47.20S 167.55 E
North Tyne 118 Kg 54.59N 2.08W
North Uist 118 Fd 57.37N 7.22W
Northumberland 118 Kf 55.15N 2.10W
Northumberland 118 Kf 55.15N 2.05W
Northumberland Islands 208 Gg 21.40S 150.00 E
Northumberland Strait 180 Lg 46.00N 63.30W
North Umpqua River 188 De 43.16N 123.27W
North Vancouver 188 Db 49.19N 123.04W
North Walsham 124 Db 52.49N 1.23 E
Northway 178 Kd 62.59N 141.43W
North West Bluff 197c Bc 16.49N 62.12W
North West Cape 208 Cg 21.45S 114.10 E
North-Western 170 Ee 13.00S 25.00 E
Northwest Frontier 148 Eb 33.00N 70.30 E
North West Highlands 110 Fd 57.30N 5.00W
Northwest Pacific Basin (EN) 106 Je 40.00N 155.00 E
North West Point 220g Ab 2.02N 157.30W
Northwest Providence Channel 184 Hl 26.10N 78.20W
Northwest Reef 220a Bb 7.59N 134.33 E
North West River 180 Lf 53.32N 60.09W
Northwest Territories 180 Hc 66.00N 102.00W
Northwich 118 Kh 53.16N 2.32W
North York Moors 118 Mg 54.25N 0.50W
North Yorkshire 118 Lg 54.15N 1.40W
Norton [Ks.-U.S.] 182 Gd 39.50N 100.01W
Norton [Va.-U.S.] 184 Fg 36.56N 82.37W
Norton [Zimb.] 172 Ec 17.53S 30.41 E
Norton Bay 178 Gd 64.45N 161.15W
Norton Sound 174 Cc 64.45N 161.15W
Norvegia, Kapp- 222 Bf 71.25S 12.18W
Norwalk [Ct.-U.S.] 184 Ke 41.07N 73.27W
Norwalk [Oh.-U.S.] 184 Fe 41.14N 82.37W
Norway 184 Dc 45.47N 87.55W
Norway (EN) = Norge 112 Gc 62.00N 10.00 E
Norway Bay 180 Hb 71.00N 104.35W
Norway House 180 Hf 53.58N 97.50W
Norwegian Basin (EN) 110 Fb 68.00N 2.00W
Norwegian Bay 180 Ia 77.45N 90.30W
Norwegian Sea (EN) = Norske Havet 110 Gc 70.00N 2.00 E
Norwegian Trench (EN) 110 Gd 59.00N 4.30 E
Norwich [Ct.-U.S.] 184 Ke 41.32N 72.05W
Norwich [Eng.-U.K.] 112 Ge 52.38N 1.18 E
Norwich [N.Y.-U.S.] 184 Jd 42.33N 75.33W
Norwich Airport 124 Db 52.40N 1.18 E
Norwood 184 Ef 39.10N 84.28W
Nosappu-Misaki 156a Db 43.23N 145.47 E
Noshappu-Misaki 156a Ba 45.27N 141.39 E
Noshiro 152 Pc 40.12N 140.02 E
Nosovaja 136 Fb 68.15N 54.31 E
Nosovka 136 De 50.54N 31.37 E
Nosratābād 144 Id 29.54N 59.59 E
Nossa Senhora das Candeias 202 Kf 12.40S 38.33W
Nossa Senhora do Livramento 204 Db 15.48S 56.22W
Noss Head 118 Jc 58.30N 3.05W
Nossob 158 Jk 26.55S 20.40 E
Nossop 172 Ce 26.55S 20.40 E
Nosy-Be 160 Lj 13.22S 48.16 E
Nosy-Be 158 Lj 13.20S 48.15 E
Nosy-Varika 172 Hd 20.35S 48.30 E
Nota 114 Hb 68.07N 30.10 E
Notch Peak 188 Ig 39.08N 113.24W
Noteć 120 Ld 52.44N 15.26 E
Notecka, Puszcza- 120 Ld 52.45N 16.00 E
Note Kemopla 219c Ab 10.55S 165.51 E
Notengo, Laguna de- 192 Ji 16.15N 98.10W
Notia Pindhos 130 Ej 39.30N 21.20 E
Nótioi Sporádhes = Dodecanese (EN) 110 Ih 36.00N 27.00 E
Nótios Evvoïkós Kólpos 130 Gk 38.20N 23.50 E
Nötö 116 Ie 60.00N 21.45 E
Noto [It.] 128 Jn 36.53N 15.04 E
Noto [Jap.] 154 Nf 37.18N 137.09 E
Noto, Golfo di- 128 Jn 36.50N 15.10 E
Notodden 114 Bg 59.34N 9.17 E
Noto-Hantō 152 Od 37.20N 137.00 E
Noto-Jima 156 Ec 37.07N 137.00 E
Notoro-Ko 156a Da 44.05N 144.10 E
Notoro-Misaki 156a Da 44.07N 144.15 E
Notranjsko 128 Ie 45.46N 14.26 E
Notre-Dame, Monts- 174 Me 48.00N 69.00W
Notre Dame Bay 180 Mg 49.50N 55.00W
Notre-Dame-de-Courson 124 Cf 48.59N 0.16 E
Notre-Dame-de-Gravenchon 124 Ce 49.29N 0.35 E
Notre-Dame-du-Lac 184 Mb 47.38N 68.49W
Notre-Dame-du-Nord 184 Hb 47.36N 79.29W
Notsé 166 Fd 6.59N 1.12 E
Notsuke-Zaki 156a Db 43.34N 145.19 E
Nottawasaga Bay 184 Gc 44.40N 80.30W
Nottaway 174 Ld 51.25N 79.50W
Notterøy 116 De 59.15N 10.25 E
Nottingham 112 Fe 52.58N 1.10W
Nottingham 118 Mh 53.05N 1.00W
Nottingham 180 Jd 63.20N 78.00W
Nottinghamshire 118 Mh 53.10N 0.55W
Nottoway River 184 Ig 36.33N 76.55W
Nottuln 124 Jc 51.56N 7.21 E
Notukeu Creek 188 Lb 49.55N 106.30W
Nouâdhibou 160 Ff 20.54N 17.01W
Nouâdhibou, Dahklet- 162 De 21.00N 16.50W
Nouâdhibou, Râs- = Blanc Cape- (EN) 158 Ff 20.46N 17.03W
Nouakchott 160 Fg 18.07N 15.59W
Nouakchott, District de- 162 Df 18.06N 15.57W
Nouamrhar 162 Df 19.22N 16.31W
Nouméa 210 Hg 22.16S 166.26 E
Nouna 166 Ec 12.44N 3.52W
Noupoort 172 Cf 31.10S 24.57 E
Nouveau-Comptoir 180 Jf 52.35N 78.40W
Nouveau-Québec, Cratère du- = New Quebec Crater (EN) 180 Kd 61.30N 73.55W
Nouvelle-Calédonie = New Caledonia (EN) 210 Hg 21.30S 165.30 E
Nouvelle-Calédonie = New Caledonia (EN) 208 Hg 21.30S 165.30 E
Nouvelle-France, Cap de - 180 Kd 62.33N 73.35W
Nouvelles-Hébrides / New Hebrides 208 Hf 16.01S 167.01 E
Nouvion 124 Dd 50.12N 1.47 E
Nouzonville 122 Ke 49.49N 4.45 E
Novabad 135 He 39.01N 70.09 E
Nová Baňa 120 Oh 48.26N 18.39 E
Nová Bystřice 120 Lg 49.02N 15.06 E
Novaci 130 Gd 45.11N 23.40 E
Nova Cruz 202 Ke 6.28S 35.26W
Nova Esperança 204 Ff 23.08S 52.13W
Nova Friburgo 202 Jh 22.16S 42.32W

Index Symbols

1 Independent Nation; 2 State, Region; 3 District, County; 4 Municipality; 5 Colony, Dependency; Continent; Physical Region; Historical or Cultural Region; Mount, Mountain; Volcano; Hill; Mountains, Mountain Range; Hills, Escarpment; Plateau, Upland; Pass, Gap; Plain, Lowland; Delta; Salt Flat; Valley, Canyon; Crater, Cave; Karst Features; Depression; Polder; Desert, Dunes; Forest, Woods; Heath, Steppe; Oasis; Cape, Point; Coast, Beach; Cliff; Peninsula; Isthmus; Sandbank; Island; Atoll; Rock, Reef; Islands, Archipelago; Rocks, Reefs; Coral Reef; Well, Spring; Geyser; River, Stream; Waterfall, Rapids; River Mouth, Estuary; Lake; Salt Lake; Intermittent Lake; Reservoir; Swamp, Pond; Canal; Glacier; Ice Shelf, Pack Ice; Ocean; Sea; Gulf, Bay; Strait, Fjord; Lagoon; Bank; Seamount; Tablemount; Ridge; Shelf; Basin; Escarpment, Sea Scarp; Fracture; Trench, Abyss; National Park, Reserve; Point of Interest; Recreation Site; Cave, Cavern; Historic Site; Ruins; Wall, Walls; Church, Abbey; Temple; Scientific Station; Railway station; Airport; Port; Military installation; Lighthouse; Mine; Tunnel; Dam, Bridge

Nova Gaia 170 Ce 10.05S 17.32 E
Nova Gorica 128 He 45.57N 13.39 E
Nova Gradiška 128 Le 45.16N 17.23 E
Nova Granada 204 He 20.29S 49.19W
Nova Iguaçu 200 Lh 22.45S 43.27W
Novaja Igirma 138 Fe 57.10N 103.55 E
Novaja-Ivanovka 130 Md 45.59N 29.04 E
Novaja Kahovka 132 Hf 46.43N 33.23 E
Novaja Kazanka 132 Pe 48.58N 49.37 E
Novaja Ladoga 114 Hf 60.05N 32.16 E
Novaja Ljalja 136 Gd 59.03N 60.36 E
Novaja Odessa 132 Gf 47.18N 31.47 E
Novaja Sibir, ostrov- = New Siberia (EN) 140 Qb 75.00N 149.00 E
Novaja Vodolaga 132 Ie 49.45N 35.52 E
Novaja Zemlja=Novaya Zemlya (EN) 140 Hb 74.00N 57.00 E
Nova Lamego 166 Cc 12.17N 14.13W
Nova Lima 202 Jh 19.59S 43.51W
Nova Londrina 204 Ff 22.45S 53.00W
Nova Mambone 172 Fd 20.58S 35.00 E
Nova Olinda do Norte 202 Gd 3.45S 59.03W
Nová Paka 120 Lf 50.29N 15.31 E
Nova Prata 204 Gi 28.47S 51.36W
Novara 128 Ce 45.28N 8.38 E
Nova Roma 204 Ia 13.51S 46.57W
Nova Russas 202 Jd 4.42S 40.34W
Nova Scotia [2] 180 Lh 45.00N 63.00W
Nova Scotia 174 Me 45.00N 63.00W
Nova Sintra 162 Cf 14.54N 24.40W
Nova Sofala 172 Ed 20.10S 34.44 E
Novato 188 Dg 38.06N 122.34W
Nova Varoš 130 Cf 43.28N 19.49 E
Nova Venécia 202 Jg 18.43S 40.24W
Novaya Zemlya (EN)= Novaja Zemlja 140 Hb 74.00N 57.00 E
Nova Zagora 130 Jg 42.29N 26.01 E
Novelda 126 Lf 38.23N 0.46W
Novellara 128 Ef 44.51N 10.44 E
Nové Mesto nad Váhom 120 Nh 48.46N 17.50 E
Nové Zámky 120 Oi 47.59N 18.11 E
Novgorod 112 Jd 58.31N 31.17 E
Novgorodka 116 Mg 57.00N 28.37 E
Novgorod-Severski 136 De 52.01N 33.16 E
Novgorodskaja oblast [3] 136 Dd 58.20N 32.40 E
Novi Bečej 130 Dd 45.36N 20.08 E
Novigrad [Yugo.] 128 He 45.19N 13.34 E
Novigrad [Yugo.] 128 Jf 44.11N 15.33 E
Novi Kričim 130 Hg 42.03N 24.28 E
Novi Ligure 128 Cf 44.46N 8.47 E
Novillero 192 Gf 22.21N 105.39W
Novion-Porcien 124 Ge 49.36N 4.25 E
Novi Pazar [Bul.] 130 Kf 43.21N 27.12 E
Novi Pazar [Yugo.] 130 Df 43.08N 20.31 E
Novi Sad 112 Hf 45.15N 19.50 E
Novi Travnik 128 Lf 44.10N 17.39 E
Novi Vinodolski 128 Ie 45.08N 14.47 E
Novoaleksandrovsk 132 Lg 45.24N 41.14 E
Novoalekseevka [Kaz.-U.S.S.R.] 132 Sd 50.08N 55.42 E
Novoalekseevka [Ukr.-U.S.S.R.] 132 If 46.16N 34.39 E
Novoaltajsk 138 Df 53.24N 83.58 E
Novoanninskij 136 Ee 50.31N 42.45 E
Novoarhangelsk 132 Ge 48.39N 30.50 E
Novo Aripuanã 202 Fe 5.08S 60.22W
Novoazovsk 132 Kf 47.05N 38.05 E
Novobirjusinski 138 Ee 56.58N 97.55 E
Novobogdanovka 132 If 47.05N 35.18 E
Novočeboksarsk 114 Lh 56.08N 47.29 E
Novočeremšansk 114 Mi 54.23N 50.10 E
Novočerkassk 136 Ef 47.25N 40.03 E
Novodevičje 114 Lj 53.35N 48.51 E
Novograd-Volynski 136 Ce 50.36N 27.36 E
Novogrudok 132 Dc 53.37N 25.50 E
Nôvo Hamburgo 206 Jc 29.41S 51.08W
Novohopërsk 132 Ld 51.06N 41.37 E
Novo Horizonte 204 He 21.28S 49.13W
Novoizborsk 116 Mg 57.43N 28.05 E
Novojenisejsk 138 Ee 58.19N 92.27 E
Novojerudinski 138 Ee 59.47N 93.30 E
Novokačalinsk 138 Ig 45.05N 131.59 E
Novokazalinsk 142 Ie 45.50N 62.10 E
Novokubansk 132 Lg 45.06N 41.01 E
Novokujbyševsk 136 Ee 53.08N 49.58 E
Novokuzneck 142 Kd 53.45N 87.06 E
Novolazarevskaja 222 Cf 70.46S 11.50 E
Novolukoml 114 Gi 54.38N 29.07 E
Novo Mesto 128 Je 45.48N 15.10 E
Novomičurinsk 114 Ji 54.02N 39.48 E
Novomihajlovka 138 Ih 44.17N 133.50 E
Novo Miloševo 130 Dd 45.43N 20.18 E
Novomirgorod 132 Ge 48.45N 31.39 E
Novomoskovsk [R.S.F.S.R.] 112 Je 54.05N 38.13 E
Novomoskovsk [Ukr.-U.S.S.R.] 136 Df 48.37N 35.16 E
Novonikolajevski 132 Md 50.55N 42.24 E
Novoorsk 136 Fe 51.24N 58.59 E
Novopokrovskaja 132 Lg 45.56N 40.42 E
Novopolock 136 Cd 55.31N 28.40 E
Novorossijsk 112 Jg 44.45N 37.45 E
Novorybnaja 138 Fb 72.50N 105.45 E
Novoržev 136 Cd 57.02N 29.20 E
Novošahtinsk 136 Df 47.47N 39.54 E
Novoselica 130 Ja 48.13N 26.17 E
Novoselje 116 Mf 58.05N 29.00 E
Novoselki 120 Ud 52.04N 24.25 E
Novoselovo 138 Ef 54.55N 91.00 E
Novosergijevka 136 Fe 52.03N 53.39 E
Novosibirsk 142 Kd 55.02N 82.55 E
Novosibirskaja oblast [3] 138 Ce 55.30N 80.00 E
Novosibirskije ostrova = New Siberian Islands (EN) 140 Qb 75.00N 142.00 E
Novosibirskoje vodohranilišče = Novosibirsk Reservoir (EN) 138 Df 54.40N 82.35 E
Novosibirsk Reservoir (EN) = Novosibirskoje vodohranilišče 138 Df 54.40N 82.35 E
Novosil 132 Jc 52.59N 37.01 E
Novosineglazovski 134 Ji 55.05N 61.25 E
Novosokolniki 136 Dd 56.19N 30.12 E
Novospasskoje 114 Lj 53.09N 47.44 E
Novotroick 136 Fe 51.12N 58.35 E
Novotroickoje 136 Hg 43.39N 73.45 E
Novoukrainka 132 Ge 48.19N 31.32 E
Novouljanovsk 114 Li 54.10N 48.23 E
Novouzensk 136 Ee 50.29N 48.08 E
Novovjatsk 114 Lg 58.31N 49.43 E
Novovolynsk 136 Ce 50.46N 24.09 E
Novovoronežski 132 Kd 51.17N 39.16 E
Novozybkov 136 De 52.32N 32.00 E
Novska 128 Ke 45.20N 16.59 E
Novy Bug 132 Hf 47.43N 32.29 E
Nový Bydžov 120 Lf 50.15N 15.29 E
Novy Jaričev 120 Ug 49.50N 24.21 E
Novyje Aneny 130 Mc 46.53N 29.13 E
Novyje Burasy 132 Oc 52.06N 46.06 E
Nový Jičín 120 Og 49.36N 18.01 E
Novy Oskol 132 Jd 50.43N 37.54 E
Novy Pogost 116 Li 55.30N 27.32 E
Novy Port 142 Jc 67.40N 72.52 E
Novy Tap 134 Mh 56.55N 67.15 E
Novy Terek 132 Oh 43.37N 47.25 E
Novy Uzen 136 Fg 43.19N 52.55 E
Novy Vasjugan 138 Ce 58.34N 76.29 E
Novy Zaj 114 Mi 55.17N 52.02 E
Nowa Dęba 120 Rf 50.26N 21.46 E
Nowa Huta, Kraków- 120 Qf 50.04N 20.05 E
Nowa Ruda 120 Mf 50.35N 16.31 E
Nowa Sarzyna 120 Sf 50.23N 22.22 E
Nowa Sól 120 Le 51.48N 15.44 E
Now Bandegān 146 Oh 28.52N 53.53 E
Nowbarān 146 Me 35.08N 49.42 E
Nowdesheh 146 Le 35.11N 46.15 E
Nowe 120 Oc 53.40N 18.43 E
Nowe Miasto Lubawskie 120 Pc 53.27N 19.35 E
Nowe Miasto-nad-Pilicą 120 Qe 51.38N 20.35 E
Nowe Warpno 120 Kc 53.44N 14.20 E
Nowfel low Shātow 146 Ne 34.27N 50.55 E
Nowgong 148 Ic 26.21N 92.40 E
Nowogard 120 Lc 53.40N 15.08 E
Nowogród 120 Rc 53.15N 21.53 E
Nowood River 188 Ld 44.17N 107.58W
Nowra 212 Kf 34.53S 150.36 E
Now Shahr 146 Nd 36.39N 51.31 E
Nowy Dwór Gdański 120 Pb 54.13N 19.06 E
Nowy Dwór Mazowiecki 120 Qd 52.26N 20.43 E
Nowy Korczyn 120 Qf 50.20N 20.50 E
Nowy Sącz 120 Qg 49.38N 20.42 E
Nowy Sącz [2] 120 Qg 49.40N 20.40 E
Nowy Targ 120 Qg 49.29N 20.02 E
Nowy Tomyśl 120 Md 52.20N 16.07 E
Noya/Anoia 126 Nc 41.28N 1.56 E
Noya / Noia 126 Db 42.47N 8.53W
Noyant 122 Gg 47.31N 0.08 E
Noyon 122 Ie 49.35N 3.00 E
Nozaki-Jima 156 Ae 33.11N 129.08 E
Nozay 122 Eg 47.34N 1.38W
Nsanje 170 Gf 16.55S 35.16 E
Nsawan 166 Ed 5.48N 0.21W
Nsefu 170 Fe 13.03S 32.07 E
Nsukka 166 Gd 6.52N 7.23 E
Ntadembele 170 Cc 2.11S 17.08 E
Ntchisi 170 Fe 13.22S 34.00 E
Ntem 158 Hh 2.10N 9.57 E
Ntoum 170 Ab 0.22N 9.47 E
Ntui 166 He 4.27N 11.38 E
Ntusi 170 Fb 0.03N 31.13 E
Nuageuses, Iles- 222 Fc 48.40S 68.58 E
Nuanetsi 158 Kk 22.40S 31.49 E
Nūbah, Jibāl an- 158 Kg 12.00N 30.45 E
Nubian Desert (EN)= Nūbiyah, Aş Şahrā' an- 158 Kf 20.30N 33.00 E
Nūbiyah, Aş Şahrā' an- = Nubian Desert (EN) 158 Kf 20.30N 33.00 E
Nucet 130 Fc 46.28N 22.35 E
Nudha 219a Ec 9.32S 160.48 E
Nueces Plain 182 Hf 28.30N 99.15W
Nueces River 182 Hf 27.50N 97.30W
Nueltin Lake 174 Jc 60.50N 99.30W
Nü'er He 154 Fd 41.06N 121.09 E
Nueva 206 Ei 55.15S 66.32W
Nueva Asunción [3] 204 Be 21.00S 60.20W
Nueva Ciudad Guerrero 192 Jd 26.35N 99.15W
Nueva Esparta [2] 202 Fa 11.00N 64.00W
Nueva Germania 204 Df 23.54S 56.34W
Nueva Gerona 190 Hd 21.53N 82.48W
Nueva Imperial 206 Fe 38.44S 72.57W
Nueva Italia de Ruiz 192 Hh 19.01N 102.06W
Nueva Ocotepeque 192 Cf 14.24N 89.13W
Nueva Palmira 204 Ck 33.53S 58.25W
Nueva Rosita 176 Ig 27.57N 101.13W
Nueva San Salvador 192 Gf 13.41N 89.17W
Nueva Segovia [3] 194 Dg 13.40N 86.10W
Nueve de Julio 206 He 35.27S 60.52W
Nuevitas 190 Id 21.33N 77.16W
Nuevitas, Bahía de- 194 Ic 21.30N 77.12W
Nuevo, Cayo- 192 Mg 21.51N 92.05W
Nuevo, Golfo- 198 Jj 42.42S 64.36W
Nuevo Berlín 204 Ck 32.59S 58.03W
Nuevo Casas Grandes 176 If 30.25N 107.55W
Nuevo Laredo 176 Jg 27.30N 99.31W
Nuevo León [2] 190 Ec 25.40N 100.00W
Nuevo Mundo, Cerro- 202 Eh 21.55S 66.53W
Nuevo Rocafuerte 202 Cd 0.56S 75.25W
Nugaal [3] 168 Hd 8.30N 48.00 E
Nugāl 168 Hd 9.30N 46.30 E
Nugālēd, Dēh- 158 Lh 7.58N 49.51 E
Nugālēd, Dōho- 168 Hd 8.35N 48.35 E
Nūgātsiaq 179 Gd 71.39N 53.45W
Nugget Point 218 Cg 46.27S 169.49 E
Nūgssuaq 179 Gd 70.30N 51.30W
Nuguria Islands 208 Ge 3.20S 154.45 E
Nuguš 134 Gj 53.05N 56.00 E
Nuhaka 218 Gc 39.02S 177.45 E
Nui Atoll 208 Ie 7.15S 177.10 E
Nuijama 116 Md 60.58N 28.32 E
Nuiqsut 178 Ib 70.20N 151.00W
Nu Jiang 140 Lh 16.31N 97.37 E
Nûk/Godthåb 224 Nc 64.15N 51.40W
Nukapu 219c Ab 10.07S 165.59 E
Nukey Bluff 212 Hf 32.35S 135.40 E
Nukhayb 144 Fc 32.02N 42.15 E
Nukhaylak 160 Jg 19.08N 26.20 E
Nukiki 219a Cb 6.45S 156.29 E
Nukuaéta 220h Ac 13.22S 176.11W
Nuku'alofa 210 Jg 21.08S 175.12W
Nukufetau Atoll 208 Ie 8.00S 178.22 E
Nukufotu 220h Bb 13.11S 176.10W
Nukuhifala 220h Bb 13.17S 176.05W
Nukuhione 220h Bb 13.16S 176.06W
Nuku Hiva, Ile- 208 Me 8.54S 140.06W
Nukulaelae Atoll 208 Ie 9.23S 179.52 E
Nukuloa 220h Bb 13.11S 176.09W
Nukumanu Islands 208 Ge 4.30S 159.30 E
Nukumbasanga 219d Cb 16.18S 179.15W
Nukunonu Atoll 208 Je 9.10S 171.53W
Nukuoro Atoll 208 Gd 3.51N 154.58 E
Nukus 142 He 42.50N 59.29 E
Nukutapu 220h Bb 13.13S 176.08W
Nukuteatea 220h Bb 13.12S 176.08W
Nulato 178 Hd 64.43N 158.06W
Nules 126 Le 39.51N 0.09W
Nullagine 210 Dg 21.53S 120.06 E
Nullagine River 212 Ed 20.43S 120.33 E
Nullarbor 212 Gf 31.26S 130.55 E
Nullarbor Plain 208 Dh 31.00S 129.00 E
Nulu'erhu Shan 152 Kc 41.40N 119.50 E
Numakawa 156a Bb 45.15N 141.51 E
Numan 166 Hd 9.28N 12.02 E
Numancia 150 Ie 9.52N 125.58 E
Numancia 126 Jc 41.47N 2.30W
Numanohata 156a Bb 42.40N 141.41 E
Numata [Jap.] 156a Bb 43.49N 141.55 E
Numata [Jap.] 154 Of 36.38N 139.03 E
Numatinna 168 Dd 7.14N 27.37 E
Numazu 154 Og 35.06N 138.52 E
Nümbrecht 124 Jd 50.54N 7.33 E
Numedal 114 Bf 60.05N 9.05 E
Numena 170 Ee 11.46S 26.31 E
Número Cinco, Canal- 204 Cm 36.44S 58.06W
Número Doce, Canal- 204 Cm 36.30S 59.08W
Número Dos, Canal- 204 Cm 36.51S 58.03W
Número Nueve, Canal- 204 Cm 36.08S 58.36W
Número Once, Canal- 204 Bm 36.28S 60.01W
Número Quince, Canal- 204 Dl 35.55S 57.45W
Número Uno, Canal- 204 Cm 36.40S 58.35W
Numfoor, Pulau- 150 Jg 1.03S 134.54 E
Nuneaton 118 Li 52.32N 1.28W
Nungarin 212 Df 31.11S 118.06 E
Nungnain Sum 152 Kb 45.45N 118.56 E
Nungo 172 Fb 13.25S 37.46 E
Nunivak 174 Cd 60.00N 166.30W
Nunkirchen, Wadern- 124 Ie 49.32N 6.53 E
Nunn 186 Df 40.45N 104.46W
Nunspeet 124 Hb 52.22N 5.46 E
Nunukan Timur, Pulau- 150 Gf 4.05N 117.40 E
Nuomin He 152 Lb 48.21N 124.32 E
Nuorgam 114 Ga 70.05N 27.51 E
Nuoro 112 Gg 40.19N 9.20 E
Nupani 219c Ab 10.04S 165.40 E
Nūq 146 Pg 30.55N 55.35 E
Nuqayr 146 Mi 27.48N 48.21 E
Nuqrah 146 Ij 25.34N 41.24 E
Nuqruş, Jabal- 164 Fe 24.49N 34.36 E
Nuqui 202 Cb 5.43N 77.16W
Nūr 146 Pg 31.25N 54.20 E
Nūr 146 Od 36.15N 52.20 E
Nura 136 Gf 48.57N 62.20 E
Nura 140 Id 50.30N 69.59 E
Nūrābād 146 Ng 30.48N 51.27 E
Nuraghe Santu Antine 128 Cj 40.29N 8.45 E
Nurata 136 Gg 40.34N 65.35 E
Nur Dağları 146 Gd 36.45N 36.20 E
Nure 128 De 45.03N 9.49 E
Nurek 136 Gh 38.25N 69.20 E
Nurhak Dağı 144 Eb 38.04N 37.29 E
Nūrī 168 Eb 18.30N 32.02 E
Nurki 138 Ie 56.42N 138.28 E
Nurlat 136 Fe 54.28N 50.48 E
Nurlati 114 Li 55.38N 48.17 E
Nurmes 114 Ge 63.33N 29.07 E
Nurmijärvi 116 Kd 60.28N 24.48 E
Nurmo 116 Jb 62.50N 22.54 E
Nürnberg 112 Hf 49.27N 11.05 E
Nurra 128 Cj 40.45N 8.15 E
Nurri, Mount- 212 Jf 31.42S 146.02 E
Nurugas 172 Bc 19.11S 18.54 E
Nurzec 120 Sd 52.33N 22.28 E
Nusa Tenggara Barat [3] 150 Gh 8.50S 117.30 E
Nusa Tenggara Timur [3] 150 Hh 9.30S 122.00 E
Nusaybin 146 Id 37.03N 41.13 E
Nushagak 178 He 58.57N 158.29W
Nushan 152 Gf 25.00N 99.00 E
Nu-Shima 156 Dd 34.10N 134.50 E
Nutak 180 Le 57.31N 62.00W
Nuttal 148 Dc 28.45N 68.08 E
Nuutele 221c Bb 14.02S 171.22W
Nuwākot 148 Gc 28.08N 83.53 E
Nuwara 148 Gg 6.58N 80.46 E
Nuwaybi 'al Muzayyinah 164 Fd 28.58N 34.39 E
Nyabing 212 Df 33.32S 118.09 E
Nyagquka/Yajiang 152 He 30.07N 100.58 E
Nyagrong/Xinlong 152 He 30.57N 100.12 E
Nyahanga 170 Fc 2.23S 33.33 E
Nyahua 170 Fc 4.58S 33.34 E
Nyainqêntanglha Feng 152 Fe 30.12N 90.33 E
Nyainqêntanglha Shan 140 Kf 30.10N 90.00 E
Nyakanazi 170 Fc 3.00S 31.15 E
Nyala 160 Jg 12.03N 24.53 E
Nyalam 152 Ef 28.15N 85.55 E
Ny-Ålesund 179 Nc 78.56N 11.57 E
Nyalikungu 170 Fc 3.11S 33.47 E
Nyamandhlovu 172 Dc 19.51S 28.16 E
Nyamapanda 172 Ec 16.55S 32.52 E
Nyamlell 168 Dd 9.07N 26.58 E
Nyamtumbo 170 Ge 10.30S 36.06 E
Nyanding 168 Ed 8.40N 32.41 E
Nyanga [3] 170 Bc 3.00S 11.00 E
Nyanga 158 Ii 2.58S 10.15 E
Nyanza [3] 170 Fc 0.30S 34.30 E
Nyanza-Lac 170 Ec 4.21S 29.36 E
Nyasa, Lake- (EN)=Niassa, Lago- 158 Kj 12.00S 34.30 E
Nyaunglebin 148 Je 17.57N 96.44 E
Nyborg 114 Ci 55.19N 10.48 E
Nybro 114 Dh 56.45N 15.54 E
Nyda 138 Cc 66.36N 72.54 E
Nyda 134 Pc 66.40N 72.50 E
Nyeboe Land 179 Gb 81.45N 56.40W
Nyêmo 152 Ff 29.30N 90.07 E
Nyeri 170 Gc 0.25S 36.57 E
Nyerol 168 Ed 8.41N 32.02 E
Ny Friesland 179 Nc 79.30N 17.00 E
Nyhammar 116 Fd 60.17N 14.58 E
Nyhem 116 Fb 62.54N 15.40 E
Nyika 158 Ki 2.37S 38.44 E
Nyika Plateau 158 Kj 10.40S 33.50 E
Nyikog Qu 152 He 30.24N 100.40 E
Nyimba 170 Fe 14.33S 30.48 E
Nyingchi 152 Ff 29.38N 94.23 E
Nyirbátor 120 Si 47.50N 22.08 E
Nyíregyháza 120 Ri 47.57N 21.43 E
Nyiri Desert 170 Gc 2.20S 37.20 E
Nyiro, Mount- 170 Gb 2.08N 36.51 E
Nyírség 120 Ri 47.50N 21.55 E
Nykøbing [Den.] 114 Ci 55.55N 11.41 E
Nykøbing [Den.] 116 Ch 56.48N 8.52 E
Nykøbing [Den.] 114 Ci 54.46N 11.53 E
Nyköping 114 Dg 58.45N 17.00 E
Nyköpingsån 116 Gf 58.45N 17.01 E
Nykroppa 116 Fe 59.38N 14.18 E
Nyland 116 Ga 63.00N 17.46 E
Nylstroom 172 Dd 24.42S 28.20 E
Nymburk 120 Lf 50.11N 15.03 E
Nymphe Bank (EN) 118 Fj 51.30N 7.05W
Nynäshamn 114 Dg 58.54N 17.57 E
Nyngan 210 Fh 31.34S 147.11 E
Nyon 128 Ad 46.23N 6.15 E
Nyong 158 Hh 3.17N 9.54 E
Nyonga 170 Fd 6.43S 32.04 E
Nyons 122 Lj 44.22N 5.08 E
Nýřany 120 Jg 49.43N 13.13 E
Nyrob 134 Hf 60.42N 56.45 E
Nyš 138 Jf 51.30N 142.49 E
Nysa 120 Nf 50.29N 17.20 E
Nysa Kłodzka 120 Nf 50.49N 17.50 E
Nysa Łużycka 120 Kd 52.04N 14.46 E
Nyslott/Savonlinna 114 Gf 61.52N 28.53 E
Nyssa 188 Ge 43.53N 117.00W
Nystad/Uusikaupunki 114 Ef 60.48N 21.25 E
Nysted 116 Dj 54.40N 11.45 E
Nytva 136 Fd 57.56N 55.20 E
Nyūdō-Zaki 154 Od 40.00N 139.35 E
Nyunzu 170 Ed 5.57S 28.01 E
Nyūzen 156 Ec 36.56N 137.30 E
Nzambi 170 Bc 3.58S 11.16 E
Nzara 168 De 4.40N 28.14 E
Nzega 170 Fc 4.13S 33.11 E
Nzérékoré 160 Gh 7.45N 8.49W
N'zeto 170 Bd 7.05S 12.50 E
Nzi 158 Gh 5.57N 4.50W
Nzilo, Barrage de- 170 Ee 10.35S 25.30 E
Nzo 166 Dd 6.16N 7.03W
Nzoro 170 Eb 3.18N 29.26 E
Nzwani/Anjouan 158 Lj 12.15S 44.25 E

O

Oa, Mull of- 118 Gf 55.35N 6.20W
Oahe, Lake- 174 Ie 45.30N 100.25W
Oahu Island 208 Lb 21.30N 158.00W
O-akan-Dake 156a Db 43.27N 144.10 E
Oakdale [Ca.-U.S.] 188 Eh 37.46N 120.51W
Oakdale [La.-U.S.] 186 Jk 30.49N 92.40W
Oakham 118 Mi 52.40N 0.44W
Oak Harbor 188 Db 48.18N 122.39W
Oak Lake 186 Fb 49.40N 100.45W
Oakland [Ca.-U.S.] 176 Gf 37.47N 122.13W
Oakland [Md.-U.S.] 184 Hf 39.25N 79.24W
Oakley [Id.-U.S.] 188 Ie 42.15N 113.53W
Oakley [Ks.-U.S.] 182 Gd 39.08N 100.51W
Oak Park 186 Mf 41.53N 87.48W
Oak Ridge 182 Kd 36.01N 84.16W
Oakridge 188 De 43.45N 122.28W
Oakville 184 Hd 43.27N 79.41W
Oamaru 216 Di 45.05S 170.59 E
Oancea 130 Ld 45.55N 28.06 E
Oani-Gawa 156 Ga 40.12N 140.16 E
Oarai 156 Gc 36.18N 140.33 E
Oaro 218 Ee 42.31S 173.30 E
Oasis 188 Hf 41.01N 114.37W
Oasis [5] 162 Hd 26.00N 5.00 E
Oates Coast 222 Jf 70.00S 160.00 E
Oaxaca [2] 190 Ee 17.00N 96.30W
Oaxaca de Juárez 176 Jh 17.03N 96.43W
Ob 140 Ic 66.45N 69.30 E
Oba 180 Jg 48.55N 84.17W
Obala 166 He 4.10N 11.32 E
Obama [Jap.] 156 Be 32.43N 130.13 E
Obama [Jap.] 154 Mg 35.30N 135.45 E
Obama-Wan 156 Dd 35.30N 135.40 E
Oban [N.Z.] 216 Ci 46.52S 168.10 E
Oban [Scot.-U.K.] 118 He 56.25N 5.29W
Obanazawa 154 Pe 38.36N 140.24 E
Obando 200 Je 4.07N 67.45W
Oban Hills 166 Gd 5.30N 8.35 E
Obeliai/Obeljaj 116 Ki 55.58N 25.59 E
Obeljaj/Obeliai 116 Ki 55.58N 25.59 E
Oberá 206 Ic 27.29S 55.08W
Oberbayern 120 Hi 47.50N 11.50 E
Oberderdingen 124 Ke 49.04N 8.48 E
Oberfranken 120 Hf 50.10N 11.30 E
Oberhausen 120 Ce 51.28N 6.51 E
Oberkirchen, Schmallenberg- 124 Kc 51.09N 8.18 E
Oberland [Switz.] 128 Bd 46.35N 7.30 E
Oberland [Switz.] 128 Dd 46.45N 9.05 E
Oberlausitz 120 Ke 51.15N 14.30 E
Oberlin 186 Fg 39.49N 100.32W
Obermoschel 124 Je 49.44N 7.46 E
Obernkirchen 124 Lb 52.16N 9.08 E
Oberösterreich=Upper Austria (EN) [2] 128 Hb 48.15N 14.00 E
Oberpfalz 120 Ig 49.30N 12.10 E
Oberpfälzer Wald=North Bohemian Forest (EN) 120 Ig 49.50N 12.30 E
Oberpullendorf 128 Kc 47.30N 16.31 E
Ober-Ramstadt 124 Ke 49.50N 8.45 E
Oberstdorf 120 Gi 47.24N 10.16 E
Oberursel (Taunus) 124 Kd 50.12N 8.35 E
Obervellach 128 Hd 46.56N 13.12 E
Oberwesel 124 Jd 50.06N 7.44 E
Ob Gulf (EN) = Obskaja guba 140 Jc 69.00N 73.00 E
Obi, Kepulauan- 150 Ig 1.30S 127.45 E
Obi, Pulau- 208 De 1.30S 127.45 E
Obi, Selat- 150 Ig 0.52S 127.33 E
Óbidos [Braz.] 200 Kf 1.55S 55.31W
Óbidos [Port.] 126 Ce 39.22N 9.09W
Obihiro 152 Pc 42.55N 143.12 E
Obilić 130 Eg 42.41N 21.05 E
Obira 156a Ba 44.01N 141.38 E
Obispos 194 Li 8.36N 70.05W
Obispo Trejo 206 Hd 30.46S 63.25W
Obitočnaja kosa 132 Jf 46.35N 36.15 E
Oblučje 138 Ig 48.59N 131.05 E
Obninsk 136 Dd 55.05N 36.37 E
Obo 160 Jh 5.24N 26.30 E
Obock 168 Gc 11.57N 43.17 E
Obojan 136 De 51.13N 36.16 E
Obokote 170 Ec 0.52S 26.19 E
Obol 114 Gi 55.24N 29.01 E
Oborniki 120 Md 52.39N 16.51 E
Obouya 170 Cc 0.56S 15.43 E
Obozerski 136 Ec 63.28N 40.20 E
Obra 120 Ld 52.36N 15.28 E
Obrenovac 130 De 44.39N 20.12 E
Obrovac 128 Jf 44.12N 15.41 E
Obrovo 120 Vd 52.27N 25.43 E
Obruchev Rise (EN) 138 Lf 52.30N 166.00 E
Obruk Platosu 146 Ec 38.02N 33.30 E
Obšči Syrt 110 Le 51.50N 51.00 E
Obskaja guba = Ob Gulf (EN) 140 Jc 69.00N 73.00 E
Ob' Tablemount (EN) 158 Ln 52.30S 42.00 E
Ōbu 156 Ed 35.01N 136.58 E
Obuasi 166 Ed 6.12N 1.40W
Obudu 166 Gd 6.40N 9.10 E
Obuhov 132 Gd 50.07N 30.37 E
Obva 134 Gg 58.35N 55.25 E
Obzor 130 Kg 42.49N 27.53 E
Oca 126 Ib 42.46N 3.26W
Oca, Montes de- 126 Ib 42.20N 3.15W
Očakov 136 Df 46.38N 31.33 E
Ocala 182 Kf 29.11N 82.07W
Očamčira 132 Lh 42.46N 41.27 E
Ocampo [Mex.] 192 Ec 28.11N 108.23W
Ocampo [Mex.] 192 Hd 27.20N 102.21W
Ocaña [Col.] 202 Db 8.15N 73.20W
Ocaña [Sp.] 126 Ie 39.56N 3.31W
Occhito, Lago di- 128 Ii 41.35N 14.55 E
Occidental, Cordillera- [Col.] 198 Ie 5.00N 76.00W
Ocean Bight 194 Kc 21.15N 73.15W
Ocean City [Md.-U.S.] 182 Ld 38.20N 75.05W
Ocean City [N.J.-U.S.] 184 Jf 39.16N 74.35W
Ocean Falls 180 Ef 52.21N 127.40W
Oceania (EN) 208 Ie 5.00S 175.00 E
Ocean Point 184 Il 26.16N 77.03W
Oceanside 182 De 33.12N 117.23W
Ocean Springs 186 Lk 30.25N 88.50W
Ocejón, Pico- 126 Ic 41.07N 3.15W
Očenyrd, gora- 134 Mb 68.05N 66.20 E
Očer 136 Fd 57.53N 54.45 E
Ochagabia / Ochagavia 126 Kb 42.55N 1.05W
Ochagavia / Ochagabia 126 Kb 42.55N 1.05W
Ochiai 156 Cd 35.02N 133.45 E
Ochiishi-Misaki 156a Db 43.10N 145.28 E
Ochil Hills 118 Je 56.23N 3.35W
Och'onjang 154 Jd 40.55N 128.50 E
Ocho Rios 194 Id 18.25N 77.07W
Ochsenfurt 120 Gg 49.39N 10.05 E
Ochtrup 124 Jb 52.13N 7.11 E
Ockelbo 114 Dd 60.53N 16.43 E
Öckerö 116 Dg 57.43N 11.39 E
Ocmulgee River 184 Fj 31.58N 82.32W
Ocna Mureş 130 Gc 46.23N 23.51 E
Ocna Sibiului 130 Hd 45.53N 24.03 E
Ocoa, Bahía de- 194 Ld 18.22N 70.39W
Oconee River 184 Fj 31.58N 82.32W
Oconto 186 Md 44.55N 87.52W
Ocosingo 192 Mi 17.04N 92.15W
Ocotal 194 Dg 13.38N 86.29W
Ocotepeque [3] 194 Cf 14.30N 89.00W
Ocotlán 190 Dd 20.21N 102.46W
Ocotlán de Morelos 192 Ki 16.48N 96.43W
Ocracoke Inlet 184 Ih 35.10N 76.05W
Ocracoke Island 184 Jh 35.09N 75.53W
Ocreza 126 Ee 39.32N 7.50W
Octeville-sur-Mer 124 Ce 49.33N 0.07 E
October Revolution Island (EN) = Oktjabrskoj Revoljuci, ostrov- 140 Lb 79.30N 97.00 E
Ocú 194 Gj 7.57N 80.47W

Index Symbols

[1] Independent Nation; [2] State, Region; [3] District, County; [4] Municipality; [5] Colony, Dependency; Continent; Physical Region

Historical or Cultural Region; Mount, Mountain; Volcano; Hill; Mountains, Mountain Range; Hills, Escarpment; Plateau, Upland

Pass, Gap; Plain, Lowland; Delta; Salt Flat; Valley, Canyon; Crater, Cave; Karst Features

Depression; Polder; Desert, Dunes; Forest, Woods; Heath, Steppe; Oasis; Cape, Point

Coast, Beach; Cliff; Peninsula; Isthmus; Sandbank; Island; Atoll

Rock, Reef; Islands, Archipelago; Rocks, Reefs; Coral Reef; Well, Spring; Geyser; River, Stream

Waterfall, Rapids; River Mouth, Estuary; Lake; Salt Lake; Intermittent Lake; Reservoir; Swamp, Pond

Canal; Glacier; Ice Shelf, Pack Ice; Ocean; Sea; Gulf, Bay; Strait, Fjord

Lagoon; Bank; Seamount; Tablemount; Ridge; Shelf; Basin

Escarpment, Sea Scarp; Fracture; Trench, Abyss; National Park, Reserve; Point of Interest; Recreation Site; Cave, Cavern

Historic Site; Ruins; Wall, Walls; Church, Abbey; Temple; Scientific Station; Railway station

Airport; Port; Military installation; Lighthouse; Mine; Tunnel; Dam, Bridge

Ocumare del Tuy	196	Cg	10.07N	66.46W
Ōda	154	Lg	35.11N	132.30 E
Oda [Ghana]	166	Ed	5.55N	0.59W
Oda [Jap.]	156	Ce	33.34N	132.48 E
Oda, Jabal-	168	Fa	20.21N	36.39 E
Ódádahraun	114a	Cb	65.09N	17.00W
Ōdai	156	Ed	34.24N	136.24 E
Odaigahara-San	156	Ed	34.11N	136.06 E
Odalen	116	Dd	60.15N	11.40 E
Ōdate	154	Pd	40.16N	140.34 E
Odawara	154	Og	35.15N	139.10 E
Odda	114	Bf	60.04N	6.33 E
Odder	116	Di	55.58N	10.10 E
Odeleite	126	Eg	37.21N	7.27W
Odemira	126	Dg	37.36N	8.38W
Ödemiş	146	Bc	38.13N	27.59 E
Odendaalsrus	172	De	27.48S	26.45 E
Odense	112	Hd	55.24N	10.23 E
Odenthal	124	Jc	51.02N	7.07 E
Odenwald	120	Eg	49.40N	9.00 E
Oder [Eur.]	110	He	53.40N	14.33 E
Oder [F.R.G.]	120	Ge	51.40N	10.02 E
Oderbruch	120	Kd	52.40N	14.15 E
Oderské vrchy	120	Ng	49.40N	17.45 E
Oderzo	128	Ge	45.47N	12.29 E
Ödeshög	114	Dg	58.14N	14.39 E
Odessa [Tx.-U.S.]	176	If	31.51N	102.22W
Odessa [Ukr.-U.S.S.R.]	112	Jf	46.28N	30.44 E
Odessa [Wa.-U.S.]	188	Fc	47.20N	118.41W
Odesskaja oblast [3]	136	Df	46.45N	30.30 E
Odet	122	Bg	47.52N	4.06W
Odiel	126	Fg	37.10N	6.54W
Odienné	160	Gh	9.30N	7.34W
Odienné [3]	166	Dd	9.45N	7.45W
Odivelas	126	Df	38.12N	8.18W
Ödmården	116	Gc	61.05N	16.40 E
Odobeşti	130	Kd	45.46N	27.03 E
Ŏdŏngk	148	Kf	11.48N	104.45 E
Odoorn	124	Ib	52.51N	6.50 E
Odorheiu Secuiesc	130	Ic	46.18N	25.18 E
Ōdose-Zaki	156a	Bc	40.46N	140.03 E
Odra	110	He	53.40N	14.33 E
Ŏdwēyne	168	Hd	9.23N	45.04 E
Odžaci	130	Cd	45.31N	19.16 E
Odžak	128	Me	45.01N	18.18 E
Odzi	172	Ec	19.47S	32.24 E
Oeiras	126	Eg	37.38N	7.40W
Oeiras [Braz.]	202	Je	7.01S	42.08W
Oeiras [Port.]	126	Cf	38.41N	9.19W
Oelde	124	Kc	51.49N	8.09 E
Oelerbeek	124	Ib	52.21N	6.38 E
Oelrichs	186	Ee	43.15N	103.10W
Oelsnitz	120	If	50.25N	12.10 E
Oelwein	186	Ke	42.41N	91.55W
Oeno Island	208	Ng	23.56S	130.44W
Oer-Erkenschwick	124	Jc	51.38N	7.15 E
Oeste, Punta-	197a	Ab	18.05N	67.57W
Oeventrop, Arnsberg-	124	Kc	51.24N	8.08 E
Ōe-Yama	156	Dd	35.27N	135.06 E
Of	146	Ib	40.57N	40.16 E
O'Fallon Creek	188	Mc	46.50N	105.09W
Ofanto	128	Ki	41.21N	16.13 E
Ofaqim	146	Fg	31.17N	34.37 E
Offa	166	Fd	8.09N	4.43 E
Offaly/Uíbh Fhailí [2]	118	Fh	53.20N	7.30W
Offenbach am Main	120	Ef	50.06N	8.46 E
Offenbach-Hundheim	124	Je	49.37N	7.33 E
Offenburg	120	Dh	48.29N	7.56 E
Offida	128	Hh	42.56N	13.41 E
Offoué	170	Bc	0.04S	11.44 E
Offranville	124	De	49.52N	1.03 E
Oficina Pedro de Valdivia	206	Gb	22.37S	69.38W
Ofidhoúsa	130	Jm	36.33N	26.09 E
Ofolanga	221b	Ba	19.36S	174.27W
Ofu	221c	Db	14.11S	169.42W
Ōfunato	154	Pe	39.04N	141.43 E
Oga	154	Oe	40.43N	141.18 E
Ogachi	156	Gb	39.05N	140.28 E
Ogaden	158	Lh	7.30N	45.00 E
Oga-Hantō	154	Oe	39.55N	139.50 E
Ōgaki	154	Ng	35.21N	136.37 E
Ogallala	182	Gc	41.08N	101.43W
Ogasawara-Shotō = Bonin Islands (EN)	140	Qg	27.00N	142.10 E
Ogawara-Ko	156a	Bc	40.45N	141.20 E
Ogbomosho	160	Hh	8.08N	4.16 E
Ogden	176	He	41.14N	111.58W
Ogdensburg	184	Jc	44.42N	75.31W
Ogeechee River	184	Gj	31.51N	81.06W
Oghāsh	146	Lc	39.10N	46.55 E
Ogi	156	Fc	37.50N	138.16 E
Ogilvie Mountains	180	Dc	65.00N	140.00W
Ogi-no-Sen	156	Dd	35.26N	134.26 E
Oginski kanal	132	Dc	52.20N	25.55 E
Oglanly	132	Sj	39.50N	54.33 E
Oglethorpe	184	Ei	31.28N	84.04W
Ogliastra	128	Dk	39.55N	9.35 E
Oglio	128	Ee	45.02N	10.39 E
Ognon	122	Lg	47.20N	5.29 E
Ogo	168	Hd	9.48N	45.35 E
Ogoamas, Bulu-	150	Hf	0.40N	120.12 E
Ogodža	138	If	52.48N	132.40 E
Ogoja	166	Gd	6.40N	8.48 E
Ogoki	180	If	51.38N	85.56W
Ogoki	180	If	51.38N	85.55W
Ogoki Reservoir	180	If	51.35N	86.00W
Ogonëk	138	Ie	59.40N	138.01 E
Ogooué	158	Hi	0.49S	9.00 E
Ogooué-Ivindo [3]	170	Bb	0.30N	13.00 E
Ogooué-Lolo [3]	170	Bc	1.00S	13.00 E
Ogooué-Maritime [3]	170	Ac	2.00S	9.30 E
Ogōri [Jap.]	156	Bd	34.06N	131.25 E
Ogōri [Jap.]	156	Be	33.24N	130.34 E
Ogosta	130	Gf	43.45N	23.51 E
Ogražden	130	Fh	41.30N	22.55 E
Ogre	114	Fh	56.50N	24.39 E
Ogre	116	Kh	56.42N	24.33 E
Ogulin	128	Je	45.16N	15.14 E
Ogun [2]	166	Fd	7.00N	3.40 E
Oguni [Jap.]	156	Fb	38.04N	139.45 E
Oguni [Jap.]	156	Be	33.07N	131.04 E
Ogurčinski, ostrov-	132	Rj	38.55N	53.05 E
Oğuzeli	146	Gd	37.00N	37.30 E
Oha	142	Qd	53.34N	142.56 E
Ohai	218	Bf	45.56S	167.57 E
Ohakune	218	Fc	39.25S	175.25 E
Ohanet	162	Id	28.40N	8.50 E
Ohansk	134	Gh	57.42N	55.25 E
Ōhara	156	Gd	35.15N	140.23 E
Ōhasama	156	Gb	39.28N	141.17 E
Ōhata	154	Pd	41.24N	141.10 E
Ohau, Lake-	218	Cf	44.15S	169.50 E
Ohey	124	Hd	50.26N	5.08 E
O'Higgins, Cabo-	221d	Bb	27.05S	109.15W
Ohio [2]	182	Kc	40.15N	82.45W
Ohio	174	Kf	36.59N	89.08W
Ohm	120	Ef	50.51N	8.48 E
Ohmberge	120	Ge	51.30N	10.28 E
'Ohonua	221b	Bc	21.20S	174.57W
Ohopoho	160	Ij	18.03S	13.45 E
Ohota	138	Je	59.20N	143.05 E
Ohotsk	142	Qd	59.23N	143.18 E
Ohotskoje more = Okhotsk, Sea of- (EN)	140	Qd	53.00N	150.00 E
Ohře	120	Kf	50.32N	14.08 E
Ohre	120	Hd	52.18N	11.47 E
Ohrid	130	Dh	41.07N	20.48 E
Ohrid, Lake- (EN) = Ohridsko jezero	110	Ig	41.00N	20.45 E
Ohrid, Lake- (EN) = Ohrit, Liqen i-	110	Ig	41.00N	20.45 E
Ohridsko jezero = Ohrid, Lake- (EN)	110	Ig	41.00N	20.45 E
Öhringen	120	Fg	49.12N	9.30 E
Ohrit, Liqen i- = Ohrid, Lake- (EN)	110	Ig	41.00N	20.45 E
Ohura	218	Fc	38.51S	174.59 E
Oiapoque	202	Hc	3.50N	51.50W
Oich	118	Id	57.10N	4.45W
Oi-Gawa	156	Fd	34.46N	138.17 E
Oil City	184	He	41.26N	79.44W
Oildale	188	Fi	35.25N	119.01W
Oiléan Baoi/Dursey	118	Cj	51.36N	10.12W
Oileán Ciarraí/Castleisland	118	Di	52.14N	9.27W
Oiléan Coarach/Mutton	118	Di	52.49N	9.31W
Oiléan Mhic Aodha/Masee, Island-	118	Hg	54.50N	5.50W
Oinoúsai	130	Jk	38.32N	26.13 E
Oinoúsai, Nísoi-	130	Em	36.45N	21.43 E
Oirschot	124	Hc	51.30N	5.18 E
Oisans	122	Mi	45.02N	6.02 E
Oise [3]	122	Ie	49.30N	2.30 E
Oise	122	Ie	49.00N	2.04 E
Oise à l'Aisne, Canal de l'-	122	Je	49.36N	3.11 E
Oisemont	124	De	49.57N	1.46 E
Oissel	124	De	49.20N	1.06 E
Oisterwijk	124	Hc	51.35N	5.11 E
Oistins	197q	Ab	13.04N	59.32W
Oistins Bay	197q	Ab	13.03N	59.33W
Ōita	152	Ne	33.14N	131.36 E
Ōita Ken [2]	154	Kh	33.15N	131.20 E
Oíti Óros	130	Fk	38.49N	22.17 E
Oituz, Pasul-	130	Jc	46.03N	26.23 E
Oiwake	156a	Bb	42.52N	141.48 E
Ojat	114	Hf	60.31N	33.05 E
Öje	116	Ed	60.49N	13.51 E
Ojika-Jima	156	Ae	33.13N	129.03 E
O-Jima	156	Be	34.00N	130.45 E
Ojinaga	190	Dc	29.34N	104.25W
Ojiya	154	Of	37.18N	138.48 E
Ojmjakon	138	Jd	63.28N	142.49 E
Ojo Caliente	192	Fb	30.25N	106.33W
Ojocaliente	192	Hf	22.34N	102.15W
Ojos del Salado, Nevado-	198	Jh	27.06S	68.32W
Ojos Negros	126	Kd	40.44N	1.30W
Ojtal	136	Hg	42.54N	73.21 E
Ojuelos de Jalisco	192	Ig	21.50N	101.35W
Oka [R.S.F.S.R.]	140	Md	55.00N	102.03 E
Oka [U.S.S.R.]	110	Kd	56.20N	43.59 E
Okaba	150	Kh	8.06S	139.42 E
Okahandja	160	Ik	21.59S	16.58 E
Okahandja [3]	172	Bd	21.30S	17.30 E
Okahukura	218	Fc	38.47S	175.14 E
Okaihau	218	Ea	35.19S	173.46 E
Okąk Islands	180	Le	57.28N	61.48W
Okanagan Lake	180	Fg	49.55N	119.30W
Okano	170	Bc	0.05S	10.57 E
Okanogan River	182	Db	48.06N	119.43W
Okapa	212	Ja	6.31S	145.32 E
Okāra	148	Eb	30.49N	73.27 E
Okarem	136	Fh	38.07N	54.05 E
Okato	218	Ec	39.12S	173.53 E
Okaukuejo	172	Bc	19.10S	15.54 E
Okavango [3]	172	Cc	18.00S	21.00 E
Okavango	158	Jj	18.53N	22.24 E
Okavango Swamp	158	Jj	19.30S	23.00 E
Ōkawa	156	Be	33.12N	130.23 E
Okaya	154	Of	36.03N	138.03 E
Okayama	142	Pf	34.39N	133.55 E
Okayama Ken [2]	154	Lg	34.50N	133.45 E
Okazaki	154	Ng	34.57N	137.10 E
Okeechobee	184	Gl	27.15N	80.50W
Okeechobee, Lake-	174	Kg	26.55N	80.45W
Okefenokee Swamp	184	Fj	30.42N	82.20W
Okehampton	118	Jk	50.44N	4.00W
Okene	166	Gd	7.33N	6.14 E
Oker	120	Gd	52.30N	10.22 E
Oketo	156a	Cb	43.41N	143.32 E
Okha	148	Dd	22.27N	69.04 E
Ókhi Óros	130	Hk	38.04N	24.28 E
Okhotsk, Sea of- (EN) = Hok-Kai	140	Qd	53.00N	150.00 E
Okhotsk, Sea of- (EN) = Ohotskoje more	140	Qd	53.00N	150.00 E
Okhthonia, Ákra-	130	Hk	38.32N	24.14 E
Oki-Daitō-Jima	152	Ng	24.30N	131.00 E
Okiep	172	Be	29.39S	17.53 E
Okinawa	156b	Ab	26.20N	127.47 E
Okinawa Islands (EN) = Okinawa-Shotō	140	Og	26.40N	128.00 E
Okinawa-Jima	152	Mf	26.40N	128.20 E
Okinawa Ken [2]	156b	Ab	26.31N	127.59 E
Okinawa-Shotō = Okinawa Islands (EN)	140	Og	26.40N	128.00 E
Okinoerabu-Jima	152	Mf	27.20N	128.35 E
Okino-Shima [Jap.]	156	Ce	32.44N	132.33 E
Okino-Shima [Jap.]	156	Bd	34.15N	130.08 E
Okino-Tori-Shima	140	Pg	20.25N	136.00 E
Oki Ridge (EN)	154	Mf	37.00N	135.00 E
Oki-Shotō	152	Nd	36.00N	132.50 E
Okitipupa	166	Fd	6.30N	4.48 E
Oki Trench (EN)	156	Dc	37.00N	135.30 E
Oklahoma [2]	182	Hd	35.30N	98.00W
Oklahoma City	176	Jf	35.28N	97.32W
Okmulgee	186	Ii	35.37N	95.58W
Oknica	130	Ka	48.22N	27.24 E
Oko	168	Fa	22.20N	35.56 E
Okob	170	Fb	2.06N	33.53 E
Okolo	170	Fb	2.40N	31.09 E
Okolona	184	Ef	38.08N	85.41W
Okondja	170	Bc	0.41S	13.47 E
Okonek	120	Mc	53.33N	16.50 E
Okoppe	154	Qb	44.28N	143.08 E
Okotoks	188	Ia	50.44N	113.59W
Okoyo	170	Cc	1.28S	15.04 E
Okrzeika	120	Re	51.40N	21.30 E
Øksfjord	114	Fa	70.14N	22.22 E
Oksino	134	Fc	67.33N	52.10 E
Okstindane	110	Hb	66.02N	14.10 E
Oktemberjan	132	Ni	40.09N	44.03 E
Oktjabrsk [Kaz.-U.S.S.R.]	112	Lf	48.40N	57.11 E
Oktjabrsk [R.S.F.S.R.]	114	Lj	53.13N	48.40 E
Oktjabrski [Bye.-U.S.S.R.]	132	Fc	52.38N	28.54 E
Oktjabrski [Kaz.-U.S.S.R.]	134	Kj	52.37N	62.43 E
Oktjabrski [R.S.F.S.R.]	134	Hh	56.31N	57.12 E
Oktjabrski [R.S.F.S.R.]	138	Ee	56.05N	99.25 E
Oktjabrski [R.S.F.S.R.]	138	Hf	53.00N	128.42 E
Oktjabrski [R.S.F.S.R.]	136	Fe	54.31N	53.28 E
Oktjabrski [R.S.F.S.R.]	114	Kf	61.05N	43.08 E
Oktjabrski [R.S.F.S.R.]	138	Kf	52.38N	156.15 E
Oktjabrski [R.S.F.S.R.]	132	Mf	47.56N	43.38 E
Oktjabrskoje	136	Gc	62.28N	66.01 E
Oktjabrskoj Revoljuci, ostrov- = October Revolution Island (EN)	140	Lb	79.30N	97.00 E
Oku	156b	Bb	26.50N	128.17 E
Ōkuchi	154	Kh	32.04N	130.37 E
Okulovka	114	Hg	58.24N	33.18 E
Okushiri	154	Oc	42.09N	139.29 E
Okushiri-Kaikyō	156a	Ab	42.15N	139.40 E
Okushiri-Tō	152	Oc	42.10N	139.25 E
Okuta	166	Fd	9.13N	3.11 E
Oku Tango-Hantō	156	Dd	35.40N	135.10 E
Okwa	158	Jk	22.26S	22.58 E
Ola	138	Ke	59.37N	151.20 E
Ólafsfjördur	114a	Ba	66.04N	18.39W
Ólafsvík	114a	Ab	64.53N	23.43W
Ola Grande, Punta-	197a	Bc	17.55N	66.08W
Olaiņe/Olajne	114	Fh	56.49N	23.59 E
Olajne/Olaiņe	114	Fh	56.49N	23.59 E
Olancha	188	Gh	36.17N	117.59W
Olanchito	194	Df	15.30N	86.35W
Olancho [3]	194	Ef	14.45N	86.00W
Öland	110	Hd	56.45N	16.40 E
Ölands norra udde	116	Gg	57.22N	17.05 E
Ölands södra grund	116	Gh	55.40N	17.25 E
Ölands södra udde	116	Gh	56.11N	16.24 E
Olanga	114	Hc	66.08N	30.38 E
Olathe	186	Ig	38.53N	94.49W
Olavarría	200	Ji	36.53S	60.20W
Oława	120	Nf	50.57N	17.17 E
Oława	120	Nf	50.57N	17.17 E
Olbernhau	120	Jf	50.40N	13.20 E
Olbia	112	Gg	40.55N	9.31 E
Olbia, Golfo di-	128	Dj	40.55N	9.40 E
Old Bahama Channel	194	Ib	22.30N	78.05W
Old Bahama Channel (EN) = Bahamas, Canal Viejo de-	194	Ib	22.30N	78.05W
Old Castile (EN) = Castilla la Vieja	126	Ic	41.30N	4.00W
Old Crow	176	Fc	67.35N	139.50W
Oldeani	170	Gc	3.21S	35.33 E
Oldebroek	124	Hb	52.26N	5.53 E
Oldenburg	120	Ec	53.10N	8.12 E
Oldenburg in Holstein	120	Gb	54.18N	10.53 E
Oldenzaal	122	Mb	52.19N	6.56 E
Old Faithful Geyser	188	Jd	44.30N	110.45W
Old Fletton	124	Bb	52.34N	0.15W
Oldham	118	Kh	53.33N	2.07W
Old Hickory Lake	184	Dg	36.18N	86.30W
Oldman River	188	Jb	49.56N	111.42W
Old Marsh Bed	212	Gd	20.55S	130.30 E
Old Mkushi	170	Ee	14.22S	29.22 E
Old Road	197d	Bb	17.01N	61.50W
Old Road Town	197c	Ab	17.19N	62.48W
Olds	180	Gf	51.47N	114.06W
Old Town	184	Mc	44.56N	68.39W
Old Wives Lake	188	Ma	50.06N	106.00W
Olean	184	Hd	42.05N	78.26W
Olecko	120	Sb	54.03N	22.30 E
Olëkma	140	Oc	60.22N	120.42 E
Olëkminsk	142	Oc	60.30N	120.15 E
Olëkminski stanovik	138	Gf	54.00N	119.00 E
Ølen	114	Ag	59.36N	5.48 E
Olenegorsk	136	Db	68.10N	33.13 E
Olenëk	140	Nb	73.00N	119.55 E
Olenëkski zaliv	138	Hb	73.10N	121.00 E
Olenica	114	Ic	66.29N	35.19 E
Olenj, ostrov-	138	Cb	72.25N	77.45 E
Olenty	132	Re	49.45N	52.10 E
Oléron, Ile d'-	110	Ff	45.56N	1.18W
Olesko	120	Ug	49.53N	24.58 E
Oleśnica	120	Ne	51.13N	17.23 E
Olesno	120	Of	50.53N	18.25 E
Olevsk	132	Ed	51.13N	27.41 E
Olga	138	Ih	43.46N	135.21 E
Olga, Mount-	212	Ge	25.19S	130.46 E
Olgastretet	179	Oc	78.30N	24.00 E
Ølgod	116	Ci	55.49N	8.37 E
Olhão	126	Eg	37.02N	7.50W
Olhovatka	132	Kd	50.17N	39.17 E
Oli	166	Fd	9.40N	4.29 E
Oliana	126	Nb	42.04N	1.19 E
Olib	128	If	44.23N	14.47 E
Oliena	128	Dj	40.16N	9.24 E
Olifantshoek	172	Ce	27.57S	22.42 E
Olifants River [Afr.]	158	Kk	24.03S	32.40 E
Olifants River [Nam.]	172	Be	25.30S	19.30 E
Olimarao Atoll	208	Fd	7.42N	145.53 E
Olimbía	130	El	37.39N	21.38 E
Ólimbos	130	Kn	35.44N	27.13 E
Ólimbos, Óros- = Olympus, Mount- (EN)	110	Ig	40.05N	22.21 E
Ólimbos Óros [Grc.]	130	Jj	39.05N	26.20 E
Olímpia	204	He	20.44S	48.54W
Olinda	202	Le	8.01S	34.51W
Olite	126	Kb	42.29N	1.39W
Oliva [Arg.]	206	Hd	32.03S	63.34W
Oliva [Sp.]	126	Lf	38.55N	0.07W
Oliva, Monasterio de la-	126	Kb	42.20N	1.25W
Oliva de la Frontera	126	Ff	38.16N	6.55W
Oliveira	204	Je	20.41S	44.49W
Oliveira dos Brejinhos	202	Jf	12.19S	42.54W
Olivença	172	Fb	11.46S	35.13 E
Olivenza	126	Ef	38.41N	7.06W
Oliver	188	Fb	49.11N	119.33W
Olivet	122	Hg	47.52N	1.54 E
Olivia	186	Id	44.46N	94.59W
Olja	132	Og	45.47N	47.35 E
Olji Moron He	154	Fb	44.16N	121.42 E
Oljutorski, mys-	140	Td	59.55N	170.25 E
Oljutorski zaliv	138	Ld	60.00N	168.00 E
Olkusz	120	Pf	50.17N	19.35 E
Ollagüe	200	Jh	21.08S	68.45W
Ollan	220d	Bb	7.14N	151.38 E
Ollerton	124	Aa	53.13N	1.01W
Olmedo	126	Hc	41.17N	4.41W
Olmos	202	Ce	5.59S	79.46W
Olney [Eng.-U.K.]	124	Bb	52.09N	0.42W
Olney [Il.-U.S.]	186	Lg	38.44N	88.05W
Olney [Tx.-U.S.]	186	Gj	33.22N	98.45W
Oloči	138	Gf	51.20N	119.53 E
Olofström	114	Dh	56.16N	14.30 E
Oloitokitok	170	Gc	2.56S	37.30 E
Oloj	138	Kc	66.20N	159.29 E
Olojski hrebet	138	Lc	65.50N	162.30 E
Olombo	170	Cc	1.18S	15.53 E
Ólomburi	219a	Ec	8.59S	161.09 E
Olomouc	112	Hf	49.36N	17.16 E
Olona	128	De	45.06N	9.21 E
Olonec	136	Dc	61.01N	32.58 E
Olonešty	130	Mc	46.29N	29.52 E
Olongapo	142	Oh	14.50N	120.16 E
Oloron, Gave d'-	122	Ek	43.33N	1.05W
Oloron-Sainte-Marie	122	Fk	43.12N	0.36W
Olosega	221c	Db	14.11S	169.39W
Olot	126	Ob	42.11N	2.29 E
Olovjannaja	138	Gf	50.56N	115.35 E
Olovo	128	Mf	44.07N	18.35 E
Olpe	120	De	51.02N	7.51 E
Olpoy	219b	Cb	14.52S	166.33 E
Olroyd River	212	Ib	14.10S	141.50 E
Olsberg	124	Kc	51.21N	8.30 E
Olshammar	116	Ff	58.45N	14.48 E
Olst	124	Ib	52.20N	6.08 E
Olsztyn	112	Ie	53.48N	20.29 E
Olsztyn [2]	120	Qc	53.50N	20.30 E
Olsztynek	120	Qc	53.36N	20.17 E
Olt [2]	130	He	44.25N	24.30 E
Olt	110	If	43.43N	24.51 E
Oltedal	116	Bf	58.50N	6.02 E
Olten	128	Bc	47.22N	7.55 E
Olteni	130	Ie	44.11N	25.17 E
Oltenia	130	Ge	44.30N	23.30 E
Olteniţa	130	Je	44.05N	26.38 E
Olteţ	130	He	44.14N	24.27 E
Oltu	146	Ib	40.33N	41.59 E
Oluanpi	140	Og	21.54N	120.51 E
Olutanga	150	He	7.22N	122.52 E
Olvera	126	Gh	36.56N	5.16W
Olym	132	Kc	52.27N	38.05 E
Olympia	176	Ge	47.03N	122.53W
Olympic Mountains	188	Dc	47.50N	123.45W
Olympus, Mount- [U.S.]	174	Ge	47.48N	123.43W
Olympus, Mount- (EN) = Ólimbos, Óros-	110	Ig	40.05N	22.21 E
Om	138	Cf	54.59N	73.22 E
Ōma	156a	Bc	41.30N	140.55 E
Oma	134	Cc	66.45N	46.20 E
Ōmachi	154	Nf	36.30N	137.52 E
Omae-Zaki	156	Fd	34.36N	138.14 E
Ōmagari	154	Pe	39.27N	140.29 E
Omagh/An Omaigh	118	Fg	54.36N	7.18W
Omaha	176	Je	41.16N	95.57W
Omak	188	Fb	48.24N	119.31W
Omakau	218	Cf	45.06S	169.36 E
Omak Lake	188	Fb	48.16N	119.23W
Oman (EN) = 'Umān [1]	142	Hg	21.00N	57.00 E
Oman (EN) = 'Umān	140	Hg	22.10N	58.00 E
Oman, Gulf of- (EN) = 'Umān, Khalīj-	140	Hg	25.00N	58.00 E
Omarama	216	Ch	44.29S	169.58 E
Omar Gambon	168	He	3.10N	45.47 E
Omaru-Gawa	156	Be	32.07N	131.34 E
Omaruru	172	Bd	21.28S	15.56 E
Omaruru [3]	172	Bd	21.30S	15.00 E
Omatako	172	Bd	21.07S	16.43 E
Omatako, Omuramba-	158	Jj	17.57S	20.25 E
Omate	202	Dg	16.41S	70.59W
Ōma-Zaki	156a	Bc	41.32N	140.55 E
Ombai, Selat-	150	Hh	8.30S	125.00 E
Ombella-Mpoko [3]	168	Bd	5.00N	18.00 E
Omberg	116	Ff	58.20N	14.39 E
Ombo	116	Ae	59.15N	6.00 E
Omboué	170	Ac	1.34S	9.15 E
Ombrone	128	Fh	42.39N	11.01 E
Ombu	152	Ee	31.18N	86.33 E
Omčak	138	Jd	61.38N	147.55 E
Omdurman (EN) = Umm Durmān	160	Kg	15.38N	32.30 E
Ōme	156	Fd	35.47N	139.15 E
Omegna	128	Ce	45.53N	8.24 E
Omeo	212	Jg	37.06S	147.36 E
Ömerköy	130	Lj	39.50N	28.04 E
Ometepe, Isla de-	190	Gf	11.30N	85.35W
Ometepec	190	Ee	16.41N	98.25W
Omhajer	168	Fc	14.19N	36.40 E
Ōmihachiman	156	Ed	35.08N	136.05 E
Omihi	218	Ee	43.01S	172.51 E
Omineca	180	Fe	56.05N	124.05W
Omineca Mountains	180	Ee	56.35N	125.55W
Omiš	128	Kg	43.27N	16.42 E
Ōmi-Shima [Jap.]	156	Cd	34.15N	133.00 E
Ōmi-Shima [Jap.]	156	Bd	34.25N	131.15 E
Omitara	172	Bd	22.18S	18.01 E
Ōmiya	152	Od	35.54N	139.38 E
Ommanney Bay	180	Hb	73.00N	101.00W
Omme Å	116	Ci	55.55N	8.25 E
Ommen	124	Ib	52.31N	6.25 E
Omø	116	Di	55.10N	11.10 E
Omo	158	Kh	4.32N	36.04 E
Omoa, Bahía de-	194	Cf	15.50N	88.10W
Omodeo, Lago-	128	Cj	40.10N	8.55 E
Omoloj	138	Ib	71.08N	132.01 E
Omolon	138	Lc	65.12N	160.27 E
Omolon	140	Rc	68.42N	158.36 E
Omono-Gawa	156	Gb	39.44N	140.04 E
Omont	124	Ge	49.36N	4.44 E
Omoto-Gawa	156	Gb	39.51N	141.58 E
Omsk	142	Jd	55.00N	73.24 E
Omskaja oblast [3]	136	Hd	56.00N	72.30 E
Omsukčan	138	Kd	62.27N	155.50 E
Omsukčanski hrebet	138	Kd	63.00N	155.10 E
Ōmu	154	Qb	44.34N	142.58 E
Omu, Vîrful-	130	Id	45.26N	25.25 E
Omulew	120	Rc	53.05N	21.32 E
Ōmura	154	Jh	32.54N	129.57 E
Ōmura-Wan	156	Ae	33.00N	129.50 E
Omurtag	130	Jf	43.06N	26.25 E
Ōmuta	154	Kh	33.02N	130.27 E
Omutinski	136	Gd	56.31N	67.45 E
Omutninsk	136	Fd	58.43N	52.12 E
Oña	126	Ib	42.44N	3.24W
Onagawa	156	Gb	38.26N	141.27 E
Onakayale	172	Bc	17.30S	15.01 E
Onaman Lake	186	Ma	50.00N	87.29W
Onamia	186	Jc	46.04N	93.40W
Onamue	220d	Bb	7.21N	151.31 E
Onaping Lake	184	Gb	46.57N	81.30W
Onatchiway, Lac-	184	La	49.03N	71.03W
Onawa	186	He	42.02N	96.06W
Onch'ŏn	154	He	38.49N	125.13 E
Oncócua	170	Bf	16.40S	13.24 E
Onda	126	Le	39.58N	0.15W
Ondangua	160	Ij	17.55S	16.00 E
Ondarroa / Ondárroa	126	Ja	43.19N	2.25W
Ondárroa / Ondarroa	126	Ja	43.19N	2.25W
Ondava	120	Rh	48.27N	21.48 E
Ondjiva	160	Ij	17.03S	15.47 E
Ondo [2]	166	Gd	7.00N	5.00 E
Ondo [Jap.]	156	Cd	34.12N	132.32 E
Ondo [Nig.]	166	Fd	7.06N	4.50 E
Ondor Sum	154	Bc	42.30N	113.00 E
Ondozero, ozero-	114	He	63.40N	33.15 E
One and Half Degree Channel	140	Ji	1.30N	73.10 E
Oneata	219d	Cc	18.27S	178.29W
Oneata Passage	219d	Cc	18.32S	178.28W
Onega	112	Jc	63.57N	38.05 E
Onega	110	Jc	63.58N	37.55 E
Onega, Lake- (EN) = Onežskoje ozero	110	Jc	61.30N	35.45 E
Onega Peninsula (EN) = Onežski poluostrov	110	Jc	64.35N	38.00 E
One Hundred Mile House	180	Ff	51.38N	121.16W
Oneida	184	Jd	43.04N	75.40W
Oneida Lake	184	Jd	43.13N	76.00W
O'Neil	182	Hc	42.27N	98.39W
Ōnejime	156	Bf	31.14N	130.47 E
Onekotan, ostrov-	140	Re	49.25N	154.45 E
Oneonta [Al.-U.S.]	184	Di	33.57N	86.29W
Oneonta [N.Y.-U.S.]	184	Jd	42.28N	75.04W
Oneroa	220p	Cb	21.15S	159.43W
Onežskaja guba	110	Jc	64.20N	36.30 E
Onežski poluostrov = Onega Peninsula (EN)	110	Jc	64.35N	38.00 E
Onežskoje ozero = Onega, Lake- (EN)	110	Jc	61.30N	35.45 E
Ongea Levu	219d	Cc	19.08S	178.24W
Ongijn-Gol	152	Hc	44.30N	103.40 E
Ongjin	152	Md	37.56N	125.22 E
Ongniud Qi (Wudan)	152	Kc	42.58N	119.01 E
Ongole	148	Ge	15.30N	80.03 E
Ongon	152	Jb	45.49N	113.08 E
Onhaye	124	Gd	50.15N	4.50 E
Oni	132	Mh	42.35N	43.27 E
Onigajō-Yama	156	Ce	33.07N	132.41 E
Onilany	158	Lk	23.34S	43.45 E
Onishibetsu	156a	Ca	45.21N	142.06 E
Onitsha	160	Hh	6.10N	6.47 E
Ōno	154	Ng	35.59N	136.29 E
Ōno	156	Cd	34.18N	132.17 E
Ono	156	Dd	34.51N	134.57 E
Ono	219d	Bc	18.54S	178.29 E
Onoda	156	Be	33.59N	131.11 E
Ōno-Kawa	156	Be	33.15N	131.43 E
Ōnohara-Jima	156	Fd	34.02N	139.23 E
Onohoj	138	Ff	51.55N	108.01 E

Index Symbols

[1] Independent Nation
[2] State, Region
[3] District, County
[4] Municipality
[5] Colony, Dependency
Continent
Physical Region
Historical or Cultural Region
Mount, Mountain
Volcano
Hill
Mountains, Mountain Range
Hills, Escarpment
Plateau, Upland
Pass, Gap
Plain, Lowland
Delta
Salt Flat
Valley, Canyon
Crater, Cave
Karst Features
Depression
Polder
Desert, Dunes
Forest, Woods
Heath, Steppe
Oasis
Cape, Point
Coast, Beach
Cliff
Peninsula
Isthmus
Sandbank
Island
Atoll
Rock, Reef
Islands, Archipelago
Rocks, Reefs
Coral Reef
Well, Spring
Geyser
River, Stream
Waterfall, Rapids
River Mouth, Estuary
Lake
Salt Lake
Intermittent Lake
Reservoir
Swamp, Pond
Canal
Glacier
Ice Shelf, Pack Ice
Ocean
Sea
Gulf, Bay
Strait, Fjord
Lagoon
Bank
Seamount
Tablemount
Ridge
Shelf
Basin
Escarpment, Sea Scarp
Fracture
Trench, Abyss
National Park, Reserve
Point of Interest
Recreation Site
Cave, Cavern
Historic Site
Ruins
Wall, Walls
Church, Abbey
Temple
Scientific Station
Railway station
Airport
Port
Military installation
Lighthouse
Mine
Tunnel
Dam, Bridge

Ono-i-Lau Islands 208 Jg 20.39S 178.42W
Onojō 156 Be 33.34N 130.29 E
Onomichi 154 Lg 34.25N 133.12 E
Onon 140 Nd 51.42N 115.50 E
Onoto 196 Dh 9.36N 65.12W
Onotoa Atoll 208 Ie 1.52S 175.34 E
Ons, Isla de- 126 Db 42.23N 8.56W
Onsala 114 Ch 57.25N 12.01 E
Onseepkans 172 Be 28.45S 19.17 E
Onslow 210 Cg 21.39S 115.06 E
Onslow Bay 182 Le 34.20N 77.20W
On-Take 156 Bf 31.35N 130.39 E
Ontake-San 156 Ed 35.53N 137.29 E
Ontario [2] 180 If 50.00N 86.00W
Ontario [Ca.-U.S.] 188 Gi 34.04N 117.39W
Ontario [Or.-U.S.] 182 Dc 44.02N 116.58W
Ontario, Lake- 174 Le 43.40N 78.00W
Ontario Peninsula 174 Ke 43.50N 81.00W
Onteniente/Ontinyent 126 Lf 38.49N 0.37W
Ontinyent/Onteniente 126 Lf 38.49N 0.37W
Ontojärvi 114 Gd 64.08N 29.09 E
Ontonagon 184 Cb 46.52N 89.19W
Ontong Java Atoll 208 Ge 5.20S 159.30 E
Ō-Numa 156a Bc 41.59N 140.41 E
Oodnadatta 210 Eg 27.33S 135.28 E
Ooidonk 124 Fc 51.01N 3.35 E
Ookala 221a Fc 20.01N 155.17W
Ooldea 210 Eh 30.27S 131.50 E
Oologah Lake 186 Ih 36.39N 95.36W
Ooltgensplaat, Oostflakkee- 124 Gc 51.41N 4.21 E
Oostburg 124 Fc 51.20N 3.30 E
Oostelijk Flevoland 124 Hb 52.30N 5.40 E
Oostende/Ostende 122 Ic 51.14N 2.55 E
Oosterhout 122 Kc 51.38N 4.51 E
Oosterschelde=East Schelde (EN) 122 Jc 51.30N 4.00 E
Oosterwolde, Ooststellingwerf- 124 Ha 53.00N 6.18 E
Oosterzele 124 Fd 50.57N 3.48 E
Oostflakkee 124 Gc 51.41N 4.21 E
Oostflakkee-Ooltgensplaat 124 Gc 51.41N 4.21 E
Oostkamp 124 Fc 51.09N 3.14 E
Oost-Souburg, Vlissingen- 124 Fc 51.28N 3.36 E
Ooststellingwerf 124 Ib 53.00N 6.18 E
Ooststellingwerf-Oosterwolde 124 Ha 53.00N 6.18 E
Oost Vieland, Vieland- 124 Ha 53.17N 5.06 E
Oost-Vlaanderen = Flanders, East- (EN) [3] 124 Fc 51.00N 3.40 E
Ootmarsum 124 Ib 52.25N 6.54 E
Opala 170 Dc 0.37S 24.21 E
Opalenica 120 Md 52.19N 16.23 E
Opanake 148 Gg 6.36N 80.37 E
Opari 168 Ee 3.56N 32.03 E
Oparino 114 Lg 59.53N 48.25 E
Opasatika 184 Fa 49.31N 82.58W
Opasatika Lake 184 Fa 49.06N 83.08W
Opasatika River 184 Fa 50.15N 82.25W
Opatija 128 Ie 45.20N 14.19 E
Opatów 120 Rf 50.49N 21.26 E
Opatówka 120 Rf 50.42N 21.50 E
Opava 120 Ng 49.57N 17.54 E
Opava 120 Og 49.51N 18.17 E
Opelika 182 Je 32.39N 85.23W
Opelousas 186 Jk 30.32N 92.05W
Opémisca, Lac- 184 Ja 49.58N 74.57W
Opheim 188 Lb 48.51N 106.24W
Ophir 178 Hd 63.10N 156.31W
Ophthalmia Range 212 Dd 23.15S 119.30 E
Opienge 170 Eb 0.12N 27.30 E
Opihikao 221a Gd 19.26N 154.53W
Opinaca 180 Jf 52.14N 78.02W
Opiscotéo, Lac- 180 Kf 53.09N 68.10W
Opladen, Leverkusen- 120 De 51.04N 7.01 E
Opobo 166 Ge 4.34N 7.27 E
Opočka 136 Cd 56.42N 28.41 E
Opoczno 120 Qe 51.23N 20.17 E
Opole 120 Nf 50.41N 17.55 E
Opole [2] 120 Nf 50.40N 17.55 E
Opole Lubelskie 120 Re 51.09N 21.58 E
Oporny 136 Ff 46.13N 54.29 E
Opotiki 218 Gc 38.01S 177.17 E
Opp 184 Dj 31.17N 86.22W
Oppa-Wan 156 Gb 38.35N 141.30 E
Oppdal 114 Be 62.36N 9.40 E
Oppenheim 120 Eg 49.51N 8.21 E
Oppland [2] 114 Bf 61.10N 9.40 E
Opportunity 188 Gc 47.39N 117.15W
Opsa 116 Li 55.31N 26.54 E
Opsterland 124 Ia 53.03N 6.04 E
Opsterland-Beetsterzwaag 124 Ia 53.03N 6.04 E
Opua 216 Dg 35.18S 174.07 E
Opunake 218 Ec 39.27S 173.51 E
Oputo 192 Eb 30.03N 109.20W
Oquossoc 184 Lc 45.04N 70.44W
Or 132 Ud 51.12N 58.33 E
Ōra 164 Cd 28.20N 19.35 E
Oradea 112 If 47.04N 21.56 E
Orahovac 130 Dg 42.24N 20.40 E
Orahovica 128 Le 45.32N 17.53 E
Orai 148 Fc 25.59N 79.28 E
Oraibi Wash 188 Ji 35.26N 110.49W
Oran 160 Ge 35.42N 0.38W
Oran [3] 162 Gb 36.00N 0.35W
Orange [Austl.] 210 Fh 33.17S 149.06 E
Orange [Fr.] 122 Kj 44.08N 4.48 E
Orange [Tx.-U.S.] 182 Ie 30.01N 93.44W
Orange [Va.-U.S.] 184 Hf 38.14N 78.07W
Orange/Oranje 158 Ik 28.38N 16.27 E
Orange, Cabo- 198 Ke 4.24N 51.33W
Orangeburg 182 Ke 33.30N 80.52W
Orange Free State/Oranje Vrystaat [2] 172 De 29.00S 26.00 E
Orange Lake 184 Fk 29.25N 82.13W
Orange Park 184 Gj 30.10N 81.42W
Orangeville 184 Gd 43.55N 80.06W
Orange Walk 190 Ge 18.06N 88.33W
Orange Walk [3] 194 Ce 17.44N 88.40W
Orango 158 Fg 11.05N 16.08W
Oranienburg 120 Jd 52.45N 13.14 E
Oranje/Orange 158 Ik 28.38N 16.27 E
Oranje Gebergte 202 Hc 3.00N 55.00W
Oranjemund 172 Be 28.38S 16.24 E
Oranjestad 202 Da 12.33N 70.06W
Oranje Vrystaat/Orange Free State [2] 172 De 29.00S 26.00 E
Oranžerei 132 Og 45.50N 47.36 E
Orapa 172 Dd 21.16S 25.22 E
Orăștie 130 Gd 45.50N 23.12 E
Orava 120 Pg 49.08N 19.10 E
Oravița 130 Ed 45.02N 21.42 E
Orayská Priehradni Nádrž 120 Pg 49.20N 19.35 E
Orb 122 Jk 43.15N 3.18 E
Orba 128 Cf 44.53N 8.37 E
Orba Co 152 De 34.33N 81.06 E
Ørbæk 116 Di 55.16N 10.41 E
Orbec 124 Ce 49.01N 0.25 E
Orbetello 128 Fh 42.27N 11.13 E
Orbetello, Laguna di- 128 Fh 42.25N 11.15 E
Órbigo 126 Gc 41.58N 5.40W
Orbiquet 124 Ce 49.09N 0.14 E
Orbost 212 Jg 37.42S 148.27 E
Örbyhus 116 Gd 60.14N 17.42 E
Órcadas 222 Re 60.40S 44.30W
Orcas Island 188 Db 48.39N 122.55W
Orchies 124 Fd 50.28N 3.14 E
Orchon→Orhon 140 Md 50.21N 106.05 E
Orcia 128 Fh 42.58N 11.21 E
Orco 128 Be 45.10N 7.52 E
Ord, Mount- 212 Fc 17.20S 125.35 E
Órdenes / Ordes 126 Da 43.04N 8.24W
Ordes / Órdenes 126 Da 43.04N 8.24W
Ordos Desert (EN)=Mu Us Shamo 140 Mf 38.45N 109.10 E
Ord River 208 Df 15.30S 128.21 E
Ordu 144 Ea 41.00N 37.53 E
Ordubad 132 Oj 38.55N 46.01 E
Ordynskoje 138 Df 54.22N 81.58 E
Ordžonikidze [Kaz.-U.S.S.R.] 134 Jj 52.25N 61.45 E
Ordžonikidze [R.S.F.S.R.] 112 Kg 43.03N 44.40 E
Ordžonikidze [Ukr.-U.S.S.R.] 132 If 47.40N 34.04 E
Ordžonikidzeabad 136 Gh 38.34N 69.02 E
Ore älv 116 Fc 61.08N 14.35 E
Orebić 128 Lh 42.58N 17.11 E
Örebro 112 Hd 59.17N 15.13 E
Örebro [2] 114 Dg 59.30N 15.00 E
Oredež 116 Nf 58.50N 30.13 E
Oregon 184 Fe 41.38N 83.28W
Oregon [2] 182 Cc 44.00N 121.00W
Oregon City 182 Cb 45.21N 122.36W
Oregon Inlet 184 Jh 35.50N 75.35W
Öregrund 116 Hd 60.20N 18.26 E
Orehov 132 If 47.34N 35.47 E
Orehovo-Zujevo 112 Jd 55.49N 38.59 E
Orel 112 Je 52.59N 36.05 E
Orel 132 Ie 48.31N 34.55 E
Orel, gora- 138 Jf 53.55N 140.01 E
Orellana [Peru] 202 Cd 4.40S 78.10W
Orellana [Peru] 202 Ce 6.54S 75.04W
Orem 182 Ec 40.19N 111.42W
Ore Mountains (EN)= Erzgebirge 110 He 50.30N 13.15 E
Ore Mountains (EN)= Krušné Hory 110 He 50.30N 13.15 E
Ören 146 Bd 37.18N 29.17 E
Orenbel 146 Hb 40.00N 39.10 E
Orenburg 112 Le 51.54N 55.06 E
Orenburgskaja oblast [3] 136 Fe 52.00N 55.00 E
Örencik 146 Cc 39.16N 29.34 E
Orense 206 Ie 38.40S 59.47W
Orense / Ourense 126 Eb 42.20N 7.51W
Orense / Ourense [3] 126 Eb 42.10N 7.30W
Oreón, Dhíavlos- 130 Fk 38.54N 22.55 E
Orepuki 218 Bg 46.17S 167.44 E
Orestiás 130 Jh 41.30N 26.31 E
Øresund 110 Hd 55.50N 12.40 E
Oreti 218 Cg 46.28S 168.17 E
Orewa 218 Fb 36.35S 174.42 E
Orford 124 Db 52.05N 1.32 E
Orford Ness 118 Oi 52.05N 1.34 E
Organyà 126 Nb 42.13N 1.20 E
Organ Needle 186 Cj 32.21N 106.33W
Orgaz 126 Ie 39.39N 3.54W
Orgejev 136 Cf 47.23N 28.50 E
Orgelet 122 Lh 46.31N 5.37 E
Orgon Tal 154 Bc 43.20N 112.40 E
Orgosolo 128 Dj 40.12N 9.21 E
Orgūn 144 Kc 32.57N 69.11 E
Orhaneli 130 Lj 39.54N 29.00 E
Orhaneli/Koca Çay 130 Lj 39.56N 28.32 E
Orhangazi 130 Mi 40.30N 29.18 E
Orhomenós 130 Fk 38.35N 22.54 E
Orhon (Orchon) 140 Md 50.21N 106.05 E
Orhy, Pico de- 126 La 42.59N 1.00W
Orichuna, Río- 196 Bi 7.30N 68.13W
Orick 188 Cf 41.17N 124.04W
Oriental 192 Kh 19.22N 97.37W
Oriental, Cordillera- [Col.] 198 Ie 6.00N 73.00W
Oriental, Cordillera- [Dom.Rep.] 194 Md 18.55N 69.15W
Oriente 206 He 38.44S 60.37W
Orihuela 126 Lf 38.05N 0.57W
Oriku 130 Ci 40.17N 19.25 E
Öri Lekánis 130 Hh 41.08N 24.33 E
Orillia 180 Jh 44.37N 79.25W
Orimattila 114 Ff 60.48N 25.45 E
Orinoco, Delta del- 202 Fb 9.15N 61.30W
Orinoco, Río- 198 Je 8.37N 62.15W
Oripää 118 Jd 60.51N 22.41 E
Orissa [3] 148 Gd 21.00N 84.00 E
Orissaare/Orissare 114 Fg 58.34N 23.05 E
Orissare/Orissaare 114 Fg 58.34N 23.05 E
Oristano 128 Ck 39.54N 8.36 E
Oristano, Golfo di- 128 Ck 39.50N 8.30 E
Orituco, Río- 196 Ch 8.45N 67.27W
Orivesi 114 Ff 61.41N 24.21 E
Orivesi 110 Ic 62.15N 29.25 E
Oriximiná 202 Gd 1.45S 55.52W
Orizaba 176 Jh 18.51N 97.06W
Orizaba, Pico de- (Citlaltépetl, Volcán-) 174 Jh 19.01N 97.16W
Orizona 204 Hc 17.03S 48.18W
Orjahovo 130 Gf 43.44N 23.58 E
Ørje 116 De 59.29N 11.39 E
Orjen 130 Bg 42.34N 18.33 E
Órjiva 126 Ih 36.54N 3.25W
Orkanger 114 Be 63.19N 9.52 E
Orkdalen 116 Ca 63.15N 9.50 E
Örkelljunga 116 Eh 56.17N 13.17 E
Orkla 116 Ca 63.18N 9.50 E
Orkney 172 De 27.00S 26.39 E
Orkney [3] 118 Kb 59.00N 3.00W
Orkney Islands 110 Fd 59.00N 3.00W
Orla 120 Me 51.35N 16.40 E
Orlândia 204 Ie 20.43S 47.53W
Orlando 176 Kg 28.32N 81.23W
Orlando, Capo d'- 128 Il 38.10N 14.45 E
Orlanka 120 Td 52.52N 23.12 E
Orléanais 122 Hf 48.40N 1.20 E
Orléans 112 Gf 47.55N 1.54 E
Orlice 120 Lf 50.12N 15.49 E
Orlické Hory 120 Mf 50.10N 16.30 E
Orlik 138 Ef 52.30N 99.55 E
Orlovskaja oblast [3] 136 De 52.45N 36.30 E
Orlovski 132 Mf 46.52N 42.06 E
Orlovski, mys- 114 Jc 67.16N 41.18 E
Orly 122 If 48.45N 2.24 E
Ormāra 148 Cc 25.12N 64.38 E
Ormes 124 Ce 49.03N 0.59 E
Ormoc 150 Hd 11.00N 124.37 E
Ormond 218 Gc 38.33S 177.55 E
Ormond Beach 184 Gk 29.17N 81.02W
Ornain 122 Kf 48.46N 4.47 E
Ornans 122 Mg 47.06N 6.09 E
Ornäs 116 Fd 60.31N 15.32 E
Orne [3] 122 Gf 48.40N 0.05 E
Orne [Fr.] 122 Me 49.17N 6.11 E
Orne [Fr.] 122 Fe 49.19N 0.14W
Orne Seamount (EN) 216 Je 27.30S 157.30W
Orneta 120 Qb 54.08N 20.08 E
Ornö 116 He 59.05N 18.25 E
Örnsköldsvik 114 Ee 63.18N 18.43 E
Oro 154 Id 40.01N 127.27 E
Oro, Río de- 204 Ch 27.04S 58.34W
Oro, Río del- 192 Ge 25.35N 105.03W
Orocué 202 Dc 4.48N 71.20W
Orodara 166 Ec 10.59N 4.55W
Orofino 188 Gc 46.29N 116.15W
Orogrande 186 Cj 32.23N 106.08W
Orohena, Mont- 221e Fc 17.31S 149.28W
Oroluk Atoll 208 Gd 7.32N 155.18 E
Orom 170 Fb 3.20N 33.40 E
Oromocto 180 Kg 45.51N 66.29W
Oron 166 Ge 4.50N 8.14 E
Orona Atoll (Hull) 208 Je 4.29S 172.10W
Orongo 221d Ac 27.10S 109.26W
Oronsay 118 Ge 56.01N 6.14W
Orontes (EN) = 'Āṣī, Nahr al- 144 Eb 36.02N 35.58 E
Oropesa 126 Ge 39.55N 5.10W
Oropesa / Orpesa 126 Md 40.06N 0.09 E
Oroqen Zizhiqi (Alihe) 152 La 50.35N 123.42 E
Oroquieta 150 He 8.29N 123.48 E
Orós 202 Ke 6.15S 38.55W
Orós, Açude- 202 Ke 6.15S 39.05W
Orosei 128 Dj 40.23N 9.42 E
Orosei, Golfo di- 128 Dj 40.15N 9.45 E
Orosháza 120 Qj 46.34N 20.40 E
Oro-Shima 156 Be 33.52N 130.02 E
Oroszlány 120 Oi 47.29N 18.19 E
Orote Peninsula 220c Bb 13.26N 144.38 E
Orote Point 220c Bb 13.27N 144.37 E
Orotukan 138 Kd 62.17N 151.50 E
Oroville [Ca.-U.S.] 188 Eg 39.31N 121.33W
Oroville [Wa.-U.S.] 188 Fb 48.56N 119.26W
Orpesa / Oropesa 126 Md 40.06N 0.09 E
Orp-Jauche 124 Gd 50.40N 4.57 E
Orqohan 152 Lb 49.36N 121.23 E
Orr 186 Jb 48.03N 92.50W
Orrefors 116 Fh 56.50N 15.45 E
Orri, Pic de l'- / Llorri 126 Nb 42.23N 1.12 E
Orsa 114 Df 61.07N 14.37 E
Orša 112 Je 54.30N 30.24 E
Orsasjön 116 Fc 61.05N 14.35 E
Orsay 124 Ef 48.42N 2.11 E
Orsjön 116 Gc 61.35N 16.20 E
Orsk 112 Le 51.12N 58.34 E
Orșova 130 Fe 44.42N 22.25 E
Ørsta 114 Be 62.12N 6.09 E
Örsundsbro 116 Ge 59.44N 17.18 E
Orta, Lago d'- (Cusio) 128 Ce 45.50N 8.25 E
Ortaca 146 Cd 36.49N 28.47 E
Ortakent 130 Kl 37.02N 27.21 E
Ortaklar 130 Kl 37.53N 27.30 E
Orta Nova 128 Ji 41.19N 15.42 E
Orte 128 Gh 42.27N 12.23 E
Ortegal, Cabo- 126 Ea 43.45N 7.53W
Ortenberg 124 Ld 50.21N 9.03 E
Orthez 122 Fk 43.29N 0.46W
Orthon, Río- 202 Ef 10.50S 66.04W
Ortigueira [Braz.] 206 Jb 24.12S 50.55W
Ortigueira [Sp.] 126 Ea 43.34N 7.44W
Ortisei / Sankt Ulrich in Gröden 128 Fd 46.34N 11.40 E
Ortiz [Mex.] 192 De 28.15N 110.43W
Ortiz [Ven.] 196 Ch 9.37N 67.17W
Ortlergruppe/Ortles 128 Ed 46.30N 10.40 E
Ortles/Ortlergruppe 128 Ed 46.30N 10.40 E
Ortolo 122a Ab 41.30N 8.55 E
Ortona 128 Ih 42.21N 14.24 E
Ortonville 186 Hd 45.19N 96.27W
Orto-Tokoj 135 Kc 42.20N 76.02 E
Örtze 120 Fd 52.40N 9.57 E
Orukuizu 220a Ac 7.10N 134.17 E
Orūmīyeh 142 Gf 37.33N 45.04 E
Orūmīyeh, Daryācheh-ye-= Urmia, Lake- (EN) 140 Gf 37.40N 45.30 E
Oruro 200 Jg 17.59S 67.09W
Oruro [3] 202 Eg 18.40S 67.30W
Orust 116 Df 58.10N 11.38 E
Orūzgān 144 Kc 32.56N 66.38 E
Orūzgān [3] 144 Kc 33.15N 66.00 E
Orval, Abbaye d'- 124 He 49.38N 5.22 E
Orvault 122 Eg 47.16N 1.37W
Orvieto 128 Gh 42.43N 12.07 E
Orville Escarpment 222 Qf 75.45S 65.30W
Orvílos, Óros- 130 Gh 41.23N 23.36 E
Orwell 124 Dc 51.58N 1.18 E
Orxois 124 Fe 49.08N 3.12 E
Orz 120 Rd 52.50N 21.30 E
Orzinuovi 128 De 45.24N 9.55 E
Orzyc 120 Rd 52.47N 21.13 E
Orzysz 120 Rc 53.49N 21.56 E
Oš 136 Hg 40.32N 72.50 E
Os 114 Ce 62.30N 11.12 E
Osa 136 Fd 57.17N 55.26 E
Oša 116 Lh 56.21N 26.29 E
Osa 120 Oc 53.33N 18.45 E
Osa, Peninsula de- 190 Hg 8.35N 83.33W
Osage 186 Je 43.17N 92.49W
Osage River 182 Id 38.35N 91.57W
Ōsaka 142 Pf 34.40N 135.30 E
Osaka 156 Ed 35.57N 137.14 E
Osaka Bay (EN)=Ōsaka-Wan 154 Mg 34.36N 135.27 E
Ōsaka-Fu [2] 154 Mg 34.45N 135.35 E
Osakarovka 136 He 50.32N 72.39 E
Ōsaka-Wan=Osaka Bay (EN) 154 Mg 34.36N 135.27 E
Osăm 130 Hf 43.42N 24.51 E
Osan 154 If 37.09N 127.04 E
Osasco 204 Hf 23.32S 46.46W
Osat 128 Nf 44.02N 19.20 E
Osawatomie 186 Ig 38.30N 94.57W
Osborne 186 Gg 39.26N 98.42W
Osburger Hochwald 124 Ie 49.40N 6.50 E
Osby 114 Ch 56.22N 13.59 E
Osceola [Ar.-U.S.] 186 Li 35.42N 89.58W
Osceola [Ia.-U.S.] 182 Ic 41.02N 93.46W
Osceola [Mo.-U.S.] 186 Jh 38.03N 93.42W
Oschatz 120 Je 51.18N 13.07 E
Oschersleben 120 Hd 52.02N 11.15 E
Oschiri 128 Dj 40.43N 9.06 E
Osen 114 Cd 64.18N 10.31 E
Osered 132 Ld 50.01N 40.48 E
Osetr 132 Kb 55.00N 38.45 E
Ōse-Zaki 154 Jh 32.38N 128.42 E
Oshamanbe 154 Pc 42.30N 140.22 E
Oshawa 180 Jh 43.54N 78.51W
Oshekehia Lake 172 Bc 18.08S 15.45 E
Oshika 156 Gb 38.17N 141.31 E
Oshika-Hantō 154 Pe 38.22N 141.27 E
Oshikango 172 Bc 17.22S 15.55 E
Ōshima 156 Fd 34.44N 139.20 E
Oshima 156 Ce 33.55N 132.11 E
Ōshima 156 Ae 33.04N 129.36 E
Ō-Shima [Jap.] 156 De 33.28N 135.50 E
Ō-Shima [Jap.] 154 Od 41.30N 139.15 E
Ō-Shima [Jap.] 154 Jh 32.04N 128.26 E
Ō-Shima [Jap.] 156 De 33.38N 134.30 E
Ō-Shima [Jap.] 156 Be 33.54N 130.27 E
Ō-Shima [Jap.] 156 Ae 32.34N 128.54 E
Ō-Shima [Jap.] 156 Ae 33.30N 129.33 E
Ō-Shima [Jap.] 156 Cd 34.10N 133.05 E
Ō-Shima [Jap.] 156 Bf 31.32N 131.25 E
Ō-Shima [Jap.] 152 Oe 34.45N 139.30 E
Oshima-Hantō 154 Pd 41.40N 140.30 E
Ōshima-Kaikyō 156b Ba 28.10N 129.15 E
Oshkosh [Nb.-U.S.] 186 Ef 41.24N 102.21W
Oshkosh [Wi.-U.S.] 182 Jc 44.01N 88.33W
Oshnavīyeh 146 Kd 37.02N 45.06 E
Oshogbo 160 Hh 7.46N 4.34 E
Oshtorān Kūh 144 Gc 33.20N 49.16 E
Oshtorīnān 146 Me 34.01N 48.38 E
Oshwe 170 Cc 3.24S 19.30 E
Osich'ŏn-ni 154 Jd 41.25N 128.16 E
Osijek 112 Hf 45.33N 18.42 E
Osilo 128 Cj 40.45N 8.40 E
Osimo 128 Hg 43.28N 13.29 E
Osinki 114 Lj 52.52N 49.31 E
Osinniki 138 Df 53.37N 87.31 E
Osipaonica 130 Ee 44.33N 21.04 E
Osipoviči 132 Fc 53.19N 28.40 E
Osječenica 128 Kf 44.29N 16.17 E
Oskaloosa 186 Jf 41.18N 92.39W
Oskarshamn 114 Dh 57.16N 16.26 E
Oskarström 116 Eh 56.48N 12.58 E
Oskélanéo 184 Ja 48.08N 75.05W
Oskino 138 Fd 60.48N 107.58 E
Öskjuvatn 114a Cb 65.02N 16.45W
Oskol 132 Je 49.06N 37.25 E
Oskū 146 Ld 37.55N 46.06 E
Oslava 120 Mg 49.05N 16.22 E
Ösling 122 Le 49.55N 6.00 E
Osljanka, gora- 134 Ig 59.10N 58.33 E
Oslo 112 Hd 59.55N 10.45 E
Oslo [2] 114 Cg 59.55N 10.45 E
Oslofjorden 110 Hd 59.20N 10.35 E
Osmānābād 148 Fe 18.10N 76.03 E
Osmancık 146 Fb 40.59N 34.49 E
Osmaneli 130 Ni 40.22N 30.01 E
Osmaniye 144 Eb 37.05N 36.14 E
Osmino 116 Mf 58.54N 29.15 E
Ošmjanskaja vozvyšennost 116 Kj 54.30N 26.00 E
Ošmjany 132 Db 54.27N 25.57 E
Ösmo 116 Gf 58.59N 17.54 E
Osmussaar/Osmussar 116 Je 59.20N 23.15 E
Osmussar/Osmussaar 116 Je 59.20N 23.15 E
Osnabrück 112 Ge 52.16N 8.03 E
Osning 124 Kb 52.10N 8.05 E
Oso, Sierra del- 192 Gd 26.00N 105.25W
Osobloga 120 Nf 50.27N 17.58 E
Osogovske Planine 130 Fg 42.10N 22.30 E
Osor 128 If 44.42N 14.24 E
Osório 206 Jc 29.54S 50.16W
Osorno 200 Ij 40.34S 73.09W
Osoyoos 180 Fg 49.02N 119.28W
Osøyra 114 Af 60.11N 5.28 E
Ospino 196 Bh 9.18N 69.27W
Osprey Reef 208 Ff 13.55S 146.40 E
Oss 122 Lc 51.46N 5.31 E
Ossa, Mount- 208 Fi 41.54S 146.01 E
Óssa, Óros- 130 Fj 39.49N 22.40 E
Ossabaw Island 184 Gj 31.47N 81.06W
Ossa de Montiel 126 Jf 38.58N 2.45W
Osse 122 Gj 44.07N 0.17 E
Ossining 184 Ke 41.10N 73.52W
Ossjøen 116 Dc 61.15N 11.55 E
Ošskaja oblast [3] 136 Hg 40.45N 73.20 E
Ossora 138 Le 59.15N 163.02 E
Östanvik 116 Fc 61.10N 15.13 E
Ostaškov 136 Dd 57.09N 33.07 E
Ostbevern 124 Jb 52.03N 7.51 E
Oste 120 Fc 53.50N 9.05 E
Ostende/Oostende 122 Ic 51.14N 2.55 E
Oster 132 Gd 50.55N 30.57 E
Oster [Ukr.-U.S.S.R.] 132 Gd 50.53N 30.55 E
Oster [U.S.S.R.] 132 Gc 53.47N 31.45 E
Osterburg in der Altmark 120 Hd 52.47N 11.44 E
Österbybruk 116 Gd 60.12N 17.54 E
Österdalälven 114 Df 60.33N 15.08 E
Østerdalen 114 Cf 62.00N 10.40 E
Østerfjorden 116 Ad 60.30N 5.20 E
Österforse 116 Ga 63.09N 17.01 E
Östergarnsholm 116 Hg 57.25N 19.00 E
Östergötland [2] 114 Dg 58.25N 15.45 E
Östergötland 116 Ff 58.25N 15.35 E
Osterholz Scharmbeck 120 Ec 53.14N 8.48 E
Österlen 116 Fi 55.30N 14.10 E
Östermark/Teuva 114 Ee 62.29N 21.44 E
Osterode am Harz 120 Ge 51.44N 10.11 E
Osterøya 114 Af 60.35N 5.35 E
Österreich = Austria (EN) [1] 112 Hf 47.30N 14.00 E
Östersjön=Baltic Sea (EN) 110 Hd 57.00N 19.00 E
Østersøen=Baltic Sea (EN) 110 Hd 57.00N 19.00 E
Östersund 112 Hc 63.11N 14.39 E
Osterwick, Rosendahl- 124 Jb 52.01N 7.12 E
Østfold [2] 114 Cg 59.20N 11.30 E
Ostfriesische Inseln=East Frisian Islands (EN) 120 Dc 53.45N 7.25 E
Ostfriesland=East Friesland (EN) 120 Dc 53.20N 7.40 E
Østgrønland=East Greenland (EN) [2] 179 Id 72.00N 35.00W
Östhammar 114 Ed 60.16N 18.22 E
Osthofen 124 Ke 49.42N 8.20 E
Östmark 116 Ed 60.17N 12.45 E
Ostrach 120 Fh 48.05N 9.25 E
Östra Silen 116 Ee 59.15N 12.20 E
Ostrava 112 Hf 49.50N 18.17 E
Ostrhauderfehn 124 Ja 53.08N 7.37 E
Ostróda 120 Pc 53.43N 19.59 E
Ostrog 132 Ed 50.19N 26.32 E
Ostrogožsk 136 De 50.52N 39.05 E
Ostrołęka 120 Rc 53.06N 21.34 E
Ostrołęka [2] 120 Rc 53.05N 21.35 E
Ostrošicki Gorodok 116 Lj 54.03N 27.46 E
Ostrov [Bye.-U.S.S.R.] 120 Vd 52.48N 26.01 E
Ostrov [Czech.] 120 If 50.18N 12.57 E
Ostrov [Rom.] 130 Ke 44.07N 27.22 E
Ostrov [R.S.F.S.R.] 136 Cd 57.23N 28.22 E
Ostrov [R.S.F.S.R.] 116 Mf 58.28N 28.44 E
Ostrovec 116 Lj 54.38N 26.06 E
Ostrovicës, Mali i- 130 Di 40.34N 20.27 E
Ostrovskoje 114 Kh 57.50N 42.13 E
Ostrowiec Świętokrzyski 120 Rf 50.57N 21.23 E
Ostrów Lubelski 120 Se 51.30N 22.52 E
Ostrów Mazowiecka 120 Rd 52.49N 21.54 E
Ostrów Wielkopolski 120 Ne 51.39N 17.49 E
Ostryna 120 Uc 53.41N 24.37 E
Ostrzeszów 120 Ne 51.25N 17.57 E
Ostsee=Baltic Sea (EN) 110 Hd 57.00N 19.00 E
Oststeirisches Hügelland 128 Jd 47.00N 15.45 E
Osttirol 128 Gd 46.55N 12.30 E
Ostuni 128 Lj 40.44N 17.35 E
Ōsumi 156 Bf 31.36N 130.59 E
Osumi 130 Ci 40.48N 19.52 E
Ōsumi-Hantō 156 Bf 31.15N 130.50 E
Osumi Islands (EN)=Ōsumi-Shotō 140 Pf 30.35N 130.59 E
Ōsumi-Shotō=Osumi Islands (EN) 140 Pf 30.35N 130.59 E
Osuna 126 Gg 37.14N 5.07W
Osveja 116 Mi 55.59N 28.10 E
Osvejskoje, ozero- 116 Mh 56.00N 28.15 E
Oswego 182 Lc 43.27N 76.31W
Oswestry 118 Ji 52.52N 3.04W
Oświęcim 120 Pf 50.03N 19.12 E
Osyka 186 Kk 31.00N 90.28W
Ōta 156 Fc 36.18N 139.22 E
Ota 156 Ed 35.56N 136.03 E
Otago [2] 218 Cf 45.00S 169.10 E
Otago Peninsula 218 Df 45.50S 170.45 E
Ōtake 154 Lg 34.12N 132.13 E
Otakeho 218 Fc 39.33S 174.03 E
Otaki 218 Fd 40.45S 175.08 E
Ōtakime-Yama 156 Gc 37.22N 140.42 E
Otanoshike 156a Db 43.01N 144.16 E
Otar 136 Hg 43.31N 75.12 E
Otaru 152 Pc 43.13N 141.00 E
Otautau 218 Bg 46.09S 168.00 E
Otava 116 Lc 61.39N 27.04 E
Otava 120 Kg 49.26N 14.12 E
Otavi 172 Bc 19.39S 17.20 E
Ōtawara 154 Pf 36.52N 140.02 E

Index Symbols

[1] Independent Nation
[2] State, Region
[3] District, County
[4] Municipality
[5] Colony, Dependency
Continent
Physical Region
Historical or Cultural Region
Mount, Mountain
Volcano
Hill
Mountains, Mountain Range
Hills, Escarpment
Plateau, Upland
Pass, Gap
Plain, Lowland
Delta
Salt Flat
Valley, Canyon
Crater, Cave
Karst Features
Depression
Polder
Desert, Dunes
Forest, Woods
Heath, Steppe
Oasis
Cape, Point
Coast, Beach
Cliff
Peninsula
Isthmus
Sandbank
Island
Atoll
Rock, Reef
Islands, Archipelago
Rocks, Reefs
Coral Reef
Well, Spring
Geyser
River, Stream
Waterfall, Rapids
River Mouth, Estuary
Lake
Salt Lake
Intermittent Lake
Reservoir
Swamp, Pond
Canal
Glacier
Ice Shelf, Pack Ice
Ocean
Sea
Gulf, Bay
Strait, Fjord
Lagoon
Bank
Seamount
Tablemount
Ridge
Shelf
Basin
Escarpment, Sea Scarp
Fracture
Trench, Abyss
National Park, Reserve
Point of Interest
Recreation Site
Cave, Cavern
Historic Site
Ruins
Wall, Walls
Church, Abbey
Temple
Scientific Station
Railway station
Airport
Port
Military installation
Lighthouse
Mine
Tunnel
Dam, Bridge

Otelu Roşu 130 Fd 45.32N 22.22 E
Otematata 218 Df 44.37S 170.11 E
Otepää/Otepja 114 Gg 58.03N 26.30 E
Otepää, vozvyšennost- / Otepää Kõrgustik 116 Lf 58.00N 26.40 E
Otepää Kõrgustik / Otepää, vozvyšennost- 116 Lf 58.00N 26.40 E
Otepja/Otepää 114 Gg 58.03N 26.30 E
Oteros 190 Cc 26.55N 108.30W
Othain 124 He 49.31N 5.23 E
Othello 188 Fc 46.50N 119.10W
Othonoí 130 Cj 39.50N 19.25 E
Óthris Óros 130 Fj 39.02N 22.37 E
Oti 158 Hh 7.48N 0.08 E
Otira 218 De 42.51S 171.33 E
Otish, Monts- 174 Md 52.45N 69.15W
Otjikondo 172 Bc 19.50S 15.23 E
Otjimbingwe 172 Bd 22.21S 16.08 E
Otjiwarongo 160 Ik 20.29S 16.36 E
Otjiwarongo 172 Bd 20.30S 17.30 E
Otjosondjou, Omuramba- 158 Ij 19.55S 20.00 E
Otjosondu 172 Bd 21.12S 17.58 E
Otmuchowskie, Jezioro- 120 Nf 50.27N 17.15 E
Otnes 114 Cf 61.46N 11.12 E
Otobe 156a Bc 41.57N 140.08 E
Otočac 128 Jf 44.52N 15.14 E
Otofuke 156a Cb 42.59N 143.10 E
Otofuke-Gawa 156a Cb 42.56N 143.12 E
Otog Qi (Ulan) 152 Id 39.07N 108.00 E
Otoineppu 156a Ca 44.43N 142.16 E
Otok 128 Me 45.09N 18.53 E
Otorohanga 218 Fc 38.11S 175.12 E
Otorten, gora- 134 If 61.50N 59.13 E
Ōtoyo 156 Ce 33.46N 133.40 E
Otra 110 Gd 58.09N 8.00 E
Otradnaja 132 Lg 44.23N 41.31 E
Otradnoje, ozero- 116 Nd 60.50N 30.25 E
Otradny 114 Mj 53.23N 51.24 E
Otranto 128 Mj 40.09N 18.30 E
Otranto, Canale d'- = Otranto, Strait of- (EN) 110 Hg 40.00N 19.00 E
Otranto, Capo d'- 128 Mj 40.06N 18.31 E
Otranto, Strait of- (EN) = Otranto, Canale d'- 110 Hg 40.00N 19.00 E
Otranto, Strait of- (EN) = Otrantos, Kanali i- 130 Bi 40.00N 19.00 E
Otranto, Terra d'- 128 Mj 40.20N 18.15 E
Otrantos, Kanali i- = Otranto, Strait of- (EN) 130 Bi 40.00N 19.00 E
Ötscher 128 Jc 47.51N 15.12 E
Ōtsu 154 Mg 35.00N 135.52 E
Ōtsuchi 154 Pe 39.21N 141.54 E
Ōtsuki [Jap.] 156 Ce 32.50N 132.41 E
Ōtsuki [Jap.] 156 Fd 35.36N 138.54 E
Otta 114 Bf 61.46N 9.32 E
Otta 220d Bb 7.09N 151.54 E
Otta 116 Cc 61.46N 9.31 E
Ottadalen 116 Bc 61.55N 8.00 E
Ottana 128 Dj 40.15N 9.05 E
Otta Pass 220d Bb 7.09N 151.53 E
Ottawa [Il.-U.S.] 186 Lf 41.21N 88.51W
Ottawa [Ks.-U.S.] 182 Hd 38.37N 95.16W
Ottawa [Oh.-U.S.] 184 Ee 41.02N 84.03W
Ottawa [Ont.-Can.] 176 Le 45.25N 75.42W
Ottawa Islands 174 Kd 59.30N 80.10W
Ottawa River 174 Le 45.20N 73.58W
Ottawa River (EN) = Outaouais, Rivière- 184 Kc 45.20N 73.58W
Ottenby 114 Dh 56.16N 16.24 E
Otterberg 124 Je 49.30N 7.46 E
Otter Creek 184 Fk 29.19N 82.48W
Otterndorf 120 Ec 53.48N 8.54 E
Otteroy 116 Bb 62.40N 6.50 E
Otter Rapids 184 Ga 50.15N 81.45W
Otterup 116 Di 55.31N 10.24 E
Ottumwa 182 Ic 41.01N 92.25W
Ottweiler 124 Je 49.23N 7.10 E
Otukpa 166 Gd 7.05N 7.40 E
Otumpa 204 Ah 27.19S 62.13W
Otuquis, Bañados de- 202 Gg 19.20S 58.30W
Otuquis, Río- 204 Cd 19.41S 58.20W
Oturkpo 166 Gd 7.13N 8.09 E
Otu Tolu Group 221b Bb 20.21S 174.32W
Otuzco 202 Ce 7.54S 78.35W
Otway, Cape- 212 Ig 38.52S 143.31 E
Otwock 120 Rd 52.07N 21.16 E
Otynja 120 Uh 48.40N 24.57 E
Ötz 128 Ec 47.12N 10.54 E
Ötztaler Ache 128 Ec 47.14N 10.50 E
Ötztaler Alpen 120 Gj 46.45N 10.55 E
Ou 148 Kd 20.04N 102.13 E
Oua 219b Ce 21.14S 167.05 E
'O'ua 221b Bb 20.02S 174.41W
Ouachita, Lake- 186 Ji 34.40N 93.25W
Ouachita Mountains 174 Jf 34.40N 94.25W
Ouachita River 182 Ie 31.38N 91.49W
Ouadane 160 Ff 20.57N 11.35W
Ouadda 160 Jh 8.04N 22.24 E
Ouaddaï 168 Cc 13.00N 21.00 E
Ouaddaï 158 Jg 13.00N 21.00 E
Ouagadougou 160 Gg 12.22N 1.31W
Ouahigouya 160 Gg 13.35N 2.25W
Ouaka 168 Cd 6.00N 21.00 E
Ouaka 158 Ih 4.59N 19.56 E
Oualata 162 Ff 17.18N 7.00W
Oualata, Dahr- 162 Ff 17.48N 7.24W
Oualidia 162 Fc 32.44N 9.02W
Ouallam 166 Fc 14.19N 2.05 E
Ouallene 162 He 24.35N 1.17 E
Ouanda-Djallé 168 Cd 8.54N 22.48 E
Ouandjia 168 Cd 8.35N 23.12 E
Ouandjia 168 Cd 9.35N 21.43 E
Ouango 168 Ce 4.19N 22.33 E
Ouangolodougou 166 Dd 9.58N 5.09W
Ouanne 122 Ig 47.57N 2.47 E
Ouarane 158 Ff 21.00N 10.00W
Ouargaye 166 Fc 11.32N 0.01 E
Ouargla 160 He 31.57N 5.20 E
Ouargla 162 Id 30.00N 6.30 E
Ouarkziz, Jbel- 158 Gf 28.00N 8.20W
Ouarra 158 Jh 5.05N 24.26 E
Ouarsenis, Djebel- 126 Ni 35.53N 1.38 E
Ouarsenis, Massif de l'- 162 Hb 35.50N 2.05 E
Ouarzazate 162 Fc 30.55N 6.55W
Ouarzazate 162 Fc 31.00N 6.30W
Oubangui 158 Ii 0.30S 17.42 E
Ouborré, Pointe- 219b Dd 18.47S 169.16 E
Ouche, Pays d'- 122 Gf 48.55N 0.45 E
Ōuchi 156 Gb 39.27N 140.06 E
Oud Beijerland 124 Gc 51.50N 4.26 E
Oude IJssel 124 Ic 52.00N 6.10 E
Oudenaarde/Audenarde 122 Jd 50.51N 3.36 E
Oudenbosch 124 Gc 51.35N 4.34 E
Oude Rijn 122 Kb 52.05N 4.20 E
Oudon 122 Fg 47.37N 0.42W
Oudtshoorn 160 Jl 33.35S 22.14 E
Oued Ben Tili 162 Fd 25.48N 9.32W
Oued el Abtal 126 Mi 35.27N 0.41 E
Oued Fodda 126 Nh 36.11N 1.32 E
Oued Lili 126 Ni 35.31N 1.16 E
Oued Rhiou 162 Hb 35.58N 0.55 E
Oued Taria 126 Mi 35.07N 0.05 E
Oued Tlelat 126 Li 35.33N 0.27W
Oued Zem 160 Ge 32.52N 6.34W
Ouégoa 219b Be 20.21S 164.26 E
Ouéllé 166 Ed 7.18N 4.01W
Ouémé 166 Fd 7.00N 2.35 E
Ouémé 158 Hh 6.29N 2.32 E
Ouen 219b Cf 22.26S 166.48 E
Ouenza 162 Ib 35.57N 8.07 E
Ouenza, Djebel- 128 Co 35.57N 8.05 E
Ouessa 166 Ec 11.03N 2.47W
Ouessant, Ile d'- 122 Af 48.28N 5.05W
Ouesso 160 Ih 1.37N 16.04 E
Ouest 166 Hd 5.20N 10.30 E
Ouest, Baie de l'- 220h Ab 13.15S 176.13W
Ouezzane 162 Fc 34.48N 5.36W
Oughter, Lough- 118 Fg 54.00N 7.29W
Ouham 168 Bd 7.00N 18.00 E
Ouham 158 Ih 9.18N 18.14 E
Ouham-Pendé 168 Bd 7.00N 16.00 E
Ouidah 166 Fd 6.22N 2.05 E
Ouistreham 122 Fe 49.17N 0.15W
Ouistreham-Riva Bella 124 Be 49.17N 0.16W
Oujda 160 Ge 34.40N 1.54W
Oujda 162 Gc 33.00N 2.00W
Oujeft 162 Ee 20.02N 13.03W
Oulainen 114 Fd 64.16N 24.57 E
Oulchy-le-Château 124 Fe 49.12N 3.21 E
Ouled Djellal 162 Ic 34.25N 5.04 E
Ouled Naïl, Monts des- 162 Hc 34.40N 3.25 E
Oulou, Bahr- 168 Cd 9.48N 21.32 E
Oulu 114 Gd 65.00N 27.00 E
Oulu/Uleåborg 112 Ib 65.01N 25.30 E
Oulu, Lake- (EN) = Oulujärvi 110 Ic 64.20N 27.15 E
Oulujärvi = Oulu, Lake- (EN) 110 Ic 64.20N 27.15 E
Oulujoki 110 Ib 65.01N 25.25 E
Oum Chalouba 160 Jg 15.48N 20.46 E
Oumé 166 Dd 6.23N 5.25W
Oumé 166 Dd 6.25N 5.30W
Oum el Bouaghi 162 Ib 35.53N 7.07 E
Oum el Bouaghi 162 Ib 35.30N 7.10 E
Oum er Rbia 158 Ge 33.19N 8.20W
Oum Hadjer 168 Bc 13.18N 19.41 E
Oumm ed Droûs Guebli, Sebkhet- 162 Ee 24.03N 11.45W
Oumm ed Droûs Telli, Sebkhet- 162 Ee 24.20N 11.30W
Ounasjoki 110 Ib 66.30N 25.45 E
Oundle 124 Bb 52.29N 0.28W
Ounianga 168 Cb 19.10N 20.30 E
Ounianga Kébir 160 Jg 19.04N 20.29 E
Ountivou 166 Fd 7.21N 1.34 E
Ouolossébougou 166 Dc 12.00N 7.55W
Oupeye 124 Hd 50.42N 5.39 E
Oupu 152 Ma 52.45N 126.00 E
Our 124 Ie 49.53N 6.18 E
Ouray 186 Cg 38.01N 107.40W
Ouray, Mount- 186 Cg 38.25N 106.14W
Ource 122 Kf 48.06N 4.23 E
Ourcq 122 Je 49.01N 3.01 E
Ourcq, Canal de l'- 122 If 48.51N 2.22 E
Ourém 202 Id 1.33S 47.06W
Ourense / Orense 126 Eb 42.20N 7.51W
Ourense / Orense 126 Eb 42.10N 7.30W
Ouricuri 202 Je 7.35S 40.05W
Ourinhos 200 Lh 22.59S 49.52W
Ouro, Rio do- 204 Ha 13.20S 48.59W
Ouro Fino 204 If 22.17S 46.22W
Ouro Prêto 202 Jh 20.23S 43.30W
Ourthe 122 Ld 50.38N 5.35 E
Ourville-en-Caux 124 Ce 49.44N 0.36 E
Ous 136 Gc 60.55N 61.31 E
Ōu-Sanmyaku 154 Pe 39.00N 141.00 E
Ouse [Eng.-U.K.] 118 Nk 50.47N 0.03 E
Ouse [Eng.-U.K.] 118 Mh 53.42N 0.41W
Oust 122 Dg 47.35N 2.06W
Outagouna 166 Fb 15.11N 0.43 E
Outaouais, Rivière- = Ottawa River (EN) 184 Kc 45.20N 73.58W
Outardes, Rivière aux- 180 Kg 49.05N 68.23W
Outat Oulad El Hajj 162 Gc 33.21N 3.42W
Outer Dowsing 118 Oh 53.25N 1.05 E
Outer Hebrides 118 Fd 57.50N 7.32W
Outer Santa Barbara Passage 188 Fj 33.10N 118.30W
Outer Silver Pit 118 Og 54.05N 2.00 E
Outjo 160 Ik 20.08S 16.08 E
Outjo 172 Ac 19.30S 14.30 E
Outlook 188 La 51.30N 107.03W
Outokumpu 114 Ge 62.44N 29.01 E
Outram Mountain 188 Eb 49.19N 121.05W
Outreau 124 Dd 50.42N 1.35 E
Out Skerries 118 Ma 60.30N 0.50W
Outwell 124 Cb 52.37N 0.14 E
Ouvéa, Ile- 208 Hg 20.35S 166.35 E
Ouvèze 122 Kk 43.59N 4.51 E
Ouyen 212 Ig 35.04S 142.20 E
Ouyou Bézédinga 166 Hb 16.32N 13.15 E
Ouzera 126 Oh 36.15N 2.51 E
Ovacık [Tur.] 146 Hc 39.22N 39.13 E
Ovacık [Tur.] 146 Ed 36.11N 33.40 E
Ovada 128 Cf 44.38N 8.38 E
Ova Gölü 130 Mm 36.16N 29.22 E
Ovakent 130 Lk 38.06N 28.02 E
Ovalau Island 219d Bb 17.40S 178.48 E
Ovalle 200 Ii 30.36S 71.12W
Oval Peak 188 Eb 48.15N 120.25W
Ovamboland 172 Bc 18.00S 16.00 E
Ovamboland 172 Bc 18.30S 16.00 E
Ovan 170 Bb 0.30N 12.10 E
Ovanåker 114 Df 61.21N 15.54 E
Ovar 126 Dd 40.52N 8.38W
Ovau 219a Cb 6.48S 156.02 E
Ovejas 194 Ji 9.32N 75.14W
Overath 124 Jd 50.57N 7.18 E
Øverbygd 114 Eb 69.01N 19.18 E
Overflakkee 122 Kc 51.45N 4.10 E
Överhalla 114 Cd 64.30N 12.00 E
Overijse 124 Gd 50.46N 4.32 E
Overijssel 124 Ib 52.25N 6.30 E
Överkalix 114 Fc 66.19N 22.50 E
Overland Park 186 Ig 38.59N 94.40W
Övermark/Ylimarkku 116 Ib 62.37N 21.28 E
Overpelt 124 Hc 51.12N 5.25 E
Overri 166 Gd 5.29N 7.02 E
Overton 188 Hh 36.33N 114.27W
Övertorneå 114 Fc 66.23N 23.40 E
Överum 116 Gg 57.59N 16.19 E
Ovidiu 130 Le 44.16N 28.34 E
Oviedo [Dom.Rep.] 194 Le 17.47N 71.22W
Oviedo [Sp.] 112 Fg 43.22N 5.50W
Oviši 116 Ig 57.34N 21.35 E
Ovo, Capo dell'- 128 Lj 40.18N 17.30 E
Øvre Årdal 114 Bf 61.19N 7.48 E
Övre Fryken 116 Ed 60.00N 13.05 E
Övre Soppero 114 Eb 68.05N 21.41 E
Ovruč 136 Ce 51.19N 28.50 E
Ovsjanka 138 Hf 53.32N 126.58 E
Owaka 218 Cg 46.27S 169.40 E
Owando 160 Ii 0.29S 15.55 E
Ōwani 154 Pd 40.31N 140.35 E
Owase 154 Ng 34.04N 136.12 E
Owatonna 182 Ic 44.05N 93.14W
Owego 184 Id 42.06N 76.16W
Owen, Mount- 218 Ed 41.33S 172.32 E
Owendo 170 Ab 0.17N 9.30 E
Owen Falls Dam 170 Fb 0.24N 33.11 E
Owensboro 182 Jd 37.46N 87.07W
Owens Lake 188 Gh 36.25N 117.56W
Owen Sound 180 Jh 44.34N 80.56W
Owens River 188 Gh 36.31N 117.57W
Owen Stanley Range 208 Fe 9.20S 148.00 E
Owl Creek Mountains 188 Ke 43.30N 108.35W
Ownay, Kowlal-e- 144 Kc 34.27N 68.22 E
Owo 166 Gd 7.11N 5.35 E
Owosso 184 Ed 43.00N 84.10W
Owyhee 188 Gf 41.57N 116.06W
Owyhee, Lake- 188 Ge 43.28N 117.20W
Owyhee Mountains 188 Ge 43.00N 116.45W
Owyhee River 182 Dc 43.40N 117.16W
Oxberg 116 Fc 61.07N 14.10 E
Oxbow 186 Eb 49.14N 102.11W
Oxelösund 114 Dg 58.40N 17.06 E
Oxford 118 Lj 51.50N 1.30W
Oxford [Eng.-U.K.] 112 Fe 51.46N 1.15W
Oxford [Ms.-U.S.] 186 Li 34.22N 89.32W
Oxford [N.C.-U.S.] 184 Hg 36.19N 78.35W
Oxford [N.Z.] 218 Ee 43.17S 172.11 E
Oxford Lake 180 Hf 54.50N 95.35W
Oxfordshire 118 Lj 51.50N 1.20W
Oxia 130 Ek 38.18N 21.06 E
Oxkutzcab 192 Og 20.18N 89.25W
Oxnard 182 De 34.12N 119.11W
Ox or Slieve Gamph Mountains 118 Eg 54.10N 8.50W
Ox or Slieve Gamph Mountains/Sliabh Gamh 118 Eg 54.10N 8.50W
Oxted 124 Bc 51.14N 0.01W
Oyabe 156 Ec 36.40N 136.52 E
O-Yama 156 Fd 34.04N 139.31 E
Ōyama [Jap.] 156 Ec 36.35N 137.18 E
Oyama [Jap.] 154 Of 36.21N 139.50 E
Ōyano 156 Be 32.35N 130.27 E
Oyapock, Fleuve- 198 Ke 4.08N 51.40W
Oyem 160 Ih 1.37N 11.35 E
Oyen 188 Ja 51.22N 110.28W
Øyeren 116 De 59.50N 11.14 E
Oykel 118 Id 57.50N 4.25W
Oyo 166 Fd 8.00N 3.50 E
Oyo [Nig.] 166 Fd 7.51N 3.56 E
Oyo [Sud.] 168 Fa 21.55N 36.06 E
Oyodo-Gawa 156 Bf 31.55N 131.28 E
Oyonnax 122 Lh 46.15N 5.40 E
Oyster Bay 212 Jh 42.10S 148.10 E
Øystese 116 Bd 60.23N 6.13 E
Özalp 146 Jc 38.39N 43.59 E
Ozamiz 150 He 8.08N 123.50 E
Ozark 184 Ej 31.28N 85.38W
Ozark Plateau 174 Jf 37.00N 93.00W
Ozark Reservoir 186 Ii 35.25N 94.05W
Ozarks, Lake of the- 182 Id 37.39N 92.50W
Ózd 120 Qh 48.13N 20.18 E
Ozeblin 128 Jf 44.35N 15.53 E
Ozernoj, zaliv- 138 Le 57.00N 163.20 E
Ozernovski 138 Kf 51.21N 156.32 E
Ozerny 132 Vd 51.08N 60.55 E
Ozersk 116 Ij 54.24N 21.59 E
Ozery [Bye.-U.S.S.R.] 120 Uc 53.38N 24.18 E
Ozery [R.S.F.S.R.] 114 Ji 54.54N 38.32 E
Ožezdy 136 Gf 48.03N 67.09 E
Ozieri 128 Dj 40.35N 9.00 E
Ozinki 136 Ee 51.12N 49.47 E
Ožogina 138 Kc 66.12N 151.05 E
Ozona 182 Ge 30.43N 101.12W
Ozorków 120 Pe 51.58N 19.19 E
Ozouri 170 Ac 0.55S 8.55 E
Ozren [Yugo.] 130 Ef 43.36N 21.54 E
Ozren [Yugo.] 128 Mg 43.59N 18.30 E
Ozren [Yugo.] 128 Mf 44.37N 18.15 E
Ōzu [Jap.] 154 Lh 33.30N 132.23 E
Ōzu [Jap.] 156 Be 32.52N 130.52 E

P

Pääjärvi 116 Kb 62.50N 24.45 E
Paama 219b Dc 16.28S 168.13 E
Pa-an → Pha-an 148 Je 16.53N 97.38 E
Paar 120 Hh 48.45N 11.35 E
Paarl 160 Il 33.45S 18.56 E
Paauilo 221a Fc 20.03N 155.22W
Paavola 114 Fd 64.36N 25.12 E
Pabbay 118 Fd 57.47N 7.20W
Pabellón, Ensenada del- 192 Fe 24.27N 107.36W
Pabellón, Punta- 206 Ff 43.16S 74.23W
Pabianice 120 Pe 51.40N 19.22 E
Pābna 148 Hd 24.00N 89.15 E
Pabrade/Pabradė 114 Fi 54.59N 25.50 E
Pabradė/Pabrade 114 Fi 54.59N 25.50 E
Pacaás Novos, Serra dos- 202 Ff 10.50S 64.00W
Pacajá, Rio- 202 Hd 1.56S 50.55W
Pacajus 202 Kd 4.10S 38.28W
Pacaraima, Serra- 198 Je 4.30N 60.40W
Pacasmayo 202 Ce 7.24S 79.34W
Paceco 128 Gm 37.59N 12.33 E
Pachala 168 Ed 7.10N 34.06 E
Pacheco 192 Eb 30.06N 108.21W
Pachino 128 Jn 36.43N 15.05 E
Pachitea, Río- 202 De 8.46S 74.32W
Pachuca de Soto 190 Ed 20.07N 98.44W
Pacific-Antarctic Ridge (EN) 222 Md 62.00S 157.00W
Pacific City 188 Dd 45.12N 123.57W
Pacific Grove 188 Eh 36.38N 121.56W
Pacífico, Océano- = Pacific Ocean (EN) 106 Ki 5.00N 155.00W
Pacific Ocean 106 Ki 5.00N 155.00W
Pacific Ocean (EN) = Kita-Taiheiyō 214 Ch 22.00N 179.00 E
Pacific Ocean (EN) = Pacífico, Océano- 106 Ki 5.00N 155.00W
Pacific Ocean (EN) = Pacifique, Océan- 106 Ki 5.00N 155.00W
Pacific Ocean (EN) = Taiheiyō 106 Ki 5.00N 155.00W
Pacific Ocean (EN) = Tihi okean 106 Ki 5.00N 155.00W
Pacific Ranges 180 Ef 50.55N 125.10W
Pacifique, Océan- = Pacific Ocean (EN) 106 Ki 5.00N 155.00W
Packsattel 128 Id 46.58N 14.58 E
Pacuí, Rio- 204 Jc 16.46S 45.01W
Pacuneiro, Rio- 204 Fa 13.02S 53.25W
Pacy-sur-Eure 124 De 49.01N 1.23 E
Paczków 120 Mf 50.27N 17.00 E
Padana, Pianura- = Po Valley (EN) 110 Gf 45.20N 10.00 E
Padang 142 Mj 0.57S 100.21 E
Padangpanjang 150 Dg 0.27S 100.25 E
Padangsidempuan 150 Cf 1.22N 99.16 E
Padangtikar, Pulau- 150 Eg 0.50S 109.30 E
Padany 114 He 63.19N 33.25 E
Padasjoki 116 Kc 61.21N 25.17 E
Padauiri, Rio- 202 Fd 0.15S 64.05W
Paddle Prairie 180 Fe 58.02N 117.50W
Paderborn 120 Ee 51.43N 8.46 E
Paderborn-Elsen 124 Kc 51.44N 8.41 E
Paderborn-Schloss Neuhaus 124 Kc 51.44N 8.42 E
Padeş, Vîrful- 130 Fd 45.40N 22.20 E
Padilla 202 Fg 19.19S 64.20W
Padina 130 Ke 44.50N 27.07 E
Padornelo, Portillo del- 126 Fb 42.03N 6.50W
Padova = Padua (EN) 128 Fe 45.25N 11.53 E
Padre, Morro do- 204 Ic 16.48S 47.35W
Padre Bernardo 204 Hb 15.21S 48.30W
Padre Island 182 Hf 27.00N 97.15W
Padrón 126 Db 42.44N 8.40W
Padua (EN) = Padova 128 Fe 45.25N 11.53 E
Paducah [Ky.-U.S.] 176 Kf 37.05N 88.36W
Paducah [Tx.-U.S.] 186 Fi 34.01N 100.18W
Padula 128 Jj 40.20N 15.39 E
Paea 221e Fc 17.41S 149.35W
Paegam-san 154 Id 40.35N 126.15 E
Paengnyong-Do 152 Ld 38.00N 124.40 E
Paeroa 216 Eg 37.23S 175.41 E
Paestum 128 Jj 40.25N 15.01 E
Paeu 219c Bb 11.22S 166.50 E
Pafuri 172 Ed 22.26S 31.20 E
Pag 128 Jf 44.27N 15.03 E
Pag 128 If 44.30N 15.00 E
Pagadian 150 He 7.49N 123.25 E
Pagai, Kepulauan- = Pagi Islands (EN) 140 Lj 2.45S 100.00 E
Pagai Selatan 150 Dg 3.00S 100.20 E
Pagai Utara 150 Cg 2.42S 100.07 E
Pagan Island 208 Fc 18.07N 145.46 E
Pagasitikós Kólpos 130 Fj 39.15N 23.00 E
Pagatan 150 Gg 3.36S 115.56 E
Pagat Point 220c Bb 13.30N 144.53 E
Page 188 Jh 36.57N 111.27W
Pagėgiai 116 Ii 55.09N 21.54 E
Paget, Mount- 222 Ad 54.26S 36.33W
Pagi Islands (EN) = Pagai, Kepulauan- 140 Lj 2.45S 100.00 E
Paglia 128 Gh 42.42N 12.11 E
Pago Bay 220c Bb 13.25N 144.48 E
Pagoda Point 140 Lh 15.57N 94.15 E
Pāgodār 146 Qh 28.10N 57.22 E
Pago Pago 210 Jf 14.16S 170.42W
Pago Pago Harbor 221c Cb 14.17S 170.40W
Pago Redondo 204 Ci 29.35S 59.13W
Pagosa Springs 186 Ch 37.16N 107.01W
Pagoua Bay 197g Ba 15.32N 61.17W
Pagwa River 186 Na 50.01N 85.10W
Pahači 138 Ld 60.30N 169.00 E
Pahala 221a Fd 19.12N 155.29W
Pahang 150 Df 3.30N 102.45 E
Pàhara, Laguna- 194 Ff 14.18N 83.15W
Pahiatua 218 Fd 40.27S 175.50 E
Pahkāing Bum 140 Lg 26.00N 95.30 E
Pahoa 221a Gd 19.30N 154.57W
Pahokee 184 Gl 26.49N 80.40W
Pahtakor 135 Fd 40.16N 67.55 E
Pahute Mesa 188 Gh 37.20N 116.40W
Païa 219b Dc 16.35S 168.12 E
Paide/Pajde 114 Fg 58.57N 25.35 E
Paignton, Torbay- 118 Jk 50.28N 3.30W
Päijänne 110 Ic 61.35N 23.30 E
Páïkon Óros 130 Fi 40.56N 22.21 E
Paila 192 He 25.39N 102.07W
Pailín 148 Kf 12.51N 102.36 E
Pailitas 194 Ki 8.58N 73.38W
Pailolo Channel 221a Eb 21.05N 156.42W
Paimio/Pemar 116 Jd 60.27N 22.42 E
Paimionjoki 116 Jd 60.25N 22.40 E
Paimpol 122 Cf 48.46N 3.03W
Painan 150 Dg 1.21S 100.34 E
Paine, Mount- 222 Mg 86.46S 147.32W
Painel 204 Gh 27.55S 50.06W
Painesville 184 Ge 41.43N 81.15W
Painted Desert 182 Ed 36.00N 111.20W
Paintsville 184 Fg 37.49N 82.48W
País do Vinho 126 Ec 41.15N 7.55W
Paisley 118 If 55.50N 4.26W
Païta 219b Cf 22.08S 166.22 E
Paita 202 Be 5.06S 81.07W
Paiva 126 Dc 41.04N 8.16W
Paj 114 If 61.43N 34.28 E
Pajala 114 Fc 67.12N 23.22 E
Pajares, Puerto de- 126 Ga 43.00N 5.46W
Pajaros, Farallon de- 208 Fb 20.32N 144.54 E
Pajaros, Punta- 192 Ph 19.36N 87.25W
Pajaros Point 197a Db 18.31N 64.18W
Pajatén 202 Ce 7.29S 77.22W
Pajde/Paide 114 Fg 58.57N 25.35 E
Pajęczno 120 Oe 51.09N 19.00 E
Pajer, gora- 136 Gb 66.40N 64.20 E
Paj-Hoj 110 Mb 69.00N 62.30 E
Pajule 170 Fb 2.58N 32.56 E
Pakanbaru 142 Mi 0.32N 101.27 E
Pakaraima Mountains 202 Fb 4.05N 61.30W
Pakharan 148 Ec 26.55N 71.55 E
Pakch'on 154 He 39.44N 125.35 E
Pakhna 146 Ee 34.46N 32.48 E
Pákhnes 130 Hn 35.18N 24.02 E
Paki 166 Gc 11.30N 8.09 E
Pakima 170 Dc 3.21S 24.06 E
Pakin Atoll 208 Gd 7.04N 157.48 E
Pakistan 142 Ig 30.00N 70.00 E
Pakleni Otoci 128 Kg 43.10N 16.23 E
Pakokku 148 Jd 21.17N 95.06 E
Pakowki Lake 188 Jb 49.22N 110.57W
Pak Phanang 148 Kg 8.21N 100.12 E
Pakrac 128 Le 45.26N 17.12 E
Pakruois/Pakruojis 114 Fi 55.57N 23.50 E
Pakruojis/Pakruois 114 Fi 55.57N 23.50 E
Paks 120 Oj 46.38N 18.52 E
Paktīā 144 Kc 33.30N 69.30 E
Pakwach 170 Fb 2.28N 31.30 E
Pakxé 142 Mh 15.07N 105.47 E
Pakxèng 148 Kd 20.10N 102.40 E
Pala 168 Ad 9.22N 14.54 E
Palacca Point 194 Kc 21.15N 73.26W
Palacios [Arg.] 204 Bj 30.43S 61.37W
Palacios [Tx.-U.S.] 186 Hl 28.42N 96.13W
Palafrugell 126 Pc 41.55N 3.10 E
Palagruža 128 Kh 42.24N 16.15 E
Palaiokastrítsa 130 Cj 39.40N 19.41 E
Palaiokhóra 130 Gn 35.14N 23.41 E
Palais, Le- 122 Cg 47.21N 3.09W
Palaiseau 124 Ef 48.43N 2.15 E
Palamás 130 Fj 39.28N 22.05 E
Palamós 126 Pc 41.51N 3.08 E
Palamuse/Palamuze 116 Lf 58.39N 26.35 E
Palamut 130 Kk 38.59N 27.41 E
Palamuze/Palamuse 116 Lf 58.39N 26.35 E
Palana 142 Rd 59.07N 159.58 E
Palancia / Palància 126 Le 39.40N 0.12W
Palància / Palancia 126 Le 39.40N 0.12W
Palanga 136 Cd 55.57N 21.05 E
Palangkaraya 150 Fg 2.16S 113.56 E
Pālanpur 148 Ed 24.10N 72.26 E
Palaoa Point 221a Ec 20.44N 156.58W
Palapye 160 Jk 22.33S 27.08 E
Palasa 150 Hf 0.29N 120.24 E
Palatka [Fl.-U.S.] 182 Kf 29.39N 81.38W
Palatka [R.S.F.S.R.] 138 Kd 60.05N 151.00 E
Palau (EN) = Belau 128 Di 41.11N 9.23 E
Palau 210 Ed 7.30N 134.30 E
Palau Islands 208 Ed 7.30N 134.30 E
Palauli 221c Aa 13.44S 172.16W
Palauli Bay 221c Aa 13.47S 172.14W
Palau Trench (EN) 214 Af 6.30N 134.30 E
Palavas-les-Flots 122 Jk 43.32N 3.56 E
Palaw 148 Jf 12.58N 98.39 E
Palawan 140 Ni 9.30N 118.30 E
Palawan Passage 150 Gd 10.00N 118.00 E
Palayan 150 Hc 15.33N 121.06 E
Pālayankottai 148 Fg 8.43N 77.44 E
Palazzo, Punta- 122a Aa 42.22N 8.33 E
Palazzolo Acreide 128 Im 37.04N 14.54 E
Palazzolo sull'Oglio 128 De 45.36N 9.53 E

Index Symbols

- 1 Independent Nation
- 2 State, Region
- 3 District, County
- 4 Municipality
- 5 Colony, Dependency
- Continent
- Physical Region
- Historical or Cultural Region
- Mount, Mountain
- Volcano
- Hill
- Mountains, Mountain Range
- Hills, Escarpment
- Plateau, Upland
- Pass, Gap
- Plain, Lowland
- Delta
- Salt Flat
- Valley, Canyon
- Crater, Cave
- Karst Features
- Depression
- Polder
- Desert, Dunes
- Forest, Woods
- Heath, Steppe
- Oasis
- Cape, Point
- Coast, Beach
- Cliff
- Peninsula
- Isthmus
- Sandbank
- Island
- Atoll
- Rock, Reef
- Islands, Archipelago
- Rocks, Reefs
- Coral Reef
- Well, Spring
- Geyser
- River, Stream
- Waterfall, Rapids
- River Mouth, Estuary
- Lake
- Salt Lake
- Intermittent Lake
- Reservoir
- Swamp, Pond
- Canal
- Glacier
- Ice Shelf, Pack Ice
- Ocean
- Sea
- Gulf, Bay
- Strait, Fjord
- Lagoon
- Bank
- Seamount
- Tablemount
- Ridge
- Shelf
- Basin
- Escarpment, Sea Scarp
- Fracture
- Trench, Abyss
- National Park, Reserve
- Point of Interest
- Recreation Site
- Cave, Cavern
- Historic Site
- Ruins
- Wall, Walls
- Church, Abbey
- Temple
- Scientific Station
- Railway station
- Airport
- Port
- Military installation
- Lighthouse
- Mine
- Tunnel
- Dam, Bridge

Paldiski 136 Cd 59.20N 24.06 E
Pale di San Martino 128 Fd 46.14N 11.53 E
Paleleh 150 Hf 1.04N 121.57 E
Palembang 142 Mj 2.55S 104.45 E
Palena 128 Ii 41.59N 14.08 E
Palencia 126 Hb 42.01N 4.32W
Palencia [3] 126 Hb 42.25N 4.30W
Palen Lake 188 Hj 33.46N 115.12W
Palenque 176 Jh 17.30N 92.00W
Palenque [Mex.] 192 Ni 17.31N 91.58W
Palenque [Pan.] 194 Hi 9.13N 79.41W
Palenque, Punta- 194 Ld 18.14N 70.09W
Palermo 112 Hh 38.07N 13.22 E
Palermo, Golfo di- 128 Hl 38.10N 13.25 E
Palestina = Palestine (EN) 144 Dc 32.15N 34.47 E
Palestina = Palestine (EN) 146 Ff 32.15N 34.47 E
Palestine 182 He 31.46N 95.38W
Palestine (EN) = Palestina 144 Dc 32.15N 34.47 E
Palestine (EN) = Palestina 146 Ff 32.15N 34.47 E
Palestrina 128 Gi 41.50N 12.53 E
Pālghāt 148 Ff 10.47N 76.39 E
Palgrave Point 172 Ad 20.28S 13.16 E
Palhoça 204 Hh 27.38S 48.40W
Pāli 148 Ec 25.46N 73.20 E
Palinuro, Capo- 128 Jj 40.02N 15.16 E
Palinuro, Centola- 128 Jj 40.02N 15.17 E
Palisades Reservoir 188 Je 43.04N 111.26W
Paliseul 124 He 49.54N 5.08 E
Palivere 116 Jf 59.00N 23.45 E
Palizada 192 Mh 18.15N 92.05W
Paljakka 114 Gd 64.45N 28.07 E
Paljavaam 138 Mc 68.50N 170.50 E
Paljenik 110 Hg 44.15N 17.36 E
Pälkäne 116 Kc 61.20N 24.16 E
Palkino 116 Mg 57.29N 28.10 E
Palk Strait 140 Ji 10.00N 79.45 E
Palla Bianca/Weißkugel 128 Ed 46.48N 10.44 E
Pallars 126 Mb 42.25N 0.55 E
Pallasovka 136 Ee 50.03N 46.55 E
Pallastunturi 114 Fb 68.06N 24.02 E
Palliser, Cape- 216 Eh 41.37S 175.16 E
Palliser, Iles- 208 Mf 15.30S 146.30W
Palma 172 Gb 10.46S 40.28 E
Palma / La Ciutat de Mallorca 112 Gh 39.34N 2.39 E
Palma, Badia de-/Palma, Bahia de- 126 Oe 39.27N 2.35 E
Palma, Bahia de-/Palma, Badia de- 126 Oe 39.27N 2.35 E
Palma, Rio- 202 If 12.33S 47.52W
Palma, Sierra de la- 192 Id 26.00N 101.35W
Palma del Rio 126 Gg 37.42N 5.17W
Palma di Montechiaro 128 Hm 37.11N 13.46 E
Palmar, Laguna del- 204 Bi 29.35S 60.42W
Palmar, Rio- 194 Lh 10.11N 71.52W
Palmar, Salto- 204 Cg 24.18S 59.18W
Palmares 202 Ke 8.41S 35.36W
Palmares do Sul 204 Gj 30.16S 50.31W
Palmarito 202 Db 7.37N 70.10W
Palmarola 128 Gj 40.55N 12.50 E
Palmar Sur 190 Hg 8.58N 83.29W
Palmas 206 Jc 26.30S 52.00W
Palmas, Cape- 158 Gh 4.22N 7.44W
Palmas, Golfo di- 128 Cl 39.00N 8.30 E
Palmas Bellas 194 Gi 9.14N 80.05W
Palma Soriano 190 Id 20.13N 76.00W
Palm Bay 184 Gk 28.01N 80.35W
Palm Beach 182 Kf 26.42N 80.02W
Palmdale 188 Fi 34.35N 118.07W
Palmeira 204 Gg 25.25S 50.00W
Palmeira das Missões 206 Jc 27.55S 53.17W
Palmeira dos Indios 202 Ke 9.25S 36.37W
Palmeirais 202 Je 5.58S 43.04W
Palmeiras, Rio- 204 Gb 15.25S 51.10W
Palmeiras de Goiás 204 Hc 16.47S 49.53W
Palmeirinhas, Ponta das- 158 Ii 9.05S 13.00 E
Palmela 126 Df 38.34N 8.54W
Palmer 178 Jd 61.36N 149.07W
Palmer Archipelago 222 Qe 64.10S 62.00W
Palmer Land (EN) 222 Qf 71.30S 65.00W
Palmer Station 222 Qe 64.46S 64.05W
Palmerston 218 Df 45.29S 170.43 E
Palmerston Atoll 208 Kf 18.04S 163.10W
Palmerston North 210 Ii 40.20S 175.17 E
Palmetto Point 197d Ba 17.35N 61.52W
Palmi 128 Jl 38.21N 15.51 E
Palmira [Col.] 200 Ie 3.32N 76.16W
Palmira [Cuba] 194 Gb 22.14N 80.23W
Palm Islands 212 Jc 18.40S 146.30 E
Palmital 204 Fg 24.39S 52.16W
Palmitas 204 Dk 33.27S 57.48W
Palmito 204 Cd 18.53S 58.22W
Palmitos 204 Fh 27.05S 53.08W
Palm Springs 188 De 33.50N 116.33W
Palmyra 144 Ec 34.33N 38.17 E
Palmyra Atoll 208 Kd 5.52N 162.06W
Palo Alto 182 Cd 37.27N 122.09W
Paloh 150 Ef 1.43N 109.18 E
Paloich 168 Ec 10.28N 32.32 E
Palomani, Nevado- 198 Jg 14.38S 69.14W
Palomar Mountain 182 De 33.22N 116.50W
Palomera, Sierra- 126 Kd 40.40N 1.12W
Palopo 142 Oj 3.00S 120.12 E
Palos, Cabo de- 110 Fh 37.38N 0.41W
Palo Santo 204 Cg 25.34S 59.21W
Palotina 204 Fg 24.17S 53.50W
Palouse River 188 Fc 46.35N 118.13W
Palpa 202 Cf 14.32S 75.11W
Palsa 116 Lg 57.23N 26.24 E
Pålsboda 116 Fe 59.04N 15.20 E
Paltamo 114 Gd 64.25N 27.50 E
Palu [Indon.] 142 Nj 0.53S 119.53 E
Palu [Tur.] 146 Hc 38.42N 39.57 E
Palu, Pulau- 150 Hh 8.20S 121.43 E
Pam 219b Be 20.15S 164.17 E
Pama 166 Fc 11.15N 0.42 E
Pâmark/Pomarkku 116 Ic 61.42N 22.00 E
Pambarra 172 Fd 21.56S 35.06 E
Pambeguwa 166 Gc 10.40N 8.17 E
Pamekasan 150 Fh 7.10S 113.28 E
Pamiers 122 Hk 43.07N 1.36 E
Pamir 140 Jf 38.00N 73.00 E
Pamir 136 Hh 37.01N 72.41 E
Pâmiut/Frederikshåb 179 Hf 62.00N 49.45W
Pamlico Sound 182 Ld 35.20N 75.55W
Pampa 182 Gd 35.32N 100.58W
Pampa del Indio 204 Ch 26.02S 59.55W
Pampa del Infierno 204 Bh 26.31S 61.10W
Pampa de los Guanacos 206 Hc 26.14S 61.51W
Pampas 202 Df 12.24S 74.54W
Pampas 198 Ji 35.00S 63.00W
Pampeiro 204 Ej 30.38S 55.16W
Pamplona [Col.] 202 Db 7.23N 72.38W
Pamplona [Sp.] 112 Fg 42.49N 1.38W
Pamukkale 130 Ml 37.47N 29.04 E
Pamukova 130 Ni 40.31N 30.09 E
Pamunkey River 184 Ig 37.32N 76.48W
Pan, Tierra del- 126 Gc 41.50N 6.00W
Pana 170 Bc 1.41S 12.39 E
Panagjurište 130 Hg 42.30N 24.11 E
Panaitan, Pulau- 150 Eh 6.36S 105.12 E
Panaitolikón Óros 130 Ek 38.43N 21.39 E
Panaji (Panjim) 142 Jh 15.29N 73.50 E
Panakhaïkón Óros 130 Ek 38.12N 21.54 E
Panamá [1] 176 Li 9.00N 80.00W
Panamá [Pan.] = Panama City (EN) 176 Li 8.58N 79.31W
Panamá = Panama (EN) [3] 194 Hi 9.00N 79.00W
Panama (EN) = Panamá [3] 194 Hi 9.00N 79.00W
Panamá, Bahía de- 194 Hi 8.50N 79.15W
Panamá, Canal de- = Panama Canal (EN) 190 Ig 9.20N 79.55W
Panamá, Golfo de- = Panama, Gulf of- (EN) 174 Li 8.00N 79.10W
Panama, Gulf of- (EN) = Panamá, Golfo de- 174 Li 8.00N 79.10W
Panama, Isthmus of- (EN) = Panamá, Istmo de- 174 Li 9.20N 79.30W
Panamá, Istmo de- = Panama, Isthmus of- (EN) 174 Li 9.20N 79.30W
Panama Canal (EN) = Panamá, Canal de- 190 Ig 9.20N 79.55W
Panama City 176 Kf 30.10N 85.41W
Panama City (EN) = Panamá [Pan.] 176 Li 8.58N 79.31W
Panamá La Vieja 194 Hi 9.00N 79.29W
Panambi 204 Fi 28.18S 53.30W
Panamint Range 188 Gh 36.30N 117.20W
Panao 202 Ce 9.49S 76.00W
Panarea 128 Jl 38.40N 15.05 E
Panaro 128 Ff 44.55N 11.25 E
Pana Tinai 219a Ad 11.14S 153.10 E
Pana-Wina 219a Ad 11.11S 153.01 E
Panay 140 Oh 11.15N 122.30 E
Pancake Range 188 Hg 39.00N 115.45W
Pančevo 130 De 44.52N 20.39 E
Pančićev vrh 130 Df 43.15N 20.45 E
Panciu 130 Kd 45.54N 27.05 E
Pancros 219b Db 15.58S 168.12 E
Panda 172 Ed 24.03S 34.43 E
Panda ma Tenga 172 Dc 18.32S 25.38 E
Pandan 150 Hd 11.43N 122.06 E
Pan de Azúcar 204 El 34.48S 55.14W
Pandeiros, Ribeirão- 204 Jb 15.42S 44.36W
Pandelis/Pandėlys 116 Kh 56.01N 25.21 E
Pandėlys/Pandelis 116 Kh 56.01N 25.21 E
Pandharpur 148 Fe 17.40N 75.20 E
Pándheon 130 Fl 40.05N 22.20 E
Pāndhurna 148 Fd 21.36N 78.31 E
Pandivere Kõrgustik / Pandivere vozvyšennost 116 Le 59.00N 26.15 E
Pandivere vozvyšennost / Pandivere Kõrgustik 116 Le 59.00N 26.15 E
Pando 206 Id 34.43S 55.57W
Pando [3] 202 Ef 11.20S 67.40W
Pandokrátor 130 Cj 39.45N 19.52 E
Pandora 194 Fi 9.45N 82.57W
Pandrup 116 Cg 57.14N 9.41 E
Pandu 170 Cb 4.59N 19.16 E
Panevėžis/Panevėžys 136 Cd 55.44N 24.22 E
Panevėžys/Panevežis 136 Cd 55.44N 24.22 E
Panfilov 136 Ig 44.08N 80.01 E
Panga 170 Eb 1.51N 26.25 E
Pangai 221b Ba 19.48S 174.21W
Pangaion Óros 130 Hi 40.50N 24.05 E
Pangalanes, Canal des- 158 Lk 22.48S 47.50 E
Pangani 170 Gd 5.26S 38.58 E
Pangani or Ruvu 170 Gc 5.26S 38.58 E
Pange 124 Ie 49.05N 6.22 E
Panggoe 210 Ge 7.01S 157.05 E
Pangi 170 Ec 3.11S 26.38 E
Pangkajene 150 Gg 4.50S 119.32 E
Pangkalanberandan 150 Cf 4.01N 98.17 E
Pangkalanbuun 150 Fg 2.41S 111.37 E
Pangkalaseang, Tanjung- 150 Hg 0.42S 123.26 E
Pangkalpinang 150 Eg 2.08S 106.08 E
Pangnirtung 176 Mc 66.08N 65.44W
Pang-Pang 219b Dc 17.41S 168.32 E
Panguitch 182 Ed 37.49N 112.26W
Panguma 166 Cd 8.24N 11.13W
Pangutaran Group 150 He 6.15N 120.30 E
Panhandle 186 Fi 35.21N 101.23W
Pania Mutombo 170 Dd 5.11S 23.51 E
Paniau 221a Ab 21.57N 160.05W
Panié, Mont- 216 Bd 20.36S 164.46 E
Pānīpat 148 Fc 29.23N 76.58 E
Paniza, Puerto de- 126 Kc 41.15N 1.20W
Panjang 150 Eh 5.29S 105.18 E
Panjang, Pulau- 150 Ef 2.44N 108.55 E
Panjgūr 148 Cc 26.58N 64.06 E
Panjim → Panaji 142 Jh 15.29N 73.50 E
Panjwīn 146 Ke 35.36N 45.58 E
Pankow, Berlin- 120 Jd 52.34N 13.24 E
Pankshin 166 Gd 9.20N 9.27 E
P'anmunjŏm 154 If 37.57N 126.40 E
Panopah 150 Fg 1.56S 111.11 E
Panorama 206 Jb 21.21S 51.51W
Panshan 154 Gd 41.12N 122.03 E
Panshi 152 Mc 42.56N 126.02 E
Pant 124 Cc 51.53N 0.39 E
Pantanal 198 Kg 18.00S 56.00W
Pantar, Pulau- 150 Hh 8.25S 124.07 E
Pantego 184 Ih 35.34N 76.36W
Pantelleria 128 Fn 36.50N 11.57 E
Pantelleria 110 Hh 36.47N 12.00 E
Pantelleria, Canale di- 128 Fn 36.40N 11.45 E
Pante Makassar 150 Hh 9.12S 124.23 E
Pantoja 202 Cd 0.58S 75.10W
Pánuco 192 Jf 22.03N 98.10W
Pánuco 174 Jg 22.16N 97.47W
Panxian 152 Hf 25.45N 104.39 E
Panyam 166 Gd 9.25N 9.13 E
Panzi 170 Cd 7.13S 17.58 E
Panzós 194 Cf 15.24N 89.40W
Pao, Río- [Ven.] 196 Dh 8.06N 64.17W
Pao, Río- [Ven.] 196 Bh 8.33N 68.01W
Paola [It.] 128 Kk 39.21N 16.03 E
Paola [Ks.-U.S.] 186 Ig 38.35N 94.53W
Paoli 184 Df 38.33N 86.28W
Paopao 221e Fc 17.30S 149.49W
Paoua 168 Bd 7.15N 16.26 E
Pápa 120 Ni 47.20N 17.28 E
Papa 221a Fd 19.13N 155.52W
Papaaloa 221a Fd 19.59N 155.13W
Papagaio, Rio- → Saturninā, Rio- 204 Ca 13.55S 58.18W
Papagaios 204 Jd 19.32S 44.45W
Papagayo, Golfo del- 190 Gf 10.45N 85.45W
Papaikou 221a Fd 19.47N 155.06W
Papakura 218 Fb 37.03S 174.57 E
Papalopapán, Rio- 192 Lh 18.42N 95.38W
Papanduva 204 Gh 26.25S 50.09W
Papanin Seamount (EN) 224 Ca 46.00N 170.00 E
Papantla de Olarte 190 Ed 20.27N 97.19W
Papar 150 Ge 5.44N 115.56 E
Paparoa Range 218 De 42.05S 171.35 E
Papa Stour 118 La 60.30N 1.40W
Papa Westray 118 Kb 59.22N 2.54W
Papeete 210 Mf 17.32S 149.34W
Papenburg 120 Dc 53.04N 7.24 E
Papenburg-Aschendorf (Ems) 124 Ja 53.04N 7.22 E
Papenoo 221e Fc 17.30S 149.25W
Papes ezers / Papes ozero 116 Ih 56.15N 20.55 E
Papes ozero / Papes ezers 116 Ih 56.15N 20.55 E
Papetoai 221e Fc 17.30S 149.52W
Papey 114a Cb 64.36N 14.11W
Paphos/Baf 146 Ee 34.50N 32.35 E
Papija 130 Kg 42.07N 27.51 E
Papikion Óros 130 Ih 41.15N 25.18 E
Papilė/Papilé 116 Jh 56.09N 22.45 E
Papilé/Papilė 116 Jh 56.09N 22.45 E
Papillion 186 Hf 41.09N 96.03W
Papua, Gulf of- 208 Fe 8.32S 145.00 E
Papua New Guinea [1] 210 Fe 6.00S 150.00 E
Papua Passage 220p Bc 21.15S 159.47W
Papuk 128 Le 45.31N 17.39 E
Papun 148 Je 18.04N 97.27 E
Pará [2] 202 Hd 4.00S 53.00W
Pará 114 Ji 54.23N 40.53 E
Pará, Rio- 198 Lf 1.30S 48.55W
Pará, Rio- 204 Jd 19.13S 45.07W
Parabel 138 De 58.43N 81.31 E
Parabel 138 De 58.40N 81.30 E
Paraburdoo 212 Dd 23.15S 117.45 E
Paracas 202 Cf 13.49S 76.16W
Paracatu 202 Ig 17.13S 46.52W
Paracatu, Rio- [Braz.] 204 Ic 17.30S 46.32W
Paracatu, Rio- [Braz.] 204 Jc 16.30S 45.04W
Paracel Islands (EN) = Xisha Qundao 140 Nh 16.30N 112.15 E
Pārachinār 148 Eb 33.54N 70.06 E
Paraćin 130 Ef 43.52N 21.25 E
Paracuru 202 Kd 3.24S 39.04W
Parada Km 329 204 Ek 32.30S 55.25W
Paradip 148 Hd 20.19N 86.42 E
Paradise [Ca.-U.S.] 188 Eg 39.46N 121.37W
Paradise [Mi.-U.S.] 184 Eb 46.38N 85.03W
Paragould 186 Kh 36.03N 90.29W
Paragua, Río- 202 Fb 6.55N 62.55W
Paraguá, Rio- 202 Ff 13.34S 61.53W
Paraguaçu, Rio- 198 Mg 12.45S 38.54W
Paraguaçu Paulista 204 Gf 22.25S 50.34W
Paraguai, Rio- 198 Kh 27.18S 58.38W
Paraguaipoa 194 Lh 11.21N 71.57W
Paraguaná, Península de- 202 Da 11.55N 70.00W
Paraguari 206 Ic 25.38S 57.09W
Paraguari [3] 204 Dg 26.00S 57.10W
Paraguay [1] 200 Kh 23.00S 58.00W
Paraguay, Rio- 198 Kh 27.18S 58.38W
Paraiba [2] 202 Ke 7.10S 36.30W
Paraíba do Sul, Rio- 198 Lh 21.37S 41.03W
Paraibuna, Represa do- 204 Jf 23.25S 45.35W
Paraibuna, Rio- 204 Jf 23.22S 45.40W
Parainen/Pargas 114 Ff 60.18N 22.18 E
Paraiso [Braz.] 204 Fd 19.03S 52.59W
Paraiso [Mex.] 192 Mh 18.24N 93.14W
Paraiso, Rio- 204 Bb 15.08S 61.52W
Parakou 160 Hh 9.21N 2.37 E
Param 220d Bb 7.22N 151.48 E
Paramaribo 200 Ke 5.50N 55.10W
Paramera, Sierra de la- 126 Hd 40.30N 4.46W
Paramithiá 130 Dj 39.28N 20.31 E
Páramo de Masa, Puerto de- 126 Ib 42.38N 3.44W
Paramušir, ostrov- 140 Rd 50.25N 155.50 E
Paraná 200 Ji 31.45S 60.30W
Paraná [2] 206 Jb 24.00S 51.00W
Paraná, Pico- 204 Hg 25.14S 48.48W
Paraná, Rio- 198 Ki 33.43S 59.15W
Paranã, Rio- 198 Lg 12.30S 48.14W
Paraná de las Palmas, Rio- 204 Cl 34.18S 58.33W
Paranaguá 200 Lh 25.31S 48.30W
Paraná-Guazú, Rio- 204 Ck 34.00S 58.25W
Paranaiba 202 Hg 19.40S 51.11W
Paranaíba, Rio- 198 Kh 20.07S 51.05W
Paranaiguara 204 Gd 18.53S 50.28W
Paranapanema, Rio- 198 Kh 22.40S 53.09W
Paranapiacaba, Serra do- 198 Lh 24.20S 49.00W
Paranapuã-Guaçu, Ponta do- 204 Ig 24.24S 47.00W
Paranavai 206 Jb 23.04S 52.28W
Parandak 146 Ne 35.21N 50.42 E
Paranéstion 130 Hh 41.16N 24.30 E
Paranhos 204 Ef 23.55S 55.25W
Paraoa Atoll 208 Mf 19.09S 140.43W
Paraopeba 204 Jd 19.18S 44.25W
Paraopeba, Rio- 204 Jd 18.50S 45.11W
Parapara 219b Ca 13.32S 167.20 E
Paraparaumu 218 Fd 40.55S 175.00 E
Paraspóri 130 Kn 35.54N 27.14 E
Parati 204 Jf 23.13S 44.43W
Paratodos, Serra- 204 Jb 14.40S 44.50W
Paratunka 138 Kf 52.52N 158.12 E
Pārāu, Kūh-e- 146 Le 34.37N 47.05 E
Paraúna 204 Gc 17.02S 50.26W
Paravae 220n Bc 10.27S 160.58W
Paray-le-Monial 122 Kh 46.27N 4.07 E
Parbati 148 Fc 25.51N 76.36 E
Parbhani 148 Fe 19.16N 76.47 E
Parchim 120 Hc 53.26N 11.51 E
Parczew 120 Se 51.39N 22.54 E
Pardo 204 Cm 36.15S 59.22W
Pardo, Rio- [Braz.] 204 Jb 15.48S 44.48W
Pardo, Rio- [Braz.] 204 He 20.10S 48.38W
Pardo, Rio- [Braz.] 204 Hf 22.55S 49.58W
Pardo, Rio- [Braz.] 204 Fi 29.59S 52.23W
Pardo, Rio- [Braz.] 202 Hh 21.46S 52.09W
Pardo, Rio- [Braz.] 202 Kg 15.39S 38.57W
Pardubice 120 Lf 50.02N 15.45 E
Parea 221e Eb 16.49S 150.58W
Parecis, Chapada dos- 198 Kg 13.00S 60.00W
Parecis, Rio- 204 Da 12.56S 56.43W
Paredes de Nava 126 Hb 42.09N 4.41W
Parelhas 202 Ke 6.41S 36.39W
Paren 138 Ld 62.28N 163.05 E
Parent 180 Kg 47.55N 74.37W
Parentis-en-Born 122 Ej 44.21N 1.04W
Pareora 218 Df 44.29S 171.13 E
Parepare 142 Nj 4.01S 119.38 E
Párga 130 Dj 39.17N 20.24 E
Pargas/Parainen 114 Ff 60.18N 22.18 E
Pargolovo 116 Nd 60.03N 30.30 E
Parham 197d Bb 17.05N 61.46W
Parhar 136 Gh 37.31N 69.23 E
Pari, Rio- 204 Db 15.36S 56.08W
Paria, Golfo de-/Paria, Gulf of- 202 Fa 10.20N 62.00W
Paria, Gulf of-/Paria, Golfo de- 202 Fa 10.20N 62.00W
Paria, Peninsula de- 196 Eg 10.40N 62.30W
Pariaguán 202 Fb 8.51N 64.43W
Pariaman 150 Dg 0.38S 100.08 E
Paria River 188 Jh 36.52N 111.36W
Paricutín, Volcán- 192 Hh 19.28N 102.15W
Parida, Isla- 194 Fi 8.07N 82.20W
Pari das Pedras 204 Ja 12.45S 44.47W
Parigi 150 Hg 0.48S 120.10 E
Parika 202 Gb 6.52N 58.25W
Parikkala 114 Gf 61.33N 29.30 E
Parima, Serra- 198 Je 3.00N 64.20W
Parinacota 206 Ga 18.12S 69.16W
Pariñas, Punta- 198 Hf 4.40S 81.20W
Paringul Mare, Vîrful- 130 Gd 45.20N 23.30 E
Parintins 200 Kf 2.36S 56.44W
Paris [Fr.] 112 Gf 48.52N 2.20 E
Paris [Il.-U.S.] 186 Mg 39.36N 87.42W
Paris [Kir.] 220g Ab 1.56N 157.31W
Paris [Ky.-U.S.] 184 Ef 38.13N 84.14W
Paris [Tn.-U.S.] 184 Cg 36.19N 88.20W
Paris [Tx.-U.S.] 182 He 33.40N 95.33W
Paris Basin (EN) = Parisien, Bassin- 110 Gf 49.00N 2.00 E
Parisien, Bassin- = Paris Basin (EN) 110 Gf 49.00N 2.00 E
Parita 194 Gi 8.00N 80.31W
Parita, Bahia de- 194 Gi 8.08N 80.24W
Parit Buntar 150 De 5.07N 100.30 E
Parkano 114 Fe 62.01N 23.01 E
Parkent 135 Gd 41.18N 69.40 E
Parker 188 Hi 34.09N 114.17W
Parker, Mount- 212 Fc 17.10S 128.20 E
Parkersburg 182 Kd 39.17N 81.33W
Parker Seamount (EN) 178 If 52.35N 151.15W
Parkes 210 Fh 33.08S 148.11 E
Park Falls 186 Kd 45.56N 90.32W
Parkland 188 Dc 47.09N 122.26W
Park Range 182 Fc 40.00N 106.30W
Park Rapids 186 Ic 46.55N 95.04W
Park River 186 Hb 48.24N 97.45W
Park Valley 188 If 41.50N 113.21W
Parma 128 Ef 44.56N 10.26 E
Parma [It.] 112 Hg 44.48N 10.20 E
Parma [Oh.-U.S.] 184 Ge 41.24N 81.44W
Parnaguá 202 Jf 10.13S 44.38W
Parnaíba 200 Lf 2.54S 41.47W
Parnaíba, Rio- 198 Lf 3.00S 41.50W
Parnamirim [Braz.] 202 Ke 8.05S 39.34W
Parnamirim [Braz.] 202 Ke 5.55S 35.15W
Parnarama 202 Je 5.41S 43.06W
Parnassós Óros = Parnassus (EN) 110 Ih 38.30N 22.37 E
Parnassus 218 Ee 42.43S 173.17 E
Parnassus (EN) = Parnassós Óros 110 Ih 38.30N 22.37 E
Párnis Óros 130 Gk 38.10N 23.40 E
Párnon Óros 130 Fl 37.12N 22.38 E
Pärnu/Pjarnu 112 Id 58.24N 24.32 E
Pärnu-Jaagupi/Pjarnu-Jagupi 116 Kf 58.36N 24.25 E
Pärnu jõgi / Pjarnu 114 Fg 58.23N 24.34 E
Pärnu laht / Pjarnu, zaliv- 114 Fg 58.15N 24.25 E
Parola 116 Kc 61.03N 24.22 E
Paroo River 208 Fh 31.28S 143.32 E
Paropamisus/Salseleh-ye Safīd Kūh 140 If 34.30N 63.30 E
Páros 130 Il 37.05N 25.09 E
Páros 130 Il 37.06N 25.12 E
Parowan 188 Ih 37.51N 112.57W
Parpaillon 122 Mj 44.35N 6.40 E
Parque Industrial 204 Jd 19.57S 44.01W
Parral 206 Fe 36.09S 71.50W
Parral, Rio- 192 Gd 27.35N 105.25W
Parras, Sierra de- 192 He 25.25N 102.00W
Parras de la Fuente 190 Dc 25.25N 102.11W
Parravicini 204 Dm 36.27S 57.46W
Parrett 118 Jj 51.13N 3.01W
Parrita 194 Ei 9.30N 84.19W
Parry, Cape - 180 Fb 70.12N 124.35W
Parry, Kap- [Grld.] 179 Jd 72.28N 22.00W
Parry, Kap- [Grld.] 179 Ec 77.00N 71.00W
Parry Bay 180 Jc 68.00N 82.00W
Parry Islands 174 Ib 76.00N 110.00W
Parry Peninsula 180 Fc 69.45N 124.35W
Parry Sound 180 Jg 45.21N 80.02W
Parsęta 120 Lb 54.12N 15.33 E
Parsons [Ks.-U.S.] 182 Hd 37.20N 95.16W
Parsons [W.V.-U.S.] 184 Hf 39.06N 79.43W
Parsons Range 212 Hb 13.30S 135.15 E
Partanna 128 Gm 37.43N 12.53 E
Parthenay 122 Fh 46.39N 0.15W
Partille 116 Eg 57.44N 12.07 E
Partinico 128 Hl 38.03N 13.07 E
Partizansk 138 Ih 43.13N 133.05 E
Partizánske 120 Oh 48.38N 18.23 E
Partizanskoje 138 Ee 55.30N 94.30 E
Paru, Rio- 198 Kf 1.33S 52.38W
Paru de Este, Rio- 202 Hc 1.10N 54.40W
Paru de Oeste, Rio- 198 Kf 1.30S 56.00W
Paruru 219a Ec 9.51S 160.49 E
Parvān [3] 144 Kb 35.15N 69.30 E
Pārvomaj 130 Ig 42.06N 25.13 E
Parys 172 De 27.04S 27.16 E
Paša 114 Hf 60.28N 32.55 E
Pasadena [Ca.-U.S.] 176 Hf 34.09N 118.09W
Pasadena [Tx.-U.S.] 186 Il 29.42N 95.13W
Paşaeli Yarımadası 130 Lh 41.20N 28.25 E
Paşalimanı Adası 130 Ki 40.28N 27.37 E
Pasangkaju 150 Gg 1.10S 119.20 E
Pāsārgād 146 Og 30.17N 52.55 E
Pasarwajo 150 Hh 5.29S 122.50 E
Pascagoula 182 Je 30.23N 88.31W
Paşcani 130 Jb 47.15N 26.44 E
Pasco 182 Db 46.14N 119.06W
Pasco [3] 202 Cf 10.30S 75.15W
Pascoal 204 Ba 13.38S 61.06W
Pascoal, Monte- 202 Kg 16.54S 39.24W
Pascua, Isla de- / Rapa Nui = Easter Island (EN) 208 Qg 27.07S 109.22W
Pas-de-Calais [3] 122 Id 50.30N 2.20 E
Pas-en-Artois 124 Ed 50.09N 2.30 E
Pasewalk 120 Jc 53.31N 13.59 E
Pasinler 146 Ib 40.00N 41.41 E
Pašino 138 De 55.11N 83.02 E
Pasión, Rio de la- 194 Be 16.28N 90.33W
Pasir Mas 150 De 6.02N 102.08 E
Pasirpengarayan 150 Df 0.51N 100.16 E
Pasir Puteh 150 De 5.50N 102.24 E
Påskallavik 116 Gg 57.10N 16.27 E
Paškovski 132 Kg 45.01N 39.05 E
Pasłęk 120 Pb 54.05N 19.39 E
Pasłęka 120 Pb 54.25N 19.50 E
Pašman 128 Jg 43.57N 15.21 E
Pasni 142 Ig 25.16N 63.28 E
Paso de Indios 206 Gf 43.52S 69.06W
Paso del Cerro 204 Ej 31.31S 55.46W
Paso de los Libres 206 Ic 29.43S 57.05W
Paso de los Toros 206 Id 32.49S 56.31W
Paso Tranqueras 204 Ej 31.12S 55.45W
Passamaquoddy Bay 184 Nc 45.06N 66.59W
Passa Três, Serra- 204 Hb 14.40S 49.30W
Passau 120 Jh 48.35N 13.29 E
Passero, Capo- 128 Jn 36.40N 15.10 E
Passo Fundo 200 Kh 28.15S 52.24W
Passo Fundo, Rio- 204 Fh 27.16S 52.42W
Passos 202 Ig 20.43S 46.37W
Pastaza, Rio- 198 If 4.50S 76.25W
Pasteur 206 He 35.08S 62.14W
Pasto 200 Ie 1.13N 77.17W
Pastora Peak 188 Kh 36.47N 109.10W
Pastoria, Laguna de- 192 Ki 16.00N 97.40W
Pastos Bons 202 Je 6.36S 44.05W
Pastrana 126 Jd 40.25N 2.55W
Paštrik 130 Dg 42.14N 20.32 E
Pasubio 128 Fe 45.47N 11.10 E
Pasvalis/Pasvalys 114 Fh 56.02N 24.28 E
Pasvalys/Pasvalis 114 Fh 56.02N 24.28 E
Pásztó 120 Pi 47.55N 19.42 E
Patagonia 198 Jj 44.00S 68.00W
Patagónica, Cordillera- 198 Ij 46.00S 71.30W
Patan 148 Hc 27.40N 85.20 E
Pātan 148 Ed 23.50N 72.07 E
Patani 150 If 0.18N 128.48 E
Pata Peninsula 220d Bb 7.23N 151.35 E
Patchogue 184 Ke 40.46N 73.01W
Pate 170 Hc 2.08S 41.00 E
Patea 218 Fc 39.46S 174.29 E
Patea 218 Fc 39.46S 174.30 E
Pategi 166 Gd 8.44N 5.45 E
Patensie 172 Cf 33.46S 24.49 E

Index Symbols

[1] Independent Nation
[2] State, Region
[3] District, County
[4] Municipality
[5] Colony, Dependency
Continent
Physical Region
Historical or Cultural Region
Mount, Mountain
Volcano
Hill
Mountains, Mountain Range
Hills, Escarpment
Plateau, Upland
Pass, Gap
Plain, Lowland
Delta
Salt Flat
Valley, Canyon
Crater, Cave
Karst Features
Depression
Polder
Desert, Dunes
Forest, Woods
Heath, Steppe
Oasis
Cape, Point
Coast, Beach
Cliff
Peninsula
Isthmus
Sandbank
Island
Atoll
Rock, Reef
Islands, Archipelago
Rocks, Reefs
Coral Reef
Well, Spring
Geyser
River, Stream
Waterfall, Rapids
River Mouth, Estuary
Lake
Salt Lake
Intermittent Lake
Reservoir
Swamp, Pond
Canal
Glacier
Ice Shelf, Pack Ice
Ocean
Sea
Gulf, Bay
Strait, Fjord
Lagoon
Bank
Seamount
Tablemount
Ridge
Shelf
Basin
Escarpment, Sea Scarp
Fracture
Trench, Abyss
National Park, Reserve
Point of Interest
Recreation Site
Cave, Cavern
Historic Site
Ruins
Wall, Walls
Church, Abbey
Temple
Scientific Station
Railway station
Airport
Port
Military installation
Lighthouse
Mine
Tunnel
Dam, Bridge

Paternò 128 Jm 37.34N 15.54 E
Paterson 182 Mc 40.55N 74.10W
Paterson Inlet 218 Bg 46.55S 168.00 E
Paterson Range 212 Ed 21.45S 122.05 E
Pathānkot 148 Fb 32.17N 75.39 E
Pathein 142 Lh 16.47N 94.44 E
Pathfinder Reservoir 188 Le 42.30N 106.50W
Pathfinder Seamount (EN) 178 Kf 50.55N 143.15W
Pathiu 148 Jf 10.41N 99.20 E
Patía, Río- 202 Cc 2.13N 78.40W
Patiāla 148 Fb 30.19N 76.24 E
Patiño, Estero- 204 Cg 24.05S 59.55W
Patio 221e Db 16.35S 151.29W
Pati Point 220c Ba 13.36N 144.57 E
Pătîrlagele 130 Jd 45.19N 26.21 E
Pativilca 202 Cf 10.42S 77.47W
Pátmos 130 Jl 37.19N 26.34 E
Pátmos 130 Jl 37.20N 26.33 E
Patna 142 Kg 25.36N 85.07 E
Patnos 146 Jc 39.14N 42.52 E
Pato Branco 206 Jc 26.13S 52.40W
Patom Plateau (EN) = Patomskoje nagorje 138 Ge 59.00N 115.30 E
Patomskoje nagorje = Patom Plateau (EN) 138 Ge 59.00N 115.30 E
Patos 200 Mf 7.01S 37.16W
Patos, Isla de- 196 Fg 10.38N 61.52W
Patos, Lagoa dos- 198 Ki 31.06S 51.15W
Patos, Laguna de los- 204 Aj 30.25S 62.15W
Patos, Ribeirão dos- 204 Gd 18.58S 50.30W
Patos, Rio dos- [Braz.] 204 Da 13.33S 56.29W
Patos, Rio dos- [Braz.] 204 Hb 14.59S 48.46W
Patos de Minas 200 Lg 18.35S 46.32W
Patosi 130 Ci 40.38N 19.39 E
Patquía 206 Gd 30.03S 66.53W
Pátrai 112 Ih 38.15N 21.44 E
Patrai, Gulf of- (EN) = Patraïkós Kólpos 130 Ek 38.15N 21.30 E
Patraïkós Kólpos = Patrai, Kulf of- (EN) 130 Ek 38.15N 21.30 E
Patricio Lynch, Isla- 206 Eg 48.36S 75.26W
Patricios 204 Bl 35.27S 60.42W
Patrocinio 202 Ig 18.57S 46.59W
Patta Island 158 Li 2.07S 41.03 E
Pattani 148 Kg 6.51N 101.16 E
Patteson, Passage- 219b Db 15.26S 168.09 E
Patti 128 Il 38.08N 14.58 E
Patti, Golfo di- 128 Jl 38.10N 15.05 E
Patton Seamount (EN) 174 Dd 54.40N 150.30W
Pattullo, Mount - 180 Ee 56.14N 129.39W
Patu 202 Ke 6.06S 37.38W
Patuākhāli 148 Id 22.16N 90.18 E
Patuca, Punta- 194 Ef 15.51N 84.18W
Patuca, Río- 190 He 15.50N 84.18W
Pătulele 130 Fe 44.21N 22.47 E
Patutahi 218 Gc 38.37S 177.53 E
Patuxent Range 222 Qg 84.43S 64.30W
Pátzcuaro 192 Ih 19.31N 101.36W
Pau 122 Fk 43.18N 0.22W
Pau, Gave de- 122 Ek 43.33N 1.12W
Paucartambo 202 Df 13.18S 71.40W
Paucerne, Río- 204 Ba 13.34S 61.14W
Pau dos Ferros 202 Ke 6.07S 38.10W
Pauillac 122 Fi 45.12N 0.45W
Pauini 202 Ee 7.40S 66.58W
Pauini, Rio- 202 Ee 7.47S 67.15W
Pauksa Taung 148 Ie 19.55N 94.18 E
Paulatuk 176 Gc 69.23N 124.00W
Paulaya, Río- 194 Ef 15.51N 85.06W
Paulding Bay 222 Ie 66.35S 123.00 E
Paulina Peak 188 Ee 43.41N 121.15W
Păuliş 130 Ec 46.07N 21.35 E
Paulistana 202 Je 8.09S 41.09W
Paulo Afonso 200 Mf 9.21S 38.14W
Paulo Afonso, Cachoeira de- 198 Mf 9.24S 38.12W
Pauls Valley 186 Hi 34.44N 97.13W
Paungde 148 Je 18.29N 95.30 E
Pavant Range 188 Ig 39.00N 112.15W
Pāveh 146 Le 35.03N 46.22 E
Pavia 128 De 45.10N 9.10 E
Pavilly 124 Ce 49.34N 0.58 E
Pavilosta/Pāvilosta 114 Eh 56.55N 21.13 E
Pāvilosta/Pavilosta 114 Eh 56.55N 21.13 E
Pavlikeni 130 If 43.14N 25.18 E
Pavlodar 142 Jd 52.18N 76.57 E
Pavlodarskaja oblast [3] 136 He 52.00N 76.30 E
Pavlof Islands 178 Ge 55.15N 161.20W
Pavlof Volcano 178 Ge 55.24N 161.55W
Pavlograd 132 Ie 48.32N 35.53 E
Pavlovka 134 Hi 55.25N 56.33 E
Pavlovo 136 Ed 55.58N 43.04 E
Pavlov Seamount (EN) 138 Lf 50.40N 162.00 E
Pavlovsk 132 Ld 50.27N 40.08 E
Pavlovskaja 136 Df 46.06N 39.48 E
Pavullo nel Frignano 128 Ef 44.20N 10.50 E
Pavuvu 219a Dc 9.04S 159.08 E
Pawa 219a Ed 10.15S 161.44 E
Pawhuska 186 Hh 36.40N 96.20W
Pawnee 186 Hh 36.20N 96.48W
Pawnee River 186 Gg 38.10N 99.06W
Pawtucket 184 Le 41.53N 71.23W
Paximádhia, Nisídhes- 130 Ho 35.00N 24.35 E
Paxoí 130 Dj 39.12N 20.10 E
Paxson 178 Jd 63.02N 145.30W
Payakumbuk 150 Dg 0.14S 100.38 E
Payas, Cerro- 194 Ef 15.50N 85.00W
Payerne 128 Ad 46.49N 6.58 E
Payette 182 Dc 44.05N 116.56W
Payette 188 Gd 44.05N 116.57W
Payne, Baie- 180 Ke 59.55N 69.35W
Payne, Lac- 180 Ke 59.30N 74.00W
Paysandú 200 Ki 32.19S 58.05W
Paysandú [2] 204 Dk 32.00S 57.15W
Pays de Léon 122 Bf 48.28N 4.30W
Pays d'Othe 122 Jf 48.06N 3.37 E
Payson [Az.-U.S.] 188 Ji 34.14N 111.20W
Payson [Ut.-U.S.] 188 Jf 40.03N 111.44W
Payzawat/Jiashi 152 Cd 39.29N 76.39 E
Pāzanān 146 Mg 30.35N 49.59 E
Pazar 146 Ib 41.11N 40.53 E
Pazarbası Burun 146 Db 41.13N 30.17 E
Pazarcık 146 Gd 37.31N 37.19 E
Pazardžik 130 Hg 42.12N 24.20 E
Pazardžik [2] 130 Hg 42.12N 24.20 E
Pazarköy 130 Kj 39.51N 27.24 E
Pazaryeri 146 Cc 40.00N 29.54 E
Pazin 128 He 45.14N 13.56 E
Pčinja 130 Eh 41.49N 21.40 E
Pea 221b Ac 21.11S 175.14W
Peabirú 204 Ff 23.54S 52.20W
Peace Point 180 Ge 59.12N 112.33W
Peace River 176 Hd 56.14N 117.17W
Peace River [Can.] 174 Hd 56.14N 117.17W
Peace River [Fl.-U.S.] 184 Fl 26.55N 82.05W
Peachland 188 Fb 49.46N 119.44W
Peach Springs 188 Ii 35.32N 113.25W
Peacock Hills 180 Gc 66.05N 110.00W
Peak District 118 Lh 53.17N 1.45W
Peake Creek 212 He 28.05S 136.07 E
Peaked Mountain 184 Mb 46.34N 68.49W
Peale, Mount- 182 Fd 38.26N 109.14W
Pearl 186 Lb 48.42N 88.44W
Pearland 186 Il 29.34N 95.17W
Pearl and Hermes Reef 208 Jb 27.55N 175.45W
Pearl City 221a Db 21.23N 157.58W
Pearl Harbor 221a Cb 21.20N 158.00W
Pearl River 182 Je 30.11N 89.32W
Pearsall 186 Gl 28.53N 99.06W
Pearsoll Peak 188 De 42.18N 123.50W
Peary Channel 180 Ha 79.25N 101.00W
Peary Land 224 Me 82.40N 30.00W
Pease River 186 Gi 34.12N 99.07W
Pebane 172 Fc 17.14S 38.10 E
Pebas 202 Dd 3.20S 71.49W
Peć 130 Dg 42.39N 20.18 E
Peca 128 Id 46.29N 14.48 E
Peças, Ilha das- 204 Hg 25.26S 48.19W
Pecatonica River 186 Le 42.29N 89.03W
Pečenežskoje vodohranilišče 132 Jd 50.05N 36.50 E
Pečenga 112 Jb 69.33N 31.07 E
Pečenga 114 Hb 69.39N 31.27 E
Pechea 130 Kd 45.38N 27.48 E
Pechora (EN) = Pečora 112 Lb 65.10N 57.11 E
Pechora (EN) = Pečora 110 Lb 68.13N 54.10 E
Pechora Bay (EN) = Pečorskaja guba 136 Fb 68.40N 54.45 E
Pechora Sea (EN) = Pečorskoje more 136 Fb 69.45N 54.30 E
Pecica 130 Ec 46.10N 21.04 E
Peckelsheim, Willebadessen- 124 Lc 51.36N 9.08 E
Pečora = Pechora (EN) 112 Lb 65.10N 57.11 E
Pečora = Pechora (EN) 110 Lb 68.13N 54.10 E
Pecora, Capo- 128 Ck 39.27N 8.23 E
Pečorskaja guba = Pechora Bay (EN) 136 Fb 68.40N 54.45 E
Pečorskoje more = Pechora Sea (EN) 136 Fb 69.45N 54.30 E
Pečory 114 Gh 57.49N 27.38 E
Pecos 182 Ge 31.25N 103.30W
Pecos 174 Ig 29.42N 101.22W
Pecos Plain 182 Ge 33.20N 104.30W
Pécs 112 Hf 46.05N 18.14 E
Pécs [2] 120 Oj 46.06N 18.15 E
Pedasí 194 Gj 7.32N 80.02W
Pedder, Lake- 212 Jh 43.00S 146.15 E
Peddie 172 Df 33.14S 27.07 E
Pededze 116 Lh 56.53N 27.01 E
Pedernales [Dom.Rep.] 194 Ld 18.02N 71.45W
Pedernales [Ven.] 196 Eh 9.58N 62.16W
Pedernales, Salar de- 206 Gc 26.15S 69.10W
Pedja jõgi 116 Lf 58.20N 26.10 E
Pêdo Shankou 152 Df 29.12N 83.26 E
Pedra Azul 202 Jg 16.01S 41.16W
Pedra Branca 202 Ke 5.27S 39.43W
Pedra do Sino 204 Kf 22.27S 43.03W
Pedra Lume 162 Cf 16.46N 22.54W
Pedras, Rio das- 204 Ia 13.30S 47.09W
Pedras Altas, Coxilha- 204 Fj 31.45S 53.35W
Pedregal 202 Da 11.01N 70.08W
Pedreiras 202 Jd 4.34S 44.39W
Pedriceña 192 He 25.06N 103.47W
Pedrizas, Puerto de las- 126 Hh 36.55N 4.30W
Pedro Afonso 202 Ie 8.59S 48.11W
Pedro Bank (EN) 194 He 17.00N 78.30W
Pedro Betancourt 194 Gb 22.44N 81.17W
Pedro Cays 190 Ie 17.00N 77.50W
Pedro Gomes 204 Ed 18.04S 54.32W
Pedro Gonzáles, Isla- 194 Hi 8.24N 79.06W
Pedro II 202 Jd 4.25S 41.28W
Pedro II, Ilha- 202 Ec 1.10N 66.44W
Pedro Juan Caballero 206 Ib 22.34S 55.37W
Pedro Leopoldo 204 Jd 19.38S 44.03W
Pedro Luro 206 He 39.29S 62.41W
Pedro Lustoza 204 Gg 25.49S 51.51W
Pedro Montoya 192 Jg 21.38N 99.49W
Pedro Osorio 206 Jd 31.51S 52.45W
Pedro R. Fernández 204 Ci 28.45S 58.39W
Pedro Severo 204 Ec 17.40S 54.02W
Pedroso, Sierra del- 126 Gf 38.35N 5.35W
Peebles 118 Jf 55.39N 3.12W
Pee Dee River 174 Lf 33.21N 79.16W
Peekskill 184 Ke 41.18N 73.56W
Peel 118 Ig 54.13N 4.40W
Peel 122 Lc 51.25N 5.50 E
Peel 174 Fc 67.37N 134.40W
Peel Sound 180 Hb 73.00N 96.00W
Peene 120 Jb 54.09N 13.46 E
Peer 124 Hc 51.08N 5.28 E
Peera Peera Poolanna Lake 212 He 26.30S 138.00 E
Peetz 186 Ef 40.58N 103.07W
Pegasus, Port- 218 Bg 47.10S 167.40 E
Pegasus Bay 216 Dh 43.20S 172.50 E
Pegnitz 120 Hg 49.45N 11.33 E
Pegnitz 120 Hg 49.29N 11.00 E
Pego 126 Lf 38.51N 0.07W
Pegtymel 138 Mc 69.47N 174.00 E
Pegu → Bago 142 Lh 17.30N 96.30 E
Pegu Yoma 140 Lh 19.00N 95.50 E
Pegwell Bay 124 Dc 51.18N 1.23 E
Pehčevo 130 Fh 41.46N 22.54 E
Pehlivanköy 130 Jh 41.21N 26.55 E
Pehuajó 206 He 35.48S 61.53W
Pei-ching Shih → Beijing Shi [4] 152 Kc 40.15N 116.30 E
Peine 120 Gd 52.19N 10.14 E
Peipsi järv = Peipus, Lake- (EN) 110 Id 58.45N 27.30 E
Peipus, Lake- (EN) = Čudskoje ozero 110 Id 58.45N 27.30 E
Peipus, Lake- (EN) = Peipsi järv 110 Id 58.45N 27.30 E
Peixe 202 If 12.03S 48.32W
Peixe, Lagoa do- 204 Gj 31.18S 51.00W
Peixe, Rio do- [Braz.] 204 Gh 27.27S 51.54W
Peixe, Rio do- [Braz.] 204 Ge 21.31S 51.58W
Peixe, Rio do- [Braz.] 204 Gb 14.06S 50.51W
Peixe, Rio do- [Braz.] 204 Fc 16.32S 52.38W
Peixe, Rio do- [Braz.] 204 Hc 17.37S 48.29W
Peixe de Couro, Rio- 204 Ec 17.21S 55.29W
Peixes, Rio dos- 204 Hb 15.10S 49.30W
Peixian (Yunhe) 154 Dg 34.44N 116.56 E
Peixoto, Represa de- 202 Ih 20.30S 46.30W
Pejantan, Pulau- 150 Ef 0.07N 107.14 E
Pëjde/Pöide 116 Jf 58.30N 22.50 E
Pek 130 Ee 44.46N 21.33 E
Pekalongan 150 Eh 6.53S 109.40 E
Pekan 150 Df 3.30N 103.25 E
Pekin 182 Jc 40.35N 89.40W
Peking (EN) = Beijing 142 Nf 39.55N 116.23 E
Pekulnej, hrebet- 138 Mc 66.30N 176.00 E
Pelabuhanratu 150 Eh 6.59S 106.33 E
Pelagie, Isole- 110 Hh 35.40N 12.40 E
Pelagonija 130 Eh 41.05N 21.30 E
Pélagos 130 Hj 39.20N 24.05 E
Pelaihari 150 Fg 3.48S 114.45 E
Pelat, Mont- 122 Mj 44.16N 6.42 E
Pelawanbesar 150 Gf 1.10N 117.54 E
Pélé 219b Dc 17.30S 168.24 E
Peleaga, Vîrful- 130 Fd 45.22N 22.53 E
Peleduj 138 Ge 59.40N 112.38 E
Pelée, Montagne- 190 Le 14.48N 61.10W
Pelee, Point- 184 Fe 41.54N 82.30W
Pelee Island 184 Fe 41.46N 82.39W
Peleliu Island 208 Ed 7.01N 134.15 E
Peleng, Pulau- 150 Hg 1.20S 123.10 E
Pelhřimov 120 Lg 49.26N 15.13 E
Pelican Lake 186 Gb 49.20N 99.35W
Pelicanpunt 172 Ad 22.54S 14.26 E
Peligre, Lac de- 194 Ld 18.52N 71.56W
Pelinaion Óros 130 Ik 38.32N 26.00 E
Pelješac 128 Lh 42.55N 17.25 E
Pelkosenniemi 114 Gc 67.07N 27.30 E
Pella 186 Jf 41.25N 92.55W
Pélla 130 Fi 40.46N 22.34 E
Pellegrini 206 He 36.16S 63.09W
Pellice 128 Bf 44.50N 7.38 E
Pellinge/Pellinki 116 Kd 60.15N 25.50 E
Pellinki/Pellinge 116 Kd 60.15N 25.50 E
Pello 114 Fc 66.47N 24.01 E
Pellworm 120 Eb 54.30N 8.40 E
Pelly 174 Fc 62.47N 137.19W
Pelly Bay 176 Kc 68.52N 89.55W
Pelly Bay 180 Ic 68.50N 90.10W
Pelly Crossing 180 Dd 62.50N 136.35W
Pelly Mountains 180 Ed 61.30N 132.00W
Peloncillo Mountains 188 Kj 32.15N 109.10W
Pelón de Nado, Cerro- 192 Jg 20.05N 99.55W
Peloponnesus (EN) = Pelopónnisos 110 Ih 37.40N 22.00 E
Peloponnesus (EN) = Pelopónnisos 130 El 37.40N 22.00 E
Pelopónnisos [2] 130 El 37.40N 22.00 E
Pelopónnisos = Peloponnesus (EN) 110 Ih 37.40N 22.00 E
Pelopónnisos = Peloponnesus (EN) 130 El 37.40N 22.00 E
Peloritani 128 Jl 38.05N 15.20 E
Peloro o Punta dl Faro, Capo- 128 Jl 38.16N 15.39 E
Pelotas 200 Ki 31.46S 52.20W
Pelotas, Rio- 206 Jc 27.28S 51.55W
Pelplin 120 Oc 53.56N 18.42 E
Pelvoux, Massif du- 110 Gg 44.55N 6.20 E
Pelym 136 Gd 59.40N 63.05 E
Pelymski Tuman, ozero- 134 Kf 60.05N 63.05 E
Pemalang 150 Eh 6.54S 109.22 E
Pemar/Paimio 116 Jd 60.27N 22.42 E
Pematangsiantar 142 Li 2.57N 99.03 E
Pemba [3] 170 Hd 5.02S 40.00 E
Pemba [Moz.] 160 Lj 12.57S 40.30 E
Pemba [Zam.] 170 Ef 16.31S 27.22 E
Pemba Channel 170 Gd 5.10S 39.20 E
Pemba Island 158 Ki 5.10S 39.48 E
Pemberton [Austl.] 212 Df 34.28S 116.01 E
Pemberton [B.C.-Can.] 188 Da 50.20N 122.48W
Pembina 182 Hb 48.58N 97.15W
Pembina 180 Gf 54.45N 114.17W
Pembina River 182 Hb 48.56N 97.15W
Pembroke [Ont.-Can.] 180 Jg 45.49N 77.07W
Pembroke [Wales-U.K.] 118 Ij 51.41N 4.55W
Pembuang 150 Fg 3.24S 112.33 E
Peña, Sierra de la- 126 Lb 42.31N 0.38W
Peña de Francia, Sierra de la- 126 Fd 40.35N 6.05W
Penafiel 126 Dc 41.12N 8.17W
Peñafiel 126 Hc 41.36N 4.07W
Peñagolosa/Penyagolosa 126 Ld 40.13N 0.21W
Peña Gorda, Cerro- 192 Gg 20.40N 104.55W
Peñalara 126 Id 40.51N 3.57W
Penalva 202 Id 3.18S 45.10W
Penamacor 126 Ed 40.10N 7.10W
Peña Nevada, Cerro- 174 Jg 23.46N 99.52W
Penápolis 204 Ge 21.24S 50.04W
Peñaranda de Bracamonte 126 Gd 40.54N 5.12W
Peñarroya 126 Ld 40.28N 0.43W
Peñarroya-Pueblonuevo 126 Gf 38.18N 5.16W
Peñas, Cabo de- 110 Fg 43.39N 5.51W
Penas, Golfo de- 198 Ij 47.22S 74.50W
Peñas, Punta- 202 Fa 10.44N 61.51W
Peñasco, Rio- 186 Dj 32.45N 104.19W
Pendé 168 Bd 8.07N 16.26 E
Pendembu [S.L.] 166 Cd 9.06N 12.12W
Pendembu [S.L.] 166 Cd 8.06N 10.42W
Pendik 130 Mi 40.53N 29.13 E
Pendjari 166 Fc 10.54N 0.51 E
Pendle Hill 118 Kh 53.52N 2.17W
Pendleton 176 He 45.40N 118.47W
Pendolo 150 Hg 2.05S 120.42 E
Pend Oreille Lake 182 Db 48.10N 116.11W
Pend Oreille River 182 Db 49.04N 117.37W
Pendžikent 136 Gh 39.29N 67.38 E
Peneda 126 Dc 41.58N 8.15W
Penedo 202 Kf 10.17S 36.36W
Penetanguishene 184 Hc 44.47N 79.55W
Penganga 148 Fe 19.53N 79.09 E
Pengcheng 152 Jd 36.25N 114.08 E
Penge 170 Dd 5.31S 24.37 E
Pengho Jiao 150 Fc 16.03N 112.35 E
Penghu Liehtao = Pescadores (EN) 152 Kg 23.30N 119.30 E
Penglai (Dengzhou) 152 Ld 37.44N 120.45 E
Pengshui 152 If 29.17N 108.13 E
Pengze 152 Kf 29.52N 116.34 E
Penha 204 Hh 26.46S 48.39W
Penhalonga 172 Ec 18.54S 32.40 E
Penibética, Cordillera- 126 Ig 37.00N 3.30W
Peniche 126 Ce 39.21N 9.23W
Penicuik 118 Jf 55.50N 3.14W
Penida, Nusa- 150 Gh 8.44S 115.32 E
Peninsula Ibérica = Iberian Peninsula (EN) 110 Fg 40.00N 4.00W
Peniscola / Peñiscola 126 Md 40.21N 0.25 E
Peñiscola / Peniscola 126 Md 40.21N 0.25 E
Penitente, Serra do- 202 Ie 8.45S 46.20W
Pénjamo 192 Ig 20.26N 101.44W
Penju, Kepulauan- 150 Ih 5.22S 127.46 E
Penmarch, Pointe de- 122 Bg 47.48N 4.22W
Penne 128 Hh 42.27N 13.55 E
Penne, Punta- 128 Lj 40.41N 17.56 E
Pennell Coast 222 Kf 71.00S 167.00 E
Penner 140 Kh 14.35N 80.10 E
Penn Hills 184 He 40.28N 79.53W
Pennines 110 Fe 54.10N 2.05W
Pennsylvania [2] 182 Lc 40.45N 77.30W
Penn Yan 184 Id 42.41N 77.03W
Penny Ice Cap 180 Kc 67.00N 65.10W
Penny Strait 180 Ha 76.35N 97.10W
Peno 114 Hh 56.57N 32.45 E
Penobscot Bay 184 Mc 44.15N 68.52W
Penobscot River 182 Nc 44.30N 68.50W
Penola 212 Ig 37.23S 140.50 E
Peñón del Rosario, Cerro- 192 Jh 19.40N 98.12W
Penong 210 Eh 31.55S 133.01 E
Penonomé 190 Hg 8.31N 80.22W
Pénot, Mont- 219b Cc 16.20S 167.31 E
Penrhyn Atoll 208 Le 9.00S 158.00W
Penrith 118 Kg 54.40N 2.44W
Penrith, Sydney- 212 Kf 33.45S 150.42 E
Pensacola 176 Kf 30.25N 87.13W
Pensacola Mountains 222 Rg 83.45S 55.00W
Pensacola Seamount (EN) 208 Lc 18.17N 157.20W
Pensamiento 204 Bb 14.44S 61.35W
Pensiangan 150 Gf 4.33N 116.19 E
Pentecôte, Ile- 208 Hf 15.45S 168.10 E
Penticton 180 Fg 49.30N 119.35W
Pentland 212 Jd 20.32S 145.24 E
Pentland Firth 118 Jc 58.44N 3.13W
Pentland Hills 118 Jf 55.48N 3.23W
Penwith 118 Hk 50.13N 5.40W
Penyagolosa/Peñagolosa 126 Ld 40.13N 0.21W
Penza 112 Ke 53.13N 45.00 E
Penzance 112 Ff 50.07N 5.33W
Penzenskaja oblast [3] 136 Ee 53.15N 44.40 E
Penzhina Bay (EN) = Penžinskaja guba 138 Ld 61.00N 163.00 E
Penžina 140 Sc 62.28N 165.18 E
Penžinskaja guba = Penzhina Bay (EN) 138 Ld 61.00N 163.00 E
Penžinski hrebet 138 Ld 62.15N 166.35 E
Peoples Creek 188 Kb 48.24N 108.19W
Peoria 176 Ke 40.42N 89.36W
Pepa 170 Ed 7.42S 29.47 E
Pepel 166 Cd 8.35N 13.03W
Peperiguaçu, Rio- 204 Fh 27.10S 53.50W
Peqini 130 Ch 41.03N 19.45 E
Pequena, Lagoa- 204 Fj 31.36S 52.04W
Pequiri, Rio- 202 Gg 17.23S 55.38W
Perabumulih 150 Dg 3.27S 104.15 E
Perak [2] 150 Df 5.00N 101.00 E
Perälä 116 Ib 62.28N 21.36 E
Perales, Puerto de- 126 Fd 40.15N 6.41W
Pérama 130 Hn 35.22N 24.42 E
Peräseinäjoki 116 Jb 62.34N 23.04 E
Perche, Col de la- 122 Il 42.30N 2.06 E
Perche, Collines du- 122 Gf 48.25N 0.40 E
Percival Lakes 212 Ed 21.25S 125.00 E
Percy Islands 212 Kd 21.40S 150.15 E
Perdasdefogu 128 Dk 39.41N 9.26 E
Perdida, Sierra- 192 Hd 27.30N 103.30W
Perdido, Monte- 110 Gg 42.40N 0.05 E
Perdido, Rio- 204 Df 22.10S 57.33W
Perdizes 204 Id 19.21S 47.17W
Perečin 120 Sh 48.44N 22.29 E
Pereginskoje 132 De 48.49N 24.12 E
Pereira 202 Cc 4.48N 75.42W
Pereira Barreto 206 Jb 20.38S 51.07W
Perejaslav-Hmelnicki 132 Gd 50.04N 31.27 E
Perejil, Isla de- 126 Gi 35.55N 5.26W
Pereljub 132 Qd 51.52N 50.20 E
Peremennyj, Cape- 222 He 66.08S 105.30 E
Peremyšliany 120 Ug 49.38N 24.35 E
Perenjori 212 De 29.26S 116.17 E
Pereščepino 132 Ie 48.59N 35.22 E
Pereslavl-Zalesski 114 Jh 56.45N 38.55 E
Peretu 130 Ie 44.03N 25.05 E
Peretyčiha 138 Ig 47.10N 138.35 E
Perevolocki 132 Sd 51.51N 54.15 E
Pergamino 206 Hd 33.53S 60.35W
Pergamon 130 Kj 39.08N 27.13 E
Perge 146 Dd 37.00N 30.10 E
Pergine Valsugana 128 Fd 46.04N 11.14 E
Pergola 128 Gg 43.34N 12.50 E
Perham 186 Ic 46.36N 95.34W
Perho 114 Fe 63.13N 24.25 E
Periam 130 Dc 46.03N 20.52 E
Péribonca, Rivière- 180 Kg 48.44N 72.06W
Perico 206 Hb 24.23S 65.00W
Pericos 192 Fe 25.03N 107.42W
Périgord 122 Gi 45.00N 0.30 E
Perigoso, Canal- 202 Ic 0.05N 49.40W
Périgueux 122 Gi 45.11N 0.43 E
Perijá, Sierra de- 198 Ie 10.00N 73.00W
Peristerá 130 Gj 39.12N 23.59 E
Perito Moreno 200 Ij 46.36S 70.56W
Perkam, Tanjung- = Urville, Cape d'- (EN) 150 Kg 1.28S 137.54 E
Perković 128 Kg 43.41N 16.06 E
Perlas, Archipiélago de las- 190 Ig 8.25N 79.00W
Perlas, Cayos de- 194 Fg 12.28N 83.28W
Perlas, Laguna de- 194 Fg 12.30N 83.40W
Perlas, Punta de- 194 Fg 12.23N 83.30W
Perleberg 120 Hc 53.04N 11.52 E
Perlez 130 Dd 45.12N 20.23 E
Perlis [2] 150 De 6.30N 100.15 E
Perm 112 Ld 58.00N 56.15 E
Përmeti 130 Di 40.14N 20.21 E
Permskaja oblast [3] 136 Fd 59.00N 57.00 E
Pernambuco [2] 202 Ke 8.30S 37.30W
Pernik 130 Gg 42.36N 23.02 E
Pernik [2] 130 Fg 42.35N 22.50 E
Perniö/Bjärnå 114 Ff 60.12N 23.08 E
Péronne 122 Ie 49.56N 2.56 E
Perote 192 Kh 19.34N 97.14W
Perpignan 112 Gg 42.41N 2.53 E
Perro, Laguna del- 186 Di 34.40N 105.57W
Perros-Guirec 122 Cf 48.49N 3.27W
Perry [Fl.-U.S.] 184 Fj 30.07N 83.35W
Perry [Ga.-U.S.] 184 Fi 32.27N 83.44W
Perry [Ia.-U.S.] 186 If 41.50N 94.06W
Perry [Ok.-U.S.] 186 Hh 36.17N 97.17W
Perry Lake 186 Ig 39.20N 95.30W
Perryton 186 Fh 36.24N 100.48W
Perryville 178 He 55.54N 159.10W
Persan 124 Ee 49.09N 2.16 E
Perşani, Munţii- 130 Id 45.40N 25.15 E
Persberg 116 Fe 59.45N 14.15 E
Persembe 146 Gb 41.04N 37.46 E
Persepolis 146 Oh 29.57N 52.52 E
Perseverancia 202 Ff 14.44S 62.48W
Persian Gulf (EN) = Al-Khalīj al-'Arabi 140 Hg 27.00N 51.00 E
Persian Gulf (EN) = Fārs, Khalīj-e- 140 Hg 27.00N 51.00 E
Perstorp 116 Eh 56.08N 13.23 E
Pertek 146 Hc 38.50N 39.22 E
Perth [Austl.] 210 Ch 31.56S 115.50 E
Perth [Ont.-Can.] 184 Ic 44.54N 76.15W
Perth [Scot.-U.K.] 118 Je 56.24N 3.28W
Perth Amboy 184 Je 40.32N 74.17W
Perth-Andover 184 Nb 46.44N 67.42W
Perth-Armadale 212 Df 32.09S 116.00 E
Perth-Fremantle 212 Df 32.03S 115.45 E
Perth-Kalamunda 212 Df 31.57S 116.03 E
Perth-Mundaring 212 Df 31.54S 116.10 E
Perthus, Col de-/Portús, Coll del- 126 Ob 42.28N 2.51 E
Perthus, Col du- 126 Ob 42.28N 2.51 E
Pertuis 122 Lk 43.41N 5.30 E
Pertusato, Capo- 122a Bb 41.21N 9.11 E
Perú [1] 200 Ig 10.00S 76.00W
Peru [Il.-U.S.] 186 Lf 41.20N 89.08W
Peru [In.-U.S.] 184 De 40.45N 86.04W
Perú, Altiplano del- 202 Df 15.00S 72.00W
Peruaçu, Rio- 204 Jb 15.11S 44.07W
Peru Basin (EN) 106 Mk 17.00S 90.00W
Peru-Chile Trench (EN) 106 Nl 20.00S 73.00W
Perugia 112 Hg 43.08N 12.22 E
Perugorria 204 Ci 29.20S 58.37W
Peruíbe 204 Ig 24.19S 47.00W
Perušić 128 Jf 44.39N 15.22 E
Péruwelz 124 Fd 50.31N 3.35 E
Pervari 146 Jd 37.54N 42.36 E
Pervomajsk [R.S.F.S.R.] 136 Ee 54.52N 43.48 E
Pervomajsk [Ukr.-U.S.S.R.] 136 Df 48.03N 30.52 E
Pervomajsk [Ukr.-U.S.S.R.] 132 Ke 48.36N 38.32 E
Pervomajski [Bye.-U.S.S.R.] 120 Vc 53.52N 25.33 E
Pervomajski [Kaz.-U.S.S.R.] 136 Ie 50.15N 81.59 E
Pervomajski [R.S.F.S.R.] 136 Ec 64.26N 40.48 E
Pervomajski [R.S.F.S.R.] 132 Sd 51.34N 54.59 E
Pervomajski [R.S.F.S.R.] 132 Lc 53.18N 40.15 E
Pervomajski [R.S.F.S.R.] 134 Ji 54.52N 61.08 E
Pervomajski [Ukr.-U.S.S.R.] 132 Je 49.24N 36.15 E
Pervouralsk 136 Fd 57.00N 60.00 E
Pervy Kurilski proliv 138 Kf 50.50N 156.50 E
Perwez/Perwijs 124 Gd 50.37N 4.49 E
Perwijs/Perwez 124 Gd 50.37N 4.49 E
Pes 114 Ig 59.10N 35.18 E
Peša 134 Cc 66.50N 47.32 E
Pesaro 128 Gg 43.54N 12.55 E
Pescadores (EN) = Penghu Liehtao 152 Kg 23.30N 119.30 E
Pescadores, Punta- 192 Ef 23.45N 109.45W

Index Symbols

[1] Independent Nation
[2] State, Region
[3] District, County
[4] Municipality
[5] Colony, Dependency
Continent
Physical Region
Historical or Cultural Region
Mount, Mountain
Volcano
Hill
Mountains, Mountain Range
Hills, Escarpment
Plateau, Upland
Pass, Gap
Plain, Lowland
Delta
Salt Flat
Valley, Canyon
Crater, Cave
Karst Features
Depression
Polder
Desert, Dunes
Forest, Woods
Heath, Steppe
Oasis
Cape, Point
Coast, Beach
Cliff
Peninsula
Isthmus
Sandbank
Island
Atoll
Rock, Reef
Islands, Archipelago
Rocks, Reefs
Coral Reef
Well, Spring
Geyser
River, Stream
Waterfall, Rapids
River Mouth, Estuary
Lake
Salt Lake
Intermittent Lake
Reservoir
Swamp, Pond
Canal
Glacier
Ice Shelf, Pack Ice
Ocean
Sea
Gulf, Bay
Strait, Fjord
Lagoon
Bank
Seamount
Tablemount
Ridge
Shelf
Basin
Escarpment, Sea Scarp
Fracture
Trench, Abyss
National Park, Reserve
Point of Interest
Recreation Site
Cave, Cavern
Historic Site
Ruins
Wall, Walls
Church, Abbey
Temple
Scientific Station
Railway station
Airport
Port
Military installation
Lighthouse
Mine
Tunnel
Dam, Bridge

Pesčany, mys- 132 Qh 43.10N 51.18 E
Pesčany, ostrov- 138 Gb 74.20N 115.55 E
Pescara 112 Hg 42.28N 14.13 E
Pescara 128 Ih 42.28N 14.13 E
Pescasseroli 128 Hi 41.48N 13.47 E
Peschici 128 Ki 41.57N 16.01 E
Pescia 128 Eg 43.54N 10.41 E
Pescocostanzo 128 Ii 41.53N 14.04 E
Peshāwar 142 Jf 34.01N 71.33 E
Peshkopia 130 Dh 41.41N 20.26 E
Pesio 128 Bf 44.28N 7.53 E
Peskovka 114 Mg 59.03N 52.22 E
Pesmes 122 Lg 47.17N 5.34 E
Pesočny 116 Nd 60.05N 30.20 E
Peso da Régua 126 Ec 41.10N 7.47W
Pesqueira 202 Ke 8.22S 36.42W
Pesqueria, Rio- 192 Je 25.54N 99.11W
Pessac 122 Fj 44.48N 0.37W
Pest [2] 120 Pi 47.25N 19.20 E
Pešter 130 Df 43.05N 20.02 E
Peštera 130 Hg 42.02N 24.18 E
Pestovo 136 Dd 58.36N 35.47 E
Petacalco, Bahía de- 190 De 17.57N 102.05W
Petah Tiqwa 146 Ff 32.05N 34.53 E
Petäjävesi 116 Kb 62.15N 25.12 E
Petal 186 Lk 31.21N 89.17W
Petalioi 130 Hl 38.01N 24.17 E
Petalioi, Gulf of- (EN) = Petalión, Kólpos- 130 Hk 38.00N 24.05 E
Petalión, Kólpos- = Petalioi, Gulf of- (EN) 130 Hk 38.00N 24.05 E
Petaluma 188 Dg 38.14N 122.39W
Pétange/Petingen 124 He 49.33N 5.53 E
Petare 202 Ea 10.29N 66.49W
Petatlán 192 Ii 17.31N 101.16W
Petatlán, Rio- 192 Fd 26.09N 107.45W
Petauke 170 Fe 14.15S 31.20 E
Petén [3] 194 Be 16.50N 90.00W
Petén 190 Fe 16.15N 89.50W
Petén Itzá, Lago- 194 Ce 16.59N 89.50W
Petenwell Lake 186 Ld 44.05N 89.45W
Peterborough [Austl.] 212 Hf 32.58S 138.50 E
Peterborough [Eng.-U.K.] 118 Mi 52.35N 0.15W
Peterborough [Ont.-Can.] 180 Jh 44.18N 78.19W
Peterhead 118 Ld 57.30N 1.46W
Peter I, Øy- 222 Pe 68.47S 90.35W
Peter Island 197a Db 18.22N 64.35W
Peterlee 118 Lg 54.46N 1.19W
Petermann Gletscher 179 Fb 80.45N 61.00W
Petermann Ranges 212 Fd 25.00S 129.45 E
Petermanns Bjerg 224 Md 73.10N 28.00W
Peter Pond Lake 180 Ge 55.55N 108.40W
Petersberg 120 He 51.35N 11.57 E
Petersburg [Ak.-U.S.] 178 Me 56.49N 132.57W
Petersburg [In.-U.S.] 184 Df 38.30N 87.16W
Petersburg [Va.-U.S.] 182 Ld 37.14N 77.24W
Petersburg [W.V.-U.S.] 184 Hf 39.01N 79.09W
Petersfield 118 Mk 51.00N 0.56W
Petershagen 124 Kb 52.23N 8.58 E
Peter the Great Bay (EN) = Petra Velikogo, zaliv- 140 Pe 42.40N 132.00 E
Petilia Policastro 128 Kk 39.07N 16.47 E
Petingen/Pétange 124 He 49.33N 5.53 E
Petit-Bourg 197e Ab 16.12N 61.36W
Petit-Canal 197e Bb 16.23N 61.29W
Petit Canouan 197n Bb 12.47N 61.17W
Petit Cul-de-Sac Marin 197e Ab 16.12N 61.33W
Petite Kabylie 126 Rh 36.35N 5.25 E
Petite Rivière de l'Artibonite 194 Kd 19.08N 72.29W
Petites Pyrénées 122 Hk 43.05N 1.10 E
Petite-Terre, Iles de la- 197e Bb 16.10N 61.07W
Petit-Goâve 194 Kd 18.26N 72.52W
Petit Martinique Island 197p Ca 12.32N 61.22W
Petit-Mécatina, Rivière du- 180 Lf 50.39N 59.25W
Petit Morin 122 Jf 48.56N 3.07 E
Petit Mustique Island 197n Bb 12.51N 61.13W
Petit Nevis Island 197n Bb 12.58N 61.15W
Petitot 180 Fd 60.14N 123.29W
Petit Saint-Bernard, Col du- 128 Ae 45.40N 6.55 E
Petit Saint Vincent Island 197n Bb 12.33N 61.23W
Petit Savanne 197g Bb 15.15N 61.17W
Petitsikapau Lake 180 Kf 54.40N 66.25W
Petkula 114 Gc 67.40N 26.41 E
Petlalcingo 192 Kh 18.05N 97.54W
Peto 190 Gd 20.08N 88.55W
Petorca 206 Fd 32.15S 71.00W
Petoskey 184 Ec 45.22N 84.57W
Petra 146 Fg 30.19N 35.29 E
Petralia Soprana 128 Im 37.47N 14.06 E
Petra Pervogo, hrebet- 135 He 39.00N 71.10 E
Petra Velikogo, zaliv- = Peter the Great Bay 140 Pe 42.40N 132.00 E
Petre, Point- 184 Id 43.50N 77.09W
Petre Bay 218 Je 43.55S 176.40W
Petrel 222 Re 63.28S 56.17W
Petrela 130 Ch 41.15N 19.51 E
Petrella Tifernina 128 Ii 41.41N 14.42 E
Petrič 130 Gh 41.24N 23.13 E
Pétrie, Récif- 216 Bc 18.30S 164.20 E
Petrikov 132 Fc 52.08N 28.31 E
Petrila 130 Gd 45.27N 23.25 E
Petrinja 128 Ke 45.27N 16.17 E
Petrodvorec 114 Gg 59.53N 29.50 E
Petrólea 202 Db 8.30N 72.35W
Petrolia 184 Fd 42.52N 82.09W
Petrolina 202 Je 9.24S 40.30W
Petrolina de Goiás 204 Hc 16.06S 49.20W
Petronanski prohod 130 Gf 43.08N 23.08 E
Petronell 128 Kb 48.07N 16.51 E
Petropavlovka 138 Ff 50.38N 105.19 E
Petropavlovsk 142 Id 54.54N 69.06 E
Petropavlovsk-Kamčatski 142 Rd 53.01N 158.39 E
Petrópolis 200 Lh 22.31S 43.10W
Petroșani 130 Gd 45.25N 23.22 E
Petrovac [Yugo.] 130 Bg 42.12N 18.57 E
Petrovac [Yugo.] 130 Ee 44.22N 21.25 E
Petrova Gora 128 Je 45.17N 15.47 E
Petrovaradin 130 Cd 45.15N 19.53 E
Petrovka 130 Nc 46.55N 30.40 E
Petrovsk 136 Ee 52.18N 45.23 E
Petrovski Jam 114 Ie 63.18N 35.15 E
Petrovsk-Zabajkalski 142 Md 51.17N 108.50 E
Petrov Val 132 Nd 50.10N 45.12 E
Petrozavodsk 112 Jc 61.47N 34.20 E
Petuhovo 136 Gd 55.06N 67.58 E
Petuški 114 Ji 55.59N 39.28 E
Petworth 124 Bd 50.59N 0.36W
Peuetsagoe, Gunung- 150 Cf 4.55N 96.20 E
Peumo 206 Fd 34.24S 71.10W
Peureulak 150 Cf 4.48N 97.53 E
Pevek 142 Tc 69.42N 170.17 E
Pevensey 124 Cd 50.48N 0.21 E
Pevensey Bay 124 Cd 50.48N 0.22 E
Peyia 146 Ee 34.53N 32.23 E
Peza 114 Kd 65.34N 44.33 E
Pézenas 122 Jk 43.27N 3.25 E
Pezinok 120 Nh 48.18N 17.16 E
Pfaffenhofen an der Ilm 120 Hh 48.32N 11.31 E
Pfaffenhoffen 124 Jf 48.51N 7.37 E
Pfalz 124 Je 49.20N 7.57 E
Pfalzel, Trier- 124 Ie 49.46N 6.41 E
Pfälzer Bergland 120 Dg 49.35N 7.30 E
Pfälzer Wald 120 Dg 49.15N 7.50 E
Pfarrkirchen 120 Ih 48.26N 12.52 E
Pfinz 124 Ke 49.11N 8.25 E
Pfinztal 124 Ke 49.02N 8.30 E
Pforzheim an der Enz 120 Eh 48.53N 8.42 E
Pfrimm 124 Ke 49.39N 8.22 E
Pfullendorf 120 Fi 47.55N 9.15 E
Pfunds 128 Ed 46.58N 10.33 E
Pfungstadt 124 Ke 49.48N 8.36 E
Pha-an 148 Je 16.53N 97.38 E
Phalaborwa 172 Ed 23.55S 31.13 E
Phalodi 148 Ec 27.08N 72.22 E
Phangan, Ko- 148 Jg 9.45N 100.00 E
Phangnga 148 Jg 8.28N 98.32 E
Phan Ly Cham 148 Lf 11.13N 108.31 E
Phanom 148 Jg 8.49N 98.50 E
Phan Rang 148 Lf 11.34N 108.59 E
Phan Thiet 148 Lf 10.56N 108.06 E
Pharr 186 Gm 26.12N 98.11W
Phatthalung 148 Kg 7.38N 100.04 E
Phayao 148 Ke 18.07N 100.11 E
Phenix City 182 Je 32.29N 85.01W
Phet Buri 148 Jf 13.06N 99.56 E
Phetchabun, Thiu Khao- 148 Ke 16.20N 100.55 E
Phichit 148 Ke 16.24N 100.21 E
Philadelphia [Ms.-U.S.] 186 Lj 32.46N 89.07W
Philadelphia [Pa.-U.S.] 176 Lf 39.57N 75.07W
Philae 166 Fe 23.35N 32.52 E
Philip 186 Fd 44.02N 101.40W
Philippeville 122 Kd 50.12N 4.33 E
Philippi 184 Gf 39.08N 80.03W
Philippi (EN) = Filippoi 130 Hh 41.02N 24.18 E
Philippi, Lake- 212 Hd 24.20S 139.00 E
Philippi Glacier 222 Ge 66.45S 88.20 E
Philippine Basin (EN) 106 Ih 17.00N 132.00 E
Philippine Islands (EN) = Pilipinas 140 Oh 13.00N 122.00 E
Philippines (EN) = Pilipinas [1] 142 Oh 13.00N 122.00 E
Philippine Sea (EN) 140 Oh 20.00N 130.00 E
Philippine Trench (EN) 106 Ii 9.00N 127.00 E
Philippsburg 124 Ke 49.14N 8.27 E
Philipsburg [Mt.-U.S.] 188 Ic 46.20N 113.08W
Philipsburg [Neth.Ant.] 196 Ec 18.01N 63.04W
Philip Smith Mountains 178 Jc 68.30N 148.00W
Philipstown 172 Cf 30.26S 24.29 E
Phillipsburg 186 Gg 39.45N 99.19W
Philpots 180 Jb 74.55N 80.00W
Phitsanulok 142 Mh 16.49N 100.15 E
Phnom Penh (EN) = Phnum Pénh 142 Mh 11.33N 104.55 E
Phnum Pénh = Phnom Penh (EN) 142 Mh 11.33N 104.55 E
Phoenix 176 Hf 33.27N 112.05W
Phoenix → Rawaki Atoll 208 Je 3.43S 170.43W
Phoenix Islands 208 Je 4.00S 172.00W
Phôngsali 148 Kd 21.41N 102.06 E
Phrae 148 Ke 18.07N 100.11 E
Phra Nakhom Si Ayutthaya 142 Mh 14.21N 100.33 E
Phrygia 130 Mk 38.30N 29.50 E
Phuket 142 Li 7.54N 98.24 E
Phuket, Ko- 148 Li 8.00N 98.20 E
Phulbani 148 Gd 20.28N 84.14 E
Phumĭ Mlu Prey 148 Lf 13.48N 105.16 E
Phumĭ Sâmraông 148 Kf 14.11N 103.31 E
Phu My 148 Lf 14.10N 109.03 E
Phuoc Binh 148 Lf 11.50N 106.58 E
Phu Quoc 148 Kf 10.13N 103.58 E
Phu Quoc, Dao- 148 Kf 10.12N 104.00 E
Phu Tho 148 Ld 21.24N 105.13 E
Piaanu Pass 220d Ab 7.20N 151.26 E
Piacenza 128 De 45.01N 9.40 E
Piana degli Albanesi 128 Hm 37.59N 13.17 E
Piana Mwanga 170 Ed 7.40S 28.10 E
Piancó 202 Ke 7.12S 37.57W
Pianguan 152 Jd 39.28N 111.32 E
Pianosa [It.] 128 Eh 42.35N 10.05 E
Pianosa [It.] 128 Jh 42.15N 15.45 E
Piaseczno 120 Rd 52.05N 21.01 E
Piaski 120 Se 51.08N 22.51 E
Piątek 120 Pd 52.05N 19.28 E
Piatra 130 If 43.49N 25.10 E
Piatra Neamț 130 Jc 46.55N 26.20 E
Piatra Olt 130 He 44.22N 24.16 E
Piaui [2] 202 Je 7.00S 43.00W
Piauí, Rio- 198 Lf 6.38S 42.42W
Piave 110 Hf 45.32N 12.44 E
Piaxtla, Punta- 192 Ff 23.38N 106.50W
Piaxtla, Rio- 192 Ff 23.42N 106.49W
Piazza Armerina 128 Im 37.23N 14.22 E
Pibor 168 Ed 8.26N 33.13 E
Pibor Post 168 Ed 6.48N 33.08 E
Pica 206 Gb 20.30S 69.21W
Picardie = Picardy (EN) 122 Je 50.00N 3.30 E
Picardy (EN) = Picardie 122 Je 50.00N 3.30 E
Picayune 186 Lk 30.26N 89.41W
Piccolo San Bernardo, Colle del- 128 Ae 45.40N 6.55 E
Picentini, Monti- 128 Jj 40.45N 15.10 E
Pichanal 200 Jh 23.20S 64.15W
Pichilemu 206 Fd 34.23S 72.00W
Pichilingue 192 De 24.20N 110.20W
Pichna 120 Oe 51.50N 18.40 E
Pichones, Cayos- 194 Ff 15.45N 82.55W
Pichucalco 192 Mi 17.31N 93.04W
Pickering 118 Mg 54.14N 0.46W
Pickering, Vale of- 118 Mg 54.10N 0.45W
Pickle Lake 180 If 51.29N 90.10W
Pickwick Lake 184 Ch 34.55N 88.10W
Pico 158 Ee 38.28N 28.20W
Picos 200 Lf 7.05S 41.28W
Pico Truncado 206 Gg 46.48S 67.58W
Picquigny 122 Ie 49.57N 2.09 E
Picton 216 Dh 41.18S 174.00 E
Picton 206 Gi 55.04S 67.00W
Pictou 180 Lg 45.41N 62.43W
Picunda 132 Lh 43.12N 40.21 E
Pidurutalagala 140 Ki 7.00N 80.46 E
Piedecuesta 202 Db 6.59N 73.03W
Piedimonte Matese 128 Ii 41.20N 14.22 E
Piedmont 174 Kf 35.00N 81.00W
Piedmont [Al.-U.S.] 184 Ei 33.55N 85.37W
Piedmont [Mo.-U.S.] 186 Kh 37.09N 90.42W
Piedmont (EN) = Piemonte [2] 128 Be 45.00N 8.00 E
Piedra 126 Kc 41.19N 1.48W
Piedra, Monasterio de- 126 Kc 41.10N 1.50W
Piedrabuena 126 He 39.02N 4.10W
Piedrafita, Puerto de- 126 Fb 42.36N 6.57W
Piedrahita 126 Gd 40.28N 5.19W
Piedras 202 Cd 3.38S 79.54W
Piedras, Punta- 206 Ie 35.25S 57.08W
Piedras, Rio de las- 202 Ef 12.30S 69.14W
Piedras Negras 176 Ig 28.42N 100.31W
Piedras Negras 194 Be 17.12N 91.15W
Piedra Sola 206 Id 32.04S 56.21W
Piekary Śląskie 120 Of 50.24N 18.58 E
Pieksämäki 114 Ge 62.18N 27.08 E
Pielach 128 Jb 48.15N 15.22 E
Pielavesi 114 Ge 63.14N 26.45 E
Pielinen 110 Ic 63.15N 29.40 E
Piemonte = Piedmont (EN) [2] 128 Be 45.00N 8.00 E
Pieniężno 120 Qb 54.15N 20.08 E
Pieni Salpausselkä 116 Lc 61.10N 27.20 E
Piennes 124 He 49.19N 5.47 E
Pienza 128 Fg 43.04N 11.41 E
Pierce 188 Hc 46.29N 115.48W
Piéria Óri 130 Fi 40.12N 22.07 E
Pierre 176 Ie 44.22N 100.21W
Pierrefitte-sur-Aire 124 Hf 48.54N 5.20 E
Pierrefonds 124 Ee 49.21N 2.59 E
Pierrelatte 122 Kj 44.23N 4.42 E
Pieskehaure 114 Dc 66.57N 16.30 E
Piešťany 120 Nh 48.36N 17.50 E
Pietarsaari/Jakobstad 114 Fe 63.40N 22.42 E
Pietermaritzburg 160 Kk 29.37S 30.16 E
Pietersburg 160 Jk 23.54S 29.25 E
Pietraperzia 128 Im 37.25N 14.08 E
Pietrasanta 128 Eg 43.57N 10.14 E
Piet Retief 172 Ee 27.01S 30.50 E
Pietrii, Virful- 130 Fd 45.23N 22.40 E
Pietroșani 130 If 43.43N 25.38 E
Pietrosu, Virful- [Rom.] 130 Ib 47.08N 25.11 E
Pietrosu, Virful- [Rom.] 110 If 47.23N 25.33 E
Pieve di Cadore 128 Gd 46.26N 12.22 E
Pigeon Island 197k Ba 14.06N 60.58W
Pigeon River 186 Lb 48.02N 89.41W
Piggott 186 Kh 36.23N 90.11W
Pigg's Peak 172 Ee 25.58S 31.15 E
Pigs, Bay of- (EN) = Cochinos, Bahía de- 194 Gb 22.07N 81.10W
Pigüé 204 Am 37.37S 62.25W
Pi He 154 Dh 32.26N 116.34 E
Pihkva järv = Pskov, Lake- (EN) 110 Id 58.00N 28.00 E
Pihlajavesi 116 Gf 61.45N 28.45 E
Pihlava 116 Ic 61.33N 21.36 E
Pihtipudas 114 Fe 63.23N 25.34 E
Piikkiö 116 Jd 60.26N 22.31 E
Piirisaar/Pirissar 116 Lf 58.23N 27.40 E
Pijijiapan 192 Mj 15.42N 93.14W
Pijol, Pico- 194 Df 15.06N 87.35W
Pikalevo 114 Ig 59.32N 34.03 E
Pikangikum 180 If 51.49N 94.00W
Pikelot Island 208 Fd 8.05N 147.38 E
Pikes Peak 182 Fd 38.51N 105.03W
Piketberg 172 Bf 32.54S 18.46 E
Pikiutdleq 179 Hf 64.45N 40.10W
Pikou 154 Ge 39.24N 122.21 E
Pikounda 170 Cb 0.33N 16.42 E
Pila 204 Cm 36.01S 58.08W
Piła 120 Mc 53.10N 16.44 E
Piła [2] 120 Mc 53.10N 16.45 E
Pila, Sierra de la- 126 Kf 38.16N 1.11W
Pilar [Arg.] 204 Bj 31.27S 61.15W
Pilar [Braz.] 202 Ke 9.36S 35.56W
Pilar [Par.] 206 Ic 26.52S 58.23W
Pilas Group 150 He 6.45N 121.35 E
Pilat, Mont- 122 Ki 45.23N 4.35 E
Pilatus 128 Cd 46.59N 8.20 E
Pilaya, Rio- 202 Fh 20.55S 64.04W
Pilcaniyeu 206 Ff 41.08S 70.40W
Pilcomayo, Rio- 198 Kh 25.21S 57.42W
Pile, Jezioro- 120 Mc 53.35N 16.30 E
Pili 130 Ej 39.28N 21.37 E
Pili 150 Hd 13.37N 123.17 E
Pilibhīt 148 Fc 28.38N 79.48 E
Pilica 120 Re 51.52N 21.17 E
Pilion Óros 130 Gj 39.24N 23.05 E
Pilipinas = Philippine Islands (EN) 140 Oh 13.00N 122.00 E
Pilipinas = Philippines (EN) [1] 142 Oh 13.00N 122.00 E
Pilis 120 Oi 47.41N 18.53 E
Pillahuincó, Sierra de- 204 Bn 38.18S 60.45W
Pillar, Cape- 212 Jh 43.15S 148.00 E
Pilna 114 Ki 55.33N 45.55 E
Pilões, Rio- 204 Gc 16.14S 50.54W
Pilões, Serra dos- 204 Ic 17.50S 47.13W
Pilón, Rio- 192 Je 25.32N 99.32W
Pilos 130 Em 36.55N 21.42 E
Pilos = Pylos (EN) 130 Em 36.56N 21.40 E
Pilot Peak 188 Hf 41.02N 114.06W
Pilot Rock 188 Fd 45.29N 118.50W
Pilsen (EN) = Plzeň 112 Hf 49.45N 13.24 E
Piltene 114 Eh 57.15N 21.42 E
Pilzno 120 Rg 49.59N 21.17 E
Pim 136 Hc 61.18N 71.57 E
Pimba 212 Hf 31.15S 136.47 E
Pimenteiras 202 Je 6.14S 41.25W
Pimža jõgi 116 Lg 57.57N 27.59 E
Pina 126 Lc 41.29N 0.32W
Pinacate, Cerro- 192 Cb 31.45N 113.31W
Pinaki Atoll 208 Nf 19.22S 138.44W
Pinamar 204 Dm 37.07S 56.50W
Piñami, Arroyo- 192 Cd 27.44N 113.47W
Pinang → George Town 142 Mi 5.25N 100.20 E
Pinar 126 Gh 36.46N 5.26W
Pinarbaşi 146 Gc 38.50N 36.30 E
Pinar del Rio 176 Kg 22.25N 83.42W
Pinar del Rio [3] 194 Eb 22.35N 83.40W
Pinarhisar 130 Kh 41.37N 27.30 E
Pinchbeck 124 Bb 52.48N 0.09W
Pincher Creek 180 Gg 49.30N 113.48W
Pinçon, Mont- 122 Ff 48.58N 0.37W
Pîncota 130 Ec 46.20N 21.42 E
Pindaíba, Ribeirão 204 Gb 14.48S 52.00W
Pindaré, Rio- 202 Jd 3.17S 44.47W
Pindaré-Mirim 202 Id 3.37S 45.21W
Pindaval 204 Dc 17.08S 56.09W
Pindhos Óros = Pindus Mountains (EN) 110 Ih 39.45N 21.30 E
Pindus Mountains (EN) = Pindhos Óros 110 Ih 39.45N 21.30 E
Pine Bluff 182 Ie 34.13N 92.01W
Pine Bluffs 188 Mf 41.11N 104.04W
Pine Creek 212 Gb 13.49S 131.49 E
Pine Falls 180 Hf 50.35N 96.15W
Pinega 136 Ec 64.42N 43.22 E
Pinega 110 Kc 64.08N 41.54 E
Pine Island Glacier 222 Of 75.00S 101.00W
Pineland 186 Jk 31.15N 93.58W
Pine Mountain [Ga.-U.S.] 184 Ei 32.51N 84.47W
Pine Mountain [U.S.] 184 Fg 36.55N 83.20W
Pine Pass 180 Fe 55.32N 122.30W
Pine Point 176 Hc 61.01N 114.15W
Pine Ridge 186 Ee 43.02N 102.33W
Pinerolo 128 Bf 44.53N 7.21 E
Pines, Isle of- (EN) = Juventud, Isla de la- 174 Kg 21.40N 82.50W
Pines, Isle of- (EN) = Pins, Ile des- 208 Hg 22.37S 167.30 E
Pines, Lake O' The- 186 Ij 32.46N 94.35W
Pinetown 172 Ee 29.52S 30.46 E
Ping 140 Mh 15.42N 100.09 E
Pingbian 152 Hg 22.56N 103.46 E
Pingchang 152 Ie 31.38N 107.06 E
Pingding 154 Bf 37.48N 113.37 E
Pingdingbu → Guyuan 154 Cd 41.40N 115.41 E
Pingdingshan 152 Je 33.41N 113.27 E
Pingding Shan 152 Mb 46.39N 128.30 E
Pingdu 154 Ef 36.47N 119.57 E
Pingelap Atoll 208 Hd 6.13N 160.42 E
Pingelly 212 Df 32.32S 117.05 E
Pinggu 154 Dd 40.08N 117.07 E
Pingguo 152 Ig 23.21N 107.34 E
Pinghu 154 Fi 30.42N 121.02 E
Pingjiang 154 Bj 28.45N 113.37 E
Pingle 152 Jg 24.43N 110.42 E
Pingli 152 Ie 32.27N 109.21 E
Pingliang 142 Mf 35.32N 106.41 E
Pinglu (Jingping) 154 Be 39.32N 112.14 E
Pingluo 142 Mf 38.56N 106.34 E
Pingma → Tiandong 152 Ig 23.40N 107.09 E
Pingnan 152 Jg 23.38N 110.23 E
Pingouins, Ile des- 222 Ec 46.25S 50.19 E
Pingquan 152 Kc 41.00N 118.36 E
Pingshan 154 Ce 38.21N 114.01 E
Pingshun 154 Bf 36.12N 113.26 E
Pingtan 152 Kf 25.31N 119.48 E
Pingtung 152 Lg 22.40N 120.29 E
Pingüicas, Cerro- 192 Jg 21.10N 99.42W
Pingvallavatn 114a Bb 64.15N 21.09W
Pingvellir 114a Bb 64.17N 21.03W
Pingwu 152 He 32.27N 104.35 E
Pingxiang [China] 152 Ig 22.11N 106.46 E
Pingxiang [China] 152 Jf 27.43N 113.48 E
Pingyang 152 Lf 27.40N 120.30 E
Pingyao 152 Jd 37.12N 112.13 E
Pingyi 154 Dg 35.30N 117.38 E
Pingyin 154 Df 36.17N 116.26 E
Pingyu 154 Ch 32.58N 114.36 E
Pingyuan 154 Df 37.10N 116.25 E
Pinhal 204 If 22.12S 46.45W
Pinhão 204 Gg 25.43S 51.38W
Pinheiro Machado 204 Fj 31.34S 53.23W
Pinhel 126 Ed 40.46N 7.04W
Pini, Pulau- 150 Cf 0.08N 98.40 E
Piniós [Grc.] 130 Fj 39.53N 22.44 E
Piniós [Grc.] 130 El 37.48N 21.14 E
Pinipel 219a Ba 4.24S 154.08 E
Pinjug 114 Lf 60.16N 47.54 E
Pinka 128 Kc 47.00N 16.35 E
Pink Mountain 180 Fe 56.06N 122.35W
Pinnaroo 212 Ig 35.16S 140.55 E
Pinneberg 120 Fc 53.39N 9.48 E
Pinnes, Ákra- 130 Hi 40.07N 24.18 E
Pinolosean 150 Hf 0.23N 124.07 E
Pinos 192 If 22.18N 101.34W
Pinos, Mount- 174 Hf 34.50N 119.09W
Pinos-Puente 126 Ig 37.15N 3.45W
Pinrang 150 Gg 3.48S 119.38 E
Pins, Cap des- 219b Ce 21.04S 167.28 E
Pins, Ile des- = Pines, Isle of- (EN) 208 Hg 22.37S 167.30 E
Pins, Pointe aux- 184 Gd 42.15N 81.51W
Pinsk 136 Ce 52.08N 26.06 E
Pinta, Isla- 202a Aa 0.35N 90.44W
Pintas, Sierra de las- 192 Bb 31.40N 115.10W
Pinto [Arg.] 206 Hc 29.09S 62.39W
Pinto [Sp.] 126 Id 40.14N 3.41W
Pintwater Range 188 Hh 36.55N 115.30W
Pio 219a Ed 10.12S 161.42 E
Pioche 188 Hh 37.56N 114.27W
Piombino 128 Eh 42.55N 10.32 E
Piombino, Canale di- 128 Eh 42.55N 10.30 E
Pioneer Mountains 188 Id 45.40N 113.00W
Pioner, ostrov- 140 Lb 79.50N 92.30 E
Pionerski [R.S.F.S.R.] 136 Gc 61.12N 62.57 E
Pionerski [R.S.F.S.R.] 114 Ei 54.57N 20.13 E
Pionki 120 Re 51.30N 21.27 E
Piorini, Lago- 202 Fd 3.35S 63.15W
Piorini, Rio- 202 Fd 3.23S 63.30W
Piotrków [2] 120 Pe 51.25N 19.40 E
Piotrków Trybunalski 120 Pe 51.25N 19.42 E
Piove di Sacco 128 Ge 45.18N 12.02 E
Pipa Dingzi 152 Mc 43.57N 128.14 E
Pipéri 130 Hj 39.19N 24.21 E
Pipestone 186 Hd 44.01N 96.19W
Pipestone Creek 186 Fb 49.42N 100.45W
Pipi 168 Cd 7.27N 22.48 E
Pipinas 204 Dl 35.32S 57.20W
Pipmouacan, Réservoir- 180 Kg 49.40N 70.20W
Piqan → Shanshan 152 Fc 42.52N 90.10 E
Piqua 184 Ee 40.08N 84.14W
Piqueras, Puerto de- 126 Jb 42.03N 2.32W
Piquiri, Rio- 206 Jb 24.03S 54.14W
Piquiri, Serra do- 204 Fg 24.53S 52.25W
Piracanjuba 204 Hc 17.18S 49.01W
Piracanjuba, Rio- [Braz.] 204 Hc 17.18S 48.13W
Piracanjuba, Rio- [Braz.] 204 Hd 18.14S 48.48W
Piracema 204 Je 20.31S 44.29W
Piracicaba 206 Kb 22.43S 47.38W
Piracicaba, Rio- 204 If 22.36S 48.19W
Piraçununga 204 Ie 21.59S 47.25W
Piracuruca 202 Jd 3.56S 41.42W
Piraeus (EN) = Piraiévs 112 Ih 37.57N 23.38 E
Pirai do Sul 204 Hg 24.31S 49.56W
Piraiévs = Piraeus (EN) 112 Ih 37.57N 23.38 E
Piraju 204 Hf 23.12S 49.23W
Pirajuí 204 He 21.59S 49.29W
Pirámide, Cerro- 198 Ij 49.01S 73.32W
Piran 128 He 45.32N 13.34 E
Pirané 206 Ic 25.43S 59.06W
Piranhas 204 Gc 16.31S 51.51W
Piranhas, Rio- 204 Gc 16.01S 51.52W
Pīrān Shahr 146 Kd 36.40N 45.05 E
Pirapora 200 Lg 17.21S 44.56W
Pirarajá 206 Jd 33.44S 54.45W
Pirate Well 194 Kb 22.26N 73.04W
Piratini 204 Fj 31.27S 53.06W
Piratini, Rio- 204 Fk 32.01S 52.25W
Piratinim, Rio- 204 Ei 28.06S 55.27W
Pirdop 130 Hg 42.42N 24.11 E
Pirenópolis 204 Hb 15.51S 48.57W
Pires do Rio 202 Ig 17.18S 48.17W
Pirgós 130 Fi 40.38N 22.44 E
Pírgos 130 El 37.41N 21.27 E
Piriápolis 204 El 34.54S 55.17W
Pirin 130 Gh 41.40N 23.30 E
Pirineos = Pyrenees (EN) 110 Gg 42.40N 1.00 E
Pirineus, Serra dos- 204 Hc 16.15S 49.10W
Piripiri 202 Jd 4.16S 41.47W
Pirissar/Piirisaar 116 Lf 58.23N 27.40 E
Piritu 196 Bh 9.23N 69.12W
Piritu, Islas- 196 Dg 10.10N 64.56W
Pirizal 204 Dc 16.16S 56.23W
Pirjatin 136 Hd 50.14N 32.30 E
Pirmasens 120 Dg 49.12N 7.36 E
Pirna 120 Jf 50.58N 13.56 E
Piron 219a Ad 11.20S 153.27 E
Pirón 126 Hc 41.23N 4.31W
Pirot 130 Ff 43.09N 22.36 E
Pirre, Cerro- 194 Ij 7.49N 77.43W
Pirrit Hills 222 Pg 81.17S 85.21W
Pirsagat 132 Pj 39.53N 49.19 E
Pīr Tāj 146 Me 35.45N 48.07 E
Pirttikyla/Pörtom 116 Ib 62.42N 21.37 E
Piru 150 Ig 3.04S 128.12 E
Pis 220d Ba 7.41N 151.46 E
Pisa 128 Eg 43.43N 10.23 E
Pisa 120 Rc 53.15N 21.52 E
Pisagua 206 Fa 19.36S 70.13W
Pisano 128 Eg 43.46N 10.33 E
Pisar 220d Cb 7.19N 152.01 E
Pisciotta 128 Jj 40.06N 15.14 E
Pisco 200 Ig 13.42S 76.13W
Pișcolt 130 Fb 47.35N 22.18 E
Písek 120 Kg 49.19N 14.10 E
Pishan/Guma 152 Cd 37.38N 78.19 E
Pish Qal'eh 146 Qd 37.35N 57.05 E
Pīshvā 146 Ne 35.18N 51.44 E
Piso Firme 204 Ba 13.41S 61.52W
Pissa 114 Ei 54.39N 21.50 E
Pisshiri-Dake 156a Ba 44.20N 141.55 E
Pista 114 Hd 65.28N 30.45 E
Pisticci 128 Kj 40.23N 16.33 E
Pistoia 128 Eg 43.55N 10.54 E
Pisuerga 126 Hc 41.33N 4.52W
Pisz 120 Rc 53.38N 21.49 E
Pita 166 Cc 11.05N 12.24W
Pitalito 202 Cc 1.53N 76.02W
Pitanga 206 Jb 24.46S 51.44W
Pitanga, Serra da- 204 Gg 24.52S 51.48W

Index Symbols

[1] Independent Nation
[2] State, Region
[3] District, County
[4] Municipality
[5] Colony, Dependency
Continent
Physical Region
Historical or Cultural Region
Mount, Mountain
Volcano
Hill
Mountains, Mountain Range
Hills, Escarpment
Plateau, Upland
Pass, Gap
Plain, Lowland
Delta
Salt Flat
Valley, Canyon
Crater, Cave
Karst Features
Depression
Polder
Desert, Dunes
Forest, Woods
Heath, Steppe
Oasis
Cape, Point
Coast, Beach
Cliff
Peninsula
Isthmus
Sandbank
Island
Atoll
Rock, Reef
Islands, Archipelago
Rocks, Reefs
Coral Reef
Well, Spring
Geyser
River, Stream
Waterfall, Rapids
River Mouth, Estuary
Lake
Salt Lake
Intermittent Lake
Reservoir
Swamp, Pond
Canal
Glacier
Ice Shelf, Pack Ice
Ocean
Sea
Gulf, Bay
Strait, Fjord
Lagoon
Bank
Seamount
Tablemount
Ridge
Shelf
Basin
Escarpment, Sea Scarp
Fracture
Trench, Abyss
National Park, Reserve
Point of Interest
Recreation Site
Cave, Cavern
Historic Site
Ruins
Wall, Walls
Church, Abbey
Temple
Scientific Station
Railway station
Airport
Port
Military installation
Lighthouse
Mine
Tunnel
Dam, Bridge

Pitangui 204 Jd 19.40S 44.54W
Pitcairn [5] 210 Og 24.00S 129.00W
Pitcairn Island 208 Ng 25.04S 130.05W
Piteå 114 Ed 65.20N 21.30 E
Piteälven 110 Ib 65.14N 21.32 E
Piteşti 112 Ig 44.51N 24.52 E
Pithiviers 122 If 48.10N 2.15 E
Pithorāgarh 148 Gc 29.35N 80.13 E
Piti 220c Bb 13.28N 144.41 E
Piti 170 Fd 7.00S 32.44 E
Pitiquito 192 Cb 30.42N 112.02W
Pitkjaranta 136 Dc 61.35N 31.31 E
Pitkkala 116 Jc 61.28N 23.34 E
Pitljar 138 Bc 65.52N 65.55 E
Pitlochry 118 Je 56.43N 3.45W
Pitomača 128 Le 45.57N 17.14 E
Piton, Pointe du- 197e Ba 16.30N 61.27W
Pit River 182 Cc 40.45N 122.22W
Pitrufquén 206 Fe 38.59S 72.39W
Pitt 180 Ef 53.40N 129.50W
Pitt Island 208 Ji 44.20S 176.10W
Pittsburg 182 Id 37.25N 94.42W
Pittsburgh 176 Le 40.26N 80.00W
Pittsfield [Il.-U.S.] 186 Kg 39.36N 90.48W
Pittsfield [Ma.-U.S.] 184 Kd 42.27N 73.15W
Pittsfield [Me.-U.S.] 184 Mc 44.47N 69.23W
Pitt Strait 218 Jf 44.10S 176.20W
Pitu 150 If 1.41N 128.01 E
Piũi 204 Je 20.28S 45.58W
Piura 200 Hf 5.12S 80.38W
Piura [3] 202 Be 5.00S 80.20W
Piuthān 148 Gc 28.06N 82.52 E
Piva 130 Bf 43.21N 18.51 E
Pivan 138 If 50.27N 137.05 E
Pivijay 194 Jh 10.28N 74.38W
Pižma [R.S.F.S.R.] 114 Lh 57.36N 48.58 E
Pižma [R.S.F.S.R.] 134 Fd 65.24N 52.05 E
Pizzo 128 Kl 38.44N 16.40 E
Pjakupur 138 Cd 65.00N 77.48 E
Pjalica 114 Jc 66.12N 39.32 E
Pjalma 136 Dc 62.27N 35.53 E
Pjana 114 Ki 55.37N 45.58 E
Pjandž 136 Gh 37.15N 69.07 E
Pjandž 140 If 37.06N 68.20 E
Pjaozero, ozero- 110 Jb 66.05N 30.55 E
Pjarnu/Pärnu 112 Id 58.24N 24.32 E
Pjarnu / Pärnu jõgi 114 Fg 58.23N 24.34 E
Pjarnu, zaliv- / Pärnu laht 114 Fg 58.15N 24.25 E
Pjarnu-Jagupi/Pärnu-Jaagupi 116 Kf 58.36N 24.25 E
Pjasina 140 Kb 73.47N 87.01 E
Pjasino, ozero- 138 Dc 69.45N 87.30 E
Pjasinski zaliv 138 Db 74.00N 85.00 E
Pjatigorsk 112 Kg 44.03N 43.04 E
Pjatihatki 132 He 48.27N 33.40 E
Pjórsá 110 Dc 63.45N 20.50W
Pjuhjajarvi, ozero- 116 Nc 61.50N 30.00 E
Pjussi/Püssi 116 Le 59.17N 26.57 E
Pkulagalid 220a Bb 7.36N 134.33 E
Pkulagasemieg 220a Ac 7.08N 134.23 E
Pkurengel 220a Ac 7.27N 134.28 E
Plá 204 Bl 35.07S 60.13W
Placentia 180 Mg 47.14N 53.58W
Placentia Bay 174 Ne 47.15N 54.30W
Placer 150 Hd 11.52N 123.55 E
Placerville 188 Eg 38.43N 120.48W
Placetas 180 Id 22.19N 79.40W
Plácido Rosas 204 Fk 32.45S 53.44W
Plačkovci 130 Ig 42.49N 25.28 E
Plačkovica 130 Fh 41.46N 22.32 E
Plainfield 184 Je 40.37N 74.25W
Plains [Mt.-U.S.] 188 Hc 47.27N 114.53W
Plains [Tx.-U.S.] 186 Ej 33.11N 102.50W
Plainview [Nb.-U.S.] 186 He 42.21N 97.47W
Plainview [Tx.-U.S.] 182 Ge 34.11N 101.43W
Plainville 186 Gg 39.14N 99.18W
Pláka, Ákra- 130 Ii 40.02N 25.25 E
Plake 130 Eh 41.14N 21.02 E
Plampang 150 Gh 8.48S 117.48 E
Planá 120 Ig 49.52N 12.44 E
Plana, Illa- / Plana o Nueva Tabarca, Isla- 126 Lf 38.10N 0.28 E
Plana Cays 194 Kb 22.37N 73.33W
Plana o Nueva Tabarca, Isla- / Plana, Illa- 126 Lf 38.10N 0.28 E
Planco, Peñón- 192 Ge 24.35N 104.15W
Plane, Ile- 126 Li 35.46N 0.54W
Planeta Rica 202 Cb 8.25N 75.35W
Planet Depth (EN) 106 Hj 10.20S 110.30 E
Planèzes 122 Ij 45.00N 2.50 E
Plankinton 186 Ge 43.43N 98.29W
Plantation 184 Gl 26.05N 80.14W
Plantaurel 122 Hk 43.04N 1.30 E
Plant City 184 Fk 28.01N 82.08W
Plasencia 126 Fd 40.02N 6.05W
Plast 136 Ge 54.22N 60.55 E
Plaster Rock 184 Nb 46.54N 67.24W
Plastun 138 Ih 44.48N 136.17 E
Plasy 120 Jg 49.56N 13.24 E
Plata, Rio de la- [P.R.] 197a Bb 18.30N 66.14W
Plata, Rio de la- [S.Amer.] 198 Ki 35.00S 57.00W
Platajai 130 Gk 38.13N 23.16 E
Platani 128 Hm 37.24N 13.16 E
Plateau [2] 166 Gd 8.50N 9.00 E
Plateau [3] 170 Cc 2.10S 15.00 E
Plateaux [3] 166 Fd 7.30N 1.10 E
Platen, Kapp- 179 Ob 80.31N 22.48 E
Plati 130 Fi 40.39N 22.32 E
Plato 202 Db 9.47N 74.47W
Platte 186 Ge 43.23N 98.51W
Platte 178 Je 41.00N 95.52W
Platte Island 158 Mi 5.52S 55.23 E
Platte River 186 Ig 39.16N 94.50W
Platteville 186 Ke 42.44N 90.29W
Plattsburgh 182 Mc 44.42N 73.29W
Plattsmouth 186 If 41.01N 95.53W
Plau 120 Ic 53.27N 12.16 E
Plauen 120 If 50.30N 12.08 E
Plauer See 120 Ic 53.30N 12.20 E
Plav 130 Cg 42.36N 19.57 E
Plavecký Mikuláš 120 Nh 48.30N 17.18 E
Pļaviņas/Pljavinjas 114 Fh 56.38N 25.46 E
Plavsk 132 Jc 53.43N 37.18 E
Playa Azul 190 De 17.59N 102.24W
Playa Noriega, Laguna- 192 Dc 29.10N 111.50W
Playa Vicente 192 Li 17.50N 95.49W
Playón Chico 194 Hi 9.18N 78.14W
Pleasanton [Ks.-U.S.] 186 Ig 38.11N 94.43W
Pleasanton [Tx.-U.S.] 186 Gl 28.58N 98.29W
Pleasant Point 218 Df 44.16S 171.08 E
Pleasant Valley 186 Fi 35.15N 101.48W
Plechý 120 Jh 48.49N 13.53 E
Pleiku 148 Lf 13.59N 108.00 E
Pleiße 120 Ie 51.20N 12.22 E
Pleniţa 130 Ge 44.13N 23.11 E
Plenty, Bay of- 208 Ih 37.45S 177.10 E
Plentywood 182 Gb 48.47N 104.34W
Pleščenicy 132 Eb 54.29N 27.55 E
Pleseck 136 Ec 62.44N 40.18 E
Plešivec 120 Qh 48.33N 20.25 E
Pleşu, Vîrful- 130 Fc 46.32N 22.11 E
Pleszew 120 Ne 51.54N 17.48 E
Plétipi, Lac- 180 Kf 51.42N 70.08W
Plettenberg 120 Je 51.13N 7.53 E
Plettenbergbaai 172 Cf 34.03S 23.22 E
Pleven 112 Ig 43.25N 24.37 E
Pleven [2] 130 Hf 43.25N 24.37 E
Plibo 166 De 4.35N 7.40W
Pliska 130 Kf 43.22N 27.07 E
Pliszka 120 Kd 52.15N 14.40 E
Plitvice 128 Jf 44.54N 15.36 E
Pljavinjas/Pļaviņas 114 Fh 56.38N 25.46 E
Plješevica 128 Jf 44.45N 15.45 E
Pljevlja 130 Cf 43.21N 19.21 E
Pljusa 114 Gg 58.25N 29.20 E
Pljusa 114 Gg 59.13N 28.11 E
Ploča, Rt- 128 Jg 43.30N 15.58 E
Ploče 128 Lg 43.04N 17.26 E
Płock 120 Pd 52.33N 19.43 E
Płock [2] 120 Pd 52.35N 19.45 E
Plöckenstein 120 Jh 48.49N 13.53 E
Ploërmel 122 Dg 47.56N 2.24W
Ploieşti 112 Ig 44.57N 26.01 E
Plomárion 130 Jk 38.59N 26.22 E
Plomb du Cantal 122 Ii 45.03N 2.46 E
Plön 120 Gb 54.10N 10.26 E
Płonia 120 Kc 53.25N 14.36 E
Płonka 120 Qd 52.37N 20.30 E
Płońsk 120 Qd 52.38N 20.23 E
Plopana 130 Kc 46.41N 27.13 E
Płoty 120 Lc 53.50N 15.16 E
Plouguerneau 122 Bf 48.36N 4.30W
Plovdiv 112 Ig 42.09N 24.45 E
Plovdiv [2] 130 Hg 42.09N 24.45 E
Plummer 188 Gc 47.20N 116.53W
Plumridge Lakes 212 Fe 29.30S 125.25 E
Plumtree 172 Dd 20.31S 27.48 E
Plungė/Plunge 114 Ei 55.56N 21.48 E
Plunge/Plungė 114 Ei 55.56N 21.48 E
Plymouth [Eng.-U.K.] 112 Fe 50.23N 4.10W
Plymouth [In.-U.S.] 184 De 41.21N 86.19W
Plymouth [Ma.-U.S.] 184 Le 41.58N 70.41W
Plymouth [Mont.] 190 Le 16.42N 62.13W
Plymouth Sound 118 Ik 50.25N 4.05W
Plzeň=Pilsen (EN) 112 Hf 49.45N 13.24 E
Plzeňská pahorkatina 120 Jg 49.50N 13.15 E
Pniewy 120 Md 52.31N 16.15 E
Pô 166 Ec 11.10N 1.09W
Po 110 Hg 44.57N 12.05 E
Po, Foci del-=Po, Mouths of the- (EN) 128 Gf 44.52N 12.30 E
Po, Mouths of the- (EN)= Po, Foci del- 128 Gf 44.52N 12.30 E
Poarta de Fier a Transilvaniei, Pasul- 130 Fd 45.25N 22.40 E
Poarta Orientală, Pasul- 130 Fd 45.08N 22.20 E
Poás, Volcán- 194 Eh 10.11N 84.13W
Pobé 166 Fd 6.58N 2.41 E
Pobeda, gora- 140 Qc 65.12N 146.12 E
Pobeda Ice Island 222 Ge 64.30S 97.00 E
Pobedy, pik- 140 Ke 42.02N 80.05 E
Pobla de Segur / la Pobla de Segur 126 Mb 42.15N 0.58 E
Pobla de Trives / Puebla de Trives 126 Eb 42.20N 7.15W
Poblet, Monasterio de- / Poblet, Monestir de- 126 Nc 41.20N 1.05 E
Poblet, Monestir de- / Poblet, Monasterio de- 126 Nc 41.20N 1.05 E
Pobrežije 130 Jf 43.56N 26.21 E
Pocahontas 186 Kh 36.16N 90.58W
Pocatello 176 He 42.52N 112.27W
Počep 132 Hc 52.57N 33.28 E
Pocerina 130 Ce 44.38N 19.35 E
Počinok 136 De 54.23N 32.29 E
Počitelj 128 Lg 43.08N 17.44 E
Pocito, Sierra del- 126 He 39.20N 4.05W
Pocito Casas 192 Dc 28.32N 111.06W
Pocklington Reef 214 Fj 11.00S 155.00 E
Poções 202 Jf 14.31S 40.21W
Poço Fundo, Cachoeira- 204 Jc 16.10S 45.51W
Poconé 202 Gg 16.15S 56.37W
Pocono Mountains 184 Je 41.10N 75.20W
Poços de Caldas 202 Ih 21.48S 46.34W
Pocri 194 Gj 7.40N 80.07W
Podborovje [R.S.F.S.R.] 132 Ih 59.32N 35.01 E
Podborovje [R.S.F.S.R.] 116 Mg 57.51N 28.46 E
Podbrezová 120 Ph 48.49N 19.31 E
Podčerje 134 He 63.55N 57.30 E
Poděbrady 120 Lf 50.09N 15.07 E
Podgajcy 120 Vg 49.12N 25.12 E
Podgorina 130 Ce 44.15N 19.56 E
Po di Volano 128 Gf 44.49N 12.15 E
Podjuga 114 Jf 61.07N 40.54 E
Podkamennaja Tunguska= Stony Tunguska (EN) 140 Lc 61.36N 90.18 E
Podlasie 120 Sd 52.30N 23.00 E
Podlaska, Nizina- 120 Sc 53.00N 22.45 E
Podlužje 130 Ce 44.45N 19.55 E
Podolia (EN) = Podolskaja vozvyšennost 110 If 49.00N 28.00 E
Podolsk 136 Dd 55.27N 37.33 E
Podolskaja vozvyšennost = Podolia (EN) 110 If 49.00N 28.00 E
Podor 166 Cb 16.40N 14.57W
Podporožje 136 Dc 60.54N 34.09 E
Podravina 128 Le 45.40N 17.40 E
Podravska Slatina 128 Le 45.42N 17.42 E
Podrima 130 Dg 42.24N 20.33 E
Podromanija 128 Mg 43.54N 18.46 E
Podsvilje 116 Mi 55.09N 28.01 E
Podujevo 130 Eg 42.55N 21.12 E
Podunajská nížina 120 Nh 48.00N 17.40 E
Podvološino 138 Fe 58.15N 108.25 E
Poel 120 Hb 54.00N 11.26 E
Poeniţa, Vîrful- 130 Gc 46.15N 23.20 E
Pofadder 172 Be 29.10S 19.22 E
Pogăniş 130 Ed 45.41N 21.21 E
Pogar 132 Hc 52.33N 33.16 E
Poggibonsi 128 Fg 43.28N 11.09 E
Pöggstall 128 Jb 48.19N 15.11 E
Pogibi 138 Jf 52.15N 141.45 E
Pogny 124 Gf 48.52N 4.29 E
Pogoanele 130 Je 44.55N 27.00 E
Pogórze Karpackie 120 Qg 49.52N 21.00 E
Pogradeci 130 Di 40.54N 20.39 E
Pograničny 138 Ih 44.26N 131.20 E
Pogrebišče 128 Fe 49.29N 29.14 E
Poguba Xoréu, Rio- 204 Ec 16.29S 54.58W
P'ohang 152 Md 36.02N 129.22 E
Pohja/Pojo 116 Jd 60.06N 23.31 E
Pohjankangas 116 Jc 62.00N 22.30 E
Pohjanlahti=Bothnia, Gulf of- (EN) 110 Hc 63.00N 20.00 E
Pohjanmaa 116 Jb 63.00N 22.30 E
Pohjois-Karjala [3] 114 Ge 63.00N 30.00 E
Pohlheim 124 Kd 50.32N 8.42 E
Pohorje 128 Jd 46.32N 15.28 E
Po Hu 154 Di 30.15N 116.32 E
Pohue Bay 221a Fd 19.01N 155.48W
Pohvistnevo 136 Fe 53.40N 52.08 E
Poiana Mare 130 Gf 43.55N 23.04 E
Poiana Ruscă, Munţii 130 Fd 45.41N 22.30 E
Pöide/Pějde 116 Jf 58.30N 22.50 E
Poie 170 Dc 2.55S 23.10 E
Poindimié 216 Cd 20.56S 165.20 E
Poindo → Lhünzhub 152 Fe 30.17N 91.20 E
Poinsett, Cape- 222 He 65.42S 113.18 E
Poinsett, Lake- 186 Hd 44.34N 97.05W
Point Arena 188 Dg 38.55N 123.41W
Point au Fer Island 186 Kl 29.15N 91.15W
Pointe-à-Pitre 190 Le 16.14N 61.32W
Pointe Duble 197e Bb 16.20N 61.00W
Pointe-Noire 197e Ab 16.14N 61.47W
Pointe Noire 160 Ii 4.48S 11.51 E
Point Hope 178 Fc 68.21N 166.41W
Point Lake 180 Gc 65.15N 113.00W
Point Lay 178 Gc 69.45N 163.03W
Point Pleasant [N.J.-U.S.] 184 Je 40.06N 74.02W
Point Pleasant [W.V.-U.S.] 184 Ff 38.53N 82.07W
Poisson-Blanc, Lac- 184 Jc 46.00N 75.44W
Poissonnier Point 212 Dc 20.00S 119.10 E
Poissy 122 If 48.56N 2.03 E
Poitevin, Marais- 122 Eh 46.22N 1.06W
Poitiers 112 Gf 46.35N 0.20 E
Poitou 122 Fh 46.40N 0.30W
Poitou, Plaine et Seuil du- 122 Gh 46.26N 0.17 E
Poivre Islands 172b Bb 5.46S 53.19 E
Poix-de-Picardie 122 He 49.47N 1.59 E
Poix-Terron 124 Ge 49.39N 4.39 E
Pojarkovo 138 Hg 49.42N 128.50 E
Pojkovski 136 Hc 60.59N 72.00 E
Pojo/Pohja 116 Jd 60.06N 23.31 E
Pojuba, Rio- 204 Ec 16.30S 54.59W
Pokhara 148 Gc 28.14N 83.59 E
Poko 170 Eb 3.09N 26.53 E
Pokoinu 220p Bb 21.12S 159.49W
Pokój 120 Nf 50.56N 17.50 E
Pokrovka 135 Lc 42.19N 78.01 E
Pokrovsk 138 Hd 61.29N 129.10 E
Pokrovskoje [R.S.F.S.R.] 132 Jc 52.38N 36.51 E
Pokrovskoje [Ukr.-U.S.S.R.] 132 Jf 47.59N 36.13 E
Pokšenga 114 Kd 64.01N 44.15 E
Pokutje 130 Ia 48.20N 25.05 E
Pola 114 Hg 58.05N 31.40 E
Polabí 120 Lf 50.10N 15.10 E
Polacca 188 Ji 35.50N 110.23W
Pola de Laviana 126 Ga 43.15N 5.34W
Pola de Lena 126 Ga 43.10N 5.49W
Pola de Siero 126 Ga 43.23N 5.40W
Polanco 204 Ek 33.54S 55.09W
Poland 220g Ab 1.52N 157.33W
Poland (EN)=Polska [1] 112 He 52.00N 19.00 E
Polanów 120 Mb 54.08N 16.39 E
Polar Plateau 222 Cg 90.00S 0.00
Polar Urals (EN)=Poljarny Ural 110 Mb 66.55N 64.30 E
Polatlı 144 Db 39.36N 32.09 E
Polch 124 Jd 50.18N 7.19 E
Połczyn Zdrój 120 Mc 53.46N 16.06 E
Pol-e Khomrī 144 Kb 35.56N 68.43 E
Pole of Inaccessibility (EN) 222 Eg 82.06S 54.58 E
Pol-e-Safid 146 Od 36.06N 53.01 E
Polesella 128 Ff 44.58N 11.45 E
Polesie Lubelskie 120 Te 51.30N 23.20 E
Polesine 128 Fe 45.00N 11.45 E
Polesje=Polesye (EN) 110 Ie 52.00N 27.00 E
Polessk 116 Ij 54.51N 21.02 E
Polesskoje 132 Fd 51.16N 29.27 E
Polesye (EN)=Polesje 110 Ie 52.00N 27.00 E
Polevskoj 136 Gd 56.28N 60.11 E
Polewali 150 Gg 3.25S 119.20 E
Poležan 130 Gh 41.43N 23.30 E
Polgár 120 Ri 47.52N 21.07 E
Pölgyo 154 Ig 34.51N 127.21 E
Poli 166 Hd 8.29N 13.15 E
Poliaigos 130 Hm 36.46N 24.38 E
Poličani 130 Di 40.08N 20.21 E
Policastro, Golfo di- 128 Jk 40.00N 15.35 E
Police 120 Kc 53.33N 14.35 E
Police - Trzebiez 120 Kc 53.39N 14.32 E
Policoro 128 Kj 40.13N 16.41 E
Poligny 122 Lh 46.50N 5.43 E
Poligus 138 Ed 61.58N 94.40 E
Polikastron 130 Fh 41.00N 22.34 E
Polikhnitos 130 Jj 39.05N 26.11 E
Polillo Islands 140 Oh 14.50N 122.05 E
Pólis 146 Ee 35.02N 32.25 E
Polist 114 Hg 58.07N 31.32 E
Polistena 128 Kl 38.24N 16.04 E
Políyros 130 Gi 40.23N 23.27 E
Poljarny [R.S.F.S.R.] 138 Mc 69.01N 178.45 E
Poljarny [R.S.F.S.R.] 136 Db 69.13N 33.28 E
Poljarny Ural=Polar Urals (EN) 110 Mb 66.55N 64.30 E
Polkowice 120 Me 51.32N 16.06 E
Pöllau 128 Jc 47.18N 15.50 E
Polle 220d Bb 7.20N 151.15 E
Pollença/Pollensa 126 Pe 39.53N 3.01 E
Pollensa/Pollença 126 Pe 39.53N 3.01 E
Pollino 110 Hh 39.55N 16.10 E
Polochic, Río- 194 Cf 15.28N 89.22W
Polock 136 Cd 55.29N 28.52 E
Polog 130 Dh 42.00N 21.00 E
Pologi 136 Df 47.28N 36.15 E
Polonina 120 Jh 48.30N 23.30 E
Polonnaruwa 148 Gg 7.56N 81.00 E
Polonnoje 132 Ed 50.06N 27.29 E
Polousny krjaž 138 Jc 69.30N 144.00 E
Polska=Poland (EN) [1] 112 He 52.00N 19.00 E
Polski Gradec 130 Jg 42.11N 26.06 E
Polski Trămbeš 130 If 43.22N 25.38 E
Polson 188 Hc 47.41N 114.09W
Poltár 120 Ph 48.27N 19.48 E
Poltava 112 Jf 49.35N 34.34 E
Poltavka 136 He 54.22N 71.45 E
Poltavskaja oblast [3] 136 Df 49.45N 33.50 E
Pöltsamaa/Pyltsamaa 114 Fg 58.39N 25.59 E
Pöltsamaa/Pyltsamaa 116 Lf 58.23N 26.08 E
Poluj 136 Hb 66.30N 66.31 E
Polunočnoje 136 Gc 60.52N 60.25 E
Polür 146 Oe 32.52N 52.03 E
Põlva/Pylva 114 Gg 58.04N 27.06 E
Polvijärvi 114 Ge 62.51N 29.22 E
Polynesia 208 Le 4.00S 156.00W
Polynésie Française=French Polynesia (EN) [5] 210 Mf 16.00S 145.00W
Pom, Laguna de- 192 Mh 18.35N 92.15W
Pomarance 128 Eg 43.18N 10.52 E
Pomarkku/Påmark 116 Ic 61.42N 22.00 E
Pombal [Braz.] 202 Ke 6.46S 37.47W
Pombal [Port.] 126 De 39.55N 8.38W
Pombo, Rio- 204 Fe 20.53S 52.23W
Pomerania (EN)= Pommern 110 He 54.00N 16.00 E
Pomerania (EN)= Pommern 120 Lc 54.00N 16.00 E
Pomeranian Bay (EN)= Pommersche Bucht 120 Kb 54.20N 14.20 E
Pomeranian Bay (EN)= Pomorska, Zatoka- 120 Kb 54.20N 14.20 E
Pomeroy 184 Ff 39.03N 82.03W
Pomio 210 Ge 5.32S 151.30 E
Pomme de Terre Reservoir 186 Jh 37.51N 93.19W
Pommern=Pomerania (EN) 110 He 54.00N 16.00 E
Pommern=Pomerania (EN) 120 Lc 54.00N 16.00 E
Pommersche Bucht= Pomeranian Bay (EN) 120 Kb 54.20N 14.20 E
Pommersfelden 120 Gg 49.46N 10.49 E
Pomona 188 Gi 34.04N 117.45W
Pomona Lake 186 Ig 38.40N 95.35W
Pomorije 130 Kg 42.33N 27.39 E
Pomorska, Zatoka-= Pomeranian Bay (EN) 120 Kb 54.20N 14.20 E
Pomorski bereg 114 Id 64.00N 36.15 E
Pomorskie, Pojezierze- 120 Mc 53.30N 16.30 E
Pomorski proliv 136 Eb 68.40N 50.00 E
Pomošnaja 132 Ge 48.14N 31.29 E
Pompano Beach 184 Gl 26.15N 80.07W
Pompei 128 Ij 40.45N 14.30 E
Pompeu 204 Jd 19.12S 44.59W
Ponape 210 Gd 6.52N 158.15 E
Ponape Island 208 Gd 6.55N 158.15 E
Ponca City 182 Hd 36.42N 97.05W
Ponce 176 Mh 18.01N 66.37W
Poncheville, Lac- 184 Ia 50.12N 76.55W
Pondcreek 186 Hh 36.40N 97.48W
Pondichery 148 Ff 11.56N 79.53 E
Pondicherry [3] 148 Ff 11.55N 79.45 E
Pond Inlet 176 Lb 72.41N 78.00W
Pond Inlet 180 Jb 72.48N 77.00W
Ponea 220n Ac 10.28S 161.01W
Ponente, Riviera di- 128 Cf 44.10N 8.20 E
Ponérihouen 219b Be 21.05S 165.24 E
Pones 220d Bb 7.12N 151.59 E
Ponferrada 126 Fb 42.33N 6.35W
Pongaroa 218 Gd 40.33S 176.11 E
Pongo 158 Jh 8.42N 27.40 E
Pongola 172 Ee 26.52S 32.20 E
Pong Qu 152 Ef 26.49N 87.09 E
Poniatowa 120 Se 51.11N 22.05 E
Ponoj 112 Kb 67.05N 41.07 E
Ponoj 110 Kb 66.59N 41.10 E
Ponomarevka 132 Sc 53.09N 54.12 E
Ponorogo 150 Fh 7.52S 111.27 E
Pons 122 Fi 45.35N 0.33W
Pons/Ponts 126 Nc 41.55N 1.12 E
Ponsul 126 Ee 39.40N 7.31W
Pont-à-Celles 124 Gd 50.30N 4.21 E
Ponta Delgada 160 Ee 37.44N 25.40W
Ponta Delgada [3] 162 Bb 37.48N 25.30W
Ponta Grossa 200 Kh 25.05S 50.09W
Pont-à-Mousson 122 Mf 48.54N 6.04 E
Ponta Porã 200 Kh 22.32S 55.43W
Pontarlier 122 Mh 46.54N 6.22 E
Pontassieve 128 Fg 43.46N 11.26 E
Pont-Audemer 122 Ge 49.21N 0.31 E
Pontaut 204 Bm 37.44S 61.20W
Pontávert 124 Fe 49.25N 3.49 E
Pontchartrain, Lake- 182 Ie 30.10N 90.10W
Pontchâteau 122 Dg 47.26N 2.05W
Pont-de-Claix, Le- 122 Li 45.07N 5.42 E
Pont-de-l'Arche 124 De 49.18N 1.10 E
Pont de Suert 126 Mb 42.24N 0.45 E
Pont-de-Vaux 122 Kh 46.26N 4.56 E
Ponte Alta 204 Gh 27.29S 50.23W
Ponte Alta, Serra da- 204 Id 19.42S 47.40W
Ponteareas / Puenteareas 126 Db 42.11N 8.30W
Ponte Branca 204 Fc 16.27S 52.40W
Pontecorvo 128 Hi 42.27N 13.40 E
Ponte de Lima 126 Dc 41.46N 8.35W
Ponte de Pedrā 204 Da 13.35S 57.21W
Ponte de Pedra 204 Ec 17.06S 54.23W
Ponte de Pedra, Rio- → Sacuriuiná, Rio- 204 Da 13.58S 57.18W
Pontedera 128 Eg 43.40N 10.38 E
Ponte de Sor 126 De 39.15N 8.01W
Pontedeume / Puentedeume 126 Da 43.24N 8.10W
Ponte Firme, Chapada da- 204 Id 18.05S 46.25W
Ponteix 188 Lb 49.49N 107.30W
Ponte Nova 202 Jh 20.24S 42.54W
Pontés e Lacerda 204 Cb 15.11S 59.21W
Pontevedra 126 Db 42.26N 8.38W
Pontevedra [3] 126 Db 42.30N 8.30W
Pontevedra, Ria de- 126 Db 42.22N 8.45W
Ponte Vermelha 204 Ed 19.29S 54.25W
Pont-Farcy 124 Af 48.56N 1.02W
Pontfaverger-Moronvilliers 124 Ge 49.18N 4.19 E
Ponthieu 122 Hd 50.10N 1.55 E
Pontiac [Il.-U.S.] 186 Lf 40.53N 88.38W
Pontiac [Mi.-U.S.] 184 Fd 42.37N 83.18W
Pontianak 142 Mj 0.02S 109.20 E
Pontian Kechil 150 Df 1.29N 103.23 E
Pontine Islands (EN) = Ponziane, Isole- 128 Gj 40.55N 13.00 E
Pontivy 122 Df 48.04N 2.59W
Pontivy, Pays de- 122 Dg 48.00N 3.00W
Pont-l'Abbé 122 Bg 47.52N 4.13W
Pont-l'Evêque 124 Ce 49.18N 0.11 E
Pontoise 122 Ie 49.03N 2.06 E
Pontorson 122 Ef 48.33N 1.31W
Pontremoli 128 Df 44.22N 9.53 E
Pontresina 128 Dd 46.28N 9.53 E
Ponts/Pons 126 Nc 41.55N 1.12 E
Pont-Sainte-Maxence 124 Ee 49.18N 2.36 E
Pont-Saint-Esprit 122 Kj 44.15N 4.39 E
Pontypool 118 Jj 51.43N 3.02W
Ponza 128 Gj 40.54N 12.58 E
Ponza 128 Gj 40.55N 12.55 E
Ponziane, Isole- = Pontine Islands (EN) 128 Gj 40.55N 13.00 E
Pool [3] 170 Bc 3.30S 15.00 E
Poole 118 Lk 50.43N 1.59W
Pool Malebo 158 Ii 4.02S 16.03 E
Poona → Pune 142 Jh 18.32N 73.52 E
Poopó 202 Eg 18.23S 66.59W
Poopó, Lago de- = Poopó, Lake- (EN) 198 Jg 18.45S 67.07W
Poopó, Lake- (EN) = Poopó, Lago de- 198 Jg 18.45S 67.07W
Poor Knights Islands 218 Fa 35.30S 174.45 E
Pôõsaspea neem / Pyzaspea 116 Je 59.15N 23.25 E
Popa Taung 148 Jd 21.08N 95.12 E
Popayán 200 Ie 2.27N 76.36W
Poperinge 122 Id 50.51N 2.43 E
Poperinge-Watou 124 Ed 50.51N 2.37 E
Popigaj 138 Gb 71.55N 110.47 E
Popigaj 138 Fb 72.55N 106.00 E
Poplar 188 Mb 48.07N 105.12W
Poplar 180 Hf 53.00N 97.18W
Poplar Bluff 182 Id 36.45N 90.24W
Poplar River 188 Mb 48.05N 105.11W
Popocatépetl, Volcán- 174 Jh 19.02N 98.38W
Popokabaka 170 Cd 5.42S 16.35 E
Popoli 128 Hh 42.10N 13.50 E
Popomanaseu, Mount- 219a Ec 9.42S 160.03 E
Popondetta 214 Di 8.46S 148.14 E
Popovo 130 Jf 43.21N 26.14 E
Poppberg 120 Hg 49.20N 11.45 E
Poppel, Ravels- 124 Hc 51.27N 5.02 E
Poprad 120 Qg 49.03N 20.19 E
Poprad 120 Qg 49.38N 20.42 E
Poptún 194 Ce 16.21N 89.26W
Por 120 Tf 50.48N 23.01 E
Porangahau 218 Gd 40.18S 176.38 E
Porangatu 204 Ha 13.26S 49.10W
Porbandar 148 Dd 21.38N 69.36 E
Porcien 124 Ge 49.40N 4.20 E
Porcos, Rio dos- 204 Ja 12.42S 45.07W
Porcuna 126 Hg 37.52N 4.11W
Porcupine 184 Ga 48.32N 81.10W
Porcupine 174 Ec 66.35N 145.15W
Porcupine Bank (EN) 110 Ee 53.20N 13.30W
Porcupine Creek 188 Lb 48.09N 106.22W
Porcupine Hills 188 Ha 50.05N 114.10W
Porcupine Plain 180 Dc 67.00N 137.30W
Pordenone 128 Ge 45.57N 12.39 E
Poreč 128 He 45.13N 13.37 E
Poreč 130 Fe 44.20N 22.05 E
Porecatu 204 Gf 22.43S 51.24W

Index Symbols

[1] Independent Nation
[2] State, Region
[3] District, County
[4] Municipality
[5] Colony, Dependency
Continent
Physical Region
Historical or Cultural Region
Mount, Mountain
Volcano
Hill
Mountains, Mountain Range
Hills, Escarpment
Plateau, Upland
Pass, Gap
Plain, Lowland
Delta
Salt Flat
Valley, Canyon
Crater, Cave
Karst Features
Depression
Polder
Desert, Dunes
Forest, Woods
Heath, Steppe
Oasis
Cape, Point
Coast, Beach
Cliff
Peninsula
Isthmus
Sandbank
Island
Atoll
Rock, Reef
Islands, Archipelago
Rocks, Reefs
Coral Reef
Well, Spring
Geyser
River, Stream
Waterfall, Rapids
River Mouth, Estuary
Lake
Salt Lake
Intermittent Lake
Reservoir
Swamp, Pond
Canal
Glacier
Ice Shelf, Pack Ice
Ocean
Sea
Gulf, Bay
Strait, Fjord
Lagoon
Bank
Seamount
Tablemount
Ridge
Shelf
Basin
Escarpment, Sea Scarp
Fracture
Trench, Abyss
National Park, Reserve
Point of Interest
Recreation Site
Cave, Cavern
Historic Site
Ruins
Wall, Walls
Church, Abbey
Temple
Scientific Station
Railway station
Airport
Port
Military installation
Lighthouse
Mine
Tunnel
Dam, Bridge

Name	Page	Grid	Lat.	Long.
Porećje	116	Kk	53.53N	24.08 E
Poreckoje	114	Li	55.13N	46.19 E
Porhov	136	Cd	57.45N	29.32 E
Pori/Björneborg	112	Ic	61.29N	21.47 E
Porion	130	Gn	35.58N	23.16 E
Porirua	216	Dh	41.08S	174.50 E
Pórisvatn	114a	Bb	64.20N	18.55W
Porjus	116	Cc	66.57N	19.49 E
Porkkala	116	Ke	59.55N	24.25 E
Porlamar	202	Fa	10.57N	63.51W
Porma	126	Gb	42.29N	5.28W
Pornic	122	Dg	47.07N	2.06W
Poronajsk	142	Qe	49.14N	143.04 E
Poronin	120	Qg	49.20N	20.04 E
Póros	130	Gl	37.30N	23.27 E
Póros	130	Gl	37.30N	23.31 E
Poroshiri-Dake	154	Qc	42.42N	142.35 E
Porosozero	114	He	62.44N	32.42 E
Porozovo	120	Ud	52.54N	24.27 E
Porpoise Bay	222	Ie	66.30S	128.30 E
Porquis Junction	184	Ga	48.43N	80.52W
Porrentruy / Pruntrut	128	Bc	47.25N	7.10 E
Porreras / Porreres	126	Oe	39.31N	3.00 E
Porreres / Porreras	126	Oe	39.31N	3.00 E
Porretta, Passo della-	128	Ef	44.02N	10.56 E
Porretta Terme	128	Ef	44.09N	10.59 E
Porsangen	110	Ia	70.50N	26.00 E
Porsangerhalvøya	114	Fa	70.50N	25.00 E
Porsgrunn	114	Bg	59.09N	9.40 E
Porsuk	146	Dc	39.42N	31.59 E
Portachuelo	202	Fg	17.21S	63.24W
Portadown/ Port an Dúnáin	118	Gg	54.26N	6.27W
Portage	186	Le	43.33N	89.28W
Portage la Prairie	180	Hg	49.57N	98.18W
Port Alberni	180	Fg	49.14N	124.48W
Portalegre	126	Ee	39.17N	7.26W
Portalegre [2]	126	Ee	39.15N	7.35W
Portales	182	Ge	34.11N	103.20W
Port Alfred	172	Df	33.36S	26.55 E
Port Alice	180	Ef	50.23N	127.27W
Port Allegany	184	He	41.48N	78.18W
Port an Dúnáin/Portadown	118	Gg	54.26N	6.27W
Port Angeles	182	Cb	48.07N	123.27W
Port Antonio	190	Ie	18.11N	76.28W
Port Arthur [Austl.]	212	Jh	43.09S	147.51 E
Port Arthur [Tx.-U.S.]	176	Jg	29.55N	93.55W
Port Arthur → Lüshun	152	Ld	38.50N	121.13 E
Port Augusta	210	Eh	32.30S	137.46 E
Port-au-Prince	176	Lh	18.32N	72.20W
Port-au-Prince, Baie de-	192	Kd	18.40N	72.30W
Port Austin	184	Fc	44.03N	83.01W
Port aux Français	222	Fc	49.25S	70.10 E
Porta Westfalica	124	Kb	52.15N	8.56 E
Port-Bergé-Vaovao	172	Hc	15.33S	47.38 E
Port-Bergé Vao Vao	172	Hc	15.33S	47.38 E
Port Blair	142	Lh	11.36N	92.45 E
Portbou/Port-Bou	126	Pb	42.25N	3.10 E
Port-Bou/Portbou	126	Pb	42.25N	3.10 E
Port Burwell [Newf.-Can.]	176	Mc	60.25N	64.49W
Port Burwell [Ont.-Can.]	184	Gd	42.39N	80.49W
Port-Cartier	180	Kf	50.01N	66.53W
Port Chalmers	218	Df	45.49S	170.37 E
Port Charlotte	182	Kf	26.59N	82.06W
Port Clinton	184	Fe	41.30N	82.58W
Port Coquitlam	188	Db	49.16N	122.46W
Port-de-Bouc	122	Kk	43.24N	4.59 E
Port-de-Paix	194	Kd	19.57N	72.50W
Port Dickson	150	Df	2.31N	101.48 E
Port Edward	172	Ef	31.03S	30.13 E
Portel [Braz.]	202	Hd	1.57S	50.49W
Portel [Port.]	126	Ef	38.18N	7.42W
Port Elgin	184	Gc	44.26N	81.24W
Port Elizabeth [S.Afr.]	160	Jl	33.58S	25.40 E
Port Elizabeth [St.Vin.]	197n	Ba	13.00N	61.16W
Port Ellen	118	Gf	55.39N	6.12W
Port-en-Bessin-Huppain	122	Fe	49.21N	0.45W
Port Erin	118	Ig	54.05N	4.43W
Porter Point	197n	Ba	13.23N	61.11W
Porterville [Ca.-U.S.]	182	Dd	36.04N	119.01W
Porterville [S.Afr.]	172	Bf	33.00S	19.00 E
Portete, Bahia de-	194	Lg	12.13N	71.55W
Port Fairy	212	Ig	38.23S	142.14 E
Port Fitzroy	218	Fb	36.10S	175.21 E
Port-Gentil	160	Hi	0.43S	8.47 E
Port Gibson	186	Kk	31.58N	90.58W
Port Harcourt	160	Hh	4.46N	7.01 E
Port Hardy	180	Ef	50.43N	127.29W
Port Hawkesbury	180	Lg	45.37N	61.21W
Porthcawl	118	Jj	51.29N	3.43W
Port Hedland	210	Cg	20.19S	118.34 E
Port Heiden	178	He	56.55N	158.41W
Porthmadog	118	Ii	52.55N	4.08W
Port Hope Simpson	180	Lf	52.30N	56.17W
Port Huron	182	Kc	42.58N	82.27W
Portile de Fier = Iron Gate (EN)	110	Ig	44.41N	22.31 E
Port-Ilić	132	Pj	38.53N	48.51 E
Portimão	126	Dg	37.08N	8.32W
Port Isabel	186	Hm	26.04N	97.13W
Portiţa	130	Me	44.41N	29.00 E
Port Láirge/Waterford	112	Fe	52.15N	7.06W
Port Láirge/Waterford [2]	118	Fi	52.10N	7.40W
Portland [Austl.]	212	Ig	38.21S	141.36 E
Portland [In.-U.S.]	184	Ee	40.26N	84.59W
Portland [Me.-U.S.]	176	Le	43.39N	70.17W
Portland [N.D.-U.S.]	186	Hc	47.30N	97.22W
Portland [N.Z.]	218	Fa	35.48S	174.20 E
Portland [Or.-U.S.]	176	Ge	45.33N	122.36W
Portland [Tx.-U.S.]	186	Hm	27.53N	97.20W
Portland, Bill of-	118	Kk	50.31N	2.28W
Portland, Promontoire -	180	Je	58.41N	78.33W
Portland Bight	194	Ie	17.57N	77.08W
Portland Island	218	Gc	39.20S	177.50 E
Portland Point	194	Ie	17.42N	77.11W
Port-la-Nouvelle	122	Jk	43.01N	3.03 E
Port Laoise/Portlaoise	118	Fh	53.02N	7.17W
Portlaoise/Port Laoise	118	Fh	53.02N	7.17W
Port Lavaca	182	Hf	28.37N	96.38W
Port Lincoln	210	Eh	34.44S	135.52 E
Port Loko	166	Cd	8.46N	12.47W
Port Louis	196	Fd	16.25N	61.32W
Port-Louis	160	Mk	20.10S	57.30 E
Port Macquarie	212	Kf	31.26S	152.44 E
Port Maria	194	Id	18.22N	76.54W
Port-Menier	180	Lg	49.49N	64.20W
Port Moller	178	Ge	55.59N	160.34W
Port Moody	188	Db	49.17N	122.51W
Port Moresby	210	Fe	9.30S	147.07 E
Port Nelson	180	Ie	57.04N	92.30W
Portneuf, Rivière-	184	Ma	48.37N	69.05W
Port Nolloth	160	Ik	29.17S	16.51 E
Port Nouveau-Québec	176	Md	58.35N	65.59W
Porto [2]	126	Dc	41.15N	8.20W
Porto [Fr.]	122a	Aa	42.16N	8.42 E
Porto [Port.]	112	Fg	41.09N	8.37W
Porto, Golfe de-	122a	Aa	42.16N	8.37 E
Porto Acre	202	Ee	9.34S	67.31W
Porto Alegre [Braz.]	200	Ki	30.04S	51.11W
Porto Alegre [Sao T.P.]	166	Ge	0.02N	6.32 E
Porto Amboim	160	Ij	10.44S	13.45 E
Porto Azzurro	128	Eh	42.46N	10.24 E
Portobelo	194	Hi	9.33N	79.39W
Porto Cedro	204	Ed	18.17S	55.02W
Porto Cervo	128	Di	41.08N	9.35 E
Porto Curupai	204	Ff	22.50S	53.53W
Porto de Moz	200	Kf	1.45S	52.14W
Porto Empedocle	128	Hm	37.17N	13.32 E
Porto Esperança [Braz.]	204	Db	14.02S	56.06W
Porto Esperança [Braz.]	204	Dd	19.37S	57.27W
Porto Esperança [Braz.]	204	Dc	17.47S	57.07W
Porto Esperidião	204	Cb	15.51S	58.28W
Porto Estrêla	204	Db	15.20S	57.14W
Portoferraio	128	Eh	42.49N	10.19 E
Port of Ness	118	Gc	58.30N	6.15W
Porto Franco	202	Ie	6.20S	47.24W
Port of Spain	200	Jd	10.39N	61.31W
Porto Fundação	204	Ea	13.39S	55.18W
Portogruaro	128	Ge	45.47N	12.50 E
Porto Lucena	204	Eh	27.51S	55.01W
Pörtom/Pirttikyla	116	Ib	62.42N	21.37 E
Portomaggiore	128	Ff	44.42N	11.48 E
Porto Mendes	204	Eg	24.30S	54.20W
Porto Moniz	162	Dc	32.51N	17.10W
Porto Moroco	204	Ea	13.24S	55.35W
Porto Morrinho	204	Dc	16.38S	57.49W
Porto Murtinho	200	Kh	21.42S	57.52W
Porto Novo [Ben.]	160	Hh	6.29N	2.37 E
Porto Novo [C.V.]	162	Bf	17.07N	25.04W
Port Orford	188	Ce	42.45N	124.30W
Porto San Giorgio	128	Hg	43.11N	13.48 E
Porto Santana	202	Hd	0.03S	51.11W
Porto Sant'Elpidio	128	Hg	43.15N	13.45 E
Porto Santo	158	Fe	33.04N	16.20W
Porto Santo Stefano	128	Fh	42.26N	11.07 E
Portoscuso	128	Ck	39.12N	8.23 E
Porto Seguro	202	Kg	16.26S	39.05W
Porto Tolle	128	Gf	44.56N	12.22 E
Porto Torres	128	Cj	40.50N	8.24 E
Porto União	204	Gh	26.15S	51.05W
Porto Válter	202	De	8.15S	72.45W
Porto Vecchio	122a	Bb	41.35N	9.17 E
Porto Velho	200	Jf	8.46S	63.54W
Portoviejo	200	Hf	1.03S	80.27W
Porto Xavier	204	Eh	27.54S	55.08W
Port Phillip Bay	212	Ig	38.05S	144.50 E
Port Pirie	210	Eh	33.11S	138.01 E
Portree	118	Gd	57.24N	6.12W
Port Renfrew	188	Cb	48.33N	124.25W
Port Rois/Portrush	118	Gf	55.12N	6.40W
Port Royal	184	If	38.10N	77.12W
Portrush/Port Rois	118	Gf	55.12N	6.40W
Port Said (EN) = Būr Sa'īd	160	Ke	31.16N	32.18 E
Port Saint Joe	182	Jf	29.49N	85.18W
Port Saint Johns	172	Df	31.38S	29.33 E
Port-Saint-Louis-du-Rhône	122	Kk	43.23N	4.48 E
Port-Salut	194	Kd	18.05N	73.55W
Port Saunders	180	Lf	50.39N	57.18W
Port Shepstone	160	Kl	30.46S	30.22 E
Portsmouth [Dom.]	196	Fe	15.35N	61.28W
Portsmouth [Eng.-U.K.]	118	Lk	50.48N	1.05W
Portsmouth [N.H.-U.S.]	182	Mc	43.03N	70.47W
Portsmouth [Oh.-U.S.]	182	Kd	38.45N	82.59W
Portsmouth [Va.-U.S.]	182	Ld	36.50N	76.26W
Portsmouth City Airport	124	Ad	50.46N	1.04W
Port Sudan (EN) = Būr Sūdān	160	Kg	19.37N	37.14 E
Port Sulphur	186	Ll	29.29N	89.42W
Port Talbot	118	Jj	51.36N	3.47W
Porttipahdantekojärvi	114	Gb	68.06N	26.33 E
Port Townsend	188	Db	48.07N	122.46W
Portugal	112	Fh	39.30N	8.00W
Portugalete	126	Ia	43.19N	3.01W
Portuguesa [2]	202	Eb	9.10N	69.15W
Portuguesa, Rio-	202	Eb	7.57N	67.32W
Portuguesa, Sierra de-	196	Bh	9.35N	69.45W
Portuguese Guinea (EN) → Guinea-Bissau (EN) [1]	160	Fg	12.00N	15.00W
Portús, Coll del-/Perthus, Col de-	126	Ob	42.28N	2.51 E
Port-Vendres	122	Jl	42.31N	3.07 E
Port-Vila	210	Hf	17.44S	168.19 E
Port Wakefield	212	Hf	34.11S	138.09 E
Port Washington	186	Me	43.23N	87.53W
Porvenir [Bol.]	204	Ba	13.59S	61.39W
Porvenir [Bol.]	202	Ef	11.15S	68.41W
Porvenir [Chile]	206	Fh	53.18S	70.22W
Porvenir [Ur.]	204	Dk	32.23S	57.59W
Porvoo/Borgå	114	Ff	60.24N	25.40 E
Porvoonjoki	116	Kd	60.23N	25.40 E
Porz, Köln-	120	Df	50.53N	7.03 E
Posada, Fiume di-	128	Dj	40.39N	9.45 E
Posadas [Arg.]	200	Kh	27.25S	55.50W
Posadas [Sp.]	126	Gg	37.48N	5.06W
Posavina	128	Le	45.00N	17.30 E
Poschiavo / Puschlav	128	Ed	46.20N	10.04 E
Pošehonje-Volodarsk	114	Jg	58.30N	39.08 E
Posets	126	Mb	42.39N	0.25 E
Posht-e Bādām	146	Pf	33.02N	55.23 E
Posio	116	Gc	66.06N	28.09 E
Posjet	154	Kc	42.39N	130.48 E
Poskam/Zepu	152	Cd	38.12N	77.18 E
Poso	142	Oj	1.23S	120.44 E
Poso, Danau-	150	Hg	1.52S	120.35 E
Posof	146	Jb	41.31N	42.42 E
Posŏng	154	Ig	34.46N	127.05 E
Pospeliha	138	Df	52.02N	81.56 E
Posse	202	If	14.05S	46.22W
Possession, Ile de la-	222	Ec	46.14S	49.55 E
Possession Island	172	Be	27.01S	15.30 E
Pößneck	120	Hf	50.42N	11.36 E
Post	186	Fj	33.12N	101.23W
Posta de San Martin	204	Bk	33.09S	60.31W
Postavy	136	Cd	55.07N	26.50 E
Poste-de-la-Baleine	180	Je	55.20N	76.50W
Poste Maurice Cortier/Bidon V	162	He	22.18N	1.05 E
Poste Weygand	162	He	24.29N	0.40 E
Postmasburg	172	Ce	28.18S	23.05 E
Postojna	128	Ie	45.47N	14.14 E
Posto Simões Lopes	204	Eb	14.14S	54.41W
Postville [Ia.-U.S.]	186	Ke	43.05N	91.34W
Postville [Newf.-Can.]	180	Lf	54.55N	59.58W
Potchefstroom	172	De	26.46S	27.01 E
Poteau	186	Ii	35.03N	94.37W
Potenza	128	Jj	40.38N	15.48 E
Potenza	128	Hg	43.25N	13.40 E
Poteriteri, Lake-	218	Bg	46.05S	167.05 E
Potes	126	Ha	43.09N	4.37W
Potgietersrus	172	Dd	24.15S	28.55 E
Potholes Reservoir	188	Fc	47.01N	119.19W
Poti	112	Kg	42.08N	41.39 E
Poti, Rio-	202	Je	5.02S	42.50W
Potigny	124	Bf	48.58N	0.14W
Potiskum	160	Ig	11.43N	11.04 E
Potnarhvin	219b	Dd	18.45S	169.12 E
Potomac	174	Lf	38.00N	76.18W
Potosí [3]	204	Ch	20.40S	67.00W
Potosí [Bol.]	200	Jg	19.35S	65.45W
Potosí [Mex.]	190	Dd	24.51N	100.19W
Potosí, Bahia-	192	Ii	17.35N	101.30W
Potosí, Cerro-	192	Ie	24.52N	100.13W
Pototan	150	Hd	10.55N	122.40 E
Potrerillos	206	Gc	26.26S	69.29W
Potrero, Rio-	204	Bc	17.32S	61.35W
Potsdam [2]	120	Id	52.30N	13.00 E
Potsdam [G.D.R.]	120	Jd	52.24N	13.04 E
Potsdam [N.Y.-U.S.]	184	Jc	44.40N	75.01W
Pott	219b	Ad	19.35S	163.36 E
Potters Bar	124	Bc	51.41N	0.10W
Pottstown	184	Je	40.15N	75.38W
Pottsville	184	Ie	40.42N	76.13W
Pouancé	122	Eg	47.45N	1.10W
Pouébo	219b	Be	20.24S	164.34 E
Pouembout	219b	Be	21.08S	164.54 E
Poughkeepsie	184	Ke	41.43N	73.56W
Poulaphouca Reservoir / Loch Pholl an Phúca	118	Gh	53.10N	6.30W
Poum	219b	Be	20.14S	164.01 E
Pourtalé	204	Bm	37.02S	60.36W
Pouso Alegre	202	Ih	22.13S	45.56W
Pouss	166	Ic	10.51N	15.03 E
Poutasi	221c	Bb	14.01S	171.41W
Poŭthĭsăt	148	Kf	12.32N	103.55 E
Poutrincourt, Lac-	184	Ja	49.13N	74.04W
Po Valley (EN) = Padana, Pianura-	110	Gf	45.20N	10.00 E
Považská Bystrica	120	Og	49.07N	18.28 E
Považský Inovec	120	Nh	48.35N	18.00 E
Povenec	114	Ie	62.51N	34.45 E
Poverty Bay	218	Gc	38.45S	178.00 E
Povlen	130	Ce	44.09N	19.44 E
Póvoa de Varzim	126	Dc	41.23N	8.46W
Povorino	132	Md	51.12N	42.17 E
Povungnituk	176	Lc	60.02N	77.10W
Povungnituk	180	Jd	60.03N	77.16W
Powassan	184	Hb	46.05N	79.22W
Powder River [Or.-U.S.]	188	Gd	44.45N	117.03W
Powder River [U.S.]	182	Fb	46.44N	105.26W
Powell	188	Kd	44.45N	108.46W
Powell, Lake-	182	Ed	37.25N	110.45W
Powell Lake	188	Ca	50.11N	124.24W
Powell River	180	Fg	49.52N	124.33W
Powers	184	Dc	45.39N	87.32W
Powers Lake	186	Eb	48.34N	102.39W
Powidzkie, Jezioro-	120	Nd	52.24N	17.57 E
Powys [3]	118	Ji	52.25N	3.20W
Poxoréu	202	Hg	15.50S	54.23W
Poxoréu, Rio- [Braz.]	204	Ec	16.32S	54.46W
Poxoréu, Rio- [Braz.]	204	Ec	16.08S	54.14W
Poya	219b	Be	21.21S	165.09 E
Poyang Hu	140	Ng	29.00N	116.25 E
Poza de la Sal	126	Ib	42.40N	3.30W
Pozanti	146	Fd	37.25N	34.52 E
Požarevac	130	Ee	44.37N	21.12 E
Poza Rica de Hidalgo	176	Jg	20.33N	97.27W
Požarskoje	154	Ma	46.16N	134.04 E
Požega	130	Df	43.51N	20.02 E
Poznań	112	He	52.25N	16.55 E
Poznań [2]	120	Md	52.25N	16.30 E
Pozoblanco	126	Hf	38.22N	4.51W
Pozo Borrado	204	Bi	28.56S	61.41W
Pozo Colorado	204	Cf	23.22S	58.55W
Pozo del Mortero	204	Bg	24.24S	61.02W
Pozo del Tigre	204	Bg	17.34S	61.59W
Pozo Dulce	204	Ai	29.04S	62.02W
Pozos, Punta-	206	Gg	47.57S	65.47W
Pozuelos	202	Fa	10.11N	64.39W
Pozzallo	128	In	36.43N	14.51 E
Pozzuoli	128	Ij	40.49N	14.07 E
Pra [Ghana]	166	Ed	6.27N	1.47W
Pra [R.S.F.S.R.]	114	Ji	54.45N	41.01 E
Prabuty	120	Pc	53.46N	19.10 E
Prachatice	120	Jg	49.01N	14.00 E
Prachin Buri	148	Kf	14.02N	101.22 E
Prachuap Khiri Khan	148	Jf	11.48N	99.47 E
Praděd	120	Nf	50.06N	17.14 E
Prades	122	Il	42.37N	2.26 E
Prado	202	Kg	17.21S	39.13W
Præstø	116	Ei	55.07N	12.03 E
Prague (EN)=Praha	112	He	50.05N	14.26 E
Praha=Prague (EN)	112	He	50.05N	14.26 E
Prahova [2]	130	Id	45.10N	26.00 E
Prahova	130	Je	44.43N	26.27 E
Praia	160	Eg	14.55N	23.31W
Praia a Mare	128	Jk	39.54N	15.47 E
Praia da Rocha	126	Dg	37.07N	8.32W
Praia Rica	204	Eb	14.51S	55.33W
Praid	130	Ic	46.33N	25.08 E
Prainha	202	Hd	1.48S	53.29W
Prairie Dog Town Fork	186	Gi	34.26N	99.21W
Prairie du Chien	186	Ke	43.03N	91.09W
Prangli	116	Ke	59.38N	24.50 E
Prānhita	148	Fe	18.49N	79.55 E
Prapat	150	Cf	2.40N	98.56 E
Prasat	148	Kf	14.38N	103.24 E
Praslin	197k	Bb	13.53N	60.54W
Praslin, Port-	197k	Bb	13.53N	60.54W
Praslin Island	172b	Ca	4.19S	55.44 E
Prasonisíon	130	Kn	35.52N	27.46 E
Prat, Isla-	206	Fg	48.15S	75.00W
Prata	202	Ig	19.18S	48.55W
Prata, Rio da-	204	Hd	18.49S	49.54W
Pratapgarh	148	Ed	24.02N	74.47 E
Prat de Llobregat / el Prat de Llobregat	126	Oc	41.20N	2.06 E
Prato	128	Fg	43.53N	11.06 E
Pratomagno	128	Fg	43.40N	11.40 E
Pratt	182	Hd	37.39N	98.44W
Prättigau	128	Dd	46.55N	9.40 E
Pratt Seamount (EN)	178	Ke	56.10N	142.30W
Prattville	184	Di	32.28N	86.29W
Pratudinho, Rio-	204	Ja	13.58S	45.10W
Pravda	135	Cf	36.50N	60.33 E
Pravda Coast	222	Ge	67.00S	94.00 E
Pravdinsk [R.S.F.S.R.]	114	Kh	56.33N	43.33 E
Pravdinsk [R.S.F.S.R.]	116	Ij	54.28N	21.00 E
Pravia	126	Fa	43.29N	6.07W
Praxedis G. Guerrero	192	Gb	31.22N	106.00W
Praya	150	Gh	8.42S	116.17 E
Prealpi Venete	128	Fd	46.25N	11.50 E
Predazzo	128	Fd	46.19N	11.36 E
Predeal	130	Id	45.30N	25.34 E
Predeal, Pasul-	130	Id	45.28N	25.36 E
Predel	128	Hd	46.25N	13.35 E
Predil, Passo del-	128	Hd	46.25N	13.35 E
Predivinsk	138	Ee	57.04N	93.37 E
Predporožny	138	Jd	65.00N	143.20 E
Pré-en-Pail	122	Ff	48.27N	0.12W
Preetz	120	Gb	54.14N	10.17 E
Pregolia	114	Ei	54.42N	20.24 E
Pregradnaja	132	Lh	43.58N	41.12 E
Preilj/Prejli	114	Gh	56.19N	26.48 E
Preissac, Lac-	184	Ha	48.25N	78.28W
Prejli/Preilj	114	Gh	56.19N	26.48 E
Prekmurje	128	Kd	46.45N	16.15 E
Prekornica	130	Cg	42.40N	19.12 E
Prekule/Priekulė	116	Ii	55.36N	21.12 E
Přelouč	120	Lf	50.02N	15.33 E
Premià de Mar/Premiá de Mar	126	Oc	41.29N	2.22 E
Premià de Mar/Premià de Mar	126	Oc	41.29N	2.22 E
Premnitz	120	Id	52.32N	12.20 E
Premuda	128	If	44.21N	14.37 E
Prenaj/Prienai	114	Fi	54.39N	23.59 E
Prenj	128	Lg	43.32N	17.52 E
Prenjasi	130	Dh	41.04N	20.32 E
Prentice	186	Kd	45.33N	90.17W
Prentiss	186	Lk	31.36N	89.52W
Prenzlau	120	Jc	53.19N	13.52 E
Preobraženije	138	Ih	42.58N	133.55 E
Preobraženka	138	Fd	60.04N	107.58 E
Preparis Island	148	If	14.52N	93.41 E
Preparis North Channel	148	Ie	15.27N	94.05 E
Preparis South Channel	150	Bd	14.45N	94.05 E
Přerov	120	Ng	49.27N	17.27 E
Prescott [Ar.-U.S.]	186	Jj	33.48N	93.23W
Prescott [Az.-U.S.]	182	Ee	34.33N	112.28W
Preseli, Mynydd-	118	Ij	51.58N	4.42W
Preševo	130	Eg	42.19N	21.39 E
Presho	186	Fe	43.53N	100.04W
Presicce	128	Mk	39.54N	18.16 E
Presidencia Roque Sáenz Peña	200	Jh	26.50S	60.30W
Presidente Epitácio	'206	Jb	21.46S	52.06W
Presidente Frei	222	Re	62.12S	58.55W
Presidente Hayes [3]	204	Cf	24.00S	59.00W
Presidente Juscelino	204	Jd	18.39S	44.05W
Presidente Murtinho	204	Fb	15.39S	53.54W
Presidente Olegário	204	Id	18.25S	46.25W
Presidente Prudente	206	Jb	22.07S	51.22W
Presidente Venceslau	204	Ge	21.52S	51.50W
President Thiers Seamount (EN)	208	Mg	24.39S	145.51W
Presidio	182	Gf	29.33N	104.23W
Presidio, Rio del-	192	Ff	23.06N	106.17W
Preslav	130	Jf	43.10N	26.49 E
Presnovka	134	Mi	54.40N	67.09 E
Prešov	120	Rh	49.00N	21.14 E
Prespa	130	Hh	41.43N	24.53 E
Prespa, Lake- (EN) = Prespansko jezero	110	Ig	40.55N	21.00 E
Prespansko jezero = Prespa, Lake- (EN)	110	Ig	40.55N	21.00 E
Presque Isle	182	Nb	46.41N	68.01W
Prestea	166	Ed	5.26N	2.09W
Přeštice	120	Jg	49.35N	13.21 E
Preston [Eng.-U.K.]	118	Kh	53.46N	2.42W
Preston [Id.-U.S.]	182	Ec	42.06N	111.53W
Preston [Ont.-Can.]	184	Gd	43.23N	80.21W
Prestonsburg	184	Fg	37.40N	82.46W
Preststranda	116	Ce	59.06N	9.04 E
Prestwick	118	If	55.30N	4.37W
Prêto, Rio- [Braz.]	202	Jf	11.21S	43.52W
Prêto, Rio- [Braz.]	204	Ha	13.37S	48.06W
Prêto, Rio- [Braz.]	204	Ic	17.00S	46.12W
Prêto, Rio- [Braz.]	204	Gd	18.44S	50.23W
Preto do Igapó Açu, Rio-	202	Gd	4.26S	59.48W
Pretoria	160	Jk	25.45S	28.10 E
Pretty Rock Butte	186	Fc	46.10N	101.42W
Preußisch-Oldendorf	124	Kb	52.18N	8.30 E
Préveza	130	Dk	38.57N	20.45 E
Prey	124	Df	48.58N	1.13 E
Prey Vêng	148	Lf	11.29N	105.19 E
Priangarskoje plato	138	Ee	57.30N	97.00 E
Priargunsk	138	Gf	50.27N	119.00 E
Pribelski	134	Hi	54.24N	56.29 E
Pribilof Islands	174	Cd	57.00N	170.00W
Priboj	130	Cf	43.35N	19.32 E
Příbram	120	Kg	49.42N	14.01 E
Price [Que.-Can.]	184	Ma	48.39N	68.12W
Price [Ut.-U.S.]	188	Jg	39.36N	110.48W
Price River	188	Jg	39.10N	110.06W
Prichard	184	Cj	30.44N	88.05W
Prickly Pear Cays	197b	Ab	18.16N	63.11W
Prickly Point	197p	Bc	11.59N	61.45W
Pridneprovskaja vozvyšennost = Dnepr Upland (EN)	110	Jf	49.00N	32.00 E
Priego	126	Jd	40.27N	2.18W
Priego de Córdoba	126	Hg	37.26N	4.11W
Priei, Măgura-	130	Fc	46.58N	22.50 E
Priekule	114	Eh	56.29N	21.37 E
Priekulė/Prekule	116	Ii	55.36N	21.12 E
Prienai/Prenaj	114	Fi	54.39N	23.59 E
Priene	146	Bd	37.40N	27.13 E
Prieska	160	Jk	29.40S	22.42 E
Priest Lake	188	Gb	48.34N	116.52W
Prieta, Peña-	126	Ha	43.01N	4.44W
Prieta, Sierra-	192	Cb	31.15N	112.55W
Prievidza	120	Oh	48.46N	18.39 E
Prignitz	120	Hc	53.00N	12.00 E
Prijedor	128	Kf	44.59N	16.42 E
Prijepolje	130	Cf	43.24N	19.39 E
Prijutovo	136	Fe	53.58N	53.58 E
Prikaspijskaja nizmennost = Caspian Depression (EN)	110	Lf	48.00N	52.00 E
Prilenskoje plato = Lena Mountains (EN)	140	Oc	60.45N	125.00 E
Prilep	130	Eh	41.21N	21.34 E
Priluki	136	De	50.36N	32.24 E
Primavera	222	Qe	64.09S	60.57W
Primeira Cruz	202	Jd	2.30S	43.26W
Primorje	116	Hj	54.56N	20.00 E
Primorsk [R.S.F.S.R.]	114	Gf	60.22N	28.36 E
Primorsk [R.S.F.S.R.]	120	Pb	54.44N	19.59 E
Primorsk [Ukr.-U.S.S.R.]	132	Jf	46.43N	36.22 E
Primorski hrebet	138	Ff	52.30N	106.00 E
Primorski kraj [3]	138	Ig	45.30N	135.30 E
Primorsko	130	Kg	42.16N	27.46 E
Primorsko-Ahtarsk	136	Df	46.03N	38.11 E
Primorskoje [R.S.F.S.R.]	116	Ld	60.22N	27.56 E
Primorskoje [Ukr.-U.S.S.R.]	130	Nd	45.59N	30.15 E
Primošten	128	Jg	43.36N	15.55 E
Primrose Lake	180	Gf	54.55N	109.45W
Prims	120	Cg	49.20N	6.44 E
Prince Albert	176	Id	53.12N	105.46W
Prince Albert Mountains	222	Jf	76.00S	161.30 E
Prince Albert Peninsula	180	Fb	72.30N	116.00W
Prince Albert Road	172	Cf	33.13S	22.02 E
Prince Albert Sound	180	Gb	70.25N	115.00W
Prince Alfred, Cape -	180	Fb	74.05N	124.29W
Prince Charles	174	Lc	67.50N	76.00W
Prince Charles Mountains	222	Ff	72.00S	67.00 E
Prince-de-Galles, Cap -	180	Kd	61.36N	71.30W
Prince Edward	158	Km	46.33S	37.57 E
Prince Edward Island [2]	180	Lg	46.30N	63.00W
Prince EdKard Island	176	Me	46.30N	63.00W
Prince Edward Islands	158	Km	46.35S	37.56 E
Prince George	176	Gd	53.55N	122.49W
Prince Gustaf Adolf Sea	174	Ib	78.30N	107.00W
Prince of Wales [Ak.-U.S.]	178	Me	55.47N	132.50W
Prince of Wales [Can.]	174	Jb	72.40N	99.00W
Prince of Wales, Cape-	174	Cc	65.40N	168.05W
Prince of Wales Island	212	Ib	10.40S	142.10 E
Prince of Wales Mountains	180	Ja	77.45N	78.00W
Prince of Wales Strait	180	Fb	72.45N	118.00W
Prince Patrick	174	Hb	76.45N	119.30W
Prince Regent Inlet	180	Ib	72.45N	90.30W
Prince Rupert	176	Fd	54.19N	130.19W
Prince Rupert Bay	197g	Ba	15.34N	61.29W
Prince Rupert Bluff	197g	Ba	15.35N	61.29W
Princes Risborough	124	Bc	51.43N	0.49W
Princess Anne	184	Jf	38.12N	75.41W
Princess Charlotte Bay	212	Ib	14.25S	144.00 E
Princess Elizabeth Land	222	Ff	70.00S	80.00 E
Princess Margaret Range	180	Ia	79.00N	88.30W
Princess Royal	180	Ef	52.55N	128.50W
Princeton [B.C.-Can.]	180	Fg	49.27N	120.31W
Princeton [Il.-U.S.]	186	Lf	41.23N	89.28W
Princeton [In.-U.S.]	184	Df	38.21N	87.34W
Princeton [Ky.-U.S.]	184	Dg	37.07N	87.53W
Princeton [Mo.-U.S.]	186	Jf	40.24N	93.35W
Prince William Sound	174	Ec	60.40N	147.00W
Príncipe	158	Hh	1.37N	7.25 E
Prineville	188	Ed	44.18N	120.51W
Prineville Reservoir	188	Ed	44.08N	120.42W
Prins Christians Sund	179	Hf	60.00N	43.10W
Prinsesse Astrid Kyst	222	Cf	70.45S	12.30 E
Prinsesse Ragnhild Kyst	222	Df	70.15S	27.30 E
Prins Harald Kyst	222	De	69.30S	36.00 E
Prins Karls Forland	179	Nc	78.32N	11.10 E
Prinzapolka	190	Hf	13.24N	83.34W
Prinzapolka, Rio-	194	Fg	13.24N	83.34W
Priora, Mount-	212	Ja	6.51S	145.58 E

Index Symbols

[1] Independent Nation
[2] State, Region
[3] District, County
[4] Municipality
[5] Colony, Dependency
Continent
Physical Region
Historical or Cultural Region
Mount, Mountain
Volcano
Hill
Mountains, Mountain Range
Hills, Escarpment
Plateau, Upland
Pass, Gap
Plain, Lowland
Delta
Salt Flat
Valley, Canyon
Crater, Cave
Karst Features
Depression
Polder
Desert, Dunes
Forest, Woods
Heath, Steppe
Oasis
Cape, Point
Coast, Beach
Cliff
Peninsula
Isthmus
Sandbank
Island
Atoll
Rock, Reef
Islands, Archipelago
Rocks, Reefs
Coral Reef
Well, Spring
Geyser
River, Stream
Waterfall, Rapids
River Mouth, Estuary
Lake
Salt Lake
Intermittent Lake
Reservoir
Swamp, Pond
Canal
Glacier
Ice Shelf, Pack Ice
Ocean
Sea
Gulf, Bay
Strait, Fjord
Lagoon
Bank
Seamount
Tablemount
Ridge
Shelf
Basin
Escarpment, Sea Scarp
Fracture
Trench, Abyss
National Park, Reserve
Point of Interest
Recreation Site
Cave, Cavern
Historic Site
Ruins
Wall, Walls
Church, Abbey
Temple
Scientific Station
Railway station
Airport
Port
Military installation
Lighthouse
Mine
Tunnel
Dam, Bridge

Priozersk	136	Dc	61.04N	30.07 E
Pripet Marshes (EN)	110	Ie	52.00N	27.00 E
Pripjat	110	Je	51.21N	30.09 E
Pripoljarny Ural=Subpolar Urals (EN)	110	Lb	65.00N	60.00 E
Prirečny	136	Db	69.02N	30.15 E
Prišib	132	Pj	39.06N	48.38 E
Prislop, Pasul-	130	Hb	47.37N	24.55 E
Pristan-Prževalsk	135	Lc	42.33N	78.18 E
Pristen	132	Jd	51.15N	36.42 E
Priština	130	Eg	42.40N	21.10 E
Pritzwalk	120	Ic	53.09N	12.11 E
Privas	122	Kj	44.44N	4.36 E
Priverno	128	Hi	41.28N	13.11 E
Privolžkaja vozvyšennost = Volga Hills (EN)	110	Ke	52.00N	46.00 E
Privolžsk	114	Jh	57.27N	41.16 E
Privolžski	132	Od	51.23N	46.02 E
Prizren	130	Dg	42.13N	20.45 E
Prizzi	128	Hm	37.43N	13.26 E
Prjaža	114	Hf	61.43N	33.37 E
Prnjavor	128	Lf	44.52N	17.40 E
Probolinggo	150	Fh	7.45 S	113.13 E
Prochowice	120	Me	51.17N	16.22 E
Procida	128	Hj	40.45N	14.00 E
Proctor Reservoir	186	Gj	32.02N	98.32W
Proddatur	148	Ff	14.44N	78.33 E
Profítis Ilías [Grc.]	130	Fm	36.53N	22.22 E
Profítis Ilías [Grc.]	130	Fj	39.50N	22.38 E
Profondeville	124	Gd	50.23N	4.52 E
Progonati	130	Ci	40.13N	19.56 E
Progranično	135	Dg	35.43N	63.12 E
Progreso [Mex.]	192	Id	27.28N	101.04W
Progreso [Mex.]	176	Kg	21.17N	89.40W
Progress	138	Hg	49.41N	129.40 E
Prohladny	132	Nh	43.45N	44.01 E
Prohorovka	132	Jd	51.02N	36.42 E
Prokopjevsk	142	Kd	53.53N	86.45 E
Prokuplje	130	Ef	43.15N	21.36 E
Proletari	114	Hg	58.26N	31.43 E
Proletarsk [R.S.F.S.R.]	136	Ef	46.41N	41.44 E
Proletarsk [Taj.-U.S.S.R.]	135	Gd	40.10N	69.31 E
Proletarski	132	Id	50.51N	35.46 E
Proletarskoje vodohranilišče	132	Mf	46.30N	42.10 E
Prome	142	Lh	18.49N	95.13 E
Promissâe, Reprêsa-	206	Kb	21.32 S	49.52W
Promissão	204	He	21.32 S	49.52W
Promyšlenny	134	Kc	67.35N	63.55 E
Pronja [Bye.-U.S.S.R.]	132	Gc	53.27N	31.03 E
Pronja [U.S.S.R.]	132	Lb	54.21N	40.24 E
Pronsfeld	124	Id	50.10N	6.20 E
Prophet	180	Fe	58.46N	122.45W
Propriá	202	Kf	10.13 S	36.51W
Propriano	122a	Ab	41.40N	8.54 E
Prorva	132	Rg	45.57N	53.13 E
Proserpine	212	Jd	20.24 S	148.34 E
Prosna	120	Nd	52.10N	17.39 E
Prosotsáni	130	Gh	41.11N	23.59 E
Prosperidad	150	Ie	8.34N	125.52 E
Prospihino	138	Ee	58.37N	99.20 E
Prosser	188	Fc	46.12N	119.46W
Prostějov	120	Ng	49.29N	17.07 E
Proszowice	120	Qf	50.12N	20.18 E
Próti	130	El	37.03N	21.33 E
Protoka	132	Jg	45.43N	37.46 E
Protva	114	Ii	54.51N	37.16 E
Provadija	130	Kf	43.11N	27.26 E
Prøven	179	Gd	72.15N	55.40W
Provence	110	Gg	44.00N	6.00 E
Provence	122	Lk	44.00N	6.00 E
Providence [Ky.-U.S.]	184	Dg	37.24N	87.39W
Providence [R.I.-U.S.]	176	Le	41.50N	71.25W
Providence, Cape-	218	Bg	46.01 S	166.28 E
Providence Bay	184	Fc	45.44N	82.18W
Providence Island	158	Mi	9.14 S	51.02 E
Providencia, Isla de-	190	Hf	13.21N	81.22W
Providenciales	194	Kc	21.49N	72.15W
Providenija	142	Uc	64.23N	173.18W
Provincetown	184	Ld	42.03N	70.11W
Provins	122	Jf	48.33N	3.18 E
Provo	176	He	40.14N	111.39W
Prozor	128	Lg	43.49N	17.37 E
Prudentópolis	204	Gg	25.12 S	50.57W
Prudhoe Bay	176	Eb	70.20N	148.25W
Prudnik	120	Nf	50.19N	17.34 E
Prüm	120	Cf	50.13N	6.25 E
Prüm	124	Ie	49.49N	6.28 E
Prune Island	197n	Bb	12.35N	61.24W
Pruntrut / Porrentruy	128	Bc	47.25N	7.10 E
Prussia (EN)	120	Pc	53.45N	20.00 E
Pruszcz Gdański	120	Ob	54.16N	18.36 E
Pruszków	120	Qd	52.11N	20.48 E
Prut	110	If	45.28N	28.14 E
Pružany	136	Ce	52.36N	24.28 E
Prvić	128	If	44.54N	14.48 E
Prydz Bay	222	Fe	69.00 S	76.00 E
Pryor	186	Ih	36.19N	95.19W
Przasnysz	120	Qc	53.01N	20.55 E
Przedbórz	120	Pe	51.06N	19.53 E
Przemyśl	120	Sg	49.47N	22.47 E
Przemyśl	120	Sg	49.45N	22.45 E
Prževalsk	142	Je	42.29N	78.24 E
Przeworsk	120	Sf	50.05N	22.29 E
Przysucha	120	Qe	51.22N	20.38 E
Psakhná	130	Gk	38.35N	23.38 E
Psará	130	Ik	38.35N	25.37 E
Psathoúra	130	Hj	39.30N	24.11 E
Pščišč	132	Kg	45.03N	39.25 E
Psebaj	132	Lg	44.07N	40.47 E
Psël	110	Jf	49.05N	33.30 E
Psérimos	130	Km	36.56N	27.09 E
Psina	120	Of	50.02N	18.16 E
Pšiš, gora-	132	Lh	43.24N	41.14 E
Pskem	135	Hd	41.38N	70.01 E
Pskent	135	Gd	40.54N	69.23 E
Pskov	112	Id	57.50N	28.20 E
Pskov, Lake- (EN)=Pihkva järv	110	Id	58.00N	28.00 E
Pskov, Lake- (EN) = Pskovskoje ozero	110	Id	58.00N	28.00 E
Pskova	116	Mg	57.47N	28.30 E
Pskovskaja oblast	136	Cd	57.20N	29.20 E
Pskovskoje ozero = Pskov, Lake- (EN)	110	Id	58.00N	28.00 E
Psunj	128	Le	45.24N	17.20 E
Ptič	132	Fc	52.09N	28.52 E
Ptolemaïs	130	Ei	40.31N	21.41 E
Ptuj	128	Jd	46.25N	15.52 E
Pua-a, Cape-	221c	Aa	13.26 S	172.43W
Puah, Pulau-	150	Hg	0.30 S	122.34 E
Puapua	221c	Aa	13.34 S	172.09W
Pucallpa	200	If	8.20 S	74.30W
Pučež	114	Kh	56.59N	43.11 E
Pucheng [China]	152	Kf	27.55N	118.30 E
Pucheng [China]	152	Id	35.00N	109.38 E
Pucho	170	Cf	17.35 S	16.30 E
Pucioasa	130	Id	45.05N	25.25 E
Pučišća	128	Kg	43.21N	16.44 E
Puck	120	Ob	54.44N	18.27 E
Pucka, Zatoka-	120	Ob	54.40N	18.35 E
Pudasjärvi	114	Gd	65.23N	27.00 E
Pudož	136	Dc	61.50N	36.32 E
Pudukkottai	148	Ff	10.23N	78.49 E
Puebla	190	Ee	18.50N	98.00W
Puebla, Sierra de-	192	Kh	19.50N	97.00W
Puebla de Alcocer	126	Gf	38.59N	5.15W
Puebla de Don Fabrique	126	Jg	37.58N	2.26W
Puebla de Guzmán	126	Eg	37.37N	7.15W
Puebla de Sanabria	126	Fb	42.03N	6.38W
Puebla de Trives / Pobla de Trives	126	Eb	42.20N	7.15W
Puebla de Zaragoza	176	Jh	19.03N	98.12W
Pueblo	176	If	38.16N	104.37W
Pueblo Libertador	204	Cj	30.13 S	59.23W
Pueblo Nuevo [Mex.]	192	Gf	23.23N	105.23W
Pueblo Nuevo [Ven.]	194	Mh	11.58N	69.55W
Pueblo Nuevo Tiquisate	194	Bf	14.17N	91.22W
Pueblo Viejo, Laguna de-	192	Kf	22.10N	97.55W
Puelches	206	Ge	38.09 S	65.55W
Puente Alto	206	Fd	33.37 S	70.35W
Puenteareas / Ponteareas	126	Db	42.11N	8.30W
Puentedeume / Pontedeume	126	Da	43.24N	8.10W
Puente-Genil	126	Hg	37.23N	4.47W
Puente la Reina	126	Kb	42.40N	1.49W
Puentelarrá	126	Ib	42.45N	3.03W
Pueo Point	221a	Ab	21.54N	160.04W
Pu'er	152	Hg	23.00N	101.00 E
Puerca, Punta-	197a	Cb	18.15N	65.35W
Puerco, Rio-	186	Ci	34.22N	107.50W
Puerco River	188	Ji	34.52N	110.05W
Puerto Abente	204	Df	22.55 S	57.43W
Puerto Acosta	202	Eg	15.32 S	69.15W
Puerto Adela	204	Eg	24.33 S	54.22W
Puerto Aisén	200	Ij	45.24 S	72.42W
Puerto Alegre	202	Ff	13.53 S	61.36W
Puerto Ángel	190	Ee	15.40N	96.29W
Puerto Arista	192	Mj	15.56N	93.48W
Puerto Armuelles	190	Hg	8.17N	82.52W
Puerto Asís	202	Cc	0.29N	76.32W
Puerto Ayacucho	200	Je	5.40N	67.35W
Puerto Ayora	202a	Ab	0.45 S	90.23W
Puerto Barrios	176	Kh	15.43N	88.36W
Puerto Bermejo	204	Ch	26.56 S	58.30W
Puerto Berrío	202	Db	6.30N	74.25W
Puerto Boyacá	202	Db	5.45N	74.29W
Puerto Caballo	204	Ce	20.12 S	58.12W
Puerto Cabello	200	Jd	10.28N	68.01W
Puerto Cabezas	190	Hf	14.02N	83.23W
Puerto Carreño	200	Je	6.12N	67.22W
Puerto Casado	206	Ib	20.20 S	57.55W
Puerto Colombia	194	Jh	10.59N	74.57W
Puerto Colón	204	Df	23.11 S	57.33W
Puerto Constanza	204	Ck	33.50 S	59.03W
Puerto Cooper	206	Ib	23.03 S	57.43W
Puerto Cortés [C.R.]	194	Fi	8.58N	83.32W
Puerto Cortés [Hond.]	176	Kh	15.48N	87.56W
Puerto Cumarebo	202	Ea	11.29N	69.21W
Puerto de Eten	202	Ce	6.56 S	79.52W
Puerto de la Cruz	162	Dd	28.23N	16.33W
Puerto de Lajas, Cerro-	190	Cc	28.59N	107.02W
Puerto del Rosario	162	Ed	28.30N	13.52W
Puerto de Mazarrón	126	Kg	37.34N	1.15W
Puerto de San José	190	Ff	13.55N	90.49W
Puerto Deseado	200	Jj	47.45 S	65.55W
Puerto de Sóller / El Port	126	Oe	39.48N	2.41 E
Puerto Escondido [Mex.]	190	Ee	15.48N	96.57W
Puerto Escondido [Mex.]	192	De	25.48N	111.20W
Puerto Esperanza [Arg.]	204	Eh	26.01 S	54.39W
Puerto Esperanza [Par.]	204	Ce	20.26 S	58.06W
Puerto Estrella	194	Lg	12.14N	71.13W
Puerto Fonciere	204	Df	22.29 S	57.48W
Puerto Francisco de Orellana	202	Cd	0.27 S	76.57W
Puerto Frey	204	Bb	14.42 S	61.10W
Puerto Gaitán	202	Dc	4.20N	72.10W
Puerto General Diaz	204	Eg	25.12 S	54.32W
Puerto Goya	204	Ci	29.09 S	59.20W
Puerto Grether	202	Fg	17.12 S	64.21W
Puerto Guaraní	204	De	21.18 S	57.55W
Puerto Heath	202	Ef	12.30 S	68.40W
Puerto Huitoto	202	Dc	0.18N	74.03W
Puerto Iguazú	206	Jc	25.34 S	54.34W
Puerto Indio	204	Eg	24.52 S	54.29W
Puerto Ingeniero Ibáñez	206	Fg	46.18 S	71.56W
Puerto Isabel	204	Dd	18.11 S	57.37W
Puerto Jesús	194	Eh	10.07N	85.16W
Puerto Juárez	176	Kg	21.11N	86.49W
Puerto la Concordia	202	Dc	2.38N	72.47W
Puerto la Cruz	200	Jd	10.13N	64.38W
Puerto Leguízamo	200	If	0.12 S	74.46W
Puerto Lempira	194	Ff	15.15N	83.46W
Puerto Libertad	190	Bc	29.55N	112.43W
Puerto Limón [Col.]	202	Dc	3.23N	73.30W
Puerto Limón [Col.]	202	Cc	1.02N	76.32W
Puertollano	126	Hf	38.41N	4.07W
Puerto López [Col.]	202	Dc	4.06N	72.58W
Puerto López [Col.]	194	Lh	11.56N	71.17W
Puerto Lumbreras	126	Kg	37.34N	1.49W
Puerto Madero	192	Mj	14.44N	92.25W
Puerto Madryn	206	Gf	42.46 S	65.03W
Puerto Magdalena	192	Ce	24.35N	112.05W
Puerto Maldonado	200	Jg	12.36 S	69.11W
Puerto Marangatú	204	Eg	24.39 S	54.21W
Puerto Mayor Otaño	204	Eh	26.19 S	54.44W
Puerto Mihanovich	204	De	20.52 S	57.59W
Puerto Montt	200	Ij	41.28 S	72.57W
Puerto Morelos	192	Pg	20.50N	86.52W
Puerto Mutis	202	Cb	6.14N	77.25W
Puerto Naranjito	204	Eh	26.57 S	55.18W
Puerto Nariño	202	Ec	4.56N	67.48W
Puerto Natales	200	Ik	51.44 S	72.31W
Puerto Nuevo	204	Ce	20.33 S	58.03W
Puerto Nuevo, Punta-	197a	Bb	18.30N	66.21W
Puerto Ordaz	202	Fb	8.22N	62.41W
Puerto Padre	194	Ic	21.12N	76.36W
Puerto Páez	202	Eb	6.13N	67.28W
Puerto Peñasco	190	Bb	31.20N	113.33W
Puerto Piña	194	Hj	7.35N	78.10W
Puerto Pinasco	206	Ib	22.43 S	57.50W
Puerto Piritu	196	Dg	10.04N	65.03W
Puerto Plata	190	Je	19.48N	70.41W
Puerto Presidente Stroessner	204	Eg	25.33 S	54.39W
Puerto Princesa	142	Ni	9.44N	118.44 E
Puerto Quijarro	204	Dc	17.47 S	57.46W
Puerto Real	126	Fh	36.32N	6.11W
Puerto Rico	176	Mh	18.15N	66.30W
Puerto Rico	174	Mh	18.15N	66.30W
Puerto Rico [Arg.]	206	Jc	26.48 S	54.59W
Puerto Rico [Bol.]	202	Ef	11.05 S	67.38W
Puerto Rico [Col.]	202	Cc	1.54N	75.10W
Puerto Rico Trench (EN)	106	Bg	20.00N	66.00W
Puerto Rondón	202	Db	6.18N	71.06W
Puerto San José	204	Eh	26.32 S	54.50W
Puerto Santa Cruz	200	Jk	50.09 S	68.30W
Puerto Sastre	206	Ib	22.06 S	57.59W
Puerto Siles	202	Ef	12.48 S	65.05W
Puerto Suárez	200	Kg	18.57 S	57.51W
Puerto Tacurú Pytá	204	Df	23.49 S	57.09W
Puerto Tirol	204	Ch	27.23 S	59.05W
Puerto Tres Palmas	204	De	21.43 S	57.58W
Puerto Triunfo	204	Eh	26.45 S	55.06W
Puerto Vallarta	190	Cd	20.37N	105.15W
Puerto Varas	206	Ff	41.19 S	72.59W
Puerto Victoria	204	Eh	26.20 S	54.39W
Puerto Viejo	194	Eh	10.26N	83.59W
Puerto Villamizar	194	Ki	8.19N	72.26W
Puerto Villazón	204	Ba	13.32 S	61.57W
Puerto Wilches	202	Db	7.20N	73.54W
Puerto Ybapobó	204	Df	23.42 S	57.12W
Puesto Monte Lindo	204	Df	23.57 S	57.12W
Pueu	221e	Fc	17.44 S	149.13W
Pugačev	136	Ee	52.03N	48.48 E
Puget Sound	188	Dc	48.00N	122.30W
Puglia = Apulia (EN)	128	Ki	41.15N	16.15 E
Pu He	154	Gd	41.21N	122.47 E
Puhja	116	Lf	58.13N	26.17 E
Puigcerdà	126	Nb	42.26N	1.56 E
Puigmal	126	Ob	42.23N	2.07 E
Puir	138	Jf	53.10N	141.25 E
Puisaye, Collines de la-	122	Jg	47.35N	3.18 E
Puisieux	124	Ed	50.07N	2.42 E
Pujehum	166	Cd	7.21N	11.42W
Pujeşti	130	Kc	46.25N	27.29 E
Puji → Wugong	152	Ie	34.15N	108.14 E
Pujiang	154	Ei	29.28N	119.53 E
Pujili	202	Cd	0.57 S	78.42W
Puka	130	Cg	42.03N	19.54 E
Pukaki, Lake-	218	Df	44.05 S	170.10 E
Pukalani	221a	Ec	20.50N	156.21W
Pukapuka Atoll [Cook]	208	Kf	10.53 S	165.49W
Pukapuka Atoll [Fr.Poly.]	208	Nf	14.49 S	138.48W
Pukaruha Atoll	208	Nf	18.20 S	137.02W
Pukatawagan	180	He	55.44N	101.19W
Pukchin	154	Hd	40.12N	125.45 E
Pukch'ŏng	152	Mc	40.14N	128.19 E
Pukega, Pointe-	220h	Ab	13.17 S	176.13W
Pukekohe	218	Fb	37.12 S	174.54 E
Pukemiro	218	Fb	37.37 S	175.01 E
Pukeuri Junction	218	Df	45.02 S	171.02 E
Pukp'yong	152	Md	37.28N	129.08 E
Pukšenga	114	Je	63.36N	41.55 E
Puksoozero	136	Ec	62.38N	40.32 E
Puksubaek-san	154	Id	40.42N	127.15 E
Pula [It.]	128	Dk	39.01N	9.00 E
Pula [Yugo.]	128	Hf	44.52N	13.50 E
Pula, Capo di-	128	Dl	38.59N	9.01 E
Pulandian → Xinjin	152	Ld	39.24N	121.59 E
Pulap Atoll	208	Fd	7.39N	149.25 E
Pulaski [Tn.-U.S.]	184	Dh	35.12N	87.02W
Pulaski [Va.-U.S.]	184	Gg	37.03N	80.47W
Pulau	150	Kh	5.50 S	138.15 E
Pulau Halura	150	Hi	10.19 S	120.11 E
Pulau Irian/New Guinea	208	Fe	5.00 S	140.00 E
Pulau Pinang	150	De	5.20N	100.20 E
Pulau Sapudi	150	Fh	7.06 S	114.20 E
Puławy	120	Re	51.25N	21.57 E
Pulborough	124	Bd	50.57N	0.31W
Pulheim	124	Ic	51.00N	6.48 E
Pulkau	128	Kb	48.43N	16.21 E
Pulkkila	114	Fd	64.16N	25.52 E
Pullman	182	Db	46.44N	117.10W
Pulo Anna Island	208	Ed	4.40N	131.58 E
Pulog, Mount-	140	Oh	16.36N	120.54 E
Pulpito, Punta-	192	Dd	26.30N	111.30W
Pulsano	128	Lj	40.23N	17.21 E
Pułtusk	120	Rd	52.43N	21.05 E
Pülümür	146	Hc	39.30N	39.54 E
Pulusuk Island	208	Fd	6.42N	149.19 E
Puluwat Atoll	208	Fd	7.22N	149.11 E
Puma Yumco	152	Ff	28.35N	90.20 E
Pumpėnai/Pumpenaj	116	Ki	55.53N	24.25 E
Pumpenaj/Pumpėnai	116	Ki	55.53N	24.25 E
Pumpkin Creek	188	Mc	46.15N	105.45W
Puná, Isla-	202	Bd	2.50 S	80.10W
Punākha	148	Hc	27.37N	89.52 E
Punaluu	221a	Fd	19.08N	155.30W
Pūnch	148	Eb	33.46N	74.06 E
Punda Milia	172	Ed	22.40 S	31.05 E
Pune (Poona)	142	Jh	18.32N	73.52 E
Pūnel	146	Md	37.33N	49.07 E
Pungan	135	Hd	40.45N	70.50 E
P'unggi	154	Jf	36.52N	128.32 E
Púngoè	172	Ec	19.50 S	34.48 E
P'ungsan	154	Jd	40.40N	128.05 E
Punia	170	Ec	1.28 S	26.27 E
Punitaqui	206	Fd	30.50 S	71.16W
Punjab	148	Fb	31.00N	76.00 E
Punjab	140	Jf	30.00N	74.00 E
Punjad	148	Eb	30.00N	74.00 E
Punkaharju	116	Mc	61.48N	29.24 E
Punkalaidun	116	Jc	61.07N	23.06 E
Puno	200	Ig	15.50 S	70.02W
Puno	202	Ef	15.00 S	70.00W
Punta, Cerro de-	190	Ke	18.10N	66.36W
Punta Alta	200	Ji	38.53 S	62.04W
Punta Arenas	200	Ik	53.09 S	70.55W
Punta Cardón	202	Da	11.38N	70.14W
Punta de Mata	196	Eh	9.43N	63.38W
Punta Gorda [Blz.]	190	Ge	16.07N	88.48W
Punta Gorda [Fl.-U.S.]	184	Fl	26.56N	82.03W
Punta Gorda [Nic.]	194	Fh	11.31N	83.47W
Punta Gorda, Bahía de-	194	Fh	11.15N	83.45W
Punta Gorda, Río-	194	Fh	11.30N	83.47W
Punta Indio	204	Dl	35.16 S	57.14W
Punta Prieta	190	Bc	28.58N	114.17W
Puntarenas	176	Ki	9.58N	84.50W
Puntarenas	194	Ei	9.00N	83.15W
Punta Róbalo	194	Fi	9.02N	82.15W
Punto Fijo	202	Da	11.42N	70.13W
Puolanka	114	Gd	64.52N	27.40 E
Puolo Point	221a	Bb	21.54N	159.36W
Puqi	152	Jf	29.43N	113.52 E
Puquio	202	Df	14.42 S	74.08W
Pur	140	Jc	67.29N	78.05 E
Puracé, Volcán-	202	Cc	2.21N	76.23W
Purari	214	Ci	7.52 S	145.10 E
Purcell Mountains	180	Fg	49.55N	116.15W
Purchena	126	Jg	37.21N	2.22W
Purdy Islands	208	Fe	2.53 S	146.20 E
Purgatoire River	186	Eg	38.04N	103.10W
Puri	148	He	19.48N	85.51 E
Purificación	190	Ed	23.58N	98.42W
Purikari neem / Purikarinem	116	Ke	59.36N	25.35 E
Purikarinem / Purikari neem	116	Ke	59.36N	25.35 E
Purmani/Puurmani	116	Lf	58.30N	26.14 E
Purmerend	122	Kb	52.31N	4.57 E
Purna [India]	148	Fd	21.05N	76.00 E
Purna [India]	148	Fe	19.07N	77.02 E
Purnač	114	Jc	67.00N	40.15 E
Pūrnia	148	Hc	25.47N	87.28 E
Purukcahu	150	Fg	0.35S	114.35 E
Puruliya	148	Hd	23.20N	86.22 E
Puruni River	196	Gi	6.00N	59.12W
Purús, Rio-	198	Jf	3.42 S	61.28W
Puruvesi	114	Gf	61.50N	29.25 E
Purwakarta	150	Eh	6.34 S	107.26 E
Purwokerto	150	Eh	7.25 S	109.14 E
Pusala Dağı	146	Ed	37.12N	32.54 E
Pusan	142	Of	35.06N	129.03 E
Pusan Si	154	Jg	35.10N	129.05 E
Puschlav / Poschiavo	128	Ed	46.20N	10.04 E
Pushi He	154	Hd	40.17N	124.43 E
Puškin	136	Dd	59.43N	30.24 E
Puškino [Abz.-U.S.S.R.]	132	Pj	39.28N	48.33 E
Puškino [R.S.F.S.R.]	114	Ih	56.02N	37.53 E
Puškino [R.S.F.S.R.]	132	Od	51.14N	46.59 E
Puškinskije Gory	116	Mh	56.59N	28.59 E
Pušlahta	114	Id	64.48N	36.33 E
Püspökladány	120	Ri	47.19N	21.07 E
Püssi/Pjussi	116	Le	59.17N	26.57 E
Pusteci	130	Di	40.47N	20.54 E
Pusteria, Val-/Pustertal	128	Gd	46.45N	12.20 E
Pustertal/Pusteria, Val-	128	Gd	46.45N	12.20 E
Pustomyty	120	Tg	49.37N	23.59 E
Pustoška	114	Gh	56.20N	29.22 E
Putao	148	Jc	27.21N	97.24 E
Putaruru	218	Fc	38.03 S	175.47 E
Putian	152	Kf	25.32N	119.01 E
Putignano	128	Lj	40.51N	17.07 E
Putila	130	Ib	48.00N	25.07 E
Putivl	132	Hd	51.22N	33.55 E
Putjatin	154	Lc	42.52N	132.25 E
Putla de Guerrero	192	Ki	17.02N	97.56W
Putna	130	Ib	47.52N	25.37 E
Putna	130	Kd	45.34N	27.30 E
Putnok	120	Qh	48.18N	20.26 E
Puto	219a	Ba	5.41 S	154.43 E
Putorana, plato- = Putoran Mountains (EN)	140	Lc	69.00N	95.00 E
Putoran Mountains (EN) = Putorana, plato-	140	Lc	69.00N	95.00 E
Puttalam	148	Fg	8.02N	79.49 E
Putte	124	Gc	51.04N	4.38 E
Puttelange-aux-Lacs	124	Ie	49.03N	6.56 E
Putten	124	Hb	52.16N	5.35 E
Putten	124	Gc	51.50N	4.15 E
Puttgarden, Burg auf Fehmarn-	120	Hb	54.30N	11.13 E
Püttlingen	124	Ie	49.17N	6.53 E
Putumayo	202	Cc	0.30N	76.00W
Putumayo, Río-	198	Jf	3.07 S	67.58W
Putuo (Shenjiamen)	154	Gj	29.57N	122.18 E
Putussibau	150	Ff	0.50N	112.56 E
Puu Kukui	221a	Ec	20.54N	156.35W
Puulavesi	110	Ic	61.50N	26.40 E
Puumala	114	Gf	61.32N	28.11 E
Puu o Umi	221a	Fc	20.05N	155.42W
Puurmani/Purmani	116	Lf	58.30N	26.14 E
Puurs	124	Gc	51.05N	4.17 E
Puuwai	221a	Ab	21.54N	160.12W
Puy, Le-	122	Ji	45.02N	3.53 E
Puyallup	188	Dc	47.11N	122.18W
Puyang	152	Jd	35.41N	115.00 E
Puy-de-Dôme	122	Ii	45.40N	3.00 E
Puy-l'Evêque	122	Hj	44.30N	1.08 E
Puymorens, Col de-	122	Hl	42.34N	1.49 E
Puyo	202	Cd	1.29 S	77.58W
Puysegur Point	218	Bg	46.10 S	166.37 E
Pwani	170	Gd	7.30 S	39.00 E
Pweto	160	Ji	8.28 S	28.54 E
Pwllheli	118	Ii	52.53N	4.25W
Pyapon	148	Je	16.17N	95.41 E
Pyhäjärvi	114	Fe	63.40N	25.59 E
Pyhäjärvi [Fin.]	114	Fe	63.35N	25.57 E
Pyhäjärvi [Fin.]	114	Ff	61.00N	22.20 E
Pyhäjärvi [Fin.]	116	Kc	62.45N	25.25 E
Pyhäjärvi [Fin.]	116	Jc	61.30N	23.35 E
Pyhäjoki	114	Fd	64.28N	24.14 E
Pyhäjoki	114	Fd	64.28N	24.13 E
Pyhäntä	114	Gd	64.06N	26.19 E
Pyhäranta	116	Id	60.57N	21.27 E
Pyhaselkä	116	Mb	62.26N	29.58 E
Pyhäselkä	114	Ge	62.30N	29.40 E
Pyhätunturi	114	Gc	67.01N	27.09 E
Pyhävesi	116	Lc	61.25N	26.35 E
Pyhävuori	116	Ib	62.17N	21.38 E
Pyhrnpaß	128	Ic	47.38N	14.18 E
Pyhtää/Pyttis	114	Gf	60.29N	26.32 E
Pyinmana	142	Lh	19.44N	96.13 E
Pylos (EN) = Pílos	130	Em	36.56N	21.40 E
Pyltsamaa/Põltsamaa	114	Fg	58.39N	25.59 E
Pyltsamaa/Põltsamaa	116	Lf	58.23N	26.08 E
Pylva/Põlva	114	Gg	58.04N	27.06 E
Pymatuning Reservoir	184	Ge	41.37N	80.30W
P'yŏngan-Namdo	154	Ie	39.20N	126.00 E
P'yŏngan-Pukto	154	Hd	40.00N	125.15 E
P'yŏnggang	152	Md	38.25N	127.17 E
P'yŏngsan	152	Md	38.20N	126.24 E
P'yongt'aek	154	If	36.59N	127.05 E
P'yŏngyang	142	Of	39.01N	125.45 E
P'yŏngyang Si	154	He	39.04N	125.50 E
Pyramiden	179	Nc	77.54N	16.41 E
Pyramid Lake	182	Dc	40.00N	119.35W
Pyramid Mountains	186	Bj	32.00N	108.30W
Pyrénées=Pyrenees (EN)	110	Gg	42.40N	1.00 E
Pyrenees (EN)=Pirineos	110	Gg	42.40N	1.00 E
Pyrenees (EN)= Pyrénées	110	Gg	42.40N	1.00 E
Pyrenees (EN)=Serralada Pirinenca	110	Gg	42.40N	1.00 E
Pyrénées-Atlantiques	122	Fk	43.15N	0.50W
Pyrénées-Orientales	122	Il	42.30N	2.20 E
Pyrzyce	120	Kc	53.10N	14.55 E
Pyšma	136	Gd	57.08N	66.18 E
Pytalovo	114	Gh	57.06N	27.59 E
Pyttegga	116	Bb	62.13N	7.42 E
Pyttis/Pyhtää	114	Gf	60.29N	26.32 E
Pyu	148	Je	18.29N	96.26 E
Pyzaspea / Põõsaspea neem	116	Je	59.15N	23.25 E
Pyzdry	120	Nd	52.11N	17.41 E

Q

Qā', Wādī al-	146	Hi	27.04N	38.34 E
Qābis	160	Ie	33.53N	10.07 E
Qābis	162	Ic	33.00N	9.30 E
Qābis, Khalīj-=Gabès, Gulf of-(EN)	158	Ie	34.00N	10.25 E
Qabr Hūd	168	Hb	16.09N	49.34 E
Qāderābād	146	Og	30.17N	53.16 E
Qādır Karam	146	Ke	35.12N	44.53 E
Qāḑub	144	Hg	12.38N	53.57 E
Qā'emshahr	146	Od	36.30N	52.55 E
Qafşah	160	He	34.25N	8.48 E
Qafşah	162	Ic	34.30N	9.00 E
Qa'fūr	128	Dn	36.20N	9.19 E
Qagan	152	Kb	49.16N	118.04 E
Qagan Moron He	154	Ec	43.13N	119.02 E
Qagan Nur	152	Jc	43.20N	112.58 E
Qagan Nur [China]	154	Hb	45.14N	124.17 E
Qagan Nur [China]	154	Bd	41.33N	113.48 E
Qagan Nur [China]	152	Jc	43.25N	114.50 E
Qagan Nur → Zhengxiangbai Qi	152	Jc	42.16N	114.59 E
Qagan Us → Dulan	142	Lf	36.29N	98.29 E
Qagchêng/Xiangcheng	152	Gf	28.56N	99.46 E
Qahar Youyi Houqi (Bayan Qagan)	154	Bd	41.28N	113.10 E
Qahar Youyi Qianqi (Togrog Ul)	154	Bd	40.46N	113.13 E
Qahar Youyi Zhongqi	154	Bd	41.15N	112.36 E
Qahd, Wādī-	146	Ii	26.13N	40.49 E
Qaidam He	152	Gd	36.48N	95.50 E
Qaidam Pendi=Tsaidam Basin (EN)	152	Fd	37.00N	95.00 E
Qala'an Naḩl	168	Ec	13.38N	34.57 E
Qalāt	144	Kc	32.07N	66.54 E
Qal'at Abū Ghār	146	Lg	30.25N	46.09 E
Qal'at al Akhḑar	144	Ed	28.06N	37.05 E
Qal 'at al Marqab	146	Fe	35.09N	35.57 E
Qal'at al Mu'aẓẓam	146	Gi	27.45N	37.31 E
Qal'at aş Şanam	128	Co	35.46N	8.21 E
Qal'at Bīshah	142	Gh	20.00N	42.36 E
Qal'at Dīzah	146	Kd	36.11N	45.07 E
Qal'at Şāliḩ	146	Lg	31.31N	47.16 E
Qal'at Sukkar	146	Lg	31.53N	46.56 E
Qal'eh Asgar	146	Qh	29.30N	56.35 E
Qal'eh Kūh	146	Mf	33.00N	49.10 E
Qal'eh Mūreh	146	Pe	35.35N	55.58 E
Qal'eh-ye Now	144	Jc	34.59N	63.08 E
Qal'eh-ye Sahar	146	Mg	31.40N	48.33 E

Index Symbols

1 Independent Nation; 2 State, Region; 3 District, County; 4 Municipality; 5 Colony, Dependency; Continent; Physical Region; Historical or Cultural Region; Mount, Mountain; Volcano; Hill; Mountains, Mountain Range; Hills, Escarpment; Plateau, Upland; Pass, Gap; Plain, Lowland; Delta; Salt Flat; Valley, Canyon; Crater, Cave; Karst Features; Depression; Polder; Desert, Dunes; Forest, Woods; Heath, Steppe; Oasis; Cape, Point; Coast, Beach; Cliff; Peninsula; Isthmus; Sandbank; Island; Atoll; Rock, Reef; Islands, Archipelago; Rocks, Reefs; Coral Reef; Well, Spring; Geyser; River, Stream; Waterfall, Rapids; River Mouth, Estuary; Lake; Salt Lake; Intermittent Lake; Reservoir; Swamp, Pond; Canal; Glacier; Ice Shelf, Pack Ice; Ocean; Sea; Gulf, Bay; Strait, Fjord; Lagoon; Bank; Seamount; Tablemount; Ridge; Shelf; Basin; Escarpment, Sea Scarp; Fracture; Trench, Abyss; National Park, Reserve; Point of Interest; Recreation Site; Cave, Cavern; Historic Site; Ruins; Wall, Walls; Church, Abbey; Temple; Scientific Station; Railway station; Airport; Port; Military installation; Lighthouse; Mine; Tunnel; Dam, Bridge

Qalīb ash Shuyūkh	144	Gd	29.12N	47.55 E
Qallābāt	168	Fc	12.58N	36.09 E
Qalmarz, Godār-e-	146	Qf	33.26N	56.14 E
Qalyūb	146	Dg	30.11N	31.13 E
Qamata	172	Df	31.58S	27.24 E
Qamdo	142	Lf	31.15N	97.12 E
Qamīnis	164	Dc	31.40N	20.01 E
Qamsar	146	Nf	33.45N	51.26 E
Qamūdah	162	Ic	35.00N	9.21 E
Qamūdah [3]	162	Ic	34.50N	9.20 E
Qânâq/Thule	224	Od	77.35N	69.40W
Qandahār	142	If	31.35N	65.45 E
Qandahār [3]	144	Kc	31.00N	65.45 E
Qandala	168	Hc	11.23N	49.53 E
Qangdin Gol	154	Cc	43.27N	115.03 E
Qanţarat al Fahş	128	Dn	36.23N	9.54 E
Qapqal	152	Dc	43.48N	80.47 E
Qaqortoq/Julianehåb	224	Nc	60.50N	46.10W
Qarā Dāgh	146	Lc	38.48N	47.13 E
Qārah	164	Ed	29.37N	26.30 E
Qarah Būlāq	146	Ke	34.32N	45.12 E
Qarah Dagh	146	Jd	37.00N	43.30 E
Qarah Tappah	146	Ke	34.25N	44.56 E
Qarānqū	146	Ld	37.23N	47.43 E
Qardo	160	Lh	9.30N	49.03 E
Qareh Āghāj	146	Ld	36.46N	48.46 E
Qareh Sū [Asia]	144	Gb	39.27N	47.30 E
Qareh Sū [Iran]	144	Hc	34.52N	51.25 E
Qareh Sū [Iran]	144	Ib	37.00N	56.50 E
Qareh Ẕīā'Od Dīn	146	Kc	38.53N	45.02 E
Qarkilik/Ruoqiang	142	Kf	39.02N	88.00 E
Qarnayn, Jazīrat al-	146	Oj	24.56N	52.52 E
Qarqan/Qiemo	142	Kf	38.08N	85.32 E
Qarqan He	140	Kf	39.30N	88.15 E
Qarqannah, Juzur-= Kerkennah Islands (EN)	158	Ie	34.44N	11.12 E
Qartājannah	128	En	36.51N	10.20 E
Qārūn, Birkat-	164	Fd	29.28N	30.40 E
Qaryat Abū Nujaym	164	Cc	30.35N	15.24 E
Qaryat al Gharab	146	Kg	31.27N	44.48 E
Qaryat al Qaddāḩīyah	164	Cc	31.22N	15.14 E
Qaryat al 'Ulyā	144	Gd	27.33N	47.42 E
Qaryat az Zarrūq	164	Cc	32.22N	15.09 E
Qaryat az Zuwaytīnah	164	Dc	30.58N	20.07 E
Qaryat Hubayn al Gharbīyah	146	Je	34.21N	42.05 E
Qaşabah, Ra's al-	146	Fh	28.02N	34.38 E
Qaşabāt, Hanshīr al-	128	Dn	36.24N	9.54 E
Qasigiánguit/Christianshåb	179	Ge	68.45N	51.30W
Qaşr al Azraq	146	Gg	31.53N	36.49 E
Qasr Al Hayr	146	Ge	34.23N	37.36 E
Qaşr al Qarahbullī	164	Bc	32.45N	13.43 E
Qaşr 'Amij	146	If	33.30N	41.45 E
Qaşr Bū Hādī	164	Cc	31.03N	16.40 E
Qaşr Burqu'	146	Gf	32.37N	37.58 E
Qasr-e Shīrīn	144	Gc	34.31N	45.35 E
Qaşr Farāfirah	160	Jf	27.15N	28.10 E
Qaşr Ḩamān	144	Ge	20.50N	45.50 E
Qaşr Qārūn	146	Dh	29.25N	30.25 E
Qaşş Abū Sa'īd	146	Bi	27.00N	27.35 E
Qatana	146	Gf	33.26N	36.05 E
Qaţar [1]	142	Hg	25.30N	51.15 E
Qaţar	140	Hg	25.30N	51.15 E
Qatlīsh	146	Qd	37.50N	57.19 E
Qaţrānī, Jabal-	146	Dh	29.41N	30.35 E
Qatrūyeh	146	Ph	29.09N	54.43 E
Qattara Depression (EN)= Qaţţārah, Munkhafaḑ al-	158	Je	30.00N	27.30 E
Qaţţārah, Munkhafaḑ al-= Qattara Depression (EN)	158	Je	30.00N	27.30 E
Qawām al Hamzah	146	Kg	31.43N	44.58 E
Qawz Abu Ḑulū'	168	Eb	16.55N	32.30 E
Qawz Rajab	168	Fb	16.04N	35.34 E
Qaysān	168	Ec	10.45N	34.48 E
Qayyārah	146	Je	35.48N	43.17 E
Qazvīn	142	Gf	36.16N	50.00 E
Qeqertarssuaq/Godhavn	224	Nc	69.20N	53.35W
Qeshm	146	Qi	26.58N	56.16 E
Qeshm	144	Id	26.45N	55.45 E
Qeydār	146	Md	36.07N	48.35 E
Qeys, Jazīreh-ye-	144	Hd	26.32N	53.58 E
Qezel	144	Gb	36.45N	49.22 E
Qian'an [China]	154	Ed	40.01N	118.42 E
Qian'an [China]	154	Hb	44.58N	124.01 E
Qianfangzi	154	Ad	40.01N	111.23 E
Qian Gorlos (Quianguozhen)	152	Lb	45.05N	124.52 E
Qian He	154	Dh	32.55N	117.10 E
Qianjiang [China]	154	Bi	30.25N	112.54 E
Qianjiang [China]	152	Ig	23.37N	108.58 E
Qianjiang [China]	152	If	29.30N	108.45 E
Qianning/Gartar	152	He	30.27N	101.29 E
Qianshan	154	Di	30.38N	116.35 E
Qian Shan	152	Lc	40.35N	123.00 E
Qiansuo	152	Hf	25.27N	100.41 E
Qianwei	152	Hf	29.08N	103.56 E
Qianxi [China]	152	If	27.03N	106.04 E
Qianxi [China]	154	Ed	40.08N	118.19 E
Qianyang (Anjiang)	152	Jf	27.19N	110.13 E
Qiaojia	152	Hf	27.00N	103.00 E
Qiaowan	152	Gc	40.36N	96.42 E
Qibilī	162	Ic	33.42N	8.58 E
Qichun (Caojiahe)	154	Ci	30.15N	115.26 E
Qidaogou	154	Id	41.31N	126.18 E
Qidong	154	Fi	31.48N	121.39 E
Qiemo/Qarqan	142	Kf	38.08N	85.32 E
Qift	146	Ei	26.00N	32.49 E
Qijiang	152	If	29.00N	106.39 E
Qijiaojing	152	Fc	43.28N	91.36 E
Qike → Xunke	152	Mb	49.34N	128.28 E
Qili → Shitai	154	Di	30.12N	117.28 E
Qilian (Babao)	152	Hd	38.14N	100.15 E
Qilian Shan	152	Gd	39.12N	98.35 E
Qilian Shan	140	Lf	38.30N	100.00 E
Qimantag	152	Fd	37.00N	91.00 E
Qimen	152	Kf	29.57N	117.39 E
Qinā	160	Kf	26.10N	32.43 E
Qinā, Wādī-	146	Ei	26.12N	32.44 E
Qin'an	152	Ie	34.50N	105.35 E
Qingchengzi	154	Gd	40.44N	123.36 E
Qingchuan	152	Ie	32.32N	105.11 E
Qingdao (Tsingtao)	142	Of	36.05N	120.21 E
Qingduizi	154	Fd	41.27N	121.52 E
Qingfeng	154	Cg	35.54N	115.07 E
Qinggang	152	Mb	46.41N	126.03 E
Qinggil/Qinghe	152	Fb	46.43N	90.24 E
Qinghai Hu=Koko Nor (EN)	140	Mf	37.00N	100.20 E
Qinghai Sheng (Ch'ing-hai Sheng)=Tsinghai (EN) [2]	152	Gd	36.00N	96.00 E
Qing He	154	Hc	42.16N	124.10 E
Qinghe/Qinggil	152	Fb	46.43N	90.24 E
Qinghe (Gexianzhuang)	154	Cf	37.03N	115.39 E
Qinghemen	154	Fd	41.45N	121.25 E
Qingjian	152	Jd	37.10N	110.09 E
Qingjiang	142	Nf	33.31N	119.03 E
Qing Jiang	152	Je	30.24N	111.30 E
Qingjiang (Zhangshuzhen)	152	Kf	28.02N	115.31 E
Qingkou → Ganyu	154	Eg	34.50N	119.07 E
Qinglong	154	Ed	40.26N	118.58 E
Qinglong He	154	Ee	39.51N	118.51 E
Qingshan	154	Ci	30.39N	114.27 E
Qingshuihe	152	Jd	39.56N	111.41 E
Qingshui Jiang	152	If	27.11N	109.48 E
Qingtian	152	Lf	28.12N	120.17 E
Qingxian	154	De	38.35N	116.48 E
Qingxu	154	Bf	37.36N	112.21 E
Qingyang [China]	154	Di	30.38N	117.50 E
Qingyang [China]	152	Id	36.01N	107.48 E
Qingyuan	152	Lc	42.06N	124.56 E
Qingyuan (Nandaran)	154	Ce	38.46N	115.29 E
Qingyun (Xiejiaji)	154	Df	37.46N	117.22 E
Qing Zang Gaoyuan=Tibet, Plateau of- (EN)	140	Kf	32.30N	87.00 E
Qin He	154	Bg	35.01N	113.25 E
Qinhuangdao	152	Kg	40.00N	119.32 E
Qin Ling	140	Mf	34.00N	108.00 E
Qinshui	154	Bg	35.41N	112.10 E
Qintong	154	Fh	32.39N	120.06 E
Qinxian	154	Bf	36.46N	112.42 E
Qinyang	154	Bg	35.05N	112.56 E
Qinyuan	154	Bf	36.29N	112.20 E
Qinzhou	152	Ig	22.02N	108.30 E
Qionghai (Jiaji)	152	Jh	19.25N	110.28 E
Qionglai	152	He	30.24N	103.28 E
Qiongzhou Haixia	140	Ng	20.10N	110.15 E
Qipan Guan	152	Ie	32.45N	106.11 E
Qiqihar	142	Oe	47.21N	123.58 E
Qīr	146	Oh	28.29N	53.04 E
Qira	152	Dd	37.02N	80.53 E
Qiryat Gat	146	Fg	31.36N	34.46 E
Qiryat Shemona	146	Ff	33.13N	35.34 E
Qiryat Yam	146	Ff	32.51N	35.04 E
Qishn	144	Hf	15.26N	51.40 E
Qi Shui	154	Ci	30.09N	115.22 E
Qishuyan	154	Fi	31.41N	120.04 E
Qitai	142	Ke	44.01N	89.28 E
Qitaihe	152	Nb	45.49N	130.51 E
Qiuxian (Matou)	154	Cf	36.50N	115.10 E
Qixia	154	Ff	37.18N	120.50 E
Qixian [China]	154	Cg	34.33N	114.46 E
Qixian [China]	154	Bf	37.23N	112.21 E
Qixian (Zhaoge)	154	Cg	35.35N	114.12 E
Qiyang	152	Jf	26.44N	111.50 E
Qizhou	154	Ci	30.04N	115.20 E
Qogir Feng=Godwin Austen (EN)	140	Jf	35.53N	76.30 E
Qog Qi	152	Ic	41.31N	107.00 E
Qog Ul	152	Kc	44.50N	116.19 E
Qohrūd, Kūhhā-ye-	140	Hf	32.40N	53.00 E
Qoltag	152	Ec	42.20N	88.45 E
Qom	142	Hf	34.39N	50.54 E
Qom	146	Ne	34.48N	51.02 E
Qomolangma Feng=Everest, Mount- (EN)	140	Kg	27.59N	86.56 E
Qomrud	146	Ne	34.43N	51.04 E
Qomsheh	144	Hc	32.00N	51.50 E
Qondūz	142	If	36.45N	68.51 E
Qondūz [3]	144	Kb	36.45N	68.30 E
Qondūz	144	Kb	37.00N	68.16 E
Qoqek/Tacheng	142	Ke	46.45N	82.57 E
Qôrnoq	179	Gf	64.30N	51.19W
Qorveh	146	Le	35.10N	47.48 E
Qoşbeh-ye Naşşār	144	Gc	30.02N	48.27 E
Qoţbābād [Iran]	146	Qi	27.46N	56.06 E
Qoţbābād [Iran]	146	Oh	28.39N	53.37 E
Qoţūr	146	Kc	38.28N	44.25 E
Qotūr	146	Kc	38.46N	45.16 E
Quadros, Lagoa dos-	204	Gi	29.42S	50.05W
Quairading	212	Df	32.01S	117.25 E
Quakenbrück	120	Dd	52.41N	7.57 E
Quanah	186	Gi	34.18N	99.44W
Quanbao Shan	152	Je	34.08N	111.26 E
Quang Ngai	148	Le	15.07N	108.48 E
Quang Tri	148	Le	21.02N	106.29 E
Quan He	154	Ch	32.55N	115.52 E
Quanjiao	154	Eh	32.09N	118.16 E
Quang Trach	148	Le	17.45N	106.27 E
Quanzhou [China]	152	Jf	26.01N	110.4 E
Quanzhou [China]	142	Ng	24.57N	118.35 E
Qu'Appelle River	180	Hf	50.27N	101.19W
Quaraí	206	Id	30.23S	56.27W
Quaraí, Rio-	204	Dj	30.12S	57.36W
Quaregnon	124	Fd	50.26N	3.51 E
Quartu Sant'Elena	128	Dk	39.14N	9.11 E
Quartz Lake	180	Jb	70.57N	80.40W
Quartz Mountain	188	De	43.10N	122.40W
Quartzsite	188	Hj	33.40N	114.13W
Quatre, Isle-	197n	Bb	12.57N	61.15W
Quatsino Sound	188	Aa	50.25N	128.10W
Qūchān	142	Hf	37.06N	58.30 E
Qué	170	Ce	14.43S	15.06 E
Queanbeyan	212	Jg	35.21S	149.14 E
Québec	176	Le	46.49N	71.13W
Québec [2]	180	Kf	54.00N	72.00W
Quebó	204	Db	14.36S	56.04W
Quebra Anzol, Rio-	204	Id	19.09S	47.38W
Quebracho	204	Dj	31.57S	57.57W
Quebradillas	197a	Bb	18.28N	66.56W
Quedas do Iguaçu	204	Fg	25.31S	52.54W
Quedlinburg	120	He	51.47N	11.09 E
Queen, Cape-	180	Jd	64.43N	78.18W
Queen Alexandra Range	222	Jg	84.00S	168.00 E
Queen Bess, Mount-	180	Ff	51.18N	124.33W
Queenborough	124	Cc	51.25N	0.46 E
Queen Charlotte Islands	174	Fd	51.30N	129.00W
Queen Charlotte Sound	180	Ef	51.30N	129.30W
Queen Charlotte Strait	174	Gd	50.40N	127.25W
Queen Elizabeth Islands	174	Ib	79.00N	105.00W
Queen Elizabeth Range	222	Kg	83.20S	162.00 E
Queen Mary Land	222	Ge	69.00S	96.00 E
Queen Maud Gulf	174	Ic	68.25N	102.30W
Queen Maud Land (EN)	222	Cf	72.30S	12.00 E
Queen Maud Range	222	Lg	86.00S	160.00W
Queens Channel [Austl.]	212	Fb	14.45S	129.25 E
Queens Channel [N.W.T.-Can.]	180	Ha	76.11N	96.00W
Queensland [2]	212	Id	22.00S	145.00 E
Queenstown [Austl.]	212	Jh	42.05S	145.33 E
Queenstown [Guy.]	196	Gi	7.12N	58.29W
Queenstown [N.Z.]	218	Cf	45.02S	168.40 E
Queenstown [S.Afr.]	160	Jl	31.52S	26.52 E
Queguay, Cuchilla del-	204	Dj	31.50S	57.30W
Queguay Grande, Río-	204	Ck	32.09S	58.09W
Queich	124	Ke	49.14N	8.23 E
Queimadas	202	Kf	10.58S	39.38W
Queiros	204	Ge	21.49S	50.13W
Quela	170	Cd	9.15S	17.05 E
Quelimane	160	Kj	17.51S	36.52 E
Quemado	186	Bi	34.20N	108.30W
Quemado de Güines	194	Gb	22.48N	80.15W
Quembo	170	De	14.57S	20.22 E
Quemoy (EN) = Chinmen	152	Kg	24.25N	118.25 E
Quemú-Quemú	206	He	36.03S	63.33W
Quepos	194	Ei	9.25N	84.09W
Quequén	206	Ie	38.32S	58.42W
Quequén Grande, Río-	204	Cn	38.34S	58.43W
Quequén Salado, Río-	204	Bn	38.56S	60.31W
Quercy	122	Hj	44.15N	1.15 E
Querétaro	176	Ig	20.36N	100.23W
Querétaro [2]	190	Ed	21.00N	99.55W
Querobabi	192	Db	30.03N	111.01W
Quesada [C.R.]	194	Eh	10.19N	84.26W
Quesada [Sp.]	126	Ig	37.51N	3.04W
Queshan	152	Je	32.42N	114.04 E
Quesnel	180	Ff	52.59N	122.30W
Quesnel Lake	180	Ff	52.32N	121.05W
Questa	186	Dh	36.42N	105.36W
Quetena	202	Eh	22.10S	67.25W
Quetico Lake	186	Kb	48.37N	91.52W
Quetta	142	If	30.12N	67.00 E
Quevas, Cerro-	192	Dc	29.15N	111.20W
Quevedo	202	Cd	1.02S	79.27W
Queyras	122	Mj	44.44N	6.49 E
Quezaltenango	176	Jh	14.50N	91.31W
Quezaltenango [3]	194	Bf	14.45N	91.40W
Quezon	150	Ge	9.14N	117.56 E
Quezon City	142	Oh	14.38N	121.00 E
Qufu	154	Dg	35.35N	116.59 E
Quianguozhen → Qian Gorlos	152	Lb	45.05N	124.52 E
Quibala	170	Be	10.44S	14.59 E
Quibaxe	170	Bd	8.30S	14.36 E
Quibdó	202	Cb	5.42N	76.39W
Quiberon	122	Cg	47.29N	3.07 E
Quiberon, Baie de-	122	Dg	47.32N	3.00W
Quiberon, Presqu'île de-	122	Cg	47.30N	3.08W
Quíbor	194	Mi	9.56N	69.37W
Quiché [3]	194	Bf	15.30N	90.55W
Quierschied	124	Je	49.19N	7.03 E
Quiha	168	Fc	13.28N	39.33 E
Quiindy	204	Dh	25.58S	57.16W
Quijarro	204	Cd	19.26S	58.08W
Quilá	192	Fe	24.23N	107.13W
Quillabamba	202	Df	12.49S	72.43W
Quillacollo	202	Eg	17.26S	66.17W
Quillagua	206	Gb	21.39S	69.33W
Quillan	122	Il	42.52N	2.11 E
Quillebeuf-sur-Seine	124	Ce	49.28N	0.31 E
Quillota	206	Fd	32.53S	71.16W
Quilnes	206	Id	34.44S	58.16W
Quilon	148	Fg	8.53N	76.36 E
Quilpie	212	Ie	26.37S	144.15 E
Quilqué	206	Fd	33.03S	71.27W
Quimari, Alto de-	194	Ii	8.07N	76.23W
Quimbele	170	Cd	6.30S	16.14 E
Quimilí	206	Hc	27.38S	62.25W
Quimome	204	Bc	17.42S	61.16W
Quimome, Río-	204	Bc	17.36S	61.09W
Quimper	122	Bf	48.00N	4.06W
Quimperlé	122	Cg	47.52N	3.33W
Quinault River	188	Cc	47.23N	124.18W
Quincy [Ca.-U.S.]	188	Eg	39.56N	120.57W
Quincy [Fl.-U.S.]	184	Ej	30.37N	84.32W
Quincy [Il.-U.S.]	182	Id	39.56N	91.23W
Quincy [Ma.-U.S.]	184	Ld	42.15N	71.01W
Quincy [Wa.-U.S.]	188	Fc	47.14N	119.51W
Quindío [3]	202	Cc	4.30N	75.40W
Quingey	122	Lg	47.06N	5.53 E
Quinhagak	178	Ge	59.45N	161.43W
Qui Nhon	142	Mh	13.46N	109.14 E
Quiñihual	204	Bm	37.47S	61.36W
Quiniluban Group	150	Hd	11.27N	120.48 E
Quinn River	188	Ff	40.25N	119.00W
Quiñones	192	De	24.22N	111.25W
Quintanar de la Orden	126	Ie	39.34N	3.03W
Quintana Roo [2]	190	Ge	19.40N	88.30W
Quinze, Lac des-	184	Hb	47.30N	79.00W
Quionga	172	Gb	10.35S	40.33 E
Quipungo	170	Be	14.45S	14.05 E
Quirigua	194	Cf	15.18N	89.07W
Quirihue	206	Fe	36.17S	72.32W
Quirima	170	Ce	10.48S	18.09 E
Quirinópolis	202	Hg	18.32S	50.30W
Quiroga	126	Eb	42.29N	7.16W
Quiros, Cap-	219b	Cb	14.56S	167.01 E
Quisiro	194	Lh	10.53N	71.17W
Quissanga	172	Gb	12.25S	40.29 E
Quissico	172	Ed	24.43S	34.45 E
Quitasueño, Banco-	190	Hf	14.20N	81.15W
Quitengues	170	Be	14.06S	14.05 E
Quiterage	172	Gb	11.45S	40.27 E
Quitéria, Rio-	204	Ge	20.16S	51.08W
Quitilipi	204	Bh	26.52S	60.13W
Quitman [Ga.-U.S.]	184	Fj	30.47N	83.33W
Quitman [Ms.-U.S.]	186	Lj	32.03N	88.43W
Quito	200	If	0.13S	78.30W
Quitovac	192	Cb	31.32N	112.42W
Quixadá	202	Kd	4.58S	39.01W
Quixeramobim	202	Ke	5.12S	39.17W
Qujiang	154	Cj	28.14N	115.46 E
Qu Jiang [China]	152	Ie	30.01N	106.24 E
Qu Jiang [China]	152	Kf	29.32N	119.31 E
Qujing	152	Hf	25.31N	103.45 E
Qul'ān, Jazā'ir-	146	Fj	24.22N	35.23 E
Qulansiyah	144	Hg	12.41N	53.29 E
Qulaybīah	162	Jb	36.51N	11.06 E
Qulbān al 'Isāwīyah	146	Gg	30.38N	37.53 E
Qulbān an Nabk al Gharbī	146	Gg	31.15N	37.26 E
Qulbān Layyah	146	Lh	29.50N	46.03 E
Qumar He	140	Lf	34 42N	95.00 E
Qumarlêb	152	Ge	34.35N	95.18 E
Qunayfidhah, Nafūd-	146	Kj	24.45N	45.30 E
Quoi	220d	Ba	7.32N	151.59 E
Quoich	180	Id	63.56N	93.25W
Quorn	212	Hf	32.21S	138.03 E
Quqên/Jinchuan	152	He	31.02N	102.02 E
Quraitu	146	Ke	34.36N	45.30 E
Qurayyāt, Juzur-	162	Jb	35.48N	11.02 E
Qurbah	128	En	36.35N	10.52 E
Qurdūd	168	Dc	10.17N	29.56 E
Qūr Laban	146	Cg	30.23N	28.59 E
Qurunbāliyah	128	En	36.36N	10.30 E
Qūş	164	Fd	25.55N	32.45 E
Qusaybah	146	Ie	34.24N	40.59 E
Quşay'ir	168	Ic	14.55N	50.20 E
Qutdligssat	179	Gd	70.12N	53.00W
Quthing	172	Df	30.24S	27.42 E
Quţū	164	Hf	18.30N	41.04 E
Quwaiz	164	He	20.27N	44.53 E
Quxian	152	Kf	28.54N	118.53 E
Qüxü	152	Ff	29.23N	90.45 E
Quyang	154	Ce	38.37N	114.41 E
Quy Chau	148	Le	19.33N	105.06 E
Quzhou	154	Cf	36.47N	114.56 E
Qyteti Stalin	130	Ci	40.48N	19.54 E

R

Ra'a as Saffānīyah	144	Gd	27.59N	48.37 E
Raab	120	Ni	47.41N	17.38 E
Raahe/Brahestad	114	Fd	64.41N	24.29 E
Rääkkylä	116	Mb	62.19N	29.37 E
Raalte	124	Ib	52.23N	6.17 E
Raamsdonk	124	Gc	51.41N	4.54 E
Raanes Peninsula	180	Ia	78.20N	86.20W
Raasay, Island of-	118	Gd	57.25N	6.04W
Raasay, Sound of-	118	Gd	57.25N	6.05W
Raasiku/Raziku	116	Ke	59.22N	25.11 E
Rab	128	If	44.45N	14.46 E
Rab	128	If	44.46N	14.46 E
Raba	142	Nj	8.27S	118.46 E
Rába	120	Ni	47.41N	17.38 E
Raba	120	Qf	50.09N	20.30 E
Rabāble	168	Hd	8.14N	48.18 E
Rabaçal	126	Ec	41.30N	7.12W
Rabat [Malta]	128	Io	35.50N	14.29 E
Rabat [Mor.]	160	Ge	34.02N	6.50W
Rabat-Salé [2]	162	Fc	34.02N	6.50W
Rabaul	210	Ge	4.12S	152.12 E
Rábca	120	Ni	47.41N	17.37 E
Rabenau	124	Kd	50.40N	8.52 E
Rabī', Ash Shallāl ar-= Fourth Cataract (EN)	158	Kg	18.47N	32.03 E
Rabiah	146	Jd	36.47N	42.07 E
Rābigh	144	Ee	22.48N	39.02 E
Rabinal	194	Bf	15.06N	90.27W
Rabka	120	Pg	49.36N	19.56 E
Rabočeostrovsk	114	Id	64.59N	34.44 E
Rabyānah, Şaḩrā'-	158	Jf	24.30N	21.00 E
Rabyānah, Wāḩāt al-= Rebiana Oasis (EN)	164	De	24.14N	21.59 E
Răcăciuni	130	Jc	46.20N	26.59 E
Racalmuto	128	Hm	37.24N	13.44 E
Răcăşdia	130	Ee	44.59N	21.38 E
Racconigi	128	Bf	44.46N	7.46 E
Race, Cape-	174	Ne	46.40N	53.10W
Race Point	184	Ld	42.04N	70.14W
Rach Gia	142	Mh	10.01N	105.05 E
Rachid	162	Ef	18.48N	11.41W
Raciąż	120	Qd	52.47N	20.06 E
Racibórz	120	Of	50.06N	18.13 E
Racine	182	Jc	42.43N	87.48W
Ráckeve	120	Oi	47.10N	18.57 E
Racos	130	Ic	46.03N	25.30 E
Råda	116	Ed	60.00N	13.36 E
Radama, Iles-	172	Hb	14.00S	47.47 E
Radan	130	Eg	43.02N	21.30 E
Rădăuţi	130	Ib	47.51N	25.55 E
Radbuza	120	Jg	49.46N	13.24 E
Radeberg	120	Je	51.07N	13.55 E
Radebeul	120	Je	51.06N	13.39 E
Radeče	128	Jd	46.04N	15.11 E
Radehov	120	Uf	50.13N	24.43 E
Radenthein	128	Hd	46.48N	13.43 E
Radevormwald	124	Jc	51.12N	7.22 E
Radew	120	Lb	54.07N	15.50 E
Radford	184	Gg	37.07N	80.34W
Radnevo	130	Ig	42.18N	25.56 E
Radolfzell	120	Ei	47.44N	8.58 E
Radom	112	Ie	51.25N	21.10 E
Radom [2]	120	Re	51.25N	21.10 E
Radomir	130	Fg	42.33N	22.58 E
Radomka	120	Re	51.43N	21.26 E
Radomsko	120	Pe	51.05N	19.25 E
Radomyšl	132	Fd	50.29N	29.14 E
Radomyśl Wielki	120	Rf	50.12N	21.16 E
Radoškoviči	116	Lj	54.12N	27.17 E
Radotín	120	Kg	49.59N	14.22 E
Radovanu	130	Je	44.12N	26.31 E
Radoviš	130	Fh	41.38N	22.28 E
Radøy	116	Ad	60.40N	5.00 E
Radstadt	128	Hc	47.23N	13.27 E
Radun	120	Vb	54.02N	25.07 E
Radunia	120	Ob	54.25N	18.45 E
Raduša	128	Lg	43.52N	17.29 E
Radvaniči	120	Ue	51.59N	24.09 E
Radviliškis	114	Fi	55.50N	23.33 E
Raḑwā, Jabal-	144	Ee	24.36N	38.18 E
Radymno	120	Sg	49.57N	22.48 E
Radziejów	120	Od	52.38N	18.32 E
Radzyń Podlaski	120	Se	51.48N	22.38 E
Rae	180	Fd	62.50N	116.00W
Rāe Bareli	148	Gc	26.13N	81.14 E
Rae Isthmus	180	Ic	66.55N	86.10W
Raesfeld	124	Ic	51.46N	6.51 E
Raeside, Lake-	212	Ee	29.30S	121.50 E
Raetihi	218	Fc	39.26S	175.17 E
Raevavae, Ile-	208	Mg	23.52S	147.40W
Raevski, Groupe-	216	Mc	16.45S	144.14W
Rāf, Jabal-	146	Hh	29.12N	39.48 E
Rafaela	200	Ji	31.17S	61.30W
Rafaï	168	Ce	4.58N	23.56 E
Rafḩā'	144	Fd	29.42N	43.30 E
Rafi	166	Fc	13.28N	4.10 E
Rāfkā	146	Qe	35.55N	57.36 E
Rafsanjān	144	Ic	30.24N	56.01 E
Räfsö/Reposaari	116	Ic	61.37N	21.27 E
Raga	160	Jh	8.28N	25.41 E
Ragay Gulf	150	Hd	13.30N	122.45 E
Ragged Island	194	Jb	22.12N	75.44W
Ragged Island Range	190	Id	22.42N	75.55W
Ragged Point	197q	Bb	13.10N	59.25W
Raglan	218	Fb	37.48S	174.52 E
Raguencau	184	Ma	49.04N	68.32W
Ragunda	114	De	63.04N	16.24 E
Ragusa	128	In	36.55N	14.44 E
Raguva	116	Ki	55.30N	24.45 E
Raha	150	Hg	4.51S	122.43 E
Raḩá, Ḩarrat ar-	146	Gi	27.40N	36.40 E
Rahad al Bardī	168	Cc	11.18N	23.53 E
Rahama	166	Gc	10.25N	8.41 E
Raḩaţ, Ḩarrat-	164	He	23.00N	40.05 E
Rahat Dağı	130	Ml	37.08N	29.49 E
Rahden	124	Kb	52.26N	8.37 E
Rāhgāmāti	148	Id	22.38N	92.12 E
Rahīmyār Khan	148	Ec	28.25N	70.18 E
Rahmanovskije Ključi	136	If	49.35N	86.35 E
Rahmet	136	Gf	49.19N	65.16 E
Råholt	116	Dd	60.16N	11.11 E
Rahouia	126	Ni	35.32N	1.01 E
Rahov	132	De	48.02N	24.18 E
Rahrbach, Kirchhundem-	124	Jc	51.02N	7.59 E
Raia	126	Df	39.00N	8.17W
Raiatea, Ile-	208	Lf	16.50S	151.25W
Raices	204	Cj	31.54S	59.16W
Rāichūr	142	Jh	16.12N	77.22 E
Raiganj	148	Hc	25.37N	88.07 E
Raigarh	148	Gd	21.54N	83.24 E
Raijua, Pulau-	150	Hi	10.37S	121.36 E
Rainbow Peak	188	Hd	44.55N	115.17W
Rainier, Mount-	174	Ge	46.52N	121.46W
Rainy Lake	182	Ib	48.42N	93.10W
Rainy River	186	Ib	48.43N	94.29W
Rainy River	186	Ib	48.50N	94.41W
Raipur	142	Kg	21.14N	81.38 E
Raisi, Punta-	128	Hl	38.11N	13.06 E
Raisio/Reso	114	Ff	60.29N	22.11 E
Raita Bank (EN)	214	Mb	25.25N	169.30W
Raja Ampat, Kepulauan-	150	Jg	0.50S	130.25 E
Rājahmundry	142	Kh	16.59N	81.47 E
Rajakoski	114	Gb	68.59N	29.07 E
Rajang	140	Ni	2.07N	111.12 E
Rājapālaiyam	148	Fg	9.27N	77.34 E
Rājasthān [3]	148	Ec	26.00N	74.00 E
Rājasthān Canal	148	Eb	31.10N	75.00 E
Rajbiraj	148	Hc	26.30N	86.50 E
Rajčihinsk	138	Hg	49.43N	129.27 E
Rajevski	134	Gi	54.04N	54.56 E
Rājgarh	148	Fc	28.38N	75.23 E
Rajgródzkie, Jezioro-	120	Sc	53.45N	22.38 E
Rajka	120	Ni	48.00N	17.12 E
Rajkot	142	Jg	22.18N	70.47 E
Raj Nāndgaon	148	Gd	21.06N	81.02 E
Rajony respublikanskogo podčinenija [Kirg.-U.S.S.R.] [3]	136	Hg	42.30N	73.50 E
Rajony respublikanskogo podčinenija [Taj.-U.S.S.R.] [3]	136	Gh	38.50N	69.30 E
Rājshāhi	148	Hd	24.22N	88.36 E
Rakahanga Atoll	208	Ke	10.02S	161.05W
Rakaia	218	Ee	43.45S	172.01 E
Rakaia	218	Ee	43.54S	172.13 E
Rakan, Ra's-	146	Ni	26.10N	51.13 E
Rakata, Pulau-	150	Eh	6.10S	105.26 E
Raka Zangbo	152	Ef	29.24N	87.58 E
Rakhawt, Wādī-	168	Ib	18.16N	51.50 E
Rakht-e Shāh	146	Mf	33.17N	49.23 E
Rakitnoje	154	Mb	45.36N	134.17 E
Rakitovo	130	Hh	41.59N	24.05 E
Rakkestad	116	De	59.26N	11.21 E
Rakoniewice	120	Md	52.10N	16.16 E
Rakops	172	Cd	21.01S	24.20 E
Rakovnicka panev	120	Jf	50.10N	13.30 E
Rakovník	120	Jf	50.06N	13.43 E
Rakovski	130	Hg	42.18N	24.58 E
Raków	120	Rf	50.42N	21.03 E

Index Symbols

[1] Independent Nation · [2] State, Region · [3] District, County · [4] Municipality · [5] Colony, Dependency · Continent · Physical Region · Historical or Cultural Region · Mount, Mountain · Volcano · Hill · Mountains, Mountain Range · Hills, Escarpment · Plateau, Upland · Pass, Gap · Plain, Lowland · Delta · Salt Flat · Valley, Canyon · Crater, Cave · Karst Features · Depression · Polder · Desert, Dunes · Forest, Woods · Heath, Steppe · Oasis · Cape, Point · Coast, Beach · Cliff · Peninsula · Isthmus · Sandbank · Island · Atoll · Rock, Reef · Islands, Archipelago · Rocks, Reefs · Coral Reef · Well, Spring · Geyser · River, Stream · Waterfall, Rapids · River Mouth, Estuary · Lake · Salt Lake · Intermittent Lake · Reservoir · Swamp, Pond · Canal · Glacier · Ice Shelf, Pack Ice · Ocean · Sea · Gulf, Bay · Strait, Fjord · Lagoon · Bank · Seamount · Tablemount · Ridge · Shelf · Basin · Escarpment, Sea Scarp · Fracture · Trench, Abyss · National Park, Reserve · Point of Interest · Recreation Site · Cave, Cavern · Historic Site · Ruins · Wall, Walls · Church, Abbey · Temple · Scientific Station · Railway station · Airport · Port · Military installation · Lighthouse · Mine · Tunnel · Dam, Bridge

Rakušečny, mys- ▶ | 132 | Qh | 42.52N | 51.55 E
Råkvåg | 114 | Ce | 63.46N | 10.05 E
Rakvere | 114 | Gg | 59.22N | 26.22 E
Raleigh [N.C.-U.S.] | 176 | Lf | 35.47N | 78.39W
Raleigh [Ont.-Can.] | 186 | Kb | 49.31N | 91.56W
Raleigh Bay ◨ | 184 | Ih | 35.00N | 76.20W
Ralik Chain ▣ | 208 | Hd | 8.00N | 167.00 E
Rama | 190 | Hf | 12.09N | 84.15W
Rama, Rio- �024 | 194 | Eg | 12.08N | 84.13W
Ramādah | 162 | Jc | 32.19N | 10.24 E
Ramaḍīn, Wādī- �024 | 146 | Ej | 24.57N | 32.34 E
Ramales de la Victoria | 126 | Ia | 43.15N | 3.27W
Ramalho, Serra do- ▲ | 204 | Ja | 13.45S | 44.00W
Ramapo Bank (EN) ▨ | 208 | Fb | 27.15N | 145.10 E
Ramatlabama | 172 | De | 25.37S | 25.30 E
Ramberg ▲ | 120 | He | 51.45N | 11.05 E
Rambervillers | 122 | Mf | 48.21N | 6.38 E
Rambi ◈ | 219d | Cb | 16.30S | 179.59W
Rambouillet | 122 | Hf | 48.39N | 1.50 E
Rambutyo Island ◈ | 208 | Fe | 2.18S | 147.48 E
Rāmhormoz | 146 | Mg | 31.16N | 49.36 E
Ramigala/Ramygala | 116 | Ki | 55.28N | 24.23 E
Ramis �024 | 168 | Gd | 8.02N | 41.36 E
Ramla | 146 | Fg | 31.55N | 34.52 E
Ramlīyah, 'Aqabat ar- ▱ | 146 | Di | 26.01N | 30.42 E
Ramlu ▲ | 146 | Ic | 13.20N | 41.45 E
Ramm, Jabal- ▲ | 146 | Fh | 29.35N | 35.24 E
Rammāk, Ghurd ar- ▦ | 146 | Ch | 29.40N | 29.20 E
Rāmnagar | 148 | Fc | 29.24N | 79.07 E
Ramnäs | 116 | Ge | 59.46N | 16.12 E
Ramón Santamarina | 204 | Cn | 38.26S | 59.20W
Ramos | 219a | Ec | 8.16S | 160.11 E
Ramos, Rio- �024 | 192 | Ge | 25.35N | 105.03W
Ramotswa | 172 | Dd | 24.52S | 25.50 E
Rāmpur | 148 | Fc | 28.49N | 79.02 E
Ramree ◈ | 148 | Ie | 19.06N | 93.48 E
Rams | 146 | Qj | 25.53N | 56.02 E
Ramsele | 114 | De | 63.33N | 16.29 E
Ramsey [Eng.-U.K.] | 124 | Bb | 52.27N | 0.07W
Ramsey [I. of M.] | 118 | Sg | 54.20N | 4.21W
Ramsey [Ont.-Can.] | 184 | Fb | 47.29N | 82.24W
Ramsey Lake ◠ | 180 | Jg | 47.20N | 83.00W
Rāmshir | 146 | Mg | 30.50N | 49.30 E
Ramsjö | 114 | De | 62.11N | 15.39 E
Ramstein-Miesenbach | 124 | Je | 49.27N | 7.32 E
Ramsund | 114 | Db | 68.29N | 16.32 E
Ramu | 170 | Hb | 3.56N | 41.13 E
Ramu �024 | 214 | Dh | 4.02S | 144.41 E
Ramvik | 114 | De | 62.49N | 17.51 E
Ramville, Ilet- ◈ | 197h | Bb | 14.42N | 60.53W
Ramygala/Ramigala | 116 | Ki | 55.28N | 24.23 E
Rana ◨ | 114 | Dc | 66.20N | 14.08 E
Rañadoiro, Sierra del- ▲ | 126 | Fa | 43.20N | 6.45W
Ranai | 150 | Ef | 3.55N | 108.23 E
Ranakah, Potjo- ▲ | 150 | Hh | 8.38S | 120.31 E
Rana Kao, Volcán- ▲ | 221d | Ac | 27.11S | 109.27W
Rana Roi, Volcán- ▲ | 221d | Bb | 27.05S | 109.23W
Rana Roraka, Volcán- ▲ | 221d | Bb | 27.07S | 109.18W
Ranau | 150 | Ge | 5.58N | 116.41 E
Rança ▲ | 128 | Lf | 44.24N | 17.22 E
Rancagua | 200 | Ii | 34.10S | 70.45W
Rance ◨ | 122 | Ef | 48.31N | 1.59W
Rancharia | 204 | Gf | 22.15S | 50.55W
Rancheria, Rio- �024 | 194 | Kh | 11.34N | 72.54W
Ränchī | 142 | Kg | 23.21N | 85.20 E
Ranchos | 204 | Cl | 35.32S | 58.22W
Ranco, Lago- ◠ | 206 | Ff | 40.14S | 72.24W
Randa | 168 | Gc | 11.51N | 42.40 E
Randaberg | 116 | Ae | 59.00N | 5.36 E
Randazzo | 128 | Im | 37.53N | 14.57 E
Randers | 114 | Dh | 56.28N | 10.03 E
Randers Fjord ▱ | 116 | Dh | 56.35N | 10.22 E
Randijaure ◠ | 114 | Kc | 66.42N | 19.18 E
Randow �024 | 120 | Kc | 53.41N | 14.04 E
Randsfjorden ▱ | 114 | Cf | 60.05N | 10.25 E
Ranérou | 166 | Cb | 15.18N | 13.58W
Ranfurly | 218 | Df | 45.08S | 170.06 E
Rangasa, Tanjung- ▶ | 150 | Gg | 3.33S | 118.56 E
Ranger | 186 | Gj | 32.28N | 98.41W
Rangiora | 218 | Ea | 43.18S | 172.36 E
Rangiroa Atoll ⌾ | 208 | Mf | 15.10S | 147.35W
Rangitaiki �024 | 218 | Gb | 37.55S | 176.53 E
Rangitata �024 | 218 | Df | 44.10S | 171.30 E
Rangitikei �024 | 218 | Fd | 40.17S | 175.13 E
Rangkasbitung | 150 | Fh | 6.21S | 106.15 E
Rangoon (EN) = Yangon | 142 | Lh | 16.47N | 96.10 E
Rangpur | 148 | Hc | 25.44N | 89.16 E
Rāniyah | 146 | Kd | 36.15N | 44.53 E
Rankin Inlet | 176 | Jc | 62.45N | 92.10W
Rankoshi | 156a | Bb | 42.47N | 140.31 E
Rannoch, Loch- ◠ | 118 | Ie | 56.41N | 4.20W
Ranobe ◨ | 172 | Gc | 17.10S | 44.08 E
Ranon | 219b | Dc | 16.09S | 168.07 E
Ranong | 148 | Jg | 9.59N | 98.40 E
Ranongga Island ◈ | 214 | Fi | 8.05S | 156.34 E
Ranova �024 | 132 | Sa | 54.07N | 40.14 E
Ransaren ◠ | 114 | Dd | 65.14N | 14.59 E
Ransiki | 150 | Jg | 1.27S | 134.12 E
Rantabe | 172 | Hc | 15.42S | 49.39 E
Rantasalmi | 116 | Mb | 62.04N | 28.18 E
Rantaupanjang | 150 | Fg | 1.23S | 112.04 E
Rantauprapat | 150 | Cf | 2.06N | 99.50 E
Rantekombala, Bulu- ▲ | 140 | Qj | 3.21S | 120.01 E
Rantoul | 186 | Lf | 40.19N | 88.09W
Ranua | 114 | Gd | 65.55N | 26.32 E
Ranyah, Wādī- �024 | 164 | He | 21.18N | 43.20 E
Raohe | 146 | Nb | 46.48N | 133.58 E
Raon-l'Étape | 122 | Mf | 48.24N | 6.51 E
Raoui, Erg er- ▦ | 162 | Gd | 29.15N | 2.00W
Raoul Island | 208 | Jg | 29.15S | 177.52W
Raoyang | 154 | Ce | 38.14N | 115.44 E
Raoyang He �024 | 154 | Gd | 41.13N | 122.12 E
Rapa, Ile- ◈ | 208 | Mg | 27.36S | 144.20W
Rapallo | 128 | Df | 44.21N | 9.14 E
Rapang | 150 | Gg | 3.50S | 119.48 E

Rapa Nui / Pascua, Isla de- = Easter Island (EN) ◈ | 208 | Qg | 27.07S | 109.22W
Raper, Cape- ▶ | 180 | Kc | 69.41N | 67.24W
Rapid City | 176 | Lf | 44.05N | 103.14W
Rapid Creek �024 | 186 | Ee | 43.54N | 102.37W
Rapid River | 184 | Dc | 45.58N | 86.59W
Räpina/Rjapina | 116 | Lf | 58.03N | 27.35 E
Rapla | 114 | Fg | 59.02N | 24.47 E
Rappahannock River �024 | 184 | Jf | 37.34N | 76.18W
Rápulo, Rio- �024 | 198 | Jg | 13.43S | 65.32W
Räqūbah | 160 | If | 28.58N | 19.02 E
Raraka Atoll ⌾ | 208 | Mf | 16.10S | 144.54W
Raroia Atoll ⌾ | 208 | Mf | 16.05S | 142.26W
Rarotonga Island ◈ | 208 | Lg | 21.14S | 159.46W
Rasa, Punta- ▶ | 198 | Jj | 40.51S | 62.19W
Ra's Abū Daraj | 146 | Eh | 29.23N | 32.33 E
Ra's Abū Rudays | 146 | Eh | 28.53N | 33.11 E
Ra's Abū Shajarah ▶ | 146 | Fa | 21.04N | 37.14 E
Ra's Ajdir | 128 | Em | 37.13N | 10.08 E
Ra's al 'Ayn | 146 | Id | 36.51N | 40.04 E
Ra's al-Barr ◨ | 146 | Dj | 31.31N | 31.50 E
Ra's al Ḥikmah | 146 | Bg | 31.08N | 27.50 E
Ra's al Jabal | 128 | Em | 37.13N | 10.08 E
Ra's al Khafjī | 146 | Mh | 28.25N | 48.30 E
Ra's al Khaymah | 144 | Id | 25.47N | 55.57 E
Ra's al Mish'āb | 146 | Mh | 28.12N | 48.37 E
Ra's al Unūf | 164 | Cc | 30.31N | 18.34 E
Ra's an Naqb | 146 | Fh | 30.00N | 35.29 E
Ra's as Sidr | 146 | Eh | 29.36N | 32.40 E
Ra's at Tannūrah | 146 | Ni | 26.42N | 50.10 E
Raya, Cape- ▶ | 180 | Lg | 47.37N | 59.19W
Raya, Bukit- ▲ | 140 | Nj | 1.32S | 111.05 E
Rayadrug | 148 | Ff | 14.42N | 76.52 E
Rayät | 146 | Kd | 36.40N | 44.58 E
Rayleigh | 124 | Cc | 51.35N | 0.37 E
Raymond [Alta.-Can.] | 186 | Ib | 49.27N | 112.39W
Raymond [Wa.-U.S.] | 188 | Dc | 46.41N | 123.44W
Raymondville | 182 | Hf | 26.29N | 97.47W
Rayne | 186 | Jk | 30.14N | 92.16W
Rayón [Mex.] | 192 | Jg | 21.51N | 99.40W
Rayón [Mex.] | 192 | De | 29.43N | 110.35W
Rayones | 192 | Ie | 25.01N | 100.05W
Rayong | 148 | Kf | 12.40N | 101.17 E
Raysūt | 144 | Hf | 16.54N | 54.02 E
Raytown | 186 | Jg | 39.00N | 94.28W
Raz, Pointe du- ▶ | 122 | Bf | 48.02N | 4.44W
Razan | 146 | Me | 35.23N | 49.02 E
Razdan | 146 | Ni | 40.28N | 44.43 E
Razdolinsk | 136 | Ee | 58.25N | 94.44 E
Razdolnaja �024 | 154 | Kc | 43.20N | 131.49 E
Razdolnaja ◈ | 154 | Kc | 43.33N | 131.55 E
Razdolnoje [R.S.F.S.R.] | 154 | Kc | 43.33N | 131.55 E
Razdolnoje [Ukr.-U.S.S.R.] | 132 | Hg | 45.47N | 33.30 E
Razgrad | 130 | Jf | 43.32N | 26.31 E
Razgrad ② | 130 | Jf | 43.32N | 26.31 E
Razī | 146 | Mc | 38.32N | 48.08 E
Razlog | 130 | Gh | 41.53N | 23.28 E
Razo | 162 | Cf | 16.37N | 24.36W
Ré, Ile de- ◈ | 110 | Hf | 46.12N | 1.25W
Reachlainn/Rathlin Island ◈ | 118 | Gf | 55.18N | 6.13W
Reachrainn/Lambay ◈ | 118 | Gh | 53.29N | 6.01W
Reading [Eng.-U.K.] | 118 | Mj | 51.28N | 0.59W
Reading [Pa.-U.S.] | 182 | Lc | 40.20N | 75.55W
Real, Cordillera- [Bol.] ▲ | 202 | Eg | 16.30S | 68.30W
Real, Cordillera- [Ec.] ▲ | 198 | If | 3.00S | 78.00W
Real Audiencia | 204 | Ca | 36.11S | 58.35W
Real del Castillo | 192 | Aa | 31.58N | 116.19W
Réalmont | 122 | Ik | 43.47N | 2.12 E
Reao Atoll ⌾ | 208 | Nf | 18.31S | 136.23W
Reatini, Monti- ▲ | 128 | Gh | 42.35N | 12.50 E
Rebais | 124 | Ff | 48.51N | 3.14 E
Rebecca, Lake- ◠ | 212 | Ee | 29.55S | 122.01 E
Rebiana Oasis (EN) = Rabyānah, Wāḥāt al- ▨ | 164 | De | 24.14N | 21.59 E
Rebollera ▲ | 126 | Hf | 38.25N | 4.02W
Reboly | 114 | He | 63.52N | 30.47 E
Rebord Manamblen ▲ | 172 | Hd | 24.05S | 46.30 E
Rebun-Dake ▲ | 154 | Pb | 45.23N | 141.02 E
Rebun Island ◈ | 156a | Ba | 45.25N | 141.01 E
Rebun-Suidō ▱ | 156a | Ba | 45.15N | 141.05 E
Rebun-Tō ◈ | 152 | Pb | 45.23N | 141.01 E
Recalde | 204 | Bm | 36.39S | 61.05W
Recanati | 128 | Hg | 43.24N | 13.32 E
Recaș | 130 | Ed | 45.48N | 21.30 E
Recherche, Archipelago of the- ▣ | 208 | Dh | 34.06S | 122.45 E
Rečica | 136 | De | 52.22N | 30.25 E
Recife | 198 | Mf | 8.03S | 34.54W
Recife, Cape- ▶ | 158 | Jl | 34.02S | 25.45 E
Recke | 124 | Jb | 52.23N | 7.43 E
Recklinghausen | 120 | Hb | 51.37N | 7.12 E
Recoaro Terme | 128 | Fe | 45.42N | 11.13 E
Reconquista | 206 | Hc | 29.09S | 59.39W
Recovery Glacier ▨ | 222 | Ag | 81.10S | 28.00W
Recreo | 206 | Gc | 29.16S | 65.04W
Recz | 120 | Lc | 53.16N | 15.33 E
Reda �024 | 120 | Ob | 54.38N | 18.30 E
Red Bank | 124 | He | 49.46N | 5.54 E
Red Bay | 180 | Lf | 51.44N | 56.25W
Red Bluff | 182 | Cc | 40.11N | 122.15W
Red Bluff Reservoir ◡ | 186 | Fj | 31.57N | 103.56W
Redbridge, London- | 124 | Ec | 51.35N | 0.05 E
Redcar | 118 | Li | 54.37N | 1.04W
Redcliff ▶ | 197c | Ab | 17.05N | 62.32W
Redcliffe, Mount- ▲ | 212 | Ee | 28.25S | 121.32 E
Red Cloud | 186 | Gf | 40.05N | 98.32W
Red Deer | 176 | Id | 52.16N | 113.48W
Red Deer [Can.] �024 | 180 | If | 50.56N | 109.54W
Red Deer [Can.] �024 | 180 | If | 52.55N | 101.27W
Redding | 176 | Jf | 40.35N | 122.24W
Redditch | 118 | Li | 52.19N | 1.56W

Ravänsar | 146 | Le | 34.43N | 46.40 E
Ravanusa | 128 | Hm | 37.16N | 13.58 E
Rävar | 146 | Qg | 31.12N | 56.53 E
Rava-Russkaja | 132 | Ce | 50.13N | 23.37 E
Ravels | 124 | Gc | 51.22N | 4.59 E
Ravelsbach | 128 | Jb | 48.30N | 15.50 E
Ravels-Poppel | 124 | Kc | 51.27N | 5.02 E
Ravenna [It.] | 128 | Gf | 44.25N | 12.12 E
Ravenna [Nb.-U.S.] | 186 | Gf | 41.02N | 98.55W
Ravensburg | 120 | Fi | 47.47N | 9.37 E
Ravenshoe | 210 | Ff | 17.37S | 145.29 E
Ravensthorpe | 212 | Ef | 33.35S | 120.02 E
Ravi �024 | 150 | Jf | 30.35N | 71.49 E
Ravnina | 136 | Dh | 37.57N | 62.42 E
Rawaki Atoll (Phoenix) ⌾ | 208 | Je | 3.43S | 170.43W
Rāwalpindi | 142 | Jf | 33.35N | 73.03 E
Rawa Mazowiecka | 120 | Qe | 51.46N | 20.16 E
Rawāndūz | 146 | Kd | 36.37N | 44.31 E
Rawdah | 146 | Ic | 35.15N | 41.05 E
Rawene | 218 | Ea | 35.24S | 173.30 E
Rawicz | 120 | Me | 51.37N | 16.52 E
Rawka �024 | 120 | Qd | 52.07N | 20.08 E
Rawlinna | 210 | Dh | 31.01S | 125.20 E
Rawlins | 182 | Fc | 41.47N | 107.14W
Rawlinson Range ▲ | 212 | Fd | 24.50S | 128.00 E
Rawson [Arg.] | 200 | Jj | 43.18S | 65.06W
Rawson [Arg.] | 204 | Bl | 34.36S | 60.04W
Rawura, Ras- ▶ | 170 | He | 10.20S | 40.30 E
Raxaul | 148 | Gc | 26.59N | 84.51 E
Raz, Pointe du- ▶ | 122 | Bf | 48.02N | 4.44W

Rede ◠ | 118 | Kf | 55.08N | 2.13W
Redenção | 202 | Kd | 4.13S | 38.43W
Redfield | 182 | Hc | 44.53N | 98.31W
Red Hill ▲ | 221b | Ec | 20.43N | 156.15W
Red Hills ▲ | 186 | Gh | 37.25N | 99.25W
Redkino | 114 | Nh | 56.40N | 36.19 E
Red Lake | 180 | If | 51.03N | 93.49W
Red Lake River �024 | 186 | Hc | 47.55N | 97.01W
Red Lakes ◠ | 182 | Ib | 48.05N | 94.45W
Red Lodge | 188 | Kd | 45.11N | 109.15W
Redmond | 182 | Cc | 44.17N | 121.11W
Red Oak | 186 | If | 41.01N | 95.14W
Redon | 122 | Dg | 47.39N | 2.05W
Redonda ◈ | 196 | Ed | 16.55N | 62.19W
Redondela | 126 | Db | 42.17N | 8.36W
Redondo ◈ | 126 | Ef | 38.39N | 7.33W
Redondo Beach | 188 | Fj | 33.51N | 118.23W
Redoubt Volcano ▲ | 174 | Dc | 60.29N | 152.45W
Red River [N.Amer.] �024 | 174 | Jd | 50.24N | 96.48W
Red River [U.S.] �024 | 174 | Jf | 31.00N | 91.40W
Red River (EN) = Hông, Sông- [Asia] �024 | 140 | Mg | 20.17N | 106.34 E
Red River (EN) = Yuan Jiang [Asia] �024 | 140 | Mg | 20.17N | 106.34 E
Red Rock, Lake- ◡ | 186 | Jf | 41.30N | 93.20W
Red Rock River �024 | 188 | Jd | 44.59N | 112.52W
Redruth | 118 | Hk | 50.13N | 5.14W
Red Sea (EN) = Aḥmar, Al Baḥr al- ▤ | 158 | Kf | 25.00N | 38.00 E
Redstone | 188 | Da | 52.08N | 123.42W
Redwater Creek �024 | 188 | Mb | 48.03N | 105.13W
Red Wing | 182 | Ic | 44.34N | 92.31W
Redwood City | 188 | Dg | 37.29N | 122.13W
Redwood Falls | 186 | Id | 44.32N | 95.07W
Ree, Lough-/Loch Rí ◠ | 118 | Fh | 53.35N | 8.00W
Reed City | 184 | Ed | 43.53N | 85.31W
Reedley | 188 | Fh | 36.24N | 119.27W
Reeds Peak ▲ | 186 | Cj | 33.09N | 107.51W
Reedsport | 182 | Cc | 43.42N | 124.06W
Reedy Glacier ▨ | 222 | Bg | 85.30S | 134.00W
Reef Islands ▣ | 208 | Hf | 10.15S | 166.10 E
Reefton | 218 | De | 42.07S | 171.52 E
Reepham | 124 | Db | 52.45N | 1.07 E
Rees | 124 | Ic | 51.46N | 6.24 E
Reese River �024 | 188 | Gf | 40.39N | 116.54W
Refahiye | 146 | Hc | 39.54N | 38.46 E
Reforma, Rio- �024 | 192 | Be | 26.56N | 108.12W
Reftele | 116 | Eg | 57.11N | 13.35 E
Reftinski | 134 | Jh | 57.10N | 61.43 E
Refugio | 186 | Hl | 28.18N | 97.17W
Rega �024 | 120 | Lc | 54.10N | 15.18 E
Regar | 136 | Dh | 38.34N | 68.13 E
Regen | 120 | Jh | 48.58N | 13.08 E
Regen �024 | 120 | Ig | 49.01N | 12.06 E
Regensburg | 120 | If | 49.01N | 12.06 E
Reggane | 160 | Hf | 26.42N | 0.10 E
Reggio di Calabria | 112 | Mh | 38.06N | 15.39 E
Reggio nell'Emilia | 128 | Ef | 44.43N | 10.36 E
Reghin | 130 | Hc | 46.46N | 24.42 E
Regina [Fr.Gui.] | 202 | Hc | 4.19N | 52.08W
Regina [Sask.-Can.] | 176 | Id | 50.25N | 104.39W
Registan (EN) = Rīgestān ▨ | 140 | If | 31.00N | 65.00 E
Registro | 204 | Ig | 24.30S | 47.50W
Registro do Araguaia | 204 | Gb | 15.44S | 51.50W
Regnitz �024 | 120 | Ig | 49.54N | 10.49 E
Regocijo | 192 | Gg | 23.35N | 105.11W
Reguengos de Monsaraz | 126 | Ef | 38.25N | 7.32W
Rehburg-Loccum | 124 | De | 52.28N | 9.14 E
Rehoboth | 172 | Bd | 23.18S | 17.03 E
Rehoboth ◨ | 172 | Bd | 23.50S | 17.00 E
Reḥovot | 146 | Tg | 31.54N | 34.49 E
Reichelsheim (Odenwald) | 124 | Ke | 49.43N | 8.51 E
Reichenbach | 120 | Jf | 50.37N | 12.18 E
Reichshof | 124 | Jd | 50.55N | 7.39 E
Reichshof-Denklingen | 124 | Jd | 50.55N | 7.39 E
Reichshoffen | 124 | Jf | 48.56N | 7.40 E
Reidsville | 184 | Hg | 36.21N | 79.40W
Reigate | 118 | Mj | 51.14N | 0.13W
Reims | 112 | Gf | 49.15N | 4.02 E
Rein = Rhine (EN) �024 | 110 | Ge | 51.52N | 6.02 E
Reina Adelaida, Archipiélago- ▣ | 198 | Ik | 52.10S | 74.25W
Reindeer ◈ | 180 | Ie | 55.34N | 103.10W
Reindeer Bank (EN) ▨ | 197p | Ac | 15.00N | 97.00 E
Reindeer Lake ◠ | 176 | Id | 57.15N | 102.40W
Reineskarvet ▲ | 116 | Cd | 60.47N | 8.13 E
Reinga, Cape- ▶ | 218 | Ea | 34.25S | 172.41 E
Reinhardswald ▲ | 124 | Fe | 51.30N | 9.36 E
Reinosa | 110 | Ha | 43.00N | 4.08W
Reitoru Atoll ⌾ | 208 | Mf | 17.52S | 143.05W
Reitz | 172 | Ee | 27.53S | 28.31 E
Rejmyra | 116 | Ff | 58.50N | 15.55 E
Rejowiec Fabryczny | 120 | Te | 51.08N | 23.13 E
Reka Devnja | 130 | Kf | 43.13N | 27.36 E
Rekarne ▣ | 116 | Ge | 59.20N | 16.08 E
Reken | 124 | Jc | 51.48N | 7.03 E
Reliance | 176 | Id | 62.42N | 109.08W
Relizane | 162 | Hb | 35.45N | 0.33 E
Remagen | 124 | Jd | 50.34N | 7.14 E
Remarkable, Mount- ▲ | 212 | Hf | 32.48S | 138.10 E
Rembang | 150 | Fh | 6.42S | 111.20 E
Remedios | 194 | Cg | 13.31N | 89.49W
Remedios, Punta- ▶ | 194 | Cg | 13.31N | 89.49W
Remedios, Rio- �024 | 194 | Mh | 11.01N | 69.15W
Rémire | 202 | Hc | 4.53S | 52.17W
Remiremont | 122 | Mf | 48.01N | 6.35 E
Remire Reef ◨ | 172b | Bb | 5.05S | 53.22 E

Remontnoje | 132 | Mf | 46.33N | 43.40 E
Remoulins | 122 | Kk | 43.56N | 4.34 E
Remscheid | 120 | De | 51.11N | 7.12 E
Rena ◠ | 114 | Df | 61.08N | 11.23 E
Rena �024 | 116 | Dc | 61.08N | 11.23 E
Renaix/Ronse | 122 | Jd | 50.45N | 3.36 E
Renard Islands ▣ | 219a | Ad | 10.50S | 153.00 E
Renaud Island ◈ | 222 | Qe | 65.40S | 66.00W
Rende | 128 | Kk | 39.20N | 16.11 E
Rendezvous Bay ◨ | 197b | Ab | 18.10N | 63.07W
Rend Lake ◠ | 186 | Lg | 38.05N | 88.58W
Rendova Island ◈ | 214 | Fi | 8.32S | 157.20 E
Rendsburg | 120 | Fb | 54.18N | 9.40 E
Renfrew | 180 | Jg | 45.28N | 76.41W
Rengat | 150 | Dg | 0.24S | 102.33 E
Rengo | 206 | Pa | 34.25S | 70.52W
Reni | 132 | Fg | 45.29N | 28.18 E
Renko | 116 | Kd | 60.54N | 24.17 E
Renkum | 124 | Hc | 51.58N | 5.45 E
Renland ▣ | 179 | Jd | 71.15N | 27.20W
Renmark | 210 | Fh | 34.11S | 140.45 E
Rennell, Islas- ▣ | 206 | Fh | 52.00S | 74.00W
Rennell Island ◈ | 208 | Hf | 11.40S | 160.10 E
Rennes | 112 | Ff | 48.05N | 1.41W
Rennes, Bassin de- ▣ | 122 | Ef | 48.05N | 1.40W
Rennesøy ◈ | 116 | Ae | 59.05N | 5.40 E
Rennick Glacier ▨ | 222 | Kf | 70.30S | 161.45 E
Rennie Lake ◠ | 180 | Gd | 61.10N | 105.30W
Reno | 176 | Hf | 39.31N | 119.48W
Reno �024 | 128 | Gf | 44.38N | 12.16 E
Renqiu | 154 | De | 38.42N | 116.06 E
Rensselaer [In.-U.S.] | 184 | De | 40.57N | 87.09W
Rensselaer [N.Y.-U.S.] | 184 | Kd | 42.37N | 73.44W
Renteria | 126 | Ka | 43.19N | 1.54W
Renton | 188 | Dc | 47.30N | 122.11W
Renwez | 124 | Ge | 49.50N | 4.36 E
Renxian | 154 | De | 37.07N | 114.41 E
Reo | 150 | Hh | 8.19S | 120.30 E
Réole, La- | 122 | Fj | 44.35N | 0.02W
Repartimento, Serra do- ▲ | 204 | Jc | 17.40S | 44.50W
Répce ◉ | 120 | Ni | 47.41N | 17.02 E
Repino | 140 | Mf | 60.10N | 29.58 E
Repong, Pulau- ◈ | 150 | Ef | 2.22N | 105.53 E
Reposaari/Räfsö | 116 | Ic | 61.37N | 21.27 E
Republic | 188 | Fb | 48.39N | 118.44W
Republican River �024 | 174 | Jf | 39.03N | 96.48W
Repulse Bay | 176 | Kc | 66.32N | 86.15W
Repulse Bay [Austl.] ◨ | 212 | Jd | 20.35S | 148.45 E
Repulse Bay [Can.] ◨ | 180 | Ic | 66.20N | 86.00W
Repvåg | 114 | Fa | 70.45N | 25.41 E
Requena [Peru] | 202 | Dd | 5.00S | 73.50W
Requena [Sp.] | 126 | Ie | 39.29N | 1.06W
Requin Bay ◨ | 197p | Bb | 12.02S | 61.38W
Requista | 122 | Ij | 44.02N | 2.32 E
Reşadiye Yarımadası ▶ | 130 | Km | 36.40N | 27.45 E
Reschenpass/Resia, Passo di- ▱ | 128 | Ed | 46.50N | 10.30 E
Resen | 130 | Eh | 41.05N | 21.01 E
Reserva | 204 | Gg | 24.38S | 50.52W
Reserve | 186 | Bj | 33.43N | 108.45W
Resistencia | 200 | Kh | 27.30S | 58.59W
Resita | 112 | Mf | 45.18N | 21.55 E
Reso/Raisio | 116 | Jc | 60.27N | 22.11 E
Reso/Raisio | 114 | Fd | 60.29N | 22.11 E
Resolute | 176 | Jb | 74.41N | 94.54W
Resolution ◈ | 174 | Mc | 61.30N | 65.00W
Resolution Island | 180 | Lc | 61.35N | 64.39W
Resolution Island ◈ | 218 | Bf | 45.40S | 166.35 E
Respublikai Soveti Socialisti Todžikiston/ Tadžikskaja SSR ② | 136 | Cf | 39.00N | 71.00 E
Respublika Sovetike Sočialiste Moldovenjaske/ Moldavskaja SSR ② | 136 | Cf | 47.00N | 29.00 E
Ressa ◠ | 132 | Ib | 54.45N | 35.10 E
Ressons-sur-Matz | 124 | Ee | 49.33N | 2.45 E
Restigouche River �024 | 184 | Na | 48.04N | 66.20W
Restinga de Sefton, Isla- ◈ | 198 | Fi | 29.49S | 53.23W
Restinga Séca | 204 | Fi | 29.49S | 53.23W
Retalhuleu | 190 | Ff | 14.31N | 91.41W
Retalhuleu | 194 | Bf | 14.31N | 91.40W
Retavas/Rietavas | 116 | Ii | 55.43N | 21.49 E
Retezatului, Munţii- ▲ | 130 | Fd | 45.25N | 23.00 E
Rethel | 122 | Kg | 49.31N | 4.22 E
Rethem (Aller) | 124 | Ld | 52.47N | 9.23 E
Réthimnon | 110 | Mh | 35.22N | 24.28 E
Retie | 124 | Hc | 51.17N | 5.05 E
Retortillo ◈ | 126 | Ga | 42.45N | 6.03W
Retournac | 122 | Kj | 45.12N | 4.03 E
Rétság | 120 | Pi | 47.56N | 19.08 E
Rettihovka | 154 | Lb | 44.10N | 132.45 E
Retz | 120 | Kg | 48.45N | 15.57 E
Retz, Pays de- ▣ | 122 | Eg | 47.07N | 1.58W
Réunion = Reunion (EN) ◨ | 160 | Mk | 21.06S | 55.36 E
Reunion (EN) = Réunion ◨ | 160 | Mk | 21.06S | 55.36 E
Reunion (EN) = Réunion ◨ | 158 | Mj | 21.06S | 55.36 E
Reus | 126 | Nc | 41.09N | 1.07 E
Reusel | 124 | Hc | 51.21N | 5.10 E
Reuss �024 | 122 | Nf | 47.28N | 8.14 E
Reut ◠ | 132 | Ff | 47.15N | 29.09 E
Reutlingen | 120 | Fh | 48.29N | 9.13 E
Reutte | 120 | Gi | 47.29N | 10.43 E
Reval (EN) = Tallinn | 114 | Fg | 59.25N | 24.45 E
Revda [R.S.F.S.R.] | 114 | Ic | 67.57N | 34.32 E
Revda [R.S.F.S.R.] | 134 | Ih | 56.48N | 59.57 E
Revel | 122 | Ik | 43.27N | 2.00 E
Revelata, Punta di- ▶ | 122a | Aa | 42.35N | 8.40 E
Revelstoke | 180 | Hf | 50.59N | 118.12W
Revermont ▲ | 122 | Lh | 46.20N | 5.25 E
Revillagigedo | 178 | Me | 55.35N | 131.23W
Revillagigedo, Islas- ▣ | 174 | Hh | 19.00N | 111.30W
Revin | 124 | Ge | 49.56N | 4.38 E
Revoljucii, pik- ▲ | 135 | Ie | 38.33N | 72.28 E
Revsundssjön ◠ | 116 | Fb | 62.50N | 15.15 E

Index Symbols

① Independent Nation	◨ Historical or Cultural Region	▱ Pass, Gap	▨ Depression
② State, Region	▲ Mount, Mountain	▤ Plain, Lowland	▦ Polder
③ District, County	▲ Volcano	▲ Delta	▱ Cliff
④ Municipality	▲ Hill	▦ Salt Flat	▦ Desert, Dunes
⑤ Colony, Dependency	▲ Mountains, Mountain Range	▲ Valley, Canyon	▦ Forest, Woods
◉ Continent	▲ Hills, Escarpment	▲ Crater, Cave	▦ Heath, Steppe
▣ Physical Region	▦ Plateau, Upland	▦ Karst Features	▱ Oasis

▦ Coast, Beach	▨ Rock, Reef	�024 Waterfall, Rapids	◡ Canal
▱ Cliff	◈ Islands, Archipelago	�024 River Mouth, Estuary	▨ Glacier
▶ Peninsula	▨ Rocks, Reefs	◠ Lake	▨ Ice Shelf, Pack Ice
▨ Coral Reef	◠ Salt Lake	▨ Sea	
◈ Island	▱ Well, Spring	◠ Intermittent Lake	▨ Ridge
▶ Cape, Point	▱ Geyser	◡ Reservoir	▱ Gulf, Bay
⌾ Atoll	�024 River, Stream	▨ Swamp, Pond	▱ Strait, Fjord

◉ Lagoon	▨ Escarpment, Sea Scarp	▲ Historic Site	◈ Airport
▦ Bank	▱ Fracture	▲ Ruins	▨ Port
▨ Seamount	▲ Trench, Abyss	▦ Wall, Walls	▨ Military installation
▨ Tablemount	▲ National Park, Reserve	▲ Church, Abbey	▨ Lighthouse
▨ Shelf	▲ Point of Interest	▲ Temple	▨ Mine
▲ Recreation Site	▲ Scientific Station	▨ Tunnel	
▨ Basin	▲ Cave, Cavern	▨ Railway station	▨ Dam, Bridge

Rewa	148	Gd	24.32N	81.18 E
Rewa ∽	219d	Bc	18.08S	178.33 E
Rewāri	148	Fc	28.11N	76.37 E
Rex, Mount- ▲	222	Qf	74.54S	75.57W
Rexburg	188	Je	43.49N	111.47W
Rexpoëde	124	Ed	50.56N	2.32 E
Rey	144	Hb	35.35N	51.25 E
Rey, Arroyo del- ∽	204	Ci	29.12S	59.36W
Rey, Isla del- ◆	190	Ig	8.22N	78.55W
Rey, Laguna del- ⊔	192	Hd	27.00N	103.25W
Rey Bouba	166	Hd	8.40N	14.11 E
Reyes, Point- ▶	188	Dg	38.00N	123.01W
Reyhanli	146	Gd	36.18N	36.32 E
Reykjalid	114a	Cb	65.39N	16.55W
Reykjanes ▶	110	Dc	63.49N	22.43W
Reykjanes Ridge (EN) ⋀	110	Dc	62.00N	27.00W
Reykjavik	112	Dc	64.09N	21.57W
Reynolds Range ⛰	212	Gd	22.20S	132.50 E
Reynosa	176	Jg	26.07N	98.18W
Reyssouze ∽	122	Kh	46.27N	4.54 E
Rež	134	Jh	57.23N	61.24 E
Rež ∽	134	Kh	57.54N	62.20 E
Rezé	122	Eg	47.12N	1.34W
Rezekne/Rēzekne	112	Id	56.30N	27.19 E
Rēzekne/Rezekne	112	Id	56.30N	27.19 E
Rezelm, Lacul- ⊔	130	Le	44.54N	28.57 E
Rezina	132	Ff	47.43N	28.58 E
Reznas, ozero- / Rēznas ezers ⊔	116	Lh	56.20N	27.30 E
Rēznas ezers / Reznas, ozero- ⊔	116	Lh	56.20N	27.30 E
Rezovo	130	Lh	41.59N	28.02 E
Reẕvān	146	Qi	27.34N	56.06 E
Rezve ∽	130	Lh	41.59N	28.01 E
Rgotina	130	Fe	44.01N	22.17 E
Rhaetian Alps (EN)=Alpi Retiche ⛰	128	Dd	46.30N	10.00 E
Rhaetian Alps (EN)= Rätische Alpen ⛰	128	Dd	46.30N	10.00 E
Rhallamane ⊠	158	Ff	23.15N	10.00W
Rhauderfehn	124	Ja	53.08N	7.34 E
Rhaunen	124	Je	49.51N	7.21 E
Rheda-Wiedenbrück	120	Ee	51.51N	8.18 E
Rheden	124	Ib	52.01N	6.01 E
Rheden-Dieren	124	Ib	52.03N	6.08 E
Rheider Land ⊠	124	Ja	53.13N	7.18 E
Rhein=Rhine (EN) ∽	110	Ge	51.52N	6.02 E
Rheinberg	124	Ic	51.33N	6.36 E
Rheine	120	Dd	52.17N	7.27 E
Rheinfall ⋎	128	Cc	47.41N	8.38 E
Rheinfelden (Baden)	120	Di	47.34N	7.48 E
Rheingaugebirge ⛰	120	Ef	50.05N	8.00 E
Rheinhessen ⊠	124	Ke	49.52N	8.07 E
Rheinisches Schiefergebirge =Rhenish Slate Mountains (EN) ⛰	110	Ge	50.25N	7.10 E
Rheinland-Pfalz=Rhineland-Palatinate (EN) ②	120	Cf	50.00N	7.00 E
Rheinsberg / Mark	120	Ic	53.06N	12.53 E
Rheinstetten	124	Kf	48.58N	8.18 E
Rhenen	124	Hc	51.58N	5.35 E
Rhenish Slate Mountains (EN)=Rheinisches Schiefergebirge ⛰	110	Ge	50.25N	7.10 E
Rheris ∽	162	Gc	30.41N	4.57W
Rheydt, Mönchengladbach-	124	Ic	51.10N	6.27 E
Rhin=Rhine (EN) ∽	110	Ge	51.52N	6.02 E
Rhine (EN)=Rein ∽	110	Ge	51.52N	6.02 E
Rhine (EN)=Rhein ∽	110	Ge	51.52N	6.02 E
Rhine (EN)=Rhin ∽	110	Ge	51.52N	6.02 E
Rhine (EN)=Rijn ∽	110	Ge	51.52N	6.02 E
Rhine Bank (EN) ⊞	206	Ji	50.30S	53.30W
Rhinelander	182	Jb	45.38N	89.25W
Rhineland-Palatinate (EN)= Rheinland-Pfalz ②	120	Cf	50.00N	7.00 E
Rhinluch ≀	120	Id	52.50N	12.50 E
Rhino Camp	170	Fb	2.58N	31.24 E
Rhiou ∽	126	Mi	35.59N	0.53 E
Rhir, Cap- ▶	162	Fc	30.38N	9.54W
Rho	128	De	45.32N	9.02 E
Rhode Island ②	182	Mc	41.40N	71.30W
Rhode Island Sound 〜	184	Le	41.25N	71.15W
Rhodes (EN) = Ródhos	112	Ih	36.26N	28.13 E
Rhodes (EN) = Ródhos ◆	110	Ih	36.10N	28.00 E
Rhodesia → Zimbabwe ①	160	Jj	20.00S	30.00 E
Rhodes Peak ▲	188	Hc	46.41N	114.47W
Rhodope Mountains (EN) = Rodopi ⛰	110	Ig	41.30N	24.30 E
Rhomara ⊠	126	Hi	35.10N	4.57W
Rhön ⛰	120	Gf	50.25N	10.05 E
Rhondda	118	Jj	51.40N	3.30W
Rhône ③	122	Ki	46.00N	4.30 E
Rhône ∽	110	Gg	43.20N	4.50 E
Rhône au Rhin, Canal du- ═	122	Lg	47.06N	5.19 E
Rhourd el Baguel	162	Ic	31.24N	6.57 E
Rhue ∽	122	Ii	45.23N	2.29 E
Rhum ◆	118	Ge	57.00N	6.20W
Rhyl	118	Jh	53.19N	3.29W
Riaba	166	Ge	3.24N	8.42 E
Riacho de Santana	202	Jf	13.37S	42.57W
Riangnom	168	Ed	9.55N	30.01 E
Riaño	126	Gb	42.58N	5.01W
Riánsares ∽	126	Ie	39.32N	3.18W
Rías Altas ≡	126	Da	43.30N	8.30W
Rías Bajas ≡	126	Db	42.30N	9.00W
Riau ③	150	Df	1.00N	102.00 E
Riau, Kepulauan-=Riau Archipelago (EN) ❖	140	Mi	1.00N	104.30 E
Riau Archipelago (EN)= Riau, Kepulauan- ❖	140	Mi	1.00N	104.30 E
Riaza	126	Ic	41.17N	3.28W
Riaza ∽	126	Ic	41.42N	3.55W
Ribadavia	126	Db	42.17N	8.08W
Ribadeo	126	Ea	43.32N	7.02W
Ribadesella	126	Ga	43.28N	5.04W
Ribagorça / Ribagorza ⊠	126	Mb	42.15N	0.30 E
Ribagorza / Ribagorça ⊠	126	Mb	42.15N	0.30 E
Ribamar	202	Jd	2.33S	44.03W
Ribas do Rio Pardo	204	Fe	20.27S	53.46W
Ribatejo ⊟	126	De	39.15N	8.30W
Ribáuè	172	Fb	14.57S	38.17 E
Ribble ∽	118	Kh	53.44N	2.50W
Ribe	114	Bi	55.21N	8.46 E
Ribe ②	116	Ci	55.35N	8.45 E
Ribécourt-Dreslincourt	124	Ee	49.31N	2.55 E
Ribeira	204	Hg	24.39S	49.00W
Ribeira → Santa Eugenia	126	Db	42.33N	9.00W
Ribeira, Rio- ∽	204	Ig	24.40S	47.24W
Ribeira Brava	162	Cf	16.37N	24.18W
Ribeira Grande	162	Bf	17.11N	25.04W
Ribeirão Prêto	200	Lh	21.10S	47.48W
Ribeirãozinho	204	Fc	16.22S	52.36W
Ribeiro Gonçalves	202	Ie	7.32S	45.14W
Ribemont	124	Fe	49.48N	3.28 E
Ribera	128	Hm	37.30N	13.16 E
Ribérac	122	Gi	45.15N	0.20 E
Riberalta	200	Jg	10.59S	66.06W
Ribnica	128	Ie	45.44N	14.44 E
Ribnitz-Damgarten	120	Ib	54.15N	12.28 E
Ricardo Flores Magón	192	Fc	29.58N	106.58W
Riccia	128	Ii	41.29N	14.50 E
Riccione	128	Gg	43.59N	12.39 E
Rice Lake ⊔	184	Hc	44.08N	78.13W
Rich	162	Gc	32.15N	4.30W
Richan	186	Jb	49.59N	92.49W
Richard Collinson Inlet ◧	180	Gb	72.45N	113.00W
Richards ◆	180	Ec	69.20N	134.35W
Richard's Bay	160	Kk	28.47S	32.06 E
Richardson	186	Hj	32.57N	96.44W
Richardson Mountains ⛰	174	Fc	66.00N	135.20W
Richardson Seamount (EN) ⊼	222	Cc	40.45S	14.10 E
Richard Toll	166	Bb	16.28N	15.41W
Rîchât, Guel er- ▲	162	Ee	21.07N	11.24W
Richel ⌵	124	Ha	53.18N	5.10 E
Richel Griend ⊔	124	Ha	53.18N	5.15 E
Richelieu	122	Gg	47.01N	0.19 E
Richer	186	Hb	49.39N	96.28W
Richey	188	Mc	47.39N	105.04W
Richfield	182	Ed	38.46N	112.05W
Richibucto	184	Ob	46.41N	64.52W
Richland	182	Db	46.17N	119.18W
Richland Center	186	Ke	43.22N	90.21W
Richmond [Austl.]	212	Id	20.44S	143.08 E
Richmond [Ca.-U.S.]	182	Cd	37.57N	122.22W
Richmond [Eng.-U.K.]	118	Lg	54.24N	1.44W
Richmond [In.-U.S.]	182	Kd	39.50N	84.54W
Richmond [Ky.-U.S.]	182	Kd	37.45N	84.18W
Richmond [N.Z.]	218	Ed	41.21S	173.11 E
Richmond [S.Afr.]	172	Cf	31.23S	23.56 E
Richmond [Tx.-U.S.]	186	Il	29.35N	95.46W
Richmond [Va.-U.S.]	176	Lf	37.30N	77.28W
Richmond, Mount- ▲	218	Ed	41.28S	173.24 E
Richmond Hill	184	Hd	43.52N	79.27W
Richmond Peak ▲	197n	Ba	13.17N	61.13W
Richthofen, Mount- ▲	186	Df	40.29N	105.57W
Rickmansworth	124	Bc	51.38N	0.28W
Ricobayo, Embalse de- ⊏	126	Gc	41.35N	5.50W
Ridā'	164	Hg	14.25N	44.50 E
Ridderkerk	124	Gc	51.52N	4.36 E
Ridgecrest	188	Gi	35.38N	117.36W
Ridgway	184	He	41.25N	78.45W
Riding Mountain ⛰	186	Fa	50.55N	100.25W
Riecito, Río- ∽	196	Bi	6.50N	68.51W
Ried ⊠	124	Ke	49.50N	8.25 E
Ried im Innkreis	128	Hb	48.13N	13.30 E
Riedlingen	120	Fh	48.09N	9.28 E
Riemst	124	Hd	50.48N	5.36 E
Ries ⊠	120	Gh	48.55N	10.40 E
Riesa	120	Je	51.18N	13.18 E
Riesco, Isla- ◆	206	Fh	53.00S	72.30W
Riesi	128	Im	37.17N	14.05 E
Riet ∽	158	Jk	29.00S	23.53 E
Rietavas/Retavas	116	Ii	55.43N	21.49 E
Rietberg	124	Kc	51.48N	8.26 E
Rietbron	172	Cf	32.54S	23.09 E
Rietfontein [Nam.]	172	Cd	21.58S	20.58 E
Rietfontein [S.Afr.]	172	Ce	26.44S	20.01 E
Rieti	128	Gh	42.24N	12.51 E
Rif ⛰	158	Ge	35.00N	4.00W
Rifle	186	Cg	39.32N	107.47W
Rifstangi ▶	110	Eb	66.32N	16.12W
Rift Valley ③	170	Gb	0.30N	36.00 E
Rift Valley ⊠	158	Kh	0.30N	36.00 E
Rīga/Riga	112	Id	56.57N	24.06 E
Riga/Rīga	112	Id	56.57N	24.06 E
Riga, Gulf of- (EN) = Rīgas jūŗas līcis ◧	110	Id	57.30N	23.35 E
Riga, Gulf of- (EN) = Riia laht ◧	110	Id	57.30N	23.35 E
Riga, Gulf of- (EN) = Rižski zaliv ◧	110	Id	57.30N	23.35 E
Rigachikum	166	Gc	10.38N	7.28 E
Rīgas jūŗas līcis = Riga, Gulf of- (EN) ◧	110	Id	57.30N	23.35 E
Rīgestān=Registan (EN) ⊠	140	If	31.00N	65.00 E
Riggins	188	Gd	45.25N	116.19W
Rigolet	180	Lf	54.10N	58.26W
Rig-Rig	168	Ac	14.16N	14.21 E
Rihand Sagar ⊏	148	Hd	24.05N	83.05 E
Riia laht = Riga, Gulf of- (EN) ◧	110	Id	57.30N	23.35 E
Riihimäki	114	Ff	60.45N	24.46 E
Riiser-Larsen-Halvøya ▬	222	De	68.55S	34.00 E
Riito	192	Ba	32.10N	114.45W
Riječki zaljev = Rijeka, Gulf of- (EN) ◧	128	Ie	45.15N	14.25 E
Rijeka	112	Hf	45.21N	14.24 E
Rijeka, Gulf of- (EN)= Riječki zaljev ◧	128	Ie	45.15N	14.25 E
Rijksmuseum Kröller-Müller ▼	124	Hb	52.06N	5.47 E
Rijn=Rhine (EN) ∽	110	Ge	51.52N	6.02 E
Rijssen	124	Ib	52.18N	6.37 E
Rijswijk	124	Gb	52.03N	4.21 E
Rika ∽	120	Th	48.08N	23.22 E
Rikā, Wādī ar- ∽	164	He	22.25N	44.50 E
Rikubetsu	156a	Cb	43.28N	143.43 E
Rikuzentakada	154	Pe	39.01N	141.38 E
Rila	130	Gg	42.08N	23.08 E
Rila ⛰	130	Gg	42.08N	23.33 E
Riley	188	Fe	43.32N	119.29W
Riley, Mount- ▲	186	Ck	31.58N	107.05W
Rilski Manastir ⛪	130	Gg	42.08N	23.20 E
Rima ∽	158	Hg	13.04N	5.10 E
Rimatara, Ile- ◆	208	Lg	22.38S	152.51W
Rimava ∽	120	Qh	48.15N	20.21 E
Rimavská Şobota	120	Qh	48.23N	20.01 E
Rimbo	114	Eg	59.45N	18.22 E
Rimé ∽	168	Bc	14.02N	18.03 E
Rimforsa	116	Ff	58.08N	15.40 E
Rimini	128	Gf	44.04N	12.34 E
Rimito/Rymättylä ◆	116	Jd	60.25N	21.55 E
Rîmnic ∽	130	Kd	45.32N	27.31 E
Rîmnicu Sărat	130	Kd	45.23N	27.03 E
Rîmnicu Vîlcea	130	Hd	45.06N	24.22 E
Rimouski	176	Me	48.27N	68.32W
Rimše/Rimšė	116	Li	55.30N	26.33 E
Rimšė/Rimše	116	Li	55.30N	26.33 E
Rinbung	152	Ef	29.15N	89.52 E
Rincón	197a	Ab	18.21N	67.16W
Rincon	196	Bf	12.14N	68.20W
Rincón, Bahía de- ◧	197a	Bc	17.57N	66.19W
Rincón del Bonete, Lago Artificial de- ⊏	206	Id	32.45S	56.00W
Rincón de Romos	192	Hf	22.14N	102.18W
Rindal	114	Be	63.03N	9.13 E
Ringe	116	Di	55.14N	10.29 E
Ringebu	116	Dc	61.31N	10.10 E
Ringerike ⊠	116	Dd	60.05N	10.15 E
Ringgold Isles ❖	208	Jf	16.15S	179.25W
Ringim	166	Gc	12.09N	9.10 E
Ringkøbing	114	Bh	56.05N	8.15 E
Ringkøbing ②	116	Ch	56.10N	8.45 E
Ringkøbing Fjord ◌	114	Bi	56.00N	8.15 E
Ringlades ,	130	Dj	39.25N	20.04 E
Ringsjön ⊔	116	Ei	55.50N	13.30 E
Ringsted	114	Ci	55.27N	11.49 E
Ringvassøy ◆	114	Eb	69.55N	19.15 E
Rínia ◆	130	Il	37.25N	25.13 E
Rinjani, Gunung- ▲	150	Gh	8.24S	116.28 E
Rinn Chathóir/Cahore Point	118	Gi	52.34N	6.11W
Rinn Dúain/Hook Head ▶	118	Gi	52.07N	6.55W
Rinteln	120	Fd	52.11N	9.05 E
Rinya ∽	120	Nk	45.57N	17.27 E
Rio Azul	204	Gg	25.43S	50.47W
Riobamba	200	If	1.40S	78.38W
Río Branco	204	Fk	32.34S	53.25W
Rio Branco	200	Jf	9.58S	67.48W
Rio Branco do Sul	204	Hg	25.10S	49.18W
Rio Brilhante	202	Hh	21.48S	54.33W
Río Bueno	206	Ff	40.19S	72.58W
Río Caribe	202	Fa	10.42N	63.07W
Río Chico	196	Dg	10.19N	65.59W
Rio Claro [Braz.]	204	If	22.24S	47.33W
Rio Claro [Trin.]	196	Fg	10.18N	61.11W
Rio Colorado	206	He	39.01S	64.05W
Río Cuarto	200	Ji	33.08S	64.20W
Rio de Janeiro	200	Lh	22.54S	43.15W
Rio de Janeiro ②	202	Jh	22.30S	42.30W
Río de Jesús	194	Gj	7.59N	81.10W
Río de Oro	194	Ki	8.57N	73.23W
Río de Oro ⊟	162	Ee	24.00N	14.00W
Río de Oro, Bahía de- ◧	162	De	23.45N	15.50W
Rio do Sul	206	Kc	27.13S	49.39W
Rio Fortuna	204	Hi	28.06S	49.07W
Río Gallegos	200	Jk	51.37S	69.10W
Rio Grande	200	Ki	32.02S	52.05W
Río Grande [Arg.]	206	Gh	53.47S	67.42W
Río Grande [Nic.]	194	Dg	12.59N	86.34W
Río Grande [P.R.]	197a	Cb	18.23N	65.50W
Rio Grande City	186	Gm	26.23N	98.49W
Río Grande de Añasco ∽	197a	Ab	18.17N	67.10W
Río Grande de Manati ∽	197a	Bb	18.29N	66.32W
Río Grande de Matagalpa ∽	190	Hf	12.54N	83.32W
Rio Grande do Norte ②	202	Ke	5.40S	36.00W
Rio Grande do Sul ②	206	Jc	30.00S	54.00W
Rio Grande Rise (EN) ⋀	106	Cm	31.00S	35.00W
Riohacha	202	Da	11.32N	72.54W
Río Hato	194	Gi	8.23N	80.10W
Río Lagartos	192	Og	21.36N	88.10W
Rio Largo	202	Ke	9.29S	35.51W
Riom	122	Ji	45.54N	3.07 E
Rio Maior	126	De	39.20N	8.56W
Río Mayo	206	Fg	45.41S	70.16W
Riom-és-Montagnes	122	Ii	45.17N	2.40 E
Rio Miranda ∽	202	Gg	19.25S	57.20W
Río Mulatos	202	Eg	19.42S	66.47W
Ríon	130	Ek	38.18N	21.47 E
Río Negro	206	Ff	40.47S	73.14W
Río Negro [Arg.] ②	206	Gf	40.00S	67.00W
Rio Negro [Braz.]	204	Dd	19.33S	56.12W
Rio Negro [Braz.]	206	Kc	26.06S	49.48W
Río Negro [Ur.] ②	204	Dk	32.45S	57.20W
Rio Negro, Pantanal do- ⩊	202	Gg	18.50S	56.00W
Rionero in Vulture	128	Jj	40.56N	15.40 E
Rioni ∽	132	Lh	42.10N	41.38 E
Rio Novo	204	Dc	16.28S	56.30W
Rio Pardo	206	Jc	29.59S	52.22W
Rio Prêto, Serra do- ⛰	204	Gd	18.18S	50.42W
Río San Juan ③	194	Eh	11.10N	84.30W
Río Segundo	206	Hd	31.40S	63.55W
Riosucio	202	Cb	7.27N	77.07W
Río Tercero	206	Hd	32.11S	64.06W
Rio Tinto	202	Ke	6.48S	35.05W
Rioverde	190	Dd	21.56N	100.01W
Rio Verde	202	Hg	17.43S	50.56W
Rio Verde, Serra do- ⛰	204	Fc	17.32S	52.25W
Rio Verde de Mato Grosso	202	Hg	18.56S	54.52W
Rio Verde do Sul	204	Ef	22.54S	55.27W
Rioz	122	Mg	47.25N	6.04 E
Řip ▲	120	Kf	50.24N	14.18 E
Ripanj	130	De	44.38N	20.32 E
Ripley [Eng.-U.K.]	124	Aa	53.02N	1.24W
Ripley [Tn.-U.S.]	184	Ch	35.44N	89.33W
Ripley [W.V.-U.S.]	184	Gf	38.49N	81.44W
Ripoll	126	Ob	42.12N	2.12 E
Ripon	118	Lg	54.08N	1.31W
Riposto	128	Jm	37.44N	15.12 E
Ripple Mountain ▲	188	Gb	49.02N	117.05W
Risan	130	Bg	42.31N	18.42 E
Risaralda ③	202	Cb	5.00N	75.45W
Risbäck	114	Dd	64.42N	15.32 E
Rīshah, Wādī- ∽	146	Kj	25.33N	44.05 E
Rī Shahr	146	Nh	28.55N	50.50 E
Rishiri	154	Pb	45.11N	141.15 E
Rishiri-Suidō 〜	156a	Ba	45.10N	141.30 E
Rishiri-Tō ◆	152	Pb	45.11N	141.15 E
Rishiri-Yama ▲	156a	Ba	45.11N	141.15 E
Rīshmūk	146	Ng	31.15N	50.20 E
Rishon Leẕiyyo	146	Fg	31.58N	34.48 E
Rising Star	186	Gj	32.06N	98.58W
Risle ∽	122	Ge	49.26N	0.23 E
Risnjak ▲	128	Ie	45.26N	14.37 E
Rîşnov	130	Id	45.35N	25.27 E
Risør	114	Bg	58.43N	9.14 E
Risoux, Mont- ▲	122	Mh	46.36N	6.10 E
Risøyhamn	114	Db	69.00N	15.45 E
Riß ∽	120	Fh	48.17N	9.49 E
Risti	114	Fg	59.03N	24.01 E
Ristiina	116	Lc	61.30N	27.16 E
Ristijarvi	114	Gd	64.30N	28.13 E
Ristna, mys- / Ristna neem ▶	116	If	58.55N	21.55 E
Ristna neem / Ristna, mys- ▶	116	If	58.55N	21.55 E
Rīsū ∽	146	Qf	33.52N	57.28 E
Ritchie's Archipelago ❖	148	If	12.14N	93.10 E
Ritidian Point ▶	220c	Ba	13.39N	144.51 E
Ritscher-Hochland ◓	222	Bf	73.20S	9.30W
Ritter, Mount- ▲	182	Dd	37.42N	119.20W
Ritterhude	124	Ka	53.11N	8.45 E
Rituerto ∽	126	Jc	41.36N	2.22W
Ritzville	188	Fc	47.08N	118.23W
Riva-Bella, Ouistreham-	124	Be	49.17N	0.16W
Rivadavia [Arg.]	206	Gd	33.11S	68.28W
Rivadavia [Arg.]	206	Hb	24.11S	62.53W
Riva del Garda	128	Ee	45.53N	10.50 E
Rivas	176	Kh	11.26N	85.51W
Rivas ③	194	Eh	11.25N	85.50W
Rive-de-Gier	122	Ki	45.22N	4.37 E
Rivera ②	204	Ej	31.30S	55.15W
Rivera [Arg.]	206	He	37.12S	63.14W
Rivera [Ur.]	200	Ki	30.54S	55.31W
River Cess	166	Dd	5.27N	9.35W
Riverdale	186	Fc	47.30N	101.22W
Riverhead	184	Ke	40.55N	72.40W
Riverina ⊠	212	Jg	35.25S	145.30 E
River Inlet	180	Ef	51.41N	127.15W
Rivers ②	166	Ge	4.50N	6.30 E
Rivers, Lake of the- ⊔	188	Mb	49.45N	105.45W
Riversdale [N.Z.]	218	Cf	45.54S	168.44 E
Riversdale [S.Afr.]	172	Cf	34.07S	21.15 E
Riverside	182	De	33.59N	117.22W
Riverton [N.Z.]	218	Bg	46.21S	168.00 E
Riverton [Wy.-U.S.]	182	Fc	43.02N	108.23W
Rivesaltes	122	Il	42.46N	2.52 E
Riviera Beach	184	Gl	26.47N	80.04W
Rivière-à-Pierre	184	Kb	46.58N	72.11W
Rivière-du-Loup	180	Kg	47.50N	69.32W
Rivière-Pilote	197h	Bc	14.29N	60.54W
Rivière-Salée	197h	Bb	14.32N	60.59W
Rivoli	128	Be	45.04N	7.31 E
Rivungo	170	Df	16.15S	22.00 E
Riwaka	218	Ed	41.05S	173.00 E
Riwoqê	152	Ge	31.13N	96.29 E
Rixensart	124	Gd	50.43N	4.35 E
Riyadh (EN)=Ar Riyāḑ	142	Gg	24.38N	46.43 E
Rize	144	Fa	41.02N	40.31 E
Rize, gora- ▲	135	Bf	37.48N	58.13 E
Rıze Dağları ⛰	146	Ib	40.30N	40.50 E
Rizhao	152	Kd	35.27N	119.28 E
Rizokarpásso → Dipkarpas	146	Fe	35.36N	34.23 E
Rižski zaliv = Riga, Gulf of- (EN) ◧	110	Id	57.30N	23.35 E
Rizzuto, Capo- ▶	128	Ll	38.53N	17.05 E
Rjabovo	116	Md	60.17N	29.01 E
Rjapina/Räpina	116	Lf	58.03N	27.35 E
Rjazan	112	Je	54.38N	39.44 E
Rjazanovski	114	Ji	55.08N	39.35 E
Rjazanskaja oblast ③	136	Ee	54.30N	40.40 E
Rjažsk	112	Ke	53.43N	40.04 E
Rjukan	114	Bg	59.52N	8.34 E
Rjuven ◓	116	Be	59.13N	7.10 E
Rkiz	162	Df	16.50N	15.20W
Roa [Nor.]	116	Dd	60.17N	10.37 E
Roa [Sp.]	126	Ic	41.42N	3.55W
Road Town	190	Le	18.27N	64.37W
Roag, Loch- ◧	118	Gc	58.16N	6.50W
Roan Antelope	170	Ee	13.08S	28.24 E
Roannais ⊠	122	Kh	46.05N	4.10 E
Roanne	122	Kh	46.02N	4.04 E
Roanoke ∽	174	Lf	35.56N	76.43W
Roanoke [Al.-U.S.]	184	Ei	33.09N	85.22W
Roanoke [Va.-U.S.]	176	Lf	37.16N	79.57W
Roanoke Rapids	184	Ig	36.28N	77.40W
Roan Plateau ◓	188	Kg	39.35N	108.55W
Roaringwater Bay ◧	118	Dj	51.25N	9.30W
Roatán	194	De	16.18N	86.35W
Roatán, Isla de- ◆	194	De	16.23N	86.30W
Robāţ	146	Qd	37.55N	57.42 E
Robāţ	146	Pg	30.04N	54.49 E
Robāt-e-Khān	144	Ic	33.21N	56.02 E
Robāt-e-Kord	146	Qf	33.45N	56.37 E
Robāt Karīm	146	Ne	35.28N	51.05 E
Robbie Bank (EN) ⊞	208	Jf	11.03S	176.53W
Robe, Mount- ▲	212	If	31.40S	141.20 E
Röbel	120	Ic	53.23N	12.36 E
Robert Lee	186	Fk	31.54N	100.29W
Roberts	204	Bl	35.09S	61.57W
Roberts, Mount- ▲	212	Ke	28.13S	152.28 E
Roberts Creek Mountain ▲	188	Gg	39.52N	116.18W
Robertsfors	114	Ed	64.11N	20.51 E
Robert S. Kerr Lake ⊔	186	Ii	35.25N	95.00W
Robertson	172	Bf	33.46S	19.50 E
Robertson Bay ◧	222	Kf	71.25S	170.00 E
Robertson Range ⛰	212	Ed	23.10S	121.00 E
Robertsport	166	Cd	6.45N	11.22W
Roberval	180	Kg	48.31N	72.13W
Robi	168	Fd	7.38N	39.52 E
Robinson Crusoe (EN) = Robinson Crusoe, Isla- ◆	198	Ii	33.38S	78.52W
Robinson Crusoe, Isla- = Robinson Crusoe (EN) ◆	198	Ii	33.38S	78.52W
Robinson Range ⛰	212	De	25.45S	119.00 E
Robinson River ∽	212	Hc	16.03S	137.16 E
Roboré	200	Kg	18.20S	59.45W
Rob Roy ◆	219a	Cb	7.23S	157.36 E
Robson, Mount- ▲	174	Hd	53.07N	119.09W
Robstown	186	Hm	27.27N	97.40W
Roby	186	Fj	32.45N	100.23W
Roca, Cabo da- ▶	110	Fh	38.47N	9.30W
Rocamadour	122	Hj	44.48N	1.38 E
Roca Partida, Isla- ✳	190	Be	19.01N	112.02W
Roca Partida, Punta- ▶	192	Lh	18.42N	95.10W
Rocas, Atol das- ⊡	198	Mf	3.52S	33.49W
Roccaraso	128	Ii	41.51N	14.05 E
Ročegda	136	Ec	62.42N	43.23 E
Rocha	206	Jd	34.29S	54.20W
Rocha ②	204	Fk	34.00S	54.00W
Rochdale	118	Kh	53.38N	2.09W
Rochechouart	122	Gi	45.49N	0.49 E
Rochedo	204	Ed	19.57S	54.52W
Rochefort [Bel.]	122	Ld	50.10N	5.13 E
Rochefort [Fr.]	122	Fi	45.56N	0.59W
Rochefort-Han-sur-Lesse	124	Hd	50.08N	5.11 E
Rochelle	186	Lf	41.56N	89.04W
Rochelle, La-	112	Ff	46.10N	1.09W
Rocher River	180	Gd	61.23N	112.45W
Roche's Bluff ⁂	197c	Bc	16.42N	62.09W
Rochester [Eng.-U.K.]	118	Nj	51.24N	0.30 E
Rochester [In.-U.S.]	184	De	41.04N	86.13W
Rochester [Mn.-U.S.]	182	Ic	44.02N	92.29W
Rochester [N.H.-U.S.]	184	Ld	43.18N	70.59W
Rochester [N.Y.-U.S.]	176	Le	43.10N	77.36W
Roche-sur-Yon, La-	122	Eh	46.40N	1.26W
Rochlitzer Berg ▲	120	Ie	51.05N	12.48 E
Rocigalgo ▲	126	He	39.35N	4.35W
Rockall ◆	110	Ed	57.35N	13.48W
Rockall Rise (EN) ⋀	110	Ed	57.00N	14.00W
Rock Creek Butte ▲	188	Fd	44.49N	118.07W
Rockefeller Plateau ◓	222	Ng	80.00S	135.00W
Rockenhausen	124	Je	49.38N	7.50 E
Rockford	182	Jc	42.17N	89.06W
Rockglen	188	Mb	49.10N	105.57W
Rockhampton	210	Gg	23.23S	150.31 E
Rock Hill	182	Ke	34.55N	81.01W
Rockingham [Austl.]	212	Df	32.17S	115.44 E
Rockingham [N.C.-U.S.]	184	Hh	34.56N	79.46W
Rock Islands	182	Ic	41.30N	90.34W
Rockland	182	Nc	44.06N	69.06W
Rocklands Reservoir ⊏	212	Ig	37.15S	142.00 E
Rockledge	184	Gk	28.20N	80.43W
Rockneby	116	Gh	56.49N	16.20 E
Rockport	186	Hl	28.01N	97.04W
Rock River ∽	186	Kf	41.29N	90.37W
Rock Sound	184	Im	24.53N	76.09W
Rocksprings	186	Fk	30.01N	100.13W
Rock Springs	182	Fc	41.35N	109.13W
Rockville [In.-U.S.]	184	Df	39.45N	87.15W
Rockville [Md.-U.S.]	184	If	39.05N	77.09W
Rockwood	184	Eh	35.52N	84.41W
Rocky Ford	186	Eg	38.03N	103.43W
Rocky Island Lake ⊔	184	Fb	46.56N	83.04W
Rocky Mount	182	Ld	35.56N	77.48W
Rocky Mountain ▲	182	Eb	47.49N	112.49W
Rocky Mountain House	180	Gf	52.22N	114.55W
Rocky Mountains ⛰	174	He	48.00N	116.00W
Rocky Point [Blz.] ▶	194	Cd	18.22N	88.06W
Rocky Point [Nam.] ▶	172	Ac	19.01S	12.29 E
Rocroi	124	Ge	49.55N	4.31 E
Rodach ∽	120	Gf	50.08N	10.52 E
Rodalben	124	Je	49.14N	7.38 E
Roda Velha, Rio- ∽	204	Ja	12.27S	45.33W
Rødberg	116	Cd	60.16N	8.58 E
Rødby	116	Dj	54.42N	11.24 E
Rødby Havn, Rødby-	114	Ci	54.39N	11.21 E
Rødby-Rødby Havn	114	Ci	54.39N	11.21 E
Roddickton	180	Lf	50.51N	56.07W
Rødding	116	Ci	55.22N	9.04 E
Rödeby	116	Fh	56.15N	15.36 E
Rodeio Bonito	204	Fh	27.28S	53.10W
Roden	124	Ia	53.09N	6.26 E
Rodeo [Arg.]	206	Gd	30.12S	69.06W
Rodeo [Mex.]	192	Ge	25.11N	104.34W
Rodeo [N.M.-U.S.]	186	Bk	31.50N	109.02W
Röder ∽	120	Je	51.30N	13.25 E
Rodez	122	Ij	44.20N	2.34 E
Rodgau	124	Kd	50.01N	8.53 E
Rodholívos	130	Gi	40.56N	23.59 E
Ródhos = Rhodes (EN)	112	Ih	36.26N	28.13 E
Ródhos = Rhodes (EN) ◆	110	Ih	36.10N	28.00 E
Rodi Garganico	128	Ji	41.55N	15.53 E
Roding ∽	118	Nj	51.31N	0.06 E
Rodna	130	Hb	47.25N	24.49 E
Rodnei, Munţii- ⛰	130	Hb	47.35N	24.40 E
Rodney, Cape- ▶	178	Fd	64.39N	166.24W
Rodniki	114	Jh	57.07N	41.48 E
Rodonit, Gjiri i- ◧	130	Ch	41.35N	19.30 E
Rodonit, Kep i- ▶	130	Ch	41.35N	19.27 E
Rodopi=Rhodope Mountains (EN) ⛰	110	Ig	41.30N	24.30 E
Rodrigues Island ◆	158	Nj	19.42S	63.25 E
Roebourne	212	Dd	20.47S	117.09 E
Roebuck Bay ◧	212	Ec	18.04S	122.15 E
Roer ∽	124	Hc	51.12N	5.59 E
Roermond	122	Lc	51.12N	6.00 E
Roeselare/Roulers	122	Jd	50.57N	3.08 E
Roes Welcome Sound 〜	180	Id	64.30N	86.45W

Index Symbols

- ① Independent Nation
- ② State, Region
- ③ District, County
- ④ Municipality
- ⑤ Colony, Dependency
- ■ Continent
- ⊠ Physical Region
- ⊟ Historical or Cultural Region
- ▲ Mount, Mountain
- ⩓ Volcano
- △ Hill
- ⛰ Mountains, Mountain Range
- ⌒ Hills, Escarpment
- ◓ Plateau, Upland
- ⌵ Pass, Gap
- ▭ Plain, Lowland
- ◣ Delta
- ⊓ Salt Flat
- ⋁ Valley, Canyon
- ◡ Crater, Cave
- ✲ Karst Features
- ⌣ Depression
- ⩍ Polder
- ◢ Desert, Dunes
- ♣ Forest, Woods
- ≀ Heath, Steppe
- ✻ Oasis
- ▶ Cape, Point
- ≡ Coast, Beach
- ◨ Cliff
- ▬ Peninsula
- ⧓ Isthmus
- ⋯ Sandbank
- ◆ Island
- ⊡ Atoll
- ✳ Rock, Reef
- ❖ Islands, Archipelago
- ⁂ Rocks, Reefs
- ✿ Coral Reef
- ⊙ Well, Spring
- ⛲ Geyser
- ∽ River, Stream
- ⋎ Waterfall, Rapids
- ⋖ River Mouth, Estuary
- ⊔ Lake
- ⊎ Salt Lake
- ◻ Intermittent Lake
- ⊏ Reservoir
- ⩊ Swamp, Pond
- ═ Canal
- ❆ Glacier
- ❄ Ice Shelf, Pack Ice
- ≋ Ocean
- ≈ Sea
- ◧ Gulf, Bay
- 〜 Strait, Fjord
- ◌ Lagoon
- ⊞ Bank
- ⊼ Seamount
- ⏏ Tablemount
- ⋀ Ridge
- ⊥ Shelf
- ∪ Basin
- ◹ Escarpment, Sea Scarp
- ⚡ Fracture
- ∇ Trench, Abyss
- ⊛ National Park, Reserve
- ▼ Point of Interest
- ✦ Recreation Site
- ◗ Cave, Cavern
- ⌂ Historic Site
- ∴ Ruins
- ▥ Wall, Walls
- ⛪ Church, Abbey
- ⛩ Temple
- ⊗ Scientific Station
- ⊶ Railway station
- ✈ Airport
- ⚓ Port
- ✪ Military installation
- ⛯ Lighthouse
- ⚒ Mine
- ∩ Tunnel
- ⌿ Dam, Bridge

Roetgen 124 Id 50.39N 6.12 E
Rogačev 132 Gc 53.09N 30.06 E
Rogačevka 132 Kd 51.31N 39.34 E
Rogagua, Laguna- 202 Ef 13.45S 66.55W
Rogaguado, Laguna- 202 Ef 12.55S 65.45W
Rogaland [2] 114 Bg 59.00N 6.15 E
Rogaška Slatina 128 Jd 46.15N 15.38 E
Rogatica 128 Ng 43.48N 19.01 E
Rogatin 120 Ug 49.19N 24.40 E
Rogers 186 Ih 36.20N 94.07W
Rogers, Mount- 184 Gg 36.39N 81.33W
Rogers City 184 Fc 45.25N 83.49W
Rogers Lake 188 Gi 34.52N 117.51W
Rogers Peak 188 Jg 38.04N 111.32W
Rogersville 184 Fg 36.25N 82.59W
Roggan 180 Jf 54.24N 79.30W
Roggeveldberge 172 Bf 31.50S 19.50 E
Roggewein, Cabo- 221d Bb 27.07S 109.15W
Rognan 114 Dc 67.06N 15.23 E
Rogozhina 130 Ch 41.05N 19.40 E
Rogozna 130 Df 43.04N 20.40 E
Rogoźno 120 Md 52.46N 17.00 E
Rogue River 188 Ce 42.26N 124.25W
Rohan, Plateau de- 122 Df 48.10N 2.50W
Rohl 168 Dd 7.05N 29.46 E
Rohrbach in Oberösterreich 128 Hb 48.34N 13.59 E
Rohrbach-lès-Bitche 124 Je 49.03N 7.16 E
Rohri 148 Dc 27.41N 68.54 E
Rohtak 148 Fc 28.54N 76.34 E
Roi, Le Bois du- 122 Kh 46.59N 4.02 E
Roi Et 148 Ke 16.05N 103.42 E
Roi Georges, Iles du- 208 Mf 14.32S 145.08W
Roine 116 Kc 61.25N 24.05 E
Roisel 124 Fe 49.57N 3.06 E
Roja 114 Fh 57.30N 22.51 E
Roja, Punta- / Rotja, Punta- 126 Nf 38.38N 1.34 E
Rojas 206 Hd 34.12S 60.44W
Rojo, Cabo- [Mex.] 190 Ed 21.33N 97.20W
Rojo, Cabo- [P.R.] 194 Nd 18.01N 67.15W
Rokan 150 Df 2.00N 100.52 E
Rokiškis 114 Fi 55.59N 25.37 E
Rokitnoje 132 Ed 51.21N 27.14 E
Rokkasho 156a Bc 40.58N 141.21 E
Rokycany 120 Jg 49.45N 13.36 E
Rokytná 120 Mg 49.05N 16.21 E
Rola Co 152 Ed 35.25N 88.25 E
Rolândia 204 Gf 23.18S 51.22W
Røldal 116 Be 59.49N 6.48 E
Rolla [Mo.-U.S.] 182 Id 37.57N 91.46W
Rolla [N.D.-U.S.] 186 Gb 48.52N 99.37W
Rolleston 218 Ee 43.35S 172.23 E
Rolvsøya 114 Fa 71.00N 24.00 E
Roma [Austl.] 210 Fg 26.35S 148.47 E
Roma [It.] = Rome (EN) 112 Hg 41.54N 12.29 E
Roma [Swe.] 114 Eh 57.32N 18.26 E
Romagna 128 Gf 44.30N 12.15 E
Romaine 180 Lf 50.18N 63.48W
Roman 130 Jc 46.55N 26.55 E
Romanche 122 Li 45.05N 5.43 E
Romanche Gap (EN) 106 Dj 0.10S 18.15W
Romang 204 Ci 29.30S 59.46W
Romang, Pulau- 150 Ih 7.35S 127.26 E
România = Romania (EN) [1] 112 If 46.00N 25.30 E
Romania (EN) = România [1] 112 If 46.00N 25.30 E
Romanija 128 Mg 43.51N 18.43 E
Roman-Koš, gora- 136 Dg 44.36N 34.16 E
Romano, Cayo- 194 Ib 22.04N 77.50W
Romanovka 138 Gf 53.14N 112.46 E
Romans-sur-Isère 122 Li 45.03N 5.03 E
Romanzof, Cape- 174 Cc 61.49N 166.09W
Romanzof Mountains 178 Kc 69.00N 144.00W
Rombas 124 Ie 49.15N 6.05 E
Romblon 150 Hd 12.35N 122.15 E
Rome [Ga.-U.S.] 182 Je 34.16N 85.11W
Rome [N.Y.-U.S.] 182 Lc 43.13N 75.28W
Rome [Or.-U.S.] 188 Ge 42.50N 117.37W
Rome (EN) = Roma [It.] 112 Hg 41.54N 12.29 E
Romeleåsen 116 Ei 55.34N 13.33 E
Romerike 116 Dd 60.05N 11.10 E
Romilly-sur-Seine 122 Jf 48.31N 3.43 E
Rommani 162 Fc 33.32N 6.36W
Romme 116 Fd 60.26N 15.30 E
Rommerskirchen 124 Ic 51.02N 6.41 E
Romney Marsh 124 Cc 51.02N 0.55 E
Romny 136 De 50.45N 33.29 E
Rømø 116 Bi 55.10N 8.30 E
Romodanovo 114 Ki 54.28N 45.18 E
Romont 128 Ad 46.42N 6.55 E
Romorantin-Lanthenay 122 Hg 47.22N 1.45 E
Romsdal 116 Bb 62.35N 7.50 E
Romsdalen 116 Bb 62.30N 7.55 E
Romsdalsfjorden 116 Bb 62.40N 7.15 E
Romsdalshorn 116 Bd 62.29N 7.50 E
Romsey 118 Lk 50.59N 1.30W
Ronas Hill 118 La 60.38N 1.20W
Ronave 220e Ba 0.29S 166.56 E
Roncador, Cayos de- 190 Hf 13.32N 80.03W
Roncador, Serra do- 198 Kg 13.00S 51.50W
Roncador Reef 208 Ge 6.13S 159.22 E
Roncesvalles 126 Ka 43.01N 1.19W
Roncesvalles o de Ibañeta, Puerto de- 126 Ka 43.01N 1.19W
Ronciglione 128 Gh 42.17N 12.13 E
Ronco 128 Gf 44.24N 12.12 E
Ronda 126 Gh 36.44N 5.10W
Ronda, Serrania de- 126 Gh 36.45N 5.05W
Ronda do Sul 204 Ch 15.57S 59.42W
Rondane 114 Bf 61.55N 9.45 E
Rønde 114 Ch 56.18N 10.29 E
Ronde, Point- 197g Ba 15.33N 61.29W
Ronde Island 196 Ff 12.18N 61.31W
Rondeslottet 116 Cc 61.55N 9.46 E
Rondon 204 Ff 23.23S 52.48W
Rondón, Pico- 202 Fc 1.36N 63.08W
Rondônia 200 Jg 10.52S 61.57W
Rondônia [2] 202 Ff 11.00S 63.00W
Rondonópolis 200 Kg 16.28S 54.38W
Rong'an (Chang'an) 152 If 25.16N 109.23 E
Rongcheng 154 Ce 39.03N 115.52 E
Rongcheng (Yatou) 154 Gf 37.10N 122.25 E
Rongelap Atoll 208 Hc 11.09N 166.50 E
Rongerik Atoll 208 Hc 11.21N 167.26 E
Rongjiang (Guzhou) 152 If 25.58N 108.30 E
Rongxian 152 Jg 22.48N 110.30 E
Rongzhag/Danba 152 He 30.48N 101.54 E
Rønne 114 Di 55.06N 14.42 E
Ronne Bay 222 Qf 72.30S 74.00W
Ronneby 114 Dh 56.12N 15.18 E
Ronnebyån 116 Fh 56.10N 15.18 E
Ronne Ice Shelf 222 Qf 78.30S 61.00W
Ronse/Renaix 122 Jd 50.45N 3.36 E
Ronuro, Rio- 198 Kg 11.56S 53.33W
Roodepoort 172 De 26.11S 27.54 E
Roof Butte 182 Fd 36.28N 109.05W
Rooiboklaagte 172 Cd 20.20S 21.15 E
Roon, Pulau- 150 Jg 2.23S 134.33 E
Rooniu, Mont- 221e Fc 17.49S 149.12W
Roorkee 148 Fc 29.52N 77.53 E
Roosendaal 122 Kc 51.32N 4.28 E
Roosevelt [Az.-U.S.] 188 Jj 33.40N 111.09W
Roosevelt [Ut.-U.S.] 188 Kf 40.18N 109.59W
Roosevelt, Mount- 180 Ee 58.23N 125.04W
Roosevelt, Rio- 198 Jf 7.35S 60.20W
Roosevelt Island 222 Lf 79.30S 162.00W
Root Portage 186 Ka 50.53N 91.18W
Ropa 120 Rg 49.46N 21.29 E
Ropar 148 Fb 30.58N 76.20 E
Ropaži 116 Kh 56.58N 24.26 E
Ropczyce 120 Rf 50.03N 21.37 E
Rope, The- 220q Ab 25.04S 130.05W
Roper River 208 Ef 14.43S 135.27 E
Roquefort 122 Fj 44.02N 0.19W
Roque Pérez 204 Cl 35.25S 59.20W
Roquetas de Mar 126 Jh 36.46N 2.36W
Roraima, Monte- 198 Je 5.12N 60.44W
Roraima, Território de- [2] 202 Fc 1.30N 61.00W
Røros 114 Ce 62.35N 11.24 E
Rorschach 128 Dc 47.30N 9.30 E
Rørvik 114 Cd 64.51N 11.14 E
Ros 132 Ge 49.39N 31.35 E
Rosa, Cap- 128 Cn 36.57N 8.14 E
Rosa, Lake- 194 Kc 20.55N 73.20W
Rosa, Monte- 110 Gf 45.55N 7.53 E
Rošal 114 Ji 55.41N 39.55 E
Rosala 116 Je 59.50N 22.25 E
Rosalia 188 Gc 47.14N 117.22W
Rosalia, Punta- 221d Bb 27.03S 109.19W
Rosalie 197g Bb 15.22N 61.16W
Rosalind Bank (EN) 194 Ge 16.30N 80.30W
Rosamond Lake 188 Fi 34.50N 118.04W
Rosamorada 192 Gf 22.08N 105.12W
Rosana 204 Ff 22.36S 53.01W
Rosário 202 Jd 2.57S 44.14W
Rosario 200 Ji 32.57S 60.40W
Rosario [Mex.] 192 Dd 26.27N 111.38W
Rosario [Mex.] 190 Cd 23.00N 105.52W
Rosario [Par.] 206 Ib 24.27S 57.03W
Rosario [Ven.] 194 Kh 10.19N 72.19W
Rosario, Arroyo- 192 Bb 30.03N 115.45W
Rosario, Bahia- 192 Bc 29.50N 115.45W
Rosario, Cayo del- 194 Gc 21.38N 81.53W
Rosario, Islas del- 194 Jh 10.10N 75.46W
Rosario, Sierra del- 192 He 25.35N 103.50W
Rosario de Arriba 192 Ab 30.01N 115.40W
Rosario de la Frontera 206 Hc 25.48S 64.58W
Rosario de Lerma 206 Gb 24.59S 65.35W
Rosario del Tala 204 Ck 32.18S 59.09W
Rosário do Sul 206 Jd 30.15S 54.55W
Rosário Oeste 202 Gf 14.50S 56.25W
Rosarito 192 Bc 28.38N 114.04W
Rosarno 128 Jl 38.29N 15.58 E
Rosas/Roses 126 Pb 42.16N 3.11 E
Rosa Seamount (EN) 190 Bc 26.12N 114.58W
Rosa Zarate 202 Cc 0.18N 79.27W
Roščino 116 Md 60.13N 29.43 E
Roscoe Glacier 222 Ge 66.30S 95.20 E
Ros Comáin/Roscommon 118 Eh 53.38N 8.11W
Ros Comáin/Roscommon [2] 118 Eh 53.40N 8.30W
Roscommon 184 Ec 44.30N 84.35W
Roscommon/Ros Comáin 118 Eh 53.38N 8.11W
Roscommon/Ros Comáin [2] 118 Eh 53.40N 8.30W
Ros Cré/Roscrea 118 Fi 52.57N 7.47W
Roscrea/Ros Cré 118 Fi 52.57N 7.47W
Rose, Pointe de la- 197h Bb 14.33N 61.03W
Roseau [Dom.] 176 Mh 15.18N 61.24W
Roseau [Dom.] 197g Bb 15.18N 61.24W
Roseau [Mn.-U.S.] 186 Ib 48.51N 95.46W
Roseau [St.Luc.] 197k Ab 13.58N 61.02W
Roseau River 186 Hb 49.08N 97.14W
Rosebery 212 Jh 41.46S 145.32 E
Rosebud 188 Lc 46.16N 106.27W
Rosebud Creek 188 Lc 46.16N 106.28W
Rosebud River 188 Ia 51.25N 112.37W
Roseburg 182 Cc 43.13N 123.20W
Rosemary Bank (EN) 118 Cb 59.15N 10.10W
Rosenberg 182 Hf 29.33N 95.48W
Rosendahl 124 Jb 52.01N 7.12 E
Rosendahl-Osterwick 124 Jb 52.01N 7.12 E
Rosendal 114 Bf 59.59N 6.01 E
Rosenheim 120 Ii 47.51N 12.08 E
Rosental 128 Id 46.33N 14.15 E
Roses/Rosas 126 Pb 42.16N 3.11 E
Roses, Golf de- / Roses, Golfo de- 126 Pb 42.10N 3.15 E
Roses, Golfo de- / Roses, Golf de- 126 Pb 42.10N 3.15 E
Roseți 130 Ke 44.13N 27.26 E
Roseto degli Abruzzi 128 Ih 42.41N 14.01 E
Rosetown 180 Gf 51.33N 108.00W
Rosetta (EN) = Rashīd 164 Fc 31.24N 30.25 E
Roseville 188 Eg 38.45N 121.17W
Roshage 114 Bh 57.07N 8.38 E
Rosica 130 If 43.15N 25.42 E
Rosières-en-Santerre 124 Ee 49.49N 2.43 E
Rosignano Solvay 128 Eg 43.23N 10.26 E
Rosignol 202 Gb 6.17N 57.32W
Roșiori de Vede 130 He 44.07N 24.59 E
Roskilde 114 Ci 55.39N 12.05 E
Roskilde [2] 116 Ei 55.35N 12.10 E
Roslagen 116 He 59.30N 18.40 E
Ros Láir/Rosslare 118 Gi 52.17N 6.23W
Roslavl 136 De 53.58N 32.53 E
Roslyn 188 Ec 47.13N 120.59W
Ros Mhic Thriúin/New Ross 118 Gi 52.24N 6.56W
Røsnæs 116 Di 55.45N 10.55 E
Rosny-sur-Seine 124 Df 49.00N 1.38 E
Rösrath 124 Jd 50.54N 7.12 E
Ross 180 Ed 62.00N 132.25W
Ross [Austl.] 212 Jh 42.02S 147.29 E
Ross [Bye.-U.S.S.R.] 120 Uc 53.16N 24.29 E
Ross [N.Z.] 218 De 42.54S 170.49 E
Ross, Cape- 150 Gd 10.56N 119.13 E
Ross, Mount- 222 Fc 49.25S 69.08 E
Rossano 128 Kk 39.34N 16.38 E
Rossan Point/Ceann Ros Eoghain 118 Eg 54.42N 8.48W
Ross Barnett Reservoir 186 Lj 32.30N 90.00W
Rosseau Lake 184 Hc 45.10N 79.35W
Rossel Island 208 Gf 11.26S 154.07 E
Rossell, Cap- 219b Ce 20.23S 166.36 E
Ross Ice Shelf 222 Lg 81.30S 175.00W
Rossijskaja Sovetskaja Federativnaja Socialističeskaja Respublika (RSFSR) [2] 136 Jc 60.00N 100.00 E
Ross Island 222 Kf 77.30S 168.00 E
Ross Lake 188 Eb 48.53N 121.04W
Rossland 188 Gb 49.05N 117.48W
Rosslare/Ros Láir 118 Gi 52.17N 6.23W
Roßlau 120 Ie 51.53N 12.15 E
Rosso 160 Fg 16.31N 15.49W
Ross-on-Wye 118 Kj 51.55N 2.35W
Rossoš 136 De 50.11N 39.39 E
Ross River 180 Ed 61.59N 132.27W
Ross Sea (EN) 222 Lf 76.00S 175.00W
Røssvatn 114 Cd 65.45N 14.00 E
Røst 114 Cc 67.31N 12.07 E
Rosta 114 Eb 69.02N 18.40 E
Rostamī 146 Nh 28.52N 51.02 E
Rostan Kalā 146 Od 36.42N 53.27 E
Rostāq 144 Hd 26.53N 53.52 E
Rösterkopf 124 Ie 49.40N 6.50 E
Rosthern 180 Gf 52.40N 106.20W
Rostock 116 He 54.05N 12.08 E
Rostock [2] 120 Ib 54.10N 12.10 E
Rostock-Warnemünde 120 Ib 54.10N 12.05 E
Rostov 136 Dd 57.13N 39.25 E
Rostov-na-Donu 112 Jf 47.14N 39.42 E
Rostovskaja oblast [3] 136 Ef 47.45N 41.15 E
Roswell [Ga.-U.S.] 184 Eh 34.03N 84.22W
Roswell [N.M.-U.S.] 176 If 33.24N 104.32W
Rot 116 Fc 61.15N 14.02 E
Rota 126 Fh 36.37N 6.21W
Rota Island 208 Fc 14.10N 145.12 E
Rotenburg (Wümme) 120 Fc 53.07N 9.24 E
Rotenburg an der Fulda 120 Ff 50.59N 9.43 E
Roter Main 120 Hf 50.03N 11.27 E
Roth 120 Hg 49.15N 11.06 E
Rothaargebirge 120 Ee 51.05N 8.15 E
Rothenburg ob der Tauber 120 Gg 49.23N 10.11 E
Rother [Eng.-U.K.] 124 Bd 50.57N 0.22W
Rother [Eng.-U.K.] 118 Nk 50.57N 0.45 E
Rothera 222 Qe 67.46S 68.54W
Rotherham 118 Lh 53.26N 1.20W
Rothesay 118 Hf 55.51N 5.03W
Rothorn 128 Cd 46.47N 8.03 E
Rothschild Island 222 Qe 69.25S 72.30W
Rothwell 124 Bb 52.25N 0.48W
Roti, Pulau- 140 Ok 10.45S 123.10 E
Roti, Selat- 150 Hi 10.25S 123.25 E
Rotja, Punta- / Roja, Punta- 126 Nf 38.38N 1.34 E
Rotnes 116 Dd 60.04N 10.53 E
Roto 212 Jf 33.03S 145.29 E
Rotoiti, Lake- 218 Ed 41.50S 172.50 E
Rotondella 128 Kj 40.10N 16.31 E
Rotondo, Monte- 122a Ba 42.13N 9.03 E
Rotoroa, Lake- 218 Ed 41.50S 172.40 E
Rotorua 218 Gc 38.09S 176.15 E
Rotorua, Lake- 218 Gc 38.05S 176.15 E
Rotselaar 124 Gd 50.57N 4.43 E
Rott 120 Jh 48.25N 13.20 E
Rottenburg am Neckar 120 Eh 48.28N 8.56 E
Rotterdam 112 Ge 51.55N 4.28 E
Rottnaälven 116 Ed 59.48N 13.07 E
Rottnen 116 Fh 56.45N 15.05 E
Rottneros 116 Ee 59.48N 13.07 E
Rottnest Island 212 Df 32.00S 115.30 E
Rottumerplaat 122 Ma 53.35N 6.30 E
Rottweil 120 Eh 48.10N 8.37 E
Rotuma Island 208 Hf 12.30S 177.05 E
Roubaix 122 Jd 50.42N 3.10 E
Roubion 122 Kj 44.31N 4.42 E
Roudnice nad Labem 120 Kf 50.26N 14.16 E
Rouen 112 Gf 49.26N 1.05 E
Rouergue 122 Ij 44.30N 2.30 E
Rouge, Rivière- 184 Jc 45.38N 74.42W
Rouillac 122 Fi 45.47N 0.04W
Roulers/Roeselare 122 Jd 50.57N 3.08 E
Roumois 122 Ge 49.30N 0.30 E
Roundup 182 Fb 46.27N 108.33W
Rousay 118 Jb 59.01N 3.02W
Roussillon 122 Ki 45.22N 4.49 E
Roussillon 122 Il 42.30N 2.30 E
Roussin, Cap- 219b Ce 21.21S 167.59 E
Routot 124 Ce 49.23N 0.44 E
Rouyn 176 Le 48.14N 79.01W
Rovaniemi 112 Ib 66.30N 25.43 E
Rovenskaja oblast [3] 136 Ce 51.00N 26.30 E
Rovereto 128 Fe 45.53N 11.02 E
Rovigo 128 Fe 45.04N 11.47 E
Rovinari 130 Ge 44.55N 23.11 E
Rovinj 128 He 45.05N 13.38 E
Rovkulskoje, ozero- 114 Hd 64.00N 31.00 E
Rovno 112 Ie 50.37N 26.15 E
Rovnoje 132 Od 50.47N 46.05 E
Rovuma = Ruvuma (EN) 158 Lj 10.29S 40.28 E
Rowa, Iles- 219b Ca 13.37S 167.32 E
Rowley 180 Jc 69.05N 78.55W
Rowley Shoals 208 Cf 17.30S 119.00 E
Roxas [Phil.] 150 Gd 10.28N 119.30 E
Roxas [Phil.] 150 Hd 11.35N 122.45 E
Roxboro 184 Hg 36.24N 78.59W
Roxburgh 218 Cf 45.33S 169.19 E
Roxen 116 Ff 58.30N 15.40 E
Roxo, Cap- 158 Fg 12.20N 16.43W
Roy [N.M.-U.S.] 186 Di 35.57N 104.12W
Roy [Ut.-U.S.] 188 If 41.10N 112.02W
Roya 122 Nk 43.48N 7.35 E
Royal Canal 118 Gh 53.21N 6.15W
Royale, Isle- 182 Jb 48.00N 89.00W
Royal Leamington Spa 118 Li 52.18N 1.31W
Royal Society Range 222 Jf 78.10S 162.36 E
Royal Tunbridge Wells 118 Nj 51.08N 0.16 E
Royan 122 Ei 45.38N 1.02W
Royat 122 Ji 45.46N 3.03 E
Roye 122 Ie 49.42N 2.48 E
Roy Hill 212 Dd 22.38S 119.57 E
Røyken 116 De 59.45N 10.23 E
Royston 118 Mi 52.03N 0.01W
Rožaj 130 Dg 42.51N 20.10 E
Różan 120 Rd 52.53N 21.25 E
Rozdol 120 Ug 49.24N 24.08 E
Rozewie, Przylądek- 120 Ob 54.51N 18.21 E
Rožišče 132 Dd 50.54N 25.19 E
Rožňava 120 Qh 48.40N 20.32 E
Rožniatov 120 Uh 48.51N 24.14 E
Roznov 130 Jc 46.50N 26.31 E
Rožnov pod Radhoštěm 120 Og 49.28N 18.09 E
Rożnów 120 Qg 49.46N 20.42 E
Rożnowskie, Jezioro- 120 Qg 49.48N 20.45 E
Rozoy-sur-Serre 124 Ge 49.43N 4.08 E
Roztocze 110 Ie 50.30N 23.20 E
Rrësheni 130 Ch 41.47N 19.54 E
RSFSR = Russian SFSR (EN) [2] 136 Jc 60.00N 100.00 E
RSFSR → Rossijskaja Sovetskaja Federativnaja Socialističeskaja Respublika [2] 136 Jc 60.00N 100.00 E
Rtanj 130 Ef 43.47N 21.54 E
Rtiščevo 136 Ee 52.16N 43.52 E
Ruacana, Quedas- 158 Ij 17.23S 14.15 E
Ruahine Range 218 Gc 39.50S 176.05 E
Ruapehu 208 Ih 39.17S 175.34 E
Ruapuke Island 216 Ci 46.45S 168.30 E
Rua Sura 219a Ec 9.30S 160.36 E
Ruatahuna 218 Gc 38.38S 176.58 E
Rubbestadneset 116 Ae 59.49N 5.17 E
Rubcovsk 142 Kd 51.33N 81.10 E
Rubeho Mountains 170 Gd 6.55S 36.30 E
Rubeshibe 154 Qc 43.47N 143.38 E
Rubežnoje 132 Ke 48.59N 38.26 E
Rubi 170 Db 2.48N 23.54 E
Rubiataba 204 Hb 15.08S 49.48W
Rubiku 130 Ch 41.46N 19.45 E
Rubio 202 Db 7.43N 72.22W
Rubio 126 Ic 41.26N 3.47W
Ruby 178 Hd 64.44N 155.30W
Ruby Lake 188 Hf 40.15N 115.30W
Ruby Mountains 188 Hf 40.25N 115.35W
Ruby Range 188 Id 45.15N 112.15W
Rucăr 130 Id 45.24N 25.10 E
Rucava 116 Ih 56.10N 21.00 E
Ruciane Nida 120 Rc 53.39N 21.35 E
Ruda 120 Of 50.10N 18.18 E
Rudabánya 120 Qh 48.23N 20.38 E
Rūdak 146 Nh 35.51N 51.33 E
Rūdān 146 Qi 27.17N 57.13 E
Ruda Śląska 120 Of 50.18N 18.51 E
Rūdbār [Afg.] 144 Jc 30.09N 62.36 E
Rūdbār [Iran] 146 Md 36.48N 49.24 E
Rüdersdorf bei Berlin 120 Jd 52.27N 13.47 E
Rüdesheim am Rhein 124 Je 49.59N 7.55 E
Rudiškes/Rūdiškės 116 Kj 54.30N 24.58 E
Rūdiškės/Rudiškes 116 Kj 54.30N 24.58 E
Rudki 120 Tg 49.34N 23.30 E
Rudkøbing 114 Ci 54.56N 10.43 E
Rudnaja-Pristan 138 Ih 44.25N 135.49 E
Rudničny 114 Mg 59.38N 52.29 E
Rudnik 130 De 44.08N 20.30 E
Rudnik [Bul.] 130 Kg 42.57N 27.46 E
Rudnik [Pol.] 120 Sf 50.28N 22.15 E
Rudnik [Yugo.] 130 De 44.08N 20.31 E
Rudnja [R.S.F.S.R.] 132 Nd 50.49N 44.36 E
Rudnja [R.S.F.S.R.] 136 De 54.57N 31.07 E
Rudno 120 Tg 49.44N 23.57 E
Rudny [Kaz.-U.S.S.R.] 136 Ge 52.57N 63.07 E
Rudny [R.S.F.S.R.] 154 Mb 44.28N 135.00 E
Rudolf, Lake-/Turkana, Lake- 158 Kh 3.30N 36.00 E
Rudolstadt 120 Hf 50.43N 11.20 E
Rudong (Juegang) 154 Fh 32.19N 121.11 E
Rudozem 130 Hh 41.29N 24.51 E
Rud Sar 144 Hb 37.08N 50.18 E
Rudyard 188 Jb 48.34N 110.33W
Rue 122 Hd 50.16N 1.40 E
Ruecas 126 Ge 39.00N 5.55W
Ruelle 122 Gi 45.41N 0.14 E
Rufā'ah 166 Ec 14.46N 33.22 E
Ruffec 122 Gh 46.01N 0.12 E
Ruffing Point 197a Db 18.45N 64.25W
Rufiji 158 Ki 8.00S 39.20 E
Rufino 206 Hd 34.16S 62.42W
Rufisque 166 Bc 14.43N 17.17W
Rufunsa 170 Ef 15.05S 29.40 E
Rugao 154 Fh 32.24N 120.34 E
Rugby [Eng.-U.K.] 118 Li 52.23N 1.15W
Rugby [N.D.-U.S.] 182 Gb 48.22N 99.59W
Rügen 110 He 54.25N 13.24 E
Rugles 124 Cf 48.49N 0.42 E
Ru He 154 Ch 32.55N 114.24 E
Ruhea 148 Hc 26.10N 88.25 E
Ruhengeri 170 Ec 1.30S 29.38 E
Rühlertwist 124 Jb 52.39N 7.06 E
Ruhner Berge 120 Hc 53.17N 11.55 E
Ruhnu, ostrov- 114 Fh 57.50N 23.15 E
Ruhnu, ostrov- / Ruhnu saar 114 Fh 57.50N 23.15 E
Ruhnu saar / Ruhnu, ostrov- 114 Fh 57.50N 23.15 E
Ruhr 120 Ce 51.27N 6.44 E
Rui'an 152 Lf 27.48N 120.38 E
Ruichang 154 Cj 29.41N 115.38 E
Ruiena/Rūjiena 114 Fh 57.54N 25.17 E
Ruijin 152 Kf 25.59N 116.03 E
Ruili 152 Gg 24.03N 97.46 E
Ruiselede 124 Fc 51.03N 3.24 E
Ruiz 192 Gg 21.57N 105.09W
Ruiz, Nevado del- 202 Cc 4.54N 75.18W
Ruj 130 Fg 42.51N 22.35 E
Rūja/Ruja 116 Kg 57.38N 25.10 E
Ruja/Rūja 116 Kg 57.38N 25.10 E
Rujan 130 Eg 42.23N 21.49 E
Rujen 130 Fg 42.10N 22.31 E
Rūjiena/Ruiena 114 Fh 57.54N 25.17 E
Ruki 158 Ih 0.05N 18.17 E
Rukwa [3] 170 Fd 7.00S 31.20 E
Rukwa, Lake- 158 Ki 8.00S 32.15 E
Rūl Dadnah 146 Qk 25.33N 56.21 E
Rülzheim 124 Ke 49.10N 8.18 E
Ruma 130 Cd 45.01N 19.49 E
Rumaylah 168 Fc 12.57N 35.02 E
Rumbek 160 Jh 6.48N 29.41 E
Rumberpon, Pulau- 150 Jg 1.50S 134.15 E
Rum Cay 190 Jd 23.40N 74.53W
Rumes 124 Fd 50.33N 3.18 E
Rumford 184 Lc 44.33N 70.33W
Rumia 120 Ob 54.35N 18.25 E
Rumigny 124 Ge 49.48N 4.16 E
Rumija 130 Cg 42.06N 19.12 E
Rumilly 122 Li 45.52N 5.57 E
Rum Jungle 212 Gb 13.01S 131.00 E
Rummah, Wādī ar- 146 Ki 26.38N 44.18 E
Rumoi 152 Pc 43.56N 141.39 E
Rumphi 170 Fe 11.01S 33.52 E
Run 124 Hc 51.40N 5.20 E
Runan 154 Ci 33.00N 114.21 E
Runanga 218 De 42.24S 171.15 E
Runaway, Cape- 218 Gb 37.32S 177.59 E
Runděni/Rundēni 116 Lh 56.14N 27.52 E
Rundēni/Runděni 116 Lh 56.14N 27.52 E
Rundu 160 Ij 17.55S 19.45 E
Rungu 170 Eb 3.11N 27.52 E
Rungwa 160 Ki 6.57S 33.31 E
Rungwa 170 Fd 7.36S 31.50 E
Runmarö 116 He 59.15N 18.45 E
Runn 116 Fd 60.35N 15.40 E
Ruokolahti 114 Gf 61.17N 28.50 E
Ruoqiang/Qarkilik 142 Kf 39.02N 88.00 E
Ruo Shui 140 Le 40.20N 99.40 E
Ruotsalainen 116 Kc 61.15N 25.55 E
Ruotsinpyhtää/Strömfors 116 Ld 60.32N 26.27 E
Ruovesi 114 Ff 61.59N 24.05 E
Ruovesi 116 Kc 61.55N 24.10 E
Rupanco 206 Ff 40.46S 72.42W
Rupea 130 Ic 46.02N 25.13 E
Rupel 124 Gc 51.07N 4.19 E
Rupert 188 Ie 42.37N 113.41W
Rupert 180 Jf 51.30N 78.48W
Rupert, Baie de- 180 Jf 51.35N 79.00W
Ruppert Coast 222 Mf 75.45S 141.00W
Rur 120 Be 51.12N 5.59 E
Rurrenabaque 200 Jg 14.28S 67.34W
Rurstausee 124 Id 50.38N 6.24 E
Rurutu, Ile- 208 Lg 22.26S 151.20W
Rušan 136 Hh 37.57N 71.31 E
Rusape 172 Ec 18.32S 32.07 E
Ruşayriş, Khazzān ar- = Rusayris, Lake- (EN) 168 Ec 11.40N 34.20 E
Rusayris, Lake- (EN) = Ruşayriş, Khazzān ar- 168 Ec 11.40N 34.20 E
Ruse 112 Ig 43.50N 25.57 E
Ruse [2] 130 If 43.50N 25.57 E
Rusețu 130 Ke 44.57N 27.13 E
Rushan (Xiacun) 154 Ff 36.55N 121.30 E
Rushden 124 Bb 52.17N 0.35W
Rushville 186 Kf 40.07N 90.34W
Rusk 186 Ik 31.48N 95.09W
Rusken 116 Fg 57.17N 14.20 E
Rusne/Rusnė 116 Ii 55.19N 21.16 E
Rusnė/Rusne 116 Ii 55.19N 21.16 E
Russel 180 Hb 73.55N 98.35W
Russell [Ks.-U.S.] 186 Gg 38.54N 98.52W
Russell [Man.-Can.] 180 Hf 50.47N 101.15W
Russell [N.Z.] 218 Fa 35.16S 174.08 E
Russell Islands 214 Fi 9.04S 159.12 E
Russellville [Al.-U.S.] 184 Dh 34.30N 87.44W
Russellville [Ar.-U.S.] 186 Ji 35.17N 93.08W
Russellville [Ky.-U.S.] 184 Dg 36.51N 86.53W
Russel Range 212 Ef 33.25S 123.30 E
Rüsselsheim 124 Eg 50.00N 8.25 E
Russian River 188 Dg 38.27N 123.08W
Russian SFSR (EN) = RSFSR [2] 136 Jc 60.00N 100.00 E
Rust 128 Kc 47.48N 16.40 E
Rustavi 136 Eg 41.33N 45.02 E
Rustenburg 172 De 25.37S 27.08 E
Ruston 182 Ie 32.32N 92.38W
Rutaki Passage 220p Bc 21.15S 159.48W
Rutana 170 Fc 3.55S 30.00 E
Rutanzige, Lac- = Edward, Lake- (EN) 158 Ji 0.25S 29.30 E
Rute 126 Hg 37.19N 4.22W
Ruteng 150 Hh 8.36S 120.27 E
Rutenga 172 Ed 21.15S 30.44 E
Rüthen 124 Kc 51.29N 8.27 E
Ruthenia (EN) 130 Ga 48.20N 23.30 E

Index Symbols

[1] Independent Nation
[2] State, Region
[3] District, County
[4] Municipality
[5] Colony, Dependency
Continent
Physical Region
Historical or Cultural Region
Mount, Mountain
Volcano
Hill
Mountains, Mountain Range
Hills, Escarpment
Plateau, Upland
Pass, Gap
Plain, Lowland
Delta
Salt Flat
Valley, Canyon
Crater, Cave
Karst Features
Depression
Polder
Desert, Dunes
Forest, Woods
Heath, Steppe
Oasis
Cape, Point
Coast, Beach
Cliff
Peninsula
Isthmus
Sandbank
Island
Atoll
Rock, Reef
Islands, Archipelago
Rocks, Reefs
Coral Reef
Well, Spring
Geyser
River, Stream
Waterfall, Rapids
River Mouth, Estuary
Lake
Salt Lake
Intermittent Lake
Reservoir
Swamp, Pond
Canal
Glacier
Ice Shelf, Pack Ice
Ocean
Sea
Gulf, Bay
Strait, Fjord
Lagoon
Bank
Seamount
Tablemount
Ridge
Shelf
Basin
Escarpment, Sea Scarp
Fracture
Trench, Abyss
National Park, Reserve
Point of Interest
Recreation Site
Cave, Cavern
Historic Site
Ruins
Wall, Walls
Church, Abbey
Temple
Scientific Station
Railway station
Airport
Port
Military installation
Lighthouse
Mine
Tunnel
Dam, Bridge

Rutherfordton	184	Gh	35.22N	81.57W
Ruthin	118	Jh	53.07N	3.18W
Rutland	184	Kd	43.37N	72.59W
Rutland ⊡	118	Mi	52.40N	0.40W
Rutland ◆	148	If	11.25N	92.10 E
Rutog	142	Jf	33.29N	79.42 E
Rutshuru	170	Ec	1.11 S	29.27 E
Rutter	184	Gb	46.06N	80.40W
Rutul	132	Oi	41.33N	47.29 E
Ruutana	116	Kc	61.31N	24.02 E
Ruvo di Puglia	128	Ki	41.09N	16.29 E
Ruvu	170	Gd	6.48 S	38.39 E
Ruvu → Pangani	170	Gc	5.26 S	38.58 E
Ruvuma ③	170	Ge	10.30 S	35.50 E
Ruvuma ∿	158	Lj	10.29 S	40.28 E
Ruvuma (EN) = Rovuma ∿	158	Lj	10.29 S	40.28 E
Ruwayshid, Wādī- ∿	146	Hf	32.41N	38.04 E
Ruwer ∿	124	Ie	49.47N	6.42 E
Ruya ∿	172	Ec	16.34 S	33.12 E
Ruyang	154	Bg	34.10N	112.28 E
Ru'yas, Wādī ar- ∿	164	Cd	27.06N	19.24 E
Ruyigi	170	Fc	3.29 S	30.15 E
Ruza ∿	114	Ii	55.39N	36.18 E
Ruzajevka [Kaz.-U.S.S.R.]	134	Mj	52.49N	67.01 E
Ruzajevka [R.S.F.S.R.]	136	Ee	54.05N	44.54 E
Ružany	120	Ud	52.48N	24.58 E
Ružomberok	120	Pg	49.05N	19.18 E
Rwanda ①	160	Ji	2.30 S	30.00 E
Ry	116	Ch	56.05N	9.46 E
Ryan	186	Hi	34.01N	97.57W
Rybachi Peninsula (EN) = Rybači, poluostrov- ▬	110	Jb	69.45N	32.35 E
Rybači	116	Ii	55.09N	20.45 E
Rybači, poluostrov- = Rybachi Peninsula (EN) ▬	110	Jb	69.45N	32.35 E
Rybačje	136	Hg	42.28N	76.11 E
Rybinsk	112	Jd	58.03N	38.52 E
Rybinskoje vodohranilišče = Rybinsk Reservoir (EN) ⊔	110	Jd	58.30N	38.25 E
Rybinsk Reservoir (EN) = Rybinskoje vodohranilišče ⊔	110	Jd	58.30N	38.25 E
Rybnica	132	Ff	47.45N	29.01 E
Rybnik	120	Of	50.06N	18.32 E
Rybnoje	136	De	54.46N	39.33 E
Rybnovsk	138	Jf	53.15N	141.55 E
Rychnov nad Kněžnou	120	Mf	50.10N	16.17 E
Rychwał	120	Od	52.05N	18.09 E
Ryd	116	Fh	56.28N	14.41 E
Rydaholm	116	Fh	56.59N	14.16 E
Ryde	124	Ad	50.43N	1.10W
Rye	118	Nk	50.57N	0.44 E
Rye ∿	118	Mg	54.10N	0.45W
Rye Bay ◐	124	Cd	50.55N	0.48 E
Ryegate	188	Kc	46.18N	109.15W
Rye Patch Reservoir ⊔	188	Ff	40.38N	118.18W
Ryes	124	Be	49.19N	0.37W
Ryfylke ⧗	116	Be	59.30N	6.30 E
Ryki	120	Re	51.39N	21.56 E
Rylsk	136	De	51.36N	34.43 E
Rymanów	120	Rg	49.34N	21.53 E
Rymättylä/Rimito ◆	116	Jd	60.25N	21.55 E
Ryn	120	Rc	53.56N	21.33 E
Ryńskie, Jezioro- ≈	120	Rc	53.53N	21.30 E
Ryōhaku-Sanchi ⛰	156	Ec	36.05N	136.45 E
Ryōsō-Yosui ═	156	Gd	35.22N	140.25 E
Ryōtsu	154	Oe	38.05N	138.26 E
Ryōtsu-Wan ◐	156	Fb	38.10N	138.30 E
Ryō-Zen ▲	156	Gc	37.46N	140.41 E
Rypin	120	Pc	53.05N	19.25 E
Ryškany	132	Ef	47.57N	27.32 E
Ryssby	116	Fh	56.52N	14.10 E
Rytterknægten ▲	116	Fi	55.06N	14.54 E
Ryūgasaki	156	Gd	35.54N	140.10 E
Ryukyu Islands (EN) = Nansei-Shotō ⁂	140	Og	26.30N	128.00 E
Ryūkyū-Shotō ⁂	152	Mf	25.30N	126.30 E
Ryukyu Trench (EN) ∨	106	Ig	25.45N	128.00 E
Rzepin	120	Kd	52.22N	14.50 E
Rzeszów	112	Ie	50.03N	22.00 E
Rzeszów ②	120	Rf	50.05N	22.00 E
Ržev	112	Jd	56.16N	34.20 E

S

Šaa, gora- ▲	132	Nh	42.39N	44.43 E
Sa'ādatābād [Iran]	146	Og	30.08N	52.38 E
Sa'ādatābād [Iran]	146	Og	30.06N	53.08 E
Sa'ādatābād [Iran]	146	Ph	28.02N	55.50 E
Sääksjarvi ≈	116	Jc	61.24N	22.24 E
Saalbach ∿	124	Ke	49.15N	8.27 E
Saale ∿	120	He	51.57N	11.55 E
Saaler Bodden ◐	120	Ib	54.20N	12.28 E
Saalfeld	120	Hf	50.39N	11.22 E
Saalfelden am Steinernen Meer	128	Gc	47.25N	12.51 E
Saaminki	116	Mc	61.52N	28.50 E
Saane ∿	128	Bd	46.59N	7.16 E
Saâne ∿	124	Ce	49.54N	0.56 E
Saanen	128	Bd	46.30N	7.15 E
Saanen-Gstaad	128	Bd	46.28N	7.17 E
Saar ∿	120	Cg	49.42N	6.34 E
Saar-Bergland ⧗	124	Ie	49.27N	6.45 E
Saarbrücken	112	Gf	49.14N	7.00 E
Saarbrücken-Dudweiler	124	Je	49.17N	7.02 E
Saarburg	120	Cg	49.36N	6.33 E
Sääre/Sjare	116	Ig	57.57N	21.53 E
Saaremaa/Sarema ◆	110	Id	58.25N	22.30 E
Saarijärvi	114	Fe	62.43N	25.16 E
Saaristomeri ≡	116	Id	60.20N	21.10 E
Saarland ②	120	Cg	49.20N	7.00 E
Saarlouis	120	Cg	49.19N	6.45 E
Šaartuz	136	Gh	37.16N	68.06 E
Saarwellingen	124	Ie	49.21N	6.49 E
Saas Fee	128	Bd	46.07N	7.55 E
Saatly	132	Pj	39.57N	48.26 E
Saavedra	204	Am	37.45 S	62.22W
Sab, Tônlé- ∿	150	Dd	11.34N	104.57 E
Saba ◆	190	Le	17.38N	63.10W
Saba ∿	116	Me	59.05N	29.10 E
Saba Bank (EN) ⊞	196	Ed	17.30N	63.30W
Šabac	130	Ce	44.45N	19.43 E
Sabadell	126	Oc	41.33N	2.06 E
Sabae	154	Ng	35.57N	136.11 E
Sabah ②	150	Ge	5.30N	117.00 E
Sab'ah, Qārat as- △	164	Cd	27.20N	17.10 E
Sabak Bernam	150	Df	3.46N	100.59 E
Sabalān, Kūhhā-ye- ⛰	140	Gf	38.15N	47.49 E
Sab'ān	146	Ii	27.04N	41.58 E
Sabana, Archipiélago de- ⁂	194	Hb	22.30N	79.00W
Sabana de la Mar	194	Md	19.04N	69.23W
Sabanagrande	194	Dg	13.50N	87.15W
Sabanalarga	202	Da	10.38N	74.56W
Sabancuy	192	Nh	18.58N	91.11W
Sabaneta	194	Ld	19.12N	70.58W
Sabaneta, Puntan- ▶	220b	Ba	15.17N	145.49 E
Sabang [Indon.]	150	Ce	5.55N	95.19 E
Sabang [Indon.]	150	Gf	0.11N	119.51 E
Şabanözü	146	Eb	40.29N	33.18 E
Săbăoani	130	Jb	47.01N	26.51 E
Sabarei	170	Gb	4.20N	36.55 E
Sab'Atayn, Ramlat as- ◢	164	If	15.30N	46.10 E
Sabatini, Monti- ⛰	128	Gh	42.10N	12.15 E
Sabaudia	128	Hi	41.18N	13.01 E
Sabaudia, Lago di- ≈	128	Hi	41.15N	13.05 E
Şabbāgh, Jabal- ▲	146	Fh	28.12N	34.04 E
Sab 'Bi 'Ār	146	Gf	33.46N	37.41 E
Sa Bec	148	Lf	10.18N	105.46 E
Şabḩā	146	Gf	32.20N	36.30 E
Sabhā	160	If	27.02N	14.26 E
Sabhā ③	164	Bd	26.00N	14.00 E
Sabhā, Wāḩāt- = Sebha Oasis (EN) 🌴	158	If	27.00N	14.25 E
Sabi ∿	158	Kk	21.00 S	35.02 E
Sabidana, Jabal- ▲	168	Fb	18.04N	36.50 E
Sabile	116	Jg	57.05N	22.29 E
Sabina ⧗	128	Gh	42.20N	12.45 E
Sabinal	192	Fb	30.57N	107.30W
Sabinal, Península de- ◆	194	Ic	21.40N	77.18W
Sabiñánigo	126	Lb	42.31N	0.22W
Sabinas	190	Dc	27.51N	101.07W
Sabinas, Río- ∿	192	Id	27.37N	100.42W
Sabinas Hidalgo	190	Dc	26.30N	100.10W
Sabine Lake ≈	186	Jl	29.50N	93.50W
Sabine Pass ≂	186	Jl	29.44N	93.52W
Sabine Peninsula ▬	180	Ga	76.25N	109.50W
Sabine River ∿	182	Ie	30.00N	93.45W
Sabini, Monti- ▲	128	Gh	42.15N	12.50 E
Şabir, Jabal- ▲	144	Fg	13.30N	44.03 E
Sabirabad	132	Pj	39.59N	48.29 E
Šabla	130	Lf	43.32N	28.32 E
Sable, Anse de- ◐	197e	Ab	16.07N	61.34W
Sable, Cape- [Can.] ▶	174	Me	43.25N	65.35W
Sable, Cape- [U.S.] ▶	174	Kg	25.12N	81.05W
Sable, Ile de- ◆	208	Gf	19.15 S	159.56 E
Sable Island ◆	174	Ne	43.55N	59.55W
Sables-d'Olonne, Les-	122	Eh	46.30N	1.47W
Sablé-sur-Sarthe	122	Fg	47.50N	0.20W
Sablūkah, Ash Shallāl as- = Sixth Cataract (EN) ⤵	158	Kg	16.20N	32.42 E
Sabonetau, Serra do- ⛰	204	Kb	15.20 S	43.50W
Sabonkafi	166	Gc	14.38N	8.45 E
Sabór ∿	126	Ec	41.10N	7.07W
Şabrātah	164	Bc	32.47N	12.29 E
Sabres	122	Fj	44.09N	0.44W
Sabrina Coast ⌇	222	He	67.00 S	119.30 E
Sabtang ◆	150	Hb	20.19N	121.52 E
Sabugal	126	Ed	40.21N	7.05W
Sabunči	132	Pi	40.27N	49.57 E
Şabyā	144	Ff	17.09N	42.37 E
Sabzevār	142	Hf	36.13N	57.42 E
Saca, Vîrful- ▲	130	Ic	46.30N	25.15 E
Sacajawea Peak ▲	182	Db	45.15N	117.17W
Sacalin, Insulă- ◆	130	Me	44.50N	29.39 E
Sacandica	170	Cd	5.58 S	15.56 E
Sacatepéquez ③	194	Bf	14.35N	90.45W
Sacavém	126	Cf	38.46N	9.05W
Sac City	186	Ie	42.25N	95.00W
Sacco ∿	128	Hi	41.31N	13.32 E
Sacedón	126	Jd	40.29N	2.43W
Săcel	130	Hb	47.38N	24.26 E
Săcele	130	Id	45.37N	25.41 E
Sachayoj	204	Bh	26.41 S	61.50W
Sačhere	132	Mh	42.20N	43.22 E
Sachigo ∿	180	Ie	55.05N	89.00W
Sachsen = Saxony (EN) ⊡	120	Ie	51.20N	13.30 E
Sachsenhagen	124	Lb	52.24N	9.16 E
Sachs Harbour	180	Eb	72.00N	125.08W
Šack [R.S.F.S.R.]	114	Ji	54.04N	41.42 E
Šack [Ukr.-U.S.S.R.]	120	Te	51.30N	24.00 E
Sackets Harbor	184	Id	43.57N	76.07W
Saco [Me.-U.S.]	184	Ld	43.29N	70.28W
Saco [Mt.-U.S.]	188	Lb	48.28N	107.21W
Sacramento ∿	174	Gf	38.03N	121.56W
Sacramento [Braz.]	202	Ig	19.53 S	47.27W
Sacramento [Ca.-U.S.]	176	Gf	38.35N	121.30W
Sacramento, Pampa del- ▭	202	Ce	8.00 S	75.50W
Sacramento Mountains ⛰	174	If	33.10N	105.50W
Sacramento Valley ▽	182	Cd	39.15N	122.00W
Sacre ou Timalacia, Rio- ∿	204	Ca	13.55 S	58.02W
Săcueni	130	Fb	47.21N	22.06 E
Sacuriuiná ou Ponte de Pedra, Rio- ∿	204	Da	13.58 S	57.18W
Sádaba	126	Kb	42.17N	1.16W
Sa'dābād	146	Nh	29.23N	51.07 E
Şa'dah	142	Gh	16.57N	43.44 E
Sada-Misaki ▶	156b	Ce	33.22N	132.01 E
Sada-Misaki-Hantō ▬	156	Ce	33.25N	132.15 E
Sadani	170	Gd	6.03 S	38.47 E
Sadao	148	Kg	6.39N	100.31 E
Saddle Mountains ⛰	188	Fc	46.50N	119.55W
Saddle Peak [India] ▲	148	If	13.09N	93.01 E
Saddle Peak [Mt.-U.S.] ▲	188	Jd	45.57N	110.58W
Sad-e Eskandar ▥	146	Pd	37.10N	55.00 E
Sadiya	148	Jc	27.50N	95.40 E
Sa'dīyah, Hawr as- ≈	146	Lf	32.00N	46.45 E
Sad Kharv	146	Qd	36.19N	57.05 E
Sado ∿	126	Df	38.29N	8.55W
Sado-Kaikyō ≂	156	Fc	37.55N	138.40 E
Sado-Shima ◆	140	Pf	38.00N	138.25 E
Sadowara	156	Be	32.04N	131.26 E
Sa Dragonera, Illa- / Dragonera, Isla- ◆	126	Oe	39.35N	2.19 E
Šadrinsk	136	Gd	56.05N	63.38 E
Saeby	114	Ch	57.20N	10.32 E
Saeh, Teluk- ◐	150	Gh	8.00 S	117.30 E
Saengcheon	154	Ie	39.55N	126.34 E
Saerbeck	124	Jb	52.11N	7.38 E
Şafá, Wādī aş- ∿	146	Pk	23.26N	55.41 E
Şafājah ⧗	146	Hi	26.30N	39.30 E
Safājah, Jazīrat- ◆	146	Ei	26.45N	33.59 E
Safané	166	Ec	12.08N	3.13W
Şafāqis = Sfax (EN)	160	Ie	34.44N	10.46 E
Şafāqis = Sfax (EN) ③	162	Jc	34.30N	10.30 E
Safata Harbour ◐	221c	Bb	14.00 S	171.50W
Säffle	114	Cg	59.08N	12.56 E
Safford	182	Fe	32.50N	109.43W
Saffron Walden	118	Ni	52.01N	0.15 E
Safi	160	Ge	32.18N	9.14W
Safi ③	162	Fc	31.55N	9.00W
Safia, Hamâda- ◢	166	Ea	23.10N	4.15W
Şafiābād	146	Qd	36.45N	57.58 E
Safid ∿	144	Hb	37.23N	50.11 E
Safid, Kūh-e ⛰	146	Lf	33.55N	47.30 E
Safonovo [R.S.F.S.R.]	114	Ld	65.41N	47.43 E
Safonovo [R.S.F.S.R.]	136	Dd	55.06N	33.14 E
Şafrā' al Asyāḩ ⩕	146	Ji	26.50N	43.57 E
Şafrā' as Sark ⩕	146	Kj	25.25N	44.20 E
Safranbolu	146	Eb	41.15N	32.42 E
Şafwān	146	Lg	30.07N	47.43 E
Saga [Jap.]	152	Ne	33.15N	130.18 E
Saga [Jap.]	156	Ce	33.05N	133.06 E
Saga [Kaz.-U.S.S.R.]	136	Ge	50.30N	64.14 E
Saga (Gya'gya)	152	Ef	29.22N	85.15 E
Sagae	156	Gb	38.22N	140.17 E
Sagaing	148	Jd	21.52N	95.59 E
Sagaing ③	148	Jd	23.30N	95.30 E
Saga Ken ②	154	Kh	33.15N	130.15 E
Sagamihara	156	Fd	35.34N	139.22 E
Sagami-Nada ≡	156	Fd	35.00N	139.30 E
Sagami-Wan ◐	156	Fd	35.15N	139.20 E
Sagan ∿	168	Fd	5.17N	36.57 E
Šagan ∿	136	He	50.37N	79.15 E
Saganaga Lake ≈	186	Kb	48.14N	90.52W
Saganoseki	156	Be	33.15N	131.53 E
Šagany, ozero- ≈	130	Md	45.45N	29.55 E
Sāgar [India]	148	Ff	14.10N	75.02 E
Sāgar [India]	142	Jg	23.50N	78.42 E
Sagara	156	Fd	34.40N	138.12 E
Sagaredžo	132	Ni	41.43N	45.16 E
Sagavanirktok ∿	178	Jb	70.20N	148.00W
Sagawa	156	Ce	33.29N	133.16 E
Sage	188	Jf	41.50N	110.56W
Saghād	146	Og	31.12N	52.30 E
Saginaw	182	Kc	43.25N	83.58W
Saginaw Bay ◐	182	Kc	43.50N	83.40W
Sagiz ∿	136	Ff	47.32N	53.45 E
Sagiz [Kaz.-U.S.S.R.]	136	Ff	48.12N	54.56 E
Sagiz [Kaz.-U.S.S.R.]	132	Rf	47.32N	53.27 E
Saglek Bay ◐	180	Le	58.30N	63.00W
Saglouc	176	Lc	62.12N	75.38W
Šagonar	138	Ef	51.32N	92.51 E
Sagone, Golfe de- ◐	122a	Aa	42.06N	8.41 E
Sagres	126	Dg	37.01N	8.56W
Sagres, Ponta de- ▶	126	Dh	37.00N	8.57W
Sagter Ems ∿	124	Ja	53.10N	7.40 E
Şagu	130	Ec	46.03N	21.17 E
Sagu/Sauvo	116	Jd	60.21N	22.42 E
Saguache	186	Cg	38.05N	106.08W
Sagua de Tánamo	194	Jc	20.35N	75.14W
Sagua la Grande	190	Hd	22.49N	80.05W
Saguenay ∿	174	Me	48.10N	69.45W
Saguia el-Hamra ⊡	162	Ed	26.50N	12.00W
Sagunto / Sagunt o Morvedre	126	Le	39.41N	0.16W
Sagunto-Grao de Sagunto	126	Le	39.40N	0.16W
Sagunt o Morvedre / Sagunto	126	Le	39.41N	0.16W
Sa'gya	152	Ef	28.53N	88.10 E
Sahagún [Col.]	202	Cb	8.57N	75.27W
Sahagún [Sp.]	126	Gb	42.22N	5.02W
Sahalin, ostrov- = Sakhalin (EN) ◆	140	Qd	51.00N	143.00 E
Sahalinskaja oblast ③	138	Jf	50.00N	143.30 E
Sahalinski zaliv ◐	138	Jf	53.45N	141.30 E
Sahara ◢	158	Hf	21.00N	6.00 E
Saharan Atlas (EN) = Atlas Saharien ⛰	158	He	34.00N	2.00 E
Sahāranpur	142	Jg	29.58N	77.23 E
Sahel ③	166	Ec	14.10N	0.50W
Sahel ⧗	158	Gg	15.40N	8.30W
Şahin	130	Jh	41.01N	26.50 E
Sāhiwāl [Pak.]	148	Eb	30.41N	72.57 E
Sāhiwāl [Pak.]	148	Eb	31.58N	72.20 E
Sahlābād	144	Ic	32.10N	59.51 E
Sahneh	146	Le	34.29N	47.41 E
Sahnovščina	132	Ie	49.09N	35.57 E
Sahova Kosa, mys- ▶	132	Qi	40.13N	50.22 E
Sahrihan	135	Id	40.40N	72.03 E
Šahrisabz	136	Gh	39.03N	66.41 E
Šahristan, pereval- ⌄	135	Ge	39.35N	68.38 E
Šahtersk [R.S.F.S.R.]	138	Jg	49.13N	142.09 E
Šahtersk [Ukr.-U.S.S.R.]	132	Ke	48.01N	38.32 E
Šahterski	138	Md	64.46N	177.47 E
Šahtinsk	136	Hf	49.40N	72.37 E
Šahty	136	Ef	47.42N	40.13 E
Sahuaripa	190	Cc	29.03N	109.14W
Sahuayo de Díaz	190	Dd	20.04N	102.43W
Šahunja	136	Ed	57.43N	46.35 E
Saḩūq, Wādī- ∿	146	Jj	25.40N	42.30 E
Šahy	120	Oh	48.05N	18.58 E
Sahyadri/Western Ghats ⛰	140	Jh	14.00N	75.00 E
Sai Buri	148	Kg	6.42N	101.37 E
Saïda	160	He	34.50N	0.09 E
Saïda ③	162	Hc	33.35N	0.30 E
Saïda, Monts de- ⛰	126	Mi	35.10N	0.30 E
Sa'īdābād	144	Id	29.28N	55.42 E
Saidaiji	156	Dd	34.39N	134.02 E
Said Bundas	168	Cd	8.35N	24.30 E
Saïdia	126	Ji	35.04N	2.13W
Saidor	214	Di	5.37 S	146.28 E
Saidu	148	Eb	34.45N	72.21 E
Saigō	156	Cc	36.13N	133.20 E
Saigon → Thanh-pho Ho Chi Minh	142	Mh	10.45N	106.40 E
Saihan Tal → Sonid Youqi	152	Jc	42.45N	112.36 E
Saihan Toroi	152	Hc	41.54N	100.24 E
Saijō	156	Ce	33.55N	133.10 E
Saikai	156	Ae	33.03N	129.44 E
Sai-Kawa ∿	156	Fc	36.37N	138.14 E
Saiki	154	Kh	32.57N	131.54 E
Saiki-Wan ◐	156	Be	33.00N	131.55 E
Sail Rock ✳	197n	Bb	12.37N	61.16W
Saimaa ≈	110	Ic	61.15N	28.15 E
Saimaa Canal (EN) = Sajmenski kanal ═	116	Mc	61.05N	28.18 E
Saín Alto	192	Hf	23.35N	103.15W
Sā īn Dezh	146	Ld	36.40N	46.33 E
Sains-Richaumont	124	Fe	49.49N	3.42 E
Saint Abb's Head ▶	118	Kf	55.54N	2.09W
Saint-Affrique	122	Ik	43.57N	2.53 E
Saint Agnes Head ▶	118	Hk	50.23N	5.07W
Saint-Agrève	122	Ki	45.01N	4.24 E
Saint Albans [Eng.-U.K.]	118	Mj	51.46N	0.21W
Saint Albans [Vt.-U.S.]	184	Kc	44.49N	73.05W
Saint Albans [W.V.-U.S.]	184	Gf	38.24N	81.53W
Saint Alban's Head → Saint Albhelm's Head ▶	118	Kk	50.34N	2.04W
Saint Albert	180	Gf	53.38N	113.38W
Saint Albhelm's or Saint Alban's Head ▶	118	Kk	50.34N	2.04W
Saint-Amand-les-Eaux	122	Jd	50.26N	3.26 E
Saint-Amand-Montrond	122	Ih	46.43N	2.31 E
Saint-André, Cap- ▶	158	Lj	16.11 S	44.27 E
Saint-André, Plaine de- ▭	122	Hf	48.55N	1.10 E
Saint-André-de-Cubzac	122	Fi	45.00N	0.27W
Saint-André-de-l'Eure	124	Df	48.54N	1.17 E
Saint-André-sur-Cailly	124	De	49.33N	1.13 E
Saint Andrews [N.B.-Can.]	184	Nc	45.06N	67.02W
Saint Andrews [Scot.-U.K.]	118	Ke	56.20N	2.48W
Saint Anne	118	Kl	49.40N	2.10W
Saint Ann's Bay	194	Id	18.26N	77.16W
Saint Ann's Head ▶	118	Hj	51.41N	5.10W
Saint Anthony [Id.-U.S.]	188	Je	43.58N	111.41W
Saint Anthony [Newf.-Can.]	180	Lf	51.22N	55.35W
Saint Arnaud	212	Ig	36.37 S	143.15 E
Saint-Aubert	184	Lb	47.14N	70.15W
Saint-Aubin-sur-Mer	124	Be	49.20N	0.24W
Saint Augustine	182	Kf	29.51N	81.25W
Saint-Augustin-Saguenay	180	Lf	51.14N	58.39W
Saint Austell	118	Ik	50.20N	4.48W
Saint-Avold	122	Me	49.06N	6.42 E
Saint Barthélemy ◆	190	Le	17.55N	62.50W
Saint Barthélemy, Canal de- ≂	197b	Bb	18.00N	63.00W
Saint Barthélemy, Kanaal Van- ≂	197b	Bb	18.00N	63.00W
Saint-Barthélemy, Pic de- ▲	122	Hl	42.49N	1.45 E
Saint Bees Head ▶	118	Jg	54.32N	3.38W
Saint-Benoit	172a	Bb	21.02 S	55.43 E
Saint-Benoît-sur-Loire	122	Ig	47.49N	2.18 E
Saint-Bonnet	122	Mj	44.41N	6.05 E
Saint-Brévin-les-Pins	122	Dg	47.15N	2.10W
Saint Brides Bay ◐	118	Hj	51.48N	5.15W
Saint-Brieuc	122	Df	48.31N	2.47W
Saint-Brieuc, Baie de- ◐	122	Df	48.38N	2.40W
Saint-Calais	122	Gg	47.55N	0.45 E
Saint-Camille	184	Lb	46.29N	70.12W
Saint Catharines	180	Jh	43.10N	79.15W
Saint Catherine, Monastery of- (EN) = Kātrīnā, Dayr- ⛪	164	Fd	28.31N	33.57 E
Saint Catherine, Mount- ▲	197p	Bb	12.10N	61.40W
Saint Catherines Island ◆	184	Gj	31.38N	81.10W
Saint Catherine's Point ▶	118	Lk	50.34N	1.15W
Saint-Céré	122	Hj	44.52N	1.54 E
Saint-Chamond	122	Ki	45.28N	4.30 E
Saint Charles	182	Id	38.47N	90.29W
Saint-Chély-d'Apcher	122	Jj	44.48N	3.17 E
Saint-Christol, Plateau de- ⏏	122	Lj	44.00N	5.50 E
Saint Christopher/Saint Kitts ◆	174	Mh	17.21N	62.48W
Saint Christopher-Nevis ①	176	Mh	17.21N	62.48W
Saint-Cirq-Lapopie	122	Hj	44.28N	1.40 E
Saint Clair, Lake- ≈	174	Ke	42.25N	82.41W
Saint Clair River ∿	184	Fd	42.37N	82.31W
Saint Clair Shores	184	Fd	42.30N	82.54W
Saint-Clair-sur-l'Elle	124	Ae	49.12N	1.02W
Saint-Claud	122	Gi	45.54N	0.28 E
Saint-Claude	122	Lh	46.23N	5.52 E
Saint-Claude	197e	Ab	16.02N	61.42W
Saint Claude	186	Gb	49.40N	98.22W
Saint Cloud	176	Je	45.33N	94.10W
Saint Croix ◆	190	Le	17.45N	64.45W
Saint Croix Falls	186	Jd	45.24N	92.38W
Saint Croix River ∿	182	Ic	44.45N	92.49W
Saint-Cyr-l'École	124	Ef	48.48N	2.04 E
Saint David Bay ◐	197g	Bb	15.26N	61.15W
Saint David's [Gren.]	197p	Bb	12.04N	61.39W
Saint David's [Wales-U.K.]	118	Hj	51.54N	5.16W
Saint David's Head ▶	118	Hj	51.55N	5.19W
Saint David's Point ▶	197p	Bb	12.01N	61.40W
Saint-Denis [Fr.]	122	If	48.56N	2.22 E
Saint-Denis [Reu.]	160	Mk	20.52 S	55.28 E
Saint-Dié	122	Mf	48.17N	6.57 E
Saint-Dizier	122	Kf	48.38N	4.57 E
Sainte-Adresse	124	Ce	49.30N	0.05 E
Sainte-Anne [Guad.]	197e	Bb	16.14N	61.23W
Sainte-Anne [Mart.]	197h	Bc	14.26N	60.53W
Sainte-Anne-des-Monts	184	Na	49.07N	66.29W
Sainte-Baume, Chaîne de la- ⛰	122	Lk	43.20N	5.45 E
Sainte-Énimie	122	Jj	44.22N	3.25 E
Sainte Genevieve	186	Kh	37.59N	90.03W
Sainte-Geneviève	124	Ee	49.17N	2.12 E
Saint Elias, Mount- ▲	174	Ec	60.18N	140.55W
Saint Elias Mountains ⛰	174	Fc	60.30N	139.30W
Saint-Elie	202	Hc	4.50N	53.17W
Sainte-Livrade-sur-Lot	122	Gj	44.24N	0.36 E
Saint-Éloy-les-Mines	122	Ih	46.09N	2.50 E
Sainte-Luce	197h	Bc	14.28N	60.56W
Sainte Luce	172	Hd	24.46 S	47.12 E
Sainte-Lucie, Canal de- = Saint Lucia Channel (EN) ≂	196	Fe	14.09N	60.57W
Sainte-Marie [Guad.]	197e	Ab	16.06N	61.34W
Sainte-Marie [Mart.]	197h	Ab	14.47N	61.00W
Sainte-Marie, Cap- = Sainte-Marie, Cape- (EN) ▶	158	Lk	25.36 S	45.08 E
Sainte-Marie, Cape-(EN) = Sainte-Marie, Cap- ▶	158	Lk	25.36 S	45.08 E
Sainte-Marie, Ile- ◆	158	Lj	16.50 S	49.55 E
Sainte-Marie-aux-Mines	122	Nf	48.15N	7.11 E
Sainte-Maure-de-Touraine	122	Gg	47.06N	0.37 E
Sainte-Maxime	122	Mk	43.18N	6.38 E
Sainte-Menehould	122	Ke	49.05N	4.54 E
Sainte-Rose	197e	Ab	16.20N	61.42W
Sainte-Rose-du-Dégelé	184	Mb	47.33N	68.39W
Sainte Rose du Lac	186	Ga	51.03N	99.32W
Saintes	122	Fi	45.45N	0.38W
Saintes, Canal des-	197e	Ac	15.55N	61.40W
Saintes, Iles des- ◆	196	Fe	15.52N	61.37W
Sainte-Savine	122	Kf	48.18N	4.03 E
Saintes-Maries-de-la-Mer	122	Kk	43.27N	4.26 E
Sainte-Thérèse	184	Kc	45.22N	73.15W
Saint-Étienne	112	Gf	45.26N	4.24 E
Saint-Étienne-du-Rouvray	122	He	49.23N	1.06 E
Sainte-Victoire, Montagne- ▲	122	Lk	43.32N	5.39 E
Saint-Félicien	184	Ka	48.39N	72.28W
Saint-Florent	122a	Ba	42.41N	9.18 E
Saint-Florent, Golfe de- ◐	122a	Ba	42.45N	9.16 E
Saint-Florentin	122	Jf	48.00N	3.44 E
Saint-Florent-sur-Cher	122	Ih	46.59N	2.15 E
Saint-Flour	122	Ji	45.02N	3.05 E
Saint Francis	186	Fg	39.46N	101.48W
Saint Francis River ∿	186	Ki	34.38N	90.35W
Saint Francisville	186	Kk	30.47N	91.23W
Saint-François	197e	Bb	16.15N	61.17W
Saint François Island ◆	172b	Bb	7.10 S	52.44 E
Saint Francois Mountains ⛰	186	Kh	37.30N	90.35W
Saint-Gaudens	122	Gk	43.07N	0.44 E
Saint George ◆	178	Fe	56.35N	169.35W
Saint George [Austl.]	212	Je	28.02 S	148.35 E
Saint George [N.B.-Can.]	184	Nc	45.10N	66.48W
Saint George [Ut.-U.S.]	182	Ed	37.06N	113.35W
Saint George, Cape - [Newf.-Can.] ▶	180	Lg	48.28N	59.16W
Saint George, Cape- [Pap.N.Gui.] ▶	214	Eh	4.52 S	152.52 E
Saint George, Point- ▶	188	Cf	41.47N	124.15W
Saint George Harbour ◐	184	Nd	43.15N	66.10W
Saint George Island ◆	184	Ek	29.39N	84.55W
Saint-Georges	184	Lb	46.10N	70.38W
Saint George's	176	Mh	12.03N	61.45W
Saint George's Bay ◐	180	Lg	48.20N	59.00W
Saint George's Channel ≂	110	Fe	52.00N	6.00W
Saint George's Channel (EN) = Muir Bhreatan ≂	110	Fe	52.00N	6.00W
Saint-Georges-du-Vièvre	124	Ce	49.15N	0.35 E
Saint-Germain-en-Laye	122	If	48.54N	2.05 E
Saint-Gervais-d'Auvergne	122	Ih	46.02N	2.49 E
Saint-Gervais-les-Bains	122	Mi	45.54N	6.43 E
Saint-Ghislain	124	Fd	50.27N	3.49 E
Saint-Ghislain-Baudour	124	Fd	50.29N	3.49 E
Saint-Gildas, Pointe de- ▶	122	Dg	47.08N	2.15W
Saint-Gilles	122	Kk	43.41N	4.26 E
Saint-Gilles-Croix-de-Vie	122	Eh	46.41N	1.55W
Saint-Girons	122	Hl	42.59N	1.09 E
Saint-Gobain	124	Fe	49.36N	3.23 E
Saint Gotthard Pass (EN) = San Gottardo, Passo del- ⌄	110	Gf	46.30N	8.30 E
Saint Govan's Head ▶	118	Ij	51.36N	4.55W
Saint Helena ⑤	160	Gj	15.57 S	5.42W
Saint Helena ◆	158	Gj	15.57 S	5.42W
Saint Helena Bay ◐	158	Il	32.45 S	18.05 E
Saint Helena Island ◆	184	Gi	32.30N	80.30W
Saint Helena Sound ≂	184	Gi	32.27N	80.25W
Saint Helens [Austl.]	212	Jh	41.20 S	148.15 E
Saint Helens [Eng.-U.K.]	118	Kh	53.28N	2.44W
Saint Helens [Or.-U.S.]	188	Dd	45.52N	122.48W
Saint Helens, Mount- ▲	188	Dc	46.12N	122.11W
Saint Helier	118	Kl	49.12N	2.07W
Saint-Hubert	124	Hd	50.03N	5.23 E
Saint-Hyacinthe	184	Kc	45.38N	72.57W
Saint Ignace	182	Kb	45.52N	84.43W
Saint Ignace Island ◆	186	Mb	48.48N	87.55W
Saint Ignatius	188	Hc	47.19N	114.06W
Saint Ives [Eng.-U.K.]	124	Bb	52.18N	0.04W
Saint Ives [Eng.-U.K.]	118	Hk	50.12N	5.29W
Saint James	186	Ie	43.59N	94.38W
Saint James, Cape - ▶	180	Ef	51.57N	131.01W
Saint-Jean	180	Kg	45.13N	73.15W
Saint-Jean, Baie de- ◐	197b	Bc	17.55N	62.51W
Saint-Jean, Lac- ≈	174	Le	48.35N	72.00W
Saint-Jean-d'Angély	122	Fi	45.57N	0.31W
Saint-Jean-de-Luz	122	Ek	43.23N	1.40W
Saint-Jean-de-Maurienne	122	Mi	45.17N	6.21 E
Saint-Jean-de-Monts	122	Dh	46.47N	2.04W
Saint-Jean-du-Gard	122	Jj	44.06N	3.53 E
Saint-Jean-Pied-de-Port	122	Ek	43.10N	1.14W
Saint-Jérôme [Que.-Can.]	184	La	48.26N	71.52W
Saint-Jérôme [Que.-Can.]	180	Kg	45.46N	74.00W

Index Symbols

- ① Independent Nation
- ② State, Region
- ③ District, County
- ④ Municipality
- ⑤ Colony, Dependency
- ■ Continent
- ⧗ Physical Region
- ⊡ Historical or Cultural Region
- ▲ Mount, Mountain
- 🌋 Volcano
- △ Hill
- ⛰ Mountains, Mountain Range
- ⩕ Hills, Escarpment
- ⏏ Plateau, Upland
- ⌄ Pass, Gap
- ▭ Plain, Lowland
- ◸ Delta
- ⊟ Salt Flat
- ▽ Valley, Canyon
- ◡ Crater, Cave
- ✷ Karst Features
- ⊍ Depression
- ⊓ Polder
- ◢ Desert, Dunes
- ♣ Forest, Woods
- ᴡ Heath, Steppe
- 🌴 Oasis
- ▶ Cape, Point
- ⌇ Coast, Beach
- ▌ Cliff
- ▬ Peninsula
- ⋈ Isthmus
- ⋯ Sandbank
- ◆ Island
- ⊙ Atoll
- ✳ Rock, Reef
- ⁂ Islands, Archipelago
- ⊛ Rocks, Reefs
- ✺ Coral Reef
- ⊚ Well, Spring
- ⛲ Geyser
- ∿ River, Stream
- ⤵ Waterfall, Rapids
- ⋖ River Mouth, Estuary
- ≈ Lake
- ⩰ Salt Lake
- ◌ Intermittent Lake
- ⊔ Reservoir
- ⋓ Swamp, Pond
- ═ Canal
- ❄ Glacier
- ❅ Ice Shelf, Pack Ice
- ≋ Ocean
- ≡ Sea
- ◐ Gulf, Bay
- ≂ Strait, Fjord
- ⊜ Lagoon
- ⊞ Bank
- ⩞ Seamount
- ⊼ Tablemount
- ⋀ Ridge
- ⊏ Shelf
- ⌣ Basin
- ⟋ Escarpment, Sea Scarp
- ⚡ Fracture
- ∨ Trench, Abyss
- ⚑ National Park, Reserve
- ★ Point of Interest
- ⛱ Recreation Site
- ◓ Cave, Cavern
- ⛫ Historic Site
- ∴ Ruins
- ▥ Wall, Walls
- ⛪ Church, Abbey
- ⛩ Temple
- ⊠ Scientific Station
- 🚉 Railway station
- ✈ Airport
- ⚓ Port
- ⊕ Military installation
- ⛯ Lighthouse
- ⚒ Mine
- ∩ Tunnel
- ⟂ Dam, Bridge

Saint Joe River 188 Gc 47.21N 116.42W
Saint John 196 Dc 18.20N 64.42W
Saint John [Can.] 174 Me 45.15N 66.04W
Saint John [Ks.-U.S.] 186 Gh 38.00N 98.46W
Saint John [Lbr.] 166 Cd 5.55N 10.05W
Saint John [N.B.-Can.] 176 Me 45.16N 66.03W
Saint John's [Atg.] 190 Le 17.06N 61.51W
Saint Johns [Az.-U.S.] 188 Ki 34.30N 109.22W
Saint Johns [Mi.-U.S.] 184 Ed 43.00N 84.33W
Saint John's [Mont.] 197c Bc 16.48N 62.11W
Saint John's [Newf.-Can.] 176 Ne 47.34N 52.43W
Saint Johnsbury 184 Kc 44.25N 72.01W
Saint Johns River 184 Gj 30.24N 81.24W
Saint Joseph [Dom.] 197g Bb 15.24N 61.26W
Saint Joseph [La.-U.S.] 186 Kk 31.55N 91.14W
Saint-Joseph [Mart.] 197h Ab 14.40N 61.03W
Saint Joseph [Mi.-U.S.] 184 Dd 42.06N 86.29W
Saint Joseph [Mo.-U.S.] 182 Id 39.46N 94.51W
Saint-Joseph [N.Cal.] 219b Ce 20.27S 166.36 E
Saint-Joseph [Reu.] 172a Bb 21.22S 55.37 E
Saint Joseph, Lake- 180 If 51.06N 90.36W
Saint Joseph Island 184 Fb 46.13N 83.57W
Saint Joseph River 184 Dd 42.06N 86.29W
Saint-Junien 122 Gi 45.53N 0.54 E
Saint-Just-en-Chaussée 124 Ee 49.30N 2.26 E
Saint Kilda 118 Ed 57.49N 8.36W
Saint Kitts/Saint Christopher 174 Mh 17.21N 62.48W
Saint-Lary-Soulan 122 Gl 42.49N 0.19 E
Saint Laurent 200 Ke 5.30N 54.02W
Saint-Laurent = Saint Lawrence (EN) 174 Me 49.15N 67.00W
Saint Lawrence 174 Bc 63.30N 170.30W
Saint Lawrence 174 Me 49.15N 67.00W
Saint Lawrence (EN) = Saint-Laurent 174 Me 49.15N 67.00W
Saint Lawrence, Gulf of- 174 Me 48.00N 62.00W
Saint-Léger-en-Yvelines 124 Df 48.43N 1.46 E
Saint-Léonard 184 Nb 47.10N 67.56W
Saint-Léonard-de-Noblat 122 Hi 45.50N 1.29 E
Saint-Lewis 180 Lf 52.22N 55.58W
Saint-Lô 122 Ee 49.07N 1.05W
Saint-Louis [Guad.] 197e Bc 15.57N 61.20W
Saint Louis [Mo.-U.S.] 176 Jf 38.38N 90.11W
Saint-Louis [Sen.] 160 Fg 16.02N 16.30W
Saint-Loup-sur-Semouse 122 Mg 47.53N 6.16 E
Saint Lucia 172 Ee 28.23S 32.25 E
Saint Lucia 176 Mh 13.53N 60.58W
Saint Lucia 174 Mh 13.53N 60.58W
Saint Lucia, Cape- 158 Kk 28.32S 32.24 E
Saint Lucia, Lake- 172 Ee 28.00S 32.30 E
Saint Lucia Channel 196 Fe 14.09N 60.57W
Saint Lucia Channel (EN) = Sainte-Lucie, Canal de- 196 Fe 14.09N 60.57W
Saint Magnus Bay 118 La 60.25N 1.35W
Saint-Maixent-l'Ecole 122 Fh 46.25N 0.12W
Saint-Malo 112 Ff 48.39N 2.01W
Saint-Malo, Golfe de- 110 Ff 48.45N 2.00W
Saint-Marc 190 Je 19.06N 72.43W
Saint-Marc, Canal de- 194 Kd 18.50N 72.45W
Saint-Marcellin 122 Li 45.09N 5.19 E
Saint Margaret's at Cliffe 124 Dc 51.09N 1.19 E
Saint Margaret's Hope 118 Kc 58.49N 2.57W
Saint Maries 188 Gc 47.19N 116.35W
Saint Martin 190 Le 18.04N 63.04W
Saint Martin, Cap- 197h Ab 14.52N 61.13W
Saint-Martin-Boulogne 124 Dd 50.43N 1.40 E
Saint-Martin-de-Ré 122 Eh 46.12N 1.22W
Saint-Martin-des-Besaces 124 Be 49.01N 0.51W
Saint Martins 184 Oc 45.21N 65.32W
Saint-Martin-Vésubie 122 Nj 44.04N 7.15 E
Saint Mary, Cape- 184 Nc 44.05N 66.13W
Saint Mary Peak [Austl.] 212 Hf 31.30S 138.35 E
Saint Mary Peak [U.S.] 188 Hc 46.40N 114.20W
Saint Mary's 118 Gl 49.55N 6.20W
Saint Marys [Austl.] 212 Jh 41.35S 148.10 E
Saint Marys [Oh.-U.S.] 184 Ee 40.32N 84.22W
Saint Marys [W.V.-U.S.] 184 Gf 39.24N 81.13W
Saint Mary's, Cape - 180 Mg 46.49N 54.12W
Saint Mary's Bay [N.S.-Can.] 184 Nc 44.25N 66.10W
Saint Mary's Bay [N.W.T.-Can.] 180 Mg 46.50N 53.47W
Saint Marys River 184 Gj 30.45N 81.30W
Saint-Mathieu, Pointe de- 110 Ff 48.20N 4.46W
Saint Matthew 174 Bb 60.30N 172.45W
Saint Matthias Group 208 Fe 1.30S 149.48 E
Saint-Maur-des-Fossés 122 If 48.48N 2.30 E
Saint-Maurice, Rivière- 180 Kg 46.21N 72.31W
Saint Michael 178 Gd 63.29N 162.02W
Saint Michaels 188 Ki 35.46N 109.04W
Saint-Michel 124 Ge 49.55N 4.08 E
Saint-Mihiel 122 Lf 48.54N 5.33 E
Saint-Nazaire 122 Dg 47.17N 2.12W
Saint Neots 124 Bb 52.13N 0.16W
Saint-Nicolas/Sint Niklaas 122 Kc 51.10N 4.08 E
Saint-Nicolas-d'Aliermont 124 De 49.53N 1.13 E
Saint-Nicolas-de-Port 122 Mf 48.38N 6.18 E
Saint-Omer 122 Id 50.45N 2.15 E
Saintonge 122 Fi 45.50N 0.30W
Saint Patrick's 197c Bc 16.41N 62.12W
Saint Paul 176 Je 44.58N 93.07W
Saint-Paul 158 Ol 38.55S 77.41 E
Saint Paul 178 Ee 57.07N 170.17W
Saint Paul 166 Cd 6.23N 10.48W
Saint Paul [Alta.-Can.] 180 Gf 53.59N 111.17W
Saint Paul [Nb.-U.S.] 186 Gf 41.13N 98.27W
Saint-Paul [Reu.] 172a Bb 21.00S 55.16 E
Saint Paul, Cape- 166 Fd 5.49N 0.57 E
Saint-Paul-lès-Dax 122 Ek 43.44N 1.03W
Saint Paul's 197c Ab 17.24N 62.49W
Saint Paul's Point 220q Ab 25.04S 130.05W
Saint-Péray 122 Kj 44.57N 4.50 E
Saint Peter 186 Jd 44.17N 93.57W
Saint Peter Port 118 Kl 49.27N 2.32W
Saint Peter's 197c Bc 16.46N 62.12W
Saint Petersburg 176 Kg 27.46N 82.38W
Saint Petersburg Beach 184 Fl 27.45N 82.45W
Saint-Pierre [Mart.] 196 Fe 14.45N 61.11W
Saint-Pierre [Reu.] 160 Mk 21.19S 55.29 E
Saint-Pierre [St.P.M.] 180 Lg 46.46N 56.12W
Saint-Pierre, Lac- 184 Kb 46.10N 72.50W
Saint Pierre and Miquelon (EN) = Saint-Pierre et Miquelon 176 Ne 46.55N 56.10W
Saint-Pierre-en-Port 124 Ce 49.48N 0.29 E
Saint-Pierre et Miquelon = Saint Pierre and Miquelon (EN) 176 Ne 46.55N 56.10W
Saint Pierre Island 172b Bb 9.19S 50.43 E
Saint-Pierre-sur-Dives 124 Be 49.01N 0.02W
Saint-Pol-de-Léon 122 Cf 48.41N 3.59W
Saint-Pol-sur-Mer 124 Ec 51.02N 2.21 E
Saint-Pol-sur-Ternoise 122 Id 50.23N 2.20 E
Saint-Pons 122 Ik 43.29N 2.46 E
Saint-Pourçain-sur-Sioule 122 Jh 46.18N 3.17 E
Saint-Quentin 122 Je 49.51N 3.17 E
Saint-Quentin, Canal de- 124 Fe 49.36N 3.11 E
Saint-Raphaël 122 Mk 43.25N 6.46 E
Saint-Rémy-de-Provence 122 Kk 43.47N 4.50 E
Saint-Rigaux, Mont- 122 Kh 46.12N 4.29 E
Saint-Riquier 124 Dd 50.08N 1.57 E
Saint Roch Basin 180 Ic 68.50N 95.00W
Saint-Romain-de-Colbosc 124 Ce 49.32N 0.22 E
Saint-Saëns 124 De 49.40N 1.17 E
Saint Sauflieu 124 Ee 49.47N 2.15 E
Saint-Savin 122 Gh 46.34N 0.52 E
Saint-Sébastien, Cap- 172 Hb 12.26S 48.44 E
Saint-Seine-l'Abbaye 122 Kg 47.26N 4.47 E
Saint-Servais, Namur- 124 Gd 50.28N 4.50 E
Saint Simon 124 Fe 49.45N 3.10 E
Saint Simons Island 184 Gj 31.14N 81.21W
Saint Stanislas Bay 220g Bb 1.53N 157.30W
Saint Stephen 180 Kg 45.12N 67.17W
Saint-Sylvain 124 Be 49.03N 0.13W
Saint Teresa Beach 184 Ek 29.58N 84.28W
Saint Thomas 184 Gd 42.47N 81.12W
Saint Thomas 190 Le 18.21N 64.55W
Saint-Trond/Sint-Truiden 122 Ld 50.49N 5.12 E
Saint-Tropez 122 Mk 43.16N 6.38 E
Saint-Tropez, Golfe de- 122 Mk 43.17N 6.38 E
Saint-Valéry-en-Caux 122 Ge 49.52N 0.44 E
Saint-Valéry-sur-Somme 122 Hd 50.11N 1.38 E
Saint-Vallier 122 Ki 45.10N 4.49 E
Saint-Venant 124 Ed 50.37N 2.33 E
Saint-Vincent 128 Be 45.45N 7.39 E
Saint Vincent 174 Mh 13.15N 61.12W
Saint-Vincent, Baie de- 219b Cf 22.00S 166.05 E
Saint-Vincent, Cap- 158 Lk 21.57S 43.16 E
Saint Vincent, Gulf- 212 Hf 35.00S 138.05 E
Saint Vincent and the Grenadines 176 Mh 13.15N 61.12W
Saint-Vincent-de-Tyrosse 122 Ek 43.40N 1.18W
Saint Vincent Island 184 Ek 29.40N 85.07W
Saint Vincent Passage 196 Ff 13.30N 61.00W
Saint-Vith / Sankt-Vith 122 Md 50.17N 6.08 E
Saint-Wandrille-Rançon 124 Ce 49.32N 0.46 E
Saint-Yrieix-la-Perche 122 Hi 45.31N 1.12 E
Saipan 220a Ad 6.54N 134.08 E
Saipan Channel 220b Ba 15.05N 145.41 E
Saipan Island 208 Fc 15.12N 145.45 E
Saira 204 Ak 32.24S 62.06W
Sairecábur, Cerro- 202 Eh 22.43S 67.54W
Saitama Ken 154 Of 36.00N 139.50 E
Saito 154 Kh 32.06N 131.24 E
Sajak 136 Hf 46.55N 77.22 E
Sajama 202 Eg 18.07S 69.00W
Sajama, Nevado de- 198 Jg 18.06S 68.54W
Sajānan 128 Dm 37.03N 9.14 E
Sajat 135 De 38.49N 63.51 E
Sajīd 164 Hf 16.52N 41.55 E
Sajir, Ra's- 168 Ib 16.45N 53.35 E
Sajmenski kanal = Saimaa Canal (EN) 116 Mc 61.05N 28.18 E
Sajn-Sand 142 Ne 44.55N 110.11 E
Sajó 120 Ri 47.56N 21.08 E
Sajószentpéter 120 Qh 48.13N 20.43 E
Sajram 135 Gc 42.18N 69.45 E
Sajzī 146 Of 32.41N 52.07 E
Saka 170 Gc 0.09S 39.20 E
Sakai 154 Mg 34.35N 135.28 E
Sakaide 156 Cd 34.19N 133.51 E
Sakaiminato 156 Cd 35.33N 133.15 E
Sakākah 144 Fd 29.59N 40.06 E
Sakakawea, Lake- 182 Gb 47.50N 102.20W
Sakala, vozvyšennost- / Sakala Kõrgustik 116 Kf 58.00N 25.30 E
Sakala Kõrgustik / Sakala, vozvyšennost- 116 Kf 58.00N 25.30 E
Sakami 180 Jf 53.18N 76.45W
Sakami, lac- 180 Jf 53.15N 76.45W
Sâkâne, 'Erg i-n- 166 Ea 20.40N 0.51W
Sakania 170 Ee 12.43S 28.33 E
Sakao 219b Cb 14.58S 167.07 E
Sakar 135 De 38.59N 63.45 E
Sakar 130 Jh 41.59N 26.16 E
Sakaraha 172 Gd 22.54S 44.32 E
Sakar-Čaga 135 Cf 37.39N 61.40 E
Sakārinah, Jabal as- 128 Do 35.45N 9.05 E
Sakartvelos Sabčata Socialisturi Respublica/ Gruzinskaja SSR 136 Eg 42.00N 44.00 E
Sakarya 144 Da 41.07N 30.39 E
Sakata 152 Od 38.55N 139.50 E
Sakchu 154 Hd 40.23N 125.02 E
Sakhalin (EN) = Sahalin, ostrov- 140 Qd 51.00N 143.00 E
Sakht Sar 146 Nd 36.53N 50.41 E
Saki 132 Hg 45.07N 33.37 E
Šakiai/Šakjaj 114 Fi 54.57N 23.01 E
Sakishima Islands (EN) = Sakishima-Shotō 140 Og 24.30N 125.00 E
Sakishima-Shotō = Sakishima Islands (EN) 140 Og 24.30N 125.00 E
Sakito 156 Ae 33.02N 129.34 E
Sakiz Boğazı 130 Jk 38.20N 26.12 E
Šakjaj/Šakiai 114 Fi 54.57N 23.01 E
Sakmara 110 Le 51.46N 55.01 E
Sakon Nakhon 148 Ke 17.10N 104.01 E
Sakrivier 172 Cf 30.54S 20.28 E
Šakša 134 Hi 54.47N 56.15 E
Saksaulski 136 Gf 47.05N 61.13 E
Sakskøbing 116 Dj 54.48N 11.39 E
Saku 154 Of 36.09N 138.26 E
Sakuma 156 Ed 35.05N 137.47 E
Sakura 156 Gd 35.43N 140.13 E
Sakurai 156 Dd 34.31N 135.50 E
Sakura-Jima 156 Bf 31.35N 130.40 E
Säkylä 116 Jc 61.02N 22.20 E
Sal 158 Eg 16.45N 22.55W
Sal 136 Ef 47.31N 40.45 E
Sal, Cay- 194 Gb 23.42N 80.24W
Sal, Punta- 194 Df 15.53N 87.37W
Sala 114 Dg 59.55N 16.36 E
Šalá 120 Nh 48.09N 17.53 E
Sala 168 Cb 17.00N 20.53 E
Salabangka, Kepulauan- 150 Hg 3.02S 122.25 E
Salaca 116 Kg 57.39N 24.15 E
Salacgriva/Salacgrīva 114 Fh 57.46N 24.27 E
Salacgrīva/Salacgriva 114 Fh 57.46N 24.27 E
Sala Consilina 128 Jj 40.23N 15.36 E
Salada 192 Hc 28.36N 103.28W
Salada, Laguna- 192 Ba 32.20N 115.40W
Saladas 206 Ic 28.15S 58.38W
Saladillo 206 Ie 35.38S 59.46W
Saladillo, Arroyo- 204 Bj 31.22S 60.30W
Saladillo Amargo, Arroyo- 204 Bj 31.01S 60.19W
Saladillo Dulce, Arroyo- 204 Bj 31.01S 60.19W
Salado, Arroyo- [Arg.] 204 Bm 36.27S 61.06W
Salado, Arroyo- [Mex.] 192 De 24.25N 111.30W
Salado, Riacho- 204 Ch 26.30S 58.18W
Salado, Río- 186 Ci 34.16N 106.52W
Salado, Río- 190 Ec 26.52N 99.19W
Salado, Río- [Arg.] 198 Ki 35.44S 57.21W
Salado, Río- [Arg.] 198 Ji 31.42S 60.44W
Salado, Río- [Arg.] 206 Ge 38.49S 64.57W
Salado, Valle- 192 He 24.47N 102.50W
Salaga 166 Ed 8.33N 0.31W
Salagle 168 Ge 1.50N 42.18 E
Salāhuddīn 146 Je 34.40N 44.00 E
Salailua 221c Aa 13.41S 172.34W
Salairski krjaž 138 Df 54.00N 85.00 E
Sălaj 130 Fb 47.10N 23.00 E
Šalakuša 114 Je 62.15N 40.18 E
Salal 168 Bc 14.51N 17.13 E
Salālah [Oman] 142 Hh 17.05N 54.10 E
Salālah [Sud.] 168 Fa 21.19N 36.13 E
Salamá 194 Bf 15.06N 90.16W
Salamanca 126 Gd 40.50N 6.00W
Salamanca [Chile] 206 Fd 31.47S 70.58W
Salamanca [Mex.] 190 Dd 20.34N 101.12W
Salamanca [N.Y.-U.S.] 184 Hd 42.11N 78.43W
Salamanca [Sp.] 112 Fg 40.58N 5.39W
Salamat 168 Cc 11.00N 20.30 E
Salamat, Bahr- 168 Bd 9.27N 18.06 E
Salamina 194 Jh 10.30N 74.48W
Salamís 130 Gl 37.58N 23.29 E
Salamís 130 Gl 37.55N 23.30 E
Salamis 146 Ee 35.10N 33.54 E
Salamīyah, Sabkhat as- 146 Pj 24.00N 53.45 E
Sālang, Tūnel-e- 144 Kb 35.19N 69.02 E
Salani 221c Bb 14.00S 171.34W
Salantai/Salantaj 116 Ih 56.05N 21.30 E
Salantaj/Salantai 116 Ih 56.05N 21.30 E
Salas 126 Fa 43.24N 6.16W
Salas de los Infantes 126 Ib 42.01N 3.17W
Salat 220d Cb 7.14N 152.01 E
Salat 122 Gk 43.10N 0.58 E
Salatiga 150 Fh 7.19S 110.30 E
Salavat 112 Le 53.25N 55.58 E
Salawati, Pulau- 208 Ee 1.07S 130.52 E
Sala y Gómez 208 Qg 26.28S 105.28W
Sala y Gómez Ridge (EN) 106 Ml 25.00S 98.00W
Salazar 204 Am 36.18S 62.12W
Salbris 122 Ig 47.26N 2.03 E
Salcantay, Nevado de- 198 Ig 13.22S 72.34W
Šalčininkai/Šalčininkaj 116 Kj 54.18N 25.30 E
Šalčininkaj/Šalčininkai 116 Kj 54.18N 25.30 E
Salda Gölü 130 Ml 37.33N 29.42 E
Saldaña 126 Hb 42.31N 4.44W
Saldanha 160 Il 33.00S 17.56 E
Saldungaray 204 Bn 38.12S 61.47W
Saldus 136 Cd 56.40N 22.31 E
Salé 162 Fc 34.04N 6.48W
Sale 212 Jg 38.06S 147.04 E
Salebabu, Pulau- 150 If 3.55N 126.40 E
Şāleḩābād 146 Me 34.56N 48.20 E
Salehard 142 Ic 66.33N 66.40 E
Saleimoa 221c Ba 13.48S 171.52W
Salelologa 221c Aa 13.44S 172.10W
Salem [Fl.-U.S.] 184 Fk 29.58N 83.28W
Salem [Il.-U.S.] 186 Lg 38.38N 88.57W
Salem [India] 142 Jh 11.39N 78.10 E
Salem [In.-U.S.] 184 Df 38.36N 86.06W
Salem [Ma.-U.S.] 184 Ld 42.31N 70.55W
Salem [Mont.] 197c Bc 16.45N 62.13W
Salem [Mo.-U.S.] 186 Kh 37.39N 91.32W
Salem [N.J.-U.S.] 184 Jf 39.35N 75.28W
Salem [Oh.-U.S.] 184 Ge 40.54N 80.52W
Salem [Or.-U.S.] 176 Ge 44.57N 123.01W
Salem [S.D.-U.S.] 186 He 43.44N 97.23W
Salem [Va.-U.S.] 184 Gg 37.17N 80.03W
Salemi 128 Gm 37.49N 12.48 E
Sälen 116 Ec 61.10N 13.16 E
Salentina, Penisola- = Salentine Peninsula (EN) 110 Hg 40.30N 18.00 E
Salentine Peninsula (EN) = Salentina, Penisola- 110 Hg 40.30N 18.00 E
Salerno 112 Hg 40.41N 14.47 E
Salerno, Golfo di- 128 Ij 40.30N 14.40 E
Salers 122 Ii 45.08N 2.30 E
Salève, Mont- 122 Mh 46.07N 6.10 E
Salgir 132 Ig 45.38N 35.01 E
Salgótarján 120 Ph 48.07N 19.49 E
Salgueiro 202 Ke 8.04S 39.06W
Salher 148 Ed 20.41N 73.52 E
Salhus 114 Af 60.30N 5.16 E
Šali 132 Nh 43.06N 45.56 E
Sali 128 Jg 43.56N 15.10 E
Salice Terme 128 Df 44.55N 9.01 E
Salida 182 Fd 38.32N 106.00W
Salies-de-Béarn 122 Fk 43.29N 0.55W
Salihli 144 Cb 38.29N 28.09 E
Salima 170 Fe 13.47S 34.26 E
Salīma, Wāḩāt- = Salimah Oasis (EN) 160 Jf 21.22N 29.19 E
Salimah Oasis (EN) = Salīma, Wāḩāt- 160 Jf 21.22N 29.19 E
Salina 128 Il 38.35N 14.50 E
Salina [Ks.-U.S.] 176 Jf 38.50N 97.37W
Salina [Ut.-U.S.] 188 Jg 38.58N 111.51W
Salina Cruz 190 Ee 16.10N 95.12W
Salinas [Ca.-U.S.] 176 Gf 36.40N 121.38W
Salinas [Ec.] 202 Bd 2.13S 80.58W
Salinas [P.R.] 197a Bc 17.59N 66.17W
Salinas, Bahía de- 194 Eh 11.03N 85.43W
Salinas, Cabo de-/Ses Salines, Cap de- 126 Pe 39.16N 3.03 E
Salinas, Punta- [Dom.Rep.] 194 Ld 18.12N 70.34W
Salinas, Punta- [P.R.] 197a Bb 18.29N 66.10W
Salinas, Río- 194 Be 16.28N 90.33W
Salinas de Hidalgo 192 If 22.38N 101.43W
Salinas Peak 186 Cj 33.18N 106.31W
Saline, Point- 196 Fg 12.00N 61.48W
Saline Island 197p Cb 12.26N 61.29W
Saline River [Ks.-U.S.] 186 Hg 38.51N 97.30W
Saline River [U.S.] 186 Jj 33.10N 92.08W
Salines, Pointe des- 197h Bc 14.24N 60.53W
Salinópolis 202 Id 0.37S 47.20W
Salins-les-Bains 122 Lh 46.57N 5.53 E
Salisbury 180 Jd 63.35N 77.00W
Salisbury [Dom.] 197g Bb 15.26N 61.27W
Salisbury [Eng.-U.K.] 118 Lj 51.05N 1.48W
Salisbury [Md.-U.S.] 182 Ld 38.22N 75.36W
Salisbury [N.C.-U.S.] 184 Gh 35.40N 80.29W
Salisbury Plain 118 Lj 51.15N 1.55W
Sălişte 130 Gd 45.47N 23.53 E
Šalja 136 Fd 57.15N 58.43 E
Saljany 136 Eh 39.35N 48.59 E
Šalkar, ozero- 132 Qd 50.35N 51.40 E
Šalkar-Jega-Kara, ozero- 132 Vd 50.45N 60.55 E
Salkhad 146 Gf 32.29N 36.43 E
Salla 114 Gc 66.50N 28.40 E
Sallent de Gállego 126 Lb 42.46N 0.20W
Salling 116 Ch 56.40N 9.00 E
Salliqueló 206 He 36.45S 62.56W
Sallisaw 186 Ii 35.28N 94.47W
Sallūm 168 Fb 19.23N 37.06 E
Sallūm, Khalīj as- = Salum, Gulf of-(EN) 164 Ec 31.40N 25.20 E
Sallyana 148 Gc 28.22N 82.10 E
Salm 124 Ie 49.51N 6.51 E
Salmās 144 Fb 38.11N 44.47 E
Salmi 114 Hf 61.24N 31.54 E
Salmo 188 Gb 49.12N 117.17W
Salmon 182 Eb 45.11N 113.54W
Salmon Arm 180 Ff 50.42N 119.16W
Salmon Bank (EN) 214 Kb 26.56N 176.28W
Salmon Falls Creek Reservoir 188 He 42.05N 114.45W
Salmon Mountain 188 Hd 45.38N 114.50W
Salmon Mountains 188 Df 41.00N 123.00W
Salmon River 174 He 45.51N 116.46W
Salmon River Mountains 182 Dc 44.45N 115.30W
Salmtal 124 Ie 49.56N 6.48 E
Salmyš 132 Sc 52.01N 55.21 E
Salo 168 Be 3.12N 16.07 E
Salò 128 Ee 45.36N 10.31 E
Salo 114 Ff 60.23N 23.08 E
Salobra, Rio- 204 De 20.12S 56.29W
Salobreña 126 Ih 36.44N 3.35W
Salomon, Cap- 197h Ab 14.30N 61.06W
Salon-de-Provence 122 Lk 43.38N 5.06 E
Salonga 158 Ii 0.10S 19.50 E
Salonika (EN) = Thessaloníki 112 Ig 40.38N 22.56 E
Salonika, Gulf of- (EN) = Thermaïkós Kólpos 110 Ig 40.20N 22.45 E
Salonta 130 Ec 46.48N 21.39 E
Salop 118 Ki 52.40N 2.50W
Salor 126 Ee 39.39N 7.03W
Salou 126 Nc 41.04N 1.08 E
Salouël 124 Ee 49.52N 2.15 E
Saloum 166 Bc 13.50N 16.45W
Salpausselkä 110 Ic 61.00N 26.30 E
Sal-Rei 162 Cf 16.11N 22.55W
Salsbruket 114 Cd 64.48N 11.52 E
Salseleh-ye Safīd Kūh/ Paropamisus 140 If 34.30N 63.30 E
Salses, Étang de- → Leucate, Étang de- 122 Il 42.51N 3.00 E
Salsipuedes, Canal de- 192 Cc 28.40N 113.00W
Salsipuedes, Punta- 194 Fi 8.28N 83.37W
Salsk 136 Ef 46.28N 41.29 E
Šalski 114 If 61.48N 36.03 E
Salso [It.] 128 Im 37.39N 14.49 E
Salso [It.] 128 Hm 37.06N 13.57 E
Salsola 128 Ji 41.37N 15.40 E
Salsomaggiore Terme 128 Df 44.49N 9.59 E
Salt 126 Oc 41.59N 2.47 E
Salta 200 Jh 24.47S 65.24W
Salta 206 Hb 25.00S 64.30W
Saltash 118 Ik 50.24N 4.12W
Salt Basin 186 Dk 31.50N 105.00W
Saltburn-by-the-Sea 118 Mg 54.35N 0.58W
Salt Cay 194 Lc 21.20N 71.11W
Salt Creek 188 Gh 36.15N 116.49W
Salt Draw 186 Ek 31.19N 103.28W
Saltee Islands/Na Sailtí 118 Gi 52.07N 6.36W
Salten 114 Dc 67.45N 15.31 E
Salt Fork Brazos 186 Gj 33.15N 100.00W
Salt Fork of Arkansas River 186 Hh 36.36N 97.03W
Salt Fork Red 186 Gi 34.30N 99.22W
Saltholm 116 Ei 55.40N 12.45 E
Saltillo 176 Ig 25.25N 101.01W
Salt Lake City 176 He 40.46N 111.53W
Salto 204 Dj 31.25S 57.00W
Salto 128 Gh 42.23N 12.54 E
Salto [Arg.] 206 Hd 34.17S 60.15W
Salto [Ur.] 200 Ki 31.23S 57.58W
Salto da Divisa 202 Kg 16.00S 39.57W
Salto del Guairá 206 Jb 24.05S 54.15W
Salto Grande 204 Hf 22.54S 49.59W
Salton Sea 174 Hf 33.20N 115.50W
Salt River [Az.-U.S.] 182 Ee 33.23N 112.18W
Salt River [U.S.] 188 Je 43.07N 111.02W
Saltsjöbaden 116 He 59.17N 18.18 E
Saltvik 114 Ef 60.17N 20.03 E
Saluafata Harbour 221c Ba 13.55S 171.38W
Saluda 184 Ig 37.36N 76.36W
Salum, Gulf of-(EN) = Sallūm, Khalīj as- 164 Ec 31.40N 25.20 E
Saluzzo 128 Bf 44.39N 7.29 E
Salvación, Bahía- 206 Eh 50.55S 75.05W
Salvador [Braz.] 200 Mg 12.59S 38.31W
Salvador [Niger] 166 Ha 23.14N 12.05 E
Salvador, Lake- 186 Kl 29.45N 90.15W
Salvador Mazza 206 Hb 22.10S 63.43W
Salvaterra de Magos 126 De 39.01N 8.48W
Salvatierra [Mex.] 192 Ig 20.13N 100.53W
Salvatierra [Sp.] 126 Jb 42.51N 2.23W
Salwa, Dawḩat as- 146 Nj 25.30N 50.40 E
Salwá Baḩrī 164 Fe 24.44N 32.56 E
Salween (EN) = Thanlwin 140 Lg 16.31N 97.37 E
Salyersville 184 Fg 37.45N 83.04W
Salza 128 Ic 47.40N 14.43 E
Salzach 120 Ih 48.12N 12.56 E
Salzburg 112 Hf 47.48N 13.02 E
Salzburg 128 Gc 47.20N 13.00 E
Salzburger Kalkalpen 128 Gc 47.35N 12.55 E
Salzgitter 120 Gd 52.05N 10.20 E
Salzkammergut 128 Hc 47.45N 13.30 E
Salzkotten 124 Kc 51.40N 8.36 E
Salzwedel 120 Hd 52.51N 11.09 E
Samadāy, Ra's- 146 Fj 25.00N 34.56 E
Samagaltaj 138 Ef 50.36N 95.03 E
Samaḩ [Lib.] 164 Cd 28.10N 19.10 E
Samaḩ [Sau.Ar.] 146 Kh 28.52N 45.30 E
Samaipata 202 Fg 18.09S 63.52W
Samalayuca 192 Fb 31.21N 106.28W
Samales Group 150 He 6.00N 121.45 E
Samalga Pass 178a Eb 52.48N 169.25W
Samālūt 164 Fd 28.18N 30.42 E
Samambaia, Rio- 204 Ff 22.45S 53.21W
Samaná 194 Md 19.13N 69.19W
Samaná, Bahía de- 190 Ke 19.10N 69.25W
Samaná, Cabo- 194 Md 19.18N 69.09W
Samana Cay 194 Kb 23.06N 73.42W
Samandağı 146 Fd 36.07N 35.56 E
Samangān 144 Kb 36.15N 67.40 E
Samani 152 Pc 42.07N 142.56 E
Samanlı Dağları 130 Mi 40.32N 29.10 E
Samar 140 Oh 12.00N 125.00 E
Samara [R.S.F.S.R.] 110 Le 53.10N 50.04 E
Samara [Ukr.-U.S.S.R.] 132 Ie 48.33N 35.12 E
Samarai 210 Gf 10.36S 150.39 E
Samarinda 142 Nj 0.30S 117.09 E
Samarkand 142 If 39.40N 66.58 E
Samarkandskaja oblast 136 Gg 40.10N 66.20 E
Sāmarrā' 144 Fc 34.12N 43.52 E
Samar Sea 150 Hd 11.50N 124.32 E
Samaru 166 Gc 11.10N 7.38 E
Samatan 122 Gk 43.30N 0.56 E
Samate 150 Jg 0.58S 131.04 E
Samba [Zaire] 170 Ec 4.38S 26.22 E
Samba [Zaire] 170 Db 0.14N 21.19 E
Samba Caju 170 Cd 8.45S 15.25 E
Sambalpur 148 Gd 21.27N 83.58 E
Sambar, Tanjung- 150 Fg 2.59S 110.19 E
Sambas 150 Ef 1.20N 109.15 E
Sambava 172 Ib 14.15S 50.10 E
Samber 122 Kd 50.28N 4.52 E
Sāmbhar 148 Fc 26.55N 75.12 E
Sambiase, Lamezia Terme- 128 Kl 38.58N 16.17 E
Samboja 150 Gg 1.02S 117.02 E
Sambor 136 Cf 49.32N 23.11 E
Samborombón, Bahía- 206 Ie 36.00S 57.12W
Samborombón, Río- 204 Dl 35.43S 57.20W
Sambre 122 Kd 50.28N 4.52 E
Sambre à l'Oise, Canal de la- 122 Je 49.39N 3.20 E
Samburg 138 Cc 67.00N 78.25 E
Samch'ŏnp'o 152 Me 34.55N 128.04 E
Samdi Dağı 146 Kd 37.19N 44.15 E
Samdŏng-ni 154 Ie 39.21N 126.14 E
Samdŭng 154 Ie 38.59N 126.11 E
Same [Indon.] 150 Ih 8.59S 125.40 E
Same [Tan.] 170 Gc 4.04S 37.44 E
Samer 124 Dd 50.38N 1.45 E
Sam Ford Fiord 180 Kb 70.40N 70.35W
Samfya 170 Ee 11.20S 29.32 E
Šamhor 132 Oi 40.48N 46.01 E
Sámi 130 Dk 38.15N 20.39 E
Sāmī Ghar 144 Kc 31.43N 67.01 E
Samīrah 146 Ji 26.18N 42.05 E
Şamli 130 Kj 39.48N 27.51 E
Samnah, Jabal- 146 Ei 26.26N 33.34 E
Samoa I Sisifo = Western Samoa (EN) 210 Jf 13.40S 172.30W
Samoa Islands 208 Jf 14.00S 171.00W
Samobor 128 Je 45.48N 15.43 E
Samojlovka 132 Md 51.10N 43.43 E
Samokov 130 Gg 42.20N 23.33 E
Samolva 116 Lf 58.16N 27.45 E
Sámos 130 Jl 37.45N 26.58 E

Index Symbols

1 Independent Nation
2 State, Region
3 District, County
4 Municipality
5 Colony, Dependency
Continent
Physical Region
Historical or Cultural Region
Mount, Mountain
Volcano
Hill
Mountains, Mountain Range
Hills, Escarpment
Plateau, Upland
Pass, Gap
Plain, Lowland
Delta
Salt Flat
Valley, Canyon
Crater, Cave
Karst Features
Depression
Polder
Desert, Dunes
Forest, Woods
Heath, Steppe
Oasis
Cape, Point
Coast, Beach
Cliff
Peninsula
Isthmus
Sandbank
Island
Atoll
Rock, Reef
Islands, Archipelago
Rocks, Reefs
Coral Reef
Well, Spring
Geyser
River, Stream
Waterfall, Rapids
River Mouth, Estuary
Lake
Salt Lake
Intermittent Lake
Reservoir
Swamp, Pond
Canal
Glacier
Ice Shelf, Pack Ice
Ocean
Sea
Gulf, Bay
Strait, Fjord
Lagoon
Bank
Seamount
Tablemount
Ridge
Shelf
Basin
Escarpment, Sea Scarp
Fracture
Trench, Abyss
National Park, Reserve
Point of Interest
Recreation Site
Cave, Cavern
Historic Site
Ruins
Wall, Walls
Church, Abbey
Temple
Scientific Station
Railway station
Airport
Port
Military installation
Lighthouse
Mine
Tunnel
Dam, Bridge

Sámos ⊡ 110 Ih 37.45N 26.48 E
Samosir, Pulau- ⊡ 150 Cf 2.35N 98.50 E
Samothrace (EN) = Samothráki 130 Ii 40.27N 25.35 E
Samothráki 130 Ii 40.29N 25.31 E
Samothráki = Samothrace (EN) ⊡ 130 Ii 40.27N 25.35 E
Sampacho 206 Hd 33.23S 64.43W
Sampaga 150 Gg 2.19S 119.07 E
Sampit 142 Nj 2.32S 112.57 E
Sampit ◁ 150 Fg 3.00S 113.03 E
Sampoku 156 Fb 38.30N 139.30 E
Sampwe 170 Ed 9.20S 27.23 E
Sam Rayburn Reservoir ◁ 186 Ik 31.27N 94.37W
Samro, ozero- ◁ 116 Mf 58.55N 28.50 E
Samsjøen 116 Da 63.05N 10.40 E
Samsø 114 Ci 55.50N 10.35 E
Samsø Bælt ◁ 116 Di 55.50N 10.45 E
Sam Son 148 Ld 19.44N 105.54 E
Samsun 142 Fe 41.17N 36.20 E
Samsun Daği ▲ 130 Kl 37.40N 27.15 E
Samtredia 132 Mh 42.11N 42.17 E
Samuel, Mount- ▲ 212 Gc 19.41S 134.09 E
Samuhú 204 Bh 27.31S 60.24W
Samui, Ko- ⊡ 140 Li 9.30N 100.00 E
Samur ◁ 132 Pi 41.53N 48.32 E
Samur-Apşeronski kanal ◁ 132 Pi 40.35N 49.35 E
Samus 138 De 56.46N 84.44 E
Samut Prakan 148 Kf 13.36N 100.36 E
Samut Sakhon 148 Kf 13.31N 100.15 E
San 160 Gg 13.08N 4.53W
San [Asia] ◁ 148 Lf 13.32N 105.57 E
San [Pol.] ◁ 120 Rf 50.45N 21.51 E
Şan'ā' 142 Gh 15.23N 44.12 E
Sana 128 Ke 45.03N 16.23 E
Sanaag ◁ 168 Hc 10.10N 47.50 E
Şanabū 146 Di 27.30N 30.47 E
Sanae ⊠ 222 Bf 70.18S 2.22W
Sanáfir ⊡ 146 Fi 27.55N 34.42 E
Sanäg ◁ 168 Hd 7.45N 48.00 E
Sanaga ◁ 158 Hh 3.35N 9.38 E
San Agustin 200 Ie 1.53N 76.16W
San Agustin 204 Cn 38.01S 58.21W
San Agustin, Cabo- ▶ 192 Be 28.05N 115.20W
San Agustin, Cape- ▶ 150 Ie 6.16N 126.11 E
Sanak Islands ⊡ 178 Gf 54.25N 162.35W
Sanalona, Presa- ◁ 192 Fe 24.53N 107.00W
San Ambrosio, Isla- ⊡ 206 Ec 26.21S 79.52W
Sanana 150 Ig 2.04S 125.08 E
Sanana, Pulau- ⊡ 150 Ig 2.12S 125.55 E
Sanandaj 144 Gb 35.19N 47.00 E
San Andreas 188 Eg 38.12N 120.41W
San Andrés ③ 190 Hf 12.35N 81.42W
San Andrés, Cerro- ▲ 192 Ih 19.48N 100.36W
San Andrés, Isla de- ⊡ 198 Hd 12.32N 81.42W
San Andrés, Laguna de- ◁ 192 Kf 22.40N 97.50W
San Andrés de Giles 204 Cl 34.57S 59.27W
San Andrés del Rabanedo 126 Gb 42.37N 5.36W
San Andres Mountains ▲ 182 Fe 32.55N 106.45W
San Andres Peak ▲ 186 Cj 32.43N 106.30W
San Andrés Tuxtla 190 Ee 18.27N 95.13W
San Andrés y Providencia ③ 202 Ba 12.30N 81.45W
Sananduva 204 Gh 27.57S 51.48W
San Angelo 182 Ge 31.28N 100.26W
San Antonio [Blz.] 194 Ce 16.30N 89.02W
San Antonio [Chile] 206 Fd 33.35S 71.38W
San Antonio [Tx.-U.S.] 176 Jg 29.28N 98.31W
San Antonio [Ur.] 204 Dj 31.20S 57.45W
San Antonio, Cabo- [Arg.] ▶ 198 Ki 36.40S 56.42W
San Antonio, Cabo- [Cuba] ▶ 174 Kg 21.52N 84.57W
San Antonio, Cabo de- / Sant Antoni, Cap de- ▶ 126 Mf 38.48N 0.12 E
San Antonio, Canal- ◁ 204 Aj 31.42S 62.15W
San Antonio, Punta- ▶ 192 Bc 29.45N 115.45W
San Antonio, Sierra de- ▲ 192 Db 30.00N 110.20W
San Antonio Abad / Sant Antoni de Portmany 126 Nf 38.58N 1.18 E
San Antonio Bay ◁ 186 Ik 28.20N 96.45W
San Antonio de Caparo 194 Lj 7.35N 71.27W
San Antonio de Cortés 194 Cf 15.05N 88.04W
San Antonio de los Baños 194 Fb 22.53N 82.30W
San Antonio de los Cobres 206 Gb 24.11S 66.21W
San Antonio del Táchira 194 Ch 7.49N 72.27W
San Antonio de Tamanaco 196 Ch 9.14N 66.03W
San Antonio Oeste 200 Jj 40.44S 64.57W
San Antonio River ◁ 182 Jf 28.30N 96.50W
Sanare 194 Mi 9.45N 69.39W
Sanary-sur-Mer 122 Lk 43.07N 5.48 E
San Augustine 186 Ik 31.32N 94.07W
Sanäw 168 Ji 17.50N 51.05 E
San Bartolomeo in Galdo 128 Ji 41.24N 15.01 E
San Baudilio de Llobregat / Sant Boi de Llobregat 126 Oc 41.21N 2.03 E
San Benedetto del Tronto 128 Hh 42.57N 13.53 E
San Benedetto Po 128 Ee 45.02N 10.55 E
San Benedicto, Isla- ⊡ 190 Be 19.18N 110.49W
San Benito [Guat.] 194 Ce 16.55N 89.54W
San Benito [Tx.-U.S.] 186 Hm 26.08N 97.38W
San Benito, Islas de- ⊡ 192 Bc 28.20N 115.35W
San Benito Abad 194 Ji 8.56N 75.02W
San Benito Mountain ▲ 188 Eh 36.22N 120.38W
San Bernardino 176 Hf 34.06N 117.17W
San Bernardino, Passo del- ⊟ 128 Dd 46.30N 9.10 E
San Bernardino Mountains ▲ 188 Gi 34.10N 117.00W
San Bernardino Strait ◁ 150 Hd 12.32N 124.10 E
San Bernardo [Arg.] 204 Bh 27.17S 60.42W
San Bernardo [Chile] 206 Fd 33.36S 70.43W
San Bernardo [Mex.] 192 Fd 25.32N 111.45W
San Bernardo, Islas de- ⊡ 194 Ji 9.42N 75.42W
San Bernardo del Viento 202 Cb 9.22N 75.57W
San Blas ③ 194 Ji 9.45N 75.10W
San Blas [Mex.] 190 Cd 21.31N 105.16W

San Blas [Mex.] 190 Cc 26.05N 108.46W
San Blas [Mex.] 192 Id 27.25N 101.40W
San Blas, Archipiélago de- ⊡ 194 Hi 9.30N 78.30W
San Blas, Cape- ▶ 182 Jf 29.40N 85.22W
San Blas, Cordillera de- ▲ 194 Hi 9.18N 79.00W
San Blas, Golfo de- ◁ 194 Hi 9.30N 79.00W
San Blas, Punta- ▶ 194 Hi 9.34N 78.58W
San Borja 202 Ef 14.49S 66.51W
San Borjas, Sierra de- ▲ 192 Cc 28.40N 113.45W
San Buenaventura 192 Id 27.05N 101.32W
Sancai ◁ 168 Fc 10.43N 35.40 E
San Carlos [Arg.] 204 Eh 27.45S 55.54W
San Carlos [Chile] 206 Fe 36.25S 71.58W
San Carlos [Mex.] 192 Ic 29.01N 100.51W
San Carlos [Mex.] 192 Je 24.35N 98.56W
San Carlos [Nic.] 194 Eh 11.07N 84.47W
San Carlos [Pan.] 194 Hi 8.29N 79.57W
San Carlos [Par.] 204 Df 22.16S 57.18W
San Carlos [Phil.] 150 Hd 10.30N 123.25 E
San Carlos [Phil.] 150 Hc 15.55N 120.20 E
San Carlos [Ur.] 206 Jd 34.48S 54.55W
San Carlos [Ven.] 202 Eb 9.40N 68.39W
San Carlos, Bahia- ◁ 192 Cd 27.55N 112.45W
San Carlos, Mesa de- ◁ 192 Bc 29.40N 115.25W
San Carlos, Punta- ▶ 192 Cc 28.00N 112.45W
San Carlos, Riacho- ◁ 204 Df 22.45S 57.53W
San Carlos, Rio- [C.R.] ◁ 194 Eh 10.47N 84.12W
San Carlos, Rio- [Ven.] ◁ 196 Bh 9.07N 68.25W
San Carlos de Bariloche 200 Ij 41.08S 71.15W
San Carlos de Bolívar 206 He 36.15S 61.06W
San Carlos de la Rápita / Sant Carles de la Ràpita 126 Md 40.37N 0.36 E
San Carlos del Zulia 202 Db 9.01N 71.55W
San Carlos de Rio Negro 202 Ec 1.55N 67.04W
San Carlos Reservoir ◁ 188 Jj 33.13N 110.24W
San Cataldo 128 Hm 37.29N 13.59 E
San Cayetano 204 Cn 38.20S 59.37W
Sancerre 122 Ig 47.20N 2.50 E
Sancerrois, Collines du- ▲ 122 Ig 47.20N 2.30 E
Sanchahe 154 Nb 44.59N 126.03 E
Sánchez 194 Md 19.14N 69.36W
Sánchez Magallanes 194 Mh 18.17N 93.59W
San Clemente [Ca.-U.S.] 182 Ce 33.26N 117.37W
San Clemente [Sp.] 126 Je 39.24N 2.26W
San Clemente del Tuyú 204 Dm 36.22S 56.43W
San Clemente Island ⊡ 188 Fj 32.55N 118.30W
Sancois 122 Ih 46.50N 2.55 E
San Cosme 204 Ch 27.22S 58.31W
San Cristóbal [Arg.] 206 Hd 30.19S 61.14W
San Cristóbal [Bol.] 204 Ba 13.56S 61.50W
San Cristóbal [Cuba] 194 Fb 22.43N 83.03W
San Cristóbal [Dom.Rep.] 194 Ld 18.25N 70.06W
San Cristóbal [Ven.] 192 Li 17.49N 94.32W
San Cristóbal [Ven.] 200 Ie 7.46N 72.14W
San Cristóbal, Bahía de- ◁ 192 Bd 27.25N 114.40W
San Cristóbal, Isla- ⊡ 198 Hf 0.50S 89.26W
San Cristóbal de las Casas 194 Fe 16.45N 92.38W
San Cristóbal Island ⊡ 208 Hf 10.36S 161.45 E
San Cristóbal Verapaz 194 Bf 15.23N 90.24W
Sancti Spiritus 190 Jd 21.56N 79.27W
Sancti Spiritus ③ 194 Hb 22.00N 79.30W
Sancy, Puy de- ▲ 122 Ii 45.32N 2.50 E
Sand 114 Bg 59.29N 6.15 E
Sand ◁ 172 Ed 22.25S 30.05 E
Sanda 156 Dd 34.53N 135.14 E
Sandai 150 Fj 1.15S 110.31 E
Sandakan 150 Gc 5.50N 118.07 E
Sandal, Baie de- ◁ 219b Ce 20.49S 167.10 E
Sandal, ozero- ◁ 114 Ie 62.25N 34.10 E
Sandane 114 Bf 61.46N 6.13 E
Sandanski 130 Ah 41.34N 23.17 E
Sandaré 166 Cc 14.42N 10.18W
Sandared 116 Eg 57.43N 12.47 E
Sandarne 116 Gc 61.16N 17.10 E
Sanday ⊡ 118 Kb 59.15N 2.30W
Sande 116 De 59.36N 10.12 E
Sandefjord 114 Cg 59.08N 10.14 E
Sandégué 166 Ed 7.59N 3.33W
Sandeid 114 Ag 59.33N 5.50 E
Sanders 188 Ki 35.13N 109.20W
Sanderson 182 Ge 30.09N 102.24W
Sandersville 184 Fi 32.59N 82.48W
Sandfontein 172 Bd 22.11S 19.58 E
Sandgate 124 Ni 51.04N 1.09 E
Sandhammaren ▶ 116 Fi 55.23N 14.12 E
Sandhamn 116 He 59.17N 18.55 E
Sand Hills ◁ 182 Kc 41.45N 102.00W
Sandia 202 Ef 14.17S 69.26W
Sandia Crest ▲ 186 Ci 35.13N 106.27W
San Diego [Bol.] 204 Bc 16.04S 60.28W
San Diego [Ca.-U.S.] 176 Hf 32.43N 117.09W
San Diego, Cabo- ▶ 198 Jk 54.38S 65.07W
Sandikli 146 Dc 38.28N 30.17 E
San Dimitri Point ▶ 128 In 36.05N 14.05 E
Sand in Taufers / Campo Tures 128 Fd 46.55N 11.57 E
Sand Lake ◁ 186 Ia 50.05N 94.39W
Sand Mountain ▲ 184 Dh 34.20N 86.02W
Sandnes 114 Ag 58.51N 5.44 E
Sandnessjøen 114 Cc 66.01N 12.38 E
Sandoa 160 Ji 9.41S 22.52 E
Sandö bank ⊡ 116 Hf 58.10N 19.15 E
Sandomierska, Kotlina- ◁ 120 Sf 50.30N 22.00 E
Sandomierz 120 Rf 50.41N 21.45 E
San Domino ⊡ 128 Jh 42.05N 15.30 E
Sandoná 202 Lc 1.18N 77.28W
San Donà di Piave 128 Ge 45.38N 12.34 E
Sandoval, Boca de- ◁ 192 Ke 24.58N 97.32W
Sandoway 148 Hd 18.28N 94.22 E
Sandown 124 Lk 50.39N 1.09W
Sandpoint 178 Mg 48.16N 116.33W
Sand Point 178 Gf 55.20N 160.30W
Sandras Daği ▲ 130 Ll 37.04N 28.51 E
Sandray ⊡ 118 Df 56.53N 7.30W
Sandspit 180 Ef 53.15N 131.50W
Sand Springs [Mt.-U.S.] 188 Lc 47.09N 107.27W

Sand Springs [Ok.-U.S.] 186 Hh 36.09N 96.07W
Sandstone [Austl.] 212 De 27.59S 119.17 E
Sandstone [Mn.-U.S.] 186 Jc 46.08N 92.52W
Sandu 152 Jf 26.08N 113.16 E
Sandusky [Mi.-U.S.] 184 Fd 43.25N 82.50W
Sandusky [Oh.-U.S.] 182 Kc 41.27N 82.42W
Sandveld ◁ 172 Cd 21.20S 20.10 E
Sandvig-Allinge 114 Di 55.15N 14.49 E
Sandvika 116 Se 59.54N 10.31 E
Sandviken 114 Bd 60.37N 16.46 E
Sandwich 118 Oj 51.17N 1.20 E
Sandwich Bay ◁ 180 Lf 53.35N 57.15W
Sandy 124 Bb 52.07N 0.17W
Sandy Cape [Austl.] ▶ 208 Gg 24.40S 153.15 E
Sandy Cape [Austl.] ▶ 212 Ih 41.25S 144.45 E
Sandy Desert ◁ 148 Cc 28.46N 62.30 E
Sandykači 136 Gk 36.32N 62.35 E
Sandy Lake 180 If 53.02N 93.14W
Sandy Lake ◁ 180 If 53.02N 92.55W
Sandy Point 184 Il 26.01N 77.24W
Sandy Point Town 196 Ed 17.22N 62.50W
Sandžak ◁ 130 Cf 43.10N 20.00 E
Sanem 124 He 49.33N 5.56 E
San Estanislao 206 Ib 24.39S 56.26W
San Esteban 194 Ef 15.17N 85.52W
San Esteban, Bahia de- ◁ 192 Ie 25.40N 109.15W
San Esteban, Isla- ⊡ 192 Cc 28.42N 112.36W
San Esteban de Gormaz 126 Ic 41.35N 3.12W
San Felice Circeo 128 Hi 41.14N 13.05 E
San Felipe [Chile] 206 Fd 32.45S 70.44W
San Felipe [Col.] 202 Ec 1.55N 67.06W
San Felipe [Mex.] 190 Bb 31.00N 114.52W
San Felipe [Mex.] 192 Ig 21.29N 101.13W
San Felipe [Ven.] 202 Ea 10.20N 68.44W
San Felipe, Cayos de- ⊡ 194 Fb 21.58N 83.30W
San Felipe, Cerro de- ▲ 126 Kd 40.24N 1.55W
San Felipe Creek ◁ 188 Hj 33.09N 115.46W
San Feliu de Llobregat / Sant Feliu de Llobregat 126 Oc 41.23N 2.03 E
San Felix, Isla- ⊡ 206 Dc 26.17S 80.05W
San Fermin, Punta- ▶ 192 Bb 30.25N 114.40W
San Fernando [Chile] 206 Fd 34.35S 71.00W
San Fernando [Mex.] 190 Bd 24.51N 98.10W
San Fernando [Mex.] 192 Ke 29.59N 115.17W
San Fernando [Phil.] 150 Hc 15.01N 120.41 E
San Fernando [Phil.] 150 Hc 16.37N 120.19 E
San Fernando [Sp.] 126 Fh 36.28N 6.12W
San Fernando [Trin.] 202 Fa 10.17N 61.28W
San Fernando, Rio- [Bol.] ◁ 204 Cc 17.13S 58.23W
San Fernando, Rio- [Mex.] ◁ 192 Ke 24.55N 97.40W
San Fernando de Apure 200 Je 7.54N 67.28W
San Fernando de Atabapo 202 Ec 4.03N 67.42W
San Fernando del Valle de Catamarca 200 Jh 28.30S 65.45W
Sanford [Fl.-U.S.] 182 Kf 28.48N 81.16W
Sanford [Me.-U.S.] 184 Ld 43.26N 70.46W
Sanford [N.C.-U.S.] 184 Mh 35.29N 79.10W
Sanford, Mount- ▲ 178 Kd 62.13N 144.09W
San Francisco [Arg.] 206 Hd 31.26S 62.05W
San Francisco [Bol.] 204 Cc 17.42S 59.38W
San Francisco [Pan.] 194 Gi 8.15N 80.58W
San Francisco [Ca.-U.S.] 176 Gf 37.48N 122.24W
San Francisco, Isla- ⊡ 192 Gf 24.50N 110.35W
San Francisco Bay ◁ 174 Gf 37.43N 122.17W
San Francisco Creek ◁ 186 El 37.59N 102.19W
San Francisco de Arriba 192 Hc 26.15N 102.50W
San Francisco de Bellocq 204 Bn 38.45S 60.01W
San Francisco de la Paz 194 Dh 14.55N 86.14W
San Francisco del Laishi 204 Ch 26.14S 58.38W
San Francisco del Oro 192 Gc 26.52N 105.51W
San Francisco del Rincón 192 Ig 21.01N 101.51W
San Francisco de Macoris 194 Ld 19.18N 70.15W
San Francisco Gotera 194 Cg 13.42N 88.06W
San Francisco Javier / Sant Francesc de Formentera 126 Nf 38.42N 1.25 E
San Francisco Mountains ▲ 188 Kj 33.59N 109.00W
San Francisco River ◁ 188 Kj 32.59N 109.22W
San Fratello 128 Il 38.01N 14.36 E
San Gabriel 204 Gi 13.50S 76.28W
San Gabriel, Punta- ▶ 192 Cc 28.25N 112.50W
San Gabriel Mountains ▲ 188 Gi 34.20N 117.45W
San Gallán, Isla- ⊡ 202 Gf 13.50S 76.28W
Sangamon River ◁ 186 Kf 40.07N 90.20W
Sangar [Iran] 146 Md 37.08N 49.02 E
Sangar [R.S.F.S.R.] 142 Oc 63.55N 127.31 E
Sangatte 124 Nh 50.56N 1.45 E
San Gavino Monreale 128 Ck 39.33N 8.47 E
Sangay, Volcán- ▲ 198 If 2.00S 78.20W
Sange 170 Ed 7.02S 28.21 E
Sangeang, Pulau- ⊡ 150 Gh 8.12S 119.04 E
San Gemini 128 Gh 42.37N 12.33 E
Sanger 188 Fh 36.42N 119.27W
Sangerhausen 120 Mf 51.28N 11.18 E
San Germán [Cuba] 194 Ic 20.36N 76.08W
San Germán [P.R.] 194 Nd 18.05N 67.03W
Sanggan He ◁ 154 Gd 40.24N 115.18 E
Sanggau 150 Fi 0.08N 110.36 E
Sangha [C.A.R.] ③ 158 Ii 1.10S 16.49 E
Sangha [Con.] ◁ 160 Ji 3.30N 16.00 E
Sanghe, Kepulauan- = 140 Oi 1.10N 125.00 E
Sanghe, Pulau- ⊡ 150 Oi 3.35N 125.32 E
Sanghe Islands (EN) = 140 Oi 3.00N 125.30 E
Sanghe, Kepulauan- ◁ 202 Db 3.00N 125.30 E
San Gil 202 Db 6.32N 73.08W
San Gimignano 128 Fg 43.28N 11.02 E
San Giovanni in Fiore 128 Kk 39.15N 16.42 E
San Giovanni in Persiceto 128 Ff 44.38N 11.11 E
San Giovanni Rotondo 128 Ji 41.42N 15.44 E
San Giovanni Valdarno 128 Fg 43.34N 11.32 E
Sangju 154 Nd 36.25N 128.10 E
Sāngli 142 Jh 16.52N 74.34 E
Sangmélima 166 Hh 11.56N 11.59 E
Sangolí 146 Pd 37.25N 54.35 E
San Gorgonio ▲ 174 Hf 34.05N 116.50W

San Gottardo, Passo del- = Saint Gotthard Pass (EN) ⊟ 110 Gf 46.30N 8.30 E
Sangradouro Grande, Rio- ◁ 204 Dc 16.24S 57.10W
Sangre de Cristo Mountains ▲ 174 If 37.30N 105.15W
San Gregorio 204 Al 34.19S 62.02W
Sangre Grande 196 Fg 10.35N 61.07W
Sangri 152 Ff 29.20N 92.15 E
Sangro, Rio- ◁ 128 Ih 42.14N 14.32 E
Sangue, Rio do- ◁ 202 Gf 11.00S 58.40W
Sangüesa 126 Kb 42.35N 1.17W
Sangyuan → Wuqiao 154 Df 37.38N 116.23 E
Sangzhi 152 Jf 29.23N 110.11 E
San He ◁ 154 Eh 33.00N 118.34 E
Sanhe [China] 154 Dd 40.00N 117.01 E
Sanhe [China] 152 La 50.30N 120.04 E
Sanhe-San ◁ 156 Cd 35.08N 132.37 E
Sanhezhen 154 Dd 31.30N 117.15 E
San Hilario [Arg.] 204 Ch 26.02S 58.39W
San Hilario [Mex.] 192 De 24.22N 110.59W
San Hipólito, Bahia- ◁ 192 Cc 26.55N 113.55W
San Ignacio [Arg.] 204 Eh 27.16S 55.32W
San Ignacio [Blz.] 190 Gf 17.10N 89.04W
San Ignacio [Bol.] 202 Ff 16.23S 60.59W
San Ignacio [Bol.] 202 Ff 13.08S 60.59W
San Ignacio [Mex.] 190 Bc 27.27N 112.51W
San Ignacio [Mex.] 192 Ff 25.55N 106.25W
San Ignacio [Par.] 206 Ic 26.52S 57.03W
San Ignacio, Isla de- ⊡ 192 Ie 25.25N 108.55W
San Ignacio, Laguna- ◁ 192 Cc 26.55N 113.15W
San Ildefonso (La Granja) 126 Id 40.54N 4.00W
San Ildefonso, Cape- ▶ 150 Hc 16.02N 121.59 E
San Ildefonso, Cerro- ▲ 194 Cf 15.31N 88.17W
Saniquelle 166 Dd 7.22N 8.43W
San Isidro [Arg.] 206 Id 34.27S 58.30W
San Isidro [Phil.] 150 Hd 11.24N 124.21 E
San Isidro de El General 190 Hi 9.22N 83.42W
Saniyah 146 If 33.49N 42.43 E
San Jacinto 194 Ji 9.50N 75.08W
San Jacinto Peak ▲ 188 Gj 33.49N 116.41W
San Jaime 204 Cj 30.20S 58.19W
San Javier [Arg.] 206 Id 30.35S 59.57W
San Javier [Sp.] 126 Lf 37.48N 0.51W
San Javier [Ur.] 204 Ck 32.41S 58.08W
San Javier, Rio- ◁ 204 Bj 31.30S 60.20W
San Javier de Loncomilla 206 Fd 35.36S 71.45W
San Jerónimo Taviche 192 Ki 16.44N 96.35W
Sanjiachang 152 Jm 24.45N 101.53 E
Sanjiaocheng → Haiyan 152 He 36.58N 100.50 E
Sanjō 154 Of 37.37N 138.57 E
San Joan de Labritja / San Juan Bautista 126 Ne 39.05N 1.30 E
San Joaquin 202 Ff 13.04S 64.49W
San Joaquin, Rio- ◁ 202 Ff 13.08S 63.41W
San Joaquin, Sierra de- ▲ 194 Ge 24.48S 56.00W
San Joaquin River ◁ 188 Fh 36.43N 121.50W
San Joaquin Valley ◁ 174 Gf 36.50N 120.10W
San Jon 186 Ji 35.06N 103.20W
San Jorge 206 Hd 31.54S 61.52W
San Jorge, Bahia de- ◁ 192 Cb 31.10N 113.15W
San Jorge, Golfo- ◁ 198 Jj 46.00S 67.00W
San Jorge, Golfo de- / Sant Jordi, Golf de ◁ 126 Md 40.53N 1.00 E
San Jorge, Rio- ◁ 194 Ji 9.07N 74.44W
San Jorge, Serrania- ▲ 204 Bn 20.01S 60.59W
San Jorge Island ⊡ 219a Dc 8.27S 159.35 E
San José ② 204 Di 34.15S 56.45W
San José ③ 194 Ei 9.40N 84.00W
San José [Arg.] 204 Ei 27.46S 55.47W
San José [Ca.-U.S.] 176 Ki 37.20N 121.53W
San José [C.R.] 194 Ei 9.56N 84.05W
San José [Mex.] 192 Jd 27.32N 110.09W
San José [Par.] 150 Hc 15.48N 121.00 E
San José [Phil.] 150 Hc 15.48N 120.59 E
San José [Phil.] 150 Hd 12.21N 121.04 E
San José, Golfo- ◁ 200 Jj 42.15S 64.10W
San José, Isla- [Mex.] ⊡ 190 Bc 25.00N 110.38W
San José, Isla- [Pan.] ⊡ 194 Hi 8.15N 79.07W
San José, Salinas de- ◁ 204 Bh 19.07S 60.54W
San José de Buenavista 150 Hc 10.46N 122.30 E
San José de Chiquitos 202 Ff 17.51S 60.49W
San José de Feliciano 204 Cj 30.23S 58.45W
San José de Gracia 192 Fb 28.08N 107.58W
San José de Guanipa 206 Id 30.14S 58.45W
San José de Jáchal 206 Gc 30.14S 68.45W
San José de las Lajas 194 Fb 22.58N 82.09W
San José del Cabo 190 Cb 23.03N 109.41W
San José del Guaviare 200 Ie 2.35N 72.38W
San José del Rosario 204 Ig 24.12S 56.48W
San José de Mayo 206 Id 34.20S 56.42W
San José de Ocuné 206 Ic 4.10N 70.20W
San José de Tiznados 196 Ch 9.23N 67.33W
San Juan ③ 200 Jj 31.00S 69.00W
San Juan [Arg.] 200 Jj 31.30S 68.30W
San Juán [Bol.] 204 Bd 18.08S 60.08W
San Juan [C.Amer.] ◁ 174 Kh 10.56N 83.42W
San Juan [Dom.Rep.] 194 Kd 18.48N 71.14W
San Juan [P.R.] 176 Mh 18.28N 66.07W
San Juan [U.S.] ◁ 174 Hf 37.18N 110.28W
San Juan, Cabezas de- ▶ 197a Cb 18.23N 65.36W
San Juan, Cabo- ▶ 158 Hh 1.10N 9.21 E
San Juan, Mar de- ◁ 126 Kd 40.24N 2.14W
San Juan, Pico- ▲ 190 Hf 21.59N 80.09W
San Juan, Punta- ▶ 221d Ab 27.03S 109.22W
San Juan, Rio- [Arg.] ◁ 206 Gd 32.17S 67.22W
San Juan, Rio- [Col.] ◁ 200 Id 4.00N 77.20W
San Juan, Rio- [Mex.] ◁ 192 Jd 25.34N 99.00W
San Juan, Rio- [Mex.] ◁ 192 Id 26.55N 99.20W
San Juan, Rio- [Ven.] ◁ 196 Eg 10.14N 62.39W
San Juan Bautista / Sant Joan de Labritja 126 Ne 39.05N 1.30 E
San Juan Bautista de las Misiones 206 Ic 26.38S 57.10W

San Juan Bautista Tuxtepec 192 Kh 18.06N 96.07W
San Juan de Colón 194 Ki 8.02N 72.16W
San Juan de Guadalupe 192 He 24.38N 102.44W
San Juan del Cesar 194 Kh 10.46N 72.59W
San Juan de Lima, Punta- ▶ 192 Hh 18.36N 103.42W
San Juan del Norte 190 Hf 10.55N 83.42W
San Juan de los Cayos 202 Ea 11.10N 68.25W
San Juan de los Lagos 192 Hg 21.15N 102.14W
San Juan de los Morros 202 Ea 9.55N 67.21W
San Juan del Rio [Mex.] 192 Ga 24.47N 104.27W
San Juan del Rio [Mex.] 190 Dd 20.29N 100.00W
San Juan del Sur 190 Gf 11.15N 85.52W
San Juan de Payara 196 Ci 7.39N 67.36W
San Juan, Isla- ⊡ 192 Fg 21.55N 106.40W
San Juanico, Punta- ▶ 192 Cd 26.05N 112.15W
San Juan Island ⊡ 188 Gb 48.32N 123.05W
San Juan Mountains ▲ 182 Fd 37.35N 107.10W
San Juan Nepomuceno [Col.] 204 Dc 26.39S 57.56W
San Juan Nepomuceno [Col.] 202 Cb 9.57N 75.05W
San Juan Nepomuceno [Par.] 204 Eh 26.06S 55.58W
San Juan y Martinez 194 Fb 22.16N 83.50W
San Julián 200 Jj 49.19S 67.40W
San Just, Sierra de- ▲ 126 Ld 40.46N 0.48W
San Justo 206 Hd 30.47S 60.35W
Sankarani ◁ 158 Gg 12.01N 8.19W
Sankt Anton am Arlberg 128 Ec 47.08N 10.16 E
Sankt Augustin 124 Jd 50.47N 7.11 E
Sankt Gallen 128 Dc 47.25N 9.25 E
Sankt Gallen ② 128 Dc 47.20N 9.10 E
Sankt Goar 120 Df 50.09N 7.43 E
Sankt Goarshausen 124 Jd 50.09N 7.44 E
Sankt Ingbert 120 Dg 49.17N 7.07 E
Sankt Johann im Pongau 128 Hc 47.21N 13.12 E
Sankt Michael im Lungau 128 Hc 47.06N 13.38 E
Sankt Michel/Mikkeli 112 Lc 61.41N 27.15 E
Sankt Moritz 128 Dd 46.30N 9.52 E
Sankt Peter-Ording 120 Eb 54.18N 8.38 E
Sankt Pölten 128 Jb 48.12N 15.38 E
Sankt Ulrich in Gröden / Ortisei 128 Fd 46.34N 11.40 E
Sankt Veit an der Glan 128 Id 46.46N 14.22 E
Sankt-Vith / Saint-Vith 122 Md 50.17N 6.08 E
Sankt Wendel 120 Dg 49.28N 7.10 E
Sankt Wolfang im Salzkammergut 128 Hc 47.44N 13.27 E
Sankuru ◁ 158 Ji 4.17S 20.25 E
San Lázaro 206 Ib 22.10S 57.55W
San Lázaro, Cabo- ▶ 190 Bc 24.48N 112.19W
San Lázaro, Sierra de- ▲ 192 Df 23.25N 110.00W
San Leandro 188 Dh 37.43N 122.09W
San Lorenzo ⊡ 190 Fe 17.44N 94.45W
San Lorenzo [Ec.] 200 Ie 1.17N 78.50W
San Lorenzo [Hond.] 194 Dg 13.25N 87.27W
San Lorenzo, Isla- [Mex.] ⊡ 192 Cb 28.38N 112.51W
San Lorenzo, Isla- [Peru] ⊡ 202 Cf 12.05S 77.15W
San Lorenzo, Rio- [Mex.] ◁ 192 Fe 25.07N 98.32W
San Lorenzo, Rio- [Mex.] ◁ 192 Fe 24.15N 107.24W
San Lorenzo de El Escorial 126 Hc 40.35N 4.09W
Sanlúcar de Barrameda 126 Fh 36.47N 6.21W
Sanlúcar la Mayor 126 Fg 37.23N 6.12W
San Lucas [Mex.] 190 Cb 22.53N 109.54W
San Lucas [Mex.] 192 Gd 22.33N 104.24W
San Lucas, Cabo- ▶ 174 Ig 22.50N 109.55W
San Lucas, Serrania de- ▲ 202 Db 8.00N 74.20W
San Lucido 128 Kk 39.18N 16.03 E
San Luis ② 206 Gd 34.00S 66.00W
San Luis [Arg.] 200 Jj 33.20S 66.20W
San Luis [Bol.] 204 Cc 17.39S 58.42W
San Luis [Cuba] 194 Jc 20.12N 75.51W
San Luis [Guat.] 194 Ce 16.14N 89.27W
San Luis [Mex.] 192 Dc 29.33N 111.05W
San Luis, Isla- ⊡ 192 Bb 29.58N 114.26W
San Luis, Sierra de- ▲ 194 Mh 11.11N 69.42W
San Luis de la Paz 192 Ig 21.18N 100.31W
San Luis del Palmar 204 Ch 27.31S 58.34W
San Luis de Palenque 202 Db 5.25N 71.40W
San Luis Gonzaga, Bahia- ◁ 192 Bc 30.00N 114.25W
San Luis Obispo 176 Gf 35.17N 120.40W
San Luis Pass ◁ 186 Il 29.05N 95.08W
San Luis Peak ▲ 186 Cf 37.59N 106.56W
San Luis Potosi ② 190 Dd 22.09N 100.59W
San Luis Potosi 190 Dd 22.09N 100.59W
San Luis Rio Colorado 190 Bb 32.29N 114.48W
San Luis Valley ◁ 182 Fd 37.25N 106.00W
Sanluri 128 Ck 39.34N 8.54 E
San Manuel [Arg.] 204 Cm 37.47S 58.50W
San Manuel [Az.-U.S.] 188 Jk 32.36N 110.38W
San Marcial, Punta- ▶ 192 Ee 25.30N 111.00W
San Marco, Capo- ▶ 128 Hm 37.30N 13.01 E
San Marcos ③ 194 Bf 15.00N 91.55W
San Marcos [Col.] 202 Cb 8.39N 75.08W
San Marcos [Guat.] 194 Bf 14.58N 91.48W
San Marcos [Hond.] 194 Cf 14.24N 88.56W
San Marcos [Mex.] 192 Ji 16.48N 99.21W
San Marcos [Mex.] 194 Dh 11.55N 86.12W
San Marcos [Tx.-U.S.] 176 Jf 29.53N 97.57W
San Marcos, Isla- ⊡ 192 Cd 27.13N 112.06W
San Marcos, Sierra de- ▲ 192 Id 26.30N 101.55W
San Marino ① 128 Gf 43.55N 12.28 E
San Marino 128 Gf 43.55N 12.28 E
San Martín ① 206 Gd 33.04S 68.28W
San Martin ③ 202 Db 3.00S 73.00W
San Martin 206 Dd 33.04S 68.28W
San Martin ⊠ 222 Qe 68.11S 67.00W
San Martin, Cerro- ▲ 222 Qe 68.11S 67.00W
San Martin, Lago- ◁ 206 Ff 48.52S 72.40W
San Martin, Rio- ◁ 202 Ff 13.08S 63.43W
San Martin de los Andes 200 Ij 40.10S 71.21W
San Martin de Valdeiglesias 126 Hd 40.21N 4.24W
San Martino di Castrozza 128 Fd 46.15N 11.48 E
San Mateo [Ca.-U.S.] 188 Dh 37.35N 122.19W
San Mateo [Ven.] 196 Dh 9.45N 64.33W

Index Symbols

① Independent Nation	■ Historical or Cultural Region	Pass, Gap	Depression
② State, Region	Mount, Mountain	Plain, Lowland	Polder
③ District, County	Volcano	Delta	Desert, Dunes
④ Municipality	Hill	Salt Flat	Forest, Woods
⑤ Colony, Dependency	Mountains, Mountain Range	Valley, Canyon	Heath, Steppe
⑥ Continent	Hills, Escarpment	Crater, Cave	Oasis
⑦ Physical Region	Plateau, Upland	Karst Features	Cape, Point

Coast, Beach	Rock, Reef	Waterfall, Rapids	Canal
Cliff	Islands, Archipelago	River Mouth, Estuary	Glacier
Peninsula	Rocks, Reefs	Lake	Ice Shelf, Pack Ice
Isthmus	Coral Reef	Salt Lake	Ocean
Sandbank	Well, Spring	Sea	Reservoir
Island	Geyser	Gulf, Bay	Shelf
Atoll	River, Stream	Swamp, Pond	Basin

Lagoon	Escarpment, Sea Scarp	Historic Site	Airport
Bank	Fracture	Ruins	Port
Seamount	Trench, Abyss	Wall, Walls	Military installation
Tablemount	National Park, Reserve	Church, Abbey	Lighthouse
Ridge	Point of Interest	Temple	Mine
Strait, Fjord	Recreation Site	Scientific Station	Tunnel
	Cave, Cavern	Railway station	Dam, Bridge

San Mateo/Sant Mateu del Maestrat 126 Md 40.28N 0.11 E
San Mateo Ixtatán 194 Bf 15.50N 91.29W
San Mateo Mountains 186 Cj 33.10N 107.20W
San Matías 204 Cc 16.22S 58.24W
San Matías, Golfo- 198 Jj 41.30S 64.15W
Sanmen (Haiyou) 152 Lf 29.08N 121.22 E
Sanmen Wan 154 Fj 29.00N 121.45 E
Sanmenxia 152 Je 34.44N 111.19 E
San Miguel [Arg.] 204 Dh 27.59S 57.36W
San Miguel [Bol.] 204 Bc 16.42S 61.01W
San Miguel [Ca.-U.S.] 188 Ei 35.45N 120.42W
San Miguel [El Sal.] 176 Kh 13.29N 88.11W
San Miguel [Pan.] 194 Hi 8.27N 78.56W
San Miguel, Golfo de- 194 Hi 8.22N 78.17W
San Miguel, Río- [Bol.] 198 Jg 13.52S 63.56W
San Miguel, Río- [Mex.] 192 Dc 29.16N 110.53W
San Miguel, Río- [Mex.] 192 Fd 26.59N 107.58W
San Miguel, Río- [S.Amer.] 204 Cd 19.25S 58.20W
San Miguel, Salinas de- 204 Bd 19.12S 60.45W
San Miguel, Volcán de- 190 Gf 13.26N 88.16W
San Miguel Bay 150 Hd 13.50N 123.10 E
San Miguel de Allende 192 Ig 20.55N 100.45W
San Miguel de Horcasitas 192 Dc 29.29N 110.45W
San Miguel del Monte 204 Cl 35.27S 58.48W
San Miguel del Padrón 194 Fb 23.05N 82.19W
San Miguel de Tucumán 200 Jh 26.49S 65.13W
San Miguel Island 188 Ei 34.02N 120.22W
San Miguel Islands 150 Ge 7.45N 118.28 E
San Miguelito 204 Bc 17.20S 60.59W
San Miguel River 186 Bg 38.23N 108.48W
San Miguel Sola de Vega 192 Ki 16.31N 96.59W
San Millán 126 Ib 42.18N 3.12W
Sanming 152 Kf 26.11N 117.37 E
San Miniato 128 Eg 43.41N 10.51 E
Sannan 156 Dd 35.04N 135.03 E
Sannār 160 Kg 13.33N 33.38 E
Sannicandro Garganico 128 Ji 41.50N 15.34 E
San Nicolás, Río- [Bol.] 204 Bc 17.08S 61.17W
San Nicolás, Río- [Mex.] 192 Gh 19.40N 105.14W
San Nicolás de los Arroyos 206 Hd 33.20S 60.13W
San Nicolás de los Garzas 192 Ie 25.45N 100.18W
San Nicolas Island 188 Fj 33.15N 119.31W
Sannikova, proliv- 138 Ib 74.30N 140.00 E
Sannio 128 Ii 41.20N 14.30 E
San'nohe 156 Ga 40.22N 141.15 E
San'nō-Tōge 156 Fc 37.06N 139.44 E
Sannūr, Wādī- 146 Dh 28.59N 31.03 E
Sanok 120 Sg 49.34N 22.13 E
Sanok-Zagórz 120 Sg 49.31N 22.17 E
San Onofre 202 Cb 9.45N 75.32W
San Pablo 142 Oh 14.04N 121.19 E
San Pablo, Punta- 192 Bd 27.15N 114.30W
San Pedro [3] 204 Dg 24.15S 56.30W
San Pedro [Arg.] 206 Jc 26.38S 54.08W
San Pedro [Arg.] 206 Hb 24.14S 64.52W
San Pedro [Arg.] 204 Ck 33.40S 59.40W
San-Pédro [I.C.] 166 De 4.44N 6.37W
San Pedro [Par.] 206 Ib 24.07S 56.59W
San Pedro, Río- [Guat.] 194 Be 17.46N 91.26W
San Pedro, Río- [Mex.] 192 Gg 21.45N 105.30W
San Pedro, Sierra de- 126 Fe 39.20N 6.35W
San Pedro Carchá 194 Bf 15.29N 90.16W
San Pedro Channel 188 Fj 33.43N 118.23W
San Pedro de Alcántara 126 Hh 36.29N 5.00W
San Pedro de Atacama 206 Gb 22.55S 68.13W
San Pedro de Lloc 202 Ce 7.26S 79.31W
San Pedro de Macorís 194 Md 18.27N 69.18W
San Pedro Mártir, Sierra de- 190 Ab 30.45N 115.13W
San Pedro Nolasco, Isla- 192 Dd 27.58N 111.25W
San Pedro Pochutla 192 Kj 15.44N 96.28W
San Pedros de las Colonias 190 Dc 25.45N 102.59W
San Pedro Sula 176 Kh 15.27N 88.02W
San Pedro Tapanatepec 192 Li 16.21N 94.12W
San Pedro Tututepec 192 Ki 16.09N 97.38W
San Pellegrino Terme 128 De 45.50N 9.40 E
San Pietro 128 Ck 39.10N 8.15 E
San Quintín 190 Ab 30.29N 115.57W
San Quintín, Bahía de- 192 Ab 30.20N 116.00W
San Rafael [Arg.] 200 Ji 34.40S 68.21W
San Rafael [Bol.] 204 Bc 16.45S 60.34W
San Rafael [Ca.-U.S.] 188 Dg 38.00N 122.31W
San Rafael [Mex.] 192 Ie 25.01N 100.33W
San Rafael [Mex.] 192 He 24.40N 102.01W
San Rafael [Ven.] 194 Lh 10.58N 71.44W
San Rafael, Cabo- 194 Md 19.01N 68.57W
San Rafael, Río- 204 Cd 18.26S 59.37W
San Rafael de Atamaica 196 Ci 7.32N 67.24W
San Rafael del Norte 194 Dg 13.12N 86.06W
San Rafael Knob 188 Jg 38.50N 110.48W
San Rafael Mountains 188 Fi 34.45N 119.50W
San Rafael River 188 Jg 38.47N 110.07W
San Ramón [Peru] 202 Cf 11.08S 75.20W
San Ramón [Ur.] 204 El 34.18S 55.58W
San Ramón, Río- 204 Bb 14.03S 61.35W
San Ramón de la Nueva Orán 206 Hb 23.08S 64.20W
San Raymundo, Arroyo- 192 Cd 26.21N 112.37W
San Remo 128 Bg 43.49N 7.46 E
Sanriku 156 Gb 39.08N 141.48 E
San Román, Cabo- 202 Ea 12.12N 70.00W
San Roque [Arg.] 204 Ci 28.34S 58.43W
San Roque [Sp.] 126 Gh 36.13N 5.24W
San Saba 186 Gk 31.12N 98.43W
Sansalé 166 Cc 11.07N 14.51W
San Salvador [Arg.] 204 Di 29.16S 57.31W
San Salvador [Arg.] 206 Id 31.37S 58.30W
San Salvador [El Sal.] 176 Kh 13.42N 89.12W
San Salvador [Par.] 204 Dg 25.51S 56.28W
San Salvador / Sant Salvador 126 Pe 39.27N 3.11 E
San Salvador (Watling) 190 Jd 24.02N 74.28W
San Salvador, Cuchilla- 204 Dk 33.56S 57.45W
San Salvador, Isla- 198 Gf 0.14S 90.45W
San Salvador, Río- 204 Ck 33.29S 58.23W
San Salvador de Jujuy 200 Jh 24.10S 65.20W
Sansanné-Mango 166 Fc 10.21N 0.28 E
San Sebastián [Col.] 194 Ji 9.13N 74.18W
San Sebastián [P.R.] 197a Bb 18.21N 67.00W
San Sebastián / Donostia 112 Fg 43.19N 1.59W
San Sebastián, Bahía- 206 Gh 53.15S 68.23W
San Sebastián, Isla- 194 Cg 13.11N 88.26W
San Sebastián de la Gomera 162 Dd 28.06N 17.06W
Sansepolcro 128 Gg 43.34N 12.08 E
San Severo 128 Ji 41.41N 15.23 E
San Silvestre 194 Li 8.15N 70.02W
San Simeon 188 Ei 35.39N 121.11W
Sanski Most 128 Kf 44.46N 16.40 E
Santa Águeda 192 Cd 27.13N 112.20W
Santa Ana 219a Fd 10.50S 162.28 E
Santa Ana [Arg.] 204 Eh 27.22S 55.34W
Santa Ana [Bol.] 204 Bc 16.37S 60.43W
Santa Ana [Bol.] 204 Cd 18.43S 58.44W
Santa Ana [Bol.] 202 Eg 15.31S 67.30W
Santa Ana [Ca.-U.S.] 182 De 33.43N 117.54W
Santa Ana [El Sal.] 176 Kh 13.59N 89.34W
Santa Ana [Mex.] 190 Bb 30.33N 111.07W
Santa Ana [Ven.] 196 Dh 9.19N 64.39W
Santa Ana, Río- 194 Li 9.30N 71.57W
Santa Ana, Volcán de- 174 Kh 13.50N 89.39W
Santa Bárbara [3] 194 Cf 15.10N 88.20W
Santa Barbara [Ca.-U.S.] 176 Hf 34.03N 118.15W
Santa Bárbara [Hond.] 194 Cf 14.53N 88.14W
Santa Bárbara [Mex.] 190 Cc 26.48N 105.49W
Santa Bárbara [Ven.] 194 Lj 7.47N 71.10W
Santa Bárbara, Puerto de- 126 Lb 42.30N 0.50W
Santa Bárbara, Serra de- 204 Fe 21.45S 53.23W
Santa Barbara Channel 188 Fi 34.15N 119.55W
Santa Barbara Island 188 Fj 33.23N 119.01W
Santa Catalina 219a Fd 10.54S 162.27 E
Santa Catalina [Col.] 194 Jh 10.37N 75.33W
Santa Catalina [Ven.] 196 Fh 8.33N 61.51W
Santa Catalina, Gulf of- 188 Gj 33.20N 117.45W
Santa Catalina, Isla- 192 De 25.40N 110.45W
Santa Catalina Island 188 Fj 33.23N 118.24W
Santa Catarina 192 Ie 25.41N 100.28W
Santa Catarina [2] 206 Kc 27.00S 50.00W
Santa Catarina, Ilha de- 198 Lh 27.36S 48.30W
Santa Catarina, Sierra- 192 Fc 29.40N 107.30W
Santa Cecília 204 Gh 26.56S 50.27W
Santa Cesarea Terme 128 Mj 40.02N 18.28 E
Santa Clara [Ca.-U.S.] 188 Eh 37.21N 121.59W
Santa Clara [Cuba] 176 Lg 22.24N 79.58W
Santa Clara [Gabon] 170 Ab 0.34N 9.17 E
Santa Clara [Mex.] 192 Fc 29.17N 107.01W
Santa Clara [Ur.] 204 Ek 32.55S 54.58W
Santa Clara, Barragem do- 126 Dg 37.30N 8.20W
Santa Clara, Isla- 206 Ed 33.42S 79.00W
Santa Clara de Saguier 204 Bj 31.21S 61.50W
Santa Coloma de Farners/ Santa Coloma de Farnés 126 Oc 41.52N 2.40 E
Santa Coloma de Farnés/ Santa Coloma de Farners 126 Oc 41.52N 2.40 E
Santa Coloma de Gramenet 126 Oc 41.27N 2.13 E
Santa Coloma de Queralt 126 Nc 41.32N 1.23 E
Santa Comba 126 Da 43.02N 8.49W
Santa Croce Camerina 128 In 36.50N 14.31 E
Santa Cruz [2] 206 Gg 49.00S 70.00W
Santa Cruz [3] 206 Fg 17.30S 61.30W
Santa Cruz [Azr.] 162 Ab 39.27N 31.07W
Santa Cruz [Azr.] 162 Bb 39.05N 28.01W
Santa Cruz [Bol.] 200 Jg 17.48S 63.10W
Santa Cruz [Braz.] 204 Dd 18.32S 57.12W
Santa Cruz [Braz.] 202 Id 0.36S 49.11W
Santa Cruz [Ca.-U.S.] 182 Cd 36.58N 122.01W
Santa Cruz [Chile] 206 Fd 34.38S 71.22W
Santa Cruz [C.R.] 194 Eh 10.01N 84.02W
Santa Cruz [Phil.] 150 Hd 14.01N 121.21 E
Santa Cruz, Isla- 198 Gf 0.38S 90.23W
Santa Cruz, Isla de- 192 De 25.17N 110.43W
Santa Cruz, Río- 206 Gh 50.08S 68.20W
Santa Cruz, Serra da- 204 Jc 17.05S 45.17W
Santa Cruz Cabrália 202 Kg 16.17S 39.02W
Santa Cruz de la Palma 162 Dd 28.41N 17.45W
Santa Cruz de la Zarza 126 Ie 39.58N 3.10W
Santa Cruz del Quiché 194 Bf 15.02N 91.08W
Santa Cruz del Sur 190 Id 20.43N 78.00W
Santa Cruz de Mudela 126 If 38.38N 3.28W
Santa Cruz de Tenerife 160 Ff 28.27N 16.14W
Santa Cruz de Tenerife [3] 162 Ee 28.10N 17.20W
Santa Cruz do Rio Pardo 204 Hf 22.55S 49.37W
Santa Cruz do Sul 206 Jc 29.43S 52.26W
Santa Cruz Island 188 Fi 34.01N 119.45W
Santa Cruz Islands 208 Hf 10.45S 165.55 E
Santadi 128 Ck 39.05N 8.43 E
Santa Elena [Arg.] 206 Id 30.57S 59.48W
Santa Elena [Arg.] 204 Bm 37.21S 60.37W
Santa Elena [Ec.] 202 Bd 2.14S 80.52W
Santa Elena, Bahía de- [C.R.] 194 Eh 10.59N 85.50W
Santa Elena, Bahía de- [Ec.] 202 Bd 2.05S 80.55W
Santa Elena, Cabo- 190 Gf 10.55N 85.57W
Santa Elena de Uairén 202 Fc 4.37N 61.08W
Santa Eugenia (Ribeira) 126 Db 42.33N 9.00W
Santa Eulalia 126 Kd 40.34N 1.19W
Santa Eulalia del Rio / Santa Eulària del Riu 126 Nf 38.59N 1.31 E
Santa Eulària del Riu / Santa Eulalia del Rio 126 Nf 38.59N 1.31 E
Santa Fe [2] 206 Hd 31.00S 61.00W
Santa Fe [Arg.] 200 Ji 31.40S 60.40W
Santa Fé [Cuba] 194 Fc 21.45N 82.45W
Santa Fe [N.M.-U.S.] 176 If 35.42N 106.57W
Santafé [Sp.] 126 Ig 37.11N 3.43W
Santa Fé de Minas 204 Jc 16.41S 45.28W
Santa Fé do Sul 204 Ge 20.13S 50.56W
Sant'Agata di Militello 128 Il 38.04N 14.38 E
Santa Helena [Braz.] 204 Gg 24.56S 54.23W
Santa Helena [Braz.] 202 Id 2.14S 45.18W
Santa Helena de Goiás 202 Hg 17.43S 50.35W
Santa Inês 202 Id 3.39S 45.22W
Santa Inés 194 Mh 10.37N 69.18W
Santa Inés, Bahía de- 192 Dd 27.00N 111.55W
Santa Inés, Isla- 198 Ik 53.45S 72.45W
Santa Isabel [Arg.] 206 Ge 36.15S 66.56W
Santa Isabel [Arg.] 204 Bk 33.54S 61.42W
Santa Isabel [Braz.] 204 Ba 13.40S 60.44W
Santa Isabel [P.R.] 197a Bc 17.58N 66.25W
Santa Isabel, Pico de- 166 Ge 3.35N 8.46 E
Santa Isabel Island 208 Ge 8.00S 159.00 E
Santa Izabel do Ivaí 204 Ff 22.58S 53.14W
Santa Juliana 204 Id 19.19S 47.32W
Santa Lucia [Arg.] 206 Gd 31.32S 68.29W
Santa Lucía [Ur.] 204 Dl 34.27S 56.24W
Santa Lucía, Esteros del- 204 Ci 28.15S 58.20W
Santa Lucía, Río- [Arg.] 204 Ci 29.05S 59.13W
Santa Lucía, Río- [Ur.] 204 Dl 34.48S 56.22W
Santa Lucia Cotzumalguapa 194 Bf 14.20N 91.01W
Santa Lucia Range 182 Cd 36.00N 121.20W
Santa Luzia 162 Cf 16.46N 24.45W
Santa Luzia, Ribeirão- 204 Fe 21.31S 53.53W
Santa Margarita 204 Bi 28.18S 61.33W
Santa Margarita, Isla de- 190 Bd 24.27N 111.50W
Santa Margherita Ligure 128 Df 44.20N 9.12 E
Santa Maria 158 Ee 36.58N 25.06W
Santa Maria 190 Cb 31.00N 107.14W
Santa Maria [Arg.] 206 Gc 26.41S 66.02W
Santa María [Bol.] 204 Bc 17.08S 61.01W
Santa Maria [Braz.] 200 Kh 29.41S 53.48W
Santa Maria [Ca.-U.S.] 182 Ce 34.57N 120.26W
Santa María, Bahía de- 192 Ee 25.05N 108.10W
Santa Maria, Cabo de- [Ang.] 158 Ij 13.25S 12.32 E
Santa Maria, Cabo de- [Port.] 126 Eh 36.58N 7.54W
Santa María, Cape- 194 Jb 23.41N 75.19W
Santa María, Cayo- 194 Hb 22.40N 79.00W
Santa María, Isla- 202a Ab 1.15S 90.25W
Santa María, Isla- 206 Fe 37.02S 73.33W
Santa María, Laguna de- 192 Fb 31.10N 107.15W
Santa Maria, Rio- [Braz.] 204 Ee 21.50S 54.53W
Santa Maria, Rio- [Braz.] 204 Ib 14.19S 46.49W
Santa María, Río- [Mex.] 192 Jg 21.37N 99.15W
Santa María, Río- [Pan.] 194 Gi 8.06N 80.29W
Santa Maria Asunción Tlaxiaco 192 Ki 17.16N 97.41W
Santa Maria Capua Vetere 128 Ii 41.05N 14.15 E
Santa Maria da Vitória 204 Ja 13.24S 44.12W
Santa María de Cuevas 192 Fd 27.55N 106.23W
Santa María de Ipire 196 Dh 8.49N 65.19W
Santa María del Oro 192 Ge 25.56N 105.22W
Santa María del Rio 192 Ig 21.48N 100.45W
Santa Maria di Leuca, Capo- 110 Hh 39.47N 18.22 E
Santa María la Real de Nieva 126 Hc 41.04N 4.24W
Santa María Zacatepec 192 Ki 16.46N 98.00W
Santa Marinella 128 Fh 42.02N 11.51 E
Santa Marta 200 Id 11.15N 74.13W
Santa Marta, Cabo de- 170 Be 13.52S 12.25 E
Santa Marta, Ria de- 126 Ea 43.42N 7.51W
Santa Marta, Serra de- → Divisões, Serra das- 202 Hg 16.40S 50.50W
Santa Marta Grande, Cabo de- 204 Hi 28.38S 48.45W
Santa Monica 182 De 34.01N 118.30W
Santan 150 Gg 0.03S 117.28 E
Santana 204 Ja 12.59S 44.03W
Santana, Coxilha de- 204 Ej 31.15S 55.15W
Santana, Rio- 204 Gd 19.43S 51.02W
Santana da Boa Vista 204 Fj 30.52S 53.07W
Santana do Livramento 206 Id 30.53S 55.31W
Santander [2] 202 Db 6.35N 73.20W
Santander [3] 126 Ia 43.10N 4.00W
Santander [Col.] 202 Cc 3.01N 76.29W
Santander [Phil.] 150 He 9.25N 123.20 E
Santander [Sp.] 112 Fg 43.28N 3.48W
Santander, Bahía de- 126 Ia 43.27N 3.48W
Santander Jiménez 190 Ed 24.13N 98.28W
Sant'Andrea 128 Lj 40.05N 17.55 E
Sant'Antioco 128 Ck 39.04N 8.27 E
Sant'Antioco 110 Gh 39.05N 8.25 E
Sant Antoni, Cap-/San Antonio, Cabo de- 126 Mf 38.48N 0.12 E
Sant Antoni de Portmany / San Antonio Abad 126 Nf 38.58N 1.18 E
Santañy / Santanyí 126 Pe 39.22N 3.07 E
Santanyí / Santañy 126 Pe 39.22N 3.07 E
Santa Olalla 126 Hd 40.01N 4.26W
Santa Olalla del Cala 126 Fg 37.54N 6.13W
Santa Paula 188 Fi 34.21N 119.04W
Santa Pola 126 Lf 38.11N 0.33W
Sant'Arcangelo 128 Kj 40.15N 16.16 E
Santarcangelo di Romagna 128 Gf 44.04N 12.27 E
Santarém [2] 126 De 39.15N 8.35W
Santarém [Braz.] 200 Kf 2.26S 54.42W
Santarém [Port.] 126 De 39.14N 8.41W
Santaren Channel 190 Id 24.00N 79.30W
Santa Rita [Braz.] 204 Cc 16.15S 59.00W
Santa Rita [Braz.] 202 Le 7.13S 35.02W
Santa Rita [Col.] 202 Ec 4.55N 68.20W
Santa Rita [Guam] 220c Bb 13.23N 144.40 E
Santa Rita [Hond.] 194 Df 15.09N 87.53W
Santa Rita [Ven.] 196 Ch 8.08N 66.16W
Santa Rita [Ven.] 194 Lh 10.32N 71.32W
Santa Rita do Araguaia 204 Fc 17.20S 53.12W
Santa Rosa [3] 194 Bf 14.10N 90.18W
Santa Rosa [Arg.] 206 Gd 31.31S 65.04W
Santa Rosa [Arg.] 200 Ji 36.40S 64.15W
Santa Rosa [Braz.] 206 Jc 27.52S 54.29W
Santa Rosa [Ca.-U.S.] 182 Cd 38.26N 122.43W
Santa Rosa [Ec.] 202 Cd 3.27S 79.58W
Santa Rosa [N.M.-U.S.] 182 Ge 34.57N 104.41W
Santa Rosa [Par.] 204 Dh 26.52S 56.49W
Santa Rosa [Ven.] 194 Mi 8.26N 69.42W
Santa Rosa [Ven.] 196 Dh 9.38N 64.18W
Santa Rosa, Mount- 220c Ba 13.32N 144.55 E
Santa Rosa de Copán 194 Cf 14.47N 88.46W
Santa Rosa de la Roca 204 Bc 16.04S 61.32W
Santa Rosa Island 188 Ej 33.58N 120.06W
Santa Rosalía 196 Bh 9.02N 69.01W
Santa Rosalía 176 Hg 27.19N 112.17W
Santa Rosalía, Punta- 192 Bc 28.40N 114.20W
Santa Rosa Range 188 Gf 41.00N 117.40W
Santa Rosa Wash 188 Ij 33.10N 112.05W
Šantarskije ostrova = Shantar Islands (EN) 140 Pd 55.00N 137.36 E
Santas Creus/Santes Creus 126 Nc 41.19N 1.18 E
Santa Sylvina 206 Hc 27.49S 61.09W
Santa Teresa [Arg.] 204 Bk 33.26S 60.47W
Santa Teresa [Mex.] 192 Ke 25.17N 97.51W
Santa Teresa [Peru] 202 Df 13.01S 72.39W
Santa Teresa, Rio- 204 Ha 12.40S 48.47W
Santa Teresa di Riva 128 Jm 37.57N 15.22 E
Santa Teresa Gallura 128 Di 41.14N 9.11 E
Santa Teresita 204 Dm 36.32S 56.41W
Santa Vitória 204 Gd 18.50S 50.08W
Santa Vitória do Palmar 206 Jd 33.31S 53.21W
Sant Boi de Llobregat/San Baudilio de Llobregat 126 Oc 41.21N 2.03 E
Sant Carles de la Ràpita/ San Carlos de la Rápita 126 Md 40.37N 0.36 E
Santee River 182 Le 33.14N 79.28W
Santeh 146 Ld 36.10N 46.32 E
San Telmo 192 Ab 30.58N 116.06W
San Telmo, Bahía de- 192 Hh 18.45N 103.40W
San Telmo, Punta- 190 De 18.19N 103.30W
Santerno 128 Ff 44.34N 11.58 E
Santerre 122 Ie 49.55N 2.30 E
Santes Creus/Santas Creus 126 Nc 41.19N 1.18 E
Sant'Eufemia, Golfo di- 128 Kl 38.50N 16.05 E
Sant'Eufemia Lamezia, Lamezia Terme- 128 Kl 38.55N 16.15 E
Sant Feliu de Guíxols 126 Pc 41.47N 3.02 E
Sant Feliu de Llobregat / San Feliu de Llobregat 126 Oc 41.23N 2.03 E
Sant Francesc de Formentera / San Francisco Javier 126 Nf 38.42N 1.25 E
Santhià 128 Ce 45.22N 8.10 E
Santiago [2] 206 Fd 33.30S 70.50W
Santiago [Bol.] 202 Gg 18.19S 59.34W
Santiago [Bol.] 204 Bd 19.22S 60.51W
Santiago [Braz.] 206 Jc 29.11S 54.53W
Santiago [Chile] 200 Ii 33.27S 70.40W
Santiago [Dom.Rep.] 176 Lh 19.27N 70.42W
Santiago [Mex.] 192 Cd 27.32N 112.49W
Santiago [Mex.] 192 Ie 25.25N 100.09W
Santiago [Pan.] 176 Ki 8.05N 80.59W
Santiago [Par.] 204 Dh 27.09S 56.47W
Santiago, Cerro- 194 Gi 8.33N 81.44W
Santiago, Río- 202 Cd 4.27S 77.36W
Santiago, Río de- 192 Ge 25.11N 105.26W
Santiago, Serranía- 204 Cd 18.25S 59.25W
Santiago de Chuco 202 Ce 8.09S 78.11W
Santiago de Compostela 126 Db 42.53N 8.33W
Santiago de Cuba 176 Lg 20.01N 75.49W
Santiago de Cuba [3] 194 Ic 20.10N 76.10W
Santiago de la Ribera 126 Lg 37.48N 0.48W
Santiago del Estero 200 Jh 27.50S 64.15W
Santiago del Estero [2] 206 Hc 28.00S 63.30W
Santiago de Papasquiaro 192 Ge 25.03N 105.25W
Santiago do Cacém 126 Df 38.01N 8.42W
Santiago Ixcuintla 190 Cd 21.49N 105.13W
Santiago Mountains 186 El 29.40N 103.15W
Santiago Pinotepa Nacional 190 Ee 16.19N 98.01W
Santiaguillo, Isla- 192 Lh 19.05N 95.50W
Santiaguillo, Laguna de- 192 Ge 24.50N 104.50W
Santiam River 188 Dd 44.42N 123.55W
Santillana 126 Ha 43.23N 4.06W
San Timoteo 194 Li 9.48N 71.04W
Säntis 128 Dc 47.15N 9.20 E
Santisteban del Puerto 126 If 38.15N 3.12W
Sant Jordi, Golf de- / San Jorge, Golfo de- 126 Md 40.53N 1.00 E
Sant Mateu del Maestrat/ San Mateo 126 Md 40.28N 0.11 E
Santo, Ile- 208 Hf 15.15S 166.50 E
Santo Anastácio 204 Ge 21.58S 51.39W
Santo André 204 If 23.40S 46.31W
Santo Ângelo 206 Jc 28.18S 54.16W
Santo Antão 158 Eg 17.05N 25.10W
Santo Antônio 206 Jc 26.03S 53.12W
Santo Antonio 166 Ge 1.39N 7.25 E
Santo Antônio de Jesus 202 Kf 12.58S 39.16W
Santo Antônio do Içá 202 Ed 3.05S 67.57W
Santo Antônio do Leverger 202 Gg 15.52S 56.05W
Santo Corazón 202 Gg 17.59S 58.51W
Santo Corazón, Río- 204 Cc 17.23S 58.23W
Santo Domingo [Cuba] 194 Gb 22.35N 80.15W
Santo Domingo [Dom.Rep.] 176 Mh 18.28N 69.54W
Santo Domingo [Mex.] 192 Bc 28.12N 114.02W
Santo Domingo [Mex.] 192 Bb 30.43N 115.56W
Santo Domingo [Mex.] 192 If 23.20N 101.44W
Santo Domingo [Nic.] 194 Eg 12.16N 85.05W
Santo Domingo, Cay- 194 Jc 21.42N 75.46W
Santo Domingo, Punta- 192 Cd 26.20N 112.40W
Santo Domingo, Río- [Mex.] 192 Kh 18.10N 96.08W
Santo Domingo, Río- [Ven.] 194 Mi 8.01N 69.33W
Santo Domingo de la Calzada 126 Jb 42.26N 2.57W
Santo Domingo de los Colorados 202 Cd 0.15S 79.10W
Santo Domingo de Silos 126 Ic 41.58N 3.25W
Santo Domingo Pueblo 186 Ci 35.31N 106.22W
San Tomé 196 Dh 8.58N 64.08W
Santoña 126 Ia 43.27N 3.27W
Santos 200 Lh 23.57S 46.20W
Santos, Sierra de los- 126 Gf 38.15N 5.20W
Santos Dumont 204 Ke 21.28S 43.34W
Santos Unzué 204 Bl 35.45S 60.51W
Santo Tirso 126 Dc 41.21N 8.28W
Santo Tomás [Bol.] 204 Cc 17.46S 58.55W
Santo Tomás [Mex.] 192 Ab 31.33N 116.24W
Santo Tomás [Nic.] 194 Eg 12.04N 85.05W
Santo Tomás, Punta- 192 Ab 31.34N 116.42W
Santo Tomé 206 Ic 28.33S 56.03W
Sant Salvador / San Salvador 126 Pe 39.27N 3.11 E
Santu Lussurgiu 128 Cj 40.08N 8.39 E
Santurce-Antiguo / Santurtzi 126 Ia 43.20N 3.02W
Santurtzi / Santurce-Antiguo 126 Ia 43.20N 3.02W
Sant Vicent del Raspeig / San Vicente de Raspeig 126 Lf 38.24N 0.31 E
Sanuki-Sanmyaku 156 Cd 34.05N 134.00 E
San Valentín, Cerro- 198 Ij 46.36S 73.20W
San Vicente [Arg.] 204 Cl 35.01S 58.25W
San Vicente [Mex.] 192 Ab 31.20N 116.15W
San Vicente [Phil.] 150 Hc 18.30N 122.09 E
San Vicente, Sierra de- 126 Hd 40.10N 4.45W
San Vicente de Cañete 202 Cf 13.05S 79.24W
San Vicente de la Barquera 126 Ha 43.26N 4.24W
San Vicente del Caguán 202 Dc 2.07N 74.46W
San Vicente de Raspeig / Sant Vicent del Raspeig 126 Lf 38.24N 0.31 E
San Vincente 190 Gf 13.38N 88.48W
San Vincenzo 128 Eg 43.06N 10.32 E
San Vito [C.R.] 194 Fi 8.50N 82.58W
San Vito [It.] 128 Dk 39.26N 9.32 E
San Vito, Capo- 128 Gl 38.11N 12.44 E
Sanya → Yaxian 142 Mh 18.27N 109.28 E
Sanyati 172 Dc 16.49S 28.45 E
San'yō 156 Bd 34.03N 131.10 E
Sanza 128 Jj 40.15N 15.33 E
Sanza Pombo 170 Cd 7.20S 16.00 E
São Bartolomeu, Rio- 204 Ic 16.48S 47.55W
São Benedito 202 Jd 4.03S 40.53W
São Bento 202 Jd 2.42S 44.50W
São Bento do Sul 204 Hh 26.15S 49.23W
São Borja 206 Ic 28.39S 56.00W
São Brás de Alportel 126 Eg 37.09N 7.53W
São Caetano do Sul 206 Kb 23.36S 46.34W
São Carlos [Braz.] 206 Kb 22.01S 47.54W
São Carlos [Braz.] 204 Ej 33.47N 55.30W
São Carlos [Braz.] 204 Ej 30.11S 55.30W
São Domingos [Braz.] 204 Ia 13.24S 46.19W
São Domingos [Gui.Bis.] 166 Bc 12.24N 16.12W
São Domingos, Rio- [Braz.] 204 Gd 19.13S 50.44W
São Domingos, Rio- [Braz.] 204 Ib 15.37S 46.14W
São Domingos, Rio- [Braz.] 204 Ia 13.24S 47.12W
São Domingos, Rio- [Braz.] 204 Fe 20.03S 53.13W
São Felix 202 Hf 11.36S 50.39W
São Félix do Xingu 202 He 6.38S 51.59W
São Filipe 162 Cf 14.54N 24.31W
São Francisco [Braz.] 204 Dd 18.45S 56.55W
São Francisco [Braz.] 202 Jg 15.57S 44.52W
São Francisco, Ilha de- 198 Lh 26.18S 48.37W
São Francisco, Rio- 198 Mg 10.30S 36.24W
São Francisco de Assis 204 Ei 29.33S 55.08W
São Francisco de Paula 204 Gi 29.27S 50.35W
São Francisco de Sales 204 Hd 19.52S 49.46W
São Francisco do Sul 206 Kc 26.14S 48.39W
São Gabriel 206 Jd 30.20S 54.19W
São Gonçalo 202 Jh 22.51S 43.04W
São Gonçalo, Canal de- 204 Fk 32.10S 52.38W
São Gonçalo do Abaeté 204 Jd 18.20S 45.49W
São Gonçalo do Sapucaí 204 Je 21.54S 45.36W
São Gotardo 204 Id 19.19S 46.03W
Sao Hill 170 Gd 8.20S 35.12 E
São Jerônimo, Serra de- 204 Ec 16.20S 54.55W
São João da Barra 202 Jh 21.38S 41.03W
São João da Boa Vista 204 Ie 21.58S 46.47W
São João d'Aliança 204 Ib 14.42S 47.31W
São João da Madeira 126 Dd 40.54N 8.30W
São João da Ponte 204 Kb 15.56S 44.01W
São João del Rei 202 Jh 21.09S 44.16W
São João de Meriti 204 Kf 22.48S 43.22W
São João do Araguaia 202 Ie 5.23S 48.46W
São João do Piauí 202 Je 8.21S 42.15W
São João dos Patos 202 Je 6.30S 43.42W
São João do Triunfo 204 Gg 25.41S 50.18W
São Joaquim 206 Kc 28.18S 49.56W
São Joaquim da Barra 204 Ie 20.35S 47.53W
São Jorge 158 Ee 38.38N 28.03W
São José da Serra 204 Eb 15.40S 55.18W
São José do Cerrito 204 Gh 27.40S 50.35W
São José do Norte 204 Fk 32.01S 52.03W
São José do Rio Pardo 206 Kb 21.36S 46.54W
São José do Rio Prêto 200 Lh 20.48S 49.23W
São José dos Campos 206 Kb 23.11S 45.53W
São José dos Dourados, Rio- 204 Ge 20.22S 51.21W
Saolat, Buku- 150 If 0.45N 127.59 E
São Leopoldo 206 Jc 29.46S 51.09W
São Lourenço 204 Ec 16.32S 55.02W
São Lourenço, Pantanal de- 202 Gg 17.45S 56.15W
São Lourenço, Rio- 202 Gg 17.53S 57.27W
São Lourenço, Serra de- 204 Ec 17.30S 54.50W
São Lourenço do Sul 206 Jd 31.22S 51.58W
São Luís 200 Lf 2.31S 44.16W
São Luís Gonzaga 206 Jc 28.24S 54.58W
São Mamede, Serra de- 126 Ee 39.19N 7.19W
São Manuel 204 Hf 22.44S 48.34W
São Manuel, Rio- 198 Kf 7.21S 58.03W
São Marcos 204 Gi 28.58S 51.04W
São Marcos, Baía de- 198 Lf 2.30S 44.30W
São Marcos, Rio- 204 Id 18.15S 47.37W
São Mateus 202 Kg 18.44S 39.51W
São Mateus, Rio- 204 Ia 13.48S 46.54W
São Mateus do Sul 204 Gg 25.52S 50.23W
São Miguel 158 Ee 37.47N 25.30W
São Miguel, Rio- 204 Ic 16.03S 46.07W
São Miguel do Araguaia 204 Ga 13.19S 50.13W
São Miguel d'Oeste 204 Fh 26.45S 53.34W

Index Symbols

[1] Independent Nation
[2] State, Region
[3] District, County
[4] Municipality
[5] Colony, Dependency
Continent
Physical Region
Historical or Cultural Region
Mount, Mountain
Volcano
Hill
Mountains, Mountain Range
Hills, Escarpment
Plateau, Upland
Pass, Gap
Plain, Lowland
Delta
Salt Flat
Valley, Canyon
Crater, Cave
Karst Features
Depression
Polder
Desert, Dunes
Forest, Woods
Heath, Steppe
Oasis
Cape, Point
Coast, Beach
Cliff
Peninsula
Isthmus
Sandbank
Island
Atoll
Rock, Reef
Islands, Archipelago
Rocks, Reefs
Coral Reef
Well, Spring
Geyser
River, Stream
Waterfall, Rapids
River Mouth, Estuary
Lake
Salt Lake
Intermittent Lake
Reservoir
Swamp, Pond
Canal
Glacier
Ice Shelf, Pack Ice
Ocean
Sea
Gulf, Bay
Strait, Fjord
Lagoon
Bank
Seamount
Tablemount
Ridge
Shelf
Basin
Escarpment, Sea Scarp
Fracture
Trench, Abyss
National Park, Reserve
Point of Interest
Recreation Site
Cave, Cavern
Historic Site
Ruins
Wall, Walls
Church, Abbey
Temple
Scientific Station
Railway station
Airport
Port
Military installation
Lighthouse
Mine
Tunnel
Dam, Bridge

Saona, Isla-	194	Md	18.09N	68.40W
Saône	110	Gf	45.44N	4.50 E
Saône-et-Loire [3]	122	Kh	46.40N	4.30 E
Saonek	150	Jg	0.28S	130.47 E
São Nicolau	204	Ei	28.11S	55.16W
São Nicolau	158	Eg	16.35N	24.15W
São Patricio, Rio-	204	Hb	15.02S	49.15W
São Paulo	200	Lh	23.32S	46.37W
São Paulo [2]	206	Kb	22.00S	49.00W
São Paulo de Olivença	202	Ed	3.27S	68.48W
São Pedro, Ribeirão-	204	Ic	16.54S	46.32W
São Pedro do Sul [Braz.]	204	Ei	29.37S	54.10W
São Pedro do Sul [Port.]	126	Dd	40.45N	8.04W
São Pedro e São Paulo, Penedos de-	198	Ne	0.56N	29.22W
São Raimundo Nonato	202	Je	9.01S	42.42W
São Romão [Braz.]	202	Ig	16.22S	45.04W
São Romão [Braz.]	204	Ed	18.33S	54.27W
São Roque	204	De	21.43S	57.46W
São Roque, Cabo de-	198	Mf	5.29S	35.16W
São Roque, Serra de-	204	Ib	14.40S	46.50W
São Sebastião	204	Jf	23.48S	45.25W
São Sebastião, Ilha de-	198	Lh	23.50S	45.18W
São Sebastião, Ponta-	158	Kk	22.05S	35.24 E
São Sebastião da Boa Vista	202	Id	1.42S	49.31W
São Sebastião do Paraiso	202	Ih	20.55S	47.00W
São Sepé	204	Fj	30.10S	53.34W
São Simão	202	Hg	18.56S	50.30W
São Tiago	158	Eg	15.05N	23.40W
São Tomé	160	Hh	0.20N	6.44 E
São Tomé	158	Hh	0.12N	6.39 E
São Tomé, Cabo de-	202	Jh	22.00S	40.59W
Sao Tome and Principe (EN) = São Tomé e Príncipe [1]	160	Hh	1.00N	7.00 E
São Tomé e Príncipe = Sao Tome and Principe (EN) [1]	160	Hh	1.00N	7.00 E
Saoura	162	Gd	27.50N	2.50W
Saoura	158	Gf	28.48N	0.50W
São Vicente	158	Eg	16.50N	25.00W
São Vicente [Braz.]	206	Kb	23.58S	46.23W
São Vicente [Braz.]	204	Ia	13.38S	46.31W
São Vicente, Cabo de-	110	Fh	37.01N	9.00W
São Xavier, Serra de-	204	Ei	29.15S	54.15W
Sápai	130	Ih	41.02N	25.42 E
Sapanca	130	Ni	40.41N	30.16 E
Sapanca Gölü	130	Ni	40.43N	30.15 E
Sape [Braz.]	202	Ke	7.06S	35.13W
Sape [Indon.]	150	Gh	8.34S	118.59 E
Sape, Selat-	150	Gh	8.39S	119.18 E
Sapele	166	Gd	5.55N	5.42 E
Sapelo Island	184	Gj	31.28N	81.15W
Şaphane	130	Mj	39.01N	29.14 E
Şaphane Dağı	130	Mj	39.03N	29.16 E
Sapiéntza	130	Em	36.45N	21.42 E
Šapkina	134	Fc	66.44N	52.25 E
Sapo, Serranía del-	194	Hi	7.50N	78.17W
Sa Pobla / La Puebla	126	Pe	39.46N	3.01 E
Saponé	166	Ec	12.03N	1.36W
Sapopema	204	Gf	23.55S	50.35W
Saposoa	202	Ce	6.56S	76.48W
Sapphire Mountains	188	Ic	46.20N	113.45W
Sapporo	142	Qe	43.03N	141.21 E
Sapri	128	Jj	40.04N	15.38 E
Sapucaí, Rio-	204	He	20.08S	48.27W
Sapulpa	182	Hd	36.00N	96.06W
Sapulut	150	Gf	4.42N	116.29 E
Sāqand	146	Pf	32.33N	55.12 E
Sāqiyat Sīdī Yūsuf	128	Cn	36.13N	8.21 E
Saqqez	144	Gb	36.14N	46.16 E
Sarāb	144	Gb	37.56N	47.32 E
Saraburi	148	Kf	14.30N	100.55 E
Saraf Doungous	168	Bc	12.33N	19.42 E
Sarafjagān	146	Ne	34.28N	50.28 E
Saragmatha = Everest, Mount- (EN)	140	Kg	27.59N	86.56 E
Saragossa (EN) = Zaragoza [Sp.]	112	Fg	41.38N	0.53W
Sarai	114	Jj	53.44N	41.03 E
Sarajevo	112	Hg	43.50N	18.25 E
Saraji Mine	212	Jd	22.30S	148.20 E
Sarakhs	144	Jb	36.32N	61.11 E
Sarakiná	130	Hk	38.40N	24.37 E
Šarakol	134	Kj	52.03N	62.47 E
Saraktaš	136	Fe	51.47N	56.18 E
Saraland	184	Cj	30.49N	88.02W
Saramati	148	Jc	25.44N	95.02 E
Saran	136	Hf	49.46N	72.52 E
Saran, Gunung-	150	Fg	0.25S	111.18 E
Saranac Lake	184	Jc	44.20N	74.08W
Saranci	130	Gg	42.43N	23.46 E
Saranda	130	Dj	39.52N	20.00 E
Sarandi	204	Fh	27.56S	52.55W
Sarandi, Arroyo-	204	Cj	30.13S	59.19W
Sarandí del Yí	204	Ek	33.21S	55.38W
Sarandí Grande	204	Dk	33.44S	56.20W
Šaranga	114	Lh	57.12N	46.34 E
Sarangani Bay	150	Ie	5.57N	125.11 E
Sarangani Islands	150	Ie	5.25N	125.26 E
Saranley	168	Ge	2.23N	42.16 E
Saransk	112	Ke	54.11N	45.11 E
Sarapul	112	Ld	56.28N	53.48 E
Sarapulskoje	138	Ig	48.50N	135.58 E
Sarare	194	Mi	9.47N	69.10W
Sararé, Rio-	204	Cb	14.51S	59.58W
Sarasota	182	Kf	27.20N	82.34W
Sarata	132	Ff	46.01N	29.41 E
Sărăţel	130	Hb	47.03N	24.25 E
Saratoga	188	Lf	41.27N	106.48W
Saratoga Springs	182	Mc	43.04N	73.47W
Saratok	150	Ff	1.24N	111.31 E
Saratov	112	Ke	51.34N	46.02 E
Saratov Reservoir (EN) = Saratovskoje vodohranilišče	110	Ke	52.50N	47.50 E
Saratovskaja oblast [3]	136	Ee	51.30N	47.00 E
Saratovskoje vodohranilišče = Saratov Reservoir (EN)	110	Ke	52.50N	47.50 E
Saravan	148	Le	15.43N	106.25 E
Sarawak [2]	150	Ff	2.30N	113.30 E
Saray	146	Bb	41.26N	27.55 E
Sarāyā	146	Fe	35.47N	35.58 E
Saraya	166	Cc	12.50N	11.45W
Sarayköy	146	Cd	37.55N	28.56 E
Sarbāz	144	Jd	26.39N	61.15 E
Sárbogárd	120	Oj	46.53N	18.38 E
Sarca	128	Ee	45.52N	10.52 E
Sarcelle, Passe de la-	219b	Cf	22.28S	167.13 E
Sarcelles	124	Ef	49.00N	2.23 E
Sarcidano	128	Dk	39.40N	9.15 E
Sardara	128	Ck	39.37N	8.49 E
Sar Dasht [Iran]	146	Kd	36.09N	45.28 E
Sar Dasht [Iran]	146	Mf	32.32N	48.52 E
Sardegna [2]	128	Cj	40.00N	9.00 E
Sardegna = Sardinia (EN)	110	Gh	40.00N	9.00 E
Sardegna, Mar di-	128	Bk	40.00N	7.30 E
Sardes	130	Lk	38.29N	28.03 E
Sardinal	194	Eh	10.31N	85.39W
Sardinata	202	Db	8.07N	72.48W
Sardinia (EN) = Sardegna	110	Gh	40.00N	9.00 E
Sardis Lake	186	Li	34.27N	89.43W
Sarektjåkkå	114	Dc	67.25N	17.46 E
Sarema/Saaremaa	110	Id	58.25N	22.30 E
Sar-e Pol	144	Kb	36.14N	65.55 E
Sar Eskand Khān	146	Ld	37.29N	47.04 E
Sar-e Yazd	146	Pg	31.36N	54.35 E
Sargasso Sea	174	Mg	29.00N	65.00W
Sargatskoje	136	Hd	55.37N	73.30 E
Sargodha	148	Eb	32.05N	72.40 E
Šargun	135	Fe	38.31N	67.59 E
Sarh	160	Ih	9.09N	18.23 E
Sarhro, Jebel-	162	Fc	31.00N	6.00W
Sāri	142	Hf	36.34N	53.04 E
Saría	130	Kn	35.50N	27.15 E
Sariçakaya	146	Db	40.02N	30.31 E
Sarigan Island	208	Fc	16.42N	145.47 E
Sarigöl	146	Cc	38.14N	28.43 E
Sarıkamış	146	Jb	40.15N	42.35 E
Sarıkaya	146	Fc	39.48N	35.24 E
Sarikei	150	Ff	2.07N	111.31 E
Sariköy	130	Ki	40.12N	27.36 E
Sarina	212	Jd	21.26S	149.13 E
Sarine	128	Bd	46.59N	7.16 E
Sariñena	126	Lc	41.48N	0.10W
Sarıoğlan	146	Fc	39.05N	35.59 E
Sarīr	164	Dd	27.30N	22.30 E
Sariwŏn	152	Md	38.30N	125.45 E
Sarıyer	146	Cb	41.10N	29.03 E
Sarj, Jabal as-	128	Do	35.56N	9.32 E
Šarja	112	Kd	58.24N	45.30 E
Sark	118	Kl	49.26N	2.21W
Sarkad	120	Rj	46.45N	21.23 E
Sarkand	136	Hf	45.25N	79.54 E
Şarkikaraağaç	146	Dc	38.04N	31.23 E
Sarkışla	146	Gc	39.21N	36.26 E
Šarkovščina	116	Li	55.22N	27.32 E
Sarköy	146	Bb	40.37N	27.06 E
Sarlat-la-Canéda	122	Hj	44.53N	1.13 E
Šarlyk	132	Sc	52.54N	54.42 E
Sarmi	210	Ee	1.51S	138.44 E
Sarmiento	200	Jj	45.35S	69.05W
Sarmizegetuza	130	Fd	45.31N	22.47 E
Särna	116	Ec	61.41N	13.08 E
Sarnen	128	Cd	46.54N	8.15 E
Sărnena Gora	130	Ig	42.35N	25.30 E
Sarnia	180	Jh	42.58N	82.23W
Sarny	136	Ce	51.21N	26.36 E
Saroako	150	Hg	2.31S	121.22 E
Sarolangun	150	Dg	2.18S	102.42 E
Saroma	156a	Ca	44.02N	143.45 E
Saroma-Ko	154	Qb	44.10N	143.40 E
Šaromy	138	Kf	54.23N	158.14 E
Saronic Gulf (EN) = Saronikós Kólpos	130	Gl	37.45N	23.30 E
Saronikós Kólpos = Saronic Gulf (EN)	130	Gl	37.45N	23.30 E
Saronno	128	De	45.38N	9.02 E
Saros, Gulf of- (EN) = Saros Körfezi	146	Bb	40.30N	26.20 E
Saros Körfezi = Saros, Gulf of- (EN)	146	Bb	40.30N	26.20 E
Sárospatak	120	Rh	48.19N	21.35 E
Sar Passage	220a	Ac	7.12N	134.23 E
Sarpinskije ozera	132	Nf	47.45N	45.00 E
Šar Planina	130	Dg	42.05N	20.50 E
Sarpsborg	116	De	59.17N	11.07 E
Sarqaq	179	Gd	70.00N	51.39W
Sarrabus	128	Dk	39.20N	9.30 E
Sarralbe	122	Ne	49.00N	7.01 E
Sarrāţ, Wādī-	128	Co	35.59N	8.23 E
Sarre	120	Cg	49.42N	6.34 E
Sarrebourg	122	Nf	48.44N	7.03 E
Sarreguemines	122	Ne	49.06N	7.03 E
Sarre-Union	124	Jf	48.56N	7.05 E
Sarria	126	Eb	42.47N	7.24W
Sarstún, Río-	194	Cf	15.54N	88.54W
Sartang	138	Ic	67.30N	133.20 E
Sartène	122a	Ab	41.37N	8.59 E
Sarthe [3]	122	Gf	48.00N	0.05 E
Sarthe	122	Fg	47.32N	0.31W
Sartu → Anda	154	Ha	46.35N	125.00 E
Sarufutsu	156a	Ca	45.18N	142.13 E
Saru-Gawa	156a	Cb	42.30N	142.00 E
Saruhanlı	146	Bc	38.44N	27.34 E
Sarukaishi-Gawa	156	Gb	39.25N	141.08 E
Sārūq	146	Me	34.25N	49.30 E
Saruyama-Misaki	156	Ec	37.18N	136.43 E
Sárvár	120	Mi	47.15N	16.56 E
Sarvestān	146	Oh	29.16N	53.13 E
Sárviz	120	Oj	46.22N	18.48 E
Saryagač	135	Gd	41.28N	69.11 E
Sarybarak	135	Hc	43.24N	71.29 E
Sary-Bulak	135	Jd	41.54N	75.47 E
Saryč, mys-	110	Jg	44.23N	33.45 E
Saryg-Sep	138	Ef	51.30N	95.40 E
Sary-Išikotrau	135	Kb	45.15N	76.25 E
Sarykamys	136	Ff	46.00N	53.41 E
Sarykamyšskoje, ozero-	136	Fg	41.58N	57.58 E
Sarykolski hrebet	135	Je	38.30N	74.15 E
Šaryn-Gol	152	Ib	49.20N	106.30 E
Saryozek	136	Hg	44.22N	77.54 E
Saryšagan	136	Hf	46.05N	73.38 E
Saryšiganak, zaliv-	135	Ca	46.35N	61.25 E
Sarysu	140	Ie	45.12N	66.36 E
Sary-Taš	136	Hh	39.44N	73.16 E
Saryžaz	135	Lc	42.54N	79.31 E
Sarzana	128	Df	44.07N	9.58 E
Sasabe	192	Db	31.27N	111.31W
Sasabeneh	168	Gd	8.00N	43.44 E
Sasa-ga-Mine	156	Ce	33.49N	133.17 E
Sasago-Tōge	156	Fd	35.37N	138.45 E
Sasamungga	219a	Cb	7.02S	156.47 E
Sasarām	148	Gd	24.57N	84.02 E
Sasari, Mount-	219a	Dc	8.11S	159.33 E
Sascut	130	Kc	46.11N	27.04 E
Sásd	120	Oj	46.15N	18.07 E
Sasebo	152	Me	33.12N	129.44 E
Saseginaga, Lac-	184	Hb	47.05N	78.34W
Saskatchewan [2]	180	Gf	54.00N	106.00W
Saskatchewan	174	Jd	53.12N	99.16W
Saskatoon	176	Id	52.07N	106.38W
Saskylah	138	Gb	72.00N	114.00 E
Sasluya, Cerro-	194	Eg	13.45N	85.03W
Sasovo	136	Ee	54.22N	41.54 E
Sassafras Mountain	184	Fh	35.03N	82.48W
Sassandra	160	Gh	4.57N	6.05W
Sassandra [3]	166	Dd	5.20N	6.10W
Sassandra	158	Gh	4.58N	6.05W
Sassari	112	Gg	40.43N	8.34 E
Sassenberg	124	Kc	51.59N	8.03 E
Sassenheim	124	Gb	52.14N	4.33 E
Sassetot-le-Mauconduit	124	Ce	49.48N	0.32 E
Saßnitz	120	Jb	54.31N	13.39 E
Sasso Marconi	128	Ff	44.24N	11.15 E
Sassuolo	128	Ef	44.33N	10.47 E
Sastobe	135	Hc	42.34N	70.03 E
Sastre	204	Bj	31.45S	61.50W
Sasyk, ozero- (Kunduk)	132	Fg	45.45N	29.40 E
Sasykkol, ozero-	136	If	46.40N	81.00 E
Sata	156	Bf	31.04N	130.42 E
Sata Cape- (EN) = Sata-Misaki	140	Pf	30.59N	130.37 E
Satakunta	116	Jc	61.30N	23.00 E
sa Talaiassa / Atalayasa	126	Nf	38.55N	1.15 E
Sata-Misaki = Sata, Cape- (EN)	140	Pf	30.59N	130.37 E
Satan, Pointe de-	219b	Dd	19.00S	169.17 E
Sātāra	148	Ee	17.41N	73.59 E
Sataua	221c	Aa	13.28S	172.40W
Satawal Island	208	Fd	7.21N	147.02 E
Satawan Atoll	208	Gd	5.25N	153.35 E
Satellite Bay	180	Fa	77.25N	117.15W
Säter	114	Df	60.21N	15.45 E
Satihaure	114	Ec	67.30N	18.45 E
Satipo	202	Df	11.16S	74.37W
Satīt	168	Fc	14.20N	35.50 E
Satka	136	Fd	55.03N	59.01 E
Šatki	114	Ki	55.11N	44.08 E
Sātmāla Range	148	Fe	19.30N	78.45 E
Satna	148	Gd	24.35N	80.50 E
Šator	128	Kf	44.09N	16.37 E
Sátoraljaújhely	120	Rh	48.24N	21.40 E
Sātpura Range	140	Jg	21.25N	76.10 E
Satsuma-Hantō	156	Bf	31.25N	130.25 E
Satsunai-Gawa	156a	Cb	42.55N	143.15 E
Satsunan-Shotō	152	Mf	29.00N	130.00 E
Sattahip	148	Kf	12.39N	100.54 E
Satulung	130	Gb	47.34N	23.26 E
Satu Mare	130	Fb	47.48N	22.53 E
Satu Mare [2]	130	Fb	47.46N	22.56 E
Satun	148	Kg	6.39N	100.03 E
Saturniná ou Papagaio, Rio-	204	Ca	13.55S	58.18W
Saualpe	128	Id	46.50N	14.40 E
Sauce	206	Ic	30.00S	58.46W
Sauce Corto, Arroyo-	204	Bm	36.55S	61.48W
Sauceda Mountains	188	Ij	32.30N	112.30W
Sauce Grande, Río-	204	Bn	38.59S	61.07W
Saucillo	190	Cc	28.01N	105.17W
Sauda	116	Be	59.39N	6.20 E
Saudade, Serra da- [Braz.]	204	Jd	19.20S	45.50W
Saudade, Serra da- [Braz.]	204	Fc	16.20S	53.53W
Sauðárkrókur	114a	Bb	65.45N	19.39W
Saudi Arabia (EN) = Al 'Arabīyah As-Su'ūdīyah [1]	142	Gg	25.00N	45.00 E
Sauer [Eur.]	120	Cg	49.44N	6.31 E
Sauer [Eur.]	124	Kf	48.55N	8.10 E
Sauerland	120	De	51.10N	8.00 E
Sauêruiná, Rio-	202	Gf	12.00S	58.40W
Sauga jõgi	116	Kf	58.19N	24.25 E
Saugatuck	184	Dd	42.40N	86.12W
Saugues	122	Jj	44.58N	3.33 E
Sauk Centre	186	Id	45.44N	94.57W
Sauk Rapids	186	Id	45.34N	94.09W
Saül	202	Hc	3.37N	53.12W
Šaulder	135	Gc	42.47N	68.24 E
Sauldre	122	Hg	47.16N	1.30 E
Saulieu	122	Kg	47.16N	4.14 E
Saulkrasti/Saulkrasty	114	Fh	57.17N	24.29 E
Saulkrasty/Saulkrasti	114	Fh	57.17N	24.29 E
Saulnois	124	If	48.52N	6.30 E
Sault	122	Lj	44.05N	5.25 E
Sault Sainte-Marie [Mi.-U.S.]	182	Kb	46.30N	84.21W
Sault Sainte-Marie [Ont.-Can.]	176	Ke	46.31N	84.20W
Saulx	122	Kf	48.45N	4.35 E
Saumarez Reefs	208	Gg	21.50S	153.40 E
Saumâtre, Étang-	194	Kd	18.35N	72.00W
Saumlaki	150	Jh	7.57S	131.19 E
Saumur	122	Fg	47.16N	0.05W
Saunders	222	Ad	57.47S	26.27W
Saunders Coast	222	Mf	77.45S	150.00W
Saurimo	160	Ji	9.38S	20.24 E
Sauro	128	Kj	40.18N	16.21 E
Sautar	170	Ce	11.09S	18.25 E
Sauteurs	197p	Bb	12.14N	61.38W
Sauveterre, Causse de-	122	Jj	44.22N	3.17 E
Sauveterre-de-Guyenne	122	Fj	44.42N	0.05W
Sauvo/Sagu	116	Jd	60.21N	22.42 E
Sauwald	128	Hb	48.28N	13.40 E
Sava	110	Ig	44.50N	20.28 E
Savage River	212	Jh	41.33S	145.09 E
Savai'i Island	208	Jf	13.35S	172.25W
Savala	132	Ld	51.06N	41.29 E
Savalou	166	Fd	7.56N	1.58 E
Savanes [3]	166	Fc	10.30N	0.30 E
Savan Island	197n	Bb	12.48N	61.12W
Savanna	186	Ke	42.05N	90.08W
Savannah	174	Kf	32.02N	80.53W
Savannah [Ga.-U.S.]	176	Kf	32.04N	81.05W
Savannah [Tn.-U.S.]	184	Ch	35.14N	88.14W
Savannah Beach	184	Gi	32.01N	80.51W
Savannakhét	142	Mh	16.33N	104.45 E
Savanna-la-Mar	190	Ie	18.13N	78.08W
Savanne	186	Kb	48.59N	90.12W
Savannes Bay	197k	Bb	13.45N	60.56W
Savant Lake	180	If	50.15N	90.42W
Savant Lake	186	Ka	50.30N	90.20W
Savaştepe	146	Bc	39.22N	27.40 E
Savdirī	168	Dc	14.25N	29.05 E
Savè	160	Hh	8.02N	2.29 E
Save [Afr.]	158	Kk	21.00S	35.02 E
Save [Fr.]	122	Hk	43.47N	1.17 E
Saveån	116	Dg	57.43N	11.59 E
Sāveh	144	Hb	35.01N	50.20 E
Săveni	130	Jb	47.57N	26.52 E
Saverdun	122	Hk	43.14N	1.35 E
Saverne	122	Nf	48.44N	7.22 E
Savigliano	128	Bf	44.38N	7.40 E
Savigsivik	179	Fc	76.00N	64.45W
Săvineşti	130	Jc	46.51N	26.28 E
Savinjske Alpe	128	Id	46.20N	14.30 E
Savinski	136	Ec	62.57N	40.13 E
Savio	128	Gf	44.19N	12.20 E
Săvîrşin	130	Fc	46.01N	22.14 E
Savitaipale	114	Gf	61.12N	27.42 E
Šavnik	130	Cg	42.57N	19.06 E
Savo	116	Lb	62.30N	27.30 E
Savo	219a	Dc	9.08S	159.48 E
Savoie [3]	122	Mi	45.30N	6.25 E
Savoie = Savoy (EN)	122	Mi	45.24N	6.30 E
Savona	128	Cf	44.17N	8.30 E
Savonlinna/Nyslott	114	Gf	61.52N	28.53 E
Savonranta	114	Ge	62.11N	29.12 E
Savonselkä	116	Lb	62.05N	27.20 E
Savoonga	178	Ed	63.42N	170.27W
Savoy (EN) = Savoie	122	Mi	45.24N	6.30 E
Şavşat	146	Jb	41.15N	42.20 E
Savsjö	114	Dh	57.25N	14.40 E
Savudrija, Rt-	128	He	45.30N	13.31 E
Savukoski	114	Gc	67.17N	28.10 E
Savur	146	Id	37.33N	40.53 E
Savusavu	216	Ec	17.34S	178.15 E
Savusavu Bay	219d	Bb	16.45S	179.15 E
Savu Sea (EN) = Sawu, Laut-	140	Oj	9.40S	122.00 E
Savuto	128	Kk	39.02N	16.06 E
Sawahlunto	150	Dg	0.40S	100.47 E
Sawai Mādhopur	148	Fc	25.59N	76.22 E
Sawākin	160	Kg	19.07N	37.20 E
Sawākin, Jazā'ir- = Suakin Archipelago (EN)	158	Kg	19.07N	37.20 E
Sawankhalok	148	Je	17.19N	99.54 E
Sawara	156	Gd	35.53N	140.29 E
Sawasaki-Hana	154	Of	37.47N	138.12 E
Sawatch Range	186	Cg	39.10N	106.25W
Sawbā = Sobat (EN)	158	Kh	9.45N	31.45 E
Sawbridgeworth	124	Cc	51.49N	0.09 E
Sawdā', Jabal as-	164	Cd	28.40N	15.30 E
Sawfajjīn	164	Cc	31.54N	15.07 E
Sawhāj = Sohag (EN)	160	Kf	26.33N	31.42 E
Sawkanah	164	Cd	29.04N	15.47 E
Sawla	166	Ed	9.17N	2.25W
Sawqirah	144	If	18.10N	56.30 E
Şawqirah, Ghubbat-	144	If	18.35N	56.45 E
Sawtooth Mountains	188	He	44.00N	115.00W
Sawu, Kepulauan-	150	Hi	10.30S	121.50 E
Sawu, Laut- = Savu Sea (EN)	140	Oj	9.40S	122.00 E
Sawu, Pulau-	140	Ok	10.30S	121.54 E
Şawwān, Ard as-	146	Gg	31.00N	37.00 E
Sax	126	Lf	38.32N	0.49W
Saxby River	212	Ic	18.25S	140.53 E
Saxmundham	124	Db	52.13N	1.30 E
Saxony (EN) = Sachsen	120	Ie	51.20N	13.30 E
Say	166	Fc	13.07N	2.21 E
Sayabec	184	Na	48.36N	67.37W
Saya de Malha Bank (EN)	158	Nj	11.00S	61.00 E
Sayago	126	Fc	41.20N	6.10W
Sayan	202	Cf	11.08S	77.12W
Sayang, Pulau-	150	If	0.18N	129.54 E
Sayaxché	194	Be	16.31N	90.10W
Saydā	144	Ec	33.33N	35.22 E
Sayḩūt	142	Hh	15.12N	51.14 E
Saylorville Lake	186	Jf	41.48N	93.46W
Säynätsalo	116	Kb	62.08N	25.46 E
Sayō	156	Dd	35.01N	134.22 E
Sayram Hu	152	Dc	44.35N	81.10 E
Sayula	192	Hh	19.52N	103.37W
Saywūn	168	Hb	15.56N	48.47 E
Sazanit, Ishull i-	130	Ci	40.30N	19.16 E
Sázava	120	Kg	49.52N	14.54 E
Sázava	120	Kg	49.53N	14.24 E
Sbaa	162	Gd	28.13N	0.10W
Sbisseb	126	Pi	35.42N	3.51 E
Sbruč	132	Ee	48.32N	26.25 E
Scaër	122	Cf	48.02N	3.42W
Scafell Pike	118	Jg	54.27N	3.12W
Scalea	128	Jk	39.49N	15.47 E
Scalone, Passo dello-	128	Jk	39.38N	15.57 E
Scammon, Laguna-	192	Bd	27.45N	114.15W
Scammon Bay	178	Fd	61.53N	165.38W
Scandinavia (EN)	110	Hc	65.00N	16.00 E
Scandinavian Highland (EN)	110	Hc	64.00N	13.00 E
Scanno	128	Hi	41.54N	13.53 E
Scansano	128	Fh	42.41N	11.20 E
Scapa Flow	118	Jc	58.54N	3.05W
Scapegoat Mountain	188	Ic	47.19N	112.50W
Ščapino	138	Ke	55.15N	159.25 E
Ščara	132	Dc	53.27N	24.44 E
Scaramia, Capo-	128	In	36.47N	14.29 E
Scarba	118	He	56.11N	5.42W
Scarborough [Eng.-U.K.]	118	Mg	54.17N	0.24W
Scarborough [Trin.]	202	Fa	11.11N	60.44W
Scarp	118	Fc	58.05N	7.05W
Scarpe	122	Jd	50.30N	3.27 E
Ščastje	132	Ke	48.44N	39.14 E
Sceaux	124	Ef	48.47N	2.17 E
Šćedro	128	Kg	43.05N	16.42 E
Ščekino	132	Jb	54.01N	37.29 E
Ščekurja	134	Jd	64.15N	60.52 E
Ščeljajur	136	Fb	65.21N	53.25 E
Scenic	186	Ee	43.47N	102.30W
Ščerbakty	136	He	52.29N	78.14 E
Schaalsee	120	Gc	53.35N	10.57 E
Schaarbeek/Schaerbeek	124	Gd	50.51N	4.23 E
Schaerbeek/Schaarbeek	124	Gd	50.51N	4.23 E
Schaffhausen	128	Cc	47.40N	8.40 E
Schaffhausen [2]	128	Cc	47.45N	8.40 E
Schagen	124	Gb	52.48N	4.48 E
Schärding	128	Hb	48.27N	13.26 E
Scharmützelsee	120	Kd	52.15N	14.03 E
Scharnhörn	120	Ec	53.57N	8.25 E
Scheeßel	124	La	53.10N	9.29 E
Schefferville	176	Md	54.47N	64.49W
Scheibbs	128	Jb	48.00N	15.10 E
Schelde	122	Kc	51.22N	4.15 E
Schelde (EN) = Escaut	122	Kc	51.22N	4.15 E
Schell Creek Range	182	Ed	39.10N	114.40W
Schenectady	182	Mc	42.48N	73.57W
Scheno	168	Fd	9.35N	39.25 E
Scherfede, Warburg-	124	Lc	51.32N	9.02 E
Scherpenheuvel-Zichem	124	Gd	50.59N	4.59 E
Scheveningen, 's-Gravenhage-	122	Kb	52.06N	4.18 E
Schiedam	122	Kc	51.55N	4.24 E
Schiermonnikoog	122	Ma	53.28N	6.15 E
Schifferstadt	124	Ke	49.23N	8.22 E
Schiffgraben	120	Hd	52.02N	11.10 E
Schifflange	124	Ie	49.30N	6.01 E
Schijndel	124	Hc	51.37N	5.28 E
Schiltigheim	122	Nf	48.36N	7.45 E
Schio	128	Fe	45.43N	11.21 E
Schipbeek	124	Ib	52.15N	6.14 E
Schladming	128	Hc	47.23N	13.41 E
Schlei	120	Fb	54.35N	9.50 E
Schleiden	120	Cf	50.32N	6.28 E
Schleiz	120	Hf	50.35N	11.49 E
Schleswig	120	Fb	54.31N	9.33 E
Schleswig-Holstein [2]	120	Gb	54.00N	10.30 E
Schlitz	120	Ff	50.40N	9.34 E
Schloß Holte-Stukenbrock	124	Kc	51.55N	8.38 E
Schloß Neuhaus, Paderborn-	124	Kc	51.44N	8.42 E
Schluchsee	120	Ei	47.49N	8.10 E
Schlüchtern	120	Ff	50.21N	9.31 E
Schmallenberg	124	Kc	51.09N	8.18 E
Schmallenberg-Bödefeld-Freiheit	124	Kc	51.15N	8.24 E
Schmallenberg-Oberkirchen	124	Kc	51.09N	8.18 E
Schmelz	124	Ie	49.26N	6.51 E
Schmida	128	Kb	48.20N	16.14 E
Schneeberg	120	If	50.36N	12.38 E
Schneeberg [Aus.]	128	Jc	47.46N	15.52 E
Schneeberg [F.R.G.]	120	Hf	50.00N	11.51 E
Schneifel	124	Id	50.16N	6.23 E
Schoberpaß	128	Ic	47.27N	14.40 E
Schoberspitze	128	Ic	47.17N	14.09 E
Schœlcher	197h	Ab	14.37N	61.06W
Schönebeck	120	Hd	52.01N	11.45 E
Schönecken	124	Id	50.10N	6.28 E
Schongau	120	Gi	47.49N	10.54 E
Schöningen	120	Gd	52.08N	10.57 E
Schoondijke	124	Fc	51.21N	3.33 E
Schoonebeek	124	Ib	52.40N	6.53 E
Schoonhoven	124	Gc	51.55N	4.51 E
Schorfheide	120	Jd	52.55N	13.35 E
Schoten	124	Gc	51.15N	4.30 E
Schotten	124	Ld	50.30N	9.08 E
Schouten Islands	208	Fe	3.30S	144.30 E
Schouwen	122	Jc	51.43N	3.50 E
Schramberg	120	Eh	48.14N	8.23 E
Schreiber	180	Ig	48.48N	87.15W
Schriesheim	124	Ke	49.29N	8.40 E
Schrobenhausen	120	Hh	48.33N	11.16 E
Schruns	128	Dc	47.04N	9.55 E
Schuls / Scuol	128	Ed	46.48N	10.17 E
Schultz Lake	180	Hd	64.45N	97.30W
Schurz	188	Fg	38.58N	118.46W
Schussen	120	Fi	47.37N	9.32 E
Schüttorf	124	Jb	52.19N	7.14 E
Schwabach	120	Hg	49.20N	11.02 E
Schwaben = Swabia (EN)	120	Gh	48.20N	10.30 E
Schwäbisch-Bayerisches Alpenvorland = Swabian-Bavarian Plateau (EN)	110	Hf	48.15N	10.30 E
Schwäbische Alb = Swabian Jura (EN)	110	Gf	48.25N	9.30 E
Schwäbisch Gmünd	120	Fh	48.48N	9.47 E
Schwäbisch Hall	120	Fg	49.06N	9.44 E
Schwalbach (Saar)	124	Ie	49.18N	6.49 E
Schwalm	120	Ff	50.45N	9.25 E
Schwalm	124	Lc	51.07N	9.24 E
Schwalmstadt	120	Ff	50.55N	9.12 E

Index Symbols

- [1] Independent Nation
- [2] State, Region
- [3] District, County
- [4] Municipality
- [5] Colony, Dependency
- Continent
- Physical Region
- Historical or Cultural Region
- Mount, Mountain
- Volcano
- Hill
- Mountains, Mountain Range
- Hills, Escarpment
- Plateau, Upland
- Pass, Gap
- Plain, Lowland
- Delta
- Salt Flat
- Valley, Canyon
- Crater, Cave
- Karst Features
- Depression
- Polder
- Desert, Dunes
- Forest, Woods
- Heath, Steppe
- Oasis
- Cape, Point
- Coast, Beach
- Cliff
- Peninsula
- Isthmus
- Sandbank
- Island
- Atoll
- Rock, Reef
- Islands, Archipelago
- Rocks, Reefs
- Coral Reef
- Well, Spring
- Geyser
- River, Stream
- Waterfall, Rapids
- River Mouth, Estuary
- Lake
- Salt Lake
- Intermittent Lake
- Reservoir
- Swamp, Pond
- Canal
- Glacier
- Ice Shelf, Pack Ice
- Ocean
- Sea
- Gulf, Bay
- Strait, Fjord
- Lagoon
- Bank
- Seamount
- Tablemount
- Ridge
- Shelf
- Basin
- Escarpment, Sea Scarp
- Fracture
- Trench, Abyss
- National Park, Reserve
- Point of Interest
- Recreation Site
- Cave, Cavern
- Historic Site
- Ruins
- Wall, Walls
- Church, Abbey
- Temple
- Scientific Station
- Railway station
- Airport
- Port
- Military installation
- Lighthouse
- Mine
- Tunnel
- Dam, Bridge

Schwalmtal 124 Ic 51.15N 6.15 E
Schwandorf 120 Ig 49.20N 12.07 E
Schwaner, Pegunungan- 150 Fg 0.40S 112.40 E
Schwanewede 124 Ka 53.14N 8.36 E
Schwarzach 120 Ig 49.24N 12.09 E
Schwarzbach 124 Je 49.17N 7.40 E
Schwarze Elster 120 Ie 51.49N 12.51 E
Schwarzer Mann 124 Id 50.15N 6.22 E
Schwarzrand 172 Be 26.00S 17.10 E
Schwarzwald=Black Forest (EN) 110 Gf 48.05N 8.15 E
Schwarzwalder Hochwald 124 Ie 49.39N 6.55 E
Schwatka Mountains 178 Hc 67.25N 157.00W
Schwaz 128 Fc 47.20N 11.42 E
Schwechat 128 Kb 48.08N 16.28 E
Schwechat 128 Kb 48.08N 16.28 E
Schwedt / Oder 120 Kc 53.04N 14.18 E
Schweich 124 Ie 49.49N 6.45 E
Schweinfurt 120 Gf 50.03N 10.14 E
Schweiz / Suisse / Svizra / Svizzera = Switzerland (EN) [1] 112 Gf 46.00N 8.30 E
Schweizer-Reneke 172 De 27.11S 25.18 E
Schwelm 124 Jc 51.17N 7.17 E
Schwerin 120 Hc 53.38N 11.23 E
Schwerin [2] 120 Hc 53.35N 11.25 E
Schweriner See 120 Hc 53.45N 11.28 E
Schwerte 124 Jc 51.27N 7.34 E
Schwetzingen 124 Ke 49.23N 8.34 E
Schwielochsee 120 Kd 52.03N 14.12 E
Schwyz 128 Cc 47.03N 8.40 E
Schwyz [2] 128 Cc 47.10N 8.50 E
Sciacca 128 Hm 37.31N 13.03 E
Scicli 128 In 36.47N 14.42 E
Ščigry 136 De 51.53N 36.55 E
Scilly, Isles of- 110 Ff 49.57N 6.15W
Scioto River 184 Ff 38.44N 83.01W
Ščirec 120 Tg 49.34N 23.54 E
Scobey 188 Mb 48.47N 105.25W
Scordia 128 Im 37.18N 14.51 E
Scoresby Land 179 Jd 71.45N 26.30W
Scoresbysund 224 Md 70.35N 21.40W
Scoresby Sund 224 Md 70.20N 23.30W
Scorff 122 Cg 47.46N 3.21W
Ščors 136 De 51.48N 31.59 E
Scotia Ridge (EN) 106 Co 57.00S 45.00W
Scotia Sea (EN) 198 Lk 57.00S 40.00W
Scotland [2] 118 Ie 56.30N 4.30W
Scotland 110 Fd 56.30N 4.30W
Scotlandville 186 Kk 30.31N 91.11W
Scotstown 184 Lc 45.31N 71.17W
Scott 180 Gf 52.27N 108.23W
Scott, Cape- [Austl.] 212 Fb 13.30S 129.50 E
Scott, Cape - [B.C.-Can.] 180 Ef 50.47N 128.25W
Scott, Mount- 188 De 42.56N 122.01W
Scott Base 222 Kf 77.51S 166.46 E
Scottburgh 172 Ef 30.19S 30.40 E
Scott Channel 188 Aa 50.45N 128.30W
Scott City 186 Fg 38.29N 100.54W
Scott Coast 222 Kf 76.30S 162.30 E
Scott Glacier [Ant.] 222 Mg 85.45S 153.00W
Scott Glacier [Ant.] 222 He 66.15S 100.05 E
Scott Inlet 180 Kb 71.05N 71.05W
Scott Island 222 Le 67.24S 179.55W
Scott Islands 188 Aa 50.48N 128.40W
Scott Peak 188 Id 44.21N 112.50W
Scott Reef 212 Eb 14.00S 121.50 E
Scottsbluff 176 Ie 41.52N 103.40W
Scottsboro 184 Dh 34.40N 86.01W
Scottsburg 184 Ef 38.41N 85.46W
Scottsdale [Austl.] 212 Jh 41.10S 147.31 E
Scottsdale [Az.-U.S.] 188 Ee 33.30N 111.56W
Scotts Head 197g Bb 15.13N 61.23W
Scottsville 184 Dg 36.45N 86.11W
Scottville 184 Dd 43.59N 86.17W
Scranton 176 Le 41.24N 75.40W
Scrivia 128 Ce 45.03N 8.54 E
Scrub Cays 194 Ia 24.07N 76.55W
Scrub Island 197b Bb 18.17N 62.57W
Ščučin 132 Dc 53.39N 24.48 E
Ščučinsk 136 Hd 53.00N 70.11 E
Ščučja 136 Nc 66.45N 68.20 E
Ščučje 136 Gd 55.15N 62.43 E
Scugog, Lake- 184 Hc 44.10N 78.51W
Ščugor 134 Hd 64.12N 57.32 E
Scunthorpe 118 Mh 53.36N 0.38W
Scuol / Schuls 128 Ed 46.48N 10.17 E
Scutari (EN) = Shkodra 112 Hg 42.05N 19.30 E
Scutari, Lake- (EN) = Shkodrës, Liqen i- 110 Hg 42.10N 19.20 E
Scutari, Lake- (EN) = Skadarsko jezero 110 Hg 42.10N 19.20 E
Seaford 118 Nk 50.46N 0.06 E
Seahorse Point 180 Jd 63.47N 80.10W
Sea Islands 182 Ke 31.20N 81.20W
Seal 180 Ie 59.04N 94.47W
Seal Island 184 Nd 43.30N 66.01W
Sealpunt 158 Jl 34.06S 23.24 E
Searcy 186 Ki 35.15N 91.44W
Searles Lake 188 Gi 35.43N 117.20W
Seaside [Ca.-U.S.] 188 Eh 36.37N 121.50W
Seaside [Or.-U.S.] 188 Dc 46.01N 123.55W
Seattle 176 Ge 47.36N 122.20W
Seaward Kaikoura Range 218 Ee 42.15S 173.35 E
Seba 150 Hi 10.29S 121.50 E
Sébaco 194 Dg 12.51N 86.06W
Sebago Lake 184 Ld 43.50N 70.35W
Sebaiera 162 Ee 24.51N 13.02W
Sebaou 126 Ph 36.55N 3.51 E
Sebastian, Cape- 188 Ce 42.19N 124.26W
Sebastián Vizcaíno, Bahía- 174 Hg 28.00N 114.30W
Sebastopol 188 Dg 38.24N 122.49W
Sebastopol (EN) = Sevastopol 112 Jg 44.36N 33.32 E
Sebatik, Pulau- 150 Gf 4.10N 117.45 E
Sebba 166 Fc 13.26N 0.32 E
Sebderat 168 Fb 15.27N 36.39 E
Sébé 170 Bc 1.02S 13.06 E
Šebekino 136 De 50.27N 37.00 E
Sébékoro 166 Dc 12.49N 8.50W
Seberi 204 Fh 27.29S 53.24W
Sebeş 130 Gd 45.58N 23.34 E
Sebeş 130 Gd 46.00N 23.34 E
Sebes-Körös 130 Dc 46.55N 20.59 E
Sebeşului, Munţii- 130 Gd 45.38N 23.27 E
Sebewaing 184 Fd 43.44N 83.27W
Sebež 132 Cd 56.19N 28.31 E
Sebha Oasis (EN) = Sabhā, Wāḥāt- 158 If 27.00N 14.25 E
Şebinkarahisar 146 Hb 40.18N 38.26 E
Sebino → Iseo, Lago d'- 128 Ee 45.45N 10.05 E
Sebiş 130 Fc 46.22N 22.07 E
Sebou 158 Ge 34.16N 6.41W
Sebring 184 Gl 27.30N 81.26W
Sebuku, Pulau- 150 Gg 3.30S 116.22 E
Sebunino 138 Jg 46.24N 141.56 E
Secas, Islas- 194 Gi 7.58N 82.02W
Secchia 128 Ee 45.04N 11.00 E
Sechura 202 Be 5.33S 80.51W
Sechura, Bahía de- 202 Be 5.40S 81.00W
Sechura, Desierto de- 202 Be 6.00S 80.30W
Seckau 128 Ic 47.16N 14.47 E
Seclin 124 Fd 50.33N 3.02 E
Secondigny 122 Fh 46.37N 0.25W
Secos, Ilhéus- 162 Cf 14.58N 24.40W
Secretary Island 218 Bf 45.15S 166.55 E
Sécure, Río- 202 Fg 15.10S 64.52W
Séda 126 Df 38.56N 8.03W
Seda 116 Kg 57.38N 25.12 E
Seda [Lat.-U.S.S.R.] 116 Kg 57.32N 25.43 E
Seda [Lith.-U.S.S.R.] 116 Jh 56.10N 22.00 E
Sedalia 182 Id 38.42N 93.14W
Sedan 122 Ke 49.42N 4.57 E
Sedanka 178a Eb 53.50N 166.10W
Sedano 126 Ib 42.43N 3.45W
Sedbergh 118 Kg 54.20N 2.31W
Seddenga 168 Ea 20.33N 30.18 E
Seddon 218 Fd 41.40S 174.04 E
Seddon, Kap- 179 Gc 75.20N 58.45W
Seddonville 218 Dd 41.33S 171.59 E
Seddülbahir 130 Ji 40.03N 26.10 E
Sedelnikovo 136 Hd 56.57N 75.18 E
Séderon 122 Lj 44.12N 5.32 E
Sédhiou 166 Bc 12.44N 15.33W
Sedini 128 Cj 40.51N 8.49 E
Šedok 132 Lg 44.13N 40.52 E
Sedom 146 Fg 31.04N 35.24 E
Sedona 188 Ji 34.52N 111.46W
Sedrata 128 Bn 36.08N 7.32 E
Sedro Woolley 188 Db 48.30N 122.14W
Šeduva 114 Fi 55.48N 23.45 E
Sée 122 Ef 48.39N 1.26W
Seeheim [F.R.G.] 124 Ke 49.46N 8.40 E
Seeheim [Nam.] 172 Be 26.50S 17.45 E
Seeis 172 Bd 22.29S 17.39 E
Seeland 128 Bc 47.05N 7.05 E
Seeling, Mount- 222 Og 82.28S 103.00W
Seelow 120 Kd 52.31N 14.23 E
Sées 122 Gf 48.36N 0.10 E
Seesen 120 Ge 51.54N 10.11 E
Seewarte Seamounts (EN) 158 Ee 33.00N 28.30W
Şefaatli 146 Fc 39.31N 34.46 E
Sefadu 166 Cd 8.39N 10.59W
Seferihisar 146 Bc 38.11N 26.51 E
Séféto 166 Dc 14.08N 9.51W
Sefid Dasht 146 Nf 32.09N 51.10 E
Sefrou 162 Gc 33.50N 4.50W
Sefuri-San 156 Be 33.26N 130.22 E
Segaf, Kepulauan- 150 Jg 2.10S 130.28 E
Ségalas 122 Ij 44.12N 2.26 E
Segamat 150 Df 2.30N 102.49 E
Segangane 126 Ii 35.10N 3.01W
Şegarcea 130 Ge 44.06N 23.45 E
Šegarka 138 De 57.16N 84.02 E
Segbana 166 Fc 10.56N 3.42 E
Segeg 168 Gd 7.40N 42.50 E
Segesta 128 Gm 37.55N 12.50 E
Segeža 112 Jc 63.44N 34.19 E
Seghe 219a Cc 8.25S 157.51 E
Seglinge 116 Id 60.15N 20.40 E
Segmon 116 Ee 59.17N 13.02 E
Segorbe 126 Le 39.51N 0.29W
Ségou 160 Gg 13.27N 6.15W
Ségou [3] 166 Dc 14.00N 6.20W
Segovia 126 Hd 40.57N 4.07W
Segovia [3] 126 Ic 41.10N 4.00W
Segovia, Río- → Coco, Río- 190 Hf 15.00N 83.08W
Segozero, ozero- 114 Jc 63.18N 33.45 E
Segré 122 Fg 47.41N 0.52W
Segre 126 Mc 41.40N 0.43 E
Seguam 178a Db 52.17N 172.30W
Séguédine 166 Ha 20.12N 12.59 E
Séguéla 166 Dd 7.57N 6.40W
Séguéla [3] 166 Dd 8.05N 6.30W
Seguin 186 Hf 29.34N 97.58W
Segula 178a Bb 52.01N 178.07 E
Segura 126 Lf 38.06N 0.38W
Segura, Sierra de- 126 Jf 38.00N 2.45W
Segura de la Sierra 126 Jf 38.18N 2.39W
Sehithwa 172 Cd 20.27S 22.42 E
Seia 126 Ed 40.25N 7.42W
Seibal 194 Be 16.27N 90.05W
Seiche 122 Eg 48.00N 1.46W
Seiland 114 Fa 70.25N 23.15 E
Seiling 186 Gh 36.09N 98.56W
Seille [Fr.] 122 Me 49.07N 6.11 E
Seille [Fr.] 124 Kh 46.31N 4.56 E
Sein, Île de- 122 Bf 48.02N 4.51W
Seinäjoki 114 Fe 62.47N 22.50 E
Seine 110 Gf 49.26N 0.26 E
Seine, Baie de la-=Seine, Bay of the- (EN) 110 Ff 49.30N 0.30W
Seine, Bay of the- (EN) = Seine, Baie de la- 110 Ff 49.30N 0.30W
Seine, Val de- 122 Jf 48.30N 3.20 E
Seine-et-Marne [3] 122 If 48.30N 3.00 E
Seine-Maritime [3] 122 Ge 49.45N 1.00 E
Seine-Saint-Denis [3] 122 If 48.55N 2.30 E
Seine Seamount (EN) 110 Ei 33.45N 14.25W
Seini 130 Gb 47.45N 23.17 E
Seistan (EN)=Sīstān 140 If 30.30N 62.00 E
Seixal 126 Cf 38.38N 9.06W
Sejaha 138 Cb 70.10N 72.30 E
Sejerø 116 Di 55.55N 11.10 E
Sejerø Bugt 116 Di 55.50N 11.15 E
Sejm 110 Je 51.27N 32.34 E
Sejmčan 138 Kd 62.52N 152.27 E
Sejny 120 Tb 54.07N 23.20 E
Sekakes 172 Df 30.04S 28.21 E
Sekayu 150 Dg 2.50S 103.54 E
Sekenke 170 Fc 4.16S 34.10 E
Seki 156 Ed 35.28N 136.54 E
Šeki 136 Eg 41.10N 47.11 E
Seki 146 Cd 36.44N 29.33 E
Sekincau, Gunung- 150 Dh 5.05S 104.18 E
Seki-Zaki 156b Be 33.16N 131.54 E
Sekoma 172 Cd 24.36S 23.58 E
Sekondi-Takoradi 160 Gh 4.53N 1.45W
Sekota 168 Fc 12.37N 39.03 E
Šeksna 136 Dd 59.13N 38.32 E
Šelagski, mys- 138 Mb 70.10N 170.45 E
Selah 188 Ec 46.39N 120.32W
Selajar, Pulau- 150 Hh 6.05S 120.30 E
Selajar, Selat- 150 Hh 5.42S 120.28 E
Selangor [2] 150 Df 3.10N 101.30 E
Selaön 116 Ge 59.25N 17.10 E
Selaru, Pulau- 150 Jh 8.09S 131.00 E
Selatan, Cape- (EN) = Selatan, Tanjung- 140 Nj 4.10S 113.48 E
Selatan, Tanjung-=Selatan, Cape- (EN) 140 Nj 4.10S 113.48 E
Selawik 178 Gc 66.37N 160.03W
Selawik Lake 178 Hc 66.30N 160.40W
Selb 120 If 50.10N 12.08 E
Selbjørn 116 Ae 60.00N 5.10 E
Selbjørnsfjorden 116 Ae 59.55N 5.10 E
Selbu 116 Da 63.13N 11.02 E
Selbukta 222 Bf 71.40S 12.25W
Selbusjøen 116 Da 63.15N 10.55 E
Selby [Eng.-U.K.] 118 Lh 53.48N 1.04W
Selby [S.D.-U.S.] 186 Fd 45.31N 100.02W
Selco 132 Ic 53.23N 34.05 E
Selçuk 146 Bd 37.56N 27.22 E
Seldovia 178 Ie 59.27N 151.43W
Sele 128 Ij 40.29N 14.56 E
Sele, Piana del- 128 Ij 40.30N 14.55 E
Selebi-Pikwe 160 Jk 22.13S 27.58 E
Selečka Planina 130 Eh 41.05N 21.35 E
Šelehov 138 Ff 52.10N 104.01 E
Selemdža 140 Od 51.49N 128.53 E
Selencia 140 Kf 33.04N 44.33 E
Selendi 130 Lk 38.45N 28.53 E
Selendi 130 Lk 38.40N 28.41 E
Selenduma 138 Ff 50.55N 106.10 E
Selenga (Selenge) 140 Md 52.16N 106.16 E
Selenge [Mong.] 152 Hb 49.25N 103.59 E
Selenge [Zaire] 170 Cc 1.58S 18.11 E
Selenge → Selenga 140 Md 52.16N 106.16 E
Selenginsk 138 Ff 51.59N 106.57 E
Selenica 130 Ci 40.32N 19.38 E
Selennjah 138 Jc 67.55N 145.00 E
Sélestat 122 Nf 48.16N 7.27 E
Selety 136 He 53.06N 73.00 E
Seletyteniz, ozero- 136 He 53.15N 73.15 E
Seleucia 146 Kf 33.05N 44.35 E
Selevac 130 De 44.30N 20.53 E
Seleznevo 116 Md 60.44N 28.37 E
Selfoss 114a Bc 63.56N 21.00W
Seli 166 Cd 8.33N 12.48W
Sélibabi 162 Ef 15.10N 12.11W
Seliger, ozero- 136 Dd 57.20N 33.05 E
Seligman 188 Ii 35.20N 112.53W
Šelihova, zaliv- = Shelikhov Gulf (EN) 140 Rc 60.00N 158.00 E
Selimağa 130 Lj 39.35N 28.33 E
Selimiye 146 Bd 37.24N 27.40 E
Selingenstadt 124 Kd 50.03N 8.59 E
Selinunte 128 Gm 37.35N 12.48 E
Selišarovo 114 Hh 56.51N 33.29 E
Seljatin 130 Ib 47.52N 25.14 E
Selje 116 Ab 62.03N 5.22 E
Seljord 114 Bg 59.29N 8.37 E
Selkirk [Man.-Can.] 186 Ha 50.09N 96.52W
Selkirk [Scot.-U.K.] 118 Kf 55.33N 2.50W
Selkirk Mountains 180 Ff 50.00N 117.00W
Sella 126 Ga 43.28N 5.04W
Sellasia 130 Fl 37.10N 22.25 E
Selle 124 Fd 50.19N 3.23 E
Selles-sur-Cher 122 Hg 47.16N 1.33 E
Sells 188 Jk 31.55N 111.53W
Selm 124 Jc 51.42N 7.28 E
Selma [Al.-U.S.] 182 Je 32.25N 87.01W
Selma [Ca.-U.S.] 188 Fh 36.34N 119.37W
Selmer 184 Ch 35.11N 88.36W
Selmet Wielki, Jezioro- 120 Sc 53.50N 22.30 E
Selon 114 Hg 58.14N 30.50 E
Selong 150 Gh 8.39S 116.32 E
Selsey 118 Bd 50.44N 0.47W
Selsey Bill 118 Mk 50.43N 0.48W
Seltz 124 Kf 48.53N 8.06 E
Selu, Pulau- 150 Jh 7.32S 130.54 E
Sélune 122 Ef 48.39N 1.26W
Selva 204 Ai 29.46S 62.03W
Selvagens, Ilhas- 158 Fe 30.05N 15.55W
Selvānā 146 Kd 37.25N 44.51 E
Selvas 198 Jf 5.00S 68.00W
Selway River 188 Hc 46.08N 115.36W
Selwyn, Détroit de- 219b Dc 16.04S 168.11 E
Selwyn Lake 180 He 60.00N 104.30W
Selwyn Mountains 174 Fc 63.10N 130.20W
Selwyn Range 208 Fg 21.35S 140.35 E
Selz 124 Ke 49.59N 8.02 E
Šemaha 132 Pi 40.39N 48.38 E
Semani 130 Ci 40.54N 19.26 E
Semara 160 Ff 26.44N 11.41W
Semarang 142 Nj 6.58S 110.25 E
Sematan 150 Ef 1.48N 109.46 E
Semau, Pulau- 150 Hi 10.13S 123.22 E
Sembakung 150 Gf 3.47N 117.30 E
Sembé 170 Bb 1.39N 14.36 E
Semberija 128 Nf 44.45N 19.10 E
Sembuan 150 Gg 0.19S 115.30 E
Semenicului, Munţii- 130 Fd 45.05N 22.05 E
Semenov 114 Kh 56.49N 44.29 E
Semenovka 132 Hc 52.11N 32.40 E
Semeru, Gunung- 140 Nj 7.58S 113.35 E
Semichi Islands 178a Db 52.42N 174.00 E
Semidi Islands 178 He 56.07N 156.44W
Semiluki 136 De 51.43N 39.02 E
Semily 120 Lf 50.36N 15.20 E
Seminoe Reservoir 188 Le 42.00N 106.50W
Seminole [Ok.-U.S.] 186 Hi 35.14N 96.41W
Seminole [Tx.-U.S.] 186 Ej 32.43N 102.39W
Seminole, Lake- 182 Ke 30.46N 84.50W
Semipalatinsk 142 Kd 50.28N 80.13 E
Semipalatinskaja oblast [3] 136 If 48.30N 80.10 E
Semirara Islands 150 Hd 11.57N 121.27 E
Semīrom 146 Ng 31.22N 51.47 E
Semisopochnoi 178a Bb 52.00N 179.35 E
Semitau 150 Ff 0.33N 111.58 E
Semiun, Pulau- 150 Ef 4.31N 107.44 E
Semizbugy 136 He 50.12N 74.48 E
Semliki 158 Kh 1.14N 30.28 E
Semmering 128 Jc 47.38N 15.49 E
Semnān [3] 144 Hb 35.00N 53.30 E
Semnān 142 Hf 35.33N 53.24 E
Semnon 122 Eg 47.54N 1.45W
Semois 122 Ke 49.53N 4.45 E
Šemonaiha 136 Ie 50.39N 81.54 E
Semporna 150 Gf 4.28N 118.36 E
Semuda 150 Fg 2.51S 112.58 E
Semur-en-Auxois 122 Kg 47.29N 4.20 E
Sên 148 Kf 12.32N 104.28 E
Senador Mourão 204 Kc 17.51S 43.22W
Senador Pompeu 202 Ke 5.35S 39.22W
Senaja 150 Ge 6.45N 117.03 E
Sena Madureira 202 Ee 9.04S 68.40W
Senanga 170 Df 16.07S 23.16 E
Senarpont 124 De 49.53N 1.43 E
Senatobia 186 Li 34.39N 89.58W
Sendai [Jap.] 142 Qf 38.15N 140.53 E
Sendai [Jap.] 154 Ki 31.49N 130.18 E
Sendai-Gawa [Jap.] 156 Bf 31.51N 130.12 E
Sendai-Gawa [Jap.] 156 Dd 35.34N 134.11 E
Sendai-Wan 154 Pe 38.10N 141.15 E
Senden 124 Jc 51.51N 7.30 E
Sendenhorst 124 Jc 51.50N 7.50 E
Senderg 146 Qi 26.52N 57.37 E
Seneca 186 Hg 39.50N 96.04W
Seneca Lake 184 Id 42.40N 76.57W
Sénégal=Senegal (EN) [1] 160 Fg 14.00N 14.00W
Sénégal=Senegal (EN) 158 Fg 15.48N 16.32W
Senegal (EN)=Sénégal [1] 160 Fg 14.00N 14.00W
Senegal (EN)=Sénégal 158 Fg 15.48N 16.32W
Sénégal Oriental [3] 166 Cc 13.30N 13.00W
Senekal 172 De 28.30S 27.32 E
Senetosa, Punta di- 122a Ab 41.33N 8.47 E
Seney 184 Eb 46.21N 85.56W
Senftenberg/Zły Komorow 120 Ke 51.31N 14.01 E
Sengata 142 Ni 0.28N 117.33 E
Sengilej 114 Lj 53.58N 48.46 E
Senguerr, Río- 206 Gg 45.32S 68.54W
Sengwa 172 Dc 17.05S 28.03 E
Senhor do Bonfim 200 Lg 10.27S 40.11W
Senica 120 Nh 48.41N 17.23 E
Senigallia 128 Hg 43.43N 13.13 E
Senirkent 146 Dc 38.07N 30.33 E
Senj 128 If 45.00N 14.54 E
Senja 110 Hb 69.20N 17.30 E
Senjsko Bilo 128 Jf 44.55N 15.03 E
Senkaku-Shotō 152 Lf 25.45N 124.00 E
Şenkaya 146 Jb 40.35N 42.21 E
Senkevičevka 120 Vf 50.29N 25.05 E
Şenkursk 136 Ec 62.08N 42.53 E
Senlin Shan 154 Kc 43.12N 130.38 E
Senlis 122 Ie 49.12N 2.35 E
Senmonorom 148 Lf 12.27N 107.12 E
Senn, Dahr Ou- 162 Ef 17.55N 11.00W
Sennestadt, Bielefeld- 124 Kc 51.57N 8.35 E
Senneterre 180 Jg 48.24N 77.14W
Senno 114 Gi 54.47N 29.41 E
Sennoj 132 Oc 52.07N 46.59 E
Senorbì 128 Dk 39.32N 9.08 E
Senqu 172 Be 28.38S 16.27 E
Sens 122 Jf 48.12N 3.17 E
Sensée 124 Fd 50.16N 3.06 E
Sensuntepeque 194 Cg 13.52N 88.38W
Senta 130 Dd 45.56N 20.05 E
Sentinel Peak 180 Ff 54.58N 122.00W
Sentinel Range 222 Pf 78.10S 85.30W
Senyavin Islands 208 Gd 6.55N 158.00 E
Şenyurt 146 Id 37.06N 40.40 E
Senzaki-Wan 156 Bd 34.25N 131.20 E
Senžarka 134 Mi 54.45N 67.50 E
Seo de Urgel / la Seu d'Urgell 126 Nb 42.21N 1:28 E
Seoni 148 Fd 22.05N 79.32 E
Seoul (EN)=Sŏul 142 Of 37.34N 127.00 E
Séoune 122 Gj 44.10N 0.41 E
Sepanjang, Pulau- 150 Gh 7.10S 115.50 E
Separation Point 218 Ed 40.47S 173.00 E
Sepetovka 136 Ce 50.12N 27.04 E
Sepik River 208 Fe 3.51S 144.34 E
Sępólno Krajeńskie 120 Nc 53.28N 17.32 E
Sepopol 120 Qb 54.15N 21.00 E
Sępopolska, Nizina- 120 Rb 54.15N 21.10 E
Septemvri 130 Hg 42.13N 24.06 E
Septentrional, Cordillera- 194 Ld 19.35N 70.45W
Septeuil 124 Df 48.54N 1.41 E
Sept-Iles 176 Md 50.12N 66.23W
Sept Iles, Les- 122 Cf 48.53N 3.28W
Sepúlveda 126 Ic 41.18N 3.45W
Sequeros 126 Fd 40.31N 6.01W
Sequillo 126 Gc 41.45N 5.30W
Sera 156 Cd 34.36N 133.01 E
Sera, Pulau- 150 Jh 7.40S 131.05 E
Šerabad 136 Gh 37.43N 66.59 E
Šerabad 135 Ff 37.22N 67.03 E
Serafettin Dağları 146 Ic 39.05N 41.10 E
Serafimovič 132 Me 49.36N 42.47 E
Serahs 136 Gh 36.30N 61.13 E
Seraidi 128 Bn 36.55N 7.40 E
Seraing 122 Ld 50.36N 5.31 E
Seram 208 De 3.00S 129.00 E
Seram, Laut-=Ceram Sea (EN) 208 De 2.30S 128.00 E
Serang 150 Eh 6.07S 106.09 E
Serasan, Pulau- 150 Ef 2.30N 109.03 E
Serasan, Selat- 150 Ef 2.20S 109.00 E
Serbia (EN) = Srbija [2] 130 Df 44.00N 21.00 E
Serbia (EN) = Srbija 110 Ig 43.00N 21.00 E
Serbia (EN)=Srbija 130 Df 44.00N 21.00 E
Şercaia 130 Id 45.50N 25.08 E
Serchio 128 Eg 43.47N 10.16 E
Serdo 168 Gc 11.58N 41.18 E
Serdoba 136 Nc 52.34N 44.01 E
Serdobsk 136 Ee 52.29N 44.16 E
Sereba 168 Gc 13.12N 40.32 E
Serebrjansk 136 If 49.43N 83.20 E
Serebrjanski 114 Ib 68.52N 35.32 E
Sered' 120 Nh 48.17N 17.45 E
Seredka 116 Mf 58.10N 28.25 E
Şereflikoçhisar 146 Ec 38.56N 33.33 E
Serein 122 Jg 47.55N 3.31 E
Seremban 150 Df 2.43N 101.56 E
Serengeti Plain 170 Fc 2.50S 35.00 E
Serenje 170 Fe 13.14S 30.14 E
Šereševo 120 Ud 52.31N 24.19 E
Seret 132 De 48.38N 25.52 E
Serfopoúla 130 Hl 37.15N 24.36 E
Sergač 136 Ed 55.33N 45.28 E
Sergeievka 154 Lc 43.23N 133.22 E
Sergeja Kirova, ostrova- 138 Da 77.10N 90.00 E
Sergejevka [Kaz.-U.S.S.R.] 136 Ge 53.51N 67.28 E
Sergejevka [R.S.F.S.R.] 154 Kb 44.20N 131.40 E
Sergino 142 Ic 62.30N 65.40 E
Sergipe [2] 202 Kf 10.30S 37.10W
Sergokala 132 Oh 42.30N 47.40 E
Sergozero, ozero- 114 Ic 66.45N 36.50 E
Seria 150 Ff 4.37N 114.19 E
Serian 150 Ff 1.10N 110.34 E
Seriana, Val- 128 De 45.50N 9.50 E
Seribu, Kepulauan- 150 Fh 5.36S 106.33 E
Sérifontaine 124 De 49.21N 1.46 E
Sérifos 130 Hl 37.09N 24.30 E
Sérifos 130 Hl 37.10N 24.30 E
Serifou, Stenón- 130 Hl 37.15N 24.30 E
Serik 146 Dd 36.55N 31.06 E
Seringapatam Reef 212 Eb 13.40S 122.05 E
Serio 128 De 45.16N 9.45 E
Šerlovaja Gora 138 Gf 50.34N 116.18 E
Sermata, Kepulauan- 150 Ih 8.10S 128.40 E
Sermilik 179 Ie 66.00N 38.45W
Sernovodsk 114 Mj 53.54N 51.09 E
Sernur 114 Lh 56.57N 49.11 E
Sernyje Vody 114 Mj 53.53N 50.59 E
Sero 146 Kd 37.33N 44.40 E
Serock 120 Rd 52.31N 21.03 E
Serodino 204 Bk 32.37S 60.57W
Serov 142 Id 59.29N 60.31 E
Serowe 160 Jk 22.23S 26.43 E
Serpa 126 Eg 37.56N 7.36W
Serpent, Vallée du- 166 Dc 14.50N 8.00W
Serpentine Lakes 212 Fe 28.30S 129.10 E
Serpent's Mouth/Serpiente, Boca de la- 202 Fa 10.10N 61.58W
Serpiente, Boca de la-/ Serpent's Mouth 202 Fa 10.10N 61.58W
Serpis 126 Lf 38.59N 0.09W
Serpnevoje 130 Lc 46.23N 28.59 E
Serpuhov 112 Je 54.55N 37.25 E
Serra, Aparados da- 204 Hi 28.45S 49.45W
Serra Bonita 204 Ib 15.13S 46.49W
Serra das Araras 204 Jb 15.30S 45.21W
Serra do Navio 200 Ke 0.59N 52.03W
Serra do Salitre 204 Id 19.06S 46.41W
Serra Dourada 204 Ka 12.50S 43.56W
Sérrai 130 Gh 41.05N 23.33 E
Serralada Pirinenca=Pyrenees (EN) 110 Gg 42.40N 1.00 E
Serrana, Banco de- 190 Hf 14.23N 80.12W
Serranilla, Banco- 190 Ie 15.50N 79.50W
Serranópolis 204 Fd 18.16S 52.00W
Serra San Bruno 128 Kl 38.35N 16.20 E
Serrat, Cap- 162 Ib 37.14N 9.13 E
Serra Talhada 202 Ke 7.59S 38.18W
Serre 122 Je 49.41N 3.23 E
Serre, Massif de la- 122 Lg 47.10N 5.35 E
Serre-Ponçon, Lac de- 122 Mj 44.27N 6.16 E
Serres 122 Lj 44.26N 5.43 E
Serrezuela 206 Gd 30.38S 65.23W
Serrinha [Braz.] 202 Kg 16.23S 39.35W
Serrinha [Braz.] 202 Kf 11.39S 39.00W
Serriola, Bocca- 128 Gg 43.31N 12.21 E
Serro 204 Kd 18.37S 43.23W
Serrota 126 Gd 40.30N 5.04W
Serrote, Rio- 204 Ee 21.27S 54.40W
Sersou, Plateau du- 126 Ni 35.30N 2.00 E
Sertã 126 De 39.48N 8.06W
Sertão 198 Lg 10.00S 41.00W
Sertãozinho 204 Ie 21.08S 47.59W
Sërtar 152 He 32.20N 100.20 E
Serti 166 Hd 7.30N 11.22 E
Serua, Pulau- 150 Jh 6.18S 130.01 E
Serui 150 Kg 1.53S 136.14 E
Serule 172 Dd 21.55S 27.19 E

Index Symbols

[1] Independent Nation
[2] State, Region
[3] District, County
[4] Municipality
[5] Colony, Dependency
Continent
Physical Region
Historical or Cultural Region
Mount, Mountain
Volcano
Hill
Mountains, Mountain Range
Hills, Escarpment
Plateau, Upland
Pass, Gap
Plain, Lowland
Delta
Salt Flat
Valley, Canyon
Crater, Cave
Karst Features
Depression
Polder
Desert, Dunes
Forest, Woods
Heath, Steppe
Oasis
Cape, Point
Coast, Beach
Cliff
Peninsula
Isthmus
Sandbank
Island
Atoll
Rock, Reef
Islands, Archipelago
Rocks, Reefs
Coral Reef
Well, Spring
Geyser
River, Stream
Waterfall, Rapids
River Mouth, Estuary
Lake
Salt Lake
Intermittent Lake
Reservoir
Swamp, Pond
Canal
Glacier
Ice Shelf, Pack Ice
Ocean
Sea
Gulf, Bay
Strait, Fjord
Lagoon
Bank
Seamount
Tablemount
Ridge
Shelf
Basin
Escarpment, Sea Scarp
Fracture
Trench, Abyss
National Park, Reserve
Point of Interest
Recreation Site
Cave, Cavern
Historic Site
Ruins
Wall, Walls
Church, Abbey
Temple
Scientific Station
Railway station
Airport
Port
Military installation
Lighthouse
Mine
Tunnel
Dam, Bridge

Name	Pg	Grid	Lat	Long
Sérvia	130	Ei	40.11N	22.00 E
Sérxü	152	Ge	32.56N	98.02 E
Seryitsi ⊕	130	Ii	40.00N	25.10 E
Seryševo	138	Hf	51.02N	128.25 E
Sesayap ≤	150	Gf	3.36N	117.15 E
Sesayap ≤	150	Gf	3.36N	117.15 E
Sese	170	Eb	2.11N	25.47 E
Seseganaga Lake ⊡	186	Ka	50.10N	90.15W
Sese Islands ⊡	170	Fc	0.20S	32.20 E
Sesfontein	172	Ac	19.07S	13.39 E
Sesheke	170	Df	17.29S	24.18 E
Sesia ≤	128	Ce	45.05N	8.37 E
Sesibi	168	Ea	20.05N	30.31 E
Sesimbra	126	Cf	38.26N	9.06W
Šešma ≤	114	Mi	55.20N	51.12 E
Sesnut ▲	116	Be	59.42N	7.21 E
s'Espalmador, Illa- / Espalmador, Isla- ⊕	126	Nf	38.47N	1.26 E
s'Espardell, Illa- / Espardell, Isla- ⊕	126	Nf	38.47N	1.27 E
Sessa Aurunca	128	Hi	41.14N	13.56 E
Ses Salines, Cap de- / Salinas, Cabo de- ⊳	126	Pe	39.16N	3.03 E
Sestao	126	Ja	43.18N	3.00W
Sesto Fiorentino	128	Fg	43.50N	11.12 E
Sesto San Giovanni	128	De	45.32N	9.14 E
Sestriere	128	Af	44.57N	6.53 E
Sestri Levante	128	Df	44.16N	9.24 E
Sestroreck	114	Gf	60.06N	29.59 E
Šešupė ≤	114	Fi	55.00N	22.10 E
Šešuvis ≤	116	Ji	55.12N	22.31 E
Sesvenna, Piz- ▲	128	Ed	46.42N	10.25 E
Sesvete	128	Ke	45.50N	16.07 E
Šeta/Šėta	116	Ki	55.14N	24.18 E
Šėta/Šeta	116	Ki	55.14N	24.18 E
Setaka	156	Be	33.09N	130.28 E
Setana	154	Oc	42.26N	139.51 E
Sète	122	Jk	43.24N	3.41 E
Sete de Setembro, Rio- ≤	204	Fa	12.56S	52.51W
Sete Lagoas	202	Jg	19.27S	44.14W
Setenil	126	Gh	36.51N	5.11W
Sete Quedas, Ilha- → Grande, Ilha- ⊕	204	Ef	23.45S	54.03W
Sete Quedas, Saltos das- = Guaíra Falls (EN) ≤	206	Jb	24.02S	54.16W
Setermoen	114	Eb	68.52N	18.28 E
Setesdal ⊠	114	Bg	59.05N	7.35 E
Setesdalsheiane ▲	116	Be	59.30N	7.10 E
Seti ≤	148	Gc	28.58N	81.06 E
Sétif	160	He	36.12N	5.24 E
Sétif [3]	162	Ib	36.05N	5.00 E
Seto	156	Ed	35.13N	137.05 E
Setonaikai = Inland Sea (EN) ▨	140	Pf	34.10N	133.00 E
Setouchi	156b	Ba	28.08N	129.20 E
Šetpe	136	Fg	44.06N	52.02 E
Settat	162	Fc	33.00N	7.37W
Settat [3]	162	Fc	33.00N	7.30W
Setté Cama	170	Ac	2.32S	9.45 E
Sette-Daban, hrebet- ▲	138	Id	62.00N	138.00 E
Settle	118	Kg	54.04N	2.16W
Setúbal	112	Fh	38.32N	8.54W
Setúbal [2]	126	Df	38.20N	8.30W
Setúbal, Baia de- ◖	126	Df	38.27N	8.53W
Setúbal o de Guadalupe, Laguna- ⊡	204	Bj	31.33S	60.35W
Seudre ≤	122	Ei	45.48N	1.09W
Seugne ≤	122	Fi	45.42N	0.32W
Seui	128	Dk	39.50N	9.19 E
Seuil-d'Argonne	124	Hf	48.58N	5.03 E
Seul, Lac- ⊡	174	Jd	50.20N	92.30W
Seulles ≤	124	Be	49.20N	0.27W
Seurre	122	Lg	47.00N	5.09 E
Sevan	136	Eg	40.32N	44.57 E
Sevan, Lake- (EN) = Sevan, ozero- ⊡	110	Kg	40.20N	45.20 E
Sevan, ozero- = Sevan, Lake- (EN) ⊡	110	Kg	40.20N	45.20 E
Sévaré	166	Ec	14.32N	4.06W
Sevastopol = Sebastopol (EN)	112	Jg	44.36N	33.32 E
Ševčenko	142	He	43.35N	51.05 E
Ševčenko, zaliv- ◖	135	Ca	46.30N	60.15 E
Sevenoaks	118	Nj	51.16N	0.12 E
Sever ≤	126	Ee	39.40N	7.32W
Sévérac-le-Château	122	Jj	44.19N	3.04 E
Severn ≤	118	Kj	51.20N	3.10W
Severn [Can.] ≤	174	Kd	56.02N	87.36W
Severn [U.K.] ≤	118	Kj	51.35N	2.40W
Severnaja Dvina = Northern Dvina (EN) ≤	110	Kc	64.32N	40.30 E
Severnaja Keltma ≤	134	Ff	61.30N	54.00 E
Severnaja Pseašho, gora- ▲	132	Lh	43.47N	40.30 E
Severnaja Sosva ≤	136	Ga	64.10N	65.28 E
Severnaja Zemlja = Severnaya Zemlya (EN) ⊡	140	Lb	79.30N	98.00 E
Severnaya Zemlya (EN) = Severnaja Zemlja ⊡	140	Lb	79.30N	98.00 E
Severn Lake ⊡	180	If	53.52N	90.58W
Severnoje [R.S.F.S.R.]	132	Nb	54.05N	52.32 E
Severnoje [R.S.F.S.R.]	138	Ce	56.21N	78.23 E
Severny	136	Gb	67.38N	64.06 E
Severnyje Uvaly = Northern Uvales (EN) ▨	110	Kd	59.30N	49.00 E
Severny Kommunar	134	Gg	58.23N	54.02 E
Severny Ledovity okean = Arctic Ocean (EN) ▨	224	Be	85.00N	170.00 E
Severny Ural = Northern Urals (EN) ▲	110	Lc	62.00N	59.00 E
Severobajkalsk	138	Ee	55.40N	109.25 E
Severočeský kraj [3]	120	Kf	50.35N	14.15 E
Severodoneck	132	Ke	48.57N	38.31 E
Severodvinsk	112	Kc	64.34N	39.50 E
Severo-Jenisejskij	138	Ed	60.28N	93.01 E
Severo-Kazahstanskaja oblast [3]	136	Ge	54.30N	68.00 E
Severo-Krymski kanal ≤	132	Ig	46.30N	34.35 E
Severo-Kurilsk	142	Rd	50.40N	156.08 E
Severomoravský kraj [3]	120	Ng	49.45N	17.50 E
Severomorsk	136	Db	69.04N	33.24 E
Severo-Osetinskaja ASSR [3]	136	Eg	43.00N	44.10 E
Severo-Sibirskaja nizmennost = North Siberian Plain (EN) ▨	140	Mb	72.00N	104.00 E
Severouralsk	136	Gc	60.09N	60.01 E
Sevier	188	Ig	38.35N	112.14W
Sevier Bridge Reservoir ⊡	188	Ig	39.21N	111.57W
Sevier Desert ⊠	188	Ig	39.25N	112.50W
Sevier Lake ⊡	182	Ed	38.55N	113.09W
Sevier River ≤	182	Ed	39.04N	113.06W
Sevilla ≤	126	Gg	37.30N	5.30W
Sevilla [Col.]	202	Cc	4.16N	75.53W
Sevilla [Sp.] = Seville (EN)	112	Fh	37.23N	5.59W
Sevilla, Isla- ⊕	194	Fi	8.14N	82.24W
Seville (EN) = Sevilla [Sp.]	112	Fh	37.23N	5.59W
Sevlijevo	130	If	43.01N	25.06 E
Sèvre Nantaise ≤	122	Eg	47.12N	1.33W
Sèvre Niortaise ≤	122	Fh	46.18N	1.08W
Sevron ≤	122	Lh	46.32N	5.16 E
Sevsk	132	Ic	52.08N	34.30 E
Sewa ≤	166	Cd	7.18N	12.08W
Seward [Ak.-U.S.]	176	Ec	60.06N	149.26W
Seward [Nb.-U.S.]	186	Hf	40.55N	97.06W
Seward Peninsula ▣	174	Cc	65.00N	164.00W
Sewell	206	Fa	34.05S	70.21W
Seyähkal	146	Md	37.09N	49.52 E
Seybaplaya	192	Nh	19.39N	90.40W
Seybaplaya, Punta- ⊳	192	Nh	19.45N	90.42W
Seybouse, Oued- ≤	128	Bn	36.53N	7.46 E
Seychelles [1]	160	Mi	4.00S	55.00 E
Seychelles Islands ⊡	158	Mi	4.35S	55.40 E
Seydän ≤	146	Og	30.01N	53.01 E
Seydişehir	146	Dd	37.25N	31.51 E
Seyðisfjörður	112	Eb	65.16N	14.00W
Seyfe Gölü ⊡	146	Fc	39.13N	34.23 E
Seyhan ≤	146	Le	35.57N	46.19 E
Seyhan ≤	144	Db	36.43N	34.53 E
Seyitgazi	146	Dc	39.27N	30.43 E
Seyitömer	130	Mj	39.34N	29.52 E
Seyla'	168	Gc	11.21N	43.30 E
Seymour [Austl.]	212	Jg	37.02S	145.08 E
Seymour [In.-U.S.]	184	Ef	38.58N	85.53W
Seymour [Mo.-U.S.]	186	Jh	37.09N	92.46W
Seymour [S.Afr.]	172	Df	32.33S	26.46 E
Seymour [Tx.-U.S.]	182	He	33.35N	99.16W
Seyne-sur-Mer, La-	122	Lk	43.06N	5.53 E
Sezana	128	He	45.42N	13.52 E
Sézanne	122	Jf	48.43N	3.43 E
Sfaktiria ⊕	130	Em	36.56N	21.40 E
Sfax (EN) = Şafāqis	160	Ie	34.44N	10.46 E
Sfax (EN) = Şafāqis [3]	162	Jc	34.30N	10.30 E
Sferracavallo, Capo- ⊳	128	Dk	39.43N	9.40 E
Sfintu Gheorghe [Rom.]	130	Id	45.52N	25.47 E
Sfintu Gheorghe [Rom.]	130	Me	44.53N	29.26 E
Sfintu Gheorghe, Bratul- ≤	130	Me	44.53N	29.36 E
Sfintu Gheorghe, Ostrovul- ⊕	130	Md	45.07N	29.22 E
Sfizef	126	Li	35.14N	0.15W
Shaan-hsi Sheng → Shaanxi Sheng = Shensi (EN) [2]	152	Id	36.00N	109.00 E
Shaanxi Sheng (Shaan-hsi Sheng) = Shensi (EN) [2]	152	Id	36.00N	109.00 E
Shaba [2]	170	Dd	8.30S	25.00 E
Sha'bah, Wādī ash- ≤	146	Ij	25.09N	41.55 E
Shabeellaha Dhexe [3]	168	He	3.00N	46.00 E
Shabellaha Hoose [3]	168	Ge	2.00N	44.40 E
Shabēlle, Webi- = Shebeli Webi (EN) ≤	158	Lh	0.12S	42.45 E
Shabestar	146	Kc	38.11N	45.42 E
Shabunda	170	Ec	2.42S	27.20 E
Shache/Yarkant	142	Jf	38.24N	77.15 E
Shacheng → Huailai	152	Kc	40.29N	115.30 E
Shackleton Coast ▣	222	Kd	82.00S	162.00 E
Shackleton Glacier ⊡	222	Lg	84.35S	176.15W
Shackleton Ice Shelf ▨	222	He	66.00S	101.00 E
Shackleton Range ▲	222	Ag	80.40S	26.00W
Shaddādī	146	Id	36.20N	40.45 E
Shädegän	146	Mg	30.40N	48.38 E
Shadwān, Jazīrat- ⊕	164	Fd	27.30N	33.55 E
Shaftesbury	118	Kk	51.01N	2.12W
Shagedu → Jungar Qi	152	Jd	39.37N	110.58 E
Shāghir Bazar	146	Ic	36.52N	40.53 E
Shag Rocks ⊕	222	Rd	54.26S	36.33W
Shāh 'Abbās	146	Oe	34.44N	52.10 E
Shah Alam	150	Df	3.05N	101.29 E
Shahdol	148	Gd	23.13N	81.18 E
Sha He [China] ≤	154	Ef	37.09N	114.46 E
Sha He [China] ≤	154	Ch	33.39N	114.38 E
Shahezhen → Linze	152	Hd	39.10N	100.21 E
Shah Jāhān, Küh-e- ▲	146	Qd	37.02N	57.54 E
Shahjahānpur	148	Fc	27.53N	79.55 E
Shah Küh ▲	146	Hb	36.35N	54.31 E
Shahmīrzād	146	Nd	35.47N	53.20 E
Shāhpūr ≤	146	Nh	29.39N	51.03 E
Shāhpūr ≤	146	Nh	32.50N	51.45 E
Shahrak	146	Md	36.14N	50.40 E
Shahr-e-Bābak	146	Pg	30.10N	55.09 E
Shahr-e Khafr	146	Oh	28.56N	53.14 E
Shahr Kord	144	Hc	32.19N	50.50 E
Shāhrüd	146	Md	37.17N	48.43 E
Shahu, Küh-e- ▲	146	Le	34.45N	46.30 E
Shāh Zeyd	146	Od	36.13N	52.22 E
Shā'ib al Banāt, Jabal- ▲	164	Fd	27.20N	33.29 E
Shā'īt, Wādī- ≤	146	Je	24.33N	33.01 E
Shakaga-Dake ▲	156	Ba	33.16N	130.53 E
Shakawe	160	Ji	18.23S	21.51 E
Shaker Heights	184	Hd	41.29N	81.36W
Shaki	146	Mc	41.11N	47.10 E
Shakotan-Dake ▲	156a	Bb	43.16N	140.26 E
Shakotan-Hantō ▣	156a	Bb	43.20N	140.28 E
Shakotan-Misaki ⊳	156a	Bb	43.23N	140.32 E
Shaktoolik	176	Dc	64.20N	161.09W
Shāl	146	Md	35.54N	49.46 E
Shala, Lake- ⊡	168	Fd	7.29N	38.32 E
Shalamzār	146	Nf	32.02N	50.49 E
Shalānbōd	168	Ge	1.40N	44.42 E
Shalar, Nahr- ≤	146	Ke	35.44N	45.45 E
Shaler Mountains ▲	180	Gb	71.45N	111.00W
Shaliuhe → Gangca	152	Hd	37.30N	100.14 E
Shaluli Shan ▲	140	Lf	30.45N	99.45 E
Shām, Bādiyat ash-= Syrian Desert (EN) ▨	140	Ff	32.00N	40.00 E
Shām, Jabal ash- ▲	140	Hg	23.10N	57.20 E
Shamattawa ≤	180	Le	55.52N	92.05W
Shambe	168	Ed	7.07N	30.46 E
Shambu	168	Fd	9.33N	37.07 E
Shamīl	146	Qi	27.30N	56.53 E
Shāmīyah ▨	140	Ff	34.00N	39.59 E
Shammar, Jabal- ▲	140	Gg	27.20N	41.45 E
Shamo, Lake- ⊡	168	Fd	5.50N	37.40 E
Shamokin	184	Ie	40.47N	76.34W
Shamrock	186	Fh	35.13N	100.15W
Shams	146	Pg	31.04N	55.02 E
Shamsī	168	Db	19.03N	29.54 E
Shamwa	172	Ec	17.18S	31.34 E
Shan [2]	148	Jd	22.00N	98.00 E
Shandan	152	Mf	38.50N	101.08 E
Shandī	160	Xg	16.42N	33.26 E
Shandian He ≤	154	Dc	42.20N	116.20 E
Shandong Bandao= Shantung Peninsula (EN) ▣	140	Of	37.00N	121.00 E
Shandong Sheng (Shan-tung Sheng) = Shantung (2) Sheng [2]	152	Kd	36.00N	119.00 E
Shandūr Pass ⊡	148	Ea	36.04N	72.31 E
Shangani	172	Dc	19.42S	29.22 E
Shangani ≤	172	Dc	18.30S	27.11 E
Shangbahe	154	Ci	30.39N	115.06 E
Shangcai	154	Ch	33.16N	114.15 E
Shangcheng	154	Ci	31.49N	115.24 E
Shangdu	152	Jc	41.31N	113.32 E
Shanggao	154	Cj	28.15N	114.55 E
Shanghai	142	Of	31.14N	121.28 E
Shanghai Shi (Shang-hai Shih) [6]	152	Le	31.14N	121.28 E
Shang-hai Shih → Shanghai Shi	152	Le	31.14N	121.28 E
Shanghang	152	Kf	25.04N	116.21 E
Shanghe	154	Df	37.19N	117.09 E
Shanghekou	154	Lc	40.26N	124.51 E
Shangnan	152	Je	33.31N	110.50 E
Shangpaihe → Feixi	154	Ci	31.42N	117.10 E
Shangqiu (Zhuji)	152	Ke	34.24N	115.37 E
Shangrao	154	Ck	28.29N	117.59 E
Shan Guan ⊡	152	Kf	27.28N	114.15 E
Shangxian	152	Je	33.55N	109.57 E
Shangyi (Nanhaoqian)	154	Bd	41.06N	113.58 E
Shangyu (Baiguan)	154	Fi	30.01N	120.53 E
Shangzhi	152	Mb	45.13N	127.15 E
Shanhaiguan	154	Gd	40.01N	119.45 E
Shanhetun	154	Ib	44.43N	127.14 E
Shan-hsi Sheng → Shanxi Sheng = Shansi (EN) [2]	152	Jd	37.00N	112.00 E
Shanmatang Ding ▲	152	Jg	24.45N	111.50 E
Shannon	218	Pd	40.33S	175.25 E
Shannon ⊕	179	Kc	75.20N	18.10W
Shannon/Aerfort na Sionainne ⊕	118	Ei	52.42N	8.57W
Shannon/An tSionainn ≤	110	Fe	52.36N	9.41W
Shannon, Mount- ▲	212	Ie	19.58S	141.30 E
Shannon, Mouth of the- ◖	118	Di	52.30N	9.53W
Shanshan (Piqan)	152	Fc	42.52N	90.10 E
Shansi (EN) = Shan-hsi Sheng → Shanxi Sheng [2]	152	Jd	37.00N	112.00 E
Shansi → Shanxi Sheng (Shan-hsi Sheng) [2]	152	Jd	37.00N	112.00 E
Shansonggang	154	Ic	42.30N	126.13 E
Shantar, Ra's- ⊳	146	Qi	26.22N	56.26 E
Shantar Islands (EN) = Šantarskije ostrova ⊡	140	Pd	55.00N	137.36 E
Shantou	142	Ng	23.26N	116.42 E
Shantung (EN) = Shandong Sheng (Shan-tung Sheng) [2]	152	Kd	36.00N	119.00 E
Shantung Peninsula (EN)= Shandong Bandao ▣	140	Of	37.00N	121.00 E
Shan-tung Sheng → Shandong	152	Kd	36.00N	119.00 E
Shanxian	154	Dg	34.47N	116.05 E
Shanxi Sheng (Shan-hsi Sheng) = Shansi (EN) [2]	152	Jd	37.00N	112.00 E
Shanyin (Daiyue)	154	Be	39.30N	112.48 E
Shanyincheng	154	Be	39.27N	112.56 E
Shaoguan	142	Mg	24.57N	113.34 E
Shaoshan	152	Jf	27.55N	112.32 E
Shaowu	152	Kf	27.21N	117.29 E
Shaoxing	142	Og	30.00N	120.30 E
Shaoyang	142	Mg	27.13N	111.31 E
Shapinsay ⊕	118	Kb	59.03N	2.51W
Shaqlāwah	146	Kd	36.23N	44.18 E
Shaqq al Ju'ayfir ▨	168	Db	15.16N	26.00 E
Shaqrā'	144	Gg	25.16N	45.42 E
Shaqū	146	Pg	27.14N	56.22 E
Sharaf	146	Jg	30.03N	43.45 E
Sharafah	168	Dc	12.04N	27.07 E
Sharafkhāneh	146	Kc	38.11N	45.29 E
Sharāh, Jibāl ash- ▲	146	Fg	30.10N	35.30 E
Sharā 'Iwah ⊕	146	Oj	25.02N	52.14 E
Shareh	146	Kd	37.38N	44.50 E
Shari	144	Lc	43.55N	144.40 E
Shāri, Buḥayrat- ⊡	146	Ke	34.43N	45.32 E
Shari-Dake ▲	156a	Db	43.46N	144.43 E
Shark Bay ◖	208	Cg	25.30S	113.30 E
Shark Bay (Denham)	212	Cg	25.55S	113.32 E
Sharm ash Shaykh	164	Fd	27.50N	34.16 E
Sharon	184	Hd	41.14N	80.31W
Sharon Springs	186	Fg	38.54N	101.45W
Sharqīyah, Aş Şaḥrā' ash- = Arabian Desert (EN) ▨	158	Kf	28.00N	32.00 E
Sharshar, Jabal- ▲	146	Dk	23.52N	39.20 E
Shary	144	Fd	27.15N	43.27 E
Shashe	172	Dd	21.24S	27.27 E
Shashemene	168	Fd	7.13N	38.36 E
Shashi	142	Nf	30.22N	112.11 E
Shashi	158	Jk	22.12S	29.21 E
Shasta, Mount- ▲	174	Ge	41.20N	122.20W
Shasta Lake ⊡	182	Cc	40.50N	122.25W
Shaṭī', Wādī ash- ≤	164	Bd	27.10N	13.25 E
Shattuck	186	Gh	36.16N	99.53W
Shaunavon	180	Gg	49.40N	108.25W
Shawan	152	Ec	44.21N	85.37 E
Shawano	186	Ld	44.47N	88.36W
Shawinigan	180	Kg	46.33N	72.45W
Shawnee	186	Lh	35.20N	96.55W
Shawneetown	186	Lh	37.42N	88.08W
Shaw River ≤	212	Dd	20.20S	119.17 E
Shāwshāw, Jabal- ▲	146	Ci	26.03N	28.56 E
Shayang	154	Bi	30.42N	112.34 E
Shaybārā ⊕	146	Gj	25.25N	36.51 E
Shaykh Ahmad	146	Lf	32.53N	46.26 E
Shaykh Fāris	146	Lf	32.05N	47.36 E
Shaykh Sa'd	146	Lf	32.34N	46.15 E
Shaykh 'Uthmān	144	Fj	12.52N	44.59 E
Shebar, Kowtal-e- ⊡	144	Kc	34.54N	68.14 E
Shebele, Wabe-= Shebeli Webi (EN) ≤	158	Lh	0.12S	42.45 E
Shebeli Webi (EN) = Shabēlle, Webi- ≤	158	Lh	0.12S	42.45 E
Shebele, Wabe- = Shebeli Webi (EN) ≤	158	Lh	0.12S	42.45 E
Sheberghān	142	If	36.41N	65.45 E
Sheboygan	186	Me	43.46N	87.44W
Shebshi Mountains ▲	158	Ih	8.30N	11.45 E
Shedin Peak ▲	180	Ee	55.50N	127.00W
Sheelin, Lough-/Loch Sileann ⊡	118	Ff	53.48N	7.20W
Sheenjek ≤	178	Kc	66.45N	144.33W
Sheep Haven/Cuan na gCaorach ◖	118	Ff	55.10N	7.52W
Sheep Mountain ▲	188	Hj	32.32N	114.14W
Sheep Range ▲	188	Hh	36.45N	115.05W
Sheerness	118	Nj	51.27N	0.45 E
Sheffield [Al.-U.S.]	184	Dh	34.46N	87.40W
Sheffield [Eng.-U.K.]	112	He	53.23N	1.30W
Sheffield [Tx.-U.S.]	186	Fk	30.43N	101.50W
Shefford	124	Bj	52.02N	0.20W
Shek Hasan	168	Fc	12.04N	35.53 E
Shek Hason	168	Gd	7.45N	40.42 E
Shelburne [N.S.-Can.]	180	Kh	43.46N	65.19W
Shelburne [Ont.-Can.]	184	Gc	44.04N	80.12W
Shelby [Mt.-U.S.]	182	Eb	48.30N	111.51W
Shelby [N.C.-U.S.]	184	Gh	35.17N	81.32W
Shelbyville [Il.-U.S.]	186	Lg	39.24N	88.48W
Shelbyville [In.-U.S.]	184	Ef	39.31N	85.47W
Shelbyville [Tn.-U.S.]	184	Dh	35.29N	86.27W
Shelbyville, Lake- ⊡	186	Lg	39.30N	88.40W
Sheldon	186	Ie	43.11N	95.51W
Sheldon Point	178	Gd	63.32N	164.52W
Shelikhov Gulf (EN) = Šelihova, zaliv- ◖	140	Rc	60.00N	158.00 E
Šelikof Strait ◖	178	Le	57.30N	155.00W
Shell	188	Ld	44.33N	107.44W
Shellbrook	180	Gf	53.13N	106.24W
Shellharbour	210	Gh	34.35S	150.52 E
Shelter Point ⊳	218	Cg	46.37S	168.25 E
Shelton	188	Dc	47.13N	123.06W
Shenandoah	186	If	40.45N	95.22W
Shenandoah Mountain ▲	184	Hf	38.58N	79.00W
Shenandoah Valley ▨	184	Hf	38.45N	78.45W
Shenchi	154	Be	39.05N	112.11 E
Shendam	166	Gd	8.53N	9.32 E
Shending Shan ▲	152	Nb	46.34N	133.27 E
Shenge	166	Cd	7.55N	12.57W
Shëngjin ⊡	130	Lm	41.49N	19.35 E
Shengze	154	Fi	30.55N	120.39 E
Shenjiamen → Putuo	152	Lf	29.57N	122.18 E
Shenmu	152	Jd	38.52N	110.35 E
Shenqiu (Huaidian)	154	Ch	33.27N	115.05 E
Shensi (EN)=Shaan-hsi Sheng → Shaanxi Sheng (Shaan-hsi Sheng) [2]	152	Id	36.00N	109.00 E
Shenton, Mount- ▲	212	Ee	28.00S	123.22 E
Shenxian	154	Ce	38.30N	115.33 E
Shenyang	142	Oe	41.48N	123.24 E
Shenze	154	Ce	38.11N	115.11 E
Shepherd, Îles-= Shepherd Islands (EN) ⊡	219b	Dc	16.55S	168.35 E
Shepherd Islands (EN) = Shepherd, Îles- ⊡	219b	Dc	16.55S	168.35 E
Shepparton	210	Fh	36.23S	145.25 E
Sheppey ⊕	118	Nj	51.24N	0.50 E
Shepshed	124	Ai	52.45N	1.17W
Sheqi	154	Bh	33.04N	112.56 E
Sherard, Cape - ⊳	180	Jb	74.36N	80.10W
Sherard Osborn Fjord ◖	179	Bd	82.10N	51.30W
Sherborne	118	Kk	50.57N	2.31W
Sherbro Island ⊕	158	Fh	7.33N	12.42W
Sherbrooke	176	Lg	45.24N	71.54W
Sherda	158	Ba	20.08N	16.45 E
Shere Hill ▲	166	Gd	9.57N	9.03 E
Sheridan [Mt.-U.S.]	188	Kd	44.47N	110.12W
Sheridan [Wy.-U.S.]	182	Gc	44.48N	106.58W
Sherman	186	Io	33.38N	96.36W
Sherman Station	184	Mc	45.54N	68.26W
Sherridon	180	He	55.07N	101.05W
Sherwood Forest ▨	118	Lh	53.10N	1.10W
She Shui ≤	154	Ci	30.52N	114.22 E
Shetland [2]	118	La	60.30N	1.30W
Shetland Islands (Zetland) ⊡	110	Fc	60.30N	1.30W
Shewa [3]	168	Fd	9.20N	38.55 E
Shewa Gimira	168	Fd	7.00N	35.50 E
Shexian	154	Bf	36.33N	113.40 E
Shexian (Huicheng)	154	Ej	29.53N	118.27 E
Sheyang (Hede)	154	Fh	33.47N	120.15 E
Sheyenne River ≤	182	Hb	47.05N	96.50W
Shiant Islands ⊡	118	Gd	57.54N	6.30W
Shibām	168	Hb	15.56N	48.38 E
Shibaminah, Wādī- ≤	144	Ie	22.12N	55.30 E
Shibata [Jap.]	154	Of	37.57N	139.20 E
Shibata [Jap.]	156	Gb	38.05N	140.50 E
Shibayama-Gata ⊡	152	Ec	36.21N	136.23 E
Shibazhan	152	Ma	42.28N	125.20 E
Shibecha	154	Rc	43.17N	144.36 E
Shibetsu [Jap.]	154	Rb	43.40N	145.08 E
Shibetsu [Jap.]	152	Pc	44.10N	142.23 E
Shibetsu-Gawa ≤	156a	Db	43.46N	145.06 E
Shibīn al Kawm	164	Fc	30.33N	31.01 E
Shibiutan ▲	156a	Ca	44.47N	142.35 E
Shibi-Zan ▲	156	Bf	31.59N	130.22 E
Shib Küh ▲	144	Hd	27.20N	52.40 E
Shibukawa	156	Fe	36.29N	139.00 E
Shibushi	156	Bf	31.28N	131.07 E
Shibushi-Wan ◖	156	Ki	31.25N	131.12 E
Shichinohe	156	Ga	40.41N	141.10 E
Shichiyo Islands ⊡	220d	Bb	7.23N	151.40 E
Shidao	152	Ld	36.51N	122.18 E
Shido	156	Dd	34.19N	134.10 E
Shidongsi → Gaolan	152	Hd	36.23N	103.55 E
Shiel, Loch- ⊡	118	He	56.50N	5.50W
Shiga Ken [2]	156	Ng	35.15N	136.10 E
Shi He ≤	154	Ch	32.32N	115.52 E
Shiheizi	152	Ec	44.18N	86.02 E
Shiiba	156	Be	32.28N	131.09 E
Shijaku	130	Ch	41.20N	19.34 E
Shijiazhuang	142	Nf	38.00N	114.30 E
Shijiusuo	154	Eg	35.24N	119.32 E
Shika	156	Ee	37.01N	136.46 E
Shikabe	156a	Bb	42.02N	140.47 E
Shikārpur	148	Dc	27.57N	68.38 E
Shiki Islands ⊡	220b	Bb	7.24N	151.53 E
Shikine-Jima ⊕	156	Fd	34.19N	139.13 E
Shikoku ⊕	140	Pf	33.30N	133.30 E
Shikoku Basin (EN) ▨	152	Oe	30.00N	135.00 E
Shikoku-Sanchi ▲	156	Ce	33.45N	133.35 E
Shikotan-Tō / Šikotan, ostrov- ⊕	138	Jh	43.47N	146.45 E
Shilabo	168	Gd	6.05N	44.45 E
Shiliguri	142	Kg	26.42N	88.26 E
Shiliu → Changjiang	148	Ne	19.20N	109.03 E
Shilla ▲	148	Fb	32.24N	78.12 E
Shillong	142	Kg	25.34N	91.53 E
Shimabara	154	Kh	32.47N	130.22 E
Shimabara-Hantō ▣	156	Be	32.45N	130.15 E
Shimabara-Wan ◖	156	Be	32.50N	130.30 E
Shimada	156	Fd	34.49N	138.09 E
Shima-Hantō ▣	156	Ed	34.25N	136.45 E
Shimane-Hantō ▣	156	Cd	35.30N	133.00 E
Shimane Ken [2]	156	Lg	35.00N	132.20 E
Shimanto-Gawa ≤	156	Ce	32.56N	133.00 E
Shimian	154	Og	29.10N	102.26 E
Shimizu [Jap.]	154	Og	35.01N	138.29 E
Shimla	142	Jf	31.06N	77.10 E
Shimoda	154	Og	34.40N	138.57 E
Shimodate	156	Fe	36.19N	139.58 E
Shimoga	142	Jh	13.55N	75.34 E
Shimo-Jima ⊕	156	Be	32.25N	130.05 E
Shimokawa	156a	Ca	44.18N	142.38 E
Shimokita-Hantō ▣	156a	Bc	41.15N	141.05 E
Shimo-Koshiki-Jima ⊕	156	Af	31.40N	129.40 E
Shimo la Tewa	170	Gc	3.57S	39.44 E
Shimoni	170	Gc	4.39S	39.23 E
Shimonoseki	152	Oe	33.57N	130.57 E
Shimono-Shima ⊕	156	Ad	34.20N	129.15 E
Shimotsu	156	Dd	34.07N	135.08 E
Shimotsuma	156	Fe	36.11N	139.58 E
Shin, Loch- ⊡	118	Ic	58.07N	4.32W
Shinano	156	Fc	36.47N	138.10 E
Shinano-Gawa ≤	156	Ff	37.57N	139.00 E
Shindand	144	Jc	33.18N	62.08 E
Shinga	170	Dc	3.16S	24.38 E
Shingbwiyang	148	Lc	26.41N	96.13 E
Shingū	152	Oe	33.44N	135.59 E
Shingwidzi	172	Cd	23.01S	30.43 E
Shinji	154	Ch	35.24N	132.54 E
Shinji-Ko ⊡	156	Cd	35.26N	132.56 E
Shinjō	156	Ga	38.46N	140.18 E
Shinkafe	166	Gc	13.05N	6.31 E
Shinminato	156	Ee	36.47N	137.04 E
Shinnanyō	156	Be	34.05N	131.45 E
Shinshiro	156	Ee	34.54N	137.30 E
Shintoku	156a	Cb	43.12N	142.55 E
Shin-tone-Gawa ≤	156	Ga	35.57N	140.27 E
Shintotsugawa	156a	Ca	43.36N	141.40 E
Shinyanga	160	Ki	3.40S	33.26 E
Shinyanga [3]	170	Fc	3.50S	33.00 E
Shiogama	156	Ga	38.19N	141.01 E
Shiojiri	156	Nf	36.06N	137.58 E
Shiono-Misaki ⊳	152	Oe	33.26N	135.45 E
Shiokubi-Misaki ⊳	156a	Bc	41.43N	140.57 E
Shio-no-Misaki ⊳	152	Oe	33.26N	135.45 E
Shipai → Huaining	154	Di	30.25N	116.39 E
Shiping	152	Bg	23.44N	102.28 E
Shipki La ⊡	148	Fb	31.49N	78.45 E
Shippegan	184	Lb	47.45N	64.42W
Shiprock	188	Kg	36.47N	108.41W
Shipshaw, Rivière- ≤	184	La	48.30N	71.15W
Shipu	154	Fj	29.17N	121.57 E
Shipugi Shankou ⊡	152	Ie	33.05N	108.15 E
Shiquan	154	Ie	33.05N	108.15 E
Shiquan He ≤	152	Be	32.28N	79.44 E
Shiragami-Misaki ⊳	156a	Bc	41.25N	140.12 E
Shirahama	156	Dd	33.30N	135.20 E
Shirakawa [Jap.]	154	Pf	37.07N	140.13 E
Shirakawa [Jap.]	156	Ee	35.36N	137.12 E

Index Symbols

[1] Independent Nation	⊟ Historical or Cultural Region	⊟ Pass, Gap	⊟ Depression	⊟ Coast, Beach	⊟ Rock, Reef
[2] State, Region	▲ Mount, Mountain	⊟ Plain, Lowland	⊟ Polder	⊟ Cliff	⊟ Islands, Archipelago
[3] District, County	▲ Volcano	⊟ Delta	⊟ Desert, Dunes	⊟ Peninsula	⊟ Rocks, Reefs
[4] Municipality	▲ Hill	⊟ Salt Flat	⊟ Forest, Woods	⊟ Isthmus	⊟ Coral Reef
[5] Colony, Dependency	▲ Mountains, Mountain Range	⊟ Valley, Canyon	⊟ Heath, Steppe	⊟ Sandbank	⊟ Well, Spring
[6] Continent	▨ Hills, Escarpment	⊟ Crater, Cave	⊟ Oasis	⊟ Island	⊟ Geyser
[7] Physical Region	▨ Plateau, Upland	⊟ Karst Features	⊟ Cape, Point	⊟ Atoll	⊟ River, Stream

⊟ Waterfall, Rapids	⊟ Canal	⊟ Lagoon	⊟ Escarpment, Sea Scarp	⊟ Historic Site	⊟ Airport
⊟ River Mouth, Estuary	⊟ Glacier	⊟ Bank	⊟ Fracture	⊟ Ruins	⊟ Port
⊟ Lake	⊟ Ice Shelf, Pack Ice	⊟ Seamount	⊟ Trench, Abyss	⊟ Wall, Walls	⊟ Military installation
⊟ Salt Lake	⊟ Ocean	⊟ Tablemount	⊟ National Park, Reserve	⊟ Church, Abbey	⊟ Lighthouse
⊟ Intermittent Lake	⊟ Sea	⊟ Ridge	⊟ Point of Interest	⊟ Temple	⊟ Mine
⊟ Reservoir	⊟ Gulf, Bay	⊟ Shelf	⊟ Recreation Site	⊟ Scientific Station	⊟ Tunnel
⊟ Swamp, Pond	⊟ Strait, Fjord	⊟ Basin	⊟ Cave, Cavern	⊟ Railway station	⊟ Dam, Bridge

Shirakawa [Jap.]	156	Ec	36.17N	136.53 E
Shirane-San [Jap.]	156	Fd	35.40N	138.13 E
Shirane-San [Jap.]	152	Od	36.48N	139.22 E
Shirane-San [Jap.]	156	Fc	36.38N	138.32 E
Shiranuka	154	Rc	42.57N	144.05 E
Shiraoi	154	Pc	42.31N	141.16 E
Shirase Coast	222	Mf	78.30S	156.00W
Shirataka	156	Gb	38.11N	140.06 E
Shirataki	156a	Cb	43.53N	143.09 E
Shīrāz	142	Hg	29.36N	52.32 E
Shirbīn	146	Dg	31.11N	31.32 E
Shire	158	Kj	17.42S	35.19 E
Shiren	154	Id	41.54N	126.34 E
Shiretoko-Dake	156a	Da	44.15N	145.14 E
Shiretoko-Hantō	156a	Da	44.00N	145.00 E
Shiretoko-Misaki	152	Qc	44.21N	145.20 E
Shīrgāh	146	Od	36.17N	52.54 E
Shiribetsu-Gawa	156a	Bb	42.52N	140.21 E
Shiriha-Misaki	156a	Db	42.56N	144.45 E
Shirikishinai	156a	Bc	41.48N	141.05 E
Shīrīn	146	Qi	27.10N	56.41 E
Shīrīn sū	146	Me	35.29N	48.27 E
Shiriya-Zaki	152	Pc	41.26N	141.28 E
Shīr Kūh	140	Hf	31.37N	54.04 E
Shirley Mountains	188	Le	42.15N	106.30W
Shiroishi	154	Pe	38.00N	140.37 E
Shirone	156	Fc	37.46N	139.00 E
Shirotori	156	Ed	35.53N	136.52 E
Shirouma-Dake	156	Ec	36.45N	137.46 E
Shirshov Ridge (EN)	138	Me	57.30N	171.00 E
Shīrvān	144	Ib	37.24N	57.55 E
Shīrvān	146	Lf	33.33N	46.49 E
Shirwan Mazīn	146	Kd	37.03N	44.10 E
Shishaldin Volcano	174	Cd	54.45N	163.57W
Shishi-Jima	156	Be	32.17N	130.15 E
Shishmaref	178	Fc	66.14N	166.09W
Shishou	152	Jf	29.42N	112.23 E
Shitai (Qili)	154	Di	30.12N	117.28 E
Shitara	156	Ed	35.05N	137.34 E
Shithāthah	146	Jf	32.33N	43.29 E
Shitou Shan	152	Ma	51.02N	125.12 E
Shivwits Plateau	188	Ih	36.10N	113.40W
Shiwa	154	Pe	39.33N	141.35 E
Shiwan Dashan	152	Ig	21.45N	107.35 E
Shiwa Ngandu	170	Fe	11.12S	31.43 E
Shiwpuri	148	Fc	25.26N	77.39 E
Shixian	154	Jc	43.05N	129.46 E
Shiyan	152	Je	32.34N	110.48 E
Shiyang He	152	Hd	39.00N	103.25 E
Shizilu → Junan	154	Eg	35.10N	118.50 E
Shizugawa	156	Gb	38.40N	141.28 E
Shizui	154	Ic	43.03N	126.09 E
Shizuishan (Dawukou)	152	Id	39.03N	106.24 E
Shizukuishi	156	Gb	39.42N	140.59 E
Shizunai	154	Qc	42.20N	142.22 E
Shizunai-Gawa	156a	Cb	42.20N	142.22 E
Shizuoka	142	Pf	34.58N	138.23 E
Shizuoka Ken [2]	154	Og	35.00N	138.25 E
Shkodra = Scutari (EN)	112	Hg	42.05N	19.30 E
Shkodrës, Liqen i-=Scutari, Lake- (EN)	110	Hg	42.10N	19.20 E
Shkumbini	130	Ch	41.01N	19.26 E
Shoal Lake	186	Fa	50.26N	100.34W
Shoal Lake	186	Ib	49.32N	95.00W
Shoal Lakes	186	Ha	50.20N	97.40W
Shōbara	154	Lg	34.51N	133.01 E
Shodo-Shima	156	Dd	34.30N	134.15 E
Shō-Gawa	156	Ec	36.47N	137.04 E
Shokanbetsu-Dake	156a	Bb	43.43N	141.31 E
Shokotsu-Gawa	156a	Ca	44.23N	143.17 E
Sholāpur → Solāpur	142	Jh	17.41N	75.55 E
Shoqān	146	Qd	37.20N	56.58 E
Shoranūr	148	Ff	10.46N	76.17 E
Shoreham-by-Sea	118	Mk	50.49N	0.16W
Shortland Islands	214	Fi	6.55S	155.53 E
Shosambetsu	156a	Ba	44.32N	141.46 E
Shoshone	188	He	42.56N	114.24W
Shoshone Mountains	182	Dd	39.15N	117.25W
Shoshone Peak	188	Gh	36.56N	116.16W
Shoshone River	188	Kd	44.52N	108.11W
Shoshong	172	Dd	23.02S	26.31 E
Shoshoni	188	Ke	43.14N	108.07W
Shotor Khūn	144	Jc	34.20N	64.55 E
Shouchang	154	Ej	29.23N	119.12 E
Shouguang	154	Ef	36.53N	118.44 E
Shouxian (Shouyang)	154	Dh	32.35N	116.47 E
Shouyang → Shouxian	154	Dh	32.35N	116.47 E
Shōwa	156	Gb	39.51N	140.03 E
Show Low	188	Ji	34.15N	110.02W
Shqiperia=Albania (EN) [1]	112	Hg	41.00N	20.00 E
Shreveport	176	Jf	32.30N	93.45W
Shrewsbury	118	Ki	52.43N	2.45W
Shropshire [3]	118	Ki	52.40N	2.50W
Shuangcheng	152	Mb	45.21N	126.17 E
Shuangjiang → Tongdao	152	If	26.14N	109.45 E
Shuangliao	152	Lc	43.30N	123.30 E
Shuangyang	152	Mc	43.31N	125.28 E
Shuangyashan	142	Pe	46.37N	131.10 E
Shucheng	154	Di	31.28N	116.57 E
Shufu	152	Cd	39.27N	75.52 E
Shuguri Falls	170	Gd	8.31S	37.23 E
Shu He	154	Eg	34.07N	118.30 E
Shuicheng	152	Hf	26.34N	104.52 E
Shuiding → Huocheng	152	Dc	44.03N	80.49 E
Shuiji → Laixi	154	Ff	36.52N	120.31 E
Shuijiahu → Changfeng	154	Dh	32.29N	117.10 E
Shuikou → Jianghua	152	Jg	24.58N	111.56 E
Shuiye	154	Cf	36.08N	114.06 E
Shuizhai → Xiangcheng	154	Ch	33.27N	114.53 E
Shūl	146	Ng	30.10N	51.38 E
Shulan	152	Mc	44.26N	126.55 E
Shule	152	Cd	39.25N	76.06 E
Shule He	140	Le	40.20N	92.50 E
Shulu (Xinji)	154	Cf	37.56N	115.14 E
Shumagin Islands	178	He	55.07N	159.45W
Shumarinai-Ko	156a	Ca	44.20N	142.13 E
Shunayn, Sabkhat-	164	Dc	30.10N	21.00 E
Shungnak	178	Hc	66.53N	157.02W
Shunyi	154	Dd	40.09N	116.38 E
Shuolong	152	Ig	22.51N	106.55 E
Shuoxian	152	Jd	39.18N	112.25 E
Shūr [Iran]	146	Oh	28.12N	52.09 E
Shūr [Iran]	146	Oh	28.33N	53.12 E
Shūr [Iran]	146	Ne	35.09N	51.30 E
Shūr [Iran]	146	Pi	26.59N	55.47 E
Shurāb	144	Ic	33.07N	55.18 E
Shūr Āb	146	Pg	31.45N	55.15 E
Shurugwi	172	Dc	19.40S	30.00 E
Shūsf	144	Jc	31.48N	60.01 E
Shūsh	146	Mf	32.12N	48.17 E
Shūsh = Susa (EN)	146	Mf	32.12N	48.17 E
Shushica	130	Ci	40.34N	19.34 E
Shūshtar	144	Gc	32.03N	48.51 E
Shuswap Lake	188	Fa	50.57N	119.15W
Shūt	146	Oe	34.44N	52.53 E
Shuwak	168	Fc	14.23N	35.52 E
Shuyang	152	Ke	34.01N	118.52 E
Shuzenji	156	Fd	34.58N	138.55 E
Shwebo	148	Jd	22.34N	95.42 E
Shwell	148	Jd	23.56N	96.17 E
Shyok	148	Fa	35.13N	75.53 E
Sia	150	Jh	6.49S	134.19 E
Siagne	122	Mk	43.32N	6.57 E
Siāh Band	144	Jc	32.25N	62.35 E
Sīah-Chashmeh	146	Kc	39.04N	44.23 E
Sīāh-Kūh	146	Oe	34.38N	52.16 E
Siak	150	Df	1.13N	102.09 E
Sialkot	142	Jf	32.30N	74.31 E
Sianów	120	Mb	54.15N	16.16 E
Siantan, Pulau-	150	Ef	3.10N	106.15 E
Siargao	150	Ie	9.53N	126.02 E
Šiaškotan, ostrov-	140	Re	48.49N	154.06 E
Siátista	130	Ei	40.16N	21.33 E
Siau, Pulau-	150	If	2.42N	125.24 E
Šiauliai	112	Id	55.53N	23.19 E
Šiauliai/Šjauljaj	112	Id	55.53N	23.19 E
Siavonga	170	Ef	16.32S	28.43 E
Siazan	136	Eg	41.04N	49.06 E
Sibā'ī, Jabal as-	164	Fd	25.43N	34.09 E
Sibaj	136	Fe	52.42N	58.39 E
Sibari, Cassano allo Ionio-	128	Kk	39.45N	16.27 E
Sibasa	172	Ed	22.56S	30.29 E
Šibenik	128	Jg	43.44N	15.53 E
Siberimanua	150	Cg	2.09S	99.34 E
Siberut, Pulau-	140	Lj	1.20S	98.55 E
Siberut, Selat-	150	Cg	0.42S	98.35 E
Sibi	148	Dc	29.33N	67.53 E
Sibigo	150	Cf	2.51N	95.55 E
Sibillini, Monti-	128	Hh	42.55N	13.15 E
Sibircatajaha	134	Lb	69.05N	64.43 E
Sibircevo	138	Ih	44.16N	132.20 E
Sibirjakova, ostrov-	138	Cb	72.50N	79.00 E
Sibiti	170	Bc	3.41S	13.21 E
Sibiu	112	If	45.48N	24.09 E
Sibiu [2]	130	Hd	45.46N	24.12 E
Sibolga	142	Li	1.45N	98.48 E
Sibsāgar	148	Ic	26.59N	94.38 E
Sibu	142	Ni	2.18N	111.49 E
Sibuguey Bay	150	He	7.30N	122.40 E
Sibut	160	Ih	5.44N	19.05 E
Sibutu Islands	150	Gf	4.45N	119.20 E
Sibutu Passage	150	Gf	4.56N	119.36 E
Sibuyan	150	Hd	12.25N	122.34 E
Sibuyan Sea	150	Hd	12.50N	122.40 E
Siby	166	Dc	12.22N	8.22W
Sibyllenstein	120	Ke	51.12N	14.05 E
Sicani, Monti-	128	Hm	37.40N	13.15 E
Sicasica	202	Eg	17.22S	67.45W
Si Chon	148	Jg	9.00N	99.56 E
Sichuan Pendi	140	Mf	30.01N	105.00 E
Sichuan Sheng (Ssu-ch'uan Sheng)=Szechwan (EN) [2]	152	He	30.00N	103.00 E
Sicilia [2]	128	Im	37.45N	14.15 E
Sicilia = Sicily (EN)	110	Hh	37.30N	14.00 E
Sicilia, Canale di-=Sicily, Strait of- (EN)	110	Hh	37.20N	11.20 E
Sicilia, Mar di-	128	Gn	36.30N	13.00 E
Sicily (EN) = Sicilia	110	Hh	37.30N	14.00 E
Sicily, Strait of- (EN)= Sicilia, Canale di-	110	Hh	37.20N	11.20 E
Sicily, Strait of- (EN)= Tūnis, Canal de-	110	Hh	37.20N	11.20 E
Sico Tinto, Río-	194	Ef	15.58N	84.58W
Sicuani	200	Ig	14.15S	71.15W
Šid	130	Cd	45.08N	19.14 E
Sidamo [3]	168	Fd	5.48N	38.50 E
Siddipet	148	Fe	18.06N	78.51 E
Side	146	Dd	36.46N	31.22 E
Sidéradougou	166	Ec	10.40N	4.15W
Siderno	128	Kl	38.16N	16.18 E
Siders/Sierre	128	Bd	46.17N	7.32 E
Šiderty	136	He	51.40N	74.50 E
Šiderty	136	He	52.32N	74.50 E
Sidheros, Ákra-	130	Jn	35.19N	26.19 E
Sidhirókastron	130	Gh	41.14N	23.23 E
Sīdī 'Abd ar Raḩmān	146	Cg	30.58N	28.44 E
Sidi Aïch	126	Qh	36.37N	4.41 E
Sidi Akacha	126	Nh	36.28N	1.18 E
Sidi Ali	126	Mh	36.06N	0.25 E
Sīdī 'Alī al Makkī, Ra's-	128	Em	37.11N	10.17 E
Sīdī Barrānī	164	Ec	31.36N	25.55 E
Sidi Bel Abbes	162	Gb	35.12N	0.38W
Sidi Bel Abbes [3]	162	Gc	34.45N	0.35W
Sidi Bennour	162	Fc	32.39N	8.26W
Sidi di Daoud	126	Ph	36.51N	3.52 E
Sidi Ifni	160	Ff	29.33N	10.10W
Sidi Kacem	162	Fc	34.13N	5.42W
Sidikalang	150	Cf	2.45N	98.19 E
Sidi Lakhdar	126	Mh	36.10N	0.27 E
Sīdī Zayd, Jabal-	128	En	36.29N	10.20 E
Sidlaw Hills	118	Ke	56.30N	3.00W
Sidmouth	118	Jk	50.41N	3.15W
Sidney [B.C.-Can.]	180	Fg	48.39N	123.24W
Sidney [Mt.-U.S.]	182	Gb	47.43N	104.09W
Sidney [Nb.-U.S.]	182	Gc	41.09N	102.59W
Sidney [Oh.-U.S.]	184	Ee	40.16N	84.10W
Sidney Lanier, Lake-	184	Fh	34.15N	83.57W
Sidobre	122	Ik	43.40N	2.30 E
Sidorovsk	138	Dc	66.35N	82.30 E
Sidra	120	Tc	53.33N	23.30 E
Sidra, Gulf of-(EN)=Surt, Khalīj-	158	Ie	31.30N	18.00 E
Sidrolândia	204	Ee	20.55S	54.58W
Siedlce	120	Sd	52.11N	22.16 E
Siedlce [2]	120	Sd	52.10N	22.15 E
Siedlecka, Wysoczyzna-	120	Sd	52.10N	22.15 E
Sieg [F.R.G.]	120	Df	50.45N	7.05 E
Sieg [F.R.G.]	124	Kd	50.55N	8.01 E
Siegburg	120	Df	50.48N	7.12 E
Siegen	120	Ef	50.52N	8.02 E
Siemiatycze	120	Sd	52.26N	22.53 E
Siĕmréab	148	Kf	13.22N	103.51 E
Siena	128	Fg	43.19N	11.21 E
Sieniawa	120	Sf	50.11N	22.36 E
Sienne	122	Ee	49.00N	1.34W
Sieradz	120	Oe	51.36N	18.45 E
Sieradz [2]	120	Oe	51.35N	18.45 E
Sieradzka, Niecka-	120	Oe	51.35N	18.50 E
Sierck-les-Bains	124	Ie	49.26N	6.21 E
Sierpc	120	Pd	52.52N	19.41 E
Sierra Blanca	186	Dk	31.11N	105.21W
Sierra Blanca Peak	182	Fe	33.23N	105.48W
Sierra Colorada	206	Gf	40.35S	67.48W
Sierra Leone [1]	160	Fh	8.30N	11.30W
Sierra Leone Basin (EN)	106	Di	5.00N	17.00W
Sierra Leone Rise (EN)	106	Di	5.30N	21.00W
Sierra Mojada	190	Dc	27.17N	103.42W
Sierre/Siders	128	Bd	46.17N	7.32 E
Siete Palmas	204	Cg	25.13S	58.20W
Siete Puntas, Río-	204	Df	23.34S	57.20W
Şieu	130	Hb	47.11N	24.13 E
Sifié	166	Dd	7.59N	6.55W
Sífnos	130	Hm	37.00N	24.40 E
Sig	162	Gb	35.32N	0.11W
Siğacik Körfezi	130	Jk	38.12N	26.45 E
Sigean	122	Ik	43.02N	2.59 E
Sighetu Marmaţiei	130	Gb	47.56N	23.53 E
Sighişoara	130	Hc	46.13N	24.48 E
Sigli	150	Ce	5.23N	95.57 E
Siglufjörður	114a	Ba	66.09N	18.55W
Sigmaringen	120	Fh	48.05N	9.13 E
Signal Peak	188	Hj	33.22N	114.03W
Signy Island	222	Re	60.43S	45.38W
Signy-l'Abbaye	124	Ge	49.42N	4.25 E
Signy-le-Petit	124	Ge	49.54N	4.17 E
Sigtuna	114	Dg	59.37N	17.43 E
Siguanea, Ensenada de la-	194	Fc	21.38N	83.05W
Siguatepeque	194	Df	14.32N	87.49W
Sigüenza	126	Jc	41.04N	2.38W
Siguiri	160	Gg	11.25N	9.10W
Sigulda	114	Fh	57.09N	24.53 E
Si He	154	Dg	35.11N	116.42 E
Sihong	154	Eh	33.28N	118.13 E
Sihote-Alin	140	Pe	48.00N	138.00 E
Sihou → Changdao	154	Ff	37.56N	120.42 E
Sihuas	202	Ce	8.34S	77.37W
Siikainen	116	Ic	61.52N	21.50 E
Siilinjärvi	114	Ge	63.02N	27.40 E
Siirt	144	Fb	37.56N	41.57 E
Sijunjung	150	Dg	0.42S	100.58 E
Sikaiana	219a	Fc	8.22S	162.45 E
Sikakap	150	Dg	2.46S	100.13 E
Sīkān	146	Lf	33.10N	47.39 E
Sikanni Chief	180	Fe	58.17N	121.46W
Sīkar	148	Fc	27.37N	75.09 E
Sikasso	160	Gg	11.20N	5.40W
Sikasso [3]	166	Dc	10.55N	7.00W
Sikéa [Grc.]	130	Gi	40.03N	23.58 E
Sikéa [Grc.]	130	Fm	36.46N	22.56 E
Sikeston	182	Jd	36.53N	89.35W
Síkinos	130	Im	36.50N	25.05 E
Sikkim [3]	148	Hc	27.50N	88.30 E
Siklós	120	Ok	45.51N	18.18 E
Sikonge	170	Fd	5.38S	32.46 E
Šikotan, ostrov- / Shikotan-Tō	138	Jh	43.47N	146.45 E
Siktjah	138	Hc	69.55N	125.10 E
Sil	126	Eb	42.27N	7.43W
Sila Grande	128	Kk	39.20N	16.30 E
Sila Greca	128	Kk	39.30N	16.30 E
Šilale/Šilalė	114	Fi	55.29N	22.12 E
Šilalė/Šilale	114	Fi	55.29N	22.12 E
Silao	192	Ig	20.56N	101.26W
Silaogou	154	Be	39.59N	113.03 E
Sila Piccola	128	Kk	39.05N	16.35 E
Silba	128	If	44.23N	14.42 E
Silchar	148	Id	24.49N	92.48 E
Šilda	132	Ud	51.47N	59.50 E
Sildagapet	116	Ab	62.05N	5.10 E
Şile	146	Cb	41.05N	29.35 E
Sile	128	Ge	45.28N	12.35 E
Šilega	136	Ec	64.03N	44.02 E
Silesia (EN)=Śląsk	110	He	51.00N	16.45 E
Silesia (EN)=Śląsk	120	Me	51.00N	16.45 E
Silet	162	He	22.39N	4.35 E
Silhouette Island	172b	Ca	4.29S	55.14 E
Silifke	144	Db	36.22N	33.56 E
Siligir	138	Gc	68.27N	114.50 E
Siling Co	140	Kf	31.50N	89.00 E
Siling Jiao	150	Ge	8.20N	115.27 E
Silisili, Mauga-	221c	Aa	13.35S	172.27W
Silistra	130	Ke	44.07N	27.16 E
Silistra [2]	130	Kf	44.07N	27.16 E
Silivri	146	Cb	41.04N	28.15 E
Siljan	114	Df	60.50N	14.45 E
Šilka	138	Gf	51.51N	116.02 E
Šilka	140	Od	53.22N	121.32 E
Silkeborg	114	Bh	56.10N	9.34 E
Sillamäe/Sillamjae	114	Gg	59.24N	27.43 E
Sillamjae/Sillamäe	114	Gg	59.24N	27.43 E
Sillaro	128	Ff	44.34N	11.51 E
Silleiro, Cabo-	126	Db	42.07N	8.54W
Sillé-le-Guillaume	122	Ff	48.12N	0.08W
Sillian	128	Gd	46.45N	12.25 E
Sillil	168	Gc	11.00N	43.26 E
Siloam Springs	186	Ih	36.11N	94.32W
Siloana Plains	170	Df	17.15S	23.10 E
Šilovo	136	Ee	54.24N	40.52 E
Silsbee	186	Ik	30.21N	94.11W
Siltou	168	Bb	16.52N	15.43 E
Šilutė/Šilute	136	Cd	55.21N	21.30 E
Šilute/Šilutė	136	Cd	55.21N	21.30 E
Silvan	146	Ic	38.08N	41.01 E
Silvassa	148	Ed	20.20N	73.05 E
Silver Bank (EN)	194	Mc	20.30N	69.45W
Silver Bank Passage	194	Lc	21.00N	70.15W
Silver Bay	182	Ib	47.17N	91.16W
Silver City	182	Fe	32.46N	108.17W
Silverdalen	116	Fg	57.32N	15.44 E
Silver Lake	188	Ee	43.06N	120.53W
Silver Spring	184	If	39.02N	77.03W
Silver Springs	188	Fg	39.25N	119.13W
Silverthrone Mountain	188	Ba	51.31N	126.06W
Silverton [Co.-U.S.]	186	Ch	37.49N	107.40W
Silverton [Tx.-U.S.]	186	Fi	34.28N	101.19W
Silves [Braz.]	202	Gd	2.54S	58.27W
Silves [Port.]	126	Dg	37.11N	8.26W
Silvi	128	Ih	42.34N	14.06 E
Silvia	202	Cc	2.37N	76.24W
Silvies River	188	Fe	43.22N	118.48W
Silvretta	128	Ed	46.50N	10.15 E
Silyānah	162	Ib	36.05N	9.22 E
Silyānah [3]	162	Ib	36.00N	9.30 E
Silyānah, Wādī-	128	Dn	36.33N	9.25 E
Sim	134	Hi	54.59N	57.41 E
Sim	134	Hi	54.32N	56.30 E
Sim, Cap-	162	Fc	31.23N	9.51W
Simanggang	150	Ff	1.15N	111.26 E
Šimanovsk	138	Hf	52.01N	127.36 E
Simao	152	Hg	22.40N	101.02 E
Simard, Lac-	184	Hb	47.38N	78.40W
Sīmareh	146	Mf	32.08N	48.03 E
Simav	146	Cc	39.05N	28.59 E
Simav	144	Ca	40.23N	28.31 E
Simav Dağ	130	Lj	39.04N	28.54 E
Simav Gölü	130	Lj	39.09N	28.55 E
Simayama-Jima	156	Ae	32.40N	128.38 E
Simba	170	Db	0.36N	22.55 E
Simbo	170	Fc	4.53S	29.44 E
Simbo	219a	Cc	8.18S	156.34 E
Simbruini, Monti-	128	Hj	41.55N	13.15 E
Simcoe	184	Gd	42.50N	80.18W
Simcoe, Lake -	180	Jh	44.27N	79.20W
Simen	168	Fc	13.25N	38.00 E
Simenti	166	Cc	13.00N	13.25W
Simeto	128	Jm	37.24N	15.06 E
Simeulue, Pulau-	140	Li	2.35N	96.05 E
Simferopol	112	Jf	44.57N	34.06 E
Sími	130	Km	36.36N	27.50 E
Sími	130	Km	36.35N	27.50 E
Simití	194	Kj	7.58N	73.58W
Simitli	130	Gh	41.53N	23.06 E
Simla → Shimla	142	Jf	31.06N	77.10 E
Şimleu Silvaniei	130	Fb	47.14N	22.48 E
Simmental	128	Bd	46.35N	7.25 E
Simmerath	124	Id	50.36N	6.18 E
Simmerbach	124	Je	49.48N	7.31 E
Simmern (Hunsrück)	120	Dg	49.59N	7.31 E
Simmertal	124	Je	49.48N	7.33 E
Simnas	116	Jj	54.20N	23.45 E
Simo	114	Fd	65.39N	24.55 E
Simojärvi	114	Gc	66.06N	27.03 E
Simojoki	114	Fd	65.37N	25.03 E
Simojovel de Allende	192	Mi	17.12N	92.38W
Simonstown	172	Bf	34.14S	18.26 E
Simpele	114	Gf	61.26N	29.22 E
Simpelejärvi	116	Mc	61.30N	29.25 E
Simplon Pass	128	Bd	46.15N	8.00 E
Simpson Desert	208	Eg	25.00S	137.00 E
Simpson Hill	212	Fe	26.30S	126.30 E
Simpson Peninsula	180	Ic	68.45N	89.10W
Simrishamn	114	Di	55.33N	14.20 E
Simsonbaai	197b	Ab	18.02N	63.08W
Simušir, ostrov-	140	Re	46.58N	152.02 E
Sina	148	Fe	17.22N	75.54 E
Sīnā'=Sinai Peninsula (EN)	158	Kf	29.30N	34.00 E
Sinabang	150	Cf	2.29N	96.23 E
Sinadaqo	168	Hd	5.22N	46.22 E
Sinai, Mount- (EN)=Mūsa, Jabal-	146	Eh	28.32N	33.59 E
Sinaia	130	Id	45.21N	25.33 E
Sinai Peninsula (EN)= Sīnā'	158	Kf	29.30N	34.00 E
Sinajana	220c	Bb	13.28N	144.45W
Sinaloa [2]	190	Cc	25.00N	107.30W
Sinaloa, Llanos de-	190	Cc	25.00N	107.30W
Sinaloa, Río-	192	Ee	25.18N	108.30W
Sinaloa de Leyva	192	Ee	25.50N	108.14W
Sinalunga	128	Fg	43.12N	11.44 E
Sinamaica	202	Da	11.05N	71.51W
Sinan	152	If	27.56N	108.11 E
Sinara	134	Kh	56.17N	62.23 E
Sīnāwin	164	Bc	31.02N	10.36 E
Sinazongwe	170	Ef	17.15S	27.28 E
Şincai	130	Hc	46.39N	24.23 E
Sincanli	146	Dc	38.45N	30.15 E
Sincé	194	Ji	9.14N	75.06W
Sincelejo	200	Ie	9.18N	75.24W
Sinch'am	154	Jc	42.07N	129.25 E
Sinch'ang	154	Jd	40.07N	128.28 E
Sinch'on	154	He	38.28N	125.27 E
Sinclair, Lake-	184	Fi	33.11N	83.16W
Sind [3]	148	Dc	25.30N	69.00 E
Sind	140	Ig	25.30N	69.00 E
Sindal	116	Dg	57.28N	10.13 E
Sindangbarang	150	Eh	7.27S	107.08 E
Sindara	170	Bc	1.02S	10.40 E
Sindfeld	124	Kc	51.32N	8.48 E
Sindi	114	Fg	58.24N	24.42 E
Sındırgı	146	Cc	39.14N	28.10 E
Sindirgi Geçidi	130	Lj	39.10N	28.04 E
Sîndominic	130	Ic	46.35N	25.47 E
Sindri	148	Hd	23.42N	86.29 E
Sinegorje	138	Kd	62.03N	150.25 E
Šine-Ider	152	Gb	48.56N	99.33 E
Sinekli	130	Lh	41.14N	28.12 E
Sinelnikovo	132	Ie	48.18N	35.31 E
Sines	126	Dg	37.57N	8.52W
Sines, Cabo de-	126	Dg	37.57N	8.53W
Sine-Saloum [3]	166	Bc	14.00N	15.50W
Singako	168	Bd	9.50N	19.29 E
Singapore / Singapura [1]	142	Mi	1.17N	103.51 E
Singapore Strait (EN)= Singapura, Selat-	150	Df	1.15N	104.00 E
Singapura / Singapore [1]	142	Mi	1.17N	103.51 E
Singapura, Selat-= Singapore Strait (EN)	150	Df	1.15N	104.00 E
Singaraja	150	Gh	8.07S	115.06 E
Singatoka	219d	Ac	18.08S	177.30 E
Sing Buri	148	Kf	14.53N	100.25 E
Singen	120	Ei	47.46N	8.50 E
Sîngeroz Băi	130	Hb	47.22N	24.41 E
Singida	160	Ki	4.49S	34.45 E
Singida [3]	170	Fd	5.30S	34.30 E
Singitic Gulf (EN) = Singitikós Kólpos	130	Gi	40.10N	23.55 E
Singitikós Kólpos = Singitic Gulf (EN)	130	Gi	40.10N	23.55 E
Singkaling Hkamti	148	Jc	26.00N	95.42 E
Singkang	150	Hg	4.08S	120.01 E
Singkawang	150	Ef	0.54N	109.00 E
Singkep, Pulau-	150	Dg	0.30S	104.25 E
Singkil	150	Cf	2.17N	97.49 E
Singleton [Austl.]	212	Kf	32.34S	151.10 E
Singleton [Eng.-U.K.]	124	Bd	50.55N	0.44W
Singleton, Mount-	212	De	29.28S	117.18 E
Singö	116	Hd	60.10N	18.45 E
Siniscola	128	Dj	40.34N	9.41 E
Sini vrăh	130	Ih	41.51N	25.01 E
Sinj	128	Kg	43.42N	16.38 E
Sinjah	168	Ec	13.09N	33.56 E
Sinjai	150	Hh	5.07S	120.15 E
Sinjaja	116	Mg	57.05N	28.33 E
Sinjajevina	130	Cf	43.00N	19.18 E
Sinjār	146	Id	36.19N	41.52 E
Sinjār, Jabal-	146	Id	36.23N	41.52 E
Sinjuža	132	Ge	48.03N	30.50 E
Sinkiang Uighur (EN) = Xinjiang Uygur Zizhiqu (Hsin-chiang-wei-wu-erh Tzu-chih-ch'ü) [2]	152	Ec	42.00N	86.00 E
Sin-le-Noble	124	Fd	50.22N	3.07 E
Sinmi-Do	154	He	39.33N	124.53 E
Sinn	124	Kd	50.39N	8.20 E
Sinn al Kadhdhāb	164	Fe	23.30N	32.05 E
Sinnamary	202	Hb	5.23N	53.00W
Sinni	128	Kj	40.08N	16.41 E
Sînnicolau Mare	130	Dc	46.05N	20.38 E
Sinnūris	146	Dh	29.25N	30.52 E
Sinnyŏng	154	Jf	36.02N	128.47 E
Sinoe [3]	166	Dd	5.20N	8.40W
Sinoe, Lacul-	130	Le	44.38N	28.53 E
Sinop	144	Ea	41.59N	35.09 E
Sinop Burun	146	Fa	42.02N	35.12 E
Sinp'o	154	Jd	40.02N	128.12 E
Sinsang	154	Ie	39.39N	127.25 E
Sinsheim	120	Eg	49.15N	8.53 E
Sint-Amandsberg, Gent-	124	Fc	51.04N	3.45 E
Sîntana	130	Ec	46.21N	21.30 E
Sint-Andries, Brugge-	124	Fc	51.12N	3.10 E
Sintang	150	Ff	0.04N	111.30 E
Sint Eustatius	190	Le	17.30N	62.59W
Sint-Gillis-Waas	124	Gc	51.13N	4.08 E
Sint Kruis	196	Bf	12.18N	69.08W
Sint Laureins	124	Fc	51.15N	3.31 E
Sint Maarten	190	Le	18.04N	63.04W
Sint Nicolaas	196	Bf	12.26N	69.55W
Sint Niklaas/Saint-Nicolas	122	Kc	51.10N	4.08 E
Sint-Oedenrode	124	Hc	51.34N	5.28 E
Sinton	186	Hl	28.02N	97.33W
Sint-Pieters-Leeuw	124	Gd	50.47N	4.14 E
Sintra	126	Cf	38.48N	9.23W
Sint-Truiden/Saint-Trond	122	Ld	50.49N	5.12 E
Sintu	168	Fd	8.12N	36.56 E
Sinú, Río-	194	Ji	9.24N	75.49W
Sinŭiju	142	Oe	40.06N	124.24 E
Sinujiif	168	Hd	8.30N	48.59 E
Sinzig	124	Jd	50.33N	7.15 E
Sió	120	Oj	46.23N	18.40 E
Siocon	150	He	7.42N	122.08 E
Siófok	120	Oj	46.54N	18.03 E
Sioma	170	Df	16.40S	23.35 E
Sion/Sitten	128	Bd	46.15N	7.20 E
Siorapaluk	179	Ec	77.39N	71.00W
Sioule	122	Jh	46.22N	3.19 E
Sioux City	176	Je	42.30N	96.23W
Sioux Falls	176	Je	43.32N	96.44W
Sioux Lookout	180	If	50.06N	91.55W
Sipalay	150	He	9.45N	122.24 E
Šipan	128	Lh	42.43N	17.54 E
Siparia	196	Fg	10.08N	61.30W
Šipčenski prohod	130	Ig	42.46N	25.19 E
Siping	142	Oe	43.11N	124.24 E
Sipiwesk	180	He	55.27N	97.24W
Sipiwesk Lake	180	He	55.05N	97.35W
Siple, Mount-	222	Nf	73.15S	126.06W
Siple Coast	222	Mg	82.00S	153.00W
Siple Island	222	Nf	73.39S	125.00W
Siple Station	222	Pf	75.55S	83.55W
Sipolilo	172	Ec	16.39S	30.42 E
Sipora, Pulau-	150	Cg	2.12S	99.40 E
Sippola	116	Ld	60.44N	27.00 E
Siqueira Campos	204	Hf	23.42S	49.50W
Siquia, Río-	194	Eg	12.09N	84.13W
Siquijor	150	He	9.13N	123.31 E
Siquisique	202	Ea	10.34N	69.42W

Index Symbols

[1] Independent Nation; [2] State, Region; [3] District, County; [4] Municipality; [5] Colony, Dependency; Continent; Physical Region; Historical or Cultural Region; Mount, Mountain; Volcano; Hill; Mountains, Mountain Range; Hills, Escarpment; Plateau, Upland; Pass, Gap; Plain, Lowland; Delta; Salt Flat; Valley, Canyon; Crater, Cave; Karst Features; Depression; Polder; Desert, Dunes; Forest, Woods; Heath, Steppe; Oasis; Cape, Point; Coast, Beach; Cliff; Peninsula; Isthmus; Sandbank; Island; Atoll; Rock, Reef; Islands, Archipelago; Rocks, Reefs; Coral Reef; Well, Spring; Geyser; River, Stream; Waterfall, Rapids; River Mouth, Estuary; Lake; Salt Lake; Intermittent Lake; Reservoir; Swamp, Pond; Canal; Glacier; Ice Shelf, Pack Ice; Ocean; Sea; Gulf, Bay; Strait, Fjord; Lagoon; Bank; Seamount; Tablemount; Ridge; Shelf; Basin; Escarpment, Sea Scarp; Fracture; Trench, Abyss; National Park, Reserve; Point of Interest; Recreation Site; Cave, Cavern; Historic Site; Ruins; Wall, Walls; Church, Abbey; Temple; Scientific Station; Railway station; Airport; Port; Military installation; Lighthouse; Mine; Tunnel; Dam, Bridge

Šira	138	Ef	54.29N	90.02 E
Sira	114	Bg	58.25N	6.38 E
Sira ∿	116	Bf	58.17N	6.24 E
Şīr Abū Nu'Ayr ◆	146	Pj	25.13N	54.13 E
Si Racha	148	Kf	13.10N	100.57 E
Siracusa=Syracuse (EN)	112	Hh	37.04N	15.18 E
Sir Alexander, Mount - ▲	180	Ff	53.56N	120.23W
Sirasso	166	Dd	9.16N	6.06W
Şirāţ, Jabal- ⛰	164	Hf	17.00N	43.50 E
Sirba ∿	166	Fc	13.46N	1.40 E
Şīr Banī Yās ◆	146	Oj	24.19N	52.37 E
Sirdalen ⧗	116	Bf	58.50N	6.40 E
Sirdalsvatn ≈	116	Bf	58.35N	6.40 E
Sire [Eth.]	168	Fd	8.58N	37.00 E
Sire [Eth.]	168	Fd	8.16N	39.30 E
Sir Edward Pellew Group ❖	212	Hc	15.40 S	136.50 E
Siret	130	Jb	47.57N	26.04 E
Siret ∿	110	If	45.24N	28.01 E
Sirevåg	114	Ag	58.30N	5.47 E
Şirhān, Wādī as- ∿	144	Ec	30.30N	38.00 E
Şiria	130	Ec	46.16N	21.38 E
Sīrīk	144	Id	26.29N	57.09 E
Sirik, Tanjong- ►	150	Ff	2.46N	111.19 E
Sirina ◆	130	Jm	36.21N	26.41 E
Sirino ▲	128	Jj	40.07N	15.50 E
Sirius Seamount (EN) ⩟	178	Gf	52.00N	160.50W
Širjajevo	132	Gf	47.24N	30.13 E
Sir James Mac Brian, Mount- ▲	180	Ed	62.08N	127.40W
Sirjān, Kavīr-e- ◢	146	Ph	29.30N	55.30 E
Sirmione	128	Ee	45.29N	10.36 E
Şırnak	146	Jd	37.32N	42.28 E
Širokaja Pad	138	Jf	50.15N	142.11 E
Široki	138	Jd	63.04N	148.01 E
Širokoje	132	Hf	47.38N	33.14 E
Sironcha	148	Fe	18.50N	79.58 E
Síros ◆	130	Hl	37.26N	24.55 E
Sirpsindiği	130	Jh	41.50N	26.29 E
Sirr, Nafūd as- ◢	146	Kj	25.15N	44.45 E
Sirrayn ◆	164	Hf	19.38N	40.36 E
Sirretta Peak ▲	188	Fi	35.59N	118.20W
Sīrrī, Jazīreh-ye- ◆	146	Pj	25.55N	54.32 E
Sirsa	148	Fc	29.32N	75.01 E
Sir Sandford, Mount- ▲	188	Ga	51.40N	117.52W
Sirte Desert (EN)=As Sidrah ⧗	158	Ie	30.30N	17.30 E
Sir Thomas, Mount- ▲	212	Fe	27.11 S	129.46 E
Širvintos	114	Fi	55.03N	25.01 E
Sir Wilfrid Laurier, Mount - ▲	180	Ff	52.48N	119.45W
Sisak	128	Ke	45.29N	16.22 E
Si Sa Ket	148	Ke	15.07N	104.19 E
Sīsakht	146	Ng	30.47N	51.33 E
Sisal	192	Ng	21.10N	90.02W
Sisante	126	Je	39.25N	2.13W
Sisargas, Islas- ❖	126	Da	43.22N	8.50W
Šišchid-Gol ∿	152	Ga	51.30N	97.10 E
Sishen	172	Ce	27.55 S	22.59 E
Sishui	154	Dg	35.40N	117.17 E
Sisian	132	Oj	39.31N	46.03 E
Sisili ∿	166	Ec	10.16N	1.15W
Sisimiut/Holsteinsborg	224	Nc	67.05N	53.45W
Siskiyou Mountains ⛰	188	Df	41.55N	123.15W
Sisŏphŏn	148	Kf	13.35N	102.59 E
Sissano	214	Ch	3.00 S	142.03 E
Sisseton	186	Hd	45.40N	97.03W
Sissonne	124	Fe	49.34N	3.54 E
Sīstān=Seistan (EN) ⧗	140	If	30.30N	62.00 E
Sīstān-e Balūchestān [3]	144	Jd	28.30N	60.30 E
Sisteron	122	Lj	44.12N	5.56 E
Sisters	188	Ed	44.17N	121.33W
Sistranda	114	Be	63.43N	8.50 E
Sitāpur	148	Gc	27.34N	80.41 E
Sitasjaure ≈	114	Dc	68.00N	17.25 E
Siteki	172	Ee	26.27 S	31.57 E
Sitges	126	Nc	41.14N	1.49 E
Sithonía ◨	130	Gi	40.05N	23.55 E
Sitia	130	Jn	35.12N	26.07 E
Sitio d'Abadia	204	Ib	14.48 S	46.16W
Sitio Nuevo	194	Jh	10.46N	74.43W
Sitka	176	Fd	57.03N	135.14W
Sitkalidak ◆	178	Ie	57.10N	153.14W
Sitna ∿	130	Kb	47.30N	27.10 E
Sitnica ∿	130	Dg	42.53N	20.52 E
Sitona	168	Fc	14.23N	37.22 E
Sitrah [Bhr.]	146	Ni	26.10N	50.40 E
Sitrah [Eg.]	146	Bh	28.42N	26.54 E
Sittard	122	Ld	51.00N	5.53 E
Sittee Point ►	194	Ce	16.48N	88.15W
Sitten/Sion	128	Bd	46.15N	7.20 E
Sittingbourne	124	Cc	51.20N	0.45 E
Sittoung	148	Je	17.10N	96.58 E
Sittwe (Akyab)	142	Lg	20.09N	92.54 E
Siuna	194	Eg	13.44N	84.46W
Siuslaw River ∿	188	Cd	44.01N	124.08W
Siva ∿	114	Mh	56.49N	53.55 E
Sivac	130	Cd	45.42N	19.23 E
Sivaki	138	Hf	52.38N	126.45 E
Sīvan ∿	144	Hd	29.51N	52.46 E
Sivas	142	Ff	39.50N	37.03 E
Sivaš, ozero- ≈	132	Ig	45.50N	34.40 E
Sivasli	130	Mk	38.30N	29.42 E
Šiveluč, vulkan- ⋀	138	Le	56.33N	161.25 E
Sivera, ozero- / Sivera ezers ≈	116	Li	55.58N	27.25 E
Sivera ezers / Sivera, ozero- ≈	116	Li	55.58N	27.25 E
Siverek	144	Eb	37.45N	39.19 E
Siverski	114	Hg	59.22N	30.02 E
Sivomaskinski	134	Kc	66.40N	62.31 E
Sivrice	146	Hc	38.27N	39.19 E
Sivrihisar	146	Dc	39.27N	31.34 E
Sivry-Rance	124	Gd	50.10N	4.16 E
Sivry Rance-Rance	124	Gd	50.09N	4.16 E
Sivry-sur-Meuse	124	He	49.19N	5.16 E
Sīwah	160	Jf	29.12N	25.31 E
Sīwah, Wāḩāt-=Siwa Oasis (EN) Ψ	158	Jf	29.10N	25.40 E
Siwalik Range ⛰	140	Jg	29.00N	80.00 E
Siwān	148	Gc	26.13N	84.22 E
Siwa Oasis (EN)=Sīwah, Wāḩāt- Ψ	158	Jf	29.10N	25.40 E
Sixaola, Río- ∿	194	Fi	9.35N	82.34W
Six Cross Road	197q	Bb	13.07N	59.28W
Six-Fours-la-Plage	122	Lk	43.06N	5.51 E
Sixian	154	Dh	33.29N	117.53 E
Six Men's Bay ◐	197q	Ab	13.16N	59.38W
Sixth Cataract (EN)= Sablūkah, Ash Shallāl as- ⤓	158	Kg	16.20N	32.42 E
Siyah-Chaman	146	Ld	37.35N	47.10 E
Siyang (Zhongxing)	154	Eh	33.43N	118.40 E
Siziwang Qi (Ulan Hua)	154	Ad	41.31N	111.41 E
Sjælland=Zealand (EN) ◆	110	Hd	55.30N	11.45 E
Sjamozero, ozero- ≈	114	Hf	61.55N	33.15 E
Sjare/Sääre	116	Ig	57.57N	21.53 E
Sjas ∿	114	Hf	60.10N	32.31 E
Sjasstroj	114	Hf	60.09N	32.36 E
Šjašupe ∿	114	Fi	55.00N	22.10 E
Šjauljaj	112	Id	55.53N	23.19 E
Šjauljaj/Šiauliai	112	Id	55.53N	23.19 E
Sjenica	130	Df	43.16N	20.00 E
Sjnjaja ∿	138	Hd	61.00N	126.57 E
Sjoa ∿	116	Cc	61.41N	9.33 E
Sjöbo	116	Ei	55.38N	13.42 E
Sjøholt	114	Be	62.29N	6.50 E
Sjujutlijka ∿	130	Ig	42.17N	25.55 E
Sjun ∿	134	Gi	55.43N	54.17 E
Sjuøyane ❖	179	Ob	80.43N	20.45 E
Skadarsko jezero = Scutari, Lake- (EN) ≈	110	Hg	42.10N	19.20 E
Skadovsk	136	Df	46.07N	32.56 E
Skælskør	116	Di	55.15N	11.19 E
Skærbæk	116	Ci	55.09N	8.46 E
Skagatá ►	114a	Ba	66.07N	20.06W
Skagen	114	Ch	57.44N	10.36 E
Skagern ≈	116	Ff	59.00N	14.15 E
Skagerrak ≀	110	Gd	57.45N	9.00 E
Skaget ▲	116	Cc	61.17N	9.12 E
Skagit River ∿	188	Db	48.20N	122.25W
Skagway	176	Fd	59.28N	135.19W
Skaidi	114	Fa	70.26N	24.30 E
Skaland	114	Db	69.27N	17.18 E
Skälderviken ◐	116	Eh	56.20N	12.40 E
Skålevik	116	Bf	58.04N	8.00 E
Skalisty Golec, gora- [R.S.F.S.R.] ▲	138	Ie	55.55N	130.35 E
Skalisty Golec, gora- [R.S.F.S.R.] ▲	138	Ge	56.20N	119.10 E
Skanderborg	114	Bh	56.02N	9.56 E
Skåne ⧗	110	Hd	56.00N	13.30 E
Skånevik	116	Ae	59.44N	5.59 E
Skänninge	116	Ff	58.24N	15.05 E
Skanör	116	Ei	55.25N	12.52 E
Skántzoura ◆	130	Hj	39.05N	24.07 E
Skara	114	Cg	58.22N	13.25 E
Skaraborg [2]	114	Cg	58.20N	13.30 E
Skärblacka	116	Ff	58.34N	15.54 E
Skārdu	148	Fa	35.18N	75.37 E
Skärhamn	116	Dg	57.59N	11.33 E
Skarnes	116	Dd	60.15N	11.41 E
Skärplinge	114	Df	60.28N	17.46 E
Skarsstind ▲	116	Cb	62.03N	8.35 E
Skarsvåg	114	Fa	71.06N	25.56 E
Skarszewy	120	Ob	54.05N	18.27 E
Skarvdalsegga ▲	116	Cb	62.09N	8.03 E
Skaryszew	120	Re	51.19N	21.15 E
Skarżysko-Kamienna	120	Qe	51.08N	20.53 E
Skasøy ◆	116	Ca	63.20N	8.35 E
Skăt ∿	130	Gf	43.44N	23.51 E
Skattkärr	116	Ee	59.25N	13.41 E
Skattungbyn	116	Fc	61.12N	14.52 E
Skaudvilė/Skaudvile	114	Fi	55.27N	22.33 E
Skaudvile/Skaudvilė	114	Fi	55.27N	22.33 E
Skaulen ▲	116	Be	59.38N	6.35 E
Skawa ∿	120	Pf	50.02N	19.26 E
Skawina	120	Pg	49.59N	19.49 E
Skee	116	Df	58.56N	11.19 E
Skeena ∿	174	Fd	54.09N	130.02W
Skeena Mountains ⛰	180	Ee	56.45N	128.40W
Skegness	118	Nh	53.10N	0.21 E
Skeidararsandur ☰	114a	Cc	63.54N	17.14W
Skeldon	202	Gb	5.53N	57.08W
Skeleton Coast ☰	172	Ac	17.50 S	12.45 E
Skellefteå	112	Ic	64.46N	20.57 E
Skellefteälven ∿	110	Ic	64.42N	21.06 E
Skelleftehamn	114	Ed	64.41N	21.14 E
Skëndërbeut, Mali i- ▲	130	Ch	41.35N	19.50 E
Skene	116	Eg	57.29N	12.38 E
Skerki Bank (EN) ⊟	162	Jb	37.45N	10.50 E
Skerries/Na Sceiri	118	Gh	53.35N	6.07W
Skerryvore ✳	118	Fe	56.20N	7.05W
Skhíza ◆	130	Em	36.44N	21.46 E
Skhoinoúsa ◆	130	Im	36.50N	25.30 E
Ski	114	Cg	59.43N	10.50 E
Skiathos	130	Gj	39.10N	23.29 E
Skiathos ◆	130	Gj	39.10N	23.28 E
Skibbereen/An Sciobairin	118	Dj	51.33N	9.15W
Skibotn	114	Eb	69.24N	20.16 E
Skidel	132	Dc	53.38N	24.17 E
Skien	112	Gd	59.12N	9.36 E
Skierniewice	120	Qe	51.58N	20.08 E
Skierniewice [2]	120	Qe	52.00N	20.10 E
Skiftet/Kihti ≀	116	Id	60.15N	21.05 E
Skikda	160	He	36.52N	6.54 E
Skikda [3]	162	Ib	36.45N	6.50 E
Skillet Fork ∿	186	Lg	38.08N	88.07W
Skillingaryd	116	Fg	57.26N	14.05 E
Skinári, Ákra- ►	130	Dl	37.56N	20.42 E
Skinnskatteberg	116	Fe	59.50N	15.41 E
Skipton	118	Kh	53.58N	2.01W
Skiptvet	116	De	59.28N	11.11 E
Skiropoúla ◆	130	Hk	38.50N	24.21 E
Skiros	130	Hk	38.54N	24.34 E
Skiros ◆	130	Hk	38.53N	24.32 E
Skive	114	Bh	56.34N	9.02 E
Skive Å ∿	116	Ch	56.34N	9.04 E
Skjærhalden	116	De	59.02N	11.02 E
Skjåk	116	Cc	61.52N	8.22 E
Skjálfandafljót ∿	114a	Cb	65.59N	17.38W
Skjeberg	116	De	59.14N	11.12 E
Skjern	114	Bi	55.57N	8.30 E
Skjern Å ∿	114	Bi	55.55N	8.24 E
Skjervøy	114	Ea	70.02N	20.59 E
Skjoldungen	179	Hf	63.20N	41.20W
Sklad	138	Hb	71.52N	123.35 E
Šklov	132	Gb	54.14N	30.18 E
Skobeleva, pik- ▲	135	Ie	39.51N	72.47 E
Skœrfjorden ≀	179	Kc	77.30N	19.10W
Škofja Loka	128	Id	46.10N	14.18 E
Skog	116	Gc	61.10N	16.55 E
Skógafoss ⤓	114a	Bc	63.32N	19.31W
Skoghall	116	Ee	59.19N	13.26 E
Skogshorn ▲	116	Cd	60.53N	8.42 E
Skokie	186	Me	42.02N	87.46W
Skole	120	Th	48.58N	23.32 E
Skópelos	130	Gj	39.07N	23.44 E
Skópelos ◆	130	Gj	39.10N	23.40 E
Skopí	130	Jn	35.11N	26.02 E
Skopin	114	Jj	53.52N	39.37 E
Skopje	112	Ig	42.00N	21.29 E
Skórcz	120	Oc	53.48N	18.32 E
Skorovatn	114	Cd	64.39N	13.07 E
Skorpa ◆	116	Ac	61.35N	4.50 E
Skørping	116	Ch	56.50N	9.53 E
Skorpiós ◆	130	Dk	38.42N	20.45 E
Škotovo	154	Lc	43.20N	132.21 E
Skotselv	116	Ce	59.51N	9.53 E
Skoura	162	Fc	31.04N	6.43W
Skövde	114	Cg	58.24N	13.50 E
Skovorodino	142	Od	53.59N	123.55 E
Skowhegan	184	Mc	44.46N	69.43W
Skradin	128	Jg	43.49N	15.56 E
Skreia	116	Dd	60.39N	10.56 E
Skreia ▲	116	Dd	60.34N	11.04 E
Skrekken ▲	116	Bd	60.13N	7.49 E
Skridulaupen ▲	116	Bc	61.55N	7.35 E
Skrimkolla ▲	116	Cb	62.23N	9.04 E
Skriveri/Skrīveri	116	Kh	56.37N	25.10 E
Skrīveri/Skriveri	116	Kh	56.37N	25.10 E
Skrunda	114	Eh	56.41N	22.00 E
Skrwa ∿	120	Pd	52.33N	19.32 E
Skudenesfjorden ≀	116	Ae	59.05N	5.20 E
Skudeneshavn	114	Ag	59.09N	5.17 E
Skuodas	114	Eh	56.17N	21.31 E
Skurup	116	Ei	55.28N	13.30 E
Skutskär	116	Gd	60.38N	17.25 E
Skvira	132	Fe	49.44N	29.42 E
Skwierzyna	120	Ld	52.35N	15.30 E
Skye, Island of- ◆	110	Fd	57.15N	6.10W
Slagelse	114	Ci	55.24N	11.22 E
Slagnäs	114	Ed	65.36N	18.10 E
Slamet, Gunung- ▲	140	Mj	7.14 S	109.12 E
Slaná ∿	120	Ri	47.56N	21.08 E
Slancy	136	Cd	59.08N	28.02 E
Slaney/An tSláine ∿	118	Gi	52.21N	6.30W
Slănic	130	Id	45.15N	25.56 E
Slănic Moldova	130	Jc	46.12N	26.26 E
Slannik ⧗	130	Jf	43.06N	26.13 E
Slano	128	Lh	42.47N	17.54 E
Slaný	120	Kf	50.14N	14.06 E
Śląsk=Silesia (EN) ⧗	110	He	51.00N	16.45 E
Śląsk=Silesia (EN) ▣	120	Me	51.00N	16.45 E
Śląska, Wyżyna- ⏏	120	Of	50.28N	18.40 E
Slate Islands ❖	186	Mb	48.34N	86.45W
Slatina	130	He	44.26N	24.22 E
Slatina ∿	120	Ph	48.32N	19.10 E
Slaton	186	Fj	33.26N	101.39W
Slave Coast ☰	158	Hh	6.00N	3.30 E
Slave Lake	180	Ge	55.17N	114.46W
Slave River ∿	174	Hc	61.18N	113.39W
Slavgorod [Bye.-U.S.S.R.]	132	Gc	53.27N	31.01 E
Slavgorod [R.S.F.S.R.]	138	Cf	53.03N	78.48 E
Slavičin	120	Ng	49.06N	17.53 E
Slavjanka	138	Ih	42.55N	131.20 E
Slavjanka ▲	130	Gh	41.23N	23.36 E
Slavjansk	112	Jf	48.52N	37.37 E
Slavjansk-na-Kubani	136	Df	45.15N	38.08 E
Slavkoje	120	Th	48.45N	23.31 E
Slavkoviči	116	Mg	57.37N	29.10 E
Slavonia (EN) = Slavonija ⧗	110	Hf	45.00N	18.00 E
Slavonia (EN)=Slavonija ▣	128	Le	45.00N	18.00 E
Slavonija =' Slavonia (EN) ⧗	110	Hf	45.00N	18.00 E
Slavonija=Slavonia (EN) ▣	128	Le	45.00N	18.00 E
Slavonska Požega	128	Le	45.20N	17.41 E
Slavonski Brod	128	Me	45.09N	18.02 E
Slavsk	116	Ii	55.01N	21.37 E
Slavuta	136	Ce	50.18N	26.52 E
Sława	120	Me	51.53N	16.04 E
Sławatycze	120	Te	51.43N	23.30 E
Sławno	120	Mb	54.22N	16.40 E
Slayton	186	Id	44.01N	95.45W
Sleaford	118	Mh	53.00N	0.24W
Slea Head/Ceann Sléibhe ►	118	Ci	52.06N	10.27W
Sleat, Sound of- ≀	118	Hd	57.10N	5.50W
Sleen	124	Ib	52.47N	6.49 E
Sleeper Islands ❖	180	Je	57.25N	79.50W
Sléibhte Chill Mhantáin/ Wicklow Mountains ⛰	118	Gh	53.02N	6.24W
Sleidinge, Evergem-	124	Fc	51.08N	3.41 E
Slesin	120	Od	52.23N	18.19 E
Slessor Glacier ❄	222	Af	79.50 S	28.30W
Slessor Peak ▲	222	Qe	66.31 S	64.58W
Slettefjell ▲	116	Cc	61.13N	8.44 E
Sletterhage ►	116	Dh	56.06N	10.31 E
Ślęża ▲	120	Mf	50.52N	16.45 E
Ślęża ∿	120	Me	51.10N	16.58 E
Sliabh Bearnach/Slieve Bernagh ▲	118	Ei	52.50N	8.35W
Sliabh Bladhma/Slieve Bloom ▲	118	Fh	53.10N	7.35W
Sliabh Eachtaí/Slieve Aughty ▲	118	Eh	53.10N	8.30W
Sliabh Gamh ▲	118	Eg	54.10N	8.50W
Sliabh Gamh/Ox or Slieve Gamph Mountains ▲	118	Eg	54.10N	8.50W
Sliabh Mis/Slieve Mish ▲	118	Di	52.10N	9.50W
Sliabh Speirin/Sperrin Mountains ⛰	118	Fg	54.50N	7.05W
Slidell	186	Lk	30.17N	89.47W
Slide Mountain ▲	184	Jd	42.00N	74.23W
Slidre ⧗	116	Cc	61.10N	9.00 E
Sliedrecht	124	Gc	51.50N	4.46 E
Slieve Aughty/Sliabh Eachtaí ▲	118	Eh	53.10N	8.30W
Slieve Bernagh/Sliabh Bearnach ▲	118	Ei	52.50N	8.35W
Slieve Bloom/Sliabh Bladhma ▲	118	Fh	53.10N	7.35W
Slievekimalta ▲	118	Ei	52.45N	8.15W
Slieve Mish/Sliabh Mis ▲	118	Di	52.10N	9.50W
Sligeach/Sligo	112	Fe	54.17N	8.28W
Sligeach/Sligo [2]	118	Eg	54.10N	8.40W
Sligo/Sligeach	112	Fe	54.17N	8.28W
Sligo/Sligeach [2]	118	Eg	54.10N	8.40W
Sligo Bay/Cuan Shligigh ◐	118	Eg	54.20N	8.40W
Slinge ∿	124	Ib	52.08N	6.31 E
Slingebeek ∿	124	Ic	51.59N	6.18 E
Slite	116	Hg	57.43N	18.48 E
Sliven	130	Jg	42.40N	26.19 E
Sliven [2]	130	Jg	42.40N	26.19 E
Slivnica	130	Gg	42.51N	23.02 E
Sljudjanka	138	Ff	51.38N	103.40 E
Slobodka	130	Mb	47.54N	29.12 E
Slobodskoj	136	Fd	58.47N	50.12 E
Slobodzeja	132	Ff	46.43N	29.43 E
Slobozia [Rom.]	130	Ke	44.34N	27.22 E
Slobozia [Rom.]	130	Ie	44.30N	25.11 E
Slochteren	124	Ia	53.12N	6.50 E
Slocum Mountain ▲	188	Gi	35.18N	117.13W
Slonim	136	Ce	53.05N	25.18 E
Sloten	124	Hb	52.54N	5.40 E
Slotermeer ≈	124	Hb	52.55N	5.40 E
Slough	118	Mj	51.31N	0.36W
Slovakia (EN)= Slovensko ⧗	110	Hf	48.45N	19.30 E
Slovakia (EN)= Slovensko ▣	120	Ph	48.45N	19.30 E
Slovečna ∿	132	Fd	51.41N	29.42 E
Slovenia (EN) = Slovenija [2]	128	Id	46.00N	15.00 E
Slovenia (EN) = Slovenija ⧗	110	Hf	46.00N	15.00 E
Slovenia (EN) = Slovenija ▣	128	Id	46.00N	15.00 E
Slovenija=Slovenia (EN) [2]	128	Id	46.00N	15.00 E
Slovenija = Slovenia (EN) ⧗	110	Hf	46.00N	15.00 E
Slovenija = Slovenia (EN) ▣	128	Id	46.00N	15.00 E
Slovenska Bistrica	128	Jd	46.24N	15.34 E
Slovenske Gorice ⛰	128	Jd	46.35N	15.55 E
Slovenské rudohorie ⛰	120	Ph	48.45N	20.00 E
Slovensko [2]	120	Ph	48.45N	19.30 E
Slovensko=Slovakia (EN) ⧗	110	Hf	48.45N	19.30 E
Slovensko=Slovakia (EN) ▣	120	Ph	48.45N	19.30 E
Slovenský kras ⛰	120	Qh	48.35N	20.40 E
Słubice	120	Kd	52.20N	14.35 E
Sluč [Bye.-U.S.S.R.] ∿	132	Ec	52.08N	27.32 E
Sluč [Ukr.-U.S.S.R.] ∿	132	Ed	51.37N	26.38 E
Sluck	136	Ce	53.02N	27.31 E
Slunj	128	Je	45.07N	15.35 E
Słupca	120	Nd	52.19N	17.52 E
Słupia ∿	120	Mb	54.35N	16.50 E
Słupsk	120	Nb	54.28N	17.01 E
Słupsk [2]	120	Mb	54.30N	17.00 E
Sly ∿	126	Nh	36.06N	1.08 E
Småland ▣	114	Dh	57.20N	15.05 E
Smålandsfarvandet ◐	116	Di	55.06N	11.20 E
Smålandsstenar	116	Eg	57.10N	13.24 E
Smalininkai/Smalininkaj	116	Ji	55.01N	22.32 E
Smalininkaj/Smalininkai	116	Ji	55.01N	22.32 E
Smallingerland-Drachten	122	Ma	53.06N	6.05 E
Smallwood Reservoir ⊡	174	Md	54.00N	64.30W
Smederevo	130	De	44.39N	20.56 E
Smederevska Palanka	130	De	44.22N	20.58 E
Smedjebacken	114	Df	60.08N	15.25 E
Smela	136	Df	49.13N	31.53 E
Smidovič	138	Ig	48.36N	133.50 E
Šmidta, ostrov- ◆	140	La	81.08N	90.48 E
Šmidta, poluostrov- ◨	138	Jf	54.15N	142.40 E
Śmigiel	120	Md	52.01N	16.32 E
Smilde	124	Ib	52.56N	6.28 E
Smiltene	114	Fh	57.28N	25.56 E
Smirnovo	134	Ni	54.31N	69.28 E
Smirnyh	138	Jg	49.45N	142.53 E
Smith	204	Bl	35.30 S	61.36W
Smith Arm ◐	180	Fc	66.15N	124.00W
Smith Bay [Ak.-U.S.] ◐	178	Ib	70.51N	154.25W
Smith Bay [Can.] ◐	180	Ja	77.15N	79.00W
Smith Center	186	Gg	39.47N	98.47W
Smithers	180	Ef	54.47N	127.10W
Smithfield [S.Afr.]	172	Df	30.09 S	26.30 E
Smithfield [Ut.-U.S.]	188	Jf	41.50N	111.50W
Smith Mountain Lake ≈	184	Hg	37.10N	79.40W
Smith Peak ▲	188	Gb	48.50N	116.39W
Smith River ∿	188	Jc	47.25N	111.29W
Smiths Falls	180	Jh	44.54N	76.01W
Smith's Knoll ⊟	118	Pi	52.50N	2.10 E
Smith Sound ◐	188	Ba	51.18N	127.48W
Smithton	210	Fi	40.51 S	145.07 E
Smjadovo	130	Kf	43.04N	27.01 E
Smjörfjoll ▲	114a	Cb	65.35N	14.46W
Smögen	116	Df	58.21N	11.13 E
Smoke Creek Desert ◢	188	Ff	40.30N	119.40W
Smokey Dome ▲	188	He	43.29N	114.56W
Smoky Bay ◐	212	Gf	32.20 S	133.45 E
Smoky Cape ►	212	Kf	30.56 S	153.05 E
Smoky Falls	180	Jf	50.03N	82.10W
Smoky Hill ∿	174	Jf	39.03N	96.48W
Smoky Hills ⛰	186	Gg	39.15N	99.00W
Smoky River ∿	180	Fe	56.11N	117.19W
Smøla ◆	114	Be	63.25N	8.00 E
Smolensk	112	Je	54.47N	32.03 E
Smolenskaja oblast [3]	136	De	55.00N	33.00 E
Smolenskaja vozvyšennost = Smolensk Upland (EN) ⏏	110	Je	54.40N	33.00 E
Smolensko, oblast de- (E) [3]	136	De	55.00N	33.00 E
Smolensk Upland (EN) = Smolenskaja vozvyšennost ⏏	110	Je	54.40N	33.00 E
Smolevičí	132	Fb	54.03N	28.02 E
Smolianica	120	Ud	52.40N	24.40 E
Smólikas Óros ▲	110	Ig	40.06N	20.55 E
Smoljan	130	Hh	41.35N	24.41 E
Smoljan [2]	130	Hh	41.40N	24.40 E
Smooth Rock Falls	184	Ga	49.20N	81.39W
Smorgon	136	Ce	54.31N	26.23 E
Smørstabbren ▲	116	Cc	61.32N	8.06 E
Smrdeš ⛰	130	Fh	41.34N	22.28 E
Smygehamn	116	Ei	55.21N	13.22 E
Smygehuk ►	116	Ei	55.21N	13.23 E
Smyley, Cape- ►	222	Qf	72.00 S	78.50W
Smyrna	184	Ei	33.53N	84.31W
Smyrna → İzmir	142	Ef	38.25N	27.09 E
Smyšljajevka	114	Mj	53.17N	50.24 E
Smythe, Mount- ▲	174	Gd	57.50N	124.59W
Snacke Point ►	197b	Bb	18.17N	62.58W
Snæfell ▲	114a	Cb	64.48N	15.34W
Snaefell ▲	118	Ig	54.16N	4.27W
Snæfellsjökull ▲	114a	Ab	64.49N	23.46W
Snag	180	Dd	62.23N	140.22W
Snake Bay Settlement	212	Gb	11.25 S	130.40 E
Snake Range ⛰	188	Hg	39.00N	114.15W
Snake River [Can.] ∿	180	Ec	65.57N	134.13W
Snake River [U.S.] ∿	174	He	46.12N	119.02W
Snake River Plain ▭	182	Ec	42.45N	114.30W
Snare ∿	180	Fd	63.15N	116.08W
Snares Islands ❖	216	Ci	48.00 S	166.35 E
Snarumselva ∿	116	Cd	59.57N	9.58 E
Snåsa	114	Cd	64.15N	12.22 E
Sneek	122	La	53.02N	5.40 E
Snekermeer ≈	122	La	53.04N	5.40 E
Snežnaja, gora- ▲	138	Lc	65.18N	165.30 E
Snežnik ▲	128	Ie	45.26N	14.36 E
Snežnogorsk	138	Dc	68.15N	87.35 E
Šnežnoje	132	Kf	47.59N	38.50 E
Śniardwy, Jezioro- ≈	120	Rc	53.46N	21.44 E
Śnieżka ▲	110	He	50.45N	15.43 E
Śnieżnik ▲	120	Mf	50.12N	16.50 E
Snigirevka	132	Hf	47.04N	32.45 E
Snillfjord	116	Ca	63.24N	9.30 E
Snina	120	Sh	48.59N	22.08 E
Snizort, Loch- ≀	118	Gd	57.30N	6.25W
Snjatyn	132	De	48.29N	25.34 E
Snøhetta ▲	110	Gc	62.20N	9.17 E
Snohomish	188	Dc	47.55N	122.06W
Snønuten ▲	116	Be	59.31N	6.54 E
Snøonipa ▲	116	Bc	61.42N	6.41 E
Snota ∿	116	Cb	62.51N	9.06 E
Snov ∿	132	Gd	51.32N	31.33 E
Snowbird Lake ≈	180	Hd	60.40N	102.50W
Snowdon ▲	110	Fe	53.04N	4.05W
Snowdonia ⧗	118	Jh	53.05N	3.55W
Snowdrift	180	Gd	62.23N	110.47W
Snowflake	188	Ji	34.30N	110.05W
Snow Hill	184	Jf	38.11N	75.24W
Snow Lake	180	Hf	54.53N	100.02W
Snow Mountain ▲	182	Cd	39.23N	122.46W
Snowshoe Peak ▲	188	Hb	48.13N	115.41W
Snowville	188	If	41.58N	112.43W
Snowy Mountain [N.Amer.] ▲	188	Fb	49.02N	119.57W
Snowy Mountain [N.Y.-U.S.] ▲	184	Jd	43.42N	74.23W
Snowy Mountains ⛰	212	Jg	36.30 S	148.20 E
Snowy River ∿	212	Jg	37.48 S	148.32 E
Snudy, ozero- ≈	116	Li	55.40N	27.15 E
Snug Corner	194	Kb	22.32N	73.53W
Snuŏl	148	Lf	12.04N	106.26 E
Snyder	182	Ge	32.44N	100.55W
Soalala	172	Hc	16.07 S	45.21 E
Soalara	172	Gd	23.35 S	43.44 E
Soanierana-Ivongo	172	Hc	16.54 S	49.34 E
Soar ∿	124	Ab	52.52N	1.17W
Şoarş	130	Hd	45.56N	24.55 E
Soavinandriana	172	Hc	19.10 S	46.43 E
Sob [R.S.F.S.R.] ∿	134	Mc	66.20N	66.02 E
Sob [Ukr.-U.S.S.R.] ∿	132	Fe	48.41N	29.17 E
Soba	166	Gc	10.59N	8.04 E
Sobaek-Sanmaek ⛰	154	Jf	36.00N	128.00 E
Sobat (EN)=Sawbā ∿	158	Kh	9.45N	31.45 E
Sobernheim	124	Je	49.48N	7.39 E
Soběslav	120	Kg	49.16N	14.44 E
Sōbetsu	156a	Bb	42.33N	140.51 E
Sobinka	114	Jh	56.01N	40.07 E
Sobolevo [R.S.F.S.R.]	132	Qd	51.59N	51.48 E
Sobolevo [R.S.F.S.R.]	138	Kf	54.17N	156.00 E
Sobolew	120	Re	51.41N	21.40 E
Sobo-San ▲	156	Be	32.47N	131.21 E
Sobradinho	204	Fi	29.24 S	53.03W
Sobral	200	Lf	3.42 S	40.21W
Sobrarbe ⧗	126	Mb	42.20N	0.05 E
Soca	204	El	34.41 S	55.41W
Soča=Isonzo (EN) ∿	128	He	45.43N	13.33 E
Sochaczew	120	Qd	52.14N	20.14 E
Soči	112	Jg	43.35N	39.45 E
Société, Iles de la-=Society Islands (EN) ❖	208	Lf	17.00 S	150.00W
Society Islands (EN)= Société, Iles de la- ❖	208	Lf	17.00 S	150.00W
Socompa, Paso- ⊔	198	Jh	24.27 S	68.18W
Socorro [Col.]	202	Db	6.27N	73.16W

Index Symbols

[1] Independent Nation	▣ Historical or Cultural Region	⊔ Pass, Gap	⌣ Depression	☰ Coast, Beach	✳ Rock, Reef	⤓ Waterfall, Rapids	═ Canal	⊚ Lagoon	◤ Escarpment, Sea Scarp	⛫ Historic Site	✈ Airport
[2] State, Region	▲ Mount, Mountain	▭ Plain, Lowland	⊞ Polder	◧ Cliff	❖ Islands, Archipelago	⊻ River Mouth, Estuary	❄ Glacier	⊟ Bank	⌇ Fracture	⁖ Ruins	⚓ Port
[3] District, County	⋀ Volcano	◣ Delta	◢ Desert, Dunes	◨ Peninsula	✴ Rocks, Reefs	≈ Lake	❅ Ice Shelf, Pack Ice	⩟ Seamount	⊽ Trench, Abyss	▥ Wall, Walls	⊛ Military installation
[4] Municipality	△ Hill	▤ Salt Flat	♣ Forest, Woods	⋈ Isthmus	✿ Coral Reef	⊜ Salt Lake	≋ Ocean	⊼ Tablemount	⚑ National Park, Reserve	✝ Church, Abbey	⚐ Lighthouse
[5] Colony, Dependency	⛰ Mountains, Mountain Range	∨ Valley, Canyon	⋎ Heath, Steppe	▦ Sandbank	⊙ Well, Spring	◯ Intermittent Lake	~ Sea	⋏ Ridge	▼ Point of Interest	⛩ Temple	⚒ Mine
■ Continent	⌓ Hills, Escarpment	◡ Crater, Cave	Ψ Oasis	◆ Island	♨ Geyser	⊡ Reservoir	◐ Gulf, Bay	⊓ Shelf	↑ Recreation Site	⊠ Scientific Station	∩ Tunnel
⧗ Physical Region	⏏ Plateau, Upland	✲ Karst Features	► Cape, Point	◎ Atoll	∿ River, Stream	⩩ Swamp, Pond	≀ Strait, Fjord	⊍ Basin	◖ Cave, Cavern	⧆ Railway station	⌿ Dam, Bridge

Socorro [N.M.-U.S.] 182 Fe 34.04N 106.54W
Socorro, Isla- 190 Be 18.45N 110.58W
Socotra (EN) = Suquṭrá 140 Hh 12.30N 54.00 E
Soc Trang 148 Lg 9.36N 105.58 E
Socuéllamos 126 Je 39.17N 2.48W
Sodankylä 114 Gc 67.25N 26.36 E
Soda Springs 188 Je 42.39N 111.36W
Söderåsen 116 Eh 56.04N 13.05 E
Söderfors 114 Df 60.23N 17.14 E
Söderhamn 114 Df 61.18N 17.03 E
Söderköping 116 Gf 58.29N 16.18 E
Södermanland [2] 114 Dg 59.15N 16.40 E
Södermanland 116 Ge 59.10N 16.50 E
Söderslätt 116 Ei 55.30N 13.15 E
Södertälje 114 Dg 59.12N 17.37 E
Södertörn 116 Ge 59.05N 18.00 E
Sodo 168 Fd 6.51N 37.45 E
Södra Dellen 116 Gc 61.50N 16.45 E
Södra Gloppet 116 Ia 63.05N 21.00 E
Södra Kvarken 116 Hd 60.20N 19.08 E
Södra-Midsjöbanken 116 Gi 55.40N 17.20 E
Södra Vi 116 Fg 57.45N 15.48 E
Soe 150 Hh 9.52S 124.17 E
Soekmekaar 172 Dd 23.28S 29.58 E
Soela, Proliv- / Soela Väin 116 Jf 58.40N 22.30 E
Soela Väin / Soela, Proliv- 116 Jf 58.40N 22.30 E
Soest [F.R.G.] 120 Ee 51.35N 8.07 E
Soest [Neth.] 124 Hb 52.10N 5.20 E
Soeste 124 Ja 53.10N 7.44 E
Soester Borde 124 Kc 51.38N 8.03 E
Soestwetering 124 Ib 51.30N 6.09 E
Sofádhes 130 Fj 39.20N 22.06 E
Sofala [3] 172 Ec 19.30S 34.40 E
Sofala, Baia de- 158 Kk 20.11S 34.45 E
Sofia [2] 130 Gg 42.43N 23.25 E
Sofia 172 Hc 15.27S 47.23 E
Sofia (EN)=Sofija 112 Ig 42.41N 23.19 E
Sofija=Sofia (EN) 112 Ig 42.41N 23.19 E
Sofijsk 138 If 52.20N 134.01 E
Sofporog 136 Db 65.48N 31.28 E
Sofrána, Nisídhes- 130 Jm 36.04N 26.24 E
Sōfu-Gan 152 Pf 29.50N 140.20 E
Sogamoso 202 Db 5.43N 72.56W
Soganlı 146 Eb 41.11N 32.38 E
Sogara, Lake- 170 Fd 5.15S 31.00 E
Sogda 138 If 50.24N 132.18 E
Sögel 120 Dd 52.51N 7.31 E
Sogeri 214 Di 9.10S 147.32 E
Sogn 116 Ac 61.05N 5.55 E
Sogndalsfjøra 116 Bc 61.14N 7.06 E
Søgne 116 Bf 58.05N 7.49 E
Sognefjell 116 Bc 61.35N 7.55 E
Sognefjorden 110 Gc 61.05N 5.10 E
Sognesjøen 116 Ac 61.05N 5.00 E
Sogn og Fjordane [2] 114 Bf 61.30N 6.50 E
Sogod 150 Hd 10.23N 124.59 E
Sogo Nur 152 Hc 42.20N 101.20 E
Sogoža 114 Jg 58.30N 39.06 E
Söğüt 130 Nj 40.00N 30.11 E
Söğütalan 130 Li 40.03N 28.34 E
Söğüt Gölü 146 Cd 37.03N 29.53 E
Sog Xian 152 Fe 31.51N 93.42 E
Soh 135 He 39.57N 71.08 E
Sohag (EN)=Sawhāj 160 Kf 26.33N 31.42 E
Sohano 214 Ei 5.29S 154.41 E
Sohŭksan-Do 154 Hg 34.04N 125.07 E
Soignies/Zinnik 122 Kd 50.35N 4.04 E
Soini 116 Kb 62.52N 24.13 E
Soisalo 116 Mb 62.40N 28.10 E
Soissonnais, Plateau du- 122 Je 49.20N 3.10 E
Soissons 122 Je 49.22N 3.20 E
Sōja 156 Cd 34.40N 133.44 E
Sojana 114 Kd 65.53N 43.30 E
Sojma 134 Ec 67.00N 51.00 E
Šojna 134 Bc 67.52N 44.08 E
Sŏjosŏn-man=Korea Bay (EN) 140 Of 39.15N 125.00 E
Sojuznoje 132 Vd 50.50N 60.10 E
Sojuz Sovetskih Socialističeskih Respublik (SSSR) [1] 142 Jd 60.00N 80.00 E
Sojuz Sovetskih Socialističeskih Respublik =USSR (EN) [1] 142 Jd 60.00N 80.00 E
Sok 136 Fe 53.25N 50.10 E
Sokal 132 Dd 50.29N 24.17 E
Šokalskogo, proliv- 138 Ea 79.00N 100.00 E
Sokch'o 152 Md 38.12N 128.36 E
Söke 144 Cb 37.45N 27.24 E
Sokele 170 Dd 9.55S 24.36 E
Sokirjany 132 Ee 48.28N 27.25 E
Sokna 114 Bf 60.14N 9.54 E
Soko Banja 130 Ef 43.39N 21.53 E
Sokodé 160 Hh 8.59N 1.08 E
Sokol 136 Ed 59.29N 40.13 E
Sokol 130 Ce 44.18N 19.25 E
Sokółka 120 Tc 53.25N 23.31 E
Sokolo 166 Dc 14.44N 6.07W
Sokolov 120 If 50.11N 12.38 E
Sokołów Podlaski 120 Sd 52.25N 22.15 E
Sokone 166 Bc 13.53N 16.22W
Sokosti 114 Gb 68.20N 28.01 E
Sokoto 160 Hg 13.04N 5.15 E
Sokoto [2] 166 Gc 12.20N 5.20 E
Sokoto 158 Hg 11.24N 4.07 E
Sokourala 166 Dd 9.13N 8.05W
Sol 168 Hd 9.20N 49.25 E
Sol 168 Hd 9.40N 48.30 E
Sol, Costa del- 126 Ih 36.46N 3.55W
Sol, Pico do- 204 Ke 20.07S 43.28W
Sola 219b Ca 13.53S 167.33 E
Sola 120 Pf 50.04N 19.13 E
Solai 170 Gb 0.02N 36.09 E
Solakrossen 116 Af 58.53N 5.36 E
Solanet 204 Cm 36.51S 58.31W
Solāpur 142 Jh 17.41N 75.55 E
Solbad Hall in Tirol → Hall in Tirol 128 Fc 47.17N 11.31 E
Solcy 136 Dd 58.09N 30.20 E
Sölden 128 Ed 46.58N 11.00 E
Soldier Point 197d Bb 17.02N 61.41W
Soldotna 178 Id 60.29N 151.04W
Solec Kujawski 120 Oc 53.06N 18.14 E
Soledad [Arg.] 204 Bj 30.37S 60.55W
Soledad [Ca.-U.S.] 188 Eh 36.26N 121.19W
Soledad [Col.] 202 Da 10.55N 74.46W
Soledad [Ven.] 202 Fb 8.10N 63.34W
Soledad, Boca de- 192 Ce 25.17N 112.09W
Soledad, Isla-/East Falkland 198 Kk 51.45S 58.50W
Soledade 206 Jc 28.50S 52.30W
Sølen 116 Dc 61.55N 11.30 E
Sølensjøen 116 Dc 61.55N 11.35 E
Solentiname, Archipiélago de- 194 Fh 11.10N 85.00W
Solenzara 122a Bb 42.16N 9.24 E
Sole Pit 118 Oh 53.40N 1.30 E
Solesmes 124 Fd 50.11N 3.30 E
Solferino 128 Ee 45.23N 10.34 E
Solgen 116 Fg 57.33N 15.07 E
Solgne 124 Ie 48.58N 6.18 E
Soligalič 114 Kg 59.07N 42.13 E
Soligorsk 136 Ce 52.49N 27.31 E
Solihull 118 Li 52.25N 1.45W
Solikamsk 136 Fd 59.39N 56.47 E
Sol-Ileck 112 Le 51.12N 55.03 E
Solimán, Punta- 192 Ph 19.50N 87.27W
Solimoes → Amazonas, Rio- =Amazon (EN) 198 Lf 0.10S 49.00W
Solingen 120 De 51.11N 7.05 E
Solińskie, Jezioro- 120 Sg 49.22N 22.30 E
Solis, Presa- 192 Ig 20.05N 100.36W
Sollebrunn 116 Ef 58.07N 12.32 E
Sollefteå 114 De 63.10N 17.16 E
Sollentuna 116 Ge 59.28N 17.54 E
Sóller 126 Oe 39.46N 2.42 E
Sollerön 116 Fd 60.55N 14.37 E
Solling 120 Fe 51.45N 9.35 E
Solms 124 Kd 50.46N 9.36 E
Solna 116 He 59.22N 18.01 E
Solnečnogorsk 114 Ih 56.10N 37.00 E
Solnečny 138 Id 60.10N 137.35 E
Sologne 122 Hg 47.50N 2.00 E
Sologne Bourbonnaise 122 Jh 46.40N 3.30 E
Solok 150 Dg 0.48S 100.39 E
Sololá 194 Bf 14.46N 91.11W
Sololá [3] 194 Bf 14.40N 91.15W
Solomon Basin (EN) 214 Ei 7.00S 152.00 E
Solomon Islands 208 Ge 8.00S 159.00 E
Solomon Islands (British Solomon Islands) [1] 210 Ge 8.00S 159.00 E
Solomon River 182 Hd 38.54N 97.22W
Solomon Sea 208 Ge 8.00S 155.00 E
Solon Springs 186 Kc 46.22N 91.48W
Solør 116 Dd 60.30N 11.55 E
Solor, Kepulauan- 150 Hh 8.25S 123.30 E
Solothurn 128 Bc 47.15N 7.30 E
Solothurn [2] 128 Bc 47.20N 7.40 E
Solotvin 120 Uh 48.38N 24.31 E
Soloveckije ostrova 114 Id 65.05N 35.45 E
Solovjevka 116 Nd 60.44N 30.20 E
Solovjevsk [R.S.F.S.R.] 138 Gg 49.54N 115.43 E
Solovjevsk [R.S.F.S.R.] 138 Hf 54.15N 124.30 E
Sölöz 130 Mi 40.23N 29.25 E
Solre-le-Château 124 Gd 50.10N 4.05 E
Solsona 126 Nc 41.59N 1.31 E
Solt 120 Oj 46.48N 19.00 E
Solta 128 Kg 43.23N 16.17 E
Soltānābād [Iran] 146 Rd 36.23N 58.02 E
Soltānābād [Iran] 146 Mg 31.03N 49.42 E
Solṭānī, Khowr-e- 146 Nh 29.00N 50.50 E
Soltāniyeh 146 Md 36.26N 48.48 E
Soltau 120 Fd 52.59N 9.50 E
Soltvadkert 120 Pj 46.35N 19.23 E
Solvang 188 Ei 34.36N 120.08W
Sölvesborg 114 Dh 56.03N 14.33 E
Solvyčegodsk 114 Lf 61.21N 46.52 E
Solway Firth 118 Jg 54.50N 3.35W
Solwezi 160 Jj 12.11S 26.24 E
Soma 146 Bc 39.10N 27.36 E
Sōma 154 Pf 37.48N 140.57 E
Somain 124 Fd 50.22N 3.17 E
Somalia (EN)= Soomaaliya [1] 160 Lh 10.00N 49.00 E
Somali Basin (EN) 106 Fi 0.00 52.00 E
Sombo 170 Dd 8.42S 20.57 E
Sombor 130 Cd 45.46N 19.07 E
Sombrerete 190 Dd 23.38N 103.39W
Sombrero 190 Le 18.36N 63.26W
Sombrero Channel 148 Ig 7.41N 93.35 E
Sombrio 204 Hi 29.07S 49.40W
Sombrio, Lagoa do- 204 Hi 29.12S 49.42W
Somcuţa Mare 130 Gb 47.31N 23.28 E
Someren 124 Hc 51.23N 5.43 E
Somero 116 Jd 60.37N 23.32 E
Somerset [3] 118 Jk 51.10N 3.10W
Somerset 118 Kj 51.00N 3.00W
Somerset 174 Jb 73.30N 93.30W
Somerset [Austl.] 212 Ib 10.35S 142.15 E
Somerset [Ky.-U.S.] 182 Kd 37.05N 84.36W
Somerset [Pa.-U.S.] 184 He 40.02N 79.05W
Somerset East 172 Df 32.42S 25.35 E
Somerton 188 Hj 32.36N 114.43W
Somerville Lake 186 Hk 30.18N 96.40W
Someş 130 Fa 48.07N 22.20 E
Someşu Mare 130 Gb 47.09N 23.55 E
Someşu Mic 130 Gb 47.09N 23.55 E
Somme [3] 122 Ie 49.55N 2.30 E
Somme 122 Hd 50.11N 1.39 E
Somme, Baie de- 124 Dd 50.14N 1.33 E
Somme, Bassurelle de la- 124 Dd 50.15N 1.10 E
Somme, Canal de la- 122 Hd 50.11N 1.39 E
Somme-Leuze 124 Hd 50.20N 5.22 E
Somme-Leuze-Hogne 124 Hd 50.15N 5.17 E
Sommen 116 Ff 58.08N 14.58 E
Sommen 114 Dh 58.00N 15.15 E
Sommepy-Tahure 124 Ge 49.15N 4.33 E
Sömmerda 120 He 51.09N 11.06 E
Somogy [2] 120 Nj 46.25N 17.35 E
Somontano Pirenaico 126 Lc 42.02N 0.20W
Somosierra, Puerto de- 126 Ic 41.09N 3.35W
Somosomo Strait 219d Bb 16.47S 179.58 E
Somotillo 194 Dg 13.02N 86.53W
Somoto 190 Gf 13.28N 86.35W
Somovo 132 Kd 51.45N 39.25 E
Sompolno 120 Od 52.24N 18.31 E
Somport, Puerto de- 126 Lb 42.48N 0.31W
Son 142 Kg 25.50N 84.55 E
Soná 194 Gi 8.01N 81.19W
Sona 120 Qd 52.33N 20.35 E
Sonaguera 194 Df 15.38N 86.20W
Sonāri, Ākra 130 Lm 36.27N 28.13 E
Sŏnch'ŏn 154 He 39.48N 124.55 E
Søndeled 114 Bg 58.46N 9.05 E
Sønderborg 114 Bi 54.55N 9.47 E
Sønder-Jylland [2] 116 Ci 55.00N 9.00 E
Sønder-Omme 116 Ci 55.50N 8.54 E
Sondershausen 120 Ge 51.22N 10.52 E
Søndre Strømfjord 224 Nc 66.59N 50.40W
Søndre Strømfjord 179 Ge 66.10N 53.10W
Søndre Upernavik 179 Gd 72.10N 55.38W
Sondrio 128 Dd 46.10N 9.52 E
Sonepat 148 Fc 28.59N 77.01 E
Song 166 Hd 9.50N 12.37 E
Songa 116 Be 59.47N 7.43 E
Songavatn 116 Be 59.50N 7.35 E
Song Cau 148 Lf 13.27N 109.13 E
Songe 116 Cf 58.41N 9.01 E
Songea 160 Kj 10.41S 35.39 E
Songeons 124 De 49.33N 1.52 E
Songhua Hu 154 Ic 43.30N 126.51 E
Songhua Jiang=Sungari (EN) 140 Pe 47.42N 132.30 E
Songjiang 152 Le 31.01N 121.14 E
Songjiang → Antu 154 Jc 42.33N 128.20 E
Songjianghe 154 Ic 42.10N 127.30 E
Sŏngjin → Kimch'aek 152 Mc 40.41N 129.12 E
Songjöng 154 Ig 35.08N 126.48 E
Songkhla 142 Mi 7.13N 100.34 E
Songling 152 Lb 48.02N 121.08 E
Songnim 154 He 38.44N 125.38 E
Songo [Ang.] 170 Bd 7.21S 14.50 E
Songo [Moz.] 172 Ec 15.33S 32.48 E
Songololo 170 Bd 5.42S 14.02 E
Songpan (Sungqu) 152 He 32.37N 103.34 E
Songsa-dong 154 Hd 39.49N 124.49 E
Song Shan 152 Je 34.31N 113.00 E
Songshuzhen 154 Ic 42.01N 127.09 E
Songueur 126 Ni 35.11N 1.30 E
Songxian 154 Bg 34.12N 112.09 E
Songzi (Xinjiangkou) 154 Ai 30.10N 111.46 E
Sonid Youqi (Saihan Tal) 152 Jc 42.45N 112.36 E
Sonid Zuoqi (Mandalt) 152 Jc 43.50N 113.45 E
Sonkari 116 Lb 62.50N 26.35 E
Sonkël, ozero- 135 Jd 41.50N 75.10 E
Sonkovo 114 Ih 57.47N 37.09 E
Son La 142 Mg 21.19N 103.54 E
Sonmiāni Bay 148 Dc 25.15N 66.30 E
Sonneberg 120 Hf 50.21N 11.10 E
Sono, Rio do- [Braz.] 202 Ie 9.00S 48.11W
Sono, Rio do- [Braz.] 204 Jc 17.02S 45.32W
Sonobe 156 Dd 35.07N 135.28 E
Sonoita 190 Bb 31.51N 112.50W
Sonoma Peak 188 Gf 40.52N 117.36W
Sonora [2] 190 Bc 29.20N 110.40W
Sonora 190 Bc 28.48N 111.49W
Sonora [Ca.-U.S.] 188 Eh 37.59N 120.23W
Sonora [Tx.-U.S.] 186 Fk 30.34N 100.39W
Sonqor 146 Le 34.47N 47.36 E
Sonsbeck 124 Ic 51.37N 6.22 E
Sonsonate 190 Gf 13.43N 89.44W
Sonsorol Islands 208 Ed 5.20N 132.13 E
Sonthofen 120 Gi 47.31N 10.17 E
Sontra 120 Fe 51.04N 9.56 E
Soomaaliya=Somalia (EN) [1] 160 Lh 10.00N 49.00 E
Soomenlaht=Finland, Gulf of- (EN) 110 Ic 60.00N 27.00 E
Soonwald 124 Je 49.56N 7.35 E
Søorværøy 114 Cc 67.38N 12.40 E
Sopi, Tanjung- 150 If 2.39N 128.34 E
Sopo 168 Dd 8.51N 26.11 E
Sopockin 120 Tc 53.50N 23.42 E
Sopot [Bul.] 130 Hg 42.39N 24.45 E
Sopot [Pol.] 120 Ob 54.28N 18.34 E
Sopron 120 Mi 47.41N 16.36 E
Sopur 148 Eb 34.18N 74.28 E
Sor 126 De 39.00N 8.17W
Sora 128 Hi 41.43N 13.37 E
Sorachi-Gawa 156a Bb 43.32N 141.52 E
Soråker 116 Gb 62.31N 17.30 E
Sorak-san 152 Md 38.07N 128.28 E
Sorano 128 Fh 42.41N 11.43 E
Soratfeld 124 Kc 51.40N 8.55 E
Sorbas 126 Jg 37.07N 2.07W
Sorbe 126 Id 40.51N 3.08W
Sörberget 116 Gb 62.31N 17.22 E
Sore 122 Fj 44.19N 0.35W
Sorel 180 Kg 46.03N 73.07W
Sorell, Cape- 212 Jh 42.10S 145.10 E
Soresina 128 De 45.17N 9.51 E
Sorezaru Point 219a Cb 7.37S 156.38 E
Sørfjorden 116 Bd 60.25N 6.40 E
Sørfold 116 Dc 67.28N 15.28 E
Sorgues 122 Kj 44.00N 4.52 E
Sorgun 146 Fc 39.50N 35.19 E
Soria 126 Jc 41.46N 2.28W
Soria [3] 126 Jc 41.40N 2.40W
Soriano [2] 204 Dk 33.30S 57.45W
Sørkapp 224 Kd 76.28N 16.36 E
Sorkh, Godār-e- 146 Pf 33.05N 55.05 E
Sorkh, Kūh-e- 146 Pf 33.05N 55.05 E
Sorkheh 146 Oe 35.28N 53.13 E
Sorø 116 Di 55.26N 11.34 E
Sorocaba 200 Lh 23.29S 47.27W
Soroči Gory 114 Li 55.24N 49.55 E
Sorocinsk 136 Fe 52.26N 53.10 E
Soroki 132 Fe 48.07N 28.16 E
Sorol Atoll 208 Fd 8.08N 140.23 E
Sorong 210 Ee 0.53S 131.15 E
Sorot 116 Mg 57.04N 28.50 E
Soroti 160 Kh 1.43N 33.37 E
Sørøya 110 Ia 70.36N 22.46 E
Sørøyane 116 Ab 62.20N 5.45 E
Sorraia 126 Df 38.56N 8.53W
Sørreisa 114 Eb 69.09N 18.10 E
Sorrentina, Penisola- 128 Ij 40.35N 14.30 E
Sorrento 128 Ij 40.37N 14.22 E
Sør Rondane 222 Df 72.00S 25.00 E
Sorsatunturi 114 Gc 67.24N 29.38 E
Sorsavesi 116 Lb 62.30N 27.35 E
Sorsele 114 Dd 65.32N 17.30 E
Sorsk 138 Ef 54.00N 90.20 E
Sorso 128 Cj 40.48N 8.34 E
Sorsogon 150 Hd 12.58N 124.00 E
Sort 126 Nb 42.24N 1.08 E
Šortandi 136 He 51.42N 71.05 E
Sortavala 136 Dc 61.44N 30.41 E
Sortland 114 Db 68.42N 15.24 E
Sør-Trøndelag [2] 114 Ce 63.00N 10.40 E
Sorum 134 Ne 63.50N 68.05 E
Sørumsand 116 De 59.58N 11.15 E
Šoša 116 Ih 56.33N 36.09 E
Sösan 154 If 36.47N 126.27 E
Sösdala 116 Eh 56.02N 13.40 E
Sos del Rey Católico 126 Kb 42.30N 1.13W
Sosna 132 Kc 52.42N 38.55 E
Sosnogorsk 112 Lc 63.37N 53.51 E
Sosnovka [R.S.F.S.R.] 132 Lc 53.14N 41.22 E
Sosnovka [R.S.F.S.R.] 114 Mh 56.18N 51.17 E
Sosnovka [R.S.F.S.R.] 114 Jc 66.31N 40.33 E
Sosnovka [Ukr.-U.S.S.R.] 132 Dd 50.15N 24.13 E
Sosnovo 116 Nd 60.31N 30.29 E
Sosnovo-Ozerskoje 138 Gf 52.31N 111.35 E
Sosnovy Bor 116 Me 59.48N 29.10 E
Sosnowiec 120 Pf 50.18N 19.08 E
Sospel 122 Nk 43.53N 7.27 E
Šostka 136 De 51.52N 33.31 E
Sosumav 172 Hb 13.03S 48.54 E
Sosva 136 Gd 59.32N 62.20 E
Sosva [R.S.F.S.R.] 136 Gd 59.10N 61.50 E
Sosva [R.S.F.S.R.] 136 Gc 63.40N 62.02 E
Sotavento [3] 162 Cf 14.40N 23.25W
Sotavento, Islas de- = Windward Islands (EN) 198 Jd 11.10N 67.00W
Sotik 170 Gc 0.41S 35.07 E
Sotkamo 114 Gd 64.08N 28.25 E
Soto la Marina 192 Jf 23.48N 98.13W
Soto la Marina, Rio- 192 Kf 23.45N 97.45W
Sotonera, Embalse de la- 126 Lb 42.05N 0.48W
Sotouboua 166 Fd 8.34N 0.59 E
Sotra 116 Ad 60.20N 5.05 E
Sotsudaka-Zaki 156b Ba 28.15N 129.10 E
Sottern 116 Fe 59.05N 15.30 E
Sotteville-lès-Rouen 122 He 49.25N 1.06 E
Sottrum 124 La 53.07N 9.14 E
Sottunga 116 Id 60.10N 20.40 E
Sotuf, Adrar- 162 De 21.42N 15.36W
Sotuta 192 Og 20.36N 89.01W
Souanké 170 Bb 2.05N 14.03 E
Soubré 166 Dd 5.47N 6.36W
Soubré [3] 166 Dd 5.47N 6.38W
Soúdha 130 Hn 35.29N 24.04 E
Souf 158 Hc 33.25N 6.50 E
Soufflenheim 124 Jf 48.50N 7.58 E
Souflion 130 Jh 41.12N 26.18 E
Soufrière 196 Ff 13.52N 61.04W
Soufrière [Guad.] 190 Le 16.03N 61.40W
Soufrière [St.Vin.] 190 Lf 13.21N 61.11W
Soufrière Bay 197g Bb 15.13N 61.22W
Soufrière Hills 197c Bc 16.43N 62.10W
Souillac 122 Hj 44.54N 1.29 E
Souilly 124 Le 49.01N 5.17 E
Souk Ahras 162 Ib 36.17N 7.57 E
Souk el Arba du Rharb 162 Fc 34.41N 5.59W
Sŏul=Seoul (EN) 142 Of 37.34N 127.00 E
Soulac-sur-Mer 122 Ei 45.30N 1.06W
Sŏul Si [2] 154 If 37.35N 127.00 E
Soultz-sous-Forêts 124 Jf 48.56N 7.53 E
Soumagne 124 Hd 50.37N 5.45 E
Soummam 126 Rh 36.44N 5.04 E
Sounding Creek 188 Ja 52.06N 110.28W
Soúnion 130 Hl 37.39N 24.02 E
Soúnion, Ákra- 130 Hl 37.39N 24.01 E
Sources, Mont aux- 158 Jk 28.46S 28.52 E
Soure [Braz.] 202 Id 0.44S 48.31W
Soure [Port.] 126 Dd 40.03N 8.38W
Sour el Ghozlane 162 Hb 36.09N 3.41 E
Souris 180 Hg 49.38N 100.15W
Souris 174 Je 49.39N 99.34W
Sous 162 Fc 30.25N 9.30W
Sous 162 Fc 30.22N 9.37W
Sousa 200 Mf 6.45S 38.14W
Sousel 126 Ef 38.57N 7.40W
Sous le Vent, Iles- = Leeward Islands (EN) 208 Lf 16.38S 151.30W
Sousse (EN)=Sūsah [3] 162 Jb 35.45N 10.30 E
Sousse (EN)=Sūsah [Tun.] 160 Ie 35.49N 10.38 E
South 172 Cf 33.03S 23.29 E
Souterraine, La- 122 Hh 46.14N 1.29 E
South Africa/Suid-Afrika [1] 160 Jl 30.00S 26.00 E
South Alligator River 212 Gb 12.15S 132.24 E
Southam 124 Ab 52.15N 1.23W
South America (EN) 106 Ck 15.00S 60.00W
Southampton 174 Kc 64.20N 84.40W
Southampton [Eng.-U.K.] 118 Fe 50.55N 1.25W
Southampton [N.Y.-U.S.] 184 Ke 40.54N 72.23W
Southampton, Cape- 180 Jd 62.08N 83.44W
Southampton Airport 124 Ad 50.55N 1.23W
Southampton Water 124 Ad 50.52N 1.20W
South Andaman 148 If 11.45N 92.45 E
Southard, Cape- 222 Ie 66.33S 122.04 E
South Auckland-Bay of Plenty [2] 218 Fb 38.00S 176.00 E
South Aulatsivik 180 Le 56.47N 61.30W
South Australia [2] 212 Ge 30.00S 135.00 E
South Australian Basin (EN) 106 Im 40.00S 128.00 E
Southaven 186 Li 35.00N 90.00W
South Baldy 186 Cj 33.59N 107.11W
South Bay 180 Jd 64.00N 83.25W
South Bend 182 Jc 41.41N 86.15W
South Benfleet 124 Cc 51.32N 0.33 E
Southborough 124 Cc 51.09N 0.15 E
South Boston 184 Hg 36.42N 78.58W
Southbridge 218 Ee 43.48S 172.15 E
South Buganda [3] 170 Fc 0.30S 32.00 E
South Caicos 194 Lc 21.31N 71.30W
South Carolina [2] 182 Ke 34.00N 81.00W
South China Basin (EN) 106 Hh 15.00N 115.00 E
South China Sea (EN)=Bien Dong 140 Ni 10.00N 113.00 E
South China Sea (EN)=Cina Selatan, Laut- 140 Ni 10.00N 113.00 E
South China Sea (EN)=Nan Hai 140 Ni 10.00N 113.00 E
South Dakota [2] 182 Gc 44.15N 100.00W
South Downs 118 Mk 50.55N 0.25W
South-East [3] 172 De 25.00S 25.45 E
South East Cape 208 Fi 43.39S 146.50 E
Southeast Indian Ridge (EN) 106 Ho 50.00S 110.00 E
Southeast Pacific Basin (EN) 106 Mp 60.00S 115.00W
South East Point [Austl.] 208 Fh 39.00S 146.20 E
South East Point [Kir.] 220g Bb 1.40N 157.10W
Southend 180 He 56.20N 103.14W
Southend-on-Sea 118 Nj 51.33N 0.43 E
Southern [Bots.] [3] 172 Cd 24.45S 24.00 E
Southern [Mwi.] [3] 170 Gf 15.30S 35.00 E
Southern [S.L.] [3] 166 Cd 7.40N 12.15W
Southern [Ug.] [3] 170 Fc 0.30S 30.30 E
Southern [Zam.] [3] 170 Ef 16.00S 27.00 E
Southern Alps 208 Ii 43.30S 170.35 E
Southern Cook Islands 208 Lg 20.00S 159.00W
Southern Cross 210 Ch 31.13S 119.19 E
Southern Desert (EN)= Janūbīyah, Aş Şaḩrā' al- 158 Jf 24.00N 30.00 E
Southern Ghats 148 Ff 10.00N 76.50 E
Southern Gilbert Islands 214 Jh 1.30S 175.30 E
Southern Guinea (EN) 158 Ii 8.00S 14.00 E
Southern Indian Lake 174 Jd 57.10N 98.40W
Southern Pines 184 Hh 35.11N 79.24W
Southern Region (EN) = Al Iqlīm al Janūbīyah [2] 168 Dd 6.00N 30.00 E
Southern Sierra Madre (EN) =Madre del Sur, Sierra- 174 Jj 17.00N 100.00W
Southern Uplands 110 Fd 55.30N 3.30W
Southern Urals (EN)=Južny Ural 110 Le 54.00N 58.30 E
Southern Yemen (EN) → Yemen, People's Democratic Republic of- (EN) [1] 142 Gh 14.00N 46.00 E
South Esk 118 Jf 56.43N 2.28W
South Fiji Basin (EN) 106 Jl 26.00S 175.00 E
South Foreland 118 Oj 51.09N 1.23 E
South Fork 188 Ge 42.26N 116.53W
South Fork Flathead River 188 Ib 48.07N 113.45W
South Fork Grand River 186 Ed 45.43N 102.17W
South Fork Kern River 188 Fi 35.40N 118.27W
South Fork Moreau River 186 Ed 45.09N 102.50W
South Fork Powder River 188 Le 43.40N 106.30W
South Fork Republican River 186 Ff 40.03N 101.31W
South Georgia/Georgia del Sur 222 Ad 54.15S 36.45W
South Glamorgan [3] 118 Jj 51.30N 3.15W
South Haven 184 Dd 42.24N 86.16W
South Honshu Ridge (EN) 106 Ig 24.00N 142.00 E
South Horr 170 Gb 2.06N 36.55 E
South Indian Basin (EN) 222 Hd 60.00S 120.00 E
South Island [F.S.M.] 220d Bc 6.59N 151.59 E
South Island [Kenya] 170 Gb 2.38N 36.36 E
South Island [N.Z.] 208 Ii 44.00S 171.00 E
South Island [Sey.] 172b Ab 9.26S 46.23 E
South Island [Sey.] 172b Bc 10.10S 51.10 E
South Korea (EN)=Taehan-Min' guk [1] 142 Of 38.00N 127.30 E
South Lake Tahoe 188 Eg 38.57N 120.01W
Southland [2] 218 Bf 45.45S 168.00 E
South Loup River 186 Gf 41.04N 98.40W
South Lueti 170 Df 16.14S 23.12 E
South Magnetic Pole (1980) (EN) 222 Ie 65.08S 139.03 E
South Malosmadulu Atoll 148a Ba 5.10N 72.58 E
South Mountain 186 Ge 42.44N 116.54W
South Nahanni 180 Fd 61.03N 123.22W
South Negril Point 190 Ie 18.16N 78.22W
South Orkney Islands (EN) 222 Re 60.35S 45.30W
South Pass 174 Ie 42.22N 108.55W
South Pass [F.S.M.] 220d Bb 7.14N 151.48 E
South Pass [U.S.] 186 Ll 28.55N 89.20W
South Platte 174 Ie 41.15N 100.45W
South Point 197a Ab 13.02N 59.31W
South Pole (EN) 222 Bg 90.00S 0.00
South Porcupine 184 Ga 48.28N 81.13W
Southport [Eng.-U.K.] 118 Jh 53.39N 3.01W
Southport [N.C.-U.S.] 184 Hi 33.55N 78.01W
South Reef 219a Ee 13.00S 160.32 E
South Ronaldsay 118 Kc 58.46N 2.50W
South Rukuru 170 Fe 10.44S 34.14 E
South Saint Paul 186 Jd 44.52N 93.02W

Index Symbols

[1] Independent Nation
[2] State, Region
[3] District, County
[4] Municipality
[5] Colony, Dependency
Continent
Physical Region
Historical or Cultural Region
Mount, Mountain
Volcano
Hill
Mountains, Mountain Range
Hills, Escarpment
Plateau, Upland
Pass, Gap
Plain, Lowland
Delta
Salt Flat
Valley, Canyon
Crater, Cave
Karst Features
Depression
Polder
Desert, Dunes
Forest, Woods
Heath, Steppe
Oasis
Cape, Point
Coast, Beach
Cliff
Peninsula
Isthmus
Sandbank
Island
Atoll
Rock, Reef
Islands, Archipelago
Rocks, Reefs
Coral Reef
Well, Spring
Geyser
River, Stream
Waterfall, Rapids
River Mouth, Estuary
Lake
Salt Lake
Intermittent Lake
Reservoir
Swamp, Pond
Canal
Glacier
Ice Shelf, Pack Ice
Ocean
Sea
Gulf, Bay
Strait, Fjord
Lagoon
Bank
Seamount
Tablemount
Ridge
Shelf
Basin
Escarpment, Sea Scarp
Fracture
Trench, Abyss
National Park, Reserve
Point of Interest
Recreation Site
Cave, Cavern
Historic Site
Ruins
Wall, Walls
Church, Abbey
Temple
Scientific Station
Railway station
Airport
Port
Military installation
Lighthouse
Mine
Tunnel
Dam, Bridge

South Sandwich Islands (EN) 222 Ad 56.00S 26.30W
South Sandwich Trench (EN) 106 Do 56.30S 25.00W
South Saskatchewan River 174 Id 53.15N 105.05W
South Shetland Islands (EN) 222 Re 62.00S 58.00W
South Shields 118 Lg 55.00N 1.25W
South Sioux City 186 He 42.28N 96.24W
South Sister 188 Ed 44.12N 121.45W
South Taranaki Bight 218 Fc 39.40S 174.15E
South Trap 218 Bg 47.30S 167.55E
South Tyne 118 Kg 54.59N 2.08W
South Uist 118 Fd 57.15N 7.24W
South Umpqua River 188 De 43.20N 123.25W
Southwell 124 Ba 53.04N 0.57W
South Wellesley Islands 212 Hc 17.05S 139.25E
South West Africa → Namibia [1] 160 Ik 22.00S 17.00E
South West Cape 212 Jh 43.34S 146.02E
Southwest Cape [N.Z.] 208 Hi 47.17S 167.27E
Southwest Cape [V.I.U.S.] 197a Dc 17.42N 64.53W
Southwest Indian Ridge (EN) 106 Fm 32.00S 55.00E
Southwest Miramichi River 184 Ob 46.50N 65.45W
Southwest Pacific Basin (EN) 106 Km 40.00S 150.00W
Southwest Pass 186 Ll 29.00N 89.20W
South West Point 197p Cb 12.27N 61.30W
South West Point 220g Ab 1.52N 157.33W
Southwest Point 194 Jb 22.10N 74.10W
Southwold 118 Oi 52.20N 1.40E
South Yorkshire [3] 118 Lh 53.30N 1.25W
Soutpansberg 172 Dd 22.58S 29.50E
Soverato 128 Kl 38.41N 16.33E
Sovetabad 135 Gd 40.14N 69.42E
Sovetsk [R.S.F.S.R.] 136 Cd 55.05N 21.52E
Sovetsk [R.S.F.S.R.] 136 Ed 57.36N 48.58E
Sovetskaja Gavan 142 Qe 48.58N 140.18E
Sovetski [R.S.F.S.R.] 136 Gc 61.20N 63.29E
Sovetski [R.S.F.S.R.] 114 Lh 56.47N 48.30E
Sovetski [R.S.F.S.R.] 116 Md 60.29N 28.40E
Sovetski, proliv- 156a Db 43.24N 145.50E
Sovetski Sojuz = Soviet Union (EN) [1] 142 Jd 60.00N 80.00E
Sovetski Sojuz → SSSR [1] 142 Jd 60.00N 80.00E
Sovetskoje 136 Ef 47.17N 44.30E
Soviet Union (EN) = Sovetski Sojuz [1] 142 Jd 60.00N 80.00E
Soviet Union (EN) = Union of Soviet Socialist Republics (EN) [1] 142 Jd 60.00N 80.00E
Sowghān 146 Qh 28.20N 56.54E
Sowie, Góry- 120 Mf 50.38N 16.30E
Sōya 156a Ba 45.28N 141.53E
Sōya-Kaikyō = La Perouse Strait (EN) 140 Qe 45.30N 142.00E
Sōya-Misaki 152 Pb 45.31N 141.56E
Soyatita 192 Fe 25.45N 107.22W
Soyo 170 Bd 6.05S 12.20E
Sož 110 Je 51.57N 30.48E
Sozopol 130 Kg 42.25N 27.42E
Spa 122 Ld 50.29N 5.52E
Spain (EN) = España [1] 112 Fg 40.00N 4.00W
Špakovskoje 132 Mg 45.06N 42.00E
Spalding 118 Mi 52.47N 0.10W
Spanish Fork 188 Jf 40.07N 111.39W
Spanish Peak 188 Fd 44.24N 119.46W
Spanish Point 197d Ba 17.33N 61.44W
Spanish Sahara (EN) → Western Sahara (EN) [5] 160 Ff 24.30N 13.00W
Spanish Town [B.V.I.] 197a Db 18.27N 64.26W
Spanish Town [Jam.] 190 Ie 17.59N 76.57W
Sparbu 114 Ce 63.55N 11.28E
Spargi, Isola- 128 Di 41.15N 9.20E
Sparks 182 Dd 39.32N 119.45W
Sparreholm 116 Ge 59.04N 16.49E
Sparta [Il.-U.S.] 186 Lg 38.07N 89.42W
Sparta [N.C.-U.S.] 184 Gg 36.30N 81.07W
Sparta [Tn.-U.S.] 184 Eh 35.56N 85.29W
Sparta [Wi.-U.S.] 186 Ke 43.57N 90.47W
Sparta (EN) = Spárti 130 Fl 37.05N 22.26E
Spartanburg 182 Ke 34.57N 81.55W
Spartel, Cap- 158 Ge 35.48N 5.56W
Spárti = Sparta (EN) 130 Fl 37.05N 22.26E
Spartivento, Capo- [It.] 110 Hh 37.55N 16.04E
Spartivento, Capo- [It.] 128 Cl 38.53N 8.50E
Spas-Demensk 132 Ib 54.24N 34.01E
Spas-Klepiki 114 Ji 55.10N 40.13E
Spassk-Dalni 138 Ih 44.37N 132.48E
Spassk-Rjazanski 114 Ji 54.27N 40.22E
Spátha, Ákra- = Spatha, Cape- (EN) 130 Gn 35.42N 23.44E
Spatha, Cape- (EN) = Spátha, Ákra- 130 Gn 35.42N 23.44E
Spearfish 182 Gc 44.30N 103.52W
Spearman 186 Fh 36.12N 101.12W
Speedway 184 Df 39.47N 86.15W
Speicher 124 Ie 49.56N 6.38E
Speightstown 196 Gf 13.15N 59.39W
Speke Gulf 170 Fc 2.20S 33.15E
Spello 128 Gh 42.59N 12.40E
Spenard 178 Jd 61.11N 149.55W
Spence Bay 176 Jc 69.32N 93.31W
Spencer [Ia.-U.S.] 182 Hc 43.09N 95.09W
Spencer [In.-U.S.] 184 Df 39.17N 86.46W
Spencer [Nb.-U.S.] 186 Ge 42.53N 98.42W
Spencer [W.V.-U.S.] 184 Gf 38.48N 81.22W
Spencer, Cape- 212 Hg 35.18S 136.53E
Spencer Gulf 208 Eh 34.00S 137.00E
Spenge 124 Kb 52.08N 8.29E
Spenser Mountains 218 Ee 42.10S 172.35E
Sperillen 116 Dd 60.30N 10.05E
Sperkhiós 130 Fk 38.52N 22.34E
Sperlonga 128 Hi 41.15N 13.26E
Sperone, Capo- 128 Cl 38.55N 8.25E
Sperrin Mountains/Sliabh Speirin 118 Fg 54.50N 7.05W
Spessart 120 Fg 49.55N 9.30E
Spétsai 130 Gl 37.16N 23.09E
Spétsai 130 Gl 37.16N 23.08E
Spey 118 Jd 57.40N 3.06W
Spey Bay 118 Jd 57.40N 3.05W
Speyer 120 Eg 49.19N 8.26E
Speyer-bach 124 Ke 49.19N 8.27E
Speyside 196 Fg 11.18N 60.32W
Spezzano Albanese 128 Kk 39.40N 16.19E
Spicer Islands 180 Jc 68.10N 79.00W
Spiekeroog 120 Dc 53.46N 7.42E
Spiess Seamount (EN) 222 Cd 54.40S 0.15E
Spiez 128 Bd 46.41N 7.42E
Spijkenisse 124 Gc 51.51N 4.21E
Spilimbergo 128 Gd 46.07N 12.54E
Spilion 130 Hn 35.13N 24.32E
Spilsby 124 Ca 53.11N 0.06E
Spina 128 Gf 44.42N 12.08E
Spinazzola 128 Kj 40.58N 16.05E
Spincourt 124 He 49.20N 5.40E
Spirit River 180 Fe 55.47N 118.50W
Spirovo 114 Ih 57.27N 35.01E
Spiš 120 Qg 49.05N 20.30E
Spišská Nová Ves 120 Qh 48.57N 20.34E
Spitak 132 Ni 40.49N 44.14E
Spitsbergen 224 Kd 78.45N 16.00E
Spitsbergen 224 Kd 78.00N 19.00E
Spittal an der Drau 128 Hd 46.48N 13.30E
Spitzbergen Bank (EN) 179 Oc 76.00N 23.00E
Spjelkavik 114 Be 62.28N 6.23E
Split 112 Hg 43.31N 16.26E
Split Lake 180 He 56.10N 96.10W
Spluga, Passo dello- 128 Dd 46.29N 9.20E
Splügenpaß 128 Dd 46.29N 9.20E
Spōgi/Špogi 116 Lh 56.02N 26.52E
Špogi/Spōgi 116 Lh 56.02N 26.52E
Spokane 176 He 47.40N 117.23W
Spokane, Mount- 188 Gc 47.55N 117.07W
Spokane River 188 Fc 47.44N 118.20W
Špola 136 Df 49.01N 31.24E
Spoleto 128 Gh 42.44N 12.44E
Spooner 186 Kd 45.50N 91.53W
Spoon River 186 Kf 40.18N 90.04W
Sporovo 120 Vd 52.25N 25.27E
Spotsylvania 184 If 38.12N 77.35W
Sprague 188 Gc 47.18N 117.59W
Sprague River 188 Ee 42.34N 121.51W
Spratly (EN) = NanKei Dao 150 Fe 8.42N 111.40E
Spray 188 Fd 44.50N 119.48W
Spreča 128 Mf 44.44N 18.06E
Spree 120 Jd 52.32N 13.13E
Spreewald 120 Je 51.55N 14.00E
Spremberg/Grodk 120 Ke 51.33N 14.22E
Sprengisandur 114a Bb 64.40N 18.07W
Springbok 160 Ik 29.43S 17.15E
Spring Creek 186 Fd 45.45N 100.18W
Springdale 186 Ih 36.11N 94.08W
Springe 120 Fd 52.13N 9.33E
Springer 186 Dh 36.22N 104.36W
Springer, Mount- 184 Ja 49.48N 74.51W
Springerville 188 Ki 34.08N 109.17W
Springfield [Co.-U.S.] 186 Eh 37.24N 102.37W
Springfield [Il.-U.S.] 176 Kf 39.47N 89.40W
Springfield [Ma.-U.S.] 182 Mc 42.07N 72.36W
Springfield [Mn.-U.S.] 186 Id 44.14N 94.59W
Springfield [Mo.-U.S.] 176 Jf 37.14N 93.17W
Springfield [N.Z.] 218 De 43.20S 171.56E
Springfield [Oh.-U.S.] 182 Kd 39.55N 83.48W
Springfield [Or.-U.S.] 182 Cc 44.03N 123.01W
Springfield [S.D.-U.S.] 186 He 42.49N 97.54W
Springfield [Tn.-U.S.] 184 Dg 36.31N 86.52W
Springfontein 172 Df 30.19S 25.36E
Spring Garden 202 Gb 6.59N 58.31W
Spring Hall 197q Ab 13.19N 59.36W
Springhill [La.-U.S.] 186 Jj 33.00N 93.28W
Springhill [N.S.-Can.] 180 Lg 45.39N 64.03W
Spring Mountains 188 Hh 36.10N 115.40W
Springs 172 De 26.13S 28.25E
Springsure 212 Jd 24.07S 148.05E
Spring Valley 186 Je 43.41N 92.23W
Spring Valley 188 Hg 39.10N 114.30W
Springville 188 Jf 40.10N 111.37W
Spruce Knob 174 Lf 38.42N 79.32W
Spruce Mountain [Az.-U.S.] 188 Ii 34.28N 112.24W
Spruce Mountain [Nv.-U.S.] 188 Hf 40.33N 114.49W
Spulico, Capo- 128 Kk 39.58N 16.38E
Spurn Head 118 Nh 53.34N 0.07E
Squamish 180 Fg 49.42N 123.09W
Squillace 128 Kl 38.47N 16.31E
Squillace, Golfo di- 128 Kl 38.45N 16.50E
Squinzano 128 Mj 40.26N 18.02E
Srbica 130 Dg 42.45N 20.47E
Srbija = Serbia (EN) [2] 130 Df 44.00N 21.00E
Srbija = Serbia (EN) 110 Ig 43.00N 21.00E
Srbija = Serbia (EN) 130 Df 44.00N 21.00E
Srbobran 130 Cd 45.33N 19.48E
Srē Âmběl 148 Kf 11.07N 103.46E
Sredinny hrebet 140 Rd 56.00N 158.00E
Sredna Gora 130 Hg 42.30N 25.00E
Srednekolymsk 138 Kc 67.27N 153.41E
Srednerusskaja vozvyšennost = Central Russian Uplands (EN) 110 Je 52.00N 38.00E
Srednesatyginski Tuman, ozero- 134 Lg 59.45N 65.25E
Srednesibirskoje ploskogorje = Central Siberian Uplands (EN) 140 Mc 65.00N 105.00E
Sredni Kujto, ozero- 114 Hd 65.05N 31.30E
Sredni Ural = Central Urals (EN) 110 Ld 58.00N 59.00E
Sredni Urgal 138 If 51.13N 132.58E
Sredni Verecki, pereval- 132 Ce 48.49N 23.07E
Srednjaja Ahtuba 132 Ne 48.43N 44.52E
Srednjaja Olëkma 138 He 55.26N 120.40E
Śrem 120 Nd 52.08N 17.01E
Sremska Mitrovica 130 Ce 44.58N 19.37E
Sremski Karlovci 130 Cd 45.12N 19.56E
Sretensk 142 Nd 52.15N 117.43E
Sri Gangānagar 148 Ec 29.55N 73.53E
Sri Jayawardenepura 148 Gg 6.54N 80.02E
Srijem 130 Cd 45.00N 19.40E
Srīkākulam 148 Ge 18.18N 83.54E
Sri Lanka 140 Ki 7.30N 80.30E
Sri Lanka (Ceylon) [1] 142 Ki 7.40N 80.50E
Srīnagar 142 Jf 34.05N 74.49E
Srivardhan 148 Ee 18.02N 73.01E
Środa Śląska 120 Me 51.10N 16.36E
Środa Wielkopolska 120 Nd 52.14N 17.17E
Srpska Crnja 130 Dd 45.43N 20.42E
Sruth na Maoile/North Channel 110 Fd 55.10N 5.40W
SSSR = Union of Soviet Socialist Republics (USSR) (EN) [1] 142 Jd 60.00N 80.00E
SSSR → Sojuz Sovetskih Socialističeskih Respublik [1] 142 Jd 60.00N 80.00E
Ssu-ch'uan Sheng → Sichuan Sheng = Szechwan (EN) [2] 152 He 30.00N 103.00E
Staaten River 212 Ic 16.24S 141.17E
Stabroek 124 Gc 51.20N 4.22E
Stack Skerry 118 Ib 59.02N 4.30W
Stade 120 Fc 53.36N 9.29E
Staden 124 Fd 50.59N 3.01E
Stadhavet 116 Ab 62.15N 5.05E
Stádjan 116 Ec 61.58N 12.52E
Stadlandet 116 Ab 62.05N 5.20E
Stadskanaal 122 Ma 53.00N 6.55E
Stadskanaal-Musselkanaal 124 Jb 52.56N 7.02E
Stadtallendorf 120 Ld 50.50N 9.00E
Stadthagen 124 Lb 52.19N 9.12E
Stadtkyll 124 Id 50.21N 6.32E
Stadtlohn 124 Ic 51.59N 6.56E
Stadtoldendorf 120 Fe 51.54N 9.39E
Staffa 118 Ge 56.25N 6.10W
Staffanstorp 116 Ei 55.38N 13.13E
Staffelsee 120 Hi 47.42N 11.10E
Staffora 128 De 45.04N 9.01E
Stafford 118 Ki 52.48N 2.07W
Stafford 118 Li 52.50N 2.00W
Staffordshire [3] 118 Li 52.55N 2.00W
Staicele/Stajcele 116 Kg 57.44N 24.39E
Stainach 128 Ic 47.32N 14.06E
Staines 124 Bc 51.26N 0.31W
Stakčín 120 Sg 49.00N 22.13E
Stalać 130 Ef 43.40N 21.25E
Stalham 124 Db 52.46N 1.31E
Stalingrad → Volgograd 112 Kf 48.44N 44.25E
Stalldalen 116 Fe 59.56N 14.56E
Stalowa Wola 120 Sf 50.35N 22.02E
Stamford [Ct.-U.S.] 184 Ke 41.03N 73.32W
Stamford [Eng.-U.K.] 118 Mi 52.39N 0.29W
Stamford [Tx.-U.S.] 186 Gj 32.57N 99.48W
Stamford, Lake- 186 Gj 33.05N 99.35W
Stampriet 172 Bd 24.20S 18.28E
Stamsund 114 Cb 68.08N 13.51E
Stanberry 186 If 40.13N 94.35W
Stancija Jakkabag 135 Fe 38.59N 66.42E
Stancija-Karakul 136 Gh 39.30N 63.50E
Standerton 172 De 26.58S 29.07E
Standish 184 Fd 44.00N 83.57W
Stanford 188 Jc 47.09N 110.13W
Stånga 116 Hg 57.17N 18.28E
Stångån 116 Ff 58.27N 15.37E
Stange 116 Dd 60.43N 11.11E
Stanger 172 Ee 29.27S 31.14E
Stanke Dimitrov 130 Gg 42.16N 23.07E
Stanley [Austl.] 212 Jh 40.46S 145.18E
Stanley [Falk.Is.] 200 Kk 51.42S 57.51W
Stanley [N.D.-U.S.] 186 Eb 48.19N 102.23W
Stann Creek 190 Ge 16.59N 88.13W
Stann Creek [3] 194 Ce 16.50N 88.30W
Stanovoje nagorje = Stanovoy Upland (EN) 140 Nd 56.00N 114.00E
Stanovoj hrebet = Stanovoy Range (EN) 140 Od 56.20N 126.00E
Stanovoy Range (EN) = Stanovoj hrebet 140 Od 56.20N 126.00E
Stanovoy Upland (EN) = Stanovoje nagorje 140 Nd 56.00N 114.00E
Stans 128 Cd 46.58N 8.22E
Stansted Airport 124 Cc 51.54N 0.13E
Stansted Mountfitchet 124 Cc 51.54N 0.12E
Stanthorpe 212 Ke 28.39S 151.57E
Stanton Banks 118 Fe 56.15N 7.50W
Staphorst 124 Ib 52.38N 6.14E
Staples 186 Ic 46.21N 94.48W
Stapleton 186 Ff 41.29N 100.31W
Stąporków 120 Qe 51.09N 20.34E
Starachowice 120 Re 51.03N 21.04E
Staraja Majna 114 Li 54.36N 48.59E
Staraja Russa 136 Dd 57.59N 31.23E
Staraja-Vyževka 120 Ue 51.27N 24.34E
Stará L'ubovňa 120 Qg 49.18N 20.42E
Stara Moravica 130 Cd 45.52N 19.28E
Stara Pazova 130 De 44.59N 20.10E
Stara Planina = Balkan Mountains (EN) 110 Ig 43.15N 25.00E
Stara Zagora 112 Ig 42.25N 25.38E
Stara Zagora 130 Ig 42.25N 25.38E
Starbuck Island 208 Le 5.37S 155.53W
Staretina 128 Kf 44.02N 16.43E
Stargard Szczeciński 120 Lc 53.20N 15.02E
Stari Begejski kanal 130 Dd 45.29N 20.25E
Starica 114 Ih 56.30N 34.56E
Starigrad 128 Kg 43.11N 16.36E
Stari Vlah 130 Df 43.23N 20.10E
Starke 184 Fk 29.57N 82.07W
Starkville 186 Lj 33.28N 88.48W
Starnberg 120 Hh 48.00N 11.21E
Starnberger See (Würmsee) 120 Hi 47.55N 11.20E
Starobelsk 136 Df 49.15N 38.58E
Starodub 136 De 52.35N 32.46E
Starogard Gdański 120 Oc 53.59N 18.33E
Starokonstantinov 132 Ee 49.43N 27.13E
Starominskaja 136 Df 46.31N 39.06E
Staroščerbinovskaja 132 Kf 46.37N 38.42E
Starosubhangulovo 134 Hj 53.06N 57.20E
Starotimoškino 114 Lj 53.43N 47.32E
Start Point 120 Jk 50.13N 3.38W
Staryje Dorogi 132 Fc 53.02N 28.17E
Stary Krym 132 Ig 45.02N 35.05E
Stary Oskol 136 De 51.18N 37.51E
Stary Sambor 132 Ce 49.29N 23.01E
Stary Terek 132 Og 44.01N 47.24E
Staßfurt 120 He 51.52N 11.35E
Staszów 120 Rf 50.34N 21.10E
State College 184 Ie 40.48N 77.52W
Staten Island (EN) = Estados, Isla de los- 198 Jk 54.47S 64.15W
Statesboro 184 Gi 32.27N 81.47W
Statesville 184 Gh 35.47N 80.53W
Stathelle 116 Ce 59.03N 9.41E
Stathmós Krioneriou 130 Ek 38.20N 21.35E
Statland 114 Cd 64.30N 11.08E
Staunton 182 Ld 38.10N 79.05W
Stavanger 112 Gd 58.58N 5.45E
Stavelot 124 Hd 50.23N 5.56E
Staveren 122 Lb 52.53N 5.22E
Stavern 116 Df 59.00N 10.02E
Stavnoje 120 Sh 48.59N 22.45E
Stavropol 112 Kf 45.02N 41.59E
Stavropolskaja vozvyšennost 132 Mg 45.10N 43.00E
Stavropolski kraj [3] 136 Eg 45.00N 43.15E
Stavrós [Grc.] 130 Fj 39.19N 22.14E
Stavrós [Grc.] 130 Gi 40.40N 23.42E
Stavroúpolis 130 Hh 41.12N 24.42E
Stawell 212 Ig 37.04S 142.46E
Stawiski 120 Sc 53.23N 22.09E
Stawiszyn 120 Oe 51.55N 18.07E
Stayton 188 Dd 44.48N 122.48W
Steamboat Springs 182 Fc 40.29N 106.50W
Stębark 120 Qc 53.30N 20.05E
Stebnik 120 Tg 49.14N 23.34E
Stedingen 124 Ka 53.10N 8.30E
Steele 186 Gc 46.51N 99.55W
Steelpoort 172 Ed 24.48S 30.12E
Steenbergen 124 Gc 51.35N 4.19E
Steen River 180 Fe 59.38N 117.06W
Steensby Inlet 180 Jb 70.10N 78.25W
Steenstrups Gletscher 179 Gc 75.15N 57.30W
Steenvoorde 124 Ed 50.48N 2.35E
Steenwijk 122 Mb 52.47N 6.08E
Ştefăneşti 130 Kb 47.48N 27.12E
Stefanie, Lake- (EN) = Chew Bahir 158 Kh 4.38N 36.50E
Stefansson 180 Gb 73.30N 105.30W
Ştefleşti, Virful- 130 Gd 45.32N 23.48E
Stege 116 Ej 54.59N 12.18E
Steiermark = Styria (EN) [2] 128 Ic 47.15N 15.00E
Steiermark = Styria (EN) 128 Ic 47.15N 15.00E
Steigerwald 120 Gg 49.40N 10.20E
Steilrandberge 172 Ac 17.53S 13.20E
Steinach 128 Fc 47.05N 11.28E
Steinbach 180 Hg 49.32N 96.41W
Steinen, Rio- 202 Hf 12.05S 53.46W
Steinfeld (Oldenburg) 124 Kb 52.36N 8.13E
Steinfort/Steinfurt 124 He 49.40N 5.55E
Steinfurt 120 Dd 52.09N 7.20E
Steinfurt/Steinfort 124 He 49.40N 5.55E
Steinfurt-Borghorst 124 Jb 52.08N 7.25E
Steinhagen 124 Kb 52.01N 8.24E
Steinhausen 172 Bd 21.49S 18.20E
Steinheim 124 Lc 51.51N 9.06E
Steinhuder Meer 120 Fd 52.28N 9.19E
Steinkjer 114 Cd 64.01N 11.30E
Steinkopf 172 Be 29.18S 17.43E
Steinshamn 116 Bb 62.47N 6.29E
Steinsøy 114 Af 61.00N 4.30E
Steirisch-Niederösterreichische Kalkalpen 128 Jc 47.45N 15.30E
Stekene 124 Gc 51.12N 4.02E
Stekolny 138 Ke 60.00N 150.50E
Stella 172 Ce 26.33S 24.53E
Stellenbosch 172 Bf 33.58S 18.50E
Stello 122a Ba 42.47N 9.25E
Stelvio, Passo dello- / Stilfser Joch 128 Ed 46.32N 10.27E
Stemwede 124 Kb 52.26N 8.26E
Stenay 122 Le 49.29N 5.11E
Stendal 120 Hd 52.36N 11.51E
Stende 116 Jg 57.10N 22.28E
Stende 116 Ig 57.40N 21.57E
Stenhouse Bay 212 Hh 35.17S 136.56E
Stenstorp 116 Ef 58.16N 13.43E
Stenungsund 116 Cg 58.05N 11.49E
Stepanakert 112 Kh 39.49N 46.44E
Stepanavan 132 Ni 40.59N 44.20E
Stephens, Cape- 218 Ed 40.42S 173.57E
Stephens, Mount- 222 Rg 83.23S 51.27W
Stephens Passage 178 Me 57.50N 133.50W
Stephenville [Newf.-Can.] 180 Lg 48.33N 58.35W
Stephenville [Tx.-U.S.] 186 Gj 32.13N 98.12W
Steps Point 221c Cb 14.22S 170.45W
Sterea Ellás kai Évvoia [2] 130 Hk 38.20N 24.30E
Sterkstroom 172 Df 31.32S 26.32E
Sterlibaševo 134 Gj 53.28N 55.15E
Sterling [Co.-U.S.] 182 Gc 40.37N 103.13W
Sterling [Il.-U.S.] 186 Lf 41.48N 89.42W
Sterling City 186 Fk 31.50N 100.59W
Sterlitamak 112 Le 53.37N 55.58E
Šternberk 120 Ng 49.44N 17.19E
Sterzing / Vipiteno 128 Fd 46.54N 11.26E
Stettin → Szczecin 112 He 53.24N 14.32E
Stettiner Haff 120 Kc 53.46N 14.14E
Stettler 180 Gf 52.19N 112.43W
Steubenville 182 Kc 40.22N 80.39W
Stevenage 118 Mj 51.54N 0.11W
Stevenson Entrance 178 Ie 57.45N 152.20W
Stevens Point 182 Jc 44.31N 89.34W
Stewart 180 Ee 55.56N 129.59W
Stewart 180 Dd 63.18N 139.24W
Stewart Crossing 180 Dd 63.18N 136.33W
Stewart Island 208 Hi 47.00S 167.50E
Stewart Islands 208 He 8.20S 162.40E
Steyerberg 124 Lb 52.34N 9.02E
Steyning 124 Bd 50.53N 0.20W
Steynsburg 172 Df 31.15S 25.49E
Steyr 128 Ib 48.03N 14.25E
Steyr 128 Ib 48.02N 14.25E
Štiavnické vrchy 120 Oh 48.15N 18.50E
Stidia 126 Li 35.50N 0.05W
Stiene 116 Kg 57.19N 24.28E
Stiens, Leeuwarderadeel- 124 Ha 53.16N 5.46E
Stigliano 128 Kj 40.24N 16.14E
Stigtomta 116 Gf 58.48N 16.47E
Stikine 174 Fd 56.40N 132.30W
Stikine Ranges 180 Ee 57.35N 131.00W
Stilfontein 172 De 26.50S 26.50E
Stilfser Joch / Stelvio, Passo dello- 128 Ed 46.32N 10.27E
Stilis 130 Fk 38.55N 22.37E
Stillwater [Mn.-U.S.] 182 Jd 45.04N 92.49W
Stillwater [Ok.-U.S.] 182 Hd 36.07N 97.04W
Stillwater Range 188 Fg 39.50N 118.15W
Stilo 128 Kl 38.29N 16.28E
Stilo, Punta- 128 Kl 38.27N 16.35E
Štimlje 130 Eg 42.26N 21.03E
Stînişoarei, Munţii- 130 Ib 47.20N 26.00E
Stinnett 186 Fi 35.50N 101.27W
Štip 130 Fh 41.44N 22.12E
Stirling 118 Je 56.07N 3.57W
Stirling Range 212 Df 34.25S 117.50E
Stjernøya 114 Fa 70.18N 22.45E
Stjørdalshalsen 114 Ce 63.28N 10.44E
Stobi 130 Eh 41.33N 21.59E
Stobrawa 120 Nf 50.50N 17.32E
Stocka 116 Gc 61.54N 17.20E
Stockach 120 Fi 47.51N 9.01E
Stockbridge 124 Ac 51.06N 1.29W
Stockerau 128 Kb 48.23N 16.13E
Stockholm 112 Hd 59.20N 18.03E
Stockholm [2] 114 Dg 59.20N 18.00E
Stockport 118 Kh 53.25N 2.10W
Stocks Seamount (EN) 198 Mg 12.15S 32.00W
Stockton [Ca.-U.S.] 176 Gf 37.57N 121.17W
Stockton [Mo.-U.S.] 186 Jh 37.42N 93.48W
Stockton Lake 186 Jh 37.40N 93.45W
Stockton-on-Tees 118 Lg 54.34N 1.19W
Stockton Plateau 182 Ge 30.30N 102.30W
Stoczek Łukowski 120 Re 51.58N 21.58E
Stöde 114 De 62.25N 16.35E
Stoëng Trêng 148 Lf 13.31N 105.58E
Stoer, Point of- 118 Hc 58.20N 5.25W
Stogovo 130 Dh 41.29N 20.39E
Stohod 120 Ve 51.52N 25.44E
Stoholm 116 Ch 56.29N 9.10E
Stoj, gora- 132 Ce 48.39N 23.15E
Stojba 142 Pd 52.49N 131.43E
Stoke-on-Trent 118 Kh 53.00N 2.10W
Stokksnes 114a Cb 64.14N 14.58W
Stokmarknes 114 Db 68.34N 14.55E
Stol 130 Fe 44.11N 22.09E
Stolac 128 Lg 43.05N 17.58E
Stolbcy 132 Ec 53.31N 26.43E
Stolberg (Rheinland) 120 Cf 50.46N 6.14E
Stolbovoj, ostrov- 138 Ib 74.05N 136.00E
Stolin 132 Ed 51.57N 26.52E
Stolzenau 124 Lb 52.31N 9.04E
Ston 128 Lh 42.50N 17.42E
Stone 118 Ki 52.54N 2.10W
Stonehaven 118 Ke 56.58N 2.13W
Stonehenge 212 Id 24.22S 143.17E
Stonehenge 118 Lj 51.11N 1.49W
Stoner 186 Bh 37.37N 108.18W
Stonewall 186 Ha 50.09N 97.21W
Stony 178 Hd 61.45N 156.35W
Stony Rapids 180 Ge 59.16N 105.50W
Stony River 178 Hd 61.47N 156.41W
Stony Stratford 124 Bb 52.03N 0.51W
Stony Tunguska (EN) = Podkamennaja Tunguska 140 Lc 61.36N 90.18E
Stör 120 Fc 53.50N 9.25E
Storå 116 Fe 59.43N 15.08E
Storå 116 Ch 56.19N 8.19E
Storå/Isojoki 116 Ee 62.07N 21.58E
Stora Gla 116 Ee 59.30N 12.30E
Stora Le 116 De 59.05N 11.55E
Stora Lulevatten 114 Ec 67.08N 19.20E
Storavan 114 Ed 65.42N 18.12E
Storby 116 Hd 60.13N 19.34E
Stord 114 Ag 59.55N 5.25E
Stordal 116 Bb 62.23N 7.01E
Store Bælt = Great Belt (EN) 110 Hd 55.30N 11.00E
Storebro 116 Fg 57.35N 15.51E
Storefiskbank = Great Fisher Bank (EN) 118 Qe 56.50N 4.00E
Store Heddinge 116 Ei 55.19N 12.25E
Store Hellefiske Bank (EN) 179 Ge 67.30N 55.00W
Store Koldewey 179 Kc 76.20N 18.30W
Store Kvien 116 Dc 61.34N 10.33E
Støren 114 Ce 63.02N 10.18E
Store Nupsfonn 116 Be 59.54N 7.08E
Store Sølnkletten 116 Dc 61.59N 10.18E
Storfjorden [Nor.] 116 Bb 62.25N 6.30E
Storfjorden [Sval.] 179 Nc 77.30N 20.00E

Index Symbols

[1] Independent Nation
[2] State, Region
[3] District, County
[4] Municipality
[5] Colony, Dependency
Continent
Physical Region
Historical or Cultural Region
Mount, Mountain
Volcano
Hill
Mountains, Mountain Range
Hills, Escarpment
Plateau, Upland
Pass, Gap
Plain, Lowland
Delta
Salt Flat
Valley, Canyon
Crater, Cave
Karst Features
Depression
Polder
Desert, Dunes
Forest, Woods
Heath, Steppe
Oasis
Cape, Point
Coast, Beach
Cliff
Peninsula
Isthmus
Sandbank
Island
Atoll
Rock, Reef
Islands, Archipelago
Rocks, Reefs
Coral Reef
Well, Spring
Geyser
River, Stream
Waterfall, Rapids
River Mouth, Estuary
Lake
Salt Lake
Intermittent Lake
Reservoir
Swamp, Pond
Canal
Glacier
Ice Shelf, Pack Ice
Ocean
Sea
Gulf, Bay
Strait, Fjord
Lagoon
Bank
Seamount
Tablemount
Ridge
Shelf
Basin
Escarpment, Sea Scarp
Fracture
Trench, Abyss
National Park, Reserve
Point of Interest
Recreation Site
Cave, Cavern
Historic Site
Ruins
Wall, Walls
Church, Abbey
Temple
Scientific Station
Railway station
Airport
Port
Military installation
Lighthouse
Mine
Tunnel
Dam, Bridge

Storfors 116 Fe 59.32N 14.16 E
Storis Passage 180 Hc 67.40N 98.30W
Storkerson Bay 180 Fb 73.00N 124.00W
Storkerson Peninsula 180 Gb 73.00N 106.30W
Storlien 114 Ce 63.19N 12.06 E
Stormarn 120 Gc 53.45N 10.20 E
Storm Bay 212 Jh 43.10S 147.30 E
Storm Lake 182 Hc 42.39N 95.13W
Stornoway 118 Gc 58.12N 6.23W
Storøya 179 Ob 80.08N 27.50 E
Storožinec 132 De 48.10N 25.46 E
Storsjøen [Nor.] 116 Dd 61.35N 11.15 E
Storsjøen [Nor.] 116 Dd 60.25N 11.40 E
Storsjön [Swe.] 116 Gd 60.35N 16.45 E
Storsjön [Swe.] 110 Hc 63.15N 14.20 E
Storsteinfjellet 114 Db 68.14N 17.52 E
Storstrøm [2] 116 Dj 55.00N 11.50 E
Storstrømmen 179 Jc 77.20N 23.00W
Storsudret 116 Hh 57.00N 18.15 E
Storuman 112 Hb 65.06N 17.06 E
Storuman 114 Dd 65.14N 16.54 E
Storvätteshågna 116 Eb 62.07N 12.27 E
Storvigelen 116 Eb 62.32N 12.04 E
Storvik 116 Gd 60.35N 16.32 E
Storvreta 116 Ge 59.58N 17.42 E
Stöttingfjället 114 Dd 64.38N 17.44 E
Stoughton 188 Nb 49.41N 103.03W
Stour [Eng.-U.K.] 124 Dc 51.18N 1.22 E
Stour [Eng.-U.K.] 118 Lk 50.43N 1.47W
Stour [Eng.-U.K.] 118 Oj 51.52N 1.16 E
Stourbridge 118 Ki 52.27N 2.09W
Støvring 116 Ch 56.53N 9.51 E
Stowmarket 124 Cb 52.11N 0.59 E
Strabane/An Srath Bán 118 Fg 54.49N 7.27W
Stradella 128 De 45.05N 9.18 E
Straelen 124 Ic 51.27N 6.16 E
Strakonice 120 Jg 49.16N 13.55 E
Straldža 130 Jg 42.36N 26.41 E
Stralsund 112 He 54.18N 13.06 E
Strand 172 Bf 34.06S 18.50 E
Stranda 114 Be 62.19N 6.54 E
Strand Bay 180 Ia 79.00N 94.00W
Strangford Lough/Loch Cuan 118 Hg 54.26N 5.36W
Strängnäs 116 Ge 59.23N 17.02 E
Stranraer 118 Hg 54.54N 5.02W
Strasbourg [Fr.] 112 Gf 48.35N 7.45 E
Strasbourg [Sask.-Can.] 188 Ma 51.04N 104.57W
Strašeny 132 Ff 47.06N 28.34 E
Straßwalchen 128 Hc 47.59N 13.15 E
Stratford [N.Z.] 218 Fc 39.21S 174.17 E
Stratford [Ont.-Can.] 184 Gd 43.22N 80.57W
Stratford [Tx.-U.S.] 186 Eh 36.20N 102.04W
Stratford-upon-Avon 118 Li 52.12N 1.41W
Strathclyde [3] 118 If 55.50N 4.50W
Strathgordon 212 Jh 42.54S 146.10 E
Strathmore 188 Ia 51.03N 113.23W
Strathmore 118 Je 56.40N 3.05W
Strathroy 184 Gd 42.57N 81.38W
Strathy Point 118 Ic 58.35N 4.01W
Straubenhardt 124 Kf 48.50N 8.30 E
Straubing 120 Ih 48.53N 12.34 E
Straumnes 114a Aa 66.26N 23.08W
Straumsjøen 114 Db 68.41N 14.30 E
Strausberg 120 Jd 52.35N 13.53 E
Strawberry Mountain 188 Fd 44.19N 118.43W
Strawberry River 188 Jf 40.10N 110.24W
Straža 212 Fg 42.15N 22.14 E
Stražica 130 If 43.14N 25.58 E
Strážiště 120 Kg 49.32N 14.58 E
Strážovské vrchy 120 Oh 48.55N 18.30 E
Streaky Bay 212 Gf 32.48S 134.13 E
Streaky Bay 212 Gf 32.35S 134.10 E
Streator 186 Lf 41.07N 88.50W
Středočeská pahorkatina 120 Kg 49.30N 14.15 E
Středočeský kraj [3] 120 Kg 49.55N 14.30 E
Středoslovenský kraj [3] 120 Ph 48.50N 19.10 E
Strehaia 130 Ge 44.37N 23.12 E
Strei 130 Gd 45.51N 23.03 E
Střela 120 Jg 49.54N 13.32 E
Strelasund 120 Jb 54.20N 13.05 E
Strelka 138 Ee 58.03N 93.05 E
Strelna 114 Jc 66.04N 38.39 E
Strenči 114 Fh 57.39N 25.38 E
Stresa 128 Ce 45.53N 8.32 E
Streževoj 138 Cd 60.42N 77.35 E
Stříbro 120 Ig 49.46N 13.00 E
Strickland River 212 Ia 6.00S 142.05 E
Strimbeni 130 He 44.28N 24.58 E
Strimón 130 Gi 40.47N 23.51 E
Strimonikós Kólpos 130 Gi 40.40N 23.50 E
Strjama 130 Hg 42.10N 24.56 E
Strofádhes, Nisoi- 130 Dl 37.15N 21.00 E
Ströhen, Wagenfeld- 124 Kb 52.32N 8.39 E
Strohgäu 124 Kf 48.50N 9.00 E
Stromberg 124 Je 49.57N 7.46 E
Stromboli 128 Jl 38.47N 15.14 E
Strömfors/Ruotsinpyhtää 116 Ld 60.32N 26.27 E
Stromness 118 Jc 58.57N 3.18W
Strömsbro 116 Gd 60.42N 17.10 E
Strömsbruk 116 Dc 61.53N 17.19 E
Strömsnäsbruk 116 Eh 56.33N 13.43 E
Strömstad 114 Cg 58.56N 11.10 E
Strömsund 114 De 63.51N 15.35 E
Strongili 138 Hm 36.58N 24.55 E
Stròngoli 128 Lk 39.16N 17.03 E
Stronsay 118 Kb 59.08N 2.38W
Stropkov 120 Rg 49.12N 21.40 E
Stroud 118 Kj 51.45N 2.12W
Struer 114 Bh 56.29N 8.37 E
Struga 130 Dh 41.11N 20.41 E
Strugi-Krasnyje 114 Gg 58.17N 29.08 E
Strule 118 Fg 54.40N 7.20W
Struma 110 Ig 40.47N 23.51 E
Strumble Head 118 Hi 52.02N 5.04W
Strumica 130 Fh 41.26N 22.39 E
Stry 136 Cf 49.14N 23.48 E
Stry 132 De 49.24N 24.13 E
Strydenburg 172 Ce 29.58S 23.40 E
Stryn 114 Bf 61.55N 6.47 E
Strynsvatn 116 Bc 61.55N 7.05 E
Strzegom 120 Mf 50.57N 16.21 E
Strzegomka 120 Me 51.08N 16.50 E
Strzelce Krajeńskie 120 Ld 52.53N 15.32 E
Strzelce Opolskie 120 Of 50.31N 18.19 E
Strzelin 120 Nf 50.47N 17.03 E
Strzelno 120 Od 52.38N 18.11 E
Strzyżów 120 Rg 49.52N 21.47 E
Stuart 184 Gl 27.12N 80.16W
Stuart 178 Gd 63.35N 162.30W
Stuart, Mount- 188 Ec 47.29N 120.54W
Stuart Bluff Range 212 Gd 22.45S 132.15 E
Stuart Lake 180 Ff 54.33N 124.35W
Stuart Range 212 Ge 29.10S 134.55 E
Stubaier Alpen 128 Fc 47.10N 11.05 E
Stubbekøbing 116 Ej 54.53N 12.03 E
Stubbenkammer 120 Jb 54.35N 13.40 E
Stubbs Bay 197n Ba 13.08N 61.10W
Štubik 130 Fe 44.18N 22.21 E
Stucka 114 Fh 56.36N 25.17 E
Studenica, Manastir- 130 Df 43.28N 20.37 E
Studholme Junction 218 Df 44.44S 171.08 E
Stugun 114 De 63.10N 15.36 E
Stuhr 124 Ka 53.02N 8.45 E
Stupino 114 Ji 54.57N 38.03 E
Stura di Demonte 128 Bf 44.40N 7.53 E
Stura di Lanzo 128 Be 45.06N 7.44 E
Sturge Island 222 Ke 67.27S 164.18 E
Sturgeon Bay 186 Md 44.50N 87.23W
Sturgeon Falls 180 Jg 46.22N 79.55W
Sturgeon Lake 186 Kb 50.00N 90.45W
Sturgis [Mi.-U.S.] 184 Ee 41.48N 85.25W
Sturgis [S.D.-U.S.] 186 Ed 44.25N 103.31W
Sturkö 116 Fh 56.05N 15.40 E
Sturt Creek 212 Fd 20.08S 127.24 E
Sturt Desert 212 Ie 28.30S 141.00 E
Stutterheim 172 Df 32.33S 27.28 E
Stuttgart [Ar.-U.S.] 186 Ki 34.30N 91.33W
Stuttgart [F.R.G.] 112 Gf 48.46N 9.11 E
Stviga 132 Ec 52.04N 27.55 E
Stykkishólmur 114a Ab 65.04N 22.44W
Styr 136 Ce 52.07N 26.35 E
Styria (EN) = Steiermark [2] 128 Ic 47.15N 15.00 E
Styria (EN) = Steiermark 128 Ic 47.15N 15.00 E
Styrsö 116 Dg 57.37N 11.46 E
Suafa Point 219a Ec 8.19S 160.41 E
Suai 150 Ih 9.21S 125.17 E
Suakin Archipelago (EN) = Sawākin, Jazā'ir- 158 Kg 19.07N 37.20 E
Suao 152 Lg 24.36N 121.51 E
Suardi 204 Bj 30.32S 61.58W
Suavanao 214 Fi 7.34S 158.44 E
Subačius/Subačjus 116 Ki 55.44N 24.53 E
Subačjus/Subačius 116 Ki 55.44N 24.53 E
Subang 150 Eh 6.34S 107.45 E
Subansiri 148 Jc 26.48N 93.49 E
Subao Ding 152 Jf 27.10N 110.18 E
Šubarkuduk 136 Ff 49.09N 56.31 E
Šubarši 132 Te 48.38N 57.12 E
Subate 116 Lh 56.01N 26.04 E
Subay', 'Urūq- 164 He 22.15N 43.05 E
Subaytilah 162 Ib 35.14N 9.08 E
Subbéticas, Cordillera- 126 Jf 38.30N 2.30W
Subei (Dangchengwan) 152 Fd 39.36N 94.58 E
Subi, Pulau- 150 Ef 2.55N 108.50 E
Subiaco 128 Hi 41.55N 13.06 E
Sublette 186 Fh 37.29N 100.50W
Subotica 130 Cc 46.06N 19.40 E
Subpolar Urals (EN) = Pripoljarny Ural 110 Lb 65.00N 60.00 E
Subugo 170 Gc 1.40S 35.49 E
Suceava 130 Jb 47.38N 26.15 E
Suceava [2] 130 Ib 47.40N 25.45 E
Suceava 130 Jb 47.32N 26.32 E
Sucha Beskidzka 120 Pg 49.44N 19.36 E
Süchbaatar → Suhe-Bator 142 Md 50.15N 106.12 E
Suchedniów 120 Qe 51.03N 20.51 E
Suchiapa, Rio- 192 Mi 16.36N 93.01W
Suchitepéquez [3] 194 Bf 14.25N 91.20W
Sucia, Bahía- 197a Ac 17.57N 67.10W
Sucio, Rio- 194 Ij 7.27N 77.07W
Suck/An tSuca 118 Eh 53.16N 8.03W
Suckling, Mount- 212 Ja 9.45S 148.55 E
Suçre [2] 202 Fa 10.25N 63.30W
Sucre [3] 202 Db 9.00N 75.00W
Sucre [Bol.] 200 Jg 19.02S 65.17W
Sucre [Col.] 202 Db 8.50N 74.43W
Suçuarana, Serra da- 204 Jb 14.25S 45.00W
Sucunduri, Rio- 202 Ge 5.30S 59.40W
Sućuraj 128 Lg 43.08N 17.12 E
Sucuriú, Rio- 202 Hh 20.47S 51.38W
Sud, Canal du- 194 Kd 18.40N 73.05W
Sud, Massif du- 194 Kd 18.25N 73.55W
Suda 114 Ig 59.11N 37.33 E
Suda 114 Ig 59.12N 37.30 E
Sudak 136 Dg 44.50N 34.59 E
Sudan 158 Ig 11.30N 15.00 E
Sudan (EN) = As Sūdān [1] 160 Jg 15.00N 30.00 E
Sudbury [Eng.-U.K.] 118 Ni 52.02N 0.44 E
Sudbury [Ont.-Can.] 176 Ke 46.30N 81.00W
Suddie 196 Gi 7.07N 58.29W
Sude 120 Gc 53.22N 10.45 E
Sudeten (EN) = Sudety 110 He 50.30N 16.00 E
Sudety = Sudeten (EN) 110 He 50.30N 16.00 E
Sudirman, Pegunungan- 150 Kg 4.12S 137.00 E
Sudočje, ozero- 135 Bc 43.25N 58.30 E
Sudogda 114 Ji 55.59N 40.50 E
Sudost 132 Hc 52.19N 33.24 E
Sud-Ouest [Burkina] [3] 166 Ec 10.30N 3.15W
Sud-Ouest [Cam.] [3] 166 Gd 5.20N 9.20 E
Sudovaja Višnja 120 Tg 49.43N 23.26 E
Südradde 124 Jb 52.41N 7.34 E
Südtirol / Trentino-Alto Adige [2] 128 Fd 46.30N 11.20 E
Sudža 132 Id 51.13N 35.16 E
Sue 158 Jh 7.41N 28.03 E
Sueca 126 Le 39.12N 0.19W
Suess Land 179 Jd 72.45N 26.00W
Suez (EN) = As Suways 160 Kf 29.58N 32.33 E
Suez, Gulf of-(EN) = Suways, Khalīj as- 158 Kf 28.10N 33.27 E
Suez Canal (EN) = Suways, Qanāt as- 158 Ke 29.55N 32.33 E
Suffolk 182 Ld 36.44N 76.37W
Suffolk [3] 118 Li 52.10N 1.05W
Suffolk 118 Ni 52.25N 1.00 E
Sufiān 146 Kc 38.17N 45.59 E
Sugana, Val- 128 Fd 46.00N 11.40 E
Suga-no-Sen 156 Dd 35.22N 134.31 E
Sugar Island 184 Eb 46.25N 84.12W
Sugarloaf Mountain 184 Lc 45.01N 70.22W
Suğla Gölü 146 Ed 37.20N 32.02 E
Sugoj 138 Kd 64.15N 154.29 E
Suguta 170 Gb 2.03N 36.33 E
Suha 130 Ke 44.08N 27.36 E
Suhai Hu 152 Fd 38.55N 94.05 E
Şuḩār 144 Ie 24.22N 56.45 E
Suhe-Bator (Süchbaatar) 142 Md 50.15N 106.12 E
Suhiniči 132 Ib 54.06N 35.20 E
Suhl 120 Gf 50.36N 10.42 E
Suhl [2] 120 Gf 50.35N 10.40 E
Suhodolskoje, ozero- 116 Nd 60.35N 30.30 E
Suhoj Log 134 Kh 56.55N 62.01 E
Suhona 110 Kc 60.46N 46.24 E
Suhr 128 Cc 47.25N 8.04 E
Suhumi 112 Kg 43.01N 41.02 E
Suhurlui 130 Kd 45.25N 27.35 E
Suiá-Missu, Rio- 202 Hf 11.13S 53.15W
Suibara 156 Fc 37.50N 139.12 E
Suichang 152 Kf 28.34N 119.15 E
Suid-Afrika/South Africa [1] 160 Jl 30.00S 26.00 E
Suide 152 Jd 37.28N 110.15 E
Suifenhe 152 Nc 44.25N 131.09 E
Suifen He 154 Kc 43.20N 131.49 E
Sui He 154 Eh 33.29N 118.06 E
Suihua 152 Mb 46.38N 126.57 E
Suijiang 152 Hf 28.37N 104.00 E
Suileng 152 Mb 47.17N 127.08 E
Suining [China] 152 Ie 30.30N 105.34 E
Suining [China] 154 Dh 33.54N 117.56 E
Suipacha 204 Cl 34.45S 59.41W
Suiping 154 Bh 33.09N 113.59 E
Suippe 122 Je 49.25N 3.57 E
Suippes 122 Ke 49.08N 4.32 E
Suir/An tSiúir 118 Gi 52.15N 7.00W
Suisse / Svizra / Svizzera / Schweiz = Switzerland (EN) [1] 112 Gf 46.00N 8.30 E
Suisse Normande 124 Bf 48.53N 0.50W
Suita 156 Dd 34.45N 135.32 E
Suixi 154 Dh 33.55N 116.47 E
Suixian 154 Cg 34.25N 115.04 E
Suiyang 154 Kb 44.26N 130.53 E
Suizhong 154 Lc 40.21N 120.20 E
Suj 152 Ic 42.12N 108.01 E
Šuja 114 If 61.54N 34.15 E
Šuja [R.S.F.S.R.] 136 Ed 56.52N 41.23 E
Šuja [R.S.F.S.R.] 114 If 61.59N 34.15 E
Sujer 134 Li 55.59N 65.47 E
Suji → Haixing 154 De 38.10N 117.29 E
Sujko Seamount (EN) 224 Ca 44.30N 170.20 E
Sujstamo 116 Nc 61.49N 31.05 E
Sukabumi 150 Eh 6.55S 106.56 E
Sukadana 150 Eg 1.15S 109.57 E
Sukagawa 154 Pf 37.17N 140.23 E
Sukaraja 150 Fg 2.23S 110.35 E
Sukeva 114 Ge 63.54N 27.26 E
Sukhothai 148 Je 17.01N 99.49 E
Suki 168 Ec 13.23N 33.58 E
Sukkertoppen/Manitsoq 179 Ge 65.25N 53.00W
Sukkozero 136 Dc 63.09N 32.23 E
Sukkur 142 Ig 27.42N 68.52 E
Sukon 150 Hg 0.56S 123.10 E
Sukses 172 Bd 21.01S 16.52 E
Suksun 134 Hh 57.07N 57.24 E
Sukumo 152 Ne 32.56N 132.44 E
Sukumo-Wan 156 Ce 32.55N 132.40 E
Sul, Baía- 204 Hh 27.40S 48.35W
Sul, Canal do- 202 Id 0.10S 49.30W
Sula [Nor.] 116 Bb 62.25N 6.10 E
Sula [Nor.] 114 Af 61.10N 4.55 E
Sula [R.S.F.S.R.] 114 Fc 67.16N 52.07 E
Sula [R.S.F.S.R.] 114 Ld 64.41N 47.46 E
Sula [Ukr.-U.S.S.R.] 132 He 49.40N 32.43 E
Sula, Kepulauan = Sulu Archipelago, (EN) 208 De 1.52S 125.22 E
Sulaimāniya 144 Gb 35.33N 45.26 E
Sulaimāniya [3] 146 Ke 35.40N 45.30 E
Sulaimān Range 140 Jf 30.30N 70.10 E
Sulak 132 Oh 43.17N 47.31 E
Sulak 136 Eg 43.17N 47.34 E
Sula Sgeir 118 Gb 59.05N 6.10W
Sulawesi/Celebes 140 Oj 2.00S 121.10 E
Sulawesi, Laut- = Celebes Sea (EN) 140 Oi 3.00N 122.00 E
Sulawesi Selatan [3] 150 Gg 4.00S 120.00 E
Sulawesi Tengah [3] 150 Hg 1.00S 121.00 E
Sulawesi Tenggara [3] 150 Hg 4.00S 122.30 E
Sulawesi Utara [3] 150 Hf 1.00N 123.00 E
Sulaymān 128 En 36.42N 10.30 E
Sulb 168 Ea 20.26N 30.20 E
Sulcis 128 Ck 39.05N 8.40 E
Suldalsvatn 116 Be 59.35N 6.45 E
Süldeh 146 Od 36.34N 52.01 E
Sulechów 120 Ld 52.06N 15.37 E
Sulęcin 120 Ld 52.26N 15.08 E
Suleja 134 Ii 55.11N 58.50 E
Sulejów 120 Pe 51.22N 19.53 E
Süleoğlu 130 Jh 41.46N 26.55 E
Sule Skerry 118 Ib 59.10N 4.10W
Sulima 166 Cd 6.58N 11.35W
Sulina 130 Md 45.09N 29.40 E
Sulina, Braţul- 130 Md 45.09N 29.41 E
Sulingen 120 Ed 52.41N 8.48 E
Sulitjelma 114 Dc 67.09N 16.03 E
Sulitjelma 114 Dc 67.08N 16.24 E
Suljukta 136 Gh 39.56N 69.37 E
Sulkava 114 Gf 61.47N 28.23 E
Sullana 200 Hf 4.53S 80.42W
Süller 130 Mk 38.09N 29.29 E
Sullivan [In.-U.S.] 184 Df 39.06N 87.24W
Sullivan [Mo.-U.S.] 186 Kg 38.13N 91.10W
Sullivan Lake 188 Ja 52.00N 112.00W
Sully-sur-Loire 122 Ig 47.46N 2.22 E
Sulmona 128 Hh 42.03N 13.55 E
Sulphur [La.-U.S.] 186 Jk 30.14N 93.23W
Sulphur [Ok.-U.S.] 186 Hi 34.31N 96.58W
Sulphur Creek 186 Ed 44.46N 102.25W
Sulphur River 186 Jj 33.07N 93.52W
Sulphur Springs 186 Ij 33.08N 95.36W
Sulphur Springs Draw 186 Fj 32.12N 101.36W
Sultandağı 146 Dc 38.32N 31.14 E
Sultan Dağları 146 Dd 38.20N 31.20 E
Sultanhanı 146 Ec 38.15N 33.33 E
Sultanhisar 130 Ll 37.53N 28.10 E
Sultānpur 148 Gc 26.16N 82.04 E
Sulu Archipelago 140 Oi 6.00N 121.00 E
Sulu Archipelago (EN) = Sula Kepulauan 208 De 1.52S 125.22 E
Sulu Basin (EN) 150 Ge 8.00N 121.30 E
Suluova 146 Fb 40.47N 35.42 E
Sulūq 164 Dc 31.40N 20.15 E
Sulu Sea 140 Ni 9.00N 120.00 E
Sulz am Neckar 120 Eh 48.21N 8.37 E
Sulzbach/Saar 124 Je 49.18N 7.04 E
Sulzbach-Rosenberg 120 Hg 49.30N 11.45 E
Sulzberger Bay 222 Mf 77.00S 152.00W
Šumadija 130 De 44.20N 20.40 E
Sumalata 150 Hf 0.59N 122.30 E
Sumāmus 146 Nd 36.50N 50.30 E
Sumanaj 135 Bc 42.37N 58.55 E
Sumatera = Sumatra (EN) 140 Mj 0.01N 102.00 E
Sumatera Barat [3] 150 Dg 1.00S 100.30 E
Sumatera Selatan [3] 150 Dg 3.30S 104.00 E
Sumatera Utara [3] 150 Cf 2.00N 99.00 E
Sumatra (EN) = Sumatera 140 Mj 0.01N 102.00 E
Šumava = Bohemian Forest (EN) 110 Hf 49.00N 13.30 E
Šumayr 164 Hf 17.47N 41.26 E
Sumba, Pulau- 140 Nj 10.00S 120.00 E
Sumba, Selat- = Sumba Strait (EN) 150 Hh 9.05S 120.00 E
Sumbar 132 Sj 38.00N 55.15 E
Sumba Strait (EN) = Sumba, Selat- 150 Hh 9.05S 120.00 E
Sumbawa, Pulau- 140 Nj 8.40S 118.00 E
Sumbawa Besar 150 Gh 8.30S 117.26 E
Sumbawanga 170 Fd 7.58S 31.37 E
Sumbe 160 Ij 11.12S 13.51 E
Sumber 152 Ib 46.21N 108.20 E
Sumbi Point 219a Cb 7.19S 157.04 E
Sumbu 170 Fd 8.31S 30.29 E
Sumburgh Head 118 Lb 59.51N 1.16W
Sumedang 150 Eh 6.52S 107.55 E
Šūme'eh Sarā 146 Md 37.18N 49.19 E
Sümeg 120 Nj 46.59N 17.17 E
Šumen 130 Jf 43.16N 26.55 E
Šumen [2] 130 Jf 43.20N 27.00 E
Sumenep 150 Fh 7.01S 113.52 E
Šumerlja 112 Kd 55.30N 46.26 E
Sumgait 112 Kg 40.33N 49.40 E
Sumgait 132 Pi 40.37N 49.37 E
Sumidouro, Rio- 204 Da 13.28S 56.39W
Šumiha 136 Gd 55.14N 63.19 E
Sumisu-Jima 152 Oe 31.40N 140.00 E
Sumkino 136 Gd 58.09N 68.21 E
Summer, Lake- [N.M.-U.S.] 186 Di 34.38N 104.26W
Summer, Lake- [N.Z.] 218 Ee 42.40S 172.15 E
Summer Lake 188 Ee 42.50N 120.45W
Summerland 188 Fb 49.39N 119.33W
Summerside 180 Lg 46.24N 63.47W
Summersville 184 Gf 38.17N 80.52W
Summerville 184 Eh 34.29N 85.21W
Summit Lake 180 Fe 54.17N 122.38W
Summit Mountain 188 Gg 39.23N 116.28W
Summit Peak 186 Ch 37.21N 106.42W
Sumoto 156 Dd 34.20N 134.54 E
Šumperk 120 Mg 49.58N 16.59 E
Sumprabum 148 Jc 26.33N 97.34 E
Sumsar 135 Hd 41.13N 71.23 E
Sumskaja oblast [3] 136 De 51.00N 34.15 E
Šumšu, ostrov- 138 Kf 50.45N 156.20 E
Sumter 182 Ke 33.55N 80.20W
Sumuştā al Waqf 146 Dh 28.55N 30.51 E
Sumy 112 Je 50.54N 34.48 E
Suna 114 Mh 57.53N 50.07 E
Suna 114 Ie 62.08N 34.12 E
Sunagawa 154 Pc 43.29N 141.55 E
Šunak, gora- 136 Hf 47.05N 72.35 E
Sunan 154 He 39.15N 125.40 E
Sunan (Hongwansi) 152 Gd 38.59N 99.25 E
Sunart, Loch- 118 He 56.45N 5.45W
Sunaysilah 146 Ie 35.35N 41.53 E
Sunburst 188 Jb 48.53N 111.55W
Sunbury 184 Ie 40.52N 76.47W
Sunchales 206 Hd 30.56S 61.34W
Suncho Corral 206 Hc 27.56S 63.27W
Sunch'ŏn [N.Kor.] 152 Md 39.25N 125.56 E
Sunch'ŏn [S.Kor.] 152 Me 34.57N 127.29 E
Sun City 188 Ij 33.36N 112.17W
Suncun → Xinwen 152 Kd 35.49N 117.38 E
Sunda, Selat- = Sunda Strait (EN) 140 Mj 6.00S 105.45 E
Sundance 188 Md 44.24N 104.23W
Sundarbans 148 Hd 22.00N 89.00 E
Sundargarh 148 Gd 22.07N 84.02 E
Sunda Strait (EN) = Sunda, Selat- 140 Mj 6.00S 105.45 E
Sunday Strait 212 Ec 16.20S 123.15 E
Sundborn 116 Fd 60.39N 15.46 E
Sundbron 116 Ha 63.01N 18.11 E
Sundbyberg 116 Ge 59.22N 17.58 E
Sunde 114 Ag 59.50N 5.43 E
Sunderland 118 Lg 54.55N 1.23W
Sundern (Sauerland) 124 Kc 51.20N 8.00 E
Sundgau 122 Ng 47.40N 7.15 E
Sündiken Dağları 146 Dc 39.55N 31.00 E
Sundridge 184 Hc 45.46N 79.24W
Sundsvall 112 Hc 62.23N 17.18 E
Sundsvallsbukten 116 Gb 62.20N 17.35 E
Sunflower, Mount- 186 Eg 39.04N 102.01W
Sungaidareh 150 Dg 0.58S 101.30 E
Sungaigerong 150 Dg 2.59S 104.52 E
Sungaiguntung 150 Df 0.18N 103.37 E
Sungai Kolok 148 Kg 6.02N 101.58 E
Sungai Lembing 150 Df 3.55N 103.02 E
Sungailiat 150 Eg 1.51S 106.08 E
Sungaipenuh 150 Dg 2.05S 101.23 E
Sungai Petani 150 De 5.39N 100.30 E
Sungai Siput 150 Df 4.49N 101.04 E
Sungari (EN) = Songhua Jiang 140 Pe 47.42N 132.30 E
Sungqu → Songpan 152 He 32.37N 103.34 E
Sungurlu 146 Fb 40.10N 34.23 E
Sunharon Roads 220b Bb 14.57N 145.36 E
Suning 154 Ce 38.25N 115.50 E
Sunja 128 Ke 45.21N 16.33 E
Sunjiapuzi 154 Ic 42.02N 126.34 E
Sunkar, gora- 135 Ib 44.12N 73.55 E
Sun Kosi 148 Hc 26.55N 87.09 E
Sunnadalsøra 116 Be 62.40N 8.33 E
Sunnan 114 Cd 64.04N 11.38 E
Sunndalen 116 Cb 62.40N 8.45 E
Sunndalsfjorden 116 Cb 62.45N 8.25 E
Sunne 114 Cg 59.50N 13.09 E
Sunnerbo 116 Eh 56.45N 13.50 E
Sunnersta 116 Ge 59.48N 17.39 E
Sunnfjord 116 Ac 61.25N 5.20 E
Sunnhordland 116 Ae 59.55N 6.05 E
Sunnmøre 116 Bb 62.20N 6.40 E
Sunnyside 188 Fc 46.20N 120.00W
Sunnyvale 188 Dh 37.23N 122.01W
Su-no-Saki 154 Fd 34.58N 139.45 E
Sun River 188 Jc 47.30N 111.25W
Sunsas, Serrania de- 204 Cc 17.57S 59.35W
Suntar 138 Gd 62.04N 117.40 E
Suntar-Hajata, hrebet- = Suntar-Khayata Range (EN) 140 Qc 62.00N 143.00 E
Suntar-Khayata Range (EN) = Suntar-Hajata, hrebet- 140 Qc 62.00N 143.00 E
Suntaži 116 Kh 56.49N 24.57 E
Sun Valley 182 Ec 43.42N 114.21W
Sunwu 152 Mb 49.27N 127.19 E
Sunyani 160 Gh 7.20N 2.20W
Sunža 132 Oh 43.26N 46.08 E
Suojarvi 136 Dc 62.04N 32.21 E
Suokonmäki 116 Kb 62.47N 24.30 E
Suolahti 114 Fe 62.34N 25.52 E
Suomenlahti = Finland, Gulf of- (EN) 110 Ic 60.00N 27.00 E
Suomenniemi 116 Lc 61.19N 27.27 E
Suomenselkä 116 Ic 62.55N 24.00 E
Suomi/Finland [1] 112 Ic 64.00N 26.00 E
Suomussalmi 114 Gd 64.54N 29.00 E
Suō-Nada 156 Be 33.50N 131.30 E
Suonenjoki 114 Ge 62.37N 27.08 E
Suontee 116 Lc 61.40N 26.35 E
Suordah 138 Ic 66.43N 132.04 E
Suozhen → Huantai 154 Ef 36.57N 118.05 E
Supamo, Rio- 196 Fi 6.48N 61.50W
Superior [Az.-U.S.] 188 Jj 33.18N 110.06W
Superior [Mt.-U.S.] 188 Hc 47.12N 114.53W
Superior [Nb.-U.S.] 186 Gf 40.01N 98.04W
Superior [Wi.-U.S.] 176 Je 46.44N 92.05W
Superior, Lake- 174 Ke 48.00N 88.00W
Supetar 128 Kg 43.23N 16.33 E
Suphan Buri 148 Kf 14.29N 100.10 E
Süphan Dağı 144 Fb 38.54N 42.48 E
Supiori, Pulau- 150 Kg 0.45S 135.30 E
Supoj 132 Ge 49.38N 31.50 E
Support Force Glacier 222 Rg 83.05S 47.30W
Suprasl 120 Tc 53.13N 23.20 E
Suprasl 120 Sc 53.12N 22.55 E
Sup'ung 152 Lc 40.27N 124.57 E
Sup'ung-chosuji 154 Hd 40.30N 125.05 E
Suq ash Shuyūkh 146 Lg 30.53N 46.28 E
Suqian 152 Ke 33.55N 118.13 E
Suq Suwayq 146 Hj 24.23N 38.27 E
Suquṭrā = Socotra (EN) 140 Hh 12.30N 54.00 E
Şūr 142 He 22.31N 59.30 E
Şūr 144 Ec 33.16N 35.11 E
Sur, Cabo- 221d Ac 27.12S 109.26W
Sur, Point- 188 Eh 36.18N 121.54W
Sura 132 Nc 53.53N 45.44 E
Sura 132 Kd 56.06N 46.00 E
Šurab 135 Hd 40.03N 70.33 E
Surabaya 142 Nj 7.15S 112.45 E
Surahammar 116 Ge 59.43N 16.13 E
Šurak 144 Id 25.43N 58.48 E
Surakarta 142 Nj 7.35S 110.50 E
Šurān 146 Ge 35.17N 36.45 E
Šurany 120 Oh 48.06N 18.11 E
Surar 168 Gd 7.29N 40.54 E
Surat 142 Jg 21.10N 72.50 E
Surat Thani 142 Li 9.06N 99.20 E
Suraž [Bye.-U.S.S.R.] 114 Hi 55.26N 30.46 E
Suraž [R.S.F.S.R.] 136 De 53.02N 32.29 E
Surčin 130 De 44.47N 20.17 E
Sur del Cabo San Antonio, Punta- 206 Ie 36.52S 56.40W
Surduc 130 Gb 47.15N 23.21 E
Sûre 120 Cg 49.44N 6.31 E

Index Symbols

[1] Independent Nation
[2] State, Region
[3] District, County
[4] Municipality
[5] Colony, Dependency
Continent
Physical Region
Historical or Cultural Region
Mount, Mountain
Volcano
Hill
Mountains, Mountain Range
Hills, Escarpment
Plateau, Upland
Pass, Gap
Plain, Lowland
Delta
Salt Flat
Valley, Canyon
Crater, Cave
Karst Features
Depression
Polder
Desert, Dunes
Forest, Woods
Heath, Steppe
Oasis
Cape, Point
Coast, Beach
Cliff
Peninsula
Isthmus
Sandbank
Island
Atoll
Rock, Reef
Islands, Archipelago
Rocks, Reefs
Coral Reef
Well, Spring
Geyser
River, Stream
Waterfall, Rapids
River Mouth, Estuary
Lake
Salt Lake
Intermittent Lake
Reservoir
Swamp, Pond
Canal
Glacier
Ice Shelf, Pack Ice
Ocean
Sea
Gulf, Bay
Strait, Fjord
Lagoon
Bank
Seamount
Tablemount
Ridge
Shelf
Basin
Escarpment, Sea Scarp
Fracture
Trench, Abyss
National Park, Reserve
Point of Interest
Recreation Site
Cave, Cavern
Historic Site
Ruins
Wall, Walls
Church, Abbey
Temple
Scientific Station
Railway station
Airport
Port
Military installation
Lighthouse
Mine
Tunnel
Dam, Bridge

Surendranagar	148	Ed	22.42N	71.41 E
Surgères	122	Fh	46.06N	0.45W
Surgut	142	Jc	61.14N	73.20 E
Surgutiha	138	Dd	63.47N	87.20 E
Surhandarinskaja oblast [3]	136	Gh	38.00N	67.30 E
Surhandarja	135	Ff	37.14N	67.20 E
Surhob	136	Hh	38.54N	70.04 E
Surigao	150	Ie	9.45N	125.30 E
Surin	148	Kf	14.53N	103.30 E
Suriname = Surinam (EN) [1]	200	Ke	4.00N	56.00W
Suripá, Rio-	194	Mj	7.47N	69.53W
Sūrīyah=Syria (EN) [1]	142	Ff	35.00N	38.00 E
Sürmaq	146	Og	31.03N	52.48 E
Surmelin	124	Fe	49.04N	3.31 E
Sürmene	146	Ib	40.55N	40.07 E
Surna	116	Cb	62.59N	8.40 E
Surnadalsøra	116	Cb	62.59N	8.39 E
Surovikino	136	Ef	48.36N	42.54 E
Surovo	138	Fe	55.39N	105.36 E
Sur-Pakri/Suur-Pakri	116	Je	59.50N	23.45 E
Surprise, Ile-	219b	Ad	18.32S	163.02 E
Surprise, Lac-	184	Ja	49.20N	74.57W
Surrey [3]	118	Mj	51.25N	0.30W
Surrey	118	Mj	51.20N	0.05W
Sursee	128	Cc	47.10N	8.07 E
Sursk	132	Nc	53.04N	45.42 E
Surskoje	114	Li	54.31N	46.44 E
Surt	160	Ie	31.13N	16.35 E
Surt, Khalīj-=Sidra, Gulf of-(EN)	158	Ie	31.30N	18.00 E
Surte	116	Eg	57.49N	12.01 E
Surtsey	114a	Bc	63.20N	20.38W
Sürüç	146	Hd	36.58N	38.24 E
Surud Ad	158	Lg	10.42N	47.09 E
Suruga-Wan	154	Og	34.55N	138.35 E
Surulangun	150	Dg	2.37S	102.45 E
Survey Pass	178	Ic	67.52N	154.10W
Sur Vjajn / Suur Väin	116	Jf	58.30N	23.20 E
Surwold	124	Jb	52.57N	7.31 E
Šuša	132	Oj	39.43N	46.44 E
Suså	116	Di	55.11N	11.46 E
Susa [It.]	128	Be	45.08N	7.03 E
Susa [Jap.]	156	Bd	34.37N	131.36 E
Susa (EN) = Shūsh	146	Mf	32.12N	48.17 E
Susa, Val di-	128	Be	45.10N	7.10 E
Sušac	128	Kh	42.46N	16.30 E
Sūsah [Lib.]	164	Dc	32.54N	21.58 E
Sūsah [Tun.] = Sousse (EN)	160	Ie	35.49N	10.38 E
Sūsah=Sousse (EN) [3]	162	Jb	35.45N	10.30 E
Susak	128	If	44.31N	14.18 E
Susaki	152	Ne	33.22N	133.17 E
Susami	156	De	33.33N	135.29 E
Susamyr	135	Ic	42.09N	73.59 E
Susanville	182	Cc	40.25N	120.39W
Suşehri	146	Hb	40.11N	38.06 E
Suseja	116	Kh	56.23N	25.00 E
Šušenskoje	138	Ef	53.19N	92.01 E
Sušice	120	Jg	49.14N	13.30 E
Susitna	178	Id	61.16N	150.30W
Suslonger	114	Lh	56.18N	48.12 E
Susoh	150	Cf	3.43N	96.50 E
Susong	154	Di	30.10N	116.06 E
Suspiro	204	Ej	30.38S	54.22W
Suspiro del Moro, Puerto del-	126	Ig	37.08N	3.40W
Susquehanna River	182	Ld	39.33N	76.05W
Susques	206	Gb	23.25S	66.29W
Sussex	184	Oc	45.43N	65.31W
Sussex	118	Mk	50.55N	0.30W
Sussex, Vale of-	118	Mk	51.00N	0.15W
Susubona	219a	Dc	8.19S	159.27 E
Susuman	142	Qc	62.47N	148.10 E
Susurluk	146	Cc	39.54N	28.10 E
Susuzmüsellim	130	Kh	41.06N	27.03 E
Šušvė	116	Ji	55.08N	23.53 E
Susz	120	Pc	53.44N	19.20 E
Sütçüler	146	Dd	37.30N	30.59 E
Suţeşti	130	Kd	45.13N	27.26 E
Sutherland	172	Cf	32.24S	20.40 E
Sutherland Falls	218	Bf	44.48S	167.44 E
Sutherlin	188	De	43.25N	123.19W
Sutla	128	Je	45.51N	15.41 E
Sutlej	140	Jg	29.23N	71.02 E
Sutton	184	Gf	38.41N	80.43W
Sutton, London-	124	Bc	51.21N	0.12W
Sutton Bridge	124	Cb	52.46N	0.11 E
Sutton in Ashfield	124	Aa	53.07N	1.16W
Sutton Scotney	124	Ac	51.09N	1.20W
Suttor River	212	Jd	21.25S	147.45 E
Suttsu	154	Pc	42.48N	140.14 E
Sutwik	178	He	56.34N	157.05W
Su'uholo	219a	Ec	9.46S	161.58 E
Suunduk	132	Ud	51.46N	58.46 E
Suure-Jaani	114	Fg	58.31N	25.29 E
Suur-Pakri/Sur-Pakri	116	Je	59.50N	23.45 E
Suur Väin / Sur-Vjajn	116	Jf	58.30N	23.20 E
Suva	210	If	18.08S	178.25 E
Suvadiva Atoll	140	Ji	0.30N	73.13 E
Suva Gora	130	Eh	41.51N	21.03 E
Suva Planina	130	Ff	43.08N	22.13 E
Suvasvesi	114	Ge	62.40N	28.10 E
Suvorov	132	Jb	54.08N	36.32 E
Suvorovo [Mold.-U.S.S.R.]	130	Mc	46.33N	29.35 E
Suvorovo [Ukr.-U.S.S.R.]	130	Ld	45.35N	29.00 E
Suvorovskaja	132	Mg	44.10N	42.38 E
Suwa	154	Of	36.02N	138.08 E
Suwa-Ko	156	Fc	36.03N	138.05 E
Suwałki	120	Sb	54.07N	22.56 E
Suwałki [2]	120	Sb	54.05N	22.55 E
Suwalskie, Pojezierze-	120	Sb	54.15N	23.00 E
Suwannee River	184	Fk	29.18N	83.09W
Suwanose-Jima	152	Mf	29.40N	129.45 E
Suwarrow Atoll	208	Kf	13.15S	163.05W
Suwayqīyah, Hawr as-	146	Lf	32.40N	46.03 E
Suways, Khalīj as-=Suez, Gulf of-(EN)	158	Kf	28.10N	33.27 E
Suways, Qanāt as-=Suez Canal (EN)	158	Ke	29.55N	32.33 E
Suwŏn	152	Md	37.16N	127.01 E
Suxian [China]	152	Ke	33.36N	116.58 E
Suxian [China]	152	Je	31.44N	113.25 E
Suzaka	156	Fc	36.39N	138.18 E
Suzdal	114	Jh	56.28N	40.27 E
Suzhou	142	Of	31.16N	120.37 E
Suzhou/Jiuquan	142	Lf	39.46N	98.34 E
Suzi He	154	Hd	41.56N	124.20 E
Suzu	152	Od	37.25N	137.17 E
Suzuka	156	Ed	34.51N	136.35 E
Suzuka-Sanmyaku	156	Ed	35.10N	136.20 E
Suzu-Misaki	154	Nf	37.28N	137.20 E
Suzun	138	Df	53.47N	82.19 E
Suzzara	128	Ef	45.00N	10.45 E
Særholthalvøya	114	Ga	70.30N	26.05 E
Svågan	116	Gc	61.54N	16.33 E
Svalbard [5]	224	Kd	78.00N	20.00 E
Svaljava	132	Ce	48.32N	22.59 E
Svalöv	116	Ei	55.55N	13.06 E
Svaneholm	116	Ee	59.11N	12.33 E
Svaneke	116	Di	55.08N	15.09 E
Svängsta	116	Fh	56.16N	14.46 E
Svanøy	116	Ac	61.30N	5.05 E
Svapa	132	Id	51.44N	34.59 E
Svappavaara	114	Ec	67.39N	21.04 E
Svärdsjö	116	Fd	60.45N	15.55 E
Svartå	116	Fe	59.08N	14.31 E
Svartälven	116	Fe	59.20N	14.35 E
Svartån [Swe.]	116	Fe	59.17N	15.15 E
Svartån [Swe.]	116	Ge	59.37N	16.33 E
Svartån [Swe.]	116	Ff	58.28N	15.33 E
Svartenhuk Halvø=Svartenhuk Peninsula (EN)	179	Gd	71.30N	55.20W
Svartenhuk Peninsula (EN)=Svartenhuk, Halvø	179	Gd	71.30N	55.20W
Svartisen	114	Cc	66.38N	13.58 E
Svatovo	136	Df	49.24N	38.13 E
Svay Riĕng	148	Lf	11.05N	105.48 E
Sveabreen	222	Cf	72.08S	1.53 E
Sveagruva	179	Nc	78.39N	16.25 E
Svealand	110	Hc	60.30N	15.30 E
Svealand	114	Dg	59.55N	15.30 E
Svedala	116	Ei	55.30N	13.14 E
Sveg	114	De	62.02N	14.21 E
Švėkšna	116	Ii	55.32N	21.30 E
Svelgen	114	Af	61.45N	5.18 E
Svelvik	116	De	59.37N	10.24 E
Švenčėneljaj/Švenčionėliai	114	Gi	55.09N	26.02 E
Švenčėnis/Švenčionys	114	Gi	55.07N	26.12 E
Švenčionėliai/Švenčėneljaj	114	Gi	55.09N	26.02 E
Švenčionys/Švenčėnis	114	Gi	55.07N	26.12 E
Svendborg	114	Ci	55.03N	10.37 E
Svendsen Peninsula	180	Ja	77.50N	84.00W
Svenljunga	114	Ch	57.30N	13.07 E
Svenska högarna	116	He	59.35N	19.35 E
Svenskøya	179	Oc	78.43N	26.30 E
Svenstavik	114	De	62.46N	14.27 E
Šventoj/Šventoji	116	Ih	56.04N	20.59 E
Šventoji	114	Fi	55.05N	24.24 E
Šventoji/Šventoj	116	Ih	56.04N	20.59 E
Sverdlovsk	142	Id	56.51N	60.36 E
Sverdlovskaja oblast [3]	136	Gd	59.00N	62.00 E
Sverdrup, ostrov-	138	Cb	74.30N	79.35 E
Sverdrup Channel	180	Ha	80.00N	96.30W
Sverdrup Islands	179	Jb	79.00N	98.00W
Sverige=Sweden (EN) [1]	112	Hc	62.00N	15.00 E
Svetac	128	Jg	43.02N	15.45 E
Svete/Svēte	116	Jh	56.40N	23.38 E
Svēte/Svete	116	Jh	56.40N	23.38 E
Sveti Naum	130	Di	40.55N	20.45 E
Sveti Nikola, prohod-	130	Ff	43.27N	22.36 E
Sveti Nikole	130	Eh	41.52N	21.57 E
Sveti Stefan	130	Bg	42.16N	18.54 E
Svetlaja	138	Ig	46.31N	138.18 E
Svetli	138	Ge	58.34N	116.00 E
Svetlogorsk [Bye.-U.S.S.R.]	136	Ce	52.38N	29.42 E
Svetlogorsk [R.S.F.S.R.]	116	Ij	54.55N	20.08 E
Svetlograd	136	Ef	45.19N	42.40 E
Svetlovodsk	132	He	49.02N	33.15 E
Svetly [R.S.F.S.R.]	136	Ge	50.51N	60.53 E
Svetly [R.S.F.S.R.]	114	Ei	54.41N	20.08 E
Svetly Jar	132	Ne	48.29N	44.46 E
Svetogorsk	114	Gf	61.07N	28.58 E
Svetozarevo	130	Ef	43.59N	21.15 E
Sviča	120	Ug	49.04N	24.06 E
Svid	114	Jf	61.13N	38.45 E
Svidník	120	Rg	49.18N	21.35 E
Svidník	120	Kg	49.23N	14.58 E
Svijaga	132	Ed	55.39N	48.28 E
Svilaja	128	Kg	43.50N	16.26 E
Svilengrad	130	Jh	41.46N	26.12 E
Svincovy Rudnik	135	Ff	37.52N	66.28 E
Svinecea Mare, Vîrful-	130	Fe	44.48N	22.09 E
Svir	116	Lj	54.50N	26.34 E
Svir	110	Jc	60.30N	32.48 E
Svirica	114	Hf	60.30N	32.54 E
Svirsk	138	Ff	53.04N	103.18 E
Svisloč	132	Dc	53.03N	24.07 E
Svisloč	132	Fc	53.27N	28.59 E
Svištov	130	If	43.37N	25.20 E
Svit	120	Qg	49.03N	20.12 E
Svitava	120	Mg	49.11N	16.38 E
Svitavy	120	Mg	49.46N	16.27 E
Svizra / Svizzera / Schweiz / Suisse = Switzerland (EN) [1]	112	Gf	46.00N	8.30 E
Svizzera / Schweiz / Suisse / Svizra = Switzerland (EN) [1]	112	Gf	46.00N	8.30 E
Svjatoj Nos, mys- [R.S.F.S.R.]	110	Jb	68.10N	39.43 E
Svjatoj Nos, mys- [R.S.F.S.R.]	138	Jb	72.45N	140.45 E
Svobodny	142	Od	51.24N	128.07 E
Svoge	130	Gg	42.58N	23.21 E
Svolvær	114	Db	68.14N	14.34 E
Svratka	120	Mh	48.52N	16.38 E
Svrljig	130	Ff	43.25N	22.08 E
Svulrya	116	Ed	60.25N	12.24 E
Svytaya Anna Trough (EN)	224	He	80.00N	70.00 E
Swabia (EN)=Schwaben	120	Gh	48.20N	10.30 E
Swabian-Bavarian Plateau (EN)=Schwäbisch-Bayerisches Alpenvorland	110	Hf	48.15N	10.30 E
Swabian Jura (EN)=Schwäbische Alb	110	Gf	48.25N	9.30 E
Swaffham	124	Cb	52.39N	0.41 E
Swain Reefs	208	Gg	21.40S	152.15 E
Swains Atoll	208	Jf	11.03S	171.05W
Swainsboro	184	Fi	32.36N	82.20W
Swakop	172	Ad	22.41S	14.31 E
Swakopmund	160	Ik	22.41S	14.34 E
Swakopmund [3]	172	Ad	22.30S	15.00 E
Swale	118	Lg	54.06N	1.20W
Swalmen	124	Ic	51.14N	6.02 E
Swanage	118	Lk	50.37N	1.58W
Swan Hill	212	Ig	35.21S	143.34 E
Swan Range	188	Ic	47.50N	113.40W
Swan River	180	Hf	52.06N	101.16W
Swansboro	184	Ih	34.36N	77.07W
Swansea [Austl.]	212	Jh	42.08S	148.04 E
Swansea [Wales-U.K.]	112	Fe	51.38N	3.57W
Swansea Bay	118	Jj	51.35N	3.52W
Swans Island	184	Mc	44.10N	68.25W
Swanson Lake	186	Ff	40.09N	101.06W
Swan Valley	188	Je	43.28N	111.20W
Swartberge	158	Jl	33.23S	21.48 E
Swarzędz	120	Nd	52.26N	17.05 E
Swastika	184	Ga	48.07N	80.12W
Swaziland [1]	160	Kk	26.30S	31.10 E
Sweden (EN)=Sverige [1]	112	Hc	62.00N	15.00 E
Swedru	166	Ed	5.32N	0.42W
Sweet Grass Hills	188	Jb	48.55N	111.30W
Sweet Home	188	Dd	44.24N	122.44W
Sweetwater	182	Ge	32.28N	100.25W
Sweetwater River	182	Fc	42.31N	107.02W
Swellendam	172	Cf	34.02S	20.26 E
Świder	120	Rd	52.08N	21.12 E
Świdnica	120	Mf	50.51N	16.29 E
Świdnik	120	Se	51.14N	22.41 E
Świdwin	120	Lc	53.47N	15.47 E
Świebodzin	120	Ld	52.15N	15.32 E
Świecie	120	Oc	53.25N	18.28 E
Świętej Anny, Góra-	120	Of	50.28N	18.13 E
Świętokrzyskie, Góry-	120	Qf	50.55N	21.00 E
Swift Current	180	Gf	50.17N	107.50W
Swift Current Creek	188	La	50.40N	107.44W
Swift River	180	Ed	60.05N	131.11W
Swilly, Lough-/Loch Suili	118	Ff	55.10N	7.38W
Swinburne, Cape-	180	Hb	71.14N	98.33W
Swindon	118	Lj	51.34N	1.47W
Swinford/Béal Átha na Muice	118	Eh	53.57N	8.57W
Świnoujście	120	Kc	53.53N	14.14 E
Swisttal	124	Id	50.44N	6.54 E
Switzerland (EN) = Schweiz / Suisse / Svizzera / Svizra [1]	112	Gf	46.00N	8.30 E
Switzerland (EN) = Suisse / Svizra / Svizzera / Schweiz [1]	112	Gf	46.00N	8.30 E
Switzerland (EN) = Svizra / Svizzera / Schweiz / Suisse [1]	112	Gf	46.00N	8.30 E
Switzerland (EN) = Svizzera / Schweiz / Suisse / Svizra [1]	112	Gf	46.00N	8.30 E
Syčevka	132	Ib	55.51N	34.15 E
Syców	120	Ne	51.19N	17.43 E
Sydfalster-Gedser	114	Ci	54.35N	11.57 E
Sydkap Ice Cap	180	Ja	76.30N	85.00W
Sydney [Austl.]	210	Gh	33.52S	151.13 E
Sydney [N.S.-Can.]	176	Me	46.09N	60.11W
Sydney→Manra Atoll	208	Je	4.27S	171.15W
Sydney-Campbelltown	212	Kf	34.04S	150.49 E
Sydney Lake	186	Ia	50.40N	94.24W
Sydney Mines	180	Lg	46.14N	60.12W
Sydney-Penrith	212	Kf	33.45S	150.42 E
Syktyvkar	112	Lc	61.40N	50.46 E
Sylacauga	184	Di	33.10N	86.15W
Sylane	114	Ce	63.02N	12.13 E
Sylarna	114	Ce	63.02N	12.13 E
Sylhet	148	Id	24.54N	91.52 E
Sylling	116	De	59.54N	10.17 E
Sylt	120	Eb	54.55N	8.20 E
Sylva	134	Hh	57.40N	56.57 E
Sylvania	188	Gi	32.45N	81.38W
Sylvania Tablemount (EN)	214	Ge	11.58N	165.00 E
Sylvan Pass	182	Ec	44.28N	110.08W
Sylvester	184	Fj	31.32N	83.49W
Sylvester, Lake-	212	Hc	18.50S	135.50 E
Sym	138	Ed	60.15N	90.02 E
Syndassko	138	Fb	73.14N	108.05 E
Synja	134	Ld	65.12N	64.45 E
Synnfjell	116	Cc	61.05N	9.45 E
Syowa	222	De	69.00S	39.35 E
Syracuse [Ks.-U.S.]	186	Fh	37.59N	101.45W
Syracuse [N.Y.-U.S.]	176	Le	43.03N	76.09W
Syracuse (EN)=Siracusa	112	Hh	37.04N	15.18 E
Syrdarinskaja oblast [3]	136	Gg	40.30N	68.40 E
Syrdarja	136	Gg	40.52N	68.38 E
Syrdarja=Syr Darya (EN)	140	Ie	46.03N	61.00 E
Syr Darya (EN)=Syrdarja	140	Ie	46.03N	61.00 E
Syria (EN) [1]	140	Ff	35.00N	38.00 E
Syria (EN)=Sūrīyah [1]	142	Ff	35.00N	38.00 E
Syriam	148	Je	16.46N	96.15 E
Syrian Desert (EN) = Shām, Bādiyat ash-	140	Ff	32.00N	40.00 E
Syrkovoje, ozero-	134	Lf	60.40N	65.00 E
Syrski	132	Kc	52.36N	39.28 E
Sysert	134	Jh	56.31N	60.49 E
Sysmä	116	Ff	61.30N	25.41 E
Sysola	136	Fc	61.42N	50.58 E
Syssleback	116	Ed	60.44N	12.52 E
Sysulp, gora-	130	Ha	48.29N	24.17 E
Syverma, plato-	140	Lc	67.00N	99.00 E
Syzran	112	Ke	53.09N	48.27 E
Szabolcs-Szatmár [2]	120	Sh	48.00N	22.10 E
Szamocin	120	Nc	53.02N	17.08 E
Szamos	130	Fa	48.07N	22.20 E
Szamotuły	120	Md	52.37N	16.35 E
Szarvas	120	Qj	46.52N	20.33 E
Szczawnica Krościenko	120	Qg	49.26N	20.30 E
Szczebrzeszyn	120	Sf	50.42N	22.59 E
Szczecin [2]	120	Kc	52.35N	14.30 E
Szczecin (Stettin)	112	He	53.24N	14.32 E
Szczecinek	120	Mc	53.43N	16.42 E
Szczeciński, Zalew-	120	Kc	53.46N	14.14 E
Szczekociny	120	Pf	50.38N	19.50 E
Szczerców	120	Pe	51.18N	19.09 E
Szczucin	120	Rf	50.18N	21.04 E
Szczuczyn	120	Sc	53.34N	22.18 E
Szczytno	120	Qc	53.34N	21.00 E
Szechwan (EN)=Sichuan Sheng (Ssu-ch'uan Sheng) [2]	152	He	30.00N	103.00 E
Szechwan (EN)=Ssu-ch'uan Sheng→Sichuan Sheng [2]	152	He	30.00N	103.00 E
Szécsény	120	Ph	48.05N	19.31 E
Szeged	112	If	46.15N	20.10 E
Szeged	120	Qj	46.16N	20.08 E
Szeghalom	120	Ri	47.02N	21.10 E
Székesfehérvár	112	Hf	47.12N	18.25 E
Szekszárd	120	Oj	46.21N	18.43 E
Szendrő	120	Qh	48.24N	20.44 E
Szentendre	120	Pi	47.40N	19.05 E
Szentes	120	Qj	46.39N	20.16 E
Szentgotthárd	120	Mj	46.57N	16.17 E
Szerencs	120	Rh	48.10N	21.12 E
Szeskie Wzgórza	120	Sb	54.14N	22.22 E
Szigetvár	120	Nj	46.03N	17.48 E
Szkwa	120	Rc	53.10N	21.45 E
Szlichtyngowa	120	Me	51.43N	16.15 E
Szob	120	Oi	47.49N	18.52 E
Szolnok	120	Qi	47.11N	20.12 E
Szolnok [2]	120	Qi	47.15N	20.30 E
Szombathely	120	Mi	47.14N	16.37 E
Szprotawa	120	Le	51.34N	15.33 E
Szreniawa	120	Qf	50.10N	20.35 E
Sztum	120	Pc	53.56N	19.01 E
Szubin	120	Nc	53.00N	17.44 E
Szydłów	120	Rf	50.35N	21.01 E
Szydłowiec	120	Qe	51.14N	20.51 E

T

Taakoka	220p	Cc	21.15S	159.43W
Taalintendas/Dalsbruk	116	Jd	60.02N	22.31 E
Taavetti	116	Ld	60.55N	27.34 E
Tab	120	Oj	46.44N	18.02 E
Tabacal	206	Hb	23.16S	64.15W
Ţabah	146	Ji	27.02N	42.08 E
Tabaqah	146	He	35.52N	38.34 E
Tabar Islands	208	Ge	2.50S	152.00 E
Ţabarqah	162	Ib	36.57N	8.45 E
Ţabas	146	Qf	33.36N	56.54 E
Tabasará, Serrania de-	194	Gi	8.33N	81.40W
Tabasco [2]	190	Fe	18.00N	92.40W
Tabasco y Campeche, Llanos de-	190	Fe	18.15N	91.00W
Tabašino	114	Lh	56.59N	47.43 E
Tābask, Kūh-e-	146	Nh	29.52N	51.49 E
Tabay	204	Ci	28.18S	58.17W
Tabelbala	162	Gd	29.24N	3.15W
Taber	180	Gg	49.47N	112.08W
Taberg	116	Fg	57.41N	14.05 E
Taberg	116	Fg	57.41N	14.05 E
Tabernacle	197c	Ab	17.23N	62.46W
Tabernas	126	Jg	37.03N	2.23W
Tabernes de Valldigna / Tavernes de Valldigna	126	Le	39.04N	0.16W
Tabiteuea Atoll	208	Ie	1.20S	174.50 E
Tabla	166	Fc	13.46N	3.01 E
Tablas	150	Hd	12.24N	122.02 E
Tablas Strait	150	Hd	12.40N	121.48 E
Tablat	126	Ph	36.25N	3.19 E
Tablazo, Bahia del-	194	Lh	10.52N	71.35W
Table Cape	218	Gc	39.06S	178.00 E
Table Rock Lake	186	Jh	36.35N	93.30W
Tabocas	204	Jb	14.39S	45.28W
Taboco, Rio-	204	Ed	19.53S	55.58W
Tabola	132	Pg	45.53N	48.20 E
Tábor	120	Kg	49.25N	14.41 E
Tabora	160	Ki	5.01S	32.48 E
Tabora [3]	170	Fd	5.20S	32.30 E
Tabory	134	Lg	58.31N	64.33 E
Tabou	160	Gh	4.25N	7.21W
Tabrīz	142	Gf	38.05N	46.18 E
Tābua	126	Dd	40.21N	8.02W
Tabuaeran Atoll (Fanning)	208	Ld	3.52N	159.20W
Tabuk	150	Hc	17.24N	121.25 E
Tabūk	142	Fg	28.23N	36.35 E
Ţaburbah	128	Dn	36.50N	9.50 E
Tabursuq	128	Dn	36.28N	9.15 E
Tabursuq, Monts de-	128	Dn	36.25N	9.05 E
Tabusintac	184	Ob	47.24N	65.02W
Tabwemasana	219b	Cb	15.22S	166.45 E
Täby	114	Eg	59.30N	18.03 E
Tacámbaro de Codallos	192	Ih	19.14N	101.28W
Tacarcuna, Cerro-	194	Ij	8.05N	77.17W
Tacarigua, Laguna de-	196	Dg	10.15N	65.50W
Tacheng/Qoqek	142	Ke	46.45N	82.57 E
Tachibana-Wan	156	Be	32.45N	130.05 E
Tachichilte, Isla de-	192	Ee	24.59N	108.04W
Tachikawa [Jap.]	156	Fb	38.48N	139.58 E
Tachikawa [Jap.]	156	Fd	35.42N	139.23 E
Táchira [2]	202	Db	7.50N	72.05W
Tachiumet	164	Bd	26.19N	10.03 E
Tachov	120	Ig	49.48N	12.40 E
Tachungnya	220b	Bb	14.58N	145.36 E
Tacinski	132	Le	48.13N	41.17 E
Tacir	130	Mi	40.32N	29.44 E
Tacloban	142	Oh	11.15N	125.00 E
Tacna	200	Ig	18.01S	70.15W
Tacna [3]	202	Dg	17.40S	70.20W
Tacoma	176	Ge	47.15N	122.27W
Tacotalpa, Rio-	192	Mi	17.50N	92.52W
Tacuaral	204	Cd	18.59S	58.07W
Tacuarembó	206	Id	31.44S	55.59W
Tacuarembó [2]	204	Ek	32.10S	55.30W
Tacuarembó, Rio-	204	Ek	32.25S	55.29W
Tacuari, Rio-	204	Fk	32.46S	53.18W
Tacuati	204	Df	23.27S	56.35W
Tadami	156	Fc	37.21N	139.17 E
Tadami-Gawa	156	Fc	37.38N	139.45 E
Tadarimana, Rio-	204	Ec	16.29S	54.31W
Tademaït, Plateau du-	158	Hf	28.30N	2.15 E
Tadine	219b	Ce	21.33S	167.53 E
Tadjeraout	162	He	21.17N	1.20 E
Tadjetaret	162	Ie	22.00N	7.30 E
Tadjourah	168	Gc	11.45N	42.54 E
Tadjourah, Golfe de-	168	Gc	11.45N	43.00 E
Tadoule Lake	180	He	58.35N	98.20W
Tadoussac	184	Ma	48.09N	69.43W
Tadžikskaja Sovetskaja Socialističeskaja Respublika [2]	136	Hh	39.00N	71.00 E
Tadžikskaja SSR/ Respublikai Soveth Socialisti Todžikiston [2]	136	Hh	39.00N	71.00 E
Tadžikskaja SSR = Tajik SSR (EN) [2]	136	Hh	39.00N	71.00 E
T'aebaek-Sanmaek	140	Of	37.40N	128.50 E
Taechon	154	If	36.21N	126.36 E
T'aech'on	154	Ie	39.55N	125.30 E
Taedong-gang	154	He	38.42N	125.15 E
Taegu	142	Of	35.52N	128.36 E
Taeha-dong	154	Kf	37.31N	130.48 E
Taehan-Haehyŏp=Korea Strait (EN)	140	Of	34.40N	129.00 E
Taehan-Min' guk=South Korea (EN) [1]	142	Of	38.00N	127.30 E
Taehuksan-Do	154	Hg	34.40N	125.25 E
Taejŏn	142	Of	36.20N	127.26 E
Tafahi Island	208	Jf	15.52S	173.55W
Tafalla	126	Kb	42.31N	1.40W
Tafassasset	158	If	21.56N	10.12 E
Tafassasset, Ténéré du-	166	Ha	21.20N	11.00 E
Taff	118	Jj	51.27N	3.09W
Tafilalt	162	Gc	31.18N	4.18W
Tafiré	166	Dd	9.04N	5.10W
Tafi Viejo	206	Gc	26.44S	65.16W
Taflan	146	Gb	41.25N	36.09 E
Tafna	126	Ki	35.18N	1.28W
Tafraout	162	Fd	29.43N	9.00W
Tafresh	146	Ne	34.41N	50.01 E
Taft	146	Pg	31.45N	54.14 E
Taftān, Kuh-e-	146	Ig	28.36N	61.06 E
Taftanāz	146	Ge	35.59N	36.47 E
Taga	221c	Aa	13.46S	172.28W
Taga Dzong	148	Hc	27.04N	89.53 E
Tagajō	156	Gb	38.18N	140.58 E
Tagama	158	Hg	15.50N	8.12 E
Taganrog	112	Jf	47.12N	38.56 E
Taganrogski zaliv	132	Kf	46.50N	38.25 E
Tagant [3]	162	Ef	18.30N	10.30W
Tagant	158	Fg	17.31N	12.07W
Tagarev, gora-	135	Ae	38.19N	57.18 E
Tagawa	156	Be	33.39N	130.48 E
Tagbilaran	150	He	9.39N	123.51 E
Tageru, Jabal-	168	Db	16.25N	27.10 E
Taggia	128	Bg	43.52N	7.51 E
Taghit	162	Gc	30.55N	2.02W
Tagil	134	Kg	58.33N	62.30 E
Tagish Lake	180	Ed	60.00N	134.00W
Tagliamento	128	He	45.38N	13.06 E
Taglio di Po	128	Ge	45.00N	12.12 E
Tagomago, Illa- / Tagomago, Isla de-	126	Ne	39.02N	1.39 E
Tagomago, Isla de- / Tagomago, Illa-	126	Ne	39.02N	1.39 E
Tagounit	162	Fd	29.58N	5.35W
Tagpochau, Ogso-	220b	Ba	15.11N	145.45 E
Tagrifat	164	Cd	29.12N	17.21 E
Taguatinga	202	If	12.25S	46.26W
Taguersimet	162	De	24.09N	15.07W
Tagula	219a	Ad	11.20S	153.00 E
Tagula Island	208	Gf	11.30S	153.30 E
Tagum	150	Ie	7.21N	125.50 E
Tagus (EN)=Tajo	110	Fh	38.40N	9.24W
Tagus (EN)=Tejo	110	Fh	38.40N	9.24W
Tah	162	Ed	27.37N	12.50W
Tahaa, Ile-	216	Kc	16.38S	151.30W
Tahakopa	218	Cg	46.31S	169.23 E
Tahan, Gunong-	140	Mi	4.39N	102.14 E
Tahanea Atoll	208	Mf	16.52S	144.45W
Tahat	158	Hf	23.18N	5.32 E
Tahe	152	La	52.22N	124.48 E
Ţāherī	146	Oi	27.42N	52.21 E
Tahgong, Puntan-	220b	Ba	15.06N	145.39 E
Tahiataš	135	Bc	42.20N	59.33 E
Tahifet	162	Ie	22.56N	5.59 E
Tahir Geçidi	146	Jc	39.52N	42.20 E
Tahiti, Ile-	208	Mf	17.37S	149.27W
Tahkuna neem / Takuna, mys-	116	Je	59.05N	22.30 E
Tahlequah	186	Ii	35.55N	94.58W
Tahoe, Lake-	188	Fg	38.54N	120.00W
Tahoua	160	Hg	14.54N	5.16 E
Tahoua [2]	166	Gb	16.00N	5.30 E

Index Symbols

- [1] Independent Nation
- [2] State, Region
- [3] District, County
- [4] Municipality
- [5] Colony, Dependency
- Continent
- Physical Region
- Historical or Cultural Region
- Mount, Mountain
- Volcano
- Hill
- Mountains, Mountain Range
- Hills, Escarpment
- Plateau, Upland
- Pass, Gap
- Plain, Lowland
- Delta
- Salt Flat
- Valley, Canyon
- Crater, Cave
- Karst Features
- Depression
- Polder
- Desert, Dunes
- Forest, Woods
- Heath, Steppe
- Oasis
- Cape, Point
- Coast, Beach
- Cliff
- Peninsula
- Isthmus
- Sandbank
- Island
- Atoll
- Rock, Reef
- Islands, Archipelago
- Rocks, Reefs
- Coral Reef
- Well, Spring
- Geyser
- River, Stream
- Waterfall, Rapids
- River Mouth, Estuary
- Lake
- Salt Lake
- Intermittent Lake
- Reservoir
- Swamp, Pond
- Canal
- Glacier
- Ice Shelf, Pack Ice
- Ocean
- Sea
- Gulf, Bay
- Strait, Fjord
- Lagoon
- Bank
- Seamount
- Tablemount
- Ridge
- Shelf
- Basin
- Escarpment, Sea Scarp
- Fracture
- Trench, Abyss
- National Park, Reserve
- Point of Interest
- Recreation Site
- Cave, Cavern
- Historic Site
- Ruins
- Wall, Walls
- Church, Abbey
- Temple
- Scientific Station
- Railway station
- Airport
- Port
- Military installation
- Lighthouse
- Mine
- Tunnel
- Dam, Bridge

Ṭaḥṭā	164	Fd	26.46N	31.28 E
Tahta-Bazar	135	Dg	35.55N	62.55 E
Tahtabrod	136	Ge	52.40N	67.35 E
Tahtakaracă pereval	135	Fe	39.17N	66.55 E
Tahtaköprü	130	Mj	39.57N	29.39 E
Tahtakupyr	136	Gg	43.01N	60.22 E
Tahtalı Dağları	146	Gc	38.46N	36.47 E
Tahtamygda	138	Hf	54.09N	123.38 E
Tahuata, Ile-	208	Ne	9.57S	139.05W
Tahulandang, Pulau-	150	If	2.20N	125.25 E
Tahuna	150	If	3.37N	125.29 E
Tai	166	Dd	5.52N	7.27W
Tai'an [China]	152	Kd	36.09N	117.05 E
Tai'an [China]	154	Gd	41.24N	122.27 E
Taiarapu, Presqu'île de-	221e	Fc	17.47S	149.14W
Taibai Shan	152	Ie	33.57N	107.40 E
Taibilla, Canal del-	126	Kg	37.43N	1.22W
Taibilla, Sierra de-	126	Jf	38.10N	2.10W
Taibus Qi (Baochang)	152	Kc	41.55N	115.22 E
Taicang	154	Fi	31.26N	121.06 E
Taichung	142	Og	24.09N	120.41 E
Taieri	218	Dg	46.03S	170.12 E
Taiga	138	De	56.04N	85.37 E
Taigonos Peninsula (EN) = Tajgonos, poluostrov-	138	Ld	61.35N	161.00 E
Taigu	154	Bf	37.26N	112.33 E
Taihang Shan	140	Nf	37.00N	114.00 E
Taihape	218	Fc	39.41S	175.48 E
Taihe [China]	154	Ch	33.11N	115.38 E
Taihe [China]	152	Jf	26.50N	114.52 E
Taiheiyō = Pacific Ocean (EN)	106	Ki	5.00N	155.00W
Taihu	152	Ke	30.26N	116.10 E
Tai Hu	140	Of	31.15N	120.10 E
Taikang	152	Je	34.00N	114.56 E
Taiki	156a	Cb	42.30N	143.16 E
Tailai	152	Lb	46.24N	123.26 E
Tailles, Plateau des-	124	Hd	50.15N	5.45 E
Taim	204	Fk	32.30S	52.35W
Tain	118	Id	57.48N	4.04W
Tainan	142	Og	23.00N	120.11 E
Tainaron, Ákra- = Matapan, Cape- (EN)	110	Ih	36.23N	22.29 E
Tain-l'Hermitage	122	Ki	45.04N	4.51 E
Taiof	219a	Ba	5.31S	154.39 E
Taipei	142	Og	25.03N	121.30 E
Taiping (Gantang)	150	Df	4.51N	100.44 E
Taiping [China]	154	Ei	30.18N	118.07 E
Taipingchuan	154	Gb	44.24N	123.11 E
Taiping Dao	150	Fd	10.15N	113.42 E
Taiping Ling	152	Lb	47.36N	120.12 E
Tairadate	156a	Bc	41.09N	140.38 E
Tairadate-Kaikyō	156a	Bc	41.10N	140.40 E
Taisei	156a	Ab	42.14N	139.49 E
Taisetsu-Zan	140	Qe	43.40N	142.48 E
Taisha	156	Cd	35.24N	132.40 E
Taishaku-San	156	Fc	36.58N	139.28 E
Tai Shan	140	Nf	36.30N	117.20 E
Taishō	156	Ce	33.12N	132.57 E
Taitao, Peninsula de- = Taitao Peninsula (EN)	198	Ij	46.30S	74.25W
Taitao Peninsula (EN) = Taitao, Peninsula de-	198	Ij	46.30S	74.25W
Taitung	152	Lg	22.45N	121.09 E
Taiwa	156	Gb	38.26N	140.52 E
Taiwan	140	Og	23.30N	121.00 E
Taiwan (Formosa)	142	Og	23.30N	121.00 E
Taiwan Haixia = Taiwan Strait (EN)	140	Ng	24.00N	119.00 E
Taiwan Strait (EN) = Taiwan Haixia	140	Ng	24.00N	119.00 E
Taixian	154	Fh	32.31N	120.08 E
Taixing	154	Fh	32.10N	120.00 E
Taiyang Shan	152	Ie	33.37N	106.26 E
Taiyetos Óros-	130	Fl	37.06N	22.18 E
Taiyuan	142	Nf	37.50N	112.37 E
Taiyue Shan	154	Bf	36.48N	112.00 E
Taizhou	154	Eh	32.29N	119.55 E
Taizhou → Linhai	152	Lf	28.52N	121.08 E
Taizhou Wan	154	Fj	28.40N	121.37 E
Taizi He	154	Gd	41.00N	122.23 E
Ta'izz	142	Gh	13.38N	44.02 E
Tăjābād	146	Pg	30.02N	54.24 E
Tajarhī	160	Be	24.21N	14.28 E
Tajgonos, mys-	138	Ld	60.35N	160.10 E
Tajgonos, poluostrov- = Taigonos Peninsula (EN)	138	Ld	61.35N	161.00 E
Tajik SSR (EN) = Tadžikskaja SSR	136	Hh	39.00N	71.00 E
Tajima	154	Of	37.12N	139.46 E
Tajimi	156	Ds	35.19N	137.08 E
Tajin	190	Ed	20.27N	97.23W
Tājirwīn	128	Cc	35.54N	8.33 E
Tajito	192	Db	30.58N	112.18W
Tajmba	138	Ed	60.22N	98.50 E
Tajmyr, ozero-	138	Ea	76.05N	98.55 E
Tajmyr, poluostrov- = Taymyr Peninsula (EN)	140	Mb	74.30N	102.30 E
Tajmyra	140	Lb	76.00N	99.40 E
Tajmyrlyr	138	Hb	72.30N	121.39 E
Tajmyrski (Dolgano-Nenecki) nacionalny okrug	138	Eb	72.00N	95.00 E
Tajo = Tagus (EN)	110	Fh	38.40N	9.24W
Tajo-Segura, Canal de Trasvase-	126	Je	39.30N	2.05W
Tajrīsh	144	Hb	38.48N	51.25 E
Tajšet	154	Nf	55.57N	98.00 E
Tajumulco, Volcán-	172	Jh	15.02N	91.54W
Tajuña	126	Je	40.10N	3.35W
Tak	148	Je	16.52N	99.08 E
Taka Atoll	214	He	11.07N	169.40 E
Takāb	146	Ld	36.24N	47.07 E
Takaba	170	Hb	3.27N	40.14 E
Takahagi	156	Pf	36.42N	140.41 E
Takahama	156	Dd	35.29N	135.33 E

Takahara-Gawa	156	Ec	36.27N	137.15 E
Takaharu	156	Bf	31.55N	130.59 E
Takahashi	154	Lg	34.47N	133.37 E
Takahashi-Gawa	156	Cd	34.32N	133.42 E
Takahata	156	Gc	38.00N	140.12 E
Takahe, Mount-	222	Of	76.17S	112.05W
Takakuma-Yama	156	Bf	31.28N	130.49 E
Takaka	218	Gd	40.51S	172.48 E
Takalous	162	Ie	23.25N	7.02 E
Takamatsu	152	Ne	34.20N	134.03 E
Takamori	156	Be	32.48N	131.08 E
Takanabe	156	Bf	32.08N	131.31 E
Takanawa-Hantō	156	Ce	34.00N	132.55 E
Takanosu	156	Gc	40.14N	140.22 E
Takaoka [Jap.]	156	Bf	31.57N	131.17 E
Takaoka [Jap.]	156	Ec	36.45N	137.01 E
Takapoto Atoll	216	Lb	15.00S	148.10W
Takapuna	218	Fb	36.48S	174.47 E
Takara-Jima	152	Mf	29.10N	129.05 E
Takarazuka	156	Dd	34.49N	135.21 E
Takaroa Atoll	216	Mb	14.28S	144.58W
Takasaki	154	Of	36.20N	139.01 E
Taka-Shima [Jap.]	156	Af	31.26N	129.45 E
Taka-Shima [Jap.]	156	Ce	32.40N	131.50 E
Takatshwane	172	Cd	22.36S	21.55 E
Takatsu-Gawa	156	Cd	34.42N	131.49 E
Takatsuki	156	Dd	34.51N	135.37 E
Takayama	154	Nf	36.08N	137.15 E
Takebe	156	Cd	34.53N	133.54 E
Takefu	154	Ng	35.54N	136.10 E
Takehara	156	Cd	34.21N	132.54 E
Takeo	156	Ae	33.12N	130.00 E
Tåkern	116	Ff	58.20N	14.50 E
Take-Shima	154	Kf	37.22N	131.58 E
Takêstān	144	Gb	36.05N	49.14 E
Taketa	156	Be	32.58N	131.24 E
Takêv	148	Kf	10.59N	104.47 E
Takhādīd	146	Mh	29.59N	44.30 E
Takhār	144	Kb	36.30N	69.32 E
Takhmaret	126	Mi	35.06N	0.41 E
Takht-e Soleimān	146	Nd	36.20N	51.07 E
Taki [Jap.]	156	Cd	35.16N	132.38 E
Taki [Pap.N.Gui.]	219a	Bb	6.29S	155.50 E
Takijuq Lake	180	Gs	66.05N	113.00W
Takikawa	154	Pc	43.33N	141.54 E
Takingeun	150	Cf	4.38N	96.50 E
Takinoue	156a	Ca	44.13N	143.03 E
Takko	156	Ga	40.20N	141.09 E
Takla Lake	180	Ee	55.30N	126.00W
Takla Landing	180	Ee	55.29N	125.58W
Takla Makan (EN) = Taklimakan Shamo	140	Kf	39.00N	83.00 E
Taklimakan Shamo = Takla Makan (EN)	140	Kf	39.00N	83.00 E
Takob	135	Ge	38.51N	69.00 E
Tako-Bana	156	Cd	35.35N	133.00W
Takolokouzet, Massif de-	166	Gb	18.40N	9.30 E
Taku	156	Be	33.19N	130.06 E
Takuan, Mount-	219a	Bb	6.27S	155.36 E
Takua Pa	148	Jg	8.52N	98.21 E
Takum	166	Gd	7.16N	9.59 E
Takuma	156	Cd	34.14N	133.40 E
Takume Atoll	208	Mf	15.49S	142.12W
Takuna, mys- / Tahkuna neem	116	Je	59.05N	22.30 E
Takutea Island	208	Lf	19.49S	158.18W
Tāla	192	Hg	20.40N	103.42W
Talah	162	Ib	35.35N	8.40 E
Talaimannar	148	Hg	9.05N	79.44 E
Talåiyeh	146	Kd	37.50N	45.00 E
Talaja	138	Kd	61.03N	152.30 E
Talak	166	Gb	18.20N	6.00 E
Talamanca, Cordillera de-	194	Fi	9.30N	83.40W
Talara	200	Hf	4.35S	81.25W
Talas	136	Ic	42.29N	72.14 E
Talas	135	Ic	44.05N	70.20 E
Talasea	212	Ka	5.20S	150.05 E
Talasski Alatau, hrebet-	135	Hc	42.10N	72.00 E
Talata Mafara	166	Gc	12.34N	6.04 E
Talaud, Kepulauan- = Talaud Islands (EN)	140	Oi	4.20N	126.50 E
Talaud Islands (EN) = Talaud, Kepulauan-	140	Oi	4.20N	126.50 E
Talavera, Isla-	204	Dh	27.32S	56.26W
Talavera de la Reina	126	He	39.57N	4.50W
Talawdī	168	Ec	10.38N	30.23 E
Talbot Inlet	180	Ja	77.55N	77.35W
Talca	200	Ii	35.26S	71.40W
Talcahuano	200	Ii	36.43S	73.07W
Tälcher	148	Hd	20.57N	85.13 E
Taldom	114	Ih	56.45N	37.32 E
Taldy-Kurgan	136	Jc	44.59N	78.23 E
Taldy-Kurganskaja oblast	136	Hf	44.00N	78.00 E
Talêh	168	Hd	9.09N	48.26 E
Tal-e Khosravī	146	Ng	30.07N	51.46 E
Talence	122	Fj	44.49N	0.36W
Ṭalesh, Kūhhā-Ye-	146	Md	37.35N	48.38 E
Talgar	135	Id	43.18N	77.13 E
Taliabu, Pulau-	150	Hg	1.48S	124.48 E
Talica	136	Gb	57.01N	63.43 E
Talimardžan	136	Gh	38.13N	65.31 E
Tali Post	168	Ec	5.54N	30.47 E
Talisajan	142	Ni	1.37N	118.11 E
Taliwang	150	Eh	8.44S	116.52 E
Talkeetna	178	Id	62.20N	150.07W
Talkeetna Mountains	178	Jd	62.10N	148.15W
Talladega	184	Di	33.26N	86.06W
Tall 'Afar	146	Jd	36.22N	42.27 E
Tallah	146	Dh	28.05N	30.44 E
Tallahassee	176	Kj	30.25N	84.16W
Tall al Abyaḍ	146	Hd	36.41N	38.57 E
Tallapoosa River	184	Di	32.30N	86.16W
Tallard	122	Mj	44.28N	6.03 E

Tällberg	116	Fd	60.49N	15.00 E
Tall Birāk at Taḥtāni	146	Id	36.38N	41.05 E
Tall Kayf	146	Jd	36.29N	43.08 E
Tall Kūshik	146	Jd	36.48N	42.04 E
Tallulah	186	Kj	32.25N	91.11W
Tālmaciu	130	Hd	45.39N	24.16 E
Talmenka	138	Df	53.51N	83.45 E
Talmest	162	Fe	31.09N	9.00W
Talnah	138	Dc	69.30N	88.15 E
Talnoje	132	Ge	48.53N	30.42 E
Talo	158	Kg	10.44N	37.55 E
Talofofo	220c	Bb	13.20N	144.46 E
Talon	138	Je	59.48N	148.50 E
Tāloqān	144	Kb	36.44N	69.33 E
Talovaja	132	Ld	51.06N	40.48 E
Talpa de Allende	192	Gg	20.23N	104.51W
Talsi	114	Fh	57.17N	22.37 E
Taltal	200	Ih	25.24S	70.29W
Taltson	180	Gd	61.24N	112.45W
Taluk	150	Cg	0.32S	101.35 E
Talvik	114	Fa	70.03N	22.58 E
Talwår	146	Md	36.00N	48.00 E
Tama	168	Cc	14.45N	22.25 E
Tamabo, Banjaran-	150	Ef	3.00N	115.30 E
Tamala	132	Mc	34.23N	7.57 E
Tamalameque	194	Ki	8.52N	73.38W
Tamale	160	Gh	9.24N	0.50W
Tamames	126	Fd	40.39N	6.06W
Tamana	156	Be	32.55N	130.33 E
Tamanaco, Rio-	196	Dh	9.25N	65.23W
Tamana Island	208	Ie	2.29S	175.59 E
Tamano	154	Lg	34.30N	133.56 E
Tamanoura	156	Ae	32.38N	128.37 E
Tamanrasset	160	Hf	22.47N	5.31 E
Tamanrasset	162	Ie	23.00N	5.30 E
Tamanrasset	158	Hf	22.03N	0.10 E
Tamar	118	Ik	50.22N	4.10W
Támara	202	Db	5.50N	72.10W
Tamara	130	Cg	42.27N	19.33 E
Tamarit de Litera/Tamarite de Litera	126	Mc	41.52N	0.26 E
Tamarite de Litera/Tamarit de Llitera	126	Mc	41.52N	0.26 E
Tamarugal, Pampa del-	206	Gb	21.00S	69.25W
Tamási	130	Dj	46.38N	18.17 E
Tamassoumit	162	Ef	18.35N	12.39W
Tamaulipas	190	Ed	24.00N	98.45W
Tamaulipas, Llanos de-	190	Ed	25.00N	98.25W
Tamaulipas, Sierra de-	192	Jf	23.30N	98.30W
Tamazula de Gordiano	192	Hh	19.38N	103.15W
Tamazunchale	190	Ed	21.16N	98.47W
Tambach	170	Gb	0.36N	35.31 E
Tambacounda	160	Fg	13.12N	15.48W
Tambara	172	Ec	16.44S	34.15 E
Tambelan, Kepulauan- = Tambelan Islands (EN)	150	Ef	1.00N	107.30 E
Tambelan, Pulau-	150	Ef	0.58N	107.34 E
Tambelan Islands (EN) = Tambelan, Kepulauan-	150	Ef	1.00N	107.30 E
Tambo	212	Jd	24.53S	146.15 E
Tambohorano	172	Gf	17.29S	43.58 E
Tambora, Gunung-	150	Gh	8.14S	117.55 E
Tambores	204	Dj	31.52S	56.16W
Tambov	112	Ke	52.43N	41.27 E
Tambovskaja oblast	136	Ee	52.45N	41.40 E
Tambre	126	Cb	42.49N	8.53W
Tambunan	150	Ge	5.40N	116.22 E
Tambura	168	Dd	5.36N	27.28 E
Tamchaket	162	Ef	17.20N	10.40W
Tame	202	Db	6.27N	71.45W
Tâmega	126	Dc	41.05N	8.21W
Tâmega	126	Dc	41.05N	8.21W
Tamel Aike	206	Fg	48.19S	70.58W
Tamesí	190	Ed	22.13N	97.52W
Tamesnar	156	Hg	21.55N	3.33 E
Tamgak, Monts-	158	Hg	19.11N	8.42 E
Tamgue, Massif du-	166	Fc	12.00N	12.18W
Tamiahua	192	Jg	21.16N	97.27W
Tamiahua, Laguna de-	190	Ed	21.35N	97.35W
Tamianglajang	150	Gg	2.07S	115.10 E
Tamil Nādu	148	Ff	11.00N	78.00 E
Tamise/Temse	124	Gc	51.08N	4.13 E
Tamitatoala, Rio-	202	Hf	11.56S	53.36W
Ţāmiyah	146	Dh	29.29N	30.58 E
Tam Ky	148	Le	15.34N	108.29 E
Tammaro	128	Ii	41.09N	14.50 E
Tammela	116	Jd	60.48N	23.46 E
Tammerfors/Tampere	112	Ic	61.30N	23.45 E
Tammisaari/Ekenäs	114	Fg	59.58N	23.26 E
Tamnaren	116	Gd	60.10N	17.25 E
Tamnava	130	De	44.25N	20.05 E
Tamou	166	Fc	12.45N	2.11 E
Tampa	176	Kj	27.57N	82.27W
Tampa Bay	182	Kf	27.45N	82.35W
Tampake-Misaki	156a	Bb	43.43N	141.20 E
Tampere/Tammerfors	112	Ic	61.30N	23.45 E
Tampico	176	Jg	22.13N	97.51W
Tampin	150	Df	2.28N	102.14 E
Tamri	162	Fc	30.43N	9.50 E
Tamsag-Bulak	152	Kb	47.14N	117.21 E
Tamsalu	114	Gg	59.10N	26.07 E
Tamsweg	128	Hc	47.08N	13.48 E
Tamu	148	Jc	24.13N	94.19 E
Tamuin	192	Jg	21.59N	98.46W
Tamuin, Rio-	192	Jg	21.47N	98.28W
Tamworth [Austl.]	210	Jh	31.05S	150.55 E
Tamworth [Eng.-U.K.]	118	Li	52.39N	1.40W
Tana [Eur.]	110	Ja	70.28N	28.18 E
Tana [Kenya]	158	Li	2.32S	40.31 E
Tana, Lake-	168	Gc	12.00N	37.20 E
Tanabe	154	Mh	33.42N	135.44 E
Tana bru	114	Ja	70.16N	28.10 E
Tanacross	178	Kd	63.23N	143.21W

Tanafjorden	114	Ga	70.54N	28.40 E
Tanaga	178a	Cb	51.50N	178.00W
Tanagro	128	Jj	40.38N	15.14 E
Tanagura	156	Gd	37.02N	140.23 E
Tanahbala, Pulau-	150	Cg	0.25S	98.25 E
Tanahgrogot	150	Gg	1.55S	116.12 E
Tanahjampea, Pulau-	150	Hh	7.05S	120.42 E
Tanahmasa, Pulau-	150	Cg	0.12S	98.27 E
Tanah Merah	150	Lh	6.05S	140.17 E
Tanakpur	148	Gc	29.05N	80.07 E
Tanalyk	134	Ij	51.46N	58.45 E
Tanami	212	Fc	19.59S	129.43 E
Tanami Desert	208	Eg	20.00S	132.00 E
Tan An	148	Lf	10.32N	106.25 E
Tanana	178	Ic	65.10N	152.05W
Tanana	174	Dc	65.09N	151.55W
Tanapag	220b	Ba	15.14N	145.45 E
Tanapag, Puetton-	220b	Ba	15.14N	145.44 E
Tanárgue, Le-	122	Kj	44.37N	4.09 E
Tanaro	128	Ce	45.01N	8.47 E
Tanba-Sanchi	156	Dd	35.15N	135.35 E
Tancheng	154	Eg	34.37N	118.22 E
Tanch'ŏn	152	Mc	40.25N	128.57 E
Tancitaro, Pico de-	190	De	19.26N	102.18W
Tanda	166	Eb	7.48N	3.10W
Tanda, Lac-	166	Eb	15.45N	4.42W
Tandag	150	Ie	9.04N	126.12 E
Tandaltī	168	Ec	13.01N	31.52 E
Tăndărei	130	Ke	44.39N	27.40 E
Tandil	200	Kj	37.20S	59.05W
Tandil, Sierras del-	204	Cm	37.24S	59.06W
Tandjilé	168	Bd	9.30N	16.30 E
Tando Ādam	148	Dc	25.46N	68.40 E
Tandsjöborg	114	Df	61.42N	14.43 E
Tandubāyah	150	Db	18.40N	28.37 E
Taneatua	218	Gc	38.04S	177.00 E
Tane-Ga-Shima	152	Ne	30.40N	130.58 E
Taneichi	156	Ga	40.24N	141.43 E
Tan Emellel	162	Id	27.28N	9.45 E
Tanew	120	Sf	50.27N	22.16 E
Tanezrouft	158	Gf	24.00N	0.45W
Tanezzuft	158	Bd	25.51N	10.15 E
Tanf, Jabal at-	146	Hf	33.30N	38.42 E
Tanga	160	Ki	5.04S	39.06 E
Tanga	170	Gd	5.30S	38.00 E
Tanga Islands	208	Ga	3.30S	153.15 E
Tangalla	148	Gg	6.01N	80.48 E
Tanganyika, Lac-	170	Fd	6.00S	29.30 E
Tanganyika, Lake- (EN)	158	Ji	6.00S	29.30 E
Tanganyika, Lake-	158	Ji	6.00S	29.30 E
Tanganyika, Lake- (EN) = Tanganyika, Lac-	158	Ji	6.00S	29.30 E
Tangará	202	Ke	6.11S	35.49W
Tangarare	219a	Dc	9.35S	159.39 E
Tangdan → Dongchuan	152	Hf	26.07N	103.05 E
Tångehgol	148	Pd	37.25N	55.50 E
Tanger = Tangier (EN)	160	Ge	35.48N	5.48W
Tanger = Tangier (EN)	162	Fb	35.45N	5.45W
Tangerang	150	Eh	6.11S	106.37 E
Tangermünde	120	Hd	52.33N	11.57 E
Tangger Yumco	140	Kf	31.00N	86.25 E
Tanggshan	142	Nf	39.35N	118.09 E
Tanggula Shan	152	Fe	33.05N	91.00 E
Tanggula Shan (Dangla Shan)	140	Lf	33.00N	92.00 E
Tanggula Shankou	152	Fe	32.42N	92.27 E
Tanggulashanqu / Tuotuoheyan	142	Lf	34.15N	92.29 E
Tang He	154	Cg	32.37N	112.57 E
Tang La	140	Kg	28.00N	89.15 E
Tangorin	212	Hc	21.47S	144.12 E
Tangra Yumco	140	Kf	31.00N	86.25 E
Tangshan	142	Nf	39.35N	118.09 E
Tanguiéta	166	Fc	10.37N	1.16 E
Tangxian	154	Ce	38.44N	114.58 E
Tangyin	154	Cg	35.54N	114.21 E
Tangyuan	152	Mb	46.45N	129.53 E
Tanhoj	138	Ff	51.33N	105.07 E
Tanhuijo, Arrecife-	192	Kg	21.07N	97.17W
Taniantaweng Shan	152	Ge	30.00N	98.00 E
Tanimbar, Kepulauan- = Tanimbar Islands (EN)	208	Ee	7.30S	131.30 E
Tanimbar Islands (EN) = Tanimbar, Kepulauan-	208	Ee	7.30S	131.30 E
Tanintharyi	148	Jf	13.00N	99.00 E
Tanjung [Indon.]	150	Gg	2.11S	115.23 E
Tanjung [Indon.]	150	Cf	1.23S	103.58 E
Tanjungbalai	150	Cf	2.58N	99.48 E
Tanjungpandan	150	Eg	2.45S	107.39 E
Tanjungpinang	150	Df	0.55N	104.27 E
Tanjungredep	150	Gf	2.09N	117.29 E
Tanjungselor	150	Gf	2.50N	117.22 E
Tankenberg	124	Ib	52.21N	6.58 E
Tanna, Ile-	208	Hf	19.30S	169.20 E
Tännäs	114	Ce	62.27N	12.40 E
Tanner, Mount-	188	Fb	49.40N	118.34W
Tanns Bugt	97	Fd	57.40N	10.15 E
Tannu-Ola	140	Ld	51.00N	94.00 E
Tanot	148	Dc	27.43N	70.22 E
Tanout	160	Hg	14.58N	8.53 E
Tanshui	152	Lf	25.10N	121.28 E
Ṭanṭā	160	Kc	30.47N	31.00 E
Tan-Tan	162	Ed	28.30N	11.02W
Tan-Tan	162	Ed	28.30N	11.00W
Tan-Tan Plage	162	Ed	28.26N	11.15W
Tanzania	160	Ki	6.00S	35.00 E
Tao, Ko-	148	Jf	10.05N	99.52 E
Tao'an (Taonan)	152	Lb	45.20N	122.46 E
Tao'er He	140	Oe	45.42N	124.05 E
Taoghe	172	Cd	20.37S	22.35 E
Tao He	152	Hd	35.50N	103.20 E

Taojiang	154	Bj	28.33N	112.05 E
Taolagnaro	160	Lk	25.01S	46.59 E
Taonan = Tao'an	152	Lb	45.20N	122.46 E
Taongi Atoll	208	Hc	14.37N	168.58 E
Taormina	128	Jm	37.51N	15.17 E
Taos	182	Fd	36.24N	105.24W
Taoudenni	160	Gf	22.42N	3.56W
Taougrite	126	Mh	36.15N	1.54 E
Taounate	162	Gc	34.33N	4.39W
Taounate	162	Gc	34.04N	4.41W
Taoura	128	Cn	36.10N	8.02 E
Taourirt	162	Gc	34.25N	2.54W
Taousa	162	Gc	31.00N	4.00W
Taoyuan	152	Lg	25.00N	121.18 E
Taoyuan	136	Cg	59.15N	25.59 E
Tapa	114	Ge	59.15N	25.58 E
Tapachula	176	Jh	14.54N	92.17W
Tapaga, Cape-	221c	Bb	14.01S	171.23W
Tapah	150	Df	4.11N	101.16 E
Tapajós, Rio-	198	Kf	2.24S	54.41W
Tapaktuan	152	Cf	3.16N	97.11 E
Tapalqué	204	Bm	36.21S	60.01W
Tapan	150	Cg	2.10S	101.04 E
Tapanahoni Rivier	202	Hc	4.22N	54.27W
Tapanlieh	152	Lg	21.58N	120.47 E
Tapanui	218	Cf	45.57S	169.16 E
Tapauá	202	Fe	5.45S	64.23W
Tapauá, Rio-	198	Jf	5.40S	64.21W
Tapenagá, Rio-	204	Cb	27.54S	60.23W
Taperas	204	Bc	17.54S	60.23W
Tapes	206	Jd	30.40S	51.23W
Tapeta	166	Dd	6.29N	8.51W
Taphan Hin	148	Ke	16.12N	100.26 E
Tapini	214	Di	8.19S	146.59 E
Tapiola, Espoo-	116	Kd	60.11N	24.49 E
Tapirai	204	Id	19.52S	46.01W
Tapirapuã	204	Db	14.51S	57.45W
Tapolca	120	Nj	46.53N	17.26 E
Tappahannock	184	Ig	37.55N	76.54W
Tappi-Zaki	154	Pd	41.18N	140.22 E
Tappu	156a	Ba	44.04N	141.52 E
Tapsuj	134	Jg	60.06N	61.30 E
Tāpti	140	Jg	21.06N	72.41 E
Tapul Group	150	Ne	5.30N	121.00 E
Tapurucuara	202	Ed	0.24S	65.02W
Taputapu, Cape-	221c	Cb	14.19S	170.50W
Tâqbostân	146	Le	34.30N	46.58 E
Taqtaq	146	Ke	35.53N	44.35 E
Taquara	206	Jc	29.39S	50.47W
Taquaral, Serra do-	204	Fb	15.42S	52.30W
Taquari	204	Fc	17.50S	53.17W
Taquari, Pantal do-	202	Gg	18.10S	56.30W
Taquari, Rio- [Braz.]	204	Hf	23.16S	49.12W
Taquari, Rio- [Braz.]	204	Gi	29.56S	51.44W
Taquari, Rio- [Braz.]	198	Kg	19.15S	57.17W
Taquari, Serra do-	204	Fb	18.18S	53.49W
Taquaritinga	204	He	21.24S	48.30W
Taquarivaí	204	Id	23.31S	49.15W
Taquaruçu, Rio-	204	Fe	21.35S	52.08W
Tar	135	Id	40.38N	73.26 E
Tara	130	Cf	43.55N	19.25 E
Tara	118	Gh	53.34N	6.35W
Tara [Austl.]	212	Je	27.17S	150.28 E
Tara [Jap.]	156	Be	33.02N	130.11 E
Tara [R.S.F.S.R.]	136	Hd	56.54N	74.22 E
Tara [R.S.F.S.R.]	138	Ce	56.40N	74.50 E
Tara [Yugo.]	130	Bf	43.21N	18.51 E
Taraba	166	Hd	8.00N	10.15 E
Tarabuco	202	Fg	19.10S	64.57W
Ṭarābulus = Tripoli (EN)	144	Ec	34.26N	35.51 E
Ṭarābulus = Tripoli (EN)	160	Ie	32.54N	13.11 E
Ṭarābulus = Tripolitania (EN)	160	Be	32.40N	13.15 E
Ṭarābulus = Tripolitania (EN)	158	Ie	31.00N	14.00 E
Taradale	218	Gc	39.32S	176.51 E
Tarāghin	160	Be	24.31N	14.26 E
Tarahumara, Sierra-	190	Cc	28.26N	106.50W
Tarakan	142	Ni	3.18N	117.38 E
Tarakan, Pulau-	150	Gf	3.21N	117.36 E
Taraklija	132	Gf	45.55N	28.41 E
Tarama Jima	152	Lg	24.40N	124.40 E
Taran, mys-	114	Si	54.59N	19.59 E
Taranaki	218	Fc	39.10S	174.40 E
Taranco	126	Ia	40.01N	3.33W
Taranga Island	218	Fa	36.00S	174.45 E
Taransay	118	Hf	57.55N	7.10W
Taranto	112	Hg	40.28N	17.14 E
Taranto, Golfo di- = (EN)	110	Hg	40.10N	17.20 E
Taranto, Gulf of- (EN) = Taranto, Golfo di-	110	Hg	40.10N	17.20 E
Tarapacá	198	Ga	19.55S	69.31W
Tarapacá	206	Ga	20.00S	69.20W
Tarapaina	219a	Ec	9.23S	161.24 E
Tarapoto	202	Cc	6.30S	76.25W
Taraqua	206	Eb	0.06N	68.28W
Tarara	219a	Bb	6.02S	155.24 E
Tarare	122	Ki	45.54N	4.26 E
Tararua Range	218	Gd	40.45S	175.25 E
Tarašča	132	Ge	49.34N	30.31 E
Tarascon-sur-Ariège	122	Hl	42.51N	1.36 E
Tarata	206	Gc	17.36S	70.02W
Tarata	202	Dg	17.27S	70.02W
Tarauacá	202	De	8.10S	70.46W
Tarauacá, Rio-	198	Jf	6.42S	69.48W
Taravao	221e	Fc	17.44S	149.19W
Taravao, Baie de-	221e	Fc	17.43S	149.17W
Taravo	122a	Ab	41.42N	8.48 E
Tarawa Atoll	208	Ic	1.25N	173.00 E
Tarawera	218	Gc	39.02S	176.35 E
Tarazit, Massif de-	158	Hf	20.00N	8.00 E
Tarazona	146	Mg	31.05N	48.18 E
Tarazona	126	Kc	41.54N	1.44W
Tarazona de la Mancha	126	Ke	39.15N	1.55W

Name	Page	Grid	Lat	Long
Tarbagataj, hrebet-🔺	140	Ke	47.10N	83.00 E
Tarbagatay Shan 🔺	152	Db	47.10N	83.00 E
Tarbat Ness ►	118	Jd	57.50N	3.40W
Tarbert [Scot.-U.K.]	118	Gd	57.54N	6.49W
Tarbert [Scot.-U.K.]	118	Hf	55.52N	5.26W
Tarbes	122	Gk	43.14N	0.05 E
Tarboro	184	Ih	35.54N	77.32W
Tarcǎului, Munţii-🔺	130	Jc	46.45N	26.20 E
Tarcoola	212	Gf	30.41 S	134.33 E
Tardenois ◻	124	Fe	49.12N	3.40 E
Tardienta	126	Lc	41.59N	0.32W
Tardoire ◹	122	Gi	45.52N	0.14 E
Tardoki-Jani, gora-🔺	138	Ig	48.50N	137.55 E
Taree	210	Gh	31.54S	152.28 E
Taremert-n-Akli ◹	162	Id	25.53N	5.18 E
Tarentaise ◻	122	Mi	45.30N	6.30 E
Tarfâ', Ra's at- ►	164	Hf	17.02N	42.22 E
Tarfâ', Wâdî aţ- ◹	164	Df	28.38N	30.43 E
Ţarfah, Jazîrat aţ- ◻	164	Hg	14.37N	42.55 E
Tarfaya	160	Ff	27.57N	12.55W
Targa ◻	126	Qi	35.41N	4.09 E
Targoviški prohod ◹	130	Jf	43.12N	26.30 E
Tărgovište	130	Jf	43.15N	26.34 E
Tărgovište [2]	130	Jf	43.15N	26.34 E
Tarhankut, mys- ►	132	Kg	45.21N	32.30 E
Tarhǎus, Vîrful-🔺	130	Jc	46.38N	26.10 E
Tarhûnah	164	Bc	32.26N	13.38 E
Tarhûni, Jabal at-🔺	164	De	22.12N	22.25 E
Ţârîba 🔺	194	Kj	7.49N	72.13W
Ţarîf	144	He	24.01N	53.45 E
Tarifa	126	Gh	36.01N	5.36W
Tarifa, Punta de- ►	126	Gh	36.00N	5.37W
Tarija	200	Jh	21.31 S	64.45W
Tarija [3]	202	Fh	21.30S	64.00W
Tarik ◻	220d Bb		7.21N	151.47 E
Tariku ◹	150	Kg	2.55S	138.26 E
Tariku-Taritatu ◻	150	Kg	2.52S	138.25 E
Tarim [P.D.R.Y.]	144	Gf	16.03N	49.00 E
Tarim [Sau.Ar.]	146	Fi	27.54N	35.24 E
Tarim Basin (EN) = Tarim Pendi ◹	140	Ke	41.00N	84.00 E
Tarime	170	Fc	1.21 S	34.22 E
Tarim He ◹	140	Ke	41.05N	86.40 E
Tarim Pendi = Tarim Basin (EN) ◹	140	Ke	41.00N	84.00 E
Tarin Kowt	144	Kc	32.52N	65.38 E
Taritatu ◹	150	Kg	2.52S	137.55 E
Tarjalan	152	Hb	49.38N	101.59 E
Tarjannevesi ◻	116	Kb	62.10N	24.05 E
Tarjat	152	Gb	48.10N	99.40 E
Tarka, Vallée de- ◻	166	Gc	14.30N	6.30 E
Tarkastad	172	Df	32.00S	26.16 E
Tarko-Sale	186	If	40.27N	95.23W
Tarkwa	166	Ed	5.18N	1.59W
Tarlac	142	Oh	15.29N	120.35 E
Tarm	116	Ci	55.55N	8.32 E
Tarma	202	Cf	11.25S	75.42W
Tarn [3]	122	Mk	43.50N	2.00 E
Tarn ◹	122	Hj	44.06N	1.02 E
Tårna ◻	120	Pi	47.31N	19.59 E
Tärnaby	114	Dd	65.43N	15.16 E
Tarn-et-Garonne [3]	122	Hj	44.00N	1.10 E
Tarnica 🔺	120	Sg	49.06N	22.47 E
Tarnobrzeg	120	Rf	50.35N	21.41 E
Tarnobrzeg [2]	120	Rf	50.35N	21.40 E
Tarnogród	120	Sf	50.23N	22.45 E
Tarnos	122	Ek	43.32N	1.28W
Tarnów	112	Ie	50.01N	21.00 E
Tarnów [2]	120	Qf	50.00N	21.00 E
Tarnowskie Góry	120	Of	50.27N	18.52 E
Tärnsjö	116	Gd	60.09N	16.56 E
Taro ◹	128	Ef	45.00N	10.15 E
Taron	219a Aa		4.28S	153.04 E
Tarongers, Costa dels- / Azahar, Costa del- ◻	126	Me	39.58N	0.01 E
Taroom	210	Fg	25.39S	149.49 E
Taroudant	162	Fc	30.29N	8.52W
Tarpon Springs	184	Fk	28.09N	82.45W
Tarquinia	128	Fh	42.15N	11.45 E
Tarra, Rio- ◹	194	Ki	9.04N	72.27W
Tarrafal	162	Cf	15.17N	23.46W
Tarragona	112	Gg	41.07N	1.15 E
Tarragona [3]	126	Mc	41.10N	1.00 E
Tarraleah	212	Jh	42.10 S	146.30 E
Tarrant	184	Di	33.38N	86.46W
Tàrrega	126	Nc	41.39N	1.09 E
Tarsus	144	Db	36.55N	34.53 E
Tart	152	Fd	37.07N	92.57 E
Tartagal	206	Hb	22.32S	63.49W
Tartaro ◹	128	Fe	45.02N	11.30 E
Tartas	122	Fk	43.50N	0.48W
Tartas ◹	138	Ce	55.37N	76.44 E
Tartu	112	Id	58.23N	26.45 E
Tartûs	144	Ec	34.53N	35.53 E
Tarumae-Yama 🔺	156a Bb		42.41N	141.23 E
Tarumizu	154	Ki	31.29N	130.42 E
Tarusa	132	Jb	54.43N	37.11 E
Tărût ◻	146	Ni	26.34N	50.04 E
Tarutino, Ko- ◻	148	Jg	6.35N	99.40 E
Tarutino	132	Ff	46.12N	29.09 E
Tarutung	150	Cf	2.01N	98.58 E
Tarvisio	128	Hd	46.30N	13.35 E
Tarvo ◹	204	Bb	15.06S	60.34W
Tarvo, Rio- ◹	204	Bb	14.47S	61.03W
Tasajera, Sierra- 🔺	192	Gc	29.35S	105.35W
Tašanta	138	Dg	49.43N	89.11 E
Tasaral, ostrov- ◻	135	Ja	46.15N	74.05 E
Tašauz	136	Fj	41.52N	59.59 E
Tašauzskaja oblast [3]	136	Fj	41.00N	58.40 E
Tasǎwah	164	Bd	26.01N	13.29 E
Tasbuget	136	Ga	44.48N	65.38 E
Tasejeva ◹	138	Gf	58.06N	94.01 E
Taseko Lake ◻	188	Da	51.15N	123.35W
Tasendjanet ◹	162	Hd	25.40N	0.59 E
Tashk, Daryâcheh-ye- ◻	144	Hd	29.45N	53.35 E
Tasikmalaya	142	Mj	7.20 S	108.12 E
Tåsinge ◻	116	Di	55.00N	10.36 E

Name	Page	Grid	Lat	Long
Tasiussaq	179	Gd	73.18N	56.00W
Taskan	138	Kd	62.58N	150.20 E
Taškent	142	Ie	41.20N	69.18 E
Taškentskaja oblast [3]	136	Gg	41.20N	69.40 E
Taškepri	136	Gh	36.17N	62.38 E
Taškeprinskoje, vodohranilišče- ◻	135	Df	36.15N	62.40 E
Tasker	166	Hb	15.04N	10.42 E
Taşköprü	146	Fb	41.30N	34.14 E
Taš-Kumyr	136	Hg	41.20N	72.14 E
Taşlıçay	146	Jc	39.38N	43.23 E
Tasman, Mount- 🔺	218	De	43.34 S	170.09 E
Tasman Basin (EN) ◻	106	Jn	43.00S	158.00 E
Tasman Bay ◻	216	Dh	41.10S	173.15 E
Tasmania ◻	212	Jh	43.00S	147.00 E
Tasmania [2]	208	Fi	43.00 S	147.00 E
Tasman Peninsula 🞀	212	Jh	43.05 S	147.50 E
Tasman Plateau (EN) ◻	106	Jn	48.00S	148.00 E
Tasman Sea ◻	208	Hh	40.00 S	163.00 E
Tâşnad	130	Hb	47.29N	22.35 E
Taşova	146	Gb	40.46N	36.20 E
Tassah, Wâdî- ◹	128	Cn	36.35N	8.54 E
Tassara	166	Gb	16.01N	5.39 E
Taštagol	138	Df	52.47N	88.00 E
Tåstrup	116	Ei	55.39N	12.19 E
Tastūr	128	Dn	36.33N	9.27 E
Tasty-Taldy	136	Ge	50.47N	66.31 E
Taşucu	146	Ed	36.19N	33.53 E
Tasújbánya	146	Kc	38.19N	45.21 E
Tata [3]	162	Fd	29.40N	8.00W
Tata [Hun.]	120	Oi	47.39N	18.19 E
Tata [Mor.]	162	Fd	29.45N	7.59W
Tataba	142	Pi	1.18 S	122.49 E
Tatabánya	120	Oi	47.34N	18.25 E
Takakoto Atoll ◻	208	Nf	17.20S	138.23W
Tata Mailau 🔺	150	Ih	8.55 S	125.30 E
Tatarbunary	132	Fg	45.49N	29.35 E
Tatarskaja ASSR [3]	136	Fd	55.20N	50.50 E
Tatarski proliv = Tatar Strait (EN) ◻	140	Qd	50.00N	141.15 E
Tatar Strait (EN) = Tatarski proliv ◻	140	Qd	50.00N	141.15 E
Tatau	150	Ff	2.53N	112.51 E
Taţawin	162	Jc	32.56N	10.27 E
Tateyama	154	Na	34.59N	139.52 E
Tathlina Lake ◻	180	Fd	60.30N	117.30W
Tathlîth	144	Fi	19.32N	43.30 E
Tatišćevo	132	Nd	51.40N	45.35 E
Tatla Lake	188	Ca	51.55N	124.36W
Tatla Lake ◻	188	Ca	51.58N	124.25W
Tatlow, Mount- 🔺	188	Da	51.23N	123.52W
Tatnam, Cape - ►	180	Ie	57.16N	91.00W
Tatra Mountains (EN) 🔺	110	Hf	49.15N	20.00 E
Tatsuno [Jap.]	156	Md	34.52N	134.33 E
Tatsuno [Jap.]	156	Id	35.58N	137.58 E
Tatsuruhama	156	Ec	37.04N	136.53 E
Tatta	148	Dd	24.45N	67.55 E
Tatui	204	If	23.21 S	47.51W
Tatum	182	Jj	33.16N	103.19W
Tatvan	144	Fb	38.30N	42.16 E
Tau	116	Ae	59.04N	5.54 E
Tau [Am.Sam.] ◻	221c Ba		14.15S	169.30W
Tau [Ton.] ◻	221b Bc		21.01 S	175.00W
Tauá	202	Je	6.01 S	40.26W
Taubaté	200	Lh	23.02 S	45.33W
Tauberbischofsheim	120	Fg	49.37N	9.40 E
Taučik	136	Fg	44.15N	51.20 E
Tauere Atoll ◻	208	Mf	17.22S	141.30W
Tauern 🔺	110	Hf	47.15N	13.15 E
Taufstein 🔺	120	Ff	50.31N	9.14 E
Tauhunu	220n Ac		10.25S	161.03W
Tauhunu ◻	220n Ac		10.25S	161.03W
Taujsk	138	Je	59.46N	149.20 E
Taukum ◻	138	Je	59.15N	150.00 E
Taujskaja guba ◻	135	Ba	59.5 S	167.13 E
Taumako ◻	218	Fc	38.52S	175.15 E
Taumarunui	186	Kh	37.34N	90.44W
Taum Sauk Mountain 🔺	204	De	20.18S	56.05W
Taunay	172	Ce	27.33 S	24.47 E
Taung	148	Jd	20.01N	95.33 E
Taungdwingyi	148	Jd	20.47N	97.02 E
Taunggyi	148	Jd	22.54N	95.48 E
Taungthonlon 🔺	148	Je	18.51N	94.14 E
Taungup	118	Jj	51.01N	3.06W
Taunton [Eng.-U.K.]	184	Le	41.54N	71.06W
Taunton [Ma.-U.S.]	120	Ef	50.10N	8.15 E
Taunus 🔺	124	Nd	50.08N	8.10 E
Taunusstein	216	De	38.41 S	176.05 E
Taupo	216	De	38.50 S	175.55 E
Taupo, Lake- ◻	114	Fi	55.16N	22.19 E
Taurage/Taurage	114	Fi	55.16N	22.19 E
Taurage/Tauragė	210	Ih	37.42 S	176.10 E
Tauranga	128	Kl	38.21N	16.01 E
Taurianova	122	Mk	43.53N	1.24 E
Taurion ◹	128	Mk	39.57N	18.13 E
Taurisano	218	Ea	35.10S	173.04 E
Tauroa Point ►				
Taurus Mountains (EN) = Toros Dağları 🔺	140	Ff	37.00N	33.00 E
Tauste	126	Kc	41.55N	1.15W
Tauu Islands ◻	208	Ga	4.45 S	157.00 E
Tauz	146	Ja	41.01N	45.35 E
Taválesh, Kûhhá-Ye- 🔺	146	Mc	38.42N	48.18 E
Tavas	146	Cd	37.34N	29.04 E
Tavas Ovasi ◻	146	Cd	37.34N	29.24 E
Tavastehus/Hämeenlinna	114	Hf	61.00N	24.27 E
Tavau/Davos	128	Dd	46.47N	9.50 E
Tavda	136	Gd	58.03N	65.15 E
Tavda ◹	140	Id	59.47N	67.16 E
Tavendroua	219b Cc		16.21 S	167.37 E
Tavernes de Valldigna / Tabernes de Valldigna				
Taveta	170	Gc	3.24S	37.41 E
Taveuni Island ◻	216	Fc	16.51 S	179.58W
Taviano	128	Mk	39.59N	18.05 E
Tavignano ◹	122a Ba		42.06N	9.33 E
Tavira	126	Eg	37.07N	7.39W

Name	Page	Grid	Lat	Long
Tavistock	118	Ik	50.33N	4.08W
Tavolara ◻	128	Dj	40.55N	9.40 E
Tavoliere 🞀	128	Ji	41.35N	15.25 E
Tavolžan	136	He	52.44N	77.30 E
Tavoy → Dawei	148	Lh	14.05N	98.12 E
Tavrićanka	154	Kc	43.20N	131.52 E
Tavropoú, Tekhniti Limni- 🞀	130	Ej	39.15N	21.40 E
Tavşan Adalari ◻	130	Jj	39.55N	26.05 E
Tavşanli	146	Cc	39.35N	29.30 E
Tavua	216	Ec	17.27 S	177.51 E
Taw ◹	118	Ij	51.04N	4.11W
Tawakoni, Lake- ◻	182	Kj	32.55N	96.00W
Tawas City	182	Kc	44.16N	83.31W
Tawau	216	Dh	41.15N	117.54 E
Tawfiqîyah	168	Ed	9.26N	31.37 E
Ţawîlah, Juzur- ◻	164	Ff	27.35N	33.46 E
Tawitawi Group ◻	150	He	5.10N	120.15 E
Ţawqar	160	Kg	18.26N	37.44 E
Ţawûq	146	Ke	35.08N	44.27 E
Tawûq Chãy ◹	146	Ke	34.35N	44.31 E
Tãwurghã', Sabkhat- 🞀	164	Cc	31.10N	15.15 E
Tawzar	162	Ic	33.55N	8.08 E
Taxco de Alarcón	192	Jh	18.33N	99.36W
Taxkorgan	152	Cd	37.47N	75.14 E
Tay ◹	118	Je	56.30N	3.30W
Tay, Firth of- ◻	118	Ke	56.28N	3.00W
Tay, Loch- ◻	118	Je	56.30N	4.10W
Tayandu, Kepulauan- ◻	150	Jh	5.30 S	132.15 E
Tayeğle	168	Ge	4.02N	44.36 E
Taylor [Nb.-U.S.]	186	Gf	41.46N	99.23W
Taylor [Tx.-U.S.]	182	Ke	30.34N	97.25W
Taylor, Mount- 🔺	182	Fd	35.14N	107.37W
Taylorville	186	Lg	39.33N	89.18W
Taymã'	164	Ed	27.38N	38.29 E
Taymyr Peninsula (EN) = Tajmyr, poluostrov- 🞀	140	Mb	76.00N	104.00 E
Tay Ninh	148	Lf	11.18N	106.06 E
Tayside [3]	118	Je	56.30N	3.40W
Taytay	150	Gd	10.49N	119.31 E
Taza [Mor.]	162	Jc	67.29N	78.41 E
Taza [Mor.]	162	Gc	34.00N	4.00W
Taza [R.S.F.S.R.]	160	Ge	34.13N	4.01W
Ţãzah Khurmãtū	138	Gf	54.55N	111.05 E
Tazawako	146	Ke	35.18N	44.20 E
Tazawa-Ko ◻	156	Gb	39.42N	140.44 E
Tazerbo Oasis (EN) = Tãzirbû, Wâḩãt al- 🞀	156	Gb	39.43N	140.40 E
Tãzirbû, Wâḩãt al- 🞀	162	Fc	30.35N	7.12W
Tazewell [Tn.-U.S.]	158	Jf	25.45N	21.00 E
Tazewell [Va.-U.S.]	184	Fg	36.27N	83.34W
Ţãziãzet 🞀	184	Gg	37.07N	81.34W
Tazin Lake ◻	162	De	20.55N	15.40W
Tãzirbû, Wâḩãt al- = Tazerbo Oasis (EN) 🞀	180	Ge	59.48N	109.05W
Tazlãu	158	Jf	25.45N	21.00 E
Tazmalt	130	Jc	46.16N	26.47 E
Tazouikert ◹	128	Qh	36.43N	4.08 E
Tazovskaja guba ◻	166	Ea	21.46N	1.13W
Tazovski	134	Qb	69.05N	76.00 E
Tazumal ◻	156	Ec	37.28N	78.42 E
Tbilisi	162	Ie	23.27N	6.14 E
Tchad = Chad (EN) [1]	194	Cg	14.00N	89.40W
Tchad, Lac- = Chad, Lake- (EN) ◻	112	Kg	41.43N	44.49 E
Tchamba [Cam.]	160	Ig	15.00N	19.00 E
Tchamba [Togo]	166	Hd	8.37N	12.48 E
Tchibanga	166	Fd	9.02N	1.25 E
Tchien	170	Be	2.51 S	11.02 E
Tchigaï, Plateau du- ◻	166	Bd	6.04N	8.08W
Tchikala-Tcholohanga	158	If	21.30N	14.50 E
Tchin Tabaraden	170	Ce	12.38S	16.04 E
Tcholliré	166	Gb	15.58N	5.50 E
Tczew	166	Hd	8.24N	14.10 E
Tea, Rio- ◹	120	Ob	54.06N	18.47 E
Teaca	202	Ed	0.30 S	65.49W
Teacapán	130	Hc	46.55N	24.31 E
Teaiti Point ►	192	Gf	22.33N	105.45W
Te Anau	220p Bb		21.11 S	159.47W
Te Anau, Lake- ◻	218	Bf	45.25S	167.43 E
Teano	216	Ci	45.15S	167.48 E
Teapa	128	Ji	41.15N	14.04 E
Te Araroa	192	Mi	17.33N	92.57W
Te Aroha	216	Eg	37.38S	178.22 E
Te Au Kura ◹	216	De	37.32S	175.42 E
Te Awamutu	218	Ea	35.10 S	173.04 E
Teberda	212	Gd	22.11 S	133.17 E
Tébessa	184	Le	41.54N	71.06W
Tébessa [3]	120	Ef	50.10N	8.15 E
Tébessa, Oued- ◹	216	Ee	38.41 S	176.05 E
Tebicuary, Rio- [Par.] ◹	216	Eg	38.50 S	175.55 E
Tebicuary, Rio- [Par.] ◹	114	Fi	55.16N	22.19 E
Tebingtinggi [Indon.]	114	Fi	55.16N	22.19 E
Tebingtinggi [Indon.]	210	Ih	37.42 S	176.10 E
Tebulosmta, gora- 🔺	128	Kl	38.21N	16.01 E
Teča ◹	122	Hi	45.53N	1.24 E
Tecate	128	Mk	39.57N	18.13 E
Tecer Dağlari 🔺	218	Ea	35.10S	173.04 E
Techirghiol	140	Ff	37.00N	33.00 E
Tecka	126	Kc	41.55N	1.15W
Tecklenburg	208	Ga	4.45 S	157.00 E
Tecomán	146	Ja	41.01N	45.35 E
Tecomate, Laguna- 🞀	146	Mc	38.42N	48.18 E
Tecoripa	146	Cd	37.34N	29.04 E
Tecpan de Galeana	146	Cd	37.34N	29.24 E
Tecuala	114	Hf	61.00N	24.27 E
Tecuci	128	Dd	46.47N	9.50 E
Tedegra ◹	136	Gd	58.03N	65.15 E
Tedori-Gawa ◹	140	Id	59.47N	67.16 E
Tedžen	219b Cc		16.21 S	167.37 E
Tedžen ◹				
Tedženstroj	170	Gc	3.24S	37.41 E
Teeli	216	Fc	16.51 S	179.58W
Teenuse jõgi / Tenuze ◹	128	Mk	39.59N	18.05 E
Tees ◹	122a Ba		42.06N	9.33 E
Tees Bay ◻	126	Eg	37.07N	7.39W

Name	Page	Grid	Lat	Long
Tefé	200	Jf	3.22 S	64.42W
Tefé, Rio- ◹	202	Fd	3.35 S	64.47W
Tefedest 🔺	162	Ie	24.40N	5.30 E
Tefenni	146	Cd	37.18N	29.47 E
Tegal	142	Mj	6.52S	109.08 E
Tegea (EN) = Teyéa ◻	130	Fl	37.27N	22.25 E
Tegelen	124	Ic	51.20N	6.08 E
Te Manga 🔺	220p Bb		21.13 S	159.45W
Tegernsee	120	Hi	47.43N	11.46 E
Tegina	166	Gc	10.04N	6.11 E
Tégoua 🞀	219b Ca		13.15 S	166.37 E
Tegucigalpa	176	Kh	14.06N	87.13W
Teguida I-n-Tessoum	166	Gb	17.26N	6.39 E
Teguldet	138	De	57.20N	88.20 E
Tehachapi	182	Fi	35.08N	118.27W
Tehachapi Mountains 🔺	188	Fi	34.56N	118.40W
Tehamiyam	168	Fb	18.20N	36.32 E
Te Hapua	216	Df	34.30S	172.55 E
Tehaupoo	221e Fc		17.49S	149.18W
Tehek Lake ◻	180	Hd	64.55N	95.30W
Téhini	166	Ed	9.36N	3.40W
Tehoru	162	Ie	24.48N	8.08 E
Tehrãn	150	Ig	3.23S	129.30 E
Tehuacán	142	Hf	35.40N	51.26 E
Tehuantepec, Golfo de- = Tehuantepec, Gulf of- (EN)	190	Ee	18.27N	97.23W
Tehuantepec, Gulf of- (EN) = Tehuantepec, Golfo de-	190	Ee	16.20N	95.14W
Tehuantepec, Isthmus of- (EN) = Tehuantepec, Istmo de- 🞀	174	Jh	16.00N	94.50W
Tehuantepec, Istmo de- = Tehuantepec, Isthmus of- (EN) 🞀	174	Jh	16.00N	94.50W
Tehuantepec Ridge (EN) ◻	174	Jh	17.00N	94.30W
Tehuata Atoll ◻	190	Ef	13.30N	98.00W
Teiga Plateau 🔺	208	Mf	16.50S	141.55W
Teignmouth	168	Db	15.38N	25.40 E
Teil, le-	118	Jk	50.33N	3.30W
Teili/Delet ◻	122	Kj	44.33N	4.41 E
Teith ◹	116	Id	60.15N	20.35 E
Teiuş	118	Je	56.14N	4.20W
Teixeira Pinto	130	Gc	46.12N	23.41 E
Tejkovo	166	Bc	12.04N	16.02W
Tejo = Tagus (EN) ◹	138	Ed	60.27N	92.38 E
Teju	132	Jc	56.50N	40.34 E
Te Kaha	110	Fh	38.40N	9.24W
Te Kao	148	Jc	27.55N	96.10 E
Tekapo, Lake- ◻	216	Eg	37.44S	177.41 E
Te Karaka	218	Ea	34.39 S	172.54 E
Tekax	218	Be	43.50S	170.30 E
Teke	216	Ea	38.28 S	177.52 E
Teke Burun [Tur.] ►	130	Mh	41.04N	29.39 E
Teke Burun [Tur.] ►	130	Ji	40.02N	26.10 E
Tekeli	130	Ji	40.02N	26.10 E
Tekes	136	Hg	44.48N	78.57 E
Tekes He ◹	152	Dc	43.10N	81.43 E
Tekeze ◹	152	Dc	43.35N	82.30 E
Tekija	158	Kg	14.20N	35.50 E
Tekiliktag 🔺	146	Ae	34.41N	22.25 E
Tekirdağ	152	Dd	36.35N	80.20 E
Tekman	144	Ca	40.59N	27.31 E
Te Kopuru	146	Ic	39.38N	41.31 E
Te Kou ◻	166	Hd	9.12N	12.48 E
Tekouiat ◹	130	Ji	40.02N	26.10 E
Tekro	162	He	22.30 E	
Te Kuiti	168	Bc	19.34N	20.57 E
Tela	216	Fc	38.20S	175.10 E
Telagh	190	Ge	15.44N	87.27W
Telataí	162	Hb	36.31N	1.18 E
Telavåg	166	Fb	16.31N	1.30 E
Telavi	116	Ae	60.16N	4.49 E
Tel Aviv [3]	146	Ff	32.05N	34.48 E
Tel Aviv-Yafo	142	Ff	32.04N	34.46 E
Telč	120	Mg	49.11N	15.27 E
Telchac Puerto	192	Og	21.21N	89.16W
Telciu	130	Hb	47.26N	24.24 E
Tele ◹	130	Db	2.48N	23.54 E
Teleac	130	Nc	46.41N	27.54 E
Telečkoje ozero ◻	138	Df	51.30N	87.45 E
Telefomin	214	Ci	5.08N	141.31 E
Telegraph Creek	180	Ee	57.54N	131.09W
Telekitonga ◻	221b Bb		20.24 S	174.32W
Telekivavu'u ◻	221b Bb		20.23 S	174.32W
Télémaco Borba	204	Gg	24.23S	50.28W
Telemark 🔺	114	Bg	59.30N	8.40 E
Telemark [3]	116	Ce	59.30N	8.45 E
Telén	206	Ge	36.15S	65.30W
Telenešty	130	Lb	47.30N	28.16 E
Teleno 🔺	126	Fb	42.21N	6.23W
Teleorman [2]	130	Ie	44.10N	25.15 E
Teleorman ◹	130	If	43.52N	25.26 E
Telerhteba, Djebel- 🔺	162	Ie	24.10N	6.51 E
Telescope Peak 🔺	188	Gh	36.10N	117.05W
Telescope Point ►	197p Bb		12.08N	61.36W
Telese	128	Ii	41.13N	14.32 E
Telfãn, Hadjer- 🔺	168	Bc	12.05N	18.57 E
Telford	118	Ki	52.40N	2.30W
Telgte	124	Jc	51.59N	7.47 E
Télimélé	166	Cc	10.54N	13.02W
Teljo, Jabal- 🔺	168	Cc	14.42N	25.56 E
Tell al Ubaid ◻	146	Lf	30.58N	46.01 E
Tellaro ◹	128	Jh	36.50N	15.06 E
Tell Atlas (EN) = Atlas Tellien 🔺	158	He	36.00N	2.00 E
Tell City	184	Dg	37.57N	86.46W
Teller	178	Fc	65.16N	166.22W
Telok Anson	150	Df	4.02N	101.01 E
Teloloapan	192	Jh	18.21N	99.51W
Telposiz, gora- 🔺	136	Fc	63.54N	59.10 E
Telsen	206	Gf	42.24S	66.57W
Telšiai/Telšjaj	136	Cd	55.59N	22.17 E

Name	Page	Grid	Lat	Long
Telšjaj/Telšiai	136	Cd	55.59N	22.17 E
Teltow	120	Jd	52.24N	13.16 E
Telukbetung	142	Mj	5.27 S	105.16 E
Telukdalam	150	Ef	4.13N	108.12 E
Telukdalem	150	Cf	0.34N	97.49 E
Téma	160	Gh	5.37N	0.01W
Temacine	162	Ic	33.01N	6.01 E
Te Manga 🔺	220p Bb		21.13 S	159.45W
Tematangi Atoll ◻	208	Mg	21.41 S	140.40W
Tembenči ◹	138	Ed	64.36N	99.58 E
Témbi [2]	130	Fj	39.53N	22.35 E
Tembilahan	150	Dg	0.19 S	103.09 E
Temblador	196	Bh	9.59N	62.44W
Tembleque	126	Ie	39.42N	3.30W
Temblor Range 🔺	188	Fi	35.30N	119.55W
Tembo	170	Cd	7.42 S	17.17 E
Tembo, Chutes- ◻	158	Ii	8.50 S	15.20 E
Tembo, Mont- 🔺	170	Bb	1.50N	12.00 E
Tembué	172	Ea	14.51 S	32.50 E
Teme ◹	118	Ki	52.09N	2.18W
Temerin	130	Df	45.25N	19.53 E
Temerloh	150	Df	3.27N	102.25 E
Teminabuan	150	Jg	1.26S	132.01 E
Temir	136	Ff	49.08N	57.09 E
Temir-Tau	132	Te	48.31N	57.29 E
Temirlanovka	135	Gc	42.36N	69.17 E
Temirtau	142	Jd	50.05N	72.56 E
Témiscaming	184	Hb	46.44N	79.06W
Témiscouata, Lac- ◻	184	Mb	47.40N	68.50W
Temki	168	Bc	11.39N	18.13 E
Temnikov	114	Ki	54.40N	43.13 E
Temo ◹	128	Cj	40.17N	8.28 E
Temoe, Ile- ◻	208	Ng	23.20 S	134.29W
Temores	192	Ed	27.16N	108.15W
Temora	188	Jj	33.25N	111.56W
Tempio Pausania	128	Dj	40.54N	9.06 E
Temple	182	Ke	31.06N	97.21W
Templeman, Mount- 🔺	188	Ga	50.43N	117.14W
Templemore/An Teampall Mór	118	Fi	52.48N	7.50W
Templin	120	Jc	53.07N	13.30 E
Tempoal, Rio- ◹	192	Jg	21.47N	98.27W
Temrjuk	132	Ih	45.15N	37.23 E
Temse/Tamise	124	Gc	51.08N	4.13 E
Temuco	200	Ij	38.44 S	72.38W
Temuka	218	Df	44.15S	171.16 E
Tena	202	Cd	0.59 S	77.48W
Tenacatita, Bahia de- ◻	192	Gh	19.10N	104.50W
Tenala/Tenhola	116	Kf	60.04N	23.18 E
Tenali	148	Ge	16.15N	80.35 E
Tenancingo de Degollado	192	Jh	18.58N	99.36W
Tenasserim [3]	148	Lf	13.00N	99.00 E
Tenasserim ◹	140	Lh	12.35N	97.52 E
Tenasserim ◹	148	Lf	12.24N	98.37 E
Tenby	118	Jj	51.41N	4.43W
Tence	122	Ki	45.07N	4.17 E
Tench Island ◻	214	Fa	1.38 S	150.42 E
Tenda, Col di- ◻	128	Bf	44.09N	7.34 E
Tendaho	168	Gc	11.38N	41.00 E
Tende	122	Nj	44.05N	7.36 E
Tende, Col de- ◻	128	Bf	44.09N	7.34 E
Ten Degree Channel ◻	148	In	10.00N	92.30 E
Tendó	156	Gb	38.22N	140.22 E
Tendrara	162	Gc	33.03N	2.00W
Tendre, Mont- 🔺	128	Ad	46.36N	6.19 E
Tendrovskaja kosa ◻	132	Gg	46.15N	31.45 E
Ténénkou	166	Ec	14.28N	4.55W
Tenente Lira, Rio- ◹	204	Db	15.56S	57.59W
Ténéré 🞀	158	Ig	17.36N	10.55 E
Ténéré, 'Erg du- ◻	166	Hb	17.35N	10.55 E
Tenerife ◻	158	Ff	28.19N	16.34W
Ténés	162	Hb	36.31N	1.18 E
Ténès, Cap- ►	162	Hb	36.33N	1.21 E
Teng ◹	148	Je	19.52N	97.45 E
Tengah, Kepulauan- ◻	150	Gh	7.30 S	117.30 E
Tengchong	152	Gg	24.59N	98.32 E
Te Nggano, Lake- ◻	214	Gj	11.45 S	160.25 E
Tenggarong	150	Gg	0.24 S	116.58 E
Tengger Shamo 🞀	140	Mf	38.00N	104.10 E
Tengiz, ozero- ◻	140	Id	50.25N	69.00 E
Tengréla	166	Dc	10.29N	6.24W
Tengréla [2]	166	Dc	10.27N	6.25W
Tengxian [China]	152	Jg	23.18N	110.49 E
Tengxian [China]	154	Dg	35.07N	117.10 E
Tenhola/Tenala	116	Kf	60.04N	23.18 E
Teniente General Rosendo M. Fraga	204	Af	23.45 S	62.09W
Tenkási	148	Fg	8.58N	77.18 E
Tenke	170	Ee	10.33 S	26.08 E
Tenkeli	138	Jb	70.01N	140.55 E
Tenkodogo	166	Ec	11.47N	0.22W
Tenna ◹	128	Hg	43.14N	13.47 E
Tennant Creek	210	Ef	19.40S	134.10 E
Tennessee [2]	182	Jd	35.50N	88.30W
Tennessee ◹	174	Kf	37.04N	88.33W
Tenneville	124	Hd	50.06N	5.32 E
Tenojoki ◹	114	Hb	70.28N	28.18 E
Tenom	150	Ge	5.08N	115.57 E
Tenosique de Pino Suárez	190	Ff	17.29N	91.26W
Tenri	156	Dd	34.36N	135.49 E
Tenryū-Gawa ◹	156	Id	34.35N	137.48 E
Tensift ◹	162	Fc	32.02N	9.21W
Ten Sleep	186	Ee	44.02N	107.27W
Tenterden	124	Cc	51.03N	0.42 E
Tenterfield	210	Ge	81.40N	16.45 E
Tenuze / Teenuse jõgi ◹	148	Ge	16.15N	80.35 E
Ten-Zan 🔺	156	Bd	33.20N	130.08 E
Teocaltiche	192	Hg	21.26N	102.35W
Teodelina	204	Bh	34.11 S	61.32W
Teodoro Sampaio	204	Ff	22.31 S	52.10W
Teófilo Otoni	200	Lg	17.51 S	41.30W
Teotepec, Cerro- 🔺	192	Ih	16.50N	100.50W
Teotihuacán ◻	192	Jh	19.44N	98.50W
Teotitlán del Camino	192	Kh	18.08N	97.05W

Tepa [Indon.]	150	Ih	7.52S	129.31 E
Tepa [W.F.]	220h	Bb	13.19S	176.09W
Te Pae Roa Ngake o Tuko ⊙	220n	Bb	10.23S	161.00W
Tepako, Pointe- ►	220h	Bb	13.16S	176.08W
Tepalcatepec, Río- ≈	192	Ih	18.35N	101.59W
Tepa Point ►	220k	Bb	19.07S	169.56W
Tepatitlán de Morelos	192	Hg	20.49N	102.44W
Tepehuanes	190	Cc	25.21N	105.44W
Tepehuanes, Río- ≈	192	Ge	25.11N	105.26W
Tepehuanes, Sierra de- ⩓	190	Cc	25.00N	105.40W
Tepelena	130	Di	40.18N	20.01 E
Tepi	168	Fd	7.03N	35.30 E
Tepic	176	Ig	21.30N	104.54W
Teplá	120	Ig	49.59N	12.52 E
Teplá ≈	120	If	50.14N	12.52 E
Teplice	120	Jf	50.39N	13.50 E
Tepoca, Bahía de- ◗	192	Cb	30.15N	112.50W
Tepopa, Cabo- ►	192	Cc	29.20N	112.25W
Te Puka ⊙	220n	Ac	10.26S	161.02W
Te Puke	218	Gb	37.47S	176.20 E
Tequepa, Bahía de- ◗	192	Ii	17.17N	101.05W
Tequila	192	Hg	20.54N	103.47W
Tequisquiapan	192	Jg	20.31N	99.52W
Ter ≈	126	Pb	42.01N	3.12 E
Téra	160	Hg	14.01N	0.45 E
Tera [Port.] ≈	126	Df	38.56N	8.03W
Tera [Sp.] ≈	126	Gc	41.54N	5.44W
Teradomari	156	Fc	37.38N	138.45 E
Terai ✕	140	Kg	26.30N	85.15 E
Teraina Island (Washington) ◆	208	Kd	4.43N	160.24W
Terakeka	168	Ed	5.26N	31.45 E
Teramo	128	Hh	42.39N	13.42 E
Terampa	150	Ef	3.14N	106.14 E
Ter Apel, Vlagtwedde-	124	Jb	52.52N	7.06 E
Terborg, Wisch-	124	Ic	51.55N	6.22 E
Tercan	146	Ic	39.47N	40.24 E
Terceira ◆	158	Ee	38.43N	27.13W
Tercero, Río- ≈	206	Hd	32.55S	62.19W
Terebovlja	132	De	49.18N	25.42 E
Terehovka	154	Kc	43.38N	131.55 E
Terek	132	Nh	43.29N	44.08 E
Terek ≈	110	Kg	43.44N	47.30 E
Térékolé ≈	166	Cb	15.07N	10.53W
Terek-Saj	135	Hd	41.29N	71.13 E
Terengganu [2]	150	De	5.00N	103.00 E
Terenos	204	Ee	20.26S	54.50W
Teresa Cristina	204	Gg	24.48S	51.07W
Teresina	200	Lf	5.05S	42.49W
Teresinha	202	Hc	0.58N	52.02W
Tereška ≈	132	Od	51.50N	46.45 E
Terespol	120	Td	52.05N	23.36 E
Teressa ◆	148	Ig	8.15N	93.10 E
Teresva ≈	132	Cf	47.59N	23.15 E
Terevaka, Cerro- ▲	221d	Ab	27.05S	109.23W
Tergnier	122	Je	49.39N	3.18 E
Terhazza	166	Ea	23.36N	4.56W
Teriberka	114	Ib	69.10N	35.10 E
Teriberka ≈	114	Ib	69.09N	35.08 E
Terlingua Creek ≈	186	El	29.10N	103.36W
Termas de Río Hondo	206	Hc	27.29S	64.52W
Terme	146	Gb	41.12N	36.59 E
Termez	142	If	37.14N	67.16 E
Termini Imerese	128	Hm	37.59N	13.42 E
Termini Imerese, Golfo di- ◗	128	Hl	38.00N	13.45 E
Terminillo ▲	128	Hh	42.28N	13.01 E
Términos, Laguna de- ◎	190	Fe	18.37N	91.33W
Termit, Massif de- ▲	166	Hb	16.15N	11.17 E
Termit-Kaoboul	166	Hb	15.43N	11.37 E
Termoli	128	Ji	42.00N	15.00 E
Termonde/Dendermonde	124	Gc	51.02N	4.07 E
Termunten	124	Ja	53.18N	7.03 E
Ternaard, Westdongeradeel-	124	Ha	53.23N	5.58 E
Ternate	150	If	0.48N	127.24 E
Ternej	138	Ig	45.05N	136.35 E
Terneuzen	122	Jc	51.20N	3.50 E
Terni	128	Gh	42.34N	12.37 E
Ternitz	128	Kc	47.43N	16.02 E
Ternois ✕	124	Ed	50.25N	2.19 E
Ternopol	112	If	49.34N	25.38 E
Ternopolskaja oblast [3]	136	Cf	49.20N	25.35 E
Terpenija, mys- ►	138	Jg	48.38N	144.40 E
Terpenija, zaliv- ◗	140	Qe	49.00N	143.30 E
Terrace	180	Ef	54.31N	128.35W
Terrace Bay	186	Mb	48.47N	87.09W
Terracina	128	Hi	41.17N	13.15 E
Terra de Basto ✕	126	Ec	41.25N	8.00W
Terra Firma	172	Ce	25.36S	23.24 E
Terråk	114	Cd	65.05N	12.25 E
Terralba	128	Ck	39.43N	8.39 E
Terra Rica	204	Ff	22.43S	52.38W
Terrassa	126	Oc	41.34N	2.01 E
Terrebonne Bay ◗	186	Kl	29.09N	90.35W
Terre-de-Bas	197e	Ac	15.51N	61.39W
Terre-de-Haut	197e	Ac	15.58N	61.35W
Terre Haute	182	Jd	39.28N	87.24W
Terrell	186	Hj	32.44N	96.17W
Terre Plaine ✕	122	Jg	47.25N	4.00 E
Terres Froides ✕	122	Li	45.30N	5.30 E
Terril ▲	126	Gh	37.00N	5.11W
Territoire de Belfort [3]	122	Mg	47.45N	6.55 E
Terry	188	Mc	46.47N	105.19W
Tersa ≈	132	Nd	50.46N	44.42 E
Terschelling	124	Ha	53.21N	5.13 E
Terschelling ◆	122	La	53.24N	5.20 E
Terschelling-West-Terschelling	124	Ha	53.21N	5.13 E
Tersef	168	Bc	12.55N	16.49 E
Terskej-Alatau, hrebet- ⩓	136	Hg	42.10N	78.45 E
Terski bereg ⌇	114	Jc	66.10N	39.30 E
Tersko-Kumski kanal ═	132	Ng	44.47N	44.37 E
Terter ≈	132	Oi	40.27N	47.16 E
Teruel	126	Kd	40.21N	1.06W
Teruel [3]	126	Ld	40.40N	0.40W
Tervakoski	116	Kd	60.48N	24.37 E
Tervel	130	Kf	43.45N	27.24 E
Tervo	116	Lb	62.57N	26.45 E
Tervola	114	Fc	66.05N	24.48 E
Tes	152	Fa	50.27N	93.30 E
Teša ≈	114	Ki	55.38N	42.10 E
Tesalia	202	Cc	2.29N	75.44W
Tesaret ≈	162	Hd	25.40N	2.43 E
Tesdrero, Cerro- ▲	192	Hf	22.47N	103.04W
Teseney	168	Fb	15.07N	36.40 E
Teshekpuk Lake ◙	178	Ib	70.35N	153.30W
Teshikaga	154	Rc	43.29N	144.28 E
Teshio	154	Pb	44.53N	141.44 E
Teshio-Dake ▲	154	Qc	43.58N	142.50 E
Teshio-Gawa ≈	154	Pb	44.53N	141.44 E
Teshio-Sanchi ⩓	156a	Ba	44.20N	142.00 E
Tesijn → Tesijn Gol ≈	140	Ld	50.28N	93.04 E
Tesijn Gol (Tesijn) ≈	140	Ld	50.28N	93.04 E
Teslić	128	Lf	44.37N	17.52 E
Teslin	180	Ed	60.09N	132.45W
Teslin ≈	180	Ed	61.34N	134.50W
Teslin Lake ◙	180	Ed	60.00N	132.30W
Teslui ≈	130	He	44.09N	24.29 E
Tesocoma	192	Ed	27.41N	109.16W
Tesouras, Rio- ≈	204	Gb	14.36S	50.51W
Tesouro	204	Fc	16.04S	53.34W
Tessala, Monts du- ⩓	126	Li	35.15N	0.45W
Tessalit	160	Hf	20.14N	0.59 E
Tessaoua	166	Gc	13.45N	7.59 E
Tessenderlo	124	Hc	51.04N	5.05 E
Test ≈	118	Lk	50.55N	1.29W
Test, Tizi n'- ⌒	162	Fc	30.50N	8.20W
Testa, Capo- ►	128	Di	41.14N	9.08 E
Teste, La-	122	Ej	44.38N	1.09W
Têt ≈	122	Jl	42.44N	3.02 E
Tetari, Cerro- ▲	194	Ki	9.59N	72.55W
Tetas, Punta- ►	206	Fc	23.31S	70.38W
Tete	160	Kj	16.10S	33.36 E
Tete [3]	172	Ec	15.30S	33.00 E
Te Teko	218	Gc	38.02S	176.48 E
Tetepare Island ◆	219a	Cc	8.45S	157.35 E
Tetěrchen	124	Ie	49.14N	6.34 E
Tetere	219a	Ec	9.25S	160.15 E
Teterev ≈	132	Gd	51.01N	30.08 E
Teterow	120	Ic	53.47N	12.34 E
Teteven	130	Hg	42.55N	24.16 E
Tetiaroa Atoll ⊙	208	Mf	17.05S	149.32W
Tetijev	132	Fe	49.23N	29.41 E
Tetjuši	114	Li	54.57N	48.49 E
Teton Peak ▲	188	Ic	47.55N	112.48W
Teton Range ⩓	188	Je	43.50N	110.55W
Teton River ≈	188	Jc	47.56N	110.31W
Tétouan	160	Ge	35.34N	5.22W
Tétouan [3]	162	Fb	35.35N	5.38W
Tetovo	130	Dg	42.01N	20.59 E
Tetri-Ckaro	132	Ni	41.33N	44.27 E
Teuco, Río- ≈	204	Bg	25.38S	60.12W
Teufelskopf ▲	124	Ie	49.36N	6.49 E
Teulada	128	Cl	38.58N	8.46 E
Teulada, Capo- ►	110	Gh	38.52N	8.38 E
Teul de Gonzáles Ortega	192	Hg	21.28N	103.29W
Teun, Pulau- ◆	150	Ih	6.59S	129.08 E
Teupasenti	194	Df	14.13N	86.42W
Teuquito, Río- ≈	204	Bg	24.22S	61.09W
Teuri-Tō ◆	156a	Ba	44.25N	141.20 E
Teutoburger Wald ⩓	120	Ee	52.10N	8.15 E
Teuva/Östermark	114	Ee	62.29N	21.44 E
Teuz ≈	130	Ec	46.39N	21.33 E
Tevai ◆	219c	Bb	11.37S	166.55 E
Tevaitoa	221e	Db	16.46S	151.28W
Tevere = Tiber (EN) ≈	110	Hg	41.44N	12.14 E
Teverya	146	Ff	32.47N	35.32 E
Teviot ≈	118	Kf	55.36N	2.26W
Tevli	120	Ud	52.19N	24.23 E
Tevriz	136	Hd	57.34N	72.24 E
Tevšruleh	152	Hb	47.25N	101.55 E
Te Waewae Bay ◗	218	Bg	46.15S	167.30 E
Tewkesbury	118	Kj	51.59N	2.09W
Têwo (Dêngkagoin)	152	He	34.03N	103.21 E
Texada Island ◆	188	Cb	49.40N	124.24W
Texarkana [Ar.-U.S.]	182	Ie	33.26N	94.02W
Texarkana [Tx.-U.S.]	176	Jf	33.26N	94.03W
Texas	212	Ke	28.51S	151.11 E
Texas [2]	186	Hf	31.30N	99.00W
Texas City	182	If	29.23N	94.54W
Texcoco	192	Jh	19.31N	98.53W
Texel	124	Ga	53.03N	4.47 E
Texel ◆	122	Ka	53.05N	4.45 E
Texel-De Koog	124	Ga	53.07N	4.46 E
Texel-Den Burg	124	Ga	53.03N	4.47 E
Texoma, Lake- ◙	182	He	33.55N	96.37W
Teyéa = Tegea (EN) ⁂	130	Fl	37.27N	22.25 E
Teza ≈	114	Jh	56.32N	41.57 E
Teze-Jel	136	Gh	37.55N	60.22 E
Teziutlán	190	Ee	19.49N	97.21W
Tezpur	148	Ic	26.38N	92.48 E
Tha-anne ≈	180	Id	60.31N	94.37W
Thabana Ntlenyana ▲	172	Dh	29.30S	29.15 E
Thabazimbi	172	Dd	24.41S	27.21 E
Thai, Ao- = Thailand, Gulf of- (EN) ◗	140	Mh	10.00N	102.00 E
Thai Binh	148	Ld	20.27N	106.20 E
Thailand (EN) = Muang Thai [1]	142	Mh	15.00N	100.00 E
Thailand, Gulf of- (EN) = Thai, Ao- ◗	140	Mh	10.00N	102.00 E
Thai Nguyen	148	Ld	21.36N	105.50 E
Thal ⁘	148	Eb	31.30N	71.40 E
Thālith, Ash Shallāl ath- = Third Cataract (EN) ≋	158	Kg	19.49N	30.19 E
Thamad Bū Ḩashīshah	164	Cd	25.50N	18.05 E
Thamarīd	168	Ib	17.39N	54.02 E
Thame	124	Bc	51.45N	0.59W
Thames	216	Eg	37.08S	175.33 E
Thames ≈	110	Ge	51.28N	0.43 E
Thames River ≈	184	Fd	42.19N	82.28W
Thamūd	144	Gf	17.15N	49.54 E
Thāna	142	Jh	19.12N	72.58 E
Thandaung	148	Je	19.04N	96.41 E
Thanh Hoa	142	Mh	19.48N	105.46 E
Thanh-pho Ho Chi Minh (Saigon)	142	Mh	10.45N	106.40 E
Thanjāvūr	148	Ff	10.48N	79.09 E
Thanlwin = Salween (EN) ≈	140	Lg	16.31N	97.37 E
Thann	122	Ng	47.49N	7.05 E
Thaon-les-Vosges	122	Mf	48.15N	6.25 E
Thap Sakae	148	Jf	11.14N	99.31 E
Thar/Great Indian Desert ⁘	140	Jg	27.00N	70.00 E
Thargomindah	212	Ie	28.00S	143.49 E
Tharrawaddy	148	Je	17.39N	95.48 E
Tharros ⁂	128	Ck	39.54N	8.28 E
Tharthār, Baḩrath- ◙	144	Fc	33.59N	43.12 E
Tharthār, Wādī ath- ≈	146	Je	33.59N	43.12 E
Thasi Gang Dzong	148	Ic	27.19N	91.34 E
Thásou	130	Hi	40.47N	24.43 E
Thásos ◆	110	Ig	40.49N	24.42 E
Thásou, Dhiavlos- ≡	130	Hi	40.49N	24.42 E
Thathlīth, Wādī- ≈	164	He	20.25N	44.55 E
Thaton	148	Je	16.56N	97.20 E
Thau, Bassin de- ◎	122	Jk	43.23N	3.36 E
Thaxted	124	Cc	51.57N	0.22 E
Thaya ≈	120	Mh	48.37N	16.56 E
Thayawthadangyi Kyun ◆	148	Jf	12.20N	98.00 E
Thayetchaung	148	Jf	13.52N	98.16 E
Thayetmyo	148	Je	19.19N	95.11 E
The Alberga River ≈	212	He	27.06S	135.33 E
The Aldermen Islands ✣	218	Gb	37.00S	176.05 E
Thebai = Thebes (EN) ⁂	164	Fd	25.43N	32.35 E
Thebes (EN) = Thebai ⁂	164	Fd	25.43N	32.35 E
Thebes (EN) → Thivai	130	Gk	38.19N	23.19 E
The Black Sugarloaf ▲	212	Kf	31.20S	151.33 E
The Borders ✕	118	Kf	55.35N	2.50W
The Bottom	196	Ed	17.38N	63.15W
The Broads ✕	118	Oi	52.40N	1.30 E
The Cheviot ▲	118	Kf	55.28N	2.09W
The Cheviot Hills ⩓	118	Kf	55.30N	2.10W
The Crane	197q	Bb	13.06N	59.26W
The Dalles	182	Cb	45.36N	121.10W
Thedford	182	Gc	41.59N	100.35W
The Entrance	212	Kf	33.21S	151.30 E
The Everglades ⋓	182	Kf	26.00N	81.00W
The Gap	188	Jh	36.25N	111.30W
The Granites	212	Gd	20.35S	130.21 E
The Hague (EN) = Den Haag /'s-Gravenhage	112	Ge	52.06N	4.18 E
The Knob ▲	184	Hc	41.14N	78.22W
The Little Minch ≡	118	Gd	57.35N	6.55W
Thelle ✕	124	De	49.23N	1.51 E
Thelon ≈	174	Jc	64.16N	96.05W
The Macumba River ≈	208	Eg	27.45S	136.50 E
The Merse ✕	118	Kf	55.50N	2.10W
The Naze ►	124	Di	51.42N	1.47 E
The Neales River ≈	212	He	28.08S	136.47 E
The Needles ▲	118	Lk	50.39N	1.34W
Theniet el Had	126	Oi	35.32N	2.01 E
Theodore	212	Kd	24.57S	150.05 E
Theológos	130	Hi	40.40N	24.42 E
The Pas	176	Id	53.50N	101.15W
The Pillories ✣	197n	Bb	12.54N	61.12W
Thérain ≈	122	Ie	49.15N	2.27 E
Thermaïkós Kólpos = Salonika, Gulf of- (EN) ◗	110	Ig	40.20N	22.45 E
Thermopilai = Thermopylae (EN) ⌒	130	Fk	38.48N	22.32 E
Thermopolis	182	Fc	43.39N	108.13W
Thermopylae (EN) = Thermopilai ⌒	130	Fk	38.48N	22.32 E
Thérouanne	124	Ed	50.38N	2.15 E
The Round Mountain ▲	212	Kf	30.27S	152.16 E
The Sandlings ✕	118	Oi	52.10N	1.30 E
Thesiger Bay ◗	180	Fb	71.30N	124.00W
The Slot → New Georgia Sound ≡	214	Fi	8.00S	158.10 E
The Solent Spithead ≡	118	Lk	50.46N	1.20W
Thessalia [2]	130	Fj	39.30N	22.10 E
Thessalia = Thessaly (EN) ✕	110	Ih	39.30N	22.10 E
Thessalía = Thessaly (EN) ▤	130	Fj	39.30N	22.10 E
Thessalon	184	Fb	46.15N	83.34W
Thessaloniki = Salonika (EN)	112	Ig	40.38N	22.56 E
Thessaly (EN) = Thessalia ✕	110	Ih	39.30N	22.10 E
Thessaly (EN) = Thessalía ▤	130	Fj	39.30N	22.10 E
The Stevenson River ≈	212	He	27.06S	135.33 E
Thet ≈	124	Cb	52.24N	0.45 E
Thetford	118	Ni	52.25N	0.45 E
Thetford Mines	184	Lb	46.05N	71.18W
The Twins ▲	218	Ed	41.14S	172.40 E
Theux	124	Hd	50.33N	5.49 E
The Valley	190	Le	18.03N	63.04W
The Warburton River ≈	212	He	27.55S	137.28 E
The Wash ◗	110	Ge	52.55N	0.15 E
The Weald ✕	118	Nj	51.05N	0.05 E
The Witties ✲	194	Ff	14.10N	82.45W
Thiaucourt-Regniéville	124	Hf	48.57N	5.52 E
Thiberville	124	Ce	49.08N	0.27 E
Thibodaux	186	Kl	29.48N	90.49W
Thief River Falls	182	Hb	48.07N	96.10W
Thiel Mountains ⩓	222	Pg	85.15S	91.00W
Thiene	128	Fe	45.42N	11.29 E
Thiérache, Collines de la- ⩓	122	Je	49.48N	3.55 E
Thiers	122	Ji	45.51N	3.34 E
Thiès	160	Fg	14.48N	16.56W
Thiès [3]	166	Bc	14.45N	16.50W
Thiesi	128	Cj	40.31N	8.43 E
Thika	170	Gc	1.03S	37.05 E
Thikombia ◆	216	Fc	15.44S	179.55W
Thillot, Le-	122	Mg	47.53N	6.46 E
Thimerais ✕	122	Hf	48.40N	1.20 E
Thimphu	142	Kg	27.28N	89.39 E
Thio	216	Cd	21.37S	166.14 E
Thionville	122	Me	49.22N	6.10 E
Thiou	166	Ec	13.48N	2.40W
Thira	130	Im	36.25N	25.26 E
Thira = Thira (EN) ◆	130	Im	36.24N	25.26 E
Thira (EN) = Thira ◆	130	Im	36.24N	25.26 E
Thirasia ◆	130	Im	36.25N	25.20 E
Third Cataract (EN) = Thālith, Ash Shallāl ath- ≋	158	Kg	19.49N	30.19 E
Thirsk	118	Lg	54.14N	1.20W
Thisted	114	Bh	56.57N	8.42 E
Thithia ◆	219d	Cb	17.45S	179.18W
Thiu Khao Phetchabun ⩓	148	Ke	16.20N	100.55 E
Thivai (Thebes)	130	Gk	38.19N	23.19 E
Thiviers	122	Gi	45.25N	0.55 E
Thlewiaza ≈	180	Id	60.28N	94.42W
Thoa ≈	180	Gd	60.31N	109.45W
Tho Chu, Dao- ◆	148	Kg	9.00N	103.50 E
Thoen	148	Je	17.41N	99.14 E
Tholen	124	Gc	51.32N	4.13 E
Tholen ◆	122	Kc	51.35N	4.05 E
Tholey	124	Je	49.29N	7.04 E
Thomasset, Rocher- ✲	208	Nf	10.21S	138.25W
Thomaston	184	Ei	32.54N	84.20W
Thomasville [Al.-U.S.]	184	Dj	32.18N	87.47W
Thomasville [Ga.-U.S.]	182	Ke	30.50N	83.59W
Thomasville [N.C.-U.S.]	184	Gh	35.53N	80.05W
Thompson	180	He	55.45N	97.45W
Thompson Falls	188	Hc	47.36N	115.21W
Thompson River [B.C.-Can.] ≈	188	Ea	50.12N	121.34W
Thompson River [U.S.] ≈	186	Jg	39.45N	93.36W
Thompson Sound ≡	218	Bf	45.10S	167.00 E
Thomsen ≈	180	Fb	73.40N	119.30W
Thomson	184	Fi	33.28N	82.30W
Thomson River ≈	212	Ie	25.11S	142.53 E
Thomson's Falls	170	Gb	0.02N	36.22 E
Thon ≈	124	Fe	49.53N	3.55 E
Thon Buri	142	Mh	13.43N	100.24 E
Thong Pha Phum	148	Jf	14.44N	98.38 E
Thongwa	148	Je	16.46N	96.32 E
Thonon-les-Bains	122	Mh	46.22N	6.29 E
Thoreau	186	Bi	35.24N	108.13W
Thornaby-on-Tees	118	Lg	54.34N	1.18W
Thornbury	216	Ci	46.17S	168.06 E
Thorney	124	Bb	52.37N	0.06W
Thornhill	118	Jf	55.18N	3.40W
Thorshavn	112	Fc	62.01N	6.46W
Thouars	122	Fh	46.58N	0.13W
Thouet ≈	122	Fg	47.17N	0.06W
Thouquet-Paris-Plage, Le-	122	Hd	50.31N	1.35 E
Thrace (EN) = Thráki ✕	110	Ig	41.20N	26.45 E
Thrace (EN) = Thráki ▤	130	Jh	41.20N	26.45 E
Thrace (EN) = Trakya ✕	110	Ig	41.20N	26.45 E
Thrace (EN) = Trakya ▤	130	Jh	41.20N	26.45 E
Thráki [2]	130	Ih	41.10N	25.30 E
Thráki = Thrace (EN) ✕	110	Ig	41.20N	26.45 E
Thráki = Thrace (EN) ▤	130	Jh	41.20N	26.45 E
Thrakikón Pélagos ≅	130	Hi	40.30N	25.00 E
Thrapston	124	Bb	52.24N	0.32W
Three Forks	182	Eb	45.54N	111.33W
Three Kings Islands ✣	208	Ih	34.10S	172.10 E
Three Kings Trough (EN) ⌵	106	Jm	32.00S	170.30 E
Three Pagodas Pass ⌒	148	Je	15.18N	98.23 E
Three Points, Cape- ►	158	Gh	4.45N	2.06W
Three Rivers	184	Ee	41.57N	85.38W
Three Sisters Islands ✣	219a	Ed	10.10S	161.57 E
Throckmorton	186	Gj	33.11N	99.11W
Throssel, Lake- ◙	212	Ee	27.25S	124.15 E
Thu Dau Mot	148	Lf	10.58N	106.39 E
Thuin	122	Kd	50.20N	4.17 E
Thule ◆	222	Ad	59.27S	27.19W
Thule/Qânâq	224	Od	77.35N	69.40W
Thule, Mount- ▲	180	Jb	73.00N	78.27W
Thun	128	Bd	46.45N	7.40 E
Thunder Bay	176	Ke	48.23N	89.15W
Thunder Bay [Ont.-Can.] ◗	186	Lb	48.24N	89.00W
Thunder Bay [Ont.-Can.] ◗	184	Fc	45.04N	83.25W
Thunder Butte ▲	186	Fd	45.19N	101.53W
Thuner See ◙	128	Bd	46.40N	7.45 E
Thung Song	148	Jg	8.11N	99.41 E
Thur ≈	128	Cc	47.36N	8.28 E
Thurgau [2]	128	Dc	47.40N	9.10 E
Thüringen [2]	120	Gf	50.40N	11.00 E
Thüringer Wald = Thuringian Forest (EN) ⩓	110	He	50.30N	11.00 E
Thuringian Forest (EN) = Thüringer Wald ⩓	110	He	50.30N	11.00 E
Thurles/Durlas	118	Fi	52.41N	7.49W
Thursday Island	212	Ib	10.35S	142.13 E
Thurso	112	Fd	58.35N	3.32W
Thurso ≈	118	Jc	58.35N	3.30W
Thurston Island ◆	222	Pf	72.06S	99.00W
Thury-Harcourt	124	Bf	48.59N	0.29W
Thusis/Tusaun	128	Dd	46.42N	9.26 E
Thuwayrāt, Nafūd ath- ⁘	146	Kj	26.00N	44.50 E
Thuy Phong	148	Lf	11.14N	108.43 E
Thwaites Iceberg Tongue ❄	222	Of	74.00S	108.30W
Thy ✕	116	Ch	57.00N	8.30 E
Thyborøn	116	Ch	56.42N	8.13 E
Tianbaoshan	154	Jc	42.57N	128.57 E
Tianchang	154	Ke	32.37N	119.00 E
Tiandong (Pingma)	152	Ig	23.40N	107.09 E
Tian'e (Liupai)	152	If	25.05N	107.12 E
Tianguá	202	Jd	3.44S	40.59W
Tianjin (Tientsin)	142	Nf	39.08N	117.12 E
Tianjin Shi (T'ien-chin Shih) [4]	152	Kd	39.08N	117.12 E
Tianjun (Xinyuan)	142	Lf	37.18N	99.15 E
Tianlin (Leli)	152	Ig	24.22N	106.11 E
Tian Ling ▲	154	Kb	44.24N	130.10 E
Tianmen	152	Je	30.40N	113.10 E
Tianmu Shan ⩓	154	Ei	30.31N	119.36 E
Tianmu Xi ≈	154	Ej	29.59N	119.24 E
Tianqiaoling	154	Jc	43.35N	129.35 E
Tian Shan ⩓	140	Ke	42.00N	80.01 E
Tianshan → Ar Horqin Qi	152	Lc	43.55N	120.05 E
Tianshifu	152	Lc	41.15N	124.20 E
Tianshui	142	Mf	34.35N	105.43 E
Tiantai	154	Fj	29.08N	121.00 E
Tianwangsi	154	Ei	31.45N	119.12 E
Tianyi → Ningcheng	152	Kc	41.34N	119.25 E
Tianzhen	154	Cd	40.24N	114.05 E
Tianzhen → Gaoqing	154	Df	37.10N	117.50 E
Tianzhuangtai	154	Gd	40.49N	122.06 E
Tiaraju	204	Ej	30.15S	54.23W
Tiarei	221e	Fc	17.32S	149.20W
Tiaret	160	He	35.20N	1.14 E
Tiaret [3]	162	Hc	34.50N	1.30 E
Tiaret, Monts de- ⩓	126	Ni	35.26N	1.15 E
Tiassalé	166	Ed	5.54N	4.50W
Tiavea	221c	Ba	13.57S	171.24W
Tib, Ra's aṭ- = Bon, Cape- (EN) ►	158	Ie	37.05N	11.03 E
Tibaji	204	Gg	24.30S	50.24W
Tibaji, Rio- ≈	204	Kf	22.47S	51.01W
Tibasti, Sarīr- ⁘	158	If	24.00N	17.00 E
Tibati	160	Ih	6.28N	12.38 E
Tiber (EN) = Tevere ≈	110	Hg	41.44N	12.14 E
Tiberina, Val- ∨	128	Gg	43.30N	12.10 E
Tibesti ⩓	158	If	21.30N	17.30 E
Tibet (EN) = Xizang Zizhiqu (Hsi-tsang Tzu-chih-ch'ü) [2]	152	Ee	32.00N	90.00 E
Tibet, Plateau of- (EN) = Qing Zang Gaoyuan ▰	140	Kf	32.30N	87.00 E
Tibidabo ▲	126	Oc	41.25N	2.07 E
Tibni	146	He	35.35N	30.49 E
Tibro	116	Ff	58.26N	14.10 E
Tibú	194	Ki	8.40N	72.42W
Tibugá, Golfo de- ◗	202	Cb	5.45N	77.20W
Tiburón, Cabo- ►	194	Ii	8.42N	77.21W
Tiburón, Isla- ◆	190	Bc	29.00N	112.25W
Ticao ◆	150	Hd	12.31N	123.42 E
Tice	184	Gl	26.41N	81.49W
Tichá Orlice ≈	120	Mf	50.09N	16.05 E
Tichit	160	Gg	18.26N	9.31W
Tichît, Dahr- ▲	162	Ff	18.30N	9.25W
Tichka, Tizi n'- ⌒	162	Fc	31.17N	7.21W
Tichla	162	Ee	21.36N	14.58W
Ticinesi, Alpi- ⩓	128	Cd	46.20N	8.45 E
Ticino [2]	128	Cd	46.20N	9.00 E
Ticino ≈	128	De	45.09N	9.14 E
Ticul	190	Gd	20.24N	89.32W
Tidaholm	114	Cg	58.11N	13.57 E
Tidan ≈	116	Ef	58.42N	13.48 E
Tiddim	148	Id	23.22N	93.40 E
Tidikelt, Plaine du- ▭	158	Hf	27.00N	1.30 E
Tidirhine ▲	162	Gc	34.51N	4.31W
Tidjikja	160	Fg	18.32N	11.27W
Tidore	150	If	0.40N	127.26 E
Tidra, Ile- ◆	158	Fg	19.44N	16.24W
Tiebissou	166	Dd	7.10N	5.13W
Tiechang	154	Id	41.40N	126.12 E
Tiel	122	Lc	51.54N	5.25 E
Tieli	152	Mb	47.04N	128.02 E
Tieling	154	Gc	42.18N	123.51 E
Tielongtan	152	Cd	35.10N	79.32 E
Tielt	122	Jc	51.00N	3.20 E
Tienba ≈	166	Dd	8.30N	7.10W
T'ien-chin Shih → Tianjin Shi [4]	152	Kd	39.08N	117.12 E
Tienen/Tirlemont	124	Gd	50.48N	4.57 E
Tiengemeten ◆	124	Gc	51.45N	5.20 E
Tientsin → Tianjin	142	Nf	39.08N	117.12 E
Tieroko, Tarso- ▲	168	Ba	20.45N	17.52 E
Tierp	114	Df	60.20N	17.30 E
Tierra Amarilla [Chile]	206	Fc	27.29S	70.17W
Tierra Amarilla [N.M.-U.S.]	186	Ch	36.42N	106.33W
Tierra Blanca	190	Ee	18.27N	96.21W
Tierra Colorada	192	Ji	17.10N	99.35W
Tierra del Fuego [2]	206	Gh	54.00S	67.00W
Tierra del Fuego ◆	198	Jk	54.00S	69.00W
Tierralta	202	Cb	8.10N	76.04W
Tiétar ≈	126	Fe	39.50N	6.01W
Tietê, Rio- ≈	198	Kh	20.40S	51.35W
Tietjerksteradeel	124	Ia	53.12N	6.00 E
Tietjerksteradeel-Bergum	124	Hb	52.17N	5.58 E
Tifariti	162	Ed	26.09N	10.33W
Tiffany Mountain ▲	188	Fb	48.40N	119.56W
Tiffin	184	Fe	41.07N	83.11W
Tifton	182	Ke	31.27N	83.31W
Tiga ◆	219b	Ce	21.08S	167.49 E
Tigalda ◆	178a	Fb	54.05N	165.05W
Tigăneşti	130	If	43.54N	25.22 E
Tighennif	126	Mi	35.25N	0.15 E
Tigil	138	Ke	57.48N	158.40 E
Tigil ≈	138	Ke	57.57N	158.20 E
Tignère	166	Hd	7.22N	12.39 E
Tigray [3]	168	Fc	14.00N	39.00 E
Tigre ▲	192	Hh	19.53N	102.59W
Tigre, Cerro del- ▲	192	Jf	23.03N	99.16W
Tigre, Rio- [S.Amer.] ≈	198	If	4.30S	74.10W
Tigre, Rio- [Ven.] ≈	196	Eh	9.20N	62.30W
Tigris (EN) = Dicle ≈	140	Gf	31.00N	47.25 E
Tigris (EN) = Dijlah ≈	140	Gf	31.00N	47.25 E
Tigrovy Hvost, mys- ►	135	Bc	43.57N	58.45 E
Tiguent	162	Df	17.15N	16.00W
Tiguentourine	162	Id	27.43N	9.33 E
Tigui	168	Bb	18.38N	18.47 E
Tigzirt	126	Qh	36.54N	4.07 E
Tīh, Jabal at- ▭	164	Fd	29.35N	34.00 E
Tīh, Şaḩrā' at- = At Tih Desert (EN) ⁘	164	Fc	30.05N	34.00 E
Tihāmat ▭	144	Ff	18.30N	41.30 E
Tihāmat Ash Shām ▭	164	Hf	19.15N	41.10 E
Tihāmat 'Asīr ▭	164	Hf	17.30N	42.20 E
Tihi okean = Pacific Ocean (EN) ≣	106	Ki	5.00N	155.00W
Tihoreck	112	Kf	45.51N	40.09 E
Tihuta, Pasul- ⌒	130	Ib	47.15N	25.00 E
Tihvin	136	Dd	59.38N	33.31 E
Tiirismaa ▲	116	Kc	61.01N	25.31 E
Tījī	164	Bc	32.01N	11.22 E
Tījirīt ✕	162	Ee	20.30N	15.00W
Tijuana	176	Hf	32.32N	117.01W
Tijucas	204	Hh	27.14S	48.38W
Tijucas, Baía do- ◗	204	Hh	27.15S	48.31W
Tijucas, Rio- ≈	204	Hh	27.15S	48.38W

Index Symbols

- [1] Independent Nation
- [2] State, Region
- [3] District, County
- [4] Municipality
- [5] Colony, Dependency
- ■ Continent
- ✕ Physical Region
- ▤ Historical or Cultural Region
- ▲ Mount, Mountain
- △ Volcano
- ⌂ Hill
- ⩓ Mountains, Mountain Range
- ⌓ Hills, Escarpment
- ▰ Plateau, Upland
- ⌒ Pass, Gap
- ▭ Plain, Lowland
- Δ Delta
- ▨ Salt Flat
- ∨ Valley, Canyon
- ◠ Crater, Cave
- ✿ Karst Features
- ◡ Depression
- ▥ Polder
- ⁘ Desert, Dunes
- ♣ Forest, Woods
- ⁙ Heath, Steppe
- ☘ Oasis
- ► Cape, Point
- ⌇ Coast, Beach
- ⌈ Cliff
- ⊓ Peninsula
- ⋈ Isthmus
- ⋯ Sandbank
- ◆ Island
- ⊙ Atoll
- ✲ Rock, Reef
- ✣ Islands, Archipelago
- ⁑ Rocks, Reefs
- ✺ Coral Reef
- ◉ Well, Spring
- ⊛ Geyser
- ≈ River, Stream
- ≋ Waterfall, Rapids
- ⋎ River Mouth, Estuary
- ◙ Lake
- ◘ Salt Lake
- ◌ Intermittent Lake
- ⊡ Reservoir
- ⋓ Swamp, Pond
- ═ Canal
- ❅ Glacier
- ❄ Ice Shelf, Pack Ice
- ≣ Ocean
- ≅ Sea
- ◗ Gulf, Bay
- ≡ Strait, Fjord
- ◎ Lagoon
- ⊟ Bank
- ⩚ Seamount
- ⊼ Tablemount
- ⋀ Ridge
- ⊏ Shelf
- ⊔ Basin
- ⌐ Escarpment, Sea Scarp
- ⌁ Fracture
- ⌵ Trench, Abyss
- ✤ National Park, Reserve
- ✦ Point of Interest
- ☀ Recreation Site
- ⊂ Cave, Cavern
- ▣ Historic Site
- ⁂ Ruins
- ▦ Wall, Walls
- ✝ Church, Abbey
- ☖ Temple
- ⊕ Scientific Station
- ⊞ Railway station
- ✈ Airport
- ⚓ Port
- ⚔ Military installation
- ⚑ Lighthouse
- ⚒ Mine
- ⊃ Tunnel
- ⫽ Dam, Bridge

Tijucas, Serra do- 204 Hh 27.16S 49.10W
Tijucas do Sul 204 Hg 25.56S 49.10W
Tijuco, Rio- 204 Gd 18.40S 50.05W
Tikal 176 Kh 17.20N 89.39W
Tikanlik 152 Ec 40.42N 87.38E
Tikchik Lakes 178 Hd 60.07N 158.35W
Tikehau Atoll 216 Lb 15.00S 148.10W
Tikei, Ile- 216 Mb 14.58S 144.32W
Tikitiki 218 Hb 37.47S 178.25E
Tikkakoski 116 Kb 62.24N 25.38E
Tikkurila 116 Kd 60.18N 25.03E
Tiko 166 Ge 4.05N 9.22E
Tikopia Island 208 Hf 12.19S 168.49E
Tikrīt 144 Fc 34.36N 43.42E
Tikšeozero, ozero- 114 Hc 66.15N 31.45E
Tiksi 142 Ob 71.36N 128.48E
Tiladummati Atoll 148a Ba 6.50N 73.05E
Tilamuta 150 Hf 0.30N 122.20E
Tilburg 122 Lc 51.34N 5.05E
Tilbury 118 Nj 51.28N 0.23E
Tilcara 206 Gb 23.34S 65.22W
Til-Châtel 122 Lg 47.31N 5.10E
Tileagd 130 Fb 47.04N 22.12E
Tilemsès 166 Fb 15.37N 4.44E
Tilemsi, Vallée du- 158 Hg 19.00N 0.02E
Tilia 162 Gd 27.22N 0.02W
Tiličiki 138 Ld 60.20N 166.03E
Tiligul 132 Gf 47.07N 30.57E
Tiligulski liman 132 Gf 46.50N 31.10E
Till 118 Kf 55.41N 2.12W
Tillabéry 166 Fc 14.13N 1.27E
Tillamook 188 Dd 45.27N 123.51W
Tillamook Bay 188 Dd 45.30N 123.53W
Tillanchong 148 Ig 8.30N 93.37E
Tillberga 116 Ge 59.41N 16.37E
Tille 122 Lg 47.07N 5.21E
Tillia 166 Fb 16.08N 4.47E
Tillières-sur-Avre 124 Df 48.46N 1.04E
Tillingham 124 Cd 50.58N 0.44E
Tillsonburg 184 Gd 42.51N 80.44W
Tilly-sur-Seulles 124 Be 49.11N 0.37W
Tiloa 166 Fb 15.04N 2.03E
Tilos 130 Km 36.25N 27.25E
Tilpa 212 If 30.57S 144.24E
Tim 132 Jd 51.37N 37.11E
Tim 132 Jc 52.15N 37.22E
Ţimā 164 Fd 26.54N 31.26E
Timagami 184 Gb 47.00N 80.05W
Timagami, Lake - 180 Jg 46.57N 80.05W
Timalacia, Rio- → Sacre, Rio- 204 Ca 13.55S 58.02W
Timane, Rio- 204 Be 20.16S 60.08W
Timan Ridge (EN) = Timanski krjaž 110 Lc 65.00N 51.00E
Timanski bereg 134 Eb 68.20N 51.45E
Timanski krjaž = Timan Ridge (EN) 110 Lc 65.00N 51.00E
Timaru 210 Ii 44.24S 171.15E
Timaševsk 136 Df 45.35N 38.58E
Timbalier Bay 186 Kl 29.10N 90.20W
Timbalier Island 186 Kl 29.04N 90.28W
Timbaúba 202 Ke 7.31S 35.19W
Timbédra 162 Ff 16.14N 8.10W
Timbó 204 Hh 26.50S 49.18W
Timbuktu (EN) = Tombouctou 160 Gg 16.46N 2.59W
Timedouine, Ras- 126 Qh 36.28N 4.09E
Timétrine 166 Eb 19.27N 0.26W
Timétrine 166 Eb 19.20N 0.42W
Tímfi Óros 130 Dj 39.57N 20.50E
Timfristós 130 Ek 38.57N 21.49E
Tîmia 166 Gb 18.04N 8.40E
Timimoun 160 Hf 29.15N 0.15E
Timimoun, Sebkha de- 162 Hd 29.00N 0.05E
Timiriș, Cap— 162 Df 19.23N 16.32W
Timirjazevo 136 Ge 53.45N 66.33E
Timiş [2] 130 Ed 45.38N 21.13E
Timiş 130 De 44.51N 20.39E
Timiskaming, Lake- 184 Hb 47.35N 79.35W
Timişoara 112 If 45.45N 21.13E
Ti-m-Merhsoï 166 Gb 18.00N 5.40E
Timmins 176 Ke 48.28N 81.20W
Timmoudi 162 Gd 29.19N 1.08W
Timms Hill 186 Kd 45.27N 90.11W
Timok 130 Fe 44.13N 22.40E
Timon 202 Je 5.06S 42.49W
Timor, Laut- = Timor Sea (EN) 208 Df 11.00S 128.00E
Timor, Pulau- 140 Oj 8.50S 126.00E
Timor Sea (EN) = Timor, Laut- 208 Df 11.00S 128.00E
Timor Timur [3] 150 Ih 8.35S 126.00E
Timor Trough (EN) 106 Ij 9.50S 126.00E
Timote 206 He 35.21S 62.14W
Timotes 202 Db 8.59N 70.44W
Timpton 138 He 58.43N 127.12E
Timrå 114 De 62.29N 17.18E
Tims Ford Lake 184 Dh 35.15N 86.10W
Tin, Ra's at- 164 Dc 32.37N 23.08E
Tinaca Point 140 Oi 5.33N 125.20E
Tinaco 196 Bh 9.42N 68.26W
Tinakula 219c Ab 10.24S 165.47E
Ti-n-Alkoum 162 Je 24.34N 10.11E
Ti-n-Amzi [Alg.] 162 He 20.32N 4.37E
Ti-n-Amzi [Niger] 166 Fb 17.54N 4.32E
Tinaquillo 196 Bh 9.55N 68.18W
Tinchebray 124 Bf 48.46N 0.44W
Tindalo 168 Ed 5.39N 31.03E
Tindari 128 Jl 38.10N 15.04E
Tindila 166 Dc 10.16N 8.15W
Tindouf 160 Gf 27.42N 8.09W
Tindouf, Hamada de- 162 Fd 27.45N 8.25W
Tindouf, Sebkha de- 162 Fd 27.45N 7.35W
Tinée 122 Nk 43.55N 7.11E
Tineo 126 Fa 43.20N 6.25W
Ti-n-Essako 166 Fb 18.27N 2.29E
Tin Fouye 162 Id 28.15N 7.45E
Tinghert, Ḩamādat- 158 If 28.50N 10.00E
Tinglev 116 Cj 54.56N 9.15E
Tingmiarmiut 179 Hf 62.25N 42.15W
Tingo Maria 202 Ce 9.10S 76.00W
Tingri (Xêgar) 152 Ef 28.41N 87.00E
Tingsryd 114 Dh 56.32N 14.59E
Tingstäde 116 Hg 57.44N 18.36E
Tingvoll 114 Be 62.54N 8.12E
Tinian Channel 220b Bb 14.54N 145.37E
Tinian Island 208 Fc 15.00N 145.38E
Tini Wells 168 Cb 15.02N 22.48E
Tinkisso 166 Dc 11.21N 9.10W
Tinnelva 116 Ce 59.34N 9.15E
Tinniswood, Mount- 188 Da 50.19N 123.50W
Tinnoset 116 Ce 59.43N 9.02E
Tinnsjo 116 Ce 59.54N 8.55E
Tinogasta 206 Gc 28.04S 67.34W
Tinos 130 Il 37.32N 25.10E
Tinos 130 Il 37.35N 25.10E
Tínou, Stenón- 130 Il 37.38N 25.10E
Tinrhert, Hamada de- 158 Hf 28.50N 10.00E
Tinrhir 162 Fc 31.31N 5.32W
Tinsukia 148 Jc 27.30N 95.22E
Tintagel Head 118 Ik 50.41N 4.46W
Tintamarre, Ile- 197b Bb 18.07N 63.00W
Ti-n-Tarabine 162 Ie 21.16N 7.24E
Tîntăreni 130 Ge 44.36N 23.29E
Tintina 206 Hc 27.02S 62.43W
Tinto 126 Fg 37.12N 6.55W
Ti-n-toumma 158 Ig 16.04N 12.40E
Tinwald 218 De 43.55S 171.43E
Ti-n-Zaouâtene 160 Hg 19.56N 2.55E
Tiobraid Árann/Tipperary 118 Ei 52.29N 8.10W
Tiobraid Árann/Tipperary [2] 118 Ei 52.40N 8.20W
Tioga 186 Eb 48.24N 102.56W
Tioman, Pulau- 150 Df 2.48N 104.11E
Tione di Trento 128 Ed 46.02N 10.43E
Tioro, Selat- = Tioro, Strait (EN) 150 Hg 4.40S 122.20E
Tioro Strait (EN) = Tioro, Selat- 150 Hg 4.40S 122.20E
Tiøtta 114 Cd 65.50N 12.24E
Tiouilit 162 Df 18.52N 16.10W
Tipasa 126 Oh 36.35N 2.27E
Tipitapa 190 Gf 12.12N 86.06W
Tipperary/Tiobraid Árann 118 Ei 52.29N 8.10W
Tipperary/Tiobraid Árann [2] 118 Ei 52.40N 8.20W
Tipton, Mount- 188 Hi 35.32N 114.12W
Tip Top Mountain 186 Nb 48.16N 85.59W
Tiptree 124 Cc 51.49N 0.45E
Tiracambu, Serra do- 202 Id 3.15S 46.30W
Tirahart 162 He 23.45N 2.30E
Tīrān 146 Nf 32.42N 51.09E
Tīrān, Maḏīq- 146 Fi 27.55N 34.28E
Tirana 112 Hg 41.20N 19.50E
Tirania 162 Ie 23.08N 9.01E
Tirano 128 Ed 46.13N 10.10E
Tiraspol 136 Cf 46.50N 29.37E
Tirat Karmel 146 Ff 32.46N 34.58E
Tire 144 Cb 38.04N 27.45E
Tirebolu 146 Hb 41.00N 38.50E
Tiree 118 Ge 56.31N 6.49W
Tiree, Passage of- 118 Ge 56.30N 6.30W
Tîrgovişte 130 Ie 44.56N 25.27E
Tîrgu Bujor 130 Kd 45.52N 27.54E
Tîrgu Cărbuneşti 130 Ge 44.57N 23.31E
Tîrgu Frumos 130 Jb 47.12N 27.00E
Tîrgu Jiu 130 Gd 45.03N 23.17E
Tîrgu Lăpuş 130 Gb 47.27N 23.52E
Tîrgu Mureş 112 If 46.33N 24.34E
Tîrgu Neamţ 130 Jb 47.12N 26.22E
Tîrgu Ocna 130 Jc 46.17N 26.37E
Tîrgu Secuiesc 130 Jd 46.00N 26.08E
Tîrguşor 130 Le 44.27N 28.25E
Tirich Mir 140 Jf 36.15N 71.50E
Tirins 130 Fl 37.36N 22.48E
Tiririca, Serra da- 204 Ic 17.06S 47.06W
Tiris 158 Ff 23.10N 13.30W
Tiris Zemmour [3] 162 Fe 24.00N 10.00W
Tirlemont/Tienen 124 Gd 50.48N 4.57E
Tirljanski 134 Ii 54.12N 58.33E
Tîrnava Mare 130 Gc 46.09N 23.42E
Tîrnava Mică 130 Gc 46.11N 23.55E
Tîrnăveni 130 Hc 46.20N 24.17E
Tírnavos 130 Fj 39.45N 22.17E
Tiro 166 Cd 9.45N 10.39W
Tirol/Tirolo = Tyrol (EN) 128 Fd 47.00N 11.20E
Tirol = Tyrol (EN) [2] 128 Fc 47.10N 11.25E
Tirolo/Tirol = Tyrol (EN) 128 Fd 47.00N 11.20E
Tiros 204 Jd 19.00S 45.58W
Tirreno, Mar- = Tyrrhenian Sea (EN) 110 Hh 40.00N 12.00E
Tirschenreuth 120 Ig 49.53N 12.21E
Tirso 128 Ck 39.53N 8.32E
Tirstrup 116 Dh 56.18N 10.42E
Tirua Point 218 Fc 38.23S 174.38E
Tiruchchirappalli 142 Jh 10.49N 78.41E
Tiruliai/Tiruliaj 116 Ji 55.44N 23.18E
Tiruliaj/Tiruliai 116 Ji 55.44N 23.18E
Tirunelveli 142 Ji 8.44N 77.42E
Tirupati 148 Ff 13.39N 79.25E
Tirza 116 Lg 57.09N 26.37E
Tisa = Tisza (EN) 110 If 45.15N 20.17E
Tis Abay 168 Fc 11.20N 37.40E
Tisdale 180 Hf 52.51N 104.04W
Tisnaren 116 Ff 58.55N 15.55E
Tisovec 120 Ph 48.42N 19.57E
Tissemsilt 162 Hb 35.36N 1.49E
Tissø 116 Di 55.35N 11.20E
Tisza 110 If 45.15N 20.17E
Tisza (EN) = Tisa 110 If 45.15N 20.17E
Tiszaföldvár 120 Qj 46.59N 20.15E
Tiszafüred 120 Qi 47.37N 20.46E
Tiszakécske 120 Qj 46.56N 20.06E
Tiszántúl 120 Qj 47.00N 21.00E
Tiszavasvári 120 Ri 47.58N 21.21E
Titao 166 Ec 13.46N 2.04W
Titarísios 130 Fj 39.47N 22.23E
Tit-Ary 138 Hb 71.55N 127.01E
Titicaca, Lago- 198 Jg 15.50S 69.20W
Titikaveka 220p Bc 21.15S 159.45W
Titlagarh 148 Gd 20.18N 83.09E
Titlis 128 Cd 46.47N 8.26E
Titograd 112 Hg 42.26N 19.16E
Titova Korenica 128 Jf 44.45N 15.42E
Titovo Užice 130 Cf 43.52N 19.51E
Titov Veles 130 Eh 41.42N 21.48E
Titov vrh 130 Dh 41.58N 20.50E
Titran 114 Be 63.40N 8.18E
Titteri 126 Pi 35.59N 3.15E
Titu 130 Ie 44.39N 25.32E
Titule 170 Eb 3.17N 25.32E
Titusville [Fl.-U.S.] 182 Kf 28.37N 80.49W
Titusville [Pa.-U.S.] 184 He 41.37N 79.42W
Tituvenaj/Tytuvėnai 116 Ji 55.33N 23.09E
Tiva 170 Gc 2.20S 39.55E
Tivaouane 166 Bc 14.57N 16.49W
Tiveden 116 Ff 58.45N 14.40E
Tiverton 118 Jk 50.55N 3.29W
Tivoli [Gren.] 197p Bb 12.10N 61.37W
Tivoli [It.] 128 Gi 41.58N 12.48E
Ţiwāl 168 Cc 10.22N 22.43E
Tiwi 170 Gc 4.14S 39.35E
Tiyo 168 Gc 14.41N 40.57E
Tizatlán 192 Jh 19.21N 98.15W
Tizimín 190 Gd 21.09N 88.09W
Tizi Ouzou 162 Hb 36.42N 4.03E
Tizi Ouzou [3] 162 Hb 36.35N 4.05E
Tiznados, Río- 196 Ch 8.16N 67.47W
Tiznit 162 Fd 29.43N 9.43W
Tiznit [3] 162 Fd 29.07N 9.04W
Tjačev 120 Th 48.02N 23.36E
Tjanšan 152 Dc 42.00N 80.01E
Tjasmin 132 He 49.03N 32.50E
Tjeggelvas 114 Dc 66.35N 17.40E
Tjeuuemeer 122 Lb 52.54N 5.50E
Tjøme 116 De 59.10N 10.25E
Tjorn 116 Df 58.00N 11.38E
Tjub-Karagan, mys- 132 Qg 44.38N 50.20E
Tjubuk 134 Jh 56.03N 60.58E
Tjuhtet 138 De 56.32N 89.29E
Tjukalinsk 136 Hd 55.52N 72.12E
Tjuleni, ostrov- 132 Og 44.30N 47.30E
Tjuleni, ostrova- 132 Qg 44.55N 50.10E
Tjulgan 136 Fe 52.22N 56.12E
Tjumen 142 Id 57.09N 65.32E
Tjumenskaja oblast [3] 136 Gd 57.00N 69.00E
Tjung 138 Hd 63.42N 121.30E
Tjup 135 Lc 42.44N 78.20E
Tjuri/Türi 114 Fg 58.50N 25.27E
Tjust 116 Gg 57.50N 16.15E
Tjuzašu, pereval- 135 Ic 42.19N 73.50E
Tkibuli 132 Mh 42.19N 42.59E
Tkvarčeli 136 Eg 42.52N 41.40E
Tlacolula 192 Ki 16.57N 96.29W
Tlacotalpan 192 Lh 18.37N 95.40W
Tlahualilo, Sierra del- 192 Hd 26.30N 103.20W
Tlalnepantla 192 Jh 19.33N 99.12W
Tlapa de Comonfort 192 Ji 17.33N 98.33W
Tlapaneco, Rio- 192 Jh 18.00N 98.48W
Tlaquepaque 192 Hg 20.39N 103.19W
Tlaxcala 190 Ee 19.19N 98.14W
Tlaxcala [2] 190 Ee 19.25N 98.10W
Tlemcen 162 Gc 34.52N 1.19W
Tlemcen [3] 162 Gc 34.45N 1.30W
Tleń 120 Oc 53.38N 18.20E
Tleta Rissana 126 Gi 35.14N 5.59W
Tletat ed Douaïr 126 Oi 35.59N 2.55E
Tljarata 132 Oh 42.06N 46.22E
Tlumač 120 Vh 48.46N 25.06E
Tłuszcz 120 Rd 52.26N 21.26E
Tmassah 164 Cd 26.22N 15.48E
Toaca, Vîrful- 130 Ic 46.55N 25.59E
Toagel Mlungui 220a Ab 7.32N 134.28E
Toamasina 160 Lj 18.10S 49.24E
Toamasina [3] 172 Hc 18.00S 48.40E
Toau Atoll 216 Lc 15.55S 146.00W
Toay 206 He 36.40S 64.21W
Toba 154 Ng 34.29N 136.51E
Toba, Danau- = Toba, Lake- (EN) 140 Li 2.35N 98.50E
Toba, Lake- (EN) = Toba, Danau- 140 Li 2.35N 98.50E
Tobago 198 Jd 11.15N 60.40W
Tobago Basin (EN) 196 Ff 12.30N 60.30W
Tobago Cays 197n Bb 12.39N 61.22W
Toba Kākar Range 148 Db 31.15N 68.00E
Tobarra 126 Kf 38.35N 1.41W
Tobejuba, Isla- 196 Fh 9.20N 60.52W
Tobelo 150 If 1.25N 127.31E
Tobermory [Ont.-Can.] 184 Gc 45.15N 81.40W
Tobermory [Scot.-U.K.] 118 Ge 56.37N 6.05W
Tōbetsu 156a Bb 43.14N 141.29E
Tobi Island 208 Ed 3.00N 131.10E
Tobin, Kap- 179 Jd 70.30N 21.30W
Tobin, Mount- 188 Gf 40.22N 117.32W
Tobin Lake [Austl.] 212 Fd 21.45S 125.50E
Tobin Lake [Sask.-Can.] 180 Hf 53.40N 103.20W
Tobi-Shima 156 Fb 39.12N 139.32E
Toblach / Dobbiaco 128 Gd 46.44N 12.14E
Toboali 150 Eg 3.00S 106.30E
Tobol 136 Ge 52.40N 62.39E
Tobol 140 Id 58.10N 68.12E
Tobolsk 142 Id 58.12N 68.16E
Tobruk (EN) = Ţubruq 160 Je 32.05N 23.59E
Tobseda 136 Fb 68.36N 52.20E
Tobyš 134 Ed 65.30N 51.00E
Tocantinópolis 200 Lf 6.20S 47.25W
Tocantins, Rio- 198 Lf 1.45S 49.10W
Tocantinzinho, Rio- 204 Ha 13.57S 48.20W
Toccoa 184 Fh 34.35N 83.19W
Toce 128 Ce 45.56N 8.29E
Tochigi 156 Fc 36.23N 139.44E
Tochigi Ken [2] 154 Of 36.50N 139.50E
Tochio 156 Fc 37.29N 138.58E
Töcksfors 116 De 59.31N 11.50E
Toco 196 Fg 10.50N 60.57W
Tocoa 194 Df 15.41N 86.03W
Toconao 206 Gb 23.11S 68.01W
Tocopilla 200 Ih 22.05S 70.12W
Tocumen 194 Hi 9.05N 79.23W
Tocuyo, Río- 194 Mh 11.03N 68.20W
Todd Mountain 184 Nb 46.32N 66.43W
Todi 128 Gh 42.47N 12.24E
Tödi 128 Cd 46.49N 8.55E
Todo-ga-Saki 152 Pd 39.33N 142.05E
Todos os Santos, Baia de- 198 Mg 12.48S 38.38W
Todos Santos 190 Bd 23.27N 110.13W
Todos Santos, Bahía- 192 Ab 31.48N 116.42W
Tofino 180 Eg 49.09N 125.54W
Tofte 116 De 59.33N 10.34E
Toftlund 116 Ci 55.11N 9.04E
Tofua Island 216 Fc 19.45S 175.05W
Toga 219b Ca 13.26S 166.41E
Tōgane 156 Gd 35.33N 140.21E
Tog Ḍarōr 168 Hc 10.25N 50.00E
Togdere 168 Hd 9.01N 47.07E
Tog-Dheer [3] 168 Hd 9.50N 45.50E
Togi 156 Ec 37.08N 136.43E
Togiak 178 Ge 59.04N 160.24W
Togian, Kepulauan- = Togian Islands (EN) 150 Hg 0.20S 122.00E
Togian Islands (EN) = Togian, Kepulauan- 150 Hg 0.20S 122.00E
Togliatti 112 Ke 53.31N 49.26E
Togni 168 Fb 18.05N 35.10E
Togo [1] 160 Hh 8.00N 1.10E
Togrog Ul → Qahar Youyi Qianqi 154 Bd 40.46N 113.13E
Togtoh 152 Jc 40.17N 111.15E
Togučin 138 De 55.16N 84.33E
Toguzak 134 Ki 54.05N 62.48E
Togwotee Pass 182 Ec 43.45N 110.04W
Tohen 168 Ic 11.44N 51.15E
Tohma 146 Hc 38.31N 38.25E
Tohmajärvi 114 He 62.11N 30.23E
Tohopekaliga, Lake- 184 Gk 28.12N 81.23W
Toi 156 Fd 34.54N 138.47E
Toijala 114 Ff 61.10N 23.52E
Toi-Misaki 154 Ki 31.26N 131.19E
Toisvesi 116 Jb 62.20N 23.45E
Tōjō 156 Cd 34.53N 133.16E
Tojtepa 135 Gd 41.03N 69.22E
Tok 178 Kd 63.20N 142.59W
Tok 120 Jg 49.43N 13.50E
Tok 132 Rc 52.46N 52.22E
Tokachi-Dake 156a Cb 43.25N 142.41E
Tokachi-Gawa 156a Cb 42.41N 143.37E
Tokachi-Heiya 156a Cb 43.00N 143.20E
Tokachimitsumata 156a Cb 43.31N 143.07E
Tōkai [Jap.] 156 Gc 36.27N 140.34E
Tōkai [Jap.] 156 Ed 35.01N 136.51E
Tokaj 120 Rh 48.07N 21.25E
Tokaj 132 Ld 51.18N 41.04E
Tōkamachi 154 Of 37.08N 138.46E
Tokanui 218 Cg 46.34S 168.57E
Tokara Islands (EN) = Tokara-Rettō 140 Og 29.35N 129.45E
Tokara-Kaikyō 154 Ki 30.10N 130.15E
Tokara-Rettō = Tokara Islands (EN) 140 Og 29.35N 129.45E
Tokashiki-Jima 156b Ab 26.13N 127.21E
Tokat 144 Ea 40.19N 36.34E
Tŏkch'ŏn 154 Ie 39.45N 126.15E
Tok-Do 154 Kf 37.22N 131.58E
Tokelau [5] 210 Je 9.00S 171.46W
Tokelau/Union Islands 208 Je 9.00S 171.45W
Toki 156 Ed 35.22N 137.11E
Tokke 116 Ce 59.00N 9.15E
Tokke 116 Be 59.27N 7.58E
Tokkuztara/Gongliu 152 Dc 43.30N 82.15E
Tokmak [Kirg.-U.S.S.R.] 136 Hg 42.49N 75.19E
Tokmak [Ukr.-U.S.S.R.] 136 Df 47.13N 35.43E
Tokomaru Bay 216 Eg 38.08S 178.20E
Tokoname 156 Ed 34.53N 136.49E
Tokoro 156a Da 44.08N 144.03E
Tokoroa 216 Eg 38.13S 175.52E
Tokoro-Gawa 156a Da 44.08N 144.04E
Toksovo 116 Nd 60.10N 30.42E
Toksu/Xinhe 152 Dc 41.34N 82.38E
Toksun 152 Ec 42.47N 88.38E
Toktogul 136 Hg 41.50N 73.01E
Toktogulskoje vodohranilišče 135 Id 41.45N 73.00E
Tokuji 156 Bd 34.11N 131.39E
Tokulu 221b Bb 20.06S 174.48W
Tokunoshima 156b Bb 27.45N 129.00E
Toku-no-Shima 152 Mf 27.45N 128.50E
Tokur 138 If 53.09N 132.50E
Tokushima 152 Ne 34.04N 134.34E
Tokushima Ken [2] 154 Mh 33.50N 134.10E
Tokuyama [Jap.] 154 Kg 34.03N 131.49E
Tokuyama [Jap.] 156 Ed 35.43N 136.27E
Tokwe 172 Ed 20.09S 31.54E
Tōkyō 142 Pf 35.40N 139.46E
Tokyo Bay (EN) = Tōkyō-Wan 154 Og 35.38N 139.57E
Tōkyō To [2] 154 Og 35.40N 139.20E
Tōkyō-Wan = Tokyo Bay (EN) 154 Og 35.38N 139.57E
Tola 140 Me 48.57N 104.48E
Tolaga Bay 218 Hc 38.22S 178.18E
Tolbazy 134 Gi 54.02N 55.59E
Tolbuhin 130 Kf 43.34N 27.50E
Tolbuhin [2] 130 Kf 43.34N 27.50E
Toledo [Blz.] 194 Ce 16.25N 88.55W
Toledo [Blz.] [3] 194 Ce 16.15N 88.58W
Toledo [Braz.] 206 Jb 24.44S 53.45W
Toledo [Oh.-U.S.] 176 Ke 41.39N 83.32W
Toledo [Phil.] 150 Hd 10.23N 123.38E
Toledo [Sp.] 112 Fh 39.52N 4.01W
Toledo [Sp.] [3] 126 Ie 39.50N 4.00W
Toledo, Montes de- 126 He 39.35N 4.20W
Toledo Bend Reservoir 182 Ie 31.30N 93.45W
Tolentino 128 Hg 43.12N 13.17E
Tolfa 128 Fh 42.09N 11.56E
Tolfa, Monti della- 128 Fh 42.10N 11.55E
Tolga 114 Ce 62.25N 11.00E
Toli 152 Db 45.57N 83.37E
Toliara 160 Lk 23.21S 43.39E
Toliara [3] 172 Gd 22.00S 44.00E
Tolima [3] 202 Cc 3.45N 75.15W
Tolima, Nevado del- 198 Ie 4.40N 75.19W
Toling → Zanda 152 Ce 31.28N 79.50E
Tolitoli 150 Hf 1.02N 120.49E
Toll 220d Bb 7.22N 151.37E
Tollarp 116 Ei 55.56N 13.59E
Tollja, zaliv- 138 Ea 76.40N 100.00E
Tolmačevo 116 Nf 58.48N 30.01E
Tolmezzo 128 Hd 46.24N 13.01E
Tolmin 128 Hd 46.11N 13.44E
Tolna 120 Oj 46.26N 18.47E
Tolna [2] 120 Oj 46.30N 18.35E
Tolo 170 Cc 2.56S 18.34E
Tolo, Gulf of- (EN) = Tolo, Teluk- 140 Oj 2.00S 122.30E
Tolo, Teluk- = Tolo, Gulf of- (EN) 140 Oj 2.00S 122.30E
Toločin 114 Gi 54.25N 29.41E
Tolosa 126 Ja 43.08N 2.04W
Tolstoj, mys- 140 Rd 59.10N 155.05E
Toltén 206 Fe 39.13S 73.14W
Tolú 202 Cb 9.32N 75.34W
Toluca, Nevado de- 174 Jh 19.08N 99.44W
Toluca de Lerdo 176 Jh 19.17N 99.40W
Tom 140 Kd 56.50N 84.27E
Toma 166 Ec 12.46N 2.53W
Tomah 186 Ke 43.59N 90.30W
Tomakomai 152 Pc 42.38N 141.36E
Tomamae 156a Ba 44.18N 141.39E
Tomanivi 219d Bb 17.37S 178.01E
Tomar 126 De 39.36N 8.25W
Tómaros 130 Dj 39.32N 20.45E
Tomaševka 132 Cd 51.33N 23.40E
Tomás Young 204 Ai 28.36S 62.11W
Tomaszów Lubelski 120 Tf 50.28N 23.25E
Tomaszów Mazowiecki 120 Qe 51.32N 20.01E
Tomatlán 192 Gh 19.56N 105.15W
Tombador, Serra do- 202 Gf 12.00S 57.40W
Tombigbee River 182 Je 31.04N 87.58W
Tomboco 170 Bd 6.45S 13.18E
Tombouctou = Timbuktu (EN) 160 Gg 16.46N 2.59W
Tombstone 188 Jk 31.43N 110.04W
Tombua 160 Ij 15.48S 11.52E
Tomé 206 Fe 36.37S 72.57W
Tomé-Açu 202 Id 2.25S 48.09W
Tomelilla 114 Ci 55.33N 13.57E
Tomelloso 126 Ie 39.10N 3.01W
Tomichi Creek 186 Cg 38.31N 106.58W
Tomie 156 Ae 32.37N 128.46E
Tominé 166 Cc 10.53N 13.18W
Tomini, Gulf of- (EN) = Tomini, Teluk- 140 Oj 0.20S 121.00E
Tomini, Teluk- = Tomini, Gulf of- (EN) 140 Oj 0.20S 121.00E
Tominian 166 Ec 13.17N 4.35W
Tomioka [Jap.] 156 Fc 36.15N 138.52E
Tomioka [Jap.] 156 Gc 37.20N 140.59E
Tomkinson Ranges 212 Fe 26.10S 129.05E
Tomma 114 Cc 66.15N 12.48E
Tommot 138 He 58.58N 126.19E
Tomo, Río- 202 Eb 5.20N 67.48W
Tomochic 192 Fc 28.20N 107.51W
Tomorit, Mali i- 130 Di 40.40N 20.09E
Tomotu Neo 219c Ab 10.41S 165.47E
Tomotu Noi 219c Bb 10.50S 166.02E
Tompa 120 Pj 46.12N 19.33E
Tompe 150 Gg 0.12S 119.48E
Tompo 138 Id 64.00N 136.00E
Tompo 138 Id 62.50N 134.47E
Tom Price 212 Dd 22.40S 117.55E
Tomsk 142 Kd 56.30N 84.58E
Tomskaja oblast [3] 138 De 58.20N 81.30E
Tomtabacken 116 Fg 57.30N 14.28E
Tomur Feng 140 Ke 42.02N 80.05E
Tom White, Mount- 178 Kd 60.40N 143.40W
Tonaki-Shima 156b Ab 26.21N 127.09E
Tonalá 190 Fe 16.04N 93.45W
Tonale, Passo del- 128 Ed 46.16N 10.35E
Tonami 156 Ec 36.38N 136.57E
Tonara 128 Dj 40.02N 9.10E
Tonasket 188 Fb 48.42N 119.26W
Tonb-e Bozorg 146 Pi 26.15N 55.03E
Tonbetsu-Gawa 156a Ca 45.08N 142.23E
Tonbridge 118 Nj 51.12N 0.16E
Tondano 150 Hf 1.19N 124.54E
Tondela 126 Dd 40.31N 8.05W
Tønder 114 Bi 54.56N 8.54E
Tone-Gawa 156 Gd 35.44N 140.51E
Tonekābon 144 Hb 36.53N 50.56E
Toney 222 Of 75.48S 115.48W
Tonga 168 Ed 9.28N 31.03E
Tonga [1] 210 Jf 20.00S 175.00W
Tongaat 172 Ee 29.37S 31.03E
Tonga Islands 208 Jf 20.00S 175.00W
Tonga Ridge (EN) 208 Jg 21.00S 175.00W
Tongariki 219b Dc 17.01S 168.37E
Tongatapu Group 208 Jg 21.10S 175.10W
Tongatapu Island 216 Fd 21.10S 175.10W
Tonga Trench (EN) 106 Kl 20.00S 173.00W
Tongbai 154 Bh 32.21N 113.24E
Tongbai Shan 152 Je 32.20N 113.14E
Tongcheng [China] 154 Di 31.04N 116.56E
Tongcheng [China] 154 Bj 29.15N 113.49E
Tongcheng → Dong'e 154 Df 36.19N 116.14E
Tongchuan 152 Id 35.10N 109.03E
Tongdao (Shuangjiang) 152 If 26.14N 109.45E
Tongde 152 Hd 35.29N 100.32E
Tongeren/Tongres 122 Ld 50.47N 5.28E
Tonggu 154 Cj 28.33N 114.21E
Tongguzbasti 152 Dd 38.23N 82.00E

Index Symbols

- [1] Independent Nation
- [2] State, Region
- [3] District, County
- [4] Municipality
- [5] Colony, Dependency
- Continent
- Physical Region
- Historical or Cultural Region
- Mount, Mountain
- Volcano
- Hill
- Mountains, Mountain Range
- Hills, Escarpment
- Plateau, Upland
- Pass, Gap
- Plain, Lowland
- Delta
- Salt Flat
- Valley, Canyon
- Crater, Cave
- Karst Features
- Depression
- Polder
- Desert, Dunes
- Forest, Woods
- Heath, Steppe
- Oasis
- Cape, Point
- Coast, Beach
- Cliff
- Peninsula
- Isthmus
- Sandbank
- Island
- Atoll
- Rock, Reef
- Islands, Archipelago
- Rocks, Reefs
- Coral Reef
- Well, Spring
- Geyser
- River, Stream
- Waterfall, Rapids
- River Mouth, Estuary
- Lake
- Salt Lake
- Intermittent Lake
- Reservoir
- Swamp, Pond
- Canal
- Glacier
- Ice Shelf, Pack Ice
- Ocean
- Sea
- Gulf, Bay
- Strait, Fjord
- Lagoon
- Bank
- Seamount
- Tablemount
- Ridge
- Shelf
- Basin
- Escarpment, Sea Scarp
- Fracture
- Trench, Abyss
- National Park, Reserve
- Point of Interest
- Recreation Site
- Cave, Cavern
- Historic Site
- Ruins
- Wall, Walls
- Church, Abbey
- Temple
- Scientific Station
- Railway station
- Airport
- Port
- Military installation
- Lighthouse
- Mine
- Tunnel
- Dam, Bridge

Tonggu Zhang [▲]	152	Kg	24.12N 116.22 E
Tong-Hae=Japan, Sea of- (EN) [■]	140	Pf	40.00N 134.00 E
Tonghai	142	Mg	24.15N 102.45 E
Tonghe	152	Mb	46.01N 128.42 E
Tonghua	142	Oe	41.43N 125.55 E
Tongjiang	152	Nb	47.39N 132.30 E
Tongjosŏn-man [≈]	140	Of	39.30N 128.00 E
Tongliao	142	Oe	43.37N 122.15 E
Tongling	152	Ke	30.49N 117.47 E
Tonglu	154	Ej	29.48N 119.39 E
Tongmun'gŏ-ri	152	Mc	40.58N 127.08 E
Tongoa [▲]	219b	Dc	16.54S 168.33 E
Tongoy	206	Fd	30.15S 71.30W
Tongren [China]	152	Hd	35.40N 102.07 E
Tongren [China]	152	If	27.45N 109.09 E
Tongres/Tongeren	122	Ld	50.47N 5.28 E
Tongsa Dzong	148	Ic	27.31N 90.30 E
Tongshan	154	Cj	29.36N 114.30 E
Tongta	152	If	21.20N 99.16 E
Tongtian He/Zhi Qu [≈]	140	Lf	33.26N 96.36 E
Tongue	116	Le	58.28N 4.25W
Tongue of the Ocean [≈]	194	Ia	24.12N 77.10W
Tongue River [≈]	182	Fb	46.24N 105.52W
Tongxian	152	Kd	39.52N 116.38 E
Tongxin	152	Id	36.59N 105.50 E
Tongxu	154	Cg	34.29N 114.27 E
Tongyu (Kaitong)	152	Fh	34.46N 119.51 E
Tongyu Yunhe [≈]	154	Fh	34.46N 119.51 E
Tongzi	152	If	28.09N 106.50 E
Tonichi	192	Ec	28.35N 109.34W
Tŏnisvorst	124	Ic	51.19N 6.28 E
Tonj	168	Dd	7.17N 28.45 E
Tonj [≈]	168	Jh	7.31N 29.25 E
Tonk	148	Fc	26.10N 75.47 E
Tonkin (EN)=Bac-Phan [≈]	140	Mg	22.00N 105.00 E
Tonkin, Gulf of- (EN) = Beibu Wan [◄]	140	Mh	20.00N 108.00 E
Tonkin, Gulf of- (EN)=Vinh Bac Phan [◄]	140	Mh	20.00N 108.00 E
Tônlé Sab, Bœng=Tonle Sap (EN) [≈]	140	Mh	13.00N 104.00 E
Tonle Sap (EN)=Tônlé Sab, Bœng- [≈]	140	Mh	13.00N 104.00 E
Tonnay-Charente	122	Fi	45.57N 0.54W
Tonneins	122	Gj	44.23N 0.19 E
Tönning	120	Eb	54.19N 8.57 E
Tôno	154	Pe	39.19N 141.32 E
Tonopah	182	Dd	38.04N 117.14W
Tonoshō	156	Dd	34.29N 134.11 E
Tonosi	194	Gj	7.24N 80.27W
Tønsberg	114	Cg	59.17N 10.25 E
Tonstad	114	Bg	58.40N 6.43 E
Tonumeia [●]	221b	Bb	20.28S 174.46W
Tonya	146	Hb	40.53N 39.16 E
Tooele	182	Ec	40.32N 112.18W
Toora-Hem	138	Ef	52.28N 96.22 E
Tootsi	116	Kf	58.34N 24.43 E
Toowoomba	210	Gg	27.33S 151.57 E
Topalu	130	Le	44.33N 28.03 E
Topeka	176	Jf	39.03N 95.41W
Topki	138	De	55.18N 85.40 E
Topko, gora- [▲]	138	Ie	57.00N 137.23 E
Topl'a [≈]	120	Rh	48.45N 21.45 E
Toplet	130	Fe	44.48N 22.24 E
Toplica [≈]	130	Ef	43.13N 21.51 E
Toplita	130	Hg	46.55N 25.20 E
Topola	130	De	44.16N 20.42 E
Topol'čany	120	Oh	48.34N 18.10 E
Topolnica [≈]	130	Hg	42.11N 24.18 E
Topolobampo	190	Cc	25.36N 109.03W
Topolobampo, Bahía de- [◄]	192	Ec	25.30N 109.05W
Topolog [≈]	130	Hd	44.56N 24.16 E
Topolovgrad	130	Jg	42.05N 26.20 E
Topozero, ozero- [≈]	110	Jb	65.40N 32.00 E
Toppenish	188	Ec	46.23N 120.19W
Toprakkale	146	Gd	37.06N 36.07 E
Top Springs	212	Gc	16.38S 131.50 E
Toquepala	202	Eg	17.38S 69.56W
Tor	168	Ed	7.51N 33.36 E
Tora [●]	220d	Ba	7.39N 151.53 E
Toraigh/Tory Island [●]	118	Ef	55.16N 8.13W
Tora Island Pass [≈]	220d	Ba	7.39N 151.53 E
Toråker	116	Gd	60.31N 16.29 E
Torbalı	146	Bc	38.10N 27.21 E
Torbat-e Heydarīyeh	142	Hf	35.16N 59.13 E
Torbat-e Jam	144	Ab	35.14N 60.36 E
Torbay	118	Jk	50.28N 3.30W
Torbay-Brixham	118	Jk	50.24N 3.30W
Torbay-Paignton	118	Jk	50.26N 3.30W
Torbay-Torquay	118	Jk	50.29N 3.29W
Torbert, Mount- [▲]	178	Id	61.25N 152.24W
Torch Lake [≈]	184	Ec	45.00N 85.19W
Torčin	120	Vf	50.44N 25.05 E
Tordesillas	126	Hc	41.30N 5.00W
Tordino [≈]	128	Hh	42.44N 13.59 E
Töre	114	Fd	65.54N 22.39 E
Töreboda	114	Dg	58.43N 14.08 E
Torekov	116	Ea	56.26N 12.37 E
Torenberg [▲]	122	Lb	52.15N 5.55 E
Torez	132	Kf	47.59N 38.41 E
Torgau	120	Kf	51.34N 13.00 E
Torgelow	120	Kc	53.38N 14.01 E
Torgun [≈]	132	Nd	50.10N 46.20 E
Torhamn	116	Fh	56.05N 15.50 E
Torhout	122	Jc	51.04N 3.06 E
Toribulu	150	Hg	0.19S 120.01 E
Torigni-sur-Vire	124	Be	49.05N 0.59W
Torii-Tôge [≈]	156	Dd	36.31N 31.39 E
Torino = Turin (EN)	112	Gf	45.03N 7.40 E
Toriparu	202	Hq	16.20S 53.55W
Tori-Shima [Jap.] [●]	156b	Bb	27.52N 128.14 E
Tori-Shima [Jap.] [●]	156b	Ab	26.35N 126.50 E
Tori-Shima [Jap.] [●]	152	Pe	30.25N 140.15 E
Torit	168	Ee	4.24N 32.34 E
Torixoreu	202	Hq	16.20S 52.26W
Torkoviči	114	Hg	58.53N 30.20 E
Törmänen	114	Gb	68.36N 27.29 E

Tormes [≈]	126	Fc	41.18N 6.29W
Tornado Mountain [▲]	188	Hb	49.58N 114.39W
Tornavacas, Puerto de- [◄]	126	Gd	40.16N 5.37W
Torneå/Tornio	114	Fd	65.51N 24.08 E
Torneälven [≈]	110	Ib	65.48N 24.08 E
Torneträsk [≈]	114	Eb	68.22N 19.06 E
Torngat Mountains [▲]	174	Md	59.00N 64.00W
Tornio/Torneå	114	Fd	65.51N 24.08 E
Tornionjoki [≈]	110	Ib	65.48N 24.08 E
Tornquist	204	An	38.06S 62.14W
Toro	126	Gc	41.31N 5.24W
Toro, Cerro del- [▲]	198	Jh	29.08S 69.48W
Toro, Isla del- [●]	192	Kg	21.35N 97.32W
Toro, Monte- / El Toro [▲]	126	Qe	39.59N 4.07 E
Toroiaga, Vîrful- [▲]	130	Hb	47.44N 24.43 E
Torokina	219a	Bb	6.14S 155.03 E
Törökszentmiklós	120	Qi	47.11N 20.25 E
Torola, Río- [≈]	194	Cg	13.52N 88.30W
Toropec	130	Id	56.31N 31.39 E
Tororo	170	Fb	0.41N 34.11 E
Toros Dağları=Taurus Mountains (EN) [▲]	140	Ff	37.00N 33.00 E
Torquato Severo	204	Ej	31.02S 54.11W
Torquay, Torbay-	118	Jk	50.29N 3.29W
Torrá, Cerro- [▲]	198	Ie	4.38N 76.15W
Torre Annunziata	128	Ij	40.45N 14.27 E
Torreblanca	126	Md	40.13N 0.12 E
Torrecilla	126	Hh	36.41N 5.00W
Torrecilla en Cameros	126	Jb	42.16N 2.37W
Torre del Greco	128	Ij	40.47N 14.22 E
Torre del Mar	126	Hh	36.44N 4.06W
Torredembarra	126	Nc	41.09N 1.24 E
Torre de Moncorvo	126	Ec	41.10N 7.03W
Torre de' Passeri	128	Hh	42.14N 13.56 E
Torredonjimeno	126	Ig	37.46N 3.57W
Torrejón de Ardoz	126	Id	40.27N 3.29W
Torrelaguna	126	Ic	40.50N 3.32W
Torrelavega	126	Ha	43.21N 4.03W
Torre Miró, Port de- / Torre Miró, Puerto de- [◄]	126	Ld	40.42N 0.05W
Torre Miró, Puerto de- / Torre Miró, Port de- [◄]	126	Ld	40.42N 0.05W
Torremolinos	126	Hh	36.37N 4.30W
Torrens, Lake- [≈]	208	Eh	31.00S 137.50 E
Torrens Creek	212	Jd	20.46S 145.02 E
Torrente de l'Horta/Torrente	126	Le	39.26N 0.28W
Torrente/Torrente de l'Horta	126	Le	39.26N 0.28W
Torrenueva	126	If	38.38N 3.22W
Torreón	176	Jg	25.33N 103.26W
Torre-Pacheco	126	Lg	37.44N 0.57W
Torre Pellice	128	Bf	44.49N 7.13 E
Tôrres	206	Kc	29.21S 49.44W
Torres [≈]	220d	Ab	7.19N 151.27 E
Torrès, Iles-= Torres Islands (EN) [●]	208	Hf	13.15S 166.37 E
Torres Islands (EN)=Torrès, Iles- [●]	208	Hf	13.15S 166.37 E
Torres Novas	126	De	39.29N 8.32W
Torres Strait [◄]	208	Ff	10.25S 142.10 E
Torres Vedras	126	Ce	39.06N 9.16W
Torrevieja	126	Lg	37.59N 0.41W
Torridon, Loch- [◄]	118	Hd	57.35N 5.50W
Torriglia	128	Df	44.31N 9.10 E
Torrijos	126	He	39.59N 4.17W
Torrington [Ct.-U.S.]	184	Hd	41.48N 73.08W
Torrington [Wy.-U.S.]	182	Gc	42.04N 104.11W
Torroella de Montgrí	126	Pb	42.02N 3.08 E
Torrox	126	Ih	36.46N 3.58W
Torsås	114	Dh	56.24N 16.00 E
Torsby	114	Cf	60.08N 13.00 E
Torshälla	114	Eb	56.29N 16.28 E
Torsö [●]	114	Db	69.20N 17.06 E
Torsö [●]	114	Cf	58.50N 13.45 E
Torto [≈]	128	Hm	37.58N 13.46 E
Tortola [●]	190	Le	18.27N 64.36W
Tortoli	128	Dk	39.55N 9.39 E
Tortona	128	Cf	44.54N 8.52 E
Tortorici	128	Il	38.02N 14.49 E
Tortosa	126	Md	40.49N 0.31 E
Tortosa, Cabo de-/Tortosa, Cap de- [►]	126	Md	40.43N 0.55 E
Tortosa, Cap de-/Tortosa, Cabo de- [►]	126	Md	40.43N 0.55 E
Tortue, Ile de la- [●]	190	Jd	20.04N 72.49W
Tortuga, Isla- [●]	192	Df	25.26N 111.55W
Tortum	146	Ib	40.19N 41.35 E
Torud	144	Pe	35.26N 55.07 E
Torugart, pereval- [◄]	140	Cd	39.50N 75.24 E
Torul	146	Hb	40.35N 39.18 E
Toruń	120	Oc	53.00N 18.35 E
Toruń [●]	120	Oc	53.00N 18.35 E
Torunos	194	Li	8.30N 70.04W
Toruńska, Kotlina- [◄]	120	Oc	53.00N 18.30 E
Torup	114	Ch	56.58N 13.05 E
Tõrva/Tyrva	114	Kg	58.00N 25.59 E
Tory Island/Toraigh [●]	118	Ef	55.16N 8.13W
Torysa [≈]	120	Rh	48.39N 21.21 E
Torzók	136	Dd	57.03N 35.01 E
Tosa	154	Lh	33.29N 133.25 E
Tosas, Puerto de- / Toses, Collada de- [◄]	126	Ob	42.20N 2.01 E
Tosashimizu	154	Lh	32.46N 132.57 E
Tosa-Wan [◄]	154	Lh	33.25N 133.35 E
Tosa-yamada	156	Ce	33.36N 133.40 E
Toscana = Tuscany (EN) [■]	128	Eg	43.25N 11.00 E
Toscano, Arcipelago- = Tuscan Archipelago (EN) [●]			
Toses, Collada de- / Tosas, Puerto de- [◄]	126	Ob	42.20N 2.01 E
Toshibetsu-Gawa [Jap.] [≈]	156a	Cb	42.54N 143.25 E
Toshibetsu-Gawa [Jap.] [≈]	156a	Ab	42.25N 139.48 E

Tôshi-Jima [●]	156	Ed	34.31N 136.52 E
To-Shima [●]	156	Fd	34.31N 139.17 E
Tosno	114	Hg	59.34N 30.50 E
Toson-Cengel	152	Gb	48.47N 98.15 E
Toson Hu [≈]	152	Gd	37.08N 96.52 E
Töss [≈]	128	Cc	47.33N 8.33 E
Tostado	206	Hc	29.14S 61.46W
Tôstamaa/Tystama	116	Jf	58.17N 23.52 E
Toto	156	Be	33.22N 130.30 E
Tosya	146	Fb	41.01N 34.02 E
Totak [≈]	116	Be	59.40N 7.55 E
Totana	126	Kg	37.46N 1.30W
Toten [◄]	116	Dd	60.40N 10.50 E
Toteng	172	Cd	20.23S 22.59 E
Tôtes	122	He	49.41N 1.03 E
Totes Gebirge [▲]	128	Nc	47.42N 13.55 E
Tótius	168	Ge	3.57N 43.58 E
Totland	124	Ad	50.40N 1.32W
Totma	136	Be	60.00N 42.45 E
Totonicapán	190	Ff	14.55N 91.22W
Totonicapán [■]	194	Bf	15.00N 91.20W
Totora	202	Eg	17.42S 65.09W
Totoras	204	Bk	32.35S 61.11W
Totota	166	Dd	6.49N 9.56W
Totoya [●]	219d	Cc	18.57S 179.50W
Totten Glacier [≈]	222	He	66.45S 116.10 E
Totton	124	Ad	50.55N 1.29W
Tottori	152	Mb	35.30N 134.14 E
Tottori Ken [■]	154	Lg	35.25N 133.50 E
Tou, Motu- [●]	220b	Bb	21.11S 159.48W
Touajil	162	Ee	21.45N 12.35W
Touat [◄]	158	Gf	27.40N 0.01W
Touba	166	Dd	8.17N 7.41W
Touba [■]	166	Bd	8.15N 7.45W
Toubkal, Jebel- [▲]	158	Gc	31.03N 7.55W
Touch [≈]	122	Hk	43.38N 1.24 E
Toucy	122	Jg	47.44N 3.18 E
Tougan	166	Ec	13.04N 3.04W
Touggourt	158	Hc	33.06N 6.04 E
Tougué	166	Cc	11.27N 11.41W
Touho	219b	Be	20.47S 165.14 E
Touïl [≈]	166	Db	35.33N 2.36 E
Toukoto	166	Dc	13.28N 9.52W
Toul	122	Lf	48.41N 5.54 E
Toulépleu	166	Dd	6.35N 8.25W
Toulon	112	Gg	43.07N 5.56 E
Toulouse	112	Gg	43.36N 1.26 E
Toulumne River [≈]	188	Eh	37.36N 121.10W
Toumodi	166	Dd	6.33N 5.01W
Toumassine, Hamada- [◄]	162	Fd	28.36N 5.01W
Toungo	166	Hd	8.07N 12.03 E
Toungoo	142	Jh	18.56N 96.26 E
Touques [≈]	122	Ge	49.22N 0.06 E
Toura	168	Bc	10.30N 15.19 E
Touraine [■]	122	Gg	47.12N 0.30 E
Touraine, Val de- [◄]	122	Hg	47.20N 1.30 E
Tourcoing	122	Jd	50.43N 3.09 E
Tour-du-Pin, La-	122	Li	45.34N 5.27 E
Touriñán, Cabo- [►]	126	Ca	43.03N 9.18W
Tourine	162	Ee	22.00N 12.15W
Tournai/Doornik	122	Jd	50.36N 3.23 E
Tournai-Kain	124	Md	50.36N 3.22 E
Tournon	122	Ki	45.04N 4.50 E
Tournus	122	Kh	46.33N 4.55 E
Touros	202	Ke	5.12S 35.28W
Tourteron	124	Le	49.32N 4.19 E
Tourterol	122	Hf	48.12N 1.56 E
Touside, Pic- [▲]	168	Ba	21.02N 16.25 E
Toussoro [▲]	168	Cd	9.02N 23.55 E
Toutouba [◄]	219b	Cb	15.34S 167.16 E
Touwrivier	172	Cf	33.20S 20.00 E
Touzim	120	Jf	50.04N 12.59 E
Tovar	194	Li	8.20N 71.46W
Tovarkovskij	132	Kc	53.43N 38.13 E
Tovdalselva [≈]	116	Cf	58.12N 8.06 E
Tove [≈]	124	Bb	52.04N 0.50W
Tôwa	156	Be	39.23N 141.15 E
Towada	154	Pd	40.35N 141.13 E
Towada-Kô [≈]	154	Pd	40.28N 140.55 E
Towanda	184	Ie	41.46N 76.27W
Tower	186	Jc	47.48N 92.17W
Towner	186	Fb	48.21N 100.25W
Townsend	188	Jc	46.19N 111.31W
Townshend, Cape- [►]	212	Kd	22.15S 150.32 E
Townsville	210	Ff	19.16S 146.48 E
Towot	168	Ed	6.12N 34.25 E
Towson	184	If	39.24N 76.36W
Towuti, Danau- [≈]	150	Hg	2.45S 121.32 E
Toxkan He [≈]	152	Dc	41.08N 80.11 E
Tôya	156a	Bb	42.39N 140.48 E
Toyah Creek [≈]	186	Ek	31.18N 103.27W
Tôya-Ko [≈]	154	Pc	42.33N 140.50 E
Toyama	142	Ni	36.41N 137.13 E
Toyama Ken [■]	154	Nf	36.40N 137.10 E
Toyama Trench (EN) [≈]	154	Nf	38.00N 138.00 E
Toyama-Wan [◄]	154	Nf	37.00N 137.15 E
Tôyô	154	Mh	33.22N 134.18 E
Toyohashi	154	Mb	34.46N 137.23 E
Toyokoro	156a	Cb	42.48N 143.28 E
Toyo'oka	152	Od	35.33N 137.54 E
Toyo'oka	154	Ng	35.33N 134.49 E
Toyota	154	Ng	35.05N 137.09 E
Toyotama	156	Ad	34.27N 129.19 E
Toyotomi	156a	Bd	45.07N 141.47 E
Toyoura	156a	Bb	34.10N 130.55 E
Trabancos [≈]	126	Gc	41.27N 5.11W
Traben Trabach	124	Oe	49.57N 7.07 E
Trabzon	142	Ee	41.00N 39.43 E
Tracadie	180	Kg	47.31N 64.55W
Trafalgar, Cabo- [►]	126	Fh	36.11N 6.02W
Tragacete	126	Kd	40.21N 1.32W
Traiguén	206	Be	38.15S 72.41W
Trail	176	He	49.06N 117.43W

Traill [●]	179	Jd	72.45N 24.00W
Trairas, Rio- [≈]	204	Hb	14.07S 48.31W
Trairi	202	Kd	3.17S 39.15W
Traisen [≈]	128	Jb	48.22N 15.46 E
Trakai/Trakaj	114	Fi	54.38N 24.57 E
Trakaj/Trakai	114	Fi	54.38N 24.57 E
Trakt	126	Oc	41.43N 2.56 E
Trakya = Thrace (EN)	110	Ig	41.20N 26.45 E
Trakya = Thrace (EN) [■]	130	Ji	41.20N 26.45 E
Tralee/Trá Lí	118	Di	52.16N 9.42W
Tralee Bay/Bá Thrá Lí [◄]	118	Di	52.16N 9.42W
Trá Lí/Tralee	118	Di	52.16N 9.42W
Trá Mhór/Tramore	118	Fi	52.10N 7.10W
Tramonti di Sopra	128	Ga	46.18N 12.47 E
Tramore/Trá Mhór	118	Fi	52.10N 7.10W
Tramping Lake [≈]	188	Ka	52.10N 108.48W
Trăn	130	Fg	42.50N 22.39 E
Tranås	114	Dg	58.03N 14.59 E
Trancoso	126	Ec	40.47N 7.21W
Tranebjerg	116	Di	55.50N 10.36 E
Tranemo	116	Eg	57.29N 13.21 E
Trang	142	Li	7.33N 99.36 E
Trangan, Pulau- [●]	150	Jh	6.35S 134.20 E
Trani	128	Ki	41.17N 16.25 E
Transantarctic Mountains (EN) [▲]	222	Lg	85.00S 175.00W
Transcaucasia (EN) [■]	110	Kg	41.00N 45.00 E
Transilvania = Transylvania (EN) [■]	110	If	46.30N 25.00 E
Transilvania = Transylvania (EN) [■]	130	Hc	46.30N 25.00 E
Transkei [■]	158	Ji	31.30S 29.00 E
Transkei [■]	172	Df	32.45S 28.30 E
Transtrand	116	Ec	61.05N 13.19 E
Transtrandsfjällen [▲]	116	Ec	61.15N 12.58 E
Transvaal [■]	172	Dd	25.00S 30.00 E
Transylvania (EN) = Transilvania	110	If	46.30N 25.00 E
Transylvania (EN) = Transilvania	130	Hc	46.30N 25.00 E
Transylvanian Alps (EN) = Carpaţii Meridionali [▲]	110	If	45.30N 24.15 E
Trants Bay [◄]	197c	Bc	16.46N 62.09W
Trapani	112	Hh	38.01N 12.29 E
Trapper Peak [▲]	188	Hd	45.54N 114.18W
Trappes	124	Ef	48.47N 2.01 E
Traralgon	212	Jg	38.12S 146.32 E
Trarza [■]	162	Jg	18.00N 15.00W
Trarza [◄]	158	Fg	17.20N 14.40W
Traşcăului, Munţii- [▲]	130	Gc	46.23N 23.33 E
Trasimeno, Lago- [≈]	128	Gg	43.10N 12.06 E
Träslövsläge	116	Eg	57.04N 12.16 E
Trás os Montes e Alto Douro [■]	126	Ec	41.30N 7.15W
Trat	148	Kf	12.13N 102.16 E
Traun	128	Ib	48.16N 14.22 E
Traun [≈]	128	Ib	48.16N 14.22 E
Traunsee [≈]	128	Hc	47.52N 13.48 E
Traunstein	120	Ii	47.53N 12.39 E
Trave [≈]	120	Gc	53.54N 10.50 E
Travemünde, Lübeck-	120	Gc	53.57N 10.52 E
Travers, Mount- [▲]	216	Dh	42.01S 172.44 E
Traverse, Lake- [≈]	186	Hc	45.43N 96.40W
Traverse City	182	Jc	44.46N 85.37W
Traverse Islands [●]	222	Ad	56.34S 27.40W
Travers Reservoir [≈]	188	Ia	50.14N 112.51W
Travesía [≈]	194	Df	15.20N 87.53W
Travnik	128	Lf	44.14N 17.40 E
Travo	112	Gf	47.23N 0.41 E
Trbovlje	128	Jd	46.10N 15.03 E
Treasurers [●]	219c	Ba	9.53S 167.09 E
Treasury Islands [●]	219a	Bb	7.22S 155.37 E
Trebbia [≈]	128	De	44.58N 9.41 E
Trebč	120	Lg	49.13N 15.53 E
Trebel [≈]	120	Ic	53.55N 13.02 E
Trebisacce	128	Kk	39.52N 16.32 E
Trebišnjica [≈]	128	Lh	42.43N 18.21 E
Trebišov	120	Rh	48.40N 21.43 E
Treblinka	120	Sd	52.40N 22.03 E
Trebnje	128	Je	45.54N 15.01 E
Trebon	120	Kg	49.01N 14.48 E
Trebońska pánev [◄]	120	Kg	49.00N 14.50 E
Trégorrois [◄]	122	Cf	48.43N 3.15W
Tregrosse Islets [●]	208	Gf	17.40S 150.45 E
Tréguier	122	Cf	48.47N 3.14W
Treherne	186	Gb	49.38N 98.41W
Treignac	122	Hi	45.32N 1.48 E
Treinta y Tres	206	Jd	33.14S 54.23W
Treinta y Tres [■]	204	Ek	33.00S 54.15W
Treis-Karden	124	Gd	50.11N 7.17 E
Trélazé	122	Fg	47.27N 0.28W
Trélew	206	Gf	43.15S 65.18W
Trelleborg	112	Hd	55.22N 13.10 E
Trélon	124	Gd	50.04N 4.06 E
Tremadog Bay [◄]	118	Gi	52.54N 4.10W
Tremblant, Mount- [▲]	174	Le	46.15N 74.34W
Tremiti, Isole-=Tremiti Islands (EN) [●]	128	Id	42.07N 15.30 E
Tremiti Islands (EN)=Tremiti, Isole- [●]	110	Hg	42.10N 15.30 E
Tremonton	188	If	41.43N 112.10W
Tremp	126	Mb	42.10N 0.54 E
Trenche, Rivière- [≈]	180	Fg	47.46N 72.58W
Trenčín	120	Oh	48.54N 18.04 E
Trenque Lauquen	206	Mh	35.58S 62.42W
Trent, Vale of- [◄]	118	Li	52.45N 1.50W
Trentino-Alto Adige / Südtirol [■]	128	Fd	46.30N 11.20 E
Trento	128	Fd	46.04N 11.08 E
Trenton [Mo.-U.S.]	186	Jf	40.05N 93.37W
Trenton [N.J.-U.S.]	176	Le	40.13N 74.45W
Trenton [Ont.-Can.]	184	Ic	44.06N 77.35W
Tréon	124	Df	48.41N 1.20 E
Trepassey	180	Mg	46.44N 53.22W
Tréport, Le-	122	Hd	50.04N 1.22 E
Tres Árboles	204	Dk	32.24S 56.43W

Tres Arroyos	200	Ji	38.22S 60.15W
Tres Bocas	204	Ck	32.44S 59.45W
Tres Caraçóes	202	Ih	21.42S 45.16W
Tres Cruces, Cerro- [▲]	192	Mj	15.28N 92.24W
Três de Maio	204	Eh	27.47S 54.14W
Tres Esquinas	202	Cc	0.43S 75.15W
Tres Isletas	204	Bh	26.21S 60.26W
Treska [≈]	130	Eh	41.59N 21.28 E
Tres Lagoas	200	Kh	20.48S 51.43W
Três Marias, Represa- [≈]	202	Jg	18.15S 45.15W
Três Montes, Peninsula- [►]	206	Eg	46.50S 75.30W
Três Passos	206	Jc	27.27S 53.56W
Tres Picos, Cerro- [▲]	198	Jh	38.09S 61.57W
Tres Picos, Cerro- [▲]	192	Li	16.36N 94.13W
Três Pontas	204	Je	21.22S 45.31W
Tres Puntas, Cabo- [Arg.] [►]	198	Jj	47.06S 65.53W
Tres Puntas, Cabo- [Guat.] [►]	194	Cf	15.58N 88.37W
Três Ranchos	204	Id	18.27S 47.47W
Três Rios	204	Kf	22.07S 43.12W
Třešt'	120	Lg	49.18N 15.28 E
Tres Valles	192	Kh	18.15N 96.08W
Tretten	114	Cf	61.19N 10.19 E
Treuchtlingen	120	Gh	48.57N 10.55 E
Treuer Range [▲]	212	Gd	23.55S 130.50 E
Treungen	116	Ce	59.02N 8.33 E
Trevi	128	Gg	42.52N 12.45 E
Tréviéres	124	Be	49.19N 0.54W
Treviglio	128	De	45.31N 9.35 E
Trevinca, Peña- [▲]	126	Fb	42.15N 6.46W
Treviño	126	Jb	42.44N 2.45W
Treviso	128	Ge	45.40N 12.15 E
Trevose Head [►]	118	Hk	50.33N 5.01W
Trgoviște	130	Fg	42.21N 22.06 E
Triagoz, Les- [●]	122	Cf	48.53N 3.40W
Triánda	130	Lm	36.24N 28.10 E
Triangle	172	Ed	21.02S 31.28 E
Triángulos, Arrecifes- [●]	192	Jg	20.57N 92.16W
Trianísia [●]	130	Jm	36.18N 26.45 E
Tribe'č [▲]	120	Oh	48.17N 18.20 E
Tribune	186	Fg	38.28N 101.45W
Tricarico	128	Kj	40.37N 16.09 E
Tricase	128	Mk	39.56N 18.22 E
Trichür	148	Ff	10.31N 76.13 E
Tri City	188	Dc	46.20N 123.15W
Trie-Château	124	De	49.17N 1.50 E
Triel-sur-Seine	124	Ef	48.59N 2.01 E
Trier	120	Cg	49.45N 6.38 E
Trier-Ehrang	124	Fe	49.49N 6.41 E
Trier-Pfalzel	124	Fe	49.46N 6.41 E
Trieste	112	Hf	45.40N 13.46 E
Trieste, Golfo di- [◄]	128	He	45.40N 13.30 E
Trieux [≈]	122	Cf	48.50N 3.03W
Trifels [●]	124	Je	49.11N 7.59 E
Triglav [▲]	110	Hf	46.23N 13.50 E
Trigno [≈]	128	Ih	42.04N 14.48 E
Trikala	130	Ej	39.33N 21.46 E
Trikhonís, Límni- [≈]	130	Ek	38.34N 21.30 E
Trikomo = Yeniboğaziçi	146	Ee	35.17N 33.52 E
Trikomon = Yeniboğaziçi	146	Ee	35.17N 33.52 E
Trikora, Puncak-	150	Kg	4.15S 138.45 E
Trilport	124	Ef	48.57N 2.57 E
Trim/Baile Átha Troim	118	Gh	53.34N 6.47W
Trimouille, La-	122	Hh	46.28N 1.02 E
Trincheras	192	Cb	28.55N 104.18W
Trincomalee	142	Ki	8.34N 81.14 E
Trindade	202	Ia	16.40S 49.30W
Trindade, Ilha da- [●]	198	Nh	20.31S 29.19W
Tring	124	Bc	51.47N 0.39W
Tringia [▲]	130	Ej	39.37N 21.25 E
Trinidad [Bol.]	200	As	14.47S 64.47W
Trinidad [Ca.-U.S.]	188	Cf	41.07N 124.07W
Trinidad [Co.-U.S.]	176	If	37.10N 104.31W
Trinidad [Cuba]	190	Id	21.48N 79.59W
Trinidad [Mex.]	192	Ec	28.25N 109.06W
Trinidad [Ur.]	206	Jd	33.32S 56.54W
Trinidad, Golfo- [◄]	206	Eg	49.55S 75.25W
Trinidad, Isla- [●]	198	Jj	39.08S 61.58W
Trinidad, Laguna- [≈]	204	Be	20.21S 61.35W
Trinidad and Tobago [■]	200	Jd	11.00N 61.00W
Trinidade Spur (EN) [≈]	106	Ci	21.00S 35.00W
Trinitapoli	128	Ki	41.21N 16.05 E
Trinity	186	Ik	30.57N 95.22W
Trinity Bay [Austl.]	212	Jc	16.25S 145.35 E
Trinity Bay [Can.]	180	Mg	48.15S 53.10W
Trinity Islands [●]	174	Se	56.33N 154.25W
Trinity Range [▲]	188	Ff	40.18N 118.45W
Trinity River [≈]	188	Df	41.11N 123.42W
Trinkitat	168	Fb	18.41N 37.43 E
Trino	128	Ce	45.12N 8.18 E
Trionto [≈]	128	Kk	39.37N 16.45 E
Trionto, Capo- [►]	128	Kk	39.37N 16.45 E
Triora	128	Bf	43.59N 7.46 E
Tripoli (EN)=Ţarābulus	160	Ie	32.54N 13.11 E
Tripoli (EN)=Ţarābulus [■]	144	Ce	34.26N 35.51 E
Tripoli (EN)=Ţarābulus [■]	160	Bc	32.40N 13.15 E
Tripolis	130	Fl	37.31N 22.22 E
Tripolitania (EN) = Ţarābulus / Ţarābulus	158	Ie	31.00N 14.00 E
Tripolitania (EN) = Ţarābulus / Ţarābulus	164	Bc	30.00N 15.00 E
Tripura [■]	148	Id	24.00N 92.00 E
Trisanna [≈]	128	Ec	47.09N 10.32 E
Tristan da Cunha [●]	158	Fi	37.05S 12.17W
Tristan da Cunha Group [●]	198	Fi	37.15S 12.30W
Triste, Golfo- [◄]	196	Bg	10.40N 68.10W
Triunfo	204	Be	20.46S 55.47W
Trivandrum	142	Ji	8.29N 76.55 E
Trivento	128	Ii	41.47N 14.33 E
Trjavna	130	Hg	42.52N 25.30 E
Trnava	120	Nh	48.22N 17.35 E
Troarn	124	Be	49.11N 0.11W

Index Symbols

Symbol	Label	Symbol	Label	Symbol	Label	Symbol	Label
[1]	Independent Nation		Historical or Cultural Region		Pass, Gap		Depression
[2]	State, Region		Mount, Mountain		Plain, Lowland		Polder
[3]	District, County		Volcano		Delta		Desert, Dunes
[4]	Municipality		Hill		Salt Flat		Forest, Woods
[5]	Colony, Dependency		Mountains, Mountain Range		Valley, Canyon		Heath, Steppe
[■]	Continent		Hills, Escarpment		Crater, Cave		Oasis
	Physical Region		Plateau, Upland		Karst Features		Cape, Point

Symbol	Label	Symbol	Label	Symbol	Label	Symbol	Label
	Coast, Beach		Rock, Reef		Waterfall, Rapids		Canal
	Cliff		Islands, Archipelago		River Mouth, Estuary		Glacier
	Peninsula		Rocks, Reefs		Lake		Ice Shelf, Pack Ice
	Isthmus		Coral Reef		Salt Lake		Ocean
	Sandbank		Well, Spring		Intermittent Lake		Gulf, Bay
	Island		Geyser		Sea		Strait, Fjord
	Atoll		River, Stream		Swamp, Pond		

Symbol	Label	Symbol	Label	Symbol	Label
	Lagoon		Escarpment, Sea Scarp		Historic Site
	Bank		Fracture		Ruins
	Seamount		Trench, Abyss		Wall, Walls
	Tablemount		National Park, Reserve		Church, Abbey
	Ridge		Point of Interest		Temple
	Shelf		Recreation Site		Scientific Station
	Basin		Cave, Cavern		Railway station

	Airport
	Port
	Military installation
	Lighthouse
	Mine
	Tunnel
	Dam, Bridge

Trobriand Islands 208 Ge 8.30S 151.05 E
Trödje 116 Gd 60.49N 17.12 E
Trofors 114 Cd 65.34N 13.25 E
Trögd 116 Ge 59.30N 17.15 E
Trogir 128 Kg 43.32N 16.15 E
Troglav [Yugo.] 128 Mg 43.02N 18.33 E
Troglav [Yugo.] 128 Kg 43.58N 16.36 E
Trøgstad 116 De 59.38N 11.18 E
Troia 128 Ji 41.22N 15.18 E
Troick [R.S.F.S.R.] 138 Ee 57.23N 94.55 E
Troick [R.S.F.S.R.] 142 Id 54.06N 61.35 E
Troickoje [R.S.F.S.R.] 138 Df 52.58N 84.45 E
Troickoje [R.S.F.S.R.] 138 Ig 49.30N 136.32 E
Troickoje [Ukr.-U.S.S.R.] 130 Nb 47.38N 30.12 E
Troicko Pečorsk 136 Fc 62.44N 56.06 E
Troina 128 Im 37.47N 14.36 E
Troisdorf 124 Jd 50.49N 7.10 E
Trois Fourches, Cap des- 162 Gb 35.26N 2.58W
Trois-Pistoles 184 Ma 48.07N 69.10W
Trois Pitons, Morne- 197g Bb 15.22N 61.20W
Trois-Ponts 124 Hd 50.22N 5.52 E
Trois-Rivières [Guad.] 197e Ac 15.59N 61.39W
Trois-Rivières [Que.-Can.] 176 Le 46.21N 72.33W
Troissereux 124 Ee 49.29N 2.03 E
Troisvierges/Ulflingen 124 Hd 50.07N 6.00 E
Trojan 130 Hg 42.53N 24.43 E
Trojanovka 120 Ve 51.21N 25.25 E
Trojanski Manastir 130 Hg 42.53N 24.48 E
Trojanski prohod 130 Hg 42.48N 24.40 E
Trojebratski 136 Ge 54.25N 66.03 E
Trollhättan 114 Cg 58.16N 12.18 E
Trollheimen 114 Be 62.50N 9.05 E
Trollhetta 116 Cb 62.51N 9.19 E
Trolltindane 116 Bd 62.29N 7.43 E
Tromba 204 Ha 13.28S 48.45W
Trombetas, Rio- 198 Kf 1.55S 55.35W
Tromelin 158 Mj 15.52S 54.25 E
Tromøya 116 Cf 58.30N 8.50 E
Troms [3] 114 Eb 69.07N 19.15 E
Tromsø 112 Hb 69.40N 19.00 E
Tron 116 Db 62.10N 10.43 E
Trona 188 Gi 35.46N 117.24W
Tronador, Monte- 198 Ij 41.10S 71.54W
Trondheim 112 Hc 63.25N 10.25 E
Trondheimsfjorden 110 Hc 63.40N 10.50 E
Tronto 128 Hh 42.54N 13.55 E
Troodos 144 Dc 34.55N 32.53 E
Tropea 128 Jl 38.41N 15.54 E
Tropeiros, Serra dos- 204 Jb 14.43S 44.33W
Tropoja 130 Dg 42.24N 20.10 E
Trosa 114 Dg 58.54N 17.33 E
Troškūnai/Troškunaj 116 Ki 55.32N 24.59 E
Troškunaj/Troškūnai 116 Ki 55.32N 24.59 E
Trostberg 120 Ih 48.02N 12.33 E
Trostjanec 122 Id 50.29N 34.59 E
Trotuş 130 Kc 46.03N 27.14 E
Trou Gras Point 197k Bb 13.52N 60.53W
Troumasse 197k Bb 13.49N 60.54W
Trout Lake [Mi.-U.S.] 184 Eb 46.12N 85.01W
Trout Lake [N.W.T.-Can.] 180 Fd 60.35N 121.10W
Trout Lake [Ont.-Can.] 180 If 53.54N 89.56W
Trout Lake [Ont.-Can.] 180 If 51.12N 93.19W
Trout Peak 188 Kd 44.36N 109.32W
Trout River 180 Lg 49.29N 58.08W
Trouville-sur-Mer 122 Ge 49.22N 0.05 E
Trowbridge 118 Kj 51.20N 2.13W
Troy [Al.-U.S.] 182 Je 31.48N 85.58W
Troy [Mo.-U.S.] 186 Kg 38.59N 90.59W
Troy [Mt.-U.S.] 188 Hb 48.28N 115.53W
Troy [N.Y.-U.S.] 182 Mc 42.43N 73.40W
Troy [Oh.-U.S.] 184 Ee 40.02N 84.12W
Troy (EN)=Truva [Tur.] 146 Bc 39.57N 26.15 E
Troyes 112 Gf 48.18N 4.05 E
Troy Peak 182 Dd 38.19N 115.30W
Trstenik 130 Df 43.37N 21.00 E
Trubčevsk 136 De 52.36N 33.46 E
Truchas Peak 186 Di 35.58N 105.39W
Trucial Coast (EN) 140 Hg 24.00N 53.00 E
Trucial States (EN) → United Arab Emirates (EN) [1] 142 Hg 24.00N 54.00 E
Truckee 188 Eg 39.20N 120.11W
Trudfront 132 Og 45.56N 47.41 E
Trudovoje 138 Ih 43.18N 132.05 E
Trufanova 114 Kd 64.29N 44.05 E
Trujillo [2] 202 Db 9.25N 70.30W
Trujillo [Hond.] 190 Ge 15.55N 86.00W
Trujillo [Peru] 200 If 8.10S 79.02W
Trujillo [Sp.] 126 Ge 39.28N 5.53W
Trujillo [Ven.] 202 Db 9.22N 70.26W
Trujillo, Rio- 192 Hf 23.39N 103.08W
Truk Islands 208 Gd 7.25N 151.47 E
Trumann 186 Ki 35.41N 90.31W
Trumbull, Mount- 188 Ed 36.25N 113.10W
Trun 124 Gf 48.51N 0.02 E
Trung Phan=Annam (EN) 140 Mh 15.00N 108.00 E
Truro [Eng.-U.K.] 118 Hk 50.16N 5.03W
Truro [N.S.-Can.] 176 Me 45.22N 63.16W
Truskavec 132 Ce 49.17N 23.34 E
Truth or Consequences (Hot Springs) 182 Fe 33.08N 107.15W
Trutnov 120 Lf 50.34N 15.54 E
Truva [Tur.]=Troy (EN) 146 Bc 39.57N 26.15 E
Truyère 122 Ij 44.38N 2.34 E
Trysil 114 Cf 61.18N 12.16 E
Trysil 116 Ec 61.25N 12.25 E
Trysilelva 116 Ee 59.23N 13.32 E
Trysilfjellet 116 Ec 61.18N 12.11 E
Trzcianka 120 Mc 53.03N 16.28 E
Trzcińsko Zdrój 120 Kd 52.58N 14.35 E
Trzebiatów 120 Lb 54.04N 15.14 E
Trzebiez, Police- 120 Kc 53.39N 14.32 E
Trzebinia-Siersza 120 Pf 50.11N 19.25 E
Trzebnica 120 Ne 51.19N 17.03 E
Trzebnicki, Wał- 120 Me 51.30N 16.20 E
Trzebnickie, Wzgórza- 120 Me 51.15N 17.00 E
Trzemeszno 120 Nd 52.35N 17.50 E
Tsaidam Basin (EN)=Qaidam Pendi 152 Fd 37.00N 95.00 E
Tsamandá, Óri- 130 Dj 39.48N 20.21 E
Tsarap 148 Fb 33.31N 76.56 E
Tsaratanana 172 Hc 16.46S 47.38 E
Tsaratanana (EN)=Tsaratanana, Massif du- 158 Lj 14.00S 49.00 E
Tsaratanana, Massif du-=Tsaratanana (EN) 158 Lj 14.00S 49.00 E
Tsau 172 Cd 20.10S 22.27 E
Tsavo 170 Gc 2.59S 38.28 E
Tses 172 Be 25.58S 18.08 E
Tsévié 166 Fd 6.25N 1.13 E
Tshabong 160 Jk 26.02S 22.06 E
Tshane 160 Jk 24.01S 21.43 E
Tshangalele, Lac- 170 Ee 10.55S 27.03 E
Tshela 160 Ii 4.59S 12.56 E
Tshesebe 172 Dd 20.43S 27.37 E
Tshibala 170 Dd 6.56S 21.28 E
Tshibamba 170 Dd 9.06S 22.34 E
Tshikapa 160 Ji 6.25S 20.48 E
Tshilenge 170 Dd 6.15S 23.46 E
Tshimbalanga 170 Dd 9.43S 23.06 E
Tshimbulu 170 Dd 6.29S 22.51 E
Tshinsenda 170 Ee 12.16S 27.55 E
Tshofa 170 Ed 5.14S 25.15 E
Tsholotsho 172 Dc 19.46S 27.45 E
Tshopo 170 Eb 0.33N 25.07 E
Tshuapa 158 Ji 0.14S 20.42 E
Tshwane 172 Cd 22.38S 22.05 E
Tsiafajavona 172 Hc 19.21S 47.15 E
Tsihombe 172 He 25.17S 45.30 E
Tsimlyansk Reservoir (EN) = Cimljanskoje vodohranilišče 110 Kf 48.00N 43.00 E
Tsinan → Jinan 142 Nf 36.35N 117.00 E
Tsinghai (EN)=Ch'ing-hai Sheng → Qinghai Sheng [2] 152 Gd 36.00N 96.00 E
Tsinghai (EN)=Qinghai Sheng (Ch'ing-hai Sheng) [2] 152 Gd 36.00N 96.00 E
Tsingtao → Qingdao 142 Of 36.05N 120.21 E
Tsiribihina 172 Gc 19.42S 44.31 E
Tsiroanomandidy 172 Hc 18.50S 46.00 E
Tsis 220d Bb 7.18N 151.50 E
Tsjokkarassa 114 Fb 69.59N 24.32 E
Tsodilo Hill 172 Cc 18.50S 21.45 E
Tsu 152 Oe 34.43N 136.31 E
Tsubame 156 Fc 37.39N 138.56 E
Tsubata 154 Nf 36.40N 136.44 E
Tsubetsu 156a Db 43.43N 144.01 E
Tsuchiura 154 Pf 36.05N 140.12 E
Tsugaru-Hantō 156a Bc 41.00N 140.30 E
Tsugaru-Kaikyō=Tsugaru Strait (EN) 140 Qe 41.40N 140.55 E
Tsugaru Strait (EN)=Tsugaru-Kaikyō 140 Qe 41.40N 140.55 E
Tsuken-Jima 156b Ab 26.15N 127.57 E
Tsukidate 156 Gb 38.44N 141.01 E
Tsukigata 156a Bb 43.20N 141.39 E
Tsukumi 156 Be 33.04N 131.52 E
Tsukura-Se 156 Af 31.18N 129.47 E
Tsukushi-Sanchi 156 Be 33.25N 130.30 E
Tsumeb 160 Ij 19.13S 17.42 E
Tsumeb [3] 172 Bc 19.00S 17.30 E
Tsumkwe 172 Cc 19.32S 20.30 E
Tsuna 156 Dd 34.26N 134.54 E
Tsuno-Shima 156 Bd 34.22N 130.52 E
Tsuru 156 Fd 35.35N 138.50 E
Tsuruga 152 Od 35.39N 136.04 E
Tsuruga-Wan 156 Ed 35.45N 136.05 E
Tsurugi 156 Ec 36.26N 136.37 E
Tsurugi-San 156 De 33.51N 134.03 E
Tsurui 156a Db 43.14N 144.21 E
Tsurumi-Dake 156 Be 33.18N 131.27 E
Tsurumi-Saki 156 Ce 32.56N 132.05 E
Tsuruoka 154 Oe 38.44N 139.50 E
Tsuruta 156 Ga 40.44N 140.26 E
Tsushima 140 Of 34.30N 129.20 E
Tsushima [Jap.] 156 Ed 35.10N 136.43 E
Tsushima [Jap.] 156 Ce 33.07N 132.30 E
Tsushima-Kaikyō=Korea, Strait (EN) 140 Of 34.40N 129.00 E
Tsuwano 156 Bd 34.28N 131.46 E
Tsuyama 154 Lg 35.03N 134.00 E
TTPI → Pacific Islands, Trust Territory of the- [5] 210 Gc 10.00N 155.00 E
Tua 126 Ec 41.13N 7.26W
Tuai 218 Gc 38.49S 177.08 E
Tuaim/Tuam 118 Eh 53.31N 8.50W
Tuakau 218 Fb 37.15S 174.57 E
Tual 150 Jh 5.40S 132.45 E
Tuam/Tuaim 118 Eh 53.31N 8.50W
Tuamotu, Iles-=Tuamotu Archipelago (EN) 208 Mf 19.00S 142.00W
Tuamotu Archipelago (EN) =Tuamotu, Iles- 208 Mf 19.00S 142.00W
Tuamotu Ridge (EN) 106 Ll 20.00S 145.00W
Tuapa 220k Ba 18.57S 169.54W
Tuapse 112 Jg 44.07N 39.05 E
Tuaran 150 Ge 6.11N 116.14 E
Tuasivi 221c Aa 13.40S 172.07W
Tuasivi, Cape- 221c Aa 13.40S 172.07W
Tuatapere 216 Ci 46.08S 167.41 E
Tuba 138 Ef 54.00N 91.40 E
Tuba City 188 Jh 36.08N 111.14W
Tubai, Ile- 208 Mg 23.18S 149.30W
Tubai-Manu → Maiao, Ile- 208 Lf 17.34S 150.35W
Tubal, Wādī at- 146 Jf 32.19N 42.13 E
Tuban 150 Fh 6.54S 112.03 E
Tubarão 206 Kc 28.30S 49.01W
Ţubayq, Jabal at- 146 Gh 29.32N 37.15 E
Tubbataha Reefs 150 Ge 8.51N 119.56 E
Tubeke/Tubize 124 Gd 50.41N 4.12 E
Tübingen 120 Fh 48.32N 9.03 E
Tubize/Tubeke 124 Gd 50.41N 4.12 E
Ţubruq=Tobruk (EN) 160 Je 32.05N 23.59 E
Tubuai Islands (EN) = Tubuai ou Australes, Iles- 208 Lg 23.00S 150.00W
Tubuai ou Australes, Iles- = Tubuai Islands (EN) 208 Lg 23.00S 150.00W
Tubutama 192 Db 30.53N 111.29W
Tucacas 202 Ea 10.48N 68.19W
Tucacas, Punta- 194 Mh 10.52N 68.13W
Tucavaca 204 Cd 18.36S 58.55W
Tucavaca, Rio- 204 Cd 18.37S 58.59W
Tuchola 120 Nc 53.35N 17.50 E
Tucholska, Równina- 120 Oc 53.40N 18.30 E
Tuchów 120 Rg 49.54N 21.03 E
Tucker Glacier 222 Kf 72.35S 169.20 E
Tucson 176 Hf 32.13N 110.58W
Tucumán [2] 206 Gc 27.00S 65.30W
Tucumcari 182 Gd 35.10N 103.44W
Tucunui 202 Id 3.42S 49.27W
Tucupido 202 Eb 9.17N 65.47W
Tucupita 202 Fb 9.04N 62.03W
Tudela 126 Kb 42.05N 1.36W
Tudia, Sierra de- 126 Ff 38.05N 6.20W
Tudmur 144 Ec 34.33N 38.17 E
Tudora 130 Jb 47.31N 26.38 E
Tuela 126 Ec 41.30N 7.12W
Tuensang 148 Ic 26.17N 94.40 E
Tuerto 126 Gb 42.18N 5.53W
Tufanbeyli 146 Gc 38.18N 36.11 E
Tufi 210 Fe 9.08S 149.20 E
Tugela 158 Kk 29.14S 31.30 E
Tug Fork 184 Ff 38.25N 82.35W
Tuguegarao 142 Oh 17.37N 121.44 E
Tugulym 134 Lh 57.04N 64.39 E
Tugur 138 If 53.51N 136.52 E
Tuhai He 154 Ee 38.05N 118.13 E
Tujiabu → Yongxiu 152 Kf 29.05N 115.49 E
Tujmazy 136 Fe 54.36N 53.42 E
Tukan 134 Hj 53.50N 57.31 E
Tukangbesi, Kepulauan-=Tukangbesi Islands (EN) 150 Hh 5.40S 123.50 E
Tukangbesi Islands (EN)=Tukangbesi, Kepulauan- 150 Hh 5.40S 123.50 E
Tukayel 168 Hd 8.05N 45.20 E
Tukayyid 146 Kh 29.47N 45.36 E
Tukituki 218 Gc 39.36S 176.56 E
Tuko Village 220n Ab 10.22S 161.02W
Tūkrah 164 Dc 32.32N 20.34 E
Tuktoyaktuk 176 Fc 69.27N 133.02W
Tukums 114 Fh 56.59N 23.10 E
Tukuringra, hrebet- 138 Hf 54.30N 126.00 E
Tukuyu 170 Fd 9.15S 33.39 E
Tula 170 Gc 0.50S 39.51 E
Tula 190 Ed 20.06N 99.19W
Tula [Mex.] 192 Jf 23.00N 99.43W
Tula [R.S.F.S.R.] 112 Je 54.12N 37.37 E
Tula de Allende 192 Jg 20.03N 99.21W
Tula Mountains 222 Ee 66.54S 51.06 E
Tulancingo 190 Ed 20.05N 98.22W
Tulare 188 Fh 36.13N 119.21W
Tulare Lake Bed 188 Fh 36.03N 119.49W
Tularosa 186 Cj 33.04N 106.01W
Tularosa Valley 186 Cj 32.45N 106.10W
Tulcán 202 Cc 0.48N 77.43W
Tulcea 130 Ld 45.10N 28.48 E
Tulcea [2] 130 Md 45.12N 29.10 E
Tulčin 132 Fe 48.39N 28.52 E
Tulelake 188 Ef 41.57N 121.29W
Tulemalu Lake 180 Hd 62.55N 99.25W
Tulgheş 130 Ic 46.57N 25.46 E
Tuli 172 Dd 21.55S 29.12 E
Tuli 172 Dd 21.48S 29.04 E
Tulia 186 Fi 34.32N 101.46W
Tulihe 152 La 50.30N 121.51 E
Tullahoma 184 Dh 35.22N 86.11W
Tullamore/An Tulach Mhór 118 Fh 53.16N 7.30W
Tulle 122 Hi 45.16N 1.46 E
Tulln 128 Kb 48.20N 16.03 E
Tulln 128 Kb 48.22N 16.03 E
Tullner Becken 128 Jb 48.25N 15.55 E
Tullow/An Tulach 118 Gi 52.48N 6.44W
Tullus 168 Cc 11.03N 24.33 E
Tully 212 Jc 17.56S 145.56 E
Ţulmaythah 164 Dc 32.43N 20.57 E
Tuloma 110 Jb 68.52N 32.49 E
Tulos, ozero- 114 He 63.35N 30.35 E
Tulsa 176 Jf 36.09N 95.58W
Tulskaja oblast [3] 136 De 54.00N 37.30 E
Tuluá 202 Cc 4.05N 76.12W
Tuluksak 178 Gd 61.06N 160.58W
Tulum 192 Pg 20.13N 87.28W
Tulum 190 Gd 20.15N 87.27W
Tulun 142 Md 54.35N 100.33 E
Tulungagung 150 Fh 8.04S 111.54 E
Tuma 114 Ji 55.10N 40.36 E
Tuma, Rio- 194 Eg 13.03N 84.44W
Tumaco 200 Ie 1.49N 78.46W
Tumaco, Rada de- 202 Cc 1.50N 78.40W
Tumacuari, Pico- 202 Fc 1.15N 64.40W
Tuman-gang 154 Kc 42.18N 130.41 E
Tumba 116 Ge 59.12N 17.49 E
Tumbarumba 212 Jg 35.47S 148.01 E
Tumbes 200 Hf 4.05S 80.35W
Tumbes [3] 202 Bd 3.50S 80.30W
Tumča 114 Hc 66.35N 31.45 E
Tumd Youqi 152 Jc 40.33N 110.32 E
Tumd Zuoqi 152 Jc 40.43N 111.06 E
Tumen 142 Oe 42.58N 129.49 E
Tumen Jiang 154 Kc 42.18N 130.41 E
Tumeremo 202 Fb 7.18N 61.30W
Tumkur 148 Ff 13.21N 77.05 E
Tummel 118 Je 56.43N 3.44W
Tummo 164 Be 23.00N 14.10 E
Tumon Bay 220c Ba 13.31N 144.48 E
Tumpat 150 De 6.12N 102.10 E
Tumu 166 Ec 10.52N 1.59W
Tumucumaque, Serra- 198 Ke 2.20N 55.00W
Tumwater 188 Dc 47.01N 122.54W
Tuna, Punta- 197a Cc 18.00N 65.52W
Tunapuna 196 Fg 10.38N 61.23W
Tunas 204 Hg 24.58S 49.06W
Tunas, Sierra de las- 192 Fc 29.40N 107.15W
Tunas Chicas, Laguna- 204 Am 36.01S 62.20W
Tunaydah 146 Cj 25.31N 29.21 E
Tunçbilek 130 Mj 39.37N 29.29 E
Tunduma 170 Fd 9.18S 32.46 E
Tunduru 170 Ge 11.07S 37.21 E
Tundža 130 Jh 41.40N 26.34 E
Tunga 166 Gd 8.07N 9.12 E
Tungabhadra 148 Fe 15.57N 78.15 E
Tungaru 168 Ec 10.14N 30.42 E
Tungnaá 114a Bb 64.10N 19.34W
Tungokočen 138 Gf 53.33N 115.34 E
Tungsten 180 Ed 62.05N 127.42W
Tungua 221b Bb 20.01S 174.46W
Tuni 148 Ge 17.21N 82.33 E
Tūnis=Tunis (EN) 160 Ie 36.48N 10.11 E
Tūnis=Tunis (EN) [3] 162 Jb 36.30N 10.00 E
Tūnis=Tunisia (EN) [1] 160 He 34.00N 9.00 E
Tunis (EN)=Tūnis 160 Ie 36.48N 10.11 E
Tunis (EN)=Tūnis [3] 162 Jb 36.30N 10.00 E
Tūnis, Canal de-=Sicily, Strait of- (EN) 110 Hh 37.20N 11.20 E
Tūnis, Khalīj- 162 Jb 37.00N 10.30 E
Tunisia (EN)=Tūnis [1] 160 He 34.00N 9.00 E
Tunja 200 Ie 5.31N 73.22W
Tunkhannock 184 Je 41.32N 75.57W
Tunliu 154 Bf 36.18N 112.53 E
Tunnhovdfjorden 116 Cd 60.25N 8.55 E
Tunø 116 Di 55.55N 10.25 E
Tunumuk 180 Ec 69.00N 134.57W
Tununak 178 Fd 60.35N 165.16W
Tunungayualok 180 Le 56.05N 61.05W
Tunxi 152 Kf 29.45N 118.15 E
Tuo He 154 Dh 33.16N 117.45 E
Tuo Jiang 152 If 28.55N 105.26 E
Tuostah 138 Ic 67.50N 135.40 E
Tuotuo He 152 Fe 34.03N 92.46 E
Tuotuoheyan / Tanggulashanqu 142 Lf 34.15N 92.29 E
Tupã 206 Jb 21.56S 50.30W
Tupaciguara 204 Hd 18.35S 48.42W
Tupai Atoll (Motu-Iti) 216 Kc 16.17S 151.50W
Tupanciretã 206 Jc 29.05S 53.51W
Tupelo 182 Je 34.16N 88.43W
Tupik 138 Gf 54.28N 119.57 E
Tupinambaranas, Ilha- 202 Gd 3.00S 58.00W
Tupiraçaba 204 Hb 14.29S 48.34W
Tupiza 202 Eh 21.27S 65.43W
Tupper Lake 184 Jc 44.13N 74.29W
Tupungato, Cerro- 206 Gd 33.22S 69.47W
Tuquan 152 Lb 45.22N 121.33 E
Túquerres 202 Cc 1.06N 77.37W
Tur 130 Fa 48.04N 22.33 E
Tura 136 Gd 57.12N 66.56 E
Tura [India] 148 Ic 25.31N 90.13 E
Tura [R.S.F.S.R.] 142 Mc 64.17N 100.15 E
Turabah [Sau.Ar.] 144 Fd 21.13N 41.39 E
Turabah [Sau.Ar.] 144 Fd 28.13N 42.59 E
Turagua, Serranías- 196 Di 7.20N 64.35W
Turakina 218 Fd 40.02S 175.13 E
Turān 146 Qe 35.40N 56.50 E
Turan 138 Ef 52.08N 93.55 E
Turana, hrebet- 138 If 51.30N 132.00 E
Turangi 218 Fc 38.59S 175.48 E
Turano 128 Gh 42.26N 12.47 E
Turanskaja nizmennost 140 Ie 44.30N 63.00 E
Turawa 120 Of 50.45N 18.05 E
Turawskie, Jezioro- 120 Of 50.43N 18.10 E
Turbaco 194 Jh 10.19N 75.25W
Turbat 148 Cc 25.59N 63.04 E
Turbo 200 Ie 8.06N 76.43W
Turcoaia 130 Ld 45.07N 28.11 E
Turda 130 Gc 46.34N 23.47 E
Tūreh 146 Me 34.02N 49.17 E
Tureia Atoll 208 Ng 20.50S 138.32W
Turek 120 Od 52.02N 18.30 E
Turenki 116 Kd 60.55N 24.38 E
Turfan Depression (EN)=Turpan Pendi 140 Ke 42.30N 89.30 E
Turgai Gates (EN) = Turgajskaja ložbina 140 Id 51.00N 64.30 E
Turgai Upland (EN) = Turgajskoje plato 140 Id 51.00N 64.00 E
Turgaj 136 Gf 49.38N 63.28 E
Turgaj 140 Id 48.01N 62.45 E
Turgajskaja ložbina = Turgai Gates (EN) 140 Id 51.00N 64.30 E
Turgajskaja oblast [3] 136 Ge 50.30N 66.00 E
Turgajskoje plato = Turgai Upland (EN) 140 Id 51.00N 64.00 E
Turgeon, Rivière- 184 Ha 50.00N 78.55W
Turgutlu 146 Bc 38.30N 27.50 E
Turhal 146 Gb 40.24N 36.06 E
Türi/Tjuri 114 Fg 58.50N 25.27 E
Turia / Túria 126 Lg 39.27N 0.19W
Túria / Turia 126 Le 39.27N 0.19W
Turiaçu, Baía de- 202 Id 1.30S 45.15W
Turiec 120 Og 49.06N 18.52 E
Turijsk 120 Ue 51.10N 24.37 E
Turimiquire, Cerro- 202 Fa 10.03N 64.00W
Turin (EN) = Torino 112 Gf 45.03N 7.40 E
Turinsk 136 Gd 58.03N 63.42 E
Turja 132 Dd 51.48N 24.52 E
Turka [R.S.F.S.R.] 138 Ff 52.57N 108.13 E
Turka [Ukr.-U.S.S.R.] 120 Tg 49.07N 23.01 E
Turkana 170 Gb 4.00N 35.30 E
Turkana, Lake-/Rudolf, Lake- 158 Kh 3.30N 36.00 E
Türkeli 146 Fb 41.57N 34.21 E
Turkestan 142 Ie 43.18N 68.15 E
Turkestanski hrebet 136 Gh 39.35N 69.00 E
Türkeve 120 Qi 47.06N 20.45 E
Turkey (EN)=Türkiye [1] 142 Ff 39.00N 35.00 E
Turkey Creek 212 Fc 17.02S 128.12 E
Turki 132 Mc 52.01N 43.16 E
Türkiye=Turkey (EN) [1] 142 Ff 39.00N 35.00 E
Turkmenistan Sovet Socialistik Respublikasy/Turkmenskaja SSR [2] 136 Fh 40.00N 60.00 E
Turkmen-Kala 135 Df 37.26N 62.19 E
Turkmenskaja Sovetskaja Socialističeskaja Respublika [2] 136 Fh 40.00N 60.00 E
Turkmenskaja SSR/Turkmenistan Sovet Socialistik Respublikasy [2] 136 Fh 40.00N 60.00 E
Turkmenskaja SSR=Turkmen SSR (EN) [2] 136 Fh 40.00N 60.00 E
Turkmenski zaliv 132 Rj 39.00N 53.30 E
Turkmen SSR (EN)=Turkmenskaja SSR [2] 136 Fh 40.00N 60.00 E
Türkoğlu 146 Gd 37.31N 36.49 E
Turks and Caicos Islands [5] 176 Lg 21.45N 71.35W
Turks Island Passage 194 Lc 21.25N 71.19W
Turks Islands 190 Jd 21.24N 71.07W
Turku/Åbo 112 Ic 60.27N 22.17 E
Turku-Pori [2] 114 Ff 61.00N 22.30 E
Turkwel 170 Gb 3.06N 36.06 E
Turlock 188 Eh 37.30N 120.51W
Turmantas 116 Li 55.42N 26.34 E
Turnagain, Cape- 218 Gd 40.30S 176.37 E
Turneffe Islands 190 Ge 17.22N 87.51W
Turnhout 122 Kc 51.19N 4.57 E
Turnov 120 Lf 50.35N 15.09 E
Turnu Măgurele 130 Hf 43.45N 24.52 E
Turnu Roşu, Pasul- 130 Hd 45.33N 24.16 E
Turočak 138 Df 52.16N 87.05 E
Turó de L'Home 126 Oc 41.45N 2.25 E
Turopolje 128 Ke 45.38N 16.07 E
Turpan 142 Ke 42.56N 89.10 E
Turpan Pendi=Turfan Depression (EN) 140 Ke 42.30N 89.30 E
Turquino, Pico- 190 Ie 19.59N 76.51W
Turrialba 194 Fi 9.54N 83.41W
Tursuntski Tuman, ozero- 134 Kf 60.35N 63.55 E
Turtas 134 Ng 58.57N 69.10 E
Turtas 134 Nf 59.06N 68.50 E
Turtkul 136 Gg 41.35N 61.00 E
Turtle Mountain 186 Fb 49.05N 100.15W
Turugart Shankou 140 Je 40.32N 75.24 E
Turuhan 138 Dc 65.56N 87.42 E
Turuhansk 138 Dc 65.49N 87.59 E
Turvânia 204 Gc 16.39S 50.09W
Turvo 204 Hi 28.56S 49.41W
Turvo, Rio- [Braz.] 204 Hd 19.56S 49.55W
Turvo, Rio- [Braz.] 204 Gc 17.46S 50.12W
Tusaun/Thusis 128 Dd 46.42N 9.26 E
Tuscaloosa 182 Je 33.13N 87.33W
Tuscan Archipelago (EN) = Toscano, Arcipelago- 110 Hg 42.45N 10.20 E
Tuscania 128 Fh 42.25N 11.52 E
Tuscany (EN) = Toscana [2] 128 Eg 43.25N 11.00 E
Tuscarora Mountain 184 Ie 40.10N 77.45W
Tuscarora Mountains 188 Gf 41.00N 116.20W
Tuščibas, zaliv- 135 Ba 46.10N 59.45 E
Tuscola 186 Lg 39.48N 88.17W
Tusenøyane 179 Oc 77.05N 22.00 E
Tuskar 132 Jf 51.40N 36.15 E
Tuskegee 184 Ei 32.26N 85.42W
Tuşnad Băi 130 Ic 46.09N 25.51 E
Tustna 116 Ca 63.10N 8.05 E
Tuszymka 120 Rf 50.09N 21.30 E
Tuszyn 120 Pe 51.37N 19.34 E
Tutajev 136 Dd 57.52N 39.32 E
Tutak 146 Jc 39.32N 42.46 E
Tuticorin 148 Fg 8.47N 78.08 E
Tutira 218 Gc 39.12S 176.53 E
Tutóia 202 Jd 2.45S 42.16W
Tutoko Peak 218 Bf 44.36S 167.58 E
Tutončana 138 Ed 64.05N 93.50 E
Tutova 130 Kc 46.06N 27.32 E
Tutrakan 130 Je 44.03N 26.37 E
Tuttle Creek Lake 186 Hg 39.22N 96.40W
Tuttlingen 120 Ei 47.59N 8.49 E
Tutuala 150 Ih 8.24S 127.15 E
Tutuila Island 208 Jf 14.18S 170.42W
Tutupaca, Volcán- 202 Dg 17.01S 70.22W
Tuupovaara 116 Nb 62.29N 30.36 E
Tuusniemi 114 Ge 62.49N 28.30 E
Tuvalu (Ellice Islands) [1] 210 Ie 8.00S 178.00 E
Tuvalu Islands 208 Ie 8.00S 178.00 E
Tuvana-i-Ra Island 216 Fd 21.00S 178.43W
Tuvana-i-Tholo Island 208 Ig 21.02S 178.49W
Tuvinskaja ASSR [3] 138 Ef 51.30N 94.00 E
Tuvutha 219d Cb 17.40S 178.48W
Ţuwayq, Jabal- 140 Gg 25.30N 46.20 E
Tuxer Alpen 128 Fc 47.10N 11.45 E
Tuxford 124 Ba 53.13N 0.53W
Tuxpan [Mex.] 190 Cd 21.57N 105.18W
Tuxpan [Mex.] 192 Hh 19.33N 103.24W
Tuxpan, Arrecife- 192 Kg 21.02N 97.13W
Tuxpan, Rio- 192 Kg 20.53N 97.18W
Tuxpan de Rodriguez Cano 190 Ed 20.57N 97.24W
Tuxtla Gutiérrez 176 Jh 16.45N 93.07W
Tuy 126 Db 42.03N 8.38W
Tuy, Rio- 196 Dg 10.24N 65.59W
Tuy An 148 Lf 13.17N 109.16 E
Tuy Hoa 148 Lf 13.05N 109.18 E
Tüyserkān 146 Me 34.33N 48.27 E
Tuz, Lake- (EN)=Tuz Gölü 140 Ff 38.45N 33.25 E
Tuz Gölü=Tuz, Lake- (EN) 140 Ff 38.45N 33.25 E
Tuzkan, ozero- 135 Fd 40.35N 67.30 E
Tūz Khurmātū 144 Fc 34.53N 44.38 E
Tuzla 128 Mf 44.33N 18.41 E
Tuzla Gölü 146 Fc 39.01N 35.50 E
Tuzlov 132 Lf 47.23N 40.08 E
Tuzluca 146 Jb 40.03N 43.39 E
Tuzly 130 Nd 45.56N 30.05 E

Index Symbols

1 Independent Nation
2 State, Region
3 District, County
4 Municipality
5 Colony, Dependency
Continent
Physical Region
Historical or Cultural Region
Mount, Mountain
Volcano
Hill
Mountains, Mountain Range
Hills, Escarpment
Plateau, Upland
Pass, Gap
Plain, Lowland
Delta
Salt Flat
Valley, Canyon
Crater, Cave
Karst Features
Depression
Polder
Desert, Dunes
Forest, Woods
Heath, Steppe
Oasis
Cape, Point
Coast, Beach
Cliff
Peninsula
Isthmus
Sandbank
Island
Atoll
Rock, Reef
Islands, Archipelago
Rocks, Reefs
Coral Reef
Well, Spring
Geyser
River, Stream
Waterfall, Rapids
River Mouth, Estuary
Lake
Salt Lake
Intermittent Lake
Reservoir
Swamp, Pond
Canal
Glacier
Ice Shelf, Pack Ice
Ocean
Sea
Gulf, Bay
Strait, Fjord
Lagoon
Bank
Seamount
Tablemount
Ridge
Shelf
Basin
Escarpment, Sea Scarp
Fracture
Trench, Abyss
National Park, Reserve
Point of Interest
Recreation Site
Cave, Cavern
Historic Site
Ruins
Wall, Walls
Church, Abbey
Temple
Scientific Station
Railway station
Airport
Port
Military installation
Lighthouse
Mine
Tunnel
Dam, Bridge

Tvååker 116 Eg 57.03N 12.24 E
Tvărdica 130 Ig 42.42N 25.54 E
Tvedestrand 114 Bg 58.37N 8.55 E
Tverca 114 Ih 56.52N 35.59 E
Tweed 118 Lf 55.46N 2.00W
Tweedsmuir Hills 118 Jf 55.30N 3.22W
Tweerivier 172 Be 25.35S 19.37 E
Twello, Voorst- 124 Ib 52.14N 6.07 E
Twente 122 Mb 52.17N 6.40 E
Twentekanaal 124 Ib 52.13N 6.53 E
Twilight Cove 212 Ff 32.20S 126.00 E
Twin Buttes Reservoir 186 Fk 31.20N 100.35W
Twin Falls 176 He 42.34N 114.28W
Twin Islands 180 Jf 53.50N 80.00W
Twin Peaks 188 Hd 44.35N 114.29W
Twisp 188 Eb 48.22N 120.07W
Twiste 124 Lc 51.29N 9.09 E
Twistringen 120 Ed 52.48N 8.39 E
Two Butte Creek 186 Eg 38.02N 102.08W
Two Harbors 186 Kc 47.01N 91.40W
Two Rivers 186 Md 44.09N 87.34W
Two Thumb Range 218 De 43.45S 170.40 E
Tychy 120 Of 50.09N 18.59 E
Tyczyn 120 Sg 49.58N 22.02 E
Tydal 114 Ce 63.04N 11.34 E
Tygda 138 Hf 53.07N 126.20 E
Tyin 116 Cc 61.14N 8.14 E
Tyin 116 Cc 61.15N 8.15 E
Tyler 182 He 32.21N 95.18W
Tylertown 186 Kk 31.07N 90.09W
Tylösand 116 Eh 56.39N 12.44 E
Tylöskog 116 Ff 58.40N 15.10 E
Tym 138 De 59.30N 80.07 E
Tymovskoje 138 Jf 50.50N 142.41 E
Tympákion 130 Hn 35.06N 24.45 E
Tynda 142 Od 55.10N 124.43 E
Tyne 118 Lf 55.01N 1.26W
Tyne and Wear [3] 118 Lg 55.00N 1.35W
Tynemouth 118 Lf 55.01N 1.24W
Týn nad Vltavou 120 Kg 49.14N 14.26 E
Tynset 114 Ce 62.17N 10.47 E
Tyra, Cayos- 194 Fg 12.50N 83.20W
Tyrifjorden 116 De 60.05N 10.10 E
Tyringe 116 Eh 56.10N 13.35 E
Tyrma 138 If 50.01N 132.10 E
Tyrnyauz 132 Mh 43.23N 42.56 E
Tyrol (EN)=Tirol [2] 128 Fc 47.10N 11.25 E
Tyrol (EN)=Tirol/Tirolo 128 Fd 47.00N 11.20 E
Tyrol (EN)=Tirolo/Tirol 128 Fd 47.00N 11.20 E
Tyrone 184 He 40.41N 78.15W
Tyrrell, Lake- 212 Ig 35.20S 142.50 E
Tyrrel Lake 180 Gd 63.05N 105.30W
Tyrrhenian Basin (EN) 110 Hh 40.00N 13.00 E
Tyrrhenian Sea (EN)= Tirreno, Mar- 110 Hh 40.00N 12.00 E
Tyrva/Tõrva 114 Fg 58.01N 25.59 E
Tyrvää 116 Jc 61.21N 22.53 E
Tysmenica 120 Uh 48.49N 24.56 E
Tyśmienica 120 Se 51.33N 22.30 E
Tysnesøy 114 Af 60.00N 5.35 E
Tysse 116 Ad 60.22N 5.45 E
Tyssedal 116 Bd 60.07N 6.34 E
Tystama/Tõstamaa 116 Jf 58.17N 23.52 E
Tystberga 116 Gf 58.52N 17.15 E
Tyszowce 120 Tf 50.36N 23.41 E
Tytuvėnai/Tituvenaj 116 Ji 55.33N 23.09 E
Tywyn 118 Ii 52.35N 4.05W
Tzanconeja, Rio- 192 Ni 16.51N 91.47W
Tzaneen 172 Ed 23.50S 30.09 E
Tzintzuntzan 192 Ih 19.38N 101.34W
Tzucacab 192 Og 20.04N 89.05W

U

Uaboe 220e Ab 0.31S 166.54 E
Uacurizal, Ilha do- 204 Dc 16.25S 56.05W
Ua Huka, Ile- 208 Ne 8.54S 139.33W
Uanukuhahaki 221b Ba 19.58S 174.29W
Ua Pou, Ile- 208 Me 9.23S 140.03W
Uaroo 212 Dd 23.00S 115.10 E
Uatumã, Rio- 198 Kf 2.26S 57.37W
Uaupés 200 Jf 0.08S 67.05W
Uaupés, Rio- 198 Je 0.02N 67.16W
Uaxactún 190 Ge 17.25N 89.29W
Ub 130 De 44.27N 20.05 E
Ubá 202 Jh 21.07S 42.56W
Übach-Palenberg 120 Cf 50.56N 6.05 E
Ubagan 136 Ge 54.23N 64.40 E
Ubaila 146 If 33.06N 40.15 E
Ubaitaba 202 Kf 14.18S 39.20W
Ubajay 204 Cj 31.47S 58.18W
Ubangi 158 Ii 0.30S 17.42 E
Ubatuba 204 Jf 23.26S 45.04W
Ubay 150 Hd 10.03N 124.28 E
Ubaye 122 Mj 44.28N 6.18 E
Ubayyiḑ, Wādī al- 144 Fc 32.34N 43.48 E
Ube 154 Kh 33.56N 131.15 E
Übeda 126 If 38.01N 3.22W
Ubekendt Ejland 179 Gd 71.10N 53.45W
Uberaba 200 Lg 19.45S 47.55W
Uberaba, Lagoa- 204 Dc 17.30S 57.45W
Uberlândia 200 Lg 18.56S 48.18W
Überlingen 120 Fi 47.46N 9.10 E
Ubiaja 166 Gd 6.39N 6.23 E
Ubiña, Peña- 126 Ga 43.01N 5.57W
Ubiratã 204 Fg 24.32S 52.56W
Ubon Ratchathani 142 Mh 15.15N 104.54 E
Ubort 132 Fc 52.06N 28.30 E
Ubrique 126 Gh 36.41N 5.27W
Ubsu-Nur (Uvs Nuur) 140 Ld 50.20N 92.45 E
Ubundu 160 Ji 0.21S 25.29 E
Učaly 136 Fe 54.20N 59.31 E
Učami 138 Ed 63.50N 96.39 E
Učaral 136 If 46.08N 80.52 E
Ucayali [3] 202 De 7.10S 75.15W
Ucayali, Rio- 198 If 4.30S 73.30W
Uccle/Ukkel 124 Gd 50.48N 4.19 E
Üçdoruk Tepe 146 Ib 40.45N 41.05 E
Ucero 126 Ic 41.31N 3.04W
Uchiko 156 Ce 33.34N 132.38 E
Uchi Lake 186 Ja 51.05N 92.35W
Uchinomi 156 Dd 34.30N 134.19 E
Uchinoura 156 Bf 31.16N 131.05 E
Uchiura-Wan 154 Pc 42.18N 140.35 E
Uchte 120 Ed 52.30N 8.55 E
Učka 128 Ie 45.17N 14.12 E
Uckange 124 Ie 49.18N 6.09 E
Uckermark 120 Jc 53.10N 13.35 E
Uckfield 124 Cd 50.58N 0.06 E
Učkuduk 136 Gg 42.10N 63.30 E
Učkurgan 135 Id 41.01N 72.04 E
Ucrainskaja Sovetskaja Socialističeskaja Respublika [2] 136 Df 49.00N 32.00 E
Ucross 188 Ld 44.33N 106.31W
Ucua 170 Bd 8.40S 14.12 E
Učur 140 Pd 58.48N 130.35 E
Uda [R.S.F.S.R.] 138 Ff 51.45N 107.25 E
Uda [R.S.F.S.R.] 140 Pd 54.42N 135.14 E
Uda [R.S.F.S.R.] 138 Ee 56.05N 99.34 E
Udačny 138 Gc 66.25N 112.20 E
Udaipur 142 Jg 24.35N 73.41 E
Udaj 132 Hd 50.05N 33.07 E
Udaquiola 204 Cm 36.34S 58.31W
Udbina 128 Jf 44.32N 15.46 E
Uddevalla 114 Cg 58.21N 11.55 E
Uddjaure 110 Hb 65.58N 17.50 E
Uden 124 Hc 51.40N 5.37 E
Udgīr 148 Fe 18.23N 77.07 E
Udhampur 148 Fb 32.56N 75.08 E
Udimski 114 Kf 61.09N 45.52 E
Udine 128 Hd 46.03N 13.14 E
Udipi 148 Ef 13.21N 74.45 E
Udmurtskaja ASSR [3] 136 Fd 57.20N 52.50 E
Udoha 116 Mg 57.58N 29.50 E
Udomlja 114 Ih 57.56N 35.02 E
Udone-Jima 156 Fd 34.28N 139.17 E
Udon Thani 148 Ke 17.25N 102.48 E
Udot 220d Bb 7.23N 151.43 E
Udskaja guba 140 Pd 55.00N 136.00 E
Udskoje 138 If 54.36N 134.30 E
Udy 132 Je 49.47N 36.35 E
Udžary 132 Oi 40.31N 47.40 E
Udzungwa Range 170 Gd 8.05S 35.50 E
Uebonti 150 Hg 0.55S 121.38 E
Uecker 120 Kc 53.45N 14.04 E
Ueckermünde 120 Kc 53.44N 14.03 E
Ueda 152 Od 36.24N 138.16 E
Uele 158 Jh 4.09N 22.26 E
Uelen 138 Oc 66.13N 169.48W
Uelzen 120 Gd 52.58N 10.34 E
Ueno 156 Ed 34.46N 136.06 E
Uere 158 Jh 3.42N 25.24 E
Ufa 112 Le 54.44N 55.56 E
Ufa 110 Le 54.40N 56.00 E
Uftjuga 114 Lf 61.28N 46.12 E
Ugab 158 Ik 21.12S 13.38 E
Ugāle/Ugale 116 Ig 57.19N 21.52 E
Ugale/Ugāle 116 Ig 57.19N 21.52 E
Ugalla 170 Fd 5.08S 30.42 E
Uganda [1] 160 Kh 1.00N 32.00 E
Ugărčin 130 Hf 43.06N 24.25 E
Ugashik 178 He 57.32N 157.25W
Ughelli 166 Gd 5.30N 5.59 E
Ugijar 126 Ih 36.57N 3.03W
Uglegorsk 138 Jg 49.05N 142.06 E
Uglekamensk 138 Ih 43.18N 133.08 E
Ugleuralski 134 Hg 58.59N 57.38 E
Uglič 136 Dd 57.33N 38.23 E
Ugljan 128 Jf 44.05N 15.10 E
Uglovoje 154 Lc 43.20N 132.06 E
Ugnev 120 Tf 50.20N 23.45 E
Ugo 156 Gb 39.13N 140.23 E
Ugolnyje Kopi 138 Md 64.42N 177.50 E
Ugoma 170 Ec 4.55S 26.50 E
Ugra 136 De 54.30N 36.07 E
Ugtal-Cajdam 152 Ib 48.25N 105.30 E
Uh 120 Rh 48.33N 22.00 E
Uherské Hradiště 120 Ng 49.04N 17.27 E
Uhlava 120 Jg 49.45N 13.23 E
Uhlenhorst 172 Bd 23.45S 17.55 E
Uhta 112 Lc 63.33N 53.40 E
Uibh Fhaili/Offaly [2] 118 Fh 53.20N 7.30W
Uig 118 Gd 57.30N 6.20W
Uige 160 Ii 7.35S 15.04 E
Uige [3] 170 Cd 7.00S 15.30 E
'Uiha 221b Ba 19.54S 174.25W
Uijec 220d Bb 7.10N 151.57 E
Uijŏngbu 154 If 37.44N 127.02 E
Uiju 154 Hd 40.12N 124.32 E
Uil 136 Ff 49.04N 54.42 E
Uil 136 Ff 48.36N 52.30 E
Uilpata, gora- 132 Mh 42.47N 43.44 E
Uinta Mountains 182 Ec 40.45N 110.05W
Uinta River 188 Kf 40.14N 109.51W
Uis 172 Ad 21.08S 14.49 E
Uisŏng 154 Jf 36.21N 128.42 E
Uitenhage 160 Jl 33.40S 25.28 E
Uithoorn 124 Gb 52.14N 4.52 E
Uithuizen 124 Ia 53.25N 6.42 E
Uithuizerwad 124 Ia 53.30N 6.40 E
Uj 136 Ge 54.20N 63.58 E
Ujae Atoll 208 Hd 9.05N 165.40 E
Ujān 146 Og 30.45N 52.05 E
Ujandina 140 Jc 68.23N 145.50 E
Ujar 138 Ee 55.48N 94.20 E
Ujarrás 194 Fi 9.50N 83.40W
Ujedinenija, ostrov- 138 Da 77.30N 82.30 E
Ujelang Atoll 208 Hd 9.49N 160.55 E
Újfehértó 120 Ri 47.48N 21.41 E
Uji 156 Dd 34.53N 135.47 E
Uji-Guntō 154 Ji 31.10N 129.28 E
Ujiie 156 Fc 36.41N 139.57 E
Ujiji 160 Ji 4.55S 29.41 E
Ujjain 142 Jg 23.11N 75.46 E
Ujunglamuru 150 Gg 4.40S 119.58 E
Ujung Pandang=Makasar (EN) 142 Nj 5.07S 119.24 E
Uk 138 Ee 55.04N 98.52 E
Ukata 166 Gc 10.50N 5.50 E
Ukeng, Bukit- 150 Gf 1.45N 115.08 E
Ukerewe Island 170 Fc 2.03S 33.00 E
Uke-Shima 156b Ba 28.02N 129.15 E
Ukhayḑir 146 Jf 32.26N 43.36 E
Ukiah [Ca.-U.S.] 182 Cd 39.09N 123.13W
Ukiah [Or.-U.S.] 188 Fd 45.08N 118.56W
Uki Ni Masi 219a Ed 10.15S 161.44 E
Ukkel/Uccle 124 Gd 50.48N 4.19 E
Ukmergė/Ukmerge 114 Fi 55.14N 24.47 E
Ukmerge/Ukmergė 114 Fi 55.14N 24.47 E
Ukraine (EN) 110 Jf 49.00N 35.00 E
Ukrainian SSR (EN)= Ukrainskaja SSR [2] 136 Df 49.00N 32.00 E
Ukrainskaja SSR/Ukrainska Radyanska Socialistična Respublika [2] 136 Df 49.00N 32.00 E
Ukrainskaja SSR=Ukrainian SSR (EN) [2] 136 Df 49.00N 32.00 E
Ukrainska Radyanska Socialistična Respublika/ Ukrainskaja SSR [2] 136 Df 49.00N 32.00 E
Ukrina 128 Le 45.05N 17.56 E
Uku 170 Be 11.25S 14.18 E
Uku-Jima 156 Ae 33.16N 129.07 E
Ula 146 Cd 37.05N 28.26 E
Ula 120 Ub 54.06N 24.20 E
Ulaidh/Ulster 118 Gg 54.30N 7.00W
Ulalu 220d Bb 7.25N 151.40 E
Ulan (Xiligou) 152 Gd 36.55N 98.16 E
Ulan → Otog Qi 152 Id 39.07N 108.00 E
Ulanbaatar → Ulan-Bator 142 Me 47.55N 106.53 E
Ulan-Badrah 154 Ac 43.58N 110.37 E
Ulan-Bator (Ulaanbaatar) 142 Me 47.55N 106.53 E
Ulanbel 136 Hg 44.49N 71.10 E
Ulan-Burgasy, hrebet- 138 Ff 52.30N 108.30 E
Ulangom 142 Le 49.58N 92.02 E
Ulanhad/Chifeng 152 Kc 42.16N 118.57 E
Ulan Hol 136 Ef 45.27N 46.46 E
Ulan Hot/Horqin Youyi Qianqi 142 Oe 46.04N 122.00 E
Ulan Hua → Siziwang Qi 154 Ad 41.31N 111.41 E
Ulan-Hus 152 Eb 49.02N 89.23 E
Ulanów 120 Sf 50.30N 22.16 E
Ulansuhai Nur 152 Ic 40.56N 108.49 E
Ulan-Tajga 152 Ga 50.45N 98.30 E
Ulan-Ude 142 Md 51.50N 107.37 E
Ulan Ul Hu 152 Fe 34.45N 90.25 E
Ulas 146 Gc 39.27N 37.03 E
Ulawa Island 214 Gi 9.46S 161.57 E
Ulbeja 138 Je 59.20N 144.25 E
Ulchin 154 Jf 36.59N 129.24 E
Ulcinj 130 Ch 41.56N 19.13 E
Uleåborg/Oulu 112 Ib 65.01N 25.30 E
Ulefoss 114 Bg 59.17N 9.16 E
Ulegej 142 Ke 48.56N 89.57 E
Ulety 138 Gf 51.22N 112.30 E
Uleza 130 Ch 41.40N 19.53 E
Ulfborg 116 Ch 56.16N 8.20 E
Ulflingen/Troisvierges 124 Hd 50.07N 6.00 E
Ulft, Gendringen- 124 Ic 51.54N 6.24 E
Ulgain Gol 152 Kb 45.31N 117.50 E
Ulhāsnagar 148 Ee 19.10N 73.07 E
Uliastai → Dong Ujimqin Qi 152 Kc 45.31N 116.58 E
Uliga 210 Id 7.09N 171.13 E
Ulindi 158 Ji 1.40S 25.52 E
Ulithi Atoll 208 Ed 9.58N 139.40 E
Ulja 138 Je 58.48N 141.40 E
Uljanovka [R.S.F.S.R.] 116 Ne 59.37N 30.55 E
Uljanovka [Ukr.-U.S.S.R.] 132 Ge 48.20N 30.13 E
Uljanovsk 136 Ee 54.20N 48.24 E
Uljanovskaja oblast [3] 136 Ee 54.00N 48.00 E
Uljanovski 136 He 50.05N 73.45 E
Uljasutaj 142 Le 47.45N 96.49 E
Ulkan 138 Fe 55.55N 107.55 E
Ulla 126 Db 42.39N 8.44W
Ullapool 118 Hd 57.54N 5.10W
Ullared 114 Ch 57.08N 12.43 E
Ulldecona 126 Md 40.36N 0.27 E
Ullsfjorden 114 Eb 69.58N 20.00 E
Ullswater 118 Kg 54.34N 2.54W
Ullŭng-Do 154 Kf 37.29N 130.52 E
Ullvettern 116 Fe 59.25N 14.15 E
Ulm 120 Fh 48.25N 10.00 E
Ulmen 124 Id 50.13N 6.59 E
Ulmeni 130 Jd 45.04N 26.39 E
Ulmu 130 Je 44.16N 26.55 E
Ulongwé 172 Eb 14.43S 34.21 E
Ulricehamn 114 Ch 57.47N 13.25 E
Ulrichstein 124 Ld 50.35N 9.12 E
Ulrum 124 Ia 53.22N 6.20 E
Ulrum-Zoutkamp 124 Ia 53.20N 6.18 E
Ulsan 152 Md 35.33N 129.19 E
Ulsteinvik 114 Ae 62.20N 5.53 E
Ulster 120 Ff 50.51N 9.59 E
Ulster/Ulaidh 118 Gg 54.30N 7.00W
Ulster Canal 118 Gg 54.27N 6.40W
Ulu 168 Ec 10.43N 33.29 E
Ulu/Uulu 116 Kf 58.13N 24.29 E
Ulua, Rio- 190 Ge 15.56N 87.43W
Ulubat Gölü 146 Cb 40.10N 28.35 E
Ulubey 146 Cc 38.09N 29.33 E
Uludağ 144 Ca 40.04N 29.13 E
Uludere 146 Jd 37.27N 42.51 E
Ulugqat/Wuqia 152 Cd 39.40N 75.07 E
Ulukışla 146 Fd 37.33N 34.30 E
Ulungur He 140 Ke 46.58N 87.28 E
Ulungur Hu 152 Eb 47.20N 87.10 E
Ulus 146 Eb 41.35N 32.39 E
Ulus Dağ 130 Lj 39.18N 28.24 E
Ulva 118 Ge 56.28N 6.12W
Ulverston 118 Jg 54.12N 3.06W
Ulverstone 212 Jh 41.09S 146.10 E
Ulvik 116 Bd 60.34N 6.54 E
Ulvön 116 Ha 63.05N 18.40 E
Ulysses 186 Fh 37.35N 101.22W
Ulytau 136 Gf 48.35N 67.05 E
Ulytau, gora- 136 Gf 48.45N 67.00 E
Uly-Žilanšik 136 Gf 48.51N 63.47 E
Uma 152 La 52.36N 120.38 E
Umag 128 He 45.25N 13.32 E
Umala 202 Eg 17.24S 67.58W
Umán 192 Og 20.53N 89.45W
Uman 136 Df 48.47N 30.09 E
Uman 220d Bb 7.18N 151.53 E
'Umān=Oman (EN) [1] 142 Hg 21.00N 57.00 E
'Umān=Oman (EN) 140 Hg 22.10N 58.00 E
'Umān, Khalīj-=Oman, Gulf of- (EN) 140 Hg 25.00N 58.00 E
Umanak 179 Gd 70.36N 52.15W
Ũmánarssuaq/Farvel, Kap- 224 Nb 59.50N 43.50W
Umatac 220c Bb 13.18N 144.40 E
Umba 136 Db 66.41N 34.17 E
Umbelasha 168 Cd 9.51N 24.50 E
Umbertide 128 Gg 43.18N 12.20 E
Umboi Island 208 Fe 5.36S 148.00 E
Umbozero, ozero- 114 Ic 67.45N 34.20 E
Umbria [2] 128 Gh 43.00N 12.30 E
Ume 172 Dc 17.15S 28.20 E
Umeå 112 Ic 63.50N 20.15 E
Umeälven 110 Ic 63.47N 20.16 E
Umm al Arānib 164 Bd 26.08N 14.45 E
Umm al Ḩayf, Wādī- 144 Hf 18.37N 53.59 E
Umm al Jamaājim 146 Ki 26.59N 45.19 E
Umm al Qaywayn 144 Id 25.35N 55.34 E
Ummanz 120 Jb 54.30N 13.10 E
Umm ar Rizam 164 Dc 32.32N 23.00 E
Umm as Samīm 144 Ie 21.30N 56.45 E
Umm aţ Ţūẕ 146 Je 34.47N 42.42 E
Umm Bāb 146 Nj 25.12N 50.48 E
Umm Bel 168 Dc 13.32N 28.04 E
Umm Buru 168 Cb 15.01N 23.36 E
Umm Dhibbān 168 Dc 14.14N 29.37 E
Umm Durmān=Omdurman (EN) 160 Kg 15.38N 32.30 E
Umm Inderaba 168 Eb 15.12N 31.54 E
Umm Kaddādah 168 Dc 13.36N 26.42 E
Umm Lajj 144 Ed 25.04N 37.13 E
Umm Naqqāţ, Jabal- 146 Fj 25.30N 34.14 E
Umm Qam'ul 146 Pj 24.47N 54.42 E
Umm Ruwābah 160 Kg 12.54N 31.13 E
Umm Sayyālah 168 Ec 14.25N 31.00 E
Umm Urūmah 146 Gj 25.46N 36.33 E
Umnak 174 Cd 58.25N 168.10W
Umne-Gobi 152 Fb 49.06N 91.43 E
Umpqua River 188 Ce 43.42N 124.03W
Umpulu 170 Ce 12.42S 17.40 E
Umsini, Gunung- 150 Jg 1.35S 133.30 E
Umtata 160 Jl 31.35S 28.47 E
Umuarama 206 Jb 23.45S 53.20W
Umurbey 130 Ji 40.14N 26.36 E
Umvukwes 172 Ec 17.01S 30.52 E
Umvuma 172 Ec 19.19S 30.35 E
Umzingwani 172 Dd 22.12S 29.56 E
Una 128 Ke 45.16N 16.55 E
Unabetsu-Dake 156a Db 43.52N 144.51 E
Unac 128 Kf 44.29N 16.08 E
Unai 202 Ig 16.23S 46.53W
Unalakleet 178 Gd 63.53N 160.47W
Unalaska 174 Cd 53.45N 166.45W
Unare, Rio- 196 Dg 10.06N 65.12W
Unauna, Pulau- 150 Hg 0.10S 121.35 E
'Unayzah 146 Fg 30.29N 35.48 E
'Unayzah 142 Gg 26.06N 43.56 E
Uncia 202 Eg 18.27S 66.37W
Uncompahgre Peak 182 Fd 38.04N 107.28W
Uncompahgre Plateau 186 Bg 38.30N 108.25W
Unden 116 Ff 58.45N 14.25 E
Underberg 172 De 29.50S 29.22 E
Under-Han 142 Ne 47.19N 110.39 E
Undjulljung 138 Hc 66.20N 124.40 E
Undu Point 219d Cb 16.08S 179.57W
Undva neem 116 If 58.25N 21.45 E
Undva neem / Kiprarenukk, mys- 116 If 58.25N 21.45 E
Uneča 132 Hc 52.50N 32.44 E
'Ung, Jabal al- 128 Dn 36.45N 9.35 E
Unga 178 Ge 55.15N 160.45W
Ungava, Péninsule d'-= Ungava Peninsula (EN) 174 Lc 60.00N 74.00W
Ungava Bay 174 Md 59.30N 67.30W
Ungava Peninsula (EN)= Ungava, Péninsule d'- 174 Lc 60.00N 74.00W
Ungeny 132 Ef 47.13N 27.50 E
Unggi 154 Kc 42.21N 130.23 E
Ungureni 130 Jb 47.53N 26.47 E
Ungwatiri 168 Fb 16.55N 36.05 E
União 202 Jd 4.35S 42.52W
União da Vitória 206 Jc 26.13S 51.05W
União dos Palmares 202 Ke 9.10S 36.02W
Uničov 120 Ng 49.49N 17.07 E
Uniejów 120 Oe 51.58N 18.49 E
Unije 128 If 44.38N 14.15 E
Unimak 174 Cd 54.50N 164.00W
Unimak Pass 178 Gf 54.35N 164.43W
Unini, Rio- 202 Fd 1.41S 61.30W
Union [Mo.-U.S.] 186 Kg 38.27N 91.00W
Union [S.C.-U.S.] 184 Gh 34.42N 81.37W
Union City 184 Cg 36.26N 89.03W
Uniondale 172 Cf 33.40S 23.08 E
Unión de Reyes 194 Gb 22.48N 81.32W
Unión de Tula 192 Gh 19.58N 104.16W
Union Island 194 Ff 12.36N 61.26W
Union Islands/Tokelau 208 Je 9.00S 171.45W
Union of Soviet Socialist Republics (USSR) (EN)= SSSR [1] 142 Jd 60.00N 80.00 E
Union Seamount (EN) 180 Eg 49.35N 132.45W
Union Springs 184 Ei 32.09N 85.49W
Uniontown 184 Hf 39.54N 79.44W
Unionville 186 Jf 40.29N 93.01W
United Arab Emirates (EN) = Al Imārāt al 'Arabīyah al Muttaḩidah [1] 142 Hg 24.00N 54.00 E
United Arab Republic (EN) → Egypt (EN) [1] 160 Jf 27.00N 30.00 E
United Kingdom [1] 112 Fe 54.00N 2.00W
United Kingdom of Great Britain and Northern Ireland [1] 112 Fe 54.00N 2.00W
United States [1] 176 Jf 38.00N 97.00W
United States of America [1] 176 Jf 38.00N 97.00W
Unity [Or.-U.S.] 188 Fd 44.29N 118.13W
Unity [Sask.-Can.] 180 Gf 52.27N 109.10W
University City 186 Kg 38.39N 90.19W
Unna 120 De 51.32N 7.41 E
Unnāb, Wādī al- 146 Gg 30.11N 36.39 E
Unnukka 116 Lb 62.25N 27.55 E
Unst 110 Fc 60.45N 0.55W
Unstrut 120 He 51.10N 11.48 E
Unterfranken 120 Fg 50.00N 10.00 E
Unterwalden nid dem Wald [2] 128 Cd 46.55N 8.30 E
Unterwalden ob dem Wald [2] 128 Cd 46.50N 8.20 E
Unuli Horog 152 Fd 35.12N 91.58 E
Ünye 144 Ea 41.08N 37.17 E
Unža 110 Kd 57.20N 43.08 E
Unzen-Dake 156 Be 32.45N 130.17 E
Uoleva 221b Ba 19.51S 174.24W
Uozu 154 Nf 36.48N 137.24 E
Úpa 120 Lf 50.22N 15.54 E
Upata 202 Fb 8.01N 62.24W
Upemba, Lac- 170 Ed 8.36S 26.26 E
Upernavik 179 Gd 72.20N 56.00W
Upin 150 Ig 2.56S 129.11 E
Upington 160 Jk 28.25S 21.15 E
Upland 124 Kc 51.18N 8.42 E
Upolu Island 208 Jf 13.55S 171.45W
Upolu Point 214 Oc 20.16N 155.52W
Upper [3] 166 Ec 10.30N 1.30W
Upper Arlington 184 Fe 40.01N 83.03W
Upper Arrow Lake 188 Ga 50.30N 117.55W
Upper Austria (EN) = Oberösterreich [2] 128 Hb 48.15N 14.00 E
Upper Hutt 218 Fd 41.07S 175.04 E
Upper Klamath Lake 182 Cc 42.23N 122.00W
Upper Lake 188 Ef 41.44N 120.08W
Upper Lough Erne/Loch Éirne Uachtair 118 Fg 54.20N 7.30W
Upper Red Lake 186 Ib 48.10N 94.40W
Upper Sandusky 184 Fe 40.48N 83.17W
Upper Sheik 168 Hd 9.57N 45.09 E
Upper Thames Valley 118 Lj 51.40N 1.40W
Upper Trajan's Wall (EN) = Verhni Trajanov val 130 Lc 46.40N 29.00 E
Upper Volta (EN) → Burkina Faso [1] 160 Gg 13.00N 2.00W
Uppingham 124 Bb 52.35N 0.43W
Uppland 116 Gd 60.00N 17.50 E
Upplands Väsby 116 Ge 59.31N 17.54 E
Uppsala 112 Hd 59.52N 17.38 E
Uppsala [2] 114 Df 60.00N 17.45 E
Upsala 186 Kb 49.02N 90.29W
Upshi 148 Fb 33.50N 77.49 E
Upton 188 Md 44.06N 104.38W
Uqbān 164 Hf 15.30N 42.23 E
'Uqlat aş Şuqūr 146 Jj 25.53N 42.15 E
Uqturpan/Wushi 152 Cc 41.10N 79.16 E
Ur 144 Gc 30.58N 46.06 E
Urabá, Golfo de- 202 Cb 8.25N 77.00W
Uracoa 196 Eh 9.00N 62.21W
Uracoa, Rio- 196 Eh 9.08N 62.20W
Uradarja 135 Fe 38.51N 66.02 E
Urad Qianqi 152 Ic 40.49N 108.37 E
Urad Zhonghou Lianheqi (Haliut) 152 Ic 41.34N 108.32 E
Uraga-Suido 156 Fd 35.15N 139.45 E
Ura-Guba 114 Hb 69.18N 32.48 E
Urahoro 156a Cb 42.48N 143.38 E
Urahoro-Gawa 156a Cb 42.44N 143.40 E
Uraj 136 Gc 60.08N 64.40 E
Urakawa 154 Qc 42.09N 142.47 E
Ural 110 Lf 47.00N 51.48 E
Ural Mountains (EN) = Uralskije gory 110 Ld 57.00N 60.00 E
Uralsk 112 Le 51.14N 51.22 E
Uralskaja oblast [3] 136 Ff 49.45N 51.00 E
Uralskije gory = Ural Mountains (EN) 110 Ld 57.00N 60.00 E
Urambo 170 Fd 5.04S 32.03 E
Uranium City 176 Id 59.34N 108.36W
Uraricoera 202 Fc 3.27N 60.59W
Uraricoera, Rio- 198 Je 3.02N 60.30W
Ura-Tjube 136 Gh 39.53N 69.01 E
Urawa 156 Og 35.51N 139.39 E
'Uray'irah 146 Mj 25.57N 48.53 E
Urayq, Nafūd al- 146 Jj 25.17N 42.25 E
Urbana [Il.-U.S.] 186 Lf 40.07N 88.12W
Urbana [Oh.-U.S.] 184 Fe 40.06N 83.45W
Urbandale 186 Jf 41.38N 93.48W
Urbania 128 Gg 43.40N 12.31 E
Urbano Santos 202 Jd 3.12S 43.23W
Urbino 128 Gg 43.43N 12.38 E
Urbino, Étang d'- 122a Ba 42.02N 9.28 E
Urbión, Picos de- 126 Jb 42.01N 2.52W
Urcel 124 Fe 49.30N 3.33 E
Urcos 202 Df 13.42S 71.38W
Urdinarrain 204 Ck 32.41S 58.53W
Urdoma 114 Lf 61.47N 48.29 E
Urdžar 136 If 47.06N 81.37 E
Uré 194 Jj 7.46N 75.31W
Ure 118 Lg 54.01N 1.12W
Uren 136 Ed 57.29N 45.48 E
Urenui 218 Fc 39.00S 174.23 E
Ures 190 Bc 29.26N 110.24W
Ureshino 156 Ab 33.06N 129.59 E
'Urf, Jabal al- 146 Ei 27.49N 32.55 E

Index Symbols

[1] Independent Nation
[2] State, Region
[3] District, County
[4] Municipality
[5] Colony, Dependency
Continent
Physical Region
Historical or Cultural Region
Mount, Mountain
Volcano
Hill
Mountains, Mountain Range
Hills, Escarpment
Plateau, Upland
Pass, Gap
Plain, Lowland
Delta
Salt Flat
Valley, Canyon
Crater, Cave
Karst Features
Depression
Polder
Desert, Dunes
Forest, Woods
Heath, Steppe
Oasis
Cape, Point
Coast, Beach
Cliff
Peninsula
Isthmus
Sandbank
Island
Atoll
Rock, Reef
Islands, Archipelago
Rocks, Reefs
Coral Reef
Well, Spring
Geyser
River, Stream
Waterfall, Rapids
River Mouth, Estuary
Lake
Salt Lake
Intermittent Lake
Reservoir
Swamp, Pond
Canal
Glacier
Ice Shelf, Pack Ice
Ocean
Sea
Gulf, Bay
Strait, Fjord
Lagoon
Bank
Seamount
Tablemount
Ridge
Shelf
Basin
Escarpment, Sea Scarp
Fracture
Trench, Abyss
National Park, Reserve
Point of Interest
Recreation Site
Cave, Cavern
Historic Site
Ruins
Wall, Walls
Church, Abbey
Temple
Scientific Station
Railway station
Airport
Port
Military installation
Lighthouse
Mine
Tunnel
Dam, Bridge

Urfa 144 Eb 37.08N 38.46 E
Urfa Platosu 146 Hd 37.10N 38.50 E
Urgal 138 If 51.00N 132.50 E
Urgel, Llanos de-/Urgell, Pla d'- 126 Mc 41.25N 0.36 E
Urgell, Pla d'-/Urgel, Llanos de- 126 Mc 41.25N 0.36 E
Urgen 154 Ab 44.45N 110.40 E
Urgenč 142 Ie 41.33N 60.38 E
Ürgüp 146 Fc 38.38N 35.56 E
Urgut 136 Gh 39.23N 67.14 E
Uri 148 Eb 34.05N 74.02 E
Uri [2] 128 Cd 46.40N 8.30 E
Uribiá 202 Da 11.42N 72.17W
Uricki 136 Ge 53.19N 65.34 E
Urique, Rio- 192 Fd 26.29N 107.58W
Urjala 116 Jc 61.05N 23.32 E
Urjupinsk 136 Ee 50.48N 42.02 E
Urk 122 Lb 52.39N 5.36 E
Urkan 138 Hf 53.27N 126.56 E
Urla 146 Bc 38.18N 26.46 E
Urlaţi 130 Je 44.59N 26.14 E
Urluk 138 Ff 50.03N 107.55 E
Urmi 138 Ig 48.43N 134.16 E
Urmia, Lake- (EN) = Orūmīyeh, Daryācheh-ye- 140 Gf 37.40N 45.30 E
Uromi 166 Gd 6.42N 6.20 E
Uroševac 130 Eg 42.22N 21.10 E
Urshult 116 Fh 56.32N 14.47 E
Ursus 120 Qd 52.12N 20.53 E
Urtazym 134 Ij 52.15N 58.50 E
Urtigueira, Serra da- 204 Gg 24.15S 51.00W
Uru, Rio- 204 Hb 15.24S 49.36W
Uruaçu 202 If 14.30S 49.10W
Uruana 204 Hb 15.30S 49.41W
Uruapan del Progreso 190 De 19.25N 101.58W
Uruará, Rio- 202 Hd 2.00S 53.38W
Urubamba, Rio- 198 Ig 10.43S 73.48W
Urubici 204 Hi 28.02S 49.37W
Urubú, Cachoeira do- 204 Ha 12.52S 48.13W
Urucará 202 Gd 2.32S 57.45W
Uruçuí 202 Je 7.14S 44.33W
Urucuia, Rio- [Braz.] 204 Jc 16.08S 45.05W
Urucuia, Rio- [Braz.] 204 Ib 15.38S 46.10W
Urucum, Serra do- 204 Dd 19.13S 57.33W
Urucurituba 202 Gd 2.41S 57.40W
Uruguai, Rio- 198 Ki 34.12S 58.18W
Uruguaiana 200 Kh 29.45S 57.05W
Uruguay [1] 200 Ki 33.00S 56.00W
Uruguay, Rio- 198 Ki 34.12S 58.18W
Urukthapel 220a Ac 7.15N 134.24 E
Urumbaba Daği 130 Lj 38.25N 28.49 E
Ürümqi 142 Ke 43.48N 87.35 E
Urup 132 Lg 44.59N 41.10 E
Urup, ostrov- 140 Qe 46.00N 150.00 E
Uruša 138 Hf 54.03N 122.55 E
Urussu 114 Mi 54.38N 53.24 E
Uruwira 170 Fd 6.27S 31.21 E
Urville, Cape d'- (EN) = Perkam, Tanjung- 150 Kg 1.28S 137.54 E
Uryū 156a Bb 43.39N 141.51 E
Uryū-Gawa 156a Bb 43.40N 141.54 E
Urziceni 130 Je 44.43N 26.38 E
Uržum 136 Fd 57.10N 50.01 E
Usa 156 Be 33.31N 131.22 E
Usa [R.S.F.S.R.] 110 Lb 65.57N 56.55 E
Usa [R.S.F.S.R.] 132 Nc 53.02N 45.18 E
Uşak 144 Cb 38.41N 29.25 E
Usakos 172 Bd 22.01S 15.32 E
Ušakovo 138 Hf 51.54N 126.35 E
Ušakovskoje 138 Nb 71.00N 178.35W
Usambara Mountains 158 Ki 4.45S 38.30 E
Usarp Mountains 222 Jf 71.10S 160.00 E
Usas Escarpment 222 Nf 76.00S 125.00W
Ušba, gora- 132 Mh 43.06N 42.40 E
Usborne, Mount- 206 Ih 51.42S 58.50W
Ušće 130 Df 43.29N 20.38 E
Usedom 120 Jb 54.00N 14.00 E
Useldange 124 He 49.46N 5.59 E
'Ushayrah 146 Kj 25.35N 45.46 E
'Ushayrah 164 He 21.46N 40.38 E
Ushibuka 156 Be 32.13N 130.01 E
Ushikubi-Misaki 156a Bc 41.08N 140.48 E
Ushimado 156 Dd 34.37N 134.09 E
'Ushsh, Wādī al- 146 Fd 27.18N 42.15 E
Ushuaia 200 Jk 54.47S 68.20W
Usingen 124 Kd 50.20N 8.32 E
Usinsk 136 Fb 65.57N 57.29 E
Üsküdar, İstanbul- 146 Cb 41.01N 29.03 E
Üsküp 146 Kh 41.44N 27.24 E
Uslar 120 Fe 51.40N 9.39 E
Üslava 120 Jg 49.54N 13.32 E
Usman 136 De 52.00N 39.43 E
Usman 132 Kd 51.54N 39.20 E
Usmas, ozero- / Usmas ezers 116 Ig 57.13N 22.00 E
Usmas ezers / Usmas, ozero- 116 Ig 57.13N 22.00 E
Usogorsk 136 Ec 63.28N 48.35 E
Usoke 170 Fd 5.06S 32.20 E
Usolje 136 Fd 59.25N 56.41 E
Usolje-Sibirskoje 138 Ff 52.47N 103.38 E
Usora 128 Mf 44.43N 18.04 E
Ussel 122 Ii 45.33N 2.19 E
USSR (EN)=Sojuz Sovetskih Socialističeskih Respublik [1] 142 Jd 60.00N 80.00 E
Ussuri 140 Pe 48.28N 135.02 E
Ussurijsk 142 Pe 43.48N 131.59 E
Usta 114 Kh 56.53N 45.28 E
Ust-Barguzin 138 Ff 53.27N 108.59 E
Ust-Bolšereck 138 Kf 52.40N 156.18 E
Ust-Cilma 136 Fb 65.27N 52.06 E
Ust-Čorna 120 Uh 48.17N 24.02 E
Ust-Donecki 132 Lf 47.39N 40.55 E
Ust-Džeguta 132 Mg 44.05N 42.01 E
Uster 128 Cc 47.20N 8.43 E
Ustevatn 116 Bd 60.30N 8.00 E
Ust-Hajrjuzovo 138 Ke 57.04N 156.50 E
Ustica 128 Hl 38.42N 13.11 E
Ustica 110 Hh 38.42N 13.10 E
Ust-Ilimsk 142 Md 58.03N 102.43 E
Ustilug 120 Uf 50.50N 24.09 E
Ústí nad Labem 120 Kf 50.40N 14.02 E
Ústí nad Orlicí 120 Mg 49.58N 16.24 E
Ustinov → Iževsk 112 Ld 56.51N 53.14 E
Ust-Išim 136 Hd 57.44N 71.10 E
Ustja 136 Ec 61.33N 42.36 E
Ust-Judoma 138 Ie 59.10N 135.02 E
Ustjurt, plato- 140 He 43.00N 56.00 E
Ustjužna 114 Ig 58.53N 36.28 E
Ustka 120 Mb 54.35N 16.50 E
Ust-Kamčatsk 142 Sd 56.15N 162.30 E
Ust-Kamenogorsk 142 Ke 49.58N 82.38 E
Ust-Kan 138 Df 50.57N 84.55 E
Ust-Kara 136 Gb 69.15N 64.59 E
Ust-Karsk 138 Gf 52.41N 118.45 E
Ust-Katav 134 Ii 54.56N 58.10 E
Ust-Kujga 142 Pc 70.00N 135.36 E
Ust-Kut 142 Md 56.46N 105.40 E
Ust-Labinsk 136 Df 45.13N 39.40 E
Ust-Luga 114 Gg 59.39N 28.15 E
Ust-Maya 142 Pc 60.25N 134.32 E
Ust-Muja 138 Ge 56.28N 115.30 E
Ust-Nera 142 Qc 64.34N 143.12 E
Ust-Njukža 138 He 56.30N 121.48 E
Uštobe 136 Hf 45.13N 77.59 E
Ust-Olenëk 138 Gb 72.58N 119.42 E
Ust-Omčug 138 Jd 61.05N 149.30 E
Ust-Ordynski 138 Ff 52.48N 104.45 E
Ust-Ordynski Burjatski nacionalny okrug [3] 138 Ff 53.30N 104.00 E
Ustovo 130 Hh 41.34N 24.47 E
Ust-Pinega 114 Jd 64.10N 41.58 E
Ust-Pit 138 Ee 58.59N 92.00 E
Ust-Port 138 Dc 69.45N 84.25 E
Ust-Požva 134 Hg 59.05N 56.05 E
Ustrzyki Dolne 120 Sg 49.26N 22.37 E
Ust-Sobolevka 138 Ig 46.10N 137.59 E
Ust-Šonoša 114 Jf 61.11N 41.20 E
Ust-Uda 138 Ff 54.10N 103.03 E
Ust-Ujskoje 134 Ki 54.15N 63.57 E
Ust-Umalta 138 If 51.42N 133.18 E
Ustupo 194 Ii 9.08N 77.56W
Usū 142 Ke 44.27N 84.37 E
Usui-Tōge 156 Fc 36.22N 138.38 E
Usuki 154 Kh 33.08N 131.49 E
Usuki-Wan 156 Be 33.10N 131.50 E
Usulután 194 Cg 13.21N 88.27W
Usumacinta 174 Jh 18.22N 92.40W
Ušumun 138 Hf 52.46N 126.37 E
Usu-San 156a Bb 42.32N 140.49 E
Usva 134 Hg 58.40N 57.35 E
Usva 134 Hg 58.17N 57.47 E
Utah [2] 182 Ed 39.30N 111.30W
Utah Lake 182 Ec 40.13N 111.49W
Utajärvi 114 Gd 64.45N 26.23 E
Utashinai 156a Cb 43.31N 142.03 E
Utata 174 Ff 50.51N 102.45 E
Ute Creek 186 Ei 35.21N 103.50W
Utembo 158 Jj 17.06S 22.01 E
Utena 114 Fi 55.29N 25.40 E
Ute Reservoir 186 Ei 35.21N 103.31W
Utete 170 Gd 7.59S 38.47 E
Uthai Thani 148 Ke 15.20N 100.02 E
Utiariti 204 Ca 13.02S 58.17W
Utica 182 Lc 43.06N 75.15W
Utiel 126 Ke 39.34N 1.12W
Utiel, Sierra de- 126 Ke 39.36N 1.08W
Utila 194 De 16.06N 86.54W
Utila, Isla de- 194 De 16.06N 86.56W
Utique 128 Em 37.04N 10.04 E
Utirik Atoll 208 Hc 11.15N 169.48 E
Utlängan 116 Fh 56.00N 15.45 E
Utljukski liman 132 If 46.20N 35.15 E
Uto 154 Kh 32.40N 130.41 E
Utö [Fin.] 116 Ie 59.45N 21.25 E
Utö [Swe.] 116 Ig 58.55N 18.15 E
Utorgoš 116 Nf 58.17N 30.15 E
Utoro 156a Da 44.06N 144.58 E
Utrata 120 Qd 52.13N 20.15 E
Utrecht [3] 124 Hb 52.05N 5.08 E
Utrecht [Neth.] 112 Ge 52.05N 5.08 E
Utrecht [S.Afr.] 172 Ee 27.28S 30.20 E
Utrera 126 Gg 37.11N 5.47W
Utsira 116 Ae 59.20N 4.55 E
Utsjoki 114 Gb 69.53N 27.00 E
Utsunomiya 142 Pf 36.33N 139.52 E
Uttaradit 148 Ke 17.38N 100.06 E
Uttarkāshi 148 Fb 30.45N 78.19 E
Uttar Pradesh [3] 148 Fc 28.00N 80.00 E
Utuado 194 Nd 18.16N 66.42W
Utukok 178 Gb 70.04N 162.18W
Utuloa 220h Ab 13.16S 176.11W
Utupua Island 208 Hf 11.20S 166.36 E
Uturoa 221e Db 16.44S 151.26W
Utva 132 Rd 51.29N 52.40 E
Uudenmaa [2] 114 Ff 60.30N 25.00 E
Uukuniemi 116 Nc 61.47N 30.01 E
Uulu/Ulu 116 Kf 58.13N 24.29 E
Uusikaupunki/Nystad 114 Ef 60.48N 21.25 E
Uusimaa 116 Kd 60.30N 25.00 E
Uva 136 Fd 56.58N 52.14 E
Uvac 130 Cf 43.36N 19.30 E
Uvalde 182 Hf 29.13N 99.47W
Uvarovo 136 Ee 52.00N 42.15 E
Uvdal 116 Cd 60.20N 8.30 E
Uvéa, Ile- 208 Jf 13.18S 176.10W
Uvelka 134 Ji 54.05N 61.35 E
Uvelski 134 Ji 54.26N 61.27 E
Uvildy, ozero- 134 Ji 55.35N 60.30 E
Uvinza 170 Fd 5.06S 30.22 E
Uvira 160 Ji 3.24S 29.08 E
Uvs Nuur → Ubsu-Nur 140 Ld 50.20N 92.45 E
Uwa 156 Ce 33.21N 132.30 E
Uwajima 152 Ne 33.13N 132.34 E
Uwajima-Wan 156 Ce 33.15N 132.30 E
Uwa-Kai 156 Ce 33.20N 132.15 E
Uwayl 168 Dd 8.46N 27.24 E
'Uwaynāt, Jabal al- = Uweinat, Gebel- (EN) 158 Jf 21.54N 24.58 E
'Uwaynat Wannin 164 Bd 28.05N 12.59 E
Uweinat, Gebel- (EN) = 'Uwaynāt, Jabal al- 158 Jf 21.54N 24.58 E
Uwekuli 150 Hg 1.25S 121.06 E
Uwi, Pulau- 150 Ef 1.05N 107.24 E
Uxin Qi (Dabqig) 152 Id 38.27N 109.08 E
Uxmal 176 Kg 20.20N 89.46W
Uyo 166 Gd 5.07N 7.57 E
Uyuni 200 Jh 20.28S 66.50W
Uyuni, Salar de- 198 Jh 20.20S 67.42W
Už [Eur.] 120 Rh 48.33N 22.00 E
Už [Ukr.-U.S.S.R.] 132 Gd 51.15N 30.12 E
Uza 116 Mg 57.47N 29.38 E
Uzbekiston Sovet Socialistik Respublikasy/Uzbekskaja SSR [2] 136 Gg 41.00N 64.00 E
Uzbekskaja Sovetskaja Socialističeskaja Respublika [2] 136 Gg 41.00N 64.00 E
Uzbekskaja SSR/Uzbekiston Sovet Socialistik Respublikasy [2] 136 Gg 41.00N 64.00 E
Uzbekskaja SSR=Uzbek SSR (EN) [2] 136 Gg 41.00N 64.00 E
Uzbek SSR (EN)= Uzbekskaja SSR [2] 136 Gg 41.00N 64.00 E
Uzbel Shankou 152 Bd 38.42N 73.48 E
Uzen 136 Fg 43.22N 52.50 E
Uzerche 122 Hi 45.25N 1.34 E
Uzès 122 Kj 44.01N 4.25 E
Uzgen 135 Id 40.44N 73.21 E
Užgorod 136 Cf 48.37N 22.22 E
Uzin 132 Ge 49.52N 30.27 E
Uzlovaja 132 Kb 54.01N 38.12 E
Uzlovoje 120 Sh 48.23N 22.27 E
Užokski, pereval- 132 Ce 49.02N 22.58 E
Uzümlü 130 Mm 36.44N 29.14 E
Uzun Ada 130 Jk 38.28N 26.42 E
Uzunagač [Kaz.-U.S.S.R.] 135 Kc 43.36N 76.19 E
Uzunagač [Kaz.-U.S.S.R.] 135 Kc 43.08N 76.20 E
Uzunköprü 146 Bb 41.16N 26.41 E
Užur 138 De 55.20N 90.00 E
Užventis 116 Ji 55.44N 22.37 E
Uzynkair, mys- 135 Bb 45.47N 59.20 E

V

Vääksy 116 Kc 61.11N 25.33 E
Vaal 158 Jk 29.24S 23.38 E
Vaala 114 Gd 64.34N 26.50 E
Vaals 124 Id 50.46N 6.01 E
Vaalwater 172 Dd 24.20S 28.03 E
Vaasa [2] 114 Fe 63.12N 23.00 E
Vaasa/Vasa 112 Ic 63.06N 21.36 E
Vaassen, Epe- 124 Hb 52.17N 5.58 E
Vabalninkas 116 Ki 55.58N 24.49 E
Vác 120 Pi 47.47N 19.08 E
Vacacai, Rio- 204 Fi 29.55S 53.06W
Vacaria 206 Jc 28.30S 50.56W
Vacaria, Rio- 204 Fe 21.55S 53.59W
Vacaville 188 Eg 38.21N 121.59W
Vaccarès, Étang de- 122 Kk 43.32N 4.34 E
Vache, Ile à- 194 Kd 18.04N 73.38W
Väddö 116 Hd 60.00N 18.50 E
Vadehavet 116 Ci 55.15N 8.40 E
Vădeni 130 Kd 45.22N 27.56 E
Vadheim 116 Ac 61.13N 5.49 E
Vadodara 142 Jg 22.18N 73.12 E
Vado Ligure 128 Cf 44.17N 8.27 E
Vadsø 112 Ia 70.05N 29.46 E
Vadstena 114 Dg 58.27N 14.54 E
Vaduz 112 Gf 47.08N 9.30 E
Værlandet 116 Ac 61.20N 4.45 E
Vaga 110 Kc 62.48N 42.56 E
Vagaj 134 Mh 56.28N 67.18 E
Vagaj 134 Nh 57.55N 69.01 E
Vågåmo 114 Bf 61.53N 9.06 E
Vaganski vrh 128 Jf 44.21N 15.30 E
Vågåvatn 116 Cc 61.50N 8.50 E
Vaggeryd 114 Dh 57.30N 14.07 E
Vaghena 219a Cb 7.25S 157.43 E
Vagil 134 Kg 59.45N 62.40 E
Vagis, gora- 138 Jf 52.20N 142.15 E
Vagnhärad 116 Gf 58.57N 17.31 E
Vågsøy 116 Ac 62.00N 5.05 E
Våh 120 Ni 47.55N 18.00 E
Vah 140 Jc 60.45N 76.45 E
Vahitahi Atoll 208 Nf 18.44S 138.52W
Vahruši 114 Mg 58.43N 50.02 E
Vahš 135 Gf 37.43N 68.49 E
Vahsel Bay → Herzog-Ernst-Bucht 222 Af 77.48S 34.39W
Vahtan 114 Lh 57.59N 46.42 E
Vaiaau 221e Db 16.52S 151.28W
Vaigat 179 Gd 70.30N 54.00W
Vaihingen an der Enz 124 Kf 48.56N 8.58 E
Vaihú 221d Ab 27.10S 109.23W
Väike-Maarja/Vjaike-Maarja 116 Le 59.04N 26.12 E
Väike-Pakri/Vjajke-Pakri 116 Je 59.50N 23.50 E
Väike Väin / Vjajke-Vjajn 116 Jf 58.30N 23.10 E
Vailala 220h Bb 13.13S 176.09W
Vailala, Pointe- 220h Ab 13.13S 176.10W
Vaileka 219d Bb 17.23S 178.09 E
Vailheu, Récif- 172 Gb 11.48S 43.04 E
Vailly-sur-Aisne 124 Fe 49.25N 3.31 E
Vainikkala 116 Md 60.52N 28.18 E
Vainode/Vajnëde 116 Ih 56.26N 21.45 E
Vairaatea Atoll 208 Nf 19.19S 139.20W
Vaison-la-Romaine 122 Lj 44.14N 5.04 E
Vaitape 221e Db 16.31S 151.45W
Vaitoare 221e Db 16.41S 151.28W
Vaitupu Island 208 Ie 7.28S 178.41 E
Vajgač, ostrov- 110 La 70.00N 59.30 E
Vajnëde/Vainode 116 Ih 56.26N 21.45 E
Vakaga [3] 168 Cd 10.00N 23.30 E
Vakfıkebir 146 Hb 41.03N 39.20 E
Vaksdal 116 Ad 60.29N 5.44 E
Val 138 Jf 52.19N 143.09 E
Vala 114 Mh 56.59N 51.16 E
Valaam 114 Hf 61.24N 30.59 E
Valaam, ostrov- 116 Nc 61.20N 31.05 E
Valahia = Walachia (EN) 110 Ig 44.00N 25.00 E
Valahia = Walachia (EN) 130 He 44.00N 25.00 E
Valais / Wallis [2] 128 Bd 46.15N 7.30 E
Valamarës, Mali i- 130 Di 40.47N 20.28 E
Valamaz 114 Mh 57.36N 52.14 E
Valandovo 130 Fh 41.19N 22.34 E
Valašské Meziříčí 120 Ng 49.29N 17.58 E
Valáxa 130 Hk 38.49N 24.29 E
Vålberg 116 Ee 59.24N 13.12 E
Valburg 124 Hc 51.55N 5.49 E
Valcabra 126 Jg 37.30N 2.43W
Vâlcëdräm 130 Gf 43.42N 23.27 E
Valcheta 206 Gf 40.42S 66.09W
Valdagno 128 Fe 45.39N 11.18 E
Valdahon 122 Mg 47.09N 6.21 E
Valdai Hills (EN) = Valdajskaja vozvyšennost 110 Jd 57.00N 33.30 E
Valdaj 136 Dd 57.59N 33.14 E
Valdajskaja vozvyšennost = Valdai Hills (EN) 110 Jd 57.00N 33.30 E
Valdarno 128 Fg 43.45N 11.15 E
Valdavia 126 Hb 42.24N 4.16W
Valdecañas, Embalse de- 126 Ge 39.45N 5.30W
Valdeganga 126 Ke 39.09N 1.40W
Val-de-Marne [3] 122 If 48.47N 2.29 E
Valdemārpils/Valdemarpils 114 Fh 57.24N 22.39 E
Valdemarpils/Valdemārpils 114 Fh 57.24N 22.39 E
Valdemarsvik 114 Dg 58.12N 16.32 E
Valdepeñas 126 If 38.46N 3.23W
Valderaduey 126 Gc 41.31N 5.42W
Valderas 126 Gb 42.05N 5.27W
Valderrama, Cienaga de- 194 Ki 8.56N 72.10W
Valderrobres/Vall-de-roures 126 Md 40.53N 0.09 E
Valdés, Península- 198 Jj 42.30S 64.00W
Valdez 176 Ec 61.07N 146.16W
Val d'Isère 122 Mi 45.27N 6.59 E
Valdivia 200 Ii 39.48S 73.14W
Valdivia Seamount (EN) 158 Hk 25.20S 6.15 E
Valdobbiadene 128 Fe 45.54N 12.00 E
Val-d'Oise [3] 122 Ie 49.10N 2.10 E
Val-d'Or 176 Le 48.07N 77.47W
Valdosta 176 Kf 30.50N 83.17W
Valdres 116 Cc 60.55N 9.10 E
Vale [Geo.-U.S.S.R.] 132 Mi 41.36N 42.51 E
Vale [Or.-U.S.] 188 Gd 44.01N 117.15W
Valea Ierii 130 Gc 46.39N 23.21 E
Valea lui Mihai 130 Fb 47.31N 22.09 E
Valea Vişeului 130 Hb 47.51N 24.10 E
Valença [Braz.] 204 Kf 22.15S 43.43W
Valença [Braz.] 202 Kf 13.22S 39.05W
Valença do Minho 126 Db 42.02N 8.38W
Valença do Piauí 202 Je 6.24S 41.45W
Valençay 122 Hg 47.09N 1.34 E
Valence [Fr.] 122 Gj 44.06N 0.55 E
Valence [Fr.] 122 Kj 44.56N 4.54 E
Valencia 200 Jd 10.11N 68.00W
Valencia 126 Le 39.30N 0.40W
València/Valencia 112 Fh 39.28N 0.22W
Valencia/València 112 Fh 39.28N 0.22W
Valencia / València [3] 126 Le 39.20N 0.50W
València / Valencia [3] 126 Le 39.20N 0.50W
València, Golf de-/Valencia, Golfo de- 110 Fh 39.30N 0.00
Valencia, Golfo de-/ València, Golf de- 110 Fh 39.30N 0.00
Valencia, Lago de- 196 Cg 10.11N 67.45W
Valencia de Alcántara 126 Ee 39.25N 7.14W
Valencia de Don Juan 126 Gb 42.18N 5.31W
Valencia-El Grao 126 Le 39.27N 0.20W
Valenciennes 122 Jd 50.21N 3.32 E
Vălenii de Munte 130 Jd 45.11N 26.02 E
Valentia/Dairbhre 118 Cj 51.55N 10.20W
Valentin 154 Mc 43.07N 134.19 E
Valentine 182 Gc 42.52N 100.33W
Valenza 128 Ce 45.01N 8.38 E
Våler 114 Cf 60.40N 11.50 E
Valera 202 Db 9.19N 70.37W
Valga 136 Cd 57.49N 26.05 E
Valge jõgi 116 Ke 59.32N 25.36 E
Valhalla Mountains 188 Gb 49.45N 117.48W
Valiente, Península- 194 Gi 9.05N 81.51W
Valier 188 Ib 48.18N 112.15W
Valinco, Golfe de- 122a Ab 41.40N 8.49 E
Valjevo 130 Ce 44.16N 19.53 E
Valka 114 Gh 57.47N 26.01 E
Valkeakoski 114 Ff 61.16N 24.02 E
Valkeala 116 Ld 60.57N 26.48 E
Valkenswaard 124 Hc 51.21N 5.28 E
Valkininkai/Valkininkaj 116 Kj 54.18N 25.55 E
Valkininkaj/Valkininkai 116 Kj 54.18N 25.55 E
Valko/Valkom 116 Ld 60.25N 26.15 E
Valkom/Valko 116 Ld 60.25N 26.15 E
Valkumej 138 Mc 69.41N 170.30 E
Valladolid [3] 126 Hc 41.35N 4.40W
Valladolid [Mex.] 190 Gd 20.41N 88.12W
Valladolid [Sp.] 112 Fg 41.39N 4.43W
Valldal 116 Bb 62.20N 7.21 E
Vall-de-Roures/Valderrobres 126 Md 40.53N 0.09 E
Vall de Uxó / La Vall d'Uxó 126 Le 39.49N 0.14W
Valle 114 Bg 59.12N 7.32 E
Valle [Col.] [3] 202 Cc 3.40N 76.30W
Valle [Hond.] [3] 194 Dg 13.30N 87.35W
Vallecas, Madrid- 126 Id 40.23N 3.37W
Valle d'Aosta / Vallée d'Aoste [2] 128 Be 45.45N 7.15 E
Valle de Cabuérniga 126 Ha 43.14N 4.18W
Valle de Guanape 196 Dh 9.54N 65.41W
Valle dei Templi 128 Hm 37.18N 13.35 E
Valle de la Pascua 202 Eb 9.13N 66.00W
Valle de los Caídos 126 Hd 40.39N 4.09W
Valle de Santiago 192 Ig 20.23N 101.12W
Valle de Topia 192 Fe 25.13N 106.25W
Valle de Zaragoza 192 Gd 27.28N 105.49W
Valledupar 202 Da 10.28N 73.15W
Vallée d'Aoste / Valle d'Aosta [2] 128 Be 45.45N 7.15 E
Vallée Jonction 184 Lb 46.23N 70.55W
Valle Hermoso 192 Ke 25.39N 97.52W
Vallejera, Puerto de- 126 Gd 40.30N 5.42W
Vallejo 182 Cd 38.07N 122.14W
Vallejo, Sierra de- 192 Gg 20.55N 105.20W
Valle Nacional 192 Ki 17.47N 96.19W
Vallenar 200 Ih 28.35S 70.46W
Vallentuna 116 He 59.32N 18.05 E
Vallès / Vallés 126 Oc 41.35N 2.15 E
Valletta 112 Hh 35.54N 14.31 E
Valley City 182 Hb 46.55N 97.59W
Valley Falls 188 Ee 42.31N 120.15W
Valleyfield 180 Kg 45.15N 74.08W
Valley Station 184 Ef 38.06N 85.52W
Valleyview 180 Fe 55.02N 117.08W
Vallgrund 114 Ee 63.12N 21.14 E
Vallhagar 116 Hg 57.20N 18.10 E
Vallimanca 204 Bm 36.21S 61.02W
Vallimanca, Arroyo- 204 Bl 35.40S 60.02W
Vallo della Lucania 128 Jj 40.14N 15.16 E
Valloires, Abbaye de- 124 Dd 50.20N 1.47 E
Vallorbe 128 Ad 46.43N 6.23 E
Valls 126 Nc 41.17N 1.15 E
Valls d'Andorra → Andorra [1] 112 Gg 42.30N 1.30 E
Vallsta 116 Gc 61.32N 16.22 E
Vallvik 116 Gc 61.11N 17.11 E
Valmaseda / Balmaseda 126 Ia 43.12N 3.12W
Valmiera 136 Cd 57.32N 25.29 E
Valmont 124 Ce 49.44N 0.31 E
Valnera 126 Ia 43.10N 3.45W
Valognes 122 Ee 49.31N 1.28W
Valois, Plaine du- 122 Ie 49.10N 2.45 E
Valoria la Buena 126 Hc 41.48N 4.32W
Valpaços 126 Ec 41.36N 7.19W
Valparaiso 184 De 41.28N 87.03W
Valparaíso 200 Ii 33.02S 71.38W
Valparaíso [Braz.] 204 Ge 21.13S 50.51W
Valparaíso [Mex.] 192 Hf 22.46N 103.34W
Valpovo 128 Me 45.39N 18.25 E
Valréas 122 Kj 44.23N 4.59 E
Vals 158 Jk 27.23S 26.31 E
Vals, Tanjung- 150 Kh 8.26S 137.38 E
Valsjöbyn 114 Dd 64.04N 14.08 E
Valtellina 128 Dd 46.10N 9.55 E
Valtimo 114 Ge 63.40N 28.48 E
Váltou, Óri- 130 Ej 39.10N 21.20 E
Valujki 136 De 50.12N 38.08 E
Valul-Lui Traian 130 Le 44.15N 28.30 E
Valverde 162 Dd 27.48N 17.55W
Valverde de Júcar 126 Je 39.43N 2.12W
Valverde del Camino 126 Fg 37.34N 6.45W
Valverde del Fresno 126 Fd 40.13N 6.52W
Vamdrup 116 Ci 55.25N 9.17 E
Våmhus 114 Df 61.08N 14.28 E
Vamizi, Ilha- 172 Gb 11.02S 40.40 E
Vammala 114 Ff 61.20N 22.54 E
Vámos 130 Hn 35.25N 24.12 E
Van 144 Fb 38.28N 43.20 E
Van, Lake- (EN) = Van Gölü 140 Gf 38.33N 42.46 E
Vanajanselkä 114 Ff 61.09N 24.15 E
Vanak 146 Ng 31.32N 51.19 E
Vanak 146 Ng 31.41N 50.52 E
Vanån 116 Fd 60.31N 14.14 E
Vanault-les-Dames 124 Gf 48.51N 4.46 E
Vanavana Atoll 208 Ng 20.47S 139.09W
Vanavara 138 Fd 60.22N 102.16 E
Van Buren [Ar.-U.S.] 186 Ii 35.26N 94.21W
Van Buren [Me.-U.S.] 184 Nb 47.09N 67.56W
Vanč 135 He 38.23N 71.29 E
Vanceburg 184 Ff 38.36N 83.19W
Vancouver [B.C.-Can.] 176 Ge 49.16N 123.07W
Vancouver [Wa.-U.S.] 182 Cb 45.39N 122.40W
Vancouver Island 174 Ge 49.45N 126.00W
Vandalia [Il.-U.S.] 186 Lg 38.58N 89.06W
Vandalia [Oh.-U.S.] 184 Ef 39.53N 84.12W
Vanderbijl Park 172 Da 26.42S 27.54 E
Vanderhoof 180 Ff 54.01N 124.01W
Vanderlin Island 212 Hc 15.45S 137.00 E
Van Diemen, Cape- 212 Gb 11.10S 130.25 E
Van Diemen Gulf 212 Gb 11.50S 132.00 E
Vandmtor, ozero- 134 Le 62.15N 65.45 E
Vändra/Vjandra 114 Fg 58.40N 25.01 E
Vänern 110 Hd 58.55N 13.30 E
Vänersborg 114 Cg 58.22N 12.19 E
Vang 116 Cc 61.08N 8.35 E
Vangaindrano 172 Hd 23.23S 47.33 E
Van Gölü = Van, Lake- (EN) 140 Gf 38.33N 42.46 E
Vangunu Island 208 Ge 8.40S 158.05 E
Van Horn 182 Ge 31.03N 104.50W
Vanick, Rio- 204 Fa 13.06S 52.52W
Vanier 180 Ha 76.00N 103.50W
Vanikolo 219c Bb 11.37S 166.58 E
Vanikolo Islands 208 Hf 11.37S 167.03 E
Vanimo 214 Ch 2.40S 141.18 E
Vanino 138 Jg 49.11N 140.19 E
Vankavesi 116 Jc 61.50N 23.50 E
Vanna 114 Ea 70.09N 19.51 E
Vännäs 114 Ee 63.55N 19.45 E
Vanne 124 Gf 48.12N 3.16 E
Vannes 122 Dg 47.40N 2.45W
Van Ninh 148 Lf 12.42N 109.14 E
Vannsjø 116 De 59.25N 10.50 E

Index Symbols

[1] Independent Nation; [2] State, Region; [3] District, County; [4] Municipality; [5] Colony, Dependency; Continent; Physical Region; Historical or Cultural Region; Mount, Mountain; Volcano; Hill; Mountains, Mountain Range; Hills, Escarpment; Plateau, Upland; Pass, Gap; Plain, Lowland; Delta; Salt Flat; Valley, Canyon; Crater, Cave; Karst Features; Depression; Polder; Desert, Dunes; Forest, Woods; Heath, Steppe; Oasis; Cape, Point; Coast, Beach; Cliff; Peninsula; Isthmus; Sandbank; Island; Atoll; Rock, Reef; Islands, Archipelago; Rocks, Reefs; Coral Reef; Well, Spring; Geyser; River, Stream; Waterfall, Rapids; River Mouth, Estuary; Lake; Salt Lake; Intermittent Lake; Reservoir; Swamp, Pond; Canal; Glacier; Ice Shelf, Pack Ice; Ocean; Sea; Gulf, Bay; Strait, Fjord; Lagoon; Bank; Seamount; Tablemount; Ridge; Shelf; Basin; Escarpment, Sea Scarp; Fracture; Trench, Abyss; National Park, Reserve; Point of Interest; Recreation Site; Cave, Cavern; Historic Site; Ruins; Wall, Walls; Church, Abbey; Temple; Scientific Station; Railway station; Airport; Port; Military installation; Lighthouse; Mine; Tunnel; Dam, Bridge

Name	Page	Grid	Lat	Long
Vanoise, Massif de la- [▲]	122	Mi	45.20N	6.40 E
Vanoua Lava, Ile- [⊕]	208	Hf	14.00S	167.30 E
Van Phong, Vung- [▨]	148	Lf	12.33N	109.18 E
Van Rees, Pegunungan- [▲]	150	Kg	2.35S	138.15 E
Vanrhynsdorp	172	Bf	31.36S	18.44 E
Vansbro	114	Df	60.31N	14.13 E
Vanse	116	Bf	58.07N	6.42 E
Vansittart [⊕]	180	Jc	65.50N	84.00W
Vantaa [S]	116	Kd	60.13N	24.59 E
Vanua Levu [⊕]	208	If	17.28S	177.03 E
Vanua Mbalavu [⊕]	216	Fc	17.14S	178.57W
Vanuatu [1]	210	Hf	16.00S	167.00 E
Vanua Vatu [⊕]	219d Cc		18.22S	179.16W
Van Wert	184	Ee	40.53N	84.36W
Van Wyksvlei	172	Cf	30.18S	21.49 E
Vao	219b Cf		22.40S	167.29 E
Vao, Nosy- [⊕]	172	Gc	17.30S	43.45 E
Vão das Almas	204	Ia	13.42S	47.27W
Vapnjarka	132	Fe	48.32N	28.46 E
Var [3]	122	Mk	43.30N	6.20 E
Var [S]	122	Nk	43.39N	7.12 E
Vara [S]	116	Ef	58.16N	12.57 E
Vara [S]	122	Df	44.09N	9.53 E
Varaita [S]	128	Bf	44.49N	7.36 E
Varakļāni/Varakļjany	114	Gh	56.36N	26.48 E
Varakļjany/Varakļāni	114	Gh	56.36N	26.48 E
Varaldsøy [⊕]	116	Ad	60.10N	6.00 E
Varale	166	Ed	9.40N	3.17W
Varallo	128	Ce	45.49N	8.15 E
Varämin	146	Ne	35.20N	51.39 E
Varangerfjorden [▨]	110	Ia	70.00N	30.00 E
Varangerhalvøya → Varanger Peninsula (EN) [▨]	110	Ia	70.25N	29.30 E
Varanger Peninsula (EN) = Varangerhalvøya [▨]	110	Ia	70.25N	29.30 E
Varano, Lago di- [▨]	128	Ji	41.53N	15.45 E
Varävi	146	Oi	27.25N	53.06 E
Varaždin	128	Kd	46.18N	16.20 E
Varazze	128	Cf	44.22N	8.34 E
Varberg	114	Ch	57.06N	12.15 E
Vardak [3]	144	Kc	34.15N	68.00 E
Vardar [S]	110	Ig	40.50N	22.50 E
Varde	114	Bi	55.38N	8.29 E
Varde Å [S]	116	Ci	55.35N	8.20 E
Vardhoúsia Óri [▲]	130	Fk	38.40N	22.10 E
Vardø [⊕]	116	Id	60.15N	20.20 E
Varel	120	Ec	53.24N	8.08 E
Varėna/Varena	114	Fi	54.15N	24.39 E
Varena/Varėna	114	Fi	54.15N	24.39 E
Värend [▨]	116	Fh	56.45N	14.55 E
Varengeville-sur-Mer	122	Ce	49.55N	0.59 E
Varenikovskaja	132	Jg	45.06N	37.37 E
Varenne [S]	122	Ff	48.24N	0.39W
Varennes-en-Argonne	122	Jf	49.14N	5.02 E
Varennes-sur-Allier	122	Jh	46.19N	3.24 E
Vareš	128	Mf	44.10N	18.20 E
Varese	128	Ce	45.48N	8.50 E
Varese, Lago di- [▨]	128	Ce	45.50N	8.45 E
Vårgårda	116	Ef	58.02N	12.48 E
Vargaši	136	Gd	55.23N	65.48 E
Vargem Grande	202	Jd	3.33S	43.56W
Varginha	202	Ih	21.33S	45.26W
Vargön	116	Ef	58.21N	12.22 E
Varhaug	116	Af	58.37N	5.39 E
Varjão	204	Hc	17.03S	49.37W
Varkaus	112	Ic	62.19N	27.55 E
Varkmö [⊕]	116	He	59.20N	18.35 E
Värmeln [▨]	116	Ee	59.30N	12.55 E
Värmland [2]	114	Cg	59.45N	13.15 E
Värmland [▨]	116	Ee	59.50N	13.05 E
Värmlandsnäs [▨]	116	Ee	59.00N	13.10 E
Varna	130	Kf	43.10N	27.35 E
Varna [Bul.]	112	Ig	43.13N	27.55 E
Varna [R.S.F.S.R.]	134	Jj	53.24N	60.58 E
Värnamo	114	Dh	57.11N	14.02 E
Varnenski Zaliv [▨]	130	Kf	43.11N	27.56 E
Varniai/Varnjaj	116	Ji	55.44N	22.17 E
Varnjaj/Varniai	116	Ji	55.44N	22.17 E
Varnsdorf	120	Oi	50.54N	14.38 E
Várpalota	120	Oi	47.12N	18.08 E
Vársec	130	Gf	43.12N	23.17 E
Varsinais-Suomi/Egentliga Finland	116	Jd	60.40N	22.30 E
Värska	116	Lg	57.58N	27.38 E
Vartašen	132	Oi	41.05N	47.29 E
Varto	146	Ic	39.10N	41.28 E
Vartofta	116	Ef	58.06N	13.38 E
Värtsilä	116	Nb	62.15N	30.40 E
Varzaneh	146	Of	32.25N	52.39 E
Varzaqān	146	Lc	38.31N	46.39 E
Varzarin, Küh-e- [▲]	144	Gc	33.24N	46.48 E
Várzea, Rio da- [S]	204	Fh	27.13S	53.19W
Várzea da Palma	204	Jc	17.36S	44.44W
Varzea Grande	202	Gg	15.39S	56.08W
Varzelândia	204	Jb	15.42S	44.02W
Varzi	128	Df	44.49N	9.12 E
Varzuga [S]	114	Ic	66.17N	36.50 E
Varzy	122	Jg	47.22N	3.23 E
Vas [2]	120	Mi	47.10N	16.45 E
Vasa/Vaasa	112	Ic	63.06N	21.36 E
Vasai (Bassein)	148	Ee	19.21N	72.48 E
Vasalemma/Vazalemma	116	Ke	59.15N	24.11 E
Vásárosnamény	120	Sh	48.08N	22.19 E
Vascão [S]	126	Eg	37.31N	7.31W
Vaşcau	130	Fc	46.28N	22.28 E
Vascoeuil	124	De	49.27N	1.23 E
Vascongadas / Euzkadi = Basque Provinces (EN) [▨]	126	Ja	43.00N	2.30W
Vascos, Montes- / Euskal Mendiak [▲]	126	Jb	42.50N	2.10W
Vasgün [S]	146	Oe	34.55N	56.30 E
Vasilevici	132	Fc	52.14N	29.47 E
Vasiliká	130	Gi	40.28N	23.08 E
Vasiljevka	132	If	47.23N	35.18 E
Vasilkov	136	De	50.12N	30.22 E
Vasilkovka	132	Je	48.13N	36.03 E
Vasiss	136	Hd	57.30N	74.55 E
Vasjugan [S]	138	De	59.10N	80.50 E
Vasjuganje [▨]	140	Jd	58.00N	77.00 E
Väska [S]	136	Ec	64.53N	45.47 E
Vaslui	130	Kc	46.38N	27.44 E
Vaslui [2]	130	Kc	46.38N	27.44 E
Vaslui [S]	130	Kc	46.41N	27.43 E
Vaslui [S]	130	Kc	46.37N	27.44 E
Vassako [S]	168	Bd	8.36N	19.07 E
Vassdalsegga [▲]	114	Bg	59.46N	7.07 E
Vassy	124	Bf	48.51N	0.40W
Västeras	112	Hd	59.37N	16.33 E
Västerbotten [2]	114	Dd	64.58N	17.28 E
Västerdaläven [S]	116	Eg	59.00N	13.05 E
Västergötland [▨]	116	Ee	58.07N	13.00 E
Västerhaninge	116	He	59.07N	18.06 E
Västernorrland [2]	114	De	63.00N	17.30 E
Västervik	114	Dh	57.45N	16.38 E
Västmanland [2]	114	Dg	59.45N	16.20 E
Västmanland [▨]	116	Fe	59.40N	15.15 E
Vasto	128	Ih	42.07N	14.42 E
Västra Silen [▨]	116	Ee	59.15N	12.10 E
Vatan	124	Cg	47.04N	1.49 E
Vatersay [⊕]	118	Fe	56.53N	7.28W
Vatican City (EN) = Città del Vaticano [1]	112	Hg	41.54N	12.27 E
Vaticano, Capo- [▶]	128	Ji	38.37N	15.50 E
Vatilau [⊕]	219a Ec		8.53S	160.01 E
Vatnajökull [⊙]	110	Ec	64.24N	16.48W
Vatneyri	114a Ab		65.35N	24.00W
Vatoa Island [⊕]	208	Jf	19.50S	178.13W
Vatomandry	172	Hc	19.20S	48.59 E
Vatra Dornei	130	Ib	47.21N	25.22 E
Vättern [▨]	110	Hd	58.25N	14.35 E
Vatu-i-Ra Channel [▨]	219d Bb		17.24S	178.29 E
Vatulele [⊕]	219d Ac		18.33S	177.38 E
Vatutino	132	Ge	49.02N	31.09 E
Vatu Vara [⊕]	216	Fc	17.28S	179.32W
Vaubecourt	124	Hf	48.56N	5.07 E
Vauclin, Pointe du- [▶]	197b Bb		14.34N	60.50W
Vaucluse [3]	122	Lj	44.00N	5.10 E
Vaucluse, Montagne du- [▲]	122	Lk	44.00N	5.22 E
Vaucouleurs	122	Lf	48.36N	5.40 E
Vaud [2]	128	Ad	46.35N	6.30 E
Vaudémont, Butte de- [▲]	122	Lf	48.30N	6.00 E
Vaughn	182	Fe	34.36N	105.13W
Vaupés [3]	202	Dc	1.00N	71.00W
Vaupés, Rio- [S]	198	Je	0.02N	67.16W
Vauvilliers	124	Ge	49.31N	4.17 E
Vaux [S]	124	Ge	49.31N	4.17 E
Vaux du Loir, Les- [S]	122	Gg	47.45N	0.25 E
Vaux-le-Vicomte [▲]	122	If	48.34N	2.43 E
Vavatenina	172	Hc	17.26S	49.12 E
Vava'u Group [▨]	208	Jf	18.40S	174.00W
Vava'u Island [⊕]	216	Ge	18.36S	174.00W
Vavoua	166	Dd	7.23N	6.29W
Vavuniya	148	Ae	8.45N	80.30 E
Vaxholm	116	He	59.24N	18.20 E
Växjö	112	Hd	56.53N	14.49 E
Vaza-Barris, Rio- [S]	202	Kf	11.10S	37.10W
Vazalemma/Vasalemma	116	Ke	59.15N	24.11 E
Vazante	202	Ig	18.00S	46.54W
Vazuza [S]	132	Ia	56.10N	34.35 E
Veadeiros, Chapada dos- [▲]	202	If	14.05S	47.28W
Vecht [S]	120	Cd	52.35N	6.05 E
Vechta	120	Ed	52.43N	8.17 E
Vechte [S]	120	Cd	52.35N	6.05 E
Vecpiebalga	116	Kh	56.57N	25.50 E
Vecsés	120	Pi	47.24N	19.17 E
Vedavågen	116	Ae	59.19N	5.12 E
Veddige	116	Eg	57.16N	12.19 E
Vedea	130	He	44.47N	24.37 E
Vedea [S]	130	If	43.53N	25.59 E
Vedeno	132	Oh	42.57N	46.05 E
Vedia	130	Bl	34.30S	61.32W
Vedrà, Isla- / Es Vedrà, Illa- [⊕]	126	Nf	38.52N	1.12 E
Veendam	120	Dc	53.06N	6.58 E
Veenendaal	124	Hb	52.02N	5.34 E
Veere	124	Fc	51.33N	3.40 E
Vega [⊕]	186	Ei	35.15N	102.26W
Vega Baja	197a Bb		18.25N	66.23W
Veganj [S]	128	Kh	43.50N	16.45 E
Vegår [S]	116	Cf	58.48N	8.47 E
Vegårshei	116	Cf	58.46N	8.48 E
Veghel	124	Hc	51.37N	5.32 E
Veglie	128	Lj	40.20N	17.58 E
Vegorritis, Limni- [▨]	130	Ei	40.45N	21.45 E
Vègre [S]	122	Fg	47.51N	0.14W
Vehmersalmi	116	Mb	62.46N	28.02 E
Vehmoor [▨]	124	If	48.54N	11.50 E
Veinge	116	Eh	56.34N	13.05 E
Veintecinco de Mayo [Arg.]	206	He	35.26S	60.10W
Veinticinco de Mayo [Ur.]	204	Dh	34.12S	56.22W
Veio [∵]	128	Gh	42.02N	12.23 E
Veisiejai/Vejsejaj	116	Jj	54.03N	23.46 E
Vejen	114	Bi	55.29N	9.09 E
Vejer de la Frontera	126	Bh	36.15N	5.58W
Vejle	114	Bi	55.42N	9.32 E
Vejle [2]	116	Ci	55.45N	9.20 E
Vejsejaj/Veisiejai	116	Jj	54.03N	23.46 E
Vel [S]	114	Kf	61.06N	42.10 E
Vela, Cabo de la- [▶]	194	Ga	12.13N	72.11W
Velas	128	Kh	42.58N	16.44 E
Velas, Cabo- [▶]	194	Hi	10.22N	85.53W
Velásquez	204	El	34.02S	54.17W
Velay, Plateaux du- [▲]	122	Jj	45.10N	3.50 E
Velaz	204	Ch	26.42S	58.40W
Velbaždski prohod [♦]	130	Fg	42.14N	22.28 E
Velbert	120	De	51.20N	7.02 E
Velddrif	172	Bf	32.47S	18.10 E
Velden am Wörthersee	128	Id	46.37N	14.03 E
Veldhoven	124	Hc	51.24N	5.24 E
Velebit [▲]	110	Hg	44.17N	15.12 E
Velebitski kanal [▨]	128	If	44.45N	14.50 E
Veleka [S]	130	Kg	42.04N	27.58 E
Velencei-tó [▨]	120	Oi	47.13N	18.36 E
Velenje	128	Jd	46.22N	15.07 E
Velestínon	130	Fj	39.23N	22.45 E
Veleta [▲]	126	Ig	37.04N	3.22W
Velez [S]	128	Lg	43.20N	18.00 E
Velež [▲]	128	Lg	43.20N	18.00 E
Vélez Blanco	126	Jg	37.41N	2.05W
Vélez de la Gomera, Peñón de- [▨]	126	Hi	35.11N	4.54W
Vélez-Málaga	126	Hh	36.47N	4.06W
Vélez Rubio	126	Jg	37.39N	2.04W
Velhas, Rio das- [S]	198	Lg	17.13S	44.49W
Velika [S]	120	Ve	51.49N	25.11 E
Velikaja-Gluša	114	Ie	62.17N	35.06 E
Velikaja Guba	138	Jg	45.29N	137.08 E
Velikaja Kema	132	Hf	47.09N	33.59 E
Velikaja Lepetiha	132	Ff	47.04N	29.52 E
Velikaja Mihajlovka	128	Je	45.13N	15.02 E
Velika Kapela [▲]	128	Je	45.11N	15.49 E
Velika Kladuša	130	Ee	44.20N	21.03 E
Velika Morava [S]	130	Ee	44.20N	21.05 E
Velika Plana	120	Sh	48.54N	22.30 E
Veliki Berezny	120	Ui	47.58N	24.04 E
Veliki Drvenik [⊕]	128	Kg	43.27N	16.09 E
Veliki Jastrebac [▲]	130	Ef	43.24N	21.26 E
Velikije Luki	112	Jd	56.20N	30.32 E
Veliki Mosty	120	Ue	50.10N	24.12 E
Veliki kanal [S]	130	Bd	45.52N	18.52 E
Veliki Ljuben	130	Tg	49.37N	23.45 E
Veliki Trnovac	130	Eg	42.29N	21.45 E
Veliki Ustjug	112	Kc	60.46N	46.20 E
Velikodolinskoje	130	Nc	46.20N	30.29 E
Veliko Gradište	130	Ee	44.46N	21.32 E
Veliko Tărnovo	112	Ig	43.04N	25.39 E
Veliko Tărnovo [2]	130	If	43.04N	25.39 E
Velikovisočnoje	136	Fb	67.16N	52.01 E
Veli Lošinj	128	If	44.31N	14.31 E
Velingara	166	Cc	13.09N	14.07W
Velingrad	130	Gg	42.01N	24.00 E
Velino [▲]	128	Hh	42.10N	13.23 E
Velino [S]	128	Gh	42.26N	12.43 E
Veliž	132	Gb	55.36N	31.12 E
Vel'ká Fatra [▲]	120	Ph	49.00N	19.05 E
Velké Meziříčí	120	Lg	49.21N	16.00 E
Vel'ký Krtíš	120	Ph	48.13N	19.20 E
Vella Lavella Island [⊕]	208	Ge	7.45S	156.40 E
Velletri	128	Gi	41.41N	12.47 E
Vellinge	116	Ei	55.28N	13.01 E
Vellore	142	Jh	14.26N	79.58 E
Velmerstot [▲]	124	Ee	51.50N	9.00 E
Velmo [S]	138	Ed	61.43N	92.25 E
Velopoúla [⊕]	130	Gm	36.55N	23.28 E
Vels	134	If	60.45N	58.45 E
Velsen-IJmuiden	124	Gb	52.28N	4.35 E
Velsk	136	Ec	61.05N	42.05 E
Veluwe [▨]	122	Lb	52.20N	5.50 E
Veluwemeer [▨]	124	Hb	52.23N	5.40 E
Velva	186	Fb	48.04N	100.56W
Velvendós	130	Fi	40.15N	22.04 E
Vema Seamount (EN) [⊠]	158	Hl	31.38S	8.19 E
Vemdalen	114	Ce	62.26N	13.52 E
Ven [⊕]	116	Ei	55.55N	12.40 E
Venable Ice Shelf [⊠]	222	Pf	73.03S	87.20W
Venado	192	If	22.56N	101.05W
Venado, Cerro- [▲]	196	Ei	6.17N	62.45W
Venado Tuerto	206	Md	33.45S	61.58W
Venafro	128	Ii	41.29N	14.02 E
Venamo, Rio- [S]	196	Fi	6.43N	61.07W
Vence	122	Nk	43.43N	7.07 E
Venceslau Brás	204	Hf	23.51S	49.48W
Venda [▨]	172	Ed	22.35S	30.45 E
Venda Nova	202	Ih	19.45S	43.50W
Vendas Novas	126	Df	38.41N	8.27W
Vendée [3]	122	Fh	46.40N	1.20W
Vendée [⊠]	122	Fh	46.40N	1.10W
Vendée [S]	122	Fh	46.19N	0.58W
Vendée, Bocage- [▨]	122	Fh	46.50N	1.20W
Vendéenne, Plaine- [▨]	122	Fh	46.30N	1.20W
Vendel	116	Gd	60.10N	17.36 E
Vendeuvre-sur-Barse	122	Kf	48.14N	4.29 E
Vendôme	122	Hg	47.48N	1.04 E
Vendrell	126	Nc	41.13N	1.32 E
Vendsyssel [▨]	116	Cf	57.20N	10.00 E
Venetia (EN) = Veneto [2]	128	Gd	45.30N	12.00 E
Venétiko [Grc.] [⊕]	130	Ei	40.05N	22.09 E
Venétiko [Grc.] [⊕]	130	Em	36.42N	21.53 E
Veneto = Venetia (EN) [2]	128	Gd	45.30N	12.00 E
Venev	132	Kb	54.22N	38.18 E
Venezia = Venice (EN)	112	Hf	45.27N	12.21 E
Venezia, Golfo di- = Venice, Gulf of- [▨]	110	Hf	45.15N	13.00 E
Venezia-Lido	128	Ge	45.28N	12.22 E
Venezia-Marghera	128	Ge	45.28N	12.44 E
Venezia-Mestre	128	Ge	45.29N	12.14 E
Venezuela [1]	200	Je	8.00N	65.00W
Venezuela, Gulf of- (EN) = Venezuela, Golfo de- [▨]	198	Id	11.30N	71.00W
Venezuela, Golfo de- [▨]	198	Id	11.30N	71.00W
Venezuelan Basin (EN) [⊠]	124	Mh	15.00N	68.00W
Vengerovo	138	Ce	55.41N	76.55 E
Veniaminof, Mount- [▲]	178	Em	56.13N	159.18W
Venice	184	Fl	27.06N	82.27W
Venice (EN) = Venezia	112	Hf	45.27N	12.21 E
Venice, Gulf of- (EN) = Venezia, Golfo di- [▨]	110	Hf	45.15N	13.00 E
Véniissieux	124	Ki	45.41N	4.53 E
Venjan	116	Ec	60.57N	13.55 E
Venjansjön [S]	116	Ed	60.55N	13.55 E
Venlo	122	Mc	51.24N	6.10 E
Venlock River [S]	212	Ib	12.15S	142.00 E
Vennesla	114	Bg	58.17N	7.59 E
Venosa	128	Ji	40.58N	15.49 E
Venosta, Val- / Vintschgau [▨]	128	Ed	46.40N	10.35 E
Venray	122	Lc	51.32N	5.59 E
Vent, Canal du- = Windward Passage (EN) [▨]	194	Lh	20.00N	73.50W
Vent, Iles du- = Windward Islands (EN) [▨]	208	Mf	17.30S	149.30W
Venta [S]	114	Eh	57.23N	21.32 E
Venta de Baños	126	Hc	41.55N	4.30W
Ventana, Cerro- [▲]	192	Fe	24.15N	106.20W
Ventersdorp	172	De	26.17S	26.48 E
Venterstad	172	Df	30.47S	25.48 E
Venticinco de Diciembre	204	Dg	24.42S	56.33W
Ventimiglia	128	Bg	43.47N	7.36 E
Ventnor	124	Ad	50.36N	1.11W
Ventotene [⊕]	128	Hj	40.45N	13.25 E
Ventspils	136	Cd	57.24N	21.33 E
Ventuari, Rio- [S]	198	Je	3.58N	67.02W
Ventura	182	De	34.17N	119.18W
Vénus, Pointe- [▶]	221e Fc		17.29S	149.29W
Venus Bay [▨]	212	Bg	38.40S	145.45 E
Venustiano Carranza	192	Mi	16.21N	92.33W
Venustiano Carranza, Presa- [▨]	192	Id	27.30N	100.40W
Ver [S]	124	Bc	51.31N	0.27W
Vera [Arg.]	206	Hc	29.28S	60.13W
Vera [Sp.]	126	Jg	37.15N	1.52W
Verá, Laguna- [▨]	204	Dh	26.05S	57.39W
Veracruz [2]	190	Ge	20.00N	96.40W
Veracruz Llave	176	Jh	19.12N	96.08W
Veraguas [3]	194	Gj	8.30N	81.00W
Verával	148	Ed	20.54N	70.22 E
Vera y Pintado	204	Bj	30.09S	60.21W
Verbania	128	Ce	45.56N	8.33 E
Verbano → Maggiore, Lago- [▨]	128	Ce	45.59N	8.40 E
Verbovski	114	Sh	55.29N	41.59 E
Vercelli	128	Ce	45.19N	8.25 E
Vercors [▲]	122	Lj	44.57N	5.25 E
Verdalsøra	114	Ce	63.48N	11.29 E
Verde, Cape- [S]	194	Jb	22.50N	74.52W
Verde, Cay- [⊕]	194	Jb	22.02N	75.12W
Verde, Costa- [▨]	126	Ga	43.40N	5.00W
Verde, Rio- [Braz.] [S]	198	Kh	23.09S	57.37W
Verde, Rio- [Braz.] [S]	202	Gf	11.54S	55.50W
Verde, Rio- [Braz.] [S]	202	Hg	19.11S	50.44W
Verde, Rio- [Braz.] [S]	202	Hh	21.12S	51.53W
Verde, Rio- [Braz.] [S]	204	Hb	15.07S	48.40W
Verde, Rio- [Braz.] [S]	204	Ca	13.33S	58.01W
Verde, Rio- [Mex.] [S]	204	Hb	19.50S	49.45W
Verde, Rio- [Mex.] [S]	192	Jj	21.37N	99.15W
Verde, Rio- [S.Amer.] [S]	192	Hg	20.42N	103.14W
Verde Grande, Rio- [S]	204	Kb	14.35S	43.53W
Verden (Aller)	120	Fd	52.55N	9.14 E
Verdigris River [S]	186	Ie	35.48N	95.18W
Verdinho, Rio- [S]	204	Gc	18.23S	50.27W
Verdon [S]	122	Lk	43.43N	5.46 E
Verdon-sur-Mer, Le-	122	Ei	45.33N	1.04W
Verdun [Fr.]	122	Le	49.10N	5.23 E
Verdun [Que.-Can.]	184	Kc	45.28N	73.34W
Verdura [S]	128	Hm	37.28N	13.12 E
Vereeniging	172	De	26.38S	27.57 E
Vereščagino	136	Fd	58.05N	54.40 E
Verga, Cap- [▶]	166	Cc	10.12N	14.27W
Vergara [Arg.]	204	Dl	35.23S	57.48W
Vergara [Ur.]	204	Ea	32.56S	53.57W
Vergara / Bergara	126	Ja	43.07N	2.25W
Vergato	128	Ff	44.17N	11.07 E
Verhnedneprovsk	132	Ie	48.39N	34.21 E
Verhnedneprovski	132	Nb	55.01N	33.21 E
Verhnedvinsk	114	Gi	55.46N	27.59 E
Verheimbatsk	138	Dd	63.20N	88.00 E
Verhne-Karabahski kanal	132	Qj	39.44N	47.57 E
Verhnespasskoje	114	Kg	58.45N	45.28 E
Verhnetulomski	114	Kg	68.36N	31.48 E
Verhnetulomskoje vodohranilišče [▨]	114	Hb	68.35N	31.00 E
Verhneuralsk	134	Ij	53.53N	59.13 E
Verhnevilujsk	138	Hd	63.20N	120.25 E
Verhni At-Urjah	138	Kd	62.38N	150.03 E
Verhni Avzjan	134	Hj	53.33N	57.33 E
Verhni Kujto, ozero- [▨]	114	Hj	65.00N	30.40 E
Verhni Most	116	Mg	57.29N	29.00 E
Verhni Tagil	134	Jh	57.22N	60.01 E
Verhni Uslon	114	Li	55.47N	48.58 E
Verhnije Sinevidnoje	120	Tg	49.02N	23.36 E
Verhojansk	142	Pc	67.35N	133.27 E
Verhojanski hrebet = Verhoyansk Mountains (EN) [▲]	140	Oc	67.00N	129.00 E
Verhotur'e	134	Jh	58.52N	60.48 E
Verhovceva	132	Ie	48.31N	34.12 E
Verhovina	130	Ib	48.08N	24.48 E
Verhovje	132	Kc	52.49N	37.14 E
Verhoyansk Mountains (EN) = Verhojanski hrebet [▲]	140	Oc	67.00N	129.00 E
Verin	126	Ec	41.56N	7.26W
Veriora	116	Lg	57.56N	27.21 E
Veríssimo, Rio- [S]	204	Hd	18.23S	48.20W
Veríssimo, Serra do- [▲]	204	Hd	19.33S	48.25W
Vermand	124	Fe	49.52N	3.09 E
Vermandois [▨]	122	Je	50.00N	3.20 E
Vermeille, Côte- [▨]	122	Jl	42.30N	3.05 E
Vermelho, Rio- [Braz.] [S]	204	Ib	14.26S	46.26W
Vermelho, Rio- [Braz.] [S]	204	Gb	14.54S	51.06W
Vermelho, Rio- [Braz.] [S]	204	Ed	19.36S	53.58W
Vermenton	122	Jg	47.40N	3.44 E
Vermilion Bay	180	Ig	49.51N	93.24W
Vermilion Cliffs [▶]	188	Ih	37.10N	112.35W
Vermilion Lake	186	Jc	47.53N	92.25W
Vermilion River [S]	184	Gb	46.16N	81.41W
Vermillion	186	He	42.47N	96.56W
Vermillion River [S]	186	He	42.44N	96.53W
Vermillon, Rivière- [S]	184	Kc	47.38N	72.59W
Vérmion Óros [▲]	130	Ei	40.30N	22.00 E
Vermont [2]	182	Mc	43.50N	72.45W
Vernal	182	Fc	40.27N	109.32W
Verneuil-sur-Avre	122	Gf	48.44N	0.56 E
Vernon [B.C.-Can.]	180	Ff	50.16N	119.16W
Vernon [Fr.]	122	He	49.05N	1.29 E
Vernon [Tx.-U.S.]	182	He	34.09N	99.17W
Vernon Óros [▲]	130	Ei	40.39N	21.22 E
Vernou	197e Ab		16.11N	61.39W
Verny	124	Ie	49.01N	6.12 E
Vero [S]	126	Mb	42.00N	0.10 E
Vero Beach	182	Kf	27.38N	80.24W
Véroia	130	Fi	40.31N	22.12 E
Verona	112	Hf	45.27N	11.00 E
Verónica	206	Ie	35.22S	57.20W
Versailles [Fr.]	122	If	48.48N	2.08 E
Versailles [In.-U.S.]	184	Ef	39.04N	85.15W
Versilia [▨]	128	Eg	43.56N	10.15 E
Veršino-Darasunski	138	Gf	52.18N	115.32 E
Veršino-Šahtaminski	138	Gf	51.16N	117.55 E
Versmold	124	Kb	52.03N	8.09 E
Vert, Cap- = Vert, Cape- (EN) [▶]	158	Fg	14.43N	17.30W
Vert, Cape- (EN) = Vert, Cap- [▶]	158	Fg	14.43N	17.30W
Vertentes, Serra das- [▲]	204	Je	20.56S	44.00W
Vértes [▲]	120	Oi	47.25N	18.20 E
Vertientes	194	Hc	21.16N	78.09W
Vertiskos Óros [▲]	130	Gi	40.50N	23.19 E
Verviers	122	Ld	50.36N	5.52 E
Vervins	124	Fe	49.50N	3.54 E
Vesanto	116	Lb	62.56N	26.25 E
Vescovato	122a Ba		42.29N	9.26 E
Vesder/Vesdre [S]	124	Kd	50.37N	5.37 E
Vesdre/Vesder [S]	124	Kd	50.37N	5.37 E
Veselí nad Lužnicí	120	Kg	49.11N	14.43 E
Veselovskoje vodohranilišče [▨]	132	Lf	47.00N	41.15 E
Vešenskaja	136	Ef	49.38N	41.46 E
Vesgre [S]	124	Df	48.53N	1.28 E
Vesijärvi [▨]	116	Kc	61.05N	25.30 E
Vesjegonsk	114	Ng	58.41N	37.16 E
Veškajma	114	Li	54.03N	47.08 E
Vesljana [S]	122	Je	49.23N	3.28 E
Vesoul	134	Gd	60.20N	54.03 E
Vessigebro	122	Mg	47.38N	6.10 E
Vest-Agder [2]	116	Eh	56.59N	12.39 E
Vestbygd	114	Bg	58.30N	7.10 E
Vesterålen [▨]	106	Bb	58.30N	6.35 E
Vesterhavet [▨]	110	Hb	68.45N	15.00 E
Vesterhavn	116	Bi	55.50N	7.30 E
Vestfjorden [▨]	116	Dg	57.08N	10.56 E
Vestfold [2]	110	Hb	68.35N	14.30 E
Vestfonna [⊙]	114	Cg	59.15N	10.10 E
Vestgrønland = West Greenland (EN) [2]	179	Oc	79.58N	20.15 E
Vestía	179	He	69.00N	49.30W
Vestmannaeyjar	204	Ge	20.23S	51.25W
Vestnes	114a Bc		63.26N	20.16W
Vestre Jakobselv	116	Eg	62.38N	7.06 E
Vestsjælland [2]	114	Ga	70.07N	29.25 E
Vestvågøy [⊕]	116	Di	55.30N	11.30 E
Vésubie [S]	116	Gb	68.15N	13.50 E
Vesuvio = Vesuvius (EN) [▲]	122	Nk	43.57N	7.12 E
Vesuvius (EN) = Vesuvio [▲]	110	Hg	40.49N	14.26 E
Veszprém	110	Hg	40.49N	14.26 E
Veszprém [2]	120	Ni	47.06N	17.55 E
Vésztő	120	Ni	47.10N	17.40 E
Vétaoundé, Ile- [⊕]	120	Rj	46.55N	21.16 E
Vetauua [⊕]	208	Hf	13.15S	167.38 E
Vété, Pointe- [▶]	219d Ca		13.25S	166.41 E
Vetka	219b Ca		13.27S	166.41 E
Vetlanda	132	Gc	52.34N	31.13 E
Vetljanka	114	Dh	57.26N	15.04 E
Vetluga	114	Mj	52.52N	51.09 E
Vetluga [S]	114	Kh	57.51N	45.46 E
Vetluga [S]	114	Kh	56.18N	46.24 E
Vetlužski [R.S.F.S.R.]	114	Kh	57.11N	45.07 E
Vetlužski [R.S.F.S.R.]	114	Kh	58.26N	45.28 E
Vetreny	138	Jd	61.43N	149.40 E
Vetrino	114	Hi	55.25N	28.31 E
Vetschau/Wětošow	120	Ke	51.47N	14.04 E
Vettore [▲]	128	Hh	42.49N	13.16 E
Vežen [▲]	130	Hg	42.45N	24.24 E
Vezere [S]	122	Gj	44.53N	0.53 E
Vezirköprü	146	Fb	41.09N	35.28 E
Viadana	128	Ef	44.56N	10.31 E
Viale	204	Bj	31.53S	60.01W
Viana	202	Jd	3.13S	45.00W
Viana del Bollo	126	Eb	42.11N	7.06W
Viana do Alentejo	126	Ef	38.20N	8.00W

Index Symbols

[1] Independent Nation	▲ Historical or Cultural Region	◢ Pass, Gap	∿ Depression
[2] State, Region	▲ Mount, Mountain	▬ Plain, Lowland	▬ Polder
[3] District, County	▲ Volcano	▬ Delta	▬ Desert, Dunes
[4] Municipality	▲ Hill	▬ Salt Flat	≋ Forest, Woods
[5] Colony, Dependency	▲ Mountains, Mountain Range	▬ Valley, Canyon	≋ Heath, Steppe
■ Continent	▲ Hills, Escarpment	▲ Crater, Cave	▲ Oasis
⊠ Physical Region	▲ Plateau, Upland	⊠ Karst Features	▶ Cape, Point

▨ Coast, Beach	▲ Rock, Reef	↯ Waterfall, Rapids	▬ Canal
▬ Cliff	▬ Islands, Archipelago	▬ River Mouth, Estuary	⊙ Glacier
▶ Peninsula	▬ Rocks, Reefs	▬ Lake	▬ Ice Shelf, Pack Ice
▬ Isthmus	▬ Coral Reef	▬ Salt Lake	▬ Ocean
▬ Sandbank	▬ Well, Spring	▬ Intermittent Lake	▬ Sea
▬ Island	▬ Geyser	▬ Reservoir	▬ Gulf, Bay
⊙ Atoll	▬ River, Stream	▬ Swamp, Pond	▬ Strait, Fjord

▬ Lagoon	▲ Escarpment, Sea Scarp	▲ Historic Site	⊕ Airport
▬ Bank	▬ Fracture	▲ Ruins	⊠ Port
⊠ Trench, Abyss	▬ National Park, Reserve	▬ Wall, Walls	⊠ Military installation
▬ Tablemount	▬ Point of Interest	▬ Church, Abbey	⊠ Lighthouse
▬ Ridge	▬ Recreation Site	▬ Temple	▬ Mine
▬ Shelf	▬ Scientific Station	▬ Tunnel	
▬ Basin	▬ Cave, Cavern	▬ Railway station	▬ Dam, Bridge

Viana do Castelo 126 Dc 41.42N 8.50W
Viana do Castelo [2] 126 Dc 41.55N 8.25W
Vianden 124 Ie 49.55N 6.16 E
Vianen 124 Hb 52.00N 5.05 E
Viangchan (Vientiane) 142 Mh 17.58N 102.36 E
Vianópolis 204 Hc 16.45 S 48.32W
Viar 126 Gg 37.36N 5.50W
Viareggio 128 Eg 43.52N 10.14 E
Viarmes 124 Ee 49.08N 2.22 E
Viaur 122 Hj 44.08N 1.58 E
Viborg 114 Bh 56.26N 9.24 E
Viborg [2] 116 Ch 56.30N 9.30 E
Vibo Valentia 128 Kl 38.40N 16.06 E
Vic 126 Oc 41.56N 2.15 E
Vicari 128 Hm 37.49N 13.34 E
Vicecomodoro Marambio 222 Re 64.16 S 56.44W
Vicente Guerrero 190 Dd 23.45N 103.59W
Vicenza 128 Fe 45.33N 11.33 E
Vichada [3] 202 Ec 5.00N 69.30W
Vichada, Rio- 198 Je 4.55N 67.50W
Vichadero 204 Ej 31.48 S 54.43W
Vichy 122 Jh 46.07N 3.25 E
Vicksburg 182 Ie 32.14N 90.56W
Vico, Lago di- 128 Gh 42.19N 12.10 E
Vic-sur-Aisne 124 Fe 49.24N 3.07 E
Vic-sur-Cère 122 Ij 44.59N 2.37 E
Victor Bay 222 Ie 66.20 S 136.30 E
Victor Harbour 212 Hg 35.34 S 138.37 E
Victoria [2] 212 Ig 38.00 S 145.00 E
Victoria 174 Hb 71.00N 114.00W
Victoria [Arg.] 206 Hd 32.37 S 60.10W
Victoria [B.C.-Can.] 176 Ge 48.25N 123.22W
Victoria [Cam.] 166 Ge 4.01N 9.12 E
Victoria [Chile] 206 Fe 38.13 S 72.20W
Victoria [Gren.] 196 Ff 12.12N 61.42W
Victoria [Mala.] 150 Ge 5.17N 115.15 E
Victoria [Malta] 128 In 36.02N 14.14 E
Victoria [Rom.] 130 Hd 45.44N 24.41 E
Victoria [Sey.] 160 Mi 4.38 S 55.27 E
Victoria [Tx.-U.S.] 176 Jg 28.48N 97.00W
Victoria/Ying zhan 142 Ng 22.17N 114.09 E
Victoria, Lake- [Afr.] 158 Ki 1.00 S 33.00 E
Victoria, Lake- [Austl.] 212 If 34.00 S 141.15 E
Victoria, Mount- [Bur.] 140 Lg 21.14N 93.55 E
Victoria, Mount- [Pap.N.Gui.] 208 Fe 8.53 S 147.33 E
Victoria, Sierra de la- 204 Fg 25.55 S 54.00W
Victoria and Albert Mountains 180 Ka 79.00N 75.00W
Victoria de Durango 176 Ig 24.02N 104.40W
Victoria de las Tunas 190 Id 20.58N 76.57W
Victoria Falls 160 Jj 17.56 S 25.50 E
Victoria Falls 158 Jj 17.55 S 25.21 E
Victoria Fjord 179 Hb 82.20N 48.00W
Victoria Land (EN) 222 Jf 75.00 S 159.00 E
Victoria Nile 158 Kh 2.14N 31.26 E
Victoria Peak [B.C.-Can.] 188 Ba 50.03N 126.06W
Victoria Peak [Blz.] 194 Ce 16.48N 88.37W
Victoria River 208 Df 15.12 S 129.43 E
Victoria River Downs 212 Gc 16.24 S 131.00 E
Victoria Strait 180 Hc 69.30N 100.00W
Victoriaville 180 Kg 46.03N 71.58W
Victoria West 172 Cf 31.25 S 23.04 E
Victorville 188 Gi 34.32N 117.18W
Victory, Mount- 212 Ja 9.10 S 149.05 E
Vičuga 136 Ed 57.15N 42.00 E
Vicuña 206 Fc 29.59 S 70.44W
Vicuña Mackenna 206 Hd 33.54 S 64.23W
Vidå 116 Cj 54.58N 8.41 E
Vidal 188 Hi 34.11N 114.34W
Vidalia 186 Kk 31.34N 91.26W
Videbæk 116 Ch 56.05N 8.38 E
Videira 206 Jc 27.00 S 51.08W
Videla 204 Bj 30.56 S 60.39W
Videle 130 Ie 44.17N 25.31 E
Vidigueira 126 Ef 38.13N 7.48W
Vidin 130 Ff 43.59N 22.52 E
Vidin [2] 130 Ff 43.59N 22.52 E
Vidisha 148 Fd 23.42N 77.47 E
Vidlič 130 Ff 43.08N 22.47 E
Vidojevica 130 Ef 43.10N 21.32 E
Vidöstern 116 Fg 57.04N 14.01 E
Vidourle 122 Kk 43.32N 4.08 E
Vidra [Rom.] 130 Jd 45.55N 26.54 E
Vidra [Rom.] 130 Je 44.16N 26.09 E
Vidsel 114 Ed 65.49N 20.31 E
Viduša 128 Mh 42.54N 18.18 E
Vidzeme 116 Kg 57.10N 26.00 E
Vidzemes Augstiene / Vidzemskaja vozvyšennost 116 Kh 56.45N 26.00 E
Vidzemskaja vozvyšennost / Vidzemes Augstiene 116 Kh 56.45N 26.00 E
Vidzy 116 Li 55.23N 26.47 E
Vie 124 Be 49.09N 0.04W
Viechtach 120 Ig 49.05N 12.53 E
Viedma 200 Jj 40.50 S 63.00W
Viedma, Lago- 198 Ij 49.35 S 72.35W
Vieille Case 197g Ba 15.36N 61.24W
Vieja, Sierra- 186 Dk 30.30N 104.40W
Viejo, Cerro- 190 Bb 30.20N 112.15W
Viekšniai/Viekšnjai 116 Jh 56.14N 22.28 E
Viekšnjai/Viekšniai 116 Jh 56.14N 22.28 E
Vielha / Viella 126 Mb 42.42N 0.48 E
Viella / Vielha 126 Mb 42.42N 0.48 E
Vielsalm 124 Hd 50.17N 5.55 E
Viels-Maisons 124 Ff 48.54N 3.24 E
Vienna [Mo.-U.S.] 186 Kg 38.11N 91.57W
Vienna [W.V.-U.S.] 184 Gf 39.20N 81.33W
Vienna (EN) = Wien 112 Hf 48.12N 16.22 E
Vienna Woods (EN) = Wienerwald 128 Jb 48.10N 16.00 E
Vienne 122 Ki 45.31N 4.52 E
Vienne [3] 122 Gh 46.30N 0.30 E
Vienne 110 Gf 47.13N 0.05 E
Vientiane → Viangchan 142 Mh 17.58N 102.36 E
Vientos, Paso de los- = Windward Passage (EN) 174 Lh 20.00N 73.50W
Vieques, Isla de- 190 Ke 18.08N 65.25W
Vieques, Pasaje de- 197a Cb 18.08N 65.40W
Vieques, Sonda de- 197a Cb 18.17N 65.25W
Vierge Point 197k Bb 13.49N 60.53W
Viernheim 124 Ke 49.32N 8.35 E
Viersen 120 Ce 51.15N 6.23 E
Vierville-sur-Mer 124 Be 49.22N 0.54W
Vierwaldstätter See = Lucerne, Lake- (EN) 128 Cc 47.00N 8.30 E
Vierzon 122 Ig 47.13N 2.05 E
Viesca 192 He 25.21N 102.48W
Viesite/Viesīte 116 Kh 56.20N 25.38 E
Viesīte/Viesite 116 Kh 56.20N 25.38 E
Vieste 128 Ki 41.53N 16.10 E
Viet Nam = Vietnam (EN) [1] 142 Mh 13.00N 108.00 E
Vietnam (EN) = Viet Nam [1] 142 Mh 13.00N 108.00 E
Viet Tri 148 Ld 21.18N 105.26 E
Vieux Fort 196 Ff 13.44N 60.57W
Vieux-Fort, Pointe du- 197e Ac 15.57N 61.43W
Vieux Fort Bay 197k Bb 13.44N 60.58W
Vieux-Habitants 197e Ab 16.04N 61.46W
Vievis/Vevis 116 Kj 54.45N 24.58 E
Viga 114 Kg 59.15N 43.42 E
Vigala 116 Kf 58.43N 24.22 E
Vigan 150 Hc 17.34N 120.23 E
Vigan, Le- 122 Jk 43.59N 3.36 E
Vigeland 116 Bf 58.05N 7.18 E
Vigevano 128 Ce 45.19N 8.51 E
Vigia 202 Id 0.48 S 48.08W
Vigía Chico 192 Ph 19.46N 87.35W
Vignacourt 124 Ed 50.01N 2.12 E
Vignemale 126 Lb 42.46N 0.08W
Vigneulles-lès-Hattonchâtel 124 Hf 48.59N 5.43 E
Vignoble 122 Lh 46.50N 5.30 E
Vignola 128 Ef 44.29N 11.00 E
Vigny 124 De 49.05N 1.56 E
Vigo 112 Fg 42.14N 8.43W
Vigo, Ria de- 126 Db 42.15N 8.45W
Vigra 116 Bb 62.30N 6.05 E
Vigrestad 116 Af 58.34N 5.42 E
Vihanti 114 Fd 64.30N 25.00 E
Vihiers 122 Fg 47.09N 0.32W
Vihorevka 138 Fe 56.12N 101.09 E
Vihorlat 120 Sh 48.55N 22.10 E
Vihren 130 Gh 41.46N 23.24 E
Vihti 114 Ff 60.25N 24.20 E
Viiala 116 Jc 61.13N 23.47 E
Viinijärvi 116 Mb 62.39N 29.14 E
Viinijärvi 116 Mb 62.45N 29.15 E
Viitasaari 114 Fe 63.04N 25.52 E
Viivikonna/Vijvikonna 116 Le 59.14N 27.41 E
Vijayawāda 142 Kh 16.31N 80.37 E
Vijvikonna/Viivikonna 116 Le 59.14N 27.41 E
Vik 114a Bc 63.25N 19.01W
Vika 116 Fd 60.57N 14.27 E
Vikarbyn 116 Fd 60.55N 15.01 E
Vikbolandet 116 Gf 58.30N 16.40 E
Viken 116 Eh 56.09N 12.34 E
Viken 116 Ff 58.40N 14.20 E
Vikenara Point 219a Dc 8.34 S 159.53 E
Vikersund 116 De 59.59N 10.02 E
Vikingbanken 118 Pa 60.20N 2.30 E
Vikmanshyttan 116 Fd 60.17N 15.49 E
Vikna 114 Cd 64.53N 10.58 E
Vikna 114 Cd 64.54N 11.00 E
Viksoyri 114 Bf 61.05N 6.34 E
Viktorija 179 Pb 80.10N 36.45 E
Vila da Maganja 172 Fc 17.18 S 37.31 E
Vila de Rei 126 De 39.40N 8.09W
Vila do Bispo 126 Dg 37.05N 8.55W
Vila do Conde 126 Dc 41.21N 8.45W
Vila do Porto 162 Bb 36.56N 25.09W
Vila Flor 126 Ec 41.18N 7.09W
Vilafranca del Maestrat / Villafranca del Cid 126 Ld 40.25N 0.15W
Vilafranca del Penedès/ Villafranca del Panadés 126 Nc 41.21N 1.42 E
Vila Franca de Xira 126 Df 38.57N 8.59W
Vila Franca do Campo 162 Bb 37.43N 25.26W
Vila Franca do Save 172 Ed 21.09 S 34.32 E
Vila Gamito 172 Eb 14.10 S 32.59 E
Vilagarcía de Arousa / Villagarcía de Arosa 126 Db 42.36N 8.45W
Vila Gouveia 172 Ec 18.03 S 33.11 E
Vilaine 122 Dg 47.23N 2.27W
Viļaka/Viljaka 114 Gh 57.14N 27.46 E
Vila Machado 172 Ec 19.17 S 34.12 E
Vilanculos 160 Kk 22.00 S 35.19 E
Viļani/Viljani 114 Gh 56.33N 26.59 E
Vila Nova da Cerveira 126 Dc 41.56N 8.45W
Vila Nova de Famalicão 126 Dc 41.25N 8.32W
Vila Nova de Foz Côa 126 Ec 41.05N 7.12W
Vila Nova de Gaia 126 Dc 41.08N 8.37W
Vilanova i la Geltrú/ Villanueva y Geltrú 126 Nc 41.14N 1.44 E
Vila Paiva de Andrada 172 Ec 18.41 S 34.04 E
Vila Pouca de Aguiar 126 Ec 41.30N 7.39W
Vila Real 126 Ec 41.18N 7.45W
Vila Real [2] 126 Ec 41.35N 7.35W
Vila-Real / Villarreal de los Infantes 126 Le 39.56N 0.06W
Vila Real de Santo António 126 Eg 37.12N 7.25W
Vilar Formoso 126 Fd 40.37N 6.50W
Vila Velha 202 Jh 20.20 S 40.17W
Vila Velha de Ródão 126 Ee 39.40N 7.42W
Vila Viçosa 126 Ef 38.47N 7.25W
Vilcabamba 202 Df 13.05 S 73.01W
Vilcabamba, Cordillera- 202 Df 13.00 S 73.00W
Vîlcea [2] 130 He 45.10N 24.10 E
Vilches 126 If 38.12N 3.30W
Vildbjerg 116 Ch 56.12N 8.46 E
Viled 114 Lf 61.22N 47.15 E
Vilejka 136 Ce 54.30N 26.53 E
Vilhelmina 114 Dd 64.37N 16.39 E
Vilhena 200 Jg 12.43 S 60.07W
Vilija 132 Db 54.55N 25.40 E
Viljaka/Viļaka 114 Gh 57.14N 27.46 E
Viljandi 136 Cd 58.22N 25.35 E
Viljany/Viļani 114 Gh 56.33N 26.59 E
Viljuj 140 Oc 64.24N 126.26 E
Viljujsk 138 Hd 63.40N 121.33 E
Viljujskoje plato = Vilyui Range (EN) 140 Mc 66.00N 108.00 E
Viljujskoje vodohranilišče 138 Gd 62.30N 111.00 E
Vilkaviškis 114 Fi 54.43N 23.02 E
Vilkickogo, ostrov- [R.S.F.S.R.] 138 Cb 73.30N 76.00 E
Vilkickogo, ostrov- [R.S.F.S.R.] 138 Ka 75.40N 152.30 E
Vilkickogo, proliv- = Vilkitski Strait (EN) 140 Mb 77.55N 103.00 E
Vilkija 114 Fi 55.03N 23.35 E
Vilkitski Strait (EN) = Vilkickogo, proliv- 140 Mb 77.55N 103.00 E
Vilkovo 132 Fg 45.23N 29.35 E
Villa Aberastain 206 Gd 31.39 S 68.35W
Villa Ahumada 190 Cb 30.37N 106.31W
Villa Altagracia 194 Ld 18.40N 70.10W
Villa Ana 204 Ci 28.29 S 59.37W
Villa Ángela 206 Hc 27.35 S 60.43W
Villa Atuel 206 Gd 34.50 S 67.54W
Villa Berthet 204 Bh 27.17 S 60.25W
Villablino 126 Fb 42.56N 6.19W
Villa Bruzual 202 Eb 9.20N 69.06W
Villa Cañas 204 Bk 34.00 S 61.36W
Villacañas 126 Ie 39.38N 3.20W
Villacarrillo 126 If 38.07N 3.05W
Villacastín 126 Hd 40.47N 4.25W
Villach 128 Hd 46.36N 13.50 E
Villacidro 128 Ck 39.27N 8.44 E
Villa Clara 204 Cj 31.50 S 58.49W
Villaclara [3] 194 Hb 22.30N 80.00W
Villa Constitución [Arg.] 206 Hd 33.14 S 60.20W
Villa Constitución [Mex.] 190 Bc 25.09N 111.43W
Villa Coronado 192 Gd 26.45N 105.10W
Villada 126 Hb 42.15N 4.58W
Villa de Arriaga 192 Ig 21.54N 101.23W
Villa de Cos 192 Hf 23.17N 102.21W
Villa de Cura 196 Cg 10.02N 67.29W
Villa de Maria 206 Hc 29.54 S 63.43W
Villa de Reyes 192 Ig 21.48N 100.56W
Villa de San Antonio 194 Df 14.16N 87.36W
Villadiego 126 Ib 42.31N 4.00W
Villa Dolores 206 Gd 31.56 S 65.12W
Villa Elisa 204 Ck 32.10 S 58.24W
Villa Flores 192 Mi 16.14N 93.14W
Villa Florida 204 Dh 26.23 S 57.09W
Villafranca del Bierzo 126 Fb 42.36N 6.48W
Villafranca del Cid / Vilafranca del Maestrat 126 Ld 40.25N 0.15W
Villafranca de los Barros 126 Ff 38.34N 6.20W
Villafranca del Panadés/ Vilafranca del Penedès 126 Nc 41.21N 1.42 E
Villafranca di Verona 128 Ee 45.21N 10.50 E
Villa Frontera 190 Dc 26.56N 101.27W
Villagarcía de Arosa / Vilagarcía de Arousa 126 Db 42.36N 8.45W
Villa General Roca 206 Gd 32.39 S 66.28W
Villa Gesell 204 Dm 37.15 S 56.55W
Villagrán 192 Je 24.29N 99.29W
Villaguay 206 Id 31.51 S 59.01W
Villa Guillermina 204 Ci 28.14 S 59.28W
Villa Hayes 206 Ic 25.06 S 57.34W
Villa Hermandarias 204 Cj 31.13 S 59.59W
Villahermosa 176 Jh 17.59N 92.55W
Villa Hidalgo 192 Gd 26.16N 104.54W
Villa Huidobro 206 Hd 34.50 S 64.35W
Villajoyosa / La Vila Joiosa 126 Lf 38.30N 0.14W
Villalba 126 Ea 43.18N 7.41W
Villaldama 192 Id 26.30N 100.26W
Villalón de Campos 126 Gb 42.06N 5.02W
Villalpando 126 Gc 41.52N 5.24W
Villamalea 126 Ke 39.22N 1.35W
Villamanrique 126 Jf 38.33N 3.00W
Villa María 200 Ji 32.25 S 63.15W
Villamartín 126 Gh 36.52N 5.38W
Villa Matamoros 192 Gd 26.50N 105.35W
Villa Media Agua 206 Gd 31.59 S 68.25W
Villamil 202a Ab 0.56 S 91.01W
Villa Minetti 204 Bi 28.37 S 61.39W
Villa Montes 200 Jh 21.15 S 63.30W
Villandraut 122 Fj 44.28N 0.22W
Villa Nueva 206 Gd 32.54 S 68.47W
Villanueva 192 Hf 22.21N 102.53W
Villanueva [Col.] 194 Kh 10.37N 72.59W
Villanueva [N.M.-U.S.] 186 Di 35.17N 105.23W
Villanueva de Córdoba 126 Hf 38.20N 4.37W
Villanueva del Arzobispo 126 Jf 38.10N 3.00W
Villanueva de la Serena 126 Gf 38.58N 5.48W
Villanueva del Fresno 126 Ef 38.23N 7.10W
Villanueva de los Infantes 126 If 38.44N 3.01W
Villanueva del Río y Minas 126 Gg 37.39N 5.42W
Villanueva y Geltrú/Vilanova i la Geltrú 126 Nc 41.14N 1.44 E
Villa Ocampo [Arg.] 206 Ic 28.28 S 59.22W
Villa Ocampo [Mex.] 190 Cc 26.27N 105.31W
Villa Ojo de Agua 206 Hc 29.31 S 63.42W
Villa Oliva 204 Dh 26.01 S 57.53W
Villa Pesqueira 192 Ec 29.08N 109.58W
Villaputzu 128 Dk 39.26N 9.34 E
Villa Ramírez 204 Bk 32.11 S 60.12W
Villarcayo 126 Ib 42.56N 3.34W
Villar del Arzobispo 126 Le 39.44N 0.49W
Villa Regina 206 Ge 39.06 S 67.04W
Villa Rosario 202 Db 7.50N 72.29W
Villarreal de los Infantes / Vila-Real 126 Le 39.56N 0.06W
Villarrica [Chile] 206 Fe 39.16 S 72.16W
Villarrica [Par.] 200 Kh 25.45 S 56.26W
Villarrobledo 126 Je 39.16N 2.36W
Villasalto 128 Dk 39.29N 9.23 E
Villa San Giovanni 128 Jl 38.13N 15.38 E
Villa San Martín 206 Hc 28.18 S 64.12W
Villasimius 128 Dk 39.08N 9.31 E
Villatoro, Puerto de- 126 Gd 40.33N 5.10W
Villa Unión [Mex.] 192 Ic 28.15N 100.43W
Villa Unión [Mex.] 190 Cd 23.12N 106.16W
Villaverde, Madrid- 126 Id 40.21N 3.42W
Villavicencio 200 Ie 4.09N 73.37W
Villaviciosa 126 Ga 43.29N 5.26W
Villazón 202 Eh 22.06 S 65.36W
Ville-de-Laval 184 Kc 45.33N 73.44W
Ville de Paris [3] 122 If 48.52N 2.20 E
Ville de Toulouse Bank (EN) 174 Hh 11.30N 117.00W
Villedieu-les-Poêles 122 Ef 48.50N 1.13W
Ville-en-Tardenois 124 Fe 49.11N 3.48 E
Villefranche-de-Lauragais 122 Hk 43.24N 1.44 E
Villefranche-de-Rouergue 122 Ij 44.21N 2.03 E
Villefranche-sur-Saône 122 Ki 45.59N 4.43 E
Ville-Marie 184 Hb 47.20N 79.26W
Villemur-sur-Tarn 122 Hk 43.52N 1.31 E
Villena 126 Lf 38.38N 0.51W
Villeneuve d'Ascq 124 Fd 50.38N 3.09 E
Villeneuve-Saint-Georges 124 Ef 48.44N 2.27 E
Villeneuve-sur-Lot 122 Gj 44.24N 0.43 E
Villeneuve-sur-Yonne 122 Jf 48.05N 3.18 E
Ville Platte 186 Jk 30.42N 92.16W
Villers-Bocage [Fr.] 124 Ee 50.00N 2.20 E
Villers-Bocage [Fr.] 124 Be 49.05N 0.39W
Villers-Bretonneux 124 Ee 49.52N 2.31 E
Villers-Carbonnel 124 Ee 49.52N 2.54 E
Villers-Cotterêts 124 Fe 49.15N 3.05 E
Villers-la-Ville 124 Gd 50.35N 4.32 E
Villers-sur-Mer 124 Be 49.19N 0.01W
Villerupt 122 Le 49.28N 5.56 E
Villerville 124 Ce 49.24N 0.08 E
Ville-sur-Tourbe 124 Ge 49.11N 4.47 E
Villeurbanne 122 Ki 45.46N 4.53 E
Villiersdorp 172 Bf 33.59 S 19.17 E
Villingen-Schwenningen 120 Eh 48.04N 8.28 E
Villmanstrand/Lappeenranta 112 Ic 61.04N 28.11 E
Villmar 124 Kd 50.23N 8.12 E
Vilnius/Vilnjus 112 Ie 54.41N 25.19 E
Vilnjus/Vilnius 112 Ie 54.41N 25.19 E
Vilok 120 Sh 48.08N 22.50 E
Vilppula 116 Kb 62.01N 24.31 E
Vils [F.R.G.] 120 Hg 49.10N 11.59 E
Vils [F.R.G.] 120 Jh 48.35N 13.10 E
Vilsandi 116 If 58.20N 21.45 E
Vilsbiburg 120 Ih 48.27N 12.21 E
Vilshofen 120 Jh 48.38N 13.11 E
Vilusi 130 Bg 42.44N 18.36 E
Vilvoorde/Vilvorde 122 Kd 50.56N 4.26 E
Vilvorde/Vilvoorde 122 Kd 50.56N 4.26 E
Vilyui Range (EN) = Viljujskoje plato 140 Mc 66.00N 108.00 E
Vimeu 124 Dd 50.05N 1.35 E
Vimianzo 126 Ca 43.07N 9.02W
Vimmerby 114 Dh 57.40N 15.51 E
Vimoutiers 122 Gf 48.55N 0.12 E
Vimperk 120 Jg 49.03N 13.47 E
Vimy 124 Ed 50.22N 2.49 E
Vina 166 Id 7.45N 15.36 E
Viña del Mar 200 Ii 33.02 S 71.34W
Vinalhaven Island 184 Mc 44.05N 68.52W
Vinalopó 126 Lf 38.11N 0.36W
Vinaròs / Vinaroz 126 Md 40.28N 0.29 E
Vinaroz / Vinaròs 126 Md 40.28N 0.29 E
Vînători 130 Hc 46.14N 24.56 E
Vincennes 182 Jd 38.41N 87.32W
Vincennes Bay 222 He 66.30 S 109.30 E
Vincente, Puntan- 220b Bb 14.56N 145.40 E
Vinci 128 Eg 43.47N 10.55 E
Vindafjorden 116 Ae 59.20N 5.55 E
Vindelälven 114 Ee 63.54N 19.52 E
Vindeln 114 Ed 64.12N 19.44 E
Vinderup 116 Ch 56.29N 8.47 E
Vindhya Range 140 Jg 24.37N 77.00 E
Vindö 116 He 59.20N 18.40 E
Vineland 184 Jf 39.29N 75.02W
Vingåker 114 Dg 59.02N 15.52 E
Vingeanne 122 Lg 47.21N 5.29 E
Vinh 142 Mh 18.40N 105.40 E
Vinhais 126 Fc 41.50N 7.00W
Vinh Bac Phan = Tonkin, Gulf of- (EN) 140 Mh 20.00N 108.00 E
Vinh Linh 148 Le 17.04N 107.02 E
Vinica [Yugo.] 130 Fh 41.53N 22.30 E
Vinica [Yugo.] 128 Je 45.28N 15.15 E
Vinita 186 Ih 36.39N 95.09W
Vînju Mare 130 Fe 44.25N 22.52 E
Vinkovci 128 Me 45.17N 18.49 E
Vinnica 112 If 49.14N 28.29 E
Vinnickaja oblast [3] 136 Cf 49.00N 28.50 E
Vinniki 132 De 49.48N 24.11 E
Vino, Tierra del- 126 Gc 41.30N 5.30W
Vinogradov 132 Ce 48.09N 23.02 E
Vinslöv 116 Eh 56.06N 13.55 E
Vinson Massif 222 Pf 78.35 S 85.25W
Vinstervåtn 116 Cc 61.20N 9.00 E
Vinstra 114 Bf 61.36N 9.45 E
Vinstra 116 Cc 61.36N 9.45 E
Vintilă Vodă 130 Jd 45.28N 26.43 E
Vintjärn 116 Gd 60.50N 16.03 E
Vinton 186 Ke 42.10N 92.00W
Vintschgau/Venosta, Val- 128 Ed 46.40N 10.35 E
Vipiteno / Sterzing 128 Fd 46.54N 11.26 E
Vipya Plateau 170 Fe 11.09 S 34.00 E
Viqueque 150 Ih 8.52 S 126.22 E
Vir 128 Jf 44.18N 15.03 E
Virac 150 Hd 13.35N 124.15 E
Viramgām 148 Ed 23.07N 72.02 E
Virandozero 114 Id 64.01N 36.03 E
Viranşehir 146 Hd 37.13N 39.45 E
Virbalis 116 Jj 54.37N 22.49 E
Vircava 116 Jh 56.35N 23.43 E
Virden 180 Hg 49.51N 100.55W
Virdois/Virrat 114 Fe 62.14N 23.47 E
Vire 122 Ff 48.50N 0.53W
Vire 122 Ee 49.20N 1.07W
Virei 170 Bf 15.43 S 12.54 E
Vireux-Wallerand 124 Gd 50.05N 4.44 E
Vîrful, Curcubăta- 130 Fc 46.25N 22.35 E
Virgin Gorda 196 Dc 18.30N 64.25W
Virginia [2] 182 Ld 37.30N 78.45W
Virginia [Mn.-U.S.] 182 Ib 47.31N 92.32W
Virginia [S.Afr.] 172 De 28.12 S 26.49 E
Virginia Beach 182 Ld 36.51N 75.59W
Virginia City 188 Fg 39.19N 119.39W
Virgin Islands 174 Mh 18.20N 66.45W
Virgin Islands of the United States [5] 176 Mh 18.20N 64.52W
Virgin Mountains 188 Ih 36.40N 113.50W
Virgin Passage 197a Cb 18.20N 65.10W
Virgin River 188 Hh 36.35N 114.18W
Virihaure 114 Dc 67.22N 16.33 E
Virkby/Virkkala 116 Kd 60.13N 24.01 E
Virkkala/Virkby 116 Kd 60.13N 24.01 E
Virmasvesi 116 Lb 62.50N 26.55 E
Virôchey 148 Lf 13.59N 106.49 E
Viroin 122 Kd 50.05N 4.43 E
Viroinval 124 Gd 50.05N 4.33 E
Viroinval-Nismes 124 Gd 50.05N 4.33 E
Virojoki 114 Gf 60.35N 27.42 E
Viroqua 186 Ke 43.34N 90.53W
Virovitica 128 Le 45.50N 17.23 E
Virpazar 130 Cg 42.15N 19.06 E
Virrat/Virdois 114 Fe 62.14N 23.47 E
Virserum 114 Dh 57.19N 15.35 E
Virsko More 128 If 44.20N 15.00 E
Virton 122 Le 49.34N 5.32 E
Virton-Ethe 124 He 49.35N 5.35 E
Virtsu 114 Fg 58.37N 23.31 E
Virudanagar 148 Fg 9.36N 77.58 E
Virvičja/Virvyčia 116 Jh 56.14N 22.30 E
Virvyčia/Virvičja 116 Jh 56.14N 22.30 E
Vis 128 Kg 43.03N 16.12 E
Vis 128 Kg 43.02N 16.10 E
Visalia 182 Dd 36.20N 119.18W
Visayan Sea 150 Hd 11.35N 123.51 E
Visby 114 Eh 57.38N 18.18 E
Viscount Melville Sound 174 Hb 74.10N 113.00W
Visé/Wezet 124 Hd 50.44N 5.42 E
Višegrad 128 Ng 43.48N 19.17 E
Višegrad 130 Jh 41.59N 26.20 E
Višera [R.S.F.S.R.] 110 Lc 59.55N 56.50 E
Višera [R.S.F.S.R.] 136 Fc 61.57N 52.25 E
Viseu [2] 126 Ed 40.45N 7.50W
Viseu [Braz.] 202 Id 1.12 S 46.07W
Viseu [Port.] 126 Ed 40.39N 7.55W
Vişeu de Sus 130 Hb 47.43N 24.26 E
Vishākhapatnam 142 Kh 17.42N 83.18 E
Visingsö 116 Ff 58.03N 14.20 E
Viskafors 116 Eg 57.38N 12.50 E
Viskan 114 Ch 57.14N 12.12 E
Viski kanal 128 Kg 43.07N 16.17 E
Vislanda 116 Fh 56.47N 14.27 E
Vislinski zaliv 120 Pb 54.27N 19.40 E
Visnes 116 Ae 59.21N 5.14 E
Višnevka 130 Lc 46.22N 28.27 E
Visoki Dečani 130 Dg 42.33N 20.16 E
Visoko 128 Mg 43.59N 18.11 E
Visokoi 222 Ad 56.42 S 27.12W
Visonggo 219d Bb 16.13 S 179.40 E
Visp 128 Bd 46.17N 7.53 E
Vissefjärda 116 Fh 56.32N 15.35 E
Vista 188 Gj 33.12N 117.15W
Visten 116 Ee 59.40N 13.20 E
Vistonías, Órmos- 130 Ii 40.58N 25.05 E
Vistonís, Límni- 130 Ih 41.03N 25.07 E
Vistula (EN) = Wisła 110 He 54.22N 18.55 E
Vištytis 116 Jj 54.27N 22.44 E
Visuvisu Point 219a Cb 7.57 S 157.31 E
Vit 130 Hf 43.41N 24.45 E
Vitebsk 112 Jd 55.12N 30.11 E
Vitebskaja oblast [3] 136 Cd 55.20N 29.00 E
Viterbo 128 Gh 42.25N 12.06 E
Vithkuqi 130 Di 40.31N 20.35 E
Vitichi 202 Eh 20.13 S 65.29W
Vitigudino 126 Fc 41.01N 6.26W
Viti Levu 208 If 18.00 S 178.00 E
Vitim 138 Ge 59.33N 112.28 E
Vitim 140 Nd 59.26N 112.34 E
Vitimski 138 Ge 58.18N 113.18 E
Vitimskoje ploskogorje 138 Gf 54.00N 114.00 E
Vitinja → Cureski prohod 130 Gg 42.47N 23.45 E
Vitjaz Strait 214 Di 5.35 S 147.00 E
Vitolište 130 Eh 41.11N 21.50 E
Vitória 200 Lh 20.19 S 40.21W
Vitoria / Vitoria-Gasteiz 126 Jb 42.51N 2.40W
Vitória da Conquista 200 Lg 14.51 S 40.51W
Vitória de Santo Antão 202 Ke 8.07 S 35.18W
Vitoria-Gasteiz / Vitoria 126 Jb 42.51N 2.40W
Vitorog 128 Lf 44.08N 17.03 E
Vitosa 130 Gg 42.33N 23.15 E
Vitré 122 Ef 48.08N 1.12W
Vitry-en-Artois 124 Ed 50.20N 2.59 E
Vitry-le-François 122 Kf 48.44N 4.35 E
Vítsi 130 Ei 40.39N 21.23 E
Vittangi 114 Ec 67.41N 21.39 E
Vitteaux 122 Kg 47.24N 4.32 E
Vittel 122 Lf 48.12N 5.57 E
Vittinge 116 Ge 59.54N 17.04 E
Vittoria 128 In 36.57N 14.32 E
Vittorio Veneto 128 Ge 45.59N 12.18 E
Vityaz Depth (EN) 106 Je 44.00N 151.00 E
Vityaz I Depth (EN) 106 Ih 11.20N 141.30 E
Vityaz II Depth (EN) 106 Kl 23.27 S 175.00W
Vityaz III Depth (EN) 106 Km 32.00 S 178.00W
Vityaz Seamount (EN) 208 Jc 13.30N 173.15W
Vityaz Trench (EN) 106 Jj 10.00 S 170.00 E
Vivarais, Monts du- 122 Ki 44.55N 4.15 E
Vivarais, Plateaux du- 122 Kj 44.50N 4.45 E
Viver 126 Le 39.55N 0.36W

Index Symbols

[1] Independent Nation
[2] State, Region
[3] District, County
[4] Municipality
[5] Colony, Dependency
Continent
Physical Region
Historical or Cultural Region
Mount, Mountain
Volcano
Hill
Mountains, Mountain Range
Hills, Escarpment
Plateau, Upland
Pass, Gap
Plain, Lowland
Delta
Salt Flat
Valley, Canyon
Crater, Cave
Karst Features
Depression
Polder
Desert, Dunes
Forest, Woods
Heath, Steppe
Oasis
Cape, Point
Coast, Beach
Cliff
Peninsula
Isthmus
Sandbank
Island
Atoll
Rock, Reef
Islands, Archipelago
Rocks, Reefs
Coral Reef
Well, Spring
Geyser
River, Stream
Waterfall, Rapids
River Mouth, Estuary
Lake
Salt Lake
Intermittent Lake
Reservoir
Swamp, Pond
Canal
Glacier
Ice Shelf, Pack Ice
Ocean
Sea
Gulf, Bay
Strait, Fjord
Lagoon
Bank
Seamount
Tablemount
Ridge
Shelf
Basin
Escarpment, Sea Scarp
Fracture
Trench, Abyss
National Park, Reserve
Point of Interest
Recreation Site
Cave, Cavern
Historic Site
Ruins
Wall, Walls
Church, Abbey
Temple
Scientific Station
Railway station
Airport
Port
Military installation
Lighthouse
Mine
Tunnel
Dam, Bridge

Vivero 126 Ea 43.40N 7.35W
Viverone, Lago di- 128 Ce 45.25N 8.05 E
Vivi 138 Ed 63.52N 97.50 E
Vivian 186 Jj 32.53N 93.59W
Viviers 122 Kj 44.29N 4.41 E
Vivo 172 Dd 23.03S 29.17 E
Vivoratá 204 Dm 37.40S 57.39W
Vivorillo, Cayos- 194 Ff 15.50N 83.18W
Viwa 219d Ab 17.08S 176.56 E
Vizcaíno, Desierto de- 190 Bc 27.40N 114.40W
Vizcaíno, Sierra- 192 Bd 27.20N 114.00W
Vizcaya / Bizkaia 126 Ja 43.15N 2.55W
Vizcaya, Golfo de- 110 Fg 44.00N 4.00W
Vizcaya, Golfo de- = Biscay, Bay of- (EN) 110 Fg 43.50N 2.30W
Vize 130 Kh 41.34N 27.45 E
Vize, ostrov- 140 Jb 79.30N 77.00 E
Vizianagaram 148 Ge 18.07N 83.25 E
Vizille 122 Li 45.05N 5.46 E
Vizinga 136 Fc 61.05N 50.10 E
Viziru 130 Kd 45.00N 27.42 E
Vižnica 132 De 48.14N 25.12 E
Vizzini 128 Im 37.10N 14.45 E
Vjaike-Maarja/Väike-Maarja 116 Lg 59.04N 26.12 E
Vjajke-Pakri/Väike-Pakri 116 Je 59.50N 23.50 E
Vjajke-Vjajn / Väike Väin 116 Jf 58.30N 23.10 E
Vjalje, ozero- 116 Ne 59.00N 30.20 E
Vjalozero, ozero- 114 Ic 66.50N 35.10 E
Vjandra/Vändra 114 Fg 58.40N 25.01 E
Vjartsilja 114 He 62.10N 30.48 E
Vjatka 110 Ld 55.36N 51.30 E
Vjatskije Poljany 136 Fd 56.14N 51.04 E
Vjatski uval 114 Lg 58.00N 49.45 E
Vjazemski 138 Ig 47.31N 134.45 E
Vjazma 112 Jd 55.13N 34.18 E
Vjazniki 114 Kh 56.15N 42.12 E
Vjeio, Rio- 194 Dg 12.17N 86.54W
Vjosa 130 Ci 40.37N 19.20 E
Vlaamse Banken 122 Ef 51.15N 2.30 E
Vlaamse Vlakte = Flanders Plain (EN) 122 Id 50.40N 2.50 E
Vlaanderen/Flandres= Flanders (EN) 110 Ge 51.00N 3.20 E
Vlaanderen/Flandres= Flanders (EN) 122 Jc 51.00N 3.20 E
Vlaardingen 122 Kc 51.54N 4.21 E
Vlădeasa, Vîrful- 130 Fc 46.45N 22.48 E
Vlădeni 130 Kb 47.25N 27.20 E
Vladičin Han 130 Fg 42.43N 22.04 E
Vladimir 112 Kd 56.10N 40.25 E
Vladimirskaja oblast 136 Ed 56.00N 40.40 E
Vladimirski Tupik 132 Hb 55.42N 33.18 E
Vladimir-Volynski 136 Ce 50.51N 24.22 E
Vladivostok 142 Pe 43.10N 131.56 E
Vlad Ţepeş 130 Ke 44.21N 27.05 E
Vlagtwedde 124 Ja 53.02N 7.08 E
Vlagtwedde-Ter Apel 124 Jb 52.52N 7.06 E
Vlahina 130 Fh 41.54N 22.52 E
Vlăhiţa 130 Ic 46.21N 25.31 E
Vlasenika 128 Mf 44.11N 18.57 E
Vlašić 128 Lf 44.19N 17.40 E
Vlašic 130 Ce 44.27N 19.35 E
Vlašim 120 Kg 49.42N 14.54 E
Vlasotince 130 Fg 42.58N 22.08 E
Vlasovo 138 Ib 70.40N 134.35 E
Vlieland 124 Ha 53.17N 5.06 E
Vlieland 124 Ka 53.15N 5.00 E
Vlieland-Oost Vlieland 124 Ha 53.17N 5.06 E
Vliestroom 124 Ha 53.17N 5.10 E
Vlissingen 122 Jc 51.26N 3.35 E
Vlissingen-Oost-Souburg 124 Fc 51.28N 3.36 E
Vloesberg/Flobecq 124 Fd 50.44N 3.44 E
Vlorë 112 Hg 40.27N 19.30 E
Vlorës, Gjiri i- 130 Ci 40.25N 19.25 E
Vlotho 124 Kb 52.10N 8.51 E
Vltava=Moldau (EN) 116 He 50.21N 14.30 E
Vöcklabruck 128 Hb 48.01N 13.39 E
Vodice 128 Jg 43.46N 15.47 E
Vodla 114 If 61.49N 36.00 E
Vodlozero, ozero- 114 Ie 62.20N 37.00 E
Vodňany 120 Kg 49.09N 14.11 E
Vodnjan 128 Hf 44.57N 13.51 E
Vodny 136 Fe 63.32N 53.20 E
Voerde (Niederrhein) 120 Ce 51.35N 6.41 E
Voeren/Fouron 124 Hd 50.45N 5.48 E
Vôge, La- 122 Mf 48.05N 6.05 E
Vogel Peak 166 Hd 8.24N 11.47 E
Vogelsberg 120 Ff 50.30N 9.15 E
Voghera 128 Df 44.59N 9.01 E
Vogtland 120 If 50.30N 12.05 E
Voh 219b Be 20.58S 164.42 E
Võhandu jõgi / Vyhandu 116 Lf 58.03N 27.40 E
Vohémar 172 Ib 13.22S 50.00 E
Vohipeno 172 Hd 22.20S 47.52 E
Vöhl 124 Kc 51.12N 8.56 E
Vohma 136 Ed 58.58N 46.45 E
Vohma 114 Lg 58.45N 46.36 E
Voi 160 Ki 3.23S 38.34 E
Voikoski 116 Lc 61.16N 26.48 E
Voinjama 160 Gh 8.25N 9.45W
Vóïon Óros 130 Ei 40.15N 21.03 E
Voire 122 Kf 48.27N 4.25 E
Voiron 122 Li 45.22N 5.35 E
Voitsberg 128 Jc 47.02N 15.09 E
Voïviis, Límni- 130 Fj 39.32N 22.45 E
Vojens 116 Ci 55.15N 9.19 E
Vojkar 134 Ld 65.38N 64.40 E
Vojmsjön 114 Dd 65.00N 16.24 E
Vojnić 128 Je 45.19N 15.42 E
Vojnilov 120 Ug 49.04N 24.33 E
Vojvodina 130 Cd 45.00N 20.00 E
Voj-Vož 136 Fc 62.56N 54.59 E
Voknavolok 114 Hd 64.57N 30.31 E
Vokré, Hoséré- 158 Ih 8.21N 13.15 E
Volary 120 Jh 48.55N 13.54 E
Volcán 194 Fi 8.46N 82.38W
Volcánica, Cordillera- 174 Ih 18.00N 101.00W
Volcano 221a Fd 19.26N 155.20W
Volcano Islands (EN)=Iō/Kazan-Rettō 140 Qg 25.00N 141.00 E
Volcano Islands (EN)=Kazan-Rettō/Iō 140 Qg 25.00N 141.00 E
Volčansk [R.S.F.S.R.] 134 Jg 59.59N 60.04 E
Volčansk [Ukr.-U.S.S.R.] 132 Jd 50.16N 37.01 E
Volčiha 138 Df 52.02N 80.23 E
Volda 114 Be 62.09N 6.06 E
Voldafjorden 116 Ab 62.10N 6.00 E
Volga 114 Jh 57.57N 38.25 E
Volga 110 Kf 45.55N 47.52 E
Volga-Baltic Canal (EN)= Volgo-Baltijski vodny put imeni V. I. Lenina 110 Jd 59.58N 37.10 E
Volga Delta (EN) 110 Kf 46.30N 47.00 E
Volga Hills (EN) = Privolžkaja vozvyšennost 110 Ke 52.00N 46.00 E
Volgo-Baltijski vodny put imeni V.I. Lenina=Volga-Baltic Canal (EN) 110 Jd 59.58N 37.10 E
Volgodonsk 136 Ef 47.33N 42.08 E
Volgo-Donskoj sudohodny kanal imeni V. I. Lenina= Lenin Canal (EN) 110 Kf 48.40N 43.37 E
Volgograd (Stalingrad) 112 Kf 48.44N 44.25 E
Volgograd Reservoir (EN) = Volgogradskoje vodohranilišče 110 Kf 49.20N 45.00 E
Volgogradskaja oblast 136 Ef 49.30N 44.30 E
Volgogradskoje vodohranilišče = Volgograd Reservoir (EN) 110 Kf 49.20N 45.00 E
Volhov 112 Jd 59.55N 32.20 E
Volhov 110 Jc 60.08N 32.20 E
Volhynia 110 Ie 51.00N 25.00 E
Volhynia (EN) 120 Uf 51.00N 25.00 E
Volissós 130 Ik 38.29N 25.55 E
Volja 134 Je 63.11N 61.16 E
Volka 120 Vd 52.43N 25.43 E
Völkermarkt 128 Id 46.39N 14.38 E
Völklingen 120 Cg 49.15N 6.51 E
Volkmarsen 124 Lc 51.24N 9.07 E
Volkovysk 132 Dc 53.10N 24.31 E
Volkovysskaja vozvyšennost 120 Uc 53.10N 24.30 E
Volksrust 172 De 27.24S 29.53 E
Vollenhove 124 Hb 52.40N 5.57 E
Vollsjö 116 Ei 55.42N 13.46 E
Volme 124 Jc 51.24N 7.27 E
Volmunster 124 Je 49.07N 7.21 E
Volna, gora- 138 Kd 63.30N 154.57 E
Volnjansk 132 If 47.54N 35.29 E
Volnovaha 132 Jf 47.37N 37.36 E
Voločajevka 2-ja 138 Ig 48.36N 134.36 E
Voločisk 132 Ee 49.31N 26.13 E
Volodarsk 114 Kh 56.14N 43.13 E
Volodarski 132 Pf 46.26N 48.31 E
Volodarskoje 136 Ge 53.18N 68.08 E
Vologda 112 Jd 59.12N 39.55 E
Vologodskaja oblast 136 Ed 60.00N 41.00 E
Volokolamsk 114 Ih 56.03N 35.58 E
Volokonovka 132 Jd 50.29N 37.52 E
Vólos 112 Ih 39.22N 22.57 E
Vološka 114 Jf 61.20N 40.03 E
Vološka 114 Jf 61.42N 39.15 E
Volosovo 114 Gg 59.28N 29.32 E
Volovec 120 Th 48.42N 23.17 E
Volovo 132 Kc 53.35N 38.01 E
Voložin 132 Eb 54.06N 26.32 E
Volquart Boons Kyst 179 Jd 70.20N 24.20W
Volsini, Monti- 128 Fh 42.40N 11.55 E
Volsk 136 Ee 52.02N 47.23 E
Volta 166 Fd 7.00N 0.30 E
Volta 158 Hh 5.46N 0.41 E
Volta, Lake- 158 Hh 7.30N 0.15 E
Volta Blanche=White Volta (EN) 158 Gh 8.38N 0.59W
Volta Noire=Black Volta (EN) 166 Ec 12.30N 4.00W
Volta Noire=Black Volta (EN) 158 Gh 8.38N 1.30W
Volta Redonda 200 Lh 22.32S 44.07W
Volta Rouge=Red Volta (EN) 158 Gh 10.34N 0.30W
Volterra 128 Eg 43.24N 10.51 E
Voltoya 126 Hd 41.13N 4.31W
Voltri, Genova- 128 Cf 44.26N 8.45 E
Volturino 128 Jj 40.25N 15.48 E
Volturno 128 Hi 41.01N 13.55 E
Volubilis 162 Fc 34.04N 5.33W
Vólvi, Límni- 130 Gi 40.41N 23.28 E
Volynskaja grjada 120 Ue 51.05N 25.00 E
Volynskaja oblast 136 Ce 51.10N 25.00 E
Volynskaja vozvyšennost 132 Dd 50.30N 25.00 E
Volžsk 136 Ed 55.55N 48.19 E
Volžski [R.S.F.S.R.] 112 Kf 48.48N 44.44 E
Volžski [R.S.F.S.R.] 114 Mj 53.28N 50.08 E
Voma 219d Bc 18.00S 178.08 E
Vomano 128 Ih 42.39N 14.02 E
Vonavona 219a Cc 8.12S 157.05 E
Vondrozo 172 Hd 22.47S 47.17 E
Von Frank Mountain 178 Id 63.33N 154.20W
Vónitsa 130 Dk 38.55N 20.53 E
Vonne 122 Gh 46.25N 0.15 E
Võnnu/Vynnu 116 Lf 58.15N 27.10 E
Voorne 124 Gc 51.52N 4.05 E
Voorschoten 124 Gb 52.08N 4.28 E
Voorst 124 Ib 52.10N 6.09 E
Voorst-Twello 124 Ib 52.14N 6.07 E
Vop 132 Hb 54.56N 32.44 E
Vopnafjörður 114a Cb 65.45N 14.50W
Vora 130 Ch 41.23N 19.40 E
Vörå/Vöyri 116 Ja 63.09N 22.15 E
Vorarlberg 120 Dc 47.15N 9.50 E
Vóras Óros 130 Ei 41.00N 21.50 E
Vorau 128 Jc 47.24N 15.53 E
Vorden 124 Ib 52.06N 6.20 E
Vorderrhein 128 Dd 46.49N 9.26 E
Vordingborg 114 Ci 55.01N 11.55 E
Voreifel 124 Jd 50.10N 7.00 E
Vorga Šor 134 Kc 67.35N 63.40 E
Vória Pindhos 130 Dj 40.20N 20.55 E
Vórioi Sporádhes, Nísoi-= Northern Sporades (EN) 110 Ih 39.15N 23.55 E
Vórios Evvoïkós Kólpos= Évvoia, Gulf of- (EN) 130 Gk 38.45N 23.10 E
Vorkuta 112 Mb 67.27N 63.58 E
Vorma 114 Cf 60.09N 11.27 E
Vormsi 116 Je 59.02N 23.05 E
Vormsi 114 Fg 59.00N 23.15 E
Vorniceni 130 Jb 47.59N 26.40 E
Vorogovo 138 Dd 60.58N 89.28 E
Vorona 132 Md 51.22N 42.03 E
Voroncovo [R.S.F.S.R.] 138 Db 71.40N 83.40 E
Voroncovo [R.S.F.S.R.] 116 Mg 57.15N 28.49 E
Voronež 112 Je 51.40N 39.10 E
Voronež 132 Kd 51.31N 39.05 E
Voronežskaja oblast 136 Ee 51.00N 40.15 E
Voronin Trough (EN) 224 Ge 80.00N 85.00 E
Voronja 114 Ib 69.09N 35.47 E
Voronovo 116 Kj 54.09N 25.19 E
Voropajevo 116 Li 55.07N 27.19 E
Vorošilovgrad 112 Jf 48.34N 39.20 E
Vorošilovgradskaja oblast 136 Df 49.00N 39.10 E
Vorotan 132 Oj 39.15N 46.43 E
Vorotynec 114 Kh 56.02N 45.52 E
Vorožba 132 Id 51.10N 34.11 E
Vorskla 132 Ie 48.52N 34.05 E
Vorsma 114 Ki 55.58N 43.17 E
Vörts järv / Vyrtsjarv, ozero- 114 Gg 58.15N 26.05 E
Võru/Vyru 136 Cd 57.52N 27.05 E
Voruh 136 He 39.52N 70.35 E
Vosges 122 Mf 48.10N 6.50 E
Vosges 110 Gf 48.30N 7.10 E
Voskresensk 114 Ji 55.22N 38.42 E
Voskresenskoje 114 Kh 56.51N 45.27 E
Voss 116 Bd 60.40N 6.30 E
Vossa 116 Ad 60.39N 5.42 E
Vossevangen 114 Bf 60.39N 6.26 E
Vostočno-Kazahstanskaja oblast 136 If 49.00N 84.00 E
Vostočno-Kounradski 136 Hf 46.58N 75.07 E
Vostočno Sibirskoje more = East Siberian Sea (EN) 224 Cd 74.00N 166.00 E
Vostočny [R.S.F.S.R.] 134 Jg 58.48N 61.52 E
Vostočny [R.S.F.S.R.] 138 Jg 48.19N 142.40 E
Vostočny, hrebet- 138 Lf 55.00N 160.30 E
Vostočny Sajan=Eastern Sayans (EN) 140 Ld 53.00N 97.00 E
Vostok 222 Hf 78.28S 106.48 E
Vostok Island 208 Lf 10.06S 152.23W
Vostrecovo 138 Ig 45.56N 134.59 E
Võsu/Vyzu 116 Ke 59.30N 25.50 E
Votkinsk 136 Fd 57.05N 53.59 E
Votkinskoje vodohranilišče = Votkinsk Reservoir (EN) 110 Ld 57.30N 55.10 E
Votkinsk Reservoir (EN) = Votkinskoje vodohranilišče 110 Ld 57.30N 55.10 E
Votuporanga 204 He 20.24S 49.59W
Vouga 126 Dd 40.41N 8.40W
Vouillé 122 Gh 46.38N 0.10 E
Voulgára 130 Ej 39.06N 21.54 E
Vouliagméni 130 Gl 37.49N 23.47 E
Voulte-sur-Rhône, La- 122 Kj 44.48N 4.47 E
Voúrinos Óros 130 Ei 40.11N 21.40 E
Voúxa, Ákra- 130 Gn 35.38N 23.36 E
Vouziers 122 Ke 49.24N 4.42 E
Voves 122 Hf 48.16N 1.38 E
Vovodo 168 Cd 5.40N 24.21 E
Voxna 116 Fc 61.21N 15.34 E
Voxnan 116 Gc 61.17N 16.26 E
Voyeykov Ice Shelf 222 Ie 66.20S 124.38 E
Vöyri/Vörå 116 Ja 63.09N 22.15 E
Vože, ozero- 114 Jf 60.35N 39.05 E
Vožega 114 Jf 60.30N 40.12 E
Vožega 114 Jf 60.33N 39.13 E
Voznesenje 114 If 61.01N 35.27 E
Voznesensk 136 Df 47.35N 31.20 E
Vozroždenija, ostrov- 135 Bh 45.05N 59.15 E
Vraca 130 Gf 43.12N 23.33 E
Vraca 130 Gf 43.12N 23.33 E
Vracha 130 Dh 41.54N 20.45 E
Vradijevka 132 Gf 47.51N 30.34 E
Vrakhiónas 130 Dl 37.48N 20.45 E
Vran 128 Lg 43.39N 17.27 E
Vrancea 130 Jd 45.50N 26.42 E
Vranica 128 Lg 43.57N 17.44 E
Vranje 130 Eg 42.33N 21.54 E
Vranov nad Topľou 120 Rh 48.54N 21.41 E
Vrăška čuka, prohod- 130 Ff 43.50N 22.23 E
Vratnica 130 Eg 42.08N 21.07 E
Vratnik, prohod- 130 Jg 42.49N 26.10 E
Vrbas 130 Cd 45.34N 19.39 E
Vrbas 128 Le 45.07N 17.31 E
Vrbno pod Pradědem 120 Nf 50.08N 17.23 E
Vrbovsko 128 Je 45.22N 15.05 E
Vrchlabí 120 Lf 50.38N 15.37 E
Vrede 172 De 27.30S 29.06 E
Vreden 124 Ib 52.02N 6.50 E
Vredenburg 172 Bf 32.54S 17.59 E
Vredendal 172 Bf 31.41S 18.35 E
Vresse, Vresse-sur-Semois- 124 Ge 49.52N 4.56 E
Vresse-sur-Semois 124 Ge 49.52N 4.56 E
Vresse-sur-Semois-Vresse 124 Ge 49.52N 4.56 E
Vretstorp 116 Fe 59.02N 14.52 E
Vrhnika 128 Ie 45.58N 14.18 E
Vries 124 Ia 53.05N 6.36 E
Vriezenveen 124 Ib 52.26N 6.36 E
Vrigstad 116 Fg 57.21N 14.28 E
Vron 124 Dd 50.19N 1.45 E
Vršac 130 Ed 45.07N 21.18 E
Vryburg 160 Jk 26.55S 24.45 E
Vryheid 172 Ee 27.52S 30.38 E
Vsetín 120 Ng 49.21N 18.00 E
Vsevidof, Mount- 178a Eb 53.07N 168.43W
Vsevoložsk 114 Hf 60.04N 30.41 E
Vstrečny 138 Lc 68.00N 165.58 E
Vtačník 120 Oh 48.42N 18.37 E
Vuanggava 219d Cc 18.52S 178.54W
Vučitrn 130 Dg 42.49N 20.58 E
Vučjak 130 Fh 41.28N 22.20 E
Vuka 128 Me 45.21N 19.00 E
Vukovar 128 Me 45.21N 19.00 E
Vuktyl 136 Fc 63.50N 57.25 E
Vulavu 219a Dc 8.31S 159.48 E
Vulcan 130 Gd 45.23N 23.16 E
Vulcan, Vîrful- 130 Fc 46.14N 22.58 E
Vulcano 128 Il 38.25N 15.00 E
Vulkaneşty 132 Fg 45.38N 28.27 E
Vulture 128 Jj 40.57N 15.38 E
Vung Tau 148 Lf 10.21N 107.04 E
Vunindawa 219d Bb 17.49S 178.19 E
Vunisea Station 216 Ec 19.03S 178.09 E
Vuohijärvi 116 Lc 61.10N 26.40 E
Vuoksa 116 Nd 60.35N 30.42 E
Vuoksa, ozero- [R.S.F.S.R.] 116 Mc 61.00N 30.00 E
Vuoksa, ozero- [R.S.F.S.R.] 116 Md 60.38N 29.55 E
Vuollerim 114 Ec 66.25N 20.36 E
Vuosjärvi 116 Ka 63.00N 25.30 E
Vuotso 114 Gb 68.06N 27.08 E
Vuranimala 219a Eb 9.05S 160.51 E
Vyborg 112 Ic 60.42N 28.45 E
Vyčegda 110 Kc 61.18N 46.36 E
Vyčegodski 114 Lf 61.17N 46.48 E
Vychodočeský kraj 120 Lf 50.10N 16.00 E
Východoslovenská nížina 120 Rh 48.35N 21.50 E
Východoslovenský kraj 120 Rg 49.00N 21.15 E
Vyg 114 Ie 63.17N 35.17 E
Vygoda [Ukr.-U.S.S.R.] 130 Nc 46.38N 30.24 E
Vygoda [Ukr.-U.S.S.R.] 120 Uh 48.52N 24.01 E
Vygozero, ozero- 110 Jc 63.35N 34.45 E
Vyhandu / Võhandu jõgi 116 Lf 58.03N 27.40 E
Vyja 114 Le 62.57N 46.42 E
Vyksa 136 Ed 55.20N 42.12 E
Vym 136 Fc 62.13N 50.25 E
Vynnu/Võnnu 116 Lf 58.15N 27.10 E
Vyrica 136 Dd 59.24N 30.19 E
Vyrnwy 118 Ki 52.45N 2.50W
Vyrtsjarv, ozero- / Vörts järv 114 Gg 58.15N 26.05 E
Vyru/Võru 136 Cd 57.52N 27.05 E
Vyša 132 Mb 54.03N 42.06 E
Vyšgorod 132 Gd 50.38N 30.29 E
Vyšgorodok 116 Mh 56.55N 28.05 E
Vyškov 120 Mg 49.17N 17.00 E
Vyškovski, pereval- 120 Th 48.38N 23.45 E
Vyšni Voloček 136 Dd 57.37N 34.32 E
Vysock 114 Gf 60.36N 28.36 E
Vysoké Tatry = Hight Tatra (EN) 120 Pg 49.10N 20.00 E
Vysokogorny 138 If 50.07N 139.10 E
Vysokogorsk 154 Mb 44.23N 135.23 E
Vysokoje 132 Cc 52.22N 23.26 E
Vysokovsk 114 Ih 56.21N 36.29 E
Vyšši Brod 120 Kh 48.37N 14.18 E
Vytebet 132 Ic 53.53N 35.38 E
Vytegra 136 Dc 61.01N 36.28 E
Vyvenka 138 Ld 60.10N 165.20 E
Vyzu/Võsu 116 Ke 59.30N 25.50 E
Vzmorje 138 Jg 47.45N 142.30 E

W

Wa 166 Ec 10.03N 2.29W
Waal 122 Kc 51.55N 4.30 E
Waalre 124 Hc 51.23N 5.27 E
Waalwijk 124 Hc 51.41N 5.04 E
Waar, Meos- 150 Jg 2.05S 134.23 E
Waardgronden 124 Ha 53.12N 5.05 E
Waarschoot 124 Fc 51.09N 3.36 E
Wabana 180 Mg 47.38N 52.57W
Wabao, Cap- 219b Ce 21.36S 167.51 E
Wabasca 180 Ge 56.00N 113.53W
Wabasca 180 Fe 58.21N 115.20W
Wabash 184 Ee 40.48N 85.49W
Wabash 174 Kf 37.46N 88.02W
Wabasha 186 Jd 44.23N 92.02W
Wabash River 186 Lh 37.46N 88.02W
Wabowden 180 Hf 54.55N 98.38W
Wąbrzeźno 120 Oc 53.17N 18.57 E
Wabu Hu 152 Ke 32.20N 116.55 E
Wachau 128 Jb 48.20N 15.25 E
Wachile 168 Fe 4.33N 39.03 E
Wachusett Seamount (EN) 208 Lh 32.00S 151.20W
Waco 176 Jf 31.55N 97.08W
Waconda Lake 186 Gg 39.30N 98.30W
Wadayama 156 Dd 35.20N 134.51 E
Wad Bandah 168 Dc 13.06N 27.57 E
Waddān 164 Cd 29.10N 16.08 E
Waddān, Jabal- 164 Cd 29.20N 16.20 E
Waddeneilanden/Friesische Inseln = Frisian Islands (EN) 110 Hc 54.00N 6.00 E
Waddeneilanden = West Frisian Islands (EN) 122 Ka 53.30N 5.00 E
Waddenzee 124 Ha 53.20N 5.30 E
Waddington, Mount- 174 Gd 51.23N 125.15W
Wadena 186 Ic 46.26N 95.08W
Wadern 124 Ie 49.32N 6.53 E
Wadern-Nunkirchen 124 Ie 49.32N 6.53 E
Wadersloh 124 Kc 51.44N 8.15 E
Wadersloh-Liesborn 124 Kc 51.43N 8.16 E
Wadesboro 184 Gh 34.58N 80.04W
Wadhams 188 Ba 51.30N 127.31W
Wādī Bīshah 144 Fe 21.24N 43.26 E
Wādī Fajr 144 Ec 30.17N 38.18 E
Wādī Ḥalfā' 160 Kf 21.56N 31.20 E
Wādī Jimāl, Jazīrat- 146 Fj 24.40N 35.10 E
Wādī Mūsā 146 Fg 30.19N 35.29 E
Wādī Shiḥan 168 Ib 18.10N 52.57 E
Wad Madanī 160 Kg 14.24N 33.32 E
Wad Nimr 168 Ec 14.32N 32.08 E
Wadowice 120 Pg 49.53N 19.30 E
Wadsworth 188 Fg 39.38N 119.17W
Wafangdian → Fuxian 152 Ld 39.38N 121.59 E
Wafrah 144 Gd 28.25N 47.56 E
Waga-Gawa 156 Gb 39.18N 141.07 E
Wagenfeld 124 Kb 52.33N 8.35 E
Wagenfeld-Ströhen 124 Kb 52.32N 8.39 E
Wageningen 124 Hc 51.57N 5.41 E
Wagēr, Qar- 168 Hc 10.01N 45.30 E
Wager Bay 174 Kc 65.26N 88.40W
Wagga Wagga 210 Fh 35.07S 147.22 E
Waghäusel 124 Ke 49.15N 8.30 E
Wagin 210 Ch 33.18S 117.21 E
Waginger See 120 Ii 47.58N 12.50 E
Wagoner 186 Ii 35.58N 95.22W
Wagon Mound 186 Dh 36.01N 104.42W
Wagontire Mountain 188 Fe 43.21N 119.53W
Wagrien 120 Gb 54.15N 10.45 E
Wągrowiec 120 Nd 52.49N 17.11 E
Wah 148 Eb 33.48N 72.42 E
Waha 160 If 28.10N 19.57 E
Wahai 150 Ig 2.48S 129.30 E
Wahiawa 214 Oc 21.30N 158.02W
Wahoo 186 Hf 41.13N 96.37W
Wahpeton 182 Hb 46.16N 96.36W
Waialeale, Mount- 221a Ba 22.04N 159.30W
Waialua 221a Cb 21.35N 158.08W
Waianae 221a Cb 21.27N 158.12W
Waiau 216 Dh 42.39S 173.03 E
Waiau 218 Ee 42.47S 173.22 E
Waiblingen 120 Fh 48.50N 9.18 E
Waibstadt 124 Ke 49.18N 8.56 E
Waidhofen/Ybbs 128 Ic 47.58N 14.46 E
Waidhofen an der Thaya 128 Jb 48.49N 15.17 E
Waigame 150 Ig 1.50S 129.49 E
Waigeo, Pulau- 208 Ee 0.14S 130.45 E
Waihi 218 Fb 37.24S 175.50 E
Waihou 218 Fb 37.10S 175.33 E
Waikabubak 150 Gh 9.38S 119.25 E
Waikare, Lake- 218 Fb 37.25S 175.10 E
Waikaremoana, Lake- 216 Eg 38.45S 177.05 E
Waikato 218 Fb 37.23S 174.43 E
Waikawa 218 Cg 46.38S 169.08 E
Waikouaiti 218 Df 45.36S 170.41 E
Wailangilala 219d Cb 16.45S 179.06W
Wailua 221a Ba 22.03N 159.20W
Wailuku 214 Oc 20.53N 156.30W
Waimamaku 218 Ea 35.34S 173.29 E
Waimanalo Beach 221a Db 21.20N 157.42W
Waimangaroa 218 Dd 41.43S 171.46 E
Waimate 218 Df 44.45S 171.03 E
Waimea [Hi.-U.S.] 221a Fc 20.02N 155.40W
Waimea [Hi.-U.S.] 221a Bb 21.57N 159.40W
Waimes 124 Id 50.25N 6.07 E
Wainfleet All Saints 124 Ca 53.06N 0.15 E
Wainganga 140 Jh 19.36N 79.48 E
Waingapu 150 Hh 9.39S 120.16 E
Waini Point 196 Gh 8.24N 59.49W
Waini River 196 Gh 8.24N 59.51W
Wainwright [Ak.-U.S.] 178 Gb 70.38N 160.01W
Wainwright [Alta.-Can.] 180 Gf 52.49N 110.52W
Waiouru 216 Eg 39.29S 175.40 E
Waipahu 221a Cb 21.23N 158.01W
Waipara 218 Ee 43.03S 172.45 E
Waipawa 218 Gc 39.56S 176.35 E
Waipiro 218 Hc 38.02S 178.20 E
Waipu 218 Fa 35.59S 174.26 E
Waipukurau 218 Gd 40.00S 176.33 E
Wairakei 218 Gc 38.37S 176.05 E
Wairarapa, Lake- 218 Fd 41.15S 175.15 E
Wairau 218 Fd 41.31S 174.03 E
Wairoa 216 Eg 39.03S 177.26 E
Wairoa 218 Fb 36.11S 174.02 E
Waitaki 218 Df 44.56S 171.09 E
Waitangi 216 Fh 43.56S 176.34W
Waitara 216 Dg 39.00S 174.14 E
Waitati 218 Df 45.45S 170.34 E
Waitemata 218 Fb 36.50S 174.40 E
Waitotara 218 Fc 39.48S 174.44 E
Waiuku 218 Fb 37.15S 174.44 E
Waiwerang 150 Hh 8.23S 123.09 E
Waiyevo 218 Fc 16.48S 179.59W
Wājid 168 Ge 3.50N 43.14 E
Wajima 154 Nf 37.24N 136.54 E
Wajir 160 Ih 1.42N 40.04 E
Waka [Eth.] 168 Fd 7.09N 37.19 E
Waka [Zaire] 170 Db 1.01N 20.13 E
Wakamatsu-Shima 156 Ae 32.54N 129.00 E
Wakasa-Wan 152 Od 35.45N 135.40 E
Wakatipu, Lake- 216 Ci 45.05S 168.35 E
Wakaya 219d Bb 17.37S 179.00 E
Wakayama 142 Pf 34.13N 135.11 E
Wakayama Ken 154 Mh 33.55N 135.20 E
Wake 156 Dd 34.48N 134.08 E
Wa Keeney 186 Gg 39.01N 99.53W
Wakefield [Eng.-U.K.] 118 Lh 53.42N 1.29W
Wakefield [N.Z.] 218 Ed 41.24S 173.03 E
Wake Island 210 Hc 19.18N 166.36 E
Wake Island 208 Hc 19.18N 166.36 E
Wakkanai 142 Qe 45.25N 141.40 E
Waku Kungo 170 Ce 11.25S 15.07 E
Wakunai 219a Ba 5.52S 155.13 E
Wakuya 156 Gb 38.33N 141.05 E
Wala 170 Fd 5.46S 32.04 E
Walachia (EN) = Valahia 110 Ig 44.00N 25.00 E
Walachia (EN) = Valahia 130 He 44.00N 25.00 E

Index Symbols

1 Independent Nation	Historical or Cultural Region	Pass, Gap	Depression	Coast, Beach	Rock, Reef	Waterfall, Rapids	Canal	Lagoon	Escarpment, Sea Scarp	Historic Site	Airport
2 State, Region	Mount, Mountain	Plain, Lowland	Polder	Cliff	Islands, Archipelago	River Mouth, Estuary	Glacier	Bank	Fracture	Ruins	Port
3 District, County	Volcano	Delta	Desert, Dunes	Peninsula	Rocks, Reefs	Lake	Ice Shelf, Pack Ice	Seamount	Trench, Abyss	Wall, Walls	Military installation
4 Municipality	Hill	Salt Flat	Forest, Woods	Isthmus	Coral Reef	Salt Lake	Ocean	Tablemount	National Park, Reserve	Church, Abbey	Lighthouse
5 Colony, Dependency	Mountains, Mountain Range	Valley, Canyon	Heath, Steppe	Sandbank	Well, Spring	Intermittent Lake	Sea	Ridge	Point of Interest	Temple	Mine
Continent	Hills, Escarpment	Crater, Cave	Oasis	Island	Geyser	Reservoir	Gulf, Bay	Shelf	Recreation Site	Scientific Station	Tunnel
Physical Region	Plateau, Upland	Karst Features	Cape, Point	Atoll	River, Stream	Swamp, Pond	Strait, Fjord	Basin	Cave, Cavern	Railway station	Dam, Bridge

Wałbrzych	112	He	50.46N	16.17 E
Wałbrzych [2]	120	Mf	50.45N	16.15 E
Walchensee	120	Hi	47.35N	11.20 E
Walcheren	122	Jc	51.33N	3.35 E
Walcott, Lake-	188	Ie	42.40N	113.23W
Walcourt	124	Gd	50.15N	4.25 E
Walcourt-Fraire	124	Gd	50.16N	4.30 E
Wałcz	120	Mc	53.17N	16.28 E
Waldböckelheim	124	Je	49.49N	7.43 E
Waldbröl	120	Df	50.53N	7.37 E
Waldeck	124	Lc	51.12N	9.05 E
Waldeck	124	Kc	51.17N	8.50 E
Waldems	124	Kd	50.15N	8.18 E
Walden	186	Cf	40.44N	106.17W
Waldfischbach-Burgalben	124	Je	49.17N	7.40 E
Waldkirchen	120	Jh	48.44N	13.36 E
Waldkraiburg	120	Ih	48.12N	12.25 E
Wald-Michelbach	124	Ke	49.34N	8.49 E
Waldnaab	120	Ig	49.35N	12.07 E
Waldorf	184	If	38.37N	76.54W
Waldrach	124	Ie	49.45N	6.45 E
Waldron	186	Ii	34.54N	94.05W
Waldshut-Tiengen	120	Ei	47.37N	8.13 E
Waldviertel	128	Jb	48.30N	15.30 E
Waleabahi, Pulau-	150	Hg	0.15 S	122.20 E
Walej, Sha'īb al-	146	Hf	33.30N	39.15 E
Wales	178	Fc	65.36N	168.05W
Wales [2]	118	Ji	52.30N	3.30W
Wales	110	Fe	52.30N	3.30W
Wales	180	Ic	67.50N	86.40W
Walewale	166	Ec	10.21N	0.48W
Walferdange	124	Ie	49.39N	6.08 E
Walgett	210	Fh	30.01 S	148.07 E
Walgreen Coast	222	Of	75.15 S	105.00W
Walhalla	186	Hb	48.55N	97.55W
Walikale	170	Ec	1.25 S	28.03 E
Walker	186	Ic	47.06N	94.35W
Walker Lake	182	Dd	38.40N	118.43W
Walkerston	212	Jd	21.10 S	149.10 E
Wall	186	Ed	44.01N	102.14W
Wallace	188	Hc	47.28N	115.56W
Wallaceburg	184	Fd	42.36N	82.23W
Wallangarra	212	Ke	28.56 S	151.56 E
Wallaroo	212	Hf	33.56 S	137.38 E
Wallary Island	212	Ic	15.05 S	141.50 E
Wallasey	118	Jh	53.26N	3.03W
Walla Walla	182	Db	46.08N	118.20W
Walldorf	124	Ke	49.20N	8.39 E
Wallenhorst	124	Kb	52.21N	8.01 E
Wallibu	197n	Ba	13.19N	61.15W
Wallingford	124	Ac	51.36N	1.08W
Wallis / Valais [2]	128	Bd	46.15N	7.30 E
Wallis, Iles- = Wallis Islands (EN)	208	Jf	13.18 S	176.10W
Wallis and Futuna (EN) = Wallis-et-Futuna [5]	210	Jf	14.00 S	177.00W
Wallis-et-Futuna = Wallis and Futuna (EN) [5]	210	Jf	14.00 S	177.00W
Wallis Islands (EN) = Wallis, Iles-	208	Jf	13.18 S	176.10W
Wallowa	188	Gd	45.34N	117.32W
Wallowa Mountains	188	Gd	45.10N	117.30W
Walmer	124	Dc	51.12N	1.24 E
Walney, Isle of-	118	Jg	54.07N	3.15W
Walnut Ridge	182	Id	36.04N	90.57W
Walpole, Ile-	208	Hg	22.37 S	168.57 E
Walrus Islands	178	Ge	58.45N	160.20W
Walsall	118	Li	52.35N	1.58W
Walsenburg	182	Gd	37.37N	104.47W
Walsrode	120	Fd	52.52N	9.35 E
Walterboro	184	Gi	32.54N	80.39W
Walter F. George Lake	184	Ej	31.49N	85.08W
Walters	186	Gi	34.22N	98.19W
Waltershausen	120	Gf	50.54N	10.34 E
Waltham	184	Ic	45.58N	76.57W
Walton-on-the-Naze	124	Dc	51.51N	1.17 E
Waltrop	124	Jc	51.38N	7.24 E
Walvisbaai/Walvis Bay [3]	172	Ad	23.00 S	14.30 E
Walvisbaai = Walvis Bay (EN)	160	Ik	22.59 S	14.31 E
Walvisbaai = Walvis Bay (EN) [5]	160	Ik	22.59 S	14.31 E
Walvisbaai = Walvis Bay (EN)	158	Ik	22.57 S	14.30 E
Walvis Bay/Walvisbaai [3]	172	Ad	23.00 S	14.30 E
Walvis Bay (EN) = Walvisbaai	160	Ik	22.59 S	14.31 E
Walvis Bay (EN) = Walvisbaai [5]	160	Ik	22.59 S	14.31 E
Walvis Bay (EN) = Walvisbaai	158	Ik	22.57 S	14.30 E
Walvis Ridge (EN)	106	El	28.00 S	3.00 E
Wama	170	Ce	12.14 S	15.34 E
Wamba	158	Ii	3.56 S	17.12 E
Wamba [Kenya]	170	Gb	0.59N	37.19 E
Wamba [Nig.]	166	Gd	8.56N	8.36 E
Wamba [Zaire]	170	Eb	2.09N	28.00 E
Wamena	150	Kg	4.00 S	138.57 E
Wami	158	Ki	6.08 S	38.49 E
Wampusirpi	194	Ef	15.15N	84.37W
Wamsutter	188	Lf	41.40N	107.58W
Wan	150	Kh	8.23 S	137.56 E
Wana	148	Db	32.17N	69.35 E
Wanaka	210	Hi	44.42 S	169.08 E
Wanaka, Lake-	218	Cf	44.30 S	169.10 E
Wan'an	152	Jf	26.32N	114.48 E
Wanapiri	150	Kg	4.33 S	135.59 E
Wanapitei Lake	184	Gb	46.45N	80.45W
Wandel Hav = Wandel Sea (EN)	179	Kb	83.00N	15.00W
Wandel Sea (EN) = Wandel Hav	179	Kb	83.00N	15.00W
Wandsworth, London-	124	Bc	51.27N	0.12W
Wanganui	216	Eg	39.56 S	175.02 E
Wanganui	218	Fc	39.58 S	175.00 E
Wangaratta	212	Jg	36.22 S	146.20 E
Wangcun [China]	152	Jd	39.58N	112.53 E
Wangcun [China]	154	Df	36.41N	117.42 E
Wangda/Zogang	152	Gf	29.37N	97.58 E
Wangdu	154	Ce	38.43N	115.09 E
Wangen im Allagäu	120	Fi	47.41N	9.50 E
Wangerooge	120	Dc	53.46N	7.55 E
Wanggameti, Gunung-	150	Hi	10.07 S	120.14 E
Wanggezhuang → Jiaonan	154	Eg	35.53N	119.58 E
Wangiwangi, Pulau-	150	Hh	5.20 S	123.35 E
Wangjiang	154	Di	30.08N	116.41 E
Wangkui	152	Mb	46.50N	126.29 E
Wangpan Yang	140	Of	30.33N	121.26 E
Wangping	152	Mc	43.18N	129.46 E
Wangying → Huaiyin	154	Eh	33.35N	119.02 E
Wani, Laguna-	194	Ff	14.50N	83.25W
Wanie-Rukula	170	Eb	0.14N	25.34 E
Wanitsuka-Yama	156	Bf	31.45N	131.17 E
Wanleweyn	168	Ge	2.35N	44.55 E
Wān Namton	148	Jd	22.03N	99.33 E
Wannian (Chenying)	154	Dj	28.42N	117.04 E
Wanning	152	Jh	18.59N	110.24 E
Wanquan	154	Cd	40.52N	114.44 E
Wansbeck	118	Lf	55.10N	1.34W
Wan Shui	154	Di	30.30N	117.01 E
Wanxian	142	Mf	30.48N	108.21 E
Wanyuan	152	Ie	32.03N	108.04 E
Wanzai	154	Cj	28.06N	114.27 E
Wanzhi → Wuhu	154	Ei	31.21N	118.23 E
Wapato	188	Ec	46.27N	120.25W
Wapiti	188	Kd	44.28N	109.28W
Wapiti	180	Fe	55.08N	118.19W
Wapsipinicon River	186	Kf	41.44N	90.20W
Waqooyi Galbeed [3]	168	Gc	10.00N	44.00 E
Warangal	142	Jh	18.18N	79.35 E
Waratah Bay	212	Jg	38.50 S	146.05 E
Warburg	120	Fe	51.30N	9.10 E
Warburger Borde	124	Lc	51.35N	9.12 E
Warburg-Scherfede	124	Lc	51.32N	9.02 E
Warburton Bay	180	Gd	63.50N	111.30W
Warburton Mission	212	Fe	26.10 S	126.35 E
Warburton Range	212	Fe	26.10 S	126.40 E
Ward	218	Fd	41.50 S	174.08 E
Warden	172	De	27.56 S	29.00 E
Wardenburg	124	Ka	53.04N	8.12 E
Wardha	148	Fd	20.45N	78.37 E
Ward Hunt Strait	212	Ja	9.25 S	149.55 E
Ware [B.C.-Can.]	180	Ee	57.27N	125.38W
Ware [Eng.-U.K.]	124	Bc	51.49N	0.01W
Waregem	124	Fd	50.53N	3.25 E
Waremme/Borgworm	122	Ld	50.42N	5.15 E
Waren [G.D.R.]	120	Ic	53.31N	12.41 E
Waren [Indon.]	210	Ee	2.16 S	136.20 E
Warendorf	120	De	51.57N	7.59 E
Warin Chamrap	148	Ke	15.14N	104.52 E
Warka	120	Re	51.47N	21.10 E
Warkworth	218	Fb	36.24 S	174.40 E
Warmbad [3]	172	Be	28.00 S	18.30 E
Warmbad [Nam.]	172	Be	28.29 S	18.41 E
Warmbad [S.Afr.]	172	Dd	24.53 S	28.17 E
Warming Land	179	Gb	81.50N	52.45W
Warmington	124	Ab	52.08N	1.24W
Warminster	118	Kj	51.13N	2.12W
Warm Springs [Nv.-U.S.]	188	Gg	38.13N	116.20W
Warm Springs [Or.-U.S.]	188	Ed	44.46N	121.16W
Warnemünde, Rostock-	120	Ib	54.10N	12.05 E
Warner, Mount-	188	Da	51.03N	123.12W
Warner Mountains	182	Cc	41.40N	120.20W
Warner Peak	188	Fe	42.27N	119.44W
Warner Robins	182	Ke	32.37N	83.36W
Warner Valley	188	Fe	42.30N	119.55W
Warnes	202	Fg	17.30 S	63.10W
Warnow	120	Ib	54.06N	12.09 E
Waroona	212	Df	32.50 S	115.55 E
Warragul	212	Jg	38.10 S	145.56 E
Warrego Range	212	Je	25.00 S	145.45 E
Warrego River	208	Fh	30.24 S	145.21 E
Warren [Ar.-U.S.]	186	Jj	33.38N	92.05W
Warren [Mi.-U.S.]	184	Fd	42.28N	83.01W
Warren [Mn.-U.S.]	186	Hb	48.12N	96.46W
Warren [Oh.-U.S.]	182	Kc	41.15N	80.49W
Warren [Pa.-U.S.]	184	He	41.52N	79.09W
Warrenpoint/An Pointe	118	Gg	54.06N	6.15W
Warrensburg	186	Jg	38.46N	93.44W
Warrenton	172	Ce	28.09 S	24.47 E
Warri	166	Gd	5.31N	5.45 E
Warrington [Eng.-U.K.]	118	Kh	53.24N	2.37W
Warrington [Fl.-U.S.]	184	Dj	30.23N	87.16W
Warrior Reefs	212	Ia	9.35 S	143.10 E
Warrnambool	210	Fh	38.23 S	142.29 E
Warroad	182	Hb	48.54N	95.19W
Warrumbungle Range	212	Jf	31.30 S	149.40 E
Warsaw [In.-U.S.]	184	Ee	41.14N	85.51W
Warsaw [Mo.-U.S.]	186	Jg	38.15N	93.23W
Warsaw [N.Y.-U.S.]	184	Hd	42.45N	78.07W
Warsaw (EN) = Warszawa [Pol.]	112	Ie	52.15N	21.00 E
Warshīkh	168	He	2.18N	45.48 E
Warstein	124	Kc	51.27N	8.22 E
Warstein-Belecke	124	Kc	51.29N	8.20 E
Warszawa [2]	120	Qd	52.15N	21.00 E
Warszawa [Pol.] = Warsaw (EN)	112	Ie	52.15N	21.00 E
Warta	110	He	52.35N	14.39 E
Waru	150	Jg	3.24 S	130.40 E
Warwich	212	Ke	28.13 S	152.02 E
Warwick	118	Li	52.25N	1.30W
Warwick [Eng.-U.K.]	118	Li	52.17N	1.34W
Warwick [R.I.-U.S.]	184	Le	41.42N	71.23W
Warwickshire [3]	118	Li	52.10N	1.35W
Wasagu	166	Gc	11.22N	5.48 E
Wasatch Range	174	He	41.15N	111.30W
Wascana Creek	188	Ma	50.40N	104.55W
Wasco	188	Fi	35.36N	119.20W
Waseca	186	Jd	44.05N	93.30W
Washburn	186	Fc	47.17N	101.02W
Washess Bay	220g	Ab	1.49N	157.31W
Wāshim	148	Fd	20.10N	76.58 E
Washington [2]	182	Cb	47.30N	120.30W
Washington [D.C.-U.S.]	176	Lf	38.54N	77.01W
Washington [Eng.-U.K.]	118	Lg	54.54N	1.31W
Washington [Ga.-U.S.]	184	Fi	33.44N	82.44W
Washington [Ia.-U.S.]	186	Kf	41.18N	91.42W
Washington [In.-U.S.]	184	Df	38.40N	87.10W
Washington [N.C.-U.S.]	184	Ih	35.33N	77.03W
Washington [Pa.-U.S.]	184	Ge	40.11N	80.16W
Washington → Teraina Island	208	Kd	4.43N	160.24W
Washington, Mount-	174	Le	44.15N	71.15W
Washington Court House	184	Ff	39.32N	83.29W
Washington Island	186	Md	45.23N	86.55W
Washington Land	179	Fb	80.15N	65.00W
Washita River	186	Hi	34.12N	96.50W
Washtucna	188	Fc	46.45N	118.19W
Wasile	150	If	1.04N	127.59 E
Wasilków	120	Tc	53.12N	23.12 E
Wasior	150	Jg	2.43 S	134.30 E
Wāsiț [3]	146	Lf	32.35N	46.00 E
Waskaganish	176	Ld	51.25N	78.45W
Wąsosz	120	Me	51.34N	16.42 E
Waspán	190	Hf	14 44N	83.58W
Wassamu	156a	Ca	44.02N	142.24 E
Wassenaar	124	Gb	52.09N	4.24 E
Wassenberg	124	Ic	51.06N	6.09 E
Wasserburg am Inn	120	Ih	48.04N	,2.14 E
Wasserkuppe	120	Ff	50.30N	9.56 E
Wassigny	124	Fd	50.01N	3.36 E
Wassuk Range	188	Fg	38.40N	118.50W
Wassy	122	Kf	48.30N	4.57 E
Waswanipi, Lac-	184	Ia	49.32N	76.29W
Watampone	142	Oj	4.32 S	120.20 E
Watansoppeng	150	Gg	4.21 S	119.53 E
Watari	156	Gb	38.02N	140.51 E
Waterbeach	124	Cb	52.16N	0.12 E
Waterberg	172	Bd	20.25 S	17.15 E
Waterbury	182	Mc	41.33N	73.02W
Water Cays	194	Ib	23.40N	77.45W
Wateree Pond	184	Gh	34.25N	80.50W
Waterford/Port Láirge	112	Fe	52.15N	7.06W
Waterford/Port Láirge [2]	118	Fi	52.10N	7.40W
Waterford Harbour/Cuan Phort Láirge	118	Gi	52.10N	6.57W
Wateringues	122	Id	50.55N	2.15 E
Waterloo [Bel.]	122	Kd	50.43N	4.24 E
Waterloo [Ia.-U.S.]	182	Ic	42.30N	92.20W
Waterloo [Il.-U.S.]	186	Kg	38.20N	90.09W
Waterlooville	124	Ad	50.52N	1.01W
Watersmeet	184	Cb	46.18N	89.11W
Watertown [N.Y.-U.S.]	182	Lc	43.57N	75.56W
Watertown [S.D.-U.S.]	182	Hc	44.54N	97.07W
Watertown [Wi.-U.S.]	186	Le	43.12N	88.43W
Waterville	182	Nc	44.33N	69.38W
Watford	118	Mj	51.40N	0.25W
Watford City	186	Ec	47.48N	103.17W
Wa'th	168	Ed	8.10N	32.07 E
Watheroo	212	Df	30.17 S	116.04 E
Watīr, Wādī-	146	Fh	29.01N	34.40 E
Watkins Glen	184	Id	42.23N	76.53W
Watling → San Salvador	190	Jd	24.02N	74.28W
Watlington	124	Ac	51.38N	1.00W
Watonga	186	Gi	35.51N	98.25W
Watou, Poperinge-	124	Ed	50.51N	2.37 E
Watrous	180	Gf	51.40N	105.28W
Watsa	160	Jh	3.03N	29.32 E
Watseka	186	Mf	40.47N	87.44W
Watsi [C.R.]	194	Fi	9.37N	82.52W
Watsi [Zaire]	170	Dc	0.19 S	21.04 E
Watsi Kengo	170	Dc	0.48 S	20.33 E
Watson Lake	176	Gc	60.07N	128.48W
Watsonville	188	Eh	36.55N	121.45W
Watt, Morne-	197g	Bb	15.19N	61.19W
Watton	124	Cb	52.34N	0.50 E
Watts Bar Lake	184	Eh	35.48N	84.39W
Wattwil	128	Dc	47.18N	9.05 E
Watubela, Kepulauan-	150	Jg	4.35 S	131.40 E
Wau	212	Ja	7.20 S	146.45 E
Waubay Lake	186	Hd	45.25N	97.25W
Wauchope	212	Kf	31.27 S	152.44 E
Wauchula	184	Gl	27.33N	81.49W
Waucoba Mountain	188	Fh	37.00N	118.01W
Waukara, Gunung-	150	Gg	1.15 S	119.42 E
Waukarlycarly, Lake-	212	Ed	21.25 S	121.50 E
Waukegan	182	Jc	42.22N	87.50W
Waukesha	186	Le	43.01N	88.14W
Waupaca	186	Ld	44.21N	89.05W
Wausau	182	Jc	44.59N	89.39W
Wauseon	184	Ee	41.33N	84.09W
Wauwatosa	186	Me	43.03N	88.00W
Wave Hill	212	Gc	17.29 S	130.57 E
Waveney	118	Oi	52.28N	1.45 E
Waver/Wavre	122	Kd	50.43N	4.37 E
Waverly [Ia.-U.S.]	186	Je	42.44N	92.29W
Waverly [Oh.-U.S.]	184	Ff	39.07N	82.59W
Waverly [Tn.-U.S.]	184	Dg	36.05N	87.48W
Waves	184	Jh	35.37N	75.29W
Wavre/Waver	122	Kd	50.43N	4.37 E
Wāw	160	Jh	7.42N	28.00 E
Wawa [Nig.]	166	Fd	9.55N	4.27 E
Wawa [Ont.-Can.]	180	Jg	47.59N	84.47W
Wawa, Río-	194	Fg	13.53N	83.28W
Wāw al Kabīr	160	If	25.20N	16.43 E
Wāw an Nāmūs	164	Ce	24.55N	19.45 E
Wāw Nahr	168	Dd	7.03N	27.13 E
Wawo	150	Hg	3.41 S	121.02 E
Wawotobi	150	Hg	3.51 S	122.06 E
Waxahachie	186	Hj	32.24N	96.51W
Waxweiler	124	Id	50.06N	6.22 E
Waxxari	152	Ed	38.37N	87.22 E
Way, Lake-	212	Ee	26.50 S	120.20 E
Waya	219d	Ab	17.18 S	177.08 E
Wayabula	150	If	2.17N	128.12 E
Wayan	188	Je	43.00N	111.22W
Waycross	182	Ke	31.13N	82.21W
Wayne [Nb.-U.S.]	186	He	42.14N	97.01W
Wayne [W.V.-U.S.]	184	Ff	38.14N	82.27W
Waynesboro [Ga.-U.S.]	184	Fi	33.06N	82.01W
Waynesboro [Ms.-U.S.]	186	Lk	31.40N	88.39W
Waynesboro [Pa.-U.S.]	184	If	39.45N	77.36W
Waynesboro [Va.-U.S.]	184	Hf	38.04N	78.54W
Waynesville [Mo.-U.S.]	186	Jh	37.50N	92.12W
Waynesville [N.C.-U.S.]	184	Fh	35.29N	83.00W
Waynoka	186	Gh	36.35N	98.53W
Waziers	124	Fd	50.23N	3.07 E
Wda	120	Oc	53.25N	18.29 E
Wdzydze, Jezioro-	120	Nc	54.00N	17.50 E
Wé	216	Cd	20.55 S	167.16 E
We, Pulau-	150	Ce	5.51N	95.18 E
Wear	118	Lg	54.55N	1.22W
Weatherford [Ok.-U.S.]	186	Gi	35.32N	98.42W
Weatherford [Tx.-U.S.]	182	He	32.46N	97.48W
Weaverville	188	Df	40.44N	122.56W
Weber	218	Gd	40.24 S	176.20 E
Webster	186	Hd	45.20N	97.31W
Webster City	186	Je	42.28N	93.49W
Webster Springs	184	Gf	38.29N	80.25W
Weda	150	If	0.21N	127.52 E
Weda, Teluk-	150	If	0.20N	128.00 E
Weddell Island	206	Hh	51.50 S	61.00W
Weddell Sea (EN)	222	Rf	72.00 S	45.00W
Wedel	120	Fc	53.35N	9.41 E
Wedgeport	184	Od	43.44N	65.59W
Wedza	172	Ec	18.35 S	31.35 E
Weed	188	Df	41.25N	122.27W
Weener	120	Dc	53.10N	7.21 E
Weerdinge, Emmen-	124	Ib	52.49N	6.57 E
Weert	122	Lc	51.15N	5.43 E
Weesp	124	Hb	52.18N	5.02 E
Wegberg	124	Ic	51.09N	6.16 E
Węgliniec	120	Le	51.17N	15.13 E
Węgorzewo	120	Rb	54.14N	21.44 E
Wegrów	120	Sd	52.25N	22.01 E
Wehni	168	Fc	12.40N	36.42 E
Weichang (Zhuizishan)	152	Kc	41.55N	117.39 E
Weida	120	If	50.46N	12.04 E
Weiden in der Oberpfalz	120	Ig	49.41N	12.10 E
Weifang	142	Nf	36.43N	119.06 E
Weihai	152	Ld	37.27N	122.02 E
Weihe	154	Jb	44.55N	128.23 E
Wei He	140	Nf	34.36N	110.10 E
Weil	124	Kd	50.28N	8.16 E
Weilburg	120	Ef	50.29N	8.15 E
Weilerbach	124	Je	49.29N	7.38 E
Weilerswist	124	Id	50.46N	6.50 E
Weilheim in Oberbayern	120	Hi	47.50N	11.09 E
Weilmünster	124	Kd	50.26N	8.21 E
Weimar [F.R.G.]	124	Kd	50.46N	8.43 E
Weimar [G.D.R.]	120	Hf	50.59N	11.19 E
Weinan	152	Ie	34.30N	109.34 E
Weingarten	120	Fi	47.48N	9.38 E
Weinheim	120	Eg	49.33N	8.40 E
Weining	152	Hf	26.46N	104.18 E
Weinsberger Wald	128	Ib	48.25N	15.00 E
Weinstraße	124	Ke	49.20N	8.05 E
Weinviertel	128	Kb	48.35N	16.30 E
Weipa	210	Ff	12.41 S	141.52 E
Weirton	184	Ge	40.24N	80.37W
Weiser	188	Gd	44.15N	116.58W
Weiser River	188	Gd	44.15N	116.59W
Weishan Hu	152	Ke	34.35N	117.15 E
Weishi	154	Cg	34.25N	114.10 E
Weishui → Jingxing	154	Ce	38.03N	114.09 E
Weiße Elster	120	He	51.26N	11.57 E
Weißenberg	124	Je	49.15N	7.49 E
Weißenburg in Bayern	120	Gg	49.02N	10.59 E
Weißenfels	120	He	51.12N	11.58 E
Weißer Main	120	Hf	50.05N	11.24 E
Weißerstein	124	Id	50.24N	6.22 E
Weißkugel/Palla Bianca	128	Ed	46.48N	10.44 E
Weiss Lake	184	Eh	34.15N	85.35W
Weißwasser/Běła Woda	120	Ke	51.31N	14.38 E
Weitra	128	Ib	48.42N	14.53 E
Weixi	152	Gf	27.13N	99.19 E
Weixian	154	Cf	36.59N	115.15 E
Weixin (Zhaxi)	152	If	27.46N	105.04 E
Weiz	128	Jc	47.13N	15.37 E
Wejherowo	120	Ob	54.37N	18.15 E
Welbourn Hill	210	Eg	27.21 S	134.06 E
Welch	184	Gg	37.26N	81.36W
Weldiya	168	Fc	11.48N	39.35 E
Weld Range	212	De	26.55 S	117.25 E
Welega [3]	168	Fd	8.38N	35.40 E
Welel	168	Ed	8.56N	34.52 E
Weligama	148	Gg	5.58N	80.25 E
Welkenraedt	124	Hd	50.39N	5.58 E
Welker Seamount (EN)	178	Ke	55.07N	140.20W
Welkite	168	Fd	8.17N	37.49 E
Welkom	160	Jk	27.59 S	26.45 E
Welland	180	Jh	42.59N	79.15W
Welland	118	Ni	52.53N	0.02 E
Welland Canal	184	Hd	43.14N	79.13W
Wellesley Islands	208	Ef	16.45 S	139.30 E
Wellin	124	Hd	50.05N	5.07 E
Wellingborough	118	Mi	52.19N	0.42W
Wellington [2]	218	Fd	40.10 S	175.30 E
Wellington [Austl.]	212	Jf	32.33 S	148.57 E
Wellington [Eng.-U.K.]	118	Jk	50.59N	3.14W
Wellington [Ks.-U.S.]	186	Hh	37.16N	97.24W
Wellington [Nv.-U.S.]	188	Fg	38.45N	119.22W
Wellington [N.Z.]	210	Ii	41.17 S	174.46 E
Wellington, Isla-	198	Ij	49.20 S	74.40W
Wellington, Lake-	212	Jg	38.10 S	147.15 E
Wellington Channel	180	Ia	75.10N	93.00W
Wells [Eng.-U.K.]	118	Kj	51.13N	2.39W
Wells [Eng.-U.K.]	118	Ni	52.58N	0.51 E
Wells [Nv.-U.S.]	182	Dc	41.07N	115.01W
Wells, Lake-	212	Ee	26.45 S	123.15 E
Wells, Mount-	212	Fc	17.26 S	127.14 E
Wellsboro	184	Ie	41.45N	77.18W
Wellsford	218	Fb	36.18 S	174.31 E
Wellton	188	Hj	32.40N	114.08W
Welmel	168	Gd	5.35N	40.55 E
Wełna	120	Md	52.36N	16.50 E
Welo [3]	168	Fc	12.00N	40.00 E
Wels	128	Ib	48.10N	14.02 E
Welshpool	118	Ji	52.40N	3.09W
Welver	124	Jc	51.37N	7.58 E
Welwitschia	172	Ad	20.21 S	14.57 E
Welwyn Garden City	118	Mj	51.48N	0.13W
Wema	170	Dc	0.26 S	21.38 E
Wemding	120	Gh	48.52N	10.43 E
Wen'an	154	De	38.52N	116.30 E
Wenatchee	182	Cb	47.25N	120.19W
Wenatchee Mountains	188	Ec	47.20N	120.45W
Wenchang	152	Jh	19.43N	110.44 E
Wenchi	166	Ed	7.44N	2.06W
Wenchit	168	Fc	10.03N	38.35 E
Wenden	124	Jd	50.58N	7.52 E
Wendeng	152	Ld	37.10N	122.01 E
Wendland	120	Gc	53.10N	11.00 E
Wendo	168	Fd	6.37N	38.25 E
Wendover	188	Hf	40.45N	114.02W
Wengyuan (Longxian)	152	Jg	24.21N	114.13 E
Wen He	154	Ef	37.06N	119.29 E
Wenling	152	Lf	28.23N	121.22 E
Wenquan	152	Fe	33.15N	91.55 E
Wenquan/Arixang	152	Dc	44.59N	81.04 E
Wenshan	152	Hg	23.22N	104.23 E
Wenshui	154	Bf	37.26N	112.01 E
Wensu	152	Dc	41.15N	80.14 E
Wensum	124	Db	52.37N	1.22 E
Wentworth	212	If	34.07 S	141.55 E
Wenxian	152	He	32.52N	104.40 E
Wenzhou	142	Og	27.57N	120.38 E
Wenzhu	152	Jf	27.00N	114.00 E
Wepener	172	De	29.46 S	27.00 E
Wépion, Namur-	124	Gd	50.25N	4.52 E
Werda	172	Ce	25.16 S	23.17 E
Werder	160	Lh	7.00N	45.21 E
Werder	120	Jc	53.40N	13.25 E
Werdohl	124	Jc	51.16N	7.46 E
Were Ilu	168	Fc	10.38N	39.23 E
Werkendam	124	Gc	51.49N	4.55 E
Werl	124	Jc	51.33N	7.55 E
Werlte	124	Jb	52.51N	7.41 E
Wermelskirchen	124	Jc	51.09N	7.13 E
Werne	124	Jc	51.40N	7.38 E
Wernigerode	120	Ge	51.50N	10.47 E
Werra	110	Ge	51.26N	9.39 E
Werribee	212	Ig	37.54 S	144.40 E
Werris Creek	212	Kf	31.21 S	150.39 E
Werse	124	Jb	52.02N	7.41 E
Wertach	120	Gh	48.24N	10.53 E
Wertheim	120	Fg	49.45N	9.31 E
Wesel	120	Ce	51.40N	6.37 E
Weser	110	Ge	53.32N	8.34 E
Weserbergland	120	Fe	51.55N	9.30 E
Wesergebirge	120	Fd	52.15N	9.10 E
Weslaco	186	Gm	26.09N	98.01W
Wesley	197g	Ba	15.34N	61.19W
Wesleyville	180	Mg	49.09N	53.34W
Wessel, Cape-	212	Hb	11.00 S	136.45 E
Wesseling	124	Id	50.50N	6.59 E
Wessel Islands	208	Ef	12.00 S	136.45 E
Wessington Springs	186	Gd	44.05N	98.34W
West Allis	186	Le	43.01N	88.00W
West Baines River	212	Gc	15 26 S	130.08 E
West Bay	186	Ll	29.00N	89.30W
West Bend	186	Le	43.25N	88.11W
West Bengal [3]	148	Hd	24.00N	88.00 E
West Berlin (EN) = Berlin (West)	112	He	52.31N	13.24 E
West Branch	184	Ec	44.17N	84.14W
West Bridgford	124	Ab	52.55N	1.07W
West Bromwich	118	Li	52.31N	1.59W
Westbrook	184	Ld	43.41N	70.21W
West Burra	118	La	60.05N	1.10W
West Caicos	194	Kc	21.47N	72.17W
West Cape	208	Hi	45.55 S	166.26 E
West Caroline Basin (EN)	106	Ii	4.00N	138.00 E
West Carpathians (EN) = Západné Karpaty	120	Og	49.30N	19.00 E
West Des Moines	186	Jf	41.35N	93.43W
Westdongeradeel	124	Ha	53.23N	5.58 E
Westdongeradeel-Holwerd	124	Ha	53.22N	5.54 E
Westdongeradeel-Ternaard	124	Ha	53.23N	5.58 E
Westeinderplassen	124	Gb	52.15N	4.30 E
West Elk Mountains	186	Cg	38.40N	107.15W
West End	184	Hl	26.41N	78.58W
Westende, Middelkerke-	124	Ec	51.10N	2.46 E
West End Village	197b	Ab	18.11N	63.09W
West Entrance	220a	Bb	7.57N	134.30 E
Westerbork	124	Ib	52.51N	6.36 E
Westerburg	124	Jd	50.34N	7.59 E
Westerland	120	Eb	54.54N	8.18 E
Westerlo	124	Gc	51.05N	4.55 E
Western [Ghana] [3]	166	Ed	5.30N	2.30W
Western [Kenya] [3]	170	Fb	0.30N	34.35 E
Western [S.L.] [3]	166	Cd	8.20N	13.00W
Western [Ug.] [3]	170	Fb	1.00N	31.00 E
Western [Zam.] [3]	170	Df	15.00 S	24.00 E
Western Australia [2]	212	Ed	25.00 S	122.00 E
Western Desert (EN) = Gharbīyah, Aş Şaḩrā' al-	158	Jf	27.30N	28.00 E
Western Dvina (EN) = Daugava	136	Cd	57.04N	24.03 E
Western Dvina (EN) = Zapadnaja Dvina	110	Id	57.04N	24.03 E
Western Entrance	219a	Bb	6.55 S	155.40 E
Western Ghats/Sahyadri	140	Jh	14.00N	75.00 E
Western Isles [3]	118	Fd	57.40N	7.10W
Western Port	212	Jg	38.25 S	145.10 E
Western River	180	Gc	66.22N	107.15W
Western Sahara (EN) [5]	160	Ff	24.30N	13.00W
Western Samoa (EN) = Samoa I Sisifo [1]	210	Jf	13.40 S	172.30W
Western Sayans (EN) = Zapadny Sajan	140	Ld	53.00N	94.00 E
Western Sierra Madre (EN) = Madre Occidental, Sierra-	174	Ig	25.00N	105.00W
Western Turkistan (EN)	140	He	41.00N	60.00 E
Westerschelde = West Schelde (EN)	122	Jc	51.25N	3.45 E
Westerschouwen	124	Fc	51.41N	3.43 E

Index Symbols

- [1] Independent Nation
- [2] State, Region
- [3] District, County
- [4] Municipality
- [5] Colony, Dependency
- Continent
- Physical Region
- Historical or Cultural Region
- Mount, Mountain
- Volcano
- Hill
- Mountains, Mountain Range
- Hills, Escarpment
- Plateau, Upland
- Pass, Gap
- Plain, Lowland
- Delta
- Salt Flat
- Valley, Canyon
- Crater, Cave
- Karst Features
- Depression
- Polder
- Desert, Dunes
- Forest, Woods
- Heath, Steppe
- Oasis
- Cape, Point
- Coast, Beach
- Cliff
- Peninsula
- Isthmus
- Sandbank
- Island
- Atoll
- Rock, Reef
- Islands, Archipelago
- Rocks, Reefs
- Coral Reef
- Well, Spring
- Geyser
- River, Stream
- Waterfall, Rapids
- River Mouth, Estuary
- Lake
- Salt Lake
- Intermittent Lake
- Reservoir
- Swamp, Pond
- Canal
- Glacier
- Ice Shelf, Pack Ice
- Ocean
- Sea
- Gulf, Bay
- Strait, Fjord
- Lagoon
- Bank
- Seamount
- Tablemount
- Ridge
- Shelf
- Basin
- Escarpment, Sea Scarp
- Fracture
- Trench, Abyss
- National Park, Reserve
- Point of Interest
- Recreation Site
- Cave, Cavern
- Historic Site
- Ruins
- Wall, Walls
- Church, Abbey
- Temple
- Scientific Station
- Railway station
- Airport
- Port
- Military installation
- Lighthouse
- Mine
- Tunnel
- Dam, Bridge

Westerschouwen-Haamstede	124	Fc	51.42N	3.45 E
Westerstede	120	Dc	53.15N	7.56 E
Westerwald ⛰	120	Df	50.40N	7.55 E
Westerwoldse A ⧅	124	Ja	53.10N	7.10 E
West European Basin (EN) ⊌	106	De	47.00N	15.00W
West Falkland/Gran Malvina, Isla- ◆	198	Kk	51.40 S	60.00W
West Fayu Island ◆	208	Fd	8.05N	146.44 E
West Fork Big Blue River ⧅	186	Hf	40.42N	96.59W
Westfriesland=West Friesland (EN) ⧗	122	Kb	52.45N	4.50 E
West Friesland (EN)=Westfriesland ⧗	122	Kb	52.45N	4.50 E
West Frisian Islands (EN) = Waddeneilanden ⬡	122	Ka	53.30N	5.00 E
Westgate-on-Sea	124	Dc	51.22N	1.21 E
West Glacier	188	Ib	48.30N	113.59W
West Glamorgan [3]	118	Jj	51.40N	3.55W
West Grand Lake ⊜	184	Nc	45.15N	67.52W
West Greenland (EN) = Vestgrønland [2]	179	He	69.00N	49.30W
West Helena	186	Ki	34.33N	90.39W
West Hollywood	184	Gm	25.59N	80.11W
Westhope	186	Fb	48.55N	101.01W
West Ice Shelf ❅	222	Ge	67.00 S	85.00 E
West Indies ⬡	190	Je	19.00N	70.00W
West Indies (EN)=Indias Occidentales ⬡	190	Je	19.00N	70.00W
West Island ◆	172b	Ab	9.22 S	46.13 E
Westkapelle	124	Fc	51.31N	3.26 E
Westkapelle, Knokke-	124	Fc	51.19N	3.18 E
West Lafayette	184	De	40.27N	86.55W
Westland [2]	218	De	43.10 S	170.30 E
West Liberty	184	Fg	37.55N	83.16W
Westlock	180	Gf	54.09N	113.52W
West Lunga ⧅	170	De	13.06 S	24.39 E
Westmalle	124	Gc	51.18N	4.41 E
West Mariana Basin (EN) ⊌	106	Ih	15.00N	137.00 E
Westmeath/An Iarmhí [2]	118	Fh	53.30N	7.30W
West Melanesian Trench (EN) ∪	214	Dh	1.00 S	150.00 E
West Memphis	182	Id	35.08N	90.11W
West Mersea	124	Cc	51.46N	0.54 E
West Midlands [3]	118	Li	52.30N	2.00W
Westminster	184	If	39.35N	76.59W
Westminster, London-	124	Bc	51.30N	0.07W
West Monroe	186	Jj	32.31N	92.09W
Westmorland ▣	118	Kg	54.30N	2.40W
West Nicholson	160	Jk	21.03 S	29.22 E
West Nueces River ⧅	186	Gl	29.16N	99.56W
Weston [Mala.]	150	Ge	5.13N	115.36 E
Weston [W.V.-U.S.]	184	Gf	39.03N	80.28W
Weston [Wy.-U.S.]	188	Md	44.42N	105.18W
Weston-super-Mare	118	Kj	51.21N	2.59W
Westoverledingen	124	Ja	53.10N	7.27 E
Westoverledingen - Ihrhove	124	Ja	53.10N	7.27 E
West Palm Beach	176	Kg	26.43N	80.04W
West Pensacola	184	Dj	30.27N	87.15W
West Plains	182	Id	36.44N	91.51W
West Point [Ms.-U.S.]	186	Lj	33.36N	88.39W
West Point [Nb.-U.S.]	186	Hf	41.51N	96.43W
Westport	210	Ii	41.45 S	171.36 E
Westport/Cathair na Mart	118	Dh	53.48N	9.32W
Westray ◆	118	Kb	59.20N	3.00W
Westree	184	Gb	47.27N	81.32W
Westrich ⧗	124	Je	49.20N	7.25 E
West Road ◐	124	Cd	50.52N	0.50 E
West Schelde (EN)=Westerschelde ∽	122	Jc	51.25N	3.45 E
West Scotia Basin (EN) ⊌	198	Kk	57.00 S	53.00W
West Siberian Plain (EN) = Zapadno-Sibirskaja ravnina ▭	140	Jc	60.00N	75.00 E
Weststellingwerf	124	Ib	52.53N	6.00 E
Weststellingwerf-Wolvega	124	Ib	52.53N	6.00 E
West Sussex [3]	118	Mk	51.00N	0.40W
West Tavaputs Plateau ⌓	188	Jf	40.00N	110.25W
West-Terschelling, Terschelling-	124	Ha	53.21N	5.13 E
West Union [Ia.-U.S.]	186	Ke	42.57N	91.49W
West Union [Oh.-U.S.]	184	Ff	38.48N	83.33W
West Virginia [2]	182	Kd	38.45N	80.30W
West-Vlaanderen = Flanders, West- (EN) [3]	124	Ec	51.00N	3.00 E
Westwood	188	Ef	40.18N	121.00W
West Wyalong	212	Jf	33.55 S	147.13 E
West Yellowstone	182	Ec	44.30N	111.05W
West Yorkshire [3]	118	Lh	53.40N	1.30W
Wetar, Pulau- ◆	208	De	7.48 S	126.18 E
Wetaskiwin	180	Gf	52.58N	113.22W
Wete	170	Gd	5.04 S	39.43 E
Wětošow/Vetschau	120	Ke	51.47N	14.04 E
Wetter ⧅	124	Kd	50.18N	8.49 E
Wetter (Hessen)	124	Kd	50.54N	8.43 E
Wetter (Ruhr)	124	Jc	51.23N	7.24 E
Wetterau ⧗	120	Ef	50.15N	8.50 E
Wetteren	122	Jc	51.00N	3.53 E
Wetzlar	120	Ef	50.33N	8.30 E
Wetzstein ▲	120	Hf	50.27N	11.27 E
Wevelgem	124	Fd	50.48N	3.10 E
Wewahitchka	184	Ej	30.07N	85.12W
Wewak	210	Fe	3.34 S	143.38 E
Wexford/Loch Garman	112	Fe	52.20N	6.27W
Wexford/Loch Garman [2]	118	Gi	52.20N	6.40W
Wexford Harbour/Cuan Loch Garman ◐	118	Gi	52.20N	6.25W
Wey ⧅	118	Mj	51.23N	0.28W
Weyburn	180	Hg	49.41N	103.52W
Weyhe	124	Kb	52.59N	8.52 E
Weyhe-Leeste	124	Kb	52.59N	8.50 E
Weymouth and Melcombe Regjs	118	Kk	50.36N	2.28W
Wezet/Visé	124	Hd	50.44N	5.42 E
Whakatane	216	Eg	37.58 S	177.00 E
Whale Cove	180	Id	62.14N	92.10W
Whalsay ◆	118	Ma	60.22N	0.59W
Whangarei	210	Ih	35.43 S	174.19 E
Wharfe ⧅	118	Lh	53.51N	1.07W
Wharton	186	Hl	29.19N	96.06W
Wharton Basin (EN) ⊌	106	Hk	19.00 S	100.00 E
Wharton Lake ⊜	180	Hd	64.00N	99.55W
Whataroa	218	De	43.16 S	170.22 E
Wheatland	188	Me	42.03N	104.57W
Wheat Ridge	186	Dg	39.46N	105.07W
Wheeler	188	Dd	45.42N	123.52W
Wheeler ⧅	180	Ke	57.02N	67.14W
Wheeler Lake ⊜	184	Dh	34.40N	87.05W
Wheeler Peak [N.M.-U.S.] ▲	182	Fd	36.34N	105.25W
Wheeler Peak [U.S.] ▲	174	Hf	38.59N	114.19W
Wheeling	182	Kc	40.05N	80.43W
Whidbey Island ◆	188	Db	48.15N	122.40W
Whitby	118	Mg	54.29N	0.37W
Whitchurch [Eng.-U.K.]	118	Ki	52.58N	2.41W
Whitchurch [Eng.-U.K.]	124	Bc	51.53N	0.50W
Whitchurch [Eng.-U.K.]	124	Ac	51.13N	1.20W
White ◆	180	Jc	65.50N	85.00W
White, Lake- ⊜	212	Fd	21.05 S	129.00 E
White Bay ◐	174	Nd	50.00N	56.30W
White Bear Lake	186	Jd	45.04N	93.01W
White Butte ▲	186	Ec	46.23N	103.19W
White Carpathians (EN) = Bílé Karpaty ⛰	120	Nh	48.55N	17.50 E
White Cliffs	212	If	30.51 S	143.05 E
White Cloud	184	Ed	43.33N	85.46W
Whitecourt	180	Ff	54.09N	115.41W
Whitefish	182	Eb	48.25N	114.20W
Whitefish Bay ◐	182	Kb	46.40N	84.50W
Whitefish Point ▶	184	Eb	46.45N	85.00W
Whitefish Range ⛰	188	Hb	48.40N	114.26W
Whitehall [Mi.-U.S.]	184	Dd	43.24N	86.21W
Whitehall [Mt.-U.S.]	188	Id	45.52N	112.06W
Whitehall [Oh.-U.S.]	184	Ff	39.58N	82.54W
Whitehall [Wi.-U.S.]	186	Kd	44.22N	91.19W
Whitehaven	118	Jg	54.33N	3.35W
Whitehorse	176	Fc	60.43N	135.03W
White Island [Ant.] ◆	222	Ee	66.44 S	48.35 E
White Island [N.Z.] ◆	218	Gb	37.30 S	177.10 E
White Lake ⊜	186	Jl	29.45N	92.30W
White Lake (EN) = Beloje ozero ⊜	110	Jc	60.11N	37.35 E
Whiteman Range ⛰	212	Ja	5.50 S	149.55 E
Whitemark	212	Jh	40.07 S	148.01 E
White Mountain	178	Gd	64.35N	163.04W
White Mountain Peak ▲	182	Dd	37.38N	118.15W
White Mountains [Ak.-U.S.] ⛰	178	Jc	65.30N	147.00W
White Mountains [U.S.] ⛰	182	Mc	44.10N	71.35W
White Mountains [U.S.] ⛰	188	Fh	37.30N	118.15W
Whitemouth Lake ⊜	186	Ib	49.14N	95.40W
Whitemouth River ⧅	186	Ha	50.07N	96.02W
White Nile (EN)=Abyaḍ, Al Baḩr al- [3]	168	Ec	12.40N	32.30 E
White Nile (EN)=Abyaḍ, Al Baḩr al- ⧅	158	Kg	15.38N	32.31 E
White Pass [N.Amer.] ⋎	178	Le	59.37N	135.08W
White Pass [Wa.-U.S.] ⋎	188	Ec	46.38N	121.24W
White River	180	Ig	48.35N	85.17W
White River	186	Fe	43.34N	100.45W
Whiteriver	188	Kj	33.50N	109.58W
White River [In.-U.S.] ⧅	184	Df	38.25N	87.44W
White River [Nv.-U.S.] ⧅	188	Hh	37.18N	115.08W
White River [Tx.-U.S.] ⧅	186	Fj	33.14N	100.56W
White River [U.S.] ⧅	188	Kf	40.04N	109.41W
White River [U.S.] ⧅	182	Hc	43.45N	99.30W
White River [U.S.] ⧅	174	Jf	33.53N	91.03W
White River [Yuk.-Can.] ⧅	180	Dd	63.10N	139.32W
White Salmon	188	Ed	45.44N	121.29W
Whitesand Bay ◐	118	Ik	50.20N	4.35W
White Sea (EN) = Beloje more ≋	110	Kb	66.00N	44.00 E
White Sea-Baltic Canal (EN) = Belomorsko-Baltijski kanal ═	110	Jc	63.30N	34.48 E
White Settlement	186	Hj	32.45N	97.27W
White Sulphur Springs	188	Jc	46.33N	110.54W
Whiteville	184	Hh	34.20N	78.42W
White Volta ⧅	158	Gh	8.38N	0.59W
White Volta (EN)=Volta Blanche ⧅	158	Gh	8.38N	0.59W
Whitewater	186	Bg	38.59N	108.27W
Whitewater Baldy ▲	186	Bj	33.20N	108.39W
Whitewater Bay ◐	184	Gm	25.16N	81.00W
Whitewater Lake ⊜	186	La	50.50N	89.10W
Whitewood	186	Ea	50.20N	102.15W
Whitianga	218	Fb	36.50 S	175.42 E
Whitmore Mountains ⛰	222	Og	82.35 S	104.30W
Whitney	184	Hc	45.30N	78.14W
Whitney, Lake- ⊜	186	Hk	31.55N	97.23W
Whitney, Mount- ▲	174	Hf	36.35N	118.18W
Whitstable	124	Dc	51.21N	1.06 E
Whitsunday Island ◆	212	Jd	20.15 S	149.00 E
Whittier	178	Jd	60.46N	148.41W
Whittlesea	212	Jg	37.31 S	145.07 E
Whittlesey	124	Bb	52.33N	0.08W
Wholdaia Lake ⊜	180	Hd	60.45N	104.10W
Whyalla	212	Hf	33.02 S	137.35 E
Wiarton	184	Gc	44.45N	81.09W
Wiawso	166	Ed	6.12N	2.29W
Wibaux	188	Mc	46.59N	104.11W
Wichita	176	Jf	37.41N	97.20W
Wichita Falls	176	Jf	33.54N	98.30W
Wichita Mountains ⛰	186	Gi	34.45N	98.40W
Wichita River ⧅	186	Gi	34.07N	98.10W
Wick	118	Jc	58.26N	3.06W
Wick ⧅	118	Jc	58.25N	3.05W
Wickenburg	188	Ij	33.58N	112.44W
Wickepin	212	Df	32.46 S	117.30 E
Wickham	124	Ad	50.54N	1.10W
Wickham Market	124	Db	52.09N	1.22 E
Wickiup Reservoir ⊏	188	Ee	43.40N	121.43W
Wickliffe	184	Cg	36.58N	89.05W
Wicklow/Cill Mhantáin	118	Gi	52.59N	6.03W
Wicklow/Cill Mhantáin [2]	118	Gi	53.00N	6.30W
Wicklow Head/Ceann Chill Mhantáin ▶	118	Hi	52.58N	6.00W
Wicklow Mountains/Sléibhte Chill Mhantáin ⛰	118	Gh	53.02N	6.24W
Wicko, Jezioro- ⊜	120	Mb	54.33N	16.35 E
Wickrath, Mönchengladbach-	124	Ic	51.08N	6.25 E
Widawa ⧅	120	Me	51.13N	16.55 E
Wide Bay ◐	212	Ka	5.05 S	152.05 E
Widefield	186	Dg	38.42N	104.40W
Widgiemooltha	212	Ef	31.30 S	121.34 E
Wi-Do ◆	154	Ig	35.38N	126.17 E
Więcbork	120	Nc	53.22N	17.30 E
Wied ⧅	124	Jd	50.27N	7.28 E
Wiehengebirge ⛰	120	Ed	52.20N	8.40 E
Wiehl	124	Jd	50.57N	7.32 E
Wieliczka	120	Qg	49.59N	20.04 E
Wielimie, Jezioro- ⊜	120	Mc	53.47N	16.50 E
Wielki Dział ▲	120	Tf	50.18N	23.25 E
Wielkopolska ▣	120	Ne	51.50N	17.20 E
Wielkopolskie-Kujawskie, Pojezierze- ◮	120	Md	52.25N	16.30 E
Wieluń	120	Oe	51.14N	18.34 E
Wien [2]	128	Kb	48.15N	16.25 E
Wien = Vienna (EN)	112	Hf	48.12N	16.22 E
Wiener Becken ⧗	128	Kc	48.00N	16.28 E
Wiener Neustadt	128	Kc	47.48N	16.15 E
Wienerwald=Vienna Woods (EN) ⛰	128	Jb	48.10N	16.00 E
Wieprz ⧅	120	Re	51.32N	21.49 E
Wieprza ⧅	120	Mb	54.26N	16.22 E
Wieprz-Krzna, Kanał- ═	120	Se	51.56N	22.56 E
Wierden	124	Ib	52.22N	6.36 E
Wieringen	124	Hb	52.56N	5.02 E
Wieringen-Den Oever	124	Hb	52.56N	5.02 E
Wieringen-Hippolytushoef	124	Gb	52.54N	4.59 E
Wieringermeer	124	Hb	52.51N	5.01 E
Wieringermeer Polder ⊔	124	Gb	52.50N	5.00 E
Wieringermeer-Wieringerwerf	124	Hb	52.51N	5.01 E
Wieringerwerf, Wieringermeer-	124	Hb	52.51N	5.01 E
Wieruszów	120	Oe	51.18N	18.08 E
Wierzchowo, Jezioro- ⊜	120	Mc	53.50N	16.45 E
Wierzyca ⧅	120	Oc	53.51N	18.50 E
Wiesbaden	112	Ge	50.05N	8.15 E
Wiese ⧅	120	Di	47.35N	7.35 E
Wieslautern	124	Je	49.05N	7.49 E
Wiesloch	120	Eg	49.18N	8.42 E
Wietingsmoor ⩩	124	Kb	52.39N	8.39 E
Wietmarschen	124	Jb	52.32N	7.08 E
Wieżyca ▲	120	Ob	54.17N	18.10 E
Wigan	118	Kh	53.32N	2.35W
Wigger ⧅	128	Bc	47.15N	7.55 E
Wiggins	186	Lk	30.51N	89.08W
Wight, Isle of- ◆	110	Fe	50.40N	1.20W
Wigry, Jezioro- ⊜	120	Tb	54.05N	23.07 E
Wigston	124	Ab	52.35N	1.06W
Wigtown	118	Ig	54.52N	4.26W
Wigtown Bay ◐	118	Ig	54.46N	4.15W
Wijchen	124	Hc	51.48N	5.44 E
Wijdefjorden ∽	179	Nc	79.50N	15.30 E
Wijk bij Duurstede	124	Hc	51.59N	5.22 E
Wil	128	Dc	47.27N	9.05 E
Wilbur	188	Fc	47.46N	118.42W
Wilburton	186	Ii	34.55N	95.19W
Wilcannia	210	Fh	31.34 S	143.23 E
Wild Coast ⌇	158	Jl	32.00 S	29.50 E
Wildeshausen	120	Ed	52.54N	8.26 E
Wild Horse	188	Jb	49.01N	110.12W
Wildspitze ▲	128	Ed	46.53N	10.52 E
Wilga ⧅	120	Re	51.50N	21.20 E
Wilhelm-II-Land ⧗	222	Ge	69.00 S	90.00 E
Wilhelminakanaal ═	124	Gc	51.43N	4.53 E
Wilhelm-Pieck-Stadt-Guben	120	Ke	51.57N	14.43 E
Wilhelmshaven	120	Ec	53.31N	8.08 E
Wilhelmstal	172	Bd	21.54 S	16.20 E
Wilkes-Barre	182	Lc	41.15N	75.50W
Wilkesboro	184	Gg	36.09N	81.09W
Wilkes Land (EN) ⧗	222	Hf	71.00 S	120.00 E
Wilkins Coast ⌇	222	Qe	69.40 S	63.00W
Wilkins Sound ∽	222	Qf	70.15 S	73.00W
Willamette River ⧅	188	Dd	45.39N	122.46W
Willandra Billabong Creek ⧅	212	If	33.08 S	144.06 E
Willapa Bay ◐	188	Dc	46.37N	124.00W
Willard	186	Ci	34.36N	106.02W
Willards, Punta- ▶	192	Cc	28.50N	112.35W
Willcox	188	Kj	32.15N	109.50W
Willebadessen	124	Lc	51.38N	9.02 E
Willebadessen-Peckelsheim	124	Lc	51.36N	9.08 E
Willebroek	124	Gc	51.04N	4.22 E
Willemstad [Neth.]	124	Gc	51.41N	4.26 E
Willemstad [Neth.Ant.]	200	Jd	12.06N	68.56W
Willeroo	212	Gc	15.17 S	131.35 E
William Bill Dannelly Reservoir ⊏	184	Di	32.15N	86.45W
Williams	182	Ed	35.15N	112.11W
Williamsburg [Ky.-U.S.]	184	Eg	36.44N	84.10W
Williamsburg [Va.-U.S.]	184	Ig	37.17N	76.43W
Williams Lake	180	Ff	52.08N	122.09W
Williamson Glacier ❄	222	He	66.30 S	114.30 E
Williamsport	182	Lc	41.16N	77.03W
Williamston	184	Ih	35.50N	77.06W
Williamstown	184	Ef	38.38N	84.34W
Willich	124	Ic	51.16N	6.33 E
Willikie's	197d	Bb	17.03N	61.42W
Willingdon, Mount- ▲	188	Ga	51.48N	116.17W
Willis Group ⬡	208	Gf	16.20 S	150.00 E
Willis Islands ⬡	222	Ad	54.00 S	38.11W
Williston [N.D.-U.S.]	182	Gb	48.09N	103.37W
Williston [S.Afr.]	172	Cf	31.20 S	20.53 E
Williston Lake ⊜	174	Gd	50.57N	122.23W
Willits	188	Dg	39.25N	123.21W
Willmar	182	Hb	45.07N	95.03W
Willoughby Bay ◐	197d	Bb	17.02N	61.44W
Willow Bunch Lake ⊜	188	Mb	49.27N	105.28W
Willowlake ⧅	180	Fd	62.42N	123.08W
Willowmore	172	Cf	33.17 S	23.29 E
Willows	188	Dg	39.31N	122.12W
Willow Springs	186	Kh	36.59N	91.58W
Wills, Lake- ⊜	212	Fd	21.20 S	128.40 E
Wills Point	186	Ij	32.43N	95.57W
Wilma Glacier ❄	222	Ee	67.12 S	56.00 E
Wilmington [De.-U.S.]	182	Ld	39.44N	75.33W
Wilmington [N.C.-U.S.]	176	Lf	34.13N	77.55W
Wilmington [Oh.-U.S.]	184	Ff	39.28N	83.50W
Wilnsdorf	124	Kd	50.49N	8.06 E
Wilseder Berg ▲	120	Fc	53.10N	9.56 E
Wilson	182	Ld	35.44N	77.55W
Wilson, Cape - ▶	180	Jc	66.59N	81.27W
Wilson, Mount- ▲	186	Ch	37.51N	107.59W
Wilson Bluff ▲	222	Ff	74.20 S	66.47 E
Wilson Lake [Al.-U.S.] ⊜	184	Dh	34.49N	87.30W
Wilson Lake [Ks.-U.S.] ⊜	186	Gg	38.57N	98.40W
Wilsons Promontory ⧗	212	Jg	38.55 S	146.20 E
Wilton River ⧅	212	Gb	14.45 S	134.33 E
Wilts ▣	118	Lj	51.20N	2.00W
Wiltshire [3]	118	Lj	51.30N	2.00W
Wiltz	122	Le	49.58N	5.55 E
Wiluna	212	Ee	26.36 S	120.13 E
Wimereux	124	Dd	50.46N	1.37 E
Winamac	184	De	41.03N	86.36W
Winburg	172	De	28.37 S	27.00 E
Winchelsea	124	Cd	50.55N	0.43 E
Winchester [Eng.-U.K.]	118	Lj	51.04N	1.19W
Winchester [In.-U.S.]	184	Ee	40.10N	84.59W
Winchester [Ky.-U.S.]	184	Ef	38.01N	84.11W
Winchester [Va.-U.S.]	182	Ld	39.11N	78.12W
Windeck	124	Jd	50.49N	7.34 E
Windemin, Pointe- ▶	219b	Cc	16.34 S	167.27 E
Winder	184	Fi	34.00N	83.47W
Windermere ⊜	118	Kg	54.22N	2.56W
Windermere [B.C.-Can.]	188	Ha	50.30N	115.58W
Windermere [Eng.-U.K.]	118	Kg	54.23N	2.54W
Windhoek	160	Ik	22.34 S	17.06 E
Windhoek [3]	172	Bd	22.30 S	17.00 E
Windischgarsten	128	Ic	47.43N	14.20 E
Wind Mountain ▲	186	Dj	32.02N	105.34W
Windom	186	Ie	43.52N	95.07W
Windom Mountain ▲	186	Ch	37.37N	107.35W
Windorah	212	Ie	25.26 S	142.39 E
Window Rock	188	Ki	35.41N	109.03W
Wind River ⧅	188	Ke	43.08N	108.12W
Wind River Peak ▲	188	Ke	42.42N	109.07W
Wind River Range ⛰	182	Fc	43.05N	109.25W
Windrush ⧅	118	Lj	51.42N	1.25W
Windsor [Eng.-U.K.]	118	Mj	51.29N	0.38W
Windsor [N.S.-Can.]	180	Lh	44.59N	64.09W
Windsor [Ont.-Can.]	180	Jh	42.18N	83.01W
Windsor Forest	184	Gj	31.58N	81.10W
Windward Islands ⬡	190	Lf	13.00N	61.00W
Windward Islands (EN)=Barlovento, Islas de- ⬡	174	Mh	15.00N	61.00W
Windward Islands (EN) = Sotavento, Islas de- ⬡	198	Jd	11.10N	67.00W
Windward Islands (EN)=Vent, Iles du- ⬡	208	Mf	17.30 S	149.30W
Windward Passage (EN)=Vent, Canal du- ∽	194	Lh	20.00N	73.50W
Windward Passage (EN)=Vientos, Paso de los- ∽	174	Lh	20.00N	73.50W
Winfield [Al.-U.S.]	184	Di	33.56N	87.49W
Winfield [Ks.-U.S.]	182	Hd	37.15N	96.59W
Wingene	124	Fc	51.04N	3.16 E
Wingen-sur-Moder	124	Jf	48.55N	7.22 E
Winisk	176	Kd	55.15N	85.12W
Winisk ⧅	174	Kd	55.17N	85.05W
Winisk Lake ⊜	180	If	52.55N	87.20W
Winkler	186	Hb	49.11N	97.56W
Winklern	128	Gd	46.52N	12.52 E
Winneba	166	Ed	5.20N	0.37W
Winnebago, Lake- ⊜	182	Jc	44.00N	88.25W
Winnemucca	182	Dc	40.58N	117.44W
Winnemucca Lake ◳	188	Ff	40.10N	119.20W
Winner	182	Hc	43.22N	99.51W
Winnett	188	Kc	47.00N	108.21W
Winnfield	186	Jk	31.55N	92.38W
Winnibigoshish, Lake- ⊜	186	Ic	47.27N	94.12W
Winnipeg	176	Je	49.53N	97.09W
Winnipeg ⧅	174	Jd	50.38N	96.19W
Winnipeg, Lake- ⊜	174	Jd	52.00N	97.00W
Winnipeg Beach	186	Ha	50.31N	96.58W
Winnipegosis	180	Hf	51.39N	99.56W
Winnipegosis, Lake- ⊜	174	Jd	52.30N	100.00W
Winnipesaukee, Lake- ⊜	184	Ld	43.35N	71.20W
Winnsboro	186	Kj	32.10N	91.43W
Winnweiler	124	Je	49.34N	7.51 E
Winona [Mn.-U.S.]	182	Ic	44.03N	91.39W
Winona [Mo.-U.S.]	186	Kh	37.06N	91.19W
Winona [Ms.-U.S.]	186	Lj	33.29N	89.44W
Winschoten	122	Na	53.08N	7.02 E
Winsen (Luhe)	120	Gc	53.22N	10.13 E
Winslow [Az.-U.S.]	182	Ed	35.01N	110.42W
Winslow [Eng.-U.K.]	124	Bc	51.57N	0.52W
Winslow Reef ✿	208	Je	1.36 S	174.57W
Winston-Salem	182	Kd	36.06N	80.15W
Winterberg	120	Ee	51.12N	8.32 E
Winter Harbour	180	Gb	75.00N	111.00W
Winter Harbour ◐	180	Gb	74.46N	110.40W
Winter Haven	182	Kf	28.01N	81.44W
Winter Park [Co.-U.S.]	186	Dg	39.47N	105.45W
Winter Park [Fl.-U.S.]	184	Gk	28.36N	81.20W
Winters	186	Gk	31.57N	99.58W
Winterset	186	If	41.20N	94.01W
Winterswijk	122	Mc	51.58N	6.44 E
Winterthur	128	Cc	47.30N	8.45 E
Winton [Austl.]	210	Fg	22.23 S	143.02 E
Winton [N.C.-U.S.]	184	Ig	36.24N	76.56W
Winton [N.Z.]	218	Cg	46.09 S	168.20 E
Wipper [G.D.R.] ⧅	120	He	51.20N	11.10 E
Wipper [G.D.R.] ⧅	120	He	51.47N	11.42 E
Wisbech	118	Ni	52.40N	0.10 E
Wiscasset	184	Mc	44.00N	69.40W
Wisch	124	Ic	51.55N	6.22 E
Wisch-Terborg	124	Ic	51.55N	6.22 E
Wisconsin [2]	182	Jc	44.45N	89.30W
Wisconsin ⧅	174	Je	43.00N	91.15W
Wisconsin Range ⛰	222	Ng	85.45 S	125.00W
Wisconsin Rapids	182	Jc	44.23N	89.49W
Wiseman	178	Ic	67.25N	150.06W
Wisła	120	Og	49.39N	18.50 E
Wisła=Vistula (EN) ⧅	110	He	54.22N	18.55 E
Wiślana, Mierzeja- ⋯	120	Pb	54.25N	19.30 E
Wiślane, Żuławy- ⩩	120	Ob	54.10N	19.00 E
Wiślany, Zalew- ◎	120	Pb	54.27N	19.40 E
Wisłok ⧅	120	Sf	50.13N	22.32 E
Wisłoka ⧅	120	Rf	50.27N	21.23 E
Wismar	120	Hc	53.54N	11.28 E
Wismarbucht ◐	120	Hc	53.57N	11.25 E
Wissant	124	Dd	50.53N	1.40 E
Wissembourg	122	Ne	49.02N	7.57 E
Wissen	120	Df	50.47N	7.45 E
Wissenkerke	124	Fc	51.35N	3.45 E
Wissey ⧅	124	Cb	52.34N	0.21 E
Witbank	160	Jk	25.56 S	29.07 E
Witchekar Lake ⊜	186	Fb	49.15N	100.16W
Witdraai	172	Ce	26.58 S	20.41 E
Witham	124	Cc	51.47N	0.38 E
Witham ⧅	118	Ni	52.56N	0.04 E
Withernsea	118	Nh	53.44N	0.02 E
Witkowo	120	Nd	52.27N	17.47 E
Witmarsum, Wonseradeel-	124	Ha	53.06N	5.28 E
Witney	118	Lj	51.48N	1.29W
Witnica	120	Kd	52.40N	14.55 E
Witputz	172	Be	27.37 S	16.42 E
Witten	120	De	51.26N	7.20 E
Wittenberg [G.D.R.]	120	Ie	51.52N	12.39 E
Wittenberg [Wi.-U.S.]	186	Ld	44.49N	89.10W
Wittenberge	120	Hc	53.00N	11.45 E
Wittenoom	212	Dd	22.17 S	118.19 E
Wittingen	120	Gd	52.44N	10.43 E
Wittlich	120	Cg	49.59N	6.53 E
Wittmund	120	Dc	53.34N	7.47 E
Wittow ⊣	120	Jb	54.38N	13.19 E
Wittstock	120	Ic	53.09N	12.30 E
Witu	170	Hc	2.23 S	40.26 E
Witu Islands ⬡	214	Dh	4.40 S	149.18 E
Witvlei	172	Bd	22.23 S	18.32 E
Witzenhausen	120	Fe	51.20N	9.52 E
Wivenhoe	124	Cc	51.51N	0.58 E
Wizard Reef ❋	158	Mi	8.57 S	51.01 E
Wizna	120	Sc	53.13N	22.26 E
Wjdawka ⧅	120	Oe	51.32N	18.52 E
W. J. Van Blommestein Meer ⊏	202	Hc	4.45N	55.00W
Wkra ⧅	120	Qd	52.27N	20.44 E
Władysławowo	120	Ob	54.49N	18.25 E
Włocławek	120	Pd	52.39N	19.02 E
Włocławek [2]	120	Od	52.40N	19.00 E
Włodawa	120	Te	51.34N	23.32 E
Włoszczowa	120	Pf	50.25N	19.59 E
Wodonga	212	Jg	36.17 S	146.54 E
Wodzisław Śląski	120	Of	50.00N	18.28 E
Woensdrecht	124	Gc	51.25N	4.18 E
Woerden	124	Gb	52.05N	4.52 E
Woerth	124	Jf	48.56N	7.45 E
Woëvre, Plaine de la- ▭	122	Le	49.15N	5.45 E
Wohlthat-Massif ⛰	222	Cf	71.35 S	12.20 E
Woippy	124	Ie	49.09N	6.09 E
Wojerecy/Hoyerswerda	120	Ke	51.26N	14.15 E
Wokam, Pulau- ◆	150	Jh	5.37 S	134.30 E
Woken He ⧅	154	Ja	46.19N	129.34 E
Woking	118	Mj	51.20N	0.34W
Wokingham	124	Bc	51.25N	0.50W
Wolbrom	120	Pf	50.24N	19.46 E
Wolcott	184	Id	43.13N	76.42W
Wołczyn	120	Oe	51.01N	18.03 E
Woldberg ◮	124	Hb	52.25N	5.55 E
Woleai Atoll ⊙	208	Fd	7.21N	143.52 E
Woleu-Ntem [3]	170	Bb	2.00N	12.00 E
Wolf, Isla- ◆	202a	Aa	1.23N	91.49W
Wolf, Volcán- Λ	202a	Ab	0.01 S	91.20W
Wolfach	120	Eh	48.18N	8.13 E
Wolf Creek	188	Ic	47.00N	112.04W
Wolf Creek ⧅	186	Gh	36.35N	99.30W
Wolfen	120	Ie	51.40N	12.17 E
Wolfenbüttel	120	Gd	52.10N	10.33 E
Wolfhagen	120	Fe	51.19N	9.10 E
Wolf Point	182	Fb	48.05N	105.39W
Wolfratshausen	120	Hi	47.54N	11.25 E
Wolf River ⧅	186	Ld	44.11N	88.48W
Wolfsberg	128	Id	46.50N	14.50 E
Wolfsburg	120	Gd	52.26N	10.48 E
Wolfstein	124	Je	49.35N	7.36 E
Wolgast	120	Jb	54.03N	13.46 E
Wolica ⧅	120	Tf	50.54N	23.12 E
Wolin	120	Kc	53.50N	14.35 E
Wolin ◆	120	Kc	53.51N	14.38 E
Wollaston	124	Bb	52.15N	0.40W
Wollaston, Islas- ⬡	206	Gi	55.40 S	67.30W
Wollaston Forland ⧗	179	Jd	74.35N	20.15W
Wollaston Lake	180	He	58.05N	103.38W
Wollaston Lake ⊜	174	Id	58.15N	103.20W
Wollaston Peninsula ⊣	174	Hc	70.00N	115.00W
Wollongong	210	Gh	34.25 S	150.54 E
Wöllstein	124	Je	49.49N	7.58 E
Wolmaransstad	172	De	27.12 S	26.13 E
Wołomin	120	Rd	52.21N	21.14 E
Wołów	120	Me	51.29N	16.55 E
Wolseley	180	Hf	50.25N	103.19W
Wolstenholme, Cap - ▶	180	Jd	62.34N	77.30W
Wolstenholme Fjord ∽	179	Ec	76.40N	69.45W
Wolsztyn	120	Md	52.08N	16.06 E
Wolvega, Weststellingwerf-	124	Ib	52.53N	6.00 E
Wolverhampton	118	Ki	52.36N	2.08W
Wolverton	118	Mi	52.04N	0.50W
Wŏnju	152	Md	37.21N	127.58 E
Wŏnsan	142	Of	39.10N	127.26 E
Wonseradeel	124	Ha	53.06N	5.28 E
Wonseradeel-Witmarsum	124	Ha	53.06N	5.28 E
Wonthaggi	212	Jg	38.36 S	145.35 E
Woodall Mountain ▲	186	Li	34.45N	88.11W
Woodbridge	118	Oi	52.06N	1.19 E

Index Symbols

[1] Independent Nation
[2] State, Region
[3] District, County
[4] Municipality
[5] Colony, Dependency
■ Continent
⧗ Physical Region
▣ Historical or Cultural Region
▲ Mount, Mountain
Λ Volcano
◭ Hill
⛰ Mountains, Mountain Range
◮ Hills, Escarpment
⌓ Plateau, Upland
⋎ Pass, Gap
▭ Plain, Lowland
◣ Delta
▤ Salt Flat
∨ Valley, Canyon
◯ Crater, Cave
✺ Karst Features
⌣ Depression
⊔ Polder
◢ Desert, Dunes
♣ Forest, Woods
〰 Heath, Steppe
⚘ Oasis
▶ Cape, Point
⌇ Coast, Beach
◧ Cliff
⊣ Peninsula
⋈ Isthmus
⋯ Sandbank
◆ Island
⊙ Atoll
✳ Rock, Reef
⬡ Islands, Archipelago
❋ Rocks, Reefs
✿ Coral Reef
◉ Well, Spring
⫪ Geyser
⧅ River, Stream
⧄ Waterfall, Rapids
⋖ River Mouth, Estuary
⊜ Lake
⊝ Salt Lake
◳ Intermittent Lake
⊏ Reservoir
⩩ Swamp, Pond
═ Canal
❄ Glacier
❅ Ice Shelf, Pack Ice
≈ Ocean
≋ Sea
◐ Gulf, Bay
∽ Strait, Fjord
◎ Lagoon
▦ Bank
⏏ Seamount
⊼ Tablemount
⩙ Ridge
⊓ Shelf
⊌ Basin
⟋ Escarpment, Sea Scarp
ϟ Fracture
∪ Trench, Abyss
⚑ National Park, Reserve
▼ Point of Interest
⇧ Recreation Site
◓ Cave, Cavern
⛫ Historic Site
⁘ Ruins
♜ Wall, Walls
✝ Church, Abbey
⛩ Temple
⊠ Scientific Station
⊞ Railway station
✈ Airport
⚓ Port
⊛ Military installation
⛯ Lighthouse
⚒ Mine
⌒ Tunnel
⌿ Dam, Bridge

Name	Page	Grid	Lat	Lon
Woodbridge Bay	197g	Bb	15.19N	61.25W
Woodhall Spa	124	Ba	53.09N	0.13W
Woodland [Ca.-U.S.]	188	Gg	38.41N	121.46W
Woodland [Wa.-U.S.]	188	Dd	45.54N	122.45W
Woodlark Island	208	Ge	9.05S	152.50 E
Wood Mountain	188	Lb	49.14N	106.20W
Woodridge	186	Hb	49.17N	96.09W
Wood River	188	Lb	50.08N	106.10W
Wood River Lakes	178	He	59.30N	158.45W
Woodroffe, Mount-	212	Ge	26.20S	131.45 E
Woods, Lake-	212	Gc	17.50S	133.30 E
Woods, Lake of the-	174	Je	49.15N	94.45W
Woods Hole	184	Le	41.31N	70.40W
Woodside	188	Jg	39.21N	110.18W
Woodstock [Eng.-U.K.]	118	Lj	51.52N	1.21W
Woodstock [N.B.-Can.]	180	Kg	46.09N	67.34W
Woodstock [Ont.-Can.]	184	Gd	43.08N	80.45W
Woodstock [Vt.-U.S.]	184	Kd	43.37N	72.31W
Woodville [Ms.-U.S.]	186	Kk	31.01N	91.18W
Woodville [N.Z.]	218	Fd	40.20S	175.52 E
Woodville [Tx.-U.S.]	186	Ik	30.46N	94.25W
Woodward	182	Hd	36.26N	99.24W
Wooler	118	Kf	55.33N	2.01W
Woomera	212	Hf	31.11S	137.10 E
Wooramel River	212	Ce	25.47S	114.10 E
Wooster	184	Ge	40.46N	81.57W
Worcester	118	Ki	52.11N	2.10W
Worcester [Eng.-U.K.]	118	Ki	52.11N	2.13W
Worcester [S.Afr.]	182	Mc	42.16N	71.48W
Worcester Range	160	Il	33.39S	19.27 E
Wörgl	222	Jf	78.50S	161.00 E
Workai, Pulau-	128	Gc	47.29N	12.04 E
Workington	150	Jh	6.40S	134.40 E
Worksop	118	Jg	54.39N	3.33W
Workum	118	Lh	53.18N	1.07W
Worland	124	Hb	52.59N	5.27 E
Wormer	182	Fc	44.01N	107.57W
Wormhout	124	Gb	52.30N	4.52 E
Worms	124	Ed	50.53N	2.28 E
Worms Head	120	Eg	49.38N	8.21 E
Wörrstadt	118	Lj	51.34N	4.20W
Wörth am Rhein	124	Ke	49.50N	8.06 E
Wörther-See	124	Ke	49.03N	8.16 E
Worthing	128	Id	46.37N	14.10 E
Worthington	118	Mk	50.48N	0.23W
Wosi	182	Hc	43.37N	95.36W
Wotho Atoll	150	Ig	0.11S	127.58 E
Wotje Atoll	208	Hc	10.06N	165.59 E
Woudenberg	208	Ig	9.27N	170.02 E
Wounnioné, Pointe-	124	Hb	52.05N	5.25 E
Wounta, Laguna de-	219b	Db	14.54S	168.02 E
Wour	194	Fg	13.38N	83.34W
Wousi	168	Ba	21.21N	15.57 E
Wowoni, Pulau-	219b	Cb	15.22S	166.39 E
Woy Woy	150	Hg	4.08S	123.06 E
Wrangel, ostrov- =	212	Kf	33.30S	151.20 E
Wrangel Island (EN)				
Wrangel Island (EN) =	140	Tb	71.00N	179.30 E
Wrangel, ostrov-				
Wrangell	140	Tb	71.00N	179.30 E
Wrangell, Cape-	176	Fd	56.28N	132.23W
Wrangell Mountains	178a	Ab	52.50N	172.26 E
Wrath, Cape-	174	Ec	62.00N	143.00W
Wray	110	Fd	58.37N	5.01W
Wreake	182	Gc	40.05N	102.13W
Wreck Reef	124	Ab	52.41N	1.05W
Wrecks, Bay of-	208	Gg	22.15S	155.10 E
Wrexham	220g	Bb	1.52S	157.17W
Wright Island	118	Kh	53.03N	3.00W
Wright Patman Lake	222	Of	74.03S	116.45W
Wrightson, Mount-	186	Ij	33.16N	94.14W
Wrigley	188	Jk	31.42N	110.50W
Wrigley Gulf	180	Fd	63.19N	123.38W
Wrocław [2]	222	Nf	74.00S	129.00W
Wrocław = Breslau (EN)	120	Me	51.05N	17.00 E
Wronki	112	He	51.06N	17.00 E
Wrotham	120	Md	52.43N	16.23 E
Wroxham	124	Cc	51.18N	0.19 E
Września	124	Db	52.42N	1.24 E
Wschodnia	120	Nd	52.20N	17.34 E
Wschowa	120	Rf	50.30N	21.18 E
Wu'an	120	Nk	51.48N	16.19 E
Wuchale	154	Cf	36.42N	114.12 E
Wuchang	168	Fc	11.31N	39.37 E
Wuchang, Wuhan-	154	Ab	44.55N	127.11 E
Wucheng (Jiucheng)	154	Ci	30.32N	114.18 E
Wuchiu Yu	152	Ag	25.09N	119.27 E
Wuchuan	154	Ad	41.08N	111.25 E
Wuchuan (Duru)	152	Jf	28.28N	107.57 E
Wuchuan (Meilù)	152	Jg	21.28N	110.44 E
Wuda	152	Jg	39.30N	106.33 E
Wudan → Ongniud Qi	152	Kc	42.58N	119.01 E
Wudao	152	Ld	39.28N	121.30 E
Wudaoliang	152	Fd	35.15N	93.14 E
Wudi	154	Df	37.44N	117.36 E
Wudil	166	Gc	11.49N	8.51 E
Wuding	152	Hf	25.36N	102.27 E
Wudu	152	Hf	33.24N	105.00 E
Wugang	152	Jf	26.48N	110.32 E
Wugong (Puji)	154	Ie	34.15N	108.14 E
Wuhai	152	Id	39.32N	106.55 E
Wuhan	142	Nf	30.30N	114.20 E
Wuhan-Hankou	154	Ci	30.35N	114.16 E
Wuhan-Hanyang	154	Ci	30.33N	114.16 E
Wuhan- Wuchang	154	Ci	30.32N	114.18 E
Wuhe	152	Ke	33.08N	117.51 E
Wuhu	142	Nf	31.18N	118.27 E
Wuhu (Wanzhi)	154	Ei	31.13N	118.23 E
Wujia He	152	Ic	40.56N	108.52 E
Wujiang	154	Fi	31.09N	120.38 E
Wu Jiang	140	Mg	29.43N	107.24 E
Wukari	160	Hh	7.51N	9.47 E
Wukro	152	Fc	13.48N	39.37 E
Wular	148	Eb	34.30N	74.30 E
Wulff Land	179	Hb	82.19N	50.00W
Wulian (Hongning)	154	Eg	35.45N	119.13 E
Wuliang Shan	152	Hg	24.00N	101.00 E
Wuliaru, Pulau-	150	Jh	7.27S	131.04 E
Wuling Shan	140	Mg	28.20N	110.00 E
Wulongbei	154	Hd	40.15N	124.16 E
Wulongji → Huaibin	154	Ci	32.27N	115.23 E
Wulur	150	Ih	7.09S	128.39 E
Wum	166	Hd	6.23N	10.04 E
Wumei Shan	154	Cj	28.47N	114.50 E
Wümme	124	Ka	53.10N	8.40 E
Wuning	154	Cj	29.17N	115.05 E
Wünnenberg	124	Kc	51.31N	8.42 E
Wünnenberg-Haaren	124	Kc	51.34N	8.44 E
Wunnummin Lake	180	If	52.55N	89.10W
Wun Rog	168	Dd	9.00N	28.21 E
Wunstorf	120	Fd	52.26N	9.25 E
Wuntho	148	Jd	23.54N	95.41 E
Wupper	120	Ce	51.05N	7.00 E
Wuppertal	120	De	51.16N	7.11 E
Wuqi	152	Id	36.57N	108.15 E
Wuqia/Uluqqat	152	Cd	39.40N	75.07 E
Wuqiao (Sangyuan)	154	Df	37.38N	116.23 E
Wuqing	154	Df	39.23N	117.04 E
Wuqing (Yangcun)	154	De	39.23N	117.04 E
Würm	124	Kf	48.53N	8.42 E
Würmsee → Starnberger See	124	Hi	47.55N	11.20 E
Wurno	166	Gc	13.18N	5.26 E
Würselen	124	Id	50.49N	6.08 E
Würzburg	112	Gf	49.48N	9.56 E
Wurzen	120	Ie	51.22N	12.44 E
Wu Shan	152	Ie	31.00N	110.00 E
Wushaoling	152	Hd	37.15N	102.50 E
Wusheng Guan	152	Je	31.45N	114.04 E
Wuski/Uqturpan	152	Cc	41.10N	79.16 E
Wusong	154	Fi	31.23N	121.29 E
Wusuli Jiang	150	Ob	48.28N	135.02 E
Wutach	120	Ei	47.37N	8.15 E
Wutai [China]	154	Be	38.43N	113.14 E
Wutai [China]	152	Dc	44.38N	82.06 E
Wutai Shan	152	Jd	39.04N	113.28 E
Wuustwezel	124	Gc	51.23N	4.36 E
Wuvulu Island	208	Fe	1.43S	142.50 E
Wuwei	154	Di	31.17N	117.54 E
Wuwei (Liangzhou)	142	Mf	37.58N	102.48 E
Wuxi [China]	142	Of	31.32N	120.18 E
Wuxi [China]	152	Ie	31.27N	109.34 E
Wu Xia	152	Je	31.02N	110.10 E
Wuxiang (Duancun)	154	Bf	36.50N	112.51 E
Wuxing (Huzhou)	152	Le	30.47N	120.07 E
Wuxue→Guangji	152	Kf	29.58N	115.32 E
Wuyang [China]	152	Jd	36.29N	113.07 E
Wuyang [China]	154	Bh	33.26N	113.35 E
Wuyang → Zhenyuan	152	If	27.05N	108.26 E
Wuyi [China]	154	Ej	28.54N	119.50 E
Wuyi [China]	154	Cf	37.49N	115.54 E
Wuyiling	152	Mb	48.37N	129.20 E
Wuyi Shan	140	Ng	27.00N	117.00 E
Wuyuan [China]	142	Me	41.08N	108.17 E
Wuyuan [China]	154	Dj	29.15N	117.52 E
Wuyuanzhen → Haiyan	154	Fi	30.31N	120.56 E
Wuzhai	154	Ae	38.54N	111.49 E
Wuzhen	154	Ai	31.42N	112.00 E
Wuzhi Shan [China]	154	Ed	40.31N	118.02 E
Wuzhi Shan [China]	152	Ih	18.54N	109.40 E
Wuzhong	152	Ie	38.00N	106.10 E
Wuzhou	142	Ng	23.32N	111.21 E
Wyalkatchem	212	Df	31.10S	117.22 E
Wyandotte	184	Fd	42.12N	83.10W
Wyandra	212	Je	27.15S	145.59 E
Wye	124	Cc	51.11N	0.56 E
Wye	118	Kj	51.37N	2.39W
Wyemandoo, Mount-	212	De	28.31S	118.32 E
Wyk auf Föhr	120	Eb	54.42N	8.34 E
Wylie, Lake-	184	Gh	35.07N	81.02W
Wymondham	118	Oi	52.34N	1.07 E
Wyndham [Austl.]	210	Df	15.28S	128.06 E
Wyndham [N.Z.]	218	Cg	46.20S	168.51 E
Wyndmere	186	Hc	46.16N	97.08W
Wynne	186	Ks	35.14N	90.47W
Wynniatt Bay	180	Gb	72.50N	111.00W
Wynyard [Austl.]	212	Jh	40.59S	145.41 E
Wynyard [Sask.-Can.]	180	Hf	51.47N	104.10W
Wyoming	184	Ad	42.54N	85.42W
Wyoming [2]	182	Fc	43.00N	107.30W
Wyoming Peak	182	Ec	42.36N	110.37W
Wyśmierzyce	120	Qe	51.38N	20.49 E
Wysoka	120	Nc	53.11N	17.05 E
Wysokie Mazowieckie	120	Sd	52.56N	22.32 E
Wyszków	120	Rd	52.36N	21.28 E
Wyszogród	120	Qd	52.23N	20.11 E
Wytheville	184	Ge	36.57N	81.07W
Wyvjlle Thomson Ridge (EN)				
Wyvis, Ben-	118	Fa	60.10N	8.00W
	118	Id	57.42N	4.30W

X

Name	Page	Grid	Lat	Lon
Xàbia / Jávea	126	Mf	38.47N	0.10 E
Xaintrie	122	Ii	45.00N	2.10 E
Xainza	152	Ee	30.50N	88.37 E
Xaitongmoin	152	Ef	29.26N	88.08 E
Xai-Xai	160	Kk	25.04S	33.39 E
Xamba → Hanggin Houqi	152	Ic	40.59N	107.07 E
Xam Nua	148	Kd	20.25N	104.02 E
Xá-Muteba	170	Cd	9.34S	17.50 E
Xangongo	160	Ij	16.46S	14.59 E
Xang Qu	152	Ef	29.22N	89.09 E
Xanten	120	Ce	51.40N	6.27 E
Xánthi	130	Hh	41.08N	24.53 E
Xanthos	146	Cd	36.20N	29.20 E
Xanxerê	206	Jc	26.53S	52.23W
Xapuri	202	Ef	10.39S	68.31W
Xar Hudag	152	Jb	45.06N	114.30 E
Xar Moron	154	Af	42.37N	111.02 E
Xar Moron He	152	Lc	43.24N	120.39 E
Xarrama	126	Df	38.14N	8.20W
Xàtiva/Jàtiva	150	Jh	7.27S	131.04 E
Xau, Lake-	172	Cd	21.15S	24.44 E
Xavantes, Reprêsa de-	204	Hf	23.20S	49.35W
Xavantina	204	Fe	21.15S	52.48W
Xavier / Javier	126	Kb	42.36N	1.13W
Xayar	152	Dc	41.15N	82.50 E
Xebert	154	Fc	44.00N	122.00 E
Xêgar → Tingri	152	Ef	28.41N	87.00 E
Xenia	184	Ff	39.41N	83.56W
Xiachengzi	154	Kb	44.41N	130.26 E
Xiacun → Rushan	154	Ff	36.55N	121.30 E
Xiaguan	152	Hf	25.32N	100.12 E
Xiahe (Labrang)	152	Hd	35.18N	102.30 E
Xiajin	154	Cf	36.57N	116.00 E
Xiamen = Amoy (EN)	142	Ng	24.32N	118.06 E
Xi'an	142	Mf	34.15N	108.50 E
Xianbin Ansha	150	Qe	9.48N	116.38 E
Xianfeng	152	If	29.41N	109.09 E
Xiangcheng	154	Bh	33.51N	113.29 E
Xiangcheng/Qagchêng	152	Gf	28.56N	99.46 E
Xiangcheng (Shuizhai)	154	Ch	33.27N	114.53 E
Xiangfan	154	Nf	32.03N	112.05 E
Xianggang/Hong Kong	142	Ng	22.15N	114.10 E
Xianghua Ling	152	Jf	25.26N	112.32 E
Xianghuang Qi (Xin Bulag)	152	Jc	42.12N	113.59 E
Xiang Jiang	140	Ng	29.26N	113.08 E
Xiangkhoang	148	Ne	19.20N	103.22 E
Xiangkhoang, Plateau de-	148	Ke	19.30N	103.10 E
Xiangquan He	152	Ce	32.05N	79.20 E
Xiangshan (Dancheng)	152	Lf	29.29N	121.52 E
Xiangshan Gang	154	Fj	29.35N	121.38 E
Xiangtan	142	Ng	27.54N	112.55 E
Xiangxiang	152	Cj	28.26N	115.59 E
Xiangyin	154	Bj	28.41N	112.53 E
Xiangyuan	154	Bf	36.32N	113.02 E
Xianju	152	Lf	28.50N	120.42 E
Xianning	152	Cj	29.52N	114.17 E
Xiannümiao → Jiangdu	154	Eh	32.30N	119.33 E
Xiantaozhen → Mianyang	154	Bi	30.22N	113.27 E
Xianxia Ling	152	Kf	28.24N	118.41 E
Xianxian	154	De	38.12N	116.07 E
Xianyang	154	Ie	34.26N	108.40 E
Xiaobole Shan	152	La	51.46N	124.09 E
Xiao'ergou	152	Lb	49.10N	123.43 E
Xiaogan	154	Bi	30.52N	113.58 E
Xiao He	154	Bf	37.38N	112.24 E
Xiao Hinggan Ling = Lesser Khingan Range (EN)	140	Oe	48.45N	127.00 E
Xiaoling He	154	Fd	40.55N	121.12 E
Xiaoluan He	154	Ed	41.36N	117.05 E
Xiaoqing He	154	Ef	37.19N	118.59 E
Xiaoshan	154	Fi	30.10N	120.16 E
Xiaowutai Shan	154	Ce	39.57N	114.59 E
Xiaoxian	154	Da	34.11N	116.50 E
Xiaoyi	154	Af	37.07N	111.48 E
Xiaoyi → Gongxian	154a	Ba	34.46N	112.57 E
Xiapu	152	Kf	26.57N	119.59 E
Xiawa	154	Dj	29.15N	117.52 E
Xiayi	154	Dg	34.14N	116.07 E
Xiazhuang → Linshu	154	Fg	34.56N	118.38 E
Xicalango, Punta-	192	Nh	19.41N	92.00W
Xichang	142	Mg	27.52N	102.15 E
Xicheng → Yangyuan	154	Cd	40.08N	114.10 E
Xicoténcatl	192	Jf	23.00N	98.56W
Xicotepec de Juárez	192	Kg	20.17N	97.57W
Xiejiaji → Qingyun	154	Df	37.46N	117.22 E
Xifei He	154	Df	32.38N	116.39 E
Xifeng	154	Hc	42.45N	124.44 E
Xifengzhen	152	Ie	35.40N	107.42 E
Xigazê	142	Kg	29.15N	88.52 E
Xi He [China]	154	Dj	29.38N	116.53 E
Xi He [China]	152	Hd	34.00N	105.03 E
Xiheying	154	Cd	39.53N	114.42 E
Xihua	154	Ch	33.48N	114.31 E
Xi Jang	140	Ng	23.05N	113.00 E
Xiji [China]	152	Id	35.52N	105.35 E
Xiji [China]	154	Ia	34.05N	114.23 E
Xi Jiang	152	Jg	23.05N	112.18 E
Xijir Ulan Hu	152	Fd	35.12N	90.18 E
Xikouzi	154	La	42.58N	120.29 E
Xiliao He	140	Oe	43.24N	123.42 E
Xiligou → Ulan	152	Gd	36.59N	98.16 E
Xilin	154	Ig	24.30N	105.05 E
Xilin Gol	154	Jb	44.00N	116.00 E
Xilin Hot → Abagnar Qi	142	Ne	43.58N	116.08 E
Xilitla	192	Jg	21.20N	98.58W
Xilókastron	130	Hc	41.04N	100.14 E
Ximiao	152	Hc	41.04N	100.14 E
Xin'an	154a	Bd	34.22N	107.03 E
Xin'anjiang	154	Ei	29.27N	119.15 E
Xin'anjiang Shuiku	152	Kf	29.25N	119.05 E
Xin'anzhen → Guannan	154	Eg	34.04N	119.21 E
Xin'anzhen → Xinyi	154	Ge	34.17N	118.14 E
Xin Barag Youqi (Altan-Emel)	152	Kb	48.41N	116.47 E
Xin Barag Zuoqi (Amgalang)	152	Kb	48.13N	118.14 E
Xinbin	154	Hd	41.44N	125.02 E
Xin Bulag → Xianghuang Qi	152	Jc	42.12N	113.59 E
Xincai	154	Ch	32.40N	114.57 E
Xinchang	154	Fj	29.30N	120.54 E
Xincheng [China]	152	Ig	24.04N	108.39 E
Xincheng [China]	154	Bf	37.57N	112.33 E
Xincheng (Gaobeidian)	154	Ce	39.20N	115.50 E
Xindi → Honghu	154	Bi	29.49N	113.28 E
Xing'an → Ankang	142	Mf	32.37N	109.02 E
Xingcheng	154	Fd	40.38N	120.43 E
Xingguo	152	Kf	26.22N	115.21 E
Xinghai	152	Gd	35.45N	99.59 E
Xinghe	154	Jc	40.53N	113.56 E
Xinghua	154	Jc	32.56N	119.49 E
Xingkai Hu = Khanka Lake (EN)	140	Pe	45.00N	132.24 E
Xinglong	154	Dd	40.25N	117.31 E
Xinglongzhen	154	Ia	46.35N	124.30 E
Xingren	152	If	25.26N	105.08 E
Xingtai	142	Nf	37.00N	114.30 E
Xingtang	154	Ce	38.26N	114.33 E
Xingu, Rio-	198	Kf	1.30S	51.53W
Xingxingxia	152	Gc	41.47N	95.07 E
Xingyang	154	Bg	34.47N	113.21 E
Xingyi (Huángcaoba)	152	Hf	25.03N	104.55 E
Xingzi	152	Dj	29.28N	116.03 E
Xinhe	154	Cf	37.32N	115.14 E
Xinhe/Toksu	152	Dc	41.34N	82.38 E
Xin Hot → Abag Qi	152	Jc	44.01N	114.59 E
Xinhuai He	154	Fg	34.23N	120.05 E
Xinhui → Aohan Qi	152	Kc	42.18N	119.53 E
Xining	142	Mf	36.37N	101.46 E
Xinji → Shulu	154	Cf	37.56N	115.14 E
Xinjian	152	Cj	28.41N	115.50 E
Xin Jiang	152	Dj	28.37N	116.40 E
Xinjiangkou → Songzi	154	Ai	30.10N	111.46 E
Xinjiang Uygur Zizhiqu (Hsin-chiang-wei-wu-erh Tzu-chih-ch'ü) = Sinkiang Uighur (EN) [2]	152	Ec	42.00N	86.00 E
Xinjin	152	He	30.25N	103.46 E
Xinjin (Pulandian)	154	Ld	39.24N	121.59 E
Xinkai He	154	Gc	43.36N	122.31 E
Xinle	154	Ce	38.15N	114.40 E
Xinlin	154	Ea	43.58N	118.03 E
Xinlitun [China]	154	Gc	42.01N	122.11 E
Xinlitun [China]	152	Ma	50.58N	126.39 E
Xinlong/Nyagrong	152	He	30.57N	100.12 E
Xinmin	154	Gc	42.00N	122.50 E
Xinpu → Lianyungang	142	Nf	34.34N	119.15 E
Xinqing	152	Mb	48.15N	129.31 E
Xintai	154	Dg	35.54N	117.44 E
Xinwen (Suncun)	154	Df	35.49N	117.38 E
Xinxian [China]	152	Jd	38.24N	112.43 E
Xinxian [China]	154	Ci	31.42N	114.50 E
Xinxiang	142	Nf	35.17N	113.50 E
Xinyang	142	Nf	32.05N	114.07 E
Xinye	154	Bh	32.30N	112.22 E
Xinyi (Xin'anzhen)	154	Ge	34.17N	118.14 E
Xinyi He	154	Eg	34.29N	119.49 E
Xinyuan/Künes	152	Dc	43.24N	83.18 E
Xinyuan → Tianjun	152	Lf	37.18N	99.15 E
Xin Zhen → Hanggin Qi	152	Ic	43.52N	127.07 E
Xinzheng	154	Bg	34.25N	113.46 E
Xinzhou	154	Ej	28.27N	119.29 E
Xinzo de Limia	126	Eb	42.03N	7.43W
Xiong Xian	154	Ce	38.59N	116.06 E
Xionyuecheng	154	Gd	40.12N	122.08 E
Xiping [China]	154	Bh	33.22N	114.00 E
Xiping [China]	152	If	28.27N	119.29 E
Xisha Qundao = Paracel Islands (EN)	140	Nh	16.30N	112.15 E
Xishuangbanna	152	Gg	22.15N	100.00 E
Xishuanghe → Kenli	154	Ef	37.35N	118.30 E
Xishui	154	Dj	30.28N	115.15 E
Xi Taijnar Hu	152	Fd	37.15N	93.30 E
Xitianmu Shan	152	Ke	30.21N	119.25 E
Xi Ujimqin Qi (Bayan Ul Hot)	152	Kc	44.31N	117.33 E
Xiuning	154	Ej	29.47N	118.11 E
Xiushui	152	Jf	29.02N	114.33 E
Xiu Shui	152	Jf	29.13N	116.00 E
Xiuwu	154	Bg	35.13N	113.27 E
Xiuyan	154	Cc	40.18N	123.10 E
Xiwanzi → Chongli	154	Cd	40.57N	115.12 E
Xixabangma Feng	152	Ef	28.21N	85.47 E
Xixian	154	Ch	32.21N	114.43 E
Xixona / Jijona	126	Lf	38.32N	0.30W
Xiyang	154	Bf	37.38N	113.41 E
Xizang Zizhiqu (Hsi-tsang Tzu-chih-ch'ü) = Tibet (EN) [2]	152	Ee	32.00N	90.00 E
Xizhong Dao	154	Fe	39.25N	121.18 E
Xochicalco	192	Jh	18.45N	99.20W
Xochimilco	192	Jh	19.16N	99.06W
Xorkol	152	Fd	39.04N	91.05 E
Xpujil	192	Oh	18.35N	89.25W
Xuanchang	154	Ei	30.56N	118.44 E
Xuande Qundao	150	Fc	17.08N	111.30 E
Xuan'en	154	Ie	30.02N	109.30 E
Xuanhan	152	Ie	31.23N	107.39 E
Xuanhua	154	Kc	40.39N	115.05 E
Xuanwei	152	Hf	26.19N	104.05 E
Xuchang	142	Nf	34.02N	113.58 E
Xuecheng (Lincheng)	154	Dg	34.38N	117.14 E
Xuefeng Shan	152	Jf	27.35N	110.50 E
Xue Shan	152	Gf	27.30N	99.55 E
Xugezhuang → Fengnan	154	Ee	39.34N	118.05 E
Xugou	154	Ea	34.37N	119.08 E
Xugui	152	Gd	35.45N	96.08 E
Xuguit Qi (Yakeshi)	154	Ig	49.16N	120.41 E
Xümatang	152	Ge	33.57N	97.00 E
Xun Jiang	152	Jg	23.28N	111.18 E
Xunke (Qike)	152	Mb	49.34N	128.28 E
Xunwu	154	Kg	24.59N	115.33 E
Xunxian	154	Cg	35.40N	114.33 E
Xupu	152	Jf	27.54N	110.35 E
Xúquer/Júcar	110	Fh	39.09N	0.14W
Xushui	154	Ce	39.02N	115.40 E
Xuwen	152	Jg	20.22N	110.10 E
Xuyi	152	Ke	32.58N	118.33 E
Xuyong (Yongning)	152	If	28.13N	105.26 E
Xuzhou	142	Nf	34.17N	117.13 E

Y

Name	Page	Grid	Lat	Lon
Ya'an	142	Mg	30.00N	102.57 E
Yabassi	166	Ge	4.28N	9.58 E
Yabe	152	Jc	40.25N	115.33 E
Yabebyry	204	Dh	27.24S	57.11W
Yabelo	168	Fe	4.53N	38.07 E
Yablonovy Range (EN) = Jablonovy hrebet	140	Nd	53.30N	115.00 E
Yabrai Shan	152	Hc	40.00N	103.10 E
Yabrīn	168	Ha	23.15N	48.59 E
Yabrūd	146	Gf	33.58N	36.40 E
Yabucoa	197a	Cb	18.03N	65.53W
Yabuli	152	Mc	44.56N	128.37 E
Yabulu	212	Jc	19.00S	146.40 E
Yacaré Cururú, Cuchilla-	204	Dj	30.30S	56.33W
Yacaré Norte, Riacho-	204	Cj	22.43S	58.14W
Yacaré Sur, Riacho-	204	Cj	22.43S	58.14W
Yachats	188	Cd	44.20N	124.03W
Yacuma, Rio-	202	Ef	13.38S	65.23W
Yacyretá, Isla-	204	Dh	27.25S	56.30W
Yadé, Massif du-	168	Bd	7.00N	15.30 E
Yadong/Chomo	152	Ef	27.38N	89.03 E
Yae-Dake	156b	Ab	26.38N	127.56 E
Yaeyama-Rettō	152	Lg	24.20N	124.00 E
Yafran	164	Bc	32.04N	12.31 E
Yağcilar	130	Lj	39.25N	28.23 E
Yagishiri-Tō	156a	Ba	44.26N	141.23 E
Yagoua	166	Ic	10.20N	15.14 E
Yagradagzê Shan	152	Gd	35.09N	95.39 E
Yaguajay	194	Hb	22.19N	79.14W
Yaguari	204	Dj	31.31S	54.58W
Yaguari, Arroyo-	204	Di	29.44S	57.37W
Yahualí	146	Fc	38.05N	35.25 E
Yahualica de Gonzáles Gallo	192	Hg	21.08N	102.51W
Yahuma	170	Db	1.06N	23.10 E
Yaita	156	Fc	36.50N	139.55 E
Yaizu	156	Fd	34.51N	138.19 E
Yajiang/Nyagquka	152	He	30.07N	100.58 E
Yakacik	146	Ed	36.05N	32.45 E
Yake-Dake	156	Ec	36.14N	137.35 E
Yakeishi-Dake	156	Gb	39.10N	140.50 E
Yakeshi → Xuguit Qi	152	Lb	49.16N	120.41 E
Yake-Yama	156	Ec	39.58N	140.48 E
Yakima	176	Ee	46.36N	120.31W
Yakima River	188	Fc	46.15N	119.02W
Yako	166	Cc	12.58N	2.16W
Yakumo	156	Pc	42.15N	140.16 E
Yaku-Shima	152	Ne	30.20N	130.30 E
Yakutat	178	Le	59.33N	139.44W
Yakutat Bay	178	Ke	59.45N	140.45W
Yala	148	Kg	6.32N	101.19 E
Yalahán, Laguna de-	192	Pg	21.30N	87.15W
Yalcubul, Punta-	192	Og	21.35N	88.35W
Yale Point	188	Mh	36.25N	109.48W
Yalewa Kalou	219b	Ab	16.40S	177.46 E
Yalgoo	212	De	28.20S	116.41 E
Yalikavak	130	Kl	37.06N	27.18 E
Yalıköy	130	Lh	41.29N	28.17 E
Yalinga	168	Cd	6.31N	23.13 E
Yaloké	168	Bd	5.19N	17.05 E
Yalong Jiang	140	Mg	26.37N	101.48 E
Yalova	146	Cb	40.39N	29.15 E
Yalu Jiang	154	Hd	39.55N	124.20 E
Yalvaç	146	Dc	38.17N	31.11 E
Yäm, Ramlat-	164	If	17.42N	45.09 E
Yamada [Jap.]	156	Be	33.33N	130.45 E
Yamada [Jap.]	154	Pe	39.28N	141.57 E
Yamada-Wan	156	Hb	39.30N	142.00 E
Yamaga	156	Be	33.01N	130.41 E
Yamagata	152	Pd	38.15N	140.15 E
Yamagata Ken [2]	156	Be	38.30N	140.00 E
Yamagawa	156	Bf	31.12N	130.39 E
Yamaguchi	154	Kh	34.10N	131.23 E
Yamaguchi Ken [2]	154	Kh	34.10N	131.30 E
Yamakuni	156	Be	33.24N	131.02 E
Yamal Peninsula (EN) = Jamal, poluostrov-	140	Ib	70.00N	70.00 E
Yamamoto	152	Ga	40.06N	140.03 E
Yamanaka	156	Ec	36.15N	136.22 E
Yamanashi Ken [2]	156	Og	35.30N	138.45 E
Yamashiro	156	Ce	33.57N	133.43 E
Yamato Rise (EN)	154	Me	39.30N	134.30 E
Yamatsuri	156	Gc	36.53N	140.25 E
Yamazaki	156	Dd	35.00N	134.33 E
Yambi, Mesa de-	202	Dc	1.30N	71.20W
Yambio	160	Jh	4.34N	28.23 E
Yambol	158	Fd	8.25N	36.00 E
Yambu Head	197a	Ba	13.09N	61.09W
Yambuya	170	Db	1.16N	24.33 E
Yame	156	Be	33.13N	130.34 E
Yamethin	148	Jd	20.26N	96.09 E
Yamma Yamma, Lake-	212	Ge	26.20S	141.25 E
Yamoto	156	Gb	38.25N	141.13 E
Yamoussoukro	166	Dd	6.49N	5.17W
Yampa River	182	Fc	40.32N	108.59W
Yampi Sound	212	Ec	16.11S	123.40 E
Yamuna	140	Kg	25.30N	81.53 E
Yamunanagar	148	Fb	30.08N	76.59 E
Yamzho Yumco	152	Ef	29.00N	90.40 E
Yanagawa	156	Be	33.10N	130.24 E
Yanahara	156	Dd	34.57N	134.05 E
Yanahuanca	202	Cf	10.30S	76.30W
Yanai	156	Be	33.58N	132.07 E
Yanam	148	Ge	16.51N	82.15 E
Yan'an	142	Nf	36.36N	109.30 E
Yanaoca	202	Hf	26.51N	101.32 E
Yanbian	152	Hf	26.51N	101.32 E
Yanbu'	144	Ee	24.05N	38.03 E
Yanchang	152	Jd	36.39N	110.03 E
Yancheng [China]	154	Bh	33.16N	120.10 E
Yancheng [China]	154	Bh	33.35N	114.00 E
Yanchi	152	Id	37.47N	107.24 E
Yande	219b	Aa	20.03S	163.48 E
Yandina	219a	Dc	9.07S	159.13 E
Yandja	170	Cc	1.41S	17.43 E
Yandua	219b	Bb	16.49S	178.18 E
Yanfolila	166	Cd	11.11N	8.08W
Yangalia	168	Cd	6.58N	21.01 E
Yangcheng	154	Bg	35.32N	112.36 E
Yangchun	152	Jg	22.11N	111.48 E
Yangcun → Wuqing	154	De	39.23N	117.04 E
Yangdôg-Qu	152	Ef	29.31N	91.18 E
Yangganga	219b	Bb	16.35S	178.35 E
Yanggang-Do [2]	154	Jd	41.15N	128.00 E

Yanggao 152 Jc 40.21N 113.47 E
Yanggeta 219d Ab 17.01S 177.20 E
Yanggu 154 Cf 36.08N 115.48 E
Yang He 154 Cd 40.24N 115.18 E
Yangi 130 Mm 36.55N 29.01 E
Yangjiang 152 Jg 21.59N 111.59 E
Yangjiazhangzi 154 Fd 40.48N 120.30 E
Yangon = Rangoon (EN) 142 Lh 16.47N 96.10 E
Yangor 220e Ab 0.32S 166.54 E
Yangqu (Huangzhai) 154 Be 38.05N 112.37 E
Yangquan 152 Jd 37.49N 113.34 E
Yangquanqu 152 Jd 37.04N 111.30 E
Yangshuo 152 Jg 24.46N 110.28 E
Yang Sin, Chu- 148 Lf 12.24N 108.26 E
Yangtze Kiang → Chang Jiang 140 Of 31.48N 121.10 E
Yangxian 152 Ie 33.20N 107.35 E
Yangxin [China] 152 Kf 29.50N 115.11 E
Yangxin [China] 154 Df 37.39N 117.34 E
Yangyuan (Xicheng) 154 Cd 40.08N 114.10 E
Yangzhou 152 Ke 32.20N 119.25 E
Yanhe (Heping) 152 If 28.31N 108.28 E
Yanji 152 Mc 42.56N 129.30 E
Yanjin 154 Cg 35.09N 114.11 E
Yankton 182 Hc 42.53N 97.23W
Yanling 154 Cg 34.07N 114.11 E
Yanqi 142 Ke 42.04N 86.34 E
Yanqing 154 Cd 40.28N 115.57 E
Yan Shan 140 Ne 40.18N 117.36 E
Yanshan [China] 154 De 38.03N 117.12 E
Yanshan [China] 152 Hg 23.38N 104.24 E
Yanshan (Hekou) 154 Dj 28.18N 117.41 E
Yanshi 154 Bg 34.44N 112.47 E
Yanshou 154 Jb 45.28N 128.19 E
Yantai 142 Of 37.28N 121.24 E
Yanutha 219d Ac 16.14S 178.00 E
Yanweigang 154 Eg 34.28N 119.46 E
Yanyuan 152 Hf 27.26N 101.32 E
Yanzhou 152 Kd 35.33N 116.49 E
Yao [Chad] 168 Bc 12.51N 17.34 E
Yao [Jap.] 156 Dd 34.38N 135.36 E
Yaodu → Dongzhi 154 Di 30.06N 117.01 E
Yaoundé 160 Ih 3.52N 11.31 E
Yapacani 202 Fg 16.36S 64.18W
Yapei 166 Ed 9.10N 1.10W
Yapen, Pulau- 208 Ee 1.45S 136.15 E
Yapen, Selat- 150 Kg 1.30S 136.10 E
Yapeyú 204 Di 29.28S 56.49W
Yap Islands 208 Ed 9.32N 138.08 E
Yapraklı 146 Eb 40.46N 33.47 E
Yapu 148 Jf 14.51N 98.03 E
Yaqian → Yuexi 154 Di 30.51N 116.22 E
Yaque del Norte, Río- 194 Ld 19.51N 71.41W
Yaque del Sur, Río- 194 Ld 18.17N 71.06W
Yaqueling 154 Ai 30.40N 111.36 E
Yaqui 174 Hg 27.37N 110.39W
Yaracuy [2] 202 Ea 10.20N 68.45W
Yaraka 210 Fg 24.53S 144.04 E
Yaralıgöz 146 Fb 41.45N 34.10 E
Yare 118 Oi 52.35N 1.44 E
Yaren 220e Ab 0.33S 166.54 E
Yari, Río- 198 If 0.23S 72.16W
Yariga-Take 156 Ec 36.20N 137.39 E
Yarīm 144 Fg 14.21N 44.22 E
Yaritagua 202 Ea 10.05N 69.08W
Yarkant/Shache 142 Jf 38.24N 77.15 E
Yarkant He 140 Ke 40.28N 80.52 E
Yarlung Zangbo Jiang 140 Lg 24.02N 90.59 E
Yarmouth [Eng.-U.K.] 124 Ad 50.41N 1.30W
Yarmouth [N.S.-Can.] 176 Me 43.50N 66.07W
Yarram 212 Jg 38.33S 146.41 E
Yarumal 202 Cb 6.58N 75.25W
Yasawa 219d Ab 16.47S 177.31 E
Yasawa Group 208 If 17.00S 177.23 E
Yashi 166 Gc 12.22N 7.55 E
Yashima 156 Gb 39.09N 140.10 E
Ya-Shima 156 Ce 33.45N 132.10 E
Yashiro-Jima 156 Ce 33.55N 132.15 E
Yasothon 148 Ke 15.46N 104.12 E
Yass 212 Jf 34.50S 148.55 E
Yassiören 130 Lh 41.18N 28.35 E
Yasugi 156 Cd 35.26N 133.15 E
Yāsūj 144 Hc 30.45N 51.33 E
Yasun Burnu 146 Gb 41.09N 37.41 E
Yatağan 146 Cd 37.20N 28.09 E
Yatate Tōge 156 Gb 40.26N 140.37 E
Yatate-Yama 156 Ad 34.12N 129.14 E
Yatenga 166 Ec 13.48N 2.10W
Yaté-Village 216 Cd 22.09S 166.57 E
Yathata 219d Cb 17.15S 179.32W
Yathkyed Lake 180 Hd 62.40N 98.00W
Yatolema 170 Db 0.21N 24.33 E
Yatou → Rongcheng 154 Gf 37.10N 122.25 E
Yatsu-ga-Take 156 Fd 35.59N 138.23 E
Yatsushiro 152 Ne 32.30N 130.36 E
Yatsushiro-Kai 156 Be 32.20N 130.25 E
Yatta Plateau 170 Gc 2.00S 38.00 E
Yauco 194 Nd 18.02N 66.51W
Yauri 202 Df 14.47S 71.29W
Yauyos 202 Cf 12.24S 75.57W
Yavari, Río- 202 Dd 4.21S 70.02W
Yavi, Cerro- 202 Eb 5.32N 65.59W
Yaviza 194 Ii 8.11N 77.41W
Yawatahama 154 Lh 33.27N 132.24 E
Yaxchilán 190 Fe 16.54N 90.58W
Yaxian (Sanya) 142 Mh 18.27N 109.28 E
Yayladağı 146 Ge 35.56N 36.01 E
Yazd 142 Hf 31.53N 54.25 E
Yazd [3] 144 Hc 31.30N 54.30 E
Yazılıkaya 146 Dc 39.13N 30.45 E
Yazoo City 186 Kj 32.51N 90.28W
Yazoo River 186 Kj 32.22N 91.00W
Ybbs 128 Jb 48.10N 15.06 E
Ybbs an der Donau 128 Jc 48.10N 15.05 E
Yding Skovhøj 116 Ch 56.01N 9.48 E
Ydre 116 Fg 57.52N 15.15 E
Ydstebøhamn 116 Ae 59.03N 5.25 E
Ye 142 Lh 15.15N 97.51 E
Yebaishou → Jianping 152 Kc 41.55N 119.37 E
Yebbi Bou 168 Ba 20.58N 18.04 E
Yébigé 168 Ba 22.04N 17.49 E
Yecheng/Kargilik 142 Jf 37.54N 77.26 E
Yech'ŏn 154 Jf 36.39N 128.27 E
Yecla 126 Kf 38.37N 1.07W
Yécora 190 Cc 28.20N 108.58W
Yēd 168 Ge 4.48N 43.02 E
Yedi Burun 130 Mm 36.23N 29.05 E
Yedseram 166 Hc 12.16N 14.09 E
Yefira 130 Fi 40.44N 22.42 E
Yegros 204 Dh 26.24S 56.25W
Yeguas 126 Hf 38.02N 4.15W
Yeha 168 Fc 14.21N 39.05 E
Yei 168 Ee 4.05N 30.40 E
Yei 168 Ee 4.40N 30.30 E
Yeji [China] 154 Ci 31.51N 115.55 E
Yeji [Ghana] 166 Ed 8.13N 0.39W
Yekepa 166 Dd 7.35N 8.32W
Yelgu 168 Ec 10.01N 32.31 E
Yélimané 166 Cb 15.07N 10.36W
Yell 110 Fc 60.35N 1.05W
Yellice Dağı 130 Mj 39.23N 29.57 E
Yellowhead Pass 180 Ff 52.50N 117.55W
Yellowknife 176 Hc 62.27N 114.21W
Yellowknife 180 Gd 62.23N 114.20W
Yellow River (EN) = Huang He 140 Nf 37.32N 118.19 E
Yellow Sea (EN) = Huang Hai 140 Of 36.00N 124.00 E
Yellow Sea (EN) = Hwang-Hae 140 Of 36.00N 124.00 E
Yellowstone 174 Ie 47.58N 103.59W
Yellowstone Lake 174 He 44.25N 110.22W
Yellowstone National Park 188 Jd 44.58N 110.42W
Yell Sound 118 La 60.33N 1.15W
Yeltes 126 Fd 40.56N 6.31W
Yelwa [Nig.] 166 Gd 8.51N 9.37 E
Yelwa [Nig.] 166 Fc 10.50N 4.44 E
Yemen (EN) = Al Yaman 142 Gh 15.00N 44.00 E
Yemen, People's Democratic Republic of- (EN) → Al Yaman 142 Gh. 15.00N 44.00 E
Yenagoa 166 Ge 4.55N 6.16 E
Yenangyaung 148 Id 20.28N 94.53 E
Yen Bay 148 Kd 21.42N 104.52 E
Yendi 166 Ed 9.26N 0.01W
Yenge 170 Dc 0.55S 20.40 E
Yengisar 152 Cd 38.56N 76.09 E
Yengo 170 Cb 0.22N 15.29 E
Yeniboğaziçi 146 Ee 35.17N 33.52 E
Yenice [Tur.] 130 Kj 39.55N 27.18 E
Yenice [Tur.] 146 Fd 36.59N 35.03 E
Yeni Erenkoy 146 Fe 35.35N 34.15 E
Yenice [Tur.] 146 Eb 41.18N 32.08 E
Yenifoça 130 Jk 38.44N 26.51 E
Yenihisar 130 Kl 37.22N 27.15 E
Yenimahalle, Ankara- 146 Ec 39.56N 32.52 E
Yenipazar 130 Ll 37.48N 28.12 E
Yenişehir 146 Cb 40.16N 29.39 E
Yenisey (EN) = Jenisej 140 Kb 71.50N 82.40 E
Yenisey Bay (EN) = Jenisejski zaliv 138 Db 72.00N 81.00 E
Yenisey Ridge (EN) = Jenisejski krjaž 140 Ld 59.00N 92.30 E
Yennádhion 130 Km 36.01N 27.56 E
Yeo, Lake- 212 Ee 28.05S 124.25 E
Yeovil 118 Kk 50.57N 2.39W
Yepes 126 Ie 39.54N 3.38W
Yeppoon 212 Kd 23.08S 150.45 E
Yerákion 130 Fm 37.00N 22.42 E
Yerbabuena 192 Hf 23.00N 103.30W
Yerer 168 Gd 7.32N 42.05 E
Yerington 188 Fg 38.59N 119.10W
Yerkesik 130 Ll 37.07N 28.17 E
Yerköy 146 Fc 39.38N 34.29 E
Yerlisu 130 Ji 40.46N 26.39 E
Yermak Plateau (EN) 179 Mb 82.00N 6.00 E
Yeroḥam 146 Fg 31.00N 34.55 E
Yerres 122 If 48.43N 2.27 E
Yerupajá, Nevado- 198 Ig 10.16S 76.54W
Yerushalayim [3] 146 Fg 31.45N 35.00 E
Yerushalayim = Jerusalem (EN) 142 Ff 31.46N 35.14 E
Yerville 124 Ce 49.40N 0.54 E
Yerwa 166 Hc 11.13N 12.53 E
Yesa, Embalse de- 126 Kb 42.36N 1.09W
Yeşan 154 If 36.41N 126.51 E
Yeşilhisar 146 Fc 38.21N 35.06 E
Yeşilırmak 144 Ea 41.24N 36.35 E
Yeşilköy 146 Cb 40.57N 29.49 E
Yeşilova 130 Ml 37.30N 29.46 E
Yeşilyurt 130 Ll 37.11N 28.17 E
Yeso 204 Cj 30.56S 59.28W
Yeste 126 Jf 38.22N 2.18W
Yetti 158 Gf 26.10N 7.50W
Ye-u 148 Jd 22.46N 95.26 E
Yeu, Ile d'- 122 Dh 46.43N 2.20W
Yèvre 122 Ig 47.13N 2.04 E
Yexian [China] 154 Ef 37.11N 119.58 E
Yexian [China] 154 Bh 33.38N 113.21 E
Yguazú, Río- 204 Eg 25.20S 55.00W
Yhú 204 Eg 24.59S 55.59W
Yí, Río- 204 Dk 33.07S 57.08W
Yialí 130 Km 36.40N 27.05 E
Yi'an 152 Mb 47.53N 125.17 E
Yiannitsá 130 Fi 40.48N 22.25 E
Yíaros 130 Hl 37.37N 24.43 E
Yibin 142 Mg 28.47N 104.35 E
Yibug Caka 152 Ee 33.55N 87.05 E
Yichang 142 Nf 30.42N 111.22 E
Yicheng [China] 154 Ag 35.44N 111.43 E
Yicheng [China] 154 Bi 31.42N 112.16 E
Yichuan 152 Jd 36.00N 110.06 E
Yichun [China] 152 Jf 27.47N 114.25 E
Yichun [China] 152 Mb 47.41N 128.55 E
Yıdılzeli 146 Gc 39.52N 36.38 E
Yidu [China] 152 Je 30.23N 111.28 E
Yidu [China] 152 Kd 36.41N 118.29 E
Yidun (Dagxoi) 152 Ge 30.25N 99.28 E
Yifag 168 Fc 12.02N 37.41 E
Yifeng 154 Cj 28.25N 114.47 E
Yığılca 146 Db 40.58N 31.27 E
Yigo 220c Ba 13.32N 144.53W
Yi He [China] 154 Bg 34.41N 112.33 E
Yi He [China] 154 Eg 34.07N 118.15 E
Yilan 152 Mb 46.18N 129.33 E
Yıldız Dağı 144 Ea 40.08N 36.56 E
Yıldız Dağları 146 Bb 41.50N 27.10 E
Yiliang 152 Hg 24.59N 103.08 E
Yimianpo 154 Jb 45.04N 128.03 E
Yimin He 152 Kb 49.15N 119.42 E
Yinan (Jiehu) 154 Eg 35.33N 118.27 E
Yinchuan 142 Mf 38.28N 106.19 E
Yindarlgooda, Lake- 212 Ef 30.45S 121.55 E
Yingcheng [China] 154 Bi 30.57N 113.33 E
Yingcheng [China] 154 Hb 44.08N 125.54 E
Yingde 152 Jg 24.13N 113.24 E
Ying He 152 Ke 32.30N 116.31 E
Yingjiang 152 Gg 24.45N 97.58 E
Yingjin He 154 Ec 42.20N 119.19 E
Yingkou 142 Oe 40.40N 122.12 E
Yingkou (Dashiqiao) 154 Gd 40.39N 122.31 E
Yingshan 154 Ci 30.45N 115.40 E
Yingshang 154 Dh 32.38N 116.16 E
Yingshouyingzi 154 Dd 40.33N 117.37 E
Yingtan 154 Dj 28.13N 117.00 E
Yingxian 154 Be 39.33N 113.10 E
Ying zhan/Victoria 142 Ng 22.17N 114.09 E
Yining/Gulja 152 Dc 43.54N 81.21 E
Yinma He 154 Hb 44.50N 125.45 E
Yinqing Qunjiao 150 Fe 8.55N 112.35 E
Yin Shan 140 Me 41.30N 109.00 E
Yi'ong Zangbo 152 Gf 29.56N 95.10 E
Yioúra 130 Hj 39.24N 24.10 E
Yipinglang 152 Hf 25.13N 101.55 E
Yiquan → Meitan 152 If 27.48N 107.32 E
Yirga Alem 168 Fd 6.44N 38.24 E
Yirol 168 Ed 6.33N 30.30 E
Yirshi 152 Kb 47.17N 119.55 E
Yishui 154 Eg 35.47N 118.38 E
Yisra'el = Israel (EN) [1] 142 Ff 31.30N 35.00 E
Yithion 130 Fm 36.45N 22.34 E
Yitong 154 Hc 43.20N 125.17 E
Yitong He 154 Hb 44.45N 125.40 E
Yitulihe 152 La 50.41N 121.33 E
Yiwu 154 Fj 29.19N 120.04 E
Yiwu/Aratürük 152 Fc 43.15N 94.35 E
Yixian [China] 154 Dj 29.56N 117.56 E
Yixian [China] 154 Fd 41.33N 121.14 E
Yixian [China] 154 Ce 39.21N 115.30 E
Yixing 154 Ei 31.21N 119.48 E
Yixun He 154 Dd 41.00N 117.41 E
Yiyang [China] 154 Dj 28.24N 117.24 E
Yiyang [China] 154 Bg 34.30N 112.10 E
Yiyang [China] 152 Jf 28.41N 112.20 E
Yiyuan (Nanma) 154 Ef 36.11N 118.10 E
Yizheng 154 Eh 32.16N 119.10 E
Yläne 116 Jd 60.53N 22.25 E
Ylikitka 114 Gc 66.08N 28.30 E
Yli-Li 114 Fd 65.22N 25.50 E
Ylimarkku/Övermark 116 Ib 62.37N 21.28 E
Ylistaro 114 Fe 62.57N 22.31 E
Ylitornio 114 Fc 66.18N 23.40 E
Ylivieska 114 Fd 64.05N 24.33 E
Ylöjärvi 116 Jc 61.33N 23.36 E
Ymers 179 Jd 73.20N 25.00W
Yngaren 116 Gf 58.50N 16.35 E
Yngen 116 Fe 59.45N 14.20 E
Ynykčanski 138 Id 60.08N 137.47 E
Yoboki 168 Gc 11.28N 42.06 E
Yobuko 156 Ae 33.33N 129.54 E
Yodo-Gawa 156 Dd 34.41N 135.25 E
Yogoum 168 Bb 17.27N 19.31 E
Yoğuntaş 130 Kh 41.50N 27.04 E
Yogyakarta 142 Nj 7.48S 110.22 E
Yoichi 154 Pc 43.12N 140.41 E
Yojoa, Lago de- 194 Df 14.50N 88.00W
Yōju 154 If 37.18N 127.38 E
Yokadouma 160 Ih 3.31N 15.03 E
Yōkaichi 156 Ed 35.07N 136.11 E
Yōkaichiba 156 Gd 35.40N 140.28 E
Yokkaichi 154 Ng 34.58N 136.37 E
Yoko 166 Hd 5.32N 12.19 E
Yokoate-Jima 152 Mf 28.50N 129.00 E
Yokohama 142 Pf 35.27N 139.39 E
Yokosuka 154 Og 35.18N 139.40 E
Yokote 152 Pd 39.18N 140.34 E
Yola 160 Ih 9.12N 12.29 E
Yolaina, Serranias de- 194 Fh 11.40N 84.20W
Yolombo 170 Dc 1.32S 23.15 E
Yom 148 Ke 15.52N 100.16 E
Yom 148 Ke 15.52N 100.16 E
Yŏmju 154 He 39.50N 124.33 E
Yomou 166 Dd 7.34N 9.16W
Yomra 146 Hb 40.58N 39.54 E
Yon 122 Eh 46.30N 1.18W
Yona 220c Bb 13.25N 144.47 E
Yonago 154 Lg 35.26N 133.20 E
Yonaguni-Jima 152 Lg 24.25N 123.00 E
Yonaha-Dake 156b Ab 26.43N 128.13 E
Yonan 154 If 37.55N 126.05 E
Yoneshiro-Gawa 156 Ga 40.13N 140.00 E
Yonezawa 152 Pd 37.55N 140.07 E
Yong 166 He 4.54N 13.12 E
Yong'an 152 Kf 25.58N 117.29 E
Yŏngan 152 Mc 41.15N 129.30 E
Yongchang 152 Hd 38.17N 102.07 E
Yongcheng 154 Dh 33.56N 116.21 E
Yongch'on 154 Jg 35.59N 127.59 E
Yongchuan 152 If 29.22N 105.59 E
Yongch'u-gap 154 Jf 37.03N 129.26 E
Yongdeng 152 Hd 36.44N 103.24 E
Yongding He 152 Kd 39.20N 117.04 E
Yŏngdŏk 154 Jf 36.24N 129.22 E
Yŏngdong 154 If 36.10N 127.47 E
Yonghung 154 Ie 39.33N 127.14 E
Yongji (Kouqian) 154 Ic 43.40N 126.30 E
Yongjing 152 Hd 36.00N 103.17 E
Yŏngju 152 Md 36.49N 128.37 E
Yongkang 152 Lf 28.51N 120.05 E
Yongle Qundao 150 Fc 16.35N 111.40 E
Yongnian (Linmingguan) 154 Cf 36.47N 114.30 E
Yongning → Xuyong 152 If 28.13N 105.26 E
Yongqing 154 De 39.19N 116.29 E
Yŏngsanp'o 154 Ig 35.00N 126.43 E
Yongsheng 152 Hf 26.41N 100.45 E
Yongshu Jiao 150 Fe 9.35N 112.50 E
Yŏngwŏl 154 Jf 37.11N 128.28 E
Yongxiu (Tujiabu) 152 Kf 29.05N 115.49 E
Yonibana 166 Cd 8.26N 12.14W
Yonkers 184 Ke 40.56N 73.54W
Yonne [3] 122 Jg 47.55N 3.45 E
Yonne 122 If 48.23N 2.58 E
Yopal 202 Db 5.21N 72.23W
Yopurga 152 Cd 39.15N 76.45 E
York 118 Lg 54.10N 1.30W
York [Al.-U.S.] 184 Ci 32.29N 88.18W
York [Austl.] 212 Df 31.53S 116.46 E
York [Eng.-U.K.] 118 Lh 53.58N 1.05W
York [Nb.-U.S.] 186 Hf 40.52N 97.36W
York [Pa.-U.S.] 182 Ld 39.57N 76.44W
York, Cape- 208 Ff 10.40S 142.30 E
York, Kap- 224 Od 76.05N 67.05W
York, Vale of- 118 Lg 54.10N 1.20W
Yorke Peninsula 212 Hf 35.00S 137.30 E
Yorkshire Dales 118 Kg 54.15N 2.10W
Yorkshire Wolds 118 Mh 54.00N 0.40W
York Sound 212 Fb 14.50S 125.05 E
Yorkton 176 Id 51.13N 102.28W
Yorktown 184 Ig 37.14N 76.32W
Yoro 194 Df 15.09N 87.07W
Yoro [3] 194 Df 15.15N 87.15W
Yoron-Jima 156b Bb 27.03N 128.26 E
Yoro-Shima 156b Ba 28.02N 129.10 E
Yorosso 166 Ec 12.21N 4.47W
Yorubaland Plateau 166 Fd 8.00N 4.30 E
Yörük 130 Ki 40.56N 27.04 E
Yosemite National Park 182 Dd 35.28N 119.33W
Yosemite Rock 198 Hi 31.58S 83.15W
Yoshida [Jap.] 156 Ce 33.16N 132.32 E
Yoshida [Jap.] 156 Cd 34.40N 132.42 E
Yoshii 156 Ae 33.18N 129.40 E
Yoshii-Gawa 156 Dd 34.36N 134.02 E
Yoshino-Gawa 156 Dd 34.05N 134.36 E
Yŏsu 152 Me 34.44N 127.44 E
Yotaú 202 Fg 16.03S 63.03W
Yōtei-Zan 156a Bb 42.49N 140.47 E
Yotvata 146 Fh 29.53N 35.03 E
Youghal/Eochaill 118 Fj 51.57N 7.50W
Youghal Harbour/Cuan Eochaille 118 Fj 51.52N 7.50W
You Jiang 140 Mg 22.50N 108.06 E
Youllemmedene 158 Hg 16.00N 1.00 E
Young [Austl.] 212 Jf 34.19S 148.18 E
Young [Ur.] 204 Dk 32.41S 57.38W
Young, Cape- 218 Je 43.42S 176.37W
Younghusband Peninsula 212 Hg 36.00S 139.30 E
Young Island 222 Ke 66.25S 162.30 E
Young's Island 197n Ba 13.08N 61.13W
Youngs Rock 220q Ab 25.03S 130.06W
Youngstown 182 Kc 41.05N 80.40W
Youshashan 152 Fd 38.04N 90.53 E
Youssoufia 162 Fc 32.15N 8.32W
Youyang 152 If 28.49N 108.45 E
Yozgat 144 Db 39.50N 34.48 E
Ypacaraí 206 Ic 25.23S 57.16W
Ypacaraí, Laguna- 204 Dg 25.17S 57.20W
Ypané, Río- 204 Df 23.29S 57.19W
Ypé Jhú 204 Ef 23.54S 55.20W
Ypoá, Lago- 204 Dg 25.48S 57.28W
Yport 124 Ce 49.44N 0.19 E
Ypres/Ieper 122 Id 50.51N 2.53 E
Yreka 182 Cc 41.44N 122.43W
Yser 122 Ic 51.09N 2.43 E
Yssingeaux 122 Ki 45.08N 4.07 E
Ystad 114 Ci 55.25N 13.49 E
Ytambey, Río- 204 Eg 24.46S 54.24W
Ythan 118 Ld 57.25N 2.00W
Ytre Arna 116 Ad 60.28N 5.26 E
Ytre Sula 116 Ac 61.05N 4.40 E
Ytterhogdal 116 Fb 62.11N 14.56 E
Ytterlännäs 114 De 63.01N 17.41 E
Yttermalung 116 Ed 60.35N 13.50 E
Ytyk-Kjuël 138 Id 62.28N 133.25 E
Yu 'Alliq, Jabal- 146 Eg 30.22N 33.31 E
Yuan'an 154 Ai 31.04N 111.39 E
Yuanbaoshan 154 Ec 42.19N 119.19 E
Yuanbao Shan 152 If 25.24N 109.11 E
Yuan Jiang [Asia] = Red River (EN) 140 Mg 20.17N 106.34 E
Yuanjiang [China] 154 Bj 28.50N 112.23 E
Yuanjiang [China] 152 Hg 23.22N 102.26 E
Yuan Jiang [China] 140 Ng 28.58N 111.49 E
Yuanling 152 Jf 28.30N 110.25 E
Yuanmou 152 Hf 25.45N 101.54 E
Yuanping 152 Jd 38.43N 112.42 E
Yuanqu (Liuzhangzhen)) 152 Jd 35.19N 111.44 E
Yuanshi 154 Cf 37.45N 114.30 E
Yuba City 182 Cd 39.08N 121.37W
Yūbari 152 Pc 43.04N 141.59 E
Yūbari-Dake 156a Cb 43.06N 142.15 E
Yūbari-Gawa 156a Bb 43.08N 141.35 E
Yūbari-Sanchi 156a Cb 43.10N 142.15 E
Yuba River 188 Eg 39.07N 121.36W
Yubdo 168 Fd 8.58N 35.27 E
Yūbetsu 154 Qb 43.13N 144.05 E
Yūbetsu-Gawa 156a Ca 44.14N 143.37 E
Yucatán [2] 190 Gd 20.50N 89.00W
Yucatán, Canal de- = Yucatan Channel (EN) 174 Kg 21.45N 85.45W
Yucatán, Península de- = Yucatan Peninsula (EN) 174 Kh 19.30N 89.00W
Yucatan Basin (EN) 190 Ge 20.00N 84.00W
Yucatan Channel (EN) = Yucatán, Canal de- 174 Kg 21.45N 85.45W
Yucatan Peninsula (EN) = Yucatán, Península de- 174 Kh 19.30N 89.00W
Yucheng 154 Df 36.56N 116.39 E
Yuci 152 Jd 37.41N 112.49 E
Yucuyácua, Cerro- 190 Ee 17.07N 97.40W
Yuda 156 Gb 39.19N 140.48 E
Yudi Shan 152 Lb 52.17N 121.52 E
Yueliang Pao 154 Gb 45.44N 123.55 E
Yueqing 152 Lf 28.08N 120.58 E
Yuexi 152 Hf 28.37N 102.36 E
Yuexi (Yaqian) 154 Di 30.51N 116.22 E
Yueyang 152 Jf 29.18N 113.12 E
Yufu-Dake 156 Be 33.17N 131.23 E
Yugan 152 Kf 28.42N 116.39 E
Yugoslavia (EN) = Jugoslavija [1] 112 Hg 44.00N 19.00 E
Yu He 154 Be 39.51N 113.26 E
Yuhuang Ding 154 Df 36.20N 117.01 E
Yuki 170 Cc 3.55S 19.25 E
Yukon 186 Hi 35.31N 97.44W
Yukon 174 Cc 62.33N 163.59W
Yukon Flats 178 Jc 66.35N 146.00W
Yukon Plateau 174 Fc 61.30N 135.40W
Yukon Territory [3] 180 Dd 63.00N 136.00W
Yüksekova 146 Kd 37.19N 44.10 E
Yukuhashi 156 Be 33.44N 130.58 E
Yule River 212 Dd 20.41S 118.17 E
Yuli/Iopnur 152 Ec 41.22N 86.09 E
Yulin [China] 142 Ng 22.39N 110.08 E
Yulin [China] 142 Mf 38.14N 109.48 E
Yuling Guan 152 Ke 30.04N 118.53 E
Yulin Jiao 140 Mh 17.50N 109.30 E
Yulongxue Shan 152 Hf 27.09N 100.12 E
Yuma [Az.-U.S.] 176 Hf 32.43N 114.37W
Yuma [Co.-U.S.] 186 Ef 40.08N 102.43W
Yuma, Bahia de- 194 Md 18.21N 68.35W
Yumare 196 Bg 10.37N 68.41W
Yumari, Cerro- 202 Ec 4.27N 66.50W
Yumbe 170 Fb 3.28N 31.15 E
Yumbi [Zaire] 170 Cc 1.53S 16.32 E
Yumbi [Zaire] 170 Ec 1.14S 26.14 E
Yumen (Laojunmiao) 142 Lf 39.50N 97.44 E
Yumenkou 152 Jd 35.42N 110.37 E
Yumenzhen 152 Gc 40.17N 97.12 E
Yumin 152 Db 45.59N 82.28 E
Yumurtalik 146 Fd 36.49N 35.45 E
Yuna, Río- 194 Md 19.12N 69.37W
Yunak 146 Dc 38.49N 31.45 E
Yunaska 178a Db 52.40N 170.50W
Yuncheng [China] 152 Jd 35.02N 111.00 E
Yuncheng [China] 154 Cg 35.35N 115.56 E
Yungas 198 Jg 16.20S 66.45W
Yungay 206 Fe 37.07S 72.01W
Yungui Gaoyuan 140 Mg 26.00N 105.00 E
Yunhe → Peixian 154 Dg 34.44N 116.56 E
Yuni 156a Bb 42.59N 141.46 E
Yunjinghong → Jinghong 152 Hg 21.59N 100.48 E
Yunkai Dashan 152 Jg 22.30N 111.00 E
Yunlin 152 Lg 23.43N 120.33 E
Yun Ling 152 Gf 27.00N 99.30 E
Yunmeng 154 Bi 31.01N 113.45 E
Yunnan Sheng (Yün-nan Sheng) [2] 152 Hg 25.00N 102.00 E
Yün-nan Sheng → Yunnan Sheng [2] 152 Hg 25.00N 102.00 E
Yunomae 156 Be 32.15N 130.57 E
Yunotsu 156 Cd 35.05N 132.21 E
Yun Shui 154 Bi 30.43N 113.57 E
Yunxian 152 Je 32.50N 110.50 E
Yunxiao 152 Kg 24.05N 117.18 E
Yunyang 152 Ie 31.00N 108.55 E
Yunzhong Shan 152 Jd 38.50N 112.27 E
Yuquan 154 Ib 45.27N 127.08 E
Yuquerí 204 Ci 28.53S 58.02W
Yura 202 Dg 16.12S 71.42W
Yura-Gawa 156 Dd 35.31N 135.17 E
Yurimaguas 200 If 5.54S 76.05W
Yuriria 192 Ig 20.12N 101.09W
Yuruarí, Río- 196 Fi 6.44N 61.40W
Yurungkax He 152 Dd 38.05N 80.20 E
Yuscarán 194 Dg 13.55N 86.51W
Yushan 154 Ej 28.41N 118.15 E
Yushan 140 Og 23.30N 121.00 E
Yu Shan 152 Kf 27.00N 116.00 E
Yushe 154 Bf 37.04N 112.58 E
Yushu [China] 154 Ib 44.50N 126.33 E
Yushu [China] 142 Lf 33.06N 96.48 E
Yushutun 152 Lb 47.06N 123.41 E
Yūsuf, Baḥr- 146 Dh 29.19N 30.50 E
Yusufeli 146 Ib 40.50N 41.33 E
Yutai (Guting) 154 Dg 35.00N 116.40 E
Yutian 154 De 39.53N 117.45 E
Yutian/Keriya 142 Kf 36.52N 81.42 E
Yuty 206 Ic 26.32S 56.18W
Yutz 124 Ie 49.21N 6.11 E
Yuwan-Dake 156b Ba 28.18N 129.19 E
Yuxi 152 Hg 24.27N 102.34 E
Yuxian [China] 152 Jd 39.49N 114.35 E
Yuxian [China] 152 Jd 38.03N 113.28 E
Yuxian [China] 154 Bg 34.09N 113.29 E
Yuxikou 154 Ei 31.26N 118.18 E
Yuyao 154 Fi 30.04N 121.10 E
Yuya-Wan 156 Bd 34.20N 130.55 E
Yuza 156 Fb 39.01N 139.53 E
Yuzawa [Jap.] 156 Fc 36.56N 138.47 E
Yuzawa [Jap.] 154 Pe 39.10N 140.30 E
Yvel 122 Dg 47.59N 2.23W
Yvelines [3] 122 Hf 48.50N 1.50 E
Yverdon 128 Ad 46.46N 6.40 E
Yvetot 122 Ge 49.37N 0.46 E
Yvette 124 Ef 48.40N 2.20 E
Yxlan 116 He 59.40N 18.50 E
Yxningen 116 Gf 58.15N 16.20 E

Index Symbols

[1] Independent Nation
[2] State, Region
[3] District, County
[4] Municipality
[5] Colony, Dependency
Continent
Physical Region
Historical or Cultural Region
Mount, Mountain
Volcano
Hill
Mountains, Mountain Range
Hills, Escarpment
Plateau, Upland
Pass, Gap
Plain, Lowland
Delta
Salt Flat
Valley, Canyon
Crater, Cave
Karst Features
Depression
Polder
Desert, Dunes
Forest, Woods
Heath, Steppe
Oasis
Cape, Point
Coast, Beach
Cliff
Peninsula
Isthmus
Sandbank
Island
Atoll
Rock, Reef
Islands, Archipelago
Rocks, Reefs
Coral Reef
Well, Spring
Geyser
River, Stream
Waterfall, Rapids
River Mouth, Estuary
Lake
Salt Lake
Intermittent Lake
Reservoir
Swamp, Pond
Canal
Glacier
Ice Shelf, Pack Ice
Ocean
Sea
Gulf, Bay
Strait, Fjord
Lagoon
Bank
Seamount
Tablemount
Ridge
Shelf
Basin
Escarpment, Sea Scarp
Fracture
Trench, Abyss
National Park, Reserve
Point of Interest
Recreation Site
Cave, Cavern
Historic Site
Ruins
Wall, Walls
Church, Abbey
Temple
Scientific Station
Railway station
Airport
Port
Military installation
Lighthouse
Mine
Tunnel
Dam, Bridge

Z

Zaajatskaja 134 Jj 52.53N 61.35 E
Zaalajski hrebet 135 Ie 39.25N 72.50 E
Zaanstad 122 Kb 52.26N 4.49 E
Žabaj 134 Nj 51.42N 68.22 E
Zabajkalsk 138 Gg 49.40N 117.21 E
Zabarjad 164 Ge 23.37N 36.12 E
Zāb-e Kūchek 146 Ke 36.00N 45.15 E
Zabīb, Ra's az- 128 Em 37.16N 10.04 E
Zabid 144 Fg 14.12N 43.18 E
Zabīd, Wādī- 144 Fg 14.07N 43.06 E
Žabinka 132 Dc 52.13N 24.01 E
Ząbkowice Śląskie 120 Mf 50.36N 16.53 E
Žabljak 130 Cf 43.09N 19.08 E
Zabłudów 120 Tc 53.01N 23.20 E
Zabok 128 Jd 46.02N 15.55 E
Zābol 144 Jc 31.02N 61.30 E
Zābol [3] 144 Kc 32.00N 67.15 E
Zabolot 116 Kk 53.56N 24.46 E
Zabolotje 120 Ue 51.37N 24.26 E
Zabolotov 130 Ia 48.25N 25.23 E
Zabré 166 Ec 11.10N 0.38W
Zábřeh 120 Mg 49.53N 16.52 E
Zabrze 120 Of 50.18N 18.46 E
Zacapa 190 Gf 14.58N 89.32W
Zacapa [3] 194 Cf 15.00N 89.30W
Zacapu 192 Ih 19.50N 101.43W
Zacatecas 176 Ig 22.47N 102.35W
Zacatecas [2] 190 Dd 23.00N 103.00W
Zacatecoluca 194 Cg 13.30N 88.52W
Zacatepec 192 Jh 18.39N 99.12W
Zacatlán 192 Kh 19.56N 97.58W
Zaccar, Djebel- 126 Oh 36.20N 2.13 E
Zacoalco de Torres 192 Hg 20.14N 103.35W
Zacualtipán 192 Jg 20.39N 98.36W
Zaculeu 194 Bf 15.21N 91.29W
Zadar 112 Hg 44.07N 15.15 E
Zadarski kanal 128 Jf 44.10N 15.10 E
Zadetkyi Kyun 148 Jg 9.58N 98.13 E
Zadi 170 Bc 4.46S 14.52 E
Zadoi 152 Fe 33.10N 94.58 E
Zadonsk 132 Kc 52.23N 38.58 E
Za'farānah 164 Fd 29.07N 32.33 E
Zafferano, Capo- 128 Hl 38.07N 13.32 E
Ẓafīr 144 He 23.07N 53.46 E
Zafra 126 Ff 38.25N 6.25W
Żagań 120 Le 51.37N 15.19 E
Žagarė/Zagare 116 Jh 56.19N 23.14 E
Zagare/Žagarė 116 Jh 56.19N 23.14 E
Zāgheh 146 Mf 33.30N 48.42 E
Zāgh Marz 146 Od 36.47N 53.17 E
Zaghrah, Wādī- 146 Fh 28.40N 34.20 E
Zaghwān 162 Jb 36.24N 10.09 E
Zaghwān [3] 162 Jb 36.25N 10.10 E
Zaghwān, Jabal- 128 En 36.21N 10.07 E
Zagora 160 Ge 30.19N 5.50W
Zagora 128 Kg 43.40N 16.15 E
Zagória 130 Dj 39.45N 20.50 E
Zagorje 128 Jd 46.05N 16.00 E
Zagorodje 120 Vd 52.15N 25.30 E
Zagórów 120 Nd 52.11N 17.55 E
Zagorsk 112 Jd 56.18N 38.08 E
Zagórz, Sanok- 120 Sg 49.31N 22.17 E
Zagreb 112 Hf 45.48N 16.00 E
Zāgros, Kūhhā-ye- = Zagros Mountains (EN) 140 Gf 33.40N 47.00 E
Zagros Mountains (EN) = Zāgros, Kūhhā-ye- 140 Gf 33.40N 47.00 E
Žagubica 130 Ee 44.12N 21.48 E
Za'gya Zangbo 152 Ee 31.55N 88.58 E
Zagyva 120 Qi 47.10N 20.12 E
Zāhedān 142 Ig 29.30N 60.52 E
Zahlah 146 Ff 33.51N 35.53 E
Zahmet 136 Gh 37.48N 62.29 E
Ẓahrān 164 Hf 17.40N 43.30 E
Zahrez Chergui 126 Pi 35.14N 3.32 E
Zailijski Alatau, hrebet- 135 Kc 43.00N 77.00 E
Žailma 136 Ge 51.32N 61.40 E
Zaire [3] 170 Bd 6.30S 13.30 E
Zaire 158 Ii 6.04S 12.24 E
Zaire 158 Ii 6.04S 12.24 E
Zaïre (Congo, Democratic Republic of the-) [1] 160 Ji 1.00S 25.00 E
Zaisan, Lake- (EN) = Zajsan, ozero- 140 Ke 48.10N 83.50 E
Zaj 114 Mi 55.36N 51.40 E
Zaječar 130 Ff 43.54N 22.17 E
Zajsan 142 Ke 47.30N 84.55 E
Zajsan, ozero- = Zaisan, Lake- (EN) 140 Ke 48.10N 83.50 E
Zak 158 Jk 29.39S 21.11 E
Zaka 172 Ed 20.20S 31.29 E
Zakamensk 138 Ff 50.23N 103.20 E
Zakarpatskaja oblast [3] 136 Cf 48.20N 23.20 E
Zakataly 136 Gg 41.38N 46.37 E
Zakháro 130 El 37.29N 21.39 E
Zākhū 144 Fb 37.08N 42.41 E
Zákinthos 130 Dl 37.47N 20.54 E
Zákinthos = Zante (EN) 110 Ih 37.47N 20.47 E
Zakinthou Dhiavlos- 130 Dl 37.50N 21.00 E
Zakopane 120 Pg 49.19N 19.57 E
Zakouma 168 Bc 10.54N 19.49 E
Žaksy 136 Ge 51.53N 67.20 E
Zala [2] 120 Mj 46.40N 16.50 E
Zala 120 Nj 46.43N 17.16 E
Zālābiyah 146 He 35.39N 39.51 E
Zalaegerszeg 120 Mj 46.50N 16.51 E
Zaláf 146 Gf 32.55N 37.20 E
Zalalövő 120 Mj 46.51N 16.36 E
Zalamea de la Serena 126 Gf 38.39N 5.39W
Zalamea la Real 126 Fg 37.41N 6.39W
Zalantun → Butha Qi 152 Lb 48.02N 122.42 E
Zalari 138 Ff 53.36N 102.32 E
Zalaszentgrót 120 Nj 46.57N 17.05 E
Zalău 130 Gb 47.12N 23.03 E
Zaleščiki 132 De 48.39N 25.44 E
Ẓalim 144 Fe 22.43N 42.10 E
Zalingei 168 Cc 12.54N 23.29 E
Zalṭan 164 Cd 28.55N 19.50 E
Zaltbommel 124 Hc 51.49N 5.17 E
Žaltidjal 130 Ih 41.30N 25.05 E
Žaltyr 136 Ge 51.35N 69.58 E
Žaltyr, ozero- 132 Qf 47.25N 51.05 E
Zamakh 144 Gf 16.28N 47.35 E
Zamami-Shima 156b Ab 26.15N 127.18 E
Zambeze = Zambezi (EN) 158 Kj 18.50N 36.17 E
Zambezi 158 Kj 18.50N 36.17 E
Zambezi (EN) = Zambeze 158 Kj 18.50N 36.17 E
Zambézia [3] 172 Fc 17.00S 37.00 E
Zambezi Escarpment 172 Ec 16.15S 30.10 E
Zambia [1] 160 Jj 15.00S 30.00 E
Zamboanga 142 Oi 6.54N 122.04 E
Zamboanga Peninsula 150 He 7.32N 122.16 E
Zambrah, Jazīrat- 162 Jb 37.08N 10.48 E
Zambrano 194 Ji 9.45N 74.49W
Zambrów 120 Sd 53.00N 22.15 E
Zambué 172 Ec 15.07S 30.49 E
Zamfara 166 Fc 12.02N 4.03 E
Zamkova, gora- 120 Vc 53.34N 25.53 E
Zamkowa, Góra- 120 Qb 54.25N 20.25 E
Zammar 146 Jd 36.47N 42.40 E
Zamora [3] 126 Gc 41.45N 6.00W
Zamora [Ec.] 202 Cd 4.04S 78.52W
Zamora [Sp.] 126 Gc 41.30N 5.45W
Zamora, Río- 202 Cd 2.59S 78.15W
Zamora de Hidalgo 190 De 19.59N 102.16W
Zamość 120 Tf 50.44N 23.15 E
Zamość [2] 120 Tf 50.44N 23.15 E
Zampa-Misaki 156b Ab 26.26N 127.43 E
Zamtang (Gamda) 152 He 32.23N 101.05 E
Zamuro, Punta- 194 Mh 11.26N 68.50W
Zamzam 164 Cc 31.24N 15.17 E
Zanaga 170 Bc 2.51S 13.50 E
Žanatas 136 Gg 43.36N 69.43 E
Zancara 126 Ie 39.18N 3.18W
Zanda (Toling) 152 Ce 31.28N 79.50 E
Zandvoort 122 Kb 52.22N 4.32 E
Zanesville 182 Kd 39.55N 82.02W
Zangelan 132 Oj 39.05N 46.38 E
Zanhuang 154 Cf 37.38N 114.26 E
Zanjān 144 Gb 36.40N 48.29 E
Zanjān [3] 144 Gb 36.35N 48.15 E
Zanjānrūd 146 Ld 37.08N 47.47 E
Žannetty, ostrov- 138 Ka 76.45N 158.25 E
Zannone 128 Hj 40.55N 13.05 E
Zante (EN) = Zákinthos 110 Ih 37.47N 20.47 E
Zanthus 212 Ef 31.02S 123.34 E
Zanzibar 160 Ki 6.10S 39.11 E
Zanzibar [2] 170 Gd 6.10S 39.20 E
Zanzibar [3] 170 Gd 6.00S 39.50 E
Zanzibar Channel 170 Gd 6.00S 39.00 E
Zanzibar Island 158 Ki 6.10S 39.20 E
Zaolin 152 Jd 39.09N 113.03 E
Zaō-San 156 Gb 38.08N 140.28 E
Zaouatallaz 162 Ie 24.52N 8.26 E
Zaoyang 154 Je 32.08N 112.45 E
Zaozerny 138 Ee 55.57N 94.42 E
Zaozhuang 152 Ke 34.58N 117.34 E
Zap 146 Jd 36.00N 43.21 E
Zapacos Norte, Río- 204 Ac 17.03S 62.23W
Zapacos Sur, Río- 204 Ac 17.03S 62.23W
Zapadnaja Dvina 114 Hh 56.17N 32.03 E
Zapadnaja Dvina = Western Dvina (EN) 110 Id 57.04N 24.03 E
Zapadna Morava 130 Ef 43.41N 21.24 E
Západné Karpaty = West Carpathians (EN) 120 Og 49.30N 19.00 E
Zapadni Rodopi 130 Hh 41.45N 24.05 E
Zapadno-Karelskaja vozvyšennost 114 He 63.40N 31.40 E
Zapadno-Sibirskaja ravnina = West Siberian Plain (EN) 140 Jc 60.00N 75.00 E
Zapadny Sajan = Western Sayans 140 Ld 53.00N 94.00 E
Západočeský kraj [3] 120 Ig 49.45N 13.00 E
Západoslovenský kraj [3] 120 Nh 48.20N 18.00 E
Zapala 200 Ii 38.55S 70.05W
Zapardiel 126 Gc 41.29N 5.02W
Zapata 186 Gm 26.52N 99.19W
Zapata, Peninsula de- 194 Gb 22.20N 81.35W
Zapatera, Isla- 194 Eh 11.45N 85.50W
Zapatosa, Cienaga de- 194 Ki 9.05N 73.50W
Zapljusje 116 Mf 58.24N 29.56 E
Zapoljarny 136 Db 69.26N 30.48 E
Zapopan 192 Hg 20.43N 103.24W
Zaporožje 112 Jf 47.50N 35.10 E
Zaporožskaja oblast [3] 136 Df 47.15N 35.50 E
Zapotitlán, Punta- 192 Lh 18.33N 94.49W
Za Qu 152 Ge 32.00N 96.55 E
Zara 146 Gc 39.55N 37.48 E
Zarāf, Baḥr az- 168 Ed 9.25N 31.10 E
Zarafšan 136 Gg 41.39N 64.10 E
Zaragoza [3] 126 Lc 41.35N 1.00W
Zaragoza [Col.] 202 Db 7.30N 74.52W
Zaragoza [Mex.] 192 Jf 23.58N 99.46W
Zaragoza [Mex.] 192 If 22.02N 100.44W
Zaragoza [Mex.] 192 Ic 28.29N 100.55W
Zaragoza [Sp.] = Saragossa (EN) 112 Fg 41.38N 0.53W
Zarajsk 114 Ji 54.47N 38.53 E
Zarand [Iran] 146 Me 35.08N 49.00 E
Zarand [Iran] 146 Qg 30.48N 56.53 E
Zarand-e-Kohneh 146 Ne 35.17N 50.30 E
Zărandului, Munţii- 130 Fc 46.10N 22.15 E
Zaranj 142 If 31.06N 61.53 E
Zarasai/Zarasaj 114 Gi 55.43N 26.19 E
Zarasaj/Zarasai 114 Gi 55.43N 26.19 E
Zárate 200 Ki 34.05S 59.02W
Zarautz / Zarauz 126 Ja 43.17N 2.10W
Zarauz / Zarautz 126 Ja 43.17N 2.10W
Zaraza 202 Eb 9.21N 65.19W
Žarcovski 114 Hi 55.53N 32.16 E
Zard Kūh 140 Hf 32.22N 50.04 E
Zardob 132 Oi 40.14N 47.42 E
Zarečensk 114 Hc 66.40N 31.23 E
Zarghat 146 Ii 26.32N 40.29 E
Zarghun 148 Db 30.31N 68.50 E
Zarghūn Shahr 144 Kc 32.51N 68.25 E
Zaria 160 Hg 11.04N 7.42 E
Žarkamys 136 Ff 47.59N 56.29 E
Žarma 136 If 48.48N 80.55 E
Zărneşti 130 Id 45.33N 25.18 E
Zarqān 146 Oh 29.46N 52.43 E
Zarrīneh 146 Kd 37.05N 45.40 E
Zarrīnshahr 146 Nf 32.30N 51.25 E
Zaruma 202 Cd 3.42S 79.38W
Zarumilla 202 Bd 3.30S 80.16W
Žary 120 Le 51.38N 15.09 E
Žaryk 136 Hf 48.52N 72.54 E
Zarzaïtine 162 Id 28.05N 9.45 E
Zasa 116 Lh 56.15N 26.01 E
Zāskar 148 Fb 34.10N 77.20 E
Zaškov 132 Ge 49.15N 30.09 E
Zaslavl 116 Lj 54.00N 27.22 E
Zaslavskoje vodohranilišče 116 Lj 54.00N 27.30 E
Zastavna 130 Ia 48.25N 25.49 E
Zastron 172 Df 30.18S 27.07 E
Žatec 120 Jf 50.20N 13.33 E
Zatišje 130 Mb 47.47N 29.48 E
Zatobolsk 134 Kj 53.12N 63.43 E
Zatoka 130 Nc 46.07N 30.25 E
Zauche 120 Id 52.15N 12.35 E
Žavadovskogo Island 222 Ge 66.30S 86.00 E
Zavāreh 146 Of 33.30N 52.29 E
Zaventem 124 Gd 50.53N 4.28 E
Zavety Ilića 138 Jg 49.02N 140.19 E
Zavidovići 128 Mf 44.27N 18.09 E
Zavitinsk 138 Hf 50.01N 129.26 E
Zavodoukovsk 136 Gd 56.33N 66.32 E
Zavodovski 222 Ad 56.20S 27.35W
Zavolžje 114 Kh 56.38N 43.21 E
Zavolžsk 114 Kh 57.32N 42.10 E
Zawidów 120 Le 51.01N 15.02 E
Zawiercie 120 Pf 50.30N 19.25 E
Zawīlah 164 Cd 26.10N 15.07 E
Zāwiyat al Mukhaylá 164 Dc 32.10N 22.17 E
Zāwiyat Masūs 164 Dc 31.35N 21.01 E
Zāwiyat Qirzah 164 Bc 31.00N 14.20 E
Zāwiyat Shammās 146 Bg 31.31N 26.24 E
Zawr, Ra's az- 146 Mi 27.26N 49.19 E
Zaya 128 Kb 48.31N 16.55 E
Zāyandeh 146 Of 32.20N 52.50 E
Zaydūn, Wādī- 146 Ej 25.53N 33.04 E
Zayü (Gyigang) 152 Gf 28.43N 97.25 E
Zaza, Río- 194 Hc 21.37N 79.32W
Zazir 162 If 19.50N 5.13 E
Zbaraž 132 De 49.42N 25.47 E
Zbąszyń 120 Ld 52.16N 15.55 E
Zborov 120 Vg 49.37N 25.09 E
Ždanichý les 120 Mg 49.05N 16.50 E
Ždanov → Mariupol' 112 Jf 47.00N 37.33 E
Ždanovsk 132 Oj 39.45N 47.33 E
Žd'árské vrchy 120 Mg 49.35N 16.03 E
Ždiar 120 Qg 49.16N 20.15 E
Zdolbunov 132 Ed 50.33N 26.15 E
Zduńska Wola 120 Oe 51.36N 18.57 E
Zealand (EN) = Sjælland 110 Hd 55.30N 11.45 E
Zebediela 172 Dd 24.19S 29.16 E
Zebēs, Mali i- 130 Dh 41.55N 20.14 E
Zebil 130 Le 44.57N 28.46 E
Zeča 128 If 44.46N 14.19 E
Zeddine 126 Nh 36.12N 1.50 E
Zedelgem 124 Fc 51.09N 3.08 E
Zeehan 210 Fi 41.53S 145.20 E
Zeeland [3] 124 Fc 51.27N 3.45 E
Zeeland 124 Fc 51.27N 3.45 E
Zeerust 172 De 25.33S 26.06 E
Zefat 146 Ff 32.58N 35.30 E
Zegrzyńskie, Jezioro- 120 Rd 52.30N 21.05 E
Zehdenick 120 Jd 52.59N 13.20 E
Zeil, Mount- 212 Gd 23.25S 132.25 E
Žeimelis/Zeimjalis 116 Jh 56.14N 23.58 E
Žeimena/Žejmena 116 Fi 54.54N 23.53 E
Zeimjalis/Žeimelis 116 Jh 56.14N 23.58 E
Zeist 122 Lb 52.05N 5.15 E
Zeitz 120 Ie 51.03N 12.09 E
Zeja 142 Od 53.45N 127.15 E
Zeja 140 Od 50.13N 127.35 E
Žejmena/Žeimena 114 Fi 54.54N 23.53 E
Zejskoje vodohranilišče 138 Hf 54.40N 127.30 E
Zěkog 152 Hd 35.00N 101.35 E
Želanija, mys- 140 Ib 76.57N 68.35 E
Zelaya [3] 194 Eg 13.00N 84.00W
Želča 116 Lf 58.18N 27.50 E
Zele 124 Gc 51.04N 4.02 E
Želechów 120 Re 51.49N 21.54 E
Zelee, Cape- 219a Ec 9.44S 161.34 E
Zelenaja Rošča 116 Md 60.08N 29.14 E
Zelenčukskaja 132 Lh 43.51N 41.34 E
Zelengora 128 Mg 43.22N 18.35 E
Zelenoborsk 136 Gc 61.29N 63.59 E
Zelenoborski 136 Db 66.50N 32.18 E
Zelenodolsk 136 Ed 55.53N 48.31 E
Zelenogorsk 136 Cc 60.12N 29.42 E
Zelenograd 114 Ih 56.01N 37.12 E
Zelenogradsk 116 Ij 54.57N 20.27 E
Zelenokumsk 136 Eg 44.23N 43.53 E
Zeletin 130 Kc 46.03N 27.23 E
Železné hory 120 Lg 49.50N 15.45 E
Železnik 130 De 44.43N 20.23 E
Železnodorožny [R.S.F.S.R.] 138 Fe 57.55N 102.50 E
Železnodorožny [R.S.F.S.R.] 114 Ei 54.23N 21.19 E
Železnodorožny [R.S.F.S.R.] 136 Fc 62.37N 50.55 E
Železnogorsk 136 De 52.21N 35.23 E
Železnogorsk-Ilimski 138 Fe 56.40N 104.05 E
Železnovodsk 132 Mg 44.08N 43.00 E
Zelfana 162 Hc 32.24N 4.14 E
Želiezovce 120 Oh 48.03N 18.40 E
Zelivka 120 Lg 49.43N 15.06 E
Željin 130 Df 43.29N 20.48 E
Zell am See 128 Gc 47.19N 12.47 E
Zell am Ziller 128 Fc 47.14N 11.53 E
Zelów 120 Pe 51.28N 19.13 E
Želtau Ajtau 135 Ib 44.30N 74.00 E
Želtyje Vody 132 He 48.23N 33.31 E
Želudok 120 Vc 53.33N 25.07 E
Zelva 120 Uc 53.04N 24.54 E
Želva 116 Ki 55.13N 25.13 E
Zelzate 122 Jc 51.12N 3.49 E
Žemaičiu Aukštuma / Zemajtskaja vozvyšennost 116 Ji 55.45N 22.30 E
Žemaiciy-Naumiestis/Žemajčju-Naumiestis 116 Ii 55.21N 21.37 E
Žemaitija 116 Ji 55.55N 22.30 E
Žemajčju-Naumiestis/Žemaiciy-Naumiestis 116 Ii 55.21N 21.37 E
Zemajtskaja vozvyšennost / Žemaičiu Aukštuma 116 Ji 55.45N 22.30 E
Zembin 116 Mj 54.24N 28.19 E
Zembretta, Ile- 128 Em 37.07N 10.53 E
Zemetčino 132 Mc 53.31N 42.38 E
Zemgale 116 Kh 56.30N 25.00 E
Zémio 168 Dd 5.19N 25.08 E
Zemmora 126 Mi 35.43N 0.45 E
Zemmour 158 Ff 25.30N 12.00W
Zemplínska Sirava, údolná nádrž- 120 Sh 48.50N 22.02 E
Zempoala 190 Ee 19.27N 96.23W
Zempoaltepec 174 Jh 17.00N 96.50W
Zemra, Djebel- 126 Pi 35.14N 3.54 E
Zemst 124 Gd 50.59N 4.28 E
Zemun, Beograd- 130 De 44.53N 20.25 E
Zengfeng Shan 154 Jc 42.25N 128.44 E
Zenica 128 Lf 44.13N 17.55 E
Zenker Seamount (EN) 222 Bc 41.00S 6.00W
Zenkov 132 Id 50.13N 34.22 E
Zenne 124 Gc 51.04N 4.26 E
Zenobia Peak 186 Bf 40.40N 108.48W
Zentsūji 156 Cd 34.14N 133.47 E
Zenzach 126 Pi 35.21N 3.22 E
Zenza do Itombe 170 Bd 9.16S 14.13 E
Žepče 128 Mf 44.26N 18.03 E
Zepu/Poskam 152 Cd 38.12N 77.18 E
Zéralda 126 Oh 36.43N 2.50 E
Zeravšan 136 Gh 39.10N 68.40 E
Zeravšan 140 If 39.22N 63.45 E
Zeravšanski hrebet 136 Gh 39.15N 68.30 E
Zerbst 120 Ie 51.58N 12.05 E
Žerdevka 136 Ee 51.53N 41.28 E
Zerind 130 Ec 46.37N 21.31 E
Zermatt 128 Bd 46.02N 7.44 E
Zernez 128 Ed 46.42N 10.07 E
Zernograd 136 Ef 46.48N 40.19 E
Zeroua 126 Ph 36.22N 3.21 E
Žešart 134 De 62.05N 49.31 E
Zestafoni 132 Mh 42.07N 43.02 E
Zeta 130 Cg 42.28N 19.16 E
Zetland → Shetland Islands 110 Fc 60.30N 1.30W
Žetybaj 136 Fg 43.34N 52.04 E
Žetykol, ozero- 132 Vd 51.05N 60.55 E
Zeune Islands 219a Bb 6.18S 155.50 E
Zeven 120 Fc 53.18N 9.17 E
Zevenaar 124 Ic 51.55N 6.05 E
Zevenbergen 124 Gc 51.38N 4.36 E
Zeydābād 146 Ph 29.37N 55.33 E
Zeydār 146 Pd 36.20N 55.53 E
Zeytinbağı 130 Li 40.23N 28.47 E
Zeytindağ 130 Kk 38.58N 27.04 E
Zêzere 126 De 39.28N 8.20W
Žežmarjaj/Žiežmariai 116 Kj 54.47N 24.36 E
Zghartā 146 Fe 34.24N 35.54 E
Zgierz 120 Pe 51.52N 19.25 E
Zgorzelec 120 Le 51.12N 15.01 E
Zhabdun → Zhongba 142 Kg 29.41N 84.10 E
Zhag'yab 152 Ge 30.40N 97.40 E
Zhangbei 154 Jc 41.13N 114.43 E
Zhangde → Anyang 142 Nf 36.01N 114.25 E
Zhangdian → Zibo 152 Kd 36.48N 118.04 E
Zhangguangcai Ling 154 Jb 45.00N 129.00 E
Zhang He 154 Cf 36.27N 114.42 E
Zhangjiakou 142 Ne 40.49N 114.57 E
Zhangjiapan → Jingbian 152 Id 37.32N 108.45 E
Zhangling 152 La 52.39N 123.31 E
Zhanglou 154 Dh 32.40N 116.47 E
Zhangping 152 Kf 25.25N 117.27 E
Zhangqiu (Mingshui) 154 Df 36.44N 117.33 E
Zhangshuzhen → Qingjiang 152 Kf 28.02N 115.31 E
Zhangwei Xinhe 154 Dg 38.13N 117.48 E
Zhangwu 152 Lc 42.23N 122.33 E
Zhangye 142 Mf 38.57N 100.28 E
Zhangzhou 142 Ng 24.38N 117.39 E
Zhangzi 152 Jd 36.04N 112.53 E
Zhan He 152 Mb 49.21N 128.07 E
Zhanhua (Fuguo) 154 Ef 37.42N 118.08 E
Zhanjiang 142 Ng 21.13N 110.23 E
Zhanyi 152 Hf 25.40N 103.46 E
Zhao'an 152 Kg 23.49N 117.10 E
Zhaodong 152 Mb 46.04N 125.56 E
Zhaoge → Qixian 154 Cg 35.35N 114.12 E
Zhaojue 152 Hf 28.02N 102.50 E
Zhaoqing 154 Jg 23.04N 112.28 E
Zhaosu/Monggolküre 152 Dc 43.10N 81.07 E
Zhaosutai He 154 Gc 42.42N 123.35 E
Zhaotong 142 Mg 27.20N 103.46 E
Zhaoxian 154 Cf 37.46N 114.46 E
Zhaoyang Hu 154 Dg 35.00N 116.48 E
Zhaoyuan [China] 154 Ff 37.22N 120.23 E
Zhaoyuan [China] 154 Hb 45.30N 125.06 E
Zhaozhou 154 Hb 45.42N 125.15 E
Zhari Namco 152 Ee 31.05N 85.35 E
Zhaxi → Weixin 152 If 27.46N 105.04 E
Zhaxi Co 152 Ee 32.12N 85.10 E
Zhecheng 154 Cg 34.05N 115.17 E
Zheduo Shankou 152 He 30.06N 101.48 E
Zhejiang Sheng (Che-Chiang Sheng) [2] 152 Kf 29.00N 120.00 E
Zhen'an 152 Ie 33.27N 109.10 E
Zhenba 152 Ie 32.37N 107.50 E
Zhenghe 152 Kf 27.20N 118.58 E
Zhenghe Qunjiao 150 Fd 10.20N 114.20 E
Zhenglan Qi (Dund Hot) 154 Cc 42.14N 115.59 E
Zhengxiangbai Qi (Qagan Nur) 152 Jc 42.16N 114.59 E
Zhengyang 154 Ci 32.36N 114.23 E
Zhengzhou 142 Nf 34.42N 113.41 E
Zhenhai 154 Fj 29.57N 121.43 E
Zhenjiang 152 Ke 32.03N 119.26 E
Zhenkang (Fengweiba) 152 Gg 23.54N 99.00 E
Zhenlai 152 Lb 45.50N 123.14 E
Zhenning 152 If 26.05N 105.46 E
Zhenping 154 Bh 33.02N 112.14 E
Zhenxiong 152 Hf 27.28N 104.52 E
Zhenyuan 152 Hg 23.52N 100.53 E
Zhenyuan (Wuyang) 152 If 27.05N 108.26 E
Zhicheng 152 Je 30.17N 111.29 E
Zhidan (Bao'an) 152 Id 36.48N 108.46 E
Zhidoi 152 Ge 34.46N 95.46 E
Zhijiang 152 If 27.32N 109.42 E
Zhi Qu/Tongtian He 140 Lf 33.26N 96.36 E
Zhiziluo → Bijiang 152 Gf 26.39N 99.00 E
Zhob 148 Db 32.04N 69.50 E
Zhongba (Zhabdun) 142 Kg 29.41N 84.10 E
Zhongba → Jiangyou 152 He 31.48N 104.39 E
Zhongdian 152 Gf 27.42N 99.41 E
Zhōngguó = China (EN) 140 Mg 35.00N 105.00 E
Zhonghua Renmin Gongheguo = China (EN) [1] 142 Mf 35.00N 105.00 E
Zhongjian Dao 150 Fc 15.52N 111.13 E
Zhongmou 154 Cg 34.45N 114.01 E
Zhongning 152 Id 37.28N 105.41 E
Zhongshan 152 Jg 22.31N 113.23 E
Zhongwei 142 Mf 37.30N 105.09 E
Zhongxian 152 Ie 30.20N 108.02 E
Zhongxiang 152 Je 31.10N 112.38 E
Zhongxing → Siyang 154 Eh 33.43N 118.40 E
Zhongye Qundao 150 Fd 11.20N 114.30 E
Zhoukoudianzhen 154 Ce 39.41N 115.55 E
Zhoukouzhen 154 Ce 33.32N 114.40 E
Zhoushan Dao 154 Gi 30.00N 122.00 E
Zhoushan Qundao 140 Of 30.00N 122.00 E
Zhuanghe 152 Ld 39.42N 122.58 E
Zhucheng 152 Kd 35.58N 119.28 E
Zhu Dao 154 Fe 39.05N 121.10 E
Zhugqu 152 He 33.46N 104.18 E
Zhuhe 154 Bj 29.44N 113.07 E
Zhuizishan → Weichang 152 Kc 41.55N 117.39 E
Zhuji 154 Fj 29.43N 120.13 E
Zhuji → Shangqiu 152 Ke 34.24N 115.37 E
Zhujiang Kou 152 Jg 22.20N 113.45 E
Zhumadian 152 Je 32.54N 114.03 E
Zhuolu 154 Cd 40.23N 115.13 E
Zhuoxian 152 Kd 39.26N 116.00 E
Zhuozhang He 154 Bf 36.36N 113.10 E
Zhuozi 154 Bd 40.52N 112.33 E
Zhuozi Shan 152 Id 39.36N 107.00 E
Zhushan 152 Je 32.16N 110.12 E
Zhuzhou 142 Ng 27.52N 113.12 E
Ziama Mansouria 162 Ib 36.40N 5.29 E
Ziar nad Hronom 120 Oh 48.36N 18.52 E
Ẓibā' 144 Ed 27.21N 35.40 E
Zibo (Zhangdian) 152 Kd 36.48N 118.04 E
Zicavo 122a Bb 41.54N 9.08 E
Židačov 120 Ug 49.17N 24.12 E
Zielona Góra 120 Le 51.56N 15.31 E
Zielona Góra [2] 120 Le 51.55N 15.30 E
Zierikzee 122 Jc 51.38N 3.55 E
Žiežmariai/Žežmarjaj 116 Kj 54.47N 24.36 E
Ziftá 146 Dg 30.43N 31.15 E
Žigalovo 138 Ff 54.48N 105.08 E
Zigana Geçidi 146 Hb 40.38N 39.25 E
Žigansk 138 Hc 66.45N 123.30 E
Zigey 168 Bc 14.43N 15.47 E
Zighan, Wāḥāt- 164 Dd 25.35N 22.06 E
Zigong 142 Mg 29.20N 104.48 E
Zigui 152 Je 31.01N 110.42 E
Ziguinchor 160 Fg 12.35N 16.16W
Žigulevsk 136 Ee 53.27N 49.29 E
Zihuatanejo 190 De 17.38N 101.33W
Zijing Shan 152 Jd 37.12N 112.50 E
Zijpenberg 124 Hb 52.04N 6.00 E
Zilālet 166 Gb 18.28N 7.48 E
Zile 144 Ea 40.18N 35.54 E
Žilina 112 Hf 49.14N 18.45 E
Žilino 116 Ij 54.55N 21.48 E
Zillah 160 If 28.33N 17.35 E
Ziller 128 Fc 47.24N 11.50 E
Zillertaler Alpen 120 Hi 47.00N 11.55 E
Žiloj 132 Qi 40.19N 50.33 E
Zilupe 114 Gh 56.25N 28.07 E
Zima 142 Md 53.55N 102.04 E
Zimapán 192 Jg 20.45N 99.21W
Zimatlán de Álvarez 192 Ki 16.52N 96.47W
Zimba 170 Ef 17.02S 26.30 E
Zimbabwe 172 Ed 20.16S 30.55 E
Zimbabwe (Rhodesia) [1] 160 Jj 20.00S 30.00 E
Zimbor 130 Gc 47.00N 23.16 E
Zimi 166 Cd 7.19N 11.18W
Zimni bereg 114 Jd 66.00N 40.45 E
Zimnicea 130 If 43.40N 25.22 E
Zimovniki 132 Mf 47.08N 42.29 E
Zina 166 Hc 11.16N 14.58 E
Zincirli 146 Gd 37.00N 36.41 E
Zinder 160 Hg 13.48N 8.59 E
Zinder [2] 166 Hb 15.00N 10.00 E
Zinga 168 Be 3.43N 18.35 E
Zingst 120 Ib 54.25N 12.50 E
Zinjibār 164 Lg 13.08N 45.23 E
Zinnik/Soignies 122 Kd 50.35N 4.04 E
Zinsel du Nord 124 Jf 48.49N 7.44 E
Zion [Il.-U.S.] 186 Me 42.27N 87.50W
Zion [St.C.N.] 197c Ab 17.09N 62.32W
Zipaquirá 202 Db 5.02N 74.01W
Zirc 120 Ni 47.16N 17.52 E

Index Symbols

[1] Independent Nation
[2] State, Region
[3] District, County
[4] Municipality
[5] Colony, Dependency
Continent
Physical Region
Historical or Cultural Region
Mount, Mountain
Volcano
Hill
Mountains, Mountain Range
Hills, Escarpment
Plateau, Upland
Pass, Gap
Plain, Lowland
Delta
Salt Flat
Valley, Canyon
Crater, Cave
Karst Features
Depression
Polder
Desert, Dunes
Forest, Woods
Heath, Steppe
Oasis
Cape, Point
Coast, Beach
Cliff
Peninsula
Isthmus
Sandbank
Island
Atoll
Rock, Reef
Islands, Archipelago
Rocks, Reefs
Coral Reef
Well, Spring
Geyser
River, Stream
Waterfall, Rapids
River Mouth, Estuary
Lake
Salt Lake
Intermittent Lake
Reservoir
Swamp, Pond
Canal
Glacier
Ice Shelf, Pack Ice
Ocean
Sea
Gulf, Bay
Strait, Fjord
Lagoon
Bank
Seamount
Tablemount
Ridge
Shelf
Basin
Escarpment, Sea Scarp
Fracture
Trench, Abyss
National Park, Reserve
Point of Interest
Recreation Site
Cave, Cavern
Historic Site
Ruins
Wall, Walls
Church, Abbey
Temple
Scientific Station
Railway station
Airport
Port
Military installation
Lighthouse
Mine
Tunnel
Dam, Bridge

Name	Page	Grid	Lat	Long
Žirje [symbol]	128	Jg	43.39N	15.40 E
Zirkel, Mount- [mountain]	186	Cf	40.52N	106.36W
Žirnovsk	136	Ee	51.01N	44.48 E
Ziro	148	Ic	27.32N	93.32 E
Zi Shui [river]	152	Jf	28.41N	112.43 E
Žitava [river]	120	Oi	47.53N	18.11 E
Žitkoviči	132	Fc	52.16N	28.02 E
Žitkovo	114	Gf	60.42N	29.23 E
Žitomir	112	Ie	50.16N	28.40 E
Žitomirskaja oblast [3]	136	Ce	50.40N	28.30 E
Zittau	120	Kf	50.54N	14.50 E
Zitterwald [mountain]	124	Id	50.27N	6.25 E
Zitundo	172	Ee	26.44S	32.49 E
Živinice	128	Mf	44.27N	18.39 E
Ziwa Magharibi [3]	170	Fc	2.00S	31.30 E
Ziway, Lake- [symbol]	168	Fb	8.00N	38.48 E
Ziyamet	146	Fe	35.22N	34.00 E
Ziyang	152	Ie	32.34N	108.37 E
Ziz	162	Gc	30.29N	4.26W
Žizdra [river]	132	Ic	53.45N	34.43 E
Žizdra [river]	132	Jb	54.14N	36.12 E
Zlatar [mountain]	130	Cf	43.23N	19.51 E
Zlaté Moravce	120	Oh	48.23N	18.24 E
Zlatibor [mountain]	130	Cf	43.40N	19.43 E
Zlatica	130	Hg	42.43N	24.08 E
Zlatica [river]	130	Dd	45.49N	20.10 E
Zlatijata [symbol]	130	Gf	43.40N	23.36 E
Zlatiški prohod [symbol]	130	Hg	42.45N	24.05 E
Zlatna	130	Gc	46.07N	23.13 E
Zlatograd	130	Ih	41.23N	25.06 E
Zlatoust	112	Ld	55.10N	59.40 E
Zlatoustovsk	138	If	52.59N	133.41 E
Zletovo	130	Fh	41.59N	22.15 E
Žliťan	164	Bc	32.28N	14.34 E
Žlobin	136	De	52.59N	30.03 E
Złocieniec	120	Mc	53.33N	16.01 E
Złoczew	120	Oe	51.25N	18.36 E
Zlot	130	Ee	44.01N	21.59 E
Złotoryja	120	Le	51.08N	15.55 E
Złotów	120	Nc	53.22N	17.02 E
Zły Komorow/Senftenberg	120	Ke	51.31N	14.01 E
Zlynka	132	Gc	52.27N	31.44 E
Zmeinogorsk	138	Df	51.10N	82.13 E
Zmeiny, ostrov- [symbol]	132	Gg	45.15N	30.12 E
Žmerinka	136	Cf	49.02N	28.05 E
Żmigród	120	Me	51.29N	16.55 E
Žmijev	132	Je	49.41N	36.20 E
Zmijevka	132	Jc	52.40N	36.24 E
Zna [river]	114	Ih	57.33N	34.25 E
Znamenka [R.S.F.S.R.]	132	Lc	52.24N	41.28 E
Znamenka [Ukr.-U.S.S.R.]	132	He	48.41N	32.40 E
Znamensk	116	Ij	54.39N	21.15 E
Znamenskoje	136	Hd	57.08N	73.55 E
Žnin	120	Nd	52.52N	17.43 E
Znojmo	120	Mh	48.51N	16.03 E
Zobia	170	Eb	2.53N	26.02 E
Zóbuè	172	Ec	15.36S	34.26 E
Žodino	132	Fb	54.07N	28.19 E
Žodiški	116	Lj	54.40N	26.33 E
Zoetermeer	124	Gb	52.04N	4.30 E
Zogang/Wangda	152	Gf	29.37N	97.58 E
Zohreh [river]	146	Mg	30.04N	49.34 E
Zolgë	152	He	33.38N	103.00 E
Zoločev [Ukr.-U.S.S.R.]	136	Cf	49.49N	24.58 E
Zoločev [Ukr.-U.S.S.R.]	132	Id	50.18N	35.59 E
Zolotaja Gora	138	Hf	54.21N	126.41 E
Zolotoje	132	He	49.40N	32.02 E
Zolotonoša	132	Jc	52.07N	36.25 E
Zolotuhino	136	He	51.45N	71.44 E
Żolymbet	160	Kj	15.23S	35.20 E
Zomba	152	Ef	28.57N	85.12 E
Zongga → Gyirong	170	Cb	4.21N	18.36 E
Zongo	144	Da	41.27N	31.49 E
Zonguldak	154	Di	30.42N	117.12 E
Zongyang				
Zonkwa	166	Gd	9.47N	8.17 E
Zonnebeke	124	Ed	50.52N	2.59 E
Zontehuitz, Cerro-	192	Mi	16.50N	92.38W
Zonúz	146	Kc	38.35N	45.50 E
Zonza	122a	Bb	41.44N	9.10 E
Zorita	126	Ge	39.17N	5.42W
Zorkassa, gora- [mountain]	135	Ge	38.01N	68.10 E
Zorleni	130	Kc	46.16N	27.43 E
Zorritos	202	Bd	3.40S	80.40W
Zorzor	166	Dd	7.47N	9.26W
Zottegem	124	Fd	50.52N	3.48 E
Zou [3]	166	Fd	8.00N	2.15 E
Zouar	160	If	20.27N	16.32 E
Zouîrât	160	Ff	22.46N	12.27W
Zouping	154	Df	36.53N	117.44 E
Zoutkamp, Ulrum-	124	Ia	53.20N	6.18 E
Zouxian	154	Dg	35.24N	116.59 E
Zóvten	130	Nb	47.14N	30.14 E
Žovtnevoje	132	Hf	46.52N	32.02 E
Zrenjanin	130	Dd	45.23N	20.23 E
Zrinska Gora [mountain]	128	Ke	45.10N	16.15 E
Zrmanja [river]	128	Jf	44.12N	15.35 E
Zruč nad Sázavou	120	Lg	49.45N	15.07 E
Zschopau [river]	120	Je	51.08N	13.03 E
Żuantobe	136	Gg	44.47N	68.52 E
Zuata, Rio- [river]	196	Di	7.52N	65.22W
Zubayr, Jazā'ir az-	164	Hf	15.05N	42.08 E
Zubcov	114	Ih	56.10N	34.31 E
Zubova Poljana	114	Ki	54.05N	42.50 E
Zudañez	202	Fg	19.06S	64.44W
Zuénoula	166	Dd	7.26N	6.03W
Zuénoula [3]	166	Dd	7.22N	6.12W
Zuera	126	Lc	41.52N	0.47W
Zufāf [symbol]	164	Hf	16.43N	41.46 E
Žufár [symbol]	140	Hh	17.30N	54.00 E
Zug [2]	128	Cc	47.10N	8.40 E
Zug [Switz.]	128	Cc	47.10N	8.30 E
Zug [W.Sah.]	162	Ee	21.36N	14.09W
Zugdidi	136	Eg	42.29N	41.48 E
Zuger See [symbol]	128	Cc	47.10N	8.30 E
Zugspitze [mountain]	128	Gi	47.25N	10.59 E
Zuid Beveland [symbol]	124	Fc	51.25N	3.45 E
Zuidelijk Flevoland [symbol]	124	Hb	52.25N	5.20 E
Zuid-Holland [3]	124	Gc	52.00N	4.30 E
Zuid-IJsselmeerpolders [3]	124	Hb	52.20N	5.20 E
Zuidlaren	124	Ia	53.06N	6.42 E
Zuid-Willemsvaart [symbol]	124	Hd	50.50N	5.41 E
Zuidwolde	124	Ib	52.40N	6.25 E
Zújar	126	Ge	39.01N	5.47W
Zújar, Embalse del- [symbol]	126	Gf	38.50N	5.20 E
Žukovka	136	De	53.33N	33.47 E
Žukovski	114	Ji	55.37N	38.12 E
Zula	168	Fb	15.14N	39.40 E
Zulia [2]	202	Db	10.00N	72.10W
Zulia, Rio- [river]	194	Ki	9.04N	72.18W
Zülpich	124	Id	50.42N	6.39 E
Zumbo	172	Ec	15.36S	30.25 E
Zundert	124	Gc	51.29N	4.40 E
Zungeru	166	Gd	9.48N	6.09 E
Zunhua	154	Dd	40.12N	117.58 E
Zuni	186	Bi	35.04N	108.51W
Zuni River [river]	188	Ki	34.39N	109.40W
Zunyi	142	Mg	27.40N	106.56 E
Zuoquan	154	Bf	37.05N	113.22 E
Zuoyun	154	Be	39.58N	112.40 E
Zupanja	128	Me	45.04N	18.42 E
Zuqāq [symbol]	164	Hf	18.04N	40.48 E
Zurak	166	Hd	9.14N	10.34 E
Zürich [2]	128	Cc	47.30N	8.30 E
Zürich, Lake- (EN) = Zürichsee [symbol]	128	Cc	47.15N	8.45 E
Zürichsee = Zurich, Lake- (EN) [symbol]	128	Cc	47.15N	8.45 E
Zurmi	166	Gc	12.47N	6.47 E
Žuromin	120	Pc	53.04N	19.55 E
Zuru	166	Gc	11.26N	5.14 E
Zuša [river]	132	Jc	53.27N	36.25 E
Zusam [river]	120	Gh	48.42N	10.45 E
Žut [symbol]	128	Jg	43.52N	15.19 E
Zutiua, Rio- [river]	202	Id	3.43S	45.30W
Zutphen	122	Mb	52.08N	6.12 E
Zuwārah	164	Bc	32.56N	12.06 E
Zvenigorodka	132	Ge	49.04N	30.59 E
Zverinogolovskoje	134	Li	54.28N	64.50 E
Zvezdny	138	Fe	56.40N	106.30 E
Zvičina [mountain]	120	Lf	50.25N	15.41 E
Zvirca	120	Uf	50.24N	24.16 E
Zvishavane	172	Ed	20.19S	30.04 E
Zvolen	120	Ph	48.35N	19.08 E
Zvornik	128	Nf	44.23N	19.07 E
Zwarte Bank = Black Bank (EN) [symbol]	124	Fa	53.15N	3.55 E
Zweibrücken	120	Dg	49.15N	7.22 E
Zweisimmen	128	Bd	46.34N	7.25 E
Zwesten	124	Lc	51.03N	9.11 E
Zwettl/Niederösterreich	128	Jb	48.37N	15.10 E
Zwickau	120	If	50.44N	12.30 E
Zwickauer Mulde [river]	120	Ie	51.10N	12.48 E
Zwierzyniec	120	Sf	50.37N	22.58 E
Zwiesel	120	Jg	49.01N	13.14 E
Zwijndrecht	124	Gc	51.50N	4.41 E
Zwischenahn	124	Kb	53.11N	8.01 E
Zwischenahner Meer [symbol]	124	Ka	53.12N	8.01 E
Zwoleń	120	Re	51.22N	21.35 E
Zwolle	122	Mb	52.30N	6.05 E
Zychlin	120	Pd	52.15N	19.13 E
Zyrardów	120	Qd	52.04N	20.25 E
Žyrjanka	138	Kc	65.45N	105.51 E
Žyrjanovsk	136	If	49.45N	84.16 E
Żywiec	120	Pg	49.41N	19.12 E

Index Symbols

Symbol	Meaning
[1]	Independent Nation
[2]	State, Region
[3]	District, County
[4]	Municipality
[5]	Colony, Dependency
■	Continent
[symbol]	Physical Region
	Historical or Cultural Region
	Mount, Mountain
	Volcano
	Hill
	Mountains, Mountain Range
	Hills, Escarpment
	Plateau, Upland
	Pass, Gap
	Plain, Lowland
	Delta
	Valley, Canyon
	Crater, Cave
	Karst Features
	Depression
	Polder
	Desert, Dunes
	Heath, Steppe
	Oasis
	Cape, Point
	Coast, Beach
	Cliff
	Peninsula
	Sandbank
	Island
	Atoll
	Rock, Reef
	Islands, Archipelago
	Rocks, Reefs
	Coral Reef
	Well, Spring
	River, Stream
	Waterfall, Rapids
	River Mouth, Estuary
	Lake
	Salt Lake
	Intermittent Lake
	Geyser
	Reservoir
	Swamp, Pond
	Canal
	Glacier
	Ice Shelf, Pack Ice
	Ocean
	Sea
	Ridge
	Gulf, Bay
	Strait, Fjord
	Lagoon
	Bank
	Fracture
	Seamount
	Tablemount
	Shelf
	Basin
	Escarpment, Sea Scarp
	Trench, Abyss
	National Park, Reserve
	Point of Interest
	Recreation Site
	Cave, Cavern
	Historic Site
	Ruins
	Wall, Walls
	Church, Abbey
	Temple
	Scientific Station
	Railway station
	Airport
	Port
	Military installation
	Lighthouse
	Mine
	Tunnel
	Dam, Bridge